Encyclopedia of
World Literature
in the 20th
Century

Encyclopedia of World Literature in the 20th Century

VOLUME 3: L–R

ST. JAMES PRESS

Steven R. Serafin, *General Editor*

Laura Standley Berger, *Project Coordinator*

Joann Cerrito, Dave Collins, Nicolet V. Elert,
Miranda Ferrara, Kristin Hart, Margaret Mazurkiewicz, Michael J. Tyrkus
St. James Press Staff

Peter M. Gareffa, *Managing Editor, St. James Press*

Mary Beth Trimper, *Production Director*
Deborah Milliken, *Production Assistant*

Cynthia Baldwin, *Product Design Manager*
Eric Johnson, *Art Director*
Pamela A. Reed, *Photography Coordinator*
Randy Bassett, *Image Database Supervisor*
Robert Duncan, Mike Logusz, *Imaging Specialists*

Susan Trosky, *Permissions Manager*
Kelly A. Quin, *Permissons Associate*

Copyright © 1999
St. James Press
27500 Drake Road
Farmington Hills, MI 48331

Encyclopedia of World Literature / Steven R. Serafin, general editor. — 3rd ed.
    p.   cm.
    Includes bibliographical references and index.
    Contents: v. 1. A-D — v. 2. E-K — v. 3. L-R — v. 4. S-Z and indexes
    ISBN 1-55862-373-6 (set). — ISBN 1-55862-374-4 (v. 1). — ISBN 1-55862-375-2 (v. 2). — ISBN 1-55862-376-0 (v. 3). — ISBN 1-55862-377-9 (v. 4).
    1. Literature, Modern—20th century—Bio-bibliography.
    2. Literature, Modern—20th century—Encyclopedias   I. Serafin, Steven.
    PN771.E5   1998
    803—dc21   98-40374
                                                           CIP

Printed in the United States of America
St. James Press is an imprint of Gale

10 9 8 7 6 5 4 3 2

BOARD OF ADVISORS

PERIODICALS USED

A&E	Anglistik & Englischunterricht	*AL*	American Literature
AAS	Asian and African Studies		Alaluz: Revista de Poesia, Narracion y Ensayo
AAW	Afro-Asian Writing	*AL&C*	African Languages & Cultures
ABnG	Amsterdamer Beiträe zur Neueren Germanistik	*ALEC*	Anales de la Literatura Española Contemporánea
ACLALSB	ACLALS Bulletin	*ALHis*	Anales de Literatura Hispanoamericana
	Actualidades: Consejo Nacional de la Cultura, Centro de Estudios Latinoamericanos "Romulo Gallegos"/Caracas, Venezuela	*ALR*	American Literary Realism, 1870-1910
		ALS	Australian Literary Studies
ADP	Arbeiten zur deutschen Philologie	*ALT*	African Literature Today
	Africa: Rivista Trimestrale di Studi e Documentazione	*AmerD*	American Drama
AfricaL	Africa: Journal of the International African Institute/Revue de l'Institut Africain International	*AmerP*	American Poetry
		AmerT	American Theatre
AfricaR	Africa Report	*AmLH*	American Literary History
AfrLJ	African Journal	*AmRev*	Americas Review
AfrLS	African Language Studies	*AN*	Acta Neophilologica
AfrSR	African Studies Review	*ANP*	Anales de la Narrative Española Contemporánea
AGald	Anales Galdosianos		
AGR	American-German Review	*AnUs*	Annual of Urdu Studies
AHR	Afro-Hispanic Review	*ANZSC*	Australian and New Zealand Studies in Canada
AICRJ	American Indian Culture and Research Journal	*APR*	American Poetry Review
AIPHOS	Annuaire de l'Institut de Philologie et d'Histoire Orientales et Slaves	*AQ*	American Quarterly
		AR	Antioch Review
AIQ	American Indian Quarterly		Arabica: Revue d'Études Arabes
AJFS	Australian Journal of French Studies	*ARD*	African Research and Documentation
AJPh	American Journal of Philology	*ArielE*	Ariel: A Review of International English Literature
AJS	American Journal of Semiotics		

ArielK	Ariel
ArO	Archív Orientální: Quarterly Journal of African, Asian, and Latin-American Studies
ArQ	Arizona Quarterly
ASch	American Scholar
ASEER	American Slavic and East European Review
	Asemka: A Literary Journal of the University of Cape Coast
ASPAC	Asian Pacific Quarterly of Cultural and Social Affairs Quarterly
ASQ	Arab Studies Quarterly
ASR	American Scandinavian Review
	Atenea: Revista de Ciencia, Arte y Literatura de la Universidad de Concepción
AUB-LLR	Analele Universității, București, Limbă și Liter“erĕ Română
AUC	Anales de la Universidad de Chile
AUMLA	AUMLA: Journal of the Australasian Universities Language and Literature Association—A Journal of Literary Criticism and Linguistics
AWR	Anglo-Welsh Review
BA	Books Abroad
BAALE	Bulletin of the Association for African Literature in English
BAC	Boletín de la Academia Colombiana
BALF	Black American Literature Forum
BalSt	Balkan Studies
BB	Bulletin of Bibliography
BeneN	Bete Noire

BEPIF	Bulletin des Etudes Portugaises et Brésiliennes
BF	Books from Finland
BHe	Baltische Hefte
BHS	Bulletin of Hispanic Studies
BlackI	Black Images: A Critical Quarterly on Black Arts and Culture
BMMLA	Bulletin of the Midwest Modern Language Association
BO	Black Orpheus
Boundary	Boundary 2: A Journal of Postmodern Literature and Culture
BRMMLA	Rocky Mountain Review of Language and Literature
BRP	Beiträge zur Romanischen Philologie
BR/RB	Bilingual Review/La Revista Bilingüe
BSIS	Bulletin of the Society for Italian Studies
BSS	Bulletin of Spanish Studies
BSUF	Ball State University Forum
BUJ	Boston University Journal
BuR	Bucknell Review
BW	Black World
CA	Cuadernos Americanos
CALC	Cahiers Algériens de Littérature Comparée
	Callaloo: A Black South Journal of Arts and Letters
CalSS	California Slavic Studies
CanL	Canadian Literature
CARHS	Canadian-American Review of Hungarian Studies
CarQ	Caribbean Quarterly

CasaA	Casa de las Américas		*CJItS*	Canadian Journal of Italian Studies
CAsJ	Central Asiatic Journal		*CL*	Comparative Literature
CASS	Canadian-American Slavic Studies		*CLAJ*	College Language Association Journal
CatR	Catalan Review		*CLAQ*	Children's Literature Association Quarterly
CBAA	Current Bibliography on African Affairs		*CLC*	Columbia Library Columns
CBC	Cesare Barbieri Courier		*CLEAR*	Chinese Literature: Essays, Articles, Reviews
CCrit	Comparative Criticism			
CCur	Cross Currents: A Yearbook of Central European Culture		*CLQ*	Colby Library Quarterly
			CLS	Comparative Literature Studies
CE	College English		*CML*	Classical and Modern Literature
CE&S	Commonwealth Essays and Studies		*CMo*	Creative Moment
CEA	CEA Critic		*CMRS*	Cahiers du Monde Russe et Soviétique
CEAfr	Cahiers d'Études Africaines		*CNIE*	Commonwealth Novel in English
CelfanR	Revue Celfan/Celfan Review		*CNLR*	CNL/Quarterly World Report
CentR	Centennial Review		*CollG*	Colloquia Germanica
CFM	Canadian Fiction Magazine		*Colóquio*	Colóquio/Letras
CFR	Canadian Fiction Review		*ColQ*	Colorado Quarterly
CFrC	Contemporary French Civilization		*CompD*	Comparative Drama
CH	Crítica Hispánica		*ComQ*	Commonwealth Quarterly
CHA	Cuadernos Hispanoamericanos			Confluencia: Revista Hispánica de Cultura y Literatura
	Chasqui: Revista de Literatura Latinoamericana		*ConL*	Contemporary Literature
ChicL	Chicano Literature			
ChinL	Chinese Literature		*ContempR*	Contemporary Review
ChiR	Chicago Review		*CP*	Concerning Poetry
CJAS	Canadian Journal of African Studies		*CQ*	Cambridge Quarterly
CJLACS	Canadian Journal of Latin American and Caribbean Studies		*CR*	Critical Review
			CRCL	Canadian Review of Comparative Literature
CJIS	Canadian Journal of Irish Studies			

CREL	Cahiers Roumains d'Études Littéraires: Revue Trimestrielle de Critique, d'Esthétique et d'Histoire Littéraires	*DSt*	Deutsche Studien
CRevAS	Canadian Review of American Studies	*DU*	Der Deutschunterricht: Beiträge zu Seiner Praxis und Wissenschaftlichen Grundlegung
Crit	Critique: Studies in Modern Fiction	*DUJ*	Durham University Journal
CritI	Critical Inquiry	*DUR*	Dublin University Review
	Critique: Revue Générale des Publications Françaises et Étrangères	*DutchS*	Dutch Studies
CritQ	Critical Quarterly	*DVLJ*	Deutsche Vierteljahrsschrift für Literaturwissenschaft und Geistesgeschichte
CS	Cahiers du Sud	*EA*	Études Anglaises
CSP	Canadian Slavonic Papers		Eco: Revista de la Cultura de Occidente
CSR	Christian Scholar's Review	*ECr*	L'Esprit Créateur
CSS	Canadian Slavic Studies	*ECW*	Essays on Canadian Writing
CTR	Canadian Theatre Review		Edebiyat: A Journal of Middle Eastern Literatures
CV II	Contemporary Verse II	*EF*	Études Françaises
Dada	Dada/Surrealism	*EG*	Études Germaniques
DASDJ	Deutsche Akademie für Sprache und Dichtung, Darmstadt, Jahrbuch	*EI*	Études Irlandaises
DeltaES	Delta: Revue du Centre d'Études et de Recherche sur les Écrivains du Sud aux États-Unis	*EinA*	English in Africa
		Éire	Éire-Ireland: A Journal of Irish Studies
	Diacritics: A Review of Contemporary Criticism	*EJ*	English Journal
	Dimension: Contemporary German Arts and Letters	*ELH*	English Literary History (formerly Journal of English Literary History)
DLB	Dictionary of Literary Biography	*ELit*	Études Littéraires
DLit	Discurso Literario: Revista de Temas Hispánicos	*ELT*	English Literature in Transition
DQ	Denver Quarterly	*ELWIU*	Essays in Literature
DQR	Dutch Quarterly Review of Anglo-American Letters		English: The Journal of the English Association
DR	Dalhousie Review	*Ensayistas*	Los Ensayistas: Georgia Series on Hispanic Thought

ES	English Studies	*GRM*	Germanisch-Romanische Monatsschrift
ESA	English Studies in Africa	*GSlav*	Germano-Slavica: A Canadian Journal of Germanic and Slavic Comparative Studies
ESC	English Studies in Canada		
	Escritura: Revista de Teoría y Crítica Literarias	*HAHR*	Hispanic American Historical Review
ETJ	Educational Theatre Journal	*HAR*	Hebrew Annual Review
ETR	East Turkic Review	*HC*	Hollins Critic
Evergreen	Evergreen Review	*HisJ*	Hispanic Journal
EᴀTL	Explicación de Textos Literarios	*Hispam*	Hispamérica: Revista de Literatura
FE	France-Eurafrique		Hispania: A Journal Devoted to the Interests of the Teaching of Spanish and Portuguese
FI	Forum Italicum		
FLS	French Literature Series	*Hispano*	Hispanófila
FMLS	Forum for Modern Language Studies	*HJAS*	Harvard Journal of Asiatic Studies
	Folio: Essays on Foreign Languages and Literatures		Horizontes: Revista de la Universidad Católica de Puerto Rico
FR	French Review	*HR*	Hispanic Review
FS	French Studies	*HSL*	University of Hartford Studies in Literature
Francofonia	Studi e Ricerche Sulle Letterature di Lingua Francese		
		HSS	Harvard Slavic Studies
FrF	French Forum	*HudR*	Hudson Review
	Frontiers: A Journal of Women Studies	*HungQ*	Hungarian Quarterly
FSt	Feminist Studies	*I&FR*	Indian & Foreign Review
GaR	Georgia Review	*I&L*	Ideologies and Literature
GerSR	German Studies Review	*Ibero*	Iberoromania
GettR	Gettysburg Review		IBLA: Revue de l'Institut des Belles Lettres Arabes
GL&L	German Life and Letters		
GN	Germanic Notes	*IBSB*	International P.E.N. Bulletin of Selected Books
GQ	German Quarterly	*IC*	Islamic Culture
GR	Germanic Review	*IFR*	International Fiction Review
		IFRev	International Folklore Review

IJMES	International Journal of Middle East Studies
IJSLP	International Journal of Slavic Linguistics and Poetics
	Imagine: International Chicano Poetry Journal
IndL	Indian Literature
IndSch	Indian Scholar
	Inti: Revista de Literatura Hispánica
IonC	Index on Censorship
IowaR	Iowa Review
IQ	Italian Quarterly
IranS	Iranian Studies: Journal of the Society for Iranian Studies
IRLI	Italianistica: Rivista di Letteratura Italiana
IS	Italian Studies
ItalAm	Italian Americana
Italianist	The Italianist: Journal of the Department of Italian Studies, University of Reading
ItC	Italian Culture
IUR	Irish University Review: A Journal of Irish Studies
IWT	Indian Writing Today
JAAC	Journal of Aesthetics and Art Criticism
JAC	Journal of American Culture
JAOS	Journal of the American Oriental Society
JapQ	Japan Quarterly
JAPS	Journal of the American Portuguese Society
JArabL	Journal of Arabic Literature

JARCE	Journal of the American Research Center in Egypt
JASO	Journal of the Anthropological Society of Oxford
JASt	Journal of Asian Studies
JATJ	Journal of the Association of Teachers of Japanese
JBalS	Journal of Baltic Studies
JBlS	Journal of Black Studies
JBRS	Journal of the Burma Research Society
JByelS	Journal of Byelorussian Studies
JCF	Journal of Canadian Fiction
JCH	Journal of Contemporary History
JCL	Journal of Commonwealth Literature
JCLTA	Journal of the Chinese Language Teachers Association
JCS	Journal of Croatian Studies
JCSR	Journal of Canadian Studies/Revue d'Études Canadiennes
JCSt	Journal of Caribbean Studies
JEGP	Journal of English and Germanic Philology
JES	Journal of European Studies
JEthS	Journal of Ethnic Studies
JFCS	Journal of Feminist Cultural Studies
JGE	Journal of General Education
JHD	Journal of the Hellenic Diaspora
JHI	Journal of History of Ideas
JIAS	Journal of Inter-American Studies
JIL	Journal of Irish Literature
JIWE	Journal of Indian Writing in English

JJS	Journal of Japanese Studies		*L&P*	Literature and Psychology
JLSTL	Journal of Literary Studies		*LAAW*	Lotus: Afro-Asian Writing
JMAF	Journal of Modern African Studies		*LALR*	Latin American Literary Review
JNALA	Journal of the New African Literature and the Arts			Landfall: A New Zealand Quarterly
JNT	Journal of Narrative Technique		*Lang&S*	Language and Style
JNZL	Journal of New Zealand Literature		*LangF*	Language Forum
JOL	Journal of Oriental Literature		*LangQ*	USF Language Quarterly
JPalS	Journal of Palestinian Studies		*LARR*	Latin America Research Review
JPC	Journal of Popular Culture		*LATR*	Latin American Theatre Review
JPrag	Journal of Pragmatics		*LBR*	Luso-Brazilian Review
JRS	Journal of Russian Studies		*LCUT*	Library Chronicle of the University of Texas
JSoAL	Journal of South Asian Literature		*LE&W*	Literature East and West
JSS	Journal of Semitic Studies		*LHY*	Literary Half-Yearly
JSSB	Journal of the Siam Society		*LitG*	Literary Griot
JSSE	Journal of the Short Story in English		*LitR*	Literary Review
JSSTC	Journal of Spanish Studies: Twentieth Century			Lituanus: Baltic States Quarterly of Arts & Sciences
JTamS	Journal of Tamil Studies		*LJ*	Library Journal
JUkGS	Journal of Ukrainian Graduate Studies		*LJGG*	Literaturwissenschaftliches Jahrbuch im Auftrage der Görres-Gesellschaft
JUkS	Journal of Ukrainian Studies			
JWIL	Journal of West Indian Literature		*LM*	London Magazine
KanQ	Kansas Quarterly		*LOS*	Literary Onomastics Studies
KFLQ	Kentucky Foreign Language Quarterly		*LPer*	Literature in Performance: A Journal of Literary and Performing Art
KFQ	Keystone Folklore			
	Kiabàrà: Journal of the Humanities		*LQ*	Literary Quarterly
KR	Kenyon Review		*LuK*	Literatur und Kritik
KRQ	Romance Quarterly (formerly Kentucky Romance Quarterly)		*LWU*	Literatur in Wissenschaft und Unterricht
			MAL	Modern Austrian Literature

MAPS	Memoirs of the American Philosophical Society		*MLS*	Modern Language Studies
MarkhamR	Markham Review		*MMisc*	Midwestern Miscellany
MAWAR	MAWA Review		*MN*	Monumenta Nipponica
MBL	Modern Black Literature		*ModA*	Modern Age
MCL	Modern Chinese Literature			Monatshefte: Für Deutschen Unterricht, Deutsche Sprache und Literatur
MD	Modern Drama			Mosaic: A Journal for the Interdisciplinary Study of Literature
MEF	Middle Eastern Forum		*MP*	Modern Philology: A Journal Devoted to Research in Medieval and Modern Literature
MEJ	Middle East Journal			
MelbSS	Melbourne Slavonic & East European Studies (formerly Melbourne Slavonic Studies)		*MPS*	Modern Poetry Studies
	Merkur: Deutsche Zeitschrift für europäisches Denken		*MQ*	Midwest Quarterly: A Journal of Contemporary Thought
MES	Middle Eastern Studies		*MQR*	Michigan Quarterly Review
MFS	Modern Fiction Studies		*MR*	Massachusetts Review: A Quarterly of Literature, the Arts and Public Affairs
MGS	Michigan Germanic Studies		*MRRM*	Monographic Review/Revista Monográfica
MHL	Modern Hebrew Literature		*MSFO*	Mémoires de la Société Finno-Ougrienne
MHRev	Malahat Review		*MSpr*	Moderna Språk
MichA	Michigan Academician: Papers of the Michigan Academy of Science, Arts, and Letters		*MuK*	Maske und Kothurn
MinnR	Minnesota Review		*MV*	Minority Voices: An Interdisciplinary Journal of Literature and the Arts
MissQ	Mississippi Quarterly		*MW*	Muslim World
ML	Modern Languages		*NAR*	North American Review
MLF	Modern Language Forum		*NConL*	Notes on Contemporary Literature
MLJ	Modern Language Journal		*NDEJ*	Notre Dame English Journal
MLN	Modern Language Notes		*NDH*	Neue Deutsche Hefte
MLQ	Modern Language Quarterly		*NDL*	Neue Deutsche Literatur
MLR	Modern Language Review			Neohelicon: Acta Comparationis Litterarum Universarum

Neophil	Neophilologus		*NTQ*	New Theatre Quarterly
NEQ	New England Quarterly		*NWR*	Northwest Review
NER	New England Review and Bread Loaf Quarterly		*NYHT*	New York Herald Tribune
NewA	New African		*NYHTBR*	New York Herald Tribune Books Review
NewC	New Criterion		*NYLF*	New York Literary Forum
NewL	New Letters: A Magazine of Fine Writing		*NYRB*	New York Review of Books
NewR	New Republic		*NYT*	New York Times
NewS	New Scholar		*NYTBR*	New York Times Book Review
NFS	Nottingham French Studies		*NYTMag*	New York Times Magazine
NGC	New German Critique: An Interdisciplinary Journal of German Studies		*NZSJ*	New Zealand Slavonic Journal
			O&C	Œuvres & Critiques
NGS	New German Studies			Obsidian II: Black Literature in Review
NHQ	New Hungarian Quarterly		*ÖGL*	Österreich in Geschichte und Literatur
NL	Nouvelles Littéraires		*OJES*	Osmania Journal of English Studies
NLH	New Literary History: A Journal of Theory and Interpretation		*OL*	Orbis Litterarum
			OLR	Oxford Literary Review
NLitsR	New Literatures Review		OnsE	One Erfdeel: Algemeen-Nederlands Tweemaandelijks Cultureel Tijdschrift
NMAL	Notes on Modern American Literature			
NME	New Middle East		*OntarioR*	Ontario Review
NMQ	New Mexico Quarterly		*OSP*	Oxford Slavonic Papers
NorS	Northern Studies		*P&R*	Philosophy and Rhetoric
NorthwestR	Northwest Review		*PA*	Présence Africaine
	Novel: A Forum on Fiction		*PAJ*	Pan-African Journal
NR	New Republic		*PakR*	Pakistan Review
NRF	Nouvelle Revue Française			Paragraph: The Journal of the Modern Critical Theory Group
NRs	Neue Rundschau			Parnassus: Poetry in Review
NS	New Statesman		*PCL*	Perspectives on Contemporary Literature

PCLS	Proceedings of the Comparative Literature Symposium
PCP	Pacific Coast Philology
PEGS	Publications of the English Goethe Society
PFr	Présence Francophone: Revue internationale de langue et de littérature
	Plaza: Revista de Literatura
PLL	Papers on Language and Literature
	Ploughshares
	Plural: Revista Cultural de Excelsior
	PMLA: Publications of the Modern Language Association of America
PoetryR	Poetry Review
PolP	Polish Perspectives
PolR	Polish Review
POMPA	Publications of the Mississippi Philological Association
PoT	Poetics Today
PPNCFL	Proceedings of the Pacific Northwest Conference on Foreign Languages
PQ	Philological Quarterly
PQM	Pacific Quarterly (Moana)
PR	Partisan Review
PRev	Poetry Review
	Prismal/Cabral: Revista de Literatura Hispánica/Caderno Afro-Brasileiro Asiático Lusitano
PRL	Puerto Rican Literature
PrS	Prairie Schooner
PSA	Papeles de Son Armandans
PSM	Philippine Studies

PSMLAB	Pennsylvania State Modern Language Association Bulletin
PStud	Portuguese Studies
QI	Quaderni d'Italianistica
QIA	Quaderni Ibero-Americani
QL	La Quinzaine Littéraire
QQ	Queen's Quarterly
QRFS	Quarterly Review of Film Studies
QRL	Quarterly Review of Literature
	Quimera: Revista de Literatura
RaJAH	Rackham Journal of the Arts and Humanities
RAL	Research in Africa Literatures
RALS	Resources for American Literary Study
RCB	Revista de Cultura Brasileña
RCEH	Revista Canadiense de Estudios Hispánicos
RCF	Review of Contemporary Fiction
RChL	Revista Chilena de Literatura
RCL	Revue de Littérature Comparée
RCLL	Revista de Crítica Literaria Latinoamericana
RC-R	Revista Chicano-Riqueña
RCSCSPL	Russian, Croatian and Serbian, Czech and Slovak, Polish Literature
REH	Revista de Estadios Hispánicos
RELC	RELC Journal
	Renascence: Essays on Value in Literature
	Renditions: A Chinese-English Translation Magazine
RevB	Revista Bilingüe

RevI	Revista/Review Interamericana		*RRWC*	Renaissance and Renascences in Western Literature
	Review: Latin American Literature and Arts		*RS*	Research Studies
RG	Revue Générale		*RSI*	Revista Storica Italiani
RH	Revue Hebdomaire		*RUO*	Revue de l'Université d'Ottawa
RHL	Revue d'Histoire Littéraire de la France		*RUS*	Rice University Studies
RHLQCF	Revue d'Histoire Littéraire du Québec et du Canada Français		*RusL*	Russian Literature
			RusR	Russian Review
RHM	Revista Hispánica Moderna		*SAB*	South Atlantic Bulletin
RI	Revista Iberoamericana		*SAD*	Studies in American Drama
RIB	Revista Interamericana de Bibliografía/ Inter-American Review of Bibliography		*SAF*	Studies in American Fiction
			SAIL	Studies in American Indian Literature
RLA	Romance Language Annual		*SAJL*	Studies in American Jewish Literature
RLC	Revue de Littérature Comparée		*SAQ*	South Atlantic Quarterly
RLJ	Russian Language Journal		*SatR*	Saturday Review
RLI	Rassegna della Letteratura Italiana		*SBL*	Studies in Black Literature
RLMC	Rivista di Letterature Moderne e Comparate		*SBR*	Swedish Book Review
RLT	Russian Literature Triquarterly		*Scan*	Scandinavica
RLV	Revue des Langues Vivantes		*ScanR*	Scandinavian Review
RMS	Renaissance & Modern Studies		*SCB*	South Central Bulletin
RNL	Review of National Literatures		*SchM*	Schweizer Monatshefte
RO	Revista de Occidente		*SCL*	Studies in Canadian Literature
ROMM	Revue de l'Occident Musulman et de la Méditerranée		*ScotIR*	Scottish International Review
			ScotR	Scottish Review
RomN	Romance Notes		*SCR*	South Carolina Review
RoR	Romanian Review		*SDR*	South Dakota Review
RPh	Romance Philology		*SEACS*	South East Asian Cultural Studies
RR	Romanic Review		*SEEA*	Slavic and East European Arts

SEEJ	Slavic and East European Journal		*SSF*	Studies in Short Fiction
SEER	Slavonic and East European Review		*SSl*	Scando-Slavica
SFC	Science Fiction Chronicle		*SSL*	Studies in Scottish Literature
SFR	Stanford French Review		*SSLit*	Soviet Studies in Literature
SHEH	Stanford Honors Essays in the Humanities		*SSMLN*	Society for the Study of Midwestern Literature Newsletter
SHR	Southern Humanities Review		*SSR*	Scottish Slavonic Review
Siglo	Siglo XX/20th Century		*StBL*	Studies in Black Literature
	Signs: Journal of Women in Culture and Society		*StIsl*	Studia Islamica
SlavonicR	Slavonic Review		*StTCL*	Studies in Twentieth Century Literature
SlavR	Slavic Review			Studies: An Irish Quarterly Review
SLitI	Studies in the Literary Imagination			SubStance: A Review of Theory and Literary Criticism
SLJ	Southern Literary Journal		*SuF*	Sinn und Form
	Slovo: Časopis Staroslavenskog Zavoda u Zagrebu		*Sur*	Revista Sur
SlovLit	Slovenská Literatúra: Revue Pre Literárnu Vedu		*SUS*	Susquehanna University Studies
SlovS	Slovene Studies		*SWR*	Southwest Review
SNNTS	Studies in the Novel		*SXX*	Secolul XX
SoQ	Southern Quarterly			Symposium: A Quarterly Journal in Modern Foreign Literatures
SoR	Southern Review (Baton Rouge, LA)		*T&K*	Text & Kontext
SoRA	Southern Review (Adelaide, Australia)		*TA*	Theatre Annual
	Southerly: A Review of Australian Literature		*TAH*	The American Hispanist
SovL	Soviet Literature		*TamR*	Tamarack Review
SPFA	Bulletin de la Société des Professeurs Français en Amérique		*TC*	Twentieth Century
SPHQ	Swedish Pioneer Historical Quarterly		*TCL*	Twentieth Century Literature
SR	Sewanee Review		*TCrit*	Texto Crítico
SS	Scandinavian Studies		*TDR*	Tulane Drama Review/The Drama Review
			TheatreQ	Theatre Quarterly

	Theoria: A Journal of Studies in the Arts, Humanities and Social Sciences
TJ	Theatre Journal
TkR	Tamkang Review
TLS	[London] Times Literary Supplement
TM	Temps Modernes
TQ	Texas Quarterly
Transatlantic	Transatlantic Review
TRev	Translation Review
TriQ	TriQuarterly
TSAR	Toronto South Asian Review
TSLL	Texas Studies in Literature and Language
TSWL	Tulsa Studies in Women's Literature
TuK	Text + Kritik: Zeitschrift für Literatur
TWQ	Third World Quarterly
TxSE	Texas Studies in English
UDQ	Denver Quarterly
UDR	University of Dayton Review
UES	Unisa English Studies
UHSL	University of Hartford Studies in Literature
UkrR	Ukrainian Review: A Quarterly Magazine Devoted to the Study of the Ukraine
UQ	Ukrainian Quarterly: Journal of East European and Asian Affairs
UR	University Review
UTQ	University of Toronto Quarterly
UWR	University of Windsor Review (Windsor, Ontario)
V&I	Voix et Images: Littérature Québécoise

VLang	Visible Language
VQR	Virginia Quarterly Review
W&L	Women & Literature
WAJML	West African Journal of Modern Languages
WAL	Western American Literature
WascanaR	Wascana Review
WB	Weimarer Beiträge
WCR	West Coast Review
	Westerly: A Quarterly Review
WHR	Western Humanities Review
WI	Die Welt dea Islams
WIRS	Western Illinois Regional Studies
WLT	World Literature Today
WLWE	World Literature Written in English
WR	Western Review
WS	Women's Studies: An Interdisciplinary Journal
WSCL	Wisconsin Studies in Contemporary Literature
WSJ	Wiener Slavistisches Jahrbuch
WSl	Die Welt der Slaven
WSlA	Wiener Slawistischer Almanach
WVUPP	West Virginia University Philological Papers
WZ	Wort in de Zeit
WZUG	Wissenschaftliche Zeitschrift der Ernst Moritz Arndt-Universität Greifswald
YCC	Yearbook of Comparative Criticism

YCGL	Yearbook of Comparative and General Literature	*Y/T*	Yale/Thestre
YES	Yearbook of English Studies	*ZAA*	Zeitschrift für Anglistik und Amerikanistik
YFS	Yale French Studies	*ZS*	Zeitschrift für Slawistik
YItS	Yale Italian Studies	*ZSP*	Zeitschrift für Slavische Philologie
YR	Yale Review		

ACKNOWLEDGMENTS

For permission to reproduce the illustrations in this edition of the *Encyclopedia of World Literature in the 20th Century,* the publisher is indebted to the following:

Abe, Kōbō, photograph by Jerry Bauer. © Jerry Bauer. Reproduced by permission.—Achebe, Chinua, photograph. AP/Wide World Photos. Reproduced by permission.—Adams, Henry S., photograph. AP/Wide World Photos. Reproduced by permission.—Adorno, Theodore W., photograph. Archive Photos, Inc. Reproduced by permission.—Agee, James, photograph. The Library of Congress.—Akhmatova, Anna Andreevna, photograph. The Library of Congress.—Albee, Edward, photograph. The Library of Congress.—Alegría, Fernando, photograph. Arte Publico Press Archives, University of Houston. Reproduced by permission.—Aleixandre, Vicente, photograph. AP/Wide World Photos. Reproduced by permission.—Algren, Nelson, photograph. The Library of Congress.—Allende, Isabel, photograph. AP/Wide World Photos. Reproduced by permission.—Amado, Jorge, photograph. AP/Wide World Photos. Reproduced by permission.—Amichai, Yehuda, photograph by John Reeves. Reproduced by permission.—Amis, Kingsley, photograph. AP/Wide World Photos. Reproduced by permission.—Anderson, Sherwood, photograph. Archive Photos, Inc. Reproduced by permission.—Angelou, Maya, photograph. AP/Wide World Photos. Reproduced by permission.—Anouilh, Jean, photograph. AP/Wide World Photos. Reproduced by permission.—Aragon, Louis, photograph. The Library of Congress.—Ashbery, John, photograph. AP/Wide World Photos. Reproduced by permission.—Atwood, Margaret, photograph. The Library of Congress.—Auchincloss, Louis, photograph by Jerry Bauer. © Jerry Bauer. Reproduced by permission.—Auden, W. H., photograph. Corbis-Bettmann. Reproduced by permission.—Audiberti, Jacques, photograph. AP/Wide World Photos. Reproduced by permission.—Azuela, Mariano, photograph. The Library of Congress.—Baraka, Imamu Amiri (LeRoi Jones), photograph. Corbis-Bettmann. Reproduced by permission.—Barnes, Djuna, photograph. UPI/Corbis-Bettman. Reproduced by permission.—Baroja, Pìo, photograph. AP/Wide World Photos. Reproduced by permission.—Barrie, Sir James M., photograph. AP/Wide World Photos. Reproduced by permission.—Barth, John, photograph. AP/Wide World Photos. Reproduced by permission.—Barthelme, Donald, photograph by Jerry Bauer. © Jerry Bauer. Reproduced by permission.—Bates, H. E., photograph. Mark Gerson Photography. Reproduced by permission.—Beattie, Anne, photograph by Jerry Bauer. © Jerry Bauer. Reproduced by permission.—Beckett, Samuel, photograph. Archive Photos, Inc. Reproduced by permission.—Behan, Brendan, photograph. AP/Wide World Photos. Reproduced by permission.—Bellow, Saul, photograph. Archive Photos, Inc. Reproduced by permission.—Benét, Stephen Vincent, photograph by Pirie MacDonald. The Library of Congress.—Bergson, Henri, photograph. The Library of Congress.—Berryman, John, photograph. AP/Wide World Photos. Reproduced by permission.—Betjeman, Sir John, photograph. Archive Photos, Inc. Reproduced by permission.—Bialik, Hayyim N., photograph. The Library of Congress.—Bierce, Ambrose, photograph. Corbis-Bettmann. Reproduced by permission.—Bishop, Elizabeth, photograph. AP/Wide World Photos. Reproduced by permission.—Blaise, Marie Claire, photograph by John Reeves. Reproduced by permission.—Blasco Ibáñez, Vicente, photograph. AP/Wide World Photos. Reproduced by permission.—Bloom, Harold, photograph by Jerry Bauer. © Jerry Bauer. Reproduced by permission.—Böll, Heinrich, photograph. Archive Photos, Inc. Reproduced by permission.—Borges, Jorge Luis, photograph. The Library of Congress.—Bowen, Elizabeth, photograph. The Library of Congress.—Breton, André, photograph. Archive Photos, Inc./AFP. Reproduced by permission.—Brookner, Anita, photograph by Jerry Bauer. © Jerry Bauer. Reproduced by permission.—Brooks, Gwendolyn, photograph. The Library of Congress.—Brutus, Dennis, photograph. AP/Wide World Photos. Reproduced by permission.—Buber, Martin, photograph. The Library of Congress.—Bullins, Ed, photograph by Marva Rae. Helen Merrill Ltd. Reproduced by permission of the photographer.—Bunting, Basil, photograph by Thomas Victor. Copyright © 1986 by Thomas Victor. All rights reserved. Reproduced by permission of the Estate of Thomas Victor.—Burgess, Anthony, photograph. AP/Wide World Photos. Reproduced by permission.—Burke, Kenneth, photograph. The Library of Congress.—Burroughs, William S., photograph. AP/Wide World Photos. Reproduced by permission.—Caldwell, Erskine, photograph. The Library of Congress.—Čapek, Karel, photograph. AP/Wide World Photos. Reproduced by permission.—Capote, Truman, photograph. The Library of Congress.—Cardenal, Ernesto, photograph by Lou Dematteis. Reuters/Corbis-Bettmann. Reproduced by permission.—Carpentier, Alejo, photograph. Archive Photos, Inc. Reproduced by permission.—Carver, Raymond, photograph. Archive Photos, Inc. Reproduced by permission.—Cather, Willa, photograph by Carl Van Vechten. The Library of Congress.—Cela, Camilio José, photograph by Jerry Bauer. © Jerry Bauer. Reproduced by permission.—Celine, Louis F., photograph. Archive Photos, Inc. Reproduced by permission.—Chandler, Raymond, photograph. The Library of Congress.—Cheever, John, photograph. The Library of Congress.—Chekov, Anton, photograph. International Portrait

Gallery/Library of Congress.—Chesterton, G. K., photograph. Archive Photos, Inc. Reproduced by permission.—Claudel, Paul, photograph. The Library of Congress.—Cocteau, Jean, photograph. AP/Wide World Photos. Reproduced by permission.—Cortázar, Julio, photograph. AP/Wide World Photos. Reproduced by permission.—Coward, Sir Noel (Peirce), photograph. AP/Wide World Photos, Inc. Reproduced by permission.—Crane, Hart, photograph by Walker Evans. The Library of Congress.—cummings, e. e., photograph. The Library of Congress.—Day Lewis, Cecil, photograph. Archive Photos, Inc. Reproduced by permission.—de Beauvoir, Simone, photograph. AP/Wide World Photos. Reproduced by permission.—de la Mare, Walter, photograph. The Library of Congress.—Derrida, Jacques, photograph. Archive Photos, Inc. Reproduced by permission.—Dickey, James, photograph. AP/Wide World Photos. Reproduced by permission.—Didion, Joan, photograph by Jerry Bauer. © Jerry Bauer. Reproduced by permission.—Doctorow, E. L., photograph by Horst Tappe. Archive Photos, Inc. Reproduced by permission.—Doolittle, Hilda, photograph. The Library of Congress.—Dos Passos, John, photograph. The Library of Congress.—Drabble, Margaret, photograph. AP/Wide World Photos. Reproduced by permission.—Dreiser, Theodore, photograph by Pirie MacDonald. The Library of Congress.—DuBois, W. E. B., photograph. The Library of Congress.—Ehrenburg, Ilya Grigoryevich, photograph. The Library of Congress.—Eliot, T. S., photograph. The Library of Congress.—Ellison, Ralph, photograph. AP/Wide World Photos. Reproduced by permission.—Elytis, Odysseus, photograph. AP/Wide World Photos. Reproduced by permission.—Farrell, James T., photograph. The Library of Congress.—Faulkner, William, photograph by Carl Van Vechten. The Library of Congress.—Fitzgerald, F. Scott, photograph by Carl Van Vechten. The Library of Congress.—Fo, Dario, photograph. © Jerry Bauer. Reproduced by permission.—Forster, E. M., photograph. Archive Photos, Inc. Reproduced by permission.—France, Anatole, photograph. The Library of Congress.—Freire, Romulo Gallegos, photograph. The Library of Congress.—Freud, Sigmund, photograph. The Library of Congress.—Frost, Robert, photograph. The Library of Congress.—Fuentes, Carlos, photograph. AP/Wide World Photos. Reproduced by permission.—Furphy, Joseph, photograph. The Library of Congress.—Gaines, Ernest, photograph. AP/Wide World Photos. Reproduced with permission.—Gaitán Durán, Jorge, photograph. The Library of Congress.—García Lorca, Federico, photograph. Archive Photos/Popperfoto. Reproduced by permission.—García Márquez, Gabriel, 1982, photograph. AP/Wide World Photos. Reproduced by permission.—Gass, William, photograph by Miriam Berkley. © Miriam Berkley. Reproduced by permission.—Genet, Jean, photograph. Archive Photos, Inc. Reproduced by permission.—Gibran, Kahlil, photograph. UPI/Corbis-Bettman. Reproduced by permission.—Gide, André, photograph. UPI/Corbis-Bettman. Reproduced by permission.—Glissant, Edouard, photograph. AP/Wide World Photos. Reproduced by permission.—Golding, William, photograph by Caroline Forbes. The Library of Congress.—Gordimer, Nadine, photograph. AP/Wide World Photos. Reproduced by permission.—Gordon, Caroline, photograph. The Library of Congress.—Gorky, Maxim, photograph. The Library of Congress.—Grass, Günter, photograph by Fred Stein. The Library of Congress.—Graves, Robert, photograph. AP/Wide World Photos, Inc. Reproduced by permission.—Greene, Graham, photograph. AP/Wide World Photos, Inc. Reproduced by permission.—Hammett, Samuel D., photograph. The Library of Congress.—Hamsun, Knut, photograph. The Library of Congress.—Handke, Peter, photograph by Jerry Bauer. © Jerry Bauer. Reproduced by permission.—Hansberry, Lorraine V., photograph. The Library of Congress.—Hardy, Thomas, photograph. Archive Photos, Inc. Reproduced by permission.—Hauptmann, Gerhart, photograph. The Library of Congress.—Head, Bessie, photograph. Reproduced by the kind permission of the Estate of Bessie Head.—Hellman, Lillian, photograph. AP/Wide World Photos. Reproduced by permission.—Hemingway, Ernest, photograph. Archive Photos, Inc. Reproduced by permission.—Housman, A. E., photograph. Archive Photos, Inc. Reproduced by permission.—Hughes, James Langston, photograph by Carl Van Vechten. The Library of Congress.—Hughes, Ted, photograph by Mark Gerson. Mark Gerson Photography. Reproduced by permission.—Hurston, Zora Neale, photograph. AP/Wide World Photos. Reproduced by permission.—Inge, William R., photograph. The Library of Congress.—Ionesco, Eugéne, photograph. The Library of Congress.—Irving, John, photograph. AP/Wide World Photos. Reproduced by permission.—Isherwood, Christopher, photograph. Archive Photos, Inc. Reproduced by permission.—James, Henry, photograph. The Library of Congress.—Jarry, Alfred, drawing by F. A. Cazalz, 1897, photograph. Corbis-Bettmann. Reproduced by permission.—Jeffers, Robinson, photograph. The Library of Congress.—Jiménez, Juan Ramón, photograph. AP/Wide World Photos. Reproduced by permission.—Johonson, James Weldon, photograph. The Library of Congress.—Jones, James, photograph. Corbis-Bettmann. Reproduced by permission.—Joyce, James (Ulysses), photograph. The Library of Congress.—Jung, Carl, photograph. The Library of Congress.—Jünger, Ernst, photograph. Archive Photos/Camera Press. Reproduced by permission.—Kafka, Franz, photograph. AP/Wide World Photos. Reproduced by permission.—Kawabata Yasunari, photograph. AP/Wide World Photos. Reproduced by permission.—Kerouac, Jack, photograph. Archive Photos. Reproduced by permission.—Killens, John O., photograph by Carl Van Vechten. The Library of Congress.—Kristeva, Julia, photograph by Jerry Bauer. © Jerry Bauer. Reproduced by permission.—Kumin, Maxine, photograph. AP/Wide World Photos. Reproduced by permission.—Kundera, Milan, photograph. Archive Photos.

Reproduced by permission.—Lagerkvist, Pär F., photograph. The Library of Congress.—Lawrence, D(avid) H(erbert), photograph. AP/Wide World Photos. Reproduced by permission.—Lessing, Doris, photograph by Jerry Bauer. © Jerry Bauer. Reproduced by permission.—Levi, Carlos, photograph. Archive Photos, Inc. Reproduced by permission.—Levi, Primo, photograph. The Library of Congress.—Lewis, Sinclair, photograph. The Library of Congress.—Lindsay, Vachel, photograph. Corbis-Bettmann. Reproduced by permission.—London, Jack, photograph. The Library of Congress.—Lowell, Amy, photograph. UPI/Corbis-Bettman. Reproduced by permission.—Lowell, Robert, photograph. The Library of Congress.—Lukács, György, photograph. Hulton-Deutsch/Corbis-Bettmann. Reproduced by permission.—Macleish, Archibald, photograph. The Library of Congress.—MacLennan, Hugh, photograph. AP/Wide World Photos. Reproduced by permission.—Maeterlinck, Maurice, photograph. The Library of Congress.—Mailer, Norman, photograph by Carl Van Vechten. The Library of Congress.—Malamud, Bernard, photograph. The Library of Congress.—Mamet, David, photograph by Brigitte Lacombe. Grove/Atlantic, Inc. Reproduced by permission.—Mann, Luiz Heinrich, photograph. The Library of Congress.—Mann, Thomas, photograph. The Library of Congress.—Mansfield, Katherine, photograph. Corbis-Bettmann. Reproduced by permission.—Marcel, Gabriel, photograph. Archive Photos, Inc. Reproduced by permission.—Marquand, John, photograph. Archive Photos, Inc. Reproduced by permission.—Masefield, John, photograph. The Library of Congress.—Maugham, W. Somerset, photograph by Carl Van Vechten. The Library of Congress.—Mauriac, François, photograph. The Library of Congress.—McCarthy, Mary, photograph. The Library of Congress.—McCullers, Carson, photograph. AP/Wide World Photos. Reproduced by permission.—McKay, Claude, photograph. The Library of Congress.—Mencken, Henry Louis, photograph. The Library of Congress.—Merrill, James, photograph. AP/Wide World Photos. Reproduced by permission.—Millay, Edna St. Vincent, photograph. The Library of Congress.—Miller, Arthur, photograph. Archive Photos, Inc. Reproduced by permission.—Miller, Henry, photograph. The Library of Congress.—Milosz, Czeslaw, photograph by Jerry Bauer. © Jerry Bauer. Reproduced by permission.—Mishima, Yukio, photograph. AP/Wide World Photos. Reproduced by permission.—Mistral, Gabriela, photograph. The Library of Congress.—Momaday, N. Scott, photograph. AP/Wide World Photos. Reproduced by permission.—Moore, Marianne, photograph. The Library of Congress.—Moravia, Alberto, photograph. The Library of Congress.—Morrison, Toni, photograph. AP/Wide World Photos. Reproduced by permission.—Mukherjee, Bharati, photograph. AP/Wide World Photos. Reproduced by permission.—Nabokov, Vladimir, photograph. AP/Wide World Photos. Reproduced by permission.—Naipaul, V. S., photograph. AP/Wide World Photos. Reproduced by permission.—Narayan, R. K., photograph. The Library of Congress.—Nemerov, Howard, photograph by Margaret Nemerov. Reproduced with permission.—Neruda, Pablo, photograph by Jerry Bauer. © Jerry Bauer. Reproduced by permission.—Nin, Anaïs, photograph. The Library of Congress.—O'Casey, Sean, photograph. The Library of Congress.—O'Connor, Flannery, photograph. Corbis-Bettmann. Reproduced by permission.—O'Hara, Frank, photograph. AP/Wide World Photos. Reproduced by permission.—O'Hara, John, photograph. The Library of Congress.—O'Neill, Eugene G., photograph. The Library of Congress.—Oates, Joyce Carol, photograph. UPI/Corbis-Bettmann. Reproduced by permission.—Odets, Clifford, photograph. AP/Wide World Photos, Inc. Reproduced by permission.—Ōe Kenzaburō, photograph. Reuters/Kyodo/Archive Photos. Reproduced by permission.—Ortega y Gasset, José, photograph. AP/Wide World Photos. Reproduced by permission.—Orwell, George, photograph. AP/Wide World Photos. Reproduced by permission.—Osborne, John, photograph. AP/Wide World Photos. Reproduced by permission.—Ozick, Cynthia, photograph. Corbis-Bettmann. Reproduced by permission.—Parra, Nicanor, photograph by Miriam Berkley. © Miriam Berkley. Reproduced by permission.—Pasolini, Pier Paolo, photograph. AP/Wide World Photos, Inc. Reproduced by permission.—Paton, Alan, photograph. The Library of Congress.—Pavlović, Miodrag, photograph by John Reeves. Reproduced by permission.—Paz, Octavio, photograph. AP/Wide World Photos. Reproduced by permission.—Percy, Walker, photograph by Jerry Bauer. © Jerry Bauer. Reproduced by permission.—Pérez Galdós, Benito, photograph. The Library of Congress.—Perse, Saint John, photograph. AP/Wide World Photos. Reproduced by permission.—Pietri, Dr. Arturo Uslar, photograph. AP/Wide World Photos. Reproduced by permission.—Pinter, Harold, photograph. AP/Wide World Photos. Reproduced by permission.—Pirandello, Luigi, photograph. AP/Wide World Photos. Reproduced by permission.—Plath, Sylvia, photograph. Corbis-Bettmann. Reproduced by permission.—Porter, Katherine Anne, photograph. Archive Photos, Inc. Reproduced by permission.—Pound, Ezra, photograph. The Library of Congress.—Pritchett, V. S., photograph by Jerry Bauer. © Jerry Bauer. Reproduced by permission.—Proust, Marcel, photograph. The Library of Congress.—Puig, Manuel, photograph by Jerry Bauer. © Jerry Bauer. Reproduced by permission.—Purdy, James, photograph. The Library of Congress.—Pynchon, Thomas R., photograph. UPI/Corbis-Bettmann. Reproduced by permission.—Quasimodo, Salvatore, photograph. Corbis-Bettmann. Reproduced by permission.—Remarque, Erich M., photograph. The Library of Congress.—Renault, Mary, photograph. AP/Wide World Photos. Reproduced by permission.—Rexroth, Kenneth, photograph. AP/Wide World Photos. Reproduced by permission.—Rice, Elmer, photograph. AP/Wide World Photos.

Reproduced by permission.—Rich, Adrienne, photograph. AP/Wide World Photos. Reproduced by permission.—Richler, Mordecai, photograph by John Reeves. Reproduced by permission.—Robbe-Grillet, Alain, photograph by Jerry Bauer. © Jerry Bauer. Reproduced by permission.—Robinson, Edwin Arlington, photograph. AP/Wide World Photos. Reproduced by permission.—Roethke,Theodore, photograph by Imogen Cunningham. AP/Wide World Photos, Inc. Reproduced by permission.—Roth, Philip, photograph. Corbis-Bettmann. Reproduced by permission.—Rukeyser, Muriel, photograph. AP/Wide World Photos. Reproduced by permission.—Rulfo, Juan, photograph. AP/Wide World Photos. Reproduced by permission.—Rushdie, Salman, photograph. Archive Photos, Inc. Reproduced by permission.—Russell, George William, photograph. The Library of Congress.—Salinger, J. D., photograph. AP/Wide World Photos, Inc. Reproduced by permission.—Sandburg, Carl, photograph. The Library of Congress.—Santayana, George, photograph. The Library of Congress.—Saroyan, William, photograph. The Library of Congress.—Sarraute, Nathalie, photograph. AP/Wide World Photos. Reproduced by permission.—Sarton, May, photograph. UPI/Corbis-Bettmann. Reproduced by permission.—Sassoon, Siegfried, photograph. The Library of Congress.—Schnitzler, Arthur, photograph. Archive Photos, Inc. Reproduced by permission.—Sexton, Anne, photograph. AP/Wide World Photos. Reproduced by permission.—Shaw, George Bernard, photograph. The Library of Congress.—Shepard, Sam, photograph. Archive Photos, Inc. Reproduced by permission.—Simenon, Georges, photograph. AP/Wide World Photos, Inc. Reproduced by permission.—Sinclair, Upton, photograph. AP/Wide World Photos, Inc. Reproduced by permission.—Singer, Isaac Bashevis, photograph. UPI/Corbis-Bettmann. Reproduced by permission.—Sitwell, Edith, photograph. UPI/Corbis-Bettman. Reproduced by permission.—Škvorecký, Josef, photograph by John Reeves. Reproduced by permission.—Snow, Charles Percy, photograph. Corbis-Bettmann. Reproduced by permission.—Snyder, Gary, photograph. AP/Wide World Photos. Reproduced by permission.—Sontag, Susan, photograph. AP/Wide World Photos. Reproduced by permission.—Soto, Pedro Juan, photograph. Arte Publico Press Archives, University of Houston. Reproduced by permission.—Soyinka, Wole, photograph. Archive Photos/Trappe. Reproduced by permission.—Spark, Muriel, photograph. AP/Wide World Photos. Reproduced by permission.—Stein, Gertrude, photograph by Carl Van Vechten. The Library of Congress.—Steinbeck, John, photograph. Archive Photos, Inc. Reproduced by permission.—Stevens, Wallace, photograph. The Library of Congress.—Strachey, Lytton, photograph by E. O. Hoppe. Corbis-Bettmann. Reproduced by permission.—Strand, Mark, photograph. The Library of Congress.—Szymborska, Wislawa, photograph. AP/Wide World Photos. Reproduced by permission.—Tate, Allen, photograph. UPI/Corbis-Bettman. Reproduced by permission.—Thomas, Dylan, photograph. AP/Wide World Photos. Reproduced by permission.—Thurber, James, photograph. AP/Wide World Photos. Reproduced by permission.—Tolkien, J. R. R., photograph. AP/Wide World Photos. Reproduced by permission.—Tremblay, Michel, photograph by Yves Renaud. Agence Goodwin. Reproduced by permission of the photographer.—Trevor, William, photograph by Kristin Morrison. Mark Gerson Photography. Reproduced by permission.—Tyler, Anne, photograph. AP/Wide World Photos. Reproduced by permission.—Unamuno, Miguel de, photograph. Corbis-Bettmann. Reproduced by permission.—Undset, Sigrid, photograph. AP/Wide World Photos. Reproduced by permission.—Updike, John, photograph. AP/Wide World Photos. Reproduced by permission.—Valéry, Paul, photograph. Archive Photos, Inc. Reproduced by permission.—Vargas Llosa, Mario, photograph. AP/Wide World Photos. Reproduced by permission.—Vidal, Gore, photograph. AP/Wide World Photos. Reproduced by permission.—Villa, José Garcia, photograph. AP/Wide World Photos. Reproduced by permission.—Vonnegut, Kurt, Jr., photograph. Archive Photos/Saga 1991 Frank Capri. Reproduced by permission.—Walcott, Derek, photograph by Jerry Bauer. © Jerry Bauer. Reproduced by permission.—Walker, Alice, photograph. Archive Photos, Inc. Reproduced by permission.—Warren, Robert Penn, photograph. The Library of Congress.—Wassermann, Jakob, photograph. Archive Photos, Inc. Reproduced by permission.—Waugh, Evelyn, photograph. Mark Gerson Photography. Reproduced by permission.—Wedekind, Frank, photograph. Hulton-Deutsch Collection/Corbis-Bettmann. Reproduced by permission.—Weiss, Peter, photograph. AP/Wide World Photos. Reproduced by permission.—Weldon, Fay, photograph. AP/Wide World Photos. Reproduced by permission.—Wells, H. G., photograph. The Library of Congress.—Welty, Eudora, photograph. AP/Wide World Photos. Reproduced by permission.—Wesker, Arnold, photograph. UPI/Corbis-Bettman. Reproduced by permission.—Wharton, Edith, photograph. AP/Wide World Photos. Reproduced by permission.—White, E. B., photograph. AP/Wide World Photos. Reproduced by permission.—White, Patrick, photograph. AP/Wide World Photos. Reproduced by permission.—Wiesel, Elie, photograph by Nancy Rica Schiff. Archive Photos, Inc. Reproduced by permission.—Wilbur, Richard, photograph. AP/Wide World Photos. Reproduced by permission.—Wilder, Thornton, photograph by Carl Van Vechten. The Library of Congress.—Williams, Tennessee, photograph. AP/Wide World Photos. Reproduced by permission.—Wilson, August, photograph. AP/Wide World Photos. Reproduced by permission.—Wodehouse, P. G., photograph. AP/Wide World Photos. Reproduced by permission.—Wolfe, Thomas, photograph by Carl Van Vechten. The Library of Congress.—Wolfe, Tom, photograph. AP/Wide World Photos. Reproduced by permission.—Woolf, Virginia, photograph. AP/Wide World Photos. Reproduced by permission.—Wright, James, photograph by Ted Wright. Reproduced by permission of the Estate of James Wright.—Wright, Richard, photograph by Carl Van Vechten. The Library of Congress.—Yeats, William Butler, photograph. The Library of Congress.—Yourcenar, Marguerite, photograph. AP/Wide World Photos. Reproduced by permission.

INTRODUCTION

This four-volume third edition of the *Encyclopedia of World Literature in the 20th Century* is designed as a comprehensive survey of significant literary activity of international scope and proportion extending from the beginning of the century to the present. The breadth and complexity of this activity demands progressive study, analysis, and evaluation, and the *Encyclopedia* serves as an inclusive and authoritative guide for this purpose. Responsive to the needs of scholarly and general readers alike, the *Encyclopedia* provides in a reference work of singular importance the most extensive treatment of information necessary to the assessment and appreciation of the growth and development of modern world literature.

The twentieth century represents a period of extraordinary literary productivity and proliferation realized within the framework of unprecedented historical transformation and challenge. The decades preceding the publication of the *Encyclopedia* have produced global transition, dominated by the impact of social and political upheaval and the redefinition of national boundaries and identities. We have witnessed events that have altered the shape of the world in which we live and the terms by which we discuss literature. Although the sociopolitical as well as cultural ramifications of these alterations have yet to fully realize themselves and be understood, we have made every effort to incorporate these developments within the context of the *Encyclopedia,* thus enhancing the reader's perception of the relationship between literature and society.

This edition is a collaborative effort to cover, in more than 2,300 article entries in four volumes, the major aspects of world literature in the twentieth century. To this end, nearly all the literatures of the world with claim to a substantial productivity within the century are discussed in survey articles. Likewise, in their relationship to the literature of the century, literary movements of consequence (e.g., expressionism, futurism, surrealism) are covered in separate topical articles, as are movements in ideas (e.g., existentialism, historicism, postmodernism). The core of the *Encyclopedia* consists of separate articles on major and representative writers incorporating salient biographical information and critical analysis of the writer's major themes and works.

Bases of Selection: The selection of individual entries represents extensive assessment and evaluation of critical recognition earned from the international literary community as well as endorsement as figures of substantial literary importance from specialists of representative national literatures. In order to fulfill its purpose as a reference work, the *Encyclopedia* attempts to be as comprehensive as possible within the limitations imposed by the span of the edition. It is also important to maintain the international scope of the *Encyclopedia.* Thus, many authors—American, British, European—who are well known to English-speaking readers do not receive individual entries but are instead treated within the survey articles of national literatures. Many of the authors receiving individual entries are from less familiar literatures who have limited exposure to English-speaking readers, and a significant number to date have not been translated into English or have not generated criticism in English of scholarly merit. For these authors, the *Encyclopedia* serves as the primary source of reference to English-speaking readers.

Omissions: Despite the scope and magnitude of the *Encyclopedia,* it is inevitable that an appreciable number of writers have been omitted. In works of this kind, with claims of a wide coverage, the inclusion of some writers as against others is of course subject to debate. Regrettably, it was not always possible to identify a specialist of sufficient expertise to prepare individual author entries or to compile and research a national literature. As a result, there is unfortunately at times insufficient coverage of writers deserving of inclusion from relatively obscure or isolated literatures.

Entries: Organization and Data—Individual author entries have been arranged into four parts: a headnote containing vital statistics; a body that includes biographical information and a critical assessment of the author's achievement; a section titled *Further Works* containing publications not mentioned in the body of the article; and a final section titled *Bibliography* comprising selective bibliographical material concerning the author and his or her work. A list of periodicals and their abbreviations cited will be found at the front of Volume 1, and an index to the entries will be included at the end of Volume 4. In a very few of the headnotes the statistics are incomplete, owing to the difficulty of obtaining conclusive confirmation from accessible, reliable sources.

Works featured in the body of the article, as well as in the *Further Works* section, carry their full title and, wherever possible, their original year of publication. In the case of authors writing in languages other than English, titles of published English translations are cited in parentheses, along with their original publication dates. Where several translations of a non-English work have been made under the same title in English, only the publication date of the earliest translation is given. With those works that have been translated under more than one English title, we have tried to feature the titles of all such translations. For non-English works that have not been translated into English, original titles will appear followed by the year of publication and the title's literal translation in parentheses.

Cross References and Pseudonyms: Extensive cross-references to other authors, literatures, and movements appear wherever appropriate in the texts of articles. Where a writer with an individual entry is referred to in another entry, at the first mention his or her last name appears in small capital letters. Likewise, where a movement with a separate entry is referred to in another entry, at the first mention the topic appears in small capital letters. The survey articles on national literatures are cross-referenced by language so that the reader will be directed to the appropriate national literature or literatures (e.g., under Bengali Literature will be found "See Bangladeshi Literature and Indian Literature").

Authors known primarily by their *non de plume* will be listed under their pseudonym (e.g., Blixen under *Dinesen,* Gorenko under *Akhmatova,* Hadjiandreas under *Tsirkas*). For the convenience of readers certain of these names have been cross-referenced, but the abiding principle in this regard has been to avoid overelaboration.

Transliterated and Romanized Languages: As an international reference work, the *Encyclopedia* attempts to be as consistent as possible with the transliteration and romanization of non-English names, most notably those in Arabic, Chinese, Japanese, and Russian. In Arabic, prefixes that are part of the surname will be retained when the surname is used for alphabetizing (e.g., 'Abd al-Hamīd ibn Hadūga under *Ibn Hadūga*). In Chinese practice, the family name comes before the given name, which usually has two elements. The family name and the first element of the given name are capitalized, and the given name is hyphenated (e.g., Kao Hsiao-sheng). Chinese names wherever necessary are cross-referenced in the index by their updated romanization (e.g., Gao Xiaosheng. *See* Kao Hsiao-sheng). In Japanese practice, the family name also comes before the given name (e.g., Ōe Kenzaburō rather than Kenzaburō Ōe). While there are many systems for transliterating Russian names, the phonetic method adopted was considered the most appropriate for a general reader, and the most easily recognizable from the viewpoint of common usage (e.g., see *Gorky*, not Gorki, Gorkii, or Gor'kiy).

Quotations: To some entries, primarily authors of international repute, the *Encyclopedia* appends a selection of critical excerpts to further enhance the reader's understanding and perception of the author's productivity and contribution to world literature. The excerpts are cited by author, source, year of publication, and page number(s).

The Contributors: These have been drawn from a wide sphere of literary authorities, both from the United States and abroad, most often based on the recommendation of the advisers in national literatures. The name of the contributor appears at the end of each article in the *Encyclopedia.*

The general editor wishes to express his appreciation, first, to the hundreds of individuals whose contributions have helped to make the *Encyclopedia* a reference work of distinction. He is most indebted to those individuals listed in the board of advisers, whose generosity of time and expertise provided proportion, balance, and consistency in the preparation of the edition. He also expresses his appreciation to Peter M. Gareffa, managing editor of St. James Press, and Laura Berger, senior editor.

Assisting the general editor, Madeline D. Murray was the senior editor and production coordinator of the *Encyclopedia.* Production editors were Sonya Collins, Victoria Eng, and Matthew Miller. Technical assistance was provided by Enercida Guererro, Ana Angelillo, and Harlan Cayetano. Editorial assistance was provided by Carina Garcia, Bonnie MacSaveny, Denise Galang, Sean O'Hanlon, Chriscita Corbin, Rachel Shook, Michelle Gonzalez, Christine Cifra, Anna Degrezia, Francesca Fiore, Rebecca Lawson, Jill Bauer, Lisa Butler, Michelle Cutler, Julie Miele, Anna Gross, Karma Cloud, Nancy Moore, Joseph Weissman, Rose Sung, Jason Berner, and Greta Wagle.

STEVEN R. SERAFIN
HUNTER COLLEGE OF THE CITY UNIVERSITY OF NEW YORK

L

LABRO, Philippe

French novelist, essayist, and journalist, b. 27 Aug. 1936, Montauban

One of the best-known writers and media personalities in modern France, L. has been regarded by American and other international anchorpersons as a respected authority on the mood of the French people and the status of their cultural life. A graduate of the well-known Lycée Janson-de-Sailly in Paris, he attended Washington and Lee University in Lexington, Virginia. where, between ages eighteen and twenty he spent two years gaining fluency in English and studying about American culture and civilization. The immensity of the American nation, in general, and the dramatic landscape of the America West are often referred to in many of his literary works. An avid reader of the classics of American literature, his travels throughout the American continent helped him to confirm the veracity of what he had learned in these texts and also to compare life in the New World with that of his native France.

L. began his career as a reporter for *Europe No. 1* (1957-58). In 1958-59 he served as a reporter for *Marie-France*, and for many years thereafter as a journalist for *France-Soir*, one of the leading Paris dailies. He also wrote articles in *Paris-Match*. Soon he expanded his newspaper undertakings by becoming active in the arena of television and cinema. During the last three decades he produced and/or directed a number of major films, notably *L'héritier* (1973; The Heir), *Le hasard et la violence* (1974; Luck and Violence), *L'alpaqueur* (1976; The Man of the Mountain Pastureland), *La crime* (1983; The Criminal Brigade), and *Ecran noir* (1997; Black Screen). Currently, L. is the chief administrative officer of RTL, France's most popular radio network. Due to his familiarity with the American scene, he is viewed by many of his countrymen as the most reliable commentator of U. S.

But it is in the domain of the novel and in the literary essay that L. will probably earn his most enduring acclaim. His novels, written in an exceptionally translucent style and with much human warmth and intensity of feeling, enjoy immense popularity in French-speaking countries. Without exception his literary works spring directly out of his personal experiences.

In *Le petit garçon* (1990; The Little Boy) L. relates a tale of an adolescent's (presumably his own) pubescent awakening as he finds himself inexplicably drawn to the charms of the opposite sex. At the same time in the background looms the Nazi occupation of France, both in the northern zone and in the so-called "free" zone. L. draws a sharp contrast between those who chose to collaborate with the German invaders and those who tried, at great risk, to save their Jewish compatriots from certain death in the concentration camps. Through the eyes of a child the reader sees a disquieting view of the world of adults.

Quinze ans (1992; Fifteen Years Old) a sequel to *Le petit garçon*, projects a dual image of the world: first, we see the ongoing emotional development of the same young man as he experiences his first real love affair; second, we have a study of the prevailing values and attitudes of adolescent males who grow up during the 1950s in the posh sixteenth arrondissement of Paris. On his first date with a somewhat older girl at a recital of the renowned pianist Wilhelm Kempf, the fifteen-year-old protagonist discovers an irresistible attraction exploding within his soul for his female companion, but, because of his inexperience and awkwardness he fails to translate his passionate feelings for her into physical consummation. But this failure does not stop the young hero from boasting about his imagined conquest with his male friends in his lycée. Once the narrator has discovered what it feels like to be really in love, he decides that in the next stage of his life he will travel—to America, the subject of subsequent novels.

In *Un début à Paris* (1994; A Beginning in Paris) the same youthful hero, having returned from his two-year adventure in the new world, embarks upon a new career as a journalist in the newspaper world of Paris. L. recaptures here the excitement of life in a capital city electrified by the Nouvelle Vague of French cinema, also by the polemics dividing the French over the events taking place in Algerian war of independence, by the stimulating life in the cafés of the Saint-Germain-des-Prés district of Paris, and by the dynamics of life led by reporters who work in the offices of *France-Soir*. The book ends just as the narrator begins his mandatory period of military service in North Africa.

La traversée (1996; Dark Tunnel, White Light), possibly L.'s finest work to date, contains two powerful personal tales about the author's "crossings" through the intersections of life, each of which is at once an autonomous and an interconnected event. At the beginning, he recounts his exhilarating sense of victory as he climbs the peak of a lofty summit in the Colorado Rockies. He feels as if he has placed himself upon the top of the world. Then in the second part of the book, by far the longest and most significant portion, he recounts, in minute detail his struggle with death in a Paris hospital where he finds himself in a desperate battle for survival: a virulent microbe has invaded his respiratory system. Thanks to the miracles of modern medicine—especially the life-support system that traverses his body—and thanks also to the impressive human support he received from his immediate family and from the highly skilled and devoted nursing staff in the intensive care unit, he witnesses not only survival but also total rebirth: Now he realizes that life is worth living because one can be spiritually nourished by the people who love us and who cherish the very breath we breathe.

L. writes in a style that is remarkable for its fluidity and clarity, this in the age of complexity and intricate experimentation practiced by the Nouveaux Romanciers, the playwrights of the THEATER OF THE ABSURD, and by the deconstructionist critics in modern France. But L.'s clarity is, in some ways, deceptive. Beneath it one encounters multifarious layers of bewilderment and dilemmas. Each of L.'s novels seems to serve as a prelude for the subsequent one. Although each novel may be read as an autonomous entity, together these works form a flowing revelation of both L.'s own evolution as a human being, and also as a literary artist. If these books expose the innermost personal feelings and experiences of the author himself, they also delineate the larger, more cosmic currents of the world within which he has developed as a man and as a creative artist.

FURTHER WORKS: *Aspects de la presse britannique* (1952); *Aspects du cinéma américain* (1953); *Un Américain peu tranquille* (1960); *Quatre fois D* (1966); *Des feux mal éteints* (1967); *Ce n'est gu'un début* (1969); *Les barricades de mai* (1969); *Tout peut arriver* (1969); *Sans mobile apparent* (1971) *L'etudiant étranger* (1986)

BIBLIOGRAPHY: Nourrissier, F., "À la gloire de l'adolescence," *Le Magazine littéraire*, 16 Jan. 1993: 93; Payot, M., "A quel écrivain appartient cet univers?," *Lire*, 208 (Jan. 1993): 114-17; Cusin, P., "Labro et son double," *Le Fiagro littéraire*, 9 Sept. 1994: 4; Kolbert, J., "L., P.: *Quinze ans*," *FR*, 68 (February 1995): 571-72; Brown, J. L., "P. L.," *WLT*, 69 (Summer 1995): 553-554; Hamon, L. E., "Six écrivains français parlent de l'Amérique: Extraits des entretiens," *France-Amérique*, 26 Oct.-1 Nov. 1996: 16-17

—JACK KOLBERT

LACAN, Jacques

French psychoanalyst and psychoanalytic theorist, b. 13 Apr. 1901, Paris; d. 9 Sept. 1981, Paris

L. studied medicine and psychiatry at the Faculté de Médecine de Paris, and in 1932 he published his doctoral thesis *De la psychose paranoïaque dans ses rapports avec la personnalité* (rev. ed., 1975, *De la psychose paranoïaque dans ses rapports avec la personnalité suivi de Premiers écrits sur la paranoïa*; the paranoiac psychosis and its relations to the personality and early writings on paranoia). In this same year, L. became clinical director of the Faculté de Médecine de Paris. In 1934 he became a member of the Société Psychanalytique de Paris, and two years later he served as staff psychiatrist at various Paris mental hospitals. During this time, he became interested in SURREALISM, founded by André BRETON, in its approach to the unconscious, and he contributed to the surrealist publication *Le Minotaure*.

From the early 1950s to his death at age eighty, L. initiated and dominated the renewal of popular interest in psychoanalysis in France. L. developed Sigmund FREUD's psychological theory to incorporate the foundations of structural linguistics. Although his theories were considered controversial, L. was generally acknowledged as one of the most influential figures in the intellectual circles of Paris. He is often associated with the structuralist movement, which included, among others, Louis Althusser (1918–1990), an interpreter of MARX, Claude LÉVI-STRAUSS, Jacques DERRIDA, and Michel FOUCAULT. These theorists and practitioners of structural analysis recognized the Swiss linguist Ferdinand de Saussure (1857–1913) as the pioneer who served as the inspiration of their methods.

In 1936, at the XIVth Psychoanalysis International Congress in Marienbad, L. made an astonishing debut into the psychoanalytic world with a speech entitled "Le stade du miroir" ("The Mirror-Phase," 1937). In this address, L. demonstrated the primordial role of "identification" in early childhood, acknowledging several phases that infants go through to acquire their own identity. What L. called the "mirror stage" is defined as the various reactions of a child placed in front of a mirror. At first a child considers the reflection a reality, exterior to himself, which he tries to catch; then, realizing there is no one behind the mirror, he stops looking for an Other; and finally he recognizes that other person as himself. In other words, from a fragmented vision of his own body he comes to perceive its global form through an exterior image. A child's primary identification with the mirror reflection, which L. qualified

as *imaginaire*, works as a source of all the child's further identifications. This fundamental discovery for psychoanalysis was further explored in another speech: "'Le stade du miroir' comme formateur de la fonction du 'je'" (1949; "The Mirror As Formative of the Function of the I," 1968), delivered in 1949 at the XVIth Congress in Zurich.

In 1953 internal conflict within the organization drove him to split from the Société de Paris and to organize the Société Française de Psychanalyse. Then, in 1964, his exclusion from the International Society led L. to create the École Freudienne de Paris. L.'s new school was designed to train future analysts. Its unorthodox methods challenged the traditional aspects of psychoanalytic training and practice. In 1980, L. dissolved his École Freudienne de Paris and formed l'École de la Cause Freudienne.

From 1951 to 1963 L. was a lecturer in psychoanalysis at St. Ann's hospital in Paris, and in 1963 he began lecturing at the École Normale Supérieure and later at the École Pratique des Hautes Études. For about twenty years, L. gave a biweekly seminar attended by a generation of French intellectuals, accounting for his great influence and reputation in France. His wide-ranging knowledge enabled him to broaden psychoanalysis to include linguistics, rhetoric, anthropology, and philosophy, as well as various scientific fields such as mathematics, solid geometry, and optics.

Throughout his career, L. advocated a return to Freud. His essential theoretical contribution to psychoanalysis consists of two main principles: *L'inconscient est le discours de l'Autre* (the unconscious is the discourse of the Other) and *l'inconscient est structuré comme un langage* (the unconscious is structured as a language). When developing his theory, L. made use of the linguistics theories of Saussure and Roman Jakobson (1896–1982) as well as the anthropological studies of Lévi-Strauss. L. was further influenced by philosophers such as Heidegger and Hegel.

In his 1953 paper "Fonction et champ de la parole et du langage" (1956; "Function and Field of Speech and Language," 1968) psychoanalytic theory is approached in terms of structuralist methodology. In this paper, L. expressed one of his major themes, "the unconscious is structured as a language" and went on to say that the instrument of psychoanalysis is speech. For that purpose, L. used the Saussurean concept of the "sign" as defined by its two components, the signifier and the signified. In order to demonstrate the mechanism by which repression works (as described by Freud), L. gave supremacy to the signifier. Faithful to Freud's institutions that the laws of dream are equivalent to those of poetry, L. attempted to interpret the poetics of the unconscious via fundamental figures of speech such as metaphor and metonymy. Metaphor occurs when interpretation results from a substitution of signifiers, whereas metonymy is ensued by the presence of the former signifier in the *chaîne signifiante* but is shadowed by the presence of a new signifier. Hence, the role of the psychoanalyst is to help the patient to repossess the lost sign and understand the process by which it has been repressed.

L.'s masterpiece *Écrits* (1966; rev. ed., *Écrits, I-II*, 2 vols., 1970; writings) is a collection of his most significant theoretical writings dealing with both psychoanalysis and language. Beginning in 1973, transcripts of L.'s lectures appeared in a multivolume series entitled *Le seminaire de J. L.*, four of which had been published in English: *Livre XI: Les quatre concepts fondamentaux de la psychanalyse, 1964* (1973; *The Four Fundamental Concepts of Psycho-Analysis*, 1978); *Livre I: Les écrits techniques de Freud, 1953–1954* (1975; *Freud's Papers on Technique, 1953–1954*, 1988); *Livre II: Le moi dans la théorie de Freud et dans la technique de la psychanalyse, 1954–1955* (1978; *The Ego in Freud's Theory and in the Technique of Psychoanalysis, 1954–1955,* 1988); and *Livre VII: L'éthique de la psychanalyse 1959–1960* (1986; *The Ethics of Psychoanalysis 1959–1960,* 1992).

With the publication of *Écrits,* L. gained international reputation as a psychoanalytical theorist. His influence was strongly felt in other disciplines such as literary criticism both in the U.S. and Latin America. In France Lacan's theories were in part incorporated into FEMINIST CRITICISM in the 1970s and 1980s, notably in regard to the works of Luce Irigaray (b. 1939), Julia KRISTEVA, and Hélène CIXOUS to explain the root of sexual identity. Other authors whose work has been influenced by L. include the French novelist Claude Ollier and the Italian novelist Paolo Volpini as well as the Polish novelist and dramatist Witold GOMBROWICZ.

Speech being the object as well as the instrument of his practice, L. himself developed a unique style in his work. He was considered a creative writer, for he was gifted with the capacity of auto criticism, which enabled him to observe the ways his analytical principles were manifested through his style. L. willingly blended various styles. He could be as abstract in his writing as Stéphane Mallarmé (1842–1898) had been, and his speech might also be rich and replete with witticisms.

An eminent and controversial figure in the psychoanalytic and intellectual worlds, L. dealt with and in orality, yet his legacy, as it must be, is in print. His *Écrits* are the conscious voice of the unconscious, the tip of the iceberg that refers us to hidden depths. In its effect on literature, poetry, and criticism, Lacanian interpretation has had a lasting effect on language itself.

FURTHER WORKS: *Télévision* (1974; *Television,* 1990); *Le séminaire: Livre XX: Encore, 1972–1973* (1975); *Le sinthome* (1976); *L., J. Travaux et interventions* (1977); *L. in italia, 1953–1978 = L. en Italie, 1953–1978* (1978; bilingual ed.); *Le séminaire: Livre III: Les psychoses, 1955–1956* (1981); *L'acte psychanalytique: Séminaire 1967–68* (1982); *Les complexes familiaux dans la formation de l'individu: essai d' analyse d'une function en psychologie* (1984); *Almanach de la dissolution* (1986); *Joyce avec L.* (1987); *Le séminaire: Livre VIII: Le transfert, 1960–1961* (1991); *Le séminaire: Livre XVII: L'envers de la psychanalyse* (1991). FURTHER WORKS IN ENGLISH: *The Language of the Self: The Function of Language in Psychoanalysis* (1968; rev. ed., *Speech and Language in Psychoanalysis,* 1981); *Écrits: A Selection* (1977)

BIBLIOGRAPHY: Palmier, J.-M, *L.* (1970); Hesnard, A., *De Freud à L.* (2nd ed., 1971); Fages, J.-B, *Comprendre J. L.* (1971); Lacoue-Labarthe, P. and Nancy, J.-L., *Le titre de la lettre* (1973); Georgin, R., *L.* (1977); Clément, C., *Vies et légendes de J. L.* (1981); Mitchell, J. and Rose, J., eds., *Feminine Sexuality: J. L. and the école freudienne* (1982); Georgin, R., *De Lévi-Strauss à L.* (1983); Dor, J., *Bibliographic des travaux de J. L.* (1984); Silhol, R., *Le texte du désir* (1984); Dor, J., *Introduction à la lecture de L.* (1985); Raglan-Sullivan, E., *J. L. and the Philosophy of Psychoanalysis* (1986); MacCannell, J. F., *Figuring L.: Criticism and the Cultural Unconscious* (1986); Andrès, M., *L. et la question du métalangage* (1987); Felman, S., *J.L. and the Adventure of Insight: Psychoanalysis in Contemporary Culture* (1987); Bowie, M., *Freud, Proust, and L.: Theory As Fiction* (1987); Muller, J. P. and Richardson, W. J., *The Purloined Poe: L., Derrida, and Psychoanalytic Reading* (1988); Grosz, E., *J. L.: A Feminist Introduction* (1990); Hogan, P. C. and Pandit, L., eds., *Criticism and L.: Essays and Dialogue on Language, Structure, and the Unconscious* (1990); Bowie, M., *L.* (1991); Smith, J. H., *Arguing with L.: Ego Psychology and Language* (1991)

—GENEVIÈVE TROUSSEREAU

LAFORET, Carmen

Spanish novelist and short-story writer, b. 6 Sept. 1921, Barcelona

After growing up in the Canary Islands, L. returned to the Spanish mainland and studied law at the universities of Barcelona and Madrid. She published her first novel, *Nada* (1945; *Nada,* 1958), when she was twenty-four. Since 1963 she has been writing mostly travel pieces, articles, and short stories.

With *Nada,* for which she won the first Nadal Prize, L. brought energy and direction to the post-civil-war novel. This highly successful and widely acclaimed work spoke eloquently for a generation wounded by war and despair. In *Nada* L. portrays the experiences of Andrea, an eighteen-year-old girl, not unlike herself, who has just arrived from the Canary Islands to study at the University of Barcelona. She stays at her grandmother's house, a microcosm of Spain, where she is surrounded by aunts and uncles, inadequate and troubled human beings, who, out of weakness and pain, inexorably destroy each other. At the end of the novel Andrea frees herself from this lugubrious environment by going off with a friend to study in Madrid.

In L.'s next novel, *La isla y los demonios* (1952; the island and the devils), she again portrays the coming to maturity of a young girl and her struggles for liberation. Contrary to what might be expected, L.'s first novel is actually a sequel to the second, for *La isla y los demonios* takes place in the Canary Islands, a few years *before* the time frame of *Nada,* and Marta, its protagonist, is two years younger than Andrea.

L.'s third novel, *La nueva mujer* (1955; the new woman), presents Paulina—a kindred spirit of Andrea and Marta—who struggles with the problems of freeing herself from an impinging society. Toward the end of the novel Paulina has a religious experience, just as L. herself did, and suddenly regains her Catholic faith.

La insolación (1963; sunstroke), the first novel of a planned trilogy that so far has not been completed, also deals with the coming of age of an adolescent. L. recounts three summers in the life of Martín, a sensitive and alienated teenager. At the end of the novel Martín is forced to leave his family and make his own way in the world.

Nada has already secured a place of honor for L. in the history of the post-civil-war novel. It is to be regretted that she has never gone beyond the scope of this book. Nevertheless, she is a fine novelist who has had great success with her character studies and her delicate portrayal of adolescence.

FURTHER WORKS: *La muerta* (1952); *La llamada* (1954); *Gran Canaria* (1961); *Paralelo 35* (1967); *La niña y otros relatos* (1970)

BIBLIOGRAPHY: Coster, C. C., "C. L.: A Tentative Evaluation," *Hispania,* 40 (1957): 187–91; Mulvihill, E. R., and R. G.Sánchez, Introduction to *Nada* (1958): ix—xv; Ullman, P. L., "The Structure of C. L.'s Novels," in Friedman, M., ed., *The Vision Obscured* (1970): 201–19; Adaro, G. Illanes, *La novelística de C. L.* (1971); Saffar, R. El, "Structural and Thematic Tactics of Suppression in

C. L.'s *Nada*," *Symposium*, 28 (1974): 119–29; Thomas, M., "Symbolic Portals in L.'s *Nada*," *ANP*, 3 (1978): 57–74; Johnson, R., *C. L.* (1981); Pérez Firmat, G., "The Dilemna of Artistic Vocation," in Brown, J., ed., *Women Writers of Contemporary Spain: Exiles in the Homeland* (1991): 26-41; Ennis, G., *Nada* (1993); Dolgins Casado, S., "Structure and Meaning in C. L.'s *Nada: A Case of Self-Censorship*," in Vidal Tibbits, M., ed., *Studies in Honor of Gilberto Paolini* (1996): 352-58

—MARSHALL J. SCHNEIDER

LAFOURCADE, Enrique

Chilean novelist and editor, b. 14 Oct. 1927, Santiago

L.'s early education was in Santiago, but in the 1950s he spent considerable time abroad: in France, where he studied art history at the Sorbonne (1954), in Italy, as the recipient of an Italian government honor fellowship (1955), and in Spain, where he served as cultural attaché in Madrid (1959–1962). During the 1960s and early 1970s, he taught at numerous American universities (Iowa, Utah, UCLA, Illinois, New Mexico, California, Columbia), returning to some schools two or three different times. Since 1972 he has remained principally in Santiago, editing the literary supplement of the Santiago newspaper *El Mercurio*, working periodically in television, and writing essays for newspapers, magazines, and books.

Due to his caustic attacks on public figures and his liberal lifestyle, L. has had a stormy public and private life. However, he retains the devotion of numerous Chilean novelists and short-story writers who make up the Chilean Generation of 1950. While some critics insist that L. "invented" the Generation of 1950, there are indications that it was a true "generation" of postwar authors who chose to reject the established *Criollista* writers and their regional-sociological approach to Chilean problems. In truth, L. organized a short-story contest and thereby gave his young colleagues the chances to express themselves. Then he published in 1954 the results of that contest in the *Antología del nuevo cuento chileno* (anthology of the new Chilean short story)—which gave many of those young writers their beginnings, including José DONOSO and Jorge EDWARDS, who are, together with L., three of Chile's leading novelists.

While numerous Chileans fled their country to avoid the conflicts with governments of the extreme left and right during the 1970s and 1980s, L. remained in Santiago, taking up battle with leaders and their decisions. Irrespective of the people in power, L. has openly voiced his opposition to many of the actions with which he disagreed. His outspokenness on social decadence is an outgrowth of L.'s nihilistic philosophy, which emerges in his fiction as his view of life. He cherishes his individuality and states that he has been a literary activist, "studying, investigating, observing, writing, commenting on, defending, attacking, exposing, traveling, giving classes, living, and . . . creating."

One of the predominant elements in L.'s prose fiction has been an utter pessimistic tone, which unites character and theme in a tight band. L.'s disillusionment with modern society, together with his nihilistic (Nietzschean) weltanschauung produces characters who, as antiheroes, become increasingly alienated, materialistic, sadistic, dehumanized, and aware of their own absurd state of existence.

Because of his narrative structures and his use of existentialist key words and titles, such as *Asedio* (1956; blockade), early critics saw L. as an existentialist, but he personally expressed in 1985 that he was incensed by any suggestion that he had ever been an existentialist or was ever influenced by that school of thought. Yet he is proud to be considered a nihilist. He feels that the world should not be portrayed in literature as simply Manichaean, as a dichotomy of good and evil.

L.'s later fiction does not appear to have varied far from his earlier molds: revolutionaries who terrorize and then go running home to mother or father when things work out badly; individuals who create their own religion, saying it is of God, but condemn or manipulate followers rather than saving them; obscenely conniving bureaucrats who usurp human freedoms; or obsessive manipulators who abuse others in the pursuit of materialistic gains as they lower themselves into the quagmire of the dilemma of modern life. Some of his novels, such as *Variaciones sobre el tema de Nastasia Filippovna y el príncipe Mishkin* (1975; variations on the theme of Nastasis Filippovna and Prince Mishkin) and *Adiós al Führer* (1982; farewell to the führer), are full of symbolism and are sometimes difficult to follow. But in *Novela de Navidad* (1965; Christmas novel), *Terroristas* (1976; terrorists), and numerous others it is easy to get caught up in the plot and his parody of the characters' causes. Often L. takes a sensationalist theme and thrusts his characters into a marasmic world that destroys them.

L. was one of the early writers to attack Latin American dictators—a theme that became popular in the "boom" period of Spanish American literature of 1965–1980—and he did it with his highly acclaimed *Fiesta del Rey Acab* (1959; *King Ahab's Feast*, 1963).

His most successful novel has been *Palomita blanca* (1971; little white dove), Chile's greatest best-seller. Chilean newspaper critics passed it off as a popular work influenced by Erich Segal's (b. 1937) *Love Story* (1970), but it is a spontaneous synthesis of the themes that L. had been elaborating in previous novels, which often lacked the human warmth, anguish, and spontaneity that *Palomita blanca* conveys. Published in several languages, it has never appeared in English. *Palomita blanca* depicts the popular optimism and the language changes occurring in Chile during the important historical period of the Allende Campaign for the presidency in 1970.

L. has worked with many innovations, but not always successfully. He has won numerous important Chilean literary prizes for his novels, such as the Municipal Prize of Santiago in 1959 for *Fiesta del Rey Acab*, the converted Gabriela Mistral Prize in 1961 for *El príncipe y las ovejas* (1961; the prince and the sheep), and in 1982 the Marí Luisa Bombal Prize in Literature. His total output of twenty novels and ten other books, most with numerous editions, has been impressive and effective, but the public is often polarized into readers who admire him and those who hate him.

FURTHER WORKS: *El libro de Kareen* (1950); *Pena de muerte* (1952); *Para subir al cielo* (1959); *Invención a dos voces* (1963); *Fábulas de L.* (1963); *Pronombres personales* (1967); *Frecuencia modulada* (1968); *En el fondo* (1973); *Salvador Allende* (1973); *Inventario I* (1975); *Buddha y los chocolates envenenados* (1977); *Nadie es la patria* (1980); *Animales literarios de Chile* (1982); *El escriba sentado* (1982); *El gran taimado* (1984); *Los hijos del arco iris* (1985); *Carlitos Gardel, mejor que nunca* (1985); *Humo hacia el sur* (1987); *Pepita de oro* (1990); *Hoy está solo mi corazón* (1990); *Mano bendita* (1993); *Crónicas de combate* (1996); *El veraneo y otros horrores* (1996); *Cuando los políticos eran inteligentes* (1996); *Cristianas viejas y limpias* (1997)

BIBLIOGRAPHY: Fleak, K., "Promotion of the Chilean Short Story", *LangQ*, 24 (1986): 31–32, 37; Godoy, E. Gallardo, *La generación del 50 en Chile: Historia de un movimiento literario* (1991)

—LON PEARSON

LAGERKVIST, Pär

Swedish novelist, short-story writer, poet, and dramatist, b. 23 May 1891, Växjö; d. 11 July 1974, Stockholm

L. grew up in Växjö, the provincial capital of Småland, in southern Sweden. His parents' pietistically inclined religious faith lent an atmosphere of security and calm restraint to his childhood home, evocatively described in the autobiographical novel *Gäst hos verkligheten* (1925; *Guest of Reality*, 1936). As an adolescent L. distanced himself intellectually from the fundamentally conservative milieu by turning to Darwin's theory and to political radicalism. Nevertheless, the conversion was an uneasy one, as L.'s lifelong preoccupation with metaphysical and religious questions attests.

Pär Lagerkvist

After studying briefly at the University of Uppsala, L. made his literary debut in 1912 (the year of STRINDBERG's death) with *Människor* (human beings), but he first attracted attention the following year with the theoretical essay "Ordkonst och bildkonst" (verbal art and pictorial art). During a visit to Paris he had become aware of new trends in the visual arts. Proposing that modern literature be revitalized through architecture-like construction analogous to CUBISM, he rejected naturalism in favor of the elevation and simplicity found in Greek tragedy, the Old Testament, and the Icelandic sagas. L.'s search for a new style is apparent in the works that followed: the prose poems of *Motiv* (1913; motifs), the short stories in *Järn och människor* (1914; iron and human beings), and most importantly, the poetry collection *Ångest* (1916; anguish). Often cited as the beginning of poetic MODERNISM in Sweden, this volume, in which startling imagery and a disjointed, EXPRESSIONISTIC style communicate the despair and pain brought on by World War I, was his true breakthrough.

L.'s early dramas also demonstrate his interest in aesthetic revolt and renewal. The essay "Modern teater: Synpunkter och angrepp" ("Modern Theatre: Points of View and Attack," 1966), published in the volume titled *Teater* (1918; theater), provides the theoretical program. Ibsen's "five long acts of words, words, words" are characterized as ineffective; L. expresses admiration for medieval drama, the plays of Shakespeare, and the work of Strindberg after the mental crisis of his "Inferno" period, all of which he views as approaching the essence of human experience through allegory and symbolism. The three short expressionistic plays *Den svåra stunden I—III* (1918; *The Difficult Hour I—III*, 1966), published in *Teater*, reveal that L. had learned a great deal from Strindberg's dramatic technique in, for instance, *A Dream Play*.

Den svåra stunden explores different individual responses to death; another play, *Himlens hemlighet* (1919; *The Secret of Heaven*, 1966), poses the question, What is the meaning of life? L. implies that while this issue preoccupies human beings, it is a matter of total indifference to the Almighty. Similarly, in the story "Det eviga leendet" (1920; "The Eternal Smile," 1954), a group of people ask God what His purpose was in creating them. The answer is that He had not meant anything in particular, but merely had done His best. L.'s pessimism is tempered by a note of affirmation: although there may be no intrinsic meaning in life, human beings are capable of creating their own meaning within a circumscribed sphere; they may find happiness through a sense of duty and solidarity with others.

A gradual movement toward the resigned acceptance of humankind's lot, combined with a more straightforward, realistic style, is apparent in the collection *Onda sagor* (1924; evil tales) and in *Gäst hos verkligheten*, which provides a key to L.'s personal and philosophical development. The drama *Han som fick leva om sitt liv* (1928; *The Man Who Lived His Life Over*, 1971) is a step toward a more realistic stage art.

L.'s works of the 1930s and 1940s are dominated by his preoccupation with the nature of evil and the crisis of humanism when confronted with the fascist threat. The theme is established in the poetry collection *Vid lägereld* (1932; at the campfire). The novella *Bödeln* (1933; *The Hangman*, 1936), which L. made into a play, also called *Bödeln* (1934; *The Hangman*, 1966), investigates the universality of evil by comparing and contrasting medieval with modern times. Two other dramas, *Mannen utan själ* (1936; *The Man without a Soul*, 1944) and *Seger i mörkret* (1939; victory

5

in darkness) express faith in the moral superiority and eventual triumph of the humanist tradition, despite the temporary victory of the powers of darkness.

Dvärgen (1944; *The Dwarf*, 1945), L.'s first nonautobiographical novel, considered by many to be his finest work, evinces a direct thematic connection with *Bödeln*. While skillfully creating a pastiche of Renaissance Italy, L. establishes his title character as a universal symbol of the evil forces within every human being—forces that may lie dormant for a while but are certain eventually to surface.

Although L. came late to the novel, that genre dominates his later production. He continued to put questions about the nature of religious faith and the meaning of life. In *Barabbas* (1950; *Barabbas*, 1951), which L. dramatized under the same title in 1953, the protagonist can neither live in accordance with the message of Jesus—"Love one another"—nor reject it out of hand. He wants to believe, but is unable to make the necessary leap of faith. This ambivalence is conveyed through antithetical symbols and images: light and darkness, life and death, love and hate. Similar paradoxes are central to the poetry collection *Aftonland* (1953; *Evening Land*, 1975), in which God is an unseen spear thrower striking down the narrator from behind, and to interlinking novels *Sibyllan* (1956; *The Sibyl*, 1958), *Ahasverus död* (1960; *The Death of Ahasuerus*, 1962), *Pilgrim på havet* (1962; *Pilgrim at Sea*, 1964), and *Det heliga landet* (1964; *The Holy Land*, 1966). The sibyl, chosen as the mouth-piece of Apollo, finds that her encounter with the irrational fills her with terror as well as ecstasy, while Ahasuerus hates the God who has condemned him to wander eternally, only to discover that his very hatred binds him forever to God.

L.'s position in 20th-c. Swedish literature is unusual. His production spans more than half a century and encompasses all major genres and many literary trends. Yet L. has had few imitators and founded no school; his early formalist experiments provided a foundation for later poets to build on, but he remained an isolated individualist. Typical of L.'s reserve is that his only speeches were on the occasion of his election to the Swedish Academy in 1940 and his receiving the Nobel Prize in 1951. L.'s works display a remarkable internal consistency. His prose style is immediately recognizable—simple, unadorned, incorporating forms from the spoken language, and at the same time strangely stylized and impersonal. The tendency toward abstraction in language complements his propensity for timeless themes.

FURTHER WORKS: *Två sagor om livet* (1913); *Sista mänskan* (1917); *Kaos* (1919); *Den lyckliges väg* (1920); *Den osynlige* (1923); *Valda sidor* (1925); *Hjärtats sånger* (1926); *Det besegrade livet* (1927); *Kämpande ande* (1930); *Konungen* (1932; *The King*, 1966); *Skrifter* (3 vols., 1932); *Den knutna näven* (1934); *I den tiden* (1935); *Genius* (1937); *Den befriade människan* (1939); *Sång och strid* (1940); *Dikter* (1941); *Midsommardröm i fattighuset* (1941; *Midsummer Dream in the Workhouse*, 1953); *Hemmet och stjärnan* (1942); *Prosa* (1945); *Dramatik* (1946); *De vises sten* (1947; *The Philosopher's Stone*, 1966); *Låt människan leva* (1949; *Let Man Live*, 1951); *Prosa* (5 vols., 1949); *Dramatik* (3 vols., 1956); *Dikter* (1965); *Prosa* (1966); *Marianne* (1967; *Herod and Mariamne*, 1968). FURTHER WORKS IN ENGLISH: *The Eternal Smile and Other Stories* (1954); *The Marriage Feast and Other Stories* (1955); *Modern Theater: Seven Plays and an Essay* (1966); *The Eternal Smile: Three Stories* (1971)

BIBLIOGRAPHY: Buchman, T. R., "P. L. and the Swedish Theatre," *TDR*, 6, 2 (1961): 60–89; Scobbie, I., *P. L.: An Introduction* (1963); Ryberg, A., *P. L. in Translation: A Bibliography* (1964); Swanson, R., "Evil and Love in L.'s Crucifixion Cycle," *SS*, 38 (1966): 302–17; Linnér, S., ed., special L. issue, supplement to *Scan*, 10, 1 (1971); Spector, R. D., *P. L.* (1973); Sjöberg, L., *P. L.* (1976); Warme, L. G., "P. L." in Jackson, W. J. H., ed., *European Writers: The Twentieth Century* (1990), vol. 10: 1677-1702; Warme, L. G., *A History of Swedish Literature* (1996): 313-20

—ROCHELLE WRIGHT

LAGUERRE, Enrique

Puerto Rican novelist, short-story writer, dramatist, essayist, and poet; b. 3 May 1906, Moca

L., an educator by profession, began his career at age nineteen and became a certified teacher two years later. In 1935 he published the novel *La llamarada* (the blaze), which brought him national and international acclaim. In 1936 he worked as a school administrator and the next year received his B.A. in education from the University of Puerto Rico. From 1937 to 1938 L. taught at Fajardo High School. The next three years he worked as an educational author for the Puerto Rican Department of Public Instruction ("School of the Air" radio series), and in 1941 he obtained his M.A. from the University of Puerto Rico. Between 1943 and 1978 L. wrote eight novels, a play, several short stories, and four books of essays. He taught at the University of Puerto Rico and at several distinguished American universities. He received two honorary doctor's degrees and was named a fellow by the American Association of Teachers of Spanish and Portuguese (1980). In 1967 L. was elected president of the Society of Puerto Rican authors and the next year he became a member of P.E.N.

In *La llamarada* L. presents a conflict between the workers of a sugar mill and the absentee owners. The protagonist, Juan Antonio Borrás, is a recent university graduate whose conscience is split between materialistic interests and the problems of the poor Puerto Rican people (*jíbaros*). In the next novel, *Solar Montoya* (1941; Montoya plantation), the *jíbaros* who attempt to grow coffee face such powerful obstacles as hurricanes, poor management, and high tariffs. Unlike the previous two novels. *El 30 de febrero* (1943; the 30th of February) takes place in an urban locale and a university environment. The plot revolves around a hunchback, Teófilo Sampedro, who must live and compete in a merciless society.

La resaca (1949; the undertow) is L.'s masterpiece and constitutes a departure in theme and technique from his previous works. It covers a period of Puerto Rican history (from 1870 to 1898) in fictional form. To read *La resaca* is to get immersed in the late colonial times of the island and to experience the despotism practiced by the Spanish rulers. An omniscient narrator tells the story.

La ceiba en el tiesto (1956; the ceiba tree in the flower pot) and *El Laberinto* (1959; *The Labyrinth*, 1960) depict the lot of Puerto Ricans living in other parts of the U.S. In *La ceiba en el tiesto* the main protagonist avoids responsibility for his involvement with a political group and seeks refuge in New York City where he leads an anonymous life. *El Laberinto* is even more a New York novel than *La ceiba en el tiesto*.

L.'s recent novels are *Cauce sin río* (1962; river bed without a river), *El fuego y su aire* (1970; fire and its air), and *Los amos benévolos* (1976; *Benevolent Masters*, 1983). *Cauce sin río* is an introspective novel. All the events of the novel are sifted through the protagonist's mind. *El fuego y su aire* continues the introspective vein. It is another novel of the quest for Puerto Rican identity. L. advances his technical experimentation in this work by the frequent use of interior monologues, perspectivism, and daring metaphors. In *Los amos benévolos* L. approaches the practice of MAGIC REALISM, a predominant trend of modern Spanish American fiction. It is an indictment against Puerto Rican nouveaux riches.

As a dramatist L. is credited with only one work, *La resentida* (1960; the resentful woman), a historical play, which was first staged in 1944.

L. is the most significant Puerto Rican novelist of the 20th c. He has thoroughly explored the culture, history, and psychology of his people. While he does not pontificate, his denunciation of Puerto Rica's evils does call for a social commitment: The Puerto Rican reader must seek better alternative for his condition. L. uses both traditional and modern techniques and does link with the Latin American narrative "boom" in his espousal of magical realism and the frequent use of interior monologues. He is both a regional and a universal writer; while unveiling Puerto Rican culture and psychology, he shows a wider vision that readers from other cultures can comprehend and even espouse.

FURTHER WORKS: *Los dedos de la mano* (1951); *Pulso de Puerto Rico, 1952–1954* (1956); *El jíbaro de Puerto Rico: Símbolo y figura* (1968); *La Poesía modernista en Puerto Rico* (1969); *Obras completas* (1974); *Palos de la cultura iberoamericana* (1977); *Proa libre sobre mar gruesa* (1996)

BIBLIOGRAPHY: González, J., "El laberinto," *Asomante*, 16 (1960): 70–76; Gastón, N. Vientos, "La novela de L., *La ceiba en el tiesto*," *Indice Cultural*, 50 (1962): 239–42; González, J., "*Cauce sin río*," *Asomante*, 19 (1963): 63–66; Morfi, A., *E. A. L. y su obra: "La resaca"; cumbre en su arte de novelar* (1964); Meléndez, C., *La generación del treinta: cuento y novela* (1972): 31–36; Zayas Micheli, L. O., *Lo universal en E. A. L.* (1974); Sánchez, O. Casanova, *La crítica social en la obra novelística de E. A. L.* (1975); Beauchamp, J. J., *Imagen del puertorriqueño en la novela* (1976): 71–160; special L. section, *Horizontes*, 38 (1976): 5–16, 27–66; Cabrera, M. García, *L. y sus polos de la cultura iberoamericana* (1978); Irizarri, E., *E. A. L.* (1982); Ortega-Vélez, R. E., *La mujer en la obra de E. A. L.* (1989); Ortega-Vélez, R. E., *La educación como niveladora social a través de la obra de E. A. L.* (1995)

—JORGE RODRÍGUEZ-FLORIDO

LA GUMA, Alex

South African novelist and short-story writer (writing in English), b. 20 Feb. 1925, Cape Town; d. 11 October 1985, Havana, Cuba

After attending secondary school, L. held a variety of jobs before beginning a career as a journalist. His active opposition to the South African government and its policy of apartheid led to periods of imprisonment, house arrest, and in 1966 exile to England, where he now lives.

L.'s writing frequently stems from personal experience as a black man and reflects his deep opposition to the South African regime. Thus, *A Walk in the Night* (1962), set in the slums of Cape Town, pictures the losing struggle to retain a fundamental humanity in the face of racial oppression. *And a Threefold Cord* (1964) is also based on life in the ghetto, while *The Stone Country* (1967) is inspired by L.'s own imprisonment and is dedicated to "the daily 70,351 prisoners in South African gaols in 1964." L.'s early political activism is reflected in *In the Fog of the Season's End* (1972), a novel based on organizing underground opposition to apartheid.

Thus L.'s literary world grimly mirrors the realities of life for nonwhites in South Africa. Crime and brutality inevitably erupt as people keenly aware of their own powerlessness find themselves in intolerable situations. Little room for sentimentality exists in such a world, yet love and even comedy can occasionally and fleetingly blossom. L. handles his settings concretely and vividly, whether a prison, shantytown, white suburbs, or, as in *Time of the Butcherbird* (1979), a new Bantu homeland to which people have been forcefully removed.

Characters in L.'s fiction are inevitably victims of society. People like Michael Adonis, a "coloured" who unjustly loses his job in *A Walk in the Night*, and Charlie Pauls, who in *And a Threefold Cord* attacks a white policeman, move outside the law because the social structure allows them no other choice. For L., this structure can only produce disease and parasitism, whether in the form of a petty criminal living off shanty people, a tough jailbird off other prisoners, or whites off the rest of the country's population. Given the vicious situation they find themselves in, moral action for L.'s characters becomes defensive, passive, and even perverted, rather than assertive and positive, as might be possible in a freer society.

Since L. is concerned with the enormous direct impact that political and social realities have on the life of his country and its people, it has been argued that his characters become artistically subordinated to the depiction of particular situations. Yet L. cannot be validly accused, as some black South African writers might be, of presenting journalistic fact in the guise of creative literature. Rather, L. comes to his subject with freshness and originality. His description of person and place is graphic, his accurate rendition of various dialects invigorating. He masterfully evokes both mood and atmosphere, and even on occasion finds humor in the midst of pathos; these qualities enable him to make some telling points about the human condition. He is considered by many critics to be one of black South Africa's most significant and successful writers.

FURTHER WORKS: *A Walk in the Night, and Other Stories* (1967); *A Soviet Journey* (1978); *Memoirs of Home: The Writings of A. L.* (1991)

BIBLIOGRAPHY: Rabkin, D., "L. and Reality in South Africa," *JCL*, 8 (1973): 54–61; Wanjala, C. L., "The Face of Injustice: A. L.'s Fiction," in Wanjala, C. L., ed., *Standpoints on African Literature* (1973): 305–22; Asein, S., "The Revolutionary Vision in A. L.'s Novels," *LAAW*: 24–25 (1975): 9–21 (also in *Phylon*, 39 (1978): 74–86; Gakwandi, A., *The Novel and Contemporary Experience in Africa* (1977): 8, 21–26; Wade, M., "Art and Morality in A. L.'s *A*

Walk in the Night," in Parker, K., ed., *The South African Novel in English: Essays in Criticism and Society* (1978): 164–91; Scanlon, P. A., "A. L.'s Novels of Protest: The Growth of the Revolutionary," *Okike,* 16 (1979): 85–93; Moore, G., *Twelve African Writers* (1980): 104–20; Abrahams, C. A., *A. L.* (1985)

—DAVID F. BEER

LAHUTI, Abulqasim

Persian and Tajik poet, b. 31 Dec. 1887, Kermanshah, Iran; d. 16 March 1957, Moscow

L. was the son of a minor Sufi (mystical) poet. He went to school in Tehran and participated in the Iranian revolution of 1905–11. After the failure of the revolution, he escaped to Baghdad (1913–15), and after returning to Iran for a while, emigrated to Istanbul (1918–20). In 1921 he led an antigovernment revolt in Tabriz. After its suppression he fled to the Soviet Union. From 1925 to 1931 L. lived in Soviet Tajikistan, where he held high administrative and Party posts. In 1931 he settled in Moscow and in 1934 became one of the secretaries of the Writers Union of the U.S.S.R. His political fortunes began to decline in 1941. From the middle of 1949 the publishing of L.'s works ceased almost completely, to be renewed only in 1954 in order to scotch published rumors in Iran about his alleged defection from Soviet Tajikistan via Afghanistan to Pakistan.

L.'s earliest poems, written at the age of sixteen, were of the Sufi character. In his first revolutionary poems (1907–11) he praised revolution as the real implementation of the spirit of Islam. L.'s main preference during this period was for the classical *ghazal,* a short lyrical or mystical poem, which, however, he filled with political and patriotic content. His finest political *ghazals,* written between 1919 and 1921, formed the main part of his first published book, *La'aliyi lahuti* (1921; divine pearls)—the title is a pun on his name; *lahuti* means "divine."

L.'s almost immediate conversion to communism after his arrival in the U.S.S.R. led his early Soviet poems, such as "Kreml" (1923; the Kremlin), to be suffused with an abstract but sincere exaltation. These poems were written mainly in a classical Persian common to Persians and Tajiks. L.'s poetry of the 1920s and 1930s pictures the Soviet Union in bright and joyous colors, contrasting it with a gloomy non-Soviet world.

During the 1930s L. emerged as one of the main Soviet poet-panegyrists of Stalin, so much so that Stalin once mocked L.'s fawning. Yet although the praise is evidently sincere, the style is dependent on the elaborate Persian classical tradition of panegyrical court poetry.

L.'s main poetic interest in the late 1920s and the 1930s was Tajikistan. The language and style of Tajik poetry at that time were still close to those of classical Persian poetry. In 1940 a special volume of his poems on Tajik topics, *Shi'rhayi tajikistani* (Tajikistani poems), was published; in these he used the Tajik vernacular to a great extent. The most outstanding among them, still regarded as one of the masterpieces of Tajik Soviet poetry, is the epic poem "Taj va bayraq" (1935; crown and banner).

With the outbreak of war with Germany in 1941, L.'s political themes shifted from a contrast of classes—triumphant proletariat

and oppressive capitalists—to patriotic ones, juxtaposing the heroic Soviet people, led by Russians, with the satanic Germans.

The late 1940s and 1950s were years of artistic decline for L. Deeply depressed by Party attacks, barred from publication, impoverished, incurably ill, the poet turned his eyes to his native country, writing nostalgic poems about Iran.

Throughout his creative life L. wrote love poems. Although mainly in the classical Persian tradition, they are spontaneous, natural, full of sincere romantic feeling. Many of them became Tajik folk songs.

L.'s influence on the development of Tajik poetry was enormous. He also had a great impact on leftist poetry in Iran in the 1940s, and although almost forgotten again from the 1950s through the 1970s, he was rediscovered once more after the upheaval at the end of the 1970s and recognized as one of the greatest modern Persian poets.

FURTHER WORKS: *Ruba'iyat* (1924); *Inqilabi surkh* (1926); *Hazar misra'* (1935); *Divan* (1939); *Divani ash'ar* (1942); *Asari muntakhab* (1946); *Surudhayi azadi va sulh* (1954); *Muntakhabi az ash'ar* (1954); *Nidayi zindagi* (1956); *Divan* (1957); *Kulliyat* (6 vols., 1960–1963); *Kulliyat* (1978); *Divan* (1979)

BIBLIOGRAPHY: Ishaque, M., *Modern Persian Poetry* (1943): 146–48; Rahman Munibur, *Post-Revolution Persian Verse* (1955): 42–51; Alavi, B., *Geschichte und Entwicklung der modernen persischen Literatur* (1964): 105–12; Machalski, F., *La littérature de l'Iran contemporain* (1965), Vol. I: 138–43; Bečka, J., in Rypka J., et al., *History of Iranian Literature* (1968): 564–66

—MICHAEL ZAND

LAING, Kojo

(born B. Kodjo Laing) Ghanaian poet and novelist (writing in English), b. 1 July 1964, Kmasi

Aside from the time he spent in attendance at the University of Glasgow in Scotland, L. has spent his entire life in Ghana. After receiving his master's degree in 1968, he worked as an administrator for a number of years in various political capacities, including a year at the seat of Government in the coastal capital of Accra. In 1980 L. was appointed Secretary to the Institute of African Studies at the University of Ghana. Five years later, in an attempt to make more time for his writing and prior to the release of his first novel, *Search Sweet Country* (1986), L. accepted the post of chief executive of St. Anthony's, a private school established by his mother in 1962.

Like many contemporary African poets, L. has combined English with his native language to form a kind of literary pidgin consisting of actual Akan words, Ghanaian English slang, and his own neologisms. The formal effect of this hybridization is to foreground the tonality of the poetry over the direct meaning of the words. It also reinforces the oral foundation of the written tradition as well as the subversive qualities of the postcolonial implementation of the colonizer's language. While L. employs this tone-infused language in all his work, *Woman of the Aeroplanes* (1988), a novel, and *Godhorse* (1989), a collection of poetry, are the best realizations of L.'s overall innovations with language.

Aside from *Godhorse*, *Search Sweet Country* is L.'s best-known work and certainly the most accessible. The vocabulary relies on the same eclectic melange of African, English, and manufactured words, but the novel is driven much more by a sense of story. Its central theme is the political and industrial modernization of Africa, and the ways in which religion—Christianity in particular—and tradition interact. While *Search Sweet Country* is just as surreal as L.'s other work, it is clearly more narrative than his other work.

Woman of the Aeroplanes is perhaps L.'s most avant-garde novel. Language preempts both narrative and character in this novel much in the same way that it does in James JOYCE's *Finnegan's Wake*. Utterance, as a result, is the single unifying principle of the book. L. uses words to create impossible, linguistic realities which bear only the vaguest resemblance to the actual world. One of the characters in this novel throws himself in the garbage can, and a lake becomes jealous of its ducks and refuses to ripple. Nevertheless, despite the surreal quality of the work, L. manages to keep the novel grounded in a tangible world full of odor, color, and texture.

In *Godhorse* the physical world takes on a particular sense of wonder and significance through mundane physical objects made magical with language. The poems in this collection are clearly informed by the NÉGRITUDE poets, though they finally function in a mode of their own. Full of imagistic and situational juxtapositions, these poems reinscribe the commonplace with a sense of animation and life. One of L.'s particularly interesting stylistic innovations is his modulation—or transliteration—of one image into another. Often this is done with a relatively concise gesture as he does in the poem "Godsdoor": "Girlfriend of the Door says: bird don't aeroplane yourself / for you make the sky move." More than mere anthropomorphism, L.'s poetry imbues simple objects like cars, chairs, and doors with an autonomy and agency of their own.

Major Gentl and the Achimota War (1992) is a novel set in 2020 A.D., which again deals with the problem of the world encroaching on an Africa struggling to maintain ties with traditions; however, in this novel technology and warfare occupy the thematic place of religion and nostalgia. L.'s surrealistic mode seems more at place in this novel than in any of his others, because it mirrors the absurdity and alienation of a technological future.

L. has been hailed by critics as one of the first "modern" writers to come out of Africa, though it seems more appropriate to suggest that he has moved past both MODERNISM and postcolonialism to reach toward a kind of global literature. All of L.'s work is marked both by his wit and his attempts to push the world toward a kind of universalized language. Because of Ghana's cosmopolitan nature, it is common for its people to intermix one language with words from another. The matrix of major and minor languages and neologisms that characterize L.'s work hybridizes two or more languages into a single word. L. believes that linguistic hybridization should be done "universally for the idea is to create one gigantic language."

BIBLIOGRAPHY: Maja-Pearce, A., "Interview with K. L.," *Wasafiri*, 6-7 (Spring-Autumn 1987): 27-29; Dakubu, M. E. K., "The Language of Being in the Poetry of B. K. L.," *Legon*, 5 (1991): 76-92

—TODD PETERSON

LAK LITERATURE
See North Caucasian Literatures

LALIĆ, Mihailo

Yugoslav novelist and short-story writer (writing in Serbian), b. 14 Oct. 1914, Trepča (near Andrijevica), Montenegro; d. 30 December 1992, Herceg Novi, Montenegro

In 1933 L. left his native Montenegro to study law in Belgrade. Before World War II he was imprisoned several times for his revolutionary activities. In 1941 he joined the partisans (anti-Fascist, procommunist guerrillas) in Montenegro, was apprehended by the chetniks (anti-Fascist, promonarchist guerrillas) and deported to a camp in Greece, but he escaped in 1943 and rejoined the partisans. He was the director of the Yugoslav news agency for Montenegro from 1944 to 1946, then held various editorial jobs in Belgrade until his retirement in 1965. He has been a member of Serbian Academy of Sciences and Arts since 1964.

The focal point of L.'s fiction is the struggle between the partisans and chetniks in Italian-occupied Montenegro during World War II. Against this background L. explores the eternal conflict between good and evil and analyzes various aspects of human nature in the face of the extreme conditions brought about by the war. L.'s tendency to equate good with the partisans and evil with the chetniks at times adversely affects the universal character of his poetic message. A distinct characteristic of L.'s writing is his striving for perfection, which prompted him to revise some of his best works after their initial publication.

In his best-known novel, *Lelejska gora* (1957; new version, 1962; *The Wailing Mountain*, 1965), L. explores the horrifying and potentially destructive effects of loneliness and despair on a partisan separated from his unit and pursued by the enemy like a wild animal. The hero, a man of honor and principle, undergoes many trials until he realizes that evil can be defeated only when one confronts it and fights it with its own weapons.

In the novel *Pramen tame* (1970; a patch of darkness), which grew out of a long short story, L. assigned the leading role to a negative hero, Riko Gizdić, a chetnik and a former policeman, a servant of many regimes. Through Riko's story L. traces the development of the chetnik movement in Montenegro and comments on its ideology.

Two later novels, *Ratna sreća* (1973; the luck of war) and *Zatočnici* (1976; champions), are the first two volumes of a planned tetralogy. Both are in the form of the protagonist's memoirs and excerpts from his diary. They span a period of some thirty years, from the Balkan wars (1912) to the early 1940s. Together with the hero, Pejo Grujović, L. ponders the fate of patriotism and the traditional values faced with the ever-growing threats and dilemmas of modern times.

In all his works, L. masterfully integrates descriptions of the rugged but majestic Montenegro countryside and the moods and emotional upheavals of his equally rugged characters. In L.'s view, society is composed of two kinds of human beings: those on the right and those on the wrong side of life. A never-ending struggle between the two antagonistic camps forms the texture of life, in which individual men either "walk tall" or break down, depending on their moral rather than physical strength.

A good stylist, writing in short, often broken sentences that appeal to the contemporary reader, and a master of minute psychological analysis, L. remains today one of the most impressive literary figures in Yugoslavia. One thing is certain: L.'s opus will remain a monumental document of the most inhuman, destructive, and tragic period in recent Yugoslav history, during which men were, in L.'s words, "like wolves to one another."

FURTHER WORKS: *Staze slobode* (1948); *Izvidnica* (1948); *Svadba* (1950); *Izabrane pripovetke* (1950); *Tri dana* (1950); *Prvi snijeg* (1951; rev. and enl. ed., 1977); *Osveta martoloza* (1951); *Usput zapisano* (1952); *Na Tari* (1952); *Zlo proljeće* (1953); *Raskid* (1955); *Tajne Bistrih voda* (1955); *Na mjesečini* (1956); *Hajka* (1960); *Gosti* (1967); *Posljednje brdo* (1967); *Sabrana dela M. L.* (10 vols., 1979)

BIBLIOGRAPHY: Hitrec, J., on *The Wailing Mountain, NYTBR*, 18 Apr. 1965: 20–21; Suhadolc, J., on *The Wailing Mountain, SEEJ*, 11 (1967): 234–35; Mihailovich, V. D., on *Posljednje brdo, BA*, 43 (1969), 132; Pribić, N., on *Lelejska gora, BalSt*, 10 (1969): 208–9; Mikašinović, B., on *Pramen tame, BA*, 45 (1971): 542; Protić, P., on *Ratna sreća, BA*, 49 (1975): 157; Eekman, T., *Thirty Years of Yugoslav Literature (1945–1975)* (1978): 126–32

—BILJANA ŠLJIVIĆ-ŠIMŠIĆ

LAMMING, George

Barbadian novelist, b. 8 June 1927, Carrington Village, Barbada

L. has told an interviewer that from his first novel, *In the Castle of My Skin* (1953), to *Natives of My Person* (1972) he was writing the same book. This statement may not do justice to the variety of his work, but all his novels are about departure and return. The roots of this theme are probably in his boyhood, when a scholarship took him from his working class village to Combermere, a school for middle-class Barbadian boys. The education he received there cut him off from the life of the village, but because of his feelings of guilt that he had betrayed his origins, he has never been at home in the new world that the school opened up to him. His books suggest that from his early teens L. has been an outsider, an exile.

This personal deracination is translated in his fiction into a metaphor for the predicament of West Indians in general, and indeed for the anomie of modern man. In his first novel L. describes the gradual alienation of a growing boy from his community. It ends with his escape into a wider world. In *The Emigrants* (1954) this escape is frustrated when a group of West Indian exiles fail to make the foreignness of London fill the void left by their separation from their native islands.

L.'s four most recent novels are about abortive attempts at returning to the islands. The problems created in the West Indies by the history of slavery and colonialism are fused with the theme of return, for L. describes not only physical journeys back, as in *Of Age and Innocence* (1958) and *Natives of My Person*, but also psychological attempts at plunging into the past to discover the forces that separate modern West Indians from themselves. Novels such as *Of Age and Innocence* and *Season of Adventure* (1960) point out the futility of trying to forge ahead politically without first taking a "backward glance" at one's beginnings.

To emphasize the complexity of his themes and the painfulness of his psychological probing, L. often uses elaborately convoluted plots, the intricacies and coincidences of which are sometimes distracting. Nevertheless, the passion of his commitment to the West Indian peasant and to all working-class people, and the vehemence of his hatred of the exploitation of these people are powerfully conveyed by the flexibility and the eloquence of his prose.

FURTHER WORKS: *The Pleasures of Exile* (1960); *Water with Berries* (1971)

BIBLIOGRAPHY: Morris, M., "The Poet as Novelist: The Novels of G. L.," in James, L., ed., *The Islands in Between* (1968): 73–85; Moore, G., *The Chosen Tongue* (1969): 12–17, 37–42, 49–57; Ramchand, K., *The West Indian Novel and Its Background* (1970): 135–49; Thiong'o, Ngugi wa, *Homecoming* (1972): 110–44; Larson, C., *The Novel in the Third World* (1976): 89–107; Petersen, K. H., "Time, Timelessness and the Journey Metaphor in G. L.'s *In the Castle of My Skin* and *Natives of My Person*," in Niven, A., ed., *The Commonwealth Writer Overseas* (1976): 283–88; Griffiths, G., *A Double Exile: African and West Indian Writing between Two Cultures* (1978): 91–96, 100–104, 135–38; Paquet, S. P., *The Novels of G. L.* (1982); Jonas, J., *Anancy in the Great House: Ways of Reading West Indian Fiction* (1990); Joseph, M. P., *Caliban in Exile: The Outsider in Carribean Fiction* (1992)

—ANTHONY BOXILL

LAMPEDUSA, Giuseppe Tomasi di

See Tomasi di Lampedusa, Giuseppe

LANDOLFI, Tommaso

Italian novelist, short-story writer, essayist, translator, and dramatist, b. 9 Aug. 1908, Pico, Frosinone; d. 7 July 1979, Rome

A graduate in Italian language and literature of the University of Florence, L. came into his own as a strikingly mature writer in the 1930s.

Immediately before World War II he was imprisoned for his anti-Fascist beliefs. His imprisonment, however, did not prevent him from writing for *Letteratura* and *Campo di Marte*, two of the most influential journals of modern writing. After his release from prison, he lived in Rome, but he frequently returned to his hometown.

As a critic and as a translator, L. wrote admirable essays on Russian literature and produced excellent translations from Russian and French. As a creative writer he was haunted throughout his career by the "mania for the impossible in literature." He wanted to obtain "from the written word what the word cannot give": the unattainable reality of the "thing."

The collection of short stories *Dialogo dei massimi sistemi* (1937; dialogue of the highest systems), although an early work, already reveals the abundance of themes—mostly polarities—and of interests running through most of L.'s literary production:

cruelty and pity, falsity and truth, death and resurrection, love, sensuality and eroticism, dreams, surrealistic imagery, linguistic parody, and experimentalism. The title story tells of a man who believes he knows the Persian language, but who, instead, invents a new language (false Persian); consequently, he is the only one who can read the work of poetry he has created.

La pietra lunare (1937; the moon stone), considered by most critics L.'s masterpiece, is a romantic, demoniac, magical, and lyrical novel. The enigmatic nature of Gurù, the female protagonist (a soft, tender, and delirious half-human, half-feral being), and the male protagonist's fascination for and repulsion from her, seem to epitomize L.'s contradictory feelings about life.

In *Le due zittelle* (1945; the two spinsters) L. plays lucidly and ironically with the possible resemblances between animal and human psychology. Two spinsters lovingly raise a monkey who at night unleashes itself and goes to the church at a nearby nunnery, where it gorges itself on the sacred hosts and horribly mimics the ritual of the mass. This farcical, humorous story takes a startlingly sinister turn when the half-serious theological discussion on whether the monkey, who has no soul, has sinned, ends with a guilty verdict in an atmosphere reminiscent of witch-hunting.

After 1950 L. moved progressively away from the well-structured story toward more loose and openly autobiographical narratives, as in *Cancroregina* (1950; cancerqueen), *Rien va* (1963; French: nothing goes), and *Racconti impossibili* (1966; impossible tales). In *Cancroregina* a mad scientist, unable to return to earth, remains in orbit and dies in that frightening dimension. Within the paradigm of science fiction, L. reveals his anguished vision of man's existence.

"La muta" (the mute girl), the first tale in *Tre racconti* (1964; three tales), is perhaps the best expression of what L. defined as his "religious, and superstitious, love for and hatred of words." The young mute girl with whom the protagonist falls in love becomes the emblem of unattainable and unbearable purity. The girl's muteness—she is uncontaminated by speech—seems to the protagonist a mark of perfection; thus, he kills her before life can find its ways to corrupt her.

One of the most learned Italian writers of the 20th c., L. was both innovative and traditional in his tastes as well as in his style. His writings bear witness to his knowledge of and love for Dante, the great Russian, French, and German writers of the 19th c., and the new literary experiences of the 20th-c. writers, especially the SURREALISTS.

FURTHER WORKS: *Il mar delle blatte, e altre storie* (1939); *La spada* (1942); *Racconto d'autunno* (1947); *La bière du pecheur* (1953); *Il principe infelice* (1954); *Ombre* (1954); *La raganella d'oro* (1954); *Ottavio di Saint-Vincent* (1958); *Mezzacoda* (1958); *Landolfo IV di Benevento* (1959); *Se non la realtà* (1960); *Racconti* (1961); *In società* (1962); *Scene della vita di Cagliostro* (1963); *Un amore del nostro tempo* (1965); *Des mois* (1967); *Un paniere di chiocciole* (1968); *Faust'67* (1969); *Gogol a Roma* (1971); *Vio-la di morte* (1972); *Del meno* (1978); *An Autumn Story* (1989); *Gogol's Wife and Other Stories*; *Words in Commotion and Other Stories* (1986)

BIBLIOGRAPHY: Brew, C. C., "The 'Caterpillar Nature' of Imaginative Experience: A Reading of T. L.'s 'Wedding Night,'" *MLN*, 89 (1974): 110–15

—MARIOLINA SALVATORI

LANGEVIN, André

Canadian novelist (writing in French), b. 15 July 1927, Montreal, Que.

L. was orphaned at the age of seven and spent five years in an institution, a bitter experience that marked him deeply. After education in a Montreal classical college he joined the newspaper *Le devoir* as messenger boy and quickly rose through the ranks. A journalist and radio producer by profession, he has written a number of novels that by their stark power and originality have singled him out as one of the most accomplished writers of his generation.

His first novel, *Évadé de la nuit* (1951; escaped from the night), strikes the note of incommunicability and despair that is sounded again and again in his fiction. As he grows up, Jean Cherteffe, an abandoned child, seeks to make contact with others, first with an alcoholic poet, then with a young woman. The poet is past help and commits suicide; Micheline dies in childbirth, and Jean takes his own life in the snow.

This apprentice work was followed by *Poussière sur la ville* (1953; *Dust over the City*, 1955), generally considered to be one of the best French-Canadian novels of the 1950s. To the psychological study of existential solitude in L.'s first novel, *Poussière sur la ville* adds a social dimension. The asbestos-mining town of Macklin provides the narrow conventional background for the unconventional drama of Alain Dubois, a young doctor who arrives with his passionate red-haired bride to set up practice. Madeleine is intemperate, impulsive, inexpressive, and quickly bored. She soon runs through the normal resources of Macklin and takes a lover, a local truckdriver. Caught by his love for his wife but unable to please or reach her, Dubois defies the town's ethics and condones the affair. The people of Macklin take revenge by separating the lovers; Madeleine attempts to shoot her lover but turns the weapon on herself instead. From the complex point of view of the sympathetic but helpless participant, Dubois records the drama in the journal that makes up the novel. The dilemma echoes CAMUS in the hero's detached suffering, his ambiguous choice, his foiled sense of justice. The style is sparse, nervous, intense, like classical French tragedy, and the winter setting is used with great symbolic effect to underscore the action.

A religious concern is grafted on L.'s fiction in *Le temps des hommes* (1956; the time of men). The orphaned hero, Pierre Dupras, is an ex-priest who has left the seminary in revolt against the senseless death of a child. In the northern wilds he seeks to rejoin the world of men but cannot make contact any better than L.'s other heroes, and, like them, he is overwhelmed by the brutality of men and the injustice of God.

Sixteen years elapsed before L.'s next novel, *L'élan d'Amérique* (1972; the American moose). During this time he wrote several plays and television dramas and a few short stories, but although he contributed a regular column on Quebec issues to *Le magazine Maclean* in the 1960s, he lived like a recluse. *L'élan d'Amérique* was heralded as a triumphant return to the mainstream of Quebec fiction. Among other things, it is a political allegory dramatizing in strong lyric images and in a new free style some of the collective traumas of the French-Canadian psyche. The protagonists are Claire Peabody, wife of an American pulp and paper magnate who represents the forces of exploitation; and Antoine, a forest guide who stands for Quebec. Their liaison is symbolized in their reactions to a giant moose that Antoine seeks to protect and Claire wishes to dominate and kill. Antoine finally shoots the animal and sends its head to Claire, who throws the head from her husband's airplane and jumps out after it.

The violence and fantasy of L.'s mature style is captured again in *Une chaîne dans le parc* (1974; *Orphan Street*, 1976), a poetic novel with autobiographical overtones. Set in east-end Montreal in 1944, it traces a few months of relative liberty in the life of an eight-year-old hero between bleak stretches in institutions for unwanted children. It is told from the boy's point of view, and movingly—and sometimes humorously—contrasts the spontaneity of childhood with the cold adult, world as Pierrot seeks "to arm himself against the mysteries of life."

Despite the sparseness of his literary production and the darkness of his palette, L.'s seriousness and his intense poetic vision have made him one of the most respected writers of fiction in contemporary Quebec.

FURTHER WORKS: *L'œil du peuple* (1957)

BIBLIOGRAPHY: Marcotte, G., *Une littérature qui se fait* (1962): 51–61; Major, J.-L., *Le roman canadien-français* (1964): 207–30; Bessette, G., *Trois romanciers québécois* (1973): 131–80; special L. issue, *ELit*, 6, 2 (1973); Pascal, G., *La quête de l'identité chez A. L.* (1977); Bond, D. J., *The Temptation of Despair: A Study of the Quebec Novelist A. L.* (1982)

—PHILIP STRATFORD

LAO KHAMHOM

(pseud. of Khamsing Srinawk) Thai short-story writer, b. 25 Dec. 1930, Khorat

L. was born into a family of rice farmers in Khorat province in northeast Thailand. After completing secondary schooling, he enrolled at the Faculty of Journalism at Chulalongkorn University, simultaneously working as a political correspondent for *Neao na* newspaper and writing occasional short stories. Following a political clampdown in 1952, which saw many writers and journalists arrested, he joined the Forestry Department, and worked in the north of Thailand. Returning to Bangkok in 1956, L. spent two years as a research assistant to an American anthropologist from Cornell University and with the money he earned from this, he bought farming land and set up a small publishing company. At the same time, he began to write short stories once more, publishing his most famous collection, *Fa bo kan* (The Sky Is No Barrier), in 1958.

Like many fellow writers, L. abandoned writing during the Sarit régime (1958-63), when freedom of expression was severely restricted, and turned to farming in Khorat. He became actively involved in politics after the overthrow of the military regime in October 1973 and was made vice chairman of the newly formed Socialist Party of Thailand. When the military returned to power following the massacre of students on 6 October 1976, he and his family fled to Sweden, where he spent several years in self-imposed exile, before returning to Thailand in 1981.

Since its first appearance in 1958, *Fa bo kan* has been reprinted more than ten times. Many of the stories in the collection appeared in English translation under the title *The Politician and Other Stories* (1973) and were also translated into other languages, including Japanese and Swedish. The stories in this collection

portray the reaction of insular-looking villagers to a rapidly changing world in which foreign-aided economic development rudely encroaches upon their isolation. In stories such as "Mo thu'an" (1958; "The Quack Doctor," 1973) and "Khon Phan" (1958; "Breeding Stock," 1973), as well as "Khaemkham" (1969; "Dark Glasses," 1973), L. portrays the downtrodden villagers' encounter with this hostile world sympathetically but unsentimentally, frequently criticizing their superstitiousness and poking gentle fun at their naivety. "Pai" (1970; "Name Tag," 1998) adopts much the same technique, the author subtly evoking the corrupting presence of American troops stationed on Thai soil during the Vietnam War, as an old lady wrongly begins to suspect that her daughter has become a prostitute.

L. was one of the first writers from a poor rural background to try to bring the reality of peasant life to an urban audience, neither sentimentalizing nor romanticizing their lives. Although his output is small, and his later works have not enjoyed the same popularity, L. remains widely regarded by fellow writers and critics alike as one of Thailand's most accomplished short-story writers. He was recently honored with the title, National Artist.

FURTHER WORKS: *Kamphaeng* (1975); *Meao* (1984); *Lom laeng* (1986); *Krateng luk liap chua lok* (1988); *Kamphaeng lom* (1990); *Praweni* (1996)

BIBLIOGRAPHY: Anderson, B. R. O'G., and Ruchira Mendiones, *In the Mirror: Literature and Politics in Siam in the American Era* (1985); Manas Chitakasem, "The Development of Political and Social Consciousness in Thai Short Stories," in Davidson, J. H. C. S, and H. Cordell, eds., *The Short Story in South East Asia: Aspects of a Genre* (1982): 63-99; Phillips, H. P., *Modern Thai Literature: With an Ethnographic Interpretation* (1987); Smyth, D., and Manas Chitakasem, *The Sergeant's Garland and Other Stories* (1998)

—DAVID A. SMYTH

LAO LITERATURE

Lao literature, which had its beginnings in poetry, reached its heights in the 16th and 17th cs. with the production of such epic poems as *Sin Xay* (partial tr., "The Sin Xai," 1967) by Thao Pangkham (fl. 1650). These poems were designed to be sung or chanted to the accompaniment of music. They contained descriptions of landscapes and accounts of love scenes and great battles.

Lao literature in the 20th c. reflects the major political changes during this period. During the first third of the century, when Laos was under French control, the *mohlam*, or traditional singers, continued to create and carry on the traditions of Lao poetry. In the 1930s and 1940s a new era in Lao literature was ushered in by young intellectuals who wrote articles in French about their own culture, language, and religion. Following the publication by Katay Don Sasorith (1904–1959) of *Comment joue-t-on le phaytong?* (1931; *The Game of Phay-Tong*, 1959), a string of articles by Lao authors appeared in French publications. Others who wrote in French included Prince Phetsarath Ratanavongsa (1890–1959), Prince Souphanouvong (b. 1912), Prince Souvannaphouma (b. 1901) and Nhouy Abhay (b. 1909).

With the rise of Lao nationalism in the 1940s, many writers began publishing in prose in their native language. Such important authors as Maha Sila Viravong (b. 1904), Thao Kéne (dates n.a.), Phouvong Phimmasone (b. 1911), and Somchine Pierre Nginn (b. 1892) wrote in Lao. By 1953 the Lao Literary Committee had begun publication of *Wannakhadisan*, a magazine devoted to articles on Lao language and culture.

During the 1940s and 1950s—both before and after independence (1954)—works appeared chronicling political events from the point of view of the Lao, albeit the elite. Prince Phetsarath published an important work in Thai, *Chao Phetsarat: Burut lek haeng Ratcha'anachak Lao* (1956; *Iron Man of Laos: Prince Phetsarath Ratanavongsa*, 1978), which provided a view of the life of a person actively involved in the modern history of Laos.

The publication in Paris of Sisouk Na Champassak's (b. 1928) *Tempête sur le Laos* (1961; *Storm over Laos*, 1961), written from the royalist point of view, added a major work of political journalism to the literature by the Lao elite in the French language.

Phoumi Vongvichit (dates n.a.), as secretary-general of the central committee of the Lao Patriotic Front (a component of the communist Pathet Lao), provided a different view of the political situation in his *Le Laos et la lutte victorieuse du peuple lao contre le néo-colonialisme américain* (1968; *Laos and the Victorious Struggle of the Lao People against United States Neo-colonialism*, 1969).

Much of the poetry composed from the late 1950s to the present reflected Lao political struggles. Poets of the major sides in the fight for Laos—communists, royalists, and neutralists—appealed to the people to join them, frequently referring to Buddhist literature and to Lao myths and legends to support their positions. Poems were also written by Lao in Western languages. An interesting collection of poems written in Lao, French, and English by Khamchan Pradith (b. 1930) was called simply *Mes poèmes* (1960; my poems).

A great amount of technical literature in Lao was produced in the 1960s, primarily to support an educational system that was now teaching more subjects in the Lao language. Textbooks were written on agriculture, education, home economics, Lao language and literature, mathematics, and science. And Buddhist works were published by the monks of Vat Phonpranao.

Popular fiction in Lao came into its own in the late 1960s and early 1970s. A group of young writers in the Vientiane area attempted to encourage reading and writing in the Lao language; the major themes of their short stories were love, the trials of war, and Lao nationalism. Much of their writing appeared in two new magazines, *Phay nam* (from June 1972) and *Nang* (from December 1972), the latter a magazine written primarily by and for women. Characteristic of the works of this group is Leng Phouphangeum's (dates n.a.) *Sivit ni khy lakhon kom* (1968; this life is like shadow theater), and Panai (a pseudonym, dates n.a.) and Douangchampa's (a pseudonym, dates n.a.) *Thale sivit* (1971; ocean of life). At the same time, socialist writers were producing works emphasizing the sufferings and struggles of Lao villagers and guerrillas in the areas of the country controlled by the Lao Patriotic Front. Such writing can be found in the short-story anthology *Kay pa* (1968; *The Wood Grouse*, 1968).

In the late 1970s two major types of publications appeared: (1) works produced in Laos under the new Lao People's Democratic Republic, including collections of short stories such as *Siang oen khong phay* (1978; whose cry for help), and collections of poems in traditional *lam* styles such as *Kon lam pativat* (1977; songs of the revolution); (2) writings by Lao refugees in the countries to which they had moved, including newsletters in Lao and English containing information about life in a new country, and articles written in English or French on Lao culture.

The horrors of war, in particular the American bombing campaign, the unjust and corrupt prerevolution regime, and the new government's success in rescuing the downtrodden were common themes in popular fiction of the 1980s in which the hero or heroine was deliberately intended to provide a role model for readers through his or her exemplary behavior. More recently stories of a less didactic nature reflecting problems such as deforestation and the legacy of unexploded bombs have begun to appear.

BIBLIOGRAPHY: Phimmasone, P., "Cours de littérature lao," *Bulletin des Amis du Royaume Lao*: Nos. 4–5 (1971): 5–70; Lafont, P.-B., "La littérature politique lao," in Lafont, P.-B., and D. Lombard, eds., *Littératures contemporaines de l'Asie du sud-est*, Colloque du XXIXe; Congrès International des Orientalistes (1974): 40–55; Phinith, S., "Contemporary Lao Literature," *JSSB*, 63 (1975): 239–50; Compton, C. J., *Courting Poetry in Laos: A Textual and Linguistic Analysis*, Northern Illinois University, Center for Southeast Asian Studies Special Report No. 18 (1979); Nguyen, N., "Lao Literature through History," in Social Science Committee of Vietnam (Hanoi), *History and Culture of South East Asia: Studies on Laos* (1981): 35–48

—CAROL J. COMPTON

LAO SHE

(pseud. of Shu Ch'ing-ch'un) Chinese novelist, short-story writer, and dramatist, b. 3 Feb. 1899, Peking; d. 24 Aug. 1966, Peking

Fatherless since early childhood, L. S. worked his way through Peking Teachers' College. After graduation he managed to support himself and his mother through a series of teaching and administrative posts. In 1924 he went to London, where he taught Chinese at the School of Oriental and African Studies.

While in London, L. S. became a great admirer of Dickens, and in 1926 he wrote his first novel, *Lao Chang te che-hsüeh* (1928; the philosophy of Old Chang), in imitation of *Nicholas Nickleby*. It was an immediate success, for in addition to being written in the lively dialect of the Peking streets, this novel was the first to introduce humor into the New Literature movement (launched in 1918). In 1930, with his literary reputation already established, he returned to China, where he continued to teach and began to write short stories.

Renewed exposure to the harsh realities of Chinese society increasingly shifted the emphasis of L. S.'s works. *Mao ch'eng Chi* (1933; *Cat Country*, 1970), is one of the bitterest satires about Chinese society ever written. L. S. considered the novel a failure and soon turned his hand again to humor. The results were the eminently successful *Li-hun* (1933; *The Quest for Love of Lao Lee*, 1948) and *Niu T'ien-tz'u chuan* (1934; *Heavensent*, 1951), which was partly modeled on Fielding's *Tom Jones*.

Lo-t'o hsiang-tzu (1938; *Rickshaw*, 1979; also tr. as *Camel Xiangzi*, 1981) is his best novel. This tragic tale, in which he attempted to show the complete bankruptcy of individualism, traces, without sentimentality, the moral ruin of an honest Peking rickshaw puller brought about by a callous, cruel society. The first American translation of this work, *Rickshaw Boy*, became a best seller shortly after its publication in 1945. This version, however, in which the translator took the liberty of providing the story with a happy ending, was not acceptable to L. S. (He was later to disapprove of the same man's translation of *Li-hun* [*Divorce*, 1948], and commissioned a new translation of the same work, *The Quest for Love of Lao Lee*.)

The outbreak of the second Sino-Japanese War (1937–45) radically altered L. S.'s writing. Essentially apolitical (he mistrusted all government officials), in 1938 he was elected head of the Chinese Writers' Anti-Aggression Association, a group formed to pull writers of all political persuasions together in the common cause of the war with Japan. L. S. became a patriotic propagandist and indulged his lifelong interest in popular forms of entertainment by writing ballads, plays, and short skits on wartime themes.

After the war, L. S. published a gigantic novel in three parts, *Ssu-shih t'ung-t'ang* (abridged tr., *The Yellow Storm*, 1951), which deals with life in Peking during the Japanese occupation of Manchuria. The first two parts, *Huang-huo* (bewilderment) and *T'ou-sheng* (ignominy), were published in 1946, while part three, *Chi-huang* (famine), was not published until 1950–51, when it appeared in serialized form. Like his wartime works, this trilogy seems dated because of its emphasis on brave patriots and sniveling collaborationists.

Between 1946 and 1949 L. S. lived in the U. S., having gone there at the invitation of the Department of State. While there, he completed a new novel that was translated and published in 1952 as *The Drum Singers*; the Chinese version of this novel has not yet appeared. When the People's Republic was established in 1949, he returned to China and held a number of important cultural posts. During these years he wrote many propagandistic works, the most successful of which was the play *Lung hsü-kou* (1951; *Dragon Beard Ditch*, 1956).

L. S. had a lifelong interest in the craft of writing. In his early collection of essays *Laoniu p'o-ch'e* (1939; an old ox and worn-out cart) he explains how he wrote much of his best work. His essays after 1949, however, are less concerned with his own writing than with teaching the craft of writing to a new generation; the most noteworthy of these later essayistic works is *Ch'u-k-'ou ch'eng-chang* (1964; spoken so well it's ready to print).

In 1966, during the Cultural Revolution, L. S. was driven to suicide by the Red Guards. Since the fall of Chiang Ch'ing (guiding hand of the Cultural Revolution) in 1976, L. S. has been officially praised, his early works republished, and his persecutors blamed, although not brought to trial.

L. S. will probably be best remembered for the excellent novels and stories he wrote during the 1920s and 1930s. These works show a warm humanitarian humor, graceful handling of the Peking dialect, deep love for China, and sympathy for the underdog, all of which will assure L. S. international readers for a very long time to come.

FURTHER WORKS: *Chao Tzu-yüeh* (1927); *Erh Ma* (1929; *Ma and Son*, 1980); *Hsiao-p'o te sheng-jih* (1931); *Kan-chi* (1934); *Ying-hai-chi* (1935); *Ko-tsao-chi* (1936); *Chien-pei 'Pien* (1940); *Kuo-chia chih-shang* (1940, with Sung Chih-ti); *Huo-ch'e-chi* (1941); *Wen Po-shih* (1941); *Kuei-ch-ü-lai hsi* (1943); *Ts'an-wu* (1943); *Mien-tzu wen-t'i* (1943); *Chung-lieh t'u* (1943); *Wang-chia Chen* (1943); *Chang Tzu-chung* (1943); *Ta-ti lung-she* (1943); *T'au-li ch'un-feng* (1943); *Shei nsien tao-le Ch'ung-ch'ing* (1943); *IIuotsang* (1944); *Tung-hai pa-shan-chi* (1946); *Wei-shen-chi* (1947); *Fang Chen-chu* (1950); *Pieh mi-hsin* (1951); *Ch-un-hua ch'iu-shih*

(1953); *Ho kung-jen t'ung-chih-men t'an hsieh-tso* (1954); *Wu-ming kao-ti yu-le ming* (1954); *Shih-wu kuan* (1956); *Hsi-wang Ch'ang-an* (1956); *Ch'a-kuan* (1957); *Fuhsing-chi* (1958); *Hung Ta-yüan* (1958); *Ch'üan-chia fu* (1959); *Nü-tien-yüan* (1959); *Pao-ch'uan* (1961); *Ho Chu p'ei* (1962); *Shen-ch'üan* (1963). FURTHER WORKS IN ENGLISH: *Two Writers and the Cultural Revolution: L. S. and Chen Jo-hsi* (1980); *Crescent Moon and Other Stories* (1985)

BIBLIOGRAPHY: Slupski, Z., *The Evolution of a Modern Chinese Writer: An Analysis of L. S.'s Fiction, with Biographical and Bibliographical Appendices* (1966); Boorman, H. L., and Howard, R. C., eds., *Biographical Dictionary of Republican China* (1970), Vol. III: 132–35; Hsia, C. T., *A History of Modern Chinese Fiction: 1917–1957* (1971): 165–88, 366–75, 546–50; Vohra, R., *L. S. and the Chinese Revolution* (1974); Kao, G., ed., *Two Writers and the Cultural Revolution: L. S. and Chen Jo-hsi* (1980): 5–34; Wang, T., *Fictional Realism in Twentieth Century China: Mao Dun, L. S., Shen Congwen* (1992)

—WILLIAM A. LYELL

LARBAUD, Valery

French novelist, poet, short-story writer, critic, and translator, b. 29 Aug. 1881, Vichy; d. 2 Feb. 1957, Vichy

The only son of wealthy parents, L. enjoyed a privileged childhood. Despite delicate health, he traveled in Spain, Italy, Germany, and Russia before he was eighteen. At school near Paris L. had already made many foreign friends. His early education and travels left a cosmopolitan stamp on his writing and his widely varied literary interests.

L.'s first book of poems, *Les portiques* (porticoes), was published in 1896 at his mother's expense. His first translation, of Coleridge's *Rime of the Ancient Mariner*, appeared in 1901, the year he enrolled at the Sorbonne for a program of English/German studies he never completed. A facile linguist with an inquiring critical mind, L. fashioned his own eclectic literary education.

L. was a highly personal writer whose work reflects four spheres of interest: the world of childhood, the feminine mystique, travel, and pursuit of the literary life. His adopted pose, that of cosmopolitan aesthete and vagabond, was emulated by contemporaries. In an era of chauvinism, he pioneered the humanistic concept of pan-European civilization.

Fermina Márquez (1911; Fermina Márquez) records L.'s recollection of school days and adolescent romance. *A. O. Barnabooth, ses œuvres complètes: C'est-à-dire un conte, ses poésies et son journal intime* (1913; poems first pub. as *Poèmes par un riche amateur*, 1908; *Poems of a Multimillionaire*, 1955; journal section tr. as *A. O. Barnabooth, His Diary*, 1924) remains L.'s most discussed work. It is a curious potpourri: a brief tale of Voltairean flavor, a collection of free verse conjuring travel memories, and a diary, all purportedly the work of a young South American millionaire. The poems, published earlier with a mock biography, are to be read as the work of an amateur. The diary, light in tone, poses a moral dilemma: the search for identity. Like André GIDE's heroes of that period, Barnabooth pursues an impossible freedom from constraint. Efforts to divest himself of possessions and conventions misfire, revealing the tragicomic complexity of his human fate and his inability to escape from his aristocratic condition. L.'s irony is felt in our last glimpse of Barnabooth, newly married.

Enfantines (1918; childlike tales) contains a half-dozen brief tales centering on childhood dreams and desires, essentially those of girls. They show L.'s gift for portraying poignant emotion with unsentimental sensitivity. Lolita-like teenagers and international show girls alike haunt L.'s reverie, extensions of his fascination with Fermina Márquez. Love for women often mingles with a near-erotic attraction to the life of the great cities.

Although devoted to individuals, and curious about alien cultures and eager to embrace them, L. never felt what we now call social consciousness. Through his translations, prefaces, and critical articles, he introduced a great number of British, American, and Spanish writers to French readers. L. is particularly celebrated for the key role he played in promoting James JOYCE's *Ulysses*, even collaborating with the author to supervise the difficult translation.

In 1957, shortly before his death, L. was named one of the ten delegates who represented France at the World's Fair in Brussels. Never a widely popular writer, but rather a modest, discerning presence in the world of letters, L. is esteemed for originality of style and vision, for his incisive critical prowess, and for having helped to introduce cosmopolitanism into French literature.

FURTHER WORKS: *Beauté, mon beau souci* (1920); *Amants, heureux amants* (1921); *Mon plus secret conseil* (1923); *Ce vice impuni, la lecture, domaine anglais* (1925); *Notes sur Maurice Scève* (1926); *Allen* (1927); *Jaune bleu blanc* (1927); *Aux couleurs de Rome* (1931); *Ce vice impuni, la lecture, domaine français* (1941); *Sous l'invocation de Saint Jérôme* (1944); *Francis Jammes—V. L.: Lettres inédites* (1947); *Lettres à André Gide* (1948); *Journal 1912–1935* (1955); *Correspondance V. L. et G. Jean-Aubry 1920–1935* (1971); *Léon-Paul Fargue—V. L.: Correspondance 1910–1946* (1971); *Le cœur de l'Angleterre, suivi de Luis Losada* (1971); *Alfonso Reyes—V. L.: Correspondance 1923–1952* (1972); *V. L.—Marcel Ray: Correspondance* (3 vols., 1979–1980)

BIBLIOGRAPHY: Jean-Aubry, G., *V. L., sa vie et son œuvre* (1949); Delvaille, B., *V. L.* (1963); Weissman, F., *L'exotisme de V. L.* (1966); O'Brien, J., *The French Literary Horizon* (1967): 193–208; D'Eaudeville, J., *V. L., européen* (1972); Alajouanine, T., *V. L. sous divers visages* (1973); Brown, J. L., *V. L.* (1981); Staay, E. van der, *Le Monologue Interieur dans L'œuvre de V. L.* (1987)

—JAMES ROBERT HEWITT

LARKIN, Philip

English poet, b. 9 Aug. 1922, Coventry; d. 2 Dec. 1985, Hull

An only son, L. spent his childhood, which he referred to as "a forgotten boredom," in Coventry. He attended St. John's College, Oxford, and became a librarian in 1943. From 1955 he was the Librarian of the University of Hull.

The North Ship (1945) was L.'s first book of poetry. It is a collection of short lyrics, usually with short lines and carefully worked-out rhyme schemes; only a small number have titles. There is a paucity of adjectives. The poems display a studied plainness, and very few of them depend on visual images or precise observation. For the most part they are sad songs of vague and general emotions.

The influence of the short lyrics of YEATS on the poems of *The North Ship* is very marked. In his introduction to the revised edition (1966), L. stated that after having been made vividly aware of Yeats's work in 1943, "I spent the next three years trying to write like Yeats . . . out of infatuation with his music. . . I used to limber up by turning the pages of the 1933. . . edition, which stopped at 'Words for Music Perhaps,' and which meant in fact that I never absorbed the harsher last poems." Reading HARDY in 1946, he declared, cured him of his infatuation with Yeats.

L.'s reputation as a poet rests on *The Less Deceived* (1955) and *The Whitsun Weddings* (1964). The poems they contain are more elaborate, richer, and more solid than those in *The North Ship*. L. makes skillful use of the tones and rhythms of ordinary speech; even the most formal poems are slightly colloquial. That they all have titles is indicative of their greater particularity and sharper focus.

When the poems have a definite setting it is the urban, English landscape of the industrial north and Midlands. L. concentrates on the ordinary, dreary, humdrum, and unfashionable. He notes the ambulances, the noisy playgrounds, the drainpipes, and the fire escapes. The people who appear in the poems are provincial, weary, poor, bleak, and dull, unaware of the futility of their lives.

The central preoccupation in L.'s work is with going away from experience. A characteristic situation is for the poet to be looking out of a train window or musing on old photographs. He often declares that he prefers loneliness and celebrates his retreat from life.

That the past is simply and absolutely past is felt as being slightly enigmatic, and this mystery informs some of L.'s best poetry. The poet seems to feel that he cannot mourn for what has happened or for lost possibilities, because nothing has any real meaning. He is filled, nevertheless, with elegiac feelings, and his intelligence is at war with this nostalgia. Any sense of tragedy is both muffled and denied. All passions in L. are mundane and deliberately muted.

The persona who speaks makes a point of his own failures, his selfishness and inability to love, his unadventurous nature, and the emptiness and insignificance of his life—but usually with a wry humor. He is a drab and unrhetorical cousin of T. S. ELIOT's J. Alfred Prufrock. Perhaps the best known of L.'s phrases is the poet's ironic description of himself entering a church: "Hatless, I take off/My cycle-clips in awkward reverence." The strength of L.'s poetry is in his capacity for metaphorical statement. This can be seen in such powerful lines as: "Why should I let the toad *work*/ Squat on my life?" and "All the unhurried day/Your mind lay open like a drawer of knives."

In recent years the urge to self-limitation appears to have carried L. to the point of not writing much poetry and to keeping his deeper feelings out of the poems he *did* write. He continued in *High Windows* (1974) to be the spectator of his own memories, but the poems were only a repetition of his old forms in which the passion was lost.

The vividness of L.'s perception of everyday English life, his ironic self-awareness, and his technical ability have caused him to be considered one of the best English poets of his generation.

FURTHER WORKS: *Jill* (1946; rev. ed., 1963); *A Girl in Winter* (1947); *All What Jazz? A Record Diary 1961–68* (1970)

BIBLIOGRAPHY: Wain, J., "Engagement or Withdrawal: Some Notes on the Work of P. L.," *CritQ*, 6 (1964): 167–78; Timms, D., *P. L.* (1973); Brownjohn, A., *P. L.* (1975); King, P. R., *Nine Contemporary Poets* (1979): 1–43; Morrison, B., *The Movement*

(1980): passim; Bloomfield, B. C., *P. L.: A Bibliography* (1980); Day, R., *L.* (1987); Salwak, D., *P. L.: The Man and His Work* (1989); Rossen, J., *P. L.: His Life's Work* (1989); Motion, A., *P. L.: A Writers' Life* (1993); Swarbrick, A., *Out of Reach: The Poetry of P. L.* (1995)

—ROBERT M. REHDER

LARSEN, Marianne

Danish poet, novelist, and prose writer, b. 27 Jan. 1951, Kalundborg

L. is one of the foremost representatives of Danish vanguard prose and poetry in the 1970s. Born in a provincial district of Zealand, she studied Chinese at the University of Copenhagen and later translated a selection of Lu Xun's poetry into Danish. Her own debut, with a collection of texts called *Koncentrationer* (1971; Concentrations), dates back to her first year at the university.

This volume, along with the following collection *Overstregslyd* (1972; crossed-out sound), marks an authoritative body of experimental prose and poetry in which dream like abstraction and surrealism come across in a language defiant of normal grammar and logic. Repressive orderly circumstances and societal norms are subjected to linguistic disruption, and the crossing of visual and auditory boundaries, as in "crossed-out sound," indicates a confrontational poetic strategy aimed at creating new and freer connections and identities.

In *Ravage* (1973; havoc) this exclusive scheme applies more directly to societal conditions as it unmasks the conflict between victims and perpetrators of political oppression. It affords an insight into revolution, love, and poetry that is indispensable for the underdogs to counter the havoc inflicted by the powers that be. *Cinderella* (1974; title in English) is a specific, gender-political deployment of these experiences.

In *Billedtekster* (1974; pictorial texts), with the subtitle "Uncalligraphy," and *Sætninger* (1974; sentences), textual and scripture-thematic under-pinnings still provide a balance for L.'s sociopolitical rejection of the entire society of commercial exploitation; her location of disorders remains a matter of combining political analysis with sensitive reflections of human loneliness. L. wishes to liberate the abandoned individual, but for the effort to take effect, she concurrently must redefine societal frames. Increasingly concrete, her texts incorporate her abstractions and leave the reader with a synthesis of political criticism and political utopianism.

In *Modsætninger* (1975; contrasts) the political analysis of societal conflicts gets the upper hand while in *Fællessprog* (1975; common language) a reborn and purified sociolinguistic synthesis is proclaimed. An attempt to further simplify these social teachings is apparent in *Det må siges enkelt* (1976; it must be said in simple terms) and in the bold political poems of *Handlinger* (1976; actions). *Hvem er fjenden?* (1977; who is the enemy?) makes no bones about the implications: This is "class poetry," as the subtitle reads, and it is unambiguous class poetry to boot.

Not abandoning the victims of technocracy and male domination, L. succeeds in reopening her political agenda for poetic inquiry. *Under jordskælvet i Argentina* (1978; during the earthquake in Argentina) is a college of photos and texts with discernible references to clashes between military rulers and rebelling masses,

yet it shows few geographical restraints. In *Jeg spørger bare* (1982; I am only asking) the questioning referenced in the title is the guiding principle in the opening part of the book—before predictable left-wing answers follow at the end. In the meantime a series of sober examples, written in different poetic and narrative modes, giving compelling testimony to the typical hardships of society's little people, especially its children.

De andre, den anden (1986; the others, the other) recalls the dichotomy between collective situations and individual attachments. Myriads of outer sensations collide with notions of intimate love. This is not individualism, though. The "other" is a figment of one's imagination—until the others offer fulfillment. *En skønne dag* (1989; one fine day) may promise precisely that; but it may also be a bittersweet indulgence in wishful thinking.

A similar ambiguity adheres to L.'s novels. *Fremmed lykke* (1990; alien happiness) submits that human progress comes with development and the recognition of otherness, but also that otherness is always alien and out of reach. It makes a formally compelling case for both possibilities.

Ranging from almost trivial verisimilitude to impenetrable abstractions, L.'s oeuvre has nothingness as its pivotal point. Her language blueprints a universe that is moving, touching, and indicative of *Lysende kaos* (1990; Shining Chaos), "open texts—registrations of transition," written with Pernille Tønesen (b.1957), and followed by *Via Media* (1993; Via Media), yet another open-ended textual dialogue between the two authors.

A different effort at collaboration, this one between L. and an Iraqi-born Danish poet, Muniam Alfaker, has resulted in *Barndommens kupé* (1994; The Compartment of Childhood), a prose narrative about an accidental encounter in a train compartment somewhere in Europe between an Iraqi man fleeing war and death and a Danish girl trying to escape despair in her foster home. Underneath their present predicaments and cultural differences lie a common ground of childhood memories; and out of their intersecting cross-cultural disorders flows a unifying dream of utopia. Plain wonder is a challenge to the unnatural boundaries behind which we live, because it is nothing, really. But its volatility is captivating, and so is the author when she allows poetry to be her political dimension and to complicate her more gullible political pronouncements, so typical of the 1970s.

As L. continues to expand her poetic vision, the titles of her poetry collections become increasingly rhythmic and challenging, as in *Chance for at danse: Sladderhistorier om at blive svimmel* (1995; Chance to Dance: Gossip Stories about Becoming Dizzy), or they alternate boldly between such instances of synaesthesia as *Skyggekalender* (1994; Shadow Calendar) and */ en venten hvid som sne* (1996; In a Waiting as White as Snow).

FURTHER WORKS: *21 digte* (1972); *Noget tegnet syv gange* (1973); *Aforismer* (1977); *Opgørelse følger* (1978); *Det kunne være nu* (1979); *Hinandens kræfter* (1980); *Der er et håb I mit hoved* (1981); *Bag om maskerne* (1982); *Dagbogsleg 1958-83* (1983, with Ib Hørlyck); *I dag og i morgen* (1983); *Kære levende* (1983); *Udvalgte digte 1969–82* (1983); *Direkte* (1984); *Pludselig dette* (1985); *Hvor du er* (1987); *I timerne og udenfor* (1987); *Giv bare kærlighed skylden* (1989); *Gæt hvem der elsker dig* (1989); *Fir stil—Fantomtid* (1991). **FURTHER WORKS IN ENGLISH:** *Selected Poems* (1982); *Galleri Virkeligheden* (1992); *Det stof drømme er gjortaf* (1992, with L. Holten)

—POUL HOUE

LASKER-SCHÜLER, Else

German poet, dramatist, essayist, and storyteller, b. 11 Feb. 1869, Elberfeld-Wuppertal; d. 22 Jan. 1945, Jerusalem

L.-S. was born in the Ruhr region as the daughter of a banker. Her ancestors include rabbis, scholars, and community leaders, and her plays *Die Wupper* (1909; the Wupper River) and *Arthur Aronymus und seine Väter* (1932; Arthur Aronymus and his fathers) lovingly reflect her family background and the lore of her native Rhineland. Soon enough, however, she turned her back on her bourgeois background and lived the life of a bohemian. With her first husband, the physician Berthold Lasker, she moved to Berlin, where she became the *magna mater* of early EXPRESSIONISM, frequenting such fabled cafés as the Café des Westens and the Romanisches Café, and befriending many members of the avant-garde. Although ten volumes of her poetry and prose had appeared by the outbreak of World War I, her material circumstances steadily worsened after the breakup of her second marriage in 1912. In 1933, the year after she had received the prestigious Kleist Prize, L.-S. fled to Switzerland. The following year she visited Palestine for the first time, but the reality of her poetic and spiritual homeland was such a shock to her that she soon returned to Zurich. Her prose work *Das Hebräerland* (1937; the land of the Hebrews) is a jumble of magnificent insights and misconceptions; like a number of her other books it was illustrated with some of her dreamily grotesque drawings. The outbreak of the war in 1939 turned her third visit to Palestine into an immigration. Her remaining years were marked by disappointment, disorientation, and destitution, for the terrestrial Jerusalem was no match for the heavenly city that she had hymned for so long, and the harsh reality of the land of the Hebrews ill accorded with her self-willed conception of primordial purity and an exemplary community. In *Ichundich* (1960; "IandI"), a curiously Faustian play she wrote in 1942, she split herself into a poet and a scarecrow. Her haunting poem "Ich weiß, daß ich bald sterben muß" (1943; I know that I must die soon) was recited at her burial on the Mount of Olives.

L.-S.'s penchant for mythmaking and mystification informed both her life and her work. When she signed some of her letters "Prince Yussuf of Thebes" or "Princess Tino of Baghdad," she was putting on poetic masks in an attempt to escape to a fantasy world and introduce a mystical strain into her person and her poetry. She also invented fanciful names for accomplished and admired friends, claimed that her son Paul (born in 1899 and probably the issue of a failed marriage) had been fathered by a Greek or Spanish prince, renamed her second husband (Georg Levin) "Herwarth Walden," and called Gottfried BENN "King Giselheer the Heathen," which is also the title of a cycle of love poems she addressed to him.

Her collections of poetry range from *Styx* (1902; Styx) to *Mein blaues Klavier* (1943; my blue piano). German did not seem to suffice her for the optimal expression of her ecstatic visions, and so she wrote some poems in a language of her own devising that she called "Mystic Asiatic." The poet's idiosyncratic language with its deep-pile texture of assonance, metaphors, neologisms, ambiguities, ellipses, and luxuriant "inward" imagery poses a challenge to readers and translators alike. L.-S.'s metaphysical longing for universal fellowship even led her to accept certain Christian ideas, and the unorthodox Judaism of this conciliatory spirit encompassed Jesus and the Madonna. Her *Hebräische Balladen* (1913; Hebrew ballads) presents an eminently personal allegorical evocation of biblical figures and legends, containing the sensual (and even sexual) imagery characteristic of so much of her poetry, notably "Mein Volk" (my people), "Versö hnung" (reconciliation), and "Ein alter Tibetteppich" (an old Tibetan carpet). However, what has been described as the oriental or exotic strain in her poetry is as much indebted to German romanticism as it is to the Song of Songs and other Eastern legends and ideas. L.-S. had great affection for eastern European Jews and their "wonder rabbis," and she yearned for *wilde Juden*—untamed, heroic Maccabean types.

L.-S., always a poet's poet, is properly ranked with Gertrud KOLMAR and Nelly SACHS as one of the greatest poets produced by German Jewry.

FURTHER WORKS: *Der siebente Tag* (1905); *Das Peter-Hille-Buch* (1906); *Die Nächte Tino von Bagdads* (1907); *Meine Wunder* (1911); *Mein Herz* (1912); *Gesichte* (1913); *Der Prinz von Theben* (1914; rev. ed., 1920); *Die gesammelten Gedichte* (1917); *Der Malik* (1919); *Die Kuppel* (1920); *Der Wunderrabbiner von Barcelona* (1921); *Theben* (1923); *Ich räume auf* (1925); *Konzert* (1932; *Concert*, 1994); *Arthur Aronymus* (1932); *Briefe an Karl Kraus* (1959); *Gedichte 1902–1943* (1959); *Verse und Prosa aus dem Nachlaß* (1961); *Prosa und Schauspiele* (1962); *Sämtliche Gedichte* (1966); *Lieber gestreifter Tiger* (1969); *Wo ist unser buntes Theben?* (1969); *Die Wolkenbrücke* (1972); *"Was soll ich hier? Exilbriefe an Salman Schocken* (1986). FURTHER WORKS IN ENGLISH: *Hebrew Ballads and Other Poems* (1980); *Your Diamond Dreams Cut Open My Arteries: Poems by E. L.-S.* (1982)

BIBLIOGRAPHY: Politzer, H., "The Blue Piano of E. L.-S." *Commentary*, 9 (1950): 335–44; Kraft, W., *E. L.-S.* (1951); Guder, G., *E. L.-S.: Deutung ihrer Lyrik* (1966); Elow, (pseud. of E. Lowins) "E. L.-S.," *Jewish Spectator*, 34 (Sept. 1969): 21–25; Gertner, M., "E.-L.-S.'s Biblical Poems," *Jewish Quarterly*, 17 (1969): 26–34; Blumenthal, B., "The Play Element in the Poetry of E. L.-S.," *GQ*, 43 (1970): 571–76; Cohn, H. W., *E. L.-S.: The Broken World* (1974); Hessing, J., "E. L.-S. and Her People," *ArielK*, 41 (1976): 60–76; Grunfeld, F. V., *Prophets without Honor* (1979): 96–145; Bauschinger, S., *E. L.-S.: Ihr Werk und ihre Zeit* (1980); Hessing, J., *E. L.-S.* (1985); Yudkin, L. I., "E. L.-S. and the Development of Jewish Expressionism," *Jewish Quarterly*, 32 (1985): 51–56; Schwertfeger, R., *E. L.-S.*; Yudkin, L. I., *E. L.-S.*; Jones, C. N., *The Literary reputation of E. L.-S.* (1994); Shedletzky, I., ed., *E. L.-S.,'s Jerusalem*

—HARRY ZOHN

LA TOUR DU PIN, Patrice de

French poet, b. 16 March 1911, Paris; d. 28 Oct. 1975, Paris

L. dedicated his life to poetry. Born into an old, aristocratic family, he grew up at Le Bignon-Mirabeau, a country estate near Paris that was to provide the themes and images of his early poems. L. received a Catholic education at Sainte-Croix in Neuilly-sur-Seine, studied literature at the Sorbonne, and enrolled in the École Libre des Sciences Politiques intending to become a lawyer. Within three years he abandoned law. Alternating between Paris and Le Bignon-Mirabeau, he channeled his energies into writing and drew inspiration from nature, contemporary life, reflection, the

Bible, and such masters as Montaigne, Dante, Saint Thomas Aquinas, Saint John of the Cross, and Rainer Maria RILKE.

The high praise accorded L.'s first published work, the romantically elusive, descriptive poem "Les enfants de Septembre" (1931; September's children), prefigured the widespread acclaim for *La quête de joie* (1933; the quest of joy), a collection of serene, predominantly religious lyrics, conceived as part of a monumental investigation of man's spirituality that was to occupy L. for over thirty years. World War II slowed down the project. Drafted into the army and taken prisoner by the Germans, he was repatriated in 1942 and reemerged three years later with the six-hundred-page *Une somme de poésie* (1946; a sum of poetry), which incorporates all previously published poems and builds them into a vast construction centered around L.'s interpretations of spirituality seen both as creativity and transcendence. Man's journey inward, redeemed through the discovery of reality beyond the self, forms the unifying theme of this intricate work. It is held together by prose interludes, by recurrent images, and by protagonists who move through a mythic universe of symbolic objects and occurrences. In *Le second jeu* (1959; the second game), written as Part II of *Une somme de poésie*, self-knowledge is attained and transcended. Man opens up to the created world and in an act of generosity that L. associated with creativity, affirms the efficacy of the community.

With *Le petit théâtre crépusculaire* (1963; the little twilight theater) and *Une lutte pour la vie* (1970; a fight for life), as well as the later *Psaumes de tous les temps* (1974; psalms of all times), L. attempts to fuse poetry with prayer, sometimes with theological statement. Here he achieves the unity of himself before God that he had sought from the beginning.

L.'s verse is lofty, rhythmic, regular, at times oratorical, although free of rigidity. It evidences a control and a consciousness of purpose that suggest the presurrealist manner. Unlike his contemporaries, L. shunned experimentation and sought to integrate the diverse functions of poetry, thus evolving a dense, finely tuned, varied style that ranges from sensual descriptions to direct statements to mythical and symbolic structures. Much of his verse is intelligible. But his later poetry, complex, grounded in religious doctrine, derives from an essentially subjective vision, which in the eyes of some critics is marred by intellectualized detail and obscurity.

FURTHER WORKS: *L'enfer* (1935); *Le lucernaire* (1936); *Le don de la passion* (1937); *Psaumes* (1938); *La vie recluse en poésie* (1938; *The Dedicated Life in Poetry*, 1948); *Les anges* (1939); *Deux chroniques intérieures* (1945); *La Genèse* (1945); *Le jeu du seul* (1946); *Les concerts sur terre* (1946); *Les contes de soi* (1946); *un bestiaire fabuleux* (n.d.); *La contemplation errante* (1948); *Noël des eaux* (1951); *Une pépinière d'arbres de Noël* (1957); *Concert eucharistique* (1972). FURTHER WORKS IN ENGLISH: *The Dedicated Life in Poetry, and The Correspondence of Laurent de Cayeux* (1948)

BIBLIOGRAPHY: Gros, L. G., *Poètes contemporains* (1944): 11–33; Spender, S., Introduction to L. *The Dedicated Life in Poetry* (1948): viii–xix; Rousselot, J., *Panorama critique des nouveaux poètes français* (1952): 191–98; Reid, J. C., "Poetry and P. de L.," *Renascence*, 7, 1 (1954): 17–29; Brereton, G., *An Introduction to the French Poets* (1956): 282–86; Jans, A., "Où en est P. de L.," *Revue générale belge* (Feb. 1960): 95–103; Kushner, E., *P. de L.* (1961)

—VIKTORIA SKRUPSKELIS

LATVIAN LITERATURE

Latvian literature, like the literatures of its two neighbors on the Baltic, Estonia and Lithuania, emerged only in the 19th c. The ground from which Latvian letters sprang had been prepared for centuries by folklore. Tribes speaking Baltic languages had settled near the Baltic Sea during the 2nd millennium B.C. Latvian and Lithuanian are the only surviving languages of this once widespread branch of Indo-European: their folk poetry has preserved many aspects of the common Indo-European heritage.

At the beginning of the 20th c. Latvian literature in the accepted sense of the word was only about half a century old. Since the appearance of the first book printed in Latvian in 1585, there had developed a tradition of religious and didactic writing—the authors being mainly German clergymen—which can hardly be classed as literature. The first literary work of merit is *Dziesmiņas* (1856; little songs), a volume of poetry and translations by Juris Alunāns (1832–1864). The significant movement of National Awakening (1859–80) laid the foundations for all literary genres except the drama. Although it did not produce a major poet, it created a body of poetry whose orientation toward a national romanticism strengthened pride in the Latvian past and hopes for a free state. During this period, a group of realistic prose writers turned out fine work, although with moralistic overtones, an example of which is the panoramic novel *Mērnieku laiki* (1879; the times of the land surveyors) by the brothers Reinis Kaudzīte (1839–1920) and Matīss Kaudzīte (1848–1926).

The interest in collecting Latvian folklore, under the inspired leadership of Krišjānis Barons (1835–1923), was perhaps the most vital seed planted during this period. The first edition of *Latvju dainas* (Latvian folk songs) appeared in eight volumes from 1894 to 1915.

In 1890 a new two-pronged era set in: neoromanticism and the socialist movement called the New Current, the latter having been prompted into existence by urgent sociopolitical problems (Russification by the tsarist regime was only one of them). The most prominent New Current writers were Jānis RAINIS and his wife Aspazija (pseud. of Elza Rozenberga-Pliekšāne, 1868–1943). In the personality and works of Aspazija we witness the interplay of the two movements dominating Latvian literature at the turn of the century. In her early dramatic works and lyrics she attacks social injustice and shows feminist tendencies. Her later writing reveals the true personality of a romantic. Her lasting achievement lies in her "lyrical autobiography," five volumes of verse (1910–33). Rainis, a many-sided and philosophically inclined writer, was conscious heir to the poetic aspirations of the National Awakening in trying to incorporate into his work the spirit and structure of the folk songs.

Jānis Poruks (1871–1911) and Fricis Bārda (1880–1919) were both influenced by German neoromanticism. Poruks is also credited with introducing psychological realism into Latvian literature with his prose works. Rūdolfs Blaumanis (1863–1908) continued the traditions of realism established during the National Awakening but he shifted the focus from the social plane of earlier realists to the human soul and thus gave his dramatic works and stories an ageless quality.

After the unsuccessful revolution of 1905 political hopes were shattered, and a change of pace occurred in Latvian literature. Writers advocated the freeing of literature from subservience to social problems, as well as the right to personal and spontaneous expression, echoing western European developments of "art for art's sake" and SYMBOLISM. These two literary movements acted only as catalysts. The Latvian adaptation had little in common with either, inclining toward impressionism in vividness of images and stressing lyrical qualities in poetry as well as prose. Thus, a period of lyrical impressionism followed the New Current. It counted among its adherents some of the finest poets in the Latvian language, for example, Kārlis SKALBE, a master of succinct lyrical expression and simplicity of form. The spirit and ethos of folklore seem to have been reborn in his deeply national poetry and fairy tales. Impressionism with aestheticist tendencies is found in the sonorous rhythmic patterns of Vilis Plūdonis (pseud. of Vilis Lejnieks, 1874–1940).

One of the finest writers of this period, Anna BRIGADERE, had "a passion for the light, color, and symbolic verities of the folk imagination" (W. K. Matthews). Out of these elements she created fairytale plays as well as childhood reminiscences, a genre that, especially with the surge of impressionism after 1905, also engaged the best creative powers of such writers as Jānis Jaunsudrabiņš (1877–1962), Antons Austriņš (1884–1934), and Jānis Akurˉters (1876–1937). The glorification of the Latvian farmstead as reflecting in its unchanging ways an eternal order reached its apogee in Edvarts VIRZA's novellength prose poem *Straumēni* (1933; the Straumēni homestead). (Even during the political exile of writers following World War II several gems of bucolic evocations have enriched Latvian literature, for instance, the autobiographical novels by the painter Margarita Kovaļevska (b. 1910), which reflect both the colorful earthiness and fantasy charged atmosphere of a fairy tale.)

Side by side with the discovery of the self and nature through impressionism, realism (often verging on naturalism) remained a powerful means of taking stock of the native land, its history and people. Following in the footsteps of the brothers Kaudzīte and their great novel about the times of the land surveyors in northern Latvia, two 20th-c. novelists put the landscape and past of southwestern Latvia and the capital city, Riga, on the literary map: Augusts Deglavs (1862–1922) with his trilogy *Rīga* (1911–22; Riga) and Jēkabs Janševskis (1865–1931) with *Dzimtene* (1921–24; homeland), also a trilogy. Their earthy style and colorful use of regional dialects engendered a whole school of novelists who attained prominence during the 1930s and continued in the same manner in exile. Prominent among these are Jaunsudrabiņš, Aīda Niedra (1898–1972), Alfrēds Dziļums (1907–1966), and Jānis Klīdzējs (b. 1914).

In the wake of World War I an independent Latvian Democratic Republic was declared and a new period of literature set in, which lasted until 1940. The literary achievement of these twenty-two years is impressive. The first decade of independence was characterized by openness to foreign influences and by an efflorescence of all the arts. French models made themselves felt in the polished prose style of Jānis Ezeriņš (1891–1924). Kārlis Zariņš's (1889–1979) fiction achieved a psychological depth and epical poise between lyricism and realism worthy of the best work of his western European contemporaries. The impact of German EXPRESSIONISM, coupled with influences from Russian IMAGISM and FUTURISM, called forth the first truly modern Latvian poets. Pēteris Ērmanis (1893–1969) stands out as a Latvian expressionist, while Aleksandrs ČAKS is doubtlessly Latvia's greatest modern poet. A born rebel and keen innovator, Čaks shocked with his first books of poetry, where he discarded rhyme in favor of rhythm and used daring and unexpected images. His best collection, *Iedomu spoguļi* (1938; mirrors of imagination), is one of the finest achievements of

Latvian poetry. Not only are his poetic means refreshingly new, but also his world—Riga and its suburbs—had never thus been celebrated in poetry before. Čaks died in Soviet-occupied Latvia at the height of his creative powers after being criticized for being unable to overcome his "bourgeois prejudices."

After the coup d'état of 1934, which brought an authoritarian government to power, instead of an international modernism, a return to indigenous traditions and a glorification of the past became the order of the day. The main figure of this school of poetry was Edvarts Virza. Renewed preoccupation with folklore resulted in experiments with folk-song meter in the poetry of Jānis Medenis (1903–1961) and a reincarnation of its spirit in the subtly balanced verse of Zinaīda Lazda (1902–1957). In fiction attempts were made to re-create the legendary Latvian past and to reconstruct the ancient religion of the Balts by, among others, Jānis Veselis (1896–1962) and Ilona Leimane (1905–1989). Aleksandrs Grīns (1895–1941) pioneered the novel-legend about the Latvian fight for freedom. Kārlis Zariņš lifted the historical novel onto a higher artistic plane.

During the 1930s, a tendency toward universalism paralleled the national and traditional aspirations, finding expression in the essays of Zenta Mauriņa (1897–1978) and in the short stories and poems of Mirdza Bendrupe (b. 1910), who was greatly influenced by FREUD and Oriental mysticism. The work of Ēriks Ādamsons (1907–1947), a major poet and short story writer, developed during the 1930s in almost direct opposition to national trends. Favoring introspection and refinement rather than focusing on the native soil, he occupies an isolated yet prominent place in Latvian letters.

Toward the end of the 1930s the mores of urban society and the psychology of love gained momentum as literary themes. They were explored and carried over into exile writing in the work of Anšlavs Eglītis (1906–1994), Valdemārs Kārkliņš (1906–1964), and Knuts Lesiņš (b. 1909), the last the author of the short-story collection *Mūžības vīns* (1949; *The Wine of Eternity*, 1957). The only dramatist of note during the 1930s was Mārtiņš ZĪVERTS, the author of more than forty plays, in which he experiments both with the form and the subject matter of modern drama, having acquired an especially high degree of perfection in handling dramatic dialogue.

Before going into exile Veronika Strēlerte (pseud. of Rudīte Strēlerte-Johansone, 1912-1995) published two collections of verse that established her as the finest artist among a host of Latvian women poets. Her polished, pliant verse lends itself well to intellectual meditation or restrained patriotic feeling. Since 1945 she has published three more poetry volumes. Andrejs Eglītis (b. 1912) gained great popularity with his patriotic verse during the war years and has continued as a national bard in exile, producing more than ten volumes of poetry.

During the German occupation (1941–45) political uncertainty and a violent reaction of disillusionment combined to produce an atmosphere unfavorable to good creative work. Nevertheless, some writers were able to add several works of great merit to Latvian literature.

After the mid-1950s a new generation of poets began to dominate the literary scene in exile. Born during the 1920s and educated in Latvian schools, they brought about a renascence of Latvian poetry by claiming Čaks as their ancestor and incorporating the lesson learned from Western experimental poetry into their work. Among the most original women poets are Velta Sniķere (b. 1920), who continues the traditional dialogue with the language of the folk songs, transposing it into a SURREALIST key; Astrīde Ivaska (b. 1926), in whose poems life appears vibrant with beauty and mystery; Aina Zemdega (b. 1924), whose emotionally charged

19

images and impressions (mainly of nature) again and again gush forth with all the immediacy and weirdness of a turbulent unconscious; Valda Dreimane (1932–1994), who likes to underscore her Latvian vision by incorporating folklore motifs in her poetry; Velta Toma (b. 1912), whose magic incantations reflect her absorption of the best current poetic developments in her homeland; and Baiba Bičole (b. 1931), who can instantaneously connect the ancient with the immediate, the rational with the irrational, the organic with the inorganic; Aina Kraujiete (b. 1923), whose poetry's most salient feature is its perfect emotional and intellectual balance. Bičole and Kraujiete, as well as Rita Gāle (b. 1925), belonged to the New York group of Latvian poets. Its most outstanding members, however, were Linards Tauns (pseud. of Alfrēds Bērzs, 1922–1963), whose visionary poetry represents the highest achievement to date in Latvian poetry in exile, and Gunars Saliņš (b. 1924), whose mythical poetic imagination ranges in time from ancient Baltic ritual to "happenings" in Greenwich Village, and in space from deep cellars with murals dripping wine, to the tops of Manhattan skyscrapers where cherubs with nylon wings sit inert before sunrise. In Olafs Stumbrs' (1931–1996) poetry exile becomes a metaphor for the poet's fate of loneliness and alienation, whereas Valdis Krāslavietis (pseud. of Valdis Grants, 1920–1994) waxes especially indignant at the sterility and aimlessness of exile existence. Juris Kronbergs (b. 1946) was born, brought up, and educated in Sweden. Nevertheless, his idiom is still flexible enough to bend to new sounds, experiences, and expression, and is still absorbent enough to soak up foreign elements without being contaminated. Also, the poems of Maija Meirāne-Šlesere (b. 1934), Sniedze Runǧe (b. 1951) and Sarma Muižniece (b. 1960) owe poetic afflatus to their double spiritual citizenship.

A breakthrough to modernism in prose among writers in exile began during the 1950s in the novels of Modris Zeberiņš (1923-1994) and Dzintars Sodums (b. 1922); it became an undeniable fact in the work of Guntis Zariņš (1926–1965), who produced six novels in rapid succession, all of which evinced an EXISTENTIAL-IST point of view and a breathless search for self-identification both as an individual and a Latvian. Ilze Šķipsna (1928–1981) and Andrejs Irbe (b. 1924) center their interest in exploring psychological states and the substratum of dreams and memories in the exile's inner life, which could not be reached by realistic prose writing. The painter Tālivaldis Ķiķauka (b. 1928) leans toward surrealism in his imaginative, exhilarating prose. The prose works of Richards Rīdzinieks (pseud. of Ervins Grīns, 1925–1979) and Aivars Ruņǧis (b. 1925) reflect various formalistic and absurdist trends of modern Western literature. Arturs Baumanis's (1905–1989) monumental epic novel *Hernhūtieši* (8 vols., 1976), about the Herrnhut religious movement in 18th-c. Livonia, is permeated with earthy humanity. The diary-like prose pieces of Benita Veisberga (b. 1928) form a direct and honest reappraisal of her life and work, an *apologia pro vita sua*.

Almost immediately after the Red Army entered Latvia in June 1940, official spokesmen declared Soviet Russian literature to be "an absolutely indispensable school for literary development in Latvia," and Latvian writers were urged to strive for the "perfection embodied in the literary experience of the first socialist state, Soviet Russia." The German occupation prevented the Soviet authorities from carrying out these policies immediately. After World War II, however, literary administrators from Moscow resumed their weeding-out process, and Latvian writing was narrowed and reduced to propagandistic functions—with tragic consequences for creativity, for actual works, and for individuals.

Following Stalin's death, especially after the Twentieth Congress of the Communist Party of the Soviet Union in February 1956, a substantial number of those intellectuals who had "taken their own song by the throat" were inspired by the possibility of expressing ideas and sentiments they had long repressed—for example, Ēvalds Vilks (1923–1976), Dagnija Cielava-Zigmonte (b. 1931), and Jezups Laganovskis (1920–1987). Harijs Heislers (1926–1985) wrote a long poem, *Nepabeigtā dziesma* (1956; *The Unfinished Song*, 1958), perhaps the first work of literature in the entire U.S.S.R. to deal strictly with the theme of banishment to Siberia. Although the literary line hardened after the 1956 "ideological revolt," partly as a consequence of events in Poland and Hungary, and later still more—after the 1968 attempt to "democratize socialism" in Czechoslovakia—some writers found it possible to deal in one way or another with subjects and themes that had been forbidden during the first ten or fifteen postwar years. Several gifted writers endeavored to lead the way toward the revival of literature. Visvaldis Lāms-Eglons (1923–1992), in spite of the obligatory admixture of Socialist REALISM, succeeded in maintaining a modicum of literary merit and in demonstrating his talent for communicating the atmosphere of a particular time and place, usually his chaos-laden native land during World War II and its aftermath. His many novels, such as *Kāpj dūmu stabi* (1960; smoke is rising), *Visaugstākais amats* (1968; the top post), *Jokdaris un lelle* (1971; a joker and a puppet), and *Mūža guvums* (1973; *A Life Reviewed*, 1979), combine psychology and social criticism and bring into Latvian fiction complex, unpredictable characters, who are first human beings and only then heroes. The fatuous positive *homo sovieticus* of "socialist" construction and facile happy ending also are completely absent from several other works, for example, the novel *Kailums* (1970; nakedness) by Zigmunds Skujiņš (b. 1926), one of those writers who have been able to straddle the literary fence by writing good literature as easily as sermonizing propaganda pieces. The central theme of several of Regīna Ezera's (b. 1930) works of fiction is the dilemma of sensitive individuals who are isolated and destroyed by the stultification and depravity of the environment. The dominant characteristics of Aivars Kalve (1937–1994), Andris Jakubāns (b. 1941), and Jānis Mauliņš (b. 1933) are indirectly expressed irony, understatement, and an incongruous juxtaposition of situations and characters. Marǧeris Zariņš's (1910–1993) narratives often shift spheres of fictional reality in the manner of PIRANDELLO. Alberts Bels (b. 1938) in his best novels—*Izmeklētājs* (1967; *The Investigator*, 1980), *Būris* (1972; the cage), and *Saucēja balss* (1973; *The Voice of the Herald*, 1980)—recaptures the spirit of experimentation by using montagelike construction and multidimensional views of events, and by attempting to express illusion, hallucination, and foreboding by syntactical distortions, blurring person and number. Herberts Dorbe (1894–1983), Jānis Kalniņš (b. 1922), Antons Stankevičs (b. 1928), and Saulcerīte Viese (b. 1932) have excelled in the neglected genre of the biographical novel.

The scope of lyrical expression was broadened especially by those poets who entered the literary scene in the 1960s. Vizma Belševica (b. 1931), whose idiosyncratic poems represent perhaps the most important achievement in contemporary Latvian poetry, was silenced by the authorities for almost ten years after the publication of her masterful poem "Indriķa Latvieša piezīmes uz Livonijas hronikas malām" (1969; "The Notations of Henricus de Lettis in the Margins of the Livonian Chronicle," 1970), which renders history with the immediacy of a news broadcast on a current—and personal—crisis. She was partially rehabilitated in the late 1970s. Her politically outspoken son Klābis Elsbergs (1959–1987), a poet par excellence himself, died under mysterious circumstances by falling out of a Soviet Writers' Union building near Riga. The "Latvian Yevtushenko", Ojārs Vācietis (1933–1983), in quite a few of his poems exalts such abstract terms as "freedom," "justice," "truth," and "human dignity," simultaneously trying to mobilize the conscience of his countrymen against the dry, dehumanizing kind of technology (and ideology).

Especially popular have been the writings of Imants Ziedonis (b. 1933), a prolific, impulsive, impatient and at times even angry poet, author of miniatures ("epiphanies") and travel notes, as well as a skilled translator. Although his poetry is not always free of Party propagandistic appeals, Ziedonis makes a great effort to assert the right of personal freedom, creative freedom, and freedom of thought, and he attempts to resurrect truths and to challenge obliquely the role of the authorities. Māris Čaklais (b. 1940), truly an intellectual poet, whose usually analytical and reflexive, and often difficult, personal, and esoteric poetry is thought out to the smallest detail, repeatedly asserts that "a human being without a past is a human being without a future."

Vitauts Lūdēns (b. 1937), a master of manipulating language and structure to achieve formal unity and profundity of vision, whether he writes about the Teutonic crusaders in the 13th c., the revolution of 1905, World War I, and the horrors of the last war, or ancient traditions and medieval folklore, always strives to convey the organic interconnection between historical periods. The answer to the meaning of history lies in the earth, specifically the Latvian soil, also for Jānis Peters (b. 1939), Imants Auziņš (b. 1937), Laima Līvena (b. 1943), and others. Knuts Skujenieks's (b. 1936) short untitled poetic fragments often allude to his sense of oppression at not being allowed to write freely and openly; in the 1960s he was sentenced to seven years in a labor camp for engaging in "anti-Soviet activities."

"A human being without a past is a human being without a future." During the Brezhnevian stagnation period, this became the motto of several other poets, notably Jānis Baltvilks (b. 1944), Ilze Binde (b. 1941), Ingvars Jakaitis (b. 1949), Velga Krile (1945–1991), Hermanis Marģers Majevskis (b. 1951), Māra Misina (b. 1949), Aivars Neibarts (b. 1939) and Mārā Zālīte (b. 1952). In Leons Briedis (b. 1949), Jānis Rokpelnis (b. 1945), Juris Helds (b. 1942) and, especially, the innovative formal virtuoso Uldis Bērzinš (b. 1949), events actually represent markers in the formarion of a particular texture of language, consisting of interacting symbolic modules that can communicate with us only after we suspend our conventional notions of how a language works.

During the second half of the 1980s, the *perestroika* period during which the nadir of stagnation yielded to nothing less than a Latvian national revival, witnessed the appearance of some exciting new works free of *Glavlit* interference, works completed years ago (though not published then) and works by previously banned authors, including those in exile. The various "realism" of the more distant as well as immediate past, be they "social," "neo" or "socialist"—from tsarist Cossack boots to Soviet tank tracks across the broken Baltic landscape—made way for a proliferation of alternative literary forms as manifested in the creative output of such younger generation writers as Amanda Aizpuriete (b. 1956), Irēna Auziņa (b. 1958), Guntis Berelis (b. 1961), Pēters Brūvers (b. 1957), Guntares Godiņš (b. 1958), Rudīte Kalpiņa (b. 1966), Aivars Kļavis (b. 1953), Valda Melgalve (b. 1955), Māris Melgalvs (b. 1957), Gundega Repše (b. 1960), Eva Rubene (b. 1962), Lelde

Stumbre (b. 1952), Inese Zandere (b. 1958), Andris Žebers (b. 1958), Rimants Ziedonis (b. 1962) and Egīls Zirnis (b. 1956).

In the aftermath of the collapse of the Soviet Union and the independence of Latvia in 1991, representatives of all genres, both newcomers and veterans, commenced uncovering in the literary output those factors of the imagination that had been in check during the more than fifty years of foreign rule.

BIBLIOGRAPHY: Virza, E., *La littérature lettonne depuis l'époque de réveil national* (1926); Johansons, A., "Latvian Literature in Exile," *SEER*, 30 (1952): 466–75; Andrups, J., and V. Kalve, *Latvian Literature* (1954); Rubulis, A., and M. J. Lahood, eds., *Latvian Literature* (1964); Rubulis, A., *Baltic Literature* (1970); Andrups, J., "Latvian Literature," in Ivask, I., and G. von Wilpert, eds., *World Literature since 1945* (1973): 449–55; Ziedonis, A., et al., eds., *Baltic Literature and Linguistics* (1973); Ekmanis, R., *Latvian Literature under the Soviets: 1940–1975*, (1978); Ekmanis, R., "Die Literatur in Lettland in den 60er und 70er Jahren," *AB*, 18 (1979): 194–370; Straumanis, A., ed. *Baltic Drama: A Handbook and Bibliography* (1981): 113–380

—ASTRID IVASK

LAUGESEN, Peter

Danish poet, art critic, and translator, b. 5 Mar. 1942, Copenhagen

L. has his origins both in the Danish province of the 1950s and the American and European postmodernist art. Born in Copenhagen, L. was reared in Odder and educated as a typographer. When he was an apprentice, he printed his own first poems on the workshop machines in his spare time. His early collections were only known to a small circle of passionate readers, friends, and fellow poets such as Dan TURÈLL, Henning Mortensen (b. 1939), and Jens Smærup Sørensen (b. 1946). As a young poet, he joined the revolutionary artists' union, the Situationistic International of Paris and Antwerpen, but was soon expelled.

After a few years in Copenhagen in the 1960s, L. moved back to Århus and settled in Brabrand. The suburb and its population of respectable families and youngsters as well as bums and drunkards became an important environment of his poems. L. printed his first collection of poems, *Landskab* (Landscape), in 1967. He was inspired by the American poet Charles OLSON's ideas on "the projective verse," by French structuralism and poststructuralism, and by anarchistic philosophy and wanted to make writing itself a liberating and extrovert activity.

According to L., the process of writing should extend the poet's and the reader's whole notion of life and undermine hierarchic thinking. He tried to let poems generate through the writing process itself. Writing on a typewriter to him was and is like playing a musical instrument—it involves and appeals to both body and soul, to thought and emotion. The typewriter's prints of the letters and syllables on the paper sheets are important and figurative, and the poem should be a kind of a score to the reader. L.'s list of works also includes a handwritten collection, *72 håndskrevne sider* (1970; 72 Handwritten Pages), that has become a much-coveted collector's item.

In addition to being an extremely prolific poet, L. has translated into Danish poems, essays, and dissertations by Charles Olson, by the Feno-Swedish surrealist Gunnar BJÖRLING, by the French poet and dramatist Antonin ARTAUD, and by the Russian anarchist Mikhail Bakunin (1814-1876). The most important of L.'s early works are *Skrift* (1969; Writing), *Katatonien* (1970; Catatonia), *Hamr&Hak* (1977; Hammer & Hack), and *Åens Skrift* (1979; The Stream's Writing). The collections seem to be various dimensions of the same lasting discovering of rhythms and forms. Both the linguistic ecology and the emerging of revolting aesthetical forms interest L. more than an artistic fulfilment of the poem itself. Poetry is a resistance to the modern political and ideological exploitation of language as well as environment. This poetic resistance is at hand in everyday language and by means of the writing process the poet sets linguistic energy free. In order to point out that creative artistic work isn't tied to individuality he has cooperated with fellow poets. On *Dobbeltskrift* (1973; Double Writing) he cooperated with Dan Turèll in various genres, mingled with scribbles and sketches.

In the 1980s and 1990s L. became widely recognized as one of the leading Danish poets. His masterly use of everyday language, his poetic cadence, his quiet humor, and the existential meditations of his works impressed readers, fellow poets, and critics. His poetry experiments with still more comprehensive forms, using hymns, jingles, quotations from songs and poems, and proverbs. Titles such as *Himmel Kærlighed Frihed* (1982; Heaven Love Freedom) and *Barnetro* (1985; The Faith of Your Childhood) indicate L.'s deliberate linguistic balancing at the edge of banality trying to open language to new meanings and metaphors. L. is always aware of the ambiguity of language and different voices, verses, and phrasings form an open poetry or what the American poet Charles Olson called "composition by field." L. writes Japanese haikus as well as blank verse and nonsense-verse and small diamond-like poems and sentences are mixed with longer narrative prosa poems, where the whole register of the Danish language has been used. Major works from the 1990s are *Milesten* (1991; Milestones), with poems to the late musician Miles Davies, *29 digte* (1991; 29 Poems), *Plettede Plusfours* (1993; Stained Plus Fours), *Deadlines* (1994; title in English), and *Kragetæer* (1995; Scribbles). Descriptions of the suburb environment and of the close surroundings and the home of the poet has always been a track in L.'s poetry, and this track has become increasingly more important.

In *Pjaltetider* (1997; Rag-Times) the title both refers to L.'s rough school days and to the present, where social losers are kept out of respectable people's sights, and art is often prostituted by public opinion, consensus, and polical correctness. Verses and words are still revolting in L.'s poems and the present climax is the large collection *Når engle bøvser jazz* (1998; Burping Angels Sing the Jazz) with poems dedicated to his American kindred spirits Olson, Allen GINSBERG, and William BURROUGHS. For many years L. has been an art critic and a collumnist at a leading paper. In 1991 he published the essays *Kunsthistorier* (Histories of Art) that decribes some of his own artistic theories. In cooperation with two musicians he has formed the band Mind-Spray, and their performances have cult status to a young audience of poetry fans.

L.'s poetry is deeply engaged in social and ecological as well as poetical questions. There are no easy solutions and answers, but in his poems L. keeps on listening to the mucic of the words and being tender with letters, syllables, and metaphors—the microcosmos of language and the links of human relations.

FURTHER WORKS: *Uden titel, eller Man kan ikke sige* (1969); *Sprogets Yoga* (1972); *Det er kun en måne af papir* (1973); *Jeg kan høre dig synge* (1973); *Guds ord fra landet* (1974); *Anarkotika* (1975); *Blues* (1977); *Den flyvende hollænder* (1977); *Stol på bumsernes klare sprog* (1978); *Skæve Stjerner* (1978); *Den automatiske pilot* (1978); *Skibets mytologiske arkitektur* (1979, with Mogens Kjær); *Telegram* (1979); *Forstad til intet* (1980); *Blækpatroner*(1983); *Pow* (1984); *Retro* (1984); *Vindens tunge* (1986); *Frø og strængler* (1988); *Nattur* (1989); *Artur på genfærd* (1989); *Indianer Joes Vandskål* (1990); *Kulttur* (1990); *Konstrueret situation* (1996)

BIBLIOGRAPHY: Thule, V. H., "Anarcho-skriften-om P. L.," in *Meddelelser fra Dansklærerforeningen*, 4 (1980): 247-50; Schnack, A., and J. G. Brandt, *80 moderne danske digtere* (1988): 141-45; Borup, A., "Der er liv allevegne. Om P. L.'s Kulttur," in Mai, A. M., ed., *Digtning fra 80'erne til 90'erne* (1994): 161-75; Knudsen, P. Ø., "Inspirationen er cn mumlende idiot," in *Børn skal ikke lege under fuldmånen. Forfatterportrætter* (1995): 139-73; Conrad, N. A., "Portraits of Danish Poets, " *Danish Literary Magazine*, 12 (1997) 12-13

—ANNE-MARIE MAI

LAURENCE, Margaret

Canadian novelist and short-story writer (writing in English), b. 18 July 1926, Neepawa, Man.; d. 5 Jan. 1987, Lakefield, Ont.

L. was born and raised in a small Manitoban town, a locale which has profoundly influenced all of her writing and which became the basis for her fictional Manawaka. She studied English literature at United College, Winnipeg. Her husband's engineering work took the couple to Africa for seven years, to what was then the British Protectorate of Somaliland and to Ghana. Five years in Vancouver were followed by a decade in England. After more than twenty years of traveling, she has returned to settle in Lakefield, a small Ontario town resembling the Neepawa of her youth.

L.'s work may be divided into two parts, by setting. Her African writing is less well known than her Canadian fiction, which is often studied in isolation. The neglect of the African work—a translation of Somali poetry and folktales, *A Tree for Poverty* (1954); a magnificent travel book, *The Prophet's Camel Bell* (1964); a novel set in Accra, *This Side Jordan* (1960); a collection of short stories, *The Tomorrow-Tamer* (1964); and a study of contemporary Nigerian dramatists and novelists, *Long Drums and Cannons* (1968)—is unfortunate, since her Canadian fiction emerges from two streams: the prairie roots, and the self-knowledge and maturity achieved abroad. Africa was the catalyst and crucible for much of L.'s work.

The five Canadian-based novels that make up L.'s Manawaka cycle re-create an entire society and constitute a portrait of human experience. Hagar Shipley, the ninety-year-old heroine of *The Stone Angel* (1964), wrestles with pride, love, and an indomitable lust for life. *The Diviners* (1974) demonstrates, through a middle-aged woman writer's experience and memory, that the past is alive in the present and is constantly being renewed, that it is a living river. The cycle also includes *A Jest of God* (1966), *The Fire-Dwellers* (1969), and *A Bird in the House* (1970).

Travel has played a major role in L.'s life and has provided her with her central metaphor—the psychic journey toward inner freedom and spiritual maturity. Journeying, strangerhood, and exile express (in her phrase) "the pain and interconnectedness of mankind." L.'s recurring themes are roots, ancestors, human complexity, acceptance of the other, and the necessity of growth.

The epic quality of L.'s fiction, and her ability to give symbolic form to social or collective life, has earned her a justified comparison with Tolstoy, while her literary vision of the two-way flow of time places her among philosophical novelists like Marcel PROUST. Her basic vision is religious, humanistic, and, more recently, increasingly political. Using her prairie region and specific historical issues, L.'s art dramatizes age-old concerns of human dignity and the need for social justice.

FURTHER WORKS: *Jason's Quest* (1970); *Heart of a Stranger* (1976); *The Olden Days Coat* (1979); *The Christmas Birthday Story* (1980); *Dance on the Earth: A Memoir* (1989)

BIBLIOGRAPHY: Thomas, C., *M. L.* (1969); Cameron, D., *Conversations with Canadian Novelists*, Vol. I (1973): 96–115; Thomas, C., *The Manawaka World of M. L.* (1975); New, W., ed., *M. L.* (1977); Woodcock, G., "The Human Elements: M. L.'s Fiction," in Helwig, D., *The Human Elements: Critical Essays* (1978): 134–61; special L. issue, *JCS*, 13, 3 (1978); special L. issue, *JCF*, No. 27 (1980); Morley, P., *M. L.* (1981); McCormick Loger, G. M. K., *New Perspectives on M. L.: Poetic Narrative, Multiculturalism, and Feminism* (1996)

—PATRICIA MORLEY

LAWRENCE, D(avid) H(erbert)

English novelist, short-story writer, poet, essayist, and dramatist, b. 11 Sept. 1885, Eastwood; d. 30 March 1930, Vence, France

L.'s early life is familiar to many, having been transmuted into the art of *Sons and Lovers* (1913). The coal-mining father, repudiated by his wife and dismissed by his children; the puritanical mother, with social and intellectual aspirations for her children; the artistic son, treasuring but also rebelling against his mother's nurturing, struggling to become an adult—these elements, the core of this novel, are the stuff of his life. His Midlands hometown in Nottinghamshire was a landscape of opposites in close proximity, village streets and coal mines immediately adjacent to lush countryside; the jarring juxtaposition marks L.'s inner landscape as well, a violent stridency alternating with the most exquisite gentleness. Throughout his life, L. railed against the ugliness of industrialization and praised the healing powers of the natural world.

In his youth L. found an intellectual forum in the Congregational Chapel's literary society, the Mechanics' Institute library, and the local socialist movement. He received his formal education in the area schools up through Nottingham University College, where he studied botany and French and trained as a teacher. After graduation in 1908 L. taught grammar school in south London and arrived on the London literary scene, thanks to the encouragement of his long-time sweetheart Jessie Chambers ("Miriam" in *Sons and Lovers*) and the interest of Ford Madox Hueffer (later Ford Madox FORD), editor of the *English Review*. Hueffer found L. a publisher for his first novel, *The White Peacock* (1911), and introduced him

to the likes of H. G. WELLS, Ezra POUND, and W. B. YEATS. The respiratory illnesses that had plagued L. since birth flared up in 1911 (he attributed this to the death of his mother the year before) and he gave up teaching to devote himself to writing under the editorial mentorship of Edward Garnett (1868–1937). In 1912 L. eloped with the wife of his former college French teacher, Frieda von Richthofen Weekley—several years his elder, daughter of a German baron, and mother of three children. L. was totally unlike Frieda in class, nationality, and temperament and thrived on these differences even as he chafed at them. Throughout his career he portrayed their fiery relationship in many autobiographical poems and stories.

From the first the eroticism of L.'s writings offended polite society. The outbreak of World War I compounded L.'s problems, since he was vociferously opposed to the war and, moreover, had a German wife. L.'s fourth novel, *The Rainbow* (1915), was banned for its alleged obscenity; the banning created further difficulties for him in getting anything published and forced him to rely on the generosity of others. John Middleton Murry (1889–1957) and Katherine MANSFIELD, with whom the Lawrences developed an intense friendship, offered him their various "little magazines" as forums for his work. An important patron was Lady Ottoline Morrell, wife of a Liberal Member of Parliament, to whose home, Garsington Manor, many literati flocked. Through her, L. formed relationships with several people—among them, Aldous HUXLEY, E. M. FORSTER, and Bertrand Russell (1872–1970)—whose aid he tried to enlist in the creation of a new, utopian society—a small community to be established outside of England and away from war by those dissatisfied with the status quo.

During the war L. tried to leave England but was not permitted to emigrate until 1919. His years of wandering began: first to Italy and Germany and then to Ceylon, Australia, New Zealand, and, ultimately, North America, beckoned by a New Mexican fan, Mabel Dodge Sterne (later Luhan, 1879–1962), with visions of "primitive" Indians and unsullied landscape. By the 1920s L. was writing and publishing frequently in spite of nagging poor health. He continually wove the ever-changing scenery and events of his life into his fiction. Toward the end of his life he flouted the censors by exhibiting his sexually and religiously provocative paintings and by bringing out in a private edition the very explicit *Lady Chatterley's Lover* (1928; authorized abridged ed., 1932; unexpurgated edition, 1959). Both were seized by the authorities (the novel would not be sold openly in the United States until 1960), and the intransigency of society, as L. saw it, kept his wrath ignited until the last. He died of tuberculosis in southern France in 1930, but his ashes are interred at his ranch outside Taos, New Mexico, where Frieda lived on until her own death in 1956.

L. had an apocalyptic vision of life, formed by his coming of age as the century was newly ended, when old orders—agricultural and rural—were passing away, and by the cataclysm of the Great War. Like Yeats, L. was interested in cycles of death and rebirth: the phoenix was his personal emblem and appears time and again in his literary and pictorial art. L.'s works are characteristically open-ended, with no definitive resolutions to the crises they depict but with the possibility of better worlds ahead. Thus, *Sons and Lovers*, L.'s third and perhaps finest novel, ends with Paul Morel's heading toward the city and a new life, after the death of his mother. As in any novel of development, this hero tries out a variety of relationships and learns from them how to create a future for himself. That future is tentative, but the guiding values are set for Paul as for the writer whose life he mirrors: reverence for nature, faith in the regenerative powers of sex, and respect for the need for separateness in every person.

In *Sons and Lovers* Paul articulates L.'s desire to break through the crust of personality to get at the "protoplasm" beneath. This desire becomes a credo in *The Rainbow*. The title change from *Paul Morel* to *Sons and Lovers* had shown L.'s attempt at seeing the universal significance of individual identities, and the search for universality marks the direction of L.'s career, culminating in fables like *The Man Who Died* (1929; first pub. as *The Escaped Cock*). Although *The Rainbow* is a family saga and novel of development, it is less realistic than symbolistic; that is, it is "about" contrasting forces: the urge toward the earth, darkness, and "blood-consciousness" (L.'s term for an instinctual, nonrational way of knowing) versus the urge toward civilization, light, and mental consciousness. The rainbow symbolizes union-in-polarity, a life firmly earth-centered but reaching toward the sky. Typically, no such union is achieved in the novel, although Ursula Brangwen comes close to knowing how she might attain it.

Ursula's story continues in *Women in Love* (1920), which L. considered a sequel to *The Rainbow* but which can actually stand alone (the two novels began as one, but L. split the work when it became unwieldy). Episodic in nature, *Women in Love* is knit together by recurring motifs and a dancelike pattern of changing partners. As in *The Rainbow*, many scenes are puzzling on surface levels of plausibility and realism but are charged with deep significance: these include Birkin's stoning of the moon and Gerald Crich's fighting with the rabbit. Yet the novel is also filled with the simplest naturalistic touches that anchor it firmly to earth, like Ursula's worry that her fingers are too fat to wear Birkin's rings. The two modes of realism and symbolism exist in a precarious but ultimately successful balance.

Whereas *The Rainbow* is historical, *Women in Love* is eschatological: the pall of war hangs over it, although the exact war is unspecified; instead, there is a pervasive feeling of destruction and doom. L. is commonly known for his depiction of intimate love relationships, but he always related this personal realm to the larger fate of society. His readings in anthropology and history (for instance, Gibbon's *Decline and Fall of the Roman Empire*) add scope to this ambitious novel, which calls for a leader to resurrect modern society from its ashes.

L. was always seeking the utopia that he called "Rananim." In his searches he produced a great deal of travel writing in two genres, novels and travel books; these are stamped with the force of L.'s idiosyncratic and often negative impressions of a particular country, even as they faithfully capture the distinctive qualities of that country. In his so-called "leadership period," in the novels *Aaron's Rod* (1922), *Kangaroo* (1923), and *The Plumed Serpent* (1926), L. recorded his observations of warring political factions in several countries. His tendency toward propagandizing, obvious in *Women in Love*, came to the fore in these novels, which are generally considered L.'s weakest. But the landscape always lives, even when the novel disappoints. And *The Plumed Serpent*, L.'s reinstatement of pre-Aztec gods into the ruling pantheon of modern Mexico, has many devotees because of its color, poetry, and religious intensity.

L. returned to the English countryside that he knew so intimately for his tenth and final novel, *Lady Chatterley's Lover*. The gamekeeper figure of his first novel, *The White Peacock*, occupies center stage in his last one, representing all the life-nurturing

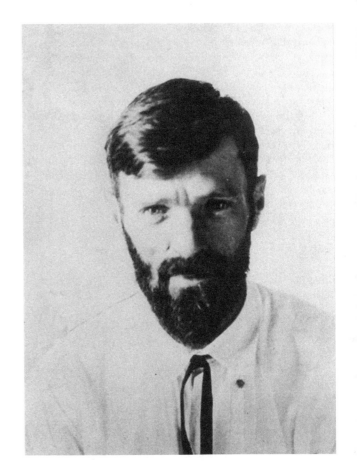

D. H. Lawrence

qualities that L., as a good romantic, associated with nature and opposed to mechanization and industrialism. The configuration of characters is the familiar Lawrentian triangle, with an earthy, brutish type in rivalry with a thin-blooded prig for the same woman: in this case, Lady Chatterley renounces her upper-class husband to marry his virile employee. L. deliberately attempted to shock society with four-letter words that he hoped would resore it to healthy sexuality; indeed, the novel preaches a gospel of sex, and in spite of the tenderness of the love affair (*Tenderness* was L.'s original choice for a title), the novel is marred by its preachiness.

L. is undoubtedly best known for his novels, in which he cuts a grand, imposing, and often windy figure. His consummate skill at incident or vignette, as evidenced in these novels, helps to explain why many readers prefer his shorter fiction. At their finest, L.'s novellas and short stories combine meticulously accurate social settings with penetrating psychological analyses. They also have a mythological or archetypal richness, sometimes made explicit, as in "Samson and Delilah" (1917), but more often left to reverberate beneath the surface, as in "The Rocking-Horse Winner" (1926). So the myth of Persephone wedded to the underworld Hades resonates in many stories, among them "The Ladybird" in *The Ladybird* (1923; Am., *The Captain's Doll*), "Fannie and Annie" (1921), and "The Blind Man" (1920).

L.'s poetry also merits attention. *Look! We Have Come Through!* (1917), his third volume, is a coherent group of confessional poems relating the harmony and conflicts of the unfolding relationship between L. and Frieda, or between any two lovers. In *Birds, Beasts and Flowers* (1923), the natural world offers paradigms for human behavior even as the poet celebrates its otherness. In fact, L.'s wonderment at the "foreignness" of all creatures, plant or animal, characterizes his entire canon and marks his reverence for the Unknown.

L. produced a large body of essayistic writing on subjects ranging from psychoanalysis to education, written in a colloquial and vibrant prose style and influenced by his extensive background readings. Especially noteworthy are his analyses of such American writers as Cooper, Hawthorne, Melville, and Poe, which were eventually revised and collected in *Studies in Classic American Literature* (1923). L. finds in this literature a twofold rhythm of disintegration of the old, European mental consciousness and the formation of a new, American passional self. At once impressionistic and persuasive, these essays are of a piece with all L.'s work in that they attempt to reform modern society and to get at the deeper meanings behind the raw data of experience.

In L. the artist and the prophet coexist. Some of L.'s works are damaged by his haranguing tone and protofascist views; L.'s most doctrinal fiction, however, typically contains the opposing viewpoint in the form of a devil's advocate or scoffer, and this viewpoint was in an important sense L.'s own. He was a questioner and doubter. His fiction's open-endedness results in great part from his unwillingness to commit himself fully to any doctrine, especially one that threatens the inviolate self. If at times his works reveal a misanthropy bordering on hysteria, and if his villains are pasteboard characters, still L. produced some of the most humane fiction and some of the most complex characters in modern literature. His greatness arises from his skill at so many literary forms; his intensity of expression; and his emphases on personal integrity, humankind's capacity for risk-taking intimacies, and the balanced polarity of instinct and reason.

FURTHER WORKS: *The Trespasser* (1912); *Love Poems and Others* (1913); *The Widowing of Mrs. Holroyd* (1914); *The Prussian Officer and Other Stories* (1914); *Twilight in Italy* (1916); *Amores* (1916); *New Poems* (1918); *Bay* (1919); *Touch and Go* (1920); *The Lost Girl* (1920); *Movements in European History* (1921, under pseud. Lawrence H. Davison); *Psychoanalysis and the Unconscious* (1921); *Tortoises* (1921); *Sea and Sardinia* (1921); *Fantasia of the Unconscious* (1922); *England, My England and Other Stories* (1922); *The Boy in the Bush* (1924, with M.L.Skinner); *St. Mawr, together with The Princess* (1925); *Reflections on the Death of a Porcupine and Other Essays* (1925); *David* (1926); *Sun* (1926; unexpurgated version, 1928); *Glad Ghosts* (1926); *Mornings in Mexico* (1927); *Selected Poems* (1928); *Rawdon's Roof* (1928); *The Woman Who Rode Away* (1928); *Collected Poems* (2 vols., 1928); *Sex Locked Out* (1929); *The Paintings of D. H. L.* (1929); *Pansies* (1929); *My Skirmish with Jolly Roger* (1929); *Pornography and Obscenity* (1929); *Nettles* (1930); *Assorted Articles* (1930); *A Propos of "Lady Chatterley's Lover"* (1930); *The Virgin and the Gipsy* (1930); *Love among the Haystacks, and Other Pieces* (1930); *Apocalypse* (1931); *The Triumph of the Machine* (1931); *Etruscan Places* (1932); *Letters* (1932); *Last Poems* (1932); *The Lovely Lady and Other Stories* (1933); *We Need One Another* (1933); *The Plays* (1933); *The Tales* (1933); *A Collier's Friday Night* (1934); *A Modern Lover* (1934); *The Spirit of Place* (1935); *Phoenix: The Posthumous Papers of D. H. L.* (1936); *Foreword to "Women in Love"* (1936); *Fire and Other Poems* (1940); *The First Lady Chatterley* (1944); *Letters to Bertrand Russell* (1948); *A Prelude* (1949); *The Complete Short Stories* (1955); *Eight Letters to Rachel Annand Taylor* (1956); *The Complete Poems* (1957); *The Collected Letters* (1962); *The Symbolic Meaning: The Uncollected Versions of "Studies in Classic American Literature"* (1962); *The Complete Poems* (1964); *The Paintings of D. H. L.* (1964); *The Complete Plays* (1965); *Phoenix II: Uncollected, Unpublished, and Other Prose Works* (1968); *L. in Love: Letters From D. H. L. to Louie Burrows* (1968); *The Quest For Rananim: D. H. L.'s Letters to S. S. Kotel iansky* (1970); *The Centaur Letters* (1970); *Letters to Martin Secker 1911–1930* (1970); *John Thomas and Lady Jane* (1972); *The Escaped Cock* (1973); *Letters to Thomas and Adele Seltzer* (1976); *The Letters* (1979 ff.)

BIBLIOGRAPHY: Carswell, C., *The Savage Pilgrimage* (1932); Lawrence, F., *Not I, but the Wind* (1934); Chambers, J. [E. T.], *D. H. L.: A Personal Record* (1935); Leavis, F. R., *D. H. L.: Novelist* (1955); Spilka, *The Love Ethic of D. H. L.* (1955); Hough, G., *The Dark Sun: A Study of D. H. L.* (1957); Nehls, E., ed., *D. H. L.: A Composite Biography* (3 vols. 1957–59); Vivas, E., *D. H. L.: The Failure and the Triumph of Art* (1960); Beal, A., *D. H. L.* (1961); Widmer, K., *The Art of Perversity: D. H. L.'s Shorter Fictions* (1962); Moynahan, J., *The Deed of Life* (1963); Roberts, F. W., *A Bibliography of D. H. L.* (1963); Daleski, H., *The Forked Flame: A Study of D. H. L.* (1965); Ford, G., *Double Measure: A Study of the Novels and Stories of D. H. L.* (1965); Sagar, K., *The Art of D. H. L.* (1966); Clarke, C., *River of Dissolution: D. H. L. and the Romantic* (1969); Cowan, J., *D. H. L.'s American Journey* (1970); Gilbert, S., *Acts of Attention: The Poems of D. H. L.* (1972); Kermode, F., *D. H. L.* (1973); Sanders, S., *D. H. L.: The World of the Major Novels* (1973); Moore, H., *The Priest of Love: A Life of D. H. L.* (1974); Delany, P., *D. H. L.'s Nightmare: The Writer and His Circle in the Years of the Great War* (1978); Meyers, J., *D. H. L.: A Biography* (1990); Fernihough, A., *D. H. L.: Aesthetics and Ideology* (1993); Thornton, W., *D. H. L.: a Study of the Short Fiction* (1993); Poplawski, P., *D. H. L.: A Reference Companion* (1996); Becket, F., *D. H. L.: The Thinker as Poet* (1997); Ellis, D., *D. H. L., Dying Game* (1998)

—JUDITH RUDERMAN

He harangues us like Carlyle, whom he resembled in many aspects; the artist in him was doubled with the rhetorician. He too sprang from a poverty-cramped, sullen, illiterate fighting-stock; he too was the favored child of a mother who represented in those surroundings a superior and pious refinement; he too was born with a suspicion of any sort of agreement, and with a conviction, often agonized, that everybody must be wrong except himself; he was born too with a faculty for exquisite sympathy for individuals and an almost sadistic relish for the sufferings of people in general . . . he too was a humorist whose sense of fun sprang from a constantly tragic sense of life; he too was a prodigious egotist, yet in himself strangely lovable and fascinating, his egotism finding relief in minatory "uplift" diatribes, and showing itself in his intolerance of the smallest self-assertion on the part of others. For L. the egotist, to whom the experience of "love" was the crucial test of individual excellence, egotism, legitimate or illegitimate, in that relation, was a central problem. He too was, in a sense in which that phrase has a meaning apart from accomplishment, "a great man," one whom to be near, whether through his writings, or directly, meant for others an enhancement of life.

Desmond MacCarthy, *Criticism* (1932), p. 248

[A]mong all English novelists, Hardy and L. have the most faithful touch for the things of nature and the greatest evocative genius in bringing them before the imagination. But there are certain definitive differences of attitude. Both Emily Brontë's and Hardy's worlds are dual, and there is no way of bringing the oppositions of the dualism together: on the one side . . . are those attributes of man that we call "human," his reason, his ethical sensibility; and on the other side is "nature"—the elements and the creatures and man's own instinctive life that he shares with the nonhuman creatures. The opposition is resolved only by destruction of the "human": a destruction that is in Emily Brontë profoundly attractive, in Hardy tragic. But L.'s world is multiple rather than dual. Everything in it is a separate and individual "other" . . . ; and there is a creative relationship between people and between people and things so long as this "otherness" is acknowledged. When it is denied— and it is denied when man tries to rationalize nature and society, or when he presumptuously assumes the things of nature to be merely instruments for the expression of himself, or when he attempts to exercise personal possessorship over people—then he destroys his own selfhood and exerts a destructive influence all about him.

Dorothy Van Ghent, *The English Novel: Form and Function* (1953), p. 252

In the relations between man and woman . . . L. called for balance or "polarity," as if between two oppositely charged entities; or he placed the marriage unit itself in balance with the world of purposive activity—so that the protagonists of his novels must also be in tune, as it were, with the world around them. In other words, they must achieve organic being through "an infinity of pure relations" with the living universe: first, with each other, through love; then with other men and women, through friendship and creative labor; and finally even with birds, beasts, and flowers, which play a vital role in all the novels.

Once this is clearly understood, his psychology begins to take on flesh and substance; it falls within a greater and essentially religious scheme of life, and draws its depth and quality from that fact. Indeed, this interpenetration of the greater universe with specific situations, of the "lifeforce" with a well-developed psychology of life, is the hallmark of Lawrentian fiction. . . .

Mark Spilka, *The Love Ethic of D. H. L.* (1955), pp. 10–11

L. continually enlarges the boundaries of our consciousness, and a judgment of his individual artistic achievement will in the long run probably depend on the extent and the worth of the new territory acquired. Of course with many novelists this kind of inquiry would be pointless. They are concerned with putting in order experiences of a kind we are already quite familiar with. L. (or Dostoevsky or, in his own way, Proust) extends our experience; and to think about a novelist of this kind at once lands us in difficulties. We cannot talk for long about technique, powers of representation or even of moral insight; for we soon find that we are dealing with ideas and mental states that we have never clearly recognized till we meet them in this particular artistic context. Of course we can set L. against traditional moral habits, as Mr. Eliot does . . . ; and of course L. comes out a heretic. To define the limits of his offences against faith and morals may be a useful thing, even highly illuminating. But the net is so wide that the essence of his work simply slips through the mesh, as Mr. Eliot knows well.

Graham Hough, *The Dark Sun: A Study of D. H. L.* (1956), p. 4

Because the form of action in the behavioral sense is easier to perceive than the structure of inward experience, a first reading of L. and even a second or third gives us little more than a chaos of incidents and scenes that, however brilliantly presented, seem to lack formal interrelationships. But persistent search for the structure of the work is at last rewarded. Synoptically we grasp the pattern of an ordered whole. We notice the first signs of nascent desire turning into clearly directed urge and notice the passional urge seeking satisfaction and succeeding or arriving at frustration; we notice the pattern of attraction and repulsion, the harmony of wills or their clash, and back of these harmonies or conflicts we notice the values that these inward commotions seek to realize and succeed or fail in realizing. And strange as it might seem, since L. is so frequently dismissed as antirational, we notice also the growth in wisdom on the part of his characters—or of what L. takes to be wisdom—and the causes for the success or failure of that growth.

Eliseo Vivas, *D. H. L.: The Failure and the Triumph of Art* (1960), pp. 225–26

On one dimension, which *The Rainbow* shares with the novels of Wells and Bennett, Ursula is the ordinary village girl whose struggle to find herself in the modern world is representatively commonplace. On a second dimension, however, a dimension rarely represented at all in the novels of Wells and Bennett, this ordinary girl is likened to a prophet from the Bible whose life-story is told as if it were of mythic or epic-scale significance. . . .

L. once described the Bible as "a great confused novel," and one is tempted, in the fashion of Oscar

Wilde, to retort that *The Rainbow* is a great confused bible. The Bible, L. adds, is not a book about God but about man alive. . . .

[T]here is considerable similarity between [James] Joyce's use of Homeric parallels in *Ulysses* and L.'s use of Biblical parallels. Even though the apparent discrepancy between the large-scaled epic heroes and heroines of antiquity and their more ordinary modern-day equivalents is played up by Joyce for effects of comedy that are different from L.'s. . . , the author of *Ulysses* is nevertheless using similar methods for similar ends. Both novelists, dissatisfied with the one-dimensional level of naturalistic fiction, create a second dimension by suggesting, through parallels, that human experience is constant rather than totally chaotic.

George Ford, *Double Measure: A Study of the*
Novels and Stories of D. H. L. (1965), pp. 133–34

Homage to the mystery of power . . . is as essential to L.'s extremely Romantic conception of poetry as to the relationship of leader and follower. And such homage necessarily precludes irony, just as the leadership novels precluded any real exploration of the complexities of self-achievement. The profound egalitarianism which, as L. recognized, is an absolute prerequisite of true democracy, permits the sort of relativism that leads to an ironic—Prufrockian—qualification of experience: "Who am I to ask the overwhelming question? Why not so-and-so?" In the aristocratic Lawrentian system, however, both leader and follower must commit themselves, without ironic reservations, to the power both apprehend as mysteriously fluent in the leader. And therefore the world-vision of both is not ironic, like that of most modern, egalitarian men, but anti-ironic, wholly concentrated on the wonder of power. . . .

In a way, then, L.'s bitterness about the war . . . made possible the writing of *Birds, Beasts and Flowers*, and, more, the success of the poems in that volume. His bitterness inspired a temporary but intense misanthropy, resulting in a contempt for the mass of mankind and a belief in the "sacred right" of a specially chosen few to guide the many. Such a leadership obsession, however incompatible with the writing of successful novels, led to the composition of visionary, anti-ironic poetry.

Sandra Gilbert, *Acts of Attention: The Poems of*
D. H. L. (1972), pp. 128–29

[L.] was not on the whole sympathetic to, or even very interested in, the avant-garde movements of his time; if we were to try to relate his innovations to those, virtually contemporary, of Hulme in England or Apollinaire in France, we should be struck at once by his apparent isolation, by the way he worked things out for himself. The formative years, for example, of André Breton, can be recounted with reference to large and well-documented movements

such as Dada and Surrealism; at a deeper level we could find affinities with L.—for example, in common apocalyptic and occult preoccupations—but L. is always working alone. His relationship to the history of ideas in his time is so far below the surface that to write it would be to engage in very delicate and also very speculative excavations. And this is true of his political as well as of his psychological and aesthetic positions.

Frank Kermode, *D. H. L.* (1973), pp. 25–26

LAXNESS, Halldór

Icelandic novelist, dramatist, essayist, and poet, b. 23 April 1902, Reykjavík; d. 1 February 1998, outside Reykjavík

L. grew up in Reykjavík and nearby Mosfellssveit, thus absorbing both urban and rural influences in his youth. He left school early in order to concentrate on writing. After traveling extensively in Europe and North America in the 1920s, he returned to Iceland, where he has since resided, the first man to earn a living as a creative writer in Icelandic.

At seventeen L. published his first novel, *Barn náttúrunnar* (1919; child of nature), and in the same year made his first journey abroad. During the following decade he struggled to develop an understanding of himself and his world, and to forge a personal style. After his first contact with the turbulent cultural life of Europe, he converted to Roman Catholicism; but after a brief novitiate in a monastery in Luxembourg, his interests again became secular.

This period brought forth L.'s first major novel, *Vefarinn mikli frá Kasmír* (1927; the great weaver of Kashmir), a semiautobiographical work that seethes with uncompromising views about the condition of modern man. Its forceful EXPRESSIONISM, outspokenness, and utter disregard of stylistic and moral conventions offended and shocked most readers, but won high praise from a minority.

While the protagonist of *Vefarinn mikli frá Kasmír* ends by rejecting the world and turning to God, L. himself went in the opposite direction. Even before he went to North America in 1927, his Catholicism was weakening; direct experiences with American capitalism and its critics (he became personally acquainted with Upton SINCLAIR) turned him into an ardent socialist. His socialism inspired *Alpýðubókin* (1929; a book for the people), an essay collection written in America but addressed to his countrymen. In it L. declares man to be the only proper human concern, and vows to dedicate his art to the destiny of his people.

During the next twenty years L. published a series of novels in which he depicts, on an epic scale, the struggle of Iceland's poor against the brutalities of nature and social oppression. In this period L. the mature novelist and master of Icelandic prose emerged. His writing combines compassion, humor, and biting social satire.

In *Sjálfstætt fólk* (2 vols., 1934–35; *Independent People*, 1946) the protagonist is a small farmer who, after many years in the service of others, has bought some land and thereby acquired independence in his own eyes and those of society. The story describes his prolonged struggle to retain this independence; this struggle makes virtual slaves of himself and his family, brings sickness and death to two wives in succession, and ends in loss of the farm in the Great Depression. Unbroken, but having achieved a new understanding of himself and society, he prepares himself for another struggle ahead. Although this novel is set in a remote corner of Iceland, it epitomizes the Icelandic farmers' thousand-year battle against nature and exploitation; it is also a parable about Iceland's development as it began to change from a semicolonial peasant society into an independent capitalist state.

The central theme of *Heimsljós* (4 vols., 1937–40; *World Light*, 1969), another important novel of the 1930s, is the function of traditional literary culture in Icelandic life, even among the poorest. The story, set in a small fishing village dominated by a local "tyrant," is about a destitute poet who is torn between the demands made on him by his love of art and beauty on the one hand, and by his hatred of social injustice on the other.

Íslandsklukkan (3 vols., 1943–46; the bell of Iceland), which appeared during the war years, when Iceland finally acquired independence, takes national culture and national destiny as its major themes. This is a historical novel, based on actual events of the early 18th c., the darkest period in Iceland's history. The ineffectual culture of the upper class, personified by the manuscript collector Arnas Arnæus, is contrasted with the more robust lifestyle of the lower classes, in the person of the invincible fisherman Jón Hreggviðsson. *Íslandsklukkan* gives a vivid picture of Icelandic life in the 18th c. Most of the inhabitants are miserable, even destitute, and great parts of the nation's most valued treasure, the Arnæus manuscript collection, go up in flames when Copenhagen is burned. Despite these conditions, there is an obstinate clinging to life, and the vivid hope of better times ahead—no signs of which, however, are to be seen. Here, as everywhere in L.'s social satire, the grimness of life is counterbalanced by deep compassion and refined humor.

In subsequent novels L. has taken his subject matter from Icelandic postwar society as well as the 11th, 19th, and early 20th cs. In the 1950s he gradually abandoned socialism, and his writing took a new direction. In autobiographical works he denounced Soviet communism and ideologies in general. His later novels are characterized by philosophical skepticism, a semimystical faith in life, and an affirmation of simple values of people who, without being selfish, tend their gardens, and look upon the great and the mighty with a condescending pity.

L. was very prolific. Apart from his novels, he published numerous plays, short stories, memoirs, and essays, as well as a volume of poetry. He used a variety of narrative techniques, but moved steadily in the direction of objective and dramatic presentation of characters and situations. His style is rich, but not easily rendered in other languages. Always unmistakably personal, it grew in complexity and idiosyncrasy during the 1940s and 1950s, but he simplified his style while retaining a subtle irony. With the partial exception of *Vefarinn mikli frá Kasmír*, L. always chose realistic themes from Icelandic life; but in his work their meaning transcends geographical and cultural boundaries.

The Nobel Prize for Literature, which he won in 1955, is a token of his international stature.

FURTHER WORKS: *Nokkrar sögur* (1923); *Undir Helgahnúk* (1924); *Kvæðakver* (1930); *Salka Valka* (2 vols., 1931–1932; *Salka Valka*, 1936); *Fótatak manna* (1933); *Straumrof* (1934); *Dagleið á fjöllum* (1937); *Gerska ævintýrið* (1938); *Vettvangur dagsins* (1942); *Sjö töframenn* (1942); *Sjálfsagðir hlutir* (1946); *Atómstöðin* (1948; *The Atom Station*, (1961); *Reisubókarkorn* (1950); *Heiman eg fór* (1952); *Gerpla* (1952; *The Happy Warriors*, 1958); *Silfurtúnglið* (1954); *Dagur í senn* (1955); *Brekkukotsannáll* (1957; *The Fish Can Sing*, 1966); *Gjörníngabók* (1959); *Paradísarheimt* (1960; *Paradise Reclaimed*, 1962); *Strompleikurinn* (1961); *Prjónastofan Sólin* (1962); *Skáldatími* (1963); *Sjöstafakverið* (1964); *Upphaf mannúðarstefnu* (1965); *Dúfnaveislan* (1966); *Islendíngaspjall* (1967); *Kristnihald undir Jökli* (1968; *Christianity at Glacier*, 1972); *Vínlandspúnktar* (1969); *Innansveitarkronika* (1970); *Yfirskyggðir staðir* (1971); *Guðsgjafaþula* (1972); *Þjóðhátíðarrolla* (1974); *Í túninu heima* (1975); *Úngur eg var* (1976); *Seiseijú, mikil ósköp* (1977); *Sjömeistarasagan* (1978); *Grikklandsárið* (1980); *Við heygarðshornið* (1981)

BIBLIOGRAPHY: Einarsson, S., "A Contemporary Icelandic Author," *Life and Letters Today*, 14, 4 (1936): 23–30; Kötz, G., *Das Problem Dichter und Gesellschaft im Werke von H. K. L.* (1966); Lange, W., "Über H. L.," *GRM*, 14 (1966): 76–89; Hallberg, P., *H. L.* (1971); Wilz, O., "Der Wikingerroman als politische Tendenzschrift: Zu H. L.s *Gerpla*," *Skandinavistik*, 1 (1971): 1–16; special L. issue, *Scan*, 2, 1 (1972); Sonderegger, S., "Rede auf H. L.," in *H. L. in St. Gallen* (1974): 9–34; Höskuldsson, S., "Women and Love in the Novels of L.," *NorS*, 6 (1975): 3–20; Pálsson, H., "Beyond the Atom Station," in Höskuldsson, S., ed., *Ideals and Ideologies in Scandinavian Literature* (1975): 317–29

—VÉSTEINN ÓLASON

LAYTON, Irving

Canadian poet (writing in English), b. 12 March 1912, Neamtz, Romania

Brought to Canada at the age of one, L. was raised in the Jewish immigrant district of Montreal. After earning a bachelor's degree in agriculture and serving in the Royal Canadian Artillery (1942–43), he studied history and political economy at McGill University, where he earned an M.A. in 1946. During the 1930s L. became known as a fiery Marxist orator, and he thought his career would be as a political analyst of world affairs. By the early 1940s, however, his poetic talent had begun to emerge, and eventually he decided to devote himself to writing poetry, while earning a living through teaching. He became one of the editors of an avant-garde poetry magazine, *First Statement*, and a founding member of Contact Press, a venture promoting contemporary poetry in Canada. In the 1940s and 1950s he published several volumes of poems and short stories that reached a small but appreciative audience.

In 1959 a commercial publisher launched L.'s first sizable collection, *A Red Carpet for the Sun*, with considerable fanfare. During the next decade L. became a controversial public figure in Canada. His dynamic presence on radio, television, and the poetry-reading circuit, and his provocative prefaces and interviews, combined with the sensational aspects of his poetry, served to create a public image of an iconoclast, an irreverent sensualist, and a relentless satirist. Most critics were distracted by this image, but those, like Northrop FRYE and George Woodcock (b. 1912), who managed to see beyond it, discovered L. to be an elegant, elegiac poet with an extraordinary range of technical ability and a complex, integrated vision. Others, like William Carlos WILLIAMS applauded the candor, vitality, and audacity of the poems.

L.'s oeuvre consists of over thirty volumes, including two collections of prose and several collected or selected editions of verse, the best of the latter to date being *The Darkening Fire* (1975) and *The Unwavering Eye* (1975). Recently retired from his professorship at York University, L. continues to travel widely and is in great demand as a speaker and reader.

L.'s early poetry displayed a Marxist orientation, and to this day he maintains an admiration for Marx the man, and his early writings. But L. was never a doctrinaire Marxist; and, particularly since the early 1950s, his denunciations of Marxism as an ideology, and especially of Russian Communism, have been a persistent strain in his poetry. Since the early 1950s, too, his work has revealed a remarkably strong affinity with Nietzschean thought. In fact, most of L.'s poetry may be read with great profit in a Nietzschean perspective.

L.'s poetry is also marked by an awareness of his Jewish heritage, sharpened in the late 1960s by the Arab-Israeli conflict. Since that time he has become increasingly concerned with Jewish themes—with the Holocaust, with anti-Semitism in the Soviet Union and elsewhere, and particularly with the historical and current relations between Jews and Christians.

In the early 1970s he embarked on a "campaign" to reclaim Jesus for the Jews and to laugh the remnants of "Xianity" out of existence. His concept of the Jew, however—"Someone/who feels himself to be/a stranger/everywhere/Even in Israel"—merges on the one hand with the figure of the poet-prophet and, on the other, with the Nietzschean superman, the heroic individualist who by selfmastery and creativity learns to extract a tragic joy from existence. This complex figure, in one guise or another, is at the center of L.'s work. Through it he explores the moral, political, and psychological dilemmas of modern man and probes the erotic and demonic depths of the human psyche, not least his own. An unflinching confrontation with reality leads L. to a sardonic view of human nature and a tragic vision of man's cosmic fate. To this he opposes an exuberant celebration of life through the redemptive agencies of imagination and love. ("Whatever else, poetry is freedom," he claims.) This world is hell indeed; but, as opposed to meek and passive acceptance of suffering, L. applauds those who passionately resist evil, despair, and death.

FURTHER WORKS: *Here and Now* (1945); *Now Is the Place* (1948); *The Black Huntsmen* (1951); *Cerberus* (1952, with L.Dudek and R.Souster); *Love the Conqueror Worm* (1953); *In the Midst of My Fever* (1954); *The Long Pea-Shooter* (1954); *The Blue Propeller* (1955); *The Cold Green Element* (1955); *The Bull Calf and Other Poems* (1956); *Music on a Kazoo* (1956); *The Improved Binoculars* (1956); *A Laughter in the Mind* (1958); *The Swinging Flesh* (1961); *Balls for a One-Armed Juggler* (1963); *The Laughing Rooster* (1964); *Collected Poems* (1965); *Periods of the Moon* (1967); *The Shattered Plinths* (1968); *Selected Poems* (1969); *The Whole Bloody Bird* (1969); *Nail Polish* (1971); *The Collected Poems of I. L.* (1971); *Engagements: The Prose of I. L.* (1972); *Lovers and Lesser Men* (1973); *The Pole-Vaulter* (1974); *Seventy-five Greek Poems* (1974); *For My Brother Jesus* (1976); *The Poems of I. L.* (1977); *Taking Sides* (1977); *The Uncollected Poems of I. L.* (1977); *The Covenant* (1977); *The Tightrope Dancer* (1978); *The Love Poems of I. L.* (1978); *Droppings from Heaven* (1979); *An Unlikely Affair: The I. L.—Dorothy Rath Correspondence* (1980);

For My Neighbours in Hell (1980); *Europe and Other Bad News* (1981); *I. L. and Robert Creeley: The Complete Correspondence, 1953-1978* (1990)

BIBLIOGRAPHY: Woodcock, G., "A Grab at Proteus", *CanL*, No. 28 (1966): 5–21; Mandel, E., *I. L.* (1969); Doyle, M., "The Occasion of I. L.," *CanL*, No. 54 (1972): 70–83; Mayne, S., ed., *I. L.: The Poet and His Critics* (1978); Van Wilt, K., "L., Nietzsche and Overcoming," *ECW*, 10 (1978): 19–42; Baker, H., "Jewish Themes in the Works of I. L.," *ECW*, 10 (1978): 43–54; Francis, W., "The Farting Jesus: L. and the Heroic Vitalists," *Contemporary Verse Two*, 3, 3 (1978): 46–51

—WYNNE FRANCIS

LEACOCK, Stephen

Canadian short-story writer, novelist, essayist, and political economist (writing in English), b. 30 Dec. 1869, Swanmore, England; d. 28 March 1944, Toronto, Ontario

L.'s upper-middle class family emigrated when he was six to Canada, where they lived an impoverished farm life in Simcoe County, Ontario. He earned a Ph.D. at the University of Chicago by 1903, and became a professor of economics and political science at McGill University, Montreal, a post he held until his retirement in 1936. A superb raconteur and speaker, he was much in demand for public appearances, and toured the British Empire in this role in 1907–8. L. was also highly regarded as a university teacher and administrator.

L.'s first book, *Elements of Political Science* (1906), long a university textbook, was his best moneymaker, but his reputation rests on his works of humor, which constitute the bulk of his output and led to the establishment of the Leacock Society and its Leacock Medal for the best book of humor published in Canada each year. L. published his first book of humor, *Literary Lapses* (1910), at his own expense. A collection of monologues, parodies, and comments on various topics, many of which he developed in later works, it shows that his singular ability to portray universal human imperfection in a way that stirs the reader to both sympathy and laughter matured early and did not appreciably progress; for it contains many pieces published previously in journals, some of which, for example "My Financial Career" (1895), he never subsequently surpassed.

Sunshine Sketches of a Little Town (1912), a comedy of pastoral sentiment, mirrored so vividly the mores of small-town life that it incensed a generation of the people of its model, Orillia, Ontario, site of L.'s summer home. *Arcadian Adventures with the Idle Rich* (1914) bubbles with fun and ripples with nonsense but also swirls with somber undercurrents of sharp irony and anger as it indicts the self-interest and the focus on money and power of the North American big city. Both works consist of linked stories; lacking the structural unity of novels, they nevertheless cohere because of their unity of tone and purpose. L.'s shorter fiction likewise succeeds more by a convincing creation of atmosphere and social environment than by the usual plot and characterization of the genre.

L. satirizes institutions, types, and patterns of behavior rather than persons. His targets include wealth, church, government, the business world, education, and con artists together with their gullible victims; these subjects reflect his deep concern that socialism, technology, and commercialism would deny human individuality and dignity.

His success as a humorist can be judged by the continued appearance in paperback editions of many works. *Nonsense Novels* (1911) and *Frenzied Fiction* (1918) parody types of popular fiction of the times, for example, the Sherlock Holmes stories; *Moonbeams from the Larger Lunacy* (1915) tackles human follies ranging from prize-novel contests to World War I; *My Discovery of England* (1922), one of his best, and like his best drawn from personal experience, laughs at topics such as Oxford University and the "public speaker."

L. wrote quickly—almost a book a year—with little concern for literary convention, but he is no glib comic, for his humor is balanced by an awareness of the deliberate evil of much human motive and act. His forté is the short impressionistic glimpse of the incongruities in human interaction. His works on the theory of humor, his criticism, and his biographies of humorists lack the imaginative spark of his creative writing, which brought him an international reputation, with translations into many languages, and made him the best-selling humorist writing in English between 1910 and 1925. L. was the successor in North American humor to the Canadian Thomas Chandler Haliburton (1796–1865) and the American Mark Twain; but whereas those reflect respectively the British and the American humorist traditions, L. speaks with a Canadian sensibility and peoples his humorous writings with distinctively Canadian characters.

FURTHER WORKS: *Baldwin, Lafontaine, Hincks: Responsible Government* (1907; rev. ed., *Mackenzie, Baldwin, LaFontaine, Hincks*, 1926); *Greater Canada, An Appeal: Let Us No Longer Be a Colony* (1907); *Behind the Beyond and Other Contributions to Human Knowledge* (1913); *Laugh with L.* (1913); *Adventures of the Far North: A Chronicle of the Frozen Seas* (1914); *The Dawn of Canadian History: A Chronicle of Aboriginal Canada* (1914); *The Mariner of St. Malo* (1914); *The Methods of Mr. Sellyer* (1914); *The Marionettes' Calendar* (1915); *Marionettes' Engagement Book* (1915); *"Q.": A Farce in One Act* (1915, with B. M. Hastings); *Essays and Literary Studies* (1916); *Further Foolishness* (1916); *The Hohenzollerns in America, with The Boshelviks in Berlin, and Other Impossibilities* (1919); *The Unsolved Riddle of Social Justice* (1920); *Winsome Winnie and Other New Nonsense Novels* (1920); *College Days* (1923); *Over the Footlights* (1923); *The Garden of Folly* (1924); *The Proper Limitations of State Interference* (1924); *Winnowed Wisdom* (1926); *Short Circuits* (1928); *The Iron Man and the Tin Woman* (1929); *Economic Prosperity in the British Empire* (1930); *The L. Book* (1930); *Wet Wit and Dry Humor, Distilled from the Pages of S. L.* (1931); *Afternoons in Utopia* (1932); *Back to Prosperity* (1932); *The Dry Pickwick and Other Incongruities* (1932); *Lahontan's Voyages* (1932); *Mark Twain* (1932); *Winsome Winnie: A Romantic Drama* (1932, with V. C. Clinton-Baddeley); *Charles Dickens: His Life and Work* (1933); *S. L.'s Plan to Relieve the Depression* (1933); *The Greatest Pages of Charles Dickens* (1934); *Lincoln Frees the Slaves* (1934); *The Perfect Salesman* (1934); *The Pursuit of Knowledge* (1934); *Humour, Its Theory and Technique* (1935); *Funny Pieces* (1936); *The Gathering Financial Crisis in Canada* (1936); *Hellements of Hickonomics, in Hiccoughs of Verse Done in Our Social Planning Mill* (1936); *The Greatest Pages of American Humour, Selected and Discussed by S. L.* (1936); *Here Are My Lectures and Stories* (1937); *Humour and Humanity* (1937); *My Discovery of the West* (1937); *Model Memoirs* (1938); *All Right, Mr. Roosevelt* (1939); *Too Much College; or, Education Eating Up Life* (1939); *Laugh Parade* (1940); *Our British Empire: Its Structure, Its History, Its Strength* (1940); *Canada: The Foundation of Its Future* (1941); *Montreal: Seaport and City* (1942; repub. as *L.'s Montreal*, 1948); *My Remarkable Uncle* (1942); *Our Heritage of Liberty: Its Origin, Its Achievement, Its Crisis* (1942); *Happy Stories, Just to Laugh At* (1943); *How to Write* (1943); *"My Old College" 1843–1943* (1943); *Memories of Christmas* (1943); *Canada and the Sea* (1944, with Leslie Roberts, Wallace Ward, and J. A. Morton); *Last Leaves* (1945); *While There Is Time: The Case against Social Catastrophe* (1945); *The Boy I Left behind Me* (1946); *The L. Roundabout* (1946); *The Bodley Head L.* (1957; Can., *The Best of L.*); *The Unicorn L.* (1960); *Caroline's Christmas* (1969); *Hoodoo McFiggin's Christmas* (1970); *Feast of Stephen* (1970); *L.* (1970); *The Social Criticism of S. L.* (1973); *Laugh with L.: An Anthology of the Best Work of S. L.* (1981); *The Penguin S. L.* (1981)

BIBLIOGRAPHY: Curry, R. L., *S. L.: Humorist and Humanist* (1959); Watters, R. E., "A Special Tang: S. L.'s Canadian Humour," *CanL*, 5 (1960): 21–32; Cameron, D. A., *Faces of L.: An Appreciation* (1967); Davies, R., *S. L.* (1970); Kimball, E., *The Man in the Panama Hat: Reminiscences of My Uncle, S. L.* (1970); Legate, D. M., *S. L.* (1970); Clever, G., "L.'s Dunciad," *SCL*, 1 (1976): 238–41; Lynch, G., *S. L.: Humour and Humanity* (1988)

—GLENN CLEVER

LEAVIS, F(rank) R(aymond)

English literary critic, b. 16 July 1895, Cambridge; d. 17 April, 1978, Cambridge

L. was educated at Emmanuel College, Cambridge, where he studied history and English. In 1932 he became Director of English Studies at Downing College, and in 1936 he was appointed Assistant Lecturer in the University and a Fellow of Downing. After 1962, when the Downing Fellowship ended, L. was a visiting professor at various British universities.

In 1932 L. helped to found *Scrutiny*, an influential journal of literary criticism, which he edited from 1932 until 1953, when it ceased publication. His wife, Q. D. (Queenie Dorothy) Leavis (b. 1906), the author of *Fiction and the Reading Public* (1932), collaborated with L. on *Scrutiny* and on a number of books.

L.'s first major publication was *New Bearings in English Poetry: A Study of the Contemporary Situation* (1932). This radical and influential work, which focused on T. S. ELIOT, Ezra POUND, and Gerard Manley Hopkins, was instrumental in establishing their reputations and defining their importance as leaders of a contemporary revolution in English poetry against what L. called the "debilitated nineteenth-century tradition."

L.'s next important critical book, *Revaluation: Tradition and Development in English Poetry* (1936), was a collection of essays that had first appeared as a series of articles in *Scrutiny*, but it was also a continuation of the argument L. had begun in *New Bearings in English Poetry*. In *Revaluation* L. turned to earlier poets, from the metaphysical poets (early 17th c.) to the Victorians, to redefine the tradition of English poetry in terms of the qualities he had already praised in Eliot and Hopkins. L.'s revaluation of the English poetic tradition elevated the metaphysical poets and Pope at the expense of Milton, Dryden, and Shelley. Along with T. S. Eliot and the American New Critics, L. helped to create the contemporary taste for metaphysical wit and complexity.

In the 1940s, L. turned his attention from poetry to the novel. Beginning in 1941, he published a series of essays on the novel in *Scrutiny*, which were later collected in *The Great Tradition: George Eliot, Henry James, Joseph Conrad* (1948). L. added an introductory chapter that began with the controversial statement, "The great English novelists are Jane Austen, George Eliot, Henry James and Joseph Conrad." Although L. later enlarged the "great tradition" to some extent, he never wavered in his conviction that the quality that distinguished the writers who belonged to it was "a vital capacity for experience, a kind of reverent openness before life, and a marked moral intensity."

In *The Great Tradition* L. illustrated his thesis with studies of George ELIOT, JAMES, and CONRAD. He believed that D. H. LAWRENCE was the 20th-c. heir to the great tradition, but he had already treated Lawrence in an earlier pamphlet, *D. H. Lawrence* (1930), and he would later devote two books to Lawrence—*D. H. Lawrence, Novelist* (1955) and *Thought, Words and Creativity: Art and Thought in Lawrence* (1976). As for Austen, Q. D. Leavis had already produced a series of *Scrutiny* articles on her work. L. did not place Dickens in his great tradition, but he did provide a final chapter on *Hard Times*, which he believed then to be the only one of Dickens's novels that was a "completely serious work of art." L. later revised this estimate, however. In *Dickens, the Novelist* (1970), written in collaboration with Q. D. Leavis, L. argued that Dickens was not only a great novelist but also a "genius of a greater kind" than Henry James.

Both as a critic and as a teacher, L. inspired dedicated disciples; but he also engaged opponents in vehement critical controversies. His passionate advocacy of the literary and moral values he espoused sometimes descended, especially in later years, to the level of strident personal battles with advocates of opposing positions (L.'s attacks on C. P. SNOW are probably the most notorious).

The importance of L.'s contribution to 20th-c. criticism cannot be denied. By his lifelong dedication to the principle that literary values cannot be separated from ethical values, his insistence upon the social relevance of literature, and his emphasis on discrimination and evaluation as central critical tasks, L. preserved the tradition of Matthew Arnold of humanistic criticism is a generally antihumanistic age.

FURTHER WORKS: *Mass Civilisation and Minority Culture* (1930); *How to Teach Reading: A Primer for Ezra Pound* (1932); *For Continuity* (1933); *Culture and Environment: The Training of Critical Awareness* (1933, with D. Thompson); *Education and the University: A Sketch for an "English School"* (1943); *The Common Pursuit* (1952); *Two Cultures? The Significance of C. P. Snow* (1962); *Anna Karenina, and Other Essays* (1967); *Lectures in America* (1969, with Q.D.L.); *English Literature in Our Time and the University* (1969); *Nor Shall My Sword: Discourses on Pluralism, Compassion and Social Hope* (1972); *Letters in Criticism* (1974); *The Living Principle: English as a Discipline of Thought* (1975); *The Critic as Anti-Philosopher: Essays and Papers* (1982); *Valuation in Criticism and Other Essays* (1986)

BIBLIOGRAPHY: Bentley, E., ed., *The Importance of Scrutiny* (1948); Buckley, V., *Poetry and Morality: Studies on the Criticism of Matthew Arnold, T. S. Eliot, and F. R. L.* (1959): 158–233; Watson, G., *The Literary Critics: A Study of English Descriptive Criticism* (1964): 205–15 and passim; Wellek, R., "The Literary Criticism of F. R. L.," in Camden, C., ed., *Literary Views: Critical and Historical Essays* (1964): 175–93; Hayman, R., *L.* (1976); Bilan, R. P., *The Literary Criticism of F. R. L.* (1979); Walsh, W., *F. R. L.* (1980)

—PHYLLIS RACKIN

LEBANESE LITERATURE

In Arabic

Benefiting from centuries of close contact with Western civilization, Lebanese writers, translators and journalists in the 19th c. were instrumental in bringing about the literary renascence of the Arabs. Yet while the efforts of the key Lebanese figures of this movement aimed mainly at reviving the classical language after a long period of decadence, the work of the writers in the 20th c. concentrated on innovation in the language of prose and poetry and on experimentation in new genres: the novel, the short story and the drama.

Poetry

During the first three decades of the 20th c. a new poetic sensibility was evident in the compositions of Bishārā al-Khūrī (1884?–1968) and Amīn Nakhla (b. 1901) in Lebanon and the Lebanese Khalīl Mutrān (1870–1949) in Egypt. Al-Khūrī's *Dīwān al-hawā wa al-shabāb* (pub. 1953; the divan of love and youth) introduced into Arabic poetry a fresh diction, a music reminiscent of the Andalusian *Muwashshahas* (strophic poems invented in Arab Spain in the late 9th or early 10th c.), and a sincerity of emotion unknown in earlier poetry. In *Dafātir al-ghazal* (1952; notebooks of love poems), Nakhla chose words with a care much like that of the French Parnassian poets, and practiced a method of composition that was to serve as a check on the rampant experiments of succeeding romantic poets. Mutrān's contributions were in the genre of narrative poetry, in his concern for organic unity, and in his experiments in new poetic forms. His *Dīwān al-Khalīl* (1908; the divan of al-Khalīl) was an early source of inspiration for the poets of the time.

Creative activity among Lebanese writers, however, was not confined to the Middle East; oppressive political and social circumstances leading up to and beyond the civil strife of the 1850s had led many prominent Christian families to emigrate, in particular to the Americas. Thus, in the first quarter of the 20th c., the literary activity called *Adab al-Mahjar* (the literature of the Americas) was initiated. The most prominent writers were members of the Society of the Pen, founded in North America by Khalīl (Kahlil) GIBRĀN in 1920, and the Lebanese and Syrian members of the Andalusian League, formed in Brazil in 1932. Whereas the Society of the Pen propagated a universal outlook and the creation of a new language capable of changing the whole conception of classical Arabic poetry, the Andalusian League retained the traditional approach and reflected Arab nationalist themes. Besides Gibrān, the most influential writers in the North were Amīn al-Rīhānī (1876–1940) and Mīkhā'īl NU'AYMA, whose efforts, along with those of Fawzī al-Ma'lūf (1889–1930), Shafīq al-Ma'lūf (b. 1905), and Ilyās Farhāt (b. 1893) of the Andalusian League, established the romantic school in Arabic poetry and had a profound influence on the course of modern Arabic literature.

Gibrān's simple, poetical prose in such works as *al-'Awāsif* (1920; the tempests), and *al-Arwāh al-mutamarridah* (1908; *Spirits Rebellious*, 1949) was the first real break from the rhyming prose of the previous centuries. His subjects were no longer those that tradition dictated, and his images and symbols erased life's dualisms and sought the unity of all existence, so aptly portrayed in his long poem *al-Mawākib* (1919; *The Processions*, 1958) and in his famous writings in English, *The Madman* (1918), *The Prophet* (1923), and *Jesus the Son of Man* (1928). In all his works he embodied his ideas about life and art, setting an example for the writers who succeeded him.

Like Gibrān, Na'ayma and al-Rīhānī devoted most of their work to new experiments in language. Although neither of them was a great poet, al-Rīhānī's prose poems in *al-Rīhāniyyāt* (4 vols., 1922–24; the Rīhāniyyāt) and Na'ayma's new simple prose in his short-story collection *Kān mā kān* (1937; once upon a time) and his poem "Akhī" (1917; my brother) were powerful examples of the new poetic idiom that Gibrān established.

In South America, aside from Fawzī al-Ma'lūf's romantic poem *'Ala bisāt al-rīh* (1929; on the magic carpet), which shows clearly the influence of the Society of the Pen, Shafīq al-Ma'lūf's *'Abqar* (1936; the valley of the muses), which explores the use of Arab mythology, and Ilyās Farhāt's original and successful attempt at the allegorical genre in *Ahlām al-rāī* (1953; the shepherd's dreams), the rest of the poets retained the style and form of classical Arabic poetry.

In Lebanon, two main schools of poetry—the romantic and the Parnassian-symbolist—emerged between 1930 and 1948. The former, an extension of the North American school, reached full bloom in the works of Ilyās Abū Shabaka (1903–1947), particularly in *Afā'ī al-firdaws* (1938; the serpents of paradise), where his spiritual conflict, intense personal experiences, and religious suffering are vividly depicted.

The Parnassian-symbolist School, headed by Sa'īd 'AQL, was a reaction against the romantic poets' sentimentality and simple common diction and a product of early French SYMBOLIST influence. As Sa'īd 'Aql declared in his introduction to *al-Majdaliyya* (1937; the Magdalen), poetry was primarily music, evoking meaning indirectly through the creation of an aesthetic atmosphere. 'Aql's influence was short-lived because the generation of committed poets that followed him, while drawing inspiration from his polished diction, had little tolerance for his aesthetic concepts.

After 1948, experimentation and innovation proceeded at a dizzying pace. In Beirut, two influential journals, *Al-ādāb* and *Shi'r*, popularized free verse and the prose poem. The leading poets of the 1950s and 1960s dropped the distinction between poetic and nonpoetic language, changing the theory and practice of Arabic poetry.

Writing in free verse, one of the greatest poets of the century, Khalīl HĀWĪ succeeded in eliminating the poetry of statement, employed symbols for maximum emotional and intellectual effects, and explored the untapped rhythms of some classical meters. His five *dīwāns* (collections), especially *Bayādir al-jū'* (1965; the threshing-floors of hunger), reflect the angst of an Arab nationalist in a period of Arab defeat. He was killed during the 1982 fighting in Lebanon.

The use of a prose medium in poetry became the preoccupation of the major poets of the 1960s, ADŪNĪS, Unsī al-HĀJJ, and Yūsuf al-KHĀL. Al-Hājj in *Lan* (1959; Never), al-Khāl in *al-Bi'r al-mahjūrah* (1958; the forsaken well), and Adūnīs in *Waqt bayn al-ramād wa al-ward* (1970; a time between ashes and roses) and *Mufrad fī sīghat al-jam'* (1975; singular in the form of plural) created a new language, liberating words from their usual meanings.

In their attempts to change the classical idiom, the 20th-c. poets drew upon the highly developed oral and written folk poetry—the verbal duels of Zaghlūl al-Dāmūr (b. 1925), and *Dūlāb* (1957; wheel) and *Laysh* (1964; why) by Michel Trād (b. 1913). Many of the leading poets, including Gibrān, 'Aql, and Hāwī, did in fact compose in the Lebanese dialect, but criticism has only recently started to explore this genre and assess its effects on these poets' works.

Fiction

The novel, short story, and drama are Western literary genres that have no developed prototypes in the Arabic literary tradition. The Lebanese, whose openness to the West predated that of their fellow Arabs, were among the first to introduce these genres into modern Arabic literature.

The early attempts at fiction, dating back to the 1870s, were either translations of and adaptations from European works, or original compositions with undue emphasis on spectacle and bald narrative rather than on plot and character development. Between 1891 and 1914 appeared the twenty-one historical novels of Jurjī Zaydān (1861–1914). These novels cultivated a new readership in the Arab world and revived a consciousness of a glorious past, which had become indistinct during the previous century.

Of more artistic value were the short stories of Kahlīl Gibrān and Mikhāīl Nu'ayma, who early in the century introduced a realistic trend into Arabic fiction. In his short story collections *'Arā'is al-murūj* (1906; *Nymphs of the Valley*, 1949) and *Al-Arwāh al-mutamarridah* and in his romantic novel *al-Ajnihah al-mutakassirah* (1912; *The Broken Wings*, 1957), Gibrān attacked outmoded social customs and religious fanaticism, and sought to demolish the causes of man's misery. On the other hand, Na'ayma, who was no less concerned about social injustices, exhorted his characters to follow the life of the mystics as a panacea for their dilemmas. His short stories and his novel, *Liqā'* (1946; encounter), are technically superior to the works of his immediate predecessors.

Realistic and naturalistic fiction finds its best expression in *Al-Raghīf* (1939; the loaf of bread), a novel by Tawfīq 'AWWĀD, which depicts the horrors of famine during World War I; in 'Awwād's short story collections *Al-Sabt al-a'raj* (1937; the lame boy) and *Qamīs al-sūf* (1964; the woolen shirt), and later on in his excellent novel *Tawāhīn Bayrūt* (1972; *Death in Beirut*, 1976), a psychological study of the problems of contemporary Lebanese society and the choices facing the Lebanese intellectual in his war against traditional values.

Two novels, Mārūn 'Abbūd's (1886–1962) *Fāris Aghā* (1959; Fāris Aghā), a successful caricature of the waning traditional values in Lebanese villages, and Emily Nasralla's (dates n.a.) *Tuyūr aylūl* (1967; September birds), a probing account of the effects of emigration on Lebanese villagers, are cited by critics as the best examples of novels portraying local color and village life.

Fiction of social protest is best exemplified in Laylā Ba'albakkī's (b. 1938) novels *Anā ahyā* (1958; I live) and *Al-Āliha al-mamsūkha*

(1960; the disfigured gods), and her short story "Safīnat hanān ila al-qamar" (1964; "A Space Ship of Tenderness to the Moon," 1967), which question the traditional subservient role of women in society and call for woman's liberation and sexual freedom.

In the 1960s and 1970s the novel reached a high stage of development in the intellectual works of Yūsuf Habshī al-Ashqar (dates n.a.), *Arba'at afrās humr* (1964; four red horses) and *Lā tanbut judhūr fi al-samā'* (1971; roots do not grow in the sky), and in Halīm Barakāt's (b. 1933) *'Awdat al-tā'ir ilā al-bahr* (1969; *Days of Dust*, 1974), a successful experiment in form, juxtaposing the events of the 1967 Arab-Israeli war and its aftermath with the Book of Genesis, and inciting the Arab intellectual to contemplate the meaning of the Arab nation's defeat.

Drama

Lebanese writers were also pioneers in the development of drama in modern Arabic literature. In 1848 Mārūn al-Naqqāsh (1817–1855) presented to a yet uncritical audience *Al-Bakhīl* (the miser), an adaptation into Arabic verse of Molière's play, marking the first step in a rich tradition of translation and adaptation of European dramas, as well as of original compositions.

By the turn of the century, however, many of the brightest Lebanese actors and play-wrights had already left Lebanon for Egypt, where similar developments in drama were taking place. This mass exodus had adverse effects on the Lebanese theater. Although some dramatists had attempted to combine drama as a mode of written literature and drama as theater art, very few successful examples before the late 1950s are recorded.

The period from 1960 until 1974, the date of the beginning of the Lebanese civil war, marked the establishment of numerous theatrical companies with varied artistic orientations.

In general, the modern Lebanese theater in the Arabic language is part of the modern theater in the West in that it freely draws upon Western theatrical techniques. Freeing itself from oratory and melodrama, it succeeds in efficiently utilizing the innovations of leading Western playwrights, actors, directors, and theoreticians.

The first major trend is represented in the productions of the National Theater, founded in 1965 by Hasan 'Alā' al-Dīn (pseud.: Shū Shū, ?–1976). This is the Lebanese boulevard theater, which depends on a central actor, uses the Lebanese dialect and occasional improvisation, and presents political and social problems in a comical fashion.

Concern for form assumes great importance in the plays of Munīr Abū Dibs (b. 1931), founder of the Modern Theater in 1960 and the Beirut School of Modern Theater in 1970. In such plays as *Al-Tūfān* (1970; the deluge) and *Yasū'* (1973; Jesus), voice, lighting, and external form take precedence over content. On the other hand, the work of the Beirut Dramatic Art Workshop, founded in 1968 by Roger 'Assāf (dates n.a.) and Nidāl al-Ashqar (dates n.a.), is less concerned with form and totally dependent on intellectual content, improvisation, and the colloquial idiom.

An excellent example of political theater is Jalāl Khūrī's (dates n.a.) *Juhā fi al-qurā al-amāmiyya* (1971; Juhā in the frontline villages), a successful play in the manner of BRECHT that established a great rapport with its audience because it deals with the concerns of the majority of the populace and faithfully comments on their strengths and weaknesses.

Additionally, critics credit Raymond Gebara's (b. 1935) *Li tamut Dasdamūna* (1970; let Desdemona die), Thérèse 'Awwād's

(b. 1933) *al-Bakara* (1973; the pulley), and Ya'qūb Chedrāwī's (dates n.a.) *A'rib mā yalī* (1970; parse the following) with important artistic innovations.

The Lebanese civil war, which has since 1974 tragically undermined most aspects of life in Lebanon, has had amazingly little effect on literary activity. Publishing houses have increased threefold. Among other things, this fact has led to the appearance of works of questionable literary merit. Even so, the period has also witnessed the publication of a number of distinguished works. Among these are Ilyās Khūrī's (b. 1948) experiments in the form of the novel, *Al-Jabal al-saghīr* (1977; the small mountain) and *Al-Wujūh al-baydā'* (1981; white faces); and Roger 'Assāf's play *Hikāyāt 1936* (1979; the stories of 1936), which revives in modern garb the role of the traditional storyteller. These works would seem to confirm that in spite of current adversities, the Lebanese literary tradition will continue to fulfill its central role in the development of modern Arabic literature.

In French

By the end of the 19th c. and the beginning of the 20th, Lebanese literature in French was quite sophisticated even by the French literary standards of the day. Novels by Jacques Tabet (1885–19??)—*L'émancipée* (1911; the emancipated)—and Georges Samné (1877–19??)—*Au pays du Chérif* (1911; in the land of Chérif), written in collaboration with Maurice Barrès (1862–1923); the plays of Chekri Ganem (1861–1929)—*Antar* (1910; Antar), which was performed at the Odéon in Paris—and Michel I. Sursock (dates n.a.)—*Le serment d'un Arabe* (1906; the oath of an Arab); and a large collection of poetic works by Jacques Tabet and others ushered in a period of "revolutionary literature" concentrating on the liberation of Lebanon and the Arab world from Ottoman domination.

During the period of the French Mandate (1920–43), however, literary themes were marked by a strong adherence to Christianity, a philosophical tendency to identify with the Phoenician rather than the Arab past, and a celebration of the friendship that many Lebanese Christians have always had with France, the "elder sister."

Aside from the influential prose of Michel Chiha (1891–1954), collected and published as *Essais* (2 vols., 1951–52; essays), poetry was the most prevalent literary genre in this period. Notwithstanding similarity in theme, the poetry of Charles Corm (1894–1963) in, for example, *La montagne inspirée* (1934; the inspired mountain), Hector Klat (1888–1976) in *Le cèdre et les lys* (1934; the cedar and the lilies), and Elie Tyanc (1885–1957) in *Le château merveilleux* (1934; the enchanted castle) exhibit a rich variety of Oriental imagery and verse forms ranging from the Alexandrine to free verse.

The work of the new generation of writers, from the 1950s to the present, is, strictly speaking, French, both in execution and appeal. The nationalistic and religious themes of the previous generation give way to a universality of vision and a successful attempt to influence the trends and movements of contemporary French literature. As in much of French poetry, a SURREALISTIC trend is evident in the works of Georges Schehadé (1910-1989) and of the younger generation, especially Nadia Tuéni (b. 1935), Hoda Adib (dates n.a.), and Christiane Saleh (dates n.a.). Schehadé's transparent imagery, of which Saint JOHN-PERSE spoke highly, Fouad Naffah's (b. 1925) constant search for the powerful word that can change the world, and Salah Stétié's (b. 1928) poetry of ideas have elicited the keen attention of French critics.

Most of the poets of this period also wrote drama and fiction, and a few published in Arabic, but none attained the renown of Schehadé, whose contributions to the avant-garde theater with such plays as *Le voyage* (1961; the voyage) and *L'émigré de Brisbane* (1965; the emigrant from Brisbane) place him side by side with BECKETT, IONESCO, GENET, and ADAMOV.

In the short story and the novel, with the exception of *L'envers de Caïn* (1959; the other side of Cain), a realistic novel by Farjalla Haïk (b. 1909), which shows the novelist's attachment to Lebanon and his concern for his country's social, political, and religious problems, only a few works in French have been produced by Lebanese writers. The recent civil war and the consequent emigration of many young Lebanese to France will no doubt have a positive impact on Lebanese writing in French.

BIBLIOGRAPHY: Sélim, A., *Le bilinguisme arabe-français au Liban* (1962); Khalaf, S., *Littérature libanaise de langue française* (1974); Salamé, G., *Le théâtre politique au Liban* (1974); Badawī, M. M., *A Critical Introduction to Modern Arabic Poetry* (1975); Jayyūsī, S., *Trends and Movements in Modern Arabic Poetry* (1977)

—ADNAN HAYDAR

LE CARRÉ, John

(pseud. of David John Moore Cornwell) British novelist, b. 19 Oct. 1931, Poole, Dorset

Le C. is the author of a series of espionage novels written in the manner of Graham GREENE. Le C. had a troubled early life. His father was in and out of legal trouble, and his mother deserted the family while le C. was still a child. The family moved frequently, and le C. attended a series of boarding schools. Eventually, his father sent him to Switzerland where he studied German language and literature at the University of Bern. In 1949 le C. joined the Royal army and served in the intelligence corps. After a short tour in the army, he resumed his education, earning a degree in modern languages at Oxford in 1956. After graduation, he was a tutor in modern languages at Eton for two years. Somewhat dissatisfied with his experience in teaching, he tried his hand at various other vocations, eventually having a successful career with the British Foreign Office, until 1964 when he resigned to work on his writing full time.

Le C.'s first two novels, *Call for the Dead* (1961) and *A Murder of Quality* (1964), are more detective stories than espionage novels, but they do introduce the character of George Smiley, around whom most of le C.'s later novels will revolve. They also introduce the central conflict that will be developed in his later work: human beings versus their institutions. Both of these novels enjoyed moderate critical and commercial success, but his literary breakthrough was his third novel, *The Spy Who Came In from the Cold* (1963).

Unlike the two preceding novels, *The Spy Who Came In from the Cold* is a solid espionage novel that introduces the world of "the Circus," le C.'s construct of the British Intelligence establishment. The novel tells a story of great complexity, but the text is tightly focused through the perceptions and psychological insights of the central character and concentrates upon internal conflict rather than external action. Through this technique, le C. achieves the psychological depth and intricate characterization that distinguish his later work. This novel was an international best-seller, and its success allowed le C. to become a full-time author. His next novel, *The Looking Glass War* (1965), was equally successful and earned him the Edgar Allen Poe Award for 1965.

The centerpieces of le C.'s work are the George Smiley books: *Tinker, Tailor, Soldier, Spy* (1974), *The Honorable Schoolboy* (1977), *Smiley's People* (1980), and *The Secret Pilgrim* (1991). The first three of these novels form a trilogy that traces the latter part of Smiley's career in "the Circus," and the fourth is a retrospect of Smiley's life of espionage. Other novels, such as *The Little Drummer Girl* (1983), and the semiautobiographical *A Perfect Spy* (1986), do not involve Smiley directly but maintain a consistent depiction of the intelligence community and a similar concentration upon character and internal conflict.

Le C.'s novels have achieved great popular success. The Smiley books are among the best-selling thrillers of all time, and seven of le C.'s novels have been made into motion pictures. His work has evolved from the relatively simple early mysteries to very complex, intricately crafted novels of great psychological depth. Rather than merely maintain a successful formula, le C. has continued to elaborate and expand upon his themes and characters. Three aspects that distinguish his work are the elaborate depth and development of his characters, the attention given to the often mundane, almost ritualistic day-to-day activities within a bureaucracy, and the consistent depiction of his principal landscape, "the Circus," which rivals Thomas HARDY's "Wessex" or William FAULKNER's "Yoknapatawpha" in its solidity. The later novels in particular have drawn significant critical attention and elevated le C. beyond consideration as merely a genre author to consideration as a successful author of "straight" fiction.

FURTHER WORKS: *A Small Town in Germany* (1968); *The Naive and Sentimental Lover* (1971); *Vanishing England* (1987, with Gareth Davies); *The Russia House* (1989); *The Night Manager* (1993); *Our Game* (1995); *The Tailor Panama* (1996)

BIBLIOGRAPHY: Sauerberg, L. O., *Secret Agents in Fiction: Ian Fleming, J. le C. and Len Deighton* (1984); Lewis, P. E., *J. le C.* (1985); Barley, T., *Taking Sides: The Fiction of J. le C.* (1986); Homberger, E., *J. le C.* (1986); Monaghan, D., *Smiley's Circus: A Guide to the Secret World of J. le C.* (1986); Wolfe, P., *Corridors of Deceit: The World of J. le C.* (1987)

—ROBERT GREENUP

LECHOŃ, Jan

(pseud. of Leszek Serafinowicz) Polish poet and essayist, b. 13 July 1899, Warsaw; d. 8 July 1956, New York, N.Y., U.S.A.

L. was born and educated in Warsaw, at that time a city under Russian domination. The major events in his life were closely linked to his nation's political fortunes. The beginning of his career as a poet (and also its peak) coincided with the euphoric early

1920s, when Poland was rejoicing in its newly regained independence. During the 1930s L. served as cultural attaché at the Polish embassy in Paris; the outbreak of World War II caught him in France. He eventually fled to the U.S., where he remained in exile as an ardent opponent of the Communist Polish government until his death by suicide.

L.'s fame as a poet, and as something of a prodigy, dates from November 1918 and the founding of the literary café Pod Pikadorem. He was one of the Skamander poets, noted as a group for their poetic verve, satirical irreverence, and their closeness to ruling circles. During the 1920s L.'s literary output was divided between highly serious poetry and buoyant satire. He served as editor of the satirical weekly *Cyrulik Warszawski* from 1926 through 1928.

The poems on which L.'s fame rests, published in two slim volumes—*Karmazynowy poemat* (1920; crimson poem) and *Srebrne i czarne* (1924; silver and black)—display his impressive mastery of classical verse forms. They reveal a troubled reaction to the Polish poetic heritage: in tone and style they are clearly linked with the great romantic tradition, but they also express a modern impatience with the constraints of solemn reverence for matters Polish imposed by that tradition. *Srebrne i czarne* adds personal themes to the public concerns explored in *Karmazynowy poemat*. The personal poems explore with somber dignity the impossibility of finding love and happiness in life. In "Lenistwo" (1924; laziness) L. proclaims: "My body torments me and my soul is repulsive," while in "Spotkanie" (1924; a meeting) Dante's shade confides in him: "There is neither heaven nor earth, no abyss and no hell./ There is only Beatrice. And she does not exist."

L.'s philosophical despair was compounded by severe psychological depression. He suffered from a serious writer's block, overcome in later life only by the powerful urge to lament Poland's fate in World War II. The poems of the 1940s show even greater technical mastery than the early work, and are no longer at odds with the ardent patriotism of the romantics.

L.'s posthumously published diary, which he kept during the 1950s, reveals a lonely hypochondriac, a man of great aesthetic sensibility, struggling desperately to overcome his writer's block. The uncharitable snobbery and fanatical patriotism expressed in the diary seem to be his way of compensating, as it were, for his failure to live up to the brilliant promise of his youthful poetry.

FURTHER WORKS: *Na złotym polu: Zbiorek wierszy* (1913); *Po różnych ścieżkach: Zbiór wierszy* (1914); *Paryż 1919: Wrażenia i wspomnienia* (1919); *Facecje republikańskie* (1919, with Antoni Słonimski); *Rzeczpospolita Babińska. Śpiewy historyczne* (1920); *Pierwsza szopka warszawska* (1922, with A. Słonimski and Julian Tuwim); *Szopka polityczna "Cyrulika Warszawskiego"* (1927, with Marian Hemar, A. Słonimski and J. Tuwim); *Szopka polityczna 1930* (1930, with M. Hemar, A. Słonimski and J. Tuwim); *Szopka polityczna 1931* (1931, with M. Hemar and J. Tuwim); *Lutnia po Bekwarku* (1942); *O literaturze polskiej* (1942); *Aria z kurantem* (1945); *Historia o jednym chłopczyku i o jednym lotniku* (1946); *Poezje zebrane 1916–1953* (1954); *Aut Caesar aut nihil* (1955); *Mickiewicz* (1955); *Poezje* (1957); *Dziennik* (3 vols., 1967–1973)

BIBLIOGRAPHY: Folejewski, Z., "J. L.'s Poetic Work," *PolR*, 1, 4 (1956): 3–7; Miłosz, C., *The History of Polish Literature* (1969): 397–98

—MADELINE G. LEVINE

LE CLÉZIO, J(ean) M(arie) G(ustave)

French novelist, b. 13 April 1940, Nice

After receiving degrees in literature from the Institute of Literary Studies in Nice, L. taught at universities in Thailand and Mexico, after which he spent four years in the Panamanian forests with the Embera Indians. Since that time he has lived in France, the U.S., and Mexico.

L. does not write avant-garde literature in the sense that phrase is used by most critics. He is not concerned with form, with the problems pertaining to the text alone, concerns that isolate literature from the world in which it is created. Hence, he is connected to none of the modern movements in French literature. He stands by himself, expressing his anguish and his quest in powerfully lyrical fiction, which breaks the traditional bounds of the novel and creates an epic of consciousness rather than of deeds.

His first novel, *Le procès-verbal* (1963; *The Interrogation*, 1964), for which he was awarded the Théophraste Renaudot Prize, depicts the quest for discovery of both himself and the world by an alienated young man who subsequently flees from both into the security of a mental hospital. This alternation of quest and flight controls the work, and it is not therefore surprising that many of L.'s subsequent novels are conceived in terms of physical or spiritual journeys: *Terra amata* (1968; *Terra Amata*, 1969), *Le livre des fuites* (1969; *The Book of Flights*, 1972), *Voyages de l'autre côté* (1975; journeys to the other side).

Throughout L.'s work his protagonists are dominated by two major influences: the sun and the sea—or occasionally water in some other form. The sun brings understanding of things that are sometimes too painful to withstand; thus, man tries to escape what the light forces him to see. But everything is focused on the sun; for L., all man's thought, and hence the structures he establishes, are created around it, for it is the source of revelation. It is reality. The complementary influence is water, which is the symbol both of woman and of death in *Le procès-verbal* and in *Le déluge* (1968; *The Flood*, 1968).

The other opposites that dominate L.'s work are the city, with its consumer goods, traffic, and noise, and the natural world of insects, plants, quiet, and so forth. All L.'s heroes have a love-hate relationship with the city (also seen as a woman). This theme is most prominent in *La guerre* (1970; *War*, 1973) and *Les géants* (1973; *The Giants*, 1975).

The same themes are taken up again in two volumes of short stories, *La fièvre* (1965; *Fever*, 1966) and *Mondo, et autres histoires* (1978; Mondo, and other stories), and are explored at length in a different way in two philosophical essays, *L'extase matérielle* (1966; the ecstasy of matter) and *L'inconnu sur la terre* (1978; the unknown man on earth).

For L. the world is a mysterious, dangerous, powerful, and wonderful place which man must struggle to understand but from which he is separated by buildings, electricity, technology, cars, words, people—an ever-increasing multitude of manmade objects from which we must escape before we can perceive the aspects of the world that are normally outside the scope of everyday reality. Madness, walking, emotion, drugs, meditation—all can and do serve to break down the barriers that confine our understanding. L. describes them all in such a way that we share every minute particle of his characters' experience: anguish, confusion, and joy. Theirs are the concerns of today—the concerns of people whose world is rapidly deteriorating to an intolerable level. And they seek solutions to this situation.

Such solutions, however, have become less violent during the course of L.'s career. Indeed, in the more recent volumes—*Voyages de l'autre côté, Mondo, et autres histories, L'inconnu sur la terre*—protagonists flee into the world of the imagination and of children, rejecting utterly the stress of modern life apparent in the earlier works. These last texts are very gentle, yet they cannot be separated from the others because there is a unity of theme throughout L.'s body of work. Indeed, these last three function in an important way both in opposition to and as a complement to the earlier work.

The juxtaposition of alternatives is a technique the author uses at all levels. In particular, one can note the instability of his subject pronouns at all times. Narration moves frequently from "I" to "you" to "he" without any apparent motivation—a technique that both alienates the reader and forces him to share the alienation of narrator and protagonist very intimately. The novels have little or no plot, and in many cases the sections within a book have no apparent order. Usually they are made up of a series of situations that illustrate a given theme from different angles. These can be complementary or contradictory, developing the theme further or offering another possibility, a different interpretation. The effect is that of a number of tableaux rather than of continuous narration. Each book is complete in itself and yet is linked to the worlds of his other books by a system of recurrent detail, repetition of images, new or further treatment of themes and problems. Hence all L.'s writings are woven together into a single growing structure in which each strand reinforces the others, and adds to their combined impact and power.

FURTHER WORKS: *Haï* (1971); *Mydriase* (1973); *Vers les icebergs* (1979); *Désert* (1980); *Trois villes saintes* (1980)

BIBLIOGRAPHY: Lhoste, P., *Conversations avec J. M. G. L.* (1971); Cagnon, M., and S. Smith, "J. M. G. L.: Fiction's Double Bind," in Federman, R., ed., *Surfiction: Fiction Today and Tomorrow* (1975): 215–26; Waelti-Walters, J., *J. M. G. L.* (1977); Le Clézio, M., "L'être sujet/objet: La vision active et passive chez L.," in Cagnon, M., ed., *Éthique et esthétique dans la littérature française du XXe siècle* (1978): 113–21; Oxenhandler, N., "Nihilism in L.'s *La fièvre*," in Tetel, M., ed., *Symbolism and Modern Literature* (1978): 264–73; Smith, S. L., "L.'s Search for Self in a World of Words," *MLS*, 10, 2 (1980): 48–58; Waelti-Walters, J., *Icare; ou, L'évasion impossible: Étude psycho-mystique de l'œuvre de J. M. G. L.* (1981)

—JENNIFER R. WAELTI-WALTERS

LEDUC, Violette

French memoirist and novelist, b. 8 April 1907, Arras; d. 28 May 1972, Faucon

L.'s best writings describe her life, which was a stormy one. She was born to an unmarried mother, a servant seduced by the son of the house, and her intense relationship with her mother was repeated in her affairs with women and in her brief marriage. After a variety of vaguely literary but unimportant jobs, she met the writer Maurice Sachs (1906–1945), whom she admired equally for

his writing and his homosexuality. He introduced her to the black market during World War II and persuaded her to write her childhood memories. These became *L'asphyxie* (1946; *In the Prison of Her Skin*, 1970), which was published on the recommendation of Albert CAMUS, after Simone de BEAUVOIR had read the manuscript. Jean-Paul SARTRE also published extracts from her writings in his periodical, *Les temps modernes*, in 1945, 1946, and 1947.

The story of L.'s adulation of Simone de Beauvoir, who treated her with great kindness, is told in *L'affamée* (1948; the starving woman), a semisurrealistic account of L.'s romantic feelings for "her" (unnamed, but obviously Beauvoir), in which factual detail merges into lyrical effusion.

L.'s mind began to give way when she was working on the novel *Ravages* (1955; *Ravages*, 1967), the book that would make her sex life public, albeit in the form of a novel. She had been a difficult person to cope with for some time. Passionate, possessive, full of complaints and appeals for sympathy, constantly in tears, lamenting the size of her nose, paying homage to prominent homosexuals such as Jean COCTEAU and Jean GENÊT, she had been buoyed up by her spontaneity, by the excitement of her emotional involvements, and by considerable resilience. But now she began to feel herself an object of general interest and censure. At the same time, her unfulfilled love for "Jacques," a rich homosexual manufacturer who admired her writing, led her to believe that she was being persecuted by a gang led by "Jacques." She traveled to take her mind off her troubles, and describes her travels in *Trésors à prendre* (1960; treasures within reach).

L. attained international literary renown—and notoriety—with *La bâtarde* (1964; *La Bâtarde*, 1965), which recounts her life up to 1944 and for which Simone de Beauvoir wrote the preface. The success of *La bâtarde* was upheld by *La folie en tête* (1970; *Mad in Pursuit*, 1971), the last volume of her autobiography to appear in her lifetime. The final volume, *La chasse à l'amour* (1973; the hunt for love), appeared posthumously, edited by Simone de Beauvoir. It brings events up to 1964.

These last two volumes contain a truly extraordinary history of paranoia seen from within. It is amazing to think that L. could have written as well as she did when her mind was so disturbed. She was obviously a born writer. Possibly, her paranoia and her writing were forms of the same solipsism. Her psychiatrist considered that her writing was therapeutic. But she did not always write well. Her novellas are curiously insubstantial in spite of a tremendous straining after emotional effect. For instance, *Le taxi* (1971; *The Taxi*, 1972) consists of a lyrical outpouring of desire from a brother and sister copulating in a cab, but it leaves no definite impression behind, and one feels that it comes to an end so soon because L. did not entirely believe in it herself. When she wrote about herself and the people she knew, she wrote at length because this was a subject she really believed in. In her autobiographical writings her surrealistic lyricism conveys an exact impression of the truth of her emotions, and the effect is immediately convincing.

It is sad that she did not have time to describe her last years, which brought her success and relative peace of mind; but her autobiography, as it is, stands as a monument to all those who are insane, ridiculous, ugly, perverse, lonely, despised, and disinherited, all of whom look at us through her eyes and ask us to remember that they are human beings.

FURTHER WORKS: *La vieille fille et le mort; Les boutons dorés* (1958; *The Old Maid and the Dead Man; The Golden Buttons, in*

The Woman with the Little Fox: Three Novellas, 1966); *La femme au petit renard* (1965; *The Woman with the Little Fox*, 1966); *Thérèse et Isabelle* (1966; *Thérèse and Isabelle*, 1967)

BIBLIOGRAPHY: de Beauvoir, S., Foreword to *The Golden Buttons* (1961): 5–6; Flanner, J., ("Genêt"), "Letter from Paris," *New Yorker* (23 Jan. 1965): 108–14; de Beauvoir, S., Foreword to *La bâtarde* (1965): v–xviii; Haynes, M., on *The Woman with the Little Fox, Nation* (23 Jan. 1967): 118–20; Brooks, P., on *Mad in Pursuit, NYTBR* (3 Oct. 1971): 4, 41; Wood, M., on *The Taxi, NYRB* (Aug. 1972): 15–16; Courtivron, I. de, "V. L.'s *L'affamée*: The Courage to Displease," *ECr*, 19, 2 (1979): 95–96

—BARBARA J. BUCKNALL

LEHTONEN, Joel

Finnish novelist, short-story writer, essayist, and poet, 27 Nov. 1881, Sääminki; d. 20. Nov. 1934, Huopalahti

Born out of wedlock and abandoned, L. became the ward of a pastor's widow and received a good education; thus, he had a double perspective, as an outcast and as a member of established society, on life in Savo, his native province in eastern Finland. His first notable work was the semiautobiographical *Mataleena* (1905; Magdalene), about his natural mother and his own early life. Sojourns in Switzerland and Italy (1907–8), France (1911–12), and North Africa and Italy again (1914) led to an admiration for French and Italian literatures (he translated Boccaccio, Stendhal, and Anatole FRANCE). During this period he wrote the travel stories of *Myrtti ja alppiruusu* (1911; myrtle and rhododendron) and the prose poems, influenced by Baudelaire, of *Punainen mylly* (1913; the red mill). At the same time, L. remained conscious of his roots, returning to Finnish themes (and using STRINDBERG's informal lyric technique) in the poems of *Rakkaita muistoja* (1911; beloved memories) and its sequel, the rowdy "little epic" on a rustic engagement party, *Markkinoilta* (1912; from the market).

In 1905 L. had bought a cottage and a piece of land near Savonlinna for an improvident half-brother, and spent many of his summers there; a keen observer of the tensions between the backwoods "savages" and their "civilized" town neighbors, L. undertook what he thought would be a "human comedy" for his home region. (He liked to compare Finnish country folk with James Fenimore Cooper's redskins, or the tribes of the Sahara.) The first volume was *Kerran kesällä* (1917; once in summer), about a composer who, returning from abroad, despairingly perceives the changes time has wrought in him and his people; it was followed by *Kuolleet omenapuut* (1918; the dead apple trees), a collection of masterful short stories, many in monologue form, dealing in part with a very recent event, Finland's civil war (January—May 1918). The artistic climax came with *Putkinotko: Kuvaus laiskasta viinarokarista ja tuhmasta herrasta* (2 vols., 1919–20; Putkinotko: an account of a lazy moonshiner and a stupid gentleman), which takes place on a single summer day before the war and minutely depicts the uneasiness of Aapeli Muttinen, a fat and sybaritic book-dealer, who has put his vacation cottage into the care of Juutas Käkriäinen, an obstinate, shiftless, and ignorant tenant farmer. The series— which has a wealth of other memorable characters: a would-be

learned barber, a nouveau-riche Swedophile, a lawyer who blindly admires German discipline, and a ludicrous enthusiast of the *Kalevala*, the Finnish national epic—came to an untimely end with the four novellas of *Korpi ja puutarha* (1923; the backwoods and the garden); here we learn that Käkriäinen has been killed "like an animal" in the civil war.

L.'s other work falls into several groups: realistic novels, where he once again considers the immediate prewar days, now against a Helsinki setting—*Sorron lapset* (1923; children of oppression) and *Punainen mies* (1925; the red man); experiments with EXPRESSIONISM and the grotesque—*Rakastunut rampa* (1922; the enamored cripple) and *Sirkus ja pyhimys* (1927; the circus and the saint); idyllic tales and reflections—*Onnen poika* (1925; the happy fellow) and *Lintukoto* (1929; the bird home), a title also referring to an imaginary land of bliss; and sometimes cruel self-analysis: the author's dog is a main character of *Rai Jakkerintytär* (1927; Rai, Jakker's daughter). L.'s pessimism received its last expression in the visionary novel *Henkien taistelu* (1933; the battle of the spirits), where a devil conducts the hero on a tour of the scenes of Finnish corruption; Helsinki—which L. detested—is the setting of the novel's finale. L. took his own life the next year; the revelatory poems of *Hyvästijättö Lintukodolle* (1935; farewell to Lintukoto) appeared posthumously.

Eino LEINO compared L. to Strindberg; in many respects, however, he is closer to Knut HAMSUN—in his inclination to occasional stylistic and emotional rhapsodies, in his devotion to his own small world, in his sardonic wit, and in his misanthropy. Yet he had a tolerance for human frailty that Hamsun may well have lacked.

FURTHER WORKS: *Perm* (1904); *Paholaisen viulu* (1904); *Villi* (1905); *Tarulinna* (1906); *Ilvolan juttuja* (1910); *Nuoruus* (1911); *Munkki-kammio* (1914); *Puolikuun alla* (1919); *Tähtimantteli* (1920); *Putkinotkon herra: Kirjeitä* 1907–1920 (1969)

BIBLIOGRAPHY: Tarkka, P., *Putkinotkon tausta: J. L. henkilöt 1901–1923* (1977), English summary: 488–505; Tarkka, P., "J. L. and Putkinotko," *BF*, 11 (1977): 239–45

—GEORGE C. SCHOOLFIELD

LEINO, Eino

(pseud. of Eino Lönnbohm) Finnish poet, dramatist, and journalist, b. 6 July 1878, Paltamo, d. 10 Jan. 1926, Tuusula

L. made his mark early. At sixteen he published a translation of a poem by Johan Ludvig Runeberg (1804–1877), the great Finland-Swedish poet. After starting studies at the University of Helsinki, he joined Helsinki literary and newspaper circles, where his elder brother Kasimir had preceded him. Having published several books of verse, he produced his masterpiece, the first volume of *Helkavirsiä* (1903; *Whitsongs*, 1978). He became an exponent of the neoromantic movement, which was strong in Finland around the turn of the century. Nearly every year until his death he brought out at least one volume, whether poetry, drama, or fiction.

L. was influenced by Goethe, Heine, and Nietzsche, but more deeply by the *Kalevala*, the Finnish national epic. His subjects are nature, love, his native land, and the quest for truth. Composed in the trochaic meter of the *Kalevala*, the ballads of the *Helkavirsiä* are denser in meaning and often more powerful than their model in their impact on the modern reader. L.'s verse is also rich in alliteration, but there is less parallelism than in the *Kalevala*. Several of the ballads present a kind of Faustian hubris, but the protagonists are more violent, more barbaric than Goethe's hero. The God-defying eponymous hero of "Ylermi" (Ylermi) is an example. In "Kouta" (Kouta) a brawny man of Lapland probes for the answer to the riddle of the universe in a supernatural wilderness. In "Tuuri" (Tuuri) the central figure pleads that death might grant him a reprieve. His plea is granted on a sardonic note. Awaking from a night of revelry with some pagan gods, he discovers that his young wife and little son have long since finished their life cycles, leaving him alone. Time has turned out to be relative, in appalling fashion. Nevertheless, the volume expresses a tragic optimism, a willing acceptance of fate, suggestive of Nietzsche's superman. Other ballads lack the metaphysical dimension. For example, "Kimmon kosto" (Kimmo's revenge) and "Räikkö Räähkä" (Räikkö the wretch) present violent episodes in a dim historical past; Räikkö betrays his village and commits suicide in remorse for collaborating with the enemy.

None of L.'s later works was to surpass his achievement in the first *Helkavirsiä*, but he demonstrated his virtuosity in other types of verse. Nor did he limit himself to Finnish themes. His play *Alkibiades* (1909; Alcibiades) his *Bellerophon* (1919; Bellerophon), a story in verse, and his various translations show his broader interests. There is a remarkable play of end rhyme, internal rhyme, and alliteration in his well-known "Nocturne" (nocturne) and in other lyrics of *Talvi-yö* (1905; winter night), as well as in the collection *Halla* (1908; frost). These titles imply a growing disenchantment with life.

His second volume of *Helkavirsiä* (1916; Whitsuntide songs) is more pessimistic and more mystical than the first. "Ukri" (Ukri) of the later volume recalls "Ylermi," indicating the persistence of L.'s preoccupations with philosophical issues. "Auringon hyvästijättö" (the sun's farewell) presents a cosmic vision with erotic overtones. In this, as in some other poems, the symbolism is obscure. An obsession with the self, with failure, and with death marks certain of the later pieces.

After 1910 people felt that L. was wasting his great talents in hackwork and a bohemian existence. The women he had love affairs with included two writers: L. Onerva (Hilja Onerva Lehtinen-Madetoja, 1882–1972) who wrote his biography; and Aino KALLAS, the noted short-story writer, who tried in vain to persuade him to write a third collection of *helkavirsiä*.

His most notable plays survive because of their lyrical qualities and their folkloric content. A fine early example is *Tuonelan joutsen* (1896; the swan of the land of death). In it Lemminkäinen (a character from the *Kalevala*) seeks to plumb the mystery of existence. Both the swan and the land of Tuonela would appear in other writings of L. He was disappointed in his effort to establish a viable theater with adaptations of the *Kalevala*. As for his many novels, they were no more than potboilers and have fallen into oblivion.

L.'s major achievement remains the ballads of *Helkavirsiä* and the lyrics of *Talvi-yö* and *Halla*. The vigor and richness of the legend poems have not been matched in Finnish literature. His command of the language is outstanding, and he skillfully applied the resources of his folk heritage to poetry for his own time. If he

had few followers, his countrymen still honor him along with the painter Gallen-Kallela and the composer Sibelius, who were also inspired by the *Kalevala*.

FURTHER WORKS: *Maaliskuun lauluja* (1896); *Kangastuksia* (1902); *Simo Hurtta* (1904); *Naamiota* (6 vols., 1905–1911); *Suomalaisia kirjailijoita* (1909); *Suomalaisen kirjallisuuden historia* (1910); *Elämän koreus* (1915); *Juhana herttuan ja Catherina Jagellonican lauluja* (1919); *Syreenien Kukkiessa* (1920); *Elämäni kuvakirja* (1925); *Kootut teokset* (16 vols., 1926–1930); *Elämän laulu* (1947); *Kirjokeppi* (1949); *Pakinat* (2 vols., 1960); *Kirjeet* (4 vols., 1961–1962); *Maailman kirjailijoita* (1978)

BIBLIOGRAPHY: Tompuri, E., ed., *Voices from Finland: An Anthology* (1947): 13–14, 21; Havu, I., *An Introduction to Finnish Literature* (1952): 64–70; Kolehmainen, J. I., *Epic of the North* (1973): 244–58; Ahokas, J., *A History of Finnish Literature* (1973): 147–66; Branch, M., Introduction to E. L., *Whitsongs* (1978): 5–20; Sarajas, A., "E. L.: 1878–1928," *BF*, 12 (1978): 40–46; Schoolfield, G. C., on *Whitsongs, SS*, 52 (1980): 341–44

—REINO VIRTANEN

LEIRIS, Michel

French autobiographer, poet, ethnographer, critic, and novelist, b. 20 April 1901, Paris; d. 30 September 1990, Saint Hiliare

From an upper-middle class family, L. began his literary career as a poet and participated in the SURREALIST movement between 1924 and 1929. In 1929, after a mental crisis and a period of sexual impotence, he underwent psychoanalysis, after which he began a new career in anthropology, participating in an ethnographical expedition to Africa (1931–33). After returning to France, L. formally studied ethnography and later became a curator at the Museum of Man in Paris. In 1937, with writer-friends Georges BATAILLE and Roger Caillois (1913–1978), he founded the College of Sociology, a group devoted to the study of social structures. He fought in North Africa in 1939 but returned to Paris during the German occupation and began writing his autobiography. During this period he became a friend of Jean-Paul SARTRE and other Resistance writers. After the war he traveled to the Antilles, to China, to Japan, and in the 1960s to Cuba, whose communist revolution he supported. He has continued actively to promote leftist political causes.

L. has long been interested in the relationship of language to dreams and the unconscious. His poetic works, such as those collected in *Mots sans mémoire* (1969; words without memory) and *Haut mal, suivi de Autres lancers* (1969; severe seizure, followed by other throws)—*Haut mal* was first published alone in 1943—and his only novel, *Aurora* (1946; Aurora), show his fascination with word games, with the associative power of language, and with private mythmaking. Writing, for L., was a means to discover how to live more fully. Indeed, one could say that his literary works constituted one long autobiographical search.

In *Miroir de la tauromachie* (1938; mirror of bullfighting) L. sets forth his aesthetic theories, inspired by Baudelaire, and based on the idea of the *corrida*. In the bullfight L. sees the solemnity of ceremony, the courage to face death, the reenactment of myth and of ritual sacrifice, and erotic overtones that must also be intrinsic to art. In *Le ruban au cou d'Olympia* (1981; the ribbon around Olympia's neck) he returns to the subject matter of *Miroir de la tauromachie*. *L'Afrique fântome* (1934; phantom Africa) incorporates L.'s ethnographical concerns into a personal journal of his trip to Africa. In his self-portrait, *L'âge d'homme* (1939; *Manhood*, 1963)—republished in 1946 with an important prefatory essay "De la littérature considérée comme une tauromachie" (published in English as "The Autobiographer as Torero")—he likens the risks of personal confession to those taken by a bullfighter in the ring. His feelings of inadequacy, his obsessions with physical flaws and infirmities, and his sexual fantasies are given poetic dimension through his meditations on the mythic figures of the biblical Judith, the archetypal man-killer, and the legendary Lucrece, the image of the wounded or punished woman.

Biffures (1948; deletions), the first of the four-volume autobiography *La règle du jeu* (*The Rules of the Game*, 1991), is a masterpiece of the genre in the way it questions both autobiographical works and the very act of writing. It is not a chronology of events; by showing how one word can evoke another and by "crossing out" or "deleting" illusory connections, L. examines the relationships among writing, history, and a mythopoetic vision of personal experience. *Biffures* focuses on his childhood and on language. In the second volume, *Fourbis* (1955; odds and ends), he discusses his preoccupation with death and celebrates loves and friendships, particularly those from the war years. The third volume, *Fibrilles* (1966; fibrils), evokes his trip to China, deals with the question of the need for political commitment, and includes an account of his 1958 suicide attempt. At the end of *Fibrilles* L. renounces what he now realizes to be an impossible project—that of bringing together all the parts of his life into a unified whole. The last volume, *Frêle bruit* (1976; frail noise), composed primarily of short texts, acknowledges the fragmentary quality of life.

L. also wrote sensitive works of ethnography and literary and art criticism, especially texts for art books. His *Brisées* (1966; *Broken Branches*, 1989) contains articles on the work of many of his friends (including Pablo Picasso, Joan Miró, and André Masson), as well as several ethnographical pieces.

FURTHER WORKS: *Simulacres* (1925); *Le point cardinal* (1927); *Tauromachies* (1937); *Glossaire, j'y serre mes gloses* (1939); *Nuits sans nuits* (1945); *André Masson et son univers* (1947, with Georges Limbour; *André Masson and His Universe*, 1947); *La langue secrète des Dogons de Sanga* (1948); *Toro* (1951); *Contacts de civilisations en Martinique et en Guadeloupe* (1955); *Bagatelles végétales* (1956); *balzacs en bas de casse et picassos sans majuscules* (1957); *La possession et ses aspects théâtraux chez les Éthiopiens de Gondar* (1958); *Vivantes cendres, innommées* (1961); *Marrons sculptés pour Miró* (1961); *Grande fuite de neige* (1964); *Afrique noire: La création plastique* 1967, with Jacqueline Delange; *African Art*, 1968); *Cinq études d'ethnologie* (1969); *Fissures* (1970); *Wifredo Lam* (1970); *André Masson: Massacres et autres dessins* (1971); *Francis Bacon; ou, La vérité criante* (1974). FURTHER WORKS IN ENGLISH: *The Prints of Joan Miró* (1947)

BIBLIOGRAPHY: Mauriac, C., *The New Literature* (1959): 61–73; Nadeau, M., *M. L. et la quadrature du cercle* (1963); Sontag, S., "M. L.'s *Manhood*" (1964), *Against Interpretation* (1966): 61–68; Boyer, A. M., *M. L.* (1974); Mehlman, J., *A Structural Study of Autobiography* (1974): 65–150; Brée, G., "M. L.: Mazemaker," in Olney, J., ed., *Autobiography: Essays Theoretical and Critical* (1980): 194–206; Hewitt, L. D., "Historical Intervention in L.'s Bif(f)ur(e)s," *FrF*, 7 (1982): 132–45

—LEAH D. HEWITT

LEÑERO, Vicente

Mexican novelist, dramatist, short-story writer, and journalist, b. 9 June 1933, Guadalajara

L. grew up in Mexico City and was graduated from the National University in civil engineering. After practicing his profession briefly, he turned to journalism and literature for his livelihood. Modest, unassuming, and deeply religious, L. has remained aloof from the literary circles in the Mexican capital. He is, nevertheless, one of the most admired intellectuals in the country today. In addition to his activities as a novelist and playwright, he has written television scripts and for several years was editor of *Claudia*, a popular women's magazine.

L.'s first novel, *La voz adolorida* (1961; the sorrowful voice), consists of a monologue of the mentally deranged protagonist, who describes his unhappy life prior to his confinement in a mental hospital. His convincing tone and the fluctuations between his moments of sanity and dementia suggest the relativity of both truth and normality. *Los albañiles* (1964; the bricklayers) is L.'s undisputed masterpiece. This novel, which won the prestigious Biblioteca Breve Prize in Spain, has the outward form of a detective story but, symbolically, the investigator's unsuccessful search for the murderer of a night watchman at a building site represents modern man's vain quest for truth. L. utilizes a wide range of avant-garde techniques designed to eliminate the omniscient narrator and create a multidimensional work of art, thus underscoring the complexities of an indecipherable, rapidly changing world. Even more structurally complex, *Estudio Q* (1965; studio Q) satirizes commercial television by portraying an actor who confuses reality with fiction while filming a play based on his biography. *El garabato* (1967; the squiggle) emerges as an antinovel that parodies L.'s preoccupation with the creative process. Like *Los albañiles*, it takes the form of a detective story, but the parallel plots of a critic seeking the solution to a moral dilemma while he reads a mediocre murder mystery suggest L.'s frustration as a writer and, perhaps, his disillusionment with the novel as a genre.

After finishing *El garabato*, L. discovered a new medium for himself in drama. Although his most successful play is his adaptation of *Los albañiles* (1970), he also initiated documentary theater in Mexico as a kind of educational vehicle. The best examples of this genre are *Pueblo rechazado* (1969; rejected people), the dramatization of the widely publicized controversy over Prior Gregorio Lemercier's introduction of psychoanalysis into a Benedictine monastery to determine aptitudes for the priesthood; and *El juicio* (1972; the trial), a representation of the 1928 trial of the accused assassins of President-elect Alvaro Obregón. The novel *Los periodistas* (1978; the journalists) demonstrates L.'s continued interest in the documentary mode, its subject being a dispute between *Excelsior*, Mexico's most prestigious newspaper, and then-President Luis Echeverría.

L.'s continued success as a nonfiction novelist has been demonstrated more recently by *la gota de agua* (1983; The drop of water) and *Asesinato, el doble crimen de los Flores Muñoz* (1985; Murder, the double murder of the Flores Muñoz), both about topical subjects in contemporary Mexico. Viewed in its entirety, L.'s œuvre has registered three successive phases: psychological realism, sophisticated avant-gardism, and a scrupulously objective art form. His awesome versatility and acute sensitivity to the complicated realities of today's world make him one of contemporary Latin America's more significant literary voices.

FURTHER WORKS: *La polvareda, y otros cuentos* (1959); *A fuerza de palabras* (1967); *V. L.* (1967); *El derecho de llorar, y otros reportajes* (1968); *La zona rosa, y otros reportajes* (1968); *Compañero* (1970); *La carpa* (perf. 1971, pub. 1974); *Los hijos de Sánchez* (perf. 1972); *Redil de ovejas* (1973); *Viaje a Cuba* (1974); *El evangelio de Lucas Gavilán* (1979); *La mudanza* (1980)

BIBLIOGRAPHY: McMurray, G. R., "The Novels of V. L.," *Crit*, 8, 3 (1966): 55–61; Robles, H. E., "Approximaciones a *Los albañiles* de V. L.," *RI*, 73 (1970): 579–99; Langford, W. M., *The Mexican Novel Comes of Age* (1971): 151–67; Foster, D. W., and V. R. Foster, eds., *Modern Latin American Literature* (1975); Grossman, L. S., "*Los albañiles*, Novel and Play: A Two-Time Winner," *LATR*, 9, 2 (1976): 5–12; Grossman, L., "*Redil de ovejas*: A New Novel from L.," *RomN*, 17 (1976): 127–30; Holzaphel, T., "*Pueblo rechazado*: Educating the Public through Reportage," *LATR*, 10, 1 (1976): 15–21; McCracken, E. M., *Mass Media and the Latin American New Novel: V. L. and Julio Cortazar* (1977)

—GEORGE R. MCMURRAY

LENZ, Siegfried

German novelist, short-story writer, dramatist, and essayist, b. 17 March 1926, Lyck (now Elk, Poland)

L., the son of a civil servant, grew up in a small Masurian town in former East Prussia; he served in the German navy during the last years of World War II. After being held as a prisoner of war for a short time by the British, he began studying philosophy as well as German and English literature at the University of Hamburg. In 1948 L. embarked upon a brief journalistic career and eventually became feuilleton editor of the newspaper *Die Welt* (1950–51), a position he relinquished to devote all his time to writing. Although not a party member, L. has been active in election campaigns on behalf of the Social Democratic Party since 1965; in 1970 Günter GRASS and L. accompanied Chancellor Willy Brandt to Warsaw for the signing of the treaty that was to effect a rapprochement between the Federal Republic and Poland.

L. became affiliated with Group 47 in the early 1950s; he subsequently fully subscribed to that group's early endeavors to create a literature of political and social concern and commitment. But L.'s four early novels, like many of his early short stories, tend to concentrate on situations of human crisis in which the protagonist is severely tested and inevitably fails. L.'s first novel, *Es waren Habichte in der Luft* (1951; there were hawks in the sky), develops the theme of guilt, frequently encountered in L.'s work, and that of

flight—in an overly symbolic fashion. *Duell mit dem Schatten* (1953; duel with a shadow), with its somewhat contrived plot and stylistic infelicities, was considered a failure by L. himself. In *Der Mann im Strom* (1957; the man in the river), the story of an aged diver, and *Brot und Spiele* (1959; bread and games), a sports novel, the respective heroes are doomed to failure; but in both novels, which are set in contemporary Germany, an element of social criticism is to be noticed.

Stadtgespräch (1963; *The Survivor*, 1965), a novel that presumably takes place in Norway during the German occupation in World War II, probes the ethical dilemma that confronts the Resistance leader Daniel when he has to choose between self-sacrifice or sacrificing the lives of innocent hostages. The limited perspective of the narrator, a member of the Resistance, is broadened by discussions among the hostages and the townspeople, who debate the political and moral consequences of Daniel's decision not to surrender. Although L. implicitly endorses the protagonist's choice as necessary for the continuation of the struggle against a dictatorial regime, the lack of a specific historical context and the tendency toward the parabolic diffuse the central moral question and diminish the novel's impact.

In his masterpiece, the novel *Deutschstunde* (1968; *The German Lesson*, 1971), L. avoids the pitfalls of too abstract a presentation and succeeds in capturing the atmosphere and milieu of a specific landscape as well as the character of its people without succumbing to the maudlin sentimentality and provincialism often to be found in the *Heimatroman*, or regional novel. Despite occasional implausibilities that arise from the first person narrative perspective, the novel is L.'s most significant artistic contribution to the so-called *Vergangenheitsbewältigung*, or coming to terms with Germany's Nazi past, even if the central conflict seems to pale in comparison to the atrocities depicted in Holocaust literature. Required to write an essay on the "Joys of Duty," the narrator, a juvenile delinquent in a reform school, recounts the dogmatic, obsessive, and, ultimately, inhumane dedication to duty of his father, a policeman in Germany's northern-most region of Schleswig-Holstein. The policeman had been charged with enforcing an edict that forbids the artist Max Ludwig Nansen (based, in part, on the expressionist painter Emil Nolde) to engage in painting. The narrator's questioning of perverted concepts of duty that continue to exist emphasizes his precarious position as an outsider. L. inverts the traditional bildungsroman to demonstrate that the vestiges of the Nazi past have not yet vanished.

The novel *Das Vorbild* (1973; *An Exemplary Life*, 1976) also poses a pedagogical problem. Three educators have been asked to select materials suitable for a representative school reader. They largely fail in their search for a both convincing and generally acceptable role model, an exemplary life to be emulated by young people. The discussions about the various suggested models and the educators' own character flaws encourage the reader of the novel to question the former and present propagation of models that may be used to manipulate youthful enthusiasm. The ambiguous outcome and the insufficient relevance of the story finally agreed upon make the novel less successful than its predecessor.

The narrator of the lengthy novel *Heimatmuseum* (1978; *The Heritage: The History of a Detestable Word*, 1981), an accomplished carpet weaver, delves deeply into both his own past and the history of his native Masuria to explain and justify his decision to set fire to the museum that he had laboriously rebuilt in West Germany after World War II. The museum was in danger of being propagandistically exploited by groups laying claim to Germany's lost eastern territories. The novel's detailed descriptions, vivid episodes, charming anecdotes, and memorable if slightly eccentric characters result in a leisurely, digressive style that lends some credence to the claim that L.'s real forté is the short story.

In fact, L.'s mastery of the short story is attested to by four collections in particular: *Jäger des Spotts* (1958; hunter of ridicule), *Das Feuerschiff* (1960; *The Lightship*, 1986), *Der Spielverderber* (1965; the spoilsport), and *Einstein überquert die Elbe bei Hamburg* (1975; Einstein crosses the Elbe near Hamburg). In the early stories the influence of Ernest HEMINGWAY, whom L. explicitly acknowledged as a model, is quite pronounced. Thus, the plot of "Jäger des Spotts" in general and the protagonist's stoic dignity in the face of defeat in particular recall Hemingway's *The Old Man and the Sea*. But L. soon began to reject Hemingway, whom he faulted for lacking social awareness and historical perspective. L.'s later short stories exhibit a wide thematic range and a great variety of narrative modes that extend from the profoundly serious to the ironic, satiric, and Kafkaesque questioning of the perception of reality. L.'s versatility as a storyteller is also evident in several collections of humorous tales, notably the tribute to his native Masuria, *So zärtlich war Suleyken* (1955; so tender was Suleyken).

Although L. is primarily considered a writer of fiction, a number of radio and stage plays demonstrate his skill as a playwright. *Zeit der Schuldlosen* (1962; time of the innocents) was especially successful in performance. In its parabolic quality and concentration on the extreme situation as a test for human morality, familiar from L.'s early fiction, the play is reminiscent of both Jean-Paul SARTRE and Albert CAMUS.

Like other writers of his generation (for example, Grass), L. is concerned with the consequences of the Nazi past for contemporary West German society. He considers the writer a witness who is called upon to voice his protest in the face of societal inequities by means of his craft—albeit without provocative stridency and within the framework of conventional narrative. L.'s social commitment, then, is tempered by his insight into the frailty of the human condition. This insight also prevents L. from adopting a moralizing tone. L.'s undoubted gifts as a storyteller, combined with his unobtrusive commitment and undiminished literary output will, in all probability, continue to secure him a place of distinction among contemporary German writers.

FURTHER WORKS: *Das Kabinett der Konterbande* (1956); *Das schönste Fest der Welt* (1956); *Wippchens charmante Scharmützel* (1960, with Egon Schramm); *Zeit der Schuldlosen—Zeit der Schuldigen* (1961); *Stimmungen der See* (1962); *Das Gesicht* (1964); *Lehmanns Erzählungen* (1964); *Flug über Land und Meer* (1967, with Seelmann Dieter); *Haussuchung* (1967); *Leute von Hamburg* (1968); *Die Augenbinde; Nicht alle Förster sind froh* (1970); *Beziehungen* (1970); *Lotte soll nicht sterben* (1970); *So war es mit dem Zirkus* (1971); *Der Geist der Mirabelle* (1975); *Wo die Möwen schreien* (1976, with Seelmann Dieter); *Der Verlust* (1981); *The Selected Stories of S. L.* (1989)

BIBLIOGRAPHY: Russ, C. A. H., "The Short Stories of S. L.," *GL&L*, 19 (1965–66): 241–51; Paslick, R. H., "Narrowing the Distance: S. L.'s *Deutschstunde*," *GQ*, 46 (1973): 210–18; Russ, C., ed. *Der Schrifsteller S. L.* (1973); Elstren, E. N., "How It Seems and How It Is: Marriage in Three Stories by S. L.," *OL*, 29 (1974): 170–79; Russell, P., "S. L.'s *Deutschstunde*: A 'North German' Novel," *GL&L*, 28 (1974–75): 405–18; Wagener, H., *S. L.* (1976); Russell, P., "The 'Lesson' in S. L.'s *Deutschstunde*," *Seminar*, 13 (1977): 42–54; Murdoch, B., and M. Read, *S. L.* (1978); Gohlmann, S. A., "Making Words Do for Paint: 'Seeing' and Self-Mastery in S. L.'s *The German Lesson*," *MLS*, 9, 2 (1979): 80–88; Bosmajian, H., "S. L.'s *The German Lesson*: Metaphors of Evil on Narrow Ground," *Metaphors of Evil* (1979): 57–81; Butler, G. P., "Zygmunt's Follies? On S. L.'s *Heimatmuseum*," *GL&L*, 33 (1979–80): 172–78

—SIEGFRIED MEWS

LEONOV, Leonid Maximovich

Russian novelist and dramatist, b. 31 May 1899, Polukhino; d. 8 August 1994, Moscow

L., whose father wrote poetry advocating social reforms, graduated from a Moscow secondary school and attended Moscow University, but did not complete his studies. He served briefly in the Red Army during the civil war. His first works show widely different influences, ranging from E. T. A. Hoffmann (1776–1822) in *Derevyannaya koroleva* (1922; the wooden queen) to Oriental poetry in *Tuatamur* (1924; *Tuatamur*, 1935), which is written in poetic prose.

One can safely assume that L. accepted the revolution without understanding the basic tenets of Marxism. Although he attempts to portray the new social order in a favorable light, his heroes are complex and have all the human frailties. They face ethical and moral dilemmas, suffer emotionally, and more than occasionally are victims of social and revolutionary changes. L. tries to understand the revolution from a sociopsychological point of view; there is also a constant antagonism between the old and the new, between the village and the city. L.'s affection for the old and the rural is more than evident: the village people in his works are pure and strong. L. shows that the new roads, factories, and plants disrupt the idyllic countryside and the cherished Russian traditions. Since the conflict between the old and the new is not to be resolved, L., through sometimes obvious or trite symbolism, tries to reconcile the differences between Hegelian *Verstandesmetaphysik* (rationality) and *Vernunftsmetaphysik* (reason). His symbolism is intricate and complex; it constantly oversteps the boundaries of any type of realism, be it social, historical, concrete, or "mature" (*zrely*), as these terms are used by exponents of SOCIALIST REALISM. Occasionally L. applies the attitudes of the past to contemporary circumstances, as in *Russky les* (1953; *The Russian Forest*, 1958), in which a girl named Polya views Red Square and Lenin's mausoleum in Moscow as national religious shrines, as someone years before might have viewed a church or a tomb of a saint, and thereupon makes a pledge to be a good girl and a communist.

L.'s language differs from that of other Soviet Russian writers in its extreme complexity and subjectivity. He makes extensive use of hyperbole, oxymoron, synesthesia, and other figures of speech, as well as various Dostoevskian devices such as STREAM OF CONSCIOUSNESS, archaisms, and colloquial neologisms. Indeed, when L. appeared on the literary scene in the early 1920s many critics, including GORKY, called him a follower of Dostoevsky.

L.'s first novel, *Barsuki* (1925; *The Badgers*, 1947), which he made into a play with the same title in 1927, is concerned with two

Russias—the prerevolutionary merchant Moscow and the Russian village during the revolution. It depicts two antagonistic brothers; Pasha, who later becomes Comrade Anton; and Semyon, who protects the village. The conflict is not resolved at the end of the novel, but L.'s sympathy remains with Semyon. A story within a story in *Barsuki*, "Pro neistovogo Kalafata" (the fierce Kalafat)—usually referred to in English as "The Kalafat Legend"—portrays a tower representing Communism (as well as any bureaucracy) being built higher and higher but at the end remaining at the same level because it is slowly sinking.

In *Vor* (1927; *The Thief*, 1931), whose action takes place in Moscow during the NEP period, L.'s psychological propensities have obvious Dostoevskian roots. Here pessimism is stronger than optimism, and idealism is trampled in the name of the road to Communism. In his next novel, *Doroga na okean* (1935; *Road to the Ocean*, 1944), which was quite controversial, L. tried to create a Communist work in which readers would actively identify themselves, through the author's appeal to their reason, with the march toward the classless society. This novel, dedicated to the whole of mankind, symbolically depicts a river merging with the "Utopian Ocean." L.'s hero, Kurilov, an ideal Communist who espouses the positive and the rational, predicts a bright future. L., however, fails to make Kurilov plausible. Despite authorial attempts to imbue him with a progressive ideology, Kurilov comes off no better than other characters in the novel.

Until 1936 L. had generally been regarded as a leading novelist, but after Gorky's death in that year, the adverse criticism that he received for his novels became unbearable, and he turned to dramatic works. His plays of the 1930s were also severely criticized, but during World War II L. wrote two plays dealing with the German invasion—*Nashestvie* (1943; *The Invasion*, 1944) and *Lyonushka* (1943; Lyonushka)—for which he received a Stalin Prize.

L.'s difficulties began again with his play *Zolotaya kareta* (1946, rev. version, 1955; the golden coach), the composition of which, in several different versions, played a major role in L.'s creative life. The play contrasts the attitudes of the older and younger generations of revolutionary Russia toward love and marriage. The first version was immediately suppressed. The revisions he was forced to make showed L. that ideological uncertainties in depicting contemporary society were not welcome by Party functionaries. Thus, in his long novel *Russky les*, L. avoids contemporary problems. He goes back to 1941–42 and describes the deforestation of Russia and the conflict between Vikhrov, an honest scientist who sincerely loves forests, and his rival Gratsiansky, a pseudoscientist. Although the novel seems primarily to depict the beauty and the usefulness of the forest, the underlying implications are more intricate and more meaningful.

In general, L.'s novels are of a Dostoevskian polyphonic nature. L's preoccupation with the individual, with *chistota* (purity), and with life that is complex, ambivalent, and irrational makes his works distinctive and understandable to a Western reader. Ultimately L. takes a moralist's position.

FURTHER WORKS: *Untilovsk* (1925); *Provintsialnaya istoria* (1927; dramatized 1928); *Usmirenie Badadoshkina* (1928); *Sarancha* (1930); *Sot* (1930; *Soviet River*, 1932); *Skutarevsky* (1932; *Skutarevsky*, 1936); *Volk* (1938); *Polovchanskie sady* (1938; *The Orchards of Polovchansk*, 1946); *Evgenia Ivanovna* (written 1938, pub. 1963); *Obyknovenny chelovek* (1940); *Metel* (1940); *Vzyatie Velikoshumska* (1945; *Chariot of Wrath*, 1946); *Begstvo Mistera*

Makkinli (1960); *Teatr: Dramaticheskie proizvedenya, stati rechi* (2 vols., 1960); *Literaturnye vystuplenia* (1966); *Literatura i vremya* (1967); *Sobranie sochineny* (10 vols., 1969–1972)

BIBLIOGRAPHY: Simmons, E. J., *Russian Fiction and Soviet Ideology: Introduction to Fedin, L., and Sholokhov* (1958): 89–161; Muchnic, H., *From Gorky to Pasternak* (1961): 276–303; Terras, V., "L. L.'s Novel *The Russian Forest,"SEEJ*, 8 (1964): 123–40; Thomson, R. B., "L. L.," *FMLS*, 2 (1966): 264–73; Plank, D. L., "Unconscious Motifs in L. L.'s *The Badgers*," *SEEJ*, 16 (1972): 19–35; Thomson, R. B., "L.'s Play *Zolotaja kareta*," *SEEJ*, 16 (1972): 438–48; Harjan, G., *L. L.: A Critical Study* (1979)

—VYTAS DUKAS

LEOPOLD, Jan Hendrik

Dutch poet, b. 11 April 1865, 's Hertogenbosch; d. 21 June 1925, Rotterdam

L. studied classical philology at the University of Leiden, where he received his doctorate in 1891, and thereafter taught classical languages in a secondary school in Rotterdam. A shy and introverted man, in the course of his uneventful life he was increasingly isolated by growing deafness. He began to publish his poetry in *De nieuwe gids* in 1893, and continued to publish in that journal. During his lifetime his work was known to a small but select circle of readers; his poetry has subsequently found a much wider audience.

L. offered a highly individual voice to Dutch poetry. More than any other Dutch poet, he profitably absorbed the strong influence of French SYMBOLISM, especially that of Verlaine. (Another influence on his poetry is Spinoza, in whom he was deeply read.) His lyrics, often individually untitled, create an intensely private universe, suggested rather than described, in which the voice of the persona often addresses a beloved woman, asleep or dead. This poetry creates a realm suggestive of sleep and dreaming, heightened by the subtle musicality of the verse. L. is a master of assonance and enjambment, and can effectively spin out a long sentence through tight rhymed stanzas in a way that intensifies the sense of the transitory that the poetry often expresses. One of his finest poems, with the Greek title "Oinou hena stalagmon" (1910; a drop of wine), uses several complex images—the offering of a drop of wine to the sea as a libation that pervades all the ocean, the fall of an unpicked apple, mentioned in a fragment of Sappho, that moves the universe—to suggest the way an impulse of the mind may move out and pervade the minds of other men. Yet for the most part, this is elusive and meditative poetry, in which the voice of the persona is never answered.

A somewhat different note is heard in the sequence of poems entitled "Oostersch" (Oriental), which first appeared in *Verzen, tweede bundel* (2 vols., 1926; verses, second collection). Beginning in 1904, L. read Persian and Arabic poetry in French and English translations, and produced his own translations (some from the *Rubaiyat* of Omar Khayyam), adaptations, and original poems in the same style. These poems counterpoint his other work: they are sharper, crisper, and more aphoristic. The note of fatalism and disillusionment L. drew from the great Persian poets can be seen as a way of responding to the delicately modulated frustration his other poems express.

Of his longer poems, *Cheops* (1915; Cheops) has been the most discussed. In its stately cadenced verse we are told how the spirit of the Pharaoh joins in his own funeral procession and moves out into the great spaces of the universe, but chooses finally to return to the tomb in the pyramid, there to remain forever. This act of voluntary inwardness can be seen as central to L.'s poetic art.

FURTHER WORKS: *Verzen* (1913); *Nabetrachtingen van een concertganger* (1929); *Verzamelde verzen* (1935); *Verzameld werk* (2 vols., 1951–1952). FURTHER WORKS IN ENGLISH: *The Flute* (1949); *The Valley of Irdîn* (1957)

BIBLIOGRAPHY: Jalink, J. M., *Eine Studie über Leben und Werk des Dichters J. H. L.* (1949); Meijer, R. P., *Literature of the Low Countries*, new ed. (1978): 271–74

—FRED J. NICHOLS

LEŚMIAN, Bolesław

(pseud. of Bolesław Stanisław Lesman) Polish poet and literary critic, b. 22 Jan. 1877, Warsaw; d. 5 Nov. 1937, Warsaw

L.'s paternal ancestors belonged to the small but not negligible group of Polish Jews who assimilated into Polish society to the point of converting to Roman Catholicism. L. spent his youth in Kiev, where he studied law and was profoundly influenced by the surrounding lush Ukrainian countryside. The years 1918–33 he spent in the towns of Hrubieszów and Zamość, where he worked as a notary public. In 1933 he was elected member of the Polish Academy of Literature.

L. was associated with the movement known as Young Poland, which followed some tenets of SYMBOLISM, Decadence, and neoromanticism. Like most truly original poets, however, he cannot be easily assigned to the trend to which he nominally belonged. L.'s poetry seems to derive from evenings spent in country meadows and cemeteries. He was a baroque romantic, or an exuberant yet melancholy author of nature poems in which dazzling verbal acrobatics and gentle humor conceal a deeply pessimistic philosophy. His early poems focus on nature, whereas the later ones tend to deal either with love or with death. His essay "Traktat o poezji" (1937; treatise on poetry) is probably the best essay ever written on L.'s own poetry. He defines poetry as a dance that has rebelled against the drabness of life, and he desires poetry to be unconstrained by the conventional meanings of words and by social and political problems.

L.'s approach to nature is unusual among the European poets of his generation. Instead of painting landscapes in verse, as so many lesser modernists have done, he adopts the point of view of animate and inanimate objects. In his poems nature looks at man and not the other way around. In the title poem of *Łąka* (1920; the meadow), a grassy flatland reminds man how he once gave it the name of meadow and how since then it has had an identity of its own.

The rustic landscapes of L.'s youth reappeared in his poetry in the form of monsters and apparitions who rejoice and grieve for reasons that defy human logic. Students of L.'s poetry have pointed out that these creatures derive from Polish folklore but that they are not simply lifted from it. In "Dusiołek" (1920; an untranslatable

neologism designating a spirit that strangles men) the downtrodden peasant Bajdała upbraids his worn-out horse and ox for not waking him up when Dusiołek tried to strangle him in his sleep, and then he also upbraids God for creating Dusiołek. This popular ballad exemplifies L.'s talent for describing fantastic yet believable creatures, as well as his poetic habit of talking back to God in a gently humorous fashion.

In *Łąka*, side by side with a cycle of erotic poems, there appears a cycle entitled "Pieśni kalekujące" (lame songs; the word *lame* translates a neologism) describing a hunchback, a man without legs who lusts after a pretty girl, and a mad cobbler. From these poems of compassion there is but a step to the death poems in *Napój cienisty* (1936; shadowy potion), which express the intuition that nothingness, rather than God, awaits man after death.

L.'s creative use of the dialects of Polish surpasses that of any poet that preceded him. He also created scores of neologisms that fit the individual poems so well that they can hardly be used in another context. L.'s verbal inventiveness contrasts sharply with his rigidly traditional versification. His sensitivity to language manifested itself also in the change of his own Germanic-sounding name Lesman to the very Polish-sounding Leśmian.

L.'s literary criticism consists mostly of book reviews published in literary magazines between 1910 and 1937, which were collected in *Szkice literackie* (1959; literary sketches). These short essays rank among the best works of criticism of his generation.

L. has never enjoyed the popularity of a poet whose verse expresses a world view or a message that is easy to identify and accept. His total output is small: three volumes of poetry published in his lifetime, and one published posthumously. His poems are short and generally unconnected with one another, and his poetic world resembles the atmosphere of Rimbaud's "The Drunken Boat," of Velemir KHLEBNIKOV's FUTURIST verse, and of Boris PASTERNAK's early volume *Sister My Life*. He is an original creator of the "artificial paradises" invoked in the preceding generation by Rimbaud. He is also one of Poland's most "Polish" poets, in the sense that the values of his poetry are locked in the Polish language and so far they have remained, for the most part, out of the reach of translators.

FURTHER WORKS: *Sad rozstajny* (1912); *Klechdy sezamowe* (1913); *Przygody Sindbada Żeglarza* (1913); *Dziejba leśna* (1938); *Wybór poezyj* (1946); *Wiersze wybrane* (1955); *Klechdy polskie* (1956); *Poezje zebrane* (1957); *Utwory rozproszone: Listy* (1962); *Poezje* (1965)

BIBLIOGRAPHY: Pankowski, M., "La révolte de B. L. contre les limites: À propos de son premier receuil *Sad rozstajny,*" AIPHOS, 15 (1960): 289–318; Pankowski, M., *L.: La révolte d'un poète contre les limites* (1967); Miłosz, C., *The History of Polish Literature* (1969): 347–51; Heller, R. S., *B. L.: The Poet and His Poetry* (1976)

—EWA M. THOMPSON

LESOTHO LITERATURE

Lesotho (formerly Basutoland) is a mountainous independent state surrounded by South Africa. The dominant language is South

Sotho. The country is remarkable for its long tradition of printed vernacular literature, uncommon in Africa, where vernaculars are usually associated with oral poetry and storytelling.

Such writing was originally encouraged by missionaries, who, as early as 1841, imported a press to print translations of the Bible (completed 1878) and religious tracts. The literary tradition begins with Azariele Sekese's (1849–1930) collection in South Sotho *Buka ea pokello ea mekhoa ea Basotho le maele le litsome* (1893; new ed., 1907; customs and proverbs of the Basuto). The most important Sotho writer is Thomas MOFOLO. His series of moralistic historical novels culminated in a genuine masterpiece, *Chaka* (written 1910, pub. 1925; *Chaka the Zulu*, 1931; new tr., 1981), which recounts the life of the great Zulu conqueror as a tragic epic. This work, widely translated, has been called by the scholar Albert S. Gérard the "first major African contribution to world literature." The publication of *Chaka* marked the beginning of modern Lesotho literature.

Another writer of this period was Mofolo's teacher, Everitt Segoete (1858–1923), who wrote a moralistic novel, *Monono ke moholi mouoane* (1910; riches are like mist, vapor). This work has the distinction of originating the most common plot in southern African writing: the trials of an innocent tribal youth encountering the dangers and temptations of Johannesburg. The South African writer Peter ABRAHAMS's *Mine Boy* (1946) is a classic example of the genre, later scornfully called the "Jim goes to the city" theme. It is also the subject of the most famous modern Lesotho novel, Attwell Sidwell Mopeli-Paulus's (1913–1960) *Blanket Boy's Moon* (1953).

During the 1930s most books published were obliged to feature the Christian ethics demanded by the missionaries, but the 1950s brought a new spate of original Lesotho writing.

The past success of vernacular publication and its established readership caused most Lesotho authors to retain their own language rather than explore English. The themes continue to parallel those that commonly inspire other writers in southern Africa. Albert Nqheku's (b. 1912) novel *Tsielala* (1959; silence, please), about Sotho workers in the gold mines, is bitterly outspoken against the racist policies of South Africa. Bennett Khaketla's (b. 1913) novel *Meokho ea thabo* (1951; tears of joy) is about the inevitable clash between the values of the rural tradition and the expectations of the city life of young migrant workers. Since his theme stresses love as a mode of selecting a bride rather than the customary arranged marriage, he presents cultural conflict in sexual as well as political terms. Khaketla and Michael Mohapi (b. 1926) have written in various genres, including drama and poetry.

Kemuele Ntsane (b. 1920) wrote a series of satiric poems that, uncharacteristically for South Sotho verse, attempt rhyme forms. He also wrote four novels, including *Makumane* (1961; tidbits) and *Bao batho* (1968; these people).

Two novels by Mopeli-Paulus—*Blanket Boy's Moon* and *Turn to the Dark* (1956), both based on his own documentary account *Liretlo* (1950; ritual murder)—are the only modern works that have achieved a widespread international readership. They strongly oppose the apartheid system. Their method of creation was unusual: they were told by the author and then written down by sympathetic translators Richard Lanham and Miriam Basner, who produced the admired English versions, to which they may have contributed new material.

The first book written directly in English was *Masilo's Adventures, and Other Stories* (1968) by Benjamin Leshoai (b. 1920).

The use of English was justified by the intention to use this book as a school reader, and it is still not certain whether this is the forerunner of the kind of English-language literature that is encountered elsewhere in Africa or whether the vigorous Sotho-language writing will predominate.

BIBLIOGRAPHY: Franz, G. H., "The Literature of Lesotho," *Bantu Studies*, 6 (1930): 45–80; Beuchat, P.-D, *Do the Bantus Have a Literature?* (1963); Mofolo, B., "Poets of Lesotho," *NewA*, 6, 2 (1967): 19–23; Gérard, A. S., *Four African Literatures* (1971): 101–81; Jordan, A. C., *Towards an African Literature* (1973), passim; Maphike, P. R. S., "On the Essay in Southern Sotho," *Limi*, 8 (1980): 35–49; Gérard, A. S., *African Language Literatures* (1981): 190–223

—JOHN POVEY

LESSING, Doris

English novelist, short-story writer, playwright and critic, b. 22 Oct. 1919, Kermanshah, Persia

L. was born in Persia, where her father worked for a bank; dissatisfied, he decided to return to England and so transported his family overland through Russia in 1925. While in England he decided to become a farmer in Southern Rhodesia (now Zimbabwe),

Doris Lessing

where she was raised. She attended both public and convent schools until age thirteen, lived on the family farm thereafter, educating herself through voracious reading, and worked as a secretary in Salisbury. Married and divorced twice, she moved to London in 1949. Her return visits to Rhodesia resulted in an excellent memoir, *Going Home* (1957), and in *Africa Laughter: Four Visits to Zimbabwe* (1992).

The Grass Is Singing (1950), her first novel, focuses on settlers in Rhodesia: Mary and Dick Turner are impoverished, unhappy, and ill-adjusted to each other and to the terrain. As they sink to a level barely above that of the natives, Mary turns inward and ignores or mistreats their workers. After she taunts their houseboy, he kills her; her emotional instability, isolation, and violation of the whites' "code" of behavior all lead to the murder.

The first four volumes of L.'s five-volume *Bildungsroman, Children of Violence—Martha Quest* (1952), *A Proper Marriage* (1954), *A Ripple from the Storm* (1958), and *Landlocked* (1965)— trace the growth of a woman whose life parallels the events of L.'s own. Martha gradually discovers and accepts her sexuality, a more complete understanding of racial tensions and relations, the appeal of communism as a panacea, and the larger world outside Rhodesia. The apocalyptic fifth volume, *The Four-Gated City* (1969), begins with Martha a new immigrant in England and ends in the 1990s with the world annihilated. Especially vivid are the descriptions of the bleak post-World War II years and the powerful, pessimistic closing chapters, in which mankind is described as rushing madly to chaos.

The sequence was interrupted by L.'s masterpiece, one of the most important works of fiction in modern literature. *The Golden Notebook* (1962) is a structurally complex work, again focusing on a woman somewhat similar to L. Anna Freeman Wulf, a writer, suffers from writer's block and schizophrenically fragments her psyche into four notebooks: black (reflecting her African youth and earlier success), red (her time as a communist), yellow (a fictionalized account of an alter ego), and blue (a diary of Anna's "real" life). These are eventually supplanted by a golden notebook, suggesting a harmonious integration of the aspects of her psyche. As part of her therapy, she writes a short, formal novel, *Free Women*, which like the first four notebooks is offered piecemeal throughout *The Golden Notebook*. As L. has repeatedly stated, the meaning of *The Golden Notebook* is in the relation of the parts to each other.

Such a complex work offers endless interpretive possibilities, and some parts seem to contradict others; L. focuses less on the precise ways individual parts are understood and more on Anna's personal hell as she struggles toward mental health. L. probes unceasingly into various forms of commitment, and many readers (both male and female) have found her account of sexual, marital, racial, political, and psychological experiences profoundly influential. Only as Anna rejects experiential and psychic isolation, especially regarding language, and moves toward integration with the larger world, this time using language publicly (that is, in a novel), can she achieve wholeness.

L.'s forays into the apocalyptic continued with *Briefing for a Descent into Hell* (1971), an "inner-space fiction" especially reflecting the thought of psychoanalyst R. D. Laing (b. 1927). One of L.'s few works with a male protagonist, *Briefing for a Descent into Hell* concerns Charles Watkins, a Cambridge University classics professor, who takes a symbolic psychic "journey" into possible past existences before he is restored to mental health

(through shock treatment) and to mundane reality: he sees himself adrift in the Atlantic following extraterrestrial contact, shipwrecked in the ruins of a prehistoric city, transported to a conference on Mount Olympus (where gods are "briefed" before descending to hell, that is, earth), and guerrilla fighting in World War II in Yugoslavia.

The Memoirs of a Survivor (1974) is also concerned with catastrophe, in this case in a city (presumably London) following a major war. The protagonist, an unnamed middle-aged woman, is strong, solitary, and suddenly responsible for twelve-year-old Emily. The two subsequent years show Emily maturing dramatically and the protagonist realizing the extent to which civilization has deteriorated; children such as Emily are naturally more flexible than those tied to a memory of what the world had been like, and a new social system based on barter, gang structure, and existence at any cost, even eating corpses, enables the children to survive. Out of such anarchy necessarily comes a new set of rules for order, one wholly divorced from memory of what had existed prior to the war.

In *The Memoirs of a Survivor* L.'s increasing concern with nonrational, intuitive forms of knowledge (influenced by the ideas of Sufism, a mystical branch of Islam, and especially the writings of Idries Shah, b. 1924) leads to a sharp contrast to the external chaos. As the protagonist focuses on a patch of bare wall, she "sees" the vacant flat next door and envisions a series of scenes from her presumed early life, when she too was called Emily. Reconciling such a fantasy life with the external horror is achieved through a symbolic rejection of precataclysmic thinking and behavior, after which the protagonist has a "vision" of an ethereal, transcendent woman who mystically "protects" her and her friends. Her willingness to discard rational, linear thinking in favor of an intuitive, extrasensory awareness enables her to reconcile the mundane and the ideal into a sublime evolutionary stage, far beyond the rational way the world is "normally" perceived.

L.'s five-volume series of "space fiction" was even further removed from her early realistic fiction: *Canopus in Argos: Archives. Shikasta* (1979), the least compelling because of its lack of character or dialogue, is a didactic and sometimes tedious sequence of reports, documents, and diaries in which various recognizable periods in Earth's history are depicted from an "objective," celestial perspective. L. suggests that galactic empires of good and evil compete for dominance over earth and other worlds, that the "substance-of-we-feeling" (akin to theological grace) has diminished on Earth, and that an emissary is sent to help Earth avoid the conflagration depicted in *The Four-Gated City*. Earth's "last days" are thus described in an allegorical, deterministic narrative in which man moves from catastrophe to catastrophe because he rejects such divine guidance.

The Marriages between Zones Three, Four, and Five (1980), while still allegorical, operates on a far more human, lyrical level. In *Shikasta* L. posits a series of "zones," with the lower numbers the more ethereal and spiritual. Hence a celestial dictum that the queen of Zone Three must marry the king of Zone Four suggests that a relatively peaceful, harmonious society merges with a more warlike, insensate one. The newlyweds must compromise their respective values, and their child brings their two worlds closer. But the king is again ordered to marry, this time to the even more barbaric queen of Zone Five, and the first queen is banished, left to wander ignominiously back to her kingdom and then up toward the heights of Zone Two.

The Sirian Experiments (1981), a midpoint between the didactic collection of documents of *Shikasta* and the emotional richness of

The Marriages between Zones Three, Four, and Five, focuses on a female member of the celestial powers who is both participant in and observer of events on Earth and other planets. A kind of emotional compromise occurs as she interacts with an even more exalted superior being, thus showing how the cosmic empires' manipulation of events on earth is balanced by the "human" qualities demonstrated by these beings.

The Making of the Representative for Planet 8 (1982), the fourth in the *Canopus* series, is a short novel about the death—through freezing—of an Earth-like planet. As all forms of life on the planet slowly adjust and mutate because of the climatic changes, the Canopean masters take an active role in the inhabitants' preparation for both the planet's extinction and their escape to a more benign world; yet the overlords too are merely pawns in some larger plan for the universe, and as the planet—and all life indigenous to it—expires, we, like the overlords, are left to wonder about justice and mercy. L.'s long afterword both connects her story to the ill-fated Scott expedition to the Antarctic and expounds on nationalism and universal "process." Lessing is as concerned with the larger cosmic picture as in the earlier novels in the sequence and as pessimistically apocalyptic in her sense of celestial, transcendent, certain doom.

The final volume in the sequence—thus far, at any rate, for L. hasn't declared the series closed—is *Documents Relating to the Sentimental Agents in the Volyen Empire* (1983), a satiric consideration of the education of an apprentice Canopean agent and his susceptibility to Rhetorical Disease. L. is astute in her handling of such issues as emotionally arousing language and other semantic approaches to otherworldly creatures' confusion about nuances of earthly propaganda. L. clearly has earthly western society in her sights as she explores impassioned political and other rhethorically excessive usage. There is, of course, a plot more centered on the celestial powers' changing spheres of influence (and consequent unreliability of documents paralleling those on earth), but her linguistic explorations remain of central interest. Though L. once acknowleged starting a sixth novel in the *Canopus* sequence, she has thus far abandoned the series, which at its best enables us to see humanity through other' eyes, at its pedantic worst dependent on a sometimes relentless sequence of documents to suggest an impersonal examination of historical epochs.

In 1983, L. attempted to see if she could publish fiction under a pseudonym ("Jane Somers") to determine whether editors and reviewers would accord the same recognition to an unknown writer as to an established one. The result were two novel, *The Diary of a Good Neighbour* (1983) and *If the Old Could* (1984), neither of which, as if to confirm L.'s conviction, received much critical or popular attention until the author's true identity was revealed. The two books deal with death and responsibility, particularly the kind of responsibility the well-off owe to those less fortunate. The title character, affectionately called Janna, is a dedicated but rather indifferent caregiver who befriends a dying woman in her nineties while simultaneously relating to an irresponsible younger woman, both of whom Janna's help but neither of whom knows how to acknowledge needed assistance. Like such earlier L.'s novels as *The Summer Before the Dark* and, to a lesser extent, *The Four-Gated City, Diary* focuses on demands on one's dedication to others as these conflict with one's own needs.

The Good Terrorist (1985) is in some respects a throwback to L.'s earlier realistic novels, with its emphases on leftist politics, family disruptions, class distinctions, and above all with uncertain male/female relations. Alice leaves her life of privilege to live in a abandoned "squat" with others of similar dedication to overthrowing the establishment. As she gradually tries to change the house into a genuine commune, with order and cleanliness as well as anarchic planning, Alice finds herself becoming the parents she has disowned. Rather masochistic in her willingness to endure privations and abuse, Alice naively endures parasitic companions, social ostracism, and opportunistic hangers-on for the sake of her poorly-analyzed cause. Completely lacking self-knowledge as well as understanding of political movements, Alice is a choice characterization of one who has chosen society's underside for no good reason aside from rebellion.

One of L.'s excellences has been her willingness to experiment with various genres othr than the realistic novel, with *The Fifth Child* (1988) her experimental foray into horror fiction. Again focusing on the family, the novel describes how an otherwise stable family is torn apart by the arrival of their fifth offspring, a boy named Ben variously described as a goblin, a monster, a troll, a Neaderthal, a genetic throwback. No one is willing to acknowledge that Ben is basically inhuman or subhuman, not a social creature accepted by anyone aside from some working-class toughs. The family has been effectively destroyed by a creature who simply cannot fit into such conventional social categories as a family. L.'s perspective in her analysis of the kinds of malaise affecting contemporary Britian, though neither Ben nor his family or others in the book rise above the two-dimensional.

In recent years, L. has produced more non-fiction than fiction. Her only full-length work of fiction, *Love, Again* (1996) is a strong work, close to *The Summer Before the Dark* in its examinatin of an older woman's effort at self-analysis. Sarah Durham, manager of a small theatre company planning to stage the story of Julie Vairon, 19th c. quadroon from Martinique who survived as an artist and composer before killing herself. The parallels between Durham and Vairon that emerge as the company takes on the project include lovers, infatuations, and suicides; Durham's emotional struggles, including the complexities of aging and her ambiguous feelings toward family, colleagues, and lovers, result in an excellent dramatization of the life of a complex woman.

African Laughter (1994), already mentioned, described four visits to Zimbabwe between 1982 and 1992 and combines the political with the personal, as when she tells of her racist brother's views and subsequent death. Her sense of Zimbabwe is bleak, given its decline and chaos, but she remains hopeful that the country can mature and survive.

The personal elements in the book prepared the way for her first two volumes (of a proposed series of three) of autobiography. *Under My Skin* (1994) covers her life from childhood in Zimbabwe until 1959, when she migrated to England with her first novel and the son from her second marriage. The work forthrightly, unsentimentally compares her early fiction with the facts of her life and is candid about her convictions, though she is rather taciturn regarding her marriages and love-affairs, and nicely captures colonial African physical and emotional life. *Walking in the Shade* (1997) covers the period till 1962 and completion of *The Golden Notebook*. Less concerned in this volume with childhood memories, L. is more explicit about her struggles to survive, about other writers, and especially about her years as a Communist, which she explains in terms of her idealistic youth and need for a cause. Though she is good in describing her disillusionment with Communism, she only hints at her later interest in mysticism and is somewhat evasive regarding children, specific lovers, and friends.

Even though L.'s form and technique have undergone radical change since her first realistic novels, she continually deals with certain ideas and themes, including psychic wholeness, the importance of nonphysical phenomena, a pessimistic sense of imminent Armageddon, and solitary, driven protagonists controlled by forces and pressures that they neither fully recognize nor understand. Less positive are her sometimes wooden style, repetitious use of similar character types and incidents, her too-obvious symbolism (especially with names), her verbosity and polemicizing, and an endlessly serious, humorless stance as a Cassandra offering prophetic warnings. Yet she is remarkably able to probe into her characters' controlling impulses, to analyze the underlying causes of the malaise infecting the modern world (especially the conflict of the personal with the universal), to offer a successive series of escape routes (which have necessarily changed as she herself has changed), and finally to indict, in a most compelling way, man's incessant surge toward self-destruction.

FURTHER WORKS: *This Was the Old Chief's Country* (1951); *Five: Short Novels* (1953); *Retreat to Innocence* (1956); *The Habit of Loving* (1957); *Fourteen Poems* (1959); *Each His Own Wilderness* (1959); *In Pursuit of the English* (1961); *Play with a Tiger* (1962); *A Man and Two Women* (1963); *African Stories* (1964); *Particularly Cats* (1967; expanded version, *Particularly Cats and More Cats* (1989; in the U. S. as *Particularly Cats. . . and Rufus*, 1991); *The Story of a Non-Marrying Man and Other Stories* (1972; pub. in the U. S. as *The Temptation of Jack Orkney and Other Stories*, 1972); *The Summer before the Dark* (1973); *A Small Personal Voice: Essays, Reviews, Interviews* (1974; expanded U. K. ed., 1994); *Stories* (1978); *Winter in July* (1966); *The Black Madonna* (1966); *Nine African Stories* (1968); *The Sun Between Their Feet* (1973); *Collected Stories* (2 vols., 1978; pub. in the U. S. As *Stories*, 1978); *Prisons We Choose to Live Inside* (1986); *The Wind Blows Away Our Words and Other Documents Relating to Afghanistan* (1987); *The D. L. Reader* (1990; pub. in the U. S., with same title but different continents, 1990, with Philip Glass); *The Making of the Representative for Planet 8* (1988); *London Observed: Stories and Sketches* (1992; pub. in the U. S. as *The Real Thing: Stories and Sketches*, 1992); *Playing the Game* (1995); *Love, Again* (1996); *Conversations* (1994; pub. in the U. K. as *Putting the Question Differently: Interviews* (1996); *Play with a Tiger and Other Plays* (1996)

BIBLIOGRAPHY: Brewster, D., *D. L.* (1965); Schlueter, P., *The Novels of D. L.* (1973); Thorpe, M., *D. L.* (1973); special L. issue, *ConL*, 14, 4 (1973); special L. section, *WLWE*, 12, 2 (1973): 148–206; Spilka, M., "L. and Lawrence: The Battle of the Sexes," *ConL*, 16 (1975): 218–40; Kaplan, S. J., *Feminine Consciousness in the Modern Novel* (1975): 136–72; Rose, E. C., *The Tree Outside the Window: D. L.'s Children of Violence* (1976); Singleton, M. A., *The City and the Veld: The Fiction of D. L.* (1977); Rubenstein, R., *The Novelistic Vision of D. L.* (1979); special L. issue, *MFS*, 26, 1 (1980); Seligman, D., *D. L.: An Annotated Bibliography of Criticism* (1981); Spiegel, R., *D. L.: The Problem of Alienation and the Form of the Novel* (1980); Draine, B., *Substance Under Pressure: Artistic Coherence and Evolving Form in the Novels of D. L.* (1983); Sage. L., *D. L.* (1983); Knapp, M., *D. L.* (1984); Bertelsen, E., ed., *D. L.* (1984); Fishburn, K., *The Unexpected Universe of D. L.* (1985); Sprague, C., and V. Tiger, eds., *Critical Essays on D. L.* (1986); Budhos, S., *The Theme of Enclosure in the Works of D. L.* (1987); Kaplan, C., and E. C. Rose, eds., *D. L.: The Alchemy of Survival* (1988); Whittaker, R., *D. L.* (1988); Myles, A., *D. L.: A Novelist with Organic Sensibility* (1991); Fahim, A. S., *D. L. And Sufi Equilibrium: The Evolving Form of the Novel* (1994); Greene, G., *D. L.: The Poetics of Change* (1994); Maslen, E., *D. L.* (1994); Rowe, M. M., *D. L.* (1994); Galin, M., *Between East and West: Sufism in the Novels of D. L.* (1997)

—PAUL SCHLUETER

As in *The Golden Notebook*, mental breakdowns of all kinds are, in part, a response to the politics of the West, the bureaucratization, the incipient fascism, the irrational violence, and to the dehumanized, propaganda- and drug-addicted culture we live in. But for Mrs. L. in 1969, madness is not merely a debilitating affliction or an escape, or even a novelist's tool. Developing particular forms of what Western man calls "madness" may be the only way out of his afflicted culture. Can anything—any persons or organizations—Mrs. L. asks in [*The Four-Gated City*], call a halt to the inevitable destruction to come, given the growth and movement about the earth of mad machines, on the one hand, and the lack of internal human commonsensical and moral controls, on the other? Her answer is unequivocally No. Our dulled apathy to the condition of daily life and to the cries of war signals what Robert Bly has called "the deep longing for death," a suicidal rush to annihilation, as though the half-drugged of us were longing for total immolation, for the relief of the end. Mrs. L., on the contrary, envisions a struggle toward life, through the use of extraordinary sensory powers by intelligence and a moral consciousness.

Florence Howe, on *The Four-Gated City, Nation*, 11 Aug. 1969, p. 117

The most considerable single work by an English author in the 1960s has been done by D. L., in *The Golden Notebook* (1962). It is a carefully organized but verbose, almost clumsily written novel, and if we were to view it solely as an aesthetic experience, we might lose most of its force. The book's strength lies not in its arrangement of the several notebooks which make up its narrative and certainly not in the purely literary quality of the writing, but in the wide range of Mrs. L.'s interests, and, more specifically, in her attempt to write honestly about women. To be honest about women in the sixties is, for Mrs. L., tantamount to a severe moral commitment, indeed almost a religious function, in some ways a corollary of her political fervor in the fifties.

While the English novel has not lacked female novelists, few indeed—including Virginia Woolf—have tried to indicate what it is like to be a woman: that is, the sense of being an object or thing even in societies whose values are relatively gentle. For her portraits, Mrs. L. has adopted, indirectly, the rather unlikely form of the descent into hell, a mythical pattern characterized by her female protagonists in their relationships with men, an excellent metaphor for dislocation and fragmentation in the sixties.

Frederick R. Karl, "D. L. in the Sixties: The New Anatomy of Melancholy," *ConL*, 13 (1972), p. 15

Indeed, what attracts men as well as women to D. L.'s fiction these days, we might conclude, is what attracted them to [D. H.] Lawrence's: namely, an autobiographical intensity by which images of the author's self are put on the line and exploited with an honesty so self-searching and unsparing as to anticipate most of our critical objections to those images: a prophetic arrogance, too, a projected self-importance by which such characters are taken as where we are now or where we should be heading. . . . And finally, there is an immersion through such characters in some regional manifestation of the fate of a whole civilization in decline . . . in which Anna [Wulf] and [Lawrence's Rupert] Birkin [in *Women in Love*] steep themselves each with a fatal yearning, yet which each also struggles to transcend. . . . [B]oth writers have made the same refusal to be cowed by the modern world's absurdities and incomprehensibilities; and surely both demand of readers the same active faith in their audacity and sincerity as pledges to authenticity—with the surprising result that Lawrence. . . and Lessing. . . have found audiences they have themselves helped to create who approach them with just such activated faith.

Mark Spilka, "L. and Lawrence: The Battle of the Sexes," *ConL*, 16 (1975), pp. 221–22

The ideal of the City stands behind everything L. has written, an expression of her firm sense of purpose, put most explicitly in an important essay, "The Small Personal Voice." There she affirms a belief in "committed" literature, in which the writer considers himself/herself "an instrument of change." . . . [T]he Armageddon of technological disaster looms there as well. . . . L. believes that mankind is at a crucial point in history and that artists must paint the possible evil as well as strengthen "a vision of good which may defeat the evil"; that is, art for society's sake. L.'s criteria for art fit her own work. Not simply an artist, she is also critic and prophet, dissecting in minute detail the faults of a society "hypnotized by the idea of Armageddon" and prophesying the calamitous results of those faults. At the same time, she attempts to delineate possible solutions to the world's problems.

Mary Ann Singleton, *The City and the Veld: The Fiction of D. L.* (1977), p. 18

[The] center of L.'s fictional universe is the perceiving mind as it translates the phenomenal world through its own experience. . . . L.'s primary orientation as a writer is thus less an aesthetic than an ideological one. It is not gracefulness of style but a steadily high level of intellectual energy and the provocative framing of ideas, embodied through deeply

felt characters experiencing both typical and unconventional life situations, that invigorate her fiction. Her continuing incorporation of a broad spectrum of social concerns ranging from Leftist politics to racial issues, female roles, sexuality, esoteric tradition, science fiction extrapolations, mid-life crises, the various insanities of contemporary life for which madness itself is the most expressive analogy, and a number of others, may obscure the fact that all of these are meaningful within the larger metaphysical coherence of her vision.

Roberta Rubenstein, *The Novelistic Vision of D. L.: Breaking the Forms of Consciousness* (1979), p. 245

In *Martha Quest* we see the adolescent Martha struggling with her dreams of selfhood and having them stunted by a patriarchal society that is so potent even her own mother betrays her. In *A Proper Marriage* we see the young mother Martha trying to overcome the crippling effects of the institution of motherhood, both as it affects her and her daughter. In the final three books of the series. . . we see a maturing woman still haunted by her mother—driven, in fact, to actual illness upon the prospects of a visit from her. We also witness L.'s ultimate solution to the politics of mother-daughter: eliminate the problem altogether by opening humanity's individual psyches to such an extent that no one would be able to control another person, nor would anyone want or feel the need to. . . . In her cataclysmic conclusion to the series, she dramatically predicts that the power plays and oppression characteristics of the nightmare repetition of motherhood can lead not only to alienated women but to the end of the world.

Katherine Fishburn, "The Nightmare Repetition: The Mother-Daughter Conflict in D. L.'s *Children of Violence*," in Cathy N. Davidson and E. M. Brower, eds., *The Lost Tradition: Mothers and Daughters in Literature* (1980), p. 215

The Four-Gated City is a chronicle of change: a chronicle which explores the evolution of human consciousness and its uneasy interrelation to a changing society; a study of the impact of social values on individual lives; and a revelation of the relative fragility of the individual as he confronts powerful social forces with which he ultimately must grapple if he or society is to survive. The ten fragments which make up the futuristic Appendix to the novel purport to have been written after the terrible catastrophe that has ended modern civilization as we know it. The fragments recount both the events leading up to the catastrophe and those that follow. . . . L. affirms that the survival of modern civilization lies in the nature of human beings and in the relations that individuals make with others. . . . Shortly after the publication of *The Four-Gated City*, L. stated in an interview . . . that one of her main concerns in writing the book was "to reach the youth." . . .For L. hope lies with the seedling-children, with those rare few who, compelled by the life force, will seek a place to grow, send out roots, join with others, and finally build new islands in the sea of chaos that is the modern world. . . . For L. the ultimate question is whether the few can succeed in forming the complex structures necessary for the survival of the many. . . . The Appendix records one possibility for the future; there is still time for a different history.

Melissa G. Walker, "D. L.'s The Four-Gated City: Consciousness and Community—A Different History," SoR, 17 (1981), pp. 117–20

LEUTENEGGER, Gertrud

Swiss novelist and poet (writing in German), b. 6 Dec. 1948, Schwyz

L. is one of the most outspokenly feminist and politically leftist novelists of the postwar generation in Switzerland. Her most important contributions are in the areas of drama and the novel, which are characterized by a combination of a highly lyrical style, autobiographical elements, and political allegory. She initially published short stories and poetry. L. was the daughter of a civil servant and was educated in Swiss schools as well as a French boarding school. She also lived in Florence, England, and Berlin, then specialized in early-childhood education, but also worked in a women's psychiatric clinic as well as being for a time the custodian of the Nietzsche House in Sils Maria. These diverse working and living experiences made her critical of Swiss society's self-perception as a well-regulated microcosm, with its unrelenting insistence on tradition and order. L. protests against deeply entrenched structures of order, normalcy, and sameness, which marginalize women, foreigners, especially the Italian working-class population in Switzerland, the mentally ill, and those with communist or socialist political leanings.

Her first novel, *Vorabend* (1975; the evening before), invokes the apocalyptic atmosphere on the eve of a political demonstration. The isolated female narrator feels alienated from her surroundings but chronicles her feelings of dread and rebellion in realistic detail on a walk through Zurich, remembering on the eve of a big protest march, which she wants to join, sudden and violent disruptions of the daily routine—a worker killed by electric current in the town square, an awakening lesbian relationship to a girlfriend in high school with the ridicule that went along with it, being a nurse in a women's psychiatric ward, where the old and the ill are kept medicated but no effort is made to reintegrate them into society or even treat them as human beings. L. voices her hope for a less hierarchical, more caring society, but her appeal is tempered by skepticism. In her second novel, *Ninive* (1977; Ninive), L. frames her plea for social innovation in a more biblical and allegorical vein. The narrative begins with a visitation, an embalmed whale is exhibited to the people of L.'s hometown, and ends with the whale's destruction. This narrative contains the childhood friendship and later love story of two communist inhabitants whose vision of a better society survives the repression of state institutions, which the whale symbolizes.

In 1977 L. began taking classes in directing for the stage at the Zurich Academy of Theater and the Arts, and interned with the noted director Jürgen Flimm in Hamburg in 1978. This experience led to the publication of a play, *Lebewohl, gute Reise* (1980; farewell, have a good trip), which deals with the struggle between Gilgamesh and Enkidu for control of the world. Their brutality is opposed but not overcome by two marginalized and abused female protagonists. The play incorporates many fantastical and surrealist elements, which tend to dominate in L.'s next novel, *Gouverneur* (1981; governor), an allegory of a Nietzschean construction project on a mountain plateau in Switzerland, far from the cities yet subject to periodic checks by teams of hostile state inspectors. The narrator wishes to find or remember the governor (God), who planned the project originally. The governor does return unexpectedly in the guise of a knife seller at the end when most of the other protagonists have been killed or victimized, and the dramatic ending leaves it open whether he has returned to help or to kill the narrator.

Two of L.'s more recent prose works, *Kommins Schiff* (1983; come onboard) and *Meduse* (1985; Medusa), demonstrate her mastery of evocative, lyrical language. While the political dimension of L.'s earlier writing is less foregrounded in these texts, they blend philosophy, fantasy, and autobiographical detail with a critique of male-female relationships in so far as they reproduce social inequalities. L. is most compelling in her ability to blend social critique and writing about everyday life in Switzerland with a richly poetic language.

FURTHER WORKS: *Wie in Salomons Garten* (1981); *Das verlorene Monument* (1985)

BIBLIOGRAPHY: Matt, B. von, "G. Ls Gouverneur," *Lesarten* (1985): 171–74; Köchli, Y. D., *Themen in der neuren schweizerischen Literatur* (1982): 12–34, 121–55

—HELGA DRUXES

LEVERTOV, Denise

American poet and essayist, b. 24 Oct. 1923, Ilford, England; d. 20 Dec. 1997, Seattle

L. was born and raised in a suburb of London. The daughter of a scholarly Russian Jewish father who had converted to Christianity and become an Anglican priest and of a Welsh mother, L. never went to school but was educated chiefly at home by her mother, the BBC Schools Programs, and private tutors. After her marriage to an American she emigrated to the U.S. in 1948 and later became a naturalized U.S. citizen. L. taught at a number of American colleges and universities and retired, a full professor, from Tufts University. She also served as poetry editor of *The Nation*. Long a political activist, especially against the Vietnam war, L. gave antiwar readings and helped in student demonstrations for that cause and others around the country.

L.'s poetry, from the first collection in 1946 to her last, shows a consistency of theme, tone, and technical control, with only moderate changes in emphasis caused by increasing maturity and concern with social injustice. Her mood is intense, ranging from tenderness to ebullience or outrage. Her subject matter is feminine without being feminist, and ranges from the smallest sensory or personal detail of domestic life to international social and military atrocities, especially those that involve children. Many of the poems concern the creative process. L.'s technique is determined by the strongly emotional impulses that generate her poems. She writes in the rhythms of speech, often excited, impulsive speech, and in open forms that often reflect physical movement; she pays great attention to precise sensory detail, and uses little metaphor, allusion, or other conspicuous rhetorical devices. She employs a significant amount of direct, emotionally charged statement, which tends to make the meanings of her poems more explicit than mysterious or multileveled. At her most successful the poem is a single swift stab of experience that implies felt ideas; at her least successful (most often in the political poems) she can be somewhat sentimental and expository.

L.'s prose analyses of her own creative process, many of them collected in *The Poet in the World* (1973), consistently explain what her poems demonstrate: a reverence for and cultivation of the initial subconscious emotional impulse and a rhythm dependent on "the cadence of the thinking-feeling process." (Although L. has often been classified with Charles OLSON and the "Projectivist" or "Black Mountain" poets, she partly rejects that classification, saying, "I've never fully gone along with Charles Olson's idea of the use of the breath.") She also favors a "semiconscious" creation of metaphor from literal details and a use of diction and reference that achieves "a fairly constant balance between the aesthetic and humane needs" of writer and reader, that is, a style neither "elitist" nor "popular." In other words, L. believes that "a poem *is* a sonic, sensuous event and not a statement or a string of ideas." Her best poems are such events. For example, in "The Curve," from *Relearning the Alphabet* (1966), L. describes a literal walk along a railroad track, and by means of sequence, selection of detail, and rhythm makes the experience represent not only the faith-doubt, hope-surprise inherent in taking a walk, but in creating a poem or at the same time discovering even wider universal meanings.

Despite L.'s British origin, she was clearly an American poet. She shared the interest in social action and personal autobiography of her American contemporaries. In technique she favored the Williams Carlos WILLIAMS side of MODERNISM, rather than the T. S. ELIOT side. What separates her most clearly from other poets who also write direct, intense poems on social and personal themes, in open forms, is her tone of gladness. Whether disappointed, reflective, or exultant, L.'s poetry is essentially *glad*.

FURTHER WORKS: *The Double Image* (1946); *Here and Now* (1957); *Overland to the Islands* (1958); *5 Poems* (1958); *With Eyes at the Back of Our Heads* (1959); *The Jacob's Ladder* (1961); *O Taste and See* (1964); *City Psalm* (1964); *Poems Concerning the Castle* (1966); *The Sorrow Dance* (1968); *Three Poems* (1968); *A Tree Telling of Orpheus* (1968); *The Cold Spring and Other Poems* (1968); *A Marigold from North Vietnam* (1968); *In the Night: A Story* (1968); *Embroideries* (1969); *Relearning the Alphabet* (1970); *Summer Poems 1969* (1970); *A New Year's Garland for My Students, MIT 1969–70* (1970); *To Stay Alive* (1971); *Footprints* (1972); *The Freeing of the Dust* (1975); *Life in the Forest* (1978); *Collected Earlier Poems 1940–1960* (1978); *Light Up the Cave* (1981); *Pig Dreams: Scenes from the Life of Sylvia* (1981); *Candles in Babylon* (1982); *Poems, 1960-1967* (1983); *Breathing the Water* (1987); *Poems, 1968-1972* (1987); *Door in the Hive* (1989); *Evening Train* (1992); *New and Selected Essays* (1992); *Tesserae: Memories and Suppositions* (1995); *Sands of the Well* (1996)

BIBLIOGRAPHY: Wagner, L., *D. L.* (1967); Wilson, R. A., *A Bibliography of D. L.* (1972); Mersmann, J., "D. L.: Piercing In,"

Out of the Vietnam Vortex (1974): 77–112; Carruth, H., "L.," *HudR*, 27 (1974): 475–80; Younkins, R., "D. L. and the Hasidic Tradition," *Descant*, 19 (1974): 40–48; Gitzen, J., "From Reverence to Attention: The Poetry of D. L.," *MQ*, 16 (1975): 328–41; Wagner, L., ed., *D. L.: In Her Own Province* (1979); Marten, H., *Understanding D. L.* (1988); Wagner-Martin, L., ed., *Critical Essays on D. L.* (1990); Gelpi, A., ed., *D. L.: Selected Criticism* (1993); Rodgers, A. T., *D. L.: The Poetry of Engagement* (1993)

—ALBERTA TURNER

LEVI, Carlo

Italian essayist, novelist, and journalist, b. 29 Nov. 1902, Turin; d. 4 Jan. 1975, Rome

From his earliest formative years, L. came into contact with socialist ideology, and by the time he had completed his university studies in medicine he was an active member of the incipient resistance to Mussolini in Turin. He was arrested in 1934, incarcerated, and then released but placed under house surveillance. A year later, he was rearrested and exiled in two isolated villages of southern Italy, first in Grassano and shortly thereafter in Galliano, in the province of Lucania. Although the distance from his native Turin was great, and even greater in terms of civilization and culture, it was here that the future author found his intellectual,

Carlo Levi

moral, and artistic nourishment. The two years of his banishment were not spent in sterile isolation but in fruitful activity. He continued his creative work as a painter—he already had a certain reputation, having exhibited in Venice—and became the physician to the villagers, sharing their sufferings with a sympathy that grew into a genuine spiritual communion.

These experiences found their expression in 1939 in an essay, *Paura della libertà* (1946; *Of Fear and Freedom*, 1958), which constitutes an impassioned demonstration of the coercive irrationality of dictatorships and an exaltation of the freedom and dignity of the individual. Creatively, these experiences bore their best fruit during the closing days of World War II, when, hiding in a room for several months in order to avoid deportation as a Jew by the retreating Nazis, they resurfaced most vividly, were set down in a short time (December 1943—July 1944), and appeared in print under the title *Cristo si è fermato a Eboli* (1945; *Christ Stopped at Eboli*, 1947). The book became the world's window on southern Italy, brought its author international recognition, and made him one of the leaders of the committed writers of NEOREALISM.

In *Cristo si è fermato a Eboli* L. gives an account of his banishment on two levels. On one, he chronicles his personal vicissitudes from the day of his arrival to that of his departure. On another, he records and comments upon the happenings, routine or startling, in the life of the villages. The private and the public dimensions are skillfully interwoven throughout the book and find their fullest convergence toward the latter part, when L. feels and acts like one of the villagers, themselves victims of Fascist oppression. L. provides us, however, with much more than a book of memories. He illustrates the tyranny of the outsiders, mainly the state functionaries, and of their local Fascist allies, the middle class of landowners and professionals, over the downtrodden farmhands, laborers, and shepherds. He gives us a gallery of portraits of individuals (such as the Fascist mayor, the town crier, and the unforgettable Giulia, who had more than a dozen pregnancies with more than a dozen men), or of groups (such as children at play, the villagers witnessing the pig doctor's operations, and the oratorical tournament). He paints colorful landscapes. He describes, always compellingly—at times elaborately, at others succinctly—everyday incidents and exceptional events, celebrations and rituals. These incidents are often endowed with a symbolic and supernal aura. He probes the inner world of the villagers, revealing their rough or gentle traits, their rudimentary but wholesome and sensitive responses to the occurrences of life, their distrust of all authority, political or religious, their continued belief in superstition and their practice of magic. The most impressive features, however, do not stem from L.'s consummate skill as a portraitist or from his perceptiveness as a diagnostician of this rural society, but from his ability to engage the intellectual, moral, and social consciousness of his readers and to make them share his own sympathies and antipathies. He accomplishes this not by the seemingly documentary presentation and the factual glossing of the reality he apprehended, but by his subjective shaping and creative contrivance of it. Hence, although difficult to categorize neatly, the book is a work of conscious literary art, closer to fiction than to document.

A similarly compassionate commitment to the lot of the victims of the impersonal state pervaded L.'s subsequent work as an editor and journalist who contributed to major Italian publications, as a politician who was elected to the senate in 1963 and served until his death, as a painter whose works sought to express arcane reality, and finally as a writer of short essays, novels, and travel accounts.

In his literary works, whether fictional or nonfictional, we find a purposiveness similar to that of *Cristo si è fermato a Eboli*. L.'s writing, in fact, was never an evasion but always stemmed from his urgent concern for the political, social, and moral issues in Italy and elsewhere. None of his subsequent works, however, elicited among the readers or the critics the response of *Cristo si è fermato a Eboli*.

L. was not a transcendent writer, but *Cristo si è fermato a Eboli* exercised an enduring influence, thematically as well as formally, on the development of post-World War II Italian fiction. Although the conditions that engendered his masterpiece have changed or are changing, it has not lost any of its broad appeal for its international readership.

FURTHER WORKS: *L'orologio* (1950; *The Watch*, 1951); *Le parole sono pietre: Tre giornate in Sicilia* (1955; *Words Are Stones: Impressions of Sicily*, 1958); *Il futuro ha un cuore antico* (1956); *La doppia notte dei tigli* (1959; *The Linden Tree*, 1962); *Un volto che ci somiglia: Ritratto d'Italia* (1960); *Tutto il miele è finito* (1960); *Quaderno a cancelli* (1979)

BIBLIOGRAPHY: Rosenberg, H., "Politics as Dancing," *Tradition of the New* (1959): 199–206; Pacifici, S., "The New Writers," *A Guide to Contemporary Italian Literature* (1962): 114–49; Heiney, D., "Emigration Continued: L., Alvaro, and Others," *America in Modern Italian Literature* (1964): 126–45; Pacifici, S., "C. L.: The Essayist as a Novelist," *The Modern Italian Novel: From Pea to Moravia* (1979): 90–98; Catani, R. D., "Structure and Style as Fundamental Expression: The Works of C. L. and Their Poetic Ideology," *Italica*, 56 (1979): 213–29

—EMMANUEL HATZANTONIS

LEVI, Primo

Italian memorialist, novelist, and short-story writer, b. 31 July 1919, Turin; d. 11 Apr. 1987, Turin

As a child L. had a vague awareness of Jewish cultural tradition; but as a chemistry student at the University of Turin he had to deal with the racial laws promulgated in 1938 by the Fascist regime. In 1943 he joined an antifascist partisan group. Captured shortly thereafter, he was deported to Auschwitz, where he survived one year thanks to a series of fortuitous circumstances. Liberated by the Russians in January 1945, his return home turned into an eight-month odyssey. He resumed his career as a chemist in Turin and also found time to write his two classic memorials. Several collections of science fiction and short stories followed at intervals until he retired in 1977 to become a full-time writer. Throughout his career he was the honored recipient of several literary prizes, including the Campiello Prize in 1963 and again in 1982 as well as the Bagutta Prize in 1967.

L.'s first memorial, *Se questo è un uomo* (1947; *Survival in Auschwitz: The Nazi Assault on Humanity*, 1961), sprang from a pressing need to recount his experience in the camp and make others participate in that experience. At the same time he documented how such a dehumanizing institution systematically deprived each individual of his and her identity and dignity, and brought about the annihilation of the internees. The astonishing revocation of his personal calamities alternates with those of a vast gallery of fellow internees, caught with striking psychological insight. His alert moral consciousness blocks any hate for the oppressors, and equally guarantees an incommensurable admiration for those who, in spite of the terrifying brutality to which they were subjected, never completely forgot they were human beings. With great skill, balance, and comprehension, L. transforms documentary fact into a profound civil and moral experience.

La tregua (1963; *The Awakening*, 1965) is a sequel. In a more tranquil tone L. portrays the absurd wanderings that he and his companions followed at Russian directive through a devastated eastern Europe. The account of the eight-month peregrinations is at once tragic, comic, and picaresque. But eventually a pessimistic view takes over. The prisoners' aimless meandering, their subjugation to blind bureaucracy, and their impotence are not only a documentation of a tragic destiny, but also an allegory of life itself. The idea emerges that the hate inherent to the camp necessarily engenders revenge and violence, and further, that the human being is perhaps living in a permanent state of war in or out of the camp. L.'s style is essential, concise, and precise. A wise use of adjectives renders a feel for the complexities and contradictory aspects of reality and human nature.

In his fictional works L. abstracted and applied this historically based thematic to modern society. If the camp was synonymous with the perversion of human reason and a concomitant perverted use of science and technology for the sake of power, then scientific and technological progress could be construed as a threat to nature and to humankind. He wrote two series of science-fiction short stories, collected in *Storie naturali* (1966; natural stories) and *Vizio di forma* (1971; vicious form). Selections from both works were published in *The Sixth Day, and Other Tales* (1990). In both series L. writes of quotidian cases where excessive technological development changes the true essence of our lives and of nature.

Taking a more positive slant, *Il sistema periodico* (1975; *The Periodic Table*, 1984) mirrors a chemist's professional life of victories and defeats scrupulously performed with precision and deep moral dedication. The obvious implication is that in the "trade" of living the same scrupulous precision and dedication are needed. This theme, together with L.'s admiration for those who choose their destiny in the face of social restrictions, is fully developed in *La chiave a stella* (1978; *The Monkey's Wrench*, 1986). *Se non ora, quando?* (1982, *If Not Now, When?*, 1989) combines the emergence of Jewish consciousness and pride with the historical documentation of action taken on the Russian front by partisan Jewish groups against retreating Nazi forces. His last book, *I sommersi e i salvati* (1986; *The Drowned and the Saved*, 1988), poses the question of how much of the camp is alive and well in our time, and how long it will remain in our memories.

L. is considered a great memorialist since the publication of *Se questo è un uomo*, and recent attentive readings of his works have revealed the full-fledged literary stature of a complex writer very attuned to the problems of the contemporary human being.

FURTHER WORKS: *L'osteria di Brema* (1975; repub. as *Ad ora incerta*, 1984; *Collected Poems*, 1988); *La ricerca delle radici. Antologia personale* (1981); *Lilit, e altri racconti* (1981; *Moments of Reprieve*, 1986); *L'altrui mestiere* (1985; *Other People's Trades*, 1989); *Racconti e saggi* (1986; *The Mirror Maker*, 1989)

BIBLIOGRAPHY: Gunzberg, L., "Down among the Dead Men: L. and Dante in Hell," *MLS*, 16 (1986): 10–28; Epstein, A., "P. L. and the Language of Atrocity," *BSIS*, 20 (1987): 31–38; McRae, M.,

Primo Levi

"Opposition and Reversal in P. L.'s *The Periodic Table*," *POMPA* (1988): 115–24; Mondo, L., "P. L.'s Muse: Curiosity," preface to *The Mirror Maker* (1989): ix–xi; Regge, T., Introduction to *Dialogo* (1989): vii–xviii; Schehr, L. R., "P. L.'s Strenuous Clarity," *Italica*, 4 (1989): 429–43; Motola, G., "The Varnish-Maker's Dream," *SR*, 98 (1990): 506–14; Sodi, R. B., *A Dante of Our Time: P. L. and Auschwitz* (1990)

—ROSARIO FERRERI

LEVINE, Philip

American poet, b. 10 Jan. 1928, Detroit, Michigan

L. was educated in the public schools in Detroit and at Wayne University (now Wayne State University). He worked at automobile plants and in various grease shops along Grand River Avenue to make enough money to live on until leaving the city for good in 1953, traveling to Palo Alto to study with Yvor WINTERS at Stanford and to Iowa City where his teachers were Robert LOWELL and John BERRYMAN, whom he favored. That industrial city of Detroit as well as Barcelona of the 1930s, both of which had entered L.'s boyhood imagination as he saw American workers struggling with the hazards and indignities of assembly line work, shaped the territory for much of L.'s poetry. The poems represent a symbolic quest to transcend the old vision that the earth belongs to no one, through a facing up to the inequalities and broken promises and to the poet's own anger.

Seeds of L.'s early naturalistic views can be seen in *Red Dust* (1971) in the references to fate, death's incontrovertible nature, and the "failures of will" he found all around him. L. expresses anger at an unresponsive universe housing the wreckage of civilized living and at a god and heaven that, if they existed, ought, L. makes clear, to provide solace and answers. The conflict that is presented through the first half of L.'s work is between the ideals of human will, aspiration, and hard work on the one hand—all that represents promise—and reality on the other. L. remains angry about the broken promise, about the discrepancy between the wish "for a new world and a new home" and people's willingness to work for it, "Putting their lives / into steel," working until they are often too tired to stand up; and he is angry about the reality of poverty, the essential uselessness of work.

The bleakness of this vision, where in *1933* (1974) the disappointments are presented as generational—a working-class father spawning a working-class son, neither of whom is able to control his destiny—gives way in *Ashes* (1979), his ninth book. L.'s quarrel is at least partly resolved when in several of the poems the speaker takes responsibility for his boyhood and the familial past. In "Salts and Oils" L.'s speaker says that his fully digesting the "filth and glory / of the palatable world" happens "because I have to grow up." The tone changes in the poems written in mid-career, humor appearing with more frequency then and in the next books. Death is presented as a part of living, and the bad that L. continues to see in the American experience is balanced against what remains good, essentially a grace and a faithfulness to one's life, no matter how darkened by the grim realities of working class necessities. Despite racism, plunder, industrial detritus, and economic inequalities, the heroes in L.'s universe stand tall: political idealists, old boxers, uncomplaining peasants, a poor black man ironically named Tom Jefferson in the collection entitled *A Walk with Tom Jefferson* (1988).

The L. line is an orthodox free-verse line, broken syntactically. The authority of the lines often appears to derive solely from establishing a length and staying with it. Their integrity is related to narrative image; the poem unfolds, the details of the story are interesting, and the line carries those details with no visible show of artistic adornment, as in William Carlos WILLIAMS. The strong narrative impulse, which the lines so effortlessly carry, comes from two obvious sources: L.'s personal past, and invention. What matters is of course artistic truth, which L. renders without fanfare and with the help from a few other literary forebears: Whitman, Keats, and Federico GARCÍA LORCA, who he has said offered him a model for "all the eloquence and fury a poet could master."

L.'s poetry will be remembered for its giving voice to the complicated lives of men and women and for making something closer to simple song than ordinary speech. The reasons for song are not usual—love and/or the beauties of nature—although beauty does matter in the world L. creates, and love is redemptive. The bright, sung conversations of the earth and the earthbound are what so many of the poems record. If some of the stories repeat—about trying to live with dignity in a very difficult century—they are worth their retelling. They continue L.'s quest for ways to understand the paradoxes of isolation and community, Godlessness and spirituality, death and beauty, tears and "deep song" (Lorca's phrase), which are synonymous with the experience of living. The territory of this poetry keeps coming back to a center—praise for the common person, an American, probably with immigrant parents, who having gotten "off the bus / at the bare junction of nothing / with nothing" manages to find a way home.

FURTHER WORKS: *On the Edge* (1963); *Not This Pig* (1968); *Pili's Wall* (1971); *They Feed They Lion* (1972); *The Names of the Lost* (1976); *Ashes: Poems New and Old* (1979); *7 Years from Somewhere* (1979); *One for the Rose* (1981); *Don't Ask* (1981); *Selected Poems* (1984); *Sweet Will* (1985); *New Selected Poems* (1991); *What Work Is* (1991); *The Simple Truth* (1994); *The Bread of Time* (1994)

BIBLIOGRAPHY: Jackson, R., "The Long Embrace: P. L.'s Longer Poems," *KR*, 11 (Fall 1989): 160-9; Buckley, C., *On the Poetry of P. L.: Stranger to Nothing* (1991)

—CAROL FROST

LÉVI-STRAUSS, Claude

French anthropologist and sociologist, b. 28 Nov. 1908, Brussels, Belgium

L.-S. was raised in Versailles and attended the University of Paris. He studied philosophy and law but found anthropology and sociology far more appealing. A teaching position at the University of São Paulo, Brazil, enabled him to do research on Brazilian native tribes, after which he taught at the New School for Social Research in New York, where he was influenced by the linguist Roman Jakobson (b. 1896). In the early 1950s L.-S. returned to France and a teaching post at the École Pratique des Hautes Études. Currently he is professor of social anthropology at the Collège de France.

L.-S. was one of an extraordinary group of French intellectuals—which included Jean-Paul SARTRE, Simone de BEAUVOIR, and Maurice Merleau-Ponty (1908–1961)—who studied in Paris during the early 1930s and shaped postwar French intellectual life. His anthropology is similar to Sir James Frazer's (1854–1941) in that he, too, seeks to extrapolate from the specific data of tribal myths universal characteristics of the human mind. As a result, L.-S. has been attacked by traditional functionalist anthropologists and lionized by interdisciplinary thinkers. For much as Marxism is applied in literary, social, economic, and political interpretation, so too L.-S.'s structural anthropology has had its impact on many disciplines, including literary study.

That structural anthropology should have an impact on literary study is not really surprising when it is noted that seeds of STRUCTURALISM have been traced as far back as Giambattista Vico (1668–1744) and subsequently Samuel Taylor Coleridge (1772–1834) by some scholars, and it is more generally acknowledged to have germinated from the work of the Swiss linguist Ferdinand de Saussure (1857–1913). He demonstrated that words take their meaning as much from their relationships to other words in a given utterance, or what he called *parole*, as they do from any outside referents or universal rules, or what he called *langue*. This view influenced both Russian and American formalist critics, who analyzed works solely on the basis of the internal relationships in a text; L.-S. does likewise, but also insists that the structure of thought underlying the relationships is universal.

This latter point is advanced most boldly by L.-S. in *Le totémisme aujourd'hui* (1962; *Totemism*, 1963) and *La pensée sauvage* (1962; *The Savage Mind*, 1966). Just as FREUD had argued that neurotics differ only in degree rather than kind from normal people, L.-S. argues in these books that primitive thought differs only in degree from modern. In other words, the medicine man is as effective within his world as the modern doctor is within his. This view was supported by the child psychologist Jean Piaget's (1896–1981) analogous claims about the child's perception of reality: it, too, is complete unto itself and not merely an incomplete or nascent form of adult perception. Hence, what L.-S. claimed about primitives (and Piaget about children) could also be applied to modern man—that he structures his world into a self-adjusting whole whose parts interrelate in such a way that to modify one modifies the whole.

But L.-S. has been faulted for not attempting to analyze modern, that is, historically conscious, man, and the task has fallen to others, especially poststructuralist and Marxist critics. The latter influenced L.-S.'s view that the necessities of life explain consciousness and ideology, not vice versa. As a result, inherited—or what are claimed to be intrinsic and thus privileged—interpretations of reality have been dismissed as ultimately fascist; that is, a given view of the world controls our own individual perceptions of it, such as the Judeo-Christian belief that man is "fallen." Thus, art must break out of its traditional conventions of genre and style (as much contemporary art in fact does). Or such privileged views must themselves become the subject of analysis, as in the work of Michel FOUCAULT and Jacques DERRIDA.

L.-S.'s fascination with underlying structures can be traced back to his early interest in geology, from which he learned that surface configurations could be fully understood only in terms of subsurface structures. In his autobiographical narrative about research on Brazilian tribes, *Tristes tropiques* (1955; *Tristes Tropiques*, 1964), which first gained him attention, L.-S. identified geology as his first love, with Marxism, psychoanalysis, and music as his three mistresses. All four, of course, stress the structural relationships among the given parts of a whole as the parameters by which manifest appearances should be understood.

L.-S. believes that the underlying structure of human thought itself is based on binary opposition. The seminal opposition in anthropology is between nature and culture: man is simultaneously natural (an animal) and cultural (a human being). Such an antinomy is incapable of resolution, or synthesis, and hence L.-S. rejects, especially in the final chapter of *La pensée sauvage*, the privileged position that the dialectical interpretation of history holds in the intellectual community. There can be no working out of a paradox through time. Nor, because the unconscious infrastructure of the mind orders reality for us more than our conscious mind, is man free to choose his fate. In also rejecting the traditional humanist and the EXISTENTIALIST faith in man's freedom of choice, L.-S. rejects too, at least implicitly, the traditional assumption about the autonomy of the artist.

Dismissing individuality, L.-S. argues instead for the universality of human thought across centuries and continents. This timeless and spaceless quality of the basic logic of humans, which by nature is polar, or binary, makes paradox the subject of myth, as well as of music, for both are free of the specific referential qualities that normally circumscribe other modes of discourse. Or conversely, myth and music are the most universal and easily translatable modes of discourse, hence the most representative of the human mind in its essence. The relationships among the various "bundles of relations" (as L.-S. calls the groupings within a whole) that compose a musical score or a myth are what finally determine

their "meaning," not the time of composition, the place of composition, or the biography of the composer.

The influence of L.-S.'s structural approach on literary study has been considerable. Traditionally, literary interpretations have been based, like history, on the diachronic unfolding of events (or signifiers in a text)—that is, changes and occurrences over a period of time. L.-S. offers his synchronic approach not as superior to, but as a complement to the diachronic approach because he wants to find and identify what is timeless and spaceless about the human mind, even if it means neglecting the particular details of a text or an author's life.

By way of demonstrating this approach in his own works, after *Le totémisme aujourd'hui* and *La pensée sauvage* L.-S. wrote a four-volume series entitled *Mythologiques*, which translates roughly as "the logic of myths." The first of these four, *Le cru et le cuit* (1964; *The Raw and the Cooked: Introduction to a Science of Mythology I*, 1969), is organized like a musical score, with "Overture," "Theme and Variation," "Sonata," etc. in place of chapters. Throughout the four volumes, as in this one, L.-S. offers a dazzling synthesis of over six hundred myths from North and South American Indian tribes, demonstrating, or rather advocating, the position that they can all be explained in terms of binary opposition and mediation—that is, an accommodation of opposites without resolution—rather than synthesis.

Despite L.-S.'s claims to the contrary, poetry and fiction can be interpreted in a similar manner, particularly when they are decidedly unique in style and/or language and thus as untranslatable into denotative and referential terms as myth or music. What structural analysis should reveal is something quite different from traditional forms of analysis, as is the case with L.-S.'s treatment of the Oedipus myth in "Les structures des mythes" ("The Structural Study of Myth," 1955), published first in English and in French as a chapter in *Anthropologie structurale* (1958; *Structural Anthropology*, 1963). Therein L.-S. rearranges diachronic elements of the plot into a synchronic score, which he interprets as a message about overvaluation and undervaluation of kinship on the one hand, and denial and acceptance of man's autochthonous origin on the other.

Another literary analysis by L.-S. (in conjunction with Jakobson) is "'Les chats' de Charles Baudelaire" (1962; "Charles Baudelaire's 'The Cats,'" 1972). If L.-S.'s reading of the Oedipus myth seems to move too far outside the text in search of universals, this essay moves too far inside its text, breaking the poem down into phonemic units about which Baudelaire could hardly have been conscious. But no matter, as far as L.-S. is concerned, for binary opposition on the linguistic model has been demonstrated even if the authors have had to murder the poem to dissect it (to paraphrase Wordsworth).

Although literary study has now moved into what is known as poststructuralism, structural analyses and analyses of structuralism continue to interest scholars. Questions about the scientific accuracy of basing studies on the model of binary opposition, and about the extent to which the social sciences can or even should contribute to a "science" of literary study testify to the vivifying influence of L.-S.'s structural anthropology on literary study.

FURTHER WORKS: *Les structures élémentaires de la parenté* (1949; *The Elementary Structures of Kinship*, 1969); *Entretiens avec C. L.-S.* (1961; *Conversations with C. L.-S.* (1969); *Mythologiques II: Du miel aux cendres* (1966; *From Honey to Ashes*, 1973); *Mythologiques III: L'origine des manières de table* (1968; *The*

Origin of Table Manners, 1978); *Mythologiques IV: L'homme nu* (1971; *The Naked Man*, 1981); *Anthropologie Structurale II* (1973; *Structural Anthropology II*, 1976); *Myth and Meaning* (1979); *The Naked Man* (1981); *Way of the Masks* (1982); *View from Afar* (1984); *Jealous Potter* (1988); *Story of Lyrx* (1995); *Suadades do Brasil: A Photographic Memoir* (1995); *Look, Listen, Read* (1997)

BIBLIOGRAPHY: Hayes, E. N., and Hayes, T., eds., *C. L.-S.: The Anthropologist as Hero* (1970); Leach, E., *C. L.-S.* (1970); Paz, O., *C. L.-S.* (1970); Macksey, R., and Donato, E., eds., *The Languages of Criticism and the Sciences of Man: The Structuralist Controversy* (1970); Bersani, J., "Is There a Science of Literature?" *PR*, 39 (1972): 535–53; Boon, J., *From Symbolism to Structuralism* (1972); Gardner, H., *The Quest for Mind: Piaget, L.-S., and the Structuralist Movement* (1973); Scholes, R., *Structuralism in Literature* (1973); Culler, J., *Structuralist Poetics* (1975); Cook, A., *Myth and Language* (1980)

—GENE M. BERNSTEIN

LEWIS, C(live) S(taples)

English novelist, poet, and essayist, b. 29 Nov. 1898, Belfast, Northern Ireland; d. 22 Nov. 1963, Oxford

Born in Ulster, L. was schooled privately and at English schools, and, having served in World War I, was elected in 1925 to a Fellowship at Magdalen College, Oxford, where he had received three First Class degrees. During the 1940s, L. was the center of the "Inklings," an informal Oxford literary group composed of his friends, notably Charles Williams (1886–1945) and J. R. R. TOLKIEN. In 1954 he was elected unanimously to the Cambridge Professorship of Medieval and Renaissance Literature, which he held until shortly before his death in 1963. His marriage at age fifty-seven to an American and her death in 1960 greatly influenced his later work.

As the autobiography of his early life, *Surprised by Joy* (1955), demonstrates, the watershed in L.'s life was his conversion to Christianity in 1929, prior to which he had maintained a dogmatic atheism and had published only two volumes of verse, *Spirits of Bondage* (1919) and *Dymer* (1926), under the name Clive Hamilton. Although the event itself was almost Pauline in its suddenness, it is clear that his thought had been changing for some time under the influence of his close study of 17th-c. poetry, of the Scottish writer George MacDonald's (1824–1905) novel *Phantastes* (which he first read as a boy), and, particularly of his conversations and arguments with his fellow dons, later to be the nucleus of the Inklings, J. R. R. Tolkien, Owen Barfield (1898-1997), Nevill Coghill (1899–1980), and H. V. D. Dyson (1896–1975).

Although L.'s postconversion work falls generally into three broad areas—religion, literary criticism, and fiction—it is underlain by the same conversative antiliberalist, antiscientific, antimodernist values. In *The Pilgrim's Regress* (1933), a thinly disguised allegory of his own conversion, his hero finds that to discover "joy" he must reject all current intellectual fads and retrace his steps until he has rediscovered right reason and the fundamental religion of his childhood; *The Problem of Pain* (1940) advances an almost fundamentalist approach to Scripture and suggests that pain may well be Satan's infecting of God's world; L.'s popular war-time radio talks

made use of post-Hegelian logic effectively disguised by common-sense diction and wartime allegory to present the case for nonsectarian Christian orthodoxy based on extranatural reason and moral law; the enormously successful *Screwtape Letters* (1942) presents the same case inversely by means of the letters of an experienced older devil to his nephew busily at work among men; *Miracles* (1947) attempts to prove that reason and the moral law exist independently of the natural world. However, probably because of both growing attacks on his use of dubious logic and his marriage, his later religious works are reflective and personal rather than argumentative and logic-crammed.

L.'s literary criticism likewise opposes classical, traditional, and purely literary values to the "personal heresies" of biographical, psychological, and impressionistic criticism. L. is at his best, however, when synthesizing literary history, as in *The Allegory of Love* (1936), *English Literature in the Sixteenth Century* (1954), and *The Discarded Image* (1964), and considerably less effective when indulging in literary polemics.

L.'s fiction is principally made up of two series of novels: a science-fiction trilogy—*Out of the Silent Planet* (1938), *Perelandra* (1943), and *That Hideous Strength* (1945)—which explores L.'s notions of Earth as cut off by sin from the rest of creation and of the destructive dehumanizing impulses of science; and the hastily written *Chronicles of Narnia—The Lion, the Witch, and the Wardrobe* (1950), *Prince Caspian* (1951), *The Voyage of the Dawn Treaders* (1952), *The Silver Chair* (1953), *The Horse and His Boy* (1954), *The Magician's Nephew* (1955), and *The Last Battle* (1956)—which present basic Christian doctrine and traditional morality by means of children's fiction. L.'s last novel, however, *Till We Have Faces* (1956), shows the same kind of tranquillity that marks all his later work. A retelling of the Cupid and Psyche myth, it suggests that in the end only faith and the bearing of one another's burdens can conquer the false delusions of scientific rationalism.

L.'s religious tracts are widely quoted and admired, largely because they summarize and reinforce the basic tenets of orthodox Christian belief and morality in a time when these values have been largely abandoned. The Narnia books especially are admired for this reason. It is not unfair to say, however, that posterity will probably view his championing of orthodoxy as the least important of his roles and regard his sound literary judgments to be of enduring worth.

FURTHER WORKS: *The Personal Heresy* (1939); *Rehabilitations* (1939); *Broadcast Talks* (1942; Am., *The Case for Christianity*); *A Preface to "Paradise Lost"* (1942); *Christian Behaviour* (1943); *The Abolition of Man* (1943); *Beyond Personality* (1944); *The Great Divorce* (1946); *Arthurian Torso* (1948, with Charles Williams); *Transposition, and Other Addresses* (1949; Am., *The Weight of Glory*); *Mere Christianity* (1952); *Reflections on the Psalms* (1958); *The Four Loves* (1960); *Studies in Words* (1960); *The World's Last Night and Other Essays* (1960; rev. and expanded ed., 1980); *A Grief Observed* (1961); *An Experiment in Criticism* (1961); *They Asked for a Paper* (1962); *Poems* (1964); *Letters to Malcolm: Chiefly on Prayer* (1964); *Screwtape Proposes a Toast* (1965); *Studies in Medieval and Renaissance Literature* (1966); *Letters of C. S. L.* (1966); *Of Other Worlds* (1966); *Christian Reflections* (1967); *Spenser's Images of Life* (1967); *Letters to an American Lady* (1969); *Narrative Poems* (1969); *Selected Literary Essays* (1969); *Undeceptions* (1971; Am., *God in the Dark*); *Fernseed and Elephants and Other Essays in Christianity* (1976); *The Dark Tower, and Other Stories* (1977); *The Joyful Christian: 127*

Readings from C. S. L. (1977); *They Stand Together: The Letters of C. S. L. to Arthur Greeves* (1979); *The Visionary Christian: 131 Readings from C. S. L.* (1981); *On Stories, and Other Essays on Literature* (1982); *C. S. L., Letters to Children* (1985); *The Essential C. S. L.* (1988); *All My Road Before Me: The Diary of C. S. L., 1922-1927* (1991)

BIBLIOGRAPHY: Green, R. L., and W. Hooper, *C. S. L.: A Biography* (1947); Kilby, C., *The Christian World of C. S. L.* (1964); Gibb, J., ed., *Light on C. S. L.* (1965); Gelbert, D., and C. Kilby, *C. S. L.: Images of His World* (1973); Carpenter, H., *The Inklings* (1978); Glover, D. E., *C. S. L.: The Art of Enchantment* (1981); Hannay, M. P., *C. S. L.* (1981); Griffin, W., *C. S. L.: A Dramatic Life* (1986); Coren, M., *The Man Who Created Narnia: The Story of C. S. L.* (1996); Gromley, B., *C. S. L.: Christian and Storyteller* (1998)

—CHARLES MOORMAN

LEWIS, Saunders

Welsh dramatist, novelist, essayist, critic, and poet (writing in Welsh and English), b. 15 Oct. 1893, Wallasey, England; d. 1 Sept. 1985, Cardiff

The son of a minister and his wife, L. was born just over the border from Wales, was raised in Liverpool, and was graduated from the university in that city, where he also pursued graduate work and published a version of his graduate research under the title *A School of Welsh Augustans* (1924). In 1926 he became president of the newly formed Welsh Nationalist Party, which post he held until 1939. In 1936 he was dismissed from his post of lecturer in Welsh at University College, Swansea, for setting fire, with two others, to a weapons and training establishment in the Llyn peninsula. From then until 1951 he lived at Llanfarian, near Aberystwyth, and contributed to various periodicals. From 1952 to 1957 he was lecturer in Welsh at University College of South Wales and Monmouthshire.

L. has been the dominant writer in Wales during the last forty years. His writings include over five hundred brochures and articles devoted to political and social concerns; several volumes of poetry; ten books and numerous articles of literary criticism; and nearly a score of dramatic works, including translations. L. has published in both Welsh and English.

His major novel, *Monica* (1930), is a *roman à thèse* intended to prove "the idea that the value of love lies in itself." L.'s drama can be divided into three types: comedies; historical plays about contemporary Europe; and plays dealing with the Wales of today. Examples of his satirical comedy are two published in one volume: *Eisteddfod Bodran; Gan bwyll* (1952; the Bodran eisteddfod; take it easy). *'Gymerwch chi sigaret?* (1958; have a cigarette?) is about espionage in eastern Europe, and *Brad* (1958; treason) deals with the attempt by German army officers to assassinate Hitler. *Yn y trên* (1965; on the train), is an allegory about present-day Wales, while *Cymru fydd* (1967; the Wales to be) highlights varieties of political opinion in Wales.

A writer of international stature, L. is both the most important literary critic and the paramount dramatist in 20th c. Wales. His criticism is renowned for its precision and historical erudition. Both the scope of his work and the subtle originality of his mind

made him a powerful spokesman for the Welsh cause and its tradition. His convictions about the Catholic faith, to which he converted in February 1932, and Welsh nationalism, of which he was a prophet and molder, provide the dominant motifs of his writing.

FURTHER WORKS: *The Eve of St. John* (1920); *Gwaed yr uchelwyr* (1922); *Williams Pantycelyn* (1927); *Ceiriog: Yr artist yn Philistia, I* (1929); *Ieuan Glan Geirionydd* (1931); *Braslun o hanes llenyddiaeth Gymraeg hyd 1535* (1932); *Daniel Owen; Yr artist yn Philistia, II* (1936); *Buchedd Garmon* (1937); *Is There an Anglo-Welsh Literature?* (1939); *Amlyn ac Amig* (1940); *Byd a betws* (1942); *Ysgrifau dydd Mercher* (1945); *Blodeuwedd* (1948); *Siwan a cherddi eraill* (1955); *Esther: Serch yw'r doctor* (1960); *Merch Gwern Hywel* (1964); *Gramadegau'r penceirddiaid* (1967); *Problemau prifysgol* (1968). FURTHER WORKS IN ENGLISH: *Presenting S. L.* (1973)

BIBLIOGRAPHY: Edwards, E., "S. L., the Dramatist," *Wales*, 2 (1958): 39; Davies, P., "The Poetry of S. L.," *Poetry Wales*, 1 (1969), 5; "S. L. for a Nobel Prize?" *The Times* (London), 28 Sept. 1970: 2; Thomas, H. B., "A Welsh Prophet," *London Tablet*, 27 Oct. 1973: 1012–14; Jones, A. R. and G. Thomas, eds., *Presenting S. L.* (1973)

—THOMAS E. BIRD

LEWIS, Sinclair

American novelist, b. 7 Feb. 1885, Sauk Centre, Minn.; d. 10 Jan. 1951, Rome, Italy

The son of a respected small-town physician, L. was reared in a comfortable, middle class home. Although he early demonstrated an anguished awareness of his own difference from both his family and his town, L.'s childhood and youth were not marked by overtly traumatic experiences. He earned a B.A. at Yale and spent the next several years in a roving apprenticeship as a journalist, exhibiting a propensity for the travel that was to become a lifelong habit, as well as verbal facility and cleverness in a variety of literary forms. His first novel, *Hike and the Aeroplane*, a boy's adventure tale written under the pseudonym of Tom Graham, appeared in 1912. L.'s success as an editor and as a writer of short stories for popular magazines enabled him to concentrate on the novel, which was his proper mode.

Between 1914 and 1919 L. published five novels. Although now deservedly forgotten except by serious students of L., they at once typify the popular fiction of their time and presage some of the very elements intrinsic to L.'s later fame: flashes of satire, an eye for significant minutiae to portray character and social scene, an ear for the quirks of American speech, and the use of disguised or projected autobiographical material. Their dominant optimism and romanticism responded to the requirements of the market L. was serving, yet also genuinely represented fundamental strains of L.'s own sensibility. The best of these early novels is *The Job* (1917), a generally realistic account of the life of a working woman in an urban setting. *The Trail of the Hawk* (1917), which treats the development of aviation, and *Free Air* (1919), inspired by a cross-country automobile trip, manifest L.'s shrewd sense for timely topics.

The appearance of *Main Street* (1920) utterly transformed L.'s career and began a decade of productivity and success that has

Sinclair Lewis

never been surpassed in American letters. *Main Street* articulated the dissatisfaction many intellectuals felt toward American life. It challenged the "happy village" myth and it excoriated jingoistic patriotism, materialism, and conformity. The town of Gopher Prairie that L. portrays in the novel is as narrow, ugly, and mean in its architecture and attitudes as the natural landscape is large and splendid. No reader, native or foreign, could possibly misunderstand the novel's message. It is announced in the preface and repeatedly reiterated in a series of episodes that demonstrate Gopher Prairie's intolerance for any kind of individualism, talent, taste, or beauty

The novel's tension and interest derives from its ambivalence toward its characters and subject. Carol Kennicott, the heroine, is clearly the author's persona and the main instrument for his exposé of Gopher Prairie's vices. Yet in her impatience, tactlessness, and inconsistency Carol is also something of a fool. Will Kennicott, her husband, embodies many of the town's worst qualities, yet his steadiness, courage, and competence as a country doctor elicit the reader's admiration. Carol's quarrel with the town is counterpointed by her marital conflicts. Thus, the novel's issues are argued simultaneously in two arenas, social and domestic, with only superficially satisfying resolutions.

Although *Main Street* was recognized even by contemporary reviewers as a flawed novel, it assumed a presence that resisted analytical criticism. Like the novels that followed, it displayed a driving narrative energy, quick turns of plot, a host of vivid, albeit flat, characters, and a wealth of telling detail, which comprise the

essence of L.'s method at its best. The writer's voice—shrill and tedious as it often became—was a new phenomenon in American literature. That voice, conveying a peculiarly timely and provocative message, virtually overnight attracted national and international attention, transforming L. into a celebrity.

Main Street was still enjoying considerable attention and lively sales when L. published *Babbitt* (1922) two years later. L. had discovered his true métier, satirical realism, and *Babbitt* represents perhaps the surest and most controlled example of L.'s craftmanship. The scene is now the invented but typical American city of Zenith in the imagined Midwestern state of Winnemac; the novel's protagonist, a middle-class businessman, could easily have been recruited from among Carol Kennicott's adversaries in Gopher Prairie. But Babbitt too is a tantalizingly ambiguous character, at once tyrant and slave, dangerous and pathetic. *Main Street* had culminated the "revolt from the village"; *Babbitt* served as a dramatic illustration of the social theories and criticism of such figures as Thorstein Veblen (1857–1929), Randolph Bourne (1886–1918), and H. L. MENCKEN.

Yet although the novel functions as a vehicle for ideas and a scathingly effective treatment of commercialism and convention—an entire society dominated by the profit motive—it also integrates the universal theme of the corruption of human dreams by the world's demands and time's passage. When Babbitt attempts his middle-age revolt against the forces he has himself created, it is far too late. Too rich, too well-fed, too experienced, and too rational to believe in heaven and hell, not talented or dedicated enough to believe in himself or his work, he can only rely on what his peers and the mass media tell him. Once he learns that they lie, he loses all capacity for faith. Perhaps Babbitt's most tragic fate is that he becomes incapable of responding to pleasure, or indeed to any powerful or authentic feeling, a condition especially ironical in a culture devoted to physical comfort and constantly in search of entertainment. This view of character, achieved in a narrative that records the world's textures, sights, and sounds in overwhelming detail, verges on mythos.

Arrowsmith (1925) is L.'s best novel of his great decade. Although much of the book satirizes various aspects of the medical establishment and again depicts the powers of hypocrisy, mediocrity, and materialism triumphant over rebels and reformers, the novel's impact derives mainly from the vibrancy of its characters and narrative conception rather than from its social revelations. Moreover, the reader is heartened by L.'s unqualified enthusiasm for science, the work's true hero. In *Arrowsmith* there is no confusion about L.'s standards or loyalties. Both the novel's literary quality and affirmative tone were recognized by the award of the Pulitzer Prize, which L. refused with considerable public ado.

The verisimilitude of *Main Street* and *Babbitt* depended upon common experience and acute observation rather than upon some special knowledge. Although *Arrowsmith* was in part inspired by L.'s family background, it also involved intensive research. From this point on in his career L. often employed the methods of the anthropologist or sociologist in writing his novels, exploring such diverse fields as hotel management, penology, and public relations.

Elmer Gantry (1927) capitalized not only upon such deliberately accumulated material but also on a volatile atmosphere in which the Scopes "Monkey Trial" and the lively presence of the evangelists Billy Sunday and Aimee Semple McPherson provided a ready context for the novel's presumably fictional characters and episodes. Inevitably, the book provoked an immediate and thunderous reaction. It is also important as a literary document, for it was the first major American novel to assault virtually the entire institution of formal religion. Yet despite the work's timeliness and the exercise of L.'s furious narrative energy and sardonic humor, *Elmer Gantry* had less impact upon the national consciousness than his previous novels. Its success was almost entirely that of scandal, not art, and such success is intrinsically transient. One of the novel's basic problems is its characterization: L. gives the reader not a single sympathetic major character.

The decade concluded with two more books: *The Man Who Knew Coolidge* (1928) and *Dodsworth* (1929). The first contains no surprises; it is one of Babbitt's speeches multiplied into 275 pages. But it does demonstrate L.'s extraordinary skill in the mode of the humorous satirical monologue—a skill unsurpassed until Philip ROTH's *Portnoy's Complaint*. *Dodsworth*, by contrast, contains relatively little satire or humor. Although L. treats the international theme with considerable intensity, the novel's fundamental concern is the deterioration of a marriage—an obvious projection of L.'s own experience. The novel's "villain," Fran Dodsworth, is a thinly disguised and acidulous portrayal of L.'s first wife, Grace, whom he divorced in 1927, while its most admirable female character, Edith Cortright, is a totally idealized version of the journalist Dorothy Thompson (1894–1961), whom L. married in 1928.

L.'s great decade was culminated by the award of the Nobel Prize for literature in 1930, the first to an American writer. The Nobel Prize also marked the apogee of L.'s prestige and artistic power. Whether because of his own fame, the exhaustion of his artistic resources, or fundamental changes in American society with the onset of the Depression, after 1930 L. moved from the center of attention to its periphery. Although he continued to publish novels at a regular rate for the next twenty years, only occasionally did his novels capture large audiences and excite discussion, as in *It Can't Happen Here* (1935), which portrays a fascist coup d'état in America, and *Kingsblood Royal* (1947), which deals with racial prejudice. Some of his fiction after 1930 attains substantial quality, but too much is bad, spoiled by sentimentality, self-imitation, and self-contradiction.

In retrospect, if L.'s best work of the 1920s falls short of the masterpieces of his contemporaries—for example, DREISER's *An American Tragedy* and FITZGERALD's *The Great Gatsby*, both published in the same year as *Arrowsmith*—his total contribution to modern American fiction must nevertheless be acknowledged as considerable. His twenty-three novels present a broad spectrum of American locales and professions and comprise a gallery of national types, an American human comedy after the examples of Balzac or Dickens. Indeed, Dickens strongly influenced L., and there are many resemblances between their work. At the very height of L.'s fame as a controversial social critic and realist, James Branch Cabell (1879–1958) shrewdly pointed out that L. was basically a romanticist who invented imaginary lands and populated them with goblins. Because of his unhappy personal life and the sharp decline of his career after winning the Nobel Prize, there is a tendency to view L. as a failure. But this is neither an appropriate nor an accurate judgment. Although his work reveals conflicting impulses—negation versus affirmation, realism versus romance, reportage versus satire—this very ambivalence is also the major reason for L.'s dynamism and appeal. At the end of his life L. is said to have repeated, "I love America—but I don't like it," a remark that conveys the essence of L.'s attitude toward his material. Whatever may be charged of L.'s defects and excesses, it must also be remembered that he worked to the very maximum of his talent,

not a credit all modern writers could claim, and that he changed the way Americans think of themselves.

FURTHER WORKS: *Our Mr. Wrenn* (1914); *The Innocents* (1917); *Mantrap* (1926); *Ann Vickers* (1933); *Work of Art* (1934); *Jayhawker* (1935); *Selected Short Stories* (1935); *The Prodigal Parents* (1938); *Bethel Merriday* (1940); *Gideon Planish* (1943); *Cass Timberlane* (1945); *The God-Seeker* (1949); *World So Wide* (1951); *From Main Street to Stockholm: Letters of S. L. 1919–1930* (1952); *The Man from Main Street: A S. L. Reader* (1953); *Main Street; Babbitt* (1992)

BIBLIOGRAPHY: Lewis, G. H., *With Love from Gracie* (1955); Schorer, M., *S. L.: An American Life* (1961); Grebstein, S., *S. L.* (1962); Schorer, M., ed., *S. L.: A Collection of Critical Essays* (1962); Sheean, V., *Dorothy and Red* (1963); Dooley, D. J., *The Art of S. L.* (1967); Griffin, R. J., ed., *Interpretations of "Arrowsmith"* (1968); Light, M., ed., *Studies in "Babbitt"* (1971); O'Connor, R., *S. L.* (1971); Lundquist, J., *S. L.* (1973); Light, M., *The Quixotic Vision of S. L.* (1975); Bloom, H., *S. L.'s Arrowsmith* (1988)

—SHELDON N. GREBSTEIN

S. L. has said of himself: "He has only one illusion: that he is not a journalist and 'photographic realist' but a stylist whose chief concerns in writing are warmth and lucidity." Such illusions are not uncommon: the scientist who prides himself on his violin-playing, the statesman who would like to be known as a poet—most men would rather think of themselves as excelling in another activity than that in which they are eminent. L.'s wish need not prevent us from adopting the general view of him, namely, that though he is a "photographic realist" and also, at times, something of a novelist or creative artist, yet after all he is primarily a satirist—unless indeed he is even more interesting as a product than as a critic of American society. Surely no one else serves so well as he to illustrate the relation between literature and a practical world: in such a world he has himself lived all his life, and such a world he portrays and holds up to ridicule and obloquy.

No small part of his effectiveness is due to the amazing skill with which he reproduces his world. His knack for mimicry is unsurpassed. He is a master of that species of art to which belong glass flowers, imitation fruit, Mme. Tussaud's wax-works, and barnyard symphonies, which aims at deceiving the spectator into thinking that the work in question is not an artificial product but the real thing. Of this art Zeuxis, who painted grapes so truly that birds came and pecked at them, is the most eminent practitioner; but L.'s standard is often little short of the Zeuxine.

T. K. Whipple, *Spokesmen* (1928), p. 208

When I re-read L. I am struck by two strong and conflicting impressions. The first impression is one of annoyance. I am annoyed by the shallowness of his writing, by his lists of places seen and things done, by his attempt to capsule whole areas of emotion and render them in a single paragraph of reportorial neighbourliness, by those caricature-characterisations that Alfred Kazin called his "brilliant equivalents" of American people. And yet, for all this initial feeling of annoyance, I come back always to a feeling of sympathy for these grotesque people he created. This second impression is one that leads me to the man himself—I think it is without any intention on L.'s part or any conscious intention on mine—to this cantankerous soul who was driven by the everlasting gospel of work and whose good heart shines through his work. All these books of his reflect back on him, but since he did not consciously intend it, the result is somehow acceptable. I feel that I can agree with Thomas Wolfe when he goes on in that account of L.-McHarg in *You Can't Go Home Again*: "In spite of the brevity of their acquaintance, George had already seen clearly and unmistakably what a good and noble human being McHarg really was. He knew how much integrity and courage and honesty was contained in that tormented tenement of fury and lacerated hurts. Regardless of all that was jangled, snarled, and twisted in his life, regardless of all that had become bitter, harsh, and acrid, McHarg was obviously one of the truly good, the truly high, the truly great people of the world."

Geoffrey Moore, "S. L.: A Lost Romantic," in Carl Bode, ed., *The Young Rebel in American Literature* (1959), pp. 72–73

Perhaps there was too much, and too much in conflict, to have made self-knowledge possible. Not many men are doomed to live with such a mixture of warring qualities as he was. Consider him at any level of conduct—his domestic habits, his social behavior, his character, his thought, his art—always there is the same extraordinary contradiction. Sloppy and compulsively tidy, absurdly gregarious and lonely, quick in enthusiasms and swiftly bored, extravagant and parsimonious, a dude and a bumpkin, a wit and a bore, given to extremities of gaiety and gloom, equally possessed of a talent for the most intensive concentration and for the maddest dishevelment of energies; sweet of temper and virulent, tolerant and abruptly intolerant, generous and selfish, kind and cruel, a great patron and a small tyrant, disliking women even when he thought he most loved them, profane and a puritan, libertine and prude, plagued by self-doubt as he was eaten by arrogance; rebel and conservative, polemicist and escapist, respectful of intellect and suspicious of intellectual pursuits, loving novelty and hating experiment, pathetically trusting in "culture" and narrowly deriding "art"; cosmopolitan and chauvinist, sentimentalist and satirist, romanticist and realist, blessed—or damned—with an extraordinary verbal skill and no style; Carol Kennicott and Doc, her husband; Paul Riesling and George F. Babbitt; Harry Lewis and Dr. E. J. Lewis or Dr. Claude B. Lewis; Harry Lewis and even Fred the miller, who never left home.

One might list these conflicting qualities in opposite columns and suggest that there were two selves in S. L.; but all these qualities existed together and simultaneously in him, and in their infinite, interacting combinations there must have been not two but six or eight or ten or two hundred selves and, because they could never be one, a large hole in the center. When he peered into that, what could we expect him to see?

Mark Schorer, *S. L.: An American Life* (1961), pp. 9–10

L., however, never lost sight of the dream; we have seen that he conjured it up in novels written at every stage of his career. It provided him with the vision of the one Eden of which he could conceive; the one great objective worth striving for, in an otherwise barren world, was an enlightened and prosperous America. Though at times he viewed its prospects pessimistically, his basic outlook was not one of disillusionment, but of romantic optimism. Even in ridiculing this optimism he added a defense of it, so that when he described his own short stories as "so optimistic, so laudatory . . . so certain that large, bulky Americans are going to do something and do it quickly and help the whole world by doing it," he added to the ironic description the thought that perhaps such optimism is an authentic part of American life. Then he confessed that he himself, though he had been labeled a satirist and a realist, was actually a romantic medievalist of the most incurable sort.

D. J. Dooley, *The Art of S. L.* (1967), p. 259

S. L. possessed the quixotic imagination, and many of his characters, who read, venture, and fancy, as he did, are inheritors of his vision. In him opposing emotions ran deep, yet surfaced quickly. Perhaps volatility goes hand-in-hand with the impulse to create a body of fiction that searches out and breaks stereotypes apart, pillories injustices, and exposes those beliefs we loosely call "myths" about the American way of living and the American character. In L., the classic struggle between illusion and reality is particularly fierce—for L.'s enemies were both the illusions he discovered in the world and the illusions his nature invented. He fought the illusions the world offered and struggled to understand the illusions his mind and emotions brought forth.

As a result, impudence, flamboyance, and audacity, at one extreme, and gloom, despair, and carelessness, at the other, characterize L.'s books. Mark Schorer and others record L.'s exuberant performances, deep angers, rantings, drunkenness, tasteless practical jokes, and contrition—the emotionalism of a distraught quixote who finds outlet in audacious gestures.

L. stubbornly adhered to a few romantic ideas, personified in his books by yearners, rebels, and builders. His central characters are the pioneer, the doctor, the scientist, the businessman, and the feminist. The appeal of his best fiction lies in the opposition between his idealistic protagonists and an array of fools, charlatans, and scoundrels—evangelists, editorialists, pseudo-artists, cultists, and boosters.

Martin Light, *The Quixotic Vision of S. L.* (1975),
p. 4

LEWIS, Wyndham

English novelist, satirist, essayist, literary critic, and polemicist, b. 18 Nov. 1882, on his father's yacht off Amherst, N.S., Canada; d. 1 March 1957, London

Son of an American eccentric and English mother whose permanent separation occurred when their only offspring was eleven years old, L. settled with his mother in England, where he attended Rugby and then the Slade School of Art (1898–1901). Despite his father's urgings that L. complete his formal education, ideally at Cornell University, L. preferred what he called the "vaster alma maters of Paris, of Munich," and other European cities in which he lived for eight years prior to his return to England in 1909. During the next decade L. became a revolutionary artist, helping to establish the movement in painting known as Vorticism, a style noted for its angularity derived from machine forms that was meant to avoid what was perceived as the weaknesses in both CUBISM and FUTURISM, kindred Continental art movements. From 1914 to 1915 L. coedited with Ezra POUND the review *BLAST* (facsimile eds., 2 vols., pub. 1981), in which he began his revolutionary activity in literature as well as in painting. L. saw heavy action during World War I; some of his more extreme political positions later in his life may have been influenced by his traumatic wartime experiences.

Always a writer who assumed numerous literary personae, L. found particularly congenial to his irascible temperament the role of The Enemy, originally the title of a literary review he edited and largely wrote (1927–29). His pose as The Enemy and some ill-advised writings in the early 1930s endorsing elements of fascism brought L. persecution and abuse. Fearing he would be thought disloyal, although he had repudiated much of his earlier profascist writings, L. and his wife left England for the U.S. and finally settled in Canada at the start of World War II. He resided in Toronto, in dire financial straits, for the war's duration. Upon his return to England, L. enjoyed a measure of public success as painter and writer. He wrote art reviews for *The Listener* until the slowgrowing brain tumor, which eventually killed him, rendered him blind. Stoic in affliction, L. produced, "substituting dictaphone for typewriter," an impressive quantity of writing in the last years of his life.

L.'s first novel, *Tarr* (1918; rev. ed., 1928), seemed notably experimental both in form and content, based, in part, on application of vorticist thought to fiction with the end of creating through satire or at least irony externalist art—"deadness is the first condition of art: the second is absence of soul, in the human and sentimental sense," as L.'s protagonist, Frederic Tarr, announces. In contrast, the other would-be artist in the novel, the German sculptor and painter Otto Kreisler, usually considered a more fully delineated character than Tarr, is the romantic sentimentalist who succumbs empathetically to the "writhing turbulent mess" of life and love. He detaches himself sufficiently only at the end of the novel to achieve a clean, well-executed suicide. According to L., Kreisler's death is simply a "tragic game," and this approach to mortality and to characters whom L. calls "machines"—puppets,

not natures—will figure prominently in L.'s later cultural theorizing and fiction.

L.'s influential work of cultural philosophy, *Time and Western Man* (1927), likewise has relevance to his subsequent narrative techniques; herein he stakes out his position opposite writers like JOYCE, PROUST, and Virginia WOOLF, whose subjectivist interior monologues and STREAM OF CONSCIOUSNESS, in L.'s opinion, portray the flux of time rather than overcome it, as he desires to do by transforming the temporal into the spatial. In novel writing L. looks to the "Great Without," with his method of external approach. Thus, L. departs radically from the impressionistic aesthetic that has dominated Anglo-American modernism. General critical agreement often supports Hugh Kenner's assessment of *Time and Western Man* as one of the dozen or so most important books of the 20th c.

L.'s most vitriolic satire against Bloomsbury intellectuals as monuments of triviality is found in *The Apes of God* (1930), presented in a distinctive prose style complementing the violent, mechanized existence of Europe between the wars. Many of L.'s crotchets are displayed in this novel in the catalogue of ridiculed persons, objects, and ideas, namely, the cult of the child, burgeoning feminism and homosexuality, militarism, and the pervasive interest within the best circles in the Freudian unconscious. On the surface, the novel resembles those of Aldous HUXLEY and Evelyn WAUGH at the same period, but L.'s style is his own, inspiring T. S. ELIOT to describe L. as the "greatest prose master of style of my generation."

Generally, *The Revenge for Love* (1937) has been judged the finest and most moving of L.'s novels. Openly political in a way reminiscent of Graham GREENE's best work, this novel achieves something unusual in L. in the emotional resonance and sympathy for the victims who fall prey to the revenge for love masterminded by the Marxists and opportunists who set the lovers up for violence and death in Spain during the civil war. The distinguished critic Fredric Jameson, in a recent provocative study of L., brilliantly summarizes what he takes to be the source of this novel's greatness, which might be extended to form the foundation of a revisionist revaluation of L.'s canon: " . . . it is precisely this reality isolation of the intelligentsia of power, it is precisely its blind imprisonment in its own world of words, which is at issue."

L. turned to largely self-critical novels with *The Vulgar Streak* (1941), wrongly neglected, and *Self-Condemned* (1954), based on his years of penurious self-imposed exile in Canada. *Self-Condemned* is a kind of cryptic war novel about how the violent forces of history transform an intellectually active scholar into a displaced person and misanthrope who finds within himself the violence he has opposed in the external world. L.'s rather autobiographical protagonist, René Harding, discovers the terrifying secret of History and ends his career in an academic "cemetery of shells" where "the Faculty had no idea that it was a glacial shell of a man who had come to live among them, mainly because they were themselves unfilled with anything more than a little academic stuffing."

L.'s most ambitious, even gargantuan, work, *The Human Age* (1955), consisting of the revised *The Childermass* (original version pub. 1928), *Monstre Gai*, and *Malign Fiesta*, and a fourth part, *The Trial of Man* (existing only as a synopsis and a draft of a first chapter), has been aptly described by Jameson as "theological science fiction." This truncated tetralogy's most enthusiastic advocate, Martin Seymour-Smith, confidently forecasts that *The Human Age* "will come to be recognized as the greatest single imaginative prose work in English of this century." That hyperbolic prophecy has yet to be fulfilled, but interest in and appreciation of L. have recently been renewed, more widely than before. With the increasing critical and popular validation of the seriousness of fantasy fiction, L.'s novels within the genre should finally find an appreciative audience. *The Human Age* examines the effects of rapid technological and media change upon former innocents, satirizes the welfare state, expresses cautionary fears of the spread of various cults, and, in short, offers a Swiftian gloss on the 20th c., its hell on material earth, and its possible projection into a future heaven where Paradise itself emulates the earth's decline and fall.

L.'s enormous and varied output all bear witness to the author's vigorous intelligence and profound imagination. He had an integrated vision in art and literature that also informed his aesthetic theory and his literary criticism. The precise nature of that vision is only now being clarified. Years ago, when L. was a conspicuously neglected writer, Anthony BURGESS noted that L. is too massive a writer to be ignored by posterity. L. must be seen as one of the most prodigiously talented modernists, whose freshness and astringency may deter us from too complete absorption in so-called POSTMODERNISM. In ideology L. is admittedly often offensive, especially to the present—sexist, fascist, homophobic, and the like—but his art, as Jameson argues, uses and transcends its ideological raw materials. L. endures as a portraitist of the violence within 20th-c. people and their words, ideas, and actions, and as an augur of the apocalyptic doom of mass civilization bereft of those strong personalities whose will and common decency are necessary to prevent the apocalypse.

FURTHER WORKS: *The Art of Being Ruled* (1926); *The Lion and the Fox: The Role of the Hero in the Plays of Shakespeare* (1927); *The Wild Body: A Soldier of Humour, and Other Stories* (1927); *Paleface: The Philosophy of the "Melting Pot"* (1929); *Satire and Fiction* (1930); *The Diabolical Principle and the Dithyrambic Spectator* (1931); *Hitler* (1931); *The Doom of Youth* (1932); *The Enemy of the Stars* (1932); *Filibusters in Barbary* (1932); *Snooty Baronet* (1932); *One-Way Song* (1933); *Men without Art* (1934); *Left Wings over Europe; or, How to Make a War about Nothing* (1936); *The Roaring Queen* (1936, withdrawn before publication; pub. 1973); *Count Your Dead: They Are Alive! or, A New War in the Making* (1937); *Blasting and Bombardiering* (1937); *The Hitler Cult* (1939); *W. L. the Artist, from "Blast" to Burlington House* (1939); *America, I Presume* (1940); *America and Cosmic Man* (1948); *Rude Assignment: A Narrative of My Career Up to Date* (1950); *Rotting Hill* (1951); *The Writer and the Absolute* (1952); *The Demon of Progress in the Arts* (1954); *The Red Priest* (1956); *The Letters of W. L.* (1964); *W. L.: An Anthology of His Prose* (1969); *W. L. on Art: Collected Writing 1913–1956* (1971); *Unlucky for Pringle: Unpublished and Other Stories* (1973): *The Essential W. L.: An Introduction to His Work* (1989); *Tarr: The 1918 Version* (1990); *Rude Assignment: An Intellectual Autobiography* (1984)

BIBLIOGRAPHY: Kenner, H., *W. L.* (1954); Tomlin, E. W. F., *W. L.* (1955); Wagner, G., *W. L.: A Portrait of the Artist as the Enemy* (1957); Holloway, J., "W. L.: The Massacre and the Innocents," *The Charted Mirror* (1960): 118–36; Pritchard, W. H., *W. L.* (1968); special L. triple issue, *Agenda*, 7, 3/8, 1 (1969–70); Chapman, R. T., *W. L.: Fiction and Satires* (1973); Materer, T., *W. L. the Novelist* (1976); Russell, J., *Style in Modern British Fiction* (1978): 123–57; Henkle, R. B., "The 'Advertised Self': W. L.'s Satire," *Novel*, 13 (1979): 95–108; Jameson, F., *Fables of Aggression: W. L., the Modernist as Fascist* (1979); Meyers, J., *W. L.: A Revaluation: New Essays* (1980); Meyers, J., *The Enemy: A Biography of W. L.* (1980)

—EDWARD T. JONES

W. L. has been seen in these pages as a contemporary neoclassicist, and it is seriously to be doubted that this neoclassical approach is positive, especially if we find it in L. Unwittingly, perhaps, he puts the case against himself: "the romantic traditional outlook . . . results in most men living in an historic past." We are too "historical," he argues; even when we satirize ourselves, we do not satirize what we are, only what we have been. We tend to laugh at the foibles of our past, and so fail to progress. Only the laugher, therefore, lives for only he, the true "person" of L.'s political ideal, sees all satirically, externally, nonromantically, in a perpetual present. Only this man is fully conscious.

This would be all very well, if the exigencies of the present time permitted it. But not only does L.'s critical position bind itself too closely to tradition to allow for the present at all, it also insists on continually assailing the present in a *parti pris* fashion. This insistence on particularities, on assailing our time and not all time, robs his satire of universality. Much of his work is contemporary in allusion, and some of it only contemporary. Is it just possible that L.'s loss in powers of observation may be due to the "apriorist heresy," to his approaching reality subjectively (not to say, romantically), selecting from it data to confirm his theories?

Geoffrey Wagner, *W. L.: A Portrait of the Artist as the Enemy* (1957), pp. 310–11

. . . Most important of all in his life's whole work is his insight into the case of twentieth century man; his unique vision of the watershed, or the abyss, of the present. Most important in his fiction is his capacity to transmit and to intensify both his insight and the judgement that passes insensibly with it, through the total unifying movement of narrative. His ideas were always developing, and his work always had to be exploratory of them. He strained his powers to the uttermost or beyond. He probably wrote too much too carelessly. There are enough bad patches and loose ends, it may be said, to prevent any of his books from being unreservedly a masterpiece. Yet there is no real doubt by now that W. L. established himself as among the great writers of the century, and among (though not equal to) Yeats, Lawrence, Eliot, and the other geniuses born in the astonishing decade of the 1880s.

John Holloway, "W. L.: The Massacre and the Innocents," *The Charted Mirror* (1960), p. 136

With *Childermass* and *Apes* [*of God*], the air thickens, along with the books, and becomes a good deal harder to breathe freely in. If, as T. S. Eliot has said of his own works, prose may deal with ideals while poetry must deal with actuality, then L.'s "poetry" of the late 1920's is, unlikely as it may at first seem, located in these two novels. Although *Childermass* takes place outside something called the Magnetic City and has been termed a philosophical fantasy, its world is still the "moronic inferno of insipidity and decay" that *Apes* renders and that contradicts whatever Utopian ideas seek to transform it. To distinguish between the critical books and the "creative" ones of these years is, of course, particularly difficult; and Eliot's distinction between prose ideals and poetic actuality must not be taken too rigidly—ideals and actuality are admirably fused in works of his own like *Four Quartets* or *The Three Voices of Poetry*. In L.'s case it is only necessary to mention the gallery of rogues and monsters through which the critical books conduct us to be reminded of how certain effects are absolutely dependent on the writer's power of satirical creation. It is perhaps somewhat harder to see how the novels, preoccupied as they are with the world as a moronic inferno, can express those rational standards and values by which the inferno is satirized and ultimately judged.

William H. Pritchard, *W. L.* (1968), p. 69

L. worked consistently hard to keep his imagination under restraint, and to transform it into polemical energy. He tried to ignore the non-cerebral elements in creativity. Perhaps he was afraid of his imagination in rather the same way as Swift (justifiably) was of his. Certainly the fierce hardness of outline that characterizes his painting and most of his prose may be seen as gaining its firmness from a need to curb and control a violent and wild passionateness of nature. Just as L. obstinately stayed "outside" the literary world, so he kept his intellect obstinately outside the animality and the emotionality of its physical residence. He laughed (brilliantly) at the intellectual implications of Lawrence and his "Dark Gods." But he did not in fact deny his own animality; rather he saw it as comic. What is unique about his writing is its comic objectivity about the existence of physicality; this is not calculated to appeal to a fashionable critic, who is after all concerned mainly to pretend to himself that, humanly he can live with himself while he produces an endless stream of shrill, derived patter. Even less will such (in Lewisian terms) automata feel impelled to examine the nature and quality of the feeling and disturbance and emotion that together made up L.'s imagination.

Martin Seymour-Smith, "W. L. as Imaginative Writer," *Agenda*, 7, 3/8, 1 (1969–70), p. 10

. . . If L. is judged as a traditional novelist, he may well appear to rank closer to writers such as Ford Madox Ford and E. M. Forster than to greater novelists such as James Joyce or D. H. Lawrence. I doubt that L.'s contribution to the novel will ever be appreciated if one claims, as do . . . most of L.'s defenders to date, that he is the equal of such giants as Pope, Swift, Lawrence, and Joyce.

T. S. Eliot observed that "It may be that the very variety of L.'s achievement, and the fact that so much of it just falls short of perfection, obscures his excellence in each kind." If L. is not to be dismissed as a volcanic but burnt-out genius, his achievement should be studied where it is most vital—in the novel. Once his work as a novelist is singled out from the variety of his other achievements, the unique nature of his art will emerge. L. is generally considered an impersonal and highly innovative writer. Yet his greatest novels reveal that his art is highly personal and traditional. His true esthetic is not found in his idiosyncratic theory of satire but in his relatively conventional and less well-known interpretation of Shakespearean tragedy. L.'s central problem as a novelist was to reconcile his satiric with his tragic vision of the world. . . . L.'s art moves between the poles of satire and tragedy. This dual movement, together with an exploration of both the destructive and creative nature of violence in this war-torn century, characterizes all of L.'s novels.

Timothy Materer, *W. L. the Novelist* (1976), pp. 22–23

Like many geniuses—and L. deserves this title—he was a multifarious man who assumed many roles. The disparate aspects of his character cannot readily be focused in a single convincing image, for the Enemy fought bitterly, yet was also a kindly and courtly friend. Though the words "quarrel" and "attack" have frequently appeared as leitmotifs in this book, they do not represent an entirely negative side of L.'s character. In most of the major disputes . . . he was morally and intellectually right. His attacks on friends like Pound, Joyce and Eliot, though personally offensive, contained penetrating and persuasive literary criticism. He was reckless about libel, but demanded honesty and efficiency from his publishers. His political judgment was seriously defective; but his open and defiant stance on artistic issues was stringent and salutary, and his blasts provided a refreshing change from the mealy-mouthed puffs that usually passed for serious criticism. Though L. was ungrateful to his patrons, his attitude was often justified by their arrogant condescension. . . .

If L., who wrote 50 books and 360 essays, had not composed political tracts, but had concentrated on perfecting his major works and devoted more time to painting, his reputation would have been much greater. He was one of the most lively and stimulating forces in modern English literature, and deserves recognition not only as a painter and writer, but also as an independent, courageous artist and a "brilliant and original observer" of contemporary society.

Jeffrey Meyers, *The Enemy: A Biography of W. L.* (1980), pp. 330–31

LEZAMA LIMA, José

Cuban poet and novelist, b. 19 Dec. 1910, Havana, d. 9 Aug. 1976, Havana

L. L. studied law at the University of Havana and was active in protests against the dictatorship, but he also studied theology and history, both of which left their mark on his literary work. During the 1930s he began publishing his poetry and immediately achieved considerable success. In 1937 he started the periodical *Verbum*, which served as the organ of the Transcendentalist group of poets, of which he was the founder. Transcendentalism was largely an attempt to go beyond the *costumbrista* tradition, which tended to deal more or less superficially with regional experience. Among other journals he founded was the highly influential *Orígenes* (1944–56), the focus of another group of poets who looked to him for leadership. L. L. held various posts in the Castro government, but his main concern was always his literary work.

This intense, imposing man, living in Havana with his mother and surrounded by his disciples, prevented by asthma from traveling as he would have liked, declared that in the creative words he produces, a man returns to the world as divine essence the air vouchsafed him as breath. Always a lover of conversation, he felt that in each word was to be found "a seed germinated by the union of the stellar and the verbal." His task, as he conceived it, was to invent a poetic reinterpretation of the world. Thus, his work is often hermetic, and he is a prime representative of the so-called neo-Baroque tendency. Many influential Hispanic poets of his era were concerned with rescuing from oblivion the great Spanish poet Luis de Góngora (1561–1627), one of whose major concerns was the use of poetic language to exhaust the possibilities inherent in a subject in order to elevate it from a mundane level to a correspondence with the archetypal. For L. L., it is more a matter of exploring the latent possibilities of language itself in the process of building a meaningful new cosmos.

It is generally agreed that L. L.'s controversial novel *Paradiso* (1966; *Paradiso*, 1974) represents the culmination of his art. Having borrowed the title from Dante, he presents a world that is anything but paradisiacal, and yet, true to his principles, he attempts to elevate his otherwise generally undistinguished characters and their equally homely daily activities to a meaningful level by continually comparing them to the deeds of gods and heroes. The critic Raymond D. Souza has noted that L. L.'s imagery often moves from a square to a circle. In Jungian terms this movement represents the transition from earthly wholeness (the square) to the heavenly sort (the circle). L. L.'s desired world is always one created by poetic language.

Accused of writing pornography, L. L. replied that at its roots his work is essentially an *auto sacramental* (religious play), a dramatic accompaniment to the means of grace. The point at issue is the notorious eighth chapter of *Paradiso*, which appears to be a somewhat obscene apology for homosexuality. This chapter, however, which stands between the two natural divisions of the work and serves as a transition between them, in reality portrays man as recently emerged in the form of undifferentiated unity, able to relate only to himself until the creation of woman. In this poet's novel the reader must avoid superficial judgments, for the work constitutes a search for primordial reality in language. It is a sensorial universe, and within it the fundamental experience is that of language as a creative force.

In the field of recent Spanish American fiction, L. L., along with Guillermo CABRERA INFANTE, has taken the lead in concentrating on the possibilities inherent in language itself. He is viewed not only as Cuba's premier modern poet but as an indispensable link between poetry and the novel.

FURTHER WORKS: *Tratados en La Habana* (1958); *Orbita de L. L.* (1966); *L. L.* (1968), *La expresión americana* (1969); *Posible imagen de J. L. L.* (1969); *La cantidad hechizada* (1970); *Esferaimagen* (1970); *Poesía completa* (1970; expanded ed., 1975); *Introducción a los vasos órficos* (1971); *Obras completas* (1975); *Cangrejos y golondrinas* (1977); *Oppiano Licario* (1977); *Cartas* (1978); *Fragmentos a su imán* (1979)

BIBLIOGRAPHY: Simón, P., ed. *Recopilación de textos sobre J. L. L.* (1970); "Focus on *Paradiso*," special section, *Review*, No. 12 (1974): 4–51; special L. section, *RI*, 41: 92–93 (1975): 465–546; Souza, R. D., *Major Cuban Novelists* (1976): 53–79; Lima, E. Lezama, "J. L. L., mi hermano," *RevI*, 8 (1978): 297–304; Ulloa, J. C., ed. *J. L. L.: Textos críticos* (1979)

—WILLIAM SIEMENS

LEZGIAN LITERATURE

See Caucasian Literatures

LI Ang

(pseud. of Shih Shu-tuan) Chinese short-story writer, novelist, and essayist, b. 1952, Lu-kang, Taiwan

L. was born in the coastal town of Lu-kang in central Taiwan, from which she draws most of her creative inspiration. In 1975 L. came to the U.S. and earned a master's degree in drama from the University of Oregon. Since returning to Taiwan, she has written several collections of stories, three novels, and numerous essays on social and political issues. L. now resides in a suburb of Taipei with her sister, a literary critic and professor of Chinese literature, Shih Shu-nü. Her other sister, Shih Shu-ching (dates n.a.), is also a well-known novelist. L. teaches in the Department of Theater at the University of Chinese Culture; she also travels extensively in between her busy schedule of teaching and participating in political activities. Her works are widely read by readers in Taiwan, Hong Kong, the People's Republic of China, and overseas Chinese communities.

Generally regarded as one of Taiwan's most talented and controversial writers, L. began her writing career at the age of sixteen, when she published her first short story, "Hua-chi" (Flower Season), dealing with a young woman's curiosity about sex at a time when such a topic was a taboo. Traditional Chinese society's aversion to discussions of sex marked her writings throughout this early period, which inevitably brought attacks upon her, especially with the 1973 publication of a short story entitled "Jen-chien shih" (Man's World), which deals with clandestine sexual activities in a college dormitory. Since then, L. has continued to deal with similar topics—sexuality, politics, and violence against women—reaching a climax with the publication of the internationally acclaimed novel

Sha-fu (1983; *The Butcher's Wife*, 1986), which won Taiwan's prestigious *United Daily News* prize for long fiction in 1983. Long before domestic abuse and violence against women became a widely recognized problem, even in the U.S., *Sha-fu* brought the issue to the attention of Taiwanese society, which, not surprisingly, subjected the author to virulent, often ad hominem attacks. The novel centers on an abusive butcher who uses food rationing to control his wife sexually and psychologically. The female protagonist, Lin Shih, is forced to prostitute herself to her husband, while women from the neighborhood pass on moral judgment and scathing criticism of her. Driven by the double oppression of marital brutality and social pressure, she eventually takes up her husband's knife and butchers him in the same fashion he slaughters pigs. Readers generally agree that this is a novel that attacks the Chinese patriarchal society, reducing the factors to two basic needs for survival, food and sex. However, what often escapes critics' attention is the group of women who not only do not come to Lin's aid, but actually aid in pushing her further into the inferno of abuses. In this sense, contrary to claims by her most severe critics, L. is not attacking Chinese men, but Chinese tradition; in her own words, this is a novel more about humanity than about women.

Although sexual politics in the Chinese context remains L. dominant theme, she is nevertheless constantly looking for ways to broaden her scope and, more importantly, keep up with the rapid social and cultural changes in contemporary Taiwan. Her second major work, *An Yeh* (1985; Dark Night), is exemplary in this regard, though it is sometimes considered to be an "artistically inferior but far more daring novel." Depicting a group of middle- and upper-class men and women in the increasingly materialistic world of cosmopolitan Taipei, *An Yeh* captures the complexities of modern life without losing sight of the issues that concern L. most: infidelity, humiliation and manipulation in the business world, and women's fate in the battlefield of sexual politics. Explicit depictions of sexual activity remain the center of controversy over this work, though L.'s detractors often ignore the parallel between sexual conquest and domination in the ruthless world of business.

L. is by no means a writer whose interest is simply to expose the dark side of society and its treatment of women through literary works. As an ardent supporter and active participant in many political rallies organized by a major oppositional party, the Democratic Progressive Party (DDP), L.'s experience as a woman in a predominantly male political milieu prompted her to compose *Pei-kang hsiang-lu jen-jen ch'a* (1996; Everyone Got to Stick Incense in the Pei-kang Burner), a collection of four linked stories. A huge scandal erupted even before the stories were published in book form, when one of them was serialized in the *Chung-kuo shih-pao*, and readers identified the characters in her story with real-life political figures. Unfortunately, the controversy obscured the core issues of L.'s work: an exploration of the intricate connection between sex and politics in post martial-law Taiwan, an examination of the role of women in the formation of a true opposition party in Taiwan's democratization process, and an investigation of the ways in which women obtain political power. Ultimately, the work forces the readers and the critics to ponder the fundamental question of feminism: whether women should empower themselves by exploiting their sexuality. Equally ignored in the debate has been the issue of recording and interpreting history, which informs much of L.'s work.

Never a writer content with pleasing the public nor someone shying away from controversy, L. can easily be considered as a catalyst of changes in bringing important social, political and cultural issues to people's attention: from her earliest work, which tackles female sexuality and fantasy, to *Sha-fu*, which deals with domestic abuse and sexual power politics, to An Yeh, which exposes the roles of sex and women in the business world, to her latest work, which questions women's role in politics. Her detractors may not be thrilled with her topics, but her contributions to Taiwan's literature and feminist causes cannot be ignored.

FURTHER WORKS: *Hua-chi* (1975); *Ai-ch'ing shih-yen* (1982); *T'a-men te yen-lei* (1984); *I-feng wei chi te ch'ing-shu* (1986); *Mi-yuan* (1991). FURTHER WORKS IN ENGLISH: *The Butcher's Wife and Other Stories* (1995)

BIBLIOGRAPHY: Ng, D., "Feminism in the Chinese Context: L. A.'s *The Butcher's Wife*," *MCL*, 4 (1988): 177-200; Yeh, M., "Shapes of Darkness: Symbols in L. A.'s Dark Night," in Duke, M., ed., *Modern Chinese Women Writers* (1989): 78-95; Goldblatt, H., "Sex and Society: The Fiction of L. A.," in Goldblatt, H., ed., *Worlds Apart* (1990): 150-65

—SYLVIA LI-CHUN LIN

LI Jui

(also romanized as Li Rui) Chinese novelist and short-story writer, b. 1950, Beijing

Coming of age during the Great Proletarian Cultural Revolution (1966-76), L. was sent to the rural area of the Lüliang Mountains in Shanxi Province in 1969. After six years there, L. worked as a laborer at a steel factory in Linfen, Shanxi. His experience in the poverty-stricken mountain villages would later become the main source of his creativity, with the Cultural Revolution serving as the ideological backdrop. In 1977 L. began working for the magazine *Shanxi Literature*, first as editorial clerk, then as director of the editorial office, and finally as assistant editor-in-chief. Currently, L. is a full-time writer and vice chairman of the Shanxi Writers' Association.

One of the most promising writers of his generation, L. is well known for his innovative use of language, his experimentation with narrative styles, and his tactful handling of political issues. He is considered a wordsmith who chooses each word carefully, and whose skillful employment of the Shanxi dialect to convey local flavor is remarkable. As an eyewitness to the devastating effects of the Cultural Revolution on the Chinese people, L. often deals with incidents concerning one of the most chaotic decades in China's history. However, unlike so many of the accusatory works that have appeared in China in recent years, L. complicates our understanding of the events by depicting complex human relations and the political system while subtly criticizing the entire communist mechanism.

L. published his first major work, *Tiu-shih ti ch'ang-ming so* (1985; The Lost Longevity Locket), in 1985, but his status as an important writer was not widely recognized until after the publication of *Hou-t'u* (1989; Fertile Earth), a collection of short stories set in the Lüliang Mountains that displays a salient minimalist characteristic requiring the reader to contemplate the complexity of his texts; what is not revealed is at least as significant as what is said. Most of these stories deal with the impoverished lives of peasants in the mountain area, with topics ranging from a sham marriage, finding a thief by way of "democratic election," and the deterioration of morality and ethics under the pressure of poverty and political changes. Most noteworthy is the parallel between political hierarchy and gender inequality, and how the former is reflected in the latter: when a villager is taken advantage of by the village head, a party cadre, the abused man can only regain his manhood via sexual dominance over a woman. Although feminist readers might object to this treatment of women, L. appears to be ridiculing Chinese men for their fragile ego, whose balance hinges upon the gain or loss of a woman. The target of L.'s criticism in these stories is actually the oppressive authority figure and the control it exerts upon impoverished villagers, be it political control by a party cadre, economic control by the haves over the have-nots, or the sexual oppression of women. The collection has been translated into Swedish by a member of the Swedish Academy.

Chiu-chih (1993; *Silver City*, 1997), a historical novel, is more ambitious, for it tells of the love/hate relationships between three generations of two families. L.'s first novel to be translated into English, it has been widely praised by reviewers in the West for its panoramic narrative scope, and for L.'s skillful juxtaposition of the vicissitudes of two families' fortunes with national political changes. Focusing on the rivalry between two clans in the fictional salt-producing locale of Silver City, the narrative moves back and forth in time to depict what is essentially a history of the Chinese Communist Party. Most noteworthy in this family saga is the female protagonist, Li Zihen, who demonstrates her determination to remain single by disfiguring her face with burning joss sticks in order to support her younger brothers and sisters. She lives her life based upon a strong personal philosophy and a "traditional" Chinese sense of morality, yet is pulled in opposite directions by various political forces, eventually becoming a revolutionary hero; later, for the same behavior, she is labeled a counter-revolutionary. By putting a personal face on the ever-changing political ideology that is the trademark of modern Chinese history, L. molds a subtle yet poignant critique of the communist system.

L.'s next two major novels belong to his "Walking Mountains" series. *Wu-feng chih shu* (1996; The Windless Tree) and *Wan-li wu-yün* (1997; The Cloudless Sky), represent a new direction in L.'s narrative strategy. What makes these two novels unique and compelling, in addition to the extraordinarily complex human relationship, is the technique of multiple first-person narratives. The story line progresses from the point of view of a number of characters, including, even, a mule and the ghost of one of the characters after he has hanged himself. Unlike the Japanese novel *Roshomon*, which provides four different versions of the same event, these two novels take the strategy a step further by having characters take turns narrating the story. The reader then pieces together the strands of information to form a unified whole. L.'s careful use of each individual's unique (and frequently self-serving) account to present an unfiltered and non-judgmental view of both the characters and the events enhances the sense of drama. This technique allows the author to question the recording of events as he exposes a dark side of Chinese politics, rural society, and, ultimately, humanity. Although in both novels L. adopts a similar narrative strategy and relies upon the use of Shanxi mountain-village dialect, he clearly intends to test the limits of his technique in the second novel, *Wan-li wu-yün*. It is as if he were trying to see how much he could challenge his readers to accept the "otherness" of his work—the dialect and the difficult task of reading and deciphering. L. is not an author who conforms to popular tastes,

which is why he has become one of the most notable writers in post-Deng China.

FURTHER WORKS: *Hung fang-tzu* (1988); *Hsüan tsei: L. J. tuan-p'ien hsiao-shuo hsüan-tu* (1988)

—SYLVIA LI-CHUN LIN

LIBERIAN LITERATURE

Liberia was founded as a nation in the 19th c. by the U.S. Congress to provide a land for freed black slaves who wished to return to West Africa. Unfortunately, the returnees, called "Americos," became a governing class as cruelly indifferent to the problems of the indigenous Africans as any colonial administration. Years of resentment culminated in a coup d'état in 1980. Restrictive rule did little for development of a significant literature.

The Liberian writing that has been published either has been highly derivative, borrowing outdated diction and form from earlier English poetry, or has drawn on the indigenous storytelling tradition. Little of incisive contemporary value has appeared.

Typical of the earlier style is the work of Roland Tombekai Dempster (1910–1965). His poems *Echoes from a Valley* (1947) and "To Monrovia Old and New" (1958) have a declamatory rhetoric and style that derive little from their supposed occasion and locality.

One unusual earlier work, unfortunately without successors, was the novel *Love in Ebony: A West African Romance* (1932) by Varfelli Karlee (b. 1900). If not of outstanding quality, it did at least deal with the issues of the African people outside the society of the Monrovian elite.

Of those writers closely linked with the oral tradition, Bai Moore (1910–1988) is the most distinguished and the most prolific. After spending time studying in Virginia, he returned to Liberia in 1938 and began to collect folktales and poems, particularly from the Golah society into which he had been born. He translated much of this material and incorporated some of it into his English-language writing. Also drawing on the oral tradition is Wilton Sankawulo (b. 1945), whose stories of the Kpelle tribe, including "The Evil Forest" (1971)—part translations, part adaptations—have been published in *African Arts*.

The problems of a writer in Liberia are exemplified by the experience Bai Moore encountered in publishing his work. His major collection of poetry, *Ebony Dust* (1963), in which he reflects on his travels in Europe, America, and Africa, had to be produced in mimeographed form. His more topical journalistic report on a true event, *Murder in the Cassava Patch* (1968), was distributed by Moore himself, who sold two thousand copies on a street corner in Monrovia. Not until it was selected as a school text were the remaining three thousand copies sold.

Despite obstacles, writers do struggle to find an outlet for their work. Doris Henries (b. 1930) is one of the more active of recent writers. She has not yet prepared a full volume of her own work, but she has been instrumental in publishing some important anthologies of Liberian writing: *Poems of Liberia: 1836–1961* (1966) and *Liberian Folklore* (1966). It must be acknowledged that this country has not yet produced a writer of the stature of those from other West African countries. Perhaps the new political situation will encourage the development of a more vital literature.

BIBLIOGRAPHY: *Liberian Writing: Liberia as Seen by Her Own Writers as Well as by German Authors* (1970); Henries, D., *The Status of Writing in Liberia* (1972); Singler, J. V., "The Role of the State in the Development of Literature: The Liberian Government and Creative Fiction," *RAL*, 11 (1980): 511–28; Gérard, A. S., *African Language Literatures* (1981): 243–46

—JOHN POVEY

LIDMAN, Sara

Swedish novelist and journalist, b. 30 Dec. 1923, Missenträsk

L. grew up in the isolated rural environment of Västerbotten, an area in northern Sweden. During adolescence she suffered from tuberculosis, which in 1937 and 1938 necessitated her confinement in a sanatorium at Häallnäs. In 1949 she completed studies in English, French, and education at the University of Uppsala.

In her late twenties L. made a stunning literary debut with a regional novel, *Tjärdalen* (1953; the tar still). Set in a northern Swedish village during the 1930s, *Tjärdalen* is not only a re-creation of the writer's own childhood, through the superbly rendered dialect and sense of place, but also a tightly structured narrative about human guilt and responsibility, with frequent biblical overtones and parallels.

In *Hjortronlandet* (1955; cloudberry land) L. combined remarkable descriptions of the far-northern environment with portrayals of intensely alive, sharply differentiated characters. Again the setting is rural Västerbotten of the 1930s. L.'s focus is on the collective, the outland marsh settlers called *öare*. L.'s strong sense of empathy with these social outcasts enables her to probe, more sharply than in *Tjärdalen*, the issue of responsibility toward those whom society has labeled unfit or incompetent.

During the 1960s L.'s horizons were broadened by trips to South Africa, Rhodesia, and Vietnam. A committed observer of what she considered the exploited and oppressed peoples in these areas of conflict, she gradually abandoned fiction in favor of subjective documentary writing. With books such as *Samtal i Hanoi* (1966; conversations in Hanoi) and *Gruva* (1968; mine), she became an influential voice of the Swedish radical left and thus a molder of Scandinavian political opinion.

L. returned to fiction in the late-1970s, with a trilogy on 19th-c. crofter life: *Dintjänare hör* (1977; your servant hears), *Vredens barn* (1979; children of wrath), and *Nabots sten* (1981; Naboth's stone). Her sweeping and masterful narrative traces the roots of the welfare state, to show how a struggle for physical survival four generations ago has led to an industrial society where adverse conditions have adapted rather than disappeared. The wrath that animates her characters can be traced ultimately to their human needs and their spiritual oppression.

L. has written about the poor in spirit and material possessions, racism in South Africa, the war in Vietnam, and inequality in the Swedish welfare state. Abstract ideologies are, however, secondary to her central subject in one work after another—the human being.

FURTHER WORKS: *Job Klockmakares dotter* (1954); *Aina* (1956); *Regnspiran* (1958; *The Rain Bird*, 1962); *Bära mistel* (1960); *Jag och min son* (1961; rev. ed., 1963); *Med fem diamanter* (1964); *Vänner och u-vänner* (1969); *Marta Marta: En folksaga* (1970); *Fåglarna i Nam Dinh: Artiklar om Vietnam* (1972)

BIBLIOGRAPHY: Gustafson, A., *A History of Swedish Literature* (1961): 559–61; Lundbergh, H., on *The Rain Bird*, *ASR*, 51, 3 (1963), 315; Borland, H. H., "S. L.'s Progress: A Critical Survey of Six Novels," *SS*, 39 (1967): 97–114; Bäckström, L., "Eyvind Johnson, Per Olof Sundman, and S. L.: An Introduction," *ConL*, 12 (1971): 242–51; Dembo, L. S., "An Interview with S. L.," *ConL*, 12 (1971): 252–57; Lagerlöf, K. E., ed., *Modern Swedish Prose in Translation* (1979): 57–58

—RAYMOND JARVI

LIHN, Enrique

Chilean poet, novelist, and short-story writer, b. 3 Sept. 1929, Santiago; d. 10 July 1988, Santiago

Born in the home of his maternal grandmother, L. lived there sporadically during what he called his "archliterary childhood," where he fell under her spell, and more importantly, under his uncle's, Gustavo Carrasco, who according to L., "was the first artist in my life." This uncle, a professor of drawing, instilled in the boy a love of art, which he later as a youth studied seriously at the School of Fine Arts as well as attending the German *lycée* in Santiago. L.'s interest in the pictorial arts never flagged—indeed, some of his books are charmingly illustrated with his own drawings, and later in life he made an amusing documentary movie in which he played a major role.

However, L.'s true artistic talents lay elsewhere, in the realm of poetry, and this he discovered early on. His first slim volume of verse, *Nada se escurre* (1949; nothing slips away), came out when he was twenty, and was followed by *Poemas de este tiempo y de otro* (1955; poems of our times and another).

La pieza oscura y otros poemas (1963; *The Dark Room and Other Poems*, 1978) established L. as a major poetic voice in Chile. Close upon the publication of this book came his next one, *Poesía de paso* (1966; occasional poetry), which brought him the prestigious Cuban award for poetry granted by La Casa de las Américas. These last two volumes received much acclaim not only in his native Chile but also abroad, in other Latin American countries, in Europe, and the U.S. In 1965 L. took his first trip to Europe, having won a UNESCO fellowship, where he traveled through various countries, being especially "obsessed," as he put it, with Italy. Later, he spent some time in Paris on a Guggenheim fellowship, and the "City of Light" figures prominently in his later collections of poems. On another tour, in 1974, this time to the U.S., he was heralded enthusiastically on college campuses where he gave readings of his poetry. This prompted various translators like Dave Oliphant in *If Poetry Is To Be Written Right* (1977) and Jonathan Cohen, John Felstiner, and David Unger in *The Dark Room and Other Poems* (1978) to publish selections of his poems in English.

From 1973 on L. held a teaching position as professor of literature at one of the branches of the University of Chile in Santiago. He also taught as visiting professor at the University of California, Irvine, in 1976, and at the University of Texas, Austin, in 1986. During the mid-1980s L. underwent a serious operation for a heart problem, and his health began to fail. He returned to Chile, where he died two years later of cancer.

Though often moody and morose in his last years, when in high spirits L. was a witty, theatrical, and highly entertaining person, charged with life and dynamism. These latter qualities are certainly reflected in his poetry, where he frequently reaches and maintains a high level of emotional intensity. Many of his poems dwell on the tragedies in life, the loss of love, the betrayal of the beloved, or sadness at death. And like many contemporary poets, L. speaks directly to the reader, employing an everyday vocabulary and a disarming conversational tone to let us know what he thinks of social and political injustice, and at the same time to cry out against his existential loneliness. In many of his poems we encounter alienation. Communication tends to break down; consequently, relationships must suffer and crack apart.

The magic of L.'s poetry resides in the subterranean, subjective dream world he depicts, dark and destructive, filled with fears and anxieties. The reader may well be shaken up by his poems, by their sweat and tears, pulsing with life. But not all of them are somber or violent; there are moments of quiet pleasure. In addition, we witness his inquiring mind at work: Most everything is called into question, even the values of poetry and those who write it. But the general impression we are left with after reading his poems is one of a world where little separates convention from nightmare and abominations.

Although one of L.'s last books of verse, *Albello aparecer de este lucero* (1983; to the fair apparition of this morning star), is punctuated with moments of hope and desire, as its title would indicate, it is also pervaded with a deep sadness, as is his *Diario de muerte* (diary of death), published posthumously in 1989. When he died, L. left some twenty volumes of verse to his credit, almost all of them scant in length but extremely rich in substance, long poems and short ones, but mainly long poems, often intensely gripping and immensely readable. Undoubtedly, L. has made his niche in the gallery of distinguished 20th-c. Chilean poets, which includes Pablo NERUDA, Gabriela MISTRAL, and Nicanor PARRA. Like them, he has attained international stature.

Besides his poetry, L. published several collections of short stories, notably *Agua de arroz* (1964; rice water), for which he received the Atenea Prize (1964) at the University of Concepción, Chile, and several novels, such as *Batman en Chile o El ocaso de un ídolo o Solo contra el desierto rojo* (1973; Batman in Chile or the sunset of an idol or alone against the red desert), *La orquesta de cristal* (1976; the crystal orchestra), and *El arte de la palabra* (1980; the art of the word). In these novels L.'s ironic sense of humor reigns supreme. Pedro Lastra (b. 1931), his close friend of long standing and collaborator on several books, published an engaging series of interviews, *Conversaciones con E. L.* (1980; 2nd ed., 1990; conversations with E. L.), packed with interesting information about the writer and his views on literature, which also includes a useful and extensive bibliography.

FURTHER WORKS: *Escrito en Cuba* (1969); *La musiquilla de las pobres esferas* (1969); *Algunos poemas* (1972); *Por fuerza mayor* (1975); *París, situación irregular* (1977); *L. y Pompier* (1978); *A partir de Manhattan* (1979); *Antologí al azar* (1981); *Estación de los desamparados* (1982); *El paseo ahumada* (1983); *Pena de extrañamiento* (1986); *Mester de juglaría* (1987); *La aparición de la Virgen* (1987); *Album de toda especie de poemas* (1989. FURTHER WORKS IN ENGLISH: *This Endless Malice* (1969)

BIBLIOGRAPHY: Lastra, P., "Las actuales promociones poéticas," *AUC*, 120 (1960): 181–92; Goic, C., "E. L. *La pieza oscura* (1955–1962)," *AUC*, 128 (1963): 194–97; special L. section, *Review*, 23 (1978): 5–37; O'Hara, E., "La poesía de E. L.," *Desde Melibea* (1980): 121–31; Rojas, W., "A manera de prefacio: *La pieza oscura* en la perspectiva de una lectura generacional," in *La pieza oscura* (2nd ed., 1984): 7–27; Cánovas, R., *L., Zurita, Ictus, Radrigan: Literatura chilena y experiencia autoritaria* (1986): 21–56; Coddou, M., *Veinte estudios sobre la literatura chilena del siglo veinte* (1989): 147–68; Lastra, P., ed., *Conversaciones con E. L.* (2nd ed., 1990)

—GEORGE D. SCHADE

LIIV, Juhan

Estonian poet, short-story and novella writer, and critic, b. 30 April 1864, Alatskivi; d. 1 Dec. 1913, Kavastu

The son of a poor peasant, L. attended a parish school and then, for only a short time, owing to ill health, a secondary school in Tartu. He subsequently became a journalist. Although he published his first poem in 1885, to earn a living he devoted his time mainly to writing prose. L. won recognition for *Kümme lugu* (1893; ten stories), which was quickly followed by the publication of novellas *Käkimäe kägu* (1893; the Käkimäe cuckoo), *Vari* (1894; the shadow), and *Nõia t'tar* (1895; the sorcerer's daughter), all written in a naturalistic, in part sentimental, forceful, and musical style. As a critic he preferred the message of humanitarian ideas and depth of feeling to a formalist "aesthetic chiseling" of the text.

A straightforward writer in both his objective fiction and his controversial criticism, occasionally a powerful realistic painter of village life, in his poetic work L. stands in the front rank of the experimental poets of northern Europe, yet his lyrical talent was little appreciated until after his death. His extant production consists of some three hundred short poems and epigrams, the best of them written during the period of his acute mental illness from 1893 until his death from tuberculosis in 1913. In 1894, depressed by persecution mania, he burned a great number of his manuscripts, including a complete collection of poems, which, according to some of his contemporaries, was a singular masterpiece. Ill and homeless, L. wandered from place to place, the drama of his life played out on moral, nationalist, mystical, and psychic planes, with him as a soothsayer of repentance, anguish, and humility.

L.'s *Luuletused* (poems), consisting of forty-five verse pieces, appeared first in 1909, then again in 1910, and, with supplementary poems, in 1919 and 1926, each time with texts edited and corrected by Gustav Suits (1883–1956) and Friedebert Tuglas (1886–1971); these editors, despite their high literary culture, introduced an Art Nouveau and impressionistic artiness foreign to L.'s style. The original versions were in many cases destroyed. After he had overcome the influence of late romanticism, L. showed great skill in developing and transforming traditional verse schemes into either dramatic or intimate yet very songlike lines with considerable range of expression, full of symbolic, sometimes mysteriously obscure meaning. L.'s diction, rich with compressed and strange imagery, defies classification because his genius, expressed in seemingly simple and yet often undefinable word-gestures, aspires to more than human significance. His verse is at once nature poetry, philosophical poetry, and civic poetry.

L.'s poems exhibited a new type of form, their "verse-sketchiness" also being a factor in his inventive, "finished-unfinished" approach. L.'s phantasms and bodings, his nonconformist, invigorating spiritual force of heart and soul played an important part in the evolution of 20th-c. Estonian poetry. His highly individual style did not produce direct followers, but indirectly he inspired almost all Estonian poets who came after him. In the Soviet Union, L. is looked upon as a "critical realist," and nearly nothing is said about his figurative as well as politically inspired messianic ideas. Prophetically, L., deploring the loss of Estonian sovereignty in the 13th c., announced the coming of a new Estonian statehood long before anybody thought it could happen.

Throughout L.'s tortured literary career, an unusually sensitive trajectory can be traced. Beginning with the brooding peasants of the work of his early period, he moved toward the emotive intensity of his years of dark derangement, creating, however, during hours of mental lucidity increasingly heavy yet intellectually provocative and ever more sonorous poems of extended clairvoyant power. Although interest in his work has grown since his death, L. still is understood only partially.

FURTHER WORKS: *Kogutud teosed* (8 vols., 1921–1935); *Valitud luuletused* (1949)

BIBLIOGRAPHY: Ivask, I., "J. L.: The Somber Forest of the Past," in Kõressaar, V., and A. Rannit, eds., *Estonian Poetry and Language: Studies in Honor of Ants Oras* (1965); Jänes, H., *Geschichte der estnischen Literatur* (1965): 64–70; Nirk, E., *Estonian Literature* (1970): 137–40, 390; Terras, V., "J. L.: An Estonian Visionary Poet," in Leitch, V. B., ed., *The Poetry of Estonia: Essays in Comparative Analysis* (1982): 29–47

—ALEKSIS RANNIT

LIND, Jakov

(pseud. of Heinz Landwirth) Austrian novelist, short-story writer, and dramatist (also writing in English), b. 10 Feb. 1927, Vienna

As a Jewish boy endangered by Nazi persecution L. left his native city in late 1938 and emigrated to Holland. Having become fluent in Dutch, he posed as a Dutchman named Jan Gerrit Overbeek and worked on a Rhine barge, later living in Germany as a laborer at a metallurgic research institute of the German aviation ministry. After the end of World War II, L. went to Palestine under the name Jakov Chaklan. In 1950 he returned to Vienna and studied acting and stagecraft at the Max Reinhardt Seminar. After working at a variety of jobs—fisherman in the Mediterranean, beach photographer in Tel Aviv, orange picker in Netanya, private detective, traveling salesman, film agent—L. went to London, where he has made his home since 1954, with periods of residence in New York and on Majorca.

L. achieved international prominence as a writer with a collection of stories entitled *Eine Seele aus Holz* (1962; *Soul of Wood*, 1964). In the title story, which is by turns horrifying and hilarious, a paraplegic Jewish youth who has been entrusted to an Austrian male nurse when his parents are deported from Vienna is abandoned on a mountainside. L.'s first novel, *Landschaft in Beton* (1963; *Landscape in Concrete*, 1966), has been described by Daniel Stern as "one of the most piercing pictures of the nihilism of this century." In it L. paints the lunatic landscape of the waning Third Reich and describes in allegorical fashion the macabre odyssey of the demented Wehrmacht Sergeant Gauthier Bachmann.

In *Eine bessere Welt* (1966; *Ergo*, 1967), an intricate scatological satire full of wicked wit and grisly humor, L. continues his relentless exploration of the cloaca of contemporary consciousness. Using his hated native country as a metaphor for the dismal state of Western society, the author describes the running fight between two German-Austrian humanoids that represent the dregs of postwar society. After several radio plays and autobiographical works L. published *Travels to the Enu: Story of a Shipwreck* (1982), his first work of fiction written in English, a novel that details a phantasmagoric journey to a utopian, paradisiac island inhabited by strange bird-men. The epistolary novel *The Inventor* (1987) presents the contrapuntal lives of two Jewish brothers born in Poland and raised in England, one of whom has invented a sort of supercomputer that will determine the distribution of the world's resources.

Alvin Rosenfeld has characterized L.'s prose style as being "somewhere between Kafka and Günter GRASS." L., however, does not regard himself as a grotesque or absurdist writer but as an old-fashioned moralist in the tradition of Peter Altenberg (1859–1919) and Karl KRAUS who describes ordinary people (though these are often more loathsome and dangerous than fanatics). His literary stance clearly is that of a survivor, and Virginia Kirkus perhaps characterizes his work best when she writes: "With a proliferation of dreamily forlorn details, a Mephistophelian grin, and a superbly insouciant style he fashions fables for our age, post-Auschwitz vaudeville."

FURTHER WORKS: *Die Heiden* (1965); *Anna Laub* (1965); *Angst* (1969); *Hunger* (1969); *Israel: Rückkehr für 28 Tage* (1972); *Der Ofen* (1973). FURTHER WORKS IN ENGLISH: *The Silver Foxes are Dead, and Other Plays* (1968); *Counting My Steps* (1969); *Numbers: A Further Autobiography* (1972); *The Trip to Jerusalem* (1973)

BIBLIOGRAPHY: Stern, D., "A Contemporary Nightmare," *SatR*, 15 June 1966: 25–26; Potoker, E. M., "A Distillation of Horror," *SatR*, 21 Oct. 1967: 35–36; Kahn, L., *Mirrors of the Jewish Mind* (1968): 231–32; Rosenfeld, A. H., "J. L. and the Trials of Jewishness," *Midstream*, Feb. 1974: 71–75; Langer, L. L., *The Holocaust and the Literary Imagination* (1975): 205–49; Swanson, R. A., "Versions of Doublethink in *Gravity's Rainbow, Darkness Visible, Riddley Walker*, and *Travels to the Enu*," *WLT*, 58, 2 (Spring 1984): 203–8; Stenberg, P., "Edgar Hilsenrath and J. L. Meet . . . ," in Gilman, S. L., et al, eds., *Yale Companion to Jewish Writing and Thought in German Culture* (1997): 642-47

—HARRY ZOHN

LINDEGREN, Erik

Swedish poet, b. 5 Aug. 1910, Luleå; d. 31 May 1968, Stockholm

L. was born and raised in northern Sweden. His family belonged to the small middle class of a mining town. L. studied philosophy and literature at the University of Stockholm but did not graduate, although he continued to study classics, psychology, and religion on his own. He was a literary reviewer for major newspapers and magazines, contributing editor of the leading literary journal, *Bonniers litterära magasin*, and from 1948 to 1950 editor of

Prisma, an experimental journal of high quality but short life. He was also a member of the Swedish Academy.

L. published poetry in small local papers during his school years. His first collection, *Posthum ungdom* (1935; posthumous youth), is characterized by irony, formal elegance, and conventionality. Present already in this work, however, is what would later become a characteristic feature of L.'s mature poetry: sudden leaps of feeling into moments of ecstasy.

Before publishing his next collection, L. studied contemporary literature, especially French SYMBOLIST and SURREALIST poetry. In 1942 he published privately a small numbered edition of *Mannen utan väg* (the man without a way), consisting of forty poems in broken sonnet form in which the only thing that remains of the original form is the number of lines. It was first acknowledged more as an admirable experiment than as a finished work of art. Over the years general opinion has changed, and the work is now recognized as sophisticated verse representing the new MODERNIST direction of poetry in Sweden. With grotesque imagery describing anxiety, brutality, and pain, L. advocates stoic acceptance of life's chaotic totality.

His next work, *Sviter* (1947; suites), containing more accessible poetry, immediately inspired a great number of imitators. L.'s fascination with Hamlet (he translated the play in 1967) is reflected in the introductory poem, "Hamlets himmelsfard" (Hamlet's ascension to heaven), where he describes a Hamlet overwhelmed by his longing for death. The poem sets the tone for many others that deal with death almost lovingly. The musical quality of L.'s poetry is evident particularly in his most anthologized poem, "Arioso" ("Arioso," 1963). *Sviter* also contains a number of prose poems in which L. takes a humorous attitude toward an absurd life. A key word in *Sviter* is "statue," used to connote lifelessness, confinement, or hollowness.

L.'s last work, *Vinteroffer* (1954; winter sacrifice), contains his most personal poetry and deals with loneliness, aging, and death. In the introductory poem, "Ikaros" (Icarus), one of his many classically inspired poems, L. describes a flight toward the limits of ecstasy, where reality is destroyed without creating new reality—a destruction of art and of the artist as well. The key word "statue" is, in *Vinteroffer*, used differently from the way it is used in *Sviter*. Here it signifies a captured movement and feeling, something lasting. Snow and winter here symbolize paralysis and death.

L.'s heritage from his paternal grandfather, a composer and music teacher, is evident from the musical quality and phraseology of L.'s poetry. L. also wrote directly for musical works, such as scenarios for several ballets. He translated Verdi's opera *Un ballo in maschera* (1950) and Mozart's *Don Giovanni* (1961), and wrote the libretto for an opera, *Aniara* (1959; Aniara), based on the work of the contemporary poet Harry MARTINSON.

L. also translated a number of important modern works into Swedish, including several plays by T. S. ELIOT, fiction by William FAULKNER, modern French poetry, and Rainer Maria RILKE's *Duinese Elegies*.

L. is one of the most important poets of modern Swedish literature. His masterpiece, *Mannen utan väg*, is one of the leading works of the new modernist movement of the 1940s. *Sviter* is equally important for the poetry of the 1950s. And as a reviewer and translator as well as a poet, L. played a major role in Swedish letters.

FURTHER WORKS: *Dikter* (1962)

BIBLIOGRAPHY: Gustafson, A., *A History of Swedish Literature* (1961): 548–51; Ekner, R., "The Artist as the Eye of a Needle," *SS*, 42 (1970): 1–13; Böhm, A., "L.'s *Mannen utan väg* und die Naturwissenschaft," *Scan*, 12 (1973): 37–42; Steene, B., "E. L.: An Assessment," *BA*, 49 (1975): 29–32; Prinz-Påhlson, G., "The Canon of Literary Modernism: A Note on Abstraction in the Poetry of E. L.," *CCrit*, 1 (1979): 155–66

—TORBORG LUNDELL

LINDGREN, Torgny

Swedish novelist, poet, and short-story writer, b. 16 June 1938, Raggsjö

L. was born in the northern province of Västerbotten, a desolate region that has produced more than its proportionate share of outstanding writers; Sara LIDMAN and Per Olov ENQUIST both hail from the same area. L. is the recipient of a number of literary prizes, among them the French *Prix Fémina Étranger* in 1986 for the novel *Bat Seba* (1984; *Bathsheba*, 1989). In 1991 he was elected to the Swedish Academy.

L.'s early works are highly critical of certain aspects of contemporary Swedish society. From his platform as a social democrat, he aims his criticism at his own party's excessive bureaucracy, the disparity between professed vision and actual practice, and the tendency to forget the everyday problems of citizens. The collection of poetry *Hur skulle det vara om man vore Olof Palme?* (1971; what would it be like to be Olof Palme?) offers examples of such censure. The collection of short stories with the long title *Skolbagateller medan jag försökte skriva till mina överordnade* (1972; school trivia, while attempting to write to my superiors) is set in a school milieu, familiar to L., who had a long career as a teacher behind him when he became a full-time writer in 1985. Here the failings of the school system are poignantly illustrated in the fates of a few students.

The novel *Skrämmer dig minuten?* (1981; does this minute frighten you?), a highly entertaining story but with treacherously buried barbs, was a popular and critical success. L.'s real breakthrough, however, came in 1982 with the novel *Ormens väg på hälleberget* (*Way of a Serpent*, 1990), a dark and powerful tale from the author's native Västerbotten. Set in the 19th c., it tells of abject poverty, ruthless exploitation, and power abuse, as the widow Thea is forced to pay her debts to the local merchant with her body, a practice her daughter inherits when Thea is worn out and no longer able to please. What raises the story to the level of great literature is L.'s highly stylized prose, a mixture of dialect and biblical and archaic turns of phrase. The effect of this style is frequently humorous in a manner that only heightens the pathos of this Job-like lamentation questioning the righteousness of the Lord. Ian Hinchliffe (b. 1952) has pointed out that "In the well-weighed words of this single slender novel L. expresses the pietism, the stoicism and melancholy which is the northern soul." The collection of short stories *Merabs skönhet* (1983; *Merab's Beauty and Other Stories*, 1990) is also set in the Arctic North and exemplifies a happy phenomenon in the Swedish literature of the 1980s: the noticeable return of fabulation, the joy of telling a good or suspenseful tale. The eleven stories are set in L.'s native province and he continues to employ—and to elaborate on—its expressive dialect. L. would again tap the resources of this Arctic region in the novel *Ljuset* (1987; the light), in which the fantastic and the darkly chaotic, pathos, and bizarre humour form a disturbing union. L. was brought up in a pietistic religious environment; as an adult he converted to Catholicism. It may not be farfetched to read into this strange story a plea for a divine order beyond human anarchy.

The Bible was one of L.'s earliest encounters with literature. In *Bat Seba* he retells the Old Testament legend of King David and Bathsheba, the beautiful wife of the warrior Uriah. The King uses his power to make her his own. The novel is the story of unbridled sensuality, possession, violence, cruelty, and tenderness. David, the Lord's Anointed, commits a number of crimes because of his love; in turn he becomes more helpless as the power of her love grows and constitutes a threat to his holiness. In an ironic reversal of roles she uses the same unscrupulous means as the king to gain her ends to secure ultimately the throne for her son Solomon. The novel can be read on several different levels, as an allegory of male versus female, as a study in the uses and abuses of power, and—as is often the case with L.'s stories—as a tale about the human being's relationship with the divine or as an exploration of the nature of God.

L. is one of the most widely translated of contemporary Swedish writers. His command of the resources of language is impressive; he is a natural storyteller, whose fantasy at times is reminiscent of the MAGIC REALISM of Latin American writers. His best stories, often set in the times of history, myth, and legend, are ultimately existential and metaphysical explorations of the human condition.

FURTHER WORKS: *Plåtsax, hjärtats instrument* (1965); *Dikter från Vimmerby* (1970); *Övriga frågor* (1973); *Hallen* (1975); *Brännvinsfursten* (1979); *Markus* (1982); *Legender* (1986); *Kärleksguden Frö* (1988); *Till sanningens lov* (1991)

BIBLIOGRAPHY: special T. L. issue, *SBR, Supplement* (1985); Algulin, I., *A History of Swedish Literature* (1989): 274–75

—LARS G. WARME

LINDSAY, Vachel

American poet, b. 10 Nov. 1879, Springfield, Ill.; d. 5 Dec. 1931, Springfield, Ill.

L. considered it significant that at birth his face had been covered by a "prophet's veil" (a caul), and indeed he was destined to become a preaching poet. Born into a family of Disciples of Christ, an evangelical sect, he grew up in a city permeated with memories of Lincoln. His primary interests at Hiram College (1897–1900) were oratory and art; but his odd study habits at the Art Institute of Chicago (1900–1903) and as an intermittent apprentice of the painter Robert Henri in New York (1904–8) lengthened the period of casting about for a career. His mother, opposed to his writing poetry, created a tension that delayed his marrying until 1925, and much of his work shows the effect of an unhealthy loneliness. On walking tours through America he sought to convince listeners of the value of beauty.

His first important poem, "General William Booth Enters into Heaven," was published in *Poetry* magazine in 1913, and launched the new poetry movement more than two decades after Walt Whitman's death. Like many of his later poems, it was elaborately

Vachel Lindsay

scored for musical instruments, and was set (in L.'s words) "to the tune that is not a tune, but a speech, a refrain used most frequently in the meetings of the [Salvation] Army on any public square to this day." He became a platform poet, declaiming his works at universities and in small towns.

L. wrote several extraordinary poems: "The Eagle That Is Forgotten" (1913), about Peter Altgeld, the reformist Democratic governor of Illinois (1893–97), who after his defeat for reelection became a symbol of martyred liberalism; "The Congo" (1914), a memorial to a Disciple missionary in Africa, which L. subtitled "A Study of the Negro Race"; "Bryan, Bryan, Bryan, Bryan" (1918), about the presidential election campaign of 1896 as seen by an adolescent; and "Abraham Lincoln Walks at Midnight" (1914), a sentimental favorite with the public. To explain his private symbolism, he made a "Map of the Universe," a drawing depicting throne mountains, fallen palaces, and so forth that, as one biographer has noted, was more a map of L.'s mind, theology, theodicy, and cosmology than of the universe. During the 1920s he became increasingly interested in Chinese hieroglyphics (i.e., pictographs), motion pictures, and Jeffersonian democracy.

The writings of H. L. MENCKEN and Sinclair LEWIS, which set the tone for the last decade of L.'s life, were partly responsible for the loss of reader interest in his exuberant, open poetry. Yet L. himself was responsible for many of his problems. He could not evaluate his own work justly, with detachment, and wrote far too much; he was never clear in his own mind just what poetry should do, or what his message was; he remained defiantly ignorant of the technical devices whereby poetry can release meaning with power. He was, nevertheless, far more than a poet of the Jazz Age (a tag that he repudiated). His bardic powers, as well as his vision of the future (*The Golden Book of Springfield*, 1920), confirm YEATS's judgment that this was a poet.

More than half a century has elapsed since L.'s paranoia led to suicide (by drinking Lysol). Current misconceptions about his character and poetical talents may be traced back to Edgar Lee MASTERS's biography, published shortly after L.'s death, which praised the strongly rhythmical poems at the expense of practically everything else L. wrote. New studies of the final works in his canon, and of the uncompleted manuscripts that he left behind, indicate that he was testing original ideas on religion, music, and Americanism. His writings continue to resist easy categorization. Moreover, his pessimism about this country's direction in the 1920s needs to be stressed; he believed, as the critic Ann Massa has written, in our "perpetual need of Lincolns." In the 1980s such a view may not be dismissed as naïve; like many other opinions held by L., it repays closer examination.

FURTHER WORKS: *The Tramp's Excuse and Other Poems* (1909); *Rhymes to Be Traded for Bread* (1912); *General William Booth Enters into Heaven and Other Poems* (1913); *Adventures While Preaching the Gospel of Beauty* (1914); *The Congo and Other Poems* (1914); *The Art of the Moving Picture* (1915); *A Handy Guide for Beggars* (1916); *The Chinese Nightingale and Other Poems* (1917); *The Golden Whales of California and Other Rhymes in the American Language* (1920); *Going-to-the-Sun* (1923); *Going-to-the-Stars* (1926); *The Candle in the Cabin: A Weaving Together of Script and Singing* (1926); *The Litany of Washington Street* (1929); *Every Soul Is a Circus* (1929); *Letters of V. L. to A. Joseph Armstrong* (1940)

BIBLIOGRAPHY: Masters, E. L., *V. L.: A Poet in America* (1935); Harris, M., *City of Discontent* (1952); Ruggles, E., *The West-Going Heart* (1959); Massa, A., *V. L.: Fieldworker for the American Dream* (1970); McInerny, D. Q., "V. L.: A Reappraisal," and Chénetier, M., "V. L.'s American Mythocracy and Some Unpublished Sources," in Hallwas J. E., and D. J. Reader, eds., *The Vision of This Land: Studies of V. L., Edgar Lee Masters, and Carl Sandburg* (1976): 29-54

—HAROLD OREL

LINNA, Väinö

Finnish novelist, b. 20 Dec. 1920, Urjala; d. 21 April 1992, Kangsala

L. was the seventh child (of ten) of a country butcher, a man known in his home region for his trusting nature and honesty; these qualities may have led to the collapse of the family finances before the father's death in 1927. After attending public school for six years, L. did odd jobs, was briefly employed as a farmhand and lumberjack, and in 1938 set out for the textile mills of Tampere, capital of L.'s native province of Häme. There he spent his spare time in libraries, discovering, among other things, Jaroslav HAŠEK'S *The Good Soldier Švejk*. Drafted in April 1940, directly after Finland's "Winter War," L. was sent to noncommissioned officers' school, and fought in the "Continuation War" with the Soviet

Union until the spring of 1943, when he was posted back to Finland as an instructor.

Following the armistice of September 1944 L. returned to Tampere and continued work in the mills until 1955; however, he had long since decided to become a writer, and in 1947 his novel, *Päämäärä* (the goal) was published. The book was a thinly disguised autobiography. Although overburdened with philosophical reflections, *Päämäärä* was treated kindly by critics, one saying that L. was a diamond in the rough. *Musta rakkaus* (1948; black love), a tale of jealousy and murder set in Tampere, revealed a marked increase in L.'s ability to portray scenes he knew. In 1957 L. brought out a much shortened version of the melodramatic narrative, but has subsequently refused to allow a new printing.

The productivity of the immediate postwar years (in which L. also wrote two unpublished volumes of verse) was succeeded by a period of depression; L. embarked upon a new novel, variously called "The Messiah" or "The Lonely One," about a tubercular factory clerk, but the project was interrupted by an emotional crisis, and was never completed: L. was unwilling to let the torso appear as a "miniature novel."

L. then began a broad epic about the war of 1941–44; the result was *Tuntematon sotilas* (1954; *The Unknown Soldier*, 1957), and L. suddenly became the most discussed author in Finland. The book follows a single platoon from the summer offensive of 1941 to the capture of Petrozavodsk on Lake Onega, then to the trench warfare in the Svir bridgehead in 1942 and 1943, and to the bloody retreat of 1944. Like Zola in *The Debacle*, L. tries to see the war from the viewpoint of the enlisted man and (much less obviously than Zola) to indicate the larger movements of history; yet the realism of his soldiers' language and behavior, his sometimes biting portraits of individual officers, and an isolated episode about the immorality of a member of the women's auxiliary corps, enraged those Finns who still were determined to regard their army in an idealized light. Shortly, however, thanks in part to Edvin Laine's film version of 1955, *Tuntematon sotilas* became not only a best seller but a national classic: its characters (who speak a variety of Finnish dialects) were familiar to the general public, and its patriotism was no longer impugned but, rather, extolled by readers who saw the novel as an encomium of the Finnish soldier's humor, independence, and unostentatious heroism. There is no question about its popular appeal. Nonetheless, the novel is in fact a complex work of art, which admits a variety of interpretations, not least on the basis of L.'s skillful interpolation of phrases from J. L. Runeberg's (1804–1877) two-part patriotic poem cycle *The Songs of Ensign Stål*. Paradoxically, L. can be taken as a representative of the very Runebergian stoicism and dutifulness he mocks, and which he has disparaged in essays and addresses; unintentionally, he has become Runeberg's substitute as a flatterer of the national ego.

L.'s other masterpiece is the trilogy *Täällä pohjantähden alla* (1959–62; here beneath the north star), the account of a family and its neighbors in a south Finnish hamlet from the 1880s until the middle 1940s. A farm laborer, Jussi Koskela, drains a bog on property belonging to the local parsonage, and comes to regard the land as his own; Jussi's son, Akseli—resentful when a new pastor, bullied by his wife, claims the fields—enters the socialist movement and becomes an officer in the Red Army during Finland's civil war of 1918. Imprisoned and almost executed during the reprisals of the victorious Whites, Akseli eventually buys the plot during the agricultural reforms of the 1920s and acquires a certain prosperity while losing his interest in politics. Of his sons, two are killed in the Winter War, and a third—a main figure in *Tuntematon sotilas*—falls in the retreat of 1944. As the suite ends, Akseli's surviving son is a well-placed farmer, the proud owner of a tractor.

Again, L. has shown himself to be a traditionalist: in his choice of the family novel as his form (used by Zacharias Topelius [1818–1898] for a widely read novella cycle about Finland's history), in his old-fashioned linear narration, in his wealth of memorable characters, in his great set pieces (for example, a roofing bee, the expulsion of a tenant farmer in midwinter, the execution of Red prisoners in 1918, the kidnapping of a Socialist politician by a band of would-be fascists in the early 1930s). Tightly controlling his cast of characters and often viewing them with affectionate humor, L. resembles such masters of the 19th-c. novel as Dickens, Theodor Fontane, and Nikolay Leskov; like L.'s war novel, his trilogy has won a broad readership both because many families in contemporary Finland can see their pasts in it, and because its technique (which has been scorned by some sophisticated critics) places no apparent difficulties in the audience's way. Yet there is much more here than meets the eye: a careful structure, a dialogue filled with hidden subtleties (although he has never written a play, L. has been called a born dramatist), and a constant tension between the author's generous humanism and the ultimate pessimism of his outlook. Save for a volume of essays, *Oheisia* (1967; appended materials), L. has been silent since the trilogy's completion, observing, with characteristic honesty, that he has delivered his message and has nothing more to say.

Aided by the brilliant translations into Swedish of N.-B. Stormbom (L.'s biographer), L.'s work has entered the general literary heritage of the North; it has also attained some popularity in eastern Europe, despite L.'s undoctrinaire political and social attitudes. He is as yet too little known in the English-speaking world.

BIBLIOGRAPHY: Laitinen, K., "V. L. and Veijo Meri: Two Aspects of War," *BA*, 36 (1962): 365–67; Varpio, Y., "V. L.: A Classic in His Own Time," *BF*, 11 (1977): 192–97; Niemi, J., "V. L.: Introduction to 'The Strike,'" *BF*, 14 (1980): 139–45

—GEORGE C. SCHOOLFIELD

LINS DO RÊGO, José

See Rêgo, José Lins do

LIPKIN, Semyon Izrailevich

Russian poet, prose writer, and translator, b. 6 Nov. 1911, Odessa

For decades highly regarded for his translations of central Asian and Caucasian poetry, it was not until the 1980s that L. became known as a major poet in his own right. Born in Odessa in 1911, L. graduated from the Moscow Institute of Engineering and Economics in 1937. While a student in Moscow, L. became acquainted with the poet Osip MANDELSTAM, an association that profoundly affected the beginning poet. L., who began to publish his verse in the late 1920s, embarked on his distinguished career as verse translator in the mid-1930s, a decision in part motivated by his refusal to subject his poetry to the political demands on literature. L. continued to write poetry, but published very little. L.'s experiences as a soldier in World War II are reflected in the prose book of

sketches *Stalingradskii Korabl'* (1943; the ship of Stalingrad) and in numerous poems. Three collections of L.'s verse appeared between 1967 and 1977, but they offered a highly selective and skewed sampling of the poet's work. L.'s courageous decision to contribute six poems to the literary almanac *Metropol'* (1979; *Metropol*, 1982) changed the course of what had been a relatively prosperous career. The publication of the almanac abroad resulted in official censure for most contributors, which included a ban on their works. L., his wife Inna LISNYANSKAYA, and Vassily AKSYONOV resigned from the Union of Writers to protest the expulsion of two younger colleagues. For L., who had been a member of the Union since 1934, this was not merely a symbolic gesture. Freed from the constraints of Soviet censorship, L. prepared a large volume of poetry that was published in the West. *Volia* (1981; freedom) collected verse written over a period of more than forty years and showed L. to be an important poet. L.'s next major publication abroad, *Kochevoi ogon'* (1984; a nomadic flame), also presents some early verse, but the emphasis is on poems written after *Volia*. In addition to these two volumes, L. published three books of prose, and his work appeared in all the major émigré periodicals. The advent of glasnost in the U.S.S.R. paved the way for L.'s reinstatement in the Union of Writers. Since 1987 L.'s work has been published by most of the leading soviet journals, including *Novyi Mir, Druzhba Narodov, Ogonek,* and *Iunost'*. The literary rehabilitation of the *Metropol* group brought L. numerous public tributes for his staunch defense of the almanac.

L.'s close association as translator for the non-Russian nationalities of the U.S.S.R. made him acutely aware of the injustices perpetrated on these peoples, including the forced migration of entire ethnic groups. Consequently, L.'s *Volia* is deeply rooted in history and religion, both taboo subjects for Soviet literature of the time. The role of the lyric persona as indicated by the poem "Ochevidets" (eyewitness) is to record and preserve the memory of the oppressed. The cycle of narrative poems *Vozhd' i plemia* (leader and tribe) refers to arrests, murders, and the secret police, all ruthlessly engineered by Stalin and his lackeys. The final poem in the cycle, "Literaturnoe vospominanie" (a literary reminiscence), recounts the degradation of Eduard Bagritsky (1895–1934), L.'s one-time mentor, whose poetic talents were corrupted by politics. Merely the titles of many poems would have prevented publication: "Bogoroditsa" (mother of God) and "Odesskaia sinagoga" (the Odessa synagogue). Given the thematics of L.'s verse, it is not surprising that before the publication of *Volia* only a small circle of friends knew L. as a poet. That circle, however, included Anna AKHMATOVA, who considered L. to be a leading poet of his generation.

L.'s *Kochevoi ogon'*, as the title suggests, highlights his interest in non-Russian themes and imagery. The volume, unlike *Volia*, emphasizes the short lyric over the long narrative poem. The poignant love poem "Est' prelest' gor'kaia v moei sud'be" (there is a bitter delight in my fate) sets the tone for the entire book, since in a larger sense it underscores both the lyric persona's gratitude for the life he has been privileged to live, yet acknowledges the difficult role he has chosen. Although death is a constant in the majority of the poems, the persona seeks solace in his belief in God. The volume closes with the narrative "Viacheslav. Zhizn' peredelkinskaia" (to Vyacheslav: life in Peredelkino), which represents a short history in verse of the writers colony located outside of Moscow. The poet Boris PASTERNAK and his young neighbor Vyacheslav Ivanov are the principal characters, but many others figure. The lyric persona is autobiographical, but not idealized, since he reproaches himself for choosing silence when friendship required action.

The novel *Dekada* (1983; a ten-day festival), L.'s fictionalized portrayal of the deportation of a non-Slavic minority from the Caucasus to Kazakhstan, should be read in conjuction with his poetry. One of the principal characters, the translator Stanislav Borodsky, is obviously modeled on L. The novel recounts the enormous losses, not only of lives, but of an entire culture. For all its sincerity, *Dekada* is not successful as a novel, and the reader wishes that L. would abandon the mask of Borodsky and tell the story without resorting to fiction. L.'s most rewarding prose book is the warm memoir of the writer Vassily Grossman (1905–1964), published as *Stalingrad Vasiliia Grossmana* (1986; Vassily Grossman's Stalingrad). Drawing on his long friendship with Grossman, as well as letters and other documents, L. reconstructs a portrait not only of a friend, but also of an entire era.

L.'s role as eyewitness and chronicler of the fate of culture had been privately acknowledged for over half a century before the publication of *Volia* initiated public recognition of a major talent.

FURTHER WORKS: *Ochevidets* (1967); *Vechnyi den'* (1975); *Tetrad' bytiia* (1977); *Kartiny i golosa* (1986); *Lira* (1989)

BIBLIOGRAPHY: "L.," in Terras, V., ed., *Handbook of Russian Literature* (1985): 255–56; Lowe, D. A., *Russian Writing since 1953: A Critical Survey* (1987), 17: 130–31

—RONALD MEYER

LISNYANSKAYA, Inna

Russian poet and translator, b. 24 June 1928, Baku, U.S.S.R. (now Azerbaijan)

L., who was born in the capital city of Azerbaijan, began to write poetry at the age of ten, although she was not from a literary family. Unbeknownst to her Jewish parents, L. was taken by her grandmother to be christened, an event that profoundly affected the young girl. L. did not attend university, even though she was invited to apply for admission to a literary institute on the merits of her early poems. A published poet in Baku since 1948, L. attracted the attention of Alexander Tvardovsky (1910–1971), the influential editor of the Moscow journal *Novyi Mir*, and in 1957 her poetry began to appear in that and other mainstream publications. L. became a member of the Union of Writers in 1957 and moved to Moscow in 1961, where she resides to the present day. Five volumes of L.'s verse were published from 1957 to 1978. In addition, L. worked as a translator of poetry, principally from Azerbaijan. The official censure of the literary almanac *Metropol* (1979; *Metropol*, 1982), to which L. had contributed seven poems, altered the course of L.'s career in the U.S.S.R. The Metropolians intended to publish an uncensored volume of works, chosen on the basis of artistic principles, rather than ideological criteria. Refused permission to publish the collection in the U.S.S.R., the writers defiantly opted for publication abroad. The majority of the participants suffered public and private harassment, which included a ban on their works, and two young writers were expelled from the Union of Writers. L., together with her common-law husband, Semyon Lipkin, and Vassily AKSYONOV, one of the principal organizers of the almanac, resigned from the Union of Writers in

protest. L. did not publish in the U.S.S.R. until 1988, when the reform policies of Gorbachev paved the way for her reinstatement into the Union. Since that time she has published widely in the leading literary journals and has been publicly acknowledged for her resolute defense of the *Metropol* group and her own artistic independence.

In her "Nechto vrode avtobiografia" (1990; something in the way of an autobiography) L. dismisses her early books as immature, but blames the censorship for the distortion of her talents in the succeeding volumes *Iz pervykh ust* (1966; right from the source) and *Vinogradnyi svet* (1978; grape light). From the beginning, L.'s poetry was marked by a distinctively un-Soviet character, since the primary emphasis is on private and not social concerns. In contrast to the "stadium" poets such as Yevgeny YEVTUSHENKO, whom detractors criticized for actively courting the crowd with political pamphlets in verse, L. has consistently eschewed rhetoric and politics in favor of lyric simplicity and intimacy. Consequently, L. has become a master of the short form, whose predominant stanzaic measure is the quatrain. However, L. does not restrict herself to the familiar territory of Russian women's verse, but invokes such ethical problems as conscience and memory.

During the ten years of nonpublication in the U.S.S.R. that followed the *Metropol* affair, two volumes of L.'s verse appeared in the émigré press: *Dozhdi i zerkala* (1983; rains and mirrors) and *Stikhotvoreniia: na opushke sna* (1984; poems: on the edge of sleep). The first volume, which collects works written over a span of more than fifteen years, reveals the full scope of L.'s poetry, in particular the religiosity that the Soviet censorship had previously found unacceptable. *Stikhotvoreniia*, too, includes poems from as early as 1966, but the vast majority date from the 1980s and unmistakably herald a new poetic voice. Perhaps L.'s enforced silence, as well as the freedom from translation work, provided the impetus. Whatever the cause, *Stikhotvoreniia* is generally considered L.'s most successful book, largely due to the unity in theme and style that is achieved. The volume is a lyrical diary in which the persona records her hopes and tragedies as woman, poet, and citizen.

Firmly grounded in the traditions of Russian lyric poetry, most notably the verse of Anna AKHMATOVA and Marina TSVETAEVA, L.'s work retains its own distinct character. The hallmarks of L.'s style are a conversational diction, a sense of self-irony, and an attention to everyday events or objects, all of which belie the gravity of the lyric persona's anguish and loss.

FURTHER WORKS: *Eto bylo so mnoi* (1957); *Vernost'* (1958); *Ne prosto liubov'* (1963); *Vozdushnyi plast* (1990)

BIBLIOGRAPHY: Heldt, B., "I. L.'s *Stikhotvoreniia: No opushke sna,*" *WLT*, 60, 1 (Winter 1986), 131; Lowe, D. A., *Russian Writing since 1953: A Critical Survey* (1987), 7, 131

—RONALD MEYER

LISPECTOR, Clarice

Brazilian novelist and short-story writer, b. 10 Dec. 1925, Chechelnik, Ukraine; d. 9 Dec. 1977, Rio de Janeiro

L. was born while her family was emigrating from Russia to Brazil. The family settled first in Recife; in 1937 they moved to Rio de Janeiro. A precocious child, she first began to compose stories at the age of six in the hope of seeing them published in the local newspapers. L. entered law school in Rio and took a job as editor at the Agência Nacional, a news agency, and at the newspaper *A noite*. While in Rio, L. came to know Lúcio Cardoso (1913–1968), Adonias Filho (b. 1915), and Cornélio Pena (1896–1958), three of the most innovative and experimental writers of the time and artists who provided L. with the kind of criticism and encouragement she needed. In 1943 L. graduated from Rio's National Faculty of Law, completed her first novel, *Perto do coração selvagem* (1944; close to the savage heart), and married a former classmate. L. and her diplomat husband lived abroad for many years, including a sojourn of eight years spent in Washington, D. C. L. separated from her husband in 1959 and, with the couple's two children, returned that same year to live in Rio de Janeiro, her permanent place of residence until her death.

L. first achieved widespread acclaim with *Laços de família* (1960; *Family Ties*, 1972), a collection of introspective, enigmatic short stories. One of her stories, "Amor" ("Love"), established her as one of the best writers of short narrative in all of Latin America. In it the protagonist, Anna, is jarred out of her sense of security by an unexpected series of epiphanies and crises. Anna then struggles vainly to balance her newly discovered self-awareness with her former unthinking complacency, but, unable to cope with the existential burden of her new, unsettling consciousness, she finally retreats into the false security of her earlier routine existence. Another well-known story in this collection, "O crime do professor de matemática" ("The Crime of the Mathematics Professor"), is a sparely written tale of guilt, obsession, and expiation in which a man attempts to atone for a crime he believes he has committed.

L.'s major breakthrough as a writer, however, came with the publication of *A maçã no escuro* (1961; *The Apple in the Dark*, 1967). Lengthy and complex, this novel is a painstaking study of the birth and abandonment of a human consciousness. Profoundly symbolic and mythic, and written in an intense, lyrical style that recalls that of Djuna BARNES, Virginia WOOLF, and Katherine MANSFIELD, *A maçã no escuro* is really an ironic quest novel, one in which the erratic antihero protagonist ends up by embracing what he initially abjured. Martim, one of the few male central characters in L.'s work, is traced from his first attempt at self-liberation, the commission of a crime, through his rejection of language on the grounds that it constitutes a specious, misleading medium of expression, and, finally, his moving toward a new apprehension of self, one crowned, ironically, by a contrite acceptance of failure and a humble desire for reintegration into society. *A maçã no escuro* advances the idea that while self-awareness is theoretically a worthy goal, it is difficult to recognize, achieve, and maintain. Indeed, it may even prove to be useless or dangerous in a society that stresses conformity in word and deed, unthinking allegiance to orthodoxy, and programmed behavior.

The themes of isolation, frustration, and uncertainty, while paramount in this work, are strongly present in L.'s other fiction as well, most notably in *A paixão segundo G. H.* (1964; *The Passion According to G. H.*, 1988) and *Água viva* (1973; *The Stream of Life*, 1989). These novels not only place L. in the mainstream of 20th-c. Western literature but, as Gregory Rabassa has observed, they also show her to have much in common with such Spanish American masters as Julio CORTÁZAR and Gabriel GARCÍA MÁRQUEZ.

A member of the revisionist school of writers that emerged in Brazil during the years immediately following World War II, L.

was instrumental in leading Brazilian fiction away from the regionalism of the sociologically oriented northeastern novel of the 1930s. Primarily on the strength of L.'s efforts, Brazilian fiction began to move toward a more psychological, intellectual, and aesthetic base, one stressing experimentation in form and aiming thematically at revealing the universal as it is embedded in the local or particular. In one sense a continuation of the "deep regionalism" already initiated by João Guimarães ROSA, L.'s fiction went even further in internalizing experience, in emphasizing the connection between language and being, between one's sense of identity and one's ability to express it verbally. As such, L. is widely regarded as one of the most important and influential writers of fiction in recent Brazilian literature.

FURTHER WORKS: *O lustre* (1945); *A cidade sitiada* (1948); *Alguns contos* (1952); *A legião estrangeira* (1964); *O mistério do coelho pensante* (1967); *A mulher que matou os peixes* (1968); *Uma aprendizagem; ou, O livro dos prazeres* (1969); *Felicidade clandestina: Contos* (1971); *A imitação da rosa* (1973); *Onde estivestes de noite* (1974); *A via crucis do corpo* (1974); *A vida íntima de Laura* (1974); *De corpo inteiro* (1975); *Visão do esplendor: Impressões leves* (1975); *Para não esquecer* (1978); *Quase de verdade* (1978); *Um sopro de vida* (1978); *A hora da estrela* (1978); *The Hour of the Star* (1986); *An Apprenticeship, or, The Book of Delights* (1986); *The Foreign Legion: Stories and Chronicles* (1986); *The Passion According to G. H.* (1988); *Soulstorm: Stories* (1989); *The Stream of Life* (1989); *Near to the Wild Heart* (1990); *Selected Cronicas* (1996)

BIBLIOGRAPHY: Bryan, C. D. B., on *The Apple in the Dark*, *NYTBR*, 3 Sept. 1967: 22–23; Moisés, M., "C. L.: Fiction and Cosmic Vision," *SSF*, 8 (1971): 268–81; Foster, D., and V. Foster, eds., *Modern Latin American Literature* (1975): Vol. 2: 484-91; Fitz, E. E., "C. L. and the Lyrical Novel: A Re-examination of *A maçã no escuro*," *LBR*, 14 (1977): 153–60; Fitz, E. E., "Freedom and Self-Realization: Feminist Characterization in the Fiction of C. L.," *MLS*, 10, 3 (1980): 51–61; Lowe, E., "The Passion according to C. L." (interview), *Review*, No. 24 (1980): 34–37; Patai, D., "C. L. and the Clamor of the Ineffable," *KRQ*, 27 (1980): 133–49; Cixous, H., *Reading with C. L.* (1990)

—EARL E. FITZ

LITERARY CRITICISM

Both the 18th and 19th cs. have been called "the age of criticism": surely the 20th c. deserves this title with a vengeance. Not only has a veritable spate of criticism descended upon us, but criticism has achieved a new self-consciousness, a much greater public status, and has developed, in recent decades, new methods and new evaluations. Criticism, which even in the later 19th c. was of no more than local significance outside of France and England, has made itself heard in countries that before seemed on the periphery of critical thought: in Italy since Benedetto CROCE, in Russia, in Spain, and, last but not least, in the United States. Any survey of 20th c. criticism must take account of this geographical expansion and of the simultaneous revolution of methods. We need some principles of selection among the mountains of printed matter that confront us.

Obviously even today much criticism is being written that is not new in approach: we are surrounded by survivals, leftovers, throwbacks to earlier stages in the history of criticism. Day-to-day book reviewing still mediates between the author and the general public by the well-tried methods of impressionistic description and arbitrary pronouncements of taste. Historical scholarship continues to be of great importance in evaluative criticism. There will always be a place for simple comparisons between literature and life: for the judging of current novels by standards of probability and accuracy of the social situations reflected in them. In all countries there are writers, and often good writers, who practice these methods marked out by 19th c. criticism: impressionistic appreciation, historical explanation, and realistic comparison. Let us recall the charming evocative essays of Virginia WOOLF, or the nostalgic vignettes of the American past by Van Wyck Brooks (1886–1963), or the mass of social criticism of the recent American novel, and allude to the contribution that historical scholarship has been making toward a better understanding of almost all periods and authors in literary history. But at the risk of some injustice an attempt will be made to sketch out what seem to be the new trends in 20th-c. criticism.

First of all, one is struck by the fact that there are certain international movements in criticism that have transcended the boundaries of any one nation, even though they may have originated in a single nation; that from a very wide perspective a large part of 20th-c. criticism shows a remarkable resemblance of aim and method, even where there are no direct historical or cultural relationships. At the same time, one cannot help observing how ingrained and almost insurmountable national characteristics seem to be: how within the very wide range of Western thought, with cross-currents from Russia to the Americas, from Spain to Scandinavia, the individual nations still tenaciously preserve their own traditions in criticism.

The new trends of criticism, of course, also have roots in the past, are not without antecedents, and are not absolutely original. Still, one can distinguish at least seven general trends that have originated in this century: (1) Marxist criticism; (2) psychoanalytic criticism; (3) myth criticism appealing to the findings of cultural anthropology and the speculations of Carl JUNG; (4) linguistic and stylistic criticism; (5) a new organistic formalism; (6) what amounts to a new philosophical criticism inspired by EXISTENTIALISM and kindred world views; and (7) the new STRUCTURALISM and its many variants.

Marxist Criticism

In taste and in theory Marxist criticism has grown out of the realistic criticism of the 19th c. It appeals to a few pronouncements made by Marx and Engels, but as a systematic doctrine it cannot be found before the last decade of the 19th c. In Germany Franz Mehring (1846–1919) and in Russia Georgy Plekhanov (1856–1918) were the first practitioners of Marxist criticism, but they were very unorthodox from the point of view of later Soviet dogma. Mehring combines Marx with Kant and Darwin: he believes, for instance, in a certain autonomy of art and praises Schiller (in a biography: *Schiller*, 1905) for escaping from the sordid realities of his time. In *Lessing-Legende* (1893; Lessing legend) Mehring attacks the academic conceptions of Lessing: he emphasizes his loneliness and opposition to the age of Frederick the Great and analyzes the social conditions of the time. But the method he employs is only vaguely sociological: Mehring had not yet grasped

Marxist dialectics. Similarly, Plekhanov draws on Darwin to argue for an innate sense of beauty, and in his discussion of the "art for art's sake" doctrine, in *Isskustvo i obshchestvennaya zhizn* (1912; *Art and Social Life*, 1953), condemns both aestheticism, as the ineffective revolt of the artist against bourgeois civilization, and purely propagandist art.

Marxist criticism as a coherent theory developed only after the victory of the revolution in Russia; Lenin is unsystematic even in his early papers, such as his attempt to make Tolstoy a representative Russian peasant who had not seen the significance of the proletariat. Marxist criticism crystallized into a coherent system only in the 1920s; but even then, in Russia, there were still a good many vacillations, diverse shadings, and compromises allowed. Leon Trotsky (1879–1940), who in *Literatura i revolyutsia* (1924; *Literature and Revolution*, 1925) sharply attacked formalism, still recognized that art is "a transformation of reality, in accordance with the peculiar laws of art," and Nikolay Bukharin (1888–1938) proposed (at the All-Union Congress of Soviet Writers, 1925) a compromise between Marxism and formalism that would allow formalism at least a subordinate position.

Among the strictly Marxist critics in the 1920s, several groups can be distinguished: those like Vladimir Pereverzev (1882–1968) who were mainly interested in giving a social explanation of literary phenomena in genetic terms; those who saw in Marxism largely a polemical weapon with which they judged all literature according to its immediate usefulness to the Party; and finally subtler critics, such as Alexandr Voronsky (1884–1935), who thought of art largely as "thinking in images," intuitive and unconscious, which only obliquely reflects the processes of society. But by 1932 all debate was suppressed; a uniform creed was devised and imposed and all the later history of Marxist criticism in Russia is really a history of the Party line and its sinuosities.

The term "SOCIALIST REALISM" applies to the loose overall theory that asks the writer, on the one hand, to reproduce reality correctly, accurately, to be a realist in the sense of depicting contemporary society with an insight into its structure; and on the other hand, to be a socialist realist, which in practice means that he is not to reproduce reality accurately, but use his art to spread socialism—that is, communism, the Party spirit, and the Party line.

Andrey Zhdanov (1892–1948) proclaimed that Soviet literature cannot be content with "reflecting" or truthfully reporting reality. It must be "instrumental in the ideological molding of the working masses in the spirit of socialism," advice that fitted Stalin's often-quoted saying that writers are "engineers of the human soul." Literature is thus frankly didactic and even idealizing, in the sense that it should show us life not as it is but as it ought to be. Good Marxist theorists understand that art operates with characters and images, actions and feelings. They focus on the concept of type as the bridge between realism and idealization. Type does not mean simply the average, the representative, but also the ideal type, the model, or simply the hero whom the reader is supposed to imitate and follow in actual life.

Georgy Malenkov, then the premier, proclaimed in a speech delivered on October 5, 1952, the "typical, to be the basic sphere of the manifestation of Party spirit in art. The problem of typicalness is always a political problem." The typical allows any and every manipulation of reality that serves the purposes of the Party: one can produce in Russia a simply cartoonlike art, almost in the manner of fairy tales, glorifying the Soviet man, or one can satirize the Russian bourgeoisie and its leftovers. Criticism is almost entirely criticism of the novel and the drama, criticism of characters and types. Authors such as Ilya EHRENBURG and Alexandr FADEEV, however orthodox in their ideology, are taken to task for not depicting reality correctly—for example, for not assigning sufficient weight to the Party or for not depicting certain characters favorably enough. Soviet criticism, especially since World War II, is, besides, highly nationalistic and provincial: foreign influences are minimized or ignored and "comparative literature" was long a blacklisted subject. The general level of artistic and intellectual standards in criticism is extremely low; even the insights of Marxism into social processes and economic motivation are hardly used. Criticism has become an organ of Party discipline.

Marxism spread abroad, especially in the 1920s, and found adherents and followers in most nations. In the United States, V. F. Calverton (1900–1940) and Granville Hicks (1901–1982) were early adherents. Hicks made a systematic though rather innocuous reinterpretation of the history of American literature from a Marxist point of view in *The Great Tradition* (1928), and Bernard Smith (b. 1906) wrote a history of American criticism, *Forces in American Criticism* (1939). The actual Marxist movement in American literary criticism was quite short-lived, but the influence of Marxist ideas extends far beyond the strict Party line writers. It is visible in certain stages of the development of Edmund WILSON and Kenneth Burke (b. 1897), for instance. Recently, more sophisticated versions of Marxism have been propounded in the U.S. Fredric Jameson's (b. 1934) *Marxism and Form* (1971) reports knowledgeably on the German Marxists, on György LUKÁCS, and on Jean-Paul SARTRE, and tries to find a bridge between Marxism and structuralism.

In England Christopher Caudwell (pseud. of Christopher St. John Sprigg, 1907–1937), who was killed in the Spanish Civil War, wrote the outstanding Marxist book *Illusion and Reality* (1937), which draws also on anthropology and psychoanalysis to diagnose the decay of individualistic civilization and the death of false bourgeois freedom. Marxist criticism revived after World War II. The many books by Raymond Williams (b. 1921), such as *Culture and Society* 1750–1950 (1958), *The Long Revolution* (1961), and *The Country and the City* (1973), are studies that use literature as documentation for social history seen in terms of the class struggle. More recently, in *Marxism and Literature* (1977), Williams has argued for a version of Marxism that would give up its determinism, the whole assumption that literature reflects reality passively, in favor of an emphasis on human creativity and self-creation. One wonders what remains of Marxism except the hatred for capitalism.

In France the influence of Marxism has been felt even more widely even on thinkers and critics such as SARTRE and Roland BARTHES, who cannot be described as orthodox Marxists. A variation of Marxist criticism was advocated by Lucien Goldmann (1913–1970), who was very close to the young Lukács. He attempted to construe "homologies" rather than prove strict causal relationships between social groups and literary attitudes. In *Le Dieu caché* (1956; *The Hidden God*, 1964) Goldmann linked Racinian tragedy and Pascal's tragic vision with the decay of the *noblesse de robe*, the nobility of lawyers and magistrates deprived of power by the absolute monarchy of Louis XIV. The tragic vision of Jansenism is considered a decisive step beyond the rationalism of Descartes and the empiricism of Hume to the critical philosophy of Kant and the dialectics of Hegel and Marx. In *Pour une sociologie du roman* (1964; *Towards a Sociology of the Novel*, 1975) Goldmann traced the "homology" between the development of 20th-c. capitalism and the novels of André MALRAUX.

Several influential new versions of Marxism applied to literature emerged in the last decades. Roger Garaudy's (b. 1913) *D'un réalisme sans rivages* (1963; of a realism without shores), praised by Louis ARAGON, argued for replacing the strict requirements of Socialist Realism by a wider conception that would allow the most diverse methods of art as long as the commitment to communism is kept. A new twist to Marxist theory was given by Pierre Macherey (dates n.a.) in *Pour une théorie de la production littéraire* (1970; *A Theory of Literary Production*, 1978). Macherey rejects the neo-Hegelian assumptions of Lukács and suggests that the ideology of a work should be defined rather by its silences, gaps, and absences. The work of art is always incomplete, irregular, decentered, contradictory, and the critic's task is to uncover these inner conflicts.

In Italy, Antonio Gramsci (1891–1937), one of the founders of the Italian Communist Party who spent the last eleven years of his life in a Fascist jail, is revered as the father of Marxist criticism. He was largely a political ideologist, but in his literary studies, collected in *Letteratura e vita nazionale* (1950; literature and national life), he tried to combine a Marxist approach with many motifs derived from the aesthetics of Croce and Francesco De Sanctis (1817–1883). The strange combination of Marxism and Croceanism is his legacy to many recent Italian critics who try to preserve the main doctrines of Croce while abandoning their idealistic basis for dialectical materialism. This is true particularly of Luigi Russo (1892–1962) and the learned literary historian Natalino Sapegno (b. 1901). Quite differently did Galvano della Volpe (1895–1968) attempt to build bridges from Marxism to the most recent semantics. His influential *Critica del gusto* (1960; *Critique of Taste*, 1978), supplemented by many erudite writings on the history of criticism, argues against the whole romantic tradition of imagination and image for an ultimately highly rationalistic reading of literature as truth and "social truth."

In Germany, Marxist criticism was reformulated in the most original ways, in combinations with many other motifs of thought. Marx's early writings, published from manuscripts only in 1935, centering on the concept of alienation, attracted the most attention. The new Marxists analyzed and debated mainly Western modernist literature and rejected the Soviet dogma of Socialist Realism. Walter BENJAMIN is usually considered a Marxist, although most of his writings on literature predate his conversion to Marxism. He started with erudite works on German romantic criticism and German Baroque tragedy. *Der Ursprung des deutschen Trauerspiels* (1928; *The Origin of German Tragic Drama*, 1977) is, however, deceptively named: instead of the origins of the German tragedy, it studies rather what Benjamin calls the "play of lament" from Shakespeare to the "fate" drama of the German romantics, emphasizing German Baroque tragedy. A new genre, different from tragedy, is defined and its method, allegory, defended. Some of Benjamin's early writings are inspired by a mystical conception of language. An original language to which all languages can be reduced is implied in his essay "Die Aufgabe des Übersetzers" (1923; "The Task of the Translator," 1968). A lengthy and difficult essay, *Goethes "Wahlverwandtschaften"* (1924–25; Goethe's *Elective Affinities*) interprets the death of the heroine, Ottilie, as mythic sacrifice. It was not until 1925 that Benjamin embraced Marxism. His later work centered on the figure of Baudelaire, who becomes for Benjamin the spokesman of the progressive alienation of man in the 19th c. With him the work of art loses its "halo" (*die Aura*) and becomes a commodity, a process described in a famous essay, "Das Kunstwerk im Zeitalter seiner technischen Reproduzierbarkeit" (1936; "The Work of Art in the Age of Mechanical Reproduction,"

1968). The fact that works of art can be reproduced freely and thus lose their uniqueness is welcomed as a sign of democratization but also mourned as presaging the imminent death of literature. But other essays, even of his Marxist stage, are only loosely related to his passionate commitment. The cycle of PROUST's novels is worked into the general scheme of the decay of the halo. But KAFKA is seen as an inventor of parables who combines the "greatest mysteriousness with the greatest simplicity." He harks back to a prehistoric world of German folklore. The famous essay "Der Erzähler: Betrachtungen zum Werk Nikolai Lesskows" (1936; "The Storyteller: Reflections on the Work of Nikolai Leskov," 1968) sketches a history of fiction in social terms, contrasting the storyteller with the novelist, the world of artisans with that of the bourgeoisie. Benjamin was one of the earliest expounders of Bertolt BRECHT and wrote perceptively on Karl KRAUS, but one can hardly speak of a coherent Marxist aesthetic.

Theodor W. ADORNO, who revived the forgotten Benjamin, was mainly a sociologist, philosopher, and theorist of modern music. But his literary criticism—*Prismen* (1955; *Prisms*, 1967), *Noten zur Literatur* (4 vols., 1958–78; *Notes on Literature*, 2 vols., 1991-92)—and *Ästhetische Theorie* (1970; aesthetic theory) show the same synthesis of Marxism, leftist Hegelianism, Freudianism, and a modern sensibility acutely conscious of the crisis of civilization, which constitute the appeal of much of the apocalyptic writings of Marxist prophets of the doom of Western civilization. In Adorno's view, the work of art criticizes reality by the very contradiction between image and external reality.

But by far the most outstanding Marxist critic was György Lukács, not only because he had an extensive knowledge of European literatures and wrote mainly in German (although a Hungarian by birth), but because of the quality and quantity of his production. Lukács began to publish before his conversion to Marxism around 1918: a book in Hungarian on modern drama; a series of sensitive essays, *Die Seele und die Formen* (1911; *Soul and Form*, 1974), and *Die Theorie des Romans* (written 1915, pub. 1920; *The Theory of the Novel*, 1971), which construes a dialectic of literary genres very much in Hegelian terms in which category and history are intrinsically connected. Lukács conceived the novel as reflecting the rise of capitalism, away from the totality of being into social and personal fragmentation. Nostalgically, the modern novel is contrasted with the ancient epic, the totality of life that today no longer exists. The book, written in a precious style, has had, with its emphasis on modern irony and the questing hero, a wide influence and is, in many respects, Lukács's best work anchored in the German aesthetic tradition. Lukács wrote many books after his conversion to Marxism occurred, including numerous political works. Volumes such as *Goethe and seine Zeit* (1947; *Goethe and His Age*, 1969), *Essays über den Realismus* (1948; essays on realism), *Der russische Realismus in der Weltliteratur* (1949; Russian realism in world literature), *Deutsche Realisten des 19. Jahrhunderts* (1951; German realists of the 19th century), and *Der historische Roman* (1955; *The Historical Novel*, 1962) combine a thorough grasp of dialectical materialism and its sources in Hegel with a real knowledge of the main German classics, considerable argumentative skill, and frequent insights into issues that are not purely political. Lukács, in his exposition of the aesthetics of Marx and Engels, manages to approximate it closely to the main tenets of German classicism, with a strong emphasis on what he calls "the great realism." Lukács tries to reinterpret German classicism as a continuation of the Enlightenment and to trace the destruction of Reason through the 19th c. The results often violate a much more complex reality, but few could deny the illuminative value of seeing Goethe and Schiller, Hölderlin and Heine through the eyes of a consistent Marxist who always looks for progressive elements and emphasizes their social implications.

The writings of Lukács preceding his return from Russia to Hungary in 1945 must be preferred: later he came under strong attack for lack of Marxist orthodoxy, and for a time conformed and indulged in purely "Cold War" polemics against the West, particularly in *Die Zerstörung der Vernunft* (1954; *The Destruction of Reason*, 1981), where Nietzsche and even the philosopher Wilhelm Dilthey (1833–1911) are made out to be protofascists. In 1956 Lukács was for a short time Minister of Education in the Nagy government and, after the suppression of the Hungarian revolt, was deported to Romania. But he was allowed to return after a few months, and, in retirement, wrote the large-scale *Die Eigenart des Ästhetischen* (2 vols., 1963; the specific nature of the aesthetic). It combined the main theses of realism—literature as the reflection of reality—with arguments for the specificity of art, an almost Aristotelian emphasis on catharsis, and an incongruous reliance on Pavlovian behaviorist signal systems.

In the satellite countries, Marxism has been imposed as a general creed. It had its early adherents before the Communist takeover, for example, the Czech Bedřich Václavek (1897–1943), a victim of the Nazi terror, who combined the commitment to Marxism with a passionate defense of modernism condemned by Lukács and official Russian literary politics. More recently, there have been other Marxist critics; in Poland, to mention only one, Henryk Markiewicz (b. 1922), and in Yugoslavia the revered Croat novelist and poet Miroslav KRLEŽA; within the framework of the Marxist scheme such writers have cultivated acute and sensitive literary criticism. Marxism in criticism has become a genuinely international movement.

Psychoanalytic Criticism

Marxism is often at its best when it serves as a device to expose the latent social and ideological implications of a work of art. Psychoanalysis serves, with its very different individualistic and irrationalistic assumptions, the same general purpose: a reading of literature behind its ostensive façade; an unmasking. FREUD himself suggested the leading motifs of psychoanalytical criticism. The artist is a neurotic who by his creative work keeps himself from a crack-up, yet also from any real cure. The poet is a daydreamer who publishes his fantasies and is thus strangely socially validated. These fantasies are to be sought in childhood experiences and complexes, and can be found symbolized in dreams, in myths and fairy tales, and even in jokes. Literature thus contains a rich storehouse of evidence for man's subconscious life, and it is no accident that Freud drew the term Oedipus complex from Sophocles' play, or interpreted *Hamlet* and *The Brothers Karamazov* as allegories of incestual love and hatred.

But in Freud the literary interest is only peripheral, and he himself always recognized that psychoanalysis does not solve the problems of art. His followers, however, have applied his methods systematically to all literature: *Imago* (1912–38) was the organ devoted to these studies, and among Freud's close followers Wilhelm Stekel (1888–1942), Otto Rank (1884–1929), Hanns Sachs (1884–1939), and others demonstrated the theories on an enormous variety of materials. Rank was interested in the interpretation of myths and fairy tales and widened the original, purely individualistic view of literature in the study of the subconscious implications in a work of art, the subconscious drives of a fictional figure, or those to be found in the biography of an author. Literary historians soon profited from psychoanalysis; for example, in 1908 Otokar Fischer (1883–1938) analyzed the dreams of the title character of Gottfried Keller's (1819–1890) *Green Henry.*

Freudian psychoanalysis spread slowly around the world. An English physician, Ernest Jones (1879–1958), who was later to write a comprehensive study of the master, was the first to give "The Oedipus Complex as an Explanation of Hamlet's Mystery" (in *The American Journal of Psychology,* 1910) and developed this thesis in *Essays in Applied Psychoanalysis* (1923) and again in *Hamlet and Oedipus* (1949). An American, Frederick Prescott (1871–1957)—whose series of articles, "Poetry and Dreams," dates back to 1912—in his study *The Poetic Mind* (1922) combined psychoanalytic insights into the nature of dreams with a highly romantic concept of the poetic process. In the United States Freudianism penetrated into strictly literary criticism after World War I. Conrad AIKEN, in *Scepticisms* (1919), was an early practitioner, and there is now a mass of psychoanalytical criticism that is not orthodox Freudian but employs the methods of psychoanalysis only occasionally and often loosely: for instance, Kenneth Burke, or Edmund Wilson, who, in the title essay of *The Wound and the Bow* (1941) uses the Philoctetes legend as an allegory for the artist's compensation for his wound; or Joseph Wood Krutch (1893–1970) with his psychoanalytical interpretation of so obvious a subject as Edgar Allan Poe. Lionel TRILLING, although deeply interested in psychoanalysis, voiced many serious reservations about this method of interpretation.

Psychoanalytical interpretations flourish in biography, not necessarily of literary figures. Much of what has been written on historical figures seems completely unverifiable but when handled with subtlety as, for example, in Leon Edel's (1907–1997) *The Life of Henry James* (5 vols., 1953–72), it can provide insights not only into psychic conflicts but into motivation and choice of themes. Another literary critic with psychoanalytical assumptions, Frederick C. Crews (b. 1933), has written monographs on E. M. FORSTER and on Hawthorne (*The Sins of the Fathers,* 1966) but later recanted his allegiance to Freudian methods, although only partially (see *Out of My System,* 1975). A new use of psychoanalysis is being propagated by Norman N. Holland (b. 1927) in such books as *The Dynamics of Literary Response* (1968), *Poems in Persons* (1973), and *Five Readers Reading* (1975). Holland investigates with methods for which he claims scientific accuracy the response of readers, which he interprets in terms of their psychic defense mechanisms, conflicts, and associations.

Technical medical analysts have rarely made an impression in literary circles, since they are usually insensitive to texts and artistic values. An exception is Ernst Kris (1900–1957), whose *Psychoanalytic Explorations in Art* (1952) shows a subtle mind conversant both with clinical method and the aesthetics of art.

Psychoanalytical criticism is in evidence in almost all countries this side of the Iron Curtain. Charles Baudoin (1893–1963), a Swiss, in his book *Le symbole chez Verhaeren* (1924; *Psychoanalysis and Aesthetics,* 1924), was an early exponent, while in France, Charles Mauron (1899–1966) was the most widely recognized adherent of the method. His book *Des métaphores obsédantes au mythe personnel* (1963; obsessive metaphors in personal myth) bears the subtitle "Introduction à la psychocritique" (introduction to psychocriticism). But much of Mauron's psychoanalysis shades off into a study of myth. In England, Herbert READ, in his *In Defence of Shelley* (1936), gave an analytical interpretation of the poet's behavior, somewhat defeating his avowed apologetic intentions, however, by his frank recital of abnormalities; and John Middleton Murry (1889–1957) interpreted D. H. LAWRENCE in terms of the Oedipus complex in a biography, *Son of Woman: The Story of D. H. Lawrence* (1931), in which he oddly vacillates between love and hate for his subject.

Myth Criticism

Out of Freudian analysis grew the Jungian version of the subconscious as a collective subconscious that serves as a kind of reservoir of the "archetypal patterns," the primordial images of mankind. Carl Gustav Jung himself was cautious about applying his philosophy to literature; he made many reservations even when he discussed James JOYCE's *Ulysses* (1922) or Goethe's *Faust.* But, especially in the Anglo-Saxon world, his caution has been thrown to the winds and a whole group of critics have developed "myth criticism," that is to say, they have tried to discover behind all literature the original myths of mankind: the Divine Father, the Earth Mother, the descent into hell, the purgatorial stair, the sacrificial deaths of the gods, etc. Modern anthropology, since Sir James G. Frazer (1854–1941), author of *The Golden Bough* (1890; rev. ed. 1900), with its new expertise on primitive civilizations, their myths and rituals, from all over the world, and the findings of the so-called Cambridge school—Gilbert Murray (1866–1957), Jane Harrison (1850–1928), and others—which studied Greek religion and the sources of Greek drama in myth, have supplied arguments and materials for this view.

In England, Maud Bodkin (1875–1967), in *Archetypal Patterns in Poetry* (1934), studied *The Ancient Mariner* and *The Waste Land,* for instance, as poems of the rebirth pattern; G. Wilson Knight (b. 1897) and Herbert Read, in their varied careers, have used Jungian concepts; C. Day LEWIS explained poetic imagery (*The Poetic Image,* 1947) in terms of the survival of mythical thinking. In the United States "myth criticism" became a great force in the 1950s; it was offered as the alternative to the New Criticism and will have to be discussed in its place.

These three trends—Marxism, psychoanalysis, myth criticism—are genuinely international ones. The resemblance between all the different movements in individual countries, which, by concentrating upon textual interpretation have reacted against 19th-c. positivism, is, however, only a general one: manifest is the preoccupation with the work of art in the modern world, its meaning and the kind of insight or knowledge it provides; and with the refinement of methods of textual analysis, whether it be focused upon details of verbal texture or upon the underlying structure of ideas. To particularize, we have to distinguish between the different national literatures and their diverse developments.

Italy

The earliest systematic reaction against the conventions of late 19th-c. criticism, its antiquarianism, its emphasis on biography, its fragmentation of the work of art, comes from an unexpected quarter—Italy. There Benedetto Croce transformed Italian criticism and, with his *Tesi fondamentali di un'estetica come scienza dell'espressione e linguistica generale* (1902; *Aesthetic as Science of Expression and General Linguistic,* 1909) influenced profoundly the course of criticism almost everywhere in the world. In Germany a school of brilliant scholars in the romance literatures (especially Karl Vossler [1872–1949]) was deeply indebted to him. In England R. G. Collingwood's (1889–1943) *Principles of Art* (1934) could be described as a Crocean aesthetics, and in the United States Joel Elias Spingarn (1875–1939) proclaimed a diluted version of Croce, *The New Criticism*, in 1911.

Croce, in an early booklet, *La critica letteraria* (1894; literary criticism), had attacked the confused state of criticism and had appealed to the model of the great 19th-c. historian of Italian literature Francesco De Sanctis, who then, as a Hegelian, was in eclipse. But only with the founding of the review *La critica* in 1903 did Croce's influence on Italian criticism become decisive. Croce's position, expounded in *Estetica*, had first a negative influence on criticism: his theory of art as intuition, which completely identifies intuition with expression, radically disposed of many traditional problems. Art for Croce is not a physical fact, but purely a matter of mind; it is not pleasure; it is not morality; it is not science, nor is it philosophy. There is no special artistic genius: there is no distinction between form and content. The common view that Croce is a "formalist" or a defender of "art for art's sake" is, however, mistaken. Art does play a role in society and can even be controlled socially, although nothing can touch the artist's original act of intuition. In his practical criticism Croce pays no attention to form in the ordinary sense, but rather to what he calls the "leading sentiment." In Croce's radical monism there is no place for rhetorical categories, for style, for symbol, for genres, even for the distinctions among the arts, since every work of art is a unique, individual intuition-expression. In Croce, the creator, the work, and the auditor are identified. The true reader becomes a poet. Criticism can do little more than remove obstacles to this identification, and pronounce that the identification has been achieved, that a work is art or non-art. Croce's theory hangs together remarkably well and is not open to objections that neglect its basis in an idealistic metaphysics. If we object that Croce neglects medium, or technique, he can answer that "what is external is no longer a work of art."

In the course of his development Croce somewhat modified his position. He came to recognize the universalizing power of art, while still insisting that art does not provide any intellectual knowledge; he retracted the romantic implications of his "expressionism," which seemed to recommend emotion and passion. Rather, he endorsed "classicity," which must not be confused with rhetorical classicism. He also redefined the role of criticism in more intellectual terms: it becomes identified with aesthetics and philosophy. The aim of criticism is the characterization of an individual author, its form is the essay. There is no literary history (except external annals and compendia), since every poet is *sui generis*. Sociological and nationalistic histories of literature as well as the idea of stylistic evolution are dismissed as external.

Croce produced a stream of essays in which he tries to define the true sentiment of each writer discussed and to judge him by his, Croce's, intuitive standard. In his short work *Goethe* (1919; *Goethe*, 1923) he completely divorces man and work from each other. Problems of philosophical truth, biographical correspondence, and intentions are dismissed. Croce can make a selection from Goethe's works and can discuss *Faust* as an album in which Goethe entered his feelings at different times of his life. There is no unity to the two parts. But this is not destructive criticism; rather, Croce argues, it removes an artificially imposed mechanism.

Similarly, in his *La poesia di Dante* (1920; *The Poetry of Dante*, 1922), Croce draws a sharp distinction between the "theological-political romance" and the structure as an abstract scheme, and the

poetry that grows around and in it. In a later work, *La poesia* (2 vols., 1935–36; *Poetry and Literature*, 1981), he elaborates with great clarity his distinction between "poetry" and "literature": while "literature" is writing in its civilizing function, involved in society, "poetry" remains unique, immediately accessible intuition-expression. In many other books of essays Croce judges Italian and foreign poets severely. In *Poesia e non poesia* (1923; *European Literature in the Nineteenth Century*, 1924), for instance, Schiller is labeled a philosophical rhetorician, not a poet. Kleist was merely striving by will power to become a poet; but he did not succeed. Walter Scott is only a hero in a history of commerce. Croce's method is particularly well exemplified in *Ariosto, Shakespeare e Corneille* (1920; *Ariosto, Shakespeare, and Corneille*, 1920). Here, the leading sentiment of Ariosto is defined as a desire for cosmic harmony, that of Corneille as the ideal of free will. In practice, his emphasis on the uniqueness of the work of art leads Croce to highly generalized and rather empty definitions.

Croce's taste is very pronounced: he despises the baroque as a form of ugliness and dislikes modern decadence (Gabriele D'ANNUNZIO), SYMBOLISM, and "pure poetry" à la Paul VALÉRY. In Croce the monistic theory led increasingly to a critical paralysis; his last books are little more than anthologies of passages, with comments on contents and feelings. Croce's great historical learning came increasingly to obscure his criticism. Literary history, psychology, biography, sociology, philosophical interpretation, stylistics, genre criticism—all are ruled out in Croce's scheme. We revert to an intuitionism which, in practice, is hard to distinguish from impressionism—which isolates appealing passages, or anthologizes arbitrarily from an unargued pronouncement of judgments.

Yet Italian criticism of the last fifty years has been almost completely dominated by Croce. Among his followers there is erudition, there is taste, there is judgment, but, on the other hand, we find no systematic analysis of texts, no *Geistesgeschichte*, no stylistics. Several critical individualities stand out, who differ often in emphasis and taste. One of these is Francesco Flora (1891–1962), author of the five-volume *Storia della letteratura italiana* (1940–42; rev. ed., 1947–49; history of Italian literature), a diffuse, florid, enthusiastic history that combines great erudition with a Crocean emphasis on intuition and individuality (but with a taste very different from Croce's). Flora loved the baroque and the decadent and wrote various books that reveal his sympathy for the viewpoint that sees poetry as metaphor and for the modernist trends, such as FUTURISM and HERMETICISM, that Croce deprecated. Flora was a colorful, sensual writer engaged in communicating the pleasure and even the voluptuousness of fine poetry, a master of evocation and description rather than a judicial critic.

Attilio Momigliano (1883–1952), although Crocean in many ways, was a sensitive psychologist and impressionistic critic, a delicate reader and interpreter of poetry, subtle, refined, even morbidly so, cautious and scrupulous. His *Storia della letteratura italiana* (1948; history of Italian literature) is a masterpiece of compression and carefully weighted characterization. Momigliano also wrote on Ariosto and, with increasing devotion, repeatedly on Alessandro Manzoni (1785–1873).

Luigi Russo was an ideologist, a theoretician, a brilliant, although violent polemicist who had great social and moral concerns at heart. As a practical critic he was at his best in his books on Giovanni VERGA and Machiavelli, rather than with poets in a strict sense. His taste tended to the impersonal and realistic. Still, it is surprising that this orthodox Crocean should have been able to turn to Marxism in his last years.

As theorist and historian of criticism, the most outstanding of the Croceans was Mario Fubini (1900–1977), who wrote a long series of studies on the history of Italian criticism and on Italian literature, mainly of the 18th c. and the romantic movement, and worked toward a solidly founded theory of criticism and literature. *Critica e poesia* (1956; criticism and poetry) shows a slow emancipation from orthodox Croceanism, especially in a learned study of the history of genre theories.

These men illustrate the enormous success Croce had in changing Italian academic scholarship. They are all literary historians, of great erudition, who still remain critics vitally concerned with the judgment of literature.

But the earliest Croceans who plunged into literary life proved unfaithful disciples. Giuseppe Antonio Borgese (1882–1952) started his career with a Crocean work, *Storia della critica romantica in Italia* (1905; history of romantic criticism in Italy), in which he propounded the odd thesis that Italian romanticism is good classicism. More and more, however, Borgese became a declamatory apocalyptic prophet of art as the "transfiguration of man and figuration of God," absorbed in such questions as the meaning of Italian literature in general (which was and is to produce a "sacred, eternal, celestial art"). In later years Borgese (he emigrated to the United States in 1931) devoted his energies to projects for a "World Constitution." Nevertheless, his collection of essays *Poetica dell'unità* (1934; poetics of unity) contains fervent polemics against Croce and his denial of a unified history of poetry, and a sketch of the history of criticism. In general, Borgese held a romantic collectivist view of literature in the Hegelian tradition.

Alfredo Gargiulo (1876–1949), an early collaborator in Croce's *La critica*, also moved away from his master's theories. While his book *D'Annunzio* (1921; D'Annunzio) was a Crocean attempt to distinguish between the maker of naturalistic myths and singer of lyrical landscapes and the decadent *poseur, La letteratura italiana nel Novecento* (1930–33; Italian literature in the twentieth century) shows Gargiulo's taste for symbolism and the Italian hermetic poets (Giuseppe UNGARETTI in particular), and many papers on aesthetics, collected in *Scritti di estetica* (1952; writings on aesthetics), argue effectively against several of Croce's central doctrines. Gargiulo developed a theory of "expressive means" that allowed him to reintroduce into aesthetics and literary theory a classification of the arts and concepts of medium and genre dismissed by Croce.

Besides the Crocean tradition, which positively or sometimes polemically at odds with the master has dominated Italian criticism, one can distinguish a second trend that is largely independent of general aesthetics and philosophy and has followed, rather, the tradition of French criticism: the psychological portrait, the close reading and tasting of a text.

Renato Serra (1884–1915), who was killed in World War I, left a few essays, letters, and diaries, which are the earliest examples of what in Italy is called "criticism of the fragment." But Serra was more a moralist, a dreamer and solitary who used criticism as self-examination, than a close student of texts. Textual, stylistic methods were developed in Italy, mainly by Giuseppe de Robertis (1888–1963), who wrote in innumerable, often tiny essays interpreting specific passages of the poets: their sound and sense, associations and implications, which surprisingly enough led him often to final obscurities and gestures toward mysticism.

Among the next generation, Gianfranco Contini (1912–1990) is the best of the close readers. He is linguistically learned and stays away from mysticism. In subject matter his range is wide, writing

as he does on the earliest Italian lyricists as well as on the latest, the most opaque, modernists. Two other linguists who developed new divergent methods of stylistic analysis are Giacomo Devoto (1897–1974) and Antonio Pagliaro (1898–1973).

Somewhat apart stand three critics, all close students of American and English literature: Emilio Cecchi (1884–1966), Mario Praz (1896–1982), and Cesare PAVESE. Cecchi's *Storia della letteratura inglese nel secolo XIX* (1915; history of English literature in the nineteenth century) never progressed beyond the first volume, devoted to the English romantics. Even here he shows his power of evocation and portraiture more in the style of Sainte-Beuve (1804–1869) or Walter Pater (1839–1894) than in the Italian tradition. In his later writings he indulges in a curious sly humor and irony and in personal, often capricious judgments. *Scrittori inglesi e americani* (1946; English and American writers) is a collection of his many essays with an emphasis on what could be called the "dark," irrational, and violent tradition in American and English literature. Cecchi also wrote on many Italian topics as a general essayist.

The starting point of Mario Praz is also English literature. His early book, *Secentismo and marinismo in Inghilterra* (1925; seventeenth-century literary style and Marinism [style of Giambattista Marino, 1569–1625] in England), devoted to Donne and Crashaw, helped to restore the two great English baroque poets to their rightful place. In many other books he studied Italian-English relations (for example, the influence of Machiavelli in England) with acumen and skill. He surveyed English literature in *Storia della letteratura inglese* (1937; history of English literature), which is much more than an excellent textbook. But with *La carne, la morte e il diavolo nella letteratura romantica* (1930; *The Romantic Agony*, 1933) Praz went beyond his specialty to a subtle study of erotic sensibility in all 19th-c. Europe, seen in terms of its sources in the Marquis de Sade and as a part of the general phenomenon of decadence. *La crisi dell'eroe nel romanzo vittoriano* (1952; *The Hero in Eclipse in Victorian Fiction*, 1956) shows a surprising change or broadening of Praz's taste: a sympathy for the idyllic, realistic art of the Biedermeier, which he traces from Dutch genre painting to the novels of Trollope, Thackeray, and George Eliot. Increasingly, in a number of essay collections, Praz tried to use the art of the essayist to define a personal taste and paint his own intellectual portrait. He studies either the psychology of the author, or the sensibility of a time, or the linkage of literature with the plastic arts. He is not so much a day-by-day critic of literature as a scholar-critic, not a theorist but a historian of sensibility and taste.

Pavese, the novelist, as a critic introduced new motifs into Italian literature. Like Cecchi, he was an admirer of American literature, or rather of one strand in it: the mystic, the dark and violent he finds in Melville and Sherwood ANDERSON. But his remarkable diary, *Il mestiere di vivere: Diario* 1935–1950 (1951; *The Burning Brand: Diaries* 1935–1950, 1961), revealed a speculative critic of high order concerned with themes usually neglected in Italian criticism: with myth become figure, with time in the novel, and with pervasive imagery similar to that of G. Wilson Knight in England. Pavese called his ideal "rustic classicism," which seems, finally, a primitivistic and naturalistic view in spite of all its sophistication.

But Pavese stands alone. The direction of recent Italian criticism seems unclear except for two facts: the dominance of Croce and Croceanism has waned, and Marxist criticism has found many recruits.

But Italy is today also full of echoes of the other European movements in criticism and aesthetics. Existentialism had wide philosophical repercussions. At least in Enzo Paci (b. 1911) it found a subtle interpreter of literature—of Novalis, Rilke, Dostoevsky, Valéry, and Thomas MANN—discussed in his *Dall'esistenzialismo al realismo* (1958; from existentialism to realism). French structuralism and more recently semiotics (which goes well beyond literary criticism in its claim to encompass all of man's symbol-making activities) have found many adherents: Cesare Segrè (b. 1928) and Umberto ECO are the outstanding names. Marcello Pagnini (b. 1921), who uses texts from English, excels in structural analyses. Among older critics, Giacomo Debenedetti (1901–1967) has, particularly since his death, emerged as a great figure. His posthumous publications, *Poesia italiana del Novecento* (1974; Italian poetry of the twentieth century), *Verga e il naturalismo* (1976; Verga and naturalism), and *Il romanzo del Novecento* (1971; the twentieth-century novel), have offered support to almost every point of view as he appeals to Henri BERGSON and Freud, Husserl and Marx as his spiritual fathers to arrive at a curiously eclectic but often highly perceptive interpretation of 19th- and 20th-c. literature, not just in Italy. Debenedetti illustrates well the Italian situation: criticism there is buffeted by winds of doctrine from almost all sides: east, west, and north.

France

France, around 1900, was the country with the strongest critical tradition. It could look back to Sainte-Beuve and Hippolyte Taine (1828–1893), who had reestablished the leadership of France in criticism during the latter half of the 19th c. In France the divorce between scholarship and criticism never became so acute as in the other countries, and there was then a flourishing "university criticism" that combined erudition with taste, usually of a conservative kind. Ferdinand Brunetière (1849–1906), a doctrinaire upholder of 17th-c. classicism who also propounded a Darwinian theory of the evolution of genres, Émile Faguet (1847–1916), an extremely versatile commentator on all periods of French literature, and Gustave Lanson (1857–1934), the author of the widely used *Histoire de la littérature française* (1894; history of French literature), were still active and influential in the early 20th c. Besides the historian-critics, the bulk of criticism was impressionist: as a theory, impressionism had been proclaimed by Jules Lemaître (1853–1914) late in the 19th c., but even he, in his later years, embraced a conservative creed that led to his sharp condemnation of Rousseau and all romanticism.

The basically rationalistic, classicist tradition of French criticism continued deep into the 20th c. and had its important revivals. Charles Maurras (1868–1952), the founder of the Action Française, had critical affiliations with the so-called École Romane. He proclaimed Latinity, reason, and conservatism as its standards and condemned the Revolution and romanticism (which strangely enough were conceived as almost identical). Pierre Lasserre (1867–1930), in *Le romantisme français* (1907; French romanticism), attacked romanticism and all its works as a disease due to the "psychopath" Jean-Jacques Rousseau, and (Baron) Ernest Seillière (1866–1955) wrote an unending series of books denouncing romanticism, Germans, and imperialism.

After World War I a purely rationalistic point of view, proclaimed to be particularly French, was restated powerfully in Julien Benda's (1867–1956) *Belphégor* (1919; *Belphégor*, 1929) and in the writings of Henri Massis (1886–1970), who had begun by

attacking Lanson and academic criticism and later wrote *La défense de l'Occident* (1925; *The Defence of the West*, 1927), a strident proclamation of Western, Latin values against everything Northern and Eastern. The widely read, largely journalistic critic Paul Souday (1869–1929) can be classed with these defenders of reason, intellectualism, and art as construction, and haters of everything vague, mystical, sentimental, romantic, symbolic, and irrational. Among more recent critics, Ramon Fernandez (1894–1944) was nearest to the conservative classicism of the Action Française. He has on many points striking affinities with T. S. ELIOT, sharing as he does Eliot's search for objectivity and impersonality. The collection of essays *Messages* (1926; *Messages*, 1927) strongly urges the claim of criticism to yield an "imaginative ontology." The metaphysical problem of being is to be solved in art, although transposed to the plane of imagination. The world of poetry is a world of quality, not a reflection of an author's psyche. Criticism should investigate the philosophical substructure of a work of art and not the biography or psychology of an author or his overt intentions. In an essay on Stendhal, Fernandez shows, for instance, how even so autobiographical an author uses private experiences only as building materials for his books. Unfortunately, Fernandez did not live up to the promise of his early work: in his last books, *Balzac* (1943; Balzac) and *Proust* (1943; Proust), he pursues philosophical themes with some moralistic obtuseness: in Balzac, he argues, intuition, conception, and expression remain unfused. In Proust, there is no way from passive impression to an external world of action, no moral progress.

But clearly the classical, rationalist, and moralist point of view, although important in the academy and in arguments on general culture, lost out to the much more powerful stream of irrationalism that flooded French criticism. One must distinguish among these irrationalisms, however, and must not obscure the strength of the classical tradition in men such as Valéry. One must recognize different strands and chronological groupings. Symbolism might be considered one central critical motif, Bergsonism another, Catholicism a third, within which, however, we must distinguish between mystical thinkers and more rationalistic neo-Thomists.

A fourth definite movement is SURREALISM and, after World War II, existentialism. Some of these classifications are not clearcut. A Catholic poet such as Paul CLAUDEL was a symbolist in his poetic theories; the Catholics Charles PÉGUY and Charles Du Bos (1882–1939) felt the strong impact of Bergson. One can speak today of a Catholic existentialism and the term Bergsonism must not always be interpreted technically; it might be combined with an interest in Freud and find ways to agree with the Church. The situation is extremely fluid, the boundary lines fluctuate. The methods of French criticism of the last fifty years are mostly intuitive and often impressionistic: its form is the essay—so much so that many critics seem never to have written a proper book. The interest in a systematic theory is small, as criticism is conceived as an art and a means of self-expression and self-discovery rather than as a body of knowledge and judgments.

Symbolism as a poetic movement was apparently on the decline since the beginning of the century, although Baudelaire, Mallarmé, and Rimbaud actually determined the course of a modern French poetry and also supplied a body of poetic doctrine. The prolific critic Remy de Gourmont (1858–1915) could be described as a popularizer of the symbolist creed, although Gourmont had nothing of Mallarmé's austerity and has often pronounced tones of elegant fin-de-siècle Decadence. His best books, such as *Le problème du style* (1902; the problem of style), with its advocacy of bright, visual, concrete writing, and his analytical skill in the "disassociation of ideas," provided important suggestions for the IMAGISM of Ezra POUND and the early criticism of T. S. Eliot.

The great poet Claudel, an intensely proselytizing Catholic, formulated a new version of symbolist poetics: image is the essence of poetry. Unlike prose, which gives us knowledge of reality, poetry provides us with an equivalent, or species of reality. The poet does not tell us what a thing is, but what it means, what is its place in the universe, which is a unity, linked by correspondences, surrounding us with "figures of eternity." Claudel's *Art poétique* (1907; *Poetic Art*, 1948) ranges from an immediate vision of God's universe to close prescriptions for the reform of French verse as reflecting the rhythm of the soul, rather than the mind, *anima* rather than *animus*.

A basically symbolist poetics was also formulated by Valéry in writings that in part date back to the 1890s but belong largely to the period between the wars. The five volumes of *Variété* (1924–44; *Variety*, 2 vols., 1927, 1938) especially carried his views on poetry to a wide audience, in a fragmentary fashion. But if we supplement these essays by many other pronouncements in lectures and notebooks, a coherent theory of poetics emerges that is both striking and original. Valéry, more radically than anybody else, asserts a discontinuity between author, work, and reader. He stresses the importance of form divorced from emotion and takes poetry completely out of history into the realm of the absolute. For Valéry, there is first a deep gulf between creative process and work. At times it seems as if Valéry were hardly interested in the work, but only in this process of creation. He did not publish for twenty years and seemed content to analyze the creativity of genius in general. His ideal was the universal man, a Leonardo da Vinci. Later he wrote subtle, introspective descriptions of the process of composing his poems, always citing evidence for the distance between the original idea, the germ that might be, in a word, a rhyme, a line, or a melody, and the finished product. For Valéry poetry is not inspiration, not dream, but a making with a mind wide-awake. Poetry must be impersonal to be perfect. Emotional art, art appealing to sensibility, seems to him always inferior. A poem should aim to be "pure," absolute poetry, free from factual, personal, and emotional admixtures. It cannot be paraphrased, it cannot be translated. It is a tight universe of sound and meaning, so closely interlocked that we cannot distinguish content and form. Poetry exploits the resources of language to the utmost, removing itself from ordinary speech by the use of sound and meter and all the devices of metaphorics. Poetic language is a language within language, language completely formalized. To Valéry poetry is both a calculus, an exercise, even a game, and a song, a chant, an enchantment, a charm. It is figurative and incantatory: a compromise between sound and meaning, which by its conventions, even arbitrary conventions, achieves the ideal work of art, unified, beyond time, absolute. This ideal is realized most fully in Mallarmé and in Valéry's own poetry.

The novel, with its plot complications and irrelevancies, and tragedy, with its appeal to violent emotions, seem to Valéry inferior genres, even not quite art. The novel is historical and hence contingent; it makes claims to truth in relation to an external reality. It can be summarized and easily changed in its details, without damage, as a poem cannot.

Valéry's ideal of poetry is absolute, frozen into the grandeur of pure form. Surprisingly enough, what seems a dense objective structure is to Valéry open to many interpretations. A work of art is essentially ambiguous. "My verses have the meaning that one gives to them," is Valéry's famous paradox, which allows even for

"creative misunderstanding." The door seems open for critical caprice and anarchy, but Valéry's own practical criticism—limited in scope mainly to authors such as Mallarmé and Poe, his "pure" poets, or to universal examples of creativity like Goethe and Leonardo da Vinci—preserves an admirable lucidity and balance. It defends a position that seems extreme in its austerity and vulnerable for its discontinuities. But it has been fruitful in asserting a central concern of modern poetics: the discovery of pure representation, the "unmediated vision," for which two other great poets of the century, Rainer Maria RILKE and Eliot, were also searching. Valéry stands alone in splendid isolation, although the affinities of his theories with Mallarmé's are obvious. In a wide perspective, he could be seen as bringing symbolism back to the classical tradition.

Proust also restated symbolist theory, with important modifications. Although these statements were often disguised in discussions of music and painting, Proust, especially in the last volume— *Le temps retrouvé* (1927; *The Past Recaptured*, 1932)—of his novel cycle *À la recherche du temps perdu* (1913–27; *Remembrance of Things Past*, 1922–32), expounds an aesthetics relevant to literature. The artist is concerned with a knowledge of "essences" recovered by involuntary memory: he fixes the fleeting qualitative side of the world in his own particular singular emotion. Symbolism and Bergsonism are reconciled. Besides, Proust occasionally commented on strictly literary matters: in his introduction to his early translations from John Ruskin (1819–1900), in curious reflections on the style of Flaubert, and in an acid attack on the biographical approach of Sainte-Beuve, *Contre Sainte-Beuve* (1954; *On Art and Literature*, 1958), discovered long after his death.

But the group that assembled around *Nouvelle revue française*, founded by André GIDE in 1909, was most influential in defining the new taste of the century. The main contributors can hardly be reduced to a common denominator, but Bergson loomed in the background with his philosophy of flux, of the concrete and the immediate. Gide himself was hardly an important critic, although his published journals are full of literary opinions, and his book *Dostoïevsky* (1923; *Dostoevsky*, 1926) searchingly probes ethical problems. The reigning spirit was Jacques Rivière (1885–1925), who died too soon to fulfill his promise. The early *Études* (1908; studies) show Rivière as the first sensitive expounder of Claudel and Gide. After his return from German captivity in World War I, as editor of *Nouvelle revue française*, he did much to spread the growing fame of Proust. He saw Proust rather as a classicist, that is, a detached observer, and interpreted him also in Freudian terms. But Rivière is not sufficiently described as a psychological critic of considerable finesse and warmth: he is a figure of psychological interest himself, a man who first grappled with religion and then attempted to find himself in a theory of sincerity toward oneself. To him criticism was self-discovery, a way toward a definition of the meaning of life, best exemplified in his essays collected under the title *Nouvelles études* (1927; *The Ideal Reader*, 1960).

Rivière was soon eclipsed by Albert Thibaudet (1874–1936), a voluminous writer who filled the *NRF* with his essays for many years and produced, besides many monographs, an unfinished work, *Histoire de la littérature française* (1937; *French Literature from 1795 to Our Era*, 1967). Thibaudet is somewhat like a modern Sainte-Beuve: he has his versatility and his aversion to clear-cut conclusions and theories. If he has a philosophical outlook, it is that of Bergsonism. He likes to surrender to the flux of impressions, to embrace a literary pantheism. He interpreted, always sympathetically, Mallarmé, Maurice Barrès (1862–1923), Valéry, and Flaubert in separate books. In his *Histoire de la littérature française* he shows his skill in surveying masses: he ranges his authors in a succession of generations and manages to suggest the chain of tradition, the flow of time. Thibaudet is haunted by the vision of a literary landscape, a "Republic of Letters." He evokes the soil, the province, the place of an author. He has a strong feeling and sympathy for regionalism, which is combined with a genuine vision of European solidarity. Sympathy, even at the expense of judgment, is Thibaudet's main trait. He even imitates the style of the writer he discusses, almost compulsively. He seems like a chameleon, elusive, indistinctive. The two books, ostensibly devoted to a theory of criticism, *Physiologie de la critique* (1930; physiology of criticism) and *Réflexions sur la critique* (1939; reflections on criticism), are hardly more than random notes. Nowhere is there an attempt to define a position: it emerges largely by implication, in his admiration for Victor Hugo and Flaubert, in his coolness to Balzac, Alfred de Vigny, and Baudelaire. A final romantic vein seems to prevail.

In his psychological probing, and his impressionistic technique, Charles Du Bos was in his early stages related to Rivière. Du Bos is much more labored, earnest, groping, yet also much wider in range. In contrast to Rivière and Thibaudet, whose horizon was almost exclusively French, Du Bos knew English and German literature well. He wrote extensively on Wordsworth, Shelley, Keats, Browning, and Pater, and produced a full-length psychological study of Byron (*Byron et le besoin de la fatalité*, 1929; *Byron and the Need of Fatality*, 1932). He studied Goethe in detail. In 1927 Du Bos became a convert and then developed a concept of literature which must be described as mystical. His English book, *What Is Literature?* (1938) hinges on key words such as "soul," "light," and "word," leading up to a "beatific vision," an ecstatic communion of the critic with the seers and sages. But this is only Du Bos's last stage: earlier he wrote much on the psychology of writers, the creative process, the concrete detail of a work of art, always with a Bergsonian fear of abstraction, a sense of life that he found also in the complexities of Henry JAMES and Robert Browning. The seven volumes of *Approximations* (1922–37; approximations), which contain some of the most distinguished criticism of the time, are also typical for the course they describe: from a worship of beauty for its own sake to a glorification of God's presence, from the pleasures of sensation to the "essence" embodied in literature.

Du Bos in his concept of poetry is related to the Abbé Henri Bremond (1865–1933), the historian of religious feeling in France, who in *Poésie et prière* (1926; *Prayer and Poetry*, 1927) and *De la poésie pure* (1926; of pure poetry) almost identified poetry with prayer, or rather with mystical exaltation.

But within the Catholic renaissance there was a more intellectual movement, neo-Thomism, Aristotelianism, which found a powerful spokesman in Jacques Maritain (1882–1973). He was the best-known convert (in 1906), the most widely influential Catholic philosopher. Criticism was only one of his many activities. Still, *Art et scolastique* (1920; *Art and Scholasticism*, 1930) and *Situation de la poésie* (1938; *The Situation of Poetry*, 1955) did much to define a neo-Thomist aesthetics. In his later book in English, *Creative Intuition in Art and Poetry* (1953), Maritain moved in the direction of straight mysticism. The argument is still neo-scholastic, but is also Neoplatonist, even visionary. The Thomist concept of making a work of art for human needs is now combined with a belief in free creation, an inner subjectivity. Maritain, the great foe of Cartesian subjectivism, ends with a hymn to intuitive subjectivity, to revelation, even to dark unconscious creation, to mystery and magic. Maritain admires not only English romantic poetry but also surrealism.

Surrealism is the extreme of irrationalism. It grew out of DADAISM and CUBISM, which found a rather halting theorist in Guillaume APOLLINAIRE just before World War I. But surrealism as a movement is largely due to the organizing and propagandizing zeal of André BRETON, who composed its first manifesto in 1924. The artist is to reveal the confusion of the world; he is to contribute to the total discredit of what is usually called reality. The poetic state implies a complete renunciation of reason. Automatic writing is its technique, the dream is its model. Complete anarchy and emancipation from reason, God, morality, are proclaimed with flamboyant rhetoric and an air of assurance that suggests the circus barker.

World War II brought a reaction against all theories of pure art, all concepts that suggest the "ivory tower" or civic irresponsibility. The watchword became *la littérature engagée*, as formulated by Jean-Paul Sartre. But Sartre was a philosopher, the main French propounder of existentialism long before the war, and he cannot be described as a simple advocate of the social responsibility of the arts, although he moved more and more in the direction of Marxism. *Qu'est-ce que la littérature?* (1947; *What Is Literature?*, 1949) is actually an impassioned plea for a metaphysical conception of art. The rights of pure poetry are recognized.

Sartre spoke well of the varying relationship between writer and public in history and discussed the American novelists of violence—William FAULKNER, John DOS PASSOS—in terms of this assertion of human freedom. But imagination is suspect to Sartre—shattered by the first real contact with the absurdity and horror of real existence. The bohemian type of artist is suspect, too. Sartre made a cruel psychoanalytical study, *Baudelaire* (1947; *Baudelaire*, 1949): in spite of all the meanness and rottenness he finds in Baudelaire, he approves his search for "being" rather than mere "existence," his defiance of destiny freely chosen. In a diffuse and turgid book about Jean GENET, *Saint-Genet, comédien et martyr*, (1952; *Saint-Genet: Actor and Martyr*, 1963), a homosexual thief and convict (as well as playwright) is the subject; Sartre identifies work and author completely and wishes to convince us that good is evil and evil good. The paradoxes of Sartre's phenomenology cannot, however, succeed in making an author on the margin of literature appear a great writer. Sartre devoted the last years of his life mainly to an enormous biography of Flaubert, *L'idiot de la famille: Gustave Flaubert de 1821 à 857* (3 vols., 1971–72; Vol. I tr. as *The Family Idiot: Gustave Flaubert, 1821–1857, Vol. I.*, 1981), which interprets him mainly in terms of Sartre's own existential psychoanalysis as a representative of the hated French bourgeoisie. Although Sartre claims "empathy," the book is actually a systematic persecution of the man from childhood to the writing of *Madame Bovary*, conceived as the "totalization" of Flaubert's development toward a fusion of his inner experience with contemporary history.

Existentialist assumptions and motifs permeate recent French criticism, which has become increasingly philosophical, metaphysical, and often gropingly obscure as a result. Two outstanding authors—not primarily concerned with literary criticism—defined the new attitude toward art most memorably. André Malraux, in his grand survey of the plastic arts, *Les voix du silence* (1951; *The Voices of Silence*, 1953) makes art appear as man's triumph over destiny. Albert CAMUS, in *L'homme révolté* (1951; *The Rebel*, 1954), sees art as a tool in man's revolt against his human condition, art as conquering even death.

The attitudes, ideas, and methods of these great writers reverberate in more strictly literary and academic criticism. There they combine with suggestions that come from the writings of Gaston Bachelard (1884–1962), a somewhat fantastic philosopher of nature who called his method psychoanalysis, but was, rather, related to Jung. He studied the traditional elements (fire, water, air, earth) in literature and traced the distortions imposed by the imagery of poets in such books as *La psychoanalyse de feu* (1938; *The Psychoanalysis of Fire*, 1964), *L'eau et les rêves* (1942; *Water and Dreams*, 1965), *L'air et les songes* (1943; air and dreams). *La poétique et l'espace* (1958; *The Poetics of Space*, 1964), and *La poétique de la rêverie* (1961; *The Poetics of Reverie*, 1969).

A whole group of French critics can be said to combine existentialist and "myth" interests in order to develop a special method they call *critique de conscience*. They aim less at analysis or judgment of works of art than at the reconstruction of the particular "consciousness" of each writer. Every writer is assumed to live in his peculiar unique world, which has certain interior structures it is the task of the critic to discover. The emphasis on different aspects and the philosophical affiliations of these critics vary. The oldest among them, Marcel Raymond (1897–1981), in his *De Baudelaire au surréalisme* (1935; *From Baudelaire to Surrealism*, 1949), traced the myth of modern poetry to its sources in Baudelaire. Raymond was interested in the claim of poets such as Mallarmé and the surrealists that words are more than symbols, that they can share in the essence of being, that the absolute is somehow incarnated in their work.

In Albert Béguin (1901–1957) the religious motivation is dominant. In his first book, *L'âme romantique et le rêve* (1939; the romantic soul and the dream), he studies German romanticism and the French writers who went the same way—Rousseau, Hugo, Gérard de Nerval (1808–1855)—and he ends with Baudelaire, Rimbaud, Mallarmé, and Proust. Béguin admired German romanticism because it recognized and affirmed the profound resemblance of poetic states and the revelations of a religious order. Romanticism and all poetry is a myth that leads into the dream, the unconscious, and finally into the presence of God. In later writings Béguin became identified with a Catholic mysticism.

Georges Poulet (1902–1992) on the other hand absorbed scholasticism, Descartes, and Bergson, and is primarily interested in the concept and feeling of time in writings and poets. His *Études sur le temps humain* (3 vols., 1949–54; Vol. I tr. as *Studies in Human Time*, 1956; Vol. II, *La distance intérieure* [1952], tr. as *The Interior Distance*, 1959) and *Les métamorphoses du cercle* (1962; *The Metamorphoses of the Circle*, 1967) trace a general history of French thought and feeling in terms of time with unparalleled ingenuity.

Jean-Pierre Richard (b. 1922) is related to Poulet in his method, although *Littérature et sensation* (1954; literature and feeling) and *Poésie et profondeur* (1955; poetry and depth) show his special interest in the perceptual life of the authors (Stendhal, Flaubert, Nerval, Baudelaire, Rimbaud) discussed. We are told, for example, that to Flaubert love is like drowning, or that the lover loses his bones, becomes like plastic paste. Sentences and observations, metaphors and scenes from all books and letters of an author are used indiscriminately to build up a scheme of his mental life, organized by leading motives and obsessions.

Somewhat apart from these critics stands Maurice BLANCHOT, the most difficult and obscure of the group, who in *L'espace littéraire* (1955; the literary space) discusses such topics as "Whether Literature Is Possible" or the "Space of Death," using Kafka, Mallarmé, and Hölderlin as his favorite examples. Blanchot arrives

at a strange nihilism: silence is the ultimate significance of literature, the only thing left to express.

Fortunately there are other more articulate and more rational critics in France. All share the general method and philosophical preoccupations, but remain committed to clarity. Claude-Edmonde Magny (?–1966) in *Les sandales d'Empédocle* (1945; the sandals of Empedocles) expounded her philosophical method, which she then applied to Kafka, Charles Morgan (1894–1958), and Sartre lucidly. Gaëtan Picon (1915–1976), in *L'écrivain et son ombre* (1953; the writer and his shadow), began a systematic exposition of a theory of literature that does seem to indicate a return to aesthetic considerations. Obviously the danger of existentialist criticism is its neglect of the work as an aesthetic fact. The work is broken up or ignored in favor of the act of creation and the mind of the poet. Except for recent American attempts to emulate the French method, the gulf between French and Anglo-American criticism has become very deep indeed.

In recent years a group of critics in Paris, usually called French structuralists, has caused a considerable stir. The group is by no means concerned only with literary criticism. An anthropologist (Claude LEVI-STRAUSS), a psychoanalyst (Jacques LACAN), a philosopher (Jacques DERRIDA), a historian of ideas (Michel FOUCAULT), an interpreter of Marx (Louis Althusser, 1918–1990), and a semiologist (A. J. Greimas, b. 1917) play major roles. Even Roland Barthes, primarily a literary critic, could also be classed as a sociologist for his *Mythologies* (1957; *Mythologies*, 1972) and *Système de la mode* (1967; system of fashion) or as a semiologist for his *Éléments de semiologie* (1964; *Elements of Semiology*, 1977). All these critics are deeply influenced by the Swiss linguist Ferdinand de Saussure (1857–1913), whose *Cours de linguistique générale* (1916; *Course in General Linguistics*, 1959) formulated the basic ideas that nourish structuralism, particularly the distinction, within the linguistic sign, between the signifier and the signified, a new terminology for the old distinction between acoustic image and concept. Saussure assumed the complete arbitrariness of the linguistic sign, from which the French new critics draw the conclusion that man is locked in the prison-house of language, that literature has no relation to reality. To speak about literature is to speak about language.

Barthes's first book, *Le degré zéro de l'écriture* (1953; *Writing Degree Zero*, 1968), argues that "the whole of literature, from Flaubert to the present day, has become the problematics of language." The zero style of writing, which he finds in Camus, Blanchot, and Raymond QUENEAU, leads finally to the silence of writing. Literature today has "the very structure of suicide."

The book *Sur Racine* (1963; *On Racine*, 1964) put Barthes at the center of controversy. He was attacked by Raymond Picard (b. 1917), a Racine specialist, in the pamphlet *Nouvelle critique ou nouvelle imposture*? (1965; *New Criticism or New Fraud*?, 1969), which occasioned Barthes's rejoinder *Critique et vérité* (1966; criticism and truth). *Sur Racine*, although generally quoted as the showpiece of structuralist criticism, is mainly psychoanalytical in approach. It is an analysis of Racine's characters and situations. The relationship between the characters is reduced to a double equation: "A has complete power over B. A loves B, who does not love A." This in turn is paralleled in the setting of the plays, where the chamber, in the shadow and silence, the seat of authority, contrasts with the antichamber, where the hero and the heroine are located until they are expelled to die. The same structure is also seen in the implied theology of Racine's plays, in which Barthes sees an identification of God and Father, Blood and Law. Picard rejected Barthes's interpretation as sheer fancy, while Barthes, in his rejoinder, defended the complete liberty of interpretation. "The justification of the critic is not the meaning of the work but the meaning of what he says about it."

Some of Barthes's positions are elaborated in *Essais critiques* (1964; *Critical Essays*, 1972). All writing is narcissistic. Reality is only a pretext. In *S/Z* (1970; *S/Z*, 1974) Barthes interpreted a story by Balzac, *Sarrasine*, very closely, devising a system of five codes, or voices, and arguing again for a distinction between a classical text such as Balzac's as "readable" (*lisible*) against a modern text he considers "*scriptible*," i.e., when the reader produces the text himself during the act of reading. In *Le plaisir du texte* (1973; *The Pleasure of the Text*, 1975) Barthes exalted the pleasure of literature, which is purely individual and unforeseeable, and surprisingly rejected all claims to establishing a science of literature on the model of linguistics.

This is, however, what several other critics aim at, particularly Tzvetan Todorov (b. 1939), a Bulgarian settled in France. He translated an anthology of the Russian formalists into French, and in *Qu'est-ce le structuralisme?* (1968; what is structuralism?) sketched the outline of a new poetics, a complete system or science of literature. Todorov announces a kind of involution. The aim of poetics "is not so much a better knowledge of the object as the perfecting of scientific discourse." "The object of poetics is precisely its method."

Roman Jakobson (1896–1982), a member of both the Russian formalist group and the Prague Linguistic Circle, provides a personal bridge from Russia via the U.S. to France. His analysis of Baudelaire's *Les chats* (written in collaboration with Claude Lévi-Strauss, published in the review *L'homme*, 1962, and reprinted in *Questions de poétique*, 1973; questions of poetics) uses linguistic categories in order to construe a grammer of poetry: that is, syntactic and morphological correlations and frequencies. He used the same method on poems as diverse as a sonnet of Shakespeare and poems by Dante, Blake, Brecht, and Fernando PESSOA. Jakobson is the closest analyst of poetry. Gérard Genette (b. 1930), in *Figures* (3 vols., 1966–72; figures), has most successfully analyzed storytelling and the technique of the novel, using Proust as his prime example.

Today one cannot foretell the positive results of the new structuralism. There is no doubt of the stimulus provided by its close analyses, ingenious analogies, and classifications. But one may question the view that literature is a branch of linguistics and that all reality is linguistic. One may doubt whether literature is a closed system. The consequences of viewing all reality as linguistic are that consciousness and personality are reduced to secondary phenomena. A radical group around the review *Tel Quel* proclaims the death of literature or reduces literature to inconsequential language games. Any humanist will reject these nihilistic and anarchical conclusions.

Spain, Portugal, and Latin America

Spain in the 19th c. had no great critical tradition. The dominant figure who survived into the 20th c., Marcelino Menéendez y Pelayo (1856–1912), was a polyhistor, an enormously productive compiler of histories of literature and ideas, rather than a critic. *Estudios de critical literaria* (1884–1908; studies in literary criticism) are historical studies rather than criticism. His general outlook is that of Catholic romanticism.

Genuine criticism began in Spain with the "Generation of '98," the group of brilliant writers who—after the catastrophe of the Spanish-American War—began to examine the reasons for the decay of Spain. These Spanish authors were preoccupied with the problem of nationality and only secondarily with strictly literary matters. Cervantes's *Don Quixote* became a national symbol that served as a rallying point for this intensive self-examination. In his *Vida de Don Quijote y Sancho* (1905; *Life of Don Quixote and Sancho*, 1927) Miguel de UNAMUNO transforms Don Quixote into a saint: the humor of the book is ignored or forgotten. The man Don Quixote steps from the pages as a living being: art and reality are constantly, determinedly confused. Américo Castro (1885–1972) interpreted Cervantes as a Renaissance man, a follower of Erasmus, in *El pensamiento de Cervantes* (1925; the thought of Cervantes), and in *España en su historia* (1948; *The Structure of Spanish History*, 1954) tried to define the Spanish national character in terms of its racial and regional elements. Salvador de Madariaga (1886–1978) also wrote on Don Quixote—*Guía del lector del Quijote* (1926; *Don Quixote: An Introductory Essay in Psychology*, 1935)—and speculated, often in essays first published in English, on Spanish creative genius (*The Genius of Spain*, 1923). The collection of essays *Shelley and Calderón* (1920) contains a remarkable essay on Wordsworth, chiding him for provinciality. Madariaga, who played a role in the League of Nations as ambassador of the Republic, and as professor of Spanish at Oxford, was a type of the new Spanish internationalist: intensely conscious of his nationality, but wide open to the world, anxious to have Spain emerge from its isolation and importance. Madariaga was a convinced liberal. On the opposite end of the political scale, Ramiro de Maeztu (1875–1936) also wrote on Don Quixote—*Don Quijote, Don Juan y la Celestina* (1926; Don Quixote, Don Juan, and La Celestina)—and produced an antidemocratic and antiliberal work, *Defensa de la hispanidad* (1934; defense of hispanism).

These two themes, hispanism and Don Quixote, are also the starting point of the most prominent literary critic Spain has produced: José Ortega y GASSET. Ortega was an immensely stimulating, versatile writer on all subjects: history, philosophy, art, and even science, love, pedagogy, and politics. Literary criticism was only a small part of his enormous activity. The early *Meditaciones del Quijote* (1914; *Meditations on Quixote*, 1961) is hardly literary criticism: it is an attack on the surface culture of Mediterranean man in the name of Germanic "profundity." Ortega studied philosophy with Hermann Cohen (1842–1918) in Marburg in 1913–14, and always preserved an intense interest not only in Kant and Kantianism, but in George Simmel (1858–1918), Max Scheler (1874–1928), Martin Heidegger (1889–1976), and especially Wilhelm Dilthey, from whom many motifs in his thought are derived.

Two small books by Ortega, both dating from 1925, are literary criticism in a narrow sense. *La deshumanaización del arte (The Dehumanization of Art*, 1948) has a somewhat sensational title: Ortega discusses not the dehumanization of art, but rather the retreat of modern art from realism. Ortega sees the common denominator of modern art and literature in the avoidance of living, natural forms, in its ambition for being art and nothing else, with no transcendental claim, and in its essential irony. The builders of modern art are Debussy, Mallarmé, Proust, Picasso, and PIRANDELLO. Although the thesis is somewhat overstated and refers particularly to the situation in the early 1920s, Ortega finely characterized the main trend of modernist art as away from personal emotion and toward abstract form. "Poetry has become the higher algebra of metaphors" is Ortega's definition of the aim of Mallarmé and the Spanish symbolists. Quite consistently he helped in the revival of Góngora, the great Spanish baroque poet, with an important essay, "Góngora" (1927; Góngora), in which his poetry (and implicitly all poetry) is defined as circumlocution, as the oblique naming of the taboo. An essay on Mallarmé (1923) defines poetry as a "determined escape from reality," a "keeping silent about the immediate names of things."

In *Ideas sobra la novela* (1925; *Notes on the Novel*, 1948) he applies substantially the same point of view to the modern novel. The novel, with a plot and action, is exhausted as a genre and is being replaced by the "static" novel, which tends not to inspire the reader's immediate interest but requires contemplation induced by its form and structure. The classic examples are Dostoevsky, whom Ortega skillfully defends for his technique and form, and Proust.

The book-length essay that created a sensation in Germany, *Pidiendo un Goethe desde dentro* (1932; "In Search of Goethe from Within," 1949), is not primarily concerned with Goethe's work. It is, rather, an attempt to show that Goethe betrayed his deepest mission by going to Weimar, that classicism, and Goethe's classicism specifically, hides life, as does his optimistic biological philosophy. The real Goethe, the Goethe from within, is a problematic character, constantly fleeing from himself, a habitual deserter of his destiny.

Ortega had a commanding position in Spanish cultural life. All other critics lacked his philosophical clarity and range. They were either impressionists or scholars. AZORÍN was the best sensitive literary critic of the early group. *Clásicos y modernos* (1913; classics and moderns) and *Los valores literarios* (1913; literary values) are collections in which he tries to define the Spanish literary tradition and to trace the history of the new movement.

Among more recent critics, the sensitive essayist Antonio Marichalar (1893–1973) is concerned largely with French and English literature. Guillermo de Torre (1900–1971) described and criticized avant-garde European literature and later, in exile in Argentina, passionately defended the freedom of the writer. His *Problematica de la literatura* (1951; problematics of literature) was deeply influenced by existentialism; he was disturbed by the problem of the engagement of the writer and the totalitarian attempt to make the writer serve the purpose of the state. The crisis of the concept of literature is de Torre's main theme, which allowed him to survey the contemporary literary situation with a deep social concern that does not lose sight of the nature and freedom of art.

Another development in Spain was a highly competent cultivation of stylistics, in part suggested by German methods, in part drawn from native sources of philology. Ramón Menéndez Pidal (1869–1968) was the teacher of all the younger Spanish literary scholars; he was a great philologist and medievalist whose *La Enpaña del Cid* (1929; *The Cid and His Spain*, 1934) is an impressive reconstruction of medieval Spanish civilization. Two younger men, of the same name though not related, stand out: Amado Alonso (1897–1952), who was primarily a philologist but wrote a model study of the Chilean poet Pablo NERUDA, *Poesía y estilo de Pablo Neruda* (1940; poetry and style of Pablo Neruda); and Dámaso ALONSO, who started the Góngora's revival with his 1927 edition of Góngora's *Soledades* (*The Solitudes*, 1931) and his elaborate study *La lengua poética de Góngora* (1935; the poetic language of Góngora), and who wrote a fine analytical book on Saint John of the Cross, *La poesìa de San Juan de la Cruz* (1942; the poetry of Saint John of the Cross), and a large book, *Poesía española: Ensayo de métodos y límites estilísticos* (1950; Spanish

poetry: essay on methods and stylistic limits), which contains studies of Garcilaso de la Vega, Fray Luis de León, Saint John of the Cross, Góngora, Lope de Vega, and Quevedo. It succeeds in defining the "uniqueness of the literary object" with flexible interpretative techniques of great sensitivity and learning. Dámaso Alonso sometimes loses sight of the critical ideal and is given to speaking of the "mystery of form" or "expressive intuition." But these vague gestures toward irrationalism rarely damage the mastery of the stylistic analyst, who must surely be one of the best in contemporary criticism, and not only in Spain.

One of Alonso's followers, Carlos Bousoño (b. 1923), has systematized the stylistic approach into a whole theory of literature in *Teoría de la expressón poética* (1952; expanded rev. ed., 1966; theory of poetic expression). In contrast to Alonso, Bousoño concentrates on syntax and vocabulary and makes elaborate analyses, particularly of the symbol and symbolism, which he then develops in *El irracionalismo poético (El símbolo)* (1977; poetic irrationalism [the symbol]).

A Catalan, Eugenio d'Ors (1882–1954), made a deep impression at first by his commentaries (*glosas*), written in Catalan and published under the pseudonym "Xènius," consisting of ironic epigrammatic journalism on almost all subjects. His books on painters (Goya, Cézanne, Picasso, and others) prepared the way for his study (published first in French, *Du baroque*, 1936; in Spanish, *Lo barocco*, 1944; the baroque). Here baroque is conceived as a form of style occurring in all periods of history: Góngora and Richard Wagner, Pope and Vico, Rousseau and El Greco, the Portuguese architecture of the 15th c., and recent poetry are all considered phases of the baroque.

Guillermo Díaz Plaja (1909–1984) is related to d'Ors: he admires him greatly, but goes his own romantic ways. His first book, *Introducción al studio del romanticismo español* (1935; introduction to the study of Spanish romanticism), was rather derivative, but his essays on the theory of literature, *La ventana del paper* (1939; the paper window); *El espíritu del barocco* (1940; the spirit of the baroque); and his studies of the Spanish lyric and of the prose poem in Spain established him as the most eminent of Spanish literary historians, who manages to combine a strongly personal, often impressionist and irrationalistic criticism with accurate learning. As the editor of the great *Historia general de las literatures hispánicas* (5 vols., 1949–58; general history of Hispanic literatures) he did not succeed so well as the older Ángel Valbuena Prat (b. 1900), whose *Historia de la literatura española* (3 vols., 1937; history of Spanish literature) is today considered the best history of Spanish literature. Valbuena Prat also wrote an important monograph on Calderón and a basic history of the Spanish theater.

In Portugal, Fidelino de Sousa Figueiredo (1889–1967) was the outstanding figure in literary criticism and history. He wrote a series of immensely learned literary histories and much, mainly psychological, criticism. He drew portraits of many Portuguese authors with great skill and understanding, in, for example, *Estudos da literatura* (5 vols., 1917–50; studies in literature). But he was also deeply concerned with the theory of literature and criticism, with the history of criticism, and with many topics of comparative literature, such as the influence of Shakespeare in Portugal. Figueiredo described his own outlook as that of a militant traditionalism and nationalism: but he did much to free Portuguese intellectual life from provincialism and local complacencies.

Every Latin American country has produced critics and criticism, mainly of the local scene. In Mexico, Alfonso REYES combined, like Figueiredo, wide-ranging learning with critical insight. Reyes wrote scholarly books on Greek criticism and Roman rhetoric; he early contributed to the revival of interest in Góngora; he showed fine understanding of Mallarmé; and he wrote a sympathetic study of Goethe. In a large theoretical book, *El deslinde* (1944; delimitation), he attempts extremely subtle though excessively scholastic definitions and delimitations that hardly suggest the universality and mobility of his mind. With Reyes, the Spanish culture of the New World has rediscovered its old universal Western spirit.

Jorge Luis BORGES, the eminent Argentine writer, is also a fine critic and essayist. He ranges widely from Argentine folk literature to old Germanic epics, and judges his Argentine contemporaries with some severity. Ricardo Rojas (1882–1957) was his main rival: his *La literature argentina* (8 vols., 1924–25; Argentine literature) established his reputation as an essayist.

There are, of course, many literary historians in different countries, among whom Pedro Henriquez Ureña (1884–1946) from the Dominican Republic may be singled out due to the availability of some of his work written in English (*Literary Currents in Hispanic America*, 1945). But Henriquez Ureña wrote most importantly on style and verse—*Seis ensayos en busca de nuestra expresión* (1927; six essays in search of our expression)— and was one of the most distinguished critics of Spanish America. In every country of the New World, the critical spirit is stirring, engaged in a needed examination of local values and in the importation of ideas from all over the world.

Russia and Eastern Europe

Russian criticism has been dominated by Marxism since 1917. But one should realize that early in the century very different points of view prevailed, and that even after 1917 a lively debate raged in Russia and a great diversity of doctrines were propounded. Uniformity was not imposed until about 1932. Russian literary criticism has a special appeal for the student of criticism, independent of the light it may throw on Russian literature itself. More sharply than anywhere in the West, Russian criticism has elaborated three irreconcilable positions: symbolism, formalism, and Marxism.

Symbolism, which came to Russia in the 1890s, adopted there a highly metaphysical and even theological and theosophic doctrine: poetry was thought of as a revelation of a supernatural existence; the poet became a possessor of occult knowledge. Some of the best-known symbolist poets, Konstantin BALMONT, Andrey BELY, and Valery BRYUSOV, wrote criticism that ranges from a vague mysticism to subtle technical investigations of meter and rhyme.

Closely related to the symbolist attitude was the cult and study of Dostoevsky, who was interpreted largely as a religious philosopher. Dmitry MEREZHKOVSKY relentlessly pursued, in his *Tolstoy i Dostoevsky* (1901; *Tolstoy as Man and Artist, with an Essay on Dostoevsky*, 1902), the antithesis between Tolstoy, "the seer of the flesh," and Dostoevsky, "the seer of the spirit," and found antithetical structures, pagan and Christian, everywhere else. Vyacheslav IVANOV interpreted Dostoevsky in a series of essays (1916–17, uncollected in Russian; *Freedom and the Tragic Life: A Study in Dostoevsky*, 1952) as a creator of myths, and his novels as tragedies. Nikolay Berdyaev (1874–1948) studied the world view of Dostoevsky in *Mirosozertzanie Dostoevskogo*, (1923; *The World Outlook of Dostoevsky*, 1934) as a philosophy of freedom in which God's existence is justified paradoxically by the existence of evil.

These were writers of Russian Orthodox background, who developed their own version of religious philosophy. Two Russian Jews, Mikhail Gershenzon (1869–1925) and Lev Shestov (pseud. of Leo Schwartzmann, 1868–1938), used similar methods to interpret literature with different assumptions; Gershenzon studied the elusive skeptical wisdom of Pushkin in *Mudrost Pushkina* (1919; Pushkin's wisdom), while Shestov searched for an amoral, irrational God and found nihilism everywhere: in Dostoevsky and Tolstoy, in Nietzsche, and CHEKHOV. *Apoteoz bezpochvennosti* (1905; the apotheosis of groundlessness) is the characteristic title of one of his books. Shestov in his late writings published in exile, in French, came very near to existentialism.

Partly in reaction to the mystique of symbolism and the growing power of Marxist criticism, a small but lively and influential group of young scholars, linguists, and literary historians organized a Society for the Study of Poetic Language in 1916, and thus founded what came to be known as the formalist movement. They flourished in the turbulent 1920s, but had to conform or were suppressed in the 1930s, They were a short episode in the history of Russian criticism, but their influence spread to Czechoslovakia and Poland and later to the United States.

One must distinguish several stages in the development of Russian formalism: an early stage of extremism that was closely allied with the rising movement of Russian futurism—Velemir KHLEBNIKOV, Vladimir MAYAKOVSKY; a middle period of consolidation and expansion; and a final crisis, breakup, and compromise with Marxism. One must also distinguish among its members: Viktor Shklovsky (1893–1984) was a firebrand, a stimulating gadfly, a crude and shrill publicist, while Boris Eikhenbaum (1886—1959), Roman Jakobson, and Yury Tynyanov (1894–1943) brought a great fund of erudition to their bold speculations. A learned scholar such as Viktor Zhirmunsky (1891–1971), on the other hand, drew ideas from his colleagues and tried to devise combinations with accepted views. Boris Tomashevsky (1886–1957), with his *Teoria literatury* (1905; theory of literature), was rather the popularizer and systematizer of the group.

The formalists, like the futurists, proclaimed poetry to be free creation, its word to be independent of reality, even "beyond sense." They at first denied the social and philosophical content of art and proclaimed its complete indifference, even, to emotions and ideas. In their first stage they were interested in one problem, that of poetic language, which they conceived of as a special language, achieved by a purposeful "deformation" of ordinary language, by what they called "organized violence" committed against it. They studied mainly the sound stratum of language: vowel harmonies, consonant clusters, rhyme, prose rhythm, and meter, drawing heavily on the results of modern linguistics, its concept of the "phoneme" developed by linguists such as Baudoin de Courtenay (1845–1929), Prince Nikolay Trubetskoy (1890–1938), and Roman Jakobson. They devised many technical methods (some even statistical), which can hardly be made comprehensible to someone without a knowledge of Russian. Slowly they saw that they had also to study composition and meaning, and finally that no poetics is complete without aesthetics and history. Shklovsky argued that the purpose of art is to shock us into an awareness of reality and that its main device to achieve this end is "making strange," making us see things from a new and surprising angle.

Another device of art is "putting on the brakes," forcing attention to the rocky road itself. Art is conceived even as a game of solitaire, or as a jigsaw puzzle. The techniques of narration—in folk tales, in the *Arabian Nights*, in the mystery and detective story, or in a novel as contrived as Sterne's *Tristram Shandy*—were analyzed by Shklovsky in *O teorii prozy* (1923; on the theory of prose), always with the emphasis on craft, on the distinction between subject and plot. Another formalist, Boris Eikhenbaum, boldly reinterpreted Gogol's *The Overcoat*. It is not a plea for our common humanity and the little man, as it was understood for a hundred years; it is, rather, a comic, grotesque story displaying the manipulation of the recital, the voice of the narrator. It has nothing to do with realism. Art is thus sharply divorced from life. Roman Jakobson asked: "Why should a poet have more responsibility for a struggle of ideas than for a battle of swords or a duel by pistols?" And he made the striking formulation: "Literary scholarship should investigate what makes literature literary"—that is, its literariness, the devices that make a work of art what it is.

Thus, the formalists rejected all biographical, psychological, and sociological methods as external. They ridiculed old-fashioned literary history as having no real subject matter, limits, or method. They tried to devise instead a historical poetics that would concentrate on the internal evolution of poetry. Poetic schools are considered as changing in a dialectical process of action and reaction, convention and revolt. Conventions wear out: the "automatization" of devices will need a new "actualization." The rise of new genres is seen as a revival of "low" forms, as a needed rebarbarization of literature. Thus, Dostoevsky glorified the sensational French *roman-feuilleton*, and Alexandr BLOK raised the gypsy song into the realm of art. The only criterion of value recognized by the formalists is novelty, the success of a work of art in changing the direction of literary evolution.

The parallelism between Russian formalism and similar movements in the West, such as the American New Criticism, is striking, especially in the common preoccupation with the language of poetry. But the Russian movement seems purely indigenous: some of its forerunners were the comparatist Alexandr Veselovsky (1838–1906), who attempted a historical poetics, and the linguist Alexandr Potebnya (1835–1891). The Russian formalists differed sharply from analogous movements in other countries. They leaned much more heavily on technical linguistics, especially phonemics. They disparaged the role of imagery and symbolism. Their concept of the work of art as a sum of devices was mechanistic. They were positivists, with a scientific ideal of scholarship—technicians who devised ingenious methods of analysis with great clarity. They preserved a strong interest in literary history and historical poetics. But they did not see the crucial problem of evaluation, left as they were with the single criterion of novelty, in the blind alley of relativism.

On many points Russian formalism was greatly improved when it was exported to Poland and Czechoslovakia. In Poland, Manfred Kridl (1882–1957) argued in favor of an "integral method" of literary studies, radically centered on the work of art. A philosopher, Roman Ingarden (1893–1970), writing in German, in *Das literarische Kunstwerk* (1931; new ed., 1960; *The Literary Work of Art*, 1973) applied Husserl's phenomenology to an analysis of the different strata of the work of art and its ontological status. He thus overcame the dichotomy of content and form and grounded the theories of formalism epistemologically. In Czechoslovakia, where Roman Jakobson settled for years, the Prague Linguistic Circle was founded (1926), partly at his instigation, and some of its members devoted themselves to literary theory. Among them Jan Mukařovský (1891–1975) was the outstanding theorist of literature. The Czechs

restated Russian formalism, rechristening it "structuralism." Structure is a term like *Gestalt*, which attempts to overcome the dualism of content and form.

While the Czechs adopted the main tenets of Russian formalism, they rejected its positivism—its methods of treating literature as an art entirely determined by language and literary scholarship as almost a branch of linguistics. The Czechs had studied Hegel, Husserl, *Gestalt* psychology, and the philosophy of symbolic forms propounded by Ernst Cassirer (1874–1945). They saw that the meaning of a work of literature is not purely linguistic, that it projects a "world" of motifs, themes, characters, plots, and even ideas. Mukařovský went beyond careful stylistic and semantic analyses to a general theory of aesthetics in which key concepts like function, structure, norm, and value point to an overall goal in a theory of semiology, of meaning in a social and historical context.

But all these promising developments were cut short by World War II and its aftereffects. In Poland and Czechoslovakia, Marxism was imposed after the war: men such as Mukařovský recanted publicly. Others, such as Jakobson and Kridl, emigrated to the United States.

The almost miraculous resurrection of Mikhail Bakhtin (1895–1975) has, however, aroused the most attention in the West. In his life he was almost a pariah: he was banished to a remote village on the frontier of Siberia from 1929 to 1936, and only in later years was he allowed to teach in Saransk in Mordvinia. He had to use pseudonyms and work in collaboration. Today N. Voloshinov's books *Froydizm* (1927; *Freudianism*, 1976) and *Marxizm i filosofia yazyka* (1929; *Marxism and the Philosophy of Language*, 1973) and Pavel Medvedev's *Formalny method v literaturovedeni* (1928; *The Formal Method in Literary Scholarship*, 1978) are ascribed to him. His *Problemy tvorchestva Dostoevskogo* (1929; expanded version, *Problemy poetiky Dostoevskogo*, 1963; *Problems of Dostoevsky's Poetics*, 1973), his study of Rabelais, *Tvorchestvo Fransua Rable a narodnaya kultura srednevyekovya i renessansa* (written 1940, pub. 1965; *Rabelais and His World*, 1968), and finally a collection of papers, *Voprosy literatury i estetiki* (1975; *The Dialogic Imagination*, 1981) established him as one of the most important literary scholars of this century.

Bakhtin starts out with formalist assumptions, recognizing the specificity of the aesthetic object, but instead of a phenomenology he elaborates a semiotic that by definition is sociological. Man constitutes himself in language from the point of view of another man and thus ultimately from the point of view of a collective, a society. Language is thus dialogue, the word has a "multiple voice." The novel, which is Bakhtin's main concern, is defined as a "consciously structured hybrid of languages." Dialogue is the fundamental form of novelistic discourse, and the elaboration of the voice of the other is for him the leading motif of the history of the novel. He traces this history, with great erudition, through the Middle Ages to the novel of Dostoevsky, which, in his view, as a "polyphonic novel" is radically different from the main tradition of the 18th- and 19th-c. full-fledged novel. Dostoevsky thus has his remote forerunners in the Mennippian satire, in medieval folktales, which in the book on Rabelais are investigated in a context of folk culture, humor, and grotesquerie, a whole strand of human behavior Bakhtin calls "carnivalesque." In the book on Rabelais, the humanist is purposely ignored. In the book on Dostoevsky the religious thinker and prophet is dismissed as Bakhtin concludes that "all points of view are made part of dialogue. There is no final word in the world of Dostoevsky." Although this conclusion seems doubtful, the book has many acute things to say about the hero, the genre, the plot composition, and the verbal style. There is a basic unity to the three books: a vision of man as maker of language in society, a view of the novel beyond the confines of the usual emphasis on the line from Defoe to Proust, and narrative as an all-human indulgence in joyous verbal communication and play.

Germany and Austria

Germany in the latter half of the 18th and early in the 19th c. produced a large body of aesthetic and critical doctrines whose influence was felt throughout the 19th c. The two brothers Schlegel, especially, carried the message of German romanticism all over the Western world. But in the later 19th c. Germany lost its leadership in criticism completely: no single German critic established, even in his own nation, a position remotely comparable to that of Sainte-Beuve or Taine in France, Matthew Arnold in England, De Sanctis in Italy, and Vissarion Grigorevich Belinsky (1811–1848) in Russia. The cleavage between university scholarship and day-by-day reviewing was in Germany greater than elsewhere. Scholarship became purely historical, factual, "objective," and deliberately refrained from judgment and criticism, although it often assumed the standards of value developed by the great German classics. On the other hand, the reviewers became journalists who lost touch with a coherent body of doctrine: either impressionism went rampant or standards of didactic usefulness, mainly based on nationalistic ideals or political attitudes, prevailed. In either case genuine literary criticism was dead.

In the 1880s, however, the movement of naturalism, introduced largely from France, stirred the stagnant waters and aroused violent debates (especially around Ibsen and Zola). Real criticism, in the sense of a definition of a new taste, was produced, even though the theories of naturalism were derivative and often very simplicist in their grasp of the nature of art.

At the dawn of the new century the naturalist movement had run its course; its most important critics had ceased publishing—for example, Otto Brahm (1856–1912), who had fought for Ibsen and Gerhart HAUPTMANN, had become a theatrical manager.

Simultaneous with the rise of German naturalism another reaction had set in against the 19th-c. tradition: that which loosely could be called symbolism. In Germany Stefan GEORGE became the leader of a group that exerted great influence on literary taste and criticism. George himself was hardly a literary critic in the strict sense of the word, but his proclamations on the prophetic mission of the artist, of the incantatory power of language, and the need of severe form and unity in a work of poetry, as well as his eulogies of Mallarmé, Verlaine, Jean Paul, and Hölderlin, became the stimulus for the criticism systematized by his circle. George's anthology *Deutsche Dichtung* (3 vols., 1901–3, ed. with Karl Wolfskehl; German poetry), which, besides single volumes devoted to Goethe and Jean Paul, admitted only a very small selection from nine 19th-c. poets, and George's translations from Dante, Baudelaire, and many recent French and English poets, held up a new ideal of taste that sharply broke with the emotionalism and didacticism of the 19th c.

George's disciples elaborated his hints and dicta into a body of criticism that for the first time, after a long period of relativism, historicism, and philological factualism, asserted a critical creed, proclaimed definite standards, and defined a tradition and taste. Unfortunately, the genuine insights of the school into the nature of

poetry are marred by the doctrinaire tone of delivery, the aristocratic pretensions, and the often comically high-pitched, almost oracular solemnity of their pronouncements.

By far the best of George's direct followers was Friedrich Gundolf (1880–1931), while the others, whatever their merits as poets or translators, seem as critics only sectarians. Thus Friedrich Wolters (1876–1930), in his *Stefan George und die Blätter für die Kunst* (1930; Stefan George and the *Blätter für die Kunst* [journal for art]), asserts, at great length, George's claims not only to poetic greatness but to the leadership of the nation and to a religious revelation in George's meeting with Maximin. Other books on George by members of the circle are also written in a tone of adoration for a religious leader; they are saints' lives and acts of the apostles rather than criticism. Gundolf's *George* (1920; George) is no less idolatrous, but succeeds, at least, in concretely describing and analyzing George's poetic achievements.

But the book on George was preceded by Gundolf's best critical work: *Shakespeare und der deutsche Geist* (1911; Shakespeare and the German mind) and *Goethe* (1916; Goethe). These are books nourished by considerable learning, in spite of Gundolf's ostentatious contempt for footnotes and acknowledgements: well-composed, finely phrased books that set, in Germany, new standards of critical judgment and analytical power. The early study of Shakespeare's influence on Germany from the English comedians of the 17th c. to the Schlegels combines criticism of the main German writers with insight into period styles. Gundolf admirably sets forth the distinction between mere borrowings and external parallels on the one hand, and deeper assimilation on the other, and penetratingly analyzes the style of translations and imitations. His harsh judgment of the naturalistic distortions of Shakespeare by the German "Storm and Stress" and of the moralism and rhetoric of Schiller are refreshingly straightforward, even though his own conception of Shakespeare divorces him too sharply from the stage. The concentration on the texts and figures, apart from biographical information and details of literary history, and the cultivated, even precious style of writing were welcome innovations after the spate of colorless books crammed with information but devoid of taste and judgment.

Gundolf's largest book, *Goethe*, shows the same qualities of insight, analytical power, organization, and finished presentation. But while the earlier book was clearly nonbiographical and antipsychological and still remained properly historical, the book on Goethe postulates some obscure synthesis of biography and criticism in a contemplation of the *Gestalt* of Goethe. In this heroically stylized figure no distinction, Gundolf argues, can be made between *Erlebnis* (experience) and work, with the result that the book again confuses life and poetry. Gundolf had studied *Das Erlebnis und die Dichtung* (1905; experience and poetry), a collection of essays, mostly dating from the 19th c., by the great historian of ideas and feelings Wilhelm Dilthey, and had absorbed his philosophy: a version of *Lebensphilosophie*, which Gundolf combined with ideas derived from Bergson. *Leben*, in Dilthey, does not mean life (*bios*), but the total *psyche*, the mental structure that fuses intellect, will, and feeling into one. The function of poetry is seen as an increase of vitality; the main criterion of judgment is emotional sincerity, engagement, personal involvement, presuming an intense *Erlebnis*. In Dilthey, this emotionalism is combined rather incongruously with a view of poetry as expressing a specific *Weltanschauung*, a popular philosophy with relativistic conclusions, as, for Dilthey, there are only three types of *Weltanschauung* (realism, dualistic idealism—what he calls *Idealismus der Freiheit* (idealism of freedom)—and monistic idealism), all illustrated in literature and all ultimately equal as to their claims to truth.

Gundolf, although influenced by Dilthey, never succumbed to the psychologism and relativism of Dilthey. He saved criticism by devising a distinction between *Urerlebnis* and *Bildungserlebnis*, in which the elementary personal experience is preferred to the cultural experience, and by a somewhat parallel scale of the lyrical, symbolical, and allegorical, in which the lyrical (which is not necessarily identical with the traditional genre) precedes the other two categories. The emphasis falls on the personal lyric, but Gundolf argued that the poet experiences differently from the ordinary man, in terms anticipating his creation, forming even while living. Gundolf construed a conflict between Goethe's titanism and eroticism, between work and life, after all. The emphasis on the lyrical, on the *daimon*, which yields fine analyses of the early poetry, and of *Werther*, does not however, obscure his insight into the structures of Goethe's objective, "symbolic" poetry and into the relation of Goethe's works to tradition and convention. Whatever objections to individual interpretations may be voiced, the book remains an impressive monument. Today we would feel that in spite of many fine discriminations the tone of adoration, the setting up of the pedestal, the arranging of the drapery becomes excessively monotonous. It is hard not to resent the idolatry that changes the eminently humane figure of Goethe into a demonic creator for creation's sake. Real insights are often drowned in a flood of verbiage repeating over and over again the same or similar antitheses.

Even more one-sided is Gundolf's portrait *Heinrich von Kleist* (1922; Heinrich von Kleist), in which Kleist is seen as "a solitary soul without nation and God," as a chaotic, even monstrous genius, great by his defiance of the time, tragic as a symbolic sacrifice. Gundolf's two-volume *Shakespeare: Sein Wesen und Werk* (1928; Shakespeare: his nature and work) is curiously neglected. It suffers from preciosity and monotony, it sees Shakespeare so completely out of the context of the time and the stage that Shakespeare's ethos is falsified; but individual observations show an insight into the poetry and its symbolism, an emphasis on what might be called the baroque in Shakespeare, which was rare at the time. Only the last essays, *Romantiker* (2 vols., 1930–31; romantics), return to more traditional methods of characterization and judgment, which, however, often are excessively unsympathetic to such volatile and elusive figures as Friedrich Schlegel.

Two other members of the George circle wrote significant literary criticism. Ernst Bertram's (1884–1957) *Nietzsche* (1918; Nietzsche) aroused much adverse comment because of its subtitle, *Versuch einer Mythologie* (attempt at a mythology), and an introduction that boldly proclaimed the aim of the critic to be the creation of a legend, an "image," a myth. But the text of the books does not go all the way into subjectivism. It interprets Nietzsche as a lonely romantic, an ambiguous, contradictory, tortured irrationalist, an "image" that has at least as much justification as more recent attempts, such as that of Walter F. Kaufmann (1921–1980) in *Nietzsche: Philosopher, Psychologist, Antichrist* (1950), to make Nietzsche a reasonable descendant of the Enlightenment.

Max Kommerell (1902–1944), in *Der Dichter als Führer in der deutschen Klassik* (1928; the writer as leader in German classicism), interpreted the whole German classical group in terms of Stefan George's ideals. Klopstock is seen as a disciple of the Greeks, absorbed in antiquity and Platonic friendships, as if he had not been a Christian. Jean Paul is pressed into the Weimar company. Schiller becomes a disciple of Goethe, and Hölderlin is exalted to a national hero, a prophet of a religious regeneration of Germany as a second Greece. The deification of Hölderlin (who, in Dilthey's *Das Erlebnis and die Dichtung*, still appears as a charming, sentimental dreamer) was stimulated by the discovery of Hölderlin's late hymns by another disciple of George's, Norbert von Hellingrath (1888–1916). He prepared a complete new edition and wrote short expositions that found greatness even in the crabbed translations from Pindar and Sophocles and the most baffling fragments from the last stage of Hölderlin's lucid life before madness beclouded his mind. But Kommerell soon broke with George, because he could not accept his intellectual dictatorship, and went his own way. We shall meet him in another context.

George, in his beginnings, attracted the Austrian poet Hugo von HOFMANNSTHAL. They shared the opposition to naturalism, the cult of form and word, but they soon drifted apart, because Hofmannsthal would not submit to the "discipline" of the George circle and had other ambitions in the theater and a very different concrete taste in literature. Hofmannsthal is only incidentally a critic; but his early articles written in his precocious youth under the pseudonym "Loris" (1891–97) define a taste that could roughly be called "decadent" in its love for Swinburne, Pater, and D'Annunzio, and assert the independence of poetry from life and its essence in form and imagery. Later, in many essays, articles, and speeches, Hofmannsthal, often impressionistically and loosely, defined his preferences in literature: for the baroque and romance traditions, for Molière, Hugo, and Balzac, Calderón and the Austrians Franz Grillparzer (1791–1872) and Adalbert Stifter (1805–1868). In literary theory, Hofmannsthal brought out the mystical. Neoplatonic implications of his symbolist aesthetics. The bulk of his later writing on literature moved, however, in generalities of a "political" nature. Thus, in the speech "Das Schrifttum als geistiger Raum der Nation" (1927; writing as a spiritual space of the nation) Hofmannsthal praises tradition against romantic caprice and warns against the worn-out ideals of the *Bildungsphilister* (cultural philistine): a "conservative revolution" is advocated, in which a high ideal of European unity is propped up by a strong consciousness of the role of old Austria as a mediator between North and South, East and West.

With Hofmannsthal two poets were associated in friendship: Rudolf Borchardt (1877–1945) and Rudolf Alexander Schröder (1878–1962). Borchardt, the translator of Dante into a special archaic German, and a learned student of antiquity and Italy, was a passionate, even stridently vociferous asserter of the great tradition. In a postscript to *Ewiger Vorrat deutscher Poesie* (1926; the permanent treasure of German poetry), an anthology of German poetry, he makes short work of the German 19th c. and such established reputations as Heine's, and in eloquent *Reden* (speeches), collected in 1955, he proclaimed his somewhat foggy ideal of a reconciliation of the German and Latin spirits, antiquity and the Middle Ages. But he was at his best in his scattered essays on Pindar and Vergil, Hartmann von Aue and Dante, Lessing, Dante Gabriel Rossetti, Hofmannsthal, and George. In spite of his dogmatic tone, Borchardt was full of sympathy with often very diverse minds, flexible, and even disconcertingly uncritical (for example, his excessive enthusiasm for Edna St. Vincent MILLAY). His violent criticism of contemporary literature and its commercial aspects, his glorification of the Prussian monarchic tradition, his total condemnation of the 18th c. and the Enlightenment, his panegyric of German romanticism and historicism, his acceptance of Croce's aesthetics, are some of the incongruous elements of his thought, fused only by his powerful temperament and brilliant eloquence.

Compared to Borchardt's violence and eccentricity, Schröder seems a modest, sensible, sober expounder of the great tradition. He is best known for his translations of Homer, Vergil, and Horace. His critical writings, in their smooth eloquence, assert persuasively the mission of the poet as the maker of language, the great comforter for the transience of our existence. The poet, in Schröder's later writings, is more and more identified with the religious leader. Schröder made an intensive study of Protestant hymns and religious poetry, while he clung to a defense of the classical heritage of Europe. Poets like Vergil, Horace, and Racine have found few admirers in modern Germany as sympathetic as Schröder, seems less a critic than a scholarly expositor of the classical-Christian heritage.

Also loosely related to this group was Rudolf Kassner (1873–1959), who began with a book of essays, *Die Mystik, die Künstler and das Leben* (1900; mysticism, artists, and life; rev. ed., *Englische Dichter*, 1922; English poets), which combines a taste for the Pre-Raphaelites with a genuine interest in mysticism. William Blake was his early hero. The imagination, which in these essays links the poet and the mystic, becomes, in Kassner's later, mostly philosophical writings, the central concept of a pantheistic world view in which physiognomies, the interpretation of outward physical signs, plays a central role. As a literary critic Kassner remains a symbolist who, however, developed special tastes for authors usually ignored in Germany: Laurence Sterne, whose feeling for time appeals to Kassner; Gogol; De Quincey; and even Thomas HARDY. Shakespeare, however, remains the exemplar of the imagination. All authors and all poetry, in the later Kassner, become only specimens to substantiate a philosophy in which oriental and mystical ideas combine to support a revival of a basically romantic view of the imagination: as a "seizure of the thing by the image," a universal system of analogy, of all-in-one. A grandiose attempt is made to abolish the distinctions between sense and spirit, the concrete and the abstract, but literature as such is lost sight of.

Parallel with what could be called the German symbolist movement, represented by Stefan George and Hofmannsthal, there arose a new classicism, or rather neoclassicism, which asserted the role of form and tradition, mainly in the drama. Paul Ernst (1866–1933) found, after a youth devoted to naturalism and Marxism, a way to a new, highly intellectual classicism. In *Der Weg zur Form* (1906; the way to form) Ernst pleads for necessity, for fate, for the coercion of form in the drama and the short story, and disparages the novel and all description and psychological analysis. Drama is interpreted as an ethical conflict; tragedy as a joyous recognition of necessity even in the perdition of the hero. An absolute morality is postulated as the basis for a renewal of tragedy. The critical creed, however, remains disconcertingly abstract, and Ernst's many articles on literary figures stay well within the bounds of conventional eclecticism.

In this general tradition of the defense of the cultural values of the German past, two writers might be listed who cultivated the form of the essay. Thomas MANN produced a long series of articles, speeches, lectures, and introductions, which either praise kindred spirits or circle around Mann's problem of the position of the artist in society or probe into the artist's psychology, often by means derived from Freud and Nietzsche. Mann's consciousness—whatever the changes of his political orientation—is definitely conservative, *bürgerlich*, although acutely aware of the limits of the bourgeois traditions. Mann's essays are too autobiographical and too monotonously engaged in developing broad antitheses to be good criticism, aside from the light they throw on Mann's art.

Another general essayist was Josef Hofmiller (1872–1933), whose *Versuche* (1909; attempts) and *Letzte Versuche* (1935; last attempts) are examples of the art of portraiture in the sense of Sainte-Beuve. His outlook was Roman Catholic, his interests widely scattered, his tone is reasonable, his exposition skillful, but the criticism seems often colorless and imperceptive.

The change of taste, the newly acquired sense of form and tradition also influenced academic German scholarship profoundly. A group of Romance scholars, especially, combined scholarship and criticism successfully. Karl Vossler, influenced by Croce's view of the language as individual creation, traced the history of the French literary language and wrote a large study of Dante's *Divine Comedy (Die göttliche Komödie*, 2 vols., 1907–10; *Medieval Culture*, 1929), which is both learnedly historical and critical. He wrote descriptive and analytical monographs on Racine, La Fontaine, Leopardi, Lope de Vega, and the Spanish poetry of solitude.

Ernst Robert CURTIUS had the most intimate relations with contemporary literature: at first as a critical importer of modern French literature into Germany, and then as a sensitive and often pioneering analyst of Proust, Joyce, and T. S. Eliot, in the collections *Kritische Essays zur europäischen Literatur* (1950; *Essays on European Literature*, 1973) and *Französischer Geist im zwanzigsten Jahrhundert* (1952; the French mind in the twentieth century). In his book *Balzac* (1923; Balzac) he reinterprets the master of realism as a Swedenborgian visionary, and his last and longest book, *Europäische Literatur und lateinisches Mittelalter* (1948; *European Literature and the Latin Middle Ages*, 1953), weighted though it is by immense erudition, aims at a critical point in establishing the unity and continuity of European literature since classical antiquity, not only in its forms and period styles but in its themes and commonplaces (*topoi*). In Curtius a concern for tradition, a feeling for the world of Latinity and for European unity, and admiration for George, Hofmannsthal, and Eliot, combine happily with great historical and rhetorical erudition.

Leo Spitzer (1887–1960) was more of a purely technical student of linguistics and stylistics; but in his wide-ranging studies of literature he developed a method of interpretation treating the word as a sign of the mind and soul that serves genuine critical purposes. Spitzer wrote much on French and Spanish literatures (Racine, Diderot, Voltaire, Proust, Cervantes, Lope de Vega) and later also interpreted poems by Donne and Keats and a story by Poe. Spitzer always worked on a small scale, with a specific text, although he was inspired by a general concept of humanism.

Erich AUERBACH also always starts with the stylistic analysis of a text, but in his *Mimesis: Dargestellte Wirklichkeit in der abendländischen Literatur* (1946; *Mimesis: The Representation of Reality in Western Literature*, 1953) he attempts a general history of realism from Homer to Proust. The book combines stylistic analysis of individual passages with literary, social, and intellectual history. Auerbach's concept of realism is very special: it means to him both a concrete insight into social and political reality and an existential sense of reality, understood tragically, as man in solitude facing moral decisions.

Compared to this distinguished group of scholar-critics in the Romance languages, the study of German literature was less affected by the new understanding of form and tradition. Oskar Walzel (1864–1944) was an eminent specialist in the history of ideas, especially of the German romantic movement, before he tried to apply stylistic criteria to literature. He discovered Heinrich Wölfflin's (1864–1945) *Kunstgeschichtliche Grundbegriffe* (1915; *Principles of Art History*, 1932), in which the Swiss art historian expounded a scheme for a definition of the difference between Renaissance and baroque in the plastic arts, and transferred these criteria to literature. Walzel attempted to show, for example, that Shakespeare belongs to the baroque, since his plays are not built in the symmetrical manner found by Wölfflin in pictures of the Renaissance. In a pamphlet, "Wechselseitige Erhellung der Künste" (1917; mutual elucidation of the arts), and in many later writings, Walzel defended the method of transferring criteria developed by art history to literary history and developed devices and stylistic methods of his own. But *Gestalt und Gehalt im Kunstwerk des Dichters* (1923; form and content in the literary work of art) shows that Walzel is rather an eclectic expositor of other people's ideas and opinions than a critic, and his many very valuable, erudite books are strongest when they concern intellectual history. Thus *Grenzen von Poesie und Unpoesie* (1937; limits of poetry and nonpoetry), in spite of its deceptively Crocean title, has nothing to do with criticism: it is a historical study of German romantic aesthetics.

Fritz Strich (1882–1963) showed that the method of Wölfflin's contraries can be applied to German classicism and romanticism. In *Deutsche Klassik und Romantik; oder, Vollendung und Unendlichkeit* (1922; German classicism and romanticism; or, perfection and infinity) Strich shows that the baroque characteristics hold true for romanticism, the Renaissance for classicism. Strich interprets Wölfflin's concepts of closed and open form as analogues to the opposition between the perfect classical form and the open, unfinished, fragmentary and blurred form of romantic poetry expressive of man's longing for the infinite. In detail, Strich is full of subtle remarks and observations, but the general scheme that assumes a sharp division in the general German movement of the late 18th c. will not withstand closer inspection. With Walzel and Strich stylistic analysis clearly passes into intellectual history, which was the preoccupation of most German academic scholars.

We have traced the revival of a sense of tradition and form and the establishment of what could roughly be called the symbolist and formalist point. But German literature soon after 1910 was convulsed by a very different movement: EXPRESSIONISM, which corresponds to futurism in Italy and Russia. Expressionism hardly produced criticism, at least in its earlier stages, but only manifestos, declarations, polemics, often vaguely and emotionally phrased: cries, oracular dicta, or mere fancies. Still, expressionism represented an important revolution in taste. Its complete rejection of tradition, its contempt for form, coupled with a rejection of naturalism and impressionism, the proclamation of a return to metaphysics, to an inner world of expression that would not, however, be the psychological analysis of an individual but the cry of a common humanity—all these are critical motifs that were thrown out unsystematically in articles, in *Charon*, in *Der Sturm*, and other short-lived periodicals, or in small booklets like Kasimir Edschmid's (1890–1966) *Über den Expressionismus in der Literatur und die neue Dichtung* (1918; on expressionism in literature and the new poetry). The versatile Austrian critic Hermann BAHR, who had written very early his *Die Überwindung des Naturalismus* (1891; the overthrow of naturalism), tried, in his *Expressionismus* (1916; *Expressionism*, 1916), to relate the whole movement to the theory of fine arts and drew on Wilhelm Worringer's (1881–1965) *Abstraktion und Einfühlung* (1911; *Abstraction and Empathy*, 1953), a book that contrasted abstract art, imposing form on nature, with organic art, fusing with the object. Expressionism appears related to Egyptian, Byzantine, Gothic, and baroque art in its rejection of the classical human form. In writers such as Rudolf Pannwitz (1881–1969), Lothar Schreyer (1886–1966), and Carl

STERNHEIM diverse irrationalist ideas are stressed: the vision of the artist and its power, the emancipation of the word, the role of myth in art. The relations to the past, to precursors or supposed precursors such as the rediscovered Georg Büchner (1813–1837), were explored only cursorily.

Among the leading expressionist poets only Gottfried BENN can be said to have practiced criticism with any continuity and coherence. He defined expressionism largely in terms of its destruction of reality and history, of its horrifying experience of the chaos of the world and the decay of values. Benn, who even passed through a period of admiration for Nazism, in later writings found a way to a position that is not very different (in criticism) from Eliot's or Mallarmé's. *Probleme der Lyrik* (1951; problems of poetry) proclaims the ideal of absolute poetry, without belief, without hope, addressed to nobody, made out of words. More sharply than any other German critic, Benn protested against the view that a poem is about feelings and must emanate warmth; he ridicules poems addressed to nature, full of similes starting with the word "like," full of names for colors with a seraphic tone of murmuring fountains, harps, night, and silence. Benn became the most radical critic of the assumptions of the German romantic lyric. He believed in form and reality somehow imposed on the original chaos of the world and ceased to be an expressionist.

While nothing like a coherent theory could come from the deliberately chaotic irrationalism of the expressionists proper, the general influence of expressionist attitudes and vocabulary was widely felt. Theatrical criticism possibly most clearly shows the expressionist mood, even when the critic rejects particular expressionist plays or theories. Alfred Kerr (1867–1948), in hundreds of reviews, written in an affected, clipped style, judged the Berlin stage for years. He outgrew his early naturalistic predilections and moved more and more in the direction of expressionism: his praise of August STRINDBERG, Frank WEDEKIND, and Carl Sternheim went with a rejection of everything classical. Kerr was constantly "bored" by Shakespeare and in his introductory pronouncements flaunts the idea (for which he looks in Heine and Oscar Wilde for predecessors) of criticism as art, even superior to creation, as the "eternizing of trash." Bernhard Diebold (1886–1945), in *Anarchie im Drama* (1920; expanded 4th ed., 1928; anarchy in the drama), discusses Georg KAISER, Wedekind, Sternheim, and Strindberg, often very critically, and the many books by Julius Bab (1880–1955) and those of Herbert Ihering (1888–1967) show the same taste; a dissatisfaction with naturalism as a misunderstanding of art, a turn toward experimentalism on the stage, whatever direction it might ultimately take. Although much of this theatrical criticism is necessarily ephemeral, it was the place where criticism as judgment was most alive in Germany.

In style and in his general sense of the world, especially his bitter hatred of commercial civilization, the great Austrian satirist Karl Kraus is related to expressionism. The periodical he wrote singlehandedly, *Die Fackel*, contains much literary criticism, mostly of a polemical sort animated by a fierce ethical pathos against all sham, written in an allusive, witty style that exploits all resources of language. His whole work is permeated by criticism, mostly directed against contemporary Austrian literature and journalism. Neither Arthur SCHNITZLER nor Franz WERFEL nor Hofmannsthal nor Bahr escaped the spearpoint of this harsh but salutary moralist.

The expressionist movement as a poetic trend was over by about 1920; it had been nourished by the moods of the war and its aftermath. After a few years of comparative normality, criticism was again transformed by an outside factor—the rising tide of

Nazism. Nazism defined a literary theory and taste that officially prevailed for the years 1933–45. One must, however, distinguish between two kinds of Nazi criticism: one is primarily racist, biological in its ideology, vaguely realistic, provincial in its taste; the other was, rather, mystical and vaguely philosophical. The first kind wanted *Heimatskunst, Blut und Boden* (national art, blood, and soil); it was idyllic, or pseudoidyllic. Long before World War I, Adolf Bartels (1862–1944) had produced a stream of histories and polemics that interpreted German literature from this point of view and specifically indulged in elaborate attacks on the Jews (and half- and quarter-Jews) in German literature.

A very erudite scholar, Josef Nadler (1884–1963), whose original affiliations were conservative and Catholic, also gave a biological interpretation of German literature. His *Literaturgeschichte der deutschen Stämme und Landschaften* (4 vols., 1922–28; literary history of the German tribes and regions; also pub. in a Nazified ed. as *Literaturgeschichte des deutschen Volkes*, 4 vols., 1938–41; literary history of the German people) was an attempt to write literary history "from below," according to the tribes, districts, and cities, always constructing "tribal souls" of the different regions, professing to read literary traits from the ancestry of the family.

Although much of his biology seems wholly fanciful and his philosophy of German history quite fantastic, Nadler had genuine merits: he revived interest in the submerged and neglected Catholic south, and he had a fine power of racy characterization and sense of locality, which is by no means useless in the study of the frequently very local German literature. In spite of the racist assumptions (and the anti-Semitism and superpatriotism, particularly blatant in the later edition), Nadler represents the curious mixture, common in academic Nazi scholarship, of pseudoscientific biology, old romantic conceptions of the national soul, and even categories derived from *Geistesgeschichte* and the history of artistic styles. Many other German literary historians who joined the Nazi movement and wrote Nazi literary history on a more sophisticated level drew ideas and concepts from almost anywhere: from mysticism and romanticism, from Stefan George and Nietzsche, but capped the ramshackle structure by an overriding concept of German art in which racist assumptions were weirdly amalgamated with philosophical and literary concepts. The special feature of this new literary criticism need hardly be described: the elimination or denigration of Jews, the contortions in fitting inconvenient but unavoidable figures such as Goethe into their pattern, the frantic search for anticipations of Nazi doctrines, the foggy, monotonous jargon, the resentful, nationalist boasting. It is a sorry chapter in the history of German scholarship, only partially excusable on grounds of political pressure.

After the end of World War II, existentialism began to dominate the German intellectual scene. Interpreted, as it popularly is, as a philosophy of despair, of "fear and trembling," of man's exposure in a hostile universe, the reasons for its spread are not far to seek. But the main work by Martin Heidegger, *Sein und Zeit* (1927; *Being and Time*, 1962) dates from an earlier period, and existentialist ideas, in a broad sense, had been familiar to the readers of Dostoevsky and Kafka since the vogue of Kierkegaard in Germany, early in the 1920s. Heidegger's own version of existentialism (as that of Karl Jaspers [1883–1969]) is actually a kind of new humanism, profoundly different from the far more gloomy French school with its dominant concept of absurdity. Heidegger's contribution to literary thinking is that of a vocabulary and an emphasis on some new concepts, such as time and mood, rather than of a strictly aesthetic and critical nature. His writings on aesthetics and his interpretations of Rilke and of Hölderlin are extremely obscure and personal. Beauty is identified with truth, poetry is prophecy.

But more important than these later writings were Heidegger's general ideas: his justification of the neglect of psychology, his dismissal of the whole subject and object relationship that had dominated German thought. Criticism found a new reason (as it found it also in Husserl's phenomenology (see Phenomenology and Literature) to turn to the object itself, and to try to interpret and understand it as such by means that could be called intuitive rather than analytical. In Heidegger's system, moreover, the three dimensions of time—past, present, and future—assume a central importance that helped to focus attention on the concept or feeling for time in literature.

Existentialism thus combined a rejection of the old positivistic factualism with distrust for *Geistesgeschichte*, sociology, and psychology. The newly flourishing textual interpretation in Germany is usually inspired by such philosophical motives. They are prominent in the writings of Max Kommerell after he had left the George circle and struck out on his own. He became adverse to easy generalizations and *Geistesgeschichte* and cultivated what in the United States would be called "close reading." In *Gedanken über Gedichte* (1943; thoughts on poems), which is mainly devoted to subtle interpretations of Goethe's lyrical poetry, the existentialist emphasis on poetry as "self-cognition" (*Selbsterkenntnis*), as the definition of a "mood" (*Stimmung*) is obvious, but it is combined, especially in Kommerell's other writings, with a remarkable grasp of the symbolic and conventional nature of art: with a defense of French tragedy, commedia dell'arte, and Calderón.

Similarly, Emil Staiger (b. 1908) combines a subtle gift of sensitive interpretation with existentialist motifs. In his *Die Zeit als Einbildungskraft des Dichters* (1939; time as the imagination of the poet) he interprets three poems by Brentano, Goethe, and Keller, in contrasts derived from Heidegger's terms. In the introduction all causal and psychological explanation, even simple description of literature, is rejected in favor of a phenomenology, of interpretation. *Grundbegriffe der Poetik* (1946; principles of poetics) is an attempt to give the three traditional genres (lyric, epic, drama) a new meaning by linking them to the three dimensions of Heidegger's time concept. The lyric is associated with the present; the epic, or rather the epical, with the past; the drama, or rather the dramatic, with the future. The weird scheme is based on an analysis of the German romantic lyric, of Homer, and of some tragedies (Sophocles, Schiller, and Kleist). It revives speculations suggested by Jean Paul and a little-known English 19th-c. critic, E. S. Dallas, but the scheme breaks down, since it has no relation to any historical meaning of the genres. Staiger had to admit that his concept of the tragic had never been purely realized in any work of poetry. In later writings (especially *Goethe*, 3 vols., 1952–56; Goethe) Staiger found a way of combining historical and stylistic methods while still expressing the new existentialist outlook, and in *Die Kunst der Interpretation* (1956; the art of interpretation) he again defended and exemplified his remarkable talent for the "close reading" of German poetry. In *Stilwandel* (1963; changes of style) Staiger collected essays on changes of style, which he interprets purely in terms of the prevailing stylistic situation.

Other critics of the age reflect the turn to the text, combined with existential philosophizing. A collection of interpretations of thirty German poets, *Gedicht und Gedanke* (1942; poem and thought), edited by Heinz Otto Burger, was a sign of the times, and even earlier Johannes Pfeiffer (1902–1970) had written a sensitive introduction to poetry, *Umgang mit Dichtung* (1936; contact with poetry). Pfeiffer's collection of essays *Zwischen Dichtung und Philosophie* (1947; between poetry and philosophy) also propounds the conception that poetry opens the hidden depths of existence. In Hans Hennecke's (dates n.a.) essays, *Dichtung und Dasein* (1950; poetry and being), the existentialist motive is also apparent, but the taste is more eclectic, and much effort goes into rather undiscriminating expositions of American and English authors of the recent past. While Hennecke is definitely a reviewer, a middleman, Otto Friedrich Bollnow (b. 1903) is a philosopher rather than a critic. In his book *Rilke* (1951; Rilke) he interprets, with great acumen, the late poetry in terms of existential philosophy: the uncanniness of the world, the precariousness of human existence, the proximity of death. A later collection of essays, *Unruhe and Geborgenheit* (1953; anxiety and security), points to an escape from existentialism into a new philosophy in which man would find refuge from his anxiety.

Walter Muschg's (1898–1966) *Tragische Literaturgeschichte* (1948; 2nd completely revised ed., 1953; tragic literary history) is also related in mood and interests to the existentialist movement. Muschg, however, criticized Heidegger's interpretations of German poetry very severely. In *Tragische Literaturgeschichte* he treats, in almost encyclopedic fashion, all the sufferings, misfortunes, and tragedies of writers and poets of all times and places, aiming not so much at a sociology of the artist as at a typology of the poet, who may have been magician, seer, singer, juggler, or priest before the modern type was established. Somewhat incongruously, the book attempts, besides, a new theory of genres of the kind envisaged by Staiger: only in Muschg the first person, the poet's "I," is associated with magic, the second with mystical identification with the "Thou," the third with myth and representation. Muschg is acutely aware of what he believes to be the tragedy of German literature: the isolation and final ineffectiveness of its classics. The argument of the book is, however, weakened by its diffuseness and all-inclusive scope. All questions of poetics and literary history are drowned out by the leading theme: a solemn, monotonous dirge over the poet's cruel fate in the world.

Somewhat apart stands Hans Egon Holthusen (b. 1913). He also is deeply influenced by existentialism, but he has found his standard of judgment in Protestant Christianity. In his four books of essays, *Der unbehauste Mensch* (1951; the homeless man), *Ja und Nein* (1954; yes and no), *Das Schöne und das Wahre* (1958; the beautiful and the true), and *Kritisches Verstehen* (1961; critical understanding) he has proved himself a genuine critic, not only an interpreter or historian of poetry. He asserts the necessity of judging, the authority of the critic, which he feels cannot be purely aesthetic. He argues against the usual German prejudice in favor of sentiment and emphasizes the role of language in poetry. The word in poetry does not "mean" anything, but posits reality. It is a reality fraught with the need for decisions and thus eminently ethical. Holthusen, firmly anchored in his faith, has judged Rilke as a propounder of false ideas (although a great poet), has welcomed the position of the later Eliot, and the passing of what he calls the "zero-point" in recent German literature: its emergence from the depth of despair. Holthusen, in his many fine essays, is not only a literary critic, but a critic of civilization deeply engaged in the present crisis of man, his loss of religion, the dangers of his predicament.

Existentialism strengthened the return to the text, but in the long run, literary values and distinctions between poetry and philosophy tend to disappear in existentialist criticism. Heidegger proclaimed the view that all great works of art say basically the same thing. But individuality and history would disappear if this were true; discrimination and hence criticism would become impossible. Existentialism, in spite of its insights into the human condition, represents an impasse for literary theory and criticism. The structure and form of a work of art are dissolved. We are back again at the identification of art with philosophy, of art with truth, which has been the bane of German criticism since, at least, the time of Schelling and Hegel. While intuitive interpretation in this philosophical sense and *Geistesgeschichte* flourish in Germany, criticism in the sense of judgment by artistic criteria, based on a coherent literary theory, supported by textual analysis, is almost nonexistent.

After existentialism and the ubiquitous Marxism, the most conspicuous new movement in literary theory is *Rezeptionsästhetik*, an aesthetics of the reader's response. Its most prominent advocate, Hans Robert Jauss (b. 1921), whose lecture "Literaturgeschichte als Provokation der Literaturwissenschaft" (1969; "Literary History as a Challenge to Literary Scholarship," 1970) provided the initial stimulus to the movement, has found many adherents and followers. His approach is not merely a demand for a history of readers' reactions, of criticisms, translations, etc., and for a study of readers' expectations and of the reading public; it also assumes a "fusion of horizons," a necessary interplay of text and recipient in which the text is assumed to be transformed by the reader. Jauss argues that the attitude of an author toward the public can be reconstructed not only from addresses to the reader or from external evidence but implicitly through the assumption, for instance, in *Don Quixote*, of a concern for chivalric romances. Jauss has done excellent research in medieval French literature and has exemplified the application of his theory on modern texts such as *Madame Bovary* or Racine's and Goethe's Iphigenia dramas. He had to engage in polemics with Marxism and has developed a whole system of aesthetics, most recently in *Ästhetische Erfahrung und literarische Hermeneutik* (1977; aesthetic experience and literary hermeneutics).

With colleagues at the University of Konstanz he organized regular symposia on poetics and hermeneutics and published voluminous proceedings (there is a selection in English, *New Perspectives in German Literary Criticism*, ed. Richard E. Amacher and Victor Lange, 1979). Among the participants, many of them technical philosophers, Wolfgang Iser's (b. 1926) work is of particular interest, since he writes on English literature. His *Der implizite Leser* (1972; *The Implied Reader*, 1974) traces the history of the English novel from Bunyan's *Pilgrim's Progress* to Joyce, Faulkner, and Beckett, showing how the role of the reader who discovers a new reality through fiction changes in history and how his role in filling out the "spots of indeterminacy" (blank spots in the text, a concept derived from Roman Ingarden) has grown precipitously in modern literature. Iser has developed his point of view in abstract writings collected as *Der Akt des Lesens* (1976; *The Act of Reading*, 1978). While the German approach throws much new light on the history of literature as an institution, it is in constant danger of arriving at a complete historical relativism, the besetting sin of the whole tradition of German historicism.

England and the United States

English and American criticism in the 20th c. have to be considered together, although conditions and developments of imaginative literature have differed widely in the two countries.

But in criticism, there was not only the intense interchange of ideas between countries with the same language; the key figures in the renewal of criticism moved from one country to the other and influenced both profoundly. Pound and Eliot were Americans who came to England in 1907 and 1914 respectively, and I. A. RICHARDS, a Cambridge don, went to Harvard University in 1931. It is no exaggeration to say that all modern criticism in the English-speaking world is derived from these three critics.

But before their points of view became dominant, much time had elapsed and many various developments had taken place. As these were very different in the two countries, we must deal separately first with pre-Eliotic criticism in England.

In England, around 1900, criticism was at a low ebb. The aesthetic movement was discredited after the trial of Oscar Wilde and survived only in the refined, though erratic essayist Arthur Symons (1865–1945). Very little criticism in the strict sense was produced, although academic literary scholarship with critical pretensions flourished. Several survivors from the 19th c. even wrote their most impressive books. George Saintsbury (1845–1933) wrote *A History of Criticism and Literary Taste in Europe* (3 vols., 1900–1904), a first attempt to map out the whole field from Plato to Pater, *A History of English Prosody* (3 vols., 1906–10), and *A History of English Prose Rhythm* (1912). Saintsbury's last major work, *A History of the French Novel* (2 vols., 1917–19), shows him at his best: directly commenting on books without any need to worry about principles or theories. Saintsbury's standards are impressionistic and vaguely historical. He always celebrates *gusto*, the joy of literature, and carries his enormous reading lightly. He has great merits in boldly surveying wide fields, and he has a taste that is open to the unusual, especially the metaphysical poetry of the 17th c. But he lacks any coherent theory, despises aesthetics, and is often slipshod, jaunty, and violently prejudiced. In contrast to Saintsbury, Sir Edmund Gosse (1849–1928) was almost entirely a portraitist and causerist who in his later years wrote voluminously for the *Sunday Times*. His works of scholarship and biographies are urbane but lack Saintsbury's edge and candor.

William J. Courthope (1842–1917) was the author of a massive *History of English Poetry* (6 vols., 1895–1910), which relates poetry to political and national ideals, with a taste that can be described as neoclassical. Oliver Elton (1861–1945) wrote a monumental work, *Survey of English Literature, 1740–1880* (6 vols., 1912–28), which is always admirably well-informed, firsthand, sane, but critically rather colorless. In philosophical brainwork and subtle analysis A. C. Bradley's (1851–1935) *Shakespearean Tragedy* (1904) superseded earlier criticism of Shakespeare. His concept of Shakespeare, colored by the Hegelian theory of tragedy, and his emphasis on character almost outside and apart from the play have been sharply criticized, but must be recognized as the most coherent and penetrating of their kind. His eloquent statement on "poetry for poetry's sake" (in *Oxford Lectures on Poetry*, 1909) defines an idealistic version of the autonomy of art. W. P. Ker (1855–1923) was primarily a medievalist of wide range who, in his later years, was engaged in a study of poetics and contributed with exceptional learning to a discussion of form, style, and genres, very unusual at that time in English scholarship.

But the most characteristic figures of English academic criticism were Sir Walter Raleigh (1861–1922) and Sir Arthur Quiller-Couch (1863–1944). Raleigh, professor of English literature at Oxford who wrote on Milton, Shakespeare, and Samuel Johnson, always disparaged theory and criticism, and praised empire builders, voyagers, and men of action. The many essays of "Q" are permeated by an even heartier air of manliness and gusto. H. W. Garrod (1878–1960), professor of poetry at Oxford, formulated the prevailing academic attitude when he wrote that criticism is best when "written with the least worry of head, the least disposition to break the heart over ultimate questions." This negative, profoundly skeptical attitude toward criticism was fashionable in England and paralyzed any criticism that went beyond "the art of praise" in rambling, usually whimsical, allusive essays.

A group of writers and intellectuals known as the "Bloomsbury group" was subtler in its tastes and finer in its sensibilities, but did not achieve any break with impressionistic criticism. None of them was primarily a literary critic. Lytton Strachey (1880–1932) started with a short, brilliant book, *Landmarks in French Literature* (1912), and wrote essays that show an exceptional, "un-English" taste in Racine and Pope, but often suffer from his brash wit. Virginia Woolf wrote sensitive, warm, evocative essays that devote attention to questions of the reading public; they are collected in *The Common Reader* (1925) and *The Second Common Reader* (1932). E. M. Forster wrote a sparkling though elementary essay, *Aspects of the Novel* (1927); some of his other essays are collected in *Abinger Harvest* (1936). There were other English essayists—for example, Desmond MacCarthy (1878–1952), F. L. Lucas (1894–1967), and Cyril Connolly (1903–1974)—who knew how to communicate the pleasures of literature and to share their sensibility. But, in general, whatever the merits of these essayists, English criticism, before the advent of Eliot and Richards, suffered from an almost complete lack of system, method, and theory, or even coherent frame of ideas and, in its taste, propounded little more than diluted romanticism.

American criticism, about 1900, differed sharply from its English counterpart. There was hardly any academic criticism to speak of, as American professors of literature were then philologists, specializing mainly in Anglo-Saxon or Chaucer. There was much impressionistic criticism, best represented by James Huneker (1860–1921), who brought the newest Parisian and German fashions from the Continent and described them in turgid, enthusiastic essays. In the background there loomed Henry James, who had gone to live in England. The *Prefaces* (1907–9) he wrote for the so-called New York edition of his novels were hardly appreciated in their time. They are the finest poetics of the novel—its point of view, its narrative techniques, its implied morality—and the most subtle, possibly oversubtle self-examination of the creative processes of a modern artist. Only Percy Lubbock (1879–1966), an English friend, in his *The Craft of Fiction* (1921), gave currency to James's insights. The *Prefaces* themselves were first made available by R. P. BLACKMUR in an edition entitled *The Art of the Novel* (1934), with a long analytical introduction.

Against the whole "genteel" tradition of American literature there arose early in the century a critical movement that could be called "radical" and had obvious affinities with the rising American naturalism. Its main spokesman was H. L. MENCKEN, who was professedly a Nietzschean and "aristocrat" in his contempt for the values of a mass civilization, but as a literary critic must be described rather as a propagandist for Theodore DREISER, Sinclair LEWIS, and other new writers—for anybody whom he considered vigorous and alive, capable of breaking with the standards of the past. Mencken, especially as editor of the *American Mercury* (1924–33), fulfilled an important function in the self-criticism of American civilization, but as a literary critic he was a boisterous polemicist of quite erratic taste. He could extol such meretricious authors as Joseph Hergesheimer (1880–1954) or James Branch

Cabell (1879–1958) and had little power of characterization and analysis.

Van Wyck Brooks fulfilled a similar function with his early criticism. In many books, especially *America's Coming-of-Age* (1915), Brooks deplored the plight of the artist in America and argued that "our writers who have possessed a vivid personal genius were paralyzed by the want of a social background," because a society whose end is impersonal cannot produce an ideal reflex in literature. In psychological studies of Mark Twain (*The Ordeal of Mark Twain*, 1920) and James (*The Pilgrimage of Henry James*, 1925) Brooks pursued his ideal of a liberal, mature America welcoming the artist and his criticism of American society. Later Brooks turned more and more to an uncritical and even sentimental glorification of American literary history, in a series of books beginning with *The Flowering of New England* (1936). They are little more than nostalgic chronicles. In *The Opinions of Oliver Allston* (1941) Brooks attacked all modern literature as pessimistic and recommended only "primary" writers, producing optimistic literature, "conducive to race-survival." His strange list of cheerful classics includes Tolstoy, Dostoevsky, and Thomas Mann.

A similar point of view was stated even more violently by Bernard De Voto (1897–1955) in *The Literary Fallacy* (1944). World War II changed a liberal critical movement to an uncritical, intolerant, even obscurantist "nativism." The earlier, broader social view of this critical movement was codified for literary history by Vernon L. Parrington (1871–1928), in his *Main Currents of American Thought* (3 vols., 1927–30). Here literature is seen, in terms resembling Taine's, as an expression of national ideals, American literature as the history of Jeffersonian democracy. In Parrington much is done for a history of political ideas, but more "belletristic" writers, such as Poe, Melville, or Henry James, are slighted.

Opposed to this general trend of radicalism was the movement of the American humanists. From various sources (mainly Matthew Arnold and French neoclassicism) they drew a view of literature as a means of personal and social order. They condemned romanticism and all its forms and recommended a literature filled with a sense of balance, ethical restraint, and measure. Paul Elmer More (1864–1937) collected his essays under the title *Shelburne Essays* (11 vols., 1904–21), to which he added a twelfth volume with the characteristic title *The Demon of the Absolute* (1928). In the early volumes More ranged widely and showed an admirable quality of judicious sympathy that earned him comparisons with Sainte-Beuve. But More's standards became more rigid with time, and the later volumes are all devoted to an attack on aestheticism, naturalism, and modernism in the name of tradition, standards, and a philosophical dualism that rigidly upheld the necessity of an "inner check" in man against all spontaneity and caprice.

More was a learned Greek scholar who wrote in his later years a history of Christian Platonism and embraced High Anglicanism. His friend and ally, Irving Babbitt (1865–1933), differed from him sharply, although he shared his general outlook. Babbitt was a much harder, cruder writer: a violent, pungent polemicist, quite secular in outlook. He was a Stoic with some interest in Buddhism and Confucianism. Babbitt, a Harvard professor of French, attacked the American factualism imported from Germany in *Literature and the American College* (1908). He recommended, with many reservations, the French critics in *The Masters of Modern French Criticism* (1912), especially Ferdinand Brunetière (1849–1906). *Rousseau and Romanticism* (1919) was a powerful antiromantic

tract mercilessly ridiculing the romantic worship of genius, passion, and nature, its misconception of man as naturally good. Babbitt's books are filled with a passionate concern for ideas and ethics; they suffer from a lack of aesthetic sensibility, an obtuseness of reading, a harsh and strident manner.

More and Babbitt found several influential adherents, among whom was Norman Foerster (1887–1972). Foerster, who had written well on earlier criticism in *American Criticism* (1929), organized the statements that for a short period (1929–30) attracted wide public attention to the humanist movement. The movement failed for obvious reasons: the social conservatism of the humanists ran counter to the temper of a nation just plunged into the Depression; their rigid moralism violated the nature of literature as an art; and their hostility to the contemporary arts cut them off from literature as a living institution. Still, the humanist movement left an imprint on the American universities. It helped to emancipate literary teaching from the old factualism and spread a concern for ideas and the relation of literature to life. It influenced many critics even when they rejected the creed itself: Eliot, F. O. Matthiessen (1902–1950), Austin Warren (1899–1986), Yvor WINTERS.

But the rejuvenation of criticism came, not only in the United States but also in England, from two Americans: Pound and Eliot. Pound preached "IMAGISM" since about 1912: a simple, colloquial poetry, in rhythms close to those of spoken language, with an eye turned to the object, "austere, direct, free from emotional slither." He had violently reacted against romantic and Victorian taste, but made, at first, little impression beyond a small following, which was joined by Eliot. Eliot had begun to write criticism in 1909, when he was at Harvard, but he established a reputation as a critic only with a collection of essays, *The Sacred Wood* (1920). It was secured, after the great success of *The Waste Land* (1922), with *For Lancelot Andrewes* (1928), which contained, in its preface, the famous declaration that he was "Royalist, Anglo-Catholic and classicist." In the meantime, I. A. Richards's *Principles of Literary Criticism* (1924) had made a profound impact. Richards had an entirely different intellectual background from Eliot, in positivistic psychology and in utilitarianism. Strangely and surprisingly, the doctrines of Eliot and Richards fused in many minds. Eliot and Richards influenced each other. In combination with F. R. LEAVIS in England, and with Cleanth BROOKS in the United States, a body of doctrines evolved that is the core of what is usually called the "New Criticism."

Pound, although highly important as the main instigator of the changes in taste, was himself hardly a critic. He was rather the maker of manifestos, a man who proclaimed his preferences and rankings, but never argued or analyzed as a critic should. Pound's occasional attempts at poetic theory are crude, and his literary history is extremely arbitrary. He had, however, the merit of drawing attention to much poetry that was little known except to specialists: Provençal, very early Italian before Dante, and Chinese. Pound conceived as an ideal of criticism the task "to define the classic." He succeeded in construing a highly selective ancestry for his own poetry and in disparaging everything that did not fit the pattern. According to Pound, there is nothing in German poetry besides the *Minnesänger* and Heine. There is nothing in French between Villon and the symbolists. In English, Milton is "the most unpleasant poet," a "thorough-going decadent," and among the English 19th-c. poets only Walter Savage Landor and Robert Browning find favor in Pound's eyes. Pound was less interested in prose; he wrote in detail only on James and Joyce. Pound had a personal interest in James's problem of the American expatriate and was one of the first fervent admirers of Joyce. He had the courage of his opinions and the boldness of a specific new taste. But his concept of poetry is very narrow and his idea of tradition is that of an agglomeration of appealing hobbies, unconnected glimpses of most diverse civilizations and styles. He often behaved like a "barbarian in a museum" (Yvor Winters).

T. E. Hulme (1883–1917) is usually coupled with Pound as a precursor of Eliot. He may have influenced Pound in the formulation of the imagist creed. But Eliot never knew Hulme, who was killed in World War I. His writings (with the exception of scattered articles) appeared only in 1924, as *Speculations*. By then Eliot's views were fully established. Hulme has been much overrated; he reflected a new taste and imported new ideas, but he had little to say that is his own. Much of his writing is straight exposition. In his most independent essay, "Romanticism and Classicism," Hulme expounds the anti-romanticism of the Action Française. Romanticism is to him the revolution, bourgeois liberalism, "spilt religion," a sentimental trust in human nature. Against this, Hulme pits classicism, which implies a belief in original sin. The contrast is then pinned to the Coleridgean distinction of imagination and fancy. Imagination is romantic, fancy classical. What is needed today is a fanciful, precise, visual poetry. Hulme makes a faltering attempt to claim Coleridge and Bergson for this kind of "classicism," but cannot succeed. He wants an imagist, metaphorical poetry, in free verse. But it is hard to see what all this has to do with Bergson and his romantic philosophy of flux (except the emphasis on the concrete) and how it can be brought in line with admiration for Byzantine mosaics, Egyptian sculpture, and the sculpture of Jacob Epstein. Apparently we have to do with different stages in the development of a young man (the writings on plastic art all date from December 1913 to July 1914) who had a long way to go toward the definition of an original point of view. But he was an important symptom.

Eliot is often similar in taste to Pound. But as a critic he is immeasurably subtler and more profound. Like Pound, Eliot reacted strongly against romanticism and Milton. He exalted Dante, the Jacobean dramatists, the metaphysical poets, and the French symbolists as the bearers of *the* tradition of great poetry. But in Eliot we are confronted not only with a change of taste. The new tradition is defended in terms of a new classicism, of a whole superstructure of ideas that appeals to the Latin and Christian tradition. It is anchored in a theory of poetry that starts with a psychology of poetic creation. Poetry is not the "overflow of powerful feelings," is not the expression of personality, but is an impersonal organization of feelings that demands a "unified sensibility," a collaboration of intellect and feeling in order to find the precise "objective correlative," the symbolic structure of a work of art. Eliot expounded a scheme of the history of English poetry that postulates a "unified sensibility" before the middle of the 17th c., especially in the metaphysical poets, and then traced its "dissociation," in the purely intellectual poetry of the 18th c. and the purely emotional poetry of the 19th. He postulated the need of reintegration, fulfilled in his own poetry (and that of other contemporaries, such as Pound). It is both intellectual and emotional; it concerns the whole man, not only the heart. But while Eliot speaks of unified sensibility, of the fusion of thought and feeling, he still insists that poetry is not knowledge of any kind. The poet is no philosopher or thinker. "Neither Shakespeare nor Dante did any thinking." A poet such as Dante, who has taken over the system of Thomas Aquinas, is preferable, in this respect, to a poet such as Shakespeare, who has picked up ideas from anywhere, or to Goethe, who has construed

his own personal philosophy. Eliot, who had earlier defended the "integrity" and autonomy of poetry, came to the recognition of a double standard in criticism: artistic and moral-philosophical-theological. "The 'greatness' of literature," he argued, "cannot be determined solely by literary standards." More and more, Eliot judged works of literature by their conformity to the tradition and to orthodoxy. The distinction between "artness" and "greatness," which again divorces form and content, grew out of Eliot's preoccupation with the question of "belief" in literature. The problem whether the reader should or must share the ideas of an author worried Eliot and Richards greatly.

Eliot took several, often conflicting, positions, at one time arguing that the reader need not agree and later coming to the conclusion that we cannot give poetic assent to anything we consider "incoherent, immature and not founded on the facts of experience" (as the poetry of Shelley appeared to Eliot). But Eliot's criticism was at its best when he could forget about "belief" and the related problem of "sincerity" (how far has the poet to believe the ideas he expresses?) and, rather, analyze the work itself. Eliot constantly stressed the role of language in poetry, which should be "the perfection of common language." Milton's language is condemned as artificial and conventional. Poetry must not lose touch with the living language. Eliot defended what used to be called prosaic poetry such as that of Dryden or Dr. Johnson. But he could think of poetry also as logic of the imagination, a sequence of images or even moments of emotional intensity. Sound and meter seem to him less central, as the "music" of poetry means to him much more than sound-patterns. It is the interplay of sound and meaning and of the secondary meanings. In "music" the poet touches the frontiers of consciousness; yet the poet is not a primitive man, but rather contains all history. Poets are related to their times; they cannot help expressing them, even their chaos, but, on the other hand, poetry is also timeless. There is a final hierarchy of the poets, an ultimate greater or less. There is an interplay between "Tradition and the Individual Talent" (1919). Tradition involves the historical sense and the historical sense to Eliot "involves a perception, not only of the pastness of the past, but of its presence." A poet should write "not merely with his own generation in his bones, but with a feeling that the whole literature of Europe from Homer on has a simultaneous existence and composes a simultaneous order." Tradition is the classical tradition descended from Greece and Rome. Rome (and such a poet as Vergil) is the indispensable link in the chain of tradition. Germany is sometimes excluded from this unity of European culture, defined as both Christian and classical. But in his later years Eliot welcomed Germany back again into the European fold and even recanted his earlier opinion, which excluded Goethe from the great classics, praising his "wisdom" and even his science.

Eliot thus construed the tradition very selectively. It converged on his practice as a poet: the bright visual imagination of Dante, the living speech of the later Shakespeare, of Donne and of Dryden, the dramatic lyricism of Donne, Browning, and Pound, the "wit" and "unified sensibility" of the metaphysical poets, the "irony" of Jules Laforgue (1860–1887), the impersonality of Mallarmé and Valéry. Much of Eliot's impact is due to his practical criticism: to his brief, dogmatic, assertive, but persuasive and subtle essays, which seem often to proceed only by his quoting a few passages and making brief comparisons.

In several lectures (for example, "The Frontiers of Criticism," 1956) Eliot slighted his own criticism, deplored the influence of some catch-phrases derived from it, and detached himself from what he called the "lemon-squeezer school of criticism." From the point of view of literary criticism, Eliot's influence declined in his later years. His interests shifted away from pure criticism, and he was apt to use literature as a document for his jeremiads on the modern world. He finally became committed to a double standard that dissolved the unity of the work of art as well as the sensibility that goes into its making and the critical act itself. But, taken in its early purity, his criticism was the most influential of the century.

Only I. A. Richards can compare with Eliot in influence. Richards differed completely in aim and method, but shared many of Eliot's tastes and, with his practical criticism, helped to define the turn toward an analysis of verbal art that prevails in English and American criticism. But Richards was primarily interested in theory, in the psychic effect of poetry on the mind of its reader. Richards did not recognize a world of aesthetic values and emotions. Rather, the only value of art is the psychic organization it imposes on us, what Richards describes as "the patterning of impulses," the equilibrium of attitudes it induces. The artist is conceived almost as a mental healer, and art as therapy. Richards was not, however, able to describe this effect of art very concretely, although he thought it would replace religion as a social force. He finally had to admit that the desired, balanced poise can be given by "a carpet or a pot, by a gesture as by the Parthenon." It does not ultimately matter whether we like good or bad poetry, as long as we order our minds. Thus Richards's theory—which is objective and scientific in its pretensions and often appeals to future advances of neurology—ends with critical paralysis: a complete divorce between the poem as an objective structure and the reader's mind.

But fortunately, Richards eluded, in practice, the consequences of his theory and came to grips with specific poetic texts by applying a theory of meaning first developed in *The Meaning of Meaning: A Study of the Influence of Language upon Thought and of the Science of Symbolism* (1923, with C. K. Ogden). In *Principles of Literary Criticism* (1924) Richards analyzed the different components of a work of art in psychological terms, into sensations, images, emotions, attitudes, and suggested standards of evaluation: a grading of poetry in terms of complexity, with a preference for a poetry of "inclusion" (a term derived from George SANTAYANA), a difficult poetry that would resist ironic contemplation. Richards's analysis of meaning, which distinguishes between sense, tone, feeling, and intention, emphasizes the ambiguities of language, the function of metaphor as central to poetry. Later, in *Coleridge on Imagination* (1934), Richards even restated the romantic theory of imagination as fusing and unifying, in which the most disparate elements of the world come together. The affinity with Eliot's "unified sensibility" is obvious; but in Richards, poetry is even more deliberately cut off from all knowledge and even reference. On the basis of a simple dichotomy between intellectual and emotive language, truth is assigned to science, while art can do nothing but arouse emotions, which must, however, be patterned, equipoised, complex, to achieve the purpose of mental ordering. Poetry at most elaborates the myths by which men live, even though these myths may be untrue, may be mere "pseudo-statements" in the light of science.

In his later essays (one collection is *Speculative Instruments*, 1955) Richards gave up his earlier reliance on neurology, but the point of view has remained in substance the same. Richards is primarily a theorist and wrote little on actual texts; but *Practical Criticism* (1929), a book that analyzes the papers of students who were set to discuss a series of poems given to them without the names of the authors, shows Richards's pedagogical talent in the teaching and analyzing of poetry. He distinguishes the various sources of misunderstanding: the difficulty of making out the plain sense of a poem, the lack of sensibility to meter and rhythm, the misinterpretation of figurative language, the critical pitfalls of stock responses, of sentimentality or hardness of heart, of ideological or technical preconceptions. Richards's technique of interpretation analyzes language, but unlike the logical positivists, it favors a great flexibility of vocabulary and trains in distinguishing shades of meaning.

This is the starting point of Richards's most gifted English disciple, William EMPSON, who, in *Seven Types of Ambiguity* (1930; rev. ed., 1953) developed, in a series of brilliant interpretations of poetic passages, a scheme that allowed him to distinguish types of ambiguity, progressing in complexity, with the increasing distance from the simple statement. Empson draws out implicit meanings, defines by multiple definitions, and pursues to the farthest ends the implications, poetic and social, of difficult, witty, metaphorical poetry. He is not only an analyst but a critic who tries to justify his own taste in poetry and disparages simple romantic emotionalism or vagueness. In his later books Empson combined this method of semantic analysis with ideas drawn from psychoanalysis and Marxism. In *Some Versions of Pastoral* (1935), a term that includes proletarian literature, *Alice in Wonderland* is psychoanalyzed, and Gray's "Elegy Written in a Country Churchyard" is interpreted as a defense of Tory conservatism. In *The Structure of Complex Words* (1951), Empson freed himself from the emotionalism of Richards and developed a concept of meaning that allows for knowledge and reference. He again displayed an amazing ingenuity in verbal analysis and an acute awareness of social implications. Terms such as "wit" or "honest" are analyzed in different contexts, in Pope or Shakespeare.

But Empson often left the realm of literary criticism for a version of lexicography and became more and more enmeshed in a private world of associations and speculations that lose contact with the text and use it only as pretext for his fireworks of wit and recondite ingenuity. His *Milton's God* (1961; rev. ed., 1965) is even further removed from literary criticism. It is an attack on Christianity and, in particular, on the conception of God the Father sacrificing His Son. Milton is praised for his picture of God in *Paradise Lost*, a God who seems to Empson "astonishingly like Uncle Joe Stalin." The poem has "barbaric power" because Milton could express "a downright horrible conception of God."

The impulses emanating from Eliot and Richards were most effectively combined, at least in England, in the work of F. R. Leavis and his disciples grouped around the magazine *Scrutiny* (1932–53). Leavis was a man of strong convictions and harsh polemical manners. In his later years he sharply underlined his disagreement with the later developments of Eliot and Richards. But his starting point is in Eliot's taste and in Richards's technique of analysis. He differed from them mainly by a strongly Arnoldian concern for a moralistic humanism. In *New Bearings in English Poetry* (1932) he criticized Victorian and Georgian poetry, and praised and analyzed the later Yeats, the early Eliot, and the newly discovered Gerard Manley Hopkins (1844–1889), whose poems had been published for the first time in 1918. *Revaluation* (1936) was the first consistent attempt to rewrite the history of English poetry from a 20th-c. point of view. Spenser, Milton, Tennyson, and Swinburne recede into the background; Donne, Pope, Wordsworth, Keats, Hopkins, Yeats, and T. S. Eliot emerge as the carriers of the great tradition.

In contrast to Eliot, Leavis admired Pope much more than Dryden and established his descent from the metaphysical poets. Like Eliot, Leavis disparaged Shelley, "as repetitious, vaporous, monotonously self-regarding, and often emotionally cheap." But he appreciated Wordsworth for his sanity (although he did not share his philosophy) and Keats for his emotional maturity. Similarly, Leavis attempted in *The Great Tradition* (1948) to establish a new selection from the English novel. The 18th-c. novelists and Scott are dismissed, as are Dickens ("a great entertainer"), Thackeray, and Meredith. Only Jane Austen, George Eliot, Henry James, Joseph CONRAD, and D. H. Lawrence survive. Leavis practiced close reading, a training in sensibility, which has little use for literary history or theory. But "sensibility" with Leavis meant also a sense for tradition, a concern for culture, for humanity. On the one hand, he rejected Marxism, and on the other, the orthodoxy of Eliot. He admired a local culture, the organic community of the English countryside.

Leavis sharply criticized the commercialization and standardization of English literary life and defended the need for tradition, for a social code and order, for "maturity," "sanity," and "discipline." But these terms are purely secular and include the ideals of D. H. Lawrence, whom Leavis interpreted to conform to a healthy tradition (see *D. H. Lawrence, Novelist*, 1955). Leavis's emphasis on the text, and even the texture of words, is often deceptive: his observations on form, technique, and language are often haphazard and arbitrary. Actually he left the verbal surface very quickly in order to define the particular emotions or sentiments an author conveys. He became a social and moral critic, who, however, insisted on the continuity between language and ethics, on the morality of form. Leavis's ultimate value criterion, "Life," remains, however, bafflingly obscure: it means antiaestheticism, realism, optimism, or just courage and devotion in turn, as, on the whole, Leavis as a resolute empiricist left his premises unexamined and displayed a complacent distrust of and even hatred for theory.

In his later writings—*Anna Karenina and Other Essays* (1967), *English Literature in Our Time and the University* (1969), *Dickens, the Novelist* (1970), *Nor Shall My Sword* (1972), *The Living Principle: English as a Discipline of Thought* (1975)—we can, however, discern a definite shift or even reversal of some of Leavis's positions. Not that he gave up his basic principles; but he distanced himself so completely from T. S. Eliot and embraced D. H. Lawrence and Blake so fervently that one can speak of a conversion to romanticism. He reinstated Dickens as one of the greatest creative writers.

Leavis managed to assemble a group of disciples, of whom many have contributed importantly to the development of English criticism. L. C. Knights (b. 1906), in *Drama and Society in the Age of Jonson* (1937) and in *Explorations* (1947), is mainly concerned with the Elizabethans. Derek Traversi (b. 1912) has interpreted Shakespeare with great sensitivity, especially in *An Approach to Shakespeare* (1938) and *Shakespeare: The Last Phase* (1954). Martin Turnell (b. 1908) has written extensively, although often loosely, on French literature; his *The Classical Moment: Studies in Corneille, Molière, Racine* (1947), *The Novel in France* (1950), *Baudelaire* (1952), and *The Art of French Fiction* (1959), which exalts Stendhal and Proust at the expense of Balzac and Flaubert, are instructive but often diffuse and erratic books. Mrs. Q. D. Leavis (1906–1981), in *Fiction and the Reading Public* (1932), supplied the arguments for the general view of the decline of modern taste and the shrinking of a cultivated audience. Marius Bewley (1918–1973), an American adherent, studied Hawthorne

and Henry James (in *The Complex Fate*, 1952) and the 19th-c. American novel (in *The Eccentric Design*, 1957). The intransigence of the group has diminished its immediate effectiveness; F. R. Leavis did not even recognize parallel efforts elsewhere. But in spite of shortcomings in sympathy, a certain provinciality, and an excessive preoccupation with the pedagogy of literature, Leavis and his group have produced fine practical criticism that has established the new taste and again justified the social role of literature in a minority culture.

Side by side with what could loosely be called Eliotic criticism, a number of English critics were active who could be labeled "neoromantic." They are men who finally appeal to an inner voice, to the subconscious mind, and who think of criticism mainly as a process of self-expression and self-discovery. Still, all have learned from Eliot and would have written quite differently without him as a model.

John Middleton Murry passed through bafflingly diverse stages in his development. He wrote a *Life of Jesus* (1926), as well as *The Necessity of Communism* (1932). Murry, once widely admired, has been losing influence steadily, as his later books are neither good biography nor good criticism, and indulge more and more in private theosophic speculation. But it seems unfair to neglect his early criticism because of the vagaries of his search for God. His book *Dostoevsky* (1916), although often quite mistaken in its interpretations, was an early attempt to see the Russian novelist as a kind of symbolist. *The Problem of Style* (1922) is remarkably similar in outlook to Eliot's early phase, although Eliot is not mentioned. There is the same emphasis on visual imagination, on metaphor as a mode of apprehension, on the transformation of emotion in a work of art which Murry calls "crystallization." His early collection of essays, *Aspects of Literature* (1920), and *Countries of the Mind* (1922), should also be classed with Eliotic criticism. But his *Keats and Shakespeare* (1925) shows a shift: it is a biographical interpretation (often sensitive and moving) of Keats's growth and struggle for maturity, of his "soul-making." The parallel with Shakespeare, however, is forced, and the tone has become fervent and often oracular. *Son of Woman: The Story of D. H. Lawrence* (1931) is a highly personal interpretation of his friend and enemy: it makes Lawrence out a weakling who willed himself into vitality. An arbitrary theosophy invaded the books *William Blake* (1933) and *Shakespeare* (1936), and there is hardly anything to be said for the dull book *Jonathan Swift* (1954).

The same fate seems to have befallen G. Wilson Knight. His early writings, especially *The Wheel of Fire* (1929), elaborate a technique of Shakespeare interpretation by leading images and clusters, by some kind of metaphorical organization. Knight still had contact with the text, a feeling for evidence, although the antithesis, tempest versus music, seems pressed too hard. But Knight's later books show a gradual deterioration of critical intelligence. The same method is applied indiscriminately to all writers: whether Pope or Wordsworth, Milton or Byron. All poetry is reduced to a conveyor of the same mystic message. The allegorical reading of Milton anticipating even details of World War II (with Hitler as Satan) and the interpretation of Byron as "the next Promethean man in Western history after Christ" (in *Byron: The Christian Virtues*, 1952), are so fantastic that they cease to be criticism or scholarship.

By far the best of these neoromantic critics was Sir Herbert Read. He advocated surrealism, psychoanalysis, and the use of the Jungian collective unconscious in literature, but basically kept a central critical insight into organic form. His *Wordsworth* (1930) pressed the theme of Wordsworth's supposed feeling of guilt because of his affair with Annette Vallon very far. In his *In Defence of Shelley* (1936) he attempted a psychoanalysis of Shelley that serves as a rather double-edged apology for his life. But the core of Read's writings is to be found in *Collected Essays on Literary Criticism* (1938) and *The True Voice of Feeling* (1953), in which a theory of organic form, of spontaneity, obscurity, myth, and dream is propounded with constant appeals to the great English romantic poets, particularly Coleridge, in whom Read found anticipations of Freudianism and existentialism. Read shows sensitivity, style, and a theoretical mind. Although he advocated surrender to the "dark unconscious," he did so sanely and clearly. His irrationalism was always tempered by a lively sense of the social role of both the arts and crafts.

F. W. Bateson (1901–1978) stood quite apart from other English critics, playing with gusto the role of a gadfly, of a polemicist who in his periodical, *Essays in Criticism*, argued with almost everybody. Bateson first wrote a short book, *English Poetry and the English Language* (1934); in it he sketched a history of English poetry as completely dependent on changes in the history of language, which alone mediates social influences on literature. A later book, *English Poetry: A Critical Introduction* (1950), rewrites the history of English poetry in terms of the audiences of the different periods. According to Bateson, the audiences are the determining causes of literary change, rather than the economic basis of society. Later Bateson abandoned his emphasis on the continuity between language and literature completely and argued against the use of linguistics in criticism, against the idea of the work of art as an artifact, against formalism, in favor of intention as a standard of judgment, and finally for a judicial criticism that would be both moral and social. *Essays in Critical Dissent* (1972) and *The Scholar-Critic* (1972) are collections of his papers.

Most recently English critics have begun to feel the impact of new speculative developments, particularly in linguistics and semantics. There are now fine technical studies of the language of poetry, such as Christine BROOKE-ROSE's *A Grammar of Metaphor* (1958) and Winifred Nowottny's (b. 1917) *The Language Poets Use* (1962). David LODGE has offered "verbal analyses" of the English novel, first in *The Language of Fiction* (1966) and then in *The Modes of Modern Writing* (1977), which sensitively uses Roman Jakobson's dichotomy of metaphor and metonymy to interpret modern novels. Frank Kermode (b. 1919) established his reputation with *Romantic Image* (1957), which argued against the whole tradition of romantic and symbolist poetics, and which saw poems in terms of imagery—concrete, organic, independent of the author's intention, created by an "excluded artist," expressing a truth resistant to rational explanation. Later, in *The Sense of an Ending: Studies in the Theory of Fiction* (1967), Kermode uses existentialist preconceptions of a rationalistic type to set literary fictions, particularly fictions of the Apocalypse, within a general theory of fiction. Kermode also wrote (for example, in *Continuities*, 1968) much about the nature of modernism as apocalyptic, becoming satirical about the new avant-garde, pop and op art, the music of silence, and other recent developments in which "the difference between art and joke is as obscure as that between art and non-art." In contrast, he sets up *The Classic* (1975) which, to be alive, today, has, however, to be accommodated to the modern reader by allegory and prophecy. Kermode shares the concern about the possibility of right reading, about the danger of sheer arbitrariness, and answers it by an appeal to "competence," a linguistic concept that shifts the problem to an elite of experts.

With these few exceptions, English criticism is still traditional, largely concerned with descriptive criticism, with the interpretation of specific texts and with literary history. George Watson (b. 1927), in *The Literary Critics* (1962), argued that it should be so, and he has found much support. John Holloway (b. 1920), the author of *The Victorian Sage* (1953), dismissed all philosophical and aesthetic speculations as abracadabra and pleaded for "calm intelligence, moderation," and "urbanity"; William W. Robson (dates n.a.), who in many ways is near to both Leavis and Bateson in his *Critical Essays* (1966), defended "criticism without principles," since criticism is not a science but a personal encounter with the works. "There is no body of established results which the next critic can build on." It would be the end of all discussion. But Continental ideas and trends have been felt in England increasingly in recent years. George STEINER, an American citizen born in Paris, living in Cambridge, England, has become their tireless, eloquent propagator in books such as *Language and Silence* (1967), *Extraterritorial* (1971), *After Babel: Aspects of Language and Translation* (1975), *On Difficulty and Other Essays* (1978), and *Heidegger* (1978). They are inspired by a strong feeling of the precariousness of traditional literary culture.

Recent American Criticism

Recent American criticism is usually lumped together under the term the "New Criticism," from the title of a book, published in 1941, by John Crowe RANSOM. It is a misleading term, since it suggests a far greater unity of purpose and doctrine than close examination of recent American critics will reveal. It is hard to find anything in common among all the more important American critics except a reaction against the impressionism or naturalism of the past and a general turn toward a closer analysis of the actual text of a work of art. But even this generalization does not hold good for many critics. It is better to distinguish, at least roughly, two main groups: those who draw on other fields (psychoanalysis, myth, Marxism, semantics) in order to bring their insights to an understanding of literature; and those who have focused single-mindedly on the work of art, have tried to develop techniques of analysis peculiarly suited to poetry, and have defended poetry as a way to a knowledge of concrete reality. The first group of writers tend to become general critics of civilization; the second have concentrated on a modern apology of poetry against science and attempted to define its peculiar nature and function. Only four critics in this second group, Allen TATE, Robert Penn WARREN, Ransom, and Cleanth Brooks, the so-called Southern critics, have had close personal relations and form a coherent group unified in its outlook and main preoccupations.

Possibly the best-known American critic (certainly in Europe) is Edmund Wilson, a critic of great versatility and facility who, in turn, applied almost every method to his texts and wrote on almost every subject. He began his career with *Axel's Castle* (1931), a book about the symbolist movement in Western literature, with chapters on Yeats, Valéry, Eliot, Proust, Joyce, and Gertrude STEIN, and a conclusion that predicted the demise of symbolism in favor of a social collective art. Although Wilson was hostile to aestheticism and decadence, his exposition of the masters of the 20th c. is sympathetic, since on the whole, he aims at conveying enjoyment and envisages rather vaguely a reconciliation of symbolism and naturalism, art and life, criticism and history. His later writings are not unified books (with the exception of an account of socialist and communist theories of history in *To the Finland Station*, 1940), but collections of essays ranging widely over modern literature. The influence of Marxism (always sharply distinguished from Stalinism) is often discernible and, more prominently, the method of psychoanalysis. *The Wound and the Bow* (1941) takes the Philoctetes story as a symbol of the relationship between the artist's wound, his neurosis, and his bow—his art— and shows with great finesse, in studies of Dickens and KIPLING, that psychoanalytical insight can be joined with literary taste. In all his many collections, from *The Triple Thinkers* (1938) to *The Shores of Light* (1952), Wilson shows his mastery of the form of the essay, his tolerant taste, his skill in exposition, his brilliance of formulation, his secular common sense, and strong social concern.

But Wilson, although highly meritorious in his general effect on a wide reading public, lacked analytical power and suffered from frequent lapses into journalistic indiscriminations and personal idiosyncrasies. With the exception of some original insights into the psychic histories of some of his subjects, Wilson ultimately is a middleman, immensely readable, intelligent, and sensitive, but lacking in a personal center and theory.

Lionel Trilling was also a general critic of civilization rather than strictly a critic of literature. He wrote excellently, with common sense and discrimination, on both Freudianism and the Kinsey Report. He began with a good though diffuse book, *Matthew Arnold* (1939), and collected his essays in *The Liberal Imagination* (1950) and *The Opposing Self* (1955). His chief concern was the relation between literature and politics. Trilling, a convinced liberal (in the American sense), was worried about the gulf between the rationality of his political convictions and the imaginative insights of modern literature. A man of modern sensibility with a taste for Henry James and Forster, to the second of whom he devoted a small book (*E. M. Forster*, 1943; 2nd rev. ed., 1965), and a dislike for naturalism, he was only able to state his problem, but could not solve it in his own terms precisely because he believed that ideas are emotions and that politics permeates literature. He finally had to come to recognize the "fortuitous and gratuitous nature of art, how it exists beyond the reach of the will alone." His fine essay on Keats shows his increasing feeling for selves conceived in opposition to general culture, for the alienation of the artist as a necessary device of his self-realization.

A similar combination of modern literary sensibility and social concern permeates the work of F. O. Mathiessen, except that his development went in the opposite direction from Trilling's. He began (after some academic research) with a sympathetic interpretation, *The Achievement of T. S. Eliot* (1935), and then produced *The American Renaissance* (1941), a long, careful study of Emerson, Thoreau, Hawthorne, Melville, and Whitman. It combines an Eliotic concern for language and diction, for symbolism and myth, with a fervent belief in the possibilities of democracy in America. Two books on Henry James pursue the old aesthetic interests, while many articles (some collected in *The Responsibilities of the Critic*, 1952) and a book (*Theodore Dreiser*, 1951) show increasingly a change of taste in the direction of realism and an overwhelming, passionately earnest concern with the social duties of the critic, in a Marxism reconciled with Christianity.

Kenneth Burke attempts the most ambitious scheme of recent American criticism: he combines the method of Marxism, psychoanalysis, and anthropology with semantics, in order to devise a system of human behavior and motivation that uses literature only as a starting point or illustration. Burke is rightly admired for the uncanny quickness of his mind, his astonishing originality in

making connections, his dialectical skill, and his terminological inventiveness. He has influenced recent criticism by his special terms and mannerisms. But judged as literary criticism, much of his work is irrelevant, and literature, more and more, is even violated and distorted in his work to serve quite extrinsic arguments and purposes.

Burke was still primarily a literary critic in *Counter-Statement* (1931), a collection of essays that contains, for instance, a brilliant comparison of Gide and Thomas Mann. But with *Permanence and Change* (1935) and *Attitudes toward History* (1937), he began to indulge in speculations on psychology and history and to discuss literature only in the sense that, with him, life is a poem and all men are poets. *The Philosophy of Literary Form* (1941) ostensibly returns to literature. It develops a "dialectical" or "dramatic" criticism interpreting poetry as a series of "strategies for the encompassing of situations," in practice as an act of the poet's personal purification. For example, Coleridge's *Rime of the Ancient Mariner* is elaborately interpreted as "a ritual for the redemption of his drug." Similarly, in *A Grammar of Motives* (1945), Keat's "Ode on a Grecian Urn" is read in terms of the identity of love and death, of capitalist individualism and Keat's tubercular fever, in almost complete disregard of the text. *A Grammar of Motives* is the first part of a trilogy (of which the second part, *A Rhetoric of Motives*, was published in 1950; the third part, *A Symbolic of Motives*, has not been finished) in which Burke attempts to construe a whole philosophy of meaning, human behavior, and action. Five terms—act, scene, agent, agency, and purpose—are used as main categories: literary illustrations abound, but the center of the whole project is elsewhere. All distinctions between life and literature, language and action disappear in Burke's theory.

Burke has increasingly lost any sense for the integrity of a work of art, the relevance of an observation or bright idea to a text. He has become imprisoned in a private world of terms and concepts, often so weirdly in opposition to ordinary usage that his speculations seem to evolve in a void. A system that plans to embrace all life ends as a baffling phantasmagoria of "strategies," categories, "charts," and "situations."

In Burke the expansion of criticism has reached its extreme limit. At the opposite pole is the group of "Southern critics," Ransom, Tate, Brooks, and Warren, who have concentrated on a close study of poetic texts and a modern apology for poetry. But it would be a mistake to think of them as aesthetes or even formalists, since their concern with poetry has social and even religious implications: they have defended Southern conservatism and have seen—as Leavis did in England—the evils of urbanization and commercialization, the need for a healthy society that alone can produce vital literature. But the Southern critics have kept their concept of culture separate from their literary criticism, since they understand that art is an autonomous realm and that poetry has its own peculiar function.

Although the theories of the Southern critics could be described as a fusion of those of Eliot and I. A. Richards, they differ from them importantly in having broken with their emotionalism. They recognize that poetry is not merely emotive language, but conveys a kind of knowledge, a particular kind of concrete presentational knowledge. Thus, the analysis of a work of art has to proceed from objectively recognizable factors of the work itself rather than from the reader's responses. Ransom, the oldest of the group, an eminent poet himself, developed the view (in *The World's Body*, 1938) that poetry conveys a sense of the particularity of the world. "As science more and more completely reduces the world to its types and forms, art, replying, must invest it again with the body." But purely physical or imagist poetry is only a first stage. "Platonic" poetry, poetry merely disguising or allegorizing truths, is bad. True poetry is like the "metaphysical" poetry of the 17th c., a new perception of the world, a new awareness of its realness, conveyed mainly by extended metaphor and pervasive symbolism. Ransom emphasized the "texture" of poetry, its seemingly irrelevant detail, although he upheld the need of an overall "structure" (a logical content). In practice, he was often, with his insistence on "texture," in danger of reintroducing the old dichotomy of form and content. In *The New Criticism* (1941) Ransom discussed Richards, Eliot, and Yvor Winters with many reservations and concluded by asking for an "ontological" critic who would treat an order of existence not created in scientific discourse. Ransom drew from Charles W. Morris (b. 1901), a logical positivist, the term "icon" to suggest the symbol in art, and, in a later paper (in *Poems and Essays*, 1955), used the Hegelian term, the "concrete universal," in an attempt to recognize the universalizing power of art while preserving the emphasis on the concrete, on metaphor, and its references to nature.

Allen Tate, like Ransom, was preoccupied with a defense of poetry against science. Science gives us abstraction, poetry concreteness, science partial knowledge, poetry complete knowledge. "Poetry alone gathers up the diverse departments of the intellect into a humane and living whole." Abstraction, mere idea, violates art. Good poetry proceeds from a union of intellect and feeling, or rather from a "tension." Tate elaborated his concept of poetry in several collections of essays, on which *On the Limits of Poetry* (1948) and *The Man of Letters in the Modern World* (1955) are the most inclusive.

Tate consistently rejected the attempt of Richards to make poetry a kind of therapy or make it take the place of religion. He sharply attacked both the scientific and the emotionally romantic view. Scientism, positivism, includes for Tate also historicism, the preoccupation with externals of the conventional literary scholar and any purely sociological approach. But literature is not taken out of society: on the contrary, Tate was deeply worried by the decay of an organic society and a religious world view, which alone, to his mind, could support a living tradition of art. Paradoxically, Tate, however, admired poetry most when it reflects the dissolution of tradition without losing its grasp of it. His essays on Poe, Emily Dickinson, T. S. Eliot, and Yeats show how these poets found personal substitutes for the old myths and symbols, while his discussion of Hart CRANE, a personal friend, serves to show the failure of the modern artist who has not found support in tradition.

Tate wrote widely, as a reviewer, mainly on modern poetry, but his interests broadened gradually to include, for instance, Dante. He became a convert to Roman Catholicism, and his later writings indicate an increasing skepticism as to the role of poetry and criticism in the modern world. Compared to the urbane, ironical, restrained Ransom, Tate was a passionate, even violent, and often polemical and personal writer.

Cleanth Brooks has been described as the systematizer and technician of the New Criticism. He has, no doubt, a sweet reasonableness and a gift for pedagogy and conciliatory formulation. His textbook, written in collaboration with Robert Penn Warren, *Understanding Poetry* (1938), has done more than any other single book to make the techniques of the New Criticism available in the classrooms of American colleges and universities and to present the techniques of analysis as something to be learned and imitated. But Brooks is not merely a popularizer and codifier.

He has his own personal theory. He has taken the terminology of Richards, deprived it of its psychologistic presuppositions, and transformed it into a remarkably clear system. It allows him to analyze poems as structures of tensions: in practice, of paradoxes and ironies.

Paradox and irony, with Brooks, are terms used very broadly. Irony is not the opposite of an overt statement, but "a general term for the kind of qualification which the various elements in a context receive from the context." It indicates the recognition of incongruities, the ambiguity, the union of opposites that Brooks finds in all good, that is, complex poetry. Poetry must be ironic in the sense of being able to withstand ironic contemplation. The method, no doubt, works best when applied to Donne or Shakespeare, Eliot or Yeats, but in *The Well Wrought Urn* (1947), a collection of analyses of poems, Brooks showed that even Wordsworth and Tennyson, Gray and Pope yield to this kind of technique. The whole theory emphasizes the contextual unity of the poem, its wholeness, its organism, while it allows a close analysis of its linguistic devices.

While Brooks is usually content to confine himself to his specialty—a masterly analysis of hidden meanings and relationships in metaphors and key words—he is also a critic, since his scheme permits him definite value judgments. Poets are ranked in terms of their success in resolving patterns of tensions, and the history of English poetry is seen in a new perspective. In *Modern Poetry and the Tradition* (1939) the romantic and Victorian ages appear as periods of decline compared to the 17th c., the greatest age of English poetry, while our own century appears as one of the revival of a properly "ironical," "tough," and complex poetry, as we find it in the later Yeats or Eliot. Brooks convincingly attacked what he calls "the heresy of paraphrase," that is, all attempts to reduce a poem to its prose content, and he has defended critical absolutism: the need of judgment against the excesses of relativism.

In *William Faulkner: The Yoknapatawpha Country* (1963) Brooks changes his method strikingly: he patiently examines the social picture, the intellectual and religious implications, and the themes and characters of Faulkner's main novels. The "formalistic" preoccupation has disappeared as is also obvious from a serious series of published lectures, *The Hidden God: Studies in Hemingway, Faulkner, Yeats, Eliot, and Warren* (1963), which announces its main topic in the title.

The fourth of the Southern critics, Robert Penn Warren, a fine novelist and poet, has published only one volume of collected criticism, *Selected Essays* (1958). The essay "Pure and Impure Poetry" states the argument for inclusive, complex, difficult (though impure) poetry memorably, and his essays on Hemingway, Thomas WOLFE, and Faulkner, and on Coleridge's *Rime of the Ancient Mariner* show his skill in symbolist interpretation, which widens into a study of the imagination and its role in the modern world.

Among the critics who cannot be called Southern, R. P. Blackmur was nearest to the general outlook of the Southern group. He was, in contrast to them, strongly influenced by Kenneth Burke and later in his career expressed dissatisfaction with their concentration on "close reading." Blackmur himself started as an extremely subtle, refined, elusive analyst, mainly of modern American poetry and Henry James. He was closely concerned with language and words, diction, imagery, rhyme and meter, and later tried to systematize his practice in a general theory of "language as gesture." "Gesture," which for Blackmur was basic to all the arts, is a term combining symbol and expression: a "cumulus of meaning" achieved by all the devices of poetry—punning, rhyme, meter, tropes. Criticism is defined as the "formal discourse of an amateur"—amateur in the sense of lover of poetry. Sympathy, identification, is required, and any external methodologies—Freudianism, Marxism, semantics—are rejected.

Increasingly, Blackmur felt the narrowness of the techniques of the New Criticism and saw that literature should, after all, be judged as a moral act in society. His perspective widened to include Dostoevsky and Tolstoy; in method, he adopted economic and psychoanalytical ideas. But in theoretical reflections he seemed not to have reached any clarity or system of his own. His essays, collected in *Language as Gesture* (1952), and *The Lion and the Honeycomb* (1955), often show a disconcerting loss of contact with the text and a random experimentation with new sets of terms and contraries: symbol, myth, form, "rational imagination," even behavior. Blackmur—just because of his great talent, versatility, and subtlety—illustrates the predicament of much recent American criticism: its involvement in a private world of concepts, feelings, and terms, groping toward a general philosophy of life on the occasion of literature, and a distrust of inherited and traditional methods that leads to reliance on purely personal perceptions and combinations. In some of Blackmur's essays the privacy of terms and feelings reached a stage of fuzziness: his supersubtlety stylistically reminds one of the last stage of Henry James, but has, in Blackmur, become so completely divorced from traditional procedures that it seems impossible to keep any interest in the solution of the riddles propounded.

While Blackmur moved into an opaque world of private ruminations, Yvor Winters could be called a lucid rationalist—a rationalist with a vengeance. Throughout his critical writings, collected under the titles *In Defence of Reason* (1947), *The Function of Criticism* (1957), *On Modern Poets* (1957), and *Forms of Discovery* (1967), Winters persecuted obscurantism and irrationalism, and bluntly stated that poetry is good only insofar as a poem makes a defensible rational statement about a given experience. Winters believed in absolute moral truths, and even in the moral content of poetry. He acidly and often vehemently attacked obscurity in modern poetry and despised the whole of the romantic tradition of spontaneous emotional expression. Poe is to Winters a bad poet and writer. Emerson, Hawthorne, and Whitman seem to him hopelessly self-indulgent, and Eliot and Ransom are both included in *The Anatomy of Nonsense* (1943). Winters admired an obscure transcendentalist poet, Jones Very (1813–1880), much more than Emerson, put Robert Bridges (1844–1930) and Sturge Moore (1870–1944) above Yeats and Eliot, and praised many minor poets. He could be easily dismissed as a crotchety doctrinaire, as a moralist similar to the new humanists.

But despite his moralism and rationalism, Winters was a "new critic," a man of modern sensibility, a fine analyst of poetry and fiction who understood that "poetic morality and poetic feelings are inseparable; feelings and technique, structure, are inseparable." Form is to him the decisive part of the moral content. He devised elaborate classifications of poetic structures and described the effects of meter well. He raised questions about the ontological status of poetry and argued against many of the theories of Eliot and Ransom. But the excessively dogmatic manner that hides a very personal and even eccentric sensibility vitiated Winters's effectiveness, which might have been very salutary as a counterweight against the irrationalism of the time. He remained alone on the fringes of the movement.

The main movement of the New Criticism reached a point of exhaustion in the 1960s. Although externally the movement was very successful in penetrating into the universities and monopolizing the critical journals, a state of stagnation set in: many imitators applied the method mechanically and unimaginatively. On some points the movement was not able to go beyond its initial narrow circle: the selection of European writers who have attracted the attention of the critics was oddly narrow and subject to the distortion of very local and temporary perspective. On the whole, the historical perspective of most critics remained very short. Literary history is still beyond the ken of the New Criticism. Also, the relations to modern linguistics and aesthetics remain unexplored. Much of the study of style, diction, and meter remains dilettantish; and aesthetics, while discussed in practice continually, remains without a sure philosophical foundation. Still, there were some hopeful signs of consolidation and expansion. William K. Wimsatt (1907–1975) in *The Verbal Icon* (1953) made an attempt to consolidate and expand the teachings of the New Criticism. He brilliantly argued against the fallacious tendency of criticism to trust the intention of the author and criticized I. A. Richards for his reliance on the emotion affecting the reader. In his epilogue to *Literary Criticism: A Short History* (1957, with Cleanth Brooks) Wimsatt made the clearest and most persuasive statement of a theory of literature that allows him to keep all three poles of literary theory: the mimetic, the emotive, and the expressionistic. The symbol, the concrete universal, remains the center of poetic theory, but ways are found to keep the relationship of poetry to morals and society intact.

The New Criticism, as a movement, has run its course. It immeasurably raised the level of awareness and sophistication in American criticism. It developed ingenious new methods of an analysis of poetry and its devices: imagery and symbol. It defined a new taste averse to the romantic tradition. It supplied an important apology of poetry in a world dominated by science. But it was unable to go successfully beyond its rather narrow confines, and it did not escape the dangers of ossification and institutionalization.

Several attempts have been made to replace the New Criticism. Among these the so-called Chicago Aristotelianism was the most distinct and most clearly organized. A group of scholars from the University of Chicago, headed by R. S. Crane (1886–1967), published a 650-page volume, *Critics and Criticism* (1952), which is, in part, devoted to very learned studies in the history of criticism and in part defends a view of literature sharply critical of the basic assumptions of the New Criticism. The role of language, metaphor, and symbol is minimized and all emphasis is put on plot and structure: Aristotle's *Poetics* serves as an inspiration for the terminology and the general scheme. In *The Languages of Criticism and the Structure of Poetry* (1953), Crane scored many polemical points against the hunters of paradoxes, symbols, and myths. But he and his followers (the most concretely critical is Elder Olson [b. 1909]) are unable to offer any positive remedies beyond the most arid classifications of hero-types, plot structures, and genres. With them, genre theory reaches more than neoclassical rigidity: for instance, Dante's *Divine Comedy* is classified as didactic and not as mimetic or symbolic. The armature of scholarship, especially imposing in the writings of the philosopher Richard McKeon (b. 1900), hides insensitivity to literary values: the professed "pluralism" and interest in the "pleasure" of literature disguises a lack of critical standards. These scholars want to arrive at them by a foolproof, mechanical way, resuscitating an Aristotelianism quite inadequate to the problems of modern literature. The whole enterprise seems an ultra-academic exercise destined to wither on the vine.

Much more successful, diverse, and stimulating was the myth criticism which, under the influence of Frazer and Jung, arose as a reaction to the New Criticism. It flourished in England and France, but in the United States it assumed a particular vitality, as it was able to absorb many of the achievements of the New Criticism, at least with its best practitioners. Myth appealed to many because it allows the discussions of themes and types, usually considered part of the "content" and thus not quite respectable to formalist critics. Huck Finn floating down the Mississippi with Jim is a "myth," and so is any truth that is generally accepted by society. "Myth" can be simply another name for ideology, *Weltanschauung*. Richard Chase (1914–1962), in *Quest for Myth* (1949), identifies all good, sublime literature with myth. But more accurately and usefully, myth means a system of archetypes recoverable in rituals and tales, or a scheme of metaphors, symbols, and gods created by a poet such as Blake or Yeats.

Among the American myth-critics we must, however, make distinctions. There are allegorizers, who find the story of redemption throughout Shakespeare or discover Swedenborgianism in the novels of Henry James. There are those who expound the private mythologies of Blake, Shelley, or Yeats as gospel truths. But there are others who are genuine literary critics. Francis Fergusson (b. 1904), in *The Idea of a Theater* (1949), uses the results of the Cambridge school to consider the theater of all ages, from Sophocles to T. S. Eliot, as ritual. Philip Wheelwright (1901–1969), in *The Burning Fountain* (1954), combines myth interest with semantics, and studies also, in a later book, *Metaphor and Reality* (1962), the sequence from literal meaning through metaphor and symbol to myth. Northrop FRYE, a Canadian, in his *Anatomy of Criticism* (1957), combines, rather, myth criticism with an attempt at an all-embracing theory of literature that is mainly a theory of genres. Frye devises an intricate scheme of modes, symbols, myths, and genres for which the Jungian archetype is the basic assumption. There are four main genres: comedy, romance, tragedy, and satire; these correspond to the four seasons: spring, summer, autumn, and winter, the rhythm of nature. The most surprising confrontations are made and the most extravagant claims for the method are put forward. Literature "imitates the total dream of man," and criticism will "reforge the links between creation and knowledge, art and science, myth and concept." Frye draws freely on the whole range of literature and interprets often sensitively and wittily (see also his *Fables of Identity: Studies in Poetic Mythology*, 1963), but he wants to discard all distinctions between good and bad works of art and ceases then to be a critic.

A recent trend of American criticism is existentialism. It hardly can be described as dependent on Heidegger or Sartre. It is rather a vocabulary, a mood, or it can be "phenomenology," an attempt at reconstructing the author's "consciousness," his relation to time and space, nature and society, in the manner of French critics such as Georges Poulet or Jean-Pierre Richard. Geoffrey Hartman (b. 1929), in his *Unmediated Vision* (1954) and *Wordsworth* (1964), traces a dialectic of perception and consciousness, and J. Hillis Miller's (b. 1928) books—*Charles Dickens: The World of His Novels* (1959), *The Disappearance of God: Five Nineteenth-Century Writers* (1963), and *Poets of Reality: Six Twentieth-Century Writers* (1965)—analyze the interior landscape or the presumed personal world of each author with great subtlety. The theme of loneliness and despair informs Murray Krieger's (b. 1923) *The Tragic Vision* (1960), in which the tragic hero (or rather "visionary") is the man of the "sickness unto death," the new nihilist. Krieger discusses Kafka, Camus, Thomas Mann, Dostoevsky,

and Melville. It is in the nature of the method that the individual work of art as an aesthetic structure is ignored and that the critic aims at discovering, rather, some inner world behind the text. The method fits the concerns of our time for answers to the ultimate questions and the interest in the personal approach of great writers to the "human condition," but the traditional issues of art and criticism are slighted.

In the last decade a group of scholars, often misleadingly referred to as the Yale School, have taken up the motifs of structuralism and theories of the French philosopher Jacques Derrida to engage in what he and they call "deconstruction." Usually Harold Bloom (b. 1930) is associated with the group, although his writings follow a quite different track. After several books of interpretations of romantic poetry—*Shelley's Mythmaking* (1959), *The Visionary Company: A Reading of English Romantic Poetry* (1961), *Blake's Apocalypse* (1963), and *Yeats* (1970), Bloom has developed a concept of the history of poetry, first expounded in *The Anxiety of Influence* (1973) and elaborated in *A Map of Misreading* (1975), *Kabbalah and Criticism* (1975), and *Poetry and Repression* (1976). Bloom interprets the history of English and American poetry from Milton to Wallace STEVENS on the analogy of Freud's "family romance." The "strong" poet revolts against his predecessors, since he cannot endure "the burden of the past" (the phrase used in the title of a book devoted to the romantic poets, *The Burden of the Past and the English Poets* [1970], by Walter Jackson Bate [b. 1918]). Bloom invents odd names—Clinamen, Tessera, Kenosis, Daemonization, Askesis, and Apophrades—to categorize the diverse strategies by which a new poet tries to cope with the "anxiety of influence." All these strategies involve inevitably a misreading or "misprision" of the prior poet. Bloom's theory is basically Freudian, but his concept of misreading links him to his colleagues (J. Hillis Miller, Geoffrey Hartman, Paul de Man [1919–1985]) who have come to completely skeptical conclusions about the very possibility of interpretation, criticism, and the notion of literature. This radical questioning of all traditional assumptions finds its support in some pronouncements of Nietzsche and in the whole long history of suspicion that many poets, critics, and philosophers have voiced against language and its ability to represent reality, to convey any truth, and to express what will forever remain ineffable.

Jacques Derrida and his followers assume that we are firmly locked within a prison-house of language, that words refer only to other words, that a text has no stable identity, origin, or end. The obvious fact that a word is not the thing signified is made to yield the view that all literature is about literature, is self-reflexive, is a mere web of "intertextuality." The difference between criticism and creative literature is denied, criticism in the old sense of evaluation is rejected, and the very concept of art dissolved in favor of the single concept of "text," or "writing," which is supposed to have preceded speaking. What remains is a concern for "rhetoric," which is not used in the old sense of the art of persuasion but as a system of tropes or figuration. It leads to reliance on etymology, in practice to punning and verbal games suggestive of the etymologizing of Heidegger, Joyce's *Finnegans Wake*, and even Dada.

Paul de Man interprets and explains modern critics in the collection *Blindness and Insight* (1971), which contains a discussion of Derrida's views of Rousseau, and in *Allegories of Reading* (1979) gives subtle and, one would assume, correct or at least plausible interpretations of Rilke, Proust, Nietzsche, and Rousseau that focus on the rhetorical or figural potentialities of language. The term "allegory" in the title, used in the sense of speaking "otherwise than one seems to speak," protects the claim for uncertainty and arbitrariness of his readings, although the distinctions and judgments made in the essays are those any traditional critic could have made.

The limitations of the New Criticism are stressed in the recent work of Geoffrey Hartman, especially in *Beyond Formalism* (1970), *The Fate of Reading* (1975), and *Criticism in the Wilderness* (1980). They display his historical learning and sensitivity but more and more embrace a new kind of creative criticism in which the priority of literary text over literary-critical text is challenged in favor of a new hybrid between criticism, inventive, witty word games, and abstract philosophizing.

These new theories, of course, have been criticized and rejected by many. Other points of view and older concepts are being defended. Gerald Graff (b. 1937), in *Literature against Itself* (1979), has surveyed the scene with a jaundiced eye, looking with disfavor even on the New Criticism as preparing the way for the aberrations of the last decade. Wayne C. Booth (b. 1921), the author of an acute book on the novel that challenged the Jamesian ideal of the absent author, *The Rhetoric of Fiction* (1961), has expounded a concept of pluralism in *Critical Understanding* (1979). It allows him, after admitting the partial truths of the theories of R. S. Crane, Kenneth Burke, and M. H. Abrams (b. 1912), a learned historian of criticism and ideas, to return to a concept of understanding that is not very different from that of the great tradition of hermeneutics descended from Friedrich Schleiermacher (1768–1834) and Dilthey. He calls it "overstanding," pleading for tolerance and sympathy for different viewpoints.

Thirty years ago there was hardly any interest in literary theory in the United States. Today there is a plethora of books that discuss the main issues of the theory of interpretation or the concept of literature and criticism from often contradictory points of view. E. D. Hirsch's (b. 1928) *Validity in Interpretation* (1967) attempts to reassert objective criticism relying on the intention of the author by drawing on the whole history of hermeneutics. His *The Aims of Interpretation* (1976) forcefully restates the arguments against antirationalism and extreme relativism. Murray Krieger has given us a *summa* of his views in *Theory of Criticism* (1976), where he elaborates and defends a scheme not too far removed from the New Criticism while making concessions to several new trends. Krieger calls it a poetics of "presence," since he wants to preserve the literary object in the context of culture without dissolving it into man's general symbol-making activity.

French structuralism has excited the most interest. There is a good expository book by Robert Scholes (b. 1929), *Structuralism in Literature* (1974), which is, however, marred by a sentimental conclusion claiming that "marriage is a sacrament of structuralism." Jonathan Culler's (b. 1944) *Structuralist Poetics* (1975), equally informative as an exposition of Continental theories, soberly proposes a concept of "literary competence" on the analogy of Noam Chomsky's (b. 1928) linguistic "competence." Fredric Jameson's *The Prison-House of Language: A Critical Account of Structuralism and Russian Formalism* (1972) is written from a strict Marxist point of view.

One has the impression that critical languages have become so diversified and mutually exclusive, held often only by small groups, that a fruitful interchange of views has become all but impossible. Grant Webster (b. 1933), in a retrospective book, *The Republic of Letters* (1979), devoted to the New Criticism and the so-called New York intellectuals (Edmund Wilson, Lionel Trilling,

et al.), adapted the thesis of Thomas S. Kuhn's (b. 1922) *The Structure of Scientific Revolutions* (1962) to argue that critical theories develop and die without any communication with preceding or succeeding rival theories he calls "charters." The end of criticism as a continuing discipline is adumbrated in this and the not so dissimilar attempt of the "deconstructionists." They all testify to the atomization of our civilization, to the breakdown of communication and thus of meaningful discourse.

Looking back at these new trends one is struck by their (however different) preoccupation with language, with the indifference to old problems of literary criticism such as the relation between art and reality and art and morals. Also, the concern for evaluation, for the distinction between art and non-art has diminished, as it has in the practice of modern art. Theory of literature is often absorbed in general linguistics or subordinated to semiotics. A gain in insight into many problems of technique and verbal surface seems often bought at the expense of generally human concerns. "Dehumanization" seems not too hasty a generalization about the newest developments in literary criticism.

For the contributions of the author of this article to literary criticism, please see separate entry.—Ed

BIBLIOGRAPHY: General. Wellek, R., *Concepts of Criticism* (1963); Wellek, R., *Discriminations: Further Concepts of Criticism* (1970); Fokkema, D. W., and E. Kunne-Ibsch, *Theories of Literature in the Twentieth Century: Structuralism, Marxism, Aesthetics of Reception, Semiotics* (1977); Magliola, R. R., *Phenomenology and Literature* (1977); Suleiman, S. R., and I. Crosman, eds., *The Reader in the Text: Essays on Audience and Interpretation* (1980); Hernadi, P., ed., *What Is Criticism?* (1981); Juhl, P. D., *Interpretation: An Essay in the Philosophy of Literary Criticism* (1981); Tompkins, J. P., ed., *Reader-Response Criticism: From Formalism to Post-Structuralism* (1981); Wellek, R., *Four Critics: Croce, Valéry, Lukács, Ingarden* (1981); Wellek, R., *The Attack on Literature, and Other Essays* (1982); Marxist Criticism. Demetz, P., *Marx, Engels, and the Poets* (1967); Baxandall, L., *Marxism and Aesthetics: A Bibliography* (1968); Solomon, M., ed., *Marxism and Art: Essays Classic and Contemporary* (1973); Jameson, F., *Marxism and Form: Twentieth-Century Dialectical Theories of Literature* (1974); Eagleton, T., *Criticism and Ideology* (1976); Eagleton, T., *Marxism and Literary Criticism* (1976); Williams, R., *Marxism and Literature* (1977); Bisztray, G., *Marxist Models of Literary Realism* (1978); Psychoanalytic Criticism. Hoffman, F. J., *Freudianism and the Literary Mind* (1945); Trilling, L., "Freud and Literature," *The Liberal Imagination* (1950): 34–57; Fraiberg, L., *Psychoanalysis and American Literary Criticism* (1960); Crews, F., ed., *Psychoanalysis and the Literary Process* (1970); Spector, J. J., *The Aesthetics of Freud* (1972); Kaplan, M., and R. Kloss, *The Unspoken Motive: A Guide to Psychoanalytic Literary Criticism* (1973); Strelka, J. P., ed., *Literary Criticism and Psychology* (1976); Orlando, F., *Toward a Freudian Theory of Literature* (1979); Myth Criticism. Philipson, M., *Outline of a Jungian Aesthetics* (1963); Vickery, J. B., ed., *Myth and Literature* (1966); Righter, W., *Myth and Literature* (1975); Strelka, J. P., ed., *Literary Criticism and Myth* (1980); Structuralism, Semiotics, Deconstruction. Ehrmann, J., *Structuralism* (1966); Macksey, R., and E. Donato, *The Languages of Criticism and the Sciences of Man: The Structuralist Controversy* (1970); Jameson, F., *The Prison-House of Language: A Critical Account of Structuralism and Russian Formalism* (1972); Broekman, J. M., *Structuralism: Moscow—Prague—Paris* (1974); Scholes, R., *Structuralism in*

Literature (1974); Culler, J., *Structurealist Poetics* (1975); Hawkes, T., *Structuralism and Semiotics* (1977); Sturock, J., *Structuralism and Since: From Lévi-Strauss to Derrida* (1979); Harari, J. V., *Textual Strategies: Perspectives in Post-Structuralist Criticism* (1979); Kurzweil, E., *The Age of Structuralism* (1980); Culler, J., *The Pursuit of Signs: Semiotics, Literature, Deconstruction* (1981); Strickland, G., *Structuralism or Criticism?* (1981); Hartman, G. H., *Saving the Text: Literature, Derrida, Philosophy* (1981); Scholes, R., *Semiotics and Interpretation* (1982); Seung, T. K., *Structuralism and Hermeneutics* (1982); Norris, C., *Deconstruction: Theory and Practice* (1982); Italy. Gorlier, C., "Contemporary Italian Literary Criticism," *LitR*, 3 (1959): 163–69; Scaglione, A., "Literary Criticism in Postwar Italy," *IQ*, 4, 13–14 (1960): 27–38; France. Girard, R., "Existentialism and Literary Criticism," *YFS*, 16 (1955–1956): 45–52; Le-Sage, L., *The French New Criticism: An Introduction and a Sampler* (1967); Fowlie, W., *The French Critic, 1549–1967* (1968); Lawall, S., *Critics of Consciousness* (1968); Simon, J. K., ed., *Modern French Criticism: From Proust and Valéry to Structuralism* (1972); Doubrovsky, S., *The New Criticism in France* (1973); Russia. Hankin, R. M., "Postwar Soviet Ideology and Literary Scholarship," in Simmons, E. J., ed., *Through the Glass of Soviet Literature* (1953): 244–89; Erlich, V., *Russian Formalism; History, Doctrine* (1955); Erlich, V., "Social and Aesthetic Criteria in Soviet Russian Criticism," in Simmons, E. J., ed., *Continuity and Change in Russian and Soviet Thought* (1955): 398–416; Ermolaev, H., *Soviet Literary Theories: 1917–34: The Genesis of Socialist Realism* (1963); Pomorska, K., *Russian Formalist Theory and Its Poetic Ambiance* (1968); Bann, S., and J. E. Bowlt, *Russian Formalism* (1973); Erlich, V., *Twentieth Century Russian Literary Criticism* (1975); Czechoslovakia. Wellek, R., "Modern Czech Criticism and Literary Scholarship," *HSS*, 2 (1954): 343–58; Wellek, R., "Recent Czech Literary History and Criticism," *Essays on Czech Literature* (1963): 194–205; Garvin, P. L., ed., *A Prague School Reader on Esthetics, Literary Structure, and Style* (1964); Matejka, J., ed., *Sound, Sign and Meaning: Quinquagenary of the Prague Linguistic Circle* (1976); Steiner, P., ed., *The Prague School: Selected Writings, 1929–1946* (1982); Germany and Austria. Bruford, W. H., *Literary Interpretation in Germany* (1952); Amacher, R. E., and V. Lange, eds., *New Perspectives in German Literary Criticism* (1979); England and the United States. Williams, O., *Contemporary Criticism of Literature* (1925); Smith, B., *Forces in American Criticism* (1939); Hyman, S. E., *The Armed Vision: A Study in the Methods of Modern Literary Criticism* (1948); O'Connor, W. V., *An Age of Criticism, 1900–1950* (1952); Stovall, F., ed., *The Development of American Criticism* (1955); Krieger, M., *The New Apologists for Poetry* (1956); Pritchard, J. P., *Criticism in America* (1956); Wimsatt, W. K., and C. Brooks, *Literary Criticism: A Short History* (1957); Leary, L., *Contemporary Literary Scholarship* (1958); Watson, G., *The Literary Critics* (1962); Sutton, W., *Modern American Criticism* (1963); Bradbury, M., *Contemporary Criticism*, Stratford-upon-Avon Studies 12 (1970); Graff, G., *Poetic Statement and Critical Dogma* (1970); Miller, D. M., *The Net of Hephaestus: A Study of Modern Criticism and Metaphysical Metaphor* (1971); Borklund, E., *Contemporary Literary Critics* (1977); Graff, G., *Literature against Itself* (1979); Webster, G., *The Republic of Letters: A History of Postwar American Literary Opinion* (1979); Lentricchia, F., *After the New Criticism* (1980); Hartman, G., *Criticism in the Wilderness* (1980); Raval, S., *Metacriticism* (1981)

—RENÉ WELLEK

LITERATURE AND EXILE

The historical phenomenon of exile, with writers among those afflicted by its cruelty, has been recorded since the first banishment from communal life by any of its ruling factions. Modern literature of exile is, however, a unique mode of writing not only in its reflections of the experience of exile, but in the patterns of expression of response to the experience.

The sheer weight of exilic history in the 20th c. undoubtedly has led to consciousness of exile as a spiritual and psychological condition not easily rooted out by favorable turns of circumstance. In addition, the constants of alienation—angst, fragmentation, and dislocation that pervade 20th c. life and art—have turned modern writing into an emphatic and invidious literature of exile.

Early literature treats exile, and its awesome threats to the sanity and equilibrium of the individual, in a manner distinct from modern literature. Ovid and Dante, in reflecting on their own and projected conditions of exile, clearly saw the phenomenon as a sentence of prosecution and persecution; their chief aim was to commute the sentence and return to their native land. Banishment was not viewed by them with ambivalence, although the necessity of acceptance of their reality produced both stoic and defiant passages of rhetoric in their work. Nineteenth-century literature of exile reflects a similar response—the exiled writer yearns for return to his banished land, but he is not destroyed by resignation to historical currency, nor is he afflicted with the disease of anomie. Émile Zola and Vicente BLASCO IBÁÑEZ are but two of these 19th-c. writers who suffered exile but who did not allow the experience to dominate their sense of history.

Twentieth-century literature, in distinction, abounds with such a sense of exilic dislocation that it subsumes geographic and historic content into a deeper psychological being. Although historic roots are at the base of modern exilic literature, the resultant tiers of expression go beyond particular history to reflect timeless and universal perception of loss. Literature of exile becomes, in the process, social history and a lyric rupture of unrecoverable moment. Whether the experience is recorded of a T'ien-ah-men (Tienanmen) Square freedom fighter who escaped into exile— Zhang Xianliang (b. 1936)—or a Spanish Civil War Loyalist who fled his country with the victory of Franco—Francisco AYALA or Benjamin Jarnes (1888–1948)—the reflections encompass a collective sense of loss as well as an immediate disjuncture of historical culture.

The 20th c.'s most horrendous example of genocide is the Holocaust, with its record of the murder of six-million Jews, but other modern genocides have occurred as well. The slaughter of the Armenians, the attempt at extinction of gypsies by Hitler's Aryan stalwarts, the execution of the Russian middle-class, the brutal massacre of Spanish Loyalists by victorious Franco squads, and the systematic killings of Kurds are among such cataclysmic events. Masterpieces that record each of these genocides are found in many languages, some native to the historic event and some observed under foreign eyes. The experience of exile is reflected in the works of these writers who lived through the upheaval of exile or observed it from a distance. At least six writers stand as exilic literary giants: Bertolt BRECHT, Thomas MANN, Vladimir NABOKOV, Isaac Bashevis SINGER, Aleksandr SOLZHENITSYN, and Elie WIESEL.

Those who did not feel the need to flee and remained in their country after the disruption and usurpation of tradition and political-social power may reflect a different attitude to events. For every Nabokov, for example, whose family lost a vast fortune with the coming of the Russian Revolution, there were those who rose to a sharing of wealth and power heretofore denied them or who gloried in the new system, as did Maxim GORKY and Ilya EHRENBURG (qq.v). Yet it is significant that both Gorky and Ehrenburg suffered exile, one before the Russian Revolution of 1917 and one several times after the Communist Party ascension to power in the U.S.S.R. The transiency in Ehrenburg's life may be seen as a variant on exilic feeling: a rooted impermanency.

Literature of exile may conveniently be schematized into categorical imperatives: political, religious, personal, and expatriate. Without question, political exile is the most quantitatively horrifying example of modern exile, but exclusive categorization is likely to provide problematic issues. The half-million citizens of Germany, Austria, and Czechoslovakia who fled their countries during the rise of Adolf Hitler and the National Socialist Party and through World War II were political refugees, for they were fleeing a national program of extinction, but their exile often had a religious cause as well. Similarly, those citizens, some of them writers, who fled Germany because of their sexual orientation may be considered political refugees since Nazi doctrine branded them as undesirable deviants and moral lepers. Thus they are political exiles at the same time that they are sexual exiles. The literature about such experiences, in whatever genres, reflects this invidious multitexture. Among such writers forced into exile, and the regions from which they fled, are: Africa—Okot P'BITEK, Camara LAYE; South Africa—Peter ABRAHAMS, Breyten BREYTENBACH, Dennis BRUTUS, Jack Cope (b. 1931), Bessie HEAD, Mazisi Kunene (b. 1930), Alex LA GUMA, Mongane Wally Serote (b. 1944); Austria—Hermann BROCH; Jakov LIND, Robert MUSIL, Joseph ROTH, Franz WERFEL, Stefan ZWEIG; China—BEI DAO, Duo Duo (b. 1951); Czechoslovakia—Pavel Kohout (b. 1928), Milan KUNDERA, Arnošt LUSTIG, Josef ŠKVORECKÝ; Germany—Theodor ADORNO, Hannah Arendt (1906–1975), Johannes R. Becher (1891–1958), Walter BENJAMIN (1892–1940), Alfred DÖBLIN, Stefan HEYM, Thomas MANN, Heinrich Mann, Herbert Marcuse (1889–1979), Nelly SACHS, Ernst TOLLER, Arnold ZWEIG; Hungary—Tamas Aczel (b. 1921), George Faludy (b. 1910), Julius Hay (1900–1975), Arthur KOESTLER, György LUKÁCS, Ferenc MOLNAR, Elie WIESEL; Argentina—Miguel BONASSO, Manuel PUIG, Luisa VALENZUELA; Chile—José DONOSO, Ariel DORFMAN, Pablo NERUDA; Colombia—Gabriel GARCÍA MÁRQUEZ; Cuba—Guillermo CABRERA INFANTE, Nicolás GUILLÉN, Heberto PADILLA, Severo SARDUY, Armando Valladares (b. 1937); Uruguay—Eduardo Galeano (b. 1904), Juan Carlos ONETTI; U.S.A.—Eldridge Cleaver (1935–1998); Poland—Stanislaw BARAŃCZAK, Marek HLASKO, Jerzy KOSINSKI, Czeslaw MILOSZ, Zdislaw Najder (b. 1930), Isaac Bashevis SINGER, Israel Joshua SINGER, Aleksander Wat (1900–1967), Adam ZAGAJEWSKI, Spain—Rafael ALBERTI, Max AUB, Luis CERNUDA, Jorge GUILLÉN, Jorge Semprun (b. 1920), Ramón SENDER; Romania—Nina Cassian (b. 1924), E. M. CIORAN, Andrei Codrescu (b. 1946); Ukraine—Vasyl Barka (b. 1908), Yuri Klen (1891–1947), Wira Wowk (b. 1920); U.S.S.R.—Yuz Aleshkovsky (b. 1929), Nina Berberova (b. 1901), Joseph BRODSKY, Ivan BUNIN, Sergey DOVLATOV, Aleksandr Galich (1919–1977), Lev Kopelev (1907–1997), Vladimir Nabokov, Irina Ratunshinskaya (b. 1954), Andrey SINYAVSKY, Aleksandr Solzhenitsyn.

Another form of exile literature is that which deals with the sense of cultural exile. Although such exile is not overtly forced on an individual (the artist may argue otherwise, in that he cannot deny his perceptions of society and a consequent ostracism for expression of such perceptions), the force of separatism is keenly felt by the individual artist who often deserts his native land when pressures become overwhelming for him. Several giants of modern literature exemplify this kind of exile—James Joyce, who found he could write only about Catholicism, Ireland, and his family by "escaping the nets" of their physical location; Samuel Beckett, who chose Paris as his home base because a troubled and parochial Ireland allowed him no vision to write; Joseph CONRAD, who self-consciously chose English as his medium of literary expression and left his native Poland at age seventeen; D. H. Lawrence, who wandered the world in search of an ideal place to write and breathe in his visionary airs; V. S. NAIPAUL, Doris LESSING, and Salman RUSHDIE, who left their birth lands redolent of colonial life for a metropolitan and more sophisticated empirical environment.

Joyce's *Ulysses* (1922) is the modern masterpiece of cultural exile-and-return in its complexly simple tale of a father and son in search of a son and father within the confines of a 24-hour walk through the mean streets of Dublin. *En attendant Godot* (1952; *Waiting for Godot*, 1954), but one example of Beckett's genius in cohering the symbolic waste of his generation's putative flames, is another instance of cultural exile in its presentation of memory and consciousness of the void of loss. Joseph Conrad's *Under Western Eyes* (1911), an early-20th-c. example of exile, treats the story of a Polish student in his czarist-occupied country who has less interest in politics and in national independence than in his personal career, but who through circumstance is forced into a choice that sends him into exile and a tormented conscience. He is subsequently forced to come to terms with an awareness of politics and community that will end his invidious disease of psychic exile.

The end of exile in the literature that treats this subject comes for some writers in the moment when the protagonist adopts a new identity, whether it be that of national citizenship, communal membership, or a more personal joining in the form of an adoption of language and customs of his new land. When the "growing pains" of a refugee are treated as domestic comedy, exile may be said to have been pushed from the center of the writer's matter, and emigration to have entered as a dominant concern. Nabokov's *Pnin* (1957) is an example of this kind of literature, as is the fiction of Sergey Dovlatov, Bharati MUKHERJEE, and I. B. Singer. Language as a gauge of the end of exile is a complex matter, for in a writer's adoption of one language over another, he or she is signaling the end of allegiance to one root and the beginning of a graft onto another. Yet loss of early roots is not always transcended in the artist's new growth. Examples may clarify the issue: Joseph Conrad chose English as his means of literary expression; in his case there was never a sense of separation from his native language, though English was his third means of expression (he knew French before he studied English). Isaac Bashevis Singer continued to write in Yiddish (with an occasional piece in English; he did not use Polish for his literary endeavors), though he lived in the U.S. for more than fifty years. Nabokov wrote in Russian and knew German and French well, but he decided to break with his past in 1941 by writing completely in English; it was in that year that his first novel in English, *The Real Life of Sebastian Knight*, took shape, signaling a break with his past that was never completely made, as Nabokov's further works showed.

Literature of exile may then be said to consist of work written by those who suffered the terrible impact of exilic experience and by those whose works treat the individious subject of exile. There is as much literature of exile treating the condition in an oblique (but pervasive) manner as there is of direct content of exilic experience. Nabokov's *Speak, Memory* (1966; orig. pub. as *Conclusive Evidence*, 1951) and Milan Kundera's *Le livre du rire et de l'oubli* (1979; *The Book of Laughter and Forgetting*, 1980) and *Nesnesitelna lehkost byti* (1984; *The Unbearable Lightness of Being*, 1984) are direct records of preserving memory before it is filtered into oblivion, yet Brecht's *Leben des Galilei* (1938; *Galileo*, 1957) and *Mutter Courage und ihre Kinder* (1939; *Mother Courage and Her Children*, 1941), Isaac Bashevis Singer's *The Slave*, and Thomas Mann's *Joseph und seine Brüder* (1933–1942; *Joseph and His Brothers*, 1934–1945) are just as intimate—if indirect—records of exilic consciousness. The experience of exile, whether immediately palpable in the work or subtly adduced through distanced modes of narrative, has changed the course of modern literature.

BIBLIOGRAPHY: Tabori, P., *The Anatomy of Exile: A Semantic and Historical Study* (1972); Spalek, J., and J. Strelka, *Deutsche Exilliteratur* (1976); Rosenfeld, A. H., *A Double Dying: Reflections on Holocaust Literature* (1980); Gurr, A., *Writers in Exile: The Creative Identity of Home in Modern Literature* (1981); Pachmuss, T., ed., *A Russian Cultural Revival: A Critical Anthology of Émigré Literature before 1939* (1981); Pike, D., *German Writers in Soviet Exile, 1933–1945* (1982); Pfanner, H. F., *Exile in New York: German and Austrian Writers after 1933* (1983); Terras, V., ed., *Handbook of Russian Literature* (1985); Seidel, M., *Exile and the Narrative Imagination* (1986); Dance, D. C., ed., *Fifty Caribbean Writers: A Bio-Bibliographical Critical Source Book* (1986); Marotos, D. C., and M. D. Hill, *Escritores de la Diaspora Cubana: Manual Biobibliografical Cuban Exile Writers: A Biobibliographic Handbook* (1986); Faulhaber, U., et al., eds. *Exile and Enlightenment: Studies in German and Comparative Literature* (1987); Ugarte, M., *Shifting Ground: Spanish Civil War Exile Literature* (1989); Tucker, M., ed., *Literary Exile in the Twentieth Century: An Analysis and Biographical Dictionary* (1991)

—MARTIN TUCKER

LITHUANIAN LITERATURE

The Lithuanians, an ancient people, speaking one of the oldest Indo-European languages, have nevertheless lacked, for most of their long history, a written literature of their own. Powerful neighbors, constantly pressing them from the south and the east against the Baltic Sea, have forced the Lithuanians to spend their best energies in the struggle for survival. Under those conditions, the literary genius of the nation was preserved in its rich and ancient folklore. The Lithuanian folk song (those that survived long enough to be recorded) concerns itself with the lyrical expression of an intimate relationship between man and nature, and with a lucid, restrained statement of man's basically tragic situation in a world ruled by sorrow and death.

The first important work of written literature came, in the middle of the 18th c., from the pen of Kristijonas Donelaitis (1714–1780), a Protestant clergyman in East Prussia. His rural epic *Metai* (written c. 1765–75, pub. 1818; *The Seasons*, 1967) describes the daily life of the Lithuanian peasant as he plods the treadmill of time

toward the hoped-for eternity in which his plain country virtue is to meet its just reward. In vigorous, earthy language Donelaitis exhorts his countrymen to resist both the oppression and the corrupt enticements coming from the alien culture of the German overlords.

The first significant writers in Lithuania proper—Simanas Daukantas (1793–1864), Simanas Stanevičius (1799–1848), and Motiejus Valančius (1801–1875)—were stimulated by the winds of romantic nationalism blowing from western Europe. Their desire was to arouse Lithuanian self-respect and to encourage allegiance to the country's indigenous cultural values.

Somewhat aloof from these stood the lonely, talented figure of Antanas Baranauskas (1835–1902), who achieved fame with his one major work, *Anykščių šilelis* (1860–61; the pine grove of *Anykščiai*), a long lyrical poem in melodious verse that sings of the past glories of a wooded spot near his home.

The groundswell of romantic nationalism produced intensified resistance against the russification policies of the tsarist regime, which in 1865 had gone so far as to proclaim a ban against Lithuanian books printed in the Latin alphabet. The lifting of the ban in 1904 released the creative energies of a large number of writers whose works established a solid foundation for the further growth of Lithuanian literature.

By far the best of the romantic poets was Maironis (pseud. of Jonas Mačiulevičius-Mačiulis, 1862–1932). His emotionally intense patriotic poems raised Lithuanian poetic diction and prosody to a new dimension. Using the language firmly, he demonstrated sure handling of the syllabo-tonic meters and great sensitivity to the nuances of relationship between rhythm, emotion, and idea. In prose, the major writer of the period was Juozas Tumas-Vaižgantas (1869–1933), who wrote chatty, colorful tales about the emerging national consciousness in the life of the Lithuanian countryside.

Their works, as well as those of Marija Pečkauskaitė-Šatrijos Ragana (1878–1933), Julija Žymantienė-Žemaitė (1845–1921), and Antanas Žukauskas-Vienuolis (1882–1958), spanned a period of crucial changes in Lithuanian history, extending from the 1905 revolution in Russia, through World War I, to the establishment of an independent Lithuanian state in 1918. Vienuolis, in fact, lived to see his country occupied by the Germans in 1940 and to become one of the Party-controlled writers in Lithuania under Soviet rule.

Vincas KRĖVĖ, however, chose self-exile when the Soviet armies returned to Lithuania in 1944. A prolific and complex writer, he distinguished himself in several genres. Nostalgia for Lithuanian antiquity inspired him to write *Dainavos šalies senu̜ žmoniu̜ padavimai* (1912; tales of the old folk of Dainava), a series of highly stylized legends dealing with heroes of times past. Present-day Lithuania led him to write realistic stories about villagers, living in close intimacy with nature, who possessed, in the author's eyes, the indefinable, deep strength that had sustained his people through countless ages. This same power figures prominently in his plays *Šarūnas* (1911; Šarūnas) and *Skirgaila* (1925; Skirgaila), which deal with crucial moments in Lithuanian history. And in a biblical epic, *Dangaus ir žemės sūnūs* (2 vols., 1949, 1963; the sons of heaven and earth), he pursued his search for the secret of human fortitude to a confrontation between man and God.

The development of poetry after Maironis went in the direction of SYMBOLISM. Jurgis Baltrušaitis (1873–1944), most of whose poetry was written in Russian, was himself a prominent member of the circle of Russian symbolists. His Lithuanian poems have the same austere clarity of vision and ascetic restraint as his Russian ones, but they also provide a rich interplay among three different language strata, consisting of Lithuanian equivalents to the Russian symbolist vocabulary, highly idiosyncratic personal linguistic constructs, and down-to-earth peasant vocabulary. In both languages, he contemplates man's relationship to eternity on the same terms.

Balys Sruoga (1896–1947), who experimented vigorously with verse forms, succeeded in combining the symbolist outlook with the imagery and diction of the Lithuanian folk song. In his verse drama Sruoga returned to classical order and clarity developing, as in the play *Milžino paunksms'* (1930; shadow of the giant), philosophical portrayals of historical figures in an atmosphere of lyrical contemplation.

Faustas Kirša (1891–1964) and Vincas MYKOLAITIS followed the Western trends of SYMBOLISM, particularly the French. They remained, however, intimately bound to the indigenous traditions, to the Lithuanian manner of translating reality into metaphor and symbol as it had developed in folklore.

Mykolaitis became widely known for his quasi-autobiographical novel *Altorių šešėly* (1933; in the shadow of the altars), in which the hero is a young priest who tries in vain to come to terms with an evanescent image of God. Mykolaitis made a similarly unsuccessful effort to meet the requirements of SOCIALIST REALISM under Soviet occupation with the novel *Sukilėliai* (1957; the rebels), dealing with the Polish-Lithuanian uprising against the Russians in 1863.

The literary traditions of Lithuania Minor (East Prussia), begun so well with Donelaitis, were continued by Vilius Storasta-Vydūnas (1868–1953) and by Ieva Simonaityteė (b. 1897). The most philosophical of Lithuanian authors, Storasta-Vydūnas constantly sought, in his many plays and other writings, to understand the ultimate meaning of man's existence in terms of mystical images of "eternal light," which is the unending principle of life and the spark of divinity in man. Simonaitytė, in her novel *Aukštujų Šimonių likimas* (1935; the destiny of the Simonys of Aukštujai), depicted the gradual disappearance of the Lithuanian ethnic minority in East Prussia during the course of centuries, under the influx of German colonists.

In the 1920s the influence of Russian FUTURISM and western European EXPRESSIONISM manifested itself in the "Four Winds" movement, so called after the title of a literary periodical edited by Kazys Binkis (1893–1942). The movement's manifesto contains all the brash statements that were so dear to the futurists: the worship of the machine age; the desire to forge and hammer out poetry like iron by an effort of rational will; contempt for "insipid romantics" and "starry-eyed symbolists." Nevertheless, Binkis's own verse remained light and lyrical in essence, since Lithuania—a land of quiet lakes and green meadows—did not offer the industrial realities necessary for the development of truly dynamic futurism. Other important members of the movement were Juozas Petrėnas-Tarulis (1896–1980) and Teofilis Tilvytis (1904–1969).

The second important literary movement of the 1920s was called the "Third Front." Third Front writers were leftists who were interested in fighting social and economic injustice and who were committed to the budding Lithuanian proletariat and to the peasantry. The most important poet in this group was Salomėja Neris (1904–1945), although her deeply lyrical, and feminine poetry, vibrant with warm personal feeling, transcended the outlines of any particular ideology. Petras Cvirka (1909–1947) wrote novels of social satire directed against the ruling Lithuanian bourgeoisie, in which he glorified the honest work of simple peasants. The literary critic Kostas Korsakas (1909–1986) and the poet Antanas Venclova (1906–1971) also played a significant role in this movement. Korsakas, Cvirka, Venclova, Neris, and Tilvytis were later to form

the nucleus of those who produced the Soviet Lithuanian literature that emerged in the aftermath of World War II.

In the 1930s Lithuanian literature came of age in the sense that art itself, as an embodiment of a personal vision of reality, became the object of primary concern. Bernardas Brazdžionis (b. 1907) believed that reality was permeated and made meaningful by the hidden presence of God. The frequent biblical references in his works create a feeling not only of Christian devotion, but also of a romantic longing for some dimly perceived, intensely desired, ultimate home for the soul. He treats nature, both in broad outlines and in minute details, as a stage setting for his poetic drama of life as a holy pilgrimage toward death. This mood is especially strengthened by Brazdžionis's skillful handling of rhythm and syntax, and by his fine sensitivity to the musical qualities of words.

The poetry of Jonas AISTIS broke new ground in the uses of poetic language. Skillfully combining plain everyday language with highly refined literary formulas, he created an intoxicating effect of a still raw, but already inspired, reality, quivering on the verge of poetic fulfillment. Much of his work consists of an intense confrontation with the values and possibilities of art itself, conveyed sometimes directly in its own terms and sometimes through poetic formulations of the themes of love, patriotism, painful human solitude, and his closeness to the Lithuanian landscape.

Other significant poets of the same time were Antanas Miškinis (1905–1983), who used the language and lyrical texture of the native folk songs to perfect a poetry of highly personal lyricism, and Kazys Boruta (1905–1965), a poet who asserted the spirit of freedom and of individual human dignity.

The prose writers in this period were strongly influenced by impressionism, especially of the Scandinavian variety. Although Ignas Šeinius (1889–1959) was to spend much of his life in Sweden, the imprint of such authors as Knut HAMSUN can already be seen in his best work, the novella *Kuprelis* (1913; the hunchback), which was written before he left Lithuania. The story tells about a gifted, physically disfigured dreamer who is doomed to vegetate in the provinces. The double psychological tension of the story consists of the desire for personal happiness and the deformity that prevents it on the one hand, and intellectual yearning versus gray reality on the other.

Antanas VAIČIULAITIS established his reputation with the novel *Valentina* (1936; Valentina); in which delicate shades of feeling in the soul of a man possessed by love are carefully integrated with summer light and evening shadow, cricket song and sudden storms, in a manner reminiscent of the French impressionist painters. Vaičiulaitis is also known for his stories of country life and for his fairy tales.

Jurgis Savickis (1890–1952) belongs among the better Lithuanian prose stylists. His outstanding qualities are brevity, precision, and a certain dry, elegant irony of understatement that he uses when describing situations fraught with possible tragic meanings. The main theme of his short stories appears to be the blindness of small men—the careerist, the bourgeois, the semi-intellectual—to the immensity of the life passing them by. Savickis spent considerable time in western Europe, in the Lithuanian diplomatic service, and had good opportunities for observing the human comedy of petty ambitions and moral inadequacies, both at home and abroad.

Other significant prose writers are Juozas GRUŠAS and Jurgis Jankus (b. 1906), as well as Liudas Dovydėnas (b. 1906). Grušas, who still lives in Soviet-occupied Lithuania, has recently shown himself a gifted play-wright. He has written historical plays as well as plays that approach the modern concept of the THEATER OF THE

ABSURD. Dovydeênas, author of the prize-winning novel *Broliai Domeikos* (1936; *The Brothers Domeika*, 1976), is a close and loving observer of Lithuanian country life.

The events of World War II and their consequences for the Lithuanian people—the German occupation, the return of the Soviets in 1944—resulted in splitting the literary community into two parts. Some writers remained in Lithuania and submitted to Communist Party dictates in art, while others withdrew to the West and were confronted with the variety, and perhaps confusion, of the literary trends prevailing there. The older writer, finding himself sometimes unable to comprehend the intellectual and artistic challenge implicit in the tragedy of his exile, often withdrew into reminiscences of home, or else allowed his bitter patriotic fervor to shape the purposes of his art.

New developments came from a generation of younger writers who, because they were only beginning to emerge by 1944, were sufficiently flexible to be able to respond to the new experiences of spiritual and artistic life that the West offered. Paradoxically, the primary source of their new inspiration must be sought still in Lithuania, in the person of Vytautas Mačernis (1920–1945). He was a gifted EXISTENTIALIST poet whose poetic visions stimulated his friends to seek new relationships between themselves, art, and reality.

The young exiles gathered around the periodical *Literatūros lankai*, which was started in Buenos Aires in 1952. Their guiding spirit at the beginning was the poet Juozas Kėkštas (1915–1981), who died in Poland. Another poet, Kazys Bradūnas (b. 1917), contributed a good deal to organizing the movement, which was to call itself the "Earth" collective.

Bradūnas's early verse was permeated with direct existential pain, born of a physical sense of loss, of sudden alienation in a strange country. Later Bradūnas deepened and at the same time sublimated his sorrow by reconstructing a Lithuanian mythology of those who lived and died on Lithuanian soil through countless ages, thus performing an unending sacrifice before the living presence of God, whether He be understood in pantheistic, pagan terms, or as the Christian God of later generations.

Alfonsas Nyka-Niliūnas (b. 1920) achieved a breakthrough in Lithuanian literary criticism by demanding that the vague, impressionistic approaches of the past be replaced by informed, systematic, and lucid literary analysis. His main contribution to the literature of exile, however, is in his poetry. Niliūnas is a highly complex, searching poet, capable of transforming philosophical quest into intense lyrical emotion, of integrating his own visions with the creative efforts of all mankind by means of subtly interconnected systems of symbolic and intellectual references. His basic position is existentialist: the recognition of reality, especially for an exile, is equivalent to the understanding of alienation.

Closely connected with the "Earth" collective were some prose writers, notably Algirdas Landsbergis (b. 1924) and Antanas Škėma (1911–1961). Landsbergis's first novel, *Kelionė* (1954; the journey), re-created the experience of war and exile on a plane on which chronological time sequence is replaced by an inner continuum of thought and feeling, as if a new mosaic were to be created from the broken pieces of reality destroyed by World War II. Landsbergis also writes short stories and plays in which his satirical intelligence is directed at the sometimes tragic inadequacies of man. One of his better-known plays is *Penki stulpai turgaus aikšteje* (1966; *Five Posts in the Market Place*, 1968).

Antanas Škėma, in his novel *Balta drobulė* (1958; the white shroud) and in a number of short stories and plays, depicts the condition of man as that of being in exile, since the logical inevitabilities that rule the universe do not provide for the principle of life, much less for the irrational urge of creativity that constitutes the divine spark of man. Therefore, the more perfect an organism, the greater is its suffering, and in man the supreme qualities of mind fulfill themselves in supreme agony. Škėma's works often contain cruel, even melodramatic, situations centered around the conflict between freedom and tyranny.

Other significant novelists are Aloyzas Baronas (1917–1980), a prolific writer of quixotic, paradoxical works that investigate man's basic values against the background of ashes left by the holocaust of World War II, and Vincas Ramonas (b. 1905), whose *Kryžiai* (1947; the crosses) depicts the traumatic encounter between the peasants of independent Lithuania and the invading Soviet ideology, borne on the backs of tanks.

Marius Katiliškis (1915–1981), in such novels as *Užuovėja* (1952; the wind shelter) and *Miškais ateina ruduo* (1957; autumn comes through the forests), evokes Lithuania in all its elemental power and shows how the people who inhabit it must live in an indissoluble bond with the soil, as if they were mere configurations upon the surface of continuing life. Then it comes as a special shock to realize that the impossible *has* happened; that these people have actually been separated from their soil; that they have become exiles, groping in vain for some meaning to their lives.

Pulgis Andriušis (1907–1976) re-creates the atmosphere of the Lithuanian countryside in lush, ornate prose, exploiting to the fullest all the resources of the language to spin a web of enchanting memory.

In drama, the exile Kostas Ostrauskas (b. 1926) has written absurdist plays. His main attention is focused upon death as an unimaginable, yet inevitable, final event in the life of both body and mind. Since no rational dialogue is possible between man's intelligence and the incomprehensible void facing it, absurdity must necessarily be the overwhelming presence in any drama purporting to depict the human condition. In such plays as *Pypkė* (1954; *The Pipe*, 1963) and *Duobkasiai* (1967; *The Gravediggers*, 1967) Ostrauskas calls for defiant reassertion of life in the face of death, even if such an act remains ultimately meaningless.

Similarly, death dominates the poetry of Algimantas Mackus (1932–1964). In his work, the condition of exile necessitates a reversal of all the meanings and values of conventional poetic language that are based upon the consciousness that an artist is at home in the world. Mackus was developing a systematic reconstruction of all basic metaphorical and semantic connotations in poetic imagery, assigning the meaning of death to terms that ordinarily mean life. The result is a shattering picture of reality as a visible expression of the ultimate void. In this context Mackus placed the specific events, feelings, and beliefs of the Lithuanian exiles. The result is an image of a deathbound community of lost men in a universe that cannot contain any meaning. Yet, in the very clarity of his dark vision, Mackus managed to lend a tragic dignity to the stature of man.

Perhaps the greatest, and certainly the most complex and subtle Lithuanian poet is Henrikas RADAUSKAS. He cannot be readily identified with any trends and movements, whether in independent Lithuania or in exile. The theme of Radauskas's poetry is ultimately art itself, whereas exile, death, nature, history, and the mythological and metaphysical aspects of man's experience constitute the component elements of an aesthetic entity called a poem—a thing of noble beauty, aloof from the lesser passions and accomplishments of man.

Another outstanding poet is Tomas Venclova (b. 1937), son of Antanas Venclova (see above), who has recently left the Soviet Union to live in the U.S. His "arid" poetry, without any surface emotionalism or "beautiful language," presents complex verbal structures of high intellectual order, full of very intricate, subtle and infinitely evocative interrelationships among all aspects of human experience in history and in art. In his work one hears echoes of Russian Acmeists and of recent "underground" Russian poets, for example, Joseph BRODSKY, as well as of "intellectual" Western poets, such as T. S. ELIOT and Ezra POUND.

The literature of Soviet-occupied Lithuania was for a long time at a low point. "Inspiration" came from the desk drawer of a Communist Party bureaucrat; questions of style and technique became subordinate to the ideological requirements of socialist realism. Only in recent years, particularly after de-Stalinization, have new talents come forward, replacing the submissive and often quite mediocre older writers.

Among the ground-breaking poetic talents was Eduardas Mieželaitis (1919–1997), winner of the All-Union Lenin Prize in Literature. In his work, attemps to convey personal experience are combined with an interest in experimenting with florid poetic diction and baroque form.

Justinas Macrinkevičius (b. 1930) searches among the ruins of sorrows long endured for the promise of the future in his own soul and in that of his people, notably in his narrative poem *Kraujas ir pelenai* (1960; blood and ashes), which describes the total destruction of a Lithuanian village by the Nazis during World War II. His historical trilogy—*Mindaugas* (1968; Mindaugas), *Katedra* (1971; the cathedral), and *Mažvydas* (1976; Mažvydas)—focuses on outstanding figures in Lithuanian history in an attempt to depict the moral crucibles of the nation, its resilience under oppression, and its determined search for a cultural and moral identity across the centuries leading toward the modern age.

Judita Vaičiūnaitė (b. 1937) and Janina Degutytė (1928–1990) are poets of genuine artistic gifts. Sigitas Geda (b. 1943) is a subtle poet of nature and of the soul, whose word-magic is permeated with symbolic references ranging from ancient myth to medieval symbolism. Mykolas Sluckis (b. 1929), Jonas Avyžius (b. 1922), Romualdas Granauskas (b. 1939), and Juozas Aputis (b. 1936) are talented writers of fiction notable especially for their bold experimentation with modern stylistic and psychological devices. Kazys Saja (b. 1932) has been successfully searching for new creative modes in the theater.

Lithuanian Literature since 1980

The postwar Soviet occupation of Lithuania divided the Lithuanian literary community into two parts: writers at home, subject to the ideological constraints of Socialist Realism, and writers forced into exile.

Poetry

The exilic community included poets Juozas Kėkštas (pseud. of Juozas Adomavičius), Kazys Bradūnas, Alfonsas Nyka-Niliūnas (pseud. of Alfonsas Čipkus), and Bernardas Brazdžionis; prose writers Algirdas Landsbergis and Antanas Škėma; and the dramatist Kostas Ostrauskas. A poet of tragic intensity is Liūnė Sutema (b. 1927), wife of the novelist Marius Katiliškis and sister of poet Henrikas Nagys. The greatest conflicts in Sutema's poetry arise from the confrontation of her own life, and that of her fellow

Lithuanian refugees, with the trauma of exile and dispossession. Similarly, the condition of exile dominates the poetry of Algimantas Mackus and Henrikas RADAUSKAS .

Within Soviet-occupied Lithuania, after de-Stalinization, talents came forward only gradually, notably Eduardas Mieželaitis, an outstanding pioneer of the new self-reliant poetry, and Justinas Marcinkevičius, who uses Lithuanian history in an attempt to depict the moral crucibles of the nation.

Judita Vaičiūnaitė, a poet of vibrant personal emotions, has explored erotic love in her verses with urban settings, and deep mythological dimensions in poetry with a prehistoric focus. Janina Degutytė is known for her deep, lyrical devotion to the land and to nature in general. Sigitas Geda is a subtle poet of nature and of the soul, whose word magic is permeated with references to ancient myth and to medieval symbolism. Notable among the recent poets are also Jonas Juškaitis (b. 1933), a master of finely tuned, complex emotions; Albinas Bernotas (b. 1934), a friend of the nature that envelops the human soul; and Marcelijus Martinaitis (b. 1936), famous for his folksy-surrealist cycle *Kukučio baladės* (1977; the ballads of Kukutis).

The younger generation born from the 1940s through the 1960s seeks a much more direct confrontation with the contemporary political situation in Lithuania, is more militant about ecology, and at the same time is immensely concerned with the mysteries of the poet's craft. Gintaras Patackas (b. 1951), a poet of many moods, can write with powerful anger against the menace of tyranny in human affairs, as he does in his latest books, *Amuletai* (1988; amulets) and *Kapitono Homero vaikai* (1989; the children of Captain Homer). Similarly, Donaldas Kajokas (b. 1953) in some poems exploits the traditionally strong presence of nature in Lithuanian poetry to reveal with a sudden and revolting clarity the ugly mutilation of the countryside by the presence of Soviet concentration camps, notably in *Tylinčiojo aidas* (1988; the echo of the silent one). In the same book Kajokas reinforces his point by depicting unendurable mystical horrors in a poem dedicated to the beauty of Bach's St. Matthew Passion.

Julius Keleras (b. 1961) is also very angry about the destruction of his nation, and the Christmas wafer in the title of his latest book, *Baltas Kalėdaitis* (1990; the white Christmas wafer), often tastes of blood and tears and of the bitter herbs of exile.

A broader view of exile is taken by Vytautas Bložė (b. 1930), who says in the preface to his book *Polifonijos* (1981; polyphonies) that he seeks "to give meaning to the universality of human existence in various planes of space and time." This he achieves by relating, in close-knit image sequences, the experiences of east European exiles to Siberia and those of Africans brought in ships to slavery, and those anywhere who weep for a lost home. He extends these visions to the historical dimension, writing in the seemingly dispassionate manner of a chronicler in the elaborately entitled *Miko Kėdainiškio laiškai sau pačiam irkti nežinomi rankraščiai rasti senų griūvančių mūrinių namų pastogėje* (1986; the letters of Mikas Kėdainiškis to himself, and other unknown manuscripts found in the attic of an old, crumbling stone house). In *Noktiurnai* (1990; nocturnes), Bložė focuses upon the poet's self-consciousness as the entire universe, petty and grand, turns around him.

Tautvyda Marcinkevičiūtė (b. 1955) in her *Tauridė* (1990; Tauris) speaks in a lyrical voice of shifting realities evocative of the world of antiquity. Antanas A. Jonynas (b. 1953), in his *Parabolė* (1984; parabola), also conveys a strong "classical" flavor in the style and mood of his verse. Markas Zingeris (b. 1947), in his *Vakaras vaikystėje* (1989; an evening in childhood), writes verses that are sad and full of ancient Jewish wisdom filtering like a mournful light through the veil of reality. Eduardas Juchnevičius (b. 1942), a graphic artist, with his book of poems entitled *Vilkolakiai* (1988; the werewolves), illustrates another recent trend in Lithuania—the crossing of boundaries between the arts.

In the last few years, some of the established poets have at least partially succumbed to a malaise, a restless wandering of the spirit and even a revulsion against writing poetry. Considered by many the voice of the nation, or at least its conscience, they were at the beginning of independence swept away into a whirlwind of political activities where they found themselves speaking with the voice of a prophet rather than that of an artist. After the political turmoil calmed down, however, many returned to their craft and have continued publishing new and interesting things. Among them, Sigitas Geda left a special mark with his *Babylono atsatymas* (1994), a collection of verse written in wide-ranging modulations of language, from tightly traditional to totally deconstructed modernistic, dealing with a constantly shifting historical entity he calls "Lithuania." Sigitas Parulskis (b. 1965) followed his bitter 1990 collection *Iš ilgesio visa tai* (It All Comes from Yearning) describing his horrible experiences while serving with the Soviet paratroopers, with *Mirusiųjų* (1994; Of the Dead), a somber, hard-eyed set of poetic meditations on life and death in the context of the Holy Writ, myth and nature.

In the meantime, a fair number of new and eager poets, mostly but not always young, have sprung up, filling their shelves with rather small booklets of fledgling verse as ambitious as it is uneven in quality. One of the very best is Gražina Cieškaitė (b. 1951), an intensely philosophical poet. Her *Auka žvaigždžių vainikui* (1991; An Offering for a Wreath of Stars) wanders through the shadowy philosophical realms of being and non-being, in the company of love and death. Korneliju Platelis (b. 1951) is another intellectual poet, but of a rather classical bent. He contemplates Western civilization with an effort at clarity of statement and complexity of thought and perception. Arturas Tereškinas (b. 1965) is a much more bitter observer. Western civilization, through his eyes in the collection *Absonia* (1996; Absonia) is a heap of malodorous ruins from which emerges a repulsive lust to live. Nijolė Miliauskaitė (b. 1950) is a gentle, simple soul with the magic gift of turning plain rye-bread and sand-between-the-toes reality into a texture of deep personal experience whose intimacy invites the mind to an equally intimate response, as in her *Uždraustas įeiti kambarys* (1995; A Room Forbidden to Enter).

One may also mention in passing Algis Balbierius (b. 1954), Romas Daugirdas (b. 1951), and Elena Karnauskaitė (b. 1964), Arnas Ališauskas (b. 1970) and especially Kęstutis Navakas (b. 1964), all talented poets of various styles and approaches to poetry.

Fiction

Prose writers are not as productive as their colleagues in poetry; in particular, there remains only a waning interest in the large novel, a genre that in the past had helped to build a high reputation for Lithuanian literature with the readers of all the former soviet republics. Among the older writers, Mykolas Sluckis and Jonas Avyžius have undertaken to explore new modes of consciousness open to an individual once free from the constrictions of Socialist Realism. Avyžius has written some powerful accounts of the violence done to Lithuanian peasantry during its enforced collectivization, and the continues to show interest in rural Lithuanian life and its problems in his two recent novels, *Degimai* (1982;

burned forest clearings) and *Sodybų tuštėjimo metas. Trečia knyga* (1988; the time of emptying homesteads).

Romualdas Granauskas and Juozas Aputis have created an intense, as it were, magical reality, seemingly plain, yet both surreal and mythical, in which to place the human soul in the crucibles of our age. Granauskas has not been very productive lately, but Aputis published two collections of short stories in his familiar style: *Gegužė and nulūžusio beržo* (1986; the cuckoo on a broken birch tree) and *Skruzdėlynas Prūsijoje* (1989; an anthil in Prussia). Richardas Gavelis (b. 1950) has recently published a sensational novel, *Vilniaus pokeris* (1990; the Vilnius poker game), in which life under communism is depicted as a filthy nightmare of mixed pornography and horror. His latest book, called *Jauno žmogaus memuarai* (1991; memoirs of a young man), portrays the hero as a dead man exploring his mind and his past life from beyond the grave. The novel *Priešaušrio vieškeliai* (1985; predawn highways) by Bronius Radzevičius (1940-1980), and his collection of short stories *Link Debesijos* (1984; toward cloudland), have left a powerful imprint upon Lithuanian prose. They do not have any elaborate or even very coherent plots, and consist instead of intensely emotional sets of episodic images subject to such tight control that, under its pressure, they begin to function like poetry, where every word acquires a symbolic meaning in the battle between the author's aesthetic discipline and his heart.

Writers in the West are subject to the inevitable attrition of time, and there is no real hope at all that the children and grandchildren of exiles will take their place, because most of them either no longer speak Lithuanian, or know it so poorly that they could not possibly write either poetry or creative fiction. Some of the older writers are still productive, however, notably Kazimieras Barėnas (b. 1908), who continues his fictional chronicles of Lithuanian life before and during World War II with the novel *Meškos maurojimo metai* (1990; the year of the roaring bear), and the dramatist Kostas Ostrauskas, with a new play, *Ars Amoris* (1991; the art of love). In general, Lithuanian cultural life in the diaspora has begun to gravitate more and more toward the home country itself. There are frequent visits by individuals, some of whom participate in cultural reconstruction of the country by teaching at academic institutions, supplying advice and material assistance to the economy, participating in worldwide conferences, held in Lithuania, of Lithuanian writers and scholars, attending national folk festivals, athletic events, and the like. The older and middle generations are increasingly regaining the feeling that "home" is the old country, and not the comfortable nests they had built in western lands over the years. Even many of the young people are more and more interested in the land of their forebears. Lithuania itself welcomes this interest and tries to involve the émigrés in its life as much as is possible. In one such effort, the émigré writers are being republished at home with increasing frequency. Among the most recent examples we find the collected works of Bernardas Brazdžionis under the title *Poezijos pilnatis* (1989; the full moon of poetry), of Kazys Bradūnas, *Prie vieno stalo* (1990; together at the table), of Henrikas Nagys, *Grižulas* (1990; the Pleiades), and of Juozas Kėkštas, *Dega vėjai* (1986; the winds are burning).

Lithuanian literature continues to develop in spite of the contingencies of exile or the lingering consequences of past Soviet occupation.

BIBLIOGRAPHY: Engert, H., *Aus litauischer Dichtung* (1935); Mauclère, J., *Panorama de la littérature lithuanienne contemporaine* (1938); Jungfer, V., *Litauen: Antlitz eines Volkes* (1948); Landsbergis,

A., Introduction to Landsbergis, A., and C. Mills, eds., *The Green Oak* (1962): 9–21; Rubulis, A., *Baltic Literature* (1970): 163–212; Šilbajoris, R., *Perfection of Exile: Fourteen Contemporary Lithuanian Writers* (1970); Šilbajoris, R., "Lithuanian Literature," in Ivask, I., and G. von Wilpert, eds., *World Literature since 1945* (1973): 456–61; Ziedonis, et al., A., eds., *Baltic Literature and Linguistics* (1973); Ciplijauskaitė, B., "Old Themes Experienced Anew in Recent Lithuanian Poetry," *JBalS*, 6, 2–3 (1975): 190–98; Vaškelis, B., "The Motif of Anxiety in the Contemporary Short Story of Lithuania," *JBalS* 6, 2–3 (1975): 162–70; Šilbajoris, R., "Forbidden Thoughts, Permitted Voices: Poets in Lithuania and in the Leningrad Underground," *Lituanus*, 23, 4 (1977): 45–54; Šilbajoris, R., Foreword to Zdanys, J., ed., *Selected Postwar Lithuanian Poetry* (1978): 7–12; Šilbajoris, R., Introduction to Skrupskelis, A., ed., *Lithuanian Writers in the West: An Anthology* (1979): 16–19; Šilbajoris, R., "Images of America in Lithuanian Prose," *Lituanus*, 27, 1 (1981): 5–19; Straumanis, A., ed., *Baltic Drama: A Handbook and Bibliography* (1981): 381–560; Bukaveckas-Vaičkonis, K., "The Development of Lithuanian Literature in the West: Two Divergent Trends," *Lituanus*, 28 (1982): 41–54; Šilbajoris, R., "Translucent Reality in Recent Lithuanian Prose," *WLT*, 57, 1 (Winter 1983): 21–24; Šilbajoris, R., ed., *Mind against the Wall: Essays on Lithuanian Culture under Soviet Occupation* (1983); Straumanis, A., ed., *Fire and Night: Five Baltic Plays* (1986); Šilbajoris, R., "Time, Myth, and Ethos in Recent Lithuanian Literature, " *WLT*, 60, 3 (Summer 1986): 432–35; Willeke, A., "Iconoclastic Voices in Lithuanian Exile Prose," *JBalS*, 17, 2 (1986): 133–43; Šilbajoris, R., "Folkloric Subtexts in Modern Lithuanian Poetry," *IFRev*, 5 (1987): 11–19; Kavolis, V., "The Radical Project in Lithuanian Émigré Literature," *Lituanus*. 34, 1 (1988): 5–17; Mandelker, A., and Reeder, R., eds., *The Supernatural in Slavic and Baltic Literature: Essays in Honor of Victor Terras* (1988); Šilbajoris, R., "Some Recent Baltic Poets: The Civic Duty To Be Yourself,"*JBalS*, 20, 3 (Fal 1989): 243–59; Šilbajoris, R., "A Look at Recent Poetry from Lithuania," *WLT*, 65, 2 (Spring 1991): 225–29; Kubilius, V., ed., *Lithuanian Literature* (1997)

—RIMVYDAS ŠILBAJORIS

LIU Ya-Tzu

Chinese poet and historian, b. 28 May 1887, Wu-chiang, Kiangsu Province; d. 21 June 1958, Peking

Born of a landholding gentry-scholar family, L. early imbibed revolutionary ideas prevalent among Chinese youth at the turn of the century. In 1906, while in Shanghai, he joined Sun Yat-sen's China Alliance and wrote inflammatory essays and poems to advocate the overthrow of the Manchu regime. His major activity in this period was the founding (1909) of the Southern Society, which grew under his leadership into a large literary organization with over one thousand members. As a veteran Kuomintang member, he made occasional forays into the political arena in the 1910s and 1920s, but fared better as writer and scholar. He was director of the Gazetteer Bureau of the Shanghai Municipality (1932–37) and supervised the publication of a series of its yearbooks and historical studies. He withdrew from active life during the Sino-Japanese War, but political differences with the Kuomintang faction under Chiang Kai-shek led to L.'s dismissal from the party (1941) and to his subsequent support of the Communist cause. He was invited to Peking by Mao Tse-tung after the Communist victory in 1949 and held various offices in the new regime until his death nine years later.

L. left to posterity a large legacy of poetic works written in the classical style, in which he showed great skill and expertise, even though it was his contention that the future belonged to the new vernacular poetry of the May Fourth era (see Chinese Literature). For almost fifty years—from his first published poems (in *Kiangsu*, a Tokyo-based Chinese periodical) in 1903 to his last poems, written in 1951—he cultivated the poetic art with devotion and diligence. His verses contain fresh ideas and powerful, overflowing emotions that best express the aspirations and ideals of the Chinese revolution. He was also adept at extempore pieces compiled for his many friends on various occasions. Whether occasional or topical, his poems abound in historical and classical allusions that bear witness to his erudition.

L. was dedicated to the memories of his friends. He not only wrote essays and poems to them, but also collected and published their writings after their deaths. Among the works he edited were those of early revolutionary martyrs. L.'s great effort, however, was directed toward the collection of Su MAN-SHU's literary remains and biographical materials, which he published in five volumes: *Man-shu ch'üan-chi* (1928–31; Man-shu's complete works). Indefatigable in his research, L. succeeded in disentangling the confused threads of his friend's life in a series of new studies. The same interest led to his compilation of *Nan-shê chi-lüeh* (1940; a short account of the Southern Society). Its title notwithstanding, the book is a comprehensive record of the activities of the Southern Society (1909–24) with a complete listing of its members. In another volume, *Huai-chiu chi* (1947; essays in remembrance of old times and friends), L. wrote fondly on some of his friends as well as on topics of current and historical interest.

During the first years of his self-imposed seclusion in Japanese-occupied Shanghai (1937–40) L. started his most ambitious project, on the history of Southern Ming (covering two decades of the mid-17th c. during which the Ming loyalists rallied in south China against the conquering Manchus), which he continued when he moved to Hong Kong (1940–41). Although the work was disrupted by the Japanese occupation of the island after Pearl Harbor and L.'s subsequent flight to the Chinese hinterland, he was able to complete and publish several articles on the subject. The entire work, however, was left unfinished.

The life and thought of L., poet and scholar, was affected by the major political upheavals of his time. Impelled by an inborn patriotism and strong ideological conviction, he plunged, if only for short periods, into the maelstroms. Using his unique experiences reinforced by ardent feelings, he created a new type of revolutionary heroic verse unsurpassed by his contemporaries. Discarding the hackneyed, pedantic classical clichés, he rescued Chinese poetry from degeneration by infusing it with a vigorous spirit and strong individualism. Not an innovator, he was rather a master of age-old poetic conventions, which he artfully transformed into new modes and into a powerful vehicle for the communication of patriotic sentiments.

L.'s influence was widespread. He was beloved of younger writers, to whom he was especially considerate and helpful, and by whom he was acclaimed modern China's great poet.

FURTHER WORKS: *Ch'eng-fu chi* (1928); *L. Y. shih-tz'u hsüan* (1959)

BIBLIOGRAPHY: Boorman, H. L., ed.,*Biographical Dictionary of Republican China* (1967), Vol. II: 421–23; Wu-chi Liu, *Su Manshu* (1972): 68–82

—LIU WU-CHI

LOBATO, Monteiro

Brazilian short-story writer and essayist, b. 18 April 1882, Taubaté
d. 4 July 1948, São Paulo

A practicing lawyer in the state of São Paulo, where he was born, L. eventually turned to farming, an occupation that, in 1914, prompted him to write a now famous letter to the newspaper *O Estado de São Paulo* in which he decried the "slash and burn" technique then so widely practiced in Brazilian agriculture. The vigorous, forthright style of that letter, and of his subsequent articles, along with his firsthand knowledge of the life of the backlander, quickly won L. a host of admirers and supporters.

Turning from nonfiction to fiction, L. wrote *Urupês* (1918; Urupês), a collection of stories and sketches that dealt realistically and often pessimistically with life as it was really lived by Brazil's uneducated and exploited rural poor. L. later became instrumental in the development of Brazil's publishing industry and even began his own, ill-fated company. Although negatively disposed toward the basic principles of MODERNISM, L. nevertheless published through his company the work of many of that movement's leading writers.

Urupês, with its fresh, distinctly Brazilian language and its iconoclastic treatment of an old but hitherto artificially rendered theme, the lives of Brazil's hinterland populace, was, ironically, cited by Oswald de ANDRADE, modernism's enfant terrible, as the true genesis of the modernist movement in Brazil, despite the fact that L.'s critical and aesthetic views were not consonant with modernist orthodoxy. Jeca Tatu, the backward, disease-ridden, and chronically abused central character of the *Urupês* stories, and a literary figure destined to become immortalized as a national type, is never depicted in a romantic or idealized fashion. By means of a realistic style, one characterized by an often fatalistic human, colorful language, and biting irony, L. portrays Jeca Tatu and his kind more as pathetic victims of an indifferent society rather than as quaintly comical rustics. This theme links *Urupês* directly with two other classic works of Brazilian literature, Euclides da Cunha's (1866–1909) *Os sertões* (1902; *Rebellion in the Backlands*, 1944) and Graciliano RAMOS's *Barren Lives*.

Believing that only by properly educating its youth could any society expect to progress and prosper, and therefore judging children's literature to be the most important and worthwhile aspect of his work, L. often commented that he wished the whole of his career had been devoted to it. His story "Lúcia; ou, A menina de narizinho arrebitado" (1921; Lúcia; or, the girl with the turned-up little nose) still ranks among the best loved and most widely read of all children's stories in Brazil.

A true patriot who argued for a renovation of his country's political processes, a firm believer in the positive aspects of material progress, and an enthusiastic advocate of all things authentically Brazilian, L. was an indefatigable idealist, innovator, and reformer. He believed in the greatness of Brazil's future, but he insisted always on a sober, honest assessment of its faults as well as its merits. L. is remembered today chiefly as the first Brazilian writer to deal honestly and truthfully with the poverty-plagued lives of Brazil's rural masses.

FURTHER WORKS: *Problema vital* (1918); *Cidades mortas* (1919); *Idéias de Jeca Tatu* (1919); *Negrinha* (1920); *A onda verde* (1921); *O Saci* (1921); *Fábulas* (1922); *O Marquês de Rabicó* (1922); *O macaco que se fez homem* (1923); *Mundo da lua* (1923); *A caçada da onça* (1924); *O cheque das raças; ou, O presidente negro* (1926); *Mr. Slang e o Brasil* (1927); *América* (1931); *O ferro* (1931); *Novas reinações de Narizinho* (1932); *Viagem ao céu* (1932); *As caçadas do Pedrinho* (1933); *História do mundo para as crianças* (1933); *Na antevéspera* (1933); *Emília no país da gramática* (1934); *Aritmética da Emília* (1935); *Contos leves* (1935); *Contos pesados* (1935); *Geografia de Dona Benta* (1935); *O escândalo do petróleo* (1936); *Memórias de Emília* (1936); *Histórias da tia Nastácia* (1937); *O poço do visconde* (1937); *Serões de Dona Benta* (1937); *O minotauro* (1939); *O picapau amarelo* (1939); *A chave do tamanho* (1942); *Urupês, outros contos e coisas* (1943); *Os doze trabalhos de Hércules* (1944); *A barca de Gleyre: Quarenta anos de correspondência literária entre M. L. e Godofredo Rangel* (2 vols., 1944–1946); *Prefácios e entrevistas* (1946); *Urupês: Contos: Notas biográficas e críticas* (1946); *Obras completas* (30 vols., 1946–1947). **FURTHER WORKS IN ENGLISH:** *Brazilian Short Stories* (1925)

BIBLIOGRAPHY: Brown, T., Jr., "Idea and Plot in the Stories of M. L.," *BRMMLA*, 27 (1973): 174–80; Foster, D., and V. Foster, eds., *Modern Latin American Literature* (1975); Brown, T., Jr., "The Poetic World of M. L.," *LBR*, 14 (1977): 230–35

—EARL E. FITZ

LODGE, David

English novelist and Literary critic, b. 28 Jan. 1935, London

L. has successfuly pursued two careers, combining the writing of novels with the teaching of English literature, primarily at Britain's University of Birmingham. L.'s fiction is often richly comic, and frequently draws upon his experiences as a Catholic and an academic.

L.'s first novel. The *Picture Goers* (1960), focuses somewhat gloomily on a group of Catholics living in a lower-middle-class district in London; L. admits that much of its style and tone can be traced to his youthful admiration for the more bluntly theological novels of Graham GREENE. With *The British Museum Is Falling Down* (1965), his third novel, L. employs a more overtly comical style, but again focuses primarily on young English Catholics struggling to cope with the requirements of their faith at a time when traditional beliefs and practices were widely believed to be in steep decline. It also features highly skilled parodies of several other well-known writers, including James JOYCE, another major influence on L.'s art.

During the early 1970s, L. was still best known for his critical writings, which included *Graham Greene* (1966), *Evelyn Waugh* (1971), and, most importantly, *The Language of Fiction* (1966), a lively and influential investigation of the function of style in the works of several accomplished writers of imaginative prose, including Austen, Dickens, and Thomas HARDY.

With his fifth novel, *Changing Places: A Tale of Two Campuses* (1975), L. began to acquire a wider readership in both Britain and North America. Its central characters are two English professors—one British and one American—who decide one academic year to exchange teaching positions and find themselves exchanging a good deal more, including spouses, in the bargain. Although the novel is largely comic in tone, and features many funny episodes, it also addresses a wide range of social and intellectual issues that had suddenly moved to the fore in the 1970s, including the sexual revolution and the future of the novel—subjects that would continue to surface in L.'s later fictions.

In *How Far Can You Go?* (1980; pub. in the U. S. as *Souls and Bodies,* 1982) L. portrays ten Catholic men and women who reassess their practices and beliefs in the wake of Vatican II. This novel, like *The British Museum Is Falling Down,* makes clear L.'s own opposition to the Church's official teachings on birth control; it suggests that many Catholics of L.'s generation were unable to form an enlightened and happy understanding of human sexuality. But as his works show, L. is not motivated by an abiding hostility to Catholicism; in fact, his stance tends to be that of a reformminded believer who recognizes that religion plays a major role in the lives of most people, many of whom have been left anxious and puzzled by recent social and theological trends, feeling "spiritually orphaned" rather than spiritually renewed.

L. continues his largely satirical portrayal of academic life in *Small World* (1984), which again features Philip Swallow and Morris Zapp, the principal figures of *Changing Places* Swallow plays a smaller role in *Nice Work* (1989), which centers on the unlikely love affair between a rather conservative, hard-nosed British businessman and a young college teacher with feminist leanings. *Nice Work* is L.'s most ambitious novel to date, combining humor and sharp social criticism while deliberately, brilliantly evoking the 19th-c. tradition of such "Condition of England" novels as Disraeli's *Sybil* (1845), and Dickens's *Hard Times* (1854).

L. is, however, very much a writer of his times; his fiction repeatedly displays a wide range of postmodern assumptions and strategies. And yet, in L.'s case, this artistic self-consciousness is not obtrusive or pretentious, perhaps because-in the tradition of literary realism—he never discounts the importance of convincing characters and well made plots. At its best, L.'s fiction provokes both laughter and thought—an uncommon achievement in any age.

FURTHER WORKS: *Ginger, You're Barmy* (1962); *Out of Shelter* (1970); *The Novelist at the Cross roads and Other Essays on Fiction and Criticism* (1971); *The Modes of Modern Writing: Metaphor, Metonymy, and the Typology of Modern Literature* (1977); *Working with Structuralism: Essays and Reviews on Nineteenth- and Twentieth-Century Literature* (1981); *Write On: Occasional Essays '65–'85* (1986); *Paradise News* (1991)

BIBLIOGRAPHY: Bergonzi, B., "D. L. Interviewed," *The Month* (Feb. 1970): 108–16; Widdowson, P., "The Anti-History Men: Malcolm Bradbury and D. L.," *CritQ,* 26, 4 (1984): 5–32; Morace, R. A., *The Dialogic Novels of Malcolm Bradbury and D. L.* (1989); Holmes, F. M., "The Reader as Discoverer in D. L.'s Small World," *Crit,* 32, 1 (Fall 1990): 47–57

—BRIAN MURRAY

LO-JOHANSSON, Ivar

Swedish novelist, short-story writer, and poet, b. 21 Feb. 1901, Ösmo; d. 11 April 1990, Stockholm

L.-J.'s parents originally belonged to the lowest of the farmworker class, the *statare,* whose lot first improved in 1945, thanks in part to L.-J., whose writing had exposed their extreme poverty and misery. At the time of L.-J.'s birth, however, they were poor crofters. L.-J. left school at the age of eleven, and aside from two winter sessions at a school in 1917 and 1920, he was self-educated. He moved to Stockholm and worked in a number of odd jobs while studying on his own, especially languages. In 1925 he left Sweden and lived for the next four years on the Continent and in England.

In 1927 L.-J. published the first of a series of travel books, *Vagabondliv i Frankrike* (vagabond life in France), in which he combines a traveler's observations with comments on society. After his only collection of poetry, *Ur klyvnadens tid* (1931; from the time of division), came his first novel, *Måna är död* (1932; Måna is dead), about a young man torn between a woman's erotic attraction and his work.

The novel *Godnatt, jord* (1933; *Breaking Free,* 1990) and three collections of short stories, *Statarna* (2 vols., 1936–37; the *statare*) and *Jordproletärer* (1941, proletarians of the earth) constitute L.-J.'s great epic about the people among whom he grew up. These are also works of cultural history, describing an environment that up to the time had not been treated in fiction. *Godnatt, jord* portrays, with both tenderness and a feeling for the beauty of nature, a young man's struggle for freedom in an oppressive social environment. Also belonging to this group of works is *Traktorn* (1943; the tractor), which with its many characters but no main protagonist, except for the machine, conforms to the ideal of a collective novel.

Like *Godnatt, jord,* the novel *Kungsgatan* (1935; King's Street) has been made into a film. Dealing with a farm boy's experiences in a big city, it created a sensation for its frank descriptions of prostitution and venereal disease. Another work that has been filmed is *Bara en mor* (1939; *Only a Mother,* 1991), one of L.-J.'s finest novels, about a young woman from the *statare* class who swims nude alone in a lonely lake on a hot summer day and is ostracized, regarded as a loose woman. In despair she marries an irresponsible man, works hard, and dies young. In this work L.-J. sides with the individual against the collective, whose narrow-minded moralism destroys the life of an innocent woman.

L.-J.'s next major group of works was a suite of autobiographical novels in which he combined the personal and the societal in a way characteristic of his sense of man as a historical figure. The first, *Analfabeten* (1951; the illiterate man), is a loving portrayal of his father. In *Gårdfariehandlaren* (1953; *Peddling My Wares,* 1995), *Socialisten* (1958; the socialist), and *Proletärförfattaren* (1960; the proletarian writer) he describes his past with both a nostalgic and a satiric tone.

L.-J. often writes about love, sex, and other forces that drive man to actions beyond reason and will. Such vices and sins are exposed in a sequence of short-story collections, many with historical settings, called *Passionssviten* (1968–72; the suite of passions), comprising seven books, among them *Girigbukarna* (1969; the misers), *Vällustingarna* (1970; the lechers), and *Lögnhalsarna* (1971; the liars). Most recently L.-J. has begun a series of memoirs: *Pubertet* (1978; puberty), for which he won the Nordic Council Literary Prize in 1979, *Asfalt* (1979; asphalt), and *Att skriva en roman* (1981; to write a novel).

L.-J. is without doubt one of the major 20th-c. Swedish writers. He is outstanding as a writer of short stories although some critics see him as uneven in that respect. He has created some of the most important and impressive novels in Swedish literature. Few writers match him in descriptions of sensual and erotic elements in life. He has an unusual sense of humor and a deep feeling for man's existential loneliness as well as an admirable talent for integrating contemporary man with history.

FURTHER WORKS: *Kolet i våld* (1928); *Ett lag historier* (1928); *Nerstigen i dödsriket* (1929); *Zigenare* (1929); *Mina städers ansikten* (1930); *Jag tvivlar på idrotten* (1931); *Statarklassen i Sverige* (1939); *Geniet* (1947); *Ålderdom* (1949); *Okänt Paris* (1954); *Stockholmaren* (1954); *Journalisten* (1956); *Författaren* (1957); *Soldaten* (1959); *Lyckan* (1962); *Astronomens hus* (1966); *Elektra: Kvinna år 2070* (1967); *Passionerna* (1968); *Martyrerna* (1968); *Karriäristerna* (1969); *Vishetslärarna* (1972); *Statarskolan i litteraturen* (1972); *Ordets makt* (1973); *Nunnan i Vadstena* (1973); *Furstarna* (1974); *Lastbara berättelser* (1974); *Dagar och dagsverken* (1975)

BIBLIOGRAPHY: Mennie, D. M., "I. L.-J.'s *Vagabondliv i Frankrike:* A Re-evaluation," in Dubois, E. T., et al., eds., *Essays Presented to C. M. Girdlestone* (1960): 219–28; Gustafson, A., *A History of Swedish Literature* (1961): 515–19; Bougnet, P., "I. L.-J. et l'épopée des ouvriers agricoles suédois," *LanM*, 63 (1969): 685–92; Paulsson, J.-A, "I. L.-J.: Crusader for Social Justice," *ASR* 59 (1971): 21–31

—TORBORG LUNDELL

LONDON, Jack

American novelist and short-story writer, b. 12 Jan. 1876, San Francisco, Cal.; d. 22 Nov. 1916, Glen Ellen, Cal.

L.'s origins are somewhat obscure. He was probably the illegitimate son of "Professor" W. H. Chaney, a wandering intellectual who claimed all knowledge as his specialty (and who later denied being L.'s father) and Flora Wellman, an unstable woman devoted to spiritualism and astrology. L.'s surname was given him by John London, who married L.'s mother eight months after L. was born.

L. grew up on the San Francisco waterfront, went to sea in the early 1890s, and took part in the Alaskan gold rush in 1896. He read widely as a child, and his later adventures prompted him to try his hand at writing. His short stories about life in the Yukon found a ready audience. His first book, the collection *The Son of the Wolf* (1900), was followed by almost fifty others over the next twenty years.

Despite the wealth he earned from his writing, L. became an earnest socialist, combining Marxism with Herbert Spencer's

Jack London

(1820–1903) theory of evolutionary progress and Nietzsche's idea of the superman. One of the works that best presents L.'s social theory is *The Iron Heel* (1908), a prophetic novel set seven hundred years in the future when fascism has triumphed and must be overthrown by L.'s protagonist. Even though most of L.'s writing rings with high adventure, it is often marred by his persistence in illustrating his social and political beliefs.

There is a sameness about L.'s novels, yet most of them remain surprisingly readable. Three are especially memorable.

The Call of the Wild (1903) is one of the most popular books ever written in the U.S. Buck, a giant pet dog, is stolen in California and shipped to the Yukon; as a sled dog, he acts out the theory of survival of the fittest. He is rescued from a succession of evil masters by the kind and admirable John Thornton. After Thornton is killed by Indians, Buck, his survival instincts now fully awakened, responds to the call of the wild and runs off to lead a wolf pack.

The Sea-Wolf (1904) further reveals L.'s fascination with wild impulses and the demands of survival. Wolf Larsen is the brutal, cynically intelligent captain of a sealing schooner, which picks up two refugees off a shipwreck, Humphrey Van Weyden and Maude Brewster. People of culture, they offer strong contrasts to the roughness of Larsen. Humphrey and Maude, pressed into service, escape from the evil captain, who is determined to assault Maude sexually, but end up stranded on a small Arctic island. Weeks later, the wreck of the schooner, with Larsen aboard, washes up. Larsen soon after dies of a brain tumor, and the two castaways are rescued.

The Sea Wolf is full of strangely unnatural dialogue, but the characterization of Larsen, along with the descriptions of the Arctic Ocean, combine to provide a powerful effect.

Martin Eden (1909) is L.'s most ambitious novel and one of his most significantly autobiographical. Eden, an uneducated, rough outsider, like L. himself, aspires to money and status through writing. He is drawn to Ruth Morse, a woman who has everything he thinks he wants a wife to have—beauty, wealth, charm. But Eden, who finds himself suddenly successful, becomes disillusioned over the meaninglessness and conformity his good fortune has brought him. He has long been a Nietzschean, but he begins to despair of any hope for valid societal change through Nietzsche's philosophy or anyone else's. His destiny is apparent: he commits suicide. (It is widely assumed that L.'s death was also a suicide.)

Some readers find L. at his best as a short-story writer. Many of his stories are too contrived, but a few, notably "To Build a Fire" (1902) and "The White Silence" (1899), are graphic and intensely suspenseful.

The limitations of L. as a writer are considerable, stemming mainly from the haste with which he wrote and his belief that ideas are more important than style. But his influence, both because of the daring way he lived and because he drew most of his story material from the world of he-men, has been considerable on such writers as Ernest HEMINGWAY, Jack KEROUAC, and Robert Ruark (1915–1965).

FURTHER WORKS: *The God of His Fathers* (1901); *Children of the Frost* (1902); *The Cruise of the Dazzler* (1902); *A Daughter of the Snows* (1902); *The Kempton-Wace Letters* (1903, with Ann Strunsky); *The People of the Abyss* (1903); *The Faith of Men* (1904); *The Game* (1905); *Tales of the Fish Patrol* (1905); *War of the Classes* (1905); *Moon-Face and Other Stories* (1906); *Scorn of Women* (1906); *White Fang* (1906); *Before Adam* (1907); *Love of Life, and Other Stories* (1907); *The Road* (1907); *Burning Daylight* (1910); *Lost Face* (1910); *Revolution, and Other Essays* (1910); *Theft: A Play in Four Acts* (1910); *Adventure* (1911); *The Cruise of the Snark* (1911); *South Sea Tales* (1911); *When God Laughs and Other Stories* (1911); *The House of Pride and Other Tales of Hawaii* (1912); *Smoke Bellew* (1912); *A Son of the Sun* (1912); *The Abysmal Brute* (1913); *John Barleycorn* (1913); *The Night-Born* (1913); *The Valley of the Moon* (1913); *The Mutiny of the Elsinore* (1914); *The Strength of the Strong* (1914); *The Scarlet Plague* (1915); *The Star Rover* (1915); *The Acorn-Planter: A California Forest Play* (1916); *The Little Lady of the Big House* (1916); *The Turtles of Tasman* (1916); *The Human Drift* (1917); *Jerry of the Islands* (1917); *Michael, Brother of Jerry* (1917); *The Red One* (1918); *On the Makaloa Mat* (1919); *Hearts of Three* (1920); *Dutch Courage, and Other Stories* (1922); *The Assassination Bureau, Ltd.* (1963); *Letters from J. L.* (1965); *J. L. Reports* (1970); *Daughters of the Rich* (1971); *J. L.'s Articles and Short Stories for the (Oakland) High School Aegis* (1971); *Gold* (1972); *The Letters of J. L.* (1988)

BIBLIOGRAPHY: Walker, F., *J. L. and the Klondike: The Genesis of an American Writer* (1966); Labor, E., *J. L.* (1974); McClintock, J. I., *White Logic: J. L.'s Short Stories* (1976); Barltrop, R., *J. L.: The Man, the Writer, the Rebel* (1976); special L. centennial tribute, *MFS*, 22, 1 (1976–77); Sherman, J. R., *J. L.: A Reference Guide* (1977); Sinclair, A., *Jack: A Biography of J. L.* (1977)

—JAMES LUNDQUIST

LOPES, Henri

Congolese novelist (writing in French), b. 12 Sept. 1937, Kinshasa, Democratic Republic of Congo

Born of mixed African and European parentage, L. attended primary school in Brazzaville and then in Bangui, and at the age of twelve was sent to France to continue his studies, which led to degrees in arts and history from the Sorbonne. In 1965 he returned to Brazzaville to teach history. Shortly thereafter he was appointed Minister of Education. He remains active in public affairs to this day. Prime Minister of the Republic of the Congo in 1973 and 1974, he has been with UNESCO since 1981 occupying increasingly responsible positions and is presently Assistant Director General, Bureau for External Relations.

Concurrently with his diplomatic activity, L. has devoted much time to writing. His first book, *Tribaliques* (1971; *Tribaliks: Contemporary Congolese Stories*, 1987), a collection of short stories, attracted attention because of the author's elegant style and talent for observation and received the Literary Grand Prize of Black Africa in 1972. These early stories already reveal L.'s lasting concern for ordinary Africans victimized by the callousness of the French and by the corruption of their own governmental officials.

As a member of the new governmental elite, L. disclosed the shortcomings of the preceding rule of Fulbert Youlou. *Tribaliques* is L.'s most clearly political work. Although L. was attracted to the Marxism prevalent among contemporary French intellectuals, he never reflected Marxist dialectics in his works. His was an idealistic communism compatible with the deep-seated humanism which permeates his writings.

Tribaliques was followed by two novels that were also favorably received due to the author's ability to capture the telling detail and to interest the reader in his characters. However, in this first cycle of writings style and structure remain quite conventional.

More striking is *Le pleurer-rire* (1982; *Laughing Cry: An African Cock and Bull Story*, 1987), a biting satire of a general who, after a coup, heads an unspecified African country. He is portrayed as an egomaniacal dictator who shows no concern at all for his people. The subject matter is not original. Other African writers of the period, such as Mongo BETI, Yambo Ouloguem (b. 1940), Ahmadou KOUROUMA, and Chinua ACHEBE, also expressed their disappointment with corruption and nepotism in post-independence African governments. *Le pleurer-rire* differs in that instead of focusing on the victims, L. lets a detached observer relate the incoherent reality, allowing readers to draw their own conclusions. This introduces a note of optimism by implying that, shown the truth, people can learn and improve matters.

The intricate structure of *Le pleurer-rire* reveals L.'s growing concern with artistic form. He views the creation of novels which merely encourage sociological and anthropological interpretation as leading African literature to a dead end. Furthermore, in the French classical tradition, he insists on the writer's duty to perfect his craft. Indeed the progression of his novels shows the work of a very conscious artist experimenting with ever new forms.

In the 1990s L.'s novels became more personal, though not autobiographical. Questions raised by his own métis origin and education dominate his *Le chasseur d'Afriques* (1990; The Hunter of Africas). The hero, André Leclerc, half black half French, is obsessed by the problems of this duality as he searches for his own place in the world. The novel tells of André's suffering because individuals on either side of his heritage do not fully recognize him as one of their own, and also shows how all his relationships, even that with his own mother, are equivocal. Language itself is a source of ambivalence. Adroitly, L. creates a complex situation in which the reader too is affected by ambiguity because objective reality and the hero's inner struggles overlap. If André finds a sort of peace, it is through his own acceptance of his status and his absorption into the ancestral African landscape. Although L. has stated the need for the African artist to leave NÉGRITUDE behind, the reader hears echoes of Léopold Sédar SENGHOR, and understands why L. keeps a photograph of himself with Senghor in his UNESCO office.

Le lys et le flamboyant(1997; The Lily and the Flame Tree) marks yet another turn in his craft. Written with verve, humor, at times almost playfully, the novel purports to be the biography of a métisse female entertainer whose whereabouts are uncertain. The story is narrated by Victor Augegneur Houang, L.'s double who, at some point, turns against L. himself. L. even appears in a third form in the novel, that of his own ghost. This play of multiple mirrors is an intriguing tour de force.

L. has proven to be a versatile, skillful writer open to artistic innovation, while remaining committed to progress in his homeland.

FURTHER WORKS: *La nouvelle romance* (1976); *Sans tam-tam* (1977); *Sur l'autre rive* (1992)

BIBLIOGRAPHY: Malanda, A. S., *H.L. et l'impératif romanesque* (1987); Yewah, E., "Dictatorship and the Press in H. L.'s *Le pleurer-rire*," *Ufahamu*, 18, 1 (1990): 82-90; Deltel, D., *H. L.: individu singulier, Afrique plurielle* (1994); Harrow, K.W., *Thresholds of Change in African Literature*(1994): 291-313; Felgine, O., "Pistes Métisses," *L'autre Afrique*, 17 (Sept. 1997): 82-83; Felgine, O., "H. L., Le temps du bilan," *L'autre Afrique*, 37 (Feb. 1998): 72-73

—NATALIE SANDOMIRSKY

LÓPEZ Y FUENTES, Gregorio

Mexican novelist, short-story writer, journalist, folklorist, and poet, b. 17 Nov. 1897, Huasteca; d. 11 Dec. 1966, Mexico City

After attending school in the state of Veracruz, L. y F. enrolled in a teachers' college in Mexico City, where he began his literary career with contributions to the review *Nosotros*. His first book, *La siringa de cristal* (1914; the crystal flute), was a collection of poems written within the orbit of MODERNISM. In 1914 he was sent to Veracruz with other students to oppose U.S. occupation of the city. He sided with Venustiano Carranza against Pancho Villa when their differences developed into military conflict. L. y F. published twelve novels, a book of short stories, and two volumes of poetry; there are many articles, stories, and sketches still uncollected in book form. As a journalist he contributed to *El universal ilustrado* and was director of *El universal* and *El gráfico*.

L. y F.'s principal novels deal with aspects of the Mexican revolution, with unassimilated and exploited groups of Indians, and with rural life, which he knew well as the son of a rancher and owner of a country store. *Campamento* (1931; bivouac) depicts an overnight encampment of soldiers of the revolution. *Tierra* (1932; land) dramatizes episodes in the life of Emiliano Zapata and his supporters between 1910 and 1920. *El indio* (1935; *El Indio*, 1937), awarded the National Prize for Literature in 1935, is the most famous and internationally known of L. y F.'s novels. In a series of selectively pertinent episodes without a structured plot, the author relates the customs, superstitions, problems, and areas of internal, external, and personal conflict of a group of Mexican Indians on the eve of the revolution in 1910.

L. y F.'s use of types rather than characters, of groups rather than individuals, of details, incidents, and episodes rather than plots, of folklore, proverbs, and popular speech rather than contrived literary language, was distinctively innovative. Using these techniques, he achieved an intensity in his fiction that has a strong emotional impact on the reader.

FURTHER WORKS: *Claros de selva* (1922); *El vagabundo* (1922); *El alma del poblacho* (1922); *Mi general* (1934); *Arrieros* (1937); *Huasteca* (1939); *Cuentos campesinos de México* (1940); *Acomodaticio* (1943); *Los peregrinos inmóviles* (1944); *Entresuelo* (1948); *Milpa, potrero y monte* (1950)

BIBLIOGRAPHY: Morton, R. F., *Los novelistas de la revolución mexicana* (1949): 95–115; González, M. P., *Trayectoria de la novela en México* (1951): 249–67; Carter, B., "The Mexican Novel at Mid-Century," *PrS*, 28 (1954): 147–50; Mate, H. E., "Social Aspects of Novels by L. y F. and Ciro Alegría," *Hispania*, 39 (1956): 287–92; Brushwood, J. S., *Mexico in Its Novel* (1970): 209–11, 215–17, 231–32

—BOYD G. CARTER

LORD, Audre

American poet, autobiographer, and essayist, b. 18 Feb. 1934, New York, N.Y.; d. 17 Nov. 1992, Christiansted, St. Croix, Virgin Islands

Though raised in a blue-collar household, L. earned a B.A. from Hunter College in New York City in 1954. After studying briefly at the National University of Mexico, she received a master's degree in library science from Columbia University in 1961. While a student, however, she was not economically secure enough to evade her working-class roots, but labored as a medical clerk, x-ray technician, social worker, ghost writer, and factory worker, all of which register in her later writings. From 1961 until 1968 L. worked as a librarian in several institutions, eventually becoming head librarian at the Town School in New York City. Through the 1970s and 1980s and until her death, L. taught at several colleges in the City University system in New York, and held an endowed chair as Thomas Hunter Professor in 1987-88. Teaching, for L., has never been a way to avoid social responsibility, but a means of realizing it. "Poets must teach what they know, if we are all to continue being," she comments in the introduction to a 1968 anthology of student work entitled *Pound*. L.'s sense of social commitment was not limited to her teaching. She was a member of the Harlem Writers Guild, Sisterhood in Support of Sisters in South Africa, and founder of Kitchen Table, Women of Color Press. Before her untimely death from liver cancer at fifty-eight, L. wrote twelve books of poetry, a novel, a memoir, and three collections of essays. She was named poet laureate of New York in 1991.

The rhythms of L.'s writings have always been symbiotic with the rhythms of her life. By 1968, having attained a position of relative socioeconomic security through her own efforts and her marriage (in 1962) to attorney Edwin Ashley Rollins, and having been awarded a National Endowment for the Arts Grant and a residency at Tougaloo College, L. was able to end her tenure as a librarian and devote her time to teaching and writing. The style and content of her first book, *The First Cities* (1968), bear the trace of her socioeconomic circumstances. Though published at the height of the Black Arts movement, *The First Cities* has very little of the confrontational, polemical momentum that energized the poetry of that period and that drives much of her later poetry. Concerned primarily with interpersonal relationships, the voice in this early poetry rides the rhythms of natural imagery and introspection with by turns a calm grace and imagistic excitement (though not excitability), inhabiting an essential—perhaps essentializing—"blackness" without declaiming an Afrocentric identity or taking an overtly race-oriented political stance.

Though she never completely leaves the romanticizing tendencies of her early work behind, as L. gains more confidence in her poetic voice, and as she becomes both more established in her own career (eventually becoming full professor at Hunter College) and more assertive in her sociosexual "difference" as a black lesbian feminist, the stance and voice of her poetry also change. Books published in the mid and late 1970s, such as *New York Head Shop and Museum* (1974) and *Black Unicorn* (1978), are still centered in the personal, but specific themes—the difficulty of lesbian love relationships, anger at racial injustice and sexism, the oppression often involved in parent-child relationships—as well as the rhetoric of the work become more public and socially engaged, tendencies that would mark the style of her poetry and prose through the remainder of her career. The publication of *Black Unicorn* also marks L.'s entry into a larger arena of literary discourse—before this, her poems had appeared in small press editions. By the mid 1970s L.'s work had begun to realize her definition of poetry as communication. "I have a duty," she stated in a 1970 interview, "to speak the truth as I see it," sparing neither the pain or joys of life as she lived it.

L.'s prose follows the social and political trajectories of her poetry. Characteristic of L.'s mature work is the stance of putting her life on the line. No book performs this ethos more compellingly than the memoir/essay *The Cancer Journals* (1980). The book chronicles L.'s battle with breast cancer, bolstered by insightful reflections on the hypocrisy and self-denial of prosthetic surgery. Along with her identity as a black lesbian feminist, L.'s mastectomy marked her "difference"—the "very difference which I wish to affirm." L. encourages women not to hide behind a cosmetically simulated "normalcy," but to become "visible to each other," breaking the oppressive silence and loneliness of "this scourge" with a bond of sisterhood, and generating greater public awareness of the seriousness and prevalence of the disease. Thus women are led to view their "bodies," their biological being as both a basis for shared experiences with other women and a medium for sociopolitical commentary deployed to "translate the silence . . . into language and action."

On the whole, L.'s poetry and prose bring together striking, sensuous, sometimes exotic and almost surrealistic imagery with a narrative straightforwardness and rhetorical directness that speak to the self in its most crucial roles as an intimate presence in interpersonal relationships as lover, mother, daughter, and friend and as a actively, sociopolitically engaged public persona.

FURTHER WORKS: *Cables of Rage* (1970); *From a Land Where Other People Live* (1973); *Coal* (1976); *Between Our Selves* (1976); *Uses of the Erotic: The Erotic as Power* (1979); *Chosen Poems Old and New* (1982); *Zami: A New Spelling of My Name* (1982); *Sister Outside: Essays and Speeches* (1984); *Our Dead Behind Us* (1986); *A Burst of Light: Essays* (1988); *Undersong: Chosen Poems Old and New* (1992); *The Marvelous Arithmetics of Distance* (1993); *The Collected Poems of A. L.* (1997)

BIBLIOGRAPHY: Bigsby, C. W. E., ed., *The Black American Writer* (1969); Vinson, J., ed., *Contemporary Poets* (1975); Tate, C., ed., *Black Women Writers at Work* (1983); Martin, J., "The Unicorn Is Black: A. L. in Retrospect," in Evans, M. ed., *Black Women Writers (1950-1980): A Critical Evaluation* (1984): 277-91; Brooks, J., "In the Name of the Father: The Poetry of A. L.," in Evans, M., ed., *Black Women Writers (1950-1980): A Critical Evaluation* (1984): 269-76; Provost, K., "Becoming Afrekete: The Trickster in the Work of A. L.," MELUS, 20, 4 (1995): 4559; Worsham, F. C., "The Poetics of Matrilineage: Mothers and Daughters in the Poetry of Aftican American Women, 1965-1985," in *Women of Color: Mother-Daughter Relationships* in *20th-Century Literature* (1996): 177-31; Braham, J., "A Lens of Empathy," in *Inscribing the Daily: Critical Essays on Women's Diaries* (1996): 56-71; Keating, A., *Women Reading Women Writing: Self-Invention in Paula Gunn Allen, Gloria Anzaldua and A. L.* (1996)

—TOM LAVAZZI

LOVELACE, Earl

Trinidadian novelist, short-story writer, and dramatist, b. 13 July 1935, Toco

L.'s family history is grounded in a love of the land and a sense of their specialness as Amerindian-African West Indians. Born in Trinidad, L. was moved shortly thereafter to Tobago where he lived with his maternal grandparents who raised him. The women in his family made an enormous investment in time and resources to encourage his development and ensure his survival in a society plagued by unemployment and racial prejudice. L. attended Scarborough Methodist Primary School in Tobago and Nelson Street Boys, R.C., in Trinidad. In Port-of-Spain, he attended the Ideal High School from 1948-1953 before moving to Centeno, Trinidad, to attend the Eastern Caribbean Institute of Agriculture and Forestry from 1962 to 1971. L. earned his M.A. in English from John Hopkins University in Baltimore, Maryland, before being awarded a Guggenheim fellowship in 1977. L.'s first job as a professional proofreader for the *Trinidadian Guardian* in 1953 merged his love for the land and his interest in writing. As a field assistant and agricultural assistant for the department of forestry from 1956 to 1966, L. learned the real and the poetic dimensions of the land and the people, which he recreates in an unmatched use of natural imagery in his fictional work. He was an employee in the Civil Service when he was given the B.P. Independence Literary Award in 1964 for his first novel, *While Gods Are Falling* (1965). In 1966 he received the Pegasus Literary Award for Outstanding Contribution to the Arts in Trinidad and Tobago. L. spent a year as writer in residence at Howard University in 1966–1967, and published *The*

Schoolmaster in 1968. Accepting a position as writer on the *Trinidad and Tobago Express Newspaper*, he moved to Port-of-Spain to divide his time between journalistic writing and the creation of fiction and dramatic work.

L.'s sense that one person's voice can make a difference in the way a community evolves imbues all of his protagonists with parts of his own life experiences. For instance, it is believed that the character Bolo in *The Wine of Astonishment* (1982) was based on a newspaper story of a man who acted out Bolo's fictional trauma in real life. In this work, L. also immortalized the social proto types that have the greatest impact on grassroots communication and change: The Badjohn, the Street Prince, and the Schoolmaster. While these figures are not new in Trinidadian culture, L. has taken them to new heights of literary artistry. *While Gods Are Falling* has become the harbinger of L.'s stylistic depiction of the question of the 20th c.: Can we successfully make the jump from a rural, agrarian culture to a technological society centered in urban populations? In *The Schoolmaster* the protagonist rapes the daughter of the man who arranges for the establishment of the school where he will reign as headmaster. The rape is also a metaphysical rape of the culture and society he does not know how to preserve. The daughter's suicide marks the death of the idyllic disposition of the inhabitants of rural Trinidad who must now try to enter the world of the latter 20th c. on their own terms. In *The Dragon Can't Dance* (1979), L. articulates the hierarchical power relationship of poor and democratic governments in postcolonial economies. The Street Prince, the Badjohn, and the Calypsonian, innovators of strategies in the tradition of the resistance of black people in Trinidad, appear here in a masterfully intricate plot dealing with the lives of people that are controlled by "carnival economies/carnival cultures" all over the globe.

L.'s collection *A Brief Conversion and Other Stories* (1988) contains previously published stories and new short fictional works. They focus primarily on the lives of people in the great migration from the countryside to the city. A significant technical difference in this collection is that the women have voices—they are better developed here as people with opinions and feelings.

While L. has written and produced many plays, *Jestina's Calypso and Other Plays* (1984) is the only published collection. These three plays are portrayals of problems L. dealt with in his newspaper editorials or in his public-service work years before: *Jestina's Calypso* parodies the argument that Trinidadian women with African physical attributes have a different but by no means lesser kind of beauty that needs to be acknowledged and appreciated. *The New Hardware Store* examines the function of capitalism in a culture-specific context through the example of a business that changes ownership after a riot. If black ownership does not positively impact on the lives of the employees or the community, can the change be considered progress? *My Name Is Village* is the archetype Village Play that challenges the concept of Western progress: Progress should have many culture-specific roles besides massive urbanization. The play is also about individuals coming of age—a father, a son, and a young woman who confront dichotomies in gender roles and the necessity of self-love before being able to love someone else. The language ascends to poetry inside the dialogue, dance, stick-fight choreography, and singing.

BIBLIOGRAPHY: Barratt, H., "Michael Anthony and E. L.: The Search for Selfhood," *ACLALSB*, 5, 3 (1980): 62–73; Green, J., "Moving Spirit-*The Wind of Astonishment* by E. L.," *Race Today* (May–June 1982): 110; Reyes, A., "Carnival: Ritual Dance of the Past and Present in E. L.'s *The Dragon Can't Dance*," *WLWE*, 24, 1 (Summer 1984): 107–20; Cager, C., "E. L.: A Bibliography," *Contributions in Black Studies: A Journal of African and Afro-American Studies*, 8 (1986–1987): 101–5; Cary, N. R., "Salvation, Self, and Solidarity in the Work of E. L.," *WLWE*, 28, 1 (Spring 1988): 103–14; Callaghan, E., "The Modernization of the Trinidadian Landscape in the Novels of E. L.," *ArielE*, 20, 1 (Jan. 1989): 41–54

—CHEZIA THOMPSON-CAGER

LOVINESCU, Eugen

Romanian critic and essayist, b. 31 Oct. 1881, Fălticeni; d. 16 July 1943, Bucharest

L. was the son of a high-school teacher. He studied Latin at the University of Bucharest, graduating in 1903, and earned a doctorate in 1909 from the University of Paris. For most of his life L. taught at prestigious secondary schools in Ploieşti, Iaşi, and Bucharest. He published in most of the literary journals of the day, brought out his own journal, *Sburătorul* (1919–22, 1926–27), and presided over a highly influential literary circle that advocated Western and democratic ideas and encouraged a modernist literature, oriented toward the cultural needs of the urban population. For this activity, as well as for his support of groups who were discriminated against (women, Jews), L. was repeatedly attacked by fascist and right-wing authorities.

L.'s central work, *Istoria literaturii române contemporane* (6 vols., 1926–29; a history of contemporary Romanian literature), strongly attacks the neoromantic traditionalism and rural glorification that characterized part of the Romanian literature of the day. He praises technical sophistication, psychological analysis, and urban subjects. Many of the best writers of the interwar period, like Ion BARBU, Camil PETRESCU, and Hortensia PAPADAT-BENGESCU, were launched by L. He provided an ideological and sociological statement of his position in *Istoria civilizaţiei române moderne* (3 vols., 1924–25; a history of modern Romanian civilization), in which he makes a forceful case for a liberal, Western-oriented development as the only hope for Romania. In both works he presents the theory of "synchronicity," the need for smaller countries to catch up with present trends in the West, rather than plod slowly through all phases of a previous development. Toward the end of his life L. wrote a cycle of critical works devoted to the Junimea, or Youth group (to which most of the great names of the 19th-c. Romanian literary revival were connected), in which he tries to describe the dialectics of ideological progress and conservation; the implication is that extreme nationalist and fascist trends should not be admitted as partners in civilized discourse.

L. was a consummate master of the polemical essay and the descriptive portrait of a writer's physical appearance; many of his most readable pages are to be found in his memoirs and his incidental criticism. His novels—some rather autobiographical, others in the historical genre—did not enjoy much success with the public. His translations from classical Latin and French and his Latin textbooks were widely used in high schools.

FURTHER WORKS: *Paşi pe nisip* (1906); *J. J. Weiss et son œuvre littéraire* (1909); *Les voyageurs français en Grèce au XIXe siècle*

(1909); *Critice* (10 vols., 1909–1929); *Gr. Alexandrescu* (1910); *Scenete și fantezii* (1911); *Costache Negruzzi* (1913); *Aripa morței* (1913); *Pagini de război* (1918); *In cumpăna vremii* (1919); *Lulu* (1920); *Gh. Asachi* (1921); *Viața dublă* (1927); *Memorii* (3 vols., 1930–1937); *Bizu* (1932); *Firu-n patru* (1934); *Bălăuca* (1935); *Mite* (1935); *Diana* (1936); *Mili* (1937); *T. Maiorescu* (2 vols., 1940); *Aquaforte* (1941); *P. P. Carp, critic literar și literat* (1942); *Antologia ideologiei junimiste* (1942); *T. Maiorescu și contemporanii lui* (2 vols., 1943–1944); *Titu Maiorescu și posteritatea lui critică* (1943); *Antologia scriitorilor ocazionali* (1943)

BIBLIOGRAPHY: Munteano, B., *Modern Romanian Literature* (1939): 168–70; Nemoianu, V., "Variable Sociopolitical Functions of Aesthetic Doctrine: L. vs. Western Aestheticism," in Jowitt, K., ed., *Social Change in Romania, 1860–1940: A Debate on Development in a European Nation* (1978): 174–207

—VIRGIL NEMOIANU

LOWELL, Amy

American poet, biographer, and literary critic, b. 9 Feb. 1874, Brookline, Mass.; d. 12 May 1925, Brookline, Mass.

Born into a distinguished Boston family, L. was a cousin of James Russell Lowell (1819–1891) and a sister of Abbott Lawrence Lowell (1855–1916), the noted astronomer. Although she was widely traveled, her childhood home, Sevenels, remained the center for her many literary and social activities.

Her dedication to poetry came late; her first volume of verse was published in 1912. In London in 1913 she met Ezra POUND and the writers associated with IMAGISM. Adopting imagist techniques, L. promoted the movement in the U.S. From 1915 to 1917 she edited an annual anthology, *Some Imagist Poets*, which included the work of D. H. LAWRENCE, Hilda DOOLITTLE, Richard Aldington (1892–1962), and John Gould Fletcher (1886–1950).

The title of her first book of poetry, *A Dome of Many-Coloured Glass* (1912), is a phrase from "Adonais," Shelley's elegy for Keats. Although conventional and sentimental, the volume reveals many of L.'s persistent themes: childhood memories, romantic longings, celebration of the natural world. It also reveals her admiration of Keats, a lifelong interest that resulted in her final work and possibly most significant contribution to literature, the massive and painstakingly detailed two-volume biography, *John Keats* (1925).

Her second book of verse, *Sword Blades and Poppy Seeds* (1914), helped to establish her in the U.S. as a controversial experimentalist in the new poetry. She promoted and publicized modernist verse, and attracted the attention of a wide audience. She used freeverse techniques, what she called "unrhymed cadence," and created "polyphonic prose," prose-poems of varied rhythms and sound patterns. Believing that poetry should be heard, she emphasized verbal effects in her verse; and in numerous poetry readings, she presented her work as performance art. Many of her poems were frankly erotic; she sought complete freedom in the choice of subject matter. She claimed that "the true test of poetry is sincerity and vitality," and her verse is often intense and dramatic. It can also seem excessively self-indulgent and merely histrionic. A recurring theme is the desire for romantic fulfillment.

Visual images predominate in her verse; L. juxtaposes clear and vivid images in order to create striking metaphors. Her sensuous and impressionistic descriptions are often celebrations of physical beauty; the natural world is animated with movement and emotion. The "white mares of the moon" rear in the night sky; fish ponds in moonlight become shimmering dragons. Fanciful, wistful, luminous, her poetry expresses her restless energy, her luxuriant imagination.

What's O'Clock (1925), a collection of lyrics published posthumously, won the Pulitzer Prize. L. was often more imitative than original, more conservative than radical, more romantic than modern. Yet she helped to create a climate in the U.S. in which artistic experimentation could flourish. Her verse can be faulted for its superficiality; D. H. Lawrence described it as "pure sensation *without concepts*." L. is often credited with having talents that are more political than poetic. Nevertheless, she remains a significant presence in modern American literature, a productive force encouraging emancipated and vigorous writing.

FURTHER WORKS: *Six French Poets* (1915); *Men, Women, and Ghosts* (1916); *Tendencies in Modern American Poetry* (1917); *Can Grande's Castle* (1918); *Pictures of the Floating World* (1919); *Fir-Flower Tablets* (1920, with Florence Ayscough); *Legends* (1921); *A Critical Fable* (1922); *East Wind* (1926); *The Madonna of Carthagena* (1927); *Ballads for Sale* (1927); *Selected Poems* (1928); *Poets and Poetry* (1930); *Complete Poetical Works* (1955)

BIBLIOGRAPHY: Damon, S. F., *A. L.: A Chronicle* (1936); Greenslet, F., *The Lowells and Their Seven Worlds* (1946); Gregory, H., *A. L.:*

Amy Lowell

Portrait of the Poet in Her Time (1958); Gould, J., *The World of A. L. and the Imagist Movement* (1975); Heymann, C. D., *American Aristocracy: The Lives and Times of James Russell, Amy and Robert Lowell* (1980): 157–279

—JO BRANTLEY BERRYMAN

LOWELL, Robert

American poet, b. 1 March 1917, Boston, Mass.; d. 12 Sept. 1977, New York, N.Y.

L. was born to an outwardly conventional, patrician New England family. Without the means to maintain their social position, however, the family was racked by internal tensions, and L. had a moody, turbulent childhood. He spent six uncomfortable years at St. Mark's School, where he studied with the poet Richard Eberhart (b. 1904) and began writing poetry, and then two years at Harvard, where he immersed himself in English literature. Then he made an abrupt break with his milieu by transferring to Kenyon College to study with John Crowe RANSOM. The fierce radical impulse in his life led L. to a passionate, although ultimately temporary, conversion to Roman Catholicism, followed by his six-month imprisonment as a conscientious objector during World War II. Thereafter, L.'s personal history was always entangled with national history. His subsequent private life was characterized by a succession of mental breakdowns, hospitalizations, and recoveries, and three literary marriages—to Jean Stafford (1915–1979), Elizabeth Hardwick (b. 1916), and Caroline Blackwood (b. 1931). He taught at the University of Iowa, Boston University, and Harvard, and over the years made a number of widely publicized political gestures (the most famous of which was his refusal in 1965 to attend the White House Festival of the Arts because of opposition to the Vietnam war). L.'s poems charted the contours of his own agonized life with ever-increasing directness and candor, and when he died of heart failure at the age of sixty, he left behind a creative output that had uniquely fused the private and public realms of his experience.

L.'s first book, *Land of Unlikeness* (1944), established him as a passionate, rebellious American literary presence. In his introduction to the volume Allen TATE noted the willed intricate formalism of L.'s poems and the consciously Catholic nature of his aesthetics and his symbolism. L. derived his title, and his inscription for the book, from Saint Bernard's idea that "as the soul is unlike God, so too it is unlike itself," dwelling in the "land of unlikeness." L. rewrote and reprinted ten of the poems in the Pulitzer Prize-winning *Lord Weary's Castle* (1946). These harsh, alliterative, and difficult early poems are heavily freighted with Christian symbolism, juxtaposing the world of grace to the secular culture of the urban wasteland. Poems like "Christmas Eve under Hooker's Statue" and "The Quaker Graveyard in Nantucket" stand as didactic indictments of American imperialism and materialism, in particular attacking the capitalist/Puritan heritage of New England. L.'s apocalyptic renunciations of a world that "out-Herods Herod" ("The Holy Innocents") provide a scathing critique of American ambition and culture.

L.'s next book, *The Mills of the Kavanaughs* (1951), reflects the defects and marks the crisis of his early style. The long narrative

Robert Lowell

monologues at the book's core are burdened by obscure allusions, a wrenching formalism, and a false rhetorical style. L.'s turn to Robert FROST and Robert Browning as models demonstrated a new interest in plot and character, but the poems' ambitions were undermined by their willful difficulty. Ironically, the book's most successful poems are translations: a pastiche from Vergil and an adaptation from Franz WERFEL. This crisis in L.'s career was both formal and religious, and thereafter he published no new book for eight years as he sought a new language and a new subject matter.

Life Studies (1959) was the major breakthrough and remains his most accomplished and influential book. The poems dispense with the symbolism and formal rigidity of the earlier work, speaking in a more intimate personal and public manner. The prose of CHEKHOV and Flaubert, as well as Williams Carlos WILLIAMS'S poetry, served as models for this flexible new style. The core of the book is composed of a long prose memoir, "91 Revere Street," and fifteen unsparingly personal poems about L.'s family and himself. These family and self-portraits are so unrelentingly and dramatically honest that the critic M. L. Rosenthal termed them "confessional poetry." The satiric prose autobiography unveils the milieu of L.'s childhood, characterizing his father as weak and ineffectual and his mother as cold, shrill, and domineering. With a delicate blend of love, disgust, and wit, the related sequence of poems moves from L.'s childhood to his middle years, exposing private humiliations and treating his own bouts with mental illness with psychological frankness. In placing the unmasked personality of the poet at the center of his volume L. deeply affected the direction of American postwar poetry. In *For the Union Dead* (1964) he continued in the confessional mode, but extended the range of his poems to include public themes.

L.'s historical imagination also led him to translating European poets. In *Imitations* (1961), which he called "a book of versions and free translations," he adapted and re-created a small anthology of poetry ranging from Homer to Boris PASTERNAK. The book shows him assimilating a range of dark and disparate voices into his own native idiom, and often the poems read as L. originals (hence his borrowing from Dryden the idea of translation as "imitation"). L.'s translations of Racine's *Phaedra* (1961) and Aeschylus' *Prometheus Bound* (1969) and *The Oresteia* (1978) also show him freely adapting and absorbing those two to his own model. By his vast effort of translation L. tried to create for himself a viable European tradition. And always this European tradition pointed back to the New World. For example, the theme of Rome, the greatness and horror of her empire, threads together L.'s translations of Horace, Juvenal, Dante, Quevedo, and Góngora in *Near the Ocean* (1967), but that imperial story also represents a parable for America.

L.'s trilogy of one-act plays, *The Old Glory* (1964), reflects his deep preoccupation with the dilemmas of the American past. The plays, unified by the emblem of the flag, dramatize the idealism and violence of the American character at three different historical stages. The first play, *Endecott and the Red Cross*, based on Hawthorne's story "The Maypole of Merrymount," evokes a gentle Puritan forced into bloodshed because of religious expediency. The second, *My Kinsman, Major Molineux*, a dramatization of Hawthorne's story, treats the American revolution in its darkest, most violent aspect. The third and strongest play, *Benito Cereno*, based on Melville's haunting novella of the same title, attacks the problem of race (and, implicitly, American foreign policy) through the story of a slave revolt. These plays dramatize the moral forces and contradictions at the heart of American history.

L.'s most extensive late work was his series of unrhymed blank verse sonnets. The original *Notebook 1967–1968* (1969) began as a verse diary, but outgrew its initial format and reappeared, heavily revised and expanded, in 1970 as *Notebook*. The loose sonnet form marks L.'s attempt to combine his formal and informal modes while meditating on both private and public themes. The scheme of *Notebook*—which he considered a single poem, intuitive in arrangement and jagged in pattern—follows the arc of the seasons. Diary entries, historical meditations, contemporary events, letters, and soliloquies were all poured into this open framework. At their weakest the sonnets read as undigested fragments; at their strongest they chart a rich autobiographical history. L. himself remained dissatisfied with the coherence of the sonnets and felt compelled continually to revise them. Three years later they again reappeared, radically metamorphosed into three new books. *History* (1973) re-creates a host of historical figures from biblical times to the present day, including a striking series of verse portraits of other writers. *For Lizzie and Harriet* (1973) contained no new poems, but reworked and regrouped poems dealing with L.'s second wife and his daughter. *The Dolphin* (1973) details L.'s move to England as he left one wife for another. The domestic plot of his subsequent marriage and the birth of his son suggests his deep compulsion to rewrite his own story. The unsparing self-revelations continue the personal mode of *Life Studies*. In L.'s final book of poems, *Day by Day* (1977), he at last abandoned the sonnet form for an irregular free verse but continued his struggle to record honestly and accurately his painful domestic history.

L.'s collected works passionately embody his own turbulent life history. At the same time they show a firm critical insight into the political and historical nature of his own era. He is the most central American poet of the postwar generation.

FURTHER WORKS: *The Voyage, and Other Versions of Poems by Baudelaire* (1968); *Selected Poems* (1976); *Collected Prose* (1987)

BIBLIOGRAPHY: Jarrell, R., *Poetry and the Age* (1953): 208–19; Mazzaro, J., *The Achievement of R. L.: 1939–1959* (1960); Staples, H. B., *R. L.: The First Twenty Years* (1962); Mazzaro, J., *The Poetic Themes of R. L.* (1965); Rosenthal, M. L., *The New Poets: American and British Poetry since World War II* (1967): 25–78; Parkinson, T., ed., *R. L.: A Collection of Critical Essays* (1968); Boyers, R., and M. London, eds., *R. L.: A Portrait of the Artist in His Time* (1970); Williamson, A., *Pity the Monsters: The Political Vision of R. L.* (1974); Yenser, S., *Circle to Circle: The Poetry of R. L.* (1975); Axelrod, S. G., *R. L.: Life and Art* (1978); Fein, R. J., *R. L.*, 2nd ed. (1979); Vendler, H., *Part of Nature, Part of Us: Modern American Poets* (1980): 125–73; Meyers, J., *R. L., Interviews and Memoirs* (1988); Mariani, P. L., *Lost Puritan: A Life of R. J.* (1994); Hart, H., *R. L. and the Sublime* (1995)

—EDWARD HIRSCH

Underneath all these poems "there is one story and one story only"; when this essential theme or subject is understood, the unity of attitudes and judgments underlying the variety of the poems becomes startlingly explicit. The poems understand the world as a sort of conflict of opposites. In this struggle one opposite is that cake of custom in which all of us lie embedded like lungfish—the stasis or inertia of the stubborn self, the obstinate persistence in evil that is damnation. Into this realm of necessity the poems push everything that is closed, turned inward, incestuous, that blinds or binds: the Old Law, imperialism, militarism, capitalism, Calvinism, Authority, the Father, the "proper Bostonians," the rich who will "do everything for the poor except get off their backs." But struggling within this like leaven, falling to it like light, is everything that is free or open, that grows or is willing to change: here is the generosity or openness or willingness that is itself salvation; here is "accessibility to experience"; this is the realm of freedom, of the Grace that has replaced the Law, of the perfect liberator whom the poet calls Christ.

Consequently the poems can have two possible movements or organizations: they can move from what is closed to what is open, or from what is open to what is closed.

Randall Jarrell, *Poetry and the Age* (1953), pp. 208–9

What seems to be happening in *The Mills of the Kavanaughs* is that L., having mastered the traditional forms, is engaging in a search for a more individualized style. That is to say, reacting against the conventional, he is preoccupied with setting for himself increasingly difficult formal problems to solve.

The direction that his ingenuity takes at this point is towards more and more complicated rhyme schemes combined, as in "Thanksgiving's Over," with a fantastically elaborate metrical pattern. This poem is almost unintelligible, partly because of the very odd religious symbolism involved, but more importantly because in this poem, L. has reached the point where decadence begins—where considerations of style and form become so obsessive as to obscure meaning and intention.

"Thanksgiving's Over" is the last poem in *The Mills of the Kavanaughs*, and it marks the climax of L.'s preoccupation with form for its own sake. In *Life Studies*, published after an interval of eight years, the structure of his poetry is much looser than anything written earlier. Just as the sense of strain, conflict and rebellion is markedly reduced as L. tends towards an acceptance of reality, so the rigidity of his early period gives way to a more informal, even casual blend of free verse and occasional rhyme. To be sure, there are a few reminders of his old contention with the order of things in such poems as "Beyond the Alps" and "Skunk Hour"; significantly, it is these poems that bear the closest resemblance on a formal level to his earlier work.

In its broadest outlines, then, the curve of L.'s development as a poet in his first two decades is from a posture of rebellion towards a position of acceptance. And the parallel tendency away from his initial formalism towards relative flexibility is not the paradox it seems, but a function of his poetic needs.

Hugh B. Staples, *R. L.: The First Twenty Years* (1962), pp. 20–21

[In *Life Studies*] the poet who emerged in 1944 as "consciously a Catholic poet" can no longer find souls to be saved. What had been L.'s religious view has turned into a soulless world of conformity. In the process, Conrad Aiken's hopes that L. might "expand his range" and try things of a "non-religious sort" have been fulfilled. R. P. Blackmur's objections to the "fractious vindictiveness" and the "nearly blasphemous" nature of the character portrayals have been resolved by their removal from his writing. However, man caught in the network of society is treated as vindictively as he was when caught in the lockstep of time. That later one is as materially destroyed as the other was spiritually. Nevertheless, in an age which likes to separate its religion from its art, the technical accomplishments of *Life Studies* may far outweigh the loss of the Christian experience.

Jerome Mazzaro, *The Poetic Themes of R. L.* (1965), pp. 118–19

. . . For L. the process of "recasting and clarification" has continued beyond *Life Studies*. *Life Studies* was the most remarkable poetic sequence to appear since Hart Crane's *The Bridge* and William Carlos Williams's *Paterson*. It may well stand as L.'s chief

accomplishment. At the same time, it presented L. himself so vulnerably and humiliatingly that only his extraordinary gifts enabled him to transcend the hysteria behind it. The transcendence made for a revolutionary achievement, but of a sort that can never be repeated by the same poet. In *For the Union Dead*, we are shown that for L. at least there is a further way, closer to the "main stream." To maintain indefinitely the violent pace of *Life Studies* would be to cultivate a poetry that not only repeated itself but also fed on, and encouraged, suicidal madness. Instead, beyond a certain point at least, L. has been working free of the intolerable burden of his self-laceration. The problem is to hold on meanwhile to what he has gained in poetic conception (the painfully alert sensibility alive to the pressure of its own anxieties and those of the age) and in its embodiment in a brilliantly improvised formal technique.

M. L. Rosenthal, *The New Poets: American and British Poetry since World War II* (1967), p. 76

L. as much as any current poet deserves systematic study in universities. He is entwined in the great moral issues of our age with compelling fullness, reacting against the savagery and barbarism of great and small wars, apprehending passionately the solitude and waste of the individual caught in a world that, in Rilke's phrase, has "fallen into the hands of men." He is in effect the poetic conscience tormented by its perception of reality and its imagination of possibilities in this most terrible of centuries, once spoken of with unconscious irony as The American Century. And he sees this century within the total web of the past and as a trouble to be seen in the major languages of the world. He is neither a temporal nor a spatial provincial. American historical life is seen as an experienced whole, and the ancestral voices of his poetry are familial, of New England, and at the same time universal spirits. His work is not national in any sense, but local and international, representing his identity as a New England writer and his obligations as a member of the international poetic community. It would be too much to ask that he embrace Oriental culture; his only provincialism resides in his faithfully European affections, and surely the legacy of Western Europe is rich—and relevant—enough to engage the energies of a lifetime.

Thomas Parkinson, "Introduction: R. L. and the Uses of Modern Poetry in the University," in Thomas Parkinson, ed., *R. L.: A Collection of Critical Essays* (1968), p. 8

All of L.'s work since *Life Studies* might be seen as an attempt to find a center for his enormously complex and self-divided personality in the act of finding a totally adequate language. Such a language would have to be at once deep and spontaneous enough to reach the innermost recesses of feeling, and versatile enough to catch all responses to the outside. The sense that, if one could find this central point, one could move the world, is not unique to L.; it is there in every poet who undertakes such a quest for the absolute language, even if he merely wishes to move the world into his poems. But in L.'s case, the claim is more serious, more philosophical, than in most, due to the movement of his work toward microcosmic-macrocosmic orderings, his psychoanalytic view of history.

Alan Williamson, Pity the Monsters: The Political Vision of R. L. (1974), p. 215

. . . By including versions of poems from all of L.'s preceding volumes (except the first, much of which was incorporated in the second), <i>History</i> testifies to and helps to establish a contextual relationship among all of these volumes that is comparable to the relationships among the poems within one of them. The book is a synecdoche for L.'s work: what his poetry is to history, <i>History</i> is to his poetry. More than this, it is L.'s most ambitious attempt to date to discover the whole of his life—which is to say its shape as well as much of its data—in a part of it.

If it still risks being lost, as one of its sections implies the <i>Cantos</i> risk being lost, "in the rockslide of history," <i>History</i> certainly better fits the conception of a book that is "one poem" than had either of the <i>Notebooks</i>. A troubling and troubled work, which takes chances that most of us did not even know could be taken, it nevertheless reassures us that L. has not lost touch with the formal desiderata of poetry, just as he has not lost touch with his earliest work. Perhaps there is little need to worry that he will ever do so. The principle that accounts for the nature of his development so far and betokens that of his future development also provides for the preservation of the shaping spirit.

Stephen Yenser, Circle to Circle: The Poetry of R. L. (1975), pp. 10–11

Although the style of L.'s art changed radically over the years, its essentially experiential character remained constant. "The thread that strings it together," he remarked, "is my autobiography"; "what made the earlier poems valuable seems to be some recording of experience and that seems to be what makes the later ones." "Experience" does not mean only what "happened" to L., for that formulation would place too much emphasis on an active but unilateral environment, and would reduce the experiencer's mind to the passive role of a transmitting lens. The mind itself is active, trembling to "caress the light." "Experience" more truly means the sum of the relations and interactions between psyche and environment. It grows from the Cartesian dualism of inner and outer, but through its interpenetrating energies abolishes the dualism. Just as experience mediates between self and world, partaking of both, so L.'s poems mediate between himself and his

world, and between his personal history and that of his readers. His poems are structures of experience. They both record his life and assume a life of their own; and as they transform the poet's life into the autonomous life of art, they reenter his life by clarifying and completing it.

Steven Gould Axelrod, R. L.: Life and Art (1978), pp. 4–5

LOWRY, (Clarence) Malcolm

English novelist, poet, and short-story writer, b. 28 July 1909, Liscard; d. 27 June 1957, Ripe

L. basically had a conventional upper-middle-class upbringing. He was sent by his businessman father to the best possible public schools, and eventually Cambridge, after which he was expected to follow in the family tradition and go into the business. At the age of seventeen, L. began drinking heavily, an activity that he hoped would allow him to escape, a motif that would run through his entire life and writing experience. L. yearned for something outside of his ruling-class provincialism, and embarked upon a lifestyle which would keep him permanently adrift.

After dropping out of school, L. convinced his father to let him see the world, and decided to go to sea. Chauffeur driven to the dock, he shipped out on a tramp steamer and embarked on a trip that would become the basis of his first novel, <i>Ultramarine</i> (1933). The story basically follows the journey of a sensitive, educated man's voyage to the Far East, and catalogues his attempts to win the favor of the proletarian crew, who resent and bully him for his lack of worldly experience. Heavily influenced by his literary contacts, <i>Ultramarine</i> reflected both the works of Conrad AIKEN and James JOYCE in style and technique, marking L.'s attraction to the difficult MODERNIST novel. While the novel contains flashes of brilliance, its critical reception was chilly.

Following this failure, L. drifted around Europe supported by his father's money. He married and divorced, and worked on various projects that would not come into completion until after his death. During this period, L. worked on <i>Lunar Caustic</i> (1968), a posthumously published work, which reflects L.'s obsession with alcohol, madness, and failure, tracing the collapse of an Englishman abroad. Waking up in a mental hospital, the central character undergoes a series of transformations on the road to recovery, finding some home truths along the way. <i>Lunar Caustic</i> is a spare and powerful novel, with a wry wit that is absent in his other works.

Unable to find a publisher, a chronically depressed L. drifted into Mexico in 1936 and began work on the first draft of his masterpiece, <i>Under the Volcano</i> (1947). A largely autobiographical novel, the story follows the tragic decline of Geoffrey Firmin who is hell bent on drinking himself into the grave. L. links the political disintegration of Mexico with the personal collapse of Firmin, who is eventually assassinated by Fascists. <i>Under the Volcano</i> is essentially a fuller exploration of L.'s own alcoholic agony and confusion bout the world at large, juxtaposing the personal, with the strange, fecund madness of the Mexican jungles.

Generally speaking, <i>Under the Volcano</i> was well received, and sold many copies in the U.S., a success L. was unable to repeat. Haunted by his Mexican experience, he began <i>Dark is the Grave Wherein My Friend Is Laid</i> (1968), but quickly abandoned it in

125

favor of heavy drinking and traveling. In 1949 L. managed to finish a 455-page film script for an adaptation of F. Scott FITZGERALD's *Tender is the Night* (1934), a project that was more of a psychological boost than an actual real achievement. Following this breakthrough, L. wrote and finished a series of short stories that would eventually be collected as *Hear Us O Lord from Heaven Thy Dwelling Place* (1961). These stories tend to dramatize the states of despair L. was most familiar with, casting his major characters into the role of social rejects plagued by artistic impotence. L.'s last novel, *October Ferry to Gabriola* (1970), outlined his life in exile in Vancouver, and like many of his works, it was published posthumously.

L. belongs to the tradition of sodden writers who favor the high modernist mode, and his place and reputation is largely an issue of dispute. With flashes of talent in his early works, L. burnt out after completing only one major novel. A compulsive autobiographer, L. turned his life into the raw materials of his own work, fulfilling a highly personal vision that eschewed most traditional novelistic forms. While L.'s work was slow to win acceptance, it was filled with a dazzling intensity that focused on questions of alienation, failure, and the compulsive need for self destruction. Though L.'s work largely went unread, he remains an interesting voice in British modernist fiction.

FURTHER WORKS: *Selected Poems of M. L.* (1962); *Selected Letters of M. L.* (1965); *M. L.: Psalms and Songs* (1975); *The Collected Poetry of M. L.* (1992)

BIBLIOGRAPHY: Day, D., *M. L., A Biography* (1973); Arac, J., "The Form of Carnival in Under the Volcano," *PMLA*, 92 (1977): 481-89; Markson, D., *M. L.'s "Volcano": Myth, Symbol, Meaning* (1978); Cross, R. K., *M. L.: A Preface to His Fiction* (1980); Binns, R., *M. L.* (1984); Salloum, S., *M. L.: Vancouver Days* (1987); Bareham, T., *M. L.* (1989)

—PAUL HANSOM

LOZI LITERATURE

See Zambian Literature

LU HSÜN

(pseud. of Chou Shu-jen) Chinese short-story writer, essayist, critic, translator, and literary theorist, b. 25 Sept. 1881, Shaoshing, Chekiang Province; d. 19 Oct. 1936, Shanghai

Born into the gentry class, rapidly declining under the Ching (Manchu) dynasty, L. H. was brought up in the twilight of a vanishing way of life. He received a traditional education before he enrolled in new-style schools in Nanking. He was sent to Japan in 1902 on a government scholarship to study medicine, but in 1905 he abruptly terminated his medical studies and decided to devote his full energies to literary endeavors. He wanted to explore the Chinese national character through his writing. After a decade of constant failure following his return to China in 1909, he was finally catapulted to literary renown in 1918 with the short story "K'uangjen jih-chi" (1918; "The Diary of a Madman," 1941),

published in *Hsin ch'ingnien*, the journal that initiated the intellectual revolution in China known as the New Culture Movement. The work has been called China's first modern story because of its use of the vernacular and its highly subjective, devastating critique of traditional culture.

Two collections of short stories followed: *Na han* (1923; *Call to Arms*, 1981) and *P'ang huang* (1926; *Wandering*, 1981)—published together in English as *The Complete Stories of Lu Xun* (1981). Between 1918 and 1936, the year he died, he also wrote sixteen volumes of essays, a collection each of personal reminiscences, prose poetry, and historical tales, some sixty classical-style poems, half a dozen volumes of scholarly research (mainly on Chinese fiction), and numerous translations of Russian, eastern European, and Japanese writers.

In 1928 L. H. settled in Shanghai, where he became the doyen of literati. Having witnessed the vicissitudes of the Chinese political situation, he turned increasingly leftist and was a founding member of the League of Left-Wing Writers in 1930. While sympathetic to the underground Chinese Communist Party, he was never a Party member. He eventually became embroiled in the internecine squabbles on the leftist front and died a tormented and alienated man. After his death, however, he was deified by Mao Tsetung as China's greatest "writer, thinker, and revolutionist" and enjoyed a renown comparable to Mao's.

L. H.'s works have often been read as scathing critiques of Chinese society and culture. His sardonic, satirical essays have been seen as effective weapons with which he launched attacks on enemies of all hues. Privately, however, he was seized with periodic spells of spiritual nihilism and seemed unable to shake off the inner ghosts of his traditional past. Thus, some of his literary works, particularly his later fiction and prose poetry, reveal a subtle lyricism and a philosophical depth unparalled in modern Chinese literature.

L. H. is known in the West chiefly for his short stories, which have been translated into more than a dozen languages. In them he succeeded brilliantly in rendering a multifaceted portrait of Chinese people caught in all their tribulations. Aside from his first modern story, "K'uang-jen jih-chi," his most celebrated story, both in China and abroad, is "Ah Q cheng-chuan" (1921; "The True Story of Ah Q," 1926), a satirical "biography" of an ignorant village laborer who experiences, with an utter lack of self-awareness, a series of humiliations and finally dies a victim of the chaos of the Republican revolution of 1911. Comparable in cultural significance to Cervantes's Don Quixote, L. H.'s Ah Q stands as a personification of the negative traits of the Chinese national character.

Less allegorical and more realistic and moving are such well-known stories as "Kung I-chi" (1919; "Kung I-chi," 1932), "Ku-hsiang" (1921; "My Native Town," 1935), "Chu-fu" (1924; "The New Year Blessing," 1936), and "Fei-tsao" (1924; "The Cake of Soap," 1941), in all of which the hypocrisy and insensitivity of upper-class intellectuals are contrasted with the suffering of the lower-class people. Nonetheless, L. H.'s own profound ambivalence toward his countrymen and his sophistication as an artist infused his stories with layers of ambiguity in both characterization and narrative technique, which defy easy ideological analysis. In most of his stories there can be found a metaphysical level, centering on an alienated loner besieged and persecuted by an uncomprehending crowd. Thus, the "philosophical" messages of L. H.'s works are much less positive than they are perceived to be in the numerous eulogistic biographies, monographs, and articles that have poured out continually from his Chinese adulators. This introspective, almost tragic, side of L. H.'s works, ignored by his admirers in China, is notably present in his classical-style poetry, his prose poetry collection *Yeh-ts'ao* (1927; *Wild Grass*, 1974), and some of his early essays.

Despite these darker and apolitical aspects of L. H.'s art and psyche, his name has been constantly used in successive political campaigns by the Chinese Communists since 1949, including the Cultural Revolution, in which his reputation remained unscathed, although his numerous disciples, friends, and scholars were purged. L. H. is still modern China's most admired and respected writer.

FURTHER WORKS: *L. H. ch'uan-chi* (20 vols., 1938); *L. H. ch'uan-chi pu-i* (2 vols., 1946, 1952); *L. H. shu-chien* (2 vols., 1952); *Diary of a Madman and Other Stories* (1990); *Selected Short Stories of L. X* (1990). FURTHER WORKS IN ENGLISH: *Ah Q and Others* (1941); *Selected Works of L. H.* (4 vols., 1956–1957); *Selected Stories of L. H.* (1960)

BIBLIOGRAPHY: Huang, S., *L. H. and the New Culture Movement of Modern China* (1957); Hsia, C. T., *A History of Modern Chinese Fiction* (1961): pp.28–54; Hsia, T. A., *The Gate of Darkness* (1968): pp.101–62; Hanan, P., "The Technique of L. H.'s Fiction," *HJAS*, 34 (1974): 53–95; Lyell, W. A., *L. H.'s Vision of Reality* (1976); Lee, L. O., "Genesis of a Writer: Notes on Lu Xun's Educational Experience," Mills, H. C., "Lu Xun: Literature and Revolution—from Mara to Marx," Doleželová-Velingerová, M., "Lu Xun's 'Medicine,'" in Goldman, M., ed., *Modern Chinese Literature in the May Fourth Era* (1977): 161–232; Semanov, V. I., *L. H. and His Predecessors* (1980); Kowallis, J. E., *The Lyrical L. X.: A Study of His Classical Style Verse* (1996)

—LEO OU-FAN LEE

LUANDINO VIEIRA, José

See Vieira, José Luandino

LUCEBERT

(pseud. of Lubertus Jacobus Swaanswijk) Dutch poet, b. 15 Feb. 1924, Amsterdam

L. was raised by his strict Calvinist grandmother on a farm near Amsterdam. His early schooling in Amsterdam was interrupted by World War II, when he was conscripted into forced labor by the occupying German army. Arrested on suspicion of sabotage, he was later released and spent the remaining years of the war in underground activities. After the war L. studied German romanticism and philosophy. He is a prolific painter, whose work has been widely exhibited in British and continental galleries.

Shortly after the liberation in 1945, L. associated himself with radical political and artistic groups in the Netherlands. One such group of artists, both painters and writers, began to react against what they considered unconscionable provincialism in Holland. Known as "De Vijftigers" (the generation of the 1950s), they incorporated various current "isms" into an invigorating, albeit somewhat formless, body of protest. An early member of De Vijftigers, L. played a crucial role in developing the concept of language as physical form—employing wordplay neologisms,

typographical tricks—which continues to be characteristic of the poetic avant-garde in the Netherlands. Because of L.'s skill as painter and poet, the amalgamation of the two forms met with considerable success.

In 1952 L. published five books of poetry: *Apocrief* (apocryphal), *De analfabetische naam* (the illiterate name), *De welbespraakte slaap* (the eloquent sleep), *De getekende naam* (the signed name), and *De amsterdarnse school* (the Amsterdam school). These books were intended as a protest against the condition of art in the postwar society. It seems as if L. offered, in these early works, the principle of disruption as his supreme credo. There are times, as in the title poem of *9000 jakhalzen zwemmen naar Boston* (1950; 9000 jackals are swimming to Boston), when he breaks up his own vision with conflicting images and words. L. learned, however, the virtue of control, the ability to organize his insight around a particular set of metaphors.

By the time of the publication of *Val voor vliegengod* (1959; trap for the lord of the flies), L., altering the emphasis of his concerns, had turned his attention to mankind's search for enduring beauty. The problems of society became, in a sense, the problems of aesthetics; where once L. showed beasts at large in society, he now detected the "lord of the flies" within each human breast as well.

Throughout the 1960s and 1970s L. devoted most of his time to painting. Although *Gedichten 1948–1963* (1965; poems 1948–1963) brought him recognition as one of the most important Dutch poets of the 20th c., he has published few books of verse since. His poems have been translated into sixteen languages, however, some fifty of them have been set to music and recorded, and adaptations of his work are regularly performed on Dutch television and radio and on the stage.

The variorum edition of L.'s poetry, *Verzamelde gedichten* (1974; collected poems), illustrated by the author, reveals a skillful practitioner of two complementary art forms. He is able to develop powerful images of the beautiful and the grotesque (concepts he finds inseparable) by combining language and line, word and color, to dissolve their apparent differences in one encompassing vision.

FURTHER WORKS: *Triangel in de jungel* (1951); *De dieren der democratie* (1951); *Van de afgrond en de luchtmens* (1953); *Alfabel* (1955); *Amulet* (1957); *Mooi uitzicht & andere kurioziteiten* (1963); *Poezie is kinderspel* (1968); *Drie lagen diep* (1969); *. . . en morgen de hele wereld* (1973); *Oogsten in de dwaaltuin* (1981). FURTHER WORKS IN ENGLISH: *The Tired Lovers They Are Machines* (1973)

BIBLIOGRAPHY: Snapper, J., *Post-War Dutch Literature: A Harp Full of Nails* (1972), passim

—LARRY TEN HARMSEL

LUGONES, Leopoldo

Argentine poet, short-story writer, essayist, and historian, b. 13 June 1874, Villa de María del Río Seco; d. 18 Feb. 1938, Isla del Tigre

L. was Argentina's most important lyric poet of the early 20th c. He left his native province of Córdoba in 1893 and moved to

Buenos Aires. Once in the capital, L. befriended Rubén DARÍO and became Argentina's premier MODERNIST poet, but he had to support himself through bureaucratic posts in the national government. L. became the director of the library of the National Council of Education after 1914 and was the Argentine representative to the Committee on Intellectual Cooperation of the League of Nations. In 1926 he won the National Prize for Literature. Turning from the socialism of his youth to advocacy of ultraconservative nationalism, he became alienated from many of his former friends. As his isolation from the Argentine intelligentsia grew, disillusionment led to emotional depression and finally suicide in 1938.

Although L.'s poetry and prose evolved gradually, there are several constant themes: love and feminine sensuality; the celebration of natural beauty in vivid landscape descriptions and a metaphysical concern about organic processes; increasing nationalism and a search for Argentine identity; a preoccupation with death linked to love; and the poet's original treatment of the symbolic imagery associated with the moon.

L. began the modernist phase of his work with *Las montañas del oro* (1897; the mountains of gold), which was influenced by French SYMBOLISM and represented an elaborate experiment with visual imagery, rhyme, and meter (especially free verse). Although *Los crepúsculos del jardín* (1905; the garden twilights) is generally considered to be L.'s most typically modernist book, his exceptional talents as a creator of metaphor and as a musical poet attuned to the subtle nuances and interplay of sound and meaning first emerge here. By filtering emotions through the eyes of a distant poetic speaker or by using natural landscapes as contrasting backgrounds rather than projections of the emotional stress felt by his characters, L. avoids maudlin sentimentality.

Most critics consider *Lunario sentimental* (1909; sentimental phases of the moon) L.'s masterpiece because its original metaphors, phantasmagoric imagery, and ironic tone anticipate facets of the vanguardist poetry of the next decade. Jorge Luis BORGES and the *Martinfierrista* group would later praise L.'s use of metaphor in this book as a direct influence on their own poetry, although they rejected his insistence on rhyme. This book also signals the culmination of L.'s youthful modernist verse. The moon is the central motif of the book, which is a potpourri of verse, one-act plays in verse and prose, prose poems, and lyrical short stories.

Odas seculares (1910; secular odes) initiated L.'s POSTMODERNIST poetry. The book's epic vision of Argentina's past, its flora and fauna, its mountains and streams, its major cities and national heroes (especially, the Argentine gaucho), commemorate the nation's centennial. "A los ganados y las mieses" (to the cattle and grainfields) stands out for its distinctive metaphors but lies within the tradition inaugurated by the Venezuelan Andrés Bello (1781–1865), in which South America's agriculture is extolled. Some of L.'s best love poetry is found in *El libro fiel* (1912; the faithful book), where L. provides an essentially romantic but philosophical view of conjugal love presented in a nostalgic tone of poignant tenderness. L. also employs popular verse forms like ballads or the Argentine *vidalita* (a sentimental folk song).

In *El libro de los paisajes* (1917; the book of landscapes), L. strips his verse of all vestiges of the exotic themes and settings common in modernist poetry to focus his attention on the flora and fauna of the region around Buenos Aires. L.'s interest in musical composition is reflected here by the use of onomatopeia, euphony, and alliteration. Many poems are modeled on symphonic forms and the orchestral tonality and range of classical musical instruments.

L.'s later poetry was of uneven quality but continued to evolve toward autobiographical lyricism in *Poemas solariegos* (1927; ancestral poems) and narrative verse in his glorification of the national spirit and past incarnated by the gaucho in the posthumously published *Romances del río seco* (1938; ballads of the dry river).

This last collection was an attempt to apply his theories of gaucho songs and verse, theories that are contained in his most important collection of essays, *El payador* (1916; the minstrel cowboy). L.'s prose includes both historical and cultural essays, but he is probably most remembered for some of his short stories. In *La guerra gaucha* (1905; the gaucho war), the narrative focus of these historical vignettes is overshadowed by a proliferation of rhetorical adornments and poetic imagery. *Las fuerzas extrañas* (1906; the strange forces) is L.'s most important contribution to fiction because it introduced science fiction to Argentine literature and surely influenced the fantastic stories of Adolfo Bioy CASARES and Borges.

L. was much more than the leading Argentine disciple of Darío's modernism. An indisputable master of metaphor and visual imagery, he was an original precursor of the essential elements of vanguardist poetry and contemporary prose in Latin America.

FURTHER WORKS: *El imperio jesútico* (1904); *Piedras liminares* (1910); *Historia de Sarmiento* (1911); *Las horas doradas* (1922); *Estudios helénicos* (1923); *Cuentos fatales* (1924); *El ángel de la sombra* (1926); *La grande Argentina* (1930); *Poesías completas* (1948); *Obras en prosa* (1962)

BIBLIOGRAPHY: Borges, J. L., *L.* (1955); Moreno, J. C., "Silence in the Poetry of L. L.," *Hispania*, 46 (1963): 760–63; Ashhurst, A. W., et al., *Homenaje a L. L. (1874-1938)* (1964); Sola González, A., "Las *Odas seculares* de L. L.," *RI*, 32 (1966): 23–51; Martínez Estrada, E., *L. L.: Retrato sin retocar* (1968); Omil, A., *L. L.: Poesía y prosa* (1968); Mudrovic, M., "The Speaker's Position in Some Poems of Machado and L.," *KRQ*, 27 (1980): 281–88

—JAMES J. ALSTRUM

LUKÁCS, György

(also known as Georg Lukács) Hungarian literary historian, critic, and philosopher (writing in Hungarian and German), b. 13 April 1885, Budapest; d. 4 June 1971, Budapest

L. was born into a wealthy Jewish family. He was a student of neo-Kantianism, and from the very first combined philosophical studies with a great interest in literature and sociology. L. studied at the universities of Budapest and Berlin. Georg Simmel (1858–1918) and Max Weber (1864–1920) were his teachers and models. After travels in Italy, he lived in Heidelberg (1912–16), where he belonged to the Max Weber circle. The publication of a collection of his essays, *Die Seele und die Formen* (1911; *Soul and Form*, 1974), established L. as a critic of international reputation.

In 1917 L. returned to Budapest, joined the Communist Party, and became people's commissar for public education in the short-lived government of the Hungarian Communist republic of 1919. After its overthrow by Horthy, L. was forced to flee to Austria, settling in Vienna.

György Lukács

When, in 1923, L. published *Geschichte und Klassenbewußtsein (History and Class Consciousness,* 1971), the Communist International charged him with "revisionism," a term that was to haunt him for the rest of his life. When a similar charge was brought against him in 1929, he withdrew from politics. From 1931 to 1933 he lived in Berlin. At the advent of Hitler he emigrated to the Soviet Union, where he worked at the Philosophical Institute of the Academy of Sciences, laying the foundations for his major works.

In 1945, at the end of World War II, L. returned to Budapest after twenty-five years of exile. He became a member of the national assembly of Hungary, which was then ruled by a postwar coalition government. He was also appointed a member of the presidium of the Hungarian Academy of Sciences and professor of aesthetics and cultural history at the University of Budapest. In 1948 the Hungarian Communist Party, although a minority, gained power and, in 1949, proclaimed Hungary a People's Republic. In the following period, in which Hungary aligned itself with the Soviet bloc, renewed accusations of revisionism caused L. again to withdraw from political life. When, in October 1956, a popular anti-Communist revolt broke out, a new coalition government under Imre Nagy declared Hungary neutral and withdrew from the Warsaw Pact. It was in this short-lived coalition government that L. served as minister of culture. Soon, however, Soviet troops suppressed the rebellion, and L. was deported to Romania. In 1957 he was allowed to return to Budapest, and with his brief political career over, he devoted himself until his death to his studies in aesthetics and ethics. L.'s death was for the most part ignored by the Communist press of eastern Europe, although he was buried in Budapest with all due Party honors.

As a literary scholar and critic, L. was primarily concerned with the historical, political, and social dynamics of a work of art. Art to L. was not simply a political tool or social documentation. In fact, he stressed the originality and freedom of the artist's imagination. He pointed out how artistic imagination reflects the reality of the historical process, elevating events and circumstances that may appear devoid of meaning to the level of symbolic significance. The outstanding feature of L.'s aesthetics is that art has the function of "a seeing, hearing, and feeling organon of humanity—of humanity in every human being." Art, therefore, plays a most important role in the development of man's consciousness of humanity; it forms an integral part of the process of freeing mankind from its state of alienation.

L.'s approach to literature was philosophical, his vision of history, Marxist, and his aesthetics, Hegelian. Hegel is the most relevant in the sense that L. adopted his view of the historical development of form in art. From Hegel and Marx L. evolved his own philosophy of history, which was formulated in *Geschichte und Klassenbewußtsein* in 1923. A major work in Marxist philosophy, this book is the integration of Marx's interpretation of history—a chronicle of man's emancipation from the class struggle—with Hegel's concept of totality. Its particular significance lies in the fact that L. had in it visualized the matrix from which his literary criticism could be evolved.

In *Die Theorie des Romans* (completed 1916, pub. 1920; *The Theory of the Novel,* 1971), which marked L.'s transition from neo-Kantianism to Hegelianism, L. related the genres of epic and novel to Western intellectual history. Epic poetry, he maintained, expressed a sense of the "extensive totality of life," as experienced in Greece at the dawn of history. The novel is regarded as "an expression of the transcendental homelessness" of modern man, its development being paralleled by the decline of religious faith and the rise of scientific ideology. *Die Theorie des Romans* was L.'s first step in formulating his theory that artistic forms can be perceived in terms of historical development.

It was after L.'s emigration to the Soviet Union that the doctrine of SOCIALIST REALISM was officially proclaimed. Under the ideological umbrella of this doctrine L. began to develop his own theory of the "great realism." Basing his theory on Lenin's epistemology in *Materialism and Empiriocritism* (1908), which posits a "real world" that is independent of the mind, L. considered art a special form of reflecting "reality that exists independently of our consciousness." The work of art, however, does not mirror reality directly, but only indirectly. Works of art that reflect reality directly were condemned by L. as "naturalistic," while those that are too far removed from reality were denounced as "formalistic." This aesthetic theory became the basis of L.'s literary criticism for the following years. His "great realism" differs from Socialist Realism in paying more attention to the classical heritage and in deemphasizing the importance of adhering to the Party line in literary works. L.'s literary taste gravitated to the writers of the 18th and 19th cs., however bourgeois they may have been, and he always opposed mere propaganda literature, an attitude for which he was to be attacked by the Party in the late 1950s.

During the 1930s L. participated in the discussion on the origins and goals of German EXPRESSIONISM that was published in the exile journal *Das Wort* and that was to become one of the most important debates in the history of Marxist aesthetics. The two major antagonists, Bertolt BRECHT and L., both vigorously opposed fascism. Brecht maintained that Communist writers must break radically with traditional forms and that they must utilize modern techniques. L. sought to employ the liberal and humanist traditions of bourgeois art as allies against fascism, condemning at the same time modern art as decadent or formalist. Thus L. denounced James JOYCE, John DOS PASSOS, and Alfred DÖBLIN for their formalism, while praising Maxim GORKY, Romain ROLLAND, and Thomas and Heinrich MANN for their realism.

In *Der historische Roman* (Russian, 1937; German, 1955; *The Historical Novel*, 1962) L. cited the historical novel, as represented by Sir Walter Scott, Balzac, and Tolstoy as the prime example of realist literature, since this type of narrative demonstrates not only the effect of historical reality upon literature but also the interrelationship of economic and social developments with literature and art. The integrity of the genre, threatened by the romanticists and the bourgeois writers after the revolution of 1848, is reestablished by Anatole FRANCE, Stefan ZWEIG, Lion FEUCHTWANGER, Roman Rolland, and Henrich Mann.

L.'s studies in European realism are characterized by questions such as "Balzac or Flaubert?" and "Tolstoy or Dostoevsky?" Making the representation of reality the criterion for his judgment, L. decided in favor of Balzac and Tolstoy. Balzac exemplifies Friedrich Engels's idea of "the triumph of realism," that is to say, a great writer cannot but portray reality, even if such reality conflicts with his ideology. In the case of Flaubert, L. is critical of the writer's preoccupation with literature as "a revelation of the inner life."

Thomas Mann, for L., is one of the great realists, "the last great bourgeois writer" and representative of German humanism. In his *Thomas Mann* (1949; *Essays on Thomas Mann*, 1964), L. traced Mann's brand of realism back to Goethe. Demonstrating in his studies—*Skizze einer Geschichte der neueren deutschen Literatur* (1953; an outline of the history of modern German literature) and *Die Zerstörung der Vernunft* (1954; the destruction of reason)—the interrelationship between political and intellectual history in German literature and philosophy, L. pointed out a progressive and a suppressive trend within German culture—rationalism and humanism as represented by Lessing, Goethe, Hegel, Heine, Marx, and Thomas Mann on the one hand, and irrationalism and barbarism as represented by the romanticists Richard Wagner and Nietzsche on the other. In these studies L. attempted to analyze the German catastrophe of 1933–45 while also formulating designs for a better future.

The last phase of L.'s writings is characterized by his opposition to manifestations of Stalinism in literature, such as the mandatory expression of Socialist Realism and political control of the artist in general. He energetically fought the "expedient character" of Stalinist theories of art, working for what he called the "liquidation of Stalinism in literature."

During these last years, he also adopted Aristotelian concepts in place of Lenin's theory of reflection. *Die Eigenart des Ästhetischen* (2 vols., 1963; the specific nature of the aesthetic), which forms part of a projected magnum opus of his later years, introduces Aristotle's definition of art as mimesis (imitation), stressing the anthropomorphic, evocative, and cathartic character of art.

Although *Zur Ontologie des gesellschaftlichen Seins* (3 vols., 1971–73; on the ontology of social existence; Vol. 1, *Marx's Basic Ontological Principles*, 1978), the first Marxist ontology written since Marx, was completed, a planned work on ethics had only been begun at his death.

World literature in Goethe's sense was always L.'s preoccupation. As one of the most important and thought-provoking Marxist theoreticians of literature and aesthetics, L. influenced decisively the philosophical writings of Ernst Bloch (1885–1977), Herbert Marcuse (1898–1979), Jean-Paul SARTRE, and Maurice Merleau-Ponty (1908–1961), among others, as well as Karl Mannheim's (1893–1947) sociology of knowledge and the literary criticism of Walter BENJAMIN, Lucien Goldmann (1913–1970), and Ernst Fischer (1899–1972). Any formalist or STRUCTURALIST school of literary criticism cannot fail to benefit from the historical perspective L. brought to the understanding of literature.

FURTHER WORKS: *Lenin: Studie über den Zusammenhang seiner Gedanken* (1924; *Lenin: A Study on the Unity of His Thought*, 1971); *Moses Hess und die Probleme der idealistischen Dialektik* (1926); *Goethe und seine Zeit* (1947; *Goethe and His Age*, 1969); *Der junge Hegel* (1948; *The Young Hegel*, 1976); *Essays über den Realismus* (1948); *Schicksalswende: Beiträge zu einer neuen deutschen Ideologie* (1948); *Karl Marx und Friedrich Engels als Literaturhistoriker* (1948); *Der russische Realismus in der Weltliteratur* (1949; partial tr. in *Studies in European Realism*, 1964); *Deutsche Realisten des 19 Jahrhunderts* (1951); *Balzac und der französische Realismus* (1952; partial tr. in *Studies in European Realism*, 1964); *Beiträge zur Geschichte der Ästhetik* (1954); *Probleme des Realismus* (1955); *Wider den mißverstandenen Realismus* (1958; *Realism in Our Time: Literature and the Class Struggle*, 1964); *Schriften zur Literatursoziologie* (1961); *Werke: Gesamtausgabe* (17 vols., 1962–1981); *Von Nietzsche zu Hitler; oder, Der Irrationalismus und die deutsche Politik* (1966); *Schriften zur Ideologie und Politik* (1967); *Ausgewählte Schriften* (4 vols., 1967–1970); *Über die Besonderheit als Kategorie der Ästhetik* (1967); *Gespräche mit G. L.: Hans Heinz Holz, Leo Kofler, Wolfgang Abendroth Pinkus* (1967; *Conversations with L.*, 1975); *Solschenizyn* (1970; *Solzhenitsyn*, 1971); *Heidelberger Philosophie der Kunst: 1912–1914* (1974); *Heidelberger Ästhetik: 1916–1918* (1975); *Politische Aufsätze* (3 vols., 1975–1977); *Entwicklungsgeschichte des modernen Dramas* (1981); *Gelebtes Leben: Eine Autobiographie im Dialog* (1981). FURTHER WORKS IN ENGLISH: *Writer and Critic, and Other Essays* (1970); *Political Writings: 1919–1929* (1972); *Marxism and Human Liberation: Essays on History, Culture and Revolution* (1973); *Essays on Realism* (1980)

BIBLIOGRAPHY: Demetz, P., "G. L. as a Theoretician of Literature," *Marx, Engels and the Poets: Origins of Marxist Literary Criticism*, rev. ed. (1967): 199–227; Sontag, S., "The Literary Criticism of G. L.," *Against Interpretation* (1969): 90–99; Lichtheim, G., *G. L.* (1970); Parkinson, G. H. R., ed., *G. L.: The Man, His Work and His Ideas* (1970); Jameson, F., "The Case for G. L.," *Marxism and Form: Twentieth Century Dialectical Theories of Literature* (1971); Bahr, E., and R. G. Kunzer, *G. L.* (1972); Mészáros, I., *L.'s Concept of Dialectic, with Biography, Bibliography and Documents* (1972); Királyfalvi, B., *The Aesthetics of G. L.* (1975); Arato, A., and P. Breines, *The Young L. and the Origins of Western Marxism* (1979); Miles, D. H., "Portrait of the Marxist as a Young Hegelian: L.'s Theory of the Novel," *PMLA*, 94 (1979): 22–35; Löwy, M., *G. L.: From Romanticism to Bolshevism* (1979); Fekete, É., and E. Karádi, eds., *G. L.: Sein Leben in Bildern, Selbstzeugnissen und Dokumenten* (1981)

—EHRHARD BAHR

G. L. is probably the only Communist philosopher and literary critic in East Europe who still has the power to interest and to teach many readers in the West. This is due entirely to his intellectual gifts and to the systematically moral vision of history that he has retained as a writer despite his many servilities to Stalin and the betrayals of his own intellectual standards that he has in times past committed as a Communist leader. L. owes his reputation entirely to the logical skill and intellectual vision with which, as a thinker rather than as a "party intellectual," he has sought to illuminate the deepest aspects of Marxism. He gives the impression that no other Communist philosopher has done for some time—that despite official avowals and mechanical formulas, here is an individual thinker who is fascinated by and thoroughly committed to Marxism as a philosophy, and who uses it for the intellectual pleasure and moral satisfaction that it gives him. Yet unlike the really noble figures in the early days of Communist history like Rosa Luxemburg, and brilliant writers like Leon Trotsky, who were truly revolutionary intellectuals . . . L. is actually a more "bourgeois" and academic humanist—who because of his inner detachment can stimulate and provoke us by his insights into a text and his formulations of an esthetic issue.

Alfred Kazin, Introduction to G. L., *Studies in European Realism* (1964), p. v

L. strikes me as seeing through to the very bones and muscles and working organs of the literary tradition where most critics are content to describe its skin; and what enables him to get this depth is his historical sense. In this he brings to literary studies something they have been short of for generations. . . .

The philosophy that underlies his own interpretations of literary history springs from the historical materialism of Marx. . . . The test of making it one's own is how one applies it, or (to come closer to the critical act itself) not how one "applies" it but rather, temporarily ceasing to be aware of Marx's idea, how one goes to work among literature; manages to find, say, family likenesses between works, or main lines of growth inside a trend, or equivalences between a trend or an individual work and things in the main life of an epoch; and *then*, this specifically critical task being done, one may recognize afresh and claim to have confirmed the deep large anterior idea: it is indeed the case at point after point that social being determines consciousness. . . .

The question is: how does the critic find or identify the social equivalent among the mass of possibles? and, once found, what sort of value can it confer on the work of art? To put the question in terms purely of evaluation . . . , how is the critic to distinguish between an intelligent conception of an epoch which, however, remains artistically inert and a work which is fully alive and effective in its own medium and thereby succeeds in having, as counterpart to its theme, a social equivalent which is historically important? That this is what L. is committed to finding,

and evaluating, shows through in many of his theoretical asides.

David Craig, "L.'s Views on How History Moulds Literature," in G. H. R. Parkinson, ed., *G. L.: The Man, His Work and His Ideas* (1970), pp. 191–95

G. L. stands as a lone and splendid tower amidst the gray landscape of eastern European and Communist intellectual life . . . No contemporary Western critic, with the possible exception of Croce, has brought to bear on literary problems a philosophic equipment of comparable authority. In no one since Sainte-Beuve has the sense of history, the feeling for the rootedness of the imagination in time and in place, been as solid and acute. . .

. . . In his works two beliefs are incarnate. First, that literary criticism is not a luxury, that is not what the subtlest of American critics has called "a discourse for amateurs." But that it is, on the contrary, a central and militant force toward shaping men's lives. Secondly, L. affirms that the work of the critic is neither subjective nor uncertain. The truth of judgment can be verified.

. . . L. has put forward a solution to the two-fold dilemma of the modern critic. As a Marxist, he discerns in literature the action of economic, social, and political forces. This action follows on certain laws of historical necessity. To L. criticism is a science even before it is an art . . . Secondly, he has given his writing an intense immediacy. It is rooted in the political struggles and social circumstances of the time. His writings on literature . . . are instruments of combat. . . . L.'s arguments are relevant to issues that are central in our lives. His critiques are not a mere echo to literature. Even where it is sectarian and polemic, a book by L. has a curious nobility. It possesses what Matthew Arnold called "high seriousness."

George Steiner, "Marxism and the Literary Critic" and "G. L. and His Devil's Pact," *Language and Silence: Essays on Language, Literatures and the Inhuman* (1970), pp. 311, 327–28, 330

L., as a thoroughgoing Hegelian idealist, may err in the *Theory of the Novel* in the direction of . . . "surplus metaphysics," but he still ranks, together with Benjamin, Adorno, and Auerbach, as one of our major critics and theoreticians in the German idealist tradition. Perhaps one of the best ways to assess his achievement is to refer to Isaiah Berlin's famous study of Tolstoy, *The Hedgehog and the Fox*, in which he sets up a typology whereby the hedgehog "knows one big thing" and the fox "knows many things." Tolstoy himself, as Berlin points out, was obviously a fox, but a fox who constantly strove (and failed) to become a hedgehog—particularly in the chapters on the philosophy of history in *War and Peace*. L., by contrast, like so many other thinkers in the Hegelian tradition, was the complete hedgehog— yet a hedgehog who tried, again and again, and without success, to become a political fox (cf. his would-be conversion to Marxism-Leninism in 1918). Whereas Tolstoy's genius lay in fastening on the infinite variety of the world and perceiving how "each given object is uniquely different from all others," L.'s talents lay in the opposite direction: he had the ability, which Tolstoy constantly longed for but never acquired, of relating everything in the world to a central, all embracing system, to a "universal explanatory principle," in Berlin's words, one that could perceive, "in the apparent variety of the bits and pieces which compose the furniture of the world," a deep and underlying unity.

David H. Miles, "Portrait of the Marxist as a Young Hegelian: L.'s *Theory of the Novel,*" *PMLA*, 94 (1979), pp. 32–33

With universities and students at or close to the center, a New Left social movement spread across the Western world and parts of the rest of the globe in the late 1960s. . . . In it the young L.'s ideas found their first extensive audience. It was not the audience which he, let alone the great majority of Marxists, had in mind. Yet, the intended audience, the industrial proletariat, had rarely been receptive. . . . Within the framework of this complex movement, only segments of its student and intellectual currents revived the young L.'s ideas. Yet the underlying source of this revival was not that his ideas provided a long-lost clue to the puzzle of how the proletariat becomes revolutionary. On the contrary, the young L.'s heirs in the 1960s reinterpreted his work as a critique of their own experience in capitalist (and socialist) society—as a contribution to their own radicalization. For at its root, the rebellion of students and intellectuals was directed against the reification of everyday life, the process by which human life is transformed under modern conditions of production into things, marketable goods, numbers. A critique of reification lay at the heart of the young L.'s work, pre-Marxist and post-Marxist. In that work, sections of the New Left grasped a vital theoretical anticipation of their own activity.

Andrew Arato and Paul Breines, *The Young L. and the Origins of Western Marxism* (1979), pp. 224

Adorno pointed out that the supreme criterion of L.'s aesthetics, "the postulate of a reality which must be depicted as an unbroken continuum joining subject and object," assumes that a reconciliation has already taken place, "that all is well with society, that the individual has come into his own and feels at home in the world." Besides, L. could not reconcile the Marxist cause with the fact that the novel of Realism he praised was a bourgeois invention. Like Marx, he hoped not to reject bourgeois achievements but to appropriate them: still, it was obviously insulting to offer Brecht and other Marxist writers the edifying examples of Scott and Balzac. But he remains an important figure for anyone who regards the relation between fiction, politics, and ideology as a crucial matter.

Denis Donoghue, "The Real McCoy: *Essays on Realism* by G. L.," *NYRB*, 19 Nov. 1981, p. 45

LUNDKVIST, Artur

Swedish poet, novelist, and essayist, b. 3 March 1906, Hagstad; d. 11 Dec. 1991, Stockholm

L. was born into relatively modest circumstances, and his formal education was not extensive. He has read widely, however, in his native Swedish as well as in nearly a dozen other languages, and his travels have taken him throughout most of the world. L. has assiduously guarded his personal and aesthetic independence by never associating too closely with any movement or any particular line of thought. He has surprised some by his lack of loyalty to social realism or organized labor movements and by his advocacy, during the 1950s and 1960s, of a political position beholden to neither the U.S. nor the Soviet Union. In 1968 he was elected a member of the Swedish Academy.

L.'s first volume of poetry, *Glöd* (1928; embers), and others of the early 1930s celebrate life, energy, and power portrayed as absolute values in lusty imagery and surging free verse. By 1932 L. had come under the influence of SURREALISM, from which he learned much about liberating mankind from its fears, apprehensions, and anxieties. The impact of L.'s surrealistic meditations can be most clearly observed in *Nattens broar* (1936; the bridges of night) and *Sirensång* (1937; siren song).

During World War II and the subsequent years of political unrest, L.'s compassion for the powerless and his sympathy for human misery became more apparent in his poetry. One of his most accomplished works is the long poem *Agadir* (1961; *Agadir*, 1979), which describes the earthquake that struck that Moroccan city in 1960. In its evocation of heroic humility in the face of dreadful fact the poem transcends the specific event that is its subject to become universal in theme. Since 1960 L. has made effective use of the prose poem in such a way that the antithetical relationships inherent in the genre emerge in bold relief.

The growing prominence of prose in L.'s writing, suggested by the prose poems, is amplified by a series of longer, more integrated narratives that approach the novel in scope. These works, written for the most part since 1970, were by no means L.'s first narrative efforts, but they have a particular power deriving from their common concern with characters who break out of established social molds—Genghis Khan, Goya, Alexander the Great, and Viking heroes—to go on journeys that extend their horizons of personal understanding.

Two other prose forms have also been especially important: the travel narrative and the critical essay. L., an inveterate traveler, has used his accounts of sojourns abroad to describe the vast range of human possibilities as well as his impressions of exotic places and people. His most significant critical essays have also had a similar purpose: the introduction of important contemporary foreign writers to the Swedish reading public. His advocacy of writers as diverse as William FAULKNER, Pablo NERUDA, and Czesław MIŁOSZ has made him one of the most insistent and articulate spokesmen for 20th-c. MODERNISM in Sweden.

L.'s most significant contributions to Swedish and world literature are not to be seen in terms of intellectual profundity or formal innovations but rather in the arresting articulation of his extremely broad interests and his genuine concern about the human condition. Both his poetry and poetics are grounded in the world of experience heightened by power of imagination. He has argued that literature should not exist for its own sake but for man's sake; it should thus defend and promote man's fundamental humanity and suggest ways in which he can become ever more humane.

FURTHER WORKS: *Naket liv* (1929); *Jordisk prosa* (1930); *Svart stad* (1930); *Atlantvind* (1932); *Vit man* (1932); *Negerkust* (1933); *Floderna flyter mot havet* (1934); *Himmelsfärd* (1935); *Drakblod* (1936); *Eldtema* (1939); *Ikarus flykt* (1939); *Vandrarens träd* (1941); *Diktare och avslöjare i Amerikas nya litteratur* (1942); *Korsväg* (1942); *Dikter mellan djur och Gud* (1944); *Skinn över sten* (1947); *Fotspår i vattnet* (1949); *Negerland* (1949); *Indiabrand* (1950); *Malinga* (1952); *Vallmor från Taschkent* (1952); *Spegel för dag och natt* (1953); *Darunga* (1954); *Liv som gräs* (1954); *Den förvandlade draken* (1955); *Vindrosor, moteld* (1955); *Vindingevals* (1956); *Berget och svalorna* (1957); *Vulkanisk kontinent* (1957); *Ur en befolkad ensamhet* (1958); *Komedi i Hägerskog* (1959); *Utsikter över utländsk prosa* (1959); *Det talande trädet* (1960); *Orians upplevelser* (1960); *Berättelser för vilsekomna* (1961); *Ögonblick och vågor* (1962); *Sida vid sida* (1962); *Drömmar i ovädrens tid* (1963); *Från utsiktstornet* (1963); *Hägringar i handen* (1964); *Texter i snön* (1964); *Sällskap för natten* (1965); *Så lever Kuba* (1965); *Självporträtt av en drömmare med öppna ögon* (1966); *Mörkskogen* (1967); *Brottställen* (1968); *Snapphanens liv och död* (1968); *Historier mellan åsarna* (1969); *Utflykter med utländska författare* (1969); *Besvärjelser till tröst* (1969); *Långt borta, mycket nära* (1970); *Himlens vilja* (1970); *Antipodien* (1971); *Tvivla, korsfarare!* (1972); *Läsefrukter* (1973); *Lustgårdens demoni* (1973); *Livsälskare, svartmålare* (1974); *Fantasins slott och vardagens stenar* (1974); *Världens härlighet* (1975); *Krigarens dikt* (1976); *Flykten och överlevandet* (1977); *Slavar för Särkland* (1978); *Sett i det strömmande vattnet* (1978); *Utvandring till paradiset* (1979); *Skrivet mot kvällen* (1980); *Babylon, gudarnas sköka* (1981); *Sinnebilder* (1982). FURTHER WORKS IN ENGLISH: *The Talking Tree and Other Poems* (1982); *Journeys in Dream and Imagination* (1991)

BIBLIOGRAPHY: Vowles, R. B., "From Pan to Panic: The Poetry of A. L.," *NMQ*, 22 (1952): 288–303; Sjöberg, L., "An Interview with A. L.," *BA*, 50 (1976): 329–36; Miłosz, C., "Reflections on A. L.'s *Agadir*," *WLT*, 54 (1980): 367–68; Sondrup, S. P., "A. L. and Knowledge for Man's Sake," *WLT*, 55 (1981): 233–38

—STEVEN P. SONDRUP

LUO LITERATURE

See Kenyan Literature and Ugandan Literature

LUSATIAN LITERATURE

The Lusatians (also known as Sorbs and Wends) are descendants of Slavic tribes who at the beginning of the first millennium occupied the territory between the Oder River on the east and the Elbe and Saale rivers on the west. Today, they constitute a separate national minority in East Germany, inhabiting the area southeast of Berlin, traditionally divided into Upper and Lower Lusatia.

From its beginnings in the days of the Reformation to the present, the literature of the Lusatians has reflected the struggle of this smallest Slavic group to preserve its cultural identity. Following a 19th-c. revival of national consciousness brought about by the romantic movement, a period of decline set in at the turn of the century. During that critical time, the continuity of Lusatian culture was preserved largely through the efforts of Catholic men of letters, such as the priests Jurij Winger (1872–1918), author of the popular historical tale *Hronow* (1893; Hronow); Mikłaẃs Andricki (1871–1908), who edited the leading Lusatian periodical, *Łužica*, between 1896 and 1904; and Jurij Deleńk (1882–1918), editor of the Catholic paper *Katolski posoł*.

World War I and its aftermath brought about a new wave of patriotism and a renewed belief in the viability of Lusatian culture. Among the leading figures of that period were the writers of fiction Jakub Lorenc-Zaлěski (1874–1939) and Romuald Domaška (1869–1945); the poets Jan Skala (1889–1945) and Józef Nowak (b. 1895); and the historian, poet, and critic Ota Wićaz (1874–1952).

After World War II Lusatian literature experienced another revival. Writers whose literary activities were restricted or altogether suppressed during the Third Reich, such as Michał Nawka (1885–1968), Mina Witkojc (b. 1893), Marja Kubašec (b. 1890), Měrćin Nowak (b. 1900), and Wylem Bjero (b. 1902), began to publish again with new vigor. These and younger writers have added new dimensions to Lusatian literature. Traditional subjects—the glorious past and village life—dealt with chiefly in poetry and short stories, have now been augmented by full-fledged novels about both life under the Nazis and contemporary social and political problems.

The most successful Lusatian novelist is Jurij Brězan (b. 1916), who also writes in German. The trilogy *Feliks Hanuš: Generacija horkich nazhonjenjow* (1958–66; Feliks Hanuš: generation of bitter experiences)—published first in German under the titles *Der Gymnasiast* (1958; the high-school student), *Semester der verlorenen Zeit* (1960; semester of lost time), and *Mannesjahre* (1966; years of maturity)—is an autobiographical and social novel dealing with the dilemma of being a Lusatian in the modern world. *Krabat; oder, Die Verwandlung der Welt* (1975; Krabat; or, the transformation of the world), a philosophical work published first in German, is a semimythical history of the Lusatian people and their strivings for an existence without fear, told from a contemporary perspective. Other novels and plays of Brězan have appeared in both Lusatian and German. Younger writers who deal with contemporary themes are Marja Mlynkowa (b. 1934), author of the collection of stories *Kostrjanc a čerwjeny mak* (1965; the cornflower and the red poppy), and the poet and translator Jurij Koch (b. 1936), whose novel *Mjez sydom mostami* (1968; between seven bridges) was adapted for the stage in 1970.

Poetry, however, remains the principal genre in Lusatian literature. Leading contemporary exponents are the literary scholar and translator Jurij Młyńk (b. 1927), whose poems are filled with love and pride for Lusatia and its culture; and Kito Lorenc (b. 1938), who writes philosophical and social poetry.

Members of the younger generation, organized in the Circle of Young Sorbian Authors, at times voice controversial and (from the official Communist viewpoint) even heretical views on various ideological issues. Most official literary and cultural activities in

Lusatia revolve around the national organization Domowina ("home-land")—banned in 1937 during the Nazi period—which has been the center of Lusatian cultural life since 1912.

Although favored by a contemporary literary boom and government subsidies, Lusatian culture is threatened by apparently benevolent but insidiously exploitive official policies and Germanization.

BIBLIOGRAPHY: Stone, G., *The Smallest Slavonic Nation* (1972); Jokostra, P., "Ein Archipel von Sprachinseln: Bericht über die Literatur der sorbischen Minderheit in der DDR," *DSt*, 15 (1977): 277–84

—LEONID RUDNYTZKY

LUSTIG, Arnošt

Czechoslovak short-story writer, novelist, and screenwriter (writing in Czech), b. 21 Dec. 1926, Prague

At an early age L. was exposed to the drastic experience of several Nazi concentration camps; toward the end of World War II he escaped from a transport train headed for Dachau. After the war he studied journalism in Prague and in 1948–49 covered the Arab-Israeli war as a radio correspondent. He continued to work for Czechoslovak Radio until 1958, then became an editor of a youth magazine, and from 1960 was a screenwriter with Czechoslovak State Film. In 1968 L. left Czechoslovakia and, following stays in Israel and Yugoslavia, settled in 1970 in the U.S. From 1971, L. taught at Iowa University, University of Nebraska, and at American University, Washington, D.C. After the fall of communism L. returned to Prague. Since September 1995, he has been editor in chief of the Czech-language version of Playboy Magazine.

L. was one of the younger writers who came to the fore during the slight political relaxation in the late 1950s and whose work signaled a break with the propagandist literature of the first half of the decade. In quick succession he published two volumes of short stories, *Noc a naděje* (1958; *Night and Hope*, 1962) and *Démanty noci* (1958; *Diamonds in the Night*, 1962; later tr., *Diamonds of the Night*, 1978), in which he examined the behavior of people under extreme pressure. L.'s approach was considerably influenced by modern American fiction, particularly that of William FAULKNER. His stories, which take place in Nazi concentration camps, on death transports, and during the turbulent last days of World War II, contain little action and only the rudiments of a plot. The characters, most of them children or old people, are sketchily drawn, since the author is less concerned with their psychological development than with their momentous reaction when faced with a moral dilemma. The crucial act of making an ethical decision under conditions of ultimate inhumanity is presented as proof that man can be destroyed but not vanquished.

The static nature of the stories, which seek to evoke an atmosphere and to explore the very essence of humanity, obliged L. to pay great attention to composition and style. The degree of sophistication that he achieved in this respect, however, sometimes unfavorably contrasted with the paucity of dramatic action. This imbalance marks some of his work in which he ventured onto other ground than that of the camp experience. Lack of action was also considered to be the main shortcoming of his next collection of short stories, *Ulice ztracených bratří* (1959; the street of lost brothers).

In the novella *Dita Saxová* (1962; *Dita Sax*, 1966) L. deals with the psychological wounds of those who survived the camps. Dita is "too young to be left to herself and too old to allow anyone to take care of her." Unable to adjust to postwar times, suffering from mistrust and loneliness, she commits suicide. Another novella, *Modlitba pro Kateřinu Horovitzovou* (1964; *A Prayer for Katerina Horovitzova*, 1973), describes both defiance and passivity in the face of death. Kateřina, a beautiful Jewish girl, is saved from the gas chamber on her arrival in the camp and allowed to join a group of rich European Jews caught by the Nazis when they had prematurely returned to Italy from their refuge in America. By deception and psychological manipulation they are gradually deprived of their wealth and reduced to sheeplike docility, with which they go to their slaughter, while Kateřina, even in the last hopeless moment, saves her dignity and humanity by the act of attacking the torturers. The novel is one of several of L.'s works that have been made into remarkable films.

New aspects of L.'s talent were revealed in *Hořká vůně mandlí* (1968; the bitter smell of almonds), which is composed of a novella and three short stories. While in the stories L. returned to subjects familiar from his earlier books, in the novella, *Dům vrácené ozvěny* (the house of the returned echo), he portrayed with great insight an unsuccessful and helpless Jewish businessman and his family as they inexorably follow the road that leads them to destruction. Set in Prague just before the war and during the early years of the Nazi occupation and war, the pitiful heroes and their small world are viewed by L. with a slightly ironic compassion.

L.'s last book published in Czechoslovakia, a novel, *Miláček* (1969; darling), is a rather tenuous love story set against the background of the first Arab-Israeli war. The matter-of-fact heroism that is supposed to lurk behind the façade of self-denigrating Jewish humor, as well as the tenderness covered up by rough talk, are in fact only too often obliterated by these devices.

L.'s first book written in exile, *Z deníku sedmnáctileté Perly Sch.* (1979; from the diary of seventeen-year-old Perla Sch.), shows L.'s mastery of style and structure. But there may be some doubt whether the subject (a Jewish prostitute in Terezín concentration camp commits a ghoulish act of revenge on a Nazi officer) is not too melodramatic to justify such refined treatment.

L. is one of the few writers who succeeded in exorcising the tragic experience of the death camps by transforming it into art. In his search for the qualities that make man indomitable, he has endowed the fate of the Jews with a universal human dimension.

FURTHER WORKS: *Můj známý Vili Feld* (1961); *Nikoho neponížíš* (1963); *Bílé břízy na podzim* (1966); *Tma nemá stín* (unpub. expanded version of short story; *Darkness Casts No Shadow*, 1977). FURTHER WORKS IN ENGLISH: *The Holocaust and the Film Arts* (1978); *The Beadle of Prague* (1983); *The Unloved* (1985); *Indecent Dreams* (1988); *Street of Lost Brothers* (1990); *Children of the Holocaust* (1995)

BIBLIOGRAPHY: Hajek, I., comp., "A. L.," in Mihailovich, V. D., et al., eds., *Modern Slavic Literatures* (1976) Vol. 2: 142-45; Sherwin, B. L., "The Holocaust Universe of A. L.," *Midstream*, Aug.-Sept. 1979: 44–48; Haman, A., "Man in a Violent World: The Fiction of A. L.," *Czechoslovak and Central European Journal*, 11 (Summer 1992): 73-80

—IGOR HÁJEK

LUXEMBOURG LITERATURE

From the early Middle Ages Luxembourg was divided into French-and German-speaking provinces. In 1659 the country lost part of its French-speaking territory to France; in 1839 the remaining French region became part of the newly established kingdom of Belgium. The people in what remained of Luxembourg speak a Moselle-Franconian dialect of German, the Luxembourg patois. Children are taught both German and French in elementary school. Thus, citizens of the Grand Duchy of Luxembourg can express themselves in three languages, and Luxembourg has three literatures.

In the Luxembourg Dialect

In the 19th c., after political autonomy had been reestablished, a nationalist spirit gave rise to a written literature in the Luxembourg dialect. Dialect writers created lyrical, epic, and satirical poetry as well as plays, mostly comedies. Michel Rodange (1827–1876) wrote the greatest book in Luxembourg dialect, the long poem *De Rénert* (1872; Reynard the fox), which has become a national epic. The playwright Andréï Duchscher (1840–1911) gave Luxembourg its first social drama, *Franz Pinell* (1899; Franz Pinell), about the conflict between a foundry owner and his workers. Batty Weber (1860–1940) wrote the first tragedy in dialect, *De Sche'fer vun Aasselburn* (1898; the shepherd of Asselborn); the hero is a historical figure who participated in the uprising of the Luxembourg peasants against the French Directoire in 1798.

Dialect literature developed along the lines of 19th-c. models during the first decades of the century and had an upsurge during the German occupation of Luxembourg in World War II, in reaction to the Nazi terror. Since World War II dialect writers have also turned to the essay, the short story, and the novel. Dialect drama was revitalized in the late 1950s by Norbert Weber (b. 1925), who introduced the techniques of the international avantgarde. The hero of his historical drama *Jean Chalop* (1963; Jean Chalop) is an alderman who was killed by the Burgundians when they penetrated the fortress of Luxembourg in 1443. Dialect theater, which had been dominated by light comedy, including musical comedy, today convincingly treats serious subjects.

In German

All the literary genres are employed by authors writing in German, but it is mainly the novelists who stress particularly Luxembourg problems. The Catholic influence has for a long time been dominant in the country, but it has also provoked criticism. In Batty Weber's novel *Fenn Kass* (1913; Fenn Kass), for example, a Catholic priest falls prey to doubt and eventually leaves the Church. Jean-Pierre Erpelding (1884–1977), in *Bärnd Bichel* (1917; Bärnd Bichel), analyzes avarice and moral degeneration. His trilogy *Adelheid François* (1936–38; Adelheid François) is concerned with the Luxembourg intellect torn between French and German cultures. His *Peter Brendel* (1959; Peter Brendel) deals with a Luxembourg peasant who nearly endorses the Nazi "blood and earth" theory; only hardship and tragedy make Brendel understand that mankind is more worthy of love than the soil.

Nicolas Hein (1889–1969), in some of the stories in the collection *Unterwegs* (1939; on the road), focuses on the sufferings of the Luxembourg intellectual in the provincial and narrow-minded atmosphere of his small country. Other of his stories relate the difficult life of Moselle wine growers. In a short novel, *Der Verräter* (1948; the traitor), Hein describes the awakening of national identity between 1830 and 1839. Historical subject matter is also treated in the posthumously published *Job, der Baumeister* (1961; Job the architect) by Paul Noesen (1891–1960), about the Swiss architect Ulrich Job, who directed the building of the Luxembourg cathedral (finished in 1621); the novel explores the religious faith of the Luxembourgers of the time. In the short novel *Kleines Schicksal* (1934: humble destiny) Joseph Funck (1902–1978) poignantly portrayed a miserly member of Luxembourg's subproletariat.

Mimy Tidick-Ulveling (b. 1892) is concerned with moral and intellectual progress toward individual freedom and responsibility, from the late Middle Ages until today. In the novel *Im Zeichen der Flamme* (1961; under the sign of the flame) she uses the trial and execution of a young woman accused of being a witch to develop these ideas. Fernand Hoffmann's (b. 1929) novel *Die Grenze* (1972; the borderline) tackles the problem of political and moral responsibility in a story about resistance to Nazi oppression. Roger Manderscheid (b. 1933), in his critical and satirical novel *Die Dromedare: Stilleben für Johann den Blinden* (1973; the dromedaries: still life for John the Blind), attacks the mediocrity of the national Spirit and human insufficiency in general. *Schumann* (1976; Schumann) by Cornel Meder (b. 1938) is the fictitious diary of a young woman teacher who lucidly analyzes her own situation, world problems, and the social and political life of Luxembourg.

The poet Paul Henkes (b. 1898) is more interested in universal than in specifically national subjects. In such works as *Ölbaum and Schlehdorn* (1968; olive tree and blackthorn), *Das Bernsteinhorn* (1973; the amber horn), and *Gitter und Harfe* (1977; grille and harp) he expresses with subtle means a profound concern for the dilemmas of Western man.

In French

Some Luxembourgers writing in French see in their choice of language a signal of their desire to assert Luxembourg's liberty and independence. The most striking of these is Marcel Noppeney (1877–1966), a poet, essayist, and polemicist, author of *Le prince Avril* (1907; Prince April) a volume of poetry in the Parnassian vein. Nicolas Ries's (1876–1941) two novels, *Le diable aux champs* (1936; the devil in the country) and *Sens unique* (1940; one way only), depict rural life in Luxembourg. Nicolas Konert's (b. 1891), novel *Folle Jeunesse* (1938; crazy youth) portrays an upstart's life in the wine-growing Moselle region in eastern Luxembourg. Joseph Leydenbach's (b. 1903) most interesting novel is *Les désirs de Jean Bachelin* (1948; the longings of Jean Bachelin); Leydenbach's protagonists are from his own upperclass background and are torn between wordly dissipation and spiritual aspiration. Albert Borschette's (1920–1976) one novel, *Continuez à mourir* (1959; go on dying), is about Nazi-occupied western Europe and the hardships suffered by Luxembourg's young men, who were forced to serve in the German army.

Paul Palgen (1883–1966), who wrote *Oratorio pour la mort d'un poète* (1957; oratorio for the death of a poet), was a sensuous, perhaps decadent poet. Edmond Dune (b. 1914), poet, playwright, and essayist, on the other hand, is a grim critic of material and intellectual pollution. In spite of the restraints he puts on his

135

feelings, he reveals himself, in *Poèmes en prose* (1973; prose poems), for instance, as a fervent lover of life, nature, and art.

BIBLIOGRAPHY: Hoffmann, F., *Geschichte der luxemburger Mundartdichtung* (2 vols., 1964–1967); Gérard, M., *Le roman français de chez nous* (1968); Hoffmann, F., *Standort Luxemburg* (1974); Kieffer, R., "Luxembourg Literature Today," *BA*, 48 (1974): 515–19; Christophory, J., *The Luxembourgers in Their Own Words* (1978); Kieffer, R., ed., *Littérature luxembourgeoise de langue française* (1980)

—ROSEMARIE KIEFFER

LUZI, Mario

Italian poet and essayist, b. 20 Oct. 1914, Florence

L. obtained a degree in literature with a dissertation on François MAURIAC and taught in various high schools in Italy. He was among the first contributors to the Italian literary journals *Frontespizio, Letteratura*, and *Campo di Marte*. He now teaches French literature at the University of Florence.

With the collections *La barca* (1935; the boat) and *Avvento notturno* (1940; nocturnal advent) L. showed himself to be one of the most interesting and original poets of the movement known as HERMETICISM. This early stage of his production is characterized by a refined, sometimes precious linguistic experimentation, which tends toward fragmentation and strong condensation of language and reveals literary influences ranging from Mallarmé to French SURREALISM.

His postwar poetry—in *Un brindisi* (1946; a toast), *Quaderno gotico* (1947; gothic note-book), *Primizie del deserto* (1952; first fruits of the desert), *Onore del vero* (1957; truth's honor)—all collected in the volume *Il giusto della vita* (1960; what is right in life), moves away from his early symbolism and opens itself to a more discursive style. This need to embrace a more narrative mode emerges more clearly in the collections *Nel magma* (1963; in the magma), *Dal fondo delle campagne* (1965; from the bottom of the fields), *Su fondamenti invisibili* (1971; on invisible foundations), and *Al fuoco della controversia* (1978; in the fire of the controversy)—now all included in the volume *Nell'opera del mondo* (1979; in the world's work).

The abandonment of his early Parnassian style, with its refinements, reflects a stronger urge to explore human relationships and existential conflicts and to debate moral truths. L. examines the Christian message, conveying it in images of the suffering of a harsh, wintry, snowy landscape, in a rural, precapitalistic world. But these images do not define a closed, dogmatic religion or an easy escape into metaphysics. L.'s religion presents itself as a witness of a suffering common to all people that is too often overlooked by the official philosophies and ideologies. Far from being a resigned act of isolation, his Christianity constitutes the difficult choice to live with other men, to divide a common burden, to share a violent desire to hope, even knowing that perhaps salvation may not occur in the course of human history. In this lucid acceptance of pain L. places himself, along with Eugenio MONTALE, in that line of Italian cultural tradition embracing the lesson of Giacomo Leopardi's (1798–1837) poem "La ginestra" ("The Broom"). This poetry is characterized by its uncompromising

denunciation of every ideological attempt to simplify the harsh history of man, by its will to penetrate the contradictions and limitations of human reality without escaping into easy consolations, and by its courage to maintain a generous pessimism, open to the tragic beauty of man.

In addition to poetry, L. has written essays and other prose works, and has done several translations—of Shakespeare, Coleridge, and Racine. His critical writings give intelligent, sensitive, and elegant analyses of Italian and European literatures and disclose strong and precise cultural preferences as well as his particular concept of the function of the poet. Through them the reader can gain a greater understanding of the development and maturation of his poetic methods and philosophy.

FURTHER WORKS: *L'opium chrétien* (1938); *Un'illusione platonica* (1941); *Biografia a Ebe* (1942); *Vita e letteratura* (1943); *L'inferno e il limbo* (1949); *Studio su Mallarmé* (1952); *Aspetti della generazione napoleonica, e altri saggi* (1956); *L'idea simbolista* (1959); *Lo stile di Constant* (1962); *Trame* (1963); *Tutto in questione* (1965); *Poesia e romanzo* (1973, with Carlo Cassola); *Libro di Ipazia* (1978). FURTHER WORKS IN ENGLISH: *For the Baptism of Our Fragments* (1992)

BIBLIOGRAPHY: Sampoli, M. S., "An Italian Contemporary Poet: M. L.," *IQ*, 6, 23–24 (1962): 3–20; Merry, B., "The Anti-Oracle in M. L.'s Recent Poetry," *MLR*, 68 (1973): 333–43; Craft, W., "M. L.," *BA*, 49 (1975): 33–40

—GOFFREDO PALLUCCHINI

LYNCH, Marta

Argentine novelist, short-story writer, and journalist, b. 8 Mar. 1925, Buenos Aires; d. 8 Oct. 1985, Buenos Aires

L. studied liberal arts at the National University of Buenos Aires where she obtained her B.A. in literature in 1952. Ten years later she was awarded the Band of Honor of the Argentine Society of Writers for her novel *La alfombra roja* (1962; the red carpet). Finished with her university studies, L. undertook a series of trips to North and Central America, Europe, Africa, the Near Orient, and the Pacific Islands. She taught literature courses, gave conferences at Argentine and foreign universities and cultural institutions, and attended numerous conventions of writers. In 1970 she formed part of the jury of a contest organized by Casa de las Américas, a Cuban publishing house formed to establish an association of Latin American intellectuals and to publish their works. L. was also very active in politics, because, to her, politics was something noble, a transcendental expression of education, and an activity involving the most central values of human existence. She was the director of the national committee of the Radical Intransigent Union Party; she was actively involved in Juan D. Perón's return to Argentina, and she was one of the few to criticize the military government for waging the Falkland Islands war against Great Britain in 1983.

L.'s record of literary production is impressive both for its quality and quantity; within one fifteen year period she produced five novels and three collections of short stories, subsequently translated into English, French, Portuguese, German, Russian, Italian, Swedish, Norwegian, and Croatian. L. is also well known in Argentina for her newspaper articles and television appearances.

She is one of the most representative of feminist writers in Argentina, along with Silvina Bullrich (b. 1915), Victoria Ocampo (1890–1979), Olga Orozco (b. 1920), and Beatriz GUIDO, a generation that renewed the Argentine narrative and lyric. L.'s literary works express her view of the condition of Argentine women as oppressed in the expression of their disquieting insights by speech patterns imposed by a prevailing patriarchal society. One of L.'s merits lies in her innovative treatment of this theme and her creation of female characters of universal significance. L. has affirmed that she began to write out of her own feelings of interior chaos and desperation. Additional motives included feelings of anguish, the need to find an appropriate language, and the wish to engage in dialogue with other writers.

L.'s most widely known novel is *La Señora Ordóñez* (1968; Mrs. Ordóñez), which went through five editions in its first year alone, and was also made into a film for television. In this novel, as in most of her other works, love is the prime mover. Like Blanca Ordóñez, many of L.'s female protagonists feel oppressed and resigned; as a result, they suffer from flawed psyches and inhabit an obsessive, enclosed world. In order to fill their spiritual emptiness, they are always in need of a lover, which often results in obsession for sexual encounters that only end in disillusionment. Fear of aging is another recurring characteristic of L.'s female figures, who sometimes experience the anguish of losing their physical attraction and with it their power to command male attention. This preoccupation was mentioned in her last letter, written shortly before L.'s suicide in 1985.

Because she was straightforward in her writing, L.'s works are a direct reflection of her thoughts. Since her novel—*Informe bajo llave* (1983; report under lock and key)—L.'s longer fiction is deeply concerned with politics. In *Informe bajo llave*, for instance, L. reveals her concern about the concentration of power in one individual, who thereby becomes dehumanized.

Although several book reviews, dissertations, and critical studies of L.'s works do exist, she has received relatively little critical attention in comparison with other major Argentine writers of her generation such as Jorge Luis Borges, Ernesto Sábato, G, and Manuel Puig. The corpus of L.'s works offers a profound inquiry into the nature of Argentine social reality as well as the mindset of Argentine women who are alienated from emotional, historical, and political realities. Her narratives are more than mere testimony or chronicle, for they transcend such categories both formally and conceptually. The problems her works concern belong to a recent past that touches even those who are either indifferent to the nation's destiny or intent on denying their own responsibility as participants in the life of the nation. As an analyst of the national reality and a voice for Argentine women, L. has made significant contributions to history by way of her writings.

FURTHER WORKS: *Al vencedor* (1965); *Crónicas de la burguesía* (1965); *Los cuentos tristes* (1966); *Cuentos de colores* (1970); *El cruce del río* (1972); *Un árbol lleno de manzanas* (1974); *Los dedos de la mano* (1976); *Apuntes para un libro de viajes* (1978); *La penúltima versión de la Colorada Villanueva* (1978); *Los años de fuego* (1980); *Toda la función* (1982); *Páginas de M. L. seleccionadas por la autora* (1983)

BIBLIOGRAPHY: Kaminsky, A. S. K., "The Real Circle of Iron: Mothers and Children, Children and Mothers in Four Argentine Novels" *LALR*, 9 (1976): 77–86; Lindstrom, N., "The Literary Feminism of M. L.," *Crit*, 20, 2 (1978): 49–58; Foster, D. W., "M. L.: The Individual and the Argentine Political Process. *La penúltima version de la Colorada Villanueva*," *Latin American Digest*, 13, 3 (1979): 8–9; Lindstrom, N., "Woman's Voice in the Short Stories of M. L.," *The Contemporary Latin American Short Story* (1979): 148–53; Birkemoe, D. S., "The Virile Voice of M. L.," *REH*, 16, 2 (1982): 191–211; Lewald, E., "Alienation and Eros in Three Stories by Beatriz Guido, M. L. and Amalia Jamilis" in Mora, G., ed., *Theory and Practice of Feminist Literary Criticism* (1982): 175–85; Lindstrom, N., "Women's Discourse Difficulties in a Novel by M. L.," *I&L*: 4, 17 (1983): 339–48; Díaz, G. J., Introduction to *Páginas de M. L. seleccionadas por la autora* (1983): 11–40; Esquivel, M., "M. L., novelista por naturaleza," *Tragaluz*, 2, 13 (1986): 17–19; Martín, C., "La señora Ordóñez o el discurso del silencio," in Arancibia, J., ed., *Mujer y sociedad en América* (1990): 85-91; Foster, D. W., "Raping Argentina: M. L.'s *Informe bajo llave*," *The Centennial Review*, 35 (1991): 663-80; Riccio, A., "Eros y poder en *Informe bajo llave de M. L.*," *Escritura*, 16 (1991): 223-29; Galván, D., "*Hacia la vejez en No te duermas, no me dejes de M. L.*," *Alba de América: Revista Literaria*, 10 (Jul. 1992): 203-14; Martínez de Richter, M., "Textualizaciones de la violencia: *Informe bajo llave de M. L. Y La rompiente de Reina Roffe*," *Siglio*, 11 (1993): 89-117; Thon, S., "El silencio en el discurso femenio: La señora Ordóñez de M. L.," *Crítica Hispánica*, 16 (1994): 395-402; Hammer, G. L., *Voces dialógicas en la narrativa de M. L. DAI* (1996)

—VIRGINIA SHEN

LYOTARD, Jean-François

French philosopher, b 10 Aug. 1924, Versailles; d. 21 Apr. 1998, Paris

L. was trained in Husserlian phenomenology at the Sorbonne; his first book, an overview of PHENOMENOLOGY, bears the traces of such a training (*La phénoménologie* [1954; phenomenology]). He started his career as a teacher in 1950 and taught at the high-school level for ten years, including two years in Constantine, Algeria, shortly before the beginning of the Algerian War (1950–1952). His shock in front of the aggressivity of French colonialism marked the beginning of his active political involvement—first in Algeria itself, then, after 1954, in the radical leftist group *Socialisme or Barbarie* (Socialism or Barbarism). After the split of the group in 1964 he joined one of the two dissident organizations, *Pouvoir Ouvrier*, until 1966 when he left the "active service of the revolution" and began an intense activity of writing: In his first major book, *Discours, Figure* (1971; discourse, figure), art, especially painting, replaces active practical political militancy. Since 1959 he has taught at the Sorbonne (1959–1966) and at the universities of Nanterre (1966–1970) and Vincennes (1970–1987). He has been a researcher at the National Center for Scientific Research (CNRS) and was the cofounder of the International College of Philosophy. He has been a visiting professor in numerous universities in the U.S., Brazil, Canada, and Germany; he is currently a professor at the University of California, Irvine.

L.'s career as a philosopher, writer, critic, and teacher spans more than four decades, and the phases of his trajectory—existentialist PHENOMENOLOGY, Marxism, Freudian psychoanalysis, POSTSTRUCTURALISM, analytic philosophy and pragmatism, Kantian philosophy—comprise almost all the major movements of postwar continental philosophy. His work appeals to a number of different disciplines: philosophy, aesthetics, psychoanalysis, political history, and theories of language.

One of L.'s privileged objects of philosophical investigation since the beginning of his career has been and remains Kant. *L'enthousiasme* (1986; enthusiasm) is an analysis of the Kantian critique of history. In *Du sublime* (1988; on the sublime) L. raises the question of interest in the Kantian sublime. His most recent book, *Leçons sur l'analytique du sublime* (1991; lessons on the analytic of the sublime), is a close reading of the section on the sublime in Kant's *Critique of Judgment*. If Kant's sublime occupies such an important place in L.'s thinking, it does so insofar as the sublime feeling (the shock of a combined pleasure and pain) stems from a failure of Imagination (the faculty of presentation) to provide a representation of its object, a failure testifying, *a contrario*, to Imagination's attempt to represent that which cannot be represented. The sublime feeling marks the disruption of thought by that which resists representation and articulation: What is at stake in L.'s analyses of Kant, and could be seen as his larger project, is to preserve the unrepresentable, the inarticulable, the heterogeneous.

It is from a philosopher's point of view—not quite that of the art critic or the art historian—that L. has approached aesthetics and, since *Discours, Figure*, regularly comments on contemporary art. For him, the artistic avant-gardes have to do with this figural space insofar as they are concerned with the shock of a presentation presenting nothing but "presence" itself. In painting, it is a question of color and matter, in music, of sounds and timbres. L. has written on such artists as Marcel Duchamp, Gianfranco Baruchello, Albert Aymé, Jacques Monory, Valério Adami, Shusaku Arakawa, and Daniel Buren. He even organized a major art exhibit in Paris in 1985 called *Les Immatériaux*, the "immaterials," which testified to this concern for matter.

The defense of the heterogeneous undertaken in *Discours, Figure* marked L.'s move from phenomenology to psychoanalysis. Indeed, it is from a psychoanalytic perspective (a reading of Freud's *Interpretation of Dreams*) rather than from a phenomenological perspective that L. analyzed the presence of the figural within discourse. *Des dispositifs pulsionnels* (1973; apparatuses of drives), *Dérive à partir de Marx et Freud* (1973; partially translated as *Driftworks*, 1984), and *Économic libidinal* (1974; libidinal economy) then extended the psychoanalytic notions of an apparatus of drives and of libidinal forces in such a way that economical, political, linguistic, and pictorial apparatuses could be approached from a libidinal perspective. What was at stake in L.'s rereading of Marx was to show that the political economy hides a libidinal economy.

However, after *Économie libidinale*, L. abandoned the libidinal perspective, and gradually elaborated a "philosophy of phrases," which reached its most complete development in *Le différend* (1984; *The Different: Phrases in Dispute*, 1988), drawing from Kant as well as from Wittgenstein's work on language. *La condition postmoderne* (1979; *The Postmodern Condition*, 1984), the book that gave him international recognition, already analyzed sociopolitical, economical, and aesthetic aspects of our contemporary society in terms of a pragmatics of narratives, hence of phrases. The phrase interests L. as an *event*, the fact that something happens, before all determination of what happens. To say "there is no phrase" is still a phrase: for there to be no phrase is impossible. To think is to link phrases, which raises the question of the incommensurability of phrases, that is, the question of the conflict—the *différend*—among possible linkages: a *différend* is a fundamental difference, unresolvable because it resists synthesis and linkage. The "philosophy of phrases," which is not a linguistic or semiotic approach of the sociopolitical, allowed L. to analyze our contemporary world in terms of phrases and of conflicts among phrases.

L., with Jacques DERRIDA, Michel FOUCAULT, and Gilles Deleuze (1925-1995), is one of the key figures in contemporary French philosophy. He consistently pushes philosophical speculation to border zones that are potentially productive for a variety of disciplines.

FURTHER WORKS: *Rudiments païens* (1977); *Instructions païennes* (1977); *Les TRANSformateurs DUchamp* (1977; *Duchamp's TRANS/formers*, 1990); *Récits tremblants* (1977); *Le mur du Pacifique* (1977; *Pacific Wall*, 1990); *Aujuste* (1979; *Just Gaming*, 1985); *L'altra casa* (1979); *La partie de peinture* (1980); *Sur la constitution du temps par la couleur* (1980); *L'histoire de Ruth* (1983); *Tombeau de l'intellectuel et autres papiers* (1984); *L'assassinat de l'expéérience par la peinture* (1984); *Le post-moderne expliqué aux enfants* (1986); *L'enthousiasme* (1986); *Que peindre? Adami, Arakawa, Buren* (1987); *Heidegger et "les juifs"* (1988; *Heidegger and "the Jews,"* 1990); *L'inhumain* (1988; *The Inhuman*, 1992); *Lectures d'enfance* (1991). FURTHER WORKS IN ENGLISH: *Perigrinations Law, Form, Event* (1988; publ. in French as *Périgrinations*, 1990); *The L. Reader* (1989)

BIBLIOGRAPHY: Gasché, R., "Deconstruction As Criticism," *Glyph*, 6 (1979): 177–215; Bennington, G., "Theory: They or We?," *Paragraph: The Journal of the Critical Theory Group*, 1 (1983): 19–27; special L. issue, *Diacritics*, 14, 3, (Fall 1984); Rorty, R., "Le cosmopolitisme sans émancipation (en réponse à J.-F.L.)," *Crit*, 456 (1985): 569–80; Carroll, D., *Paraesthetics: Foucault, L., Derrida* (1987): 23–52, 155–84; Bennington, G., "*L.—Writing the Event*" (1988); Carroll, D., "L'invasion française dans la critique américaine de letters," *Crit*, 491 (1988): 263–79; Ruby, C., *Les archipels de la différence: Foucault, Derrida, Deleuze, L.* (1990); special L. issue, *ECr*, 31, 1 (Spring 1991); Readings, B., *Introducing L.* (1991)

—ANNE TOMICHE

M

MACAULAY, Rose

English novelist, essayist, and poet, b. 1 Aug. 1881, Rugby; d. 30 Oct. 1958, London

The families from whom M. was descended on both sides belonged to an interrelated intellectual complex. Between her father's teaching appointments at Rugby and Cambridge, the family spent seven years on the Mediterranean shore near Genoa, where the children lived an unceremonious free outdoor life; a "gauche tomboy" of thirteen when they returned to England, she found the life there painfully restricting. But in the intellectual atmosphere of Somerville College, Oxford, she became lively and outgoing. She studied history, specializing in the 17th c.—her lifelong favorite. Going with her family to a small university town in Wales, she found these three years an exile; her first novel, *Abbots Verney* (1906), presents what was to be her main theme: the conflict between the alert and adventurous mentality and the dull and ungenerous. From 1913 on, London and its literary life became her ambience. During World War I, after much self-questioning, she entered upon an attachment with a married man that lasted until his death in 1942. For much of her adult life she found spiritual support in the Anglican Church.

The last of M.'s twenty-two novels, *The Towers of Trebizond* (1956)—some find it her best—was published fifty years after her first. She also produced two books of verse; three books of literary criticism, including *The Writings of E. M. Forster* (1938), a friend and fellow Cantabridgian; several books of light, satirical essays; a weekly column in *Spectator* during part of the interwar period, and other journalism; and three remarkable books combining travel and history. *They Went to Portugal* (1946) presents the experiences of a great variety of English visitors to that country during seven centuries; in *Fabled Shore* (1949) all the past of Spain is with her on a trip in 1947 around the Iberian coasts in a battered car; in *Pleasure of Ruins* (1953) she considers the fear and fascination that the world's many ruins have inspired.

Abbots Verney and her fourth novel, *The Valley Captives* (1911) illustrated the cruelty that can result from ignorance. Her second, however, *The Furnace* (1907), introduced a theme that arose from her childhood in Italy and reappeared importantly in several later novels, including *The Lee Shore* (1912): the possibility of leading a simple, generous, delighted life outside the superfluities and limiting thought of mundane society. Her wit became more sophisticated in *The Making of a Bigot* (1914), with the relentless logic of its charmingly absurd plot. The horror of the war, its numbing of sympathies, and the need to work for a negotiated armistice were the themes of the courageous *Non-Combatants and Others* (1916).

International fame came with *Potterism* (1920), which satirizes, with a carefully controlled style, the senselessness of the popular press and of gushing lady novelists. By this time M. was considered one of the leading wits of London. *Dangerous Ages* (1921), which sensitively treats the lives of several women, won the Fémina-Vie Heureuse prize, a French award given to British writers in the 1920s and 1930s. The brilliant *Told by an Idiot* (1923) presents the history of upper-middle-class England through three generations. *Orphan Island* (1924) is a comic South Seas tour de force. M.'s interest in the 17th c. produced the strong historical novel *They*

Were Defeated (1932); here again, extremists at both ends defeat moderates. A similar conflict, but conceived as light comedy, is found in *Going Abroad* (1934), laid in the Spanish Basque country. *And No Man's Wit* (1940) gives a rueful retrospective of the Spanish Civil War as World War II menaces; *The World My Wilderness* (1950) shows the moral destitution at the end of World War II.

The Towers of Trebizond brings together the themes, the erudition, the depth, and the comedy of all of M.'s work. Laurie's journey takes place on two levels: on a realistic one and on one of witty fantasy, of charade. As she travels along the Turkish coast, mulling over her extramarital love affair, which has alienated her from the Church of England, a poem emerges that envisions the old Byzantine city projected as the Church transcendent, ever there but ever beyond.

FURTHER WORKS: *The Secret River* (1909); *Views and Vagabonds* (1912); *The Two Blind Countries* (1914); *What Not: A Prophetic Comedy* (1918); *Three Days* (1919); *Mystery at Geneva* (1922); *A Casual Commentary* (1925); *Catchwords and Claptrap* (1926); *Crewe Train* (1926); *Keeping Up Appearances* (1928; Am., *Daisy and Daphne*); *Staying with Relations* (1930); *Some Religious Elements in English Literature* (1931); *They Were Defeated* (1932; Am., *The Shadow Flies*); *Milton* (1934); *Personal Pleasures* (1935); *I Would Be Private* (1937); *Life among the English* (1942); *Letters to a Friend* (1961); *Last Letters to a Friend* (1962); *Letters to a Sister* (1964)

BIBLIOGRAPHY: "Miss M.'s Novels," *TLS*, (12 May 1950): 292; Annan, N., "The Intellectual Aristocracy," in Plumb, J. H., ed., *Studies in Social History* (1955): 241–87; Nicolson, H., et al., "The Pleasures of Knowing R. M.," *Encounter*, March 1950: 23–31; Lockwood, W. J., "R. M.," in Hoyt, C. A., ed., *Minor British Novelists* (1967): 135–56; Swinnerton, F., "R. M.," *KR*, 29 (1967): 591–608; Bensen, A. R., *R. M.* (1969); Smith, C. B., *R. M.: A Biography* (1972); Passty, J., *Eros and Androgyny: The Legacy of R. M.* (1988); Emery, J., *R. M.: A Writers' Life* (1991)

—ALICE R. BENSEN

MACCAIG, Norman

Scottish poet, b. 14 Nov. 1910, Edinburgh; d. 23 Jan. 1996, Edinburgh

M., brought up in his native city, received an honors M.A. in classics from Edinburgh University. After many years of schoolteaching and having made his mark as a poet in the 1960s, he was made Fellow in Creative Writing and Lecturer in English Studies at Edinburgh University. Later he became Reader in Poetry at the University of Stirling.

Although M. is city-born and city-bred, his roots are largely elsewhere; although not a Gaelic speaker, he thinks of himself as "threequarter Gael." His poetry, he feels, was shaped by a combination of classical training and what he calls the "extreme formality" of Celtic art. In form, theme, and tone his poems are marked by restraint, and with few exceptions they do not exceed a page in length. He abstains almost entirely from the kind of Scots vocabulary cultivated by the "Lallans" poets.

His poetic world is not the public one of social commitment or indignation, nor one of strong emotions. In several poems he speaks about his own art with gentle irony, but sometimes also in self-defense or self-assertion, wanting to make it clear that he looks upon himself, not as a Blake or a Hieronymus Bosch but rather as a Breughel who takes note of "unemphatic marvels": every kind of object penetrates his vision and is made welcome.

Geographically M.'s world is restricted: the setting of his poems is either Edinburgh or (rather more frequently) the West Highlands (the exceptions are a handful of poems set in Tuscany and New York). His landscapes are either small-scaled and intimately observed, or majestic depictions of wide spaces, distant horizons, monumental hills and mountains. Few of his poems are, however, purely descriptive: a recurring pattern is for a landscape to turn into a mindscape, into an observation on the speaker's own situation. In this regard, the critic is tempted to see the influence of Robert FROST. Often the center of interest is the poet himself; but in a number of poems it is instead other people: admired Highland characters, eccentrics, or occasionally individuals who are seen ironically or even attacked, usually because they represent pomposity or abused power. Whoever or whatever M. studies, his poems usually give impressions of the here and now; he seldom pries into roots and beginnings or explores history on a wide scale.

M.'s descriptions of animal life are sensitive yet unsentimental; they often deal with ordinary creatures: a goat, a crow, a house sparrow. Here as elsewhere, M. demonstrates his facility at metaphor making, at times rather too obtrusively. While his images are often memorable, occasionally they become a little too ingenious and the thought they convey rather too precious, particularly in the love poems, which often relate feelings of frustration, of insuperable separation, sometimes expressed in terms of physical distance.

Anthropomorphizing metaphors are numerous in M.'s verse. Objects of nature, animals, sometimes even abstractions are often portrayed as individualized human types. At times the comparison is focused on a particular physical characteristic or mental state.

Some of M.'s creative processes and devices are present in his first two volumes of verse, although he chooses to disregard them, considering them exercises in a pretentiously abstruse modernist manner. But after that—with the exception of some relapsing in his fourth collection, *The Sinai Sort* (1957)—he has stuck tenaciously to his own ideals of style and theme. He cannot be said to have developed in any striking manner. He speaks engagingly of his verse as "fairly low-falutin'." He distrusts big words, the flaunting of extreme feelings, "the fake, the inflated, the imprecise, and the dishonest." On guard against such phenomena, he can speak ironically both about himself and others; but his poems, for the most part, are celebrations of the natural dignity of people and places and expressions of an unorthodox, unsolemn credo of joy in the manifoldness of the created world.

FURTHER WORKS: *Far Cry* (1943); *The Inward Eye* (1946); *Riding Lights* (1955); *A Common Grace* (1960); *A Round of Applause* (1962); *Measures* (1965); *Surroundings* (1966); *Rings on a Tree* (1968); *A Man in My Position* (1969); *Selected Poems* (1971); *The White Bird* (1973); *The World's Room* (1974); *Tree of Strings* (1977); *Old Maps and New: Selected Poems* (1978); *The Equal Skies* (1980)

BIBLIOGRAPHY: Press, J., *Rule and Energy* (1963): 172–81; special M. section, *Akros*, 3, 7 (1968): 21–47; Fulton, R., "Ishmael among the Phenomena: The Poetry of N. M.," *ScotIR*, 5, 8 (1972): 22–27 (repr. in R. Fulton, *Contemporary Scottish Poetry: Individuals and Contexts* [1974]: 69–87); Scott, M. J. W., "Neoclassical M.," *SSL*, 10, 3 (1973): 135–44; Porter, W. S., "The Poetry of N. M.," *Akros*, 11, 32 (1976): 37–53; Frykman, E., "*Unemphatic Marvels*": *A Study of N. M.'s Poetry* (1977); Keir, W., "The Poetry of N. M.," *ScotR*, No. 21 (1981): 27–32

—ERIK FRYKMAN

MACDIARMID, Hugh

(pseud. of Christopher Murray Grieve) Scottish poet and essayist, b. 11 Aug. 1892, Langholm; d. 9 Sept., 1978, Edinburgh

The son of a rural postman, M. grew up in the Border region of Scotland. Although his formal education was brief, he received encouragement early from excellent teachers who recognized his talent and continued to correspond with him. After leaving school at fourteen, he supported himself as a journalist while concentrating his real interest on poetry. As an editor and publisher of his own journal (*The Scottish Chapbook*, 1922–23) and three collections of modern Scottish verse (*Northern Numbers*, 1920–22) he was a key figure in the literary and cultural movement called the Scottish Renaissance; his journalistic prose defined and supported it, and his early poetry was its greatest achievement. Both a nationalist and a communist, M. joined political activism with his interest in cultural change, serving as a town councillor and justice of the peace, helping to found the National Party of Scotland, and running for various offices. During the 1930s he lived an isolated life on Whalsey, a small island in the Shetlands. In his later years he returned to the Borders. He remained active in cultural and political affairs and traveled extensively, including trips to Russia and China.

M.'s poetry shows great technical variety, developing from brief, intense lyrics in dense Scots through long poetic sequences to increasingly long and difficult philosophical poems in English. Major themes are the dialectic nature of reality; the relationships among Scotland, self, and poetry; human aspiration toward higher consciousness; and the nature of the creative act. The personal and political concerns running through his work reflect his sense of the artist's struggle to penetrate and reveal the unknown and the social need to free all people from economic constraints. His technical experimentation focused largely on vocabulary and imagery; both show his interest in using the widest resources of sound and meaning in both Scots and English. His dominant images—the Scottish thistle, the Celtic snake, water, and stones—represent changing ways to symbolize a complex modern vision of reality.

M.'s early Scots lyrics were an experiment aimed at reviving the language. He wrote a "synthetic" Scots: by using Scots vocabulary from any time or region, he sought to assimilate into literature the full range of Scottish life. Reacting against a limited and sentimental tradition, he called for an intellectual poetry showing a mastery of style and thought. His first two volumes of poetry, *Sangschaw* (1925) and *Penny Wheep* (1926) consist primarily of brief lyrics that gain their musical and thematic effects from the sounds and significance of Scots. M. believed that the Scottish vernacular was unique in its capacity to effect swift and subtle shifts in tone and to render uncanny spiritual and pathological perceptions. In his early poems unusual images, often extremely compressed and densely packed, are joined with words chosen for their multiple significance or for their precise expression of unusual moods in order to create such effects. Characteristically assuming a stance outside ordinary experience, these poems often convey wry humor, pathos, or a startling unease through subverting conventional assumptions. Frequently moving between the cosmic and the minute, they extend the Scottish experience to the universe, while recurrent images of seas, darkness, the moon, and the night sustain the sense of being outside conventional vision. Many of these lyrics depend on rare words or complex images to effect a sudden insight or alternative mode of seeing.

M.'s interest in expressing the whole of Scottish experience led to a series of increasingly longer poems. His first and greatest long poem, *A Drunk Man Looks at the Thistle* (1926), retains early techniques. Combining intense lyrics with descriptive and philosophic passages, it carries the use of dense Scots and swift shifts of mood into an extended poetic sequence with a large and inclusive vision of life. Composed of many loosely related sections forming thematic and tonal sequences and climaxes, *A Drunk Man Looks at the Thistle* embodies M.'s commitment to join unity and diversity. Its unity derives from a single image capable of endless transformations and containing paradox and contradiction. The thistle, Scotland's national emblem, symbolizes for M. what he considers the fundamental Scottish character: a yoking of contraries and freedom in passing from one mood to another, which has been called the "Caledonian antisyzygy." The poem's key themes focus on a union of various poles of experience: life and death, evolution and decline, self and world, bestiality and beauty. Other key ideas are the struggle of the human soul for higher vision, the poet's special burden as center of creative energy, and Scotland's need to rise above sentiment and commercial values. These themes unite in a distinctly modern statement of the nature of reality as complex, contradictory, and endlessly transformational.

In *To Circumjack Cencrastus* (1930) M. attempted to use his early techniques for a new purpose: rather than contraries and struggle he wished to express the unity underlying all change. Cencrastus, the curly snake, is the Celtic image of eternity. M. was less able, in *To Circumjack Cencrastus*, to sustain a sense of unity through a single image, but the poem indicates important changes in style and theme. His last long poem in a lyric mode, it shows M.'s increasing interest in Gaelic culture, in direct expression of ideas, and in the use of English.

In the 1930s M. moved from a consistent line of lyric development to wide-ranging experiments in style and theme. After *To Circumjack Cencrastus* several volumes of shorter pieces appeared: *First Hymn to Lenin* (1931), *Scots Unbound* (1932), *Stony Limits* (1934), and *Second Hymn to Lenin* (1935). Along with Scots lyrics in the early style, these volumes include a series of poems on his own origins in Langholm, in Dumfriesshire, explicitly political poems, and long philosophical poems in English. Many return to speculation on the nature of reality, the creative act, and the role of Scotland in history. M.'s interest in Gaelic values appears in several philosophical poems as well as translations from the Gaelic. In *Stony Limits* M. also experimented with using obscure and technical English vocabulary to express modern complexity. His most fundamental change was a shift in emphasis from sound to content. This shift parallels an increasing detachment from personal experience and emotion and a commitment to poetry of thought. After 1935 M. wrote almost no lyrics and almost nothing

in Scots. His major late works include the long poem *The Kind of Poetry I Want* (1961)—sections of it had been previously published in his autobiography, *Lucky Poet* (1943)—and *In Memoriam James Joyce* (1955), which were apparently intended to be parts of a single gigantic work, *Mature Art*, never published. These pieces, which he calls "poetry of fact," contain lengthy quotations, lists of names and facts, and obscure words and references. Extended images are embedded in long discursive commentaries. They explore the nature of poetry, art, and world languages, aspiring to an encyclopedic inclusiveness of detail. Like Ezra POUND's *Cantos* they aim at what M. calls "opening out" and taking in more and more of reality. He continued as well to write individual pieces, such as *Dìreadh I, II, III* (1974), a group of three poems, using nature images and developing sustained ideas. Nearly all of M.'s late work, which continued to appear into the 1970s, was written in the 1930s.

In addition to original poems, M. did verse translations, edited books and journals, and wrote short stories, biographies, autobiography, and an enormous body of polemical prose. In *Lucky Poet*, an autobiography of his intellectual life, he attempted a synthesis of his vast and varied interests, chiefly Scottish nationalism, communism, language, and the nature and function of poetry. His own early poetry is influenced by traditional Scottish folk songs and ballads and John Jamieson's (1759–1838) *Etymological Dictionary of the Scottish Language* (1808). His late work is more allied with the looser rhythms and massed detail of Whitman and Pound. Other important influences, formal and intellectual, include Dostoevsky, Lev Shestov (1866–1938), Vladimir Solovyov (1853–1900), John MacLean (1879–1923), the Scots communist-nationalist, Paul VALÉRY, James JOYCE, Francis George Scott (1880–1958), the Scottish composer, and Charles Doughty (1843–1926). In turn he influenced a generation of Scots poets who joined in the aims of the Scottish Renaissance, which called for a return to the pre-Robert Burns Scottish tradition of William Dunbar (1460?–1520?) and Robert Henryson (1430?–1506?), characterized by intellect, sophistication, distinctive nationality, and links with international literary trends. His influence remains in current Scottish poetry in the vernacular, and his commitment to long poems on native tradition has influenced such contemporary Irish poets as John Montague (b. 1929) and Seamus HEANEY. M.'s work compares with that of T. S. ELIOT, W. B. YEATS, and Pound as a major statement of the modern condition.

FURTHER WORKS: *Annals of the Five Senses* (1923); *Contemporary Scottish Studies* (1926; enlarged ed., 1976); *Albyn, or Scotland and the Future* (1927); *At the Sign of the Thistle* (1934); *Scottish Scene* (with L. G. Gibbon, 1934); *Scottish Eccentrics* (1936); *The Islands of Scotland* (1939); *A Kist of Whistles* (1947); *Cunningham Graham* (1952); *Francis George Scott* (1955); *Three Hymns to Lenin* (1957); *The Battle Continues* (1957); *Burns Today and Tomorrow* (1959); *Collected Poems* (1962; rev. ed., 1967); *The Company I've Kept* (1966); *A Lap of Honour* (1967); *The Uncanny Scot* (1968); *Early Lyrics* (1968); *A Clyack-Sheaf* (1969); *Selected Essays* (1969); *More Collected Poems* (1970); *Selected Poems* (1970); *The H. M. Anthology* (1972); *A Political Speech* (1972); *Metaphysics and Poetry* (1975); *Complete Poems* (1978)

BIBLIOGRAPHY: Leavis, F. R., "H. M.," *Scrutiny*, 4 (1935), 305; Daiches, D., "M. and Scottish Poetry," *Poetry*, 72 (1948): 202–18; Scott, T., "Some Poets of the Scottish Renaissance," *Poetry*, 88 (1956): 43–47; Wittig, K., *The Scottish Tradition in Literature*

(1958): 281–88; Duval, K., and S. G. Smith, eds., *H. M.: a Festschrift* (1962); Buthlay, K., *H. M.* (1964); Glen, D., *H. M. and the Scottish Renaissance* (1964); National Library of Scotland *H. M., Catalogue No. 7* (1967); M. special and Scottish poetry double issue, *Agenda*, 5, 4/6, 1 (1967–68); Glen, D., ed. *H. M.: A Critical Survey* (1972); special issue, *Akros*, 12: 34–35 (1977); Wright, G., *M.: An Illustrated Biography* (1977); special M. issue, *Chapman 22*, 5, 4 (1978); Gish, N., "An Interview with H. M.," *ConL*, 20, 2 (1979): 135–54; Boutelle, A., *Thistle and Rose: A Study of H. M.'s Poetry* (1980); Scott, P. H., and A. C. Davis, eds., *The Age of M.* (1980)

—NANCY K. GISH

Such a socially effective idiom is what M. has always been looking for. He is thus related analogically, rather than linealogically, to earlier Scots poetry. The Border Ballads set out to inspire a bundle of cattle thieves to the hazards of a life of murder, robbery, and rape. The complex sonorities of Dunbar, on the other hand, were addressed to the king and his contingent noblemen. Hence the difference between these two types of verse. M.'s public is of another kind altogether. His purpose lies with "the wisest and learnedest of mankind, who have this one great gift of reason, to answer solidly or to be convinced." The people he wishes to influence are the scientists, administrators, and scholars of his time. In their hands lies the fate of the world and it is their present insensitivity to those diabolical and illogical influences, explicit only in art, that today endangers humanity. He is therefore anxious to persuade them of the finally objective importance of the aesthetic exploration. [1957]

Burns Singer, "Scarlet Eminence," in Duncan Glen, ed., *H. M.: A Critical Survey* (1972), p. 41

What M. seems to be adumbrating in *The Kind of Poetry I Want*—it is nowhere made sharp and definite—is a poetry which is highly organised in parts, but not prescriptively with regard to the whole. It is not so much an organism as a colony, a living and in one sense formless association of organisms which share a common experience. Shape and architectonics are not so important as the quick movements of the thought—the feelers in the water, moved partly by the surrounding currents and partly by their own volition and partly in response to the movement of neighbor tentacles—while a succession of images, illustrations, and analogies is presented to it. As zoologists may argue whether a colony is an organism, critics may hesitate to say that the kind of *poetry* M. wants is a kind of *poem*. A movement towards a more "open" conception of the poem than has prevailed in the modern period is however gaining ground, and I see no reason why we should deny ourselves, for love of architectonics, the ingredient and emergent pleasures of a poetry in evolution. [1962]

Edwin Morgan, "Poetry and Knowledge in M.'s Later Work," in Duncan Glen, ed., *H. M.: A Critical Survey* (1972), pp. 201–2

It is not only M.'s happy use of his native tongue and his folk song rhythms that suggest Hopkins. There is his overt expression of the "red opinions" that the Jesuit confided to a private letter. Thus, the Scotsman writes a lyric to "The Dead Liebknecht," the Spartacist victimized by the Germans, and celebrates the idol of the Russian communists in more than one hymn to Lenin. There is also M.'s evident delight in nature's wilder inscapes—trees and waters, earth and sky, the uncertain or headlong movement of a mountain stream, the moon like a weird pale crow above the spinning earth, the tough willows that never come down from their stormy moods; there is his hurrahing in the Hebridean harvest as he watches the herring fishers, when the catch swims in as if of its own accord. And there is the counterpart of Hopkins' darker humours, when sand churns in his ears, the grave of all mankind opens before him, and he groans that no man can know his own heart until life's tide uncovers it.

Babette Deutsch, *Poetry in Our Time* (1963), pp. 343–44

M. had never recognised this kind of absentee landlordism of the spirit: one of the aspects of his achievement worth stressing is the way he has got most of himself onto the page even preoccupations one may dislike. The contemplative centre we value so much in Eliot and Edwin Muir is there, but also the coarser activity, the sparks from the rim of the wheel. Pride, humour, contrariness; patriotism, hatred, nostalgia; love, lust, longing: there is no contemporary poem more varied in mood than *[A] Drunk Man Looks at the Thistle*. And since there is no achievement without an accompanying technique, the poem is a showpiece of M.'s early virtuosity, like [Pound's] *Hugh Selwyn Mauberley*, another poem in which a poet examines the civilisation he is involved with.

John Montague, "The Seamless Garment and the Muse," *Agenda*, 5, 4/6, 1 (1967–68), p. 27

When M. came back to Scotland after military service in the eastern Mediterranean and started to write (just at the point when Eliot, Pound, Joyce, and the mature Yeats were bringing out their crucial work), he set himself, deliberately, to remake a style for poetry in his country. He took words and phrases from folksong, dictionaries, and his native speech, and he also took symbols and forms from Continental writers (Dostoevsky, Rilke). Many of his earlier lyrics are exercises, he was trying out a whole gamut of styles, in the way of so many modern artists (Eliot, Picasso, Stravinsky). But his own vision starts to emerge—a very modern sense of the world as an arena of conflict, a site of organic evolution, where vital instability is a permanent condition of life and human nature, human feelings, are always mixed and ambiguous.

David Craig, "A Great Radical: H. M., 1892–1978," *Marxism Today*, 23, 2 (1979), p. 57

Again and again in the lyrics in *Sangschaw* (1925) and *Penny Wheep* (1926), M. suggests a multidimensional view of reality by contrasting our usual viewpoint with a God's-eye-view of the universe; this cosmic outlook simultaneously shrinks the world to socially manageable proportions and suggests the imaginative majesty of man who is capable of possessing the cosmos through creativity alone. M. used God as an instantly accessible image of a meaningful universe and avoided the theological stereotype. For example, the God of "Crowdieknowe" is no awesome patriarch but an odious observer who has to contend with the truculent force of humanity in the shape of the Langholm locals who are unwillingly resurrected. . . . The faith that the mature M. put in scientific insights was already present in the early lyrics. In "The Eemis Stane" he saw a poignancy in the spectacle of the planet earth trembling in space. . . . That visionary approach could be extended to almost mystical levels, but for M. even the most puzzling elements of existence still deserved a human solution.

Alan Bold, "Dr. Grieve and Mr. M.," P. H. Scott and A. C. Davis, eds., *The Age of M.* (1980), p. 46

In M.'s case it isn't simply a question of his changing his mind from time to time, though of course he has done that like everybody else, nor—in spite of some important similarities with Whitman . . . —is it a question of Whitmanesque largeness. Self-contradiction is for him a mode of poetic awareness. This fact is easily obscured if we look at his work chronologically and chart carefully the different phases in his career. If we do that we will talk of his earliest quasi-mystical poetry in English, his perfectly wrought little lyrics in Scots, and his later massively discursive poems in what might be called a lexicographical English. We will distinguish between these, and say which we prefer and why. But if we take a comprehensive, synchronistic view of M.'s work we begin to see certain kinds of unity amid all this diversity. And two things will emerge. The first is that the counterpointing of unity and diversity is central to his poetic character. And the second is that such a counterpointing is bound up with M.'s view of the nature of the Scottish literary character.

David Daiches, "H. M. and the Scottish Literary Tradition," in P. H. Scott and A. C. Davis, eds., *The Age of M.* (1980), p. 60

MACEDONIAN LITERATURE

Macedonian literature in the 20th c. has been produced in two totally diverse social and political periods. The first period was characterized by the lack of freedom: until 1914 Macedonia was part of the Ottoman Empire; from 1918 to 1941 it belonged to the Kingdom of the Serbs, the Croats, and the Slovenes, and was known as Southern Serbia or Vardar Province; while during World War II it was under German, Bulgarian, and Italian occupation. From 1945 it enjoyed relative autonomy within the Federal Republic of Yugoslavia, whereas complete autonomy was achieved in 1991 by the establishment of the Republic of Macedonia.

From the second half of the 19th c. to the early 1920s artistic literature underwent a transformation from romanticism to realism, but classicistic, sentimental, and naturalistic elements, as well as a profound influence of folk literature, which had a long and fruitful tradition, were also of primary importance. The ideological founder of the modern Macedonian standard language was Krste Petkov Misirkov (1874-1926), who expounded his ideas about language in his book *Za makedonskite raboti* (1903; On Macedonian Issues). His basic views were incorporated into the modern Macedonian standard language (phonetic orthography, the Cyrillic alphabet, and western Macedonian dialects), which was inaugurated by the 1945 Macedonian Constitution.

In 1900 Vojdan Pop Georgiev Černodrinski (1876-1951) and his theater group *Skrb i utjeha* (Care and Comfort) performed the first truly Macedonian play *Makedonska krvava svadba* (A Macedonian Bloody Wedding), which was distinguished by romantic idealism and naturalistic directness in the presentation of events. The most significant authors of the 1920s and 1930s were the dramatists Nikola Kiril Majski (1880-1962), Risto Krle (b. 1900), Anton Panov (1906-1968), and Vasil Iljoski (1920-1995) and the poet Kočo Racin (1908-1943), who also wrote critical essays and short stories as well as the first Macedonian novel, *Afion* (Opium), the manuscript of which has been lost. The literary works of the time dealt with social and moral problems of the present and recent past. Literature was under the strong influence of folk art, as well as critical, descriptive, and social realism. In 1937 Vasil Iljoski wrote the first Macedonian comedy *Čorbadži Teodos* (Merchant Teodos). Racin's collection of poems *Beli mugri* (1939; White Dawns) became a programmatic basis for modern poetry and a paradigmatic example of the standard Macedonian language. Literature produced during and immediately after World War II was utilitarian in function. When the war ended, several authors—Aco Šopov (1923-1982), Blaže Koneski (b. 1921), and Slavko Janevski (b. 1920), among others—sought to overcome the regressive SOCIALIST REALISM that was being promoted under the influence of communist ideology.

In 1944 Aco Šopov published the first collection of poems *Pesni* (Poems) in liberated Macedonia. In the next year the first literary journal in free Macedonia, *Nov den*, was launched. In 1947 Jovan Boškovski (1920-1968) published the first collection of short stories entitled *Rastrel* (Execution by Firing Squad). After the historic rift between Tito and Cominform in 1948, the ideologically and poetically canonized socialist realism diminished in importance and was replaced by MODERNISM.

Poetry

The early 1950s marked a radical turning point in Macedonian poetry, which culminated in a polemic between the traditionalist and modernist poets. The social and political environment was now more democratic, and there was a turn from collective to individual consciousness and a subjective understanding of history and literary subjects. Modernism enriched poetic diction at the prosodic and semantic levels. Modernist poetry is thus full of self-referential utterances, in which the problems of human endangerment, the reason for existence, and creativity in general gained the upper hand. The predominantly imagery-based poetry was replaced by a conceptual poetry that was characterized by complicated metaphors and diverse symbolism based on global or national artefacts. Poetic utterances and images became more and more dense and sometimes completely hermetic, and therefore, difficult to decipher semantically. Important collections of poems included Aco Sopov's *Pesni za makata i radosta* (1952; Poems about Misery and Joy) and *Veterot nusi ubavo vrene* (1955; The Wind Carries Nice Weather); Gane Todorovski's (b. 1929) *Trevozni zvuci* (1953; Exciting Sounds) and *Spokoen cikor* (1956; A Placid Step); Blaže Koneski's *Vezilka* (1955; Embroiderness); Mateja Matevski's (b. 1929) *Dozjive* (1956; Rains); and Slavko Janevski's *Leb I kamen* (1957; Bread and Stone). The poetry of the 1960s was distinguished by mature individual expression, stylistic clarity, and a more elaborate versification system, which Mateja Matervski enriched with free verse conceived in a modern fashion. In the 1960s a search began for a "universal poem" that was to synthesize modern poetic diction, local civilization and authenticity, and archetypal imagination. It was to become a link between the past and the present. As a result, pictures of national history were revived, and myths, legends, folklore, rituals, magic elements, archetypes, and pagan customs were reestablished. The topics included individual and collective identity, various aspects of alienation, patriotism, returning to one's roots, fatalism and attitude towards man and nature. The diction is characterized by complicated semantics, simultaneous speech, polyphonic structures, hermeticity, metatextual fragments, and colloquial speech. The most authentic collections of poems of the day were Radovan Pavlovski's (b. 1937) *Suša, svadba* (1961; A Drought, A Wedding, and Removals), Petre M. Andreevski's (b. 1934) *Ni na nebo ni na zemja* (1962; Neither in Heaven Nor on Earth), Mihail Rendžov's (b. 1936) *Strav* (1976; Fear), Vlada Urošević's (b. 1934) *Zvrezdena terazija* (1973; A Star-Lit Scale), Bogomil Đuzel's (b. 1939) *Alheniske ruža* (1963; An Alchemic Rose), as well as Aco Šopov's *Nebidnina* (1963; Nonexistence) and *Gatač vo pepelta* (1970; The Ash Soothsayer), Gane Todorovski's *Apoteoza na delnikot* (1964; Apotheosis to a Working Day), and Slavko Janevski's *Evangelie po itar Pejo* (1966; The Gospel According to Sly Pejo). Since the 1980s, poets of the younger generation have been pressing for a rational, constructive, organized, logical, consciously concrete, and realistic poetry, as well as for experimentation in language and expression. Recognizable poetic opuses were made by Atanas Vangelov (b. 1946), Eftim Kletnikov (b. 1946), Katica Ćulavkova (b. 1950), and somewhat older Jovan Pavlovski (b. 1937), who introduced scientific vocabulary and the topic of death into Macedonian poetry with *Identitet* (1974; Identity) and *Oksidiranja* (1983; Oxidation). The Struga Poetry evenings, a world renowned festival held every year in Struga, where the Crni Drin empties into Ohrid Lake, has played a prominent role in the development of Macedonian poetry.

The Short Story

Published in 1870, Rajko Žinzifov's (1839-1877) "Prošedba" (A Walk) was the first short story in Macedonian literature. Marko Cepenkov (1829-1920) collected and analyzed a plethora of folk short stories. The rise of short-story writing began after World War II. Between the two wars Kočo Racin wrote, in Croatian and Serbian since Macedonian was banned, short prose texts of marginal value. However, linguistic and stylistic limitations were soon overcome, and the polemic between the traditionalists and the modernists resulted in a more pronounced lyricism, individualism, and diversity in short-story writing. Authors experimented with language and style, autobiographical elements were connected with the meditative, the picturesque with the symbolic, and the realistic intertwined with the imaginary. Important short-story collections among the transformations of literary expression included Blaže Koneski's *Lozje* (1955; A Vineyard), Slavko Janevski's *Klovnove I luđe* (1956; Clowns and People), Živko Čingo's (1936-1987) *Paskvelija* (1963; Paskvelija), Petre M. Andreevski's *Sedmoit dan* (1964; The Seventh Day), and Vlada Urošević's *Znaci* (1969; Signs). Important changes took place during the 1960s, when metonymic and metaphoric expression replaced the mimetic. The Macedonian short story showed signs of a pronounced tendency towards the fantastic, magic, and surrealist expression. This was practiced by authors of the older generation, notably Janevski, Čingo, Andreevski, and Urošević, the younger generation, notably Vase Mančev (b. 1949) and Mitko Madžunkov (b. 1943), as well as emerging authors such as Dragi Mihajlovski (b. 1951), Dimitar Duracovski (b. 1952), Aleksandar Prolopiev (b. 1953), and Venko Andonovski (b. 1964). Irony, the grotesque, allegory, exploration of the possibilities of the various genres, disharmonious structures, and demolished reality gained in importance. The younger writers leaned towards the postmodernist way of writing in which they saw the poetic challenges of their time.

The Novel

Slavko Janevski published the first Macedonian novel, *Selo zad sedumte jaseni* (A Village Behind Seven Ash-Trees) in 1952. The dynamic development of the Macedonian novel went from folklore to psychological realism. Individual works usually tackled historical themes from various periods. The leading writers in the 1960s were Janevski, Vlado Maleski (1919-1984), Dimitar Solev (b. 1930), and Metodija Fotev (b. 1932), who at that time primarily treated themes from World War II. In the 1960s and 1970s the realistic method was enriched by a more critical approach towards reality; humor, satire, and the grotesque are exceptional in Vladimir Kostov's *Svadbata na Mara* (1968, Mara's Wedding); as is the neorealism in Jovan Pavlovski's *To Radiovce vo koe pađam dlaboko* (1972; That Abyss into Which I'm Falling Deep). On the basis of the screenplay of his own film, Boškovdki wrote the historical action novel *Solunskite atentatori* (1962; Assassins from Solun). Živko Čingo wrote the lyric novel *Golemata voda* (1971; Big Water), while Vlada Urošivić tried his hand at fiction in *Vkusot na praskite* (1965, The Taste of Peaches). Taško Georgievski (b. 1935) introduced the topic of the exodus of Macedonians from Aegean Macedonia in a series of novels of which the most outstanding are *Crno seme* (1966; The Black Seed) and *Ramna zemja* (1981; A Flat Country). Božin Pavlovski (b. 1942) promoted the modern approach to the novel, while the style of Petre M. Andreevski is characterized by a rich imagination based on magic and fantastic elements that are used to deal with historic events, as in his novels *Pirej* (1980; Weed), *Skakulci* (1984; Grasshoppers), and *Nebeska Timjanova* (1990; Nebeska Timjanova). Kole Čašule (b. 1921) introduced the political novel in *Konzulski pisma* (1991; The Prostate Juices), which takes place in Moscow during Gorbachov's *perestroika*. The most impressive novelistic opus is that of Slavko Janevski, which includes a multivolume historical chronicle. Janevski's most prominent novels are *Tvrdoglave* (1970; The Stubborn), the trilogy *Mirakuli na grozomorata* (1984; The Miracles of Horrors), *Devet Kerubinove vekovi* (1986; A Cherub's Nine Centuries), *Čudotvorci* (1988; Wonderworkers), *Rulet so sedum brojke* (1989; Roulette with Seven Figures), and *Kontinent Kukulino* (1996; The Continent of Kukulino), which has a fascinating mythical basis, a symbolic vision of history, and a manneristic style proving that Macedonian is a language of high aesthetic value and functions in the most complicated of semantic and syntactic expression.

Drama

During the second half of the 20th c. the production of drama encompassed elements of descriptive and psychological realism, existentialist drama, THEATER OF THE ABSURD, and POSTMODERNISM. In *Čest* (Honor), published in 1953, Vasil Iljoski approached psychological realism, while Kole Čašule mastered the technique in *Vejka na vetrot* (1957; A Branch in the Wind) and *Crnila* (1961; The Color Black). Čašule's play *Vitel* (1967; The Whirl) was the first existentialist drama in Macedonian literature, while *Paritura za eden Miron* (1968; A Score for a Miron) introduced theater of the absurd. He also heralded the postmodernist dramatic concept. Modernist concepts were also promoted by Tome Arsovski (b. 1928) in *Paradoksot na Diogen* (1961; Diogenes' Paradon) and by Branko Pendovski (b. 1927) in *Pod piramida* (1974; Under a Pyramid). Goran Stefanovski (b. 1952) improved dramatic expression in *Divo meso* (1979; Proud Flesh) and showed himself as a postmodernist in his first work in dramatic form *Jane Zadrogaz* (1974), as well as in some of his later texts *Crna dupka* (1987; The Black Hole), *Saraevo* (1993; Sarajevo), and *Bahanalii* (1996; Bacchanalia). Jordan Plevneš (b. 1953), with his symbolic and surrealistic dramatic vision *Erigon* (1982), takes the foremost place in Macedonian drama production. Plays by Čašule, Stefanovski, and Plevneš have been translated into foreign languages and performed abroad the U.S., Great Britain, Russia, France, the Netherlands, Denmark, Poland, Croatia, Slovenia, and the Federal Republic of Yugoslavia. Taking their place as leading writers of the promising younger generation are Venko Andonovski, Saško Nasev (b. 1966), Dejan Dukovski (b. 1969), and Jugoslav Petrovski (b. 1969). They all write plays of the postmodernist type, which are dominated by irony, the grotesque, and the absurd; their fragmented dramatic texts range from a new type of farce to melodrama. As far as the subject matter is concerned, Macedonian drama production is characterized by a critical view of historical events and the current social and political infrastructure. At the center of all of these dramatic events is an individual who is either confronted with a totalitarian regime or is in search of the reason for his existence, which is jeopardized by various types of alienation.

BIBLIOGRAPHY: Holton, M., and G. W. Reid, eds., *Reading the Ashes: An Anthology of the Poetry of Modern Macedonia* (1977); Urošević, V., "Macedonian Poetry between Yesterday and Today," *CP*, 17 (Fall 1984): 157-63; Cvetanovski, S., "Developments and Qualitative Trends in the New Macedonian Short Prose," *WLT*, 63 (Summer 1989): 428-32; Osers, E., ed., *Contemporary Macedonian Poetry* (1991)

—BORISLAV PAVLOVSKI

MACGOYE, Marjorie Oludhe

Kenyan poet and novelist (writing in English), b. 12 Oct. 1928, Southampton

M. was born as Marjorie King, the only child in a working-class family, in the English port city of Southampton. In 1954, at the age of twenty-six, she moved to Kenya as a missionary bookseller with the Church Missionary Society, the mission arm of the Anglican Church. M. worked for the Society in Nairobi until 1960, when she married Daniel Oludhe Macgoye. She took Kenyan citizenship following independence in 1963, living and writing in East Africa ever since. She lived in Kisumu during the 1960s and in Dar es Salaam during the early 1970s, before settling in Nairobi after 1975.

Despite her British roots, M. made a conscious choice to adopt a thoroughly Kenyan identity early in her career, in the process denying herself of many of the trappings of white privilege. She rarely followed the typical missionary path, choosing to live in Pumwani, among Nairobi's poor, rather than on the mission compound on Nairobi Hill. When she married a Luo husband, it was at a time when interracial marriages were not unheard of in Kenya, but were more likely to occur between a European and a member of the Kenyan elite; Daniel Macgoye was a junior civil servant at the time of their marriage. M.'s writing is consequently grounded in the sensibilities of someone who has deliberately adopted a Kenyan, in particular a Luo, cultural identity. Almost all her works concern themselves in one way or another with the dynamics of coming to terms with a new life, a theme that appears on both personal and societal levels.

M.'s creative energies have been divided almost equally between poetry and novels. The title piece in *Song of Nyarloka and Other Poems* (1977) is a lengthy and complex three-thousand-line poem that explores questions of cultural identity using two dominant metaphors: *Nyarloka*, which is the Luo term given to a woman who leaves her home to join a husband's clan across a body of water, and *nyawawa*, the Luo tradition of creating loud noises to drives out an evil that has entered the family compound. M. herself is a *nyarloka* of sorts, but the poem goes on to argue that all African women are in such a situation, and (more broadly) that Kenyan society itself is in such a position, having crossed into a new, modern era of rapid change. The poem suggests the changes and crossings, migrations and hybridizing influences that have been the reality in East Africa throughout history. As a result, the practice of *nyawawa* is doomed to failure, since one can never completely remove external influences.

M. is acutely conscious of the failures and bitterness of missed opportunities and mistakes in forming new societies. The tragic massacre of innocent bystanders following a tense visit to Kisumu by Kenya's then-President Jomo Kenyatta in October 1969, for instance, appears in *Song of Nyarloka* as well as in some other works. M. draws heavily on metaphors of birth—including barrenness, abortion and miscarriage—to apply either to political events or to the creative process itself.

M.'s best-known novel, the Sinclair Prize-winning *Coming to Birth* (1986), is about the transformation of the naive Luo girl Paulina into a mature and self-aware woman. There are various births in the story, some of them literal, but the more important developments in the novel are the metaphorical birth of Paulina as a whole person and the coming to birth of Kenya as a nation. M. again draws parallels between the personal and the political in *The Present Moment* (1987), a slightly more complex but highly satisfying novel set in a home for the elderly (known as "The Refuge") in a poor section of Nairobi. The novel traces the lives of seven of these women through a series of flashbacks, dreams, and reminiscences. The present moment, the novel suggests, is the result of the overlapping experiences of many ordinary individuals, "separately enfolded" in each others' lives.

A strong moral commitment undergirds M.'s life and works, and she has also published nonfiction works that do not hesitate to challenge what she sees as the shortcomings of her adopted society. Her signature poem, "A Freedom Song," included in *Song of Nyarloka and Other Poems*, criticizes the practice of hiring poor relatives on unfavorable terms as nannies, something M. refers to as "domestic slavery." *Moral Issues in Kenya: A Personal View* (1996) takes on the topics of the legitimacy of traditional cultural practices, sexuality, corruption, and gender roles in contemporary Kenya.

Critical recognition of M.'s work was somewhat slow in coming, thanks in large part to her complicated personal identity. Critics had a hard time knowing how to classify this writer, who defies many of the standard categories for East African writers. M. is not African by birth, but rather by choice, and yet her works show that she cannot be placed in the same category as many other writers of European descent, such as Isak DINESEN or Elspeth Huxley (1907-1997). Because of her life and her writings, M. has earned renown and credibility among Kenyan readers. She is regularly cited for her influence in the writing community in organizing regular readings during the late 1970s in the downtown bookstore that she managed. Partly because of the significance of her most important works, and partly because of the way these works and her life highlight the complexity of cultural identity in East Africa of the late 20th c., M. must be seen as a central figure in the region's literary history.

FURTHER WORKS: *Growing Up at Lina School* (1971); *Murder in Majengo* (1972); *The Story of Kenya* (1986); *Street Life* (1987); *Victoria* (1993); *Homing In* (1994); *Chira* (1997); *Make It Sing and Other Poems* (1998)

BIBLIOGRAPHY: Bukenya, A., *Notes on M. M.'s Coming to Birth* (1988); Gurnah, A., "Suffering with Stoicism: Kenyan Histories," *TWQ* (January 1988): 973-78; Nasta, S., ed., *Motherlands: Black Women's Writing from Africa, the Caribbean and South Asia* (1991)

—J. ROGER KURTZ

MACHADO, Antonio

Spanish poet, b. 26 July 1875, Seville; d. 22 Feb. 1939, Collioure, France

Educated at the Institution of Free Learning of Madrid, Spain's most innovative, progressive, and liberal school, where the influence of the German philosopher Karl Christian Friedrich Krause (1781–1832) was strong, M., one of Spain's greatest poets, wrote the most representative poetry of the Generation of '98. His brother Manuel (1874–1947) was also a poet. In 1909 M. married a sixteen-year-old girl, Leonor, who died three years later. In the 1920s he again sought personal happiness and a poetic muse through Guiomar, the other great love of his life. A teacher as well as a writer, he was an ardent antifascist and supporter of the Republic. He wrote poetry about war and peace, including a moving elegy on the death of GARCÍA LORCA. He died, a victim of the civil war, in a foreign land.

Not unaware of the MODERNIST innovations, M. himself utilized them only briefly, early in his career, although on deeper levels much of his poetry continued to be SYMBOLIST and modernist. His early poetry is often autobiographical, and he used typically Andalusian symbols like the lemon tree. In *Soledades, galerías, y otros poemas* (1907; *Solitudes, Galleries, and Other Poems*, 1987), an expanded edition of *Soledades* (1903; *Times Alone*, 1983), he showed that poetry, for him, was a profoundly spiritual enterprise. Solitude, in this collection, is conveyed through a fusing of the poet's soul and the landscape, of inner and outer realities. His themes include a lack of illusion and of love, nostalgia for childhood as memory becomes the mirror of time, the stirrings of an existential anguish, and a paradoxical hope. Dream and fantasy spur on his quest for love and his lifelong search for God through time, symbolized as a fountain or flowing water, the flow of life into death.

In *Campos de Castilla* (1912; *The Castilion Camp*, 1982), which one critic called the "poetic breviary of the Generation of '98," M. is an outstanding interpreter of the Spanish soul. Based on five years he spent in the province of Soria, which represented the essential Castilian spirit for him, this volume combines images of earth and countryside with patriotic fervor. M. attempts to rouse his countrymen from their complacency as he shows a once great nation fallen on evil days. Still, the austere and melancholy Castilian landscape is symbolized by the sturdy oak; and whatever the bitterness and injustices suffered by its inhabitants, there remains a special kind of beauty. M. fuses a personal emotion with objective description, searching for love, for a metaphysical God, and for values that may no longer exist. Exploring the tragic sense of life, M. also meditates on the philosophy of Henri BERGSON.

Included in *Campos de Castilla* is "La tierra de Alvargonzález" ("The House of Alvargonzález," 1961), M.'s one great effort at the Spanish ballad form. Set in a rugged mountain area of Soria, it depicts greed, patricide and vengeance. Two older brothers, scheming and evil, resent the virtuous and loving younger brother. Eventually the assassins, unable to stay away from the scene of their father's murder, fall to their deaths. Infused with the ideas and imagery of the passing of time, dream, mystery, the supernatural, and brooding terror, the poem stresses tragic fate.

In *Nuevas canciones* (1924; new songs) M. develops the theme of love, combining the sensual and the colorful, against background images of gray olive trees, blue mountains, brown oaks, and white lightning. Expanding a series of proverbs and songs he first published in a new version of *Campos de Castilla* included in *Poesías completas* (1917; rev. eds., 1928, 1933, 1936, 1965, 1970; complete poetry), M. experiments with a kind of Japanese haiku form. Life is a path without guidance, and M. becomes a "perpetual sailor of the eternal earth." Love, life and death, dream and reality, and dual personality are themes of these epigrammatic and at times satirical and skeptical poems.

In addition to plays written in collaboration with his brother Manuel, M. also wrote penetrating prose memoirs: *Juan de Mairena: Sentencias, donaires, apuntes y recuerdos de un profesor apócrifo* (1936; *Juan de Mairena: Epigrams, Maxims, Memoranda, and Memoirs of an Apocryphal Professor*, 1963). The invented, "apocryphal" professor Mairena, critic and moralist, whom M. labels his "philosophical alter ego" and who died young, offers philosophy, irony, humor, poetic anguish, and an explanation of M.'s existential outlook. Mairena rejects the power of pure reason and science and examines the problem of existence and death. Skeptical but not dogmatic, Mairena and M. explore literature, truth, liberty, politics, language, and philosophic works, although they also lampoon philosophers as of little use in an "apocryphal" world. Lacking God and Christ, M. in his solitude turns to man and nature.

Portions of *Los complementarios* (1972; the complementaries), written from 1912 on, were published over a period of years, in spite of M.'s prohibition. In part a diary, which enhances his reputation as a moral and ethical man, it also contains poetry and prose of various kinds, anecdotes, political and philosophical writings, and perceptive literary criticism.

M. combined the traditional and the modern. A dreamer, he wove his poems from landscape and memory, as he explored the hidden secrets in man's soul. Called "luminous and profound" by Rubén DARÍO, M. rejected verbal pyrotechnics for a spiritual search for eternity, but his poetry is delicate as well as profound. The poet yearned for immortality, but his poetry, which he defined as the "essential word in time," could not provide him with a faith in God. A good and modest man, stoical in the face of lost love and life's blows, he asserted, in spite of his resigned pessimism, the spirit and dignity of man. In sincere, simple, and evocative words, M. proclaimed: "The essence of all noble fighters is never the certainty of victory but the fervent desire to deserve it."

FURTHER WORKS: *Canciones del alto Duero* (1922); *Juan de Mañara* (1927, with M. Manuel); *Las adelfas: La Lola se va a los puertos* (1930, with M. Manuel); *La guerra* (1937); *El hombre que murió en la guerra* (1947); *Obras completas de Manuel y A. M.* (4 vols., 1947); *Cartas de A. M. a Miguel de Unamuno* (1957); *Cartas de A. M. a Juan Ramón Jiménez* (1959); *Prosas y poesías olvidadas* (1964); *Poesías completas* (1973). FURTHER WORKS IN ENGLISH: *Zero* (1947, bilingual); *Eighty Poems of A. M.* (1959, bilingual); selected poems in A. J. McVan, *A. M.* (1959); *Castilian Ilexes* (1963); *Still Waters of the Air* (1970); *I Go Dreaming Roads* (1973); *Sunlight and Scarlet* (1973); *Del Camino* (1974); *Selected Poems of A. M.* (1978); *The Dream below the Sun: Selected Poems of A. M.* (1981, bilingual); *Selected Poems* (1982, bilingual)

BIBLIOGRAPHY: Trend, J. B., *A. M.* (1953); Serrano Poncela, S., *A. M.: Su mundo y su obra* (1954); Zubiría, R. de, *La poesía de A. M.* (1955); McVan, A. J., *A. M.* (1959); Cobos, P. de, *Humor y pensamiento de A. M. en la metafísica poética* (1963); Tuñón de Lara, M., *A. M.: Poeta del pueblo* (1967); Sánchez Barbudo, A., *Los poemas de A. M.* (1969); Gullón, R., *Una poética para A. M.* (1970); Cobb, C. W., *A. M.* (1971); Aguirre, J. M., *A. M.: Poeta simbolista* (1973); Valverde, J. M., *A. M.* (1975); Luis, L., *A. M.: Ejemplo y lección* (1975); Schulman, I. A., "A. M. and Enrique González Martínez: A Study in Internal and External Dynamics," *JSSTC*, 4 (1976): 29–46

—KESSEL SCHWARTZ

MACHAR, Josef Svatopluk

Czechoslovak poet and essayist (writing in Czech), b. 29 Feb. 1864, Kolín; d. 17 March 1942, Prague

Son of a miller's foreman, M. grew up in Prague. After abandoning the study of law, he took a clerical job at a financial institution in Vienna. While living there, he wrote for a number of

Czech literary reviews and associated with progressive writers who opposed the Hapsburg regime. In 1916 he was imprisoned in Vienna—he wrote of this experience in *Kriminál* (1918; *The Jail*, 1921). Returned to Prague before the end of World War I, in 1918 he became inspector general in and cultural adviser to the newly created Czechoslovak army. An idealist and man of strong views, he gave up his post after five years, as well as some valuable friendships, including that with President T. G. Masaryk, because of numerous disagreements over both public and personal matters.

M.'s strongly argumentative personality is reflected in all his works. He represented realism in Czech poetry, and his verse is sober, terse, and factual—very different from the emotionalism and ornate verbosity of the school of Svatopluk Čech (1846–1908) and Jaroslav Vrchlický (pseud. of Emil Frída, 1853–1912). His three volumes of subjective lyrical poems, *Confiteor* (1887–92; Latin: I confess), express M.'s disillusionment after an unhappy love affair, a disillusionment that in part led to his attacks on the morals of contemporary society. Gloom also marks a number of poems in *Čtyři knihy sonetů* (1903; four books of sonnets). The political lyrics of *Tristium Vindobona* (1893; Latin: Vienna elegy) convey a nostalgia similar to that of the exiled Ovid; aware of a writer's responsibility to his nation, M. deplored flaws in the national character and inveighed against the evils in Czech public life.

Two of M.'s best volumes of poetry can be described as feminist: *Zde by měly kvést růže* (1894; roses should bloom here) contains lyrical portraits of suffering women humiliated by an insensitive, narrow-minded society; *Magdaléna* (1894; *Magdalen*, 1916), a novel in verse, subtly presents a young reformed prostitute's vain effort to rehabilitate herself in a world of provincial pharisees, political careerists, and snobbish egoists.

Golgata (1901; Golgotha), in which M. sets patriotism and religion in the context of the historical development of mankind, anticipates his magnificent cycle *Svědomím věků* (9 vols., 1906–26; the conscience of the ages). Unable to find a true ideal in the present, M. here tries to formulate the lessons man can learn from the past. Strongly influenced by Nietzsche, M. is pessimistic as he finds the aristocratic paganism of the ancient world superior to democratic, austere, and sense-suppressing Christianity. In the ancient world M. discovers his ideal of a strong personality, a fully integrated individual. One of his last important books of poetry, *Tristium Praga* (1926; Prague elegy), however, sounds a more optimistic note.

M. was also a well-known journalist, and his prose is characterized by the same sobriety, eloquence, and pugnacity as his poetry. Among his numerous prose works, *Konfese literáta* (2 vols., 1902; the confessions of a writer) is outstanding. Other important essayistic works are *Řím* (1907; Rome), a collection of polemical essays on classical antiquity, Christianity, Roman Catholicism, among other subjects; *Katolické povídky* (1901; Catholic stories), a collection of short fiction that gives vent to his strong anti-Catholic feelings; *Antika a křesťanství* (1919; the ancient world and Christianity); *Pod sluncem italským* (1918; under the Italian sun), a travel book; *Čtyřicet let s Aloisem Jiráskem* (1931; forty years with Alois Jirásek), a collection of correspondence.

A prolific writer, M. was a leading member of the important Czech literary generation of the 1890s. With his rather pessimistic, frequently satirical and polemical poetry and prose, he brought social evils to the attention of a wide public.

FURTHER WORKS: *Bez názvu* (1889); *Letní sonety* (1891); *Zimní sonety* (1892); *Jarní sonety* (1893); *Podzimní sonety* (1893); *Třetí kniha lyriky* (1892); *Pêle-mêle* (1892); *1893–1896* (1897); *Boží bojovníci* (1897); *Výlet na Krym* (1900); *Knihy fejetonů II* (1901; repr. as *Za rána*, 1920); *Knihy fejetonů I* (1902; repr. as *Trofeje*, 1903, 1920); *Stará próza* (1902); *Satiricon* (1903); *Próza z let 1901–1903* (1904); *Hrst beletrie* (1905); *Vteřiny* (1905); *V záři helenského slunce* (1906); *Jed z Judey* (1906); *Próza z let 1904–1905* (1906); *Próza z r. 1906* (1907); *Veršem i prózou* (1908); *Klerikalismus mrtev!* (1910); *Krajiny, lidé a netopýři* (1910); *Barbaři* (1911); *Pohanské plameny* (1911); *Apoštolové* (1911); *Českým životem* (1912); *Nemocnice* (1913); *Význam Volné myšlenky v českém národě* (1914); *Krůpěje* (1915); *Životem zrazeni* (1915); *Franz Josef* (1918); *O Habsburcích* (1918); *Vídeň* (1919); *Třicet roků* (1919); *Vídeňské profily* (1919); *Časové kapitoly* (1920); *Vzpomíná se . . .* (1920); *V poledne* (1921); *Oni* (1921); *On* (1921); *Krůčky dějin* (1926); *Kam to spěje?*(1926); *Na křižovatkách* (1927); *Pět roků v kasárnách* (1927); *Oni i já* (1927); *Zapomínaní i zapomenutí* (1929); *Při sklence vína* (1929); *Dvacet pohlednic z Kysiblu* (1931); *Dva výlety do historie* (1932); *Peníze* (1932); *Filmy* (1934); *Na okraj dnů* (1935); *Rozmary* (1937); *První dějství* (1939)

BIBLIOGRAPHY: Harkins, W. E., *Anthology of Czech Literature* (1953): 142–44; French, A., *Czech Poetry* (1973): 315; Novák, A., *Czech Literature*, (1976): 233–36

—B. R. BRADBROOK

MACLEISH, Archibald

American poet, dramatist, and essayist, b. 7 May 1892, Glencoe, Ill.; d. 20 April 1982, Boston, Mass.

Archibald MacLeish

After taking degrees at Yale and at Harvard Law School, M. studied independently and wrote poetry in France (1923–28); there, Ernest HEMINGWAY, James JOYCE, and Saint-John PERSE became his personal friends. During the 1930s M. wrote lucid essays for *Fortune* magazine. Under Roosevelt he became Librarian of Congress (1939–44) and Assistant Secretary of State (1944–45). Following an affiliation with UNESCO (1946–49), M. taught poetry at Harvard (1949–62) and Amherst (1963–67).

Under the spell of the SYMBOLISTS, M.'s early works, such as *Streets in the Moon* (1926), are introspective and filled with archetypal patterns. Often his poems are responses to cultural giants like Shakespeare or FREUD; sometimes, to modern masters like Charles Baudelaire. Not only significant cultural achievements but also verse forms and dramatic structures find their analogues in these as well as later works; *Conquistador* (1932), winner of a Pulitzer Prize, repeats Dante's terza rima in an assonant pattern so that the *Inferno* is felt as the force behind Cortez's monumental journey through Mexico; in *The Hamlet of A. M.* (1928), in part a reply to *The Waste Land* of T. S. ELIOT, marginal annotations to Shakespeare's play make M.'s anxieties seem recapitulations of Hamlet's.

Responding to social and political issues during the Depression and World War II, M. wrote verse any concerned adult can grasp— like "Speech to Those Who Say Comrade" (1936). He wrote radio scripts and documentary films, and in *Land of the Free—U.S.A.* (1938) photographs of disgruntled Americans are counterpointed against a poem asking if the American Dream has failed. *Freedom Is the Right to Choose* (1951) is a selection of essays answering that

the "American experiment" is the very belief in the worth of mankind. The "original documents" of democracy, however, must be deciphered, restored from beneath the palimpsest of their prostitutions, argues *Frescoes for Mr. Rockefeller's City* (1933). Finally, in *Actfive, and Other Poems* (1948), the false gods are exposed: science as miracle worker, the state as a savior, crowd consciousness as a center of existence. Instead, there persists the "responsible man" of "flesh and bone."

Archetypal images and the paradigms of masterpieces also give substance to M.'s plays. Typical of his radio plays is *The Fall of the City* (1937), in which citizens are paralyzed before a huge enemy in hollow armor. *J. B.* (1958) depicts modern man as a Job who can resist all loss and yet retain his love of life. Memorable in this Pulitzer Prize-winning play is the framework: a mock quarrel between a clown and a peanut vendor, wearing God and Satan masks. *Herakles* (1967) dramatizes the plight of a scientist struggling to remain a humanist; earlier, in *Nobodaddy* (1926), M. had represented Cain as the prototype of a man wrestling against superstition, and in the long poem *Einstein* (1929) M., skillfully blending puzzlement and awe, had suggested the ultimate limitations of natural science. During the 1970s M. reiterated his central motifs: *Scratch* (1971) is a political *J. B.* and *The Great American Fourth of July Parade* (1975) is an affirmation of democracy written on the occasion of the bicentennial celebration.

Throughout his career M. regarded himself as an aesthetician. In the famous "Ars Poetica" (1926) he wrote, "A poem should not mean/But be." By 1955 (in the essay "The Proper Pose for Poetry") this symbolist stance was converted into the view that "the poem is an action, not an urn," and by 1964 (in the essay "The Gift Outright") into the concept that poetry is "a speaking voice," the embodiment of each poet's unique synthesis of body, mind, and feeling. For M., a poem therefore has a definite tone and tempo—the adagio of "Immortal Autumn" (1930), for instance, or the scherzo of "The End of the World" (1926). Whatever M.'s music, though, his central purpose is clear: to mend the breach between the ancients and the moderns, between "private worlds" and "the public world," between mankind and the "unanswering universe."

FURTHER WORKS: *Songs for a Summer's Day* (1915); *Tower of Ivory* (1917); *The Happy Marriage, and Other Poems* (1924); *The Pot of Earth* (1925); *New Found Land* (1930); *Poems 1924–1933*, (1933); *Panic* (1935); *Public Speech* (1936); *Air Raid* (1938); *America was Promises* (1939); *Union Pacific* (1939); *The Irresponsibles* (1940); *The Next Harvard* (1941); *The American Cause* (1941); *A Time to Speak* (1941); *American Opinion and the War* (1942); *A Time to Act* (1943); *Colloquy for the States* (1943); *The American Story* (1944); *Poetry and Opinion* (1950); *The Trojan Horse* (1952); *Collected Poems 1917–1952*, (1952); *This Music Crept by Me upon the Waters* (1953); *Songs for Eve* (1954); *Poetry and Journalism* (1958); *The Secret of Freedom* (1959); *Three Short Plays* (1961); *Poetry and Experience* (1961); *The Collected Poems of A. M.* (1962); *The Dialogues of A. M. and Mark Van Doren* (1964); *The Eleanor Roosevelt Story* (1965); *An Evening's Journey to Conway, Massachusetts* (1967); *The Wild Old Wicked Man, and Other Poems* (1968); *A Continuing Journey* (1968); *Champion of a Cause* (1971); *The Human Season* (1972); *New and Collected Poems, 1917–1976* (1976); *Riders on the Earth* (1978); *Six Plays* (1980)

BIBLIOGRAPHY: Waggoner, H. H., "A. M. and the Aspect of Eternity," *CE*, 4 (1943): 402–12; Sickels, E., "A. M. and American Democracy," *AL*, 15 (1943): 223–37; Beach, J. W., *Obsessive Images: Symbolism in Poetry of the 1930's and 1940's* (1960), passim; Falk, S. L., *A. M.* (1965); Goodwin, K. L., *The Influence of Ezra Pound* (1967): 175–83 and passim; Gianakaris, C. J., "M.'s *Herakles*: Myth for the Modern World," *CentR*, 15 (1971): 445–63; Smith, G., *A. M.* (1971)

—BEN MCKULIK

MACLENNAN, Hugh

Canadian novelist and essayist, b. 20 March 1907, Cape Breton Island, N.S.; d. 7 Nov. 1990, Montreal

After a Scots-Presbyterian upbringing, M. studied at Dalhousie University, where he excelled in classics. He received graduate degrees at Oxford University and at Princeton University. Since he joined the McGill University faculty in 1951, teaching and writing have been the chief activities of an outwardly uneventful life. Widely read abroad, M. is not without recognition in Canada, where he has won several awards for his contributions to Canadian literature.

Set in Halifax during World War I, M.'s first novel, *Barometer Rising* (1941), deals with the disastrous explosion in the harbor of a munitions ship bound for the European theater of war. Revelations in the lives of M.'s symbolic characters coincide with this watershed event in the emergence of Canadian nationhood. It dramatizes the need for a national identity that includes an independent, mediating role in international affairs. Several elements of the novel were to become characteristic of M.'s art: the well-realized sense of place, the echoes of Greek myth that reverberate behind the narrative, and the somewhat contrived plot.

Two Solitudes (1945) deals with the uneasy coexistence of French and English Canada, the two solitudes of the title. Up to the death of wise old Athanase Tallard, the seigneur who typifies the French Canadian, the epic story is masterfully told, recalling HARDY and Balzac at their best. The second part, however, suffers from characters that are more symbolic than real and from the intrusion of M.'s views on war, social change, and the impact of other cultures on Canada. Perhaps the most remarkable quality of the book lies in its overarching historical and geographical imagination.

The setting of *Each Man's Son* (1951) is a coal-mining town on Cape Breton Island, M.'s birthplace. Departing from the sweeping concerns of previous novels, M. minutely examines the relationship between a doctor and the young boy whose life he wishes to shape. Beyond the question of willful manipulation of one personality by another, the book has much to say about the lingering effects of puritanism on Canada. In craftsmanship *Each Man's Son* marks a considerable advance. The technique of telling the story as filtered through the consciousness of several characters no longer impairs overall unity, while character and situation are handled with a new deftness and assurance.

The Return of the Sphinx (1967) continues the story of *Each Man's Son*. In the polarized 1960s, though, the solution to the French-English dilemma envisioned in *Two Solitudes*, an ethnic pluralism based on mutual respect and protection of differences, seems an impossibility. After several ultimately optimistic books on Canada's problems, M. suggested here that Canada is under a curse that renders its future enigmatic. A novel of its time, *The Return of the Sphinx* skillfully weaves cogitation on the forces of history with fictional episodes illustrating the manifestations of such forces. Such are the gulfs separating parents from children and those separating the generation of the Great Depression from the post-World War II generation.

In his four volumes of collected essays, M. frequently elaborates on such matters as the Canadian identity problem, the prospects for revitalizing society through Christianity, the relationship between Canada and the U.S., and the transcending question of purpose in life. Undistracted by the need to invent fictional vehicles for thought, M. is often more cogently persuasive in his essays.

Despite their conservative and occasionally uncertain technique, M.'s novels as a whole constitute an impressive achievement. He has pointed a new direction for Canadian fiction through his original treatment of Canadian themes and his attempt to define the moral and ideological dimensions of the Canadian mind.

FURTHER WORKS: *Oxyrhynchus: An Economic and Social Study* (1935); *The Precipice* (1948); *Cross Country* (1949); *Thirty and Three* (1955); *The Watch That Ends the Night* (1959); *Scotchman's Return, and Other Essays* (1961); *Seven Rivers of Canada* (1961; expanded ed., *Rivers of Canada*, 1974); *The Colour of Canada* (1967); *The Other Side of H. M.: Selected Essays Old and New* (1978); *Voices in Time* (1980)

BIBLIOGRAPHY: McPherson, H., "The Novels of H. M.," *QQ*, 60 (1953–1954): 186–98; Wilson, E., *O Canada* (1965): 59–80; Buitenhuis, P., *H. M.* (1969); Morley, P., *The Immoral Moralists: H. M. and Leonard Cohen* (1972); Mathews, R., "H. M.: The Nationalist Dilemma in Canada," *SCL*, 1 (1976): 49–63; Staines, D., "Mapping the Terrain," *Mosaic*, 11 (1978): 137–51; Cameron, E., *H. M.: A Writer's Life* (1981)

—JOHN H. FERRES

MACNEICE, Louis

Anglo-Irish poet, radio dramatist, critic, and novelist, b. 12 Sept. 1907, Belfast, Northern Ireland; d. 3 Sept. 1963, London

Son of a bishop of the Anglican Church, M. early established his special affinity for pivotal groups of friends. At Sherbourne Preparatory School in Dorset and Marlborough College in Wiltshire, his first small group of intimates included the future poets Bernard Spencer (1909–1963) and John Betjeman (b. 1906). At Merton College, Oxford, where he excelled in classics and philosophy, he added Stephen SPENDER and W. H. AUDEN to his circle.

The chronology of M.'s poetry reflects the international currents of his era; the budding, then disillusioned liberalism of his personal experience tends to mirror the rather repentant liberalism of the 1940s. His association with other poets caused him to be labeled a member of the group, yet he fulfilled his early promise and became a distinctively original writer.

M. was coeditor with Stephen Spender of *Oxford Poetry: 1929*. His first volume, *Blind Fireworks*, appeared in the same year; it displayed the philosophic bent of his mind and the wit of his expression. More surprisingly, the poems "Neurotics" and "Middle Age" describe a moribund culture at the moment of its death throes with a witty bathos rather than with pathos.

Poems (1935) appeared after he had become a "junior member of the Auden-Isherwood-Spender literary axis" and before he had visited Iceland with Auden—see *Letters from Iceland* (1937). With C. DAY LEWIS in place of Christopher ISHERWOOD, these four young British poets, grouped by the critics as the "Proletarian Poets," predicted the doom of contemporary culture, in a breezy manner set to jazz tunes. But hardly had he become a member of the left-of-center proletarian poets (all themselves upper-class) than Barcelona was bombed (December 7, 1937), and he confessed in *Autumn Journal* (1939) that vague, diffuse good will would be ineffectual against the screaming radio voices of Mussolini and Hitler. At the outbreak of World War II he volunteered for the Royal Navy but was rejected because of poor eyesight, and instead served as a London fire watcher. In 1941 he began writing radio dramas for the BBC, continuing his services as a scriptwriter and producer for fourteen years.

The Dark Tower, and Other Radio Scripts (1947) and *Persons from Porlock, and Other Plays for Radio* (1969) contain the best of his verse plays—which were often produced with stunning casts, including Laurence Olivier, and with music by Benjamin Britten or William Walton. M. defended radio verse drama by the claim that, since poetry began with Homeric bards and Icelandic skalds shouting over banqueting guests, squalling babies, fighting dogs, and snoring oldsters, it could triumph over the interruptions of radio transmission.

Hugh MacLennan

M.'s sense of the failure of liberalism led inevitably to *The Last Ditch* (1940). Thus, when, in *Plant and Phantom* (1941) he attacks monism, the intellectual argument has the emotional overtone of despair of any attempt at establishing an orderly world. In *Springboard* (1945) he frankly describes the prewar liberal as a kind of ethical "Bottleneck," so high-minded he will fight only for pure motives. *Holes in the Sky: Poems 1944–1947* (1948) shows the poet caught in the straitjacket of an improvisational style suitable for stating the old social criticisms with tongue in cheek but inadequate for new themes.

Ten Burnt Offerings (1952) contains the best writing of the mature, reflective M. Longer, structurally more complex, more substantial in theme than his earlier work, and often religious in topic and tone, these poems are also richer and more deeply moving than the old flippant ditties. This and the last two volumes published in his lifetime are often marked by mystical vision. The final seven poems of *Visitations* (1958) practice the "immediate experience of mystery." *Solstices* (1961), taking its title from the semiannual points at which the sun is farthest from the celestial equator, represents the cyclical motion of M.'s career: classical scholar, teacher of Greek, very modern poet of social and political satire, prolific writer of radio plays, and then, at the end, once again back to the classics.

The Burning Perch, published posthumously in 1963, is the most eschatological of M.'s poetry. The bird flutters on a burning perch. Is it only supreme egotism that shrilly demands the world's attention to its midget dilemma? Clearly the budgerigar represents a world on fire with no place to escape. But in the final poem, "Memoranda to Horace," M. reveals his sense of literary kinship to the classical poet's polished style of sophisticated satire, moving like Horace in "court circles" and yet maintaining his independence of thought.

FURTHER WORKS: *Roundabout Way* (1932, under pseud. Louis Malone); *The "Agamemnon" of Aeschylus* (1936; tr. from Greek); *Out of the Picture: A Play in Two Acts* (1938); *Zoo* (1938); *The Earth Compels: Poems* (1938); *I Crossed the Minch* (1938); *Modern Poetry: A Personal Essay* (1938); *Selected Poems* (1940); *The Poetry of W. B. Yeats* (1941); *Christopher Columbus: A Radio Play* (1944); *Springboard: Poems 1941–1944* (1944); *Collected Poems: 1925–1948* (1949); *Goethe's Faust* (1951; tr. with Ernst Stahl); *Autumn Sequel* (1954); *Traitors in Our Way* (1957); *Eighty-five Poems* (1959); *Astrology* (1964); *The Mad Islands and The Administrator* (1964); *Varieties of Parable* (1965); *The Strings Are False: An Unfinished Autobiography* (1965); *Collected Poems* (1966); *One for the Grave: A Modern Morality Play* (1968)

BIBLIOGRAPHY: Spender, S., "Songs of an Unsung Classicist," *SatR* (7 Sept. 1963): 25–33; Auden, W. H., "L. M.: 1907–1963," *Listener* (24 Oct. 1963): 646; Smith, E. E., *L. M.* (1970); McKinnon, W. T., *Apollo's Blended Dream: A Study of the Poetry of L. M.* (1971); Moore, D. B., *The Poetry of L. M.* (1972); Brown, T., *L. M.: Sceptical Vision* (1975); Coulton, B., *L. M. in the BBC* (1980)

—ELTON E. SMITH

MADAGASCAR LITERATURE
See Malagasy Literature

MADHUBUTI, Haki R.

(born Don L. Lee) American poet, critic, and essayist, b. 23 Feb. 1942, Little Rock, Arkansas

Though M. has a strong acedemic background, his experience in the nonacademic, professional, and blue-collar world, as well as the instability of his early family life, temper a poetry that is aesthetically sophisticated but energized by close contact with the sociopolitical realities of the lives of minorities in America. M.'s father deserted the family when M. was very young, and his mother died an alcoholic when M. was sixteen. Despite domestic insecurity, in the late 1960s, M. received an A.A. degree from Chicago City College, and an M.A. from the University of Illinois, Chicago Circle; in 1984 he was awarded an M.F.A. from the University of Iowa. Since 1984 M. has been a professor of English at Chicago State University. Before embarking on his teaching career, however, which began in 1968 with a one-year residency at Cornell University, M. worked at a number of odd jobs in Chicago. In the mid to late 1960s he served as an apprentice curator at the DuSable Museum of African-American History, a stock clerk for Montgomery Ward, a post office clerk, and a junior executive for Spiegel Incorporated. However, throughout his career, M. has remained committed to the education and unification of the black community and to the promotion of socially conscious African-American

writers. He is, for example, founder and editor of *Black Books Bulletin* and Third World Press (1967), and contributing editor to *Black Scholar* and *First World*; he also founded the Institute of Positive Education (which he directed until 1991)—an organization concerned with black nation building—and is a founding member of the Organization of Black American Culture Writers' Workshop. M. has been a member of the African Liberation Day Support Committee and the Executive Council of the Congress of African People. As M.'s sense of self became more African-centered, he shed what he considered his "slave name," and, in 1973, began to publish under the Swahili name Haki R. Madhubuti.

The most significant features of M.'s poetry, however, are not only its African-American centeredness and its insights into the lives of everyday minorities, but also its desire to convey a global awareness of socio-economic struggle; throughout his poetry, the "realenemy"—"a poem to complement other poems"—M. wants his readers to realize is not so much a function of race, but class: the ideological/economic Other of international politics, global capitalism, and consumerism. The targets of M.'s social criticism are not only the "white" power structure, but also and fundamentally minorities—primarily African-Americans—who are unaware of their social-political position and their own culpability with the system that oppresses them. M.'s critique of the unquestioned black life and his celebration of enlightened African-Americanness are means of exposing the "realenemy" and empowering a particular racial group (his own) to rise, intelligently, against it.

Think Black (1967), M.'s first volume of poetry, deals with such themes as African-American self-definition and determination, concern for the education and enlightenment of the community, and the celebration of African-American womanhood. Most striking is the volume's vibrant tracing of the ambiguous and fractured contours of the dual consciousness resulting from a growing awareness of what it means to be a racial/ethnic/economic "other." Prosodically, the patchwork style and diction, ranging from street slang to rhymed verse, articulates the (productive) confusion of a voice straddling multiple territories. In figuring this linguistic and social mobility, black artists are at once a threat to the status quo and a mooring post for black culture, tethering old values to new ones, as M. comments in the introduction to *Think Black*. "Back Again, Home (confessions of an ex-executive)," for example, merges the personal with the political, deploying autobiography to stage detrimental effects of living one's life outside the "true" self: the speaker recalls how, though he was successful in business, he rarely spoke and often looked ill. He had to return to his ethnic roots, his community (from which he had been "Ostracized"), and learn to become "BLACK AGAIN" before he could find his voice, before poetry—before "real" words—could happen. On a similar note, "The Self-Hatred of Don L. Lee" uses direct language and very thin, one-two syllable lines to figure the suppression of an inner, "all black" self squeezing through the seems of an "outer," culturally diluted self (re)manufactured to meet the needs of tokenism. *Think Black* expresses concerns that will remain constant throughout M.'s poetry. In "The Long Reality" M. networks the global and the local, imaging a communal bond that cuts across racial, ethnic, and geographical boundaries. Using rhymed verse to broach an anti-Anglo-American theme—criticism of U.S. involvement in the Vietnam War—he calls for "Viet-brothers" to join with "black brothers" in the struggle for freedom and ownership of their own land.

Much of M.'s earlier poetry is formally experimental. The title poem of *Don't Cry, Scream* (1969), for example, phonemically imitates saxophone riffs opposite marginal directions for the vocal improvisations. Formal disruption is sometimes the vehicle for aggressively anti-white, stereotypically derisive, and sexist commentary, as in the poem "Malcolm Spoke / Who Listened?," from the same volume, which parodies white upper middle class coeds and Jews. M.'s social critique, however, spares neither black nor white—the poem also castigates blacks who wear, rather than practice, their culture; M.'s values are essentially conservative. Family, tradition, conventional notions of womanhood, the importance of racial memory, and, especially in later poems, the urgent need to shore up language against the eviscerating effects of popular culture are themes that resonate throughout M.'s work.

The poetry in *Killing Memory, Seeking Ancestors* (1987), though as didactic and direct as earlier work, is more measured in its rhythms and less confrontational formally. The title poem of the book, for example, critiques the breakdown of family values, economic exploitation, and the erosion of African-American cultural traditions in an even, authoritative voice, more concerned with chastising and teaching—putting poets and language on the right track—than with verbal assault; M. is careful to examine such issues as poverty and broken families on a global scale, from Latin America to Lebanon, emphasizing a bond of brotherhood wherever people are oppressed. The poems in *Killing Memory*, however, are no less critical of the African-American community, which often suffocates itself in superficialities of dress and makeup, and no less clear about what the community needs and expects from its artists: framers of wisdom, models of critical thinking, questioners of unjust deeds; skilled writers who remember their roots and can reinterpret traditions in light of current needs.

Poetry, for M., is more than the formal arrangement of words on a page. It is didactic, conservationist, and empowering. Poetry can revitalize "word and world"; it can itself be a reservoir of strength, transferring energy from a deep, cultural, ancestral "source" to the poet's immediate environment. As praxis, poetry must be activist in spirit, socially and politically conscious, and always in a state of (self-critical) readiness to cut through the debris of consumerism and bad consciousness stifling lost or neglected selves.

FURTHER WORKS: *Black Pride* (1968); *For Black People (and Negroes Too)* (1968); *We Walk the Way of the New World* (1970); *Directionscore: Selected and New Poems* (1971); *Dynamite Voices: Black Poets of the 1960s* (1971); *From Plan to Planet; Life-Studies; The Need for Afrikan Minds and Institutions* (1973); *Book of Life* (1973); *Enemies: The Clash of Races* (1978); *Earthquakes and Sun Rise Missions: Poetry and Essays of Black Renewal, 1973-1983* (1984); *Say That the River Turns: The Impact of Gwendolyn Brooks* (1987); *Kwanza: A Progressive and Uplifting African American Holiday* (1987); *Black Men—Obsolete, Single, Dangerous?: Afrikan American Families in Transition: Essays in Discovery, Solution and Hope* (1990); *Why L.A. Happened: Implications of the '92 Los Angeles Rebellion* (1993); *Claiming Earth: Race, Rage, Rape, Redemption: Blacks Seeking a Culture of Enlightened Empowerment* (1994); *GroundWork: Selected Poems of H. R. M.* (1996)

BIBLIOGRAPHY: Shands, A. O., "The Relevancy of Don L. Lee as a Contemporary Black Poet," *BW*, 21, 8 (1972): 35-48; Miller, E. E., "Some Black Thoughts on Don L. Lee's Think Black! Thunk by a Frustrated White Academic Thinker," *CE*, 34 (1973): 1094-1102; Mosher, M., *New Directions from Don L. Lee* (1975); Harris, W. J., "Militant Singers: Baraka, Cultural Nationalism and M.," *MV*, 2, 2 (1979): 29-34; Johnson, L. A., "'Ain'ts,' 'Us'ens,' and 'Mother-Dear': Issues in the Language of M., Jones, and Reed," *JBS*, 10 (1979): 139-66; Thompson, J. E., "The Public Response to H. R. M., 1968-1988," *LitG*, 4, 1-2 (1992), 16-37

—TOM LAVAZZI

MADSEN, Svend Åge

Danish novelist, b. 2 Nov. 1939, Århus

After having studied Danish and mathematics at the University of Århus from 1958 to 1961, M. made his debut in the mid-1960s with four experimental works. They were strongly influenced by the French *nouveau roman* of Alain ROBBE-GRILLET and Michel BUTOR and aimed at subverting the traditional novel genre in an attempt to formulate M.'s own concept of reality in a new form.

In his later works M. increasingly employs existing popular novel genres but disclaims their ability to describe reality. Instead he emphasizes playfulness and the fictitious basis, using the novel as a linguistic, cognitive model. With the years, M. has moved from the hermetic and exclusive to an open style somewhat more accessible, but without abandoning his persistent probing into the insecurity of modern life. In recognition of his prominent position in modern Danish literature the Danish Academy awarded him its Literature Prize in 1972.

The point of departure for M.'s oeuvre is a theory that a literary work should not attempt to recreate reality but rather create its own reality. To write fiction means to establish an identity through language, both that of the author and the reader, and even the characters of the narrative only exist inasmuch as they are able to build up their identity through their own story. This theory is exemplified in the extreme in *Tilføjelser* (1967; additions), a novel published as a cassette in five separate volumes with different narrators, who nevertheless comment on one another and quote from M.'s earlier books. It is up to the reader to choose the order of reading and thus to establish an identity through the text.

Already in M.'s first novel, *Besøget* (1963; the visit), he experiments with various narrative perspectives offering the reader different possibilities of leading the totally abstract story to a conclusion. In the "non-novel" *Lystbilleder* (1964; pictures of lust) the basic situation is described again from various viewpoints. It is apparently done to define the concept of lust but actually to allow the author to experiment with narrative angles, with identity changes, and, above all, with various styles and language itself. The work is atomized into seemingly absurd episodes that might serve as elements of a puzzle to create coherence. A similar technique is used in the short-story collection *Otte gange orphan* (1965; eight times orphan). In the first seven stories seven mentally abnormal conditions are portrayed in deliberately monotonous language that follows certain given rules. However, in the eighth story complete linguistic anarchy prevails as a reflection of the impossibility of the narrator—and the reader—to make any sense of chaos.

The second phase of M.'s writings is signaled formally by a shift from first-person to third-person narration. The narrator and the protagonists no longer create their own fixed version of reality; rather it is the structure of a given novel type that determines the language, action, and thought of the characters. At the same time

M. abandons verbal abstraction and stylistic puritanism in favor of humor and imagination.

Whereas the five volumes in *Tilføjelser* are mutually contradictory, five coherent novels executed in five different traditional genres make up *Sæt verden er til* (1971; if the world exists). The one-track search for the self has been replaced by a susceptibility, the ambiguity of which illustrates that the world is indeed changeable, that life can be experienced in many different ways. Still, the reader has to make an existential, Kierkegaardian choice, as in *Dage med Diam eller Livet om natten* (1972; *Days with Diam, or, Life at Night*, 1994), which has two titles. The novel can only be read when the reader constantly chooses between two possibilities. According to a specific system 63 short-story fragments can be combined into 32 completed texts, each with its own outlook on life—M.'s background as a mathematician shines through here as well as in other works.

In M.'s later novels the experiments serve to stir social and political awareness. The plot of the colossal two-volume pseudodocumentary *Tugt og utugt i mellemtiden* (1976; *Virtue and Vice in the Middle Time*, 1992) is located in contemporary Århus. The novel is, in fact, a succinct political and social analysis of Denmark during the 1970s, supposedly written after the year 2000 by a writer who, to understand that period better, makes use of its favorite novel genres: the love story and the detective novel.

In the tradition of Balzac and Zola, M. allows characters from previous works to resurface in later books. Thus, in *Se dagens lys* (1980; see the light of day) many threads go back to the previous *Tugt og utugt i mellemtiden*. This new work too is a science-fiction story, set in a society completely guided by a computer, which at regular intervals moves the characters around from one family to the next, constantly providing new challenges and new encounters with people. Openness and freedom have been introduced, loneliness and monotony abolished. As the only restriction one is not allowed to see again one's fellow beings; one thing is prohibited: love as a repetition. M.'s artistic coup is his intertwinement of capitalist consumer society and dogmatic, restrictive socialism as two ways of expressing the same nightmare.

In *Lad tiden gå* (1986; let time pass) M. has widened the scope from his earlier focus on the question of identity to a more universal existentialist discussion. The concept of repetition resurfaces again but only increases the confusion and suffering that is humankind's lot. If one tampers with time, death is also being eliminated and thereby that which could make our lives meaningful. Besides death, M. tells us, only art is able to create meaning in absurdity.

The search for truth is the only thing that unites the 126 characters in M.'s next tragicomic novel *At fortælle menneskene* (1989; to tell human beings), in which he expands the microcosm of his native Århus into a timeless realm of total abstraction. The characters appear and disappear seemingly without any logical reason, intermarry, or change names and sex on the spur of the moment. However, in spite of the unpredictable behaviour and fantastic metamorphoses of the characters, as well as the insane twists of plot, M. demonstrates that it is precisely language that creates coherence in chaos and helps us to overcome hopelessness and human wickedness.

M. is one of the most sophisticated, speculative writers of modern Danish literature but, at the same time, also one of the most imaginative. Besides novels and short stories. M. has also written dramas and radio and television plays focusing on the same issues as in his prose, but it is as a novelist that he proves himself to be a writer of international rank.

Reading M. presents an intriguing challenge. His demands on the reader are enormous. Like no one else in contemporary Scandinavian literature, he is able to juggle with language, turn concepts upside down, bend words, and create puns. His oeuvre abounds with intellectual subtlety, and it is the main objective of his writing to implicate the reader and thus his fellow humans in an artistic experience. But whereas the world was nothing but fiction, according to M.'s earlier works, now fiction not only establishes our identity but has become the basis for an existential process that might help us to answer some of the perpetual questions about art, faith, and eternity.

FURTHER WORKS: *Et livstykke og andre stykker* (1967); *Liget og Lysten* (1968); *Tredje gang så ta'r vi ham . . .* (1969); *Maskeballet* (1970); *Jakkels vandring* (1974); *Hadets bånd* (1978); *Narrespillet om Magister Bonde og Eline Mortensdatter* (1978); *Slægten Laveran* (1988); *Mellem himmel og jord* (1990); *Jagten på et menneske* (1991); *Eden gave* (1992); *Slægten Laveran* (1992); *Syvaldves galskab* (1993)

BIBLIOGRAPHY: Schmidt, K., *Mandlighedens positioner, Studie i S. Å. Ms forfatterskab* (1982)

—SVEN HAKON ROSSEL

MAETERLINCK, Maurice

Belgian dramatist, poet, and essayist (writing in French), b. 29 Aug. 1862, Ghent; d. 6 May 1949, Nice, France

After earning a law degree in 1885, M. went to Paris, where he became familiar with the poetry of Verlaine, Rimbaud, Villiers de l'Isle Adam, and Mallarmé. M.'s long liaison with the actress-singer Georgette Leblanc was followed by his marriage to Renée Dahon (1919). He won the Nobel Prize for literature in 1911.

M.'s collection of poems *Serres chaudes* (1889; hothouses) showed his affinity to SYMBOLISM: repetition of words, images, and sonorities; protracted silences; imperceptible tonal nuances ushering in soul-scapes tinged with discord; variety of color ranges; and a dreamy ambience broken by the intrusion of aggressive feelings.

M.'s early plays brought symbolism into the theater and can be considered precursors of modern avant-garde drama. Language, setting, lighting, and gesture flow into one central image. Their impact has a cumulative effect on the audience: the nuances and emotions become painful, until the weight of the experience becomes almost unbearable. The exteriorization of the protagonists' moods and feelings is effected by their physical demeanor and by the incantatory quality of their speech. M.'s dialogue relies heavily on repetition of sounds and phrases that frequently take on the power of a litany; the original function of language—its supernatural and religious characteristics—is thus revived. Gone are the platitudes and banalities of everyday speech. Words are no longer used in their habitual sense but usher in a world of magic, arousing a multitude of associations and sensations that act and react viscerally upon the onlooker—not by brash or obvious means, but rather by imposed restraints, nuances, and subtleties.

La princesse Maleine (1889; *Princess Maleine*, 1894), which Octave Mirbeau (1850–1917) called a masterpiece, is a symbolic drama incarnating the worlds of nightmare and joy. Its themes are the inexorable march of fate and man's feeble attempt to circumvent destined misfortunes; it is also a dramatic fairy tale, and as such it permitted M. to inject a sense of timelessness into the characters.

L'intruse (1890; *The Intruder*, 1894), a play about death, is constructed almost exclusively on inner states. The actors remain virtually immobile throughout the performance; their gestures, pared down to the barest suggestions of movement, underscore by their restraint the mounting terror of the situation. The dialogue is sparse, taking on at times the solemnity of a religious chant. Divested of personal elements, the characters take on mythical qualities. They flay each other on stage in the subtlest of ways, compelled to do so by some invisible network of fatal forces.

Les aveugles (1890; *The Blind*, 1894) is metaphysical in dimension and dramatizes what psychologists call the "dying complex." A sense of isolation, loneliness, and fear pervades the atmosphere. With no real plot, its strength and beauty lie in its concise language, economy of gesture, and emotional restraint. Suspense consists in waiting; in this sense it may be likened in theme to BECKETT's *Waiting for Godot*.

For M., as for Emerson, whose influence upon him was great, the poet is a superior being, a "representative" man: intuitive, inspired, and imaginative. Through his art, the poet gives form to the realities experienced in his unconscious and to the spiritual forces discovered within his depths. Influenced also by Plato, Swedenborg, and the medieval Flemish mystic Jan van Ruysbroeck (1293–1381), whose *The Adornment of the Spiritual Marriage* M. translated (1891), M. suggested that the world was to be perceived not through the intellect but through the senses. It was man's obligation to ascend the spiritual ladder, from sightlessness to illumination and from constriction of the soul to its liberation.

Pelléas et Mélisande (1892; *Pelléas and Mélisande*, 1894), M.'s greatest theatrical success, was first staged by Lugné-Poë in an innovative production that emphasized the play's dreaminess and mystery. Its central theme is the birth and burgeoning of love and the destruction of the protagonists by passion. The fairy-tale structure, with its obstacles, its inexplicable appearances and disappearances, its unaccountable dangers, and its concern with fate and death, was the perfect vehicle for this symbolic drama.

M. wrote three plays for marionettes, having been drawn to this form by the ambiguity and mystery of these wooden creatures—their simultaneous helplessness and power, their archetypal and collective nature: *Alladine et Palomides* (1894; *Alladine and Palomides*, 1896), *Intérieur* (1894; *Interior*, 1899), and *La mort de Tintagiles* (1894; *The Death of Tintagiles*, 1896).

M.'s plays henceforth became more conventional and realistic: *Aglavaine et Sélysette* (1896; *Aglavaine and Selysette*, 1897), in which love becomes an instrument of destruction; *Ariane et Barbe-Bleu* (1901; *Ariadne and Barbe-Bleu*, 1901), a feminist play; *Monna Vanna* (1902; *Monna Vanna*, 1903), a play set in the 15th c. about self-sacrifice as a regenerative force; and *Marie Magdaleine* (1909; *Mary Magdalene*, 1910), a liturgical drama.

L'oiseau bleu (1909; *The Blue Bird*, 1909), first performed in Moscow (1907) and then in Paris (1911), was an enormous success. The play dramatizes a creation myth—the spiritual awakening of children—and reveals M.'s preoccupation with theosophy and the unconscious.

A philosopher and mystic, M. wrote essays that reflect his profound understanding of the mysteries of matter and the need of modern man for unfathomable domains in his overly scientific, mechanized, and industrial society. *Le trésor des humbles* (1896;

Maurice Maeterlinck

The Treasure of the Humble, 1897) is a metaphysical inquiry into themes such as the value of silence and secrecy as being essential to the well-being of the soul. *La vie des abeilles* (1901; *The Life of the Bee*, 1901) draws parallels between the bee and man; each bee carries out his precise function in terms of the evolution of the group. *La vie des termites* (1926; *The Life of the White Ant*, 1927) is a very pessimistic work: M. compares man's future existence with that of the termite, who inhabits a world of darkness, feeds on its own dejecta and dead, and lives in a collective and utilitarian society.

To the extent that M.'s plays are based on symbols, gestures, and ritual they may be considered precursors of the THEATER OF THE ABSURD. Like Antonin ARTAUD, M. looked upon theater as a sacred ceremony. His dialogue, like Samuel BECKETT's, is stripped to its essentials, pared of its conventional meanings. In his mystical writings too he anticipated a trend of the later 20th-c.: the need for the mysterious and religious in a technological world.

FURTHER WORKS: *Les sept princesses* (1891; *The Seven Princesses*, 1894); *Douze chansons* (1896); *La sagesse et la destinée* (1898; *Wisdom and Destiny*, 1898); *Sœur Béatrice* (1901; *Sister Beatrice*, 1901); *Le temple enseveli* (1902; *The Buried Temple*, 1902); *Joyzelle* (1903; *Joyzelle*, 1906); *Le double jardin* (1904; *The Double Garden*, 1904); *L'intelligence des fleurs* (1907; *The Intelligence of the Flowers*, 1907); *La mort* (1913; *Death*, 1911); *L'hôte inconnu* (pub. 1917; *The Unknown Guest*, 1914); *Deux contes* (1918); *Le bourgmestre de Stilmonde* (1918; *The Burgomaster of Stilemonde*, 1918); *Les fiançailles* (pub. 1922; *The Betrothal*,

1918); *Le miracle de Saint-Antoine* (pub. 1919; *A Miracle of St. Anthony*, 1917); *Le grand secret* (1921; *The Great Secret*, 1922); *Le malheur passe* (pub. 1925; *The Cloud That Lifted*, 1923); *La puissance des morts* (pub. 1926; *The Power of the Dead*, 1923); *Marie Victoire* (1927); *La vie de l'espace* (1927; *The Life of Space*, 1928); *Juda de Kérioth* (1929); *La grande féerie* (1929); *La vie des fourmis* (1930; *The Life of the Ant*, 1930); *Avant le grand silence* (1934; *Before the Great Silence*, 1935); *Devant Dieu* (1934); *Princesse Isabelle* (1935); *La grande porte* (1939); *L'autre monde* (1942; *The Great Beyond*, 1947); *Bulles bleues, souvenirs heureux* (1948); *Jeanne d'Arc* (1948); *Théâtre inédit I* (1959). FURTHER WORKS IN ENGLISH: *Old Fashioned Flowers, and Other Open-Air Essays* (1905); *Chrysanthemums, and Other Essays* (1907); *Life and Flowers* (1907); *The Measures of the Hours* (1907); *The Inner Beauty* (1910); *On Emerson, and Other Essays* (1912); *Hours of Gladness* (1912); *News of Spring, and Other Nature Studies* (1913); *Our Eternity* (1913); *Poems* (1915); *The Wrack of the Storm* (1916); *The Light Beyond* (1917); *Mountain Paths* (1919); *Ancient Egypt* (1925); *The Magic of the Stars* (1930); *The Supreme Law* (1934); *Pigeons and Spiders; The Water Spider; The Life of the Pigeon* (1935); *The Hour Glass* (1936)

BIBLIOGRAPHY: Harry, G., *M. M.* (1910); Bithell, J., *Life and Writings of M. M.* (1913); Taylor, U., *M. M.* (1914); Halls, W. D., *M. M.: A Study of His Life and Thought* (1960); Donneux, G., *M. M.* (1961); Postic, M., *M. M. et le symbolisme* (1970); Knapp, B. L., *M. M.* (1975); Valency, M., *The End of the World: An Introduction to Contemporary Drama* (1980): 62–83; Lambert, C. J., *The Empty Cross: Medieval Hopes, Modern Futility in the Theatre of M. M.* (1990); Compère, G., *M. M.* (1990)

—BETTINA L. KNAPP

MAGDALENO, Mauricio

Mexican novelist, short-story writer, dramatist, essayist, and critic, b. 13 May 1906, Villa del Refugio

M. developed emotionally and matured intellectually during the violence-ridden period of the Mexican revolution, an epochal upheaval that was to influence much of his literary production. The years he spent in Spain in the early 1930s sharpened his critical acumen and tempered his nationalism with cosmopolitan cultural assimilations, evident in collections of essays such as *Vida y poesía* (1936; life and poetry) and *Tierra y viento* (1948; land and wind). Back from Spain in 1934, M. cofounded the important theatrical group Today's Theater, which presented social dramas. Since that time he has concentrated primarily on fiction and the essay.

M.'s masterpiece, and the best Mexican novel of the 1930s, is *El resplandor* (1937; *Sunburst*, 1944), the action of which, although set in the 1920s, reflects the revolutionary fervor of the Cárdenas regime (1934–40). The collective protagonist is an impoverished Otomí Indian community exploited by corrupt politicians and generations of wealthy landowners. Departing from the usual straightforward style and linear structure of his Mexican contemporaries, M. presents flashbacks into the remote past, which serve to explain the present-day situation, and uses innovative techniques such as STREAM OF CONSCIOUSNESS and dream sequences, which broaden both the aesthetic and psychological dimensions of the

novel. The cyclical recurrence of hope, betrayal, and violence in the lives of the Indians not only underscores the social protest theme but also suggests a pessimistic view of the historical process. Although *El resplandor* is occasionally marred by verbose descriptions and tendentious rhetoric, it effectively dramatizes the failure of the revolution to integrate the oppressed Indian into the mainstream of Mexican society.

Cabello de Elote (1949; Blondie) depicts a Mexican town on the eve of and during World War II. The protagonist of this popular novel is a blonde mestiza whose Indian heritage frustrates her attempts to attain the social prestige she so ardently desires. M. adroitly utilizes contrasting montage structures and surrealistic probes of the subconscious in order to highlight racial dichotomies and capture the confusion of a rapidly evolving society. Aesthetic cohesion and dramatic impact suffer, however, because the proliferation of characters and events, although not without interest, obscures the psychological development of the central figure.

M. stands out as an innovative regionalist whose works reflect a profound understanding of modern Mexico and an intuitive insight into the universal human experience.

FURTHER WORKS: *Mapimí 37* (1927); *Teatro revolucionario mexicano: Pánuco 137, Emiliano Zapata, Trópico* (1933); *Campo Celis* (1935); *Concha Bretón* (1936); *Rango* (1941); *Sonata* (1941); *La tierra grande* (1949); *El ardiente verano* (1954); *Ritual del año* (1955); *Las palabras perdidas* (1956); *El compromiso de las letras* (1958); *La voz y el eco* (1964); *Retórica de la Revolución* (1978); *Escritores extranjeros en la Revolución* (1979)

BIBLIOGRAPHY: Stanton, R., "The Realism of M. M.," *Hispania* 24 (1939): 345–53; Morton, F. R., *Los novelistas de la Revolución mexicana* (1949): 207–13; Brushwood, J. S., *Mexico in Its Novel* (1966): 19–21: 217–18; Carter, B. G., "*El resplandor* de M.: Su estructura clásica," *Revista mexicana de cultura* (25 Feb. 1968): 1–2; Sommers, J., *After the Storm: Landmarks of the Modern Mexican Novel* (1968): 23–33; Parle, D. J., "Las funciones del tiempo en la estructura de *El resplandor* de M.," *Hispania*, 63 (1980): 58–68

—BOYD G. CARTER

al-MĀGHŪT, Muhammad

Syrian poet, dramatist and journalist, b. 1934, Syria

Well known in the fields of Arabic poetry, drama, and journalism, the Syrian-born M. lived in self-imposed exile for many years in Lebanon, where he was an early and active proponent of MODERNISM in literary movements dating from the late 1950s. Self-educated, M. has familiarized himself with foreign literatures in translation, but looked for inspiration to such maverick figures in the Arabic poetic tradition as Al-Hutay's (d. 678) and Abū Nuwās (d. 810). He now enjoys success as a screen writer in collaboration with the popular Syrian comedian Durayd Lahham (b. 1933), and resides for the most part in Damascus.

Huzn fi daw' al-qamar (1959; grief in the moonlight), M.'s first volume of poems, was an experiment in the form of prose-poetry. Most notably, the book launched a new satiric voice in Arabic poetry, which had been little disturbed by self-directed irony or much intimation that humor and absurdity are implict in the business of making poems. Often jeopardized by their political beliefs, Arab poets had maintained a sober view of their artistic missions; M.'s roguish persona was the antithesis of the poet-prophet, guilty of a panoply of misdemeanors against virtually every social convention. Yet, however irreverent, M.'s poetry can by no means be considered "decadent" or trival. Even in the images of defeat and self-indulgence, deprecation of the self merges with criticism of society—not in the tone of facile indictment, but with a naked cry from the heart.

M.'s first volume of poems had contained curiously powerful elegies for his adopted country, Lebanon; the second, *Ghurfah bi-malāyān judrān* (1964; a room with millions of walls), presented an image of the Arab world as a prison from which no one escapes: a room with millions of walls. The subject matter was the defeated Arab, homeless and downtrodden; the underlying concern was the Arab's perception of history. A society numbed with nostalgia for its past victories and heroes had produced a literature in which cynicism and despair were anathema and in which it was mandatory to graft an optimistic postscript onto each poem. In contrast, M.'s poetic purpose was clearly ignited by concerns of the immediate, physical, and known and loved world, not an envisaged better one of the future or, for that matter, of the past.

In his next volume of poems, *Al-farah laysa mihnatī* (1970; joy is not my profession), M. reached artistic maturity in both language and form. The poems are shorter and more tightly structured, no longer suffering from stretches of hastily developed ideas, and the curious images achieve maximum impact. The tragic leitmotiv continues to be the theme of the beloved country, depicted by turns as betrayer and betrayed, yet finally indifferent to its lesser denizens. These poems demonstrate yet more clearly that M.'s "country" is the Arab nation, which offers a precarious sense of identity. The betrayal experienced is that of Arab by Arab, the people by its governments, and ultimately, "man's inhumanity to man."

Though he is a prolific and popular playwright, only two of M.'s plays have been published, the most noteworthy being *Al-'Usfur; al-ahdab* (1967; the hunchbacked bird). In this surrealistic work, an odd assortment of characters is imprisoned for obscure misdeeds in an unknown cage in a nameless desert: an allegory for the capricious practices of political imprisonment imposed by suppressive regimes. M.'s unpublished plays show greater mastery of characterization and form, with fewer intrusive monologues.

His volumes of poetry are few, but it is as a poet that M. has made his most significant literary contribution. With the publication of his work in the late 1950s, the poet as antihero invaded the newly emerging modern Arabic poem. M.'s use of poetic language is also remarkable: it juxtaposes the modern idiom with literary Arabic in a startling manner, giving maximum effect to unusual images and intentionally mixed metaphors. In both poetry and drama, this electric imagery spotlights serious social themes, leavened generously with satire. The result is an oeuvre that is by turns realistic and surrealistic, preposterous and tragic—an exceedingly rare blend in Arabic literature.

FURTHER WORKS: *M. al-M. al-āthār al-kāmilah* (1973); *Al-Muharrij* (1973); *Sa'khūnu watanī* (1987)

BIBLIOGRAPHY: Allen, R., ed. *Modern Arabic Literature* (1987): 187–92; Asfour, J. M., "Adonis and M. al-M.: Two Voices in a Burning Land," *JArabL*, 20 (1989): 20–30; Asfour, J. M., and A., Burch, "M. al-M. and the Surplus Man," *Edebiyat*, 1, 2 (1989): 23–40; Asfour, J., and A. Burch, *Joy Is Not My Profession: Selected Poems of Muhammad al-Maghut* (1994)

—JOHN M. ASFOUR

MAGIC REALISM

"Magic realism" does not refer to a specific literary movement or period of modern Western literature. Long before Spanish American critics began labeling the prose works of certain authors as magic realist, there was a coalescence of diverse cultural perspectives and conceptions in Latin America which foreshadowed the invention and use of this literary expression. The modern perception of the reality found in Latin America was the result of a unique fusion of the beliefs and superstitions of different cultural groups that included the Hispanic conqueror, his *criollo* (creole) descendants, the native peoples, and the African slaves. The shared experiences of each one of these groups colored the accounts of America's discovery and colonization by both native and European chroniclers. In addition to his erroneous preconceptions and utopian images of the New World, the European chronicler often patterned his narrative on the *Libros de caballerías* (books of chivalry), which related fantastic and incredible feats realized by fictional heroes. Little distinction was made between fact and fiction within the traditions of European Renaissance historiography and rhetoric. By relying on the oral storytelling traditions of their ancestors' fables and myths as the primary source for their history, the native chroniclers also combined truth and fantasy. Today, many critics often note that magic realism, like myth, also provides an essentially synthetic or totalizing way of depicting reality.

Franz Roh (1890–1965), a German art critic, first mentioned magic realism in his book *Nach Expressionismus: Magischer Realismus: Probleme der neusten europäischen Malerei* (1925; after expressionism: magic realism: problems of the newest European painting), which was partially translated into Spanish in 1927 and appeared in ORTEGA Y GASSET's journal, *Revista de Occidente*. Although Massimo BONTEMPELLI and others around the Italian journal '*900* also advocated a "magic realism," the term never found general favor among European critics and was soon discarded. In Roh's original conception, magic realism was considered to be synonymous with postexpressionist painting (1920–25), which was thought to be magical because it revealed the mysterious elements hidden in everyday reality. Even when applied to literature, magic realism never signified for Roh the mixture of fantasy and reality. It was firmly grounded in daily reality and expressed man's astonishment before the wonders of the real world.

The Venezuelan writer Arturo USLAR PIETRI was the first Latin American to speak of magic realism, but he did not mention Roh in his book, *Hombres y letras de Venezuela* (1948; men and letters of Venezuela). His use of the term essentially agreed with Roh's formulation and was applied to a few Venezuelan short stories that contained strange characters and themes based on real life situations and were written in a poetic prose style. Soon afterward, the Cuban writer Alejo CARPENTIER talked about "marvelous American reality" in the prologue to his novel *El reino de este mundo* (1949; *The Kingdom of This World*, 1957). Carpentier emphasized the importance of the American cultural experience and history in his notion of "marvelous American reality." Later, in *Tientos y diferencias* (1964; touches and differences), Carpentier had to concede that the marvelous aspects of reality were not limited to America. Carpentier criticized SURREALISM as an artificial invention of a reality that already contained many intrinsic marvels of its own. He conceived "marvelous American reality" as a moment of awareness akin to poetic epiphany and based on a faith in the miraculous that allowed the writer to convey to his readers through the characters a vision of the fantastic features of reality. The conceptions of magic realism posited by Carpentier and Uslar Pietri corresponded to a transitory phase of their own fiction and critical theories of the narrative art.

The critic Ángel Flores (b. 1900) popularized the term among critics in a famous essay "Magical Realism in Spanish American Fiction" (1955). He widened the scope of its original meaning and applied it to a very diverse group of writers, which included Jorge Luis BORGES and Miguel Ángel ASTURIAS. Magic realism was simplified to mean an amalgam of the real and the fantastic. The Mexican critic Luis Leal (b. 1907) posed some objections to Flores's definition of magic realism and returned to Roh's original conception by stressing that the phrase meant an attitude toward reality in which the poetic or mysterious facets of daily life stood out and all fantastic elements were excluded. Many critics now consider Uslar Pietri, Carpentier, and Asturias as the initial theoreticians and exponents of magic realism because of their common insistence on its mimetic and regionalist aspects.

Although the concept of magic realism has been extended to some younger writers such as the Colombian Gabriel GARCÍA MÁRQUEZ and the Mexican Juan RULFO, lately, its ambivalence and inexactness have been attacked by a score of critics who favor replacing it with a more precise exegetical term. Some view magic realism as a technique for creating or inventing a fantasy that is made to appear verisimilar. This view in turn implies a relativist concept of the real that can be distorted or manipulated through shifts in the narrative point of view. Here, the traditional emphasis on mimesis in magic realism is replaced by genesis or the artistic re-creation of reality. Virtually all critics now agree that magic realism constitutes a narrative tendency that is distinct and separate from fantastic literature. Many would also agree that magic realism is a thematic rather than a structural term because its usefulness for literary analysis is so imprecise. For some critics magic realism has been construed as a cultural or ontological view of reality that Latin Americans readily accepted while they sought autonomy from European prose models in the first half of the 20th c.

BIBLIOGRAPHY: Ben-Ur, L. E., "El realismo mágico en la crítica hispanoamericana," *JSSTC*, 4 (1976): 149–63; Flores, Á., "Magical Realism in Spanish American Fiction," *Hispania*, 38 (1955): 187–92; Leal, L., "El realismo mágico en la literatura hispanoamericana," *CA*, 153 (1967): 230–35; Merrell, F., "The Ideal World in Search of Its Reference: An Inquiry into the Underlying Nature of Magical Realism," *Chasqui*, 4 (1975): 5–17; Yates, D. A., ed., *Fantasía y realismo mágico en Iberoamérica* (1975)

—JAMES J. ALSTRUM

MAHFŪZ, Najīb

Egyptian novelist and short-story writer, b. 10 Dec. 1911, Cairo

M. is the Arab world's most famous novelist, and he has also made contributions to the short story and drama. Born in Cairo, he has spent his entire life in Egypt, much of it as a civil servant within the cultural sector. At the University of Cairo M. studied philosophy, and it was while he was contemplating entering a graduate degree program that he began to write the series of short stories that appeared in his first collection, *Hams aljunūn* (1939; whisper of madness).

The stories in this earliest collection show clearly what has remained one of M.'s principal concerns: the individual and the question of the nature of the absurd. Following this volume however, M. pursued an earlier interest in the history of ancient Egypt by writing three novels set in that period and even made plans for a whole series of such works. It is the immense gain of the modern Arabic novel that he changed his mind and turned his attention to the circumstances of his own contemporaries within the older quarters of Cairo itself. The series of novels that appeared during the late 1940s and early 1950s demonstrated the maturity of the realistic novel in Arabic literature. This was a period of tremendous political unrest in Egypt, with terrorism and assassination being clear signs of the social turmoil preceding the revolution of 1952. M.'s novels succeed in capturing the atmosphere of these times, and no more brilliantly than in *Zuqāq al-Midaqq* (1947; *Midaq Alley*, 1966), *Al-Qāhira al-jadīda* (1946; modern Cairo), and *Bidāya wa nihāya* (1951?; *The Beginning and the End*, 1985). This series of novels was to culminate in a huge project that took M. five years to complete, the monumental *Al-Thulāthiyya* (1956–57; the trilogy), consisting of three novels, *Bayn al-Qasrayn* (1956; *Palace Walk*, 1990), *Qasr al-Shawq* (1956; *Palace of Desire*, 1991), and *Al-Sukkariyya* (1957; *Sugar Street*, 1992), each named after a different quarter of Cairo. This huge work of over fifteen hundred pages presents three generations of the family of 'Abd al-Jawwād, seen during the period 1917–44. As the narrative moves from one part of Cairo to another, we witness through the infinite care and subtlety that M. applies to his task the way in which this family is a microcosm of the forces of change within Egyptian society as a whole.

M. has said that this work was completed just before the 1952 revolution, in which King Farouk was overthrown, and that he was uncertain about publishing it until the nature of the revolution itself was clearer. The publication of *Al-Thulāthiyya* brought him instant fame and the State Prize for Literature. In 1959 the newspaper *Al-Ahrām* serialized his most controversial work, *Awlād hāratinā* (*Children of Gebelawi*, 1981), which caused a sufficient outcry among the conservative religious establishment to prevent its publication in book form in Egypt (it was published in Lebanon in 1967). An allegory concerning the development of the great religions and man's attitude to them, it surveys the careers of Adam, Moses, Jesus, and Muhammad before posing in the fifth section the question of the relationship between science and religion, strongly implying that the former has destroyed the latter. While this work was satisfyingly controversial, it was not a success from a literary point of view: the level of allegory was too inconsistent and the major purpose of the entire work—to suggest that science might be the cause of the destruction of religion—was too obvious.

During the 1960s M. wrote another series of novels in which he is more concerned with the individual in society than he was in his earlier work. Descriptions are more economical than previously, the symbolism is more pronounced, and there is much use of interior monologue and STREAM OF CONSCIOUSNESS. Outstanding among these works are *Al-Liss wa al-kilāb* (1961; *The Thief and the Dogs*, 1984), with its scarcely veiled criticism of the fair-weather socialists and opportunists within society; and *Tharthara fawq al-Nīl* (1966; *Adrift on the Nile*, 1993), in which a houseboat symbolizing Egypt itself is the setting for the meetings of a group of intellectuals and artists who have retreated from society because they feel that they have no role to play. The final novel in this series, *Mīrāmār* (1966; *Miramar*, 1978), is a yet franker exposé of corruption in the public sector of Egypt, but the kind of exploitation that M. describes seems insignificant in the wake of the circumstances surrounding the defeat by Israel in the 1967 Six-Day War.

Following this disaster, M. addressed himself to the issue of civic responsibility and the maintenance of values in a series of lengthy short stories, often cyclical in form, which were published in collections between 1967 and 1971. The publication of his novels had been interspersed previously with a few short-story collections, of which *Dunyā Allāh* (1963; God's world) and *Khamārat al-Qiṭṭ al-Aswad* (1968; Black Cat Tavern), contain some of the best examples of M.'s contributions to this genre.

In 1971 M. surveyed the course of his career and the intellectual life of Egypt in the first half of this century in a work entitled *Al-Marāyā* (1972; *Mirrors*, 1977), purportedly a series of fifty-five vignettes but actually a commentary on education, morals, religion, international relations, and a whole host of other topics. This work was to mark a new direction in M.'s writing, away from the social realism of the pre-1967 period towards a number of new directions. During the 1970s and 1980s M. adopted a newly terse, sardonic, and richly allusive style to address himself in a number of works to local Egyptian issues. Perhaps most interesting of all have been M.'s attempts to reflect the priorities of some of his novelistic colleagues by invoking names and themes heavily associated with particular genres of writing from the classical period of Arabic narrative, as in *Rihlat ibn Farrumah* (1983; *The Journey of Ibn Fattouma*, 1992).

In October 1994 M. was attacked with a knife by a follower of one of the popular Islamic movements in Egypt and narrowly escaped death. Since that time his already reduced output has been radically affected, and yet that has not prevented him from publishing—almost as an act of defiance—one of his most interesting and cryptic works, *Asda; al-sirah al-dhatiyyah* (1996, Echoes of Autobiography), a fascinating blend of personal anecdotes and evocations of the mystical writings of earlier centuries.

M.'s style has changed relatively little during the course of his career, and his vocabulary is quite small in comparison with some other writers of fiction in the Arab world today. His mastery of the use of language to create scene and mood, more expansive in his realistic period, more economical and symbolic during the 1960s, is complete and has allowed him to create some memorable pages of Arabic fiction. When the history of 20th-c. Arabic fiction comes to be written, he will undoubtedly be regarded as the first Arab novelist to bring full mastery to the genre and to produce works of world stature.

FURTHER WORKS: *'Abath al-aqdār* (1939); *Radūbīs* (1943); *Kifāḥ Ṭībā* (1944); *Khān al-Khālīlī* (1946); *Al-Sarāb* (1948); *Al-Summān wa al-kharīf* (1962; *Autumn Quail*, 1985); *Al-Ṭarīq* (1964; *The Search*, 1987); *Bayt say' al-sum'a* (1965); *Al-Shaḥḥādh* (1965; *The Beggar*, 1986); *Taht al-mazalla* (1969); *Hikāya bilā bidāya wa lā nihāya* (1969); *Shahr al-'asul* (1971); *Al-Hubb tahta al-matar* (1973); *Al-Jarīma* (1973); *Al-Karnak* (1974; *Al-Karnak*, 1984); *Hadrat al-muhtaram* (1975; *Respected Sir*, 1986); *Hikāyāt hāratinā* (1975; *Fountain and Tomb*, 1988); *Qalb al-layl* (1975); *Malhamat* *al-harāfīsh* (1977; *The Harafish*, 1994); *Al-Hubb fawqa hadbat al-haram* (1979); *Al-Shaytān ya'iz* (1979); *'Asr al-hubb* (1980); *Afrāḥ al-qubba* (1981; *Wedding Song*, 1984); *Layālī alf layla* (1982; *Arabian Nights and Days*, 1995); *Ra'aytu fīmā yarā al-nā'im* (1982). FURTHER WORKS IN ENGLISH: *God's World* (1973); *The Time and the Place and Other Stories* (1991)

BIBLIOGRAPHY: Le Gassick, T., "The *Trilogy* of N. M.," *MEF*, 39, 2 (1963): 31–34; Milson, M., "N. M. and the Quest for Meaning," *Arabica*, 17 (1970): 177–86; Allen, R., "Mirrors by N. M.," *MW*, 62, 2 (1972): 115–25, and 63, 1 (1973): 15–27; Somekh, S., *The Changing Rhythm: A Study of N. M.'s Novels* (1973); Sakkut, H., "N. M.'s Short Stories," and Le Gassick, T., "An Analysis of *Al-Hubb tahta al-matar*," in Ostle, R. C., ed., *Studies in Modern Arabic Literature* (1975): 114–25, 140–51; Milson, M., "Reality, Allegory and Myth in the Work of N. M.," *AAS*, 11 (1976): 157–79; Allen, R., "Some Recent Works of N. M.," *JARCE*, 14 (1977): 101–10; Allen, R. M. A., *The Arabic Novel: An Historical and Critical Introduction* (1982): 55–62, 101–7; Mikhail, M., *Studies in the Short Fiction of M. and Idris* (1992); El-Enany, R., *N. M.: The Pursuit of Meaning* (1993)

—ROGER ALLEN

MAHON, Derek

Irish poet, b. 23 Nov. 1941, Belfast

M. spent his early years in Belfast, but left there to go to Dublin to attend Trinity College, from which he received a B.A. in 1965. Since graduation, M. has divided his time between England and Ireland, but in common with many modern Irish writers he has spent more of his adult life abroad than at home.

Irish poets have always been obsessed by all those objects and persons that are visibly there in front of them: parts of landscapes, modern buildings, lovers, and parents. However, even though all these are present as themes in M.'s poetry, they do not dominate his work as they do the work of others. Instead, one of M.'s great concerns, following in the footsteps of Samuel BECKETT, a fellow Protestant and Trinity alumnus, is absence. In his best-known poem, "A Disused Shed in Co. Wexford," which appears in *The Snow Party* (1975), he feels that it is the poet's responsibility to provide the dead, in both human and nonhuman forms, with a voice, because people who are no longer alive and objects that are no longer used are essences crying out to be given a voice for "their deliverance" from silent agony.

The silent Ireland that is so attractive to M. stands in stark contrast to the living Ireland in which he grew up, and which he is unable to come fully to terms with. He is clearly uncomfortable in Belfast, his hometown, and has written little about his childhood there, or his family, or the Troubles. Unlike his contemporaries Seamus HEANEY, James Simmons (b. 1933), and Michael Longley (b. 1939), M. refuses to lend his poetic gifts to the inflamed political situation in the North, and steers well clear of it. In the poem "Afterlives" (in *The Snow Party*) he admits that after five years of destruction he can "scarcely recognize the places I grew up in," and wonders if he "had lived it bomb by bomb" might he "have grown up at last and learnt what is meant by home." M. rebukes himself for abandoning Belfast, though he is uncertain he would have found a sense of community had he remained there.

M.'s language is as eclectic as his themes, and over and over he has proven himself to be wonderfully inventive and dexterous. Like W.H. AUDEN and Louis MACNEICE, who have exercised a strong influence on his work, he possesses a remarkable ability to introduce original contrasts, and to vary his syntax and diction, without ever appearing to be merely seeking to be clever. In his most recent collections, M. has taken on new landscapes and themes—downtown New York in *The Hudson Letter* (1996), and Ireland at the end of this century in *The Yellow Book* (1998). In both collections, M. has employed traditional poetic forms to describe the chaos of contemporary life, and the results are spectacular, both formally and thematically.

FURTHER WORKS: *Night-Crossing* (1968); *Ecclesiastes* (1970); *Beyond Howth Head* (1970); *Lives* (1972); *The Man Who Built His City in Snow* (1972); *Light Music* (1977); *The Sea in Winter* (1979); *Poems 1962–1978* (1979); *The Hunt by Night* (1982); *The Chimeras* (1982); *A Kensington Notebook* (1984); *High Time* (1985); *The School for Wives* (1986); *Selected Poems* (1991); *Journalism: Selected Prose* (1997)

BIBLIOGRAPHY: Carpenter, A., "Double Vision in Anglo-Irish Literature," in Carpenter, A., ed., *Place, Personality, and the Irish Writer* (1977): 173–89; Donnelly, B., "From Nineveh to the Harbour Bar," *Ploughshares*, 6, 1 (1980): 131–37; Deane, S., *Celtic Revivals* (1985): 156–65; Deane, S., *A Short History of Irish Literature* (1986): 227–47

—EAMONN WALL

MAILER, Norman

American novelist, essayist, journalist, and screenwriter, b. 31 Jan. 1923, Long Branch, N. J.

M. had a conventional upbringing by a supportive family in a middle-class section of Brooklyn, N. Y. While at Harvard M. became so infused with literature and with the idea of creating great literary works which would attract acclaim that he began to write fiction. Upon graduation in 1943 M. entered the army and served in the Pacific.

M.'s writing has increasingly focused upon his life, lived broadly in a variety of realms: a prominent public personality, M. cofounded *The Village Voice* newspaper (1955); campaigned to be mayor of New York City (1969); actively participated in political protest and cultural dissent; launched several conspicuous literary feuds; acted in a few films; was arrested several times, most notoriously for stabbing his wife (1960); and has flamboyantly been married six times.

The Naked and the Dead (1948), M.'s first novel, was a great critical success and launched M.'s career. It depicted the past and present lives of an ethnically diverse group of soldiers involved in a South Pacific campaign during World War II. The novel displays the influence of several American social realists: James T. FARRELL in the overall style; John DOS PASSOS in the flashback technique, called in the novel the "Time Machine," and in the authorial

perspective and structure; John STEINBECK in the propensity for elaborate imagery and metaphorical allusions.

Barbary Shore (1951), a more ambitious novel, was a critical failure: whereas his first novel grew out of America's general wartime experience, his second grounded itself in the particular political and philosophical concerns of the American left, reflecting such contemporary events as the Alger Hiss trial. The influence of F. Scott FITZGERALD is apparent in the stylized grafting of an Arthurian allegory (of the search for the Grail) upon the Stalinist-Trotskyite affinities of the residents of a Brooklyn rooming house.

In *The Deer Park* (1955), a novel about the Hollywood community (building upon M.'s observations as an unsuccessful screenwriter in 1949), M. began to demonstrate his notion that the sexual qualities of fictional characters might be connected to their moral nature; the novel was influenced by M.'s belief in the prototypical masculinity that he saw as existing in the fiction of Ernest HEMINGWAY and Henry MILLER. Because of the personal aspect of the novel's themes, M. held the work in high esteem; when it was rejected by six publishers before ultimately appearing in print to ambiguous reviews, M. experienced a sense of depression, an artistic turbulence in keeping with the indecisive and derivative nature of his early work.

M.'s resurgence occurred with *Advertisements for Myself* (1959), a bold and idiosyncratic work in which he not only assembled a retrospective of his literary career, but interpreted his work through a vitalized critical commentary. He announced his desire to stimulate "a revolution in the consciousness of our time" accordingly, he affirmed his confidence that "it is my present and future work which will have the deepest influence of any work being done by an American novelist in these years." Evident in this work transcending generic classification is M.'s sense of himself as being exemplary of his age—a figure of dramatic individuality and dynamic creative vigor who would embody through literature the great themes of the era. Also characteristic are his increasing interest in EXISTENTIALISM, his reliance upon evocative contemporary material, and his utilization of paradoxical metaphors to accommodate his philosophical formulations: thus, in the essay "The White Negro" (originally published in 1957), M. presents the "psychopathic hipster," whom he sees as being inherently creative and in tune with life, in opposition to the conventional citizen, whom he views as being repressed and alienated.

An American Dream (1965) expresses many of M.'s themes in mature fictional form: the war between God and the Devil for possession of the earth; sex as an encompassing metaphor for time and theology; the literary form of history; the viability of paranoia; the underlying morality and creativity behind deviant behavior. The protagonist, Rojack (a war hero who is a former politician and television talk-show host), does not achieve genuine heroic stature until he murders his wife and frees himself from the oppressive influence of the economic and political institutions with which he has previously been involved. Newly receptive to the poetic guidance of the moon, he attains individual fulfillment and expression of his personal being by gradually sloughing off the skins of conventional American existence. Central to this novel is M.'s prevailing conviction that any person in the United States is "a member of a minority group if he contains two opposed notions of himself at the same time."

A novel reminiscent stylistically of William BURROUGHS and thematically of William FAULKNER, *Why Are We in Vietnam?* (1967) offers a frenetic Alaskan bear hunt as a metaphor for the

American involvement in southeast Asia. M.'s desire to exert an "influence" upon his time and to shape his history through literary vision resulted in *The Armies of the Night* (1968), which won a Pulitzer Prize and a National Book Award. This is a novelistic description of his participation in (and arrest during) the actual 1967 march on the Pentagon. M.'s use of the third person to relate a narrative in which he himself emerges as the protagonist excited the imagination of a decade eager to achieve immediacy and straightforwardness; it exerted a considerable influence upon the style of popular writing called the "New Journalism."

Fueled by his success, M. continued to explore the state of society from his own tempestuous vantage point. He twice interpreted Presidential contests—in *Miami and the Siege of Chicago* (1968) and *St. George and the Godfather* (1972). *The Prisoner of Sex* (1971), M.'s response to the feminist movement, proposed that gender might determine the way a person perceives and orders reality. *The Fight* (1975) analyzed the bout between Muhammad Ali and George Foreman as a metaphorical joust between cosmic animism and death.

M.'s account of the life and execution of the convict Gary Gilmore, the Pulitzer Prize–winning *The Executioner's Song* (1979), is an impressive and dramatic work that is both fiction and journalism. Drawing on actual interviews and records, M., for the first time, submerges himself in another's tale, with the result that M.'s own world vision is convincingly established.

M.'s efforts to project himself into other realms of experience resulted in *Ancient Evenings* (1983), his massive contemplation on spiritualism, death, and life in ancient Egypt. *Tough Guys Don't Dance* (1984) displays M. in his more customary individualistic mystery genre form. M.'s two major novels of the 1990s demonstrate his consistent willingness to take artistic risks, exploring the extensive conspiritorial network of the Cold War and the CIA in *Harlot's Ghost* (1991) and attempting an iconoclastic meditation on Jesus Christ in *The Gospel According to the Son* (1997).

Although M. has frequently announced his intention to create the ultimate novel of our age, it may well be that his body of work, when considered together, reflects most keenly the volatile state of the American nation. Often infuriating—reveling in a stylish nonconformity and a self-indulgence that often conceal a fundamental conservatism of values and a desire for popular adulation—flawed, poetic, crass, brilliant, M. has succeeded in making our contemporary era the "time of his time."

FURTHER WORKS: *Deaths for the Ladies (and Other Disasters)* (1962); *The Presidential Papers* (1963); *Cannibals and Christians* (1966); *The Bullfight* (1967); *The Deer Park: A Play* (1967); *The Short Fiction of N. M.* (1967); *The Idol and the Octopus* (1968); *Of a Fire on the Moon* (1971); *On the Fight of the Century: King of the Hill* (1971); *Maidstone: A Mystery* (1971); *Existential Errands* (1972); *Marilyn: A Biography* (1973); *The Faith of Graffiti* (1974); *Genius and Lust: A Journey through the Major Writings of Henry Miller* (1976); *Some Honorable Men* (1976); *Of Women and Their Elegance* (1980); *Pieces and Pontifications* (1982); *The Time of Our Time* (1998)

BIBLIOGRAPHY: Schulz, M., *Radical Sophistication* (1969): 69–110; Tanner, T., *City of Words* (1971): 344–71; Braudy, L., ed., *N. M.: A Collection of Critical Essays* (1972); Poirier, R., *N. M.* (1972); Kazin, A., *Bright Book of Life* (1973); Adams, L., *A Bibliography of N. M.* (1974); Solotaroff, R., *Down M.'s Way* (1974); Zavarzadeh,

Norman Mailer

M., *The Mythopoeic Reality: The Postwar American Nonfiction Novel* (1976): 153–76; McConnell, F. D., *Four Postwar American Novelists* (1977): 58–107; Bufithis, P., *N. M.* (1978)

—GEOFFREY GREEN

MAIS, Roger

Jamaican novelist, short-story writer, dramatist, poet, and journalist, b. 11 Aug. 1905, Kingston; d. 20 June 1955, Kingston

M., a passionate advocate of cultural and political nationalism, is a central figure in the development of modern Caribbean literature. One of eight children, M. spent part of his childhood on a coffee plantation in the Blue Mountains to which his family moved in 1912. Here he was taught mainly at home by his mother. When he later returned to Kingston, M. attended Calabar High School for three years. He earned the terminal certificate, the Senior Cambridge, in 1922.

M. turned increasingly to writing after brief careers as civil servant, photographer, education officer, insurance salesman, overseer, and horticulturist, among others. As a journalist, he was an editor for *Jamaica Tit-Bits*, a short-lived Jamaican publication, and continued in this career with the Daily Gleaner, the ranking local newspaper. The turmoil of the 1930s, characterized by labor riots and strikes, led M. to reject eventually the politics and social values of his middle-class background; radicalized by the events of 1938, he became unabashedly nationalist.

Much of M.'s writing was in the short-story genre, a choice that widened his audience. M. brought nationalist criteria to these stories—of which there are some one hundred—insisting on nationalist authenticity to the "real" Jamaica. This meant subject shifts to underprivileged characters, with realistic portrayal of their social environment. The majority of these stories were published in the popular *Public Opinion*, the organ of the People's National Party (PNP), one of the two Jamaican political parties. Others appeared in *Focus* (Jamaica) and *Bim* (Barbados), and some were broadcast on the B.B.C.'s *Caribbean Voices* program. In 1942 M. personally financed the publication of two collections of stories, *Face and Other Stories* and *And Most of All Man*.

M.'s poems also hold a significant place in Caribbean literature. Crafted and eloquent, poems such as "All Men Come to the Hills" (1940) and "Men of Ideas" (1948) are anthologized with frequency.

As a dramatist, M. created over thirty stage and radio plays. The plays were written during a period of furious creativity alongside poetry, including *Masks and Paper Hats* (perf. 1943), *Hurricane* (perf. 1943), and *Atalanta in Calydon* (perf. 1950). Only two of M.'s plays were published. *The Potter's Field* (1950) and *The First Sacrifice* (1956). By 1951 M. had won ten first prizes in West Indian literary competitions.

M. gained notoriety in 1944 when he published the anticolonial essay "Now We Know" in *Public Opinion*. He particularly blamed Winston Churchill for "hypocrisy and deception" toward the colonies. M. was accused of sedition, and jailed by the colonial court for six months. His political act of resistance and defiance earned him the stature of hero among the people.

It is his achievement as a novelist, however, that marks his literary eminence. His first novel, *The Hills Were Joyful Together* (1953), startled readers with its daring content and form, serving to expose the injustices in his society, particularly as experienced by the poor. As a work of social realism, the novel was seen as brutally honest in its representations. Stylistically, it was a tour de force, for it had successfully fused the mode of social realism with an experimental one—a new format suitable to represent the different cultural textuality of the Caribbean "yard" culture. M. showed himself ahead of his time in his second novel, *Brother Man* (1954), in which he intuited the cultural significance of Rastafarianism, the indigenous religion that was then strongly denigrated by the middle class. Allegorical, the novel reworked older biblical myth to symbolize the Rasta character, Brother Man, as a Christ figure. *Black Lightning* (1955), his last published novel, was M.'s least typical narrative. Philosophic, and poetically affective, it dramatized the dilemma of the artist in society, one beset by his own hubris and duality.

M., partly through frustration with his native Jamaica, which he found filled with "philistines"—"Why I Love and Leave Jamaica" (1952)—journeyed to England in August 1952 to continue writing and painting. Later, while residing in France, M. began a novel (*In the Sight of This Sun*) that was never completed. M. became ill with cancer and returned to Jamaica in 1954. Until his death in 1955, M. mainly painted. His unpublished works in typescript, at the Mais Special Collection of the University of the West Indies, include the plays *Atalanta at Calydon, Ordinary People* (perf. 1943), *George William Gordon* (perf. 1949), *Apollo in Delos* (perf. 1950), and *Samson* (perf. 1950), and the critical and theoretical manuscript *Form and Substance in Fiction* (wr. 1942–1943).

M. was a journalist, poet, fiction writer, dramatist, and painter who dedicated his life to art and to achieving nationalism in Jamaica, a colonized country. He saw the major task of writers as that of creating national culture and identity. His influence continues in the "new" literature that finds its sources in the indigenous peoples, culture, and language of the now postcolonial society. M. was awarded the Order of Jamaica posthumously in 1978.

FURTHER WORKS: *Another Ghost in Arcady* (1942); *The Seed in the Ground* (1943); *Blood on the Moon* (1950); *Storm Warning* (1950)

BIBLIOGRAPHY: Hearne, J., "R. M.—A Personal Memoir," R. M. Supplement, *Daily Gleaner* (Jamaica), (10 June 1966): 2; Carr, W. I., "R. M.—Design from a Legend," *CarQ*, 13 (1967): 3–28; Creary, J., "A Prophet Armed: The Novels of R. M.," in James, L., ed., *The Islands in Between* (1968): 50–63; Ramchand, K., "The Achievement of R. M.," *The West Indian Novel and Its Background* (1970): 179–88; Lacovia, R. M., "R. M.: An Approach to Suffering and Freedom," *Blacki*, 1 (1972): 7–11; Brathwaite, E., Introduction to *Brother Man* (1974): v–xxi; D'Costa, J., *R. M*, (1978); Morris, D., Introduction to *The Hills Were Joyful Together* (1981): iii–xxii; Hawthorne, E. J., "Power from Within: Christianity, Rastafarianism, and Obeah in the Novels of R. M.," *Journal of West Indian Literature*, 2,2 (Oct. 1988): 23–32; Hawthorne, E. J., *The Writer in Transition: R. M. and the Decolonization of Caribbean Culture* (1989)

—EVELYN J. HAWTHORNE

MAJEROVÁ, Marie

Czechoslovak novelist and short-story writer (writing in Czech), b. 1 Feb. 1882, Uvaly; d. 16 Jan. 1967, Prague

M.'s writing, with its ideological bent toward socialism, was shaped by the experiences of her working-class childhood and adolescence. Her first years were spent in Prague. In 1894 the family moved to Kladno, a major center of heavy industry based on coal and iron ore. There the intellectually precocious girl discovered the joys of reading and assimilated the defiant spirit of nascent Czech proletarian consciousness. In the cosmopolitan atmosphere of Vienna, where she moved with her husband, M. turned to writing and also participated in the general strike of 1905. Under the influence of the Czech poet Stanislav Kostka Neumann (1875–1947), she was first drawn to social anarchism. A stay in Paris—the writers, including Romain ROLLAND she met there; the lectures she heard—led to a decisive break with the politics of anarchism, later recorded in her second novel, *Náměstí Republiky* (1914; Place de la République). In 1908 she officially joined the Czech Social Democratic Party and in 1921 was a founding member of the Communist Party of Czechoslovakia. In 1947 the Czechoslovak government awarded her the title of National Artist.

M.'s first novel, *Panenství* (1907; virginity), deals with the fashionable fin-de-siècle issue of woman's virginity in the grim social context of the proletarian condition. In spite of its melodramatic dénouement, the novel shows originality in its characterization and use of atmosphere. The central crisis of the plot places the heroine, a spirited servant girl, between two equally strong imperatives. Her devotion to an impoverished young journalist prompts her secretly to offer her virginity to a senile rake in exchange for enough money to obtain medical care for her consumptive beloved. When the sacrificial instant is upon her, the body's instinct for health prevails, and she runs away with her honor intact.

M.'s interest in the woman question never waned. In a collection of short stories, *Mučenky* (1921; the women martyrs), she casts an ironic but compassionate eye on the fate of middle-class women trapped by the hypocrisies of the double standard of sexual morality and by their own romantic delusions.

M.'s masterpiece is the novel *Siréna* (1935; *The Siren*, 1953). It is a chronicle of three generations of the Hudec family, iron and coal workers of Kladno. The theme of generations interacts with the historical and social background. The action, which begins in the 1850s and ends around 1918, illustrates the region's progression toward industrialization, with the accompanying emergence of class consciousness among the workers, who take their time shedding the more individualistic guild attachments. The dominant personality of a woman spans the life of the three generations: Hudcovka's village roots prove a solid foundation for her role as daughter-in-law, wife, and mother of workers and rebels. The linguistic texture of this novel is rich and varied, with M. drawing on the resources of the regional idiom. Her description of the 1905 strike, which briefly closed all the coal mines of the Austrian Empire, has the raw, convincing quality of an eyewitness account.

M. was a prolific writer of novels, short stories, and feuilletons whose lifelong commitment to socialism earned her the reputation of being the leading Czech SOCIALIST REALIST. Her writings are widely translated in all socialist countries. Her major novel *Siréna*, however, stands on its own as a fine example of pure realism.

FURTHER WORKS: *Povídky z pekla a jiné* (1907); *Plané milování* (1908); *Nepřítel v domě* (1909); *Dcery země* (1910); *Červené kvítí* (1911); *Rézinka* (1912); *Čarovný svět* (1913); *Zlatý pramen* (1918); *Z luhů a hor* (1919); *Ze Slovenska* (1920); *Dojmy z Ameriky* (1920); *Nejkrásnější svět* (1923); *Zázračná hodinka* (1923); *Den po revoluci* (1925); *Pohled do dílny* (1929); *Bruno* (1930); *Přehrada* (1932); *Parta na křižovatce* (1933); *Africké vteřiny* (1933); *Kde je Charlie?* (1934); *Květná neděle* (1936); *Výlet do Československa* (1937); *Havířská balada* (1938; *Ballad of a Miner*, 1960); *Robinsonka* (1940); *Město ve znamení ohně* (1940); *Nespokojený králíček* (1946); *Deset tisíc kilometrů nad Sovětským svazem* (1948); *Cesta blesku* (1949); *Pravda veliké doby* (1950); *Sebrané spisy* (19 vols., 1952–1961)

BIBLIOGRAPHY: Mihailovich, V. D., et al., eds., *Modern Slavic Literatures* (1976), Vol. II: 148–51; Novák, A., *Czech Literature* (1976): 285–88

—MARIA NĚMCOVÁ BANERJEE

MAJOR, Clarence

American novelist, poet, short-story writer, lexicographer, and critic, b. 31 Dec. 1936, Atlanta, Georgia

In addition to being a writer adapt in several genres, M. is also a painter and photographer. Moving from Atlanta to Chicago at a young age, by his teens M. had become fascinated by impressionist art. M. entered the Art Institute of Chicago, but soon found that his interests and talents were geared more toward literature than visual art; his early training in visual arts has stayed with him, however, and has influenced the formal and presentational quality of his literary works. M. founded and edited *Coercion Review* (1958-61), and, after moving to New York in 1966, participated in the Umbra Workshop (though never formally becoming a member). In 1967 M. began teaching in high schools in the New York City area, and publishing anthologies of his students' work; M. also became an associate editor of the *Journal of Black Poetry* during the 1960s, completed his first published the novel *All-Night Visitors* (1969), and embarked on his first major editorial job, the anthology *New Black Poetry* (1969). In the mid-1970s M. helped found the Fiction Collective to publish and publicize the works of more experimental writers who were being ignored by the mainstream presses. Since then, M. has been employed as a steel worker, a newspaper reporter, and has taught at several universities; since 1989 he has been a professor of English at University of California at Davis. M. has published twelve volumes of poetry, eight novels, a collection of short stories, edited six anthologies of poetry and fiction, written a work of literary criticism, and compiled a dictionary of African-American slang. The variety of M.'s interests and experiences, his concern for promoting the work of others, and his interdisciplinary leanings underlie the vital aesthetic presence of has literary achievements.

M.'s best work is formally experimental as well as socially and politically engaged, evincing a Brechtian, self-reflexive edge. While M.'s first novel, *All-Night Visitors*, is experimental by default in that the original manuscript was cut by one-half, "poetically" emphasizing the surreal, psychosexual aspects of scenes, but excising passages that developed character motivation, his second novel, *NO* (1973), best demonstrates the avant-garde style that would become M.'s hallmark. Generic conventions of fiction, such as narrative point of view and character development, as well as the linguistic integrity of the novel are challenged. A third-person point of view becomes a first-person voice, and character identities collapse into one another; as in *All-Night Visitors*, psychosexual imagery dominates (blood, human excrement, sexual organs), but racism emerges more sharply as a theme. The page space itself breaks the conventions of block print and functions as a canvas, a visual field of irregular word and line spacing, italics, capitalization, various type fonts, and hand drawing, enacting the central character's confusion about his own identity in a world of stifling racial stereotypes and socioreligious prohibitions. The novel makes us (uncomfortably) aware of the role of language and cultural codes in constructing our experience of the world and a sense of ourselves (our "selves").

Emergency Exit (1979), like *NO*, deconstructs narrative structure (this time through a digressive, episodic structure) while parodying sociocultural conventions. In the novel the Ingram family, living in a small Connecticut town, is compelled (along with other residents) by local statute to adhere to social customs deriving from antiquated, Anglocentric romance traditions. Though more Swiftian in intent then *NO*, as in the former novel the narrator's and characters' voices often blend, and the "text" itself is a assemblage of verbal and visual material, including lists, schedules, catalogues, charts, epigraphs, poems, paintings, and word and image collages. As in *NO*, *Emergency Exit* demonstrates the manner in which sociocultural discourses construct the nature of our experience—our being in the world—to the point of no (except through disruptive articulations arising from a state of urgency) exit.

M.'s poetry also evidences a stylistic restlessness and sociopolitical awareness. *Swallow the Lake* (1970) traverses a wide territory of styles—from straightforward narratives and personal lyrics to more opaque literary constructs—and themes—from the private (personal relationships) to the public (the inequities of war and racial conflict). The poems in *Swallow the Lake* and later volumes, such as *Symptoms & Madness* (1971) and *Parking Lots* (1992), a collaborative work with illustrations by Laura Dronzek, put the sociocultural status quo on trial both in their form and content, suggesting that social change means first and foremost a change of mind, an alteration in the way we think and the means through which we perceive and articulate our world.

Perhaps M.'s belief in the close relationship between language and identity has led to his interest in lexicography. The *Dictionary of Afro-American Slang* (1970) presents slang usage as a way of cutting against and through hegemonic discourse, as well as opening a space for marginalized voices. M. also indicates how the texture of American English is being actively altered by verbalizations from nontraditional sources.

Although M. had a regular column in the *American Poetry Review* from 1973 to 1976, he is perhaps best known as a critic for his collection of essays and reviews, *The Dark and Feeling: Black American Writers and Their Work* (1974), in which M. comments on the social and formal constraints that African-American novelists have had to struggle against; he also discusses the Black Arts movement in the 1960s and its impact on his own prosody. The second and third sections of the collection contain book reviews and biocritical sketches of African-American authors, and the closing section contains primarily interviews and the first of his *American Poetry Review* columns, "On Censorship," a polemical response to a local newspaper's condemnation of a 1972 poetry reading M. gave in northwestern Connecticut. The book is significant not so much for its commentary of other writers as its limning of M.'s aesthetic and sociopolitical orientation.

M.'s work continues to play a significant role in postmodern, and especially African-American literature. His formally exploratory poetry and prose, his sometimes direct and sometimes parodic criticism of ideology (depending on the genre he is working within), and his celebration and promotion of the writings of other minority authors make M.'s multifaceted, genre-bending works a vital presence in the African-American literary scene.

FURTHER WORKS: *The Fires That Burn in Heaven* (1954); *Love Poems of a Black Man* (1965); *Human Juices* (1966); *Private Line* (1971); *The Cotton Club* (1972); *The Syncopated Cakewalk* (1974); *Reflex and Bone Structure* (1975); *Inside Diameter: The France Poems* (1985); *My Amputations* (1986); *Such Was the Season*(1987); *Surfaces and Masks* (1987); *Some Observations of a Stranger at Zuni in the Latter Part of the Century* (1988); *Painted Tuille: Woman with Guitar* (1988); *Fun & Games* (1990); *Parking Lots* (1992); *Dirty Bird Blues: A Novel* (1996)

BIBLIOGRAPHY: Klinkowitz, J., "Notes on a Novel-in-Progress: C., "M.'s *Emergency Exit*," *BALF*, 13 (1979): 46-50; Bolling, D., "A Reading of C. M.'s Short Fiction," *BALF*, 13 (1979): 51-56; Mackey, N., "To Define an Ultimate Dimness: Deconstruction in C. M.'s Poems," *BALF*, 13 (1979): 61-68; Bradfield, L. D., "Beyond Mimetic Exhaustion: The *Reflex and Bone Structure* Experiment," *BALF*, 17 (1983): 120-23; McCaffery, L., and J. Kutnik, "Beneath a Precipice: An Interview with C. M.," *Some *Other Fluency: Interviews with Innovative American Authors* (1996): 241-64

—TOM LAVAZZI

MAKSIMOVIĆ, Desanka

Yugoslav poet, translator, short-story writer, novelist, travel writer, and children's-book writer (writing in Serbian), b. 16 May 1898, Rabrovica (near Valjevo); d. 12 Feb. 1992, Belgrade

M. grew up in Brankovina and Valjevo, in an area where the people were strongly aware of the Serbian national heritage and heroic traditions. She studied comparative literature, world history, and history of art at the University of Belgrade (1919–23) and in Paris (1924–25). Upon graduation she was appointed a high-school teacher in Belgrade and remained in that position until her retirement in 1953. Recipient of innumerable literary awards and honors, she has been a member of Serbian Academy of Sciences and Arts since 1959.

In her very first collection, *Pesme* (1924; poems), M. emerged as a sensitive lyric poet, fascinated with nature, of which she has felt an integral part and in which she has confided and searched for joy, beauty, and comfort ever since. M.'s prewar poetic work includes mainly love and descriptive poems in which the poet confesses her own youthful anxieties and curiosity in front of the great mysteries of life and love. As she matured M. widened the scope and depth of her preoccupations, and her poetry came to have a more universal character. The suffering of her nation in World War II inspired a series of beautiful, humane patriotic poems, of which *Krvava bajka* (1946; *A Legend of Blood*, 1962), occasioned by the German massacre of school-boys in Kragujevac in 1941, is the best known and most widely translated.

M. reached her peak in the 1960s and 1970s. The collection *Tražim pomilovanje* (1964; I plead for mercy), subtitled "Lyrical Discussions with Tsar Dushan's Medieval Code of Laws," glorifies forgiveness and compassion as the most noble of human virtues. Among those for whom the poet pleads are both the oppressed and the oppressors, the humble and the vain, the naïve and the sly, the poor and the rich, women, monks, soldiers, sinners, and dreamers—all her fellow human beings. In the collection *Nemam više vremena* (1973; my time is running short) the aging poet meditates on death and dying and reminisces about the passing of her loved ones. With calm resignation, M. accepts death as a component of life and prepares herself for the last journey, which for her means returning to nature and merging with eternity.

Like many great literary figures, M. does not belong to any specific 20th-c. literary movement or fad. Anything that might have influenced her is filtered through the prism of her own talent and her strong poetic individuality and is fully and harmoniously integrated in an entirely original poetic whole. With its accent on love, beauty, and universal ethical principles, her poetry, written in a superb style, represents M.'s most valuable contribution to Serbian literature. In addition, she has presented to Yugoslav readers many outstanding Slavic and French writers in excellent translations, and has been a prolific and popular author of literature for children and young adults. Besides poetry, she wrote several novels and many short stories for young people, all of which abound with lyricism and with beautiful descriptions of nature. They are aimed not only at entertaining young readers but at developing in them ethical values and love and respect for their fellow human beings.

M.'s travel books, *Praznici putovanja* (1972; the festive days of traveling) and *Snimci iz Švajcarske* (1978; snapshots from Switzerland), provide a valuable insight into the poet's personality. In both of them M. focuses her attention on her favorite subjects: the people whom she met during her many travels, and the natural beauties of the places she visited.

One of the few best-selling poets of our nonpoetic era, her opus has become an integral part of Serbian national culture.

FURTHER WORKS: *Zeleni vitez* (1930); *Ludilo srca* (1931); *Gozba na livadi* (1932); *Kako oni žive* (1935); *Nove pesme* (1936); *Oslobodjenje Cvete Andrić* (1945); *Pesnik i zavičaj* (1946); *Otadžbina u prvomajskoj povorci* (1949); *Izabrane pesme* (1950); *Otadžbino, tu sam* (1951); *Otvoren prozor* (1954); *Strašna igra* (1954); *Miris zemlje* (1955); *Izabrane pjesme* (1958); *Buntovan razred* (1960); *Zarobljenik snova* (1960); *Govori tiho* (1961); *Pesme* (1963); *Pesme* (1964); *Pesme* (1965); *Pesme* (1966); *Pesme* (1966); *Deset mojih pesama* (1967); *Pesme* (1967); *Stihovi* (1967); *Vratnice* (1968); *Ne zaboraviti* (1969); *Sabrana dela* (7 vols., 1969); *Verujem* (1969); *Pradevojčica* (1970); *Izabrane pesme* (1972); *Izbor iz dela* (1974); *Letopis Perunovih potomaka* (1976); *Pesme iz Norveške* (1976); *Pjesme* (1977); *Ničija zemlja* (1979); *Izbrana dela: Poezija* (5 vols., 1980). FURTHER WORKS IN ENGLISH: *Greetings from the Old Country* (1976, bilingual)

BIBLIOGRAPHY: Klančar, A. J., on *Nove pesme, BA*, 11 (1937), 512; Petrov, A., on *Tražim pomilovanje, IBSB*, 15 (1964): 267–68; Mihailovich, V. D., on *Tražim pomilovanje, BA*, 40 (1966), 355; Matejić, M., on *Neman više vremena, BA*, 48 (1974): 395–96; Surdučki, M., Preface to D. M., *Greetings from the Old Country* (1976): ix–xiv; Šljivić-Šimšić, B., on *Letopis Perunovih potomaka, WLT*, 51 (1977): 305–6; Eekman, T., *Thirty Years of Yugoslav Literature (1945–1975)* (1978): 25–26

—BILJANA ŠLJIVIĆ-ŠIMŠIĆ

MALAGASY LITERATURE

In Malagasy

Written literature in the Malagasy language dates back to the mid-19th c. and the creation of an alphabet for the Malagasy language in 1823. Shortly afterwards, European missionaries began to found schools to teach the Malagasy to read and write in their own language. The first major publication, the Malagasy Bible followed in 1835. The first periodical, a religious journal entitled *Teny Soa* commenced publication in 1866, reaching a circulation of 3,000 by 1875. Several other religious magazines issued by European missionary presses made their appearance in the course of the 19th c., notably *Ny Isankeritaona, Ny Mpanolo-Tsaina, Ny Resaka, Ny Mpamafy*, and *Sadaizan 'ny tanora. Ny Gazety Malagasy* and *Vaovaom-panjakana* belong to the growing number of secular Malagasy-language journals emerging during the same period. These journals provided reading and writing opportunities for Madagascar's growing literate population and inaugurated a tradition of writing for local journals that persisted well into the 20th c.

The most significant Malagasy-language publications in the 19th c. were historical, religious, or ethnographic in orientation. Literary writing in Malagasy began to flourish after the onset of French colonial rule in 1896, despite the application of a decree enforcing the French language as the sole medium of communication in Madagascar's schools. Aspiring writers found a forum for their works in a new generation of secular magazines that were unaffiliated with the European missions or the French colonial administration. Several writers in the early decades of the 20th c. combined their creative activity with journalism and the editing of literary journals, notably Edouard Andrianjafintrimo (1881-1972), Jasmina Ratsimiseta (1890-1946), and Justin Rainizanabololona (1861-1938). Poetry, the short story, and serialized novels were the most suited to publication in this setting, and became increasingly dominant. Many poets of the colonial period such as Ester Razandrasoa (1893-1931), Samuel Ratany (1901-1926), and J. H. Rabekoto (1902-1932) were known only in Madagascar's small literary journals. Most literary texts were, however, never published outside of these journals so that actual book publications do not begin to give an idea of the vibrant literary culture in early-20th-c. Madagascar.

Sentimental and gothic themes were popular in the early novels. Andriamatoa Rabary's (1864-1947) *Nivoah and Rafanoela* (1933; Rafaniola's Exit) is typical of this style. Auguste Rajaonarivelo (1890-1957) deviates from this trend with his more ethnographic and sympathetic portrayal of a particular Malagasy ethnic group in his novel *Bina* (1933; Bina). The early 20th c. witnessed the development of a distinctive and Malagasy dramatic form combining the traditional dances of the *hira gasy* with French music hall. Social commentary and romance featured in plays such as Dondavitra's (pseud. of Charles-Aubert Razafimahefa, 1880-1936) *Peratra Mahavariana* (perf. 1906; The Magic Ring). Rodlish (pseud. of Arthur Razakarivony, 1897-1967) became the most popular of the playwrights of the early colonial period with *Ranomody* (1926; The Whirlpool) and *Sangy mahery* (1936; Violent Games). Other dramatists such as Tselatra Rajaonah (1863-1931) and Naka Rabermanantsoa (1892-1943) are still remembered as major figures in the vibrant dramatic life of early-20th-c. Madagascar, even though their numerous plays were never published in book form. Hymnbooks published by the missions exercised a considerable influence on Malagasy poetry, and resulted in the emergence of a new written poetry rather unlike the traditional *hain-teny*, the oral poetry of the Malagasy. Justin Rainizanabololona, playwright, journalist, and poet, is credited with codifying the new system of Malagasy versification. Jean Narivony (dates n.a.) produced the earliest anthology of poetry, *Amboara voafantina* (1926; Selected Poems) in conjunction with his uncle Rodlish, the playwright. The colonial period was increasingly associated with the development of a nostalgic and melancholy poetry expressing the pain of lost independence. Ny Avana Ramanantoanina (1891-1940) who wrote in this mode is often considered one of Madagascar's greatest poets. His collected works are available in *Anthologie* (1992; Anthology) published posthumously.

The nostalgic tradition continued in the later colonial period in the works of poets like Fredy Fajaofera (1902-1968), the author of *Kintan 'ny mamatonalina* (1930; Midnight Star) and *Sahondran 'avoko* (1931; Two Flowers). Identical sentiments are also evident in the poetry of Dox (pseud. of Jean Verdi Razakandriana, 1913-1979), the author of *Ny Hirako* (1940; My Songs), *Izy mirahavavy* (1946; The Two Sisters), *I Mavo handray fanjakana* (1958; When Mavo Came to Power), *Telomiova* (1965; Tricolor), and *Folihala*

(1968; Spider), among other works. Clarisse Ratsifandrihamanana (b. 1926) inclines towards a more political kind of poetry in her works written after independence in 1960: *Fahavaratra* (1960; The Rainy Season), *Tamberintany* (1961; Vertigo), and *Aritory* (1977; Awake at Night). Emilson Andriamalala (b. 1918) became the dominant novelist of the 1960s and 1970s with *Fofombadilo* (1963; My Fianceé), *Hetraketraka* (1964; Violence), and *Ilay Vohitry ny Nofy* (1972; Legendary City). In comparison to prose and poetry, few plays have been published in contemporary times. However, the dramatic forms pioneered in the early 20th c. by writers like Rodlish remain popular in performance, as do the songs and dances of the more traditional *hira gasy*.

In French

Prior to 1896, and the imposition of French colonial rule in Madagascar, the prospects appeared promising for a growing tradition of Malagasy-language writing, sponsored by European Protestant missionaries. With the advent of French colonial administrators, however, and their determination to promote the French language, literary writing in French gradually gained prominence over the older tradition of Malagasy-language literature. A single author dominates Malagasy writing in French in the early colonial period, Jean-Joseph RABEARIVELO. The first French-language texts produced in colonial Madagascar are his early collections of poetry, *La coupe de cendres* (1924: Cup of Ashes), *Sylves* (1927: Woods), and *Volumes* (1928; Volumes). While Rabearivelo's decision to write in French might have been construed as a betrayal of his native tongue at the time, his work in fact shares parallels with the Malagasy-language poetry of the colonial period. Despite its French symbolist trappings, his poetry communicates a despondency typical of Malagasy and their culture to foreign rulers. Furthermore, for Rabearivelo, writing in French did not supplant composition in Malagasy. Indeed, he was to confirm his continuing commitment to Malagasy-language writing in his last and best-known collections of poetry, *Presque-songes* (1935; Near Dreams) and *Traduit de la nuit* (1936; Translations from the Night), both written in bilingual French-Malagasy format. He also produced a translation of Malagasy traditional poetry, *hain-teny*, into French, *Vielles chansons des pays d'Imerina* (1967; Old Songs from the Merina Country).

Two other poets are associated with the later colonial period. Jacques RABEMANANJARA and Flavien Ranaivo (b. 1914) seem typical of writers belonging to the black cultural movement, NÉGRITUDE in their responses to colonialism. Rabemananjara, more so than Ranaivo, identified with leaders of the Négritude movement like Léopold Sédar SENGHOR during his student days in Paris. Political sentiment is manifest in the vigorous poetry of *Rites millénaires* (1955; Ancient Rites), *Antsa* (1956; Eulogy), *Lamba* (1956; Malagasy Shawl), and *Antidote* (1961; Antidote), where Rabemananjara expresses his devotion to the Malagasy nation and to the cause of its political emancipation. Ranaivo's nationalism, on the other hand, is more cultural than political. The mood in *L'ombre et le vent* (1947; Shadow and Wind), *Mes chansons de toujours* (1955; Songs for All Time), and *Le retour au bercail* (1962; Return to the Fold) is tranquil and lighthearted in a style adapted from the elusive question and answer form of the Malagasy *hain teny*. Like Rabearivelo, Ranaivo undertook his own translation of the *hain-teny* into French in a later publication, *Hain-teny présentés et transcrits du malgache par Flavien Ranaivo*

(1975; Hain-teny Presented and Transcribed from Malagasy by Flavien Ranaivo).

In Rabemananjara's plays, *Les dieux malgaches* (1947; Malagasy Gods), *Les boutriers de l'aurore* (1957; Vessels of the Dawn), *Agape des dieux Tritriva* (1957; Feast of the Tritriva Gods), the style derives from French classical tragedy while the subject matter relates to popular Malagasy myths and tradition had been earlier pioneered by Rabearivelo in his two plays, *Imaitsoanala, fille d'oiseau* (1935; Imaitsoanala, Daughter of a Bird) and *Aux portes de la ville* (1936; At the City Gates). However, neither Rabearivelo nor Rambemananjara's plays in French ever gained the popularity enjoyed by the unpublished Malagasy-language plays of the colonial period. Few novels were published in French during the entire colonial period. Edouard Bezoro's (dates n.a.) *La soeur inconnue* (1932; The Unknown Sister), considered one of the earliest examples of prose from Francophone Africa, is the singular exception. The exact identity of the author has never been confirmed, and appears all the more suspect in the light of the novel's overt identification with the aims of French colonialism and its condemnation of aspects of Malagasy culture. By contrast, Rabearivelo's novel, *L'interférence* (1988; Interference), originally written in 1928 and containing explicit criticism of French colonial activity in Madagascar, was to remain unpublished for the next sixty years.

In 1972 the government attempted to restore writing in Malagasy to its former prominence in Madagascar. The decision to make Malagasy the primary language of instruction and communication however coincided with the onset of a period of economic decline on the island nation. The growing political and economic crisis between 1985 and 1992 gave birth to new generation of Malagasy writers concerned more about the climate of social decay than with cultural nationalism. Writing in French became one means, among others, of effecting social criticism or signifying opposition to specific government policy. Michèle RAKOTOSON, the best-known writer of this new generation, has written three short narratives, *Dadabe et autres nouvelles* (1984; Dadabe and Other Stories), *Le bain des reliques* (1988; Awash in Relics), and *Elle au printemps* (1996; She, in the Spring). She is also the author of two plays *La maison morte* (1991; The Dead Home) and *Un jour, ma mémoire* (1991; Remembrance, One Day). Her plays, like Jean-Luc Raharimanana's (b. 1967) *Le prophète et le président* (1991; The Prophet and the President), project in sparse action and striking language the absurd reasoning of unidentified dictators. David Jaomanoro's (b. 1953) *La retraite* (1990; Retreat) deals with the pressures of poverty on the urban poor. Raharimanana's short stories in *Lepreux* (1992; Leprous) and *Lucarne* (1996; Skylight) focus on similar issues as he recounts an extreme inhumanity propelled by poverty. Charlotte Rafenomanjato (b. 1936) differs somewhat from these other writers in her more symbolic presentation of social injustice and upheaval in the novel *Le cinquième sceau* (1993; The Fifth Seal), and in the concentration on the power of tradition in *La pétale écarlate* (1991; Scarlet Petal). Rabemananjara continues to write, but has been in exile since the 1970s. The themes of his recent lyric poetry in works like *Rien qu'encens et filigrane* (1987; Only Incense and Filigree) clearly contrasts with the pessimism and emphasis on poverty and social decline reflected in the works of the younger generation of Malagasy writers.

BIBLIOGRAPHY: Gérard, A., "The Birth of Theater in Madagascar," *ETJ*, 6 (1973): 362-64; Wake, C., "J.-J. Rabearivelo—A Poet before Négritude," in Wright, E., ed., *The Critical Evaluation of African Literature* (1973): 149-72; Breier, U., "Rabearivelo,"

Introduction to African Literature (1979): 99-104; Gérard, A., *African Language Literatures* (1981); Rajemisa-Raolison, R., *Les poètes malgaches d'expression française* (1983); Bemananjara, Z., and Ramamonjisoa, S.-A., "Malagasy Literature in Madagascar," in Andrzejewski, B., W., S. Pitaszewicz, and Tyloch, W., eds., *Literatures in African Languages: Theoretical Issues and Sample Surveys* (1985): 426-57; Adejunmobi, M., "African Language Writing and Writers: A Case Study of Jean-Joseph Rabearivelo and Ny Avana in Madagascar," *ALC*, 7 (1994): 1-18; Ramarasoa, L., *Anthologie de la littérature Malgache d'expression Française des années*, 80 (1994); Adejunmobi, M., *J.-J. Rabearivelo, Literature and Lingua Franca in Colonial Madagascar* (1996)

—MORADEWUN A. ADEJUNMOBI

al-MALĀ'IKA, Nāzik

Iraqi poet and critic, b. 23 Aug. 1922, Baghdad

M. comes from a cultured, literary family, and her mother, Um Nizār al-Malā'ika, was herself a poet. She studied first at the Higher Teachers' Training College in Baghdad, then at the University of Wisconsin, where she obtained an M.A. in literature in 1956. Both as poet and critis M. enjoys an eminent place in modern Arabic literature. Her courage, her genuine creative energy, and her pioneering spirit enabled her to launch, at the end of the 1940s, in conjunction with her compatriot Badr Shākir AL-SAYYĀB, the freeverse movement, which is the most radical revolution ever in the form of the Arabic poem.

For over fifteen centuries formal Arabic poetry had sustained the monorhymed, two-hemistich form characterized by a fixed number of feet in each line and by symmetry and balance. Influenced by readings in foreign poetries, 20th-c. Arab poets launched a sustained effort to break the domination of this form and create their own. It was M. and al-Sayyāb who eventually succeeded in this, building on earlier contemporary experiments. The freeverse movement was launched with the publication of M.'s second collection, *Shazāyā wa ramād* (1949; sharpnel and ashes), which had eleven freeverse poems and a preface in which M. elucidated the advantages of this new form. The most heated debate in the history of Arab poetics ensued in the 1950s, in which M. took a leading role on the side of free-verse writing; at the same time, she produced some of the most original poems of the period, thus giving concrete proof of her argument. By the end of the 1950s, M.'s theories on poetry, which she published in consecutive articles, had developed greatly in sophistication and depth. The publication of her collected articles, *Qadaya 'l-shi'r al-mu'āsir* (1962; issues in contemporary poetry), was a major event, producing yet again a heated argument against some of the principles she laid down to secure free verse against what she believed to be its inherent chaotic freedom. The appearance of this book showed how necessary it was to reexamine the bold free-verse venture.

M.'s studies abroad helped her formulate her critical method based on the concepts of the NEW CRITICISM which concentrates on the literary work itself rather than on its sources and effects, or on the poet's social and psychological background.

It was also in the early 1950s that M. advocated a revolutionary feminist stance. In two resounding lectures that shocked the audience of the time, "Al-mar'a baina 'l-tarafain, al-salbiyya wa 'l-akh-lāq'" (1953; woman between passivity and positive morality),

and "Al-tajzi'iyya fi 'l-mujtama' al-Arabī" (1954; fragmentation in Arab society), she expounded, with unrivaled skill and incisiveness, her argument concerning women's historical grievances in a patriarchal, oppressive society, and her faith in woman's capacity to excel in all avenues of artistic and intellectual life. Although her religious revivalism since the late 1960s has introduced a moralistic streak into her writings, her faith in women's capabilities has never weakened.

In its eloquence, terseness of language, and strength of structure, M.'s poetry stems from the heart of the Arab poetic tradition, but in all other respects she is highly innovative. Her poetry passed through three phases: Throughout the 1940s it was introverted and characterized by romantic sorrow and despair; in her second phase, lasting throughout the 1950s and most of the 1960s, she produced her best and greatly modernized poetry, which demonstrated a wide versatility of themes and a great originality in the manipulation of form, diction, and metaphor. At the end of the 1960s M. turned to a more conservative approach, writing on Islamic and nationalistic themes and resorting often to the two-hemistich form. Some of her poetry during this phase acquired an ardent tone of Islamic piety.

In her best poetry M. is versatile, inventive, and unique, producing poems of high quality that lay bare the general dilemma of life in the Arab world and, while preserving a personal approach to universal problems, often explore the predicament of the human condition in general. M.'s vocabulary is senusous, fresh, and unadulterated by use, and in many of her poems, which include some of the religious poems she wrote in the 1970s, she employs a diction of ecstasy and ardor. There is a search for original metaphors and for rare epithets in her work, and she can string them together in ways that produce aesthetic rapture. In several poems she resorts to the use of verbal paradoxes, but in others, such as "Al-shakhs al-thānī" (1951; the second person) and "Al-za'ir al-ladhī lam yaji'" (1952; the visitor who never came), both poems in *Qarārat al-mawja* (1958; the trough of the wave), she employs broad paradoxes of wit that inform the whole poem, modifying dramatically our preconceived concepts of things. She also uses complex symbols, some, as in her poem "Al-uf'uwān" (1948; the serpent), entertaining double interpretation, where the personal and the communal are merged.

M. has worked as a university lecturer and professor, spending many years at the University of Kuwait, from which she took an early retirement. A festschrift was published in her honor in Kuwait in 1985, edited by 'Abdallah al-Muhanna (dates n.a.), containing twenty articles on her work.

M. has kept a diary all her life. When and if it is published, it should illuminate many aspects of Iraqi and Arab cultural, social, and political experience during a great part of the 20th c., offered from the point of view of one of its most brilliant Arab women writers.

There is much to be learned from M.'s deep concern for and love of poetry, her delicate ear for the music of verse, her great confidence and courage, her steadfast adherence to her artistic and moral principles, and, above all, her technical precision, her adroit handling of language and metaphor, and her great thematic range.

FURTHER WORKS: *'Āshiqat al-layl* (1947); *Shir'r Alī Mahmūd Tāhā* (1965); *Shajarat al-qamar* (1968); *Ma'sāt al-hayāt wa ughniyat al-insān* (1970); *Almajmū'a 'l-kāmila* (2 vols., 1971); *Al-tajzi'yya fi 'l-mujtama' al-'Arabī* (1974); *Yughayyiru alwanahu 'l-bahr* (1977); *Li 'l-salāt wa 'l-thawra* (1978)

BIBLIOGRAPHY: Rossi, P., "Impressions sur la poésie d'Iraq. Jawahiri, Mardan, N. al-M., Bayati," *Orient*, 12 (1959): 199–212; Stewart, D., "Contacts with Arab Writers," *Middle East Forum*, 37 (Jan. 1961): 19–21; Martinez, M. L., "N. al-M." *Cuadernos de la Biblioteca Espanola de Tétuar*, (1964), Vol. 2: 75–82; Rejwan, N., "Rejecting Europe's Cultural Influence: Protest of an Iraqi Poetess," *Jewish Observer and Middle East Review*, 15, 22 (3 March 1966): 16–17; Wiett, G., *Introduction à la littérature arabe* (1966): 302–3; Moreh, S., "N. al-M. and al-shi'r al-hurr in Modern Arabic Literature," *AAS*, 4 (1968): 57–84; Vernet, J., *Literatura árabe* (1968): 212–45; Montavez, P. M., "Aspectos de la actual literatura femina árabe," *Almenara*, 1 (1971): 85–110; Altoma, S., "Postwar Iraqi Literature: Agonies of Rebirth," *BA*, 46 (1972): 211–13; Badawi, M. M., *A Critical Introduction to Modern Arabic Poetry* (1975): 143–44: 225–26: 228–30; Moreh, S., *Modern Arabic Poetry* 1800–1970: *The Development of Its Forms and Themes under the Influences of Western Literature* (1976): 213–15 and passim; Fernea, E. W., and Bezirgan, B. Q., eds., *Middle Eastern Muslim Women Speak* (1977): 331–49; Jayyusi, S. K., *Trends and Movements in Modern Arabic Poetry* (1977), Vol. 1: 557–60: 672–73; Montavez, P. M., *Literatura iraqui contemporanea*, 2nd ed. (1977): 65–68, 155–56, 373–85; Berque, J., *Cultural Expression in Arab Society Today* (1978), passim; Abdul-Hai, M., *Tradition and English and American Influence in Arabic Romantic Poetry* (1982): 27–29: 110–12, 119; Ayyad, S., and Witherspoon, N., *Reflections and Deflections: A Study of the Contemporary Arab Mind through Its Literary Creations* (1986): 135–37

—SALMA KHADRA JAYYUSI

MALAMUD, Bernard

American novelist and short-story writer, b. 26 April 1914, Brooklyn, N.Y.; d. 18 Mar. 1986, New York, N.Y.

Born to Russian-Jewish immigrant parents, M. spent his childhood and much of his adult life in New York. He attended City College, where he received his B.A. in 1936. After working for several years as a clerk for the Bureau of the Census in Washington, D.C., M. returned to New York, teaching evening high school and earning his M.A. in English from Columbia University in 1942. In 1949 he accepted a position in the English Department at Oregon State University, where he remained for the next twelve years. In 1961 he joined the faculty of Bennington College, Vermont. He served as a visiting lecturer at Harvard University and traveled extensively in Europe.

M.'s fiction, although difficult to classify, often has its roots in the Jewish experience—both ancient and modern. His prose style alternates between surrealistic fantasy (his stories have been compared to the paintings of Marc Chagall) and detailed realism. The themes of suffering, redemption, and moral responsibility recur throughout his work, from his early short stories to his latest novels.

M.'s first novel, *The Natural* (1952), stands apart as his only work without Jewish characters or background. Nevertheless, the theme of suffering and the myth of salvation, which dominate much of M.'s later fiction, are central to the novel. Here, however, M. presents a vision of man defeated rather than renewed. Roy Hobbs, the novel's mythical baseball hero, does not possess the sense of moral responsibility that redeems many of M.'s later

Jewish characters. Roy fails to learn from his experiences, and the novel ends on a note of loss and despair.

In relation to M.'s subsequent fiction, *The Natural* appears uneven and overly reliant on its mythological allusions and structure. *The Assistant* (1957), by contrast, is one of M.'s most satisfying achievements. The novel is pessimistic in tone and starkly realistic in its presentation of the bleak, urban world of New York City. Imprisoned within his failing grocery store, Morris Bober, like many of M.'s Jewish immigrants, struggles against the overpowering forces of his environment. But the book's focus is on Frank Alpine, the grocer's assistant, who undergoes a transformation from victimizer to helper and from Christian to Jew. More than anything else in the novel, Frank's conversion represents M.'s belief in man's capacity for renewal and for self-creation.

A New Life (1961), as the title indicates, continues M.'s exploration of the theme of redemption. S. Levin, the novel's protagonist, journeys from his native New York to the Northwest in search of a new beginning as a college English instructor. Levin, the archetypal Jewish schlemiel, is more bungler than moral hero, and his exploits at Cascadia College are more comic than serious. But like Frank Alpine, Levin grows and changes and ultimately learns to accept the weight of moral entanglement.

Similarly, Yakov Bok, the hero of *The Fixer* (1966)—the novel for which M. received both the National Book Award and the Pulitzer Prize—comes to understand that the path to true redefinition of self is difficult and intricate. The novel represents the culmination of M.'s earlier themes and motifs and is considered by many to be his most successful effort. Here the metaphor of man imprisoned is translated into physical reality, and the story of Bok (based on the famous Mendel Beiliss case in tsarist Russia) becomes the perfect vehicle for M.'s themes of redemptive suffering, moral growth, and the acceptance of one's fate.

M.'s two novels of the 1970s, *The Tenants* (1971) and *Dubin's Lives* (1979), take greater risks and make greater demands on the reader than his previous works. Although they both demonstrate M.'s willingness to strike out in new directions, neither contains the rich and complex view of human existence presented in his earlier novels and stories. *The Tenants* ironically and pessimistically depicts the bitter and fatal struggle between two writers: one Jewish, the other black. The issue is once again man's moral involvement with his fellow man, but M. concludes The *Tenants* with an image of apocalyptic destruction. With *Dubin's Lives*, M. departed from all but the slightest connection with the Jewish experience, as well as with former themes. The motif of death and resurrection is present, but only in relation to the artistic and sexual endeavors of William Dubin, the novel's central figure. Intricate in its exposition of the character of Dubin, the novel contains some of M.'s finest prose but remains somewhat confined within its limited thematic concerns.

Perhaps M.'s greatest achievement lies in his short stories, especially those collected in his first volume, *The Magic Barrel* (1958), for which M. received his first National Book Award. The most successful of these—"The Magic Barrel" and "The Last Mohican," for example—possess a haunting magical quality that brings the reader to an understanding of the mystery of human existence. M. writes of misery and suffering, yet there remains throughout these stories the suggestion of fragile optimism.

At the center of M.'s fiction is the possibility of human growth, of man's ability to transcend old, unsatisfactory roles and to create new, more positive ones. In his finest works, of which *The Assistant, The Fixer*, and several of the early short stories are the best examples, there is a carefully balanced view of existence: an understanding of man's defeats and an appreciation of his triumphs. M. remains one of the few contemporary authors who has made us feel the richness of his moral imagination and the force of his affirmative vision.

FURTHER WORKS: *Idiots First* (1963); *A M. Reader* (1967); *Pictures of Fidelman: An Exhibition* (1969); *Rembrandt's Hat* (1973); *God's Grace* (1982)

BIBLIOGRAPHY: Richman, S., *B. M.* (1966); Meeter, G., *B. M. and Philip Roth: A Critical Essay* (1968); Field, L., and J. Field, eds., *B. M. and the Critics* (1970); Pinsker, S., *The Schlemiel as Metaphor: Studies in the Yiddish and American Jewish Novel* (1971): 87–124; Ducharme, R., *Art and Idea in the Novels of B. M.: Toward "The Fixer"* (1974); Cohen, S., *B. M. and the Trial by Love* (1974); Field, L., and J. Field, eds., *B. M.: A Collection of Critical Essays* (1975); Astro, R., and J. Benson, eds., *The Fiction of B. M.* (1977); M. special issue, *SAJL*, 4, 1 (1978); Avery, E., *Rebels and Victims: The Fiction of Richard Wright and B. M.* (1979); Alter, I., *The Good Man's Dilemma: Social Criticism in the Fiction of B. M.* (1981)

—STEVEN J. RUBIN

MALAWIAN LITERATURE

Formerly the British Central African Protectorate and member of the defunct Federation of Rhodesia and Nyasaland (1953-63), Malawi became independent on July 6, 1964 and a republic in the following year. However, postindependence up to 1994 Malawi was a one-party state run by the dictator, Dr. Hastings Kamuzu Banda, whose reign came to an end when he was defeated in the first democratic general elections since the end of British rule. The nature of British colonial policy as well as of the postcolonial dictatorship, to a large extent, determined the form and content of Malawian writing. The production of writing in the country is as old as the earliest acquisition of literacy by Malawians, but even so, it is really in the late 1920s, with the encouragement of enlightened missionaries and such organizations as the African Literature Society, that Malawian writers began to write in earnest. During the 1930s the Chinyanja sections of the literary competition organized by the International African Institute based in London attracted such excellent work that it ended up being published in Europe, most notably the novels *Mnyamboza* (1949) and *Headman's Enterprise* (1949) by Samuel Ntara (b. 1905).

Ntara's work stands out as the most significant of its time, but one has to acknowledge that he was but one of the many writers who wrote in local languages: Yao, Lomwe, Tumbuka, Tonga, Sena, and Nkonde, among others. That tradition received a boost with the formation of the Northern Rhodesia and Nyasaland Publication Bureau in the late 1940s, which was aimed at improving literacy by providing locally produced reading material. Although it often supported work promoting specific government policies, it also allowed room for genuinely creative work to be published. Nevertheless, by the time of independence little English-language literature had been produced. There are number of complex reasons for this, one of which was the small size of the local market for literature in general, but also the lack of higher

Bernard Malamud

education facilities in the country. Until the establishment of the University of Malawi in 1965, Malawians traveled to South Africa, Uganda, and Zimbabwe—and in some cases to the U.S. and Britain—for higher education.

It was through one of such educational migrants, Legson Kayira (b. 1940), that Malawi was to boast of the first significant postcolonial piece of creative writing. He published *I Will Try* in 1965, an autobiographical account of his journey from Northern Malawi to the U.S. in search of higher education. Though it is of doubtful literary merit, according to a number of critics, it is a monumental national treasure and its political significance was made more obvious when it was banned by the Banda regime. In his subsequent novels, *The Looming Shadow* (1967), *Jingala* (1969), and *The Civil Servant* (1971), Kayira examines the relationship between tradition and modernity, focusing on such themes as the role of Christianity and the city in the transformation of indigenous cultural identities. In his most overtly political novel, *The Detainee* (1974), he portrays the suffering inflicted on ordinary people by a dictator similar to Banda. Kayira's contribution to the development of Malawian writing has been immense, his international stature being an important source of inspiration to aspiring writers. This is also true of Aubrey Kachingwe (dates n.a.), whose first and only novel, *No Easy Task* (1966), suggested to aspiring Malawian writers that the Heinemann African Writers Series was indeed within the reach of Malawian talent and was not just a preserve of East and West African writers. The novel tells the story of the struggle against colonial rule and the heroism of both ordinary people and their leaders, conveying with an informing vividness the tragic dimensions of the process of decolonization and liberation.

When in 1967, David Rubadiri (b. 1930) published his novel *No Bride Price*, it was another feather in the national cap. The novel, set in Uganda, examines the corruption of power in a post-colonial African state and it is also regarded as one of the first attempts to explore the troubled relations between East African Asians and indigenous African communities. The novel is evidently an accomplished effort, but even more salutary an achievement is Rubadiri's poetry. Poems such as "An African Thunderstorm" (1963) and "Stanley Meets Mukasa" (1976), written long before his novel, are among the most anthologized poems in African literature. He, like Kayira, spent most of the years of the dictatorship in exile. Desmond Dudwa Phiri (dates n.a.), a contemporary of Rubadiri and Kachingwe, began writing in Tumbuka, a local language, before switching to English, with his play, *The Chief's Bride*—first performed in Dar es Salaam 1964 and published in 1968. Phiri has, in addition, published extensively on Malawian political history. Another writer of the same cultural and political generation as Rubadiri, Kachingwe, and Phiri is Murry William Kanyama Chiume (b. 1929) who, like Phiri, began his career writing in Tumbuka, and later produced *Kwacha: An Political Biography* (1975) and *The African Deluge* (1978), a novel. It is also important to record that Chiume has also written in Kiswahili, some of which has been published in Tanzania where he spent his years of exile from 1964 to 1994.

Other writers who wrote in voluntary or forced exile are Frank Chipasula (b. 1950) and Walije Gondwe (b. 1936). Chipasula's *Visions and Reflections* (1973) is the first collection of poetry in English by a Malawian poet. It explored questions of cultural conflict between Africa and the West and also subtly addresses issues of power and leadership, a theme that must have made the regime so visibly uncomfortable as to make Chipasula flee the country in fear of his life. While in exile, he published an excellent anthology of southern African poetry, *When My Brothers Come Home* (1984), and also two collections of his own poetry, *O Earth Wait for Me* (1984) and *Whispers in the Wings* (1991). The most distinctive feature of Chipasula's poetry is his subtle blending of the private and public into a political love poetry in which the usurpation of power by the Malawian dictator is not simply a matter of the corruption of the public space, but also of the poet's most intimate sense of self. Malawi's first woman novelist, Walije Gondwe is the author of *Love's Dilemma* (1985), *Second-hand* (1988), *Love Match* (1989), *Double Dating* (1994), and *I Still Miss Him* (1993), as well as a children's book, *Guitar Wizard* (1993). Principally, her books are in the vein of popular fiction, focusing mostly on romantic love, but her treatment of the theme brings questions of cultural authenticity into the frame, giving her characters a rare depth of psychological and cultural formation in the genre. Gondwe's male counterpart within Malawi is Aubrey Kalitera (dates n.a.) whose brand of popular fiction has attracted some in-depth international critical attention. His publications include *A Taste of Business* (1976), *Why Father, Why* (1982), *Why Mother, Why* (1983), and *Why Son, Why* (1983).

The founding of the University of Malawi in 1965 was a great stimulant to literacy production; in the early 1970s, the Writers Group was formed with the aim of bringing students and teachers together for discussion of their creative work. The workshop included Frank Chipasula, Jack Mapanje (b. 1944), Steve Chimombo (b. 1945), Felix Mnthali (b. 1933), Paul Tiyambe Zeleza (b. 1955),

James Ng'ombe (dates n.a.), Dede Kamkondo (dates n.a.), and Ken Lipenga (dates n.a.), among others, some of whom were also involved with the University Traveling Theater. A number of local magazines served as outlets for the writers' work, notably *Odi*, *Kalulu*, *Outlook*, *Muse*, and *Umodzi*. The weekly *Malawi News* also regularly carried short stories and poems, providing a useful commercial outlet for the emerging writers. In addition, the Writers' Corner and Theater of the Air on Malawi Broadcasting Corporation Radio served as important cultural sites for writers. The diverse poetic voices of the period have been collected in Anthony Nazombe's (b. 1955) edition entitled *Haunting Winds* (1990), which includes a number of emerging poets like Lupenga Mphande (dates n.a.). However, not all Malawian writers writing within the country during the Banda regime were associated with the University of Malawi: Edson Mpina, a bank clerk in Blantyre city, astonished the Malawian literary establishment when he won the 1981 Commonweath Poetry Prize with his poem "Summer Fires" (1983). Since then, he has produced *Raw Pieces* (1986) and *Malawi Poetry Today: An International Telephone Conversation with Paul Engle* (1986), as well as a novel, *The Low Road to Death* (1991). But his forte remains a certain untutored autonomy of point of view that focuses on the fauna and flora of Malawi.

The major poets writing from within the country during the years of the dictatorship are Jack Mapanje, Steve Chimombo, and Felix Mnthali. Mnthali's *When Sunset Comes to Sapitwa* (1980) is a meditative and sonorous philosophical exploration of the metaphysical basis of power. In contrast, Mapanje's *Of the Chameleon and the Gods* (1981) offers an originality of satirical dissection of corrupt power that uses humor as a vehicle for making a perceptive comment on the moral and intellectual foundation of Banda's oppressive regime. In 1987 Mapanje was detained and spent four years in prison without ever being tried, and the collection he produced after being released from prison, *The Chattering Wagtails of Mikuyu Prison* (1993), is less satirical than his earlier work, but equally political, as it is a reflective record of his experience of the dehumanizing conditions of prison life during Banda's era. Mapanje has won a number of international awards for his writing and is one of the most internationally renowned Malawian writers. Chimombo's *Napolo Poems* (1987) uses the local myth of the serpentine destructive fore of Napolo to weave a mythopoesis that provides him with a language through which to engage with the exestential and political aspects of life under the dictator. He also published two long poems, *A Referendum of the Forest Creatures* (1993), an allegorical record of the period leading to the 1993 United Nations-sponsored referendum on the one-party state, and *Breaking the Beadstrings* (1995), which celebrates Malawian womanhood and aligns itself with the struggle for equal relations of gender in the country. Chimombo has also written fiction and drama. In his novel, *The Basket Girl* (1990), adapted from an earlier short story, he explores the link between class and gender in contemporary Malawi.

Ken Lipenga is one of the best short-story writers of his generation, as is evident from his collection, *Waiting for A Turn* (1981), which demonstrates the writer's interest in the interplay between the fictional and the real. An important short-story anthology is *Namaluzi* (1984), edited by James Ng'ombe and Lupenga Mphande. However, it is Paul Aeleza who at the age of twenty-two gave Malawi its first short-story collection, *Night of Darkness and Other Short Stories* (1976), a volume that covers a wide range of cultural settings as well as human situations, from the comic to the tragic and the village to the city. If the short-story collection is less overtly political, his novel *Smouldering Charcoal* (1990) is in contrast much more so. It offers the possibility of a socialist solution to Malawi's postcolonial dictatorship. Dede Kamkondo and James Ng'ombe are also among the significant fiction writers in Malawi. Ng'ombe's *Sugarcane with Salt* (1989) dwells on the cultural transformation caused by an increasingly hybrid cultural formation within postcolonial Malawi. Kankondo's novels, *Children of the Lake* (1987), *The Truth Will Out* (1987), and *For the Living* (1989), show a great interest in contemporary issues, particularly questions of growing up in the city and trying to come to terms with corruption and hypocrisy. Other fictional works of note include Tito Banda's (b. 1950), *Sekani's Solution* (1979) and *A Bitter Disapproval* (1987); Dennis M'Passou's (b. 1935) *Murder in the Interest of the Church* (1985) and *A Pig in the Coffin* (1991); and Willie Zingani's (b. 1954) *From the Phone Booth* (1985).

Chimombo's play, *The Rainmaker* (1978), is one of the most ambitious Malawian dramatic works. As in *Napolo Poems*, in the play Chimombo examines suffering and redemption through and epic machinery based on the Malawian myth about Mbona's martyrdom. In addition to Chimombo's *The Rainmaker,* other notable plays include Chris Kamlongera's (dates n.a.) *Love Potion*, Innocent Banda's (b. 1948) *Cracks*, and Joe Mosiwa's (dates n.a.) *Who Will Marry Our Daughter*, all of which were published in James Gibbs's edition entitled *Nine Malawian Plays* (1979). The development of drama and the theater in the country has been taken a step further through the effort of Du Chisiza (dates n.a.) who set up a well-organized full-time professional theater, Wanyakhumbata Ensemble Theater, in the mid-1980s. His plays, which concentrate on local contemporary themes, some of them political and others more social and moralistic, have been published as *Barefoot in the Heart and Other Plays* (1993).

Although constricted by years of dictatorship, Malawi has a vibrant literary scene that is steadily developing into a rich and distinctive local idiom of cultural and creative expression. The international recognition of a number of the writers shows that it is a literature that speaks not only to the immediate and local, but also to universal concerns, in particular, the quest for freedom.

BIBLIOGRAPHY: Smith, A., *East African Writing in English* (1989); Lindfors, B., *Kulankula: Interviews with Writers from Malawi and Lesotho* (1989); Vail, L., and L. White, *Power and the Praise Poem* (1991); Roscoe, A., and M.-H., Msiska, eds., *The Quiet Chameleon: Modern Poetry from Central Africa* (1992); Msiska, M.-H., "Geopoetics: Subterraneanity and Subversion in Malawian Poetry," in A. Gurnah, ed., *Essays on African Writing* (1995), Vol. 2: 73-99; Kerr, D., *African Popular Theatre* (1996); Msiska, M.-H., and P. Hyland, eds., *Writing and Africa* (1997)

—MPALIVE-HANGSON MSISKA

MALAY LITERATURE
See Malaysian Literature and Singapore Literature

MALAYALAM LITERATURE
See Indian Literature

MALAYSIAN LITERATURE

In Malay

Fiction

Modern writing in the Malay language began in the 19th c. with the works of Abdullah bin Abdul Kadir Munshi (1796–1854), but it was not until the 1920s that truly modern literature took shape. Short stories and novels appeared that were no longer the classical *hikayat* fairy tales of princes and princesses but works depicting true-to-life characters facing the problems of contemporary society. *Hikayat Faridah Hanum* (1925; the story of Faridah Hanum) by Syed Sheikh al-Hady (1867–1934) was the prototype of early Malay novels. An adaptation of an Egyptian novel, the characters and setting were therefore not Malayan. Still, it focused on the chief preoccupation of the Malayan elite at the time: to resolve the sociocultural conflicts arising from the confrontation between traditional culture and modern Western civilization. The main message was that the ethics of Islam, especially pertaining to relationships between the sexes, could not be compromised.

Many Malay novels until the outbreak of war in the Pacific in 1942 carried a similar message: the best defense against the problems of modern life is strict observance of the Islamic moral code. While there continued to be novels with foreign settings, Malay fiction had shifted to local scenes and situations. A love story is set against the background of urban life, often portrayed as full of evil. Surprisingly, criticism of old customs and outdated beliefs did not find fertile ground among Malay novelists, as it did among Indonesian novelists writing in Malay (Indonesian) at the same time.

During the 1930s publication of novels in Malay became widespread. About half were short penny-novels telling romantic stories. Many were more serious, concerned with moral questions and national aspirations. *Putera Gunung Tahan* (1936; the prince of Mount Tahan) by Ishak Haji Muhammad (b. 1910) and *Mari kita berjuang* (1940; let us struggle) by Abdullah Sidik (1913–1973) are representative. *Putera Gunung Tahan* satirizes the attitudes of the British colonial rulers toward their subjects. *Mari kita berjuang* is a straightforward narrative aimed at inspiring young Malayans to be self-reliant economically and politically.

The rise of the short story in the 1920s and 1930s coincided with the proliferation of magazines and newspapers in Malay. Many were simple romantic tales interlaced with moral teachings. The leading short-story writer of the period was Abdul Rahim Kajai (1894–1943).

During the Japanese occupation (1942–45) literary production almost ceased. The end of the war ushered in a period of nationalist struggle, first for cultural identity and later for political independence. New importance was placed on Malay language and literature. At first, however, novels continued prewar traditions. The moralistic novels of Ahmad Lutfi (1911–1966), like *Bilik 69* (1949; room 69) and *Joget moden* (1949; modern dance) were reminiscent of *Hikayat Faridah Hanum*, although they presented contemporary situations and spicy bedroom scenes. Ahmad Bachtiar (1902–1961) continued the prewar trend of the historical novel with nationalist overtones, while Salleh Ghani (dates n.a.) in *Seruan merdeka* (1949; the call of freedom) and Hamdan (dates n.a.) in *Barisan Zubaidah* (1950; the Zubaidah movement), treated nationalism in a more contemporary way.

A truly fresh approach to the novel did not appear until the late 1950s, and during the 1960s writing became more sophisticated. Abdul Samad Said (b. 1935), for instance, wanted to make Malay writing more realistic. His graphic portrayal of Singapore slum life in *Salina* (1961; Salina) brought a new dimension to fiction: the purpose of the novel is not to moralize but to capture contemporary society. While *Hikayat Faridah Hanum* and the novels of Ahmad Lutfi reflected fears that Malay traditions were losing out to the modern way of life, the new novels lay bare contemporary social injustices. *Tak ada jalan keluar* (1962; there is no way out) by Suratman Markasan (b. 1930) presents a typical moral compromise: a divorcée resorts to prostitution so that her children can have a better future. *Desa pingitan* (1964; nurturing village) by Ibrahim Omar (b. 1936) and *Angin hitam dari kota* (1968; dark wind from the city) by A. Wahab Ali (b. 1941) are two prize-winning novels that deal with the conflicts between urban and rural values.

A prolific writer in the 1960s, who by the 1970s had become the leading fiction writer, is Shahnon AHMAD. His novels mostly deal with controversial issues of the day. *Rentong* (1965; burned to ashes) and *Ranjau sepanjang jalan* (1966; *No Harvest but a Thorn*, 1972) are about the hard life of rural rice farmers, while *Protes* (1967; protest) raises touchy religious issues.

Women writers brought a new perspective to Malay fiction. Salmi Manja's (b. 1936) youthful novel *Hari mana bulan mana* (1960; which day, which month) depicts a woman's everyday experiences in a changing society. Adibah Amin's (b. 1934) *Seroja masih di kolam* (1968; the lily is still in the pond) focuses on the difficulties women face in trying to eschew traditions. Khadijah Hashim's (b. 1945) novel *Merpati putih terbang lagi* (1971; the white dove flies again) rearticulates the age-old Malayan ideal of honesty and goodness surmounting all obstacles.

While novelists have grappled with language and narrative techniques, they have not been able to deal successfully with new social experiences: the multiethnicity of the Malaysian population, political processes, and economic problems are hardly touched on.

The short story has played a more important role than the novel. Moralizing tales yielded to new trends during the 1950s, spurred on by a radical group known as Asas '50 (generation of the 1950s). Writers like Keris Mas (b. 1922), Awam-il-Sarkam (b. 1918), Wijaya Mala (b. 1923), Hamzah Hussein (b. 1927), and Asmal (pseud. of Abdul Samad bin Ismail, b. 1924), began to deal realistically with social problems. Anticolonial sentiments also appeared, but the main concern was the injustices suffered by the urban poor, rural peasants, and fishermen. The members of Asas '50 were political activists, but they were also concerned with the improvement of literary techniques and a more penetrating approach to themes.

The influence of Asas '50 continued into the mid-1960s. Asmal's "Ingin jadi pujangga" (1959; aspiring poet) is a self-caricature of the young writers who, in trying to live up to the ideals of serious writing, fall prey to their own artificialities. Asmal's "Ah Kau masuk syurga" (1959; Ah Kau goes to heaven) exposes the tendency of Malayans to accept symbols rather than substance. Keris Mas's collection *Patah tumbuh* (1962; continuity) shows not only the progress in Malay short-story writing after the war but also the writer's view of events that led to independence.

By the mid-1960s, the leading short-story writers were Abdul Samad Said and Shahnon Ahmad. Themes were still mainly social, but now set against the problems of a newly independent nation. Short-story writers portrayed emergent types: corrupt politicians, statusconscious civil servants, university-educated social climbers.

Younger writers like Mohd. Affandi Hassan (b. 1940), S. Othman Kelantan (b. 1938), Ali Majod (b. 1940), Azizi Abdullah (b. 1942), and the women writers Khadijah Hashim and Fatimah Busu (b. 1943) have broadened the horizons of the short story and evinced a more polished technique. Since the late 1960s social themes have been balanced by a more introspective and penetrating look at human life.

Poetry

The first attempts to break away from traditional *syair* and *pantun* verse forms were made in the early 1930s. The new poetic expression, collectively called *sajak*, was influenced by the rise of modern poetry in Indonesia in the 1920s and 1930s. Although it took hold slowly, *sajak* bloomed after World War II. The early *sajak* poems often expressed Malayan nationalism in romantic terms.

Asas '50 viewed the *pantun* and the *syair* as too rigid for the philosophy the group advocated: they favored the free-verse expression of the *sajak*. The *sajaks* of Usman AWANG and Mahsuri Salikon (b. 1927) became models for younger writers. Usman Awang's collection *Gelombang* (1961; waves) is representative of modern poetry of the time. The early *pantun* forms, the later free verse, his preoccupation with freeing himself from the shackles of tradition, his opposition to colonialism, and his concern for social justice are clearly arrayed chronologically in this volume. His second collection, *Duri dan api* (1969; thorns and fire), shows his ease with the free-verse forms and at the same time his widening vision, moving beyond his homeland.

There was a time when some poets thought that free verse was a license to experiment without constraint; this concept brought about the phenomenon of *sajak kabur* (obscure poems) in the 1950s and early 1960s. *Sajaks* proliferated: there was hardly a magazine or newspaper that did not print them.

Poets debuting since the late 1960s and the 1970s have had the advantage of greater education, including some knowledge of foreign literatures. Muhammed Haji Salleh (b. 1942), Firdaus Abdullah (b. 1944), Kassim Ahmad (b. 1933), Latif Mohidin (b. 1941), Zurinah Hassan (b. 1949), and Baharuddin Zainal (b. 1939) are among those who have written serious works of poetry. Poetry has moved away from social and political problems, concentrating instead on personal, philosophical, and aesthetic themes. A woman poet, Zanariah Wan Abdul Rahman (b. 1940), using traditional imagery, has written about the dilemmas of a young girl in love. Even in religious poems, thunderous exhortations and evangelistic fervor have given way to a more philosophical expression.

Drama

Malay drama in the 20th c. has had varied sources: it springs from folk-ritualistic drama, from the traditional shadow play, from the popular theater called the *bangsawan* (plays on romantic or historical themes interspersed with songs and comic sketches), and from the Western plays that were introduced through the schools. Before World War II the *bangsawan* was the main form of urban theater and the main expression of the rising urban culture. Traditional folk performances continued to thrive in the villages.

Modern Malay theater started with school performances, during the colonial period of Shakespeare and other European dramatists. During the Japanese occupation *sandiwara* plays, similar to *bangsawan* but with contemporary themes, to some extent replaced the *bangsawan*; this form of theater was inspired by Indonesian drama. Not until the 1950s was there a deliberate effort to create truly Malayan (later Malaysian) plays. The result was not only plays with modern social themes, but also, following the *bangsawan*, themes drawn from the historical and legendary past. The latter is usually referred to as *purbawara*. Shahrum Hussein (b. 1919) has written plays about past heroes, such as *Si bongkok Tanjung Puteri* (1961; the hunchbacked warrior of Tanjung Puteri) and *Tun Fatimah* (1964; Tun Fatimah [the woman warrior of old Malacca]). Mustapha Kamal Yassin (b. 1925) has dealt with contemporary subjects. His *Atap genting atap rembia* (1963; tiled and thatched roofs) attacks those who put status and wealth above love in marriage. Ali Aziz (b. 1935), in *Hang Jebat menderhaka* (1957; Hang Jebat rebels), tried to apply techniques of Shakespearean tragedy to the duel between two blood brothers: Hang Tuah, who upholds the cardinal Malayan traditional value of unquestioning loyalty to the sultan; and Hang Jebat, who rebels for the sake of justice. Usman Awang's *Muzika Uda dan Dara* (1976; the musical play of Uda and Dara), a simple tale of unrequited love between two young villagers, has been presented as a musical play as well as a dance drama.

Since the late 1960s, dramatists like Syed Alwi (b. 1930) and Nordin Hassan (b. 1929) have experimented with techniques from the traditional drama: images reflected on a screen, as in the shadow play, have been used for special effects or to convey a character's past experiences. And drama in the round often uses the techniques of traditional dance theater like the *randai*.

In Chinese

Before the Pacific War writings in Chinese echoed those of China proper. Early Chinese writers in Malaya had migrated from China, and sentiments expressed were mainly directed at the homeland. In the 1930s, after the Japanese invaded China, nationalism dominated the writing of overseas Chinese. Chinese writing had to go underground during the Japanese occupation of Malaya (1942–45). From prison Siew Yang (dates n.a.) and Chin Chung (dates n.a.) wrote clandestine anti-Japanese works.

The early postwar years saw a revival of literary activity, but writing in Chinese again suffered a setback after the communist insurrection of 1948. Between 1948 and 1957 hardly any literary activity took place, partly because of the local situation and partly because of the break in communication with China.

The desire to produce a truly *Ma-hoa*, or Malaysian Chinese, literature was nurtured in the years following independence in 1957. Young writers who had grown up in Malaysia realized that *Ma-hoa* literature should have its own identity, but the legacy and influence of classical Chinese literature remained formidable.

The preferred genre of Chinese literature in Malaysia has been the short story. Between 1945 and 1965, works were mostly anticolonial and antifeudal. They reflected the life of the middle and lower classes. Since 1965 Malaysian settings and problems specifically related to the country have characterized Chinese writing in Malaysia.

In Tamil

Tamil writing in Malaysia began with religious poetry toward the end of the 19th c. The first Tamil novel was Venkitarattinam's (dates n.a.) *Karunacakaran; allathu, Kathalinmatchi* (1917; Karunacakaran; or, the glory of love). Short stories appeared during the 1930s, coinciding with the proliferation of Tamil newspapers. Many of the stories were moralizing. During this period those writing for local publications were in constant contact with developments in the homeland in south India. The influence of the Indian Tamil journal *Manikkodi* brought new themes into Malaysian Tamil short stories: political, economic, and social questions were raised.

Poetry has dominated Tamil literature in Malaysia. And the majority of poems until the 1940s were religious in content. Since the 1950s Tamil poetry had a variety of themes, ranging from social reform and patriotism to romantic love, nature, and the mother tongue.

Short stories became more numerous in the 1950s. The periodical *Tamil necan* regularly published stories by Suba Narayanan (b. 1938) and Bairoji Narayanan (b. 1931). Contact with the Tamil homeland still provided the literary guide for local writers. S. Vadivelu's (b. 1929) stories show an unusual ability to create a vivid setting; his stories that take place during the Japanese occupation are especially notable. Short stories now have a variety of themes: politics, education, economics, citizenship problems, family organization, human relationships, alcoholism, and national unity.

Only in 1958, a year after Malaysian independence, did the Association of Tamil Writers in Malaya come into being. By the 1960s there was a marked shift in Tamil literature toward Malaysian themes and problems. S. Vadivelu, who has continued to be a leading figure, published the collection of stories *Irunda ulagam* (1970; dark world) dealing with the problems of the Indian community in Malaysia.

In English

Literature in English can be called Malaysian after Malaysian writers began to write a distinctive literature in English. Before that there was only writing in English with a Malayan setting, written both by foreigners living in the country and by locals. Of the former, the most notable is Anthony BURGESS, who served as an education officer toward the end of British rule and wrote *The Malayan Trilogy* (1956–59). Gregory de Silva (dates n.a.) with *Sulaiman Goes to London* (1938), Chin Kee Onn (b. 1908) with *Malaya Upside Down* (1946), Ooi Cheng Teck (dates n.a.) with *Red Sun over Malaya: John Man's Ordeal* (1948), and Gurchan Singh (dates n.a.) with *Singa The Lion of Malaya* (1959) represent the latter.

The seeds of Malaysian literature in English were sown by natives who used English because it was the language of their education, and hence the only language they were proficient in. Although some of them were conscious of their dilemma—inheriting a colonial culture while the country was readying itself for independence—they still could not shake off the influence of English. The best they could do was to adopt certain Malayan elements in their writings.

Wang Gungwu (b. 1930) was one of the early writers who attempted to forge a Malayan identity while using English; the poems in his collection *Pulse* (1950) have a definite Malayan quality. There were others like Wang Gungwu, but they could not sustain their creativity, and after a year or two they would stop publishing. Of the few who continued writing consistently, the leading poets have been Ee Tiang Hong (b. 1933), Wong Phui Nam (b. 1936), and Muhammed Haji Salleh. Ee Tiang Hong is fond of writing about different places in Malaysia. In "Heeren Street, Malacca" (1968), for example, he sees the old Baba Chinese culture, a relic of a past age, coming face to face with modern times. His early poems are collected in *I of the Many Faces* (1960). His tone became more critical of society as years went by. Wong Phui Nam excels in beautiful descriptions. Muhammed Haji Salleh, who studied in England and first wrote in English, now writes in Malay.

In prose, there are almost no novels, but short stories appear regularly in both popular magazines and more serious journals, like *Tenggara* and *Lidra*. Of the novels, *Scorpion Orchid* (1976) by Lloyd Fernando (b. 1926) is the best. Innovative in form, it deals with that period when the struggle for independence was not a clear-cut issue for the English-educated elite.

BIBLIOGRAPHY: Osman, Mohd. Taib bin, *An Introduction to the Development of Modern Malay Language and Literature* (1961); Kirkup, J., Introduction to A. Majid and O. Rice, eds., *Modern Malay Verse* (1963): vii—xiv; Subramaniam, M., "Growth of Modern Tamil Literature in Malaysia," *Proceedings of the First International Conference-Seminar of Tamil Studies* (1969), Vol. II: 304–8; Dhandayudham, R., "The Development of the Tamil Short Story in Malaysia," *JTamS*, No. 3 (1973): 7–16; Osman, Mohd. Taib bin, "Classical and Modern Malay Literature," *Handbuch der Orientalistik*, 3, 3, 1 (1976): 116–86; Zainal, B., "A Guide to Malay Literature (1970–1976)," *Tenggara*, 8 (1976): 70–79; Ali, A. Wahab, "The Role of Literature in Transmitting National Values: Malaysia," in R. J. Bresnahan, ed., *Literature and Society: Cross-Cultural Perspectives* (1977): 32–42; Bennett, B., "The Subdued Ego: Poetry from Malaysia and Singapore," *Meanjin*, 37 (1978): 240–46; Ismail, Y., "The National Language and Literature of Malaysia," in A. Q. Perez, et al., eds., *Papers from the Conference on the Standardisation of Asian Languages, Manila, Philippines, December*, 1974 (1978): 16–21, 93–103; Hong, E. T., "Malaysian Poetry in English: Influence and Independence," *PQM*, 4 (1979): 69–73; Simms, N., "The Future of English as a Poetic Language in Singapore and Malaysia," *CNLR*, 2, 2 (1979): 9–13; 3, 1 (1980): 10–14; and 3, 2 (1980): 8–12; Wong, S., "The Influence of China's Literary Movement on Malaysia's Vernacular Chinese Literature in the 1930's," *TkR*, 10 (1980): 517–34

—MOHD. TAIB BIN OSMAN

MALERBA, Luigi

(pseud. of Luigi Bonardi) Italian novelist, poet, screenwriter, and journalist, b. 11 Nov. 1927, Berceto, Parma

M. is a prolific writer who for over three decades has excelled in fiction, poetry, children's books, scriptwriting for cinema and television, literary criticism, and journalism. He is one of the original founders and, unquestionably, one of the most important writers to emerge from the experimental and avant-garde literary movement "Gruppo 63." From his first work critics noticed the author's remarkable talent and originality in using humor, language, eccentric characters, and metaliterary narrative strategies to illustrate the contradictions between the world of words—with their various ambiguities and possible meanings—and the world of reality. M.'s linguistic features as well as his totally fantastic and absurd stories found a match only in the equally outstanding cerebral literary divertissements of Giorgio Manganelli (1922–1990)—also a master of the art of dwelling on "nonsense." Hardly by chance, both writers were fans of Lewis Carroll, Laurence Sterne, James JOYCE, Eugène IONESCO, and the Marx brothers.

Throughout over twenty works M. has demonstrated himself to be an exceptional narrator whose writings are rooted in a myriad of applications of wit, irony, plurilinguism (dialectal and standard Italian), irrational thinking, mental gymnastics, absurd situations, arbitrary social conventions, obsessions, dreams, violence, mental and physical cruelty, perversions, madness, mythology, suspense, and postmodern historical settings ranging from Roman and Greek history to late 20th-c. Italy. His works are also comic demonstrations of how the more one tries to give meaning to what we call reality the more one becomes entangled in a web of doubt, ambiguity and paradox.

La scoperta dell'alfabeto (1963; The Discovery of the Alphabet), *Il serpente* (1966; *The Serpent*, 1968), and *Salto mortale* (1968, *What is Buzzing?*, 1969) can be seen as a trilogy illustrating the author's interests in narrating a variety of issues linked to the topic of communication, which is often burdened by absurd arguments and irrational rationalizations. In his first novel an older illiterate man's excitement about learning to read and write disappears after he learns to recognize approximately one hundred words; the more he learns the more he becomes frustrated as he questions the logic of the alphabet and of language in general. With the appearance of *Il serpente* critics became strong supporters of M.'s nontraditional narrative skills and inventiveness

Il serpent, whose metaphoric title refers to both the slippery nature of the meaning of words and consequently of the art of writing and narrating a story, is an entertaining metalinguistic and metafictional mind boggling antidetective novel. Through first-person narration and numerous monologues we witness the surreal adventures of a protagonist who falls in love with a girl whom he calls Miriam, becomes jealous of her, kills her, cannibalizes her, and then speaks to her while she is in his stomach. A police investigation then reveals that the girl never existed. Like words that can be erased or statements that can be contradicted so too M.'s characters can suddenly change and disappear under the reader's eyes. In *Salto mortale* there is plenty of confusion created by the mere fact that several characters have the same name Giuseppe. M.'s unreliable narrators often frustrate the reader with incongruous and contradictory statements, ambiguities, disorder, uncertainties, and paradoxes. M.'s unorthodox narrative strategies continue in his next novel that, which some readers who did not appreciate his irony considered obscene and even desecrating.

Il protagonista (1973; The Protagonist) is a "phallus-centered" narrative that recalls Alberto Moravia's *Io e lui* (1971; *The Two of Us*, 1972)—both dealing with the male genital organ as protagonist. M.'s protagonist is a megalomaniac who uses eroticism and a variety of social transgressions as a means to grasp reality. In the opening pages the "capoccia" (the "head") is described as an antenna. Once he falls in love with Elisabetta and her twin sister—who does not exist—he embarks on a surrealistic and perverted self-searching odyssey that leads him to extreme actions such as violating a mummy, a public statue, and a dead body.

M.'s experiments with postmodern historical novels began in the 1970s with *Il pataffio* (1973; Pataffio) and *Le rose imperiali* (1974; Imperial Roses) and continued throughout the 1990s. In *Il fuoco greco* (1989; The Greek Fire) M. uses a variety of historical settings that allow him to discuss, in different eras, universal themes of violence and the thirst for and abuses of power. Byzantium provides the backdrop for this political murder-mystery story, filled with sexual intrigues and conspiracies that see ambassadors, rulers, writers, servants, and political enemies, all involved in accusing, suspecting, fighting, betraying, and murdering, in order to control a secret weapon. At the center of the novel there is a fascinating dialogue involving the writer Lippas—clearly meant to represent the author—who claims that he does not know how the story will end but does know that the novel will end when he decides that it is time for it to end.

Il pianeta azzurro (1986; The Blue Planet), set in the years of terrorism in Italy in the late 1970s, is M.'s longest and most political novel. It is also the author's most metafictional mystery story about power, criminal activities, and corruption. The main story deals with the search for truth and with Demetrio's obsession with wanting to kill a corrupt "Professor" linked to underground political activities. The narration progresses within a mixture of four narrative voices: the author's, the narrator's, the main protagonist's, and a commentator's, as well as with frequent references to a diary and to a discovered manuscript. The numerous references to greedy politicians and to corrupt governments, as in *Il fuoco greco*, establish obvious analogies with the political situation of the Italy of the 1980s. This type of postmodern pastiche of past and present continues in *Le maschere* (1995; The Mask). Set in Rome during the 16th c., this novel centers on a power struggle among cardinals, politicians and spies who are trying to prevent the election of a foreign pope, Adrian from Utrecht, considered to be too religious. M.'s usual well documented historical research is in the background of this colorful story about a city at the mercy of personal interests, hate, immorality, hypocrisy, clergymen, prostitutes, politicians, and the plague.

In *Itaca per sempre* (1997; Ithaca Forever) M. develops a psychological conflict between Ulysses and Penelope and their son Telemachus. Unlike the Homeric Odysseus, M.'s hero is very human and so sensitive that he often cries. Ulysses, like many of M.'s characters, cannot distinguish between fiction and reality and up to the final page he is not certain if he can remain in Ithaca after being told by his wife that she has known his true identity from the first day that he arrived on the island, dressed as a pauper. The originality of this text lies primarily in M.'s suggestion that Ulysses, a great storyteller, and not Homer, may have been the real author of the *Iliad* and the *Odyssey*, and in M.'s exploiting a familiar literary myth in order to stage a modern psychological drama about marital problems.

In his collections of short stories, just as in his novels, M. demonstrates masterfully controlled language, inventiveness of themes and of eccentric characters, and, equally important, a capacity to entertain readers with a variety of fantastic stories that at the same time are clear manifestations of literariness. In the 1980s one of M.'s most discussed texts was *Diario di un sognatore* (1981; Diary of a Dreamer), a collection of 350 short dreams, all of which were carefully transcribed—as the author has maintained in interviews—one every day without any interpretation. Or is this just another of M.'s brilliant ironic demonstrations of different levels of reality present in the possible worlds of fiction? Regardless of the authenticity of the dreams the text is a fascinating collection of microstories by an outstanding writer who has never stopped narrating about the pleasures of verbal divertissements and of the art of storytelling.

Even when M. appears to be having fun playing cat and mouse with his readers he never neglects to entertain them with his fabulous stories that are clearly rooted in our contemporary reality. Without being too political or ideological M. remains an exceptional fabulist socially committed in his endeavors to illustrate the many contradictions of modern society.

FURTHER WORKS: *Salto mortale* (1968); *Le rose imperiali* (1974); *Le parole abbandonate* (1977); *Pinocchio con gli stivali* (1977); *Il pataffio* (1978); *Dopo il pescecane* (1979); *Le galline pensierose* (1980); *Storiette tascabili* (1984); *Testa d'argento* (1988); *Cina Cina* (1985); *Le pietre volanti* (1992); *Il viaggiatore sedentario* (1993); *Che vergogna scrivere* (1996)

BIBLIOGRAPHY: Almansi, G., "M. and the Art of Story-Telling," *Quaderni d'italianistica*, 2 (1980): 157-70; Brouwear-van Vethoven, O., "M. and the Nouveau Roman in Italy," *Critics in Translation*, 1 (1976): 39-45; Cannon, J., *Postmodern Italian Fiction: The Crisis of Reason in Calvino, Eco, Sciascia, M.* (1989); Koelb, C., "Nietzsche, M., and the Aesthetics of Superficiality," *Boundary*, 2 (Fall 1983): 117-32; West, R., "The Poetics of Plenitude: M.'s *Diario di un sognatore*," *Italica*, 63 (1984): 201-13

—ROCCO CAPOZZI

MALGONKAR, Manohar Dattatray

Indian novelist, short-story writer, and journalist (writing in English), b. 12 July 1913, Bombay

Educated at Karnatak College, Dharwar, M. then attended Bombay University, receiving a B. A. (honours) degree in English and Sanskrit in 1936. From 1935 to 1937, he arranged tiger shoots for maharajahs and worked as a professional big-game hunter. He held the post of cantonment executive officer, Government of India, 1937 to 1942. As a career military man, he served in the Maratha Light Infantry, worked on the British Army's general staff during World War II, and rose to the rank of lieutenant colonel. From 1953 to 1959 M. owned the Jagalbet Manganese Mining Syndicate, and since 1959 he has farmed a remote estate in Jagalbet, Belgaum District, Maharashtra. He has twice run, unsuccessfully, for the Indian Parliament.

In 1948 M. began writing stories for All-India Radio and *The Illustrated Weekly of India*. One need only look at his background to understand that M.'s writing is based largely on the values of the aristocracy—both Indian and British. His novels and stories have been severely criticized for dealing with the elite and ignoring the reality of India's dirt and poverty. His first two novels, *Distant Drum* (1960) and *Combat of Shadows* (1962), largely romantic tales of action and intrigue, fail most obviously in character development. His longer narratives tend to be strong in idea, but somewhat weak in execution.

This defect is particularly apparent in *A Bend in the Ganges* (1964), which deals with the violence of the 1947 partition and faults Gandhi for setting unrealistic expectations as a political expedient. M.'s best novel, *The Princes* (1963) deals with the absorption of the princely states into modern India at the time of independence, but is also a successful *Bildungsroman*. *The Devil's Wind* (1972), an engrossing historical novel, presents the Sepoy Mutiny of 1857 through the eyes of Nana Sahib, leader of the revolt.

M. has also written three works of Indian history, more than fifty short stories, at least a hundred articles, and several film scripts, one of which, *Spy in Amber* (1971), was fashioned into a novel by his daughter. Although M.'s writing deals with an era now past, his work has value as historical fiction, written from a distinctly feudal point of view no longer celebrated by Indian writers attuned to India's contemporary problems.

FURTHER WORKS: *Kanhoji Angray, Maratha Admiral* (1959); *Puars of Dewas Senior* (1963); *The Chhatrapatis of Kolhapur* (1971); *Toast in Warm Wine* (1974); *In Uniform* (1975); *Line of Mars* (1979); *The Last Maharani of Gwalior* (1987)

BIBLIOGRAPHY: Gemmill, J. P., "Three by M. M.," *Mahfil*, 3 (1966): 76–84; Amur, G. S., *M. M.* (1973); Dayananda, Y. J., "The Novelist as Historian," *JSoAL*, 10 (1974): 55–67; Asnani, S. M., "A Study of the Novels of M. M.," *LHY*, 16 (1975): 71–98; Dayananda, J. Y., *M. M.*, (1975); Jayashri, I., "Women versus Tradition in the Novels of M. M.," *Triveni*, 45, 2 (1976): 73–80; Amur, G. S., "M. M. and the Problems of the Indian Novelist in English," in Mohan, R., ed., *Indian Writing in English* (1978): 37–46; Pradhan, N. S., "M. M.: *A Bend in the Ganges*," in Pradhan, N. S., ed., *Major Indian Novels: An Evaluation* (1986): 135-54; Rajagopalachari, M., *The Novels of M. M.* (1990); Rao, C. M., *M. M. and a Portrait of the Hero in His Novels* (1993); Bomer, K. H., "Fact in Fiction: The Indian Army in the Novels of M. M.," in Bindella, M. T., and G. V. Davis, eds., *Imagination and the Creative Impulse in the New Literatures in English* (1993): 41-55

—JANET M. POWERS

MALI LITERATURE

Vast, sparsely populated, predominantly agricultural, Mali has an illustrious history going back to medieval times. Under French rule the territory was called French Sudan. An independent nation since 1960, Mali has launched various campaigns to fight illiteracy, educating the masses in both French and Bambara, a Mandé language spoken by the largest ethnic group in the country. As literacy increases, interest in the arts grows as well. The rich oral tradition has given rise to theater groups. Since the early 1970s the government-owned publishing company, Editions Populaires, has published historical, anthropological, and literary works. It limits publication to noncontroversial subject matter, however, emphasizing the glorification of the past rather than the examination of the present with a critical eye.

Among the most renowned African historians is Amadou Hampaté Bâ (1920–1991), who has published important works in the field of African religion and Islamic theology. Having developed an Arabic script for the Fulani language, Bâ published *Kaidara* (1965; Kaidara), a traditional allegorical poem in a bilingual Fulani/French edition.

Emphasis upon history and Mali's rich oral tradition is also apparent in the work of Bâ's contemporary, Djibril Tamsir Niane (b. 1920), who was born either in Mali or northern Guinea and whose ancestors were Malinké *griots* (oral historians). Niane's version of the Malinké epic *Soundjata; ou, L'épopée mandingue* (1960; *Sundiata: An Epic of Old Mali*, 1965) retells the legend of the crippled boy who grew up to become an outstanding military and political leader and rule the Mali Empire (1230–55). In the introduction to the epic, Niane emphasizes the importance of the *griot*; "We are vessels of speech, we are the repositories that harbor secrets many centuries old."

A younger generation has taken up the same tradition of glorifying the past. Massa Maken Diabaté (b. 1936) has rewritten the Sundiata legend as *Kala Jata* (1965; Kala Jata). Combining his talents as a poet and an anthropologist, Diabaté uses words and expressions in the Malinké language interspersed within the French text in an attempt to capture the rhythms of Malinké poetry.

Seydou Kouyaté Badian (b. 1928) is known as a poet, playwright, and novelist. His novel *Sous l'orage* (1963; under the storm) examines the conflict between generations in a changing society. When two lovers challenge their parents by deciding to marry, they involve the entire village in the conflict. Badian has also turned to African history for inspiration. His play *La mort de Chaka* (1962; the death of Chaka) treats the theme of the Zulu king first presented in literature by the Lesotho writer Thomas MOFOLO, in his novel *Chaka* (1925; *Chaka the Zulu*, 1931), written in the Bantu language South Sotho.

Drawing upon ancient Mali history to challenge modern perceptions of Africa's past, Yambo Ouologuem (b. 1940) published an important and controversial novel, *Le devoir de violence* (1968; *Bound to Violence*, 1971), in which he created the fictional African kingdom of Makem, ruled by the violent despots of the Saif dynasty. He advances the thesis that violence and slavery existed long before the colonial powers' scramble for the continent. The first African novel to receive the Renaudot Prize in France, *Le devoir de violence* has been attacked by critics for its brutality, eroticism, and alleged plagiarism. Ouologuem uses violence to shock the reader. In addition, he blends legend with realism, African and Arabic expressions with French. He forces the reader to react to his prose, to come to grips with his expression of the eternal problem of man's inhumanity to man.

Mali is committed to affirming a rich cultural tradition. Its writers today reveal a genuine commitment to studying the present and the past and to synthesizing the old and the new.

BIBLIOGRAPHY: Larson, C., *The Emergence of African Fiction* (1972), passim; Rubin, J. S., "Mali: New Writing from an Ancient Civilization," *SBL*, 4, 3 (1973): 15–18; Olney, J., "Of Griots and Heroes," *SBL*, 6, 1 (1975): 14–17; Diawara, G., "Literature and the New Generations," *LAAW*, 31 (1977): 114–17; Singare, T., "*Où* en sont les lettres maliennes?" *Études maliennes*, 22 (1977): 1–23; Palmer, E., *The Growth of the African Novel* (1979): 199–220; Decraene, P., "Le Mali: Tradition, arts et littérature," *FE*, 294 (1980): 34–37

—MILDRED MORTIMER

MALINKÉ LITERATURE
See Mali Literature

MALINOVSKI, Ivan

Danish poet, b. 18 Feb. 1926, Copenhagen; d. 5 Nov. 1989, Copenhagen

M. lived in Sweden during the German occupation of Denmark and afterward studied Slavic languages at the University of Århus, 1947–52. He has written for numerous newspapers and magazines and has translated such writers as BRECHT, ENZENSBERGER, GARCÍA LORCA, NERUDA, PASTERNAK, and CHEKHOV. In 1970 M. received the Prize of the Danish Academy.

M. made what he considers his debut as a poet at a relatively mature age with *Galgen-frist* (1958; respite from the gallows), having disavowed his first two collections of poems from the 1940s. His closest literary affinities are to the Swedish MODERNISTS of the 1940s—Karl Vennberg (b. 1910), Erik LINDEGREN, and Gunnar EKELÖF—rather than to contemporary Danish poets. M. shares with the Swedish poets their rigor of expression, formal density, deep pessimism, and criticism of capitalist society.

Galgenfrist occupies a central position in M.'s oeuvre. The basis of these modernist poems is a total nihilism that leaves no room for any metaphysics, in contrast to most postwar Danish modernist writing. M. shows a complete distrust of any belief, theory, or ideology. This very attitude, according to M., may serve as a starting point for truthful artistic creativity.

One might expect this extreme nihilism to be at odds with M.'s Marxist-oriented criticism of society. To M., however, the two attitudes are not mutually exclusive; rather, they are a necessary outcome of our painful reality and as such constitute the fruitful tension that gives impetus to M.'s poetic creativity. He distinguishes between an objective inhumanity and a subjective human experience; when the suffering caused by the inhuman forces becomes unbearable, the human being will revolt.

Åbne digte (1963; open-ended poems) and *Romerske bassiner* (1963; Roman pools), with their portrayal of a repressive society and their treatment of contemporary events, are explicitly political. M.'s Marxist orientation, however, is only part of an EXISTENTIALIST attitude. It is the fundamantal dichotomies of the human condition that M. has put into literary form. In *Romerske bassiner* a collage technique is used to describe society through its own distorted language. The cliché-ridden language of radio, magazines, advertisements, and speeches is captured in all its fraudulence and meaninglessness.

M.'s most prevalent technique has been described as a "strategy of opposition," whereby the compressed antithetical form reflects the antinomy between subjective and objective forces. *Poetomatic* (1965; poetomatic) is an accomplished structure of abrupt, irreconcilable opposites. The closed, aphoristic form is not easily accessible, but it aptly underscores the sense of discontinuity and nothingness. M.'s fast-growing reputation testifies to his success in finding an appropriate form for the complex experiences of modern man.

FURTHER WORKS: *Ting* (1945); *De tabte slag* (1947); *Vejen* (1954); *Glemmebogen: Femten digtere i dansk gendigtning* (1962); *Med solen i ryggen* (1963); *De tomme sokler* (1963); *Leve som var der en fremtid og et håb* (1968); *Misnøje til skade for mandstugten: Et digtudvalg* (1969); *Samlede digte* (1970); *Kritik af tavsheden* (1974); *Vinterens hjerte* (1980)

BIBLIOGRAPHY: King, C., *An Introduction to I. M.* (1975);

—CHARLOTTE SCHIANDER GRAY

MALLEA, Eduardo

Argentine novelist, short-story writer, and essayist, b. 14 Aug. 1903, Bahía Blanca; d. 14 Aug. 1982, Buenos Aires

M.'s father, a physician, instilled in his son a love of humanity and a respect for the downtrodden. M. first studied law in Buenos Aires, before finding his true vocation in literature. Central in his life and in his fiction is his impassioned, anguished search for what he calls the real Argentina, the Argentina that lies beneath the

surface of the ostentation, materialism, and false values he sees enshrined in his country. M. has been a lifelong contributor to the newspaper *La nación* and directed its literary supplement for many years. He has also written frequently for the prestigious journal *Sur*.

At the beginning of his career M. was influenced by the European avant-garde writers of the 1920s. His first work, *Cuentos para una inglesa desesperada* (1926; stories for a desperate Englishwoman), revealed aesthetic sensitivity and refinement. More than stories, the narrations in this volume are poetic expressions in prose of moods and feelings, couched in delicate and at times affected language. Before M. wrote his first novel, he published *Historia de una pasión argentina* (1937; history of an Argentine passion), a seminal essay that stands as his intellectual and philosophical credo. It contains many themes that were to appear in M.'s fiction, the most important being his concept of the two Argentinas—the visible Argentina and the invisible one. The visible is the pretentious, artificial, and hypocritical veneer that the country lives with from day to day; the invisible is the heart, the genuine soul of the country, its true but hidden values.

M. is an intellectual and psychological novelist who sees man's anguish resulting more from a struggle of forces within his own psyche than from external, environmental ones. In this sense, novels such as *Fiesta en noviembre* (1938; *Fiesta in November*, 1966) and *La bahía de silencio* (1940; *The Bay of Silence* 1944) represent the counterpoise to the *criollista* novel, or novel of the land that held sway in Spanish America from about 1920 to 1940, in which hostile nature was the protagonist and man its helpless victim. M. is an existential writer who penetrates to the inner core of man's feelings and states of mind to reveal his basic loneliness, lack of communication, and alienation. In *Fiesta en noviembre*, inspired by the murder of Federico GARCÍA LORCA during the Spanish Civil War, M. juxtaposes two distinct and ironically incompatible narratives: the frivolous party given by Señora Rague, and the Kafkaesque kidnapping and execution of a young poet. The autobiographical *La bahía de silencio*, which established M. as one of the most important writers in Argentina, represents his struggle to affirm his social ideals in the face of an impersonal and uncaring public. The torment and disillusion of Martín Tregua as he views his misguided Argentina forms the central theme of the novel.

In *Todo verdor perecerá* (1941; *All Green Shall Perish*, 1966) the cold, arid, and reticent nature of Agata and Nicanor Cruz leads to their ultimate destruction. Emotional withdrawal appears as a leitmotif in many of M.'s novels and stories and as the central theme in *Chaves* (1953; *Chaves*, 1966), a brief, intense novel about a sawmill worker whose inexorable taciturnity is symptomatic of profound grief and frustration.

M. is as fine a short-story writer as he is a novelist. *La sala de espera* (1953; the waiting room) consists of seven independent stories unified spatially by their setting at a train station, where each of the protagonists awaits the train back to Buenos Aires, back to a life of pain and despair.

There is little external action in most of M.'s fiction; it is almost static, the conflicts arising from the inner turmoil of the characters. Instead of movement in the form of a linear narrative, the reader senses a tension, a stress, an internal struggle between reason and emotion, or between will and feeling. M.'s characters are unhappy, unfulfilled, and isolated souls; his women are cold and distant, indifferent, ungiving, haughty, "alone in their aloneness." The people in his fiction are seeking to find themselves, to find their own set of values, whether it be in crass Buenos Aires, as in the case of Jacobo Uber in the story "La causa de Jacobo Uber, perdida"

(1936; "The Lost Cause of Jacob Uber," 1966), or in the inner provinces, as with the wealthy Román Ricarte in *Las águilas* (1943; the eagles).

M.'s style is original, distinctive, and highly suitable for the penetrating analysis of character on which his fiction depends. His language, expansive rather than succinct or precise, can be heavy, dense, and inclined toward the abstract, but it can also be lyrical and poetic. At his best, M. uses ingenious linguistic play to capture the intensity and subtlety of his intellectual and emotional world.

M.'s place in Spanish American literature is secure. Although he is perhaps too cerebral ever to be a popular novelist, he has examined human emotions with great understanding and sensitivity.

FURTHER WORKS: *Conocimiento y expresión de la Argentina* (1935); *Nocturno europeo* (1935); *La ciudad junto al río inmóvil* (1936); *Meditación en la costa* (1939); *El sayal y la púrpura* (1941); *Rodeada está de sueño* (1944); *El retorno* (1946); *El vínculo* (1946); *Los enemigos del alma* (1950); *La torre* (1951); *Notas de un novelista* (1954); *El gajo de enebro* (1957); *Simbad* (1957); *Posesión* (1958); *La raza humana* (1959); *La vida blanca* (1959); *Las travesías* (2 vols., 1961–1962); *La representación de los aficionados: Un juego* (1962); *La guerra interior* (1963); *El resentimiento* (1966); *La barca de hielo* (1967); *La red* (1968); *La penúltima puerta* (1969); *Gabriel Andaral* (1971); *Triste piel del universo* (1971); *En la creciente oscuridad* (1972); *Los papeles privados* (1974). FURTHER WORKS IN ENGLISH: *All Green Shall Perish* (1966; contains three novellas and four short stories)

BIBLIOGRAPHY: Dudgeon, P., *E. M.: A Personal Study of His Work* (1949); Chapman, A., "Terms of Spiritual Isolation in E. M.," *MLF*, 37: 1–2 (1952): 21–27; Polt, J. H. R., *The Writings of E. M.* (1959); Peterson, F., "Notes on M.'s Definition of Argentina," *Hispania*, 45 (1962): 621–24; Lichtblau, M., *El arte estilístico de E. M.* (1967); Rivelli, C., *E. M.: La continuidad temática de su obra* (1969); Lewald, E. H., *E. M.* (1977)

—MYRON I. LICHTBLAU

MALLET-JORIS, Françoise

(pseud. of Françoise Lilar) Belgian novelist, poet, short-story writer, and memoirist (writing in French), b. 6 July 1930, Antwerp

Daughter of a Belgian statesman and of the writer Suzanne Lilar (b. 1901), M.-J. now resides in France with her third husband; she has four children. Her conversion to Catholicism had a great impact on her life. An editor for the Grasset publishing house, M.-J. also serves on the juries of the Fémina Prize and the Goncourt Academy.

Since the publication, when she was seventeen, of a book of verse, M.-J.'s production has been steady and varied. Besides the novels and memoirs that have won her wide public recognition, M.-J. has translated English books and has written children's stories, song lyrics, prefaces for classics, and historical novels. Relatively unconcerned by problems of form, M.-J. admits that style is not of primary importance in her work, and she is resolutely opposed to the imitation of contemporary fads and NEW NOVEL innovations.

Le rempart des béguines (1951; *The Illusionist*, 1952) had a *succès de scandale* because of its lesbian theme, while the detached directness of the young author's approach suggested echoes of *Les liaisons dangereuses* by Choderlos de Laclos (1741–1803). *La*

chambre rouge (1955; *The Red Room*, 1956), a sequel, continues focusing on the evolution of an adolescent facing a disillusioning adult world.

The title of *Les mensonges* (1956; *House of Lies*, 1957) emphasizes a theme that is becoming predominant in M.-J.'s work: the conflict between the characters' inner nature, hidden from others and even from themselves, and their social roles. This preoccupation slowly unfolds in *L'Empire Céleste* (1958; *Café Céleste*, 1959) until the main character, forced to act in accordance with the image others have of him, is faced with nothing but a mask. Winner of the Fémina Prize, this novel reveals an increased technical mastery in its handling of a great many characters of extreme diversity.

In *Le jeu du souterrain* (1973; *The Underground Game*, 1975) M.-J. deemphasizes precisely drawn descriptions, adopts a more fragmented technique, and conveys a much lighter atmosphere tinged with irony: a writer's relative failure in productive creativity has a humorous counterpart in the modest archaeological find that crowns another man's endless years of solitary underground labor. *Allegra* (1976; Allegra) portrays with deft and convincing touches the type of heroine often found in M.-J.'s world. Completely herself, Allegra is unaware that her innocence looks suspicious in a society used to compromises and role playing. Counterpointed with Allegra's instinctive nonconformism, the theme of women's guilt whenever they deviate from what is normally expected of them becomes more explicit than in earlier works.

M.-J. has been compared to Flemish painters for the precision and realism of her settings, and to Balzac for her adroit handling of a wide social spectrum. Already evident in her first novel, M.-J.'s talent over the years has consistently matured; the scope of her social observation has widened as well as deepened. There has been no sudden transformation in her narrative technique, which has remained fairly traditional, although it does not rely on introspection and leaves a margin of ambiguity behind everyone's actions. Rather pessimistic in outlook, most of M.-J.'s characters retain, nevertheless, a dynamic resilience and an intuitive belief in the value of living. The pursuit of authenticity and the search for identity may be the unifying trend in M.-J.'s world, while her lucid observation of human frailties makes M.-J. essentially a moralist. Her interest in people, men as well as women, of varying backgrounds and personalities may have ensured her success as a novelist.

FURTHER WORKS: *Poèmes du dimanche* (1942); *Cordélia* (1956; *Cordelia, and Other Stories*, 1965); *Les personnages* (1961; *The Favourite*, 1962); *Lettre à moi-même* (1963; *A Letter to Myself*, 1964); *Marie Mancini, le premier amour de Louis XIV* (1964, *The Uncompromising Heart: A Life of Marie Mancini, Louis XIV's First Love*, (1966); *Les signes et les prodiges* (1966; *Signs and Wonders*, 1967); *Trois âges de la nuit* (1968; *The Witches*, 1969); *La maison de papier* (1970; *The Paper House*, 1971); *J'aurais voulu jouer de l'accordéon* (1976); *Jeanne Guyon* (1978); *Dickie-Roi* (1979); *Un chagrin d'amour et d'ailleurs* (1981)

BIBLIOGRAPHY: Reck, R. D., "M.-J. and the Anatomy of the Will," *YFS*, 24 (1959): 74–79; Delattre, G., "Mirrors and Masks in the World of M.-J.," *YFS*, 27 (1961): 121–26; Crosland, M., *Women of Iron and Velvet: French Women Writers after George Sand* (1976): 180–91; Detry, M., *M.-J.: Dossier critique et inédits* (1976); Rumeau-Smith, M., "Rôles, images et authenticité dans *Allegra* de F. M.-J.," *SPFA* (1980–1981): 91–102

—YVONNE GUERS-VILLATE

MALOUF, David

Australian novelist, poet, short-story and novella writer, autobiographer, librettist, and essayist, b. 20 Mar. 1934, Brisbane, Queensland

Born of a Lebanese Christian father and Jewish-English mother of Portuguese extraction, M. is a first-generation Australian. He grew up in a middle-class extended family with grandparents and aunts who either did not speak English or who were manifestly different in a Brisbane that was, until the 1960s, essentially monocultural. The son of migrants, M. identified strongly with his new culture. Educated at the University of Queensland, he worked as a teacher of secondary and later tertiary students in both Britain and Australia, and subsequently became a full-time author, living and writing in both Sydney and Tuscany.

A formal poet with a lyrical and philosophical bent, M.'s early volumes, *Bicycle and Other Poems* (1970) and *Neighbours in a Thicket* (1974), create a neoromantic world where the child and the past are intrinsically more vivid and alive than jaded, bourgeois adults—a theme that he pursues more trenchantly in novels like *Johnno* (1975), *The Great World* (1990), and *Conversations at Curlow Creek* (1996). In his poetry's focus on the unremarkable domestic detail, and the sensuousness of unlovely postwar, subtropical Brisbane, he drew inspiration from American poets Robert LOWELL, and Wallace STEVENS as well as Russian poet Osip MANDELSHTAM in making the subject of his poetry the luminosity of ordinary daily experience.

M.'s Brisbane was constructed in contradistinction to a nationalist literature that focused on the outback and, if on urban life, then that of the larger more cosmopolitan Sydney and Melbourne. His fiction, most notably *Johnno, The Great World*, and *Harland's Half-Acre* (1984), serves to inscribe a pre-1960s Brisbane and environs as an innocent monoculture, which was vanishing and which had rarely been the subject of fiction, and certainly not part of the national stereotypes. His work as an artist is to give it shape and meaning, to create it. Its characteristic old-style architecture (timber houses built on poles) enables a multifaceted, Freudian (though internally contested) analysis of the dynamics of repression in an Anglo-Celtic conformist Protestant/Catholic community. The larger-than-life Dionysiac rebel, a creature of 1960s youth rebellion, is doomed to self-immolation, while his doppelgänger castigates himself for his timidity and is simultaneously uncomfortably aware of his symbiosis with the dissident. M.'s autobiography, *12 Edmonstone Street* (1986), is a remarkable series of fictional essays that meditate on difference, on the body and memory, and on the role of geography at the microcosmic level of domestic spaces, as well as in more geographical terms, in defining the mind.

Although he has always resisted identification as a multicultural or ethnic writer, a resistance based on a refusal to be limited to and by the ghetto, M. has written movingly of the experience of crossing cultural divides and of the arrogant assumptions made by those who claim cultural superiority. Perhaps his most celebrated novel, *An Imaginary Life* (1978), which creates an imagined account of Ovid's life in exile among the "barbaric" Getae, and simultaneously interrogates wolf-boy literature, is an elegant poetic exploration of the falsity of the distinction between civilized and barbarian, human and animal, and argues for the interconnectedness of all living things. Similarly, *Remembering Babylon* (1996) examines, and with full consciousness of the postcolonial issues, the intersections between Aboriginal and white Australia and has as a central character a white convict who has been brought up as an Aborigine. He is preoccupied in both novels about metalinguistic matters, and in particular, the inadequacies of language to encompass experience and cultural difference, and for this reason has sometimes been criticized for aestheticizing the politics of postcolonialism.

M. in many of his novels and poems has taken up an adversarial stance on one of the key icons of 20th-c. Australian nationalism, the Anzac myth. In his novel, *Fly Away Peter* (1982), he mobilizes poetic prose to demonstrate the unthinking and dangerous innocence of the Anzacs who enlisted for World War I and to create contrasting worlds, the wetlands of the antipodes and the infernal trenches, linked by bird-life not limited to either reality and existing beyond the fabricated animosities of men. In *The Great World*, a novel that details the atrocities of Changi and the Burma Railway, it is prisoners of war who are the focus rather than soldiers, and M. refuses to demonize the Japanese. Moments of illumination in M.'s fiction typically involve a point of liminality where the boundaries between different realities—outside and inside realities, physical or spiritual, animate or inanimate—metamorphose one into another in a free and often erotic exchange.

M. has emerged as an opera librettist of note, his most ambitious one being a collaboration with composer Richard Meale in adapting Patrick WHITE's *Voss* for the Australian Opera in 1986. M. is the recipient of numerous literary awards, including the Pascall Prize (1988), Gold Medals from the Australian Literary Society in 1975 and 1982, the Miles Franklin Award (1991), and the New South Wales and Victorian Premier's Award for Fiction in 1978, 1986, and 1987, as well as the Commonwealth Prize (1991) and France's *Prix Femina Etranger* (1991). *Remembering Babylon* was nominated for the 1993 Booker Prize and won the IMPAC prize in 1996.

FURTHER WORKS: *Poems 1976-1977* (1977); *First Things Last* (1981); *Selected Poems* (1981, 1982); *Child's Play* with *Eustace and the Prowler* (1982); *Antipodes* (1985); *Blood Relations* (1987); *Mer de Glace* (1990); *Poems 1959-1989* (1992); *Baa Baa Black Sheep* (1993)

BIBLIOGRAPHY: Hergenhan, L. "Discoveries and Transformations: Aspects of D. M.'s Work," *ALS*, 11 (1984): 328-41; Neilson, P., *Imagined Lives: A Study of D. M.* (1990); Hansson, K., *Sheer Edge: Aspects of Identity* (1991); Indyk, I., *D. M.* (1993); Nettlebeck, A., *Provisional Maps: Critical Essays on D. M.* (1993); Nettlebeck, A.: *Reading D. M.* (1995)

—FRANCES DEVLIN GLASS

MALRAUX, André

French novelist and essayist, b. 3 Nov. 1901, Paris; d. 23 Nov. 1976, Paris

The son of separated parents, M. early established his independence by leaving school to frequent Parisian literary and artistic circles of the post-World War I period. In a spirit of adventure, he abruptly went to Cambodia in 1923 and was arrested for the theft of art treasures from a temple; he stayed on in Indochina to edit an anticolonial newspaper in Saigon. In 1936 he commanded an international air squadron on the Loyalist side during the Spanish

Civil War. When World War II erupted, M. disappeared into the French underground and later joined General de Gaulle's 1945–46 government as Minister of Cultural Affairs. Recognized since 1928 as a major novelist, M. devoted the last several decades of his life to writing voluminously on art and also to publishing his personal reminiscences. In both literature and politics, M. proved to be one of the most prominent and controversial figures of the 20th c.

M. wrote quickly and was not given to rewriting for polished effect. His style is alternately reportorial and poetic; his characters speak in the vernacular of fighting men, yet sometimes sound like philosophers. In their structure, M.'s novels rely heavily on cinematic technique, with sudden "fade-outs" and abrupt transitions of scene, time, and place.

Two major influences on the young M. were Dostoevsky, whose psychological complexities he sought to capture in his own characters, and Nietzsche, who had portrayed the human will as an almost tangible force. M. was also fascinated by T. E. Lawrence, the British soldier-adventurer-writer known as "Lawrence of Arabia."

At the heart of M.'s work one senses not only a personal dynamism but the underlying tensions that motivated him to write. We are witness to a fierce struggle between the egocentric, rugged individualist—a romantic 19th-c. "conquering hero" type—and the modern hero who becomes increasingly aware of his isolation unless he recognizes his identity as a social and political being with an obligation to pursue collective action and international brotherhood.

M.'s first published novel, *Les conquérants* (1928; *The Conquerors*, 1929), deals with the revolutionary uprisings in Canton, Hong Kong, and Shanghai in 1925. Although he had only briefly visited China at that time, *Les conquérants* was generally, if erroneously, considered to be a documentary novel of events in which he had personally participated. Its hard-hitting journalistic style and vivid descriptions of revolutionary activity do create a "documentary" flavor, and the novel abounds in action and violence, but M. was actually seeking to create a gallery of human portraits to probe why and how men will fight for a given cause.

In particular, he contrasts the pure anarchist with the methodical and calculating revolutionary "organizer," and juxtaposes the sincere, dedicated revolutionary with his cynical, ruthless, and opportunistic counterpart. The central figure, Garine, is something of a cross between these two extremes. Sympathetic to the downtrodden, he believes that men must be manipulated and molded by a leader if they are to attain their collective goals. He has commitment but lacks idealistic fervor, and is, one senses, potentially a dangerous totalitarian tyrant. Despite his devotion to the revolutionary cause, Garine remains a self-centered individualist who never attains a true feeling of communal brotherhood.

The same characteristics are exhibited by the hero of *La voie royale* (1930; *The Royal Way*, 1935), another foreign adventurer in the Far East who wants to "leave a scar on the map." Perken becomes involved in a scheme to unearth Cambodian art treasures in order to sell them and obtain money for supplying a native tribe with modern weapons to fight off the colonial French, who would bring "civilization" to the jungle. He dies realizing that there are no true "causes," no authentic heroism, only solitary individuals who in the end die solitary deaths. *La voie royale* is based in part on M.'s own experience but also seems to derive from Joseph CONRAD's *Heart of Darkness*, transcending the framework of the adventure tale to deal with the very meaning of life and death.

In *La condition humaine* (1933; *Man's Fate*, 1934, also pub. as *Storm in Shanghai*, 1934) M. returns to the Chinese revolution of the 1920s, exploring in still greater depth the reasons men fight and

die for what they believe. It is in this novel that a strongly positive new element enters his philosophical thinking. Kyo, the Eurasian hero, discovers that death can be "conquered" in a sense if a man gives his life for the good of a communal cause, and, in so doing, acquires a deep personal experience of brotherhood and fraternity. While the "human condition" described by the 17th-c. philosopher Pascal (from whom M. took his title) is bleak, tragic, and meaningless without the grace of God, M. sees man's fate as lofty and meaningful when we consciously choose a course of action that transcends destiny and earns for us our individual human dignity. This expression of a new, agnostic, and altogether contemporary tragic humanism, along with M.'s positing of the "absurd," make him a precursor of SARTRE, CAMUS, and EXISTENTIALISM.

On a grander scale than in his previous novels, *L'espoir* (1937; *Man's Hope*, 1938, as pub. as *Days of Hope*, 1938) once more embodies the basic stylistic characteristics and philosophical dialectic that marked both *La condition humaine* and *Les conquérants*. *L'espoir* records the early months of the Spanish Civil War, which eventually led to the victory of Generalissimo Francisco Franco. M.'s novel, however, ends on a note of hope that the fraternal spirit of the antifascist forces in Spain may yet triumph. Although he may have written *L'espoir* at least partly for its propaganda effect, and while it is a rather sprawling novel, it is also a powerful and epic work of fiction, adding to M.'s stature as a novelist of international importance.

When M. published *Les voix du silence* (1951; *The Voices of Silence*, 1953), followed by an impressive series of other volumes on painting and sculpture, he was attacked by art critics and historians for his unorthodox views and his cryptic, often paradoxical, commentary. In essence, M. was writing less about art per se than about the rise and fall of civilization and the destiny of mankind. Continuing the dialogue of his novels, M. advances the theory that the artist is a hero who triumphs over chaos by imposing form, meaning, and truth, and that art is our key to earthly immortality. It is art, M. believes, that defines man's continuity from civilization to civilization.

Great anticipation preceded the publication of what had been rumored to be M.'s "memoirs" but he perversely called the first volume of his personal recollections *Anti-mémoires* (1967; *Anti-Memoirs*, 1968). Devoid of the customary anecdotes and gossip, and bypassing the author's childhood and youth completely, *Antimémoires* defies the conventions of autobiography. As a challenge to accepted notions of "reality," M. also juggles fact and fiction by interspersing excerpts from his novels. In lieu of following normal chronology, he dates certain chapters with several different years (for example, "1934 Saba/1965 Aden"), in order to alert the reader that his thoughts on certain civilizations are not just past impressions or just present impressions but rather a literary distillation of both. The result is an astonishing tour de force, highly demanding on the reader, but creating a unique, extratemporal "surreality" of almost mythic proportions.

Just as M.'s life had become a legend in his own time, he sought to re-create that life in legendary fashion by circumventing the devices of traditional literary memoirs. Subsequent volumes of his personal recollections include memorable portraits of such diverse personalities as Léopold Sédar SENGHOR, Pablo Picasso, and M.'s political idol, de Gaulle.

"What then is the relationship between a man and the myth that he embodies?" M. teasingly asks in one of these last volumes. Throughout his colorful and stormy career, M. remained a resolutely private person, letting his public image grow to fantastic proportions with neither comment nor denial. Widely admired as an adventurer, soldier, novelist, essayist, and statesman, he was nonetheless frequently attacked as a hypocrite, opportunist, even charlatan. Because he had fought side by side with communists, and wrote sympathetically about them, M. was believed to have been himself a communist. Yet despite his prorevolutionary stance, M. was fundamentally simply antifascist. He early saw the Soviet Union as a police state, and long before his postwar diatribes against official Russian communism, such anti-Stalinist attitudes are apparent in his novels.

M. remains the prototype of his own fictional hero: the man who repeatedly defies death as a means of asserting and confirming his indomitable faith in life. *Les voix du silence* and *Antimémoires* are recognized as two of the most original and provocative works of nonfiction of our time; *La condition humaine*, which won the Goncourt Prize in 1933, continues to be acknowledged as one of the indisputedly great novels of this century.

FURTHER WORKS: *Lunes en papier* (1921); *La tentation de l'Occident* (1926; *The Temptation of the West*, 1961); *Le temps du mépris* (1935; *Days of Wrath*, 1936); *Les noyers de l'Altenburg* (1943; *The Walnut Trees of Altenburg*, 1952); *Esquisse d'une psychologie du cinéma* (1946); *La psychologie de l'art* (3 vols., 1947–1950): *Le musée imaginaire, La création artistique, La monnaie de l'absolu* (*The Psychology of Art*, 3 vols., 1949–1950: *Museum without Walls, The Creative Act, The Twilight of the Absolute*); *Saturne* (1950; *Saturn: An Essay on Goya*, 1957); *Le musée imaginaire de la sculpture mondiale* (3 vols., 1952–1954); *La métamorphose des dieux* (1957; *The Metamorphosis of the Gods*, 1960); *Le triangle noir* (1970); *Les chênes qu'on abat* (1971; *Felled Oaks: Conversation with de Gaulle*, 1972); *Oraisons funèbres* (1971); *Paroles et écrits politiques 1947–1972* (1973); *La tête d'obsidienne* (1974; *Picasso's Mask*, 1976); *Lazare* (1974; *Lazarus*, 1977); *L'irréel* (1974); *Hôtes de passage* (1975); *L'intemporel* (1976); *La corde et les souris* (1976); *Le miroir des limbes* (1976); *L'homme précaire et la littérature* (1977); *Le surnaturel* (1977)

BIBLIOGRAPHY: Frohock, W. M., *A. M. and the Tragic Imagination* (1952); Blend, C. D., *A. M.: Tragic Humanist* (1963); Lewis, R. W. B., ed. *M.: A Collection of Critical Essays* (1964); Righter, W., *The Rhetorical Hero: An Essay on the Aesthetics of A. M.* (1964); Langlois, W. G., *A. M.: The Indochina Adventure* (1966); Wilkinson, D., *M.: An Essay in Political Criticism* (1967); Horvath, V., *A. M.: The Human Adventure* (1969); Kline, T. J., *A. M. and the Metamorphosis of Death* (1973); Greenlee, J. W., *M.'s Heroes and History* (1975); Lacouture, J., *A. M.* (1975); de Courcel, M., ed., *M.: Life and Work* (1976); Hewitt, J. R., *A. M.* (1978); special M. issue, *TCL*, 24, 3 (1978); "A.M.: Metamorphosis Imagination," special M. issue, *NYLF*, No. 3 (1979)

—JAMES ROBERT HEWITT

One may well agree with Marcel Savane's judgment that *Man's Hope* will endure into the twenty-first century as one of the best revelations to later readers of what it meant to live in the twentieth. But if so, it will survive more by its value as a document than as a piece of literature, and by its appeal to the comprehending intellect rather than to the emotions. Its confusions, its loose ends, its diffuseness, may

even increase its documentary interest. In its consciousness of what the fighting was about, *Man's Hope* towers above the book that is inevitably compared with it, *For Whom the Bell Tolls*. But Hemingway's book has the tight unity, the coherence, the constant emotional tension, and the finish, that M.'s does not. The difference is that Hemingway intended a novel while M. intended a novel and something more. The books are thus not entirely commensurable. If M.'s book outlasts Hemingway's, all that will be proved is that novels are not necessarily the most durable of books.

Wilbur M. Frohock, *A. M. and the Tragic Imagination* (1952), p. 125

La condition humaine is not a novel of ideas, although it forces one to think. It is even less a novel of propaganda. The Chinese revolution in Shanghai provides it with its general theme, but it is in no way dependent upon a historical framework for its major interest. Balzac would have described the city of Shanghai, its geography and appearance, its motley crowd of natives and foreign traders, its smells, and some of its shops and houses. Tolstoy might have written at length of the great and small causes that had brought about the revolt and of the way in which events had been determined. M.'s method, like that of most moderns, makes greater demands on the reader's brain. Nowhere is the confused skein of factions and assassinations and plots unraveled for his benefit. The traditional disorder of history is scrupulously respected. M. relates the struggle as an actor in those events and not as an omniscient and reflective spectator. The contemporary public, which has lived through one or more wars, is learning daily, through the press and the radio, how disconnected and futile are most of the events in which they are forced to take an interest, do not balk at the efforts they are asked to make. They know too well that men are not heroes curbing fate at will and that betrayals, contradictions, and dissonances are the common occurrence of any war, civil or foreign.

Henri Peyre, *The Contemporary French Novel* (1955), p. 197

His early novels (*Les conquérants, La voie royale*) are perhaps even a little excessive in their lyrical praise of the adventurer. No wonder Gaëtan Picon calls him and his generation romantic. But even in his later and more mature works, he consciously shuns the analytical novel, both introspective and retrospective. His is a literature of the present, a literature of "extreme situations," as Sartre calls it; a literature of war and death, in which evil, as represented by the sadistic will to degrade, remains pure and consequently redeemable. In the revealing preface to *Le temps du mépris*, M. fervently takes issue with the cerebral (and pathologically impartial) kind of novelist who, obsessed by the notion of individualism and individual antagonisms, forever explores the "inner world" of his characters, but neglects to find solidarity in common action.

Victor Brombert, *The Intellectual Hero: Studies in the French Novel 1880–1955* (1961), p. 166

The word "lucid," which M. sometimes applies to the heroes of his early novels, has frequently been applied to M. himself. Nonetheless, when we come to examine the meaning of his text, we find that he is very far from lucid as this word is generally understood in France. All the words that M. loves so well, that he uses over and over and over again—fraternity, destiny, fate, eternity, centuries-old, millennary—are just the resonant type of word that sets us dreaming. Whatever precise contents these words may originally have had is soon dissipated by incessant reiteration. Yet there is something in these vague and shapeless words, and in the emotions that are clustered around them, that is essential to M.'s meaning. M. truly believes—and he has become increasingly explicit on this point in his later writings—that the really important, fundamental aspects of human experience are mysteries that cannot be elucidated but only revealed. Death is a mystery; human fraternity, a mystery; art, a mystery; and behind them all, the great impenetrable mystery of man himself. "The word 'to know' as applied to human beings has always stupefied me. I believe that we know no one." But we do have, according to M., an immediate intuition of this mystery in certain moments that transcend our normal experience of life. And the vague abstractions, progressively depleted of rational content during the unfolding of a M. novel, are suddenly brought to life at the end, by the impact of approaching death. Death gives the dimension of the absolute to that which was relative, the depth of eternity to that which was transient. And the emotional illumination is reinforced by the strange nocturnal lighting effects that are characteristic of so many of M.'s climactic scenes.

Germaine Brée and Margaret Guiton, *The French Novel from Gide to Camus* (1962), p. 189

Essentially, it is the idea of the chaos of appearance or the chaos of the world as given by creation that makes it possible for M. to find unity in all artistic creation, whether it be religious or secular in nature. "All art," he declares, "seems to begin with a struggle against chaos." If art is also the expression of the artist's feeling about the universe, it follows that in M.'s philosophy the artist begins by feeling that the universe is chaotic, at least as it appears on the surface. This is no less true for the artist whose inspiration is religious in nature than for one for whom there is only man. For the former, the chaotic nature of appearance hides a truth "beyond," which he seeks to attain and, in one way or another, to manifest. The religious artist, then, takes the apparent chaos and orders it in terms of the truth that is the dominant value in his life. For the nonreligious artist, there may well be no order behind the chaos except

what he can impose in terms of artistic truth as he sees it; this will be a human order, one determined by man's desires. Malraux dramatized this by his now famous remark on the Greek acanthus. The acanthus, he said, is a stylized artichoke; it is what an artichoke would have been if man had been God. This is nothing other than a restatement of Baudelaire's *dictum*, "The primary business of an artist is to substitute man for nature."

Charles D. Blend, *A. M.: Tragic Humanist* (1963), p. 149

M.'s career begins in mystery with the expedition to Indo-China, the obscure affair of the missing statues, a short term of imprisonment, and a plunge into Eastern politics. The details of these matters are still unknown to us, but it is their resonance that counts. With all their shadow and uncertainty they nevertheless suggest a purity of adventure. M. entered the European consciousness not as a writer but as an event, as a symbolic figure somehow combining the magical qualities of youth and heroism with a sense of unlimited promise. Here was no longer an air of defeat or fatigue, the melancholy self-deprecating "Hamlet" figure, but an insatiable cultural pirate, ransacking the four corners of the earth for some mysterious yet significant end, a last incarnation of "Faustian man." . . .

Such a symbolic existence, at a high level of self-consciousness, has complex responsibilities, above all the painful one of remaining true to itself. And no paradox of M.'s career has more puzzled and inflamed both critics and admirers than the particular metamorphosis that has transformed the novelist of violence into a critic and curator, or the ardent revolutionary into a fixture of the established order.

William Righter, *The Rhetorical Hero: An Essay on the Aesthetics of A. M.* (1964), pp. 2–3

It is important to bear in mind that it is an *individual* that M. would reintegrate into the society of men—a being who is fully aware of his stature as a man and who, by conscious choice, is willing to dedicate himself to elevating all men to a level of human dignity. This explains why all of M.'s heroes are intellectuals who have broken with a society in which they themselves suffered humiliation or in which dignity was denied their fellow men; they are lucid heroes, conscious of their world, and activated by a desire to either escape from the imperfect world into which they were born or to refashion it.

M.'s individual is born of a break with what he considers a world in need of rectification—a world conceived as a prison from which he must escape in order to forge his own destiny. M. himself is perhaps the chief protagonist of his own works. Whether the individual be a man of action or an artist, his origin is the same: he is born of a rupture with the world he has inherited. This world might be the political structure of society in the case of the former, or the world of pictures in the case of the latter.

Violet Horvath, *A. M.: The Human Adventure*
(1969), p. 107

MALTESE LITERATURE

In the first two decades of the 20th c. the Maltese language was still without a standard orthography. A group of Maltese writers formed an association that in 1920 became known as the Academy of Maltese Writers. The Academy's aims were to establish a standardized orthography for the language—which would facilitate matters for all writers—and to advance Maltese literature. The success of the Academy was largely due to its journal, *Il-Malti*, which started publication in 1925. At the same time it often acted as training ground for the younger generations of writers. Through the Academy's efforts great strides were made in the development of Maltese literature, and its task was facilitated because of educational progress and social change. The early 20th c., therefore, may by called the ripening period of literature in Maltese.

Political independence from Great Britain was attained in 1964, which serves as a dividing line in the history of Maltese literature. Preindependence literature was mainly concerned with the search for a national identity and therefore veered towards traditional elements. It is dominated by a spirit of romanticism and by the figure of Mgr. Carmelo PSAILA, commonly known as Dun Karm and Malta's National Poet. Postindependence literature, on the other hand, dealt largely with the conflict between the individual and society and steered towards the fundamental needs of the self. It is characterized mainly by a spirit of radicalism and modernism, and dominated largely by the Movement for the Promotion of Literature, founded in 1967.

Poetry

Maltese romantic poetry in the 20th c. is dominated by Dun Karm, a pillar of the Academy. His poetry transcends the particular to perceive the universal and in the process thoughts become unmediated perception. Dun Karm often found poetic expression in his solitude, which was eventually accompanied by a high degree of spiritual balance. His poetry reflects a background of village life crowned with an atmosphere of family feeling and it also portrays the Maltese countryside with a perceptive imagination. It synthesizes the popular culture of the Maltese, which is quite evident from its rural characteristics that furnish a local identity. Dun Karm also explored poetically Malta's history to confirm its cultural and national identity. At the same time some of his best poems illustrate an inner journey of sentimental and moral experience. Thus, his poetry exhibits great subjectivity but it also expresses his country's collective aspirations. Both the personal and the national sentiments are treated from a deep religious viewpoint that discusses existentialism. The spiritual crisis in his masterpiece, *Il-Jien u Lihinn Minnu* (1938; The Self and Beyond it), is analyzed in universal human terms that illuminate man's existence and insist on the inexplicability of the relations between God and man except for the latter's absolute acceptance of the former's hidden power. In theme and subject matter, as well as in

style (mostly imagery, meter, and diction), a group of poets, most of them active members of the Academy, came under his influence, notably Ġorġ Pisani (b. 1909), Ġorġ Chetcuti (b. 1914), Mattew Sultana (b. 1918), Vincent Ungaro (b. 1919), Dun Frans Camilleri (1919-1990), Ġuże Chetcuti (b. 1921), Ġuże Cardona (1922-1988), and Pawlu Aquilina (b. 1929).

Romanticism, as a broad movement in the history of Maltese consciousness, found another outlet in another group of poets (most of whom are also Academy members) who do not fall under the direct influence of Dun Karm. Chief among these are Ružar Briffa (1906-1963), Karmenu Vassallo (1913-1987), Anton Buttigieg (1912-1983), and Ġorġ Żanut (1908-1990). Their poetry is characterized by a unique form of sensibility, each poet with his own particular form: Briffa's poetry represents spontaneity and raw feelings; Vasallo's excitability and at times even irascibility; Butigieg's affection and tenderness; and Żammit's realization and understanding. In a very broad sense the work of Briffa and Vassallo is poetry of anguished sentiment and that of Buttigieg and Żanut poetry of intimate descriptions. However, they are all engaged in the extraordinary enterprise of seeking the deep yearnings of man's heart. The power of the creative mind is autonomous. Each of these poets assumes that the imagination can perceive reality and re-create it as truth.

With these came others most of whom are Academy members: Wallace P. Gulia (b. 1926), Amante Buontempo (b. 1920), Alfred Massa (b. 1938), Mary Meylak (1905-1975), Alfred Palma (b. 1939), V. M. Pellegrini (b. 1911), and Michael Buttigieg (b. 1916), as well as Maltese writers living in Australia. Most of these poets continued writing well into the last years of the 20th c. despite the new wave of poetry. Self-consciousness very often is a central characteristic of these romantics. Their subjectivity, grounded in common experience, poetically exalts the ordinary decencies that hold people together. Such romanticism, prevalent in human nature, is an aesthetic phenomenon whose achievement is imposing in 20th-c. Maltese literature.

With the arrival of the Movement poets, such as Victor Fenech (b. 1935), Daniel Massa (b. 1936), Achille Mizzi (b. 1939), Mario Azzoparki (b. 1944), Philip Sciberrras (b. 1945), Oliver FRIGGIERI, and Doreen Michallef (b. 1949), poetry moved in a new direction because the poets shared a different set of principles about the nature of poetry and a new attitude to their readers. Most of the time they were antiromantic and antisentimental and no longer believed in the power of the Muse as did the romantics. They did not write for a poetry-loving audience, and neither did they act as the people's spokesman—except for Friggieri later on. They adopted a conscious unaffectedness in their tone which often invited the reader to agree with their judgement. Movement poems, however, were full of ambiguity and rather thin in images, yet the few images they had still presented a perception that dragged its own associational appeal. In the 1970s the Movement was already disbanded, but the poets continued writing in isolation into the 1990s, each with his own characteristics. Most of them joined the Academy, which had by now an aura of permanency because of its literary tradition. At first, some of this poetry revealed an ironic distrust of all that was traditional, but that distrust was mingled with sentiments of direct experience as if the new poets' personal engagement was showing the inadequacy of conventional language.

These poets all use distinctly individual voices. Their poetry does not avoid experimentation but generally eschews the cultivation of stylistic idiosyncrasy. In the decades following the 1960s, they set forth in divergent directions, but still they represent the continuation of the modernist tradition. Other poets who emerged on the scene include Marjanu Vella (1927-1988), Liliam Sciberras (b. 1946), Jane Micallef (b. 1945), Raymond Mahoney (b. 1949), Joe Friggieri (b. 1946), Rena Balzan (b. 1946), Trevor Zahra (b. 1947), and Joe Zammit Ciantar (b. 1942). There also developed an interest in narrative verse with Oliver Friggieri's *Pawlu ta' Malta* (1985; Malta's Paul) and *L-Ghanja ta' Malta* (1989, The Song of Malta) in which the poet raises a voice for the nation; and Charles Briffa's (b. 1951) *Temenos* (1990), which is a narrative poem that presents the poet's imaginative nobility of his ancestors.

Drama

Maltese drama in the 20th c. inherited from the previous century the *teatrin* or the village theater in which melodrama and the farce flourished. As a result, drama did not develop with the same pace as the other genres. However, there were some dramatists in the first half of the 20th c. who attempted serious drama. One of the promoters of the *teatrin* was Ninu Cremona (1880-1972) who in 1913 moved to classical drama. His poetic play, *Il-Fidwa tal-Boliewa* (1913; The Farmers' Ransom), is set in 15th-c. Malta when the islands were under a feudal lord who was a greedy despot. Excessive oppression led to the inhabitants' insurrection, which overthrew the despot's government. As a consequence the poor locals had to refund in full the money paid for the possession of the islands. But all this is only the sociohistorical backdrop of the love drama of the village girl, Roži—young, beautiful, respectable, and loyal—who is engaged to be married to the patriotic seaman, Pietru—strong, heroic, devoted, and altruistic. The bride-to-be is abducted by a brutish landlord and Pietru must save her. He does so and all evil elements are romantically destroyed. The love drama, however, merges into the nationalistic crisis so that Pietru's rescue of the helpless heroine on the white steed symbolizes the farmers' redemption from the oppressor's yoke.

The next exponent of classical drama was Erin Serracino Inglott (1904-1983). His three poetic plays, *Ir-Rahaheb* (1941; The Monk), *Il-Barrani* (1942; The Outsider), and *Il-Kenjoti* (1942; The Iscariot), highlight the aspect of the outsider in him: as a creative artist he considers himself to be contemporary social themes. Serracino Inglott, however, treated universal themes in these plays. Classical drama continues with Oliver Friggieri who takes up the national issue against the formidable French at the end of the 18th c.

By the middle of the 20th c. ranting melodrama was firmly removed from the scene and a type of social realism was allowed to make itself at home, at first intermingled with subjectivity and romanticism and later in a more objective manner. Ivo Muscat Azzopardi (1893-1965) and Ġorġ Aquilina (b. 1911) claim as dramatists to grapple with society's problems, but they do so in a rather subjective manner to present a sublime idealization. Their works exploit the social implications of realism as they aim to rid the stage of histrionics replacing them with a more natural style. However, they allow their own subjective consciousness to intrude into the action.

Objective reality is effectively dealt with in the plays of Ġuże Diacono (b. 1912). As a realist Diacono aims at the presentation of concrete facts. His plays, notably *Salib Haddiehor* (1960; Other People's Troubles), Enwieh Marbula (1965; Chained Souls), *L-Ewwel Jien* (1972; I Come First), and his television serial *Il-Madonna taċ-Ċoqqa* (1978; Our Lady of the Hood) are not

intellectual—instead, they are unromantic and objective in their treatment of the themes. Diacono's intention is to analyze not man's hidden motive but the tangible results of those hidden motives, and he skillfully avoids oversentimentalism. Consequently, his language is full of self-control and it lacks emotive values. There is very little inner spiritual tension and emotional relationship among his characters. He is not interested in speculation, but it is the concrete world that provides him with material for his dramatic performances. Diacono's realism does not allow the characters to control their own context. It turns them into objects and thus his theater presents types and not individuals, emphasizing the context and not the characters.

But the 1950s also saw the birth of psychological realism in the modern literary theater with the dramatic output of Francis EBEJER, who wrote in Maltese and English and attained international esteem. His ideals were upheld by both the Academy (to which he belonged) and the Movement. He wrote many plays from 1950 until his death, the best known being *Vaganzi tas-Sajf* (1962; Summer Holidays), *Boulevard* (1964; Boulevard), *Menz* (1967; Menz), *Il-Hadd fuq il-Bejt* (1973; Sunday on the Roof), *L-Imnarja Żmien il-Qtil* (1973; Imnarja Is a Time for Killing), *L-Imwarrbin* (1973; The Cliffhangers), *Hitan* (1974; Walls), and *Il-Ġahan ta' Bingemma* (1985; The Jester of Bingemma). He also wrote many radio and television plays, and the televised serial *Id-Dar tas-Soru* (1997-1978, The Nun's House) was a major success. The emergence in the last decades of the 20th c. of other dramatists, such as Oreste Calleja (b. 1946) and Alfred Sant (b. 1948), both members of the Movement for the Promotion of Literature, ensured dramatic continuity while providing new efforts on stage that involve unique debate on man's condition.

Fiction

The novel came to the Maltese shores via Italy in the form of the historical romantic novel, which was compatible with the local mentality. History was a source of national pride and fiction (including novels and short stories) gave vent to wishful thinking, so the historical novel was an obvious favorite form of literary expression. In the beginning of the 20th c. the novel had two branches: the popular—which appealed to and was comprehensible to the general population—and the literary—which was involved in healthy experimentation that withstood the test of time and scholarship. The literary novel ushered in the social novel that often assumed a reformist role and later developed into the political, psychological, and sociopsychological novels.

The literary historical novel in Maltese has three structurally distinct kinds: the fictionalized history, the romantic fantasy, and the historical fiction. The period novel that represents fictionalized history makes historical characters and actions form the basis of the novel. Ġuże Muscat Azzopardi (1853-1927) is the major exponent of this types of fiction. His best-known novel is *Nazju Ellul* (1909, Ignatius Ellul), which emphasizes the political situation during the French period in Malta by revealing social preoccupation and national concern, but it includes a fictionalized love tragedy. Similarly, Agostino Levanzin (1872-1955) in his *Is Sahhar Falzun* (1908-12; Falzon the Warlock) aims at historical instruction through literary means. The romantic fantasy, on the other hand, is a period novel that depicts a historical romance in which the past is simply used as a sensational and dramatic backdrop for adventurous exploits. Guże Galea (1901-1978) in his *Ragel bil-Ghaqal* (1943;

A Witty Man) depicts the hero's adventures on the Mdina bastion and in his hideout on Comino as the Maltese islands are being threatened by pirates. And Ninu Muscat Fenech (1854-1910) in his *Ġorġ il-Bdot* (1927; George the Navigator) presents a plot based during the era of the Knights of Malta. Finally, historical fiction includes the period novel that puts fictitious characters and actions within a historical background. The difference between the romantic fantasy and historical fiction is that in the former history is represented in an exciting way, whereas in the latter it is authentic. A. E. Caruana's (dates n.a.) *Ineż Farruġ* (1889; Agnes Farug), Galea's *San Ġwann* (1939; St. John's Cathedral), and Ġuże Aquilina's *Taħt Tliet Saltniet* (1938; Under Three Rules) are all examples of historical fiction. Eliciting patterns from history was full of significance, and it aroused a sense of patriotism.

After the historical novel came the social novel with novelists and short-story writers such as Victor Apap (b. 1913), Ġuże Bonnici (1907-1940), Paul P. Borg (b. 1949), Wistin Born (1910-1986), Lina Brockdorff (b. 1918), Joseph J. Camilleri (b. 1928), Albert M. Casola (1915-1974), Ġuże Chetcuti, Ġwann Marno (1886-1941), Alfred Massa, Mary Meylak, Ivo Muscat Azzopardi, Ġuże Orlando (1898-1962), Ġorġ Pisani, Alfred Sant, Michael Spilteri (b. 1917), Paul Xuereb (1923-1995), Ġorġ Zammit (1908-1990), and Temi Zammit (1864-1935). The essential interest of the literary historical novel is nationalism, and the general aim of the contemporary social novel is awareness of the present. One glorifies the past to understand the present, the other tries to understand the present as a preparation for the future. Eventually, the dwelling on the collective political theme for patriotic involvement gave way to a preoccupation with social hardships, and the social novel started demanding more interpenetration of plot, character, and moral theme. And as the social novel's offshoot developed into a psychological inquiry the interpenetration of character and theme became an essentiality. Novelists like Rena Balzan, Ġuże Ellul Mercer (1897-1961), Oliver Friggieri, Frans Sammut (b. 1945), Francis Ebejer, Lino Spiteri (b. 1938), and Trevor Zahra all explored the sociopsychological novel.

Serious Maltese fiction has often been concerned with portraying life, and its audience was mainly recruited from among those who were chiefly interested in social change and in qualifying human conditions. Looking at the efforts of the 20th c., it becomes clear that local fiction has been depicting the spread of insecurity among the Maltese people: the historical and social novels reproduce most of the anxiety and fear that results from a nation's political fate, and the sociopsychological novel renders an aura of uncertainty and worry that are part of human nature. Even on a small island like Malta the novel does not prosper only in a stable and harmonious society: insecurity is often thematically productive. However, most modern novelists view life sharply and critically, but they do not want to distort or caricature it. Their work is more of a comment and when they view the past of Maltese society their aim is mainly to lay judgement by their point of view or attitude.

Even children's fiction flourished especially through the indefatigable efforts of Trevor Zahra. Other juvenile writers include: Charles Casha (b. 1943), Carmel G. Cauche (b. 1944), Charles Briffa, Ġorġ Malia (b. 1957), Mary Puli (b. 1930), George Peresso (b. 1939), and Joe Zammit Ciantar.

By the end of the 20th c. Maltese literature took an unpredictable course, depending not on any corporate intellectual and/or artistic effort but on individual genius. Thus, contemporary Maltese literature must content itself with a moderate amount of scattered talents. Each genre tend to stress something. The poetry of the last decades reveals an important fact: the Maltese poet is utterly aware that he is a full-time member of the global community. He has to be sensitive to the events and moods experienced outside his shores, but at the same time he has to confirm his Mediterranean identity. The novelist also becomes very sensitive and finds himself in solidarity against a structure of social injustice. Theatregoers still seek entertainment, but they have come to appreciate the lasting work of thoughtful, serious writers.

BIBLIOGRAPHY: Aquilina, J., "Malta's Current Contribution to Commonwealth Literature," in Goodwin, K. L., ed., *National Identity* (1968): 104-14; Arberry, A. J., ed., *A Maltese Anthology* (1960); Briffa, C., and Mallia, G., *Trevor Zahra: A Childhood of Delight* (1992); Eberjer, F., *The Bilingual Writer as Janus* (1989); Falzon, G., "The Savage Mind of Mario Azzopardi," in Azzopardi, M., *Naked as Water* (1996): xi-xiii; Friggieri, O., "In Search of a National Identity: A Survey of Maltese Literature," in Hopkins, K., and van Roekel, R. eds., *Crosswinds: An Anthology of Post-War Maltese Poetry* (1980): i-xxxiv; King, B., "Francis Ebejer," in Kirkpatrick, D. L., ed., *Contemporary Dramatists* (1988): 138-40; Massa, D., "Contemporary Maltese Literature," in *ComQ*, 2, 7 (1978): 11-26; Serracino Inglott, P., Introduction to Massa, D., ed., *Limestone 84: Poems from Malta* (1978): 1-9

—CHARLES BRIFFA

MAMEDKULIZADE, Djalil

Azerbaijani journalist, short-story writer, and dramatist, b. 22 Feb. 1866, Nakchichevan; d. 4 Jan. 1932, Baku

M. taught school and studied law before finding his true vocation as a journalist and social critic. In 1906 in Baku he founded the weekly *Molla Nasreddin*, in which he perfected the satirical-realist style that became the hallmark of his finest stories and plays of the pre-Soviet period. After the Russian Revolution he lived for a time in Tabriz, in northern Iran. Returning home in 1922, he revived *Molla Nasreddin* and continued writing, but he could not adjust completely to the new political and cultural order. Although the Soviet state has acknowledged his remarkable gifts, it has found his cosmopolitan views and independent stance often incompatible with its ideal of the proletarian writter.

M.'s reputation rests primarily upon his editorship of *Molla Nasreddin*. Named after the half-legendary sage who made the rich and powerful the butt of his wit, it achieved an influence unrivaled by any similar publication in the Muslim world before World War I. Nonconformist and radical, M. attacked all forms of conservatism, but reserved special venom for the Shiite Muslim clergy, whose ignorance and depravity he held responsible for the backwardness of Azerbaijani society.

From his first collection of stories, *Danabash kendinin ehvalatlary* (1894; events in the village of Danabash), to the pieces written after 1922 M. carried on the realist tradition of 19th-c. Azerbaijani prose. His instrument was the spoken language; his subject matter, the peasantry. To portray the daily sufferings and aspirations of ordinary people, he used the simple narrative form of the popular tale, which he honed in editorials and sketches written for *Molla*

Nasreddin. The natural, outwardly impassive flow of the narrative and the tightly controlled selection of details, quite new to Azerbaijani prose, are reminiscent of CHEKHOV and de Maupassant. Despite the obvious aim of social criticism, these stories are never didactic. M.'s substle art did not allow direct commentary; an ironic intonation here and a satirical wink there were enough to convey his intent.

Although he called them "comedies," M.'s plays were in reality serious meditations on the meaning of life. The two most important—*Ölüller* (1909; the victims) and *Deliyighinjagy* (1922; the assembly of the mad)—have an atmosphere of religious fanaticism and moral degradation that warps the human personality and undermines the general good. The "victims" and the "madmen" are the pious who in the name of religion ignore the most elemental rules of civilized behavior toward their fellow men, while the "normal" are those who flout the mores of Muslim society in the service of fundamental human values. As in his stories, M. used clarity, humor, and understatement to achieve his ends.

M. made two lasting contributions to Azerbaijani prose and drama: a realistic style that combined simplicity and satire; and complex characterization, such as that of the heroes of his plays, who, although keen observers of society, are of natures too flawed to change it.

FURTHER WORKS: *Sechilmish eserleri* (2 vols., 1951–1954)

BIBLIOGRAPHY: Bennigsen, A., *"Molla Nasreddin* et la presse satirique musulmane de Russie avant 1917," *CMRS*, 3 (1962): 505–20; Caferoglu, A., "Die aserbeidschanische Literatur," *Philologiae turcicae fundamenta*, 2 (1964), 679: 684–85

—KEITH HITCHINS

MAMET, David

American dramatist and screenwriter, b. 30 Nov. 1947, Chicago, Ill.

The title of one of M.'s plays, *A Life in the Theater* (perf. 1977, pub. 1978), epitomizes his career. He attended the Neighborhood Playhouse School of the Theater and was graduated in 1969 from Goddard College, where he was later artist in residence. At Yale and the University of Chicago he has taught drama and playwriting. He has served as artistic director for both the St. Nicholas Theater Company and the Goodman Theater in Chicago. Among his awards are an "Obie" in 1976 for the best new American plays produced off-Broadway, *American Buffalo* (perf. 1975, pub. 1977) and *Sexual Perversity in Chicago* (perf. 1974, pub. 1978) and the New York Drama Critics Circle Award in 1977 for *American Buffalo* as the best American play of the year. Lately he has turned to writing for radio, television, and films.

M. first gained recognition with *The Duck Variations* (perf. 1972, pub. 1978). Critics immediately made comparisons to BECKETT and PINTER because of the play's lurking air of menace, its aphasic dialogue, and its limited palette of characters and props. But his early plays are less derivative than they are assertive: they announce M.'s talent for quickly and deftly etching a character's desperate pain and tenuous sense of self. Whether dealing with the panic people feel at mutual commitment (*Sexual Perversity in*

Chicago) or with the ironic awareness that "business" is "people taking *care* of themselves" (*American Buffalo*), M. proves that the way characters talk causes them both to perform self-destructive actions and to fix themselves in frustration.

Because M., like Voltaire, believes that language conceals feelings, he strives in three recent plays to lay bare his characters' hearts, but in a language that modulates from merciless profanity through querulousness to abstract poetry. Originally a radio play, *The Water Engine* (perf. 1977, pub. 1978) also satirizes the commercial ethic, but it demonstrates that the system corrupts the hearts of heroes and villains alike. M. raises the ante in *A Life in the Theater.* Confronting two actors, professionally adept at disguise, he discovers that only attitudes constitute their core. And *The Woods* (perf. 1977, pub. 1979) abstractly suggests the flight from intimacy felt by two lovers ignorant about their hearts.

M.'s admirers credit him with the subtlest ear for language among living American dramatists. Any event in his characters' lives results directly from that person's particular habits of using language. Because friendship and loyalty form the nexus of our social lives, M. focuses on these themes, which he conveys through fragmented structures. But none of these characteristics accounts for the empathy, understanding, and affection that M. has for his characters and that the audience feels for both them and him.

FURTHER WORKS: *Lakeboat* (perf. 1970, pub. 1981); *Reunion* (perf. 1976, pub. 1979); *Dark Pony* (perf. 1977, pub. 1979); *The Revenge of the Space Pandas; or, Binky Rudich and the Two-Speed Clocks* (perf. 1977, pub. 1978); *Mr. Happiness* (1978); *Glengarry Glen Ross* (1984); *House of Games* (1988); *Oleanna* (1992)

BIBLIOGRAPHY: Eder, R., "D. M.'s New Realism," *NYTMag* (12 March 1978): 40–47; Storey, R., "The Making of D. M.," *HC*, 16, 4 (1979): 1–11; Ditsky, J., "'He Lets You See the Thought There' The Theater of D. M.," *KanQ*, 12, 4 (1980): 25–34

—JAMES B. ATKINSON

MAMMERI, Mouloud

Algerian novelist, essayist, dramatist, and translator (writing in French), b. 28 Dec. 1917, Traourt-Mimoun; d. 26 Feb. 1989, Algiers

After attending the local primary school of his Berber village, where he learned French, M. pursued his studies in Rabat, Morocco, in Algiers, and in Paris. During World War II he fought in Algeria and later in Europe after the liberation of North Africa. After the war M. worked as a teacher. In 1957 he went to Morocco, returning after Algeria achieved independence in 1962 to Algiers, where he has been professor of ethnology at the University of Algiers and director of a research center at the Bardo Museum.

M. belongs to the first wave of major Algerian Francophone authors, called by some the "generation of '52"—for the year in which M. and Mohammed DIB published their first novels. M.'s novel, *La colline oublié* (the forgotten hill), is set in a remote Kabyle village in the late 1930s and early 1940s. The book is presented in the form of a diary kept by Mokrane Chaalal. Near the end of the book, the diary breaks off and the narrator intervenes to tell what happens thereafter. The novel provides interesting socio-logical insights into such local customs as fertility rites and vendettas based on the male-honor code.

The action of M.'s second novel, *Le sommeil du juste* (1955; *The Sleep of the Just*, 1958), takes place during World War II; in it we see the notions of independence and an Algerian entity begin-ning to stir in the minds of the young Kabyles. M. shows greater technical mastery in this novel than in his first, which had numer-ous subplots; here he limits the number of major characters and increases the density of action. Much of *Le sommeil du juste* consists of a long letter the main character, Arezki, writes to his old French schoolteacher. The letter, like the novel in general, is an indictment of the inequality imposed by the colonial system.

M.'s third novel, *L'opium et le bâton* (1965; opium and the stick), although in some ways less unified in creative vision than M.'s earlier works, is nevertheless his most successful. It is an ambitious fresco of the liberation struggle in Algeria, presenting particular moments of the revolution.

In *La traversée* (1982; the crossing)—an impressionistic novel that makes frequent use of dreams, letters, and diary entries—the notion of "crossing" is explored on four levels; the title and theme of a controversial political fable by the journalist Mourad, which causes his resignation; an actual Sahara crossing; the trajectory of a human life; and the inexorability of historical movements. Mourad, cynical and alienated, tries to recover his Berber roots, but dies of a fever on arriving in his native village.

The evolution of M.'s protagonists—within each book, as well as from book to book—has been from rural security toward a vaster but more fragmented cosmopolitan humanism. Even as his pro-tagonists have become more disenfranchised, M. has become increasingly aware of the implications of their loss and increasingly involved in a quest to preserve the cultural roots some of his younger characters have forsaken.

M.'s later works have addressed the possible decline of Berber civilization, owing to a worldwide trend toward uniformity of culture. In 1969 M. brought out *Les isefra: Poèmes de Si Mohand-ou-Mhand* (the *isefra*: poems of Si Mohand-ou-Mhand), a large bilingual collection of the traditional nine-line *isefra* by the great Kabyle wandering bard (1845–1906), who sang of, among other things, Kabylia's degeneration after French colonization. In 1980 M. published an anthology, *Poèmes kabyles anciens* (old Kabyle poems). A play, *Le banquet* (1973; the banquet), preceded by an essay entitled "La mort absurde des Aztèques" (the absurd death of the Aztecs), deals ostensibly with Cortés's destruction of Montezu-ma and his people, but it also explores ethnocide in general and the dual threat that European colonialism and Arab-Muslim national-ism pose to the traditional values of Kabyle society.

BIBLIOGRAPHY: Dembri, M. S., "L'itinéraire du héros dans l'œuvre romanesque de M. M.," *CALC*, No. 3 (1968): 79–99; Ortzen, L., ed., *North African Writing* (1970): 1–3, 90–99; Mortimer, M., "M. M. Bridges Cultural Worlds," *AfricaR*, 16, 6 (1971): 26–28; Yetiv, I., *Le thème de l'aliénation dans le roman maghrébin d'expression française, 1952–1956* (1972): 114–33; Déjeux, J., *Littérature maghrébine de langue française* (1973): 180–208; Adam, J., "Le jeune intellectuel dans les romans de M. M.," *RUO*, No. 46 (1976): 278–87; Déjeux, J., "*La colline oubliée* (1952) de M. M., un prix littéraire, une polémique politique," *O&C*, 4, 2 (1979): 69–80

—ERIC SELLIN

David Mamet

MANDELSHTAM, Osip Emilevich

(often spelled Mandelstam in English) Russian poet and prose writer, b. 15 Jan. 1891, Warsaw, Poland; d. 27 Dec. 1938, near Vladivostok

From an assimilated middle-class Jewish family, M. grew up in St. Petersburg, where his family had moved when he was very young and where he received a classical education at the Tenishev School. He spent the greater part of the years 1907–10 in western Europe, discovering the French SYMBOLISTS in Paris, visiting Italy and Switzerland, and studying Old French literature at Heidelberg University. In 1911, while at St. Petersburg University, he joined Nikolay GUMILYOV and Anna AKHMATOVA in launching Acmeism. During World War I and the Russian Revolution, in which he took no active role, M. continued to write, publish, and travel within Russia. During the civil-war years, he worked briefly for Anatoly Lunacharsky's (1875–1933) Education Ministry in Moscow and traveled to Kiev, Georgia, and the Crimea.

Although he was able to publish until 1928, M. supported himself during the 1920s largely by translating and by writing children's books. His arrest in May 1934 was connected with his poem denouncing Stalin as a "peasant slayer." At the end of his three-year term of exile in Voronezh, he was at first allowed to return to Moscow, then banished to its outskirts. The months before his second arrest in May 1938 were spent in search of work and money from sympathetic friends. Sentenced to five years at hard labor for counterrevolutionary activities, he was sent to a transit camp near Vladivostok, where, according to an official notice, he died two months later, of heart failure.

In the spare, traditionally structured verses of his first book, *Kamen* (1913; *Stone*, 1973), he is the poet of a confrontation between the universal emptiness, palpably evoked, and the fragile, yet indestructible pattern of individual, artistic consciousness. In their preoccupation with poetry itself, M.'s first poems evoke a primordial silence, from which both music and the word are born. The poet's terror before the abyss of eternity and his feeling of impotence over not possessing sufficient language are counterbalanced by the serene assertion of his own significance and the word he has to speak. He embraces the "poverty" of the tangible world as the raw material from which enduring art is made. His poems about famous buildings are celebrations of man's ability to overcome both the "cruel weight" of matter and the emptiness of space.

In the longer, more richly imagistic poems of his second collection, *Tristia* (1922; Latin: sad things [from Ovid]), M. continued to be the poet of civilization. St. Petersburg, Rome, Florence, Moscow, Venice, Troy, Siena, Theodosia in the Crimea— all appear as emanations of an integral and timeless "world culture" (centered in the Mediterranean, as the birthplace of Christianity), the longing for which he would later give as his definition of Acmeism. His tragic sense of the meaning of Russia's cataclysmic years is reflected in his poetry on the death of his beloved St. Petersburg. Yet, even as he re-creates the Ovidian theme of a poet's exile from his native city, he affirms the inevitable homecoming inherent in the survival of the "blessed, meaningless word" of poetry, an absolute aesthetic value, eternally new, eternally repeated. In the image of poetry as a plow churning up the layers of time, M. expressed his faith in the survival of the positive values created by each age.

But in *Stikhotvorenia 1921–25* (1928; *Poems 1921–25*, 1973), containing some of M.'s most profound philosophical meditations on time and the age, the concept of creative time is opposed and overshadowed by the image of inimical time: the "Age-Ruler." The painful ambivalence of the poet, who wishes to belong to his own age yet cannot escape his internal estrangement from it, gives rise to repeated images of personal diminution and of the encroaching poetic muteness that would, in fact, envelop him from 1926–1930.

M.'s later poetry, contained in the two "Moskovskie tetradi" (1930–34; Moscow notebooks) and the three "Voronezhskie tetradi" (1935–37; Voronezh notebooks), was not published in his lifetime and survived only through the efforts of his widow, Nadezhda Yakovlevna Mandelshtam (née Khazin, 1899–1980). The stature of this large (over two thirds of his poetic output) and varied body of work has attained only belated recognition. Closely linked with M.'s personal fate, it centers upon the struggle of the poet, who is "not a wolf by blood," against the relentless "age-wolfhound." The possibility of survival is strongly linked with place. St. Petersburg-Leningrad has become a coffin. Armenia, which M. visited in 1930, becomes in his poetry an "outpost of Christendom"; yet the purity and vitality of this "land of the Sabbath" sustains him only temporarily, before his return to "Buddhist Moscow," the inert, menacing landscape of the Soviet era, where defiant assertions of his continued existence alternate feverishly with the resigned certainty of his impending exile and death. If his deserted, "quiet as paper" Moscow apartment represents the city's silencing of his voice, it is not a final defeat. In exile, he insists upon his "moving lips" as the symbol of his poetic immortality. Locked in the plains of his Voronezh exile, he preserved a vision of the waters and mountains of his ideal Hellenic landscape, "man's place in the universe."

The substantial body of M.'s prose writings, which include his autobiographical evocation of prerevolutionary Russia, "Shum vremeni" (1925; "The Noise of Time," 1965), the surrealistic Petersburg tale "Egipetskaya marka" (1928; "The Egyptian Stamp," 1965), and a number of critical-philosophical essays, displays the brilliance and originality of his poetry. Linked by countless conceptual and imagistic threads to his poetry, to which they provide a vital gloss, they demonstrate the essential unity of M.'s creative oeuvre.

M. stands alongside Boris PASTERNAK, Marina TSVETAEVA, and Anna Akhmatova as one of the great voices of 20th-c. Russian poetry. His many-layered verse, built upon a complex system of verbal and euphonic echoes and a broad network of literary and historical allusion, yields its fullness only to that ideal, culturally literate "reader in posterity," whom M. envisioned in an early essay. The survival of his work is ensured by the sheer beauty and power of the language in which he conducted his lifelong defense of culture against barbarism and fixed the image of history's fragile "victim," the indestructible poet.

FURTHER WORKS: *Sobranie sochineny* (3 vols., 1964–71); *Stikhotvorenia* (1974). FURTHER WORKS IN ENGLISH: *The Prose of O. M.* (1965); *The Complete Poetry of O. E. M.* (1973); *Selected Poems* (1973); *Selected Poems* (1975); *Selected Essays* (1977); *Selected Works* (1977); *O. M.* (1977); *Journey to Armenia* (1977); *The Complete Critical Prose and Letters* (1979)

BIBLIOGRAPHY: Terras, V., "Classical Motives in the Poetry of O. M.," *SEEJ*, 3 (1966): 25–67; Mandelstam, N., *Hope against Hope* (1970); Brown, C., *M.* (1973); Mandelstam, N., *Hope Abandoned* (1974); Nilsson, N. A., *O. M.: Five Poems* (1974); Broyde, S., *O. M. and His Age* (1975); Rayfield, D., "M.'s Voronezh Poetry," *RLT*, II (1975): 323–62; Baines, J., *M.: The Later Poetry* (1976); Taranovsky, K., *Essays on M.* (1976); Harris, J. G., Introduction to *The Complete Critical Prose and Letters* (1979): 3–49; Leiter, S., "M.'s Moscow: Eclipse of the Holy City," *RusL*, 7, 2 (1980): 167–97

—SHARON L. LEITER

MANGER, Itsik

Yiddish poet, b. 28 May 1901, Czernowitz, Austro-Hungarian Empire (now Chernovtsy, Ukraine); d. 20 Feb. 1969, Tel Aviv, Israel

M. was born in the Bukovina region. His father, a tailor and "a storyteller, a compulsive rhymster who often drowned his sorrow in the wine cellar," hardly ever earned enough to support his family. His mother "filled the house with folk songs and songs of the Yiddish theater." M. attended the Czernowitz high school for two years, but was expelled because he could not "endure the discipline." He then served several years in the Austrian army.

M. wrote his first poems in German, but from 1921 on he wrote exclusively in Yiddish. In 1928 he went to Warsaw, and his first collection of poems, *Shtern oyfn dakh* (1929; stars on the roof), appeared the following year. His whimsy and tender lyricism, and the touch of the grotesque in his work won him immediate acceptance and popularity. Many of his poems were set to music.

M. was in Paris at the time it fell to the Nazis. He escaped to Marseille and tried, in vain, for many months to get to Palestine. He finally reached London, and in 1951 came to New York. He was officially received by the American Poetry Society in 1961.

His years in the U.S. were difficult. M. was alone, desperate, and embittered. The title of his last collection of poetry, published in New York, was, significantly enough, *Shtern in shtoyb* (1967; stars in the dust). He became ill in New York and was invited by the Israeli government to settle in Israel as a guest of the state. He suffered a stroke and died in 1969.

M. occupies a place apart in modern Yiddish poetry. Despite MODERNIST, impressionist, EXPRESSIONIST, and FUTURIST trends in Yiddish poetry of the day (in Poland, the Soviet Union, and the U.S.), he remained "old-fashioned" and classical in his versification. Yet his imagery was dramatically explosive, nightmarishly surrealistic, expressing not only the dilemma but the "sweat of the soul-anguish" (M.'s evaluation of Franz KAFKA) of modern man. He is at once lucidly simple yet maturely sophisticated; naïve yet wondrously wise; soberly observant yet obsessed by the most phantasmagoric visions; alert to the tragic social misery of the present yet steeped in the past. He carries the weight of countless generations who nurtured him.

In a certain way he can be likened to the master humorist of Yiddish literature, Sholem Aleichem: both obliterated the boundary between a smile and a tear. Each sums up the sadness, wisdom, skepticism, and hope of his epoch. Both describe the bizarre nightmare of an era in the life of their people with compassion and forgiveness, and both possess the uncanny wisdom of approaching the edge of despair and drawing back on a narrow path of faith in man and affirmation of life.

M. saw his poetry as a mission entrusted to him, whose purpose, as he rides the "winged colt," Pegasus, fusing "vision with music," is to reach that elusive goal where "beauty wipes away the tears of all pain and anguish." He saw himself as the distilled continuum of centuries of Yiddish folk singers and writers—especially the "Broder Singers" at the end of the 19th c. and Abraham Goldfaden (1840–1908), the "father" of the Yiddish theater. He often uses their idiom and style—a creative and wise ruse of simplicity—to convey the most sophisticated and complex images and ideas. The effect of this synthesis is often startling: he is at once familiar and frighteningly strange, seemingly transparent and obscure, obliterating the thin line between wakefulness and dream.

M. goes back to the very headwaters of the Jewish mythos, creating a new biblical epos—in *Khumesh-lider* (1935; songs of the Pentateuch), the eight poems of the "Rut" (1935; Ruth) cycle, and *Megile-lider* (1936; songs of the Book of Esther). His biblical personages, however, even the Patriarchs, look, act, and speak as if they emerged out of an eastern European shtetl. Even the landscape is more Slavic than Asian. He makes the biblical characters and their relationships contemporary. With the removal of the patina of history and the hyperbole of the biblical text, they become not only more intimate and homey, they become us—modern people grappling with everlasting problems and interrelationships, and painfully trying to understand the sense—if any—of life.

M. achieved a complete conquest and/or denial of time (very like, in a sense, Marc Chagall's biblical figures portrayed as shtetl Jews). M. realized the same purpose in his whimsical novel *Dos bukh fun gan-eydn* (1939; *The Book of Paradise*, 1965), a tongue-in-cheek sad and dreamy depiction of heaven. The sardonic quality is heightened because Everyman's hometown, with its foibles and evils and drollness, is so easily recognizable in this mock-paradise.

M. carried within him the creativity of a people—past, present, and future. He was in eternal combat with the dark shadows of his moods and fears, and he sought not only to give them substance, but also to dissipate them through "vision and music," the two ever-reverberating strings of his poetic instrument, a fantastic hybrid of an old lyre and a dreamlike flute of tomorrow.

FURTHER WORKS: *Lamtern in vint* (1933); *Felker zingen* (1936); *Demerung in shpigl: Lid un balade* (1937); *Velvl Zbarzher shraybt briv tsu Malkhele der sheyner* (1937); *Noente geshtaltn* (1938); *Volkens ibern dakh: Lid un balade* (1942); *Hotsmakh-shpil* (1947); *Der shnayder-gezeln Note Manger zingt* (1948); *Gezamelte shriftn* (1950); *Medresh Itsik* (1951); *Lid un balade* (1952); *Noente geshtaltn, un andere shriftn* (1961)

BIBLIOGRAPHY: Leftwich, J., "M.: Wandering Poet," *Menorah Journal*, Spring 1952: 55–80; Rais, E., and Jassine, D., "Poésie yiddish: I. M.," *Évidences*, No. 32 (1953): 34–38; Madison, C., *Yiddish Literature* (1968): 317–18; Biletzky, I. C., *Essays on Yiddish Poetry and Prose Writers of the Twentieth Century* (1969): 195–206; Liptzin, S., *The Maturing of Yiddish Literature* (1970): 232–38

—ITCHE GOLDBERG

MANHIRE, Bill

New Zealand poet and short-story writer, b. 27 Dec. 1946, Invercargill

M. was reared in New Zealand's southern extremities. His parents were in the hotel trade, and he lived as child in a succession of small towns in Otago and Southland, before eventually the family settled in Dunedin. M. studied English literature at the University of Otago, and then in the early 1970s spent three years in London where he wrote a dissertation on the Norse sagas. Returning to New Zealand in 1973, he took up a job at Victoria University in Wellington where he still teaches today.

His earliest publication was the concrete poem *Malady* (1970), developed in collaboration with the major New Zealand painter Ralph Hotere. The two have worked together on a number of projects since, among them M.'s first standard volume, *The Elaboration* (1972). The poems in this and the book that followed, *How to Take Off Your Clothes at the Picnic* (1977), introduced a style preternaturally evolved and distinctive. Brief, faintly mannered, always exquisitely finished, these enigmatic lyrics quickly won a discerning audience, even though readers were quite often puzzled about how to proceed with their resisting surfaces.

The poetry scene in which M. first emerged was still strongly informed by a landscape-based, realist nationalism. In this climate M.'s emphatically untransparent and language-oriented practice appeared out of left field, and early readers were sometimes reproachful about this flaunting of the local frame of reference. An outsider image was further enforced by M.'s apparent difference from the other young poets around him, much of whose noisy and groundbreaking work was characterized by a semiconfessive candor. Nonetheless, M. is a poet of his generation, in as much as the young writers of the 1970s sexualized New Zealand poetry, and oversaw a transfer of poetic energy from landscape and issues of cultural identity to domestic interiors and the politics of intimacy. M. is also a poet of desire and its vicissitudes. If he can also be a baffling poet, it is because the terms in which he investigates the arena of personal relations are so hesitant, language-bound, and skeptical. The connections towards which his lovers aspire are constantly dissolving into repetition and misrecognition, though the tone remains bemused and comical and the voice fastidiously polite.

The summit of the first phase of M.'s career comes with *Good Looks* (1982), a book containing some of his simplest work—a suite of poems addressed to children—but featuring, too, his densest and most formidable writing to date. Like poems by Ian WEDDE from this same late-1970s moment, the key texts have a recapitulatory feel, returning to the strategies of the previous decade with a critical, even satirical eye. At the same time, a newly explicit acknowledgment in several of these poems of the role of a mourned father clarifies complex emotional structures governing new and old poems alike. The effect is richly transferential: the story of a poetic generation and the unraveling of its confidence in a poetics of display is laminated onto a personal account of the unraveling of a symbolic contract and its mortgage on desire. Showcasing, too, M.'s sophisticated reading of the intimate relations of reader and text, these poems accommodate with seeming ease the most complex of psychoanalytic and other theoretical elaborations. To what extent this speaks of a self-conscious immersion in psychoanalytic theory it would be unlike M. to say. However, it seems as likely that this apparent distillation of the findings of the Freudian century comes by way of his reading of poetics and poetry.

A selected poems, *Zoetropes* (1984), was followed by two further volumes of new work. *Milky Way Bar* (1990) and *My Sunshine* (1996), in some ways more accessible than earlier books, have both won significant prizes and been widely appreciated. The more personal and amorous poems have thinned out, with M. preferring to work at the more explicitly playful end of his repertoire of language routines: dictionary games, elliptical mock-narratives, witty pastiches of popular culture with a strong emphasis on arbitrary formal principles. At times the poems stretch out to greater length than previously, and *My Sunshine*, in particular, is at its strongest in these longer excursions.

Also in this more recent period M.'s short fiction has come increasingly into focus; a major collection has come out under two different titles, in Britain as *South Pacific* (1994) and in New Zealand as *Songs of My Life* (1996). M.'s prose narratives frequently make use of comic techniques familiar from his verse: lists, accretions of tiny fragments, instruction manuals, role-playing games. But he also writes with well-tuned economy in more naturalistic modes. His prose is more local in its emphasis than his poetry, and more explicitly intrigued by the implications of its postcolonial context.

M.'s creative writing program at Victoria University attracts young writers nationwide, and the roster of talent emerging from it, in fiction as well as poetry, represents a major contribution to New Zealand literature. His own reputation continues to grow: among living New Zealand writers M. is acknowledged with Allen CURNOW as one of the most important New Zealand poets of the 20th c.

FURTHER WORKS: *Dawn/Water* (1979, with Ralph Hotere); *Sheet Music: Poems 1967-1982* (1996)

BIBLIOGRAPHY: Crisp, P., "Pavlova and Wrists: The Poetry of B. M.," *Islands*, 7 (1978), 189-95; Lauder, H., "The Poetry of B. M.," *Landfall*, 147 (1983): 299-309; Barbour, D., "Writing through the Margins: Sharon Thesen's and B. M.'s Apparently Lyrical Poetry," *ANZSC*, 4 (1990): 72-87; Newton, J., "The Old Man's Example: M. in the Seventies," in Williams, M., and M. Leggott, eds., *Opening the Book* (1995): 162-87

—JOHN NEWTON

MANICOM, Jacqueline

Guadeloupen novelist, b. 1935, Point-à-Pitre, d. 1976, Paris, France

M. was born in Guadeloupe to a large, poor family. M.'s parents, who were originally from India, had settled in Guadeloupe before her birth. Despite the family's poverty, M. went on to study both medicine and law. She practiced as a midwife in hospitals in both France and Guadeloupe, and became a founding member of the women's group Choisir, which advocated for women's reproductive rights. A politically engaged and outspoken Marxist, M. worked for both the legal and sexual emancipation of women. M. was married and had two children. She committed suicide in Paris in 1976, although for several years, her death was reputed to have been accidental.

M. published only two works in her lifetime, one novel, *Mon examen de blanc* (1972; My Exam in White), and one fictionalized diary, *La graine* (1974; The Seed). Both works are heavily autobiographical, centering on M.'s experiences with racial and sexual prejudice in the professional world and on strategies of domination used against women and people of color.

M.'s first work , *Mon examen de blanc*, is the most famous and widely studied of her works. The novel is an examination of the effects of racism on people of color—a fact made explicit by the title, *Mon examen de blanc*, which is a French Caribbean idiom meaning to behave as though one were white. M.'s novel reveals the ways in which racism is conflated with sexism, resulting in a feminization of the nonwhite races. This feminization serves as a strategy to ensure passivity on the part of the nonwhites—a strategy M. also sees operatives in the French-colonial relationship with Guadeloupe. With this laying bare of the relationship between race, gender and colonialism, *Mon examen de blanc* becomes an investigation of the processes of domination and resistance, not just in Guadeloupe, but everywhere.

M.'s protagonist, Madévie, a young, mulatto physician from Guadeloupe, is a character whose very constitution allows an interrogation of the three-fold process of domination which M. sees at work in the relationship between France and Guadeloupe. A doctor in a Point-à-Pitre hospital, Madévie is one of the only nonwhite members of the hospital's medical staff, and one of the only female doctors. The race and gender composition of the hospital reveals the inequalities inherent in French departmental rule, illustrating the way in which Guadeloupe's incorporation as a French department did little for the island except allow the continued control of money and power by the French.

But M. goes further than mere implication, probing the psychology of all characters in the novel in order to demonstrate the impact of such power imbalances on the relations between the French and the native population, between white people and people of color, and between men and women. All interpersonal relationships in the novel are presented as male-female, even those relationships that are purely platonic; thus, M. is able, again, to affirm the power dynamic operative in all relationships.

Madévie's relationship with her coworkers is represented through her friendship with Cyril, a fellow doctor. This relationship, constituted on Madévie's side by a fear that Cyril does not regard her as a competent physician, and on Cyril's side by a compulsion to buy Madévie gifts to cover over the fact that he makes substantially more than she does, mirrors the neo-colonial relationship between Guadeloupe and the metropole. Madévie embodies the French projection onto the people of Guadeloupe that they are inferior, and Cyril embodies the French attempt to buy acquiescence through promises of material gain. Additionally, since Cyril's gifts consist of art and music, they can be read as the promise of cultural "betterment" made by France to its former colonies.

Mon examen de blanc also deals with the racism and sexism operative in the metropole. Madévie goes to France to study and while there becomes involved with a white French man, named Xavier. She eventually becomes pregnant—a fact which recalls Frantz Fanon's (1925-1961) theories of "lactification," or the imposed desire of black race to "whiten" itself through sexual contact with the white race. M.'s novel rejects this desire with Madévie's abortion of the "white" fetus—an act which goes against the wishes of Xavier. His proposed solution to Madévie's pregnancy is marriage immediately followed by divorce—a proposal which demonstrates the desire of the white man to possess and control the body of the black women without treating her as a legitimate partner. This relationship, therefore, figures racism and sexism as a part of France and not just Guadeloupe.

The treatment of power and domination are continued in M.'s second work, *La graine*, which explores the hierarchies of dominance active in the medical community. Much more focused on economic and professional issues than the first work, *La graine* nonetheless echoes many of M.'s earlier thematic concerns. That this work was a scathing critique of the medical profession is evident in the fact that M. was reduced to emptying bedpans in the hospital where she worked after the novel's publication.

Like many Francophone writers, M. examines the crisis of identity which is the result of colonial domination. The power of M.'s fiction, however, is in its understanding and depiction of the detrimental effect of prejudice on both the dominator and the dominated. Furthermore, where many writers are content to simply expose and interrogate issues of racism, sexism and authoritarianism, M. ensured that her texts were as politically engaged as she was, calling openly for resistance to oppression, and figuring that resistance at both the narrative and thematic levels.

BIBLIOGRAPHY: Zimra, C., "Patterns of Liberation in Contemporary Women Writers," *L'Esprit Créateur*, 17 (1977): 103-14; Zimra, C., "Society's Mirror: A Sociological Study of Guadeloupe's J. M.," *PFr*, 19 (1979): 143-56; Wilson, B., "Sexual, Racial, and National Politics: J. M.'s *Mon examen de blanc*," *JWIL*, 1 (1987): 50-57

—DAYNA L. OSCHERWITZ

MANIU, Adrian

Romanian poet, dramatist, and essayist, b. 6 Feb. 1891, Bucharest; d. 20 April 1968, Bucharest

Son of a lawyer, M. studied law at the University of Bucharest, but soon after graduation he dedicated himself exclusively to an artistic career. For a short period he frequented the SYMBOLIST circle of Alexandru Macedonski (1854–1920), and together with such leading figures as Tristan Tzara and Ion PILLAT, founded and edited several journals, among which the most influential was *Gîndirea*. Between 1928 and 1946 he was an art inspector for the State Cultural Commission and regularly contributed to the art columns of several leading magazines. After 1948 his work was banned and he disappeared, for political reasons, from Romanian public life. Shortly before his death he was "rehabilitated" and allowed to publish a volume of poetry, significantly entitled *Cîntece tăcute* (1965; silent songs).

M.'s early poetry was characterized by an avant-garde, iconoclastic spirit, especially in *Salomeea* (1915; Salome). The caustic tone of his poems is reminiscent of such modernists as Jules Laforgue (1860–1887) and the young T. S. ELIOT, and remained a constant trait throughout M.'s literary career. *Lîngă pămînt* (1924; near the earth) bore the traditionalist mark of *Gîndirea* but was not free of parodic and self-parodic undertones. With *Drumul spre stele* (1930; road to the stars) and *Cîntece de dragoste şi moarte* (1935; songs of love and death), M. achieved a harmonious synthesis between his traditionalism and modernism. He made such skillful use of his interest in painting, and especially in iconography, that he was generally regarded as the leading Romanian IMAGIST poet. Many of his poems capture states of anxiety and forebodings of decomposition, in the guise of threatening landscapes.

Between 1922 and 1929 M. wrote several plays, such as *Meşterul* (1922; the master-builder), based on Romanian legends and fairy tales and informed by a populist ideology. It was his poetry, however, especially his prose-poems, such as *Jupînul care făcea aur* (1930; the man who would make gold), in which he combined startling pictorial imagery with sarcastic antilyricism, that established him as one of the most complex artistic personalities in contemporary Romanian literature.

FURTHER WORKS: *Figurile de ceară* (1912); *Din paharul cu otravă* (1919); *Dinu Păturică* (1925, with Ion Pillat); *Tinerţe fără bătrîneţe* (1926, with Ion Pillat); *Lupii de aramă* (1929); *Cartea ţării* (1934); *Focurile primăverii şi flăcări de toamnă* (1935); *Versuri* (1938); *Scrieri* (2 vols., 1968)

BIBLIOGRAPHY: Munteanu, B., *Panorama de la littérature roumaine contemporaine* (1938): pp.293–97

—MIHAI SPARIOSU

MANN, Heinrich

German novelist, dramatist, and essayist, b. 27 March, 1871, Lübeck; d. 12 March, 1950, Santa Monica, Cal., U.S.A.

Generally overshadowed by his brother Thomas MANN, M. has been one of the least familiar of important 20th-c. German writers to English-speaking readers. He was the eldest son of a prominent Lübeck grain merchant and his Brazilian-born wife. After early forays into bookselling, publishing, and painting, he visited France, and lived for five years (1893–98) in Italy, the setting for much of his writing. As a self-supporting writer he lived in Munich and, after 1928, in Berlin. In 1931 he was named president of the Prussian Academy of the Arts, Division of Literature, a post he was

Heinrich Mann

forced to leave in 1933, when the Nazis assumed power. The exiled author, an active antifascist, resided in France until it was occupied in 1940; he then emigrated to southern California. In 1949 he received the first National Prize of the German Democratic Republic. Shortly before his sudden death, he was offered the presidency of the East German Academy of the Arts.

M.'s debt to 19th-c. French literature and culture is immediately evident in his first important work, *Im Schlaraffenland* (1900; *In the Land of Cockaigne*, 1925). The novel is modeled along the lines of Maupassant's *Bel Ami:* its protagonist, Andreas Zumsee, also resembles the ambitious heroes of Stendhal and Balzac. The naïve young man from the provinces penetrates the superficial and modish elite society of Berlin, which M. satirically exposes as morally decadent and aesthetically vulgar.

M.'s other early novels, influenced by Flaubert and Nietzsche, deal with the perverted vitalism and hectic eroticism of both the bohemian and bourgeois elements of capitalist society. *Professor Unrat* (1905; *Small Town Tyrant*, 1944) follows the career of a pompous, repressed schoolmaster in Wilhelminian Germany, who, having fallen in love with a low-life *chanteuse*, manages to corrupt his Baltic home town. In 1930 this satire of a petty tyrant was filmed, with significant changes, as *The Blue Angel* (directed by Josef von Sternberg, with Emil Jannings and Marlene Dietrich); in this form it is the internationally best-known of M.'s works.

M.'s masterpiece is his satirical novel *Der Untertan* (1918; *The Patrioteer*, 1921). It is the first book of a trilogy—also including *Die Armen* (1917; *The Poor*, 1917) and *Der Kopf* (1925; *The Chief*,

1925)—about Prussian militarism and imperialism. Full of grotesque caricature, it follows the rise of the opportunist Diedrich Hessling, unmasking along the way the corruption of the Social Democrats, the impotence of the liberals, and the moral bankruptcy of the bourgeoisie. After many early failures, M. finally achieved great literary fame with this novel.

During his years of exile in France, M. wrote what some consider to represent the pinnacle of his work: *Die Jugend des Königs Henri Quatre* (1935; *Young Henry of Navarre*, 1937) and *Die Vollendung des Königs Henri Quatre* (1937; *Henry, King of Navarre*, 1939). The two novels offer a historically accurate and psychologically detailed portrait of the 16th-c. French king (M. also endowed him with many of his own traits). In this humanist of another time, M. found a model defender of tolerance and social equity. The novels are an optimistic demonstration of how political ideals can find pragmatic realization. Rather than attacking contemporary society with the sharp satire typical of his early work, M. here uses the high-minded realism of his historical pageant to address the abstract issues of power.

M. is an uneven, sometimes impatient writer. While his short narratives—above all the celebrated novella *Pippo Spano* (1905; Pippo Spano), a tragic farce about the isolation of the artist in bourgeois society—are often powerful, his translations—for example his 1905 translation of *Les liaisons dangereuses* by Choderlos de Laclos (1741–1803)—and his plays are less successful. His essays are brilliant: written at the height of Franco-German hostility, his controversial essay "Zola" (1915; Zola), on the crusading French writer, pleads for a socially committed art. Numerous essays written during World War II argue the cause of democracy. In 1945 he published his autobiographical meditations, *Ein Zeitalter wird besichtigt* (1945; reviewing an epoch).

Throughout his life M. and his younger brother Thomas influenced each other, sometimes criticizing, sometimes championing the other's work. Thomas's early literary success and Heinrich's early difficulties exacerbated their jealous competitiveness. During World War I, M. had been almost alone in denouncing the German intellectuals' support of the war. At that time Thomas referred to his brother as a *Zivilisationsliterat* ("cultural man of letters"), a derogatory term that demeans the cosmopolitan, overtly political orientation of his brother's world view and his art. But Thomas later acknowledged M.'s greater political sagacity.

A lifelong critic of authoritarianism, militarism, and bourgeois complacency, a supporter of the 1918 revolution in Germany, a friend of socialism (although never a communist), M. is more and more recognized as one of the most acute political critics of his day. His early writing, with its feverish tempo, anticipates EXPRESSIONISM, and all his work is aimed at his fellow Germans; his art, however, unlike his brother's, is not rooted in the German romantic tradition, but rather in the spirit of the French tradition of reason.

FURTHER WORKS: *In einer Familie* (1894); *Das Wunderbare* (1897); *Ein Verbrechen, und andere Geschichten* (1898); *Die Göttinnen* (1903; *Diana*, 1929); *Die Jagd nach Liebe* (1903); *Flöten und Dolche* (1905); *Eine Freundschaft* (1905); *Mnais und Ginevra* (1906); *Schauspielerin* (1906); *Stürmische Morgen* (1906); *Zwischen den Rassen* (1907); *Die Bösen* (1908); *Das Herz* (1910); *Die kleine Stadt* (1909; *The Little Town*, 1930); *Die Rückkehr vom Hades* (1911); *Schauspielerin* (1911); *Die große Liebe* (1912); *Madame Legros* (1913); *Auferstehung* (1913); *Brabach* (1917); *Bunte Gesellschaft* (1917); *Drei Akte* (1918); *Macht und Mensch* (1919); *Der Weg zur Macht* (1919); *Der Sohn* (1919); *Die Ehrgeizige*

(1920); *Die Tote, und andere Novellen* (1921); *Diktatur der Vernunft* (1923); *Das gastliche Haus* (1924); *Der Jüngling* (1924); *Abrechnungen* (1925); *Kobes* (1925); *Liliane und Paul* (1926); *Mutter Marie* (1927); *Eugenie; oder, Die Bürgerzeit* (1928; *The Royal Woman*, 1931); *Sie sind jung* (1929); *Sieben Jahre* (1929); *Die große Sache* (1930); *Geist und Tat* (1931); *Ein ernstes Leben* (1932; *The Hill of Lies*, 1934); *Das öffentliche Leben* (1932); *Die Welt der Herzen* (1932); *Der Haß* (1933); *Es kommt der Tag* (1936); *Lidice* (1943); *Mut* (1943); *Der Atem* (1949); *Empfang bei der Welt* (1956); *Eine Liebesgeschichte* (1953); *Unser natürlicher Freund* (1957); *Traurige Geschichte von Fried rich dem Großen* (1960); *Friedrich der Große* (1961); *Briefe an Karl Lemke und Klaus Pinkus* (1964); *Thomas Mann-H. M. Briefwechsel* (1965); *Gesammelte Werke* (18 vols., 1965–1978); *Verteidigung der Kultur* (1971)

BIBLIOGRAPHY: Weisstein, U., *H. M.: Eine historisch-kritische Einführung in sein dichterisches Werk* (1962); Schröter, K., *H. M.* (1967); Linn, R. N., *H. M.* (1967); Banuls, A., *H. M.* (1970); Winter, L., *H. M. and His Public* (1970); Roberts, D., *Artistic Consciousness and Political Conscience: The Novels of H. M. 1900–1938* (1971); Hamilton, N., *The Brothers M.* (1978)

—MARION FABER

MANN, Thomas

German novelist, short-story writer, and essayist, b. 6 June 1875, Lübeck; d. 12 Aug. 1955, Zurich, Switzerland

M. was the son of the patrician-burgher, Consul and later Senator of the Free City of Lübeck, Johann Heinrich Mann and his wife Julia, née da Silva Bruhns, of German and Portuguese stock, a southern element in his inheritance to which he often ascribed the burgher-artist conflict in himself. It also is a recurring theme in his works. A much younger brother Viktor wrote the story of the family *Wir waren Fünf* (1949; we were five). After the death of M.'s father in 1891 and the liquidation of his old and once prosperous firm of grain merchants, his widow, with the three youngest children, moved to Munich. Upon finishing—with difficulties—his Lübeck school, Thomas followed them. In Munich he worked for a short time in an insurance company and registered as an external student at the Technical University with the intention of becoming a journalist. After some of his early writings had been published, he traveled, spending some considerable time in the company of his older brother HEINRICH in Italy, particularly in Rome and Palestrina. There, in 1897, he wrote a substantial part of his first novel, *Buddenbrooks* (1901; *Buddenbrooks*, 1924), which was to establish him as a major writer (it was completed in Munich in 1900). Before that he had written several novellas and, for a short time, belonged to the editorial staff of the satirical magazine *Simplizissimus*.

In 1905 he married Katia Pringsheim, who came from a wealthy family of bankers and scholars of Jewish extraction. He undoubtedly expected the marriage to settle his marked sexual ambivalence. Still, homoerotic love retained a place in his life and played a role in many of his works. Katia bore him six children, three boys and three girls, all of them gifted, particularly the eldest son, Klaus (1906–1949), who became a writer.

Thomas Mann

With the exception of *Buddenbrooks*, all M.'s major works were written during the years of his married life, which, after Hitler had come to power in Germany, turned into years of exile. Its stations were Switzerland, the south of France, and from 1938 on, the U.S. He spent some months as visiting professor at Princeton and then lived for ten years as an American citizen in his own house in Pacific Palisades, California. After the war he visited Europe on several occasions, particularly Germany. He finally chose Switzerland as his domicile living in Kilchberg near Zurich. Among the many literary honors he received, the most distinguished was the Nobel Prize in 1929.

The history of the German novel culminates in M.'s work. He restored to German prose literature the international status that it had not enjoyed since the time of Jean Paul (1763–1825) and the romantics. His name is bound to appear, together with those of PROUST and JOYCE, in any discussion of the modern novel in Europe. The intellectual and spiritual features of his epoch are clearly recognizable in his writing, which represents that moment in the development of literary realism when its fundamental humanistic assumptions were called into question. Yet whereas his illustrious contemporaries such as Proust or Joyce expressed this predicament through the very form of their writing, M. preserved the outward conventions of realistic fiction but charged them with a new irony. From the outset his work is pervaded by the sense that art has become suspect if not impossible. Even his seemingly most conservative creation, his first novel, *Buddenbrooks*, fascinated its most sophisticated readers by the internal contrast between the meaning of the story—the decline, indeed the collapse, of the burgher tradition—and the telling of it in a manner that, by virtue of the faithful obedience to the inherited form, seems to intimate the unruffled integrity of that civilization. When an avant-garde woman artist from Munich had finished reading *Buddenbrooks*, she said to M.: "I was not bored by your novel, and with every page I read I was astonished that I was not bored." She was both not bored and astonished at not being bored because of the tension produced by that ironical juxtaposition.

The autobiographical character of *Buddenbrooks* is unmistakable, so much so that the Lübeck house of the family Mann became a kind of national monument. Destroyed by bombs during World War II, the "Buddenbrooks House" was rebuilt after the war in its original form and persists in being a tourist attraction, testimony to the enduring fame of the novel. It is safe to say that no other German work of fiction, on this level of artistic refinement, with the exception of Goethe's *Werther*, took with such spectacular success the very hurdle which in this case is its theme: the incompatibility of aesthetic sensibility and robust health, indeed, the separation of art from those for whom, after all, it is meant: the general public. For the historically inevitable decline of all Buddenbrook-like businesses, dignified by the name of a respected family and conducted by the successive heirs, does in this novel not appear to be solely determined by economic and social causes; with the Buddenbrooks, at least, it is accompanied, internally even caused, by the emergence of a consciousness that is more complex and troublesome than is good for the simple and tough practices of commerce. Would Hamlet ever have made an effective king? Thomas, the last owner of the firm of Buddenbrooks, is a kind of merchant Hamlet. He is certainly the most interesting of the three generations we come to know before his only child, Hanno, a precocious musical talent, dies—and dies as much of the inability to live as of typhoid fever.

If *Buddenbrooks* is the story of the fall of a family, it is, at the same time, M.'s first allegory of the Fall of Man. The Buddenbrooks are doomed because, in the person of Thomas, they have come to know; and it is no whim of literary ornamentation that invokes the memory of Hamlet in the novella that followed upon *Buddenbrooks: Tonio Kröger* (1903; *Tonio Kröger*, 1914). "There is something I call being sick of knowledge . . . ," says Tonio, "when it is enough for a man to see through a thing in order to be sick to death of it—the case of Hamlet . . ." This is also, attuned to his burgher existence, the case of Thomas Buddenbrook, just as it is the case of the burgher-artist Tonio Kröger. Only love, as Tonio comes to see in the end, could save him from the curse of his intellectual-aesthetic detachment and overcome his inability to "live." But when love comes to Gustav von Aschenbach, the artist hero of M.'s next novella, *Der Tod in Venedig* (1913; *Death in Venice*, 1925), and invades the insulated sphere of his exquisite artistry, the hopeless love for the boy Tadzio destroys the lover. This is the consummation of the-tragic sense that until then dominated M.'s experience of his "vocation" as an artist.

It was exactly this tragic sense of life that, during the years of World War I, M. passionately defended against any form of "Western" rationalism, enlightenment, or political "progress." He went so far as to interpret the war as Germany's defense against the intellectual conspiracy of the West to impose its shallow philosophy of life upon Germany—a country resolved to protect the spirit of music, irony, and the tragic profundities from the threatening encroachments of the rhetorical politics of reason. The enemy within Germany was the liberal-radical intellectual for whom M.

coined the name "Zivilisationsliterat," the literary propagandist of those elegantly aggressive "political virtues." The living embodiment of the "Zivilisationsliterat" was his own brother Heinrich, his rival for literary honors and intimate friend of many years. Thus, for M., the most formidable and catastrophic event of the first decades of the 20th c. turned partially into a fraternal battle. Its fascinating record is the book of more than six hundred pages, *Betrachtungen eines Unpolitischen* (1918; *Reflections of a Nonpolitical Man*, 1983). The title is not quite as ironical as it seems. It is the burden of the book that politics is held to be the domain of "the West," indeed of M.'s Westernized brother, while he himself, like the "true" Germany, is unpolitical, imbued with musical intimations of the futility of political change. At the same time, the book ends of a note of irony. M. himself, simply as a man of literature, will have contributed, he confesses, to what is historically inevitable in any case: the transformation of Germany into a political and democratic country.

The writing of *Betrachtungen eines Unpolitischen* took up all M.'s literary energies during the years of the war. He himself called the strenuous effort it demanded his "military service." The problems clamoring for a solution, or rather the oppressions of the soul crying out for an articulate liberation, made it impossible for him to become engaged in a work of the imagination. This book is, in M.'s own words, the "work of an artist whose existence was shaken to its foundations, whose self-respect was brought into question, and whose troubled condition was such that he was completely unable to produce anything else." It is the work that fills the great literary vacuum of his career between 1912 and 1924, between *Der Tod in Venedig* and *Der Zauberberg* (1924; *The Magic Mountain*, 1927).

Der Zauberberg is clearly the work of the same intelligence that was responsible for *Betrachtungen eines Unpolitischen*, but also of an imagination that has reconquered its freedom from the stifling intellectual and spiritual disquiet. At times it has the serenity of a late summer day in the mountains that are its setting: a Swiss sanatorium in the Alps. As soon as one realizes—perhaps by recognizing in their utterances verbatim quotations from *Betrachtungen*—that two of the main figures of *Der Zauberberg*, the antagonists Settembrini and Naphta, closely resemble, at least with regard to their casts of mind, respectively, the "Zivilisationsliterat" of *Betrachtungen* and its author, one also fathoms with pleasurable surprise the depth of self-irony that M. has gained: Settembrini is a most amiable version of the once hated stranger to the musical and tragic depths, while Naphta, his bitter, resentful, and altogether unpleasant opponent, is, in his convictions, quite close to the M. of those wartime reflections. Naphta's suicide stands for the end of a long phase in M.'s life. Nothing now prevented a reconciliation of the two brothers.

Der Zauberberg is also the ironical consummation of the dominant genre of the 19th-c. German novel, the *Bildungsroman*, always the story of a young man's intellectual and sentimental education. While, for instance, Goethe's Wilhelm Meister or Gottfried Keller's Grüner Heinrich set out on their life-journey with highly problematical natures and move toward increasing firmness of character and acceptance of their places in human society, the unheroic hero of *Der Zauberberg*, Hans Castorp, enters the story as an unproblematical, perfectly "adjusted" young engineer and receives his unnerving initiation at the hands of a sick community, representative of the moral and intellectual chaos of the modern world. He, too, in an exalted moment of his story, has a vision of the good life, but the vision remains a dream dreamt at the threshold of death in a mountain-desert of snow and ice, a dream without hope of ever coming true either amid the eccentricities of this alpine "pedagogical province" (to use a term from *Wilhelm Meister*) or down in the "flatland" of bourgeois triviality. Hans Castorp, too, like the hero of every *Bildungsroman*, finally enters life again, but life is death on a battlefield of Flanders. Thus, *Der Zauberberg* is the most radical reversal of the educational optimism that is at the core of every *Bildungsroman*.

Mario und der Zauberer (1930; *Mario and the Magician*, 1930) is written in a manner that was to be developed on the grandest scale in *Doktor Faustus* (1947; *Doctor Faustus*, 1948). Although it is a novella in its own right, it is also a political allegory, the highly particularized and even grotesque portrayal of a social cataclysm: the subjugation of individual wills within an amorphous society "on vacation" from its disciplined commitments, which is finally forced into uniformity. The tyrant, in this case, is the theatrically displayed vulgar will of a hypnotist—read *duce*. The rebellion of violated human dignity comes too late and, therefore, issues in catastrophe.

In *Doktor Faustus*, M.'s persistently warring opposites, life and spirit, society and art, have come together at last—not in the harmony of a good life, but in the unison of hell. Both are doomed. In this extraordinary work—a work of old age, but, ironically, distinguished among M.'s productions by a youthful luxuriance of invention and composition that would usually suggest the storm-and-stress period of a writer—a musical Tonio Kröger, demonically enhanced in stature and destiny, is no longer confronted, as the young writer Tonio Kröger was, by "Life" in its lovable innocence, but by a life that, tired of its own blue-eyed banality, has "spiritualized" itself and entered, like the artist himself, into an alliance with the forces of "the deep that lieth under." For this is what, under Hitler, has become of the Germany that, thirty years before, had been the unjustly besieged and immoderately loved hero of *Betrachtungen eines Unpolitischen*.

M.'s most despairing book was, however, preceded by his most serene achievements: the Joseph tetralogy, *Joseph und seine Brüder* (1933–42; *Joseph and his Brothers*, 1934–45), of which the first two volumes, *Die Geschichten Jaakobs* (1933; *The Tales of Jacob*, 1934) and *Der junge Joseph* (1934; *The Young Joseph*, 1935) appeared in Germany, while the third and fourth volumes, *Joseph in Ägypten* (1936; *Joseph in Egypt*, 1938) and *Joseph der Ernährer* (1943; *Joseph the Provider*, 1945) had to be published abroad, after M. had written his classic rejection of Nazism in his 1937 letter to the University of Bonn upon having been deprived of his honorary doctorate. In between those volumes he wrote the Goethe novel *Lotte in Weimar* (1939; *The Beloved Returns*, 1940). Both works are distinguished by an amazing combination of encyclopedic knowledge, enduring inspiration, and eminent literary skill. Although biographically *Joseph und seine Brüder* looks like the imaginative outcome of the writer's émigré existence reflected in his mind's flight back to the wellsprings of the myth, it is at the same time the poetically realized hope of which *Doktor Faustus* despairs: the hope of a life that is friend to the spirit, and of a spirit that is no deserter from life. The biblical story of the dreamer, who also is the interpreter of dreams, and who, estranged from his crudely wakeful brothers, is reunited with them in their hour of need as the provider of bread, has been retold and vastly enlarged by M. with an artistic intelligence and graceful irony that, rainbowlike, spans the gulf between ancient myth and modern psychology, divine and human comedy. With this work M. definitely settled in the rank of those writers whom Stendhal praised as

the most excellent for "kindling that delicious smile that is a sign of the highest intellectual pleasure."

In the end of the smile turned to laughter—in the enlarged version of a fragment that he abandoned in 1911 in order to write *Der Tod in Venedig* (because, he said, he could at that time not sustain the consistently parodistic tone of voice), namely, *Die Bekenntnisse des Hochstaplers Felix Krull* (1922; enlarged ed., 1936; finished version of Vol. I, 1954; *Confessions of Felix Krull, Confidence Man*, 1955). In this unfinished book art takes its revenge upon "life" for all that it had had to suffer, but this time with unrestrained gaiety and scandalous insolence at the expense of a world that genius may at least deceive, even if it can teach it nothing. After this masterly extravagance M. devoted his last words to the memory of Friedrich Schiller in *Versuch über Schiller* (1955; *On Schiller*, 1958), the poet to whom literature meant little except as an expression of concern for the spiritual fate of mankind.

FURTHER WORKS: *Der kleine Herr Friedemann, und andere Novellen* (1898); *Tristan* (1903; *Tristan*, 1925); *Fiorenza* (1906); *Königliche Hoheit* (1909; *Royal Highness*, 1916); *Herr und Hund* (1918; *Bashan and I*, 1923); *Gesang vom Kindchen* (1919); *Wälsungenblut* (1921); *Erzählungen* (2 vols., 1922); *Gesammelte Werke* (15 vols., 1922–1935); *Rede und Antwort* (1922); *Bemühungen* (1925); *Pariser Rechenschaft* (1926); *Unordnung und frühes Leid* (1926; *Disorder and Early Sorrow*, 1929); *Die Forderung des Tages* (1930; *Order of the Day*, 1942); *Lebensabriß* (1930; *A Sketch of My Life*, 1960); *Leiden und Größe der Meister* (1935); *Ein Briefwechsel* (1937; *An Exchange of Letters*, 1937); *Dieser Friede* (1938; *This Peace*, 1938); *Achtung, Europa!* (1938); *Die vertauschten Köpfe: Eine indische Legende* (1940; *The Transposed Heads: A Legend of India*, 1941); *Das Gesetz* (1944; *The Tables of the Law*, 1945); *Ausgewählte Erzählungen* (1945); *Adel des Geistes: Sechzehn Versuche zum Problem der Humanität* (1945; *Essays of Three Decades*, 1947); *Leiden an Deutschland* (1946); *Neue Studien* (1948); *Die Enstehung des "Doktor Faustus": Roman eines Romans* (1949; *The Story of a Novel: The Genesis of "Doctor Faustus,"* 1961); *Michelangelo in seinen Dichtungen* (1950); *Der Erwählte* (1951; *The Holy Sinner*, 1952); *Altes und Neues* (1953); *Die Betrogene* (1953; *The Black Swan*, 1954); *Nachlese, Prosa 1951–1955* (1956); *Briefe an Paul Amann, 1915–1952* (1959); *T. M. an Ernst Bertram, 1910–1955* (1960); *T. M.-Karl Kerenyi, Gespräch in Briefen* (1960); *Gesammelte Werke* (12 vols., 1960); *Briefe, 1889–1955* (3 vols., 1961–1965); *T. M.-Robert Faesi: Briefwechsel* (1962); *Reden und Aufsätze* (2 vols., 1965); *T. M.-Heinrich Mann: Briefwechsel, 1900–1949* (1968); *Hermann Hesse-T. M. Briefwechsel* (1968; *The Hesse/M. Letters, 1910–1955*, 1975); *T. M. und Hans Friedrich Blunck: Briefwechsel und Aufzeichnungen* (1969); *T. M.: Briefwechsel mit seinem Verleger Bermann-Fischer, 1932–1955* (1973); *Notizen* (1973); *Gesammelte Werke* (13 vols., 1974); *Essays* (3 vols., 1977); *T. M.-Alfred Neumann Briefwechsel* (1977); *Tagebücher* (4 vols., 1977–1980; abridged tr., *Diaries: 1918–21/1933–39*, 1982); *Werkausgabe* (20 vols., 1980 ff). **FURTHER WORKS IN ENGLISH:** *Children and Fools* (1928); *Three Essays* (1929); *Past Masters, and Other Papers* (1933); *Stories of Three Decades* (1936); *Freud, Goethe, Wagner* (1937); *Order of the Day: Political Essays and Speeches of Two Decades* (1942); *Listen, Germany!* (1943); *Last Essays* (1959); *Stories of a Lifetime* (1961); *Letters of T. M., 1889–1955* (1970); *An Exceptional Friendship: The Correspondence of T. M. and Erich Kahler* (1975)

BIBLIOGRAPHY: Weigand, H. J., *T. M.'s Novel "Der Zauberberg"* (1933); Brennan, J. G., *T. M.'s World* (1942); Neider, C., ed., *The Stature of T. M.* (1947); Hatfield, H., *T. M.* (1951; rev. ed., 1962); Lindsay, J. M., *T. M.* (1954); Jonas, K. W., *Fifty Years of T. M. Studies: A Bibliography* (1955); Faesi, R., *T. M.* (1955); Stresau, H., *T. M. und sein Werk* (1955); Nicholls, R. A., *Nietzsche in the Early Work of T. M.* (1955); Lion, F., *T. M.* (1955); Thomas, E. H., *T. M.: The Mediation of Art* (1956); Mayer, H., *Leiden und Größe T. M.s* (1956); Kantorowicz, A., *Heinrich und T. M.* (1956); Kaufmann, F., *T. M.: The World as Will and Representation* (1957); Mann, E., *The Last Year of T. M.* (1958); Heller, E., *The Ironic German: A Study of T. M.* (1958); Altenberg, P., *Die Romane T. M.s* (1961); Hatfield, H., ed., *T. M.: A Collection of Critical Essays* (1964); Lukács, G., *Essays on T. M.* (1965); Feuerlicht, I., *T. M.* (1968); Bürgin, H., and Mayer, H.-O., *T. M.: A Chronicle of His Life* (1969); Kahler, E., *The Orbit of T. M.* (1969); Gronicka, A. von, *T. M.: Profile and Perspective* (1970); Bauer, A., *T. M.* (1971); Hollingdale, R. J., *T. M.: A Critical Study* (1971); Reed, T. J., *T. M.: The Uses of Tradition* (1974); Apter, T. E., *T. M.: The Devil's Advocate* (1979); Hatfield, H., *From "The Magic Mountain": M.'s Later Masterpieces* (1979); Winston, R., *T. M.: The Making of an Artist, 1875–1911* (1981)

—ERICH HELLER

T. M.'s *Dr. Faustus* and the cycle of *Joseph* novels are a remarkable achievement to represent the mature work of a single writer. They form a monumental recapitulation and systematization of the subject-matter of his earlier period. What were previously études, capriccios and sonatas have become whole symphonies. This formal development, however, is not just a formal matter; it never is in the work of really significant artists. The symphonic complications and syntheses issue from a widening, deepening and generalizing of the content of M.'s original subject-matter. The growing formal complexity is dictated by the inner logic of his early themes. The characters, their relationships and experiences tended towards universality. If one looks at his early writing, one can see how little his development may be understood in formal terms. True, he starts off with a large novel which is pronouncedly universal in character, *Buddenbrooks*. In a certain sense it strikes all the notes of his later critique of capitalist society. And yet, compared even with later short stories, the first novel is much sparser, much less polyphonic.

It is along these lines that one should view M.'s development. The *Joseph* cycle and *Dr. Faustus* mark the culmination. They form a mature *œuvre* of a very special type. They were specifically conditioned by the epoch in which they were conceived, that is by the culture of the imperialist period and its particular German variant. [1948]

Georg Lukács, *Essays on T. M.* (1965), p. 47

M. never conceived of progress in terms of a simple break with the past. His interest in the forward movement of history always embraced equally the notion of return. Particularly in *The Magic Mountain* and *Joseph* special significance attaches therefore to the conception of the circular motion of time, implying the double process of return to a point of departure and advance from it. Its attraction for M. lay also in its inverse suggestion of the proximity of progress and reaction—a theme of *Doktor Faustus*. The preoccupation with the idea of return, linked to the search for a basis of advance, corresponds to this belief in an earlier tradition of middle-class culture, which is "classical" in his definition of the term as a "basic type" in the sense rather of Goethe's "Urphänomen"— "a primal type moulded by the patriarchs of the race, in which later life will recognize itself, in the footsteps of which it will walk, a myth, that is to say, for the type is mythical, and the essence of the mythical is return, timelessness, the eternally present" [*Adel des Geistes*]. "That which has once been lived is weak, it must be lived a new, strengthened in the sphere of the spirit"—the quotation from *Lotte in Weimar* implies the dual aspect involved in M.'s relationship to the middle-class culture of an earlier period, the process at once of leave-taking and renewal.

R. Hinton Thomas, *T. M.: The Mediation of Art*
(1956), pp. 16–17

T. M.'s responsible and zealous love for the full growth, the pure form and representation of mankind came into conflict with the glowing love for his own people for which he had labored in the *Reflections [of an Unpolitical Man]*. But this love for man that made him choose the martyrdom of the exile is not foreign to the love which is at the roots of vicarious suffering—this religious aspect of artistic representation, the experience of the writer who spends his life in the Inferno of the human soul. . . .

This search for the soul, a religion of self-concern, is the animating power in the concern with and for the soul of man as the center of T. M.'s work. It gives the artist's approach to human life legitimacy, vigor, and warmth because the self finds itself and is consummated only as it finds its way into the life of others. Thus is begotten a spirit of infinite sympathy in which the respect for the dignity of man and the compassion for him in his "eminent" exposure are one. In communicating to us this sense for man's great predicament as it is experienced in the elations and agonies of the soul, the artist may contribute his mite to a new ethos in a new covenant.

Fritz Kaufman, *T. M.: The World as Will and Representation* (1957), pp. 237–38

Regarded as a whole, M.'s career is a striking example of the "repeated puberty" which Goethe thought characteristic of the genius. In technique as well as in thought, he experimented far more daringly than is generally realized. In *Buddenbrooks* he wrote one of the last of the great "old-fashioned" novels, a patient, thorough tracing of the fortunes of a family.

The novel, far from naturalistic in spirit, demonstrates his mastery of the techniques of naturalism and impressionism: elaborate accounts of the dinners, the bank balances, and the ailments of the Buddenbrooks alternate with swift evocations of mood. Primarily—and hence no doubt its enormous popularity—the novel tells a story in a solid, conventional, unilinear way. From *The Magic Mountain* on, the secure ground of the nineteenth-century novel has been left for good. Daring experiments with the same sense, lack of interest, for long periods, in narration as such, and mythical associations are characteristic. In the climactic chapter of *The Beloved Returns* M. uses the technique of the stream of consciousness, which he ventures to apply to the mind of Goethe. Still more audacious is the attempt, in *Doctor Faustus*, to render in words the spirit and the impact of both actual and imaginary works of music. All of the later novels are in some sense experimental. M. says somewhere that the great novel transcends the limits of the genre; this, like so many of his general statements, probably refers primarily to his own work.

Henry Hatfield, *T. M.*, rev. ed. (1962), pp. 2–3

T. M.'s development as a novelist comprises the whole development of modern narrative prose. He began his career with a book that, though marked by the destiny of modern art, still resembled the traditional realistic novel. Indeed, he has gone on using the comfortably circumstantial, digressive manner of the nineteenth-century novel right up into the latest, "structuralist" stages of his work—even in this last summing-up, his *Faust*. Yet what a long way from *Buddenbrooks* to *Doctor Faustus*! All that has happened to us, to the world, to art, during the last half-century, can be read in the course of this journey.

M.'s whole *œuvre*, we have said, must be regarded as a single, consistent creation because, throughout, there may be felt in it an unconscious or semi-conscious tendency toward a structural unity of the whole. It is a dynamic macrocosm, a more and more dense and comprehensive complex of developing motifs, exhibiting as a whole a fugal character such as is otherwise found only in single novels or works of art. Just as each work gains increasing symbolic richness by the use and intensification of a leitmotif and the fusing of several leitmotifs, so on a larger scale the work as a whole exhibits the progressive exfoliation and metamorphosis of one single all-pervasive theme. . . .

The lifelong central theme of M.'s books has been an inquiry into the function of art and the artist, of culture and the intellectual in modern society.

Erich Kahler, *The Orbit of T. M.* (1969), pp. 22–23

This, then, is T. M.'s solution: The arcane magic of a dialectical process enabled the author without recourse to black art or a devil's pact to carry forward

his immense life's work to ever more startling achievements. He reached a high point in the novel that holds the key to the triumph of the modern artist over seemingly insurmountable difficulties. In writing this "book of the end" [*Doctor Faustus*], M. has, in fact, made a new beginning for the novel. He proved that this form of art is indeed still possible, perhaps not in its traditional aspect, but as a work that combines self-conscious artistry with intensity of feeling and Romantic irony with objective epic narration. M. demonstrated that the modern novel, on its multiple interrelated levels, can offer the reader the sophisticated pleasure of an oratorio, magically recreated in words, together with as unsophisticated and popular a thrill as an eyewitness account of betrayed love avenged by murder in a streetcar.

André von Gronicka, *T. M.: Profile and Perspectives* (1970), pp. 15–16

Perhaps it is precisely culture, M.'s use of traditional means, which sticks in the throat. For the critic harrowed by harsh realities, T. M.'s cultural language may seem too coherent, too readily disponible, his technique too sovereign. Altogether he has something too much like mastery. And mastery is unpalatable in a world the critic believes is unmastered.

Yet the mastery was not easy. It was an achievement, demanding all the creative effort that word implies. M.'s culture was not complacent—only the legend of the solemn polymath makes it seem that—nor was it exhaustive or static. It was purposefully acquired, personally turned, and subtly used. Over a long lifetime it also acquired, inevitably, its own coherence of theme and substance; but this personal synthesis was incidental to M.'s work as an artist, using materials like any other artist. If the result is open to objection in principle, then it is doubtful whether any culture can subsist. The order established by art seldom rests on an ideally ordered world. It nevertheless has a value in proportion as the artist has taken issue with the disorder of the real world—we have seen how conscientiously T. M. did that—and contributed, by whatever means, to understanding it. For understanding is the first small step towards control.

T. J. Reed, *T. M.: The Uses of Tradition* (1974), p. 414

T. M. tried to state every claim in the devil's favour. He hoped, with a would-be humanism, that an investigation of evil's force and fascination would result in refreshing disgust with evil, that evil, once exposed, would shrivel in sunlight and crumble in the hands of the clear-eyed. This hope, however, is the point against which his novels, stories and essays move. As he boldly underlines the sometimes grotesque, sometimes elegant course the daemonic and decadent take, the dark river of corruption fails to reveal an unqualified ugliness; unflaggingly it glows with an hypnotic iridescence and flows with a silky vitality that promises rich and good things.

M. had to face the crisis of morality, the transformation of values he found in the works of Schopenhauer, Nietzsche and Freud. A person could no longer be seen as governed primarily by consciousness, nor could human impulses be supposed to be educable and enlightened. The will to live was not simply a prudent desire to survive; it was a will to power, constantly in conflict with other wills which in turn seek power. . . . Genius and creativeness, even in their brightest, most liberating forms, were not simple children of light, but were born of energies that are themselves amoral and which, in their unusually excessive strength, are akin to the daemonic.

This is the basic world picture M. inherited from Schopenhauer and Nietzsche, and his own moral development can be seen as a result of the tension between these philosophers' opposing recommendations of which value-systems should function within this world.

T. E. Apter, *T. M.: The Devil's Advocate* (1979), pp. 1–2

MANNER, Eeva-Liisa

Finnish poet, dramatist, novelist, short-story writer, and translator, b. 5 Dec. 1921, Helsinki; d. Jan. 1995, Helsinki

M.'s formal education stopped after junior high school. She worked for an insurance company from 1940 to 1944 and for a publisher from 1944 to 1946. Since then she has been a full-time writer and translator of numerous works—by, among others, HESSE, KAFKA, Büchner, and Shakespeare. Shy and retiring, partly because of illness, unmarried, she lives in Tampere, the second city of Finland, but has traveled widely in southern Europe, especially Andalusia, Spain, a region that is evoked in several of her works.

Although M. published two collections of poems and one of short stories between 1944 and 1951, it was not until the verse collection *Tämä matka* (1956; rev. ed., 1963; this journey) that she received wide recognition. It was one of the most successful among the works of the 1950s that reacted against traditionalism in Finnish poetry. With the poets of the 1950s M shares an elaborately structured, freely associative IMAGISM and a rejection of strict form.

For M., the ideal poet possesses a wisdom transcending knowledge, like the ancient Greek philosophers. She shares with her generation an interest in Chinese mysticism, adding to it astrology, troubadour poetry, and other esoteric studies, but she uses these subjects allusively to express her own views. Music is important to her; she develops synesthetic visions suggested by composers like Bach, Haydn, Mozart, or Webern and models her poems on musical forms, discovering polyphonic structures in the universe.

According to M., sterile intellectualism has all but annihilated the Western world; the poem "Strontium" (strontium), in *Orfiset laulut* (1960; orphic songs) states: "strange smokes are rising/ invisible ashes are raining/bartering death./ For they, the Skilled Ones,/ are almost destroying the whole world/although it is half dream." The poems "Descartes" (Descartes) and "Spinoza" (Spinoza) in *Tämä matka* criticize these philosophers, but M. is not an

antiintellectual poet. She says in the essay "Moderni runo" (1957; modern poetry): "The new form, as I understand it, requires that the reader's . . . reason participate in the movement of the poem."

To M., established religions are cold and hostile systems, a part of the "logical disorder" that destroys the "magical order" of the world; this view is expressed in her novel *Tyttö taivaan laiturilla* (1951; the girl on the pier of heaven) and the poem "Lapsuuden hämärästä" (from the twilight of childhood) in *Tämä matka*. She understands the poor and the humble, who appear in her poems on Andalusia, and she has a quiet, slightly whimsical sense of humor, prevalent especially in her most recent book of poems, *Kamala kissa* (1976; that horrible cat).

M. has also written several plays, of which the dreamy and lyrical *Eros ja Psykhe* (1959; Eros and Psyche), although never a great success, has been repeatedly performed.

Although the general trend of Finnish poetry has changed more than once since M. published her principal works, the span of her interests, the depth and intensity of her intellect and feeling, and her mastery of language make her one of the foremost Finnish poets of our time.

FURTHER WORKS: *Mustaa ja punaista* (1944); *Kuin tuuli ja pilvi* (1949); *Kävelymusiikkia pienille virtahevoille* (1957); *Oliko murhaaja enkeli* (1963, under pseud. Anna September); *Niin vaihtuivat vuoden ajat* (1964); *Uuden vuoden yö* (1965); *Toukokuun lumi* (1966); *Kirjoitettu kivi* (1966); *Poltettu oranssi* (1968); *Fahrenheit 121* (1968); *Varjoon jäänyt unien lähde* (1969); *Paetkaa purjet kevein purjein* (1971); *Varokaa voittajat* (1972); *Kuolleet vedet* (1977); *Viimeinen kesä* (1977); *Runoja 1956–1977* (1980)

BIBLIOGRAPHY: Dauenhauer, R., "The Literature of Finland," *LitR*, 14, 1 (1970): 9–10; Ahokas, J. A., "E.-L. M.: Dropping from Reality into Life," *BA*, 47 (1973): 60–65; Sala, K., "E.-L. M.: A Literary Portrait," in Dauenhauer, R., and Binham, P., eds., *Snow in May: An Anthology of Finnish Writing 1945–1972* (1978): 58–59

—JAAKKO A. AHOKAS

MANNING, Olivia

English novelist and short-story writer, b. 1915, Portsmouth; d. 23 July 1980, Isle of Wight

Daughter of a commander in the Royal Navy, M. grew up in Portsmouth. In 1939 she married Reginald Donald Smith, whose work as a producer for the BBC took the couple to many countries. Eventually settling in London, M. avoided publicity but wrote prolifically on a wide variety of subjects, including history—*The Remarkable Expedition* (1947; Am., *The Reluctant Rescue*), an account of Stanley's rescue of Emin Pasha; travel—*The Dreaming Shore* (1950), about a visit to Ireland; and pets—*Extraordinary Cats* (1967). She also wrote articles for many periodicals. In 1976 she was appointed Commander of the Order of the British Empire.

M.'s first novel, *The Wind Changes* (1937), is set in Dublin just before the English-Irish truce of 1920. Its principal characters—an artist, a writer, and a revolutionary—carry on an emotional war that serves as counterpoint to the larger struggle. The book received mixed reviews, but in retrospect, it displays M.'s major characteristics: emphasis on sensuous detail, and an antiromantic point of view that portrays individuals as mirrors of common venality and confusion.

M.'s literary reputation was firmly established with her Balkan Trilogy, whose major characters, Harriet Pringle, a sensitive young wife, and Guy Pringle, a thoughtless young professor working for an official British cultural program in a foreign country, are fictional portraits of the author herself and her husband. The young couple's problems of learning to understand each other are compounded by the economic and political uncertainties of the first years of World War II. *The Great Fortune* (1960) introduces Harriet to Bucharest, a city exotic, gay, and still friendly to the British, and ends with the barely mentioned fall of Paris. *The Spoilt City* (1962) traces the day-to-day rumors and the terrifying disintegration that lead to the German occupation. *Friends and Heroes* (1965) takes place in Athens, to which the Pringles and their compatriots have fled, revealing the gradual involvement and suffering of the Greeks and ending with the fall of Crete and yet another escape, this time to Alexandria.

A convincing portrayal of civilian life in wartime, the trilogy produces a cumulative impression of a nonstructured world, a literary slice of life, without definite beginning, climax, or resolution of conflicts—only flow. Harriet concludes at the end of the first book that "the great fortune is life," and at the end of the third book that the couple's remaining together is the only certainty they can expect. In the late 1970s M. extended the Pringles' adventures to a Levant Trilogy: *The Danger Tree* (1977), *The Battle Lost and Won* (1978), and *The Sum of Things*, published posthumously in 1981; the six volumes are called collectively *The Fortunes of War*.

While M.'s precise observations capture the sights, sounds, smells, and moods of many exotic settings, the objective tone she uses with autobiographical material—home-town, childhood, marital experiences, international acquaintances—barely masks a strong antiromantic point of view. None of her "friends and heroes" is either a true friend or heroic. *A Different Face* (1953) makes postwar Coldmouth (Portsmouth) the chief cause of an expatriate's depression. In *The Play Room* (1969; Am., *The Camperlea Girls*) M.'s schoolgirl-spokesman suffers the nagging claims of a self-pitying mother (only slightly improved from the mother in the short stories in *A Romantic Hero*, 1966); with her brother (named for the author's brother) is exposed to an elderly transvestite and a macabre "play room" (based on an actual vacation incident); and understands too late the strangeness of the rich and beautiful classmate who dies in a rape-murder.

The total effect of M.'s artistry is realism that is ironically sympathetic, uncomfortably persuasive.

FURTHER WORKS: *Growing Up* (1948); *Artist Among the Missing* (1949); *School for Love* (1951); *The Doves of Venus* (1955); *My Husband Cartwright* (1956); *The Rain Forest* (1974)

BIBLIOGRAPHY: Rees, G., on *The Wind Changes, Spectator* (30 April 1937): 832–34; Jones, H. M., on *The Wind Changes, SatR* (9 April 1938): 12; Alpert, H., on *The Doves of Venus, SatR* (18 Nov. 1956): 18–19; Bostwick, J., on *The Great Fortune, SatR* (22 July 1961): 24; Morris, R. K., *Continuance and Change: The Contemporary British Novel Sequence* (1972): 24–49; Trickett, R., on *The Battle Lost and Won, TLS* (24 Nov. 1978): 1358; Milton, E., on *The Battle Lost and Won, Christian Science Monitor* (9 April 1979): B7

—ESTHER M. G. SMITH

Katherine Mansfield

MANSFIELD, Katherine

(pseud. of Kathleen Beauchamp) English short-story writer, b. 14 Oct. 1888, Wellington, New Zealand; d. 9 Jan. 1923, Fontainebleau, France

Much of M.'s early life was a rebellion against her origins: her birth in provincial and unsophisticated Wellington, her philistine upbringing by a banker father and a genteel mother, with all the concomitant restrictions placed upon her as a daughter in a pretentious colonial household. The result was enthusiastic withdrawal to a school for girls in London, a determination to be a woman writer in a man's world, and a loosening of moral and societal restrictions to permit experimentation with premarital affairs, with lesbianism, with abortion—in short, with a way of life antithetical to her upbringing.

Paradoxically, the last portion of her short career was devoted to exploring her roots proudly by re-creating in fiction the New Zealand of her brother "Chummie"—killed at the front in World War I—her beloved grandmother, her parents, and particularly the little girl and young woman who resembles so powerfully the developing M. Perhaps this psychological need for identification with place owes much to the tormented, gypsylike existence of M.'s mature years when a combination of eventually fatal illnesses forced her from the uncongenial climate of England to medical exile on the French Riviera, in Switzerland, in Italy, and elsewhere, seeking the healing sun, but without the company of friends, family, or even of her husband, John Middleton Murry (1889–1957). For many of these latter years, she relived in her memories and her fiction the childhood period of belonging to a land, a family, and a distinct culture.

Although M. wrote about one hundred stories, her fame rests on fewer than twenty wrought with precise and calculated craftsmanship. James JOYCE had earlier made the "epiphany" his trademark. M. independently used the technique repeatedly and effectively in her best stories. Her heroes and heroines are presented to the reader at a climactic, or at least psychologically traumatic, moment in their lives, when they see incisively into the mystery of their being. Bertha Young in "Bliss" (1918) approaches the abyss of her husband's infidelity; Mr. Salesby in "The Man without a Temperament" (1920) becomes painfully aware that his relationship to his wife has deteriorated to "rot"; and, in "The Stranger" (1920) Mr. Hammond, like Gabriel Conroy in Joyce's "The Dead," must forever after feel more a "stranger" to his own wife than does the dying male acquaintance on the ship as he expires in Mrs. Hammond's arms. Her most memorable fiction is thus devoted to subtle but momentous alterations in marital and family relationships—changes long in the coming but necessitated and focused by the revelatory instant.

Like Anton CHEKHOV, whose work M. revered, she is most at home with the short sketch, the quiet vignette, in which little occurs on the surface. Insects drone, nature dozes, a character daydreams of past or future. But both character and reader are, often unwittingly, involved through the magic of image, symbol, word rhythm, repetitive patterns of gesture, color, sound, in a transformation that brings one or both to a new level of awareness of reality.

Because M.'s reality was abnormally bleak—her creative years full of physical pain and weakness, loneliness, exile, jealousy, frustration, alienation—her protagonists ordinarily reflect the bitter world of their creator. There are few happy characters in M.'s stories. Death and consciousness of class impinge on young Laura's rapture in "The Garden Party" (1921); time and age wear down the two sisters in "The Daughters of the Late Colonel" (1920); and in "Marriage à la Mode" (1921) the whole brittle underpinning of England's smart set is shown to be crumbling.

M. misses greatness as a writer of fiction, although in a few stories she comes very close. Her importance lies in her willingness to discard the stuffy post-Victorian drawing room of fiction for the modernist approach in which she excelled. She used the tools of psychology, not mechanically but creatively, to examine characters from within as well as without, concentrating on spirit rather than material circumstance. In her best work she surely attains her aim of tunneling beneath life's ostensible ugliness to reveal the beauty beneath.

FURTHER WORKS: *In a German Pension* (1911); *Prelude* (1918); *Je Ne Parle Pas Français* (1920); *Bliss, and Other Stories* (1921); *The Garden Party, and Other Stories* (1922); *The Dove's Nest, and Other Stories* (1923); *Poems* (1924); *Something Childish, and Other Stories* (1924); *The Journal of K. M.* (1927); *The Letters of K. M.* (1928); *The Aloe* (1930); *Novels and Novelists* (1930); *Stories by K. M.* (1930); *The Scrapbook of K. M.* (1937); *Collected Stories* (1945); *K. M.'s Letters to John Middleton Murry, 1913–1922* (1951); *Journal of K. M., Definitive Edition* (1954)

BIBLIOGRAPHY: Murry, J. M., *The Autobiography of John Middleton Murry: Between Two Worlds* (1936); Berkman, S., *K. M.: A Critical Study* (1951); Daly, S., *K. M.* (1965); Magalaner, M., *The Fiction of K. M.* (1971); Alpers, A., *The Life of K. M.* (1980); Hanson, C., and A. Gurr, *K. M.* (1981)

—MARVIN MAGALANER

MAŃSI LITERATURE
See Finno-Ugric Literatures

MAO Tun

(pseud. of Shen Yen-ping) Chinese novelist and short-story writer, b. 25 June 1896, Tung-hsiang, Chekiang Province; d. 27 March 1981, Peking

M. T. came from a small-town, middle-class family and was educated in the big cities. After graduation from the junior division of the National Peking University, he worked in the editorial office of the Commercial Press, one of the large publishing houses in Shanghai. In 1921 he became editor of the company's *Hsiao-shuo yüeh-pao*, a monthly that published fiction. He was also one of the founding members, in 1920, of the Literary Research Association. With the support of the Association members, *Hsiao-shuo yüeh pao* soon became a leading literary periodical of the time (1921–32); many important works of modern Chinese fiction, including those of M.T. himself, were published in it.

M. T.'s most popular novels are the trilogy *Shih* (1930; eclipse)—consisting of *Huanmieh* (disillusion), *Tung-yao* (vacillation), and *Chui-ch'iu* (pursuit)—which depicts in successive stages the tensions and struggles of young Chinese intellectuals prior to Nationalist victory in China; *Hung* (1930; rainbow), detailing the adventures of an innocent and intelligent girl thrust into the maelstrom of life in a complex society; and *Tzu-yeh* (1933; *Midnight*, 1957), his best-known novel, about the filth and corruption of the business and industrial communities in metropolitan Shanghai. He also published several story collections, which include "Ch'un ts' an" (1932; "Spring Silkworms," 1956) and "Lin-chia p'u-tzu" (1932; "The Shop of the Lin Family," 1956). Both stories narrate with sympathy and pathos the sufferings respectively of peasants and small-townsfolk.

During the Sino-Japanese War (1937–45) M. T. joined the exodus of Chinese intellectuals to the southwest interior. His important works of this period are the novels *Fu-shih* (1941; corrosion) and *Shuang-yeh hung szu erh-yüeh hua* (1943; frosted leaves as red as flowers in February), and the play *Ch'ingming ch'ien hou* (1945; before and after the spring festival).

M. T. shared the modern Chinese writers' interest in politics, which was often inseparable from literature. Although he was not a member of the Communist Party early in his career, he had pronounced leftist tendencies and associated with authors who were ardent in their denunciation of the Nationalist government. After the founding of the People's Republic in 1949, he rose high in the literary hierarchy of the new regime and was elected chairman of the All-China Federation of Literary Workers (later called the Chinese Writers' Union). For sixteen years (1949–65) he was Minister of Culture in the Communist government. Beginning in 1951, he also served as editor of *Chinese Literature*, an official literary organ of Communist China, published in several languages for foreign readers. But he did little creative writing beyond revising and reissuing his earlier works in the ten-volume *M. T. wen-chi* (1958–61; M. T.'s collected works). He survived the purges of the intellectuals during the Cultural Revolution, but the most productive period of his life as a writer was long past.

A faithful chronicler of his time, M. T. recorded in a realistic manner the men and events of modern Chinese society, focusing on its ugliness and evils and on class distinctions that separate the rich from the poor. He analyzed with meticulous care the disruptive social and political forces that plunged the country into chaos in the most critical years prior to the socialist revolution that ushered in the Communist regime. After the establishment of the People's Republic, his political activities and administrative duties all but superseded his role as the most accomplished and versatile author of modern China.

FURTHER WORKS: *Yeh ch'iang-wei* (1929); *San-jen hsing* (1931); *Lu* (1932); *Hua hsiatzu* (1934); *M. T. tuan-p'ien hsiao-shuo chi* (1934); *Su-hsieh yü sui-pi* (1935); *Yin-hsiang kan-hsiang hui-i* (1936); *To-chiao kuan hsi* (1936); *Ti-i chiai-tuan ti ku-shih* (1945); *Wei-ch'ü* (1945); *Su-lien chien-wen lu* (1947). **FURTHER WORKS IN ENGLISH:** *Spring Silkworms and Other Stories* (1956)

BIBLIOGRAPHY: Liu Wu-chi, "The Modern Period, 1900–1950," supplement to Giles, H. A., *A History of Chinese Literature*, enlarged ed. (1967): 490–92; Hsia, C. T., *A History of Modern Chinese Fiction* (1971): 140–64: 350–59; Berninghausen, J., "The Central Contradiction in Mao Dun's Earliest Fiction," and Chen, Y., "Mao Dun and the Use of Political Allegory in Fiction: A Case Study of His 'Autumn in Kuling,'" in Goldman, M., ed., *Modern Chinese Literature in the May Fourth Era* (1977): 233–59: 261–80; Gálik, M., *The Genesis of Modern Chinese Literary Criticism* (1980): 191–213; Průšek, J., "M. T. and Yü Ta-fu," in Lee, O., ed., *The Lyric and the Epic: Studies of Modern Chinese Literature* (1980): 121–77

—LIU WU-CHI

MAORI LITERATURE

See New Zealand Literature and Pacific Islands Literatures

MARAINI, Dacia

Italian novelist, poet and essayist, b. 13 Nov. 1936, Florence

The second of three daughters of the famous ethnologist Fosco and Sicilian princess Topazia Alliata, M. spent her first years in Japan where her father was doing research. Her parents' refusal to recognize Mussolini's "Republic of Salò" cost the family two years in concentration camps, from 1943 to 1945. Upon her return to Italy M. lived for several years in Bagheria, in Sicily, where her mother's family owned the famous Villa Valguarnera. She began writing in her school journal and continued writing fiction and poetry. Her first publication was *La vacanza* (1962; *The Holiday*, 1966). In almost forty years of incessant writing activities M. has published more than ten novels and several books of poetry, theater

works, and essays on cultural and literary studies. She has written for important Italian newspapers and magazines such as *Corriere della Sera*, *L'Unità*, and *Noi Donne*. M. has taught creative writing, hosted a television show on writing, and coordinates the *Fondazione Alberto Moravia*, a foundation dedicated to the memory of her famous companion, Alberto MORAVIA.

This impressive activity has made M. by far one of the most famous Italian women writers and certainly among the most translated. Along with all her literary work M. has established a reputation as one of the leading feminists in Italy. Her social and political engagement with the Feminist movement has always been tightly connected to her creative writing.

M.'s literary work can be divided into three periods. The first period, from 1962 to 1970, produced *La vacanza* (1962; The Vacation) and *L'età del malessere* (1963; *The Age of Malaise*, 1963); in these novels psychological issues are investigated already with a feminist bent. The characters are always young women facing moral issues such as abortion, as in *L'età del malessere,* a play portraying the struggle of women against a corrupt male society where women are used exclusively for domestic labor and physical pleasure, and where family ties reveal their incongruence as well as their oppression of women as mothers, wives, and daughters.

M.'s writing from 1970 to 1989 represents a period of stronger political engagement, of "Women's Lib," of active participation in social activities regarding women's rights in the realms of abortion, divorce, and family, and of the establishment of the *"Telefono rosa,"* ("pink telephone"), an association for battered women. M. was very active in several theatrical activities, culminating in the opening of a feminist theater, *Il teatro della Maddalena*, as well as the publication of more than ten feminist plays, still performed throughout the world, such as *Maria Stuarda* (Mary Stuart), *Solo le prostitute si sposano in maggio* (Only Prostitutes Marry in May), and *I Sogni di Clitennestra* (Clytemnestra's Dreams). Leading her fiction writing during this period was *Memorie di una ladra* (1973; *Memoirs of a Female Thief*, 1974). It is the story of a thief M. met in her prison investigations and with whom the author shared royalties for the publication of her adventures. The book reveals how Roman minor delinquency, often provoked by genuine poverty, a sense of desperation, and lack of social structures, and not adequately treated by social services, results in the basic impossibility of rehabilitation. In 1974 M. also published a collection of feminist poetry, *Donne mie*, and another of interviews on theater, *Fare teatro*. In 1975 *Donna in guerra* (*Woman at War*, 1989) appeared. Written in the form of a diary, it relates Vannina's painstaking process of emancipation from her husband, emancipation which also means the painful but necessary choice of aborting his child, of deciding to have an affair with a younger man, and then watching the man die of a terrible illness. Vannina has to take a position against the whole conservative and oppressing society—of which the father of the young man is highly symbolic.

M.'s works of the 1980s include *Diario di Piera* (1980; Piera's Diary), written with actress Piera Degli Esposti, which chiefly narrates a problematic mother-daughter relationship and the actress's inability to bring to term her pregnancies, always terminated in abortion. The year 1981 saw the publication of *Lettere a Marina* (*Letters to Marina*, 1988), an epistolary novel revolving around the unveiling of youthful traumas and the unrequited lesbian love of Bianca, ending in madness. In 1984 *Il treno per Helsinki* (The Train) and *Isolina: la donna tagliata a pezzi* (*Isolina*, 1994) were published. In the latter work, which describes an investigation of a famous unsolved murder case of a lower-class girl in 1900s Verona, the author explicitly admits of her sadness in describing not only the mystery of this unsolved case of violence upon a woman but the misery permeating the society of the time, ruled by assertive Piedmontese officers.

In the third period, the last decade of the 20th c., M. experiments with historiographic metafiction in *La lunga vita di Marianna Ucrìa* (*The Silent Duchess*, 1992) and with autobiographical fiction in *Bagheria* (1993; *Bagheria*, 1995). In the former novel, inspired by the portrait of an ancestor, M. deals with the structural issues of historiographic metafiction as well as with the metaphorical silence surrounding women in 18th-c. Italy. The difficulty of speaking up for women prevents the voicing of childhood traumas, such as Marianna's rape perpetrated by the uncle who later becomes her husband. Only with the coming of a later age, and also by leaving Sicily, can Marianna begin her journey toward self-awareness and be the sole person responsible for her actions, including the one of keeping a beautiful younger lover all for herself. M.'s love for Sicilian culture, food traditions, and landscape is at its peak, masterfully recreating for the readers the sense of Oriental mystery that brings Europe closer to the East. In 1991 her collection of poetry *Viaggiando con passo di volpe* (*Traveling in the Gait of a Fox*, 1992) won the Premio Mediterraneo and Premio Città di Penna.

Voci (1994; *Voices*, 1994) is an investigation of the thriller genre, based on the true story of a murder in Rome. The reporter Micaela unveils a story of violence and of the silencing of abused, raped, and mistreated women. Another epistolary novel, *Dolce per sé* (1997; Sweet for Itself) is significantly titled after a verse of Giacomo Leopardi's *Ricordanze* and describes the end of an affair between Vera and Edoardo. Vera writes letters to Edoardo's niece Flavia, a little girl often portrayed as Red Riding Hood, a symbol of eternal innocence and of the nostalgia for lost years. Vera's correspondence ultimately affirms her devotion to love and youth. Love is for the most part the topic of Flavia's letters in which unfolds the nine-year-long love story between Vera and Edoardo, who is a renowned violinist fifteen years younger than Vera is seeing other women and searching for a life with children of his own. The character of Vera—a writer and playwright—seems to draw upon the personal experience of M.

Personal memoirs, fiction, and essaystic annotations make *Dolce per sé* a summation of M.'s narrative production. *E tu chi eri?* (1998; And Who Were You?), originally published in 1973, moreover provides a collection of interviews with twenty-six artists about their childhoods.

As a result of her social commitment and of her personal conviction to discuss the condition of women M.'s works, especially the fictional and the theatrical ones, deal mainly with women's issues. Nonetheless all of her work also provides an implacable analysis of Italian society during the latter half of the 20th c.

FURTHER WORKS: *Crudeltà all'aria aperta* (1966); *Viva l'Italia* (1973); *Donne mie* (1974); *La donna perfetta* (1975); *Don Juan* (1976); *Mangiami pure* (1978); *Il ricatto a teatro e altre commedie* (1979); *Suor Juana* (1980); *Il bambino Alberto* (1981); *Dimenticato di dimenticare* (1982); *Lezioni d'amore e altrecommedie* (1982); *Stravaganze* (1987); *Veronica, meretrice e scrittora* (1992); *Cercando Emma* (1993); *Clandestino a bordo* (1996); *Searching for Emma* (1998)

BIBLIOGRAPHY: Santangelo, G., "D. M./Marianna Ucrìa: Tessere la memoria sotto lo sguardo delle chimere," *Italica*, 73, 3 (1996): 410-28; Brooke, G., "Sicilian Philomela: Marianna Ucrìa and the Muted Women of Her Time," *Italian Culture*, 13 (1995): 201-11; Merry, B., *D. M. and her Place in Contemporary Italian Literature* (1993); Ballaro, B., "Making the Lesbian Body: Writing and Desire in D. M.'s *Lettere a Marina*," in Benedetti, L., et al., eds., *Gendered Contexts: New Perspectives in Italian Cultural Studies* (1996): 177-78; Amoia, A., "D. M.: The Designing Woman," in *Twentieth-Century Italian Women Writers: The Feminine Experience* (1996): 86-99; Wood, S., "The Silencing of Women: The Political Aesthetic of D. M.," in *Italian Women's Writing 1860-1994* (1995): 216-31; Cannon, J., "Rewriting the Female Destiny: D. M.'s *La lunga vita di Marianna Ucrìa*," *Symposium*, 49, 2 (1995): 136-46; O'Healy, A., "Filming Female 'Autobiography': M., Ferreri, and Piera's Own Story," in Miceli-Jeffries, G., ed., *Feminine Feminists: Cultural Practices in Italy* (1995): 190-298; Masland, L., "In Her Own Voice: An Irigarayan Exploration of Women's Discourse in *Caro Michele* (Natalia Ginzburg) and *Lettere a Marina* (D. M.)," *Canadian Review of Comparative Literature*, 21, 3 (1994): 331-40; Golini, V., "Italian Women in Search of Identity in D. M.'s Novels," in *International Women Writing: New Landscapes of Identity* (1995); Anderlini, S. "Prolegomena for a Feminist Dramaturgy of the Feminine: Interview with Dacia Maraini," *Diacritics*, 2-3 (1991): 148-60; Lazzaro-Weis, C., *From Margins to Mainstream: Feminism and Fictional Modes in Italian Women's Writing, 1968-1990* (1993); Tamburri, A. J., "D. M.'s *Donna in guerra*: Victory or Defeat?" in Aricò, S. L., ed., *Contemporary Women Writers in Italy: A Modern Renaissance* (1990): 138-51

—STEFANIA LUCAMANTE

MARAN, René

Martinican poet, novelist, and biographer, b. 15 Nov. 1887, Fort-de-France; d. 8 May 1960, Paris, France

M. started writing poetry while he was still in high school in Bordeaux, France, where he had been sent by his parents when he was about six years old. By the age of sixteen he was already publishing poems, and before leaving for Equatorial Africa in 1909 to serve as a colonial officer, his first volume *La maison du bonheur* (1909; home of happiness), had appeared to be followed by *La vie intérieure* (1912; the inner life). These collections and *Le livre du souvenir* (1958; the book of remembrance) constitute M.'s major poetic works. His main themes include love, the loneliness of a sensitive mind, and the inevitability of sorrow and its acceptance with fortitude. His quest for the right word and for the perfect rhythm and rhyme was almost fanatical, yet he did not sacrifice sense to sound.

Between 1912 and 1958 M. wrote mainly fiction, essays, and biographies. He returned to France in 1923, making his home in Paris. He was, in the 1920s, in contact with the New Negro movement in the U.S. Thus, in 1924 he was invited to be a judge in a literary contest organized by *The Crisis* (the house organ of the NAACP) and in 1926 to participate in the Albert and Charles Boni Novel Competition. Through articles and radio talks he promoted, in France and many other European countries, the writings of the New Negro authors. M.'s Friday evening receptions at his Paris home in the 1930s not only helped to bring black intellectuals into contact with men and women of letters from other parts of the world, but also provided a forum for discussion that fostered the emergence of NEGRITUDE.

M.'s first novel, *Batouala, véritable roman nègre* (1921; *Batouala*, 1922), won the enviable Goncourt Prize in 1921. *Batouala* was the first attempt by a black writer to present an objective picture of the African in literature. Whether the attempt succeeded or failed is still an open question. What is certain is that, when it was published, *Batouala* with its preface, which attacked the French *method* (as distinct from *principle*) of colonization in Africa, was as controversial as M.'s own ambivalent attitude toward his African ancestral roots. Some critics commended his exposure of the dehumanizing effects of the French method of colonization in Africa—with its excessive taxation, forced labor, and attempts to make Africans renounce their customs and traditions—but condemned his portrayal of the African chief Batouala and his people as unmitigatedly primitive. Some agents and admirers of the French colonial administration saw the preface of *Batouala* not only as a misrepresentation of French activities in Africa but also as anti-French ammunition in the hands of Germany and other enemies of France. Others saw the portrayal of the African life style—characterized by idleness, cannibalism, and excessive sexual appetite—as justification for the colonization of Africa.

M. continued his attack on the French method of colonization in his later works. *Le Tchad de sable et d'or* (1931; Chad of sand and gold) demonstrated Africans' need for the protection of Europe. *Livingstone et l'exploration de l'Afrique* (1938; Livingstone and the exploration of Africa) celebrated David Livingstone's exploits.

M.'s perception of Africa and its reality was colored by his French upbringing. A great stylist, he saw himself first and foremost as a French writer. His writing, especially his poetry, is dominated by the stoic philosophy of Marcus Aurelius.

FURTHER WORKS: *Le visage calme* (1922); *Le petit roi de Chiméerie* (1924); *Djouma, chien de brousse* (1927); *Le cœur serré* (1931); *Le livre de la brousse* (1934); *Les belles images* (1935); *Savorgnan de Brazza* (1941); *Bêtes de la brousse* (1942); *Les pionniers de l'empire* (3 vols., 1943–1955); *Mbala lééphant* (1944); *Peines de cœur* (1944); *Un homme pareil aux autres* (1947); *Bacouya le cynocéphale* (1953); *Félix Eboué, grand homme et loyal serviteur* (1957); *Bertrand du Guesclin* (1961)

BIBLIOGRAPHY: Vandérem, F., "Le Prix Goncourt," *La revue de France*, 1 (1922): 386–91; Cook, M., *Five French Negro Authors* (1943): 123–48; M. R., *Hommage à* (1965); Kesteloot, L., *Black Writers in French: A Literary History of Negritude* (1974): 75–79 and passim; Hausser, M., *Les deux Batouala de R. M.* (1975); Ikonné, C., "R. M. and the New Negro," *CLQ*, 15, 4 (1979): 224–39; Ade, F. O., "R. M. devant la critique," *O&C*, 3: 2–4, 1 (1979): 143–55

—CHIDI IKONNÉ

MARATHI LITERATURE

See Indian Literature

Gabriel Marcel

MARCEL, Gabriel

French philosopher, dramatist, and critic, b. 7 Dec. 1889, Paris; d. 8 Oct. 1973, Paris

After extensive travels with his diplomat father, M. took a degree in philosophy at the Sorbonne (1910) and afterward taught in secondary schools for a number of years. Later he worked for two Paris publishing houses, and was drama and music critic for various periodicals. His early publications included plays, essays, and critical articles, and in 1927 his *Journal métaphysique (Metaphysical Journal*, 1952) won him attention as a serious philosopher. Already acquainted with the works of Kirkegaard and the German philosopher Karl Jaspers (1883–1969), he crystallized his own religious thinking and, in 1929, embraced Catholicism. Recipient, over the years, of a goodly number of awards and prizes in France and abroad, M. was elected to the Academy of Moral and Political Sciences in 1952, named to other prestigious organizations, and invited to lecture all over the world. Some of his personal reminiscences can be found in *En chemin vers quel éveil?* (1971; en route toward what awakening?).

M. is usually identified as a "Christian existentialist" despite his repudiation of the term (he preferred Christian-Socratic). He insisted that his philosophical writings were not intended to constitute a closed "system" nor to be considered treatises in the usual sense. Often in the form of journals, collected essays, or public lectures, they are concerned with human existence and the search for authentic being and personal transcendence. In them M. offers critiques of several contemporary philosophical systems and points to the irreligion of our age. He distinguishes between modern man's obsession with "having"—both in the Christian sense of the "flesh" and its wants, and in the sense of the desire for possession in our technocratic world—and striving for "being," necessary elements of which include love for and direct and open communication with others, the more fully to find one's authentic self. Being is a "mystery," experienced and felt through involvement even in a "broken world." This mystery of being cannot be analyzed, just as faith in God is felt through concrete experience, not through abstract "proofs." M. considered his *Positions et approches concrètes du mystère ontologique* (1933; *Philosophy of Existence*, 1948; repr. as *The Philosophy of Existentialism*, 1961) the most succinct expression of his contribution to contemporary thought.

M. insisted, however, that in order fully to understand his philosophy one must know his plays, for he viewed them as the concrete revelation of his metaphysical thought. Although he refused to call them thesis plays—in the sense that he had no wish to impose any ready-made truth on his public—it is nonetheless true that he intended them to free the individual spectator from whatever opinions or prejudices might keep him from having access to his self or communication with others. The plays therefore aim at a spiritual and intellectual renewal for the audience and as a result are heavily intellectual. They do not always escape the wordiness of even indirectly didactic theater of a metaphysical thrust. They too frequently lack a true dramatic dynamic and rely on the last act or scene's making all the rest clear. They deal with arresting personalities, however—souls in exile, as M. called them. Especially absorbing in this respect are *Un homme de Dieu* (1925; *A Man of God*, 1958), *La chapelle ardente* (1925; *The Funeral Pyre*, 1958; later retitled *The Votive Candle*, 1965), and *Le chemin de Crête* (1936; *Ariadne*, 1958).

While M.'s perception of the difficulties of the human condition in the modern world is in some ways akin to that of Jean-Paul SARTRE and other atheistic EXISTENTIALISTS, his faith militates against his searching for "being" without a sense of hope.

FURTHER WORKS: *La grâce* (1911); *Le palais du sable* (1913); *Le seuil invisible* (1914); *Le cœur des autres* (1921); *L'iconoclaste* (1923); *Le quatuor en fa dièse* (1925); *Trois pièces: Le regard neuf, Le mort de demain, La chapelle ardente* (1931); *Le monde cassé* (1933); *Être et avoir* (1935; *Being and having*, 1949); *Le fanal* (1936); *Le dard* (1938); *La soif (Les cœurs avides)* (1938); *Du refus à l'invocation* (1940; *Creative Fidelity*, 1964); *Homo viator* (1944; *Homo Viator: Introduction to a Metaphysic of Hope*, 1951); *L'horizon* (1945); *La métaphysique de Royce* (1945; *Royce's Metaphysics*, 1956); *Théâtre comique* (1947); *Vers un autre royaume: L'émissaire et Le signe de la croix* (1949); *La fin des temps* (1950); *Le mystère de l'être* (2 vols., 1951; *The Mystery of Being*, 2 vols., 1950–1951); *Les hommes contre l'humain* (1951; *Man against Mass Society*, 1952); *Rome n'est plus dans Rome* (1951); *La dimension Florestan* (1952); *Le déclin de la sagesse* (1954; *The Decline of Wisdom*, 1954); *Mon temps n'est pas le vôtre* (1955); *Croissez et multipliez* (1955); *L'homme problématique* (1955; *Problematic Man*, 1967); *Théâtre et religion* (1958); *Présence et immortalité* (1959; *Presence and Immortality*, 1967); *L'heure théâtrale de Giraudoux à Jean-Paul Sartre* (1959); *Fragments philosophiques, 1909–1914* (1962; *Philosophical Fragments and The Philosopher and Peace*, 1965); *La dignité humaine et ses assises existentielles* (1964; *The Existential Background of Human*

Dignity, 1963); *Auf der Suche nach Wahrheit und Gerechtigkeit* (1964; *Searchings*, 1967); *Regards sur le théâtre de Claudel* (1964); *Paix sur la terre: Deux discours, une tragédie* (1965); *Le secret est dans les îles: Le dard, L'émissaire, La fin des temps* (1967); *Pour une sagesse tragique et son au-delà* (1968; *Tragic Wisdom and Beyond*, 1973); *Entretiens Paul Ricœur, G. M.* (1968; in *Tragic Wisdom and Beyond*, 1973); *Percées vers un ailleurs: L'iconoclaste, L'horizon, suivi de L'audace en métaphysique* (1973)

BIBLIOGRAPHY: Ricœur, P., *G. M. et Karl Jaspers: Philosophie du mystère et philosophie du paradoxe* (1947); Chénu, J., *Le théâtre de G. M. et sa signification métaphysique* (1948); Gallagher, K. T., *The Philosophy of G. M.* (1962); Cain, S., *G. M.* (1963); Miceli, V., *Ascent to Being: G. M.'s Philosophy of Communion* (1965); Troisfontaines, R., *De l'existence à l'être: La philosophie de G. M.*, new ed. (1968); Widner, C., *G. M. et le théisme existentiel* (1971)

—RUTH B. YORK

MARECHAL, Leopoldo

Argentine novelist, poet, and dramatist, b. 11 June 1900, Buenos Aires; d. 26 June 1970, Buenos Aires

M., like his celebrated contemporary Jorge Luis BORGES, began his career as an avant-garde, ULTRAIST poet in the Buenos Aires of the 1920s and only much later achieved lonely distinction (and some notoriety) as a writer of fiction. His father was a worker who died in the influenza epidemic of 1918, and his maternal grandfather had been an exiled Paris Communard; M. regarded himself as a revolutionary, first as a socialist and later an an ardent supporter of Juan Perón. He made his living for many years as a schoolteacher and journalist and between 1944 and 1955 held various public posts, including the Cultural Directorship of the Argentine Ministry of Education.

M.'s identification with Peronism was to isolate him from most of the dominant writers of his generation and led to a decade of almost complete seclusion following Perón's fall in 1955 and to general critical neglect of his work, including the monumental city novel *Adán Buenosayres* (1948; Adam Buenosayres). The appearance of a second, slighter, novel, *El banquete de Severo Arcángelo* (1965; the banquet of Severo Arcángelo) an immediate popular and critical success, has stimulated a reassessment of M.'s position among Argentine writers of the 20th c.

Unlike his fiction, M.'s poetry received early and continuing recognition. His development was from the self-consciously MODERNIST free verse of *Días como flechas* (1926; days like arrows), characterized by a perhaps too great reliance on startling metaphor, to a more ordered and formal poetry, metaphysical in theme, and in manner often closely related to the tradition of the Spanish past. *Odas para el hombre y la mujer* (1929; odes for man and woman) was awarded first prize in a competition sponsored by the municipality of Buenos Aires. M.'s religious conversion in the early 1930s is reflected in the austerity of the collections *Cinco poemas australes* (1937; five southern poems) and *El centauro* (1940; the centaur), which together with *Sonetas a Sophia, y otros poemas* (1940; sonnets to Sophia, and other poems) won for M. in 1941 the coveted National Prize in poetry.

The classicism and restraint of the later poetry hardly prepared M.'s readers for the immense novel *Adán Buenosayres*, begun in

Paris in 1930 and written and rewritten during the following eighteen years. Julio CORTÁZAR, who greeted its publication as "an extraordinary event in Argentine letters," also conceded, "Seldom has a book appeared that is less coherent." Autobiographical and fantastic by turns, Rabelaisian in parts and tender in others, scatological and eschatological often at the same time, it is a mélange of dreams, jokes, metaphysics, farce, and history. One early reviewer complained that *Adán Buenosayres* employed more bad words than *Ulysses*, and indeed it is with the comic epic of James JOYCE that its closest affinities are found. As in *Ulysses*, a story of the present, or near present, is overlaid upon Greek myth, a device that M. used again in his play *Antígona Vélez* (1965; Antigone Vélez).

By comparison, the less ambitious later novels *El banquete de Severo Arcángelo* (which won the Forti Glori prize in 1966) and *Megafón; o, La guerra* (1970); Megafón; or, war) are more coherent, although still strange, blends of farce, melodrama, and religious allegory. In Argentina they have been well received.

M. is perhaps less well known by English-speaking readers than any other Latin American writer of comparable stature. Aside from the poems "Cortejo" (1937; "Cortège," 1942) and "El centauro" (1939; "The Centaur," 1944), almost nothing by, and very little about, M. is presently available in English. The curious reader who wishes to encounter one of the most surprising and often rewarding writers of this hemisphere has no recourse but to turn to the original.

FURTHER WORKS: *Los aguilochos* (1922); *Laberinto de amor* (1936); *Historia de la calle Corrientes* (1937); *Vida de Santa Rosa de Lima* (1943); *La rosa en la balanza* (1944); *El viaje de la primavera* (1945); *La alegropeya* (1962); *Cuaderno de navegación* (1966); *Las tres caras de Venus* (1966); *El poema de Robot* (1966); *La batalla de José Luna* (1970); *Don Juan* (1978)

BIBLIOGRAPHY: Marechal, L., *Las claves de "Adán Buenosayres" y tres artículos de Julio Cortázar, Adolfo Prieto, Graciela de Sola* (1966); Andrés, A., *Palabras con L. M.* (1968); Coulson, G., *M.: La pasión metafísica* (1974); Kuehne, A., "M.'s Antígona: More Greek than French," *LATR*, 9, 1 (1975): 19–27; Gordon, A., "Dublin and Buenos Aires, Joyce and M.," *CLS*, 19 (1982): 208–19

—AMBROSE GORDON

MARECHERA, Dambudzo

Zimbabwean novelist, poet, dramatist, and short-story writer, b. 4 June 1952, Vengere Township, Rusape, d. 18 Aug. 1987, Harare

M. was raised in the Vengere township ghetto near Rusape. When M. was eleven, his father while walking home was struck by a car and died. Three years later, M., his mother, and his eight siblings, were evicted from their home. M. attended mission schools through Form 6 when he sat for exams. His results being exceptional, he was awarded a scholarship to the University of Rhodesia where he studied English literature beginning in 1972. After being expelled in 1973 for participating in political activities, M. fled to Botswana, and then to England where he gained political asylum and was awarded a scholarship to attend New College at Oxford University. M. studied at Oxford from 1974 through 1976,

when he was expelled from the University. He remained in Britain, sleeping on friends' floors, while writing his first book, *The House of Hunger* (1978), which was awarded the Guardian fiction prize in 1979. With the success of his first book, M. briefly became writer-in-residence at the University of Sheffield in 1979. Until M. left England in 1982, he supported himself by writing articles, stories, and reviews to supplement a grant from the Arts Council. M. returned to Harare to assist Christ Austin with his film, *The House of Hunger*, and remained in Harare living with friends and on the streets until his death in 1987 from an AIDS-related pulmonary disorder.

M.'s first collection of short stories, *The House of Hunger*, like his other works, is largely autobiographical. The collection's well crafted, stark language is both unrelenting and unforgiving. The collection's nihilistic brutality provides readers with M.'s untempered view of ghetto life while exploring the values that exist when individuals are confined within a system of duality and oppression. M., the stories seem to demonstrate, believes the inevitable result is a type of collective insanity.

In his second book, *Black Sunlight* (1980), which was initially banned in Zimbabwe, M. again confronts the collective condition while exploring the conflicted individual. In *Black Sunlight* M. suggests parallels between the political transformation in Zimbabwe and the transformation of the self, both ending in nihilism. Important for M. are conflicts of language. Fully aware of the impossibilities of language and an admirer of the American beat writers, M. uses language in general and satire in particular to react against power structures, be they white or black.

M.'s third book, *Mindblast* (1984), which was the last to be published during his lifetime, is an amalgamation of shorter works that continue to explore both social order and language. Published by a small Zimbabwean press, it consists of three plays, two stories, some poetry, and a memoir. The memoir, the strongest piece in the collection, explores his wanderings through the Harare township after his return from Britain.

The Black Insider (1990), published posthumously, has themes similar to *Black Sunlight* and might in fact be an earlier draft of *Black Sunlight*. The collection, also printed by a small Zimbabwean press, provides archival material for scholars interested in M.'s development, since the collection informs *Black Sunlight*. It also presents a more realistic view of Zimbabwean life. The collection, however, has little value when compared to M.'s first two works.

M.'s importance will undoubtedly grow as *The House of Hunger* and *Black Sunlight* become more widely known. His nihilistic perspective informs both colonial and post-colonial literature by providing a brutal and unabashed look at an Africa in transition. No one escapes M.'s political and satirical attacks, including the African male. M.'s unique and commanding voice speaks to a period of great importance in Zimbabwe.

FURTHER WORKS: *Cemetery of the Mind: Collected Poems of D. M.* (1992); *Scrapiron Blues* (1994)

BIBLIOGRAPHY: Caute, D., *The Espionage of Saints: Two Essays on Silence and the State* (1986); Veit-Wild, F., "D. M.: A Preliminary Annotated Bibliography," *Zambezia*, 14, 2 (1987): 121-29; Veit-Wild, F., ed., *D. M. 4 June 1952-18 August 1987: Pictures. Poems. Prose. Tributes* (1988); Foster, K., "The Soul for the Starving: D. M.'s *House of Hunger*," *JCL* 27, 1 (1992): 58-70; Veit-Wild, F., *D. M.: A Sourcebook on His Life and Work* (1992)

—ALAN TINKLER

MARI LITERATURE
See Finno-Ugric Literatures

MARÍN CAÑAS, José

Costa Rican novelist and short-story writer, b. 1904; d. 14 Dec. 1980, San José

M. C., one of Costa Rica's most famous novelists, has also made contributions as a short-story writer, dramatist, and essayist. Due to the financial ruin of his family, he did not complete university studies and had to support himself as a baker, stevedore, merchant, violist, movie distributor, and radio broadcaster. Except for three years spent in Spain when he was a teenager, he resided in San José all of his life and made a living as a journalist after founding the newspaper *La Hora* (1933). One of his most important novels was serialized in this paper: *El infierno verde* (1935; green hell). Throughout his life, he wrote hundreds of articles and chronicles. One cause of bitterness was the loss of his job as a professor of journalism at the University of Costa Rica for lack of an advanced degree. However, he received several distinctions during his life, including the Magón National Award for Literature (1967) and the Pío Viquez Award for Journalism (1970). In addition, M. C. was a member of the Costa Rica Academy of Language and served as president of the Hispanic Culture Institute.

M. C. uses the elements of the chronicle to create short stories and novels and is the first Costa Rican author to reconstruct a historical event of his country: *Coto, la guerra del 21 con Panamá* (1934; Coto, the war of 21 with Panama), a collection of essays. With this work he also breaks from the folkloric and picturesque trend of his national literature.

In *Los bigardos del ron* (1929; the marginal society of rum) M. C. pictures the life of the lowest stratum of society, and does so with humanity, lyricism, and poetic feeling. The author shares the suffering of his characters and anticipates hope and beauty in spite of the darkness of their lives. He denounces the system with sympathy and humor, at times reaching the frontiers of the absurd. With this work, M. C. initiates the picaresque genre in Costa Rica.

In *Pedro Arnáez* (1942; Pedro Arnáez), his masterpiece, M. C. shows clear and graphic perspectives on the land and its suffering people through multiple levels of narration. The expression is direct and subjective, following the story of a man in search of himself. Pedro Arnáez is an exceptional character: idealistic, mysterious, humane, always confronting with strength adverse circumstances. M. C., in this novel, perceives chaos everywhere and makes obvious the inequities between the rural setting and the urban one in El Salvador. Humanity does not exist. Society is ruthless and meaningless. Life is uneasy, and the only redeeming factor is love. Revolution to liberate the masses cannot succeed.

M. C., as the most important author of his generation in Costa Rica, depicts with vigor and skill the uncertainty of fate in Central America. The masses do not know where to go and cannot avoid failure. They live and die without understanding the system, as shown especially in *Pedro Arnáez* and *El infierno verde*, the author's favorite works. In denouncing social, political, and economic evils and dilemmas, however, M. C. does not chastise anyone in particular, in spite of the severity of his exposition, and his final message is that we must not live in an isolated exercise but in function of the well-being of others.

FURTHER WORKS: *Lágrimas de acero* (1929); *Como tú* (1929); *Tú, la imposible* (1931); *Pueblo macho: o, Ensayos sobre la guerra civil española* (1937); *Tierra de conejos* (1971); *Ensayos* (1972); *Realidad e imaginación* (1974); *Valses nobles y sentimentales* (1981)

BIBLIOGRAPHY: "M. C. y *Pedro Arnáez,*" *La República* (19 Jan. 1969): 13; Erickson, M., "Los clásicos y la joven literatura costarricense," *La República* (11 April 1971): 9; Castegnaro, E., "M. C., periodista y escritor," *La Hora* (10 Dec. 1971): 4; Tovar, E., "J. M. C.," *La Nación* (26 Aug. 1973): 10; Duverrar, R., Introduction to *Los bigardos del ron* (1978): 7–24; Cerutti, F., *Recuerdo de J. M. C.* (1981); Marín, M., "M. C. y el relato histórico," *Revista Revenar*, 3, 6 (1983): 26–29

—INÉS DÖLZ-BLACKBURN

MARINETTI, Filippo Tommaso

Italian critic, journalist, novelist, poet, and dramatist (also writing in French), b. 22 Dec. 1876, Alexandria, Egypt; d. 2 Dec. 1944, Bellagio

The son of a prominent Italian lawyer residing in Egypt, M. moved to Paris in his early youth, while his family returned to Italy, and spent his formative years studying at the Sorbonne, where he received a degree. Later he attended the University of Pavia and graduated from the law school of the University of Genoa.

He began to write in French, and his first literary production includes, among other things, an epic poem, *La conquête des étoiles* (1902; the conquest of the stars). In 1905 M. moved to Milan and founded *Poesia*, an international journal of poetry that was partly committed to the propagation of French SYMBOLISM and Decadence but also accepted the work of Italian writers of the younger as well as the older generation. In connection with that review M. also organized a group of "poètes incendiaires," which can be regarded as one of the first rallies of FUTURISM. All the innovative ferment of M.'s work was to break out a few years later with the publication of the first manifesto of futurism, which appeared almost simultaneously in French in *Le Figaro* (February 20, 1909) as "Manifeste du futurisme" ("The Founding and Manifesto of Futurism," 1972), and in Italian in *Poesia* (February—March 1909). It was followed by other "technical" proclamations of the futurist theory, as applied to literature and the arts—for example, "Manifesto tecnico della letteratura futurista" (1912; "Technical Manifesto of Futurist Literature," 1972).

M. advocated, among other things; daring and temerity, action and aggressiveness, militarism and patriotism, and open rebellion against all traditional forms of culture. He called for the liquidation of all values and institutions of the past and exalted modern dynamism and industry, the myth of the machine, and the unrestrained cult of the individual.

In the fields of poetry and other creative writing M. urged the dismantling of syntax, the abolition of punctuation, and the adoption of unorthodox typographical devices and techniques that would assure the reader's attention and participation—the style he called *parole in libertà* (words freed). These ideas, some of which were inherent in the development of modern irrationalism, M.

attempted to exemplify in subsequent writings and particularly in the novel *Mafarka le futuriste: Roman africain* (1909; Mafarka the futurist: African novel), first published in French, a work whose overt iconoclasm and avowal of heroic vitalism has at times suggested definition in terms of "political" propaganda.

Both in his manifestos on the theater and in his "syntheses" (short dramatic pieces) M., rejecting the analytical pedantry of psychological drama and the static and diluted style of the stage of his time, aimed at revolutionizing the values and conventions of the traditional theater with ideas and methods whose seminal originality and vitality opened the way to a new age of experimentation in the performing arts.

M. also attempted to apply the principles of futurism, intended as a living doctrine and a global theory, to all aspects of social, cultural, and political life, even to the extent of actively supporting the policies of Mussolini and his Fascist regime.

Beyond his colorful and controversial activity as propagandist and committed writer, however, M.'s prominence remains confined mainly to his original function as ideologue and spokesman of one of the first avant-garde movements in 20th-c. art and literature. In this sense it can be said that his futurist manifestos represent his main literary contribution and can justifiably be valued for their special role in establishing a new "genre" that effectively blends the rhetoric of slogans and theoretical pronouncements with timely insights and highly innovative ideas for the development of all art forms.

FURTHER WORKS: *D'Annunzio intime* (1903); *Destruction: Poèmes lyriques* (1904); *La momie sanglante* (1904); *Le roi Bombance: Tragédie satirique en 4 actes* (1905); *La ville charnelle* (1908; It., *Lussuria-velocità*, 1920); *Les dieux s'en vont, D'Annunzio reste* (1908); *Poupées électriques* (1909); *Uccidiamo il chiaro di luna!* (1911); *Le futurisme: Théories et mouvement* (1911); *Le monoplan du pape* (1912); *La battaglia di Tripoli* (1912); *Manifeste technique de la littérature futuriste* (1912); *I manifesti del futurismo* (1914); *Guerra sola igiene del mondo* (1915); *Come si seducono le donne* (1917); *Scelta di poesie e parole in libertà* (1918); *I manifesti del futurismo* (4 vols., 1919); *8 anime in una bomba: Romanzo esplosivo* (1919); *Democrazia futurista: Dinamismo politico* (1919); *Elettricità sessuale* (1919); *Al di là del comunismo* (1920); *L'alcova d'acciaio* (1921); *Il tamburo di fuoco* (1922); *Gli amori futuristi* (1922); *Gli indomabili* (1922); *Futurismo e Fascismo* (1924); *Scatole d'amore in conserva* (1927); *Prigionieri e vulcani* (1927); *L'oceano del cuore* (1928); *Primo dizionario aereo italiano* (1929); *Il suggeritore nudo* (1930); *Novelle colle labbra tinte* (1930); *Futurismo e novecentismo* (1931); *Il paesaggio e l'estetica futurista della macchina* (1931); *Ali d'Italia* (1931); *Il fascino dell'Egitto* (1933); *Poemi simultanei futuristi* (1933); *L'aeropoema del Golfo della Spezia* (1935); *L'originalità napoletana del poeta Salvatore di Giacomo* (1936); *Il poema africano della divisione "XXVIII ottobre"* (1937); *Patriottismo insetticida* (1939); *Il poema non umano dei tecnicismi* (1940); *Carlinga di aeropoeti futuristi di guerra, collaudata da F. T. M.* (1941); *Canto eroi e macchine della guerra mussoliniana* (1942); *Quarto d'ora di poesia della X Mas* (1945); *Teatro* (3 vols., 1960); *Il teatro della sorpresa* (1968); *Teoria e invenzione futurista* (1968); *La grande Milano tradizionale e futurista; Una sensibilità italiana nata in Egitto* (1969); *Lettere ruggenti* (1970); *Poesie a Beny* (1971); *Collaudi futuristi* (1977); *M. futurista: Pagine disperse, documenti e antologia critica* (1977). FURTHER WORKS IN ENGLISH: *Selected Writings* (1972); *Short Plays* (1973)

BIBLIOGRAPHY: Trillo, R. Clough, *Futurism* (1961); Martin, M. W., *Futurist Art and Theory* (1968); Apollonio, U., ed., *Futurist Manifestos* (1973); Darío, R., "M. and Futurism" [tr. of 1909 article], *DQ*, 12 (1977): 147–52; Bronner, S. E., "F. T. M.: The Theory and Practice of Futurism," *BUJ*, 25 (1977): 48–56; Festa-McCormick, D., "M.'s Murder of the Moonlight and the Kinetics of Time," *Centerpoint*, 2 (1977): 50–54; Tindall, C., and Bozzolla, A., *Futurism* (1980)

—A. ILLIANO

MARINKOVIĆ, Ranko

Croatian novelist, short-story writer, and dramatist, b. 22 Feb. 1913, Vis

M. belongs to the generation of Croatian writers who became active on the eve of World War II. It was during this period of an intensive political crisis that the representatives of the so-called modern objectivism but also those of the Marxist, sociorealistic "reflection theory" appeared on the Croatian literary scene. Modern objectivism was similar to classical realism, being enriched by artistic experience of early modernism and contemporary, primarily expressionist tendencies. At this time M. graduated from the Zagreb Faculty of Philosophy and—together with Ivan Dončević (b. 1909)—started to publish the literary revue *Dani i ljudi* (1935).

M.'s first literary efforts were chronicles of his native island of Vis, published by Miroslav KRLEŽA in 1939, and the play *Albatros* (perf. 1939; Albatross). Immediately after the outbreak of World War II he was interned at Clabria, El Shat. After the war he returned to Zagreb, where he was the head of the Croatian National Theater's drama division. From 1951 until his retirement he was a professor at the Zagreb Academy of Dramatic Art.

M. became popular as a writer only after the war: he first published the realistic stories *Proze* (1948; Proses), in which he depicted the provincial life of his native island. His second book was the collection of symbolic and realistic stories entitled *Ruke* (1953; The Hands), in which he unmasked the collective mental state and the social psychosis by means of a psychoanalysis of human conflicts and misunderstandings between individuals and the society. In his miracle play, *Glorija* (1955; Gloria), he focused upon an individual's conflict with the dogmatized consciousness and reactivated the old motive of man's spiritual and physical dualism. The same topic can be found in his vaudeville *Politeia ili Inspektorove spletke* (1977; Politeia or the Inspector's Intrigues) and in the satirical play *Pustinja* (1980; The Desert).

M.'s artistically most distinguished and most popular work is his urban, conspicuously intellectualistic novel *Kiklop* (1966; Cyclop), which made him one of the most prominent Croatian novelists. In this erudite work the author depicted the mental atmosphere of Zagreb, especially of its bohemian element on the eve of World War II. The novel is characterized by modern narration, psychological description of characters, subtle irony, and black humor.

In much of his fiction M. uses original, individual expressive procedures—puns and a number of literary allusions and citations. Such a "poetics" includes also his "antinovel" *Zajednička kupka*

(1980; Joint Bathing). In the novel *Never More* (1993; title in English) he deals again with the pathology of the period and the existential drama of an individual in war. M.'s world consists of characters plagued by inner conflicts, rambling between the spiritual and the material. At the same time, these characters are highly individual, independent from the real world. They are mostly marginal and witty eccentrics, intellectual exhibitionists, and protagonists of a contemporary "human comedy." Both the provincial and the urban Zagreb settings are viewed through the same satiric and grotesque prism and by bizarre details interrelated with each other by means of a penetrating and attractive imagination. In such a way the commonplace reality with its provincial or bourgeois characters is being transformed into a unique, interesting and original microcosm of eccentrics, in which every pathological phenomenon, including war, turns out to be an expected consequence of the mental status in a cannibalistic age.

M. is a master in playing with language: he unremittingly explores the possibilities and combinations of narrative forms on all linguistic and semantic levels. It is in his prose that he achieved the finest expression of subtle irony, which stands for his superior critical attitude, his attitude towards life and his weltanschauung. As a fiction writer of unusual expressive power and a distinctly intellectual profile, M. also wrote theater criticism and essays on theater and film. The most popular are his collections of essays *Geste i grimase* (1951; Gestures and Grimaces) and *Nevesele oči klauna* (1986; The Clown's Unhappy Eyes).

BIBLIOGRAPHY: Vaupotić, M., *Hrvatska suvremena književnost*: *Contemporary Croatian Literature*(1966): 116-18; Šicel, M., *Hrvatska književnost* (1982): 207-15; Frangeš, I., *Povijest hrvatske književnosti* (1987): 361-66; Milanja, C., *Hrvatski roman 1945-1990* (1996): 26-31; Jelčić, D., *Povijest hrvatske književnosti* (1997): 302-3

—DUBRAVKA SESAR

MARKANDAYA, Kamala

(pseud. of Kamala Purnaiya Taylor) Indian novelist (writing in English), b. 1924, Chimakurti

Born into a Madhwa Brahmin family of south India, M. was educated at various schools there and attended Madras University. She later worked as a journalist and moved to England, where she married. M. has been writing steadily since the publication of her widely acclaimed first novel, *Nectar in a Sieve* (1954), which has been translated into seventeen languages.

Nearly all of M.'s writing deals with the conflict between East and West or its more subtle form: tension between tradition and modernity in Indian life styles. In her novels British and urban elements are portrayed as agents of dynamic change, whereas nativeborn and village folk manifest cohesive but static social structures. *Nectar in a Sieve* conveys a romantic view of the Indian villager struggling against unending poverty. Yet at core, M. lacks familiarity with village life and writes more successfully, in *A Handful of Rice* (1966), of the overcrowded conditions and the angry young men that are the results of migration to the cities.

Two Virgins (1973) is an absorbing *Bildungsroman*, which explores the minds of two sisters as they encounter a rapidly changing external world as well as the puzzling internal world of

emotions and growing sexuality. M. departs from her usual themes in *The Nowhere Man* (1972), which depicts the plight of an aged Indian merchant living in London and caught in the backlash of anti-Asian feeling fueled by Pakistani and Indian immigration. *The Golden Honeycomb* (1979) is a historical novel of intrigues and shattered ideals in a princely state around 1900.

M. has shown an admirable willingness to tackle a number of contemporary issues, to the extent that her writing may be considered socioliterature. Indeed, her conscious use of sociological imagery has increased as her writing has matured; wherever possible, she concentrates on demolishing stereotypes in favor of presenting truth. The assignment of roles according to gender is a major concern in her work. M.'s novels intelligently illustrate the major social issues confronting India and its citizens, beginning with the struggle for independence. Most are superb stories as well.

FURTHER WORKS: *Some Inner Fury* (1955); *A Silence of Desire* (1960); *Possession* (1963); *The Coffer Dams* (1969)

BIBLIOGRAPHY: Shiv, K., "Tradition and Change in the Novels of K. M.," *BA*, 43 (1969): 508–13; Rao, K. S. N., "K. M.: The Novelist as Craftsman," *IWT*, 8 (1969): 32–40; Harrex, S. C., "A Sense of Identity: The Novels of K. M.," *JCL*, 6 (1971): 68–78; Adkins, J. F., "K. M.: Indo-Anglican Conflict as Unity," *JSoAL*, 10 (1974): 89–102; Shimer, D. B., "Sociological Imagery in the Novels of K. M.," *WLWE*, 14 (1975): 357–70; Rao, K. S. N., "Religious Elements in K. M.'s Novels," *ArielE*, 8, 1 (1977): 35–50; Prasad, H. M., "The Quintessence of K. M.'s Art," *ComQ*, 3, 9 (1978): 173–85

—JANET M. POWERS

MARKISH, Peretz

Yiddish poet, novelist, and dramatist, b. 7 Dec. 1895, Polone, Russia; d. 12 Aug. 1952, Moscow, Russia

M. was born and raised in a town in Volhynia. War and revolution were the crucible of M.'s life and work. He served in the tsar's army in World War I, was wounded at the front, and was thought for a time to have perished in the Ukrainian pogroms of 1918–19. In 1921 M. left the Soviet Union for Warsaw, where he launched the Yiddish EXPRESSIONIST group Di khalyastre (The Gang) with Melech Ravitch (1893–1976) and Uri Zvi GREENBERG. Wanderlust took him to Berlin, Paris, London, and Palestine, but Poland remained the center of his intense literary activity until he returned to the Soviet Union in 1926. Soon thereafter he came under vicious attack for maintaining ties with the "bourgeois reactionary circles in the West" and for "misrepresenting Soviet reality." Although M. bravely challenged his critics, he eventually submitted to Party control and subjected his own works to self-censorship and ideological revision. In 1939 he was awarded the Order of Lenin. M.'s response in his writings to the Nazi conquest of Poland was immediate and profound, but these intensely Jewish works could not be published until his country entered the war. Arrested on January 27, 1949, during the purge of the Jewish cultural figures, he was shot in the Lubyanka Prison on August 12, 1952.

For M., the revolution meant freedom from the neoromantic, melancholy, and stylized verse that had dominated Yiddish poetry of the previous decade; it meant the physical freedom to travel and work wherever he chose, striking roots nowhere. The titles of his earliest collections of poetry best illustrate this mood: *Shveln* (1919; thresholds), *Pust un pas* (1919; idle), *Shtiferish* (1919; mischievous), and *Stam* (1921; just like that). By the time he left for Poland, he had become the poetic voice of the revolution in Yiddish literature.

Influenced by two very different strands of Russian MODERN-ISM—FUTURISM and Acmeism—M. introduced a new Yiddish poetics: inverted syntax, the use of regional and unusual words, wild metonymies instead of metaphors, assonance, and wrenched rhyme. His most dazzling lyric poems applied classical forms (notably the sonnet) to such modernist themes as the city, chaos, and technology. Throughout his career, M. favored a dramatic, exclamatory style, which he managed to combine with long descriptive passages. This tension between classical form and modernist theory, between egocentric pathos and the need to chronicle the historical present, between the lyric and the epic, is at the heart of M.'s achievement.

The balance shifted from one period to another. M.'s early poetry was an exalted, personal celebration of the present, with its boundless possibilities. When he tried to capture the shtetl of his childhood in the narrative poem *Volin* (written 1918, pub. 1921; Volhynia), the people were portrayed dispassionately and as lacking all sense of the present moment. In his expressionist period (1921–26), external reality existed only to the extent that it was reflected within the poet's own ego—and reality could be anything from Ukrainian pogroms to the Eiffel Tower. In *Di kupe* (1921; the corpse heap), for instance, his major expressionist work, the poet is overwhelmed by the physicality of the pogrom, by the revolting smell of decomposing bodies. The egocentric vision allowed for no temporal development. Each poem captured a single moment, and even the poetic "I" had no biographical past: he was society at large or every "I" reading the poem.

M.'s narrative poem *Brider* (1929; brothers) marked a turning point and synthesis. M. returned to the shtetl setting to show it transformed by human experience. In the tale of two Jewish brothers who gave their lives to the revolution, a sense of history was achieved through highly figurative language, haunting repetitions, a fusion of lyric and narrative, high and low diction. Most innovative was M.'s elliptic throwing together of detail instead of a full narrative development. The social, political, and generational aspects of this theme received a more sustained, if more conventional treatment in M.'s first novel, *Dor oys dor ayn* (1929; generations come and go).

The 1930s were essentially a period of consolidation and revision. M. adapted his more popular works for the Soviet Yiddish theater, then in its heyday, and saw an impressive number of his works appear in Russian translation.

In his last, most tragic period, M. became the supreme elegist of Polish Jewry. In his finest poem, *Tsu a yidisher tentserin* (written 1940, pub. 1959; to a Jewish dancer), he treated the unfathomable tragedy through the fate of a single victim, the artistic embodiment of her people. Less successful were his all-encompassing epic poem *Milkhome* (1948; war) and his novel about the Warsaw Ghetto uprising, *Trot fun doyres* (written 1947–48; pub. [in censored version] 1966; the tread of generations). In 1948 M. wrote a

defiant elegy for his close friend Solomon Mikhoels, the preeminent actor and director of the Yiddish theater whom the Soviet secret police had just murdered. With its total poetic control and classical locutions, this poem is a fitting requiem for all of Soviet Yiddish culture.

FURTHER WORKS: *In mitn veg* (1919); *Nokhn telerl fun himl* (1919); *Farbaygeyendik (eseyen)* (1921); *Radio* (1922); *Der galaganer hon* (1922); *Nakhtroyb* (1922); *Farklepte tsiferblatn* (1929); *Nit gedayget* (1931); *Vokhnteg* (1931); *Gezamlte verk* (3 vols., 1933–1937); *Eyns of eyns* (1934); *Dem balegufs toyt* (1935; also pub. as *Anshl der zalyaznik*); *Oyfgang afn Dnyeper* (1937); *Lider vegn Shpanye* (1938); *Foterlekhe erd* (1938); *Dertseylungen* (1939); *Di naye mishpokhe* (1939); *Mikhoels* (1939); *Poemen vegn Stalinen* (1940); *Roytarmeyishe balades* (1940); *Dor oys dor ayn*, Vol. 2 (1941); *A toyt di kanibaln!* (1941); *Farn folk un heymland* (1943); *Yerushe* (1959); *Der fertsikyoriker man* (1978)

BIBLIOGRAPHY: Shmeruk, C., "Yiddish Literature in the U.S.S.R.," in Kochan, L., ed., *The Jews in Soviet Russia since 1917* (1970): 232–68; Markish, E., *The Long Return* (1978); Roskies, D. G., "The Pogrom Poem and the Literature of Destruction," *NDEJ*, 11 (1979): 89–113

—DAVID G. ROSKIES

MARQUAND, J(ohn) P(hillips)

American novelist, b. 10 Nov. 1893, Wilmington, Del.; d. 16 July 1960, Newburyport, Mass.

Born into New England literary society, M. majored in chemistry at Harvard. After graduation he took up magazine editing for *The Boston Transcript* and later worked in advertising and journalism following his military service as an artillery lieutenant during World War I. Married three times, M. had two sons and a daughter.

M. began his career by writing popular, melodramatic tales like the Mr. Moto stories, and costume romances like *The Black Cargo* (1925) and *Haven's End* (1937). *The Late George Apley* (1937), a satiric rendering of upper-class Bostonian traditions, made him known as a serious novelist, set the tone of subsequent works, and won him a Pulitzer Prize in 1938. *Wickford Point* (1939) employs the same setting to explore the career of a slick, popular writer from a decaying New England family through M.'s favorite narrative techniques of ironic point of view and flashback. Similarly, *H. M. Pulham, Esq.* (1941) is the portrait of a Boston businessman, the symbol of a vanishing order, who ineffectually rebels against social class and customs.

Turning to other cities and professions for subjects, M. continued to build on the theme of American social manners in his novels. *So Little Time* (1943) suggests the unrelenting passage of time in the life of a middle-aged playwright. Following an inferior war novel, *Repent in Haste* (1945), *B. F.'s Daughter* (1946) reveals the effects of the wartime mood on big business and the Washington bureaucracy. In the postwar *Point of No Return* (1949) M. revived his earlier brilliance in satire and sociological study: a successful banker realizes too late in his career that the competitive ethics of

J. P. Marquand

(1949); *Stopover, Tokyo* (1957); *Life at Happy Knoll* (1957); *Timothy Dexter Revisted* (1960)

BIBLIOGRAPHY: Hicks, G., "M. of Newburyport," *Harper's* (April 1950): 105–8; Brady, C. A., "J. P. M.," in Gardner, H. C., ed., *Fifty Years of the American Novel, 1900–1950* (1952): 107–34; Kazin, A., "J. P. M. and the American Failure," *Atlantic,* (Nov. 1958): 152–54; Gross, J. J., *J. P. M.* (1963); Holman, C. H., *J. P. M.* (1965); Bell, M., *M.: An American Life* (1979); Green, G., "J. M.: The Reluctant Prophet," *NER,* 2 (1980): 614–24

—LYNN DEVORE

MARQUÉS, René

Puerto Rican dramatist, short-story writer, novelist, essayist, and poet, b. 4 Oct. 1919, Arecibo; d. 22 March 1979, San Juan

After earning an agronomy degree in 1942, M. attended the University of Madrid, where he took courses in literature. In 1949 he received a Rockefeller grant to study theater arts at Columbia University, and upon returning to Puerto Rico he began a literary career that would make him the island's best-known contemporary man of letters.

M.'s basic preoccupation as a writer was Puerto Rico's political future. An outspoken advocate of independence, he abhorred the domination of his homeland by the U.S., which has led to the industrialization of the island's agricultural economy and to the contamination of its Hispanic culture. M. also condemned his fellow countrymen who barter their national identity for economic gain.

Most critics agree that M. will be remembered primarily as a dramatist whose works revitalized the modern Puerto Rican theater. His most popular play is *La carreta* (perf. 1951, pub. 1963; *The Oxcart,* 1969), which depicts the plight of peasants who leave their farm in search of a better life, first in San Juan and then in New York. After suffering the dehumanizing misfortunes of slum life, they return to the land they never should have abandoned.

M.'s most highly acclaimed critical successes were *Un niño azul para esa sombra* (1958; a blue child for that shadow) and *Los soles truncos* (1959; *The House of the Setting Suns,* 1965). *Un niño azul para esa sombra* is a poetic tragedy of an alienated child whose suicide results from the rift between his Americanized mother and his revolutionary father. The color blue symbolizes idealism; the shadow, Puerto Rico's submission to American influence. In *Los soles truncos* two guilt-ridden old maids relive the past on the day of their sister's death. A series of flashbacks explains their mental torment, a metaphor of the collective guilt weighing on the Puerto Rican psyche. The theme of purification is suggested when the sisters set fire to their decaying mansion to prevent American entrepreneurs from converting it into a hotel.

Innovations in M.'s theater include striking visual and auditory effects as well as abrupt temporal and spatial dislocations. M. also injected elements of pantomime, farce, and THEATER OF THE ABSURD into his dramas in order to poeticize his political ideas. His last plays treat biblical themes that draw parallels between past and present-day situations and thus deny temporal progression.

M.'s short stories are considered second only to his theater, a fine example of this genre being the prize-winning "Tres hombres junto al río" (1960; "Three Men near the River," 1978), in which

American business have left him spiritually bankrupt. The past in inaccessible; he can only complete a dead life.

In *Melville Goodwin, U.S.A.* (1951) M. pictures the military world through the eyes of a journalist and achieves a double-edged irony that reflects both the shallowness of the reporter's medium and deceit among the Army's higher echelons. More purely in the tradition of Sinclair LEWIS, *Sincerely, Willis Wayde* (1955) brutally relates the lack of morality and character in the life of an American entrepreneur. M.'s last important and most autobiographically interesting novel, *Women and Thomas Harrow* (1958), is the story of a successful playwright and his three marriages. M. again uncovers spiritual mediocrity in American society.

M. was one of the most consistently popular and best-selling social novelists of his age. His thorough and detailed canvases of America, the grace of his parody and irony, and the power of his themes about the conflict between the individual and conformity speak of an artistic vision and sensibility fundamental to American literature.

FURTHER WORKS: *Prince and Boatswain* (1915); *The Unspeakable Gentleman* (1922); *Four of a Kind* (1923); *Lord Timothy Dexter* (1925); *Do Tell Me, Doctor Johnson* (1928); *Warning Hill* (1930); *Ming Yellow* (1935); *No Hero* (1935); *Thank You, Mr. Moto* (1936); *Think Fast, Mr. Moto* (1937); *Mr. Moto Is So Sorry* (1938); *Mr. Moto Takes a Hand* (1940); *Don't Ask Questions* (1941); *Last Laugh, Mr. Moto* (1942); *It's Loaded, Mr. Bauer* three Indians drown a white man to test the validity of, and ultimately destroy, the resurrection myth.

Although M. has been labeled a pessimist because of the adversity most of his protagonists experience, he was, in reality, an optimist who considered man capable of change once he is made aware of his foibles. His incessant search for new artistic horizons lent universal dimensions to his work, elevating it above most social-protest literature written in Spanish.

FURTHER WORKS: *Peregrinación* (1944); *El hombre y sus sueños* (1946); *El sol y los MacDonald* (1947); *Juan Bobo y la Dama de Occidente* (1955); *Otro día nuestro* (1955); *La muerte no entrará en palacio* (1956); *La víspera del hombre* (1957); *Carnaval afuera, carnaval adentro* (1960); *La casa sin reloj* (1960); *En una ciudad llamada San Juan* (1960); *El apartamiento* (1964); *Mariana; o, El alba* (1965); *Sacrificio en el Monte Moriah* (1969); *David y Jonathan* (1970); *Tito y Berenice* (1970); *Vía crucis del hombre puertorriqueño* (1970); *Ensayos (1953–1971)* (1971); *Inmersos en el silencio* (1976); *La mirada* (1976)

BIBLIOGRAPHY: Dauster, F., "The Theater of R. M.," *Symposium*, 18, 1 (1964): 35–45; Shaw, D. L., "R. M.'s *La muerte no entrará en palacio:* An Analysis," *LATR*, 2, 1 (1968): 31–38; Siemens, W. L., "Assault on the Schizoid Wasteland: R. M.'s *El apartamiento*," *LATR*, 7, 2 (1974): 17–23; Holzaphel, T., "The Theater of R. M.: In Search of Identity and Form," in Lyday, L. F., and Woodyard, G. W., eds., *Dramatists in Revolt: The New Latin American Theater* (1976): 146–66; Rodríguez-Seda, A., "Puerto Rican Narrative: Aspects of Frustration," *PCL*, 2, 2 (1976): 53–62; Pilditch, C., *R. M.: A Study of His Fiction* (1977); Martin, E. J., *R. M.* (1979)

—GEORGE R. MCMURRAY

MARSHALL, Paule

American novelist and short-story writer, b. 9 Apr. 1929, Brooklyn, N.Y.

Born to parents who had emigrated from Barbados, M. graduated from Brooklyn College in 1953. As a journalist for the publication *Our World*, she was sent to the West Indies and to Brazil, experiences she would exploit in her fiction. In the course of the 1960s, she received recognition in the form of prizes and fellowships from the Guggenheim Foundation, the Ford Foundation, the National Institute of Arts and Letters, the National Endowment for the Arts, and the Yaddo Corporation. In 1984 she received the Before Columbus Foundation American Book Award.

In spite of these institutional honors, M. endured a period of relative neglect from serious literary critics; more recently, however, M. has begun to receive the sort of recognition her impressive, if not notably large, body of work deserves. The neglect perhaps had something to do with the fact that M. did not fit easily into the most available categories. Although a black novelist, and fully capable of militant responses to what she perceived as racism, M. could not in her work easily be identified with any political line; moreover, her West Indian background, marking her as a member of a minority within a minority, presented difficulties to any critic who might be less interested in the individual talent or, for that matter, in the complexities of that mysterious phenomenon we call "race" than in sweeping generalizations about the significance of black

literature. And, although a woman writing eloquently about women, M. did not in her work reflect a narrowly or mechanically ideological (and therefore predictable) feminism; this is not to deny, of course, that what might be called a humane feminism, at once critical and compassionate in its portrayal of relationships between the sexes, makes itself felt as an informing presence in her work.

At the center of each of M.'s first three novels is a remarkable female character. Selina, the protagonist of *Brown Girl, Brownstones* (1959), grows from childhood to young womanhood; Merle, in *The Chosen Place, the Timeless People* (1969), is a strongly defined woman in her forties; Avey Johnson, in *Praisesong for the Widow* (1983), is a widow in her sixties. In these three novels M. has thus given us portraits of three women at three major passages in their lives.

She has also placed these women in clearly defined fictional worlds, the interaction of individual and environment being one of her compelling concerns. In *Brown Girl, Brownstones* the environment extends from the protagonist's family outward to Brooklyn's Barbadian community as a whole. M.'s portrayal of that community, filtered through the consciousness of a protagonist who must define herself in part by rebelling against it, impresses the reader by its balance of the critical and the sympathetic; M. sees more than her character does. But the portrayal of life within the family is the novel's greatest strength; a casual reading might stress Selina's relation to her father, but it may well be that the mother-daughter relationship constitutes the novel's richest and most resonant achievement. M. has said that the conversations she overheard in her own mother's kitchen have been a major resource in the development of her narrative art.

The Chosen Place, the Timeless People, set on a fictional island that bears more than a fleeting resemblance to Barbados, puts a personal portrayal of the character Merle ("the most alive of my characters," says M.) against a panorama of island society that reflects not only the struggles of the present, but also the legacy of an imperialist past, a past that itself remains chillingly present; this novel also includes M.'s most ambitious attempt to deal with relationships involving characters of different races.

Praisesong for the Widow affirms openly what may be implicit in the earlier novels: that environment, for M., is as much spiritual as social and historical. Avey Johnson's discovery of her spiritual identity through rediscovering the link to her African heritage, the experience arising out of what was to have been a Caribbean pleasure cruise, provides the organizing theme of the novel. But the power of the book stems not from its abstract theme, but from its rhythms and textures; the novel is saturated with the rituals, traditions, folk and formal literatures, and art forms (especially dance, a major motif in M.'s work) of African, Caribbean, and African-American cultures.

In her first novel, M. explored the experience of the West Indian immigrant to the U.S., opening up a subject area that had received little previous exposure in American fiction. In her second novel, she brought a group of American characters to a fictional island in the Caribbean. Both novels placed M. clearly and firmly within the realistic tradition in fiction. In her third novel, although her capacity for social observation remained undimmed. M. ventured beyond realism into the realm of the mythic; she proved still capable of surprising us.

The placing of women's experience within varying and specific cultural contexts, especially contexts reflecting African origins, may be M.'s primary concern as an artist, but some of the most memorable characters in her fiction are men. Selina's father in *Brown Girl, Brownstones* and Avey's husband in *Praisesong for the Widow* are especially impressive achievements in the art of characterization. And it is worth noting that they differ dramatically from each other; M. doesn't work from a simplified model of the male. *Soul Clap Hands and Sing* (1961), a collection of four short novels, each featuring a male protagonist/view-point character, confirms this aspect of M.'s talent.

In the fall of 1991 M.'s long-awaited fourth novel appeared. Set in both New York and the West Indies, *Daughters* finds its moral focus in Ursa, daughter of a West Indian father and an American mother, while introducing a cast of characters comparable in range and complexity to that of *The Chosen Place, the Timeless People*. Through such characteristic concerns as the explorations of tensions—especially daughter-parent tensions—within the family, the articulation of the family within the larger social setting, the probing of relationships that refuse to fit neatly within preestablished categories, and the affirmation of the continuing power and presence of folk culture as a force and source in black life, American and West Indian, set against images of a past that is at once and inextricably historical and mythic, M. undertakes her most ambitious examination of the politics of male-female relationships and of the sexual dimensions of the political. Although the novel begins with an abortion, it is typical of M.'s art that, rather than degenerating into an occasion of ideological orthodoxy, the abortion here becomes a dynamic, complex, and by no means unambiguous organizing symbol of the novel as a whole.

M. has recently begun to receive the critical recognition denied her earlier in her career; most of the incisive commentary on her fiction dates from the 1980s. The recognition is deserved, because M. is unquestionably one of the gifted American writers of her generation. But its significance goes beyond that. Because M. has refused to be pigeonholed, the recognition she receives suggests that we may be ready to expand our notions of what constitutes African-American fiction or the feminist novel. M. is one of those writers to whom we turn in search of our humanity.

FURTHER WORKS: *Reena, and Other Stories* (1983)

BIBLIOGRAPHY: Brown, L., "The Rhythm of Power in P. M.'s Fiction," *Novel*, 7 (1974): 159–67; Christian, B., *Black Women Novelists: The Development of a Tradition, 1892–1976* (1980): 80–137, 239–53; Schneider, D., "A Feminine Search for Selfhood: P. M.'s *Brown Girl, Brownstones*," in Bruck, P. and W. Karrer, eds., *The Afro-American Novel since 1960* (1982): 53–73; Collier, E., "The Closing of the Circle: Movement from Division to Wholeness in P. M.'s Fiction," in Evans, M., ed., *Black Women Writers* (1950–1980): *A Critical Evaluation* (1984): 295–315; McCluskey, J., "And Called Every Generation Blessed: Time, Setting, and Ritual in the Works of P. M.," in Evans, M., ed., *Black Women Writers (1950–1980): A Critical Evaluation* (1984): 316–34; Christian, B., *Black Feminist Criticism: Perspectives on Black Women Writers* (1985): 103–18, 149–58; Spillers, H. J., "*Chosen Place, Timeless People*: Some Figurations on the New World," in Pryse, M., and Spillers, H. J., eds., *Conjuring: Black Women, Fiction, and Literary Tradition* (1985): 151–75; Willis, S., *Specifying: Black Women Writing the American Experience* (1987): 53–82; Busia, A., "What Is Your Nation? Reconstructing Africa and Her Diaspora through P. M.'s *Praisesong for the Widow*," in Wall, C. A., ed., *Changing Our Own Words* (1989): 196–211; Russell, S., *Render Me My Song: Afro-American Woman Writers from Slavery to the Present* (1990): 144–50; Kubitschek, M. D., *Claiming the Heritage: African-American Women Novelists and History* (1991): 69–89

—W. P. KENNEY

MARSMAN, Hendrik

Dutch poet and critic, b. 30 Sept. 1899, Zeist; d. 21 June 1940, English Channel

Only M.'s death sets his biography apart from those of many other middle-class, university-trained professional literati. He served brief and relatively unsuccessful stints as editor of a literary journal and newspaper critic, which failed to further his ambition to play a leadership role in the world of letters. Such influence as he did exert, especially over minor talents, was based more on his often forceful reviews, in which he developed his programmatic opinions. In 1921 and 1922 M. made an extensive journey through Germany, and later he lived for more than a decade on the Mediterranean: in Italy, Spain, and France. The political developments in Germany in the 1930s aroused his opposition to fascism, and when Hitler's troops invaded the Netherlands in May 1940, he decided to seek sanctuary in England. The ship on which he was making the crossing from the French port of Bordeaux was sunk by a German submarine, and M. drowned.

A selection of M.'s earliest poems, which had appeared in various journals since 1919, was published in the volume *Verzen* (1923; verse), followed some years later by a more extensive collection, *Paradise regained* (1927; title in English). These texts were dominated by a pseudoexpressionistic style, which reflected M.'s perception of such German poets as Herwarth Walden (1878–1941) and Hermann Kasack (1896–1966). In essence, M.'s lyric stance was impressionistic and individualistic in this so-called "vitalistic" phase, whose end he proclaimed in 1933.

Actually, he had abandoned this style in his poetry several years earlier. Even in the 1927 volume, occasional works had foreshadowed the new direction of his poetry in a basically romantic preoccupation with loneliness and death. The earlier tendency toward exaggerated diction gave way to a simpler and more colloquial mode of expression. The principal yield of this second phase was collected in *Porta Nigra* (1934; Latin: Black Gate)—the title derives from the monumental "black gate" built by the Romans in the city that is now Trier, West Germany—which won a prestigious official literary award. Thematically related to these poems was one of M.'s few attempts at fiction, the novel *De dood van Angèle Degroux* (1933; the death of Angèle Degroux).

After a period of reduced literary productivity, from about 1936 on M. reasserted his prominent position in the Dutch world of letters with his poetry and criticism, and with another novelistic venture, written in collaboration with Simon VESTDIJK, *Heden ik, morgen gij* (1937; today I, tomorrow thou). But the most important work by far of these years, and of M.'s entire creative career, was the collection of verse *Tempel en kruis* (1940; temple and cross). In a variety of poetic forms, M. addressed himself to the dual roots of Western civilization in Greek antiquity and Christian religion. While acknowledging early Christianity as a positive force, he subscribed to the Nietzschean idea of its progressive decline into sterile dogmatism. On the other hand, the spirit of antiquity appeared to M. as a vital and enduring civilizing influence.

Tempel en kruis, the last work to be completed by M., was one of the very few successful lyric statements concerning the advent of fascism, because it avoided the pitfall of explicit politicizing. Instead, M. sublimated his misgivings about the political trends of his day in a grandiose vision of the civilization whose continued existence was threatened by the totalitarian and collectivistic movements that were sweeping Europe. M.'s death as a victim of World War II not only added a note of personal tragedy to his literary concern over the fate of Western culture but also deprived Netherlandic literature of a major lyric talent.

FURTHER WORKS: *Penthesilea* (1925); *De anatomische les* (1926); *De vliegende Hollander* (1927); *De lamp van Diogenes* (1928); *De vijf vingers* (1929); *Witte vrouwen* (1930); *Voorpost* (1931); *Kort geding* (1931); *Herman Gorter* (1937); *Menno ter Braak* (1939); *Verzameld werk* (3 vols., 1938); *Brieven over literatuur* (1945, with Simon Vestdijk); *Verzameld werk IV* (1947); *H. M. voor de spiegel* (1966); *De briefwisseling tussen P. N. van Eyck en H. M.* (1968); *Ik zoek bezielden* (1978)

BIBLIOGRAPHY: Meijer, R. P., *Literature of the Low Countries* (1978): 316–21

—EGBERT KRISPYN

MARTIN DU GARD, Roger

French novelist and dramatist, b. 23 March 1881, Neuilly-sur-Seine; d. 23 Aug. 1958, Bellême

M.'s father was a lawyer in Paris, and the long legal tradition in M.'s family is reflected in the careful preparation and documentation that went into M.'s novels. M. devoted himself almost exclusively to his writing, choosing to work in isolated country retreats, where he kept huge files of documentation on his characters and on historical events. An extremely ambitious writer who modeled himself after Tolstoy and sought to write epic novels like *War and Peace*, M. set such high standards for himself that he destroyed several completed manuscripts and could not complete his last novel, *Le journal du Colonel de Maumort* (Colonel de Maumort's diary), to his satisfaction. M. was awarded the Nobel Prize for literature in 1937.

M. made his literary debut with *Devenir!* (1909; to become!), a novel about a selfish, ambitious young writer who fails to measure up to his own expectations. Both the protagonist, André Mazarelles, and the plot of *Devenir!* are remarkably similar to those of *The Immoralist* (1902) by André GIDE. M. and Gide had a long, close friendship, which is revealed in their letters published in *Correspondance* (2 vols., 1968; correspondence) and in M.'s *Notes sur André Gide* (1951; *Recollections of André Gide*, 1953). M. shared with Gide, twelve years his senior, many literary and social concerns, although their approaches to writing were totally different. While Gide wrote directly and passionately, revealing much of himself in his fictional works, M. sought to remain impersonal and objective and strove for a transparent style in the manner of Flaubert.

M.'s first major novel was *Jean Barois* (1913; *Jean Barois*, 1949), the story of a young man's attempt to free himself from religion and spread the doctrine of rationalism and scientific truth. *Jean Barois*, which quickly became a best seller, provides one of the most accurate and moving accounts of the Dreyfus Affair, a series of events that shattered French political and social life. In writing *Jean Barois*, M. sought to innovate by eliminating the third person omniscient narrator and relating events directly through dialogue (as in the theater) and through documentation (excerpts from speeches and newspaper articles dealing with the Dreyfus Affair). With the novel, M. succeeded in the very goal that the unsuccessful protagonist of his first novel had set for himself: the creation of a new kind of novel that combines historical and psychological truth. The circumstances of Barois's death, which takes place in the same house and the same bed where his father had died at the beginning of the novel, give the work its cyclical unity. M. himself never had a feeling for religion, but in *Jean Barois* and in the sixth volume of *Les Thibault* (8 vols., 1922–40; Vols. 1–6, *The Thibaults*, 1939; Vols. 7–8, *Summer 1914*, 1941), M. powerfully depicts the comfort and solace that Christianity offers to those who are about to die.

Les Thibault, an eight-volume novel that traces the lives of two very different brothers from adolescence to adulthood, is undoubtedly M.'s masterpiece. It consists of *Le cahier gris* (1922; the gray notebook), *Le pénitencier* (1922; the penitentiary), *La belle saison* (1923; the springtime of life), *La consultation* (1928; the consultation), *La sorellina* (1928; the sorellina), *La mort du père* (1929; the father's death), *L'été1914* (1936; summer 1914), and *Épilogue* (1940; epilogue). In depicting the two brothers—Jacques, the maladjusted adolescent who seeks purity and eventually joins the socialist revolutionary movement, and Antoine, the older, more conformist, hard-working doctor who seeks change through evolution—M. actually depicted two conflicting aspects of his own personality: his sense of rebellion and his need for order. The conflict between the two brothers and their ultraconservative, egotistical bourgeois father provides the focus for the first two volumes of the series. Although both brothers are extremely critical of their father's harsh authoritarian ways, they begin to recognize his reflection in themselves as they grow older. Many disgruntled adolescents of the 1920s identified with Jacques and wrote letters to M. empathizing with his young protagonist. Yet M. himself judged Jacques harshly and ironically, stating that Jacques "lived and died like an idiot." M. identified most closely with the older brother Antoine, and it is Antoine who, in his diary in the last volume, *Épilogue*, delivers the final message of humanism and hope for the betterment of humanity in a new (socialist) society.

An automobile accident in 1931 in which he and his wife were injured led M. to reexamine his plans for the rest of *Les Thibault*. He decided to reduce the scope of his epic novel and change its very nature from a primarily psychological study to a historical study of the events that led to the outbreak of World War I during the summer of 1914. In the penultimate volume of the series, *L'été 1914*, Jacques, the young writer who has become an adamant pacifist, tries desperately and feverishly to avert a war. Using a technique similar to his documentation in *Jean Barois*, M. lengthily explores the negotiations and diplomatic missions that immediately preceded World War I. He sought to prove that World War I could easily have been avoided if only the socialist-pacifists had published certain revealing documents. The war, with its unnecessary bloodshed and the subsequent destruction of the entire European way of life, is shown to have been the result of blind nationalism and selfish propaganda on the part of political leaders on both sides.

M.'s one serious drama, *Un taciturne* (1932; a silent man), which explores the tragic consequences of the hero's discovery of his own latent homosexuality, was not as well received as

M.'s novels, although its powerful confrontation scenes are dramatically effective.

M. did not write about extraordinary individuals; his goal was to reflect life itself, with its tedium and complexities, to present life in the rough as it appears to ordinary people. His frank explorations of the moral issue of euthanasia and the question of suicide in *Jean Barois* and in *Les Thibault* make his works relevant to the moral debates of the 1980s.

By stressing the emptiness of life led in isolation and insisting on the need for the individual to become involved with the collectivity, M. anticipated the writings of André MALRAUX, Jean-Paul SARTRE, and M.'s friend and admirer Albert CAMUS. Like the EXISTENTIALISTS who followed, M. dealt with man's need to define himself, to discover his own identity through action in a world without God. The recent publication of M.'s personal correspondence, *Correspondence générale* (2 vols., 1980; general correspondence), which reveals a passionate yet puritanical man who concealed his personality under a self-imposed literary strait-jacket, will certainly lead to a better appreciation of M., the moralist and the man.

FURTHER WORKS: *L'abbaye de Jumièges: Étude archéologique des ruines* (1909); *L'une de nous* (1910); *Le testament du père Leleu* (1920; *Papa Leleu's Will*, 1921); *La gonfle, farce paysanne* (1928); *La confidence africaine* (1930); *Vieille France* (1933; *The Postman*, 1954); *Souvenirs autobiographiques et littéraires* (1955); *Œuvres complètes* (2 vols., 1955)

BIBLIOGRAPHY: Lalou, R., *R. M.* (1937); Brodin, P., *Les écrivains français d'l'entre-deux-guerres* (1942): 183–201; Magny, C.-E., *Histoire du roman français depuis 1918* (1950): 305–50; Camus, A., "R. M." (1955); *Lyrical and Critical Essays* (1968): 254–87; Brombert, V., *The Intellectual Hero: Studies in the French Novel 1880–1955* (1961): 94–118; Boak, D., *R. M.* (1963); Schalk, D., *R. M.: The Novelist and History* (1967); Savage, C., *R. M.* (1968); Howe, I., "M.: The Novelty of Goodness" (1968); *The Decline of the New* (1970): 43–53; Taylor, M., *M.: "Jean Barois"* (1974); Fernandez, D., "M. sans corset," *L'express* (12 April 1980): 86–88

—DEBRA POPKIN

MARTÍN GAITE, Carmen

Spanish novelist, short-story writer, essayist, and poet, b. 8 Dec. 1925, Salamanca

M. G. enjoyed a liberal upbringing and enlightened education, unusual for a Spanish female of her generation. Thanks to living in the medieval university town of Salamanca, M. G. found it relatively easy to complete a university degree in Romance philology in 1949. As Salamanca was quickly occupied by the Franco forces early in the Spanish Civil War (1936-39), the area experienced no prolonged conflict or devastation, and M. G. escaped adolescent wartime trauma marking most writers of her generation.

Literary interests and membership in writers' groups date from her university days; she married fellow writer Rafael SÁNCHEZ FERLOSIO in 1953 and bore one son and one daughter, both of whom died tragically in separate accidents—profound emotional upheavals echoed in M. G.'s subsequent fiction. In 1972 M. G.

completed a doctorate in history at the University of Madrid, specializing in Spanish 18th-c. studies, with a dissertation on a misunderstood politician: *El proceso de Macanaz: historia de un empapelamiento* (1969; Macanaz's Trial: Attack by Paper), republished as *Macanaz, otro paciente de la Inquisición* (1975; Macanaz, Another Victim of the Inquisition). Another period treatise investigates *El Conde de Guadalhorce: su época y su labor* (1983; The Count of Guadalhorce: His Epoch and His Work). Submersion in popular culture of times past led to *Usos amorosos del dieciocho en España* (1972; *Love Customs in 18th-Century Spain*, 1991). An enormously successful and popular spin-off, *Usos amorosos de la postguerra española* (1987; Love Customs of Spain's Postwar Era), portrays courtship rituals, marriage, adultery, concubinage, and other male-female relations during M. G.'s youth, allowing readers to contrast the "war of the sexes" in two periods, different yet dismayingly similar. *Agua pasada* (1993; Water under the Bridge) contains literary criticism following an initial autobiographical essay, and a section of meditations on time's passing.

M. G.'s early fiction appeared during the postwar vogue of neorealist "social literature" in Spain during the 1950s and 1960s; initial works reflect the movement's characteristic techniques and (to a lesser extent) its themes—predominantly socioeconomic protest with underlying political intent. Strict postwar censorship forced writers to disguise opposition as "objective" observation, muffling criticism which remained implicit in selections of uniformly problematic situations. Unlike other "social" writers, M. G. regularly tackles feminist issues, focusing on gender roles and restrictions rather than social class and economic injustice. In the postneorealist period of the 1970s and thereafter, M. G. and numerous others turn increasingly to formal and linguistic experimentation.

The novelette *El balneario* (1954; The Spa), M. G.'s first noteworthy narrative, deploys a drab, middle-aged female protagonist in a surrealistic, Kafkaesque atmosphere, provoking hallucinatory perceptions and paranoid reactions before revealing that the entire experience, including bizarre behaviors by other characters in the isolated, decaying, mysterious hotel, has been a dream. Like this initial success, most of M. G.'s fiction foregrounds female characters, subtly underscoring feminine repression and constraints imposed by a patriarchal society and reactionary, totalitarian regime. Although never a professed feminist, she paints women's "unliberated" condition from adolescence through menopause and decrepitude with resolute realism, and detailed temporal, historical, socioeconomic, and political-geographic backgrounds, without sentimentality or exaggeration, but also without pulling punches. Rooting her portraits in autobiographical experience and that of female friends and acquaintances, M. G. presents ambience of enclosure, interiors, and domestic space reflecting Spain's tradition of *encierro* (encloisterment of women) that dates back to Arabic harems and medieval convents. Frequent hints at imprisonment and claustrophobia are no accident, as seen in *Entre visillos* (1954; *Behind the Curtains*, 1990), *Las ataduras* (1960; Bonds), and *El cuarto de atrás* (1978; *The Back Room*, 1983), all depicting feminine confinement. *Ritmo lento* (1963; Slow Motion), M. G.'s only novel with a male protagonist, likewise involves enforced enclosure: an alienated intellectual is confined to an insane asylum.

M. G., an exceptionally lucid essayist, has written engagingly and persuasively of Spanish women's centuries of marginalization and relegation to positions as observers. *Desde la ventana: enfoque femenino de la literatura española* (1987; From the Window:

Feminine Focus on Spanish Literature) argues that Spanish women's typical situation is *ventanera*—"at the window," restricting perspectives on life in the larger world beyond—which elucidates the titles of *Entre visillos* and *El cuarto de atrás*, together with her less successful *Fragmentos de interior* (1976; Indoor Views)—perspectives of characters "confined" to the same large apartment. *Retahilas* (1974; Skeins [of Discourse]) offers a similarly passive, spectator's view of events: a mature woman, separated from her husband, spends the night with her nephew in a death-watch beside their dying grandmother. *Las ataduras*, both novelette and title story of the collection, portrays the "ties" binding women to domestic spaces—even the more privileged, bright, and rebellious. The protagonist, seeking freedom, runs away to Paris with her professor, an unconventional French intellectual, subsequently finding herself abandoned with two small children and obliged to return, unmarried and penniless, to her parents in Spain.

Like fictions of Josefina Aldecoa (b. 1926)—the only feminist approaching comparable artistry—M. G.'s stories present dilemmas facing Spanish women under a regime which prepared them exclusively as wives and mothers, limiting access to careers, professions or independent existence and condemning them to boredom, lifelong dependency, and mental inertia. Parallel to this recurring theme, she presents the desperation of women facing spinsterhood, the tedious existence of old maids—a major subtheme in works from *Behind the Curtains* to *Nubosidad variable* (1992; Partly Cloudy). The latter counterposes the lives of two high school friends, one a "career woman," successful psychiatrist—and lonely, frustrated female; the other an aspiring writer who married, sacrificed her ambitions, bore several children, then was abandoned by a philandering husband fixated on younger women. Reencounter after thirty years produces joyous reunion as each friend recognizes her ideal interlocutor and eager listener following decades of not really being heard. M. G.'s essays often illuminate her fiction, and *La búsqueda de interlocutor y otras búsquedas* (1973; The Search for an Interlocutor and Other Searches) theorizes that every author writes for an ideal interlocutor (implied reader) with complete expression being possible only when that ideal is realized.

La reina de las nieves (1994; The Snow Queen) continues and amplifies fairy-tale allusions prevalent in *El cuarto de atrás* and *Nubosidad variable*, contrasting women's options: conventional marriage versus unconventional independence as an unmarried, struggling writer. Several fairy tales written for adolescent girls reiterate similar choices, as exemplified in *El castillo de las tres murallas* (1982; The Triple-Walled Castle), *El pastel del diablo* (1985; The Devil's Cake) and *Caperucita en Manhattan* (1990; Little Red Riding Hood in Manhattan), all promoting feminine independence. *Lo raro es vivir* (1996; What's Strange Is Living), whose protagonist takes refuge in archival research following her mother's death, investigates the life of an extraordinary 18th-c. adventurer. The protagonist's historical discoveries parallel discoveries concerning her parents' relationship—the use of parallel or dual, intersecting plot-lines is among M. G.'s signature techniques.

M. G.'s greatest critical and popular success, *El cuarto de atrás*, combines autobiographical content with elements of the fantasy novel, while analyzing "growing up female" under the Franco dictatorship. Echoing her exploration of male-female relationships in *Usos amorosos de la postguerra*, this novel depicts feminine entrapment by conventions, blending a fictitious frame-narrative with recollections that include historical names and events. Combining postmodern narrative techniques and shifting realities which undermine epistemological presuppositions, *El cuarto de atrás* offers virtuoso mastery of novelistic form and theory while providing intimate and personal memories and insights. M. G. at her best excels both as storyteller and stylist. Presently Spain's leading woman writer, she has accumulated prizes ranging from the early Nadal (1957) to the National Prize for Literature, the Anagram Essay Prize, Prince of Asturias Prize for letters, Castilla and León Letters Prize, and the National Prize for Letters (1994). M. G. has articulated women's concerns with eloquence, elegance and impact unsurpassed in the Spanish language.

FURTHER WORKS: *Ocho siglos de poesía: antología bilingüe* (1972, with Andrés Ruiz Tarazona); *A rachas* (1976); *Cuentos completos* (1978); *El cuento de nunca acabar: apuntes sobre la narración, el amor y la mentira* (1983); *Dos relatos fantásticos* 1986); *Lo que queda enterrado* (1987)

BIBLIOGRAPHY: Lipman-Brown, J., *Secrets from the Back Room: The Fiction of C. M. G.* (1987); Manteiga, R., C. Galerstein, and K. McNerney, eds., *Feminine Concerns in Contemporary Spanish Fiction by Women* (1988); Lipman-Brown, J., ed., *Women Writers of Contemporary Spain: Exiles in the Homeland* (1991); Chittenden, J., " *El cuarto de atrás* as Autobiography," *Letras Femeninas*, 12, 1-2 (1986): 7884; Servodidio, M., and M. L. Welles, eds., *From Fiction to Metafiction: Essays in Honor of C. M. G.* (1983); Pérez, J., " *Nubosidad variable*: C. M. G. and Women's Word," *Inti*, 40 (Autumn 1994): 301-15; Pérez, J., "Structural, Thematic, and Symbolic Mirrors in *El cuarto de atrás* and *Nubosidad variable* of C. M. G.," *SCRev*, 12, 1 (Spring 1995): 47-64

—JANET PÉREZ

MARTÍNEZ ESTRADA, Ezequiel

Argentine essayist, poet, critic, short-story writer, and dramatist, b. 14 Sept. 1895, San José de la Esquina; d. 4 Nov. 1964, Bahía Blanca

For some thirty years (1915–46) M. E. held various positions in the Argentine postal system. His literary work was probably influenced by such factors as economic pressures that trapped him in the bureaucratic routine of this job, a childless marriage, the frequently unenthusiastic critical reception of his work, extended travels (1961–62) in Castro's Cuba, and perhaps most of all, the experience of witnessing Argentina's steady drift toward reaction, dictatorship, and loss of national purpose.

Like many Latin Americans, M. E. began his literary career as a poet, although it was as an essayist that he was to achieve wide acclaim. The six volumes of verse published between 1918 and 1929 gained him only a modicum of recognition, but he won the National Prize for Literature for the collection *Humoresca y títeres de pies ligeros* (1929; humoresque and light-footed puppets).

M. E.'s position as one of Latin America's leading writers rests chiefly on a series of brilliant essays, in which he relentlessly probed Argentine history, character, and values. The first and most celebrated of these works, *Radiografía de la pampa* (1933; X-Ray of the Pampa*, 1971), appeared at a time of economic depression and political instability. But in analyzing Argentina's plight M. E.

chose to examine certain deep-lying historical, geographic, and social factors, suggesting that there exists a basic dysfunction in Argentine culture, born of a decadent medieval Spanish tradition that prolonged itself in the New World. In his assessment of geographic factors he found—as the Spanish thinker ORTEGA Y GASSET had found earlier—that the vast, featureless pampa impeded normal social relationships and infused in the people intense feelings of solitude. The illusion of glory that motivated the conquistador, the belief in progress and plenty, typical of the 19th-c. positivist, and the dream of the immigrant that the New World was indeed a promised land, have, in M. E.'s iconoclastic view, served chiefly to obscure the real characteristics of Argentine life—solitude, resentment, frustration, aloofness, and subterfuge. Not surprisingly, when *Radiografía de la pampa* first appeared, many critics attacked it mercilessly; in recent decades, however, it has come to be considered M. E.'s masterpiece and his special contribution to Argentine letters.

Several other essays of M. E. are worthy of note, although it has been pointed out that virtually all of his later works are, in a sense, footnotes to *Radiografía de la pampa*. In the *Cabeza de Goliat* (1940; Goliath's head) he dissects the metropolis of Buenos Aires, which he describes as a "Goliath's head" on the body of a dwarf. This essay is especially rich in striking images: at one point the city and its inhabitants are likened to prisoners in a jail whose jailer has disappeared, and on another page the railroad system is compared to an octopus whose head is in the city but whose tentacles suck the sustenance out of the rich hinterland.

In *Muerte y transfiguración de Martín Fierro* (2 vols., 1948; death and transfiguration of Martín Fierro) M. E. continued his analysis of Argentine rural life by focusing on the genesis, development, and mythification of the gaucho hero. In two short, highly charged essays, *Qué es esto?* (1956; what's this?) and *Exhortaciones* (1957; exhortations), he decries the fact that the post-Perón governments were guided more by a desire to return to normality than by the conviction that the nation needed basic, if not radical, changes in its political, economic, and social order.

M. E. also published a number of literary studies, several plays, and a series of well-regarded novellas and short stories.

M. E. occupied a very special position among Argentine writers of his generation in that he became a genuine mentor for younger writers. Moreover, his radical critique of society transcends national boundaries and has thus established him as one of Latin America's most provocative and stimulating essayists.

FURTHER WORKS: *Oro y piedra* (1918); *Nefelibal* (1922); *Motivos del cielo* (1924); *Argentina* (1927); *Sarmiento* (1946); *Panorama de las literaturas* (1946); *Los invariantes históricos en el Facundo* (1947); *El mundo maravilloso de Guillermo Enrique Hudson* (1951); *Sábado de gloria* (1956); *Cuadrante del pampero* (1956); *Marta Riquelme* (1956); *Tres cuentos sin amor* (1956); *Tres dramas* (1957); *El hermano Quiroga* (1957); *Las 40* (1957); *La tos y otros entretenimientos* (1957); *Heraldos de la verdad* (1958); *Coplas de ciego* (1959); *Mensaje a los escritores* (1959); *Análisis funcional de la cultura* (1960); *Diferencias y semejanzas entre los países de la América Latina* (1962); *El verdadero cuento del tío Sam* (1963); *Realidad y fantasía en Balzac* (1964); *Antología* (1964); *Mi experiencia cubana* (1965); *La poesía afrocubana de Nicolás Guillén* (1966); *Martí, revolucionario* (1967); *Para una revisión de las letras argentinas* (1967); *En torno a Kafka, y otros ensayos* (1967); *Meditaciones sarmientinas* (1968); *Leopoldo Lugones: Retrato sin retocar* (1968); *Leer y escribir* (1969)

BIBLIOGRAPHY: Murena, H. A., *El pecado original de América* (1954): 43–65: 105–29; Ghiano, J. C., "M. E. narrador," *Ficción*, No. 4 (1956): 139–48; Sebreli, J. J., *M. E.: Una rebelión inutil* (1960); Stabb, M. S., "E. M. E.: The Formative Writings," *Hispania*, 49, 1 (1966): 54–60; Adam, C., *Bibliografía y documentos de E. M. E.* (1968); Earle, P., *Prophet in the Wilderness: The Works of E. M. E.* (1971); Maharg, J., *A Call to Authenticity: The Essays of E. M. E.* (1977)

—MARTIN S. STABB

MARTÍNEZ SIERRA, Gregorio and María

Spanish dramatists, novelists, essayists, poets. Gregorio b. 6 May 1881, Madrid; d. 1 Oct. 1947, Madrid. María b. 28 Dec. 1874, San Millán de la Cogolla; d. 28 June, 1974, Buenos Aires, Argentina

María M. S., in all probability the principal writer in this unusual literary partnership, wanted all works, whether written by her alone or in collaboration with her husband, to be published under Gregorio's name. Gregorio, an important theatrical director and producer as well as a writer, founded and managed Spain's most avant-garde and prestigious theatrical company of the period, the Compañía Lírico-Dramática Gregorio Martínez Sierra. With leading lady Catalina Bárcena, the actress for whom Gregorio eventually left María, the company toured Europe and the Americas for five years during the 1920s with an international repertory that included works by Shakespeare, Dumas, and Shaw, as well as M. S. In the 1930s Gregorio spent several years in Hollywood supervising film versions of his plays and writing scripts for movie companies. When the Spanish Civil War (1936–39) began, Gregorio and Catalina moved to Buenos Aires, Argentina, where they lived until returning to Madrid only weeks before Gregorio's death in 1947. In the pre-civil war period, María remained in Spain to write. She also took an active role in Spanish politics and in the nascent feminist movement. During the Republic (1931–36) she was elected Socialist deputy to the Cortes (parliament). After the civil war she lived in Switzerland and France before settling in 1952 in Buenos Aires, her home until her death at exactly ninety nine and a half years of age.

Although M. S. also wrote novels, short stories, essays, and poetry, it is as a dramatist that he is best remembered. M. S.'s most successful play, *Canción de cuna* (1911; *The Cradle Song*, 1917), remains a standard inclusion in the modern international repertory. This delicate play features cloistered nuns who adopt a foundling, and illustrate poignantly the author's reverence for motherhood. Yet despite the admiration for nuns depicted in this and in several other plays, such as *El reino de Diós* (1916; *The Kingdom of God*, 1923) and *Lirio entre espinas* (1911; *A Lily Among Thorns*, 1930), M. S. did not favor the cloistered life. In all of his plays women are happiest when actively expressing their social impulses. In works that focus principally on women M. S. favored a balance of physical, emotional, and spiritual participation in life and effectively blended idealism with realism. Unaware, perhaps, of María's major contribution to the M. S. signature, some critics have chided Gregorio for a lack of masculine vigor and worldly sophistication; others strongly defend the optimism and healthy enthusiasm for life so strongly associated with his works.

Despite an insistence that women are essentially mothers and that maternity is the loftiest expression of femininity, M. S. was a staunch apologist for women's rights. His feminism, individual and personal, relates almost exclusively to the social situation of the Spanish woman of the early 20th c. The feminist heroines of the plays (never members of an organization for women's rights) are diplomatically aggressive as they charmingly push for equality of responsibilities as well as of rights. In *Cada uno y su vida* (1924; to each his own) and *Seamos felices* (1929; let's be happy), for example, they contend that women have as much duty as men to support the family materially. It is interesting to note, moreover, that rather than claim as theirs the moral standard associated with the men of the period, these feminists insist that both sexes adhere to the more stringent code of behavior expected of women. M. S. repeatedly advocated careers for women, particularly in education, medicine, and the social services. The ideal career, M. S. suggests, is the professional collaboration of husband and wife, as illustrated in *Amanecer* (1915; dawn) and *Sueño de una noche de agosto* (1918; *The Romantic Young Lady*, 1923). This ideal of professional collaboration was one that Gregorio and María lived for many years and partially accounts for the frequency with which it appears in their works.

FURTHER WORKS: *Tú eres la paz* (1906; *Ana María*, 1921); *Primavera en otoño* (1911); *Mamá* (1913); *El amor brujo* (1915; music by Manuel de Falla); *El sombrero de tres picos* (1916; music by Manuel de Falla); *Obras completas* (14 vols., 1920–1930); *Mujer* (1925); *Triángulo* (1930; *Take Two from One: A Farce in Three Acts*, 1931). FURTHER WORKS IN ENGLISH: *The Plays of G. M. S.* (2 vols., 1923)

BIBLIOGRAPHY: Gardner, M., Introduction to *Sueño de una noche de agosto* (1921): vii–xxv; Douglas, F., "G. M. S.," *Hispania*, 5, 5 (1922): 257–68, and 6, 1 (1923): 1–13; Martínez Sierra, M., *Gregorio y yo* (1953); O'Connor, P. W., *Women in the Theater of G. M. S.* (1967); O'Connor, P. W., *G. and M. M. S.* (1977)

—PATRICIA W. O'CONNOR

MARTINICAN LITERATURE
See French-Caribbean Literature

MARTÍN-SANTOS, Luis

Spanish novelist and short-story writer, b. 11 Nov. 1924, Larache, Morocco; d. 21 Jan. 1964, San Sebastián

M.-S. was educated at the Marian Brothers School in San Sebastián. He studied medicine at the University of Salamanca and was a medical researcher as well as a surgeon. His interest turned to psychiatry, which he studied both in Spain and Germany, and he became the director of the Psychiatric Asylum of San Sebastián. At the time of his death, as a result of an automobile accident, he was considered a significant figure in contemporary psychiatry.

M.-S. was also an avid fiction reader, particularly of JOYCE, PROUST, MANN, and SARTRE. While a student, he was active in a

literary group whose members came into their own as writers in the 1960s.

M.-S.'s *Tiempo de silencio* (1962; *Time of Silence*, 1964), a major novel whose structure has been compared to that of Joyce's *Ulysses*, appeared at a time when Spanish fiction was still mired in repetitive social-realist themes. Set in Madrid in 1949, the novel has a protagonist who becomes involved in a series of misadventures as he attempts to carry out his medical research. The desperate conditions of social and professional life in the post-civil-war era are revealed through multiple narrative points of view. The protagonist's "travels" bring him to the dead end of both personal and national silence. The work attained instant critical praise, with prime attention given to its intellectual and poetic depths blended with an ironic and satiric perspective.

Apólogos, y otras prosas inéditas (1970; apologues, and other unpublished prose works), a collection of some of M.-S.'s short fiction and sketches of other planned works, was published posthumously. It includes a tale about bullfighting (a recurrent image in M.-S.'s works), in which the narrator attempts to decipher the crucial importance to Spanish life of this diversion. Another story offers an insight into Basque mentality. Fragments of a novel that was to be called *Tiempo de destrucción* (1975; time of destruction) were also published.

M.-S.'s brief career was of considerable consequence. His one novel represented a significant breakthrough in modern Spanish fiction. Following the stylistic paths opened by the early works of Camilo José CELA and Rafael SÁNCHEZ FERLOSIO, he surpassed them to achieve a fiction of intellectual rage, which has since been widely imitated.

FURTHER WORKS: *Dilthey, Jaspers y la comprensión del enfermo mental* (1955); *Libertad, temporalidad y transferencia en el psicoanálisis existencial* (1964)

BIBLIOGRAPHY: Díaz, J. W., "L. M.-S. and the Contemporary Spanish Novel," *Hispania*, 51 (1968): 232–38; Seale, M. L., "Hangman and Victim: An Analysis of M.-S.'s *Tiempo de silencio*," *Hispano*, 44 (1972): 45–52; Rey, A., *Construcción y sentido de "Tiempo de silencio"* (1977); Caviglia, J., "A Simple Question of Symmetry: Psyche as Structure in *Tiempo de silencio*," *Hispania*, 60 (1977): 452–60; Anderson, R. K., "Self-Estrangement in *Tiempo de silencio*," *REH*, 13 (1979): 299–317

—IRWIN STERN

MARTINSON, Harry

Swedish poet, novelist, and essayist, b. 6 May 1904, Jämshög, d. 11 Feb. 1978, Gnesta

M. lost his father early, and in 1910 his mother emigrated to America, leaving the boy and his sisters to become wards of the home parish. His childhood was marked by hard work, unfeeling guardians, and several attempts to run away. At the age of sixteen M. went to sea and worked for seven years as a stoker, with periods of vagabondage in South America and India. After contracting tuberculosis, he settled in Sweden, married Helga Swartz (who began a writing career in 1933 as Moa Martinson [1890–1964]), and established himself as a writer with the "vitalist-primitivist" literary group Fem Unga. In 1934 he attended the writers' conference in the Soviet Union from which he returned politically disillusioned. During the 1939–40 Winter War between Finland and the U.S.S.R. he volunteered on the Finnish side. M. never completely regained his health, and after his divorce and remarriage he spent most of his life in Gnesta. He was the recipient of a number of major literary prizes. In 1949 he became the first self-educated writer of working-class background to be elected to the Swedish Academy; in 1954 he received an honorary doctorate at the University of Göteborg; and in 1974 he shared the Nobel Prize in literature with Eyvind JOHNSON.

M.'s poetry is characterized by a masterful use of language, bold innovations, and a brilliant employment of metaphors and similes in playful juxtapositions that are always based on an astonishing precision of observation. As a nature poet, he has few if any equals. In his early collection *Nomad* (1930; nomad) he formulates his particular philosophy of acceptance of the gentle forces in life and nature. In *Passad* (1945; trade winds) he hails the trade winds as a symbol of openness, undogmatic mobility, and the fresh renewing forces of humanity, as opposed to the mechanized "tyranny of the engineers." His "nomadic" philosophy is here deepened to include the conquest of inner distances in meditative quietism of a Taoist brand.

M.'s strong interest in the natural sciences enabled him to join in a single vision the small detail and the universal whole. His criticism of man's heedless use of modern technology, which made him an early spokesman for ecological concerns, is given powerful expression in the chilling verse epic *Aniara* (1956; *Aniara: A Review of Man in Time and Space*, 1963). This cycle of 103 cantos is a science-fiction epos of technological triumph and catastrophe, a tragic and horrifying vision of a future: earth has become uninhabitable through man's hubris about conquering nature, and the off-course spaceship becomes a symbol of modern man's alienation. Of central importance in *Aniara* is the Mima, a highly advanced computer/robot with a soul that is a source of distraction and consolation for the spaceship passengers.

M.'s prose works display the same virtuosity as his poetry in the use of the Swedish language. *Resor utan mål* (1932; travels without destination) and *Kap Farväl* (1933; *Cape Farewell*, 1934) present kaleidoscopic impressions of his years at sea and sojourns on different continents. In the novel *Nässlorna blomma* (1935; *Flowering Nettle*, 1936) and its sequel, *Vägen ut* (1936; the way out), M. gives a moving and unsentimental account of his difficult childhood and adolescence, making a lasting contribution to the autobiographical "proletarian" literature of the period. Two collections of lyrical philosophical essays, *Midsommardalen* (1938; the midsummer valley) and *Det enkla och det svåra* (1930; the simple and the difficult) excel in nature descriptions, and in *Verklighet till döds* (1940; reality to death) M. settles his personal account with Soviet ideology. Many of M.'s concerns—his advocacy of tolerance, pacifism, and humaneness, his admiration of Oriental philosophy, and his love of the Swedish countryside—find a mature synthesis in the novel *Vägen till Klockrike* (1948; *The Road*, 1955). This book about tramps and vagrants is a mixture of philosophical dialogue, satire, rhapsodic lyricism, social criticism, autobiography, and allegory; it marks a high point in M.'s writing.

M. was recognized from the very beginning as a truly original literary genius. Over the years he consolidated his position as one of Sweden's best-loved and most widely read authors. His linguistic innovations, often presenting insurmountable difficulties to his

translators, may be an obstacle to a full appreciation of M. abroad, but the message of his works is of universal concern.

FURTHER WORKS: *Spökskepp* (1929); *Svärmare och harkrank* (1937); *Den förlorade jaguaren* (1941); *Cikada* (1953); *Gräsen i Thule* (1958); *Vagnen* (1960); *Utsikt från en grästuva* (1963); *Tre knivar från Wei* (1964); *Dikter om ljus och mörker* (1971); *Tuvor* (1973); *Längs ekots stigar* (1978); *Doriderna* (1980). FURTHER WORKS IN ENGLISH: *Friends, You Drank Some Darkness: Three Swedish Poets* (1975)

BIBLIOGRAPHY: Johannesson, E. O., "*Aniara:* Poetry and the Poet in the Modern World," *SS*, 32 (1961): 185–202; Steene, B., "The Role of the Mima: A Note on M.'s *Aniara*," in Bayerschmidt, C. F.and Friis, E. J., eds., *Scandinavian Studies: Essays Presented to Henry Goddard Leach* (1965): 311–19; Bergmann, S. A., "H. M. and Science," *Proceedings of the Fifth International Study Conference on Scandinavian Literature* (1966): 99–120; Sjöberg, L., "H. M.: Writer in Quest of Harmony," *ASR*, 60 (1972): 360–71; "H. M.: From Vagabond to Space Explorer," *BA*, 48 (1974): 476–85; Sjöberg, L., "The 1974 Nobel Prize in Literature: Eyvind Johnson and H. M.," *BA*, 49 (1975): 407–21; Brennecke, D., "Beardsley und der Mimarob," *Skandinavistik*, 6 (1976): 37–50

—LARS G. WARME

MAS'ADĪ, Mahmūd

Tunisian dramatist, novelist, essayist, and politician, b. 28 Jan. 1911, Tazerka

Born in the village of Tazerka, where he attended the Koranic school, the young M. then left for Tunis to attend high school, first at a national institution, Al-Sadiqiya, and later at a French *lycée*. In Paris, at the Sorbonne, M. studied Arabic language and literature. When he returned to Tunisia in 1947, upon successful completion of his studies, he became a regular and noted contributor to *Al-Mabāhith*, a literary journal that actively espoused the nationalist agenda against the colonial order. Shortly after Tunisia's independence, M. became a minister of education, a position he held for ten years (1958–1968). He is generally credited with democratizing and secularizing the educational system in Tunisia.

M. was among the first Tunisian writers to have enjoyed the benefits of a bilingual education. Along with his profound knowledge and refined appreciation of classical Arabic literature, his thorough assimilation of French language, literature, and philosophy, especially EXISTENTIALISM, have further sharpened his speculative and philosophical bent. Since his early writings, in particular in the fields of language and aesthetics, M. has consistently gone against the grain. While his contemporaries sought to establish a national literary tradition by drawing on local and oral literatures, and to simplify Arabic grammar and syntax in the name of MODERNISM and identity, M.'s idea of *asāla*, by contrast, began by advocating a return to the linguistic rigor, purity, and elegance of classical Arabic, and a revamping and updating of archaic knowledge as well as rhetorical and aesthetic forms, to express a modern consciousness.

M.'s popular fame as Tunisia's premier Arabic writer rests mainly on the critical success of his play *Al-Sudd* (wr. 1942, pub.

1955; the dam). His narrative *Haddatha Abū Hurayra. . . qāla* (wr. 1939, pub. 1973; thus spake Abu Hurayra. . . he said) and his essay collection *Mawlid al-nisyān, wa-ta'ammulāt ukhrā* (wr. 1941, pub. 1974; the birth of oblivion, and other essays)—all Nietzschean titles—have received less critical attention mainly because of the hermetic and esoteric nature of their subject matter and their archaic and arcane language. Although it expounds a tragic vision of the world, his oeuvre stands as a testimony to human greatness in the face of adversity and other vicissitudes.

Al-Sudd is an existential drama revolving around the eternal poles of essence and existence. Ghaylān, who symbolizes rationality and intellect, is determined to build a dam in defiance of Sahabbā', the goddess of aridity, and against the council of his own wife Maymūnah (a symbol of love and intuition). Upon completion of this project, and as predicted, disaster befalls earth, and the couple is forever separated. Ghaylān ascends heavenward with Mayārā, the Egeria who helped him erect the dam, while Maymūnah is seen descending into earth. They leave behind an intelligent mule tied to a rock, as a symbol of permanence and rebirth. However, for M. a plot is mainly a pretext to explore the meaning of life and the secret of being.

This philosophical speculation is further pursued in *Mawlid al-nisyān, wa-ta'ammulāt ukhrā*. In these essays, very much in the vein of Jean-Paul SARTRE's brand of existentialism, M.'s man is posited as a free agent in a godless world responsible for his own actions and master of his own destiny. Whether they are called Ghaylān, Sindbad, or Abū Hurayra, all of M.'s characters are questers, idealists, and wanderers. They are relentlessly driven by a desire to seek the absolute. This is particularly true of Abū Hurayra, the protagonist of the narrative *Haddatha Abū Hurayra. . .qāla*, who bears the same name as Prophet Muhammad's close companion.

In many respects, Abū Hurayra is M.'s spokesman and alter ego, and certainly the best proponent of his existential metaphysics. In this stylistically uncompromising text, M. couches contemporary philosophical preoccupations in a blend of such archaic narrative forms as *hadīth*—or extemporaneous accounts and propositions, in the fashion of Prophet Muhammad's—and *khabar* or literary history which, unlike the sacred discourse of *hadīth* refers to lay and profane knowledge. More than any other text, *Haddatha Abū Hurayra. . . qāla* exemplifies M.'s elaborate style and highly metaphorical language that often remains abstruse to the point of incomprehensibility.

Reading M. is a demanding and arduous undertaking: His oeuvre demands of his readers exorbitant concentration and comprehension; but if successfully carried through, this effort yields immense insight and delight. M.'s oeuvre seems to revolve around a paradox—that a contemporary sensitivity can be couched in an archaic form. Within the universal and ahistorical framework of his oeuvre one does indeed find symbols that are open to social and political interpretations, some of which are indeed of acute relevance to current events in Tunisia and in the Arab world as a whole.

BIBLIOGRAPHY: Khatibi, A., *Le roman maghrébin* (1968): 37–41; Ghazi, F., *Le roman et la nouvelle en Tunisie* (1970); Zmerli, S., *Figures tunisiennes: Les contemporains et les autres* (1972); Fontaine, J., *Vingt ans de littérature tunisienne 1956–1975* (1977); Ostle, R. C., "M. al-M. and Tunisia's 'Lost Generation,'" *JArabL*, 8 (1977): 153–66; Baccar, T., and Garmadi, S., eds., *Écrivains de Tunisie* (1980): 11–54; Naser, A. Belhaj, *Quelques aspects du roman tunisien* (1981); Fawsi, A., *Arabic Literature in North Africa: Critical Essays and Annotated Bibliography* (1982); Allen, R., ed., *Modern Arabic Literature* (1987): 211–14

—HÉDI ABDEL-JAOUAD

MASAOKA Shiki

(pseud. of Masaoka Tsunenori) Japanese poet, diarist, critic, essayist, and journalist, b. 14 Oct. 1867, Matsuyama; d. 19 Sept. 1902, Tokyo.

After studying philosophy and Japanese literature for two years at the University of Tokyo, M. left to become the haiku (traditional seventeen-syllable verse form) editor of the newspaper *Nippon*, from whose pages he launched his reform of the haiku in 1892. In 1895 he went to China as a war correspondent for *Nippon* but became so ill (with tuberculosis) on the return trip that he nearly died. For the rest of his life M. was an invalid.

Nevertheless, he managed to lead a very active literary life from his sickbed. In 1897, he and his disciples founded the literary journal *Hototogisu*. The next year he launched a reform of the tanka (traditional thirty-one-syllable verse form) similar in aim to his earlier reform of the haiku, and also turned his attention to autobiographical essays.

When M. began his career, the haiku and the tanka had come to be regarded as frivolous pastimes incapable of expressing the complexities of modern life. The necessary premise of M.'s haiku reform, as well as his most important contribution as a critic, was his insistence on the potential of the haiku and the tanka as serious literature. The second pillar of M.'s haiku reform was his commitment to realism as the aim of literature. His reevaluation of the 18th-c. poet Yosa Buson (1716–1783) in the light of the ideal of realism was responsible for Buson's reputation today as one of the greatest haiku poets. His most important writings on haiku are *Dassai sho-oku haiwa* (1892; talks on haiku from the otter's den), *Haikai taiyō* (1895; the essence of haikai), and *Haijin Buson* (1897; the haiku poet Buson).

At first M.'s poems (both his haiku and tanka) were derivative. Later they became efforts to depict real scenes from nature or daily life, and finally, in the last few years of his life, he created a literary persona, a semifictional "I," who became the central character of his most affecting works while he still retained the realism of his earlier works. The recurring theme of his later work, especially of the two diaries that he published in his last two years, *Bokujū itteki* (1901; partial tr., "A Drop of Ink," 1975) and *Byōshō rokushaku* (1902; a six-foot sickbed), is the juxtaposition of M.'s own suffering mortality with the ongoing life of nature and the human world. The prose style he used in these works had been developed through his experiments with the short essay beginning in 1898 and later influenced a significant number of Japanese novelists, including NATSUME Sōseki and SHIGA Naoya. Thus, as well as having brought haiku into the modern age and having established the dominant tone of the modern tanka, M. was instrumental in the evolution of modern Japanese prose style.

There is no room to doubt M.'s crucial importance as a critic and charismatic literary figure who inspired an entire generation of haiku poets. On the other hand, there has been a wrong-headed tendency for critics and scholars (now beginning to change) to question his merits as a poet and virtually ignore the diaries and essays. M.'s excellence as a writer lies in neither his poetry nor his prose but in writing that is on the border between the two. The two diaries mentioned above best exemplify this style, in that they combine qualities of the classical Japanese poetic diary with the self-revelation of modern autobiography.

FURTHER WORKS: *Shiki zenshū* (25 vols., 1975–1978). FURTHER WORKS IN ENGLISH: *Peonies Kana: Haiku by the Upsasak Shiki* (1972)

BIBLIOGRAPHY: Brower, R. H., "M. S. and Tanka Reform," in Shively, D. H., ed., *Tradition and Modernization in Japanese Culture* (1971): 379–418; Keene, D., "S. and Takuboku," *Landscapes and Portraits: Appreciations of Japanese Culture* (1971): 157–70; Beichman-Yamamoto, J., "M. S.'s *A Drop of Ink*," *MN*, 30 (1975): 291–302; Ueda, M., "M. S.," *Modern Japanese Haiku: An Anthology*: 3–8: 25; Beichman, J., *M. S.* (1982)

—JANINE BEICHMAN

MASEFIELD, John

English poet, novelist, and dramatist, b. 1 June 1878, Ledbury; d. 12 May 1967, Abingdon

Born in Herefordshire, in the rural English west, M. was orphaned at thirteen and became a cadet on the training ship

John Masefield

Conway; after rounding Cape Horn on a sailing vessel, he left his ship and the sea at New York City in 1895. Attracted to writing by his reading of Chaucer, Keats, Shelley, and Shakespeare, M. returned to England in 1897, worked for the Manchester *Guardian*, and produced a succession of little-noticed books, beginning with *Salt-Water Ballads* (1902). In 1911 *The Everlasting Mercy*, an astonishing rhymed narrative about a tavern brawler converted to the Christian life, brought M. sudden fame; *Dauber* (1913) and two other long narrative poems appeared before World War I. From his war experience came the much-praised prose history *Gallipoli* (1916) and the poem "August 1914" (1914), followed by reflective sonnets and five other long narratives, including *Reynard the Fox* (1919) and *King Cole* (1921). M. lived out his long life quietly with his family near Oxford. In 1930 he was named Poet Laureate and became an eloquent advocate for the speaking of verse.

Critical and popular opinion tend to agree that M.'s twenty-two novels and fifteen plays are less likely to survive than his poetry. Most successful of his novels are probably the children's story *The Midnight Folk* (1927) and the sea tale *The Bird of Dawning* (1933), while the three-act folk melodrama *The Tragedy of Nan* (1909), influenced by J. M. SYNGE, has been his best-liked play.

Reynard the Fox reveals M.'s skill in storytelling and in painting the countryside and a gallery of country portraits. Part I of the poem introduces a cross section of society in the participants and onlookers at a traditional fox hunt. Part II takes the reader on the exciting hunt itself, at the end of which the fox has become the hero and escapes, while the killing of another fox, a stranger to the reader, sends the hunters home happy. This vivid pageant, even more than the tragic Cape Horn epic *Dauber* or the quietly magical *King Cole*, is often believed to have won M. the Laureateship.

In most of his work M. celebrates his country and countrymen—the English heritage and landscape; English people, arts, and games; the English soldier, ship, and sailor. His chief dedication is to the English spirit rather than to the sea and the common man of his early writing. For him Saint George, not John Bull, is the symbol of the nation he strives to interpret, and the spirit of Saint George shines brightest in the brief lyrics and these longer narratives that are most likely to live: *The Everlasting Mercy, Dauber,* "August 1914," *Gallipoli,* and *Reynard the Fox.* M.'s work is uneven, partly because of its sheer volume, but it is hard to see, as the critic Newman Ivey White has pointed out, how one can avoid assigning him a lasting place in early-20th-c. English literature without rejecting the whole tradition of English poetry

FURTHER WORKS: *Ballads* (1903); *A Mainsail Haul* (1905); *Sea Life in Nelson's Time* (1905); *On the Spanish Main* (1905); *A Tarpaulin Muster* (1907); *Captain Margaret* (1908); *Multitude and Solitude* (1909); *The Tragedy of Pompey the Great* (1910); *Ballads and Poems* (1910); *Martin Hyde* (1910); *A Book of Discoveries* (1910); *Lost Endeavour* (1910); *The Street of Today* (1911); *William Shakespeare* (1911); *Jim Davis* (1911); *The Story of a Round-House* (1912); *The Widow in the Bye Street* (1912); *The Daffodil Fields* (1913); *Philip the King* (1914); *The Faithful* (1915); *John M. Synge* (1915); *The Locked Chest; The Sweeps of Ninety-Eight* (1916); *Good Friday* (1916); *Sonnets and Poems* (1916); *The Old Front Line* (1917); *Lollingdon Downs* (1917); *Rosas* (1918); *Collected Poems and Plays* (1919); *Right Royal* (1920); *Enslaved* (1920); *Esther and Berenice* (1922); *Melloney Holtspur* (1922); *The Dream* (1922); *Selected Poems* (1922); *A*

King's Daughter (1923); *The Taking of Helen* (1923); *Collected Poems* (1923; rev. eds., 1932, 1946); *Recent Prose* (1924; rev. ed., 1932); *Shakespeare and Spiritual Life* (1924); *Sard Harker* (1924); *With the Living Voice* (1925); *The Trial of Jesus* (1925); *Collected Works* (4 vols., 1925); *ODTAA* (1926); *Tristan and Isolt* (1927); *The Coming of Christ* (1928); *Midsummer Night* (1928); *Poems* (1929); *Easter* (1929); *The Hawbucks* (1929); *The Wanderer of Liverpool* (1930); *Chaucer* (1931); *Minnie Maylow's Story* (1931); *Poetry* (1931); *A Tale of Troy* (1932); *The Conway* (1933); *End and Beginning* (1933); *The Taking of the Gry* (1934); *The Box of Delights* (1935); *Victorious Troy* (1935); *Poems: Complete Edition* (1935; rev. ed., 1953); *Eggs and Baker* (1936); *A Letter from Pontus* (1936); *The Square Peg* (1937); *The Country Scene* (1937); *Dead Ned* (1938); *Tribute to Ballet* (1938); *Live and Kicking Ned* (1939); *Some Verses to Some Germans* (1939); *Some Memories of W. B. Yeats* (1940); *Basilissa* (1940); *In the Mill* (1941); *The Nine Days Wonder* (1941); *Gautama the Enlightened* (1941); *Conquer* (1941); *A Generation Risen* (1942); *Land Workers* (1942); *Wonderings* (1943); *New Chum* (1944); *A Macbeth Production* (1945); *Thanks before Going* (1946); *A Book of Both Sorts* (1947); *Badon Parchments* (1947); *A Play of St. George* (1948); *On the Hill* (1949); *In Praise of Nurses* (1950); *Selected Poems* (1950); *St. Katherine of Ledbury, and Other Ledbury Papers* (1951); *So Long to Learn* (1952); *The Bluebells* (1961); *Old Raiger* (1964); *Grace before Ploughing* (1966); *In Glad Thanksgiving* (1967); *Letters of J. M. to Florence Lamont* (1979)

BIBLIOGRAPHY: Simmons, C., *Bibliography of J. M.* (1930); Spark, M., *J. M.* (1953); Drew, F., *Contributions to Bibliography of J. M.* (1959); Handley-Taylor, G., *J. M., O.M.: A Bibliography* (1960); Lamont, C., *Remembering J. M.* (1971); Drew, F., *J. M.'s England* (1973); Sternlicht, S., *J. M.* (1977); Babington Smith, C., *J. M.: A Life* (1978)

—FRASER DREW

MASING, Uku

Estonian poet and essayist, b. 11 Aug. 1909, Raikküla; d. 25 April 1985, Tartu

After studying theology and Semitic languages, M. taught in the department of theology at the University of Tartu from 1933 to 1940. During this early period he was associated with the famous Arbujad (Soothsayers) group of poets. Since the Soviet takeover of Estonia in 1940 M. has remained silent as a poet, but three books by him have been published in the West.

M.'s first book of poetry, *Neemed vihmade lahte* (1935; promontories into the gulf of rains), remains his most esteemed and bestknown work. In his three subsequent books, M. has continued to explore visionary mystical themes in alternately lyrical and prophetic veins. Exactingly and intimately, M., a neosymbolist, celebrates details of nature, particularly flowers, trees, birds, clouds, winds, and stars. Yet he is most original in his steady reaching upward through interstellar space for the hand of God. One of the most cosmopolitan and complex of Estonian poets, M. uses musical free verse as well as traditional forms for his often

symbolic and occasionally surreal poetic style. He is noted for coining words and for employing manneristic and archaic expressions.

Neemed vihmade lahte consists of fifty-one poems, whose titles are given only in the table of contents, allowing the text to be read as one extended work. M. centers the book in the mystical search for a full, steady, and unbroken consciousness of God's presence. Along the way M. experiences both joyous intimacy and complete faith in God, as well as anger at and despair over God's distantness from man. He portrays God at one point as a listless and decadent ruler shut behind gates of tourmaline in a drug-induced dream. Yet he realizes and admits, "We may long for angel's wings, but the stubborn urge of Thy slaves, O God, is powerless to hold Thy vision."

M.'s hallucinatory tableaux, spiritual themes, and allusive style often remind critics of William Blake, Gerard Manley Hopkins, Rabindranath TAGORE, whom he translated, and T. S. ELIOT. Like them, M. envisions life from the vantage point of eternity, as in *Piiridele pyydes* (1974; straining toward limits), where he feels "I am damned like an elevator which gets stuck between two floors for all eternity." Yet he goes on to advise devotion to the severest asceticism of Jesus, Buddha, and Lao Tzu. With this universal mysticism and poetic vision M. ranks among the finest modern religious poets.

FURTHER WORKS: *Džunglilaulud* (1965); *Udu Toonela jõelt* (1974)

BIBLIOGRAPHY: Oras, A., *Acht estnische Dichter* (1964): 9–19; Ivask, I., "The Main Tradition of Estonian Poetry," in Kõressaar, V. and Rannit, A., eds., *Estonian Poetry and Language* (1965): 292–96; Mägi, A., *Estonian Literature: An Outline* (1968): 48–54; Leitch, V. B., "Religious Vision in Modern Poetry: U. M. Compared with Hopkins and Eliot," *JBalS*, 5 (1974): 281–94; Ivask, I., "U. M.: A Poet between East and West," *JBalS*, 8 (1977): 16–21

—VINCENT B. LEITCH

MASON, Bobbie Ann

American short-story writer and novelist, b. 1 May 1940, Mayfield, Kentucky

M. grew up on a small dairy farm in western Kentucky. Upon graduating from the University of Kentucky with a B.A. in English, she worked briefly for Ideal Publishing Company in New York City as a writer for *Movie Stars, Movie Life*, and *T.V. Star Parade* magazines. After this immersion in popular culture, M. earned an M.A. in English at the State University of New York at Binghamton and a Ph.D. at the University of Connecticut. Her doctoral dissertation was a study of the novel *Ada* by Vladimir NABOKOV, whose influence on her own fiction she readily acknowledges. In 1971 M. began teaching at Mansfield State College in Pennsylvania, but she resigned her position there in 1978 to devote full time to writing. While at Mansfield State, M. published two scholarly books—one on Nabokov and the other on female detectives (like Nancy Drew) in adolescent fiction. M.'s first published stories appeared in the *New Yorker* in 1980.

M. collected sixteen stories in her first volume of fiction, *Shiloh and Other Stories* (1982). Most of these stories are set in small

Kentucky towns (termed ruburbs by one reviewer) where fast-food restaurants and television talk shows war against country ways and traditional wisdom. Culture shock threatens personal identity and divorce splinters families. In the title story, for example, an injured truck driver takes up needlepoint while his wife pumps iron. In an attempt to shore up their crumbling marriage, they take an ironic second honeymoon to the Shiloh battlefield. In "Graveyard Day" a divorced mother laments the fact that families now change memberships as casually as clubs. One story in the collection, "Detroit Skyline, 1949," moves away from Kentucky and from contemporary time to dramatize a young girl's puzzling journey of initiation.

M.'s first novel, *In Country* (1985), merges coming of age and coming home from war. The adolescent protagonist, Sam Hughes, grows up as she finds out about the combat in Vietnam that killed her father even before she was born. Meanwhile, Sam's uncle and other Vietnam veterans make their peace with a society that is still embarrassed by the war. By culminating in a pilgrimage to the newly constructed Vietnam Memorial in Washington, D.C., the novel deftly blends personal anguish and national tragedy.

As its title suggests, the novel *Spence + Lila* (1988) is a straightforward love story. Lila, an energetic farm woman, has breast cancer, but she still nurtures her husband and children. In a hospital surrounded by sterile technology and grim omens of death, her abiding pastoral values provide sustenance and hope.

Many of the stories in *Love Life* (1989) continue M.'s focus on cultural dislocations and strained relationships. "Hunktown" portrays a laid-off factory worker who aspires to be a country music star, and "Marita" displays a battle over abortion between a mother and her pregnant daughter. "Big Bertha Stories," written while M. was working on *In Country*, dramatizes personal and social disruptions resulting from the Vietnam War that still linger in America many years later. The protagonist is a troubled war veteran who tries to order his chaotic world by telling stories to his young son. These narratives, like the war experience, begin exuberantly but break off in pain and confusion.

M.'s fictional domain has typically been a troubled zone between the Old South and the New. Her prize-winning stories display a highly charged mix of popular and high culture, rural simplicity and urban sophistication. M.'s work has been compared to the minimalist fiction of Raymond CARVER, but even as she ably documents the confusion in her postmodernist ruburbs, she still seeks a vision of order and unity with the natural world.

FURTHER WORKS: *Nabokov's Garden* (1974); *The Girl Sleuth* (1974); *Feather Crowns* (1993); *Midnight Magic* (1998)

BIBLIOGRAPHY: Ryan, M., "Stopping Places: B. A. M.'s Short Stories," in Prenshaw, P. W., ed., *Women Writers of the Contemporary South* (1984): 283-94; Wilhelm, A. E., "Making Over or Making Off: The Problem of Identity in B.A.M.'s Short Fiction," *SLJ*, 18 (Spring 1986): 76-82; White, L., "The Function of Popular Culture in B.A.M.'s *Shiloh and Other Stories* and *In Country*," *SoQ*, 26 (Summer 1988): 69-79; Barnes, L. A., "The Freak Endures: The Southern Grotesque from Flannery O'Connor to B. A. M.," in Logsden, L., ed., *Since Flannery O'Connor: Essays on the Contemporary Short Story* (1987): 133-41; Giannone, R., "B. A. M. and the Recovery of Mystery," *SSF*, 27 (1990): 553-66

—ALBERT WILHELM

MASTERS, Edgar Lee

American poet, novelist, biographer, dramatist, historian, and essayist, b. 23 Aug. 1868, Garnett, Kan.; d. 5 March 1950, Melrose Park, Pa.

M. spent most of his early life in small Illinois towns; his careers in law and literature combined the interests of his father, an attorney and sometime politician, and his mother, interested in music, literature, and religion. Largely self-taught, M. spent a year at Knox College. He began writing verse pseudonymously for several newspapers in Chicago, moving there in 1890, and he was admitted to the bar in 1891; eight of the following twenty-five years as a successful attorney were spent as a partner of Clarence Darrow. The first of M.'s more than fifty books, a compilation of verse published under a pen name, appeared in 1898; he published several other volumes of verse and seven unproduced plays by 1915, when the English critic John Cowper POWYS cited him as one of three significant new American poets. For several years he had also been contributing verse to William Marion Reedy's St. Louis *Mirror*; Reedy's introducing M. to J. W. Mackail's (1859–1949) translations in *Select Epigrams from the Greek Anthology* influenced him to write first-person epitaphs of ordinary small-town people, subsequently published as *Spoon River Anthology* (1915). As his fame grew, M. gave up law and moved to New York. A fellowship M. received in 1946, the first awarded by the Academy of American Poets, helped make up for his by then diminished reputation and income, but poor health forced him to spend his last years in convalescent homes.

Spoon River Anthology went through seventy editions by the time of M.'s death; it has served as source material for plays, an opera, and dramatic readings, and it has been translated into many languages. The book—244 dramatic monologues, mostly in free verse—was both a critical and popular success. The book faithfully depicts characters representa-tive of various small-town social levels and occupations, all sharing a sense of frustration at their dreary, unfulfilled, confined lives. Although it seemed to some, in the dying days of the "genteel tradition," unnecessarily defeatist and even obscene, M. stated elsewhere that his aim had been "to awaken the American vision [and] love of liberty." As with Whitman, M. succeeded not only in dramatizing this vision but also in shocking through the honesty of his portrayals. M. was less successful with *The New Spoon River* (1922); its 321 portraits were repetitious and too polemical and violent.

M.'s many other volumes of verse include *Towards the Gulf* (1918), worth noting because of a long tribute to Reedy. *Domesday Book* (1920) dramatized reactions to a young woman's death; *The Fate of the Jury* (1929), subtitled "An Epilogue to *Domesday Book*," continued the narrative, focusing on members of a coroner's jury. None of these other volumes (mostly dramatic narratives or collections of shorter lyrical work) received much praise; nor did his novels, although *Mitch Miller* (1920) was compared to *Tom Sawyer*.

But his nonfictional prose did attract attention, partly because of his sometimes iconoclastic handling of familiar subjects. Of his six biographies—including *Vachel Lindsay* (1935), *Whitman* (1937), and *Mark Twain* (1938)—*Lincoln the Man* (1931) was the most controversial because of his attempt to destroy the "Lincoln myth": he accused Lincoln of chicanery, laziness, and other vices, and as a

Democratic partisan he emphasized Stephen A. Douglas's posthumous stature. M.'s book on LINDSAY, by contrast, was praised for its scholarship and sympathy.

Aside from *The Sangamon* (1942), in the "Rivers of America" series, his most important prose work was his autobiography, *Across Spoon River* (1936). A candid and eccentric work—he indexes fifteen love affairs but never mentions Clarence Darrow at all—it is a revealing, tormented love-hate account of his small-town heritage, family, wives and lovers, careers, and changing fortunes. It is thus a valuable, unrestrained account of a particularly lively period in American history and culture.

The sheer amount and variety of M.'s writing—much verse has never been collected, he tried every poetic form and technique, and he treated a vast array of topics—necessarily resulted in unevenness, repetitiveness, and superficiality. At his worst he produced mere magazine verse. Yet his best work supersedes changes in literary fashion and even his own frequent lapses in taste, style, and technique. His prolific versatility and occasional successes give him a permanent place among 20th-c. writers.

FURTHER WORKS: *Maximilian: A Play* (1902); *The New Star Chamber, and Other Essays* (1904); *The Blood of the Prophets* (1905); *Althea: A Play* (1907); *The Trifler: A Play* (1908); *The Leaves of the Tree: A Play* (1909); *Songs and Sonnets* (1910); *Eileen: A Play* (1910); *The Locket: A Play* (1910); *The Bread of Idleness: A Play* (1911); *Songs and Sonnets, Second Series* (1912); *Songs and Satires* (1916); *The Great Valley* (1916); *Toward the Gulf* (1918); *Starved Rock* (1919); *The Open Sea* (1921); *Children of the Market Place* (1922); *Skeeters Kirby* (1923); *The Nuptial Flight* (1923); *Mirage* (1924); *Selected Poems* (1925); *Lee: A Dramatic Poem* (1926); *Kit O'Brien* (1927); *Levy Mayer and the New Industrial Era* (1927); *Jack Kelso: A Dramatic Poem* (1928); *Lichee Nuts* (1930); *Gettysburg, Manila, Acoma* (1930); *Godbey: A Dramatic Poem* (1931); *The Serpent in the Wilderness* (1933); *The Tale of Chicago* (1933); *Dramatic Duologues: Four Short Plays in Verse* (1934); *Richmond: A Dramatic Poem* (1934); *Invisible Landscapes* (1935); *Poems of People* (1936); *The Golden Fleece of California* (1936); *The Tide of Time* (1937); *The New World* (1937); *More People* (1939); *Illinois Poems* (1941); *Along the Illinois* (1942); *The Harmony of Deeper Music: Posthumous Poems* (1976)

BIBLIOGRAPHY: Flanagan, J., "The Spoon River Poet," *SWR*, 38 (1953): 226–37; Hartley, L., *Spoon River Revisited* (1963); Earnest, E., "Spoon River Revisited," *WHR*, 21 (1968): 59–65; Flanagan, J., *E. L. M.: The Spoon River Poet and His Critics* (1974); Burgess, C. E., "E. L. M.: The Lawyer as Writer," and Russell, H., "After Spoon River: M.'s Poetic Development 1916–1919," in Hallwas, J. E. and Reader, D. J., eds., *The Vision of This Land: Studies of Vachel Lindsay, E. L. M., and Carl Sandburg* (1976): 55–73: 74–81; Masters, H., *E. L. M.: A Biographical Sketchbook about a Famous American Author* (1978); Primeau, R., *Beyond Spoon River: The Legacy of E. L. M.* (1980); Burgess, C. E., "Maryland-Carolina Ancestry of E. L. M.," *GrLR*, 8-9 (1982-83): 51-80; Harveson, R. D., "The Kindred Spirits of William James and E. L. M.," *Midamerica* (1983): 85-98; Wrenn, J. H., *E. L. M.* (1983); Burgess, C. E., "E. L. M.'s Paternal Ancestry: A Pioneer Heritage and Influence," *WIRS* (1984): 32-60; Burgess, C. E., "Ancestral Lore in *Spoon River Anthology*: Fact and Fancy," *PLL*, 20 (1984): 185-204; Krauth, L., "'A Visioned End': E. L. M. and William Stafford," *Midamerica* (1984): 90-107; Noe, M., "The Johari Window: A Perspective on the *Spoon River Anthology*," *Midamerica* (1986): 49-60; Burgess, C. E., "Spoon River: Politics and Poetry," *PLL*, 23 (1987): 347-63; Chandran, K. N., "Revolt from the Grave: *Spoon River Anthology* by E. L. M.," *MQ*, 29 (1988): 438-47; Murphy, P. D., "The Dialogical Voices of E. L. M.'s *Spoon River Anthology*," *StHum*, 15 (1988): 13-32; Burgess, C. E. "Some Family Source Material for *Spoon River Anthology*," *WIRS*, 13 (1990): 80-89; Hardwick, E., "Wind from the Prairie," *NYRB*, 38 (Sept. 1991)

—PAUL SCHLUETER

MASTRONARDI, Lucio

Italian novelist, b. 28 June 1930, Vigevano; d. 29 April 1979, Vigevano

M. was the son of schoolteachers; his father was from the Abruzzi region, and his mother from Vigevano, near Milan. Professionally, he followed in his parents' footsteps, but in time he became disenchanted with teaching and looked to writing as the chief object of his lonely and troubled life. M. suffered from a serious neurotic condition that eventually led to his suicide.

The town of Vigevano, with its thriving shoe industry and enterprising inhabitants, forms the nucleus of M.'s work. It is a nucleus rich in sociological interest, which takes on added value as a microcosm of provincial life in the industrialized north. *Il calzolaio di Vigevano* (1962; the shoemaker of Vigevano), the first part of what might be called a trilogy about life in Vigevano, was originally published in 1959 in Elio VITTORINI'S avant-garde review *Il menabò*. The work explores the obsession with material success through the depiction of the experiences of a shoe-factory worker who rises to become a small entrepreneur. A novella with a heavy infusion of Milanese dialect, *Il calzolaio di Vigevano* reflects the type of linguistic experimentation through which Carlo Emilio GADDA and Pier Paolo PASOLINI sought to recapture the immediacy and pristine flavor of the spoken language.

In *Il maestro di Vigevano* (1962; the schoolteacher of Vigevano) M.'s own experiences as a teacher, enriched by a mordant satire often laced with humor, are used to expose the stifling environment, the bureaucracy, and the formalistic pedagogy of elementary education. The dreary atmosphere of a small town, with its monotonous life and puppetlike parade of familiar faces, contributes to the portrayal of the protagonist's sterile existence, which he tries to escape by daydreaming and with absurd erotic fixations. *Il meridionale di Vigevano* (1964; a southerner in Vigevano) offers another, and equally deft, exercise in formal experimentation. The main character is a southern bureaucrat whose quest for social acceptance meets with deep-seated prejudices against southern Italians. The discordant mixture of Milanese and Neapolitan dialects points to the postwar immigration of southern Italians to the north, bringing to light the problems of social adjustment in an unreceptive environment.

M.'s last work, *A casa tua ridono* (1971; your own family is laughing at you), with its fragmented narrative, is more attuned to the trends of STRUCTURALIST narrative. Superseding the story of a misfit in the industrial setting of a large city is the steady, albeit oblique, effort to delve into the consciousness of the main character and to highlight those incidents that define his distorted psyche.

M.'s critical recognition in Italy stems from his experimentation with language and his incisive, satirical treatment of life in a social environment dominated by material gains and technological advancement.

FURTHER WORKS: *L'assicuratore* (1975).

—AUGUSTUS PALLOTTA

MATEVOSSIAN, Hrant

Armenian novelist, short-story writer, and screenwriter, b. 13 March 1935, Ahnitsor

Often compared to Vahan Totovents (1894–1938), the American-educated Soviet Armenian writer who wrote about rural life in a previous generation, M. is the most widely praised contemporary Armenian prose writer. After receiving a degree from the Apovian Institute, he graduated from the Moscow School of Scenarists in 1967, and now works for the Hayfilm studio in Armenia.

Sociopolitical phenomena have occupied a large place in Armenian literature since the turn of the century, when the population (not yet massacred and dispersed) was under Turkish rule. The "noble peasant" was used by such writers as Siamanto (pseud. of Adom Yarjanian, 1878–1915) and Eroukhan (pseud. of Ervand Srmakeshkhanlian, 1870–1915) not only to personify the victim of oppression but to symbolize energy and hope. The peasants in M.'s fiction, although no longer in danger of losing life and property, are in peril of seduction by the evil metropolis. Erevan has replaced Constantinople as the lure. While Eroukhan's themes were tragic, like his time, M.'s concerns are agrarian and his style has lyrical and light touches.

M.'s career began with assignments from the literary periodicals *Sovetagan kraganootioon* and *Kragan tert* to write feature stories and essays on agricultural students reclaiming land. His fresh style and his treatment of the underlying social problems drew immediate praise, and he continued his pastoral themes in fiction. But whereas Totovents's stories of rural life were bathed in sweet nostalgia, M.'s work is both more contemporary and more mythic. In his short novel *Menk enk mer sareruh* (1965; we are our mountains) a seemingly commonplace quarrel among shepherds over stolen sheep becomes an allegory of truth versus hypocrisy in a tale told without any moralizing. In the story "Komesh" (1978; the buffalo) a female water buffalo in heat, roaming the countryside in search of a male, symbolizes the Armenian nation's will to survive and to do creative work. Use of pagan images is typical of M.'s work. His themes, his portrayals of rites of passage and crisis, and his characters fall within the naturalistic tradition but always have mythic overtones.

In his most famous work, the short-story collection *Narinch zampiguh* (1964; *The Orange Herd*, 1976), the wild red mountain horses are reminiscent of the red horses used by Eghishe CHARENTS to symbolize the spirit of the revolution, and of the Pegasus poems of Daniel VAROUJAN, in which the winged horse is symbolic of freedom. M.'s horses, however, are not political; their mystery is more Freudian and surreal.

In the Armenian short story plot is usually secondary to characterization. M. has followed this practice but has given greater psychological depth to his characters than earlier writers. M.'s villages, although microcosms of the universe, are firmly linked to real villages of the past in the same way that M. is linked to older Armenian literary traditions.

FURTHER WORKS: *Okostos* (1967); *Dsareruh* (1978); *Mer vazkuh* (1978).

—MARZBED MARGOSSIAN

MATUTE, Ana María

Spanish novelist and short-story writer, b. 26 July 1925, Barcelona

Born into a middle-class family, M. attended a religious school until the outbreak of the Spanish Civil War. The war left an indelible mark on her life: she suddenly discovered that "the world was hunger, the world was hate. It was also the desire for justice; and it was egotism, fear, horror, cruelty, and death." M. published her first story in 1942—during what she called the horrors of peace—working in an atmosphere of indifference, censorship, and fear. To protest "against all that represents oppression, hypocrisy, and injustice" was the objective that underlay her decision to devote herself to writing.

The civil war is a recurring theme in M.'s novels. Sometimes it serves only as the background to the action—as in *Pequeño teatro* (1954; little theater)—but often it is at the center of the work—as in *En esta tierra* (1955; in this land), a revised version of the censored *Las luciérnagas* (the fireflies), and *Los hijos muertos* (1958; *The Lost Children*, 1965).

The Cain and Abel theme, present in M.'s first novel, *Los Abel* (1948; the Abel family), and in *La torre vigía* (1971; the watchtower), among others, receives its strongest and most artistic treatment in *Fiesta al Noroeste* (1959; celebration in the Northwest), one of her best novels. The frame of the plot is the accidental death of a child caused by the arrival of a puppeteer; this device serves to introduce the protagonist, whose life is told in retrospect in two stages: his own evocation of childhood and family, and his confession to a priest of his sins of pride, wrath, envy, and avarice. This technique, as well as the themes in the novel—social injustice, solitude, the impossibility of communication, alienation—is characteristic of the style of M., a style rich in rhetorical figures, colorful descriptions, striking and contrasting images, and lyric exaltation.

M.'s most ambitious work is the trilogy *Los mercaderes* (the merchants), comprising *Primera memoria* (1960; *School of the Sun*, 1963), *Los soldados lloran de noche* (1964; soldiers cry at night), and *La trampa* (1969; the trap). Together these novels present a vast panorama of Spain from 1936 to the late 1960s. Her subjects are the basic philosophical and existential dilemmas and conflicts of man. *Primera memoria*, set against the background of the civil war and a country divided by hatred, is told from the perspective of a fourteen-year-old girl who feels only fear and abhorrence for the world of adults. Many of the characters also appear in *Los soldados lloran de noche*, which deals with the continuing bloody war. In *La trampa* the war has ended, and an authoritarian government has seized power. Hatred still divides Spain, and corruption and degeneration pervade every area of life.

M. has published several books of short stories, similar to her novels in their themes and settings. Children and adolescents are often the main characters, as in the collections *Los niños tontos* (1956; the stupid children) and *Algunos muchachos* (1968; a few kids); they are seen as lonely and alienated victims of the cruelty and incomprehension of adults. M. has also written excellent short stories for children.

Although her style has been faulted for rhetorical excesses, most critics place M. among the leading contemporary Spanish novelists. She has been awarded many literary prizes and her books have been translated into twenty-two languages.

FURTHER WORKS: *El tiempo* (1957); *Paulina, el mundo y las estrellas* (1960); *El arrepentido* (1961); *Historias de la Artámila* (1961); *El país de la pizarra* (1961); *Tres y un sueño* (1961); *Libro de juegos para los niños de los otros* (1961); *A la mitad del camino* (1961); *Caballito loco* (1962); *El río* (1963); *El polizón del Ulises* (1964)

BIBLIOGRAPHY: Alborg, J. L., *Hora actual de la novela española* (1958), Vol. I: 181–90; Couffon, C., "Una joven novelista, A. M. M.," *CHA*, 44, (1961): 52–55; Jones, M., *The Literary World of A. M. M* (1970); Nora, E. de, *La novela española contemporánea* (1970), Vol. III: 264–73; Sobejano, G., *Novela española de nuestro tiempo* (1970): 366–80; Weitzner, M., *The World of A. M. M.* (1970); Díaz, J. W., *A. M. M.* (1971)

—MARÍA-LUISA OSORIO

MAUGHAM, W(illiam) Somerset

English novelist, dramatist, and short-story writer, b. 25 Jan. 1874, Paris, France; d. 15 Dec. 1965, Cap Ferrat, France

M.'s father was the solicitor for the British embassy in Paris. His mother died when he was eight, and after his father died, when M. was ten, the boy was sent to England to live with relatives. He took a medical degree but never practiced. With the publication of the novel *Liza of Lambeth* (1897) he began a sixty-five-year writing career. Although he never achieved true greatness in any genre, he nevertheless earned a place in the history of the English novel, drama, and short fiction.

Written under the influence of the English and French realists, especially Guy de Maupassant, *Liza of Lambeth* was based on M.'s experiences as a medical student in the slums of London. Although he followed this good first novel with seven more, it was not until *Of Human Bondage* (1915) that he produced another significant fictional work. Highly autobiographical, this *Bildungsroman* has come to be considered M.'s most important work. In tracing the life of a young man from childhood to maturity, M. demonstrates the importance of truth, beauty, and goodness, and, under the influence of Spinoza, reveals how reason can be subjugated by emotion. In this novel M. expressed more strongly than in any of his other works the central concern of his writing: the importance of the physical, intellectual, and spiritual freedom of the individual.

In *The Moon and Sixpence* (1919) M. presented a portrait of the artist as a man possessed by an inescapable impulse to paint and for whom freedom can come only when he expresses his inner vision

W. Somerset Maugham

through the act of creation. *Cakes and Ale* (1930), M.'s most skillfully written work, is both a masterful satire on the world of art and society and a study of those who find freedom amid social restrictions. M.'s last important novel, *The Razor's Edge* (1944), anticipates the interest in Indian mysticism of the 1960s through its hero's search for spiritual liberation in Vedanta.

M. wrote thirty-two plays; from 1908, when he suddenly had four plays running simultaneously in London, to 1933, he was a dominant dramatist in Europe and America. Although his plays generally lack the thematic substance of his fiction, some are excellently crafted examples of comedies of manners and will continue to be performed. *Our Betters* (1917) is a penetrating satiric treatment of the London upper-class milieu and the enterprising American women who marry into it. *The Circle* (1921), M.'s best play, is a shrewd examination of social façades and restrictions in English life, and here, as in many of his plays, he uses marriage as a metaphor for the individual's contract with society as a whole. *The Constant Wife* (1926) is an Ibsenesque treatment of the state of marriage as it exists among the British upper classes, and as it is especially restricting for women. In his penultimate play, *For Services Rendered* (1932), M. abandoned the comic mode to present a blistering attack on war profiteers and jingoists and to present a strong argument for pacifism.

M.'s more than one hundred short stories are among the best in English. Many follow the pattern of Maupassant's tales, with the reader given a shock in the final lines, but M. uses the form to explore a great variety of themes and situations. "Rain" (1921) is an effective study of sexuality, repression, and hypocrisy, and "The Letter" (1924) skillfully delineates the mores and ethos of British colonialism at its height. M. is best known for these stories set in the Far East, but others—for example, "The Alien Corn" (1931), "Virtue" (1931), "Sanatorium" (1938), and "The Kite" (1947)—perceptively explore psychological, sociological, moral, and philosophical themes.

Although M.'s lack of innovation in form has led critics and scholars generally to ignore him, his craftsmanship and skill as a storyteller has made him one of the world's most widely read authors. His stature as a serious writer should increase as his work is examined more thoroughly.

FURTHER WORKS: *The Making of a Saint* (1898); *Orientations* (1899); *The Hero* (1901); *Mrs. Craddock* (1902); *A Man of Honour* (1903); *The Merry-Go-Round* (1904); *The Land of the Blessed Virgin* (1905); *The Bishop's Apron* (1906); *The Explorer* (1907); *The Magician* (1908); *Lady Frederick* (1911); *Jack Straw* (1911); *Mrs. Dot* (1912); *Penelope* (1912); *The Tenth Man* (1913); *Landed Gentry* (1913); *Smith* (1913); *The Land of Promise* (1913); *The Unknown* (1920); *The Trembling of a Leaf* (1921); *Caesar's Wife* (1922); *East of Suez* (1922); *On a Chinese Screen* (1922); *Home and Beauty* (1923); *The Unattainable* (1923); *Loaves and Fishes* (1924); *The Painted Veil* (1925); *The Casuarina Tree* (1926); *Ashenden* (1928); *The Sacred Flame* (1928); *The Gentleman in the Parlour* (1930); *The Bread-Winner* (1931); *Six Stories Written in the First Person Singular* (1931); *The Book Bag* (1932); *The Narrow Corner* (1932); *Ah King* (1933); *Sheppey* (1933); *Altogether* (1934; Am., *East and West*); *Don Fernando* (1935); *Cosmopolitans* (1936); *Six Comedies* (1937); *Theatre* (1937); *The Favourite Short Stories* (1937); *The Summing Up* (1938); *The Round Dozen* (1938); *Christmas Holiday* (1939); *Princess September and the Nightingale* (1939); *France at War* (1940); *Books and You* (1940); *The Mixture as Before* (1940); *Up at the Villa* (1941); *Strictly Personal* (1941); *The Hour before the Dawn* (1942); *The S. M. Sampler* (1943); *The Unconquered* (1944); *Then and Now* (1946); *Creatures of Circumstance* (1947); *Catalina* (1948); *Great Novelists and Their Novels* (1948; rev. enlarged ed., *Ten Novels and Their Authors*, 1954; Am., *The Art of Fiction*); *Quartet* (1948); *Here and There* (1948); *East of Suez* (1948); *A Writer's Notebook* (1949); *Trio* (1950); *The M. Reader* (1950); *The Complete Short Stories* (1951); *The Vagrant Mood* (1952); *Encore* (1952); *The Collected Plays* (1952); *The World Over* (1952); *The Selected Novels* (1953); *The Partial View* (1954); *Mr. M. Himself* (1954); *The Travel Books* (1955); *The Best Short Stories* (1957); *Points of View* (1958); *Purely for My Pleasure* (1962); *Husbands and Wives* (1963); *The Kite, and Other Stories* (1963); *Selected Prefaces and Introductions* (1963); *The Sinners* (1964); *Essays on Literature* (1967); *M.'s Malaysian Stories* (1969); *Seventeen Lost Stories* (1969); *A Baker's Dozen* (1969); *A Second Baker's Dozen* (1970); *Plays* (3 vols., 1970)

BIBLIOGRAPHY: Mander, R., and J. Mitchenson, *Theatrical Companion to M.* (1955); Cordell, R., *S. M.: A Biographical and Critical Study* (1961); Brander, L., *S. M.: A Guide* (1963); Naik, M. K., *W. S. M.* (1966); Barnes, R. E., *The Dramatic Comedy of W. S. M.* (1968); Calder, R. L., *W. S. M. and the Quest for Freedom* (1972); Curtis, A., *The Pattern of M.* (1974); Dobrinsky, J., *La jeunesse de S. M.* (1975); Raphael, F., *S. M. and His World* (1976)

—ROBERT L. CALDER

MAURIAC, Claude

French novelist and essayist, b. 25 April 1914, Paris

M., son of Nobel laureate François MAURIAC, grew up in close contact with many of France's most prestigious writers. His own activities, especially his six years as private secretary to Charles de Gaulle and his reviewing assignments for *Le Figaro* and *Le monde*, vastly expanded his circle of celebrated acquaintances. The value for M. of his relations with the great political and literary figures of his era is among the principal messages of his major recent publication, nine volumes of extracts from the journals he began to keep as an adolescent.

M.'s importance derives from his contributions to developing the NEW NOVEL in France. His principal fictional work is a series of four novels that feature Bertrand Carnejoux as their protagonist: *Toutes les femmes sont fatales* (1957; *All Women Are Fatal*, 1964), *Le dîner en ville* (1959; *The Dinner Party*, 1960), *La marquise sortit à cinq heures* (1961; *The Marquise Went Out at Five*, 1962), and *L'agrandissement* (1963; the enlargement). Striking technical experiments characterize the form of all four works, while preoccupation with human experience of time creates their thematic unity. The tetralogy's first novel presents Bertrand and his thoughts on four different days across a span of sixteen years; its last unfolds during the few seconds necessary for a stoplight to pass through two cycles of red, yellow, and green. To this temporal compression corresponds an expansion of devices for depicting the almost unimaginable variety of external and internal events that constitute any given moment of human existence.

By common consent, M.'s most successful novels are the tetralogy's second and third volumes. *Le dîner en ville* consists of the thoughts and words of eight characters around a dinner table at Bertrand's expensive Paris apartment. All eight characters are fully individualized, although no authorial intervention ever names or otherwise identifies them. The novel is rich in the kinds of unspoken conversation whose name M. retroactively made for the overall title for all four Bertrand Carnéjoux novels: *Le dialogue intérieur* (interior dialogue). *La marquise sortit à cinq heures*, responding to the challenge of Paul VALÉRY'S celebrated statement that he (Valéry) could never write a sentence as banal as "La marquise sortit à cinq heures," both illustrates how the New Novel has transformed our concept of narrative statements and exemplifies M.'s personal vision of time as an endless present. The novel's characters observe a Paris intersection during a single evening hour, but the text makes the intersection's eight centuries of history as significant as the sixty minutes actually depicted. This vision of the past's living participation in the present is also crucial to the form M. has chosen for publishing his diaries. Grouped by subject instead of by date, the three thousand pages of printed journals juxtapose chronologically disconnected entries in continuous reiteration of the message communicated by the journal's collective title, *Le temps immobile* (stationary time).

M.'s concern with time places him in the great tradition of French literature epitomized by Marcel PROUST, yet his innovative representations of characters' simultaneous perceptions and thought processes link him with the central names in recent experimental fiction. His critical works, especially *L'alittérature contemporaine* (1958; *The New Literature*, 1959), are invaluable to study of how and why the New Novel came into being.

FURTHER WORKS: *Introduction à une mystique de l'enfer* (1938); *La corporation dans l'état* (1941); *Aimer Balzac* (1945); *Jean Cocteau* (1945); *La trahison d'un clerc* (1945); *Malraux* (1946); *André Breton* (1949); *Conversations avec André Gide* (1951; *Conversations with André Gide*, 1965); *Proust*, (1953); *Hommes et idées d'aujourd'hui* (1953); *L'amour du cinéma* (1954); *Petite littérature du cinéma* (1957); *La conversation* (1964); *L'oubli* (1966); *Théâtre* (1968); *De la littérature à l'alittérature* (1969); *Une amitié contrariée* (1970); *Un autre de Gaulle* (1971; *The Other de Gaulle*, 1973); *Le temps immobile* (1974); *Les espaces imaginaires* (1975); *Et comme l'espérance est violente* (1976); *La terrasse de Malagar* (1977); *Une certaine rage* (1977); *Aimer de Gaulle* (1978); *Le Bouddha s'est mis à trembler* (1979); *L'éternité parfois* (1978); *Un cœur tout neuf* (1980); *Laurent Terzieff* (1980); *Le rire des pères dans les yeux des enfants* (1981)

BIBLIOGRAPHY: Johnston, S. L., "Structure in the Novels of C. M.," *FR*, 38 (1965): 451–58; Mercier, V., *The New Novel from Queneau to Pinget* (1971): 315–62; Roudiez, L. S., *French Fiction Today* (1972): 132–51; Boschett, S. M., "Silence as an Element of Dialogue in C. M.," *IFR*, 7, 1 (1980): 35–38

—SANDY PETREY

MAURIAC, François

French novelist, poet, essayist, critic, and dramatist, b. 11 Oct. 1885, Bordeaux; d. 1 Sept. 1970, Paris

M., who is best known as a Catholic writer, came from a home divided in religious background. His father, a freethinker, died when M. was not yet two years old. His mother, a devout Catholic influenced by Jansenist thought, gave M. a distinctly pious education. His attendance from the age of five at the Catholic College of Grand-Lebrun, taught by the Marist Fathers, turned him toward introspective self-analysis and scrupulosity. The mature writer never ceased to acknowledge his grateful recognition of this early tutelage and the preservation from evil it afforded him.

M. likewise was ambivalent in his attitude toward his childhood surroundings. He always loved Malagar, the family estate bought by his great-grandfather, whose formula was "order, work, economy." M.'s novels are filled with the atmosphere of the Landes, the region of marsh and pine near Bordeaux. This fact has led some critics to call M. a regionalist writer. Yet one of M.'s chief themes was his rebellion against the bourgeois farmers—his bitter criticism of the tenaciousness with which they clung to material goods and of their avaricious spirit. In politics he was likewise severe toward middle-class conservatism.

M.'s early literary influences are many. Often they reflect his personal relationship and debt to the writers rather than a detached objective judgment on his part. *Mes grands hommes* (1950; *Men I Hold Great*, 1952) has as chapter headings the names of Pascal, Molière, Voltaire, Rousseau, Chateaubriand, Maurice de Guérin (1810–1839) and his sister Eugénie de Guérin (1805–1848), Balzac, Flaubert, Maurice Barrès (1862–1923), André GIDE, Graham GREENE, and others. M. also wrote studies on Racine and Marcel PROUST, and the poet and novelist André Lafon (1883–1915). The French names predominating in such a list are indicative of his nationalistic orientation. The variety and number of the types represented suggest the rich complexity of M.'s mind.

François Mauriac

Of all these writers, Pascal seems foremost in his influence on M. A sensitive Christian intellectual, deeply conscious primarily of his direct relationship with a personal God, Pascal is a type attractive to M., whose spiritual ordeal resembles that of the great 17th-c. writer. The constant, absorbing consciousness of God's presence and the concomitant anxiety about the conscious conflict between nature and grace are Pascal's legacy to M.

To this must be added M.'s admiration for Proust and for the subtle psychological explorations that mark Proust's work. When critics called M. the greatest French novelist since Proust, they were no doubt allying the two because of their poetic style, their reliance on remembrance of things past, and their use of interior monologue. Yet Proust's interior world never revolves about a personal God.

Although M.'s first publication was a book of poetry, *Les mains jointes* (1909; clasped hands), it was with his novels that M. was to achieve fame. His first novel, *L'enfant chargé de chaînes* (1913; *Young Man in Chains*, 1963), was followed by, among others, *La robe prétexte* (1914; *The Stuff of Youth*, 1960), *La chair et le sang* (1920; *Flesh and Blood*, 1955), and *Le fleuve de feu* (1923; *The River of Fire*, 1954). The first novel shares with its immediate successor a considerable sentimentality and reflects M.'s enthusiasm at the time for religious and romantic literature. But gradually M. developed control over his material. Using adolescent boys as central figures in his early novels, and depicting their maturation, he satirizes bourgeois society and focuses on the struggle of spirit and flesh, with profound reflections on the conflict between piety and the world—themes he never completely abandoned in his mature work.

Le baiser au lépreux (1922; *A Kiss for the Leper*, 1950) is the first of M.'s better-known novels. Here the theme that became closely identified with M.—the distrust of human love—first made a notable appearance. For M., each person is marked by isolation; the novelist seems deeply convinced of the futility of human love in people's attempts at communion with another. Ultimately, as many of M.'s novels demonstrate, the human heart finds its solace in confrontation with the "Other," with God alone.

"Those who love us form us," M. reflects in *Le jeune homme* (1926; the young man). The restraints that love puts upon us sometimes result in rebellion. The same theme in a different context, family love, is seen at its epitome in *Génitrix* (1923; *Genetrix*, 1950).

M. once wrote: "The Desert of Love' might serve as the title for my entire work." With the work bearing this title began the publication of M.'s three greatest novels: *Le désert de l'amour* (1925; *The Desert of Love*, 1929); *Thérèse Desqueyroux* (1927; *Thérèse*, 1928), and *Le nœud de vipères* (1932; *Viper's Tangle*, 1933; also tr. as *The Knot of Vipers*, 1951).

In *Le désert de l'amour* Maria Cross, a self-centered young widow, deliberately provokes the passions of both her physician, Dr. Courrèges, and his adolescent son, Raymond. Viewed again after an interval of seventeen years, the trio has found love a place of solitude rather than union, a place of utter desolation, a temporary oasis inevitably to become a mirage.

In *Thérèse Desqueyroux* the futility of passion is pictured through the complex character of a strong young woman who finds her marriage to a complacent, coarse landowner intolerable. She becomes his would-be murderess, but her innermost feelings are surrounded by an atmosphere of mystery, and her conversion is both an artistic and a moral problem for M. He is confronted with the paradox of Thérèse, who is desperately seeking freedom at the cost of murder, yet who is unable to acknowledge her guilt in terms of repentance.

Before M. wrote the third novel of this distinguished trio, he seemed to have resolved the tragic struggle between passion and conscience that had marked his earlier writing, where nature itself seems allied with pagan sensuality against God. No reconciliation had appeared possible for M. when he wrote the essay "Souffrances du pécheur" (1928; sufferings of the sinner)—later published together with "Bonheur du chrétien" (1929; joy of the Christian) under the title *Souffrances et bonheur du chrétien* (1931; *Anguish and Joy of the Christian Life*, 1964). In "Souffrances du pécheur" he expresses the Jansenist paradox in his opening sentence: "Christianity makes no provision for the flesh. It suppresses it." However, the retraction of this extreme statement, "Bonheur du chrétien," was hailed by Charles du Bos (1882–1939) as the record of a conversion, a peace treaty achieved within M. himself. In "Bonheur du chrétien" M. acknowledges "Souffrances du pécheur" as the rebellious outpourings of a man who "accuses the Author of life of failing to make provision for the flesh, and the Author of life takes vengeance by overwhelming this soul and this body in his love to the point that he confesses the law of the spirit to be, indeed, the law of the flesh."

It may be that M.'s newly achieved serenity of spirit provided the creative stimulus for *Le nœud de vipères*, which is probably his greatest work. It is written almost entirely in the first person from the point of view of Louis, an embittered old man, whose determination to keep his money from his wife and children is motivated

not by miserliness but by a sense of abandonment. His children and his illegitimate son are engaged in a counterplot against him. He finally realizes he has pursued an illusion and dies just as he discovers that the few loves he has known are revelations of the one true Love. *Thérèse Desqueyroux* is artistically admirable because of M.'s restraint in introducing the intervention of the supernatural. *Le nœud de vipères* also serves as a synthesis of characteristic M. themes: the bourgeois family as an institution, the mediocrity of innumerable Christians, the disillusionment seemingly inevitable in human love, the isolation of the individual.

Several later novels—*Galigaï* (1952; *The Loved and the Unloved*, 1952), *Les anges noirs* (1936; *The Mask of Innocence*, 1953), and *L'agneau* (1954; *The Lamb*, 1955)—are marked by the theme of isolation, but only once in the remainder of his writing did M. show comparable achievement. This was in his *La Pharisienne* (1941; *Woman of the Pharisees*, 1946), where his theme is the subtlety of a complacent Christian's hypocritical self-delusion, which results in the spiritual destruction of the "woman," Brigitte Pian. The novel is powerful, although perhaps less moving than *Le nœud de vipères*.

The fictional world M. created is acknowledged to be sharply limited; it exists only in the particular atmosphere he creates. His style is highly poetic—rhythmic, economical, full of suggestion. Of the poetry of the novel M. said: "There is little danger in the novel's invading the rest of literature. I believe that only poetry counts and that only through the poetical elements enclosed in a work of art of any genre whatever does that work deserve to last. A great novelist is first of all a great poet. Both Proust and Tolstoy were because their power of suggestion was boundless."

M.'s work as a dramatist, beginning with *Asmodée* (1937; *Asmodée; or, The Intruder*, 1939), never achieved the success of his novels. Indeed, his plays tend now to seem dated in comparison with the drama of metaphysical freedom that was being written at the same time by other playwrights. His characters often seem starkly outlined, without the nuances of background that enrich the novels; the "atmosphere" is lost. This is particularly true of *Asmodée*, in which the conflict of characters seems at times implausible. His best play is *Les mal aimés* (1945; the badly loved), a drama of frustrated love, which has a classically sharp construction.

M.'s religious writings are searching, at times anguished, always highly relevant to the troubled times in which he lived. Best among them is probably *Le fils de l'homme* (1958; *The Son of Man*, 1960), a meditation on the life of Christ. It is less controversial than his *Vie de Jésus* (1936; *Life of Jesus*, 1937), which emphasizes the human qualities of Christ.

As a journalist he made his mark in the columns of *Le Figaro* and in *La table ronde*. His collected articles. *Journal* (5 vols., 1934–51; journal), include some of the best of M.'s prose.

The highest tribute to M.'s art came with his winning of the Nobel Prize for literature in 1952. He is held by many to be the greatest French novelist of his time.

FURTHER WORKS: *L'adieu à l'adolescence* (1911); *De quelques cœurs inquiets: Petits essais de psychologie religieuse* (1920); *Préséances* (1921; *Questions of Precedence*, 1958); *Le mal* (1924; *The Enemy*, 1952); *La vie et la mort d'un poète* (1924); *Orages* (1925); *Bordeaux* (1926); *Proust* (1926); *Fabien* (1926); *La province* (1926); *La rencontre avec Pascal* (1926); *Le tourment de Jacques Rivière* (1926); *Destins* (1928; *Destinies*, 1929; also tr. as *Lines of Life*, 1957); *Le roman* (1928); *La vie de Racine* (1928);

Trois récits (1929); *Dieu et Mammon* (1929; *God and Mammon*, 1936); *Voltaire centre Pascal* (1930); *Trois grands hommes devant Dieu* (1930); *Ce qui était perdu* (1930; *That Which Was Lost*, 1951); *Commencement d'une vie, suivi de Bordeaux; ou, L'adolescence* (1931); *Jeudi saint* (1931; *The Eucharist: The Mystery of Holy Thursday*, 1944); *L'affaire Favre-Bulle* (1931); *Blaise Pascal et sa sœur Jacqueline* (1931); *René Bazin* (1931); *Pèlerins de Lourdes* (1933); *Le mystère Frontenac* (1933; *The Frontenacs*, 1961); *Le romancier et ses personnages* (1933); *Le drôle* (1933; *The Holy Terror*, 1964); *La fin de la nuit* (1935; *The End of the Night*, in *Therese: A Portrait in Four Parts*, 1947); *Plongées* (1938); *Les maisons fugitives* (1939); *Les chemins de la mer* (1939; *The Unknown Sea*, 1948); *Le sang d'Atys* (1941); *Ne pas se renier* (1944); *La rencontre avec Barrès* (1945); *Sainte Marguerite de Cortone* (1945; *Saint Margaret of Cortona*, 1948); *Le bâillon dénoué* (1945); *Du côté de chez Proust* (1947; *Proust's Way*, 1947); *Passage du malin* (1948); *Journal d'un homme de trente ans* (1948); *Terres franciscaines: Actualités de St-François d'Assise* (1950); *Le sagouin* (1951; *The Weakling*, 1952); *La pierre d'achoppement* (1951; *The Stumbling Block*, 1952); *Le feu sur la terre* (1951); *Lettres ouvertes* (1952; *Letters on Art and Literature*, 1953); *Écrits intimes* (1953); *Paroles catholiques* (1954; *Words of Faith*, 1955); *Le pain vivant* (1955); *Bloc-notes, 1952–1957* (1958); *Mémoires intérieurs* (1959; *Mémoires Intérieurs*, 1960); *Nouveaux bloc-notes, 1958–1960* (1961); *La vie de Racine* (1962); *Ce que je crois* (1962; *What I Believe*, 1963); *De Gaulle* (1964; *De Gaulle*, 1966); *Nouveaux mémoires intérieurs* (1965); *Nouveaux bloc-notes, 1961–1964* (1965); *D'autres et moi* (1966); *Mémoires politiques* (1967); *Un adolescent d'autrefois* (1969; *Malteverne*, 1970); *Derniers bloc-notes, 1968–1970* (1971); *Correspondance André Gide-F. M., 1912–1950* (1971); *Correspondance F. M.-Jacques-Émile Blanche, 1916–1942* (1976); *Œuvres romanesques et théâtrales complètes* (1978 ff). FURTHER WORKS IN ENGLISH: *Therese: A Portrait in Four Parts* (1947); *Second Thoughts: Reflections on Literature and Life* (1961); *Cain, Where Is Your Brother?* (1962)

BIBLIOGRAPHY: Heppenstall, R., *The Double Image* (1947): 45–63; O'Donnell, D., [Conor Cruise O'Brien], *Maria Cross: Imaginative Patterns in a Group of Modern Catholic Writers* (1952): 3–37; Simon, P. H., ed., *M. par lui-même* (1953); Robichon, J., *F. M.* (1953); Jarrett-Kerr, M., *F. M.* (1954); Peyre, H., *The Contemporary French Novel* (1955; new ed., *French Novelists of Today*, 1967): 101–22; Moloney, M. F., *F. M.: A Critical Study* (1958); Turnell, M., *The Art of French Fiction* (1959): 287–360; Alyn, M., *F. M.* (1960); Jenkins, C., *M.* (1965); Flower, J. E., *Intention and Achievement: An Essay on the Novels of F. M.* (1969); Smith, M. A., *F. M.* (1970); Kushner, E., *M.* (1972); Lacouture, J., *F. M.* (1980); Scott, M., *M.: The Politics of a Novelist* (1980)

—ANITA MARIE CASPARY, I. H. M.

M.'s originality as a novelist lies in his Catholic vision of the world, in his analysis of love and especially of middle-aged women and adolescents led by a love affair to explore the bitter depths of love. It lies, too, in his craftsmanship, which, conscious and subtle as it is, contrives to leave in the novel the element by which it is most likely to challenge time—poetry.

Love hallowed by the sacrament of marriage and embellished by the devotion of the Christian couple to the service of God is hardly a theme for Catholic novelists. Happiness does not interest a creator. The radiating joy of lovers who might find an absolute in physical love is the foe M. pursues relentlessly. . . . To him, desire is always hideous. "It transforms the person who draws near us into a monster that is no longer like him. Nothing then stands any longer between us and our accomplice." His married women have, of course, ceased to expect any pleasure or joy. No mutual esteem, no admiration ever precedes or prolongs physical love. Love is nothing but a delusion that makes us feel our loneliness more acutely, or a fleeting sadistic impulse to humiliate our partner. More often still, with M., love is the inordinate power to torment us with which we have suddenly invested another creature.

Henri Peyre, *The Contemporary French Novel* (1955), pp. 118–19

The lucidity of the literary tradition in which he writes barred M. from the linguistic and structural exploration of a Joyce or the syntactical freedoms of a Faulkner, but he is no less concerned than they with the dark and lawless forces which well up from man's inmost being. Equally with them he testifies to modern man's recognition of the mystery of his nature. Unlike most contemporary novelists of the unconscious, however, M. has not been content merely to chart the ebb and flow of psychic currents. His identifying procedural trait has been his projection of himself *qua* artist into the full stream of the action which he narrates. The reader of a M. novel never escapes the presence of the novelist who is at the same time a poet of extreme lyric sensibility. [Ramon] Fernandez's declaration that a novel is, above all, the bringing to light of the interior world of the novelist is highly relevant to his manner of creation. No more than that of Dostoievski, or of his contemporary, Bernanos, is M.'s a reportorial art. His characters do not have their literal counterparts in the world of everyday experience. Here he breaks with the naturalistic tradition with which in so many ways he is closely identified. He is primarily the chronicler not of human actions separate and distinct from himself but of his own real and imagined life.

Michael F. Moloney, *F. M.* (1958), pp. 121–22

The truth is that in M. religion is translated not simply into concrete, but into physical terms. I think that we can go on to conclude that "passion" and "belief" are made of the same stuff, that though "belief" clearly implies a religious nuance which is not present in "passion," "belief" is nevertheless a form of "passion" as "passion," is a form of "belief." While it is true that "passion" may provide "belief" with its driving power and "belief" may colour "passion," there is generally a conflict between the two, a conflict which is never resolved because the novelist does not wish to resolve it. His religion is not the source of harmony or unity; it is the disruptive element that creates the drama which is at the heart of all his work.

We can appreciate now the force of his statement that "this religion was *imposed* on me at birth," and the felicity of the image of the tide ebbing and flowing round the "central rock" and recoiling to form "whirlpools." The "whirlpools" are the conflicts which threaten the individual: the conflicts between love of God and love of the creature; between the Church and the world; between the individual and his environment; the individual and the family; the individual and the community.

Martin Turnell, The Art of French Fiction (1959), p. 288

It is certain . . . that with a certain feverish yet precisely evocative quality of style, immediately involving the physical in the metaphysical, M. has enriched the contemporary novel with a rare and distinctive tone. And it might seem that in such works as *Le désert de l'amour* and *Thérèse Desqueyroux*—perhaps also *Genitrix, Le nœud de vipères* and, of the plays, *Les mal aimés*—he has produced imaginative writing of lasting importance. That the Catholic novelist should achieve permanence through the more rebellious or troubled of his writings may well appear paradoxical, but this is hardly new in Catholic writing and M. himself has come to believe that, ultimately, the paradox is only an apparent one. Insofar as the value of the testimony is a function of the quality of the art, he is probably right. In the longer perspective, his contribution to his faith is not only to have maintained it in its public application against opposition from whatever quarter, but to have produced writings which—through the reality of their tensions—bear witness to the continuance of the Christian sense of life as an element in the culture of his time.

Cecil Jenkins, M. (1965), p. 114

M.'s aims and intentions as a novelist during some forty years of writing have been to exemplify to others his own firm conviction that mankind is assured of God's love. . . . Yet against this stands his description of a particular segment of bourgeois society with its families decaying and doomed to extinction. This is the problem stated in its simplest terms and one of which M. becomes increasingly aware in the course of his career. Implied values are not sufficient, particularly for the demanding Catholic critic, yet as a novelist M. is very aware of the danger of didactic literature. His attempts to incorporate his personal faith in the public statements that are his novels are various: the semi-autobiographical account of his relationship with Social Catholicism as a young man, the harsh castigation of the attitude of mind which raises material values over spiritual ones,

the idealized portrait of a family in *Le mystère Frontenac*, or the allegory of Christ's passion in *L'agneau*. Too frequently, however, such attempts are doomed to fail and M. is open to the accusation of having implanted a particular view and in consequence of having falsified his picture of society. In order to avoid the charge of didacticism or of manipulation, therefore, the Catholic element of the novel must be included in such a way that it is an essential part of the structure of the book which without it would crumble.

J. E. Flower, Intention and Achievement: An Essay on the Novels of F. M. (1969), pp. 6–7

Throughout M.'s work we have observed three predominant themes, all of them present in the personality of this most subjective of writers. First, there is the essential element of tension and conflict: sometimes between Cybele and God, passionate and pagan love of nature versus religious faith; sometimes between God and Mammon, worldliness and sensual passion combating the desire for purity and saintliness. Second, we have the desperate loneliness and solitude of the individual, unable to communicate with others, even those most beloved. We recall in this regard M.'s own admission that "desert of love" might well serve as title of his entire work. Third, there is the flagellation of bourgeois smugness, social conformity, and lack of true Christian compassion a theme first appearing in the early *Préséances* but cropping up in most of the later works, particularly in that savage *Nœud de vipères*.

Maxwell A. Smith, F. M. (1970), p. 158

MAURITIAN LITERATURE

For a long time, Mauritius, in the Indian Ocean—or Île de France, as it was called until it was ceded by France to Britain in 1814—remained culturally a distant province of France. During the first part of the 19th c. the group of the Oval Table, led by Thomi Pitot de la Beaujardière (1779–1857), reflected the style of the popular French poet and song writer Pierre-Jean de Béranger (1780–1857). The first poet to depart from exclusively French themes and style was François Chrestien (1767–1846), whose *Le bobre africain* (1822; the African guitar) even included poems in Creole.

The "father of Mauritian poetry," Léoville L'Homme (1857–1928), and the more important poet Robert Edward Hart (1891–1954) gradually moved from romanticism to SYMBOLISM. Over the course of thirty-three volumes, Loys Masson (1915–1969) achieved the transition to SURREALISM in poetry, while his *Le notaire des Noirs* (1961; the notary of Les Noirs) was a high point in the Mauritian novel. In poetry, Malcolm de Chazal (1904–1981) followed André BRETON's surrealism, notably in *Sens plastique* (1947; plastic sense), while André Masson (b.1927) veered toward esoteric themes, and Édouard J. Maunick (b.1934) emphasized the

African element in the inspired lyrics of *Ensoleillé vif* (1977; sunstruck alive). In fiction, Marcel Cabon (1912–1972) depicted indigenous life with realism and authenticity, even using local phrases occasionally in the novel *Namasté* (1965; Namasté).

Beginning with *Folklore de l'Île Maurice* (1888; folklore of Mauritius)—a collection of works, some in Creole, gathered by Charles Baissac (1831–1892), a white ethnographer—tales and *sega* (a local musical form) songs in Creole have been an important component of Mauritian literature. It took René Noyau (b.1912), however, to "decolonize" such tales—that is, to use Creole as a challenge to French cultural ascendancy—and to assert the claims of the folk tradition in *Tention caïma* (1971; beware, crocodile), reworkings of folktales in Creole. Today, Dev Virshsawmy (b. 1940) is the major champion of Creole literature as a means of achieving cultural unity and as an alternative to the belleslettres of the French-speaking elite. His best-known work, *Li* (1976; him), a play whose production was banned by the government then in power, blends cultural and political satire. Another Creole writer, Renée Asgarally (b.1942), also denounced social barriers in *Quand montagne prend difé . . .* (1977; when the mountain catches fire . . .).

Writing in English has always been on a limited scale, although English is the official administrative and school language, even since independence in 1968. Two worthy writers have emerged: Azize Asgarally (b.1933), whose plays, mostly political and metaphysical, earned him an international reputation before he turned to writing in Creole with *Ratsitatane* (1980; Ratsitatane), a play about the Malagasy leader of a 19th-c. revolt of native workers; and Deepchand Beeharry (b. 1927), whose novel *That Others Might Live* (1976) graphically evokes the plight of Indian indentured workers at the turn of the century.

Mauritian literature in English seems to have little future. There remains a strong French tradition—more than eighty percent of literary publications are still in French—but Creole writing is assuming an increasingly important position.

BIBLIOGRAPHY: Prosper, J.-G., ed., *Mauritius Anthology of Literature in the African Context* (1977); Hazareesingh, K., ed., *Anthologie des lettres mauriciennes* (1978); Prosper, J.-G., *Histoire de la littérature mauricienne de langue française* (1978); Furlong, R., ed., "La production littéraire à l'Île Maurice," special issue, *Journal of the Mauritius Institute of Education*, No. 3 (1979); Fabre, M., "Mauritian Voices: A Panorama of Contemporary Creative Writing in English," *WLWE*, 19 (1980): 121–37; Fabre, M., and D. Fabre, Quet, D. "A Checklist of Mauritian Creative Writing in English (1920–1980)," *WLWE*, 19 (1980): 138–43

—MICHEL FABRE

Mauritian Literature since 1980

The assumption that the official language of Mauritius, English, is the language of government, business, commerce, and education, while French is the literary language, had been challenged in recent years, especially during the 1990s, by the increasing use of both English and Creole by creative writers. French continues to flourish, but the inclusion of seven English-language writers (out of thirty-one) in the important anthology *Au tour des femmes* (1995; To the Turn of Women), which at first sight seems to be a French-language book, is significant. The publication less than two years later of the first collection of Mauritian writing in English, *Mauritian*

Voices (1997), containing work by twenty-three poets and story writers, confirms that English has become a viable alternative to French for a number of imaginative writers in Mauritius.

However, in containing work by older authors famous for their writings in French, such as Jean Georges Prosper (b. 1933) and Régis Franchette (dates n.a.), as well as young writers also publishing in French, notably Rajen Bablee's (dates n.a.), the author of the novel *La solitude de Dieu* (1995; The Solitude of God) from the French-language press *La maison de Mécènes*, founded in 1991, *Mauritian Voices* demonstrates that Mauritian authors are not faced with an either/or choice about the language they employ. They can use both English and French—as well as Creole—depending on the circumstances. Referring to his poems in *Mauritian Voices*, Jean Georges Prosper said that he needed the rhythms of English for certain types of writing; French rhythms were much less appropriate.

Mauritius now seems much more fertile ground for nurturing writing in English than in the past. Consider the case of Isshack Hasgarally's long novel in English about World War II, *When Blooms the Talipot*. Hasgarally began his novel in 1956 but abandoned it for many years, eventually returning to it in the 1980s thanks to the encouragement of his writer friend Bhisma Dev Seebaluck (dates n.a.), who is represented in *Mauritian Voices*. Hasgarally's novel was finally published in 1994.

There are several reasons for the emergence of English as a literary language in the recent past. The British Council, somewhat dormant for more than two decades after Mauritian independence, has become very active in the 1990s, inviting writers from Britain to visit schools and run creative writing workshops for young authors. Altogether more dramatic was the unexpected international success of Lindsey Collen's (dates n.a.) second novel, *The Rape of Sita* (1993), following its ban by the Mauritian government on the grounds that it would cause religious offense. More poetic as well as more formally daring than her first novel, *There Is a Tide* (1990), *The Rape of Sita* was recognized as a fine literary achievement by the judges of the Commonwealth Writers Prize for 1994, naming it the best book in the African section. Although born in South Africa, Collen has lived in Mauritius for many years and also writes in Creole. *The Rape of Sita*, with its strong feminist analysis, is profoundly Mauritian while being accessible to readers everywhere. This is the first Mauritian book in English to achieve international recognition in the way that some French-language writers have done. Another recent prize-winning novel in English is Bhageeruthy Gopaul's (dates n.a.) *The Changing Pattern* (1995), a historical saga about the indentured laborers brought to Mauritius from India in the 19th c. This, too, has been an encouragement to other Mauritians to develop the imaginative potential of English.

As a more favorable environment for English-language writing develops, the short story is the most popular form, although poetry has attracted several gifted writers such as Ramish Ramdoyal (who also writes in Creole), Sushilla Gopaul, Roshan Soomoodra, and especially Shakuntala Hawoldar, whose *Hymms from Beau Bois and Other Poems* (1994) is a particularly impressive achievement and establishes her as the leading story writers in English, as Chintamanee Chummun, whose collection *I Remember* appeared in 1993, but particularly exciting at the moment is the emergence of a group of young women writers of considerable promise: Garry Naw (pseud. of Bernadette Cheung Haw Sing), Meera V. Pillay, Kamini Ramphul, and Brinda Runghsawmee (dates n.a.).

—PETER LEWIS

MAUROIS, André

(pseud. of Émile Herzog) French biographer, novelist, and historian, b. 26 July 1885, Elbeuf; d. 9 Oct. 1967, Neuilly

M. was born into a family of Jewish industrialists who had fled Alsace after the Franco-Prussian War (1870) and taken refuge in Normandy, where they owned a woolen mill at Elbeuf. He was a brilliant student at secondary school in Rouen, where he came under the influence of a famous teacher who wrote under the name ALAIN. Young M.'s fluency in English led to his appointment during World War I as liaison officer with the British. The result was a series of sketches entitled *Les silences du colonel Bramble* (1918; *The Silence of Colonel Bramble*, 1920), which was an instant success in both France and England.

Peacetime found M. back at the family mill. But the success of *Les silences du Colonel Bramble* whetted his appetite for writing and attracted him to England. His next success was *Ariel; ou, La vie de Shelley* (1923; *Ariel: The Life of Shelley*, 1924), a light-hearted biography. Readers were delighted, but not so the critics. M.'s accuracy was attacked. Since *Ariel* was not intended as a work of scholarship, these attacks were manifestly unfair, but thereafter his biographies adhered to academic standards.

M.'s next important biography was *La vie de Disraëli* (1927; *Disraeli: A Picture of the Victorian Age*, 1928). Asked if he saw himself in the prime minister of Jewish background, he replied "sometimes," but M. remained outside formal religion. For his biography of Byron, *Don Juan; ou, La vie de Byron* (1930; *Byron*, 1930), he studied his subject's poetry carefully.

M.'s first biography of a French figure was *Lyautey* (1931; *Lyautey*, 1931), about the empire builder and Marshal of France. Many others followed: *Chateaubriand* (1938; *Chateaubriand: Poet, Statesman, Lover*, 1938); *À la recherche de Marcel Proust* (1949; *Proust: The Portrait of a Genius*, 1950), a meticulous study; *Lélia; ou, La vie de George Sand* (1952; *Lelia: The Life of George Sand*, 1953); *Olympio; ou, La vie de Victor Hugo* (1954; *Olympio: The Life of Victor Hugo*, 1956); and *Les trois Dumas* (1957; *The Titans: A Three-Generation Biography of the Dumas*, 1957). He returned to an English subject with *La vie de Sir Alexander Fleming* (1959; *The Life of Sir Alexander Fleming, Discoverer of Penicillin*, 1959). Next came *Adrienne; ou, La vie de Mme de La Fayette* (1961; *Adrienne: The Life of the Marquise de La Fayette*, 1961), and finally *Promethée; ou, La vie de Balzac* (1964; *Prometheus: The Life of Balzac*, 1965). All these biographies are distinguished by their delightful style; meticulously researched, they present vivid and realistic portraits of their subjects.

M. channeled his craft into history in *Histoire d'Angleterre* (1937; *The Miracle of England*, 1937), *Histoire des États-Unis* (2 vols., 1943; *The Miracle of America*, 1944), and *Histoire de la France* (1947; *The Miracle of France*, 1948). These works had all the charm lacking in the usual histories, and they won an enthusiastic readership.

Meanwhile M. was writing novels. *Ni ange, ni bête* (1919; neither angel nor beast), written during World War I, was inferior to *Les silences du colonel Bramble*. Fortunately, three major novels followed. All dealt with marital problems: *Bernard Quesnay* (1926; *Bernard Quesnay*, 1927), is a story of love among industrialists; *Climats* (1928; *Atmosphere of Love*, 1929) relates the story of a man's two successive marriages; *L'instinct du bonheur* (1934; *A Time for Silence*, 1942) is his one truly happy novel. A later

novel, *Les roses de septembre* (1956; *September Roses*, 1958), is the story of an old man's loves.

These activities as novelist, biographer, and historian would have satisfied most men, but M. was a man of extraordinary energy. He also wrote short stories, short biographies, children's books, literary criticism, and science fiction. He was an indefatigable lecturer on the writer and his problems.

In 1929 he received an invitation from Princeton to teach there for a semester. Subsequently his interest in America never flagged. When France fell, he and his wife escaped to the U.S., where he lectured at University of Kansas City and Mills College. He joined the Book-of-the-Month Club jury, and his varied contacts resulted in books about America and in defense of France. He saw his role as a sort of bridge between France and the Anglo-Saxon cultures.

When M. returned to France after World War II, he helped in the reconstruction with tongue and pen. He was already a member of the French Academy (1939), but new honors came to him.

M.'s place in the pantheon of letters is not yet sure. As a novelist he competed with distinguished compeers. His histories, too, have an uncertain position. But as a biographer he is unsurpassed. His studies will long be consulted by specialists. He tried to do everything well. As he once said: "I am never satisfied to do a hasty or improvised job when asked to write or speak."

FURTHER WORKS: *Le général Bramble* (1918; *General Bramble*, 1922); *Les bourgeois de Witzheim* (1920); *Les discours du docteur O'Grady* (1922); *Dialogues sur le commandement* (1924; *Captains and Kings: Three Dialogues on Leadership*, 1925); *Arabesques* (1925); *Les Anglais* (1926); *Meipe* (1926; *Mape: The World of Illusion*, 1926); *Conseils à un jeune Français partant pour l'Angleterre* (1927); *La conversation* (1927; *Conversation*, 1930); *Petite histoire de l'espèce humaine* (1927); *Un essai sur Dickens* (1927; *Dickens*, 1935); *Études anglaises* (1927); *Le chapitre suivant* (1927; *The Next Chapter: The War against the Moon*, 1927); *Rouen* (1927); *Deux fragments d'une histoire universelle* (1928); *Aspects de la biographie* (1928; *Aspects of Biography*, 1929); *Voyage au pays des Articoles* (1928; *A Voyage to the Island of the Articoles*, 1929); *Contact* (1928); *Le pays des trente-six mille volontés* (1928; *The Country of Thirty-six Thousand Wishes*, 1930); *Fragments d'un journal de vacances* (1928); *Le côté de Chelsea* (1929; *The Chelsea Way; or, Marcel in England: A Proustian Parody*, 1930); *Relativisme* (1930); *Patapoufs et Filifers* (1930; *Fatapoufs and Thinifers*, 1940); *Sur le vif—L'exposition coloniale de Paris* (1931); *Tourgueniev* (1931); *Le peseur d'âmes* (1931; *The Weigher of Souls*, 1931); *L'Amérique inattendue* (1931); *Proust et Ruskin* (1932); *Le cercle de famille* (1932; *The Family Circle*, 1932); *L'Anglaise et d'autres femmes* (1932; *Ricochets: Miniature Tales of Human Life*, 1935); *Mes songes que voici* (1933); *Introduction à la méthode de Paul Valéry* (1933); *Chantiers américains* (1933); *Édouard VII et son temps* (1933; *The Edwardian Era*, 1933); *Sentiments et coutumes* (1934); *Voltaire* (1935; *Voltaire*, 1932); *Magiciens et logiciens* (1935; *Prophets and Poets*, 1935; enlarged ed. pub. as *Points of View*, 1968); *Premiers contes* (1935); *La machine à lire les pensées* (1937; *The Thought-Reading Machine*, 1938); *Un art de vivre* (1939; *The Art of Living*, 1940); *Discours de réception à l'Académie Française* (1939); *États-Unis 39* (1939); *Journal d'un voyage en Amérique* (1939); *Les origines de la guerre de 1939* (1939); *Tragédie en France* (1940; *Tragedy in France*, 1940); *Études littéraires* (2 vols., 1941–44); *Frédéric Chopin* (1942; *Frederic Chopin*, 1942); *Mémoires* (1942; *I Remember, I Remember*, 1942); *Cinq visages de l'amour* (1942; rev.

ed., *Sept visages de l'amour*, 1946; *Seven Faces of Love*, 1944); *Toujours l'inattendu arrive* (1943); *Espoirs et souvenirs* (1943); *Eisenhower* (1945; *Eisenhower, the Liberator*, 1945); *Franklin: La vie d'un optimiste* (1945; *Franklin: The Life of an Optimist*, 1945); *Terre promise* (1945; *Women without Love*, 1945); *Études américaines* (1945); *Washington* (1946; *Washington: The Life of a Patriot*, 1946); *États-Unis 46* (1946; *From My Journal*, 1948); *Journal d'un tour en Suisse* (1946); *Conseils à un jeune Français partant pour les États-Unis* (1947); *Retour en France* (1947); *Les mondes impossibles* (1947); *Quand la France s'enrichissait* (1947); *Rouen dévasté* (1947); *Journal d'un tour en Amérique Latine* (1948; *My Latin-American Diary*, 1953); *Alain* (1950); *Les nouveaux discours du docteur O'Grady* (1950; *The Return of Doctor O'Grady*, 1951); *Le dîner sous les marroniers* (1951); *Cours de bonheur conjugal* (1951; *The Art of Being Happily Married*, 1953); *Ce que je crois* (1951); *Destins exemplaires* (1952); *La vie de Cecil Rhodes* (1953; *Cecil Rhodes*, 1953); *Lettres à l'inconnue* (1953; *To an Unknown Lady*, 1957); *Portrait de la France et des Français* (1955); *Aux innocents les mains pleines* (1955); *Hollande* (1955); *Périgord* (1955); *Discours prononcé à l'Académie Française pour la réception de Jean Cocteau* (1955); *Robert et Elizabeth Browning* (1955); *Louis XIV à Versailles* (1955); *La France change de visage* (1956); *Lecture mon doux plaisir* (1957; *The Art of Writing*, 1960); *Dialogue des vivants* (1957); *Portrait d'un ami qui s'appelait moi* (1959); *Pour piano seul: Toutes les nouvelles d'A. M.* (1960); *Histoire parallèle: Histoire des États-Unis de 1917 à 1961* (4 vols., 1962, with Louis Aragon; also pub. as *Les deux géants: Histoire des États-Unis et de l'URSS de 1917 à nos jours*, 1962–64; *From the New Freedom to the New Frontier: A History of the United States from 1917 to the Present*, 1963); *De Proust à Camus* (1963; *From Proust to Camus: Profiles of French Writers*, 1966); *Choses nues* (1963); *Histoire d'Allemagne* (1965; *An Illustrated History of Germany*, 1966); *De Gide à Sartre* (1965); *Lettre ouverte à un jeune homme sur la conduite de la vie* (1965); *Au commencement était l'action* (1966); *Soixante ans de ma vie littéraire* (1966); *D'Aragon à Montherlant* (1967); *La conquête de l'Angleterre par les Normands* (1967); *Les illusions* (1968). FURTHER WORKS IN ENGLISH: *A Private Universe* (1932); *Women of Paris* (1955); *A M. Reader* (1949); *Collected Stories of A. M.* (1967)

BIBLIOGRAPHY: Droit, M., *A. M.* (1953); Suffel, J., *A. M.* (1963); Keating, L. C., *A. M.* (1965); Kolbert, J., "The Worlds of A. M.," *SUS,* 7 (1965): 215–30; Kolbert, J., "A. M.'s Esthetics of Biography," *BRMMLA,* 20 (1967): 45–51; Lemaitre, G., *M.: The Writer and His Work* (1968); *Exposition organisée à l'occasion du dixième anniversaire de la mort d'A. M.* (1977)

—L. CLARK KEATING

MAXIMIN, Daniel

Guadeloupean novelist, b. 1947, Point-à-Pitre

Born in Guadeloupe, M. received his university degree in education and went on to become a teacher, writer and literary critic. In the early part of his career M. worked closely with the journal *Présence Africaine*, the foremost literary journal of African and Caribbean writing. M.'s contributions to the journal were often critical studies of the writings of other black authors, and the

exposure such critical interrogation provided M. to such writings greatly influenced his own literary work.

M. first appeared as a force in Antigen literature in the early 1980s, with the publication of his first novel, *L'isole soleil* (1981; *Lone Sun*, 1989). This novel introduced many of the characters, events, and themes which would form the basis of his work. Presented as the writing of a novel within a novel, *L'isole soleil* has as its narrative frame the efforts of a young woman from Guadeloupe to document her family history from the 18th c. to the present day.

The epigraph of the novel presents Guadeloupe as an island of "four races, seven languages and dozens of bloods" and announces the narrative goal of the text—to simultaneously document the multiple threads of Guadeloupe's past and to weave those threads into a living present. This goal is achieved through the act of writing, which constitutes the internal narrative being composed by the character/narrator of Marie-Gabriel and the substance of the novel itself.

As noted, writing performs a double function in M.'s text, documenting the past and actualizing the present. The function of documentation is, itself, achieved through Marie-Gabriel's historical research, which is composed of her own, original writings, and of (real and fictive) journals, poems, proverbs, testimonies, songs, and biographies written by others. Thus, intertextuality plays a central role in *L'isole soleil*, drawing attention to the power of writing, by using already written texts to represent the past. Furthermore, this inclusion of other texts which range from French poetry to Creole proverbs functions as a concretization of the hybrid past which Marie-Gabriel attempts to retrace.

The second function of writing, that of actualizing the present, also occurs doubly in the text; Marie-Gabriel creates a new identity for herself through her recognition of the past, and M. promises a similar process of renewal for Guadeloupe itself. In this way M. aligns himself quite closely with the many other post-colonial writers and theorists who see language as the vehicle for self-actualization and agency, especially for those who have, until recently been denied both. What M. attempts to illustrate in *L'isole soleil* is, therefore, the ability of the individual and the nation to bring themselves into being by inscribing themselves into language. The double act of writing present in the text—the novel within a novel—is M.'s way of accomplishing this inscribing at both the fictional and actual levels.

M.'s second novel, *Sourfrières* (1987; Sulphur Mines), incorporates many of the same characters and concerns found in *L'isole soleil*. This novel, named for the active volcano found on Guadeloupe, also figures Marie-Gabriel as its central character, and also places the act of writing in a position of dominance within the text, repeating the gestures of hybridity and intertexuality found in M's earlier work. In many respects, the volcano, which becomes a character in the novel through its depiction in a fictional play entitled "The Dance of the Volcano Woman," embodies the gesture of speaking and writing the subject into existence which is presented thematically in *L'isole soleil*. The volcano's imminent eruption, present as a threat and promise from the beginning of the text, constitutes both the destruction of all structures and meanings that have been imposed upon the island, and the possibility of rebirth and renewal in the aftermath of such an effacement.

With this second novel, then, M. complicates the role of history in the building of a new Caribbean identity. He makes clear the fact that history, as it has been presented, is an imposed history, the history of the colonizer. Rebirth, therefore, must be predicated on the absolute erasure of this history, and the creation of a new one.

This gesture of eruption, which the novel links to revolution and political upheaval as well as enunciation, recalls the process of rebuilding history engaged in by Marie-Gabriel in *L'isole soleil*. Read together, these two novels elucidate M.'s position on the relation of past to present, and suggest that the true past of Guadeloupe must be built on the ashes of the imposed past—it must be created as part of the performance of the new identity of the island and its inhabitants.

M.'s third novel, *L'ile et une nuit* (1996; The Island and One Night) again centers on Marie-Gabriel is again, but in this work, she is more a presence or consciousness than a character. Like *Soufrières*, *L'ile et une nuit* is set against the force of an act of nature, this time a hurricane which sweeps across the island during one night destroying everything in its path. In many ways, M.'s third work is an extension of his second; the violence of the hurricane parallels that of the volcano, and the threat and promise of both forces are the same—the simultaneous effacement and rebirth of the identity of the island. However, this novel, in its refusal to conform, even at a superficial level, to the conventions of genre announces the literary parallel to the new cultural identity which M.'s two previous novels have explored.

The concerns of M.'s novels, concerns about language and history and the role of both in creating and sustaining identity, are central to the process of resistance in which Guadeloupe and nearly all former colonies have been engaged in recent years. The goal of such resistance is the absolute liberation of these former colonies from the political and symbolic domination imposed upon them for the past two centuries. M.'s novels present this act of resistance through their exploration of writing and history, and through their destruction of literary convention. Ultimately, M. seeks not only to advocate the creation of a new Guadeloupe, but to embody that creation.

BIBLIOGRAPHY: Taleb-Khyar, M. B., "*L'isole soleil* de D. M.: Une Écriture d'histoires, une histoire d'écritures," *Francofonia*, 22 (1992): 131-41; Scharfman, R., "Rewriting the Césaires: D. M.'s Caribbean Discourse," in Condé, M., ed., *L'Heritage de Caliban* (1992): 233-45; Yoder, L.W., "Developing Identity in the Caribbean: Writing about History in the Novels of D. M.," in Ryan-Ransom, H., ed., *Imagination, Emblems and Expressions: Essays on Latin American, Caribbean and Continental Culture and Identity* (1993): 109-25; Bongie, C., "The (Un)Exploded Volcano: Creolization and Intertextuality in the Novels of D. M.," *Callaloo*, 17 (1994): 627-42; Murdoch, H. A., "(Dis)Placing Marginality: Cultural Identity and Creole Resistance in Glissant and M.," *RAL*, 25 (1994): 81-101

—DAYNA L. OSCHERWITZ

MAYAKOVSKY, Vladimir Vladimirovich

Russian poet and dramatist, b. 19 July 1893, Bagdadi (now Mayakovsky), Georgia; d. 14 April 1930, Moscow

M., Soviet poet laureate and major revolutionary artist, was born the son of a forest ranger in Georgia. After the sudden death of his father in 1906, the family moved to Moscow, where M. became involved in the Bolshevik movement. By the age of sixteen the youth had been arrested three times for antitsarist activities. While serving five months of a prison term in solitary confinement, he began to write verses and decided to suspend Party work to pursue an education. With his talent for drawing, M. won entrance in 1910 to the Moscow School of Painting, Sculpture, and Architecture. Here he met the radical painter-poet David Burlyuk (1882–1967). With the support of Burlyuk, who first recognized M.'s poetic genius, M. plunged into a literary career in the ranks of the cubo-futurists (see FUTURISM). This group of highly inventive writers, with their avid interest in avant-garde painting, sought to free the arts from academic traditions. Their flamboyant public performances created scandals across Russia, and M.'s association with this artistic modernism led to his expulsion from the Moscow School. A leading member of the artistic avant-garde, M. lived the life of a café bohemian. When the Bolsheviks took power in Russia in 1917, he enthusiastically welcomed the event. The poet-rebel now sought to become a poet of revolution.

M.'s literary debut took place in the notorious futurist collection *Poshchechina po obshchestvennomu vkusu* (1912; a slap in the face of public taste), which contained the famous manifesto of the same title. Despite the massive quantity and diversity of the art that followed, M.'s work as a whole consistently describes a persona closely identifiable with the poet himself. His first separate publication took the emphatic title *Ya!* (1913; "I," 1933); in essence it is a four-part portrait in verse. Like all of M.'s poetry, *Ya!* is striking in its manipulation of imagery. Cosmic and religious motifs take an irreverent tumble as the pain of the persona parallels his vividly distorted vision of urban life. The year 1913 also marked the premiere of his first play, the "monodrama" *Vladimir Mayakovsky, Tragedia* (*Vladimir Mayakovsky, a Tragedy*, 1963), in which he performed the title role. The play, a summation of many motifs and ideas in M.'s early lyrics, highlights the recurrent theme of the poet-martyr.

Among the finest vehicles of M.'s persona are his long poems (*poemy*). The first was *Oblako v shtanakh* (1915; "The Cloud in Trousers," 1933)—one of several dedicated to Lily Brik (1891–1978), wife of the critic Osip Brik (1888–1945)—which offers a vivid exposé of the torment of unrequited love. The work is also significant for its juxtaposition of sharply intense personal emotions with revolutionary challenges to do away with the old love, art, society, and religion. The hyperbolic sensitivity characteristic of M.'s persona acquired a well-known form in the early long poem *Fleyta-pozvonochnik* (1915; "The Backbone Flute," 1960), and the theme of love merged with that of the stages of life in the long work *Lyublyu* (1922; "I Love," 1960). In *Voyna i mir* (1916; war and universe), a text interspersed with bars of music, the poet confronts the horrors of war with a glimpse of utopia. Conflict also arises in *Chelovek* (1916; "A Man," 1975), when the persona's persistent pull toward the future is countered by the forces of philistinism. The clichéd existence of everyday life (*byt*) is a constant enemy in M.'s world view and plays a major role in his superb long poem dedicated to love, *Pro eto* (1923; "About This," 1965).

M.'s art has a strong utilitarian dimension. During World War I he wrote a series of satirical "hymns" for the journal *Novy satirikon* and designed posters. After the 1917 revolution he sketched and captioned propaganda posters for ROSTA, the Russian telegraph agency. He wrote political verses, poem-marches, children's poetry, and commercial jingles for state enterprises. His *Misteria-buff* (1918; 2nd version, 1921; *Mystery-Bouffe*, 1933), considered the first Soviet play on a current topic, is a modern morality play that, in its parody of Noah's Ark, reveals the superiority of the "unclean" (the proletariat) over the "clean" (the bourgeoisie). Two later plays, the satires *Klop* (1928; *The Bedbug*, 1960) and *Banya* (1929; *The Bathhouse*, 1963) were banned temporarily because they dealt critically with bureaucratic corruption and hypocrisy in early Soviet Russia. The plays also bring on stage representatives of the communist future. M. wrote many topical poems for Soviet papers, and traveled to western Europe, the U.S., and Mexico and a Soviet representative. These trips resulted in a series of articles and poems.

A master of realized metaphor and unusual literary images, M. was also fascinated by the art of film. He wrote several film scenarios, and sequences in many of his poems recall film techniques. Along with imaginative use and choice of imagery, the originality of M.'s work lies in its wealth of verbal play, neologisms, innovative rhymes and rhythms. Linked in part to the declamatory "velvet bass" of his recitation methods, M.'s style reflects an effort to bring art closer to the content and cadences of normal speech. Peppering his texts with crude phrases, slogans, and advertisements of the day, he mixes rhythm patterns, regularly employs accentual verse, and heightens prosodic features with typesetting styles like the "short column" and "staircase" arrangements of verse lines on the page. His emphasis upon concrete images and rich sound textures lends a special tactile quality to his writing. While motifs of movement enhance the dynamism of his work, those of fire, water, and stars share the poetic field with heavy metals, weapons, and machines.

A sense of the monumental pervades M.'s poetry. It fills the emotions of his hulking persona and underlies his glorification of common Soviet citizens as well as his testimonial *Vladimir Ilyich Lenin* (1924; "Vladimir Ilyich Lenin [A Poem]," 1939). A pride equal to the epic event of the October Revolution evinced in *Khorosho!* (1927; "Good!," 1939) remains undiminished in a later poem dedicated to a Soviet passport, *Stikhi o sovetskom pasporte* (1930; "Soviet Passport," 1938). As part of the new symbolics, M. frequently engaged his lyric "I" with the concept of "we." For the long poem *150 000 000* (1921; partial tr., "150,000,000," 1949), the population figure of the Soviet state in 1919, an entire nation is claimed as the author of a poem. Yet the voice in the verse remains unmistakably M.'s. Audacious political agitator, irreverent destroyer of old myths, or delicate cloud in trousers, his poetic "I" stands ultimately alone in its own hyperbole. Like the title of his last, unfinished work, the poem *Vo ves golos* (1930; "At the Top of My Voice," 1940), the song of the poet approaches the tension of a cry.

M.'s career was surrounded by sharp controversy. As editor of the futurist journals *Lef* (1923–25) and *Novy lef* (1927–28) he was embroiled in debates over matters of formalism. In 1930 he abruptly joined the dominant proletarian writers organization RAPP. A few months later M., who had earlier condemned in verse, in "Sereyu Yeseninu" (1926; "To Sergei Yessenin," 1965), the suicide of the poet Sergey YESENIN, took his own life.

M. is a major writer of this century, and since 1935, when Stalin proclaimed indifference to M.'s works a crime, his place in Soviet literary history has been assured. Aspects of his work have been admired by other great Russian writers, such as Boris PASTERNAK, Anna AKHMATOVA, and Maxim GORKY. He has had a strong influence on later generations of Soviet poets, as well as on such foreign writers as Louis ARAGON and Pablo NERUDA.

FURTHER WORKS: *Kak delat stikhi?* (1926; *How Are Verses Made?*, 1970); *Moe Otkrytie Ameriki* (1926); *Ispania, Okean; Gavana; Meksita; Amerika* (1926); *Kon-ogon* (1928; *Timothy's Horse*, 1970); *Polnoe sobranie sochineny* (12 vols., 1934–38); *Polnoe sobranie sochineny* (12 vols., 1939–49); *Polnoe sobranie sochineny* (13 vols., 1955–61); *Novoe o M.* (1958); *M.—khudozhnik* (1963); *Izbrannye proizvedenia* (2 vols., 1963); *Sobranie sochineny* (8 vols., 1968); *Semya M. v pismakh* (1978); *Sochinenia* (3 vols., 1978); *Izbrannye sochinenia* (2 vols., 1982). FURTHER WORKS IN ENGLISH: *M. and His Poetry* (1945); *The Bedbug, and Selected Poetry* (1960); *M.* (1965); *The Complete Plays of V. M.* (1968); *Electric Iron* (1971); *V. M.: Poems* (1972); *Essays on Paris* (1975)

BIBLIOGRAPHY: Jakobson, R., "*On a Generation That Squandered Its Poets*" (1931), in Brown, E. J., ed., *Major Soviet Writers* (1973): 7–32; Bowra, C. M., "The Futurism of V. M.," *The Creative Experiment* (1949): 94–127; Muchnic, H., *From Gorky to Pasternak* (1961): 185–275; Humesky, A., *M. and His Neologisms* (1964); Stahlberger, L., *The Symbolic System of M.* (1964); Woroszylski, W., *The Life of M.* (1970); Shklovsky, V., *M. and His Circle* (1972); Brown, E. J., *M.: A Poet in the Revolution* (1973); Jangfeldt, B., *M. and Futurism*: 1917–1921 (1976); Miller, A., tr., *V. M.: Innovator* [collection of essays] (1976); Barooshian, V., *Brik and M.* (1978)

—JULIETTE R. STAPANIAN

MAYRÖCKER, Friederike

Austrian poet, prose writer, and dramatist, b. 20 Dec. 1924, Vienna

M. grew up in Vienna and first attended a business school. From 1942 to 1945 she was drafted as a helper in the Luftwaffe. At the same time she trained to be an English teacher. She served in this capacity from 1946 until 1969, when she became a full-time author. She began writing at an early age, and her first poems appeared in print in 1946. In 1954 she met the poet Ernst JANDL, and their friendship has provided many collaborations. She has been on several reading tours throughout Europe as well as the U.S. and Russia. She has won numerous prizes for her work, including the Theodor Körner Prize (1963), the Georg Trakl Prize for poetry (1977), and the Great Austrian State Prize (1982). She still resides in Vienna.

M. is perhaps the most consequential experimental writer living in Austria. At an early age, she was influenced by prewar avant-garde literary movements, especially SURREALISM, and her early texts from about 1944 to 1965 were thus somewhat simple and derivative. They were collected in her first important work, *Tod durch musen* (1966; death through muses). After this initial period of exploration M. went on to develop her own personal style. In such works as *Minimonsters traumlexikon* (1968; minimonster's dream dictionary), *Fantom fan* (1971; title in English), and *Je ein umwölkter gipfel* (1973; each a cloud-covered peak) she presented structural principles that she has applied quite consistently in all her remaining works. She begins with bits of personal remembrances, experiences, and feelings to which she adds other linguistic material collected from a variety of sources (and which she puts down through the years on pieces of paper). Her works consist of a grand collage of all of these elements, which she subjects to a series of permutations, repetitions, and other manipulations reminiscent of concrete poetry. The result is a text that does not easily fit into one of the standard genres, and which displays rich simultaneous interrelationships between dream and reality. As she further refined her style, recognizable characters began to appear, like in *Das licht in der landschaft* (1975; the light in the landscape) or *Fast ein frühling des markus m.* (1976; almost a spring of Markus M.), and one can discover some bits of narrative, but she has always steadfastly avoided the traditional devices of plot and character development.

In the late 1960s and 1970s, M. wrote a large number of radio plays. The most important works are the collection *Fünf mann menschen* (1971, with Ernst Jandl; five man humans), *Message comes* (1975; title in English), and *Schwarmgesang* (1978; swarm song). Like her other texts, these plays contain no recognizable plots or protagonists but instead explore the possibilities of acoustic and linguistic montage.

In the late 1970s and into the 1980s, a change became apparent in M.'s writing. Such works as *Heiligenanstalt* (1978; asylum for saints), *Die abschiede* (1980; farewells), *Reise durch die nacht* (1984; *Night Train*, 1992), and *Mein herz, mein zimmer, mein name* (1988; my heart, my room, my name) are less hermetic than the earlier works and have thus accounted for a new popularity and recognition among critics and readers. In addition, these works are permeated by a certain degree of sadness and lamentation. They discuss the themes of aging, deteriorating personal relationships, and identity crises centering on the profession of writing. Yet amidst the pessimism in these highly personal writings one can still discern a glimmer of hope.

M. is one of the most famous authors on the contemporary Austrian scene. While some of her works might be too opaque for many, she has been able in recent years to find a wide readership that shares with her the quest to maintain personal identity in an increasingly dehumanized mass society.

FURTHER WORKS: *Larifari* (1965); *Metaphorisch* (1965); *Texte* (1966); *Sägespäne für mein herzbluten* (1967); *Sinclair sofokles der babysaurier* (1971); *Arie auf tönernen füszen* (1972); *Blaue erleuchtungen* (1972); *In langsamen blitzen* (1974); *Augen wie schaljapin bevor er starb* (1974); *Meine träume ein flügelkleid* (1974); *Schriftungen: oder gerüchte aus dem jenseits* (1975); *Rot ist unten* (1977); *Heisze hunde* (1977); *Lütt' koch* (1978); *Ausgewählte gedichte 1944 1978* (1979); *Tochter der bahn* (1979); *Friederike mayröcker: ein lese buch* (1979); *Pegas das pferd* (1980); *Schwarze romanzen* (1981); *Treppen* (1981); *Bocca della verità* (1981); *Ich, der rabe und der mond* (1981); *Gute nacht, guten morgen: gedichte 1978–1981* (1982); *Im nervensaal* (1983); *Magische blätter* (1983); *Das anheben der arme bei feuersglut* (1984); *Rosengarten* (1985); *Das herzzerreißende der dinge* (1985); *Das jahr schnee* (1985); *Configurationem* (1985); *Winterglück: gedichte 1982–1986* (1986); *Der donner des stillhaltens* (1986); *Magische blätter II* (1987); *Blauer streusand* (1987); *Zittergaul* (1989); *Aus einem stein entsprungen: aus einem verwandtschaftshimmel* (1989); *Gesammelte prosa 1949–1975* (1989); *Magische blätter III* (1991)

BIBLIOGRAPHY: Acker, R., "Ernst Jandl and F. M.: A Study of Modulation and Crisis," *WLT* 55, 4 (Autumn 1981): 597–602; Bjorklund, B., "Radical Transformation and Magical Synthesis: Interview with F. M.," *LitR*, 25, 2 (Winter 1982): 222–28; special M. issue, *TuK*, 84 (October 1984); Schmidt, S., ed., *F. M.* (1984); Bjorklund, B., "The Modern Muse of F. M.'s Literary Production," in Daviau, D.G., ed., *Major Figures of Contemporary Austrian Literature* (1987): 313–36

—ROBERT ACKER

MCCARTHY, Cormac

American novelist, b. 20 July 1933, Providence, Rhode Island

Born Charles Joseph McCarthy, Jr., M. was reared in Knoxville, Tennessee, where he was first exposed to the people and places that occupy his earliest works. His family was stable and financially secure, especially compared to those in the rural areas of the region. He was raised a Roman Catholic, educated in Catholic Schools, entering the University of Tennessee in 1951. He left school in 1953 to join the U. S. Air Force, where he spent much time reading and studying. Returning to the university in 1957, he enrolled in Robert Daniel's fiction writing course. At the University of Tennessee he was awarded the Ingram-Merrill Award for creative writing. Two of his short stories—"Wake for Susan" (1959) and "A Drowning Incident" (1960)—were published in the university's literary magazine the *Phoenix*. He left the university to pursue a writing career without completing a degree just after beginning work on *The Orchard Keeper* (1965). Throughout his writing career, M. traveled extensively, taking a two-year tour of Europe between 1966 and 1968, living in Chicago, Knoxville, and settling in El Paso, Texas. He has received many scholarships and grants, including a Rockefeller Foundation Grant and a Guggenheim Fellowship. He received the National Book Award and the National Book Critics Circle Award for *All the Pretty Horses* (1992).

M.'s first novel, *The Orchard Keeper*, inaugurates the theme of psychic landscape, in which a main character's relationship to nature is deeply personal and interpretive. The novel main narrative centers on young John Wesley Rattner as he comes of age in the rugged mountains of eastern Tennessee. Two ancillary narrative strands involve: first, Marion Sylder, who kills John Wesley's brutal father and hides the body in an insecticide pit in a peach orchard; and second, Arthur Ownby, who discovers the body and keeps watch over it for seven years. The novel involves an artful merging of romantic and naturalist themes, suggesting that nature is primitive, dark, brutal, yet fragile and personally transformative. His second novel *Outer Dark* (1968) derives its title from Matthew 8:9-12, as Christ predicts that the faithless are destined to wander in outer darkness. The novel primarily involves two characters: Culla Holme and his sister Rinthy, who have incestuously conceived a child. Driven by shame, Culla abandons the child in the woods telling Rinthy that it died at birth. Within the typological context of Judeo-Christian mythology, Culla becomes the symbol of fallen humanity, a Cain figure, condemned to wander aimlessly in the outer darkness.

Child of God (1975), based upon an actual murder case in the Knoxville area, continues the theme isolation and abandonment, as does *Suttree* (1979), which deals with the same themes, similar characters, but on a much larger and more developed scale, anticipating finally the possibility of redemption. Many of M.'s works are driven by a preoccupation with the shaping influence of the past and are meticulously researched. This is particularly the case with *Blood Meridian; or, The Evening Redness in the West* (1985). This novel is a culmination of M.'s darkest vision of the human landscape. In a rare interview with Richard B. Woodward in the *New York Times Magazine*, M. said that "There's no such thing as life without bloodshed. . . . I think the notion that the species can be improved in some way, that everyone could live in harmony, is a really dangerous idea." *Blood Meridian* traces the scalp hunting expeditions of John Joel Glanton against the Apache Indians in 1849 and 1850. The narrative centers around a young dispossessed fourteen-year-old boy and his involvement with Glanton and the mysterious, intellectually sophisticated, and Satan-like Judge Holden. The boy becomes an accomplice in the brutality of the gang, struggles for years to redeem himself psychologically, and in a final scene that echoes Faust, the boy, now a man, gives into darkness as the Judge "gathered him in his arms against his immense and terrible flesh and shot the wooden bar latch home behind him."

This Manichean struggle between the forces of darkness and light, brutality and kindness, love and hate, order and disorder, inform all of M.'s works, and are balanced tenuously in the first two novels of M.'s border trilogy, *All the Pretty Horses* and *The Crossing* (1994). Both novels involve characters who journey into landscapes that are simultaneously geographical and psychic, objectively physical and intensely personal, landscapes that mirror in description the struggles of nomadic young characters in search of spiritual identity and meaning. All of M.'s works figure the landscape as character, as a kind of consciousness through which human beings come to understand themselves in the context of a fallen world. M.'s later works echo the possibilities first posited in *Suttree*, exploring the potential for redemption and the mysterious power of grace that may be found if searched for. M.'s novels are remarkable for their depth, complexity, narrative innovation, and artful use of language. They draw from and recontextualize the deepest and most resonant of Western literary and philosophical traditions. They are variously drawn from his experiences as a child roaming the rural regions of Tennessee, from his Catholic upbringing, and from his extensive reading in classical, English, and American literature. Critics and reviewers have continually noted in his works the influence of the Bible, Dante, Herman Melville, Mark Twain, Joseph CONRAD, and William FAULKNER. His novels on the surface display a dark sometimes bleak and unforgiving naturalism, and his characters are driven by internal and external forces that operate just beyond the realm of comprehension. But the allegorical dimension present in his works suggests a typological practice not dissimilar to American Puritans such as Cotton Mather and Jonathan Edwards, a practice in which the mysterious dynamics of grace and redemption provide order to a fallen often hellish world.

FURTHER WORKS: *The Stonemason: A Play in Five Acts* (1994)

BIBLIOGRAPHY: Luce, D., *Perspectives on C. M.* (1993); Bell V., *The Achievement of C. M.* (1988); Woodward, R. B., "Venomonus Fiction," *NYTM*, 19 Apr. 1992: 6, 28-29

—STEVEN FRYE

MCCARTHY, Mary

American novelist, short-story writer, and critic, b. 21 June 1912, Seattle, Wash.; d. 25 Oct. 1989, New York, N.Y.

Orphaned by the 1918 influenza epidemic, M. was raised successively by two sets of rich but austere grandparents, one Catholic and one Protestant. She attended Catholic, public, and Episcopal schools and graduated Phi Beta Kappa from Vassar College in 1933. She then worked as an editor and theater critic (for *Partisan Review*) and briefly taught English at two American women's colleges. She was married four times, the second time to literary critic Edmund WILSON, with whom she had her only child.

M.'s fiction, often described as witty, sophisticated, and savagely satiric, was distinguished by a relentlessly frank analysis of sexuality, political commitment, social pretense (especially in artists and intellectuals), and the effects of the modern world on people with middle-class values. Her first book, *The Company She Keeps* (1942), was a collection of loosely linked stories, some admittedly autobiographical, about a woman who decides to get a "fashionable" divorce, join a literary-political coterie, and go through analysis. *The Oasis* (1949) was a short novel about a well-meaning but incompetent utopian society of artists and intellectuals.

The Groves of Academe (1952) told of an incompetent liberal professor who spreads the rumor that a Joseph McCarthy-style of witch hunt is behind moves to dismiss him; other liberals support him (on political rather than academic grounds), and he remains while the college president is forced to resign—a satiric inversion of justice and freedom that questioned the authenticity of the liberals' integrity and intellectualism. In *A Charmed Life* (1955) the central character returns with a new husband to the artists' colony in which the novel is set, is seduced by her former husband, and dies en route to an abortionist; with little plot, this book contains long digressions on art and literature and ruthless dissections of character. *The Group* (1963), M.'s most famous work, concerns eight Vassar graduates of M.'s own class who find their lives in turmoil regarding sex, politics, and art.

Birds of America (1971) was M.'s only comic—albeit sharply satiric—novel; it was told by a youth whose mother refuses to accept modern conveniences, although she changes husbands and lifestyles with impunity. Gradually the boy's naïve beliefs—beliefs in people's innate goodness, in nature's benevolence, in truth itself—are shattered, and only after these abstractions are eliminated can he really understand his mother's lack of sympathy with "progress," for this kind of "progress," M. would have us believe, leads man to the same danger of extinction identified with the birds of the novel's title. *Cannibals and Missionaries* (1979), a topical work unlike any of M.'s earlier fiction, concerned a hijacked airliner and two groups of hostages, liberal human-rights activists and wealthy art collectors. Although tied-in to current events, this novel was not convincing as realistic political fiction because of M.'s confused handling of character relationships and responses to terrorism.

M.'s critical writing, by contrast, was consistently evocative of particular settings and concepts, whether this was in an autobiographical work, such as her fine *Memories of a Catholic Girlhood* (1957), her books on Venice and Florence, or her various theater essays. In more recent years she turned to political reportage, with short but brilliant analyses of Vietnam and Watergate.

M.'s strengths as a novelist are a cold, calculating eye for hypocrisy, a piercing, honest examination into motivation, a pervasive sense of wit and intelligence, and a fine style; her weaknesses include forced polemics, philosophical digressions, stereotyped, repetitive characters, and a poor sense of structure (especially in regard to the endings of her novels). These strengths and weaknesses combined make her nonfiction especially effective as topical commentary yet make her fiction often appear more like extended polemical, satiric, and philosophical exercises than like works concerned with plot, structure, and character.

FURTHER WORKS: *Sights and Spectacles: 1937–1956* (1956; repub. and expanded as *Sights and Spectacles: Theatre Chronicles 1937–1958* [1959] and *Theatre Chronicles 1937–1962* [1963]); *Venice Observed* (1956); *The Stones of Florence* (1959); *On the Contrary: Articles of Belief 1947–1961* (1961); *The Humanist in the Bathtub* (1964); *Vietnam* (1967); *Hanoi* (1968); *The Writing on the Wall and Other Literary Essays* (1970); *Medina* (1972); *The Mask of State: Watergate Portraits* (1974); *The Seventeenth Degree* (1974); *Can There Be a Gothic Literature?* (1975); *Cast a Cold Eye* (1978); *Ideas and the Novel* (1980); *The Hounds of Summer and Other Stories* (1981); *Occasional Prose* (1985); *How I Grew* (1987); *Never Too Old to Learn* (1988); *Conversations with M. M.* (1993); *Intellectual Memoirs: New York, 1936-1938* (1992); *Between Friends: The Correspondence of Hannah Arendt and M. M., 1949-1975*

BIBLIOGRAPHY: Niebuhr, E., "The Art of Fiction XXVII: M. M.," *Paris Review*, 27 (1962): 58–94; Schlueter, P., "The Dissections of M. M.," in Moore, H. T., ed., *Contemporary American Novelists* (1964): 54–64; Auchincloss, L., *Pioneers and Caretakers: A Study of Nine American Women Novelists* (1965): 170–86; Aldridge, J., *Time to Murder and Create: The Contemporary Novel in Crisis* (1966): 95–132; McKenzie, B., *M. M.* (1966); Grumbach, D., *The Company She Kept: A Revealing Portrait of M. M.* (1967); Stock, I., *M. M.* (1968); Widmer, E., "Finally a Lady: M. M.," in French, W., ed., *The Fifties* (1970): 93–102; Gelderman, C. W., *M. M.: A Life* (1988); Brightman, C., *Writing Dangerously: M. M. and Her World* (1992)

—PAUL SCHLUETER

MCCULLERS, Carson

American novelist, short-story writer, and dramatist, b. 19 Feb. 1917, Columbus, Ga.; d. 29 Sept. 1967, Nyack, N.Y.

M. was herself as peculiar and egocentric a person as any of her characters. An overindulgent mother encouraged her from her earliest years to behave exactly as she chose, and at the age of thirteen she was accustomed to hearing the catcall "freak!" from her schoolmates. In later years her determination to succeed as a writer and her bisexual proclivity so undermined her husband's self-esteem that he was driven to suicide, and M. refused not only to mourn her husband but even to pay the cost of having his ashes sent from France for interment in the U.S. In short, M. was an eccentric, self-centered woman, preoccupied with money, with literary success, and with the satisfaction of her own emotional needs. No one else was quite real to her.

But the failings of M.'s life were the material of her art, and all of her characters share her egocentricity and suffer the pangs of its attendant loneliness. Indeed, egocentricity and loneliness are facts of the human condition for them, not personal failings, and M.'s fiction has in consequence an air of stark, existential angst. Her view of the human condition is especially clear in her first novel, *The Heart Is a Lonely Hunter* (1940). The main character is a deaf-mute who receives uncomprehendingly the confidences of four characters who mistakenly think him sympathetic, and the deaf-mute in turn confides his heartaches to a man who is feeble-minded as well as mute, extending the line of meaningless communication. The novel is successful because its plain, grave style suits its rigid architecture, and because its characters touch the heart. M.'s second novel, *Reflections in a Golden Eye* (1941), is less successful. Its characters are Krafft-Ebing grotesques, clearly beyond M.'s ken, and its style tends toward the portentously abstract—a failing toward which M.'s work always tends, but more egregiously so in this novel than elsewhere.

The long story "The Ballad of the Sad Café" (1943) is M.'s most startling work. Its grotesqueries include a brooding, two-fisted Amazon, a hunchbacked confidence man, and a climactic wrestling match between the Amazon and her former husband. But the effect of the story is more archetypal than grotesque, for an anonymous narrator recounts the story in a folk idiom, and an *envoi* recasts the events of the story into vast, analogical terms. Many critics think it is M.'s finest work.

Yet *The Member of the Wedding* (1946) vies with "The Ballad of the Sad Café" for literary distinction. Its central character, Frankie Addams, is a motherless tomboy who decides to become a member of her brother's wedding in an attempt to be someone more than herself. Reality eventually compels her accommodation to selfhood, but not before a world of adolescent loneliness is laid out for the reader with bittersweet realism and marvelous delicacy. M. adapted this story for the stage at the suggestion of her friend Tennessee WILLIAMS, and the Broadway production of *The Member of the Wedding* had a successful run in 1950–51. It is considered today one of the outstanding adaptations from a novel in the history of the American theater. M. was not able to repeat the theatrical success of *Member* with her subsequent play, *The Square Root of Wonderful* (1956), however, and declining health made it impossible for her to maintain the quality of her earlier fiction in her final novel, *Clock without Hands* (1961).

M.'s work is often compared to that of Eudora WELTY, Flannery O'CONNOR, and Katherine Anne PORTER, somewhat to its disadvantage. M.'s artistry is less sophisticated than that of these other writers, to be sure, and her understanding of the dark corners of the mind is certainly less astute than theirs. But M.'s writing is distinguished from her fellow Southerners' work by an empathy for the disaffiliate so profound that she is his preeminent spokesman in modern American literature. No one has written more feelingly than she about the plight of the eccentric, and no one has written more understandingly than she about adolescent loneliness and desperation.

FURTHER WORKS: *The Ballad of the Sad Café: The Novels and Stories of C. M.* (1951); *Sweet as a Pickle and Clean as a Pig* (1964); *The Mortgaged Heart* (1972)

BIBLIOGRAPHY: Hassan, I., "C. M.: The Alchemy of Love and the Aesthetics of Pain," *MFS*, 5 (1959): 311–26; Evans, O., *The Ballad of C. M.* (1966); Edmonds, D., *C. M.* (1969); Graver, L., *C. M.*

(1969); Carr, V. S., *The Lonely Hunter: A Biography of C. M.* (1975); Cook, R. M., *C. M.* (1975); Kiernan, R. F., *Katherine Anne Porter and C. M.: A Reference Guide* (1976)

—ROBERT F. KIERNAN

MCGUANE, Thomas

American novelist, essayist, and screenwriter, b. 11 Dec. 1933, Wyandotte, Michigan

M. came from a working-class family, Irish in background and cultural heritage. In his youth, he spent time in the Northern Rockies and the Florida Keys, and from his unpretentious roots he developed a fondness for storytelling, humor, sports, and the outdoors. He earned his B.A. at Cranbrook, Michigan State University in 1962 and an M.F.A. from Yale School of Drama in 1965. He also studied under Wallace STEGNER in the creative writing program at Stanford University.

M.'s first novel, *The Sporting Club* (1969), is set in the mountains of northern Michigan. The novel explores the manners, behaviors, and the comic misadventures of a group of wealthy "sportsmen" and the society they form within the confines of their elaborate hunting and fishing lodge. The novel is satirical in nature and replete with references to Hemingway-type heroes, as these highly urbane, wealthy, would be "hunters" attempt to find meaning and identity in a world that seems to increasingly deny the possibility of traditional heroism. *The Bushwhacked Piano* (1971) and *Ninety-Two in the Shade* (1973) continue in the same satirical, irreverent, even farcical manner. All of these novels, though they are comical, betray a romantic reverence for the rejuvenative power of nature and the debilitative effects of urbanization.

Similar issues—the virtues of nature and landscape, the angst and confusion of postmodern culture—inform *Panama* (1972), a novel dealing with the dark decline of a rock musician; *Nobody's Angel* (1982), which is set in the cattle-country of Montana; *Something to Be Desired* (1985), a novel dealing with a Montana man searching for personal and financial security; *Keep the Change* (1989), which explores the life of an artist; and *Nothing But Blue Skies* (1992), a bleak but oddly comical story of a Montana real estate developer searching for a lost sense of personal identity. In *An Outside Chance* (1980) M. collects essays dealing with sports but in doing so grapples with abstract and sometimes mysterious philosophical concerns such as the role of human beings in relation to the wilderness, and the value of hunting as a means of integrating with nature. M. has also written a number of film scripts, including *Rancho Deluxe* (1974) and *The Missouri Breaks* (1976).

M.'s novels are noticeably contemporary in their irreverent and colloquial style, comic tone, and lean and terse use of language. These stylistic elements, however, mask the pervasive influence of Western literary traditions as well as a deep philosophical complexity. Comic irreverence clothes characters that confront a fragmented culture and a bleak and twisted world. M. is by no means an "academic" writer, and as such he cannot easily be classified as postmodern. But his works suggest a concern for the social, political, and personal affects of a culture devoid of clear and distinct cultural values and definitions. In M.'s novels a comic outlook offers one of the only possible opportunities for redemption. M.'s work in general attempts to provide context and meaning

Carson McCullers

to the apparent confusion of contemporary life in America. M. manages quite successfully merge the strong influence of a literary tradition with a preoccupation with the concerns of contemporary American culture. In form and style his works bear the mark of his extensive reading, which included writers such as Cervantes and Rabelais as well as later American novelists like Mark Twain and William FAULKNER. But his novels, rooted firmly in the novel of manners, deal primarily with late-20th c. concerns, especially the malaise and angst that plague many Americans from the 1960s forward. Not unlike Wallace Stegner, M. is often classified as a Western "regionalist," since his novels emphasize the importance of Western landscape and geography. But the personal dilemmas faced by his characters emerged from their failed attempt to establish roots. M.'s novels are remarkably intricate, personal, and psychological. But the individuals that people his stories are intimately linked with social context. The fragmentation of mainstream culture, the emergence of counterculture, the radicalization of politics, are major concerns in M.'s works.

BIBLIOGRAPHY: Klinkowitz, J., *The New American Novel of Manners: The Fiction of Richard Yates, Dan Wakefield, and T. M.* (1986); Morris, G. L., "How Ambivalence Won the West: T. M. and the Fiction of the New West," *Critique*, 32 (Spring 1991): 180-89; Westrum, D., *T. M.* (1992)

—STEVEN FRYE

Claude McKay

MCKAY, Claude

Jamaican-American poet, novelist, short-story writer, and journalist, b. 15 Sept. 1889, Sunny Ville, Jamaica; d. 22 May 1948, Chicago, Ill.

M. came from a petit-bourgeois agricultural family; his father claimed Ashanti origins, his mother, Madagascan. Both were Baptists, but M. was more strongly influenced by the rationalism of his brother, who was his teacher and guardian for some years, and of Walter Jekyll, a British expatriate writer who was his literary mentor and patron.

Undecided on a career, M. joined the Jamaica Constabulary in 1911 but gained release after a year upon the publication of poems first in the *Daily Gleaner* (Kingston) and then in two small volumes, *Songs of Jamaica* (1912) and *Constab Ballads* (1912), through the efforts of Jekyll. M. was hailed as the "Robert Burns of Jamaica," an undeserved sobriquet, since his work lacked the philosophical content of the Scot and M. himself deprecated dialect—which he henceforth rejected except for disparagement of characters.

In 1912 he left Jamaica forever, although it remained for him the main source of inspiration and a constant and Edenic frame of reference. Its many shortcomings he rigorously overlooked: as in the poem "North and South" (1920), Jamaica (and the other West Indian islands) represented the antithesis of the degeneration, impersonality, and racial antagonism of North American cities. Although he entered Tuskegee Institute and then Kansas State

College, he soon left both; he worked as railroad waiter between New York and Pittsburgh, and did odd jobs in Harlem before joining the leftist literary circles in New York. He was associate editor of *The Liberator*, but a contretemps over the paper's position on the race-versus-class issue precipitated his resignation. Meanwhile, his "If We Must Die" (1919), occasioned by the 1919 race riots in several American cities, had made M. the leading poet of the "black belt." His *Spring in New Hampshire* (1920) and *Harlem Shadows* (1922)—again suggesting the antithesis of country and city—established his position as a leader of the Harlem Renaissance.

In 1922 M. visited Russia and addressed the Third International. While there he produced two works both written in English, then translated into and published in Russian, and later retranslated into English: *Sudom lyncha* (1922; *Trial by Lynching*, 1977) and *Negry v Amerike* (1923; *The Negroes in America*, 1979). The first was M.'s initial volume of short fiction and developed themes that are to be found also in the poetry but more clearly in the subsequent prose: the horrendous treatment of black people in America, the uncertain role of the mulatto, and the "use" made of blacks.

The Negroes in America, a work of popular sociology that is really a superior form of journalism, indicated what the neo-Marxist M. thought his Russian hosts and readers would appreciate. It nonetheless contains many astute observations: M. suggested that the 1920s was the age of Negro art and race consciousness (some years before Alain Locke's [1886–1954] similar declaration); that race liberation and women's liberation are inextricable; that black and white workers must appreciate their common interests; that the black middle class can not be trusted with the black masses' welfare; that whites' fears of blacks' sexuality is psychologically revealing.

After his "magic pilgrimage" to Russia, M. drifted around Europe and North Africa. His *Home to Harlem* (1928), the first of a genre of realistic novels of urban black life written by a black, was a great success, although it was censured by W. E. B. DUBOIS for catering to the "prurient interests" of whites. M. responded that he was giving a realistic picture of black life.

In 1934 M. returned to the U.S., but his long absence and his recantation of his Communist beliefs distanced him from his former associates. *Banana Bottom* (1933), a nostalgic idyll of Jamaica, and *Gingertown* (1932), a collection of short stories, represented a retreat from proletarian, or "protest," literature and suggested that M. was writing for yet another audience. His conversion to Catholicism in 1945 further isolated him from his political and social origins.

In his last years he became a Catholic apologist, wrote *My Green Hills of Jamaica* (pub. 1980), and completed a large cycle of poems (all in the sonnet form that he most readily worked in), which remain unpublished, as do two unfinished and unsatisfactory novels.

The reputation of M. rests principally on *Selected Poems* (1953), which reprints the best work of his earlier volumes, excluding the dialect verse. Although he is associated now with the Harlem Renaissance, ironically he was abroad during the whole of that movement's vital decade.

FURTHER WORKS: *Banjo* (1929); *Harlem: Negro Metropolis* (1940)

BIBLIOGRAPHY: Gayle, A., Jr., *C. M.: The Black Poet at War* (1972); Cooper, W., ed., *The Passion of C. M.* (1972); Wagner, J.,

Black Poets of the United States (1972): 211–81; Giles, J. R., *C. M.* (1976); McLeod, A. L., "Memory and the Edenic Myth: C. M.'s *Green Hills of Jamaica*," *WLWE*, 18 (1979): 245–54; McLeod, A. L., "C. M.'s Adaptation to Audience," *Kunapipi*, 2, 1 (1980): 123–34

—A. L. MCLEOD

MCMURTRY, Larry

American novelist, essayist, and screenwriter, b. 3 June 1936, Wichita Falls, Tex.

Long regarded as an interesting and promising regional writer, M. has won both a solid reputation as a serious novelist and a wide popular audience for his work. He grew up on a ranch outside Archer City, Texas, where he listened to his uncle's and grandfather's tales of the Old West. Except for a semester at Stanford, he was educated in Texas, and he wrote his first four books while working as a college English instructor there. In 1970 he bought a rare-book store in Washington, D.C., and relocated. Since buying a ranch in Texas, M. divides his time between the two, with occasional trips to California; besides being an extremely prolific novelist, he is a book scout and a screenwriter.

M.'s first three novels are set in Texas and are preoccupied with the passing away of the Old West and its values; the protagonists, generally adolescents, struggle to find identities in an increasingly confusing and diminished world. Lonnie, the first-person narrator of *Horseman, Pass By* (1961), has to choose whether to model himself on his grandfather Homer, a cattle rancher and representative of pioneer virtue; his step-uncle Hud, a rake with few moral scruples, representative of the new Texas; or hired hand Jesse, a drifting cowboy. Torn between love of the land and the desire to escape, Lonnie also has to cope with emerging sexuality that has no outlet. In *Leaving Cheyenne* (1963), a story about a lifelong triangular love affair, told in first-person narratives by each of the protagonists, the two males escape for a while when they are young, but are drawn back to their home country by their attachment to the same woman—who marries someone else. Unlike the first two novels, *The Last Picture Show* (1966) is set in town, not the country, has an omniscient narrator, and is frequently satiric; again the adolescent protagonists must cope with loneliness, the desire to escape, often-frustrated sexuality, and mostly inadequate adults.

Critics interested in Southwestern fiction paid these books some attention, but even though all three were adapted as films—and two of the films were critical and popular successes—they did little to win M. wide recognition.

After writing directly about his ambivalence about Texas, present and past, in the collection of essays called *In a Narrow Grave* (1968), M. produced his "urban trilogy," three novels of contemporary Houston: *Moving On* (1970), *All My Friends Are Going To Be Strangers* (1972), and *Terms of Endearment* (1975). All three have young adult protagonists who seek fulfillment in marriage and love affairs without finding much. These novels are less tightly structured than M.'s early work, perhaps reflecting the characters' deracinated lives. Critics generally faulted the shapelessness while continuing to praise M.'s sense of place, his characterization, and his dialogue.

In 1975 M. announced his intention to abandon Texas as a setting for his fiction, and he did so in his next three novels: *Somebody's Darling* (1978), set in Hollywood, *Cadillac Jack* (1982), set in Washington, D.C., and *The Desert Rose* (1983), set in Las Vegas. These novels have more protagonists who are mature in years—if not in feelings—than the early work, and the characters have to grapple with partings and endings, of friendships, love affairs, and careers.

M.'s next novel, *Lonesome Dove* (1985), is a great American Western, the book that finally made M. famous, garnering universally favorable reviews, smashing popular success, and a Pulitzer Prize. Like M.'s early fiction, *Lonesome Dove* contains tension between nostalgia and antinostalgia. The main characters are both touchingly vulnerable human beings and larger-than-life heroes—and heroines—in their ability to cope with adversities like snakes, hail storms, life in a sod hut, kidnaping by Indians, and the U.S. Cavalry. The main plot is classically Western, a cattle drive from Texas to Montana undertaken by two ex-Texas Rangers who have made their state too civilized to have any use for them. However, neither protagonist is sure of the ultimate point of the journey. There are no climactic confrontations between good and evil, no satisfactory resolutions for any of the lovers, and finally no sense that the heroes' exploits will even be remembered very long. A number of the most engaging characters die, to be buried in shallow graves with fragile wooden signs. The tension between romance and antiromance helps make *Lonesome Dove* M.'s most richly satisfying book to date. Its commercial success—enhanced by its adaptation as a television miniseries in 1989–has ensured all of M.'s subsequent work a place on the best-seller list.

Since *Lonesome Dove*, M. has followed a pattern of alternating novels of the new and old West. In the contemporary Texas novels, he chronicles the middle age of characters from his earlier fiction: the protagonists of *The Last Picture Show* in *Texasville* (1987), Danny Deck from *All My Friends* in *Some Can Whistle* (1989). While the first book is comic, the second finally tragic, both are loosely structured, both explore random, senseless violence, both are sympathetic to the characters' efforts to connect to one another, and both are rich in detail—often satiric—about contemporary Texas. The novels of the Old West, *Anything for Billy* (1988) and *Buffalo Girls* (1990), are much less romantic than *Lonesome Dove*, although each features a "legendary" Western character, Billy the Kid and Calamity Jane respectively. M.'s Billy is a sad kid with a character disorder, and he's not even a good shot. M.'s Calamity is an engaging survivor, but falling into alcoholism and making up stories about her past, including a nonexistent love affair with Wild Bill Hickock and an imaginary daughter. Perhaps the most interesting theme in both novels is M.'s speculation about how the West of legend was created. The narrator of *Anything for Billy* is a dime novelist from Philadelphia, intent on writing Billy's life, whose prior fiction is almost all fabrication. Calamity has also been approached by a dime novelist; more importantly, she goes to London with Buffalo Bill's show, which misrepresents the frontier even as that frontier is passing away. All four of these novels achieved respectful reviews and some popular success, though none generated as much enthusiasm as *Lonesome Dove*.

M. has achieved solid popularity among general readers and wide attention from reviewers. His reputation as a serious American—not just regional—novelist is growing. M.'s sense of place, of regional details, and of speech patterns and character types may still be most acutely accurate when he writes about Texas and the

West. M.'s themes—how we can know the past and measure the present against it, how men and women and parents and children and friends can connect to one another, how people cope with change and loss in an indifferent and randomly violent world— are universal.

FURTHER WORKS: *Film Flam: Essays on Hollywood* (1987); *The Evening Star* (1992)

BIBLIOGRAPHY: Peavy, C. D., "A. L. M. Bibliography," *WAL*, 3 (1968): 235–48; Landess, T., *L. M.* (1969); Crooks, A. F., "L. M.— A Writer in Transition," *WAL*, 7 (1972): 151–55; Schmidt, D., ed., *L. M.: Unredeemed Dreams* (1978; 2nd ed., 1981); Ahearn, K., "L. M.," in Erisman, F., and Etulain, R. W., eds., *Fifty Western Writers: A Bio-bibliographical Sourcebook* (1982): 280–90; Rafferty, T., "The Last Fiction Show," *The New Yorker* (15 June 1987): 91–94; Adams, R. M., "The Bard of Wichita Falls," *NYRB* (13 Aug. 1987): 39–41

—SARAH ENGLISH

MCNALLY, Terrence

American dramatist and screenwriter, b. 3 Nov. 1939, St. Petersburg, Florida

M. credits Elaine May with demonstrating to him that behavior, not dialogue, is the dramatist's essential task. That knowledge, plus his experiences as a journalist, an actor, and a stage manager at the famed Actors Studio, has contributed to M.'s successful career writing for Broadway. He has won Tony Awards for the book of *Kiss of the Spider Woman* (1993) and *Ragtime* (1998), an Obie and a Dramatists Guild Hull Warriner Award for *Bad Habits* (1974), and an Emmy Award for *Andre's Mother* (1995). He has also won two Guggenheim Fellowships, a citation from the American Academy of Arts and Letters, a William Inge Award, and a Rockefeller Grant. He has taught playwriting at Julliard and is vice president of the Dramatists Guild.

Music is an essential element of M.'s work, not only as background and atmosphere but also as an integral component of the play's construction. Obviously in such plays as *Master Class* (1995) about diva Maria Callas, the plot revolves around music as she works with students and shares her talent. But more, the play uses music as an entree to art in general, a way of speaking to the necessity for art as a means of dealing with emotion, as a mode for expressing personal vision. It is also a treatise on the consequences to those who dare to achieve the greatest heights in art.

In other works music becomes the source for shared meanings, for the common ground of experience. The actor's speeches take on the musical forms of arias, duets, sonatas, even marches, and flow in legatos or startle in staccatos. The dialogue and the structure has a rhythm; the movements between actors take on the appearance of dance as they come together, move apart, and carefully circle, as in *Frankie and Johnny in the Clair de Lune* (1987). Certainly this devotion to melodic elements has led to M.'s success in writing the librettos for *The Rink* (1985), *Kiss of the Spider Woman*, and *Ragtime*.

Death is frequently the motivating factor in M.'s plays—the reason for writing as well as the reason for character behavior.

AIDS has been the shadow behind much of M.'s work, if not an actual factor of the action. In *A Perfect Ganesh* (1993) the death of sons becomes the death of the soul for two women until they face troubling truths about the nature of prejudice and learn to live with them. Katherine and Margaret are confronted with death on the massive scale of human misery, putting their individual losses into perspective.

Perhaps M.'s most popular work is *The Ritz* (1976), a madcap romp through a New York bathhouse. The homosexuality that M. feels is impossible to ignore in modern writing is here of the "in-your-face" variety. The emphasis on physical buffoonery is unusual in M.'s work, with near misses, mistaken identities, cross-dressing, and chase scenes.

It's Only a Play (1986) is a satiric look at show business in which the practice of theater reviewing with its make-or-break impact is pilloried. However, even though the focus is the critic, the pettiness of the characters representing actors, directors, and dramatists is an important element of the play. Even those not intimately acquainted with the theater and its workings can find amusement here with the names of stage icons bandied about as the subject of insider gossip.

M. writes sophisticated works that provoke self-awareness and social reflection. He is a master of technique, using a variety of structures that keep his work vital and absorbing. His appreciation and knowledge of the classics in music and literature shine through to enrich each piece. In all his plays one theme is constant, even amid the humor—humans long for intimacy yet erect barriers to discourage it. M. demonstrates the destructiveness of those barriers, encouraging his audiences to break them down.

FURTHER WORKS: *Next* (1968); *Tour* (1968); *Botticelli* (1968); *Sweet Eros* (1969); *Cuba Si!* (1969); *Witness* (1969); *Noon* (1969); *Last Gasps* (1970); *Bringing It All Back Home* (1970); *Where Has Tommy Flowers Gone?* (1972); *Whiskey* (1973); *The Lisbon Traviata* (1986); *Lips Together, Teeth Apart* (1992); *Love! Valour! Compassion!* (1995); *Corpus Christi* (1998)

BIBLIOGRAPHY: DiGaetani, J. L., *A Search for a Postmodern Theater: Interviews with Contemporary Playwrights* (1991); Corliss, R., "Success is His Best Revenge," *Time*, 23 August 1993: 73; Bryer, J. R., ed., *The Playwright's Art: Conversations with Contemporary American Dramatists* (1995); Kolin, P. C., and Kullman, C. H., eds., *Speaking on Stage: Interviews with Contemporary American Playwrights* (1996); Zinman, T. S., ed., *T. M.: A Casebook* (1997)

—BEVERLY BRONSEN SMITH

MCPHERSON, James A(lan)

American short-story writer, b. 16 Sept. 1943, Savannah, Georgia

M. is one of the most notable African-American writers to come into prominence during the late 1960s and throughout the 1970s. He is without doubt one of the most accomplished short-story writers in contemporary American literature. His early collection, *Hue and Cry* (1969), garnered the highest critical acclaim and won him the *Atlantic Monthly* "Firsts Award" in 1969, a National

Institute of Arts and Letters Grant, and a Rockefeller Grant in 1970. His stories also won him a Guggenheim Fellowship in 1972. His second collection of stories, *Elbow Room* (1977), earned him the Pulitzer Prize in 1977, along with a prestigious MacArthur Foundation Award in 1981.

Many of the stories in *Hue and Cry* are autobiographical and reflect incidents from his childhood, adolescence, and early adulthood. "A Matter of Vocabulary" comes out of his own boyhood experience as a potato bagger in a supermarket in Savannah, Georgia, a skill he likens to learning the craft of fiction: "Putting things together in just the right combination" became "an education in literary form." He transformed his later experience working on the railroad into "On Trains" and one of his most poignant novellas, "A Solo Song: For Doc." "Gold Coast," the first story he published in the *Atlantic Monthly* in 1968, came out of an actual job he had as a janitor in an apartment building in Cambridge, Massachusetts. His sympathetic portrayal of the wrecked lives of the alcoholic custodian, Mr. Sullivan, and his demented wife, established M. as a writer of deep emotional and psychological dimensions. Many of the stories in *Hue and Cry* document the lives of isolated and deeply lonely people: loneliness also became a major theme in many of his later stories in *Elbow Room*.

"All the Lonely People" deals with problems of self-identity as the main character struggles with what may be his latent homosexual feelings, a theme that Jerry, in the title story, must also eventually face. Though racism runs throughout most of the stories, it rarely becomes their main focus. M. includes it as a crucial element of most of the stories in *Hue and Cry*, but focuses on the common "human" difficulties that members of both races share within the context of a racist, sexist, and homophobic society. Much of the violence in these stories comes from characters unable to articulate the disturbing ambiguity of their own feelings about sexuality, race, and injustice.

Elbow Room is generally less pessimistic than *Hue and Cry*, though their themes are identical. Although more irony and humor appear in these stories, there is also a greater emotional and psychological range in their portrayal of character. "The Story of a Dead Man" delineates the roguish peccadillos of Billy Renfro, but he could just as well be white, Italian, or Chicano. However, M. unapologetically includes, as few writers do, the determining influences of his characters' geographical and cultural backgrounds. He leaves it to the reader to decide how crucial those influences may or may not be. Several stories in this collection deal with the older generations' inability or unwillingness to change. "The Faithful" shows Reverend John Butler, also a barber, refusing to learn new techniques of barbering and preaching and, thus, losing both his customers and his congregation. The last two stories in *Elbow Room*—"A Sense of Story" and the title story—deal with postmodern topics such as the necessary fictions that people need to tolerate the suffering in their lives and the overwhelming racial injustice that makes the lives of both African Americans and bigoted whites unbearably complicated and agonizing.

M.'s stories also show evidence of a keenly perceptive legalistic mind, since he also graduated from Harvard Law School in 1968. "The Act of Prostitution," "Problems of Art," and "A Sense of Story" concern the lives of lawyers and judges and brilliantly demonstrates how the law regularly fails those who often need it most. Indeed, the title of *Hue and Cry* comes from a book about the history of English law and alludes to the "hue and cry" that should publicly be raised after a felony is committed. M. later earned an

M.F.A. degree from the University of Iowa, where he taught not only creative writing but also in that school's law school. Some of the violence he witnessed in the African-American communities he lived in become subject matter for some of his more remarkable stories, such as "The Story of a Scar" and the almost surrealist slapstick elements of "The Silver Bullet."

M. has been criticized by some groups of African-American literary critics because he has not defined his racial themes as forcefully as such writers as Alice WALKER or Toni MORRISON. His work does not highlight the distinctive characteristics of the black experience. He claimed, in speaking of *Hue and Cry*, that "this collection of stories can be read as a book about people: old, young, lonely, homosexual, confused, used, discarded, wronged. As a matter of fact, certain of these people happen to be black, and certain of them happen to be white; but I have tried to keep the color part of most of them far in the background, where these things should rightly be kept."

There were expectations that M. would someday finish a novel he had reportedly been working on since the late 1970s, and critics were surprised when his highly acclaimed memoir entitled *Crabcakes* appeared in 1998. *Crabcakes* is not only his favorite food but became his version of Proust's madeleine cake, the taste of which opens the floodgates of his past, the actual subject of *Crabcakes*. The structure of the memoir is also Proustian insofar as it rejects a linear time frame and is built, rather, on a serial format. Each section is both a recollection and a meditation on the significance of that memory. M. does not follow a temporal plot line but, rather, mixes past and present according to the spiritual importance of certain epiphanic moments. He intermixes words and expressions from Latin, French, Italian, and Japanese with their English equivalents, discovering that sometimes there is no exact equivalent, for instance, for the Latin word "communitas" in English. The sections of the book are not numbered and become, at times, linguistic exercises in learning how English is incapable of expressing certain abstract spiritual realities. M.'s experiences in Japan and its language convince him that much of human "reality" is a linguistic one, and that perception in unavoidably conditioned by language itself. Though the task is often overwhelming, M.'s continuous and devoted task is to create some kind of meaningful connection between and among human beings of all races.

FURTHER WORKS: *Railroad: Trains and Train People in American Culture* (1976)

BIBLIOGRAPHY: Wallace, J., "The Politics of Style in Three Stories by J. A. M.," *MFS*, 34 (Spring 1988): 17-26; Beavers, H., *Wrestling Angels into Song: The Fictions of Ernest J. Gaines and J. A. M.* (1996)

—PATRICK MEANOR

MECKEL, Christoph

German poet and novelist, b. 12 June 1935, Berlin

M. is one of the most prolific and versatile writers of the postwar generation, comparable to Günter GRASS. The son of the poet and theater critic Eberhard Meckel (1907–1969), M. went to school in Freiburg, Munich, and Paris with the aim of becoming a graphic artist. Afterward, he traveled widely, and lived in Berlin, Provence, Africa, southern Europe, and Mexico, and taught German literature at Oberlin College, Ohio University, and the University of Texas.

M. chronicled his education as a visual artist and as a traveler in an autobiographical essay, *Bericht zur Entstehung einer Weltkomödie* (1985; account of the evolution of a world comedy). In the late 1950s, M. published several surrealist poetry collections, and received eight literary prizes between 1958 and 1974. His poetry collection *Wildnisse* (1962; wildernesses) evokes apocalyptic visions influenced by Goya and Bosch. The trilogy of poems *Säure* (1979; acid), *Souterrain* (1984; basement), and *Anzahlung auf ein Glas Wasser* (forthcoming; down payment on a glass of water) describes cyclical troubles in a love relationship. The main character of the short novel *Tullipan* (1965; tullipan) embodies the genesis of the writing process for M.: A fantastical personage enters the author's study and claims his attention. This motif is continued in the short novel *Die Gestalt am Ende des Grundstücks* (1975; *The Figure on the Boundary Line*, 1983), in which a vagrant appears at a Mexican villa, where the author is an invited guest, then gradually draws the author into a friendship until he adopts his way of life and disappears with him over the boundary line of the property, of what is knowable. The novel *Licht* (1978; light) analyzes a male-female love relationship that begins to dissolve and thematizes deception and self-deception and the importance of memory for overcoming disaster. One of M.'s strongest works is the novel *Suchbild* (1981; visual puzzle), which is an accounting of the writer father's involvement with Nazi ideology. It represents one of the best examples of the spate of postwar German novels of generational conflict as they appeared in the mid-to late 1970s.

The fantasy novels *Der wahre Muftoni* (1982; the real Muftoni) and *Plunder* (1986; junk) are playful fairy tales about objects and actions that resist integration into a society ruled by materialism. The short biography *Sieben Blätter für Monsieur Bernstein* (1986; seven prints for Monsieur Bernstein) tells of the author's encounter and eventual friendship with a Holocaust survivor in southern France. M.'s drawings attempt to express with a childlike simplicity the horror of the Nazi concentration camps, while his writing tries to commemorate the victim's suffering.

M. celebrates the redemptive power of imagination and memory, and combines a high level of realistic description with fantastical writing that attempts to subvert the ordered universe of time and space.

FURTHER WORKS: *Tarnkappe* (1956); *Hotel für Schlafwandler* (1958); *Nebelhörner* (1959); *Moë* (1959); *Manifest der Toten* (1960); *Im Land der Umbramauten* (1961); *Die Noticen des Feuerwerkers Christopher Magalan* (1966); *Der glückliche Magier* (1967); *Der Wind, der dich weckt, der Wind im Garten* (1967); *Bei Lebzeiten singen* (1967); *Die Balladen des Thomas Balkan* (1969); *Eine Seite aus dem Paradiesbuch* (1969); *Werkauswahl* (1970); *Lieder aus dem Dreckloch* (1972); *Tunifers Erinnerungen* (1980)

BIBLIOGRAPHY: Middleton, C., "A New Visual and Poetic Fantasy," *TLS* (28 April 1961): 269; Brackert-Rausch, G., "C. M." in Nonnenmann, K., ed., *Schriftsteller der Gegenwart* (1963): 221–27; Maier, W., "C. M.,"*Leserzeitschrift*, 4 (1963): 12–15; Segebrecht, W., "C. M.s Erfindungen," *Merkur* 20 (1966): 80–85; Segebrecht, W., "C. M. als Erzähler," *Der glückliche Magier* (1967): 7–25; Reinig, C., "C. M." in Kunisch, H., ed., *Handbuch der deutschen Gegenwartsliteratur* 64–65 (1970)

—HELGA DRUXES

MEGGED, Aharon

Israeli novelist, short-story writer, and dramatist, b. 18 Aug. 1920, Wolozabek, Poland

M. emigrated to Palestine with his parents as a child in 1926, and, except for periods of service abroad, has always lived in Palestine (later Israel). He early established himself as a journalist and editor, started writing children's stories in the 1940s, and published his first collection of stories for adults, *Ruah yamim* (spirit of the times), in 1950. Since then, he has produced a regular succession of plays, stories, and novels, increasingly favoring this last genre.

From his first novel, *Hedva vaaniy* (1954; Hedva and me), M.'s work has been concerned with the social fabric of the emergent Israeli society, seeing how quickly pioneering idealism has turned sour. In this work, town is contrasted with country, in the guise of Tel Aviv vis-à-vis the kibbutz. The naive young people from the collective settlement are converted by their parents and parents-in-law into the grasping and vacuous materialists now populating the young State of Israel. The form adopted is the early picaresque novel, and the context is the social satire appropriate to the form. M. conscripts an allusive, literary language replete with echoes and phrases from the classical literature. Although the story is presented as a first person narrative, as conveyed by the simple but harassed Shlormik, the tone adopted is that of the ironic observer.

M.'s social satire was to deepen into bitter parody, Kafkaesque SURREALISM, and, as in his recent work, notably in *Foiglman* (1987; Foiglman), into desperate nostalgia. The novels are well made, typically reserving the principal elements in the denouement to the finale, as in a detective story. The narrator's stance continues to be that of marginal individual, of observer, specifically the observer of modern Israel and the current Jewish situation, reduced to functional paralysis. Sometimes the brilliance of the metaphor is sustained throughout the course of the novel, as in *Hahay al hamet* (1965; *The Living on the Dead*, 1970), where the narrator is used for failure to comply with the terms of his contract and produce a biography. It is he who is living on the dead (as a biographer), but he is also unable to flourish in his vocation as a writer until his name has been cleared. He can not produce the work, as the biographee has disappointed him, in that his mythical life has proven a lie. But neither can he yet move on to something else, as this is all that he has to feed on, at the moment.

The preeminent theme in this prolific output is disappointed idealism. The fate of the narrator is linked to the national fate. In *Foiglman* the death of the eponymous central figure represents, for the narrator, the death of the people (or of Yiddish or of the diaspora); something more is happening than the specific event, in its implications and suggestion. Like the hero of *Hahay al hamet*, the narrator here. Professor Zvi Arbel, is not sure that he will be able to proceed with his historical research (here, on Petluria) and bring it to a conclusion. For all the humor and zest of the writing, M.'s book seems to comprise a dirge, an act of mourning for a nation.

M.'s writing continually recognizes the compulsiveness in the act of writing, long after the rational justification for the word seems to have departed. M.'s heroes are always acting against their better, or their rational judgment and rather in accordance with some inner force. The narrator in *Foiglman* continues to pursue the Yiddish poet, into and beyond the grave. The detached observer finds himself plunged into commitment.

FURTHER WORKS: *Yisrael haverim* (1956); *Miqreh haksil* (1959; *Fortunes of a Fool*, 1962); *Habrihah* (1962); *Hahayim haqzarim;* (1972; *The Short Life*, 1980); *Haatalef* (1975); *Heinz uvno veharuah haroah* (1976); *Asahel* (1978; *Asahel*, 1982); *Masa beav* (1980); *Hagamal hameofef vedabeshet hazahav* (1982); *Yom haor shel anat* (1992); *Gaaguim leolga* (1994); *Avel* (1996)

BIBLIOGRAPHY: Yudkin, L. I., *Escape into Siege: A Survey of Israeli Literature Today* (1974): 173–74; Feinberg, A., "An Interview with A. M." *MHL*, 8: 3–4 (Spring-Summer 1983): 46–52; Lotau, Y., "Sweet Revenge," *MHL*, 9: 3–4 (Spring-Summer 1984): 67–68

—LEON I. YUDKIN

MEHREN, Stein

Norwegian poet, essayist, dramatist, and novelist, b. 16 May 1935, Oslo

M. is one of Norway's strongest lyrical talents of recent times. His university studies in philosophy and biology, combined with his position as secretary to an art collector, have contributed to the high intellectual awareness and logical consistency of his work, while his experience as a ski instructor and guide have strengthened his love of nature and his feeling for the concrete image.

M.'s many poems have a resonance, beauty, and poetic magic that carry the reader along even when interpretation becomes difficult. A lover of words and ideas, he has attempted to go his own way to find his view of life and the human being. Longing for the inexpressible, for childhood, and for direct experience is joined in his poetry with philosophical reflections on the situation of modern man.

In *Gjennom stillheten en natt* (1960; through the silence one night) M. created bold comparisons and nature images while revealing feelings of unrest, alienation, and unreality. He has also always been preoccupied with problems of language. In *Hildring i speil* (1961; reflected illusion), he shows how language not only distorts experience but also creates expectations that life cannot fulfill.

In his subsequent poetic works, M.'s field expands to include all of European tradition. With daring linguistic inventiveness, he attacks all forms of prejudice and false assumptions in modern society, everything that makes the human being alien to himself and the world.

M.'s essays, which deal with modern isolation, neurosis, and fear, but which also emphasize the positive virtues of nature and love, parallel his lyrics. In *Aurora, det niende mørke* (1971; Aurora, the ninth darkness) and *Kongespillet* (1971; the royal game) M. mixes poems, essays, and aphorisms to show a romantic preference for a mythical explanation of the world and a mythical path to wisdom and at the same time to oppose the modern tendency toward the demythologizing of society.

M.'s novels deal with people's struggles to find their way through modern ideological difficulties. Both *De utydelige* (1972; the vague ones) and *Titanene* (1974; the titans) deal with the same three intellectuals from Oslo and their attempts to avoid the pitfalls of fixed ways of thinking. For M., ideologies are modern illusions that lead people away from themselves and their fellow men. One must seek freedom and self-awareness by going one's own way.

M.'s drama *Narren og hans hertug* (1968; the fool and his duke) deals with an actual historical revolt of the 1400s but seeks timeless psychological and political insights into the phenomenon of revolt in general. Idealism, immaturity, and ineffectiveness are reflected in the fool, Fastelan, who leads the revolt, and in the people, while the leaders, who hold fast to power in spite of momentary urges to allow justice to hold sway, symbolize the sophistication of power.

All of M.'s works are meant to give strength and freedom—to the reader, to his characters, and to himself—to break the grip of the times on us, and to save our deepest thoughts from destruction by the modern world.

FURTHER WORKS: *Alene med en himmel* (1962); *Mot en verden av lys* (1963); *Gobelin Europa* (1965); *Tids alder* (1966); *Vind runer* (1967); *Maskinen og menneskekroppen: En pastorale* (1970); *Veier til et bilde* (1971); *Den store frigjøring* (1973); *Dikt for enhver som våger* (1973); *Kunstens vilkår og den nye puritanismen* (1974); *En rytter til fots* (1975); *Menneske bære ditt bilde frem* (1975); *Den store søndagsfrokosten* (1976); *Det opprinnelige landskapet* (1976); *Det trettende stjernebilde* (1977); *Myten og den irrasjonelle fornuft* (2 vols., 1977–1980); *Vintersolhverv* (1979); *50 60 70 80* (1980)

BIBLIOGRAPHY: Naess, H., "S. M.: Dialectic Poet of Light and Dreams," *BA*, 47 (1973): 66–69

—WALTER D. MORRIS

MEHRING, Walter

German poet, satirist, novelist, essayist, and dramatist, b. 29 April 1896, Berlin; d. 3 Oct. 1981, Zurich, Switzerland

After being expelled from secondary school for "unpatriotic conduct," M. studied art history and in 1916 published his first poems in the EXPRESSIONIST journal *Der Sturm*. He was one of the founders of the Berlin DADA movement, and in the early days of the Weimar Republic his songs and skits were performed in a number of Berlin cabarets. During most of the 1920s M. lived in Paris, working as a correspondent for German publications, including *Die Weltbühne*, the leading periodical of the intellectual left. Immediately after the Reichstag fire M. fled Berlin; ten of his books were burned by the Nazis. Until the annexation of Austria in 1938 M. was a correspondent in Paris and Vienna for an exiles' newspaper. He was interned several times in Vichy, France, but escaped and eventually reached the U.S. In the 1950s M. returned to Europe, choosing to live in Switzerland. In spite of his reputation as a leading literary figure in prewar Germany, M. was largely ignored by postwar writers and critics. He continued to publish—reminiscences, a book of essays on "painters, connoisseurs, and collectors," new collections of earlier work—but in 1976 the disappearance of an eight-hundred-page manuscript, a semifictional autobiography, proved to be the "greatest catastrophe" of a life marked by loss and calamity.

In the 1920s M. published several volumes of poetry. Inspired by François Villon, Heinrich Heine, traditional German folk songs and ballads, Baroque poetry, and American jazz, his poems captured the rhythms of life in bustling modern cities and attacked prejudice, injustice, and hypocrisy in pre-Hitler Germany. He was one of the chief creators of the modern German chanson and pioneered in developing the montage poem and what he called "verbal ragtime." The songs in the plays of Bertolt BRECHT reveal a substantial (unacknowledged) debt to M.

In 1929 M.'s play *Der Kaufmann von Berlin* (the merchant of Berlin) was a theatrical and political scandal. The play savagely exposed the shameless profiteering that had occurred during the inflation of 1923 and pointed up the pervasiveness of anti-Semitism in German society.

In exile M. wrote the satirical novel *Müller: Chronik einer deutschen Sippe von Tacitus bis Hitler* (1935; chronicle of a German tribe from Tacitus to Hitler), in which he mocked the Nazis' ideal of racial purity by tracing a "Germanic" family tree back to Roman times and showing how peoples of different racial stocks had met and mingled on German territory. In the poetic cycle "Briefe aus der Mitternacht" (1944; separate book pub., 1971; "Odyssey out of Midnight," 1944) M. depicts the stages of his exile in a world that has fallen into the grip of evil. The counterpoint to this apocalyptic vision is his love for the woman who accompanied him during much of his odyssey, either in person or in his thoughts. In *Die verlorene Bibliothek* (1952; *The Lost Library*, 1951), first published in English translation, M. summons up memories of his father's library, left behind when he fled Vienna, in order to reconstruct a highly subjective intellectual history of the Western world.

Throughout his career M. opposed bourgeois complacency and greed, and political extremism of all kinds. As a believer in the power of the word, he pointed out the falsehoods in propaganda and stereotyped thought and speech. Neither his poetry nor his prose writings have received the critical attention they deserve, either as documents of their time or as literature of enduring value. M.'s poetry appears readily accessible, but it is actually highly intricate in form and sophisticated in content. Most of M.'s prose works lack a clear narrative thread; with their webs of images, allusions, and associations they seem at first to be Dadaistic or impressionistic jottings. Careful analysis, however, reveals an elaborate inner structure.

FURTHER WORKS: *Die Frühe der Städte* (1918); *Das politische Cabaret* (1919); *Das Ketzerbrevier* (1921); *Wedding-Montmartre* (1923); *Europäische Nächte* (1924); *In Menschenhaut, aus Menschenhaut, um Menschenhaut herum* (1924); *Westnordwestviertelwest* (1925); *Neubestelltes abenteuerliches Tierhaus* (1925); *Algier; oder, Die 13 Oasenwunder* (1927); *Paris in Brand* (1927); *Gedichte, Lieder und Chansons* (1929); *Sahara* (1929); *Arche Noah SOS* (1930); *Die höllische Komödie* (1932); *. . . und euch zum Trotz* (1934); *Die Nacht des Tyrannen* (1938); *Timoshenko, Marshal of the Red Army* (1942); *George Grosz* (1946); *Edgar Degas* (1946); *Verrufene Malerei* (1958); *Der Zeitpuls fliegt* (1958); *Berlin-Dada* (1959); *Morgenlied eines Gepäckträgers* (1959); *Neues Ketzerbrevier* (1962); *Kleines Lumpenbrevier* (1965); *Großes Ketzerbrevier* (1974); *Werke* (1978 ff.); *Wir müssen weiter: Fragmente aus dem Exil* (1979). FURTHER WORKS IN ENGLISH: *No Road Back* (1944, bilingual)

BIBLIOGRAPHY: Schwab-Felisch, H., "W. M.: Dichter am Rand der Zeit," *Der Monat* (July 1953): 403–6; Pesel, P., "'Und sie werden mich also nicht hören:' Versuch über W. M.," *Deutsche Rundschau*, 85 (1959): 1090–95; Geuner, R., "W. M.: Provokation durch Satire," *Gegenspieler* (1969); Denker, K. P., "Staatenlos im Nirgendwo: W. M.," *Akzente*, 22 (1975): 258–73; Serke, "W. M.: Schüsse mitten ins deutsche Gemüt," *Die verbrannten Dichter* (1979): 98–113; Hansen, T., "W. M.s antifaschistische Romane: Ein Beitrag zur politischen Prosa im Exil," in Elfe, W. et al., eds., *Deutsche Exilliteratur: Literatur im 3. Reich* (1979): 132–40

—KRISHNA WINSTON

MEIRELES, Cecília

Brazilian poet, b. 7 Nov. 1901, Rio de Janeiro; d. 9 Nov. 1964, Rio de Janeiro

Orphaned at the age of three, M. was raised by her maternal grandmother in Rio de Janeiro. By the time she graduated from normal school in 1917 M. had already demonstrated a strong enthusiasm for music and foreign languages. In later years, she became a noted orientalist as well. In 1934 M. delivered a series of lectures on Brazilian literature at the universities of Lisbon and Coimbra, and in 1935 she taught at the newly formed University of the Federal District. In 1940 she lectured on Brazilian literature and culture at the University of Texas. As a teacher, which she was for most of her adult life, M. did much to promote educational reforms and to foster the construction of children's libraries in Brazil.

M. began composing simple rhymes and songs even in grade school. Her first book of poems, *Espectros* (1919; specters), was published when she was eighteen. During the 1930s, M. matured as an artist. One of her most respected works, *Viagem* (1938; voyage), won the coveted poetry prize of the Brazilian Academy of Letters. Often mystical in tone and consistently universal in scope, *Viagem* ranks among the most significant of all Brazil's MODERNIST poetic achievements. *Vaga música* (1942; vague music) reflects a rather disillusioned, skeptical, and world—weary author, as do *Mar absoluto* (1945; absolute sea) and, to a lesser degree, *Retrato natural* (1949; natural portrait), a work in which the commonplaces of everyday life come to the fore.

The high point of M.'s career as a poet is *Romanceiro da inconfidência* (1953; song-book of the revolution), a long and inspired narrative poem that, by presenting in closely interlocking patterns several different perspectives on the same subject matter, blends the style of the medieval Portuguese troubadour with a chronicler's sense of people and event. Widely held to be M.'s most original and imaginative work, this challenging poem is a paean to liberty and, in its entirety, amounts to a virtual apotheosis of "Tiradentes" (the dentist who was the leader of the aborted revolt) and his confederates, the men involved in the ill-fated independence movement of 1789.

Often counted among the Brazilian modernists, M.'s best work really places her more squarely in the SYMBOLIST tradition. Unlike the more radical modernists, such as Mário de ANDRADE and Oswald de ANDRADE, M. did not advocate a total break with the Portuguese language's rich poetic traditions. Rather, she synthesized what were essentially established forms and metrical patterns with new images and the modernist's world view. The result, eclectic in nature, was a corpus of poetic works outstanding in their musicality, their fluidity, and their evocative power.

Much of M.'s poetry is intensely personal and reflects a quest for self-discovery in which certain motifs recur, especially those involving the sea, space, and solitude. M.'s lyric poetry is characteristically visual in essence. M. tended to praise the simple beauties of the natural world while rebuking mankind for its selfishness, egoism, and vanity. A pure poet, M.'s poems, which resist strict classification, cut back and forth across the arbitrary divisions of time and fashion.

FURTHER WORKS: *Nunca mais . . . e Poema dos poemas* (1923); *Baladas para El-Rei* (1925); *Criança: Meu amor* (1933); *Poetas novos de Portugal* (1944); *Rui: Pequena história de uma grande vida* (1949); *Problemas de literatura infantil* (1950); *Amor em Lenoreta* (1952); *Doze noturnos da Holanda, e O aeronauta* (1952); *Pequeno oratório de Santa Cecília* (1955); *Pistóia, cemitério militar brasileiro* (1955); *Panorama folclórico dos Açores* (1955); *Canções* (1956); *Giroflé, giroflá* (1956); *Romance de Santa Cecília* (1957); *A rosa* (1957); *Obra poética* (1958); *Metal rosicler* (1960); *Poemas escritos na Índia* (1961); *Antologia poética de C. M.* (1963); *Solombra* (1963); *Escolha o seu sonho* (1964); *Crônica trovada da cidade de Sam Sebastiam* (1965); *Inéditas* (1967); *Poesia* (1967). FURTHER WORKS IN ENGLISH: *C. M.: Poems in Translation* (1977, bilingual)

BIBLIOGRAPHY: Nist, J., *The Modernist Movement in Brazil* (1967): 190–204; Coutinho, A., *An Introduction to Literature in Brazil* (1969): 187, 224, 244; Martins, W., *The Modernist Idea* (1970): 13, 108–9; Keith, H., and R. Sayers, Introduction to *C. M.: Poems in Translation* (1977); García, R., "Symbolism in the Early Works of C. M.," *RomN*, 21 (1980): 16–22; Sadlier, D. J., "Metaphor and Metamorphosis: A Study of the Sea Imagery in C. M.'s *Mar absoluto*," *KRQ*, 27 (1980): 361–70

—EARL E. FITZ

MEJÍA VALLEJO, Manuel

Colombian novelist, short-story writer, and poet, b. 23 Apr. 1923, Jericó, Antioquia; d. 23 July 1998, Bogota

M. V. is currently the best-known Antioquian short-story writer and one of the major contemporary narrators in Colombia. He attended the Bolivariana University in Medellín, Colombia, studied sculpture and drawing at the Institute of Fine Arts of Medellín, and completed courses in journalism in Venezuela and Guatemala. He taught literature at the University of Antioquia and directed the university journal *Editorial Universitaria*. M. V. has also worked as a journalist in Venezuela and Central America, and contributed articles to the newspapers *El Tiempo* and *El Espectador* of Bogotá. To date he has published four volumes of short stories and five novels. M. V. was the first foreigner to be awarded the Eugenion Nadal Award in Barcelona, Spain, in 1963, for his novel *El día señalado* (1964; the appointed day), and the National Novel Award in 1973 for *Aire de tango* (1973; air of tango). He has been judge and guest in numerous national and international literary contests. At present he writers for national and foreign newspapers and journals, and lives in Medellín, Antioquia.

M. V. belongs to the group of novelists associated with the period known as La Violencia (1946–1964), who are characterized by their critical vision of national economic, social, and political life. Although many novels of La Violencia have been criticized for their documentary style, immediacy, and lack of creative essence, M. V.'s works have been praised for their ingenious use of literary devices such as his method of converging separate plot lines within a single work and his symbolic depictions of various psychological states. His earlier novels and short stories were noted for their tendency to idealize lyrically landscapes overloaded with sentimentalism, and he is considered a continuation of the Antioquian literary tradition embodied by Tomás CARRASQUILLA. M. V.'s prose is always vigorous and pleasant. Like other writers of his era, M. V. is greatly interested in everyday life and social milieu. The novelist himself has said that he wrote his first novel, *La tierra éramos nosotros* (1945; the land used to be ours), on the basis of characters he had known on his parents' farm. In this work the first person narrator-protagonist tells the story of his youth with innocence and honesty and writes in an immediate present of his life among impoverished peasants who inhabit the land of Antioquia and who must face life as victims of both the natural and the human order. With fresh and authentic realism the novel presents a complex psychological problem of Colombian people: being confused and puzzled during the steps of social transition, not knowing where to go or what to do, and ignorant of the history that has produced them.

M. V.'s masterpiece, *El día señalado*, is an example of the multiple facets of his artistry as a novelist. The literary symbolism, imagery, and complex structure of the novel invite readers to become involved in the development of the story in a Faulknerian fashion. This extensive novel depicts the trauma of the period of La Violencia as experienced in a remote small town in Colombia. During this era of tremendous political unrest in Colombia, approximately three hundred thousand Colombians died as victims of either Progovernment or antigovernment terrorism. The novel is essentially patterned on the psychology of its characters, who are human types inescapably tied to a fatal destiny. M. V. captured vividly the authentic spirit and atmosphere of La Violencia as well as the exploitation and hypocrisy that the country endured during this period of social and political turmoil. Unlike other novels of this period, M. V. incorporated social, economic and political sources without describing in an overly graphic manner scenes of physical conflict.

One needs to have knowledge of the historical context of La Violencia in Colombia to understand much of *El día señalado*, in which the spirit of violence functions as the driving force behind the atmosphere and action of the novel. The fear, the memory of death, the authoritarianism, the despoilment of land and persons, the official complicity, and the traditional violence of a small cockfighting town are so rendered by M. V. as to become emblematic of the social, moral, psychological, political, and economic decomposition of the nation. *El día señalado* is the most outstanding of the more than forty novels of La Violencia written in Colombia in the 1950s and 1960s. The novel successfully unifies many elements in its treatment of the topic, while undermining an ideological interpretation of La Violencia by showing that the determining factor of this period is not, in fact, partisan politics, but banal acts of human irrationality.

In spite of having won significant literary awards at the national and international levels, M. V.'s works still remain little studied by foreign critics and scholars in comparison with Gabriel GARCÍA

MÁRQUEZ, the Colombian Nobel Prize winner. Through his tense and vivid style and effective treatment of rural life. M. V. has been able to call attention to the fact that some of the most important novels of the last few decades can be fully understood only if readers are sensitive to the social conditions amid which novelists have forged new intellectual realities.

FURTHER WORKS: *Tiempo de sequía* (1957); *Al pie de la ciudad* (1958); *Cielo cerrado* (1963); *Cuentos de zona tórrida* (1967); *Las noches de la vigilia* (1975); *Prácticas para el olvido* (1977); *Las muertes ajenas* (1979); *Tarde de verano* (1981); *El viento lo dijo* (1981); *Memoria del olvido: poemas y dibujos de M. M. V.* (1990)

BIBLIOGRAPHY: Carlos, A. J., *"El día señalado," Hispania*, 48 (1965): 947–48; Núñez Segura, J. A., *Literatura colombiana; sipnosis y comentarios de autores representativos* (1967): 572–73; Rodríguez, B. Ávila, *"El día señalado de* M. M. V.: cuentos-base y funcionamiento de dos ejes narrativos," *Thesaurus*, 31, 2 (1976): 358–66; Sánchez López, L. M., *Diccionario de escritores colombianos* (1978): 295–96; Mena, L. I., "La función de los prólogos en *El día señalado* de M. M. V." *Hispam*: 25–26 (1980): 137–46; Bedoya, L. I., *La novela de La Violencia en Colombia. El día Señalado de M. M. V.* (1981); Williams, R. L., *M. M. V. Una decada de la novela colombiana* (1981): 77–89; Williams, R. L., *The Colombian Novel, 1844–1987* (1991); Tang-Cuadrado, C., *De la narrativa de la violencia: M. M. V.*, in *DAI*, 1, 2 (1992)

—VIRGINIA SHEN

MELO NETO, João Cabral de

Brazilian poet, b. 9 Jan. 1920, Recife, Pernambuco

Born into a traditional family, M. N. spent his childhood on a sugarcane plantation and studied in Catholic schools. In 1941 he published his first essay on poetry. He moved to Rio de Janeiro in 1942 and entered the foreign service. M. N. served in Europe and Latin America; his sojourns in Spain clearly influenced his work. In 1968 he was elected to the Brazilian Academy of Letters. M. N. has received numerous awards, including the prestigious Camões Prize (1990) for lifetime literary achievement in Portuguese and the twelfth (1992) Neustadt International Prize for Literature (University of Oklahoma).

Chronologically, M. N. coincides with Brazil's so-called "Generation of '45," who perceived excesses in modernist free verse and proposed neoparnassian solutions. M. N. shared with this group a formal rigor and discipline in the most general sense, but he opposed their cult of the sonnet, focus on psychic states, and bias for an elevated poetic lexicon. M. N.'s verse is based on things, objects, tangible reality, and a belief in the materiality of words rather than romantic inspiration. He advocates rationality in composition instead of a conventional lyricism of self-expression. M. N. is a leading exponent of new objectivity in postwar Latin American poetry but commonly connects his language of objects to real settings and social facts.

In *Pedra do sono* (1942; sleep stone) visual imagery and the plasticity of language are valued over any emotive content or message. This early poetry of dream states and spirits has evident elements of SURREALISM. *O engenheiro* (1945; the engineer)

abandons the initial taste for the surreal and offers the poem as a calculated function, as a fully constructed artifact. M. N. works systematically against the picturesque, sentimentalism, and irrationalism, seeking, above all, awareness of the objects that shape modern consciousness. Setting the standard for the collections to follow, the poetry is functionally architectanic and exhibits geometric rigor, with careful modification and manipulations of semantics. The three sections of *A psicologia da composicão* (1947; the psychology of composition) all constitute metapoetry, contemplations of verse making. The subtitle of the third poem, "Antiode"—"against so-called profound poetry"—reflects the poet's rejection of intuition and passion in favor of calculated composition in the lineage of Poe. The values of exactness and balance are maintained throughout.

M. N. next turns to regional settings for his severe verse. Avoiding superfluous sentimental cadences, he sharpens his perception of human situations and landscapes in a very nominal poetry. He is socially aware and depicts abject living conditions with sober precision while remaining faithful to literary principles. *O cão sem plumas* (1950; the plumeless hound) is a long poem, sinuous like the river it describes. Less figurative is *O rio* (1954; the river), where M. N. uses folk narrative; the full subtitle reads "story of the voyage that the Capibaribe River makes from its source to the city of Recife." Public discourse is also foregrounded in the dramatic verse of *Morte e vida Severina* (1955; death and life of Severina), M. N.'s best-known work. A refugee from drought walks toward the city and finds death at every turn, but he finally encounters hope in a birth in a riverside slum. *Morte e vida Severina* had great success as a musical with settings by poet-composer Chico BUARQUE and won international recognition at the university festival in Nancy, France (1966). The dramatic verse was published in *Duas águas* (1956; dual waters) alongside the long poem "Uma faca só Lamina" (a knife all blade), another meditation on writing, in which the knife is a symbol of poetic language.

References to Castille and Andalusia are frequent in M. N.'s titles of the 1960s and again in *Sevilha Andando* (1989, Seville walking). Harsh realities are often seen through a dry, laconic language. In *A educação pela pedra* (1966; education by stone), stone symbolism figures prominently in the questioning of self. There is a further distillation of subjectivity and affectivity in a search for a durable objective lucidity. *Museu de tudo* (1975; museum of all), *A escola das facas* (1980; the school of knives), and *Agrestes* (1985; ruralities) contain mostly shorter poems. Although this later work may appear to be more casual and personal (the first person, so rare earlier, is much more frequent), there is no concession to sentimental rhetoric or the vice of confessionalism.

Most critics agree that M. N. is a singular case in Brazilian literature. He is a Valéry-like figure who has had a broad impact. His antilyrical aesthetic of self-containment especially influenced concrete poetry, poets of song, regional poets, and all those who value rigor over emotivity. A well-conceived volume of his poetry, *Selected Poetry 1937-1990* (1994), has appeared in English translation. With the publication of his complete works, *Obra completa* (1994), co-edited with his wife, poet Marly de Oliveira, M. N. confirmed his place as the most important poet to emerge in Brazil after MODERNISM.

FURTHER WORKS: *Os três mal amados* (1943); *Paisagens comfiguras* (1955); *Quaderna* (1960); *Serial* (1961); *Dois parlamentos* (1961); *Auto do frade* (1985); *Crime na Calle Relator* (1987)

BIBLIOGRAPHY: Nist, J. A., *The Modernist Movement in Brazil* (1967): 179–90; Dixon, P., "The Geography-Anatomy Metaphor in J. C. de M. N.'s *Morte e vida severina,*" *Chasqui*, 11, 1 (Nov. 1981): 33–48; Reckert, S., "João Cabral: From Pedra to Pedra," *Psstud*, 2 (1986): 166–84; Zenith, R., "J. C. de M. N.: An Engineer of Poetry," *LALR*, 15, 30 (July-Dec. 1987): 26–42; Peixoto, M., "J. C. de M. N.," in Stern, I., ed. *Dictionary of Brazilian Literature* (1988): 196–99; special M. N. issue, *WLT*, 65 (Autumn, 1992); Perrone, C. A., *Seven Faces: Brazilian Poetry since Modernism* (1996)

—CHARLES A. PERRONE

MEMMI, Albert

Tunisian-French novelist, essayist, and poet (writing in French), b. 15 Dec. 1920, Tunis

M., a Tunisian Jew who resides in Paris, is Tunisia's foremost writer in French. Born in Tunis, M. attended first the Rabbinical School and then the Jewish Alliance School, and later the prestigious Lycée Carnot. His philosophy studies at the University of Algiers were interrupted by World War II. During the German occupation of Tunisia, M. was interned in a concentration camp, an experience accounted for in his first novel. After the war, he went to Paris to pursue his Philosophy degree at the Sorbonne. Upon his return to Tunis in 1949, he taught philosophy and practiced psychology. He also wrote for local newspapers and journals until Tunisia's independence in 1956, when he left again for Paris, where he still teaches and resides. His work is a crisscross between fiction and philosophical speculations.

His early writings, tinged with a Sartrian brand of existential anguish, reflect, in the autobiographical mode, his childhood and adolescent experiences, a time marked by a cleavage between his traditional milieu and family-oriented upbringing, and an aggressive but seductive modernity embodied by the European and particularly the French presence in his country of birth. M. is a man of two worlds. East and West, and two cultures, Tunisian and French. This dual heritage is the stuff of his fiction and of his philosophical writings.

His first novel, *La statue de sel* (1953; *The Pillar of Salt*, 1955), describes both the precariousness of his early life in the Jewish quarter in Tunis, with its psychological and material insecurities—M.'s mother was illiterate, and his father was a saddler—and the transition, both traumatic and salutary, from his traditional milieu to the discovery of modern European civilization and the outside world. Narrated in the bildungsroman fashion, *La statue de sel* deals, above all, with the difficulty of being at once an oriental Jew, a Tunisian, and a colonized. This threefold alienation is emblematized in the protagonist's hybridized French-Western, Jewish, and Arabic name: Alexandre Mordechaï Benillouche. The hero's predicament is that of the North African intellectual who is caught in the bind between many contradictory worlds: orient/occident, colonizer/ colonized, conformity/individuality. Dissatisfied with his plight, the narrator repudiates his past and leaves for Argentina—his El Dorado—to seek a new and better life.

In his second novel, *Agar* (1955; *Strangers*, 1960), M. continues his preoccupation with the conflict between cultures. However,

he explores this thematic from the point of view of the couple. Upon completion of his medical degree, the narrator, a Tunisian like M., returns to Tunis with his French bride. His family's resentment of the intruding foreign woman and the latter's inability to adapt to her husband's native culture and traditions prove to be insurmountable and ultimately tear the couple apart. *Agar* may be read as a case study of mixed marriages because the encounter with the other is examined in all its social, psychological, and political implications as a marriage of two culturally and mentally antithetical worlds East and West.

His third novel, *Le scorpion: ou, la confession imaginaire* (1969; *The Scorpion; or, The Imaginary Confession*, 1971), follows a long periods devoted to theoretical and philosophical questions already adumbrated in his earlier fiction. In *Le scorpion* M. broadens the scope and thematic of his two first novels as he delves, with poetic detachment, into the collective unconscious of a Tunisian society caught in transition between its aspiration for modernity and its nostalgia for time-honored traditions and values. This stream-of-consciousness novel, narrated by at least three voices, explores such social and psychological themes as patriarchy and the inevitable Oedipus complex as well as artistic problematics such as the relationship of fiction to reality.

Although still an integral part of his itinerary of self-discovery, M.'s fourth novel, *Le Désert, ou la vie et les aventures de Jubair Ouali El-Mammi* (1977; the desert, or the life and adventures of Jubair Ouali El-Mammi), is markedly different in theme and conception from his earlier novels, especially of *La statue de set*. It is a novel of maturity, wisdom, and irony. The self-discovery theme that marks his earlier fiction is explored here in the collective mode. Set in the 15th c., *Le désert* is a minisaga of the El-Mammi's mythical dynasty—that which he refers to as the kingdom within—whose descendant is the narrator. M. focuses his search on his cultural heritage, a kind of autobiography in the plural, and taps techniques of Maghrebian traditional and oral storytelling techniques.

Like *Le désert*, M.'s latest novel, *Le pharaon* (1988; the pharaoh), is an archaeological investigation of the Tunisian psyche (the narrator is an archaeologist by profession). The story evolves along two parallel lines, personal and collective. The narrator is caught between his nationalist aspirations—Tunisia's independence—and his desire to maintain his ties with his newly acquired French culture, between his love for his wife and children—who stand for stability, tradition, the mother, and the mother country (Tunisia), on the one hand, and his infatuation with Carlotta, his seductive mistress (France) on the other hand. At the end, the narrator chooses to leave his native city for the cosmopolitan anonymity of Paris. In many respects, *Le Pharaon* is a revisitation and an updating of the major themes and preoccupations of his earlier fiction.

M. puts to good use this autobiographical material in his sociological and philosophical essays to explore the problematics of colonialism and other forms of oppression such as racism, dominance, and dependency. With his first major philosophical essay, *Portrait du colonisé, précédé du Portrait du colonisateur* (1957; *The Colonizer and the Colonized*, 1965), M. emerged as one of the main theoreticians of colonialism and decolonization. Based on concrete situations and firsthand acquaintance with the colonial experience, M. expounds a sociology of oppression in which colonizer and colonized are not only perceived and treated as each other's foil but seem to share, in a dialectical fashion, a common predicament. M. proposed foresightedly that alienation, a by-product of the colonial situation, would perdure well after independence.

Portrait du colonisé, précédé du Portrait du colonisateur was also the blueprint for a series of other psychological and sociological types where forms of oppression and dependency are scrutinized. In *Portrait d'un juif* (1962; *Portrait of a Jew*, 1962) and its sequel, *La libération du Juif* (1966; *The Liberation of the Jew*, 1966), as in his other philosophical writings, personal observations—that which M. calls *l'expérience vécue* or life experience—and theoretical speculations are interrelated activities. His fourth major essay, *L'homme dominé* (1968; *Dominated Man*, 1968), is a synthesis of his earlier findings: We are presented here, under the same rubric of oppression and domination, with portraits as varied as that of the Jew, the servant, the black, and the woman. M. examines these types in a Hegelian fashion. In his essay *Juifs et Arabes* (1974; *Jews and Arabs*, 1975), M.—who considers himself a Jew Arab—delves into the complex psychology of Arab-Jewish relations both from the perspectives of a sociologist and a polemist. This paradigmatic approach to the question of dependence/independence and oppressed/oppressor is also the subject of his essay *La dépendance: Esquisse pour un portrait du dépendant* (1979; *Dependence*, 1984). His latest Philosophical essay, *Le racisme: Description, définition, traitement*, (1982; racism: description, definition, treatment), examines the roots of racism and the psychological motivations of the racist. Like Jean-Paul SARTRE in *Anti-Semite and Jew*, M expounds in this essay a theory of racism by focusing on the portrait of the perpetrator, the racist, rather than the victim.

In addition to being the author of essays and fiction, M. is the main contributor to two important anthologies: *Anthologie des écrivains maghrébins d'expression française* (1964; anthology of Maghrebian writers of French expression) and *Anthologie des écrivains français du Maghreb* (1969; anthology of French writers of the Maghreb). He is also the author of a book of poems, *Le mirliton du ciel* (1990; the reed pipe of the sky). M.'s poetry dwells mainly on the interior landscapes of his Tunisian youth.

M. is credited not only with putting Maghrebian literature in French on the world literary map but also for his role as a leading theoretician of Maghrebian letters and ethos. He was the leading Maghrebian novelist and thinker to use a critical discourse theory was then the sole apanage of Western thinkers—to regain intellectual initiative and assert North African identity.

BIBLIOGRAPHY: Sartre, J.-P., "Portrait du colonise," *Les Temps Modernes*, 13: 137–38 (July-Aug. 1957): 289–92; Khatibi, A., *Le roman Maghrébin* (1968): 71–77; Yetiv, I., *Le thème de l'aliénation dans le roman maghrébin d'expression française* (1972): 145–201; Déjeux, J., *Littérature maghrébine de langue française* (1973): 301–31; Yetiv, I., "Du scorpion au désert: A. M. Revisited," *StTCL*, 7, 1 (Fall 1982): 77–87; Monego, J. P., *Maghrebian Literature in French* (1984): 90–107; Roumani, J., *A. M.* (1987)

—HÉDI ABDEL-JAOUAD

MENCKEN, H(enry) L(ouis)

American essayist, political and social commentator, and literary critic, b. 12 Sept 1880, Baltimore, Md., d. 29 Jan. 1956, Baltimore, Md.

M. grew up in the pace of small-city life, enjoying the "great protein factory of the Chesapeake," and later rejecting the allure of literary New York for quiet amenities and old friends. At age eleven he forsook, in his words, "Christian Endeavor" and became "contumacious of Holy Men and resigned to Hell." After graduating from Baltimore Polytechnic Institute, he continued to study literature with a private tutor. In 1899 his father died, and M. went to work immediately as a newspaperman with the *Baltimore Herald*. Here his study of "life" rather than the liberal arts allowed him to "lay in all the worldly wisdom of a police lieutenant, a bartender, a shyster lawyer, and a midwife." He rose to the position of editor in chief, but switched to the *Baltimore Sunpapers* in 1906 and retained his connection with them for a lifetime. In 1908 he began doing book reviews for *Smart Set*, and by 1914 he was editing the magazine with George Jean Nathan (1882–1958) as well as writing monthly articles of five thousand words. This prodigious schedule lasted until 1923, when he launched the *American Mercury*; his work now became increasingly political, and his reputation as the scourge of public men grew to national proportions. His characteristic skepticism caused him to be somewhat eclipsed during the intensely committed period of the Great Depression, but he continued to comment unfavorably on the political scene while also pursuing his lifelong interests in the American language. He reported vigorously until suffering a stroke in 1948.

M.'s mind is an amalgam of Nietzschean exaltation and deadly comic skepticism about human progress. Great artists can create ecstatic experience for the few, but most men are trapped by their own smallness. M. spent his career anatomizing the "booboisie," the benighted joiners who fear and despise excellence in the arts and life. On a more abstract level, he rejected the pursuit of truth and attacked all forms of idealism. His critical work was accomplished in a razzle-dazzle style: one part Carlyle's outrageous diction, a second part Swift's abuse, and a final measure of nativist American plain talk reminiscent of Mark Twain.

M.'s range and relish for ideas and events are seemingly boundless: philosophy and literature, politics and popular culture, language and religion are explored with enthusiasm and relentless wit. *George Bernard Shaw: His Plays* (1905) and *The Philosophy of Friedrich Nietzsche* (1908) established his learning, but his manner of employing knowledge in the essay form is his distinctive attribute. As a literary critic he is neither original nor in any way systematic, yet his finest essays are keenly sensitive to the writer's special gifts and place in culture. In *A Book of Prefaces* (1917) he captures Theodore DREISER's talent for "depicting the spirit in disintegration" and humorously analyzes his clumsy prose. Of the latter M. says "there are no charms of style to mitigate the rigours of these vast steppes and pampas of narration." When M. turns to the fate of American literature in "The National Letters," published in *Prejudices: Second Series* (1920), he employs a cultural argument—or more properly a tirade. American literature is "thin and watery" because of the national fear of ideas; this quality in turn is traced to democratic conformity and plutocratic domination. Such a diatribe is typical of M. and tends to draw us away from the texture of literature and into a criticism of life: one genteel critic's "lack of humor is almost that of a Fifth Avenue divine"; another moralistic type "tries to save Shakespeare for the right thinking by proving that he was an Iowa Methodist."

M.'s rough-and-tumble debunking is most effective when used on politicians, Elks Club members, and high-minded reformers. In *A Carnival of Buncombe* (1956), a collection of essays on the American presidency, as well as in numerous other political pieces,

M. exposes the self-importance and inconsequence of men in the arena. In a 1921 essay called "The Archangel Woodrow," Woodrow Wilson is described as a "pedagogue gone mashugga." In *A Carnival of Buncombe* Harding's windy, confused writing and thinking are labeled "Gamalielese." Calvin Coolidge's intelligence is compared to that of a "cast-iron lawn dog." The New Deal is dismissed as a "milch cow with 125,000,000 teats." This tradition of abuse is also found in "On Being an American," published in *Prejudices: Third Series* (1922). Here the idea of American civilization as the greatest clown show on earth is by no means as arresting as the style. M. the social critic becomes a Tocqueville lost in the funhouse of insulting language. Our selfishness is a matter of keeping a "place at the trough." America is a "glorious commonwealth of morons," a "paradise of back-slappers, of democrats, of mixers, of go-getters." Elsewhere in his six volumes of *Prejudices* (1919–27) M. swings at chiropractors, Southern culture, professors, farmers, fundamentalists, and reformers of all shades. These last he calls "wowsers"—people with a "divine commission to regulate or improve the rest of us."

M.'s more reflective longer works are no less controversial; in *Treatise on the Gods* (1930) religion is a con game; in *The American Language* (1919; rev. and enlarged ed., 1936) scholarship coexists with lively excursions into national bigotry, prudery, and stupidity.

While sometimes provincial and noisy, M. is a continuing resource for social critics, despisers of cant, and all lovers of extravagant language. He assaulted public issues with a penetrating style unrivaled in the American essay form.

FURTHER WORKS: *Ventures into Verses* (1903); *The Gist of Nietzsche* (1910); *What You Ought to Know about Your Baby* (1910, with Leonard Keen Hirshberg); *Men versus Man* (1910, with Robert Rives La Monte); *The Artists* (1912); *Europe after 8:15* (1914, with George Jean Nathan); *A Book of Burlesques* (1916); *A Little Book in C Major* (1916); *Pistols for Two* (1917, with George Jean Nathan); *Damn! A Book of Calumny* (1918); *In Defense of Women* (1919); *The American Credo* (1920); *The Literary Capital of the United States* (1920); *Heliogabalus* (1920, with George Jean Nathan); *Americana 1925* (1925); *Notes on Democracy* (1926); *Americana 1926* (1926); *James Branch Cabell* (1927); *Menckeneana: A Schimpflexikon* (1928); *Making a President* (1932); *Treatise on Right and Wrong* (1933); *The Sunpapers of Baltimore* (1937, with others); *Happy Days, 1880–1892* (1940); *Newspaper Days, 1899–1906* (1941); *A Dictionary of Quotations* (1942); *Heathen Days, 1890–1936* (1943); *The American Language, Supplement I* (1945); *Christmas Story* (1946); *The Days of H. L. M.* (1947); *The American Language, Supplement II* (1948); *A M. Chrestomathy* (1949); *The Vintage M.* (1955); *Minority Report: H. L. M.'s Notebooks* (1956); *The Bathtub Hoax, and Other Blasts and Bravos from the Chicago Tribune* (1958); *H. L. M. on Music* (1961); *Letters* (1961); *H. L. M.'s Smart Set Criticism* (1968); *A Choice of Days* (1981)

BIBLIOGRAPHY: Manchester, W., *Disturber of the Peace: The Life of H. L. M.* (1950); Wilson, E., "M.'s Democratic Man," *The Shores of Light* (1952): 293–98; Cooke, A., Preface to *The Vintage M.* (1955): v–xii; C., Angoff, *H. L. M.: A Portrait from Memory* (1956); Adler, B., *H. L. M.: The M. Bibliography* (1961); Nolte, W. H., *H. L. M.: Literary Critic* (1966); Wagner, P. M., *H. L. M.* (1966); Stenerson, D., *H. L. M.: Iconoclast from Baltimore* (1971);

H. L. Mencken

Cooke, A., "H. L. M.: The Public and the Private Face," *Six Men* (1977): 93–133; Fecher, C. A., *M.: A Study of His Thought* (1978); Dorsey, J., ed., *On M.* (1980)

—DAVID CASTRONOVO

MENON, Vallathol Narayana

Indian poet and translator (writing in Malayalam), b. 16 Oct. 1878, Chennara; d. 13 March 1958, Cochin

Born in the state of Kerala, M., usually known in India as Vallathol, studied Malayalam and Sanskrit, and Ayurvedic medicine. In 1902 he married and worked for a time as editor of the literary journal *Atmaposhini*. Around 1910 he became deaf. In 1927 M. started the Kerala Kalamandalam, a school for the training of performers of the traditional dance-drama known as Kathakali. He participated in the World Peace Conference at Warsaw in 1950 and later visited England, Russia, China, Singapore, and Malaya.

Along with N. Kumaran Asan (1873–1924) and Ulloor Parameswara Iyer (1877–1949) M. was responsible for ushering in a romantic renascence in Malayalam literature. They began as imitators of the neoclassical tradition of the 19th c., but in the first quarter of the 20th they changed the trends chiefly through their *khanda kavyas* (short narratives) and *bhava kavyas* (lyrics).

M. was a prolific writer. In addition to verses on medicine and critical reviews, he has to his credit a substantial body of translations from Sanskrit into Malayalam. His reputation, however, rests largely on his poetry, which falls into two main groups: the narrative poems, such as *Chitrayogam* (1912; the strange union), *Bandhanastanaya Aniruddhan* (1914; Aniruddha in captivity), and *Magdalana Mariam* (1921; "Mary Magdalene," 1980); and the lyrics, mostly collected in *Sahitya manjari* (11 vols., 1916–70; cluster of literary flowers). These lyrics are written in a simple diction using mostly Dravidian meters, and cover a wide variety of themes such as political freedom, social equality, religious tolerance, domestic happiness, and the appreciation of the beauty of nature. His best poems are melodious and full of sensuous imagery. His later poems are marked by an increasing awareness of the plight of the poor.

A patriot, a humanist, a rebel with an insatiable zest for life, never an ascetic, always an optimist, M. embodies in his writings the tropical splendors of the land of his birth as well as the irrepressible adaptability of his people and the vibrant melody of their language.

FURTHER WORKS: *Badhiravilapam* (1910); *Ganapati* (1913); *Sishyanum makanum* (1918); *Kochu Sita* (1926); *Grantha viharam* (1927); *Acchanum makalum* (1941); *Vallathol Russiayil* (1951); *Abhivadyam* (1957). FURTHER WORKS IN ENGLISH: *Selected Poems* (1978); *The Song of the Peasants* (1978)

BIBLIOGRAPHY: George, K. M., *A Survey of Malayalam Literature* (1968): 151–57; Chaitanya, K., *A History of Malayalam Literature* (1971): 235–48; George, K. M., *Western Influence on Malayalam Language and Literature* (1972): 120–30; Hrdayakumari, B., *Vallathol* (1974); Paniker, K. A., *A Short History of Malayalam Literature* (1977): 50–53; Sarma, S., et al., eds., *Vallathol: A Centenary Perspective* (1978)

—K. AYYAPPA PANIKER

MEREZHKOVSKY, Dmitry Sergeevich

Russian novelist, poet, dramatist, critic, and religious and social thinker, b. 14 Aug. 1865, St. Petersburg (now Leningrad); d. 7 Dec. 1941, Paris, France

After taking a degree in philosophy at St. Petersburg University, M. married the poet Zinaida HIPPIUS. Active in literary and religious circles, M. assisted in the establishment of the Religious Philosophical Meetings and founded the journal *Novy put* in 1903. In 1920 he and his wife fled the U.S.S.R. and settled in Paris.

M. began as a poet in the tradition of Russian populism but abandoned civic idealism to initiate the SYMBOLIST movement with his collection of verse *Simvoly* (1892; symbols) and the manifesto *O prichinakh upadka i o novykh techeniakh sovremennoy russkoy literatury* (1893; on the reasons for the decline and on new trends in contemporary Russian literature), in which he advocated mystic content, symbols, and artistic impressionism as the primary elements of the new art. In his verse he expressed his aristocratic outlook, his love of beauty, and his attraction to the attributes of Greek and Roman antiquity. Yet poetry was too constraining to

permit full expression of M.'s ideas, and aestheticism could not long suppress his innate religiosity.

In his many essays and his excellent study *L. Tolstoy i Dostoevsky* (2 vols., 1901–2; *Tolstoy as Man and Artist, with an Essay on Dostoievski*, 1902) M. attempted to resolve the contradiction between the human virtues of Hellenic paganism and Christ's spirituality. Renouncing "historic" Christianity, he formulated his apocalyptic Christianity of the Third Testament, in which a synthesis would occur when history had come to an end. M. supported the revolutionary movement of 1905, and in his essays of the period, especially those in *Le tsar et la révolution* (1907; the tsar and the revolution), written with his wife and Dmitry Filosofov (1872–1940), which was published only in French, *Gryadushchy Kham* (1906; the coming Ham), and *Ne mir, no mech* (1908; not peace, but a sword), he called for a religious revolution to overthrow all forms of church and state and to establish a religious social order and the Kingdom of God on earth.

M.'s first trilogy of historical novels, *Smert bogov: Yulian Otstupnik* (1896; *The Death of the Gods,* 1901; later tr., *Julian the Apostate*, 1929), *Voskresshie bogi: Leonardo da Vinci* (1901; *The Romance of Leonardo da Vinci, the Forerunner*, 1902; later tr., 1928) and *Antikhrist: Pyotr i Alexey* (1905; *Peter and Alexis*, 1906; later tr., 1931), which mark the apogee of his career and for which he is renowned in the West, not only surpasses his other belles-lettres in artistic merit, but also occupies a central position among his religiophilosophical works. He gives brilliant re-creations, lavishly embellished with archaeological details and enlivened by the introduction of numerous historical characters and incidents, of three dynamic eras: the reign of the 3rd-c. Roman emperor Julian the Apostate, the Renaissance, and the reign of Peter the Great. At the same time he invests the genre of the historical novel with philosophical argumentation. The primary aim of these novels is to show the conflict between Christianity and paganism in the past, to reveal why attempts at reconciliation failed, and to allow M. to present his panacea for the problem. Similarly, in his later historical novels, *Alexander I* (1913; Alexander I) and *Chetyrnadtsatoe dekabrya* (1918; combined and abridged as *December the Fourteenth*, 1923), *Rozhdenie bogov: Tutankamon na Krite* (1925; *The Birth of the Gods*, 1926), and *Messia* (1928; *Akhnaton, King of Egypt*, 1927), as well as in his dramas, M. disseminated his latest socio-religious views in the guise of fiction.

As an émigré M. remained an outspoken opponent of Soviet Communism. Turning from belles-lettres after 1925, he continued to elaborate his religious thought in collections of aphorisms and in a series of biographies, primarily those of Christian saints and religious thinkers. Although he complained of being misunderstood both in Russia and Western Europe, M.'s recognition of modern man's spiritual dilemma and his efforts to find a solution to it add universal significance to his work.

FURTHER WORKS: *Stikhotvorenia, 1883–1887* (1888); *Novye stikhotvorenia, 1891–1895* (1896); *Vechnye sputniki* (1897); *"Ottsy i deti" russkogo liberalizma* (1901); *Stikhotvorenia, 1888–1902* (1902); *Lyubov silnee smerti* (1902); *Sobranie stikhov, 1883–1903* (1904); *Pushkin* (1906); *Gogol i chort* (1906); *Prorok russkoy revolyutsii* (1906); *Teper ili nikogda* (1906); *Pavel I* (1908); *Makov tsvet* (1908, with Zinaida Hippius and Dmitry Filosofov); *V tikhom omute* (1908); *M. Y. Lermontov: Poet sverkhchelovechestva* (1909); *Sobranie stikhov, 1883–1910* (1910); *Bolnaya Rossia* (1910); *Lermontov; Gogol* (1911); *Polnoe sobranie sochineny* (17 vols., 1911–13); *Polnoe sobranie sochineny* (24 vols., 1914); *Bylo i budet: Dnevnik 1910–1914* (1915); *Dve tayny russkoy poezii: Nekrasov i Tyutchev* (1915); *Zavet Belinskogo* (1915); *Budet radost* (1916); *Zachem voskres* (1916); *Nevoenny dnevnik, 1914–1916* (1917); *Ot voyny k revolyutsii* (1917); *Perventsy svobody* (1917); *Romantiki* (1917); *Tsarevich Alexey* (1920); *Tsarstvo Antikhrista* (1921, with Z. Hippius, D. Filosofov, and Vladimir Zlobin); *Tayna tryokh: Egipet i Vavilon* (1925); *Napoleon* (1929; *Napoleon: A Study*, 1929); *Tayna zapada: Atlantida-Evropa* (1930; *The Secret of the West*, 1933); *Iisus neizvestny* (2 vols., 1931; *Jesus the Unknown*, 1933; *Jesus Manifest*, 1935); *Pavel, Avgustin* (1936); *Frantsisk Assissky* (1938); *Zhanna d Ark* (1938); *Dante* (1939); *Luther* (1941); *Pascal* (1941); *Calvin* (1942). FURTHER WORKS IN ENGLISH: *Daphnis and Chloe* (1905); *The Life Work of Calderon* (n.d.); *The Life Work of Henrik Ibsen* (n.d.); *The Life Work of Montaigne* (n.d.); *The Life Work of Pliny the Younger* (n.d.); *The Life Work of Flaubert* (n.d.); *The Life Work of Marcus Aurelius* (n.d.); *The Life Work of Dostoievski* (n.d.); *The Acropolis* (n.d.); *Joseph Pilsudski* (1921); *The Menace of the Mob* (1921); *Michael Angelo, and Other Sketches* (1930)

BIBLIOGRAPHY: Chuzeville, J., *D. M.* (1922); Matlaw, R. E., "The Manifesto of Russian Symbolism," *SEEJ*, 3 (1957): 177–91; Schmourlo, A., de, *Le pensée de M.* (1957); Bedford, C. H., *The Seeker: D. S. M.* (1975); Rosenthal, B. G., *M. and the Silver Age* (1975)

—C. HAROLD BEDFORD

MERI, Veijo

Finnish novelist, short-story writer, dramatist, poet, and essayist, b. 31 Dec. 1928, Viipuri (now Vyborg, Russia)

Son of a noncommissioned officer in the Finnish army who was promoted to commissioned rank for conspicuous gallantry during the war of 1941–44, M. grew up in garrison towns and graduated from secondary school in 1948, but did not pursue his studies further. Since the publication of his first collection of short stories, *Ettei maa viheriöisi* (1954; so that the earth might not grow green), he has devoted himself entirely to literature. He was awarded the Finnish government's Sillanpää Prize for Literature in 1963, the government's Pro Finlandia Medal for artistic merit in 1967, the Nordic (Scandinavian) Council Literary Prize in 1973, and the honorary title of Artist Professor in 1975.

M. has stated that he was deeply marked by the wartime atmosphere in which he grew up; in the preface to the novel *Manillaköysi* (1957; *The Manila Rope*, 1964), for instance, he writes, in an ironic vein satirizing patriotic bombast: "Our generation had also been morally trained to be soldiers. . . . Life is a short and simple thing and requires of every individual that he live and die fearlessly for his country on land, on the sea, and in the air." M. indicates in this statement, by slight twists on patriotic rhetoric, that he does not take war and life in general quite so seriously as most people do. The adjective "absurd" has often been applied to his works; they are, however, not like BECKETT's or IONESCO's. His characters are often energetic and articulate. But misunderstandings and lack of proper communication frustrate their efforts and lead to confused situations or sudden eruptions of violence. Such events may be taken humorously; M. himself says about humor in

his essay "Huumorista ja humoristeista" (1968; on humor and humorists): "It is a bad mistake to think that humor is tragedy that falls flat. One-hundred-percent-effective tragedy is humor. When a person is shy and weak and cannot run very well, and, in spite of that, he is roughed up and chased, that is humor (Chaplin)."

War and military life, which are frequent subjects in M.'s earlier works, give him ample opportunity to describe meaningless violence which is rendered even more absurd by an insistence on rigid regulations—a nuisance that can be skillfully bypassed in peacetime, as in the novel *Yhden yön tarinat* (1967; the tales of one night), but is positively dangerous in war, as in another novel, *Sujut* (1961; quits), in which the main character is sentenced and nearly shot by his own officers because he fights efficiently, but not according to regulations.

Relations between the sexes play a larger part in M.'s works on civilian life than in those on war, as in, for example, the short-story collection *Sata metriä korkeat kirjaimet* (1969; letters one hundred meters high), the title story of which was adapted for the stage as *Sano Oili vaan* (1974; just say Oili), and the novel *Jääkiekkoilijan kesä* (1980; the summer of an ice-hockey player). These relations are somewhat less frustrating than others described by M., for the partners often achieve an enjoyable sexual union; nevertheless, they find it difficult, if not impossible, to have a life together, not so much because of emotional incompatibility as because of difficulties arising from their surroundings. In some of M.'s works, the realistic depiction of characters and actions is at times interrupted by sudden visions of dreamlike landscapes, conceived not as symbols or metaphors but rather as projections of the character's psychic processes.

In recent years M. has published three collections of poems: *Mielen lähtälasku* (1976; the countdown of the mind), *Toinen sydän* (1978; another heart), and *Ylimpänä pieni höyhen* (1980; uppermost a small feather). His verse is a natural offshoot of his prose style: nonrealistic, although not fantastic images are combined with views of everyday life into a personal vision of the world.

M.'s nonfictional work covers a variety of subjects: his travels, people he has met, and famous figures of the past. His well-documented biography of the great 19th-c. Finnish writer who published under the pseudonym Aleksis Kivi (1834–1872), *Aleksis Stenvallin elämä* (1973; enlarged ed., 1975; the life of Aleksis Stenvall), was adapted for the stage as *Aleksis Kivi* (1974; Aleksis Kivi). Because of the conjectural elements in it, this work elicited adverse criticism from some literary scholars.

M. belongs to the generation of writers of the 1950s, who brought about considerable changes in Finnish literature, although they did not have a common program or literary theory. While no mere entertainer, M. is probably the most popular among them, as well as the most prolific through the present day. With his rough humor and his penetrating view of the absurdities of everyday life, he has contributed to demolishing a number of myths and taboos—especially about war and sex.

FURTHER WORKS: *Irralliset* (1959); *Vuoden 1918 tapahtumat* (1960); *Tilanteita* (1962); *Peiliin piirretty nainen* (1963); *Suomen paras näyttelijä* (1963); *Tukikohta* (1964); *Sotamies Jokisen vihkiloma* (1965); *Everstin autonkuljettaja* (1966); *Kaksitoista artikkelia* (1968); *Suku* (1968); *Neljä näytelmää* (1970); *Kersantin poika* (1971); *Morsiamen sisar ja muita novelleja* (1972); *Leiri* (1972); *Kuviteltu kuolema* (1974); *Kaksi komediaa* (1978); *Goethen tammi* (1978); *Tuusulan rantatie* (1981)

BIBLIOGRAPHY: Bolgár, M., and C. Sylvian, Afterword to V. M.'s *Une histoire de corde* [French tr. of *Manillaköysi*] (1962): 139–45; Laitinen, K., "Väinö Linna and V. M.: Two Aspects of War," *BA*, 36 (1962): 365–67; Starkmann, A., "Ein großer finnischer Erzähler: Drei Werke V. M.s wurden ins Deutsche übersetzt," *Die Welt der Literatur*, 14 Sept. 1967: 1–2; Stormbom, N.-B., "V. M. and the New Finnish Novel," *ASR*, 55 (1967): 264–69; Dauenhauer, R., "The Literature of Finland," *LitR*, 14, 1 (1970): 18–22; Ahokas, J. A., "The Short Story in Finnish Literature," in Dauenhauer, R., and P. Binham, eds., *Snow in May: An Anthology of Finnish Writing 1945–1972* (1978): 35–37

—JAAKKO A. AHOKAS

MERRILL, James

American poet, novelist, dramatist, and essayist, b. 3 March 1926, New York, N.Y.; d. 2 Feb. 1995, Tucson, Ariz.

M.'s father, Charles E. Merrill, was a wealthy financier and founder of America's premier investment firm. This accident of fate was decisive in two ways: it allowed M. the luxury of cultivating a considerable poetic talent without any other career or any financial restraints, and the connection to fabulous wealth helped to develop in him a sense of the extraordinary—the mythical. Educated in both America and Europe, beginning with undergraduate years at Amherst College (B.A., 1947), M. worked hard at

James Merrill

the traditional stanzaic patterns, meter, and rhyme of English poetry. He studied music and classical and modern languages and read extensively in literature and the arts.

While he has worked with success at both drama—*The Immortal Husband* (1956); *The Bait* (1960)—and the novel—*The Seraglio* (1957), *The (Diblos) Notebook* (1965)—M. has most distinguished himself as a lyric poet in the pure sense of poetry as rooted in musical expression. Although his sheer mastery of prosody was evident from the earliest volumes—*The Black Swan* (1946), *First Poems* (1951), *The Country of a Thousand Years of Peace* (1959)—their highly formal and, to some extent, hermetic poems revealed the strain of imposing the traditional forms of prosody on contemporary English. M. persisted in his poetic craftmanship, and several volumes later—by the time of *The Fire Screen* (1969) and *Braving the Elements* (1972)—critics and award committees agreed that he had become a master of lyric expression. Many critics feel he is the finest lyric voice in America today, and some have claimed him to be the finest lyric poet since YEATS.

Until recently M.'s themes have been the familiar ones of lyric poetry: autobiography, nature, the particularities of time and place (especially his several homes), the adventures of travel, the stages of love and death, the ecstasies and agonies of encounter and departure, and his memory of literature and the other arts. His approach to these themes is essentially a combination of 17th-c. English metaphysical poetry, the great romantic odes, and French SYMBOLISM: nature and the arts are both symbolic of the spirit, words carefully chosen and used are pregnant with presences; meditated on long enough through symbols and words, nature reveals transcendent messages, and a series of lovers or landscapes coalesce into a platonic essence. Several of the poems in *Braving the Elements*—"Willoware Cup," "Up and Down"—and *Divine Comedies* (1976)—"Lost in Translation"—are masterpieces in the genre. These lyrics are so multifaceted and highly polished that they reflect almost any light the reader brings to them.

In addition to this lyric voice, M. has long cultivated a narrative voice in verse: long, discursive narrative poems like "From the Cupola" (1963), "Days of 1935" (1972), and "Days of 1971" (1972). These poems, which like his plays and novels compound myth and biography—sometimes indistinguishably—have found their fulfillment recently in a three-volume visionary epic: *The Book of Ephraim* (printed in *Divine Comedies*), *Mirabell: Books of Number* (1978), and *Scripts for the Pageant* (1980). In this extraordinary but flawed work, M., through the medium of a Ouija board, communicates with the dead and with the spirits and forces of the universe, including God Biology. In an endlessly unfurling mock-heroic pageant, M. has all his questions about the nature of the universe and the evolution of life answered. The epic, whose three parts are published together under the title *The Changing Light at Sandover* (1982), delineates dazzling contemporary analogies to Dante's vision while gathering into itself practically every form of the pop-spiritualism of modern times, including ESP, reincarnation, mediums, astrology, and numerology.

In its autobiographical dimensions, the epic serves as M.'s poetics—revisiting at length the scenes and personae of his life—as well as the first epic with a specifically homosexual content. On another level, it is one of the few apocalyptic epics since the Bible to respond to the evolving modes—from animism through monotheism to the mysteries of contemporary science—of man's spiritual awareness. Ironically, to achieve this vision, M. has surrendered his miraculous poetic craft by accepting the mechanistic dictates of the Ouija board. But lyric poems contained within the epic as well as several published subsequently indicate that M.'s lyric voice is still masterfully mature: it is somewhat looser and therefore broader in its scope; somewhat less hermetic and therefore closer to the luminous wisdom of the greatest lyricism.

FURTHER WORKS: *Short Stories* (1954); *Selected Poems* (1961); *Water Street* (1962); *Nights and Days* (1966); *The Yellow Pages* (1974); *From the First Nine: Poems 1946–1978* (1982)

BIBLIOGRAPHY: Yenser, S., on *Braving the Elements, Poetry*, 122 (1973): 163–68; Sáez, R., "J. M.'s Oedipal Fire," *Parnassus*, 3, 1 (1974): 159–84; Kalstone, D., "J. M.," *Five Temperaments* (1977): 77–128; Yenser, S., on *Mirabell, YR*, 68 (1979): 556–66; Vendler, H., "V Work," *New Yorker*, 3 Sept. 1979: 95–105; Howard, R., *Alone with America*, enl. ed. (1980): 386–441; Lehman, D., and C. Berger, *J. M.: Essays in Criticism* (1982)

—RICHARD SÁEZ

MERWIN, W(illiam) S(tanley)

American poet and translator, b. 30 Sept. 1927, New York, N.Y.

Son of a Presbyterian minister, M. grew up in Scranton, Pennsylvania, and attended Princeton (A.B., 1947), where R. P. BLACKMUR was his mentor. M. moved to Europe in 1949 to work as a tutor; in 1950 he tutored Robert GRAVES's son. In London (1951–54), he did translations of Spanish and French classics for the BBC Third Programme. Returning to America in 1956, M. wrote plays for The Poets' Theatre in Cambridge, Massachusetts, and served as poetry editor of *The Nation* (1961–63) before going again to France. Since 1968 he has lived in the U.S.

M.'s poetry reveals a Wallace Stevens-like quest for harmony, for a satisfactory statement of the relationship of man's order to natural order. His work, therefore, is process-oriented, as the motifs of the aborted journey and of the inadequately defined experience suggest. In his early work, for example, *A Mask for Janus* (1952), M.'s search is inhibited by his virtuosity in traditional, inherited techniques and forms. His skepticism about the possibility of a reconciliation between man and nature produce the bleakness of vision and the humorlessness in his poetry.

M. wrote in the essay "On Open Form" (1967) that poetry requires "an unduplicative resonance, something that would be like an echo except that it is repeating no sound. Something that always belonged to it; its sense and its conformation before it entered words . . . poetry seems to have to keep reverting to its naked condition, where it touches on all that is unrealized."

In *The Drunk in the Furnace* (1960), M. broke away from traditional poetic structures and conventions and began to compose poetry better suited to his personal vision. The new style, marked by colloquialism and syntactical structures that permitted greater ambiguity, strikingly resembles that of Robert FROST. *The Moving Target* (1963), which won the National Book Award, confirmed the new direction M. had taken. In his indictment of "a society whose triumphs one after the other emerge as new symbols of death, and that feeds itself by poisoning the earth," M. bears comparison to Robinson JEFFERS.

Miner's Pale Children (1970) and *Houses and Travelers* (1977) include numerous stories and sketches that contain mythic, fabulous, and legendary elements in a prose style that is essentially

poetic. M. has also been a prolific translator of works both classic and esoteric.

Although M. has published widely in various journals and continues to appear in *The New Yorker*, he has not received much attention from the general public, who may find his sobriety and sophistication to be more vexatious than solacing. Most other poets and the critics, however, have praised M.'s craft and intellect. Useful comparisons and contrasts between M.'s work and that of others remain to be made before M.'s final position in American letters will be defined.

FURTHER WORKS: *The Dancing Bears* (1954); *Green with Beasts* (1956); *Darkling Child* (1956, with Dido Milroy); *Favor Island* (1957); Lope Felix de Vega Carpio, *Punishment without Vengeance* (1958, trans.); *The Poem of the Cid* (1959, trans.); *Spanish Ballads* (1960, trans.); *The Satires of Persius* (1960, trans.); *The Gilded West* (1961); *The Life of Lazarillo de Tormes* (1962, trans.); *The Song of Roland* (1963, trans.); *The Lice* (1967); *Three Poems* (1968); *Selected Translations: 1948–1968* (1968); *Animae* (1969); *Transparence of the World: Poems of Jean Follain* (1969, trans.); *Voices: Selected Writings of Antonio Porchia* (1969, trans.); Pablo Neruda, *Twenty Love Poems* (1969, trans.); *The Carrier of Ladders* (1970); *Writings to an Unfinished Accompaniment* (1973); *Asian Figures* (1973, trans.); Osip Mandelstam, *Selected Poems* (1974, trans. with Clarence Brown); *The Compass Flower* (1977); *Sanskrit Love Poems* (1977, trans. with J. Moussaief-Masson); Euripides, *Iphigenia at Aulis* (1978, trans. with George E. Dimock, Jr.); *Selected Translations: 1968–1978* (1979); *Finding the Islands* (1982); *Unframed Originals: Recollections* (1982); *Opening the Hand* (1983); *From the Spanish Morning* (1985); *W. S. M.: Essays on Poetry* (1987); *The Rain in the Trees* (1988); *Lost Upland* (1992); *The Second Four Books of Poems* (1993); *Travels* (1993)

BIBLIOGRAPHY: Benston, A. N., "Myth in the Poetry of W. S. M.," in Hungerford, E., ed., *Poets in Progress* (1962): 179–204; Howard, R., *Alone with America: Essays on the Art of Poetry in the United States since 1950* (1969): 349–81; Atlas, J., "Diminishing Returns: The Writings of W. S. M.," in Shaw, R. B., ed., *American Poetry since 1960: Some Critical Perspectives* (1973): 69–81; Davis, C. C., "Time and Timelessness in the Poetry of W. S. M.," *MPS*, 6 (1975): 224–36; Watkins, E., "W. S. M.: A Critical Accompaniment," *Boundary 2*, 4 (1976): 187–200; Christhilf, M., "W. S. M.: The Poet as Creative Conservator," *ModA*, 23 (1979): 167–77; Contoski, V., "W. S. M.: Rational and Irrational Poetry," *LitR*, 22 (1979): 309–320; Christhilf, M. M., *W. S. M.: The Mythmaker* (1986); Brunner, E. J., *Poetry as Labor and Privilege: The Writings of W. S. M.* (1991)

—ARTHUR B. COFFIN

MÉSZÖLY, Miklós

(pseud. of Miklós Molnár) Hungarian short-story writer, novelist, essayist, dramatist, and poet, b. 19 Jan. 1921, Szekszárd

Educated in his native town and at Pázmány University in Budapest, M. finished his Ph.D. in law and started writing short stories. Sent to fight on the Russian front in World War II, he became a prisoner of war. After his return from the Soviet Union, he worked as an editor in Szekszárd and published a collection of short stories entitled *Vadvizek* (1948; marshy tracts). When communist dictatorship started in Hungary in 1948, M. became one of the most consistent critics of the political system. Because of his intransigence, he had serious difficulties earning a living. In 1951–1953 he worked for a puppet-show theater in Budapest. Since he was not allowed to publish anything but fairy tales intended for children, his stories written before the outbreak of the revolution of October 1956 were published only later, in the collection *Sötétet jelek* (1957; ominous signs). They reflect memories of the war and draw a dark picture of totalitarianism. "A stiglic" (1954; the goldfinch) is about mass deportations, and *Magasiskola* (1967; the estate), a short novel which had to wait eleven years before it was published, presents power as a force inevitably alienated from human values.

After 1956 M. was allowed to publish, but was constantly attacked by the political authorities for his pessimism. His novel *Az atléta halála* (1966; the death of an athlete) was published first in French as *Mort d'un athléte* (1965) and then in Hungarian. The message of his works is certainly at odds with communist ideology: Life is viewed from the perspective of death. The title story of *Jelentés öt egérröl* (1967; *Report on Five Mice*, 1983), written in 1958, is a grotesque parable about cruelty. In *Az atléta halála*, a book that was also translated into German in 1966 and into Danish in 1967, the wife of an athlete tries to write a biography of her husband, who died under mysterious circumstances; in *Saulus* (1968; Saulus) the death of Jesus makes the hero examine his values and lose his old identity; and in *Film* (1976; film) history appears as an endless process of deaths caused by political terror.

Many of M.'s short stories focus on the shifting interpretations of the history of central Europe and suggest that the very concept of history is illegitimate, since it depends on the knowledge of the future. In "Öregek, halottak" (1973; the old and the dead) the past becomes the object of constant distortion; in "Térkép Aliscáról" (1973; a map of Alisca) the legacy of the author's native town is interpreted as a long series of incidents that have left no trace; in "Magyar novella" (1979; a Hungarian novella) Jamma, a boy who was shot at the age of five, becomes a legendary figure whose story is reinterpreted after each war; and in "Lóregény" (1982; "A Tale of Horses," 1986) a question is asked about the legitimacy of all teleological constructs, including the story about the Resurrection.

M.'s early works are marked by an interest in the fantastic and the parabolic, whereas his later phase—anticipated by the short story "Film, az Emkénél" (1964; a film, near the Emke café)—is characterized by an interrelationship between autobiography and fiction. The haunting memories of the war reappear in several stories, including "Lesiklás" (1976; downhill), and the first-person narration often goes together with an emphasis on the difficulties of storytelling and with a technique somewhat reminiscent of the French NEW NOVEL, as, for instance, in the title story of the collection *Alakulások* (1975; transformations), or in "Levél a völgyból" (1985; a letter from the valley), a self-reflexive meditation centered around texts by Pierre Reverdy and Ludwig Wittgenstein.

In the 1970s and 1980s M.'s goal became to blur the distinction between object and subject, narrated and narrator. This is especially true of *Merre a csillag Jár* (1985; where the star moves), a collection of stories and verse. *Megbocsátás* (1984; forgiveness), a short novel, is not the author's latest work, but it can be regarded as one of his finest achievements, a synthesis of the best qualities of his art. The style of this short novel is laconic, the narrator is detached, yet the modality of the storytelling is elegiac. In the

absence of teleology, life appears as a mosaic of fragments that are seen or visualized with exceptional clarity.

In the 1950s M. was a solitary figure who ignored the aesthetics of SOCIALIST REALISM. A character of great moral and artistic integrity, he kept the impulse of experiment and innovation alive in Hungarian fiction in the darkest period of Hungarian history. No other single writer has made a more consistent, sustained, and significant contribution to Hungarian prose over the last fifty years.

FURTHER WORKS: *Hétalvó puttonyocska* (1955); *Fekete gólya* (1960); *Ablakmosó* (1963); *Bunker* (1964); *A hiú Cserépkirálykisasszony* (1964); *Hajnalfa* (1964); *Az elvarázsolt tűzoltózenekar* (1965); *Pontos történetek útközben* (1970; rev. ed., 1989); *A tágasság iskolája* (1977); *Érintések* (1980); *Esti térkép* (1981); *Sutting ezredes tündöklése* (1987); *A pille magánya* (1989); *Volt egyszer egy Közép-Európa* (1989); *Wimbledoni jácint* (1990)

BIBLIOGRAPHY: Jastzebska, J., *Personnages tragiques et grotesques dans la littérature hongroise contemporaine* (1989): 75–96

—MIHÁLY SZEGEDY-MASZÁK

MÉTELLUS, Jean

Haitian novelist, poet, dramatist, and essayist, b. 30 Apr. 1937, Jacmel

M. was born in Jacmel, the second most important city in Haiti, after Port-au-Prince. His father was a baker and his mother was a dressmaker. M.'s parents, one a member of the black bourgeoisie and the other a member of the powerful mulatto bourgeoisie, represented in and of themselves the split inherent in the population of Haiti. Thus, from the experiences within his own family, M. developed a keen sense of Haitian history, identity, and difference, all of which are reflected in his work. M. lived in Haiti and worked as a math teacher until he was forced into exile in 1957. From there, he went to Paris, where he studied medicine. M. remains in Paris, where he is a practicing neurologist and speech pathologist.

M. has been an extremely prolific writer, producing not only literary works but also historical and political books and essays, as well as medical research. His first literary contributions were poems, published initially in various journals and subsequently in book-length poetry collections, the first of which was *Au Pipirite Chantant* (1978; To the Singing Bird). This collection and those that followed contain both long and short poems that treat the various themes present in all of M.'s work: the Haitian landscape; the people and history of Haiti; the question of political engagement; the nature of literary and artistic creation; the role of the artist in society. Furthermore, the range of M.'s creative talent is evident in his poetry, which treats subjects as varied as female beauty and the life and death of Malcolm X. Five other collections of M.'s poetry have been published: *Tous ces chants sereins . . .* (1980; All These Serene Chants); *Hommes de plein vent* (1981; Men of the wind); *Voyance* (1984; Sight); *Jacmel* (1991), and *Voix nègres* (1991; Black Voices).

Although his talent as writer spans several genres, M. is best known for his novels. He has, to date, published eight novels that can be divided into two broad categories—those that deal with

Haiti and those that deal with Europe—demonstrate M.'s commitment to political action, his talent for capturing the diversity of the human condition, and his close ties to his native land, despite a nearly forty-year period of exile. M. has published five works that can be considered to be Haitian novels: *Jacmel au crépuscule* (1981; Jacmel at Dusk), *La famille Vortex* (1982; The Vortex Family), *L'année Dessalines* (1986; The Year of Dessalines), *Les cacos* (1989; The Cacos), and *Louis Vortex* (1992; Louis Vortex).

Jacmel au crépuscule is a political allegory that recounts the rise and fall of Pisquette, a street merchant from Jacmel. Pisquette rises to prominence by winning the national lottery, then falls back into poverty and despair as a result of the prejudice and hypocrisy that rule the town. Set in 1956, the novel alludes to the rise and fall of President Magloire of Haiti, who came to power in 1950 amid the promise of a new regime, but who was ultimately overthrown in 1956 as a result of his decadence and his lack of connection with the Haitian people.

Perhaps the most striking aspect of *Jacmel au crépuscule* is the way in which it is constructed. Told largely through the voices of the various (fictional) inhabitants of Jacmel, the novel takes on the character and dimension of oral history, and becomes a vehicle for M. to present people of Haiti from all classes, colors, and backgrounds. This use of multiple voices is prevalent in M.'s fiction and in his theater, and it embodies the democratic principles for which M. has long been a champion. As much as a political allegory, *Jacmel au crépuscule* is also a sociological study, documenting the lives and concerns of everyday Haitians.

Three of M.'s four remaining Haitian novels form a saga chronicling the members of a single, fictional Haitian family—the Vortex family—from the period 1949 to 1960. This eleven-year span covers events beginning with the election of President Magloire and ending with establishment of the Duvalier regime. M. uses this turbulent backdrop to explore the impact of politics on the lives of the people of Haiti. Through the more than three hundred characters presented in the saga, M. examines the problems and concerns faced by people from all walks of life. In addition, M. explores the impact of exile on the individual, presenting characters who are forced by the political situation to flee the country. Like *Jacmel au Crépuscule*, the Vortex saga combines political criticism with sociological investigation, providing insight into Haitian society, and into the effects of political upheaval on any society.

M.'s European novels differ from his Haitian novels in more than their setting. *Une eau forte* (1983; A Strong Current), *La parole prisonnière* (1986; Imprisoned Speech), and *Charles Honoré Bonnefoy* (1990; Charles Honoré Bonnefoy) all deal with more intellectual and aesthetic concerns than M.'s Haitian texts. A common theme in these works is the nature and function of artistic creation, a theme also common to M.'s poetry.

With the publication of his three plays, *Anacona* (1986; Anacona), *Le pont rouge* (1991; The Red Bridge), and *Colomb* (1992; Columbus), M. expanded his literary repertoire as well as his thematic range. These three plays, all of which deal with pre-20th-c. Haitian history, provide an insight into the devastating effects of colonialism and slavery on the Caribbean, and chronicle the resistance of "new world" inhabitants, from the Indians to the slaves, against such oppression. Taken with all of M.'s other works, the plays complete an ensemble which proves M. to be one of the most productive and poignant writers of the Francophone world.

BIBLIOGRAPHY: Deschamps, A., "J. M.: Poète, romancier, dramaturge," *Nouvelles du Sud*, 1 (1985): 87-89; Taleb-Kyar, M., "J. M.," *Callaloo*, 15 (1992): 338-41; Naudillon, F., "La Saga des Vortex de J. M.," *Litteréalité* , 7 (1995): 81-99; Naudillon, F., *J. M.*(1997)

—DAYNA L. OSCHERWITZ

MEXICAN LITERATURE

Mexican literature in the 19th c. was dominated by romanticism, a movement well suited to the national character as well as to the historical situation of the time. Toward 1880 realist and MODERNIST writers reacted against the excesses of the romanticists, occupying the literary stage for approximately the next thirty years. Although both of these schools would leave their mark on future generations, it was the aesthetically oriented elite-minded modernist poets such as Manuel Gutiérre Nájera (1859–1895), Salvador Díaz Mirón (1853–1928), Amado NERVO, and José Juan Tablada (1871–1945) who produced works of the most lasting literary value. Influenced by the French Parnassians and SYMBOLISTS, these writers emphasized perfection of form while experimenting with new metrical rhythms in order to enhance the flexibility and musicality of the Spanish language. They also sought to revitalize Spanish American literature by injecting exotic or fantastic elements, thus rendering its content more cosmopolitan and universal.

The political regime of Porfirio Díaz, which was overthrown by the revolution of 1910, coincided with the domination of Mexican education by positivism, a scientifically oriented philosophy imported from France. In 1908 Justo Sierra (1848–1912), Mexico's leading intellectual of the time, rejected positivism for the more subjective philosophy of Henri BERGSON, and the following year there appeared a group of writers known as the Atheneum of Youth, who sought not only to strengthen Mexican ties with classical European thought but also to create a culture more in tune with the realities of Mexican life. The literature of the thirty years between 1915 and 1945 is characterized by two basic trends: in fiction, the realistic dramatization of social issues; and in poetry, the search for innovative forms.

Fiction

The Mexican Revolution and its aftermath provided the warp and woof of many novels, the best of which was *Los de abajo* (1916; *The Underdogs*, 1929) by Mariano AZUELA. This naturalistic epic captures the immediacy of the revolution in a montage of fast-moving scenes depicting the initial enthusiasm, the brutality, and the eventual disillusionment of its exhausted peasant participants. Although often referred to as an epic, it also conveys the author's disenchantment with the revolution, which he suspects will be betrayed by a new class of oppressors. Another fine account of the revolution is *El águila y la serpiente* (1928; *The Eagle and the Serpent*, 1930) by Martín Luis GUZMÁN, whose role as Pancho Villa's secretary enabled him to observe the manipulation of power by leading figures of the movement.

The most outstanding political novel of this period is Guzmán's *La sombra del caudillo* (1929; in the leader's shadow), a roman à clef based on a power struggle during the regime (1924–28) of President Plutarco Elías Calles. *Indigenista* fiction, which describes the lives of oppressed Indians, is best represented by *El resplandor* (1937; *Sunburst*, 1944) by Mauricio MAGDALENO, and

El indio (1935; *El Indio*, 1937) by Gregorio LÓPEZ Y FUENTES. José Rubén ROMERO's excellent picaresque novel *La vida inútil de Pito Pérez* (1938; *The Futile Life of Pito Pérez*, 1967) satirizes the society that emerged after the Revolution.

Mexican fiction of the 1940s and 1950s was characterized by universal themes and structural innovations reflecting the intellectual and social impact of World War II. Most representative of this period are four gifted writers: José Revueltas (1914–1976), who focused on human suffering and injustice in works such as *El luto humano* (1943; *The Stone Knife*, 1947); Agustín YÁÑEZ, whose *Al filo del agua* (1947; *The Edge of the Storm*, 1963) is considered a landmark novel because of its Freudian analysis of repressed villagers just before the revolution of 1910; Juan RULFO, whose complex masterpiece *Pedro Páramo* (1955; *Pedro Páramo*, 1959) evokes the past of a ghost town and its corrupt political boss; and Juan José ARREOLA, a cosmopolitan humorist known above all for his impeccably stylized philosophical tales collected in *Confabulario* (1952; *Confabulario, and Other Inventions*, 1964).

During the past twenty years an unprecedented explosion of talent in fiction has tended to overshadow other genres in Mexico. Carlos FUENTES has emerged not only as the nation's leading novelist but also as a major figure of international stature. His experiments with a wide variety of techniques and his broad knowledge of philosophy and other literatures have enhanced his ability to capture the Mexican experience in universal terms. Two of Fuentes's finest novels are *La muerte de Artemio Cruz* (1962; *The Death of Artemio Cruz*, 1964), in which a dying Mexican tycoon relives the existential decisions of his life that ultimately determine his essence; and *Terra Nostra* (1975; *Terra nostra*, 1976), a quest for the origins of absolute authority in Hispanic America through an insightful examination of European culture.

After Rulfo, Arreola, and Fuentes, Mexico's most important living writers of fiction are Vicente LEÑERO, Salvador ELIZONDO, Gustavo SAINZ, and José AGUSTÍN. Leñero shares Fuentes's preoccupation with literary technique, as evidenced by *Los albañiles* (1964; the bricklayers), a fascinating murder mystery with profound social and philosophical overtones. Like Fuentes, Elizondo is a cosmopolitan man of letters whose most intriguing novel, *Farabeuf* (1965; Farabeuf), demonstrates his ability to assimilate foreign philosophies and techniques such as those of the NEW NOVEL. Sainz and Agustín typify the Onda (Wave), a movement of young, irreverent writers of the 1960s whose works mock the time-honored values of the establishment. Typical examples of the Wave are Sainz's *Gazapo* (1965; *Gazapo*, 1968) and Agustín's *De perfil* (1966; from the side). Now more mature, these two authors are continuing to impress their reading public with avant-garde portraits of disoriented youths caught up in the chaotic life of the burgeoning Mexican capital.

Many other novelists have contributed to the enrichment of contemporary Mexican fiction. In works such as *Las muertas* (1977; the dead ones) and *Dos crímenes* (1979; two crimes) Jorge IBARGÜENGOITIA demonstrates his mastery of irony by portraying characters trapped in a labyrinthine world beyond their comprehension. Unlike Ibargüengoitia, who fabricates clear, well-constructed plots, Sergio Fernández (b. 1926) relies on stylistic devices likely to appeal to the more sophisticated reader. His novels, a fine example of which is *Los peces* (1968; the fish), express the disillusionment and alienation so characteristic of life in a modern metropolis. In his complex, prize-winning *Palinuro de México* (1977; Palinuro of Mexico) Fernando del Paso (b. 1935) utilizes classical myth as a point of departure for his treatment of the

massacre by army troops of demonstrating students in Tlatelolco Square in 1968. Mexico's best-known living female novelist, Elena PONIATOWSKA, has sensitively captured the atmosphere of the Mexican Revolution in her fine novel *Hasta no verte Jesús mío* (1969; farewell, my Jesus), which dramatizes an uneducated woman's experiences during the uprising. And, although hardly known for his literary artistry, Luis SPOTA is Mexico's most popular writer, having published more than twenty best sellers on subjects ranging from bullfighting and wetbacks to the Tlatelolco tragedy and urban guerrilla warfare. One of Spota's most successful novels is *Casi el paraíso* (1956; *Almost Paradise*, 1964), an ingeniously structured satire of Mexico's shallow, hypocritical nouveaux riches.

During the 1960s, Mexico's principal representative of the "boom" in Latin American prose fiction was Carlos FUENTES, whose universal themes and avant-garde techniques typified the outstanding writers of that period. Mexican fiction of the "postboom," that is, the fiction of the past two decades, is characterized not only by the continued publication of established writers, but also by the appearance of numerous younger writers who have profited from the examples set by their predecessors, but who have not necessarily followed in their footsteps. In general, perhaps as a result of the 2 October 1968 massacre of student protesters in Mexico City's Tlatelolco Square, there currently seems to be less emphasis on self-conscious narration and metafiction and more on the representation of social reality, on the recreation of history, and, as John Brushwood has indicated, on a return to telling a story. But according to Danny Anderson, the reality depicted by the "postboom" writers is far more complex than that of traditional realism, which perhaps explains in part another characteristic of the period, namely, the wide diversity of themes.

In recent years Fuentes has enhanced his reputation as Mexico's best novelist. In 1987 he was awarded the Cervantes Prize, the most prestigious literary award given in the Hispanic world. Since the publication of *Terra nostra* (1975; *Terra Nostra*, 1976), his monumental inquiry into Spanish history and culture, four more novels have appeared. *Una familia lejana* (1980; *Distant Relations*, 1982) explores the cultural ties linking the old and new worlds; the dramatic vehicle here is the mysterious relationship between two families, one French and one Mexican, with the same surname. *Gringo viejo* (1985; *The Old Gringo*, 1985) is a lyrical speculation about what happened to the American writer Ambrose BIERCE, who disappeared in Mexico during the Revolution. Fuentes's most ambitious text since *Terra Nostra* is *Christobal nonato* (1987; *Christopher Unborn*, 1988), an hallucinatory vision of Mexico in 1992, the quincentennial of Columbus's discovery of the New World. The protagonist and principal narrator is a fetus whose omniscience affords the reader a series of apocalyptic glimpses of a nation plagued by grinding poverty, exploding population, incredible pollution, and an invasion by gringos determined to prevent Mexico's oil fields from falling into communist hands. For his latest novel, *La campaña* (1990; the campaign), Fuentes has turned to early 19th-c. Argentina to chronicle the epic struggle of that nation for independence from Spain.

Among the other writers of the 1960s who have maintained a high profile into the 1990s are Sergio Galindo (1926–1993) and Fernando DEL PASO. An inspired creator of tense, dramatic situations, Galindo won an important literary prize for his psychological novel *Otilia Rauda* (1986; *Otilia Body*, 1994). Del Paso writes long, difficult texts praised by the critics but read only by sophisticated readers. Two examples of these are *Palinuro de México* (1977; Palinuro of Mexico), a digressive meditation on politics, philosophy, and language; and *Noticias del imperio* (1987; news of the empire), a historical novel set in the 1860s during the Hapsburg intervention in Mexico.

Gustavo SAINZ and José AGUSTÍN, the two leading representatives of *la onda*, (the wave), a group of irreverent young writers of the 1960s, have emerged as major literary voices today. Language becomes a predominant factor in Sainz's *La princesa del Palacio de Hierro* (1974; *The Princess of the Iron Palace*, 1987), the monologue of a frivolous young woman detailing her escapades with a circle of hedonistic companions, whereas *Fantasmas aztecas: Un pre-texto* (1982; Aztec phantoms: a pre-text) is a brilliant piece of self-conscious fiction based on the excavation of the Aztec Templo Mayor (Main Temple), in the heart of Mexico City. Agustín's two most important novels during the past decade are *Ciudades desiertas* (1982; deserted cities) and *Cerca del fuego* (1986; near the fire). The former reflects the author's negative views of the U.S., where he has lectured at many universities. In *Cerca del fuego* Augustín's most important work to date, the narrator, having recovered from a six-year bout with amnesia, confronts the chaotic ambience of Mexico City at the end of President José López Portillo's term of office (1976–1982).

Prominent practitioners of the nonfiction novel, Elena PONIATOWSKA and Vicente LEÑERO also began their careers in the 1960s. Leñero's ventures into this genre include *Los periodistas* (1978; the journalists), an engrossing chronicle of a dispute between *Excélsior* (Mexico's most prestigious newspaper) and then President Luis Echeverría, and *La gota de agua* (1983; the drop of water), the entertaining account of Leñero's predicament when the supply of water to his home is shut off.

Now embedded in the Mexican collective subconscious, the Tlatelolco massacre has, not surprisingly, produced what some critics have labeled "the novel of Tlatelolco," typified by works such as *El gran solitario de palacio* (1968; alone in the palace) by René Avilés Fabila (b. 1935), *Con él, conmigo, con nosotros tres* (1971; with him, with me, with us three) by Maria Luisa Mendoza (b. 1931), *La plaza* (1972; the square) by Luis SPOTA, and *La invitación* (1972; the invitation) and *Crónica de la intervención* (1982; chronicle of the intervention) by Juan García Ponce (b. 1932).

As indicated previously, numerous young writers began their careers during the "postboom." Although they reveal a profound sensitivity to conditions in Mexico, their fields of reference encompass the entire globe. Their imaginary worlds are also fraught with subtle meanings designed to stimulate and challenge their readers. Names high on the list of these writers include Arturo AZUELA, Ignacio SOLARES, Homero Aridjis, Hugo Hiriart (b. 1942), Francisco Prieto (b. 1942), Héctor Manjarrez (b. 1945), Luis Arturo Ramos (b. 1947), and Alberto Ruy Sánchez (b. 1951). Two works are especially worthy of note: Hiriart's *Cuadernos de Gofa* (1981; notebooks of Gofa), a densely structured philosophical novel that questions the validity of Western civilization by play fully creating a fictious oriental nation (Gofa), and Aridjis's *1492: Vida y tiempos de Juan Cabezón de Castilla*, (1985; *1492: The Life and Times of Juan Cabezón de Castile*, (1991), which portrays a fourth-generation *converso* (a Jew converted to Christianity) whose narration recreates the bizarre period of Spanish history that prefigured the discovery of America.

During the past decade, women have achieved increasing prominence among Mexican writers of fiction. Elena GARRO, who became known during the 1960s, has published several poetic novels about complex human relationships, as has María Luisa Puga (b. 1944). Others have written best-sellers, including *Arráncame*

la vida (1985; put an end to my life) by Angeles Mastretta (b. 1949), *Como agua para chocolate* (1989; *Like Water for Chocolate*, 1992) by Laura Esquivel (b. 1950), and *La insólita historia de la santa de Cabora* (1990; the unusual story of the Saint of Cabora) by Brianda Domecq (b. 1942). A more serious postmodernist writer, Carmen Boullosa (b. 1954) has published a total of five novels, two of which are *Son vacas, somos puercos* (1991; They are cows, we are pigs), a historical work; and *La milagrosa* (1993; The miraculour one), set in contemporary Mexico.

Finally, to underscore the diversity of contemporary Mexican fiction, mention should be made of the new gay and proleterian subgenres, represented respectively by Luis Zapata (b. 1951) and Armando Ramírez (b. 1950). Influenced by the mass media and popular culture, these two writers use Mexico City as their setting and street vernacular as their medium to document the most shocking aspects of daily life.

Poetry

The works of Enrique GONZÁLEZ MARTÍNEZ and Ramón López Velarde (1888–1921) best exemplify the poetry of the post-modernist period (1915–22). González Martínez's famous poem "Tuércele el cuello al cisne" (1911; "Wring the Neck of the Swan," 1958) expresses his desire to replace the superficial artistry of modernism with a movement of deeper philosophical content symbolized by the meditative owl; and "La suave patria" (1919; "Gentle Fatherland," 1943) by López Velarde represents a richly symbolic, impressionistic mural that not only captures the soul of Mexican life but also marks a complete break with the preceding generation.

The most significant avant-garde schools of poetry are the Estridentistas (the Strident Ones), who flourished 1922–27 and whose tenets reflect Italian futurism and Spanish ULTRAISM, and the Contemporáneos (Contemporaries), who flourished 1928–31, a group of talented poets consisting of Jaime Torres Bodet (1902–1974), Xavier VILLAURRUTIA, Salvador NOVO, Carlos PELLICER, and José Gorostiza (1901–1973). Inspired by Tablada, González Martínez, and López Velarde, as well as by numerous European writers, the Contemporáneos ignored social problems and concentrated on aesthetic questions, such as the manipulation of free verse and the creation of fresh imagery. The most memorable of the works produced by this school is Gorostiza's long poem *Muerte sin fin* (1939; *Death without End*, 1969), which conveys an EXISTENTIALIST awareness of, and fascination with, nothingness. In a somewhat similar vein, Villaurrutia's *Nostalgia de la muerte* (1938; nostalgia of death) views death as a previous form of life, a kind of limbo or womb to which man longs to return.

The undisputed leader of postvanguardist poetry, a movement dating back to the late 1930s, is Octavio PAZ, Mexico's most esteemed living author. The underlying theme in Paz's work is the quest for a better world, a vaster and more magnificent world in which time is obliterated and man no longer experiences existential anguish. This quest is perhaps best expressed in the poem *Piedra de sol* (1957; *Sunstone* 1963), which records life's endless cycles of ecstatic moments and their inevitable collapse in the face of everyday banality. Also characteristic of Paz's verse is his use of surrealistic imagery to capture a dialectical reality generated by opposites, such as life and death, the real and the masked self, progressive and static time.

Outstanding contemporaries of Paz are Efraín Huerta (1914–1982) and Alí Chamucero (b. 1918), the former for his masterful use of popular language to depict the modern metropolis, the latter for his remarkable perfection of form and evocative leitmotifs. During the 1950s four exceptionally gifted poets began their careers: Rubén Bonifaz Nuño (b. 1923), Jaime García Terrés (b. 1924), Jaime SABINES, and Rosario CASTELLANOS. Despite their many differences, these writers share a number of traits, including the description of everyday life, the rejection of rhetorical language, a belief in the supremacy of the metaphor, and a preoccupation with solitude and time. The poets of the 1960s present themes similar to those of their immediate predecessors, but their imagery suggests the influence of SURREALISM, and their styles tend to be more literary and subjective. Prominent representatives of this generation are Marco Antonio Montes de Oca (b. 1932), José Emilio PACHECO, and Homero Aridjis (b. 1940).

Winner of the 1990 Nobel Prize in literature, Octavio PAZ was for decades Mexico's leading poet and most esteemed man of letters. Although in hislater works he repeated many of his previous themes, his imagery remained fresh and his style impeccable. As Steven Bell observes, Paz assimilated the modern age of Western civilization only to reject its decadence and dehumanization. Idealist and mystic, he was concerned above all with language, which he used to capture a kind of paradisiacal ecstasy outside the temporal realm. His principal themes included existential solitude, death, physical love, the passing of time, and the creative process. Paz was fascinated by Mexico's pre-Columbian past but was influenced more by oriental philosophy and surrealism. He was essentially a dialectic poet; his poems achieve dynamic movement through the use of binary oppositions, which he seeks to synthesize into a luminous moment of vision. Later collections include *Pasado en claro* (1975; *A Draft of Shadows*, 1979), which represents a search for self-knowledge, *Vuelta* (1976; return), written upon his return to Mexico after years of absence, and *Arbol adentro* (1987; tree inside), a group of verses conceived since the publication of *Vuelta*.

Contrasting sharply with Paz are Efraín Huerta and Jaime SABINES. Known for his sardonic tone, colloquial language, and unflagging Marxism, Huerta has had considerable influence on the younger generation. Sabines also uses popular language, but he is especially preoccupied with human solitude and the dehumanizing aspects of urban life. His *Mal tiempo* (1972; bad weather) and *Nuevo recuento de poemas* (1983; new recount of poems) helped to win him the National Prize for Literature in 1983. Another major poet is Marco Antonio de Oca (b. 1932), explorer of the mysteries of human existence through brilliant surrealistic imagery.

Frank Dauster states that because of the Tlatelolco massacre, the 1985 earthquake, and the economic depression of the 1980s, Mexican poetry has become increasingly pessimistic. Dauster also sees two major strands of poets since Tlatelolco: those concerned with philosophical issues and those committed to a social agenda. A member of the first group, José Emilio PACHECO is a versatile, widely admired poet who unveils the poetic in everyday life. He also poeticizes his metaphysical concerns with time, death, and a decaying world in collections such as *Irás y no volverás* (1973; you will go and won't return) and *Los trabajos del mar* (1983; the works of the sea). His *Miro la tierra: Poemas (1983–1986)* (1986; I look at the earth: poems, 1983–1986) elicited praise for its anguished depiction of the earthquake.

Other poets of considerable merit include Rubén Bonifaz Nuño, known for his metaliterary and love verses, Rosario CASTELLANOS, who sought to define her role as a woman in a male-dominated society, Homero Aridjis, compared frequently to Paz because of his

surrealistic and erotic imagery, and Elsa Cross (b. 1946), who has found inspiration in existential English and Italian poets.

The Essay

The essay has been a source of cultural enrichment in Mexico throughout the 20th c. The group known as the Atheneum of Youth included such masters as the eminent professor and philosopher Antonio Caso (1883–1946), who inspired the younger generation to abandon positivistic materialism for spiritual values; the political activist and mystical thinker José Vasconcelos (1882–1959), whose famous treatise *La raza cósmica* (1925; the cosmic race) views Latin America as a kind of melting pot for the emergence of a new race; and Alfonso REYES, the brilliant stylist and cosmopolitan humanist.

The first in a long series of essays on the Mexican character is *El perfil del hombre y la cultura en México* (1934; *Profile of Man and Culture in Mexico*, 1962) by Samuel Ramos (1897–1959). According to Ramos, Mexicans should strive for a more universal culture but, at the same time, for a culture that expresses the national soul and will. He inspired a group of thinkers known as the Hyperion, which, under the leadership of the well-known philosopher Leopoldo Zea (b. 1912), continued his investigations of what it means to be Mexican. The most significant examination of this subject is Octavio Paz's *El laberinto de la soledad* (1950; *The Labyrinth of Solitude*, 1961), a penetrating psychological study of the effects of the past on his fellow countrymen's search for identity in the 20th c. Paz is also a perceptive analyst of Mexican politics, his most original and interesting pieces having appeared in *Posdata* (1970; *The Other Mexico*, 1972). And his contributions to literary criticism are evidenced by his recent founding of two journals of exceptionally high quality: *Plural* (1971) and *Vuelta* (1976).

In the area of the essay Mexico has a rich tradition dating back to the 19th c., and since the Revolution the relative freedom of press has encouraged the dissemination of ideas. The older practitioners of the genre, of whom Paz is the most universally known, have often demonstrated an interest in broad subjects such as *lo mexicano* (Mexican essence) whereas, as seen below, the younger generation responds to more immediate circumstances. After the massacre of Tlatelolco, Paz published *Posdata* (1970; *The Other Mexico*, 1972), in which he sees the massacre in mythical terms, relating it to the Aztec ritual of human sacrifice. Paz has also written prolifically on literature and international politics; examples include *Tiempo nublado* (1983; cloudy times), a pessimistic view of the arms race, *Pequeña crónica de grandes días* (1990; short chronicle of great days), about the fall of communist governments in eastern Europe, and *Sor Juana Inés de la Cruz, o Las trampas de la fe* (1982; *Sor Juana Inés de la Cruz, or The Traps of Faith*, 1988), a study of Mexico's 17th-c. nun-poet.

Martin Stabb asserts that Tlatelolco has served as a unifying theme for recent Mexican essayists. Carlos Fuentes, whose essays are almost as widely read as those of Paz, reacted strongly to the massacre in his *Tiempo mexicano* (1972; Mexican time), proclaiming the bankruptcy of Mexico's political system. Thus he (along with others of the younger generation) is not interested in mythical explanations of Tlatelolco, but rather in the conditions that precipitated the tragic loss of life. In this same collection Fuentes attacks Mexico's infatuation with economic development, which he believes will make Mexico City into another Los Angeles, with the accompanying environmental problems. His most recent work, *Valiente mundo nuevo* (1990; valiant new world), speculates on the role of culture in the search for solutions to Latin America's numerous problems.

Soon after the massacre of Tlatelolco, Carlos Monsiváis (b. 1938), an accurate barometer of the times, published a book of essays entitled *Diás de guardar* (1970; days to remember), in which he attacked the political establishment, defended the changing values of young intellectuals, and pronounced the Mexican Revolution dead. In a subsequent volume, *Amor perdido* (1978; lost love), however, he took Mexican youth to task for its emulation of American culture. Now Mexico's second most important essayist (after Octavio Paz), Monsiváis published *Entrada libre: Crónicas de la sociedad que se organiza* (Chronicles of a society being organized) in 1987, which contains opinions about the nation's upheavals during the 1980s.

Another major essayist, Gabriel Zaid (b. 1934), is a kind of Mexican Ralph Nader, but humorous and intellectual. In his *Como leer en bicicleta* (1975; how to read while riding a bicycle) he pokes fun at both the political right and left, and in his next book, *El progreso improductivo* (1979; unproductive progress), he deplores, among other things, the uprooting of peasants who move to the overcrowded capital to get rich and purchase a weekend country home.

Additional voices that have contributed to the wealth of ideas in contemporary Mexico are Cosío Villegas (1898–1976), a historian fascinated with the interaction between the youth movement and the government, Jorge Ibargüengoitia, whose wry humor, like Zaid's, masks a serious intent, and Juan García Ponce and Alberto Dallal (b. 1932), both of whom defend the ideals of the younger generation.

Drama

Mexican playwrights produced little of significance prior to 1928, when the experimental Ulises Theater was formed by Xavier Villaurrutia, Salvador Novo, and Celestino Gorostiza (1904–1967). These talented writers, together with their famous colleague Rodolfo USIGLI, eventually emerged as the creators of the modern Mexican theater. Perhaps the most noteworthy drama of this period is Usigli's *El gesticulador* (1943; the impostor), a gripping portrayal of the Mexican identity crisis that would be explored in greater depth by Octavio Paz. *El gesticulador* also illustrates the role of myth in Mexican history, that is, the emergence of a charismatic figure who embodies the Mexican Revolution and thus attains mythical stature.

In the second half of the century, Mexican theater developed a repertoire of works focusing on both national and universal issues. A leading playwright was Emilio CARBALLIDO, whose works range from the realistic comedy of manners to a more poetic drama characterized by the irrational and the fantastic. His masterpiece, *Yo también hablo de la rosa* (1966; *I Too Speak of the Rose*, 1971) is representative of much of his production. *Los frutos caídos* (1956; the fallen fruit) by Luisa Josefina HERNÁNDEZ is typical of her representations of the emptiness and futility of middle-class life, and Elena GARRO combines a magical, poetic reality with elements of social protest in her best plays, *La mudanza* (1959; the move) and *Los perros* (1965; the dogs).

The works of three additional playwrights have continued to broaden the aesthetic scope of the Mexican stage. Vicente Leñero has achieved considerable success as the initiator of documentary theater, a genre that seeks to educate the public by constructing dramatic plots on materials taken from the news media and court records. A notable example is *El juicio* (1972; the trial), a taut representation of the 1928 trial and conviction of President-Elect Alvaro Obregón's assassins. In contrast to this objective art form, Carlos Fuentes's *Todos los gatos son pardos* (1970; all the cats are dark) has imaginatively probed Mexico's mythical past in order to explain present-day phenomena. And absurdist works such as *Nada como el piso 16* (1977; nothing like the sixteenth floor) by Maruxa Vilalta (b. 1932) satirize the effects of alienation in a complex, urbanized society.

Although Mexican drama still has not achieved the level of prestige generally accorded prose fiction, since World War II the genre has made steady gains. During the 1960s, Carballido emerged as the leading dramatist, a rank he still holds today; he is the founder of the country's most important theater journal, *Tramoya*, and the author of more than one hundred plays. Unlike many of his colleagues, Carballido is not overtly political, but rather, as critic Diana Taylor states, considers culture as fundamental to the people's struggle for liberation. Thus in his opinion Mexican theater should become a cultural instrument for debate and evolutionary change. A master of symbolic expression, Carballido has experimented with a wide variety of avant-garde techniques. Although his plays often deal with Mexican issues, they exude both personal and universal resonances. Two of his recent successes are *Fotografías en la playa* (1980; photographs on the beach), in which an egocentric family reveals some embarrassing secrets, and *Tiempo de ladrones: La historia de Chucho El Roto* (1983; time of thieves: the story of Chucho El Roto), an epic about a 19th-c. Mexican Robin Hood.

After Carballido, Luisa Josefina Hernández and Vicente Leñero are generally considered to be Mexico's most important dramatists. The trajectory of Hernández's career follows that of Carballido, her early works representing realistic psychological portraits of stifling provincial life and her later creations evolving innovative, experimental forms appropriate for a broader range of subjects. Typical of her more recent work is *La calle de la gran ocasión* (1981; the street of the grand occasion), which presents seven fast-moving dialogues covering a broad range of social issues. Leñero has continued writing historical documentaries, as illustrated by his *Martirio de Morelos* (1983; Morelos's martyrdom), which questions official versions of history. His *Alicia, tal vez* (1985; Alice, perhaps), on the other hand, launches a scathing feminist attack on the exploitation of women both in the home and in the workplace.

In the late 1960s a group of young dramatists began to participate in theater workshops under the direction of Carballido, Hernández, and Leñero. Although they have not achieved success comparable to that of their mentors, several are still active today. These dramatists present a pessimistic view of Mexican life; their subjects range from political corruption—the single most important theme—to sadism, machismo, isolation, the generation gap, and escape from an unbearable reality to one that is even worse. Their language tends to be realistic, often crude, and their structures fragmented, designed more than likely to capture an unstable reality created by, or imposed on, their hapless protagonists. Important names of this group are Jesús González Dávila (b. 1941), Oscar Villegas (b.1943), Willebaldo López (b. 1944), Oscar Liera (b. 1946), Tomás Espinosa (b. 1947), and Carlos Olmos (b. 1947).

Mexican literature in the 20th c. reveals a remarkable sensitivity to national realities, reflecting above all the upheaval wrought by the revolution of 1910 and the changes brought about by the urban growth of the post-World War II years. This sensitivity is further illustrated by the great quantity of essays, poetry, and fiction protesting the massacre of students in 1968. Mexican literature during the last twenty years reveals an astonishing number and variety of practitioners of all genres. If this panorama appears chaotic, it is also promising because it demonstrates the artistic vitality of a nation devastated by recent disasters. Though uneven, the quality of the works discussed here is generally high. In the early 1990s, Mexico appears to be making substantial gains, both politically and economically, and the publishing industry is thriving. One might assume that the vibrant literature of the past two decades is a prelude to even better things to come.

BIBLIOGRAPHY: Martínez, J. L., ed., Introduction to *The Modern Mexican Essay* (1965): 3–19; Brushwood, J. S., *Mexico in Its Novel* (1966); Millán, M., del C. *Diccionario de escritores mexicanos* (1967); Nomland, J. B., *Teatro mexicano contemporáneo (1900–1950)* (1967); González Peña, C., *History of Mexican Literature*, 3rd ed. (1968); Leal, L., *Panorama de la literatura mexicana actual* (1968); Sommers, J., *After the Storm: Landmarks of the Modern Mexican Novel* (1968); Langford, W. M., *The Mexican Novel Comes of Age* (1971); Usigli, R., *Mexico in Its Theater* (1976); Debicki, A. P., ed., Introduction to *Antología de la poesía mexicana moderna* (1977): 11–30; Larson, R., *Fantasy and Imagination in the Mexican Narrative* (1977); Agustín, J., "Contemporary Mexican Fiction," *University of Denver Occasional Papers*, No. 1 (1978): 15–29; Puga, M. L., *Literaturay sociedad* (1980); Brushwood, J. S., *La novela mexicana (1967–1982)* (1984); Foster, D. W., *Estudios sobre teatro mexicano contemporáneo: Semiología de la competencia teatral* (1984); Robles, M., *La sombra fugitiva: Escritoras en la cultura nacional* (1985); Young, D. J., "Mexican Literary Reactions to Tlatelolco 1968," *Latin American Research Review*, 20, 2 (1985): 71–85; Duncan, J. A., *Voices, Visions, and a New Reality: Mexican Fiction since 1970* (1986); Ruffinelli, J., "Al margen de la ficción: Autobiografía y literatura mexicana," *Hispania*, 69, 3 (Sept. 1986): 512–20; Bell, S. M., "México," in Foster, D. W., ed., *Handbook of Latin American Studies* (1987): 381–401; Dauster, F. N., *The Double Strand: Five Contemporary Mexican Poets* (1987); Klahn, N., and J. Fernández, eds., *Lugar de encuentro: Ensayos críticos sobre poesía mexicana actual* (1987); McMurray, G. R., *Spanish American Writing since 1941: A Critical Survey* (1987): 68–75, 86–95, 159–62, 164–68, 216–20, 239–57; Stabb, M. S., "The New Essay of Mexico: Text and Context," *Hispania*, 70, 1 (Mar. 1987): 47–61; González, A., *Euphoria and Crisis: Essays on the Contemporary Mexican Novel* (1990); Anderson, D. J., "Cultural Conversation and Constructions of Reality: Mexican Narrative and Literary Theories after 1968," *Siglo* 8: 1–2 (1990–1991): 11–31; Burgess, R. D., *The New Dramatists of Mexico 1967–1985* (1991); Taylor, D., *Theater of Crisis: Drama and Politics in Latin America* (1991): 1–63, 148–80

—GEORGE R. MCMURRAY

MEYER, E. Y.

(pseud. of Peter Meyer) Swiss novelist, short-story writer, essayist, and dramatist (writing in German), b. 11 Oct. 1946, Liestal

M. grew up in Pratteln and Biel. He studied history and philosophy at the University of Bern, but then decided to become a secondary-school teacher in 1971. While teaching, he began to write. Since his first works were successful, he gave up teaching in 1974. He has won several literary prizes, including the Swiss Schiller Foundation Prize (1984). He now lives in Bern.

M.'s works are known for their exactitude of description, which he achieves through complicated syntactical structures, and for their philosophical musings on the meaning of life. His early works are marked by a predominance of the dark and morbid sides of existence, but he has gradually worked his way through to a more harmonious concept of the world.

All of the characters in his first work, *Ein reisender in sachen umsturz* (1972; a traveler in matters of subversion), a collection of short stories, feel apprehensive in unreal situations from which they can find no escape. In the novel *In trubschachen* (1973; in Trubschachen) the narrator's visit to a small idyllic Emmental village turns into a gruesome discovery of disease, decay, and trepidation, and ends with his rejection of Kant's famous dictum that fulfillment of duty is to be the governing factor in our lives. In the stories in *Eine entfernte ähnlichkeit* (1975; a distant resemblance) we are presented with the idea that we are never able to perceive reality as it is. In all three works there is a central problem—the fear of death and the fear of madness. M.'s protagonists wander through a world governed by anonymous threats and loss of direction. Everything seems to be disintegrating around them. M. also explores these and related philosophical issues in several essays, some of which have been published under the title *Die Hälfte der erfahrung* (1980; one half of experience).

A partial solution to his dilemma of existence and a more positive outlook on life can be found in M.'s best work to date, his novel *Die rückfahrt* (1977; the return trip). The protagonist, Berger, no doubt an alter ego for M., is a teacher who decides to give up his profession for the sake of writing. He barely escapes death in a traffic accident, and during his recuperation he reflects on the reason for his existence and comes to the realization, through conversations with his doctor, an artist, and a monuments official, that it is only through the creative energy of art that we can hope to overcome the fear of death and the meaninglessness of life in the technological age. One must study the artistic creations of the past and the world of nature in order to live more fully in the present. A justification for life is not to be found in the mechanical fulfillment of duty in a well organized society but in a search for new interpretations of the world through art. M. thereby criticizes Swiss and all capitalist societies.

In his plays M. explores similar philosophical themes. *Sundaymorning* (1981; title in English) deals, in dialect, with the significance of art in the contemporary world and with our relationship to nature. *Das system* (1983; the system) questions our standard concepts about the perception of reality.

M.'s comparatively small oeuvre has earned him the respect of critics and a wide readership in the German-speaking countries. His precise language and his critique of accepted norms have made him one of the most important contemporary Swiss writers.

FURTHER WORKS: *Plädoyer—für die erhaltung der vielfalt der natur beziehungsweise für deren verteidigung gegen die ihr drohende vernichtung durch die einfalt des menschen* (1982)

BIBLIOGRAPHY: Pender, M., "The Tenor of German-Swiss Writing in the Nineteen-Seventies: E. Y. M." *NGS*, 8, 1 (1980): 55–69; von Matt, B., ed., *E. Y. M.* (1983); Wietlisbach, C., *Kritische Betrachtungen zu E. Y. Ms "In Trubschachen" und "Die Rückfahrt"* (1987);

Durrer, M., *Lebenohne Wirklichkeit—Schreiben gegen das Untergehen: 3 Studien zum erzählerischen Werk E. Y. Ms* (1988)

—ROBERT ACKER

MEYRINK, Gustav

(born Gustav Meyer) Austrian novelist and short-story writer, b. 19 Jan. 1868, Vienna; d. 4 Dec. 1932, Starnberg, Germany

M. was the illegitimate son of a Bavarian actress and a Swabian baron. After secondary schooling in Munich and business college in Prague, he joined a Prague banking firm. A growing interest in the occult and the esoteric led him to the study of the cabala, yoga, and Rosicrucianism. In 1902 M. went bankrupt; he subsequently left Prague for Vienna, and after a year moved on to Munich, making a not always easy living from his literary endeavors. From 1911 until his death M. made his home in Starnberg, near Munich.

M., best known for his novel *Der Golem* (1915; *The Golem*, 1928), began his literary career as a contributor to the satirical weekly *Simplicissimus*, in which his first published story appeared in 1901. The collection *Des deutschen Spießers Wunderhorn* (3 vols., 1913; the German philistine's magic horn) shows M. a mordant critic of society. Through caricature and parody that abound in grotesque and fantastic elements, he unmasks the spiritual hollowness and philistine mediocrity of bourgeois civilization, with its narrowminded prejudices; the military and jingoism are favorite targets of his caustic wit. This satirical verve is, however, only one aspect of M.'s cultural criticism, which springs from his grave concern over the despiritualization of life in the name of positivism and materialism. His turning toward the realities of man's inner life, his interest in the mysteries of esoteric teachings and the occult, must be seen as its complementary aspect.

Der Golem, the novel that made M. famous, can be read on two levels. It can be taken as a mystery, in which M., with an unerring flair for effect, fuses sensational, fantastic, grotesque, and nightmarish elements to create the uncanny atmosphere of a horror story, whereby the old Prague ghetto acquires a mysterious life of its own. But it can also be read as a novel of initiation, as the dream story of Athanasius Pernath's awakening to a higher life according to the mysteries of the cabala.

The theme of spiritual awakening is central to M.'s other novels as well. They can be characterized as esoteric novels of education, depicting rites of passage to a higher, cosmic awareness, inspired by a variety of arcane teachings: yoga in *Das grüne Gesicht* (1916; the green face), Taoism in *Der weiße Dominikaner* (1921; the white Dominican), alchemy and tantrism in *Der Engel vom westlichen Fenster* (1927; the angel of the west window). In his quest for spiritual self-knowledge, the elect often becomes conscious of the greater possibilities within himself through the experience of living past lives, identifying himself with different manifestations of unique spiritual states of being.

Beginning with *Das grüne Gesicht* M. adopted an ever more pronounced attitude of initiate and prophet, to the detriment of the literary qualities of the later novels, which often show a certain lack of balance between didactic intention and artistic realization. His earlier works, however, notably his short stories, show M. at his best, as a master of fantasy.

FURTHER WORKS: *Der heiße Soldat* (1903); *Orchideen* (1904); *Das Wachsfigurenkabinett* (1907); *Jörn Uhl und Hilligenlei* (1908); *Der Sanitätsrat* (1912, with Roda Roda); *Bubi* (1912, with Roda Roda); *Die Sklavin aus Rhodos* (1912, with Roda Roda); *Die Uhr* (1914, with Roda Roda); *Der Kardinal Napellus* (1915); *Fledermäuse* (1916); *Der Löwe Alois, und andere Geschichten* (1917); *Walpurgisnacht* (1917); *Gesammelte Werke* (6 vols., 1917); *Der violette Tod, und andere Novellen* (1922); *An der Schwelle des Jenseits* (1925); *Die heimtückischen Champignons, und andere Geschichten* (1925); *Meister Leonhard* (1925); *Das Haus zur letzten Laterne* (1973)

BIBLIOGRAPHY: Sperber, H., *Motiv und Wort bei M.* (1918); Frank, E., *G. M.: Werk und Wirkung* (1957); Bithell, J., *Modern German Literature 1880–1950* (1959): 72–74; Schwarz, T., "Die Bedeutung des Phantastisch-Mystischen bei G. M.," *WB*, 12 (1966): 716–19; Schödel, S., "Über G. M. und die phantastische Literatur," in Burger, H. O., ed., *Studien zur Trivialliteratur* (1968): 209–24; Abret, H., *G. M., conteur* (1976); Russack, N. W., "A Psychological Interpretation of M.'s *The Golem*," Hall, G., et al., eds., *The Shaman from Elko: Papers in Honor of Joseph L. Henderson on His Seventy-Fifth Birthday* (1978): 157-64; Aster, E., *Personalbibliographie von G. M.* (1980); Pollet, J.-J., "G. M.: L'Enjeu de l'Occultisme," *Recherches Germaniques*, 16 (1986): 101-18; Jennings, L. B., "M.'s *Der Golem*: The Self as the Other," Coyle, W., ed., *Aspects of Fantasy: Selected Essays from the Second International Conferences on the Fantastic in Literature and Film* (1989): 55-60; Mitchell, M., "G. M.," Daviau, D., ed., *Major Figures of Austrian Literature 1918-1938* (1995): 261-95

—FRIEDHELM RICKERT

MICHAUX, Henri

Belgian poet and essayist (writing in French), b. 24 May 1899, Namur; d. 23 Oct. 1984, Paris

M. grew up in Brussels. An introspective child out of step with reality, by his own account estranged from his parents, he discovered early his imaginative gifts, read extensively, and for a while felt a deep affinity with several mystical writers. But he was also drawn to scientific literature, and prepared to study medicine; then, at the age of twenty-one, signed up as a sailor. A reading of Lautréamont's (1846–1870) *Maldoror* rekindled M.'s desire to write and inspired his first essays, published by the Brussels review *Le disque vert*. In 1924, having settled in Paris, M. began painting. To support himself he worked as teacher and secretary and in 1938–39, as coeditor of the mystical review *Hermès*. Despite extended travels, he kept abreast of the Parisian artistic movements and for a while frequented the SURREALISTS. Since the death of his wife in 1948 M. has lived in profound solitude in Paris, writing and painting.

M.'s work stems from psychological, not aesthetic concerns. It seeks access to man's inner realm and focuses on the experience of existing in a flawed universe. *Qui je fus* (1927; who I was), M.'s first full-length work, a mixture of poetry, prose, and prose poems, opposes the inchoate flux within the self to the outer space of fixed forms, codes, and orderly processes and opts for the former as the ground of poetry. *Écuador* (1929; *Ecuador: A Travel Journal by H. M.*, 1970), a journal of travel in South America, is a work of severed contacts. It traces M.'s personal trajectory away from the experiences of the journey, which he found disappointing. *Un barbare en Asie* (1933; *A Barbarian in Asia*, 1949), M.'s second book of reportage, recounts a more successful trip to the Far East. It retains the picturesqueness of a travelogue, and through a series of essays on ideas and attitudes creates a narrative of visual and moral perception where facts are used as a point of departure for self-analysis. The work signaled M.'s break with Western culture, hastened by his discovery of Hindu spirituality.

Mes propriétés (1929; my properties) opened an era of exploration of mental and psychic phenomena that extends through five collections, ending with *L'espace du dedans* (1944; *Selected Writings: The Space Within*, 1951), a selection of tales, verse, and prose poems from the 1927–40 period. Originating in the will to extend consciousness, these highly charged, fluid texts explore unconscious drives, wishes, impulses, and emotional turbulences and define the self as a momentary point of balance amid divergent forces, threatened by both inner formlessness, that is, nonbeing, and external restraints. To the latter M. opposes the gesture of refusal. He structures his poems so as to negate the world and creates imaginary zones—places of change, of births and deaths of various objects, of shifting relationships, of rising tensions, which are reworked into concrete manifestations of inner states, into dream images, myths, monsters, allegorical figures, animal species.

In M.'s work internal projections also assume human shapes, bearing the name of Plume, among others. Plume, the bewildered protagonist and victim of tragicomic adventures, represents man's alienation and serves as an artistic mask ensuring painless exchanges between the poet and the outside world. While the Plume stories relieve tensions through humor, other texts of this period maintain a turbulent, aggressive tone. Rhythms surge, strike, hammer; images explode under pressure; sentences are pushed beyond the limits of conventional syntax, giving rise to moments of extreme tension between thought and language. M. puts to the test the very possibility of verbal articulation.

The imaginary voyages of *Ailleurs* (1948; elsewhere) impose order upon mental chaos through the creation of a narrative. Here M. portrays half-real, half-imaginary lands, inhabited by semicorporeal creatures whose life and gestures reenact man's inner conflicts. In the earlier *Au pays de la magie* (1941; in the land of magic), the workings of the poetic mind are explored. Opening up to humanitarian concerns, *Ici Poddema* (1948; Poddema calling) captures the horrors of contemporary society. Taken together, these imaginary voyages hold a mirror up to human strengths and aberrations; while maintaining a spirit of play, they propose a serious reevaluation of human nature.

M.'s poetry written between 1940 and 1948 brings together two notions: creativity and power. In 1940 he fled to southern France to escape the German occupation and there pursued a course of internal resistance that surfaced in the commitment to human values of his wartime poems. *Épreuves-exorcismes* (1945; trials-exorcisms) pits poetic language against the war, unfolding a passionate litany of human suffering and directing anathemas against man's demonic skills. It transforms the desire to oppose into the very act of opposition, giving birth to a poetry of concentrated will, of action. Poets, M. believed, can reach a threshold of intensity beyond which thoughts and feelings assume power. Their poems become actions undertaken against evil, explosive charges

introduced into the very center of suffering, acts of magical taliation. To M., they are also a healing response to life's hurts, a means to achieve liberation.

Beginning in 1948 Promethean attitudes gave way to a more willing acceptance of the world, and ultimately to serenity. Written in response to his wife's death, *Nous deux encore* (1948; two of us still) expresses the pain of loss in plaintive, lyric notes. *Face aux verrous* (1954; facing the bolts) and especially the later *Vents et poussières* (1962; winds and dusts) temper anguish into aphorisms where only occasional sharp tones betray the underlying pressures. *Meidosems* (1948; Meidosems [a fictitious nationality invented by M.]), which is about spiritual aspiration, conveys a sense of man's limits. Despite the new tone of his work in this period, the thrust to extend boundaries persists, reflected in M.'s evocations of the world beyond or in his visionary poems, which present human experience as a continuum. Essays on poetry, graphic arts, and dreams complement M.'s imaginative production of the postwar period, demonstrating his range and his understanding of the creative processes.

M.'s discovery of the drug mescaline in the mid-1950s ushered in a decade of experimentation with hallucinogenic substances and opened the door in M.'s work to a variety of transcendent states: ecstasy, limitless expansion, soaring, the experience of infinity or of total involvement with the universe. Undertaken in a spirit of scientific inquiry, these experiments produced five major works, among them *Misérable miracle* (1956; *Miserable Miracle*, 1963) and *L'infini turbulent* (1957; turbulent infinity), in both of which objective analysis and lyrical evocation fuse to close the gap between science and poetry. Lucid even while under the influence of drugs, M. demystifies experience. But he also struggles to remain a visionary and thus takes consciousness to its furthest limits. *Paix dans les brisements* (1959; peace among the windbreaks) is the most interesting mescaline text. It creates a sense of plenitude by bringing into a perfect symbiotic relationship prose commentary, poems, and drawings.

M.'s work embraces a hundred variations ranging from free verse to clinical studies of drug-induced states to painting. It developed independently and achieved an extraordinary degree of freedom from existing literary forms. Restless, spasmodic, in constant pursuit of experiences, it accelerated the pace of poetic language and, by insisting that flights of the imagination are a proper instrument of inquiry, extended the boundaries of both knowledge and poetry.

FURTHER WORKS: *La nuit remue* (1935); *Voyage en Grande Garabagne* (1936); *La ralentie* (1937); *Plume, précédé de Lointain intérieur* (1938); *Peintures* (1939); *Arbres des tropiques* (1942); *Je vous écris d'un pays lointain* (1942); *Exorcismes* (1943); *Labyrinthes* (1944); *Le lobe des monstres* (1944); *Apparitions* (1946); *Peintures et dessins* (1946); *La vie dans les plis* (1949); *Poésie pour pouvoir* (1949); *Passages* (1950); *Tranches de savoir, suivi de Secret de la situation politique* (1950); *Mouvements* (1951); *Connaissance par les gouffres* (1961; *Light through Darkness*, 1963); *Les grandes épreuves de l'esprit et les innombrables petites* (1966; *The Major Ordeals of the Mind and the Countless Minor Ones*, 1974); *Parcours* (1966); *Vers la complétude: Saisie et dessaisies* (1966); *Façons d'endormi, façons d'éveillé* (1969); *Poteaux d'angle* (1971); *Émergences-resurgences* (1972); *En rêvant à partir des peintures énigmatiques* (1972); *Bras cassé* (1973); *Moments: Traversées du champ* (1973); *Moriturus* (1974); *Par la voie des rhythmes* (1974);

Face à ce qui se dérobe (1976); *Saisir* (1979). **FURTHER WORKS IN ENGLISH:** *H. M.* (1967)

BIBLIOGRAPHY: Belaval, Y., *H. M.: Une magie rationelle* (1951); Bertelé, R., *H. M.* (1957); Bréchon, R., *M.* (1959); Leonhart, K., *H. M.* (1967); Bowie, M., *H. M.: A Study of His Literary Works* (1973); La Charité, V., *H. M.* (1977); Velinsky, L. A., *From the Gloom of Today to New Greatness of Man: Itinerary by H. M., Builder of New Poetry* (1977)

—VIKTORIA SKRUPSKELIS

MIHARDJA, Achdiat Karta
See Achdiat Karta Mihardja

MILLAY, Edna St. Vincent

American poet, b. 22 Feb. 1892, Rockland, Maine; d. 19 Oct. 1950, Steepletop (near Austerlitz), N.Y.

M. wrote poetry long before she went to college and won several prizes from *St. Nicholas Magazine*. She received a solid education at Barnard and Vassar colleges. "Renascence" (1912), her first major poem, was written when she was only nineteen years old, in the year widely regarded as the one that marked the dawning of a poetic renascence in both England and the U.S.—the same year that the magazine *Poetry* was launched by Harriet Monroe (1860–1936). Simple diction masked her wonderment and love of "The How and Why of all things, past, and present, and forevermore": the poem, published in the anthology *The Lyric Year*, made her famous. Subsequent volumes of poetry preached hedonism, anger that death should be so powerful, and love of the arts ("On Hearing a Symphony by Beethoven," 1928). Her tone was that of a young girl new to a big city (New York) who was shocked by its evil but had decided to master its tempo. Despite their bravura, her lyrics communicated a girlish innocence that won her large audiences.

M. admired classical poets like Catullus, but observed nature closely. Her work with the Provincetown Players and her experiments with verse drama (notably *Aria Da Capo*, 1920) made her a Greenwich Village celebrity. Her libretto for *The King's Henchman* (music by Deems Taylor, produced in 1927) was a serious contribution to American opera. She won the Pulitzer Prize in 1922 for *The Harp-Weaver, and Other Poems*; married Eugen Jan Boissevain the following year; and moved in 1925 to a farm in the Berkshires.

During the 1920s M. was tremendously excited by the Sacco-Vanzetti case, wrote several poems on the subject, and pleaded with the government of Massachusetts to commute the death sentence. What began as a concern with social injustice broadened, with the appearance of *Conversation at Midnight* (1937), into a consideration of international problems. Much of her later poetry was censured by critics as didactic and journalistic, and she agreed that she had not learned how to convert the ideals of a beleaguered democratic world into poetry of the first order. Her final years were spent fighting illness, personal disappointment, and a declining reputation.

A brief revival followed the posthumous publication of *Collected Poems* (1956). Over a longer period she has attracted new

Edna St. Vincent Millay

generations of readers. Many of her books remain in print, and her recordings of poems are widely available. In general, however, critics during the last three decades have chosen either to belittle M.'s self-dramatizations as immature and period-dated, or to ignore her entirely. But the record shows that she was the most exciting American woman poet since Emily Dickinson, and a distinguished contributor to both the lyric and the sonnet traditions.

FURTHER WORKS: *Renascence* (1917); *A Few Figs from Thistles* (1920); *The Lamp and the Bell* (1921); *Second April* (1921); *Two Slatterns and a King* (1921); *Poems* (1923); *Distressing Dialogues* (1924); *The Buck in the Snow and Other Poems* (1928); *Poems Selected for Young People* (1929); *Fatal Interview* (1931); *The Princess Marries the Page* (1932); *Wine from These Grapes* (1934, with George Dillon); *Flowers of Evil* (tr. of Baudelaire, 1936); *Huntsman, What Quarry?* (1939); *Make Bright the Arrows* (1940); *Collected Sonnets* (1941); *The Murder of Lidice* (1942); *Letters of E. St. V. M.* (1952); *Mine the Harvest* (1954)

BIBLIOGRAPHY: Atkins, A., *E. St. V. M. and Her Times* (1936); Sheean, V., *The Indigo Bunting: A Memoir of E. St. V. M.* (1951); Gurko, M., *Restless Spirit: The Life of E. St. V. M.* (1962); Brittin, N. A., *E. St. V. M.* (1967); Gould, J., *The Poet and Her Book: A Biography of E. St. V. M.* (1969); Cheney, A., *M. in Greenwich Village* (1975); Nierman, J., *E. St. V. M.: A Reference Guide* (1977)

—HAROLD OREL

Arthur Miller

MILLER, Arthur

American dramatist, essayist, and novelist, b. 17 Oct. 1915, New York, N. Y.

Son of a well-to-do New York Jewish couple, the young M. was an indifferent student who devoted his attention chiefly to sports. It was not until entering the University of Michigan that he developed an interest in writing. He received his B.A. degree from Michigan in 1938 and spent the next five years as a script writer for NBC, CBS, and the Federal Theatre Project. M. won the Theatre Guild National Award for his play *The Man Who Had All the Luck* in 1944 and soon earned a reputation as a major new American playwright with his successful drama *All My Sons* (1947) which won the New York Drama Critics' Circle Award. In 1956 M. was called before the House Committee on Un-American Activities and was asked to identify colleagues who were suspected of communist activities. He refused and was found in contempt of Congress in 1957, although his conviction was reversed by the U.S. Court of Appeals in the following year. It was also in 1956 that M. married the film actress Marilyn Monroe, a marriage that he dramatized in *After the Fall* (1964). They were divorced in 1961. In 1958 M. was elected to the National Institute of Arts and Letters, winning its Gold Medal for Drama in 1959. He was elected to a four-year term as president of PEN, the international literary association, in 1965. A prolific essayist, M. has articulated his views on literature both in writing and in scores of interviews.

M.'s minor early works—more than thirty plays written for production in colleges, on radio, and in amateur theaters—advanced the ethical concepts and social themes that were later to dominate his major plays. They exhibited as well M.'s penchant for dramatizing the father-son relationships that are central to most of his mature works. Among these early works is M.'s only novel, *Focus* (1945), a narrative that explores the nature of prejudice and anti-Semitism.

The ideas somewhat imperfectly expressed in M.'s early works reached fruition in *All My Sons*, a powerful drama of betrayal and disloyalty within a father-son relationship. The major advance here over M.'s previous playwriting is the achievement of a style of dialogue that allows its characters to convey and explore ideas with a minimum of explicit moralizing or declaiming of principles. In this play, M. proved himself a master in capturing the rhythms of middle-American speech, including its slang and clichés, and in imbuing such realistic, pedestrian dialogue with considerable dramatic power. The play's chief flaw is its weak ending, a denouement that calls attention to the essentially melodramatic devices of the plot. The father's suicide, for example, seems weakly motivated.

M.'s next play remains perhaps his finest. *Death of a Salesman* (1949), often called the most outstanding modern tragedy, received numerous awards, including the Pulitzer Prize for drama and the New York Drama Critics' Circle Award. It substantiates M.'s thesis—advanced repeatedly in essays and interviews—that the common man is an apt subject for contemporary tragedy. In *Death of a Salesman*, M. achieved the remarkable feat of heightening realistic, everyday speech to a level of eloquence bordering on the poetic. The play's dialogue powerfully expresses the thoughts and feelings of characters who are essentially inarticulate, relying upon repetition, rhythm, and other poetic techniques in place of extensive vocabulary.

Of all M.'s plays, *The Crucible* (1953) is the one most clearly focused upon social commentary. A drama of the 1692 Salem witch trials in colonial Massachusetts, it is often said to be M.'s allegorical commentary on the McCarthy-era persecution of suspected communists, a witch hunt of which M. himself was to become a victim three years later. Thus, *The Crucible* confirmed M.'s reputation as a topical playwright and crusader against social injustice. The play is, however, a viable drama in its own right, apart from its applicability to the red-baiting of the early 1950s. Its topic is the phenomenon of mass hysteria and its effect upon a heroic figure who chooses death rather than submit to the injustice spawned by that hysteria.

Most of M.'s work is to some extent autobiographical; his plays frequently portray characters and situations derived from his own past. The most purely autobiographical is *After the Fall*, a quasi-EXPRESSIONISTIC exercise in guilt and self-discovery that most critics have seen as M.'s apologia for his own life. The parallels between the play's hero-narrator, Quentin, and M. himself are inescapable—especially in their reference to the HUAC hearings and to M.'s marriage to Marilyn Monroe (Maggie in the play). The latter subject especially brought critical scorn upon M. for the frank exposure of his relationship with the actress, who had died only two years earlier. Despite the critical attention given to *After the Fall*, it is one of M.'s weaker plays. It is marred by the excessive narration of its hero; its supporting characters are but vaguely sketched; and Quentin's pseudopoetic monologues frequently seem convoluted and pretentious, serving only to obscure the narrative line rather than elucidate it.

By his own admission, M. has been strongly influenced by the plays of Henrik Ibsen. He greatly admires the Norwegian dramatist's ability to objectify human situations and relationships in terms of actions and deeds, rather than in mere declamation and philosophical pronouncements. Nevertheless, M. is a decidedly American playwright—one whose settings and characters are redolent of modern American life. This is attributable principally to M.'s facility with dialogue and his keen ear for ethnic and regional speech. More than any other American dramatist, M. has captured the rhythms and syntax of a wide range of the American people and has rendered their speech both expressive and dramatic.

M.'s heroes—whether from the Midwest, from colonial Salem, or from the Brooklyn waterfront—appear before us as husbands and fathers caught in familial crises. They are portrayed as common folk, struggling to define their existence within the limitations imposed upon them by hostile—or at least indifferent—social and domestic forces. Although they are little people—salesmen, longshoremen, policemen—their creator has often endowed them with tragic stature. They are as fixed and uncompromising in their exertion of self-will as were the Greek heroes in their exercise of hubris. M. has brought the common man within the reach of tragedy.

FURTHER WORKS: *Situation Normal* (1944); *A Memory of Two Mondays* (1955); *A View from the Bridge* (1955); *Collected Plays* (1957); *The Misfits* (1961); *Incident at Vichy* (1965); *I Don't Need You Any More* (1967); *The Price* (1968); *The Creation of the World and Other Business* (1973); *The Portable A. M.* (1977); *The Theater Essays of A. M.* (1978); *Chinese Encounters* (1979, with Inge Morath); *The American Clock* (1980); *Collected Plays, Vol. II* (1981)

BIBLIOGRAPHY: Welland, D., *A. M.* (1961); McAnany, E. G., "The Tragic Commitment: Some Notes on A. M.," *MD*, 5 (1962): 11–20; Prudhoe, J., "A. M. and the Tradition of Tragedy," *ES*, 43 (1962): 430–39; Weales, G., "A. M.: A Man and His Image," *TDR*, 7, 1 (1962): 165–80; Huftel, S., *A. M.: The Burning Glass* (1965); Murray, E., *A. M., Dramatist* (1967); Corrigan, R. W., ed. *A. M.: A Collection of Critical Essays* (1969); Hayman, R., *A. M.* (1970); Nelson, B., *A. M.* (1970); Moss, L., *A. M.*, rev. ed. (1980)

—JACK A. VAUGHN

MILLER, Henry

American novelist, essayist, travel writer, and dramatist, b. 26 Dec. 1891, New York, N.Y.; d. 7 June 1980, Pacific Palisades, Cal.

Born of middle-class German-Americans, M. spent his early years, as he puts it, getting an education on the streets of Brooklyn. He worked at innumerable jobs: for the Atlas Portland Cement Company, in his father's tailor shop, for the U.S. Bureau of Economic Research, for Western Union, and for the Queens County Park Department, among many others. He sold prose-poems ("mezzotints") door to door, ran a speakeasy, and wrote three still-unpublished novels. He lived in Europe (mostly Paris) in the 1930s under impoverished circumstances, doing odd jobs, and writing prolifically work that, for years, was published almost exclusively by the Obelisk Press, Paris. After an extended stay in

Henry Miller

Greece, M. returned to America following the outbreak of war. Until his death he lived in California (mostly Big Sur)—writing, painting water colors, and revisiting Europe numerous times. In 1957 he was elected to the National Institute of Arts and Letters.

M.'s major literary achievement is a pair of "autobiographical" trilogies: *Tropic of Cancer* (1934), *Black Spring* (1936), and *Tropic of Capricorn* (1939); and *The Rosy Crucifixion: Sexus* (1949), *Plexus* (1953), and *Nexus* (1960). These books, plus *Quiet Days in Cli chy* (1956), fictionalize M.'s life in a kind of free-form *Bildungsroman*, a loosely connected, anecdotal narrative. They depict an aging expatriate American writer who bears M.'s name and experience, divides his thoughts and energies between intoxicating Paris and frenzied New York, and discovers that the world is generally uncongenial to his sensitivities and needs. A "lost generation" writer of what might be called the second phase, Paris of the Depression, M. uses themes—cadging for food, shelter, and sex; attacks on such bourgeois values as work and marriage; denunciations of traditional art and literature—and imagery—wild, exuberant, often shockingly frank—that together represent a savage, nihilistic (and at times enormously funny) revulsion against a world of stupidity and ugliness.

The contradiction on which these books depend is that the picaro, gaining knowledge of the world's endless frustrations, squalor, and disasters, attains a disproportionate sense of triumph for each small victory in daily survival. Another meal, a free bed, a beautiful sky, a warm and willing female body—from these emerge a free-spirited exuberance for life, a sense of initiation and self-liberation, despite the world and his own instincts. The mask of alienation slips often, revealing a would-be eternal outsider whose exile is self-imposed, a buffoon-lecher who spouts wisdom in the guise of foolishness, while seducing, indiscriminately, virgins and whores.

M. called his fiction "auto-novels," and maintained that, like his protagonist, the work is natural, spontaneous, uncontaminated by reason or recollection. Yet M. was as much craftsman as free-spirited artist, and his "spontaneous" effects are calculated: the first-draft manuscript of *Tropic of Cancer* was three times the length of the published version, and M. rewrote the book three times. And despite his scorning of critics (whom he called "bastards" and for whom, to throw them "off the track," he planted lies in his autobiographical chronology, published in *The H. M. Reader* [1959], edited by his friend Lawrence DURRELL), he expended enormous energy on criticism: *Hamlet* (2 vols., 1939, 1941, with Michael Fraenkel); *The Plight of the Creative Artist in the United States of America* (1944); *Patchen: Man of Anger and Light* (1947); *The Books in My Life* (1952); *The Time of the Assassins: A Study of Rimbaud* (1956); plus a huge, never-completed study of D. H. LAWRENCE, *The World of Lawrence: A Passionate Appreciation* (1980).

Since the 1960s, when all of M.'s controversial writings were finally published in America, his reputation has declined. No longer underground, M.'s fiction lost first its influence and then its popularity. The world of sexual freedom, anarchism, and Oriental philosophy he helped to create no longer finds him shocking—or even particularly relevant. Now, or soon, we will be able to take his measure as artist, rather than as cause. A likely point of emphasis should be his peculiarly American posture—iconoclastic, self-educated, naturalistic, strongly antipathetic toward modern industrial society. M.'s powerful imagistic language, the lyrical intensity with which he endows our daily activities, and his brilliant re-creation of the bum's rejection of society are among those features of his work that will insure him a continuing readership.

FURTHER WORKS: *Aller Retour New York* (1935); *Money and How It Gets That Way* (1938); *Max and the White Phagocytes* (1938); *The Cosmological Eye* (1939); *The World of Sex* (1940; rev. ed., 1957); *The Wisdom of the Heart* (1940); *The Colossus of Maroussi* (1941); *Sunday after the War* (1944); *The Air-Conditioned Nightmare* (1945); *Obscenity and the Law of Reflection* (1945); *Maurizius Forever* (1946); *Of, by, and about H. M.* (1947); *Remember to Remember* (1947); *The Smile at the Foot of the Ladder* (1948); *Nights of Love and Laughter* (1955); *A Devil in Paradise* (1956); *Big Sur and the Oranges of Hieronymus Bosch* (1957); *The Red Notebook* (1958); *The Intimate H. M.* (1959); *Stand Still Like the Hummingbird* (1962); *Lawrence Durrell and H. M.: A Private Correspondence* (1963); *H. M. on Writing* (1964); *Letters to Anaïs Nin* (1965); *Selected Prose* (1965); *Writer and Critic: A Correspondence with H. M.* (1968, with William A. Gordon); *My Life and Times* (1971); *H. M. in Conversation with Georges Belmont* (1972); *Insomnia; or, The Devil at Large* (1974); *Letters of H. M. and Wallace Fowlie* (1975); *The Nightmare Notebook* (1975); *H. M.'s Book of Friends: A Tribute to Friends of Long Ago* (1976); *Sextet* (1977); *Correspondance privée 1935–1978* (1980, with Joseph Delteil)

BIBLIOGRAPHY: Porter, B., ed., *Happy Rock: A Book about H. M.* (1945); Durrell, L., and Perlès, A., *Art and Outrage: A Correspondence about H. M.* (1959); Baxter, A. K., *H. M., Expatriate* (1961); Wickes, G., ed., *H. M. and the Critics* (1963); Widmer, K., *H. M.* (1963); Wickes, G., *H. M.* (1966); Dick, K. C., *H. M.: Colossus of One* (1967); Gordon, W. A., *The Mind and Art of H. M.* (1967); Hassan, I., *The Literature of Silence: H. M. and Samuel Beckett* (1968); Nelson, J. A., *Form and Image in the Fiction of H. M.* (1970); Mitchell, E. B., ed., *H. M.: Three Decades of Criticism* (1971); Mathieu, B., *Orpheus in Brooklyn: Orphism, Rimbaud, and H. M.* (1976)

—ALAN WARREN FRIEDMAN

MILLIN, Sarah Gertrude

South African novelist, biographer, and diarist (writing in English), b. 3 March 1888, Zagar, Lithuania; d. 16 July 1968, Johannesburg

M.'s Jewish parents emigrated to South Africa when she was five months old. The family settled on alluvial diamond diggings on the Vaal River near Kimberley. M. spent her early years keenly observing the diggers whose lives were to form the major inspiration for her fiction. Her disapproval of the racial mixing she saw on the river developed into a lifelong obsession with miscegenation. In latter life she turned her back on the liberal tradition established by her fellow writers in South Africa and became instead a supporter of apartheid and of white supremacy in southern Africa. An interest in the work of her husband, Philip Millin, a barrister and judge, led to her familiarity with the law courts of Johannesburg. She attended trials and based some of her plots on them.

At the end of a long life, M. claimed that she had provided South African literature with "bulk." Apart from fifteen novels and a volume of short stories, *Two Bucks without Hair* (1957), interest in politics and history resulted in a two-volume biography of the famous Boer soldier and statesman Jan Smuts, *General Smuts* (1936), another biography, *Cecil Rhodes* (1933), and an autobiography, *The Night is Long* (1941), which she saw as a prelude to her ambitious, 1,600-page *War Diary* (6 vols., 1944–48).

M. chose a dynastic structure for several novels *God's Stepchildren* (1924), *King of the Bastards* (1949), and *The Burning Man* (1952). *God's Stepchildren*, her most popular work, covers four generations of South African life, and the theme of biological destiny is prominent. In the somber, tragic world of her novels miscegenation is the physical manifestation of original sin. Sometimes M.'s characters are disgraced by poor and demanding relations, whose connections with darker people are economic rather than sexual, as in *The Jordans* (1923). The belief in superior or inferior genes, however, is germane to M.'s world view.

M.'s numerous female characters are striking for their emotional strength and their ruthlessness. They will often stop at nothing to indulge an obsession. In *Mary Glenn* (1925) M. describes feminine ambition in a small provincial town. Typically, Mary marries for social advantage and not for love. Many of M.'s women are haunted by the fear of spinsterhood; the dread of remaining sexually unfulfilled poisons their lives.

M. sees money as the driving force in modern society. Her characters come from the deprived classes of South Africa. They are landless, uneducated, temperamentally unstable—social outcasts, poor whites, half-breeds, or simply "bastards" (that is, people of mixed race). In M.'s fiction, crimes are committed and lives blighted over trifling sums of money. Even if the economic problem is solved, M.'s protagonists are frequently unable to arrive at self-determination. Guilt, fear, or an innate self-destructiveness prevent them from rising above an inferior background.

Despite her color prejudice, incorporated in a deterministic world view, M.'s fiction is of a distinguished caliber. She writes in a tragic mode, achieving real poignancy in a style that is at once plain and forceful. She is a master of dialogue and situation, and her portraits of the poor and degenerate families who eked out a living in a provincial and rural South Africa during the first decades of the 20th c. are both emotionally compelling and authentic.

FURTHER WORKS: *The Dark River* (1919); *Middle-Class* (1921); *Adam's Rest* (1922); *The South Africans* (1926); *An Artist in the Family* (1928); *The Coming of the Lord* (1928); *The Fiddler* (1929); *Men on a Voyage* (1930); *The Sons of Mrs. Aab* (1931); *What Hath a Man?* (1938); *South Africa* (1941); *The Herr Witchdoctor* (1941; Am., *The Dark Gods*); *The People of South Africa* (1951); *The Measure of My Days* (1955); *The Wizard Bird* (1962); *Goodbye, Dear England* (1965); *White Africans Are Also People* (1966)

BIBLIOGRAPHY: Snyman, P. P. L., *The Works of S. G. M.* (1955); Rubin, M., *S. G. M.: A South African Life* (1977); Rabkin, D., "Race and Fiction: *God's Stepchildren* and [William Plomer's] *Turbott Wolfe*," in Parker, K., ed., *The South African Novel in English: Essays in Criticism and Society* (1978): 77–94; Sarvan, C., and L. Sarvan, "*God's Stepchildren* and *Lady Chatterley's Lover*: Failure and Triumph," *JCL*, 14, 1 (1979): 53-57; Coetzee, J. M., "Blood, Flaw, Taint, Degeneration: The Case of S. G. M.," *ESA*, 23 (1980): 41–58

—JEAN MARQUARD

MIŁOSZ, Czesław

Polish poet, novelist, essayist, and critic (also writing in English), b. 30 June 1911, Seteiniai (Szetejnie), Lithuania

M. is Polish although his native country is Lithuania. From the 14th to the 18th cs., Poland and Lithuania were part of the same commonwealth ruled by the Polish king, who was also the Lithuanian grand prince. Owing to intermarriage and cultural assimilation, many Lithuanian families eventually became ethnically Polish; M.'s family was one of them.

M. began to publish poetry when he was a law student at the University of Wilno (Vilnius). From 1946 to 1951 he served as a Polish diplomat in Washington and Paris, but in 1951 he broke with the Communist government of Poland, and after spending nine years in France came to the U.S. Since that time he has been a professor of Slavic languages and literatures at the University of California at Berkeley. In 1978 he received the Neustadt Prize, and in 1980 the Nobel Prize for literature. In connection with the Nobel Prize he was asked about his plans for the future, to which he replied: "I intend to continue my private occupation of translating the Bible from Hebrew and Greek into Polish."

M. has written poetry, novels, short stories, philosophical and literary essays, and political pamphlets. Most of his works are in Polish, but some were written in English. His autobiography

Czesław Miłosz

Rodzinna Europa (1959; *Native Realm: A Search for Self-Definition*, 1968) speaks about the formation of an intellectual amid the social and political upheavals that took place in eastern Europe during the first part of the 20th c. It succeeds in demonstrating the psychological differences between the intellectuals of eastern and western Europe.

Notwithstanding the variety of his occupations and activities, M. has remained primarily a poet. His poetry is crisp, laconic, and cerebral, and it often verges on rhythmical prose, especially in the middle and later periods. The essentials of M.'s poetic style have not changed much over the years. His determination as a poet to use the smallest possible number of words to express an idea or an emotion has contributed to making him one of the great stylists of Polish literature. Some of his poems indicate that he has been influenced by the Manichean vision of the world. Throughout his life, M. has had a profound interest in nature; this interest was reflected in his early poetry in the portrayals of the Lithuanian countryside, and in later poetry in the landscapes of California.

M.'s poetic themes have been nature, philosophy, Poland and Lithuania, and himself. In contrast to many of his contemporaries in Poland and abroad, he has been more interested in thoughts than in words, and he has sought to provide definitions of things, events, and people rather than the impressions of them. In this he is a born classicist, differing sharply from the FUTURISTS, the impressionists, and other modernist poets of his time.

Traktat poetycki (1957; the poetic treatise) is M.'s most significant poetic work. The dry title hides a dynamic content. It is a spirited defense of poetry in an age in which most significant writing has been done in prose. In verse, M. argues that poetry is essential for every human community wanting to survive as a community. It alone is capable of condensing the community's experience in a form that is understandable to all. Following his thesis, M. surveys Polish history from 1918 to the 1950s. He deals with poets, thinkers, and sacrifices, rather than with governments and political declarations. In this work, M. tries to express the experience of his lifetime, that is to say, the experience of a Pole who lived in independent Poland between the two world wars, survived the war and lived on afterward, and who eventually came to view his native country from a geographical and emotional distance. *Król Popiel, i inne wiersze* (1962; King Popiel, and other poems) contains the famous "Ballada" (ballad) commemorating the inhabitants of Warsaw who had been decimated by the uprising of 1944. "Gdzie wschodzi słońce i kędy zapada" (1974; partial tr., "From the Rising of the Sun," 1978) is a poem in rhythmical prose in which M. comes to terms with his own personal victories and defeats.

Of M.'s prose works, *Zniewolony umysł* (1953; *The Captive Mind*, 1953) has enjoyed the greatest popularity. It tells the story of four eastern European intellectuals who adapted themselves to the Communist system while at the same time preserving their belief in their own personal integrity. This book resembles the French writer Julien Benda's (1867–1956) *The Treason of the Intellectuals* (1927) in decrying the betrayal of reason by 20th-c. intellectuals.

The novel *Dolina Issy* (1955; *The Issa Valley*, 1981) deals with M.'s childhood in Lithuania. Old Lithuania, which M. describes in this work, was a rural country in which Poles, Lithuanians, and Jews lived and died in obscurity, their conflicts ignored or misunderstood by conquerors from the East and observers from the West. In the novel, a boy lives with his grandparents on a small country estate. He absorbs the adults' conversations about wars and uprisings, and he watches the dark passions and evil obsessions they try to conceal from him. As often happens in books about rural life, the peaceful milieu of the boy's childhood conceals an undercurrent of unresolved psychological conflicts. While shedding a tear over a world that is no more, M. provides a glimpse into the dark side of human nature. Another novel, *Zdobycie władzy* (1955; *The Seizure of Power*, 1955), deals with quite different subject matter: the Communist takeover of Poland.

In recent years, M. has published two books of essays, *Emperor of the Earth: Modes of Eccentric Vision* (1977) and *Ogród nauk* (1979; the garden of learning), that contain his critique of contemporary Western culture. M. feels that the spiritual ingredient of this culture, conceived in ancient Israel, Greece, and Rome, has all but disappeared in the Western world. It has been preserved on the frontiers of Western culture, however, in countries such as Poland and some of the other eastern European nations. M.'s *The History of Polish Literature* (1969), a critical and historical work of taste and style, has become an indispensable reference tool to English-speaking students of Polish literature.

FURTHER WORKS: *Poemat o czasie zastygłym* (1933); *Trzy zimy* (1936); *Ocalenie* (1945); *Światło dzienne* (1953); *Gucio zaczarowany* (1965); *Wiersze* (1967); *Widzenie nad zatoką San Francisco* (1969; *Visions from San Francisco Bay*, 1982); *Miasto bez imienia* (1969); *Prywatne obowiązki* (1972); *Człowiek wśród skorpionów: Studium o Stanisławie Brzozowskim* (1972); *Gdzie wschodzi słońce i kędy zapada* (1974); *Ziemia Ulro* (1977); *Utwory poetyckie:*

Poems (1976); *Księga Psalmów* (1979); *Nobel Lecture* (1981). FURTHER WORKS IN ENGLISH: *Selected Poems* (1973; rev. ed., 1981); *Bells in Winter* (1978)

BIBLIOGRAPHY: Folejewski, Z., "C. M.: A Poet's Road to Ithaca between Worlds, Wars and Poetics," *BA*, 43 (1969): 17–24; Contoski, V., "C. M. and the Quest for the Critical Perspective," *BA*, 47 (1973): 35–41; Schenker, A. M., Introduction to C. M. *Utwory poetyckie: Poems* (1976): xv–xxvii; Bayley, J., "Return of the Native," *NYRB*, 25 June 1981: 29–33; Stone, J., "C. M., Child and Man," *NYTBR*, 28 June 1981, 7: 16–19; Zweig, P., on *The Issa Valley*, *NYTBR*, 28 June 1981, 7, 29

—EWA M. THOMPSON

MIMOUNI, Rachid

Algerian novelist (writing in French) b. 20 Nov. 1945, Boudouaou (formerly Alma); d. 12 Feb. 1995, Paris, France

Born into a poor peasant family, M. was educated in Algeria (B.S., 1968) and Montreal. He taught economics at the National Institute of Industrial Protection and Development and the University of Algiers.

M. is one of the most widely read novelists in Algeria. His ten works, which have earned him numerous literary prizes such as the prize of Franco-Arab friendship, the prize of the French Academy, and the Albert Camus Prize, cast a highly critical but lucid gaze on postindependence Algeria. They reflect the profound disillusionment and bitterness of a generation that came of age during the revolution, only to witness the betrayal of its ideals after independence.

M.'s first two novels, *Le printemps n'en sera que plus beau* (1978' Springtime Will Only Be More Beautiful) and *Une paix a vivre* (1983; A Peace to Be Lived), which were published in Algeria, went almost unnoticed. Although the first novel is the only one set during the Algerian revolution, the betrayal of revolutionary ideals is the underlying theme of all his successive works, which portray a traumatized society unable to heal from its scars. The second work, which was heavily censored, treats the early months of independence and the difficulties resulting from learning to live again after war.

Le fleuve détourné (1982; The Diverted Stream), which was published in Paris, established M.'s literary reputation. Disenchanted with the state publishing monopoly and censors in Algeria, M. published all his successive works in France. It is not by chance that these works are much more virulent than the early ones. Unlike many other postindependence novels that sing the praises of the revolution in order to legitimate the ruling FLN political party, in *Le fleuve détourné* the returning martyr of the revolution, who has been declared dead, becomes a disturbing ghost who represents the hiatus between past and present, ideals and reality. He is a victim of historical amnesia for he cannot recover his identity in a corrupt and oppressive society that has diverted the ideals for which he fought.

In *Tombéza* (1984; Tombeza) the monstrous protagonist becomes both the victim and the executioner, a symbol of the horror and violence at the heart of contemporary Algeria. With each successive novel M. shows us more and more how Algerian society is not only paralyzed by its past, but also by the lack of a viable political alternative.

Set in a remote Algerian village, *L'honneur de la tribu* (1989; *The Honor of the Tribe*, 1992), is a fable that addresses the attachment to the past and the onslaught of modernity. By dealing with a forgotten Algeria, M. does not only look back but also forward, acutely conscious that any attachment to the past must be linked up with a future that has a people's interests at heart.

Both the pamphlet *De la barbarie en général et de l'intégrisme en particulier* (1992; On Barbarism in General and Fundamentalism in Particular) and the novel *La malédiction* (1993; The Curse) attack the rise of fundamentalism in Algeria, which M. considers the greatest danger in Algeria today. Nevertheless, in the pamphlet, M. also harshly criticizes the thirty-year FLN dictatorship that he blames for state corruption, economic disaster, social paralysis, and the rise of fundamentalism. In *La malédiction* M. provides a grim portrait of the fundamentalist takeover of Algeria in 1991 and the ensuing civil war. More importantly, he shows how the current crisis in Algeria stems from unresolved conflicts and ambiguities of the Algerian revolution.

To the end, M. refused to let terrorist threats on his life force him into exile. However, when the lives of his children were at stake, M. was forced to leave Algeria, which he did on December 31, 1993, going into hiding with his family in Morocco. His radio broadcasts for Radio Medi I in Tangiers from January 1994 to January 1995 were published posthumously as *Chroniques de Tanger* (1995; Chronicles from Tangiers). They give us M.'s last insights as a social commentator of events in Algeria and the world.

Unlike many other Francophone Algerian writers who sought exile early on in France, M. remained in Algeria until 1994, contending that the problems of a society had to be addressed from within. That is why, like Rachid BOUDJEDRA, he published a tract against the FIS (Islamic Salvation Front), believing that intellectuals in Algeria had a moral obligation and a social responsibility to address fundamentalism, while, at the same time, realizing that such an act could easily result in a death sentence. M. was a writer of great integrity and courage, an advocate of Voltairian tolerance in *a fin de siècle* marked by barbary and obscurantism.

FURTHER WORKS: *La ceinture de l'ogresse* (1990; *The Ogre's Embrace*, 1993); *Une peine à vivre* (1991)

BIBLIOGRAPHY: Nair, S., "R. M., un homme libre," *Les Temps Modernes*, 460 (1984): 917-30; Fabre, T., "L'Algérie traumatisée," *Esprit*, 152-53 (1989): 68-77; 917-30; Gafaiti, H., "M. entre la critique algérienne et française," *Itinéraires et Contacts de Cultures* (1991): 26-34; Abu-Haidar, F., "Algeria Unmasked: The Fiction of R. M. (1945-1995)," *TWQ*, 16, 2 (1995): 326-29

—DANIELLE MARX-SCOURAS

MĪNA, Hannā

Syrian novelist and short-story writer, b. 1924, Lattakia

M. is Syria's most prominent novelist and one of the most acclaimed contemporary Arab authors of this genre. Born to a poor family in Lattakia, M. started working at the age of twelve after completing his elementary degree, the only degree he has. He worked in several jobs, one of which was as a workman with a sailor, an occupation that appeared repeatedly in his writings later, and which won him the title "the novelist of the sea." M. also worked as a journalist for twelve years, and was one of the founders of the Arab Writer's Union in 1951. M. was imprisoned nine times because of his political activities, and lived in exile for ten years in China and Hungary. Since 1969 he has been working as an adviser on publications and translations at the ministry of education in Damascus. In 1968 M. was awarded the State's Encouragement Prize in Syria, and in 1990 he received Sultan Oweiss' Literary Prize, a distinguished award in the Arab world. Several of his novels have been translated into Russian, Chinese, Hungarian, and French.

M.'s first three novels established him as a novelist of Socialist REALISM. This sense of commitment is to remain with him throughout his literary career. *Al-Masābīh al-zurq* (1954; blue lamps) examines the effects of World War I on Lattakia. The title refers to Lattakia's inhabitants who paint their window panes blue to divert the attacking planes. M. states that he was influenced by Najīb MAHFŪZ'S *Zuqāq al-Midaqq* (1947; *Midaqq Alley*, 1966) while writing this novel. Like Mahfūz's novel, it takes a quarter in Lattakia to stand for the whole country. M.'s second novel, *Al-shirā' wa-al-'asifa* (1966; the sail and the storm), deals with confronting history in an indirect manner by facing it symbolically through nature. The sail represents the determination of human beings in confronting the storm, which is French colonialism. This novel brought M. immediate recognition in the Arab world, and it was often compared to Ernest HEMINGWAY's *The Old Man and the Sea* (1952). In *Al-thalj ya'tī min al-nāfidha* (1969; the snow comes in through the window) M. tackles the life of a political activist and how he faces an unjust society. M. believes in a socialist revolution that would enable humanity to prosper in a homogeneous universe. His realistic style embodies the dialectical materialistic concept of history where individuals struggle against odd circumstances. Although his first novel suffered artistically for its inability to synthesize the individual with his community, the other novels show M.'s stylistic development in the treatment of the individual who becomes in fact Everybody in her or his struggle against social oppression and injustice.

Class conflict is a major theme in M.'s entire literary oeuvre. *Al-Shams fī yawm ghā'im* (1973; the sun on a cloudy day) depicts this conflict within a single family where the unnamed bourgeois intellectual "youth" sympathizes and suffers with the working class. He believes that his father, by dealing with the colonizer, contributes to the misery of the underprivileged class. However, the youth's calls for progressive change are doomed to failure because of his family's class position. This novel is an outcry for the liberation of the human soul from the shackles of outmoded concepts and traditions. Such liberation from within is a prerequisite step in the liberation of one's country.

Baqāyā suwar (1974; fragments of pictures) and *Al-Mustanqa'* (1977; the swamp) established M. as a master of the autobiographical novel. The novels present the suffering and displacement of M.'s family in the 1920s and 1930s respectively. Although told through a child's eyes, the novels blend successfully the personal with the general to show the effects of the world's economic crisis in Syria.

M.'s literary corpus gives a faithful picture of the historical period in Syria after World War I. While M. sets most of his novels in the past, he is in fact commenting on the present, showing that social struggle is necessary for a better and prosperous future at all times. Although M.'s style had suffered at the beginning of his career from its overemphasis on the political and ideological message, he was able in his later works to blend these messages artistically where the dialectics of fear and courage, of weakness and strength, of failure and achievement are worked out in a profound and natural manner to show the complexity of human nature. M.'s poetic language, his usage of symbol and myth, his mastery of the internal monologue and free association, his employment of time as a main factor for change are demonstrated with great skill and convey his vision of an optimistic future. Although M. understands quite correctly the unavoidable clash between freedom and necessity, his ultimate commitment is to humanity itself. Hence his message is universal, and his position as one of the pillars of modern Arabic literature seems to be beyond doubt.

FURTHER WORKS: *Nazim Hikmat wa-qadāyā ada-biyyah wa-fikriyyah* (1971); *Man yadhkur tilka al-ayyām* (1974, with Attār Najāh); *Al-yātir* (1975); *Al-abnūsah al-baydā'* (1976); *Al-marsad* (1980); *Hikāyat Bahhār* (1981); *Al-duqul* (1982); *Al-marfa' al-ba'id* (1983); *Al-rabī wa-al-kharif* (1984); *Ma' sāt Dimetrio* (1985); *Al-qitāf* (1986); *Hamāmah Zarqā fi al-suhub* (1988); *Nihāyat rajul shujā* (1989); *Al-wallā'ah* (1990); *Fawq al-jabal wa-taht al-thalj* (1991); *Al-Rahio'inda al-Ghurub* (1992); *Hiwarat wa-ahadith fi al-hayah wa-al-kitabah al-riwa'iyyah* (1992); *Al-Hujum tuhakim al-qamar* (1993); *Hadatha fi bitakhu* (1995)

BIBLIOGRAPHY: Allen, R., *The Arabic Novel* (1982): 72–74; Allen, R., ed., *Modern Arabic Literature* (1987): 219–24

—SABAH GHANDOUR

MINANGKABAU LITERATURE

See Indonesian Literature

MIRÓ, Gabriel

Spanish novelist, short-story writer, and essayist, b. 28 July 1879, Alicante, d. 27 May 1930, Madrid

M. took a degree in law after studies at the universities of Valencia and Granada, but his education as a writer came from elsewhere: the Spiritual Exercises at the Jesuit-run school he attended in Orihuela, which trained his sensual imagination; his uncle's academy for painters (in Alicante), where he was taught that the eye should be a veritable camera obscura; Pérez GALDÓS's noninstitutional Christianity; the critic and novelist Juan Valera's (1824–1905) aestheticism; years of reading and seeing for a blind friend. Because M. requires closer attention than many readers are willing to give, he never achieved the popular success that would enable him to live from his writing, and he had to support himself by taking various positions in Alicante, Barcelona, and Madrid.

M.'s densely populated "city" novel about the clergy and people of Oleza (Orihuela rearranged) was published as two books,

Nuestro Padre San Daniel: Novela de capellanes y devotos (1921; *Our Father San Daniel: Scenes of Clerical Life*, 1930) and *El obispo leproso* (1926; the leper bishop). Dozens of characters painted as in enamel; many episodes; lengthy flashbacks and side flashes; morbid Catholic orthodoxy and traditionalism against life-serving Christianity and progressivism—all are presented through a technique of such intense linguistic concentration, heavy with nouns and metaphors, poor in verbs, that at the end one feels enveloped by a vast series of shimmering mosaics, with time held poignantly at bay.

"There is only one heroism, to see the world as it is and to love it," a remark of Romain ROLLAND's, was appropriated by M. as his own ethical and aesthetic principle. The absence of love and the presence of human suffering and cruelty, most often physical and depicted by M. with chilling candor, are therefore his most obsessive subjects, beginning with his first mature work, *Del vivir* (1904; about being alive), an account of the visit by Sigüenza, M.'s alter ego, to a leper colony. M.'s general characteristics here did not change in later works: an almost intolerable pathos attenuated by gentler modes of irony and wit, as well as outright comedy and the expression of astonishment (*pasmo*) that what is there is there (antisubjectivism). These qualities are notable in the numerous short pieces—anecdotes devolving into meditations—brought together in *Libro de Sigüenza* (1917; Sigüenza's book) and in the neo-Parnassian heroism of M.'s last book, *Años y leguas* (1928; years and leagues), where Sigüenza takes spiritual possession, through the word, of the days and places of his youth: the towns and trails, mountains and valleys, and peasant characters of the region around Alicante.

Although not a practicing Catholic, the adult M. retained a lifelong loving obsession with the Church's liturgies, lore, and teachings, especially the doctrines of the incarnate word and transubstantiation, seen in *El humo dormido* (1919; the sleeping smoke) as elaborate human inventions satisfying the need for the illusion of transcendence and obscuring the truth of radical alienation. M.'s works abound with cases of orphanhood, estrangement, separation, and unprovoked cruelty. In *Figuras de la Pasión del Señor* (2 vols., 1916–17; *Figures of the Passion of Our Lord*, 1924) M. shows the Disciples in their anxiety as they face the loss of Christ their transcending mediator, and Christ himself as He is abandoned by God to utterly human agony on the cross.

M. did not share with his contemporaries, the so-called Generation of '98, their abiding preoccupation with the "problem of Spain." Rather, exploiting the most idiosyncratic resources of the Spanish language, he set forth the problem of man, and in so doing achieved a power of expression unique and unsurpassed in Spanish prose.

FURTHER WORKS: *Nómada* (1908); *La novela de mi amigo* (1908); *La palma rota* (1909); *El hijo santo* (1909); *Las cerezas del cementerio* (1910); *Del huerto provinciano* (1912); *Los amigos, los amantes y la muerte* (1915); *El abuelo del rey* (1915); *Dentro del cercado* (1916); *El ángel, El molino, El caracol del faro* (1921); *Niño y grande* (1922); *Obras completas* (1 vol., 1943)

BIBLIOGRAPHY: Guillén, J., "Adequate Language: *G. M.*," *Language and Poetry: Some Poets of Spain* (1961): 157–97; Casalduero, J., "G. M. y el cubismo," *Estudios de literatura* (1962): 219–66; Vidal, R., *G. M.: Le style, les moyens d'expression* (1964); King, E. L., Introduction to G. M., *El humo dormido* (1967): 15–53;

Macdonald, I., *G. M.: His Private Library and His Literary Background* (1975); Landeira, R., *An Annotated Bibliography of G. M.* (1900–1978) (1978); Ramos, V., *G. M.* (1979)

—EDMUND L. KING

MISHIMA Yukio

(pseud. of Hiraoka Kimitake) Japanese novelist, short story writer, dramatist, and essayist, b. 14 Jan. 1925, Tokyo; d. 25 Nov. 1970, Tokyo

M., the son of a government official, was raised mainly by his paternal grandmother, who hardly permitted the boy out of her sight. This fact has frequently been cited to explain both his fragility and oversensitivity as an adolescent.

In 1944, the year in which he entered Tokyo University, his first book, *Hanazakari no mori* (the forest in full bloom), was published. In 1945 he took his physical examination for military service, but was rejected.

In 1946 M. met KAWABATA Yasunari. The older novelist took an interest in his work and not only introduced him to the literary world but recommended his stories to important magazines. M. continued his law studies at Tokyo University, but found after graduation in 1947 that he could not combine a career as a civil servant with that of a writer; he resigned his post in the finance ministry in 1948 to devote himself entirely to his writings. M. was not an avant-garde writer and showed relatively little interest in the work of foreign contemporary writers; he drew greater inspiration from premodern literature, both Japanese and Western. His absorption with classical Japanese literature sets him off from other writers of his generation.

Kamen no kokuhaku (1948; *Confessions of a Mask*, 1968) was the novel that established M.'s literary reputation. In the opinion of some critics, this is his best work. It describes in thinly disguised form M.'s childhood memories, his life as a student, and his wartime experiences It is a record of the significant steps in the development of the narrator's awareness that he would have to wear a mask before the world because of his abnormal sexual preferences.

The central character of M.'s next major novel, *Ai no kawaki* (1950; *Thirst for Love*, 1969), is Etsuko, a woman who has become the mistress of her late husband's father. M. admitted that he had written this novel under the influence of François MAURIAC, and it is not difficult to detect similarities between Etsuko and various Mauriac protagonists. But the climactic moments when Etsuko gashes the back of the young man she loves as he cavorts at a festival, or when in the final scene she kills him, continue the mood of *Kamen no kokuhaku*. Etsuko's victim is the strong, sunburned youth untroubled by intellectual concerns who seemed to embody for M. the most attractive aspect of traditional Japan.

Perhaps M.'s finest novel is *Kinkakuji* (1956; *The Temple of the Golden Pavilion*, 1959). The central incident, the burning of the celebrated temple by a deranged monk, was inspired by an actual event of 1950. M.'s concern here was not with uncovering the facts but with establishing circumstances that would make the act seem logical and even inevitable.

Many of M.'s later novels were intended as experiments. In the unsuccessful *Kyōko no ie* (1959; Kyoko's house) he apportioned different aspects of his life among the four main characters in the

Gabriel Miró

detached manner of a "study in nihilism," to use his description. He followed this with the less ambitious but nearly flawless *Utage no ato* (1960; *After the Banquet*, 1963), a story so closely based on the personal life of a well-known politician that M. lost the ensuing suit for invasion of privacy.

Even as he was writing these novels, M. wrote many short stories and novellas. His best novella, *Yūkoku* (1960; *Patriotism*, 1966), describes the suicides of a young army officer and his wife. This was the first manifestation of M.'s absorption with the February 26, 1936, army coup, when young officers attempted to wrest power from the politicians in the name of the emperor. M. contrasted the purity of their motives with the greed of the old politicians and businessmen. His fascination with their ideals led him to emulate them.

His plays, especially those included in *Kindai nōgaku shū* (1956; *Five Modern Nō Plays*, 1957), were the finest written in Japan in the postwar years. M.'s plays were cast in many idioms, and their contents ranged from contemporary events to themes inspired by the Nō dramas and the tragedies of Euripides and Racine. His best full-length play was *Sado kōshaku fujin* (1965; *Madame de Sade*, 1967), of which he wrote: "I felt obliged to dispense entirely with the usual, trivial stage effects, and to control the action exclusively by dialogue; collisions of ideas had to create the shape of the drama, and sentiments had to be paraded throughout in the garb of reason." The play was clearly in the tradition of Racine, M.'s favorite among Western dramatists. Each of the six women of the play stands for a particular kind of feminine

Mishima Yukio

personality as it reacts to the offstage presence of the Marquis de Sade.

M.'s last work of fiction, the tetralogy *Hōjō no umi* (1969–71; the sea of fertility), is loosely based on an 11th-c. Japanese tale of dreams and reincarnation. In his own opinion, this was the grand summation of his work as a novelist. The first volume, *Haru no yuki* (1969; *Spring Snow*, 1972), evoked the world of the aristocracy in 1912. This story, told with exceptional beauty of style and detail, was an expression of the feminine ideals of Japan. The second volume, *Homba* (1969; *Runaway Horses*, 1972), by contrast, describes the masculine ideals of the way of the Japanese warrior. It takes place in the 1930s, and its protagonist, the stern young Isao, is the reincarnation of the rather effeminate protagonist of *Haru no yuki*. In *Homba* M. gave his most powerful expression of the themes of loyalty and devotion to Japanese ideals that had occupied him since *Yūkoku*.

The third volume, *Akatsuki no tera* (1970; *The Temple of Dawn*, 1973), is divided into two parts: the first is set in southeast Asia, where we first see the Thai princess who is the reincarnation of Isao; the second takes place in Japan after World War II, when the old values of society have been corrupted. The last volume, *Tennin gosui* (1971; *The Decay of the Angel*, 1974), carries the story into the future, and describes the conflict between the reincarnation of the Thai princess and the one man who has observed the four transformations of the being whose decay presages his end. The novel concludes with a superbly written scene that casts doubt on the reality of the events described in the four volumes. In the end

we discover that the "sea of fertility" may be as arid as the region of that name on the moon, although it seems to suggest infinite richness.

On the day that M. delivered the final installment of *Tennin gosui* to his publisher he and members of his private "army" broke into the headquarters of the Japanese Self-Defense Force. He unsuccessfully harangued a crowd of soldiers, and soon afterward committed *seppuku* in the traditional manner, apparently in the hopes of inducing the Japanese to reflect on what they had lost of their cultural heritage. The incident created an immense sensation, but M.'s reputation was to be determined not by this act but by the brilliant works in many genres he wrote during his short life. Long before his suicide he had established himself as the first Japanese writer whose fame was worldwide.

FURTHER WORKS: *Kinjiki* (1951–1953; *Forbidden Colors*, 1968); *Manatsu no shi* (1953; *Death in Midsummer*, 1966); *Yoru no himawari* (1953; *Twilight Sunflower*, 1958); *Shiosai* (1954; *The Sound of Waves*, 1956); *Shizumeru Taki* (1955); *Shiroari no su* (1956); *Shi wo kaku shōnen* (1956; *The Boy Who Wrote Poetry*, 1977); *Bitoku no yoromeki* (1957); *Rokumeikan* (1957); *Bara to kaizoku* (1958); *Ratai to ishō* (1959); *Yoroboshi* (1960; *Yoroboshi: The Blind Young Man*, 1979); *Kemono no tawamure* (1961); *Utsukushii hoshi* (1962); *Gogo no eikō* (1963; *The Sailor Who Fell from Grace with the Sea*, 1965); *Watakushi no henreki jidai* (1964); *Kinu to meisatsu* (1964); *Mikumano mōde* (1965); *Eirei no koe* (1966); *Suzaku-ke no metsubō* (1967); *Hagakure nyūmon* (1967; *The Way of the Samurai*, 1977); *Wa ga tomo Hittorā* (1968; *My Friend Hitler*, 1977); *Taiyō to tetsu* (1968; *Sun and Steel*, 1970); *Bunka bōei ron* (1969)

BIBLIOGRAPHY: Keene, D., *Landscapes and Portraits: Appreciations of Japanese Culture* (1971): 204–25; Kimball, A. G., *Crisis in Identity and Contemporary Japanese Novels* (1973): 75–93; Keene, D., "The Death of M.," in Dillon, W. S., ed., *The Cultural Drama: Modern Identities and Social Ferment* (1974): 271–87; Nathan, J., *M.: A Biography* (1974); Miyoshi, M., *Accomplices of Silence: The Modern Japanese Novel* (1974): 141–80; Scott-Stokes, H., *The Life and Death of Y. M.* (1974); McCarthy, P., "M. Y.'s *Confessions of a Mask*," in Tsuruta, K. K. and T. E. Swann, eds., *Approaches to the Modern Japanese Novel* (1976): 112–28; Ueda, M., *Modern Japanese Writers and the Nature of Literature* (1976): 219–59; Yamanouchi, H., *The Search for Authenticity in Modern Japanese Literature* (1978): 137–52

—DONALD KEENE

MISTRAL, Gabriela

(pseud. of Lucila Godoy Alcayaga) Chilean poet, b. 7 April 1889, Vicuña; d. 10 Jan. 1957, Hempstead, N.Y.

As a young woman M. worked as a rural schoolteacher in various parts of Chile; she went to Mexico in 1922 as an educational consultant. In 1925 she joined the Chilean diplomatic service, representing Chile in Spain, Portugal, France, Brazil, and the U.S. M.'s first literary triumph came in 1914, when a group of sonnets, "Sonetos de la muerte" (sonnets of death), won a prize in Santiago. In 1945 she received the Nobel Prize for literature.

The major themes throughout M.'s work are the humanistic ones of love and respect for all people, especially children, women, and country folk. Another important motif is admiration for the natural world, which she often presents in specifically American or Chilean contexts and which she describes with great detail and clarity. Many of her poems reflect a preoccupation with death and with the passing of time, expressed at first, in *Desolación* (1922; desolation), as a blunt cry of personal anguish and in later works as a theme of universal application.

In *Desolación* M. describes herself as the "rural schoolteacher," a strong, compassionate woman dedicated to her work. In a brief section on nature she presents both such universal subjects as mountains, clouds, rain, stars, pine trees, and autumn, and specific places—Patagonia, and Iztaccíhuatl in Mexico. In the first section of *Desolación*, "Vida" (life), Christian faith is the main theme, and biblical imagery is abundant. The most important parts of the book deal with death as a dark, quiet, and impenetrable barrier separating people into two parallel worlds. The section "Dolor" (pain) includes the three autobiographical "Sonetos de la muerte," which reflect M.'s own feelings of loneliness and despair as she confronts the loss, by suicide, of the man she loved. These sonnets take the form of a spiritual monologue directed at the beloved. They promise that, after the death of the poet, the dark and cold image of death will become, for all eternity, a "sunny land" in which roses and lilies, symbols of hope beyond death, grow from decay and spread pollen over the earth. In the final sonnet M. alludes to her own selfish prayers, asking for the death of the beloved should he share his love with another woman. She expresses faith in a forgiving God who understands the exclusive nature of her love.

Many of the poems in *Ternura* (1924; tenderness) deal with children and the world as seen by them. This collection demonstrates M.'s ability to write simple yet elegant verse. She describes the precariousness of a young child's life, in which death is as near as sleep. A major section in *Ternura*, "Canciones de cuna" (cradle songs), has a pronounced melodic verse form, with a refrain. These lullabies focus on maternal love and care, and contain frequent references by M. to "my child," reflecting her deep longing for children of her own. The group "Cuentamundo" (tales of the world) contains descriptions of simple things basic to a complex world: air, light, water, animals, fruit.

M. continued her inventory of these basics in *Tala* (1938; devastation). In the "Materias" (matter) section she writes of bread, salt, water, rainfall, and air in the same manner as in *Ternura*. The opening of *Tala* is a group of somber personal poems focusing on the death of the poet's mother, in which M. expresses, through Christian imagery, belief in spiritual life after death. In other poems in *Tala* there are views of the Chilean landscape, the Caribbean Sea, tropical sun, and corn growing.

M.'s interest in nature continued in the collection *Lagar* (1954; wine press), in which her descriptions of nature are extended to areas as distant as Uruguay, Cuba, and California.

Intertwined throughout both *Tala* and *Lagar* are two contrasting worlds—the timeless and the evanescent. M. suggests that freedom from the confines of time, change, and rational cause-and-effect relationships is both desirable and inevitable. Escape from changes due to the passing of time can be found in constant elements in nature: the eternal air and sea, the centuries-old plants native to America. Another form of escape from the rational effects of the passing of time may be found in an irrational approach to life. In the section called "Locas mujeres" (mad women) in *Lagar* M. sketches

women who find entrance to a timeless existence through obliteration of memory and logic by means of insanity—a state similar to death.

In the metaphysical poems of *Tala* and *Lagar* M. suggests that life is a mysterious pilgrimage leading to death, which she portrays as a final and complete liberation from the confines of both time and the rational world. Time, measured by each person as a succession of permanent memories, can bring people to a negation of the present, if they desire only to relive and eternalize moments remembered from the past. M. implies that she herself was caught in this paradox, for she describes herself poetically as wanting things she has never had or no longer has. It is the continuous presence of the past that makes the women of the poems "La abandonada" (the abandoned woman), "La humillada" (the humiliated woman), and others in *Lagar* seek refuge in irrationality or in death. M. traces a mystical progression, from harmony with the permanence of nature, from irrationality, or from death, to liberation from the earthly limits of time and to a sense of becoming part of a greater, mysterious, yet compelling universe.

In her work M. reveals a great understanding of and concern for humanity. The problems of individuals are presented specifically, although these same problems may be extended to a universal interpretation. Her love of nature is basic to her metaphysical poetry, in which the earth is found to be an unchanging source of hope and security. Death, seen in her early work as an enemy, is, in *Tala* and *Lagar*, a source of mystical beauty.

FURTHER WORKS: *Lecturas para mujeres* (1923); *Rondas para niños* (1930); *Nubes blancas* (1930); *La Oración de la maestra* (1930); *Antología* (1941); *Poemas de las madres* (1950); *Poesías completas* (1958); *Motivas de San Francisco* (1965); *Antología de G. M.* (1967). FURTHER WORKS IN ENGLISH: *Selected Poems of G. M.* (1957)

BIBLIOGRAPHY: Pinilla, N., *Biografía de M* (1946); Molina, J. Saavedra, *G. M.: Su vida y su obra* (1946); Iglesias, A., *G. M. y el modernismo en Chile* (1950); Figueira, G., *G. M.: Fuerza y ternura de América* (1952); Guevara, M. Ladrón de, *G. M.: Magnificent Rebel* (1962); Torres-Rioseco, A., *G. M. (una profunda amistad, una dulce recuerdo)* (1962); Vásquez, M. Arce de, *G. M.: The Poet and Her Work* (1964); Preston, M. C. A., *A Study of Significant Variants in the Poetry of G. M.* (1964); Taylor, M. C., *G. M.'s Religious Sensibility* (1968)

—CATHERINE VERA

MITTELHOLZER, Edgar

Guyanese novelist, b. 16 Dec. 1909, New Amsterdam; d. 6 May 1965, Farnham, England

M. was born in what was then British Guiana to mixed-blood, middle-class parents who, he claims, were bitterly disappointed in his swarthy complexion. Educated at the local secondary school, he seemed destined for a career in the civil service. He determined early on to become a writer, however, and worked at various times as a customs officer, meteorological observer, cinema inspector, journalist, and hotel receptionist to support himself while he wrote. He left for England in 1948 to become a professional novelist.

Although M.'s first novel, *Corentyne Thunder* (1941), is of considerable historical significance in the West Indies, since it was the first work of fiction to deal in depth with the Guyanese peasantry, it went largely unnoticed because of World War II. His second, *A Morning at the Office* (1950; Am., *Morning in Trinidad*), however, attracted much attention not only to M. himself but more generally to English-Caribbean writing, which was beginning to appear in London and New York. The analysis of race and class in these early works and the massive interpretation of Guyanese history in his Kaywana trilogy—*Children of Kaywana* (1952; repub. as two volumes, *Children of Kaywana* and *Kaywana Heritage*, 1976), *The Harrowing of Hubertus* (1954; Am., *Hubertus*; repub. as *Kaywana Stock*, 1959), and *Kaywana Blood* (1958; Am., *The Old Blood*)—no doubt helped to establish race and history as basic themes in West Indian writing. A more general assessment of his twenty-five books indicates, however, that West Indian society is less intrinsic to his works than such concerns as the situations of the strong and the weak in society, and such problems as those caused by "racial, cultural and psychic disorientation," referred to by the critic Michael Gilkes as "the Divided Consciousness."

These themes are explored on a very personal level in M.'s autobiography *A Swarthy Boy* (1963), on a social and historical level in the works mentioned above and in such others set in the West Indies as *A Tale of Three Places* (1957) and *Latticed Echoes* (1960), and on a very didactic level in such novels set in England as *The Weather in Middenshot* (1952) and *The Aloneness of Mrs. Chatham* (1965). As his career as a novelist progressed, M. became less interested in depicting people and more interested in expounding his ideas. The world of his West Indian novels, created with some understanding and sympathy, accommodates more organically his themes of strength, weakness, and disorientation than does the English world of his later novels, which is merely a framework into which these themes are obsessively forced.

In the majority of his novels, from the first to the last, M.'s characters resort to suicide as the only satisfactory way to cope with the anguish caused by disorientation and alienation. The reader of M.'s work who has come to recognize so many of M.'s own interests and obsessions in his characters is hardly surprised to learn that M. burned himself to death in a manner similar to that used by a character in his last novel, *The Jilkington Drama* (1965).

While M.'s work at its worst descends to obsessively haranguing the reader to accept an extreme and warped vision of the world, at its best it does lay bare the anguish of an intense and passionate personality.

FURTHER WORKS: *Shadows Move among Them* (1951); *The Life and Death of Sylvia* (1953; repub. as *Sylvia*, 1963); *The Adding Machine* (1954); *My Bones and My Flute* (1955); *Of Trees and the Sea* (1956); *The Weather Family* (1958); *With a Carib Eye* (1958); *A Tinkling in the Twilight* (1959); *The Mad MacMullochs* (1959, under pseud. H. Austin Woodsley); *Eltonsbrody* (1960); *Thunder Returning* (1961); *The Piling of Clouds* (1961); *The Wounded and the Worried* (1962); *Uncle Paul* (1963)

BIBLIOGRAPHY: Cartey, W., "The Rhythm of Society and Landscape (M., Carew, Williams, Dathorne)," *New World*, Guyana Independence Issue (1966): 97–104; Birbalsingh, F. M., "E. M.: Moralist or Pornographer?" *JCL*, No. 7 (1961): 88–103; Howard, W. J., "E. M.'s Tragic Vision," *CarQ*, 16, 4 (1970): 19–28; James, L., Introduction to *Corentyne Thunder* (1970): 1–6; Gilkes, M., *Racial Identity and Individual Consciousness in the Caribbean Novel* (1975): 5–35; Gilkes, M., "E. M.," in King, B., ed., *West Indian Literature* (1979): 95–110; Gilkes, M., *The West Indian Novel* (1981): 41–85

—ANTHONY BOXILL

MIYAZAWA Kenji

Japanese poet and writer of children's stories, b. 27 Aug. 1896, Hanamaki; d. 21 Sept. 1933, Hanamaki

M. went to an agricultural college and taught at an agricultural school. Both institutions had been established to meet the special need of his region, Iwate, which suffered from chronic crop failures because of the harsh climate and backward agricultural methods. A devout Buddhist of an activist sect, M. resigned from his school in 1926 and turned to farming to put his teachings into practice. During the next few years he forced himself to subsist on a poorer diet than even the local farmers were used to, and ruined his health.

M.'s scientific training, Buddhist vision, and concern for the plight of the local farmers, combined with his hallucinatory imagination, sense of drama, and humor, resulted in a highly distinctive body of work. His poems are laced with precise technical terms and vivid descriptions, but they seldom become trivial or simply curious, supported as they are by a larger view of life, a combination of Buddhist pantheism and the belief that science can solve all problems. At the center of his poetic world is the poet himself, presented as an *asura* (a Sanskrit word), in Buddhist belief a contentious, arrogant, malevolent giant somewhere between a human and a beast. As described in the title poem of his first book, *Haru to shura* (1924; spring and asura), M.'s *asura* is unenlightened and restless. Still, M.'s poetic self is far from being egotistic. Even when he describes himself, he externalizes the description. More often, he is concerned with people and phenomena: his dead sister, a bull enjoying himself in the night mist, a horse that died from overwork, a tired farm boy, the movement of clouds, a rainstorm, a country doctor. It is the depth and range of M.'s mind apparent in such poems that make him outstanding.

The stories M. wrote for children share similar qualities, here often extended in a fantastic way. M. describes a great variety of animals and objects, such as a slug, a cat, a fox, a nighthawk, a lark, an ant, a frog, a birch tree, a constellation, and an electric pole, as if he let them project their qualities onto himself, rather than projecting his emotions onto them. The stories are often stark, sometimes brutal. Even where compassion is the theme, the resolution of the conflict of the story is usually realistic and credible.

M. wrote prolifically, and although he revised many of his poems and stories, a good number of them give the impression of being roughhewn and unfinished. Not widely known while alive, he is now considered one of the three or four greatest poets, and surely the most imaginative writer of children's stories, of 20th-c. Japan.

FURTHER WORKS: *M. K. zenshū* (15 vols., 1973–1977); *M. K. zenshū* (16 vols., 1979–1980). **FURTHER WORKS IN ENGLISH:** *Winds from Afar* (1972); *Spring and Asura: Poems of K. M.* (1973).

—HIROAKI SATO

MŇAČKO, Ladislav

Czechoslovak novelist, journalist, dramatist, and poet (writing in Slovak), b. 29 Jan. 1919, Valasské Klobouky; d. 24 Feb. 1994, Bratislava, Slovakia

M. is of working-class origin and had no formal higher education. When the Nazi occupation of Czechoslovakia began, he joined the partisans operating in the mountains that lie between Moravia and Slovakia. After the war he embarked on a varied and tumultuous literary career. In 1967 M. traveled to Israel despite being expressly forbidden by his government to do so. As a result he was deprived of citizenship. Nevertheless, he returned to Czechoslovakia in 1968, but left again when the U.S.S.R. forcibly stamped out the reforms instituted by the Dubček regime. The novel *Die siebente Nacht* (pub. in German, 1968; *The Seventh Night*, 1969) is his account of the 1968 invasion of Czechoslovakia. Since 1968 M. has been living in western Europe.

In the early 1950s M. started to write that particular blend of reportage and fiction for which he has become known. His reportage uses techniques of fiction, and his fiction has substantial factual content.

As a roving reporter M. explored neglected regions of Czechoslovakia and brought back vivid, and sometimes deeply disturbing, reports of the problems people had to cope with in the building of socialism in remote and impoverished parts of the country.

M. achieved his greatest success as a novelist with the publication of *Smrt' sa volá Engelchen* (1959; *Death Is Called Engelchen*, 1961). In this clearly autobiographical book (which was made into a successful film) he returned to his experience as a partisan during the Nazi occupation. He did not present the war in the simplistic terms common to most Czech and Slovak fiction of the period. Instead, he dealt with the demoralization and brutalization brought about by war and affecting both the Nazis and the partisan fighters.

A special problem facing the partisans was that of not jeopardizing the lives of the civilian population, who were subject to dreadful punishment for aiding them. The proceeds from *Smrt' sa volá Engelchen* were donated to the surviving inhabitants of Ploština, which was destroyed by the Nazis in reprisal for just such aid to the partisan group of which M. had been a member.

Although a convinced Communist, M. grew more and more disllusioned with Communist Czechoslovakia. In *Oneskorené reportáže* (1962; belated reportages) M. shows the perversion of the revolutionary spirit in the 1950s. The book presents a stark description of the great suffering inflicted on innocent people by the government and by local Party chiefs under the flimsiest pretexts. M. did not exempt himself from guilt, as he too had contributed to bringing about the debasement of more humane goals. *Oneskorené reportáže* was meant as a warning against the repetition of similar outrages and was written to reestablish trust among men. It was one of the most widely read books of the postwar era.

Ako chutí moc (1968; *The Taste of Power*, 1967) widened the rift between M. and the Novotný group, which had developed with the publication of *Oneskorené reportáže*. President Novotný felt he was being caricatured in this new novel about the gradual corruption of a revolutionary leader. The story is one of a man who started out as an idealistic revolutionist and ended as a venal politician. The novel is also a condemnation of a system that has failed, one that has devoured many of its children.

In his lively journalistic style, M. exposed evils that at that time few other writers dared to tackle.

FURTHER WORKS: *Partyzáni* (1945); *Piesne ingotov* (1950); *Mosty na východ* (1952); *Bubny a činely* (1954); *Živá voda* (1954); *Vody Orava* (1955); *Marxova ulica* (1957); *D'aleko je do Whampoa* (1958); *Aj taký človek* (1960); *Kde končia prašné cesty* (1963); *Dlouhá bílá přerušovaná čára* (1965; tr. into Czech from the manuscript); *Nočný rozhovor* (1966); *Der Vorgang* (1970; tr. into German from the manuscript); *Súdruh Münchhausen* (1972)

BIBLIOGRAPHY: Součková, M., *A Literary Satellite* (1970): 150–53; Hájek, I., comp., "L. M.," in Mihailovich, V. D., et al., eds., *Modern Slavic Literatures* (1976), Vol. II: 154–57

—IGOR HÁJEK

MO Yen

(or Mo Yan; pseud. of Kuan Mo-yeh) Chinese novelist, short-story writer, and essayist, b. Mar. 1956, Kao-mi County, Shantung Province

M. is one of China's most prolific and versatile contemporary writers, known primarily for his contributions to "Hsün-ken wen-hsüeh" (root-seeking literature), which flourished in the mid 1980s. M.'s early education was interrupted by the Cultural Revolution in 1965. He spent the next ten years working in the fields and later at a cotton plant. The experience was not a total waste, for M. acquired valuable first-hand knowledge about hardships in life and distinguished himself with some penetrating treatments of the cruel and degenerated conditions of humankind. At the age of twenty, M. enlisted in the People's Liberation Army. It was not until 1984 that he was admitted to the department of literature at the PLA Academy of Arts, and subsequently the graduate program at Peking Normal University. His teenage memories, his military experience, and his academic training all provided major ingredients for his art.

M.'s early writings followed a realist path commonly taken by almost all post revolution fiction writers in China. "Ch' un-yeh yü fei-fei" (1981; spring drizzles), for example, deals with the monotonous life of a soldier in a realist light. M.'s artistic breakthrough did not come until after he was enrolled in the PLA Academy of Arts. With the appearance of his prize-winning "T' ou-ming te hung-lo-po" (1985; transparent carrots) M. entered a most prolific as well as versatile phase. His popularity was reconfirmed with the appearance of his first full-length novel, *Hung kao-liang chia-tsu* (1986; *Red Sorghum*, 1993). (Part of the novel was later made into an equally popular film, "Hung kao-liang" [1987; the red sorghum], by Chang I-mou, which won the Golden Bear Award at the West Berlin Film Festival in 1988.) The period between 1985 and 1989 saw M. in a burst of creativity, with the publication of "Chin-fa ying-er" (1985; the golden-haired infant), "Paocha" (1985; explosions), "Mao-shih huei-t' sui" (1987; collected anecdotes about cats), "Hung huang" (1987; red locusts), *Tien-t'ang suan-t' ai chih ko* (1988; a song of garlic in Paradise County), *Shih-san pu* (1989; the thirteenth step), "Ni te hsing-wei shih wo-men kan-tao k'ung-chü" (1989; your behaviour horrifies us), and other works. Whereas he achieved almost instant fame in 1985 as one of the contemporary writers in search of national roots, his more experimental pieces (such as "Huan-le" [joy] and "Hung-huang") attracted rather negative criticisms. Although the change in readers' response was not unrelated to the gradual inward turn of his narrative, as M. probed sociopolitical pressures on his protagonists, but ideological campaigns in favour of positive treatment of reality since 1986 also had something to do with the adverse criticisms he received. He has nevertheless kept up with his writing, and his latest novel, Shih-ts' ao chia-tsu (the herbivorous family), is scheduled to be published soon.

Like other root-seeking writers, M. chooses for his milieu his native village, Kao-mi Tung-pei hsiang, Shantung, despite his disclaimer that the place is more fictional than real. The location is known for the unique behaviour of its inhabitants. Among other things, the villagers are extremely robust and individualistic, presumably as a result of the adverse environment and the turbulent age they live in. The orphan child in "T' ou-ming te hung-lo-po," Grandpa in Hung kao-liang chiatsu, Kao Ma (tall horse) in Tian-t'ang suan-t' ai chih ko, and the protagonist in "Hung huang" are but a few examples of his indomitable characters. (By contrast, the contemporary world is peopled by soft and greedy weaklings.) To M., writing should be an unreserved and unimpeded dissemination of human energy, and these rugged characters clearly serve as vehicles for such unrestrained expression. These characters derive their vitality from their intuitive, almost animalistic, mode of life and, in some cases, their unorthodox behaviour, including their herbivorous diet ("Hung huang").

Related to the concept of the individual is the family, be it extended or nuclear. M.'s works invariably consider how an individual fares in a familial context. Characteristically, his characters are found trapped in a clan that is on the road to decline, and some revitalization is in order (for example, in Hung kao-liang chia-tsu, "Pao-cha," and "Hung-huang"). To highlight the crisis of the family, especially in the modern context, M. often puts families in a rural setting, but increasingly under the threat of urban forces. The Prize-winning "Pai-kou ch'iu-ch'ien chia" (1985; the white dog and the swing) deals with the return of an intellectual to his native village to find his childhood girlfriend married to a deaf-mute and leading the life of a common peasant. The reunion induces much remorse in him over the gap that has developed between himself and his friend. To M. an individual acquires identity through his or her relations with the family just as much as through individual efforts. Thus, to know a person, it is necessary to play one character against another as well as one family against another. The idea of doubles is thus often fully exhausted. One character is, for instance, described as defiant while the other is depicted as docile (Tian-t'ang suant' ai chih ko). Furthermore, one dead character's identity may be given to his neighbour after the latter is given plastic surgery (with the dead man's head being sewn on to his body) in a funeral parlor (Shih-san pu).

M.'s works are mainly about quests for identity in terms of relationships. These quests are conducted in the context of traditional kinship systems and against the backdrop of an increasingly bureaucratized and commercial society in contemporary China.

FURTHER WORKS: Explosions and Other Stories (1991)

BIBLIOGRAPHY: Chou, Y. H., "Romance of the Red Sorghum Family," MCL, 5 (1989): 1–20; Zhang, J., "Red Sorghum," Film Quarterly, 42, 3 (Spring 1989): 41–43

—YING-HSIUNG CHOU

MOBERG, Vilhelm

Swedish novelist and dramatist, b. 20 Aug. 1898, Algutsboda; d. 8 Aug. 1973, Väddö

M.'s forebears were soldiers and small farmers in the province of Småland, in southern Sweden. Largely self-educated, M. worked in the glassblowing industry and as a farm laborer before turning to journalism in his early twenties. The critical and popular success of Raskens (1927; the Rask family), a carefully documented novel based on family tradition about the daily life of a soldier and his family in late-19th-c. rural Småland, enabled M. to concentrate on literary endeavors.

In the partly autobiographical trilogy comprising Sänkt sedebetyg (1935; Memory of Youth, 1937), Sömnlös (1937; Sleepless Nights, 1940), and Giv oss jorden! (1939; The Earth Is Ours, 1940) one volume translation of complete trilogy, The Earth Is Ours, 1940—the protagonist Knut Toring's inability to find happiness either in the rural Småland of his youth, where he lacks intellectual stimulation, or in Stockholm, where he feels cut off from his roots, becomes a metaphor for existential homelessness. The final volume culminates in an impassioned plea for the defense of humanitarian principles against encroaching fascism, a theme M. expands on in the historical novel Rid i natt! (1941; Ride This Night!, 1943), which M. dramatized in 1942.

Soldat med brutet gevär (1944; partial tr., When I Was a Child, 1956) also incorporates considerable autobiographical material, but the focus is on social history rather than psychological conflict. By tracing the influences of various social and political movements on his fictional alter ego, Valter Sträng, M. portrays the confrontation between the innate conservatism of rural culture and the political radicalism that accompanied rapid industrialization in the early 1900s.

M.'s best-known work is the four-volume epic about mid-19th-c. emigration to America: Utvandrarna (1949; The Emigrants, 1951), Invandrarna (1952; Unto a Good Land, 1954), Nybyggarna (1956; The Settlers, 1978), and Sista brevet till Sverige (1959; Last Letter Home, 1961). In Utvandrarna M.'s representative characters, a group of Småland peasants, collectively illustrate the historical causes of emigration: poverty, religious persecution, and the desire for personal freedom and social betterment. While never abandoning documentary realism, M. places increasing emphasis in the later volumes on the psychological cost of the uprooting. The work connects thematically both with the Knut Toring trilogy and with Din stund på jorden (1961, dramatized 1967; A Time on Earth, 1965), in which the protagonist is a Swedish-American of M.'s own generation.

M. wrote more than thirty plays, primarily folk comedies set in rural Småland, such as Marknadsafton (1929; market day eve) and Änkeman Jarl (1940; Jarl the widower); or serious contemporary dramas about moral or social issues, like Vår ofödde son (1945; our unborn son) and Domaren (1957; the judge). In Scandinavia M. was also known for speaking out in defense of individual freedoms and for his attacks on corruption in government. Before his death he had completed two volumes of Min svenska historia (1970, 1972; A History of the Swedish People, 1972).

M.'s strengths are his straightforward narrative style and epic breadth combined, in his best works, with penetrating psychological insight and a lyricism rooted in the natural rhythms of the language. Like other working-class writers of his generation, he deliberately set out to tell about the people from whom he came, and his works are important documents of social history. Still the most widely read serious novelist in Sweden today, he is also among the few Swedish writers to have achieved international renown.

FURTHER WORKS: *I vapenrock och linnebyxor* (1921); *Kassabrist* (1925); *Hustrun* (1928); *Bröllopssalut* (1929); *Långt från landsvägen* (1929); *De knutna händerna* (1930); *A. P. Rosell, bankdirektör* (1932); *Mans kvinna* (1933); *Våld* (1933); *Kyskhet* (1936); *Jungfrukammare* (1938); *En löskekarl* (1940); *Hundra gånger gifta* (1941); *Sanningen kryper fram* (1943); *Segerstedtstriden* (1945); *Brudarnas källa* (1946); *Gudens hustru* (1946); *Den okända släkten* (1950; rev. ed., 1968; *The Unknown Swedes*, 1988); *Fallet Krukmakaregatan* (1951); *Det gamla riket* (1953); *Att övervaka överheten* (1953); *Lea och Rakel* (1954); *Därför är jag republikan* (1955); *Komplotterna* (1956); *Dramatik* (3 vols., 1957); *Nattkyparen* (1961); *Sagoprinsen* (1962); *Förrädarland* (1968); *Berättelser ur min levnad* (1968); *I egen sak* (1984); *Vårplöjning och andra berättelser* (1990)

BIBLIOGRAPHY: Winther, S. K., "M. and a New Genre for the Emigrant Novel," *SS*, 34 (1962): 170–82; Moberg, V., "Why I Wrote the Novel about Swedish Emigrants," *SPHQ*, 17 (1966): 63–77; Alexis, G. T., "Sweden to Minnesota: V. M.'s Fictional Reconstruction," *AQ*, 18 (1966): 81–94; Holmes, P. A., "Symbol, Theme and Structure in *Utvandrarromanen*", in Lagerroth, E. and B., eds., *Perspektiv på Utvandrarromanen* (1971): 239–48; Orton, G. and Holmes, P., "Memoirs of an Idealist: V. M.'s *Soldat med brutet gevär*," *SS*, 48 (1976): 29–51; McKnight, R., *M.'s Emigrant Novels and the Journals of Andrew Peterson: A Study of Influences and Parallels* (1979); Holmes, P., *V. M.* (1980); Warme, L. G., *A History of Swedish Literature* (1996): 335-39

—ROCHELLE WRIGHT

MODERNISM

In its general sense as applied to literature and art, "modernism" connotes change and innovation, a break with the past, a rejection of the traditional and conventional, and a search for new means of expression. In the 20th c. the word has been loosely used to describe art and literature which broke from the dominant 19th-c. modes of romanticism and realism and which, in the case of literature, experimented with language and form, found new subject matter, was antimimetic, and frequently self-consciously delved into the inner states of the writer.

"Modernism," however, is more narrowly applied to specific literary movements in Latin America and Europe, the most prominent being the *modernismo* of Spanish America. It has been customary to date Spanish American modernism from the publication in Chile of a collection of stories and poems entitled *Azul* (1888; blue) by the Nicaraguan writer Rubén DARÍO. In fact, although *Azul* was a landmark of the movement and although Darío was the first to use the term, the modernist writings of the Cuban José Martí (1853–1895) and the Mexican Manuel Gutiérrez Nájera (1859–1895), as well as works by the Cuban poet Julián del Casal (1863–1893) and the Colombian poet José Asunción Silva (1865–1896) predate *Azul*. Nevertheless, Darío is the central figure of the movement.

Spanish American modernism originated in a dissatisfaction with the provincial Hispanic tradition of poetry and perhaps also from a loss of religious faith. The modernists desired to free Spanish American poetry from didactic purposes and to make it more cosmopolitan. They first turned for inspiration to the French Parnassians—Leconte de Lisle (1818–1894), José Maria de Hérédia (1842–1905), Catulle Mendès (1843–1909)—with their emphasis on concision, color, form, metrical perfection, and emotional detachment, and their "art for art's sake" theory derived from Théophile Gautier. French SYMBOLISM—Verlaine, Rimbaud, Malarmé—also exerted a strong influence, adding musical flow, verbal hermeticism, conceptual complexity, synesthetic imagery, and a mystical undercurrent to the modernist esthetic. The examples of Victor Hugo, Charles Baudelaire, and Edgar Allan Poe also had an influence on Spanish American modernism.

In Darío's work the modernist tendency is epitomized. He wrote in highly literary language, experimented with unusual meters, added color and innovative imagery to Spanish-language verse, and enriched his texts with classical and mythological allusions and philosophical undertones.

The leading Argentine modernist poet was Leopoldo LUGONES, whose verse was influenced by Hugo and Jules Laforgue (1860–1887). Lugones and other major modernist poets—the Mexican Amado NERVO, the Uruguayan Julio HERRERA Y REISSIG, the Bolivian Ricardo Jaimes Freyre (1868–1933), the last of whom used Nordic themes, and the Peruvian José Santos CHOCANO—reflect awareness not only of symbolism and other vanguardist tendencies but also sensitive and intelligent identification with New World problems and cultures; although they looked to Europe (but not Spain), they also tried to be essentially American.

The Mexican poet Enrique GONZÁLEZ MARTÍNEZ is considered by many the transitional figure between modernism and postmodernism in Spanish American poetry. While his verse is marked by Parnassian and symbolist elements, his sonnet "Tuércele el cuello al cisne" (1911; "Wring the Neck of the Swan," 1958), in which he replaces the swan, the symbol of elaborate modernist rhetoric, with the wise owl, is seen by many critics as signaling the end of the modernist period. Among postmodernists who broke away from the ornate language of Darío and his contemporaries were the Mexican Ramón López Velarde (1888–1921), who wrote with linguistic brilliance about the corruption of the city and about erotic subjects, and the Chilean poet Gabriela MISTRAL, a Nobel Prize winner.

Spanish American prose writers also participated in the modernist movement. The Uruguayan José Enrique RODÓ was the foremost essayist of the group; in *Ariel* (1900; *Ariel*, 1922) and other works he pleads for spiritual values in a materialistic world. The Venezuelan novelist Manuel Díaz Rodríguez (1871–1927), in *Ídolos rotos* (1901; broken idols) and *Sangre patricia* (1902; patrician blood), wrote in highly chiseled prose on symbolic themes. The Guatemalan literary journalist Enrique Gómez Carillo (1873–1927) kept the New World's Hispanic public abreast of modernist and vanguardist developments in Europe.

The Spanish American War and the arrival of Darío in Europe in 1898 hastened the impact of modernism in Spain. The war caused intellectuals to reassess Spanish culture, and Darío's innovations had an influence on such writers as Juan Ramón JIMÉNEZ; the poet and dramatist Francisco Villaespesa (1877–1936), who popularized the movement in Spain; and Manuel Machado (1874–1947), a poet who combined Andalusian folklore with the musicality of modernism. The impact of Spanish American modernism, with its roots in symbolism, was also felt in Portugal, where its most eminent representative was the poet Eugénio de Castro (1869–1944).

The term "modernism" has also been used to describe specific avant-garde literary manifestations in countries outside of Spanish America—in particular, Russia, the Ukraine, the Swedish-speaking part of Finland, and Brazil.

In Russia the term is identified with the "decadent" foreign influences (primarily French) of the turn of the century and is used more or less interchangeably with symbolism. Pioneered by Dmitry MEREZHKOVSKY, with the mystical philosophy of Vladimir Solovyov (1853–1900) as a precursor, Russian modernism was dominated in its early phase by the poets Konstantin BALMONT, Valery BRYUSOV, and Fyodor SOLOGUB. and later by Alexandr BLOK, Andrey BELY, and Vyacheslav IVANOV. The movement was notable for its aesthetic individualism tinged with anarchism and for its rejection of moralizing realism in literature. In the Ukraine the relaxation of censorship after the revolution of 1905 led to a period of modernism influenced by symbolism and the concept of art for art's sake. While continuing to deal with Ukrainian subject matter, particularly village life and the role of the intelligentsia in the Ukraine, modernist prose writers and poets searched for new forms. In the 1920s the Soviet government put a stop to the development of modernist writing in the Ukraine, imposing the strictures of socialist ideology.

Finland-Swedish modernism came about around the time of Finland's independence from Russia (1917), the victory of the Whites in the 1918 civil war, and the establishment of the Republic of Finland (1919), when an atmosphere of optimism was pervasive. Poetry was freed from traditional rhyme and meter and came under the influence of such avant-garde movements as DADAISM and SURREALISM. Edith SÖDERGRAN introduced modernism into Finland-Swedish poetry and had an enormous influence on later Finland-Swedish and Swedish poets. Along with her, Elmer DIKTONIUS, Gunnar BJÖRLING, and Rabbe ENCKELL were the leading modernist poets, while Hagar Olsson (1893–1978), in her criticism, fiction, and drama, epitomizes Finland-Swedish modernist prose writing.

Modernism in Brazil (see also Brazilian Literature) had almost no links with the Spanish American modernism of the turn of the century. Coming somewhat later than Darío's brand of modernism, it had its sources in FUTURISM, EXPRESSIONISM, and CUBISM; gathering momentum during the first decades of the century, Brazilian modernism was proclaimed and celebrated at a series of sessions on the arts called the Modern Art Week, held in 1922 in São Paulo. Its tenets were that art (all art, not just literature) was to utilize native and folkloric sources, that the Brazilian vernacular rather than "classical" Portuguese was to be used, and avant-garde movements of Europe and North America were to be adapted to Brazilian themes. (A later development was the idea that Brazilian literature was to be free from foreign influences.) Modernism dominated all the arts in Brazil until after World War II, and its influence is still felt.

Monteiro LOBATO's early stories and critical writings are of great importance to the beginnings of Brazilian modernism. Its outstanding exponent, however, was Mário de ANDRADE, who in his poetry, fiction—in particular, *Macunaíma* (1928; Macunaíma)— and essays embodied the iconoclastic spirit of the movement. The essayist José da Graça ARANHA was the strongest defender of the modernists. Oswald de ANDRADE, one of the organizers of the Modern Art Week, in his poetry and prose exemplifies the modernist idiom—informal, irreverent, exalting the primitive. One faction

of modernism was highly nationalistic and somewhat fascistic; Ricardo CASSIANO, a member of this group, wrote *Martim Cererê* (1928; Martim Cererê), the epic poem of the modernist movement.

To mention outstanding writers of Brazilian modernism is to list all the outstanding writers of the first half of the century. Major poets include Manuel BANDEIRA, who became the leader of the Rio de Janeiro modernists; Cecília MEIRELES, considered by many to be the most important woman poet writing in Portuguese; Carlos Drummond de ANDRADE, one of the greatest of Latin American poets; Jorge de Lima (1895–1951), from the Northeast, who wrote excellent Negro poetry and religious verse; and the younger João Cabral DE MELO NETO, who carried on the regionalist orientation of the movement.

The Northeast developed its own form of modernism, particularly in the regional novel. The seminal influence was the anthropologist and novelist Gilberto FREYRE, who dealt with the distinctive culture of the region. Jorge AMADO, Graciliano RAMOS, and José LINS DO RÊGO were the outstanding modernist novelists of the Brazilian Northeast, while João GUIMARÃES ROSA, innovative in style and technique, wrote of the region of Minas Gerais. There is hardly a Brazilian writer today who has not in some way been touched by the modernism of the 1920s, 1930s, and 1940s.

BIBLIOGRAPHY: Goldberg, I., *Studies in Spanish American Literature* (1920); Craig, G. D., *The Modernist Trend in Spanish American Poetry* (1934); Spender, S., *The Struggle of the Modern* (1963); Davison, N. J., *The Concept of Modernism in Hispanic Criticism* (1966); Nist, J., *The Modernist Movement in Brazil* (1967); Howe, I., ed., *The Idea of the Modern in Literature and the Arts* (1968); Anderson, R. R., *Spanish American Modernism: A Selected Bibliography* (1970); Chiari, J., *The Aesthetics of Modernism* (1970); Martins, W., *The Modernist Idea* (1970); Bradbury, M., and J. McFarlane, *Modernism 1890–1930* (1974); Forster, M. H., ed., *Tradition and Renewal: Essays on Twentieth-Century Latin American Literature and Culture* (1975); Ackroyd, P., *Notes for a New Culture: An Essay on Modernism* (1976); Bender, T. K., et al., *Modernism in Literature* (1977); Faulkner, P., *Modernism* (1977)

—BOYD G. CARTER

MODIANO, Patrick

French novelist, dramatist, and screenwriter, b. 30 July 1945, Boulogne-Billancourt

Although M. was born after the end of World War II, many of his writings reflect his fascination with the humiliating German occupation of France. A winner of more literary prizes than almost any other French novelist of his generation, M. enjoys a wide audience in the French-speaking world. Many of his books have been translated into English and other languages. His father, an eastern European Jew, lived an underground life during World War II and survived miraculously during the Holocaust by dealing in the black market. M.'s mother, Luisa Colpeyn, was a Belgian actress who had moved to Paris during the occupation where she married his father. The couple had two children, Patrick and Rudy; the latter was M.'s closest childhood friend. His death at an early age haunted the author throughout his existence, and most of his major works are dedicated to his brother. After the liberation of

France, M.'s father became a successful financier and business-man. The taciturnity of his father concerning his past and the separation of his parents when he was eighteen years old in 1963 were the basis for the obsessive themes of M.'s later works. During an itinerant, unstable youth, M.'s attended various schools, the most important of which was the Collège Saint Joseph in Thônes (Haute-Savoie) during 1960–1962, after which he received the baccalaureate degree at the prestigious Lycée Henri IV in Paris. After a year of study at the University of Paris in 1965–1966, M. abandoned further education to become a creative writer. Two years later, when he was twenty-three, Gallimard published M.'s first novel, *La Place de l'Étoile* (1968; the Place de l'Étoile), a work that not only won him instant fame but also two literary prizes, the Prix Roger Nimier in 1968 and the Prix Féelix Fénéon in 1969.

In *La Place de l'Étoile* M. reveals several recurrent traits of his unique art: a mélange of historical veracity (the setting is the German occupation of Paris of 1940–1945) and of fictional inventiveness; also transparent is stylistic lucidity that paradoxically expresses an atmosphere of vague mystery. The novel depicts both flagrant anti-Semitism and a fascination with the beauty of Judaic values and virtues. The protagonist, Raphael Schlemilovitch (the very name suggests in Yiddish a buffon who never succeeds at anything), is tormented by his love/hate relationships with his Jewish heritage. M.'s second novel, *Ronde de nuit* (*Night Rounds*, 1971) appeared in 1969. Once again the setting is the sinister world of Paris under German control, an infernal place governed by the Gestapo and characterized by countless police raids, incorporating dramatic shifts from examples of French collaborators to fighters of the French Resistance movement. Perhaps M.'s best known novel is his third work, *Les boulevards de ceinture* (*Ring Roads*, 1974), published in 1972, a novel for which he was awarded the prestigious Grand Prix du Roman (1972) of the French Academy. The protagonist is obsessed with an old photograph of his missing father; he eventually locates him, a pitiful and despicable Jew who is being hunted by the Nazis because of his black-market activities.

M. shifts the time and setting of his fourth novel, *Villa Triste*, (1975; *Villa Triste*, 1977), from the Paris of 1940–1945 to a fashionable spa on the French side of the Lake of Geneva during the early 1960s. The eighteen-year-old narrator seeks incessantly to resuscitate the emotions of a lost past and to make relive a disappeared villa in which he had spent many joyous days of childhood. In 1977, M. published his fifth novel, *Livret de famille* (family book or album). Here one of his most frequently used themes—that of memories-becomes for this author a useful device that allows him to blend pure autobiography with pure fiction. One year later, in 1978, M. published another novel, *Rue des boutiques obscures* (*Missing Person*, 1980). For this work M. finally won France's most coveted literary prize, the Prix Gon-court (1978), a fact that guaranteed that this work would become a best-seller almost overnight. M. poses this question: What sort of things does a dead human being leave behind after death? An old photograph, a birth certificate, a few letters and documents, several memories. But all of these begin to fade away with the passage of time. Life is like an echo that eventually becomes total silence. The central character, an employee with a private detective agency, begins to recognize his own personal traits in those of the missing person he has been trying to find—we suspect that the protagonist is the same man for whom he has been searching. The tone of uncertainty and mystery constitutes one of the unique characteristics of M.'s prose fiction.

A marked resemblance unites his three novels *Une jeunesse* (1981; youth), *Memory Lane* (1981; title in English), and *De si braves garçons* (1982; such good fellows): these three works deal with the memories of events that all occurred some twenty years earlier. In the latter work, M. emphasizes the disparity between what each of twelve boys dreamed of becoming and the actual reality of their destinies twenty years later.

During the 1990s, M.'s composition of novels continued with unabated regularity. These recent novels are constructed around a common theme, one that preoccupied the writer in his earlier works: the way memories of mysterious events that had taken place in the remote past continue to haunt, even to shape one's life many years after the fact. How do these strange, at times even magical experiences perpetuate themselves throughout the innermost recesses of today's events and those of the future? Two especially riveting novels on this subject merit special consideration here because they rank among M.'s finest achievements: *Voyage de noces* (1990, Honeymoon), and *Du plus loin de l'oubli* (1996, As far as one gets from forgetfulness). In the first of these novels M. reminds himself of a baffling event from the World War II years of the German occupation of France: while hitchhiking along a Côte d'Azur highway, a generous, kindly couple offered the narrator a ride and proved to be unusually helpful to him at a trying epoch of his life. Many years later he reads in an Italian newspaper an article about a mysterious suicide by a woman named Ingrid Riguad. It suddenly occurs to him that the latter was the very same person who had earlier offered him his ride and lifted him out of utter despondency. As the narrator begins to write his novel about this bewitching incident, he reflects on the nature of fiction and comes to comprehend how novels are really the amalgamation of factitious episodes and the genuinely authentic experiences lived by the novelist. In the second novel, M. utilizes an influential and nearly indecipherable encounter of some thirty years ago to come to grips with the meaning of his existence today. In his groping analyses of the shimmering flashes of light and darkness of a distant past, he penetrates into the innermost substratum of memory. In all of his novels, the underlying tone is similar: the author deliberately creates fascinating unanswered and unanswerable questions that haunt both the writer and the reader.

Noteworthy is M.'s collaboration with the internationally renowned director Louis Malle in one of the most successful French films of the last two decades: *Lacombe, Lucien* (1974; Lacombe, Lucien, 1975).

Among the contemporary writers of France, M. stands virtually apart from the dominant post-World War II literary trends. And unlike many of the novels published by the other trailblazing innovators, M.'s works are highly readable. He relates an interesting story and does so in a style easy to understand. In many respects, he continues the tradition of classical French literature. His works seem simple, orderly, and are devoid of unnecessary stylistic ornateness; they are generally brief, compact, and sensibly structured. The ambience painted in them is contemporary: bars, cafées, modern cities, travel and tourism, resorts that are very much in vogue. M.'s works reflect the rapid pace and fragmentation of modern human existence. His characters conduct their lives in a hallucinatory atmosphere of uncertainty, mystery, amnesia, alienation, rootlessness. The combination of these ingredients lends to M.'s texts an aura of magical poetry.

FURTHER WORKS: *Interrogatoire* (1976, with Emmanuel Berl); *Quartier perdu* (1984); *Une aventure de Choura* (1986); *Dimanches* *d'août* (1986); *Une fiancée pour Choura* (1987); *Vestiaire de l'enfance* (1988); *Fleurs de ruine* (1991)

BIBLIOGRAPHY: Chassequet-Smirgel, J., "La Place de l'Étoile de M.," in *Pour une psychanalyse de l'art et de la créativité* (1971): 217–55; Rambures, J.-L. de, "Comment travaillent les écrivains. P.M.: Apprendre à mentir," *Le Monde*, 24 May 1974: 24; Magnan, J. -M, "Un apatride nommé M.," *Sud*, 19 (3rd trimester 1976): 120–31; Bersani, J., "M., agent double" *NRF*, 1976, 298 (Nov. 1977): 78–84; Morel, P. -J, "Une dissertation de M.," *Les Nouvelles Littéraires* (18 Nov. 1982): 37–38; Nettlebeck, C. W., and P. A. Hueston, "Anthology As Art, P. M.'s *Livret de famille*," *AJFS*," 21 (May-Aug. 1984): 213–23; Richter, S., "Silhouetten von P. M.," *WB*, 31, 10 (1985): 1710–20; Nettlebeck, C. W., and P. A. Hueston, *P. M., Pièces d'identité: Écrire l'entretemps* (1986); Prince, G., "Re-Remembering M., or Something Happened," *Substance*, 49 (1986): 35–43; Warehime, M., "Originality and Narrative Nostalgia: Shadows in M.'s *Rue des boutiques obscures*," *FrF*, 12, 3 (Sept. 1987): 335–45; Bridges, V., and S. Barbour, "P. M.: *Quartier Perdu*," *YFS*, 1 (1988): 259–83; O'Keefe, C., "P. M.'s *La Place de l' Étoile*: Why Name a Narrator 'Raphael Schlemilovich'?" *LOS*, 15 (1988): 67–74; Golsan, R., "Collaboration, Alienation, and the Crisis of Identity," in Ayock, W., and M. Schoenecke, *Film and Literature* (1988): 16–123; Prince, G., "P. M.," in Brosman, C. S., ed., *DLB: French Novelists since 1960* (1989): 147–53; Boyarin, J., "Europe's Indian, America's Jew: M. and Vizenor," *Boundary II* (Fall 1992), Vol. 19, 3: 197-222

—JACK KOLBERT

MOFOLO, Thomas

Lesotho novelist (writing in South Sotho), b. 2 Aug. 1875, Khojane, Basutoland (now Lesotho); d. 8 Sept. 1948, Teyateyaneng

When M. was five, his Christian parents moved to the Qomoqomong Valley, Quthing District. There M. met the black Christian missionary teacher whose devotion to education M. was to idealize in the figure of Reverend Katse in the novel *Pitseng* (1910; Pitseng). M. became a houseboy to Alfred Casalis, who was the head of the Bible school, the printing press, and the book depot in Morija. Recognizing M.'s potential, Casalis sent him to the Bible School and then to the teachers' college, from which M. received certification. Casalis also encouraged him to write.

M.'s first novel, *Moeti oa bochabela* (1907; *The Traveller of the East*, 1934), had first been serialized in *Leselinyana*, a Sotho journal. It is probably the first novel by a black to be published in southern Africa. Set in Basutoland, the action of the morality tale centers around the quest of the young protagonist, Fekisi, for the causes of the presence of evil in the world. Although he does not find the answer, his journey ends in his ascent to a Christian heaven where all is honesty and virtue.

In this novel Christian morality is idealized, while that of the African is shown to be in decline. M. tried to integrate African values with Christian values in a harmonious synthesis; Christianity for him was a way of restoring the purity of ancient African civilization.

The plot of *Pitseng*, M.'s second novel, concerns the marriage between two young Christianized Africans. In showing the moderation, discipline, and patience of both Alfred and Aria, qualities

that make their marriage bond secure, M. alluded to marriage as the symbol of the relationship between the Church and Christ. Much emphasis is given to the character portrayal of the simple people who live in the secluded valley of Pitseng. In contrast to the virtue and piety of Alfred and Aria, M. pictures the hypocrisies of many other Christian Africans, black and white. M. here focuses on the discrepancy between the teachings of Christianity and the behavior of many Christians.

M.'s masterpiece, *Chaka* (1925; *Chaka the Zulu*, 1931; new tr., 1981), the last of his three novels, was written in 1910, but it was considered unsuitable for publication by M.'s only recourse, the missionary press, which did not alter this position for fifteen years. Disillusioned, M. gave up writing at thirty-five and devoted the next years to building a successful business. In 1937 he retired to his farm. But he was not to be allowed to enjoy it. M.'s farm was expropriated in 1940 when the government proceeded to enforce a prohibition of the Land Act of 1914—that a black could not own land that abuts the property of a white. Thus victimized by the whites and having lost the financial security obtained by years of work, he became a broken man. His last years were redeemed from grim poverty only by a small pension.

Chaka, a dramatic departure from M.'s earlier books, is the tragic study of a man who, once accustomed to the gratifications of power, can no longer live according to common morality. The novel is based on the history of an African conqueror, the "black Napoleon," who in the early 19th c. amassed an army of close to a million Zulu warriors and ruled over half of Africa, from the Congo to South Africa. In M.'s version, Chaka becomes evil when he succeeds to the chiefdom at his father's death; from that point on Chaka develops from a moral man into a monster. He sinks into the dark world of sorcery and paganism, bartering his soul for power. There is no turning back for Chaka, and he goes on to extraordinary success on the battlefields. But the code of power and violence by which he lives in the end devours him as well, when he is assassinated by his two half-brothers.

The appeal of Chaka is mythic; about him is the light of the fallen prince; he is Satan, Tamburlaine, and Faust. Although he destroys himself, his is a magnificent adventure. There is poetry in his evilness, fascination in his decline. Chaka chose the way of power, violence, cruelty. M. was attracted to another way—that of love and trust in humanity—but he understood the frustration and rage at the root of Chaka's evilness, and as an African he could even glory in Chaka's magnificent conquests.

Soon after its publication *Chaka* was a best seller in Africa, both in South Sotho and in other African and European-language editions, and M., who by then had long stopped writing, enjoyed its success.

M., both in the virtues he exhibited during his lifetime and in the themes he conveyed through his novels, belongs to a transitional African period, one in which conflict between traditional and modern values resulted in a painful distortion of both value systems. His work illustrates the tragic irony that angels as well as monsters are swallowed up when violence overtakes the African terrain.

BIBLIOGRAPHY: Kunene, D. P., *The Works of T. M.: Summaries and Critiques* (1967); Gérard, A. S., *Four African Literatures: Xhosa, Sotho, Zulu, Amharic* (1974): 125–30; Mphahlele, E., *The African Image*, rev. ed. (1974): 206–10: 223; Ikonné, C., "Purpose versus Plot: The Double Vision of T. M.'s Narrator," in Heywood, C., ed., *Aspects of South African Literature* (1976): 54–65; Burness,

D., ed., *Shaka, King of Zulus* (1976), passim; Swanepoel, C. F., "Reflections on the Art of T. M." *Limi*, 7 (1979): 63–76

—MARTIN TUCKER

MOHANTY, Gopinath

Indian novelist and short-story writer (writing in Oriya), b. 1 April 1914, Cuttack

M. was born into an aristocratic landowning family, the ninth and youngest child of his parents. He earned an M.A. in English literature at Ravenshaw College in Cuttack and then entered government service as a subdeputy collector under the British administration. While holding a variety of jobs in his home state of Orissa, he came into contact with a cross section of different groups, particularly the Adibasis, a tribal people. He mastered the Adibasi language, and has often used Adibasi words and phrases in his novels. He was further inspired, if not influenced, by the literary achievement of his elder brother, Khanu Charan Mohanty (b. 1906), a novelist of high repute. M. is a polyglot, a man of culture, and also a keen observer of human nature. He received the Sahitya Akademi Award in 1955 and the highest Indian literary prize, the Jnanpith Award, in 1974.

M.'s major novels are *Paraja* (1945; subjects), *Amritara santan* (1949; son of the nectar), *Danapani* (1955; bread and butter), and *Mati matal* (1964; *matal* soil). The central theme of *Paraja* is the exploitation of the poor by landlords. *Amnitara santan* deals with the Kondha, an Adibasi tribe, and focuses on the life of a village woman. In *Danapani* M. lays bare the hypocrisy of a "town man," showing how he exploits people, including his wife, in his ambition to rise to high position. *Mati matal* is an in-depth study of the nature of an individual and his efforts to come to terms with the environment and with changing society.

M. has also written numerous short stories; two of the best known are "Ghasara phula" (1957; flower of grass) and "Na mane nahin" (1968; name not remembered).

M. brought glory to the Oriya language and raised its status among other Indian languages. He has great insight into human nature. His special contribution is his depiction of the Adibasis' way of life, which no writer had done before. His awareness of changing times and values is evident in his work. Above all, he is an outstanding craftsman.

FURTHER WORKS: *Managahirara chhasa* (1940); *Dadi Buddha* (1944); *Harijana* (1948); *Sarata babunka gali* (1950); *Rahura chhaya* (1952); *Dwipatra* (1954); *Sapana mati* (1954); *Naba badhu* (1956); *Chhai alua* (1956); *Sarala Mahabharata* (1956); *Siba bhai* (1958); *Poda kapala* (1958); *Mahapurusa* (1958); *Mukti Pathe* (1958); *Apahancha* (1961); *Tantrikar* (1963); *Ranadhandola* (1963); *Dipang jyoti* (1965); *Utkala mani* (1967); *Gupta ganga* (1967); *Pahanta* (1970); *Udanta khai* (1971); *Akash sundari* (1972); *Analanala* (1973). FURTHER WORKS IN ENGLISH: *Ants, and Other Stories* (1979)

BIBLIOGRAPHY: Mansinha, M., *History of Oriya Literature* (1962): 268–70; Mohanty, J. M., *There Where Trees Flower* (1980): 62–79

—BIJAY KUMAR DAS

MOLDOVIAN LITERATURE

The literature of the former Moldavian Soviet Socialist Republic must be treated as distinct from that of Romania. Created in 1940 by a merger of the former Romanian province of Bessarabia (1918-40) and the small Moldavian Autonomous Soviet Socialist Republic, which had been organized in 1924 east of the interwar Soviet-Romanian border, the Moldavian S.S.R., except during World War II, was completely incorporated into the Soviet political and social system. In literature the symbol of the incorporation was the adoption of a modified Cyrillic alphabet; a version of this alphabet had been in use since 1924 in the Moldavian A.S.S.R., but this tiny region—created as a symbol of the Soviet intention to reacquire Bassarabia—did not produce any literature of consequence. Although Moldavian writers have been fully integrated into Soviet cultural life, and their theme and methods have reflected Soviet rather than Romanian realities.

The major themes of poetry immediately after World War II were patriotism and the building of socialism; the epic, well suited to civic poetry, was the favorite genre. The work of Emilian Bukov (b. 1909) and Andrei Lupan (b. 1912) was typical, for in it ideological and social considerations prevailed over aesthetic requirements. Since the 1950s subject matter and means of expression have diversified, as illustrated in the poetry of Emil Lotianu (b. 1936). His work runs the gamut from civic to love poetry, conveying sentiment and conviction through striking images.

Fiction has generally followed the same evolution as poetry. At first, the peasant and his adjustment to collectivized society was the dominant theme, but in the 1950s other heroes and new techniques came to the fore. The first Moldavian novel, Emilian Bukov's *Kresk etazhele* (1952; The Floors Grow), dealt with the urban working class, and Adriadna Shalar's (b. 1923) novel *Neastymper* (1961; Restlessness) described the spiritual formation of the new generation. One of the major innovators in prose has been Ion Drutse (b. 1928), whose novels, among them *Balade din kympie* (1963; Ballads of the Steppes), pursue the fortunes of the peasantry between the world wars. Telling his stories in the laconic, figurative language reminiscent of popular fables, he displays a keen appreciation for the material and psychological foundations of village life.

Moldavian drama reached maturity more slowly than poetry and prose. The first important Moldavian play, *Lumina* (1948; Light), by Andrei Lupan, was typical of the early preoccupation of dramatists with the broad social problems and their relative lack of interest in individual psychology and experimentation with form. Ion Drutse's *Kasa mare* (1962; The Festive Room) was a promising new departure. The story of a young wife whose soldier-husband has been killed at the front, it probes with sympathy and insight her inner struggle with loneliness and suggests some universal truths about the purity of the human conscience.

Between the 1960s and the collapse of the Soviet Union in 1991 Moldavian literature continued to be strongly influenced by trends in Soviet literature as a whole. Although a revival of interest in the cultural heritage of the Moldavians and an emphasis on its essentially Romanian character found expression in prose and poetry, political tension between the Soviet Union and Romania limited their influence. One of the leading representatives of the new tendencies was Ion Drutse, whose novel, *Belaia tserkov'* (1983; The White Church), is a remarkably sympathetic portrayal of the customs and mentality of the 18th-c. Moldavian village. Since 1991, when Moldova (as the country is now called) declared independence, the national revival has quickened. Regular contacts with Romania have reinforced the Romanian character of Moldovian literature, but the decades of Soviet predominance has left its mark, and a specific Moldovian sense of identity remains in place.

—KEITH HITCHINS

MOLNÁR, Ferenc

Hungarian dramatist, novelist, short-story writer, and journalist (also writing in English), b. 12 Jan. 1878, Budapest; d. 1 April 1952, New York, N. Y., U.S.A.

Son of a physician, M. studied law in Budapest and Geneva but soon began writing feuilletons and novels. In 1896 he joined the editorial staff of *Budapesti napló* and later that of several other newspapers. His early writings gained wide recognition, and he soon became a prominent dramatist and novelist. During World War I M. was a war correspondent. In the 1920s his plays achieved worldwide fame. He spent many years abroad, and in 1939 left Hungary permanently because of the menace of fascism. He settled in New York City and continued writing—sometimes in English—until his death.

As a journalist, M. valued keen observation, precise description, suave mischievousness, and wit. His urbane, vibrant short stories, mainly featuring lovelorn men and cunning women engaged in the battle of sexes, are meticulously constructed. His novels are characterized by clever plots and stylistic brilliance, although their range is rather narrow. Only the early *A Pál-utcai fiúk* (1907; *The Paul Street Boys*, 1927) is a masterpiece. It is a moving, realistic tale about youngsters playing adults. M. depicts their nobility, innocence, camaraderie, and love of freedom, but also their innate cruelty. Their gang life is an allegory of a problem-ridden age. M.'s insights into young people's psyches, his sympathies with their boundless hopes and dreams, are communicated to the reader in a succinct, poetic style.

M.'s chief contribution to world literature was as a dramatist. He was a natural playwright with a mesmerizing, unerring dramatic instinct, originality, and dazzling technique and craftsmanship. His whimsical, sophisticated drawing-room comedies show the influence of Oscar Wilde, of the French boulevard playwrights, and of SHAW, SCHNITZLER, and PIRANDELLO. M. achieved a felicitous synthesis of realism and romanticism, cynicism and sentimentality, the profane and the sublime. His elegant, satiric plays about manners, frailties, and illusions are built on precisely timed, sparkling dialogue.

M.'s first great success was *Az ördög* (1907; *The Devil*, 1908), a comedy in which the devil forces two people together who might have remained virtuous without him. From powdered dandies and scheming ladies, M. turned to thugs and simple servants in his next play, *Liliom* (1909; *Liliom*, 1921), his most famous work. Staged worldwide and filmed, both the play and its Americanized musical version, *Carousel* (1946), are classics. Combining naturalism and fantasy, this touching allegory examines the problem of redemption while portraying human suffering in Budapest's underworld. Liliom, a tough barker at an amusement park, marries Juli, a naïve

servant. Failing in his efforts to steal and kill for money, he commits suicide. At a celestial court, he learns that after purging himself for sixteen years, he could gain salvation by one good deed. After his probation he returns to earth, but when his daughter refuses his gift, a stolen star, Liliom strikes her in exasperation, although the girl says the slap felt like a caress. Thus, the incorrigible sinner is escorted back to hell as irredeemable. Liliom is M.'s paradoxical Everyman, Juli the eternal female ideal.

M. developed one of his favorite themes, the contrast of relative and absolute truth, of illusion and reality, by using actors as characters in two of his most famous plays. *A testőr* (1910; *The Guardsman*, 1924), a sparkling comedy, presents the predicament of an actor who feels he is not loved for what he is and needs to masquerade as what he believes his wife wants. Using his histrionic powers to impersonate the guardsman (his new "rival"), he sets out to seduce his own wife. In *Játék a kastélyban* (1926; *The Play's the Thing*, 1927), the distinctions between theater and life are again blurred. The play is a dazzling, mercilessly cynical farce proving that our lives are mere role-playing.

Equally entertaining are his facile farces portraying romance among the aristocracy. *A hattyú* (1921; *The Swan*, 1929) is a witty satire about a princess who is compelled to forsake genuine love because of family obligations. Elaborating on a similar theme in *Olympia* (1928; *Olympia*, 1928), M. assails the cruelty of aristocracy toward the common man.

M. achieved international fame by amusing audiences everywhere for five decades. Instead of conveying social messages, this prolific, imaginative, witty writer aimed merely to entertain by transforming his colorful, stormy personal experience into effective works of art. M. excelled as an observer, a storyteller, and a humorist. A master of stagecraft, he provided escape and gaiety in an illusory world in which conflicts were amenable to solution.

FURTHER WORKS: *Magdolna és egyéb elbeszélések* (1898); *A csókok éjszakája és elbeszélések* (1899); *Az éhes város* (1901); *Egy gazdátlan csónak története* (1901; *The Derelict Boat*, 1924); *A doktor úr* (1902; *The Lawyer*, 1927); *Éva* (1903; *Eva*, 1924); *Józsi* (1904); *Gyerekek* (1905); *Egy pesti lány története* (1905); *Rabok* (1908; *Prisoners*, 1924); *Muzsika* (1908); *Ketten beszélnek* (1909; *Stories for Two*, 1950); *Pesti erkölcsök* (1909); *Hétágú síp* (1911); *A farkas* (1912; *The Wolf*, 1925); *Ma, tegnap, tegnapelőtt* (1912); *Báró Márczius és egyéb elbeszélések* (1913); *Kis hármaskönyv* (1914); *Az aruvimi erdő titka és egyéb szatirák* (1916); *A fehér felhő* (1916; *The White Cloud*, 1927); *Egy haditudósito emlékei* (1916); *Farsang* (1917; *Carnival*, 1924); *Ismerősök* (1917); *Úri divat* (1917; *Fashions for Men*, 1922); *Andor* (1918); *Széntolvajok* (1918); *Szinház* (1921); *Égi és földi szerelem* (1922; *Launzi—Heavenly and Earthly Love*, 1923); *A vörös malom* (1923; *The Red Mill*, 1928); *Az üvegcipő* (1924, *The Glass Slipper*, 1925); *A gőzoszlop* (1926; *The Captain of St. Margaret's*, 1945); *Riviera* (1926; *Riviera*, 1927); *Összes munkái* (20 vols., 1928); *Egy kettő, három* (1929; *The President*, 1930); *A jó tündér* (1930; *The Good Fairy*, 1932); *Harmonia* (1932); *Valaki* (1932; *Arthur or Somebody*, 1952); *Csoda a hegyek közt* (1933; *Miracle in the Mountain*, 1947); *A zenélő angyal* (1933; *Angel Making Music*, 1935); *Az ismeretlen lány* (1934); *A cukrászné* (1935; *Delicate Story*, 1941); *Nagy szerelem* (1935); *A királynő szolgálólánya* (1936; *The King's Maid*, 1941); *Delila* (1937; *Blue Danube*, 1952); *A zöld huszár* (1937); *Őszi utazás* (1939); *Panoptikum* (1942; *Waxworks*, 1952); *A császár* (1942; *The Emperor*, 1942); *The Blue-Eyed Lady* (1942);

Farewell My Heart (1945); *Szivdobogás* (1947; *Game of Hearts*, 1952); *Companion in Exile: Notes for an Autobiography* (1950). **FURTHER WORKS IN ENGLISH:** *Husbands and Lovers* (1924); *Plays of M.* (1927); *The Plays of F. M.* (1929; repr. as *All the Plays of M.*, 1937); *Romantic Comedies: Eight Plays* (1952)

BIBLIOGRAPHY: Chandler, F. W., "Hungarian and Czech Innovators: M. and the Čapeks," *Modern Continental Playwrights* (1931): 438–53; Gassner, J., "M. and the Hungarians," *Masters of the Drama* (1945): 478–81; Behrman, S. N., "Playwright: F. M." (1946), *The Suspended Drawing Room* (1965): 191–253; Gergely, E. J., *Hungarian Drama in New York: American Adaptations 1908–1940* (1947): 9–60: 181–90; Middleton, G., "F. M.," *These Things Are Mine* (1947): 363–69; Reményi, J., *Hungarian Writers and Literature* (1964): 348–62; Györgyey, C., *F. M.* (1980); Sárközi, M., *Szinhá az egész világ: M. F. regényes élete* (1995); Györgyey, C., "Merely a Player?," *NHQ*, 143 (1996): 117-121

—CLARA GYÖRGYEY

N. Scott Momaday

MOMADAY, N(atachee) Scott

American poet, novelist, and short-story writer, b. 27 Feb. 1934, Lawton, Okla.

As a writer M. has explored the ways of being both a contemporary Native American and a member of a heritage that includes European as well as Indian ancestry. His lifelong concern with the influence of myth and ritual upon the fates of individuals figures largely in his highly autobiographical novels, short stories, and memoirs. Of Kiowa origin, M. was raised in the Navajo and Jemez Indian traditions of Arizona and New Mexico. Both parents had academic backgrounds and influenced M.'s interests in tribal identity and the inherent tension between the Anglo-American and Native American cultures. Between 1936 and 1943 M. lived with his family on Navajo reservations, learning the Navajo language but returning periodically to the Oklahoma Kiowa country in a conscious attempt to deepen his ancestral roots through communion with the land. During World War II he was exposed for the first time to the wider American culture when both parents took jobs in war-related industries. The imaginative world of sports stars, war heroes, and movie stars would affect him as profoundly as would his immersion in Kiowa and Navajo cultures. After graduating in political science from the University of New Mexico in 1958, M. spent a year teaching speech at a reservation school, where he found time to develop his poetry. He was accepted into the creative-writing program at Stanford University the following year, where Yvor WINTERS became his mentor. M. received an A.M. from Stanford in 1960, and a Ph.D. in 1963. Thereafter he remained an English teacher and writer at the University of California at Santa Barbara, 1962–1969; Berkeley, 1969–1972 (English and comparative literature); and since 1972 at Stanford.

For his first major work, *House Made of Dawn* (1968), M. was awarded—as the first Native American—a Pulitzer Prize. Concerned with the heartbreak and disillusionment of Abel, a young World War II veteran, the novel explores the contradictions apparent when he attempts to live in the Anglo world of a Los Angeles relocation center, and, later, when he attempts an interracial relationship with a visiting white woman on the San Ysidro reservation. M. involves his protagonist in the spectrum of violent confrontation, misdirected anger, and prejudiced reaction existing between the bifurcated world of Indian and urban Anglo culture. Paralleling this tensive world, however, is a positive treatment of the imaginative world of contemporary Native American culture. Characters such as the grandfather, who comes to represent the continuity of Pueblo tradition through his evocation of nature imagery and stories of tribal origin, and the Mexican priest of the village, whose Catholic tradition mixes with Indian mythology, serve to articulate the search for personal and tribal identity that lies at the heart of this novel. Central to the thought of *House Made of Dawn* is the prescription that the survival of a people is dependent upon the continual revaluation of their identities.

A journey to his ancestral graves in the Kiowa homeland left M. with a determination to present Kiowa oral tradition in *The Way to Rainy Mountain* (1969). The sense of separation he felt at his grandfather's graveside, where his past seemed to lie in oblivion, led him on an intensive search for the stories and storytellers of tribal tradition. This quest he regarded as necessary to better understand his identity, but also as a necessary act of retrieval, because many Indian oral traditions were in danger of extinction. Characteristic of M. in this memoir is his focus on the lives of the storytellers by means of descriptive character detail, his concern for a subjective accounting of his own thoughts while in pursuit of folkloric detail, and, finally, his careful reading of the mythic stories and legends. Structurally, *The Way to Rainy Mountain* reflects the polymorphic approach of a writer who would see the landscape of his past through many eyes. Twenty-four triads of mythical, historical, and personal narratives are framed by a prologue and epilogue, the entire work preceded by an explanatory introduction. Two poems of mythical origins lend further perspective to the whole, the first dealing with tribal origins, the second predicting the end of traditional Kiowa culture. The entire work offers a multiplicity of tones as well, running from the restrained, matter-of-fact approach of the prologue, which deals with the development and decline of the oral tradition, to the highly rhythmic archaic power of the first poem, which tries to evoke the manifold forces of nature beyond the grasp of poetic language. *The Way to Rainy Mountain* attempts to meld an Indian tradition of "geopiety," a theology of the land, with a recognition of the significance of the past—dying and yet alive—that will sustain a revaluation of individual and tribal identity.

In *The Names: A Memoir* (1976), M. continues an exploration of the physical and spiritual presence of the land as a supportive force in Native American life. More unified in structure and tone than *The Way to Rainy Mountain*, it documents the history and lore of his own family ancestry, which includes Kiowa Indians and white Kentucky tobacco farmers; M. regards both cultural groups as rooted in the cultivation and appreciation of the land. He was significantly influenced by the Danish writer Isak DINESEN, who focused on the connection between the land and the people of Africa in her autobiographical *Den afrikanske farm* (1937; *Out of Africa*, 1937) and *Skygger på græsset* (1960; *Shadows on the Grass*, 1960). Although M. has called *The Names* "an evocation of the American landscape," time as much as place is evoked through the conviction that the ancestral spirits surround the writer, that they are part of his present being.

M.'s poetic collections include prose poetry as well as more formal techniques and concern subjects familiar to his prose works. Social criticism of modern industrialism and nuclear-arms development also appear, as well as moments of humorous verse on dark subjects; more lyrical poetry confronting the problems of loneliness and separation reflects a Native American pursuit of song and formulaic charms as a necessary response to life's vicissitudes.

Most characteristic of M.'s writings as a whole is his integration of personal quest with a more general search for tribal redefinition. He has said before a group of Native American scholars, "We are what we image. Our very existence consists in our imagination of ourselves." As a writer, M.'s words become products of self-knowledge, part of the imaginative life that must now serve the contemporary Native American, who has "at last stepped out of the museum that we have made of his traditional world."

FURTHER WORKS: *The Journey of Tai-me* (1967); *Colorado: Summer, Fall, Winter, Spring* (1973); *Angle of Geese and Other Poems* (1974); *The Colors of Night* (1976); *The Gourd Dancer* (1976); *A Coyote in the Garden* (1988); *Ancestral Voice* (1989); *The Ancient Child* (1989); *In the Presence of the Sun: A Gathering of Shields* (1991); *The Native American: Indian Country* (1993)

BIBLIOGRAPHY: Hylton, M. W., "On the Trail of Pollen: M.'s *House Made of Dawn*," *Crit*, 14, 2 (1972): 60–69; Trimble, M. S., *N. S. M.* (1973); McAllister, H. S., "Be a Man, Be a Woman: Androgyny in *House Made of Dawn*," *AIQ*, 12 (1975): 14–22; Strelke, B., "N. S. M.: Racial Memory and Individual Imagination," in Chapman, A., ed. *Literature of the American Indians*

(1975): 348–57; Evers, L. J., "Words and Place: A Reading of *House Made of Dawn*," *WAL*, 11 (1977): 297–320; Dickinson-Brown, R., "The Art and Importance of N. S. M.," *SoR*, 14 (1978): 31–45; Kerr, B., "The Novel As Sacred Text: N. S. M.'s Mythmaking Epic," *SWR*, 63, 2 (1978): 172–79; Berner, R. L., "N. S. M.: Beyond Rainy Mountain," *American Indian Culture and Research Journal*, 3, 1 (1979): 57–67; Fields, K., "More Than Language Means: Review of N. S. M.'s *The Way to Rainy Mountain*," *SoR*, 6 (1979): 196–204; Velie, A. R., "Post-Symbolism and Prose Poems: M.'s Poetry," *Four American Indian Literary Masters* (1982): 11–31; Schubnell, M., *N. S. M.: The Cultural and Literary Background* (1985); Antell, J. A., "M., Welch, and Silko: Expressing the Feminine Principle through Male Alienation," *AIQ*, 12, 3 (Summer 1988): 213–20; Wild, P., "N. S. M.: Gentle Maverick," *American West*, 25 (1988): 12–13

—WILLIAM OVER

MON, Franz

(pseud. of Franz Löffelholz) German poet and dramatist, b. 6 May 1926, Frankfurt am Main

M. studied history, philosophy, and German at the University of Frankfurt, where he received his doctorate in 1955. He is now the business manager of a textbook publishing house in Frankfurt.

M. can be classified as one of the leading concrete poets, since the content of his experimental works is language itself. As is the case with most avant-grade writers, M. has compiled extensive theoretical texts to explain and justify his approach. Most of these have appeared in the anthology *texte über texte* (1970; texts about texts). Here M. argues that we can know reality only through language. Yet this language has stored up historical ideas and conventions that are no longer valid. To rid ourselves of these incrustations and to achieve a clearer perception of present-day reality, it is therefore necessary to analyze this language by isolating its parts and performing experiments on them. For example, one can recombine bits of language in montage fashion, one can stretch the syntax of the sentence to unmanageable lengths, or one can create optical images using letters, words, parts of words, or sentences. Through such playful procedures one can hope to begin understanding how language works and how it influences our perception of the world.

M. began writing in the surrealist tradition, and his early poems were full of grotesque images. He quickly moved, however, to a more radical experimentation with language in his first major collection of concrete texts, *artikulationen* (1959; articulations). In subsequent collections he refined and expanded his technique. In *sehgänge* (1964; paths of vision), for example, he manipulates given texts according to set procedures: expansions through grammatical associations or similarities of sound, rearrangement of words, or the creation of pictures and new words from parts of the text. In his *lesebuch* (1967; reader) he creates sentences that are so long as to be uninterpretable, thus forcing readers to concentrate on the form, or the creates sentences that are syntactically straightforward but which have such bizzare images that the reader is baffled by the semantic connotations. In all these works the combination of linguistic elements not usually found together in language usage or the creation of new linguistic forms are supposed to give us a heightened insight into the relationship between language and reality.

M.'s most famous work is *herzzero* (1968; heart zero). The book contains two parallel texts that are collages of sentences, words, colloquial speech, and familiar sayings. Readers are instructed to mark in the book; with a pencil they are to connect passages that belong together, with a pen they are to improve or supplement the texts, and with a felt-tipped pen they are to cross out superfluous texts. Readers thus actively restructure their own language-reality and in so doing interpret the world in a new light.

In the late 1960s and early 1970s, M. wrote several radio plays where he applied the same principles and techniques of language experimentation. The pieces have no plot or theme, except to examine language. These acoustic montages and permutations came to be viewed as paradigms for the then popular genre of the "new radio play."

M.'s influence on German literature was intense but short. He argued cogently for a rethinking of our linguistic consciousness and for a responsible use by authors of their medium. His contributions to the concrete school are considerable, and he will be remembered for his ingenuity and innovation, even if his theories found no long-lasting support or confirmation.

FURTHER WORKS: *movens* (1960); *protokoll an der kette* (1961); *verläufe* (1962); *weiss wie weiss* (1964); *rückblick auf isaac newton* (1965); *5 beliebige fassungen eines textes aus einem satz* (1966); *animal nur das alphabet gebrauchen* (1967); *text mit 600* (1970); *aufenthaltsraum* (1972); *maus in mehl* (1976); *hören und sehen vergehen oder in einen geschlossenen mund kommt eine fliege* (1978); *fallen stellen* (1981); *hören ohne aufzuhören 03 arbeiten 1952–1981* (1982)

BIBLIOGRAPHY: Brüggemann, D., "Die Aporien der konkreten Poesie," *Merkur*, 2 (1974): 148–65; Waldrop, R., "Songs and Wonderings," *CL*, 4 (1975): 344–54; special M. issue, *T+K,* 60 (1978); Hedges, I., "Concrete Sound: The Radio Plays of F. M.," *Dada*, 12 (1983): 60–69

—ROBERT ACKER

MONENEMBO, Tierno

(pseud. of Tierno Saïdou Diallo) Guinean novelist (writing in French), b. 21 July 1947, Porédaka

M. was reared in the Futa Jallon mountains near Mamou, on the railway line between Kankan and Kindia. He obtained his baccalaureate in Conakry with a major in biology. He fled Sékou Touré's dictatorship in 1969 and went on to study science at the universities of Dakar and Abidjan. He narrowly escaped extradition to Guinea in 1973 and migrated to France where he completed a doctorate in biochemistry at Lyons University. M. taught science in Algeria and Morocco for seven years before accepting a position at the Honfleur High School in Normandy. In 1987, as France was trying to resume relations with the new regime after Sékou Touré's death in 1984, the French Government facilitated M.'s return to his country to give a series of conferences after eighteen years in exile. In 1994 M. spent several months in Brazil researching his fifth novel, *Pelourinho* (1995; Pelourinho).

M.'s six novels, all published in Paris by the prestigious Editions Seuil, could be seen as an ongoing project on narrative experimentation. M's novels are forever more challenging or disconcerting, depending on the reader's ability to adapt to the narrators' dislocated discourse.

Les crapauds-brousse (1979; The Bush Toads, 1983) and *Les ecailles du ciel* (1986; The Scales of the Sky) were inspired by the responsibility to bear witness to the suffering of his compatriots abandoned to Sékou Touré's totalitarian regime in Guinea. M. had to explain to Guinean writers of the *Nouvelle ecole* (New School) the Fulani sources for the titles of his first two novels: according to Fulani mythology, the bush toad, formerly a chosen creature, owes its ugliness to his betrayal of God, and the "scales of the sky" are one of the signs of universal disaster. M.'s "bush toads," best represented by Dioulidé, are fearful intellectuals who are unable to provide leadership because they cannot communicate with the people. In his second novel the "scales of the sky" may serve as a metaphor for the obscurantism that seizes a whole population whose only defense against political oppression is drunkenness. S. Garnier classified M. among the masters of the poetics of rumor in the wake of the two great Congolese protest writers TCHICAYA U'TAMSI and Sony Labou TANSI. Rumors liberate the crowd's inventiveness and grant the right to judge the State. Rumors restore women's participation in events. The "horizontal" spread of rumors thus escapes the "vertical" control of the hierarchy.

However, Garnier warns of the danger of too much discourse fragmentation at the expense of fictional figures, in particular in M.'s next novel *Un rêve utile* (1991; A Useful Dream). This third novel offers the reader disjointed insights into a young African exile in Loug—alias Lyons—and his perilous escape from Guinea to Senegal and France. The narrative focuses on the refugees' ability to fare and even care for each other against all odds. The mixture of migrant survival slang and African words—dishes, trees, musical instruments and singers, as well as cultural landmarks such as the epic *Soundjata* or the historic figures of Shaka and Queen Pokou—makes the reading somewhat turbulent.

Although the next two novels are more detached from Guinea as literary location, African culture remains at the core of M.'s fiction. In *Un Attiéké pour Elgass* (1993; A Serve of Attiéké for Elgass), the remembrance of events in people's memory is more important than the unfolding of the events themselves, but at least the characters are more easily identifiable. The long day of wandering through the sprawls of Abidjan introduces yet another community of Guinean refugees, albeit suspiciously cheerful, as though everyone had something to conceal. The supposed *frères-pays* (brothers from home) are prompted to unveil their hypocrisy, in particular Badio. Yet the book does not end with this *brother*'s dramatic trial—Aunty Assiki's interruptions take over, differentiated from Badio's discourse by a mere dash. The narrative then invokes an eschatological figure, half-siren, half-snake, whose role is to proclaim the finality of all human enterprises. This apocalyptic discourse may be meant to absolve Badio by making the other characters share his guilt. Indeed, the last page reveals the depravity of his "little sister" and supposed victim.

In venturing in other locations for his fiction, M.'s subtle use of narrative voices seems to offer variations on a similar catharsis of a guilt complex. *Pelourinho*, the "pilgrimage" of an African writer in search of his "cousins" among the riff-raff of Salvadore de Bahia in Brazil, introduces a double psychoanalytic analysis. The two narrators, a young thug and an old blind lady reluctantly confess their misdeeds to Escritore (and the reader). Both villains turn out to be related and to have been the mutual cause of their misery. Yet again, the delinquent, named after his forefather, the slave who had refused to accept his master's name, Innocenzio, is indeed innocent, not guilty of the worse crime he has been confessing throughout the book: the murder of the African intent upon finding Africanity in Brazilian culture. With *Pelourinho*, M. is shifting the responsibility for evil from the political or historical trauma (dictatorship or slavery) to the realization of personal accountability.

Cinéma (1997; Cinema) has been described as a repeat of *Pelourinho* in its search for Africa's vanished grandeur. If so, the audacity required by the heirs of Samory Touré, who opposed French colonization in the 19th c., has to be updated. Shattered by the news that he is an adopted child, Binguel takes refuge in Mamou's cinema with his older friend and mentor, Bintê, nicknamed Oklahoma Kid. Eager to administer justice, Binguel looks for a culprit and elects his pedantic and negligent mentor. The inhabitants of Mamou, as much as the reader, are left to ponder Binguel's show of initiative. Now that Sékou Touré has been dead for fourteen years (Binguel's age in *Cinéma*), M. may be devising a new perception of his compatriots, in particular those who have survived within the borders of Guinea.

The story "Dieu-la-Garde" (1994; God Keep Her), which shows a Fulani village's cultural predicament between Islam, traditional magic and government industrialization of nomadic people, testifies to M.'s ability to write a typical African tale, rich in poetry, suspense, political conscientiousness and humor. However, M. chose to challenge his reader to rediscover such qualities in a shambles of narrative techniques that aim to give priority to the narrators' fragmented experience of life over the logical unfolding of events. The reader is thus called to draw the lessons to be learnt from the tribulations of M.'s fleeting yet resilient African characters.

BIBLIOGRAPHY: Malanda A.-S., "T. M.: Littérature et transhumance," *PA*, 144 (1987): 47-58; Gasster, S., "The Novels of T. M.: A World in Disintegration" *Callaloo*, 15 (1992): 1110-12; Garnier, X., "Poétique de la rumeur : l'exemple de T. M.," *Cahiers d'études africaines*, 35 (1995): 889-96; special M. section, *Notre Librairie*, 126 (1996): 80-116

—BLANDINE STEFANSON

MONGOLIAN LITERATURE

Mongolian literature begins with Chinggis Khan (Genghis Khan) in the early 1200s and the famous *Secret History of the Mongols*, an imperial chronicle of family genealogy and conflict. The later centuries of internal warfare were not conducive to writing or preserving literature. Not until the introduction of Lamaist Buddhism in the late 1500s did an upsurge occur. The next centuries saw a prodigious output of translations from Tibetan sacred scriptures, but only rarely histories or epics.

There was a widespread and popular oral literature, which encompassed: central Asian story cycles, some from Indian sources; didactic literature; stories, poems, legends; and particularly heroic epics, lengthy verse compositions about mighty heroes, their steeds, beautiful heavenly daughters, marvelous palaces, and the many-headed mangus, the monster of Mongolian folklore. In the last decades of the 19th c. collectors of folklore and epics began to transcribe many of these long works, saving them from extinction as old cultural ways yielded to incursions of the West.

At the fall of the Manchu (Ch'ing) dynasty under revolutionary pressures around 1910, the new government of the Chinese Republic was no longer able to exert effective control over its more distant provinces; Inner Mongolia, beyond the Great Wall, heavily settled with Chinese agriculturalists, remained part of the Republic, but Outer Mongolia cast off its ties to the Manchus and declared itself autonomous.

Outer Mongolian Literature

The proclaiming in 1924 of the Mongolian People's Republic, the first political satellite of the U.S.S.R., with its attendant socialization and collectivization of the economy, led to the creation of a new literature of SOCIALIST REALISM, in line with similar developments in the U.S.S.R. itself. The creation of an educational system, where none had existed before (except for training for the religious hierarchy), presented young Mongols with the possibility of becoming writers, artists, and intellectuals.

Dashdorjiin Natsagdorj (1906–1937), called the founder of modern Mongolian literature, is known for fiction, drama, poetry, and translations. His poem "Minii nutag" (1933; "My Native Land," 1967) is almost an anthem for Mongolia and is known to everyone. He wrote a libretto for an opera on native Mongolian themes, *Uchirtai gurvan tolgoi* (the three hills of sorrow), which was first produced in 1934 and is still performed regularly in Ulan Bator. Another important achievement is his short story "Tsagaan sar ba khar nulims" (1932; New Year's and bitter tears), which compares the life of a rich landlord's daughter with that of a poor servant girl.

Tsendiin Damdinsüren (b. 1908) is a noteworthy poet, translator, literary critic, and scholar. His first success was *Gologdson khüükhen* (1929; the rejected girl), the first Mongolian novel, a story of class struggle in the feudal countryside and the changes in a poor hired girl's life brought about by the revolution. It was considerably influenced by traditional folklore. His most famous poem is probably "Buural iiji minii" (1934; my grayhaired mother), a letter-dialogue whose theme is the tender affection between mother and son. He contributed to scholarship by editing an immensely important anthology, *Monggol uran jokiyal-un degeji jagun bilig* (1959; the hundred best selections of Mongolian literature), revealing hitherto unsuspected depth and richness in the literature of his country. He also published a study of the Geser epic, which appeared in Russian under the title *Istoricheskie korni Geseriady* (1957; historical bases of the Geser cycle).

Chadraavolyn Lodoidamba's (1917–1970) famous adventure novel *Altaid* (1949–51; in the Altai range) which, typically for Mongolian fiction, focuses more on exciting events than on character development, was followed by *Tungalag Tamir* (1962; the transparent Tamir River), the latter made into a successful motion picture. The dean of academics, Byamba Rinchen (1905–1977), wrote a three-volume historical novel, *Üüriin tuya* (1951–55; the ray of dawn), a detailed and historically accurate reconstruction of prerevolutionary times, treating battles, trials, social structure, shamanism, love and politics.

A number of other versatile authors have all written poetry, short stories, novels, and plays: Bökhiin Baast (b. 1921), Shanjmyatavyn

Gaadamba (b. 1924), Püreviin Khorloo (b. 1917), Erdenebatyn Oyuun (b. 1913), Dashzevegiin Sengee (1916–1959). Sengiin Erdene (b. 1929) became a spokesman for his generation with his lyrical novels, whose heroes have some psychological depth.

Inner Mongolian Literature

Although in the mid- and late-19th c. there were noted writers of Inner Mongolian origin and residence, their works formed part of a general Mongolian culture. Nonetheless, such writers as Khesigbatu (1849–1916), Güleranja (1820–1851), Gelegbalsan (1846–1923), Injannashi (1837–1892), and Ishidanzanwangjil (1854–1907) were important forerunners of a 20th-c. Inner Mongolian literature.

During the period when the young Mongolian People's Republic was launching Communism, the Inner Mongolian region of China was struggling with factions of Chinese nationalism (later to result in the split between Nationalists and Communists), a struggle followed by hegemony by Japan until the end of World War II. Among young Mongolian nationalists sent to Japan for education was the essayist and poet Saichungga (later known as Na. Sainchogtu, b. 1914).

After the Chinese Communist victory in 1949, writers in Inner Mongolia, still heavily Chinese in settlement (ten to one in some areas), were permitted as a minority to publish in their native script. One figure who kept old traditions alive was the bard Pajai (1902–?), an original poet as well as a singer of epic poems.

During the Cultural Revolution in the 1960s it was difficult to secure information about literary figures and publications, a situation that holds true even today. The continued use of traditional script in Inner Mongolia now acts as a barrier to literary exchange with the Mongolian People's Republic, where a modified Cyrillic alphabet is used. And the decades-long Sino-Soviet tensions have played their roles, too. Inner Mongolian literature today is largely a vehicle for socialist thought, dominated by the Chinese (Han) educational and administrative system.

BIBLIOGRAPHY: Poppe, N., *Mongolische Volksdichtung* (1955); Gerasimovich, L. K., *History of Modern Mongolian Literature (1921–1964)* (1970); Heissig, W., *Geschichte der mongolischen Literatur*, Vol. II (1972)

—JOHN R. KRUEGER

MONTAGUE, John

Irish poet and short-story writer, b. 28 Feb. 1929, Brooklyn, N.Y., U.S.A.

M. spent the first four years of his life in New York City before moving to County Tyrone, Northern Ireland, where he was raised by his paternal aunts. He received his B.A. in English from University College, Dublin (1949), his M.A. in English from Yale University (1952), and his M.F.A. from the University of Iowa (1955). In common with many Irish writers, M. has spent much of his adult life outside Ireland, though almost all of his work has remained Irish-centered. However, unlike the work of many of his contemporaries, M.'s work has been strongly influenced by the

poets of other countries, and by modern American and French poets in particular.

Although M. is usually associated with the group of northern Irish poets who emerged in the late 1960s—Seamus HEANEY, Derek MAHON, and Michael Longley (b. 1939)—his work is perhaps better understood if it is considered in relation to that of his own contemporaries—Thomas KINSELLA, Anthony Cronin (b. 1926), and James Liddy (b. 1934)—all of whom graduated from University College, Dublin, in the late 1950s and early 1960s, and became part of a stable of poets whose work was published by Liam Miller's Dolmen Press. All of these poets, influenced by Patrick KAVANAGH, believed that Irish poetry had to be rescued from the post-Celtic twilight slumber it had fallen into, and be reborn by combining Irish material with more experimental forms.

The dominant themes present in M.'s first four collections of poems, *Forms of Exile* (1958), *Poisoned Lands* (1961), *A Chosen Light* (1967), and *Tides* (1970), are Irish history, mythology, and place, and M.'s exploration of his more private self as revealed in his relationships with his family and lovers. In contrast with William Butler YEATS's, M.'s view of the Irish past is both anti-heroic and anti-Yeatsian. The Irish landscape may well be beautiful to look at, but it is also full of poisons—lovelessness, hatred, and loneliness. In one of his best early poems, "The Siege of Mullingar, 1963," published in *A Chosen Light*, M., to his delight, discovers that religious oppression, which is at the heart of many of Ireland's problems, is being obliterated by the forces of change that emerged in the 1960s and he declares, parodying Yeats's "September 1913" (1914), that "Puritan Ireland is dead and gone, a myth of O'Connor and O'Faolain."

The outbreak of the troubles in Northern Ireland in 1969 forced M. to reexamine his career as a poet and his relationship with the North. *The Rough Field* (1972) is a collage in which old and new poems are set side by side with quotations, epigraphs, and wood-cuts, all of which are used to describe the collapse of the North as a civilization. Although M. empathizes with the Catholic national-ists, he does not believe that a vibrant province will emerge from the battle for equality and reform. His poems of this period are remarkably successful as art, but also because they represent the most sustained attempt by a modern Irish writer to describe a region, and a people, in its moment of collapse. *The Dead Kingdom* (1984) is M.'s most personal and perhaps his greatest work to date. The book is structured around a journey from Cork, where M. now lives, to Fermanagh/South Tyrone, where he spent much of his youth, and is a meditation on personal and national history.

M.'s style has changed little throughout his career. From its beginning, he has basically written in two forms—poems with vigorous, longer, Yeatsian lines, and poems with short lines, often just two words, of the type that one will encounter in the poetry of William Carlos WILLIAMS. The former is a feature of southern Irish poetry, while the latter dominates Northern verse, and shows that M. can be easily accommodated within either tradition. Published in 1995, M.'s *Collected Poems* was greeted with acclaim in both Ireland and in the United States. A feature of this volume is an important new poetic sequence, *Border Sick Call*, an account of a journey M. made with his brother along the border between Northern Ireland and the Irish Republic.

FURTHER WORKS: *The Old People* (1960); *Death of a Chieftain* (1964); *All Legendary Obstacles* (1966); *Patriotic Suite* (1966); *Home Again* (1967); *Hymn to the Omagh Road* (1968); *Small Secrets* (1972); *The Cave of Night* (1974); *O'Riada's Farewell*

(1975); *A Slow Dance* (1975); *The Great Cloak* (1978); *Selected Poems* (1982); *Mount Eagle* (1988); *An Occasion of Sin* (1992)

BIBLIOGRAPHY: Kersnowski, F., *M.* (1975); Carpenter, A., "Double Vision in Anglo-Irish Literature," in Carpenter, A., ed., *Place, Personality, and the Irish Writer* (1977): 173–89; Deane, S., *Celtic Revivals* (1985): 146–86; Deane, S., *A Short History of Irish Literature* (1986): 227–47

—EAMONN WALL

MONTALE, Eugenio

Italian poet, b. 12 Oct. 1896, Genoa; d. 13 Sept. 1981, Milan

M. spent his childhood and early adult years in Genoa and the Cinque Terre, a rugged marine area on the Ligurian coast that figures prominently in his first collection of poetry, *Ossi di seppia* (1925; *Cuttlefish Bones*, 1990). In 1915 he began the serious study of singing. Although he had already dabbled a bit in verse by then, he did not commit himself entirely to the writing of poetry until he abandoned his operatic career in 1916. He was drafted during World War I, returning to his family home in 1919, where he remained for the next ten years. In 1929 he took on the directorship of the Vieusseux Research Library in Florence and held this post until 1938, when he was dismissed because of his refusal to join the Fascist Party. M. spent the years of World War II in Florence, during which time he made a living by translating French, English, American, and Spanish works, and by contributing to various literary journals. In 1948 the poet was hired by the Milanese newspaper *Corriere della sera* and remained active in journalism until 1967. His collected essays, short stories, and travel pieces are all the fruit of his years as a journalist. M. was given the honorary position of Senator for Life in 1967 and won the Nobel Prize for literature in 1975.

M.'s first published poetry, "Accordi" (1922; chords), was a series of seven poems that sought to imitate the sounds of musical instruments. This impressionistic phase was soon replaced, however, by the "countereloquence" of *Ossi di seppia*. Although this volume contains many poems that speak of the rocky landscape and ever-present Mediterranean of Liguria, it is clear that M.'s real interest is not in the representation of the physical world but rather in the search for some metaphysical and cognitive certainties in the midst of what he feels is an obdurately uncertain reality. This search is carried out in a pared-down, harsh poetic style that avoids the inherent lyricism of the Italian language. The title points, therefore, not only to its thematic center—the sea and the marine atmosphere surrounding it—but also to M.'s stylistic ideal of a honed, essential poetry.

M.'s second volume, *Le occasioni* (1939; *The Occasions*, 1987), also contains in its title an indication of its origins and goals, "occasions" being those rare, private moments of illumination that are best re-created in brief "flashes" of lyric. The central series of the collection—"Mottetti" (motets)—is made up of twenty very short love poems written to and about a beloved woman who is now absent from the poet's life, but who provides him with continued hope for success in his search for meaning. In this volume M. suppresses any discursive, descriptive elements in favor of an elliptic, allusive style, somewhat analogous to T. S. ELIOT's "objective correlative."

The third collection, *La bufera, e altro* (1956; *The Storm, and Other Poems*, 1978, 1985), develops fully the figure of the beloved, who is now called Clizia, and who is the bearer of transcendental salvation to the poet as well as to the war-torn world. This is a much less "hermetic" volume than the second, for M. here is deeply involved in the "storm" of the directly experienced historical events of the 1940s, even though he is still pursuing his own personal dream of fulfillment through love. The poet experiments with traditional poetic forms, most notably the sonnet, in a continuing dedication to the creation of a powerful style.

M.'s three late collections—*Satura* (1971; *Satura*, 1998), *Diario del '71 e del '72* (1973; diary of '71 and '72), and *Quaderno di quattro anni* (1977; *It Depends: A Poet's Notebook*, 1980)—represent a new direction, for they are written in a prosaic, satiric style, providing an ironic commentary on the first three volumes. They find much of their inspiration in the poet's daily life, in current events, and in retrospective self-evaluation. The "Xenia" series of *Satura*, poems written to his wife, who was called Mosca, are exquisite examples of the way in which language can be used to express great emotion in an understated, even humorous manner while losing none of its power to move and enthrall. The critical edition of M.'s poetry, *L'Opera in versi* (1980; Work in verse), which includes both early and late poems that were never before published, gives a complete overview of M.'s poetic production.

M.'s poetry, although superficially related to HERMETICISM, representative poets of which are Giuseppe UNGARETTI and Salvatore QUASIMODO, does not belong to any school. It is rather the product of a lifelong dedication to poetry understood as the solitary pursuit of knowledge and perfected form. M. is a master in pointing to the uncertainties, ambiguities, and moral complexities of our century. His difficult poetry does not offer any sure solutions to the existential and spiritual problems with which it deals, but rather finds its abiding power in its unforgettable formal beauty, its incisive, profoundly intelligent first-person voice, and its commitment to the importance of the individual, to what M. has called "daily decency," and to the essential seriousness of artistic creation.

FURTHER WORKS: *La casa dei doganieri, e altri versi* (1932); *Finisterre* (1943); *Quaderno di traduzioni* (1948); *Farfalla di Dinard* (1956; *Butterfly of Dinard*, 1971); *Auto da fé* (1966, rev. ed. 1995); *Fuori di casa* (1969); *La poesia non esiste* (1971); *Nel nostro tempo* (1973; *Poet in Our Time*, 1976); *Trentadue variazioni* (1973); *Sulla poesia* (1976); *Tutte le poesie* (1977; rev. ed. 1991). FURTHER WORKS IN ENGLISH: *Poems* (1959); *Poesie di M.* (1960, bilingual); *Poesie/Poems* (1964, bilingual); *Selected Poems* (1965, bilingual); *Provisional Conclusions* (1970); *New Poems* (1976); *The Second Life of Art: Selected Essays* (1982); *L'Opera in versi* (1980); *Quaderno genovese* (1983); *Trentadue variazioni* (1987); *Prose e racconti* (1995); *Diario postumo* (1996); *Otherwise: Last and First Poems of E. M.* (1984)

BIBLIOGRAPHY: Cambon, G., "E. M.'s 'Motets': The Occasions of Epiphany," *PMLA*, 82 (1967): 471–84; Pipa, A., *M. and Dante* (1968); Cary, J., *Three Modern Italian Poets: Saba, Ungaretti, M.* (1969; rev. ed., 1993); Singh, G., *E. M.: A Critical Study of His Poetry, Prose and Criticism* (1973); Almansi, G., and B. Merry, *E. M.: The Private Language of Poetry* (1977); Huffman, C., "Structuralist Criticism and the Interpretation of M.," *MLR*, 72 (1977): 322–34; West, R. J., *E. M.: Poet on the Edge* (1981); Cambon, G., *E. M.'s Poetry: A Dream in Reason's Presence* (1982); Huffman, C., *M. and the Occasions of Poetry* (1983);

Becker, J., *E. M.* (1986); Biasin, G. P., *M., Debussy, and Modernism* (1989)

—REBECCA J. WEST

MONTEIRO LOBATO

See Lobato, Monteiro

MONTES-HUIDOBRO, Matías

Cuban dramatist, short-story writer, novelist, poet, and essayist, b. 26 Apr. 1931, Sagua la Grande, Villa Clara

M.-H. received his secondary and postsecondary education in Havana, where he obtained a doctorate in education (1952). His first publications appeared in the journal *Nueva generación* in 1949. During the first three years of the Castro regime, M.-H. gained increasing notoriety. He wrote theater criticism for *Lunes de Revolución* and won literary prizes. However, on 27 November 1961, he left for the U.S. First, he taught high school Spanish in Meadville, Pennsylvania, from 1962 to 1964. Then, he moved to Honolulu, where he was a professor of Spanish at the University of Hawaii from 1964 to 1997. After his retirement, he moved to Miami, Florida.

M.-H. has written more than twenty plays, seven of them while living in Cuba. *Sobre las mismas rocas* (1991; Over the Same Rocks) won the Prometeo Award in 1951. Although the action of the play takes place in the U.S., the immediate reality of the location and of the characters, whose names are letters of the alphabet, can be questioned. In *Los acosados* (1960; The Harrassed) a man and a woman are beset by poverty, illness, and unemployment. Their character portrayal, as alienated figures, is a paradigm of many of M.-H.'s subsequent works. *La botija* (1959; The Jug) won the J. A. Ramos Prize and is an indictment of the corrupt Batista government and a vindication of the Cuban people. *El tiro por la culata* (1960; Shooting from the Hip) shows the exploitation of the poor by the rich, using original techniques that include abrupt character changes. *Gas en los poros* (1961; Once Upon a Future, 1996) is a Caribbean tragedy. A daughter takes the life of her mother who, in turn, had sided with the Batista regime and had become a tyrant at home. *La madre y la guillotina* (1973; *The Guillotine*, 1975), written in Cuba, shows the climate of fear and intimidation that prevailed among the middle class and other sectors of society. Characters self-destruct and suffer because of lack of mutual trust and ideological differences. *La sal de los muertos* (1971; The Salt of the Dead), also written in Cuba, is symbolic of the island nation. Family members await the death of the corrupt grandfather to inherit his fortune.

Since his arrival in the U.S., M.-H. has written more than a dozen plays. In *Ojos para no ver* (1974; Eyes for Not Seeing) Solavaya, the dictator, and María, his oppressed subject, are embodiments of the Cuban situation. In *La navaja de Olofé* (1982; Olofé's Razor) the action takes place in Santiago de Cuba and M.-H. re-creates the Changó myth in the characterization of a couple, mother and son, who engage in an incestuous relationship. *Exilio* (1988; Exile) takes place in New York. There, five characters—two couples and a single person—relive three historical moments: the exile caused by the Batista dictatorship, the Castro

regime, and the life of the New York of the 1980s. *Su cara mitad* (1992; Your Better Half, 1991) is a Cuban-American play, more so, perhaps than *Exilio*. Like in *Exilio*, there are two couples and a friend. After having abandoned Cuba, the main characters have a hard time at adaptation.

M.-H. has published many narrative works. Some of his short stories appeared in well known Cuban journals, such as *Bohemia*, *Carteles*, and *Revista Universidad de las Villas*. In the U.S. he published a collection of short stories, *La Anunciación y otros cuentos cubanos* (1967; The Annunciation and Other Cuban Stories). In it there are stories written in Cuba and in the U.S. From 1975 to 1996 M.-H.'s stories appeared in numerous anthologies. The characters in most of his narratives are portrayed with psychological depth; they face an uncertain future and must cope with frustration and failure.

Many of M.-H.'s stories show great insights in the depiction of feminine characters, religious syncretism, and the Cuban political situation. However, it is in the novel where M.-H. shows a greater mastery of narrative techniques. *Desterrados al fuego* (1975; Qwert and the Wedding Gown, 1992) won an honorary mention and was published by the Fondo de Cultura Económica in Mexico. It narrates the adventures of a Cuban couple upon their arrival in the U.S. The couple must face loneliness and alienation in their effort to assimilate to a new society. They have to confront a lack of linguistic ability and the affirmation (or lessening thereof) of their Cuban identity. They have to make some sense of the cultural chaos that surrounds them and find peace.

M.-H.'s first poem, "El campo del dueño" (1950; The Field of the Owner), was published in *Nueva generación*. But it was not until he came to Hawaii that he renewed his interest in the genre. Since 1965 M.-H. has published more than one hundred poems in newspapers, magazines, journals, and anthologies. The content of his creations is varied and includes life in exile, family relationships, linguistic performance, human love, the representation of otherness, and the excesses of Western technology. Most of his poetry is included in the volume *Nunca de mí te vas* (1997; You Never Will Leave from Me), the title taken from a verse of a poem dedicated to his deceased mother. M.-H. has also contributed hundreds of articles, notes, and reviews in the area of literary criticism. As an essayist, he is known for his monumental studies on Cuban and Puerto Rican theater: *Persona: vida y áscara en el teatro cubano* (1973; Persona: Life and Mask in Cuban Theater) and *Persona: vida y máscara en el teatro puertorriqueño* (1984; Persona: Life and Mask in Puerto Rican Theater).

M.-H. has promoted and preserved Cuban letters in the U.S. In his fiction, plays, and poems he has captured the essence of exile. Without falling into diatribe he has opted for creativity in language and experimentation in technique. His innovations are daring but rooted in the best traditions of Spanish, Cuban, and Latin American literatures. Through his writings he has amply asserted his talents and found his own persona in a culture other than his own.

FURTHER WORKS: *La vaca de los ojos largos* (1967); *Superficie y fondo de estilo* (1971); *Segar a los muertos* (1975); *Hablando en chino* (1977); *Obras en un acto* (1991); *Fetuses* (1991); *Funeral en Teruel* (1991); *La diosa del Iguazú* (1995)

BIBLIOGRAPHY: González-Cruz, L., "Selected Poems and Interview," *LALR*, 2, 4 (1974): 163-70; Colecchia, F., "M.-H.: His Theater," *LATR*, 13, 2 (1980): 77-80; Febles, J., "La desfiguración enajenante en *Ojos para no ver*," *Crítica Hispánica*, 4, 2 (1982):

127-36; Siemens, W., "Parallel Transformations in *Desterrados al fuego*," *Término*, 2, 6 (1984): 17-18; González-Pérez, A., "Magia, mito y literatura en *La navaja de Olofé*, *RIB*, 42, 2 (1992): 635-44; Rodríguez-Florido, J., "La otredad en la poesía de M.-H.," *Diáspora*, 3 (1994): 78-90; Febles, J., and A. González-Pérez, eds., *M.-H. Acercamiento a su obra literaria* (1997)

—JORGE J. RODRÍGUEZ-FLORIDO

MONTHERLANT, Henry de

French novelist, dramatist, essayist and poet, b. 21 April 1896, Paris; d. 21 Sept. 1972, Paris

M. lied about the date of his birth by one year (1896 instead of 1895) to make himself younger and by one day (21 April instead of 20 April) to have his birthday coincide with the legendary date of the founding of Rome. He also chose the date of his death by committing suicide on the day of the autumnal equinox. These choices are typical of his deliberate efforts to shape his biography and give a heroic dimension to an otherwise rather uneventful and protected life devoted mainly to reading and writing. They also indicate to what extent Rome and a particular idea about Roman stoicism took hold of his imagination. It had started very early, since at nine he wrote a "Roman" novel inspired by Henryk SIENKIEWICZ's *Quo Vadis?* In conformity to his wish, his ashes were scattered over the ruins of the Forum in Rome.

Since M.'s writings are often autobiographical and always marked by his egotistical personality, the books he wrote are inseparable from the various events and experiences of his life. Conversely, some of his books had a decisive influence on the course of his life. An only child, M. was born into a conservative, aristocratic family and educated in private Catholic schools. This experience, marked by a passionate friendship for a boy who was schoolmate, which caused his dismissal at seventeen from the École Saint-Croix, was to be the source of many fictional transmutations. It inspired his first book, *La relève du matin* (1920; the morning relief), a collection of lyrical essays published at his own expense but immediately greeted as a work of great promise. The same incident provided the subject matter of what many consider M.'s best play, *La ville dont le prince est un enfant* (1951; *The Fire That Consumes*, 1980). It finally inspired a long novel, *Les garçons* (1969; *The Boys*, 1974), published three years before M.'s death.

M. had been declared unfit for military service, and he kept away from the front during three years, completing his education by vast reading. In the last months of World War I he managed, through family connections, to be attached to an infantry regiment. He was wounded by a bursting shell on 6 June 1918. This very limited experience allowed him to use war as the background of his first novel, *Le songe* (1922; *The Dream*, 1962). The hero, Alban de Bricoule, a fictional double of the author, is the prototype of later M. heroes: he enjoys only the sensual love of his undemanding mistress, Douce; through his indifference he tortures Dominique Soubrier, a bright, beautiful, and athletic girl whom he finally rejects because she does love him in a sentimental way and has followed him to the front as a nurse. Alban's friendship for Stanislas Prinet, which has brought him to the front, means much more to him than his love for women. But he displays the same kind of sadism toward his comrade, whom he reprimands for being a weak, clumsy, sentimental bourgeois. When Prinet is killed, Alban regrets his cruelty and sinks into a depression. This apparently tough character, who takes pride in his strength and independence, is in fact totally dependent on other human beings yet afraid of making lasting commitments. At the end of the book, he is utterly alone and cut off from society.

This brilliant novel is also one of the first in the post-World War I period to present an EXISTENTIALIST hero, who, thrown into exceptional circumstances, rejects the conventional values of his education, discovers himself in the face of impending death during a bombardment, and makes decisive choices. M., who had played soccer and enjoyed cross-country running, celebrated athletes and praised the moral values bred by the practice of sport in *Les Olympiques* (1924; enlarged ed., 1938; the Olympic Games). *Les bestiaires* (1926; *The Bullfighters*, 1927; later tr., *The Matador*, 1957) is a novel based on M.'s early experience when he visited Spain before the war. Once again Alban de Bricoule is the protagonist, an adolescent who "merits" the love of a Spanish girl, Soledad, by overcoming his fear and killing a particularly mean bull; but he rejects her love after his victory. M., however, transcends this rather thin plot by giving the bullfight a dimension of mythical timelessness by associating it with the ancient Mithraic cult.

In 1925, after the death of his grandmother, with whom he had lived since his parents' death ten years earlier, M. sold all his belongings and left France. He traveled in Spain, Italy, and North Africa for the next ten years. In *Les voyageurs traqués* (1927; the hunted travelers) he described the "metaphysical crisis" he underwent. It consisted mainly of an encounter with the absurd leading to nihilism and despair. Alternating his moods, M. at times abandoned himself to a strong impulse toward asceticism, renunciation, detachment, and indifference and then practiced absolute self-indulgence, acting as an apologist of sensual pleasure.

The lesson he drew from this crisis and its resolution is summed up in an important volume of essays, *Service inutile* (1935; useless service), which made a strong impression on the young Albert CAMUS. While emphasizing the folly of all human ambitions and the vanity of all human undertakings in tones reminiscent of the Book of Ecclesiastes, M. preaches a philosophy of action.

He had managed to surmount his emotional crisis by writing two long novels. *La rose de sable* (1968; the desert rose)—part of which had earlier been published as *L'histoire d'amour de la rose de sable* (1954; *Desert Love*, 1957)—is a condemnation of French colonialism as M. had observed it in North Africa. He had finished it by 1932 but postponed its publication for fear of further hurting his country's tottering prestige. It was published in its entirety five years after the end of the Algerian war. The book is disappointing for the lack of inventiveness in its form and the timidity of its content. *Les célibataires* (1934; *Perish in Their Pride*, 1936; later tr., *The Bachelors*, 1960), on the other hand, in which M. created two unforgettable characters—pitiful aristocrats modeled on his own uncle and great-uncle—is a masterpiece of craftsmanship full of incisive humor, subtlety, and verve.

In 1934 M. met a twenty-three-year-old girl from a respectable middle-class family. During the next two years they were engaged, had a liaison, broke off, were several times on the point of getting married before they finally separated in 1936. This young woman was to be the model for the main female character, Solange Dandillot, and the central thread of a four-volume novel under the general title of *Les jeunes filles: Les jeunes filles* (1937; *The Young Girls*, 1938), *Pitié pour les femmes* (1936; *Pity for Women*,

1938)—these first two English translations published together in one volume—*Le démon du bien* (1937), and *Les lépreuses* (1939)—these last two published together in English as *Costals and the Hippogriff* (1940); the tetralogy was later translated as *The Girls* (1968). Costals, the hero of the novel, a libertine, shares many of M.'s traits and opinions. He is a creative writer, believes that sensuality should be kept separate from love, and does not think that the dignity and honesty of frank voluptuousness is compatible with the traditional marriage relationship, at least for men and women of outstanding gifts. The novel exalts the joy of artistic creation and attacks "shop-girl morality," sentimentality, the cult of suffering, and romantic love. It is often irritating and even deliberately infuriating, but it illustrates a point that has often been made since by feminist writers: women have created themselves in the image that men have of them. It is the virtuoso performance of a consummate craftsman who exploits all forms of narrative technique with great verve. The novel was an immediate best seller; its *succès de scandale* gave M. a widespread notoriety.

By 1939 M. had become a legendary figure, and his shrewdly provocative statements contributed to his image as an anticonformist and a maverick in French literature not unlike Rousseau in his time. He was contributing articles to both the communist and the conservative press, and he was praised by both the left and the right.

The publication of *Le solstice de juin* (1941; the June solstice) tarnished M.'s image and irretrievably damaged his reputation. The title refers to 24 June 1940, the date on which the French signed the armistice after being defeated by Nazi Germany. The essays entitled "Épuration" (purification) and "Les chenilles" (caterpillars) represent what is most objectionable in the book. In them M. gives vent to his contempt for Christianity and expresses satisfaction at the victory of the solar wheel (swastika) over the cross.

After the war M. was blacklisted by the National Committee of Writers (C.N.E.) and as a result did not play any role in the moral and ideological debates of postwar France. But he did pursue a glorious career as a playwright, a career that had started during the war with the immensely successful premiere of *La reine morte* (1942; *Queen after Death*, 1951) in December 1942 at the Comédie Française.

Whether his plays are set in the contemporary period—*Fils de personne* (1943; *No Man's Son*, 1951), *Demain il fera jour* (1949; *Tomorrow the Dawn*, 1951)—or classified as "costume" tragedies and set in 14th-c. Portugal—*La reine morte*; 15th-c. Italy—*Malatesta* (1946; *Malatesta*, 1951); or 15th-c. Spain—*Le maître de Santiago* (1947; *The Master of Santiago*, 1951)—M. always gives expression to his own many contradictory selves. He was never more personal than in his plays, and yet he preserved the appearance of objectivity, since he could not be totally identified with any single character.

The pessimism and nihilism earlier present in his essays and novels are exacerbated in the aging heroes of his plays. In *Fils de personne* and *Demain il fera jour* the theme of the conflict between a haughty and rigid father and his mediocre illegitimate son is apparently borrowed from the author's personal situation (he had an illegitimate son himself). M.'s plays are psychological and devoted to the exploration of proud, cruel, ruthless, lonely, self-deceiving, and world-weary protagonists. They are characterized by a great economy of means, tightly woven plots, and a sumptuous language verging sometimes on bombast. They have been criticized for being too static, too stylized, too remote from modern tastes. Many critics consider them in the tradition of the classic French theater of Racine and Corneille. Others emphasize the modernity of their themes and more particularly their preoccupation with the absurdity of life.

In spite of unpleasant personality traits, frankly repellent aspects of his ideology, and some obvious shortcomings in his works, M. holds an important place in contemporary French literature as a consummate craftsman both in fiction and drama. He is one of the great French prose writers, in the tradition of Rousseau, Chateaubriand, and Maurice Barrès (1862–1923).

FURTHER WORKS: *Chant funèbre pour les morts de Verdun* (1924); *Aux fontaines du désir* (1927); *La petite Infante de Castille* (1929); *L'exil* (1929); *Hispano-mauresque* (1929); *Pour une vierge noire* (1932); *Mors et vita* (1932); *Encore un instant de bonheur* (1934); *Pasiphaë* (1936); *L'équinoxe de septembre* (1938); *Fils des autres, un incompris* (1944); *Notes sur mon théâtre* (1950); *Celles qu'on prend dans ses bras* (1950); *Coups de soleil* (1950); *Le fichier parisien* (1952); *Textes sous une occupation* (1953); *Port-Royal* (1954); *Un voyageur solitaire est un diable* (1955); *Brocéliande* (1956); *Carnets années 1930 à 1944* (4 vols., 1947–1956); *Don Juan* (1958); *Romans et œuvres de fiction non théâtrale* (1959); *Le cardinal d'Espagne* (1960); *Le chaos et la nuit* (1963; *Chaos and Night*, 1964); *Discours de réception à l'Académie Française* (1963); *Essais* (1963); *La guerre civile* (1965; *Civil War*, 1967); *Va jouer avec cette poussière* (1966); *Un assassin est mon maître* (1971); *Théâtre* (1972); *La marée du soir 1968–71* (1972). FURTHER WORKS IN ENGLISH: *Selected Essays* (1961)

BIBLIOGRAPHY: Faure-Biguet, J. N., *Les enfances de M.* (1941); Sipriot, P., *M. par lui-même* (1953); Chiari, J., *The Contemporary French Theatre* (1958): 205–22; Perruchot, H., *M.* (1959); Norrish, P. J., "M.'s Conception of the Tragic Hero," *FS*, 14 (1960): 18–37; Beer, J. de, *M.; ou, L'homme encombré de Dieu* (1963); Cruickshank, J., *M.* (1964); Guicharnaud, J., *Modern French Theater from Giraudoux to Genet* (1967): 98–116; Batchelor, J., *Existence and Imagination: The Theatre of H. de M.* (1967); Johnson, R. B., *H. de M.* (1968); Grover, F. J., "The Inheritors of Maurice Barrès," *MLR*, 64 (1969): 529–45; Mason, H. T., "M.," in Fletcher, J., ed., *Forces in Modern French Drama*, (1972): 68–85; Robichez, J., *Le théâtre de M.* (1973); Sipriot, P., *Album M.* (1979)

—FREDERIC J. GROVER

It is noteworthy that *no one* of M.'s works paints for us a man-to-man conflict; coexistence is the great living drama, but it eludes him. His hero always stands alone before animals, children, women, landscapes; he is the prey of his own desires (like the queen in *Pasiphaë*) or of his own demands (like the master of Santiago in *The Master of Santiago*), but there is never anyone at his side. Alban in *The Dream* has a comrade: he disdains Prinet alive, and becomes excited about him only over his corpse. M.'s works, like his life, admit of only one consciousness....

M.'s lofty indifference to all causes and his preference for the pseudo-sublime are illustrated in *The Dead Queen* and *The Master of Santiago*. In these dramas, both significant in their pretentiousness, we see two imperial males who sacrifice to their empty pride women guilty of nothing more than being human: for punishment one loses her life, the other her soul. Once again, if we ask in the name of what, the author haughtily answers: in the name of nothing. He did not want the King to have too clear motives of state for killing Inès, for then this murder would be only a commonplace political crime. [1949]

> Simone de Beauvoir, *The Second Sex* (1953),
> pp. 210, 213

If one day, we rediscover the commonplace truth that there is such a thing as a literary art, just as there is a pictorial or a musical art, and if writers—they alone are guilty in this—finally stop treating "literature" with contempt (it sometimes returns the favor), then M.'s works will provide proof that the rare fusion of irony and majestic writing was also part of the art of our age.

> André Malraux, in a letter dated October 19, 1952,
> to French Radio and Television (R.T.F.) for a
> radio program on M.: "Fifteen Evenings with M."

M. is for me the very model of a certain clan of French writers (Chateaubriand, Barrès), and I flatter myself that I am one of them. A common trait unites the members of this group, which includes such fraternal enemies as Aragon and Malraux. Since I consider myself a part of the family, I hope I may be forgiven for saying that this element of kinship is based on a kind of imposture. The word is not intended here in its sinister sense, as in the title of Molière's *Tartuffe* (*Tartuffe; or, The Impostor*). Don Juan too is an impostor and that is the kind of deceit I have in mind, the deceit of style. Writers of that breed all strive for effect and cocky posturing, for music and the advantageous pose.

> François Mauriac, "Bloc-notes," *Figaro*, 8 March
> 1960, p. 16

M. emphasizes the fact that "the tragedies of the Ancients were tragedies not only among members of the same family but between the different selves making up any single individual." This latter form of tragic characterisation plays a dominant part in most of M.'s plays. Ferrante, in *The Dead Queen*, is tempted to do good yet finally does evil. He does so partly in order to "cut the fearful knot of contradictions" within himself so that he can learn at last who he really is. La Soeur Angélique, in *Port-Royal*, suffers from self-division in an acute form as she battles with the fear of losing her faith. . . . *Le Cardinal d'Espagne* follows the same pattern. Cardinal Cisneros, the principal character, has a nature split into two warring parts. One element in him withdraws into his religion in reaction to the vanity of human life; another enjoys power, particularly the power of life and death over his fellow-men.

> John Cruickshank, *M.* (1964), p. 112

Style is a quality that seldom ranks very high in the contemporary critic's scale of values: but it would be impossible to discuss M. the novelist without considering his achievement as a modern master of the French language. His prose style is uncommonly rich and various—tart, idiomatic, incisive, when he attacks some typical or controversial issue; measured, euphonious, poetic, when he deals with wider and less transitory themes. . . . Like every genuine style, that of M. is no mere adventitious decoration, but arises from his subject as he enlarges and develops it. M.'s efforts as a controversialist should never blind us to the fact that he is primarily an accomplished artist. *The Girls* may be read as a deliberately controversial book—an attack on "the cult of woman," on the place that Woman has come to occupy in the modern European world; and as such it may have helped to break down many masculine taboos and phobias. But it is also an imaginative work of art, which, having absorbed and digested its subject matter, presents us with something far more valuable and lasting. . . . So long as literature continues to play a part in our lives, M.'s story of *Les jeunes filles* is a book that will retain its youthful freshness.

> Peter Quennell, Introduction to *The Girls* (1968),
> p. 15

"I am a poet," says M., "and only a poet." Why do critics with unusual stubbornness—whether it is to praise or damn him—continue to see in M. first of all a thinker? . . . They talk too much about ethics concerning him and never enough about aesthetics, which in fact informs everything in his work. His work is essentially dramatic, based on conflict and contrast. The contrast is everywhere: in words, images and themes. . . . It is this law of contrast that brings M. to unite voluptuousness and chastity, life and death, desire and renunciation. The famous *alternance* [i.e., alternation] is a principle of art before it became a principle of life. This aesthetic principle of conflict explains why M. came quite naturally to the theater. Actually, he had started his writing career at eighteen with a play, *L'exil*. The same aesthetic law governs a novel like *Les jeunes filles*, in which the male and female principles are set in conflict by means of a comic method that is but another form of dramatic art. . . . This writer, in whom everyone tries to find the man and the thinker, needs more than any other to be exposed to "formalist" types of criticism. He has nothing to lose from this critical approach, which on the contrary will establish his greatness and endurance.

> Jacqueline Piatier, "M. et la contradiction," *Le
> monde*, 19 April 1969, 17

The despair occasioned by the recognition of the absurdity of human existence has led writers like Camus and Sartre to propound a new humanism to palliate the anguish of modern man. M.'s response, however, is a purely personal code of ethics. Recognizing that there is no reward for man either on this earth or in another life, M. has set up as a *raison d'être* the superior qualities which characterize his hero. His search for an answer to the problem facing the twentieth century of how to live, and for what reasons to live, when all traditional philosophical systems have proved inadequate, has led M. to his concept of the hero. This lucid individual, having rejected all hope of immortal life or of recompense in this life, having realized the vanity of all human things, must still go forward, must accomplish, despite the absurdity of man's destiny. Thus, he attempts to make his experiences as intense and as varied as possible. . . . Responsible only to himself, he goes forward to meet his destiny, heedless of others. Whatever wrongs he may commit are justified if they serve him in his quest for self-realization. Recognizing that human existence is essentially tragic, the hero cannot content himself with his despair, but must act in order to find deliverance.

> Lucille Becker, *H. de M.: A Critical Biography*
> (1970), pp. 114–15

We may discern dramatically important links between parent and child in all but four of M.'s plays and in all the important ones. . . . If Georges [in *Fils de personne*], Ferrante [in *La reine morte*], and Alvaro [in *Le maître de Santiago*] express in varying degree the anguished fear of betrayal by their progeny, it is more than the simple disappointment of a father. These children strike at something fundamental in the parent himself. . . . Inès [in *La reine morte*] represents for Ferrante a weakness to which he is in danger of consenting, and Georges abandons Gillou in *Fils de personne* because the latter does not give back to him a satisfactory image of himself. Just as Ferrante seeks to discover his own identity and in so doing strikes at his children, so are Georges and Alvaro seeking their true self-image in those they have brought into the world. Alvaro's love of God, says M., is "love for the idea he has of himself"; so is his love of Mariana. . . . In acting thus, these fathers are acting against themselves. . . . Thereby they relate to another great theme in M.—the theme of suicide.

> H. T. Mason, "M.," in John Fletcher, ed., *Forces in Modern French Drama* (1972), pp. 82–84

MOORE, Brian

Irish-Canadian novelist, b. 25 Aug. 1921, Belfast, Northern Ireland

Raised as a Catholic in Belfast, M. emigrated to Canada in 1948. Although now a Canadian citizen, he has lived in he U.S. since 1959. Thus, he has had access to three cultures, and his novels accordingly explore Irish, Canadian, and American life. M.'s reputation was established with his first novel, *The Lonely Passion of Judith Hearne* (1955), a remorselessly realistic study of the

disintegration of a Belfast spinster. In the novels that have followed it, M. has by and large continued his commitment to the techniques of realism.

M.'s first two novels—the second was *The Feast of Lupercal* (1957; repub. as *A Moment of Love*, 1960)—presented the entrapment of his characters within the religious and familial structures of Belfast Catholic life. Later novels reveal a complex reaction to this concern with entrapment. Much of M.'s work deals with the guilt feelings of the person who liberates himself from religious values and stable cultural traditions. These guilt-ridden characters may be Irish-born writers living in the U.S., as in *An Answer from Limbo* (1962) and *Fergus* (1970); or they may be unfaithful wives who have renounced their Catholicism, as in *I Am Mary Dunne* (1968) and *The Doctor's Wife* (1976). These novels present central characters free from belief and from the demands of a life conducted according to traditional values, but isolated in a despair that is sometimes suicidal. In the short novel *Catholics* (1972) M. created a brilliant variation on this theme by presenting the orderly and beautiful life of Irish monks in a remote island monastery presided over by an abbot who has lost his faith and who lives daily in despair at its loss. A longing for the discarded Latin liturgy of Catholicism suffuses the book, and the abbot, who does not rebel against anything, is in his suffering a kind of saint.

M.'s work, in its diversity of setting and its preoccupation with substantial themes, is a serious contribution to the literature of the latter half of the 20th c. Considered both an Irish and a Canadian novelist, he has created a fictional world that expresses the painful condition of the culturally displaced and the religiously alienated. His novels, no matter the setting, are always realized with greatest particularity. Yet beyond the satisfying realistic surfaces of his novels lie expressions of the powerful and insoluble conflicts between freedom and security, personal fulfillment and love, religious belief and suicidal despair.

FURTHER WORKS: *The Luck of Ginger Coffey* (1960); *The Emperor of Ice-Cream* (1965); *The Revolution Script* (1971); *The Great Victorian Collection* (1975); *The Mangan Inheritance* (1979); *The Temptation of Eileen Hughes* (1981)

BIBLIOGRAPHY: Dahlie, H., *B. M.* (1969); Flood, J., *B. M.* (1974); McSweeney, K., "B. M.: Past and Present," *CritQ*, 18 (1976): 53–66; Scanlan, J., "The Artist-in-Exile: B. M.'s North American Novels," *Éire*, 12 (1977): 14–33; Shepherd, A., "Place and Meaning in B. M.'s *Catholics*," *Éire*, 15 (1980): 134–40

—JEANNE A. FLOOD

MOORE, George

Anglo-Irish poet, novelist, dramatist, and essayist, b. 24 Feb. 1852, Moore Hall, County Mayo, Ireland; d. 20 Jan. 1933, London

After a haphazard education, with considerable freedom to do as he pleased, and equipped with a lively imagination and a sound knowledge of the racing stables, M. at eighteen was left with an adequate income and no professional training. In 1873, after spending a few years in London, he went to Paris to study painting, soon finding himself on the periphery of the group of French impressionists. Most of his fiction reflects his interest in and knowledge of painting.

The practical result of these studies and friendships was *Modern Painting* (1893), mainly essays he had contributed to *The Speaker*. Without talent for painting and having been introduced between 1877 and 1880 to some of the French writers associated with the naturalist movement in fiction and the SYMBOLIST movement in poetry, M. turned to writing. *Flowers of Passion* (1878) and *Pagan Poems* (1881), in the main poor imitations of Baudelaire, showed M. he had no great talent in this genre. He wrote *A Modern Lover* (1883; rev. as *Lewis Seymour and Some Women*, 1917) in imitation of Zola, and there followed such volumes as *A Mummer's Wife* (1885), *A Drama in Muslin* (1886), and *Spring Days* (1888), each in various ways a modification of Zola's manner.

Even in these early years of his career M. was dissatisfied with what he considered the surface psychological portraiture in the French novel and in the work of, among other English writers, Fielding. He was already searching for a way of expressing states of mind and emotions more subtly and penetratingly. In *Esther Waters* (1894), his greatest success, his use of the impressionistic painter's techniques and his counterpointing of tones showed a marked shift away from the naturalistic manner. Some of his early short stories, as in *Celibates* (1895), are in a sense exercises in subtle psychological portraiture.

M.'s lifelong interest in the short story is demonstrated in *"Minor Keys" G. M.'s Uncollected Short Stories* (1982). This volume and the five volumes of short stories published in his lifetime make a convincing case for him as a major writer in this genre.

In midcareer, with *Evelyn Innes* (1898) and *Sister Teresa* (1901), M. carried the search for a new technique still further by adapting to fiction Wagner's innovations in music. His subject often became the private inner life in conflict with the public life. His techniques increasingly borrowed from painting and music. The effects of these experiments on his fiction are next seen in the short-story collection *The Untilled Field* (1903) and the novel *The Lake* (1905), written during the ten-year period of his return to Ireland. This period is recorded in his novelistic autobiography, *Hail and Farewell* (3 vols., 1911–14). As this work reveals, M. clashed with other leaders of the Irish literary renaissance, and he soon realized that this movement could no longer serve his interests and talents.

From about 1915 to 1933 M. published most of his work in expensive limited editions. His later work, that of the "melodic line," is thus little known. The complex, supple style is perhaps best illustrated by his brilliant novel *The Brook Kerith* (1916) and his prose epic *Héloïse and Abélard* (1921).

Although M.'s career after about 1915 has received little attention, it was, despite his illness and exhaustion, very active and fruitful. By refusing to deal significantly with the problem of modern times, as he had done during the earlier phases of his career, he lost many readers. Much of the later work was misjudged as being insufficiently original but relying too heavily on translations of classical and biblical stories, biographies, and histories. But M.'s "re-creations" did have claim to originality in the same sense as the classical dramatists' individual treatments of well-known myths. Thus, *The Brook Kerith* is a re-creation of biblical history, *Héloïse and Abélard* of biography, *The Pastoral Loves of Daphnis and Chloe* (1924) of myth, *Ulick and Soracha* (1926) of Irish history, and *Aphrodite in Aulis* (1930) of the Greece of the 5th c. B.C.

M. also played an important role in the development of the modern drama. Early in his career he became very knowledgeable in practical aspects of the theater. He contributed significantly to the Independent Theatre, which performed Ibsen, and later was instrumental in helping to launch the Irish Literary Theatre; and he wrote a number of very competent plays.

M. will probably be longest remembered for his novels, his essays, his imaginative autobiographical writings, and, above all, for being one of the most influential molders of taste of the last two decades of the 19th c. and forerunner of many modern techniques in the novel and short story.

FURTHER WORKS: *Martin Luther* (1879, with Bernard Lopez); *Literature at Nurse; or, Circulating Morals* (1885); *Confessions of a Young Man* (1886); *A Mere Accident* (1887); *Parnell and His Island* (1887); *Mike Fletcher* (1889); *Impressions and Opinions* (1891); *Vain Fortune* (1892); *The Strike at Arlingford* (1893); *The Bending of the Bough* (1900); *Diarmuid and Grania* (1901, with W.B. Yeats); *Memoirs of My Dead Life* (1906); *The Apostle* (1911; final version, *The Passing of the Essenes*, 1930); *Esther Waters* (play, 1913); *A Story-Teller's Holiday* (1918); *Avowals* (1919); *The Coming of Gabrielle* (1920); *In Single Strictness* (1922; rev. as *Celibate Lives*, 1927); *Conversations in Ebury Street* (1924); *Peronnick the Fool* (1924); *The Making of an Immortal* (1927); *Letters to Edouard Dujardin, 1886–1922* (1929); *A Communication to My Friends* (1933); *Letters to John Eglinton* (1942); *Letters to Lady Cunard* (1957); *G. M. in Transition: Letters to T. Fisher Unwin and Lena Milman, 1894–1910* (1968); *G. M. on Parnassus: Letters (1900–1933) to Secretaries, Publishers, Printers, Agents, Literati, Friends and Acquaintances* (1982)

BIBLIOGRAPHY: Morgan, C., *Epitaph for G. M.* (1935); Hone, J. M., *The Life of G. M.* (1936); Nejdefors-Frisk, S., *G. M.'s Naturalistic Prose* (1952); Brown, M., *G. M.: A Reconsideration* (1955); Cunard, N., *G. M.* (1956); Collet, G.-P., *G. M. et la France* (1957); Gilcher, E., *A Bibliography of G. M.* (1970); Dunleavy, J. E., *G. M.: The Artist's Vision, the Storyteller's Art* (1973); Gerber, H. E., "G. M.," in Finneran, R. J., ed., *Anglo-Irish Literature: A Review of Research* (1976): 138–66; Farrow, A., *G. M.* (1978)

—HELMUT E. GERBER

MOORE, Marianne

American poet, translator, and essayist, b. 15 Nov. 1887, Kirkwood, Mo.; d. 5 Feb. 1972, New York, N.Y.

After graduating from Bryn Mawr in 1909, and from the Carlisle (Pennsylvania) Commercial College in 1910, M. taught commercial subjects at the United States Indian School in Carlisle. She began publishing poems in periodicals in 1915. She moved to New Jersey in 1916, to Manhattan in 1918, to Brooklyn in 1929, and back to Manhattan in 1966. She worked in a private school and in the New York Public Library until 1925, when she was appointed acting editor of *The Dial*, becoming editor the following year, a position she held until 1929. Thereafter she lived as a free-lance poet, translator, reviewer, and critic, receiving many recognitions of excellence, culminating in her selection in 1955 for membership in the American Academy of Arts and Letters.

M.'s first volume, entitled simply *Poems* (1921), was published by friends, without M.'s prior knowledge. Although she chose to omit almost half of the 1921 poems from her *Complete Poems* (1967), her most characteristic qualities were visible from the start—astringently judgmental wit, fastidious intellectual detachment, cryptic or eccentric associational logic, and a prosody that was syllabic rather than metrical, rhyming lightly when it rhymed at all, and rigorously regular in its stanzaic designs, although a persistent habit of revising earlier poems, sometimes radically, subsequently obscured that regularity. While not prosaic, the voice was that of elegantly lucid prose, given to quoting passages from other sources, not for purposes of allusion but because M. found the phrasing attractive or appropriate for her own purposes.

Early reviewers were not sure what to make of M., although Ezra POUND, T. S. ELIOT, and William Carlos WILLIAMS were sympathetic. But *Observations* (1924) received the Dial Award, and *Selected Poems* (1935), by appearing in London and New York editions, indicated that she was receiving international recognition, a fact confirmed by the appearance of French, Spanish, German, and Italian translations of her poems. And *Collected Poems* (1951) received a National Book Award, a Pulitzer Prize, and the Bollingen Prize.

By the time of the 1951 *Collected Poems*, three things of importance for M. had happened—the outbreak of war in 1939, an eight-year commitment to translating *The Fables of La Fontaine* (1954), and her mother's death in 1947, when M. herself was sixty. Mary Warner Moore appears to have been M.'s closest friend (M. never married); M. kept a notebook of her mother's sayings, and regarded her as almost a collaborator. Her involvement with La Fontaine may have been a means of keeping herself alive as a writer through a time of deep personal loss; she apparently wrote no poems of her own during these years, and her later poems satisfied her less than her earlier ones.

World War II seems to have forced, or at least hastened, M. to a personal reassessment which was fundamentally religious in nature (she was a lifelong member of the Presbyterian Church) and which becomes especially visible in her books of the 1940s—*What Are Years?* (1941) and *Nevertheless* (1944)—although some of the poems registering that reassessment were written before the war's actual outbreak. In "Virginia Britannia" (1935) and "The Pangolin" (1936), which later appeared in *What Are Years?*, the frequently caustic and intolerant brilliance of her treatment of the human in her earlier work has yielded almost entirely to a deeper, more complex affirmation of understanding, acceptance, and affection. "Virginia Britannia" is a poem about colonization in all its ruthlessness and arrogance, and also in its courage and creativeness, inextricably interlocked in the burden of history. "The Pangolin" juxtaposes anteaters—graceful, humble, self-effacing, admirably adapted to survive without aggressiveness—against men, their absurd, aggressive, creative, humorous, vulnerable, engaging, and imperfectly admirable cousins—juxtaposes, and accepts the less graceful of the two. "Virginia Britannia" is elegiac. "The Pangolin" ruefully comic, but both are deeply human in a way that had not been much evident in M.'s earlier work.

"What Are Years?" (1940), which opens its volume, and "In Distrust of Merits" (1943), which closes *Nevertheless*, are clearly wartime poems, and in them affirmation deepens to an impassioned and tragic identification with the world of pain and responsibility.

Marianne Moore

"What Are Years?" has to do with the reality and the mystery of human courage, affirming that freedom of the spirit exists only in the context of a confining necessity. But "In Distrust of Merits" finds even such moral formulations inadequate in the face of a devastating sense of personal involvement in and sin-ridden responsibility for the intolerable facts of war. In a 1961 *Paris Review* interview with Donald Hall, M. said it was hardly a poem at all, and in a way she was right; the intolerable remains intolerable, not reduced or reducible to aesthetic form. But in that respect, "In Distrust of Merits" is comparable with Eliot's "The Waste Land," Picasso's "Guernica," and the monument at Treblinka. It seems safe to suppose, on the strength of these poems of the 1930s and 1940s, that M.'s permanence is assured among the poets of this century, and perhaps of any century.

FURTHER WORKS: *Marriage* (1923); *The Pangolin and Other Verse* (1936); *Rock Crystal* (1945); *Predilections* (1955); *Selected Fables of La Fontaine* (1955); *Like a Bulwark* (1956); *O to Be a Dragon* (1959); *A M. M. Reader* (1961); *The Absentee* (1962); *Puss in Boots, The Sleeping Beauty & Cinderella* (1963); *The Arctic Ox* (1964); *Tell Me, Tell Me: Granite, Steel and Other Topics* (1966); *Selected Poems* (1969); *The Complete Poems*, rev. ed. (1981)

BIBLIOGRAPHY: Engel, B. F., *M. M.* (1964); Tambimuttu, M. J., ed., *Festschrift for M. M.'s Seventy-Seventh Birthday* (1964); Nitchie, G. W., *M. M.: An Introduction to the Poetry* (1969); Abbott, C. S., *M. M.: A Reference Guide* (1978); Stapleton, L.,

M. M.: The Poet's Advance (1978); Borroff, M., *Language and the Poet: Verbal Artistry in Frost, Stevens, and M.* (1979): 80–135; Costello, B., *M. M.: Imaginary Possessions* (1981)

—GEORGE W. NITCHIE

MORAND, Paul

French novelist, short-story writer, poet, and essayist, b. 13 March 1888, Paris; d. 24 July 1976, Paris

M. was born into a bourgeois family with artistic, political, and literary connections and with whom he early on had the opportunity to begin the extensive travels that were to dominate his life and his works. His studies at the Faculty of Law of the University of Paris and the School of Political Sciences, interrupted by a year at Oxford, his travels, and his military service, were completed just before World War I, and he became a diplomat. Named to posts around the world, he continued in this profession until the end of World War II, when the provisional government removed him because of his connection with the Vichy government; he did not return to diplomacy until 1953. He retired in 1955. While one can say that his autobiography is in much of what he wrote in the way of travel notes, chronicles, and essays, one can consult in particular *Mes débuts* (1934; my beginnings), in which he describes his family background and early years; *Papiers d'identité* (1931; identity papers), a miscellany of reflections and impressions; *Le visiteur du soir* (1949; evening visitor), reminiscences of Marcel PROUST, in which the sentimental side of M. is revealed; and *Venises* (1971; Venices), which contains memories of his whole life.

M. began his literary career with two volumes of poetry, *Lampes à arc* (1920; arc lamps) and *Feuilles de température* (1920; temperature charts), both striking in their modernism. These were followed by three books of short stories, *Tendres stocks* (1921; *Green Shoots*, 1923), and *Ouvert la nuit* (1922; *Open All Night*, 1923), and *Fermé la nuit* (1923; *Closed All Night*, 1924), which solidified his reputation as an extremely fastidious portrayer of telling details and a stylist with some of the preciosity one associates with his friend Jean GIRAUDOUX.

M.'s style is more subdued in his first novel, *Lewis et Irène* (1924; *Lewis and Irene*, 1925), which has a feminist theme; in *L'Europe galante* (1926; *Europe at Love*, 1927), satirical sketches of eroticism in postwar Europe; in *Rien que la terre* (1926; *Nothing but the Earth*, 1927); and in *Champions du monde* (1930; *World Champions*, 1931)—all of which show his fine skills of observation. The cosmopolitan aspect of his work is reflected in *Magie noire* (1928; *Black Magic*, 1929), a description of blacks in Africa and America; his highly successful place-sketches like *New York* (1930; *New York*, 1930) and *Londres* (1933; *A Frenchman's London*, 1934); or his numerous essays on travel, full of picturesque images, rapid descriptions, and silhouettelike characters.

One critic sees his *Bouddha vivant* (1927; *The Living Buddha*, 1928), a novel contrasting Europe and Asia, as a pivotal work, and it is true that its themes are more serious than in his earlier work, as are the subjects and techniques of his later novels and novellas, such as *Hécate et ses chiens* (1954; Hecate and her dogs) and *La folle amoureuse* (1956; the mad woman in love), where one finds more thoughtful, more psychologically probing portrayals. These, his historical studies, and his *Venises* are considered by many to be his best.

Although dismissed by certain detractors as a superficial cosmopolitan, too rapid, too aloof, or too ironic to be taken very seriously, M. was nevertheless a moralist in the French sense of the word—a close observer of a commentator on his times. And there is no denying the fact that both his observations and his manner have had an influence on a younger generation of French writers.

FURTHER WORKS: *Poèmes, 1914–1924* (1924); *La fleur double* (1924); *Rain, Steam, Speed* (1926); *Le voyage* (1927); *L'innocente à Paris; ou, La jolie fille de Perth* (1927); *U.S.A.* (1927); *Paris-Tombouctou* (1928); *Hiver caraïbe* (1929); *À la Frégate* (1930); *Conseils pour voyager sans argent* (1930); *1900* (1931; *1900 A.D.*, 1931); *Air indien* (1932; *Indian Air: Impressions of Travel in South America*, 1933); *Flèche d'Orient* (1932; *Orient Air Express*, 1932); *L'art de mourir, suivi de Le suicide en littérature* (1932); *Paris de nuit* (1933); *Paris to the Life: A Sketchbook*, 1933); *Rococo* (1933); *Paysages méditerranéens* (1933); *France la doulce* (1934; *The Epic-Makers*, 1935); *La femme agenouillée* (1934); *Rond-point des Champs-Elysées* (1934); *Bucarest* (1935); *La route des Indes* (1936; *The Road to India*, 1937); *Les extravagants* (1936); *Apprendre à se reposer* (1937); *Le réveille-matin* (1937); *Méditerranée, mer des surprises* (1938); *L'heure qu'il est* (1938); *Isabeau de Bavière, femme de Charles VI* (1938); *Réflexes et réflexions* (1939); *Chroniques de l'homme maigre, suivi de Propos d'hier* (1941); *L'homme pressé* (1941); *Feu monsieur le duc, avec Bug O'Shea* (1942); *Vie de Guy de Maupassant* (1942); *Petit théâtre* (1942); *Propos de 52 semaines* (1942); *Excursions immobiles* (1944); *Adieu à Giraudoux* (1944); *Montociel, rajah aux Grandes Indes* (1947; *Montociel, Rajah of Greater India*, 1962); *Journal d'un attaché d'ambassade, 1916–17* (1948); *Giraudoux, souvenirs de notre jeunesse* (1948); *L'Europe russe annoncée par Dostoïevsky* (1948); *Le flagellant de Séville* (1951; *The Flagellant of Seville*, 1953); *L'eau sous les ponts* (1954); *Fin de siècle* (1957); *Le prisonnier de Cintra* (1958); *Le lion écarlate, précédé de La fin de Byzance* (1959); *Bains de mer, bains der rêve* (1960); *Fouquet; ou, Le soleil offusqué* (1961); *Le nouveau Londres* (1962); *Majorque* (1963); *La dame blanche des Habsbourg* (1963); *Tais-toi* (1965); *Mon plaisir en littérature* (1967); *Ci-gît Sophie Dorothée de Celle* (1968); *Mon plaisir en histoire* (1969); *Les écarts amoureux* (1974); *L'allure de Chanel* (1976); *Lettres à des amis et à quelques autres* (1978). FURTHER WORKS IN ENGLISH: *East India and Company* (1927)

BIBLIOGRAPHY: Lemaître, G., *Four French Novelists* (1938): 301–92; Guitard-Auviste, G., *P. M.* (1956); Thiébaut, M., "P. M., l'amour et la vitesse," *Entre les lignes* (1962): 107–29; Sarkany, S., *P. M. et le cosmopolitisme littéraire* (1968); Schneider, M., *M.* (1971)

—RUTH B. YORK

MORANTE, Elsa

Italian novelist and poet, b. 18 Aug. 1918, Rome; d. 25 Nov. 1985, Rome

Daughter of a Sicilian father and an Emilian mother, M. left home at the age of eighteen. In 1941 she married Alberto MORAVIA

—they were later divorced. In 1943, during the German occupation, she lived the desperate life of a refugee in the countryside near Cassino, where she experienced that rural world of the south that plays an important part in her fiction. M. has lived most of her life in Rome, although she has traveled all over the world.

With her first two novels, *Menzogna e sortilegio* (1948; *House of Liars*, 1951) and *L'isola di Arturo* (1957; *Arturo's Island*, 1959), M. defined her literary universe: a world filtered through memory, a private, magical world whose jealously guarded dreams and obsessions cultivated in the secret silence of the heart are ever threatened by the encroachment of external reality. In *Menzogna e sortilegio* this conflict is depicted through the vicissitudes of three generations of a family—their obsessive dreams, brooding silences, narcissistic theatricality, and feudal stubbornness. *L'isola di Arturo* re-creates the painful maturation of a child caught between the attachment to his luminous fantasies, to the world of his private island, and an increasing awareness that this beauty is destined to dissolve. The narrator is Arturo himself, who, looking back at his life with a more adult consciousness, still oscillates between the tempting fantasies of his childhood and his new awareness.

To say that M. in these two novels develops a narrative style dominated by the magic, mythical dimension of the imagination does not do full justice to her literary strategies. She proceeds in her writing through a slow accumulation of details that balances the fantastic with a wide-ranging realism. M. herself rejects an interpretation of her work that stresses only the mythical, fantastic elements.

The theme of the conflict between a private, fantastic world and an external historical reality continues to dominate her later work. In *Il mondo salvato dai ragazzini* (1968; the world saved by the children), a collection of poems, popular songs, and a one-act play, it acquires more precise connotations than earlier: those who do not accept the logic of power and domination and whose innocent dreams can find no place within social norms, those whose innocence is the source of anarchic rebellion, inevitably come into conflict with the violent institutions and ideologies of society.

In *La storia* (1974; *History: A Novel*, 1977) the conflict between "outsiders" and institutions, society, and history is analyzed in a blend of the fantastic, the fairy tale, and the devices of the popular historical novel. Through the story of a timid schoolteacher, Ida Ramundo, her two sons, and many other defenseless characters, set during World War II and the immediate postwar period, M. condemns the arrogant falsifications of official history, which would like to present itself as a glorious process, but which in reality has been a long series of violent acts, persecutions, and injustices.

FURTHER WORKS: *Le bellissime avventure di Caterí dalla trecciolina* (1941); *Il gioco segreto* (1941); *Alibi* (1958); *Le straordinarie avventure di Caterina* (1959); *Lo scialle andaluso* (1963)

BIBLIOGRAPHY: Brennan, M., on *House of Liars, New Yorker*, 9 Feb. 1952: 106–9; Hicks, G., on *Arturo's Island, SatR*, 15 Aug. 1959, 16; Ferrucci, F., "E. M.: Limbo without Elysium," *IQ*, 7: 27–28 (1963): 28–52; McCormick, E. A., "Utopia and Point of View: Narrative Method in M.'s *L'isola di Arturo* and Keyserling's *Schwüle Tage*," *Symposium*, 15 (1963): 114–30; Spender, S., on *History: A Novel, NYRB*, 28 April 1977: 31–34

—GOFFREDO PALLUCCHINI

Alberto Moravia

MORAVIA, Alberto

Italian novelist, short-story writer, dramatist, and essayist, b. 28 Nov. 1907, Rome; d. 26 Sept. 1990, Rome

Born of well-to-do middle-class parents, M. was stricken with osteomyelitis at the age of nine and spent the next several years of his life bedridden and under treatment in sanatoriums. A precocious writer, he began working on his first major novel, *Gli indifferenti* (1929; *The Indifferent Ones*, 1932; new tr., *The Time of Indifference*, 1953), at the age of eighteen. In 1941 he married the novelist Elsa MORANTE, from whom he was later divorced. Except for a period of exile in the Abruzzi region in 1943, M. has always lived in Rome, the city intimately associated with most of his fiction.

Always sharply critical of the middle class (the object of bitter irony in many of his stories), M. has stated that Marxism is one of the two main poles of his thought; Freudianism is the other. From his earliest works to his most recent, M.'s themes, characters, and ideas have remained remarkably constant.

M. has identified the main theme of all his writing as the "relationship between man and reality." The perspective from which he views this relationship is that of sexuality—indeed, for him, the relationship itself is sexual. The reality is the dehumanized, capitalist world that the bourgeoisie has created, a nightmare that causes lifelong anguish in every individual. His characters are shown to be creatures of their instincts, governed by the forces of a mysterious bond between sex and money, the root of their alienation and torment.

Gli indifferenti, with its portrayal of the despair of the individual who is trapped in what would later come to be known as "the absurd," may be considered the first European EXISTENTIALIST novel. It was an immediate success, despite its harsh description of the decadence and rot of the middle-class society of its day. M. has readily concurred with critics who claim that he has continued to rewrite this first book, for the seeds of virtually all his later works were sown here. In character types, there is the typical impotent intellectual hero who suffers from boredom and self-disgust and who is pitted against a virile, successful rival; there are the women who are presented as prey to their sexuality, either as unconsciously voluptuous seductresses or as pitiful but disgusting aging mistresses and courtesans.

Variations on the women of *Gli indifferenti* have figured prominently in M.'s fiction. Two of M.'s best-known novels, *La romana* (1947; *The Woman of Rome*, 1949) and *La ciociara* (1957; *Two Women*, 1958), trace the awakening consciousness of three women who slowly come to an understanding of their own nature and of the meaning of life. In *La romana* we watch the sixteen-year-old Adriana, a naïve, unconsciously sensual girl of the working class, become a prostitute because she discovers that she "likes love and money and the things that money can buy." At the core of the experiences she narrates is her existentialist crisis and her recurring feeling of despair, spawned by a sense of shame at her life. When we leave her at age twenty-one, she has learned to accept herself and all humanity with its entangled strands of evil, violence, and suffering; she can now look to the future with hope for happiness.

For the two women in *La ciociara* redemption comes through suffering. The war experiences of the middle-class businesswoman and her daughter in this novel are closely based on M.'s own experiences as a refugee in the Abruzzi during World War II. The two women finally break out of their "tomb of indifference and wickedness" and take up life again at a moment when they are able to feel grief and compassion. Through his description of the brutal, dehumanizing forces of war we see M.'s belief that man is man because he suffers most cogently illustrated. This novel is also probably the most poignant expression of M.'s view of the human condition.

Among the hundreds of short pieces of fiction M. has written, the 130 stories in the *Racconti romani* (1954; *Roman Tales*, 1957) and *Nuovi racconti romani* (1959; *More Roman Tales*, 1964) are probably his best known. Originally published as a regular newspaper feature, they charmed readers all over Italy, but most especially the Romans, who saw themselves and their daily activities reflected in these brief, thumbnail sketches of working-class characters in everyday situations.

Most critics and readers of M. consider his earlier short works to be his finest, however. In three of these stories M. excels in portraying adolescents during a time of crisis in the painful period of growing up. "Inverno di malato" (1930; "A Sick Boy's Winter," 1954), is a delicately melancholy tale about a middle-class boy under treatment in a sanatorium, who tries to seduce a naïve but willing fourteen-year-old patient. His feelings of shame and guilt, combined with the tormenting despair at his unimproved condition, are rendered with masterful sensitivity. Both *Agostino* (1945; *Agostino*) and *La disubbedienza* (1948; *Luca*)—published together in English as *Two Adolescents* (1950)—relate the anguish of loss of purity and the intense suffering of a boy confronted with an harsh

reality so different from his ideals. The intimate drama of fifteen-year-old Luca's initiation into the mysteries of sexual union in *La disubbedienza* provides a sequel to the story of thirteen-year-old Agostino's desperate but futile attempts to experience sex.

M. has not received the critical acclaim for his essays, plays, and travel books that he had for his stories and novels. Indeed, these do remain minor works. However, his collected essays provide clear summaries of his ideas, and are provocative and stimulating if at times highly questionable or even outrageous. M.'s plays are generally elaborations of a broad thesis and embodiments of themes that are not always as fully explored in his fiction. In his travel books M. has written some memorable passages of impressions of people and life styles in the various countries he has visited.

Throughout his career M. has been a figure of controversy. He has, however, remained faithful to his inner vision and in so doing has reflected the main preoccupations of 20th-c. thought. An expert storyteller, he is widely recognized as a master of plot and description.

FURTHER WORKS: *La bella vita* (1935); *Le ambizione sbagliate* (1935; *Wheel of Fortune*, 1937; repub. as *Mistaken Ambitions*, 1955); *L'imbroglio* (1937); *I sogni del pigro* (1940); *La mascherata* (1941; *The Fancy Dress Party*, 1952); *L'amante infelice* (1943); *L'epidemia: Racconti surrealistici e satirici* (1944); *La cetonia* (1944); *Due cortigiane, e Serata di Don Giovanni* (1945); *L'amore coniugale, e altri racconti* (1949; *Conjugal Love*, 1951); *Il conformista* (1951; *The Conformist*, 1951); *I racconti* (1952); *Il disprezzo* (1954; *A Ghost at Noon*, 1955); *Teatro* (1958; *Beatrice Cenci*, 1966, tr. of one play in the vol.); *Un mese in U.R.S.S.* (1958); *La noia* (1906; *The Empty Canvas*, 1961); *Saggi italiani* (1960, with Zolla Elémire); *Un'idea dell'India* (1962) *L'automa* (1963; *The Fetish, and Other Stories*, 1964); *L'uomo come fine e altri saggi* (1964; *Man as an End*, 1965); *L'attenzione* (1965; *The Lie*, 1966); *Il mondo è quello che è* (1966); *L'intervista* (1966); *Una cosa è una cosa* (1967; *Command and I Will Obey You*, 1968); *La rivoluzione culturale in Cina* (1967; *The Red Book and the Great Wall*, 1968); *Il dio Kurt* (1968); *La vita è gioco* (1969); *Il paradiso* (1970; *Bought and Sold*, 1973; repub. as *Paradise and Other Stories*); *Io e lui* (1971; *Two: A Phallic Novel*, 1972); *A quale tribù appartieni?* (1972; *Which Tribe Do You Belong To?*, 1974); *Un altra vita* (1973; *Lady Godiva and Other Stories*, 1975; also tr. as *Mother Love*, 1976); *Al cinema* (1975); *Boh* (1976; *The Voice of the Sea and Other Stories*, 1978); *La vita interiore* (1978; *Time of Desecration*, 1980); *Un miliardo di anni fa* (1979); *Cosma e i briganti* (1980); *Impegno controvoglia: Saggi, articoli, interviste—trentacinque anni di scritti politici* (1980). FURTHER WORKS IN ENGLISH: *Bitter Honeymoon and Other Stories* (1956); *The Wayward Wife and Other Stories* (1960)

BIBLIOGRAPHY: Lewis, R. W. B., "A. M.: Eros and Existence," *The Picaresque Saint: Representative Figures in Contemporary Fiction* (1956): 36–56; Pacifici, S., *A Guide to Contemporary Italian Literature* (1962): 29–56; Dego, G., *M.* (1966); Rimanelli, G., "M. and the Philosophy of Personal Existence," *IQ*, 41 (1967): 39–68; Heiney, D., *Three Italian Novelists: M., Pavese, Vittorini* (1968): 1–82; Ragusa, O., "A. M.: Voyeurism and Storytelling," *SoR*, 4 (1968): 127–41; Radcliff-Umstead, D., "M.'s Indifferent Puppets," *Symposium*, 24 (1970): 44–54; Ross, J. and D. Freed, *The Existentialism of A. M.* (1972); Kibler, L., "The Reality and Realism of A. M.," *IQ*, 65 (1973): 3–25; Cottrell, J., *A. M.* (1974)

—JANE E. COTTRELL

MORDVIN LITERATURE
See Finno-Ugric Literatures

MORENO-DURAN, Rafael Humberto

Colombian novelist and short-story writer, b. 7 Nov. 1946, Tunja

M.-D. studied law and political science at the National University of Colombia in Bogotá. He has been associated with a number of journals published in Spain and Latin America, and since 1989 has directed the Latin American edition of *Quimera*. Like other POSTMODERNISTS, he has spent much of his life in Europe. A man of broad culture, he is most fascinated by the classical era and its revival and reinterpretation in 18th-c. Europe, particularly the salon society. He speaks approvingly of "the ironic and demythologizing, irreverent and festive climate of the 18th c."

M.-D. is known for his postmodernist tendencies. In his case these involve a greater concentration on language as such than on the topic at hand and, correspondingly, a certain HERMETICISM. M.-D. places great value on the principle of ambiguity, the effect of which is to deny validity to anything purporting to be an authoritative discourse. Nevertheless, his latest novel, *Los felinos del canciller* (1987; the chancellor's felines), is a good deal less hermetic than his earlier works, even while continuing to concentrate on the philological concerns of both characters and narrator. At the same time, wit of the linguistic variety has become more prominent in his fiction.

In his early novels the author placed great emphasis on the role of women in society, having concluded that all the significant novels of Colombia concentrated on concerns inherent to the life of women. While his short stories written from a woman's perspective appear to many readers to ring true, some feminist critics claim to find them somewhat inauthentic in this regard.

His first book was an ambitious essay, *De la barbarie a la imaginación* (1976; from barbarity to imagination), which set the tone for his subsequent fiction. Although he had completed first drafts of the novels in his trilogy known as *Femina Suite* (woman suite) by 1976, they were published between 1977 and 1983. The first, *Juego de damas* (1977; game of checkers, literally "ladies' game"), has as its framework a party that is reminiscent of the 18th-c. salons, albeit in parodic fashion. The characters recall their student days, including their abortive attempt to mount an armed rebellion against the government, but, in postmodern fashion, the most important activity in the text is clearly its various forms of discourse. Rather than narrate events, M.-D. tends to allow his characters to recreate them in lengthy dialogues. Alvaro Pineda-Botero has commented that M.-D.'s characters and situations serve not as the revelation of a supposed external reality but as a framework for the true motive of the discourse, which is language and culture.

The text of *El toque de Diana* (1981; reveille, or Diana's touch) also continually calls attention to itself. The central characters are highly sophisticated people who converse in several languages. The two most prominent are a general, whose career has just come to an end, and his wife, the owner of an elegant millinery shop. At one point she offers her opinion that style controls culture. Even so, in this work, as in the first of the trilogy, culture tends to be reduced to sexuality.

Within M.-D.'s hermetic style in the trilogy, the reader perceives an increasing emphasis on humor, most notably in the sexual realm, and often involving a multiform satire on cultural forms. At one point in *Finale capriccioso con madonna* (1983; capricious finale with Madonna), a Colombian male finds himself in bed with his Arabic ex-wife and his Jewish lover, their three bodies forming a triangle. The narration of the event plays on the cabala and other esoterica, and at the same time suggests that this may be a parody of the *convivencia* or codwelling of three religious groups under Alphonse X in 12th-c. Spain. In this novel, too, all of culture is reduced to style and sexuality.

The ostensible topic of *Los felinos del canciller* is Latin American diplomacy. In its opening pages the years of violence in Colombia (1948–1958 and beyond) have begun, ironically in Bogotá, which has always taken pride in calling itself "the Athens of South America." The protagonist is in New York, exercising a diplomatic career, when he receives the news of violence in the halls of the Colombian legislature in Bogotá. He then rehearses his family's history through several generations by means of flashbacks. Subsequently he returns home to uncover some of the family's more profound secrets. As Raymond L. Williams has noted, the key activity in the work is manipulation, both of people and of language. The narrator comments, "Politics and philology were the same thing in this country. In the beginning was the word, and the word was made with power." In this work, as in *Los felinos del canciller*, language is sexualized as surely as sex is equated with philological exercises.

M.-D.'s finely crafted short stories were published as *Metropolitanas* (1986; metropolitan women) and *Epístola final sobre los cuáqueros* (1987; final epistle on the Quakers). The latter won the National Short Story Prize (1987). His stories often deal with the attempts made by European women to come to terms with a maledominated world. The best of those in *Metropolitanas* is "Perpetua" (Perpetua), the narrator of which is an Italian woman who has suffered greatly from the ravages of World War II as well as her late husband's infidelity. Ultimately she creates an identity for herself within the boundaries of the eternal feminine principle, because, as she perceives the situation, time is irredeemably cyclical. True to M.-D.'s tendencies, she does so largely through double entendres, both conscious and unconscious.

M.-D. is currently preparing what he calls a "literary biography" entitled "La augusta sílaba" (the august syllable) and a novel, "El caballero de La Invicta" (the knight of La Invicta).

M.-D. has developed a public image as the writer's writer. His readership, in contrast to that of Gabriel GARCÍA MÁRQUEZ, consists largely of a relatively small group of people interested in innovative fiction.

BIBLIOGRAPHY: Jaramillo, J. E., "*Los felinos del canciller*: Una crítica de las fundaciones," in Pineda-Botero, A., and R. L. Williams, eds., *Deficciones y realidades* (1989): 255–68; Pineda-Botero, A., *Del mito a la posmodernidad* (1990): 184–93; Siemens, W. L., "M.-D.: 'Perpetua' y la cartografía de la feminidad," in Oyarzún, K., ed. *The Latin American Short Story* (1990): 98–105; Williams, R. L., *The Colombian Novel, 1844–1987* (1991): 196–204

—WILLIAM L. SIEMENS

MORGENSTERN, Christian

German poet, critic, and translator, b. 6 May 1871, Munich; d. 31 March 1914, Merano, Italy

M. was born into a family of artists; because of family difficulties his education beyond secondary school was limited to one year at Breslau University. He moved to Berlin in 1894, working as a professional writer, contributing literary, drama, and art criticism to important journals in Germany and Austria. He soon joined the group of writers and artists known as the Friedrichshagen circle, so named after the Berlin suburb where its founders, the Hart brothers, lived, and where meetings were held. Through the Harts—Heinrich (1855–1906) and Julius (1859–1930)—M. met many of Berlin's intellectual elite. His interest in theater led him to found a theatrical journal, *Das Theater* (1903–5), during the time he worked for the publisher Bruno Cassirer. Between 1897 and 1903 M. was also active as a translator, being particularly commended for his renditions of Ibsen.

M. considered poetry a sacred mission and regarded himself as a serious poet, but he also believed that humor and seriousness grew from common roots. While his first collection, *In Phantas Schloß* (1895; in fancy's castle), combined humor and fantasy, subsequent early works struck a more serious, romantic, and melancholy note. However, in *Galgenlieder* (1905; *The Gallows Songs*, 1964), his most enduring volume, M. reverted to a satiric voice to express his rejection of literary naturalism. Written during a period of skepticism, the poems play with language and present objects in a grotesque and surreal manner as a protest against man's manipulation of nature.

Most of the poetry he published between 1910 and 1914 had religious overtones and reflected his growing cosmic awareness, which extended even to the love lyrics for his wife in *Ich und Du* (1911; I and you). An exception to this preoccupation with religion and mysticism was *Palmström* (1910; Palmström), in which humor with a philosophical twist was directed at a complacent materialist society.

Although his serious writing was underrated in his lifetime, the depth of M.'s thought places him above most other German neoromantic poets. His tendency toward introspection and philosophy, including German and Oriental mysticism, was reinforced by long rest periods necessitated by tuberculosis. He acknowledged the influence of Nietzsche and Schopenhauer, of the controversial cultural philosopher Paul de Lagarde (1827–1891), and of the linguistic theorist Fritz Mauthner (1849–1923). Others have seen links in his humorous poetry with the satiric works of Clemens Brentano (1778–1842) and Wilhelm Busch (1832–1908), and with SYMBOLISM, DADAISM, and SURREALISM. M.'s last book, *Wir fanden einen Pfad* (1914; we found a path), was dedicated to Rudolf Steiner (1861–1925), founder of the anthroposophy movement, who was also his final mentor.

FURTHER WORKS: *Horatius travestitus* (1897); *Auf vielen Wegen* (1897); *Ich und die Welt* (1898); *Ein Sommer* (1900); *Und aber rundet sich ein Kranz* (1902); *Melancholie* (1906); *Einkehr* (1910); *Palma Kunkel* (1916); *Stufen* (1918); *Der Gingganz* (1919); *Der Melderbaum* (1920); *Epigramme und Sprüche* (1920); *Klein Irmchen* (1921); *Über die Galgenlieder* (1921); *. . . Daß auch sie einst Sonne werde* (1923); *Mensch Wanderer* (1927); *Die Schallmühle* (1928); *Meine Liebe ist groß wie die weite Welt* (1936); *Böhmischer Jahrmarkt* (1938); *Das aufgeklärte Mondschaf* (1938); *Wer vom Ziel nicht weiß, kann den Weg nicht haben* (1939); *Klaus Burrmann der Tierwelt Photograph* (1941); *Zeit und Ewigkeit* (1942); *Ausgewählte Gedichte* (1945); *Flugsand und Weidenflöten* (1945); *Stilles Reifen* (1945); *Mann muß aus einem Licht fort in das andre gehn* (1948); *Liebe Sonne, liebe Erde* (1949); *Egon und Emilie* (1950); *Quellen des Lebens hör ich in mir singen* (1951); *Sausebrand und Mausbarbier* (1951); *Ein Leben in Briefen* (1952); *Das Mondschaf* (1953; *The Moonsheep*, 1953); *Vom offenbaren Geheimnis* (1954); *Die drei Hasen* (1959); *Aphorismen und Sprüche* (1960); *Der Spielgast* (1960); *Alles um des Menschen Willen* (1962); *Eine Auswahl der schönsten Galgenlieder in deutscher und englischer Sprache* (1964); *Der Sündfloh* (1965); *Gesammelte Werke* (1965); *Kindergedichte* (1965); *Heimlich träumen Mensch und Erde* (1967); *Versammlung der Nägel* (1969); *Gedenkausgabe 1871–1971* (1971); *Sämtliche Dichtungen* (16 vols., 1971–1979); *Alle Galgenlieder* (1972); *Galgenlieder: Der Gingganz* (1973); *Gesammelte Werke* (1974); *Palmström: Palma Kunkel* (1974); *Das große C.-M.-Buch* (1976). FURTHER WORKS IN ENGLISH: *The Three Sparrows and Other Nursery Poems* (1968); *The Great Lalula and Other Nonsense Rhymes* (1969); *The Daynight Lamp and Other Poems* (1973); *Selected Poems of C. M.* (1973)

BIBLIOGRAPHY: Bauer, M., *C. M.s Leben und Werk* (1933; 2nd ed., 1954); Hiebel, F., *C. M.: Wende und Aufbruch unseres Jahrhunderts* (1957); Beheim-Schwarzbach, M., *C. M. in Selbstzeugnissen und Bilddokumenten* (1964); Walter, J., *Sprache und Spiel in C. M.s Galgenliedern* (1966); Gumtau, H., *C. M.* (1971); Hofacker, E. P., *C. M.* (1978)

—EVELINE L. KANES

MORI Ōgai

(pseud. of Mori Rintarō) Japanese novelist, short-story writer, and critic, b. 17 Feb. 1862, Tsuwano; d. 9 July 1922, Tokyo

M. followed his father by taking up a career in medicine, studying new Western scientific techniques, largely imported from Germany, which were taught in Tokyo in the 1870s. After joining the army, M. was sent to Germany to observe hygienic practices. He remained in Europe from 1884 to 1888, and on his return, fired by a new-found love for German literature and philosophy, began to pursue a double career as a writer and a bureaucrat that was to continue throughout his life. M. eventually obtained the rank of Surgeon General of the Japanese army, but his creative writing activities put him, along with his contemporary, NATSUME Sōseki, in the forefront of the writers of his generation.

Shortly after his return from Germany, M. wrote a trilogy of stories about his German experiences. The first of these, "Maihime" (1890; "The Girl Who Danced," 1964), chronicles the activities of a young Japanese in Europe who falls in love and then abandons his German mistress. The story, for all of its romantic trappings, concentrates on the conflict between self-fulfillment and social duty, a theme that finds repercussions in virtually every important M. work.

M.'s enthusiasms then turned to the preparation of a series of translations of works by Hans Christian Andersen, Goethe, Heine, and Kleist, among many others. He also did research in German aesthetic theory. M. wrote a number of stories and essays in the years that followed, but his first sustained period as a writer began in 1909, when, late in his forties, he began a series of novels and stories that allowed him to explore his own experience against the background of a rapidly modernizing society. The first of them, *Vita sexualis* (1909; *Vita Sexualis*, 1973), sketches with trenchant irony his development of feelings for the opposite sex. The second, *Seinen* (1910; youth), recounts the spiritual adventures of a young man struggling to become a novelist in modern Tokyo. In the third novel, *Gan* (1911; *Wild Geese*, 1959), M. creates as his heroine a woman caught between traditional and modern ways of behavior. She and the protagonist, a young student bound for study in Germany, are attracted to each other but never manage to meet in any meaningful way; her loneliness forces the woman to come alive to the forces of life that well up within her.

The protagonist of *Seinen* declares that art can only grow from a sense of the past, and by 1912 M. showed his commitment to this position in a series of historical stories and novels usually judged as his finest work. Among these, "Sanshō dayū" (1914; "Sanshō Dayū," 1952), a moving story, set in medieval times, of two children taken into slavery, shows M.'s ability to infuse traditional narrative with acute psychological and philosophical insight. Another notable story, "Kanzan Jittoku" (1915; "Han Shan and Shi Te," 1971) tells the legend of two Chinese Zen recluses with humor and wisdom. M.'s masterpiece is doubtless *Shibue Chūsai* (1916; Shibue Chūsai), the biography of a Confucian scholar and doctor who lived from 1805 to 1858, the period just prior to the modernization of Japan. M. reconstructs the details of the scholar's life, and, as he does so, shows his own affinities with this earlier figure, revealing both his and his subject's views on life in an intimate and compelling fashion.

M. continued to write and translate important works from European literature, including a number of Ibsen plays and Goethe's *Faust*. Although failing health caused him to curtail his activities, he continued to do research and writing until shortly before his death.

M.'s reputation is founded not only on his literary and critical works but also on a widespread admiration for the quality of the life that he led. His understanding of modern European culture, with its restless search for truth in an era when science was replacing metaphysics, helped him delineate the same changes in Japan. M.'s ironic detachment, which led him to an austere and poetic sense of philosophical resignation, reveals an atmosphere of moral courage that combines traditional Confucian virtue with modern sophistication.

FURTHER WORKS: *Omokage* (1889); *Utakata no ki* (1890; *Utakata No Ki*, 1974); *Kamen* (1909); "Hannichi" (1909; "Half a Day," 1974); "Hanako" (1910; "Hanako," 1918); *Ikutagawa* (1910); "Asobi" (1910); "Mōsō" (1911; "Delusion," 1970); *Hyaku monogatari* (1911); "Ka no yo ni" (1912; "As If," 1925); "Sakai jihen" (1914; "The Incident at Sakai," 1977); "Yasui Fujin" (1914; "The Wife of Yasui," 1977); *Oshio Heihachirō* (1915); "Takasebune" (1915; "Takase-bune," 1918); *Izawa Ranken* (1916); *Zenshū* (53 vols., 1951–1956)

BIBLIOGRAPHY: Miyoshi, M., *Accomplices of Silence: The Modern Japanese Novel* (1974): 38–54; Rimer, J. T., *M. Ō* (1975); Johnson, E. W., "Ōgai's *The Wild Goose*," in Tsuruta, K. and T. Swann, eds., *Approaches to the Modern Japanese Novel* (1976): 129–47; Rimer, J. T., *Modern Japanese Fiction and Its Traditions* (1978): 138–61;

Bowring, R., *M. Ō. and the Modernization of Japanese Culture* (1979)

—J. THOMAS RIMER

MÓRICZ, Zsigmond

Hungarian novelist, dramatist, and short-story writer, b. 30 June 1879, Tiszacsécse; d. 4 Sept. 1942, Budapest

Born in a small village in eastern Hungary, M. grew up among peasants, and although his mother, a descendant of impoverished Calvinist clergymen, instilled in him a respect for book learning, the adult M. identified more closely with his ambitious and hardworking peasant father. After attending some of the best church-run schools in provincial Hungary, M. enrolled in the Theological Seminary of Debrecen, but then switched to law, although he quit before receiving a degree. In 1900 he moved to Budapest and for a number of years made a meager living as a journalist and as a clerk in a government office. He also began to write essays and children's stories. In 1903, with a grant from a Hungarian learned society, he undertook a tour of the Hungarian countryside, collecting folktales and poetry in remote villages. This pioneering field trip, which may be compared with his compatriot Béla Bartók's researches into folk music, also begun around this time, signaled a turning point in his life as a writer. Not being interested in scholarship, M. did not publish his finds but the material he gathered—its spirit more than the narrative riches—fed his creative vein for many years to come.

With a poignant story in the manner of CHEKHOV about the dignity of the rural poor, "Hét krajcár" (1909; "Seven Pennies," 1962), M. established his name in Hungarian literature, and within a few years he came to be known as a modern master. He managed to incorporate the crises and conflicts of his personal life into his works, without making any of them transparently autobiographical. He was married twice, both times unhappily (his first wife committed suicide); in his novels male-female relationships are invariably tempestuous. Although M. was among the literary innovators who were associated with the modernist periodical *Nyugat*—between 1929 and 1933 he was one of the editors of the journal—at the time of his death in 1942 he was a father figure to Hungary's increasingly influential populist writers.

In M.'s mature fiction we encounter a new type of peasant: brooding, complex, violence-prone, a far cry from the docile and comically hapless figures familiar from earlier literature. His first important novel, *Sárarany* (1910; golden mud), shocked many people because in it the poverty and backwardness of the Hungarian village is described without palliative idealizations. The novel's peasant hero, a disturbingly robust, aggressive man with a huge appetite for life, was even more shocking. M.'s early conservative critics labeled him—disparagingly of course—a "naturalist"; the sexual excesses of his characters, as well as the hints about biological determinism, were seen as evidence of a suspiciously radical, Zolaesque tilt. In truth, detached, slice-of-life naturalism was alien to M.'s temperament. He was attracted to the darker side of social and psychological reality, but an ingrained sense of morality also made him a passionate crusader for social justice. A quintessential realist, M. was nevertheless partial to strongly emotive language; he filled in background with bold colors and favored romantic hyperbole when depicting moments of high drama. Perhaps his most successfully realized novel, *A fáklya* (1918; *The Torch*, 1931), the story of a well-meaning though flawed Calvinist minister who tries to enlighten his narrow-minded parishioners, ends with a spectacular barn fire that claims the lives of hundreds of villagers, including the hero's.

M. was just as interested in the provincial middle class and the gentry as he was in the peasantry. The daydreaming, hopelessly frustrated heroine of *Az Isten háta mögött* (1911; behind God's country) has been called the Hungarian Madame Bovary; indeed, references to Flaubert's characters are made throughout the novel. Two more mature works, *Kivilágos kivirradtig* (1926; until daybreak) and *Úri muri* (1928; gentry roistering), also present a devastating picture of life in the Hungarian provinces. Descriptions of endless and almost desperate drinking and carousing, of arrogant posturing and nostalgic daydreaming, suggest not only the decadence of the gentry but the utter hollowness of its life style.

A far mellower and more serene novel, which has become a children's classic in Hungary, is *Légy jó mindhalálig* (1920; *Be Faithful unto Death*, 1962). Despite temptations, the earnest adolescent hero of this novel remains unaffected by the cruelties and corruptions of the adult world. M. himself, as he grew older, became more pessimistic about the possibility of reforming entrenched social institutions and alleviating social inequities. For example, his novel *Rokonok* (1932; the relatives), is a bitter exposé of machinations and cover-ups in high places.

M.'s most ambitious undertaking as a writer was the historical trilogy *Erdély* (1922–35; Transylvania), perhaps the most splendid historical novel in Hungarian literature. In it he pits two Transylvanian princes against each other—one a sober and effective compromiser, the other an anarchic and charismatic fighter. In addition to a host of fascinating characters, the trilogy also offers a rich tapestry of 17th-c. eastern European civilization.

M.'s most lasting achievements are his novels; as a playwright he was less successful (his works for the stage include adaptations of his popular novels). On the other hand, he was a master of the short story. Indeed his best stories—for example, "Barbárok" (1932; "Brutes," 1962) and "A világ végén már szép és jó" (1938; "Everything Is Good at the End of the World," 1966)—have a balladlike terseness and intensity that his longer fiction lacks. Toward the end of his life M. befriended a young girl, a waif from the outskirts of Budapest who, when the author first met her, was about to commit suicide. M. wrote a number of stories about her harsh life, and through her learned a great deal about the urban poor. An avid note-taker and listener, M. was bent on discovering new worlds even in old age. He may have begun his career surveying peasant life only, but in time just about every stratum of Hungarian society fell under his careful, implacable scrutiny.

FURTHER WORKS: *Sári bíró* (1910), *Kerek Ferkó* (1913); *Mese a zöld füvön* (1915); *Nem élhetek muzsikaszó nélkül* (1916); *Szegény emberek* (1918); *Búzakalász* (1924); *Pillangó* (1925); *Forró mezők* (1929); *Esőleső társaság* (1931); *Az asszony közbeszól* (1934); *A boldog ember* (1935); *Rab oroszlán* (1936); *Életem regénye* (1939); *Árvácska* (1941); *Rózsa Sándor a lovát ugratja* (1941); *M. Z. összegyűjtött művei* (7 vols., 1953–1959); *Színművei* (1956); *M. Z. hagyatékából* (1960); *Regényei és elbeszélései* (12 vols., 1961–1965)

BIBLIOGRAPHY: Reményi, J., *Hungarian Writers and Literature* (1964): 326–40; Klaniczay, T., J. Szauder, and M. Szabolcsi,

History of Hungarian Literature (1964): 199–205; Nagy, P., "How Modern Was Z. M.?" *NHQ*, No. 77 (1980): 29–42

—IVAN SANDERS

MOROCCAN LITERATURE

In Arabic

As a French Protectorate, from 1912 until it gained its independence in 1956, Morocco produced little creative writing. The important Arabic works that were written during that period were mostly religious or historical texts. Creative writing was more or less restricted to poetry and short didactic prose narratives. Being geographically distant and politically isolated from the Middle East, the literary *Nahda* (Renaissance), which began in Egypt and the Levant in the 19th c., did not immediately reach Morocco. During the first half of the 20th c., the rise of the *Salafiyya* (Return to the Past) movement, which glorified classical Arabic literature, discouraged any innovation in creative writing.

It was not until the middle of the 20th c. that the short story emerged, to be followed shortly afterwards by the novel. It is generally agreed that the autobiographical novel *Fī al-Tufūla* (1957; 1968; On Childhood) by Abdelmajid Benjelloun ('Abd al-Majīd ibn Jallūn, 1919-1981), describing life during the Protectorate, is a landmark in the development of Arabic fictional writing in Morocco. Benjelloun wrote his novel in the 1940s. It was serialized before it was published in book form and the author awarded the Morocco Prize for Literature and Art in 1969. A diplomat and educationalist, Benjelloun was also a poet. He wrote a number of works in French, explaining Morocco, its history and society to a Western readership. Benjelloun paved the way for younger French-educated academics, such as Mohammed Aziz Lahbabi (Muhammad 'Azīz al-Habābī, 1922-1993) and Abdallah Laroui ('Abd Allāh al-'Arwī, b. 1933), who were also bilingual writers. Lahbabi was a cofounder of the Union of Maghrebi Writers. He is best remembered for his novels *Jīl al-Dama'* (1967; The Generation of Thirst) and *Iksīr al-Hayāt* (1974; The Elixir of Life). Laroui, a historian, wrote a number of works in French on the history of the Maghreb, some of which have been translated into English. His novel *Al-Ghurba* (1971; Exile) is one of the first works of Arabic fiction in the Maghreb to deal with the theme of alienation.

It was Mubārak Rabī' (b. 1935) who gave Arabic fictional writing a new verve. Rabī' is well known for his two novels *Al-Tayyibūn* (1971; The Good Folk), awarded a special prize by the Tunisian Ministry of Culture and Information, and *Rifqat al-Silāh wa al-Qamar* (1976; The Companions of Arms and the Moon). The latter, which focusses on the 1973 Arab-Israeli War, won the prize of the Arabic Language Academy of Cairo. Perhaps the name that is more readily associated with the novel and short story is that of 'Abd al-Karīm GHALLĀB. One of his earliest novels, *Dafannā al-Mādī* (1966; We Have Buried the Past), which won the literary prize of the Moroccan Ministry of Culture (1968), has been translated into several languages. Ghallab is a prolific writer who is still producing fictional works along with younger contemporaries, foremost among them Mohamed BERRADA, Idris al-Khuri (b. 1939), Mohamed ZAFZAF, and Mustafa al-Misnawi (b. 1953). Women have yet to make their mark on Moroccan literature. To date the two most important exponents of Arabic writing are Khannāta Bannūna (b. 1940) and Leila Abouzeid (b. 1950) who introduce assertive women characters into their works. A writer who deserves special mention is Mohammad Choukri (b. 1935) whose autobiographical novel, *Al-Khubz al-Hāfī*, appeared in English first, translated by Paul BOWLES as *For Bread Alone* (1973). Choukri had recorded the novel for Bowles in Moroccan dialectal Arabic. It was not published in Arabic until 1982.

Poetry has been written in Morocco throughout the present century, reaching peaks of excellence with the works of 'Abd al-Karīm al-Tabbāl (b. 1931) and Muhammad Bannīs (b. 1948). These two poets, along with Muhammad al-Habīb al-Furqānī (b. 1922) and Muhammad al-Sabbāgh (b. 1930) among others, write innovative verse marked by a vividness of imagery. The phrasing and rhythm which characterize their compositions are free of the rigid strictures of the meters of classical Arabic poetry. Al-Tabbāl uses different rhyme schemes to create different moods and musical intonation. His poetry is full of oxymora, like sadness-happiness, youth-old age, and darkness-light. Al-Furqānī is another poet who resorts to the use of oxymora. His poems are politically charged, and the views expressed in them have landed him in prison on more than one occasion, both before and after independence. Al-Sabbāgh, who has been greatly influenced by modern Spanish poetry, published his first collection *El árbol de fuego* (1953; The Fire Tree) in Spanish before it appeared in Arabic a year later. He has published several collections of poems and short stories, some for children. Bannīs, a keen follower of poetic trends both in the Arab world and the West, has brought to modern Arabic poetry his own distinct fusion of imagery and meaning. Another well-known poet is Hasan al-Turaybiq (b. 1945) who writes poetry in verse. One of his best known verse plays is *Bayna al-Amwāj wa al-Qarāsina* (1982; Among Waves and Pirates).

Morocco has a wealth of oral literature in both Arabic and Berber, consisting of narratives poems, and proverbs, a great part of which has yet to be published. It is this rich Arabic and Berber folklore which is at the core of Moroccan theater, and especially the plays of Tayeb Saddiki (pseud. of Al-Tayyib al-Saddīqī, b. 1938). Dramatist, producer, and actor, Saddiki's contribution to the establishment and development of a national theater in Morocco is immeasurable. Fluent in French and Arabic, both literary and dialectal, Saddiki's audiences seem to determine the languages he presents his plays in. A promoter of different types of theater, including educational, experimental and touring theater, he has adapted several plays by well known Western dramatists, from Shakespeare to IONESCO. Saddiki's fame, however, rests on his ability to draw on the traditional oral legends and poetry of his country and to turn them into plays for modern audiences. In the preface to his play *Les Sept grains de beauté* (1991; The Seven Beauty Spots) he mentions how as a child he used to pass daily by story-tellers in market places. It is they who fired his imagination and whose stories provide the raw material for his plays.

Another dramatist who has been influenced by oral narratives is 'Abd al-Haqq al-Zarwālī (b. 1952). Al-Zarwali has perfected the art of the one-hander where audiences are faced with one actor performing an entire play, evocative of the role of the storyteller in the market place. Fādil Yūsuf (b. 1949) is one of the more interesting voices in Moroccan theater today. Yusuf is a firm believer in the power of live theater in influencing audiences and shaping their ideas. His plays, notably *Hallāq Darb al-Fuqarā'* (1978; The Barber of the Poor People's Alley) and *Su'ūd wa Inhiyār Marrākush* (1980; The Rise and Fall of Marrakesh) have

proved popular with audiences. 'Abd al-Karīm Berrashīd (b. 1943), like Saddiki, is a dramatist, producer, and actor. Among his best-known plays are *Fawst wa al-Amīra al-Sal'ā'* (1977; Faust and the Bald Princess) and *'Utayl wa al-Khayl wa al-Bārūd* (1977; Othello, the Horses and Gunpowder).

In French

The first attempt at Francophone novel writing is, *Mosaïques ternies* (1932; Tarnished Mosaics) by Benazous Chatt (dates n.a.). It was reprinted in 1991 and the author's name given as Abdelkader Chatt. The novel, which is partly autobiographical, describes with nostalgia Moroccan traditions and customs that were being eroded by the advent of modernity. The francophone novel, however, did not become a full-fledged genre until the 1950s. Ahmed Sefrioui's (b. 1915) first novel, *La boîte à merveilles* (1954; The Box of Wonders), describes an idyllic childhood in Fez in the early decades of the 20th c. Sefrioui had made his name with a collection of short stories, *Le chapelet d'ambre* (1949; The Amber Rosary), with the stories strung together like beads in a rosary.

It was Driss CHRAÏBI who was the first writer to make Moroccan Francophone literature globally known. His first novel, *Le passé simple* (1954; *The Simple Past*, 1990), an autobiographical work, condemns colonialism, antiquated religious practices, patriarchal customs, and the taboo-laden societies that do nothing to eradicate them. Narrated in the first person, Chraïbi's attack is directed against the domineering, cruel father who subjects his long-suffering wife and other members of his family to his relentless cruelty. The novel ends with the hero leaving Morocco for France. In his second novel, *Les boucs* (1955; *The Butts*, 1983), Chraïbi describes the daily struggle of North African immigrants trying to survive in France by doing the most menial jobs, amid endless hostility and ill-treatment from the host society. In *Succession ouverte* (1962; *Heirs to the Past*, 1972), a sequel to *Le passé simple*, the narrator tries to make amends for his earlier actions, and returns briefly to Morocco for his father's funeral. Chraïbi is one of the most prolific Maghrebi writers. His output comprises short stories also, but it is the novel which seems to be his favorite medium of expression, and a platform from which he voices his views. Chraïbi's impassioned entry into Moroccan literature came as a sharp contrast to the sobriety of Sefrioui, and for a time his was the only iconoclastic voice in Moroccan literature. He was later joined by younger writers voicing virulent attacks on their society, notably Mohammed Khaïr-Eddine (1941-1995), and Abdelhak Serhane (b. 1950). Khaïr-Eddine was already known as a poet before he published his first novel *Agadir* (1967; Agadir), where the narrator, finding destruction everywhere, caused by the 1960 earthquake, is desperate to leave for France. Like Chraïbi before him, Khair-Eddine in this novel denounces the political climate and religious practices in his country. His cry of anguish and desperation becomes even stronger in subsequent novels. Serhane's first novel, *Messaouda* (1983; *Messaouda*, 1986), is a diatribe against the antiquated customs of his people which stunt the individual growth and development of children. This view is repeated in his second novel, *Les enfants des rues étroites* (1986; The Children of Narrow Streets). In *Le deuil des chiens* (1998; The Bereavement of Dogs) he introduces the character of the brutal father. The novel is narrated by a woman who, with her three sisters, is chased out of the family home by their stepmother. The sisters go their separate ways to fend for themselves. Ten years later the central character and two of her sisters reunite to tell their father what happened to them. But by then he is dead, and the sisters recount their stories, standing around his fly-infested dead body.

Abdelkebir KHATIBI's first novel, *La mémoire tatouée* (1971; The Tatooed Memory), is an autobiographical account of a decolonized person who has a conversation with Nietsche. In *Amour bilingue* (1983; *Love in Two Languages*, 1990), he focuses again on decolonization, mainly from a linguistic perspective. Tahar BEN JELLOUN published several novels, collections of short stories, poems, and scholarly works before his novel *La nuit sacrée* (1987; *Sacred Night*, 1989) won the Goncourt Prize and made his name internationally known. In this and in his earlier novel, *L'enfant de sable* (1985; *Sand Child*, 1987), Ben Jelloun concentrates on the theme of ambiguous sexual identity. The two works deal with alienated, dispossessed individuals, ill-treated by life and their own society.

One of the best-known women Francophone writers is Noufissa Sbaï (b. 1946) who in *L'enfant endormi* (1987; The Sleeping Child) describes three young women fighting for their right to be recognized as individuals in a society which still views women as dependent on men. Halima Ben Haddou (dates n.a.) in *Aïcha la rebelle* (1982; Aïcha the Rebel) makes a strong stand against colonial oppression which her country had to endure. Physically handicapped, Ben Haddou, through her central character Aïcha, voices an impassioned cry for not being able to lead a normal life. Another important writer is Leïla Houari (b. 1958). She moved to Belgium with her family where she wrote her two novels *Zeïda de nulle part* (1985; Zeïda from Nowhere) and *Quand tu verras la mer* (1988; When You See the Sea), both from the perspective of a young Moroccan woman trying to make sense of the two opposing cultures which have been imposed on her. Houari's writing is often classified under the rubric Beur literature, the name usually given to the works of children of North African immigrants in France and Belgium. A writer of Moroccan origin, whose work can be referred to as immigrant or Beur literature, is Paul Smaïl (dates n.a.). His first novel, *Vivre me tue* (1997; Living Kills Me), has been well received in France where he lives. A first-person narrative, it describes in lyrical language the problems facing a young man of Maghrebi origin who wants to be treated as a human being in his own right.

Several well-known novelists began their literary careers as poets, notably Khaïr-Eddine and Ben Jelloun. Lahbabi published several collections of poetry, notably *Les chants d'espérance* (1952; Songs of Hope) and *Misères et lumières* (1958; Wretchedness and Light). But the name that has become synonymous with Francophone poetry in Morocco is that of Abdellatif Laabi (b. 1942). Laabi began writing poetry in his early twenties, cofounding the Francophone literary journal *Souffles* (1966), and its Arabic counterpart *Anfās*, with fellow poets Khaïr-Eddine and Mostafa Nissaboury (b. 1943). A bilingual writer, Laabi has translated most of his Francophone poetry into Arabic, and translated Arabic poetry into French, including an anthology of Palestinian poetry (1970). Taking a firm stand for the freedom of the individual, and fighting for free speech landed Laabi in prison in 1972. While in prison, he published his well-known volumes of poetry, *L'arbre de fer fleurit* (1974; The Iron Tree in Bloom), *Le règne de barbarie* (1976; The Rule of Barbarity), and *Chroniques de la citadelle d'exil* (1978; Chronicles from the Citadel of Exile), the latter two volumes include poems as well as letters from prison. His volume of poetry, *Sous le bâillon* (1981; Gagged), was published after his release in 1980. But perhaps one of his most moving works is *Le chemin des ordalies* (1982; The Road of Ordeals), an account of prison life and the torture to which he was subjected.

Among the few women who have contributed to the corpus of Moroccan Francophone poetry is Rachida Madani (b. 1951) with her forceful assertion of the female self, *Femme je suis* (1981; I Am a Woman); and Selma El Melhi (b. 1949) with her two collections, *Vie trahie* (1988; A Life Betrayed) and *A l'ombre du papyrus* (1990; In the Shade of the Papyrus). Saïda Menebhi (1952-1977) was imprisoned because of her left-wing views, and died as a result of a hunger strike. She left a considerable number of poems and letters, written in prison, which were posthumously published under the title *Poèmes, lettres et écrits de prison* (1978; Poems, Letters and Writings from Prison).

One of the first Moroccan dramatists is Ahmed Belhachmi (1927), whose play *L'oreille en écharpe* (1956; The Ear in a Scarf), dealing with the problems of a mixed marriage between a Moroccan man and a French woman, was published without his permission. He reworked the play and titled it *Le rempart du sable* (1962; The Sand Rampart), before publishing it under the pseudonym Farid Faris. Several well-known novelists and poets have written plays, including Khatibi, *Le prophète dévoilée* (1979; The Veiled Prophet), about the 8th c. Hakīm ibn Hishām, known as *al-muqanna'* (the veiled); Ben Jelloun, *Entretien avec Monsieur Saïd Hammadi* (1984; Interview with Mr. Said Hammadi) and *La fiancée de l'eau* (1984; The Water Fiancée); Laabi, *Le baptême chacaliste* (1987; The Jackal's Baptism). Tayyeb Saddiki has written and produced several plays in French. Another important playwright is Nabyl Lahlou (b. 1945) whose plays are produced in the Maghreb and France.

In Other Languages

Apart from Sabbāgh, whose first book appeared in Spanish, there are several Moroccans who use Spanish as their medium of expression. With the presence of Moroccans in Italy, short stories in Italian are finding their way into anthologies. Yet works in Spanish or Italian are still too sporadic and negligible in number to constitute a distinct literary "school." The language that is gaining ground among Moroccans is Dutch. Moroccan immigration to the Netherlands began during the 1960s. There are at present more than 200,000 Dutch-domiciled Moroccans, the majority originating from Berber-speaking areas in northern Morocco. In 1989 a young woman, Zohra Zarouali (b. 1971), published an autobiographical novel, *Amel, een Marokkans meisje in Nederland* (Amel, A Moroccan Girl in the Netherlands). In this work Zarouali draws attention to the difficulties encountered by young women living in a traditional Moroccan home within a Dutch environment. This novel marks the beginning of Moroccan writing in Dutch.

Zarouali has since published two more novels, *Amel en Faisel* (1994; Amel and Faisel) and *Sanae* (1997; Sanae). The former, which is a sequel to her first novel, describes Amel's life as a married woman, while the latter, is yet another exposé of the life of Dutch-domiciled Moroccan women, as experienced by the eponymous Sanae. A novel that has received a great deal of critical acclaim is *De Weg naar het noorden* (1995; The Way to the North) by Naima El Bezaz (b. 1974). It appeared while the author was still a law student at the University of Leiden. The novel, dealing with the plight of illegal immigrants, is constructed as a journey. It charts the adventures of a young Moroccan who leaves Meknes, where El Bezaz herself was born, and travels through Spain, France, and Belgium. He eventually arrives in the Netherlands illegally where one evening, coming out of a bar, he is confronted by a jeering group of Dutch youth who taunt him with insults. In the fight that follows he is fatally wounded. Another novel that has been well received is *Hoezo bloodmooi!* (1995; It is Bloody Beautiful!) by Hans Sahar (b. 1974). Hans is a pseudonym which the author has adopted to be able to survive in the world of street crime and drug pushers that his novel so vividly evokes.

Dutch writing by Moroccans has come into its own in a relatively short time. The number of novels and collections of short stories are on the increase, with works such as Hafid Bouazza's (b. 1970) story collection entitled *De voeten van Abdullah* (1996; Abdullah's Feet) and Abdelkader Benali's (b. 1975) novel entitled *Bruilott aan zee* (1996; A Wedding by the Sea) (novel). There are also several volumes of poetry, among them *Mijn vormen* (1994; My Forms) by Mustafa Stitou (b. 1974) who is a great admirer of the cinema, as can be seen in his poems dealing with cinematic themes. As the majority of Moroccans in the Netherlands are Berber-speaking, works are now appearing in Tarifit Berber, the language spoken in the Rif region of northern Morocco. Among recently published works are Mohamed Chacha's (b. 1955) novel *Rez ttabu ad teffegh tfuct* (1997; Break the Taboo and the Sun Will Appear), and collections of poetry, notably Ahmed Essadki's (b. 1959) *Re'yad n thmuth* (1997; The Earth's Scream).

BIBLIOGRAPHY: Khatibi, A., *Écrivains marocains. Du Protectorat à 1965. Anthologie* (1974); Ben Jelloun, T., *La mémoire future, anthologie de la nouvelle poésie du Maroc* (1976); Cherif-Chergui, A., Introducción to *Literatura y pensamiento marroquíes contemporáneos* (1981): xvii-xxxvii; Gontard, M., *Violence du texte—La littérature marocaine de langue française* (1981); Farhat, A., *Aswat Thaqafiyya min al-Maghrib* (1984); Al-Awfi, N., *Muqarabat al-Waqi fi 'il-Qissa al-Qasira al-Maghribiyya* (1987); Azrawil, F., *Mafahim Naqd al-Riwaya fi 'l-Maghrib* (1989); Dahgmoumi, M., *Al-Riwaya al-Maghribiyya wa 'l-Taghayyur al-Ijtima'i* (1991); Déjeux, J., *La littérature maghrébine de language française* (1992); Gontard, M., *Le moi étrange—littérature marocaine de langue française* (1993); Al-Wazzani, H., *Dalil al-Kuttab al-Maghariba* (1993 Directory of Moroccan Writers)

—FARIDA ABU-HAIDAR

MORRIS, Mervyn

Jamaican poet, b. 1937, Kingston, Jamaica

Born in Kingston, M. attended Munroe College and went on to the then fledgling University College of the West Indies where he studied English. After winning a Rhodes Scholarship to Oxford University in 1958 M. returned to Jamaica in 1961 and began what has been a career as an academic at the University of the West Indies.

M., although not a prolific poet—having published just four slim volumes of poetry over a twenty-five-year period—remains one of the more important poets of the West Indies after Edward Kamau BRATHWAITE and Derek WALCOTT. M. distinguishes himself from these two major poets through his constant fascination with the poem as a carefully pruned moment of irony and insight, through his capacity to explore themes of everyday domesticity, and through his almost complete lack of interest in the more typical themes of postcolonial identity that have marked the work of many of his contemporaries. Before the appearance of his first collection,

The Pond, in 1973, M. had been writing poetry seriously for more than ten years, publishing a number of poems in various anthologies and journals. In these poems and in most of his poetry since M. is fascinated by the exploration of irony through verse. Exhibiting a keen eye for detail and for the ambiguities of a given moment, M.'s verse is a study in carefully-wrought poetic form. M.'s interest in politics does not gravitate towards polemics, but towards the almost detached and dispassionate eye of the observer—the observer, that is, protected by the mask of irony. Consistently, M. writes poems about masks, and, committed to the idea that the poem is a perfectly constructed mask behind which lies a wealth of ideas and riches, his verse poetry remains free of ideological simplicity even as it tackles such troubling themes as race and sexuality, as well as the problems faced by writers in the process of creating verse.

M. shows his preoccupation with the interior life in poems such as "For A Son," "The Day my Father Died," and "Little Boy Crying," which are all witty constructions that explore quite personal themes of domestic existence. But he is also interested in the activities of the artist/writer in society. Many of his poems tackle this irony-loaded concern, including one of his most effective poems, "Valley prince," which looks at the figure of a tragically insane jazz-ska musician from the 1960s as a prototype for the sometimes beleaguered and deeply isolated artist figure in West Indian society. We see also in *The Pond* an interest in the love poem. But this interest is marked by a quality of detachment that M. cultivates with care and consistency. As a result there is a certain intensely controlled and contrived quality to the love lyric that makes it wholly modern and self-reflexive. In his more political poems such as "For Consciousness" and "Afro Saxon," M. tackles the very difficult issues of political commitment and the sometimes disingenuous ways of some political types. In these poems M. reveals a political reticence about strongly held ideologies and a bitter distaste for those who demand a certain political engagement from writers and artists.

Shadowboxing, M.'s second collection, is in many ways an extension of the ideas that he developed in *The Pond*. His poems tend to be easily categorized along lines like family poems, love poems, political poems, and poems about art and the artist, and these categories hold well in this second collection, which is even more determined than the first to explore the details of contemporary Jamaican life. The most important metaphor for the collection is found in the title poem, which points to the poet's fascination with the sparring game that he is playing with himself. The poet is boxing with his shadow and producing work that amounts to the sometimes complex dialogue between the self and the imagination. *Shadowboxing* reveals that M.'s works are literally extensions of each other, and the most important development in this work is a movement towards and even tighter control of form and line. This culminates in the extremely tightly-honed style of M.'s most recent collection, *The Examination Center*—a collection that is far more mature than the earlier volumes and one in which M. is willing to make bold statements about the masking qualities inherent in the act of writing poems. In one poem in this collection, he refers to irony as a cancer, and there is a sense in which M. is constantly struggling with the inclination towards distance and irony. M.'s politically oriented poems do not figure greatly *The Examination Center*, but there is much here to suggest that M. is seeking to find the most compact way of exploding ideas into words.

Preceding *The Examination Center* was M.'s third collection of poetry, his Easter narrative *On Holy Week* (1975), which is a retelling of the story of Jesus at the moment of his crucifixion. M.'s. interest in themes like doubt and uncertainty is an important factor in the architecture and the ideological underpinnings of this collection of poems that are really a string of related narratives. In this work, M.'s interest in the metaphysical questions of faith and belonging in a largely religious setting makes him unique in the context of West Indian poetry. M. is an important poet because his distinctive style and his interest in the poem as a contained unit, rather than an expansive epic-making unit, are unique in West Indian poetry. But his importance is most significant in the work he has done with other poets, particularly those working in performance who recognize the shift in language values and the significant shift in ideological values that have taken place. Further, M.'s poems exploring themes directly related to Jamaica—ideas of race, identity, and class—remain pivotal works that show no hesitation in challenging certain preconceived norms in society. Ultimately, it is fair to say that M. adds a significantly important dimension to the range of poetic voices that have emerged from the region in the last thirty years of the 20th c.

BIBLIOGRAPHY: Panton, G., "The Tennis-Playing Poet," *Sunday Gleaner*, 25 (May 1975): 23, 31; Baugh, E., "Since 1960: Some Highlights," in King, B., ed., *West Indian Literature* (1979): 90-93; Salick, R., "Balanced in Pain: A Study of the Male/Female Relationship in the Poetry of M. M.," *JWIL*, 1 (1986): 23-32

—KWAME DAWES

MORRIS, Wright

American novelist, essayist, critic, and short-story writer, b. 6 Jan. 1910, Central City, Nebr.

M. attended public schools in Chicago and studied at Pomona College in California, but left without graduating. After extensive travel in America and Europe—a long stay in Paris was artistically influential—he settled in California. He won Guggenheim awards in photography in 1942, 1946, and 1954. A member of the National Institute of Arts and Letters and of the American Academy of Arts and Sciences, M. received the National Book Award for the novel *The Field of Vision* (1956). He has honorary degrees from Westminster College (1968) and the University of Nebraska (1968). Since 1962 he has taught English at San Francisco State University.

My Uncle Dudley (1942), M.'s first novel, blends photographic realism and frontier nostalgia with overtones of myth. A jalopy full of social misfits heading eastward is observed through the eyes of a young man whose uncle, the group's leader, personifies the triumph of frontier independence over the contemporary wasteland. *The Man Who Was There* (1945) and *The World in the Attic* (1949) reveal M.'s eye for the minutiae of place, his ear for the mundane in dialogue. In sentences both stripped and evocative M. depicts characters who summon the past against the present in moods ranging from nostalgia to existential nausea. *The Works of Love* (1951), dedicated to Sherwood ANDERSON, recounts the plight of another "grotesque," a small-town nonentity who defies puritan philistinism and bigotry. In *The Deep Sleep* (1953) M. works within the strict unities of place and time, crisscrossing them with kaleidoscopic flashbacks and multiple points of view. *The Huge*

Season (1954) multiplies camera angles and truncates episodes to reveal the futility of the Jazz Age as seen in a handful of its aging children. Here M.'s earlier themes—mother domination, the ambivalence of love, the tyranny and richness of the past—are expanded and deepened. Landscape and inanimate objects increasingly take on a conscious life of their own, assuming both a dramatic and thematic role.

In midcareer M. focused on courage as the obverse of personal failure. *The Field of Vision* captures in a sequence of vividly realized monologues the reactions to a bullfight of five unfulfilled spectators whose memories of each other are stirred by its violence. *Ceremony in Lone Tree* (1960) is the account of a family gathering in a Nebraska ghost town on the occasion of its lone inhabitant's ninetieth birthday. Over M.'s flat landscape and the prosy exchanges of the trapped characters hangs a faint air of heroism. Perhaps the sole exception to this thematic pattern is his popular success *Love among the Cannibals* (1957), a sex comedy less evocative and mythical than brutally satirical.

What a Way to Go (1962), *Cause for Wonder* (1963), and *One Day* (1965) are expanded moments in what M. calls "durable experience," T. S. ELIOT's "still point in a turning world." *In Orbit* (1967) re-creates a single day of mindless violence in the life of a sexual predator whose exploits arouse his neighbors' secret envy. Both picaresque and mythic, *Fire Sermon* (1971) dramatizes a boy's difficult choice between the values of an urban hippie couple and the aging plainsman he reveres. The struggle for release from the past continues in M.'s nineteenth novel, *The Fork River Space Project* (1977).

In 1981 M. won an American Book Award for *Plains Song: For Female Voices* (1980), a "chanted" lament for three generations of Midwestern women in their painful confrontation with a dying tradition. *Will's Boy: A Memoir* (1981) reconstructs the first thirty years of M.'s own life set against a bleak, even harsh, Midwestern heritage; it is rendered in a spare, emotionally powerful style.

M. has also produced a sizable body of essays on American society and culture, several distinguished photographic collections, and literary criticism highly revealing of his own artistic ends and means.

Despite the quantity and quality of M.'s work, his archetypal vision of the American Middle West, and his uniquely ironic "signature," the popular response to his more than twenty volumes continues to lag behind critical estimates, which place him alongside Saul BELLOW, Bernard MALAMUD, and Ralph ELLISON, leading novelists of America's "middle" generation. A chronicler of the American Dream in all its revealed absurdity and angst, M. salvages from the past a sense of the timeless, the heroic, and the real. These are the qualities he celebrates in the midst of the contemporary clichés and artifices his characters always reject before they discover the strength and freshness of ongoing life. Plainspoken Westerners, small communities on the plains, simple artifacts, and puzzled, groping, ordinary lives—M. sees in such ingredients a "functional and classic purity."

FURTHER WORKS: *The Inhabitants* (1946); *The Home Place* (1948); *Man and Boy* (1951); *A Bill of Rites, a Bill of Wrongs, a Bill of Goods* (1968); *God's Country and My People* (1968); *W. M.: A Reader* (1970); *Green Grass, Blue Sky, White House* (1970); *War Games* (1971); *Love Affair: A Venetian Journal* (1972); *Here is Einbaum* (1973); *A Life* (1973); *About Fiction* (1975); *Real Losses, Imaginary Gains* (1976); *Earthly Delights, Unearthly Adornments: American Writers as Image Makers* (1978)

BIBLIOGRAPHY: Trachtenberg, A., "The Craft of Vision," *Crit*, 4 (1961–62): 41–45; Booth, W. C., "The Shaping of Prophecy: Craft and Idea in the Novels of W. M.," *ASch*, 31 (1962): 608–26; Klein, M., *After Alienation* (1964): 196–246; Madden, D., *W. M.* (1964); Knoll, R. E., *Conversations with W. M.: Critical Views and Responses* (1977); Crump, G. B., *The Novels of W. M.: A Critical Interpretation* (1978)

—JOHN G. HANNA

MORRISON, Blake

British poet and journalist, b. 8 Oct. 1950, Burnley, Lancashire

M. was born in Lancashire but spent most of this boyhood in Yorkshire, where both his mother and father were doctors. He attended the University of Nottingham and received a Ph.D. from the University of London in 1978. M. worked for many years as a reviewer and editor on several London dailies. In the 1980s M. first established his reputation as a critic and anthologist. His critical study, *The Movement* (1980), focused on the literary school of that name, which flourished in England in the 1950s and whose central figure was Philip LARKIN. M. is thorough and fair in his consideration of this period of poetry, and his study still remains authoritative. Indeed, it is unique in considering the fiction of the 1950s in the same context as the poetry and seeing them as participating in similar stylistic modes. M.'s monograph *Seamus Heaney* (1982) was the first serious book-length study of the Irish poet, and set the tone for future commentary by focusing on HEANEY's melding of primal earthiness and postmodern self-consciousness. Heaney was the pivotal figure as well in *The Penguin Anthology of Contemporary British Poetry* (1982), which M. coedited with Andrew Motion (b. 1952), and which brought public attention to a new generation of British and Irish poets unafraid to celebrate language and no longer captive to the 1960s cult of the self.

M.'s own poetry was somewhat obscured by his prominence as critic, but in *Dark Glasses* (1984) he attempts several poems in an elliptical or metaphysical mode, seeing experience through the obscure lenses cited in the title, as well as "The Inquisitor" a long poem about spying and knowledge somewhat similar to John Hollander's (b. 1929) *Reflections on Espionage* (1976). While astute in its satire on politics and business and intriguing in its occasional obscurity, "The Inquisitor" is limited by its reliance on political headlines of two or three years before its publication. *The Ballad of the Yorkshire Ripper and Other Poems* (1987) is M.'s most successful book of poetry, deftly mixing narrative and observation. In "On Sizewell Beach" an atmospheric description of a middle-class seaside resort is joltingly interrupted by the prospective running over of a young girl by a speeding driver; the reader is genuinely glad when the death is averted at the end of the poem. Locality and anecdote provide the backbone for "Prosperina in the Oilfields," which adeptly give the feeling of a place or an event. "Night Mail" and "Superstore" effortlessly conjure the romance of daily life. The title poem continues M.'s interest in crime, this time on a far more brutal level than the white-collar crime of "The Inquisitors." The terrible deeds of the mass-murderer Peter Sutcliffe are related with a measure and cadence that metaphorically emblematizes the way the community itself comes to terms with the crimes. The poem is rendered in a Yorkshire vernacular that is occasionally opaque to non-Yorkshiremen but lends the poem's language both jocular verve and archetypal depth.

In the 1990s M. wrote largely nonfiction. *And When Did You Last See Your Father?* (1993), a memoir of M.'s youth focusing on his father, a Yorkshire general practitioner, is a charmingly told and resonant work that has the depth of a novel, though the clarity of tone achieved by M. would have been hard to achieve in fictional mode. It is a work of sharp observation and deep moral integrity; M.'s empathy with his father as he lies dying in hospital, his jaundiced though affectionate recounting of his father's many minor scams and con-schemes, and his rivalries with his father (especially over women) are all memorable. M.'s casualness of tone allows him to range wide on subject matter, from medicine to sports, as he evokes his father's ordinary yet unforgettable journey through life. By writing about his father, M. writes a kind of concealed autobiography, as well as an informal history of growing up in the north of England in the 1950s and 1960s.

M. continued in the nonfiction genre in *As If* (1997), a chronicle of the Bulger murder in Liverpool, where a two-year-old boy was killed by two ten-and-a-half year-old boys. M. comes out sharply against a punitive stance towards the defenders, arguing that to try them as adults would merely be serving our own retributive needs and the cries of a conservative Establishment for toughness and discipline. M. makes a complex, almost syllogistic argument: what outrages us about the Bulger murder is the fact that a child was killed, that an innocent soul was dragged unwillingly into the imputed general criminality of adulthood, but to try the two murderers as adults would be murdering childhood twice over, letting the idea of childhood lapse entirely by having child-murderers tried by harsh adult standards. Not that M. is insensitive to the victim of the crime, or abandons him in the service of this thesis; M.'s pages on the victim's mother are among the most searing in the book, and are rendered so vividly to make them impossible to read and digest unemotionally. Importantly, M. questions his own role as observer, and delves into his own memories in order to lucidly situated his own perspective.

As If highlights M.'s austerity, integrity, and breadth of thought, all evident in the various genres in which he has chosen to write during his career. M. is one of those astonishingly versatile literary figures, more common in Britain and the Commonwealth countries than the U.S., whose range and achievement in a variety of genres tend to mask a substantial achievement in poetry.

FURTHER WORKS: *Too True* (1998)

BIBLIOGRAPHY: Harrison, R., and P. Barry, eds., *New British Poetries: The Scope of the Possible* (1993); Kennedy, D., *New Relations: The Refashioning of British Poetry, 1980-1994* (1996)

—NICHOLAS BIRNS

MORRISON, Toni

American novelist, b. 18 Feb. 1931, Lorain, Ohio

Unlike her Southern-born parents, M. grew up in the North relatively unscarred by racial prejudice. A good student and omnivorous reader, she received degrees in English from Howard and Cornell universities. Besides a novelist, M. has been a dancer and actress, a teacher, and an editor; she has also been a member of

Toni Morrison

both the National Council on the Arts and the American Academy and Institute of Arts and Letters. M. has actively used her influence to defend the role of the artist and strongly encourage the publication of other black writers.

M.'s first novel, *The Bluest Eye* (1970), established the pattern of her later, more complex works of fiction: it is set in the black community of a small, Midwestern town, and its characters are all black. Here M. fulfills the need she felt existed for literature about the "nobody"—in this case, an ugly little girl whose imagination convinces her that her life would be happy if only she had blue eyes. Her second novel, *Sula* (1973), again has a female protagonist, whose flouting of society's mores earns her its condemnation. Both novels show a sensitivity that has become M.'s hallmark.

Song of Solomon (1977) won the National Book Critics' Circle Award for fiction and established M. as an important American writer. The book traces Milkman Dead's efforts to recover his "ancient properties", the family roots so important to M.; it also develops M.'s concern with signs of other-worldly portent, which can be seen in *Sula*. M.'s *Tar Baby* (1981) moved in a new direction: although it, too, is strongly reliant on myth, the setting has shifted to the Caribbean, and there are several important white characters. The protagonist is a new type: a highly educated young black woman whose white orientation prevents her from achieving a committed relationship with the black man she loves. Less emphasis is placed on narrative than in M.'s earlier novels, and the characters reveal themselves increasingly through their own words and actions.

M.'s best-selling novel *Beloved*, a finalist for the National Book Award and the National Book Critics' Circle Award, won the Pultizer Prize for fiction in 1988. In the following year M. was named Robert Goheen Professor in the Humanities at Princeton University. Published in 1992, M.'s inventive love story entitled *Jazz* was followed by the publication in 1998 of the ambitious and highly praised *Paradise*. Set primarily in the all-black town of Ruby, Oklahoma, founded in the aftermath of the Civil War, the novel traces the history of the imaginary utopia while exploring the tensions between the descendants of early settlers and a collective of women living in an abandoned mansion who come to represent the appearance of evil that threatens the existence of the earthly "paradise." In 1993 M. became the first African-American to be awarded the Nobel Prize for literature.

M. is at the forefront of the group of intelligent, articulate black American woman novelists who began writing after the Black Power movement of the 1960s. M. universalizes the pain and beauty of the black experience, thus making it accessible to all readers. In so doing, in little over a decade M. has made herself a powerful voice in American literature.

FURTHER WORKS: *Playing in the Dark: Whiteness and the Literary Imagination* (1992); *The Nobel Lecture in Literature, 1993* (1994); *Conversations with T. M.* (1994); *The Dancing Mind* (1996)

BIBLIOGRAPHY: Bischoff, J., "The Novels of T. M.: Studies in Thwarted Sensitivity," *SBL*, 6 (1975): 21–23; Ogunyemi, C. O., "Order and Disorder in T. M.'s *The Bluest Eye*," *Crit*, 19 (1977): 112–20; Lounsberry, B., and G. A. Hovet, "Principles of Perception in T. M.'s *Sula*," *BALF*, 13 (1979): 126–29; Atlas, M. J., "A Woman Both Shiny and Brown: Feminine Strength in T. M.'s *Song of Solomon*," *SSMLN*, 9 (1979): 8–12; Blake, S. L., "Folklore and Community in *Song of Solomon*," *MELUS*, 7 (1979): 77–82; Christian, B., "Community and Nature: The Novels of T. M.," *JEthS*, 7 (1979): 65–78; Weever, J. de, "The Inverted World of T. M.'s *The Bluest est Eye and Sula*," *CLAJ*, 22 (1979): 402–14; Otten, T., *The Crime of Innocence in the Fiction of T. M.* (1989); Harris, T., *Fiction and Folklore: The Novels of T. M.* (1993); Furman, J., *T.M.'s Fiction* (1996); Peterson, N. J., ed., *T. M.: Critical and Theoretical Approaches* (1997); Peach, L., ed., *T. M.* (1998)

—JOAN BISCHOFF

MOZAMBICAN LITERATURE

De facto racial segregation in colonial Mozambique resulted in the founding of three social clubs: the first, established in 1920, was made up almost entirely of mestizos; the second, founded in 1932, was composed of blacks; and the third, established in 1935, had a membership of native-born whites. The mestiço club, which eventually came to be known as the African Association, through *O brado africano*, its official news organ, promoted some of the first literary efforts by Africans in the form of poems and stories in Portuguese, with an occasional work in Ronga, one of the major Bantu languages of southern Mozambique. The Association of Mozambique's Native Sons, made up exclusively of so-called second-class whites, or Europeans born in the colony (beginning in the 1960s a few token blacks and mestizos were admitted as members), published *A voz de Moçambique* as its official newspaper. This newspaper and others, like *Itinerário*, became important outlets for for the literary efforts of members of the three racial communities.

The Associative Center of the Colony's Negroes published no newspaper, but it did harbor a unique component known as the Secondary School Studies Nucleus. Eduardo Mondlane (1920–1969), the American-educated economist who headed the Mozambican Liberation Front (FRELIMO) until his assassination, founded the Nucleus in the early 1960s as an intellectual training ground for many of the militants, like Samora Machel, who would lead the rebellion against colonial rule. The Nucleus also served as a meeting place for writers.

Mozambique's acculturated literature, written in Portuguese, but from an African perspective, got under way with the posthumously published *Sonetos* (1949; sonnets) of Rui de Noronha (1909–1943) and the likewise posthumous *Godido, e outros cantos* (1952; Godido, and other short stories) by João Dias (1926–1949). But in the absence of a coordinated sociocultural movement, as in Angola, and of a Creole-African ethos, present in Angola's capital city of Luanda, the literary scene in Mozambique was fragmented and unsure.

Beginning in the 1950s the subject of Mozambican literature versus literature for its own sake reached the level of often heated debate, a debate that reached its peak in the late 1960s. Euro-Mozambicans, members of a white-dominated intellectual and literary clique in the city of Lourenço Marques (now Maputo), struggled with their own provincialism while denouncing black specificity and proclaiming a cultural universality that transcended ethnic, geographical, and political boundaries. But as the tide of national liberation swept across Portugal's colonial empire, advocates of a politically committed, Mozambican literature came forward to contest art for art's sake. Ironically, from the ranks of Euro-Mozambican intellectuals emerged a few writers who did assure themselves a place in the history of Mozambican literature. Thus, Rui Knopfli (b. 1932), in his *Mangas verdes com sal* (1969; green mangoes with salt), produced "art" poems that express aspects of a black cultural reality through the codification of the tensions and ambivalences of the European born in Africa.

Some Euro-Mozambicans may have been appalled by what they saw as Noémia de Sousa's (b. 1927) stammering artlessness, but they could not help take note of her full-throated, frequently moving poetry of African revindication. But Sousa, one of sub-Saharan Africa's first female writers, never published a book of her poems, and her poetic voice became silent when, in the 1950s, she went into voluntary exile.

Meanwhile, José Craveirinha (b. 1922) was gaining attention with his vigorous poems, collected in *Chigubo* (1965; chigubo [a traditional Ronga dance]) and *Karingana ua karingana* (1974; a Ronga phrase roughly equivalent to "once upon a time"). Craveirinha's militancy, couched in the style of NEGRITUDE, earned him an honored place among Mozambican nationalists, and his poetic phrasing and sensitivity brought him the respect and admiration of Euro-Mozambicans.

Craveirinha emerged as *the* poet of Mozambique; his counterpart in fiction was Luís Bernardo Honwana (b. 1942), whose short stories, such as those in *Nós matamos a cão tinhoso* (1964; *We Killed Mangy-Dog, and Other Mozambique Stories*, 1969), are artful elaborations of colonial social realities in the rural and semirural south. Some of Honwana's stories are clearly autobiographical; all play on the contradictions inherent in the relationship between the colonized and the colonizer. Both Craveirinha and Honwana were imprisoned in the 1960s for alleged subversive activities. Their status as political prisoners further enhanced their works in the eyes of many readers; but their literary production was an isolated case in the generally depressed cultural climate of Mozambique in the decade or so before independence.

In 1963, with the outbreak of the war of independence, literary activity became even more fragmented as militant writers fled into exile, joined their guerrilla compatriots in the bush, were imprisoned as subversives, or simply became discreetly mute. Liberal, if not militant Euro-Mozambicans, who generally opposed the Portuguese dictatorship and its colonial policies, often collaborated with black and mestizo dissidents, at least on the level of civil rights. And this concern for individual freedoms and democratic institutions led some members of the European circle to take part in a kind of cultural resistance that incorporated elements of a more committed African perspective and that ultimately embraced the cause of Mozambican nationalism.

Meanwhile, a small corpus of patriotic and combative literature was being published in exile and distributed abroad and in the liberated zones of northern Mozambique. Chief among these combative writers was Marcelino dos Santos (b. 1929), who also wrote some of his pamphleteering but frequently powerful and widely anthologized poetry under the pseudonym Kalungano.

Unlike what occurred in Angola, independence in Mozambique did not bring about a flurry of literary activity. With the flight of most Euro-Mozambican intellectuals, the preindependence publishing base was all but obliterated, and the lines of literary continuity became tenuous. There were, however, isolated and often curious cases of literary activity. Orlando Mendes (1916–1990), for example, a white Mozambican and a prolific writer, published two volumes of patriotic poems, stories, and plays under the title of *País emerso* (1975, 1976; a country emerged). And in 1975, the year of Mozambican independence, a startling find was made in the form of a number of poems written by one Mutimati Bernabé João, presumably a guerrilla fighter who had died in battle. The poems, published under the title *Eu o povo* (1975; I, the people) were actually the product of António Quadros (b. 1933), a Portuguese who had come to Mozambique in 1964 and who had actively participated in the cosmopolitan cultural activities of the circle of Euro-Mozambican intellectuals. Despite what would seem to amount to a hoax, the poems stand as something of a monument to the idea that there can be such a thing as "good" political literature; and Quadros, who has never openly admitted to being the author and who, in fact, uses several different names, continues to live and work in Mozambique.

Even without a coordinated literary thrust, there was considerable literary activity in Mozambique. This activity was not limited to the major cities, and much of it took the form of grassroots organizing by the government and FRELIMO, the ruling party. Literary contests for students and workers resulted in the publication of prize-winning, albeit mainly technically weak poems and stories. Their amateurishness notwithstanding, these works contributed to the propagation of a taste for literature among a populace that was just beginning to learn to read, and they helped form a base upon which a more substantial literature could be built. And finally, in December 1980, the proclamation of the Association of Mozambican Writers set the stage for that more coordinated effort from which, Mozambicans hope, will emerge a national literature of universal appeal. If one new voice of recognizable merit has emerged since independence, it is that of Luís Patraquim (b. 1953), whose poems, collected in the small volume *Monção* (1980; monsoon), qualify him as Craveirinha's heir in terms of artistic quality.

Another heir to Craveirinha is Eduardo White (b. 1963), one of several poets who came of age after independence and who have been innovative in ways that can be described as tropicalist and sensualist. *O país de mim* (1989; the country that comes from me) exemplifies White's ability to fashion sensual love poetry around themes that evoke the land, the Indian Ocean, and nationhood.

Other rising stars among poets of the 1990s are Filomone Meigos (b. 1960), Armando Artur (b. 1962), and Nelson Saúte (b. 1967). They, like Patraquim and White, might be called transcultural poets, meaning that despite their keen sense of place and love of country they do not restrict themselves to national or regional language, images, and themes. Filomone Meigos, who spent a year at the famed Writers Workshop at the University of Iowa, published his first book of poems with the provocative, trilingual title of *Poemakalashinlove* (1995).

With respect to innovative language and new forms for new contents, several postcolonial writers of prose fiction stand out. Two who have experimented most successfully with language and new modes of storytelling are Mia Couto (b. 1955) and Ungulani Ba Ka Khosa (b. 1957). Couto, born into a Portuguese settler family, has been contemporary Mozambique's most prolific and successful novelist and short-story writer. As of 1994 he had published one novel and four books of short stories and chronicles, most of which have been translated into six languages, including English. *Vozes anoitecidas* (1986) was published as *Voices Made Night* (1990) and *Cada homen é uma raça* (1990) as *Every Man Is a Race* (1994).

Ba Ka Khosa, of Tsonga ethnicity, molds language into new hybrid forms and recreates ancient myths and legends in the phantasmagoric tales in *Ualalapi* (1987) and *Orgia dos loucos* (1990; an orgy of madmen). As might be expected, the success of Ba Ka Khosa's and Mia Couto's literary output has influenced a number of emerging fiction writers in Mozambique.

Indeed, with the end, in 1992, of the more than ten-year Mozambican civil war, literary activity not only increased, but the works produced have tended to be less circumstantial. The bloody conflict gave rise to more than a few literary works, at least two of which are especially worthy of note. In 1988 Eduardo White published *Homoine*, a collection of eight poems. The volume's title is the name of a village where an especially horrific massacre occurred. What came to be known as a "literature of calamity and emergency" also produced *Dumba nengue* (1987; *Run for Your Life!*, 1989), by Lina Magaia (b. 1946).

Peace and the turn to multi-party democracy have helped bring about a cultural climate in which veteran and emerging writers increasingly have taken an attitude of, if not exactly art for art's sake, artists need to learn their craft. This greater attention to the art of writing has resulted in studied experimentalism and new literary paradigms. With the encouragement of such veteran writers as Craveirinha and with the support of the Writers Association and other entities, including growing literary scholarship and criticism, a substantial cultural establishment has emerged in postcolonial Mozambique.

BIBLIOGRAPHY: Moser, G. M., *Essays in Portuguese African Literature* (1969), passim; Honwana, L. B., "The Role of Poetry in the Mozambican Revolution," *LAAW*, No. 8 (1971): 148–66; Hamilton, R. G., *Voices from an Empire: A History of Afro-Portuguese Literature* (1975): 163–229; Burness, D., *Fire: Six Writers from Angola, Mozambique, and Cape Verde* (1977); Hamilton, R. G., "Cultural Change and Literary Expression in Mozambique," *Issue*, 8, 1 (1978): 39–42; Burness, D., ed., *A Horse of White Clouds: Poems from Ilosphone Africa* (1989); Burness, D., ed., *Echoes of the Sunbird: An Anthology of Contemporary African Poetry* (1993); Hamilton, R. G., "Portuguese-Language Literature," *A History of Twentieth-Century African Literatures* (1993): 240-84; Hamilton, R. G., in Owomoyela, O., ed., "The Audacious Young Poets of Angola and Mozambique," *RAL*, 26, 1 (1995): 85–96

—RUSSELL G. HAMILTON

MPHAHLELE, Ezekiel (Es'kia)

South African novelist, short-story writer, and essayist (writing in English), b. 17 Dec. 1919, Pretoria

Born in the slums of Pretoria, M. lived as a child on poor farms, then, as a teenager, returned to the urban life of Marabastad, the locale of his autobiography. He obtained a certificate in 1940 to teach English and Afrikaans in Johannesburg. In 1952 he was dismissed from his post because he protested apartheid. After working as a journalist, he left South Africa in 1957 to live in Nigeria. He moved to Nairobi, Kenya, in 1963 to teach English at University College; he also journeyed to England, the U.S., and France. The first draft of M.'s novel *The Wanderers* (1971) served as his dissertation for his degree from the University of Denver. He then moved to the University of Pennsylvania, where he taught English. He left that post in 1977 to return to his native land and changed his first name from Ezekiel to its corresponding African form, Es'kia. M. now teaches at the Center for African Studies of Witwatersrand University, on its Soweto campus.

M.'s views of human life have remained remarkably consistent. Always concerned about human rights, he has tried to avoid simplistic answers to the enormous racial problems of South Africa. His autobiography, *Down Second Avenue* (1959), exemplifies his wish to see people as human beings, not as "victims of political circumstance".

M.'s autobiographical novel *The Wanderers* is a lyric cry of pain for the many rootless black exiles who wander across the African continent searching for a new home. The protagonist, Timi Tabane, is a journalist forced to flee South Africa because he exposed the activities of a slave farm to which blacks were abducted and where they were beaten and murdered. Timi becomes an exile in more ways than just physically; he feels his alienation in free Nigeria and Kenya and in his job as a high-school teacher in eastern Africa; he even becomes alienated from his wife and children. Only in the tragic death of his son, who had joined an underground movement in South Africa, does a sense of catharsis and new resolution take hold in him.

In his second novel, *Chirundu* (1980), M. portrays an ambitious, self-made politician in a fictional country resembling Zambia. Chirundu, minister of transport and public works, is determined to gain power and wealth. He ends up in jail on a charge of bigamy brought by his first wife. Chirundu's "fall", however, is regarded by him as a boon to come later in the form of support by his tribal people, since bigamy is not recognized as a crime by his tribe. M. uses the bigamy trial to explore questions of modernism and tribalism, and of individualism and communal responsibility.

M. has also published three collections of short stories. *The Living and the Dead* (1961) and *In Corner B* (1967) portray life both in the urban slums and on the estates of wealthy English and Boer families. These stories are more charged with violence and with sexual imagery than M.'s other narrative work.

M.'s first critical study, *The African Image* (1962; rev. ed., 1974), is another attempt to gain perspective on himself and on his role as writer in a land torn by the struggle for political and human rights. In this book he attempts to reconstruct the image of the African as seen by white and black writers.

M.'s study *Voices in the Whirlwind* (1972) is a series of six essays on black culture. He expands his discussion of "African" to include black American and West Indian cultures. He remains conscious of the many differences among black men, just as he had earlier remained unconvinced by NEGRITUDE. In the "whirlwind" created by the new awareness of black art and literature, M. sees education as the single most important force.

M. is also well known as an editor of many distinguished periodicals. His *African Writing Today* (1967), an anthology, is highly regarded, both for its comprehensiveness and for his illuminating introductions.

FURTHER WORKS: *Man Must Live, and Other Stories* (1947)

BIBLIOGRAPHY: Cartey, W., *Whispers from a Continent* (1969): 27–38: 110–22; Duerden, D. and C. Pieterse, eds., *African Writers Talking* (1972): 95–115; Olney, J., *Tell Me, Africa* (1973): 26–79; Barnett, U. A., *E. M.* (1976); Roscoe, A., *Uhuru's Fire: African Literature East to South* (1977): 225–34; Moore, G., *Twelve African Writers* (1980): 40–66; Tucker, M., on *Chirundu, Worldview*, June 1982: 25–26

—MARTIN TUCKER

MROŻEK, Sławomir

Polish dramatist, b. 26 June 1930, Borzęcin

In 1950, when M. was an architecture student in Cracow, he began to publish cartoons in the daily press. The volume of ministries *Słoń* (1957; *The Elephant*, 1962) won him the prestigious award of the literary review *Przegląd kulturalny* in 1957. The first collection of his plays, *Utwory sceniczne* (theatrical works) came out in 1963. These and other plays have often been performed in his native Poland and in many American and European cities. Since the early 1960s M. has lived mainly in France, and he is now a French citizen.

M. belongs to the tradition of the THEATER OF THE ABSURD, which in Poland goes back to the plays of Stanisław Ignacy WITKIEWICZ and Witold GOMBROWICZ. Unlike these two, however, M. is an intensely moral writer. His basic technique consists of reducing political programs and social theories to the dimensions of one family or one man, and demonstrating what they entail for

those individuals who have to pay the price for their implementation. His imagery partakes heavily of war, chase, and flight. His plays have few characters, often only two or three. The plays are brief. The language is simple, lively, and easy to translate, and the action proceeds swiftly to an absurdist end.

M.'s first play, *Policja* (1958; *The Police*, 1967), is a theatrical parable of a political system that manufactures fake political dissenters, whom it then proceeds to destroy for the sake of keeping the system functioning. In *Strip-tease* (1961; *Striptease*, 1972) an anonymous Hand deprives two citizens of their possessions, their clothes, and finally, their lives. In *Na pełnym morzu* (1960; *Out at Sea*, 1967) three shipwrecked individuals discuss the methods of survival at sea. At the end, the weakest of them agrees to be killed and devoured by the other two in order to assure their survival. In *Karol* (1963; *Charlie*, 1967) an old man and his grandson visit an optician to buy a pair of glasses, but instead they take away the optician's own glasses and nearly shoot him to death. In *Indyk* (1963; the turkey) and *Śmierć porucznika* (1963; death of a lieutenant) the meaning of the play emerges out of a web of ironic allusions to Polish romantic literature. *Emigranci* (1975; *Emigrés*, 1978) is a dialogue between the two refugees who room together even though they have little in common: one is a writer who has fled from his native country in search of intellectual freedom, and the other is a worker who has gone abroad with the hopes of making a fortune. In the course of their hostile verbal exchanges, they gradually discover the bondage created by interpersonal relationships. They have both fled from political oppression only to find out that there exist other limitations to man's freedom and that it is often impossible to escape them.

M.'s best-known play, *Tango* (1964; *Tango*, 1968), dramatizes the psychological situation in which bohemian and permissive parents produce in their son so strong a longing for fixed meanings that he decides to "reform" the world by force. Instead of turning to Marxist-inspired ideologies (a course of action common in the West), Artur turns to the ideologies of the national past (as has often been the case in Communist-dominated eastern Europe). He is finally defeated by the vulgar opportunist Edek, who emerges out of the turmoil as the new lawgiver to the society.

M.'s basic dramatic situation is that of the cornered man, or the man who has been manipulated by others to such a degree that he becomes their victim. Like Gogol in his attitude toward Akaky Akakievich in *The Overcoat*, M. both sympathizes with and laughs at the victims in his plays. Doubtless there is in his schlemiels a bit of the "Polish complex," the Poles often viewing themselves as victims of their stronger and more ruthless neighbors. M.'s plays can also be read as satires on totalitarian regimes, especially on their eastern European variety, or as commentaries on the theory of Alfred Adler that a desire for power is the motivating force behind all human behavior. Some plays lend themselves best to the political interpretation—*Policja, Męczeństwo Piotra Ohey's* (1959; *The Martyrdom of Peter Ohey*, 1967), *Strip-tease*—others to the psychological one—*Emigranci, Na pełnym morzu, Karol, Tango*.

FURTHER WORKS: *Opowiadania z Trzmielowej Góry: Satyry* (1953); *Półpancerze praktyczne: Satyry* (1953); *Polska w obrazach: Satyry* (1957); *Maleńkie lato: Powieść* (1959); *Wesele w Atomicach: Opowiadania* (1959); *Postępowiec: Satyry* (1960); *Ucieczka na południe: Powieść satyryczna* (1962); *Kynolog w rozterce* (1962); *Racket baby* (1962); *Deszcz* (1962; *The Ugupu Bird*, 1968); *Zabawa* (1963; *The Party*, 1967); *Czarowna noc* (1963; *Enchanted Night*,

1967); *Opowiadania* (1964); *Dom na granicy* (1967); *Testarium* (1967; *The Prophets*, 1972); *Poczwórka* (retitled *Drugie danie*; unpub. in Polish, perf. 1968; *Repeat Performance*, 1972); *Przez okulary S. M.* (1968); *Vatzlav: Sztuka w 77 odsłonach* (written c. 1969, unpub. in Polish, perf. 1978; *Vatzlav: A Play in 77 Scenes*, 1970); *Dwa listy, i inne opowiadania* (1970); *Utwory sceniczne nowe* (1975)

BIBLIOGRAPHY: Kott, J., "M.'s Family," *Encounter* (Dec. 1965): 54–58; Czerwinski, E. J., "S. M.: Jester in Search of an Absolute," *CSS*, 3 (1969): 629–45; Krynski, M. J., "*Tango and an American Campus*," *PolR*, 15 (1970): 14–16; Stankiewicz, M. G., "S. M.: Two Forms of the Absurd," *ConL*, 12 (1971): 188–203; Galassi, F. S., "The Absurdist Vision of S. M.'s *Strip-tease*," *PolR*, 17 (1972): 74–79; Kejna-Sharratt, B., "S. M. and the Polish Tradition of the Absurd," *NZSJ*, 1 (1974): 75–86

—EWA M. THOMPSON

MUDIMBE, V(alentin) Y(ves)

Congolese novelist, b. 8 Dec. 1941, Jadotville (now Likasi)

M. completed his primary and secondary education in what is now the Democratic Republic of Congo. As many French-language writers of his generation, he went to Europe to complete his higher education. One of the most prolific contemporary African writers, M. also is well versed in philosophy, anthropology, psychoanalysis, linguistics, theology, philology, and art history.

Of M.'s many poetical works, the most well known are *Déchirures* (1971; Lacerations), *Entretailles* (1973; Between Sizes), and *Les fuseaux, parfois* (1974; Spindless, Sometimes). His poetry privileges the theme of déchirure (tearing apart), is articulated within the framework of a philosophical questioning, and cannot be dissociated from the his attempts to redefine the conditions that make possible the emergence of an African personality. The relationships between the subject and the production of knowledge are crucial in his work—fiction, poetry and essays—offering new insights that highlight the specificity of African culture.

The philosophical essays, *L'autre face du royaume* (1973: The Other Side of the Kingdom) and *L'odeur du père* (1982; The Smell of the Father), are a continuation of M.'s reflection on the position of the subject and its relationship with the construction of knowledge. Among the issues raised in these essays are the legitimacy of the Occident's representations of Africa and the possibility of writing about the Other. M. elaborates on the conditions that could help develop an authentic African discourse liberated from the cultural impositions of the Occident. If M. is cautious towards the imported values colored by Western ideology, he is also critical of African cultural productions articulated within the framework of oppositional dialectics that define culture in terms of tradition and modernity. In his recent publications written in English, including the *Invention of Africa* (1988), *Parables and Fables* (1991), *The Idea of Africa* (1994), and *Tales of Faith* (1997), the author continues to devote his intellectual endeavors to enriching the scholarship about African history and civilization.

M.'s novels explore the dynamics of social science discourse about Africa. As a creative experience, novels have helped M. to embrace a wider perspective on redefining African subjectivity. In his first novel *Entre les eaux* (1973; *Between Tides*, 1991), the author traces the itinerary of a Zairian priest, Pierre Landu, during the years that followed the independence of the country. Landu decides to join a Marxist guerrilla group to fight against the injustices of both the Church and the central government. Jailed because of his criticism of the rebels, then liberated, he marries Kaayona, a woman living on the margins of society who is unable to compromise when it comes to marital issues. When Landu finds out that his wife is pregnant, he joins a Cistercian monastery and becomes "Brother Matthew Mary of the Incarnation." In *Between Tides* as in his subsequent works, M. continues to examine the ambivalent position of a figure who draws from two different cultural heritages. Pierre Landu's drama can be explained by his incapacity to bridge between his "traditional" culture and his Western education.

Unlike in his first novel, in his second work *Le bel immonde* (1976; *Before the Birth of the Moon*, 1989), M. adopts a more objective vision to deal with the problems of corruption and exploitation that have torn apart his native country. The novel revolves around the relationship between a high state official and a prostitute. Power and illusion determine the attitudes of both characters whose romantic relationship is characterized by rupture, satire and disillusionment.

In his novel entitled *L'écart* (1979; *The Rift*, 1993) M. questions the possibility of writing and establishes a break with his previous creative esthetics. This work combines two heterogeneous texts in order to oppose the genres of the novel and the journal. The double function of the "preface" is to introduce Ahmed Nara's journal writing while questioning the nature and the effectiveness of the novel as a genre. M. outlines a two dimensional failure, then: the commentator's unsuccessful attempts to write a biography of Nara, and Nara's failure to create a novel.

M.'s work is a reevaluation of NÉGRITUDE and a continuous intellectual questioning of the contradictory nature of material and ideological productions. His goal is to determine the cultural and social conditions necessary for the production of an effective critical, contradictory yet autonomous reflection on African postcolonial societies. Unlike the proponents of Négritude and their revivalist estheticism that seeks solutions to African problems in a historical past, M.'s position reflects the contradictions and ambiguities of a modern Africa in search of its fragmented identity. His creative work goes beyond the conventional Négritude philosophy, taking into consideration the diverse cultural productions that have shaped the intellectual and ideological landscape of African societies in recent years. It outlines, for example, the capacity of the Négritude movement to awaken and empower an "African consciousness" at a time when Zaire fell prey to intellectual amnesia. M. evokes the mythical dimensions of Négritude while questioning its poetical and ideological effectiveness.

Even though M. is under recognized in the literary field, his scholarship has contributed enormously to the development of African studies in Africa as well as in Europe, and in the U.S. where he is currently teaching.

BIBLIOGRAPHY: Wauthier, C., *L'Afrique des africains* (1977); Salien, F., *Mélanges d'articles critiques sur le roman africain* (1985); Mouralis, B., *V. Y. M. ou le Discours, l'Ecart et l'Ecriture* (1988)

—MOHAMMED HIRCHI

MUHAMMADIEV, Fazluddin Aminovich

Tajik short-story writer and novelist, b. 15 June 1928, Samarqand; d. 10 June 1986, Dushawa

For a while, after completing high school, M. attended the Moscow Aviation Department. Then, following his father's death, he returned to Samarqand and worked on the farm. Between 1947 and 1949 he was a contributing correspondent to *Tojikiston-i Surkh*. In 1951 he graduated from the Central Komsomol in Moscow and joined the Communist Party. From 1951 to 1960 he served in various positions in a number of journals and newspapers, including *Zanon-i Tojikiston* and *Sado-i Sharq*. In 1962 he graduated from the Institute of Literature in the Name of Gorky in Moscow and became the editor of the satiric journal, *Khorpushtak* (1962-64). From 1964 to 1981 he served in a number of high-level Tajikistan-related positions, producing documentaries. From 1981 to the end of his life, M.'s time was dedicated to creative writing.

Although he started as a simple reporter, he quickly elevated himself to the level of a credible author. His first story, "Parcha-i Ostin" (1955; The Sleeve Piece), was enthusiastically received and, thereafter, many stories dealing with social and civilizational issues appeared. These stories were eventually published as a collection entitled *Muhojiron* (1956; The Immigrants). M.'s sensitivity to the needs of the rank and file of the collectives harks back to his *Rais-i Nav* (1955; The New Boss). In *Fattoh ve Muzaffar* (n.d.; Fattah and Muzaffar) he clearly states that managers must be accountable; if inadequate, they must be dismissed.

M. understood Soviet society, especially the psychology and the ethical norms that related the workers to each other and to the bosses. He understood their positions and thought patterns and knew how they would react in a given situation. His skill in this respect reveals itself, on an international level, in his "Mo, Noriniyonim" (1977; We Are the Narynis) in which he portrays the life of the Kyrgyz writers on the occasion of the Kyrgyz/Tajik literary decade.

M. not only traveled extensively, especially to the isolated hamlets of the republic, but maintained lasting friendships with the workers at Norak, Roghun, and Berghozi. "Shira-i Zamin" (1981; The Essence of the Earth), "Oin-i Muqaddas" (1982; The Sacred Custom), and "Savolu Javobho-i Enajon Boimatova" (1986; The Questions and Answers of Ainajan Baimatova) collectively reflect M.'s assessment of the industrialization process.

Investigation of the complex inner aspects of life was M.'s goal from the beginning. "Maktub-i Dust," (1958; The Friend's Letter), "Savdo-i Umr" (1958; The Zest for Life), "Arzamas" (1960; Arzamas), and "Roh" (1962; The Road) are indicative of his sincere intent. Following Karim Hakim (1905-1942) and Pulod Tolis (1929-1961), he skillfully depicts humor that reflects problems arising from the clash between tradition and modernization. "Tir-i Khokkhurda" (1958; The Soiled Arrow), his only science fiction story, is an example.

M.'s novella, *Odamon-i Kuhna* (1963; Traditional Folks), deals with the generation gap as well as with social ills like bribery and sponging on society. When the translation of this novella appeared in *Druzhba Narodov*, the Tajik writer was ranked among the best Soviet writers of the time.

Religion, or lack of need for one, plays a prominent role in M.'s works. He regards religion as a one-sided, superficial aspect of life.

He ascribes the new and old in life to a complex set of circumstances rather than to religion, which he considers a historical stage. The religious, to him, are those in society who ignore the future for the lure of the past. M.'s characters, even though aged, are people of today. They see the present as a consequence of events leading up to it. Therefore, they can joke about sober Muslim traditions. For instance, when they reach sixty-three, the age of the Prophet Muhammad when he died, rather than reciting the Holy *Qur'an*, they listen to the news of man's conquest of space.

In his historical novella, *Zaynabbibi* (1964; Zaynabbibi), M. shows how blind obedience of religious dicta can result in unsavory consequences. He proves that religion can dull a person's creative intellect and limit his worldview. To him the greed of the *bai*-feudal system that treated women like chattel was a direct outcome of Islam. His exemplary *Dar On Dunyo* (1965; In the Other World) views the subject of the Hajj pilgrimage from a satirical perspective. In it M. argues that the Muslims' main motivation for undertaking the pilgrimage is the elevation of their social standing. Thus, after a thorough examination of the *rivoyats*, legends, and stories on which the religion of Islam is based, the narrator, Qurban Majidov, becomes more devoted to his socialist homeland and Communist ideology than ever.

In *Palata-i Kunjaki* (1974; The Corner Ward) M. deals with complex psychological and social problems such as the common ancestry of all the Soviet peoples. Similarly, in *Odamon-i Kuhna* and *Zaynabbibi* he examines the role of Tajik women in society. Zaynabbibi, for instance, is a worthless woman ignored by everyone in the feudal society; but, after the Revolution, she rises to the directorship of the executive committee of the *rayon*. The main character of *Palata-i Kunjaki*, Khiromon, displays a unique sense of understanding of the problems with which the modern Tajik woman has to cope.

Unlike many of his peers, M. was active during the years of stagnation—from the mid-1960s to the early 1980s. His "Prokrurho-i Narm Dil ve Duzdon-i Shirdil" (n. d.; Soft Prosecutors Versus Bold Thieves) is a portrayal of the inability of the government inspectors to check the excesses of individuals trusted with public property. In this respect M. was especially effective because he could draw on his talent and resources as a journalist and express the problem on both the urban and rural levels. His contributions between 1962 and 1964, when he wrote for the satirical journal *Khorpushtak*, are indicative of his talent in this area. Indeed, at that time, he brought many writers with a satirical bent to the journal and helped them focus their writings on current issues in the republic.

M.'s last two novellas, *Shoh-i Zhapon* (1981; King of Japan) and *Varta* (1983; Precipice), measure the Tajik workers' worth and place in the community as well as living conditions, thought patterns, and spiritual world. The major characters in both works recognize the significance of being responsible individuals.

A talented and progressive writer, M. influenced Tajik prose between 1960 and 1980, establishing a new and fresh direction. Among the Tajik authors, M. was in a category of his own. Although an ardent socialist, he was not a conformist. Instead, he was a vociferous critic of the truthfulness and fairness of principles and dicta. Consequently, he criticized aspects of socialism that were not true to the behest of the early leaders as harshly as he denounced Islamic dicta that were not congruent with a well-balanced life. Many Tajik writers, including Urun Kuhzod (b. 1937), Sattor Tursun (b. 1946), and Saif Rahimov (b. 1953), have benefited from M.'s untiring efforts to improve Tajik prose literature.

FURTHER WORKS: *Povesti i Rasskazi* (1976); *Osor-i Muntakhab,* (2 vols., 1978-80); *Duston* (1985); *Uglovaya Palata* (1988)

BIBLIOGRAPHY: Qodiri, A., *Adibon-i Tojikiston* (1966): 136-39; Tabarov, S., *Hayot, Adabiyyot, Realizm* (1966); Nabiyev, A., *Ijod-i Badii, Inson ve Zamon* (1983); Saifullaev, A., "M.," in *Ensaiklopidio-i Soveti-i Tojik,* (1983), Vol. 4: 623-24; Baqozoda, J., *Navisanda ve Ideal-i Zamon* (1987); Nabiyev, A., "M.," in *Ensaiklopedio-i Adabiyyot ve San'at-i Tojik* (1989), Vol. 2: 380-83

—IRAJ BASHIRI

MUIR, Edwin

Scottish poet, critic, essayist, translator, and novelist, b. 15 May 1887, Deerness, Orkney Islands; d. 3 Jan. 1959, Cambridge, England

At fourteen M. moved with his family from the Orkneys to Glasgow. His parents and two brothers soon died, and he supported himself by office work. In spite of ill health and emotional shock, he read widely, joined discussion groups, and in 1913 began writing for A. R. Orage's (1873–1934) *New Age*. After his marriage in 1919 to Willa Anderson (1890–1970), he moved to London, where he worked as assistant to Orage and wrote criticism and reviews. Not until he underwent psychoanalysis in 1920–21, after which he spent four years on the Continent, did he recover from his early trauma and begin to write poetry. At the same time, he and his wife began their long series of translations from Continental writers, which was to lead eventually, with the publication in 1930 of *The Castle*, to their introducing Franz KAFKA to English-language readers. On their return home, M. also published an increasing amount of his own work, including several volumes of poems; collections of critical essays; a study in fiction theory, *The Structure of the Novel* (1928); three novels; and the first version of his autobiography, *The Story and the Fable* (1940). His return to the Continent, as director of the British Institute in Prague from 1945 to 1948 and in Rome from 1948 to 1949, gave him material for poems included in his last two volumes, *The Labyrinth* (1949) and *One Foot in Eden* (1956), and for additions to *The Story and the Fable*, now published as *An Autobiography* (1954). His final, posthumously published work, *The Estate of Poetry* (1962), is a collection of the Charles Eliot Norton lectures he gave at Harvard in 1955–56, and his *Collected Poems* were published in 1965.

From the first, M.'s work as a poet was shaped more by his life experience and his own sensibility than by current literary trends. The verse in *First Poems* (1925), for example, was distinguished for its visionary power rather than for the wit and technical innovation so characteristic of the 1920s. Similarly, as each succeeding volume appeared, it was the increasing range and force of this vision that slowly won him recognition. For while the childhood memories and dream images of *First Poems*, with their intimations of some transcendent good, remained constants in his poetry, other, darker images entered as well. These images, derived from his Glasgow years, his stay on the Continent, and his immersion, as a translator, in European culture, all reflected, like

Kafka's, the deep and growing anxieties of the time. Like Kafka's, too, they touched the imagination of readers beginning to sense the imminence of unimaginable horror.

Yet paradoxically, because M. was now reflecting on his past to write many of his poems and to prepare his autobiography, it was in this dark period that for the first time he was able to look back on his life and see it as a whole, where right and wrong each had a place. As a result, although the symbols of fear, frustration, and betrayal that had dominated his poems from the difficult *Variations on a Time Theme* (1934) until *The Narrow Place* (1943) continued to recur in his last three volumes of verse, *The Voyage* (1946), *The Labyrinth*, and *One Foot in Eden*, a growing number of poems in each of these later books showed a new openness. The strength he drew from his marriage, a restored faith in the natural harmony he had known as a child, the persistent intuitions of his dreams, and an increasingly deep, if unorthodox, religious sense all worked to counter-balance the forces of terror and inhumanity he saw gathering in the world about him. Even after the shock of witnessing the over-throw of the democratic government in Prague in 1948, he could still write the radiantly affirmative lines that appear in *One Foot in Eden*. Here the dark, the wrong, is not diminished, but it is included and thereby undone, in poems that establish M. beyond question as one of the major figures of modern English poetry.

At the same time, M. wrote several prose works of primary importance. His autobiography, an account of the inner as well as the outer events of his life, is a masterpiece of the genre. As the story of his first years in the Orkneys, where the ordinary and the fabulous blended together seamlessly, through the destruction of that harmony in Glasgow, to the recovery of a still deeper sense of wholeness, the autobiography documents a spiritual journey from faith through loss to new faith, justified at the end by a full recognition of evil. Further, it provides the single most valuable commentary on M.'s poetry. M.'s critical writings, too, provide insight into his poetry, but they are equally significant in their own right as balanced, perceptive, and humane discussions of a wide range of literature. As the title of his best-known collection, *Essays on Literature and Society* (1949; 2nd ed., 1965) suggests, it was his particular virtue as a critic to view literature in relation to the way human beings live and the values they hold.

Seen now against the background of his time, M.'s entire work becomes continually more impressive. In everything he wrote, there is an acute awareness of the dislocations of society in this century, of the assaults of the mechanized and the impersonal on the free human spirit, and of that spirit's miraculous capacity to endure. But above all, in his poetry M. created not only the haunting images necessary to show the times their face, but also glimpses of a reconciliation made credible by his awareness of the world's wrong and his unfailing humility before the mysteries of our being.

FURTHER WORKS: *We Moderns: Enigmas and Guesses* (1918); *Latitudes* (1924); *Chorus of the Newly Dead* (1926); *Transition* (1926); *The Marionette* (1927); *John Knox: Portrait of a Calvinist* (1929); *The Three Brothers* (1931); *Six Poems* (1932); *Poor Tom* (1932); *Scottish Journey* (1935); *Social Credit and the Labour Party* (1935); *Scott and Scotland: The Predicament of the Scottish Writer* (1936); *Journeys and Places* (1937); *The Present Age* (1940); *The Scots and Their Country* (1946); *Prometheus* (1954); *Collected Poems 1921-1951* (1957); *Selected Poems* (1965); *Selected Letters* (1974); *Uncollected Scottish Criticism* (1981)

BIBLIOGRAPHY: Hall, J. C., *E. M.* (1956); Blackmur, R. P., "E. M.: 'Between the Tiger's Paws,'" *KR*, 21 (1959): 419–36; Hamburger, M., "E. M.", *Encounter* (Dec. 1960): 46–53; Butter, P. H., *E. M.* (1962); Mellown, E. W., *Bibliography of the Writings of E. M.* (1964; augmented ed., 1970, with Hoy, P.; Butter, P. H., *E. M.: Man and Poet* (1966); Muir, W., *Belonging: A Memoir* (1968); Huberman, E., *The Poetry of E. M.* (1971); Wiseman, C., *Beyond the Labyrinth: A Study of E. M.'s Poetry* (1978); Knight, R., *E. M.: An Introduction to His Work* (1980)

—ELIZABETH HUBERMAN

MUJICA, Elisa

Colombian novelist, short-story writer, biographer, essayist, and writer of children's books, b. 21 Jan. 1918, Bucaramanga; d. 21 Apr. 1984, Córdoba

M. has often written of her birthplace, Bucaramanga, although she and her family moved to Bogotá when she was eight. At age fourteen she began to work at the Ministry of Communications in order to support herself and help her family; much of her later fiction is set in claustrophobic office worlds that suffocate youth and talent. From 1936 to 1943 she worked as a private secretary and from 1943 to 1945 as a secretary at the Colombian Embassy in Quito, Ecuador. From 1952 to 1959 she lived in Madrid and assisted José Pérez de Barradas in his monumental study of the Gold Museum in Bogotá. Upon her return to Colombia in 1959, M. was appointed bank manager (the first woman to hold such a position in Colombia) of the Agrarian Bank in Sopó, and later as a library director. She was the first woman to be elected to membership in the Colombian Academy of Language in 1984, and she has received many other prizes and honors. In 1998 she was the recipient of Colombia's most prestigious award, the Cross of Boyacá.

M. wrote her first novel at the age of eleven, and she has continued to write prolifically. Her first story was published in 1947. For some thirty years, M.'s weekly book reviews and commentaries about culture and literary events appeared in major Bogotá newspapers such as *El Tiempo* and *El Espectador*. Her first published novel, *Los dos tiempos* (1949; The Two Times), analyzes the difficult life experiences of a lonely young woman who is unable to find a congenial place in the world, a woman whose intelligence, independence and commitment to left-wing political activism marginalize her from conventional society. M.'s second and best-known novel, *Catalina* (1963; Catalina), published in Spain as part of the 1962 Esso Literary Prize, has been republished (1998) and celebrated in Colombia. It tells the story of a young woman, Catalina Aguirre, born in Bucaramanga, who progresses from youthful innocence and idealism to highly developed survival skills and greater self-awareness. A third novel, *Bogotá de las nubes* (1984; Bogotá of the Clouds), also focuses on the life of a young woman, Mirza, who struggles to find some happiness in a repressive situation. All three novels are about the painfulness and limitedness of options available to ambitious young women in various strata of Colombian society. They all analyze aspects of a process of gradual increased awareness of social realities that leaves the main protagonist stripped of her illusions but freed of

inappropriate expectations, clear-eyed and independent, her own woman at last, solitary though that may be.

M.'s many short stories focus on a wider range of topics, from the effects of an atom bomb to the claustrophobia of office environments, or belief in the supernatural. M.'s first volume of collected stories, *Angela y el diablo* (1953; Angela and the Devil), includes many tales of desolation and nostalgia for past hopes, as well as the often-anthologized title story, which evokes the presence of the famous nun, Mother Castillo, whose life is the subject of a later study by M. entitled *Sor Francisco Josefa de Castillo* (1991; Sister Josefa de Castillo). M. also published two studies of Saint Teresa of Avila, *La aventura demorada: ensayo sobre Santa Teresa de Jesús* (1962; The Delayed Adventure: Essay on Saint Teresa of Jesus) and *Introducción a Santa Teresa* (1981; Introduction to Saint Teresa). A second collection of M.'s short fiction, *Arbol de ruedas* (1972; Tree of Wheels), depicts lonely people who are alienated by tediousness and pettiness in their boring, poorly remunerated office jobs, men and women who are unable to work out their relationships with others, but whose imaginations often soar, sometimes into bizarre and truly fantastic beliefs. In a number of the stories obsessions become reality, and the rational is left behind. This is true of M.'s third collection of stories as well, *La tienda de imágenes* (1987; The Image Shop), although desolation, misery, loneliness, and death pervade most of the tales. A few anecdotes based upon historical occurrences are included, which cross over into the style and subject matter of many of M.'s books for children, where she retells incidents of Colombian history and collects stories from oral tradition. *La expedición botánica contada a los niños* (1978; The Botanical Expedition Told to Children) tells the story of José Celestino Mutis's botanical discoveries.

M.'s interest in oral history, legends, folktales, and the history of neighborhoods has led to a series of popular books. In *Las altas torres del humo* (1985; The High Towers of Smoke) M. collects and discusses stories told to her by an illiterate storyteller in Boyacá, Margarita Parra. Her fascination with the colonial center of Bogotá has led to a number of collections of neighborhood legends and historical commentaries: *La Candelaria* (1974; La Candelaria), *Cuentos para niños de la Candelaria* (1993; Stories for Children of La Candelaria), and the sumptuously illustrated *Las casas que hablan: Guía histórica de la Candelaria de Santafé de Bogotá* (1994; Houses That Speak: Historical Guide to La Candelaria of Santafé de Bogotá) describes the old part of the city street by street, weaving history and anecdotes together into a vivid impression of a living city.

M. wrote novels and stories about the difficulties and injustices in women's lives long before feminism was in vogue, but it is only in recent years that her books have received substantial critical acclaim and only in 1998 that her best-known novel, *Catalina*, has been republished and distributed widely for the first time.

FURTHER WORKS: *Pequeño bestiario* (1981); *José Celestino y el dragón* (1985)

BIBLIOGRAPHY: Araújo, H., "Dos novelas de dos mujeres," *Signos y mensajes* (1976): 125-28; Ordoñez, M., "E. M.: El recuerdo de Catalina," in Laverde, M., et al., eds., *Voces insurgentes* (1986): 47-67; Ordoñez, M., "E. M. novelista: del silencio a la historia por la palabra," *RCLL*, 13, 26 (1987): 123-36; Truque, S., ed., *E. M. en sus escritos* (1988); Agosín, M., "Ausencia y presencia en *Catalina* de E. M.," *RIB*, 38, 4 (1988): 513-16; Araújo, H., "Mujeres novelistas," *La Scherezada criolla: Ensayos sobre escritura femenina y latinoamericana* (1989): 125-60; Ordoñez, M., "One Hundred Years of Unread Writing: Soledad Acosta, E. M., and Marvel Moreno," in Bassnett, S., ed., *Knives and Angels: Women Writers in Latin America* (1990): 132-44; Ordoñez, M., "E. M.," in Marting, D., ed., *Escritoras de Hispanoamerica* (1992): 362-74; Berg, M., "Las novelas de E. M.," in Jaramillo, M., et al., eds., *Escritura y diferencia: Escritoras colombianas del siglo XX* (1995): 208-28; Forero-Villegas, Y., "Un ejemplo de narrativa moderna de los años cuarenta: el discurso femenino de E. M. en su novela *Los dos tiempos*," in Jaramillo, M., et al., eds., *Literatura y diferencia: escritoras colombianas del siglo XX* (1995): 191-207; Berg, M., "Three Catalinas," in Forbes, F., et al., eds., *Reflections on the Conquest of America. Five Hundred Years After* (1996): 163-70

—MARY G. BERG

MUJICA LÁINEZ, Manuel

Argentine novelist, short-story writer, biographer, poet, and essayist, b. 11 Sept. 1910, Buenos Aires; d. 21 April 1984, Córdoba

A member of his country's cosmopolitan elite and related to noted literary figures of Argentina's past, M. L. was educated in Buenos Aires and in France. Although he attended law school, he did not complete his studies and in 1932 began what was to become a lifelong association with the leading Latin American newspaper, *La nación*, on which he served as reporter, art critic, and travel chronicler.

M. L. began publishing short poems and tales in 1927. His first book, *Glosas castellanas* (1936; Castilian variations), was an evocation of old Spain, in the spirit of the Spaniard AZORÍN. M. L.'s compatriot, the novelist Enrique Larreta (1875–1961), inspired his first full-length fictional work, the historical novel *Don Galaz de Buenos Aires* (1938; Don Galaz of Buenos Aires). M. L. considers both books, which reveal his ongoing concern with time, preparatory works. He did not establish a reputation as a writer of fiction until 1949. In the 1940s he became well known for his biographies of celebrated Argentines. He published *Canto a Buenos Aires* (1943; ode to Buenos Aires), which still sells as a gift volume; edited a number of works by 19th-c. Argentine writers; and produced the first of his "urban albums" (texts accompanied by etchings or photos).

The linked tales of *Aquí vivieron* (1949; here they lived) were followed by the collection of stories *Misteriosa Buenos Aires* (1950; mysterious Buenos Aires), both organized chronologically according to historical periods, from the 16th to 20th cs. Then four major works firmly established M. as the author of what has been called the "saga of Buenos Aires," which records, nostalgically and critically, the decadence of Argentina's wealthy and cultured elite. *Los ídolos* (1953; the idols) presents the poeticized memories of a bachelor in three related novelettes. In the novel *La casa* (1954; the mansion), M. L.'s best-known and perhaps best work, the house itself relates the downfall of one society family. Another novel, *Los viajeros* (1955; the travelers), deals with a family related to the one in *La casa*; these people perish while dreaming of a grand tour of Europe. *Invitados en El Paraíso* (1957; guests at Villa Paradise)

follows the elite to its dissolution with the introduction of bohemian elements in the wake of World War II. M. L., who during this period had become a member of the Argentine Academy of Letters, developed a technique of his own, which includes having settings of sumptuous decay, making paintings "come to life," establishing links between his plots, and using repeated motifs and an elegant Spanish devoid of regional features.

His prestige in Argentina assured, M. L. turned to topics of universal interest. *Bomarzo* (1962; *Bomarzo*, 1969), the "autobiography" of an Italian Renaissance prince, who speaks from a 20th-c. perspective and who is "reincarnated" in the person of M. L. himself, shared the Kennedy Novel Prize of 1964 with Julio CORTÁZAR's *Hopscotch. Bomarzo*'s international recognition was enhanced by the opera by Alberto Ginastera based on it. *El unicornio* (1965; the unicorn), narrated by a French fairy, evokes the time of the Crusades.

M. L. continued to depict splendor and decadence, but his ironic view of history became more and more humorous, especially in the linked novellas *Crónicas reales* (1967; royal chronicles), which relates the exploits of an imaginary European dynasty, and *De milagros y de melancolías* (1969; of miracles and melancholies), episodes in the evolution of a hypothetical Latin American city. The satire is less boisterous in the picaresque novel *El laberinto* (1974; the labyrinth), about life in Spain and colonial America under the Habsburgs, and *El viaje de los siete demonios* (1974; the tour of the seven devils), which depicts a hellish recruiting drive through time and space. M. L.'s essentially pessimistic view of humanity's sameness is attenuated by a smiling compassion and a stress on beauty. Tidbits of history and an "I was there" technique are common in these works, and well-known motifs of literature and art are consciously recycled.

After his formal retirement from *La nación* M. L. returned to Argentine settings in his creative writing. *Cecil* (1972; Cecil) is his dog's view of his master and the latter's creative process. The novels *Sergio* (1976; Sergio) and *Los cisnes* (1977; the swans) depict contemporary Argentine society with its frustrations, including sexual ones. Sexual problems also play a role in the novel *El gran teatro* (1979; the great theater), set in pre-Perón Buenos Aires. Here, real-life dramas are played out in the opera house simultaneously with the drama on the stage.

Although M. L. uses unusual topics and narrators, he is not an innovator, but rather a traditional writer. He has updated the techniques of the Spanish AMERICAN MODERNISTS of the turn of the century with a considerable dose of social satire. Like Jorge Luis BORGES, M. L. represents an Argentina that considers itself European. Thus, his work is as appealing abroad as it is in Argentina itself.

FURTHER WORKS: *Miguel Cané (Padre)* (1942); *Vida de Aniceto el Gallo* (1943); *Vida de Anastasio el Pollo* (1948); *Cincuenta sonetos a Shakespeare* (1963); *Bomarzo* [bilingual libretto] (1967); *Obras completas* (3 vols., 1978–1980); *El brazalete y otros cuentos* (1978); *Los porteños* (1979)

BIBLIOGRAPHY: Carsuzán, M., Introduction to *M. M. L.* (1962): 7–56; Ghiano, J., Introduction to M. M. L., *Cuentos de Buenos Aires* (1972): 5–62; Schanzer, G. O., "The Four Hundred Years of Myths and Melancholies of M. L.," *LALR*, 1, 2 (1973): 65–71; Font, E., *Realidad y fantasía en la narrativa de M. M. L.* (1976);

Villena, L., *Antología general e introducción a la obra de M. M. L.* (1976): 11–33; Cruz, J., *Genio y figura de M. M. L.* (1978)

—GEORGE O. SCHANZER

MUKHERJEE, Bharati

Indian novelist, short-story writer, and prose writer (writing in English), b. 27 July 1940, Calcutta

Born into a well-to-do family, M. earned her B.A. in English at the University of Calcutta (1959) and her M.A. at the University of Baroda (1961) before attending the University of Iowa Writing Workshop, where she met her husband, Canadian novelist Clark Blaise (b. 1940). After marrying, they lived in Toronto and Montreal. M. taught English at McGill University before moving to the U.S. Her first novel, *The Tiger's Daughter* (1972) satirized Indian society from the vantage point of a Vassar-educated expatriate married to an American. With irony and insight, M. records Tara's attempt to reconcile two worlds, Indian and Western, neither of which she can inhabit completely.

In her second novel, *Wife* (1975), M. details the daily life of Dimple Basu, whose training as a devoted Indian wife fails to prepare her for life in New York City. Unable to fit into the Indian community and lacking a sense of self, Dimple becomes increasingly alienated, even from her husband. Caught in a cage of an urban apartment, the protagonist bursts her bounds in a single act of violence. Although M. portrays urban America as disorienting and dehumanizing, she also condemns the Indian cultural ideal of the passive woman for whom marriage and husband worship are the only acceptable goals.

The Middleman and Other Stories (1988), which won the National Book Critics Circle Award, is a collection of hard-nosed, bitter stories of immigrants to the U.S. from the Middle East, the Caribbean, and various parts of Asia. In sometimes shocking turns of plot, M. successfully represents the difficulties of Third World peoples adjusting to a fast-paced, mercenary society, as well as Americans who respond with insults, indifference, or sometimes curiosity. Set in Canada, her earlier collection of stories, *Darkness* (1985), similarly explores hostility between various ethnic minorities and the dominant culture. M.'s intelligent vision and startling vignettes fully measure the poorly aligned "hoops" of the immigrant experience. Her acerbic analysis of postcolonial life in the West, rendered in stark language and a tough-guy tone, bars no punches.

In *Jasmine* (1989), however, M. reaches new heights of narrative incandescence, creating a chameleonlike character capable of the fluidity demanded by contemporary American society. Born Jyoti in the Punjab, she first becomes Jasmine, a devoted wife who loses her husband to Hindu-Sikh communalism. Though Jasmine is bent on coming to the U.S. to commit *sati*, a widow's voluntary suicide, her survival instinct prevails, and she instead tries on several different lives, metamorphosing next into Jazzy and then Jane. Life in the urban Indian community proves as stifling as life in rural Iowa; California and a yuppie marriage offer alternatives. M. penetrates American life with daggerlike observations that simultaneously reveal and dissect the paradoxical emptiness and

Bharati Mukherjee

energy of U.S. society. Contrasts between the coping mechanisms of Du, an adopted Vietnamese teenager, and those of the first-person narrator spell out divergent yet parallel tracks for a common journey. History and identity are linked in a more substantial way in M.'s last two novels. *The Holder of the World* (1994) transports a Puritan woman from 17th-c. Salem to the Coromandel coast of India, along with the clipper ships and trade ventures that bound the two colonies together. Reversing Jasmine's metamorphosis, Hannah is transmogrified into the beloved of an Oriental prince. In *Leave It to Me* (1997), Devi Dee, abandoned in India and adopted in the U. S., seeks out the California counterculture and her biological mother. Quick to condemn the fluid lives of 1960s offspring, M. brings a curiously Puritan sensibility to bear on her version of Southern California life, although she couches it in terms of *karma*.

M., who has also written several prose works, has a genius for social critique. Although her writing is anything but subtle, it challenges because her characters are always thinking, always commenting on the insanity of the lives they lead. Sometimes outrageous, yet endlessly interesting, M.'s creations cause the reader to brush away improbabilities and concentrate instead on the peculiarities of a society that demands cultural gymnastics for mere survival. One also comes away from her work with a new appreciation for the ingenuity necessary in those forced to leap several centuries by emigrating to the West at this moment in time.

As a bright, new voice in Indo-American fiction, M. covers some of the same territory as Salman RUSHDIE in *The Satanic Verses* (1988), but differently. Her rendition of the immigrant experience, in a spare, clean prose style, is less of a verbal tour de force—it is a tour de force of improbable plots and astonishing characters. M., too, requires of the reader a willing suspension of disbelief, though not to the extent of Rushdie's magic REALISM. Yet, her novels and short stories, read cumulatively, cause the reader to ponder thoroughly the transformations required of so many Third World citizens suddenly transported to Disneyland.

FURTHER WORKS: *Days and Nights in Calcutta* (1977, with Clark Blaise); *The Sorrow and the Terror: The Haunting Legacy of the Air India Tragedy* (1987, with Clark Blaise); *Political Culture & Leadership in India: A Study of West Bengal* (1992)

BIBLIOGRAPHY: "Oh, Calcutta," *TLS*, 29 June 1973, 736; Vaid, K. B., "Wife," *Fiction International*, 4–5 (1975): 155–57; Desai, A., "Outcasts," *LM*, 25: 9–10 (1985–1986): 143–46; Nazareth, P., "Total Vision," *CanL*, 110 (1986): 184–91; Raban, J., "The Middleman," *NYTBR*, 19 June 1988, 1, 22–23; Ward, E., "Notes from a New America," *Book World*, 3 July 1988, 3, 9; Connell, M., J. Grearson, and T. Grimes, "An Interview with B. M.," *IowaR*, 20 (1990):7-32; Wickramagamage, C., "Relocation as Positive Act: The Immigrant Experience in B. M.'s Novels," *Diaspora*, 2 (1992): 171-200; Nelson, E., ed., *B. M.: Critical Perspectives* (1993); Fakrul, A., *B. M.* (1995); Iyer, N., "American/Indian: Metaphors of the Self in B. M.'s *The Holder of the World*," *Ariel*, 27 (1996): 29-44; "B. M.: Espatriation, Americanality, and Literary Form," in Strummer, P., and C. Balme, eds., *Fusion of Cultures?* (1996): 111-18

—JANET M. POWERS

MULISCH, Harry

Dutch novelist, short-story writer, dramatist, poet, essayist, librettist, and journalist, b. 29 July 1927, Haarlem

In his early adult life M. was actively engaged in national and international political affairs, feeling especially attracted to the principles of Cuba's Fidel Castro whom he visited on at least one occasion. Later in life he withdrew from practical politics to dedicate his time entirely to literature, increasing his knowledge of philosophy and history in order to expand even further his impressive list of publications and ensuing rewards. The emphasis in successive works gradually moved from politically inspired themes to more purely philosophical ones. Throughout his oeuvre, World War II has strongly influenced his thinking and writing.

In his early novels and short stories M. primarily explored the relationship between literature and empirical reality. In *Voer voor psychologen* (1961; Food for Psychologists) the emphasis in this quest is on his personal position and involvement in novel writing. His debut novel was *Archibald Strohalm* (1952; Archibald Strohalm), in which he contrasts two visions concerning the relationship between artistic creation and reality. The narrator-protagonist, personifying the artist, comes to the conclusion that the realist, Archibald, had to fail for the artist—the redeemer—to succeed. The creation theme would, to a larger or lesser degree, remain a prominent motive in M.'s oeuvre.

A controversy relative to an aspect of M.'s work in the beginning and still persisting today, and as his fame grew in a magnified form, concerns his claim to the cosmic scope of his subject. His so-called magnum opus, *De ontdekking van de hemel* (1992; The

Discovery of Heaven, 1996), was, for this reason, nationally and internationally, alternately extolled as the most important Dutch novel of the 20th c. and condemned as a fabricated and artificially contrived work of art. In this nine-hundred-page narrative angels in heaven "create" a human being, Quinten Quint, whom they considered ideally suited to bring the tables with the ten commandments that God himself had inscribed and given to Moses back to heaven because humanity had failed in God's mission and intentions with the world. The very title and theme description reveal the potential controversy in the writer's aspirations. However, judged on the basis of popularity with the general reading public and the plausibility of the action and the presentation of the characters, M.'s partly autobiographical *De aanslag* (1982; *The Assault*, 1986) is a much more convincing book.

A secondary theme in M.'s work is Freudian identification of erotic love and death or destruction. It is most tangibly exploited in *Het stenen bruidsbed* (1959; *The Stone Bridal Bed*, 1962), one of M.'s most popular novels. The title gives expression to the two elements of the title in a cryptic, yet comprehensible way, the "stone" referring to the bombed city and death, and the "bridal bed" to new life. In M.'s view the two are inseparable, two sides of the same coin. The protagonist is a British pilot during World War II who after the war returns to Dresden, the city that he had first helped destroy. The love affair the pilot, Corinth, initiates with a German woman is his attempt to negate his earlier act as a pilot. The description of the bombardment is in the form of Homeric songs, which means that familiarity with the classics is a requirement for the full understanding of the novel. In addition to this reference, there are other intertextual allusions, notably to James JOYCE's *Ulysses*, more specifically Molly Bloom's well-known monologue. Cross-references greatly enhance the cryptic character of M.'s work. It is noteworthy that in *De aanslag* the numerous symbolical connotations do not interfere with the narrative and are not a condition for the understanding of it. *Het stenen bruidsbed* as well as *De ontdekking van de hemel* can be regarded as experiments of a philosophical nature or, in other words, examples of myth creation, a technique commonly used by writers of postmodern literature.

FURTHER WORKS: *Chantage op het leven* (1953); *De diamant* (1954); *Het mirakel* (1955); *Het zwarte licht* (1956); *De versierde mens* (1957); *Tanchelijn* (1960); *De knop* (1960); *Voer voor psychologen* (1961); *Wenken voor de Jongste Dag* (1967); *Paralipomena Orphica* (1970); *De verteller verteld* (1971); *Over de affaire Padilla* (1971); *Soep lepelen met een vork* (1972); *Oidipous Oidipous* (1972); *Woorden, woorden, woorden* (1973); *De vogels: Drie balladen* (1974); *Bezoekuur* (1974); *Mijn getijdenboek* (1975); *Kind en kraai* (1975); *Tegenlicht* (1975); *Volk en vaderliefde* (1975); *De wijn is drinkbaar dank zij het glas* (1976); *De taal is een ei* (1976); *Axel* (1977); *Verzamelde verhalen 1947–1977* (1977); *Wat poëzie is* (1978); *Paniek der onschuld* (1979); *De compositie van de wereld* (1980); *De mythische formule* (1981); *De pupil* (1987); *Oedipus als Freud: naar aanleiding van Jung* (1988)

BIBLIOGRAPHY: Mathijsen, M., *De werken van H. M.* (1952); special M. issue, *Bzzltin*, 14 (1986); special M. issue, *Propria Cures*, 1 (1987); Anbeek, T., *Geschiedenis van de Nederlandse literatuur 1885-1985* (1990); Kok, A., ed., *M. en de wetenschap: naar aanleiding van "De ontdekking van de hemel" van H. M.* (1995)

—MARTINUS A. BAKKER

MÜLLER, Heiner

German dramatist, b. 9 Jan. 1929, Eppendorf; d. 30 December 1995, Berlin

After World War II M. was employed briefly as a civil servant, and then worked as a journalist. In 1954 and 1955 he was a technical assistant in the East German Writers' Union. Thereafter he learned theater craft at the Maxim Gorki Theater in East Berlin. During the late 1950s, M. wrote three plays with his wife Inge Müller (1925–1966). They were awarded the Heinrich Mann Prize in 1959 for their joint efforts. After 1959 M. devoted himself primarily to his writing, but in 1970 he became a theatrical advisor for the Berlin Ensemble, and from then until his death he was actively involved in producing and directing stage productions of his own works and those of other dramatists. By 1987, he had become the most widely performed playwright in the German Democratic Republic. In 1984 he became a member of the East German Academy of Arts; he took office as that organization's final president in 1990. Among the awards that he received for his literary and theatrical accomplishments were the Mühlheim Drama Prize (1979), the Georg Büchner Prize (1985), the Kleist Prize (1990), and the European Theatre Prize (1991).

From the East German point of view, M. Was a problematic figure. Although recognized by his critics as an important dramatist, he remained an outsider until the early 1980s, and much of his work was suppressed until then. The theoretical direction of his plays was often sharply discouraged by the East German regime, and productions of his dramas were always more successful in the West than they had been in East Germany.

Die Korrektur (1957; the revision), a play about the troublesome contradictions caused by the political demand for complete cooperation among the classes, and *Der Lohndrücker* (1958; the wage cutter) were among the first of the East German dialectic dramas. (The dialectic movement refused to whitewash negative aspects of early socialist reconstruction, but also declined to criticize them.)

M. was strongly influenced by Bertolt BRECHT. In form, M.'s early plays are a continuation of Brecht's didactic drama and the agitprop theater of the 1920s. M., however, went further in presenting unpleasant realities of postwar East Germany than Brecht was willing to go. This fact is especially apparent in *Der Lohndrücker*, which treats material Brecht rejected as being too negative.

Der Lohndrücker examines East German reconstruction in a difficult era. The play portrays bad working conditions and a form of labor competition that generated sabotage, jealousy, and general worker unrest. The drama's "positive hero" adapts to this world but recognizes that it can be made better. He therefore works harder than the others and produces more. By thus increasing the demanded quota, he unintentionally pushes down the wages. Yet his nonideological striving is simply an attempt to better the standard of living through increased production.

Although *Der Lohndrücker* was initially praised, the dialectic theater soon lost headway because of its treatment of sensitive topics. M.'s other openly dialectic dramas were systematically suppressed. Even *Der Bau* (1965; the construction project), perhaps M.'s best early play, based on the novel *Spur der Steine* (1964; trace of the stones) by Erik Neutsch (b. 1931), was not staged until 1980.

Attempting to salvage the dialectic theater in a disguised form, M. turned to abstractions based on classical mythology. Despite the change in approach, however, his concerns remained the same. The best of the mythological dramas is *Philoktet* (1966; Philoctetes), in which M. changed the traditional Philoctetes (who was abandoned wounded by the Greeks, then coerced into fighting when it became apparent that he was needed) into a man who refused to return to the Trojan War because he has recognized the futility of militarism.

In later works, as for example *Hamletmaschine* (1977; *Hamletmachine*, 1984), M. used harsh and abrasive symbols to intensify the drama: bits and pieces of rotting corpses, Hamlet's threat to choke the palace with royal excrement by stopping up the toilet with his mother's corpse, and Ophelia's macabre striptease after she emerges from a coffin are a few examples.

In the plays that were written after *Hamletmaschine*, M. continued to offer deliberately jarring variations on his basic themes: betrayal (especially of the revolution and thereby humanity as a whole), violence, the misuse of power, and the death of the body coupled with the life of the voice. From *Der Auftrag: Erinnerung an eine Revolution* (1979; the assignment: memory of a revolution), a work that combines the general motif of betrayal with problems inherent in a projected revolt of the Third World, to *Germania 3 Gespenster am totem Mann* (1996; Germania 3 ghosts by the dead man), his plays emphasizes the bloody trail of history, focusing on everyday human experience, the struggles of life under dictatorship, and the destruction of hope, while suggesting that hope can be renewed only through the dissolution of society. The works of his final decade reflect a conscious creative synthesis of planned and accidental elements, daringness and arbitrariness in the contrasting and combining of language, perception, and dramatic imagery. The manner in which he exploits these devices ultimately made him the only truly world-class dramatist to emerge from the otherwise bleak landscape of dramatic production in the German Democratic Republic.

FURTHER WORKS: *Der Klettwitzer Bericht* (written 1959); *Herakles 5* (1966); *Das Laken* (1966); *Ödipus Tyrann* (1966); *Prometheus* (1968); *Horizonte* (1969); *Großer Wolf; Halbdeutsch* (1970); *Die Weiberkomödie* (1970); *Macbeth* (1971); *Der Horatier* (1972); *Geschichten aus der Produktion* (2 vols., 1974); *Zement* (1974; *Cement*, 1979); *Die Umsiedlerin; oder, Das Leben auf dem Lande* (1975); *Theater-Arbeit* (1975); *Traktor* (1975); *Stücke* (1975); *Mauser* (1976; *Mauser*, 1976); *Die Schlacht; Traktor; Leben Gündlings Friedrich von Preußen; Lessings Schlaf Traum Schrei* (1977); *Germania Tod in Berlin* (1977); *Mauser* (collection, 1978); *Der Auftrag: Erinnerung an eine Revolution* (1980); *Der Aufrag. Der Bau. Herakles 5. Todesanzeige* (1981); *Rotwelsch* (1982); *Gerzstück* (1983); *Germania Tod in Berlin. Der Auftrag* (1983); *Die Bauern. Macbeth. Mühlheimer Rede* (1984); *Bildbeschreibung* (1985); *Gesammelte Irrtümer* (3 vols., 1986-94); *Stücke: Texte über Deutschland* (1989); *Ein Gespräch* (1989, with Erich Fried); *Kopien* (2 vols., 1989); *Ein Gespenst verläßt Europa* (1990); *Die Lage der Nation* (1990); *Jenseits der Nation* (1991); *Gedichte* (1992); *Krieg ohne Schlacht* (1992); *Mommsens Block* (1993); *Der Lohndrücker und Die Umsiedlerin auf dem Lande* (1995); *prophezeiung—Traumwald* (1995, with Pier P. Pasolini); *Auschwitz kein Ende. Die zweite Epiphanie. Ein leichter Tod* (1995, with Gerhard Ortinau); *Philoktet. Ein Brief an Mitko Gotscheff. Traumtext* (1995); *Last Voyage. Krieg der Viren* (1996, with Mark Lammert); *Ich bin ein Landvermesser* (1996, with Alexander Kluge); *Ich schulde der Welt einen Toten* (1996, with Alexander Kluge); *Hamletmachine and Other Texts for the Stage* (1984); *Theatremachine* (1995)

BIBLIOGRAPHY: Fehervary, H., "H. M.s Brigadenstücke," *Basis*, 2 (1971): 103–40; Schivelbusch, W., "Optimistic Tragedies: The Plays of H. M.," *NGC*, 2 (1974): 103–14; Bernhardt, R., "Antikrezeption im Werk H. M.s," *WB*, 22, 3 (1976): 83–122; Bathrick, D. and A. Huyssen, "Producing Revolution: H. M.'s *Mauser* as Learning Play," *NGC*, 8 (1976): 110–21; Schlechter, J., "H. M. and Other East German Dramaturgs," *Y/T*, 8: 2–3 (1977): 152–54; Milfull, J., "'Gegenwart und Geschichte' H. M.s Weg von *Der Bau zu Zement*," *AUMLA*, 48 (1977): 234–47; Schulz, G., *H. M.* (1980); Teraoka, A. A., *The Silence of Entropy or Universal Discourse: The Postmodernistic Poetics of H. M.* (1985); Schmidt, I., and F. Vassen, *Bibliographie H. M.* (2 vols., 1993, 1995); Fischer, G., ed., *H. M.: Contexts and History* (1995); Kalb, J., *The Theatre of H. M.* (1998)

—LOWELL A. BANGERTER

MUNGOSHI, Charles

Zimbabwean novelist, poet, dramatist, translator, and short-story writer (writing in Shona and English), b. 2 Dec. 1947, Manyene

Born and reared in what was then known as Manyene Tribal Trust, M. left his rural home in 1959, when he began Standard Four at Daramombe boarding school. From there he went on to St. Augustine's Secondary School where his literary and theatrical talents were first noticed and encouraged. In 1966, his final year of school, M.'s first story was published in *African Parade* magazine. Since then, his career has revolved almost entirely around literature: first as an invoicing clerk for Textbook Sales in Salisbury (now Harare), then as an editor for the Literature Bureau and for Zimbabwe Publishing House. He also held the prestigious post of writer-in-residence at the University of Zimbabwe from 1986 to 1987. Through these posts as well as through his literary influence, M. has played an important role in fostering the talent of Zimbabwe's next generation of writers.

Having finished school at Form 4, M. has less formal education that most Zimbabwean writers of his and later generations. However, he has continued to hone his writing skills through self-education and practice. He has thus become not only the most prolific writer of his country, but, according to many of his contemporaries, also the best.

M.'s first novel, *Makunun'unu Maodzamwoyo* (Deep Considerations of a Rotting Heart), won first prize in the Literature Bureau Competition for the best Shona novel of 1969, and was published in 1970. He went on to publish a collection of short stories in English, *Coming of the Dry Season*, in 1972. One story, "The Accident," caused the book to be banned in Rhodesia (now Zimbabwe) by the oppressive Literature Bureau. When the book was reintroduced in Zimbabwe after independence, it received wide acclaim. Like the Shona novel, M.'s stories capture the clash between the older generation and the younger one, between traditional Shona culture and Zimbabwe's educated youth. He uses psychological realism to depict the breakdown of his characters, all of whom are emotionally flawed. M. has been credited, in fact, with introducing the psychological novel in Shona, with *Ndiko Kupindana Kwamazuv* (How Time Passes) in 1975.

In the same year M. published his most well-known work, the English novel *Waiting for the Rain*, winning the Rhodesian Pen

Prize in 1976. The novel develops the theme M. introduced in his short stories: the disintegration of the family. Here he uses naturalism to exploit the landscape's effect on his character's psyches, implicitly condemning Rhodesia's relocation of blacks onto barren land. With a plot that covers only two and a half days, M.'s vision slowly takes in every detail, transforming them into dense, image-filled sentences.

In 1980, the year of Zimbabwean independence, M. came forth with *Some Kinds of Wounds and Other Short Stories*. While the subject matter in these stories is not altogether different from those of his earlier collection, here M. delves much deeper into the inner thoughts of his unique characters. He goes even further in his collection of stories entitled *Walking Still* (1997). Most Zimbabwean literature in English has taken place in the past, often during colonialism or the *chimurenga*. With *Walking Still*, M. jumps to the present, tackling issues like AIDS, homosexuality, interracial relationships, and neocolonialism.

M.'s talent is not limited to fiction; he is also well known for his poetry, collected in *The Milkman Doesn't Only Deliver Milk* (1981), for his retelling of Shona folk tales in English, presented in both *Stories from a Shona Childhood* (1989) and in *One Day, Long Ago: More Stories from a Shona Childhood* (1991), which won the 1992 Noma Award. Moreover, at least in Zimbabwe, he has earned renown with his plays: *Inongova Njakenjake* (1980; Each Does His Own Thing) and the unpublished *Dog Eat Dog*.

Readers, both in and out of Zimbabwe, best know M. for his work in English; his Shona works, though prize-winning, have suffered critical neglect. However, it precisely for his decision to use both languages equally that M. proves noteworthy. In 1987 he published *Tsanga Yembeu*, the Shona translation of NGUGI WA THIONG'O's *A Grain of Wheat* (1967), bringing the work of one of Africa's most famous writers to the attention of Shona readers. Through both this translation and his own Shona novels and plays, M. has furthered the goal set out by Ngugi: African literature in African languages.

FURTHER WORKS: *Kunyarara Hakusi Kutaura?* (1983); *The Setting Sun and the Rolling World* (1989)

BIBLIOGRAPHY: Zimunya, M. B., *Those Years of Drought and Hunger* (1982): 59-93; McLoughlin, T. O., "Black Writing in English from Zimbabwe," in Killam, G. D., ed., *The Writing of East and Central Africa* (1984): 100-19; Wild, F., *Patterns of Poetry in Zimbabwe* (1988): 79-88; Veit-Wild, F., *Survey of Zimbabwean Writers: Educational and Literary Careers* (1992); Veit-Wild, F., *Teachers, Preachers, Non-Believers: A Social History of Zimbabwean Literature* (1993): 267-300

—KATRINA DALY THOMPSON

MUNĪF, ʻAbd al-Rahman

(also spelled Abdelrahman Munif) Saudi novelist, b. 1933, Jordan

M. has come to a career in creative writing relatively late in life, but during the 1970s and 1980s he published a large number of novels that are significant additions to the contemporary tradition of Arabic fiction. Born in Jordan of mixed Saudi-Jordanian parentage, he studied law in both Damascus and Cairo before going to

Yugoslavia to complete a doctorate in petroleum economics. He began a career in oil marketing and edited the Iraqi journal *Al-Naft wa-al-Tanmiya*. While in Baghdad, he became a close colleague of the great Palestinian littérateur Jabrā Ibrāhīm JABRĀ, who seems to have served as a catalyst for M.'s decision to embark upon a writing career. In this context it is interesting to note that Jabrā and M. have written a joint novel, *'Ālam bi-lā kharā' it* (1982; world without maps). After living for several years in France, M. currently resides in Damascus.

M.'s novels reflect the wide variety of his experiences. The theme of oil and politics impinges into the narrative of *Sibāq al-masāfāt al-tawīla: rihla ilā al-sharq* (1979; long-distance race: a trip to the East), set during the period of Mossaddeg's prime-ministership in Iran in the 1950s. The impact of the discovery of oil on the Gulf region of Saudi Arabia and its effect on the indigenous population provides the context for what is the most ambitious novelistic project in Arabic to date, M.'s monumental quintet, published under the general title *Mudun al-milh* (cities of salt). It includes *Al-Tīh* (1984; *Cities of Salt*, 1987), *Al-Ukhdūd* (1985; *The Trench*, 1991), *Taqāsīm al-layl wa-al-nahār* (1988; *Variations on Night and Day*, 1993), *Al-Munbatt* (1988; the hobbled), and *Bādiyat al-zulumāt* (1988; desert of gloom). The alienation of the individual within modern Arab societies is reflected in several works, including his first published novel, *Al-Ashjār wa-ghtiyāl Marzūq* (1973; the trees and Marzūq's assassination), *'Ālam bi-lā kharā' it*, and most notably *Sharq al-Mutawassit* (1977; pub. in French as *A l'est de la Méditerranée*, 1985), one of the most harrowing portraits to date of the fate of an Arab intellectual imprisoned in his homeland and pressured while studying abroad and of the measures taken by the governmental apparatus against his family members during his absences. The detailed description in *Mudun al-milh* of the impact of oil exploration on the fragile desert environment clearly reflects M.'s deep concern for the ecology of an area of the world that he personally holds very dear; the same theme is intensified in an earlier work, *Al-Nihāyāt* (1978; *Endings*, 1988), where the traditional life of a desert community and the delicate natural balance that forms the basis of its life-style and values is portrayed in a work that provides descriptive passages of climate, animals, and people of quite unique quality.

M. has contributed to the tradition of modern Arabic fiction through his choice of themes and the unique contexts in which many of his novels are placed. Beyond this lie his experiments in the area of narrative itself. Like many of his contemporaries among Arab novelists, M. has resorted to pastiches and even quotations from earlier narrative sources as a means of linking the speakers in his Arabic novels of today with the earlier tradition of Arabic narrative, but several of his novels (and most notably *Al-Nihāyāt* and the five-volume *Mudun al-milh*) also make it clear that in crafting his narratives he is intent on replicating the narrative techniques of traditional storytellers: the lengthy asides, the provision of more than one version of many events, and, above all, an apparent lack of concern with time or the relative importance of one event over another, all the more carefully crafted because of the narration's very insouciance. Readers of M. find themselves forced to follow the priorities of his narrators, which often appear at odds with those of their counterparts in much Western fiction. Therein lies not a little of the originality of this most individual voice in modern Arabic fiction.

FURTHER WORKS: *Qissat hubb mājūsiyya* (n.d.); *Hīna taraknā al-Jisr* (1976)

BIBLIOGRAPHY: Allen, R., *The Arabic Novel* (1982; rev. ed. 1994): 92–94, 121–22, 222–30; Allen, R., *Modern Arabic Literature* (1987): 224–28; Allen, R., "Incorporating the Other," *The World and I* (Feb. 1989): 378–87; Siddiq, M., "The Contemporary Arabic Novel in Perspective," *WLT*, 60, 2 (Spring 1986): 206–11; Siddiq, M., "Cities of Salt," *The World and I* (Feb. 1989): 387–92

—ROGER ALLEN

MUNK, Kaj

(born Petersen) Danish dramatist and essayist, b. 13 Jan. 1898, Maribo; d. 4 Jan. 1944, Silkeborg

M. was born on the island of Lolland. Having lost both parents at an early age, he was taken in by a small landowner, Peter Munk, and his wife and was formally adopted by them in 1916. The pietistic atmosphere of the home left a strong mark on M., influencing his decision to study theology at the University of Copenhagen, where he received a degree in 1924. He was ordained as a minister the same year and found a position as a pastor of the small community of Vedersø in western Jutland, where he remained until the time of his arrest and murder by Gestapo agents during the German occupation of Denmark.

Beginning shortly after World War I, M. wrote close to sixty plays, as well as numerous essays and sermons. To the Danish stage, then dominated by naturalism, he wanted to bring back elevated drama in the spirit of Shakespeare. Dominant features in his writing are a deep Christian faith and a fervent admiration for the strong-willed man of action. This worship of the man of power, coupled with the political chaos in the wake of the Treaty of Versailles, led to M.'s rejection of democracy as a political possibility and his advocacy of authoritarianism. But he was first and foremost a religious idealist who saw the tragedy of man symbolized in the conflict between God and man, between good and evil. With very few exceptions M.'s plays present an idealized hero who challenges the authority of God.

Although initially a failure when performed at the Royal Theater in Copenhagen, *En idealist* (1928; *Herod the King*, 1953) is one of the best of M.'s so-called dictatorship dramas. It tells of Herod, King of the Jews, who aspires to become independent of all authority. He is the greatest of M.'s heroic characters—strong, sly, and willing to play for the highest stakes, even the death of his wife Mariamne, who personifies nobility of mind, love, and compassion. After doing away with her, he has triumphed over all men. But he is unable to win over God, and the play culminates in a meeting between Herod and the Virgin Mary with the Christ child.

I brændingen (1929; in the breakers), dramatically weak but poetically alive, describes a seventy-year-old professor, modeled on the great Danish critic Georg Brandes (1842–1927), who is an idealist with negative tendencies. His contempt of his fellow human beings and his anti-Christian attitude bring about his fall. *Cant* (1931; *Cant*, 1953), a historical drama about Henry VIII of England and Anne Boleyn, was his first major success on stage. The title refers to a special type of hypocrisy: the embellishment of egotistical deeds with insincere excuses and pious phrases in order to gain a reputation for goodness. The king is presented as a ruthless despot who cleverly disguises his desires as divine commands and who becomes self-deluded in his belief in his own lies. The play, while well constructed, lacks psychological depth and shows M.'s limited understanding of the complexities of the mind.

Although Christianity and admiration for the exceptional human being are common denominators in M.'s dramas, one group of plays puts the religious issue in the fore-ground. *Ordet* (1932; *The Word,* 1953), a modern miracle play, is set among the peasants in West Jutland. It is probably the best known among M.'s works and possesses great dramatic force. Dealing with the problem of faith, it poses the question of whether God can still fill a person with such a strong belief that miracles are possible. A young woman, Inger, dies in childbirth but is brought back to life by a Christ figure, Johannes, with the help of an innocent girl. The biblical drama *De udvalgte* (1933; the chosen ones) describes the doubts, sins, and fall of King David, who is saved through his belief in God. M.'s last religious drama, *Egelykke* (1940; *Egelykke,* 1954), set in 1805–8, is about Danish romantic poet, minister, and theologian N. F. S. Grundtvig (1783–1872)—his crisis and the finding of his vocation.

During the 1930s the political unrest in the world began to undermine M.'s world view, and he reevaluated his concept of the hero. In *Sejren* (1936; the victory) and *Han sidder ved smeltediglen* (1938; *He Sits at the Melting Pot,* 1953), both political dramas, he tries to settle accounts with his position toward dictatorship. The second play is a violent protest against the Nazi persecution of the Jews; its central theme rests on the assumption that the Christian spirit can influence the lives of men. For the first time M. chooses a weak man as his hero: Professor Mensch at the beginning is willing to sacrifice everything for Germany, even the truth. At the end, he recognizes his horrendous mistake.

During the German occupation of Denmark M. showed great courage: the historical play *Niels Ebbesen* (1942; *Niels Ebbesen,* 1944) and the curtain raiser *Før Cannae* (1943; *Before Cannae,* 1953) are unequivocal attacks on the occupying power.

M. helped revitalize the Danish theater by his rejection of the shallow naturalistic drama and his attempts—very much in the romantic tradition—to replace it with a more spiritually significant drama.

FURTHER WORKS: *Rub og stub* (1922); *Vederø-Jerusalem retur* (1934); *Os bærer den himmelske glæde* (1934); *10 Oxfordsnapshots* (1936); *Knaldperler* (1936); *Liv og glade dage* (1936); *Pilatus* (1937); *Himmel og jord* (1938); *Filmen om Christiern den anden* (1938); *Dette dødsens legeme* (1938); *Fugl fønix* (1939), *Tempelvers* (1939); *Navigare necesse* (1940); *Sværg det, drenge* (1941); *Ved Babylons floder* (1941; *By the Rivers of Babylon,* 1945); *Med ordets sværd* (1942); *Det unge Nord* (1942); *Foråret så sagte kommer* (1942); *Med sol og megen glade* (1942); *Småbyens sjæl* (1943); *Danmark* (1943); *Tre prædikener* (1943); *Den skæbne ej til os* (1943); *Jesus' historier* (1943); *Apostlenes gerninger* (1943); *Den blå anemone* (1943); *Sømandsvise* (1943); *Ewalds død* (1943; *The Death of Ewald,* 1949); *8 nye digte* (1944); *Et norsk digt om Norge* (1944); *Tre tusinde kroner* (1946); *I Guds bismer* (1946); *Så fast en borg* (1946); *Sangen til vor ø* (1946); *Alverdens-Urostifterne* (1947); *Ansigter* (1947); *Landlige interiører i lollandsk bondemål* (1948); *Kardinalen og kongen* (1948); *Kærlighed* (1948); *Naturens egne drenge* (1948); *Diktatorinden* (1948); *Mindeudgave* (9 vols., 1948–1949); *Puslespil* (1949); *Det onde liv og den gode Gud* (1951); *Vers on syndefaldet* (1951); *Julevers fra Landets Kirke på Lolland* (1956). FURTHER WORKS IN ENGLISH: *K. M.: Playwright, Priest, and Patriot* (1944); *Four Sermons* (1944)

BIBLIOGRAPHY: Schmidt, R., "K. M.: A New Danish Dramatist," *ASR,* 21 (1933): 227–32; Thompson, L., "The Actuality of K. M.'s Dramas," *BA,* 15 (1941): 267–72; Thompson, L., "A Voice Death Has Not Silenced," *BA,* 18 (1944): 126–27; Bang, C. K., "K. M.'s Autobiography," *ASR,* 33 (1945): 45–50; Keigwin, R. P., Introduction to *Five Plays by K. M.* (1953; 2nd ed., 1964): 9–21; Arestad, S., "K. M. as a Dramatist (1898–1944)," *SS,* 26 (1954): 151–76; Harcourt, M., "K. M.," *Portraits of Destiny* (1969): 1–47

—MARIANNE FORSSBLAD

MUNRO, Alice

(formerly Alice Laidlaw) Canadian short-story writer (writing in English), b. 10 July 1931, Wingham, Ontario

Among the best short-story writers in English, M. has made the form her only genre, but for occasional nonfictional pieces. M. was born into a family of modest means: M.'s father bred silver foxes during the Depression while her mother, a former school teacher, attempted various means to contribute to the family's support. Educated in local schools and at the University of Western Ontario, M. married and moved to Vancouver in 1951, raising three daughters. Her first stories were published in periodicals (*Montrealer, Chatelaine, Canadian Forum, Queen's Quarterly, Tamarack Review*) and broadcast on the Canadian Broadcasting Corporation during the 1950s and 1960s. Her first short-story collection, *Dance of the Happy Shades* (1968), includes many of these stories, covering a thirteen-year compositional span. Divorced and remarried after returning to Ontario in 1972, M. lives in Clinton, near Wingham.

Although her earliest stories display a strong attraction to the romantic and gothic (revealing an acknowledged influence of American Southern writing), M.'s most characteristic early material is derived from her childhood experience of rural southwestern Ontario. Focusing sharply on its textures—sights, sounds, smells— M. creates characters whose recollections, often the first-person narrators', probe both the nature of being and, most especially, of the mysteries of human relations and connections. These are people rooted in a particular place: Huron County, Ontario. The autobiographical dimension, seen in stories such as "Boys and Girls" and "The Peace of Utrecht," in *Dance of the Happy Shades,* and in the whole of *Lives of Girls and Women* (1971), privileges M.'s own childhood generally and her relations with her parents most particularly. Throughout, M. displays an ability to make the ordinary extraordinary, showing "People's lives," in a phrase from *Lives of Girls and Women* (putatively a novel but actually interconnected short stories), to be "deep caves paved with kitchen linoleum." Thus her art works—at its most essential—through her deftly precise probing of what she has called the surfaces of life; its mysteries are found in their most profound forms during its most commonplace occasions.

Variously seen as a feminist, magic realist, or metafictionalist— the latter especially after her next volume, *Something I've Been Meaning To Tell You: Thirteen Stories* (1974)—M. disavows all labels, preferring instead to let her stories speak for themselves, and so for her. A meticulous stylist, M. works and reworks stories to the very last moment. In one instance, *Who Do You Think You Are?*

(1978; pub. in the U.S. as *The Beggar Maid*, 1979), she almost went beyond publication. She had the book, in page proofs, pulled from the presses for restructuring. These reworkings take a variety of forms but most frequently involve shifts in point of view and, particularly, in the shaping and sharpening of story endings to offer more a sense of closure rather than any conclusive insight. The variety and extent of her compositional efforts have been made evident by her papers, collected at the University of Calgary.

Although many critics saw M. revisiting the material treated in *Lives* in *Who Do You Think You Are?*, the later volume displays far greater technical skill and detachment, and, most significantly, its insights are far more qualified and, finally, ambivalent. This ambivalence has been central to M.'s subsequent collections. It is not an attitude of uncaring, or of ennui, though; rather, what M. offers in such stories as "Chaddeleys and Flemings" and "The Moons of Jupiter" in *The Moons of Jupiter* (1982) might be called an ambivalence over ever really being able to identify, know, understand, and relate the myriad details and insights that affect a person's life. These stories reveal a writer whose art is borne by the mysteries of being, and who has no expectation of gathering them together conclusively anymore, but who finds herself driven to try, and then try again, anyhow.

During the late 1970s and early 1980s, M.'s stories began to appear first in American periodicals, most regularly in *The New Yorker*. These stories have made up the bulk of M.'s last three collections. *The Moons of Jupiter, The Progress of Love* (1986), and *Friend of My Youth* (1990). In them, she has retained her concern with personal materials—as in the title stories of each collection, each of which displays M.'s longstanding concern with daughter-parent (especially-mother) relations, derived from her own experience—yet they also suggest different directions, like the psychology of a murder-suicide (and how one reacts to such an occurrence) in "Fits" (from *The Progress of Love*) or, more unusually, in the 19th-c.-recreated gothic atmosphere which is "Meneseteung" (from *Friend of My Youth*).

But the significance of M.'s most recent work lies less with its subjects than with its style, for she has taken the first-person retrospective technique seen in her first two books—largely a matter of a past event seen from the perspective of the present—and pushed it to its logical extremes. Thus the stories in the last two collections juggle various points in time—and events—seen as each impinges on a central focal point, whether an event or a particular insight. This involves breaks and shifts in the narrative, which fragment it and, as well, perpetually reminds one of the partiality of any human understanding, and of its fundamental relativity.

Three of M.'s volumes have been awarded Canada's highest literary prize, the Governor-General's Award for Fiction (1968, 1978, and 1986), she has been runner-up for the Booker Prize, and in 1990 she received the Canada Council Molson Prize for lifetime contributions to her country's cultural life. Not for every taste, M.'s stories may be said to have a certain sameness about them that strikes some as repetitious, whatever momentary understandings they offer. Even so, her ultimate significance is as a writer of dazzling ability and irreproachable integrity, a person whose stories, above all else, communicate the textures, uncertainties, and mysteries of being, of being human, and, finally (with Munrovian paradox), of just being a human being.

FURTHER WORKS: *The A. M. Papers: First Accession* (1986); *The A. M. Papers: Second Accession* (1987); *Open Secrets* (1994); *Selected Stories* (1996)

BIBLIOGRAPHY: MacKendrick, L. K., ed., *Probable Fictions: A. M.'s Narrative Acts* (1983); Miller, J., ed., *The Art of A. M.: Saying the Unsayable* (1984); Thacker, R., "A. M.: An Annotated Bibliography," in Lecker, R. and J. David, eds., *The Annotated Bibliography of Canada's Major Authors* (1984), Vol. 5: 354–414; Dahlie, H., "A. M. and Her Works," in Lecker, R., J. David, and E. Quigley, eds., *Canadian Writers and Their Works, Fiction Series* (1985), Vol. 5: 215–56; Martin, W. R., *A. M.: Paradox and Parallel* (1987); Blodgett, E. D., *A. M.* (1988); Carrington, I., de Papp, *Controlling the Uncontrollable: The Fiction of A. M.* (1989); Hoy, H., "'Rose and Janet': A. M.'s Metafiction," *CanL*, 121 (Summer 1989): 59–83; Rasporich, B. J., *Dance of the Sexes: Art and Gender in the Fiction of A. M.* (1990)

—ROBERT THACKER

MURAKAMI Haruki

Japanese novelist, short-story writer, essayist, and translator, b. 12 Jan. 1949, Kyoto

M. grew up in Ashiya, Hyogo, as an only child. Both his parents were Japanese literature teachers in high school. Out of youthful rebellion against his parents, M. decided not to read Japanese literature; instead, he began reading cheap American paperbacks easily obtainable in the port town Kobe's secondhand bookstores. In 1968 he moved to Tokyo to study theater at Waseda University. But he hardly went to school because the late 1960s in Japan saw the height of student uprisings, and many universities, including Waseda, were occupied by leftist students and were forced to close down. In 1974 M. and his wife opened a jazz bar, which they managed until 1981, when M. decided to make a living solely by his writing. In between, in 1975, he did graduate from Waseda.

Without a doubt M. is the most successful writer of *jun bungaku* (serious literature) in modern Japan. His books have sold by the millions, forcing him into the role of cultural icon of contemporary Japan. Though there are many factors that may account for his popularity, one thing seems clear—his books have spoken for a new generation. Just as a decade before, ŌE Kenzaburō and ABE Kōbō offered a new language to the generation of existentialists unsatisfied with the peculiar Japanese aesthetics of TANIZAKI Jun'ichirō and KAWABATA Yasunari, M. has offered a new language to a new generation of Japanese. Just as many of the postwar Japanese writers had begun writing out of the existentialist vacuum left by World War II, M. began writing out of the vacuum of the 1970s that was left by the collapse of the counterculture of the 1960s. A persistent sense of loss pervades his works. At the same time, his writings struggle against the ever-threatening, all-engulfing silence in which we pretend to communicate.

M. first attracted attention in 1979 when he won the Gunzō New Writer's Award with his first novel, *Kaze no uta o kike* (1979; *Hear the Wind Sing*, 1987). This work introduced to Japanese literature bold stylistic innovations inspired by the works of two contemporary American writers, Kurt VONNEGUT and Richard Brautigan (1935–1984): brief chapters, insertions of seemingly unrelated stories, deadpan humor, a hint of science fiction, and the overall light touch eluding the introverted seriousness that had pervaded modern Japanese fiction. In it he also introduced the two main characters that inhabit the trilogy consisting of this first novel and the two that followed, *Sen kyūhyaku nanajū san nen no pinbōru* (1980; *Pinball 1973*, 1988) and *Hitsuji o meguru bōken* (1982; *A Wild Sheep Chase*, 1989): "I" and a friend, or alter ego, called "Rat."

Many of M.'s works revolve around a dualism of the self as well as a dualism of the world: "I" in search of a truer self in a dual world of "reality" and the "other world." His fourth novel, *Sekai no owari to hādoboirudo wandārando* (1985; *Hard-Boiled Wonderland and The End of the World*, 1991), is no exception. This highly allegorical work has a parallel structure of two seemingly unrelated stories alternatively narrated chapter by chapter, yet eventually forming an intricately related story of two worlds: a postmodern computer society and a fairyland of death and tranquillity where "I" is separated from his "Shadow"—his "heart" and reality. This work won the Tanizaki Prize (1985).

In his next novel, *Noruwei no mori* (1987; *Norwegian Wood*, 1989), M. departed from his previous experimental styles and presented a youthful love story in a convincing realism of his own, filled with lyrical gentleness, explicit sexual scenes, and ever haunting threats of death, insanity, and suicide.

M. has also published six collections of short stories, more than a dozen nonfiction writings, often in collaboration with illustrators or photographers, as well as translations of works by F. Scott FITZGERALD, Truman CAPOTE, Raymond CARVER, John IRVING, Paul Theroux (b. 1941) and Tim O'Brien (b. 1946).

Mainly because of his immense popularity, some critics regard M.'s works as the epitome of a postmodern consumer product, strategically packaged and marketed for mass consumption. Some bemoan the perceived lack of political engagement in his works. Others find his style too "Americanized." Yet despite the predictable criticism, his works show an imaginative power able to represent the new, vital transnational culture of contemporary Japan without ever forfeiting the author's serious moral and spiritual concerns. The postmodern outlook of his work may baffle readers accustomed to the more traditional literature of modern Japan, yet his fresh treatment of such traditional themes as love, death, and self does place him at the forefront of a tradition called "modern Japanese literature" that began over a century ago.

FURTHER WORKS: *Zō kōjō no happīendo* (1983); *Kangarū biyori* (1983); *Chūgoku iki no surou Bōto* (1983); *Nami no e. nami no hanashi* (1984); *Murakami asahidō* (1984); *Hotaru naya o yaku sonota no tanpen* (1984); *Hitsuji otoko no kurisumasu* (1985); *Kaiten mokuba no deddo hīto* (1985); *Rangeruhansutō no gogo* (1986); *Panya saishūgeki* (1986); *Murakami asahidō no gyakushū* (1986); '*The Scrap'natsukashi no 1980 nendai* (1987); *Hi izuru kuni no kōjō* (1987); *Za sukkotto fittsugerarudo bukku* (1988); *Dansu dansu dansu* (1988); *Murakami asahidō haihō!* (1989); *TV p$imacr;puru* (1990); *Toi taiko* (1990); *Uten enten* (1990); *M. H. zen sakuhin 1979–1989* (8 vols., 1990–)

BIBLIOGRAPHY: Arensberg, A., on *A Wild Sheep Chase*, *NYTBR* (3 Dec. 1989): 82; Leithauser, B., "A Hook Somewhere," *New Yorker* (4 Dec. 1989): 182–87; Seigle, S. S., on *A Wild Sheep Chase*, *JASt*, 49 (1990): 161–63; Melville, J., on *A Wild Sheep Chase*, *TLS* (16 Nov. 1990): 1233

—HOSEA HIRATA

MURDOCH, Iris

English novelist and essayist, b. 15 July 1919, Dublin, Ireland

M. was born of Anglo-Irish parents but grew up in London. She earned first-class honors at Somerville College, Oxford, in 1942, served as an assistant principal in the British Treasury from 1942 to 1944, and was an administrative officer for UNRRA in Belgium and Austria from 1944 to 1946. She then returned to Oxford and in 1948 was appointed a fellow and tutor in philosophy at St. Anne's College. She is married to the novelist and critic John Oliver Bayley (b. 1925).

M.'s early publications were in philosophy. Her first work, *Sartre, Romantic Rationalist* (1953), gave evidence of literary concerns however, and it was here that she began developing her definitions of the novel. Later essays, especially "The Sublime and the Beautiful Revisited" (1960) and "Against Dryness" (1961), establish her argument that the prevalence of the current philosophies of EXISTENTIALISM and linguistic empiricism is the reason modern consciousness is dominated by either neurosis or convention. M. feels that the contemporary novel reflects these two states of mind and is usually a "small, compact, crystalline, self-contained myth about the human condition" or a "loose journalistic epic, documentary or possibly even didactic in inspiration." Further, the "crystalline" novel is solipsistic, while the "journalistic" novel lacks vitality. Both sustain fantasy at the expense of imagination. The modern novel M. argues, must rediscover reality, must deal with solipsistic man, the nature of love and freedom, and man's behavior in times of contingency, that is, under conditions where chance and accident make unexpected demands on his moral judgments.

M.'s novels are not essentially philosophical, nor are they strict codifications of her literary criteria, but they do deal with solipsistic man, contingency, and the nature of freedom and love. Often M. uses gothic elements to create a twilight-of-the gods atmosphere in which a demonic figure is intent on imposing his system while other characters project their fantasies upon him in an attempt to give meaning and structure to their lives. *The Flight from the Enchanter* (1956) depicts such a demonic figure, Mischa Fox, and his influence on an assortment of alienated characters who not only are drawn to his enchanted world but also must escape it. *The Unicorn* (1963), M.'s most obviously gothic novel, describes the entry of characters from the world of convention into a medieval world of contingency, presided over by a recluse named Hannah. She is a scapegoat, a Christ-figure, a prisoner, and perhaps a murderess—her identity is a fiction created by the characters around her. Here existential concepts of freedom undergo a severe testing. *The Time of the Angels* (1966) focuses on a time of spiritual desolation in a world bereft of moral contexts and has as its main character an atheist priest who believes that the death of God has "set the angels free."

A number of M.'s novels can be broadly classified as domestic comedy. *A Severed Head* (1961) is this type of comedy contained in myth. A Medusa figure, Honor Klein, an anthropologist, involves a conventional male in a messy life of random pairings, passion, incest, and suicide. A complicated plot and overly self-conscious characters do not prevent this work from being a witty comment on moral responsibility. *The Bell* (1958) is set in a lay religious community that has attempted to create the sort of moral order society at large lacks. Here, the richly drawn characters, in contending with the dark side of human nature, discover something of love and the limits of human goodness. Some of M.'s domestic comedies have broader contexts and are more loosely structured. *The Nice and the Good* (1968) contains a large number of questing males, lovers, scholars, refugees, demons, and mystics, and deals with scandals, suicides, blackmail, violence, and the occult. Set in both London and the country, it is one of M.'s most successful treatments of love and the recognition of "otherness." *The Sacred and Profane Love Machine* (1974), another provocative if sometimes implausible work of this type, has at its center a love triangle. Through extensive use of dreams M. again comments on the problem of reality, the need for people to create fictions about one another, and the inability of most to handle emotional reality.

The Black Prince (1973), winner of the James Tait Black Memorial Prize for fiction, is one of M.'s finest works. It is experimental, containing prefaces and postscripts. The narrator is an excessively self-conscious and sterile writer who creates art only after a passionate love awakens his dark Eros. The art he creates brings destruction but also succeeds in helping him to retreat from his work until he finally becomes a true artist—"the lover who, nothing himself, lets other things be through him."

The 1980s and 1990s have continued M.'s philosophic emphasis and her productivity, though her acknowledging her Alzheimer's disease in 1997 may mean an end to her prolific career. The first word of *Nuns and Soldiers* (1980) is "Wittgenstein," who has frequently been mentioned in critiques of M.'s work; the protaganist, dying on Christmas Eve, hosts friends who intrude possessively between lovers, a widow, and others. *The Philosopher's Pupil* (1983) offers a didactic battle between good and evil, and *The Good Apprentice* (1985) is similarly allegorical though more concerned with the protagonist's suffering. *The Message to the Planet* (1989) deals with an influential writer who has disappeared but who has to rescue a dying, impoverished poet. Though parts of the plot parallel M.'s own life, her familiar philosophic concerns, such as the possibility of genius being touched with madness, are paramount. And *Jackson's Dilemma* (1995), her 26th and possibly final novel, is a "mystic farce" combined with psychological thriller. Jackson, an archetypally indispensable butler who may be divine, is able to bring order into the complex relationships in a fashionable but chaotic home filled with upper-class twits. The novel is funny in an eccentric manner, but M. does offer a complex if convoluted set of relationships to indicate various underlying levels of significance.

M.'s books in recent decades have grown longer and more turgid, though with a correspondingly greater concern for her characters' growth and breadth. As her books have grown more philosophical, they have also sometimes seemed less interesting as fiction, with recent characters less memorable than those from the 1960s. Yet until recently she has remained a fertile, vigorous writer, meticulously detailed and with dense, unromantic perspectives on her characters' lives, who are not tragic, merely pathetic or terrible. Comedy helps the reader to see how limited they are as they are trapped by the ideas she forces upon them. At her best, she is entertaining and intellectually challenging, at her worst, she is overtly abstract and obscure.

M.'s occasionally predictable patternings and elaborate plots sometimes undercut her stated intention to free characters to be themselves. Yet her wit, imagination, and comic inventiveness, her talent for brilliant scene-making and rich characterization, combined with a compelling moral vision, make her a major figure in 20th-c. fiction.

FURTHER WORKS: *Under the Net* (1954); *The Sandcastle* (1957); *An Unofficial Rose* (1962); *The Italian Girl* (1964); *A Severed Head* (play, 1964, with J. Priestley); *The Red and the Green* (1965); *Bruno's Dream* (1969); *A Fairly Honourable Defeat* (1970); *The Sovereignty of Good* (1970); *An Accidental Man* (1971); *The Three Arrows, and The Servants and the Snow* (1973); *A Word Child* (1975); *Henry and Cato* (1976); *The Sea, the Sea* (1978); *Art and Error* (1980); *Nuns and Soldiers* (1980); *Acastos* (1986); *Above the Gods* (1987); *The Book and the Brotherhood* (1987); *Metaphysics as A Guide to Morals* (1993); *The Green Knight* (1994)

BIBLIOGRAPHY: O'Connor, W. V., *The New University Wits and the End of Modernism* (1963): 54–74; Byatt, A. S., *Degrees of Freedom: The Novels of I. M.* (1966); Wolfe, P., *The Disciplined Heart: I. M. and Her Novels* (1966); Rabinovitz, R., *I. M.* (1968); Gerstenberger, D., *I. M.* (1975); Scholes, R., *Fabulation and Metafiction* (1979): 56–74; Dipple, E., *I. M.: Work for the Spirit* (1982); Gordon, D. J., *I. M.'s Fables of Unselfing* (1995); Antonacci, M., and W. Schwelker, eds., *I. M. and the Search for Human Goodness* (1996)

—LINDSEY TUCKER

MURPHY, Richard

Irish poet, b. 6 Aug. 1927, Galway

Born into an Anglo-Irish Protestant (Ascendancy) family, M. traveled widely in his youth and early adulthood. Fascinated with the boat life in the west of Ireland, he has lived most of his life since 1959 in Cleggan and the nearby islands, including High Island, purchased by M. in 1969. During the 1970s he was a visiting poet at Colgate, Princeton, Bard College, and the University of Iowa.

M. has been called the poet of two traditions. In some of his early poems in *The Archaeology of Love* (1955) and especially in *The Woman of the House* (1959), he expresses a fondness and deep respect for the "Big House" (that is, the Ascendancy class), while accepting the decline of its traditions. *The Battle of Aughrim* (1968), a long narrative poem, represents M.'s most complex study of his Anglo-Irish Protestant background. On the other hand, M., in the poem "Sailing to an Island" (1955), describes his difficult and painful initiation into the primitive, Catholic life of the islands in the west of Ireland. That initiation became complete with the writing of "The Last Galway Hooker" (1961) and "The Cleggan Disaster" (1963), narrative poems that record M.'s acceptance for himself of the harsh experiences of fishermen and of peasants and his desire to preserve their simple traditions.

M.'s poetry has been characterized by its detached observation, its physical energy, and its classical simplicity. In *High Island* (1974), however, the poems—while capturing in content and imagery the violence of the island life, the itinerant life of Irish tinkers, and the poet's own youth in Ceylon—are more self-exploratory than his earlier work. They examine the poet's relationship to the harsh realities he has chosen as subject matter, as well as his difficulties with language and craft in expressing his conflicts and discoveries.

M. is the most important Irish poet since YEATS to write about the fading Anglo-Irish culture and the primitive life of the Irish peasant. M.'s encounter with the two traditions is less visionary than Yeats's, but his poetry creates a vivid impression of the Ascendancy pleasure ground of his youth and the primitive, harsh landscape of his maturity.

FURTHER WORKS: *Sailing to an Island* (1963); *The Battle of Aughrim, and The God Who Eats Corn* (1968); *High Island: New and Selected Poems* (1974); *Selected Poems* (1979)

BIBLIOGRAPHY: Longley, E., "Searching the Darkness: R. M., Thomas Kinsella, John Montague, and James Simmons," in Dunn, D., ed., *Two Decades of Irish Writing* (1975): 118–53; Kersnowski, F., *The Outsiders: Poets of Contemporary Ireland* (1975): 93–98; Harmon, M., ed., *R. M.: Poet of Two Traditions* (1978); Kilroy, M., "R. M.'s Connemara Locale," *Éire*, 15, 3 (1980): 127–34

—RICHARD F. PETERSON

MURRAY, Les

Australian poet and essayist, b. 1938, Nabiac

M. lived a secluded life as child, inspired by the land and animals in the farming district of Bunyah, New South Wales, where his parents labored on his grandfather's farm. At the age of twelve his mother died after suffering a miscarriage; his father was unable to cope with the loss, and M. was left to fend for himself.

As early as 1954 M. considered becoming an artist, and in 1957 after an unsuccessful attempt to enlist in the air force, he went to the University of Sydney. There he was surrounded by philosophers, activists, writers, and poets such as Geoffrey Lehmann (b. 1940), who in particular would become important to M.'s poetic growth. M.'s rural upbringing as well as his Gaelic ancestry soon became major thematic concerns of his poetry and prose; in addition, after marrying a Roman Catholic in 1962 and being baptized in that faith in 1964, his earlier Calvinist antimaterialism and austerity fused with Catholic precepts.

In 1965 M. and Lehmann produced a collection of poems, *The Ilex Tree*, which won the Grace Leven Prize for poetry. Influenced by Lehmann to use his rural background as a subject of his poetry, M. wrote *The Weatherboard Cathedral*, published in 1969, in which emerges his ideology that the Australian identity is best portrayed by the bush rather than the urban landscape. *Poems Against Economics* (1972) turns toward political concerns, advancing M.'s hope for the Australian Commonwealth Party, of which he was directly involved. While the party was unable to achieve success, M. was gaining literary recognition as a poet and essayist, and editor of *Poetry Australia*. In 1975 M. purchased a portion of his family's land in Bunyah although he did not yet relocate there.

M.'s poetic sensibility traces back to the 1890s, a time of nationalism and optimism, when Australia was beginning to see itself as a country with a distinct geography and culture. In 1976 *The Vernacular Republic* became M.'s first collected works to be published, a magnificent assemblage of poems that draws the character of the landscape and its people. M.'s attendance upon a "vernacular republic" and its rendering of Australian culture put him at odds with the modernist movement of the 1960s and 1970s, which M. believed to be more akin to a European and American

tradition, and the conflict that ensued between M. and the modernists would occupy a prominent place in his essay writing.

In *The Peasant Mandarin* (1978) M. extends his literary and political ideology as an incisive critic of books and writers; his controversial essays and reviews espouse his convictions that cultural loyalty is invested in both a distinct dialect and environment and that these factors embody the true Australian spirit. In lieu of this belief, he maligns modernism and feminism as misguided tenets. In "The Australian Republic" he avers that the colonial education system does not represent the people, because it administers an imperialist view. In the chapter "The Lore of High Places" M. pays homage to the large variety of Aboriginal languages and the use of indigenous dialect that is akin to the geography of the land, taking on mythical proportion. In the verse novel *The Boys who Stole the Funeral* (1980)—which also won the Grace Leven Prize—M. borrows Aboriginal material for his own writing, which tells the story of a Caucasian youth who flees the city to find deeper fulfillment and values in bush life. *Persistence in Folly* (1984), M.'s second collection of prose articles, proceeds with the subjects examined in *The Peasant Mandarin*, particularly his desire for Australia to become a republic. In the essay "The Human-Hair Thread" M. explores the sources of his own works, particularly his wielding of Aboriginal culture and art, and the Jindyworobak movement, the poetic tradition of which he followed, blending Aboriginal and European features in their poetry.

In 1986 M. relocated to his country home in Bunyah. In *Blocks and Tackles* (1989)—essays and articles from 1982 to 1990—M. uses his literary shrewdness to probe the internal devices of poetry as seen in "Poems and Poesies" and "Poemes and the Mystery of Embodiment." *Dog Fox Field* (1990) and *Translations from the Natural World* (1992) recover the provincial heritage of language and poetry that was once found in newspaper verse and "singsong" rhyme. *The Paperbark Tree* (1992) comprises an assortment of prose writing from *The Peasant Mandarin*, *Persistence in Folly*, *Blocks and Tackles*, and *The Australian Year* (1985).

M. has won numerous awards for his poetry and prose and has been recognized in Australia and abroad as a poet in great mastery of language, rhythm, and idiom. Poetry for M. became a location in which a metaphorical landscape restores the self to a history that is both collective and personal. Like W. B. YEATS, who M. greatly admired, M. conjures magical images of the land and its people and keeps steady their history. However, his prescriptions tend to idealize a singular way of life thereby excluding the concerns of those in the changing map of Australia.

BIBLIOGRAPHY: Bourke, L., *A Vivid Steady State: L. M. and Australian Poetry* (1992)

—LISA TOLHURST

MUSCHG, Adolf

Swiss novelist, dramatist, and essayist (writing in German), b. 13 May 1934, Zurich

M. is one of the best-known contemporary Swiss-German authors. After studying German and English at the University of Zurich, he received his doctorate in 1959. He taught secondary school in Zurich until 1962, and then served as a guest lecturer at several Swiss and foreign universities. In 1970 he became a professor of German literature at the Federal Technical University in Zurich. He has won several awards, including the Swiss Schiller Foundation Prize (1965), the Conrad Ferdinand Mayer Prize (1968), and the Hermann Hesse Prize (1974). He now lives in Kilchberg.

M. began his literary career in the mid-1960s, and his first novel, *Im sommer des hasen* (1965; in the summer of the hare), was an immediate success. Six men are given the task of spending half a year in Japan to record their impressions, but in the course of the novel we can learn more about the Swiss mentality than about Japanese culture. Years later M. reintroduced the theme of examining Switzerland from afar (a device very popular with contemporary Swiss authors) in *Baiyun oder die freundschaftsgesellschaft* (1960; Baiyun or the friendship society). The death of the head of a Swiss delegation to China causes the other members of the group to comment at length on their own culture and proclivities.

It soon became clear that M. was to have as his central theme the nature of Switzerland and the problems of the middle class, from which he came. He examines this nexus from a critical, committed standpoint in a finely tuned and exactly polished language. Sometimes his language becomes too complicated, however, and this detracts from the thematic concerns of his works. This was the case with his next two novels, *Gegenzauber* (1967; counter magic), which deals with the futile attempts to prevent an old building from being demolished, and *Mitgespielt* (1969; playing along), where a teacher and his pupils become involved in a murder.

M. is particularly interested in the role of the intellectual and the artist in contemporary life. In the novel *Albissers grund* (1974; Albisser's reason) he explores why a high-school teacher becomes involved in the student protests of the late 1960s and why the teacher shoots his psychiatrist, the only person who is trying to help him understand his new relationship to politics. In *Das licht und der schlüssel* (1984; The Light and the Key, 1988) a vampire and expert on fine paintings, Constantin Samstag, discusses the positive effects of art. Several of the stories in *Der turmhahn* (1987; the tower rooster), on the other hand, demonstrate how life can be destroyed by art. In all these works M. indirectly examines his own position in society as a writer who is concerned with social issues. He investigates the historical dimensions of this same problem in his play *Die aufgeregten von goethe* (1971; the excited ones by Goethe), which portrays the famous German writer's reaction to the French Revolution, and in his biography *Gottfried Keller* (1977; Gottfried Keller), which describes in great detail the life and times of the well-known 19th-c. Swiss author. Finally, in his essay *Literatur als therapie?* (1981; literature as therapy?) he states that art, in the form of literature, is necessary for him as an intellectual to come to terms with the problems in life.

M. has also inspected the parameters of Swiss society in several collections of short stories: *Fremdkörper* (1968; foreign bodies), *Liebesge-schichten* (1972; love stories), *Der blaue mann* (1974; Blue Man & Other Stories, 1983), *Entfernte bekannte* (1976; distant acquaintances), and *Leib und leben* (1982; body and life). Many scholars claim that he is at his linguistic best in these shorter formats. In general the stories deal with the Swiss malaise of alienation from society, which is often metaphorically expressed as sickness and disease (another common feature of contemporary Swiss-German letters). The many characters feel powerless to act or express themselves in an environment that inhibits personal growth, and they are thus forced to resign themselves to the status quo.

M.'s honest explorations of his own metier and his open confrontation with the social ills of Switzerland (and paradigmatically of the whole industrialized world) have earned him fame far beyond the Swiss borders.

FURTHER WORKS: *Rumpelstilz* (1968); *Das kerbelgericht* (1969); *Papierwände: aufsätze über japan* (1970); *High fidelity oder ein silberblick* (1973); *Kellers abend* (1975); *Von herwegh bis kaiseraugst: wie halten wir es als demokraten mit unserer freiheit?* (1975); *Besuch in der schweiz* (1978); *Noch ein wunsch* (1979); *Besprechungen 1961–1979* (1980); *Die tücke des verbesserten objekts* (1981); *Übersee* (1982); *Ausgewählte erzählungen 1962–1982* (1983); *Unterlassene anwesenheit* (1984); *Empörung durch landschaften: vernönftigue drohreden* (1985); *Goethe als emigrant: auf der suche nach dem grüunen bei einem alten dichter* (1986); *Dreizehn briefe mijnheers* (1986); *Deshima: filmbuch* (1987); *Die schweiz am ende, am ende die schweiz: erinnerungen an mein land vor 1991* (1990)

BIBLIOGRAPHY: Waidson, H., "The Near and the Far: The Writings of A. M.," *GL&L*, 28 (July 1975): 426–37; Ricker-Abderhalden, J., ed., *Über A. M.* (1979); Voris, R., *A. M.* (1984); Ricker-Abderhalden, J., "An Interview with A. M.," *StTCL*, 8, 2 (Spring 1984): 233–48; Ossar, M., "Das Unbehagen in der Kultur: Switzerland and China in A. M.'s *Baiyun*," in Acker, R., and Burkhard, M., eds., *Blick auf die Schweiz* (1987): 113–30

—ROBERT ACKER

MUSIL, Robert

Austrian novelist, dramatist, and essayist, b. 6 Nov. 1880, Klagenfurt; d. 15 April 1942, Geneva, Switzerland

The son of a professor of engineering and a high-strung, sensuous mother, M. was early given to experiences of isolation and withdrawal. Sent to military school at the age of eleven, he graduated as a second lieutenant but quickly rejected the army for the study of engineering at the Technical University in Brno, where his father taught. Only then did he become acquainted with the German literature of his day, with the French SYMBOLISTS, with Nietzsche, and with Emerson. M. graduated as an engineer in 1901 and, after spending a year as an assistant at the Technical University in Stuttgart, turned to the study of philosophy and experimental psychology at the University of Berlin, at the same time pursuing his interest in literature, especially in the German romantics.

M.'s personal life remained difficult. He was financially dependent on his parents, who objected to M.'s liaison with a working-class girl. Only his marriage in 1911 to a Jewish painter brought him a measure of happiness.

M. completed his studies with his dissertation on the physicist and philosopher Ernst Mach (1838–1916), *Beitrag zur Beurteilung der Lehren Machs* (1908; rpt. with additions, 1980; a contribution toward a critical judgment of Mach's philosophy). Unwilling to become a university lecturer (he turned down an assistantship at the University of Graz) and unable to make a living by his pen, M. accepted a position as a librarian at the Technical University in Vienna (1911–14). From February to August 1914 he was an editor of *Die neue Rundschau* in Berlin. He was called up at the outbreak of World War I and served as an officer on the Italian front. Discharged because of illness, M. served as an editor of a military newspaper. He returned to civilian life and to Vienna at the end of the war and was for some years a civil servant in the ministries of foreign affairs and defense, while at the same time writing.

For a short while M. experienced a modest degree of prosperity. After 1924 he turned entirely to writing, becoming dependent on advances from his publisher and later on occasional help from a circle of friends. In 1938 he emigrated to Switzerland. During his last years he lived in poverty and died virtually forgotten.

M.'s work represents a lifelong preoccupation with the ethical human being in whose character rigidity, disproportion, and polarities have been overcome for the sake of genuine wholeness and integration. His first novel, *Die Verwirrungen des Zöglings Törleß* (1906; *Young Törless*, 1955), has as its setting a military school, like the one M. himself attended. While the foreground is filled with the brutalities and humiliations endemic to the milieu, the real theme of the novel is the development of a teenager who for the first time encounters his unconscious and his creative energies. At first he fails to understand his intense emotions, but in his painful process of self-discovery he comes to terms with the conflict between reason and logic on the one hand and his emotional and imaginative faculties on the other, gaining insight into a possible fusion of these two aspects of his psyche. The immediate success of this first novel was due not only to M.'s bold treatment of the subject but even more so to his insight into human motivation, his rich symbolism, and his succinct style.

The search for new, integrated identities is also the theme of the slim volume *Vereinigungen* (1911; unions)—comprising the two stories "Die Vollendung der Liebe" ("The Perfecting of a Love," 1966) and "Die Versuchung der stillen Veronika" ("The Temptation of Quiet Veronika," 1966)—some seventy pages on which M. had worked to the point of exhaustion for two and a half years. Being totally concerned with the portrayal of the feelings and thoughts of his heroines, M., in a radical experiment, did away with plot and perspective, rendering their inner lives through a succession of metaphors arranged with the greatest of precision. He thus paired ambiguity and icy rationality into a new whole. Even though M. considered *Vereinigungen* one of his best works, because of its hermetic quality it did not meet with popular success.

The failure of *Vereinigungen* caused M. to turn to a more objective genre. In a series of essays that appeared in liberal periodicals he dealt with problems in art, aesthetics, politics, and ethics posed by the complexities of modern civilization. Apart from the interruptions of the war, M. continued to write on questions of the day well into the mid-1920s.

With his return to civilian life and to creative writing at the end of the war, M. singled out the theater as the most rigid cultural institution. Hence his plays were to ventilate the stage and make it more receptive to new ideas. Both *Die Schwärmer* (1921; the enthusiasts) and *Vinzenz und die Freundin bedeutender Männer* (1923; Vinzenz and the girlfriend of important men), the first a serious drama, the second a comedy, contrast the inauthenticity of bourgeois life, as it is evidenced in the institution of marriage and in the professions, with a new kind of man, an isolated individual, indifferent to all conventions, dependent only on his inner motivation, and because of his freedom able to love others, even if only for a short period. While the strident tone and the intensity especially of *Die Schwärmer* again made the public reject the plays, they are

an important milestone in M.'s work. For the first time he introduced irony and satire into his portrayal of the bourgeoisie.

As if trying to show that he could also write in a more traditional manner, M. produced a collection of stories published under the title *Drei Frauen* (1925; three women), consisting of "Grigia" ("Grigia," 1966), "Die Portugiesin" ("The Lady from Portugal," 1966), and "Tonka" ("Tonka," 1966), in which he reverts to a more conservative form. Drawing on his own experiences during the war, among them a constant awareness of death and an intense longing for a distant love, M. created three male protagonists who are all isolated and inactive outside their familiar environment. Each of these heroes achieves a heightened state of understanding through the mediation of a woman.

The first volume of the novel *Der Mann ohne Eigenschaften* (1930–43; partial tr., *The Man without Qualities*, 1953) was immediately hailed as a great and unusual work. The publication of a second volume coincided with the coming of the Third Reich (1933). M.'s widow published the finished chapters of the third part, found among M.'s papers, in 1943. Against the pattern of the modern world, the regularity of statistics, of science, and of technology, the hero of the novel, Ulrich, experiences his ego only as a point of intersections of impersonal functions. Having lost all ambition, he cannot take his qualities, of which he has many and very good ones, seriously; they belong more to each other than they belong to him. Like his creator M., Ulrich has been in turn a soldier, an engineer, and a mathematician. His skeptical attitude, the result of his scientific training, make him critical of all culture. His citizenship in "Kakanien" (M.'s name for the old Austro-Hungarian monarchy), whose contradicting cultures and multiple nationalities mirror the disintegration of the 20th c., is another aspect of his floating kind of life.

Ulrich's search for a more authentic and meaningful life is the theme of the novel. His conversations with a group of Austrian politicians and intellectuals gathered together for the so-called *Parallelaktion*, a patriotic undertaking ostensibly planned to celebrate the sixtieth anniversary of the ascension to the throne of the aging emperor Franz Josef, to occur in 1918, are an attempt to give new meaning to the crumbling culture of the 19th and by implication also of the 20th c. Although the discussants are divided between those who rule and want to maintain the status quo and those who rebel and want to destroy it, both parties suffer from a lack of ideas aggravated by the emptiness of their personal lives and by their susceptibility to "great" and aggressive solutions.

A corollary to Ulrich's weak and fragmented sense of identity, however, is expressed in his sense of "possibility"—that is, his notion that imagination is as significant as reality, his conscious utopianism—which arises precisely from his intellectual freedom and mobility. It causes him to contemplate life as a laboratory, to consider fusing polarities for the sake of a life that is fulfilling both intellectually and emotionally. He is more open than his partners in the patriotic action to memories of a state of love and of union with the world and with others. Thus, his suggestion at the end of Volume I for an inventory of the historical evidence for such a state (a task that would be undertaken with the precision of science)—to be done by the "general secretariat of precision and soul"—would represent an attempted reordering of society.

The rejection of Ulrich's suggestion by his friends suggests that the chances for such a reform do not exist. Ulrich's fulfillment thus depends on his meeting his sister Agathe, whose existence M. has kept secret in Volume I. It is the encounter with the human being that is most like him and yet not like him, the near-twin of the opposite sex, that causes Ulrich to reconcile his fragmented ego. In his closeness to Agathe, Ulrich's dominant intellect and his suppressed feeling unite, and from his tendencies toward activity and amorality he turns toward inactivity and rest. The second part of the novel is made up of Ulrich's and Agathe's conversations regarding a new morality. Together they search for a state in which the individual is enhanced, in which his ego rises and does not fall until they both experience the "other state," in which the borders and limits between human beings slowly diminish. The question of how Ulrich's and Agathe's relationship would end has never been adequately resolved, since M. never finished the novel.

The style of *Der Mann ohne Eigenschaften* represents the highest achievement of M. as a writer. It is forever open, rejecting all firm norms, all systems. In an infinite range of possibilities it forever balances opposites, hovering between subjectivity and truth, between imagination and reality, between logic and the affective emotion, between unequivocality and the metaphor. What M. calls irony is the stylistic rendering of the profound relationship that exists between opposites. It is expressed in every chapter, page, and line, indeed in every figure of speech and in every metaphor.

M.'s work, in the intensity of his fusion of imagination and precision, is a profound attempt in modern literature to create a new man, to move mankind toward new life forms, to regain a lost potential for the sake of a richer and more rewarding life.

FURTHER WORKS: *Rede zur Rilke-Feier* (1927); *Nachlaß zu Lebzeiten* (1927); *Über die Dummheit* (1937); *Briefe nach Prag* (1971); *Tagebücher* (1976); *Gesammelte Werke* (1978); *Briefe 1901–1942* (1981). FURTHER WORKS IN ENGLISH: *Five Women* (1966)

BIBLIOGRAPHY: Dinklage, K., ed., *R. M., Leben, Werk, Wirkung* (1960); Arntzen, H., *Satirischer Stil: Zur Satire R. M.s im "Mann ohne Eigenschaften,"* (1960); Pike, B., *R. M.: An Introduction to His Work* (1961); Kaiser, E. and E. Wilkins, *R. M.: Eine Einführung in das Werk* (1962); Dinklage, K., ed., *R. M.: Studien zu seinem Werk* (1970); Roth, M.-L., *R. M.: Ethik und Aesthetik: Zum Theoretischen Werk des Dichters* (1972); Reniers-Servranckx, A., *R. M.: Konstanz und Entwicklung von Themen, Motiven und Strukturen in den Dichtungen* (1972); Appignanesi, L., *Femininity and the Creative Imagination: A Study of Henry James, R. M., and Marcel Proust* (1973); Williams, C. E., *The Broken Eagle: The Politics of Austrian Literature from Empire to Anschluss* (1974): 148–86; Peters, F. G., *R. M.: Master of the Hovering Life* (1978); Luft, D. S., *R. M. and the Crisis of European Culture 1880–1942* (1980); Arntzen, H., *Kommentar sämtlicher zu Lebzeiten erschienener Schriften ausser dem Roman "Der Mann ohne Eigenschaften"* (1980)

—WILHELM BRAUN

When an author promises to furnish a positive construction with his work, he exposes himself to an examination not only of his poetic but also of his intellectual capacity. M. once suggested that the following words be added to the graduation certificate with which he wanted to leave German literature: "Behavior unusual, talent tender, even though inclining to excesses." But the critics noticed one day that

his novel [*The Man without Qualities*] was the greatest experiment in the philosophy of history and the most relentless criticism of *Weltanschauung* since Voltaire's *Candide*. Thus some justice has been done to M.; because he wanted much more than to write a novel, more than to tell the story of the decline of Kakanien and more than to offer criticism regarding the obsolete ideas of his time.

But he did not want—and that is what he is reproached for sometimes—to go beyond his competence. He was always conscious of the fact that the poet cannot and should not penetrate into a philosophical system.

He did not go for the "whole," but gave models and prototypes, partial solutions, not *the* solution. He did not want to communicate only about reality, but also include possibility. Or as his hero Ulrich once expressed himself, "to take in the open horizon, from where life is fitted to the spirit."

Ingeborg Bachmann, "Ins tausendjährige Reich," *Akzente*, No. 1 (1954), pp. 50–51

In a world in which facts are so preponderant, in the aridity of feelings that follows from that, the appeal to the emotions is a very understandable resistance-reflex. When everything overflows with energy, when economics is more important than the human being, the workbench more important than the worker who stands at it, then one longs for a soul that like moist winds blows from the sea into the dryness. If one, however, wants to speak of a task, it can only consist of carrying benevolent feelings into the world, into the world as it is, with its facts that overpower men, with its troubles and sorrows, its hundredfold difficulties that harden the heart, but not of retreating out of this state into the "other," and of making a poem out of one's own life, torn out of any inconvenient reality. But precisely this, the world-denying sinking into the other state, into private life, not shrinking like that of the petit bourgeois, but blossoming like a fairy tale, of an overflowing feeling of love, tenderness and happiness—that is what M. lets his hero Ulrich try. He chooses the motif of the brother-sister love as a most favorable condition because the exclusion of any social aspect is given through the prohibition of the relationship as necessary. That is the secret that removes it from the world. But in the nature of the twin sister, mystically similar, so deeply related to his own nature, Ulrich continuously experiences himself, his own ego in the mirror of the other character.

Ernst Fischer, "Das Werk R. M.s," *SuF*, 9, 5 (1957), pp. 894–95

Whatever R. M., the great Austrian writer, touched, was or became difficult. Simplicity was not for him: in style, thought, or life. But the M. touch, which turns everything into subtlety, complexity, ambiguity, is not, like the Midas touch, a curse. It is an honest awareness that life is difficult—or, as we read in Rilke, whom M. revered, "There are no classes for beginners in life"—and that a mere simplistic acceptance of that fact will lessen the difficulty.

But the fascination of what is difficult does not, as Yeats would have it in an early poem, dry the sap out of the veins, whatever it may do to spontaneous joy. Besides, difficulty in M. is always both there and not there. He is not like the phony weight lifter who grunts and snarles as he lifts a weight which may be heavy, but not all that heavy; he is rather like a master juggler who would make us forget how hard his cavalierly performed feats are if we did not notice with anxiety the fearful swelling of his jugular vein.

John Simon, Afterword to *Young Törless* (1964),
p. 175

[In *Vereinigungen*] each situation unites contradictions and in each moment numerous ego possibilities meet each other—a few emerge into the light, most of them stay in the shadow; repression is found next to enticement, revolt next to apathy; there are no irrevocable divisions between yesterday and today, between good and evil; rather everything has only a functional value, dependent upon circumstances and connections as well as upon the use that is made of it. Reality is accidental, and often it remains imponderable why this or that constellation becomes firm in order to fit itself to some set of circumstances. Whatever characteristics exist next to each other seem to be born to oppose each other; the challenge through contrast, however, results in a union originating out of this tension. At the same time, effect and countereffect are so closely connected, so braided into unity "that it would be in vain . . . to want to determine . . . phases of development." This mutual development does not form a succession but a togetherness. The one exists only through the other, events outside and within man create a complimentary relationship. Thus "infidelity may be union in a deeper interior zone."

Gerhart Baumann, *R. M.: Zur Erkenntnis der Dichtung* (1965), p. 133

M.'s is notoriously a world in political collapse, the end of a great empire; but more central to his poetic writing (at times he makes one think of a prose Rilke) is the sense of a world in metaphysical collapse, a universe of hideously heaped contingency, in which there are nonetheless transcendent human powers. These he represents always by the same complex and various image of eroticism, which reaches its fullest expression in the big novel. *The Man without Qualities* has among its themes nymphomania, incest, and sex murder, not at all for their prurient interest but as indices of the reaches of consciousness. Moosbrugger, the murderer, thinks, when he is not killing, that he is by his personal effort holding together the world; the story of the love between Ulrich, the book's hero, and his sister was, according to M., to take us to the

"farthest limits of the possible and unnatural, even of the repulsive"; and yet if one theme can be called central in *The Man without Qualities* it is this one, and nobody could think M. anything but overwhelmingly serious in his treatment of it. Erotic ecstasy is beyond good and evil ("all moral propositions refer to a sort of a dream condition that's long ago taken wing") and exemplifies the power of our consciousness to cross the borderline formerly protected by what are now the obsolete fortresses of traditional ethics and metaphysics.

Frank Kermode, Preface to R. M., *Five Women*
(1966), p. 9

M. intended not to be one of those old-fashioned novelists who refuse to take the decisive step into the twentieth century. Since he was unable to perceive a divinely ordained narrative order in existence, M. believed that he could not allow himself to create a traditional novel with a plot. M. consciously decided that his novel, *The Man without Qualities*, should not follow "the law of this life, for which one yearns," that is to say, it should not present a series of actions in a unidimensional order. In fact, his novel had to be written precisely against the psychological grain of the old-fashioned reader who yearns for a plot. *The Man without Qualities*, lacking a plot, is not a novel of action but rather the supreme example in Western literature of the novel of ideas. So, too, is Ulrich a protagonist who exists not at all through his actions but mainly through his ideas, which seem to be constantly "spreading out as an infinitely interwoven surface."

Frederick G. Peters, *R. M.: Master of the Hovering Life* (1978), pp. 189–190

The poetry of *Bilder* (images) (in *Nachlaß zu Lebzeiten*) pertains not only to the practice in words but to the experience in living. It is a question of how words seize existence, of their ambiguous and complex richness, of how to integrate subjectivity and emotion into the world from which they are excluded. The question is less to know and to distinguish than to experience reality and its mechanisms in all its profundity, both visible and hidden, and to show its numerous facets and variations. One sees throughout *Bilder* a man, avidly anxious to meet the phenomena, to penetrate life, to restore authenticity to things. The exterior facts are seized with meticulous precision, which is again found everywhere in the description of persons, of women in particular, of nature, of scenes with animals. M. evokes the houses of a market square, with their identical structures, the details of doors and portals, the architecture of administrative buildings in Vienna, the monuments, the behavior of men and animals. He narrates life with its eroticism, its needs, its complications, its battles, and its failures.

Marie-Louise Roth, *R. M.: Biographie et écriture*
(1980), pp. 101–2

Strangely enough, certain interpreters have seen in the portrayal of the afterglow of the old monarchy at the Danube in this novel [*The Man without Qualities*] either a bitter satire or a hymn to this state completely free of any criticism. A more serious investigation of the chapters in question makes this seeming contradiction understandable and eliminates it. It appears that M. softens the irony of his description so much with love, or, conversely, has intermingled the approving portrayal with so much fine irony that they both merge into one another. The unconditional supporters of the old state see only one side of the presentation, and the unconditional opponents only the other side.

Even further, if one investigates the novel more precisely, one finds that the problem of Kakanien is treated exactly like all other problems. Both the pro and anti-Kakanien attitudes are represented by positive and negative ideas and bearers of ideas. The "World-Austrian" impulses of Diotima are, for example, the fantastic hopeless chimeras of a slightly overwrought unsuspecting lady, while the not less pro-Kakanien ideas of her husband, Sektionschef Tuzzi, have not only common sense but also the strength of a decisive and conclusive conviction. The importance that such a consequent thinker and great intellect as M. puts upon precision and truth excludes from the beginning any kind of oversimplification and any kind of black and white representation that would tend to incline towards untruth.

Joseph P. Strelka, "Der Nachglanz der alten Monarchie bei R. M.," *M. Forum*, 6, 1 (1980), 69–70

MUSTAGHĀNMĪ, Ahlām

Algerian poet, novelist, and essayist (writing in Arabic), b. 1953, Algiers

M.'s early literary contributions were in the field of poetry reflecting the author's strong determination to express her opinion freely. She approaches taboo subjects, whether political or sexual, directly, without ambiguity or hesitation. The poems reveal the author's socialist inclinations and her support for liberation movements. She is particularly preoccupied with the Palestinian problem, manifested in her novel *Dhākiratu'l-Jasad* (1993; The Body's Memory). The writer is concerned with political freedom, the emancipation of women, and the elimination of oppression in its various forms. M. defies many of her society's customs and traditions, unconcerned by the consequences of her attitude. She seems to take pleasure in playing "l'enfant terrible," an attitude that spills into her novel. The choice of a man protagonist/narrator in *Dhākiratu'l-Jasad* hides in fact a capricious woman who manipulates the action and the characters like a puppet handler.

Though writing and publishing in the postindependence period, M. dwells on Algeria's colonial history, particularly the plight of the Algerian workers in France. In order to convey the past in her novel she relies heavily on flashbacks, oscillating between past and present. She considers events with the eyes of a child who lost her father in the war of independence and later, with the outlook of a young woman consumed by nostalgia and the loss of a father she hardly knew. The novel is generally a reevaluation of the war of independence, its realities and its failure to fulfill its promises. The present which is shaped by the events of the past, the positive and the negative ones, is severely criticized, yet accepted with a certain fatalistic resilience.

M.'s fiction fills a very small space in the huge gap of Algerian woman novelists. For the first few decades following independence, the sole name seen in Arabic fiction writings was that of Zuhīr WANĪSĪ, who contributed two collections of short stories and a novel, *Min Yawmiyyāt Mudarrisa Hurra* (1979; Memoirs of an Independent Teacher), which is more an historical text than a fiction work. Therefore, M.'s *Dhākiratu'l-Jasad* can rightly be considered the first Arabic novel in Algeria. This phenomenon forces us to wonder about the reasons for the paucity of Arabic novels generally and Algerian women novelists writing in Arabic, in particular. In spite of the proliferation of short stories since the 1940s thanks to the press of the Association of the Muslim 'Ulama of Algeria, particularly al-Basā'ir, and the high percentage of educated women, the Algerian Arabic novel continues to progress at a very slow pace. More than three decades after independence and with an education policy that is equally accessible to men and women, long fiction works should have made their appearance on the literary scene by the end of the 1980s.

FURTHER WORKS: *Algérie: femmes et écritures* (1985)

BIBLIOGRAPHY: Déjeux, J., *La Littérature Algérienne Contemporaine* (1975):107; Bamia, A. A., "Dhākirat al-Jasad: A New Outlook on Old Themes," *RAL*, 28 (1997): 85-93

—AIDA A. BAMIA

MUTIS, Alvaro

(pseud.: Alvar de Mattos) Colombian poet and novelist, b. 25 Aug. 1923, Bogotá

Although M. was born in Bogota, his family is from the Tolima province of Colombia, and the landscape of this area is important to much of his work. M.'s father was a government official and diplomat, and M. attended elementary and secondary school in Brussels. Upon returning to Colombia, he attended secondary school in Bogota but never finished his studies. He took refuge in Mexico in 1956 because of a lawsuit brought against him in Colombia. In Mexico he was incarcerated for over a year in 1959–1960. He has resided in Mexico since 1956, and in 1989 he received the Aztec Eagle for his contributions to Latin American letters.

M.'s first book was a volume of poetry, *La balanza* (1948; the balance), written in collaboration with Carlos Patiño (dates n. a.). M. formed part of a group that has been called the *Mito* poets, after a magazine that published many of their works. The *Mito* poets did not break completely with the tradition of Colombian poetry (represented most immediately by the preceding *Piedra y Cielo* or Stone and Sky group), but they did break with much of the traditional rhetoric. In M.'s case, the widening of poetic horizons resulted from his early assimilation of French SURREALISM.

The most salient feature of M.'s work, and the one that distinguishes it from that of other Colombian poets, is the presence of a character who acts as an authorial double. This character, Maqroll el Gaviero, appears in several poems of M.'s first two collections, and comes into his own in a series of poems, "Resena de los hospitales de ultramar" (review of hospitals overseas), contained in his third volume, *Los trabajos perdidos* (1965; the lost works). The importance of Maqroll is firmly established by the title of M.'s collected poems, *Summa de Maqroll el Gaviero (1947–1970)* (1973; summa of Maqroll el Gaviero). Maqroll is an inveterate traveler marked by solitude and an outsider's view of common human experience. His obsessions (which are those of all of M.'s early poetry) include trains, coffee plantations, sea and river voyages, hospitals and illnesses, and lovers. This poetry is more narrative than most Latin American poetry, and it succeeds in recreating a world (a tropical landscape) much as would a novel. M. avoids strict meter in his poetry, but tends towards a Whitmanesque extension and to the prose poem. His fourth volume of poetry, *Caravansary* (1981; caravansary), also extends the biography of Maqroll, and is a mixture of poetry and prose.

Although avowedly apolitical, M. is enthralled with the spectacle of certain periods of monarchic rule. This is obvious in his more recent poetry, especially *Crónica regia y Alabanza del reino* (1985; royal chronicle and in praise of the kingdom). The first part of this volume explores different aspects of the life and legacy of King Philip II of Spain. The second section contains poems that reflect M.'s experiences in the Andalucía region of Spain. These poems, as well as those of *Un homenaje y siete nocturnos* (1986; an homage and seven nocturnes), make no mention of Maqroll and depart from the ahistorical melancholy of this character for a sense of spiritual completion.

M.'s early prose work, *Diario de Lecumberri* (1960; Lecumberri diary), is a series of testimonial pieces that reflect M.'s experiences while incarcerated in Mexico. The stories recount incidences of prison life and are written in straightforward prose laced with Mexicanisms. M.'s second extensive prose work is a novella, *La mansión de Araucaima* (1973; Araucaíma mansion). Subtitled "Relato gótico de tierra caliente" (gothic story from the hot lands), the novella extends M.'s obsession with characters on the margins of society and returns to the tropical landscape of his poetry. The novella's short chapters read like prose poems, and the emphasis on the grotesque betrays M.'s attentive reading of the Spanish novelist and dramatist Ramón del VALLE INCLÁN.

M.'s more recent narrative centers on the protagonist of his early poetry, Maqroll el Gaviero. These novels are among his most mature works, and they add considerable depth to the character known only fragmentarily in the poetry. The machinations of plot are of little interest, as M. concentrates his lyrical energy on Maqroll's philosophical reveries. *La nieve del almirante* (1986; the admiral's snow) is particularly interesting as it contains a diary ostensibly written by Maqroll during a voyage up a large tropical river. This setting links the novel to a large body of Latin American travel literature extending from the chronicles of the Iberian conquistadors to many important modern novels.

M. has published a number of short stories of which "El último rostro" (1978; the last face) is of special import. Dealing with the last days in the life of Simón Bolívar, this story was used as a starting point by M.'s close friend Gabriel GARCÍA MÁRQUEZ for his novel *El general en su laberinto* (1989; *The General in His Labyrinth*, 1990).

M. is among the most gifted stylists in Latin America today. His poetry, linked to the best of the Colombian tradition, is of continental importance, distinguished by its exploration of the tropical landscape and its narrative depth. While M.'s reputation is based primarily on his poetry, his later novels, contemplative and complex, are written in exquisitely crafted prose.

FURTHER WORKS: *Los elementos del desastre* (1953); *Poemas* (1978); *Poesía y prosa* (1981); *La verdadera historia del flautista de Hammelin* (1982); *Los emisarios* (1984; *Abel Quezada, la comedia del arte* (1985, with Carlos Monsivais); *Historia natural de las cosas* (1985); *Obra literaria* (1985); *Sesenta cuerpos* (1985); *Ilona Ilega con la lluvia* (1987); *La muerte del estratega* (1988); *Tras las rutas de Maqroll el Gaviero: 1981–1988* (1988); *La última escala del tramp steamer* (1989); *Un bel morir* (1989); *Amirbar* (1990). FURTHER WORKS IN ENGLISH: *Maqroll: Three Novellas* (1992)

BIBLIOGRAPHY: Barnechea, A., and Oviedo, J. M., "La historia como estética: entrevista con A. M.," in *Poesía y prosa* (1981): 576–97; Elzaguirre, L., "A. M. o la transitoriedad e la palabra poética," *Inti*: 18–19 (1983–1984): 83–105; Romero, A., "Los poetas de Mito," *RI*, 50 (1984): 689–755; Cobo Borda, J. G., "Dos poetas de Mito: A. M. y Fernando Charry Lara," *RI*, 51: 130–31 (Jan.-June 1985): 89–102; Garganigo, J. F., "Aproximaciones a la poesía de A. M.: un viaje inacabado a través del texto," *Revista de la Universidad Central*, 3, 23 (1985): 181–93; Sucre, G., *La máscara, la transparencia: Ensayos sobre poesía hispanoamericana*, rev. ed. (1985): 320–30; O'Hara, E., "*Los emisarios*: Respuestas que son preguntas," *RCLL*, 11, 24 (1986): 263–68; Jaramillo Zudvago, J. E., "El espacio en blanco, el envés de un dios, *Los elementos del desastre*," in CELAM, eds., *Presencia de Dios en la poesía latinoamericana* (1988): 309–19

—BEN A. HELLER

MYERS, L(eopold) H(amilton)

English novelist, b. 6 Sept 1881, Cambridge; d. 8 April 1944, London

Son of F. W. H. Myers, a noted Cambridge intellectual, M. was educated at Cambridge but left without taking a degree. M. passed much of his life disengaging himself from various social and ideological circles with which he was successively associated, ranging from upper-class English snobs through Bloomsbury and Chelsea aesthetes to pro-Soviet communists. Sometimes called a misanthrope, M. reserved his chief distaste usually for the materialism of his own privileged class after his youthful submersion in its pleasures and pursuits. Of considerable importance to his fiction was a mystical experience M. had as a young man in a Chicago hotel room, for the theme of a spiritual quest persists throughout his canon. Despite a generally happy marriage to an extremely wealthy woman and the comfort of two daughters, M. suffered periodic bouts of deep depression in his later years and finally committed suicide. It is regrettable that, shortly before his death, M. destroyed all copies of an autobiography in progress and urged his friends, who were often compliant, to destroy their letters from him. These materials might have shed additional light on a distinguished, provocative, but ultimately mysterious man of letters.

M.'s first novel, *The Orissers* (1922), which required nearly twelve years to reach its final form, presents in overly schematic fashion the difficulties of the sensitive and isolated moral individual caught in an unsatisfactory materialist society. As epigraph to the novel M. included Sir Francis Bacon's description of the Illusions of the Tribe, Den, Market, and Schools and then examined the role of such illusions in the lives of the novel's characters. This early work, rather reminiscent of E. M. FORSTER's *Howard's End*, stresses the inherent value of ideas and the inner life, which can encourage and deepen a sense of vocation—a theme M. continued to find congenial.

M.'s next novel, *The Clio* (1925), somewhat resembling lightweight Aldous HUXLEY, takes place on "probably the most expensive steam yacht in the world," which sails up the Amazon, where the wealthy passengers confront the jungle, South American revolutions, and the shallowness of their own supposed civilization. Absurdity on this ship of fools is redeemed only by the wit and intelligence revealed in the dialogue.

Although shorter than his other novels, *Strange Glory* (1936) contributes to the unfolding quasi-mystical vision in M.'s fiction. It is set in the bayous of Louisiana—M. habitually eschewing the home grounds of England and traditional British society as source material. M.'s characters negotiate between two curious species of mysticism in this novel: one a sort of nature worship and the other a rarefied form of idealistic communism. Perhaps as much as mysticism, M. informs his novel with myth, defined in the Jungian sense as a turning point in consciousness, with the end being to submit to destiny—finding a place in the world rather than finding oneself, or perhaps finding one through the other.

M.'s masterpiece is the tetralogy, published finally in a collected volume under the title of the first book, *The Near and the Far* (1943). The immediate model for the work is doubtless Arthur Waley's translation of Lady Murasaki's 11th-c. Japanese masterpiece *The Tale of Genji*, with its study of love and intrigue conducted in a highly polished and civilized manner. The tetralogy comprises *The Near and the Far* (1929), *Prince Jali* (1931), *Rajah Amar* (1935)—these three novels were collected as a trilogy under the title *The Root and the Flower* (1935)—and *The Pool of Vishnu* (1940). Taken together these novels demonstrate M.'s ability to transcend the "low, dishonest decade," as W. H. AUDEN termed the 1930s. Set in an imaginary 16th-c. India during the reign of Akbar, as his two sons, Daniyal and Salim, struggle for succession, *The Near and the Far* represents a profound philosophical novel about the convergence in one country of Christianity, Buddhism, Islam, and Hinduism, as well as depiction of the clash of other more secular sanctions and persuasions, including sexuality, militarism, aestheticism, and humanism. M. attempts to take measure of the spiritual dimensions of human nature and to gauge the possibilities of the self's and civilization's honorable survival. Many readers perceived the contemporary relevance of M.'s tetralogy. With his interest in the issues of history and man's place in the world, M. keeps returning to the question of what is worthwhile and how it can be achieved. Beneath all of India's divisions and diversities M. shows the unity possible through modes of feeling and standards of value more fundamental than any of the things over which the country is divided.

The first three books of the tetralogy were widely read and critically acclaimed; the fourth was generally considered inferior to its predecessors and overly abstract. Years ago M. attracted much attention from the critics associated with *Scrutiny* for his satire on the Bloomsbury group shown not so obliquely in *Rajah Amar* as Prince Daniyal's Pleasance of the Arts, and this vein has not yet been exhausted. With the current veneration of Bloomsbury's loving friends, other aspects of the tetralogy seem due for renewed attention after an extended period of neglect. If a return to an awareness of sacred order in life is imminent, then M. the moralist should speak once more to readers. M. remains stimulating and complex in his political ideas, aphoristically memorable, stylistically graceful, and often numinous in his spiritual insights, a combination of excellence rarely found in British novelists of this or any other century.

FURTHER WORKS: *Arvat: A Dramatic Poem* (1908)

BIBLIOGRAPHY: Simon, I., *L. H. M.* (1948); Bantock, G. H., *L. H. M.: A Critical Study* (1956); Hartley, L. P., Introduction to *The Near and the Far* (1956): 1–6; Gupta, B. S., "L. H. M.'s Treatment of Buddhism in *The Near and the Far,*" *RLV*, 37 (1970): 64–74; Grant, R. A. D., "Art versus Ideology: The Case of L. H. M.," *CQ*, 6 (1974): 214–40; Cockshut, A. O. J., *Man and Woman: A Study of Love and the Novel, 1740–1940* (1978): 181–85; Rao, V. A., "*The Near and the Far*: A Note on the Structure," *RLV*, 44 (1978): 275–84

—EDWARD T. JONES

MYKOLAITIS, Vincas

(pseud.: Putinas) Lithuanian poet and novelist, b. 6 Jan. 1893, Pilotiškės; d. 7 June 1967, Kačerginė

M. studied for the Roman Catholic priesthood in Seinai and took his vows in 1915, while a refugee in Russia, where he and many other Lithuanians retreated from the German advanced during World War I. During his stay in Petrograd, M. was influenced by the Russian SYMBOLISTS, particularly the philosopher-poet Vladimir Solovyov (1853–1900), whose aesthetics M. later studied in Switzerland (1918–22). After additional study of art in Munich, he was appointed to a teaching position at the University of Kaunas, Lithuania, in 1923.

While still in the seminary, M. had begun to have doubts about his religious calling. During his study abroad, his uncertainty developed into a conflict between the vocation of a priest and that of a poet. Another element was added to this inner struggle when M. fell in love with one of his students. These conflicts are reflected in his novel *Altorių šešėly* (1933; in the shadow of the altars). In 1935 the couple were secretly married, and in 1936 M. was excommunicated, although in his later years he became reconciled with the Catholic Church.

It was during his years at the University of Kaunas that M. first established a reputation as a poet. His main collections of verse of that period are *Tarp dviejų aušrų* (1927; between two dawns) and *Keliai ir kryžkeliai* (1936; roads and crossroads).

The key emotional elements in M.'s poetry are repression, rebellion, and intense yearning to reconcile his priestly vows with the poet's need for a fuller life. His success as a poet derived from his ability to sublimate these contradictory impulses in poetic structures of balanced tension, expressing his turbulent feelings in pithy, disciplined poetic language. The early influences of the Russian symbolists nourished in M. a vague existential longing and—as, for example, in the famous poem "Stella Maris" (Latin: star of the sea) in *Raudoni žiedai; Kunigaikštis Žvainys* (1917; red blossoms; Prince Žvainys)—turned his eyes towards evening horizons, the sea, and the stars as radiant points of unreachable perfection. These spacious, abstract settings in themselves became the symbols of a philosophical quest after the meaning of God. The visage of God in M.'s poetry underwent cyclical changes: from that of a cold and distant ruler, removed from human suffering by the vast, dark cosmic distances, to one of a sorrowful Christ, carved by peasant hands, contemplating man's fate on an empty roadside under the starry skies. In the service of this elusive unknown God, M. alternated between grand gestures of revolt and worshipful tenderness. Images of nature complement these transitory states of mind as vibrant spring gives way to gloomy autumn, mountain heights, to shadowy depths. Affection for the warm and sinful earth is counterpointed by moments of cosmic solitude. Love seeks its difficult path between similar antitheses, often appearing in the form of struggle between the ardent and the pious heart. In his last years, M. was caught in still another painful dichotomy: between gropings towards a "socialist consciousness" and the insistent returns of the God who will not be ignored. Stylistically, M. enriched Lithuanian poetry by his use of fresh and original rhythms, and by his extraordinary musicality of language.

M.'s novel *Altorių šešėly* established the psychological genre in Lithuanian fiction. Liudas Vasaris, the semiautobiographical protagonist of this work, for many years huddles unhappily as a novice priest in the "shadow of the altars," trying at the same time to squelch the fires of erotic temptation and to warm the cooling embers of his love for God. As a budding poet he finds his passionate, suffering soul can see beauty only as it is reflected in troubled, imperfect Creation, not as it exists in the perfection of God. He yearns for a woman's love and for the challenge of the affairs of the world. With the encouragement of a devoted woman, Liudas leaves the priesthood, rebelling not against God but against the earthly law of the Church. *Altorių šešėly* provoked bitterness and shock in conservative and Catholic Lithuanian circles; only now has it become accepted on the strength of M.'s stature as a literary figure.

After World War II M. had to adjust some of his past views to the demands of the Communist regime. His second important novel, *Sukilėliai* (1957; the rebels), shows clear signs of his efforts to stay within the ideological framework of SOCIALIST REALISM. It is the story of another young priest who makes a conscious decision to leave the contemplative life, joining the tumult of the Lithuanian uprising against the Russians in 1863. Despite M.'s efforts to give credit to the "progressive influences of Russian democratic thought" that inspired the rebellion, the novel was frowned upon by Soviet authorities. The theme was too reminiscent of Lithuania's present situation to give the Communist censors much peace of mind.

FURTHER WORKS: *Raštai* (2 vols., 1921); *Valdovas* (1930); *Naujoji lietuvių literatūra*, Vol. I (1936); *Krizė* (1937); *Literatūros etiudai* (1937); *Lietuviškoji tematika Adomo Mickevičiaus kūryboje* (1949); *Sveikinu žeme* (1950); *Rūsčios dienos* (1952); *Vakarėj žaroj* (1959); *Raštai* (8 vols., 1959–1962); *Būties valanda* (1963); *Langas* (1966); *Poezija* (2 vols., 1973)

BIBLIOGRAPHY: Jungfer, V., "V. M.-P. und Krėvė," *Litauen: Antlitz eines Volkes* (1948): 296–314; Grinius, J., *V. M.-P. als Dichter* (1964); Sietynas, A., "The Condition of Free Prisoner: Poetry and Prose of V. M.-P.," *Lituanus*, 11, 1 (1965): 48–63

—RIMVYDAS ŠILBAJORIS

MYRIVILIS, Stratis

(pseud. of Stratis Stamatopoulos) Greek novelist and short-story writer, b. 30 June 1892, Sykamia, Lesbos; d. 9 Sept. 1969, Athens

M. was old enough to fight in the Balkan wars of 1912–13 and also to observe at close range the critical events that preceded and followed the 1922 Greek catastrophe in Asia Minor. All three of his novels and several of his short stories draw their inspiration from those experiences of war and political and social conflict. He was very active as a publisher and journalist, first on his native island of Lesbos (also called Mytilene), later in Athens. Between 1936 and 1951 M. was the general program director of the Greek National Radio and wrote for newspapers. In the 1950s he visited America and described his impressions in a series of newspaper articles. He was a member of the Academy of Athens.

M.'s first collection of short stories, *To kokkino vivlio* (1915; rev. ed., 1952; the red book), and the first and best-known of his novels, *I zoi en tafo* (1924; rev. ed., 1930; *Life in the Tomb*, 1977), show him to be a great craftsman in the tradition of Greek demoticism (that is, the literary movement that worked for the promotion of the vernacular over the purist language in literature and education). The novel is a Greek equivalent, broadly speaking, of the antiwar novels of Erich Maria REMARQUE and Ernest HEMINGWAY. The main character of the story, Sergeant Kostoulas, gradually loses faith in the purpose of the Balkan wars, in which he had initially volunteered to fight, and is quite disillusioned when he dies. A diary he leaves behind describes his life in the trenches. This is supposedly found and published by a friend (the first-person narrator). The book combines stark realism with lyrical descriptions of nature and human feeling.

In M.'s second novel, *I dhaskala me ta hrissa matia* (1933; *The Schoolmistress with the Golden Eyes*, 1951), which may be seen as the center link in a loose trilogy of novels, the chief character, Leonis Drivas, returns to his native Mytilene from the war his country has lost in Anatolia, unharmed in body but badly affected in spirit. His mental convalescence is long, hampered by the shallow, naïve, or cynical attitudes of the island society, people whom the war seems to have taught nothing. Drivas is, moreover, divided between loyalty to a friend killed in the war and passion for that man's window, Sappho, the schoolmistress of the title.

Here, and also in his third novel, *I panaghia i ghorghona* (1949; *The Mermaid Madonna*, 1959), M. mixes realistic narration and description with a lyrical, almost sensuous feeling for nature, and with detailed psychological analysis of some of the more significant characters. This work deals with the settlement on Mytilene of a group of Greek refugees from Anatolia. In time, they acquire roots in the new soil, although some among them will not relinquish easily the dream of going back to their old homes. Against this background M. weaves the story of Smaragdhi (the name means "emerald girl"), a foundling, believed by the people to be of supernatural origin. She is an ideal as well as a source of torment for the men of her village, and chooses, at the end, to become a devotee of the Virgin, the Mermaid Madonna, whose icon (depicting her as half human and half fish) oversees and protects the village. The use of myth to deepen the understanding of history as well as to relieve the characters of some of the burden of the past, a technique that characterizes M.'s mature period, is also found in his novella *O Vassilis o Arvanitis* (1943; Vassilis the Albanian), a portrait of a Zorba-like character who, pushed by an irresistible lust for life, commits the inevitable hubris that leads to ruin.

To some critics, M. was particularly successful as a short-story writer. Important collections, like *To prassino vivlio* (1935; the green book), *To ghalazio vivlio* (1939; the blue book), the revised version of *To kokkino vivlio*, and *To vissini vivlio* (1959; the purple book), in fact, contain some of the best-crafted specimens of the genre in modern Greek literature. In one of his most memorable stories, "To sakki" (the sack), in *To prassino vivlio*, a middle-aged soldier of World War I carries, on his return journey, a sack with his brother's bones, which others mistake for hardtack, a luxury in those days when even bread had become scarce. The macabre as well as humorous discovery of the sack's real contents elicits, in both narrator and reader, feelings of sympathy and admiration for the poor soldier's faithfulness in carrying out a promise to his mother: to find and bring home for proper burial the remains of his younger brother, killed in battle in an earlier year of the war.

It is not for dealing with great spiritual questions (in the manner, let us say, of Nikos KAZANTZAKIS or for thematic and stylistic variety that M. is to be remembered, but instead for his rich and varied elaboration of the Greek vernacular, his talent for vivid characterization, and the interplay in his works of realism and myth. Ideologically, he remained inward-looking, from his early "angry" days to his later embrace of a wider Hellenic tradition. His overall significance lies in the role he played in realizing better than most of his predecessors the ideals of demoticism: to cultivate the popular language as a literary instrument and to provide a realistic picture of modern Greek society.

FURTHER WORKS: *O arghonaftis* (1936); *Traghoudi tis yis* (1937); *Mikres foties* (1942); *Ta paghana* (1944); *O Pan* (1946); *Ap'tin Elladha* (1956); *Pteroenta* (1964)

BIBLIOGRAPHY: Mirambel, A., "S. M., romancier de la Grèce des légendes et de la réalité," *Mercure de France*, No. 1165 (1960): 90–112; Dimaras, C. T., *A History of Modern Greek Literature* (1972), passim; Politis, L., *A History of Modern Greek Literature* (1973), passim; Doulis, T., *Disaster and Fiction: Modern Greek Fiction and the Asia Minor Disaster of 1922* (1977), passim; Rexine, J. E., on *Life in the Tomb*, *WLT*, 51 (1977): 661

—GEORGE THANIEL

N

Vladimir Nabokov

NABOKOV, Vladimir

(pseud. until 1940: V. Sirin) Russian-American novelist, short-story writer, memoirist, essayist, critic, translator, and poet, b. 23 April 1899, St. Petersburg; d. 2 July 1977, Montreux, Switzerland

N. was born into an ancient aristocratic family; his father was a prominent liberal politician and scholar. The Nabokovs were forced to leave Russia after the Bolsheviks took power in 1917, but young N.'s first books of poetry appeared before he emigrated to England. N. graduated from Cambridge in 1922 and moved to Berlin (1922–37), where his verse, stories, plays, and novels established his Russian reputation. His misleadingly simple prose style was noted by every critic. N.'s alienated and obsessive heroes, his harsh treatment of his characters, and his avoidance of popular social and political topics led most Russian critics to brand him "un-Russian" and an outsider.

Leaving Nazi Germany, N. moved to Paris, where he and his wife lived from 1937 to 1940. In May 1940 N. fled to the U.S. where he became a teacher of Russian language and literature, notably at Cornell University from 1948 to 1958. His lectures,

published as *Lectures on Literature* (1980) and *Lectures on Russian Literature* (1981), became very popular among students. N. continued to pursue his avocations of chess, tennis, and lepidopterology, all of which figure prominently in his works. Although he spoke English almost as early as he had Russian and French, he switched to English for his writing only in the 1940s. He published stories in the *New Yorker*, and his novel *The Real Life of Sebastian Knight* (1941) marked the final turning point. *Bend Sinister* (1947) followed, but it was the sensational publication of *Lolita* (1955) that made N.'s name and fortune in popular terms.

N. retired from teaching and in 1960 moved to Montreux, Switzerland (retaining his American citizenship), where he lived until his death. During the years in Switzerland he translated, or oversaw translations, of nearly all of his Russian works into English. He also translated two English works back into Russian: *Speak, Memory* (1966; orig. pub. as *Conclusive Evidence*, 1951; *Drugie berega*, 1954) and *Lolita* (*Lolita*, 1967). Moreover, all of his Russian works were reissued in the original, making his two separate but interrelated bodies of writing known all over the world—except in the U.S.S.R., where none of his works had ever been permitted to appear.

N. is one of the few writers who are major figures in two languages; moreover, both his Russian and his English styles have been lauded by fellow writers and critics. Although his poetry is not considered his highest achievement, it is clear that from his first book, *Stikhi* (1916; verse) to his last collection, *Stikhi* (1979; verse), including his poems in English (*Poems and Problems*, 1970), his poetry served as a stylistic laboratory. The richly metaphorical language of his poems is vital to the structure of his prose. His lines are alive with metaphor, and key image clusters play important roles not only in foreshadowing but in developing themes and characterization.

N.'s short stories are often elegantly poetic and as neatly structured as sonnets. The three Russian collections, *Vozvrashchenie Chorba* (1930; the return of Chorb), *Soglyadatay* (1938; the eye), and *Vesna v Fialte* (1956; spring in Fialta), were among the last things N. put into English—in collections not corresponding exactly to the originals in content, notably *Tyrants Destroyed* (1975), *A Russian Beauty, and Other Stories* (1975) and *Details of a Sunset, and Other Stories* (1976). Some are seemingly conventional character studies, with Russian émigré heroes. Others are set in fantastic worlds of the sort that later developed into *Pale Fire* (1962). In his stories as in his other fiction N. liberally uses puzzles, anagrams, allusions, and fatidic dates, challenging readers to penetrate beyond the apparent meaning of the work and discover more subtle designs. N. forces one to be more than a passive receiver of information. The reader must use all his faculties of perception, memory, and imagination if he wants to participate in the discoveries N.'s fictional world offers.

The theme of memory is the key to his first novel, *Mashenka* (1926; *Mary*, 1970) and many of N.'s other novels. The hero, Ganin, learns that his first love is soon to arrive in Berlin, and decides to renew their relationship, even though she is now married. But after spending days remembering his childhood in Russia, reliving the development of his love, and doing this all with a wealth of very specific sensory detail (typical of N.), he realizes that he has recaptured that lost time the only way humans can, and therefore does not confront Mary when she arrives. Man is unique because in his consciousness, with his retrospective faculty, he can conquer time and space.

The burlesque *Korol, dama, valet* (1928; *King, Queen, Knave*, 1968) is a rather mechanical series of variations on themes from *Madame Bovary*. Among N.'s books it was the only one he changed substantially when translating it. The bumbling hero of *Zashchita Luzhina* (1930; *The Defense*, 1964) is a monomaniac chess master; images of the board gradually take over his entire life. His ultimate defense against the moves of these images is suicide. The subject matter of this novel is well suited for N.'s use of repeated and anticipatory images. In his English foreword N. mocks the "careful reader" by saying he will notice specific passages containing what N. calls a significant system of chess-board images. However, for seventeen years no reviewer, critic, or scholar noticed that the images that N. specifies do not in fact occur in the novel. N. the illusionist, like a magician or chess player, loved such misdirections.

Kamera obskura (1932; *Laughter in the Dark*, 1938) deals with literal blindness and moral blindness, and foreshadows in some ways *Lolita*. *Podvig* (1932; *Glory*, 1971) tells the story of a Russian émigré who decides to return secretly to his homeland; the faculty of memory and what it re-creates is again vital. In *Otchayanie* (1934; *Despair*, 1937; rev. ed., 1966) N.'s obsessed first-person narrator believes he has discovered his physical double and plots to commit the perfect murder. Hermann's madness becomes clear to the reader in spite of his efforts to deny it. N.'s world is filled with moral degenerates disguised as intelligent and witty characters; his seemingly objective treatment of these figures led some critics to the erroneous conclusion that N. could create only cold and inhuman characters, and that he had no feelings about them himself.

The late 1930s was the creative climax of N.'s Russian career. *Priglashenie na kazn* (1938; *Invitation to a Beheading*, 1959), first published serially in the leading Paris émigré journal, *Sovremennye zapiski*, describes the sentencing, incarceration, and apparent execution of a man named Cincinnatus. It has usually been interpreted as a purely political novel, a Kafkaesque spoof of 20th-c. totalitarian regimes. In fact, it was N.'s first achievement of what he called "fairytale freedom." The setting of the novel seems very concrete, but on close examination it is another planned mirage; no specific place or time is ever mentioned. With difficulty one can deduce that it takes place in an imaginary future so distant that matter itself has almost worn out and all invention has ceased. The prison described is a prison in imagination only, and the book is about the creative process of writing a book. The liberating power of fantasy and imagination becomes one of N.'s main themes. The longest of N.'s Russian novels, *Dar* (1937–38; *The Gift*, 1963), also first published in *Sovremennye zapiski*, is about a poet; in it N. strives to show what creative imagination, wedded to memory, can accomplish. It is also a kind of encyclopedia of Russian literature, teeming with allusions and parodies, and written in N.'s most dazzling style.

The Real Life of Sebastian Knight marks N.'s shift to English. The central problem of the novel is how one determines the true identity of another person, and how one puts that into words. In *Bend Sinister* N. returns to a fantasy land and political themes, with the process of novel-writing itself a key concern. As in *Invitation to a Beheading*, the ancient symbols of the soul, lepidoptera, are used to suggest life beyond what humans regard as the real world. The setting is a vaguely Slavic world of mediocre absolutism, but in general, references to the totalitarianism of the Communist U.S.S.R. are quite rare in N.'s works. No other Russian writer could have

written memoirs, as N. did in *Speak, Memory*, that dismiss the revolution in passing, treating it as a minor interruption in butterfly hunting.

Lolita eclipsed N.'s earlier American novels. While it was first rejected by many publishers, and later attacked by critics from many pulpits, it has come to be recognized not as a pornographic book but as a poetically written love story, whose hero suffers from an obsession: the desire to possess "nymphets," as he terms a rare type of barely adolescent girl. Humbert Humbert, the condemned hero-narrator, is a mixture of comic and tragic features, as is the whole novel. In his urbanity, wit, and erudition he is attractive; but as usual in N., one must go beyond what the narrator tells one to what he lets slip. N. allows Humbert to apologize for his actions profusely, but he also makes him a madman and a murderer, who in moments of lucidity realizes exactly how he destroyed Lolita's childhood. N.'s foreign-eye view of American life is alternately comic and lyric, poetic and satirical.

Because its incompetent hero, an émigré professor of Russian, is so lovable, *Pnin* (1957) is often seen as the warmest and most affectionate of N.'s books. *Pale Fire* (1962) is perhaps his most experimental. Its core is an epic poem, and this is surrounded by Introduction, Commentaries, and Index, written by a mad and footnote-drugged narrator named Charles Kinbote. The structure of the narrative is so complex that critics cannot agree about the true identity of the narrator, or which characters have a "real" existence in the book. It is N.'s paradox that the madman's world, Zembla, an imaginary world, is the most realistic and vivid world in the book. N. calls into question the very nature of reality and our ability to perceive it. *Pale Fire* cannot be read in the usual linear manner, nor does it make complete sense except on subsequent readings.

This is also true of N.'s longest and most complex work, *Ada; or, Ardor: A Family Chronicle* (1969). N.'s two worlds, Russia and America, are joined in a fantasy antiworld where normal Earth geography, chronology, and history are mixed in delightful and informative ways. The hero and heroine turn out to be, on close reading, brother and sister, and their lifelong sexual passion for each other provides the sensational element in an otherwise learned and poetic novel containing dissertations on such subjects as the nature of time and space. In *Transparent Things* (1972) N. goes beyond normal time to use characters who have already died, but who in another dimension watch over the living. *Look at the Harlequins!* (1974) was N.'s attempt to recapitulate both his Russian and American careers in fictional form, using a variety of styles, each imitating his own style at various stages of his sixty-year-long career.

N.'s literary translations and criticism form a significant part of his work. He wrote an insightful critical study called *Nikolai Gogol* (1944). He practiced his carefully worked-out theory of literal translation in *The Song of Igor's Campaign: An Epic of the Twelfth Century* (1960) and Lermontov's *A Hero of Our Time* (1958). His four-volume edition of Pushkin's *Eugene Onegin* (1964; rev. ed., 1975), with translation, copious commentaries, and interpolated essays, is a unique gift from one culture to another. Many of his essays and his iconoclastic, scrupulously *written* interviews were collected in *Strong Opinions* (1973).

A brilliant style is partly a function of imagination, and it is probably the concept of imagination that is the key to most of N. He celebrates it, as he celebrates liberty, language, love, and beauty. He asserts the sanctity of individual human life. He prizes wit, and his own wit is always directed against those who by normal moral standards deserve it: people who do not love, destroyers of freedom, preachers of mediocrity, anyone who maims or kills to force his ideas on other human beings, people who are ignorant of themselves or the physical and intellectual world around them. N. has no sermons. He loathed propaganda fiction. But these values are constants in his world.

FURTHER WORKS: *Dva puti* (1918); *Gorny put* (1923); *Izobretenie valsa* (1938; *The Waltz Invention*, 1966); *Three Russian Poets: Selections from Pushkin, Lermontov, and Tyutchev* (1944); *Nine Stories* (1947); *Stikhotvorenia 1929–51* (1952); *N's Dozen: A Collection of Thirteen Stories* (1958); *Poems* (1959); *The Eye* (1965); *N.'s Quartet* (1966); *Lolita: A Screenplay* (1974); *The N.—Wilson letters 1940–1971* (1979)

BIBLIOGRAPHY: Dembo, L. S., ed., *N.: The Man and His Work* (1967); Field, A., *N.: His Life in Art* (1967); Proffer, C. R., *Keys to "Lolita"* (1968); Appel, A., Jr., ed., *The Annotated "Lolita"* (1970); Appel, A., Jr., and Newman, C., eds., *N.: Criticism, Reminiscences, Translations, and Tributes* (1970); Rowe, W. W., *N.'s Deceptive World* (1971); Field, A., comp. *N.: A Bibliography* (1973); Fowler, D., *Reading N.* (1974); Mason, B. A., *N.'s Garden: A Guide to "Ada"* (1974); Proffer, C. R., ed., *A Book of Things about V. N.* (1974); Updike, J., *Picked-Up Pieces* (1975): 191–222; Lee, L. L., *V. N.* (1976); Bodenstein, J., *The Excitement of Verbal Adventure: A Study of V. N.'s English Prose* (1977); Grayson, J., *N. Translated* (1977); Quennell, P., ed., *V. N.: A Tribute* (1979); Schuman, S., *V. N.: A Reference Guide* (1979); Pifer, E., *N. and the Novel* (1980); Rowe, W. W., *N.'s Spectral Dimension* (1981); Rivers, J. E., and Nicol, C., eds., *N.'s Fifth Arc: N. and Others on His Life's Work* (1982); Boyd, B., *V. N.: The Russian Years* (1990); Boyd, B., *V. N.: The American Years* (1991)

—CARL R. PROFFER

Under thorough scrutiny Sirin proves for the most part to be an artist of form, of the writer's device, and not only in that well-known and universally recognized sense in which the formal aspect of his writing is distinguished by exceptional diversity, complexity, brillance and novelty. All this is recognized and known precisely because it catches everyone's eye. But it catches the eye because Sirin not only does not mask, does not hide his devices, as is most frequently done by others (and in which, for example, Dostoevsky attained startling perfection) but, on the contrary, because Sirin himself places them in full view like a magician who, having amazed his audience, reveals on the very spot the laboratory of his miracles. This, it seems to me, is the key to all of Sirin. His works are populated not only with the characters, but with an infinite number of devices which, like elves or gnomes, scurry back and forth among the characters and perform an enormous amount of work. They saw and carve and nail and paint, in front of the audience, setting up and clearing away those stage sets amid which the play is performed. They construct the world of the book and they function as indispensably

important characters. Sirin does not hide them because one of his major tasks is just that—to show how the devices live and work. [1937]

Vladislav Khodasevich, "On Sirin," in Alfred Appel, Jr., and Charles Newman, eds., *N.: Criticism, Reminiscences, Translations, and Tributes* (1970), p. 97

As a literal image and overriding metaphor, the mirror is central to the form and content of N. novels. If one perceives *Pale Fire* spatially, with John Shade's poem on the "left" and Charles Kinbote's Commentary on the "right," the poem is seen as an object to be perceived, and the Commentary becomes the world seen through the distorting prism of a mind, a monstrous concave mirror held up to an objective "reality." The narrator of *Despair* (1934) loathes mirrors, avoids them, and comments on those "monsters of mirrors," the "crooked ones," in which a man is stripped, squashed, or "pulled out like dough and then torn in two." N. has placed these crooked reflectors everywhere in his fiction: Doubles, parodies and self-parodies (literature trapped in a prison of amusement park mirrors), works within works, mirror-games of chess, translations ("a crazy-mirror of terror and art"), and language games. He manipulates the basic linguistic devices—auditory, morphological, and alphabetical, most conspicuously the latter. In *Pale Fire*, Zemblan is "the tongue of the mirror," and the fragmentation or total annihilation of the self reverberates in the verbal distortions in *Bend Sinister*'s police state, "where everybody is merely an anagram of everybody else," and in the alphabetical and psychic inversions and reversals in *Pale Fire*.

Alfred Appel, Jr., "*Lolita*: The Springboard of Parody," in L. S. Dembo, ed., *N.: The Man and His Work* (1967), pp. 107–8

One of the commonest words in the Nabokovian lexicon is fate. It is fate who wills the unity of all things, who prompts the little unity of alliteration and the other poetic devices of sound repetition so common in the prose ot N., who seeks out for words of one language unsuspected cousins in another language, who provides that abundance of Pasternakian and Lermontovian coincidence which informs the novels. In his translation of Lermontov's novel *A Hero of Our Time* Nabokov refers to all these lucky encounters and overheard conversations as "the barely noticeable routine of fate." N.'s account of his own life in *Speak, Memory* is a kind of diary of the workings of fate. Fate is really one of the guises of the muse of N.

If we turn to one of the larger elements of N.'s art, the structure of the character relationships, we find fate busily at work, inevitably with the same result, since fate has only one passion—the passion for unity. In these character relationships we begin, typically, with an apparent duality, which is then reduced to unity—two men who in the course of the novel strangely coalesce. "The only real number is one, the rest are mere repetition." The central position in the novel is usually occupied by the charismatic figure of some poet or novelist of genius. The other figure is the person in the foreground, usually the narrator, whose entire function consists in surrounding the genius at the middle. He researches this genius, seeks him out, comments upon him and in fact draws his existence from him. We know the character at the center only through the efforts of our narrator and guide, who is himself a sympathetic but a less interesting, less gifted, and somehow flawed, incomplete figure.

Clarence Brown, "N.'s Pushkin," in L. S. Dembo, ed., *N.: The Man and His Work* (1967), pp. 201–2

His passion for exactitude is necessarily coupled with a love of synonymy. Without a large bag of words, the wordman is incapable of providing the right word for the right occasion. When there are semantic equals, rhythm and sound determine choice. If *whin* won't fit, *gorse* or *furze* might do. If it is a time for Elizabethan flyting and digladiation, one may grow wrathful with an unctuous mome and let fly *cudden* and *dawkin* and *mooncalf*. If it is a matter, say, of Kinbote's catamites and urning-yearnings, it helps to have *ingle* and *gunsil, bardash* and *pathic*, in verbal reserve. Most of N.'s resources, of course, are not at all rare or recherché. He is a master of the familiar word. But when he does embrace a neglected one, "it lives again, sobs again, stumbles all over the cemetery in doublet and trunk hose, and will keep annoying stodgy gravediggers" as long as literature itself endures.

Peter Lubin, "Kickshaws & Motley," in Alfred Appel and Charles Newman, eds., *N.: Criticism, Reminiscences, Translations, and Tributes* (1970), pp. 190

I have expressed in print my opinion that he is now an American writer and the best living; I have also expressed my doubt that his aesthetic models—chess puzzles and protective colorations in lepidoptera—can be very helpful ideals for the rest of us. His importance for me as a writer has been his holding high, in an age when the phrase "artistic integrity" has a somewhat paradoxical if not reactionary ring, the stony image of his self-sufficiency: perverse he can be, but not abject; prankish but not hasty; sterile but not impotent. Even the least warming aspects of his image—the implacable hatreds, the reflexive contempt—testify, like fortress walls, to the reality of the siege this strange century lays against our privacy and pride.

As a reader, I want to register my impression that N. does not (as Philip Toynbee, and other critics, have claimed) lack heart. *Speak, Memory* and *Lolita* fairly bulge with heart, and even the less ingratiating works, such as *King, Queen, Knave*, show, in the interstices

of their rigorous designs, a plenitude of human understanding. The ability to animate into memorability minor, disagreeable characters bespeaks a kind of love. The little prostitute that Humbert Humbert recalls undressing herself so quickly, the fatally homely daughter of John Shade, the intolerably pretentious and sloppy-minded woman whom Pnin undyingly loves, the German street figures in *The Gift*, the extras momentarily on-screen in the American novels—all make a nick in the mind. Even characters N. himself was plainly prejudiced against, like the toadlike heroine of *King, Queen, Knave*, linger vividly, with the outlines of the case they must plead on Judgment Day etched in the air; how fully we feel, for example, her descent into fever at the end. And only an artist full of emotion could make us hate the way we hate Axel Rex in *Laughter in the Dark*. If we feel that Nabokov is keeping, for all his expenditure of verbal small coin, some treasure in reserve, it is because of the riches he has revealed. Far from cold, he has access to European vaults of sentiment sealed to Americans; if he feasts the mind like a prodigal son, it is because the heart's patrimony is assured. [1970]

John Updike, "A Tribute," *Picked-Up Pieces* (1975), pp. 221–22

N.'s haunting magic rests precisely in the telling—in his particular combination of sounds works, ideas. . . . The mechanisms . . . are both subtle and complex. For N.'s world breathes with a teasing and unseen deception. Describing himself as a Russian writer, he has aptly emphasized "the mirror-like angles of his clear but weirdly misleading sentences."

A faintly Russian coloration further contributes to the "live iridescence" of N.'s English prose. His writings evince a unique perspective on especially these two languages and cultures.

But N.'s uniquely controlled "reality" is surely his most mysterious product. Elusive inter-echoes, from line to line, from book to book, subtly expand. Systematic networks of ironic foreshadowings produce a background unsettling in its depth. Hidden levels of meaning effect a striking range of dimension.

Nabokovian "reality" also illustrates his belief that imagination is a form of memory. His narrators . . . view and present their stories throught the lenses of their own imaginations. Memory and imagination systematically overlap. And the clear, vivid results of their purposely blurred interaction consistently make up for a negation of time.

William Woodin Rowe, *N.'s Deceptive World* (1971), pp. 151–62

In his fiction N. is always concerned with both a world and a world apart, with an objective reality on which we can more or less agree ("There is no Zembla") and a consciousness which creates a subjective world of its own ("There is not only a Zembla, but I am its king"). The conflict between these two worlds may be that between art and life, as in *Bend*

Sinister, or that between the present and the past, as in *Pnin*. The extremely complex relationship of these two sets of realities is the mark of N.'s most advanced fiction; earlier European fiction like *King, Queen, Knave* does not employ it, or employs it, as in *Despair*, in a comparatively simple fashion. The idea reaches its apotheosis in *Ada*, where the world is wholly reimagined, and it is our Terra that is the dream—or the nightmare.

The real complexities of N.'s art lie in the grazing, mirroring, adjacent planes of objective and subjective "realities," and in the complicated statements about consciousness, art, and imagination. With these inter-actions we must be very careful. But there are few major artists whose emotional appeals are so direct and unambiguous, and whose favorites are so obviously meant to awe us with their heroics of deed and perception.

Douglas Fowler, Reading N. (1974), p. 202

N. has often been celebrated for his brilliance as a stylist; but it is important to recognize that this brilliance, perhaps most centrally in *Ada*, is not ornamental, as in some of his American imitators, but the necessary instrument of a serious ontological enterprise: to rescue reality from the bland nonentity of stereotypicality and from the terrifying rush of mortality by reshaping objects, relations, existential states, through the power of metaphor and wit, so that they become endowed with an arresting life of their own. An incidental samovar, observed in passing, "expressed fragments of its surroundings in demented fantasies of a primitive genre." Lucette drowning sees her existence dissolve in a receding series of selves and perceives that "what death amounted to was only a more complete assortment of the infinite fractions of solitude." Van Veen, driving through the Alps to his first rendezvous with Ada after a separation of fifteen years, sees from his flesh (to borrow an apposite idiom from Job) the palpable reality of time as his recent telephone conversation with Ada and his view of the landscape around him are transformed in the alembic of consciousness into a summarizing metaphor.

Robert Alter, "Ada, or the Perils of Paradise," in
Peter Quennell, ed., V. N.: A Tribute (1979),
pp. 105–6

NÁDAS, Péter

Hungarian novelist, dramatist, and essayist, b. 14 Oct. 1942, Budapest

Considered an exquisitely refined intellectual writer, N. is actually one of the few novelists and dramatists of his generation without university training. He had intentions of becoming a chemist but dropped out of school and turned to photojournalism instead. During the late 1960s and early 1970s, N. worked as an editor, reader, and drama consultant, but soon thereafter became a

self-supporting writer. In the early 1980s, he left Budapest and settled in Gombosszeg, a tiny village in south-western Hungary.

N.'s first two volumes of short stories, *A biblia* (1967; the Bible) and *Kulcskereső játék* (1969; finding the key—a game), are almost wholly retrospective, dealing with children's perspectives of the grim early 1950s in Hungary. What makes these often autobiographically inspired stories particularly tense and ironic is that the young protagonists in question are the privileged children of powerful communist officials. N.'s own father had been a high-ranking party functionary. With great sensitivity and fitnesse N. depicts these children's easy identification with the values of the "new class," but he also suggests early stirrings of moral awareness.

In *Egy családregény vége* (1977; the end of a family novel), his first mature work of fiction, the author again assumes the point of view of a child growing up in Stalinist Hungary. Here the father is a dour and fanatical state-security officer who falls victim himself to one of the purges of the time. However, *Egy családregény vége* is much more than a political novel. By his own admission N. is attracted to the kind of literature that fuses "historical fact and fancy, myth, intuition, physicality and intellectuality." Thus, the shabby reality of daily life in a police state is transfigured in the child-hero's mind into thrilling suspense stories, and the boy's grandfather, an even more seductive spinner of tales, regales his grandson with fascinating and often bizarre stories about their Jewish ancestors, tracing the family back to biblical times. Indeed this "family novel," until its sudden and strangely inconclusive end, becomes a capsule history of the Jewish people.

In his second monumental novel, *Emlékiratok könyve* (1986; book of memoirs), N. remains faithful to the confessional mode and once more weaves a very intricate yarn. But like some of the extravagant postmodern fabulists, he is more interested in subtle narrative and thematic correspondences, recurrences, and even subtler stylistic parodies than in the stories themselves. The novel alternates between the recollections of a young Hungarian writer finding himself passionately in love with another man, a German poet, in East Berlin, and the memoirs of a character of his own creation, an overrefined, turn-of-the-century aesthete. There is a third voice, toward the end of the novel that of the narrator's childhood friend who, after the protagonist's return to his homeland and death several years later, concludes the memoir by describing his friend's last years, offering his own, seemingly far more objective and matter-of-fact version of their friendship.

A penetrating, analytical writer, N. is also a creator of elaborately literary prose. In highly cerebral essays and meditations, collected in *Játéktér* (1988; playing field) and *Égi és földi szerelem* (1991; heavenly and earthly love), or in more openly autobiographical reminiscences—*Évkönyv* (1989; yearbook)—he is just as likely to sketch out character, unravel motives, resort to myth and parable as he is in his fiction. His dramas, on the other hand, are stylistically more austere, narratively more static. He has written three plays—*Takarítás* (1977; housecleaning), *Találkozás* (1979; *Encounter*, 1988), *Temetés*, (1980; funeral)—and all three are virtually plotless rituals of initiation and purification.

Yet even in his most stylized and abstract pieces N. remains a probing, sympathetic intellectual who longs for synthesis and harmony, a fusion of immanence and transcendence, of "heavenly and earthly love." Actually, human sexuality is a particularly important concern, including unconventional forms of sexuality, which are also seen as attempts to merge opposites.

In the past two decades N. has turned from promising innovator to a recognized master of Hungarian prose. Moreover, *Emlékiratok*

Könyve, which has been or is being translated into a number of languages, established him as a major central European literary figure.

FURTHER WORKS: *Leírás* (1979); *Nézőtér* (1983); *Talált cetli* (1992)

BIBLIOGRAPHY: Sanders, I. on *Egy családregény vége, WLT*, 52, 3 (Summer 1978): 496; Maszák, M. Szegedy, "P. N.," *The Hungarian P. E.N.*, 27 (1986): 44–45; Sanders, I., on *Emlékiratok Könyve, WLT*, 61, 2 (Spring 1987): 322–23

—IVAN SANDERS

NAGAI Kafū

(pseud. of Nagai Sōkichi) Japanese novelist, short-story writer, essayist, and critic, b. 3 Dec. 1879, Tokyo; d. 10 April 1959, Tokyo

As a young man, N. was sent by his father to the U.S. and to France to learn the banking trade, but his love of the traditional Kabuki theater and of Japanese and French literature caused him upon his return to Japan in 1908 to take up a career as novelist, professor of French literature, literary editor, and translator, most notably of French symbolist poetry.

In an early masterpiece, the novel *Sumidagawa* (1909; *The River Sumida*, 1965), N. already shows certain of the hallmarks of his mature style, which include an ability to create an ironic view of the present reflected through an appreciation of the beauties of traditional urban Japanese culture, an elegant and elegiac prose style, and an interest in the nuances of the erotic lives of his characters, many of them from the demimonde. N. came to write about such supposedly degraded persons because he felt they represented the truth about society; for him, middle-class respectability represented an essential falsehood.

From the beginning of his career, N. showed great skill in capturing nuances in characterization and setting. In *Sumidagawa*, N. achieved a consonance of setting, mood, and character that set him apart and ahead of all other writers of his generation. In that novel, the sections on the Kabuki theater are particularly vivid. N. continued to adapt certain elements from this theatrical form to his fiction, including the use of surprising happenings and of characters with unusual and colorful personalities.

In 1916 N., increasingly disillusioned with the reactionary policies of the Japanese government, abandoned public life after the death of his father, never again assuming any kind of public position. He continued to write about the byways of contemporary Japanese culture, finding lyric impetus in the erotic world of the geishas and mistresses who functioned in perhaps the only area of life that remained resistant to change in a rapidly modernizing Japan. In an oblique fashion, N. served as a sort of cultural critic through his evocation, half lyrical, half ironic, of a vanishing lifestyle that represented for him a time when Japanese culture had been of a piece. In this one regard, his attitude of irony and detachment resembles that of his mentor, the novelist Mori ŌGAI.

Of N.'s many pre-World War II works, *Bokutō kidan* (1937; *A Strange Tale from East of the River*, 1965) is perhaps the finest, a remarkable evocation of the atmosphere of a poor section of Tokyo, written as a story within a story, in which the protagonist, a novelist, has an affair with a prostitute while composing his own story about an affair with a prostitute. A brilliant command of detail

combined with a sense of evanescence allows N. to produce a striking evocation of psychology, time, and place. N.'s treatment of the liaison mixes introspection, literary reference, and acute observation with an expression of his own intense disdain for the forces of order in society.

During the war years N. refused to cooperate with the government authorities; because of his fiercely independent attitude he became something of a culture hero after 1945. In his short stories written during the postwar period, N. continued to examine changes in Japan with an aristocratic and acerbic eye.

N. continues to be appreciated for his brilliant, evocative style as well as for the special atmosphere and psychological insight of all his works. In spite of the charges of decadence that have often been brought against him, he is, in his own way, a moralist.

FURTHER WORKS: *Amerika monogatari* (1908); *Furansu monogatari* (1909); *Kazagokochi* (1912); *Udekurabe* (1917; *Geisha in Rivalry*, 1963); *Okamezasa* (1918); *Ame shōshō* (1921); *Enoki monogatari* (1931); *Odoriko* (1944); *Towazugatari* (1945); *Zenshū* (24 vols., 1948–53). **FURTHER WORKS IN ENGLISH:** *Kafū the Scribbler: The Life and Writings of N. K., 1879–1959* (1965)

BIBLIOGRAPHY: Seidensticker, E., *Kafū the Scribbler: The Life and Writings of N. K., 1879–1959* (1965); Ueda, M., *Modern Japanese Writers and the Nature of Literature* (1976): 26–53; Rimer, J. T., *Modern Japanese Fiction and Its Traditions* (1978): 138–61

—J. THOMAS RIMER

NAGIBIN, Yury Markovich

Russian short-story writer, b. 3 Apr. 1920, Moscow; d. 17 June 1994

Perhaps the most distinguished contemporary Russian short-story writer, N. has also made his mark as an essayist and screenwriter. He grew up in a family of the Moscow intelligentsia and came by his love of literature early. After training at the Institute of Cinematography, he volunteered for service at the front during World War II and suffered a concussion in battle. He then worked as a war correspondent until 1945. For the next few years, he covered farm and village life for a newspaper. Several of these writings led to screen-plays. By the mid-1950s, N. was looked on as one of the most promising young Russian writers. Since then, he has published in virtually every Soviet literary journal. He has traveled widely abroad, appeared frequently on Soviet television, and become one of the most prominent and widely published Soviet writers.

Despite N.'s many essays, reviews, and screen-plays, it is as a short-story writer that he is best known. He has dealt with a wide range of subjects: war, children, sports, hunting and fishing, village life, art, life abroad, love, and historical personalities. N. began publishing at the outbreak of World War II, and the tone of his war stories is in keeping with the mood of the times. They are thoroughly patriotic, but suggest in their style and craftsmanship that their author is gifted. Much the same can be said about his stories of farm and village life in the late 1940s.

N. has said that the main theme of his stories is that of awakening, discovery: There turns out to be more to a person than one has thought; one sees into a person or thing as one has not seen before; appearances are deceptive, and one should not accept life at face value. This theme is present but less apparent in N.'s early stories about war and reconstruction. It was not until the 1950s that he hit his stride. Stories such as "Zimnii dub" (1953; "Winter Oak," 1955) and "Komarov" (1953; "Komarov," 1955) show his facility in portraying children. *Chistye prudy* (1962; Clear Ponds) and other collections are devoted largely to N.'s poignant memories of his youth. Stories about sports recall his days as a promising athlete. And stories about hunting and fishing, such as those in *Pogonya, Meshcheriskie byli* (1964; the chase, Meshchera stories), are made up largely of the vivid descriptions N. is noted for. Much of N.'s fiction treats love affairs, as in "Olezhka zhenilsya" (1965; "Olezhka Got Married," 1979), and marriage, as in "Il'in den'" (1972; "Elijah's Day," 1979).

N. remarked that until 1960 he took all his stories from life, from what he had seen and heard, and that it was not until "Ekho" (1960; "Echo," 1961) that he relied on imagination. Since then, his imagination has come more and more into play, and his stories on historical figures are among his richest. Starting with "Kak byl kuplen les" (1972; "A Deal in Timber," 1982), N. has published fictional biographies of the Russian writers Avvakum Petrovich (1620 [or 1621]–1682), Vasily Kirillovich Trediakovsky (1703–1768), Aleksandr Sergeevich Pushkin (1799–1837), Anton Antonovich Delvig (1798–1831), Fedor Ivanovich Tyutchev (1803–1873), Apollon Aleksandrovich Grigorev (1822–1864), Afanasy Afanasevich Fet (Shenshin) (1820–1892), Nikolay Semenovich Leskov (1831–1895), Ivan Alekseevich BUNIN, and Innokenty Fedorovich ANNENSKY, as well as Christopher MARLOWE, Stanislav PRZYBYSZEWSKI, August STRINDBERG, and Ernest HEMINGWAY and the composers Tchaikovsky, Rachmaninoff, and Bach. Many of these are included in the collection *Ostrov liubvi* (1977; *Island of Love*, 1982). The motif that runs through them all is that art calls for great sacrifices. Although the stories are based on the factual lives of personages, N. mixes fact with fiction. As a rule, the story takes place on a single day when the main character is moved to reflect on his life in an interior monologue and make a discovery. The language recalls the idiom of the period in question. The central theme or discovery is that the world of artists is quite different from that of others. It is hard for the two worlds to understand each other, but civilization needs both. In writing about artists who were not adequately recognized, N. does not overlook their shortcomings or the strengths of those who opposed them.

Although N. has written as independently as one could in the Soviet Union without being silenced, he has spoken up even more since 1985. His moving recollections of a boy in his largely autobiographical "Vstan' i idi" (1987; "Stand Up and Walk," 1988) throw a new light on his earlier memories of childhood. Other recent fiction has taken a caustic, satirical turn.

Despite N.'s stature and popularity at home, he has received less attention abroad than a number of other Soviet writers. There are several reasons. He has not made news—he has not been arrested, officially reprimanded, or exiled. By and large, he has chosen to write about the eternal rather than about ephemeral topics of the day. And the forms that come naturally to him are the short story and the *povest'* (tale or novella), whereas the foreign audience may prefer novels.

N. has won many readers with his artistry and breadth. He is unusually skilled as a stylist and craftsman and is perhaps more aware of literary tradition than any other contemporary Russian writer. His eye for detail and the strength of his epiphanies are exceptional. And perhaps no other recent Russian writer has written about so many different subjects. N. has gradually become a spokesman for the Russian intelligentsia and for its permanence amid shifting ideologies.

FURTHER WORKS: *Chelovek s fronta* (1943); *Bol' shoe serdtse* (1944); *Dve sily* (1944); *Zerno zhizni* (1948); *Gosudarstvennoe delo* (1950); *Gospodstvuiushchaia vysota* (1951); *Partiinoe poruchenie* (1951); *Rasskazy* (1953); *Trubka* (1953); *Vsegda v stroiu* (1953); *Rasskazy o voine* (1954); *Malchiki* (1955); *Rasskazy* (1955); *Skalistyi porog* (1955); *Zimnii dub* (1955); *Na ozerax* (1957); *Rasskazy* (1957); *Boi za vysotu* (1958); *Chelovek i doroga* (1958); *Na ozere Velikom* (1958); *Skalistyi porog* (1958); *Poslednii shturm* (1959); *Pered prazdnikom* (1960); *Druz'ia moiliudi* (1961); *Rannei vesnoi* (1961); *Ekho* (1964); *Razmyshleniia o rasskaze* (1964); *Dalekoe i blizkoe* (1965); *Na tikhom ozere i drugie rasskazy* (1966); *Nochnoigost'* (1966); *Zelenaia ptitsa s krasnoi golovoi* (1966); *Ne dai emu pogibnut'* (1968); *Chuzhoe serdtse* (1969); *Perekur* (1970); *Zabroshennaia doroga* (1970); *Pereulki moego detstva* (1971); *Nepobedimyi Arsenov* (1972); *Izbrannye proizvedeniia* (1973); *Moia Africa* (1973); *Ty budesh' zhit'* (1974); *V aprel'skom lesu* (1974); *Pik udachi* (1975); *Literaturnye razdum'ia* (1977); *Berendeev les* (1978); *Rasskazy o Gagarine* (1978); *Zabroshennaia doroga* (1978); *Odin na odin* (1979); *Tsarskosel'skoe utro* (1979); *Zamolchavshaia vensa* (1979); *Sobranie sochinenii v 4-kh tt.* (1980); *Nauka dal'nikh stranstvii* (1982); *Ne chuzhoe remeslo* (1983); *Moskovskaia kniga* (1985); *Lunnyi svet* (1986); *Muzykanty* (1986); *Pushkin na iuge* (1986); *Moskva . . . . kak mnogo v etom zvuke* (1987); *Poezdka na ostrova* (1987); *Sovetskie pisateli, stranitsy tvorchestva* (1987); *Chelovek s fronta* (1988); *Ispytanie* (1988); *Vdali muzyka i ogni* (1989); *Vstan' i idi* (1989). FURTHER WORKS IN ENGLISH: *Each for All* (1945); *Dreams* (1955); *Trubka* (1955); *Dreams* (1958); *The Pipe* (n. d., 1958?); *Selected Short Stories* (1963); *The Peak of Success, and Other Stories* (1986); *Unwritten Story by Somerset Maugham* (1988).

BIBLIOGRAPHY: Hager, R., "Die Evolution des 'literarischen Menschenbildes im Erzählschaffes Sergej Antonovs, Jurij Nagibins und Vladimir Tendrjakovs der 50-er Jaher," *ZS*, 20 (1975): 214–25; Porter, R. N., "The Uneven Talent of Jurij N.," *RLJ*, 32, 113 (1978): 103–13; Porter, R. N., "Jurij N.'s Istoricheskie rasskazy," *RLJ* 34, 118 (1980): 127–35; Schefski, H. K., "Y. N.: Children and the Retreat from Collective Identity," *SSR*, 4 (Spring 1985): 99–106; Sampson, E. D., "The Poacher and the Polluter: The Environmental Theme in N.," in Connolly, J. W., and S. I. Ketchian, eds., *Studies in Russian Literature in Honor of Vsevolod Setchkarev* (1986): 222–32; Goscilo, H., "Introduction," and Cochrum, E., "Biography," in Goscilo, H., ed., *The Peak of Success, and other Stories* (1986): 9–26, 27–33

—RICHARD N. PORTER

NAGY, Lajos

Hungarian short-story writer, novelist, and essayist, b. 5 Feb. 1883, Apostag; d. 28 Oct. 1954, Budapest

The illegitimate son of a housemaid, N. lived with his farm-laborer grandparents until the age of six. The "shame" of his origin and the first experiences of his awakening consciousness left their marks both on his life and his art. Eager to break away from the kind of life he was born into, he untiringly worked to get an education. He studied law, worked as a tutor with an aristocratic family, and, for a short period, as a civil servant. From 1912 on he made his living as a writer, often under severely strained financial circumstances.

In 1919, at the time of Béla Kun's short-lived communist regime, N. favored Kun's administration. The Hungarian Commune, however, which established a classification of writers, relegated him to second-class status. Yet N. was one of those few writers who, after the collapse of Béla Kun's government, were unwilling to listen to the siren song of the Christian Nationalists. On the contrary, he responded to Horthy's counterrevolutionary regime with remarkable personal courage. In *Képtelen természetrajz* (1921; an improbable bestiary) he attacked human selfishness, violence, and stupidity with the unmistakable images of animal allegory; *Találkozásaim az antiszemitizmussal* (1922; my encounters with anti-Semitism) is a spirited defense of the Jews being persecuted by the Horthy government.

N. always went his way alone. Although a socialist, he did not join the Social Democratic Party. Although as a writer he was aware of his intellectual affinity to the period's most important literary circle, the group around the magazine *Nyugat*, he did not associate himself with these writers, who viewed him with a mixture of respect and aversion.

N. published several novels and a monthly magazine, *N. külövéleménye* (N.'s dissent), written entirely by himself, but he was at his best in the short story. In his first stories, "Özvegy asszonyok" (1908; windows) and "Egy délután a Grün irodában" (1910; an afternoon in the Grün office), the problems that were to become the central concerns of his later work are already present: the recognition that women are commonly treated as objects; the power of the sex drive; and the conflict between the rich and the poor, in which N.'s stand is unequivocally anticapitalist without romanticizing the poor.

In the 1920s, the naturalistic realism of N.'s work was modified by EXPRESSIONISM. Some of his most significant stories—for instance, "Napirend" (1927; agenda), "Razzia" (1929; raid), "Január" (1929; January), "A lecke" (1930; the lesson), "Bérház" (1931; tenement), and "Anya" (1931; mother)—show the influence of the cult of the proletarian, the "new factualism" of German literature, the writings of Upton SINCLAIR and John DOS PASSOS, and the new cinematic montage technique.

In *Kiskúnhalom* (1934; Kiskúnhalom), which is about one day in his native village, N. turned away from expressionism. This synthesis of literature and sociology, reportage and Freudian analysis, can, in contemporary terms, be called an "antinovel." That airless dustbowl of a Hungarian village, according to N., can be described only by portraying the pettiness, hatred, hopeless poverty, and rigid oppression of its inhabitants. N.'s precise, cold descriptions resemble the articles in a technical journal; but the impact of the novel is achieved by exactly this method. *Kiskúnhalom* is the archetype of the sociological novel, the "village-exploring" fiction, that was to become an important genre in Hungary.

In the summer of 1934 N. was one of the two Hungarian writers invited to Moscow to attend the First Congress of Soviet Writers. For him, the journey was a disappointment. This disappointment became the main theme in his series of reports, *Tizezer kilométer Oroszország földjén* (1934; ten thousand kilometers in Russia).

In 1945 N. joined the Communist Party and became the feuilletonist for *Szabad Nép*, the central organ of the Party in

Hungary. In 1948 he was awarded the highest literary honor of the country. Yet he recognized the impossibility of writing honestly about current problems. He escaped into the past—into his own past—and began working on his autobiography; the first volume *A lázadó ember* (the rebel) was published in 1949.

At the first Congress of the Hungarian Writers' Association, in 1950, a leading Party functionary characterized N. as a "coffeehouse writer," one who "can view and portray the world only through the window of a coffeehouse." This official attack spelled the end of N.'s writing career; the second volume of his autobiography, *A menekülő ember* (the fugitive), was rejected by the state publishing house and was not published until after his death in 1954, during the short-lived, comparatively liberal government of Imre Nagy.

N. is the most important Hungarian short-story writer of the first half of the 20th c. Although he urged social change, his work is basically and deeply pessimistic. It is characterized by an exceptional talent for observation, by scathing irony, and by a deep-rooted respect for truth.

FURTHER WORKS: *Az asszony, a szeretöje és a férje* (1911); *A szobalány* (1913); *Egy leány, több férfi* (1915); *Egy berlini leány* (1917); *Az Andrássy-út* (1918); *A jó fiú* (1919); *Fiatal emberek* (1920); *Vadember* (1926); *Egyszerüség* (n.d.); *Három magyar város* (1933); *Utcai baleset* (1935); *Budapest Nagykávéház* (1936); *A falu álarca* (1937); *Három boltoskisasszony* (1938); *Egy lány a századfordulón* (1940); *A fiatalúr megnösül* (1941); *Pincenapló* (1945); *A tanitvény* (1945); *A falu* (1946); *A három éhenkórász* (1946); *Emberek, állatok* (1947); *Január* (1948); *Farkas és bárány* (1948); *Új vendég érkezett* (1954); *Válogatott elbeszélések* (3 vols., 1956); *Válogatott karcolatok* (1957); *Iró, könyv, olvasó, Tanulmányok és cikkek* (2 vols., 1959); *N. válogatott müvei* (1962)

BIBLIOGRAPHY: Aczel, T., and Méray, T., *The Revolt of the Mind* (1959): 21–33; Klaniczay, T., J. Szauder, and M. Szabolcsi, *History of Hungarian Literature* (1964); Erdei, F., *Information Hungary* (1968): 796–97

—TAMAS ACZEL

NAIDU, Sarojini

Indian poet (writing in English), b. 13 Feb. 1879, Hyderabad; d. 2 March 1949, Lucknow

The precocious eldest child of an eminent, highly Westernized family, N. began to write English poetry as a child. In 1895 she went to study at King's College, London, where she became friends with the critic Edmund Gosse (1849–1928) and later at Girton College, Cambridge, where she was introduced to members of the famous Rhymer's Club by the critic Arthur Symons (1865–1945). She returned to India in 1898, and because of her family's position in the vanguard of India's intellectual and literary renascence, she came into close contact with many of the country's most prominent writers, political figures, and reformers. She continued to write poetry until the period of World War I, then abruptly stopped. The remainder of her life was spent as an active political worker for the Indian National Congress Party. A close friend and confidante of Mahatma Gandhi, N. also campaigned vigorously for women's rights in India.

Gosse had advised N. to eschew Anglo-Saxon themes in her poetry and to concentrate on subjects from her native India. That she heeded this advice is evident in her first volume of poems, *The Golden Threshold* (1905), published in England and boasting an introduction by Symons. It is replete with descriptive pieces on snake charmers, dancers, weavers, and palanquin-bearers, as well as Indian flora and monuments. The book was well received, and N. was immediately given the epithet "nightingale of India."

Her second collection, *The Bird of Time* (1912), included an enthusiastic foreword by Gosse, who noted that the poems in this volume express a "graver music" than her earlier ones, for they treat such themes as melancholy, death, and bereavement. Others take the form of Indian folk songs and present ardent religious sentiment mixed with patriotic fervor.

The third collection, *The Broken Wing* (1917), contains a number of poems dedicated to Indian patriots, including N.'s father, G. K. Gokhale, and Mahatma Gandhi. Others are the usual sorts of descriptions of Indian cities, festivals, and monuments that were already considered standard fare in N.'s verse. The last section of this volume, however, is given over to a sequence of twenty-four poems entitled "The Temple: A Pilgrimage of Love," which is considered by many as N.'s foremost literary achievement. Here the beloved expresses a wide spectrum of emotions in relationship to her lover: the ecstasy of union, the sadness of separation, anguish over supposed infidelity, and finally silence and acceptance. The poems are replete with images of withered leaves, crushed fruit, and trampled, broken stones and clay lamps. The final section of the cycle identifies the lover with the Almighty and depicts in vivid, violent imagery the inevitability of death.

In 1961 N.'s daughter published a small collection of poems written between July and August 1927 under the title *The Feather of the Dawn*. Many of these are patriotic expressions written to Indian leaders; others are passionate love songs addressed to the god Krishna; and still others portray scenes from Indian life, festivals, and flora. In terms of style, technique, and sentiment, these poems are not notably distinguishable from those found in the earlier collections.

The heir to a tradition of English poetry started by another Indian woman, Toru Dutt (1856–1877), N. initially attracted a great deal of attention in Britain because of her remarkably idiomatic and technically accomplished verse. She offered Edwardians an unprecedented view of Indian exotica which they could readily understand and with which they could easily identify. As her later poetry became suffused with patriotic themes and a seeming preoccupation with death, she began to fall out of favor with the British literary establishment. The reason for her sudden absence from print after 1917 has been the subject of a great deal of speculation. Some suggest that she had developed a certain morbidity in outlook, whose roots were to be found in her personal life, which as a result prevented her from writing. Others submit that she was stunned into silence by the overwhelming popularity of her countryman, Rabindranath TAGORE, winner of the 1913 Nobel Prize for Literature. Still others point out that her thoroughgoing commitment to the Indian nationalist movement did not allow her the necessary time and solitude required to write poetry. Evidence suggests that all three reasons, and possibly others, contributed to her withdrawal from the literary scene.

Today N.'s poetry is generally ignored in the West. In India N.'s poetry has recently become the subject of reevaluation by critics of Indian writing in English, some of whom suggest that many of N.'s poems are among the most distinguished written in India during the 20th c.

FURTHER WORKS: *The Gift of India* (1914); *The Sceptered Flute* (1943)

BIBLIOGRAPHY: Dastoor, P., *S. N.* (1961); Iyengar, K., *Indian Writing in English* (1962): 173–87; Sengupta, P., *S. N.: A Biography* (1966); Mokashi-Puneka, S., "A Note on S. N.," *Critical Essays on Indian Writing in English* (1972): 72–82; Blackwell, F., "Krishna Motifs in the Poetry of S. N. and Kamala Das," *JSoAL*, 13: 1–4 (1977–1978): 9–14; Ramamurti, K., "The Indianness of S. N.'s Poetry," *IndSch*, 1, 2 (1979): 101–9; special N. issue, *OJES*, 16, 1 (1980)

—CARLO COPPOLA

NAIPAUL, Shiva

Trinidadian novelist, short-story writer, essayist, and travel writer, b. 25 Feb. 1945, Port Of Spain, Trinidad; d. 13 Aug. 1985, London

While N. lived for a long time in the shadow of his famous brother V. S. NAIPAUL, his fiction, essays, and travel books are persuasive evidence that he found his own voice. N. was an indifferent science student at Trinidad's Queen's Royal College, his brother's alma mater, but found his stride at the rival St. Mary's College and won an Island Scholarship for study at Oxford where he read politics, psychology, and Chinese language and literature. N.'s love-hate relationship with Trinidad gives some of his work its distinctive tension. Trinidad gave him a neurotic sense of entrapment, but it was also the stimulus and source of his artistic sensibilities.

His first two novels, *Fireflies* (1970) and *The Chip-Chip Gatherers* (1973), are stinging satires of Trinidad's dying Hinduism in the first decades of the 20th c. *Fireflies* also satirizes the colonial society on the threshold of universal suffrage in an effective blending of pathos and humor. Ramsaran's decaying trucks in *The Chip-Chip Gatherers* are a metaphor of the moribund Hindu community and the equally derelict colonial society depicted in both novels. N.'s women characters are engaging. Sushila of *The Chip-Chip Gatherers*, for instance, is not the stereotypical Hindu female; she is instead a fragile woman, despite her abrasiveness, terrified of losing her sexuality, her only asset in her circumscribed world.

North of South: *An African Journey* (1978) traces N.'s travels through East Africa, which he depicts as a brutal and brutalizing region. His criticism is aimed at both blacks and Europeans who are described as self-serving, coarse racists. N. argues that the meeting of Africans and Europeans has had tragic consequences for both races largely because of mutual intolerance. He also condemns East Africa's Asians, but they are not individualized and tend to be either caricatures or stereotypes. *Black and White* (1980), republished in 1980 as *Journey to Nowhere: A New World Tragedy*, N.'s study of the 1978 Jonestown massacre in Guyana, remains one of the best books on the subject. The book is a penetrating analysis of the making of the reverend Jim Jones and his disaffected disciples, and an illuminating exploration of Southern California and Guyana's corrupt politics of the 1970s. One of the book's most interesting arguments is that Jones subconsciously hated blacks because of his relentless exploitation of impending racial terror.

N.'s third novel, *A Hot Country* (1983), republished in 1984 as *Love and Death in a Hot Country*, was written after his traumatic sojourn in Guyana. The novel is dominated by N.'s darkened vision, and his portrait of Cuyama—the fictional Guyana, a dark void in which cynicism and banditry have become an ideology—and the men and women trapped in its political darkness is compellingly candid.

Beyond the Dragon's Mouth (1984) is a collection of short stories as well as magazine and newspaper articles. The best stories demonstrate N.'s ability to call up concrete images of the Trinidadian setting. "The Dolly House" (1974) is a charming story of lost innocence. Clara, the story's central intelligence, is described with an uncommon understanding of a woman's emotional life as N. traces her journey from child-bride to cynical woman, victim of a selfish husband. "Victim of Ramadan" (1980) is N.'s frightening account of his encounter with Islamic fundamentalism in Morocco. His description of Morocco as a repressive, zealot-ridden police state is conveyed in tense, vigorous prose. Of the three pieces on India, "The Sanjay Factor" (1981) is the most effective. The essay traces the rise of Sanjay Gandhi, autocratic son and heir to the Gandhi dynasty, and is a sustained and persuasive analysis of what N. describes as the shallowness of Indian politics.

"My Brother and I," published posthumously in *An Unfinished Journey* (1986), discusses his troubled relationship with his brother. He explains that the expectations and terrors that dominated his difficult childhood were shaped by his older brother's achievements and his attempts to measure up to those achievements. He insists that his writing vocation was not a conscious decision to imitate his brother; however, his description of the catalyst that launched his writing career reminds one of V. S. Naipaul's own beginning. The incomplete "An Unfinished Journey" is a sensitive account of N.'s rapport with two Sri Lankans who befriended him on his journey to Australia. The tone of this essay is refreshingly mellow, lacks N.'s characteristic bite, and is probably his intuition of the common frailty he shares with the two Sri Lankans. The tone is also prophetically elegiac, for N. would live for only six more months. N.'s journalism and travel writing are often acerbic, but this is a defense mechanism, one feels, against his sense of deracination, the doppelgänger that seems to have hounded him.

Although some critics have compared N.'s fiction with his brother's and found it wanting, other commentators have noted his humor and fine ear for dialogue. Although it tends to focus on the self-destructive characteristics of human beings, N.'s work is on the whole engaging and vital.

BIBLIOGRAPHY: Moss, J., "*Fireflies* by S. N.," *WLWE*, 12 (Apr. 1973): 117-19; Niven, A., "A Sophisticated Talent," *JCL*, 8 (June 1973): 131-33; Questel, V., "Literary Jackals on the Make," *Tapia*, 3 (1973): 6-7; Chancellor, A., "S. N.," *Spectator*, 24 Aug. 1985: 17-18; Maja-Pearce, A., "The Naipauls on Africa: An African View," *JCL*, 20 (1985): 111-17; Poynting, J., "Limbo Consciousness: Between India and the Caribbean," *TSAR*, 5 (Summer 1986): 205-21; Jacobs, J., "Writing in the Margin: S. N.'s *A Hot Country*," *Theoria*, 70 (Oct. 1987): 55-65; Wheatcroft, G., "Writers and Comparisons: Salman Rushdie and S. N.," *Encounter*, 75 (Sept. 1990): 38-40; Barratt, H., "S. N.," in Sander, R., and B. Lindfors, eds., *DLB*, Vol. 157 (1996): 218-26

—HAROLD BARRATT

V. S. Naipaul

NAIPAUL, V(idiadhar) S(urajprasad)

Trinidadian novelist and essayist, b. 17 Aug. 1932, Chaguanas

N., whose grandfather had come from India to the Caribbean as an indentured laborer, completed his early education in Port of Spain, Trinidad, and, after emigrating to England, was graduated from Oxford in 1954. These facts are of considerable importance for understanding N.'s progressive alienation from the three cultures that shaped him, his disaffection from any particular literary community or tradition, and his concern with political and moral freedom, exile, and the quest for order. These are the themes that, in one way or another, find their way into his writing.

Such themes are but thinly articulated in the first three novels. In *Miguel Street* (written 1954, pub. 1959) they are parceled out among several dozen inhabitants of a slum street in Port of Spain. Their activity on the street is perceived through the intelligence of the young narrator—a street "rab" of rare sensitivity and humanity who is able to transmit something poignant and comic, but at the same time profound, about lives governed by poverty, frustration, aborted ambition, and superstitious fatalism.

N.'s next two novels focus on a single protagonist. They, too, generate their satire and irony from the culturally and racially disordered world of Trinidad. In *The Mystic Masseur* (1957) the naïve Ganesh Ramsumair, through a concatenation of chance, island superstition (*obeah*), autodidacticism, and corruption, rises to become first a popular masseur, then a mystic, writer, pundit, politico, and finally a representative to the legislature. Inevitably, Ganesh loses his stature as cult figure and hero of the people, and, capping his progress, anglicizes his name to G. Ramsay Muir.

In *The Suffrage of Elvira* (1958) Surujupat Harban's shaky course to the legislature careers through the comic intrigue, boondoggling, and logrolling that accompanies democracy's rise in Trinidad and its first general election. "Pat" sells out totally to win the seat, and, winning, disowns all those factions that helped him—Hindu, Muslim, black. For the fascination of power that transports him from Trinidad's backward counties to the capital, he surrenders honesty, innocence, and wonder.

N., in these rather slight novels, seems clinically accurate about the logical progression from self-abasement to self-advertisement to selfishness; he is scrupulous in rendering the motives of the little man who must flog his egotism in order to succeed in a care-little, do-nothing, failure-prone society.

A House for Mr. Biswas (1961) was N.'s first major novel, and perhaps the best novel yet to emerge from the English-speaking Caribbean. This feat was achieved by linking one of the most notable characters in contemporary fiction with the extraordinary multiethnicity of Trinidad. Epic in conception and panoramic in execution, the novel spans three generations of West Indian Hindus and centers on Mohun Biswas, a poor, diligent Brahman, and his quest for a house of his own. *A House for Mr. Biswas* is nothing less than a small odyssey. From his inauspicious, unlucky birth, through childhood misfortunes, a too-hasty marriage, years of domination by in-laws (the power-hungry, status-seeking Tulsis), to his success as a journalist, the purchase of the house, and his death by cardiac arrest, Mr. Biswas moves through life confronting and overcoming exhaustion and loss. In the course of his forty-three years he is flogged, duped, thwarted, maligned, robbed, humiliated, frustrated, defeated, sickened, and frightened; yet he remains throughout stoic and hopeful. The house, when it at last becomes his, has come not only to symbolize his yearning for freedom and identity but his triumph over the lovelessness, waste, and chaos of his society.

Six years later—after traveling in the Americas and India and writing books about the experience—N. published his most profound book to date, *The Mimic Men* (1967). It is a novel of colonial disintegration on a par with George ORWELL's *Burmese Days* and E. M. FORSTER's *A Passage to India*; but its focus is on the disintegration of the natives rather than that of the colonialists.

The "mimic men" of the title refer to men of older cultures who have been educated to be mimics of contemporary cultures. Consequently, such a man is deprived of the authenticity of living in terms of one's own culture. The novel explores the rise to and fall from power of Ralph Singh, a West Indian Hindu. At forty, having exhausted his roles as friend, countryman, lover, son, husband, student, businessman, politician, and diplomat, he now writes his autobiography. Living in a London hotel, he strives to obtain from the "inaction" imposed upon him the "final emptiness."

Born on the island of "Isabella" and educated in England, Singh, the imperfectly Westernized Hindu, drives toward wealth and power, always under the illusion that he is free to choose, although in reality he can never overcome his past or his heritage. The novel is a monumental study of the evils and perversions of double-faced colonial exploitation, but it is also a profound study of a single life, drained by the flux of history, defeated by personal, social, political, and cultural forces, and fated for shipwreck.

An inveterate traveler and confirmed expatriate, N., always in search of new settings for his themes, offers a most searching

evaluation of several important themes in *In a Free State* (1971). The volume's three stories—ranging in tone from farce to tragedy, and in locale from Washington, D.C., to a fictional African state—are linked by the themes of freedom and exile. They are framed by two excerpts from N.'s journals, which also brood on these themes, seeing them as basic to his existence. The longest (and title) story of the volume, tells of the growing fears and ultimate neurotic collapse of two British colonials (a man and a woman) as they travel by car across a small African nation in the throes of revolution. Seeking order, safety, and freedom, Bobby and Linda experience only disillusion and the claustrophobic confinement of an English compound in the heart of Black Africa.

Guerrillas (1975) continues the theme of *In a Free State*, but the virulence of colonialism—its self- and universal destructiveness—has been translated to a nameless, if prototypical Caribbean island just on the verge of realizing its infection. To the island—divided racially, politically, and economically—comes Peter Roche, a white South African liberal who is hired as a kind of public relations liaison between the Establishment and Jimmy Ahmed, the half-caste leader of the revolutionary group. Within the ideological struggles of these two men—one who "cannot see the future," and the other who seems to hold it in the palm of his hand—N. constructs variations on the evils and disasters that liberalism, colonialism, and militancy have wrought. Every man is a guerrilla, he suggests, fighting his own war.

The nihilism of N.'s recent novels is not solely the result of the author's private pessimism; it grows out of history, out of the colonial dilemma and paradox. Colonialism leads to decay, decay to revolution, revolution to chaos and rootlessness, then back again to revolution. It is of course the individual, caught up in this dialectic, who suffers. Such is the major theme of *A Bend in the River* (1979), N.'s tenth novel. Isolated at "a bend in the river," Salim, an East African of East Indian origin, an expatriate trying to build his life out of the rubble left by postindependence revolution, finds that such "freedom" plunges him further into spiritual, cultural, and inevitably political imprisonment. His false hopes of constructing anything—a new life or new self—are scrapped for the matter of merely surviving in, and then escaping from a country that is suspiciously like Zaire with a crude, energetic, insane president that uncomfortably resembles Mobutu.

N.'s five most recent novels paint a bleak, but compelling and realistic picture of the colonial experience: of the betrayers and of the betrayed who in turn become the betrayers. One, he seems to say, may accept the order of things, the other may create the chaos, but neither, alas, is able to create order. N.'s treatment of so complex a theme, and his fluid, challenging ideas on other problems fundamental to our times, have made him one of the most original and thoughtful writers of the postwar period.

FURTHER WORKS: *The Middle Passage* (1962); *Mr. Stone and the Knights Companion* (1964); *An Area of Darkness: An Experience of India* (1964); *A Flag on the Island* (1967); *The Loss of El Dorado: A History* (1969); *The Overcrowded Barracoon: Selected Articles 1958–1972* (1972); *India: A Wounded Civilization* (1977); *The Return of Eva Perón, with The Killings in Trinidad* (1980); *Among the Believers: An Islamic Journey* (1981)

BIBLIOGRAPHY: Walsh, W., *A Manifold Voice: Studies in Commonwealth Literature* (1970): 62–85; Ramchand, K., *The West Indian Novel* (1970): 189–204; Theroux, P., *V. S. N.: An Introduction to His Work* (1972); Hamner, R. D., *V. S. N.* (1973); Walsh, W.,

V. S. N. (1973); Morris, R. K., *Paradoxes of Order: Some Perspectives on the Fiction of V. S. N.* (1975); White, L., *V. S. N.: A Critical Introduction* (1975); Boxill, A., "The Paradox of Freedom: V. S. N.'s *In a Free State,*" *Crit,* 18 (1976): 81–91; Hamner, R. D., ed., *Critical Perspectives on V. S. N.* (1977); Morris, R. K., "Shadow into Substance: V. S. N.'s *The Mimic Men,*" in Morris, R. K., ed., *Old Lines, New Forces* (1977): 131–50

—ROBERT K. MORRIS

NAŁKOWSKA, Zofia

Polish novelist, short-story writer, and dramatist, b. 10 Nov. 1884, Warsaw; d. 17 Dec. 1954, Warsaw

Daughter of a renowned scholar, N. grew up in an intellectual, progressive, and sophisticated milieu. She was introduced early to philosophical ideas and modern literary trends that influenced her creative work from the start and left their mark on her *Weltanschauung* as well as on her political stances at different times of her life. A prolific writer, N. started her career with the publication of modernistic verse, but abandoned the genre for prose—mainly the novel and the short story, later the drama.

The novel *Kobiety* (1906; *Women,* 1920) is typical of N.'s approach to the theme of women's emancipation, seen as the right to love and to experience the dark mysteries of sex—which, however, her cerebral heroines invariably fail to understand. The theme, treated by N. philosophically, realistically, or as a psychological experiment, never ceased to fascinate her throughout her writing career; but historical events—World War I, Poland's regaining of independence, World War II and the German occupation of Poland, and the postwar political situation there—developed in turn other themes, relegating feminism to a secondary interest.

Rumblings of the approaching worldwide upheaval are reflected in N.'s earlier works in the revolutionary activities of her male protagonists, but these works chiefly explore the "battle of sexes." They are written in the fin-de-siècle spirit and the ornamental style of "Young Poland," the Polish counterpart of the SYMBOLIST, and especially the Decadent movements of the period. Some critics accused her of psychologism—applying psychological conceptions to the interpretation of historical events—and of exaggerated philosophical thinking, which often deprive N.'s characters of warmth and realistically motivated behavior.

N.'s most significant work dates from the 1920s and 1930s. Her style by then had acquired simplicity and lucidity, and her characters had become less self-centered and more psychologically realistic. She has a penchant for *romans à these*: her plots tend to serve as illustrations of her favorite maxims, which are also clearly spelled out in characters' remarks or the narrator's asides, such as "one dies at just any random moment of life," or "we really are what we appear to be in the eyes of other people." Some maxims reappear in different novels. Yet, an element of social awareness and a desire to probe deeper into the complexities of life and human relationships lend authenticity even to N.'s far-fetched aphorisms.

While N.'s two plays, *Dom kobiet* (1930; the house of women) and *Dzień jego powrotu* (1930; *The Day of His Return,* 1931), still focus primarily on the vicissitudes of the human condition, her best novel, *Granica* (1935; the boundary) is different. The boundary of the title is the farthest limit of the compromise an individual can make with his conscience without jeopardizing his identity. However, since everyone is a pawn in the social "scheme" to which he belongs by birth, occupation, or financial situation, the line is certain to be gradually approached and eventually crossed. This being N.'s fatalistic premise, the plot ends in total catastrophe. *Granica* can be, and was, viewed as an indictment of the social order, symbolically dividing the protagonists into inhabitants of the upper floors and those of the cellars in an apartment house; or as an affirmation of the Bible's pronouncement that the wages of sin (in this case the seduction of a servant girl) is death.

N. met with success and recognition at practically all stages of her artistic career, especially in the final stage of her life and work following the global catastrophe of World War II, when she became a deputy to the Polish Diet and member of the Commission for the Investigation of Nazi Crimes. The latter position resulted in the publication of her documentary, *Medaliony* (1946; medallions), awesome in its stark realism. N.'s work was shaped as much by her sensitivity to social ills and her intellectual curiosity as by her talent. It also faithfully reflects the stormy historical events and the variegated literary trends of her entire lifetime.

FURTHER WORKS: *Książę* (1907); *Koteczka albo białe tulipany* (1909); *Rówieśnice* (1909); *Narcyza* (1910); *Węże i róże* (1915); *Tajemnice krwi* (1917); *Hrabia Emil* (1920); *Charaktery* (1922); *Romans Teresy Hennert* (1924); *Dom nad łąkami* (1925); *Małżeństwo* (1925); *Choucas* (1927); *Niedobra miłość* (1928); *Między zwierzętami* (1934); *Niecierpliwi* (1939); *Węzły życia* (1948; enlarged ed., 2 vols., 1950–1954); *Pisma wybrane* (1954; enlarged ed., 2 vols., 1956); *Widzenie bliskie i dalekie* (1957); *Dzienniki czasu wojny* (1970); *Dzienniki* (3 vols., 1975–1976)

BIBLIOGRAPHY: Kridl, M., *A Survey of Polish Literature and Culture* (1956): 495–97, 503; Miłosz, C., *The History of Polish Literature* (1969): 431–32; Krzyżanowski, J., *A History of Polish Literature* (1978): 624–27

—XENIA GASIOROWSKA

NAMORA, Fernando Gonçalves

Portuguese novelist, short-story writer, and poet, b. 15 April 1919, Condeixa; d. 31 Jan. 1989

N. was raised in rural central Portugal. While studying medicine at the University of Coimbra, he was the director of several small literary reviews, in which he published his first poems. N.'s works reflect his professional experiences as a rural and urban physician, as well as his interest in the role of the intellectual in a politically repressed society.

N.'s first volume of poetry, *Relevos* (1938; reliefs), displayed the confessional tone of the Presença literary group. His *Terra* (1941; soil) was the initial volume in the major series of Portuguese neorealist poetry collectively titled *Novo Cancioneiro* (new songbook). In 1959 he published his collected poems, *As frias madrugadas* (the cold dawns), to be followed by another volume of poetry, *Marketing* (1969; title in English). But N. himself has recognized his lack of a true poetic bent and has more successfully cultivated fiction.

As sete partidas do mundo (1939; the world's seven parts) and *Fogo na noite escura* (1943; fire in the dark night) are autobiographical novels, treating respectively his adolescent years at a

Coimbra high school and the members of his circle at the university at the time of their graduation during World War II. The technique of both works reflects N.'s interest in psychological detail and in the then-growing importance of the neorealist movement. *A casa da malta* (1945; the transient's house) is a complex yet well-developed narrative in which the author presents the lives of poor, wandering rural types.

In his novels of the 1950s N. turned to more existential preoccupations, through his presentation of the exploitation of tungsten miners during World War II and also that of farmers and rural workers. While *O trigo e o joio* (1954; *Fields of Fate*, 1970) is a whimsical tale of rural life, his most provocative work of this period was the novel *O homem disfarçado* (1957; the masked man), a penetrating portrait of the medical profession in Portugal.

N.'s two very notable companion volumes of short fiction, *Retalhos da vida de um médico* (1949, 1963; sketches of a doctor's life; Vol. I tr. as *Mountain Doctor*, 1956), poignantly portray characters who not only are physically ill but also, owing to their chronic misery, have been emotionally and mentally dehumanized. Among N.'s more recent novels, *Os clandestinos* (1972; the clandestine ones), is a striking view of the struggles of his own generation of Portuguese intellectuals under harsh dictatorial repression. He has also written popular biographies of figures of Portuguese medical history, a short history of the neorealist movement in Portugal, and commentaries on contemporary topics.

N.'s works have followed the prevalent trends of modern Portuguese literature, but his doctor's point of view has given his fiction a distinctive narrative voice.

FURTHER WORKS: *Mar de sargaços* (1940); *Minas de S. Francisco* (1946); *A noite e a madrugada* (1950); *Deuses e demónios da medicina* (1952); *Cidade solitária* (1959); *Domingo à tarde* (1961); *Esboço histórico do neo-realismo* (1961); *Aquilino Ribeiro* (1963); *Diálogo em Setembro* (1966); *Um sino na montanha* (1968); *Os adoradores do sol* (1971); *Estamos no vento* (1974); *A nave de pedra* (1975); *Cavalgada cinzenta* (1977); *Encontros* (1979); *Resposta a Matilde* (1980); *O rio triste* (1982)

BIBLIOGRAPHY: Gil, I. M., "La obra novelística de F. N.," *CHA*, 105 (1958): 325–32; Rogers, W. G. on *Fields of Fate, NYTBR*, 22 March 1970: 38; Ares Montes, J. on *Os adoradores do sol, Ínsula*, 270 (1972), 14

—IRWIN STERN

NARANJO, Carmen

Costa Rican poet, novelist, short-story writer, and essayist, b. 1931, Cartago

N. is one of the most distinguished and best-known Costa Rican writers and public figures of the 20th c. The first of her books of poetry was published in 1961, but she soon became more acclaimed for her innovative prose. *Los perros no ladraron* (1966; the dogs did not bark) received the Costa Rican National Aquileo Echeverria Prize in 1966; *Caminoa al mediodia* (1968; on the way to noon) and *Responso por el niño Juan Manual* (1971; requiem for the boy Juan Manuel) won the Central American Floral Games in

1967 and 1968, respectively; *Hoy es un large dia* (1974; today is a long day) was awarded the Editorial Costa Rica Prize; *Diario de una multitud* (1974; diary of a multitude) received the EDUCA Prize in 1974; and *Ondina* (1985; Ondina) won the EDUCA Prize in 1982. N. has also pursued a successful career in public administration, serving in both national and international organizations: in the Costa Rican Social Security System, as ambassador to India (1972–1974), as minister of culture, youth, and sport (1974–1976), and as Costa Rica's UNICEF representative in Guatemala and Mexico (1978–1982). In 1982 she became director of the Museum of Costa Rican Art, and since 1984 she has headed the Central American University Publishing House.

N.'s fiction and poetry reflect her double life as an administrator and as a writer. She writes of the inner workings of the bureaucratic system, and of the spiritual resources of the human beings who live in this materialistic society, numbed by daily routines. *Los perros no ladraron* depicts one day in the life of a middle-level bureaucrat who becomes aware of the extent to which he is trapped in the system. *Memorias de un hombre palabra* (1968; memories of a word man), like the essays of *Cinco temas en busca de un pensador* (1977; five themes in search of a thinker), explores the paralyzing fatalism, passivity, and other negative emotional states that are reactions to conventional society.

N.'s interest in women characters is apparent in all of her books. In *Sobrepunto* (1985; overpoint), the central character is a woman who struggles to define her identity. As in previous novels, N. explores the roles women play in Latin American society and analyzes the extent to which women are free to control their own destinies.

Another topic of recurrent concern to N. in her poems and in her fiction is the role of marginalized people. Both *Diario de una multitud* and *Homenaje a don Nadie* (1981; homage to Mr. Nobody) speak of all human beings as vulnerable to emotional and social deprivation: Anyone can become a Nobody, unloved, ignored, and unrecognized, even those who appear to have successful community identities. This is related to N.'s frequently expressed (especially in *Diario de una multitud and Sobrepunto*) anxiety that public images of Costa Rica as an exemplary democracy may lead to insufficient concern for the poor and underprivileged.

Ondina, Nunca hubo alguna vez (1984; once upon never), and *Mi guerilla* (1984; my guerilla) emphasize the need to recognize the a lmbiguity and complexity of Latin American reality, which may best be described in bizarre and surreal imaginative metaphors. *Responso por el niño juan Manuel*, too, stresses the role of imagination in interpreting reality. However, N. does not suggest that there are magical or mystical solutions to the problems she discusses in her fiction and poetry.

Both in her public career and in her writing, N. has emphasized concern for individual human beings. Her poetry and her fiction celebrate the human capacity for love, hate, compassion, imagination, and occasional heroism. Increasingly, N. is recognized as a major voice in 20th-c. Latin American literature.

FURTHER WORKS: *América* (1961); *Canción de la ternura* (1964); *Hacia tu isla* (1966); *Misa a oscuras* (1967); *Idioma de invierno* (1972); *Por las páginas de la Biblia y los caminos de Israel* (1976); *Cultura* (1978); *Estancias y días* (1985); *El caso 117,720* (1987); *Mujer y cultura* (1989); *Otro rumbo para la rumba* (1989); *Ventanas y asombros* (1990); *En partes* (1994). FURTHER WORKS IN ENGLISH: *Five Women Writers of Costa Rica: N., Odio, Oreamuno, Urbano, Vallbona* (1978)

BIBLIOGRAPHY: Cruz Burdiel de López, M., "Estudio de tres cuentos de C. N.," *Kañina*, 41 (1975): 101–10; Urbano, V., "C. N. y su voz plena en *Canción de la ternura*," *Káñina*, 1, 2 (1977): 5–31; Arizpe, L., "Interview with C. N.: Women and Latin American Literature," *Signs*, 5, 1 (1979): 98–110; Minc, R., and Méndez-Faith, T., "Conversando con C. N.," *RI*, 51: 132–33 (July-Dec. 1985): 507–10; Martincz, L. I., *C. N. y lu nurralive feminina en Costa Rica* (1987); Pićon Garfield, E., "La luminosa ceguera de sus días: Los cuentos 'humanos' de C. N.," *RI*, 53: 138–39 (Jan.-June 1987): 287–301; Rubio, P., "C. N.," in Marting, D. E., ed., *Spanish American Women Writers* (1990): 350–59; Mondragón, A., *Cambios estéticos y nuevos proyectos culturales en Centroamérica* (1994)

—MARY G. BERG

NARAYAN, R(asipuram) K(rishnaswamy)

Indian novelist, short-story writer, and essayist (writing in English), b. 10 Oct. 1906, Madras

R. K. Narayan

Of all Indian novelists writing in English, N. is the best known to Westerners. Born of an old Brahmin family that moved to Mysore when he was young, N. learned in school the language that was to become the medium of his own reading and writing (his first languages were Tamil and Kannada). His higher education was acquired at Maharajah's College (now part of the University of Mysore), from which he graduated in 1930. N. burst on the literary scene with the publication of the novel *Swami and Friends* (1935) and since then has produced a continuous stream of novels, short stories, and essays. Early in his career, N. received encouragement from Graham GREENE.

Over the years N. has contributed several hundred short stories and sketches to the Madras newspaper *Hindu*. In 1960 he received the Sahitya Akademi Award for *The Guide* (1958). Recent work has involved shortened modern prose versions in English of India's great epics, the *Mahabharata* (1978) and the 13th-c. Tamil poet Kamban's version of the *Ramayana* (1972). *Gods, Demons, and Others* (1964) contains similar prose versions of shorter sacred tales. N. has also written two travel books on Karnataka state, *Mysore* (1939) and *The Emerald Route* (1977).

N.'s novels appear at first to be gently humorous stories of Indian family life set in an imaginary town called Malgudi, where nothing of consequences happens and life goes on as usual. Despite their deceptively simple prose style, however, N.'s novels are in fact complex artistic statements adhering closely to the canons of classical Indian literature. His heroes, generally middle-class types— a printer, a teacher, a student, a sweet-vendor—usually struggle against sudden movements of fate and ensuing ethical dilemmas. Through self-discipline and self-conquest, each hero eventually attains a spiritual insight that enables him to ignore his material circumstances; spiritual knowledge thus renders further action unnecessary. The story usually ends on a note of resolution or harmony in which the equilibrium of life in Malgudi is preserved.

The Man-Eater of Malgudi (1961) involves a taxidermist, an anomaly in Hindu society, who is literally a demon erupted into a hitherto peaceful world. His role as an elemental force of disorder requires that he be eliminated by an equally potent force—divine fate. Appropriately, the demon-taxidermist oversteps his own limits and unintentionally kills himself. Margayya, in *The Financial Expert* (1952), is unable to comprehend the complexities of land banks and credit unions, and instead builds his own financial empire out of a little black box and later out of elegant offices on Market Road. When all his depositors demand their capital at once, the hero is ruined and returns to his humble seat under the banyan tree, wiser for having experienced a foolish attachment to wealth.

Most of N.'s novels also deal with deep conflicts between the traditional way of life and forces emanating from contact with the West. Malgudi changes in the course of N.'s career; the intensity of such conflicts deepens along with India's own predicaments in the real world. *Mr. Sampath* (1949; Am., *The Printer of Malgudi*, 1957), deals with the financial killing to be made in the newly developing film industry. In *The Guide* a tourist guide builds a career for a Bharata Natyam dancer. After the would-be impresario is jailed for forging the dancer Rosie's signature, he eventually makes his way to a village where he is mistaken for a holy man. Gradually he accepts this role; he is forced into fasting to placate the gods after the monsoon rains fail to come, and he dies as a result.

N.'s more recent writing takes into consideration the rapid changes occurring in contemporary India. *A Painter of Signs* (1976) presents an independent woman family planning expert who confounds a more conventional hero. Offspring who study abroad and others who insist on choosing their own spouses appear in greater numbers, upsetting the traditional ways of Malgudi. N.'s heroes continue to behave in ways that lead to turmoil, yet almost always manage to find their way back to accommodation with a society existing in several centuries simultaneously.

Although in N.'s fiction the gap between action and consequence is great, this disparity serves to point up the Hindu world view and man's incapacity to influence events. The Western view, insistent on cause-and-effect logic, never prevails, yet N.'s reconciliation of opposites is always surprising, often humorous, and spiritually ennobling. His characters, moreover, meet frustration with unfailing optimism, so that N.'s novels seem to mirror India in every aspect.

FURTHER WORKS: *The Bachelor of Arts* (1937); *The Dark Room* (1938); *Malgudi Days* (1941); *Dodu and Other Stories* (1944); *Cyclone and Other Stories* (1944); *The English Teacher* (1945; Am., *Grateful to Life and Death*, 1953); *An Astrologer's Day and Other Stories* (1947); *Waiting for the Mahatma* (1955); *Lawley Road and Other Stories* (1956); *My Dateless Diary* (1960); *Next Sunday: Sketches and Essays* (1960); *The Sweet-Vendor* (1967; Am., *The Vendor of Sweets*, 1971); *A Horse and Two Goats and Other Stories* (1970); *My Days* (1974); *Reluctant Guru* (1975); *A Painter of Signs* (1976); *Malgudi Days* (1982); *The Ramayana: A Shortened Modern Prose Version of the Indian Epic, Suggested by the Tamil Version of Kamban* (1972); *Under the Banyan Tree and Other Stories* (1987); *The Mahabharata: A Shortened Modern Prose Version* (1989); *A Writer's Nightmare: Selected Essays 1958-1988* (1989); *My Days: A Memoir* (1990); *A Story-Teller's World: Stories, Essays, Sketches* (1990); *The World of Nagaraj* (1990); *The Grandmother's Tale and Selected Stories* (1994); *Talkative Man* (1994); *A Tiger for Malgudi* (1994); *Malgudi Days II* (1998)

BIBLIOGRAPHY: Gerow, E., "The Quintessential N.," *LE&W*, 10 (1966): 1–18; Narasimhaiah, C. D., "R. K. N.: The Comic as a Mode of Study in Maturity," *The Swan and the Eagle* (1969): 135–58; Holmstrom, L., *The Novels of R. K. N* (1973); Kaul, A. N., "R. K. N. and the East-West Theme," in Mukherjee, M., ed., *Considerations* (1977): 43–65; Vanden Driesen, C., "The Achievement of R. K. N.," *LE&W*, 21 (1977): 51–64; Harrex, S. C., "R. K. N.: Some Miscellaneous Writings," *JCL*, 13, 1 (1978): 64–76; Walsh, W., *R. K. N.: A Critical Appreciation* (1982); Kain, G. R., *R. K. N.: Contemporary Critical Perspectives* (1993); McLeod, A. L., ed., *R. K. N.:Critical Perspectives* (1994)

—JANET M. POWERS

NARBIKOVA, Valeria

Russian novelist, b. 24 Feb. 1958, Moscow

N. graduated from Moscow's Gorky Literary Institute in the early 1980s. In addition to her literary persona, she is a well-known artist and has exhibited her paintings widely in Russia, Western Europe, and the U.S. Her Muscovite origins are apparent in her use of that city's distinctive argot in her fiction, and in her aesthetic affinities with the work of other prominent figures associated with the Moscow postmodern avant-garde scene of the 1970s and 1980s, including the writer and artist Vladimir Sorokin (b. 1955) and the conceptualist painter Il'ia Kabakov. Her work also shows similarities with the fiction of Andrei Bitov (b. 1937), her teacher at the Literary Institute.

Although N. began writing during the Brezhnev "era of stagnation," the profoundly experimental nature of her style and thematics all but ensured that she would be published only in the subsequent, glasnost period. Even in the relatively liberal atmosphere of Gorbachev's U.S.S.R., however, she was a controversial figure. Her first published work, the short novel *Ravnovesie dnevnykh i nochnykh zvezd* (1988; The Equilibrium of Light of Diurnal and Nocturnal Stars), attracted vociferous critical attention for its "erotic" imagery and its seemingly impenetrable narrative. The novel's many sexual scenes and references, though couched in N.'s characteristically verbose, opaque narrative style, were considered especially scandalous from the pen of a Soviet woman writer. The novel also provoked the ire of conservative critics with its conflation of religious and sexual imagery. However, the work—and her entire subsequent output—is in fact more centrally concerned with language, specifically the gross inadequacies of traditional Soviet and Russian verbal culture as a medium for human intercourse and personal expression.

The poetics of N.'s works are distinguished by virtuoso verbal play. Her texts abound in intricate puns, extended metaphors, pages-long, circular dialogues, and fragmentary streams of consciousness. Her character names are typically either linguistically dense mouthfuls (Chiashchiazhyshyn, Evdandukta, Snanduliia) or deformed literary/historical allusions (Dodostoevsky, Toest'lstoi). Among the most common devices in her prose is a transgressive juxtaposition of images from the respective poles of binary pairs such as high culture/low culture, male/female, sacred/profane, and East/West. Collectively, her novels and stories comprise an intricate network of densely layered images in which elements from each of her signature realms—the sexual, the literary, the spiritual, the ecological, and the artistic—interact in endless textual and narrative permutations.

N.'s narratives typically involve a series of short, often circular journeys made by a pair of lovers or, more commonly, the members of a love triangle, who are depicted in complicated sexual configurations and living arrangements. Frequent settings and destinations include museums, art studios, unfinished buildings, train compartments, and airplanes. Natural settings, especially seashores and forests, figure prominently, frequently as sites for sex. N.'s use of natural and religious metaphors to describe sexual acts testifies to her belief in an essential connection between sex and nature, and their status as forces spiritually superior to language and culture.

Like many other representatives of Russian women's writing, for example Ludmila PETRUSHEVSKAYA and Tatyana TOLSTAYA, N. professes no allegiance to "women's prose" (zhenskaia proza) as such. Nevertheless, many of the thematic and stylistic currents that run through her fiction evoke ideas central to feminist (especially French) theory: the iconic power of nature and the body; idealization of the prelinguistic imaginary; and a critically ironic stance towards Western thought, canons, and linear rationality. N's narrators explicitly attack ossified verbal structures in ironic tangents about, for example, Russian grammatical gender, the process of naming objects and children, and especially the discrete units of Soviet and Russian verbal culture—aphorisms, cliches, slogans, poems, and songs. Common to her entire oeuvre is an aggressively deconstructive impulse towards the extreme logocentrism of Soviet culture. On both a stylistic and expository level N. exposes and subverts the abuse of language and logic as ideologically justified instruments of violence against human creativity, romantic love, and ecological purity.

Despite the prevalence in N.'s fiction of such textbook postmodernist strategies as nonlinear narrative, intertextuality, and ironic self-referentiality, her persistent, if indirect, assertion of a coherent worldview—together with an implicit prescription for redemption—places her at odds with the hardcore postmodernist rejection of the viability of value systems. Her work is part of a larger trend within Russian cultural production that goes beyond mere ironic or nihilistic deconstruction of obsolete value matrices and signifying systems, and implies the desirability of seeking new ones.

FURTHER WORKS: *Okolo ekolo. . . : Povesti* (1992); *Izbrannoe ili Shepot shuma* (1994)

BIBLIOGRAPHY: Azhgikhina, N., "Razrushiteli v poiskakh very," *Znamia*, 9 (1990): 223-27; Pittman, R., "V.N.'s Iconoclastic Prose," *FMLS*, 28, 4 (1992): 376-89; Goscilo, H., "Domostroika or Perestroika? The Construction of Womanhood in Soviet Culture under Glasnost," in Lahusen, T., ed., *Late Soviet Culture* (1993): 233-55; Peterson, N., "Games Women Play: The 'Erotic' Prose of V. N.," in Goscilo, H., ed., *Fruits of Her Plume* (1993): 165-83; Chernetsky, V. "EPIGONOI, or Transformations of Writing in the Texts of V. N. and Nina Iskrenko," *SEEJ*, 38, 4 (1994): 655-76; Rudova, L., "A Mindset of Present Russia: V. N.'s Fiction," *RCSCSPL*, 39, 1 (1996): 79-94

—SETH GRAHAM

NASTASIJEVIĆ, Momčilo

Serbian poet, short-story writer, and dramatist, b. 6 Oct. 1894, Gornji Milanovac; d. 13 Feb. 1938, Belgrade, Yugoslavia (now Serbia)

N. was one of the most original and innovative writers in Serbian literature between the two world wars. Born in Gornji Milanovac, he became a high school teacher and spent most of his life in that capacity in Belgrade, where he died in 1938. He was also an accomplished violin player.

N. started out as a short-story writer and dramatist, but later turned more toward poetry. His collection of short stories, *Iz tamnog vilajeta* (1927; from the dark province), drew immediate attention to the critics for N.'s unusual approach to reality and his unique utilization of the language. His best play, *Medjulško blago* (1927; the treasure of Medjulug), showed similar tendencies. But it was in poetry that he achieved his full potential. Between his first collection, *Pet lirskih krugova* (1932; five lyric cycles), and his last, *Pesme* (1938; poems), lies a brief but intensive creative period. There are two posthumous collections as well, *Rane pesme i Varijante* (1939; early poems and variants) and *Sedam lirskih krugova* (1962; seven lyric cycles).

N. is perhaps the most enigmatic of Serbian poets. He developed independently of literary groups and movements, always endeavoring to create his own idiom. His unique style is characterized by extremely concise, ascetic, archaic, and often cryptic expressions, by which he enriched the modern language and tried to fathom the spiritual and religious character of his people. He drew heavily from folklore and the distant past, as well as from his deeply religious, even mystical outlook on life. He was often preoccupied with metaphysical and moral questions, which he tried

to resolve through his own highly individualistic and hermetic art. As a poet, he remained a loner, understood and admired at first mainly by his closest friends. Lately, however, he has begun to exert consider able influence on younger Serbian poets and to be studied extensively by critics.

BIBLIOGRAPHY: Petrov, A., "Orphean Inspiration in Recent Serbian Poetry," *Literary Quarterly*, 2 (1966): 159–70; Kragujević, T., *Mitsko u N. delu* (1976); Milosavljević, P., *Poetika M. N.* (1978); Goy, E. D., "The cycle 'Večernje' from the *Pet lirskih krugova* by M. N.," *Serbian Studies*, 1, 3 (1981): 31–49; Goy, E. D., "The Cycle 'Jutarnje' from the *Pet lirskih krugova* by M. N.," *Southeastern Europe*, 9: 1–2 (1982): 53–69; Goy, E. D., "The Cycle 'Bdenja' from the *Pet lirskih krugova* of M. N.," *Serbian Studies*, 4: 1–2 (1987): 29–51; Goy, E. D., "M. N.'s 'Gluhote' and 'Reči u kamenu,'" *SSR*, 8 (Spring 1987): 40–55; Vladiv, S. M., "The 'Lyrical Drama' of M. N.: Problems of Poetics and Translation," *NZSJ*, 1 (1988): 51–66

—VASA D. MIHAILOVICH

NATSUME Sōseki

(pseud. of Natusme Kin'nosuke) Japanese novelist, b. 5 Jan. 1867, Tokyo; d. 9 Dec. 1916, Tokyo

N. (usually called Sōseki) was born to a family that had fallen on hard times as a result of the Meiji Restoration. His parents were embarrassed at having a child late in life and tried unsuccessfully to have him adopted, and he was left permanently with a feeling of being unwanted. After a brilliant career as a student of English at Tokyo Imperial University, he abandoned his native city and accepted a series of rural teaching positions. In 1900 the government sent him to England for further study of English. He returned to Japan in early 1903, after having suffered a nervous breakdown. Nerves and ulcers were to plague him for the rest of his life. Although he decided, while in England, to become a creative writer rather than a literary scholar, he took a position as professor of English literature at Tokyo University, succeeding the American writer Lafcadio Hearn (1850–1904). In 1907 N. resigned his professorship to become literary editor of the newspaper *Asahi shimbun*. The ensuing decade was a period of intense literary activity until the very moment of his death from ulcers in 1916.

N.'s work can be divided into several groups representing stages in his developing philosophy. He began with experimental works, trying several fictional techniques. His first major work was *Wagahai wa neko de aru* (1905; *I Am a Cat*, 1961), a satire depicting modern Japanese society as seen from the point of view of a cat. The idea for this story was apparently derived from E. T. A. Hoffmann's (1776–1822) *Kater Murr*. At the time he wrote this book N. was still developing his narrative style, and it is not so much a unified novel as a loosely related series of amusing episodes poking fun at many aspects of Japan's modernization.

Another work from this experimental phase is *Kusamakura* (1906; *Unhuman Tour*, 1927; new tr., *Three-Cornered World*, 1965). N. said this was intended as a novel in the manner of a haiku. In one sense he uses the work to contrast Western and Eastern aesthetic values, arguing that the West emphasizes the individual while the East denies individuality. N. also said that his broader intention with *Kusamakura* was simply to leave an impression of beauty in the reader's mind.

Shortly after joining the newspaper staff and devoting himself to writing full time, there appeared his first trilogy, composed of *Sanshirō* (1908; *Sanshiro*, 1977), *Sorekara* (1909; *And Then*, 1978), and *Mon* (1909; *Mon*, 1972). In these works he introduced themes he consistently used throughout his career. One is initiation, usually taking the form of a youth who comes to Tokyo and learns to deal with adult life in the modern world. As these young men struggle to come to terms with life, they end up making decisions or taking actions, and then have to live with their consequences for the rest of their lives. Usually the consequence is feeling guilty of having been greedy or selfish. Where, asks N., can man find solace to assuage this feeling of guilt? In this trilogy he suggests love and religion to relieve the burden of guilt.

N.'s second trilogy consists of *Higan sugi made* (1910; until after the spring equinox), *Kōjin* (1912–13; *The Wayfarer*, 1967), and *Kokoro* (1914; *Kokoro*, 1941; new tr., 1957). In these works the mood is darker, as N. probes more deeply the themes of loneliness, alienation, and guilt. The avenues of relief he offers here are much less hopeful than the ones presented in earlier works. In *Kōjin*, Ichirō, the central figure, declares that the only solutions to modern man's dilemma are suicide, insanity, and religion. In exploring insanity, N. more clearly defines his philosophy: man must learn to surrender his own self to something larger.

Kokoro is probably the best and certainly the most widely read of all of N.'s novels. Here again he shows that mistrust and selfishness lead to betrayal, guilt, and alienation, which are the normal condition of modern man. N. also reflects on the merits of suicide as a means of atonement, and the theme of initiation is prominent, as in earlier works. N.'s narrative technique here is still fragmentary, but it is also highly imaginative. The first part tells of the youthful narrator going to college in the city and being exposed to modern life. The second part shows the youth at home in the country caring for his dying father, and traditional Japanese life is contrasted to the modern. The third part is in the form of a long letter and suicide note from Sensei, the youth's mentor and also a surrogate father figure. With stark simplicity N. presents the unendurable loneliness of the modern intellectual, which cannot be breached either by the ties of love and family or by intellectual companionship.

At the time of his death N. had completed several hundred pages of the novel *Meian* (1916; *Light and Darkness*, 1971). Since the work is incomplete, we have no way of knowing for certain how he would have ended it. Critical opinion is sharply divided. Some feel that the characters are headed for the same sort of gloomy dilemma we see in N.'s earlier works. Others say that he had come to terms with life by developing his philosophy of "sokuten kyoshi," which means to seek heaven by abandoning the self. Certainly, egoism or the burden of self-consciousness is at the heart of all the problems N.'s characters struggle with.

It is no exaggeration to say that N. has been the single most popular writer in Japan in the 20th c. Not only do his works give expression to the social and moral problems faced by Japan as it became Westernized and modernized; he also introduced a philosophical approach to literature. This represents a remarkable development, since traditionally fiction had been considered only frivolous and entertaining. N. raised it to the level of a serious medium for artistic expression and philosophical thought.

FURTHER WORKS: *Botchan* (1906; *Botchan*, 1970); *Yokyoshu* (1906); *Gubijinso* (1908); *Kusa awase* (1908); *Shihen* (1910); *Garasudo no naka* (1915); *Michikusa* (1915; *Grass on the Wayside*, 1969)

BIBLIOGRAPHY: McClellan, E., "An Introduction to Sōseki," *HJAS*, 20 (1959): 150–208; Viglielmo, V. H., "An Introduction to the Later Novels of N. S." *MN*, 19 (1964): 1–36; Eto, J., "N. S.: A Japanese Meiji Intellectual," *ASch*, 34 (1965): 603–19; McClellan, E., *Two Japanese Novelists: Sōseki and Tōson* (1969): 3–69; Yu, B., *N. S.* (1969); Miyoshi, M., *Accomplices of Silence: The Modern Japanese Novel* (1974): 55–92; Doi, T., *The Psychological World of N. S.* (1976); Jones, S., "N. S.'s *Botchan*: The Outer World through Edo Eyes," in Tsuruta, K., and T. Swann, eds. *Approaches to the Modern Japanese Novel* (1976): 148–65; Viglielmo, V. H., "Sōseki's *Kokoro*: A Descent into the Heart of Man," in Tsuruta, K., and T. Swann, eds. *Approaches to the Modern Japanese Novel* (1976): 166–79; McClain, Y., "Sōseki: A Tragic Father," *MN*, 33 (1978): 461–69

—KOHL W. STEOGEB

NAYLOR, Gloria

American novelist and essayist, b. 25 Jan. 1950, New York, New York

N. was born to parents who had been Mississippi cotton sharecroppers before moving to New York City shortly before N.'s birth, at which time they joined the urban working class. N. herself became a part of that same working class upon high school graduation, although she coupled this work with her part-time Jehovah's Witnesses' ministry, which she began upon joining the church at age eighteen. In 1974 N. left New York City and moved first to North Carolina, then to Florida, where she became a full-time minister, although she still depended on working-class jobs in order to support herself. In 1975 she left the Jehovah's Witnesses and returned to New York City, where she began her college studies. In 1981 N. received her bachelor's degree in English from Brooklyn College. In 1983 she was awarded a master's degree in Afro-American Studies from Yale University. Since receiving her graduate degree, N. has combined her writing career with several visiting positions at various institutions of higher learning. In 1990 she also began her own production company, One Way Productions.

N. is perhaps best known for her first novel, *The Women of Brewster Place* (1982), for which she won the American Book Award and the Distinguished Writer Award from the Mid-Atlantic Writers' Association. This first work sets the stage for N.'s continued interest in women's relationships with one another and in their search for inner strength. *The Women of Brewster Place* tells the separate tales of seven African-American women who all live in the same ghetto in a Northern city that remains unnamed. N. deals with a variety of personalities in this novel, from Cora, the unwed mother of several children who continues to engage in casual sexual liaisons in order to bear even more "doll baby" children, to the lesbian outcasts, Lorraine and Theresa. With each of the seven women, N. presents a view of the individual that erases stereotypical images of the various characters. The author places great emphasis on the ability of these women to come together from their own strength sources and to help one another, in a variety of ways, to rise out of the despair of Brewster Place. N. makes it clear that men have been of no good use to these women; the characters themselves show that they can indeed move ahead without men in their lives. While there is plenty of tragedy in *The Women of Brewster Place*, there is also the underlying positive theme of sisterhood prevailing through all the pain and anger.

The Women of Brewster Place begins for N. a series of novels interrelated by both theme and character. The first novel's character Kiswana Browne, a young woman who has changed her name from Melanie and chosen to leave behind the comforts of her upper-middle-class family in Linden Hills to embrace what she sees as her true heritage, serves as a bridge of sorts to N.'s second novel, *Linden Hills* (1985). *Linden Hills*, which originally served as N.'s master's thesis, examines upper-class African-American family structure as a betrayal of one's true roots. Following the patterns of Dante's *Inferno*, N. creates the community of Linden Hills as a modern-day hell. The community is structurally parallel to the physical dimensions of the fictitious inferno, and the novel is full of symbolic evil and greed. At the center of both the tale and the symbolism is the wealthy, mean-spirited mortician Luther Nedeed. Although Nedeed is allegorically critical to N.'s story, his wife Willa, known almost exclusively as Mrs. Nedeed in the story, becomes the story's focus in much the same way as the women in N.'s previous novel. While trapped in the cellar of her home, Willa discovers traces of her predecessors—the wives of Luther's father, grandfather, and great-grandfather, each also known in her lifetime as only Mrs. Nedeed. Willa pieces these traces of information together and finds the strength to rise out of her own personal hell to reclaim her rightful place among the living once again. N. leaves the reader with the definite feeling that women can triumph on an individual basis and, again, that a certain sense of sisterhood can help the individual on her journey.

N. continues the theme of empowered women with *Mama Day* (1988), a novel set in both the fictitious barrier island Willow Springs and New York City. It is the setting of Willow Springs that brings N.'s themes of African-American history deeply into play in this work. Willow Springs is the home of Mama Day and, thus, a deep sense of matriarchy. It is also the center of a world of conjuring and a world of belief systems that hinge intricately upon family history, in this case, the two-hundred-year-old history of the island's ownership by African-Americans. *Mama Day* clearly follows the pattern of Shakespeare's *The Tempest*. One of the main characters is named Ophelia, although she goes more often by the name Cocoa. Another main character, and Cocoa's husband ultimately, is George, whose portrayal is most interesting for the fact that it is a strongly positive portrayal. Although N. has shown a few positive male figures before this novel, this is the first work in which a major male character is portrayed in such a light. However, the focus of the novel is very deliberately once again on the strength of women. *Mama Day* is indeed the story of strong female forces, even from the historical sense of the story, where a slave woman is the one responsible for taking possession of the island for the rest of the island's African-American population and for their descendants.

Mama Day's George links this novel to N.'s fourth work, *Bailey's Cafe* (1992), which is set some fifty years before *Mama Day*. It is in *Bailey's Cafe* that George is born under very strange circumstances. George's mother Mariam is a teenaged Ethiopian girl who underwent genital mutilation in her homeland and insists that, despite the fact of her being pregnant, she is a virgin. N. also continues the theme of sisterhood in this novel, with the character Eve acting as both a mothering and a healing source for the various

abused and violated women who find their way to her "boarding house." Using a longstanding tradition of Southern American writers, N., though not herself Southern, fills *Bailey's Cafe* with a variety of odd personalities, including Miss Maple, a transvestite Ph.D. from Stanford University. There are many biblical references in this novel as well as a distinct blues theme interlaced with the other themes of the work. Somewhat new to this work is N.'s treatment of women victimizing other women; this acts in juxtaposition to the sisterhood and empowerment themes.

The Men of Brewster Place (1998) brings the author full circle, at least in terms of setting. This fifth novel takes place in the same ghetto area as does *The Women of Brewster Place* and includes further stories of the characters from that first novel. N. focuses in this recent novel, however, with seven men from Brewster Place, telling their stories in much the same fashion that she told the women's stories earlier. The character Ben, who is murdered in *The Women of Brewster Place*, comes back to life to become a narrating part of *The Men of Brewster Place*. While she remains interested in women's lives in this latest novel, N. makes a concerted attempt in this work to deal positively with African-American men's lives and issues, something that is not often seen in the works of African-American women authors.

Though N. seems to have come to an end of the usefulness of some themes and characters with this fifth of her interconnected novels, there is no doubt that her writing career will continue to flourish and that her focus on self-empowerment will continue to permeate her works. She holds a distinct place of honor in American literature in general and in African-American literature specifically, a place she assuredly will not be ready to relinquish for a very long time. There is still much work N. can do with her major themes and concerns. In addition, N. has proven herself quite capable of carrying on traditions normally typical of Southern American literature. Surely this is an area she will further explore in future works.

BIBLIOGRAPHY: Gates, H. L., Jr., and K. A. Appiah, eds., *G. N.: Critical Perspectives Past and Present* (1993); Fowler, V. C., *G. N.: In Search of Sanctuary* (1996); Harris, T., *The Power of the Porch: The Storyteller's Craft in Zora Neale Hurston, G. N., and Randall Kenan* (1996); Yohe, K. A., "G. N.," in Andrews, W. L., et al., eds., *The Oxford Companion to African American Literature* (1997): 527-29

—TERRY NOVAK

NAZARETH, Peter

Ugandan novelist and critic, b. 27 Apr. 1940, Kampala

N. has a complex personal history, and his life trajectory is in many ways itself a metaphor for the cultural hybridity, the border crossings and migrations, and the multilayered reality of identity that constitute so much of Africa's postcolonial reality. Not surprisingly, these issues relating to identity and migration feature as prominent themes in N.'s creative works and in his prolific literary criticism.

N. was born and reared in Uganda. His parents came from Goa, the former Portuguese colony on India's western coast, although his mother's side of the family had emigrated to Malaysia. Being Goan in East Africa at this time in history implied a cultural difference from the indigenous African population as well as from other Asian groups in the region. After obtaining a degree in English from Makerere University College in 1962 and a postgraduate diploma in English studies from Leeds University in 1966, N. worked in Uganda's ministry of finance for seven years. He left the country to accept a fellowship at Yale University in 1973, around the same time that the Idi Amin government expelled all Asians from Uganda. From Yale he went to the University of Iowa, first as an honorary fellow in the International Writing Program, later as visiting lecturer, and eventually as a tenured professor of English and Afro-American and world studies.

N. has been variously described as a Ugandan writer, as a writer of the "Indian diaspora," as an African of Goan origin, or as a Goan from Africa—all of these being identities that he readily claims. Probably because of this legacy, N.'s creative and critical works tend to focus on questions of origins, influence, and genealogy. The genealogy and mutual influence of ideas, especially in the colonial and postcolonial settings, are favorite topics.

N.'s first novel, *In a Brown Mantle* (1972), was prescient in predicting the expulsion of Asians from Uganda before it actually happened. The main character, Joseph D'Souza, is a Goan from the fictional nation of Damibia who takes up his pen while in a cold and lonely exile in London in order to reexamine his past and come to terms with personal and communal failures. His second novel, *The General Is Up* (1984), also focuses on a Goan community in "Damibia," featuring a protagonist who is unsure whether to align himself with Goans or the broader Ugandan community, and who in the end is forced into exile by the corrupt politics of "the General."

N.'s creative writing output includes a wide range of poetry, short stories, and plays, beginning from his early years as a student at Makerere. He studied there in an era when Makerere was Africa's leading institution of higher education, producing the next generation of leaders in all fields, including literature. He was a contemporary and schoolmate of NGUGI Wa Thiong'o, Jonathan Kariara (b. 1935), Rebecca Njau (dates n.a.), David Rubadiri (b. 1930), and other key pioneers of African literature. For five years N. edited *Penpoint*, the college literary magazine, and contributed regularly to the early issues of *Transition*, an important independent journal of society and culture.

N. is important in East Africa's literary history as one of its earliest and most consistently productive critical voices. His *Literature and Society in Modern Africa* (1972) is one of the first collections of critical essays from the region, and it reflects the figures and topics that were most relevant at the time. Foremost among these is the role of the writer in relation to society and politics; N. argues that African writers must transcend traditional disciplinary boundaries, diving into questions of politics and economics. The collection was later reissued under the title *An African View of Literature* (1974).

In later critical writings N. focuses on the trickster figure, who is a stock character in various African literary traditions, as a metaphor for both writers and writing in the postcolonial setting. Entire texts may be tricksters, he argues, inviting readings that subvert the hegemonic status quo. In this respect N. focuses on Andrew SALKEY, Francis EBEJER, and Ishmael REED as paradigmatic examples of writers who have created trickster texts.

N.'s writings have been published around the world and translated into ten languages. He is an important figure among the so-called "first generation" of postcolonial writers from East Africa, with both his creative and his critical works focusing on the key questions of cultural identity in a postcolonial setting.

FURTHER WORKS: *Two Radio Plays* (1976); *African Writing Today* (1981); *The Third World Writer: His Social Responsibility* (1978)

BIBLIOGRAPHY: Thumboo, E., "A Conversation between P. N. and Edwin Thumboo on Transformations of Oral Cultures in the Third World," *PQM*, 7, 2 (1982): 93-101; Irby, C., "Goan Literature from P. N.: An Interview," *Explorations in Ethnic Studies*, 8, 1 (Jan. 1985): 1-12; Tucker, M., "P. N.," in Tucker, M., ed., *Literary Exile in the Twentieth Century* (1991): 508-10; Elder, A., "Indian Writing in East and South Africa: Multiple Approaches to Colonialism and Apartheid," in Nelson, E., ed., *Reworlding: The Literature of the Indian Diaspora* (1992): 115-39; Nelson, E., ed., *Writers of the Indian Diaspora: A Bio-Bibliographical Critical Sourcebook* (1993); Parekh, P., ed., *Postcolonial African Writers: A Bio-Bibliographical Critical Sourcebook* (1998)

—J. ROGER KURTZ

NAZRUL ISLAM

Indian poet, short-story writer, novelist, and dramatist (writing in Bengali), b. 14 May 1899, Churulia; d. 29 Aug. 1976, Dacca, Bangladesh

N. enlisted in the Indian Army in 1917 and served in Karachi and later Iraq during World War I. During this time he came into contact with a *maulvi*, or Muslim religious teacher, in the same regiment, with whom he read the works of the Persian poet Hafiz (1327–1390). This poetry had a profound effect on N. It was at about this time that he assumed the honorific title of Kazi (a type of Muslim judge), which remained with him throughout his life. He returned to India in 1918 and in 1922 published his first major poem, "Vidrohi" ("The Rebel," 1963). Its appearance was considered a major literary event, and the poem made its author an instant celebrity. That same year N. established *Dhumketu*, a radical weekly newspaper in which he published anti-British editorials and essays. The newspaper was closed down, and eventually N. was jailed for a year by the British for sedition. During the 1920s and 1930s he continued to write and to participate actively in numerous leftist political organizations. In 1942, however, he suffered a complete mental breakdown as a result of syphilis contracted while he was in the army. Never recovering his mental facilities, he lived in seclusion in Calcutta until 1974, at which time he moved to Dacca, where he died.

N. published a number of volumes of fiction, plays, and essays, which exhibit his commitment to leftist ideology. He was first and foremost a poet, however. The publication of "Vidrohi" has been described by critics as a monumental event in Bengali literature. In this poem he displays a keen sense of self-assurance, even arrogance, in proclaiming himself a rebel-hero, a destroyer of oppression (that is, by the British) and of outmoded, conservative ideals. As a result of this work N. became known as the "rebel poet" of Bengal. In that the Bengali poetry of this period was dominated by the ethereal, other-worldly verse of Rabindranath TAGORE, N.'s compositions, replete with political activism and Marxist ideology, came as a surprise to Bengali intellectuals. It is also significant that N. was a peasant, and, to an extent, used rustic diction in his poetry.

He was, in addition, a Muslim, and many of his poems are replete with allusions to Islamic history, heroes, and culture, facts that did not go unnoticed by the predominantly Hindu literary circles of Calcutta.

Most of N.'s early poems, especially those in his first collection, *Agni vina* (1922; lute of fire), are hyperbolical, enthusiastic expressions of patriotic sentiment. Numerous volumes followed in rapid succession, notably *Bhangar gan* (1924; songs of destruction), *Biser banshi* (1924; flute of poison), and *Pralay shikha* (1924; flames of destruction), which were proscribed by the British authorities. These are filled with volatile nationalist sentiments in which the poet exhorts patriots to drive the British from the motherland and demands that the downtrodden masses take up arms against their capitalist exploiters.

In addition to patriotic works, N. also wrote numerous love songs, called *ghazals*, a genre popular in Persian and Urdu literature, which he is credited with having introduced into Bengali. A proficient singer and guitarist, he set many of these compositions, which number about 3,300, to music. Many of these poems deal with the requited love. Such love poems can also be read metaphorically as the human soul's expressions of love toward God.

N. continues to be one of the most popular poets of Bengal. He is sometimes criticized for the rather narrow scope of his poetic themes and his facile use of prosody, but while some of his poems may seem dated, his songs exhibit a timeless appeal that assures his position as one of the greatest lyric poets in 20th-c. Indian literature.

FURTHER WORKS: *Vyathar dan* (1921); *Chayanat* (1923); *Dolan campa* (1923); *Jhine phul* (1923); *Rajbandir jabanbandi* (1923); *Rikter vedan* (1924); *Citta nama* (1925); *Puver haoay* (1925); *Samyavadi* (1925); *Sancita* (1925); *Durdiner yatri* (1926); *Sarvahara* (1926); *Namaskar* (c. 1926); *Bandhan hara* (1927); *Phani manasa* (1927); *Shat bhay campa* (1927); *Sindhu hindol* (1927); *Bulbul, Part I* (1928); *Zinzir* (1928); *Nirjhar* (c. 1928); *Cakravak* (1929); *Cokher catak* (1929); *Sandhya* (1929); *Candrabindu* (1930); *Jhilimili* (1930); *Mrtyu-khuda* (1930); *N. gitika* (1930); *Pralayankar* (c. 1930); *Kuhelika* 1931); *Nazrul swarlipi* (1931); *Putuler biye* (1931); *Shiuli mala* (1931); *Aleya* (1932); *Ban giti* (1932); *Siraj* (1932); *Sur saqi* (1932); *Zulfikar* (1932); *Gul bagica* (1933); *Sonali swapan* (1933); *Ganer mala* (1934); *Giti shatadal* (1934); *Sur mukur* (1934); *Suro lipi* (1934); *Rudramangal* (c. 1935); *Maktab sahitya* (1936); *Jivaner jay yatra* (1939); *Nutan cand* (1945); *Maru bhaskar* (1950); *Bulbul, Part II* (1952); *Sancayan* (1957); *Shesh sougat* (1958); *Dhumketu* (1962); *Yugbani* (1970). FURTHER WORKS IN ENGLISH: *Selected Poems of Kazi N. I.* (1963); *The Rebel, and Other Poems of Kazi N. I.* (1974); *The Fiery Lyre of N. I.* (1974)

BIBLIOGRAPHY: Rahman, M., *N. I.* (1955); Chaudhury, S., *Introducing N. I.* (1965); Chakravarty, B., *Kazi N. I.* (1968); Haldar, G., *Kazi N. I.* (1974)

—CARLO COPPOLA

NDAO, Cheikh Aliou

Senegalese novelist, poet, short-story writer, and dramatist (writing in Wolof and French), b. 1933, Bignona

N. possesses a rich mixture of ethnicities: Manding, Wolof, Serer, and Toucouleur. He was reared in the Casamance region of Senegal, and later attended high school in the capital city of Dakar. He left for France in 1956 and studied English at the University of Grenoble from 1958 to 1962. He spent time in Wales before returning to Senegal in 1965, where he taught English in Thies, Saint Louis, and Dakar. He received a Fulbright Fellowship in 1971 to teach in the U.S. at Oakland City College and De Pauw University in Indiana. He currently lives in Senegal, where he participates actively in African writers' organizations.

N. is one of Senegal's most prolific and well-known authors. He is well respected for his commitment to writing in Wolof, Senegal's main language. He believes that Wolof-language literature develops and preserves the language, which has been neglected by Senegalese institutions that utilize French as a medium of communication. He also includes a number of Wolof words in his French-language works, as in the title of his novel *Mbaam dictateur* (1997; Donkey Dictator). He generally uses indigenous languages rather than French to designate African cities and creations. His collection of stories in Wolof, *Jigéen, Faayda* (1997; Woman, Dignity), portrays the internal conflicts of a woman who discovers that her beloved husband has secretly married a second wife. Sensitive to the effects of polygamy on women and yet respectful of traditional practices, N. delicately explores the details of family relationships. N.'s concentration on personal dilemmas in order to shed light on the political is seen in his French-language play, *L'exil d'Albouri* (1969; The Exile of Albouri), which was first directed by N. in Grenoble. It is set during the French invasion of Senegal in 1890 and focuses on the internal conflicts of the historical character King Albouri, who chooses to flee his homeland and join Malian resistance rather than fight the French armies. As in many of his works N. demonstrates a broad knowledge of African histories and traditions. Performed throughout Africa and Europe, N.'s plays often deal with the intimate lives of characters who struggle for dignity as they suffer from the changes imposed by colonization.

N.'s works often recall images from indigenous African traditions. The title of his first collection of poetry, *Kaïrée* (1962; Kairée), was chosen because it derives from an African language rather than Arab or French. His second collection of poetry, *Mogariennes* (1970; Mogariennes), is a contraction created by N. of the historical Malian towns of Mopti and Bandiangara. B.'s novel *Buur Tileen, Roi de la Medina* (1972; Buur Tileen, King of the Medina) looks at indigenous caste systems. The novel is the first in a trilogy that includes the *Excellence vos épouses* (1983; Excellence, Your Spouses) and *Un bouquet d'épines pour Elle* (1988; A Bouquet of Thorns for Her).

N.'s works demonstrate a creative melange of history, attention to detail, complexity of characterization, and rich social commentary. His mastery of several genres in two languages is impressive, as is his project of making literature accessible to the Senegalese readers who understand Wolof and not French. In the future N. plans to translate his plays into Wolof and then direct them for a Senegalese audience, thereby making his creative productions available to those who cannot read.

FURTHER WORKS: *La décision* (1967); *Le fils de l'Almamy*(1973); *La case de l'homme* (1973); *L'île de Bahila* (1975); *Le marabout de la sécheresse* (1979); *Du sang pour un trône* (1983); *Lolli—Taataan* (1990); *Bàkku Xalis*(1994); *Buur Tileen* (1993)

BIBLIOGRAPHY: Bobb, D, *The Plays and Fiction of C. A. N.*(1982); Kane, M., *Roman africain et tradition* (1982): 310, 354; Blair, D.,

Senegalese Literature: A Critical History (1984): 90-91; Diop, B. "C. A. N.: Je m'addresse a mes copains," *Notre Librarie*, 81 (1985): 94-97; Morgan, J., *Theatre and Drama in Francophone Africa* (1994): 152-63

—ELLIE HIGGINS

NDEBELE, Njabulo S.

South African poet, short-story writer, and essayist (writing in English) b. 4 July 1948, Western Native Township (Johannesburg)

Born in the same year that Afrikaner nationalists gained state power on a platform of white supremacy, N. grew up in an African community in Charterston Township outside of Nigel on the East Rand. Charterston's residents were forcibly relocated and the impact of this collective trauma on N. finds varied expression in his writing. In his award-winning *Fools and Other Stories* (1983), N. re-creates the lost urban milieu of his youth, while in "A Home for Intimacy" (1996), he ponders the personal and national ramifications of the injustice of forced removal. In addition to depicting the quotidian life of a township erased from the map by apartheid's planners, the stories in *Fools* focus on the small but socially significant African middle class into which N. himself was born. N.'s class background allowed him to escape the stultifying effects of so-called Bantu education. Unlike many of the young black writers who emerged in the early 1970s, N. benefitted from an excellent high school education. After his schooling at an elite institution in Swaziland, N.'s career became increasingly peripatetic: undergraduate studies in Lesotho followed by further studies abroad at the universities of Cambridge and Denver. N. has noted that enforced distance from his troubled homeland enabled him to engage with it successfully in fiction. Distance also served N. as an essayist. It was while teaching in Lesotho in the mid- through late 1980s that N. achieved prominence as a literary critic, cultural theorist, and public intellectual.

N. first became known for poems that he published during the black cultural renaissance of the 1970s in such journals as the *Classic* and *Staffrider*. Most of N.'s early poetry seems devoid of the overtly political preoccupations that inform so much of the work of his peers. Instead of clashes between oppressor and oppressed and of ringing assertions of black pride—commonplaces of Anglophone black poetry of the 1970s—what one chiefly finds in N.'s early texts are images of children, not radicalized children precociously committed to political struggle, but anonymous children who experience nameless fears as they confront the alien world of adults. Nonetheless, one poem, the much-anthologized "Revolution of the Aged" (1981) evinces an engagement with the harsh realities of racial domination. A terse parable of the imposition of white minority rule on the black majority and of the inevitable resistance against it, "Revolution of the Aged" is couched in a folkloric idiom that dovetails with the organic transformation that the poem's speaker advocates.

In its thematic and formal dimensions "Revolution of the Aged" can be regarded as a pivotal text in N.'s corpus. The figure of the patient and aged speaker whose wisdom is "wooled in the truth of proverbs" is analogous to the trope of the storyteller whose textured mode of representing social reality N. champions against that of

stark protest writing in "Turkish Tales and Some Thoughts on South African Fiction" (1984). During the apartheid years, much black South African literary expression in English was devoted to exposing and indicting the nation's system of legalized racial segregation. In literature the urge to document and protest the iniquity and inequities of apartheid resulted in the predominance of literary works preoccupied with the dual spectacle of suffering and of the struggle to overcome it. As for literary criticism, it often considered "irrelevant" literature which was not motivated by a protest imperative. In a series of closely argued essays published throughout the decade, N. contended that literary and critical writing by black South Africans had reached an aesthetic and political dead end. South African protest literature, N. claimed, tended either to construct a hollow heroism or to reinforce the victimization that the writing ostensibly sought to challenge. Arguing that no aspect of the life of the oppressed should be deemed unworthy of representation, N. insisted that black writing should reveal the complex ways in which blacks resisted the encroachments of the apartheid state upon their lives. The focus of literary practice thus ought to shift from the static arena of spectacular confrontation and unremitting suffering to the sphere of "the ordinary": the multifarious realm of people's relatively autonomous everyday lives.

Perhaps one of the richest instances in South African literature of the 1980s of the kind of writing that N. advocates in his essays is his own collection, *Fools and Other Stories*. With the exception of the novella that gives the collection its title—the story of an idealistic teenager who wishes to improve his people's lot and of his disillusioned and failed predecessor in that role—none of the stories in *Fools* explicitly engages apartheid. While not altogether absent from the stories, racial oppression is strategically understated in favor of an exploration of the internal resources, strengths, and problems of black communities. Typically, the central consciousness of these stories is a child. Thus, we have stories about a boy struggling to define an identity for himself among his peers, about a boy awed by a mysterious old prophetess, about the relationship between a boy and his gifted uncle, and about a boy who rebels against his parents' materialistic middle-class mores. To read these stories after immersing oneself in much black writing of the 1970s and early 1980s is to become aware of a fresh voice portraying the complex social totality of black South African life in novel ways. "Death of a Son" (1987) also breaks with the codes and canons of protest writing. Instead of making the death of a child the focus of the narrative as a writer of protest fiction might have done, N. subordinates it to the story of the parents who must simultaneously find ways of coping with the terrible loss of their infant son, of wrestling with the breakdown of their relationship, and of continuing to deal with the rigors of life under apartheid

N.'s essays and fiction were met with considerable wariness on the part of many progressive practitioners and commentators of South African culture in the highly polarized political climate of the 1980s. By 1990, however, the African National Congress had abandoned its official dictum that culture should be "a weapon of the struggle" to embrace a popularized version of N.'s theses on literature and cultural politics. In that same year N. returned to South Africa where for the past eight years he has pursued a distinguished career as a university administrator while also occupying important positions in various public institutions. Currently, he is Vice Chancellor at the University of the North. N.'s assumption of an administrative career in higher education at a time of nation-building may account for the relative paucity of his production in the 1990s. The only new creative work he has published since returning home is a collection of stories for children, and by comparison with the 1980s his essayistic output has been small. Nonetheless, N.'s wide-ranging oeuvre—on literature and literary politics, on the conditions of cultural production, on language and cultural institutions, and on the aims and spirit of a new national culture—continues to serve as a vital reference point for any discussion of South Africa's postapartheid culture in the making.

FURTHER WORKS: *Rediscovery of the Ordinary: Essays on South African Literature and Culture* (1992); *Bonono and the Peach Tree* (1993); *South African Literature and Culture: Rediscovery of the Ordinary* (1994)

BIBLIOGRAPHY: Bunn, D., and J. Taylor, *From South Africa: New Writing, Photographs, and Art* (1987); Vaughan, M., "Storytelling and Politics in Fiction," in Trump, M., ed., *Rendering Things Visible: Essays on South African Literary Culture* (1990): 186-204; de Kok, I., and K. Press, *Spring is Rebellious: Arguments about Cultural Freedom by Albie Sachs and Respondents* (1990); Brown, D., and B. Van Dyk, eds., *Exchanges: South African Writing in Transition* (1991); O'Brien, A., "Literature in Another South Africa: N.'s Theory of Emergent Culture," *Diacritics*, 22 (1992): 67-68

—DAVID ALVAREZ

NDEBELE LITERATURE
See Zimbabwean Literature

NECATİGİL, Behçet

Turkish poet and translator, b. 16 Apr. 1916, Istanbul; d. 13 Dec. 1979, Istanbul

N. is one of Turkey's most highly esteemed poets. His life, which he spent almost entirely in Istanbul, was uneventful. After graduating from the Istanbul College for Teachers, he became a teacher of Turkish literature, briefly serving at the Kars Lycée, followed by many years at Istanbul's Kabatas Lycée and the Institute for Education, until his retirement in 1972. He enjoyed fame as a teacher of literature. Many of his students became major writers.

N.'s poetic career was devoted, as he observed, "to the private experiences of a citizen of median income from birth to death, to his real and imagined life in the triangle of home–family–close relations." Although he concentrated on daily living and ordinary subjects, his aesthetics emphasized formal innovation and an unusual style. Most critics characterize him as a consistent poet with a predictable world of his own. His unconventional use of the Turkish language, especially in his later work, occasionally made him difficult to understand and inaccessible. Nonetheless, his reputation as a major modern poet has remained high since the 1950s. His complete works, *Bütün eserleri*, published in seven volumes in the 1980s, continue to enjoy estimable sales. After his

death, his family established the N. Poetry Prize, which has been awarded annually since 1980.

A leading writer of radio plays, N. collected them in four volumes, *Yıldızlara bakmak* (1965; stargazing), *Gece aşevi* (1967; night diner), *Üç turunçlar* (1970; three bitter oranges), and *Pencere* (1975; window). Among his contributions are *Edebiyatımızda Isimler Sözlüğü* (1960; who's who in Turkish literature)—which he saw through many editions and which has been updated several times since his death—and *Edebiyatımızda Eserler Sözlüğü* (1979; guide to literary works), which contains the synopses of 750 novels, short-story collections, and plays by 220 Turkish writers. He also compiled a small dictionary of mythology. A selection of his essays and other prose pieces were collected in *Bile/Yazdı* (1979; even/wrote). He translated more than twenty books, including works by Heinrich Heine (1797–1856), Knut Hamsun, Miguel de UNAMUNO, and Heinrich BÖLL. The poems he translated were posthumously collected in a volume entitled *Yalnızlık bir yağmura benzer* (1984; loneliness resembles the rain).

In a poetic career that spanned four and a half decades beginning with the publication of his first poem in the influential journal *Varlık* in 1935, N. remained staunchly independent, shunning the literary schools and movements of his time. From the outset he turned a cold shoulder to the sentimental romanticism of his predecessors and most of his contemporaries. His first collection, *Kapalı Çarşı* (1945; grand bazaar), explores the life of the man in the street in a matter-of-fact and engaging style. His books that came out in quick succession in the 1950s—*Çevre* (1951; environment), *Evler* (1953; houses), *Eski toprak* (1956; old soil), and *Arada* (1958; in between)—refined this aesthetic approach in depicting the minutiae of ordinary life in objective terms, although the poet was able to augment his simple, direct statements with subjective symbols and asides.

Dar Çağ (1960; narrow age) marked a turning point: N. began to experiment with a new kind of poetry of intellectual search and abstract formulations. *Yaz dönemi* (1963; summer term) is a prismlike collection in which N. creates a brave new world of discovered and invented relationships. In some ways similar to Wallace STEVENS, N. appeared to marshal his creative energy to transforming visions and revisions of reality in the quest for higher meanings.

With *Divançe* (1963; little divan) N. returned briefly to the quintessence of classical Ottoman verse, whose hallmarks were abstract conceits, pure imagery, and a dominant euphony. Here N. not only captures the aesthetic values of his esoteric classical heritage but also succeeds in modernizing it and putting on it his own individualistic imprint. His later books, *İki başına yürümek* (1968; twosome solitary walk), *En/Cam* (1970; out/come), *Zebra* (1973; zebra), and *Kareler aklar* (1975; squares and whites), are indefatigable quests for paradoxical relationships between objects, actions, emotions, and concepts. In these collections, N. forged new configurations of shapes and juxtaposed time and appearances into subjective formulations of what he saw or imagined. The syntax is sometimes dismembered, with phrases clipped and words employed out of context. Each poem, however, has a surface repose and a symmetry, proving that N. was one of Turkey's most meticulous practitioners of the poetic art.

In 1976 he published his selected poems, *Sevgilerde* (in loves), from the period 1935–1965. The culmination of his later work appeared in two collections, *Beyler* (1978; messieurs) and *Söyleriz* (1980; we shall tell), where his cubistic approach and formal purity were crowned by a much richer vocabulary. The eventual synthesis worked out by this superior craftsman is, in some ways, reminiscent of Paul VALÉRY. Few Turkish poets have ever offered deeper insights into living experiences, into enigmas, into the life of the imagination with any comparable combination of intellectual complexity and smooth lyricism.

BIBLIOGRAPHY: Pazarkaya, Y., *B. N.: Gedichte* (1972)

—TALAT SAIT HALMAN

NEGOIŢESCU, Ion

Romanian critic and poet, b. 10 Aug. 1921, Cluj; d. 9 Feb. 1993

After graduating from secondary school in Cluj, N. majored in literature and philosophy at the University of Cluj, after studying under Lucian BLAGA at Sibiu, where with Stefan Augustin DOINAŞ and others he organized a literary and ideological group that in a flamboyant manifesto (1943) opposed the cultural policies of fascism. After 1947 N.'s work was virtually banned from publication, and he was imprisoned for political reasons between 1961 and 1964. After 1965 he was allowed to publish again and served briefly on the editorial staffs of several literary journals, but he continued his activities of cultural and political dissidence and was subject to harassment and press attacks. Since 1980, N. lived in Cologne and Munich, Germany.

N. was influenced by German romanticism and French SURREALISM. From the beginning, as it later became clear, his purpose was to rewrite Romanian literary history from the point of view of a modern lyrical sensitivity such as had been formed between the two world wars. Most of his critical volumes, from *Scriitori moderni* (1966; modern writers) to *Analize şi sinteze* (1976; analyses and syntheses), are collections of fragments of a large historical work, the plan of which he published in an article in 1968. N.'s critical method mixes archetypal elements with empathetic and impressionist procedures; it aims primarily at discovering lyrical and irrational nuclei around which the work is organized. The approach worked best in the study of Mihai Eminescu (1850–1889), Romania's great romantic poet, where it led to the rejection of the sentimental and nostalgic strata of Eminescu's work, which were familiar to the public and had been officially emphasized for decades, in favor of a visionary and eruptive substructure apparent in the posthumously published work of the poet. In discussing contemporary literature, N. has vigorously defended aesthetic values against social and political criteria. He considers his work a continuation of that of Eugen LOVINESCU and thus a defense of competence and objective truth against topical interests.

After his self-exile to Germany, N. was active politically, critiquing not only the communist regime, but also the whole mentality and orientation of Romanian culture; most of his articles were collected in *In cunoştinţă de cauză* (1990; In Full Awareness); a volume of memoirs was begun but remained unfinished. Only partially finished was N.'s intended masterwork, a two-volume history of Romanian literature, full of original insights and challenging critical judgments.

N. also published several volumes of hermetic and erotic poetry, as well as an early surrealist story. His work synthesizes the aesthetic consciousness of Romanian culture in its attempt to offer an alternative to the politicization of human relations.

FURTHER WORKS: *Povestea tristă a lui Ramon Ocg* (1941); *Sabasios* (1968); *Poezia lui Eminescu* (1968); *Eugen Lovinescu* (1970); *Poemele lui Balduin de Tyaormin* (1970); *Însemnări critice* (1970); *Lampa lui Aladin* (1971); *Moartea unui contabil* (1972); *Engrame* (1975); *Un roman epistolar* (1975, with Radu Stanca); *Alte însemnări critice* (1980); *Istoria literaturii románe* (1991); *Scriitori contemporani* (1994); *Straja dragonilor* (1994)

BIBLIOGRAPHY: Nemoianu, V., on *Engrame, BA*, 50 (1976): 388–89; Nemoianu, V., "Romanian Revolutions," *TLS*, 8 July 1977, 824; Nemoianu, V., on *Un roman epistolar, SEEJ*, 23 (1979): 315–16

—VIRGIL NEMOIANU

NÉGRITUDE

Négritude emerged in Paris around 1934, among a group of Caribbean and African students including Aimé CÉSAIRE from Martinique and Léopold Sédar SENGHOR from Senegal. The word itself first appeared in print in Césaire's poem *Cahier d'un retour au pays natal* (1939; *Memorandum on My Martinique*, 1947; later tr., *Return to My Native Land*, 1969). It was only after World War II, in the late 1940s and 1950s, however, that the term and the concept acquired extensive currency. In the minds of its founders, Négritude was a reaction against the French colonial policy of assimilation and especially against the readiness of the older generation to accept assimilation as a goal. Négritude writers asserted instead the existence of an independent African culture and sought to define its distinctive values. They argued that all cultures have distinctive characteristics owing to biological differences between the races.

Although the term has been applied, often very loosely, to a wide variety of French-speaking black writers, there has never been a Négritude school. The concept itself has very little substance, in fact, outside its use by its main founders, Senghor and Césaire, and a few of their contemporaries, such as Léon Gontran DAMAS and Birago DIOP. It is Senghor alone who has, since the end of World War II, consistently developed and expounded Négritude as an ideology in his poetry, speeches, and essays. He has listed and defined the fundamental, permanent values of African culture— emotion, rhythm, religious spirit, community—contrasting them with the European values of reason, skepticism, and individualism.

At first, Senghor viewed these characteristics as conflicting opposites, with the virtue of creativity on the African side. Jean-Paul SARTRE, in his important essay on Négritude, "Orphée noir" (1948; *Black Orpheus*, 1963), therefore described it as an "antiracist racism." Senghor was, however, more inclined by temperament to reconciliation, and increasingly stressed the complementarity and interdependence of cultures and their evolution toward the "civilization of the universal."

While Césaire, too, stresses some of the African values invoked by Senghor (especially the African's essential quality of emotion as opposed to the European's reason), he has concentrated more on attacking the European stereotype of the black man as a cultural

359

and racial inferior and the black man's readiness to acknowledge this stereotype. In his poetry Césaire presents the black man as much closer to the natural, real world than the white man, and therefore as much more vital and creative. Unlike Senghor, Césaire has not sought to develop Négritude as an ideology and has even tended to avoid the use of the term itself.

Since the 1960s, Négritude has been increasingly criticized by black writers. This criticism has been partly directed against the Négritude definition of African culture, which is seen as being too simplistic and too close to Western racist ideologies, but also against the conservative and neocolonialist politics considered to derive from Senghor's concept of Négritude. It is now being acknowledged, however, that during the 1950s Négritude was very influential in changing black, as well as white, attitudes toward the black peoples of Africa and the Caribbean; Sartre was therefore right to see it, in his 1948 essay, as a crucial but passing historical phenomenon.

BIBLIOGRAPHY: Jahn, J., *Muntu: An Outline of Neo-African Culture* (1961); Jahn, J., *Neo-African Literature: A History of Black Writing* (1969); Moore, G., "The Politics of Negritude," in Pieterse, C., and D. Munro, eds., *Protest and Conflict in African Literature* (1969): 26–42; Adotevi, S., *Négritude et négrologues* (1972); Kesteloot, L., *Black Writers in French: A Literary History of Négritude* (1974); Steins, M., "La Négritude: Un second souffle?" *Cultures et Développement*, 12 (1980): 3–43; Irele, A., *The African Experience in Literature and Ideology* (1981)

—CLIVE WAKE

NELLIGAN, Émile

Canadian poet (writing in French), b. 24 Dec. 1879, Montreal, Que.; d. 18 Nov. 1941, Montreal, Que.

Born of an Irish father and French-Canadian mother, N. received a typical 19th-c. classical education. But he dropped out of a Jesuit college at the age of seventeen to devote himself to poetry.

Quebec's first *poète maudit*, N.'s meteoric career was compressed into three years, beginning with the publication of his first poem, "Rêve fantasque" (1896; fantastic dream), which showed his predilection for dream landscapes. In August 1899, schizophrenic, N. entered the mental hospital where he remained until his death.

The apogee of N.'s career was his recitation of "Rêve d'artiste" ("A Poet's Dream," 1960) and "La romance du vin" ("The Poet's Wine," 1960) in May 1899 at a public meeting of the École Littéraire of Montreal, from which he was borne triumphantly on the shoulders of his fellow poets. A first collection of poems, *É. N. et son œuvre* (1904; É. N. and his work) appeared thanks to the efforts of a writer friend, Louis Dantin (pseud. of Eugène Seers, 1865–1945).

Little development marks the 175 poems constituting N.'s corpus, all of which were published in *Poésies complètes, 1896–1899* (1952; complete poems, 1896–1899). The teenager quickly mastered prosody, experimenting with unusual feminine rhymes in his favorite forms, the sonnet and the rondel. The melancholy "Soir d'hiver" ("Winter Evening," 1960) haunts the reader with its verbal melodies. Music, in fact, is a constant theme in N.'s poetry, as is

evident in "Tombeau de Chopin" (Chopin's tomb) and "Pour Ignace Paderewski" (for Ignace Paderewski). In "Vieux piano" (old piano) it is associated with memories of childhood and his mother's playing. Above all, N.'s poetry aspires to the state of music, exhibiting the SYMBOLIST penchant for synaesthesia in works like "Rythmes du soir" (rhythms of evening).

Despite some Parnassian exoticism and objectivity in the cycle "Pastels et porcelaines" (pastels and porcelains), N.'s poetry is essentially private, the external landscapes composed of artifacts reflexively mirroring his emotions. His objective correlatives correspond, like Baudelaire's, to a black spirit.

N. makes a personal myth of his despair, charting a journey between the heights and the abyss. In his most famous sonnet, "Le vaisseau d'or" ("The Golden Ship," 1960), the ship, his "heart," which he calls "that work of art," falls into the abyss of dream, locus of death and poetry. The paradoxes of Baudelairean romanticism abound: cradle and grave are confounded in "Devant mon berceau" (in front of my cradle), a lament for lost childhood. The interrelationship of creation and destruction, life and death, is located in his repeated symbols: piano, ship of life, chapel, garden of childhood, black virgin, crows.

N.'s obsession with death and madness has assumed the proportions of a national myth in French Canada in light of its development by younger poets, fascinated with the state of life-in-death. Within the poetic movements of the turn of the century N. developed his own imagery and form and determined the direction of modern poetry in Quebec. He was its first great poet.

FURTHER WORKS: *Poèmes choisis* (1966); *Oeuvres complètes I: Poésie complètes; II: Poèmes et textes d'asile, 1900-1941* (2 vols., 1991). FURTHER WORKS IN ENGLISH: *Selected Poems* (1960); *The Complete Poems of E. N.* (1983)

BIBLIOGRAPHY: Dantin, L., *Gloses critiques* (1931): 179–99; Lacourcière, L., Introduction to *Poésies complètes* (1952): 7–38; Bessette, G., *Les images en poésie canadienne-française* (1960): 215–75; Wyczynski, P., *É. N.* (1967); Mezei, K., "Lampman and N.: Dream Landscapes," *CRCL*, 6 (1979): 151–65; Mezei, K., "É. N.: A Dreamer Passing By," *CanL*, 87 (1980): 81–99

—BARBARA GODARD

NEMEROV, Howard

American poet, critic, and novelist, b. 1 March 1920, New York, N.Y.; d. 5 July 1991

N. was graduated from Harvard University in 1941, served briefly as a flyer in World War II, and since that time has taught at a number of colleges and universities, including Bennington, Brandeis, and Washington University in St. Louis. In 1963–64 N. was consultant in poetry to the Library of Congress. He has received many literary awards, and in 1977 was inducted into the American Academy and Institute of Arts and Letters.

Although he is competent and prolific in many genres, N. is best known as a poet. His fictions are, for the most part, entertaining and forgettable: typical is the novel *The Homecoming Game* (1957), which was adapted for the screen as *Tall Story*.

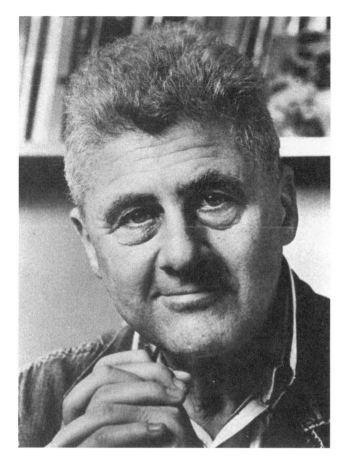

Howard Nemerov

N.'s early poetry draws heavily on biblical themes and is obsessed with the presence of death. At the same time, however, it displays wit, iconoclasm, and an almost haughty technical virtuosity. N.'s attention to formal alignments of verse (sonnets, quatrains, couplets, villanelles, and sestinas) in *Guide to the Ruins* (1950) becomes a kind of obsession. Virtually every poem follows a program to its appointed end. Because of N.'s formalism, many critics treated him harshly in the decades of the beat poets Allen GINSBERG and Lawrence Ferlinghetti (b. 1919) and of formlessness. The critic M. L. Rosenthal mutes his criticism by calling him an "independent," working apart from the trends and movements of his time, but recognizing N.'s distinct modernity.

N. has composed a number of superb dramatic monologues, in which he tries to capture the temper of the present by using a voice from the mythic past. One of his best-known works in this genre is "Lot Later," in *The Next Room of the Dream* (1962). In this lengthy, rambling, chatty disquisition the biblical character Lot ruminates about the destruction of Sodom and Gomorrah ("the whole/Outfit went up in smoke"), and about his own predicament ("neither permitted the pleasure of his sins/Nor punished for them"). Several of N.'s publications in the 1960s are conceived as poetic dramas, exploring philosophical and aesthetic themes without using any of the poetic forms that had been his mainstay.

In *The Western Approaches* (1975) N. returned to the formalism of his earlier years. Here, however, it is a conscious eccentricity, adapted to precise effect. N. asserts that technology, the preoccupation of the Western mind, represents a profound abstraction, an approach for rediscovering a sense of wonder at the infinite mysteries of the universe.

The musical technology of J. S. Bach is N.'s subject in "Playing the Inventions" in *The Western Approaches*. The "perfect courtesy of music" provides a parallel to poetic thought: it cannot exist without form, it cannot be paraphrased, it cannot know "except by modeling what it would know." This poem combines sensual and intellectual delight, describing shadow-dappled pages of music where the accidents of wind and sun expand upon the incidents of the composer's imagination to create a beatific dream world. There the centuries that separate the poet from the composer "are for a while as thought/Dissolved in the clear streams of your songs."

Science and technology, for N., are not necessarily opposed to human values. The need to catalogue the natural world, to build knowledge by increments, to test, challenge, and probe, to assay proof and root out doubt—these activities arise out of the same spirit that fears the dark, that embraces ritual or superstition, that seeks faith. The two faculties, reason and faith, are not necessarily at war; N. suggests that we do our culture and our intellect a disservice when we worship one at the expense of the other.

Western humanity, at its best, begins by tinkering with the mechanics of an entity (a poem, a miracle, a fugue, a rocket), and ends with the nervous, uncertain belief that there is more to know. As a consummate technician of poetry, N. illuminates the mind's progress from ignorance to knowledge to recognition of a wider ignorance. This progress has always been his subject.

FURTHER WORKS: *The Image & the Law* (1947); *The Melodramatists* (1949); *Federigo; or, The Power of Love* (1954); *The Salt Garden* (1955); *Mirrors and Windows* (1958); *A Commodity of Dreams* (1959); *New and Selected Poems* (1960); *Ender* (1962); *Poetry and Fiction* (1963); *Journal of the Fictive Life* (1965); *The Blue Swallows* (1967); *The Winter Lightning: Selected Poems* (1968); *Stories, Fables and Other Divisions* (1971); *Reflexions on Poetry & Poetics* (1972); *Gnomes and Occasions* (1973); *The Collected Poems of H. N.* (1977); *Figures of Thought* (1978); *Sentences* (1980)

BIBLIOGRAPHY: Rosenthal, M. L., *The Modern Poets* (1960): 255–62; Hungerford, E. B., ed., *Poets in Progress* (1962): 116–33; Meinke, P., *H. N.* (1968); Duncan, B., ed., *The Critical Reception of H. N.* (1971); Donoghue, D., *Seven American Poets from MacLeish to N.* (1975): 250–88; Labrie, R., *H. N.* (1980)

—LARRY TEN HARMSEL

NÉMETH, László

Hungarian novelist, dramatist, essayist, and translator, b. 18 April 1901, Nagybánya (now Baia-Mare, Romania); d. 3 March 1975, Budapest

A physician by training, N. burst on the literary scene in 1925 with a prize-winning short story about the death of a peasant woman, "Horváthné meghal" (Mrs. Horváth dies). Although he grew up in Budapest, N. came from a peasant background, and his knowledge of village life stood him in good stead: his best novels have a rural setting and delve into peasant psyches. Indeed, during the 1930s, after he had made a name for himself as a polemicist as well as a novelist and playwright, the Hungarian populists looked to N. as the potential ideologist of their movement. But direct involvement in politics was alien to N.'s temperament. Never lacking for disciples and partisans, N. clashed often with his fellow writers and the literary establishment. For a time in the 1930s he edited a periodical, *Tanu*, which was one of those curious ventures not entirely unprecedented in Hungarian literature: a journal written by one man. On the eve of World War II N. formulated his most controversial ideas on race and ethnic viability, for which he was attacked both from the left and the right. After the war he virtually disappeared from the literary scene and for several years earned his living by teaching and translating. Toward the end of his life, however, he was acclaimed both at home and abroad as one of the leading figures in modern Hungarian literature.

N. was a man of bold vision. Basing his ideological conviction on an odd mixture of Nietzschean elitism and Christian and socialist egalitarianism, he became an advocate of a "revolution of quality," that is, a moral revolution. The basic tenet of his writing is that life's deep-seated ills can be remedied only by moral example. Before and during World War II N. rejected both capitalism and communism, believing that the real revolution must take place within the individual's consciousness. This ethical impulse informs virtually all of his novels and plays, which deal invariably with the noble and tragic struggle of individual genius against mass stupidity and intolerance. The names alone of the historical personages around whom he built some of his dramas—Galileo, Jan Hus, Mahatma Gandhi—indicate the nature of his theme.

In subtler, more provocative ways, his novels exemplify the same outlook. The nonconformist hero of *Emberi színjáték* (1929; the human comedy) becomes a Nietzschean moral hero; and the heroines of *Égető Eszter* (2 vols., 1956; Eszter Égető) and *Irgalom* (1965; compassion), although realistically conceived, are symbols of human goodness and endurance. The father of four daughters, N. had a predilection for strong female characters. The novel *Gyász* (1935; mourning), for example, is the finely wrought story of a proud peasant widow whose grief over her husband's death turns into an awe-inspiring obsession. And N.'s best novel, *Iszony* (1947; *Revulsion*, 1965), is about a cold, virginal, but highly sensitive woman's tragic marriage to a jovial, sensuous man. *Bűn* (1936; *Guilt*, 1966) is N.'s most "Russian" novel. The title refers to the guilt felt by thoughtful members of the upper class—here represented by a wealthy intellectual—in the face of social inequality.

Marxist critics have dismissed N.'s ethical-ideological conviction as illusionary utopianism. In his later years N. came to accept Hungarian-style communism. But even in his final works the redeeming power of solitary moral exemplars remains strong.

FURTHER WORKS: *Ember és szerep* (1934); *Kocsik szeptemberben* (1937); *Alsóvárosi búcsú* (1939); *A minőség forradalma* (4 vols., 1940–1943); *Lányaim* (1942); *Kisebbségben* (2 vols., 1942); *Magam helyett* (1943); *A Medve utcai polgári* (1943); *Társadalmi drámák* (2 vols., 1958); *Történelmi drámák* (2 vols., 1963); *A kísérletező ember* (1964); *Kiadatlan tanulmányok* (2 vols., 1968); *N. L. munkái* (1969 ff.)

BIBLIOGRAPHY: Kerényi, K., "On L. N.," *HungQ*, 3 (1962): 33–38; Reményi, J., *Hungarian Writers and Literature* (1964): 394–401; Stillwell, R., on *Revulsion, SatR* (12 March 1966): 36; Ozsvath, Z., "L. N.'s *Revulsion:* Violence and Freedom," *CARHS*, 6 (1979): 67–77; Sanders, I., "Post-Trianon Searching: The Early Career of L. N.," in Király, B. K., P. Pastor, and I. Sanders, eds., *Total War and Peacemaking: A Case Study on Trianon* (1982)

—IVAN SANDERS

NENETS LITERATURE
See Finno-Ugric Literatures

NEOREALISM

The term "neorealism," first coined by the critic Arnaldo Bocelli (1900–1976) in 1930, describes a movement in modern Italian literature, cinema, and figurative arts. The term has subsequently—and less precisely—been applied by critics writing on other European literatures to identify similar tendencies.

Never organized into a school with specific aesthetic norms or recognized leaders, neorealism was a movement of hybrid components, internal ambiguities, and indistinct contours. Therefore, setting chronological limits and identifying chief representatives are quite difficult. In general terms, neorealism can be defined as a trend most important during the period 1930–55 and characterized by a pervasive preoccupation with social issues.

After the opening decades of the century there was a marked return in the Western world to forms of realism: in Russia, coinciding with the Bolshevik revolution, from the cinematic work of Sergey Eisenstein (1898–1948) and Vsevolod Pudovkin (1893–1953) to the establishment of Socialist REALISM; in Germany, with the literary suggestions of the "new factualism" of the 1920s; in England, with the documentaries of John Grierson (1898–1972) and Basil Wright (b. 1907) depicting the world of the workers. These movements led to seemingly endless polemics in Europe on the function of art as a mode of social commitment, from Jean-Paul SARTRE to the present. Within this shared framework, however, neorealism shows unique characteristics ascribable to factors peculiar to the Italian situation: opposition to the Fascist regime and to the bourgeois complicity in it, together with rebellion against the aristocratic view of art as self-sufficient and detached from the conflicts of the real world.

The aim of neorealism was to describe authentically the human condition, the social and political milieu, and the role of the intellectual in it. What results is a tragic sense of human existence, marked by solitude and the absence of communication. The solitude is perceived not elegiacally but historically, with war seen as a deformation, a vision of what man has made of man. From this effort at objectivity, there follows the discovery of a social perspective—a perspective typically focused on the lower classes, with their immediate problems and disarticulated language. Fascism, World War II, and the Resistance all molded the neorealist stance. This era gave rise to a belief in the possibility of creating at least the illusion of a radical revolt against the past and a significant metamorphosis of consciousness—in order to create a new society from zero, to create a new culture.

In literature, the neorealists advocated that the writer be politically involved, at least in terms of healing the traditional rupture between literature and the masses, between the written word and the spoken word. Reality should be approached through a narrative mode following the models of Ernest HEMINGWAY, Russian realists like Isaak BABEL and Alexandr FADEEV, and the Italian writers Cesare PAVESE and Elio VITTORINI, who were also responsible for introducing the American novel into Italian culture. The result should be a documentary literature, in which facts are viewed as protagonists, a literature that would reject lyrical expression and would instead use an immediate, antirhetorical, spoken, dialectal language. Writers who in varying degree exemplify such a literature are Vasco PRATOLINI, Francesco JOVINE, Italo CALVINO, Beppe FENOGLIO, Ignazio SILONE, Carlo LEVI, Giuseppe BERTO, Domenico REA, Silvio Micheli (b. 1911), Renata Viganò (1900–1976), and Oreste Del Buono (b. 1923).

Perhaps it was in the cinema that neorealism attained its most eloquent form. Films like *Roma, città aperta* (1945; *Rome, Open City*) and *Paisà* (1946) by Roberto Rossellini (1906–1977), *Ladri di biciclette* (1948; *Bicycle Thieves*) by Vittorio De Sica (1902–1974), *La terra trema* (1948) by Luchino Visconti (1906–1976), and *Sciuscià* (1946; *Shoeshine*) by De Sica and Cesare Zavattini (1902–1989), among others, have become exemplary of and synonymous with that movement. They were instrumental not only in the expansion of cinematic art but also in the projection of a particular image of Italy to the world.

BIBLIOGRAPHY: Pacifici, S., *A Guide to Contemporary Italian Literature: From Futurism to Neorealism* (1962): 114–49, 226–50; Armes, R., *Patterns of Realism: A Study of Italian Neo-Realist Cinema* (1971)

—ANTONINO MUSUMECI

NEPALESE LITERATURE

Around forty different languages are spoken in the kingdom of Nepal. Modern literature is published in Nepali (Nepal's national language), Maithili, Hindi, Newari, Tibetan, and several minority hill languages, while Sanskrit and Tibetan are sacred languages of scripture.

Newari is the local language of the Kathmandu Valley, where a rich urban culture flourished during the medieval period. Newari literature dates back to the 11th c., and it continues to develop and prosper in the Valley towns. Maithili is spoken in southern Nepal, and across the border in India: it too has both a medieval and a modern literature. As the national language and the regional lingua franca, however, Nepali has the most developed modern literature by far. Most Nepali writers have been higher-caste Hindus or Newars.

The earliest specimens of written Nepali are 13th-c. inscriptions and royal edicts from far western Nepal. Up until the 19th c., most authors of Nepali texts were pandits versed in the arts of Sanskrit composition who often depended upon royal patronage. Therefore, most old Nepali texts are translations of Sanskrit classics, heroic poems praising Nepal's kings, or devotional poems. Most now consider the Nepali rendering of the Ramayana produced by Bhanubhakta Acharya (dates n.a.) during the 1840s the first text of modern Nepali literature. However, Nepali literature is essentially a 20th-c. phenomenon.

Poetry

The first modern poet of note was Lekhnath Paudeltayal (1884-1965), a Brahman educated in Banaras. He was inspired by traditional Indian themes and is most highly praised for *Ritu Vichara* (1916; Reflections on the Seasons) and *Taruna Tapasi* (1953; The Young Ascetic). The first of these consists of six cantos of one hundred rhyming couplets, each describing one of the seasons. In *Taruna Tapasi* a poet sits beneath a tree, mourning the loss of his wife, and the spirit of the tree appears before him to offer consolation in the form of a long homily based on its silent observation of human life. This older style of poetry still has its adherents, among whom Madhab Prasad Ghimire (b. 1919) is probably the most loved.

Lekhnath Paudeltayal was followed by Balkrishna Sama (1903-1981) and Lakshmiprasad Devkota (1909-1959). Sama's work is colored by his reading of English literature, agnosticism, and democratic leanings, and his major contributions were his dramas, particularly *Mutuko Vyatha* (1929; Heart's Anguish), *Mukunda-Indira* (1937; Mukunda and Indira), *Prahlad* (1938; Prahlad), and *Andhavega* (1939; Blind Impulse). His poetry often expressed humanistic views that were radical for their time. The foundations of Nepali drama laid by Sama have been built upon in later years by accomplished playwrights such as Bijay Malla and Ashesh Malla (dates n.a.).

Lakshmiprasad Devkota's early poetry was influenced by the romantic English poets, particularly Wordsworth, and it dwelled on the goodness of humble people, the lost innocence of childhood, and rapturous descriptions of the beauties of nature. In 1936 Devkota published *Muna-Madan* (Muna and Madan), a verse narrative that is still the most popular book in Nepali. Its theme was borrowed from an old Newari folklore about a trader who travels to Tibet to seek his fortune. Devkota wrote a number of similar romances in the years that followed, and also produced epics (*mahakavya*) such as *Shakuntala* (1945; Shakuntala), a reworking of a classical fable, and *Sulochana* (1946; Sulochana), the story of a young woman of Kathmandu. He synthesized Greek and Indian mythology in the epics *Mayavini Sarsi* (1967; Circe the Enchantress) and *Prometheus* (1971; Prometheus). Devkota lived for most of his life in relative poverty and was prone to bouts of depression: a period spent in a mental asylum in 1939 later inspired the famous prose poem entitled "Pagal" (1953; "Crazy," 1980).

During the 1940s, Gopalprasad Rimal (1916-1973) called for the removal of the autocratic Rana regime in a series of exquisite poems such as *Amako Sapna* (1942; A Mother's Dream). Both before and after the fall of the regime in 1951, poets such as Siddhichara Shreshtha and Kedar Man Vyathit (dates n.a.) also made contributions on considerable importance. During the 1960s poetry began to develop in a different direction. Mohan Koirala (b. 1926) made a conscious effort to introduce MODERNISM by rejecting most of the conventions of earlier poetry. Koirlara's most famous poem is "Sarangi" (1961; The Fiddle), in which the sorry plight of a young minstrel whose songs no longer attract an audience is made to represent the lot of the poor and lowly classes of Nepal.

During the 1960s and 1970s, Nepali poets experimented more widely. A new movement, Tesro Ayam (Third Dimensionalism), attempted to redefine the purpose and nature of writing. Its effect was to intellectualize much of the poetry of the period, and a number of works appeared, such as the poems of Bairagi Kainla and Ishwar Ballabh (dates n.a.), which are now considered classics.

The influence of this movement fell upon other poets, who began to adopt new techniques.

The emergence of Bhupi Sherchan (1936-1989) brought further changes. Sherchan had produced two volumes of poetry full of Marxist rhetoric in earlier years, but his third collection, *Ghumne Mechmathi Andho Manche* (1969; A Blind Man on a Revolving Chair), has been one of the most important influences of recent years, because its satirical and ironic poems were composed in much plainer language. Since 1970, Nepali poetry has reassumed its earlier role as a medium for the expression of dissent, although these are of course not its only themes, and has regained the linguistic clarity of the work of its earlier poets.

Fiction

Short stories are the predominant genre of Nepali fiction, though the genre was not established fully until the 1930s. Guruprasad Mainnali's (1900-1971) "Naso" (1935; The Pledge) was probably the first modern Nepali short story, but Mainali's finest story is undoubtedly his "Paralko Ago" (1938; A Fire of Straw), which tells the tale of a quarrel between a farmer, Chame, and his wife, Gaunthali, in a tone of sympathy and humor. Although Mainali published only eleven short stories in all, they left a lasting mark on Nepali fiction.

Pushkar Shamsher's (1902-1961) stories are praised for their dramatic structure and convincing characterizations. The most famous is "Pariband" (1938; The Coincidence), in which an innocent man is convicted of murder due to an unfortunate combination of circumstances. Bishweshwar Prasad Koirala (b.1915), better known as B. P. Koirala, was the third major story writer of the 1930s and 1940s: as leader of the Nepali Congress Party, he was in the forefront of the struggle against the Rana regime.

All of the first generation of modern Nepali writers began by publishing their works in a Kathmandu journal, *Sharada*. The changes that occurred in Nepali literature during the *Sharada* era were born of an intellectual enlightenment and the growth of political consciousness as new cultural and political influences began to filter in from the outside world. Typical early stories contained portrayals of poverty, opposition to superstition and ossified tradition, and critical comment on the social status of women. Many Nepali authors began to write stories from a Marxist standpoint, or to draw attention to a specific social issue. Such stories multiplied during the period of freedom that followed the fall of the Ranas. Numerous stories by Ramesh Bikal (b. 1932) are clear examples of this Socialist REALISM.

During the 1950s, writers became familiar with the great figures of world literature and philosophy and an element of psychological analysis became important in the Nepali story. Several writers began to suggest that the old moral certainties could no longer remain unquestioned. In B. P. Koirala's "Karnelko Ghoda" (1949; The Colonel's Horse), for instance, the sexually frustrated young wife of an elderly man becomes infatuated with his horse. In the next decade the founders of the Tesro Ayam movement argued that Nepali literature was still two dimensional or "flat" and that the vocabulary and the very purpose of literature required reassessment and redefinition. The result of this can be seen most clearly in Indra Bahadur Rai's (dates n.a.) story "Hami Jastai Mainaki Ama" (1964; Maina's Mother Is Just Like Us), which is a collage of scenes and images without a linear plot.

Several innovative writers began to publish their stories after the 1960s. Parijat and other leftist writers formed Ralpha, a group

with progressive social attitudes that attempted to bring art and literature to ordinary people. In later years groups of young writers attempted to generate change with other politicized literary initiatives. Contemporary writers have stripped their literature of the last vestiges of sentimentalism and traditional beliefs.

Very few full-length novels have been written in Nepali to date, though several accomplished short novels have been published. *Basai* (A Place to Live) by Lilabahadur Kshetri (b. 1932), published in 1957, tells the story of a family that is dispossessed by corrupt landlords and moneylenders. B. P. Koirala produced a number of important novels, notably *Teen Ghumti* (1969; Three Turning Points) and *Sumnima* (n.d.; Sumnima), both of which revolve around a central female character. Parijat's 1962 novel *Shirishko Phul* (The Mimosa Flower) represented a turning point in the development of Nepali fiction, and was the first work of one of its greatest writers. This novel describes the development of a strange relationship between a morally corrupt ex-Gurkha soldier and a highly unorthodox Nepali woman. The most important contemporary novelist is Dhruba Chandra Gautam (dates n.a.).

BIBLIOGRAPHY: Abhi Subedi: *Nepali Literature, Background and History* (1978); Rubin, D., *Nepali Visions, Nepali Dreams: The Poetry of Lakshmiprasad Devkota* (1980); Pradhan, K., *A History of Nepali Literature* (1984); Hutt, M., *Himalayan Voices: An Introduction to Modern Nepali Literature* (1991); Hutt, M., *Modern Literary Nepali: An Introductory Reader* (1997)

—MICHAEL HUTT

NERUDA, Pablo

(pseud. of Neftalí Reyes Basualto) Chilean poet, b. 12 July 1904, Parral; d. 23 Sept. 1973, Santiago

Although N. did not receive the Nobel Prize for literature until 1971, he was already considered to be the most important Spanish American poet of the 20th c. because of his innovative techniques and contributions to most major trends and formal developments of the genre.

After his mother's death when he was just a month old, N.'s family moved to Temuco. N. attended schools there and came to Santiago to study French at the University of Chile. By his twentieth birthday N. had already published several books of poetry, including the international best seller, *Veinte poemas de amor y una canción desesperada* (1924; *Twenty Love Poems and a Song of Despair*, 1969), which established his reputation.

N. soon obtained an appointment in the Chilean diplomatic service and was sent to Burma as Chilean consul in Rangoon. While in the Far East (1927–31) N. completed the first volume of *Residencia en la tierra* (1933; *Residence on Earth*, 1946; later tr., 1973). After returning to Chile in 1933, N. was reassigned to Buenos Aires, where he befriended the Spanish poet Federico GARCÍA LORCA. When N. was named Chilean consul in Barcelona in 1934, García Lorca and other Spanish poets of the Generation of 1927 hailed him as a major voice of Hispanic poetry. N. published his second *Residencia en la tierra* (1935; *Residence on Earth*, 1946; later tr., 1973) volume in Spain.

After the outbreak of the Spanish Civil War, N. changed the course of his life and poetry. Beginning with his book *España en el corazón* (1937; *Spain in the Heart, in Residence on Earth, and*

Pablo Neruda

Other Poems, 1946), N.'s poetry became less personal and depicted the sociopolitical concerns of man from a socialist ideological perspective. N. partipated actively in leftist political causes until he announced his membership in the Chilean Communist Party in 1945. As early as 1938, N. had organized support for the Spanish Republic and found asylum for Spanish refugees in Chile. While still a diplomat assigned to Mexico City, N. provoked the ire of pro-Nazi groups because of his public support of the Soviet Union. N. was assaulted by Nazis in Cuernavaca in 1941, and his poem praising the defenders of Stalingrad produced such controversy that he was forced to relinquish his diplomatic post.

N. visited the Incan ruins of Macchu Picchu in 1943 and was inspired to write his acclaimed poem, *Alturas de Macchu Picchu* (1943; *The Heights of Macchu Picchu*, 1967), which was later incorporated into *Canto general* (1950; general song). His last volume of *Residencia en la tierra* (1947; *Residence on Earth*, 1973) contained poems written between 1935 and 1945. N. was elected to the Chilean senate in 1946, and when he denounced the government's anticommunist witch hunt, he was indicted and forced to flee his country in 1949 as a political exile. During this period he traveled extensively, finished *Canto general*, and met Matilde Urrutia, who later became his wife and inspired most of his mature love poetry. While in exile, N. was awarded the Stalin Prize for literature and the Lenin Peace Prize. He returned to Chile in 1952.

N.'s work cannot be easily classified within a single movement or style because it constantly changed and evolved as the personal and historical circumstances of his life and world were altered. Most critics arrange N.'s poetry according to different cyles or periods of development. Nevertheless, there are thematic and stylistic constants present throughout his work. His themes include an obsession with the sensual and material objects of the natural world and human society; an interest in both the frustration and enjoyment of material and erotic pleasures, especially in relation to telluric forces and the organic cycle of nature; a heroic view of the poet as a spokesman for the voiceless; recurring mythical archetypes; and the illogical association of images as found in dreams and the subconscious. N. assumed varying poetic personae or masks, eventually voicing not only his personal concerns but also the universal aspirations of the common man of the Third World for social justice, dignity, and respect. In style, N. made use of a wide range of techniques: the expansive employment of hermetic metaphors and polysemic imagery; chaotic enumerations of concrete objects; reiteration, alliteration, and interior rhyme; an alternating application of free unpunctuated verse and more conventional metric forms and syntax; and shifts in point of view and tone expressed by multiple voices.

Veinte poemas de amor y una canción desesperada is now considered to be a classic of Hispanic erotic poetry. It represented the highest achievement of N.'s early poetry because it marked his first successful attempt to write a book with a central theme and cohesive vision. Although the book still retained some trappings of the MODERNIST style, it initially shocked some critics because of its prosaic language and explicit celebration of amorous ecstasy, lovemaking, and heartbreak. This book led to a series of subsequent volumes dedicated to erotic themes, in which woman is represented as both an alluring seductress and man's vital link with mother-earth and the cycles of nature. N. broadened and enriched his vision of love in *Cien sonetos de amor* (1959; one hundred love sonnets) and *Los versos del capitán* (1952; *The Captain's Verses*, 1972).

Tentativa del hombre infinito (1926; attempt for the infinite man) is now regarded as one of N.'s major works, although it was misunderstood and overlooked for many years by the critics. It represented an important transitional phase between the lucid, more conventional lyricism of *Veinte poemas de amor y una canción desesperada* and the dense hermetic language of *Residencia en la tierra*. As the book's title implied, it signified a bold new experiment and a departure from N.'s earlier poetry. Here, N. attempted to create a new poetic system, which better reflected the poet's inner torment, together with an anguished vision of a disordered and disintegrating cosmos. This book marked the first use of interior monologue in N.'s poetry, as he broke with conventional punctuation, syntax, rhyme, and stanzaic organization.

The first volume of *Residencia en la tierra* initiated a period in N.'s poetry that critics have called his *Residencia* cycle. Most poems of Volume I were written in the Far East at a time of loneliness and personal crisis. Although critics have often viewed the three volumes of the cycle as a unit because of their apparent continuity, one can discern differences in emphases and style as well as a progressive shift in tone in each book, as the poet moved from existential pessimism to resignation and, ultimately, to an optimistic faith in a political solution for the world's problems. "Galope muerto" ("Dead Gallop," 1946), the introductory poem of Volume I, set the pessimistic tone of frustration for the entire book as well as providing its central theme, a vision of life in perpetual disintegration driven on a whirlwind dash toward death and oblivion.

Volume II of the *Residencia* cycle signaled a shift in poetic diction and posture. Interior monologue was replaced by a dialogue with the reader, as the poet came to realize the necessity of communicating with an audience and assumed a more public voice and declamatory style. The introspective soulsearching and dense language of the first volume was supplanted by a lighter, more digressive style and a more extroverted outlook. The poet spoke more directly to his reader and became more resigned to life's vicissitudes and less guilty about his inability to find an explanation for life's paradoxes. The images became more realistic and less "purely poetic." This movement away from a private, lyrical stance in Volume II toward a public voice and narrative style would become more pronounced as N.'s work evolved.

The publication of the third *Residencia* volume consummated the cyclical evolution of N.'s poetry: he turned away from egocentric angst toward an open espousal of social concern and ideological commitment. The poem "Las furias y las penas" ("The Furies and the Sorrows," 1973) was a poetic confession that the author's verse had changed as both his personal circumstances and the world itself had become transformed during two turbulent decades in which humanity had witnessed economic depression, the Spanish Civil War, the outbreak of World War II, and the triumph over fascism. Because of its marked political character, the last volume of the *Residencia* cycle was the most controversial: N. sought to persuade the reader that his new-found ideological commitment offered the only solution for a world in turmoil.

N.'s next major work, *Canto general*, was even more explicitly political and autobiographical, but many critics consider it to be N.'s masterpiece because of the artistry with which he effectively communicated his theme of the historic quest and epic struggle of the Latin American for social justice from time immemorial to the moment of the poet's own persecution and exile for his political ideas. The book's obvious Marxist content was presented in the lucid narrative style of the epic, whereby each canto could be read like a chapter from a novel and contained its own theme but was linked sequentially and thematically to the entire poem. Cinematic effects and the documentary character of a newsreel are achieved by shifting multiple narrators who dramatize events or disclose factual information at opportune moments through their narrative commentaries. N. recreated and mythified Latin American history in accordance with Marxist philosophy, attempting to raise the reader's social consciousness and enlist his support for the Communist cause. These shifts in point of view created a distancing effect that enabled N. to make his arguments more convincing.

The publication of *Odas elementales* (1954; *Elementary Odes*, 1961) inaugurated a new cycle in N.'s poetry. It also marked another break with his previous poetics, as he turned from the grandiose and heroic tone of the epic poem to a humorous and occasionally sardonic exaltation of the most banal objects and aspects of daily life. His language became more plainspoken and apparently artless and free of any ideological purpose. Through his odes, N. finally was able to write for the people. The odes departed from the classic tradition of employing only welldefined metric forms. They were written in free verse with a thematic orientation both lyrical and public in character. By writing about ordinary objects like fruits and vegetables, he made these subjects worthy of the solemn and serious tradition of the ode. N. wrote in a jocular and benign tone, implicitly mocking the tradition of the conventional ode. N. wrote three more books of odes, his writing becoming for the first time an act of sheer pleasure and entertainment free of soul-searching or explicit ideological commitment.

One of his major works, *Estravagario* (1958; *Extravagaria*, 1972) began the last stage of N.'s poetry, in which he returned to egocentric concerns, self-indulgence, and frivolous individuality. Like Whitman, N. wrote a song about himself, but in an irreverent tone of self-parody and criticism of his own life and works. The book was unashamedly personal in the poet's return to some of the earliest themes of his poetic repertory. He used humor to mock his own previously held conception of the poetic artist as a hero endowed with special gifts. In N.'s new antipoetry the poem was viewed as an entertaining word game. Rhetoric and graphic effects complemented one another. The poet's personal experience was made ironic and his work desanctified. Through *Estravagario* N. was able to extricate himself from his own literary tradition of personal and social concerns, while pointing toward the varied directions the books of his final decade would take. Among the more salient tendencies of N.'s last decade of poetry are his politically committed verse with touches of didacticism and satire; the simple, humorous poetry of everyday living; the antipoetic and parodic strophes devoted to the theme of the absurd; and the more solemn and prophetic lyricism present in his work since "Alturas de Macchu Picchu." Often these diverse tendencies would converge and overlap in different books as N. furiously sought to bring his poetic outpouring full circle before succumbing to cancer in 1973.

FURTHER WORKS: *Crepusculario* (1923); *El habitante y su esperanza* (1926); *Anillos* (1926); *El hondero entusiasta* (1933); *Las uvas y el viento* (1954); *Viajes* (1955); *Nuevas odas elementales* (1956); *Tercer libro de odas* (1957); *Navegaciones y regresos* (1959); *Canción de gesta* (1960; *Song of Protest*, 1976); *Las piedras de Chile* (1961); *Cantos ceremoniales* (1961); *Plenos poderes* (1962; *Fully Empowered*, 1976); *Memorial de Isla Negra* (5 vols.: *Donde nace la lluvia*; *La luna en el laberinto*; *El fuego cruel*; *El cazador de raíces*; *Sonata crítica*; 1964; *Isla Negra: A Notebook*, 1981); *Arte de pájaros* (1966); *Una casa en la arena* (1966); *Fulgor y muerte de Joaquín Murieta* (1967; *The Splendor and Death of Joaquín Murieta*, 1972); *La Barcarola* (1968); *Las manos del día* (1968); *Fin del mundo* (1969); *Aún* (1969); *Comiendo en Hungría* (1969); *La espada encendida* (1970); *Las piedras del cielo* (1970); *Geografía infructuosa* (1972); *La rosa separada* (1972); *Incitación al Nixoncidio y alabanza de la revolución chilena* (1973; *A Call for the Destruction of Nixon and Praise for the Chilean Revolution*, 1980); *El mar y las campanas* (1973); *Jardín de invierno* (1974); *El corazón amarillo* (1974); *Libro de las preguntas* (1974); *Elegía* (1974); *Defectos escogidos* (1974); *2,000* (1974); *Confieso que he vivido: Memorias* (1974; *Memoirs*, 1977); *Elrío invisible: Poesía y prosa de juventud* (1980). FURTHER WORKS IN ENGLISH: *Three Spanish American Poets: Pellicer, N., Andrade* (1942); *Three Material Songs* (1948); *Selected Poems* (1961); *Twenty Poems* (1967); *We Are Many* (1967); *A New Decade: Poems 1958–1967* (1969); *P. N.: The Early Poems* (1969); *New Poems: 1968–1970* (1972); *Selected Poems of P. N.* (1972); *Five Decades: Poems 1925–1970* (1974)

BIBLIOGRAPHY: Alonso, A., *Poesía y estilo de P. N.* (1940); Alazraki, J., *Poética y poesía de P. N.* (1965); Loyola, H., *Ser y morir en P. N.* (1967); Ellis, K., "Poema XX, a Structural Approach," *RomN*, 11 (1970): 507–17; Riess, F. J., *The Word and the Stone: Language and Imagery in N.'s "Canto general,"* (1972); "Focus on P. N.'s *Residence on Earth*," special section *Review*, No. 11 (1974): 6–37; Kauffmann, L., "N.'s Last Residence: Translations and Notes on Four Poems," *NewS*, 5 (1975): 119–41; Rodríguez Monegal, E., *N.: El viajero inmóvil* (1977); Camacho Guizado, E., *P. N.: Naturaleza, historia y poética* (1978); Rosales, L., *La poesía de N.* (1978); Costa, R., de, *The Poetry of P. N.* (1979); Alegría, F., "The State and the Poet: An Art of Resistance," *PCP*, 15 (1980): 1–9; Felstiner, J., *Translating N.: The Way to Macchu Picchu* (1980); Durán, M. and M. Safir, *Earth Tones: The Poetry of P. N.* (1981); Santi, E. M., *P. N.: The Poetics of Prophecy* (1982)

—JAMES J. ALSTRUM

By becoming a political poet, N. faced a serious dilemma: how to meet his obligation as a militant, which demanded from him simplicity and social realism in literature, and at the same time maintain the hermetic beauty of his surrealist art. He would have to either purify his poetry of all decadent elements or give up revolutionary militancy. He could not, of course, follow either of these paths. In *Canto general* he openly condemned the poetry of his youth—everything written before *España en el corazón*—and proclaimed his faith in the social function of art. He would be a popular poet, to be sure, optimistic, dynamic in his expression of the world of the future. Nevertheless, in the purest and deepest zone of his poetry, N. continued to be a surrealist and, as a consequence, remained incomprehensible for the masses. It would be a serious error to doubt his sincerity, as it would be to believe that his political message fell on deaf ears because of the complex literary form in which it is expressed. . . .

Fernando Alegría, *Las fronteras del realismo: Literatura chilena del siglo XX* (1962), pp. 184–85

The N. we have come to expect is a poet in which one of the essentials of great poetry, continual surprise and revelation *in the language itself*, is always present. The typical *form* which that revelation assumes in his work is that of the unexpected coupling of qualities, or of the discovery of unexpected analogies and "irrational" relationships—"a swan of felt," "rawhide tranquility," an "explosion of feathers," "a proletariat of petals and bullets," "destitute bread." In many ways N. seems to be the poet of the adjective. Generally, adjectives simply add or subtract. N.'s multiply—or, better yet: transform; and they do this by discovering new qualities in *objects*. . . . Perhaps the best way to put it is to say that N. is the poet of the transformation of nouns.

Thomas McGrath, "The Poetry of P. N.," *Mainstream*, 15, 6 (1962), p. 44

There are so many N.s, so many manners—his early apprenticeship to Modernism, the wild and sometimes incoherent extravagance of his three *Residencias*, the prophetic and incantatory tone of his *Canto general*, the political travelogues in *Las uvas y el viento*, the intimacy and humour of the three books of Odes, and then the lucidity and serenity of all he has written since *Estravagario* in 1958. He has always been not so much looking for a new style as discarding his previous one, like a worn lizard skin. For this reason, everyone has his own N.; and for this reason, his work has provoked the whole gamut of criticism, from hatred to idolatry, to all of which he is indifferent. He has to be taken whole, or not at all. But there is such a lot to take! What N. has done is to keep bursting at the seams, breaking the sound barrier, swallowing the world whole and regurgitating it in an endless stream of poems that he seems to leave behind him like footprints—one might as well mix the metaphor, for N. certainly would not hesitate to do so. He has not bothered to write much *about* poetry; he has too much poetry on the boil all the time. . . .

Alastair Reid, "A Visit to N.," *Encounter*, Sept. 1965, p. 67

Each important book, each distinct period of N.'s poetic career produced not only *poetry* but also a *persona*. . . In the course of his long career, N. has projected several distinct personae in his poetry: the lost boy amidst the west winds of the hostile city in his first book, *Crepusculario*; the enthusiastic soldier who is enraptured by the contemplation of infinite space . . . the new American Bécquer who reveals the melancholy and desperate art of adolescent love to several generations; the unrestrained and disconnected poet of *Tentativa del hombre infinito* . . . the somnambulistic, terrified spectator of a world undergoing a permanent process of disintegration, which *Residencia en la tierra* documents; the witness who has seen the blood in the streets and creates a deliberately impure poetry to transmit the stupor and hope of *España en el corazón*; the narrator who rises from the nourishing sand and the ocean to sing the glory and the misery of Latin America in *Canto general*; the satisfied and amorous traveler of the world who orders his poetic duties in *Las uvas y el viento*; the popular poet who plays the guitar of the poor man in order to sing . . . [in] *Odas elementales* . . . the contemplative poet who turns his gaze more and more toward his own life and lets loose the powerful forces of memory in the autobiographical book that is the culmination of his poetry [*Los versos del capitán*].

Emir Rodríguez Monegal, *El viajero inmóvil: Introducción a P. N.* (1966), p. 20

The tendency to self-imitation makes the *Canto general* a watershed in the development of his poetry; it synthesizes much of the previous work and clarifies abiding associations between major images which N. had not fully worked out in his earlier poetry. Finally, the *Canto general* provides him with a set of themes that he never abandons, especially the social, historical and political phenomena set down in the poem. . . . The reason why he refuses to forgo these themes is that N. has always sought to discover in his poetry the nature of man: to do this, he has to find his way back to an understanding of how man is related to nature.

Frank Riess, *The Word and the Stone: Language and Imagery in N.'s "Canto general"* (1972), p. 164

N. was a poet of many styles and many voices, one whose multitudinous work is central to almost every important development in twentieth-century Spanish and Spanish American poetry. He was once referred to as the Picasso of poetry, alluding to his protean ability to be always in the vanguard of change. And he himself has often alluded to his personal struggle with his own tradition, to his constant need to search for a new system of expression in each book. N. was, until very recently in his later years, a poet perpetually in revolution against himself, against his own tradition.

René de Costa, *The Poetry of P. N.* (1979), p. 1

NERVO, Amado

Mexican poet, b. 27 Aug. 1870, Tepic; d. 24 May 1919, Montevideo, Uruguay

A student of theology and jurisprudence, N. practiced briefly as a lawyer in provincial Mazatlán before moving to Mexico City, where he worked as a journalist from 1894 to 1898. The publication of his naturalistic novel *El bachiller* (1895; the bachelor of arts) quickly established his name in Mexican literary circles. N. contributed to the famed MODERNIST *Revista azul*, a magazine that reflected the influence of the French SYMBOLISTS. In 1900, as a member of the Mexican press, he traveled to Paris, where he met the famous modernist poet Rubén DARÍO. In 1905 N. entered the diplomatic corps, serving as secretary of the Mexican legation in Madrid (1905–18) and minister to Argentina and Uruguay (1919).

Although he wrote short stories in the fantastic vein, such as *Cuentos misteriosos* (1921; mysterious tales), and literary criticism, including a long study on the Mexican poet Sor Juana Inés de la Cruz (1651–1695), N. is recognized primarily as a poet. His evolution as a writer can be seen in three periods. His verse written prior to 1900—*Perlas negras* (1898; black pearls) and *Poemas* (1900; poems)—reflects the strong influence of the Mexican writer Manuel Gutiérrez Nájera (1859–1895) and the preoccupation of the early modernists with Parnassian poetic themes and forms. Even at this early stage, however, in poems such as "A Kempis" (1898; A Kempis) N. exhibited an abiding interest with spiritual concerns.

N.'s second and most prolific period coincides with his stay in Europe and his association with Darío. In collections such as *Los jardines interiores* (1905; the inner gardens), *En voz baja* (1909; in a low voice), and *Serenidad* (1914; serenity), N. became increasingly introspective; modernist pomp yielded to metaphysical anguish. The death of Ana Cecilia Luisa Dalliez, the woman he loved, inspired his best-known book, *La amada inmóvil* (1920; the motionless lover), a collection of poems that reflects the intense personal anguish caused by the loss of his beloved and marks the last period in his evolution. N's preoccupation with death, his growing pantheism, and his progression toward simplicity are clearly evidenced in *El estanque de los lotos* (1919; the lotus pond), his last collection of poetry.

Together with Gutiérrez Nájera, N. is considered Mexico's most important writer of the modernist period. Prolific and varied, N. exerted considerable influence on Mexican literature.

FURTHER WORKS: *Místicas* (1898); *El donador de almas* (1899); *La hermana agua* (1901); *El éxodo y las flores del camino* (1902); *Lira heroica* (1902); *Almas que pasan* (1906); *El glosario de la vida vulgar* (1916); *El diablo desinteresado* (1916); *El diamante de la inquietud* (1917); *Una mentira* (1917); *Un sueño* (1917); *Elevación* (1917); *Plentitud* (1918; *Plenitude*, 1928); *El sexto sentido* (1918); *Amnesia* (1918); *Parábolas, y otros poemas* (1918); *El arquero divino* (1922); *Obras completas* (2 vols., 1967). FURTHER WORKS IN ENGLISH: *Confessions of a Modern Poet* (1935)

BIBLIOGRAPHY: Meléndez, C., *A. N.* (1926); Wellman, E. T., *A. N.: Mexico's Religious Poet* (1936); Montellano, B. O., de *Figura, amor y muerte de A. N.* (1943); Leal, L., "La poesía de A. N.," *Hispania*, 43 (1960): 43–47; García Prado, C., "A. N.," *Américas*, 22, 10 (1970): 9–14

—EDWARD MULLEN

NESİN, Aziz

(pseud. of Mehmet Nusret Nesin) Turkish satirist, short-story writer, novelist, and dramatist, b. 1915, Istanbul; d. 6 July 1995

Born into a lower-middle-class family, N. first received traditional Muslim education and then was admitted to the Orphans' School on account of his family's poverty. He later enrolled in military colleges. N. began his professional writing career as a journalist in 1944, when he resigned his military commission. Two years later, in collaboration with the short-story writer Sabahattin Ali (1907–1948), he began publishing a highly popular satirical magazine of leftist leanings, *Marko Paşa*, which was closed several times by the authorities, only to reappear under a different name. Struggling to earn a living in these early years, N. also worked as a grocer, photographer, bookseller, and accountant. On account of his socialism, he was prosecuted several times, and was sentenced to prison terms in 1947 and 1950.

A period of silence until 1954 was followed by a second beginning of N.'s prolific career. The next two years saw the publication of a novel, *Kadın olan erkek* (1955; the man who became a woman) and four volumes of short stories. The title story of *Fil Hamdi* (1956; Fil Hamdi) earned the Italian Golden Palm Award (1956). "Fil Hamdi," along with the title story of *Kazan töreni* (1957; ceremony for a boiler)—a story for which he won the Golden Palm Award for the second year running—are satirical masterpieces dwelling on the absurdities of officialdom. The helplessness of the individual against the ridiculous but powerful bureaucracy is a major theme of N.'s stories: "İnsanlar uyanıyor" (1969; people are waking up), tells, with pathos and humor, of how a paroled political convict comes to terms with life after prison. N.'s stories about the absurdities of everyday life and habits are more overtly comic.

Most of N.'s novels are conceived as lengthier versions of his short stories and reflect his interest in satire over plot. He excels in presenting types rather than developing characters. *Zübük* (1961; Zübük) tells the story of a charlatan from the viewpoint of several characters cheated by him. In some works of fiction N. also successfully employs the narrative techniques of the tale in creating a version of humorous parable.

N. has written numerous plays, ranging from farces to existentialist dramas. The exuberance that marks his satires is noticeably absent from his best-known plays, which examine the loneliness and meaninglessness of life. *Çiçu* (1969; Çiçu) reveals the near total alienation of a man who is capable of living only with his plants, pets, and inflatable doll.

N.'s childhood experiences served to heighten his awareness of the pathetic and ludicrous aspects of human life at the mercy of social forces. In his memoirs, *Böyle gelmiş böyle gitmez* (2 vols., 1966, 1972; *Istanbul Boy*, 2 vols., 1977, 1979), he focuses on the contrasts between the lifestyles of the rich and the poor; between the enormous piety of his parents and the profligate degeneracy in the side streets of a metropolis in transition; and between the traditionalism of the lower middle class and the rapid modernization undertaken by the newly established republic. His later confrontations with officialdom reinforced his idealism. N.'s piercing satire derives from the tension between his profound social commitment and the extravagant way in which he portrays absurd situations.

N.'s work appeals to a broad range of readership. Along with Yaşar KEMAL, he is one of the two best-selling authors in Turkey. N.'s work has been translated into twenty-five languages and has won various foreign prizes. Because of the particular cultural context and N.'s special sense of humor, however, his work does not lend itself easily to translation into English.

FURTHER WORKS: *Azizname* (1948); *Geriye kalan* (1948); *İt kuyruğu* (1955); *Yedek parça* (1955); *Düğülü mendil* (1955); *Damda deli var* (1956); *On dakika* (1957); *Koltuk* (1957); *Gol kralı* (1957); *Toros canavarı* (1957); *Deliler boşandı* (1957); *Hangi parti kazanacak* (1957); *Ölmüş eşek* (1957); *Bir sürgünün hatıraları* (1957); *Erkek Sabahat* (1957); *Mahallenin kısmeti* (1957); *Havadan sudan* (1958); *Bay düdük* (1958); *Nazik âlet* (1958); *Memleketin birinde* (1958); *Biraz gelir misiniz* (1958); *Gıdıgıdı* (1958); *Nutuk makinesi* (1958); *Kördöğüşü* (1959); *Aferin* (1959); *Az gittik uz gittik* (1959); *Mahmut ile Nigar* (1959); *Saçkıran* (1959); *Bir şey yap Met* (1959); *Ah biz eşekler* (1960); *Gözüne gözlük* (1960); *Hoptirinam* (1960); *Bir koltuk nasıl devrilir* (1961); *Yüz liraya bir deli* (1961); *Biz adam olmayız* (1962); *Namus gazı* (1964); *Sosyalizm geliyor savulun* (1965); *Canavar* (1965); *Rıfat bey neden kaşınıyor* (1965); *İhtilâli nasıl yaptık* (1965); *Şimdiki çocuklar harika* (1967); *Poliste* (1967); *Vatan sağolsun* (1968); *Düdükçülerle fırçacıların savaşı* (1968); *Üç karagöz oyunu* (1969); *Tut elimden Rovni* (1970); *Hadi öldürsene* (1970); *Merhaba* (1971); *Leylâ ile Mecnun* (1972); *Hayvan deyip de geçme* (1973); *Tatlı Betüş* (1974); *Bu yurdu bize verenler* (1975); *Borçlu olduklarımız* (1976); *Surname* (1976); *Seyyahatname* (1976); *Pırtlatan bal* (1976); *Duyduk duymadık demeyin* (1976); *Yaşar ne yaşar ne yaşamaz* (1977); *Dünya kazan ben kepçe* (1977); *Büyük grev* (1978); *Tek yol* (1978); *Beş kısa oyun* (1979)

BIBLIOGRAPHY: Halman, T. S., "Turkish Literature in the 1960s," *LitR*15 (1972): 387–402

—AHMET Ö. EVIN

NETHERLANDS LITERATURE

Dutch Literature

At the beginning of the 20th c. the literature of the Netherlands was still dominated by the artistic ideals and methods of the Beweging van Tachtig (Movement of the Eighties)—the literary and spiritual upheaval that in the 1880s had raised Dutch culture from the slough of mediocrity in which it had been sunk for close to two centuries. The program of this movement, although enunciated with all the polemic violence of which brash youth is capable, had been strangely indecisive, being indebted both to Zola's naturalism and to the impressionism of French painting. It was also strongly influenced by English romantic poetry. The poems of Jacques Perk (1859–1881), dead at the age of twenty-two, borrowed from Shelley, and Herman Gorter's (1864–1927) *Mei* (1889; May), one of the principal monuments of the movement, was modeled on Keats's *Endymion*. The aesthetics of the Movement of the Eighties, particularly in poetry, constituted a highly unstable compound, and it was bound to dissolve.

As the 20th c. got under way, Willem Kloos (1859–1938) proved to be the only one of the Eighties group who clung stubbornly to the radical individualism that had originally characterized the movement. Albert VERWEY came to stress more and more the opposed values of the communal—the claims of society and brotherhood as opposed to those of the individual. Frederick van EEDEN sought spiritual direction first in Thoreau, later in Roman Catholicism; and Gorter turned to communism, as did Henriette Roland Holst van den SCHALK. The individual and the community—the tension between these concepts is, to be sure, found at all times and in all places, at least in the West, but it has always had a particular thematic prominence in Dutch culture. The intransigent individualism cultivated by the Beweging van Tachtig was bound to be followed by a reaction.

In style as well as in theme, lyric poetry in the first quarter of the century developed away from the belated romanticism of Tachtig. Verwey, partly under the influence of his German friend Stefan GEORGE, moved in the direction of symbolism, as did such younger poets as J. H. LEOPOLD, Pieter Cornelis BOUTENS, and Adriaan Roland HOLST. A chastened classicism of expression also manifested itself in Leopold and Boutens (both of whom were classical scholars), and the influence of W. B. YEATS was as important for Roland Holst as that of George was for Verwey. Classicism is also a feature of the poetic work of Jacobus Cornelis Bloem (1887–1966), who was associated with Verwey and Verwey's journal *De beweging*; Bloem explored the themes of nostalgia and regret.

Poetry has historically been the dominant form in the literature of the Netherlands, in contrast to the Flemish part of Belgium, where fiction has been more eminent. There are exceptions, of course: Multatuli (pseud. of Eduard Douwes Dekker, 1820–1887), author of the novel *Max Havelaar* (1860; *Max Havelaar*, 1868), the only giant figure in Dutch literature between the 17th c. and the 1880s; or Simon VESTDIJK in our own time. Still, in the 20th c. the old pattern has been basically repeated. The poetic dramas of van Eeden proved essentially for the study alone; the only significant dramatist of the early 20th c. was Herman HEIJERMANS, whose *Op hoop van zegen* (1901; *The Good Hope*, 1928) enjoyed great popularity in the early years of the century. Heijermans was a naturalist, but, like his coeval Gerhart HAUPTMANN, he made occasional excursions into the fantastic, as, for example, in *Uitkomst* (1907; deliverance).

The greatest Dutch novelist of the early part of the century was Louis COUPERUS. Although he had many affinities with the Movement of the Eighties, he remained, as both artist and man, somewhat aloof from the group. His early novel *Eline Vere* (1889; *Eline Vere*, 1892) was markedly naturalistic; later works such as *Van oude mensen, de dingen die voorbijgaan* (1906; *Old People and the*

Things That Pass, 1918) and *De boeken der kleine zielen* (4 vols., 1901–3; *The Books of the Small Souls*, 1914) revealed more subtle gifts of psychological perception. Couperus was a notable stylist, occasionally "precious" in a fin-de-siècle manner, but clearly a master of verbal art. His oeuvre also includes a series of historical novels set in antiquity at the time of its decadence.

The curious alliance of naturalism and aestheticism that Couperus was able to effect in so masterful a way is also to be noted in *Een liefde* (1888; a love) by Lodewijk van DEYSSEL and in the fiction of Marcellus Emants (1848–1923). Van Deyssel, the ideologue and polemicist of the Movement of the Eighties, was also the dominant—and representative—critic of Dutch letters in the late 19th and early 20th cs. His judgments, which were violent, abusive, and often unjust, nevertheless did much to clear away the sentimentality and obtuseness of the 19th-c. heritage; his methods, which were impressionistic and subjective, left much to be corrected by his critical successors.

Among other prose writers, Arthur van SCHENDEL is eminently deserving of mention. In *Het fregatschip Johanna Maria* (1930; *The Johanna Maria*, 1935), *De waterman* (1933; *The Waterman*, 1963), and many other novels he proved a distinguished stylist and a painstaking craftsman, with considerable psychological profundity.

The period between the two world wars was, in Holland as elsewhere in the West, the age of triumphant high modernism. Kloos and Verwey continued as significant poets, but the dominant figures in poetry were Roland HOLST, Martinus NIJHOFF, Hendrik MARSMAN, and Gerrit ACHTERBERG. Nijhoff had connections with the artistic movement known as De Stijl. Marsman was the leader of an important school of EXPRESSIONISM; his death on a ship torpedoed by the Germans in 1940 robbed 20th-c. Dutch poetry of one of its most vital presences. Achterberg, who emerged in the 1930s, was perhaps an even greater poet; had he written in a more widely known language, he would probably enjoy an international reputation as a major figure. His achievement rests on a delicate tension among a number of opposed elements: verbal experimentation versus a traditional sense of form, thematic limitation (his virtually sole theme is communication with the dead beloved) versus imagistic variety, colloquial versus technical vocabulary. In many ways he is a modern metaphysical poet.

Other important poets of the interwar period include Jan SLAUERHOFF, Victor van Vriesland (1892–1974), Anton van Duinkerken (pseud. of Willem Anton Asselberg, 1903–1968), Jan Greshoff (1888–1971), and Anthonie Donker (psued. of Nicolaas Anthonie Donkersloot, 1902–1965). Another prolific and significant poet was Simon Vestdijk, but he, unquestionably the greatest writer of 20th-c. Holland, is better known for his work as a novelist. Vestdijk was extremely prolific, producing a huge number of novels and collections of short stories and poetry, as well as numerous essays on philosophy, music, and other subjects and in literary criticism. The variety of his novelistic production is also impressive, ranging from the autobiographical *Anton Wachter* cycle (1934–50), with its clear relation to PROUST, to a number of historical novels with diverse settings, to contemporary realistic works such as *De koperen tuin* (1950; *The Garden Where the Brass Band Played*, 1965), to metaphysical fantasies such as *De kellner en de levenden* (1949; the waiter and the living ones). The metaphysical and the psychological are perhaps the constants of his oeuvre: his first historical novel, *Het vijfde zegel* (1937; the fifth seal), aims at accuracy as a re-creation of the life and times of El Greco; later work in this genre, such as *Rumeiland* (1940; *Rum Island*, 1963) uses history as an agency for creating myth. Vestdijk's

late Victor Slingeland trilogy—*Het glinsterend pantser* (1956; the shining armor), *Open boek* (1957; open book), and *De arme Heinrich* (1958; poor Heinrich)—explores in depth the preoccupation with music that is one of the recurrent themes of his work, the work of an author who, as one critic remarked, wrote "faster than God can read."

Were his work internationally known, Vestdijk might rank with MANN, JOYCE, and KAFKA, and Proust. Within the Dutch framework he was for some time before World War II associated with the group around the periodical *Forum*, headed by the essayist Menno ter BRAAK and the novelist and essayist Edgar du PERRON. The *Forum* group, manifesting again the familiar Dutch dialectic, emphasized the claims of the social, communal, and ethical as opposed to those of the intransigently individual. Vestdijk's position was less simplified and clearcut than that of his friends. Neither ter Braak nor du Perron survived the first year of World War II: the former committed suicide on learning of the Nazi invasion of the Netherlands; the latter died of a heart attack during an air raid. Like Marsman's, their deaths constituted a severe loss for Dutch letters.

Other important novelists of the period between the wars include the poet Slauerhoff, Frans Coenen (1866–1936), Ferdinand BORDEWIJK, Top Naeff (1878–1953), and Jeanne van Schaik-Willing (b. 1895), the last of whom also wrote plays. Bordewijk's *Karakter* (1938; *Character*, 1966) is one of the most impressive novels of the period between the wars. In nonfictional prose, in addition to the *Forum* group, there was the philosopher and historian Johan Huizinga (1872–1945), a towering figure in 20th-c. Dutch culture.

Note should be taken of Anne Frank's (1929–1945) *Het achterhuis* (1947; *The Diary of a Young Girl*, 1952), which retains its considerable personal and historical, although largely extra-literary, interest as an account of a gifted and sensitive adolescent's experiences during the Nazi occupation.

Achterberg remained the most influential poet during the decades following World War II, but other poets also established themselves: the "moderate surrealist" Eduard Hoornik (1910–1970), who also wrote plays and an epic entitled *Matthaeus* (1937; Matthaeus), and the Catholic Bertus Aafjes (b. 1912). (It is worth noting that, even in contemporary Dutch poetry, a specifically Christian orientation, either Catholic or Calvinist, continues to be a significant factor.) The 1950s witnessed a poetic revolution of sorts, with the advent of the group called Vijftigers ("Writers of the Fifties"): the analogy with the Movement of the Eighties is clear. These young poets—chief among them Gerrit Kouwenaar (b. 1923), Remco Campert (b. 1929), Jan Elburg (b. 1919), LUCEBERT, and Bert Schierbeek (b. 1918)—distanced themselves from contemporary society and literary tradition alike, seeking to achieve above all immediacy, sincerity, and totality of expression. They proved hospitable to foreign influences, among them those of such American poets as William Carlos WILLIAMS and Marianne MOORE. To their number should be added the name of the somewhat older Leo Vroman (b. 1915), who now lives and works in the U.S.

Lucebert has proven perhaps the most talented of the group, Campert perhaps the wittiest. Another gifted experimental poet of similar orientation is Simon Vinkenoog (b. 1928). Mention should also be made of the short-lived Hans Lodeizen (1924–1950), whose radically associational poems clearly anticipated those of the experimental poets of the 1950s. More traditional poets include Vasalis (pseud. of Margaretha Drooglever Fortuyn-Leenmans,

b. 1909) and Ellen Warmond (pseud. of Pieternella Cornelia van Yperen, b. 1930).

The Vijftigers did not constitute a school or even, really, a movement. As one of their spokesmen, Kouwenaar, has noted, it was really more a case of a number of young literary artists moving independently in the same general direction—a direction defined by a break with traditional conceptions of form, by a strong concern with the unconscious, by a distinct antiintellectualism, and by a high degree of individualism. Their poetry has some links with DADAISM, SURREALISM, and expressionism, particularly in its distrust of bourgeois society, but it differs in its absence of program, in its radical lack of belief in anything at all.

Nevertheless, Vijftiger poetry retains from earlier generations the concept of the poem as an autonomous verbal artifact rather than an unmediated expression of the author's personality. As in other Western literatures, the 1960s and 1970s saw a progressive erosion of this sense of the autonomy and integrity of the work of art. Some of the more recent Dutch poets who epitomize this tendency are J. Bernlef (pseud. of Hendrik Jan Marsman, b. 1937; not to be confused with the older poet Hendrik Marsman), Herman Hendrik ter Balkt (b. 1938), Hans van Waarsenburg (b. 1943), Frank Koenegracht (b. 1945), and Sjoerd Kuyper (b. 1952).

Contemporary Dutch drama has not achieved real distinction. Hoornik fails to reach it, both in his earlier poetic drama and in such later, realistic work as *Het water* (1957; the water). Absurdism, as exemplified by Schierbeek's *Een groot dood dier* (1963; *A Big Dead Beast*, 1963), does not rise above the fashionable. Perhaps the best Dutch dramatist of the age is the popular Jan de Hartog (b. 1914), whose *Schipper naast God* (1942; *Skipper Next to God*, 1949) and *Het hemelbed* (1943; *The Fourposter*, 1947) achieved notable commercial success even outside the boundaries of the Netherlands.

The giant figure of the late Simon Vestdijk continues to dominate Dutch fiction, but other currents began to manifest themselves from the late 1940s on—in the work of Maria Dermoût (1888–1962), whose belated literary career began with the publication of *Nog pas gisteren* (1951; *Only Yesterday*, 1959) and who evoked life in the Indies with lyrical nostalgia, and in that of Anna BLAMAN, whose EXISTENTIALIST novels include *Eenzaam avontuur* (1948; lonely adventure) and her masterpiece, *Op leven en dood* (1954; *A Matter of Life and Death*, 1974). Blaman's frank treatment of such themes as homosexuality caused controversy at the time.

Blaman seems, however, downright decorous in the light of the themes and treatments favored by the younger novelists who made their debuts in the 1950s, chief among them Willem Frederik Hermans (1921–1995) and Gerard Cornelis van het Reve (b. 1923). They share a vision of unrelieved bleakness and negativism, and motifs of violence, betrayal, and degradation permeate their work. The dream of a better society, so strong an impulse in Dutch civilization from the 17th c. down to the writers of the *Forum* group of the 1930s, is in their novels vehemently exposed as no more than a dream. Hermans's best work is probably *De donker kamer van Damocles* (1958; *The Dark Room of Damocles*, 1962). Like his earlier novel, *De tranen der acacia's* (1949; the tears of the acacias), it is set in Holland at the time of the Nazi occupation and is preoccupied with murder, violence, and intense sexuality. Society is seen as wholly a sham. Van het Reve, who now prefers to càll himself Gerard Reve, made his debut with *De ondergang van de familie Boslowits* (1946; the fall of the Boslowits family); in this work and in *De avonden* (1947; the evenings) he expressed a

comparable negativism. Another writer much concerned with dark and tragic themes is Harry MULISCH, whose most important work to date is *Het stenen bruidsbed* (1959; *The Stone Bridal Bed*, 1962), dealing with the fire-bombing of Dresden near the end of World War II. In other works, such as *Het zwarte licht* (1956; the black light), Mulisch differs from Hermans and van het Reve in a free use of fantasy.

Impulses of rejection and rebellion, conspicuously present in the poetry of the Vijftigers, are the dominant element in the novels written by the generation born in the 1920s, the generation that came to maturity during the war and the Nazi occupation. The obsessively sexual and frequently scatological fictions of Jan Wolkers (b. 1925) carry these impulses to a kind of extreme. Even in his best works, *Een roos van vlees* (1963; *A Rose of Flesh*, 1967) and *Turks fruit* (1969; *Turkish Delight*, 1974), a self-indulgent desire to shock weakens the general effect. (The rebellion syndrome is particularly strong in Wolkers as a result of a strict Calvinist upbringing.) Self-indulgence, a flaw in Wolkers, becomes a principle of being in Jan Cremer (b. 1940), *whose Ik, Jan Cremer* (1964; *I, Jan Cremer*, 1966) was hailed by some critics as a bold document of self-revelation and censured by others as an exercise in adolescent narcissism.

The stance of revolt has to some extent hardened into a literary convention, and negativism has become almost a conditioned reflex. There were some signs of change, however, in the fiction of Heere Heeresma (b. 1932), as in that of the somewhat older Adriaan van der Veen (b. 1916) and Hella Haasse (Hélène Serafia Haasse, b. 1918). The vision of life in Heeresma's novel *Een dagje op het strand* (1962; *A Day at the Beach*, 1967) is undeniably bleak, but the work possesses an awareness of human relationships that frees it from the solipsism that marks much contemporary Dutch fiction. The same observation can be made with regard to van der Veen's work, particularly *Het wilde feest* (1952; *The Intruder*, 1958) and *Doen alsof* (1960; *Make Believe*, 1963), and to Haasse's—*De scharlaken stad* (1952; *The Scarlet City*, 1954), a historical novel, and *De ingewijden* (1957; the initiated). Margo Minco (b. 1920), who is married to the poet Bert Voeten (b. 1918), dealt movingly with the persecution of the Jews in German-occupied Holland in her short novel *Het bittere kruid* (1957; *Bitter Herbs*, 1960).

The current situation in Dutch letters is rather static. There is much activity and a high degree of cosmopolitanism, but the revolutionary drives of the 1950s and 1960s have spent their force, and no countermovement has yet asserted itself. No new Multatuli has appeared on the scene, no new Couperus or Vestdijk. Lucebert is giving more time to his painting and Wolkers to his sculpture.

As previously observed, Dutch literature presents a kind of dialectic between the claims of the individual and the claims of the community. It is, in the 20th c. as in the 17th, the natural expression of a culture in which the polarity is felt with particular force. The Dutch have old and strong traditions of respect for personal freedom and of tolerance of diverse viewpoints, but they are also used to living under circumstances of population density that enforce an awareness of the claims of community. Add to that the sense of mutual dependency aroused by the centuries-long and continuing battle with the sea. Add to that the fact that Holland has always been, preeminently, a bourgeois country, with the pressures toward conformity that the adjective implies. Add, finally, that the two main religious traditions, Calvinist and Catholic, can both be rigid, dogmatic, and authoritarian. There are good historical reasons for the Dutch to be especially aware of the conflicts between the individual and the community. The defense of the individual occasioned the rebellious outburst of van Deyssel and the other Tachtigers as well as the antisocial gestures of so many later Dutch writers. A sense of communal responsibility was as central to the thought of the *Forum* group in the 1930s as it was to Pieter Corneliszoon Hooft (1582–1647) or Hugo Grotius (Huig de Groot, 1583–1645) in the 17th c.

The greatest Dutch writers hold the claims of individual and community in delicate balance. In the play *Lucifer* (1654; *Lucifer*, 1898), the 17th-c. masterpiece of Joost van den Vondel (1587–1679), greatest of Dutch poets, the hero-villain is Lucifer—archrebel but also Prince of Darkness. His individualistic rebellion is titanic, but the evil to which it is dedicated leads the reader to question the validity of uncontrolled individualism. Multatuli's titanic satirical rage is triggered equally by communal irresponsibility and by the desecration of individual rights. In our own century the greatest novelists, Couperus and Vestdijk, have probed the relationship with profundity, sympathy, and insight. It is likely to remain the great theme of Dutch literature.

BIBLIOGRAPHY: Verschool, A. R., *Silt and Sky: Men and Movements in Modern Dutch Literature* (1950); Weevers, T., *Poetry of the Netherlands in Its European Context* (1960); Flaxman, S. L., "The Modern Novel in the Low Countries," in Peyre, H., ed., *Fiction in Several Languages* (1968): 141–61; Snapper, J. P., *Post-War Dutch Literature: A Harp Full of Nails* (1971); Krispyn, E., ed., Introduction to *Modern Stories from Holland and Flanders* (1973): ix–xii; Bulhoff, F., ed., *Nijhoff, van Ostaijen, "De Stijl": Modernism in the Netherlands and Belgium in the First Quarter of the 20th Century* (1976); special Holland issue, *RNL*, 8 (1977); Meijer, R. P., *Literature of the Low Countries*, new ed. (1978)

—FRANK J. WARNKE

Dutch Literature since 1980

It is possible to present Dutch literary history as a dialectic movement between schools that emphasize individuality and those that stress the claims made by the community. A similarly valid approach would be to refer to the history of Dutch literature as a continuously fluctuating movement between realism and romanticism in various forms. In both cases the oscillating motion can be seen as a process relating directly to a basic quality of Dutch culture, namely the awareness of the Dutch of their responsibility to the community while maintaining at the same time their individual rights. The geographic circumstances of diminutive land size and proximity to water require them to be literally and figuratively "down to earth," a quality that is reflected in Dutch literature through the ages.

Ton Anbeek describes this motion between realism and romanticism in a variety of terms, such as "a tendency from literature oriented on reality" to literature that is "like an adventure on paper." A few synonyms for the latter term he uses are "a concentration on language as material of the writer," "prose in which the relationship between novel and reality becomes more problematic," "unrealistic," "antimimetic." The few decades immediately preceding 1980 can also, on this basis, be divided into two periods representing both extreme forms, namely the 1950s on the one hand and the two following decades until 1980 on the other. Following this classification, the former period is primarily seen as

a period in which romanticism in a very modern sense of the word dominated realism and the second as a period in which several prominent authors, directly or indirectly, protested the attitude of their immediate predecessors by purposefully writing in a style that resembles traditional realism.

The writers of the 1950s, generally described as experimentalists, regarded undermining the traditional mimetic form of writing—the custom of truthfully representing "reality"—their primary aim. Several young writers such as Remco Campert, Lucebert, and Simon Vinkenoog were united in their expressed aim to "release Dutch literature of its provincialism."

During the 1960s the pendulum can be said to have swung to the opposite extreme although it seems that the time of organized schools basically ends with the movement of the 1950s. We do find realism, albeit a very depressing, "existentialist" form of it, return in full force by means of the works of famous writers such as Jan Wolkers and Willem Frederik Hermans. Their work, for its traditional style, can be regarded as the continuation of realism similar to the work of authors such as Anna BLAMAN and Gerard Cornelis van het REVE from an earlier period. Both Wolkers and Hermans have a dim view of humanity: in the words of Wolkers, "Man is a pathetic species. If there were only animals, one could believe in God. Man spoils everything"; and in Hermans's, no more optimistic, "[People] want to be put to sleep by fairy tales and the more blood is spilt in the process, the more they believe in them."

After 1960 it is no longer possible to speak in terms of Dutch literature of schools or movements. If realism and romanticism are regarded as the poles between which Dutch literature oscillates, it can be said that both forms have been present since that time and that representatives of both forms are still very active in the late 1990s. Writers in which both forms are present in equal measure are among the most successful and widely read of the present era.

One of the most important representatives of the realistic writers, though not well received by the critics, is Maarten t'Hart (b. 1944), author of such works as *Het vrome volk* (1975; The Pious People), *Een vlucht regenwulpen* (1978; A Flight of Curlews), and *Het woeden der gehele wereld* (1997; The Raging of the Whole World), and the collection of essays *Wie God verlaat heeft niets te vrezen* (1997; He Who Leaves God Has Nothing to Fear). The sarcasm relative to religion and specifically his own strict upbringing can be read even in the very titles. Hart makes no secret of the fact that, in his books, he tries to create situations that his readers recognize themselves and characters with whom they can identify. The fact that his characters often become caricatures and may appear stilted is a major point of criticism of his work but still does not disqualify them from being labeled realistic.

As popular and no less realistic but of better critical reception than Hart's work are Wolkers's novels and short stories. The fact that Wolkers is also a successful painter and sculptor is clearly visible in his detailed, descriptive style. He shares with Hart an urge to continually satirize the perceived narrowmindedness in religiously conservative people, including members of his own family and hometown Maassluis. In several of his most popular books, including *Kort Amerikaans* (1962; American Cut), *Terug naar Oegstgeest* (1965; Back to Oegstgeest), and *Turks Fruit* (1969; Turkish Delight), World War II forms the backdrop to the narrative. In his subsequent works such as *Zwarte bevrijding* (1995; Black Liberation) and *Mondriaan op Mauritius* (1997; Mondriaan on Mauritius) autobiographical facts play an ever diminishing role.

Although Willem Frederik Hermans in his earlier works introduces certain elements that cannot be perceived as realistic per se, he is, like Hart and Wolkers, basically a narrative writer. In many of his most popular books he takes World War II as the background against which he gives form to his existentialist worldview. The recipient of many prizes for literature, Hermans must be counted among the greatest writers in Dutch literary history. He believes that there is no pattern or plan in life: everything that happens, happens by accident; there is no "higher" power controlling the world, and communication between people, without exception, leads to misunderstanding and even war; the periods between wars are merely pauses between "normal" times. This is clearly demonstrated from his first major novel *Het behouden huis* (1955; The Preserved House) to *Ruisend gruis* (1995; Rustling Gravel). His most successful and most popular works are *De donkere kamer van Damocles* (1958; The Dark Room of Damocles), *Herinneringen van een engelbewaarder* (1971; Memories of a Guardian Angel), and *Onder Professoren* (1975; Among Professors).

In the substantial group of prominent modern authors whose work contains certain postmodernist, nonmimetic qualities but who should still be considered writers of realistic literature, a special place is claimed by A. F. T. Van der Heijden (b. 1951). Van der Heijden made his debut in 1979, then calling himself Canaponi, with *De draaideur* (1979; The Revolving Door). The nontraditional element already present in this book, while less prominent than in later works, is the phenomenon of multilayeredness, the quality that in French is called "une texte pluriel." The trilogy *De tandeloze tijd* (The Toothless Time) consists of *De slag om de Blauwbrug* (1938; The Battle of the Blue Bridge), *Vallende ouders* (1983; Falling Parents) and *De gevarendriehoek* (1985; The Danger Triangle). The three "layers" that are brilliantly intertwined relate simultaneously to the author's youth in his hometown, Geldrop, in the South of the Netherlands, to his life as a student in the city of Nijmegen, and, finally, to life in Amsterdam.

Van der Heijden's name is often associated with the Magazine *De Revisor* together with those of other authors whose work is frequently referred to as "ideeënromans" (novels of ideas). Van der Heijden's *De Sandwich* (1986; The Sandwich) constitutes a reflection on his own time although various other analyses are possible. The title is an indication of the structure that underlies the work: it relates to his own life as well as to society in a general sense. In an indirect way a reflection on the function, the possibilities and impossibilities of a work of art, is also incorporateded into the narrative. Each of Van der Heijden's novels can, in addition, be considered as a psychological search for the writer's own identity and sociologically as a commentary on his own time. Several aspects of Van der Heijden's work are reminiscent of Marcel PROUST's *A la recherche du temps perdu* and, less obviously, of compatriot Simon VESTDIJK's work.

Van der Heijden is certainly not the only author with a tendency towards philosophizing or in whose work the concept of time and the individual's place in it constitute crucial elements. This problem is presented in Frans Kellendonk's (1951-1990) novel *Mystiek Lichaam* (1986; Mystical Body). Other well-known works by the same author are *De halve wereld* (1989; Half the World), a collection of commentaries, and his *Het complete werk* (1992; Complete Works). Kellendonk is one of the first exponents of homosexuality in Dutch literature. After the publication of *Mystiek lichaam* Kellendonk was accused of anti-Semitism, an accusation to which he meaningfully commented that critics who read this in his novel were unable to distinguish the author and his work.

Of special interest is the fact that at the time of the so-called Kellendonk lecture, one in a series of lectures commemorating the life and work of well-known authors, one of the speakers was Gerrit Krol (b. 1934), a contemporary of Kellendonk and kindred spirit who, in *Een ongenode gast* (1964; An Uninvited Guest), deals directly with the problem of time, possibly to some extent influenced by Milan KUNDERA's *The Unbearable Lightness of Being* and ideas on the eternal repetition of phenomena. The theme of Krol's speech was the relationship between art and reality. Krol based his thesis on the philosophy, very popular in modern Dutch literature, that even the most so-called realistic story only appears realistic. Krol, who by his own testimony often based his philosophy on Zen Buddhist principles, compared literature with archery: the Zen archer first shoots, blind-folded, and then draws the bull's eye around the place of the hit; writing a novel is no different, for the reality is created by the words, not the other way around. Krol's description of the function of art can be applied to most contemporary Dutch authors: what happens in art may appear highly artificial but the "truth" in literature is found in the story itself, not in the truth of the surrounding reality. For writing the "most beautiful, clearest and most elegant Dutch thinkable," Krol received the prestigious literary Busken Huet prize in 1996.

By far the most important and, by now, internationally renowned Dutch author who also deals with the problem of time and relativity, is Harry Mulisch. Already in his *Hoogste tijd* (1985; High Time) time is a crucial factor. In its five acts, the composition of this novel is based on the construction of the classical play. The principal character is offered a role in a play, the theme of which deals with Shakespeare's *The Tempest*, a title that, meaningfully, also refers to time; in the last act of *High Time*, the actor who played the part of the protagonist comes to life and thus takes a step towards "reality" in the sense that he has moved from one "reality" to another. This belief that art creates reality instead of the other way around is already, in a subtle way, the theme in Mulisch's famous *De aanslag* (1982; The Assault) and quite explicitly also in *De ontdekking van de hemel* (1992; The Discovery of Heaven). In this novel Mulisch succeeds in making the theory that time can indeed be bridged by art quite plausible. The novel has probably come closer than any Dutch novel before it to winning the Nobel Prize for literature.

Nonrealistic or antimimetic literature after 1980 in the Netherlandic context is frequently identified with postmodernist writing. The Dutch critic Anbeek finds it most practical for the Dutch situation to subscribe to the theory that claims that postmodernism includes all writing that deviates in any way from "straightforward naive or memetic realism." Taken this broad there are many Dutch authors whose work can be categorized under the heading "Postmodernism." Other critics have defined postmodernism as a prose whose emphasis is on the artistic component more than on the realistic part and that is sociologically explained as a reaction to the desperate social and cultural situation in the world. Writers do not appear to believe any longer in the possibility of representing in "straightforward" narrative a world that is chaotic and totally out of control. It follows naturally that a devastated world will be described in fragmentized, often obscure and enigmatic, though not necessarily ineffective, writing. Many texts, both in prose and poetry, take the art of writing itself as their central theme. Well-known among these are the works of Doeschka Meijsing (b. 1947) with *De beproeving* (1990; The Ordeal), Nicolaas Matsier (b. 1949) with *Gesloten huis* (1994; Closed Home), and Oek de Jong (b. 1952) with *Cirkels in het gras*(1985; Circles in the Grass) and *Een man die in de toekomst springt* (1997; A Man Who Jumps into the Future), both full of symbolism and intertextual references. This group belongs to the authors who, in the magazine *De Revisor*, explicitly concentrated on the formal structure of the novel.

Two just slightly older authors who should not go unmentioned in this context are Willem Brakman (b. 1922), who received the very prestigious P.C. Hooft prize for his complete oeuvre and whose individualistic style can serve as a model for Dutch postmodernist writing, and Gerrit Krol, whose *Het gemillimeterde hoofd* (1967; The Millimetered Head) became a model of the earlier mentioned fragmented style of writing. The novels of Cees Nooteboom (b. 1933), particularly *In Nederland* (1986; In the Netherlands) are examples of novels in which parody and pastiche, often considered examples of postmodernist writing, are the basic ingredients. The so-called *Revisor*-authors did not hesitate to refer to internationally renowned postmodernist authors Jorge Luis BORGES, Vladimir NABOKOV, and Witold GOMBROWICZ as their sources of inspiration and models.

Possibly because of their experimental character and thus lending themselves better to comparative study, the books of authors categorized as antimirmetic always get more attention of literary critics than the more traditional or realistic ones, although the latter significantly outnumber the former. Several women writers whose books can, in general terms, be described as realistic are writers of historical novels. The most prominent among these is Hella Haasse. Although she wrote most of her books before 1980, she published some major works in the 1990s, including *Ogenblikken in Valois* (1996; Moments in Valois), a collection of autobigraphical texts and essays, and *Zwanen schieten* (1997; Hunting Swan). Her development as a writer of historical novels from the traditional, 19th-c. ones modeled after Sir Walter Scott's to her very modern ones parallels the development of literature in general over the latter half of the 20th c.: one more among several reasons why her books and essays constitute very exciting and rewarding reading.

The next most prominent writer, one who belongs entirely to the period from 1980 to the late 1990s, is Nelleke Noordervliet (b. 1945). Among the ten major novels she has published during this period, the most important is *Tineke of De dalen waar het leven woont* (1987; Tineke or the Valleys Where Life Lives), a mainly fictional diary by the wife of 18th-c. author Multatuli. Her novel *Uit het paradijs* (1997; From Paradise), in contrast to the majority of her works, is not a historical novel but a contemporary family novel written in an exceptionally clear and captivating style. Other historical novels by the same author that were very well received are *Millemorti* (1989; Millemorti) and *Het oog van de engel* (1991; The Eye of the Angel).

Comparable in more than one respect to the previous two authors is Margriet de Moor (b. 1941). Her works, mainly historical novels and short stories, were all written during the 1990s. *Eerst grijs dan wit dan blauw* (1991; First Grey Then White Then Blue) earned her the respected AKO prize for Literature. Both *De Virtuoos* (1993; The Virtuoso), located in 18th-c. Italy, and *Hertog van Egypte* (1996; Count of Egypt) give witness of Moor's well-structured style and her awareness of and sensitivity to a person's inability to really know her fellow human beings.

Moor shares her interest in the psyche of people with feminist activist Renate Dorrestein (b. 1954), past editor of the feminist periodical *Opzij*. Since 1983, when she made her debut with *Buitenstaanders* (Outsiders), she has published more than fifteen works, all of which have the role of woman in society as their subject. In *Het hemelse gerecht* (1991; Heavenly Judgment) and *Een sterke man* (1994; A Strong Man) the emphasis is on her main interest, feminism. *Heden ik* (1993; Me Today) deals with the disease ME, which she herself suffers chronically. In 1998, she wrote *Een hart van steen* (A Heart of Stone). Connie Palmen (b. 1955) has so far written only two novels but has nevertheless already earned herself a place in the row of successful Dutch female writers. Her two novels *De wetten* (1991; The Laws) and *De vriendschap* (1994; The Friendship) have certain postmodernist tendencies insofar as they deal with the dilemma related to the choice between body and soul, language and reality, and social responsibility and individuality. For *De vriendschap* (The Friendship) she was awarded the AKO prize for literature in 1995.

Tessa de Loo's (b. 1947) first book, *De meisies van de suikerfabriek* (1983; The Girls from the Sugar Factory), a collection of short stories, was an immediate success with both the critics and the general public as is apparent from the two literary prizes she received for it. With her subsequent works *Isabella* (1989; Isabella) and *De tweeling* (1993; The Twins) she has not quite been able to repeat this success.

There are three more female writers who deserve mentioning. In the first place there is Mensje van Keulen (b.1946) with her novel *De rode strik* (1994; The Red Ribbon) and her children's book *Pas op voor Bez* (1996; Watch out for Bez). Secondly there is Yvonne Keuls (b. 1931), notable for her novel *Lowietjes Smartegeld, of het gebit van mijn moeder* (1995; Lowietje's Compensation, or My Mother's Dentures). Keuls also dealt with current social problems such as drugs addiction and youth crime. The works of Helga Ruebsamen (b. 1934) concludes the list of female writers. She published the short story *De dansende kater* (1991; The Dancing Tomcat) and the novel *Het lied en de waarheid* (1997; The Song and the Truth).

The list of authors whose work may contain some elements of modernist and even postmodernist qualities but who should yet be classified as primarily realistic is headed by those who base their narratives on travel experiences. The publications of popular writer Adriaan van Dis (b. 1946) are examples of this. He made his debut with *Nathan Sid* (1983; Nathan Sid). The autobiographical element is betrayed by the spelling of the names of author and protagonist. For his novel *Indische Duinen* (1994; Indian Dunes) Dis received the Gouden Uil prize for literature. He also wrote several reports on his extensive travels in addition to some novels in which the relationship between parents and son forms the basic theme.

An author who, based on his age and the dates of publication of the majority of his novels, belongs to a previous generation, is Gerard Reve. However, in 1996 his long-awaited magnum opus *Het boek van het Violet en de Dood* (The Book of the Violet and Death) was published. Somewhat ironically it was not as radically different from his previous work as the author had made the public believe in advance, the emphasis again falling on his homosexual relationship with his lifelong partner. In the course of the last decades of the 20th c. Reve published fifteen works, many in the form of letters, his most successful style.

Two authors who can be grouped together on the basis of their themes, philosophy, and style are Grunberg (b. 1971) and Zwagerman (b. 1963). Both are preoccupied with the concept of erotic love, on which they appear to have an anything but traditional view. The love relationships in Zwagerman's books always appear doomed to failure as is the case in *De buitenvrouw* (1994; The Outside Woman) and *Chaos en rumoer* (1997; Chaos and Noise). Grunberg also does not believe that normal love relationships, including the physical part, exist. In his most successful novel, *Figuranten* (1997; Extras), three young people, one female and two male, who hardly understand one another, spend their lives halfheartedly doing nothing in particular. At the end of a dubious friendship they can point at absolutely nothing they have accomplished. This very successfully portrayed situation undoubtedly reflects an important element of postmodernist thinking, but one which, from a different angle, can also be dubbed realistic. Refreshingly traditional by comparison is Thomas Rosenboom's (b. 1956) *Gewassen vlees* (1994; Washed Meat), a very substantial historical novel. His short stories and novels give expression to a very individualistic view on the construction of works of art. Typical of Rosenboom is his sensitivity to words that, in his case, has led to language that can be described as somewhat baroque and archaic, yet very effective.

A very special group of authors whose work is classified as realistic is formed by refugees from Mediterranean countries who have permanently settled in the Netherlands. The best-known among these is Kader Abdolah (b. 1954), a political refugee from Iran who has lived in the Netherlands since 1988. In the Dutch newspaper *Trouw* he wrote, "I resist oppression in Iran by writing in Dutch. I describe the history of a nation. It is my way of fighting. In this way I try to resurrect the dead, to take back what dictatorship has taken away from me." Since 1993 he has published two collections of short stories and a novel titled *De reis van de lege flessen* (1997; The Journey of the Empty Bottles). Hafid Bouazza (b. 1970) is a refugee from Morocco who uses Dutch litereture to attack the laws of Islam. His *De voeten van Abdullah* (1996; The Feet of Abdullah) met with immediate success.

In poetry it is not feasible to differentiate movements of schools at the end of the 20th c. as was possible in, for instance, the case of the writers of the 1950s. In the 1980s and 1990s it is certainly not possible to identify a group of artists inspired by an influential leader, who, on the basis of an explicit program, were inspired by a desire to change the status quo, and whose poems reflected this program, explicitly or implicitly. The tendency in modern poetry is to express and reflect the apparent brokenness of modern society more directly than is the case with prose in which a greater variety of styles, philosophies, and forms exists. The poetic stage in the 1950s was dominated by the experimentalists, the 1960s basically constituting a reaction to the extreme forms of irreality verbalized poetically by the experimentalists.

The tendencies most noticeable in the 1970s and the poets who most distinctly gave poetic expression to them are still the most active ones in the 1980s and 1990s with very few new sounds being heard. Remnants of experimentalism as well as of the reactions to this are still the most discernable and palpable at present. Of these poets J. Bernlef, Judith Herzberg (b. 1934), Gerrit Komrij (b. 1944), Gerrit Kouwenaar (b. 1923), K. Schippers (b. 1936) are the most prominent. Bernlef, whose total output comprises about fifty publications, made his debute in 1963 and has published most of his books between 1980 and the present. In 1997 he published *Achter de rug. Gedichten. 1960-1990* (Behind Me: Poems 1960-1990), an anthology of three decades of poetry. It is noteworthy that only in 1984, with the publication of *Hersenschimmen* (Phantasms), the public at large began to appreciate him. Bernlef has also published novels; for *Publiek geheim* (1987; Public Secret) he received the AKO prize for literature. Judith Herzberg published her first book of poems in 1963, but like Bernlef she published most of her total work between 1980 and 1997. Her poems are characterized best by the adjectives "accessible" and "moving." Jewish, she lives alternately in Israel and the Netherlands. Gerrit Kouwenaar began his literary career as a member of the Fifties experimentalists. He was a cofounder of the periodical *De Revisor*, the official mouthpiece of the members of the Fifties movement. He published

De tijd staat open (1996; Time is Open) and was rewarded several prestigious prizes during his literary career, including the *Prize for Netherlandic Literature* in 1989 for his complete oeuvre. His poetry is generally considered quite cryptic and in that sense representative of postmodernist writing. Finally, a poet who remained more "faithful" to the principles of the poets of the Fifties is K. Schippers (b. 1936), whose publications include *Vluchtig eigendom* (1993; Volatile Ownership), a collection of essays *De vermiste kindertekening* (1995; The Missing Children's Drawing), and a book of previously unpublished postmodernist poems in 1980 entitled *Een leeuwerik boven een weiland* (A Lark over a Meadow).

—MARTINUS BAKKER

Frisian Literature

Frisian, the West Germanic language that is most closely related to English, has three branches: West Frisian (Netherlands), and East and North Frisian (Germany). West Frisian, in spite of past suppression, now has official rights in the Netherlands. Its literature, dating back to the 11th c., reached its first peak in the 17th c., but declined in the 18th and 19th cs., when, with some notable exceptions, it was shallow, unaesthetic, and provincial.

At the beginning of the 20th c., however, a new wind began to blow across Friesland. Its freshness and vigor was perhaps most obvious in the graceful poems and lyrical fiction of Simke Kloosterman (1876–1938). *De Hoara's fan Hastings* (1921; the Hoaras of Hastings), her best novel, poignantly depicts the relations between the rich Frisian landowners and the poor, dependent farm workers who, at the turn of the century, were beginning to assert their rights.

The new wind was also evident in the spontaneous poetry of Hendrika Akke van Dorssen (pseud.: Rixt, 1887–1978), whose collected poetry was published in *De gouden rider* (1952; the golden rider). A broader talent was discernible in the short stories and novels of Reinder Brolsma (1882–1953), who focused on the lives of little people and in his best novels painted a broad and colorful canvas of Frisian life in the early decades of the century.

The Young Frisian Movement, launched in 1915 by the determined nationalist Douwe Kalma (1896–1953), produced a national awakening and a vigorous literary renaissance. Kalma, who began his literary career as a critic who roundly denounced the mediocrity and provincialism of 19th-c. literature, was a poet, dramatist, translator, and literary historian. Owing to his efforts, Frisian literature has gained intellectual breadth. Kalma's poetic art is perhaps most impressive in *Keningen fan Fryslân* (2 vols., 1949–51; kings of Friesland), a series of epic dramas in blank verse that began with *Kening Aldgillis* (King Aldgillis), published separately in 1920. His lyric poetry, largely in the classical tradition, has grandeur and shows great technical skill but suffers somewhat from a dreamy vagueness and an overuse of both archaisms and neologisms.

Another significant figure in the Young Frisian Movement was Rintsje Piter Sybesma (1894–1975), who in *Ta de moarn* (1927, toward morning) showed himself to be a firstrate sonneteer. Douwe Hermans Kiestra (1899–1970) was a vigorous poet of the soil, and Jelle Hindriks Brouwer (1900–1981) wrote verse that is sonorous and well crafted. Obe Postma (1868–1963), although not of the Young Frisian school, won high praise from Kalma. His quiet and unpretentious poetry is rich in suggestiveness and imagery. Fedde

Schurer (1898–1968), who in his early work was influenced by the aestheticism of the Young Frisian school, became the most popular and widely read poet of his time. Much of his verse centers around national, social, and religious themes.

Around 1935 a few of the younger poets began to break away from the Young Frisian tradition both in themes and in poetic idiom. Johannes Doedes de Jong (b. 1912) wrote the innovative and refreshing volume *Lunchroom* (1936; lunchroom). Douwe Annes Tamminga (b. 1909), in *Balladen en lieten* (1942; ballads and songs) and other volumes, cast aside the lofty, ornate language of the Young Frisians in favor of the more virile language of the people, which he carefully refined into durable art.

Some talented novelists appeared during the interwar period. Ulbe van Houten (1904–1974) is known especially for *De sûnde fan Haitze Holwerda* (1939; the sin of Haitze Holwerda), a novel that probes moral conflicts. Nyckle J. Haisma (1907–1943), who like Van Houten wrote a good many short stories, is remembered for his moving novel *Peke Donia, de koloniaal* (2 vols., 1937–40; Peke Donia, the colonial), about the alienation of a Frisian returned from the Dutch East Indies.

After World War II significant innovative poets were Germant Nico Visser (b. 1910) and Sjoerd Spanninga (pseud. of Jan Dykstra, b. 1906). Visser's work reflects postwar disillusionment and pessimism; Spanninga's, on the other hand, introduced an exotic flavor into Frisian verse.

After the demise in 1968 of the important but conservative literary journal *De tsjerne* (founded in 1946 by Fedde Schurer), Frisian letters increasingly showed the impact of a twofold emancipation already underway: from traditional moral codes, especially in sexual matters; and from the influence of the national movement. Emphasis shifted from the romantic to the psychological, from the realistic to the abstract, from the conventional to the experimental, from the rural to the cosmopolitan.

Perhaps no figure contributed so greatly to these changes as Anne Sybe Wadman (b. 1919), who is not only an incisive literary critic but also an able essayist, novelist, and short-story writer, whose works often attack social evils. In the novel *De smearlappen* (1963; the scoundrels) he did much to open the way for a frank treatment of sex.

Ypk fan der Fear (pseud. of Lipkje Beuckens Post, b. 1908) in her boldly conceived fiction often features women who are physically handicapped, mentally disturbed, or mystically religious. Ype Poortinga (b. 1910) has published poetry, short stories, novels, and seven volumes of Frisian folk tales. His best work is probably *Elbrich* (2 vols., 1947–49), a historical novel set in the 16th c., centering on the quest of a nobleman for the ideal woman. Rink van der Velde (b. 1932) is a prolific and popular novelist. Several of his works of fiction are set outside Friesland, in such countries as France, Greece, Czechoslovakia, and Israel. His best novel to date is *De fûke* (1966; the trap), in which he vividly portrays the tenacious resistance of a lone Frisian fisherman to Nazi terror.

Perhaps the most talented of the younger writers is Trinus Riemersma (b. 1938), whose work displays both high intelligence and honesty. His first novel, *Fabryk* (1964; factory), which caused a considerable stir because of its sexual explicitness, deals with a factory worker who feels himself estranged, lonely, and helpless amid modern cultural and technological forces. Riemersma's works, often experimental in form, usually center around problems of religion or sex. Durk van der Ploeg (b. 1930) is a novelist preoccupied largely with human weakness and failure, with physical and mental decay, and with death itself.

In contemporary poetry, which in language and form continues to show the influence of the experimentalists of the 1950s, there is much of the same pessimism found in fiction. It is well represented by the work of Jan Wybenga (b. 1917), whose doleful subjects are deserted villages and deteriorating cities, autumn and winter, dissolution and death. The verse of Daniël Daen (pseud. of Gerben Willem Abma, b. 1942) has a philosophic bent. Much of it, although it has universal overtones, concentrates upon himself and constitutes an attack on the strictures imposed upon him as a youth in a conservative family. Much more positive and optimistic is Tiny Mulder (b. 1918), whose buoyant and playful poems are often a joyous paean to life.

Contemporary Frisian literature reflects artistic and intellectual movements from elsewhere in the world.

BIBLIOGRAPHY: Fridsma, B. J., "Frisian Literature," in J. T. Shipley, ed., *Encyclopedia of Literature* (1946): 317–24; Poortinga, Y., "Die westfriesische 'schöne' Literatur nach dem Kriege," *Friesisches Jahrbuch*, 30 (1955): 180–93; Harris, E. H., *The Literature of Friesland* (1956); Fridsma, B. J., "Frisian Poetry," in A. Preminger, et al., eds., *Encyclopedia of Poetry and Poetics* (1965): 301–2; Brouwer, J. H., "A Committed Lot: Frisian Writers," *Delta*, 8, 4 (1965–1966): 39–45

—BERNARD J. FRIDSMA, SR.

NETHERLANDS ANTILLES LITERATURE

See Dutch-Caribbean Literature

NEW NOVEL

During the years immediately following World War II French literature was dominated by Albert CAMUS, André MALRAUX, and Jean-Paul SARTRE. Camus's *La peste* (1947; *The Plague*, 1948) is an expression of faith in human solidarity; Malraux's work on the philosophy of art, *Les voix du silence* (1951; *The Voices of Silence*, 1953), extols universal brotherhood; and Sartre's *Les chemins de la liberté*; (3 vols., 1945–49; *The Roads to Freedom*, 3 vols., 1947–51) points out that freedom is meaningful only when accompanied by social commitment. For these writers, literature was a tool to make people aware of their human condition and of the problems of the contemporary world.

Concurrently, another group of writers began questioning the purpose of literature as interpreted by Camus, Malraux, and Sartre. What is really the essence of writing fiction? they asked. Is the writer above all a philosopher, social critic, visionary? Or is the writer's genuine function simply to write, to combine words into patterns on the blank piece of paper? Gradually the focus shifted from content to form, and the process of writing itself became the chief subject of exploration. The first New Novels were Samuel BECKETT's *Molloy*, (1951; *Molloy*, 1955) and Alain ROBBE-GRILLET's *Les gommes* (1953; *The Erasers*, 1964).

In addition to Beckett and Robbe-Grillet, the novelists most frequently associated with this new trend in fiction are Michel BUTOR, Marguerite DURAS, Claude MAURIAC, Claude OLLIER,

Nathalie SARRAUTE, Claude SIMON, and Philippe SOLLERS, the last also a critic and one of the founders, in 1960, of the influential journal *Tel Quel*, which in its early years was closely associated with the New Novel writers. While these are highly individualistic writers, they nevertheless have enough in common to justify categorization as New Novelists. Still, no theory applies equally well to all of them. Moreover, each writer's work has evolved considerably. For instance, there is little in common between Simon's first novel, *Le tricheur* (1945; the trickster) and his most recent one, *Les Géorgiques* (1981; the Georgics).

Nevertheless, all the New Novelists would probably agree that the true writer has no particular message or insight to convey to the world. In *Pour un nouveau roman* (1963; *For a New Novel*, 1965) Robbe-Grillet states that for him the term "New Novel" is associated with all those who are exploring new forms. The New Novelists believe that writing is a perpetual quest. The work of the novelist is equivalent to that of the laboratory scientist. Without specifically attempting to do so, each may stumble upon a key that will open a door to a better world. This, however, would always be a secondary achievement, since the central one has to be the research itself.

The New Novelists are ambivalent toward literary tradition, comprehending their role within it at the same time they desire the freedom to look at the world in a direct, unobstructed way. The New Novel is frequently referred to as the *école du regard*, since vision is customarily perceived as the most objective of the senses, permitting the writer to define as far as humanly possible what is his situation in the world. The New Novelists all share the desire to see reality without the intermediary of learned responses. Moreover, they all agree that the natural world simply *is* and that the only way we can learn to understand it better is through detailed description. A willow does not weep, but its leaves have an infinite variety of colors and shapes that the writer can observe, describe, and relate to images that compose his own mental universe. Description, then, is a key word in the New Novel; however, the distance is great indeed between the geometric surfaces of Robbe-Grillet and the metaphorical, expanding descriptions in the novels of Beckett, Butor, and Simon.

As description becomes gradually more important, characters and plot cease to dominate the novel. Above all, the hero is dethroned, and in his place we find antiheroes who frequently parody the narrator's quest. This is true, for instance, in Beckett's *Molloy*, Butor's *La modification* (1957; *A Change of Heart*, 1959), and Simon's *La route des Flandres* (1960; *The Flanders Road*, 1961).

While the New Novelists reject the traditional plot, with incidents following upon one another and building to a climax, their books nevertheless are filled with stories and anecdotes. These stories, however, are not intended to reproduce the real world, recapture the past, and mirror society. An anecdote may be repeated several times, often in contradictory fashion, leaving the reader without a firm grasp as to what is happening. Moreover, since chronology has been dispensed with, the reader is unable to fix events in time, or even decide whether a given event is supposed to have taken place or is merely a figment of the imagination of the narrator or protagonist.

The New Novel has been closely associated with theory, and several of its proponents, including Robbe-Grillet, Butor, and to a lesser extent Sarraute, have written commentary on their own fiction. One of the leading theoreticians is Jean RICARDOU, author of *Problèmes du nouveau roman* (1967; problems of the new novel), *Pour une théorie du nouveau roman* (1971; for a theory of the new novel), and *Le nouveau roman* (1973; the new novel).

While the theory is a reflection on the fiction for these writers, it is by no means an attempt to set up absolute rules. On the contrary, while fiction stimulates theory, theory will in turn inspire new experiments in fiction, in a dialectical pattern.

Although essentially a French phenomenon, the New Novel has made its appearance in other countries. In England, Rayner HEPPENSTALL, who wrote two studies of Raymond ROUSSEL—one of the forerunners of the New Novelists—used its techniques in his novels *The Woodshed* (1962) and *The Connecting Door* (1962). The English writer Christine BROOKE-ROSE, a resident of France, has employed a variation of New Novel methods in much of her fiction. In the 1960s Spanish American writers such as the Argentines Julio CORTÁZAR and Ernesto SÁBATO and the Mexican Carlos FUENTES, among others, produced what could be considered New Novels in the formal sense, but with the metaphysical overtones and linguistic and structural innovations that distinguish contemporary Latin American fiction.

The New Novel demands from its readers a high degree of participation. Without the support of a dependable narrator, a central plot, and characters with comprehensible histories, the reader frequently feels lost. All one has is a skeletal structure inviting the reader to explore but not to create an artificial coherence. Instead, the reader is asked to accept the book as it is, delve into its internal structure, and work through the intricate analogies formed in the narrator's mind. In proportion to the work he is willing to put in, his own creativity is set in motion, until in the end the distinction between writer and reader is blurred, and the reader becomes creator of his own novel.

BIBLIOGRAPHY: Janvier, L., *Une parole exigeante: Le Nouveau Roman* (1964); Robbe-Grillet, A., *For a New Novel* (1965); Astier, P., *La crise du roman français et le nouveau réalisme* (1968); Sturrock, J., *The French New Novel: Claude Simon, Michel Butor, Alain Robbe-Grillet* (1969); Mercier, V., *The New Novel from Queneau to Pinguet* (1971); Heath, S., *The Nouveau Roman: A Study in the Practice of Writing* (1972); Roudiez, L., *French Fiction Today: A New Direction* (1972)

—RANDI BIRN

NEW ZEALAND LITERATURE

Aside from 18th-c. ships' logs and travel accounts, New Zealand literature begins with the stories and poems in colonial newspapers. Predictably trite and conventional, these prepare the way for the novels, diaries, and collections of verse of the late 19th c. The accents of Tennyson and the sentiments of Kipling are prominent. Yet among the descriptions of sublime landscape and romantic Maori are works in which unexpected shifts are occurring in the structures of ideas and apprehensions of the colonial world. In the work of F. E. Maning (1811-1883), Samuel Butler (1835-1902), George Chamier (1842-1915), and Katherine MANSFIELD we find a conscious effort to adjust, or even to recast or subvert, inherited conventions in order to explore and dramatize the dislocations and discontinuities of colonial life.

Samuel Butler's *Erewhon* (1872) questions not only the ideology of the time but also the validity of reason and the scope of language, disclosing the underlying anxieties and revaluations of colonial writing. At the beginnings of New Zealand literature, then, we find writing that recognizes an inherent instability in the turns of language and the tropes of landscape as well as writing grounded in the grand narratives of religion and empire, the importation of cultural myths, the faith in reason and progress. This unsettling looks forward not only to the exile Mansfield who carried her various "unhousings" with her to Europe and produced a fiction of radical instability but also to Maurice Duggan (1922-1974), Allen CURNOW, and Janet FRAME.

Katherine Mansfield addressed the problem of how to write nonprovincial literature as a late-colonial New Zealander by reversing the migration which had traded intellectual for material capital, that is, by journeying back to Europe. There she wrote the small body of modernist-impressionist stories that permanently established her reputation. As noted by Vincent O'SULLIVAN, what distinguishes her work is the quality of discomposure everywhere, Mansfield's writing is too various in its styles and too fickle in its loyalties to be circumscribed by nationalism. She takes the modern writer's condition in literature, as in the world, as being without secure footholds, deeply implicated in the dislocation of all those who find themselves between worlds. She is a feminist and a social satirist, as well as the author of sentimental stories of a New Zealand childhood. She developed a specific variety of the modernist manner of registering consciousness in musical form and wrote stories in the style of the "horse and saddle school" fashionable in the *Sydney Bulletin*.

Frank SARGESON, who had tried unsuccessfully in Europe to write in the modernist manner, chose to return to "wild" New Zealand to make himself over as a cartographer of the post-settler experience. Mansfield had remarked that New Zealand writing would only be able to respond adequately to the place when it had become more "artificial." Sargeson opted for a way of writing that seemed authentic by virtue of its rooting in the language and customs peculiar to the life of the place. In retrospect, however, it is clear how constructed and "artificial" Sargeson's authentic New Zealandness was all along. Even the early stories with their baffled outback narrators and pared back demotic contain gothic moments, narrative excesses, hints of far more flamboyant sexual identities than those adopted by the inarticulate blokes who people the stories.

The other key figure of the modernist-nationalist period of the 1930s and 1940s was Allen Curnow. For a long time it was a matter of faith that New Zealand poetry began around 1933 with Curnow, although there were minor figures, notably Ursula Bethell (1874-1945) and R. A. K. Mason (1905-71), who prepared the way among the Victorian plangencies, colonial bluster, Georgian prettiness, and the warblings of lady poets. Not surprisingly, this is a view that has come under sharp scrutiny and attack since the mid-1980s. Most recently, Michele Leggott (b. 1956) has challenged Curnow's treatment of women poets, offering writing communities and buried female lineages in place of his phalanx of masculine poets.

Curnow can be read as a poet who set out to "invent" New Zealand and founded a literary tradition with his own generation as the originating point. But he is also the poet who senses the futility in the exercise of nation-making, the inadequacy of words to those "adventures, in search of reality" they are obliged to undertake, the distances to cover before terms like tradition can have any substantial meaning in a newly settled world. Mansfield felt she had to leave colonial Wellington in order to become a writer. A generation later Sargeson made himself into a writer after several false starts in Europe by choosing to return home where he set about fashioning an art that reflected the limitations of New Zealand experience.

Both choices show the strain involved in being a serious writer in a country with little appreciation for literature. It was not until after World War II that Janet Frame demonstrated that a novelist could be both international and a New Zealand writer at the same time.

Frame's work involves a powerful criticism of New Zealand society—its conformity and narrowness. Yet her writing is never as limited by its national focus as is Sargeson's. She concentrates on a local and immediate world only to open up universal concerns. Loneliness, bafflement in the face of the human situation, wondering about existence and meaning, the threat of nuclear war, and the closeness of madness to what is called "normality"—these are the preoccupying subjects of her early fiction. Yet the romantic-modernist reading of her work that sees her setting the artist as the gifted victim against an unredeemably puritan and bourgeois society is inadequate to the range and complexity of her later work. Increasingly, Frame's subject is the word-world. In her 1988 novel, *The Carpathians*, the inhabitants of a small town are deluged by fragments of the alphabet. Bits and pieces of language shower down on them, graphically signaling the existential and linguistic collapses that lie behind the seeming certainties of suburban life.

Curnow's writing similarly effects a transition from an early stress on the reality that is "local and special" to a highly self-conscious word play. The development of Curnow's poetry traces a line of increasing scepticism about whether the world can be represented in language at all. His career also spans the successive generations of New Zealand's postcolonial literature from the poets of the 1930s, such as Charles Brasch (1909-1973) and Denis Glover (1912-1980), who imported English modernism into New Zealand and established local adaptations through the Auckland "academic" poets—Kendrick SMITHYMAN, C. K. Stead (b. 1932), Keith Sinclair (1922-1993)—to the postmodernists of the 1990s—Wystan Curnow (b. 1939), Bill MANHIRE, Michele Leggott, Gregory O'Brien (b. 1961).

Allen Curnow's Abrahamic status in New Zealand poetry has not produced a neat genealogy of scions. Even the admiring sons eventually found it necessary to resist the father, and women poets have staged a long opposition from Eileen Duggan (1894-1972) and Robin Hyde (1906-1939) in the 1930s to Michele Leggott in the 1990s. The most dramatic refusal of sonship was that of James K. Baxter (1926-1972). Sometimes dismissed as a bardic balladeer, romantic outsider, and Catholic hippy, Baxter is a poet who uses masks to dramatize his lover's quarrel with his country and the world. If facility and easy social satire weakened the verse of his middle years, the later work achieves greatness by the taut lucidity of its compulsive brooding on death, love, and meaning and by the tense doubt behind the effort to salvage what might still be used among the icons, myths, and gods.

Keri HULME's novel, *The Bone People* (1983), reflected the cultural reorientations of the 1980s, away from Eurocentrism and settler nationalism with its masculine bias towards alternative spirituality and Maori presence. Yet in using Maori culture to represent New Zealand as a "shining land" possessed of special destiny beneath the layers of colonial false consciousness, Hulme revisits colonial themes dating back at least as far as the late 19th c. If Frame's late fiction depicts New Zealand as a realm of simulacra in which the claims of the Pakeha to authenticity constitute a further plundering of the original inhabitants, Hulme's novel, for all its eclectic borrowings, seeks to construct a "real" New Zealand to replace the one Sargeson fashioned fifty years earlier.

The Bone People was part of the "Maori Renaissance" of the 1970s and 1980s, a period of cultural and political assertiveness by

Maori people. A movement that began around 1970s with the stories of Witi Ihimaera (b. 1944) and Patricia GRACE, full of lyrical nostalgia for the old ways of Maori life, gathered sharp political focus in the 1980s, especially in Ihimaera's epic novel, *The Matriarch* (1986). By the 1990s the energies of the movement had dispersed, not in the sense that Maori cultural or political assertiveness had lessened in intensity but in the growing diversity of Maori writing. This was displayed above all in Alan DUFF's bitter evocation of urban Maori life, *Once Were Warriors* (1990).

The most durable among the generation born at the end of the 1940s who came to maturity in the late 1960s—Bill Manhire, Sam Hunt (b. 1946), and Ian WEDDE—has been Manhire. His poetry, laminated with implication but refusing self-disclosure, has received both critical acclaim and popular recognition. Through his prestigious creative writing course at Victoria University and his widely disseminated insistence on a way of writing that does not rely on florid ornamentation, self-revelation, or loud self-consciousness about the national question, Manhire has influenced a remarkable body of young writers associated with Victoria University Press.

Writers such as Elizabeth Knox (b. 1959), Jenny Bornholdt (b. 1960), Damien Wilkins (b. 1963), and Emily Perkins (b. 1970) are interested in New Zealand because it constitutes the material to hand: particular and worthy of exploration, but not special by virtue of distance or dullness. They don't expect to find anything in New Zealand that doesn't exist unspectacularly elsewhere. Cody in Perkin's short story "Not Her Real Name" reads international magazines and discovers "There's a whole bunch of American women out there writing about stuff she can relate to." For these, New Zealand's isolation is mythical not because of air travel and the availability of the *New Yorker* magazine but because, like everywhere else, New Zealand is as much an imagined as a real world. Realities that are "local and special" are invented not discovered.

BIBLIOGRAPHY: McCormick, E. H., *New Zealand Literature: A Survey* (1959); Curnow, W., ed., *Essays on New Zealand Literature* (1973); Pearson, B., *Fretful Sleepers and Other Essays* (1974); Stead, C. K., ed., *In the Glass Case: Essays on New Zealand Literature* (1981); McNaughton, H., *New Zealand Drama* (1981); Jones, L., *Barbed Wire & Mirrors: Essays on New Zealand Prose* (1987 rev. ed., 1990); Williams, M., *Leaving the Highway: Six Contemporary New Zealand Novelists* (1990); Evan, P., *Penguin History of New Zealand Literature* (1990); Sturm, T. L., ed., *The Oxford History of New Zealand Literature in English* (1987; rev. ed. 1998); Williams, M., and Leggott, M., eds., *Opening the Book: New Essays on New Zealand Writing* (1995)

—MARK WILLIAMS

NEXØ, Martin Andersen

(original family name Andersen) Danish novelist and short-story writer, b. 26 June 1869, Copenhagen; d. 1 June 1954, Dresden, East Germany

N. was one of the first Danish writers of proletarian background. He lived in poverty in Copenhagen for the first eight years of his life; his family then moved to the town of Nexø on the island of Bornholm, whose name he later (1894) adopted as his own. There he worked as a farmhand and later as a cobbler. He received some further education and briefly worked as a teacher.

N.'s early novels reflect fin-de-siècle taste, but *Dryss* (1902; waste) is also a protest against the age's introversion and decadence. During 1894–96 he traveled in Italy and Spain, and his encounter with the proletariat there renewed his solidarity with the lower classes. In his short stories of this period that solidarity is expressed in some sharply edged portrayals of extreme poverty and social injustice. In the 1930s N. recalled the formative years of his life in an admirable memoir, *Erindringer* (4 vols., 1932–39; tr. of Vols. 1–2, *Under the Open Sky*, 1938).

His first major work was *Pelle erobreren* (4 vols., 1906–10; *Pelle the Conqueror*, 4 vols., 1913–16), and an Oscar-winning movie, a film version of volume 1, gave N.'s classic work a renaissance. Pelle is a poor boy whose childhood years on Bornholm bear a resemblance to N.'s. As a young man Pelle experiences the misery of the exploited workers in Copenhagen; he becomes a trade unionist and strike leader, and eventually he leads his proletarian followers to a momentous victory. The first part of the book seems very authentic, but its utopian ending lacks verisimilitude.

Critics have maintained that N. is best when he omits his political convictions, but that view warrants revision: some of N.'s best short stories are permeated by social indignation and read as convincing arguments against capitalistic society. The truth is rather that N. is a fairly limited writer who reached excellence only when he depicted those fates or milieus that he knew from experience. It is correct—and common—to call him a first-rate social realist, but it should not be overlooked that his works also contain symbolic structures and numerous references to the lore of the rural proletariat. Pelle, for example, besides being a very real person who engages in a struggle for social equality, is also the folktale hero who conquers all obstacles and fulfills a dream of happiness.

N.'s next major work, *Ditte menneskebarn* (5 vols., 1917–21; *Ditte: Girl Alive*, 1920; *Ditte: Daughter of Man*, 1922; *Ditte: Towards the Stars*, 1922), once more records the life of a child of the rural proletariat; like Pelle, she moves to Copenhagen, where she quite literally works herself to death at an early age. The book offers a starker picture of the ghastliness of poverty than does *Pelle erobreren*, but it is a mistake to assume that N. had lost his optimistic vision of the proletariat's march toward the light. Ditte's suffering is not meaningless, but rather a sacrifice for the sake of future generations. As with *Pelle erobreren*, this novel has mythical overtones.

The remainder of N.'s fiction is uneven in quality. Some of his short stories are excellent. More ambitious is the novel *Morten hin røde* (3 vols., 1945, 1948, 1957; Morten the red), which reveals its author's growing radicalism. In 1922, after a trip to the Soviet Union, N. had joined the Communist Party. *Morten hin røde* shows how social democrats like Pelle have adopted bourgeois values. Morten, a childhood friend of Pelle's, is, on the other hand, a man who remains true to the revolutionary ideals of his class. This novel, which never was finished, lacks the vividness of the earlier works.

The older N. was primarily a political activist. His numerous articles reflect his engagement in the political and humanitarian issues of his day. His views did not make him popular in Denmark, and he spent the years after World War II in the German Democratic Republic. Although theory-oriented Marxists may find flaws in N.'s works, he remains an immensely popular author in communist countries.

FURTHER WORKS: *Skygger* (1899); *Det bødes der for* (1899); *En moder* (1900); *Muldskud* (3 vols., 1900, 1924, 1926); *Familien Frank* (1901); *Soldage* (1903; *Days in the Sun*, 1929); *Af dybets lovsang* (1908); *Barndommens kyst* (1911); *Lykken* (1913); *Bornholmer noveller* (1913); *Under himlen den blå* (1915); *Folkene på Dangården* (1915); *Dybvandsfisk* (1918); *Lotterisvensken* (1919); *De tomme pladsers passagerer* (1921); *Mod dagningen* (1923); *Digte* (1926; rev. enl. ed., 1951); *Midt i en jærntid* (2 vols., 1929; *In God's Land*, 1933); *To verdener* (1934); *Mod lyset* (1938); *Et skriftemål* (1946); *Hænderne væk!* (1953); *Taler og artikler* (3 vols., 1954–1955); *Breve fra M. A. N.* (3 vols., 1969–1972)

BIBLIOGRAPHY: Slochower, H., *Three Ways of Modern Man* (1937): 105–44; Berendsohn, W. A., *M. A. N.s Weg in die Weltliteratur* (1949) *M. A. N. als Dichter und Mensch* (1966); Koefoed, H. A., "M. A. N.: Some Viewpoints," *Scan*, 4 (1965): 27–37 "M. A. N.: A Symposium," special section, *Scan*, 8 (1969): 121–35; Le Bras-Barret, J., *M. A. N.: Écrivain du prolétariat* (1969); Ingwersen, F., and N. Ingwersen, *Quests for a Promised Land: The Works of M. A. N.* (1984); Rossel, S., *A History of Danish Literature* (1992): 311-14

—NIELS INGWERSEN

NEZVAL, Vítězslav

Czechoslovak poet (writing in Czech), b. 26 May 1900, Biskoupky; d. 6 April 1958, Prague

N.'s childhood and adolescence were spent in the Moravian village of Šemkovice, where his father was a schoolteacher. He developed an early interest in musical composition and wrote poetry seriously by the time he was sixteen. His first publication was a confessional prose piece, "Jak se mnou příroda zahovořila" (1919; how nature began talking to me), in the student journal of his secondary school in Třebíč.

He arrived in Prague in 1920 and immediately plunged into its vibrant literary life. In 1922 he joined the newly formed avant-garde group Devětsil (Nine Powers), soon becoming one of its most passionate spokesmen. Named in honor of all the nine Muses, this association of poets, artists, and critics sought a radical transformation of society by way of a revolution in the arts. When the internal debate between the young proletarian poet Jiří WOLKER and the leader of Devětsil, the brilliant art theoretician Karel Teige (1900–1951) broke into the open, N. joined in with a spirited defense of fantasy and formal experimentation. His first volume of poetry, *Most* (1922; the bridge), was a display of verbal pyrotechnics, evincing an imagination untrammeled by logic or convention. In his second collection, *Podivuhodný kouzelník* (1922; marvelous magician), he records the poet's descent from the daylight of the modern city, with its violent social struggles, into the nurturing darkness of a subjective underworld. This book, recognized by Devětsil as a fulfillment of its theories, gave an additional impetus to the nascent movement of poetism, whose main theses Teige and the poet Jaroslav SEIFERT were then in the process of formulating.

N.'s magician showed the way to a complete liberation of the human spirit, including liberation from the psychological oppression of fear and guilt. It heralded this revolution by the unleashing of the carnival mood of spontaneous playfulness. Czech poetism, like its precursors Italian and Russian FUTURISM, delighted in film, sport, the music hall, and all other manifestations of speed and technological virtuosity, which were the hallmarks of the still young and cocky 20th c. In the same year as Teige coined the name for the new movement, N. contributed to it his own manifesto, *Papoušek na motocyklu* (1924; parrot on a motorcycle). Throughout the 1920s, N. participated in all the activities of poetism, while publishing thirteen volumes of original poetry.

N.'s two poetic masterpieces belong to the end of this period. The long poem *Edison* (1928; Edison) is probably the most explosive example of free verse in the Czech language. Like *Podivuhodný kouzelník, Edison* is a work about a quest. Its protagonist is the American inventor, seen as the symbol of the external anxiety that propels mankind to seek to change and manipulate nature. The poem pits Edison's restlessness against the illusion of an ever-expanding American landscape, as if seen from a speeding train. Breaking loose from the constraints of traditional metrics and the tyranny of the habitual end rhyme, N. achieves rhythmic intensity by charging his lines with the dynamo of anaphoric repetition and the hypnotic frequency of verbal parallelism. *Básně noci* (1930; poems of the night), a collection of lyric rhapsodies united by the leitmotif of the contrast between light and darkness, rivals *Edison* in the power and originality of its imagination. Here, the magic of the speaker's intonation yields a rich harvest of startling visual effects.

In the 1930s, under the influence of his readings and translations from French poets, as well as eye-opening visits to Paris, N. discovered SURREALISM. As revolutionary as Czech poetism, surrealism had the advantage of being a truly international movement. Moreover, it had incorporated FREUD'S discoveries about dreams into its comprehensive and quasi-scientific doctrines about the layers of consciousness. In 1934 N. founded the Czech branch of surrealism with the poet Konstantín Biebl (1898–1951) and the painter Toyen (pseud. of Marie Čermínová, 1902–1980). He published his own manifesto, *Surrealismus v Č.S.R.* (1934; surrealism in the Czechoslovak Republic) and invited the French leaders of the movement, André BRETON and Paul ÉLUARD, to bring their "theses of hope" to Prague. At the 1934 Congress of Writers in Moscow, N. defended the surrealist positions as a synthesis of discipline and freedom.

The finest example of N.'s surrealist poetry is the cycle *Praha s prsty deště* (1936; Prague with Fingers of Rain, 1971), published a year after his first volume of surrealist verse, *Žena v množném čísle* (1935; woman in plural), which was inspired by and dedicated to Paul Éluard. The Prague cycle creates a polythematic image of the city whose "mysterious order" the poet-lover discovers after awakening her dormant beauty by the fiat of his magic invocation.

In 1938, after the Munich agreement, N. disbanded the Czech surrealist group, in a public show of solidarity with the Communists, whose political, if not literary, ranks he had joined as early as 1924. He now considered them as the undisputed leaders of the struggle against fascism. N. spent the war years in Nazi-occupied Prague, having declined the option of exile. While his writing was banned, he turned to painting. After the liberation of Czechoslovakia, he assumed a leading position among those writers who welcomed the Communist regime. His poetic cycle *Zpěv míru*

(1950; *Song of Peace*, 1951), which asserted the justice of the Soviet position in the Korean conflict, was acclaimed in his country and the U.S.S.R. A year earlier N. had published *Stalin* (1949; Stalin), a poetic biography that marks his literary nadir. The only poems that rise above the level of propaganda in this last period of his life are those collected in the book *Chrpy a města* (1955; cornflowers and towns). Many of them were inspired by a return to France and echo the playfulness of his prewar writing.

N. was the most prolific, versatile, and elemental poet of the 20th-c. Czech avant-garde. He has been criticized for his lack of intellectual discipline and for his refusal to give up his posture of perpetual boyhood. But even his critics admit that he is one of the supreme magicians of the Czech word, who wielded the power of the original metaphor with an intensity unmatched since Karel Hynek Mácha (1810–1836).

FURTHER WORKS: *Pantomima* (1924); *Falešný mariáš* (1925); *Wolker* (1925); *Abeceda* (1926); *Básně na pohlednice* (1926); *Diabolo* (1926); *Karneval* (1926); *Menší růžová zahrada* (1926); *Nápisy na hroby* (1927); *Akrobat* (1927); *Blíženci* (1927); *Dobrodružství noci a vějíře* (1927); *Manifesty poetismu* (1928); *Zidovský hřbitov* (1928); *Hra v kostky* (1928); *Kronika z konce tisíciletí* (1929); *Smuteční hrana za Otokara Březinu* (1929); *Silvestrovská noc* (1930); *Chtěla okrást Lorda Blamingtona* (1930); *Jan ve smutku* (1930); *Posedlost* (1930); *Slepec a labut'* (1930); *Snídaně v trávě* (1930); *Strach* (1930); *Dolce far niente* (1931); *Schovávaná na schodech* (1931); *Signál času* (1931); *Tyranie nebo láska* (1931); *Milenci v kiosku* (1932); *Pan Marat* (1932); *Pět prstů* (1932); *Skleněný havelok* (1932); *Jak vejce vejci* (1933); *Zpáteční lístek* (1932); *Monaco* (1934); *Sbohem a šáteček* (1933); *Neviditelná Moskva* (1935); *Věštírna delfská* (1935); *Anička skřítek a slaměný Hubert* (1936); *Frivolní báseň pro slečnu Marion* (1936); *Řetěz štěstí* (1936); *Ulice Gît-le-Cœur* (1936); *52 hořkých balad věčného studenta Roberta Davida* (1936); *Absolutní hrobař* (1937); *Josef Čapek* (1937); *Moderní básnické směry* (1937); *V říši loutek* (1937); *100 sonetů zachránkyni věčného studenta Roberta Davida* (1937); *Matka naděje* (1938); *Pražský chodec* (1938); *70 básní z podsvětí na rozloučenou se stínem věčného studenta Roberta Davida* (1938); *Historický obraz* (1939); *Manon Lescaut* (1940); *Óda na smrt Karla Hynka Máchy* (1940); *Pět minut za městem* (1940); *Loretka* (1941); *Balady Manoně* (1945); *Historický obraz: Část I—III* (1945); *Rudé armádě!* (1945); *Svábi* (1945); *Valerie a týden divů* (1945); *Veselohra s dvojníkem* (1946); *Veliký orloj* (1949); *Dílo* (38 vols., 1950–1970); *Z domoviny* (1951); *Křídla* (1952); *Věci, květiny, zvířátka a lidé pro děti* (1953); *Dnes ještě zapadá slunce nad Atlantidou* (1956); *O některých problémech současné poesie* (1956); *Sloky o Praze* (1956); *Čtvero pozdravení* (1957); *Nebylo marné žít a umírat* (1957); *Veselá Praha* (1957); *Zlatý věk* (1957); *Moderní poesie* (1958); *Šípková růže* (1958); *Z mého života* (1959); *Jiřímu Wolkrovi* (1959); *Nedokončena* (1960)

BIBLIOGRAPHY: French, A., *The Poets of Prague* (1969): 29–119; Martin, G., Introduction to *Three Czech Poets: V. N., Antonín Bartušek, Josef Hanzlík* (1971): 11–14; Novák, A., *Czech Literature* (1976): 319–31; Banerjee, M. N., "N.'s *Prague with Fingers of Rain*: A Surrealistic Image," *SEEJ*, 23 (1979): 505–14; Hansen-Löve, C., "Die Wurzeln des tschechischen Surrealismus: V. N.," *WSIA*, 4 (1979): 313–77; French, A., "Wolker and N.," in Rechcigl, M., ed., *Czechoslovakia Past and Present* (1968), Vol. 2: 983–992

—MARIA NĚMCOVÁ BANERJEE

NGUGI WA THIONG'o

(formerly James Ngugi) Kenyan novelist, dramatist, and essayist (writing in English and Gikuyu), b. 5 Jan. 1938, Limuru

After receiving a B.A. in English at Makerere University College (Uganda) in 1964, N. worked briefly as a journalist in Nairobi before leaving for England to pursue graduate studies at the University of Leeds. Upon returning to Kenya in 1967, he taught at the University of Nairobi, eventually becoming head of the literature department, a position he held until 1978, when he was put in detention for nearly a year by the Kenyan government. After being released, he was not reinstated in his university post, and in 1982 he elected to live in exile in Britain and the U.S. In recent years he has taught at Yale, Smith, Amherst, and New York University.

N. is known best for his novels, which have focused on colonial and postcolonial problems in Kenya. *Weep Not, Child* (1964), the first novel in English to be published by an East African, tells the story of a young man who loses his opportunity for further education when his family is torn apart by the violence of the Mau Mau rebellion. *The River Between* (1965), written during N.'s undergraduate years, deals with an unhappy love affair in a rural community divided between Christian converts and non-Christians; the hero is a young schoolteacher who is trying to unite his people through Western education. Both books end tragically, emphasizing the difficulty of reconciling the old with the new in a society undergoing the trauma of cultural and political transition.

N.'s later novels, written after Kenya attained independence, concentrate on the legacy of colonialism in a new nation-state. In *A Grain of Wheat* (1967) the people who sacrificed most during the liberation struggle discover that their future has been blighted by their past and that the fruits of independence are being consumed by predatory political leaders. *Petals of Blood* (1977) carries this theme further by indicting wealthy landowners as well as politicians who capitalize on the miseries of others, thereby perpetuating economic inequality and social injustice. N. always sides with the poor, weak, and oppressed, exposing the cruelties they suffer in an exploitative neocolonial world. *Caitaani mūtharaba-Inī* (1980; *Devil on the Cross*, 1982), an allegorical novel written in Gikuyu, is an effort to make peasants and workers aware of the powerful political forces that shape their lives. His allegory entitled *Matigari*—published in Gikuyu in 1986 and in English in 1987—tells of a rebel's singleminded quest for truth and justice in a misruled society rife with greed and corruption.

N.'s plays display the same gradual shift from colonial cultural concerns to contemporary social preoccupations. The early plays deal mainly with conflicts between parent and child and between the old and the new, but N. later teamed up with Micere Githae-Mugo (b. 1942) to write *The Trial of Dedan Kimathi* (1977), a dramatization of an episode in the career of Kenya's most prominent Mau Mau leader, and in 1977 he coauthored with Ngugi wa Mirii (b. 1951) *Ngaahika ndeenda* (1980; *I Will Marry When I Want*, 1982), a play in Gikuyu that depicts social, economic, and religious exploitation in the Gikuyu highlands. It was the staging of the latter play in Limuru, his hometown, that led to N.'s incarceration for nearly twelve months. Although no formal charges were ever filed against him, he apparently had offended members of the ruling elite in Kenya.

N.'s essays express very clearly and concisely the ideas that have animated his fiction and drama. *Homecoming: Essays on*

African and Caribbean Literature, Culture and Politics (1972) places emphasis on coming to terms with the past and resisting colonial domination. *Writers in Politics* (1981; rev. ed., 1992) speaks of the postcolonial struggle for a patriotic national culture and outlines the writer's role in combating political repression. *Detained: A Writer's Prison Diary* (1981) provides a detailed account of his own involvement in efforts to increase the political awareness of his people. *Barrel of a Pen: Resistance to Repression in Neo-Colonial Kenya* (1983) speaks of the continuing conflict between artists and rulers in a society not yet free of the cultural and economic bonds of colonialism.

In recent years N. has been increasingly concerned with issues relating to language and culture. His prison experience had convinced him of the need to continue writing in his mother tongue rather than in English, a colonial language many Kenyans had not mastered. His book *Decolonising the Mind: The Politics of Language in African Literature* (1986) argued that African writers should express themselves in indigenous languages in order to reach the African masses. *Moving the Centre: The Struggle for Cultural Freedoms* (1993) took the argument a step further, recommending that African and other Third World nations ought to resist Western domination by creating their own distinct spheres of culture. And *Penpoints, Gunpoints and Dreams: The Performance of Literature and Power in Post-Colonial Africa* (1998) explored once again the vexed relationship between art and political power in contemporary Africa, where writers are often seen as enemies of the state.

N. remains East Africa's most articulate social commentator, someone whose works accurately reflect the tone and temper of his time and place.

FURTHER WORKS: *The Black Hermit* (1968); *This Time Tomorrow* (c. 1970); *Secret Lives* (1976)

BIBLIOGRAPHY: Roscoe, A., *Uhuru's Fire: African Literature East to South* (1977): 170–90; Githae-Mugo, M., *Visions of Africa: The Fiction of Chinua Achebe, Margaret Laurence, Elspeth Huxley and N.* (1978), passim; Moore, G., *Twelve African Writers* (1980): 262–88; Robson, C. B., *N.* (1980); Killam, G. D., *An Introduction to the Writings of N.* (1980); Gurr, A., *Writers in Exile: The Creative Use of Home in Modern Literature* (1981): 92–121; Killam, G. D., ed., *Critical Perspectives on N.* (1984); Bafdolph, J., *N.: L'homme et l'oeuvre* (1991); Nwandwo, C., *The Words of N: Towards the Kingdom of Woman and Man* (1992); Indrasena Reddy, K., *The Novels of Achebe and N.: A Study in the Dialectics of Commitment* (1994)

—BERNTH LINDFORS

NGUYỄN Công Hoan

Vietnamese novelist and short-story writer, b. 6 March 1903, Bắc-ninh; d. 6 June 1977, Hanoi

Scenes N. witnessed in French Indochina—first as a boy aware of the plight of peasants pitilessly exploited by village bullies and greedy, corrupt mandarins; later as a teacher assigned to different areas of the country—he incorporated into some twenty novels and over three hundred short stories. N., who began writing in the

1920s, became one of the most accomplished representatives of social realism in modern Vietnamese literature.

N.'s finest works, which offer insight into Vietnam's outmoded customs and the life of the peasantry and the urban middle class, appeared before the 1945 revolution. His most important novel, *Bước đường cùng* (1938; *Impasse*, 1963), portrays the miserable existence of a poor, debt-ridden peasant whose life is constantly threatened by natural disasters. The protagonist dares to rise up against his enemies: the landlords, the usurers, the petty local officials. This book was banned by the colonial administration.

N. is at his best when, using clear and witty language, he lashes out against injustices and corruption condoned by the French administration and against injustice and oppression in his feudal and colonial society. He treats bribery, for example, in about ten stories.

In N.'s novels plot is secondary to theme and style. For example, family conflicts, occasioned by the influence of Confucian ethics, are analyzed through skillfully constructed dialogue, as in *Cô giáo Minh* (1936; teacher Minh). Whether he portrays an audience unwittingly forcing an actor to prolong his jokes at the very time when his father is about to die, or a rickshaw boy getting stuck on New Year's Eve with a penniless prostitute as his passenger, or a mother leaving her child home to go out with her lover, N. exposes the meanness, wickedness, and deceit of people around him.

After 1954, when the French were defeated and a Communist government was established in North Vietnam, N.'s central themes became nationalism and socialist construction. In 1957 he was elected president of the Vietnam Writers' Association in Hanoi.

FURTHER WORKS: *Kiếp hồng nhan* (1923); *Những cảnh khốn nan* (1932); *Ông chủ* (1934); *Bà chủ* (1935); *Kép Tư Bền* (1935); *Tấm lòng vàng* (1937); *Tơ Vương* (1938); *Lá ngọc cành vàng* (1938); *Tay trắng, trắng tay* (1940); *Chiếc nhẫn vàng* (1940); *Nợ nần* (1940); *Lệ Dung* (1944); *Đồng-chí Tư* (1946); *Xổng cũi* (1947); *Tranh tối tranh sáng* (1956); *Hỗn canh hỗn cư* (1961); *Đống rác cũ* (1963)

BIBLIOGRAPHY: Durand, M. M. and Nguyễn-Trần Huân, *Introduction à la littérature vietnamienne* (1969): 197; Hoàng Ngọc-Thành, *The Social and Political Development of Vietnam as Seen through the Modern Novel* (1969): 222–30; Bùi Xuân-Bảo, *Le roman vietnamien contemporain* (1972): 218–28; Trương Đình Hùng, "N. C. H. (1903–1977): A Realist Writer," *Viet Nam Courier* (Oct. 1977): 26–29

—DINH-HOA NGUYEN

NGUYỄN TUÂN

(pseud. Nhất Lang) Vietnamese essayist, short-story and novella writer, literary critic, and translator, b. 10 July 1910, Hanoi; d. 28 July 1990, Hanoi

N. T. started writing in 1938 for several Hanoi newspapers and magazines such as *Tiểu-thuyết thư bảy, Tao-đàn, Hà-nội Tân-văn*, and *Trung-Bắc Chủ-nhật*. His most successful work was *Vang bóng một thời* (1940; echoes of a past era), in which like the artist of an ancient painting N. T. recreated the picture of traditional life in Vietnam, a well designed picture presented in eleven vignettes, each with its own features and colors. Through "Những chiếc ấm đã" (terra-cotta kettles), "Chén trà trong sương sớm" (a cup of tea in early dew), "Một cảnh thu muộn" (late autumn), and other stories in this volume, the reader perceives the leisurely peaceful Vietenamese way of life, the simple and confident life-style of a Confucianist and Taoist society, represented by the laureates of literary examinations who indulged in orchid collecting, chrysanthemum planting, and alcohol drinking. The first essay, for example, is about two tea addicts, one of whom is an old beggar, like his companion drinker a real connoisseur of the art of tea brewing. *Tuỳ bút* (1941; essays) can be considered as "echoes of the present era": N. T. laid bare his cynicism, whether he wrote about the air-raid siren, about life in Thanh-hoá, about his native town, about a wife expecting to give birth to twins, or about a Buddhist monk not quite detached from earthly life.

In the serialized novel *Thiếu quê-hương* (1943; lacking a native land) a restless young man feels the urge to travel constantly, just like N. T. himself. Indeed he confesses his own hereditary peripateticism in his travelogue *Một chuyến đi* (1941, a journey); in this essay N. T. shows that he simply wishes to move on and on without interruption, but the stop in Hongkong, where he took part in moviemaking, was described in humorous details—when a friend had to go to pass water in a famous hotel but showed more concern for the tip expected by the attendant, or when the Chinese music in the adjoining room made him down three cups of strong alcohol. *Nhà bác Nguyễn* (1940; Nguyen's house), as a short novel, presents charming sketches of typically Vietnamese life in a suburb, on a train, in the streets, and the like. But N.T. most excels in relating his trips to geisha houses and to opium dens: In *Chiếc lư đồng mắt cua* (1941; the copper incense burner) he depicts Thông Phu, a proud chess champion who runs a geisha house and whose heart attack, which he suffered when he lost a game, left him paralyzed and bedridden, and Bao, a Hanoi rake who took a geisha as his concubine. *Ngọn đèn dầu lạc* (1941; the peanut-oil lamp) is a two-part reportage on opium smokers, filthy and cynical characters pushed into inveterate lying, selfish behavior, and extortions just to satisfy their toxic habit.

N. T.'s remarkable talent was even more clearly shown after he had joined the ranks of resistance fighters in the anti-French war (1946–1954). After 1945 he abandoned his hedonistic and arrogant individualism as well as certain negative, doubtful literary tendencies. Both in *Đường vui* (1949; fun road) and in *Tình chiến-dịch* (1950; campaign sentiment) he related his experience in traveling with the troops, an opportunity for him to express his hatred for the enemy and his love for his people.

Between the late 1950s and the 1960s, his writings kept praising the beauty of his motherland—as he had already started doing in *Sông Đà* (1960; Da River)—and singing the unity of north and south in the anti-U.S. struggle: His essays assumed a clearly anti-American thrust. After being half jocular, half blase—a mixture of cynicism and melancholic frustration—to help readers relive the past glory of a tranquil and complacent intellectual Vietnam of yore, N. T.'s style after 1945 had turned more positive in describing the exciting days of the anti-U.S. war "for national salvation" or the guerilla fighters in South Vietnam. N. T. was undeniably a master in the use of his native tongue, whose cadence and rhythm amidst lyric expansiveness he knew how to fully exploit. He qualifies as the greatest essayist in Vietnamese literature.

FURTHER WORKS: *Tóc chị Hoài* (1943); *Nguyễn* (1945); *Chúa Đàn* (1946); *Thắng càn* (1953); *Bút-ký đi thăm Trung-Hoa* (1955); *Tuỳ-bút kháng-chiến và hoà-bình* (2 vols.; 1955, 1956); *Hà-nội ta đánh Mỹ giỏi* (1972); *Ký* (1976); *Tuyển-tập Nguyễn Tuân* (1981–82)

BIBLIOGRAPHY: Xuân-Bảo Bùi, *Le roman vietnamien contemporain* (1972), 269: 345–357; Nguyễn-Trần Huan, "The Literature of Vietnam, 1954–1973," in Tham Seong Chee, ed., *Essays on Literature and Society in Southeast Asia* (1981): 333–34; Huỳnh Sanh Thông, "Main Trends of Vietnamese Literature between the Two World Wars," *The Vietnam Forum*, 3 (Winter-Spring 1984): 99–125; Durand, M. M., and Nguyễn-Trần Huân, An *Introduction to Vietnamese Literature* (1985), passim

—DINH-HOA NGUYEN

NHẤT-LINH

(pseud. of Nguyễn Tường-Tam) Vietnamese novelist and short-story writer, b. 25 July 1906, Hai-duong; d. 7 July 1963, Saigon

N.-L. was one of the founders, in 1933, of the "Self-Reliant" group, which rejected traditional Vietnamese literature. He was also a social reformer and a political leader. He served as foreign minister in the Vietminh-dominated government of the Democratic Republic of Vietnam, took part in the negotiations with the French, and at the time of partition chose to live in South Vietnam. He committed suicide while a political prisoner of the Ngo Dinh Diem regime.

N.-L. began writing early: the short stories "Nho phong" (1926; the scholars' tradition) and "Người quay tơ" (1927; the spinner) appeared before his three-year stay in Paris (1927-30) as a student. These romantic and traditional stories contrast with his later works, which are realistic, patriotic, and revolutionary.

N.-L.'s most famous novel, *Đoạn tuyệt* (1934; break-off), is a sophisticated and resolute work championing individual freedom and the pursuit of happiness. The heroine, Loan, is ill-treated by a superstitious, cruel, and greedy mother-in-law; Loan, who kills her husband by accident, is acquitted because she is seen as a victim of the conflict between traditions and the new concept of women's rights. The title of the book pinpoints the movement away from the oppressive paternalistic kinship system.

The novels N.-L. wrote between 1935 and 1942 all depict the weaknesses of Vietnamese family and social structures. His characters, struggling for changes in their own lives and in society, rebel against age-old traditions. *Lạnh lùng* (1937; loneliness) tells the story of a young widow in love with her son's tutor. The happiness she feels in the tutor's arms cannot last, since she is afraid of social ostracism. In *Đôi bạn* (1938; two friends), a sequel to *Đoạn tuyệt*, N.-L.'s revolutionary ideals are evident. Patriotic zeal and anticolonialism are equated with dreams of individual freedom and a youthful thirst for heroic action.

In collaboration with Khái-Hưng (pseud. of Trần Khánh-Giư, 1896–1947), N.-L. wrote two excellent novels: *Gánh hàng hoa* (1934; the florist's load), about the innocent love of a young florist, and *Đời mưa gió* (1936; a stormy life), which depicts the life of a girl who, emancipated from the shackles of traditional clan life, has to become a prostitute to earn her rights as an individual.

N.-L.'s style is alternately poetic and precise. In a work like *Lạnh lùng* it is a model of clarity, precision, and balance.

FURTHER WORKS: *Anh phải sống* (1933, with Khái-Hưng); *Tối tăm* (1936); *Hai buổi chiều vàng* (1937); *Bướm trắng* (1941); *Nắng thu* (1948); *Xóm Cầu mới* (1958); *Dòng sông Thanh-thuỷ* (1961); *Mối tình "Chân"* (1961); *Thương chồng* (1961); *Viết vàđọc tiểu-thuyết* (1961)

BIBLIOGRAPHY: O'Harrow, S., "Some Background Notes on N.-L. (Nguyễn Tương Tam, 1906–1963)," *France-Asie*, 22 (1968): 205–20; Durand, M. M. and Nguyễn-Trần Huân, *Introduction à la littérature vietnamienne* (1969), passim; Hoàng Ngọc-Thành, *The Social and Political Development of Vietnam as Seen through the Modern Novel* (1969): 182–204; Bùi Xuân-Bào, *Le roman vietnamien contemporain* (1972): 164–83: 364–72

—DINH-HOA NGUYEN

NICARAGUAN LITERATURE

See Central American Literature

NICHOLS, Grace

Guyanese poet (writing in English and Creole), b. 1950, Guyana

N. was reared in Guyana and went to Britain to live in 1977. Her volume *I Is a Long-Memoried Woman* (1983) won the Commonwealth Poetry Prize in 1983 and was made shortly thereafter into a video dramatization.

In her poetry N. explores the African heritage in the Caribbean, the plight of women, and Caribbean characters in exile. She explodes myths and stereotypes in her writing as is most evident in her volume *The Fat Black Woman's Poems* (1984) in which societal standards of beauty are explored and critiqued.

As a poet concerned with language N. says she loves the battle with language that is part and parcel of her craft. She writes in both standard English and Creole, but admits to participating in the movement to reclaim and explore the language heritage of the Caribbean. She finds Creole a vibrant language with expressions that have no equivalent in standard English. In the late 1980s and 1990s N. confirmed her reputation as a major contemporary Caribbean poet with collections as *Leslyn in London* (1984), *Whole of a Morning Sky* (1986), *Lazy Thoughts of a Lazy Woman and Other Poems* (1989), and *Sunrise* (1996).

FURTHER WORKS: *Trust You Wriggly* (1981); *Baby Fish and Other Stories from Village to Rainforest* (1983); *Come into My Tropical Garden: Poems for Children* (1988)

BIBLIOGRAPHY: Burnett, P., *The Penguin Book of Caribbean Verse in English* (1986): 348-49, 428; Cudjoe, S. R., ed., *Caribbean Women Writers: Essays from the First International Conference* (1990): 283-89

—ADELE S. NEWSON

NÍ DHOMHNAILL, Nuala

Irish poet, b. 16 Feb. 1952, Lancashire, England

Born in England, N. was reared in the Irish-speaking areas of County Kerry and County Tipperary. She studied Irish and English at University College, Cork and was part of a lively group of poets centered around the literary magazine *Innti*, edited by Michael Davitt (b. 1950), which became the launching pad for the careers of a generation of poets writing in the Irish language. Her first two collections, *An Dealg Droighin* (1981) and *Féar Suaithinseach* (1984), both won the Seán Ó Riordáin Award and the Irish Arts Council Prize for Poetry; however, it wasn't until her work was first published in English—translated by N. and Michael Hartnett (b. 1941)—that she began to widen her audience in both Ireland and internationally. *Selected Poems: Rogha Dánta* (1986) is a watershed in modern Irish poetry, and has been followed by other equally brilliant collections, notably *Pharoah's Daughter* (1990), with translations by many of Ireland's most important contemporary poets, and *The Astrakhan Cloak* (1992), translated by Paul MULDOON. N.'s achievement has led to renewed interest in poetry written in Irish, has revolutionized how poetry in Irish is written, and has widened the thematic possibilities available to Irish poets, writing in both Irish and English. Along with Eavan Boland (b. 1944), N. represents the vanguard of a brilliant generation of women who have transformed contemporary Irish poetry.

The Irish language itself is central to N.'s aesthetic. She is aware that writing in Irish involves taking a calculated risk as it renders the search for an audience more difficult, given that few people outside of Ireland can read the language. However, it is a risk that must be taken as Irish provides the route to her imagination, as is made clear in "The Language Issue," her major poem of her literary purpose: "I place my hope on the water / in this little boat / of the language, the way a body might put / an infant / in a basket of intertwined / iris leaves." By writing in Irish N. seeks to recover the voice of the Irish woman, one which was stolen by centuries of colonization, both by a male-dominated Catholic Church and by the British. She is inspired by the ancient Gaelic society, which survived into the 17th c., in which women enjoyed greater legal rights and independence than they have enjoyed at any point since. N. locates in Irish mythology powerful women, often goddesses and queens, who are full of power, fertility, and knowledge, but whose role in the Irish psyche was undermined and destroyed by patriarchal systems, Roman and English, introduced from outside. In her poems ancient goddesses become human, modern, and very relevant.

In Irish literary and nationalist discourse Ireland has frequently been symbolized by the figure of the woman. This abstract figure has usually been shown as either sorrowful, as a result of the loss of land, children, or nation, or as a distant, angelic, virginal figure. In N.'s work Irish women are taken from the realm of the abstract and are made human again—full of desires, failures, and hopes. Furthermore, she proves herself to be the great love poet of her generation in a verse in which she manages to bring together so dexterously the allusive and the direct: "When you rise in the morning / and pour into me / an unearthly music / rings in my years." In addition, N. is, like many Irish poets, a great poet of place. She is not concerned so much with exploring Dublin, where she now lives, as she is with rendering into language the landscape of the West Kerry where she was reared, and in particular those points where the ocean meets the land. In a short period of time N. has made an enormous impact on Irish poetry.

BIBLIOGRAPHY: Haberstroh, P., *Women Creating Women: Contemporary Irish Women Poets* (1996); Consalvo, D. M. "The Lingual Ideal in the Poetry of N. N.," *Eire-Ireland*, 30, 2 (Summer 1995): 148-61; Kiberd, D., *Inventing Ireland* (1995): 568-625; Murphy, M., "The Elegiac Tradition," in Brophy, J., and E. Grennan, eds., *New Irish Writing* (1989): 141-51

—EAMONN WALL

NIGERIAN LITERATURE

In addition to oral art, which has been produced in the course of the centuries in the more than two hundred languages and dialects spoken by a population of nearly eighty million, Nigeria has been a prolific producer of written poetry, which began in the Muslim north, in the Arabic language, in the 15th c. The late 18th c. saw the emergence of *ajami* type literature—that is, literature written in Arabic script used for the transliteration of such non-Arabic languages as Fula and Hausa.

In Hausa

Hausa, which is the main language of northern Nigeria, became all the more important as Western missionaries adapted the Roman alphabet to it for printing. In the 1930s the Literature Bureau at Zaria encouraged young literati to create prose fiction in Hausa: one of these early writers, who signed himself Abubakar Bauchi, was to become the first prime minister of independent Nigeria as Sir Abubakar Tafawa Balewa (1912–1966). Nevertheless, poetry has remained the most widely practiced and respected genre, with such talented authors as Sa'adu Zungur (1915–1958), Mudi Sipikim (b. 1930), and Mu'azu Hadejia (1920–1955). Formal drama, which had been initiated in the 1930s by Abubakar Imam (b. 1911), does not seem to be very popular, although it is practiced by a few members of the younger generation, such as Shu'aibu Makarfi (dates n.a.) and Umaru A. Dembo (b. 1945). Significantly, the Hausa have produced hardly any imaginative writing in English.

In Yoruba

Literacy was brought to the Yoruba of western Nigeria in the mid–19th c. by one of their own, Samuel Crowther (1809–1891), a freed slave who had been educated in Sierra Leone; he put the language in writing in order to translate the Bible. Although Yoruba was used for writing purposes from the late 19th c. on, especially in local newspapers, it did not reach its literary maturity until Daniel O. Fagunwa (1910–1963) had his first, highly original works of prose fiction printed in the 1950s; often described as "romances," these are traditional oral tales woven onto a central narrative thread, and slightly modernized to bring them in harmony with the moral tenets of Christianity. One of them was translated into English by Wole SOYINKA as *The Forest of a Thousand*

Daemons (1968). Novels closer to Western models were produced almost simultaneously by Chief Isaac O. Delano (b. 1904). Two distinct trends were thus initiated: one, originating in the rich store of local lore, was pursued by Gabriel E. Ojo (1925–1962), Olaya Fagbamigbe (b. 1930), Ogunsina Ogundele (b. 1925), and D. J. Fantanmi (b. 1938). The other, which seeks to reflect the problems of contemporary life, has on the whole been less successful: its main representatives is Femi Jeboda (b. 1933). But while most of those writers were trained as schoolteachers, after independence Yoruba literature was enriched by the emergence of a number of university-educated authors who gave it greater complexity: Adeboye Babalola (b. 1926), a playwright and a well-known student of oral art, Adebayo Faleti (b. 1935), a versatile writer who has been active in narrative poetry and prose as well as in drama, and Afolabi Olabimtan (b. 1932). Yet another strikingly original Nigerian contribution to African literature is the dramatic genre known as the "Yoruba opera" because of the strong admixture of music and dance. Rooted in the biblical plays that were performed in mission schools in the 1930s, it made its real beginning in the early 1940s when Hubert Ogunde (b. 1916) founded his concert Company; he produced a satirical play with definitely political overtones that became well known throughout West Africa, and his example was soon followed by E. Kola Ogunmola (1925–1973) and his traveling theater, whose outlook was conspicuously Christian and moralizing. The most widely known representative was Duro Ladipo (1931–1978), who was chiefly inspired by Yoruba myths and historical legends: his company was famed even in Europe, and several of his works were translated into English (*Three Yoruba Plays*, 1964).

In English

While the Yoruba had started creating a written art in their own language by the middle of the century, they, unlike the Hausa, also contributed significantly to the emergence and growth of Nigerian literature in English. Until the late 1950s, this had been represented only by the mediocre versifying of Denis Osadebay (b. 1911). The first Nigerian writer to reach international fame was Amos TUTUOLA, whose first piece of prose fiction, *The Palm-Wine Drinkard and his Dead Palm-Wine Tapster in the Dead's Town* (1952) was enormously successful throughout Western countries, not only because of the author's highly idiosyncratic style but also because of the striking originality of the tale itself, which was derived, in fact, from the oral tradition and from Daniel O. Fagunwa's own recordings of it. Timothy M. Aluko (b. 1918) with *One Man, One Wife* (1959) inaugurated a series of satirical novels of a more conventional type, which constitute an imaginative chronicle of the evolution of Nigerian society and mores. And on the occasion of independence in 1960, Wole Soyinka produced *A Dance of the Forests*, a powerful drama in which elements drawn from the Yoruba tradition are combined to convey a message of national unity.

Besides Yoruba folklore and satirical wit, modern Nigerian literature is also rooted in a different, urban form of popular art: the so-called "Onitsha chapbooks" of the Igbo people. Written in substandard but often picturesque English, printed mostly in the Igbo market town of Onitsha, these became exceedingly popular among the Igbo lower middle class during the 1950s. It was as a purveyor of such subliterary pamphlets that Cyprian EKWENSI made his beginnings with a mawkish novelette, *When Love Whispers* (1948); but his *People of the City* (1954) made him known throughout the English-speaking world as the novelist of Nigerian city life. Although there are nearly ten million Igbo people in southeastern Nigeria, hardly any creative writing has been produced in the vernacular in spite of the efforts of Peter Nwana (dates n.a.) with *Omenuko* (1933; Omenuko) and, three decades later, of Leopold Bell-Gam (dates n.a.) with *Ije Odumodu jere* (1963; Odumodu's travels).

There is no doubt that the element that was chiefly responsible for giving Nigerian writing the decisive impetus that was to win for Nigeria undisputed leadership in black African literature in English was the cluster of initiatives that were taken around 1960 in the university town of Ibadan. The university college had been created in 1947. Ten years later its English department had become a hatching place for young writers, who could find an outlet for their youthful efforts in the student magazine *The Horn.* Contributors from 1957 to 1960 included John Pepper CLARK-BÈKEDEREMO (formerly John Pepper-Clark), Christopher OKIGBO, Wole Soyinka, and several other Ibadan students and graduates. While these were trying their hand in *The Horn,* two Germans, Janheinz John (1918–1973) and Ulli Beier (b. 1922), launched (also in 1957 at Ibadan) a literary periodical named *Black Orpheus* after the title of Jean-Paul SARTRE's famous preface to Léopold Sédar SENGHOR's *Anthologie de la nouvelle poésie négre et malgache de langue française* (1948; anthology of the new black poetry in the French language). The journal's first task was to make available, to African readers of English, the already abundant amount of creative writing that had been produced in French during the 1950s in Africa and in the West Indies. After a few issues, however, original African contributions in English became more and more numerous, coming not only from Nigeria but also from elsewhere in West Africa and other parts of the continent. These two modest streams coalesced more or less formally when Ulli Beier founded (still at Ibadan) the Mbari Club, the name of which (meaning a certain kind of shrine) was suggested by the novelist Chinua ACHEBE; while spreading to other parts of Nigeria (Duro Ladipo founded a Mbari Club in his hometown of Oshogbo), Mbari generated its own publishing firm and issued, between 1961 and 1964, several plays, novels, and collections of poetry by writers who now appear as the founding fathers of modern English-language literature in Africa.

By the time the civil war broke out in 1966, Nigeria could boast impressive achievements in creative writing. Poetry was dominated by Christopher Okigbo, who was killed during the Biafra war; his two slender collections, *Heavensgate* (1962) and *Limits* (1964), contain poems of exceptional excellence, some of which had previously appeared in *The Horn* and in *Black Orpheus;* they focus on familiar areas of experience, such as nostalgia for the African past, the sociopolitical problems of the present, and the eternal theme of the nature of love; but in spite of their social and historical relevance, they are first and foremost works of art, whose incantatory quality owes much to the music of Igbo oral art, even though Okigbo's techniques in the use of imagery may have been partly derived from English poetry of the generation of YEATS and ELIOT. Another promising poet was Michael Echeruo (b. 1937), who seems to have given up poetry in favor of scholarship and criticism after his only collection, *Morality* (1968).

During the early years of independence, drama was entirely dominated by Wole Soyinka, who easily outclassed James Ene Henshaw (b. 1924), a popular author of "well-made" comedies such as *This Is Our Chance* (1956), and even his contemporary John Pepper Clark-Bèkederemo, whose *Song of a Goat* (1961) was

more successful perhaps as poetry than as tragedy; Clark soon turned to the study of his native Ijaw folk tradition, editing its oral epic and giving it dramatic shape in *Ozidi* (1966). But it was Soyinka who chronicled—not only in dramatic terms, but also in his novel *The Interpreters* (1965)—Africa's dizzy descent toward the murky depths of despotism or anarchy. Whereas his 1960 play *A Dance of the Forests* had been a celebration calling on traditional myth and performance practice, *Kongi's Harvest* (1967) and *Madmen and Specialists* (1971), "enriched" by direct experience of civil war, were, as Soyinka himself put it, "an ironic expression of horror at the universal triumph of expediency and power lust."

Meanwhile, the vitality and attractiveness of Yoruba culture were illustrated in a very odd way in *The Imprisonment of Obatala and Other Plays* (1966), whose author, who called himself "Obotunde Ijimere," was none other than Ulli Beier, translating into modern drama in English episodes from Nigerian folklore. Until the late 1970s Yoruba playwrights maintained a privileged (although by no means monopolistic) position in Nigerian drama, with such younger authors as Ola ROTIMI and Wale Ogunyemi (b. 1939).

In the making of the Nigerian novel, however, Igbo writers, led by Chinua Achebe, provided the main impetus. Achebe's early novels either explored the weakness that had caused the traditional society to collapse so easily under the impact of Europe—*Things Fall Apart* (1958), *Arrow of God* (1964)—or else analyzed the inner culture clash tormenting the Westernized African—*No Longer at Ease* (1960). In some way, the conflict between native tradition and imported novelty was basic to the Nigerian novel of the early 1960s; some writers—like Onuora Nzekwu (b. 1928), Ntieyong U. Akpan (b. 1924), and Obi Egbuna (b. 1938), who is also a play-wright—chose to lament, sometimes in a humorous way, the disappearance of age-old customs and beliefs, while others—such as Timothy M. Aluko and Vincent C. Ike (b. 1931)—chose to welcome the winds of change.

In the mid-1960s, while a number of other young Igbo novelists—Nkem Nwankwo (b. 1936), Flora NWAPA, and especially Elechi AMADI with his second novel, *The Great Ponds* (1969)—turned to the tribal past for literary inspiration, setting their stories in rural communities that had little or no contact with the outside world, the moral, social, and above all political deliquescence of the country was increasingly preoccupying the more sensitive observers. Frank criticism of the corruption of the leading classes, which had played a peripheral role in some of Ekwensi's novels—*Jagua Nana* (1961), *Beautiful Feathers* (1963)—and in *The Voice* (1964), the strange allegorical and experimental novel of Ijaw writer Gabriel OKARA, became the main theme of more ambitious works with ironic titles such as Achebe's *A Man of the People* (1966) or Aluko's *Chief the Honourable Minister* (1970).

The Biafra war thus broke out in an atmosphere of disillusionment. Its traumatic impact made itself felt throughout Nigeria's literature with unprecedented intensity. The death of Okigbo was felt as a symbol of Africa destroying the best of her own substance in old-fashioned tribal quarrels. Some of the major writers turned to new modes of expression: while Clark voiced his despair in poetry—*Casualties: Poems 1966–1968* (1970)—Achebe gave up the novel in favor of poetry—*Beware, Soul Brother and Other Poems* (1971)—and the short story—*Girls at War and Other Stories* (1972); besides *Madmen and Specialists*, Wole Soyinka expressed his own concern and experience in an autobiography, *The Man Died: Prison Notes* (1972) (as did Elechi Amadi with *Sunset in Biafra: A Civil War Diary* [1973]), in poetry in *A Shuttle in the Crypt* (1972), and in his second novel, *Season of Anomy* (1973).

With John Munonye's (b. 1929) novel *A Wreath for the Maidens* (1973) and Flora Nwapa's novel *Never Again* (1974), it became clear that the civil war was on its way to becoming a mere literary cliché. It had nevertheless provided genuine inspiration for a younger generation of writers, who had been in their twenties when it broke out. These included Sebastian O. Mezu (b. 1941), with *Behind the Rising Sun* (1971), and Kole Omotoso (b. 1943), with *The Combat* (1972). But the restoration of peace in 1970, the comparative orderliness maintained by moderate military regimes, and the economic prosperity resulting from the discovery of oil also had their literary aftermath throughout the 1970s. For the new generation of writers, born in the 1940s, who had little knowledge of the colonial regime and of the struggle for independence, who were thoroughly urbanized and found traditional mores and ideas totally irrelevant to life in a modern society, who had attended one or several of Nigeria's eighteen universities and/or foreign institutions of higher learning as a matter of course, and for whom the rapid growth of the educational system had prepared a sizable public of literate readers, the Biafra war belonged to an outdated tribal past, the obsolete tensions of which were profitably manipulated by foreign capitalist interests. What they regarded as the elitist posture of their elders, who had been trying to graft their own work onto a venerable but alien tradition ranging from Shakespeare through Jane Austen to Yeats and Eliot, was as anachronistically irrelevant as their alleged veneration for the so-called "African" values, the legends, the memories, the myths, and the superstitious creeds of a society that Nigeria, they felt, had outgrown.

Although a playwright of such exceptional ability as Ola Rotimi successfully managed, in *The Gods Are Not to Blame* (1968) and in ensuing plays, to put modern scenic techniques and the manipulation of dramatic space to the service of a type of inspiration that remained recognizably Yoruba, the novel outpaced both drama and poetry in the 1970s. Given the rebellious outlook of the post-civil-war generation, it is not surprising that they should have chosen for their masters, guides, and models, two writers whom academic criticism had hitherto regarded as comparatively minor: Cyprian Ekwensi, the founder of the urban novel, and John Munonye, whose many novels, from *The Only Son* (1966) to *Bridge to a Wedding* (1978), had mostly been devoted to recording the condition of the common man. This revulsion from profundity led to a literature that was at the same time popular and populist, and whose diffusion was greatly helped by the multiplication of private publishing houses, aiming, perhaps, to fill the void created by the destruction of Onitsha during the civil war. Since 1956 Ogali A. Ogali (b. 1935) had been one of the most prolific purveyors of popular reading, and during the 1970s there were many who shared with him the rewards of this profitable branch of the entertainment business. Some of the novelists who had already emerged before the civil war, such as Nkem Nwankwo, Obi Egbuna, and Vincent C. Ike, turned their satirical glance toward the ebullient urban society of the new Nigeria, and so did (although with angrier overtones) the younger writer Femi OSOFISAN in his novel *Kolera Kolej* (1975) and especially in his various plays, such as *The Chattering and the Song* (1975), which "offers a model of the new society as well as a condemnation of the old" (Gerald Moore). But others, like Isidore Okpewho (b. 1941) in *The Victims* (1970), I. N. C. Aniebo (b. 1939) in *The Journey Within* (1978), and many of their generation—for instance, Charles Njoku (dates n.a.) in *The New Breed* (1978) or Festus IYAYI in *Violence* (1979)—chose to offer a realistic depiction of the common town dweller's experiences and ordeals, as did Nigeria's first woman playwright, Zulu

Sofola (1935–1995). The theme of the culture clash and the motif of the "been-to" (returnee), both of which had been prominent in pre-civil-war writing, received new dimensions with *The Edifice* (1971) by Kole Omotoso, who has since become one of the dynamic leaders of the new Nigerian literature, and with *Second Class Citizen* (1976) by Buchi EMECHETA, whose later novels gave ever more compelling voice to the new militancy of African womanhood.

As the 1980s dawned, it was clear that Nigerian literature, having outgrown its pioneering period, still remained the herald and the model it had been (although with Kenya close on its heels): it provided articulate evidence that this enormous, populous, and resourceful new republic had at last joined the modern society of nations, the modern world of industrialization and urbanization, with its standardized universal conflicts and tensions taking the place of the futile idealizations, the pointless nostalgia, the small-scale, parochial-tribal confrontations that had provided earlier writers with their usual subject matter.

BIBLIOGRAPHY: Laurence, M., *Long Drums and Cannons: Nigerian Dramatists and Novelists 1952–1966* (1968); Klíma, V., *Modern Nigerian Novels* (1969); King, B. ed., *Introduction to Nigerian Literature* (1971); Roscoe, A. A., *Mother Is Gold: A Study in West African Literature* (1971); Obiechina, E., *An African Popular Literature: A Study of Onitsha Market Pamphlets* (1973); Udeyop, N. J., *Three Nigerian Poets* (1973); Lindfors, B., ed., *Critical Perspectives on Nigerian Literature* (1976); Momodu, A. G. S., and U. Schild, eds., *Nigerian Writing: Nigeria as Seen by Her Own Writers as Well as by German Authors* (1976); Emenyonou, E., *The Rise of the Igbo Novel* (1978); Baldwin, C., comp., *Nigerian Literature: A Bibliography of Criticism, 1952–1976* (1980); Booth, J., *Writers and Politics in Nigeria* (1981)

—ALBERT S. GÉRARD

Nigerian Literature since 1970

Because war is such a dramatic action that provides for easy historical periodizations, it is now habitual to see the Nigerian Civil War (1967-1970) as a turning point in the short history of modern Nigerian liteerature in English. That war duly brought about its own literature, but it produced no new social or political beginnings, and if at all it started as a revolutionary war, it ended in victory for the forces of reaction that were to be found on both sides, and which came together more formidably than before.

The oil boom of the 1970s magnified all the social, moral, and economic wantonness of the prewar years, festering an unreal middle class whose ethics was consumerism, not productivity. The military sat tight in government and occupied its time building monuments to illusions of prosperity. More than the Civil War, it is this culture of collective self-abandon that forms the social action against which Nigerian literature since then has in several ways been a long reaction.

New and younger writers emerged to criticize the dissolute national life, and to reject what they perceived as the misplaced commitment of the earlier writers—Chinua Achebe, Wole Soyinka, Christopher OKIGBO, J.P. CLARK-BEKEDEREMO—who had started the modern literary tradition.

Nigerian literature since the late 1970s has been characterized by reevaluations, rewritings and redefinitions of the writer himself and his social role, of the matter to write about and its manner, and of the writer's relationship with his audience. The new writer is thus no longer one seeking aesthetic affects and spiritual values, but one striving to make his work have social effects. The older writers still dominate the scene, but such is the changed social environment that they too have somewhat modified their aesthetic stands.

Social expansion in Nigeria in the last two decades has been phenomenal, and so has literature; indeed, the 1980s might later come to be seen as the beginning of another literary renaissance. The prominent features of this expansion are a growth of the reading public brought about by the astronomical increase in the 1970s of schools and school populations, followed by a mushrooming of universities in which departments of English are usually quite large; the growth of a local publishing industry to provide both educational and leisure-reading materials for the ever-increasing literature populations; and the rapid expansion of the newspaper industry, especially in the early 1980s, manned in the main by academics and intellectuals who see a natural affinity between journalism and creative writing.

Before 1970, there were five universities in the country, four of them situated in the southern parts. Twenty years later the number has risen to more than twenty, with about eight in the northern parts. From its beginning to the present, modern Nigerian literature has remained tied to the universities. Thus, the expansion and spread of these institutions has meant the establishment of more potential centres of literary activity. The growth of an indigenous publishing industry has had two important effects on literature: easier access to publication by all and encouragement of new authors (the Association of Nigerian Authors has also played a prominent role in this); and the growth of popular literature side by side with the steady development of the elitist one. The newspapers have also played a major role by offering employment to needy young writers and by creating arts and culture pages where old and new works are regularly reviewed and talked about. What all this has meant is an outward and downward expansion in modern Nigerian literature—a making available of serious literature beyond academic journals, beyond its traditional home in the universities. To these trends may be added one other significant development: the rise of female writers in all three genres. Thus, the new aesthetic of social engagement, the situation of women, plus the call for a transethnic or "national" literature all combine to make current Nigerian literature a literature of issues.

Poetry

Poetry has taken the lead in the literary efflorescence. There are new and original ideas about the nature, function, and form of poetry, which also inform the practice; older poets have been challenged by younger ones, male and female; and such is poetry's popularity that there are now three living generations of poets in Nigeria.

Wole Soyinka, awarded the Nobel Prize for literature in 1986, followed up his 1976 one-poem volume *Ogun Abibiman with Mandela's Earth and Other Poems* (1988). In the latter, Soyinka continues his incipient concern with continental-racial emancipation by devoting the first section to the South African struggle centered around Nelson Mandela, then a Prometheus figure chained to the rocks of Robben Island. There is another section on the perennial evil of "cannibal leadership" in Africa. The two volumes are doubly political: They treat political subjects and the poet's

revival of the idioms and styles of oral political poetry is an act of renewing and passing on, in usable form, an inherited tradition.

Also quite political is J. P. Clark-Bekederemo's *State of the Union* (1985), a collection in which the poet shrugs off his earlier aloofness and equanimity, to make direct and committed statements.

The descent by poets from the metaphysical, twilight zones of gods and myths to the lower, broader plain of history and mortals is most emphatic in the second generation of poets. These younger poets, who started being heard in the early 1980s, consider that broader plain where nothing is hidden and everything is material as the proper dwelling place of poetry. These poets are concentrated around the old universities at Ibadan and Nsukka; the Ibadan group is however the more successful. Its most important members are Niyi Osundare (b. 1947), Odia Ofeimun (b. 1950), and Tanure OJAIDE.

An intellectual and university teacher of peasant background, Osundare had his higher education at Ibadan, Leeds, and Canada. He is a declared socialist, is uneasy in the elitist culture that the university institution in Nigeria has spawned, and is perpetually at war with the preceding poetic. Emotional and intellectual commitment to the peasantry and urban proletariat, clarity of expression, and the borrowing of folk idioms and saws constitute his poetic. His *The Eye of the Earth* (1986) was a joint winner of the Commonwealth Poetry Prize in 1986, and his *Waiting Laughters* (1990) won the Noma Award for 1991. *Moonsongs* (1988) is a collection of highly lyrical verse on a very intense mystical experience. In spite of his political aesthetic, Osundare is an artist who is very much concerned with the craft of poetry; in his poetry one can discern a great struggle to find English equivalents for the ample cadences of the music of his very tonal Yoruba language, with the verbal technology of orality meeting and diffusing with the "restructured consciousness" of literacy.

Ofeimun is also of peasant background and a socialist. Ofeimun is a restless man; he has been a teacher, a postgraduate student of political science, a private secretary to a major politician, and a journalist. In his two volumes to date—*The Poet Lied* (1980) and *A Handle for the Flutist* (1986)—Ofeimun does not consciously address the proletariat; instead, he has developed a muscular poetic idiom of hard-hitting tropes inspired by marxist historicism. Ofeimun's poetry succeeds in its efforts to be "national"; it is intellectual poetry of substantial individual talent, but it lacks reverberations and echoes in any particular tradition.

Ojaide is also a university teacher and critic. He is a quiet worker who has produced six volumes of verse so far; the first, *Children of Iroko*, was published in 1973. He is very sensitive to the cultural contradictions inherent in the office of the literary poet in a prevalently oral society, and how to overcome such conflicts has been a major burden of his poetry. His *Labyrinths of the Delta* (1986) gathers up all these themes and articulates them in a most economic manner. He has a strong but quiet voice; the conflicts he writes about are personalized, thus revealing the psychological dimensions attendant on the conflicts between politics and poetic imagination.

Molara Ogundipe-Leslie (b. 1940) is the most important female poet so far, though she has published only one slim volume, *Sew the Old Days and Other Poems* (1985). She graduated with honors in English at Ibadan in 1963, is vastly read, and has taught for several years at Ibadan. Ogundipe-Leslie has a mastery of tone, form, and language that shows evidence of long practice. In her poetry, militant feminism is expressed with deceptive simplicity and ease. She is thoroughly steeped in her Yoruba oral tradition and in western and oriental (haiku) traditions of poetry. In fact she tries to develop a new form, *Firí* ("eye-flash poem") based on haiku and IMAGISM. Ogundipe-Leslie possesses a freshness of vision that disturbs male-gender ways; she is introspective, playful, and ironic, and reminds one most of Emily Dickinson.

Drama

While Nigerian theater is still dominated by the now titanic figure of Soyinka, there have been significant developments in recent years: Attempts have been made to extend the modern theater in Nigeria beyond the universities; private theater companies now exist; two younger dramatists have firmly established their own names; the lone female dramatist of the 1970s, Zulu Sofola, has been joined by another, Tess ONWUEME.

Soyinka's plays of the 1980s are *Opera Wonyosi* (1980), *A Play of Giants* (1984), and *Requiem for a Futurologist* (1985), but his *The Road and Death and the King's Horseman* have seen revivals on the stage, while the Jero plays continue to be popular. *Opera Wonyosi, A Play of Giants*, and *Requiem* are comic satires, again on the type and moral quality of leaderships in Africa. *A Play of Giants* is a particularly lively and humor-laden piece, although the reader-spectator must remember to separate the illusion on the stage from the horrific reality of Idi Amin's rule in Uganda. It is a play to which W. B. Yeats's line "Gaiety transfiguring all that dread" could serve as epigraph, and which teaches that the term "political relevance" has more than one meaning.

After a long period of absence, Clark-Bekederemo has returned to the stage in a double way: With his wife he now codirects his own theater (PEC Theater), and he has produced six new plays, three of which are a trilogy called *The Bikoroa Plays* (1987). The strong sense of locale and the tragic pessimism of his earlier plays are still present, although a beguiling simplicity has been added.

Between Soyinka and Clark-Bekederemo at one end and the two younger dramatists at the other stands Ola ROTIMI whose dramaturgy has always tended toward the realistic and the popular. *If* (1981) and *Hopes of the Living Dead* (1989) view society through the bifocal lenses of humanism and socialism. In the latter, the inmates of a leper colony struggle to organize themselves into a union so as to assert their humanity rather than remain content as objects of charity. An accomplished theater director who seeks instant communication with his audience, Rotimi's forte lies in uncomplicated plots, suspense, sharp-edged dialogue, and "heavy" characters.

Femi OSOFISAN and Bode Sowande (b. 1947) are the two outstanding dramatists of the younger generation. Like the younger poets, they too believe in committed art. Osofisan is the more fecund and energetic, being also a newspaper columnist and popular short-story writer, a poet who has published a collection of poems (as Okinba Launko, *Minted Coins*, 1988), and a regular academic at Ibadan. All these creative activities constitute different aspects of one long endeavor to fuse elitist and popular literature in Nigeria. Propelled by the myth of dialectic materialism, and opposing its archetypes of reason and social consciousness to those of the irrationality, blindness, and necessity of the tragic mythos, Osofisan has been rewriting some canonical Nigerian tragedies: Soyinka's *The Strong Breed as No More the Wasted Breed* (1982), and Clark-Bekederemo's *The Raft as Another Raft* (1988). This Nigerian Brecht has also recast local myths and history on the stage. His unpublished *Esu and His Vagabond Minstrels* (perf.

1986) is a political promotion of the Yoruba Esu as essentially an incarnation of the democratic spirit—in opposition to Soyinka's promotion of Ogun, the god who incarnates the tragic essence. In his most successful play to date, *Morountodun* (1982), Osofisan also rereads local myth and history along socialist revolutionary lines. But the intertextual character and interpellatory forms of his plays tell us to pay less attention to the ideologue in Osofisan and more to the artist in him, for it is in the latter that his real revolutionary endeavor lies.

Also a lecturer in drama at Ibadan, Bode Sowande has leaned more on the television in his own social crusade. He also founded a theater company that produces his own plays. His major plays to date are collected in *Farewell to Babylon* (1979) and *Flamingo and Other Plays* (1986). Clearly, the urge to reach a wider audience, plus the reformist zeal, have combined to influence the matter and manner of Sowande's plays: They are usually on subjects such as leadership problems, unemployment, and corruption, while his approach is that of the theater as a mirror of society. In the last play in the second collection, Sowande attempts a new kind of dramaturgy in which the Yoruba storytelling theater is enlarged, through the play-within-a-play technique, into a kind of opera.

Fiction

Narrative prose has diversified much, in response to the political whirlpool and other social undercurrents of the last two decades. The political uniformity enforced by prolonged military rule has engendered a stronger sense of national identity, thereby inviting the call for a "national literature" to underscore it; the old historical, cultural, and social differences that produced "ethnic literatures" persist, overlaid by the polarization of the entire society into the two economic classes of classical Marxism. This possible replacement of "ethnic literature" by "class literature" has found support in the rise of female novelists.

Achebe's *Anthills of the Savannah* (1987) is the most important novel yet produced in the labor for the great Nigerian novel. It takes off from where *A Man of the People* (1966) left off, and, if the former is on the blind necessity of military intervention, *Anthills of the Savannah* is on the double and triple irony of that intervention. Achebe in the novel gives a prominent place to a female character who survives the destruction of the male protagonists and takes on the role of priestess and healer to the grieving nation. The novel is a reflective one in which both author and characters are seeking to understand the banal misuse of power to produce absurd effects.

Kole Omotoso was also educated at Ibadan and in the U.K. and is a scholar of Arabic literature. A prolific writer of short stories and short novels, he is an inveterate experimenter. He made his mark early with the novel *The Edifice* (1971), and his most significant work so far is also an experimental novel, *Just before Dawn* (1988). This work mixes elements of historical and fictional discourse to reveal how the present (of Nigeria) came to be. It is many stories in one, and the author has had to resort to a metonymic technique in which historical fragments imbricate. In this, he may have hit upon a correct strategy for handling politics and getting the attention of a significant segment of the Nigerian audience, which responds more vigorously to factual narratives. Indeed, both *Anthills of the Savannah and Just before Dawn* have to be read as the fictional obverse of the "national literature" coin, the other side being the personal accounts by military men, politicians, and other public officials of their roles in the political history of the nation.

The second—and main—trend is the old one in which the novel in Nigeria has been reflecting distinct group and/or ethnic, cultural, and historical identities. One novelist in this category who belongs to the first generation but still needs introduction is Elechi AMADI. A physicist by education and an ex-military man, Amadi is an odd-man-out novelist in Nigeria. In his three characteristic novels—*The Concubine* (1966), *The Great Ponds* (1969), and *The Slave* (1978)—he deals with a rural past still untouched by colonialism; he is totally apolitical; and he holds not a tragic but a pessimistic view of life. Amadi is very conversant with the rural life he depicts so evocatively, and his subject is the gods and the fiery passions that rule the lives of the villagers. His latest novel, *Estrangement* (1986), is on a contemporary and "national" subject, but, both on its own and in comparison with earlier ones, it is weak.

Two of the younger novelists deserve mention: T. Obinkaram Echewa (b. 1940) and Ben OKRI. Echewa's two novels so far, *The Land's Lord* (1976), awarded the English Speaking Union Literature Prize in 1976 and *The Crippled Dancer* (1986), are about the world of his Ibo people, depicted in all its plenitude and chaotic vitality. Echewa concentrates on ordinary lives and their little, but no less significant, acts of failure and success. This focus has not come too soon, for a phenomenological depiction of the small politics of everyday life has received only secondary attention in the Nigerian novel.

By the age of nineteen, Okri had the manuscript of his first novel ready. He grew into adolescence in the now notorious 1970s and, judging by the vision projected in his first three works, simultaneously into despair. The heroes (antiheroes, really) of the first two novels, *Flowers and Shadows* (1980) and *The Landscapes Within* (1982), are still in their teens, early victims who are not even allowed to grow into adulthood before disillusionment sets in. He followed this with a collection of short stories, *Incidents at the Shrine* (1986), after which he changed the direction of his art completely. *Stars of the New Curfew* (1988), an other short-story collection, is written in the MAGICREALISM mode of Gabriel GARCIA MÁRQUEZ and Salman RUSHDIE. If that book is a tentative but confident excursion into the supernatural world of African ontology, his next novel, *The Famished Road* (1991) and winner of the Booker Prize, is a narrative tour de force in the same mode. The hero is an *abiku*, or spirit child, who, in his combined roles as witness, participant, and narrator, embodies the novel's central theme: the transforming powers of imagination. Written in the sensuous language of poetry, *The Famished Road* reconnects with the inherited cultural imagination of the oral narratives that had been forced into retreat by the realistic mode in the African novel. But in Okri, that inherited imagination has found a powerful voice and is striking back by exposing the limitations of realism in dealing with the African universe. This novel also demonstrates that, contrary to prevalent belief, the free, autonomous imagination can be as responsive to social pains and ills as the one tied to commitment and relevance.

In the 1960s, Flora Nwapa was the only female novelist in Nigeria; now there are five who have published at least two full-length novels each: Nwapa, Buchi EMECHETA, Adora Ulasi (b. 1932), Ifeoma Okoye (b. 1945), and Zaynab Alkali (b. 1950). All of them except Ulasi are writing about the condition of women in a society of tyrannical patriarchal cultures and values. However, it is doubtful if they can be said to be writing from the "feminist" or "womanist" perspective. As of now, in Nigeria, women's movements tend either to be frustrated by the male-dominated government or assimilated into existing male institutions. There is no distinct female movement to provide the necessary political platform from which a theory and practice of feminist literature can emerge to challenge the patriarchal order. Moreover, a sizable sophisticated female audience is lacking; the majority of educated women wittingly or unwittingly subscribe to the prevalent social ideology, of which the feminine mystique forms a part. Thus, most of the novels by these female writers revolve around the conflict between that mystique (love, home, children), which glorifies woman, and its hidden ideology, which subjugates women socially and economically. In Nwapa's novels—*Efuru* (1966), *Idu* (1970), *One Is Enough* (1981), and *Women Are Different* (1986)—for instance, the heroines fail to live up to the feminine myth but, as if in compensation, succeed in storming the economic fortress occupied by men. And in *Women Are Different*, Nwapa preaches that marriage and childbearing are not the only ways for a woman to live "fully and fruitfully."

Buchi Emecheta is by far the most militant and progressive of the female novelists and, with seven adult novels already published, also the most prolific. The prolificness and militancy are partially explained by her permanent abode in Britain and her training in sociology. Where other female novelists plead for understanding or argue for equality on male terms, she is for outright emancipation. She sees women's oppression in materialist terms: Women are an oppressed socioeconomic class. In her early novels, paying a bride price is the same thing as buying a slave. In the later novels—the ironically entitled *The Joys of Motherhood* (1979), and *Double Yoke* (1982)—the heroines are transiting from the condition of wife-equals-slave to that of liberation. Here female subjectivity and sexuality are no longer traps for cooperating in the "myth of woman"; it instead finds expression in prostitution, a materialist weapon for gaining materialist emancipation.

There is neither a political platform nor a body of literary theory to give these novels an identity other than that of female authorship. However, in focusing on the injustices inherent in the fundamental experiences of love and sex, marrying and raising a family, working and feeding, it is the female novelists who, more than the male, are revealing that colonialism and neocolonialism are also internal conditions that have been contributing their own share to the dysfunctional politics so prevalent at the national level.

The major diversification in fictional prose has been in autobiography and biography, and the one and only important practitioner of both so far is Soyinka. His autobiographical work *Ake, The Years of Childhood* (1981) is a dramatist's recreation of life in a Yoruba town caught on the knife-edge of change in the 1930s and 1940s. *Ake* is definitely one of the best prose narratives in English from Africa in this century. *Isara: A Voyage around Essay* (1989) is a son's recuperation (based on actual papers left behind) of a certain period in his father's life: that period when the few young men of education were beginning to assert themselves strongly and initiate changes in the affairs of their small communities. This fictional biography gives us an insight into how the emergent educated class began to displace the old political class. These two works reveal possibilities for other genres of imaginative writing in Africa; they also point to the kind of material to look for in linking literature and society in Africa. That link has so far been more speculated upon and theorized about by critics than researched into.

The last decade has witnessed an exhilarating growth and expansion in Nigerian literature. It has been a period of drive and confident expansiveness in which, paradoxically, the more some writers tried to subsume the literature under one social cause or the other, the more it established its own autonomy. The 1990s promise to be a period of consolidation of that tradition.

BIBLIOGRAPHY: Chinweizu, O. Jemie, and Madubuike, I., *Toward the Decolonization of African Literature* (1980); Achebe, C., *The Trouble with Nigeria* (1983); Ogunbiyi, Y., ed., *Perspectives on Nigerian Literature: 1700 to the Present* (2 vols., 1988); Jeyifo, B., ed., *Wole Soyinka: Art, Dialogue and Outrage* (1988); Otokunefor, H. C., and O. M. Nwodo, eds., *Nigerian Female Writers: A Critical Perspective* (1989); Wren, R. M., *Those Magical Years: The Making of Nigerian Literature at Ibadan, 1948–1966* (1991)

—WOLE OGUNDELE

NIJHOFF, Martinus

Dutch poet and dramatist, b. 20 April 1894, The Hague; d. 26 Jan. 1953, The Hague

N. studied law in Amsterdam and later Dutch literature in Utrecht, and served as editor of *De gids* from 1926 to 1933. His poetry began to appear at the time of World War I, and he established himself as one of the most eminent Dutch literary figures of his time.

His poetry, notable for its lucidity, is carefully crafted: N. sometimes reworked already published poems. In his earlier work he makes effective use of the sonnet. Later in his career he often used looser forms, and in the verse dramas that absorbed much of his literary energy later in his life he developed a flowing verse line closer to the conversational.

A central theme in his work is the confusion of individual lives in contrast to a higher or deeper order, perhaps that established by God. This sharply etched poetry, never vague or indefinite, is full of unexpected images: the moon as a muffled sun, a satyr offering currants to the infant Christ, Saint Sebastian removing his arrows and finding himself in a modern Dutch landscape. It is poetry informed by a sense of disquiet, at times of anguish, and a recurring thematic action is breaking, both in the sense of giving way and of breaking through.

N.'s early inspiration was often religious, although the nature and degree of his belief has been a much discussed subject. Related to this impulse is the frequent return to the theme of the dead mother, a subject handled in a sensitive yet unsentimental way. N.'s later lyrics become more sensual although without losing the delicacy of tone and feeling of the earlier poems. They are more musical, and music enters as a theme. The tone of his best poems is that of a dark romanticism, where life and death exist as attractive counterweights.

Of his longer poems, *Awater* (1934; "Awater," 1954) and *Het uur U* (1942; H-hour) are the most noteworthy. Both are concerned with the unexpected effect the passage of a stranger has on the emotional lives of others, a heightening of emotions not without surrealistic overtones. Each poem leaves the reader with a sense that some breach in the order of things has been accomplished. The failure of the narrator and of others to make any but the most fleeting contact with the passing stranger is related to the theme of leaving others and of being left, a theme that recurs in the shorter poems as well.

N. was also a popular and effective writer of verse drama. His most important work of this kind is the series of three plays for Christmas, Easter, and Pentecost respectively written during World War II and later collected under the title *Het heilige hout* (1950; the sacred wood): *De ster van Bethlehem* (1942; the star of Bethlehem), *De Dag des Heren* (1949; the Lord's Day), and *Des Heilands tuin* (1950; the Savior's garden). He has also been much admired for his translations, notably of Euripides' *Iphigenia in Tauris* and T. S. ELIOT's *The Cocktail Party*.

FURTHER WORKS: *De wandelaar* (1916); *Pierrot aan de lantaarn* (1919); *Vormen* (1924); *De pen op papier* (1926); *De vliegende Hollander* (1930); *Gedachten op dinsdag* (1931); *Halewijn* (1933); *Nieuwe gedichten* (1934); *Een idylle* (1940); *Verzameld werk* (3 vols., 1954–1961)

BIBLIOGRAPHY: Sötemann, A. L., "'Non-spectacular' Modernism: M. N.'s Poetry in Its European Context," in Bulhof, F., ed., *N., Van Ostaijen, De Stijl* (1976): 95–116; Fokkema, D. W., "N.'s Modernist Poetics in European Perspective," in Fokkema, D. W., et al., eds., *Comparative Poetics* (1976): 63–87

—FRED J. NICHOLS

NIN, Anaïs

American diarist, novelist, and critic, b. 21 Feb. 1903, Paris, France; d. 14 Jan. 1977, Los Angeles, Cal.

After a cosmopolitan childhood in Europe, N. came to the U.S. with her Danish mother and two brothers in 1914, following the desertion of the father, the Cuban-born composer-pianist Joaquin Nin. Largely self-educated, she spent her youth reading and keeping a journal, which she initially wrote in French and did not begin to write in English until she was seventeen. In 1923 she married Hugh Guiler, who later became known as an engraver and filmmaker under the name of Ian Hugo; N. reproduced a number of his engravings in her fiction and appeared in his early films. During the 1930s N. lived in Paris, where she became the confidante and promoter of such writers as Henry MILLER, Lawrence DURRELL, Antonin ARTAUD and of the psychologist Otto Rank, with whom she worked as a lay analyst. Returning to the U.S. at the outbreak of World War II, she set up her own printing press when publishers refused her work, and in the 1940s and 1950s she became allied with such younger writers as Robert DUNCAN, Gore VIDAL, and James Leo Herlihy (1927-1993). Following the success of the publication of the first volume of *The Diary* (7 vols., 1966–80), N. became a much sought-after public speaker. In 1973 she was the subject of a documentary film, *Anaïs Observed*.

Although a highly poetic style and emphasis upon psychological reality are the distinguishing features of all of N.'s writing, if viewed chronologically her fiction also presents a movement from the inner to the outer, from the subjective to the objective, which dramatizes her general conviction that self-realization must precede social commitment. *House of Incest* (1936), her first fictional work, is a surrealistic prose poem wherein a self-obsessed narrator encounters fragments of herself in a desperate quest to find the core of her identity; *Collages* (1964), N.'s last work of fiction, is a loosely connected series of portraits of a wide variety of characters, and the prevailing tone is a combination of social criticism and good humor.

Published collectively under the title of *Cities of the Interior* (1959; enlarged version, 1974), five novels constitute the central core of N.'s fiction: *Ladders to Fire* (1946), *Children of the Albatross* (1947), *The Four-Chambered Heart* (1950), *A Spy in the House of Love* (1954), and *Solar Barque* (1958; enlarged and pub. as *Seduction of the Minotaur*, 1961). Designed to explore the nature and causes of discontent in four basic female types, the series illustrates N.'s grounding in contemporary psychological theory as well as the extent to which such theory was grounded in the four-humors psychology of the past. The problem of each female type is to reconcile her basic nature with the image she has projected and to admit to her own responsibility for the conflict between the two. At the same time, N.'s concern is to demonstrate the limitations of type-casting and the need to recognize that each type represents merely the ascendancy of one aspect of woman, who is in actuality a composite.

In keeping with general trends in early-20th-c. fiction, N.'s novels utilize limited point of view, STREAM OF CONSCIOUSNESS, and association rather than sequence as a structural principle, but she employs these devices to an extreme that makes her work very different from that of Virginia WOOLF, James JOYCE, or Ernest HEMINGWAY. Characterized by the elimination of all sociological details or sense of historical time, N.'s method of composition has more in common with modern trends in music and the pictorial arts, analogues that she herself emphasizes in her literary manifesto, *The Novel of the Future* (1968).

It is, however, *The Diary of A. N.* that is her masterpiece and her most significant contribution. Covering the years from 1931 to 1977, based on the original private journal N. kept during this period, and including correspondence and photographs, *The Diary* provides fascinating insights into her development as a woman and artist, although because it is a highly edited version of the original, *The Diary* should not be read as a biographical document but rather as a work of art. Each volume has a controlling theme and is structured as an aesthetic whole, while the series itself reflects the movement from inner to outer which characterizes her fiction. Internally, the art of *The Diary* lies in the quality of N.'s prose, which is rich and rhythmic to the point of incantation; its literary merits also derive from N.'s sense of the dramatic: individuals and scenes are vividly and concretely realized; conversations are presented in dialogue form; episodes are narrated in the present tense; lengthy observations are juxtaposed with cryptic comments; related themes are introduced after the fashion of subplots; and finally, the N. persona herself is a multifaceted protagonist whose various selves are continually in conflict with each other. Aside from the contemporaneity of the issues N. addresses, it is this dramatic flair which makes *The Diary* seem so immediate, and which in turn distinguishes it from other memoirs and journals.

Also characterized by its presentness is *A Woman Speaks: The Lectures, Seminars, and Interviews of A. N.* (1975), wherein are represented N.'s attitudes toward current trends in general and toward the women's liberation movement in particular. Dissociating herself from the political activism of feminists, N. advocates journal keeping as a preliminary requirement for a liberated self, to be followed by cooperation with men in the interests of mutual growth—ideas she also explores in *In Favor of the Sensitive Man* (1976).

Anaïs Nin

Influenced by D. H. LAWRENCE, about whom she wrote her first critical work, *D. H. Lawrence: An Unprofessional Study* (1932), all of N.'s writing has an erotic quality. In the early 1940s, however, she wrote a series of specifically sexual pieces, which were edited and published posthumously as *Delta of Venus* (1977) and *Little Birds* (1979). Although the quality is uneven, these pieces do as a whole illustrate in a subtle way N.'s contention that women's writing about sex differs from men's and that the difference between pornography and erotica lies in the poetic quality of the latter.

Largely ignored until the 1960s, N. is today rightly regarded as one of the leading women writers of the 20th c., and the one who has done most to pioneer and perfect a distinctly feminine mode of perception and articulation. She has also become a source of inspiration for those who would respond creatively to the self-destructive features of our time and who would see obstacles as challenges and life as an adventure.

FURTHER WORKS: *Winter of Artifice* (1939); *Under a Glass Bell* (1944); *Realism and Reality* (1946); *On Writing* (1947); *Timeless and Other Early Stories* (1977); *Linotte: The Early Diary of A. N. 1914–1920* (1978); *The Early Diary of A. N.: Volume Two, 1920–1923* (1982)

BIBLIOGRAPHY: Evans, O., *A. N.* (1968); Hinz, E., *The Mirror and the Garden: Realism and Reality in the Writings of A. N.*, rev. ed. (1973); Zaller, R., ed., *A Casebook on A. N.* (1974); Spencer, S.,

Collage of Dreams: The Writings of A. N. (1977); Knapp, B., *A. N.* (1978); special N. issue, *Mosaic*, 11, 2 (1978); Cutting, R., *A. N.: A Reference Guide* (1978); Franklin, B., and D. Schneider, *A. N.: An Introduction* (1979); Bair, D., *A. N.: A Biography* (1995)

—EVELYN J. HINZ

NIÑO, Jairo Aníbal

Colombian novelist, poet, short-story writer, and dramatist, b. 5 Sept. 1941, Moniquirá, Boyacá

N. spent his childhood and adolescence under the terror of "La Violencia" (1946-64), a period in which the nation was beset by terror, assassinations, and bloodshed as a consequence of the ideological discrepancies between the Liberal and the Conservative parties as well as human irrationality. N. has been professor at the University Javeriana and the National Pedagogical University in Bogotá. He also served as Vice Director of Communications of Colcultura, and directed the National Library until 1990, when he retired from the last of his public services. At present he lives in Bogotá and devotes himself to creative writing.

In 1966 N.'s play *El monte calvo* (1966; The Bold Mountain) won the first prize in the First National Festival of University Theater, and in the following year the same play received an award at the World Festival of Theater in Nancy, France. With Esteban Navajas and Sebastián Ospina he founded the Workshop of Dramatic Art in 1975. Under his direction, the workshop produced various outstanding plays. Although the workshop only lasted three years, it contributed a great deal to the development of contemporary theater in Colombia, due to the collective efforts of the members, the critical nature of the group, and its well-selected stage settings. N. has also received awards for his plays *El golpe de estado* (1969; The Coup D'état) and *Las balas de lata o el baile de los arzobispos* (1968; The Tin Bullets or the Dance of the Archbishops), and as well for his screenplay *Efraín González*.

N. belongs to the generation affiliated with the New Theater of Colombia. By means of revolutionary and subversive techniques, the New Theater advocates a new aesthetic concept, urging the audience to become more sensitive to the national reality. N. offers a unique feature for his critical vision of the national economic, social, and political life, especially in his depiction of governmental corruption, exploitation of the privileged classes, and the misfortune of the underdogs. N.'s early plays are more didactic and documentary, with more political intention than the pursuit of aesthetics, while his latter works lean toward the fantastic without losing their political and social implications. Although N.'s plays are often noted for their documentary style, immediacy, and excessive political essence, they also have been praised for their ingenious use of literary devices such as his symbolic re-creations of various psychological states, and his mastery use of stage effects to convey specific messages. A typical example is *El sol subterráneo* (1978; The Underground Sun), which was based on the massacre of banana workers in 1928. The play was written from the perspective of the present, recalling the bloodstained historical event several decades later. By presenting ideological characters that represent opposing dramatic situations: outsider versus insider, oppressor versus oppressed, and symbolic and effective stage resources, N.

successfully denounces the abuse of the national government and the exploitation of the foreign fruit company.

N.'s most acclaimed play is *El monte calvo*, which examines the physical and psychical traumas that the Korean War left in the Colombian people. Centered on a mutilated veteran and a depraved military, the play is written in the absurdist style of Samuel BECKETT's *Waiting for Godot* with humorous and satirical dialogues that make fun of the absurd participation of Colombia in the Korean War as a result of foreign imposition. The play explicitly denounces the alienation of the soldiers, and the indifference of the Colombian government that ignores the traumatized and mutilated veterans. It also criticizes the ignorance of common people who allow themselves to be deceived by a false and empty slogan of patriotism.

As a poet, N. has published *La alegría de querer: poemas de amor para niños* (1986; The Happiness of Loving: Poems of Love for Children), which was granted the Misael Valentino Award in Cuba; and *Preguntario: poemario para niños* (1988; Questionnaire: Book of Poems for Children), in which he recalls childhood memories with tenderness and emotion. N. has published numerous works for children, most notably *Zoro* (1977), which received the First National Award Enka for Children's Literature in 1977. Acclaimed for their expressive vitality and imaginative, boundless potential, N.'s stories create an impression of freshness and spontaneity. He often creates a world of fantasy, where sensitive beings speak a poetic and musical language. The fictional characters communicate a strong sense of intimacy, as evidenced in *La hermana del Principito* (1997; The Sister of the Little Prince) and *Los papelas de Miguela* (1997; The Papers of Miguela). N. believes that children are capable of having faith in life, living out their dreams, and creating fantastic worlds. N. has won international recognition since he received the Iberoamericano Award, Chamán, in Mexico in 1990. In 1993 he was granted the Chuchilo Canario Award of Narration in Spain. In 1996 N. received the Caracol Al Mérito Award from the Mexican Association of Narrators.

Another remarkable aspect of N.'s fiction for children is his mastery and skillful incorporation of classical texts in his writings, as illustrated in the collection entitled *Toda la vida* (1989; All the Life). However, although N. has created texts with literary antecedents and sources based on intertextuality, his ability and skill of introducing characters within national context, and incorporating new styles, forms, and narrative situations to the classical texts are original and go beyond parody and other literary devices. For this reason N.'s works are praised not only for their great poetic sensibility and tenderness, but also for their social and political criticism that denounces the abuse of power. It is precisely this fusion of his stylistic mastery and his essence as a conscious writer that places him among the most significant contemporary writers in Latin America.

FURTHER WORKS: *Alguien muere cuando nace el alba* (1965); *Los inquilinos de la ira* (1973); *Nosotros los comueros* (1973); *Triqui, triqui, triqui, tran* (1973); *La madriguera* (1978); *El manantial de las fieras* (1981); *Los andariegos* (1983); *El músico del aire* (1991); *Razzgo, Indo y Zag* (1991); *El árbol de los anhelos: relato para niños de la Constitución política de Colombia, 1991* (1992); *El obrero de la alegría* (1992); *El quinto viaje* (1992); *El cuento distancias* (1993); *El inventor de lunas* (1995); *Dalia y Zazir* (1996); *Orfeo y la cosmonauta* (1995); *De las Alas Caracolí*

(1996); *Historia y Nomeolvides* (1996); *Aviador Santiago* (1997); *El nido más bello del mundo* (1997)

BIBLIOGRAPHY: Arévalo, G., "J. A. N.: trabajador del teatro colombiano," in *Materiales para una historia del teatro en Colombia* (1978): 546-63; González, P., *El Nuevo Teatro en Colombia, DAI* (1981); "Entrevista con J. A. N.," *Actuemos*, 2 (1982): 2-8; Ovadía Andrade, R., *El Nuevo Teatro en Colombia, DAI* (1982); Jaramillo, M. M., *El Nuevo Teatro Colombiano y la colonizacón cultural* (1987); Shen, V., *El Nuevo Teatro de Colombia: la ideología y la dramaturgia en Enrique Buenaventura, Carlos José Reyes y J. A. N., DAI* (1988); Jaramillo, M. M., *Nuevo Teatro Colombiano: arte y política* (1992); Bravo de Del Risco, N., "Elementos fundamentales de la intertextualidad en la narrativa de J. A. N.," *Litterae*, 6 (Aug. 1996): 75-92

—VIRGINIA SHEN

NISHIWAKI Junzaburō

Japanese poet, essayist, and translator, b. 20 Jan. 1894, Ojiya; d. 5 June 1982, Ojiya

Born to a well-established family in a rural town in Niigata, N. first aspired to become a painter. Though his true passion lay in art and literature, he was persuaded to study economics at Keiō University in Tokyo upon his father's death. Nonetheless, at college he read widely in foreign literatures and began to write poems in Latin, French, and English. In 1922 Keiō University sent N., then a lecturer at Keiō, to Oxford University to study English literature. In his three-year sojourn in England, N. encountered not only the poetry of T. S. ELIOT and *Ulysses* (1922) by James JOYCE, but various movements of MODERNISM that were pouring in from the continent.

N.'s first book was a collection of his English poems entitled *Spectrum*, published in London in 1925. Back in Japan with his newlywed British wife, N. became professor of literature at Keiō, teaching Old and Middle English, history of English literature, and lingustics. N. soon attracted poets and intellectuals interested in modernism and began to contribute poems and essays to modernist magazines. In 1929 N. published *Chōgenjitu shugi shiron* (1929; surrealist poetics), an influential collection of papers exploring and reexamining the notion of surrealist poetry. In this book N. did not merely introduce SURREALISM but tenaciously pursued the notion of poetry itself by tracing the surrealist rupture of images through the history of Western poetry since antiquity.

In 1933, at the age of thirty-nine, N. published his first collection of poems written in Japanese, albeit with a Latin title: *Ambarvalia* (1933; Ambarvalia). The poems collected in this volume proved to be truly ground-breaking in the history of modern Japanese poetry. The places evoked in the poems were not in Japan but somewhere in Europe—Greece, Rome, London, Paris—and time freely traveled between the ancient and modern worlds. Images and their surrealistic juxtapositions were clearly in the foreground, effectively eliminating any trace of the sentimentality that N. had despised in much of modern Japanese poetry. In sum, this work revolutionized the concept as well as the language

of modern Japanese poetry by boldly incorporating a language of translation.

The luminous modernist language of *Ambarvalia* all but disappears in his second collection of Japanese poems, *Tabibito kaerazu* (1947; no traveler returns), published after a long silence precipitated by World War II. Many regard this work as N.'s return to Eastern poetics with the sentiment of *mujō* (transience) at its core. Not only the tone set by the sentiment of loneliness and transience but also the quasi classical language of the poem suggests a return to tradition. It is divided into one hundred and sixty-eight sections of varying length—from a single word to over forty lines—forming a loosely orchestrated whole that somehow resembles a *renga* (Japanese linked verse) sequence. However, the compelling beauty evoked by the entire poem does not simply come from N.'s nostalgic return to Japanese aesthetics but from his inimitable employment of repetitions, complex intertextuality, sudden imagistic and linguistic leaps, humor, and from his profound sense of lyricism that is simultaneously earthly and heavenly.

With his next collection, *Kindai no gūwa* (1953; modern fables), N.'s poetry comes to maturity. From the mode set by this work, all his subsequent poetic works do not diverge significantly except that his later works become increasingly lengthy. In this work one senses his unique, if not chaotic, fusion of opposing elements—frivolous and serious discourses, East and West, modern and ancient worlds, concrete images and abstract concepts—being encased in a most deftly crafted enclosure that is neither purely lyrical nor discursive.

With his keen interest in Joyce's linguistic experimentation, N.'s later works begin to resemble the polyglot text of *Finnegans Wake* (1939), though N.'s central tone of mujō never disappears in his freewheeling linguistic play. In the years between the age of sixty and his death at the age of eighty-eight, N.'s poetic production increased to an astonishing magnitude: ten volumes of poetry expanding over about one thousand pages. His text flowed on as a stream of consciousness, incorporating incessant insertions of allusions, of images of loneliness and eternity.

N. was also well known for his translations of works of such writers as Joyce, Eliot, D. H. LAWRENCE, Stéphane Mallarmé (1842–1898), Shakespeare, and Chaucer. His erudition in world literature from antiquity to modern and in linguistics was lengendary. He was awarded a doctorate in philosophy for his dissertation *Kodai bungaku josetsu* (1948; an introduction to ancient literature) from Keiō University.

After Hagiwara SAKUTARO, to whom N. admitted indebtedness, N. commanded an uncontested position as the most respected leader of modern Japanese poetry. N.'s influence on the younger generation of poets is enormous. N. showed them the possibility of a poetry that is first and foremost a linguistic construct free from sentimentality. Yet the uniqueness of his poetic world remains unchallenged. Nurtured by his formidable learning, N.'s poetry brought an unprecedented intellectual and intertextual depth to modern Japanese poetry. At the same time, his clear imaging of often banal objects and voices only strengthened his distinctive lyricism.

FURTHER WORKS: *Dai san no shinwa* (1956); *Ushinawareta toki* (1960); *Hōjō no megami* (1962); *Eterunitasu* (1962); *Hōseki no nemuri* (1963); *Raiki* (1967); *Jōka* (1969); *Rokumon* (1970); *Jinrui* (1979); *N. J. zenshū* (12 vols., 1982–1983). FURTHER WORKS IN ENGLISH: *Gen'ei: Selected Poems of N. J.* (1991); *The Poetry and Poetics of N. J.* (1993)

BIBLIOGRAPHY: Keene, D., *Dawn to the West: Japanese Literature of the Modern Era* (1984), Vol. 2: 323–35; Hirata, H., "Return or No-Return: N.'s Postmodernist Appropriation of Literary History, East and West," in Dissanayake, W. and Bradbury, S., eds., *Literary History, Narrative, and Culture* (1989): 122–31; Claremont, Y., "A Turning Point in N. J.'s Poetic Career," *The Journal of Oriental Society of Australia* (1990): 21–35

—HOSEA HIRATA

DER NISTER

(pseud. [Yiddish, "the concealed one"] of Pinkhes Kahanovitsh) Yiddish novelist and short-story writer, b. 1 Nov. 1884, Berdichev, Ukraine; d. 4 June 1950, a labor-camp hospital, U.S.S.R.

N. received a traditional Jewish education but also read widely in Russian. His spiritual and literary development was greatly influenced by his older brother, a Bratzlaver Hasid, who is reflected in the character of Luzi in N.'s magnum opus the novel *Di mishpokhe Mashber* (2 vols., 1939, 1948; the Mashber family). His first book, *Gedanken un motivn* (1907; thoughts and motifs), a collection of short poetic prose pieces, contains the universal themes that recur in his later works: man's divine-satanic duality, the eternal contradiction between aspiration and reality, and the ebb and flow of human emotion. *Hekher fun der erd* (1910; higher than the earth) represents an attempt to write modern Kabbalistic tales.

N. left Soviet Russia in 1921 for Berlin, where he published *Gedakht* (2 vols., 1922–23; imagined), the first collection of his visionary and fantastic tales. He revived the Hasidic symbolic tale created by Rabbi Nachman of Bratzlav (1772–1811) and developed a very distinctive style in Yiddish literature, one synthesizing the Jewish mystical tradition with world mythology. Influenced by Russian SYMBOLISM, N. integrated its characteristic symbols, verb inversions, and lyrical effects into his Yiddish writing. The hypnotic rhythms of his long sentences and their special musicality, his archaic diction and the repeated use of "and" demand and hold the reader's attention and usher him into a surrealistic atmosphere.

N. returned to the Soviet Union in 1926 and contributed to those publications still open to "fellow-traveling" writers. He also produced works for children and translations into Yiddish, literary activities he had begun during his residence in Kiev (1918–20). With the triumph of the "proletarian" critics in 1929, his work was violently condemned. He ceased publishing for a time. His last symbolist story, the complex "Unter a ployt" (1929; "Under a Fence," 1977), is both a concealed protest against regimentation of the arts and a tortured self-accusation for abandoning his symbolist art.

N. subsequently conceived a literary stratagem to rescue his artistic conscience as well as his existence as a Soviet writer. His family saga, *Di mishpokhe Mashber*, appeared on the surface to comply with the tenets of realism but it still served the author's intimate aesthetic, philosophical, and Jewish national purposes. It absorbed much from his symbolist period. This novel, perhaps the greatest work of Soviet-Yiddish prose, was conceived as the portrait of a traditional society in dissolution: N. intended to depict eastern European Jewry from the 1870s to the Russian Revolution. The two published volumes (the third may exist in manuscript),

however, cover less than a year of the 1870s in the most Jewish town of the Ukraine, Berdichev. The depiction of Jewish life, particularly of the Bratzlaver Hasidim, is deeply sympathetic rather than critical. The novel's chief protagonists are the same anguished seekers found in the earlier tales.

N. perished in the liquidation of Yiddish writers following the suppression of Jewish cultural life in the Soviet Union in 1948.

FURTHER WORKS: *Gezang un gebet* (1912); *Mayselekh in ferzn* (1918); *A bove-mayse; oder, Di mayse mit di melokhim* (1921); *Motivn* (1922); *Fun mayne giter* (1929); *Dray hoyptshtet* (1934); *Karbones* (1943); *Der zeyde mitn eynikl* (1943); *Heshl Ansheles* (1943); *Inem okupirtn Polyn* (1945); *Dersteylungen un eseyen* (1957)

BIBLIOGRAPHY: Shmeruk, K., "D. N.'s 'Under a Fence': Tribulations of a Soviet Yiddish Symbolist," in Weinreich, U., ed., *The Field of Yiddish: Studies in Language, Folklore and Literature, Second Collection* (1965): 263–87; Madison, C. A., *Yiddish Literature: Its Scope and Major Writers* (1968): 415–23; Liptzin, S., *A History of Yiddish Literature* (1972): 199–203; Shmeruk, C., "Yiddish Literature in the U.S.S.R.," in Kochan. L., ed., *The Jews in Soviet Russia since 1917* (1978): 242–80

—EUGENE ORENSTEIN

NIZAN, Paul

French novelist and essayist, b. 7 Feb. 1905, Tours; d. 23 May 1940, Saint-Omer

The son of a middle-class mother and of a father who had worked his way up from the proletariat, N., according to his friend Jean-Paul SARTRE, may have lived out this class conflict all of his short life. The two were classmates at secondary school and at the École Normale Supérieure in Paris, where N. excelled in philosophy. He flirted briefly with fascism and religion, but soon gravitated to the Communist Party, where he remained until he resigned in the wake of the Hitler-Stalin Pact in 1939. N. was killed by a stray bullet early in World War II.

A voyage to Aden in 1926 resulted in his first book, *Aden-Arabie* (1931; *Aden-Arabie*, 1968), an account of his youthful flight to the East that turns into a bitter attack on European capitalism. This was followed by *Les chiens de garde* (1932; *The Watchdogs*, 1971), a polemic in which he argued that philosophy as such does not exist, only philosophies as expressions of a class or an age.

Antoine Bloyé (1933; *Antoine Bloyé*, 1973), the story of a laborer who rises to the middle class only to discover the emptiness of his life, is a rare example of a successful proletarian novel. Although written from a Marxist perspective, it does not view existence as determined solely by economic considerations; the unconscious and its dreams, religion, and the libido play their roles as well. *Le cheval de Troie* (1935; *The Trojan Horse*, 1975) is a political novel, the account of an attempt to organize the workers of a provincial town. Although it rises above the stereotypical strategies of SOCIALIST REALISM, the novel was not well received.

La conspiration (1938; the conspiracy) better illustrates N.'s strengths. It is an ironic but sobering look at the follies of intellectual youth who act out their inarticulate rebellion against family and society in irresponsible ways. Thanks in part to the ambiguity of its point of view, it becomes as much a novel about the rites of passage into modern capitalist society as it is a plot of passwords and betrayal and an indictment of the void at the heart of bourgeois life.

N.'s brief career disproves the notion held by some critics that commitment to an ideology makes it impossible to write well. His books are being republished and read again today, after a period of oblivion.

FURTHER WORKS: *Les matérialistes de l'antiquité* (1936); *Chronique de septembre* (1939); *P. N., intellectuel communiste* (1967); *Pour une nouvelle culture* (1971)

BIBLIOGRAPHY: Sartre, J. -P., *Situations* (1965): 115–73; Ginsbourg, A., *P. N.* (1966); Lcincr, J., *Le destin littéraire de P. N. et ses étapes successives* (1970); Redfern, W. D., *P. N.: Committed Literature in a Conspiratorial World* (1972); Nizan, H., and A. Cohen-Solal, *P. N., communiste impossible* (1980); Ory, P., *N.: Destin d'un révolté* (1980); Suleiman, S. R., "The Structure of Confrontation: N., Barrès, Malraux," *MLN*, 95 (1980): 938–67

—RANDOLPH RUNYON

NOONUCCAL, Oodgeroo

(pseud. of Kath Walker) Australian poet and storyteller, b. 3 Nov. 1920, Minjerriba (North Stradbroke Island) Queensland; d. 16 Sept. 1992, Moongalba

Brought up in the traditional manner on an island off the southern coast of Queensland, N. (then known as Kath Walker—she changed her name in 1988 as a protest against Australian bicentennial celebrations) was initiated into the European world via a primary school education, and subsequently, after raising her two children alone, a secretarial course. Although proficient in both cultures, her primary identity was as an Aboriginal, and from an early age, she was active in civil liberties groups (including the Communist Party of Australia). She was especially active in support of the referendum of 1967, which delivered to Aborigines the suffrage that, in those states where it had existed, had been eradicated under the Australian Constitution in 1901, and also in the politics of land rights and conservation. She also served on a variety of arts and social services boards, including the Federal Council for the Advancement of Aborigines and Torres Strait Islanders and the Aboriginal Advancement League, to press for the civil rights of her people. She established a school, Moongalba, for the advancement of her people, and enjoyed a significant national and international reputation as an assertive and charismatic artist and black activist. As the first poet of her race to be published in English, she has been inspirational to a younger generation of writers.

In a 1950s and 1960s Australia that was comparatively wealthy but very complacent and content, and fearful of communism, N.'s satiric and polemical verse was a shock. She speaks plainly and bluntly about her people's economic mistreatment in poems like

"Aboriginal Charter of Rights" from *We Are Going* (1964). This poem is notable for its firm and seemingly confident assertion of rights that did not constitutionally exist at that point. She implicitly attacks the practice of Christianity in Australia and charges government and welfare with bureaucratic paternalism and with relegating her culture to the margins and to a permanent underclass. To white Australia at the time, it was seditious, and certainly dangerously socialist in tone. It was easy for the formalist aesthetes of the academic establishment of the day to denigrate her poetry as propagandist and regressive in its craft, as the influence of an older bush balladry was clearly evident in it. This manifesto and other poems in the same vein made a plea for human rights and Christian rights to be extended to Aborigines, and pointed to a long list of cultural practices of a discriminatory kind. At times her poetry works more obliquely, as in her much anthologized poem, "We Are Going," which nostalgically contrasts a demoralized present with an implied precontact golden age when the tribes are represented as having been in harmony and identity with every feature of their environment. In poems like "No More Boomerang" she is laconically satiric about the "advances" of white civilization, which are contrasted unfavorably with traditional values. Many poems lament the passing forever of a lifestyle and values that she perceives to be in the best interests ecologically of the land she loves and of all Australians.

N.'s poetry has always been controversial, and her critics have sometimes come from her own people. Mudrooroo, the leading black-identified intellectual of his generation, is appreciatively critical of her work, viewing her less as a poet than as a polemicist (he invents the term "poetemics" for her work), and points out that the genres she uses are those internalized as a result of her white education. However, he urges that her use of simple metres and diction are part of her enduring appeal to both her own people and to a more numerous readership of educable white readers. Other critics, informed by postcolonial theory, have pointed to whether the critical frameworks of the mainstream are appropriately applied to her work, and cite features of the verse that are not visible to white readers entailing the use of Aboriginal forms of rhetoric. Some point to the performance dimension of her art and its roots in mythic ritual and political oratory.

Although she was committed to exposing the dispossession of Aboriginal society by the white "invaders," she avoided the role of victim and worked actively and resistantly to build Aboriginal pride, identity, and solidarity. An important aspect of her educational program was her commitment to writing down stories of her almost traditional growing up at Minjerriba, and recovering and illustrating—in a delicate and accomplished traditional manner—the myths and stories of her own people and place for a younger generation of both black and white readers.

She has been awarded honorary doctorates by Griffith and Macquarie Universities and the Queensland University of Technology. In 1967 she won the Jessie Lichfield Award for Literature, and in 1977 the Fellowship of Australian Writers Patricia Weickhardt Award and the Mary Gilmore Award. Her work has the rare distinction in Australia of being continually reprinted and of having struck a note of optimistic hope for a self-respecting Aboriginality that remains potent decades later.

FURTHER WORKS: *The Dawn is at Hand* (1966); *My People: A Kath Walker Collection* (1970); *Stradbroke Dreamtime* (1972; rev.

ed., 1993); *Father Sky and Mother Earth* (1981); *Little Fella: Poems by Kath Walker* (1987); *Kath Walker in China* (1988); *The Rainbow Serpent: O. N. and Kabul Oodgeroo Noonuccal* (1990); *My People: Oodgeroo* (1990); *Shoemaker* (1994)

BIBLIOGRAPHY: Beier, U., ed., *Quandamooka: The Art of Kath Walker* (1985); Narogin, M., *Writing from the Fringe* (1990); Knudsen, E. R., "Fringe Finds Focus: Developments and Strategies in Aboriginal Writing in English," in Capone, G., B. Clunies-Ross, and W. Senn, eds., *European Perspectives: Contemporary Essays on Australian Literature* (1991); Indyk, I., "Assimilation or Appropriation: Uses of European Literary Forms in Black Australian Writing," *ALS*, 15 (1992): 249-60; Sykes, R., *Murawina: Australian Women of High Achievement* (1993); Shoemaker, A., ed., *O.: A Tribute* (1994); Cochrane, K., with a contribution by J. Wright, *O.* (1994)

—FRANCES DEVLIN GLASS

NOOTEBOOM, Cees

Dutch novelist, poet, and short-story writer, b. 13 July 1933, The Hague

N. received his education at convent schools in the south of the Netherlands. Although he lives in Amsterdam, he has always spent large parts of the year traveling abroad. This is reflected in his travel stories, and many of his novels are set in foreign countries. Since 1967 he has been employed as the editor of the travel and poetry sections of *Avenue*, one of Holland's main magazines, for which he has also translated works by a number of foreign poets.

Poetry forms an important part of N.'s oeuvre. Although his poetry debut, *De doden zoeken een huis* (1956; the dead are looking for a house), is, stylistically, not as strong as his later poems, it already contains some of the main themes of his later work: time and, related to that, death. There has been a definite development in his poetical style; his poetry has become much more sober, notably in the volume *Gesloten gedichten* (1964; closed poems). In his work, time is seen as an extension of death, while death is the result of time. The rhythm of time, expressed in the natural order of day/ night and change of seasons is connected with death and human mortality. In this, the poet is an observer; he does not express reality by his presence, but by his observations.

The same themes can be recognized in N.'s novels. He made his literary debut with the novel *Philip en de anderen* (1955; *Philip and the Others*, 1990), for which he was awarded the Anne Frank Prize (1957). It is the poetic account of a journey during which the main character explores the world and his inner self. The theme of time, so important in his later work, is already present. The novel *Rituelen* (1980; *Rituals*, 1983), for which he was given the Mobil Oil Pegasus Prize (1982), finally brought him deserved recognition. Its complex chronological structure, however, as well as its philosophical ideas, does not make it an easily accessible novel. The central themes of time and death are, again, all-important, while the title refers to the means by which the characters try to get a grasp on chaos and time. The rituals by which people live denote a higher order, a continuity that transcends ordinary lives. In *Een lied*

van schijn en wezen (1981; *A Song of Truth and Semblance*, 1984) N. deals with another major theme in his work, the relationship between the author and his created characters, between reality (time) and semblance (the world). If, N. wonders, the world is semblance only, why add to it something that is even more semblance, namely the world created by the author? The novel *In Nederland* (1984; *In the Dutch Mountains*, 1987), which was awarded the Multatuli Prize (1985), is set in a fictive Holland, which stretches from the north to the south of Europe. The story is told by a foreigner, an outsider, which produces a detachment in perspective also found in much of N.'s other work.

A large part of N.'s total oeuvre consists of travel literature. N. developed the genre in Dutch literature and is its undisputed master. N. has traveled extensively, and his stories are often very personal accounts of exotic and less faraway places, as in *Een avond in Isfahan* (1978; an evening in Isfahan). He mixes his travel stories with a large dose of history, notably in *Berlijnse notities* (1990; notes of Berlin).

Many of the central themes of his work are recurrent in all genres in which he has written. Because his work is often very philosophical, and his intricate play with time and space make his books not easily approachable, he is not read by the general public. However, his significance for Dutch literature is apparent. He cannot be classified under any particular literary movement, which contributes to making his work timeless.

FURTHER WORKS: *De verliefde gevangene* (1958); *De zwanen van de Theems* (1958); *Koude gedichten* (1959); *Het zwarte gedicht* (1960); *De koning is dood* (1961); *De ridder is gestorven* (1963); *Een middag in Bruay* (1963); *Een nacht in Tunesie* (1965); *Een ochtend in Bahia* (1968); *De Parijse beroerte* (1968); *Gemaakte gedichten* (1970); *Bitter Bolivia/Maanland Mali* (1971); *Open als een schelp, dicht als een steen* (1978); *Nooit gebouwd Nederland* (1980); *Voorbije passages* (1981); *Mokusei!* (1982); *Gyges en Kandaules* (1982); *Aas* (1982); *Waar je gevallen bent, blijf je* (1983); *Vuurtijd, ijstijd* (1984); *De zucht naar het Westen* (1985); *De brief* (1988); *Het gezicht van het oog* (1989); *De wereld een reiziger* (1989); *Het volgende verhaal* (1991)

—WIJNIE E. DE GROOT

NORDBRANDT, Henrik

Danish poet, b. 21 Mar. 1945, Frederiksberg/Copenhagen

At the University of Copenhagen N. has studied—independently—sinology since 1966, Turkish since 1969 (he has adapted Turkish poems and tales into Danish), and Arabic since 1975. Since his first journey to Greece in 1967, he has spent most of his life abroad, particularly in Asia Minor. A selection of articles and essays from N.'s stay here has been published as *Breve fra en ottoman* (1978; letters from an ottoman). N. earns a living as a free-lance journalist with various Danish newspapers and as a producer for Radio Denmark. He has received numerous awards, among them the Literature Prize of the Danish Academy in 1980.

The longing for greater openness than modern, rationalist civilization can provide and an attempt to dispel human isolation caused by a sense of inconstancy and absence even when close to natural objects or human beings has been a general theme in N.'s writing since his debut collection, *Digte* (1966; poems). The volume is dominated by fragmented modernist imagery conveying feelings of death and decay. Nevertheless, already in this volume N. is successful in overcoming any stereotype of modernist poetry by merging acute observations with a romantic longing triggered by a sense of loss and instability, which is expressed in stanzas of exquisite beauty. The style is simplified, and the poetic technique further refined in *Miniaturer* (1967; miniatures). The metaphoric compactness—still retaining a penchant for the decadent—is replaced by sinuous musical sequences frequently around one static nucleus.

With the volume *Syvsoverne* (1969; the sluggards) the worship of beauty is replaced by an increased awareness of total emptiness and a focusing on the poet's painful experience of loneliness even amidst a throng of other people, a sense of isolation that reaches a climax in the collection *Opbrud of ankomster* (1974; departures and arrivals). The previous nervousness has been replaced by a simple yet sonorous tone, the abrupt verses by lingering garlandlike structures.

Whereas nature and the seasonal changes are thoroughly integrated in N.'s earlier collections, the experience of love forces itself to the foreground as a—at least momentary—way out of the poet's present, desolate state, and a series of passionate, albeit melancholy love poems dominate the two next volumes, *Ode til blæksprutten* (1975; de to the octopus) and *Glas* (1976; glass). Together the three volumes from 1974 to 1976 constitute a Mediterranean trilogy with nature still present-Greek islands and Turkish landscapes—but only as secondary points of orientation.

A philosophical and metaphysical tone becomes noticeable in the small but crucial collection entitled *Guds has* (1977; *God's House*, 1979), describing the poet's attempt at holding on to the flighty but precious moments of happiness amidst restlessness, to establish meaning in life at least for a time. But already in *Istid* (1977; ice age) from the same year and the volume *Spøgelseslege* (1979; ghost games), much of the weariness and desperation from the previous works are found again, but now they are expressed with classical calm, perhaps resignation, as well as humor.

An orientation toward current conditions is increasingly present in N.'s poetry, particularly in the volume *Istid*, with a series of topics from the alienating, technological reality of the Nordic welfare state. This orientation dominates the poems in *Forsvar for vinden under døren* (1980; defense for the wind under the door), focusing on a number of ecological themes. Thus N. confesses his reasons for leaving Denmark. In *Armenia* (1982; Armenia), which describes the genocide in Armenia in 1915, history is incorporated as a bogey of the destructive forces in humans. On the other hand, *84 digte* (1984; 84 poems) and, in particular, *Under mausolæet* (1987; under the mausoleum) mark, as the title of the latter volume indicates, a return to N.'s fascination with death and suffering on a more personal level. No direct cause is given, unless a subtle yet bitter reference to a finished love affair offers an indirect explanation.

Thus N. once again captures his favorite themes. Inspired by the 20th-c. Greek poetry of Constantine CAVAFY, and the medieval Turkish poetry of Ymus Emre, N. blends the concrete and the mystical, East and West, past and present. His oeuvre constitues a series of infinitely varied poems sustained by glowing sensuality, sometimes in the form of subtle philosophical speculation, sometimes as precise registrations of the external world, observations that are almost a rebellion against the worship of beauty in N.'s

poetry. External and internal are interwoven in a splendidly composed tapestry. It constitutes a romantic world, yet one of burning relevance that voices not only the poet's own destiny but also an all-encompassing, breath-taking attempt at reaching humankind as a whole.

N.'s evocative mastery of language and style is conspicuous already from his first book. With every new collection he has further consolidated his exceptional position or rather uniqueness as the most accomplished Danish poet of his generation. N. is a solitary figure in Danish lyrical poetry, alien to any relativity of values, to experiments in so-called "systemic" or "concrete" poetry, and to polemic and political attacks. As an indication of his status as an author, several selections of his poetry have already been issued, among them *Udvalgte digte* (1981; selected poems).

FURTHER WORKS: *Omgivelser* (1972); *Rosen fra Lesbos* (1979); *Finckelsteins blodige bazar* (1983); *Violinbyggernes by* (1985); *Håndens skælven i november* (1986); *Nissan flytter med* (1988); *Tifanfaya* (1990). FURTHER WORKS IN ENGLISH: *Selected Poems* (1978)

BIBLIOGRAPHY: Bredsdorff, T., *Med andre ord. Om H. N.'s roetiske sprog* (1996)

—SVEN HAKON ROSSEL

NORÉN, Lars

Swedish poet and dramatist, b. 9 Apr. 1944, Stockholm

Next to Göran Sonnevi (b. 1939), N. is the outstanding poet of his generation in Sweden. As a dramatist, he has been more successful internationally than any other Swede except August STRINDBERG. Raised in the southernmost part of Sweden, N. has spent most of his mature life in Stockholm, where he still lives.

Starting out as a poet already in 1963, at the age of nineteen, N. employs a verbose, psychedelic kind of poetry in early collections like *Encyklopedi* (1966; encyclopedia) and *Stupor* (1968; stupor), where hallucinatory poems reflect a chaotic, schizophrenic experience of life. Adhering to a modernistic tradition represented by poets like Rainer Maria RILKE, Paul CELAN, and Hölderlin, N.'s visionary talent and pregnant use of imagery characterize collections like *Revolver* (1969; revolver), *Order* (1978; order), and *Hjärta i hjärta* (1980; heart in heart). N.'s tendency to break through emotional barriers by means of "inflamed" imagery and shock effects is as apparent as his ability to create moods of an abstract, lucid beauty.

As a dramatist, N. is well known, especially in northern Europe. He has written some thirty plays, almost all of them after 1980. After a cool reception of the Renaissance drama *Fursteslickaren* (1973; the prince licker), N. achieved his first success as a dramatist with *Modet att döda* (1980; the courage to kill), depicting a traumatic oedipal parent-child relationship, a recurring theme in N.'s dramatic work.

The breakthrough came in 1982 with the publication of *Natten är dagens mor* (the night is mother of the day), where N.'s black humor helped to alleviate the play of its claustrophobic impact. (In 1984 an English version of the play, entitled *Night Is Mother to the Day*, was performed at the Yale Repertory Theatre in New Haven,

Connecticut.) Being the first part of what may be seen as a family trilogy, the play was followed by *Kaos är granne med Gud* (1982; chaos is the neighbor of God), while the concluding part is called simply *Stillheten* (1986; the stillness). Like Eugene O'NEILL's *Long Day's Journey into Night*—a drama that has had a tremendous impact on him—N.'s family trilogy is highly autobiographical.

In the six-hour drama *Nattvarden* (1985; the communion) two brothers demonstrate their contrasting attitudes to their recently dead mother, present on the stage in the form of an urn, while in *Höst och vinter* (1989; autumn and winter), which opened in Copenhagen, the family interaction concerns two daughters and their parents. *Hebriana* (1989; Hebriana), first presented in the Hague, and *Endagsvarelser* (1990; one-day creatures), which had its premiere in Kassel, Germany, are thematically related. Both plays deal with representatives of a middle-aged "lost generation," caught between their own hopeful past (the spring of 1968) and the darkening future.

N.'s play entitled *Och geoss skuggorna* (1991; and grant us the shadows) opened in Oslo as *En dag längre än livet* (a day longer than life). It is a play about Eugene O'Neill, his third wife, and his two sons. Set in the living room of the O'Neills on a grim October day in 1949 (O'Neill's sixty-first birthday) from morning to dusk, the play intentionally mirrors *Long Day's Journey into Night*, demonstrating how the family interaction described in that play (set in 1912) is ironically and fatefully repeated thirty-seven years later. As a semidocumentary "sequel play" to O'Neill's autobiographical masterpiece, *Och ge oss skuggorna* is probably unique in world drama.

While N.'s earlier plays are family-oriented, his later plays demonstrate a growing concern for society at large. In *Löven i Vallombrosa* (perf. 1991; The leaves in Vallombrosa) and *Tiden är vårt hem* (perf. 1992; Time is our home), the spiritual discomfort of those living in a welfare state are voiced in Chekhovian polyphony.

In the "Dantean" *En sorts Hades* (1994; A kind of Hades), staged in 1996, and *Personkrets 3:1* (1997; personal circle 3:1), a six-hour play touring Sweden in 1997-98, N. has attracted, and shocked, large audiences with his "reports" about the outcasts in (Swedish) society.

N. has also written a number of radio plays. In recent years he has directed some of his own plays as well as plays by others.

Both as a poet and—especially—as a dramatist, N. has been astoundingly prolific. In his dramatic universe the unity of time and place has a thematic value, stressing the characters' ambivalent feeling that they are at once close to each other and imprisoned with one another. Confrontation is inevitable, separation—a key word with N.—necessary. As with O'Neill, the audience is asked to face the often strenuous interaction between the characters for a considerable time: four hours or more. Writing in a therapeutic era, N. depicts the "true" workings behind what is pretended. Roleplaying, projections, and double-bind mechanisms abound in his psychoanalytically inspired oeuvre, which demonstrates a marked ear for subtextual innuendos.

FURTHER WORKS: *Syrener, snö* (1963); *De verbala resterna av den bildprakt som förgår* (1964); *Biskötarna* (1970); *Solitära dikter* (1972); *Viltspeglar* (1972); *I den underjordiska himlen* (1972); *Kung Mej och andra dikter* (1973); *Dagliga och nattliga dikter* (1974); *Dagbok augusti-oktober 1975* (1976); *Nattarbete* (1976); *Den ofullbordade stjärnan* (1979); *Akt utan nåd* (1980); *Orestes* (1980); *En fruktansvärd lycka* (1981); *Underjordens leende* (1982); *Demoner* (1984); *Tre borgerliga kvartetter* (1992); *De döda pjäserna* (4 vols. 1995); *Radiopjäser 1971-1995* (1996)

BIBLIOGRAPHY: Algulin, I., *A History of Swedish Literature* (1989): 276–79, 280–82; Törnqvist, E., "Strindberg, O'Neill, N.: A Swedish-American Triangle," *The Eugene O'Neill Review*, 15, 1 (1991): 65–76

—EGIL TÖRNQVIST

NORTH CAUCASIAN LITERATURES

The languages of the Caucasus (exclusive of isolated Indo-European and Turkic areas) are usually classified by linguists in three groups: Southern (or Kartvelian, of which Georgian is the only written member). North-western (or Abkhaz-Adyghe, including also Abaza and Kabardian), and Northeastern (or Nakh-Daghestan; this large group comprises twenty-nine spoken languages, of which only Chechen, Ingush, Avar, Dargin, Lak, Lezgin, and Tabasaran have been accorded the status of literary languages).

Until the 20th c. the literary heritage of the North Caucasian peoples was composed almost exclusively of oral epics (the "Nart" cycles in particular among the Abkhaz, Adyghes, and Kabardians) and folklore of a highly imaginative type. Attempts at writing in several languages were made in an adapted Arabic alphabet, but these were minimal except in Daghestan, where literary works were composed as early as the 18th c. The late 19th c. and the early 20th witnessed a sudden development in written literature throughout most regions of the North Caucasus. In Daghestan the Dargin poet Sukur Kurban (1842–1922), the Lak poet Mallei (186?–190?) and the Avar poet Mahmud (1870–1919) may be considered the founders of their native belles-lettres. The Abkhaz national poet Dimitri Gulia (1874–1960) published his first work in 1912, effectively establishing the literary form of his language, which was given further impetus by the newspaper he began in 1919, *Apsny*, in which young Abkhaz writers obtained their first exposure. Bekmurza Pachev (1854–1936) published his work in Kabardian at the beginning of the 20th c., utilizing an alphabet of his own invention. One of the first dramas to be written in any North Caucasian language was *Makhadjiry* (1920; Makhadjiry), by the Abkhaz author Samson Chanba (1886–1937).

With the reconquest of the North Caucasus by the Russians in 1921, after a brief period of independence begun in 1918, the emerging generation of writers was, for the most part, constrained to utilize its talents to further the ends of communist propaganda. Despite the extraordinary difficulties of these first years of Soviet rule, a number of writers did manage to contribute works to their native literatures that avoided political saturation. Works by the Chechen writer Saidbek Baduev (1904–1943), for example, included a collection of stories, *Maccalla* (1925; hunger), a play, *Daj nizamoš* (1929; the law of the fathers), and a novel—the first in Chechen—*Petimat* (1930; Petimat), about the life of his mountain people. In Daghestan, a group of poets made their first appearance in print during the 1920s, among them the Avar Zagid Gadjiev (b. 1898), the Dargin Sagid Abdullaev (1903–1952), the Lak Mugutin Charinov (1893–1937), and the Lezgin Alibek Fatakhov (1910–1935). In Kabardian, an interesting play on folk themes from the heroic epics, *Korigot* (193?; Korigot), was written by P. Shekikhachev (1879–1937). During the 1930s many of the most talented and promising young writers were purged by Stalin and either executed or sent to labor camps, where the majority died. Among these were the gifted Adyghe poet Akhmet Khatkov (1901–1937), as well as Chanba, Fatakhov, Charinov, and Shekikhachev.

Little original work of literary value was produced during World War II, although Gulia's novel *Kamachich* (1940; Kamachich) achieved great success in Abkhazia. The Chechen and Ingush peoples were deported to Central Asia immediately after the war, suffering extremely high mortality; they were not permitted to return to the Caucasus until after Stalin's death. Since that time more creative literature has begun to appear throughout the North Caucasus, although ideological restrictions continue to be applied forcibly. In Chechen, Nadjmuddin Muzaev's (b. 1913) novels *Orgona tollosko* (1965; in the valley of the Orgun) and *Dogdoxara üpara* (1971; the power of wishes) are worthy of note. Although he has demonstrated unswerving subservience to the Party line in both his public statements and in his writing, the nonpolitical poems, sketches, and reminiscences of the Avar author Rasul Gamzatov (b. 1923) rank among the best literary productions of the North Caucasus and have achieved wide popularity throughout the Soviet Union.

BIBLIOGRAPHY: "The Literature and the Arts of Soviet Daghestan" (special issue), *SovL*, 10 (1980)

—LEONARD FOX

NORTHERN SOTHO LITERATURE

See South African Literature: In Pedi

NORWEGIAN LITERATURE

Norway began the 20th c. with a newly obtained independence and with literary bravura. The struggle for national identity, beginning with independence from Denmark in 1814, and culminating in the dissolution of the union with Sweden in 1905, had left the country free from foreign domination for the first time since the Middle Ages. The poets Henrik Wergeland (1808–1845) and Johann S. Welhaven (1807–1873) had extolled national ideals and goals; the novelists Jonas Lie (1833–1908) and Alexander Kielland (1849–1906) had critically examined Norwegian social structure; and the dramatists Bjørnstjerne Bjørnson (1832–1910) and Henrik Ibsen (1828–1906) had won international fame. By the 1890s Norway's literary output matched that of any other nation in quality.

As was true with their predecessors, modern Norwegian writers have been greatly influenced by their country's rugged landscape; the ancient granite mountains, fertile valleys, fjords, and sea coasts. Nature may sometimes symbolize romantic escape or danger, but it may also represent mystical and religious feelings, the possibilities of human development, and national identity.

Modern Norwegian literature often reflects a fierce desire for personal and political independence, which may range from defiant self-reliance to sensitive, considerate social consciousness. There is a long tradition of writing by women that describes the struggle of women for liberation and for equality with men. A sense of

history is also pervasive; the Viking times, the Middle Ages, the domination by the Hanseatic League and by Denmark, and the struggle for independence are common themes, as are disillusionment with modern industrialization and despair at war and at the growing alienation of modern man.

Norway has two languages: the dominant *bokmål* ("book language," formerly called, and still commonly referred to among its users as *riksmål*, "state language"), of Dano-Norwegian origin, which is somewhat more urban; and *nynorsk* ("new Norwegian," formerly known as *landsmål*, "rural language"), fashioned in the 19th c. by Ivar Aasen (1813–1896) and Aasmund Vinje (1818–1870) from various Norwegian dialects, which is centered more in the rural, "country interest." Compromises and spelling reforms have brought the languages closer together, until today both are truly Norwegian and representative.

Fiction

Outstanding among the new writers of fiction in the 1890s were Knut HAMSUN and Hans Kinck (1865–1926). Both eschewed the older generation, sought rural "truths," rejected themes from classical antiquity, neglected the church and other traditional cultural mores, worshiped life in a Nietzschean sense, and opposed enveloping materialism. As part of general European neoromanticism, they embraced art for art's sake as opposed to social criticism, and sought to describe inner, psychological life. Kinck was the more intellectual, with a tendency to preach and to solve conflicts, while Hamsun was a consummate story teller and ironic stylist. Hamsun never forsook his aristocratic, antidemocratic ideas that led him to criticize America and the West and to remain spiritually close to Germany, even to the extent of supporting Nazism. In the novels *Pan* (1894; *Pan*, 1920), and *Markens grøde* (1917; *Growth of the Soil*, 1920) he produced powerful, almost mythical characters who made their own worlds outside society.

Other novelists who emerged in the 1890s whose productive careers lasted well into the 20th c. were Peter Egge (1869–1959), Johan BOJER, and Gabriel Scott (1874–1958). Egge wrote stories about his native region of Trøndelag, his best work being *Hansine Solstad* (1925; *Hansine Solstad*, 1929), a novel portraying a working woman struggling to survive while resisting corruption. Bojer described the Trøndelag crofter fishermen in *Den siste Viking* (1921; *The Last of the Vikings*, 1923), one of the finest Norwegian novels of the sea. Scott, more poetic and spiritual, is best known for *Jernbyrden* (1915; *The Ordeal*, 1935), which has been compared to Hamsun's *Markens grøde*.

By the turn of the century, the symbolic and neoromantic movements were giving way before the new realism. In the vanguard were four female authors whose themes were the struggles of women for emancipation and emotional, intellectual, and spiritual independence: Ragnhild Hølsen (1875–1908), Nini Roll Anker (1873–1942), Barbra Ring (1870–1955), and Regine Normann (1867–1939). Anker's *Det svake kjøn* (1915; the weak sex), is typical. The early works of Sigrid UNDSET dealt with similar themes, but gradually her interest in detail and historical accuracy led her to studies of the sagas, folklore, and the Norwegian Middle Ages. The result was *Kristin Lavransdatter* (3 vols., 1920–22; *Kristin Lavransdatter*, 3 vols., 1923–27), regarded by many as the greatest novel in Norwegian. Set in the 13th c. and containing finely drawn characters, the novel follows the relationship of

Kristin to her father and her husband until her martyrdom during the Black Death epidemic; psychologically compelling are the heroine's struggles between the urge to obedience and the desire for happiness, between the earthly and the spiritual.

Contemporary with Undset were Olav DUUN, Kristofer UPPDAL, and Johan FALKBERGET, all of humble Trøndelag origin, a background pervasive in their works. Uppdal's *Dansen gjennom skuggeheiman* (10 vols., 1911–24; the dance through the realm of the shadows) treats the transformation of farmers into factory workers and the rise of the labor unions. Falkberget's novels deal mostly with the exploited miners of his native Røros. Many think of Duun as the giant of 20th-c. Norwegian literature. His *Juvikfolke* (6 vols., 1918–23; *The People of Juvik*, 6 vols., 1930–35) covers four hundred years but concentrates on the period from 1814 to the start of the industrial era in Norway in the early 20th c. It portrays the moral development of a family from blind, ruthless individualism to ethical and social responsibility.

Although World War I did not have a strong psychological effect on Norway, there was still some weakened faith in the future, increasing social criticism, and growing fear of industrialization and urbanization. During the 1920s the socialist journal *Mot dag*, edited by Sigurd HOEL and Erling Falk (1887–1940), attracted many excellent writers attuned to social and psychological themes, as did the more conservative *Vor verden* under Ronald FANGEN. A great stimulus to Norwegian writing and understanding was *Den gule serie*, edited by Hoel, whose appearance in 1929 first brought to Norway translations of Franz KAFKA, François MAURIAC, Graham GREENE, William FAULKNER, Ernest HEMINGWAY, and other major foreign writers.

In the 1930s, Hoel's works and those of Tarjei VESAAS began to enjoy wide acceptance. At the same time, several new novelists came into their own, among them Cora Sandel (1880–1974), Inge Krokann (1893–1962), and Aksel SANDEMOSE. In addition to his essays, criticism, and editing, Hoel wrote sensitive, thoughtful novels influenced by FREUD and Kafka, and reflecting disenchantment with the world. Typical are his novel of childhood, *Veien til verdens ende* (1933; the road to the end of the world), and of psychoanalysis, *Fjorten dager før frostnettene* (1935; fourteen days before the frosty nights). Sandel's ironic novels about the talented and ambitious Alberte follow the heroine from a cruel and insensitive home milieu to Paris, where she flowers as an artist. Sandemose is an impressive story teller, at best in his psychological analysis of a criminal's childhood in *En flyktning krysser sitt spor* (1933; *A Fugitive Crosses His Tracks*, 1936) and of an amoral manipulator of people in *Det svundne er en drøm* (1946; the past is a dream). Krokann's historical novels set in Oppdal reflect the efforts of native leaders to unify their people against foreign oppression. Vesaas is a lyrical, symbolic writer who celebrates the human need for compassionate communication. A fine example is *Is-slottet* (1963; *The Ice Palace*, 1966), a tender story of friendship between two young girls.

With the exception of Hamsun and a handful of others, the Norwegian literary world joined in the fight against Nazism. After the war, bookstalls were flooded with versions of what had happened. From concentration camps came two books of high literary quality, Odd Nansen's (1901–1973) secret diary of Grini and Sachsenhausen, *Fra dag til dag* (1946; *From Day to Day*, 1949), and Petter Moen's (1901–1944) posthumously published *Dagbok* (1949; *Diary*, 1951), written for the most part in solitary confinement. Sigurd Evensmo's (b. 1912) war novels, which deal

with the struggle for integrity and loyalty in the face of torture, can be read as social history, while Kåre HOLT's highly successful *Det store veiskillet* (1949; at the crossroads) analyzes the possible courses open to young Norwegians during the war, emphasizing decision and responsibility.

The 1950s were years of experimentation, exemplified by the masterful short stories of Vesaas, Nils Johan Rud (1908–1993), and particularly Johan BORGEN. Finn CARLING and Solveig CHRISTOV investigated the moral and psychological implications of dreams, while Finn Bjørnseth (1924–1973) wrote of the ethical and mythical components of physical love. Agnar Mykle's (1915–1994) novel *Sangen om den røde rubin* (1956; song of the red ruby) contained such explicit sexuality that he was tried on charges of pornography, although he was acquitted. Jens BJØRNEBOE investigated the misuse of power in education, medicine, law, and government.

In 1964 Norwegian literature received a new stimulus from a ruling by the Norwegian Cultural Council that insured a minimum sale for all new Norwegian belles lettres. A new generation without memories of the Depression and of World War II began to write on the issues of the day: imperialism, under-developed countries, starvation, environmental pollution, women's liberation, and Vietnam. Among those who are of a revolutionary bent are Dag SOLSTAD, Tor Obrestad (b. 1938), and Espen Haavardsholm (b. 1945). Solstad's novels examine late-capitalistic man, confused and caught by social forces, struggling toward socialism. Obrestad's *Sauda! Streik!* (1972; Sauda! strike!), a fictional-documentary account of the smelting plant strike in Sauda in 1970, draws lessons from the writings of Lenin. Haavardsholm's stories and essays involve the alienated individual who is exploited by the power structure.

Many contemporary writers, such as Mona Lyngar (1944–1993), Gunnar Lunde (b. 1944), and Øystein Lønn (b. 1936), regard modern alienation as something absurd, but they offer no political solutions. Alfred Hauge (1915–1986) seeks Christian EXISTENTIALIST answers for people in crisis who must choose the right path to salvation. In literature written about women by women, Bjørg Vik (b. 1935), Karin Bang (b. 1928), and Bergljot Hobæk Haff (b. 1925) stand out in their descriptions of love, marriage, exploitation, and victimization. Vik's *Elsi Lund* (1993; Elsi Lund), offers an excellent study of the sexual awakening of young girls. In *Dinas bok* (1989; Dina's Book), Herbjørg Wassmo (b. 1942) portrays a powerful, complicated, and unconventional woman, who attains her goals but also suffers from feelings of guilt. Liv Køltzow (b. 1945) shows the power of women when they become politically active in *Hvem bestemmer over Bjørg og Unni?* (1972; Who Decides What Happens to Bjørg and Unni?).

Despite the new trends, many excellent writers stay closer to traditional writing. Both Finn Alnæs (1932–1991) and Knud Faldbakken (b. 1941), for instance, describe modern people who are guided by more conventional goals in ambition and love. Faldbakken's *Til verdens ende* (1992; To the End of the Earth) follows Columbus's exciting voyage through the eyes of a crew member.

Terje Stigen (b. 1922) continues his prolific production of novels dealing with World War II and guilt. *Bak våre masker* (1983; Behind Our Masks) involves the leading character in a painful course of self-discovery. Similarly, in Erlan Kiøsterud's (b. 1922) *Det brente språket* (1988; The Burned Language), a couple gradually come to terms with the horrors they have experienced in the war.

Kjartan Fløgstad (b. 1944) has written with sympathy, understanding and humor about the working classes and against political trickery and corruption. *Dalen Portland* (1977; The Portland Valley) and *Kniven på strupen* (1992; The Knife in the Throat), written in picaresque style, satirize contemporary Norwegian society.

Jostein Gadder's (b. 1952) *Sofies Verden* (1991; Sofie's World), and immensely popular novel about childhood and youth, has sold over two million copies worldwide.

Drama

At the beginning of the 20th c., permanent, successful theaters were established in Oslo, Bergen, Trondheim, and Stavanger, providing opportunity for native dramatists. Several writers from other fields tried their hands at drama with varying success. Knut Hamsun's plays have a lyrical tone; *Munken Vendt* (1902; Monk Vendt) owes much to Ibsen's *Peer Gynt* in its excellent treatment of the wanderer motif. Technical difficulties often hindered the production of Hans Kinck's excellent dramas. Peter Egge, Nils Collett Vogt (1864–1937), and Nils Kjær (1870–1924), produced good psychological plays.

Of paramount importance before World War I was Gunnar Heiberg (1857–1929), who continued the psychological, moral, and political problem drama set in a middle-class milieu that Ibsen had begun. Heiberg's thirteen plays almost all shock either by their eroticism or their social criticism. In *Kjærlighetens tragedie* (1904; *The Tragedy of Love*, 1921), the heroine kills herself in despair of attaining unremitting carnal satisfaction, while the hero of *Jeg vil verge mit land* (1912; I will defend my country) ends his life in dissappointment over the concessions made by Norway to Sweden in 1905.

Between the wars, Helge Krog (1889–1962) followed the Ibsen-Heiberg tradition with logical, dialectical attacks on society reminiscent of Bernard Shaw. His plays often involve erotic conflicts. In *Underveis* (1931; *On the Way*, 1939) and *Opbrudd* (1936; *Break-Up*, 1939) women play progressive, positive roles in an outmoded, corrupt male society. Krog's contemporary, Nordahl GRIEG, wrote powerful revolutionary dramas: *Vår ære og vår makt* (1935; *Our Power and Our Glory*, 1971) attacks the exploitation of seamen during World War I, while *Nederlaget* (1937; *Defeat*, 1944), about the Paris Commune of 1871, analyzes the correct use of power.

German EXPRESSIONISM influenced the dramas of Ronald Fangen. His *Den forjættede dag* (1926; the promised day), *Syndefald* (1920; the fall), and *Fienden* (1922; the enemy) show how the coldness, emptiness and spiritual homelessness of modern life can result in criminal behavior. Johan Borgen, Arnulf ØVERLAND and Sigurd Christiansen (1891–1947) produced excellent dramas dealing with the problem of self-fulfillment. Øverland's *Gi meg ditt hjerte* (1930; give me your heart), contrasts intellect and sensuality, while Borgen's *Høit var du elsket* (1937; greatly were you loved) shows how hypocrisy can keep people from being themselves. Christiansen's *Offerdøden* (1919; the sacrificial death) is a highly ethical drama, Ibsen-like in its demand for heroic honesty.

Among the more traditional postwar dramatists in the Ibsen-Heiberg-Krog tradition are Victor Borg (1916–1996), Arne Skouen (b. 1913), Hans Heiberg (1904–1978), Finn Havrevold (1905–1988), Helge Hagerup (b. 1933), and Alex Kielland (1907–1963). They deal with moral decisions, capitalistic exploitation, postwar

superficiality, and the conflict of generations. Kielland's plays, such as *Han som sa nei* (1959; he who said no), about a soldier's duty to obey, have aroused international attention.

There has also been much experimentation in the theater. The disintegration of middleclass society and of the traditional image of reality, together with the influence of foreign dramatists such as STRINDBERG, LAGERKVIST, ELIOT, BRECHT, IONESCO, and BECKETT have contributed to the new theater. In this avant-garde drama there is usually stylization of milieu and character, action and dialogue, with the search for symbols representing general truths; the plays often contain verses, music, song, dance, and pantomime.

The first Norwegian dramatist after the war to experiment with new form was Odd EIDEM in *Spillet om Bly-Petter* (1946; the play about Bly-Petter), a strongly stylized drama, not bound to time or place, with the main character representing the oppressed proletariat. Tormod Skagestad's (b. 1920) poetic dramas, *Under treet ligg øksa* (1955; the axe lay under the tree), and *I byen ved havet* (1962; in the city by the sea), as well as his radio plays, are general, timeless, and symbolic, involving the use of chorus and allegory. Jens Bjørneboe's satirical musical, *Til lykke med dagen* (1965; many happy returns), clearly inspired by Brecht, sharply and satirically attacks the prison system. Finn Carling's *Gitrene* (1966; bars), *Slangen* (1969; the snake), and *Skudd* (1971; shot) treat biblical themes in highly unusual ways. Stein MEHREN's complicated, difficult *Narren og hans hertug* (1968; the fool and his duke), a historical drama that is meant to have contemporary significance, has dramatic appeal in spite of its heavy intellectual content.

At the forefront of modern experimentation in the drama are Paal-Helge Haugen (b. 1945) and Edvard Hoem (b. 1949). Hoem's *God natt, Europa* (1982; Good Night, Europe), a dream-play about contemporary Europe, and Haugen's *Inga anna tid, ingen annan stad* (1986; No Other Time, No Other Place), which deals with liberation from the past, both use music not only as an accompaniment, but also as a dominant part in the plots.

Cecilia Løveid (b. 1951) and Bjørg Vik have written dramas depicting women's struggles in modern society. Løveid's works are full of eroticism, irony, and humor. Her radio play, *Måkespisere* (1983; Sea Gull Eaters) is the tragedy of a young woman who dreams of becoming a great actress. Vik's *To akter for fem kvinner* (1974; Two Acts for Five Women) offers five different women's roles in sharp contrast with one another.

Poetry

In the 1890s the lyric poetry of Nils Collett Vogt, Sigbjørn Obstfelder (1866–1900) and Vilhelm Krag (1871–1933), liberated fancy and imagination, and portrayed moods, reveries, and "soul-life." This melancholy and alienation gave way about 1905 to a fullblooded flowering of new poetry, realistic in attitude, subjects, and language. The highly popular Herman Wildenvey (1886–1959) was a word artist full of humor and warmth, a happy troubador, summer's poet of beauty, but also mature and sometimes melancholy. The verse of Olaf BULL, one of the greatest Norwegian poets of the 20th c., is more profound and symbolic than Wildenvey's. His themes are the passing of time, the relationship of life and art, and often erotic passion.

The poetry of the 1905 generation also had a strong local character. Alf Larsen (1885–1967), Tore Ørjasæter (1886–1968), Olav Aukrust (1883–1929), and Olav Nygard (1884–1924) sang of the sea, the coastal lands, and the mountains, combining a love of nature with deep religious feeling, earthly passion, and mystical ecstasy.

Arnulf Øverland (1889–1968) was a contemporary of the 1905 generation, but more influenced by World War I and by social problems. Well-educated, sophisticated, a socialist, and atheist, Øverland became a leader of his people. His simple but meaningful poems are objective and warm, with subdued passion and sometimes a touch of grandeur.

In the 1920s, regional tradition continued in the verse of Jakob Sande (1906–1967) and Louis Kvalstad (1905–1952), who wrote romantically about nature, particularly the sea. Gunnar Reiss-Andersen (1896–1964), like Bull and Wildenvey, was elegant, witty and sophisticated, while Halldis Moren Vesaas (1907–1995) and Einar Skœraasen (1900–1966) show a love of home and happiness in close, trusting relationships. In contrast, Aslaug Vaa's (1889–1965) poetry about Telemark is abstract and tense, reflecting her moods and conflicts.

The 1930s brought greater depth to the continued trend toward concrete, everyday language. Rolf JACOBSEN first praised and later criticized the new technology, factories, and metropolitan life. Like Jacobsen, Claes Gill (1910–1973) was a stylistic innovator: images pile up in an illogical, associational sequence; his treatment of love, art, and death is very effective. Emil Boyson (1897–1979) favored timeless and universal themes, as evidenced especially in his fine translations from many periods and languages.

During World War II a great deal of poetry was written; much of it was circulated illegally and dealt with anti-Nazi themes, political and social ideals, and postwar goals, but also with problems created by the war, such as human debasement and fear. Nordahl Grieg's war poems, in particular, are well remembered.

Since 1945 there has been a great variation in motifs and styles. Around 1950 symbolic modernism came to Norway. At the forefront were Tarjei Vesaas, Peter R. Holm (b. 1931) and Stein Mehren. They use free rhythms, suggestive sounds, new, unexpected connections and sentence combinations, and sometimes language freed from conventional syntax. Mehren is perhaps the most restless, seeking, questioning one, concerned with poetry as a means of learning and perception. The movement declined in the early 1960s, to be replaced by concretists such as Jan Erik Vold (b. 1939), who have experimented with deliberately simple and naïve language and unusual typographical arrangement.

The changeover from symbolism to realism can also be seen in some of the social and political poets of the 1960s. Whereas many of them remained somewhat esoteric in their use of irony, satire, and metaphor, others, such as Tor Obrestad, eschewed subtle effects in order to speak directly and clearly to the masses.

Among those holding to traditional verse forms and themes have been Inger Hagerup (1905–1985) with her biblical motifs and folk-songs; Tor Jonsson (1916–1951), full of strong contrasts and longing, expressing hope for a better future; Alf Prøysen (1914–1970), great song writer, social realist, and smiling satirist; and André BJERKE, whose sensitive artistry in poems about children, love, adventure, art, and nature have marked him as one of the great contemporary poets.

The 1970s saw ever-increasing amounts of poetry published. There was also a great variety in theme and subject matter. It has been suggested that much of this output is not of high quality, and that an effort on the part of Norwegian publishers and critics is necessary to bring some order out of the chaos. Part of the difficulty can be traced to the government's support of belles lettres.

One of the themes that has often appeared in recent poetry is the combination of a love of tradition with a fear of modern change. Poets react with humor, fantasy, and sometimes terror to the threat of decay, destruction, and loss. Sigmund Skard (1903–1995) has given excellent voice to these thoughts in his glimpses of the world that contrast sharply with his love of simple Norwegian tradition. Einar Økland (b. 1940) is strongly critical of politics and politicians while at the same time presenting attractive descriptions of life in western Norway. Two others who see the world on the brink are Annie Riis (b. 1955) and Liv Lundbert (b. 1944).

Three notable poets of the 1970s are Paal-Helge Haugen (b. 1945), who, in clear, precise language, attempts to understand "the world" and to come to terms with it; Frank Stubb Micaelsen (b. 1947), whose poems show a connection between people and things throughout history, suggesting a mystical unity of all matter; and Ove Røsbak (b. 1960), whose strong, robust poems with their eagerness for life and love show excellent talent and promise.

With the deaths of Paal Brekke (1923–1993) and Rolf Jacobsen, two of the central figures in post-war Norwegian literature have been lost. Together with Georg Johanessen (b. 1931), they introduced modernism into Norwegian poetry. Brekke was a translator, editor, critic, and poet. In his last work *Ostinato* (1994; Ostinato), he showed the stubborn use of counter-motifs that characterize the poet-critic.

Bjørn Aamot (b. 1944) has been called the last classical worker's poet, but his poetry has also embraced many other subjects such as language and nuclear physics. In *ABC Dikt* (1994; ABC Poems) he shows both wit and wisdom in observations about human nature arranged playfully in alphabetical order.

Among those poets concerned about the future of the world in a nuclear age, Arild Stubhaug (b. 1948) stands out, particularly in *På veg til våpenhuset* (1995; Towards Storing the Weapons). Through the use of historical, philosophical, and biblical motifs, Stubhaug searches for ways to end modern conflicts, to achieve peace.

BIBLIOGRAPHY: Bach, G., *The History of Scandinavian Literatures* (1938): 11–87; Koht, H., and S. Skard, *Voice of Norway* (1944); Christiansen, H., *Norwegische Literaturgeschichte* (1953); Beyer, H., *A History of Norwegian Literature* (1956); Downs, B. W., *Modern Norwegian Literature 1860–1918*, (1966); Jorgensen, T., *History of Norwegian Literature* (1970); Rossel, S. H., *A History of Scandinavian Literature, 1870–1980* (1982)

—WALTER D. MORRIS

NOSSACK, Hans Erich

West German novelist, essayist, poet, and dramatist, b. 30 Jan. 1901, Hamburg; d. 2 Nov. 1977, Hamburg

Son of a merchant, N. studied philosophy and law, then held jobs as a factory worker, traveling salesman, and journalist before reluctantly joining his father's business.

An important and distinguished writer to whom recognition was denied until relatively late in his career, N. did not see his first work published until 1947. Proscribed from publishing by the Nazis because of former left-wing affiliations, N. continued to write clandestinely, but lost all his manuscripts during the Allied bombing raids on Hamburg in 1943. The ensuing physical and emotional devastation marked the turning point in N.'s life, for by associating Hamburg's fate with his own, he effectively freed himself from the coils of the past. The situation was graphically and soberly recorded in "Der Untergang" (the destruction), a piece from *Interview mit dem Tode* (1948; interview with death)—republished as *Dorothea* (1950; Dorothea)—in which N. recognized and welcomed the chance to make a complete break with a bankrupt society.

It is this theme of the total rejection of the past, of release from societies inimical to the real development of man—and the implications of this idea for the whole question of personal identity—that forms the nucleus of his work.

In his early—and only—volume of verse, *Gedichte* (1947; poems), N. explores the inner man and his motivations, and clearly enunciates his belief in moral and intellectual integrity. N. believed in pushing out to the very limits of experience, into the unknown and uncertain, into "extraterritoriality," as he called it. In *Spätestens im November* (1955; *Wait for November*, 1982) protest against the conventional and the norm is seen as the first step toward self-fulfillment, even though the outcome ends in disaster. The very fact that a stale and meaningless pattern of existence has been recognized as such and questioned was sufficient for N. The important thing was to have the courage to be oneself, to be an individual.

This concern also dominates N.'s three plays—*Die Rotte Kain* (1949; the band of Cain), *Die Hauptprobe* (1956; the main test), and *Ein Sonderfall* (1963; a special case)—which, however, despite the strength and clarity of their language and, in the case of the last two, the tragicomic effects, never enjoyed popular or critical success.

The brilliant novel *Unmögliche Beweisaufnahme* (1959; *The Impossible Proof*, 1968) deals with the problem of trying to live by two different realities: what man really is, and the image society has of man. The "account" takes the form of a trial in which communication between a judge and a defendant is reduced to a minimum, in a witty and often ironic dialogue, as the two realities are explored. This failure of understanding that occurs between these two men is seen by N. as a consequence of the increasing bureaucratization and institutionalization of society against which N. believed it was his duty to warn—and he did so repeatedly.

The distinction between what is real and unreal became increasingly blurred in N.'s work, his characters moving in mysterious and strange settings that were at one and the same time tangible and recognizable yet also vaguely unfamiliar. This precarious focus was cleverly broadened in *Der jüngere Bruder* (1958; the younger brother) to examine not only the protagonist's own nebulous identity and relationship to others but also to juxtapose a physically recognizable Europe with disturbingly out-of-focus elements.

The ever-present tendency to fuse the real and the unreal in surrealistic or mythical forms reached a climax in *Nach dem letzten Aufstand* (1961; after the last revolt), which comprises an often bewilderingly rich mixture of complex time and space elements welded together to create an alliance between this world and the other more mysterious one, in which there is a highly stylized reflection of postwar Germany's dilemmas. Protest against frozen attitudes, the quest for self-realization, and the attempt to create a new mythology out of our reality also characterize the important *Der Fall d'Arthez* (1968; *The D'Arthez Case*, 1971), while N.'s sense of comic satire was ably demonstrated in *Dem unbekannten Sieger* (1969; *To the Unknown Hero*, 1974), which attacks the

sterile systematizing of politicohistorical reality, a process N. believed denied the essential spontaneity and multidimensionality of man's experiences.

In the few years before his death, N. returned to his main themes with increasing urgency and subtlety. *Die gestohlene Melodie* (1972; the stolen melody) took the question of outsiderness a stage further, dealing with "remigrants," that is, those who had actually returned from the "other side" of being, but whose newly acquired awareness now excluded them from the familiar. In *Bereitschaftsdienst* (1973; emergency service) the feasibility of the act of suicide was seen as an apparent way out, although confusingly it was not so much extinction that was sought, but escape from the sterility of conventional norms and atrophied social forms. N.'s last novel, *Ein glücklicher Mensch* (1975; a happy man), assembled most of N.'s driving concerns to form a quintessential statement of his intellectual position.

In cool, lucid, and restrained prose, this "dispassionate visionary" portrayed with striking forcefulness man's precarious and threatened condition, his inner loneliness and basic unrelatedness. His works are inner explorations, attempts to reach the emotional centers that lie within us and to examine the manifold possibilities of human existence that lie in the pursuit of individual freedom.

An understanding of N.'s artistic purpose and *Weltanschauung* can be obtained by reading his essays, the most important of which are contained in *Die schwache Position der Literatur* (1966; the weak position of literature), in which N.'s special moralistic stance, somewhat akin to Albert CAMUS's, is well defined, and in *Pseudoautobiographische Glossen* (1971; pseudoautobiographical glosses).

N. was a percipient and relentless critic of his society who, through reasoned and always quiet argument, never wavered from his firm conviction that the solution to man's problems lies within man himself, and that all he, as a writer, could do was "to render an account."

FURTHER WORKS: *Nekyia: Bericht eines Überlebenden* (1947); *Publikum und Dichter* (1950); *Der Neugierige* (1955); *Die Begnadigung* (1955); *Spirale: Roman einer schlaflosen Nacht* (1956); *Über den Einsatz* (1956); *Begegnung im Vorraum* (1958); *Freizeitliteratur: Eine Fastenpredigt* (1959); *Das kennt man* (1964); *Sechs Etüden* (1964); *Das Testament des Lucius Eurinus* (1964); *Das Mal, und andere Erzählungen* (1965); *Der König geht ins Kino* (1974); *Um es kurz zu machen* (1975); *Dieser Andere: Ein Lesebuch mit Briefen, Gedichten, Prosa* (1976)

BIBLIOGRAPHY: Kasack, H., "Rede auf den Preisträger," *Jahrbuch der deutschen Akademie für Sprache und Dichtung* (1961): 79–89; Boehlich, W., Afterword to *Der Untergang* (1963): 55–60; Keith-Smith, B., "H. E. N.," in Keith-Smith, B., ed., *Essays on Contemporary German Literature* (1966): 63–85; Prochnik, P., "Controlling Thoughts in the Work of H. E. N.," *GL&L*, 19 (1965): 68–75; Prochnik, P., "First Words: The Poetry of H. E. N.," *MLR*, 64 (1969): 100–110; Schmid, C., ed., *Über H. E. N.* (1970)

—PETER PROCHNIK

NOUVEAU ROMAN

See New Novel

NOVÁS CALVO, Lino

Cuban short-story writer, novelist, poet, and journalist, b. 22 Sept. 1905, Grañadas del Sol, Galicia, Spain; d. 24 Mar. 1983, New York, N.Y., U.S.A.

N.C. is one of the most important short-story writers in Cuba's literary history. He was an illegitimate child, born in northwestern Spain to a poor Galician family, and was only seven years old when his mother sent him to Cuba to live with an uncle. There, he experienced a life of economic difficulties as he lived with different families, working, out of necessity, in many different jobs throughout the island. In 1926 he went to New York but soon returned to Cuba "with more scratches than dollars." From this experience he acquired sufficient knowledge of the language to later read and translate works by BALZAC, Aldous HUXLEY, and William FAULKNER, and Ernest HEMINGWAY's *The Old Man and the Sea* (1959), at the author's request. After returning to Cuba, N. C. found employment as a taxi driver, an experience he recaptures in several of his stories, especially in "La noche de Romón Yendía" ("The Dark Night of Ramón Yendía"). This first-hand knowledge of life among the working classes, and the precarious existence of being poor in Cuba, became and important aspect of his world of fiction. Like N. C. himself, most of his characters are individuals who confront social and economic hardships, are haunted by a sense of not belonging, and must struggle for permanence in a world of change.

N.C.'s debut as a writer was the publication of nine poems in *Revista de Avance* under the pseudonym Lino Maria de Calvo. "El camarada" (1928; comrade) and "Proletario" (1928; proletariat) signal the emergence in Cuban literature of a proletarian poetic voice, a perspective also found in his first short story "Un hombre arruinado" (1929; a ruined man), where N.C. explores the psychological profile of a man whose materialism has isolated him from meaningful human contact. He was immediately singled out by other writers and editors, and rose from being a taxi driver without formal education to being a member of the Cuban intellectual circle.

Though N.C. was Spanish by birth, his short stories are uniquely Cuban. He experimented, especially, with the vibrant dialogue and the poetic stylization of colloquial Cuban speech. Aware of the new currents in literary expression, N C developed a literary style that was influenced by the great writers of his time, by poetic vanguard movements, and by the vibrant force of popular Cuban figures and colloquial language that were in vogue in the vernacular and burlesque theater during the 1920s. He was also particularly interested in Sherwood Anderson's techniques, as well as in Maxim GORKY, Joseph CONRAD, John STEINBECK, and others.

In 1931 N.C. traveled to Spain as a correspondent for *Orbe*, a period that proved to be very important for him as a writer. During this time, he published three short stories in *Revista de Occidente*, contributed to other Spanish journals, became secretary for the literary section of the Ateneo of Madrid, began to write a novel, *El negrero: Vida novelada de Pedro Blanco Hernández de Trava* (1955; the slave trader, a novelized biography of Pedro Blanco de Trava), and published *Un experiment en el Barrio Chino* (1936; an experiment in the red-light district). During the Spanish Civil War, in 1937, N. C. was wrongly accused of writing articles against the miners of Asturias; he spent one night in prison, facing possible execution the next day, but he was released when the charges

against him could not be proven. With the collapse of the Spanish Republic in 1939, N. C. fled to France and then, with the help of friends, returned to Cuba. There he worked as an editor and translator for *Ultra*, a journal directed by Fernando Ortiz, and, years later, for *Bohemia*.

Between 1942 and 1945, N. C. was awarded a degree in journalism by the National School of Journalism in Havana and received several literary awards: the Hernández Catá Prize for the short story (1942), the National Prize for the short story by the Cuban ministry of education (1944), and the Varona Prize for journalism for his book *No sé quién soy* (1945; I don't know who I am). A year later he published a second collection of short stories, *Cayo canas* (1946; palm key), in which like in most of his fictional work, the narrative goes beyond traditional patterns and comes closer to the short novel. N. C.'s style became also strongly influenced by cinematographic techniques, in which emotions are not described, but are suggested through a series of images.

During the 1950s, the sociopolitical difficulties on the island and a general lack of interest in intellectual pursuits brought on a period of dissolusionment for N. C. during which his fictional production declined. In 1960, a year after the triumph of the Cuban revolution, N. C. sought political asylum at the Colombian embassy in Havana. Resettled in the U.S., N.C. worked for *Bohemta libre*, and from 1967 to 1974 taught at Syracuse University. During these last years, he wrote several short stories for journals. Several of these were later published, with some of his previous work, in *Maneras de contar* (1970; narrative modes). In this second period of his productive career, N.C. followed the same narrative style and preoccupations of his earlier work, now including conflicts surrounding the Cuban revolution. N.C. continued to articulate basically the same sense of disorientation and irrationality that always accompanied his vision of the human being as a victim of social and psychological conditions.

But N. C.'s main contributions to Latin American literature belong to his earlier writings when he, and later Alejo CARPENTIER, were the writers mostly responsible for the establishment of a modern tradition in Cuban prose fiction and the emergence of the Cuban short story as a mature and universal genre. Though N. C. was a prolific writer both in fiction and journalism, only part of his fiction has been published in collections. Several of his short stories have been translated into English and published in anthologies. Many of those that first appeared in journals in Cuba and in Spain are still unpublished in book form, while others have been lost.

FURTHER WORKS: *La luna nona y otros cuentos* (1942); *El otro cayo* (1959)

BIBLIOGRAPHY: Portuondo, J. A., "L.N.C. y elcuento hispanoamericano," *CA*, 35, 5 (Sept.–Dec. 1947): 245–63; Souza, R. D., "L.N.C. and the 'Revista de Avance,'" *Journal of Inter-American Studies*, 10, 2 (April 1968): 232–43; Gutiérrez, A. dela Solana, *Maneras de narrar: Contraste de L.N.C. y Alfonso Hernández Catá* (1972); special N. C. issue, *Symposium*, 29, 3 (Fall 1975); Ben-Ur, L., "La época española de N. C.: 1931–1939," *Chasqui*, 6, 3 (May 1977): 69–76; Clinton, S., "The Scapegoat Archetype As a Principle of Composition in N. C.'s 'Un dedo encima,'" *Hispania*, 62, 1 (Mar. 1979): 56–61; Souza, R. D., "The Early Stories of L. N. C. (1929–1932): Genesis and Aftermath," *KRQ*, 26, 2 (1979):

221–29; Souza, R. D., *L. N. C.* (1981); special N. C. issue, *Symposium*, 29, 4 (Winter 1985); Roses, L. E., *Voices of the Storyteller: Cuba's L. N. C.* (1986)

—JULIA CUERVO HEWITT

NOVO, Salvador

Mexican poet, dramatist, and essayist, b. 30 July 1904, Mexico City; d. 10 Jan. 1974, Mexico City

In 1917 N. attended Mexico City National Preparatory School with Xavier VILLAURRUTIA, Jaime Torres BODET, and Jose GOROSTIZA. In 1922 he met Pedro Henríquez Ureña (1884–1946) and became his protégé. In 1924 he was appointed the editorial chief of the Mexican ministry of education. Three years later he cofounded the Ulysses Theater and codirected with Villaurrutia *Ulysses* magazine. From 1930 to 1933 he held the History of Theater Chair at the National Conservatory. In 1933–1934 he worked as a recorder at the Seventh Panamerican Conference in Montevideo. N. received in 1946 the City of Mexico Prize for his essay "Nueva grandeza mexicana" (new Mexican grandeur). From 1937 to 1943 he wrote for the magazine *Hoy*. In 1946 he became director of the theater department of the National Institute of Fine Arts, a post he held until 1952. That same year he was elected a full member of the Mexican Academy of Language (a branch of the Spanish Royal Academy), and in 1965 was appointed the official historian of Mexico City.

N. wrote XX *poemas* (1925; XX poems), which he characterized as "visual poems." They satirize the monotonous, mechanized, impersonal characteristics of daily life. The twenty poems of *Espejo* (1933; mirror) recall his lost childhood. Like most of N.'s poetry, *Espejo* is extremely ironical and even cynical. In *Nuevo amor* (1933; new love) N. resumes the theme of dehumanization and develops it to the fullest, especially in the poem "Elegía" (elegy). *Nuevo amor* is considered N.'s ultimate poetry book by most critics. Love, a predominant theme in this collection, is "spiritual" not carnal. In 1934 N. published two volumes of poetry: *Seamen Rhymes* (title in English, bilingual ed.) and *Poemas proletarios* (proletarian poems). Other books of poetry are *XVIII sonnets* (1955; XVIII sonnets) and *Poesía* (1961; poetry), which includes previously published as well as unpublished poetry.

N. wrote over twenty dramatic pieces, some intended for children: *Don Quijote* (1947; Don Quixote) and *Astucia* (1948; astuteness). Others were composed as simple dialogues: *El tercer Fausto* (1934; Faust the third), *El Joven II* (1951; young man II), and *Didálogos* (1956; dialogues). Among his short plays are *Divorcio* (1924; divorce) and *La señorita Remington* (1924; Miss Remington). N.'s four major plays are *La culta dama* (1950; the educated lady), *Yocasta o cassi* (1961; Yocasta or almost), *La guerra de las gordas* (1963; the war of the fat women), and *A ochio columnas* (1965; at eight columns). *La culta dama* is a satire against Mexican high-class values. It indicts rich women who indulge themselves in volunteer works of mercy at the expense of their family duties. *Yocasta o casi* is a more cosmopolitan work. It draws from Greek mythology and modern psychology while presenting an alienated actress who must live out her role both in

life and on stage. *La guerra de las gordas* is based upon pre-Columbian Mexican history. Moquihuix, king of Tlatelolco and his wife, Chalchiuhnenetzin, get entangled with Axayacatl, king of Tenochtitlan. The play depicts the end of the Tlatelolco kingdom. A *ocho columnas* is a dramatic denouncement of career opportunism and based Mexican journalism.

N. was a prolific essayist. He published over twenty nonfiction prose works. Among these, the most famous is *Nueva grandeza mexicana* (1946; *New Mexican Grandeur*, 1967). This book has undergone several editions and has been frequently translated. It is a first person, comprehensive overview of Mexico City's neighborhoods, famous restaurants, movies, and play houses as well as architectural landmarks.

N.'s writing is exceptionally diverse. His poetry, plays, and essays bridge the gap between generations of writers. His poetry is decidedly ironical and iconoclastic and encompasses various literary modes: MODERNISM, SURREALISM and POST-MODERNISM. N. the essayist captures in an original and passionate manner Mexican culture, literature, and history. N. the dramatist is a pivotal figure in Mexican theater. He excelled as a director and producer of many plays where, again, social criticism and a satirical view of life do not pass unnoticed.

FURTHER WORKS: *Return Ticket* (1928; title in English); *Jalisco-Michoacán: Doce días* (1933); *Décimas en el mar* (1934); *En defensa de lo usado y otros ensayos* (1938); *Diez lecciones de técnica de actuación teatral* (1951); *Este y otros viajes* (1951); *14 sonetos de navidad y año nuevo* (1955–1968); *El teatro inglés* (1960); *Breve historia de Coyoacán* (1962); *Cuauhtémoc* (1962); *Letras vencidas* (1962); *Breve historia y antología sobre la fiebre amarilla* (1964); *In ticiteicatl o El espejo encantado* (1965); *México: imagen de una ciudad* (1967); *La ciudad de México del 9 de junio al 15 de julio de* 1867 (1967); *Cocina mexicana, o Historia gastronómica de la ciudad de México* (1967); *México* (1968); *Apuntes para una historia de la publicidad en la ciudad de México* (1968); *Un año, hace ciento: la ciudad de México en 1873* (1973); *Historia de la aviación en México* (1974)

BIBLIOGRAPHY: Dauster, F., "La poesía de S.N.," *CA*, 3, 116 (May–June 1961): 209–33; Arce, D. N., "Nómina bibliográfica de S.N.," Boletín *de la Biblioteca* Nacional, 2a, época 13, 4 (1962): 61–89; Kuehne, A., "La realidad existencial y 'la realidad creada' en Pirandello y S.N." *LATR*, 2, 1 (Fall 1968): 5–14; Magaña-Esquivel, A., *S.N.* (1971); Muncy, M., *S.N. y su teatro: estudio crítico* (1971); special N. issue, *Reflexión*: 3–4 (1975); Roster, P., *La ironía como método de análises: la poesía de S.N.* (1978); Forster, M., "S.N. como prosista," in Bleznick, D. W. and J. O. Valencia, eds., *Homenaje a Luis Leal* (1978): 129–43

—JORGE RODRÍGUEZ-FLORIDO

NOVOMESKÝ, Laco (Ladislav)

Czechoslovak poet and journalist (writing in Slovak), b. 27 Dec. 1904, Budapest, Hungary; d. 4 Sept. 1976, Bratislava

The evolution of N.'s poetic talent and the recognition his work currently enjoys are both intertwined with the vagaries of his lifelong career as a leading activist of the Slovak Communist Party. N. received his early education in Hungary. His family left for Slovakia in 1919. In 1923 N. graduated from the Teacher's College in Modra, Slovakia. He had published his first poem in 1921, and by the time he entered Bratislava University, in 1923, he was a regular contributor to the radical journal *Mladé Slovensko*.

N. joined the Communist Party of Slovakia in 1925. Two years later he published his first volume of poems, *Nedel'a* (1927; Sunday). It was followed, in the next decade, by three more books of poems. During these years, N. served the Party as a journalist and cultural propagandist, working in close collaboration with the Communist leader Klement Gottwald (1896–1953) on the editorial board of the Party organ *Rudé právo*. In the divisive debate at the Fifth Party Congress in 1929, N., together with his fellow Slovak Vladimír Clementis (1902–1952), threw their support behind Gottwald's position of militant opposition to the Versailles-created Czechoslovak Republic. In 1934 he attended the First Congress of Soviet Writers in Moscow.

In 1939, after the breakup of the Czechoslovak Republic, N. left Prague for Slovakia, there to participate in the underground life of the Slovak Communist Party. The Politburo sent him to London in 1943, with the mission of explaining the aims of the incipient Slovak uprising to the president-in-exile, Eduard Beneš. From London N. flew to Moscow, where he remained until his return to Slovakia in January 1945, after it was liberated from the Nazis.

Between 1945 and 1950 N. was a prominent participant in the cultural politics of the Party and his country. But in 1950 he was accused of "bourgeois nationalism," an official term for the separatist, anti-Czech tendencies that the Party in Slovakia had previously encouraged. In 1951 N. was imprisoned. He was released at the end of 1955 and allowed to live and even publish quietly in Prague. His official rehabilitation came in 1963, followed by national honors.

N. played an important role in the traumatic year 1968. After giving a cautious endorsement to the reforms put into effect, he broke ranks with the vast majority of Czechoslovak writers and called for an end of the Prague experiment with democracy, even before the Soviet military intervention. Until his withdrawal from public life in 1970 for reasons of health, N. remained a vocal supporter of the policies of "normalization" of the Husák regime. He was a Lenin Prize winner and a Hero of the U.S.S.R.

N.'s poetic legacy is contained in the two volumes of his collected poems, *Bdsnické dlelo* (1971, poetic works), which include all the prewar and postwar cycles of verse. In his earliest poems, N. had been primarily the poet of the proletarian suburbs, celebrating, in an aggressively prosaic idiom, man-made things and mankind's irrepressible quest for happiness. The 1930s brought more linguistic sophistication to his poetry and, here and there, the occasionally daring stab of a SURREALISTIC image. In the last cycle published before the war, the native Slovak rural strain asserts itself in poems of uncomplicated sensuality.

Villa Teréza (1963; Villa Teréza), the most important cycle of poems, was written by N. after the Communists came to power in his country. It is an ironic meditation about the individual in history, dedicated to the memory of Vladimir Antonov-Ovseenko, the hero of Red Petrograd, who later became a Soviet nonperson. N. had known him in the 1920s as the Soviet envoy to Czechoslovakia during the presidency of T. G. Masaryk. In this cycle of poems, N.'s historical subject has a very personal subtext.

N.'s literary achievement is that of a minor but authentic poet. He will also be remembered for the crucial role he has played in his

country's recent history. His life exemplifies the evolution of an official Communist writer from the youthful time when poetry and revolution seemed to be one, to the sobering realities and the historical compromises of entrenched political power.

FURTHER WORKS: *Pred nedel'ou* (written 1924–26, pub. 1971); *Znejúce ozveny* (written 1924–32, pub. 1969); *Romboid* (1932); *Marx a slovenský národ* (1933); *Manifesty a protesty* (written 1924–37, pub. 1970); *Čestná povinnost* (written 1933–44, pub. 1968); *Otvorené okna* (1936); *Slávnost istoty* (written 1938–44, pub. 1970); *Svätý za dedinou* (1939); *Zväzky a záväzky* (written 1945–50, pub. 1972); *Komunizmus v slovenskej národnej idei* (1946); *Pašovanou ceruzkou* (1948); *Hviezdoslav* (1949); *Výchova socialistického pokolenia* (1949); *T. G. Masaryk* (1950); *Do mesta 30 min.* (1963); *Samodtia' a iné* (1964); *Nezbadaný svet* (1964); *Dobrý deň, vám* (1964); *Dom, kde žijem* (1966); *Otvorená kronika: Scenár o živote a diele Vladimíra Clementisa* (1969); *Z piesní o jednote* (1971); *O literatúre* (1971); *Z úrodných podstát človečích* (1976)

BIBLIOGRAPHY: Banerjee, M. N., on *Básnické dielo*, *BA*, 47 (1973), 185; Mihailovich, V. D., et al., eds., *Modern Slavic Literatures* (1976), Vol. II: 172–75

—MARIA NĚMCOVÁ BANERJEE

NU'AYMA, Mīkhā'īl

(also spelled Mikhail Naimy) Lebanese poet, critic, essayist, dramatist, and biographer (writing in Arabic and English), b. 1889, Biskinta; d. 28 Feb. 1988, Beirut

N. attended the Russian elementary school that the Russian Imperial Orthodox Palestine Society had founded in 1899 in the village. In 1902 he qualified for admission to the Russian training college in Nazareth, and in 1906 he obtained a scholarship at the Diocesan Seminary in Poltava, Ukraine. After completion of a four-year course in 1911, N. left for the U.S. and became a student at the University of Washington, Seattle, where he received degrees in law and in English literature in 1916. After the completion of his studies, N. left for New York to join the Arab literary circle with whom he had become acquainted through correspondence. He made a living working at the Russian military mission to the U.S., until Russia withdrew from the war in November 1917 and N. was called up for active service. He was sent to France, where he spent the last week of the war on the frontline. While waiting for transport back to the U.S., he was allowed to follow courses in French language and literature at the University of Rennes. In 1919 N. returned to New York. Together with friends he founded the society of the Pen. He gave it a charter and was its first secretary. To earn his livelihood, he became a traveling salesman, refusing to pursue a career in any of the fields open to him on the basis of his academic qualifications. In 1932 he left the U.S. for Lebanon, where he lived for the remainder of his life.

The spiritual development of N. can be divided into various phases. His destination seemed to be the clergy, but if he had ever cherished such thoughts he abandoned them during his stay in

Poltava. The splendor displayed by the church may have affected his negative decision. Tolstoy's socialist ideas were more in accordance with his feelings. In Seattle he came into contact with the Theosophical Society and in 1925 he came to read Vivekananda's Raya Yogo and the Bagavatgita. Reincarnation and the purification of the soul were then to occupy a paramount place in his writings and literature.

The literary work of N. fills thirty-two volumes in Arabic. Two works were published originally in English and were later translated into Arabic. His work includes poetry, narrative prose, drama, biography, autobiography, literary criticism, and essay writing. He wrote his first poem in Russia, before 1911, his first critique in 1913, his first story in 1914. In 1917 he published, in New York, his play *al-Ābā' wa-al-banūn* (parents and children), which had been serialized in the literary magazine *al-Funūn*. It is the only work N. published in the U.S.

In 1923 *al-Ghirbāl* (the sieve), a volume of critical essays, was published in Cairo, where N. had contacts with the young and angry Dīwān group of 'Abbās Mahmūd al-'Aqqād (1889–1964) and Ibrāhīm al-Māzinī (1890–1949). *Al-Marāhil* (stages), another volume of essays, appeared in 1933 in Beirut. It contains only one essay on a literary subject, the other essays dealing with other subjects. N.'s biography *Gibrān Khalīl Gibrān. Hayātuhu, mawtuhu, adabuhu, Fannuhu* (1934; *Kahlil Gibran: His life and His Work*, 1950) produced a shock among Gibran's admirers. Instead of a eulogy N. had produced a book revealing the weaknesses of Gibran. N. defended his choice by comparing the book to John Bunyan's (1628–1688) *The Pilgrim's Progress* (1684), seeing Gibran's life as a struggle against the forces of evil. In Arabic literary history it is the first *biographie romancée*, a genre that owes its renown to writers like André MAUROIS, Lytton STRACHEY, and Stefan ZWEIG.

N. has written more than eighty stories, which he collected in volumes like *Kān mā kān* (1937; once upon a time), *Akābir* (1956; notables), and *Abū Battah* (1959; the fat-calved man), also in volumes of miscellaneous content. He also wrote long pieces of narrative prose, among which *The Book of Mirdad* (1948), which he later translated into Arabic as *Kitāb Mirdād* (1952). N. considered this work as the summit of his thought. It is a book of metaphysical instruction that he wanted to leave behind as a spiritual guidebook for humankind. But N.'s most impressive piece of work may be his autobiography, *Sab'ūn* (3 vols., 1959–1960; seventy), covering three phases of his life; his early youth in Biskinta, Nazareth, and Poltava; his stay in the U.S.; and his return to Lebanon. Not limiting the biography to his own life, he gives vivid portrayal of the people around him and of the milieu in which he lived.

Lebanon respects N. as one of its great authors. In the wider field of Arabic literature he deserves to be celebrated as one of the critics, authors, and poets who have linked Arabic literature with the Western (Russian and English) narrative forms, and who have introduced ideas of romanticism—such as the poet as creator, priest, and propher—into Arabic literature.

FURTHER WORKS: *Zād al-Ma'ād* (1936); *Hamsh al-Jufūn* (1943); *al-Awthān* (1946); *Karam 'alā darb* (1946); *Liqā'* (1946; *Till We Meet ...* 1957); *Sawt al-'ālam* (1948); *Mudhakkirāt al-Arqash* (1949; *Memoirs of a Vagrant Soul*, (1952); *al-Nūr wa-al-Dayjūr* (1950); *Fī mahabb ar-rīh* (1953); *Durūb* (1954); *Ab'ad min Mūskū wa-min Washintun* (1957); *al-Yawm al-akhīr* (1963); *Hawāmish* (1965); *Ayyūb* (1967); *Yā ibn Ādam* (1969); *al-Majmū'ah al-kāmilah* (8 vols., 1970–1974); *Fī a-ghirbā al-jadīd* (1972); *Mukhtārāt* (1972); *Nagwā al-ghurūb* (1973); *Min wahy al-Masīh* (1974); *Wamadāt. Shudhūr wa-amthāl* (1977)

BIBLIOGRAPHY: Naimy, N., *M.N. An Introduction* (1967); Gabrieli, F., "L'autobiografia did M. N.," *Oriente Moderno*, 49 (1969): 381–87; Nijland, C., *M.N. Promoter of the Arabic Literary Revival* (1975); Matar, N. I., "Adam and the Serpent: Notes on the Theology of M.N.," *JArabL*, 11 (1980): 56–61; Nijiland, C., "M.N.: The Biography of Gibran and the Autobiography," *al-Arabiyya*, 15 (1982): 7–15; Allen, R., ed., *Modern Arabic Literature* (1987): 237–44; Ghaith, A., *La pensēe religieuse chez Gubrān Halil Gubran et M.N.* (1990)

—CORNELIS NIJLAND

NUŠIĆ, Branislav

Yugoslav dramatist, short-story writer, novelist, and essayist (writing in Serbian), b. 8 Oct. 1864, Belgrade; d. 19 Jan. 1938, Belgrade

N. grew up in Belgrade and studied law there. Subsequently he held a number of government and diplomatic posts in the Serbian ministries of foreign affairs and education and later served as director of several state subsidized theaters in Belgrade, Novi Sad, Skopje, and Sarajevo.

N. was both a prolific and versatile author. Aside from his sizable fictional oeuvre, his twenty-five volumes of collected works include practically every kind of dramatic composition, from farce to tragedy. His early historical patriotic plays *Knez Ivo od Semberije* (1902; Duke Ivo of Semberia) and *Hadži Loja* (1908; Hadž Loja), several lachrymose romantic pieces, and the tragedy *Nahod* (1923; the foundling) initially enjoyed some popularity, but ultimately failed to survive the test of time. Only when N. turned to comedy did his dramatic talent attain its fullest potential. A satirist of the first rank, he revealed a true panorama of the late-blossoming Serbian bourgeois society plagued by abuses of political, bureaucratic, and police power, the peddling of influence, greed for money, and the craving for advancement and honors. Such memorable plays as *Narodni poslanik* (1883; the member of parliament), *Sumnjivo lice* (1887; the suspicious individual), *Protekcija* (1889; favoritism), *Običan čovek* (1900; an ordinary man), *Svet* (1906; the world), and *Put oko sveta* (1910; a trip around the world), all written in pre-World War I Serbia, display his satirical powers. His satirical bite increased in the interwar period, when he completed *Gospodja ministarka* (1931; the cabinet member's wife), *Ožalošćena porodica* (1934; the bereaved family), *UJEŽ* (1935; acronym for Association of Yugoslav Emancipated Women), and *Pokojnik* (1937; the late departed), in which the picture of the well-known social ills of the new south Slav state, Yugoslavia, was amply augmented by a devastating satirical comment upon more universal human foibles.

Among N.'s nondramatic prose writings, of particular note are his three volumes of short stories—*Pripovetke jednoga kaplara* (1886; tales of a corporal), *Listići* (1889; leaflets), and *Ramazanske večeri* (1898; Ramazan evenings)—and the novel *Opštinsko dete* (1902; the municipal child), characterized by a wealth of humorous detail, lively characters, and the authenticity of its Serbian provincial petit-bourgeois milieu. Although in both his dramatic and fictional works N. occasionally succumbed to his audience's thirst for easy comic effects and laughter for its own sake, his work still remains a striking exposé of that upstart segment of the Serbian bourgeois society that sacrificed everything to its frenzied pursuit of wealth, privilege, political influence, and fashion.

FURTHER WORKS: *Pučina* (1901); *Autobiografija* (1924); *Analfabeta* (1935); *Sabrana dela* (25 vols., 1966)

BIBLIOGRAPHY: Barac, A., *A History of Yugoslav Literature* (1955): 206–8; Kadić, A., *Contemporary Serbian Literature* (1964): 37–40; Nikolić, M., "Die Entstehung des serbischen Nationaltheaters im 19. Jahrhundert," *MuK*, 12 (1966): 203–9

—NICHOLAS MORAVČEVICH

NWAPA, Flora (Nwanzuruaha)

Nigerian novelist, short-story writer, and writer of children's books (writing in English), b. 13 Jan. 1931, Oguta; d. 16 Oct. 1993, Enugu

Born in Eastern Nigeria to Igbo parents who were both teachers, N. was early influenced by the storytelling tradition and songs of her community. More formally, N. received her B.A. from University College, Ibadan in 1957 and a diploma in education from the University of Edinburgh in 1958, leading to her career as a teacher. Married and with three children, N.'s affection for young people has been instrumental in shaping her writing. Another major influence was the eruption of the Biafran crisis, during which N. and her family, along with other Igbo, had to leave Lagos. N.'s support of Biafra curtailed her fictional productions, as after the war, from 1970 to 1975 N. served as Minster for Health and Social Welfare for the East Central State. In 1975 N. decided to pursue her writing full-time; however, the isolation of such a life led her also to develop her own publishing company, the Tana Press.

The freedom of her own press allowed N. to focus on publishing children's books, producing eight volumes herself between 1979 to 1981. Many of these are quite simple works, such as *My Tana* and *My Animal Colouring Book*, published in 1979, followed by *My Tana Alphabet Book* and *My Animal Number Book*, published in 1981. N.'s children's stories are simple tales that incorporate Nigerian elements and generate moral and ethical values. Those texts published by N. incorporate illustrations appropriate to Nigeria, which has not always been true of such works published abroad. An exceptional example of N.'s children's fiction is *MammyWater* (1979), which draws upon the skills N. established

in her adult fiction to bring to life a water deity drawn from traditional oral elements in Eastern Nigeria. This work illustrates N.'s ability to alter and thereby renew the meaning of traditions from precolonial Africa. In common with N.'s novels it presents strong female characters not limited by patriarchal views of women, most notably in MammyWater herself, the water goddess Ogbuide or Uhamiri who also figures in much of N.'s adult fiction. The *Adventures of Deke* (1980) retells the story of *MammyWater* more simply.

N.'s novels focus on women confronting two central tensions: first, the centrality of their roles at the heart of social and cultural traditions, but constrained by male dominance, and second, the shifts in those cultural attitudes as Nigeria moved into independence. The characters belie such a simple template, however, as N. draws a wide range of characters, from shrewd market women to wise mothers and wives to independent urban business women. This focus on women has led N. to engage in stylistic techniques that have also been seen as African in origin; her writing incorporates storytelling and community conversation that shapes judgments, encourages consensus, and marks socialization.

N.'s first novel, *Efuru* (1966), is set in the rural community in which N. herself grew up. Through the eponymous protagonist, who is childless in a culture that sees women as primarily mothers, the novel asks how a person can balance individual desires and communal demands, and what happens when one cannot conform to social expectations. At first criticized for its very fidelity to Nigerian ambiance, the novel is now celebrated for its founding position in African literature and for its rich representation of female characters. The novel has spawned many responses, some critics seeing Buchi EMECHETA's *Joys of Motherhood* (1979) as a direct response to it.

The civil war around Biafra colors *Never Again* (1975), a short, almost documentary novel that captures the feeling of war. N.'s short stories also explore military conflict; her first collection, *This Is Lagos* (1971), contains several stories set during the 1966 military coup. The social effects of war on women are more fully developed in *Wives at War* (1980). This volume reveals the changes women's roles underwent during the period of upheaval. *One is Enough* (1981), N.'s first major work after the war, reveals the extent of the revolution. Far more overtly feminist, the protagonist of this novel, Amaku, has moved away from the rural and culturally embedded protagonist of *Efuru*. Amaku shares many of the desire of N.'s earlier characters, but when circumstances conspire against her she does not succumb as in *Idu* (1970), but launches forth on her own path with great aplomb and success. This novel has been criticized for the corrupt practices it depicts; but again, this seeming weakness is a strength, as N.'s work avoids easy answers in the interest of developing awareness of possibilities and flaws in the postcolonial climate.

As one of Nigeria's first female writers, as one of the first black African women to gain an international reputation, and as a publisher, N. is an important literary figure. N.'s focus on women's issues and their place in a cultural milieu helped break down the restricted and stereotypical representations of women in Africa, and continues to demand reconsideration. N.'s incorporation of folk traditions and oral elements into her writing helped pave the way for future writers interested in orature. Her untimely death from pneumonia was a loss to the literary world.

FURTHER WORKS: *Emeka—Driver's Guard* (1972); *The Golden Wedding Jubilee of Chief and Mrs. C. I. N.* (1980); *The Miracle*

Kittens (1980); *Journey to Space* (1980); *Women Are Different* (1986); *Cassava Song & Rice Song* (1986); *The Lake Goddess* (1995)

BIBLIOGRAPHY: Wilentz, G., "The Individual Voice in the Communal Chorus: The Possibility of Choice in N.'s Efuru," *ACLALSB*, 7, 4 (1986), 30-36; Sample, M., "In Another Life: The Refugee Phenomenon in Two Novels of the Nigerian Civil War," *MFS*, 37, 3 (1991): 445-54; Wilentz, G., *Binding Cultures: Black Women Writers in Africa and the Diaspora* (1992): 3-37; special N. issue, *RAL*, 26, 2 (1995); Ezeigo, T. A., "Gender Conflict in N.'s Novels," in Newell, S., ed., *Writing African Women: Gender, Popular Culture and Literature in West Africa* (1997): 95-115

—VICTORIA CARCHIDI

NYANJA LITERATURE
See Malawian Literature

NYORO-TORO LITERATURE
See Ugandan Literature

O

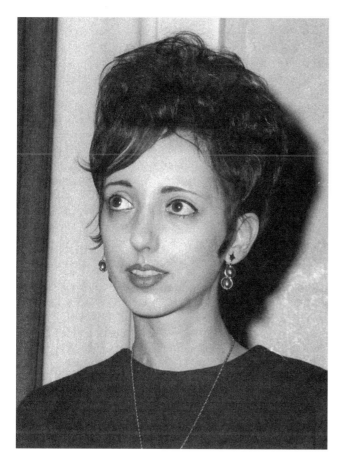

Joyce Carol Oates

OATES, Joyce Carol

American novelist, short-story writer, critic, poet, and dramatist, b. 16 June 1938, Millersport, N.Y.

O. grew up in a rural area near Lockport, New York. Her family background is bluecollar Catholic. She graduated with a B.A. in English from Syracuse University, and received her M.A., also in English, at the University of Wisconsin. She is a recipient of the O. Henry Special Award for Continuing Achievement (1967) among other awards. After teaching English at the University of Windsor in Ontario, Canada, for a number of years, she accepted a post at Princeton University.

O. is an extraordinarily versatile and prolific writer. Among her best works are her short stories. Since her first collection, *By the North Gate* (1963), she has published many short stories, both traditional and experimental in form. *The Wheel of Love* (1970) is her best-known collection. Typically, her characters find that love brings anguish and bitterness rather than fulfillment. "Accomplished Desires" (1968) depicts a student who marries the professor of her dreams, only to learn she is still unhappy. "How I Contemplated the World from the Detroit House of Correction and Began

My Life Over Again" (1969) concerns a teenager alienated from her suburban parents, who runs away from home and turns to shoplifting, drugs, and prostitution. "In the Region of Ice" (1965) shows an isolated student demanding that his nun-professor be a Christian. "Where Are You Going, Where Have You Been?" (1966) is an allegory that applies existential initiation rites to the biblical seduction myth. O.'s stories are replete with realistic details and plausible characters. Frequently, they have violent resolutions.

Her novels, too, more often than not, are resolved by violent death. O. believes her fiction reflects a contemporary American society in which an ordinary day can suddenly be filled with horror. Each novel of her early trilogy—*A Garden of Earthly Delights* (1967), *Expensive People* (1968), and *them* (1969), the last of which won a National Book Award—ends in murder or suicide. Whether rich or poor, the male protagonists act out their frustrations savagely.

Not all of O.'s works are violent. When she satirizes the university world in *Unholy Loves* (1979) she delineates with psychological realism college administrators and professors vying to identify with a famous visiting poet. *Do with Me What You Will* (1973) contains a rare heroine for O.: Elena achieves self-actualization through love, and feels that she has a chance for happiness.

A recurrent O. theme is the loss of the American Eden. Like Thoreau, whom she admires, she decries the destruction of the natural world and the related decay of moral fiber. In her poem "Dreaming America" (1973) she shows the loss of game animals and then a time when teenagers do not realize what is missing. Her ambitious gothic saga, the novel *Bellefleur* (1980), depicts six generations of a mythic American family. The Bellefleurs wantonly slaughter deer, exploit people and the land, and at times metamorphose into animals or disappear entirely. *Angel of Light* (1981), dedicated to the "Lost Generations," is a complex political novel set in the late 1970s, which dramatizes the alienation of the American people from those in positions of power.

O. is emerging as a great writer who illuminates contemporary American life with dazzling versatility. Her best short stories are masterpieces in the tradition of Nathaniel Hawthorne and Flannery O'CONNOR. Her fiction reveals an America peopled with inarticulate, violent men and unliberated, passive women. Her countrysides are replete with decimation; her polluted cities reflect racial and class tensions, as papers and dust blow through desolate streets. The world she portrays shows little social cohesion; this fragmented society is a result of a loss of spirituality and sense of community. Her vision is chilling, yet as a chronicler of narcissism and of consequent chaos, O. acts as an instrument of cultural synthesis in her assessment of modern life.

FURTHER WORKS: *With Shuddering Fall* (1964); *Upon the Sweeping Flood* (1966); *Women in Love and Other Poems* (1969); *Anonymous Sins and Other Poems* (1969); *Wonderland* (1971); *The Edge of Impossibility: Tragic Forms in Literature* (1972); *Marriages and Infidelities* (1972); *Angel Fire* (1973); *The Hostile Sun: The Poetry of D. H. Lawrence* (1973); *Love and Its Derangements and Other Poems* (1974); *Miracle Play* (1974); *New Heaven, New Earth: The Visionary Experience in Literature* (1974); *The Hungry Ghosts: Seven Allusive Comedies* (1974); *Where Are You*

Going, Where Have You Been?: Stories of Young America (1974); *The Goddess and Other Women* (1974); *The Seduction and Other Stories* (1975); *The Assassins: A Book of Hours* (1975); *The Poisoned Kiss and Other Stories from the Portuguese* (1975); *The Fabulous Beasts* (1975); *Childwold* (1976); *The Triumph of the Spider Monkey* (1976); *Crossing the Border: Fifteen Tales* (1976); *Night-Side: Eighteen Tales* (1977); *Season of Peril* (1977); *Son of the Morning* (1978); *All the Good People I've Left Behind* (1979); *Women Whose Lives Are Food, Men Whose Lives Are Money* (1978); *Cybele* (1979); *Three Plays* (1980); *A Sentimental Education: Stories* (1981); *Contraries: Essays* (1981); *Contraires: Essays* (1981); *Invisible Woman: New and Selected Poems 1970–1982* (1982); *A Bloodsmoor Romance* (1982); *The Profane Art* (1983); *Last Days* (1984); *Mysteries of Winterthorn* (1984); *Wild Saturday and Other Stories* (1984); *Solstice* (1985); *Wild Nights* (1985); *Raven's Wing* (1986); *On Boxing* (1987); *You Must Remember This* (1987); *The Assignation* (1988); *The Time Traveler* (1989); *American Appetites* (1989); *I Lock My Door Upon Myself* (1990); *Because It Is Bitter, and Because It Is My Heart* (1990); *The Rise of Life on Earth* (1991); *Where Is Here?* (1992); *Black Water* (1992); *What I Lived For* (1994); *Haunted* (1994); *Zombie* (1995); *American Gothic Tales* (1996); *Tenderness* (1996); *First Hope* (1996); *Will You Always Love Me? and Other Stories* (1996); *We Were the Malvaneys* (1996); *Man Crazy* (1997); *My Heart Laid Bare* (1998)

BIBLIOGRAPHY: Burwell, R., "J. C. O. and an Old Master," *Crit*, 15 (1973): 48–57; Grant, M., *The Tragic Vision of J. C. O.* (1978); Urbanski, M., "Existential Allegory: J. C. O.'s 'Where Are You Going, Where Have You Been?'" *SSF*, 15 (1978): 200–203; Phillips, R., "J. C. O.: The Art of Fiction LXXII," *Paris Review*, 74 (1978): 198–226; Creighton, J., *J. C. O.* (1979); Wagner, L. W., *Critical Essays on J. C. O.* (1979); Franks, L., "The Emergence of J. C. O.," *NYTMag*, 27 July 1980: 22 ff.

—MARIE OLESEN URBANSKI

ŌBA Minako

Japanese novelist, short-story writer, essayist, and poet, b. 11 Nov. 1930, Tokyo

O. refers to herself as a "vagrant spirit," reflecting a life of wandering. As a child she changed schools fourteen times due to her father's transfers as a Navy doctor. An avid reader, she explored both the Japanese classics and masterpieces of world literature in translation. At age fourteen, in 1945, she assisted atomic bomb victims in Hiroshima, a physical and mental landscape of despair, which at once shadows her writing with gloom and illuminates it with the inner strength gained from this experience. O. entered Tsuda Women's College in 1949, majoring in literature and drama. In 1955 she married "on the condition that I continue to write" and accompanied her husband, a representative for Alaska Pulp Company, to Sitka, Alaska, where she lived from 1959 to 1970. O. left periodically to study art and literature at the University of Washington and the University of Wisconsin, and to travel in the U.S. The pristine and fertile landscape of southeast

Alaska and the harmony of traditional Native Alaskan life styles contributed to her rich plant and animal imagery and to her concept of the human being as one small component of the biosphere. O.'s American experience, including her exposure to the doubts raised by U.S. involvement in Vietnam, increased her tendency to question the established order, strengthened her ability to perceive the relativism of so-called truths, and nurtured a flexible acceptance of other races and cultures. O. returned to Japan, not to put down roots, but with the determination to live her life as she wanted. She continues to travel widely and to write prolifically. In 1987 O. and Kōno Taeko (b. 1926) became the first women to sit on the selection committee of the coveted Akutagawa Prize in literature. O. was inducted into the National Academy of Arts (Geijutsuin) in 1991.

When O., a frustrated housewife, submitted "Sanbiki no kani" (1968; "The Three Crabs," 1978) to a literary magazine, she won immediate acclaim as recipient of the Gunzō New Writer Award and the Akutagawa Prize for new talent in serious fiction. A repulsion for society's hypocrisy and the spiritual isolation of the individual are themes that form the basis of her later work. Rejecting the "coherence" of Western literature with its emphasis on structure and plot, O. has developed her own form, a kind of nonform, a spontaneous flow of thoughts and images permitting maximum freedom of time and space. O.'s work is recognized for its intellectual and witty dialogues, graphic and sensuous imagery, sensitivity, and lyricism. O. is a master of simile and metaphor in which plant and animal imagery is used to strip man of his artificial clothing and housing, to lay bare our physical and mental state. More important than individual images is the manner in which they symphonize. This may be said of O.'s stories and novels, as well.

In *Garakuta hakubutsukan* (1975; the junk museum), recipient of the Prize for Women's Literature, O. focuses upon three women of diverse ethnicity, who, uprooted from their homeland, drift to a small Alaskan town. It is their individuality that is the key to their identity. They have attained their freedom, but at the cost of a certain loneliness.

O.'s protagonists are generally couples, with a focus on the female role. As in "Yamauba no bishō" (1976; "The Smile of a Mountain Witch," 1982), traditionally expressionless women are depicted as the center of consciousnes, as O. explores the price of suppressing fundamental thoughts and feelings to the point that one is anesthetized by social norms.

In *Katachi mo naku* (1982; formlessness and solitude), awarded the Tanizaki Prize for leading writers, O. seeks a state beyond the established "form" of marriage, dispelling the myths that have given shape to this institution. Through multiple images of characters and scenes, O. depicts man as a timeless component in a natural process.

The fundamental nature of the relationship between heterosexual couples and the search for female identity is explored further in a series of autobiographical novels, *Kiri no tabi* (2 vols., 1980; journey through the mist) and *Nakutori no* (1985; of singing birds), which won the Noma Literary Prize. Critic M. N. Wilson describes *Kiri no tabi* as a female-centered bildungsroman representing an ongoing resistance to social integration, a continuous "unbecoming" of what others would have us be.

Umi ni yuragu ito (1989; lines that drift through the sea) recipient of the Kawabata Prize, finds the protagonists of *Nakutori no* revisiting a small town in Alaska. The narrator follows the thread of life, not attempting to untangle or determine its course, relating tales in such a way that the past lives in the present, Japanese legends merge with Tlingit myths, characters from literature are juxtaposed to "real life" acquaintances, and dreams and reality are intertwined. As in Japanese linked verse, these episodes are loosely connected in an unrestricted realm of time and space.

In 1979 O. taught a modern literature seminar at the University of Oregon, resulting in *Oregon yume jūya* (1980; Oregon, ten nights of dreams), a free expression of subconscious perception, as found in *Yume jūya* (1907; *Ten Nights of Dreams*, 1974) by Natsume Soseki (1867–1916). In these essays O. discusses with wit and humor differences between eastern and western culture and differences in world view brought about by language.

O.'s feminist voice, sensitive cross-cultural comparisons, anecdotal style, and tendency to glide freely between different periods in time are seen in the biography *Tsuda Umeko* (1990; Tsuda Umeko), awarded the Yomiuri Literary Prize. After being raised and educated in the U.S., Umeko (1865–1929) returned to Japan and established Tsuda Women's College, creating the opportunity for students such as O. to acquire the education and self-confidence necessary to contribute to and find self-fulfillment in a society dominated by men.

O.'s work is distinguished by its fresh and immediate perception of life, its uninhibited expression of ideas, and its treatment of all aspects of life as part of a continuum, in which past and present, hope and despair, humans, plants and animals, self and other, lose their distinction in an exploration of the possibility of a new state of freedom and harmonious existence beyond established social systems.

FURTHER WORKS: *Funakuimushi* (1970); *Yūreitachi no fukkatsusai* (1970); *Uo no namida* (1971); *Sabita kotoba* (1971); *Tsuga no yume* (1971); *Kokyūo hiku tori* (1972); *O.-shū* (1972); *Shikai no ringo* (1973); *Yasōno yume* (1973); *Aoi kitsune* (1975); *Urashimasō* (1977); *Samete miru yume* (1978); *Aoi chiisana hanashi* (1978); *Hana to mushi no kioku* (1979); *Tankō* (1979); *Onna no danseiron* (1979); *Oregon yume jūya* (1980); *Shima no kuni no shima* (1982); *Watashi no erabu watashi no basho* (1982); *Yume o tsuru* (1983); *Bōshi no kiita monogatari* (1983); *Yumeno* (1984); *Yōbaidō monogatari* (1984); *Onna, otoko, inochi* (1985); *Dorama* (1985); *O. no taketori monogatari, Ise monogatari* (1986); *Miomotegawa* (1986); *Kagami no naka no kao* (1986); *O. no ugetsu monogatari* (1987); *Ōjo no namida* (1988); *Ikimono no hanashi* (1988), *Mahō no tama* (1989); *Niji no hashizume* (1989); *Shinshūotogisūshi* (1990); *O. zenshū* (10 vols., 1990–1991). FURTHER WORKS IN ENGLISH: *The Woman's Hand, Gender and Theory in Japanese Women's Writing* (1996)

BIBLIOGRAPHY: Chambers, M., "Fireweed," *JapQ*, 28 (1981): 403–27; Tanaka, Y., Introduction to *This Kind of Woman* (1982): ix–xxv; Lippit, N. M., and Selden, K. I., eds., *Stories by Contemporary Japanese Women Writers* (1982); xxii, 182–96, 218; Chambers, M., "O. M.: rebirth in Alaska," *JapQ*, 38 (1991): 474–83; Wilson, M. N., "Becoming or (Un)Becoming: the Female Destiny Reconsidered in O. M.'s Narratives," in Schalow, P. and J. Walker, eds., *The Woman's Hand, Gender and Theory in Japanese Women's Writing* (1996): 19-40, 293-328; Wilson, M. N., *Gender is Fair Game, (Re)Thinking the (Fe)Male in the Works of O. M.* (1998)

—KAREN COLLIGAN-TAYLOR

O'BRIEN, Edna

Irish novelist, short-story writer, dramatist, and screenwriter, b. 15 Dec. 1930, Tuamgraney

After growing up in the rural west of Ireland, O. attended the Pharmaceutical College in Dublin from 1946 to 1950. Married in 1951, she moved with her husband and two sons to London in 1959. Since her divorce in 1964, O. has remained in England. The author of several novels and short-story collections, she has also written for theater and films and in 1976 published *Mother Ireland*, a study of Irish culture and society.

The major characteristic of O.'s fiction is its frank portrayal of emotional and sexual relationships (her works usually have been censored in her native country). Her first three novels, *The Country Girls* (1960), *The Lonely Girl* (1962)—filmed (1964) with screenplay by O. under the title *The Girl with Green Eyes*, and later republished under that title—and *Girls in Their Married Bliss* (1964), form a trilogy about Caithleen Brady's painful journey from an awkward teenager growing up in the repressive atmosphere of rural Catholic Ireland to a young woman wounded by a bad marriage and forced to face her self-doubts and loneliness.

Her subsequent novels, with the exception of *A Pagan Place* (1970)—made into a play in 1973—which returns to the difficulties of childhood in the west of Ireland, explore the loneliness, suffering, and bitterness endured by women who have experienced emotional failure and betrayal in their relationships with men. *August Is a Wicked Month* (1965), perhaps O.'s best-written novel, with its wasteland imagery and atmosphere, and *Casualties of Peace* (1966), with its main character murdered in a case of mistaken identity, are particularly bleak studies of female isolation. *Night* (1972), whose heroine, Mary Holligan, recalls her history of emotions, desires, and loves, manages to reconcile life's pain with its promise, but *Johnny I Hardly Knew You* (1977) marks a return to a harsher world and vision, as its female victim turned avenger murders her younger lover for the past betrayals of her other loves.

O.'s collections of short stories, *The Love Object* (1960), *A Scandalous Woman* (1974), and *Mrs. Reinhardt* (1978), also develop a pattern of childhood disappointment and adult betrayals. Taken together, her novels and short stories, usually told from a personal viewpoint that has become more experimental in the later fiction, reveals a deepening probe into the desires, commitments, and betrayals of women who search for love and find a terrible sense of loss and loneliness at the end of their quest.

FURTHER WORKS: *A Nice Bunch of Flowers* (1963); *Zee and Co.* (screenplay, 1971); *Seven Novels and Other Short Stories* (1978); *Virginia: A Play* (1981)

BIBLIOGRAPHY: McMahon, S., "A Sex by Themselves: An Interim Report on the Novels of E. O.," *Éire*, 2, 1 (1967): 79–87; Kiely, B., "The Whores on the Half-Doors," in Edwards, O. D., ed., *Conor Cruise O'Brien Introduces Ireland* (1969): 148–61; Eckley, G., *E. O.* (1974); Snow, L., "'That Trenchant Childhood Route?' Quest in E. O.'s Novels," *Éire*, 14, 1 (1979): 74–83

—RICHARD F. PETERSON

O'BRIEN, Flann

(pseud. of Brian O'Nolan) Irish novelist, dramatist, and journalist, (writing in English and Gaelic), b. 5 Oct. 1911, Strabane; d. 1 April 1966, Dublin

Both of O.'s parents came from County Tyrone; because of the father's position as a customs and excise officer, the family moved frequently to various parts of Ireland. O. was the third child in a family of twelve that eventually settled in Dublin and environs. He was educated at Blackrock College and University College, Dublin.

As Brian O'Nolan (or, in its Irish form, Briain Ó Nualláin) O. spent much of his adult life as a civil servant in Dublin, chafing at the restrictions of his position and eventually losing it. As Myles na gCopaleen (or Gopaleen)—the name means "Myles of the little horse (or pony)"—he had an even longer career writing "Cruiskeen Lawn," a column for the *Irish Times*, mostly in English, sometimes in Gaelic, and even in French. His plurality of names, like his adroit shifts in languages, mirrored a multifaceted talent and a variety of literary modes, all of which came to a premature end when he died of cancer in his fifty-fifth year.

At Swim-Two-Birds (1939) established O.'s reputation and brought praise from James JOYCE, who called him a "real writer, with the true comic spirit." It remains one of the few examples of experimental modernism in Irish prose literature. Failure to have his second novel published during the war years embittered O., and he retreated from the audacities of his first novel, thereafter continuing to write comic works, but with neither the structural complexities nor the stylistic intricacies of *At Swim-Two-Birds*. He reacted against Joyce as well, publishing "A Bash in the Tunnel" (1951), an unusual critical essay on Joyce, and resurrecting Joyce as a character in the novel *The Dalkey Archive* (1964)—as a bartender and writer of religious tracts.

The amount of time that elapsed between the publication of *At Swim-Two-Birds* and the three other novels in English published under the Flann O'Brien pseudonym—*The Hard Life* (1961), *The Dalkey Archive*, and the posthumously published *The Third Policeman* (1967)—attest to the difficulty of his literary career. The last novel duplicates material from its immediate predecessor and appears to be the lost manuscript rejected in 1940, from which O. had already cannibalized. A fifth novel, *Slattery's Sago Saga*, existed for years only as a rumor, but seven chapters were unearthed and published in 1973.

The missing decades between *At Swim-Two-Birds* and *The Hard Life* were years in which the Myles-of-the-little-horse persona dominated, not only in the scurrilous and hilarious columns but also on the stage—and in the Irish language. As Myles he wrote *An béal bocht* (1941; *The Poor Mouth*, 1973), which because of its complex Irish puns was long considered untranslatable, and his first drama, *Faustus Kelly* (1943), which was produced at the Abbey Theatre. Regardless of the artistic medium or the operative language, everything written by Brian-Flann-Myles reveals an irreverent comic touch veering from frivolity to satiric bitterness.

Although some critics, primarily in Ireland, relegate *At Swim-Two-Birds* to the status of an oddity and prefer the later works, his international reputation rests essentially on that novel-within-a-novel-within-another-novel. The multiple frame, the diabolism, the conspiracy of the fictional characters against their creator, the fiendish speculations on human folly, the unexpected transcendence of folly and fate—these features characterize this unusual

work. His later novels abandon complex plot structure for linear narrative but retain the wildly comic tone, the agony of despair, the pretended indifference that underlines an acceptance of futility, the lugubriousness that nonetheless hints at religious miracle, and the skillful blend into near-plausible fantasy that characterize the first novel.

Satiric and cynical, outrageous and outlandish, O.'s world is remembered for the small-town Irish politics with the devil stuffing the ballot boxes, the smoke-filled rural kitchens with obese pigs jammed in the doorframe, the cracks in the ceiling that are maps of hell, the bicycles that take on the human characteristics of their owners, the Irish uncles who attempt to convince the Pope to provide public conveniences for women who, having consumed "gravid water," fall to their death through the floorboards, and James Joyce writing for the Catholic Truth Society. These diverse elements locate O. within the Irish comic tradition, and he persisted as a jaundiced commentator on the Irish nation that emerged in the 20th c.

FURTHER WORKS: *The Best of Myles* (1968); *Stories and Plays* (1973); *The Various Lives of Keats and Chapman and The Brother* (1976); *A. F. O. Reader* (1978)

BIBLIOGRAPHY: Wain, J., "To Write for My Own Race," *Encounter*, July 1967: 71–85; O'Keeffe, T., ed., *Myles: Portraits of Brian O'Nolan* (1968); Benstock, B., "The Three Faces of Brian Nolan," *Éire*, 3, 3 (1968): 51–65; Janik, D. I., "F. O.: The Novelist as Critic," *Éire*, 4, 4 (1969): 64–72; Lee, L. L., "The Dublin Cowboys of F. O.," *WAL*, 4 (1969): 219–25; Clissmann, A., *F. O.: A Critical Introduction to His Writings* (1975); Power, M., "F. O. and Classical Satire: An Exegesis of *The Hard Life*," *Éire*, 13, 1 (1978): 87–102

—BERNARD BENSTOCK

O'CASEY, Sean

(born John Casey; name Gaelicized, first as Sean Ó Cathasaigh) Irish dramatist, autobiographer, and essayist, b. 30 March 1880, Dublin; d. 18 Sept. 1964, St. Marychurch, England

Much of O.'s life was fraught with controversy, including the facts of his biography. He began his autobiography with "In Dublin, sometime in the early eighties, on the last day of the month of March" (even the date is erroneous), a purposely vague beginning to the story of "Johnny/Sean Casside" in a novelized version. O. had previously set his birth year ahead in order to pass as a young new playwright to qualify for the Hawthornden Prize when he was forty-six. His first play had been staged by the Abbey Theatre in Dublin three years earlier, when its author was still earning his meager living with a pick and shovel.

O. was actually born into reasonably comfortable circumstances, the last of thirteen children; the previous two had also been christened John, and both had died in infancy. His parents were lower-middle-class Protestants, but with the death of the father when O. was only six, the family became progressively poorer but never less proud. Eventually, he lived alone with his aged mother, her sole means of support during years in which he remained

Sean O'Casey

mostly unemployed. Impaired eyesight during childhood kept him away from school; at times tutored by his schoolteacher sister, he was essentially self-taught from books he bought or stole. During his thirties he wrote poems, songs, and journalistic political pieces, learned Irish and joined the Gaelic League, and served as secretary for various organizations, primarily the Irish Citizen Army, the militant arm of the tradeunion movement. He broke with the Nationalist cause because he insisted on a socialist base for its political activities, and despite his bourgeois origins he strongly identified with the working class, remaining a lifelong communist. From 1918 on he persisted in submitting plays to the Abbey Theatre, all of them rejected until *The Shadow of a Gunman* (1923) was produced; it brought instant success to him and the theater, probably saving the Abbey from bankruptcy and eventually rescuing O. from manual labor.

The next two plays, *Juno and the Paycock* (1924) and *The Plough and the Stars* (1926), confirmed O.'s reputation and are still considered his greatest, although the latter caused a recurrence of Abbey riots (there had previously been disturbances over plays by YEATS and SYNGE). While the voice of a Nationalist leader can be heard outside a pub extolling patriotic bloodletting, a happy-go-luckless prostitute is present within peddling her wares. When Nationalists in the audience erupted in anger at the idea of the flag of the Citizens Army being brought into a pub and at the portrayal of an Irish woman as a prostitute, William Butler Yeats announced from the stage the apotheosis of a new Irish genius. In 1926 O. went to London for the opening of *Juno and the Paycock* and the

Hawthornden Prize, and married a young Irish actress. The rejection of *The Silver Tassie* (1928) by the Abbey (and Yeats in particular) in 1928 changed the residence in England into permanent self-exile, and in 1938 he moved his wife and two sons to Devon, where his daughter was born the next year. From his Tor Bay-area vantage point O. surveyed events in Ireland with interest, wrote plays, essays, and autobiographies, and received visitors from all over the world; his vintage years were tragically marred by the premature death of his son Niall. His turbulent love affair with Ireland and the Abbey Theatre and his numerous quarrels with both persisted throughout, and two of his comic self-personifications—guises of a Socratic gadfly and a raucous voice insisting on joy in life, good drama, and working-class ideals—provided titles for books of fugitive essays, *The Flying Wasp* (1937) and *The Green Crow* (1956).

The twenty-two plays (plus a recently published early rejected play) constitute the primary corpus of O.'s creativity. Directly or obliquely most of the plays mirrored the historical events in Ireland (and the world at large) during O.'s lifetime: the first four major Dublin-set tragicomedies deal with the era of the "Troubles" (*The Shadow of a Gunman*), the civil war (*Juno and the Paycock*), the Easter Rising (*The Plough and the Stars*), and World War I (*The Silver Tassie*).

Two later plays have an English setting: *Within the Gates* (1934), a morality play about the economic depression set in Hyde Park, and *Oak Leaves and Lavender* (1946), a drama of the Battle of Britain set in rural England, with two Irishmen as its protagonists. The latter is among O.'s most outspoken propaganda pieces, along with *The Star Turns Red* (1940), which hypothesized for Ireland an ultimate confrontation between communist and fascist forces based on the circumstances of the Spanish Civil War. His most personal drama, *Red Roses for Me* (1943), is also his most successful political statement in favor of militant trade unionism; it is based on his own experiences during the 1911 railway strike, which had previously served as plot material for the rejected play, *The Harvest Festival* (written 1918–19, pub. 1980).

The Abbey triumphs of the 1920s established O. as a presumed master of naturalistic drama, a designation he was never comfortable with, and it was not until the EXPRESSIONIST second act of *The Silver Tassie* that he demonstrated his bent for experimentation. His ear for working-class Dublin speech, the settings in the slums, the depiction of tenement life during periods of upheaval and hardship had fixed critical assumptions of "photographic realism," but these plays were also distinguished for the ironic juxtapositions of the tragic and the comic. Having learned his craft from reading such diverse authors as Shakespeare and Dion Boucicault (1820?–1890), O. did not hesitate to mix genres and styles, and to deploy strong elements of the melodramatic. During the 1940s and 1950s he wrote several joyous and bitter comedies, beginning with *Purple Dust* (1940), in which two English businessmen make magnificent fools of themselves in attempting to restore a Tudor mansion in Ireland, losing their mistresses to militant and romantic Irish workmen, and their manor and lives to an apocalyptic flood. *Cock-a-Doodle Dandy* (1949) and *The Drums of Father Ned* (1958) are also set in rural Ireland—priest-ridden, puritanical, and bourgeois—where only an occasional free spirit, several strong-minded women, and some amorous young people can break free and possibly upset the apple cart. The most libertine and licentious comedy, however, is *Figuro in the Night* (1961), written when O. was already an octogenarian, a parable extolling the Mannequin Pis running amock in theocratic Dublin. In *The Bishop's Bonfire* (1955) O. dissected what he viewed as constricted Irish society in a drama that retains some of his zesty comic elements, but is essentially his most somber play.

Rivaling his dramatic output is his alternate career as a dynamic and caustic writer of autobiographies that transcend the genre to include aspects of the novel, imaginative fictions, and the expository essay. *I Knock at the Door* (1939), *Pictures in the Hallway* (1942), and *Drums under the Windows* (1945) are poignant, exciting, and often poetic, many of the incidents paralleling those of the plays. *Inishfallen, Fare Thee Well* (1949) marks a transition as the playwright leaves Ireland, and it points toward the later volumes of commentary and criticism in which O. indulged in acerbic observations and opinions, as well as verbal high jinks. *Rose and Crown* (1952) and *Sunset and Evening Star* (1954) are filled with warmth, compassion, good humor, and a healthy dollop of sentimentality. (The six volumes were republished as *Mirror in My House*, 2 vols., 1956).

O.'s reputation as Ireland's premier dramatist and a major figure in 20th-c. literature has consolidated since his death in 1964, although productions of any but his major plays are not as frequent as his fixed position deserves. The vagaries of fantasy, the controversial political and anticlerical elements, the subtle balances of comic and tragic, the broad nature of slapstick comedy and melodrama, and the difficulty of reproducing the mellifluous and mordant Irish speech remain inhibiting factors, yet the technological advances in stage machinery reduce some of the technical problems of production: several productions have been innovative in enacting the vast deluge that covers the stage at the end of *Purple Dust*, for instance. *Mirror in My House* has recently become an increasingly important component of O.'s body of work, and an alternate reputation has been developing for him as a fanciful chronicler of his time and a writer of creative autobiography. Despite the negative attitudes of various detractors, there are few who would deny that O. has achieved a permanent position in literary history as the creator of such immortal characters as Captain Boyle, "Joxer" Daly, and Fluther Good to share the world stage with Falstaff and Tartuffe.

FURTHER WORKS: *Windfalls* (1934); *Collected Plays* (4 vols., 1949–1951); *Behind the Green Curtains* (1961); *Feathers from the Green Crow* (1962); *Under a Colored Cap* (1964); *Blasts and Benedictions* (1967); *The S. O. Reader* (1968); *The Letters of S. O.* (2 vols., 1975, 1980); *The Harvest Festival* (written 1919, pub. 1979)

BIBLIOGRAPHY: Krause, D., *S. O.: The Man and His Work* (1960); Hogan, R., *The Experiments of S. O.* (1960); McCann, S., ed., *The World of S. O.* (1966); Ayling, R., ed., *S. O.* (1969); O'Casey, E., *Sean* (1971); Mikhail, E. H., ed., *S. O.: A Bibliography of Criticism* (1972); Mikhail, E. H., and J. O'Riodran, eds., *The Sting and the Twinkle: Conversations with S. O.* (1974); *S. O. Review* (1974–); Kilroy, T., ed., *S. O.: A Collection of Critical Essays* (1975); Benstock, B., *Paycocks and Others: S. O.'s World* (1976); Smith, B. L., *O.'s Satiric Vision* (1978); Ayling, R. and Durkin, M., eds., *S. O.: A Bibliography* (1978); Murray, C., ed., special O. issue, *IUR*, 10, 1 (1980)

—BERNARD BENSTOCK

O. is a master of knockabout in this very serious and honourable sense—that he discerns the principle of disintegration in even the most complacent solidities, and activates it to their explosion. This is the energy of his theatre, the triumph of the principle of knockabout in situation, in all its elements and on all its planes, from the furniture to the higher centres. If *Juno and the Paycock*, as seems likely, is his best work so far, it is because it communicates most fully this dramatic dishiscence, mind and world come asunder in irreparable dissociation—"chassis" (the credit of having readapted Aguecheek and Belch in Joxer and the Captain being incidental to the larger credit of having dramatised the slump in the human solid).

Samuel Beckett, *The Bookman*, 86 (1934), p. 111

The manifest fact is that O. is a baroque dramatic poet in a largely trivial and constricted theatre given over to neat construction and small-beer feeling. He is as baroque, as lavish and prodigal, as were Marlowe, Shakespeare, Jonson, and John Webster. He belongs to the spacious days of the theatre. And since he will not make himself smaller for anything as inconsequential to him as material success, the theatre will simply have to be made larger if O. is to have his rightful place . . .

He was formed as a writer neither by educational institutions nor by the theatre but by a turbulent life equally remote from the academy and the stage. It has never been possible to subjugate him to either institution. Nor could he accept the rule of any established dramatic form. Realistic group drama suited his needs in *The Shadow of a Gunman*, family drama in *Juno and the Paycock*, mass drama in *The Plough and the Stars*. His passion forced him to adopt expressionism in *The Silver Tassie* and choral drama in *Within the Gates*. Rather simplified drama was his natural mode in *The Star Turns Red* when he polarized the world into revolutionary and counterrevolutionary factions. A lyrical realism was proper to his elegaic mood when he commemorated the great Transport Strike of 1913 in *Red Roses for Me*. A turbulent fantasy was the inevitable choice for his desire to assert the claims of nature against cowardice in *Cock-a-Doodle Dandy* . . .

Neither in tragedy nor comedy can he be circumspect, cautious, or calculating. His artistry remains pure self-expression and spins everything out of his emotion and immediate observation.

John Gassner, *The Theatre in Our Time* (1954), pp. 244–45

S. O.—whose own youth was bitter—believed that life was a joyful inspiration that should never be tarnished by anything that even remotely resembled a sense of sin. He believed in the dignity of freedom and the liberty of joy; nothing, one imagines, would have given him more pleasure than an opportunity of joining God in declaring that Nietzsche was dead. He was a man of powerful vision and enormous energy, the most irrational yet likeable voice in twentieth-century theatre. An early and most vocal member of the Disestablishment, he was unable to resist sitting targets but he knocked them with brilliance and built alternatives with fierce integrity and considerable compassion. He added several new dimensions to the theatre, influenced many of the best contemporary dramatists of whom one can think, and wrote the most brilliant dialogue of our time.

Don't be misled by those who say that he was out of touch with Ireland. He wasn't. His plays have real relevance for they go back, in modern dress, to investigate the archaic, hypocritical and furtively puritanical thinking of the Irish past which still so strongly influences the mildly sophisticated thinking of the Irish present. Some day our society will change, broaden, solidify, and the old crawthumpers will be safely stored away and something approaching honesty will take the place of compromise in our politics, our religion and our thought. Then we will realise the extent of his genius. Or will we?

Kevin Casey, "The Excitements and the Disappointments," in Sean McCann, ed., *The World of S. O.* (1966), p. 233

But it was faith in life, love for his family and friends, and belief in a cheerful destiny that kept him going through a life of indigence and several personal catastrophes. He was affectionate, generous, and loyal towards those he loved and respected. His hatreds were confined to people and institutions that, in his opinion, impeded or impaired the normal joyousness of human existence. Among the advertising cards inside a Second Avenue bus in New York I was once surprised and delighted to find a quotation from O.: "I have found life an enjoyable, enchanting, active and sometimes terrifying experience, and I've enjoyed it completely. A lament in one ear, maybe, but always a song in the other." This turned out to be a quotation from one of the hundreds of personal letters he wrote to hundreds of anonymous admirers, particularly in the United States, of which he was especially fond. O. was a believer; it is a temptation to misuse a religious term and call him an Old Believer. That was his strength as a writer. The fire was in his hatred. The strength was in his love.

He was a frail man, afflicted all his life with ulcerated eyes that resulted in almost total blindness in his last years. He suffered from lumbago that made movement painful; he had bronchial and respiratory troubles that consigned him to nursing homes repeatedly. But he left a prodigious body of exuberant work. Beginning at the age of 38, when his first writings were published ("Songs of the Wren" and "The Story of Thomas Ashe") he wrote twelve full-length plays, fifteen one-act plays, six volumes of autobiography and four volumes of poems, short stories, reviews, articles and jeremiads. Although the literary forms changed, the basic point of view remained consistent.

Brooks Atkinson, Introduction to *The S. O. Reader* (1968), pp. xi–xii

In his beginning and in his ending, words were the weapons of his idealism and discontent. Words for him were a delight and a defense, a way of playing with dramatic images and developing his workingclass values, a way of compensating for his lack of formal education; but ultimately and of necessity words were a way of defending himself in an Ireland torn by economic and political revolt, religious conflict and literary backbiting. If he was poor in material things, he could be rich, even profligate with words. In some of his earliest extant letters he is in his most characteristic moods when as a St. Lawrence O'Toole piper in 1910 he defends the glory of the ancient Irish war pipes, in English and later in Gaelic; and when as an unemployed railway laborer in 1913 he defends Irish freedom and socialism in a letter to the *Irish Worker* that is subtitled, "A Challenge to Verbal Combat." He was to spend the rest of his life piping the tragicomic music of Irish life and seeking verbal combat whenever honor was at stake. He was incapable of turning away from a fight; he courted conflict, even when it was apparent that he would probably win the argument but lose the battle. As he once wrote about himself in later years in the persona of "The Green Crow": "Some Latin writer once said, 'If a crow could feed in quiet, it would have more meat.' A thing this Green Crow could never do: it had always, and has still, to speak and speak while it seeks and finds its food, and so has had less meat than it might have had if only it had kept its big beak shut." Suffering in silence would have been an unbearable sign of humiliation and defeat—to him the ultimate despair, and a sin against the Holy Ghost which he never committed.

David Krause, Introduction to *The Letters of S. O., Volume I*, 1910–1941 (1975), p. ix

O. was a "realist": his plays and his prose works present a picture of life as he saw it, with the exploited working class engaged in constant struggle not only against their capitalist and imperialist masters but also against their own human weaknesses and petty meannesses. But he was not a "naturalist." His realistic picture is constantly modified by the introduction of allegorical or mythological characters and incidents. Because the culture he writes about is Christian and largely Catholic, many of these "imaginary" elements take the form of, or are presented in language derived from, the Christian religious iconography. Because he was an Irishman (who had in his youth been a keen member of the Gaelic Revival movement) he also reflects the prevailing divine machinery of the pre-Christian Gaelic legends.

John Arden, "Ecce Hobo Sapiens: O.'s Theatre," in T. Kilroy, ed., *S. O.: A Collection of Critical Essays* (1975), p. 65

O.'s achievement, for all the unevenness and occasional failures, can be fully comprehended only by approaching his work as the product of a sensitive and well-read man, to be evaluated within the broad context of the English literary tradition that he knew so well and of modern developments in world theatre, and not merely the context of Dublin or even Anglo-Irish culture. He was a conscious literary artist, aware of what he was doing and what was going on in the world at large. His profound identification with the consciousness of Dublin, and of the Dublin proletariat in particular, is a characteristic that cannot be ignored, of course; but, at best—and this is more often than is usually recognised—his plays and prose works project a deeply realised experience of Irish life on a universal plane. If it is wrong to view James Joyce merely in parochial or regional terms, then it is equally absurd to approach O. as a provincial writer in any narrow sense, or, because of the proletarian background to his writings, to label him, even appreciatively, as a wild, untutored primitive. He was, from first to last, a deliberate and pioneering dramatic artist and his style and technique, constantly adapted and modified to display basic recurrent themes in new and theatrically exciting ways, invites analysis by virtue of its variety and originality. Criticism of O. as a playwright, therefore, should bear in mind that his command of stagecraft was no happy accident but the result of a lifetime's sustained exploration of diverse modes of dramatic expression.

Ronald Ayling, *Continuity and Innovation in S. O.'s Drama* (1976), pp. vi–vii

Flannery O'Connor

OCCITAN LITERATURE
See French Literature

O'CONNOR, Flannery

American novelist and short-story writer, b. 25 March 1925, Savannah, Ga., d. 3 Aug. 1964, Milledgeville, Ga.

O.'s life was in many ways tightly circumscribed. With the exception of two years spent at the University of Iowa acquiring a Master of Fine Arts degree, she spent her entire life in her native Georgia, the first thirteen years in Savannah, and the remainder in Milledgeville, where she lived on a farm with her mother. In part, the circumscription of O.'s life was due to illness, for she was a victim after 1950 of disseminated lupus, a debilitating blood disease. Yet O. knew nothing of self-pity: her attitude toward her illness was distinctly cavalier, and she liked to affect a broad, down-home manner in an apparent parody of her provincial existence. Nor was O. a recluse. She regularly issued invitations to friends and correspondents to visit her in Milledgeville, and she numbered Caroline GORDON, John HAWKES, Robert LOWELL, Katherine Anne PORTER, Andrew Lytle (1902–1995), and Robert Fitzgerald (1910–1985) among her friends and callers. Nor was O. a dropout from the cultural mainstream. She read carefully such

contemporary thinkers as Pierre Teilhard de Chardin (1881–1955), Hannah Arendt (1906–1975), and Jacques Maritain (1882–1973), and she read with discernment such formidable novelists as Vladimir NABOKOV, Muriel SPARK, and Henry JAMES.

But O. knew that her strength was in her roots, and all but two of her stories are set among the cities, towns, and farms of the Piedmont region, where "Jesus Saves" signs punctuate a landscape too often squalid and mean. Drawing on that intermixture of squalor and backwoods Protestantism, O. wrote stories in which ill-favored characters are engaged in an unsettling relationship with God, who tends to erupt into their lives violently and unexpectedly. Humor attends her macabre stories of God and man, for many of O.'s characters exult in their malfeasance and delight us with their unregenerate willfulness. Nonetheless, O. was herself a deeply religious Roman Catholic (a "hillbilly Thomist," she once called herself), and her characters ultimately risk condemnation for their disbelief.

O.'s two novels, *Wise Blood* (1952) and *The Violent Bear It Away* (1960), are both studies in disbelief and the saving ways of grace. Hazel Motes of *Wise Blood* goes so far as to preach the "Church without Christ," believing himself liberated from his childhood obsession with sin and Jesus, and determined to free others from the tyranny of Christian faith. Motes cannot sustain his defiance of Christ, however, and he finally embraces a life of penance as grotesque as his defiance of God had been. Marion Tarwater, the protagonist of *The Violent Bear It Away*, is a mirror-opposite of Motes, for Tarwater accepts an early call to prophetic ministry without genuine faith in his calling. Like Motes in *Wise Blood*, Tarwater comes finally to faith, but through an acceptance of his prophetic burden rather than through a rejection of it. Ironically, it is in committing murder that both Motes and Tarwater suddenly know their identities and their conversions to Christ: in O.'s fictive world, the ways of grace are eccentric as well as salvific.

O.'s short stories are not so explicitly theological in framework or in reference as her novels, and the protagonists of the short stories tend to suffer abrupt revelations about themselves rather than revelations of God. But in stories such as "The Geranium" (1946), "The Artificial Nigger" (1955), and "Everything That Rises Must Converge" (1961), the protagonists experience dark nights of the soul as profound as those of Motes and Tarwater; in stories such as "Good Country People" (1955), "The Life You Save May Be Your Own" (1953), and "A Good Man Is Hard to Find" (1953), violence erupts as shatteringly as the violence of God erupts in the novels, and it is never clear that the violence in such stories is *not* of God, for O.'s stories are always open to theological interpretation.

In many ways, O.'s short stories are more successful than her novels. *Wise Blood* and *The Violent Bear It Away* are thinly textured at best, whereas the short stories are typically thick with incident; moreover, the frigidly unsentimental tone of O.'s fiction tends to cloy in the novels, while it remains startling and effective in the more brief compass of the stories. The bite of O.'s humor is more successful in the stories than in the novels, too, for in the span of the novels the humor cumulates with an oddly saddening effect, while in the stories it remains crisp and morally authoritative, entirely an agent of the mixed effect that is O.'s aesthetic signature. Indeed, the incongruity between style and subject in O.'s fiction—a kind of poker-face she turns to the extraordinary—is what distinguishes O.'s vision from that of such kindred writers as Carson MCCULLERS and Tennessee WILLIAMS.

If O. was not the ignorant provincial that she sometimes pretended to be, she was still less the backwoods natural she is sometimes thought to have been. As her collected letters, published as *The Habit of Being* (1979), make clear, she was a conscious craftsman, not unsophisticated in technique, and she had a masterful sense of the nuances of manners and social class, a fine sense of timing, and an exact ear for speech. Her prose may seem artless to the casual glance, but its rhythms are precisely modulated, its vocabulary is concretely evocative, and its tone is marvelously calculated to embrace dark humor and religious exultation alike. Her body of work is small, consisting of only thirty-one stories, two novels, and some speeches and letters, but her achievement is major, transcending both the religious beliefs and the regionalism that so deeply inform her work.

FURTHER WORKS: *A Good Man Is Hard to Find, and Other Stories* (1955); *Everything That Rises Must Converge* (1965); *Mystery and Manners: Occasional Prose* (1969); *The Complete Stories of F. O.* (1971)

BIBLIOGRAPHY: Friedman, M. J., and Lawson, L. A., eds., *The Added Dimension: The Art and Mind of F. O.* (1966); Driskell, L. V., and Brittain, J. T., *The Eternal Crossroads: The Art of F. O.* (1971); Feeley, K., *F. O.: Voice of the Peacock* (1972); Muller, G. H., *Nightmares and Visions: F. O. and the Catholic Grotesque* (1972); Orvell, M., *Invisible Parade: The Fiction of F. O.* (1972); May, J. R., *The Pruning Word: The Parables of F. O.* (1976); McFarland, D. T., *F. O.* (1976); Shloss, C., *F. O.'s Dark Comedies: The Limits of Inference* (1980)

—ROBERT F. KIERNAN

O'CONNOR, Frank

(pseud. of Michael O'Donovan) Irish short-story writer, novelist, dramatist, literary critic, biographer, and translator, b. 17 Sept. 1903, Cork; d. 10 March 1966, Dublin

O.'s early years, the subject of his *An Only Child* (1961), the first of two autobiographies, were spent in terrible poverty. Although he had to leave school in his early teens, he continued his studies, especially of the Irish language and culture, and became active in politics. But after fighting on the losing Republican side in the Irish civil war and spending a year in an internment camp, he turned away from politics. In his second autobiography, *My Father's Son* (1969), O. describes his frustrations as a librarian in Cork and the controversies during his early literary career in Dublin. He became a director of the Abbey Theatre in 1935 but resigned after W. B. YEATS's death in 1939 and devoted his energies to writing. After a decade of struggling against Irish provincialism, O. went to America, where he taught at several universities during the 1950s. In his later years O. received long-overdue acclaim in Ireland and abroad as one of the world's finest short-story writers.

Although he also published translations from the Irish, as well as a biography, two novels, and several books of literary criticism, O. has been recognized and honored mainly for his short stories. Most of the stories in *Guests of the Nation* (1931), his first volume, are reflections of his war experiences. In *Bones of Contention* (1936) the focus is on peasant characters at odds with authority. In *Crab-Apple Jelly* (1944), one of his best collections, and *The Common Chord* (1948) O. concentrates on lonely, isolated characters, their frustrations and failures, and their occasional triumphs of the spirit. In later collections, *Traveller's Samples* (1951) and *Domestic Relations* (1957), the stories are dominated by first-person narratives, often told humorously by Larry Delaney, a spokesman for O., about the problems of growing up in Ireland.

In *The Lonely Voice* (1962), an influential study of the modern short story, O. points out that the proper subject matter for the short story, because it is a solitary art intended for the solitary reader, is the lonely, even outlawed individual who appears so frequently in Irish, American, and Russian fiction. Although he believes that the short story developed from the oral tradition, he sees the modern story as dominated by a detached, objective point of view that often makes narrative approach the mode of dramatic art.

A member of a generation that also produced Liam O'Flaherty (1896-1984) and Sean O'Faoláin (1900-1991), O. is generally regarded as Ireland's most important writer of short fiction. At their best, his stories illuminate the loneliness endured by those isolated from society by their own sensitivity, desire, or sense of failure. While several of his masterpieces are written in a detached manner, most of his stories are first-person narratives that capture the human voice speaking. O.'s popularity is largely dependent upon the charm and humor of his narrators, but his reputation as a master of the short-story form is based on his ability to write with objectivity and with insight into the lonely characters who populate his fictional world.

FURTHER WORKS: *The Saint and Mary Kate* (1932); *Three Old Brothers* (1936); *The Big Fellow: A Life of Michael Collins* (1937); *Dutch Interior* (1940); *Towards an Appreciation of Literature* (1945); *Irish Miles* (1947); *The Art of the Theatre* (1947); *The Road to Stratford* (1948; rev. ed., *Shakespeare's Progress*, 1960); *Leinster, Munster, and Connaught* (1950); *The Stories of F. O.* (1952); *More Stories* (1954; rev. ed., *Collection Two*, 1964); *The Mirror in the Roadway* (1956); *Stories by F. O.* (1956); *The Backward Look: A Survey of Irish Literature* (1967); *Collection Three* (1969); *A Set of Variations* (1969); *Collected Stories* (1981); *The Cornet-Player Who Betrayed Ireland* (1981)

BIBLIOGRAPHY: Sheehy, M., ed., *Michael/Frank: Studies on F. O.* (1969); Matthews, J., *F. O.* (1976); Wohlgelernter, M., *F. O.: An Introduction* (1977); Tomory, W., *F. O.* (1980); Chatalic, R., "F. O. and the Desolation of Reality," in Rafroidi, P. and Brown, T., eds., *The Irish Short Story* (1980): 189–204; Averill, D., *The Irish Short Story from George Moore to F. O.* (1981): 227–305; Peterson, R. F., "F. O. and the Modern Irish Short Story," *MFS*, 28 (1982): 53–67

—RICHARD F. PETERSON

ODETS, Clifford

American dramatist and screenwriter, b. 18 July 1906, Philadelphia, Pa.; d. 14 Aug. 1963, Los Angeles, Cal.

O.'s parents were originally of the working class, but his father became the owner of a printing plant after the family moved to the Bronx in 1912, and O. grew up in a comfortable, middle-class milieu. He dropped out of high school in 1923 to become an actor but his essentially unsuccessful experiences with the Theatre Guild (1923–27), Harry Kemp's Poets' Theatre (1925–27), Mae Desmond and Her Players (1927–31), and the Group Theatre (1930–35) caused him to give up the stage. His subsequent career as a dramatist reflects major trends in American playwriting of the next three decades: O. wrote proletarian, social–problem plays in the 1930s, plays dealing with loneliness and personal disorientation in the late 1930s and early 1940s, and psychological dramas for the Broadway stage in the late 1940s and early 1950s. In 1961 O. received the Drama Award of the American Academy of Arts and Letters.

O.'s best plays were produced between 1935 and 1937. *Waiting for Lefty* (1935), a one–act play in the agitprop tradition, is concerned with the situation of striking taxicab drivers. It took first prize from a field of 220 entries in the New Theatre–New Masses Theatre Contest as well as winning the George Pierce Baker Drama Prize at Yale. The play, while depicting a specific strike, offers a vigorous and searching commentary on the overall labor and social unrest of the times.

I've Got the Blues (1935), later retitled *Awake and Sing!* (1935), displays at its best O.'s talent for psychological characterization and for well-balanced tragicomedy. The play portrays the tensions of three generations of a working-class Jewish family living

Clifford Odets

together in a Bronx apartment. *Awake and Sing!* and *Paradise Lost* (1935) both deal with the lives of families whose very existence is threatened by the economic problems of the Great Depression. *Awake and Sing!* is the stronger play in that its characters are more convincingly developed and tend to be less stereotypical than those in *Paradise Lost*. Both plays demonstrate clearly O.'s fine ear for Jewish-American idiom and his ability to record it credibly. *Till the Day I Die* (1935), an agitprop play about the problems of communists in Nazi Germany, was hastily (and carelessly) written and produced hurriedly so that it might be part of a double bill. It was paired first with *Waiting for Lefty* and later with *Awake and Sing!* Some crudely presented elements in this play (for example, the smashing of Ernst Tausig's hand by a sadistic SS trooper) were refined and used productively in subsequent plays such as *Golden Boy* (1937), which, like the latter plays *The Big Knife* (1948) and *The Country Girl* (1950), is concerned with the unconscionable exploitation of talent. *Golden Boy*, the story of a sensitive violinist who is forced by economic necessity to go into professional boxing, thereby destroying his hands, retains many of the proletarian overtones of O.'s earliest work.

Of O.'s middle group of plays, *Night Music* (1940) is the most sensitive and the one with the greatest artistic integrity. It deals with homelessness and loneliness, presenting these themes with delicacy, although at times too romantically. *Rocket to the Moon* (1938) and *Clash by Night* (1941) are dependent for their development upon the hackneyed and formulaic love triangle. Only intermittently do they rise above banality.

The Big Knife is the most vitriolic of O.'s late plays. It demonstrates O.'s anger and disenchantment with Hollywood and the film industry—he had written the scripts for *The General Died at Dawn* (1937), *None But the Lonely Heart* (1944), which he also directed, *Deadline at Dawn* (1946), and *Humoresque* (1946), and would later write the screenplays for *The Sweet Smell of Success* (1957), *The Story on Page One* (1960), which he directed, and *Wild in the Country* (1961). *The Country Girl* is psychologically more profound than most of his earlier plays, save *Awake and Sing!* It focuses on the battle of an aging actor with alcoholism and on the struggle of his younger wife to help him overcome his problem and to remain loyal to him despite her romantic attraction to his director.

O.'s final stage play, *The Flowering Peach* (1954), a warm and witty allegory based on the biblical story of Noah and the flood, is one of his stronger works. In it he returns to the theme of preserving the family during times of great strain.

O.'s early contributions to proletarian drama in the U.S. belong to the best of that genre. His later work, while highly competent, was not charged with the energy, vitality, or verisimilitude of his purely proletarian plays. O.'s anger in *The Big Knife* is relatively trivial compared to his anger in a play like *Waiting for Lefty*, while *The Flowering Peach* is a comfortable, mellow play, one of resignation rather than of rebellion.

FURTHER WORKS: *Rifle Rule in Cuba* (1935, with Carleton Beales); *I Can't Sleep* (1936); *The Silent Partner* (1936); *Six Plays by C. O.* (1939); *The Time is Ripe* (1988)

BIBLIOGRAPHY: Shuman, R. B., *C. O.* (1962); Murray, E., *C. O.: The Thirties and After* (1968); Mendelsohn, M. J., *C. O.: Humane Dramatist* (1969); Weales, G., *C. O.: Playwright* (1971); Shuman, R. B., "C. O.: A Playwright and His Jewish Background," *SAQ*, 71 (1972): 225–33; Cantor, H., *C. O.: Playwright—Poet* (1978); Brenman-Gibson, M., *C. O., American Playwright: The Years from 1906 to 1940* (1981); ; Weales, G., *O., the Playwright* (1985); Miller, G., *C. O.* (1989); Demastis, W. W., *C. O.: A Research and Production Sourcebook* (1991); Miller, G., *Critical Essays on C. O.* (1991)

—R. BAIRD SHUMAN

ODIO, Eunice

Costa Rican poet, essayist, and short-story writer, b. Oct. 1922, San José; d. May 1974, Mexico City

One of the most remarkable Costa Rican poets of the 20th c., O. began to write very early in her life and started to publish her poems in 1945 in the journal *Repertorio Americano* of San José. She was awarded the prestigious "15th of September" prize for poetry for her volume *Los elementos terrestres* (the elements of earth), which was published in Guatemala in 1948. O. became a Guatemalan citizen, and continued to write poems, many of which were published only after her death in an anthology she edited herself, called *Territorio del alba y otros poemas* (1974; territory of dawn and other poems). She wrote her second book, *Zona en territorio del alba* (zone in the territory of dawn) between 1946 and 1948 and it was published in 1953 in Argentina, where it was much acclaimed. A year later, she completed a very long poem called *El*

trásito de fuego (1957; path of fire), which was published in San Salvador. After her move to Mexico in 1955, she worked as a reporter for *El Diario de Hoy* and wrote articles for many different journals. O. spent over two years in the U.S., and wrote extensively about the experience of exile. As well as poetry and essays, she wrote at least three stories in her later years, one of which, *El rastro de la mariposa* (1968; the trace of the butterfly), was published in booklet form.

O.'s poetry evolved over the course of her writing life from traditional verses in the early and mid-1940s to mystical-sensual-biblical allusion in *Los elementos terrestres* of 1948, to techniques of SURREALISM and other vanguard movements in *Zona en territorio del alba* of 1953, and finally to the lyric allegory of *El tránsito de fuego* of 1957 and subsequent poems and stories. Her early poems assimilate and use traditional lyric forms and often outspokenly advocate political activism, particularly in regard to the Spanish Civil War. *Los elementos terrestres*, a collection of eight long poems in free verse, derives its unity from the repeated lyrical insistence on natural cyclical process: night and day, the seasons, the rhythms of birth and death, love, and poetic creation. Allusions and interwoven paraphrases of the Song of Songs, Job, Genesis, and the Psalms intensify the fusion of mysticism and sensuality.

Zona en territorio del alba is far more experimental in form and in ideas. The book collects a varied series of poems in free verse about such themes as the importance of childhood, friendship, and the various artistic media: poetry, dance, and music. *El tránsito de fuego*, usually considered to be O.'s culminating masterwork, is an extensive poem, nearly five hundred pages long, in the form of an allegorical drama with many participant voices and choruses. The central plot revolves around the effort to understand Ion, the creator of the cosmos. O.'s passion for the creation and elaboration of myths culminated in her celebration of a cult to the Archangel Michael, dramatized in one of her best-known poems, "Arcangel Michael" (archangel Michael).

O. has been widely recognized as a poet of extraordinary lyric intensity. Her poems celebrate creation, imagination, erotic love, and, above all, light. Her major poems have been interpreted in many different ways, but it is mainly the luminous harmony of her verse that impresses the reader.

FURTHER WORKS: *Los trabajos de la catedral* (1971); *En defensa del castellano* (1972); *Antología: Rescate de un gran poeta* (1975); *La obra en prosa de E. O.* (1980); *E. O. en Guatemala* (1983); *Obras completas de E. O.* (1996). FURTHER WORKS IN ENGLISH: *Five Women Writers of Costa Rica: Naranjo, O., Oreamuno, Urbano, Vallbona* (1978)

BIBLIOGRAPHY: Liscano, J., "Eunice hacia la mañana," *Antología* (1975): 27–65; Huerta, E., "Deslindades costarricences," *Ancora*, 31 July 1977: 3–10; Vallbona, R. de, "E. O.: rescate de un poeta," *RIB* 31, 2 (1981): 199–214; Vallbona, R. de, "Estudio valorativo de la obra de E. O.," *Atenea*: 1–2 (1985): 91–101; Albán, L., "E. O.: una mujer contra las máscaras," *RI*, 53: 138–39 (Jan.-June 1987): 325–30; Burdiel de las Heras, M. C., "La poesía bíblica y E. O.," *Foro literario*, 17 (1987): 42–50; Duverrán, C. R., "E. O.: su mundo transfigurado," *Andromeda*, 3 (1987): 2–5; Vallbona, R. de., "E. O.," in Marting, D. E., ed., *Spanish American Women Writers* (1990): 382–93

—MARY G. BERG

ŌE Kenzaburō

Japanese novelist, short–story writer, and essayist, b. 31 Jan. 1935, Ōsemura (now Uchiko–cho)

Ō. was born and raised in an isolated rural region of the small island of Shikoku. He made his literary appearance in 1957 while still a student at Tokyo University. His early works, published between 1957 and 1963, express his sense of the degradation, humiliation, and disorientation caused by Japan's surrender at the end of World War II. Since 1964 his writing has focused on themes of madness and idiocy, themes that give expression to his personal experience as the father of a brain-damaged child and that are metaphors for the human condition. Ō. has a strong sense of social involvement, which began with the anti-American Security Treaty protests in 1960, and which encompasses his role as an antinuclear spokesman, involvements in radical causes, and numerous essays on political and social topics. Given Ō.'s commitment to social action as a way of authenticating his existence, it is not surprising that his literary mentors include Jean-Paul SARTRE, Albert CAMUS, and Norman MAILER.

One of the finest of Ō.'s early stories is "Shiiku" (1958; "Prize Stock," 1977), in which the hero is propelled from the innocent world of childhood into adulthood by various acts of madness ranging from the madness of war to the temporary insanity of his father, who murders a prisoner of war with an ax. Other early stories, such as "Kimyō na shigoto" (1957; an odd job) and "Shisha no ogori" (1957; "Lavish Are the Dead," 1965), also have protagonists who are alienated and disoriented in a world where gratuitous degradation and abuse are commonplace. Ō.'s heroes fight back with hostility and rebellion, or escape into fantasies and perverse sex.

In 1964 Ō. simultaneously published *Kojinteki na taiken* (1964; *A Personal Matter*, 1968) and *Hiroshima nooto* (1964; Hiroshima notes), both dealing with madness-producing events. The latter is an essay about the public madness of nuclear warfare. The former is more personal, a fictional account of coming to terms with the birth of a brain-damaged son. This novel was followed by several stories outlining other possible relationships between the corpulent father and the idiot son.

Although many would argue that Ō. is the finest writer in Japan today, he has been criticized by those who feel his rage against complacency is out of line in view of Japan's prosperity. Others criticize his style for being so rough it sometimes sounds as though his novels have been ineptly translated into Japanese from some other language. These complaints aside, Ō. has achieved and maintained an impressive level of literary excellence. In 1994 Ō. received the Nobel Prize for Literature.

FURTHER WORKS: *Megumushiri kouchi* (1958; *Nip the Buds, Shoot the Kids*, 1995); *Warera no jidai* (1959); *Seinen no omei* (1959); *Sakebigoe* (1962); *Nichijō seikatsu no bōken* (1963); *Man'en gannen no futtobōru* (1967; *Silent Cry*, 1974); *Warera no kyōki o iki nobiru michi o oshieyo* (1969); *Teach Us to Outgrow Our Madness*, (1972); *Kōzui wa waga tamashii ni oyobi* (1973); *Pinchiranna chōsho* (1976)

BIBLIOGRAPHY: Rabson, S., "A Personal Matter," in Tsuruta, K., and T. Swann, eds., *Approaches to the Modern Japanese Novel* (1976): 180-98; Iwamoto, Y., "The 'Mad' World of Ō. K.," *JATJ*, 14 (1979): 66–83; Wilson, M. N., "Ō.'s Obsessive Metaphor, Mori

Kenzaburō Ōe

the Idiot Son: Toward the Imagination of Satire, Regeneration, and Grotesque Realism," *JJS*, 7 (1981): 23–52

—STEPHEN W. KOHL

OGOT, Grace

Kenyan short-story writer and novelist (writing in English), b. 1930, Central Nyanza

O. is an important member of Kenya's "first generation" of writers, being one of a handful of Kenyans to produce major works of fiction in the early and mid-1960s. She has been diverse and versatile in her writing and in her other professional careers alike, building high public profiles in each. Trained as a nurse in Uganda and England, O. worked for a time in public health at Kisumu's Maseno Hospital as well as in the student health office at Makerere University College in Uganda. She was later a scriptwriter and broadcaster for the BBC Overseas Service, a public relations officer for Air India, a diplomat (serving as a delegate to UN General Assembly in 1975 and as a member of Kenya's delegation to UNESCO in 1976), and a businesswoman. She was a founding member and the first president of the Writers' Association of Kenya. Later, O. entered the world of Kenyan politics, serving as a nominated member of parliament and as an assistant minister in the Ministry of Culture and Social Services.

O.'s first major work was the novel *The Promised Land* (1966), which is increasingly coming to be recognized as an important founding text in Kenya's postcolonial literary history. This is the first novel by a Kenyan woman writer, the first to feature a complex female protagonist, and it is the first to offer a fully sympathetic portrayal of women's concerns. The story is of Nyapol, a young Luo woman who, following her marriage to a sympathetic but somewhat inept husband, refuses to conform to the passive role that is expected of her. She follows her husband on an ill-advised emigration to Tanzania, where they lose their possessions and dignity. The husband comes down with an inexplicable illness, and it is only Nyapol's strengths and instincts that pull them out of their mess. This is the story of a woman transcending her loneliness and isolation—much of which results from her status as a woman—in order to reach a "promised land" of wholeness.

Women's lives and dilemmas are central in practically all of O.'s work. Although she insists in interviews that she does not set out to write as a woman per se, O. also argues that one should portray society "as it is," and in this sense much of her writing exposes the inequities of gender relations within Kenya.

O. features a strong historical consciousness in much of her writing. *Land without Thunder* (1968), for instance, is a collection of short stories focusing on moments in Kenyan history ranging from precolonial days through mission hospitals and colonialism, to the plight of young women in contemporary Nairobi. *The Strange Bride* (1989), a novel, is the English translation of O.'s rendition of a Luo myth about a mysterious woman who appears among the people of Got Owaga. The novel originally appeared in Luo under the title *Miaha* (1983). While her Compatriot Ngugi Wa THIONG'O is more widely known for promoting writing in indigenous African languages, this has been something O. has also promoted and practiced throughout her career. In addition to Miaha, she has written stories and children's works in her Luo mother tongue. Addressing the topic in a 1983 interview with Don Burness, O. said, "It is our duty to adult literate Kenyans to have works of literature in their mother tongue, not just books on how to plant onions."

The bulk of O.'s contribution to Kenyan literature is as a short-story writer. Her stories originally appeared in significant publications *East Africa Journal*, *Transition*, *Présence Africaine*, and *Black Orpheus*. Many of these have since been anthologized in a wide range of venues, particularly in collections of world literature or international women's fiction.

Although the volume of O.'s literary production decreased as she became increasingly involved in business and political enterprises, the overall impact of O.'s writings and her status as the first significant woman writer from Kenya have earned her a central place in the region's literary history.

FURTHER WORKS: *The Other Woman and Other Stories* (1976); *The Graduate* (1980); *The Island of Tears* (1980); *Ber Wat* (1981); *Aloo Kod Apul-Apul* (1981); *Simbi Nyaima* (1983)

BIBLIOGRAPHY: Conde, M., "Three Female Writers in modern Africa: Flora Nwapa, Ama Ata Aidoo and G. O.," *PA*, 82 (1972): 132-43; Lindfors, B., "Interview with G. O.," *WLWE*, 18 (1979): 57-68; Mwanzi, H., *Notes on G. O.'s Land without Thunder* (1982); Burness, D., "G. O.," *Wanasema: Conversations with African Writers* (1985); Reid, M., "Conflict or Compromise: The Changing Roles of Women in the Writings of Rebekah Njau and G. O.," *MAWAR*, 5 (1990): 51-55; Achufusi, I., "Problems of Nationhood in G. O.'s Fiction," *JCL*, 26 (1991): 179-87; Flanagan, I., "African Folk Tales as Disruptions of Narrative in the Works of G. O. and Elspeth Huxley," *WS*, 25 (1996): 371-84

—J. ROGER KURTZ

O'HARA, Frank

American poet and art critic, b. 27 June 1926, Baltimore, Md.; d. 25 July 1966, Mastic Beach, N. Y.

O. received his B.A. in 1950 from Harvard, where he met the poet John Ashbery (b. 1927) and helped found the Cambridge Poets' Theater. In 1951 he received an M.A. in English from the University of Michigan as well as a Major Hopwood Award for poetry. Having moved to New York, he worked briefly at the Museum of Modern Art, wrote for *Art News* and other publications, and became part of several artistic and literary circles that included the poet Kenneth Koch (b. 1925), the painters Larry Rivers, Franz Kline, Willem de Kooning, Jackson Pollock, Robert Motherwell, and Helen Frankenthaler, and the composer Ned Rorem. In 1955 O. rejoined the museum, eventually becoming associate curator of painting; he organized several major exhibitions and wrote the catalogues for them. O. was relatively unknown as a poet during his lifetime (he died young from injuries sustained after being struck by a car), and his present reputation owes much to efforts of poet friends and students.

O. worked in several genres: poetry, poem-painting collaborations, plays, and film. His poetry, however, is the most substantial in volume, range, and achievement. He began with relatively straightforward and formally traditional short lyrics—a period of "muscleflexing," as Ashbery called it. Nevertheless, even these early works differ from the production of other poets at the time. Instead of learning from the dominant school of T. S. ELIOT and Wallace STEVENS, O. modeled his procedures and tone on an individual mox of "underground" sources: Gertrude STEIN, William Carlos WILLIAMS, W. H. AUDEN, Pierre REVERDY, Guillaume APOLLINAIRE, Vladimir MAYAKOVSKY, Federico GARCÍA LORCA, Boris PASTERNAK, and Arthur Rimbaud. O. strove to unify SURREALISTIC technique with American colloquial poetic diction. The early work, not surprisingly, consists largely of worshipful imitations and arguments and agreements with O.'s models. Nevertheless, O. transcended his apprenticeship to make a poetry that did not hide its debts, yet remained his own.

O. treated an astonishingly large number of subjects—art, trashy films, cityscapes (mainly New York), the demimonde, as well as more usual lyrical themes. Love and friendship figure in much of his work. Many of the poems are addressed to friends; friends are very often characters in the poems. He is happy and vivacious in a new affair, resigned or hurt or foolishly hopeful at a break-up. Yet, contrary to the charges often made against him, O. does more than merely record; his selection of detail comments indirectly.

Despite his many subjects, one theme, generally unstated, has great significance for O.'s technique: the value of intensely experiencing the moment and unwillingness to contemplate, to impose order by distancing, as preventing full participation in the moment. O.'s poems give the illusion of automatic writing, writing, when in fact their speed and spontaneity result from craft. From the DADAISTS and surrealists, O. learned how to include objects bound not by verisimilitude or logic but by psychic association with the event. In Gertrude Stein he had a model for re-creating the mind's language as it receives perceptions and before it begins to shape them into grammatical form, and he extended many of her innovations: coordination rather than subordination, to emphasize the simultaneity of multiple perceptions; syntactic but logically irrelevant conjunctions; suppressed pronoun references, radically condensed syntax, and "floating" modifiers that create at least two readings of the same semantic unit. Yet O.'s surface is much more dense than Stein's: complex images follow one another more quickly, and there is little repetition. If one compares Stein's surface to the open spaces and two-dimensional emphasis of cubist art, O.'s analogue is to the restless, intricate surfaces of "action" painters like Pollock, for whom O. proselytized in his art criticism.

O.'s commitment to capturing sensation almost for its own sake has its successes and dangers. At their best, the poems are fast, intimate, and reveal a persona of great wit and complexity. When they fail, they seem orphically incomprehensible, mere exercises in constructing complex images, or simply too personal, so "in" they have confused even O.'s friends. It is no coincidence that O.'s best-known works are also his more comprehensible: "Chez Jane" (1952), "On Rachmaninoff's Birthday (Quick! a last poem before I go)" (1953), the James Dean elegies (1955–56), "To the Film Industry in Crisis" (1955), "Rhapsody" (1959), "The Day Lady Died" (1959), and many of the lyrics titled "Poem." Long works like "Second Avenue" (1953) and "Biotherm" (1961–62) tend to collapse from their length and extreme density. Such generalizations are dangerous, however; critics and sophisticated readers are discovering meaningful threads in O.'s difficult poems.

FURTHER WORKS: *A City Winter and Other Poems* (1952); *Oranges* (1953); *Meditations in an Emergency* (1957); *Stones* (1958, with Larry Rivers); *Jackson Pollock* (1959); *Odes* (1960); *Second Avenue* (1960); *The New Spanish Painting and Sculpture* (1960); *Awake in Spain* (1960); *Try! Try!* (1960); *Lunch Poems* (1964); *The General Returns from One Place to Another* (1964); *Franz Kline: A Retrospective Exhibition* (1964); *Love Poems (Tentative Title)* (1965); *Robert Motherwell* (1965); *David Smith* (1966); *Nakian* (1966); *In Memory of My Feelings* (1967); *The Collected Poems of F. O.* (1971); *The Selected Poems of F. O.* (1973); *Hymns to St. Bridget* (1974, with Bill Berkson); *Art Chronicles, 1954–1966,* (1975); *Early Writing, 1946–1951* (1975); *Standing Still and Walking in New York* (1975); *Poems Retrieved* (1977); *Selected Plays* (1978)

BIBLIOGRAPHY: Berkson, B., "F. O. and His Poems," *Art and Literature*, No. 12 (1967): 53–63; Koch, K., "All the Imagination Can Hold," *New Republic*: 1–8 (Jan. 1972): 23–25; Vendler, H., "The Virtues of the Alterable," *Parnassus*, 1, 1 (1972): 9–20; Perloff, M., *F. O.: Poet among Painters* (1977); Meyer, T., "Glistening Torsos, Sandwiches, and Coca-Cola," *Parnassus*, 6, 1 (1977): 241-57; Smith, A., Jr. *F. O.: A Comprehensive Bibliography* (1979)

—STEVEN SCHWARTZ

Frank O'Hara

O'HARA, John

American novelist and short-story writer, b. 31 Jan. 1905, Pottsville, Pa.; d. 11 April 1970, Princeton, N. J.

The eldest of eight children of a prosperous doctor, O. had a privileged youth. But at the time he was admitted to Yale University, his father died, and O. lost financial security. O. had to leave school; he worked as a reporter and clerk in Pennsylvania and New York and began publishing stories in *The New Yorker* in 1928. A successful writer by 1934, O. took up film-script writing in Hollywood and by the mid-1950s had received numerous honors, including the National Book Award.

O.'s first and perhaps best novel, *Appointment in Samarra* (1934), chronicles the destructive effects of money, sex, and social status in the life of a wealthy Cadillac dealer and introduces the fictional world of Gibbsville, the center of O.'s Pennsylvania settings for dramatizing the themes of love, failure, and death in almost half of his stories. The ironic tales of *The Doctor's Son, and Other Stories* (1935) intricately detail a wide range of Gibbsville characters and relationships. The central focus of *A Rage to Live* (1949), while it also documents social history among the rich of the state capital from 1900 to 1920, is a woman's inability to control her passion and the tragic end of her marriage. In *Ten North Frederick* (1955) O. studies the subtleties of existence that bring a leading, well-adjusted citizen to ruin and suicide.

John O'Hara

Life in the worlds of Broadway and Hollywood is a major O. concern. The roman à clef *Butterfield 8* (1935) recreates the events behind the suicide of the beautiful celebrity, Star Faithfull, through the eyes of the protagonist-narrator and O.'s alter ego, Jimmy Malloy. This persona figures as well in the minor *Hope of Heaven* (1938) and later in the three novellas of *Sermons and Soda Water* (1960), which feature the subject of loneliness. O.'s stories of a second-rate nightclub singer collected as *Pal Joey* (1940) represent a triumph of American vernacular; the book was made into a successful Broadway musical shortly after its publication. Numerous short stories in *Files on Parade* (1939), *Pipe Night* (1945), and *Hellbox* (1947) effectively satirize various stage and screen personalities and situations. Although weak in structure and characterization, the Hollywood novel *The Big Laugh* (1962) offers authentic American idiom and bawdy humor.

O.'s later works include a minor academic novel, *Elizabeth Appleton* (1963), and the expansive *The Lockwood Concern* (1965), which covers a family dynasty over four generations. The book's center, George Lockwood, compulsively drives his son to crime and thus disintegrates the heritage. *The Instrument* (1967) revolves about a parasitic playwright and his relationship to a star actress, and *Lovely Childs: A Philadelphian's Story* (1969) deals with a 1920s celebrity heiress and her playboy husband. By the time of his death, O. had completed *The Ewings* (1972), the tale of a young lawyer making his fortune during World War I, and was working on a sequel, also posthumously published, entitled *The Second Ewings* (1977).

As a social commentator O. wrote in the tradition of Theodore DREISER and F. Scott FITZGERALD, laying life in the United States bare through a deft ear for American dialogue, accurate details, and penetrating glimpses into the human heart. While now unfashionable in the opinion of some readers, O. will remains a professional and poignant chronicler of the American scene from 1900 to 1970.

FURTHER WORKS: *Here's O.* (1946); *All the Girls He Wanted* (1949); *The Farmers Hotel* (1951); *Sweet and Sour* (1954); *A Family Party* (1956); *The Great Short Stories of O.* (1956); *Selected Short Stories* (1956); *Three Views of the Novel* (1957, with Irving Stone and MacKinlay Kantor); *From the Terrace* (1958); *Ourselves to Know* (1960); *Assembly* (1961); *Five Plays* (1961); *The Cape Cod Lighter* (1962); *49 Stories* (1963); *The Hat on the Bed* (1963); *The Horse Knows the Way* (1964); *Waiting for Winter* (1966); *And Other Stories* (1968); *The O. Generation* (1969); *The Time Element and Other Stories* (1972); *Good Samaritan and Other Stories* (1974); *"An Artist Is His Own Fault": J. On Writers and Writing* (1977); *Selected Letters of J. O.* (1978)

BIBLIOGRAPHY: Trilling, L., "J. O. Observes Our Mores," *NYTBR* (18 March 1945): 1, 9; Carson, E. R., *The Fiction of J. O.* (1961); Grebstein, S., *J. O.* (1966); Walcutt, C. C., *J. O.* (1969); Farr, F., *O.* (1973); *J. O. Journal* (1977–); MacShane, F., *The Life of J. O.* (1981)

—LYNN DEVORE

OJAIDE, Tanure

Nigerian poet, essayist, and critic (writing in English), b. 24 Apr. 1948, Okpara

O. had his early education at St. George's Grammar School, Obinomba, where he received his West African School Certificate in 1965. After two more years at the Federal Government College, Warri, he left for the University of Ibadan where he graduated with a bachelor's degree in English in 1971. He earned an M.A. in creative writing in 1979 and a Ph.D in English in 1982 from Syracuse University in the U.S. He returned to teach in Nigeria at the University of Maidugri from 1982 to 1989. Before his present position as professor of English at the University of North Carolina at Charlotte, he taught at Whitman College, in Walla Walla, Washington as Visiting Johnston Professor of Third World Literatures in 1989-90 and NEH Professor of the Humanities at Albright College, Reading, in Pennsylvania in 1996-97.

O. is an accomplished critic, scholar, and essayist, but is best known internationally as a poet internationally. His numerous poetry awards include the Africa Regional Commonwealth Poetry Prize (1987), the BBC Arts and Africa Poetry Award (1988), the All-Africa Okigbo Poetry Prize (1988, 1997), and the Association of Nigeria Authors Poetry Prize (1988, 1994).

"I Want To Be An Oracle," declared O. in one of his recent essays. That declaration of weighty responsibility started finding feet and form when his first volume of poetry, *Children of Iroko & Other Poems*, published in 1973. It marked O. as a poet whose cultural and political launching pad was as firm as his thematic trajectories were clear. Even though the new voice had in its tentative timbre the echoes of the resources of the first generation of Nigerian poets such as Wole SOYINKA, John Pepper CLARK-BEKEDEREMO, and particularly Christopher OKIGBO, it was clear that the preponderant facility was different, and would grow increasingly so. The parabolic wit of indigenous African oral expression was applied to humanitarian concerns, from tell-tale local injustice to other forms of universal oppression or deprivation abroad. While this passion for humanity has remained unchanged through seven other volumes of poetry, O.'s voice and feet have grown firmer and steadier. It is now a free-flowing, linguistically open, elegant poetry where massive cultural resources are deployed without any ostensive laboring, and ease. His collective output read together could create a Whitmanesque Nigerian *cosmos* that is unconfined by idiosyncratic patriotic fervor, because his canvass overflows into where ever his knowledge and travels have taken his keen vision and vatic humanity—the U.S., Israel, Vietnam, Italy, Netherlands, and Mexico. To understand O. requires that his African oracular mask and burden be read generically, indeed, as one might read Walt Whitman's generic singular.

Somewhat ambivalent and ambidextrous regarding past and present, oppressor and oppressed, with attentive eyes for human failings, O.'s *Labyrinths of the Delta* (1986), reconstructs Africa's tragic history of contact with duplicitous "conquistadors." It turns out in the vision of the poet that dueling with indigenous legendary tyrants like Ogiso is neither different nor easier than dueling with the "conquistadors," or the local tyrants of the new dispensation. It is a world of treachery and internecine chicanery among Africans often symbolically and allegorically drawn out in brutal and violent animal contests. The only hope is the visionary, altruistic, ascetic, warrior-poet whose other complement is expressed in the brief, doomed leadership of General Murtala Mohammed who the poet mourns and celebrates in "The Death of the Warrior." In all this, the disadvantaged is the poet's ward.

O. sees and characterizes the national murk in sharp, dolorous outlines in *The Eagle's Vision* (1987). The tyrant's grip is still firm on the throat of a hapless and bewildered populace that in the desperation to survive periodically submits itself to use. *Poems* (1988) is a complementary miscellany to that volume, while *The Endless Song* (1989) and *The Fate of Vultures* (1990) are redefinitive whorls of the poet's vision and his unchanging role of exceptional priestly monitor. Being of the people, the poet fights, at times, to rise above what afflicts the people. In *Endless Love*, the poet finds time for eulogizing foreign kindred creative spirits, and as well time to play gushing inamorato for a mysterious woman called Ita. *The Fate of Vultures* is a delicate but still unflinching gaze at tyranny at work and a somewhat self-critical and visionary self-examination.

Blood of Peace (1991) and *Daydream of Ants* (1997) judged by consistency in quality confirm O. as a premier modern African poet. One will find in his poetry a special mechanics in which the rich idiom of the folk melds with that of the streets and that of the Western-educated modern African sage to yield an elegant, sure-footed, and smooth moving verse. Like Chinua ACHEBE, Africa's leading novelist, O.'s vision draws from a closeness with the Earth and a certainty of private destiny which inspirits the word and the fabrics of the craft. His cosmos and his serious identification with that cosmos is as real as his ubiquitous grandmother, Amreghe, and Uhaghwa, his god of songs. His succinctly expressed understanding of the African poet in *Poetic Imagination in Black Africa* (1996) also sums up his own work: "The poet's conception of himself . . . encourages him to assume a didactic role—to be a

teacher . . . to be a teacher, the poet assumes a traditional African role . . . sage, priest, prophet, or even God's representative on earth."

FURTHER WORKS: *Great Boys* (1997)

BIBLIOGRAPHY: Bamikunle, A., "The Stable and the Changing in Nigerian Poetry : T. O.'s Search for a Poetic Voice, *WLWE*, 32-33 (1992-93): 56-71; Sallah, T., "The Eagle's Vision: The Poetry of T. O.", *RAL*, 26 (1995): 20-29; Ogede, O., "Poetry and Repression in Contemporary Nigeria," *ALT*, 20 (1996): 62-72

—CHIMALUM NWANKWO

OKAFOR, Chinyere Grace

Nigerian poet, dramatist, novelist, and critic (writing in English), b. May 1953, Arochukwu

With a father gifted in storytelling and mother gifted in crafts and music, O.'s talent seems natural, but it was relegated by academic pursuit. Primary education was largely in rural settings before she attended Rosary High School, Awgu, and Queen's School, Enugu. She obtained a B.A. in English from the University of Nigeria, Nsukka (1975), a Pg.D in theater from University College, Cardiff (1977), an M.A. in African studies from the University of Sussex, Brighton (1979), and a Ph.D. in English from the University of Nigeria. Her postdoctoral work in African cultural studies was at Cornell University in the U.S. Her teaching experience includes tenure at the Universities of Port-Harcourt, Benin, and Swaziland. She teaches oral and written African literature and researches gender and traditional dramatic forms. Winning of two Rockefeller Humanist-in-Residence Fellowships in 1991 (Hunter College and Cornell University) to continue an ongoing research into the poetics of African festival drama from a gender perspective attests to her ability as an academic and researcher.

O.'s debut as a writer was in 1991 with her winning of the third place in the Women's Research and Documentation Center (WORDOC) short-story competition and publication of a story that demonstrates a new direction while showing links with the previous generation. Subsequently, she received a special award in 1994 from the Association of Nigerian Authors (ANA) for distinguished performance as a writer in the three genres—drama, poetry, and prose. The prose entry was described as "a political and gender conscious collection in which the author's story telling talent, sense of appropriate form and insight into character and motivations are put to effective use." The award paved her way into the publishing arena. Her play, *The Lion and the Iroko* (1996), with the flavor of Wole SOYINKA's *The Lion and the Jewel* (perf. 1959, pub. 1963), along political and gender lines, used "chilling but vibrant scenes" to rehearse "what tomorrow's anger may well turn out to be." Her plays embody an optimistic vision lucidly communicated through satire, quick-fire dialogue, humor and setting that promotes spatial and communal relationship with the audience.

From Earth's Bedchamber is a collection of forty-eight poems "that are forcefully lethal in focus and thematic appraisal." Earth is the persona whose symbolism extends to pottery in fourteen poems. Directly invoking womanness in "Song of di Flower Woman," the proud and celebrative persona challenges her adversaries, "No be woman nyash, wey you pass come." Pidgin, symbolism, and local imagery are part of her style in traversing a wide canvas which includes war zones and love scenes. Many of her poems are performance-oriented employing dialogue and characters. She also provides symbolic graphic representations to aid verbal communication. The optimistic tenure of her writings echoes in the resilience of the persona whose last graphic representation emphasizes the inconclusive nature of the conflict that underlines the poems.

He Wants to Marry Me Again . . . (1996) contains stories with multilayered meaning portrayed through humor, dialogue, flashbacks, and pidgin that reveal well motivated characters who tackle empowerment and oppression. The majority of her characters are ordinary people and women with clear perspectives and strong sense of identity. O. aims to contribute "positively to society in any environment" she finds herself because "all forms of oppression—class, racial, or gender—instinctively bring tears and then anger" to her heart. Her stories are "eloquent tribute to the fulfilment of her life's purpose."

O. is close to working out a crisp personalised and lucidly individuated style. Her experience as a dramatist no doubt influences her narrative and poetic style which incorporates a lot of dialogue while the symbolic tenure of her prose is a sign of her poetic impulse. Her winning of the 1996 "Outstanding Finalist Award" in the Bertram's V. O. Literature of Africa Awards in Johannesburg, South Africa, with her manuscripts of a novella, *Ogini's Choice*, and a short-story collection, *Scar of Freedom,* as well as her 1998 Rockefeller Award as a resident writer at the Bellagio Center in Italy indicate that this new and courageous talent who is proficient in the three genres of literature is fast developing an authentic and compelling signature.

FURTHER WORKS: *Campus Palavar and Other Plays* (1996)

BIBLIOGRAPHY: Benson P., "Recent African Writing . . . .," *LitR*, 34 (1991): 429-31; Ige T., "Unrepentant Feminist," *The Week*, 19 Dec. 1994: 33; Iyayi, F., Preface to *He Wants to Marry Me Again.* . . . (1996): 6-9; Olaide S., "Straight from Earth's Bowel," *Nigerian Tribune*, 3 July 1996: 6

—OBIOMA NNAEMEKA

OKARA, Gabricl

Nigerian poet and novelist (writing in English), b. 24 April 1921, Bumodi

O. attended school in Umuahia and then worked as a printer and bookbinder in Lagos and Enugu. In 1956 he studied journalism in the U.S. at Northwestern University and then became involved in information-media work, once as editor of the newspaper *Nigerian Tide.*

O.'s first poems were published in the maiden issue of *Black Orpheus* (1957), an influential Nigerian literary magazine that later carried some of his fiction, translations of Ijaw myths, and experimental verse. His poetry and fiction have also appeared in numerous anthologies and literary publications outside of Nigeria and have won him an international reputation as one of Nigeria's most innovative stylists.

O.'s poetry tends to be simple, lyrical, and polyrhythmic. He writes free verse disciplined by subtly controlled metrics and amplified by sharply defined images and richly ambiguous symbols. In his early poetry he frequently combined native and nonnative imagery (oil palm and snowflake, drum and piano) as a metaphoric way of communicating the confused psychological state of the Westernized African. He was one of the first African writers to introduce into English verse uncompromisingly literal translations of metaphors, idioms, and philosophical concepts from an African vernacular language. His most recent poetry is his most explicitly political, reflecting his intense personal reaction to the horrors of the Nigerian-Biafran conflict (1967–70). The first collection of his poetry, *The Fisherman's Invocation* (1978), was awarded the Commonwealth Poetry Prize.

Although O. originally made his mark as a poet, he is perhaps better known as the author of *The Voice* (1964), an imaginative novel written in an unorthodox prose style simulating idiomatic expression in Ijaw. *The Voice* is a moral allegory about man's quest for faith, truth, and the meaning of life in a corrupted world. An idealistic hero discomfits leaders in his village by initiating a search for coherent moral values. Soon he is expelled from the village and sent into exile, but he defies the ban, returns home, and confronts those in power who had sought to obstruct his quest. He is put to death, but his words and deeds have made an impact on his people. A moral revolution has begun.

Some critics have been harsh on the radical verbal and syntactical innovations O. introduced in *The Voice*, but others think the strangeness of the style superbly suited to the strangeness of the tale. The unnatural inversions and neologisms tend to enhance the hallucinatory, dreamlike quality of the protagonist's quest, giving it an appropriate parabolic flavor. It is a poet's concern for form, awareness of symbol, and sensitivity to language that make O.'s novel a brilliant literary achievement.

O.'s experimental style and poetic vision place him in the forefront of the movement to indigenize African literature by investing it with local sonority as well as pan-African significance.

BIBLIOGRAPHY: Anozie, S. O., "The Theme of Alienation and Commitment in O.'s *The Voice,*" *BAALE*, 3 (1965): 54–67; Shiarella, J., "G. O.'s *The Voice*: A Study in the Poetic Novel," *BO*, 2: 5–6 (1970): 45–49; Palmer, E., "G. O.: *The Voice,*" *An Introduction to the African Novel* (1972): 155–67; Webb, H., "Allegory: O.'s *The Voice,*" *EinA*, 5, 2 (1978): 66–73; Egudu, R. N., "A Study of Five of G. O.'s Poems," *Okike*, 13 (1979): 93–110; Scott, P., "G. O.'s *The Voice*: The Non-Ijo Reader and the Pragmatics of Translingualism," *RAL* 21, 3 (1990): 75-88

—BERNTH LINDFORS

OKIGBO, Christopher

Nigerian poet (writing in English), b. 16 Aug. 1932, Ojoto; d. Aug. 1967, near Nsukka

O. studied in Umuahia and then went on to study classics at Ibadan University. Between 1956 and 1962 he worked in business and in government and as a teacher and a librarian. In the Nigerian-Biafran conflict (1967–70), he joined the Biafran army as a major in July 1967 and was killed in action the following month.

O. began to attract attention in 1962, when three publications of his appeared: a sequence of poems in Nigeria's influential literary magazine *Black Orpheus*; a pamphlet, entitled *Heavensgate*, in a poetry series published in Ibadan; and a long poem, *Limits*, in the

Ugandan cultural magazine *Transition*. (*Limits* appeared independently in 1964.) During the next few years O. continued to contribute poetry to *Black Orpheus* and *Transition*.

In his earliest verse—"Moonglow" and "Four Canzones," written between 1957 and 1961—one finds echoes of T. S. ELIOT, Ezra POUND, Gernard Manley Hopkins, and other modern poets, echoes that O. deliberately evoked in order to give greater sonority to the verbal music he was intent on creating. As he matured and discovered his own distinctive poetic idiom, the greatest influence on him may have been Peter Thomas (b. 1928), an English poet who taught at the University of Nigeria at Nsukka for several years and encouraged O. through discussion and enthusiastic readings of successive drafts of his poems. O. was also remarkably responsive to instrumental music, both African and Western, and he incorporated in his verse motifs inspired by symphonies, songs, and traditional percussive rhythms. Many critics have noted that O.'s work may appeal to the ear more than to the eye, for subtle nuances of sound meant more to him than mere certainties of sense.

In *Heavensgate* O. began to speak in a poetic voice informed by a judicious blend of African and Western poetic elements. This mature verse tends to be difficult, cryptically allusive, and sinuously musical, yet it achieves remarkably vivid pictorial effects by juxtaposing fresh images and compressing ideas into spare, metaphorical statements that have the lucidity of proverbs. *Heavensgate*, which O. said was originally conceived as an Easter sequence, traces the spiritual journey of a celebrant through several levels of ritual.

In *Limits* the same poet-protagonist sets out on a mystical quest for something unattainable and loses himself to his obsession. *Distances* (1964), described by O. as "a poem of homecoming," deals with the psychic and spiritual fulfillment that the writer must achieve before he can create. *Silences* (1965), inspired by tragic events in Nigeria and the Congo, is a poetic investigation of the music of mourning, with drums symbolizing the spirits of the ancestors. The poems in *Path of Thunder* (in *Black Orpheus*, 1968) reflect O.'s pessimistic response to the tensions in Nigeria in the mid-1960s, a crisis that he felt presaged war and possibly his own death. His last poems, by far his most political utterances, indicate that he was moving toward a less oblique mode of expression that could articulate moral and patriotic concerns in images accessible to the ordinary reader.

O. believed that his poems, although written and published separately, were organically related and could be read as one poetic statement. After his death, final versions of his poems, which he had himself edited, were published in the collection *Labyrinths with Path of Thunder* (1971). It has been reported that he had been working on a novel before his death, but the manuscript of this venture into prose apparently was lost during the Nigerian-Biafran war.

O.'s work defies easy explication and rational analysis. He was often more concerned with the resonance of sound and symbol than he was with communicating an intelligible meaning. His imagination played upon the rich suggestiveness of rhythm, image, and allusion, creating a subtle fusion of curiously disparate associations. He found trenchancy in obscurity, precision in ambiguity, form in formlessness. These qualities make him the most modern of African poets.

BIBLIOGRAPHY: Whitelaw, M., "Interview with C. O.," *JCL*, 9 (1970): 28–437; Anozie, S. O., *C. O.* (1972); Izevbaye, D. S., "O.'s Portrait of the Artist as a Sunbird: A Reading of *Heavensgate*," *ALT*, 6 (1973): 1–13; Udoeyop, N. J., *Three Nigerian Poets: A Critical Study of the Poetry of Soyinka, Clark and O.* (1973): 101–57; Anafulu, J. C., "C. O., 1932–1967; A Bio-bibliography," *RAL*, 9 (1978): 65–78; Achebe, C., Preface to Achebe, C., and D. Okafor, eds., *Don't Let Him Die: An Anthology of Memorial Poems for C. O. (1932-1967)* (1978): v-ix; Nwoga, D. I., *Critical Perspectives on C. O.* (1982); Scott, P., "G. O.'s *The Voice*: The Non-Ijo Reader and the Pragmatics of Translingualism," *RAL*, 21, 3 (1990): 75-88

—BERNTH LINDFORS

OKRI, Ben

Nigerian novelist and short-story writer, b. 1959 in Minna, delta region of Nigeria

Born in Nigeria, O. spent the first seven years of his life in England, where his father studied law. The family returned to Lagos, where they struggled as O.'s father practised among the poor—an experience that provided O. with firsthand material for his fiction. O. returned to England in 1978, where he studied literature at the University of Essex, was a Fellow in Creative Arts at Trinity College, Cambridge, and took up residence in London. This early and long-term relocation and acculturation away from Africa is somewhat unusual among African writers. But O.'s work remains steeped in indigenous West African images and oral forms, especially those of Yoruba culture, an influence that he has chosen and transformed.

All of this mixture of experience, culture, and travel contributed to O.'s production of his masterpiece, *The Famished Road* (1991), which won the Booker Prize of its year of publication. It has been called the classic magical realist novel of West Africa. The novel is set in a Nigeria on the eve of independence along with the construction of modern communications, roads and cars, photography, and electricity. The lives of Azaro and his poverty-stricken parents are touched destructively by the corrupt political parties who use dishonest, ruthless, and violent means to try to win support. However, the story is simultaneously situated in the world of the dream, of the nightmare, of the dead, of those waiting to be born, and crucially, linking up with the circularity of time, of those *abiku* babies, with their repeated deaths and rebirths. Azaro, the protagonist through whose eyes the bulk of the novel unfolds, is himself an *abiku* baby of ambiguous existence.

The road of the novel's title is many things. It is the danger of curiosity and adventurousness that can kill the restless traveller. It is colonial degradation, the African past and the road of life of the universal human condition and a way into the transformations of the future. What is clear, notwithstanding the labyrinth within which the road symbolism is constructed, is that in O.'s society edges blur between tradition and change, old and new, science and magic. There is no simple linear modernization as the road encroaches on the bush. The spirits dwell as much in the past as the present, on the road as much as in dreams or the spirit world itself, or even the bush. The spirits are, in fact, everywhere. Once they have recovered from the shock of the new technology, the spirits will adapt to it. They even take sides in the fight for votes within the new party politics. All of this is in the mode of the magical realist's ironic inversion of reality, where the spirits are a routine part of the mundane everyday, and electric light, gramophones, and photography constitute the awesome and the unbelievable.

There is, however, a fundamental distinction between everyday reality among ordinary people, and the ironic mode of the writer and intellectual, who have had a far more thoroughgoing Western experience and who look on the culture's uneven development with self-knowledge and some distance. It is the character of the photographer in the novel who most represents O.'s position. He is on the margins, a complex and challenging figure. He is postmodernist in the overtones of ironic, multiple readings of reality within a global framework. He shares with radical postcolonials the perception of oppression and a commitment to resisting it.

O.'s first novel, *Flowers and Shadows* (1980), written when he was only eighteen, is on the other hand firmly within the tradition of the conventions of Realism. It critiques the excesses of the corrupt rich classes governing and plundering newly independent Nigeria. It is obviously a still immature work. While his second novel, *The Landscapes Within* (1982; rev. ed., *Dangerous Love*, 1996), covers similar ground, we see O. beginning to experiment with form. It is, however, in his two collections of short stories *Incidents at the Shrine* (1986)—which won the Commonwealth Prize for Africa in 1987—and *Stars of the New Curfew* (1988), both of which were inspired primarily by the horrors of the Biafran civil war, that the search for a new and experimental technique with which to express his vision is forcefully present.

O. has yet to build on the extraordinary achievement of *The Famished Road*, however. The fiction becomes trapped in the labyrinth of its own formula when repeated in its sequel, *Songs of Enchantment* (1993), or in his next novel, *Astonishing the Gods* (1995).

FURTHER WORKS: *An African Elegy* (1992); *Birds of Heaven* (1995)

BIBLIOGRAPHY: Jeyifo, B., "B. O." in Ogunbiyi, Y., ed., *Perspectives on Nigerian Literature: 1700 to The Present*, vol. 2 (1988): 227-28; Gates, H. L., Jr., "Between the Living and the Unborn," *NYTBR*, (13 August 1989): 3, 20; Niven, A., "Achebe and O.: Contrasts in the Response to Civil War," in Bardolph, J., ed., *Short Fiction in the New Literatures in English* (1989): 277-83; Wilkinson, J., *Talking with African Writers* (1992): 76-89; Gorra, M., "The Spirit Who Came to Stay," *NYTBR*, (10 October 1993): 24; Ogunsanwo, O., "Intertextuality and Post-Colonial Literature in B. O.'s *The Famished Road*," *RAL*, 26, 1 (1995): 30-39; Quayson, A., " Esoteric Webwork as Nervous System: Reading the Fantastic in B. O.'s Writing," in Abdulrazak Gurnah, A., ed., *Essays on African Writing* (1995): 144-158; Cooper, B., *Magical Realism in West African Fiction: Seeing with a Third Eye* (1998): 67-114

—BRENDA COOPER

OKUDZHAVA, Bulat Shalvovich

Russian poet, balladeer, novelist, and screen-writer, b. 9 May 1924, Moscow; d. 12 June 1997

During World War II, at the age of eighteen, O. volunteered for service in the Soviet army and was later wounded. In 1950 he completed his education at Tbilisi State University and became a village schoolteacher. He began writing verse in 1953, and a few

years later joined the editorial staff of *Literaturnaya gazeta*, the major Soviet cultural newspaper, in Moscow. By 1960 O. had already gained a reputation as a composer (and performer with guitar) of nonconformist ballads, a genre that subsequently brought him international fame as well as official condemnation at home. He has given concerts not only in the USSR but also in Poland and western Europe. He visited the U.S. for the first time in 1979. In the 1960s O. also began writing fiction, and in recent years he has concentrated on historical novels.

O.'s first collection of verse, *Lirika* (1956; lyrics), was later dismissed by the poet as immature. In the volumes *Ostrova* (1959; islands), *Vesyoly barabanshchik* (1964; the happy drummer), and *Mart velikodushny* (1967; generous March) the basic themes of O.'s poetry emerged: abhorrence of war, compassion and hope for ordinary human beings, tenderness toward youth and women, love of Moscow with its joys and sorrows. All these emotions are expressed in unpretentious, conversational language, in contrast to the stilted Soviet officialese. O. developed and reinforced these themes in dozens of short poems set to simple tunes, several of which have been published in the U.S.S.R., but which primarily exist on tape recordings that circulated privately inside the country and were clandestinely sent abroad, where many were published and reproduced on phonograph discs.

O. is considered to be the pioneer among contemporary national bards of *magnitizdat* ("publishing by tape recorder," a term derived from *samizdat*: uncensored, "self-published" typewritten pages). He ranks in popularity with Vladimir Vysotsky (1938–1980) and Alexander Galich (1919–1977), but he avoids their explicit and biting political satire, preferring gentle humor, subtle irony, and allegory in his statements about the quality of Soviet life. For example, in one of his most famous songs, "Pro chyornogo kota" (1964; "The Black Cat," 1966), he creates the image of a malevolent authority whom none dares oppose.

O.'s first work of fiction was the novella *Bud zdorov, shkolyar!* (1961; *Lots of Luck, Kid!*, 1963). Based on his frontline experiences as a young soldier, it is filled with antimilitarism. Like his many poems about the cruelty and senselessness of war, it provoked official criticism for "mawkish pacifism." Actually, the work belongs to the vanguard of post-Stalinist realism, which rejected the pompous patriotism and spurious pathos of canonical SOCIALIST REALISM. In his later fiction O. has turned his attention to historical themes, skillfully juxtaposing authentic figures from early 19th-c. Russia with memorable imaginary heroes, such as the comic bungler in *Bedny Avrosimov* (1969; poor Avrosimov), which first appeared in a literary magazine and was later published under the title *Glotok svobody* (1971; gulp of freedom).

O. continues the humanitarian tradition in Russian literature. He reflects reality sincerely and articulates the genuine moods and aspirations of his fellow countrymen. In particular, his lyrical songs have ensured him the lasting respect and affection of people at home and abroad who value the age-old quest for truth and justice so characteristic of unfettered Russian writing.

FURTHER WORKS: *Po doroge k Tinatii* (1964); *Proza i stikhi* (1964); *Front prikhodit k nam* (1965); *Proza i poezia* (1968); *Mersi; ili, Pokhozhdenia Shipova* (1971); *Arbat, moy Arbat* (1976); *Puteshestvie diletantov* (1976; *Nocturne*, 1978). FURTHER WORKS IN ENGLISH: *Sixty-five Songs/65 pesen* (1980, bilingual)

BIBLIOGRAPHY: Mihajlov, M., *Moscow Summer* (1965): 104–14: 195–96; Langland, J., T. Aczel, and L. Tikos, eds., *Poetry from the*

Russian Underground (1973): 241-44; Sosin, G., "Magnitizdat: Uncensored Songs of Dissent," in Tökés, R. L., ed., *Dissent in the USSR* (1975): 276–309; Smith, H., *The Russians* (1976): 411–12; Brown, D., *Soviet Russian Literature since Stalin* (1978): 98–105; Rishina, I., "I Am Not Abandoning History" (interview), *SSLit*, 15, 4 (1979): 74–81; Svirsky, G., *A History of Post-War Soviet Writing* (1981): 351–67

—GENE SOSIN

OLBRACHT, Ivan

(pseud. of Kamil Zeman) Czechoslovak novelist and short-story writer (writing in Czech), b. 6 Jan. 1882, Semily; d. 30 Dec. 1952, Prague

Son of the politically liberal writer Antal Stašek (pseud. of Antonín Zeman, 1843–1931), O. began his career as a journalist for the Social Democratic press. After attending a meeting of the Third International in Moscow, he became a Communist and edited the Czechoslovak Party newspaper *Rudé právo* during most of the 1920s. He always set aside time for creative writing, however, and during the 1930s, his richest period, he devoted himself entirely to literature. He spent the war with a partisan group and was active in postwar politics as a member of the National Assembly and the Central Committee of the Czechoslovak Communist Party.

The psychological novel *Podivné přátelství herce Jesenia* (1918; the peculiar friendship of the actor Jesenius) is typical of his early writings. It uses the Dostoevskian *Doppelgänger* theme to point up the opposing forces of individualism and anarchy. In *Anna proletářka* (1925, rev. eds., 1928, 1946; Anna the proletarian) this opposition metamorphoses into individualism versus the workers' movement. This novel about a rural servant girl who goes to the city and becomes involved in organizing the general strike of 1920 exists in three quite different versions, each exemplifying a distinct stage in O.'s development. In the first he highlights the heroine's inner struggles; in the second he expands on the historical events surrounding the strike; and in the final version he turns Anna into a socially aware, SOCIALIST REALIST heroine whose Social Democrat husband betrays the workers. All three versions show the pronounced influence of GORKY.

O. came into his own with *Nikola Šuhaj loupežník* (1933; *Nikola Šuhaj, Robber*, 1954) and *Golet v údolí* (1937; *The Bitter and the Sweet*, 1965), both set in the Carpathians. In the former he begins with the true story of a local outlaw, but by skillfully combining the elemental with the monumental, he creates a kind of Robin Hood, a character of mythical dimensions, who fights for freedom and social justice against impossible odds. In the latter, three short stories of the Jewish Diaspora, he depicts ghetto life with great humor and sympathy, showing equal interest in realistic, even naturalistic, portrayals of its daily squalor and in mystical evocations of the Old Testament ethos that rules the lives of the inhabitants. These two volumes reveal an eye for local color and an ear for poetic diction completely lacking in his earlier work; they are ballads in prose and exhibit a consummate balance of documentary and fantasy.

Although the concerns in these two works do not differ essentially from those in, say, *Anna proletářka*, O. treats them less tendentiously. O.'s claim to recognition rests not so much on his

social novels, which have faded with the events they portray, as on his studies of the social outcast, the archetypal outsider.

FURTHER WORKS: *O zlých samotářích* (1913); *Žalář nejtemější* (1916); *Pátý akt* (1919); *Obrazy ze soudobého Ruska* (2 vols., 1920–1921); *Devět veselých povídek z Rakouska i republiky* (1927); *Zamřížované zrcadlo* (1930); *Dvě psaní a moták* (1931); *Země bez jména* (1932); *Hory a staletí* (1935); *Biblické příběhy* (1939); *Ze starých letopisů* (1940); *Dobyvatel* (1947); *O mudrci Bidpajovi a jeho zvířatkách* (1947); *Spisy* (15 vols., 1947–1961)

BIBLIOGRAPHY: Opelík, J., "O.s reife Schaffensperiode," *ZS*, 12 (1967): 20–37; Kunstmann, H., *Tschechische Erzählkunst im 20. Jahrhundert* (1974): 71–76; Novák, A., *Czech Literature* (1976): 284–85; Harkins, W. E., "The art of O.'s novel *Nikoja Šuhaf the bandit*," in Rechcígl, M., ed., *Czechoslovakia Past and Present* (1968), Vol. 2: 993-1001

—MICHAEL HEIM

OLESHA, Yury Karlovich

Russian novelist, short-story writer, and dramatist, b. 3 March 1899, Yelisavetgrad (now Kirovograd); d. 10 May 1960, Moscow

O. grew up in Odessa in a family of Polish origin. In 1922 he went to Moscow, where he made his literary debut with poems published in a railway workers' newspaper. His novel *Zavist* (1927; *Envy*, 1936) immediately established his reputation and made him one of the most controversial Soviet writers. It was followed by a fairy-tale account of the revolution, *Tri tolstyaka* (1928; *The Three Fat Men*, 1964), a number of short stories, and several plays.

O. found it more and more difficult to publish or even to write in the increasingly restrictive atmosphere of the 1930s. Announcing that the building of a new Soviet order was not his theme, he pleaded at the First Congress of Soviet Writers (1934) for a greater humanism in Soviet letters. But as the 1930s advanced, his published work became more and more fragmentary, and he busied himself writing film scenarios. After 1938 O. disappeared from the literary scene almost completely, and it was not until the "thaw" following Stalin's death that his works were again published. An interesting volume of reminiscences and reflections, *Ni dnya bez strochki* (1965; *No Day Without a Line*, 1979), was published posthumously.

O.'s masterpiece is *Zavist*, which deals in a symbolic and EXPRESSIONISTIC style with the conflict between the old and new orders in Soviet life. Its hero, Kavalerov, longs for personal fame, success, and love, all of which he finds unattainable in Soviet society. Rejecting the new socialist order, which is personified by Andrey Babichev, a complacent and philistine food commissar who has perfected a new sausage and is trying to open a chain of cheap soup kitchens, Kavalerov sides with those who preach a "conspiracy of feelings" in the name of such emotions as love, ambition, and jealousy. After the conspiracy's failure, he attempts to salve his wounded ego in the suffocating embraces of a fat widow.

This comic novel has a rare freshness and originality of visual imagery. In a poet's prose rich in metaphors, similes, and conceits, O. rejects both the old and new orders—the one for its lack of progress and concern for social welfare, the other because it is too mechanical and unfeeling.

Influenced by the French philosopher Henri BERGSON, O. saw an irreparable dichotomy in life between the mechanical and the biological. Such is the theme of his stories "Lyubov" (1928; "Love," 1949) and "Vishnyovaya kostochka" (1930; "The Cherry Stone," 1934). In the latter the possibility of a synthesis is indicated when the architects of a new steel and concrete building remember to provide for a garden in their plans.

"Liompa" (1928; "Liompa," 1967) contrasts a dying man for whom the world has become a collection of meaningless names and a child for whom it is it is a bright chaos of nameless objects.

O. made a free adaptation of his *Zavist* as a play, entitled *Zagovor chuvstv* (1930; *The Conspiracy of Feelings*, 1932). Although popular, the play lacks the freshness and incisiveness of the novel. Stronger is his original drama, *Spisok blagodeyany* (1931; *A List of Assets*, 1963), a fairly sensitive psychological portrayal of a Soviet actress who is destroyed by her attraction to the West.

The first critics of O.'s work took his writing as a negative comment on Soviet reality of the 1920s and early 1930s. Although this is undoubtedly true, it becomes increasingly clear that his expressionistic fiction fits into the context of Western literature of the period and that its universal theme is applicable to both Soviet and Western society.

Although O. never fulfilled the promise of his first brilliant novel, we can now see that he is one of the most vivid exponents of the European "vitalist" current of the 1920s. His profoundly philosophical work remains as readable and fresh as when it was written.

FURTHER WORKS: *Vishnyovaya kostochka* (1931); *Zapiski pisatelya* (1932); *Izbrannye sochinenia* (1956); *Povesti i rasskazy* (1965); *Pesy; Stati o teatre i dramaturgii* (1968). FURTHER WORKS IN ENGLISH: *The Way-ward Comrade and the Commissar* (1960; repub. as *Envy, and Other Works*, 1967); *Love and Other Stories* (1967); *The Complete Short Stories and The Three Fat Men* (1979)

BIBLIOGRAPHY: Struve, G., *Soviet Russian Literature, 1917–1950* (1951): 98–106: 219–30, 246–49; Brown, E. J., *Russian Literature since the Revolution* (1963): 84–94; Alexandrova, V., *A History of Soviet Literature* (1964): 188–202; Nilsson, N. A., "Through the Wrong End of Binoculars: An Introduction to Y. O.," *SSl*, 11 (1965): 40–68; Harkins, W. E., "The Theme of Sterility in O.'s *Envy*," *SlavR*, 25 (1966): 443–57; Maguire, R. A., *Red Virgin Soil* (1968): 338–44; Beaujour, E. K., *The Invisible Land: A Study of the Artistic Imagination of Y. O.* (1970)

—WILLIAM E. HARKINS

OLIVER, Mary

American poet, essayist, b. 10 Sept. 1935, Maple Heights, Ohio

O. spent her childhood in Ohio and has lived most of her adult life in Provincetown, Rhode Island, two geographical locations which figure prominently in her work, as sources for poems of natural history and description. Educated at Ohio State and at Vassar, O. has taught at Case Western Reserve, Bucknell University, the University of Cincinnati, Sweet Briar College, and Bennington College.

O. is known for her poetic contributions to American nature writing in the form of short lyrical poems about flora, fauna, the cosmos, weather, the seasons. *American Primitive*, which won the Pulitzer Prize in 1984, owe debts (in sharp observation and embrace of nature) to Emerson, Frost, Whitman, Hopkins, Williams, and John Muir, while revealing her own distinctive voice: plain-spoken, sensual, fresh, earthy, happy to forgo abstractions in favor of whatever is physical, tangible, tastable, available to the body. Subsequent books, including *Dream Work* (1986) and *House of Light* (1990) deepen this aesthetic into a visionary poetry of human communion with earth's "divinity." In her collection of essays, *Blue Pastures* (1995), she writes of learning from Whitman, "within the lit circle of his certainty, and his bravado," that "the poem is a temple—or a green field—a place to enter, and in which to feel."

In a characteristic poem, a solitary person unsentimentally but with passionate curiosity, observes what the non-human creatures of the world are up to, what they look like, how they move and eat and sleep, what complex truths they so surprisingly and simply embody. A poem will often concentrate its attentions on a single species (which gives the poem its title), making her life's work an encyclopedia of the natural world: "Mussels," "Raccoons," "Mushrooms," "The Kookaburras," "Vultures," "Egrets," "Skunk Cabbage," "The Plum Trees," Moccasin Flowers," "Lilies," "Opossum," "The Hermit Crab," "Morning Glories," "Pipefish." The poems are likely to take place during the course of an unhurried "all day" or "all night," chronicling, as the busy human world recedes, how waterfalls "unspool," how black ants climb over peonies "boring their deep and mysterious holes," how goldenrod plants toss in the wind "on their airy backbones," how crows broadcast the slaughter of one of their own by the "fat and drowsy" owl, how the sheets of moss "except that / they have no tongues / lecture . . . about spiritual patience."

Despite reminders of dissolution and death, O. finds in the natural world abundant consolation for fear, pain, frenzy, frustration, injustice. She finds means to resist ambition, self-pity, shame, the undertow of unhappy memory. A look at the fading roses in late summer, for instance, results in a resolve to strive for no less than "unstinting happiness," unvexed by daily turmoil or questions of the afterlife. A day's worth of attention to the humble grasshopper stiffens a resolve to merge idleness with blessedness, to understand life's brevity, to find a worthy purpose for one's "wild and precious life."

O. is hailed as one of the indispensable U.S. poets writing after WWII. She won the National Book Award in 1992 for *New and Selected Poems*. *White Pine* (1994) and *West Wind* (1997) include prose poems, denser and more discursive than the lyrics, but consistent in subject and sensibility. She makes a particularly American contribution to the traditions of pastoral poetry and Romantic nature poetry. Although she resists gendered readings of her work, feminist critics have found there a poetic consciousness unalienated from nature and the (female) body. She has written two handbooks for writers of poetry—*A Poetry Handbook* (1994) and *Rules for the Dance* (1998).

FURTHER WORKS: *No Voyage* (1963); *The River Styx, Ohio* (1972); *Twelve Moons* (1978)

BIBLIOGRAPHY: Alford, J. B., "The Poetry of M. O.," *Pembroke Magazine*, 20 (1988): 283-8; McNew, J., "M. O. and the Tradition of Romantic Nature Poetry," *ConL* 30 (1989): 59-77; Bonds, D. S.,

"The Language of Nature in the Poetry of M. O.," *WS*, 21 (1992): 1-15; Fast, R. R., "Moore, Bishop, and O.," *TCL*, 39 (1993): 364-79; Graham, V., "'Into the Body of Another': Mary Oliver and the Poetics of Becoming Other," *PLL*, 30 (1994): 352-72

—SARA LUNDQUIST

OLIVERI I CABRER, Maria-Antònia

Spanish novelist, short-story writer, and screenwriter (writing in Catalan), b. 4 1946, Manacor, Mallorca

O.'s novels show a great variety of themes, styles, and tone, and can be grouped loosely into three main categories, with some overlap: family/generational, mythological/fantastic, and detective. Her first novel, *Cròniques d'un mig estiu* (1970; Chronicles of a Half Summer), traces the coming of age of a Mallorcan youth, juxtaposed with the destruction of his town by tourists and developers. A similar background for *Cròniques de la molt anomenada ciutat de Montcarrà* (1972; Chronicles of the Oft-Named City of Montcarrà) provides a setting for a three-generational history of a working-class family, focusing on the women. Both time and points of view are fragmented in this complex work, which incorporates popular sayings, songs, and figures from the Mallorcan "Rondalles" (folktales) into the plot. These legendary figures lend the novel a mythological quality, one that will be seen in later works. For example, *El vaixell d'iràs i no tornaràs* (1976; The Ship That Never Returns) is the symbolic journey of a timeless society beset by monsters from legend that nonetheless resemble certain political entities. The conformism and complacency of the majority is overcome by the bravery and persistence of a woman who comes of age as she confronts the evil powers in a series of magical adventures. *Punt d'arròs* (1979; Knit/Purl) also portrays a woman's search for self, but against a more realistic background; the novel begins with a quotation from Virginia WOOLF, whose work O. translated, and it offers homage to the British novelist.

O.'s most compelling work, *Crineres de foc* (1985; Manes of Fire), encompasses the epic, a family chronicle and the founding of a town, science fiction, fantasy, and psychological and sociological studies. Using a contrapuntal technique that also appears in other novels, O. weaves together two related stories that explain each other as she explores the need for self-identification in women and in peoples. Estel and the townspeople of El Claper all struggle to hold on to their visions, dreams, identities, and autonomy in the face of the powerful and dominating men who would control them. O. bases the struggle for freedom on the eight-pointed symbol of the "rosa dels vents" or nautical compass, sending her heroes on a quest in which they meet up with the eight "tribes" represented by the winds of the Mediterranean—Xaloc, Mestral, Tramuntana, etc. The symbolism demonstrates how O. draws on her island heritage to elaborate a theme of universal value.

In the1980s O. joined in forming a collective of writers who took the name Ofèlia Dracs and published several books of stories based on specific genres, notably detective works. One of the stories she contributed to this effort, "On ets, Mònica?" ("Where Are You, Mònica?," 1992), gave birth to the female detective Lònia Guiu, who would develop into the protagonist of three

novels. *Estudi en lila* (1985; *Study in Lilac*, 1987) addresses the crime of rape and its aftermath as well as unexplained violent deaths. The author contrasts the reactions of two victims of sexual assault: a fashionable, fortyish antique seller and a very young and vulnerable Mallorcan. The detective, Mallorcan as well, weaves together the stories of these two women, who come to her detective agency by very different means. The role of the hard-boiled, feminist detective as mediator and problem-solver continues in *Antípodes* (1988; *Antipodes*, 1989), which takes its name from the dual setting in Australia and Mallorca. Crimes against women are on a larger scale here, as Lònia uncovers a network of trafficking in women as well as the usual murders. The protagonist's human side is also developed further; in addition to adding to her lipstick collection, she falls in love, is jilted, joins an ecology movement, and learns that her faithful sidekick Quim is gay. In *El sol que fa l'ànec* (1994; *Blue Roses for a Dead . . . Lady?*, 1998), the last novel in this genre to date, the crimes discovered by Lònia are against children as well as women. Here, O. humanizes her protagonist even more; at times Lònia is ill-tempered, foul-mouthed, worried about getting old, and flirtatious. The title, literally untranslatable, comes from words of a deformed song and is a clue to the mystery. O. has used this masculine genre successfully and realistically: Lònia takes her lumps and has to defend herself against violence and danger, while learning in real life about the feminist values she always heard about: solidarity, cooperation, tolerance to differences, and self-identification. At the same time O. uses the conventions of the genre without falling into its cliches.

In the 1990s O. returned to the disfunctional family relationships she had portrayed earlier and to the complicated postfeudal Mallorcan society. *Joana E.* (1992; Joana E.) is cast in the first person and goes back and forth from the ending point—Joana's bizarre second marriage—to her earliest childhood memories. *Amor de cans* (1995; Dog Love) portrays a family of sisters, poeticizing the otherness of the one who does not fit into genteel Mallorcan society.

O. has won many prizes for her work and is now at the middle of her career. She has metafictionalized herself in the Lònia novels, to the delight of her public, who anxiously awaits further tales of the feisty detective.

FURTHER WORKS: *Coordenades espai-temps per guardar-hi les ensaimades* (1975); *Les illes* (1975); *Figues d'un altre paner* (1979); *Vegetal i Muller qui cerca espill* (1982); *Margalida, perla fina* (1985); *Que patines, Laura?* (1985); *El pacaticu* (1988); *Tríptics* (1989); *Negroni de Ginebra* (1993); *La dida* (1996)

BIBLIOGRAPHY: Pérez, J., "Metamorphosis as a Protest Device in Catalan Feminist Writing: Rodoreda and O.," *CatR*, 2, 2 (1987): 181-98; McNerney, K., "Catalan Crazies: The Madwomen in M.-A.'s O.'s Attic," *CatR*, 3, 1 (1989): 137-44; McNerney, K., "Crossing Parallel Lines: M.-A. O.'s Fiction," *RLA* (1990): 536-39; Pérez, J., "Plant Imagery, Subversion, and Feminine Dependency: Josefina Aldecoa, Carmen Martín Gaite, and M.-A. O.," *In the Feminine Mode* (1990): 78-100; Hart, P., "The Mystery as Midwife: An Interview with M.-A. O.," *The Armchair Detective* (1992): 330-34; Mandrell, J., "'Experiencing Technical Difficulties'": Genre and Gender, Translation and Difference: Lourdes Ortiz, M.-A. O., and Blanca Alvarez," *JNT*, 27, 1 (1997)

—KATHLEEN MCNERNEY

OLLIER, Claude

French novelist, critic, radio dramatist, and poet, b. 17 Dec. 1922, Paris

O. first went to law school and worked in the business world before he devoted himself entirely to literature in 1955. He had started writing short stories as early as 1946. His first novel, *La mise en scène* (1958; the setting), a book of violence and mystery, which also began his first quartet of novels won the Médicis Prize. *Le maintien de l'ordre* (1961; *Law and Order*, 1976), *Été indien* (1963; Indian summer), and *L'échec de Nolan* (1967; Nolan's defeat) are the other volumes in the quartet.

According to O., all his novels are detective stories; for him, the primordial relationship of man and the world is one of terror. He writes methodically, making use of scientific jargon. Proponents of the new French criticism have praised his concept of contemporary *écriture* (writing)—his use of elaborate and intricate poetic devices, metric relations, assonance, and rhythmic superimpositions.

In 1971 O. participated in a colloquium at Cerisy devoted to the NEW NOVEL. He was at the time deeply involved in the writing of a second quartet of science-fiction-like New Novels, which he worked on for a decade. The first volume was *La vie sur Epsilon* (1972; life on Epsilon). In *Enigma* (1973; enigma) the vocabulary is Freudian. In *Our; ou, Vingt ans après* (1974; Ur; or, twenty years later), he uses literary texts as examples of cultural phenomena acquired automatically by the collective unconscious. He has voluminous notebooks describing his dreams and has said, "My most fertile inventions are those that arise out of periods of drowsiness or sudden awakening, at the end of dreams." This modern-day Jules Verne creates fables permeated by the writings of JOYCE, KAFKA, and the SURREALISTS. O. is also sensitive, perhaps more than anyone else, to the haunting, unreal world of Raymond ROUSSEL. In *Fuzzy sets* (1975; title in English) the forceful influx of the psychoanalytic theories of Jacques Lacan (1901–1981) are evident. In the fictional process, the author pinpoints criss-crossing influences determined by psychological conflicts originating in early childhood and contained in the unconscious, as well as those conflicts "born of belonging to a given social class or cultural sphere." The novels of the two quartets, to which O. gave the overall title *Le jeu d'enfant* (child's play), constitute a global, monumental work built on a "spiraloid structure."

In his North African colonial travelogue-novel, *Marrakch Medine* (1979; Marrakch Medine), which won the 1980 France-Culture Prize, he stresses dialectical materialism. And in the introduction to his *Souvenirs écran* (1981; screen memories) he scrupulously, "clinically" traces the relationship of films to his own childhood. At the same time, he tightly links his own experience as a novelist with parallel practices evidenced in the films of the New Wave from 1958 to 1968. In the same vein, O. has written a number of radio plays and film scripts, which he considers to be "satellites" constituting an important part of his overall "network."

O. not only attempts to revolutionize fiction through the ever-changing manipulation of scientific techniques, erudite organization, and precise mathematical devices; he also strives to widen the "open" meaning of the linguistic, rhetorical, and narrative process in the "new New Novel": scorning the linear plot, he weaves his words on the page almost as if they had a physical weight. Language looms on paper and seems to change shape visually. His sonorities throb within our inner ear, thereby creating a new world

of meaning through, he says, "expansion, deception, and riddle." Thus, for the serious reader, the impact of O.'s entire opus is that of an appealing, propelling, 21st-c. strangeness, stemming from the efforts of poets such as Mallarmé and VALÉRY, thrusting past present materialism toward an abstract approach to visions of the future.

FURTHER WORKS: *La mort du personnage* (1964); *L'attentat en direct* (1965); *Régression* (1965); *Cinématographe* (1965, with Jean-André Fieschi); *Navettes* (1967); *La relève* (1968); *Luberon* (1969); *Réseau de blets rhizomes* (1969); *Le dit de ceux qui parlent* (1969); *Pèlerinage* (1969); *La fugue* (1969); *Les dires des années 30* (1970); *L'oreille au mur* (1971); *Une bosse dans la neige* (1971); *La recyclade* (1971); *Our-Musique* (1975); *Réseau Ollier Navettes* (1975); *Opérettes entre guillemets* (1977); *Loi d'écoute* (1979); *Computation* (1979); *Détour* (1980); *Bon entendeur* (1980, in *Agrafes*, with others); *Nébules* (1981); *Mon double à Malacca* (1982)

BIBLIOGRAPHY: Ricardou, J., *Pour une théorie du nouveau roman* (1971): 159–99; Foucault, M., "Le langage de l'espace," Noguez, D.," 'Plus qu'un Borgès français,'" and Ricardou, J., "Textes 'mis en scène,'" in Ouellet, R., ed., *Les critiques de notre temps et le nouveau roman* (1972): 118–27; Roudiez, L., *French Fiction Today* (1972): 233–58; Houppermans, J., "Quelques rails (C. O., Roussel)," in Grivel, C., ed., *Écriture de la religion/Écriture du roman* (1979): 195–210; Cali, A., *Pratiques de lecture et d'écriture: O., Robbe-Grillet, Simon* (1980); Steisel, M.-G, "O. ou l'Orient; Orient or O.," *CELFAN*, 2, 1 (1982): 20–23

—MARIE-GEORGETTE STEISEL

OLSEN, Tillie

American novelist, short-story writer, and critic, b. 13 Jan. 1912 or 1913, Omaha, Neb.

The year of O.'s birth is uncertain. Her parents were Russian Jews who had fled to the U.S. after the 1905 revolution, and her father remained active in labor and leftist struggles, becoming secretary of the Nebraska socialist party. Although she dropped out of high school in the eleventh grade, O. continued her education through assiduous reading at public libraries and observation on her working-class jobs. A number of the "lost" writings by women that she helped to bring out of obscurity in the 1970s were works she initially discovered as a very young woman exploring libraries and second-hand bookshops. O. was also a labor activist, and was arrested organizing Midwestern packinghouse workers, as well as in the general strike in San Francisco, where she moved in the mid–1930s and has lived ever since. Since the 1950s, she has held a number of writing fellowships and visiting teaching positions on the faculties of such institutions as Stanford, Amherst, MIT, and the University of Minnesota.

If the career of any single writer can be said to epitomize an entire movement and moment in literary history, O.'s represents the impact of feminism on American literature in the second half of the 20th c. Her fiction centers on the limitations that our culture places on women's lives and the ways that class and race, as well as gender, shape female experience. In her critical writing, too, O.

focuses on both the restrictions on women as creative artists and their achievements despite those restrictions.

O.'s lifelong commitment to working-class, racial-justice, and peace movements informs her literary work, but, along with the effort of rearing four children and doing paid labor as well, it cut severely into the time and inner space she had available for writing. Her literary career is thus divided into two parts, separated by twenty years devoted almost exclusively to family, "everyday" jobs, and political life. In the earlier period, the 1930s, she published journalism, poetic prose drawn from her activist experience, and, in the 1934 *Partisan Review*, a short story that was the beginning of the novel *Yonnondio: From the Thirties* (1974) that she was to publish, still incomplete, some forty years later, and to reissue, enriched and augmented, but still unfinished, in 1994. It was not until the mid–1950s that O. began to write fiction again. Her three short stories from those years, "I Stand Here Ironing," "Hey Sailor, What Ship?," and "O Yes," offer realistic glimpses into the experience of working-class women, men, and children through use of experimental modernist techniques of narration. These three loosely connected stories are collected in a volume, *Tell Me a Riddle* (1961), along with O.'s novella of that title.

The novella "Tell Me a Riddle," which won the O. Henry Award for the best American short story of 1961, focuses on the last months in the life of an elderly Russian Jewish immigrant woman, a political activist who survived the revolution of 1905 only to witness the erosion of her own possibilities for a full life into the stifling experience of American working-class wife and motherhood. Embittered by the demands her experience has made on her, the dying woman's stream-of-consciousness is studded with the texts of suppressed idealism, the socialist humanism of her youth, in which she has never ceased to believe; these are words that make a vivid, ironic contrast with the ugly, self-satisfied world of America in the 1950s by which she is surrounded.

O.'s other fictional works include "Requa-I" (1971)—another long story—and *Yonnondio*, the novel begun in the 1930s and revised—though not completed—by the author in her maturity. *Yonnondio* is a narrative of the migrations of a working-class Midwestern family, with special attention to the way that the job and joblessness shape relationships between the sexes and the generations, as the violence of the workplace and the economy of which it is a part translates into domestic violence, marital rape, and child neglect.

As a critic, O. concentrates on the power of "circumstances," particularly race, class, and gender, to cut off creativity. *Silences* (1978) starts from her own experience as a "first generation" working-class writer and a woman and proceeds to elaborate a theory about the relation of material conditions to culture. O.'s efforts to make the work of such nearly forgotten authors as Rebecca Harding Davis (1831–1910) and Agnes Smedley (1890–1950) available to a new generation of feminist readers derives from this same sense of the social obstacles to creation and the great value of what is accomplished in spite of those obstacles.

FURTHER WORKS: *Mother to Daughter, Daughter to Mother: A Daybook and Reader* (1984)

BIBLIOGRAPHY: Rosenfelt, D., "From the Thirties: T. O. and the Radical Tradition," *FSt*, 7, 3 (Fall 1981): 371–406; Orr., E. N., *T. O. and a Feminist Spiritual Vision* (1987); Coiner, C., "Literature and Resistance: The Intersection of Feminism and the Communist Left in Meridel LeSueur and T. O.," in Davis, L. J. and Mirabella, M. B., eds., *Left Politics and the Literary Profession* (1990): 162–85; Fishkin, S. F., "The Borderlands of Culture: Writing by W. E. B. DuBois, James Agee, T. O., and Gloria Anzaldua," in Sims N., ed., *Literary Journalism in the Twentieth Century* (1990): 133–82; Pearlman, M. and Werlock, A. H. P., *T. O.* (1991); Hedges, E. and S. F. Fishkin, *Listening to Silences* (1994); Nelson, K. H. and N. Huse, eds., *The Critical Response to T. O.* (1994); Pfaelzer, J., "T. O.'s Tell Me a Riddle: The Dialectics of Silence," *Frontiers*, 15, 2 (1994): 1-22; Frye, J., *T. O.: A Study of the Short Fiction* (1995); Coiner, c., *Better Red: The Writing and Resistance of T. O. and Meridel LeSueur* (1995); Roberts, N. R., *Three Radical Women Writers: Class and Gender in Meridel LeSueur, T. O., and Josephine Herbst* (1996)

—LILLIAN S. ROBINSON

OLSON, Charles

American poet and essayist, b. 27 Dec. 1910, Worcester, Mass.; d. 10 Jan. 1970, New York, N.Y.

Best known as the author of the *Maximus Poems*, O. was the central figure of the Black Mountain school of poetry in the 1950s. His early poems and polemical essays attempt to define an American poetical tradition rooted in the innovations of Ezra POUND and William Carlos WILLIAMS. His essays, his letters, his teaching at Black Mountain College (1951–56), and the *Maximus Poems* themselves became the focal point for a number of post war poets, such as Robert CREELEY, Robert DUNCAN, and Edward Dorn (b. 1929), who sought an alternative to the closed poetic forms that academic criticism had made fashionable.

After receiving B.A. and M.A. degrees from Wesleyan University, O. prepared for an academic career. He entered the Harvard American Studies program. Although he left without taking a degree, O.'s research on Herman Melville was later published as *Call Me Ishmael* (1947). O.'s study of Melville examined the Shakespearean sources of *Moby-Dick* and Melville's attempt to fashion a mythological system from the tragic figure of King Lear and the materials of American history.

Following a brief political career in the Roosevelt administration, O. began his poetic career. From 1946 to 1950, O. developed a political approach to poetry, and his use of poetry as a didactic instrument tended to divide his audience into disciples and detractors. From Pound, whom O. visited regularly at St. Elizabeths Hospital, O. derived a "spatial" sense of history, an understanding of the continuity of the past in the present. According to O., Pound's egotism allowed him to treat Western culture as contemporaneous with himself, but limited him to a nostalgic recovery of tradition. What was needed was a sense of place, a "polis," for which the poet could make himself useful and from which he could rediscover a sense of man more comprehensive than that offered by the Western traditions.

O. adopted the sense of the local from Williams's poetry, although he thought Williams's treatment of Paterson sentimental. Pound and Williams both had a profound influence on O.'s manifesto "Projective Verse" (1950), which argued for a "postmodern" poetics based on "open" verse forms. According to O., the poem is a "field of action," a process where energy is transferred from the poet by means of the poem to the reader. The poem is not an object that comments on nature but is continuous with nature and, like any other natural object or event, should have an immediate "kinetic" effect on the reader.

In the first volume of *The Maximus Poems* (1960), O. finds in Gloucester, Massachusetts, the "polis" he will address, teach, and learn from. Constructed as a series of letters, these poems attempt to define the stance of Maximus as he confronts his city and as O. confronts the voices of the American poetic tradition. In addressing his city, Maximus takes in his experience of it, criticizes its politics and rituals, argues for a new vision of politics, and turns to historical records in order to discern its origins and to recover the meaning immanent in its founding. Throughout, Maximus employs a variety of poetic forms as a commentary on the use of poetic languages and an attempt to dissolve himself in an almost Emersonian way into the experience of the city as a spatial or "horizontal" entity.

In *Maximus Poems IV, V, VI* (1968), Maximus explores the "vertical" dimension by turning inward. Literally, his attention shifts inland from the fishing village of Gloucester to the failed farming community of Dogtown. At the same time, his introduction of JUNGIAN archetypes plunges him into an examination of his relations to mother figures, and this personal concern is reflected cosmologically in the turn to Algonquin and Hittite myths of genesis, nurturance, and rebirth. The narrower political, economic, and historical concerns of the first volume are displaced by intense sexual conflict and by wide-ranging speculation on geology, philosophy, and myth. The letter forms are replaced by several long meditations stitched together by fragments and notes, reflecting Maximus's attempt to stitch together the once unified but now disparate realms of self, world, and cosmos.

The Maximus Poems, Volume III (1975) is formally even more difficult than the second volume. Compiled posthumously, the work purports to be Maximus's "Republic." While critics disagree about the nature of this "Republic," all seem to agree that this volume is the weakest of the three. "Maximus" is discarded halfway through, and O. confronts his readers as his autobiographical self. His interest in mythology now appears obsessional as well as idiosyncratic, and the sexual and generational conflicts in those myths are exaggerated in the service of confession, as O. strains to unite himself with father and mother. The pervasive sense of loss and isolation in O.'s work, which gave urgency to his didacticism in volume I and his eccentric and passionate interest in arcane lore in volume II, begins to feed on itself in volume III as O. returns continually to autobiographical material in obsessive acts of reparation.

Since O.'s death his early poems have been reprinted in *Archaeologist of Morning* (1973) and his papers collected at the University of Connecticut continue to be published. Important and necessary tracing of O.'s sources has been done, and this research has helped make O.'s often obscure and difficult poetry more accessible. In addition to their intrinsic worth, O.'s poems and essays are themselves among the most useful commentaries on American modernism.

FURTHER WORKS: *Y & X* (1948); *Mayan Letters* (1953); *In Cold Hell, in Thicket* (1953); *The Distances* (1960); *Human Universe and Other Essays* (1965); *Proprioception* (1965); *Selected Writings* (1967); *Pleistocene Man* (1968); *Causal Mythology* (1969); *Letters for Origin* (1970); *The Special View of History* (1970); *Poetry and Truth* (1971); *Additional Prose* (1974); *The Post Office* (1975); *C. O. and Ezra Pound: An Encounter at St. Elizabeths* (1975); *The Fiery Hunt and Other Plays* (1977); *Muthologos* (1978)

BIBLIOGRAPHY: Altieri, C., "From Symbolist Thought to Immanence: The Ground of Post-modern American Poetics," *Boundary*, 2 1 (1973): 605–41; Perloff, M. G., "C. O. and the "'Inferior Predecessors': 'Projective Verse' Revisited," *ELH*, 40 (1973): 285–305; Butterick, G. F., *A Guide to the Maximus Poems of C. O.* (1978); Paul, S., *O.'s Push* (1978); Hallberg, R., von, *C. O.: The Scholar's Art* (1978); Christensen, P., *C. O.: Call Him Ishmael* (1979); Byrd, D., *C. O.'s Maximus* (1980)

—JOHN FRANZOSA

ONDAATJE, Michael

Canadian poet and novelist, b. 12 Sept. 1943, Colombo, Sri Lanka

O., one of the most influential writers of the contemporary period in Canada, has been recognized for his innovative work in two genres, poetry and prose fiction. He left Sri Lanka at the age of eleven, completing his secondary schooling in England before moving to Canada in 1962. He earned B. A. and M. A. degrees in English literature from the University of Toronto and Queen's University, Kingston, respectively. Since 1971, O. has taught at Glendon College, York University, in Toronto.

O.'s first poetry collection, *The Dainty Monsters* (1967), published when the author was only twenty-four years old, reveals an impressive maturity. Its short, intensely visual domestic lyrics startle the reader with their sharp-edged imagery. This quality is honed in the later volume *Rat Jelly* (1973), which contains a number of O.'s best-known poems: "Spider Blues," "King Kong Meets Wallace Stevens," "Rat Jelly," and "White Dwarfs." Many of these poems meditate self-consciously on art, especially on the paradoxical notion of creativity as a violent act of "freezing" the flux of lived experience. O.'s most recent poems, however, collected in *Secular Love* (1984), show a more expansive, meditative tone, though the painfully sharp imagery is still there.

In 1970, O. was awarded Canada's highest literary prize, the Governor General's Award, for *The Collected Works of Billy the Kid: Left-Handed Poems* (1970). This work was probably the most influential poetic work of that decade in Canada, since it explored a fabricated version of a historical figure, the American outlaw William Bonney, through a daring, experimental mixture of poetry and prose.

In the late 1970s, O. continued this generic experimentation in *Coming through Slaughter* (1976), a poetic novel whose short, stabbing paragraphs and visual effects again showed Canadian readers a fresh innovator at work. O. recreates another historical figure, the legendary New Orleans jazz musician Buddy Bolden, in order to meditate on the meeting of order and chaos, violence and creativity. In his prose works of the 1980s, O. took these concerns in two different directions, the autobiographical and the sociopolitical. In *Running in the Family* (1982), O. turned to his own Sri Lankan family as the source of historical fictionalizing; in so doing he forged a hybrid genre: the fictionalized (auto) biography. In his most recent novel, *In the Skin of a Lion* (1987), the alternative history is that of those nearly forgotten, marginalized working-class immigrants in Canada who worked on large public projects.

More than any other Canadian writer working today, O. has brought to the literature of this country a cosmopolitan breadth of subject matter and a taste for stylistic and generic innovation. Like other contemporary writers dubbed postmodernist, he has moved the previously marginalized and excluded (process as opposed to product, popular culture, the outlaw, the immigrant) into the center of the reader's viewing frame. The fears of his earlier poetry, that art freezes and disempowers, are implicitly answered in this act of celebrating the undervalued.

FURTHER WORKS: *The Man with Seven Toes* (1969); *Elimination Dance* (1978); *There's a Trick with a Knife I'm Learning To Do: Selected Poems* (1979); *Tin Roof* (1982); *The English Patient* (1992)

BIBLIOGRAPHY: Solecki, S., "Making and Destroying: M. O.'s *Coming through Slaughter* and *Extremist Art,*" *ECW*, 2 (1978): 24–47; Solecki, S., "Nets and Chaos: The Poetry of M. O., " in David, J., ed., *Brave New Wave* (1978); Scobie, S., "His Legend a Jungle Sleep: M. O. and Henri Rousseau," *CanL*, 76 (1978): 6–21; Solecki, S., ed., *Spider Blues: Essays on M. O.* (1986); York, L. M., *The Other Side of Dailiness: Photography in the Works of Alice Munro, Timothy Findley, M. O., and Margaret Laurence* (1987): 93–120

—LORRAINE M. YORK

O'NEILL, Alexandre

Portuguese poet, b. 19 Dec. 1924, Lisbon; d. 21 Aug. 1986, Lisbon

O., a major figure in Portuguese surrealism, was born and raised in Lisbon, but from early childhood spent summer vacations in Amarante, a charming, ancient town on the River Tâmega in the north. Two notable events from his earliest years were the flight to France of a great uncle, José Vahia, an opponent of Salazar, which came to have a certain influence on the poet's later political development, and the unexpected death of his grandmother, Maria O'Neill, a republican, suffragette, and well-known author of children's books, which left him, aged nine, with a sense of the mystery of death. As an adolescent, he followed the progress of the Spanish Civil War and was distraught at news of Franco's victory in 1939.

O.'s first published poems appeared in newspapers and magazines beginning in 1942. During the years 1947-48, along with Mário Cesariny (b. 1923), now considered Portugal's leading surrealist figure, he helped to found the first surrealist group of Lisbon. His first chapbook, *A Ampola Miraculosa (*1948; The Miraculous Vial), resulted from this association. However, when organizing his complete poems more than thirty years later, O. excluded all these early works, beginning the volume with *Tempo de Fantasmas* (1951; Time of Phantoms). Nine further volumes culminated in the *Poesias Completas 1951-1981* (1982; Complete Poetry 1951-1981). This was followed, just a month before his death, by the publication of *O Princípio de Utopia, o Princípio de Realidade, seguidos de Ana Brites, Balada tão ao Gosto Popular Português & Vários Outros Poemas* (1986; The Beginning of Utopia, the Beginning of Reality, Followed by Ana Brites, a Ballad So Much to the Portuguese Taste). In 1990 a revised and augmented version of *Poesias Completas* appeared. Other works by O. include two books published in Italy, *Portogallo mio Rimorso* (1966; Portugal, My Remorse) and *Made in Portugal* (1978), whose titles suggest the mixture of rueful sentiment and ironic criticism he felt for his homeland. In addition, the author published two volumes of prose writings and organized various anthologies,

including a collection of Carl SANDBURG's poetry, some of which he translated himself.

In 1952, after being dismissed from his position as a functionary in a large commercial pension fund for political reasons, he entered the world of advertising as a freelancer. The concision, manipulation, and word-play central to the language of advertising made its way into O.'s poetry, both as technical ploy and as butt of his ironic attacks. Irony clearly became the central force in his work, and nothing escaped his penetrating wit and deflating gibes. With an ironic, sometimes mordant humor as his constant companion, in both his poetry and his conversation, he persistently challenged the conventional, the "normal," the accepted. Although an impish, implacable foe of bourgeois complacency and of all unexamined expressions of received "wisdom," his delight in puncturing social pomposity and pretense did not prevent him from mocking himself, as well.

SURREALISM, with its professed goal of total freedom for man and for art, provided a good starting point for O. However, he never felt obliged to abide by any credo and remained suspicious of all restrictions, limitations, classifications, and artificial boundary lines. He joyously attacked all shibboleths, including those of politics and poetry. In one of his verses, for example, he counsels himself to "struggle against the beautiful" and to remember that "the rule is to have no rule." In fact, though still considered a major exponent of surrealism, O. incorporates many styles, views, and techniques in his work. Almost always linguistically playful, his poetry with its leanings toward satire and burlesque, also manifests influences from symbolism and even romanticism. Since he will not allow aesthetic, moral, political, or logical presuppositions to inhibit him, O.'s poetry has tremendous variety, originality and inventiveness. Whether drawing from romanticism, symbolism, surrealism, concretism, or POSTMODERNISM, O., always human and always doubtful, mocked and distrusted all "isms" alike.

FURTHER WORKS: *No Reino da Dinamarca* (1958); *Abandono Vigiado* (1960); *Poemas com Endereço* (1962); *Feira Cabisbaixa* (1965); *De Ombra na Ombreira* (1969); *As Andorinhas Não Tem Restaurante* (1970); *Entre a Cortina e a Vidraça* (1972); *A Saca de Orelhas* (1979); *Uma Coisa em Forma de Assim* (1980); *As Horas Já de NúmerosVestidas* (1981)

BIBLIOGRAPHY: Rocha, C., Prefácio to *Poesias Completas 1951-1981* (1982): 9-29; Ramos Rosa, A., "A. O., or the Dialectics of Sleep and Reality," *Cóloquio*, 93 (1986): 124-26; Martinho, F. J. B., "A. O. and Pessoa," *Cóloquio*, 97 (1987): 48-56; Coelho, J. F., "Carta-Elegia Para A. O.," *Cóloquio*, 100 (1987): 108-10 Mendonca, F., "An Unpublished Poem of A. O.," *Cóloquio*, 108 (1989): 63-65; Bom, L., "A. O.—A Biographical Chronology, 1924-1953," *Cóloquio*, 113 (1990): 13-30

—ALEXIS LEVITIN

O'NEILL, Eugene

American dramatist, b. 16 Oct. 1888, New York, N.Y.; d. 27 Nov. 1953, Boston, Mass.

O.'s early life provided material for his dramas. The son of a famous actor, James O'Neill, he, along with the rest of his family, accompanied his father on tour. From ages seven to fourteen he was

Eugene O'Neill

educated in Roman Catholic schools. After renouncing Catholicism, he attended a nonsectarian preparatory school and studied for a year at Princeton University. Events of special importance to his work included early voyages as a merchant seaman, interspersed with periods of beachcombing in Buenos Aires, and followed (1911–12) by a period of drinking and destitution on the New York waterfront. At this time O. suffered emotional depression and attempted suicide. He then stayed with his family in Connecticut, but was forced by the onset of tuberculosis to spend six months in a sanatorium. It was there that he determined to become a playwright. He had been reading widely, including some works of Nietzsche and plays by STRINDBERG—who would become his most important model—Ibsen, and WEDEKIND. By 1914 he had become a working playwright, and in 1916 *Bound East for Cardiff* was produced by the Provincetown Players. After this success, O. lived for periods in the bohemian atmosphere of Greenwich Village in New York, which provided settings and characters for the plays. O.'s three stormy marriages were reflected in the relationship of the sexes in his dramas. O. was awarded the Nobel Prize for literature in 1936. A progressive disease of the nervous system forced him to stop writing in 1943.

O.'s plays fall into chronological groupings through which the changes and development of his art may be traced. According to their dates of composition, three groups emerge: those plays written from 1913 to 1925, 1926 to 1933, and 1939 to 1943. From his first to his final work, O.'s major characters—those with whom the author identified—are tormented misfits, searching for their lost selves or "souls." They are all, in some way, failed poets and dreamers who envision another world or life where they can, or once did, find fulfillment, innocence, relief from guilt and conflict. Throughout his first, highly prolific period O. looked upon this dream as an affirmation of human dignity—of the stubborn, often mystical, instinct for hope that keeps us alive, even when logic calls for despair. Death itself becomes a grand gesture, a ritual celebration of freedom, escape, or homecoming.

Of O.'s apprenticeship (1913–18) the most important plays are the one-act *Bound East for Cardiff* (written 1914, pub. 1916) and *Beyond the Horizon* (written 1918, pub. 1920). O. said that *Bound East for Cardiff* contained "the germ of the spirit, life-attitude of all [my] more important future work." The play broke with tradition in that it had no real plot; it depicted a badly injured seaman who, on his deathbed, reveals his simple values of courage and friendship, and his dream of some day owning a farm, a dream that made the drudgery of life at sea worthwhile.

Beyond the Horizon, O.'s first important full-length play, is the story of two brothers, the elder a practical realist and the younger a poetic idealist. His dreams about romantic love and the pastoral life keep the younger brother at home on the family farm, which he is incapable of managing. Poverty and tuberculosis kill him, but he dies joyfully affirming his idealism, his life-giving dream of some day voyaging beyond the horizon, and his final freedom in death. He leaves behind him, however, a bitter wife and an angry brother who must live on, coping with a bleak reality. Alternate indoor and outdoor settings represented, O. said, the rhythmic "alternation of longing and of loss"—a rhythm that was to flow through subsequent plays. *Beyond the Horizon* won the Pulitzer Prize (1920) and high praise from critics; it presaged a new era of serious art in the American theater.

Between 1918 and 1925 O. wrote fifteen plays. In 1920 and 1921 alone, he completed *Anna Christie* (pub. 1922) which won a Pulitzer Prize, *The Emperor Jones* (pub. 1921), and *The Hairy Ape* (pub. 1922).

Anna of *Anna Christie* is a prostitute who regains her lost innocence when her father, an ex-sailor, takes her to live with him aboard his coal barge. To Anna the sea and the fog come to represent freedom and cleanliness; to her father they represent fate, mystery, impending danger. The play ends with Anna's marriage to a sailor to whom, also, the sea represents freedom and hope. (But O. pointed out that this was not intended to be a happy ending; the mystery and the danger would remain.)

The hero of *The Emperor Jones* begins life as a Pullman porter, who through luck and exploitation of the natives becomes ruler of an island in the West Indies. When his subjects rebel, he becomes a fugitive, pursued through the jungle to the beat of a drum in pulse rhythm. Scenes from his racial and personal history flash before him, stripping him down to the essentials of himself and of the past that shaped him. Jones dies in the end, and his death is a ritual expiation of guilt, but not all the guilt is his, and he dies on his own terms, in "the height of style."

Death as the grand gesture of ultimate escape and "belonging" is the finale, also, of *The Hairy Ape*. The protagonist, Yank, is a brawny stoker in the hold of an ocean liner, where he is proud of his occupation and his strength. His self-image is destroyed, however, when he hears a wealthy young woman call him, with revulsion, a "hairy ape." As a result he seeks vengeance on the society that he thinks has rejected his brute strength. His attempts fail, however, and in frustration and anger he goes to the zoo and harangues a real ape in a cage, with whom he identifies. In a fierce embrace, his "brother," the ape, kills him. The ape escapes and as Yank slips to the floor of the cage, O. comments that "perhaps the Hairy Ape at last belongs." Both *The Emperor Jones* and *The Hairy Ape* were highly effective dramaturgical experiments, using EXPRESSIONIST techniques to project the characters' feelings and the symbolic meaning of the action.

In most of the plays from the remaining years of this first period O.'s "dreamers" find the resolution of conflict and the peace they long for in mystical union or oneness with all life. To gain this unity with the whole they must sacrifice their individuality—not a very realistic solution for many of O.'s characters nor for the majority of his audiences. Most of these plays were failures, depending too heavily upon philosophical ideas derived from Nietzsche and Schopenhauer, Taoism, and psychoanalytic allusions to JUNG and FREUD. *All God's Chillun Got Wings* (written 1923, pub. 1924) created a sensation as the anguished love story of a black man and the white woman to whom he abases himself. *The Great God Brown* (written 1925, pub. 1926) is an intricate and confusing drama of masks in which the hero tries to find himself between conflicting self-images and conflicting forces of materialism and idealism, paganism and Christianity. *Marco Millions* (written 1923–25, pub. 1927) is a huge, spectacular pageant portraying Marco Polo as an American Babbitt who confronts the mysticism of the East with total incomprehension. *Lazarus Laughed* (written 1925–26, pub. 1927) was another enormous pageant, in which Lazarus has been reborn to bring the joyful tidings that there is really no death.

The only drama from this period that continues to be produced with popular success is *Desire under the Elms* (written 1924, pub. 1924). In this play O. moved away from mysticism and attempts at poetical diction to rustic New England dialect. It is a violent tale of a hard, realistic father in opposition to his dreamer-son. The characters are all rugged farm people, of Puritan stock, driven by the desire for sex, money, and vengeance but also by the need for warmth, love, and beauty. Even after the son has been intimate with his father's young wife, and she has murdered their child, the lovers feel that some-how their love transcends the reality of their crime and its imminent punishment. By suggesting that the characters of *Desire under the Elms* are victims of a wronged brooding maternal spirit that has demanded revenge and expiation, O. attempted to give them tragic stature. Although the two lovers go rapturously toward prison, the old father remains to work out his lonely destiny on the barren, rocky land.

He is a precursor of the protagonists of the plays written between 1926 and 1932. For them the long struggle for fulfillment and freedom ends in self-punishment or resignation. There is no ideal or transcendent world. Guilt is inescapable, and conflict ends only with the end of desire. The important plays of this period are *Strange Interlude* (written 1926–27, pub. 1928), which also won a Pulitzer Prize, and *Mourning Becomes Electra* (written 1929–31, pub. 1931).

Strange Interlude is a STREAM-OF-CONSCIOUSNESS novel in dramatic form. It consists of nine acts and takes five hours to perform, but it was the greatest popular success of O.'s career. The characters reveal their hidden motives in asides, exposing their Oedipal fixations or other drives and forces as described by Freud, Jung, and Schopenhauer. The central figure is Nina Leeds, a woman who must exploit the male characters in order to fulfill her needs for a father, lover, husband, and son. The action of the play ceases only when Nina, all passion spent, gives up hope of fulfilling these needs and accepts old age. Her rebellion against sexual

repression made the play seem shocking and revolutionary in its day. Now, however, it seems dated and often melodramatic.

Mourning Becomes Electra is O.'s version of the tragedy of the house of Atreus, set in 19th-c. New England. This trilogy (made up of *Homecoming, The Hunted*, and *The Haunted*) interprets, in psychoanalytic terms, the familiar story of the murder of Agamemnon and its consequences. The action centers around Lavinia (Electra), who avenges her father's murder by persuading her brother, Orin (Orestes) to kill her mother's (Christine-Clytemnestra) lover; the murder is followed by the suicide of the mother, and subsequently, of Orin when he discovers that he has an incestuous passion for his sister. Shouldering the family guilt, Lavinia locks herself in the family mansion to live with and be hounded by the ghosts of the past.

In a few weeks in 1932, O. wrote his only comedy, the highly successful *Ah, Wilderness!* (pub. 1933). Its nostalgic portrayal of middle-class American family life was based in part on O.'s family memories of his Connecticut days. Here the poetic dreamer is an adolescent boy in the throes of romantic love, whose introduction to sex and the adult world is treated with humor and sympathy.

O. was becoming increasingly preoccupied with his own past. In 1933 *Days without End* (pub. 1934) was completed only after many laborious drafts, each with a different ending. It is a drama of inner conflict, in which two actors play the two selves of the protagonist. One self is a gentle idealist who adores his wife; the other is a satanic mocker who hates her and life. The conflict is finally resolved in the love of Christ, as the hero returns to Catholicism. The conclusion was not very convincing, and the play was a theatrical failure. Although some critics saw in it O.'s return to his childhood faith, this was not the fact. Throughout his career, before and after *Days without End*, O. expressed his ambivalence toward Christianity in a longing to believe, on the one hand, and blasphemous contempt, on the other.

In 1935 O. began work on a cycle of eleven plays, to be called *A Tale of Possessors Dispossessed*. Its theme was the destructiveness of American greed and materialism, as seen in the two-hundred-year history of an Irish-American family. The cycle was never completed. Only two plays have survived: *A Touch of the Poet* (written 1935–43, pub. 1957) is the most finished; *More Stately Mansions* (written 1935–43, pub. 1964) was a lengthy rough draft, posthumously revised and shortened by its editors.

In his final productive period O. completed *The Iceman Cometh* (written 1939, pub. 1946), *Long Day's Journey into Night* (written 1940–41, pub. 1956), the one-act *Hughie* (written 1941–42, pub. 1959), and *A Moon for the Misbegotten* (written 1943, pub. 1952). In all these plays the characters long, still, for some kind of peace or fulfillment, but now any "dream" they have is a self-deceptive lie. Yet life is bearable to them only by virtue of these "pipe-dreams," and by the pity and sympathy they come to feel for one another. When death comes, it is no longer a grand gesture or a mystical experience, but simply a relief, a giving up.

The Iceman Cometh and *Long Day's Journey* reflect O.'s experiences in 1911–12, and his mood of depression at that time. *The Iceman Cometh* concerns a group of drunken derelicts (based on people O. knew on the waterfront and in Greenwich Village) who spend their time in the back room of Harry Hope's saloon on the lower west side of New York City. They live in an aura of alcohol and illusions about what they once were and hope to become again. These illusions are shattered when Hickey, a salesman whom they admire, appears as a messiah, offering them peace of mind if they will face reality and test their plans to rehabilitate themselves. They fail the test, and in despair are no longer able to forget their inadequacies in alcohol—until they discover that their quasiredeemer is himself living a lie; is, indeed a madman and a murderer. Then they can again find solace and community in drinking with their cronies, in Hope's back room. For three characters, however, there can be no solace but death. Two of these, Hickey and a young ex-anarchist named Parritt, have destroyed women they loved—one a wife, the other a mother. They convince themselves for a while that their crimes were justified, but when the horror of what they have done comes through to them, death is the only expiation. The third of these, Larry, thinks of himself as a philosopher, a detached observer of the others. Events show him, however, that his supposed detachment is actually a hopeless paralysis of will from which death can be the only release.

When read, the play seems to be repetitious as each character recites his own "pipedream" and subsequent disillusionment, and as the plots parallel each other. On the stage, however, and under good direction, the repetition becomes, as O. intended, an excitingly dramatic "theme and variations." The play typifies, also, another favorite device of O.'s: it begins as a comedy with the characters objectively portrayed as clowns; later, when their inner selves are revealed, they become pathetic and even tragic.

Long Day's Journey Into Night is O.'s agonized portrait of his own family, here called the Tyrones. The events take place in 1912. Edmund (the young O. himself) is staying with his family in Connecticut, before entering the tuberculosis sanatorium. O. reveals his mother's drug addiction and its effect upon the family relationships. Beginning on a note of affection and humor, the tone of the play changes to pain and bitterness as the father, the mother, and the two brothers reveal the secret springs of their own characters and the mixed love, hate, and guilt they feel toward the others. They shout recriminations at each other, then confess their own guilt and beg for forgiveness. Through it all the mother (called Mary) wanders in a morphine haze, in each scene regressing farther into the past where she thought she had once known peace, freedom, and innocence. *Long Day's Journey* is the most consistently powerful of all O.'s work.

The hauntingly effective one-act play, *Hughie*, continues the theme of *The Iceman Cometh; A Moon for the Misbegotten* continues the family history. In *Hughie* a small-time gambler cannot endure his life without someone to believe the lie that he was once in the "big time." In *A Moon for the Misbegotten*, James Tyrone, Jr., who represented O.'s older brother in *Long Day's Journey*, has been devastated by his mother's death and his guilt feelings toward her. He is a desperate alcoholic wreck. For a brief time he finds comfort in the arms of a large earthy woman who loves him, and who as a mother surrogate gives him a kind of absolution. In the end, however, the best she can hope for him is that he die in his sleep, and soon.

O. brought passion and art to the American stage. He believed that drama should attempt to project on the stage the deepest truths about human character and its relationship to the "mystery" of things. This subjective point of view led him to use a stylized rather than a literal approach to production. He employed such devices as the monologue and the aside; abstract, symbolic sets; symbolic masks, makeup and costumes; thematic repetition of spoken phrases, actions, and theatrical effects; and archetypal motifs drawn from mythology and religion. He was not above using old plot devices from melodrama or vaudeville if they served his purpose.

The depth of O.'s thought, and his knowledge of philosophy and psychology have been questioned, as has his use of language and

the quality of his imagination. He is universally honored, however, for his skillful dramaturgy and especially for the emotional truth and intensity of some of his plays. Of these the ones most likely to survive as classic repertory are his one comedy, *Ah, Wilderness!;* his paean to the "pipe-dream," *The Iceman Cometh*; and his family confessional, *Long Day's Journey into Night*. Other plays are, and will continue to be revived experimentally now and then, but these three have already become a part of the American dramatic heritage.

FURTHER WORKS: *Thirst and Other One-Act Plays* (1914); *Before Breakfast* (1916); *The Long Voyage Home* (1917); *The Moon of the Caribbees* (1918); *In the Zone* (1919); *The Rope* (1919); *Where the Cross is Made* (1919); *The Dreamy Kid* (1920); *The Straw* (1921); *Gold* (1921); *Diff'rent* (1921); *The First Man* (1922); *Welded* (1924); *The Fountain* (1926); *Dynamo* (1929); *Lost Plays, 1913–15* (1950); *Plays of E. O.* (3 vols., 1955); *Ten "Lost" Plays* (1964); *Children of the Sea, and Three Other Unpublished Plays* (1972); *Poems 1912–1944* (1980); *E. O. at work* (1981); *"The Theatre We Worked For": The Letters of E. O. to Kenneth Macgowan* (1982); *The Letters of E. O. to Kenneth Macgowan* (1982); *Chris Christophersen* (1982)

BIBLIOGRAPHY: Clark, B. H., *E. O.* (1926; rev. ed., 1947); Winther, S. K., *E. O.: A Critical Study* (1934; rev. ed., 1961); Engel, E. A., *The Haunted Heroes of E. O.* (1953); Falk, D. V., *E. O. and the Tragic Tension* (1958; rev. ed., 1982); Bowen, C., *Curse of the Misbegotten* (1959); Cargill, et al., O., eds., *O. and His Plays* (1961); Alexander, D., *The Tempering of E. O.* (1962); Gelb, A., and B. *O.* (1962); Leech, C., *E. O.* (1963); Gassner, J., ed., *O.: A Collection of Critical Essays* (1964); Raleigh, J. H., *The Plays of E. O.* (1965); Sheaffer, L., *O., Son and Play-wright* (1968); Tiusanen, T., *O.'s Scenic Images* (1968); Törnqvist, E., *A Drama of Souls: Studies in O.'s Super-Naturalistic Technique* (1969); Bogard, T., *Contour in Time: The Plays of E. O.* (1972); Sheaffer, L., *O., Son and Artist* (1973); Chabrowe, L., *Ritual and Pathos: The Theater of O.* (1976); Carpenter, F. I., *E. O.*, rev. ed. (1979); Chothia, J., *Forging a Language: A Study of the Plays of E. O.* (1979); Floyd, V., ed., *E. O.: A World View* (1979)

—DORIS V. FALK

The dialogue of *The First Man* . . . proves in reading so tasteless and dreary that one does not see how one could sit through it.

But E. O. has another vein in which he is a literary artist of genius. When he is writing the more or less grammatical dialogue of the middle-class characters of his plays, his prose is heavy and indigestible even beyond the needs of naturalism. People say the same things to one another over and over again and never succeed in saying them any more effectively than the first time; long speeches shuffle dragging feet, marking time without progressing, for pages. But as soon as Mr. O. gets a character who can only talk some kind of vernacular, he begins to write like a poet. [1922]

Edmund Wilson, "E. O. and the Naturalists," *The Shores of Light* (1952), pp. 99–100

That he is the foremost dramatist in the American theatre is . . . generally granted. His eminence is predicated on the fact that no other has anywhere near his ability to delve into and appraise character, his depth of knowledge of his fellow man, his sweep and pulse and high resolve, his command of a theatre stage and all its manifold workings, and his mastery of the intricacies of dramaturgy. His plays at their best have in them a real universality. His characters are not specific, individual and isolated types but active symbols of mankind in general, with mankind's virtues and faults, gropings and findings, momentary triumphs and doomed defeats. He writes not for a single theatre but for all theatres of the world.

George Jean Nathan, "O.: A Critical Summation," *American Mercury*, Dec. 1946, p. 718

At one time he performed a historic function, that of helping the American theatre to grow up. In all his plays an earnest attempt is made to interpret life; this fact in itself places O. above his predecessors in American drama and beside his colleagues in the novel and poetry. He was a good playwright insofar as he kept within the somewhat narrow range of his own sensibility. When he stays close to a fairly simple reality and when, by way of technique, he uses fairly simple forms of realism or fairly simple patterns of melodrama, he can render the bite and tang of reality or, alternatively, he can startle and stir us with his effects . . . But the more he attempts, the less he succeeds. *Lazarus Laughed* and *The Great God Brown* and *Days without End* are inferior to *The Emperor Jones* and *Anna Christie* and *Ah, Wilderness!*

Eric Bentley, "Trying to Like O.," *KR*, 14 (1952), p. 488

O. was a faulty craftsman; he was not a sound thinker . . . Yet to dwell on these shortcomings . . . is to confess one's own inadequate and bloodless response to the world we live in . . . O. not only lived intensely but attempted with perilous honesty to contemplate, absorb and digest the meaning of his life and ours. He possessed an uncompromising devotion to the task he set himself: to present and interpret in stage terms what he had lived through and thought about—a devotion unique in our theatre . . . O.'s work is more than realism. And if it is stammering— it is still the most eloquent and significant stammer of the American theatre. We have not yet developed a cultivated speech that is either superior to it or as good.

Harold Clurman, on *Long Day's Journey into Night, Nation*, 3 March 1956, pp. 182–83

Compassion produced by a full understanding of man's circumstances and man's essential nature, a compassion which beggars analysis, is O.'s final achievement in theatre. The action of each of the four last plays rests in a tale to be told, a tale that is essentially a confession made in hope of absolution. Although the confessional tale is often plotless, often

nothing more than a dream, it is a way of reaching out in the dark, of finding pity long denied to old sorrow.

The introspective qualities of the last plays account for their essential lyricism. When *The Iceman Cometh* was first produced in 1946, under the somewhat ponderously reverential conditions that O.'s "return" to the New York theatre necessarily occasioned, it brought with it, from producers and reviewers, charges that O. was indulging himself by refusing to cut the work. [Lawrence] Langner tells of a time during rehearsals when he timidly reminded O. that the same point had been made 18 times. O. told him "in a particularly quiet voice, 'I *intended* it to be repeated eighteen times!'" Although it was obviously not a matter of calculated intention, O. did not indulge in such repetition without full awareness of its theatrical consequences. Like many of his earlier efforts, the repetition not only in *The Iceman Cometh* but in *Long Day's Journey into Night* is essential to the lyric mode of the work, for in these plays O. became the poet he had earlier so often lamented he could not be.

Travis Bogard, *Contour in Time: The Plays of E. O.* (1972), pp. 408–9

As *Mourning Becomes Electra* was derived from the *Oresteia* in plot and structure, it had a considerable aesthetic distance from the audience. Its pathos was consequently muted, the tragic effect too removed. The fate equivalent could have its full impact only when cast in an intrinsically modern idiom. And not until *Long Day's Journey into Night*, written a decade later, did O. cast it in such an idiom. By then his philosophical outlook had turned despairing, a state of mind that worked against any spiritual triumph of the characters. But by purely aesthetic means he was able to bring about a greater release of tragic pathos than ever before. In the very defeat of man in the life struggle there was an exultation.

The fact is that O. achieved nothing less than a renaissance of an art form long thought dead. Since funeral orations have been delivered many times over the petrified body of tragedy, a renaissance is just what his work amounts to. The orations have usually been delivered by scholars and critics with a strictly Aristotelian or moral perspective, but O.'s perspective was more from the Nietzschean or aesthetic side. Through the magic of ritual and pathos he evoked the tragic emotions in the theater as of old. In varying degrees, depending on the play, he made the audience feel what life was in its essence, not think about how to deal with it in its detail. To instruct or shake the opinions of an audience—the aim of political theater—is no mean feat. Still it is less difficult and in the long run even less relevant than to move an audience to catharsis.

Leonard Chabrowe, *Ritual and Pathos—the Theater of O.* (1976), pp. xxii-xxiii

There is an element in his dialogue not captured by the traditional approaches of literary analysis. This element is movement. There is a constant pendulum movement between several polarities in O.'s dialogue: between such polarities as fear and laughter, love and hatred, tragedy and comedy, aversion and sympathy, search and finding, heroism and baseness, self-deception and honesty. The result of this movement is a grotesque, grand language of the stage, even in the apparently most traditional or realistic of his plays. This is the feature that makes O. modern even today, in this new age of drama after Samuel Beckett.

Timo Tiusanen, "O.'s Significance: A Scandinavian and European View," in Virginia Floyd, ed., *E. O.: A World View* (1979), p. 66

O.'s drama found an audience in the late 1950s. At first sight, it seems remote from the dominant serious drama of this period, the post-realist drama that stemmed from Beckett's *Waiting for Godot*. A further wave of successful revivals of the late plays early in the 1970s suggests that O.'s appeal in 1956 was not, as might have been supposed, that of a voice from the past briefly resuscitated, but that of a voice speaking directly to audiences now. It is not a quaint voice but an urgent one that we hear, one that sounds both of and outside of its own time and presents us with pressing questions about our own being. O.'s writing differs from the ephemeral writing of those contemporaries of his who might seem to share his conventions because, in his drama, word and word, word and stage image, interact within a developing pattern of meaning, startling us, as members of the audience, with their echoic quality, informing us with their mutual suggestiveness, compelling us to see contrasts and new relationships.

Jean Chothia, *Forging a Language: A Study of the Plays of E. O.* (1979), p. 185

ONETTI, Juan Carlos

Uruguayan novelist and short-story writer, b. 1 July 1909, Montevideo; d. 30 May 1994

O. spent his first twenty years in his native Uruguay, but then moved to Buenos Aires, Argentina, where he worked quite successfully as a journalist. Despondent at the Argentine social and political situation, he returned in 1954 to Uruguay, where he spent some time as a librarian. Although not well known abroad then, he won the National Prize for Literature in Uruguay in 1962. The political changes in the 1970s in Uruguay resulted in his going into exile in Spain, where he has lived since 1975, winning the prestigious Critics' Prize in 1979 for his novel *Dejemos hablar al viento* (1979; let's speak with the wind) and Spain's highest literary award, the Miguel de Cervantes Prize, in 1980.

Many of O.'s existential novels and short stories are set in the fictional town of Santa María, a locale that is a microcosm of an absurd world. Most of his protagonists lead anguished, alienated, or frustrated lives in a sad and sordid world populated by unhappy people and corrupted by absurd values. His characters often live only through the remembrance of things past and—unfulfilled

sexually, politically, socially, or morally—find death to be the only solution to a life of defeat.

O.'s first novel, *El pozo* (1939; the pit), viewed by many critics as the first truly modern Spanish American novel because it gives expression to a peculiarly Spanish American mixture of dream and reality, explores the nightmarish world of its protagonist, Eladio Linacero. A solitary being who had dreamed of utopia, Linacero recalls his rape of an innocent girl, his moral degradation, and his nightly self-torture, although his confession gives him, briefly, self-awareness and an imagined potential for a different existence.

Tierra de nadie (1941; no-man's-land), stresses the sexual frustration and political disillusionment of an entire generation. Diego de Aránzuru, a typically ambiguous and ambivalent Onetti creation, abandons the legal profession to search in vain for meaning in life and love in an absurd universe indifferent to his needs.

Para esta noche (1943; for tonight) explores the world of dreams in a city under siege. Osorio, fleeing with the teenage daughter of the man he denounced to an enemy police agent, is himself killed. Again O. depicts a cynical, cruel, sterile world of moral indifference and lack of faith.

La vida breve (1950; *A Brief Life*, 1976), stylistically innovative, again portrays a world of hatred and frustration. The narrator, Brausen, unhappy with his married life, his routine, and his mediocrity, and seeking a "brief life" to transcend nothingness, invents a fantasy existence for himself as Díaz Grey, the protagonist of a screenplay he is writing, who is no more authentic than his inventor.

In a series of short novels set in Santa María, O. continued to dwell on earlier subjects: existentially isolated people who live in the past in *Los adioses* (1954; the good-byes); a man who is sexually obsessed with a prostitute in *Una tumba sin nombre* (1959; later title, *Para una tumba sin nombre*; [for] a nameless tomb); a guilt-ridden protagonist who accepts responsibility for the death of his brother and a young girl in *La cara de la desgracia* (1960; misfortune's face).

El astillero (1961; *The Shipyard*, 1968), an ironic allegory, presents in detail the frustrated and absurd life of Larsen, a middle-aged ex-owner of a whorehouse who, seeking escape from failure, works in Jeremías Petrus's rusting shipyard. Without a meaningful present or future—he fantasizes about managing the shipyard and having a relationship with Petrus's mad daughter—Larsen ends his wasted life in unheroic defeat, much as the shipyard, devoured by decay, will also disappear. *Juntacadáveres* (1964; the body collector) is about Larsen's earlier life as brothel owner, the psychologically troubled prostitutes and clients, and, despite Larsen's attempts to alter the situation, the closing of the brothel.

O.'s protagonists search in vain for an unattainable ideal love, which could give meaning to their absurd, alienated, and irrational lives. Betrayed and defeated, they often create imaginary doubles to obtain surcease from an unattractive world. This failure of escape through fantasy, reflecting the disintegration of modern urban life, often leads his characters to suicide.

A master in fusing fantasy and realism and in dealing with the mythopoetic faculties of creation, O., using a fluid style that some have compared to FAULKNER's, gives aesthetic expression to metaphysical preoccupations, as he ponders the human condition and the destiny of man.

FURTHER WORKS: *Un sueño realizado y otros cuentos* (1951); *El infierno tan temido* (1962); *Tan triste como ella* (1963); *Jacob y el otro, y otros cuentos* (1965); *Tres novelas* (1967); *Cuentos completos* (1967); *La novia robada, y otros cuentos* (1968); *Novelas cortas completas* (1968); *Obras completas* (1970); *La muerte y la niña* (1973); *Cuentos completos* (1974); *Tiempo de abrazar* (1974); *Réquiem por Faulkner* (1975)

BIBLIOGRAPHY: Jones, Y. P., *The Formal Expression of Meaning in J. C. O.'s Narrative Art* (1969); Gómez Mango, L., ed., *Entorno a J. C. O.* (1970); Deredita, J., "The Shorter Works of J. C. O.," *SSF*, 8 (1971): 112–22; Ruffinelli, J., *O.* (1973); "Focus on J. C. O.'s *A Brief Life*," special section Review, No. 16 (1975): 5–33; Giacomán, H. F., ed., *Homenaje a J. C. O.* (1974); Kader, D., *J. C. O.* (1977)

—KESSEL SCHWARTZ

ONWUEME, (Osonye) Tess

Nigerian dramatist (writing in English), b. 1955, Ogwashi-Ukwu

O. was born into an Igbo-speaking family in the Delta area of midwestern Nigeria. She received her university preparatory education for the West African School Certificate at Mary Mount College, Agbor, near Ogwashi-Ukwu, about fifty miles from the great Niger River. She graduated with distinction in 1972. She moved on to the University of Ife where she received a degree in English in 1979 and an M.A. in literature with stress in Francophone and Anglophone African literatures in 1982. In 1987 she earned a Ph.D. in English with an emphasis on African drama from the University of Benin, Nigeria. O. was an athletic and keen sports enthusiast in her late teens, and placed first and second repeatedly in the many hurdles and long jump meets in which she participated. As an African woman from a conservative and republican Igbo culture, she appeared to sense and anticipate early in life other forms of hurdles before her.

Never far from the rich cultural circumstances of her rural Igbo origins in her early school years, her career as a dramatist and theater practitioner has benefitted immensely from that background. She broke into the drama scene when she won the Association of Nigerian Authors Prize for drama in 1985 with one of her first plays, *The Desert Encroaches*. That socially critical play with its allegorical underpinnings set the tone for the multithematic thrust of her future dramaturgic engagements. Since then, her plays have attracted various kinds of recognition in Nigeria, the United Kingdom, and in the U.S. At least a dozen of those plays have not only been published, but have enjoyed very successful stage outings and runs in public and university theaters.

In *Tell It to Women* (1994) O. affirms her position as the leading female dramatist from Africa. The sweep and range of that play is epical, and the compelling execution of its multiperspectival thought is reminiscent of the best aspects of Shavian and Brechtian drama. The atmosphere strains with the tethered worries and pain in the worlds of Ibsen and CHEKHOV. This ambitious play is filled with shibboleth crumbling dynamic characters who attempt to revise, shape, and redirect history with their lifestyles and social engagement by forcing or attempting to force a collision of disparate values and interests. The range of interaction stretches from the formal and ruminative to the placardal and iconoclastic. This is a drama whose politics of relevance and meaning also reminds one of

the old dramaturgic dictates of socialist realism but tempered and mollified with a sensibility and humanity that is peculiarly African at its best. The unfailing ubiquitous instruments of a performative indigenous African drama within an equally unfailing and deathless folk ambience in a very modern frame mark this work as any watershed work defines all important artistic careers. Decidedly womanist, without the abrasive exclusivism and truculence of the culturally alienated, *Tell It to Women* entertains while it intrigues, fascinates, provokes, or annoys and even torments the conscience. The vision is that of one who understands cultural complexity and recursiveness and the ineffectual nature of ideological conflict.

Tell It to Women followed backwards takes us to other noteworthy productions of this engaging dramatist. The fissures in the system and world of O.'s drama, like badly broken glass, will submit to no easy mending. The medicine is as bitter to swallow as the illness is grave to contemplate. In *Broken Calabash* (1984), *Mirror for Campus* (1987), *Barn Empty Barn and Other Plays* (1986), *A Hen Too Soon* (1983), *The Artist's Homecoming* (1986), *A Scent of Onions* (1986), *Some Day Soon* (1991), *Parables for a Season* (1990), and *The Reign of Wazobia* (1988) the feathers of the indigenous culture and values are ruffled violently in their cannulae, and so many questions are raised about what should be preserved or discarded from the trove of the past or the tidal waves of new ways and times. And there are questions raised about power, about agency, about voice and about silence. In the process of rectification there are often symbolic tourneys in which the new and the young fight the old and jaded in jostles for preeminence in realignment and progress. Sometimes the lines are not always clear with regard to notions of community and identity, and of friend or foe, neither are combat strategies clear or flawless. *Legacies* (1989) proffers some answers—women fight women, and men fight women in switching tags for justice. The ambition of *Tell It to Women* branches forward into new ambitious questions regarding the injury of slavery, and the haunting division of the black cosmos with its unspoken sensitivities in *The Missing Face* (1997). *Riot in Heaven* (1996) takes the drama of race and oppression right through heaven's gate. It confirms that O.'s dramaturgic canvass has no boundaries. It is mythopoeic, and it is cosmohistorical or in the words of Eugene B. Redmond, "a soular system."

O.'s plays cry out humanely for love and justice, equity and fairness, and that dignity and integrity associated with fundamental human rights as lived experience rather than political theory and utopian projection. It remains important to draw attention to the ebullience of O.'s creative will, and the indefatigable manner in which she has served the world a variety of somewhat appetizing drama always constructed with a comprehensive assemblage of resources from her treasury of Igbo ecology and cosmology. O.'s statements clearly indicate that she writes to heal, and the candor of that sentiment is unquestionable. It is not without good reason that NGUGI wa thiong'o declared in the foreword to *Tell It to Women* that "her drama and theater are a feast."

FURTHER WORKS: *Cattle Egret Versus Nama* (1986)

BIBLIOGRAPHY: Otokunefo, H., and O. Nwodo, *Nigerian Female Writers: A Critical Perspective* (1987); Chukwuma, H., "Nigerian Female Authors: 1970 to the Present," *Matatu*, 2, 1 (1987): 23-46; Redmond, E., *Drumvoices Revue*, 1, 12 (1991-92): 53-58; Ebeogu, A., "Feminism and the Mediation of the Mythic in Three Plays by T. O.," *LitG*, 3, 1(1992): 97-111; Dunton, C., *Make Man Talk True: Nigerian Drama Since 1970* (1992): 94-107; Nwachukwu-Agbada,

J. O. J., *WLT*, 66 (Summer 1992): 464-67; Obafemi, O., *ALT*, 19 (1995): 84-98

—CHIMALUM NWANKWO

OREAMUNO, Yolanda

Costa Rican novelist, short-story writer, and essayist, b. 8 Apr. 1916, San José d. 8 July 1956, Mexico City, Mexico

Best known for her short stories and for her novel *La ruta de su evasión* (1948; the route of their escape), O. is one of the most prominent Costa Rican writers of the 20th c. Born in San José, O. was twenty when she published her first stories. Many of her stories and essays appeared in *Repertorio Americano*, of San José, a journal edited by O.'s mentor and friend Joaquín García Monge (1881–1958). In 1940, O.'s novel *Por tierra firme* (for native land) won the novel prize of the Congress of Spanish American writers sponsored by Farrar and Rinehart, but the manuscript was lost and never published. A second novel, *Casta sombría* (dark race), was also lost, but several fragments of it were printed in *Repertorio Americano*. After a bitter divorce and loss of custody of her son, O.'s health declined, and she was ill for much of the remainder of her life. "México esmío" (Mexico is mine), one of her most remarkable texts, appeared in 1945, "Valle alto" ("High Valley," 1978) was published in 1946, and in 1947 O. sent two novels to a literary contest in Guatemala. In 1948 she won the prestigious "15th of September" prize for the best novel of the year in Guatemala for *La ruta de su evasión*; the other novel manuscript, *De ahora en adelante* (from now on) was lost. O., who had left Costa Rica in 1943, became a Guatemalan citizen. She lived in Guatemala and later in Mexico, where she continued to write novels and stories, many of which were still unpublished at the time of her death in 1956.

Since her death, the publication of several volumes of her collected stories, essays, letters, and novel chapters has brought her wider recognition and admiration than she enjoyed during her life time. A new edition in 1984 of O.'s only extant complete novel, *La ruta de su evasión*, has met with extensive praise for the skill with which O. combines interior monologues, realistic description, and fantasy. The novel explores the inter-dynamics of the Vasco family through analysis of the motives of the women characters, their dreams and their aspirations. Many of O.'s better-known stories, such as "Las mareas vuelven de noche" (1971; "The Tide Returns at Night," 1978) and "Valle alto," are also written in surreal, powerful prose, the images stacked against each other, sensuous and poetic, bypassing rational logic of cause and effect.

Much of O.'s fiction is fragmentary and poetic, obsessed with time and with the definition of identity. Although her stories are set around the world, in Bogotá and Carthage and Hong Kong as well as in a mythic, mysterious Mexico or generic Central America, autobiographical elements are woven throughout O.'s fiction, and her tone of personal passion is convincing. She writes with hallucinatory intensity of the complexity of male-female relationships and of the simultaneous multiplicity of motives behind even the simplest of social acts. O.'s published work is not extensive, but it is highly accomplished and varied, ranging from humorous satire to poetic allegory. As her work has become more available to a reading public, she has become one of the most highly esteemed Costan Rican writers of the century.

FURTHER WORKS: *A lo largo del corto camino* (1961); *Relatos escogidos* (1977). **FURTHER WORKS IN ENGLISH:** *Five Women Writers of Costa Rica: Naranjo, Odio, O., Urbano, Vallbona* (1978)

BIBLIOGRAPHY: Ramos, L., "Y. O. en mi recuerdo eviterno," in Chase, A., ed., *A lo largo del corto camino* (1961): 331–42; Urbano, V., *Una escritora costarricense: Y. O.*(1968); Vallbona, R., *Y. O. presentado por Rima de Vallbona* (1972); Femández, R., "En busca de Y. O.," *Revista de Excélsior* (7 March 1976); Bellver, C. G., "On 'The Tide Returns at Night'," in Urbano, V., ed., *Five Women Writers of Costa Rica* (1978): 77–78; Vallbona, R., "La ruta de su evasión de Y. O.: Escritura proustiana suplementada," *RI*, 53: 138–39 (Jan.-June 1987): 193–217; Schrade, A., "Y. O.," in Marting, D. M., ed., *Spanish American Women Writers* (1990): 394–406; Vallbona, R., *La narrativa de Y. O.* (1996)

—MARY G. BERG

ORIYA LITERATURE
See Indian Literature

ORTEGA Y GASSET, José

Spanish philosopher and essayist, b. 8 May 1883, Madrid; d. 18 Oct. 1955, Madrid

O. was the son of José Ortega Munilla (1856–1922), a noted journalist and novelist, and the grandson of Eduardo Gasset, the founder of the newspaper *El imparcial*. He attended a Jesuit school in Málaga and the University of Madrid, where he received his doctorate in 1904. In 1906 he went to Leipzig and Berlin. Later he spent a year in Marburg, where he studied with Hermann Cohen (1842–1918), the Neo-Kantian philosopher. From 1910 to 1936 he was professor of metaphysics at the University of Madrid.

Eager to contribute to the creation in Spain of a climate suited to philosophical and systematic thought, O. sought to reach the public that did not attend universities by means of newspapers, journals, and public lectures. Two of his most significant social and political works, *España invertebrada* (1922; *Invertebrate Spain*, 1937) and *La rebelión de las masas* (1930; *The Revolt of the Masses*, 1932) were first published in installments in the periodical *El sol* (1920 and 1922). His lecture series on "What Is Philosophy?" in 1929 attracted a surprisingly large and varied audience. In 1916 he began the publication of a one-man review, *El espectador*, whose eight volumes appeared at irregular intervals from 1916 to 1934. In 1923 he founded the prestigious *Revista de Occidente*, which was decisive in the intellectual and artistic formation of many writers of his generation.

O.'s first trip to Buenos Aires in 1916 marked the beginning of his influence among Latin American writers. Throughout his life he made lecture tours to North and South America and to various

European countries. O. lived outside Spain during the civil war and did not return until 1949.

O.'s works are extremely varied, for they reflect his constant interest in all the elements of his "circumstance." He wrote on philosophical, political, social, historical, and literary topics; he described the landscape of Castile, the phenomenology of love, the writings of AZORÍN, Pío BAROJA, and Marcel PROUST, the painting of Velázquez and Goya. In his preoccupation with the problem of Spain and the changes of values in modern technological society, he continued to develop some of the themes of the "Generation of 1898." Like Antonio MACHADO, Miguel de UNAMUNO, and Azorín, O. wanted to "save" the reality of Spain, to elevate even the humblest aspects of that world to their fullest meaning. But whereas the "Generation of 1898" effected the literary transformation of the Spanish landscape and of Spanish psychology and history, O.'s confrontation of these circumstances led him to his central philosophical conceptions: perspectivism and historical or vital reason.

The formula "I am myself plus my circumstances"—stated in his first book, *Meditations del Quijote* (1914; *Meditations on Quixote*, 1961) and fully elaborated in *El tema de nuestro tiempo* (1923; *The Modern Theme*, 1933)—not only expresses the relation of the individual to his physical and cultural environment but forms the basis of the theory that the point of view is one of the components of reality. This theory must be distinguished from any purely psychological relativism; for O. perspective refers not only to the subject but to reality itself. As he wrote in the essay "Verdad y perspectiva" (1916; truth and perspective): "Truth, the real, the universe, life—whatever you want to call it—breaks into innumerable facets . . . each one of which faces a certain individual." Each point of view is unique and indispensable. Each person, nation, and historical period is an irreplaceable organ for the discovery of truth. The coincidence of two points of view can only mean that the object of focus is an abstraction and not reality; the real, the concrete, can only be grasped through infinite, diverse perspectives.

In *El tema de nuestro tiempo* O. argued in favor of a vital reason that, unlike the abstract reason of rationalism, would concern itself with the ever-changing phenomena of life. The modern theme is the need to place reason within the vital or biological sphere; thought is a biological function, and it is also the tool one must use in order to live. Reason is *not* a special gift to be employed at leisure; reason is something we must have recourse to in order to make our way in that "uncertain repertory of possibilities and difficulties" presented to us by the world, as he expressed it in *Ideas y creencias* (1940; ideas and beliefs).

In *¿Qué es filosofía?* (1929; *What Is Philosophy?*, 1960) and *Historia como sistema* (1941; *Toward a Philosophy of History*, 1941; repub. as *History as a System*, 1961), works that show the influence of EXISTENTIALIST ideas and vocabulary, O. defines human life as the radical reality because all other realities occur within it. And that reality is no specific thing: it cannot be fixed and defined; it is precisely the evasion of all definition. A person is neither a body nor a soul (which are both "things") but a series of choices and actions—a drama. Life is not given to us already formed; on the contrary, it consists of continuously deciding what we are to do and be. This constant and constitutive instability is freedom. We are necessarily free. Since life has no stable, definable form, the only possible way of understanding anything human, whether personal or collective, is by telling a story, by relating its history.

José Ortega y Gasset

Vital reason is the same as historical reason. "Man does not have a nature but a history." Historical reason adapts itself to the fluid course of life and situates the individual in relation to his specific environment; it is therefore more rigorous, more demanding, more "rational" than abstract reason.

Although O. views life as radically problematical and uncertain, he also portrays it as an immense festive or "sporting" phenomenon. He differentiates between a primary activity that is spontaneous, disinterested, and creative, and a secondary one that responds to demands imposed from without. The first, an effort we make for the sheer delight of making it, is sport; the second, necessary, dependent, utilitarian, and mechanized, is work. Since life itself serves no ulterior purpose, its highest products—scientific and artistic creations, political and moral heroism, religious sainthood—are the result of a playful, superfluous expenditure of energy (*El tema de nuestro tiempo*). It is in this sense that one should understand O.'s statements, in *La deshumanización del arte* (1925; *The Dehumanization of Art*, 1948), about the essentially ironical and playful nature of the new art, an art that claims to have no transcending consequences.

Whether considering it as insecurity or as play, O. defends life's flexibility and diverseness from all rigid schemes and rules. In the name of life values he attacks the superstitious deification of reason and culture. Art, science, philosophy, and ethics are interpretations or clarifications of life and should never be elevated to ends in themselves. In his political and social works—*España invertebrada, La rebelión de las masas, En torno a Galileo* (1933; *Man and*

Crisis, 1958), *El hombre y la gente* (1957; *Man and People*, 1957)—O. sees society as a constant threat to individual authenticity. In the social realm, originally spontaneous acts become mere customary usages, empty gestures. O. often speaks of society as a fossilization of life, a mineralized excrescence of human existence. Against the danger of this degradation, O. asserts, in *Ensimismamiento y alteración* (1939; self-absorption and otherness), the need continually to absorb one's circumstances, to retreat from the accumulated mass of cultural forms in order to make unique and personal responses.

O.'s simplistic and mechanical division of society into elites and masses makes his sociology unacceptable. His unwillingness to integrate the various aspects of his thought into a coherent system, as well as certain important contradictions and inconsistencies, has left some of his ideas—especially those on modern art—open to misinterpretation. Outside of Spain he is known for his least impressive works (*La rebelión de las masas*, for example). O.'s significant contributions to existentialism are to be found in the development of the concepts of perspectivism and historical or vital reason.

FURTHER WORKS: *Vieja y nueva política* (1914); *Personas, obras y cosas* (1916); *Ideas sobre la novela* (1925; *Notes on the Novel*, 1948); *La redención de las provincias y la decadencia nacional* (1931); *Rectificación de la república* (1931); *Pidiendo un Goethe desde dentro* (1932; "In Search of Goethe from Within," 1949); *Misión de la universidad* (1932; *Mission of the University*, 1966); *Estudios sobre el amor* (1939; *On Love: Aspects of a Single Theme*, 1957); *Teoría de Andalucía, y otros ensayos* (1942); *Del imperio romano* (1946; *Concord and Liberty*, 1963); *Obras completas* (11 vols., 1946–69); *Papeles sobre Velázquez y Goya* (1950; in *Velázquez, Goya, and The Dehumanization of Art*, 1972); *La idea de principio en Leibniz y la evolución de la teoría deductiva* (1958; *The Idea of Principle in Leibniz and the Evolution of Deductive Theory*, 1971); *Prólogo para alemanes* (1959); *Una interpretación de la historia universal* (1960; *An Interpretation of Universal History*, 1973); *Pasado y porvenir para el hombre actual* (1962); *Unas lecciones de metafísica* (1966; *Some Lessons in Metaphysics*, 1970); *Epistolario* (1974). FURTHER WORKS IN ENGLISH: *The Dehumanization of Art, and Other Writings on Art and Culture* (1956); *The Origin of Philosophy* (1967); *Meditations on Hunting* (1972; tr. of prologue to *Veinte años de caza mayor* by E. Figueroa and Alonso Martínez, Conde de Yebes, pub. 1943); *Phenomenology and Art* (1975)

BIBLIOGRAPHY: Livingstone, L., "O. y G.'s Philosophy of Art," *PMLA*, 67 (1952): 609–54; Stern, A., "O. y G., Existentialist or Essentialist?" *La torre*, 4 (1956): 388–99; Ferrater Mora, J., *O. y G.: An Outline of His Philosophy* (1957); Gaete, A., *El sistema maduro de O.* (1962); Sebastian, E. G., "J. O. y G.," *Hispania*, 46 (1963): 490–95; Read, H., "High Noon and Darkest Night: Some Observations on O. y G.'s Philosophy of Art," *JAAC*, 23 (1964): 43–50; Weber, F., "An Approach to O.'s Idea of Culture," *HR*, 32 (1964): 142–56; Drijoune, L., *La concepción de la historia en la obra de O. y G.* (1968); Morón Arroyo, C., *El sistema de O. y G.* (1968); Marías, J., *J. O. y G.: Circumstance and Vocation* (1970); McClintock, R., *Man and His Circumstances: O. as Educator* (1971); Niedermayer, F., *J. O. y G.* (1973); Silver, P., *O. as Phenomenologist: The Genesis of "Meditations on Quixote"* (1978)

—FRANCES WYERS

ORTESE, Anna Maria

Italian novelist, short-story writer, poet, and journalist, b. 13 June 1914, Rome

O. grew up, in squalid circumstances, in several towns in southern Italy and later in Tripoli, Libya; from 1928 until the start of World War II she resided with her family in Naples. During the war she lived in various cities and towns in central and northern Italy, and after the war continued to move from place to place. Poor health, poverty, and inferior formal education marred her childhood. She spent most of her time at home, reading mainly such foreign authors as Edgar Allan Poe, Robert Louis Stevenson, and Hans Christian Andersen, from whom she first learned of life as a kind of poetic vision.

O.'s first publication was a poem, "Manuele" (1933; Manuele), written at the death of her twenty-year-old brother, killed in a naval accident. It created such enthusiasm among young poets that Alfonso GATTO said: "[The] poem makes her a new UNGARETTI, the man of sorrows."

A few years later O. started writing short stories for the prestigious journal *L'Italia letteraria*. These stories—lyrical visions and private dreams—captured the attention of many writers, particularly of Massimo BONTEMPELLI, the father of "MAGIC REALISM," who collected and published them under the title *Angelici dolori* (1937; angelic sorrows). In this book, which is the history of a life of "solitude," O. intertwines her life and her family's with the lives of such characters as American Indians or with fantastic adventures and dreams. These stories are a poetic amalgam of reality and fabulation. *Angelici dolori* is fundamental to the understanding of the rest of O.'s work.

Il mare non bagna Napoli (1953; *The Bay Is Not Naples*, 1955) received both national and international recognition. Translated into many languages, it contains touching stories of Neapolitan poverty. For example, "La città involontaria" ("Involuntary City") is a description, realistic yet compassionate, of a decrepit military barracks in which homeless people—like O. herself—live in subhuman conditions. She has been accused of "desecrating Naples," but it is truer to say that, as in the story "Il silenzio della ragione" ("Silence of Reason"), O.—together with a group of younger writers around the Neapolitan journal *Sud*—participates in the sorrows of her people and dreams of a better future for them.

In his remarks written for the jacket of *Il mare non bagna Napoli*, Elio VITTORINI called O. "a gypsy absorbed in a dream." The "gypsy" (who had moved, and would move until 1975, from city to city in search of the financial stability she never had) always felt "poor and simple." It may be indicative of her lifelong "solitude" that in her fascinating fable-novel *L'iguana* (1965; the iguana) the "iguana"—Estrellita, the poor little faithful servant—works all her life for a rich family (who pay her not with money but with little stones) and lives otherwise isolated in the "absolute darkness" of a cellar.

Although O.'s works have been acclaimed by many critics and although several were translated into a number of languages, writing has not made her financially comfortable. Her major novel *Il porto di Toledo* (1975; the port of Toledo) cost her five years of strenuous effort. A profound reworking of nine stories in *Angelici dolori*, it is a lyrical work of mythopoeic power. Toledo is a metaphor for Naples, and O. incorporates her life and times from childhood to the end of World War II in a synthesis of reality and dreamlike transformation, hope and disappointment.

O. emphasizes these same ideas in her latest novel, *Il cappello piumato* (1979; the feathered hat), which is set in Milan in the aftermath of World War II. The narrator scrutinizes the interior lives of a "poor and simple" group of young intellectuals, whose efforts to preserve their belief in love and politics end in the complete failure of their dreams.

FURTHER WORKS: *Poesie* (1939); *L'infanta sepolta* (1950); *I giorni del cielo* (1958); *Silenzio a Milano* (1958); *Poveri e semplici* (1967); *La luna sul muro* (1968); *L'alone grigio* (1969); *Il treno russo* (1983); *Il mormorio di Parigi* (1986); *Estivi terrori* (1987); *La morte del folletto* (1987); *In sonno e in veglia* (1987); *La lente scura: scritti di viaggio* (1991); *Il cardillo addolorato* (1993); *Alonso e i visionari* (1996); *Il paese e la notte* (1996)

BIBLIOGRAPHY: Nouat, R., "Le méridionalisme dans la littérature italienne d'aujourd'hui," *Critique*, No. 139 (1958): 1045–58; Ragusa, O., "Women Novelists in Postwar Italy," *BA*, 33 (1959): 5–9; Brandon-Albini, M., *Midi vivant* (1963): 141–43; Pautasso, S., "Une approche de la littérature italienne," *Les lettres nouvelles*: 3–5 (1976): 7–31: 144–56

—M. RICCIARDELLI

ORWELL, George

(pseud. of Eric Blair) English novelist, essayist, and social critic, b. 23 Jan. 1903, Motihari, India; d. 21 Jan 1950, London

O. was born in Bengal, the second child of Richard Walmesley Blair and Ida Mabel Limonzin. At the age of four he returned with his family to England, and four years later began his education by attending St. Cyprian's Preparatory School in Sussex until the age of thirteen. He then went by scholarship to Eton, where, after four and a half years, he completed his formal schooling. Following Eton, O. joined the Imperial Police in Burma in 1922; after serving for five years he resigned from the service. In 1928 O. decided definitely to become a writer and devoted the remainder of his life to that occupation. In 1933 he assumed the pseudonym by which he would sign all his publications.

O., who was primarily a novelist, nevertheless accomplished some of his best writing in autobiographical nonfiction and the polemical essay. These forms better served his strong sociopolitical concerns and the moral temper that led his contemporaries to call him the conscience of his age.

O.'s early work of the 1930s consists of social novels dealing largely with middle-class English life, and books of autobiographical reportage, drawn from his active involvement in the poverty and war that dominated the decade.

O.'s first book, *Down and Out in Paris and London* (1933), shows him to be a keen observer and penetrating social analyst, committed to recording accurately and imaginatively the plight of the poverty-stricken laborer and tramp on the Continent and in England. O.'s point of view in this book, that of the involved and sympathetic observer, reflects O.'s life style of subjecting himself to personal hardship in the interests of championing the underdog.

The Road to Wigan Pier (1937), in which the social protest is voiced even more articulately, was written for Victor Gollancz's

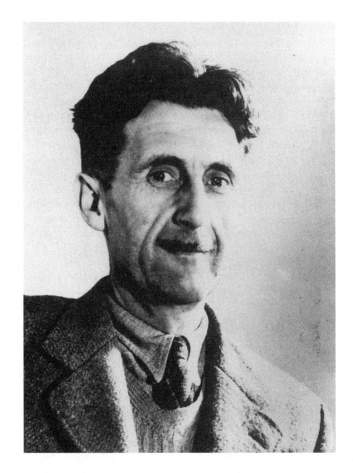

George Orwell

Left Book Club as an exposé of the depressed living conditions of workers in the north of England. It contains a disturbingly sharp lengthy criticism of the weaknesses of contemporary socialism and socialists. Although O. belonged to the left, he remained to the end of his life an uncompromising individualist and political idealist, maintaining that the ends of socialism must be justice and freedom.

O.'s involvement in the Spanish Civil War as a common soldier attested to his need to act upon his political ideals. His experiences in Spain produced *Homage to Catalonia* (1938), still considered one of the best books in English on the Spanish war. The book records O.'s initiation into the international political turmoil of the late 1930s, and foreshadows his later political fiction. Many of O.'s attributes as a writer are evident in this personal account of life at the front and ideological conflict behind the lines. O. captures the image of war and its absurdities in the plain and vivid prose style that was to become so highly praised. Although the book is pervaded by O.'s disillusionment about the capability of party politics, its theme expresses O.'s abiding faith in the decency of the common man.

O.'s fiction of the same period is less distinguished. *Burmese Days* (1934) is O.'s sole novel related to his experiences in Burma. Like *A Clergyman's Daughter* (1935), *Keep the Aspidistra Flying* (1936), and *Coming Up for Air* (1939), *Burmese Days* depicts protagonists who are victims of their social environments and their own inner frustrations and doubts. In these novels O. deals with lonely, unhappy, sometimes oppressed people, with people who are nostalgic for the past because they live in the gray world of failure, religious doubt, poverty, or boredom.

Although linked thematically with much modern fiction, the early novels are technically unimpressive and fall far short of the achievements of writers like Aldous HUXLEY, D. H. LAWRENCE, and James JOYCE. O. had not yet found the literary medium that would express his most compelling vision of society.

In the 1940s O. set out "to make political writing an art," and in two estimable works of fiction he accomplished what he spoke of as the fusion of "political purpose and artistic purpose into one whole."

Animal Farm (1945), a political satire in the form of an animal fable, depicts the revolt of barnyard animals against their farmer oppressors and the establishment of an autonomous socialistic state. The original ideals of the animals rapidly degenerate at the hands of the pigs, who assume dictatorial power and turn the society into a police state. The animals—except for the pigs, of course—are returned to a bondage and misery more severe than they had initially suffered. Clearly an allegory of the Russian Revolution and particularly of the Stalinist regime, the novel avoids a narrow topicality by suggesting the disappointing aftermath of more than one revolution. O. directs his satire at a universal human condition, that is, that all political radicalisms inevitably become reactionary when based on power and power alone.

In 1949 O. published *1984*, his second political novel and last major work. This antiutopian novel was influenced by O.'s reading in H. G. WELLS, Yevgeny ZAMYATIN, Arthur KOESTLER, and Aldous Huxley. Precipitated by the international phenomenon of the rise of totalitarian states and the long, hard years of World War II, *1984* is a protest against the fearful direction in which O. believed the modern world was moving. Undoubtedly O. again wrote with the Stalinist regime in mind, but the machinery of his not so imaginary society is also drawn from the English scene of the war and postwar years.

The effectiveness of *1984* derives in part from an immediately recognizable reality, one whose atmosphere extends beyond any specific totalitarian state and includes even aspects of the so-called free societies. The book exposes the horror of totalitarianism whatever the form. O.'s pessimism is apparent throughout, and the final emotional and intellectual capitulation of the protagonist, another Orwellian victim, to Big Brother and the authority of the state is depressing rather than tragic. Yet O.'s purpose was to shock his readers into an awareness of the disastrous results of absolute power. Less a prophecy than a warning, the novel exists as a continual reminder to contemporary Western man that he is dangerously close to losing not only his freedom but the very attributes that make him human.

O.'s sense of social and political responsibility is as apparent in his early essay "A Hanging" (1931) and the many periodical contributions of almost twenty years as it is in *1984*. The first extensive collection of his major essays, *Critical Essays* (1946; Am., *Dickens, Dali and Others*), includes some of his most perceptive commentaries on important social and cultural issues of his time.

It has been said that in O.'s later work, and especially in his final novel, he registers a profound disillusionment about contemporary liberalism and that *1984* suffers aesthetically from an attitude of defeatism. Yet it has been equally observed that despite the pessimism of *1984*, O. never relinquished his commitment to

Western liberal values, which include the freedom of mind and the sense of responsibility to acknowledge and to rectify social oppression whatever its nature, wherever it may appear, and to speak with an unadulterated truth of the ever-present threat of political totalitarianism in the 20th c.

Like Albert CAMUS, O. was convinced that the contemporary writer must become involved, must take sides, with a sincerity that becomes the *sine qua non* of literary effectiveness. Few modern writers have been as assiduous as O. in devoting their lives and creative efforts to the cause of freedom and social amelioration. This commitment is the dominant force in all of his work.

FURTHER WORKS: *Inside the Whale and Other Essays* (1940); *The Lion and the Unicorn: Socialism and the English Genius* (1941); *The English People* (1947); *Shooting an Elephant and Other Essays* (1950); *England, Your England* (1953; Am., *Such, Such Were the Joys*); *The O. Reader: Fiction, Essays, and Reportage* (1956); *Selected Essays* (1957); *Collected Essays* (1961); *The Collected Essays, Journalism and Letters of G. O.* (4 vols., 1968)

BIBLIOGRAPHY: Brander, L., *G. O.* (1954); Hollis, C., *A Study of G. O.* (1956); Rees, R., *G. O.: Fugitive from the Camp of Victory* (1961); Voorhees, R., *The Paradox of G. O.* (1961); Woodcock, G., *The Crystal Spirit: A Study of G. O.* (1966); Oxley, B., *G. O.* (1967); Aldritt, K., *The Making of G. O.* (1969); Gross, M., ed. *The World of G. O.* (1971); Stansky, P., and W. Abrahams, *The Unknown O.* (1972); Steinhoff, W., *G. O. and the Origins of "1984"* (1975); Williams, R., *O.* (1975); Stansky, P. and Abrahams, W., *O.: The Transformation* (1980); Crick, B., *G. O.: A Life* (1981)

—WAYNE WARNCKE

Mr. O. is a revolutionary who is in love with 1910. This ambivalence constitutes his strength and his weakness. Never before has a progressive political thinker been so handicapped by nostalgia for the Edwardian shabby-genteel or the under-dog. It is this political sentimentality which from the literary point of view is his most valid emotion. *Animal Farm* proves it, for it truly is a fairy story told by a great lover of liberty and a great lover of animals. The farm is real, the animals are moving. At the same time it is a devastating attack on Stalin and his "betrayal" of the Russian revolution, as seen by another revolutionary.

Cyril Connolly, on *Animal Farm*, *Horizon*, Sept. 1945, p. 215

The gist of O.'s criticism of the liberal intelligentsia was that they refused to understand the conditioned nature of life. He never quite puts it in this way but this is what he means. He himself knew what war and revolution were really like, what government and administration were really like. From first-hand experience he knew what Communism was. He could truly imagine what Nazism was. At a time when most intellectuals still thought of politics as a nightmare abstraction, pointing to the fearfulness of the nightmare as evidence of their sense of reality, O. was using the imagination of a man whose hands and eyes and whole body were part of his thinking apparatus.

Lionel Trilling, Introduction to *Homage to Catalonia* (1952), pp. xvi–xvii

I am at the moment engaged in trying to write a longer and better sketch of Eric [Blair, O.'s real name] than the one I wrote shortly after his death in which I try to show that his value consists in his having taken more seriously than most people the fundamental problem of religion. *Nineteen Eighty-Four*, for example, is more than a pessimistic prophesy. The crisis of the book is when the hero, under torture, says: "Do it to Julia, don't do it to me." Eric was appalled, like the saints, by the realization that human nature is fundamentally self-centered; and in *Nineteen Eighty-Four* the triumph of the totalitarian state is not complete until it has been demonstrated to the last resister that in the last resort he would sacrifice the person he loves best in order to save his own skin.

Richard Rees, Letter to Malcolm Muggeridge (March 8, 1955) in Miriam Gross, ed., *The World of G. O.* (1971), p. 167

O. was too solitary to be a symbol and too angry to be a saint. But he succeeded in becoming a writer who set down, in the purest English of his time, the thoughts and fantasies of an individual mind playing over the common problems of our age. What made him exceptional—and more than a little eccentric in the eyes of his contemporaries—was the fact that he also tried to work out his theories in action and then to give his actions shape in literature. The triad of thought, act and artifact runs through the whole of O.'s writing life. . . . Like Dr. Johnson, so many of whose attitudes he shared, he is likely to hold his place in English literature not only for what he wrote, but also for the man he was and for the fundamental honesties that he defended.

George Woodcock, *The Crystal Spirit: A Study of G. O.* (1966), p. 5

It is surely a permissible exaggeration to say that from first to last O., like George Eliot, was always writing the same novel. Not simply are his works marked by the same tone and style, but each one represents with variations the same troubled situation which he tries, without quite succeeding, to bring to an intellectually and emotionally satisfying outcome. Stated most generally, this central situation is a hidden or overt rebellion against a way of life accepted by most but intolerable to the protagonists. These, as O. sees them, are victims of forces they are never strong enough to oppose with any show of equality. Good is defeated by evil; the bully wins. Because of his constancy to this theme we can detect

the seeds of *1984* in all O.'s published fiction, beginning with *Burmese Days*, his first novel.

William Steinhoff, *G. O. and the Origins of "1984"* (1975), p. 123

The key to O. as an individual is the problem of identity. Educated as he was to a particular consciousness, the key to his whole development is that he renounced it, or attempted to renounce it, and that he made a whole series of attempts to find a new social identity. Because of this process, we have a writer who was successively many things that would be unlikely in a normal trajectory: an imperial police officer, a resident of a casual ward, a revolutionary militiaman, a declassed intellectual, a middle-class English writer. And the strength of his work is that in the energy of his renunciation he was exceptionally open to each new experience as it came. . . . O. could connect as closely and with as many different kinds of people as he did, precisely because of his continual mobility, his successive and serious assumption of roles. When he is in a situation, he is so dissolved into it that he is exceptionally convincing, and his kind of writing makes it easy for the reader to believe that this is also happening to himself. The absence of roots is also the absence of barriers.

Raymond Williams, *O.* (1975), pp. 87–88

OSBORNE, John

English dramatist, b. 12 Dec. 1929, London; d. 24 Dec. 1994

Twenty-five years after *Look Back in Anger* (1956) opened at the Royal Court Theatre in London, making "angry young man" the standard label for the alienated and frustrated postwar generation and introducing a new language and a new hero into the genteel traditions of British drama, O. published his autobiography, *A Better Class of Person* (1981). Although the book ends with the opening night of *Look Back in Anger*, it nevertheless gives O. the opportunity to refute many of the biographical fallacies he claims critics have perpetrated upon his work. O., a socialist, an antinuclear activist, antiroyalty and antichurch, asserts in his book the strong influence of the view of Thomas de Quincy (1785–1859) on the necessity of always tearing away the "decent drapery" that hides the moral ulcers and scars from British sensitivity. O.'s new hero in *Look Back in Anger*, Jimmy Porter, is, like O., educated and married above his working-class origins and has little in the way of positive positions. In spite of the absence of good, brave causes, he feels the need to penetrate the indifference and apathy of the world surrounding him and to view its inherent wickedness as sufficient justification for his own vitriolic responses to it.

O. also refutes the common criticism that his works are essentially dramatic monologues delivered by the central characters who inhabit a world of dramatic nonentities. But it is precisely in the creation of these exceptional heroes, neurotic but self-aware, that O. has achieved his most notable successes.

John Osborne

In *The Entertainer* (1957), Archie Rice, the embodiment of the moribund traditions of both British music-hall comedians and, metaphorically, the British Empire, attacks his father, wife, and children in a series of domestic scenes, which are surrounded by vaudeville "turns." Although critics often point to this play and to *Luther* (1961), with its twelve scenes and a narrator, as examples of the influence of Bertolt BRECHT's epic theater, O.'s plays differ from that mode in their appeal much more to feelings than to reason.

Inadmissible Evidence (1964), perhaps O.'s most accomplished play, has as its hero a loquacious and philandering lawyer, Bill Maitland, who exists for himself only to the extent that he remains an object in the existence of others. The dreamlike opening scene with Maitland on trial for committing an obscenity, namely, his life, sets in motion a sequence of scenes that show the hero gradually abandoned by family, colleagues, and friends. In turn, these characters exist for the audience only as indicators of Maitland's progressive alienation. In the course of the play he increasingly relates to the outside world by means of the telephone.

The typical O. hero—Jimmy Porter, Archie Rice, Bill Maitland—talks in a language of bitter metaphors appropriate to his respective personal and social world. These protagonists are nostalgic for some golden age that was denied them, and envious of youth. They are incapable of living on a moment-to-moment basis with the people and situations surrounding them. The eponymous heroes of *Epitaph for George Dillon* (1958, with Anthony Creighton) and

Luther share in comparable dilemmas. In *Luther* the hero and play are dominated by the central metaphor of purgation, which joins personal and theological themes. The hero, who is continually preoccupied with stomach disorders and the need to evacuate his bowels, likewise desires to purge the Church. He differs from other O. heroes in having a positive program. George Dillon, a writer who compromises his dubious standards, anticipates a subsequent writer-hero, Laurie of *The Hotel in Amsterdam* (1968). But Laurie is successful and surrounded by a balanced and mutually adjusted group of three couples. In this play, O. broke out of his prior mold; no longer is one character dominant and the others existing merely in terms of their interactions with his personal universe. And the hero, no longer looking back, now adjusts himself to the present. Yet even a play published in the same year, *Time Present* (1968), in ironic contrast with its title, has as its central character an actress, Pamela, whose values are dominated by those of her father, a famous actor who dies offstage during the course of the drama.

The earlier plays depend on central characters with ambivalent values who await some outside force that will expose them: Archie Rice has his Tax Man, Bill Maitland, his Law Society Board; and Alfred Redl, the central character of *A Patriot for Me* (1965), fears the revelation of his homosexuality. A more dynamic interchange among several characters and a more secure treatment of exposition are developments in O.'s dramaturgy of the late 1960s and 1970s.

During the 1960s O. ventured into screenwriting, often working with the director Tony Richardson, his partner in Woodfall Productions; his screenplay for *Tom Jones* (1963) won an Academy Award. In the 1970s he began writing dramas for television with varying degrees of success.

O.'s place in the history of British drama is secure. His plays introduced a series of new attitudes and relevant themes into a theatrical tradition stagnating under the limitations of a 19th-c. view of the "well-made play." His muscular, aggressive dialogue, alive to the nuances of contemporary feelings and sensitive to the dramatic needs of the play, opened new experiences for audiences. Frequent successful revivals of O.'s major works testify to his success in both challenging and yet appealing to modern sensibilities.

FURTHER WORKS: *The World of Paul Slickey* (1959); *A Subject of Scandal and Concern* (1960); *Plays for England: The Blood of the Bambergs; Under Plain Cover* (1963); *A Bond Honoured* [from Lope de Vega] (1966); *The Right Prospectus* (1968); *Very Like a Whale* (1970); *West of Suez* (1971); *Hedda Gabler* [from Henrik Ibsen] (1972); *A Sense of Detachment* (1972); *The End of Me Old Cigar, and Jill and Jack* (1974); *The Gift of Friendship* (1974); *A Place Calling Itself Rome* [from Shakespeare's *Coriolanus*] (1975); *The Picture of Dorian Gray* [from Oscar Wilde] (1975); *Watch It Come Down* (1976); *You're Not Watching Me, Mummy, and Try a Little Tenderness: Two Plays for Television* (1978)

BIBLIOGRAPHY: Taylor, J. R., *Anger and After* (1964): 37–58; Hayman, R., *J. O.* (1968); Brown, J. R., ed., *Modern British Dramatists* (1968): 47–57: 117–21, and passim; Banham, M., *O.* (1969); Carter, A. V., *J. O.* (1969); Trussler, S., *The Plays of J. O.: An Assessment* (1969); Brown, J. R., *Theatre Language* (1972): 118–57 and passim; Worth, K., *Revolutions in Modern English Drama* (1972): 67–85; Anderson, M., *Anger and Detachment* (1976): 21–49 and passim

—HOWARD B. WOLMAN

OSHAGAN, Hagop

(born Hagop Kiufejian) Armenian novelist, short-story writer, critic, and dramatist, b. 1883, Soelez, Turkey; d. 17 Feb. 1948, Aleppo, Syria

The first modern Armenian critic concerned with combining ethnological studies with literature and linguistics, O. first gained recognition as a writer with his frank, earthy fiction, then earned notoriety for his iconoclastic reviews, debunking contemporary literary idols. Championing a literature of Armenian imagery and content, he urged writers and critics to find spiritual and cultural regeneration through a national literature.

O. was educated at the seminary at Armash, Turkey, where he acquired fluency in French and German. He was fired from his first teaching job in his home village by a puritanical school board after the publication of his short story "Aracheen artsounk" (1902; the first tear). Familiar with the works of FREUD, O. believed that sexuality was the root of every human impulse. Such sexually explicit writing as his had not been seen before, and has seldom been matched since, in Armenian literature.

The material for the stories in O.'s first collection, *Khonarneruh* (1921; the humble ones), was gathered when he was forced to work as a wandering teacher. Village characters, much like those of Telkadintsi (pseud. of Hovaness Haroutiunian, 1860–1915) and Rouben Zartarian (1874–1915), animate his narratives.

In 1914 in Istanbul O. cofounded the literary magazine *Mehian* with the writers Daniel VAROUJAN, Gosdan Zarian (1885–1969), and Aharon Dadourian (1887–1965). Their work soon became the standard for contemporary Armenian literature. The influence of Nietzsche and Schopenhauer was apparent in their manifesto, which stressed a literature of ideas instead of mere reportage and realistic description, and poetry above ideas: "Art should be concerned with beauty, truth, and the ideal, and the proper themes pursued by the Armenian writer should be national."

O.'s admiration for and the influence of the work of DOSTOEVSKY, BALZAC, and PROUST is evident in his three-volume romanfleuve *Menatsortatsuh* (1931–34; those who remained). The three books—*Arkantee jampov* (via the uterus), *Ariunee jampov* (via the blood), and *Tezhokhkee jampov* (via hell)—trace the development of an Armenian town up until the 1915 massacre through the lives of some of its inhabitants, who are either Armenian victims or Turkish murderers. Psychological motivation in character development and a baroque style are the two distinct characteristics of O.'s novels, such as *Dzag bedooguh* (1929; the pot with the hole), *Haji Murad* (1933; Haji Murad), and *Haji Abdullah* (1934; Haji Abdullah). His plays, the best known of which is *Stepanos Siunetsi* (1936; Stepanos of Siunik), were more literary than dramatic successes.

Most of O.'s writing was inaccessible to the general reader because of his convoluted style. Although his work reflects the national ethos, clarity and simplicity are secondary to his lush language and imagery. In his literary criticism, collected in *Hamabadker arevmedahay kraganootian* (10 vols., 1945–82; panorama of western Armenian literature), he claims that his ambition was the "discovery of my nation" and that "literature can free itself of morality but not of its bloodline." His own writing was true to those precepts.

FURTHER WORKS: *Khorhoortneroo mehianuh* (1922); *Erp badanee en* (1925); *Suleiman Effendi* (1936); *Meenchev oor* (1936); *Erkenkee*

jampov (1936); *Hye kraganootioon* (1942); *Erp merneel keedenk* (1944); *Spiurkuh ev eerav panasdeghdsootioonuh* (1945); *Vegayootioon muh* (1945)

—MARZBED MARGOSSIAN and DIANA DER HOVANESSIAN

OSOFISAN, Femi

Nigerian dramatist, literary critic, and novelist (writing in English), b. 15 June 1946, Ijebu Ode

O. is one of the most prolific and most successful of the Nigerian writers in what has been described as the post-(Wole) SOYINKA, post-(Chinua) ACHEBE generation. After studying in Dakar and Paris, O. received his Ph.D. in French from the University of Ibadan in 1975. His first published work was a novel, *Kolera Kolej* (1975), but he is primarily a dramatist as well as a literary critic. His doctoral dissertation was entitled "The Origins of Drama in West Africa: A Study of the Development of Drama from the Traditional Forms to the Modern Theatre in English and French."

Kolera Kolej, named after a university that became an autonomous state because its home country saw that expedient as the most convenient way of dealing with an outbreak of cholera on the campus, is characteristic of O.'s strategy of using his art to expose the social problems in his society: disease, political corruption and opportunism, and totalitarianism. The same preoccupation marks his plays, for the performance of which he founded the Kakaun Sela Kompany at the University of Ibadan, where he is a professor of modern languages and dramatic arts. O. is currently the head of the department of dramatic arts.

Among his best-known works are *Once Upon Four Robbers* (1980) and *Morountodun* (1982). The former was inspired by the spate of public executions of armed robbers in the postcivil-war years in Nigeria. In it O. argues through a group of armed robbers about to be publicly executed that the structural inequities in the society, not individual perversities, were responsible for violent crimes. At the end the audience is posed the choice of siding with the authorities represented by the soldiers, or with the oppressed represented by the robbers. *Morountodun* is based on a Yoruba myth in which a patriotic princess (Moremi) sacrificed herself to win her society's deliverance from foreign marauders. In the play, however, O. revises the myth such that the heroine (Titubi) starts out with the intention of sacrificing herself on behalf of the elite pitted against the workers, but in the end switches her allegiance to the workers.

Although O. expresses admiration for the generation of writers before him, dedicating *The Chattering and the Song* (1977) to Soyinka and Christopher OKIGBO, he yet criticizes them for what he considers their elitism, escapism, and failure to grapple meaningfully with reality, signaled by their preoccupation with an elite audience, and their use of mythological materials. Such materials are legitimate, in his view, only for the sort of use he put them to in *Morountodun*—to effect their own unmasking and undermining. He identifies himself as one of the heirs to Cyprian EKWENSI, the popular Nigerian novelist, without whom he says literature would have remained the property of the privileged. These writers, according to him, are marked by "primal intention," if not by achievement, and for them literature is an active catalyst of social change, a vehicle for articulating and influencing this dynamic process of evolution.

Writing in 1985, the Nigerian leftist critic Biodun Jeyifo accepted the characterization of *The Chattering and the Song* as the most revolutionary play ever written in Nigeria, with the caveat, though, that Nigerian theater is not particularly revolutionary. But although warmly embraced by the left, O. disavows doctrinaire Marxism and refrains from the often combative rhetoric of his Marxist compatriots. Yet the agenda he promotes in his works, his undisguised antipathy for tradition and "animist gods," and his critical statements argue his close ideological affinity with them. He also shares the significant influence of Bertolt BRECHT, which critics have observed in African Marxist writers, especially in his use of sung commentaries, a discursive debate strategy, and other devices that undermine the stage as an arena for illusion. A combination of a keen sense of theater, incisive social analyses and criticism, and a lively sense of humor characterizes his plays, for which he has thrice been honored with the annual literature prize of the Association of Nigerian Authors.

FURTHER WORKS: *A Restless Run of Locusts* (1975); *Beyond Translation* (1985); *The Genre of Prose Fiction: Two Complementary Views* (1986, with Adebayo Williams); *Midnight Hotel* (1986); *A Farewell to Cannibal Rage* (1986); *Another Raft* (1988); *Birthdays Are Not for Dying and Other Plays* (1990)

BIBLIOGRAPHY: Enekwe, O. O., "Interview with F. O.," *The Greenfield Review*, 8: 1–2 (Spring 1980): 76–80; Emmanuel, I., "O. on His Ambitions," *Concord Weekly* (14–21 Jan. 1985): 35; Akpederi, J., "A Chat with F. O." *African Guardian* (27 Mar. 1986): 42; Amuta, C., "Contemporary Contradictions and the Revolutionary Alternative: *Once Upon Four Robbers* and *Morountodun*," *The Theory of African Literature* (1989): 167–75

—OYEKAN OWOMOYELA

OSORGIN, M. A.

(pseud. of Mikhail Andreevich Il'in or Ilyin) Russian novelist, journalist, and short-story writer, b. 7 Oct. 1878, Perm; d. 27 Nov. 1942, Chabris, France

The son of a circuit-court judge, O. took a degree in law at Moscow University. As a lawyer he served the poor, published political brochures, and joined the terroristic, anti-Marxist Socialist-Revolutionary Party. During the December 1905 uprising O. was arrested, serving six months in solitary confinement. He was able to escape to Italy in 1906, where he was drawn to the anarchism espoused by the Maximalist wing of the Socialist-Revolutionary Party. From Italy he contributed to a variety of Russian periodicals, using the pseudonym Osorgin (his mother's maiden name). He also wrote a book on Italy, joined the Freemasons, and established a friendship with Maxim GORKY. Returning to Russia in 1916, O. worked as a war correspondent, skillfully eluded the police, supported the February Revolution, published more political brochures "for the people," and contributed to and edited numerous democratic periodicals, all of which were finally closed down during the first months of 1918. During the next few years he published two collections of stories, translated Gozzi's *Princess Turandot* for theater director E. V. Vakhtangov (1883–1922), and became editor of a bulletin for the All-Russian Famine Relief Committee (a group that Lenin mistrusted)—leading to O.'s

arrest and imprisonment, exile to Kazan, and finally in 1922 deportation to Berlin. O. worked for Kerensky's newspaper *Dni* in Germany, then moved to Paris where he wrote for P. N. Miliukov's *Poslednie novosti* until 1940. During his years in France, O. wrote for numerous émigré periodicals and published a dozen works of fiction. He avoided the anti-Bolshevik chorus of his fellow émigrés, frequently praised Soviet novels in his book reviews, and tended more and more to live as a recluse. In June of 1940, O. left Paris for the unoccupied zone, finally settling down in the village of Chabris. Now old, ill, and poverty-stricken, O. nevertheless continued to write, sending articles both to the U.S. and to Scandinavia. After all of France was occupied in 1942, O. was jailed for a short period as a suspected communist, and died the same year.

In addition to writing news articles, O. contributed stories, sketches, criticism, and reviews to the newspapers for which he worked. Most of the novels he published were first serialized in such newspapers. During his life, O. published some 2,300 items in over 100 Russian émigré periodicals—under at least 50 different pseudonyms ("Osorgin" being the most common). He published twenty books, of which six appeared posthumously. Two collections of stories that met with considerable success were *Tam, gde byl schastliv* (1928; there where I was happy) and *Chudo na ozere* (1932; miracle on the lake). Most of these stories are narrated by the author and are obviously autobiographical, whether labeled as such or not. Though often humorous, they also tend to be nostalgic—first of all for Russia, for the birch forests and wide rivers of O.'s childhood, and, secondly, for Italy, where O. lived almost as a native for ten years. Not an experimenter except for one or two later works, O. was primarily a follower of traditional realistic narrative, employing a lyrical yet pure style pleasing to the Russian ear. Although his manner was that of conservative NEOREALISM, his views were often nonconformist. For instance, he lacked all interest in Christianity and seldom mentioned it in his writings.

Nature as the subject of O.'s many sketches was not limited to the nostalgic "birch-tree" school of writing. He also wrote about his small vacation cottage in a French village and its garden, which he so carefully tended. After eight or ten years, some thirty of O.'s feuilletons on this theme were collected under the title *Proisshestviia zelenogo mira* (1938; events of the green world). Here the major motif was the superiority of the country to the city, which O.'s Russian readers found congenial.

O. was best known for his novel *Sivtsev Vrazhek* (1928; *Quiet Street*, 1930), set in Moscow in the years 1917–1918. It became a best-seller in its American edition. The philosopher-protagonist, who represents the author, takes an existentialist view of the failure of the February Revolution to prevent the Bolshevik coup, concluding that all who had been responsible for the first revolution were in some sense also responsible for the second. O. expressed the view in this novel and in many of his later writings that he accepted both revolutions completely (even if he did not always agree with their tactics), and he regretted only that the October Revolution had rejected him by deporting him. He would rather live in Russia, even though he faced possible execution there, than live safely in bourgeois France.

O.'s only other novel to appear in English translation was *Povest' o sestre* (1931; *My Sister's Story*, 1931)—in which the author creates a believable intellectual woman of the fin de siècle period who refuses to accept the double standard in her failed marriage. She is based on O.'s own sister, Olga, who died in 1907.

The novel of his that O. liked best was *Vol'ny kamenshchik* (1937; Freemason). Relatively innovative in both style and subject, the novel treats an ordinary man, a Russian émigré, whose children speak French rather than Russian and whose marriage is falling apart. He finds the materialism of French society vastly tiresome and seeks to escape it by following the Masonic path to moral perfection. He only partly succeeds in this. The novel is not greatly didactic, while being virtually unique in its sympathetic presentation of Masonic philosophy.

Although O.'s dream of returning to Russia seemed hopeless, several of his short pieces were published in the Soviet Union in the 1960s and 1970s. Then in the late 1980s, seven major novels by him appeared in a variety of periodicals and books. *Sivtsev Vrazhek* appeared in three editions of up to 150,000 copies, and *Povest' o sestre* in two. This phenomenon attests to the fascination of Soviet intellectuals with the Russian émigrés of the first wave. More than that, it exhibits a particular fondness for O., who has implicitly been invited home by his fellow Russians—who have not forgiven O. for what he did, but rather have asked him to forgive them for what they did.

FURTHER WORKS: *Ocherki sovremennoi Italii* (1913); *Prizraki* (1917); *Skazki i neskazki* (1918); *Iz malen'kogo domika* (1921); *Veshchi cheloveka* (1929); *Svidetel' istorii* (1932); *Kniga o kontsakh* (1935); *Povest' o nekoei devitse* (1938); *V tikhom mestechke Frantsii* (1946); *Po povodu beloi korobochki* (1947); *Pis'ma o neznachitel'nom* (1952); *Vremena* (1955); *Zametki Starogo Knigoeda* (1989). FURTHER WORKS IN ENGLISH: *Selected Stories, Reminiscences and Essays* (1982)

BIBLIOGRAPHY: Nazaroff, A., "Moscow Life during the Revolution," *NYT* (19 Oct. 1930): 8; MacAfee, H. on *My Sister's Story, YR*, 21, 3 (Mar. 1932): vi–x; Gurvitch, G., "In Memory of Brother M. A. O.," *Masonic Club Rossia* (N.Y.), Bulletin 1 (Apr. 1943): 13–15; "Ilyin, M. A.," in Harkins, W., ed., *Dictionary of Russian Literature* (1959), 150; "O., M. A.," in Florinsky, M., ed., *McGraw-Hill Encyclopedia of Russia and the Soviet Union* (1961): 403; Hagglund, R., "The Russian Émigré Debate of 1928 on Criticism," *SlavR*, 32, 3 (1973): 515–26; Barmache, N., D. Fiene, and T. Ossorguine, comps., *Bibliographie des œuvres de Michel Ossorguine* (1973); Fiene, D., "M. A. O.—The Last Mohican of the Russian Intelligentsia," *RLT*, 16 (1979): 93–105; Fiene, D., ed., *Selected Stories, Reminiscences and Essays*, (1982); Sorokin-Vasiliev, O. on *Selected Stories, Reminiscences and Essays, SlavR*, 43, 1 (1984): 161; "O., M. A.," in Terras, V., ed., *Handbook of Russian Literature* (1985): 324

—DONALD M. FIENE

OSSETIC LITERATURE

Written literature in Ossetic, an Iranian language spoken by some 500,000 people of the central Caucasus in the North Ossetic Republic, came into being only at the beginning of the 19th c.; the earliest texts were translations of Christian liturgical books. But there is much evidence for the existence of a rich oral poetry in preliterate times, namely, the rich folklore of the present-day Ossets. Particularly important is the cycle of heroic legends about the Narts, superhuman beings who in mythical antiquity inhabited the plains north of the Caucasus. These legends are widespread

over the whole of the north Caucasian area, but their Iranian origin is unquestionable.

The first Ossetic poet known by name is Mamsyraty Temyrbolat (1843–1898). His younger contemporary, Khetägkaty Kosta (1859–1906) is, however, usually regarded as the "father" of Ossetic literature and the creator of the literary language. Among writers of this period, Gädiaty Seka (1855–1915) wrote short stories that portray, with harsh realism, the unrelenting struggle for existence among the people of the Caucasian mountains. For the development of social realism and for Ossetic prose in general these stories have been of great significance. Gädiaty Seka also wrote lyric poetry.

The new cultural currents that came in the wake of tsarist conquests in the 19th c. brought about a profound change in the spiritual life of the Ossets. The break with the centuries-old traditions of tribal society became a frequent theme in the new literature. For the Ossets, as for the other peoples of the Caucasus, the 20th c. has been an era of national and cultural awakening, which is reflected especially in the growth of a varied literary production. Most genres of modern European literature—the novel, the short story, the drama, the essay—have taken root, and foreign literary works have been translated. Among those who began writing at the beginning of the century were Kotsoity Arsen (1872–1944), who as a journalist and short-story writer exerted considerable influence upon the formation of the new literature; and Britiaty Elbyzdyqo (1881–1923), the first dramatist of importance.

The Russian revolution and the policies of the Soviet regime led to great changes in Ossetic literature. The abolishment of illiteracy resulted in a large expansion of the reading public; literature took on an enormously important role in national life. In the biggest towns theaters were built, thereby encouraging original dramatic works. The founding of research institutes, and in recent years of a North Ossetia university, not only was of significance to the scholarly world but also became a major incentive to cultural activities and national consciousness.

In general, Ossetic literature has followed the pattern of that of other peoples of the former Soviet Union. Themes have been sought in Caucasian situations at the time of the revolution and, later, of the collectivization. World War II made its special thematic demands. At the same time, traditional oral poetry and episodes from national history have been a vitalizing force, and it is tempting to talk about a national-romantic vein, which has become more vigorous in the last decades. A prominent figure among the pre-World War II writers was Dzanaity Ivan (pseud.: Niger; 1896–1947), who tried his hand at most literary genres and, like most of his colleagues, was actively engaged in promoting education.

The postwar period has seen a steady increase in literary output. Thanks to improved material conditions, the demand for didactic literature has decreased. Lyric poetry is apparently much in vogue; the depiction of personal problems is more freely admitted. Literature has reached a higher degree of formal sophistication. Questions of national and cultural identity and the role of writers in a modern society are intensely debated. The strengthening of national feeling has led to enthusiasm for historical and mythological themes. A representative writer of the post-war period, Dzhusoity Nafi (b. 1925), is a dynamic humanist who, besides being a literary historian, has written both novels and lyric poetry and translated Pushkin and Greek drama into his mother tongue.

The Ossets are a small linguistic community; their language is not widely known, and their books are rarely translated. Literary works are written for a limited public with a somewhat uniform taste. As with other small groups, literature has to face the danger of parochialism and a restricted aesthetic scope. Yet, Ossetic literature has succeeded in meeting the cultural needs of the people and in invigorating their sense of historical continuity and national identity.

—FRIDRIK THORDARSON

OSTAIJEN, Paul van

Belgian poet, short-story writer, and essayist (writing in Flemish), b. 22 Feb. 1896, Antwerp; d. 18 March 1928, Miavoye-Anthée

O. never finished his secondary education. While working as a clerk for the city of Antwerp, he began contributing to periodicals. Involvement with local politics forced him to flee abroad, and from 1918 to 1921 he lived in Berlin. On his return to Belgium he managed to eke out a living from his poetry and journalism, before dying of tuberculosis at the age of thirty-two.

O. made his literary debut with *Music-Hall* (1916; title in English), a volume of poems that were written when he was about eighteen. The book was immediately influential because its new vocabulary and rhythms were related to a new theme in Flemish poetry: the metropolis.

O.'s promise was fulfilled in his second volume of poems, *Het sienjaal* (1918; the signal). All the previous qualities, now openly joined by a strong humanist and apostolic credo, were developed into a verbal torrent typical of the heyday of German EXPRESSIONISM. Striking individual lines and images blend into a paean to humanity and a newly blossoming earth. An important document in the development of expressionist poetry, the book set the tone for many of O.'s contemporaries.

O. seemed assured of a respectable and successful career, but during his years in Berlin, he essayed to redefine humanitarian expressionism and began writing the kind of poetry for which he is famous. Having experimented with cocaine and witnessed a revolution, he wrote in 1921 the tormented pages of *De feesten van angst en pijn* (*Feasts of Fear and Agony*, 1976). Not published until 1952, the volume is a haunting farewell to the past, testimony to the turmoil and pain of the present, and a dire prophecy of the future.

Having met and studied the work of kindred spirits of DADA-ISM, O. published *Bezette stad* (1921; occupied city), a bitter and incisive indictment of war. A highly unusual poetic document, it describes the horror and desolation of war, as well as the cowardice of terrified citizens and the cynicism of the "State, Church, and Monarchy Corporation." Typographically, the texts explode from the page—poetic shrapnel of a generation that could no longer be deceived by slogans of any kind.

O.'s social criticism after 1921 was primarily continued in masterly tales he called "grotesques." Acerbic, absurdly reasoned, these satires have lost none of their force. Reminiscent of the writings of Swift and KAFKA, they present a world out of joint and and a society quite happily unaware of this condition. Some were printed during his lifetime, but most were published in posthumously issued collections that pleased few people.

O.'s poetic adventure continued in a series of texts that have become basic to modern Flemish poetry. He explained his objectives and techniques in a number of essays, and put his basic theory of thematic lyricism and association into practice in a series of masterful poems that were not printed in book form until the posthumously issued *Gedichten* (1928; poems). These profoundly simple and musical poems describe the mystery of the common and

the commonplace of the metaphysical. Outstripping conventions and traditions, they reflect O.'s lifelong dilemma: the limitations of expression make it impossible to capture the primordial secret of existence and of nature. Truth lies in the attempt.

O. educated his countrymen to the significant innovations of modern culture in a series of essays that included both literary topics and discussions of the visual arts. He prepared one of the first translations of Kafka and wrote the only known Dadaistic film script, although it was never realized.

In his quest for the pure poem, in his cerebral and vitriolic satires, and in his important essays on the arts and literature, O. showed himself always ahead of the avantgarde. A major contribution to 20th-c. literature, his work reaches far beyond the confines of his native Flemish tongue to assure him a foremost and irrevocable place in the literary vanguard of this century. His poetry and prose are only now being accorded their proper prominence both in Belgium and in the wider context of European literature.

FURTHER WORKS: *De trust der vaderlandsliefde* (1925); *Het bordeel van Ika Loch* (1926); *Vogelvrij* (1928); *Intermezzo* (1929); *Het eerste boek van Schmoll* (1929); *Kri012 proza* (2 vols., 1929–31); *De bende van de Stronk* (1932); *Diergaarde voor kinderen van nu* (1932); *Self-Defense* (1933); *Verzameld werk* (4 vols., 1952–56). FURTHER WORKS IN ENGLISH: *Patriotism Inc. and Other Tales* (1970); *The First Book of Schmoll: Selected Poems 1920–1928* (1982)

BIBLIOGRAPHY: Beekman, E. M., *Homeopathy of the Absurd: The Grotesque in O.'s Creative Prose* (1970); Beekman, E. M., "Blue Skiff of the Soul: The Significance of the Color Blue in P. v. O.'s Poetry," *DutchS*, 1 (1974): 113–17; Hadermann, P., "P. v. O. and Der Sturm," in Bulhof, F., ed., *Nijhoff, v. O., "De Stijl"* (1976): 37–57; Beekman, E. M., "The Universal Hue: P. v. O.'s lyrisme à thème," *Dutch Crossing* (London), No. 13 (1981): 42–80; Beekman, E. M., "Dada in Holland," in Paulsen, W. and Hermann, H. G., eds., *Sinn aus Unsinn: Dada International* (1982): 229–47

—E. M. BEEKMAN

OSTROVSKY, Nikolay Alexeevich

Russian novelist, b. 16 Sept. 1904, Vilia, Ukraine; d. 22 Dec. 1936, Moscow

Son of a poor worker, before his fifteenth birthday O. was already a member of the Komsomol (Communist Youth League) and, by 1924, a member of the Communist Party. In 1919, during the civil war, without telling his family, he volunteered for the front. A year later he was seriously wounded and partially lost his vision. He continued to take an active part in the work of the Komsomol in his native Ukraine until he was found to be suffering from an incurable form of arthritis, which slowly debilitated him. Bedridden from 1927 until his death, he completely lost his sight in 1928. Thus began his career as a writer.

O.'s literary fame rests upon a single work, the novel *Kak zakalyalas stal* (1935; *The Making of a Hero*, 1937; also tr. as *How the Steel Was Tempered*, 1952), although, with the assistance of other writers and secretaries, he managed to complete the first part of a contemplated trilogy, *Rozhdennye burey* (1936; *Born of the*

Storm, 1939). By the process of creating and writing, O. courage-ously kept up the struggle for life in the face of enormous physical handicaps.

By his own admission, when planning *Kak zakalyalas stal* O. attempted to "couch facts in literary form." His explicit wish was to provide young Soviet people with "memoirs in the form of a story." The main characters of the novel are all based on people the author knew; moreover, Pavel Korchagin, the protagonist, is an autobio-graphical portrait, "made from my brain and my blood," O. later said to an interviewer. The story unfolds during the decade preced-ing the October revolution, the civil war, the years of NEP (New Economic Policy), and the first Five-Year Plan, that is, during a stormy revolutionary period. In Pavel Korchagin, O. created a young revolutionary whose character, as the title clearly indicates, is tempered and directed as he begins to live and work for an idea—that of communism. The details of Korchagin's life and struggle closely parallel those of the author's; the novel even ends at the moment the manuscript of the novel Korchagin has written is accepted for publication.

In the Soviet Union, Pavel Korchagin was viewed as a sort of "hero of our time." The novel, which was deliberately promoted by Soviet critics in a literary propaganda campaign, attracted wide-spread attention. The personality of its author and the physical handicaps he valiantly sought to overcome contributed to making O. a legend in his own lifetime. Although the literary merits of the novel are far from outstanding, the book became a Soviet classic.

FURTHER WORKS: *Sobranie sochineny* (3 vols., 1967–68). FUR-THER WORKS IN ENGLISH: *Hail, Life! Articles, Speeches, Letters* (1955)

BIBLIOGRAPHY: Karavayeva, A., Introduction to *How the Steel Was Tempered* (1952): 5–23; Van der Eng-Liedmeier, A., *Soviet Literary Characters* (1959): 113–16; Alexandrova, V., *A History of Soviet Literature* (1963): 43–44; Struve, G., *Russian Literature under Lenin and Stalin, 1917–1953*, (1971): 287; Slonim, M., *Soviet Russian Literature: Writers and Problems, 1917–1967* (1973): 181–83

—NADJA JERNAKOFF

O'SULLIVAN, Vincent

New Zealand poet, short-story writer, novelist, dramatist, and editor, b. 28 Sept. 1937, Auckland

O. was born and educated in Auckland. He attended Catholic schools and was, for a time, educated by the Jesuits. After Auckland University he went to Oxford, returning later to New Zealand. He has taught at Waikato and Victoria Universities and spent time in Australia.

New Zealand writers have often lapsed from religious belief into writing, generally from Protestantism. This accounts for the secular temper of much New Zealand writing, the stern stress on realism, and the preference for an unadorned style (as though self-conscious or artificial writing is associated with irresponsible metaphysics). O. is among a smaller group of writers who have come from Catholicism. The effects of a catholic background are still noticeable in the writing, but in distinct ways. The style tends to be less pared, the use of metaphor and symbol more exuberant. Rejecting the cold insularities of New Zealand Catholicism, he nevertheless retains the richness of the language.

O.'s writing, in the several genres he has mastered, is character-ized by the elaborate use of symbol, metaphor, and figurative language. Without indulging in metafictional game-playing, he continually explores the interfusing of fiction with what we call fact. The world, for O. is able to be apprehended chiefly by way of the "mythic imagination." He is a realist, but an exuberant prose-stylist and a highly inventive poet.

This looking both ways enriches the poles of the dualisms he entertains (and with which he entertains us). The quotidian is untranscendable, but it can only be experienced by way of the shimmering representations of the mind. In the "Butcher" poems—*Butcher & Co* (1977) and *The Butcher Papers* (1982)—he invents a demotic and basely appetitive figure, a post-colonial Falstaff, who nevertheless shows glimmerings of larger moral and existential concerns. In *Brother Jonathan, Brother Kafka* (1980) he drama-tizes the irresolvable argument between flesh and spirit in favor of neither party.

O. began publishing poetry in the early 1960s under the influence both of James K. BAXTER and the Wellington poets and the Auckland poets associated with Allen CURNOW. He has a broader social concern, an ethical inquisitiveness, and a more marked predilection for satire than the latter, but he avoids the formal impatience that sometimes debilitates the work of the former. Arvidson observes that his work possesses "a centripetal energy that manifests itself in the variety and invention of constant creativity." This is particularly true of *The Pilate Tapes* (1986).

O. has enjoyed a long and distinguished career as a short-story writer. From *The Boy, the Bridge & the River* (1978) to *Palms and Minarets* (1992) his stories continue the criticism of a materialistic and conventional society that marks so much New Zealand fiction. O., however, brings a new dimension to the antipuritan crusade. He opposes neither religious belief nor, as Janet FRAME does, the isolate splendors of the artistic imagination, but a complex interest in the necessary fictions with which we invest our ordinary lives. These "fictions" are the residual signs and energies of a culture once in touch with the transcendent, now adrift; they lift his characters towards, not revelation but contemplation of the absurd condition itself. The narrative dance between vision and mundanity is found concentrated in *Selected Stories* (1992).

O. has written two novels. *Miracle: A Romance* (1976) is a satire that invests the busy secular world of modern New Zealand with religious myths and typologies. The effect is less finely rendered and nuanced than his major novel, *Let the River Stand* (1993). The latter revisits the themes, familiar stories, and even the characters of classic New Zealand fiction with a finely controlled ironic distance, a narrative mode in which the coarser voice of O.'s satire has been delicately edged.

O. has also had a significant career as a dramatist, notably with *Shuriken* (1985), *Jones & Jones* (1989), and *Billy* (1990). In addition, he is one of New Zealand's most important scholarly editors. He has edited *An Anthology of Twentieth Century New Zealand Poetry* (1970) and, with Margaret Scott, the multivolume *Collected Letters of Katherine Mansfield* (1984). His criticism includes a book-length study of James K. Baxter and an incisive monograph on Katherine MANSFIELD, *Finding the Pattern, Solving the Problem* (1989).

O. has made his reputation in a wide number of fields, as editor and critic as well as poet, dramatist, and fiction writer. He is an important Australasian poet and a major New Zealand writer in each of the genres, major not only because of the range and force of his work but also because he stands slightly outside the modernist-nationalist mainstream of his generation and questions its power as well as its assumptions.

FURTHER WORKS: *Our Burning Time* (1965); *Revenants* (1969); *Bearings* (1973); *From the Indian Funeral* (1976); *Dandy Edison for Lunch* (1981); *The Rose Ballroom* (1982); *Survivals* (1985); *The Snow in Spain* (1990); *Selected Poems* (1992)

BIBLIOGRAPHY: Arvidson, K. O., "Curnow, Stead and O.: Major Sensibilities in New Zealand Poetry," *JNZL*, 1 (1983): 31-48; Black, S., "Ways of Seeing: V. O.'s *Shuriken*," *Landfall*, 40, 1 (1986): 57-75; Cusack, G.,"V. O.'s Prose,' *Landfall*, 35, 4 (1981): 444-52; David Dowling, "The Poetry of V. O.," *Landfall*, 35, 4 (1981): 435-42

—MARK SULLIVAN

OTERO, Blas de

Spanish poet, b. 15 Mar. 1916, Bilbao; d. 12 July 1979, Madrid

Together with Victoriano Cremer (b. 1908), José Hierro (b. 1922), Eugenio G. de Nora (b. 1923), and Gabriel CELAYA, O. formed the group of major poets who came to prominence during post-Civil War, Francoist Spain. Following earlier education with the Jesuits in Bilbao, O. took a degree in law from the University of Valladolid; but he never practiced law and instead went on to study literature in Madrid.

While most of the giants of pro-Republic, prewar poetry were either dead or in exile, O., along with Celaya especially, became identified as the most significant voice of Marxist-oriented liberalism and as the leading literary protester against injustice, oligarchy, and dictatorship. Although he visited the Soviet Union and China, stayed in Castro's Cuba for four years, and declared sympathy for North Vietnam, O. is not fundamentally a political poet. At the center of his best work are the Spaniards of his time and the conditions of their common life. In O. this so-called "social poetry" is generally not to be confused with the social REALISM, which by decree treats only certain sectors of reality in specified manners.

Both in theory and practice O. at his best writes about what he personally feels strongly and sincerely. In often technically perfect and difficult poems, his treatment of suffering and outraged humanity becomes experience, not mere allusion or commentary. But such compositions of midcentury such as the sonnets "La tierra" (1950; the earth) and "Hombre" (1958; "Man," 1972) reveal what may be the more fundamental basis of his work: the post-World War II, existentialist questioning about the nature of God and the world he made, and the inquiry into the lot of humankind forced to live the horrors that history consistently revisits upon men, women, and children. In this context the Spanish Civil War, World War II, and the broken lives and countries of their aftermath are merely the portion of mortal misery that it has been O.'s lot to experience firsthand and to transform into his poetry. *Angel fieramente humano*

(1950; fiercely human angel) and *Redoble de conciencia* (1951; drumroll of conscience), particularly in their reedition and augmentation in 1958 as *Ancia*, may contain the best of the O. being described here.

After O's death, there was a memorial service to him in Las Ventas bullring of Madrid, which some 40,000 attended. It is probable that those who went were attracted by the persona of O. as author of the "A la inmensa mayoría" (1955; "To the Immense Majority," 1972), the dedicatory opening poem of *Angel fieramente humano*. In a 1968 interview O. explained that even though his poetry was not the stuff around which mass audiences come to center themselves, it treated the vital concerns of the great majority of people. Now some sixteen years after Franco's death and the firm establishment of prosperous democracy in Spain, it seems that O.'s public reputation is some-what on the wane. The anti-Francoism with which he was identified is largely irrelevant today. But the perdurance of O. will have nothing to do with Franco, but with his tremendously sensitive representation of human life as experienced during one of its epically trying periods.

FURTHER WORKS: *Cuatro poemas* (1941); *Cántico espiritual* (1942); *Poesías en Burgos* (1943); *Antología y notas* (1952); *Pido la paz y la palabra* (1955); *En castellano* (1959); *Esto no es un libro* (1963); *Que trata de España* (1964); *Mientras* (1970); *Historias fingidas y verdaderas* (1970); *Verso y prosa* (1974); *Todos mis sonetos* (1977); *Correspondencia sobre la edición de "Pido la paz y la palabra"* (1987). FURTHER WORKS IN ENGLISH: *Twenty Poems of B. de O.* (1964); *Selected Poems of Miguel Hernaández and B. de O.* (1972)

BIBLIOGRAPHY: Llorach, E. Alarcos, *La poesía de B. de O.* (1963); King, E. L., "B. de O.: The Past and Present of the Eternal," in Ferrán, J. and D. Testa, eds., *Spanish Writers of 1936* (1973): 125–33; Barrow, G. R., "Autobiography and Art in the Poetry of B. de O.," *HR*, 48 (1980): 213–30; Mellizo, C. L. Salstad, eds., *B. de O.: Study of a Poet* (1980); Barrow, G. R., "Notions of Nowhere: A Poet in Francoist Spain," *MRRM*, 2 (1986): 111–25; Barrow, G. R., *The Satiric Vision of B. de O.* (1988); McDermott, P., "B. de O.: Cultural Memory in a Time of Silence: Alternative Voices *En castellano*," *Antípodas*, 2 (1989): 97–116

—STEPHEN MILLER

OTTIERI, Ottiero

Italian novelist, b. 29 March 1924, Rome

O. received a doctoral degree in languages and literature from the University of Rome in 1948, but his main interest was always in psychoanalysis. When he moved to Milan, he sought work that would allow him to put his interest in social psychology to use. After having worked for a few years for a publisher, O. accepted a position in the public and human relations department of the Olivetti company. It is rather difficult to label his work as that of a realist, sociologist, essayist, moralist, psychoanalyst, or of a neurotic. O. is an extremely prolific writer and his writings show all of these characteristics and demonstrate that he is equally talented in creating masterful images, both naturalistic and psychoanalytical, in his fiction as in his poetry. And just as he was an excellent observer of the socio-economic and alienating problems that afflicted workers in the early years of industrialization in Italy, O. is also an outstanding examiner of man's preoccupation (or obsession) with his inner-self, solitude, love-hate relationships, neuroses, sickness, and awareness.

A highly autobiographical writer, O. has drawn most of his material from his own experiences. For his early novels he relied extensively on his work at Olivetti. *Tempi stretti* (1957; hard times) initiated the trend called "Literature and Industry," which received wide attention primarily because it was expected to bring linguistic innovations to literature, as well as a new view of alienation and other problems of an industrial society. *Tempi stretti* was acclaimed as an excellent inside view of workers in large factories around Milan. The novel focuses on their daily problems—mechanical, sociopolitical, and personal: on the production line, in commuting, at union meetings, in organizing strikes, and even in their most intimate moments at home.

From diaries he kept for nearly ten years O. drew the material for *Donnarumma all'assalto* (1959; *The Men at the Gate*, 1962), and *La linea gotica* (1963; the gothic line), both dealing with attempts at industrializing southern Italy and with the resulting clashes between the modern, technologically advanced north and the backward, poverty-stricken south. The psychologist's narration is based on O.'s frustrating experience as administrator of psychological and technical-skills tests to job applicants (mostly poor and illiterate) at a factory about to open in a small town near Naples. The author's pungent, ironic criticism is directed both at industry for its ridiculous hiring practices and at the government for not having prepared the south for industrialization. Using characters like Donnarumma, who aggressively demands a job while refusing to fill out an application, and portraying people who cannot cope with an eight-hour workday or with any form of organization, O. demonstrates that workers have to be educated and trained before they can function in modern industry.

With *L'irrealtà quotidiana* (1966; everyday unreality) O. began a series of semiconfessional and documentary novels dealing with JUNGIAN therapy, with clinics, and often with his own neuroses, his fears of impotence, and his excessive drinking and smoking. O. has stressed that writing can be a form of self-therapy—see especially *Il campo di concentrazione* (1972; the field of concentration [or concentration camp]).

O.'s predilection for dramatic dialogues and monologues are particularly evident in *Contessa* (1978), a drama narrated through the first-person point of view of a woman who spends (just like the author) half of her life dialoguing with her psychoanalyst. Elena Miuti suffers from frigidity and tries to overcome it by having relations with numerous partners, seeking from them pleasure and affection. Her analyst, Dr. Calligaris, far from providing a cure, becomes one of the main characters with whom she is in constant conflict. *Contessa* is the story of an existence reduced to deadly boredom and emptiness, and to a sum of futile efforts in attempting to escape this mental state. In Elena's sickness O. portrays a universal condition of modern society in which men and women struggle to communicate and to interact without success.

Il poema osceno (1996; The obscene poem) and *Una tragedia milanese* (1997; A Milanese tragedy) could very well be the point of arrival of a journey that began with the psychological narratives and poems in the days of *La corda corta*. In more recent works O. has made extensive use of dialogues and theatrical elements which

prevail over the reliance on plots and descriptions for telling a story. In *Il poema osceno*, Pietro Muojo, a mature poet, and his sister Vera are always surrounded by friends and lovers who seem to ensnare them in a merry-go-round of conversations and sexual relations. Through the manic depressive Pietro, O. discusses mental illness, sex, and, surprisingly, a certain hate for literature. Sex and death are also at the center of *Una tragedia milanese*. Here the main protagonist is a famous plastic surgeon, Prof. Antonio, married to Marietta. The surgeon chases after his younger secretary Ennia and it is not long before their relationship becomes entangled with the sexual stories of patients and of their respective lovers.

In the last four decades O. has constantly described neuroses, conflicts in personal relationships, mental illness, and preoccupation with death while underlining an empty feeling of solitude and a certain pessimism that there is no cure from all of these social and mental problems. Whether writing about industrialization or emotional disorder, O. always offers astute analyses of central problems of contemporary society.

FURTHER WORKS: *Memorie dell'incoscienza* (1954); *I venditori a Milano* (1960); *L'impagliatore de sedie* (1964); *I divini mondani* (1968); *Il pensiero perverso* (1971); *Contessa* (1976); *La corda rotta* (1978); *Di chi è la colpa* (1979); *I due amori* (1983); *Il divertimento* (1984); *L'infermiera di Pisa* (1991); *Il palazzo e il pazzo* (1993); *Diario del seduttore passivo* (1995)

BIBLIOGRAPHY: Rossi, J., On *Tempi stretti*, *BA*, 33 (1959): 334; De Bellis, A. C., on *I divini mondani*, *BA*, 43 (1969): 582; Fantazzi, C., on *L'irrealtà quotidiana*, *BA*, 41 (1967): 338; Fantazzi, C., on *Contessa*, *WLT*, 51 (1977): 75–76

—ROCCO CAPOZZI

ØVERLAND, Arnulf

Norwegian poet, essayist, short-story writer, and dramatist, b. 27 April 1889, Kristiansund; d. 25 March 1968, Oslo

Ø. came from a family of limited means, but he nevertheless finished secondary school, after which he studied literature and philosophy at the University of Oslo. He was particularly influenced by the Swedish writers August STRINDBERG and Hjalmar SÖDERBERG. The events of World War I led him to become an active member of the Norwegian Communist Party, which he remained until he was disillusioned by the Moscow trials of the 1930s. He early warned of the danger represented by Hitler, and during the Nazi occupation of Norway in World War II, his poems of defiance were widely circulated. As a result, Ø. was arrested and in 1942 sent to the Sachsenhausen concentration camp. After the war Ø. was invited to live at Grotten, a government-supported residence for outstanding artists.

Ø.'s first published collection of Poetry was *Den ensomme fest* (1911; the lonely party). In it, as well as in all his subsequent collections, he deals with such universal themes as life, death, and love. Some of this poetry is extremely introspective; there is often irony directed at self, but also poignant expressions of the bitter loneliness of youth.

In *Brød og vin* (1919; bread and wine) Ø. moved away from his introspection and expressed a deep commitment to social justice.

He makes extensive use of biblical motifs but employs them in such a manner that the message of the Norwegian Lutheran State Church appears as only one of several possible readings of the Bible. His aim is to awaken his audience not to the needs of the soul but to the material, emotional, and intellectual needs of human beings in a cruel and unjust world. In *Berget det blå* (1927; blue mountain) he used motifs from legend and folktale in order to achieve a similar effect.

Ø.'s masterwork as a poet is the collection *Hustavler* (1929; rules for living), which represents a synthesis of his early introspection and his later social commitment. The major theme is death, thoughts of which had long been familiar to the author because of his having suffered from pulmonary tuberculosis.

Ø.'s radical political stance, as well as his atheism, had made him unacceptable to large segments of the Norwegian population. World War II changed this public attitude, however, and the poet now became a symbol of patriotism. His war poetry was collected in *Vi overlever alt!* (1945; we will survive anything!) and *Tiblake til livet* (1946; back to life).

Ø. also presented his social and political views in essays and public lectures, and he is one of the foremost essayists in Norwegian literature. His lecture "Kristendommen—den tiende landeplage" (1933; Christianity—the tenth scourge) led to a trial for blasphemy in 1933. He was acquitted, but the so-called blasphemy paragraph in the criminal code was, as a result of the case, strengthened in order that it might cover similar situations in the future.

In the period after World War II Ø. battled with equal energy against a move to unify Norway's two official languages—the more urban *bokmål* and the more rural *nynorsk*—as well as against modernism in poetry. His lecture "Tungetale fra Parnasset" (1953; speaking in tongues heard from Parnassus) precipitated one of the liveliest debates in Norwegian cultural history.

Ø. is less important as a dramatist and short-story writer than as a poet and essayist. His two plays, *Venner* (1917; friends) and *Gi mig ditt hjerte* (1930; give me your heart), suffer from the author's lack of theatrical experience. The many short stories are thematically connected with the rest of his oeuvre and often satirize the same follies Ø. attacked in his essays.

Ø.'s best poetry is among the best in Norwegian literature. This holds true for both some of his poems of social commitment and many of those that deal with universal themes. Above all, Ø. was a man who refused to be silenced and whose words will continue to live.

FURTHER WORKS: *De hundrede violiner* (1912); *Advent* (1915); *Den hårde fred* (1916); *Deilig er jorden* (1923); *Gud planter en have* (1931); *Jeg besværger dig* (1934); *Samlede dikt* (2 vols., 1936); *Noveller i utvalg* (1939); *Er vårt sprog avskaffet?* (1940); *Ord i alvor til det norske folk* (1940); *Det har ringt for annen gang* (1946); *Samlede dikt* (3 vols., 1947); *Norden mellem øst og vest* (1947); *Nøitralitet eller vestblokk* (1948); *Hvor ofte skal vi skifte sprog?* (1948); *Nordiske randstater eller atlantisk fred* (1949); *Bokmålet—et avstumpet landsmål* (1949); *Fiskeren og hans sjel* (1950); *Har jorden plass til oss?* (1952); *I beundring og forargelse* (1954); *Riksmål, landsmål og slagsmål* (1956); *Sverdet bak døren* (1956); *Om Gud skulde bli lei av oss* (1958); *Verset—hvordan blir det til* (1959); *Den rykende tande* (1960); *Jeg gikk i rosengården: Kjærlighetsdikt i utvalg* (1960); *Samlede dikt IV* (1961); *På Nebo bjerg* (1962); *Hvor gammelt er Norge?* (1964); *Møllerupgåsens liv og himmelfart, og andre troverdige beretninger* (1964); *Livets minutter* (1965); *De hundrede fioliner: Dikt i utvalg* (1968)

BIBLIOGRAPHY: Beyer, H., *A History of Norwegian Literature* (1956): 317–18; Boardman, P., "A. Ø.: Patriot, Religious Atheist, Poet Laureate," *Norseman*, 3 (1964): 71–74; Beyer, E., "Die norwegische Literatur nach 1900," *SchM*, 45 (1965): 473–83; Anon., "Er war immer unbequem: Zum Tode des norwegischen Dichters A. Ø.," *Ausblick*, 19 (1968): 17–20; Houm, P., "A. Ø.," *ASR*, 61 (1973): 268–72

—JAN SJÅVIK

OWEN, Wilfred

English poet, b. 18 March 1893, Oswestry; d. 4 Nov. 1918, Landrécies, France

A true Shropshire lad, O. was born and raised on the Welsh border of rural England. He was a dreamy, sickly, somewhat bookish child, pampered and favored by his intensely devoted, rigidly Calvinist mother. Indeed, he never fully escaped the pull of either his mother's affection or her religion. Growing up to become an excellent amateur botanist, O. would later write that a visit to Broxton by the Hill at the age of ten first confirmed his poetic vocation. He wrote copiously, and his early poems are steeped in the romanticism of Keats and Shelley. After his education at the Birkenhead Institute, Liverpool, and the Technical College, Shrewsbury, he worked as an assistant at Dunsden vicarage (it was here he first suffered a crisis of faith) and spent two years teaching English in France (1913–15).

During World War I O. enlisted in the Artists' Rifles, was commissioned in the Manchester Regiment, and was assigned to the French battlefields. After several months at the front he finally suffered intolerable nervous stress, diagnosed as "neurasthenia," as a result of spending several days in a heavily shelled position staring at the scattered remnants of another officer's body. Sent to the Craiglockhart War Hospital to recover, he soon met the poet Siegfried SASSOON, who encouraged him to write about the reality and outrage of war. This new subject matter—and the radical style that it required—liberated O.'s work, and almost all of his major poems were written during an intensely creative period from August 1917 to September 1918. In August 1918 he was sent back to France and, one week before the armistice, he was killed in action.

Before his death O. had begun to put together a small collection of poems, only four of which appeared in print during his lifetime. He also left the first draft of what has become one of the most celebrated literary prefaces in English poetry, published in *The Poems of W. O.* (1931). O.'s preface stated flatly that he was not concerned with "heroes," or with any other generalized abstractions like "glory" or "honor." Rather, as he said, "My subject is War, and the pity of War. The Poetry is in the pity." O. was shocked by the harshness of modern warfare and scandalized by the ironic discrepancy between what soldiers actually endured in the trenches and the English civilian's sentimental ideas about the war. His poems set out to dismantle once and for all any idealized or patriotic stereotypes of war by showing its terrible, brutal, dehumanizing reality. Two central principles predominate in O.'s most characteristic work: anger at the senseless destruction of war, and compassion or pity for the helpless, inarticulate victims that it drives to madness and death. The furious note of protest that prevails in such didactic poems as "Dulce et Decorum Est" (pub. 1920) and "Spring Offensive" (pub. 1920) is only balanced by the elegiac tone of such laments for the dead as "Anthem for Doomed Youth" (pub. 1920) and "Strange Meeting" (pub. 1919). Either directly or indirectly, all of O.'s work testifies to the terrible effects of war on ordinary soldiers.

O.'s characteristic poetic technique was to infuse new life into traditional forms by relying on highly sensuous imagery. His concentrated, almost homoerotic descriptions of exhausted, maimed, and slaughtered male bodies give a palpable immediacy to his poetry. At the same time his consistent use of half rhyme (or pararhyme) creates a sense of discordance, delay, and frustration that is ideally suited to his subject matter. This matching of consonant assonance and vowel dissonance is especially powerful at echoing and conveying one of O.'s principle themes: that the war keeps young men from ever living out or fulfilling their lives. The slaughter and destruction of youth is always his first and final subject.

O.'s reputation has grown slowly but significantly since Edith SITWELL and Siegfried Sassoon first put together a volume of twenty-three poems from his surviving manuscripts, *Poems* (1920). This volume was supplanted by the textually more accurate and expanded 1931 volume, *The Poems of W. O.*, edited, with a "Memoir," by Edmund Blunden (1896–1974). It was this collection that significantly influenced the English political poets of the 1930s: W. H. Auden, Stephen Spender, and C. Day LEWIS. O.'s audience was further enlarged when Benjamin Britten set some of the major poems to music in his *War Requiem*, which captures something of the intense anger and enormous sympathy for the suffering of young soldiers that flows through the poetry. O. is unquestionably the most important and central English poet associated with the Great War.

FURTHER WORKS: *The Collected Poems* (1963); *Collected Letters* (1967); *W. O.: War Poems and Others* (1973)

BIBLIOGRAPHY: Welland, D. S. R., *W. O.: A Critical Study* (1960); Owen, H., *Journey from Obscurity* (3 vols.: 1963–65); Bergonzi, B., *Heroes' Twilight: A Study of the Literature of the Great War* (1965): 121–35; White, W., *W. O.: A Bibliography* (1967); Silkin, J., *Out of Battle: The Poetry of the Great War* (1972): 197–248; Stallworthy, J., *W. O.: A Biography* (1974); Hibberd, D., *W. O.* (1975)

—EDWARD HIRSCH

OYONO, Ferdinand

Cameroonian novelist (writing in French), b. 14 Sept. 1929, N'Goulémakong, near Ebolowa

O.'s mother, a fervent Roman Catholic, left her husband because although professing to be a Catholic he continued to practice polygamy. O. was a choirboy and studied the classics with a priest; when he obtained his primary-school diploma, his father suddenly took pride in his son's education, sending him to the lycée of Ebolowa and urging him to study in France. Before going to France, O. worked for missionaries as a houseboy, a situation that

served as the source of inspiration for his first novel, *Une vie de boy* (1956; *Boy!*, 1970). After receiving his diploma from the lycée of Provins near Paris, O. went on to study law and government administration. He has held several government positions.

O.'s three novels are rich in autobiographical material. *Une vie de boy* is the ironic tale of an innocent young African, Toundi, who works as a servant for a white missionary. After the missionary's death, Toundi is transferred to the service of the Commandant Decazy and his wife, a beautiful white woman whom Toundi idolizes, but who treats him with utter contempt. Like Voltaire's Candide, Toundi has an optimistic, easy-going nature and an unspoiled enthusiasm for life. His naïve frankness and sense of trust contrast sharply with the carefully calculated hypocrisy of the other Africans, who, while pretending to be subservient and obedient toward their masters, openly express their disgust and dissatisfaction when in their own private circles. Toundi's gradual awakening to the injustice of his colonial masters is pathetically demonstrated toward the end of the novel, but that awakening occurs too late for Toundi to save his own life.

His sad death is made known to the reader in an epilogue in which O., in his own voice, purports to be offering the reader Toundi's own diary. Since the narrative is presented as a translation into French from the unsophisticated houseboy's native Ewondo, its style is extremely simple and direct. *Une vie de boy* was one of the first novels to challenge openly the European's claim to being superior to the African.

In O.'s second novel, *Le vieux nègre et la médaille* (1956; *The Old Man and the Medal*, 1967), the satire is aimed not only at the whites but also at those blacks who fawn over and cringe before their masters. Meka, the old man of the title, is to be presented with a medal for his service to the administration. As naïve as Toundi, Meka is equally comical in his desire to impress his white superiors. His realization that he has been exploited also occurs late in the novel. Following the award ceremony, when Meka accidentally wanders into the white section of town, he finds himself suddenly imprisoned as a prowler and begins to rebel. He recognizes the meaninglessness of the sacrifices of his land to the Church mission and of his two sons, who died fighting in the French army. In the end Meka rejects European civilization and Christianity as he seeks to regain his original African identity.

O.'s third novel, *Chemin d'Europe* (1960; road to Europe) is his most ambitious. The subject is the many problems and frustrations a young native encounters when he seeks permission from the colonial authorities to study in Europe. *Chemin d'Europe* marks a departure from O.'s first two novels because it is sophisticated in tone and broader in scope. The protagonist, Aki Barnabas, is disillusioned and cynical from the start. He bitterly resents both Europeans who try to impose their culture upon Africans and those Africans who refuse to admit the need for change. Although skillfully written, this novel lacks the warmth, freshness, and humor of O.'s first two works.

O., committed to exposing the evils of colonialism, encouraged Africans to regain their native values. By blending humor with pathos, he awakens the reader to the oppression endured by blacks in the French African colonies just before those colonies gained their independence.

FURTHER WORKS: *Le pandémonium* (c. 1971, unpublished)

BIBLIOGRAPHY: Diop, D., on *Une vie de boy* and *Le vieux nègre et la médaille*, *PA*, 11 (1956): 125–27; Moore, G., "F. O. and the

Colonial Tragicomedy," *PA*, 18, 2 (1963): 61–73; Mercier, R., and M. Battestini, and S. Battestini, *F. O.* (1964); Brench, A. C., *The Novelists' Inheritance in French Africa* (1967): 47–63; Makward, E., Introduction to *Boy!* (1970): v–xvi; Linneman, R., "The Anticolonialism of F. O.," *YFS*, 53 (1976): 64–77; Storzer, G. H., "Narrative Techniques and Social Realities in F. O.'s *Une vie de boy* and *Le vieux nègre et la médaille*," *Crit*, 19, 3 (1978): 89–101

—DEBRA POPKIN

OZ, Amos

Israeli short-story writer, novelist, and essayist, b. 4 May 1939, Jerusalem

From a family of scholars and teachers, O. was educated at the Hebrew University, Jerusalem. At the age of fifteen he left home to settle at the Kibbutz Chulda, where to this day he divides his time between writing, farming, and teaching. After serving with a tank unit in the Six-Day War (1967) and the Yom Kippur War (1973), he published many articles and essays on the Arab-Israeli conflict, campaigning for a compromise based on mutual recognition and a Palestinian homeland in the West Bank and Gaza.

O.'s first collection of short stories, *Artsot hatan* (1965; *Where the Jackals Howl, and Other Stories*, 1981), was followed by a novel about loneliness on the kibbutz, *Makom acher* (1966; *Elsewhere Perhaps*, 1973), and his most widely known novel, *Michael sheli* (1968; *My Michael*, 1972), a tragic, loveless love story set in Jerusalem. His most demanding and controversial works—*Ad mavet* (1971; *Unto Death: Crusade and Late Love*, 1975), consisting of two novellas, and *Lagaat bamayim lagaat baruach* (1973; *Touch the Water, Touch the Wind*, 1974)—mark a turn from realistic style and subject matter toward surrealistic, archetypal studies of the deeper roots of Israeli loneliness, violence, and yearning for death. In the three novellas making up *Har haetsah haraah* (1976; *The Hill of Evil Counsel*, 1978) O. returns to a realistic mode but probes still more deeply into the Jewish soul, mentally in exile although physically at home. *Sumchi* (1978; Sumchi) is a child's tale of lonely adventure and love, and *Beor hatchelet haazah* (1979; under the blazing light) a collection of literary, ideological, and political essays. O.'s works have been translated into eighteen languages.

Unlike many Jewish writers—who portray the modern Jew as an uprooted stranger or prodigal son who, by repudiating his heritage, has turned into a self-centered materialist and his life into a wasteland devoid of dream, myth, and value—O. believes that the sabra's wanderlust, estrangement, and cynical ennui derive precisely from the mythic aura of Israel, the haunting presence of visionary forefathers, and the hovering shadow of their messianic dreams. The Earth Mother, under whose aegis Zionist fathers hoped to begin anew and heal the diseased spirituality of exilic Judaism, is portrayed as worshiped with the same sacrificial zeal as the forsaken Heavenly Father had been earlier. The ironic smile O.'s idealistic heroes wear is the scornful sneer of the apocalyptic redeemer poisoned by an exalted ideal he cannot renounce, disillusioned with the sun-washed cities and cultivated fields of his homeland because of his yearning for a home somewhere over the rainbow. Tied to an age-old dream whose modest realization he

disdains, O.'s sabra remains, like his forefathers in the Diaspora, divorced from earthly reality and relations.

In *Artsot hatan*, *Makom acher*, and *Michael sheli* O. dramatizes the ironic tragedy of real human estrangement—husbands from wives, parents from children, individuals from social bonds—arising from obsessive playing of archetypal roles, such as the Wandering Jew, dictated by a collective heritage from which Israelis believe themselves liberated. In *Ad mavet* and *Lagaat bamayim lagaat baruach* O. suggests, with none too subtle symbolic allusions, that his alienated protagonists are acting out in modern dress the role of crucifying and crucified saviors in a crusade against the world, the flesh, and the devil, a situation all the more ironic and tragic for being incarnate in men whose fathers yearned to touch the earth. In *Har haetsah haraah* O. suggests that to heal these "dream-crucified" children, Judaism must realize that there is no grace but the tender touch of a woman's hand, no redeemed life but the brief, finite, imperfect present, and no rest from lonely wandering save in the real embrace of real wives, parents, friends. Instead of the old dreams of redemption, O. calls for the little wonders achieved here and now by people committed to simple, everyday realities.

FURTHER WORKS: *Mnuchah nchonah* (1982)

BIBLIOGRAPHY: Kazin, A., on *Touch the Water, Touch the Wind*, *SatR/World* (2 Nov. 1974): 38; McElroy, J., on *Unto Death: Crusade and Late Love*, *NYTBR* (26 Oct. 1975): 4; Porat, Z., "The Golem from Zion: Exile and Redemption in A. O.'s Legends of Israel," *Ariel* (Jerusalem) 47 (1978): 71–79; Bayley, J., on *The Hill of Evil Counsel*, *NYRB* (20 July 1978): 35; Yudkin, L. I., "The Jackal and the Other Place: The Stories of A. O.," *JSS*, 23 (1978): 330–42; Vardi, D., "On A. O.: *Under the Blazing Light*," *MHL*, 5, 4 (1979): 37–40; Mojtabi, A. G., on *Where the Jackals Howl*, *NYTBR* (26 Apr. 1981): 3

—ZEPHYRA PORAT

OZICK, Cynthia

American novelist, short-story writer, and essayist, b. 17 Apr. 1928, New York, N.Y.

O. is one of the most significant, and most self-consciously "Jewish," literary voices to emerge in the past three decades. Born in New York City, O. received her B.A. in English from New York University and her M.A. from Ohio State. Equally at home with fiction and the literary essay, O. has published four novels, *Trust* (1966), *The Cannibal Galaxy* (1971), *The Messiah of Stockholm* (1987); and *The Puttermesser Papers* (1997) four collections of short fiction, *The Pagan Rabbi* (1971), *Bloodshed* (1982), *Levitation: Five Fictions* (1982), and *The Shawl* (1989); and three collections of essays. *Art and Ardor* (1983), *Metaphor and Memory* (1988) and *Fame and Folly* (1996).

O. is the case of a writer who blossomed late (she blames her long, fruitless apprenticeship on an early fascination with the art novel of Henry JAMES), but who has gradually emerged as the dominant voice for new directions in Jewish-American writing. If contemporary Jewish-American literature often seems dominated

Cynthia Ozick

by those either estranged from or hostile to their Jewish roots, O. is a noteworthy exception. She is an observant Jew, a tireless student of Jewish ideas, and a fierce supporter of the State of Israel.

For O., it is essential that the Jewish-American writer think, and even dream, in centrally Jewish ways; and she goes on to define "centrally Jewish" as "whatever touches on the liturgical." The result has been a series of fictional works that pit Pan against Moses, unbridled passions against the fences of law. Moments in her first long and largely unsuccessful novel, *Trust*, intimate these themes; the stories in *The Pagan Rabbi* make them breathtakingly clear.

For many years O. so worried about the idol-making possibilities of fiction—in both her essays and her own fiction—that critics began to worry about her obsessive self-abnegation. Not since Hawthorne has a writer seemed so fatally attracted to the demonic, to the "pagan." However, *Metaphor and Myth* makes it clear that at least some imaginative work can be numbered on the side of the angels and that literature itself need make no apology for its potential as an abiding, even necessary, moral force.

O. continues to grow as an artist, but even at the midpoint of her career it seems safe to say that she will be regarded as a first-rate short-story writer and as one of America's most provocative literary essayists.

BIBLIOGRAPHY: Wisse, R., "American Jewish Writing, Act II," *Commentary*, 61 (1976): 40–45; Rosenfeld, A., "C. O.: Fiction and the Jewish Idea," *Midstream*, 23 (1977): 76–81; Walden, D., ed., *The World of C. O.* (1987); Epstein, J., "C. O., Jewish Writer," *Commentary*, 77 (1984): 64–69; Bloom, H., ed., *C. O.: Modern Critical Views* (1986); Pinsker, S., *The Uncompromising Fictions of C. O.* (1987); Lowin, J., *C. O.* (1988); Standberg, V., *Greek Mind/Jewish Soul: The Conflicted Art of C. O.* (1994); Cohen, S., *C. O.'s Comic Art* (1994)

—SANFORD PINSKER

P

PA CHIN

(pseud. of Li Fei-kan) Chinese novelist, b. 25 Nov. 1904, Chengtu

One of the most popular writers of 20th-c. China, P. C. experienced the social turmoil that accompanied the birth of modern China and produced a generation of youth committed to revolution. Despite his upper-class family background he was a self-professed anarchist and found political inspiration in the writings of Pyotr Kropotkin (1842–1921) and of Emma Goldman (1869–1940), with whom he corresponded. His literary influences came from Russian fiction (he later translated works by GORKY, Turgenev, and Tolstoy). After returning from France, where he lived from 1927 to 1929, he turned to social and political novels, which he produced prolifically during the 1930s and 1940s. After the Communist victory in 1949 he remained on the mainland; he was made a vice-chairman of the National Committee of the All China Federation of Literary and Art Circles and was given other assignments by the government. He was, however, persecuted during the Cultural Revolution in the late 1960s. Since his recent rehabilitation he has been twice nominated for the Nobel Prize in literature, and in 1981 was elected acting chairman of the Chinese Writers' Association. He was awarded the Dante International Prize by the Italian government in 1982.

P. C.'s first novel, *Mieh-wang* (1929; destruction), is noted more for its social message than for its literary excellence. The main character, Tu Ta-hsin ("Tu Big Heart"), hates the existing government so much that he plots its overthrow. Eventually he commits suicide after failing to assassinate a garrison commander. *Hsin sheng* (1931; new life), another political novel about revolution, is distinguished by its portrayal of a Chinese "dangling man," Li Leng. A masochistic sufferer, despairing and alienated, Li finally finds himself in the anarchists' cause and dies for it.

P. C.'s most acclaimed work is the *Chi-liu* (turbulent stream) trilogy, comprising *Chia* (1931; *The Family*, 1958), *Ch'un* (1937; spring), and *Ch'iu* (1939; autumn). It traces the fortunes of the Kao family during the early 20th c., when old and new values clashed, and it treats comprehensively such related themes as frustrated young love, the low status of women, concubinage, enmity between parents and children, and harsh treatment of the young. Of the three novels in the trilogy, *Chia* is the most widely known and is considered one of his finest works. All three, however, were extremely popular with the readers of the 1930s and 1940s, who easily identified with the characters.

During the Sino-Japanese War (1937–45) P. C. at first supported the war effort by writing about the activities of patriots in the trilogy *Huo* (1938–43; fire). Despite the lack of exciting battles or moving love scenes, the trilogy is memorable for P. C.'s concentration on the emotions of patriotic men and women whose idealism and fiery zeal are symbolized by the title itself.

P. C.'s loss of enthusiasm for the war can be seen in *Hsiao-jen, hsiao-shih* (1947; little people, little events), a collection of short stories written during the war in which he stripped the war of its glamour and described the "little people" exactly as they were. His pessimism about China grew as the war dragged on and was further reflected in *Tissu ping-shih* (1945; ward number four), a novelette about the inhuman conditions in a substandard hospital in the interior.

P. C.'s harshest attack on the war and the Nationalist government, however, was in *Han yeh* (1947; *Cold Nights*, 1978), regarded, along with *Chia*, as one of his two masterpieces. Set in Chungking at the end of World War II, *Han yeh* portrays the strained and deteriorating relationships among a mother, a son, and a daughter-in-law, against a background of the social weariness and ennui that pervaded China in the 1940s. In addition to the realistic presentation of the grim realities in wartime Chungking, *Han yeh* is notable in its exploration of human motives and behavior.

Because of the Communist Party's rigid control of literature, P. C. wrote little after 1949. His visits to Korea in the early 1950s, however, led to his writing about the Chinese who fought there in *Ying-hsiung ti ku-shih* (1954; *Living Among Heroes*, 1954). Adopting a cautious attitude toward the government, he revised many of his pre-1949 works, excising references to anarchism and changing some endings.

During the height of the Cultural Revolution in the late 1960s P. C. was silenced. When he resumed writing in the late 1970s he produced more than sixty essays on a variety of topics and translated two volumes of Alexandr Herzen's (1812–1870) memoirs. Most recently he has been working on a novel about an elderly intellectual couple during the Cultural Revolution.

In his heyday P. C. was regarded as a counselor to the young. He probed the dynamics of social institutions during a time of radical change, and through the medium of fiction he eloquently communicated his vision of China's character. With the passing of time, many of the issues he wrestled with will lose their immediacy, and his works will be judged more on purely aesthetic grounds—and found to be of high artistic quality.

FURTHER WORKS: *Ssu-ch'ü-ti t'ai-yang* (1930); *Ai-ch'ing-ti san-pu-ch'u* (3 vols., 1931–1933); *Hai ti meng* (1932); *Li-na* (1934); *Ch'i yüan* (1945); *P. C. wen-chi* (14 vols., 1959–1962)

BIBLIOGRAPHY: Chen, T., "P. C. the Novelist," *Chinese Literature*, No. 6 (1963): 84–92; Lang, O., *P. C. and His Writings* (1967); Hsia, C. T., *A History of Modern Chinese Fiction* (1971): 237–56: 375–88; Mao, N. K., "P. C.'s Journey in Sentiment: From Hope to Despair," *JCLTA*, 11 (1976): 131–37; Mao, N. K., *P. C.* (1978)

—WINSTON YANG

PACHECO, José Emilio

Mexican poet, novelist, short-story writer, translator, essayist, and literary critic, b. 30 June 1939, Mexico City

P. is one of Mexico's most prolific and talented contemporary writers. He began publishing creative works in 1955 at the age of seventeen and has continued, unabated, producing literary works and literary criticism. P. has traveled widely, and he has taught and lectured throughout North America and Europe. In 1985 he was inducted into the Colegio de México as that institution's youngest member.

P. is viewed by critics as a premier poet. His poetry is found in nine collections, the first of which is *Los elementos de la noche* (1963; elements of the night). It contains poems written from 1958 to 1963 and is notable for its maturity, complex treatments of external reality, interplay of time planes, introspective musing, and solitude. *Los elementos de la noche* included various of P.'s "approximaciones," translations into Spanish of English and French poets, thus establishing P. as a literary translator, a vocation in which he has excelled. His second collection, entitled *El resposo del fuego* (1966; the resting fire), is in large part a continuation of the themes and preoccupations found in *Los elementos de la noche*. Dedicated to P.'s friend Mario VARGAS LLOSA, *El reposo del fuego* is divided into three cantos and focuses on nature and mortality, centering on the primary images of fire, wind, and water to inform a striking poetic reality.

In 1969, P. won the prestigious National Poetry Prize for his *No me preguntes cómo pasa el tiempo* (1969; don't ask me how the time flies). With this collection P.'s poetry enters a new cycle. Poetry itself becomes an object of examination—poetic language, poetic truth, poetic reality. Irony, coupled with a critical and existential worldview, becomes an organizing principle. This new cycle is extended and intensified with *Irás y no volverás* (1973; you'll go and not return), a collection of verse written from 1967 to 1972. Amidst a kaleidoscopic array of utopic visions, notes of nobility and hope, desperation and disenchantment, P. finds poetic images in an international landscape, treating such diverse places as Illinois, Canada, Montevideo, and Rio de Janeiro.

Islas a la deriva (wr. 1973–1975; islands on course), P.'s fifth collection, appeared in 1976, followed by *Desde entonces* (1980; since then). In 1980 P. also published *Tarde o temprano* (sooner or later). This collection brought together the poems of all the previous collections into one volume.

Los trabajos de mar (1983; labours of the sea) represents a compilation of fifty-two poems that treat a large variety of topics. P.'s penchant for writing poems to and about other poets and artists is evident. There are numerous works treating Greek antiquity. More recently, P. has published the collections, *Miro la tierra* (1986; I look at the earth) and *Ciudad de la memoria* (1989; city of memories). These combined works contain most of P.'s poetry written during the 1980s, treating history and the human condition.

In addition to his poetry, P. is widely respected for his prose, particularly his short stories, which, according to P., are a "complement" to his poetry. He has published four major collections, several of which have grown in the number of stories they include with subsequent editions. His first collection, *La sangre de Medusa* (1958; blood of Medusa), was republished and greatly expanded in 1990. The later publication contains stories written from 1956 to 1984. It is a retrospective of works written mostly in youth and subsequently retouched and revived by a more mature author. *El viento distante* (1963; rev. ed., 1969; the distant wind) contains eight stories; these narratives, all of which have children or adolescents as protagonists, served to establish P. as a major short-story writer. His subsequent collection. *El principio del placer* (1972; the pleasure principle), not only furthered this reputation, but it earned P. the prestigious Xavier Villaurrutia Prize in 1973. Critics tend to divide P.'s short narratives into two thematic fields: youth (its problems, viewpoints and evolution) and the fantastic. Within those themes is the preoccupation with time—its passage, past in the present, and temporal play.

P.'s two novels also merit comment. His first, *Morirás lejos* (1967; you will die far from here), won the Magda Donato Prize in 1968. It is a complicated work, which intertwines a variety of texts and has the central theme of the historical persecution and annihilation of Jews. *Las Batallas en el desierto* (1981; desert battles) is a short but incisive treatment of Mexico City in the late 1940s. Based on P.'s penchant for nostalgia, the author tries to come to terms with his personal past and the new Mexico City.

Aside from P.'s stature as a poet and prose writer, he has produced a large body of other works, including screenplays for movies and television. In collaboration with Arturo Ripstein (dates n.a.), he wrote *El castillo de la pureza* (1972; the castle of purity), which won the Ariel Prize. He won the Silver Goddess Award for *El santo oficio* (1974; the holy office), also written with Ripstein. In addition, P. is a literary translator of considerable stature, having translated into Spanish such authors as BECKETT, PINTER, PIRANDELLO, Tennessee WILLIAMS, Rimbaud, and many others. P. has also been responsible for a large number of literary anthologies, special editions, prologues, essays, and articles on literary topics. He has contributed (beginning in 1957) to numerous journals and newspaper literary supplements such as *Estaciones, México en la Culture, Revista de la Universidad de México, La Cultura en México, Excélsior, Plural, Vuelta,* and *Proceso*. For this work he won the National Prize for Journalism in 1980.

P. is a major figure in Mexican letters. As a scholar, literary critic, and creative writer, P. is a principal personage in contemporary Latin American literature. His literary output has been astonishing both in terms of quantity and quality.

FURTHER WORKS: *Giménez Botey* (1964); *Al margen* (1976); *Ayer es nunca jamás* (1978); *Jardín de niños* (1978); *Breve antología* (1980); *Prosa de la calvera* (1981); *Fin de sigle y otros poemas* (1984); *Alta traición: antología poética* (1985)

BIBLIOGRAPHY: Campos, M. A., "J. E. P. o la palabra que se va," *El Rehilete*, 3a, 34 (1971): 57–61; Hoeksema, T., "J. E. P. Signals from the Flames," *LALR*, 3, 5 (1974): 143–56; Díez, L. A., "La narrativa fantasmática de J. E. P.," *TCrit*, 2, 5 (1976): 103–14; Gullón, A. M., "Dreams and Distance in Recent Poetry by J. E. P.," *LALR*, 6, 11, (1977): 36–42; Duncan, J. A., "The Themes of Isolation and Persecution in J. E. P.'s Short Stories," *Ibero-Amerikanisches Archiv*, 4, 3 (1978): 243–51; Báez, et al., Y. Jiménez de, *Ficción e historia: La narrativa de J. E. P.* (1979); Duncan, J. A., "The Novel As Poem and Document: J. E. P.'s *Morirás lejos,*" *Ibero-Amerikanisches Archiv*, 6, 4 (1980): 277–92; Cluff, R. M., "Immutable Humanity within the Hands of Time: Two Short Stories by J. E. P.," *LALR*, 10, 20 (Spring–Summer 1982): 41–56; García Rey, J. M., "La poesía de J. E. P. o las palabras que dicta el tiempo," *CHA*, 380 (1982): 472–84; Villena, de, L. A., *J. E. P.* (1986); Verani, H. J., *J. E. P. ante la crítica* (1987)

—SAM L. SLICK

PACIFIC ISLANDS LITERATURE

The literature of the Pacific Islands comprises fiction, poetry, and drama produced by the island populations of the Pacific Ocean, from Guam in the north to New Zealand in the south, Papua New Guinea in the west to French Polynesia and Rapanui/Easter Island in the east. Australian Aboriginal and Maori literatures are major bodies of written work but can be discussed more productively in relation to their respective national settings. While there are significant cultural and historical differences across the rest of the island groups, their modern literature has been produced under broadly similar conditions of colonialism and tends to reveal similar patterns of adapting oral narrative to print texts, asserting a local identity against Western influences, and exploring ways of being that combine cultural tradition with modern society.

To a large extent indigenous vernacular cultural expression continues to be oral and performative, but there is some literary writing in Fijian, Samoan, Tongan, Kanak, Maohi, Hawaiian, and Chamorro as well as in other smaller language groups (well over 1,000 across the whole region). However, the economics of publishing and forces of history favor writing in the more widespread colonial languages of French and English, particularly the latter. For various reasons (origins in British-sourced education and publishing systems, and in university departments of English literature) Pacific literature as an area of formal study has been constructed mainly around the Anglophone southwest of Oceania—predominantly represented by the journal *Mana* and Albert WENDT's two anthologies, *Lali* (1980) and *Nuanua* (1995). However, there is significant work in English in Hawaii and a growing output in recent times from Micronesia.

Until recent times, though, the writing of Western travelers and sojourners about the islands of Oceania was taken to be the literature of the Pacific: adventures at sea, such as Charles Bernard Nordhoff (1887-1947) and James N. Hall's (1887-1951) *The Hurricane* (1936) or their trilogy of the *Bounty* mutiny (1932-34); yarns of traders dealing with mad, drunk, or vicious whites and unpredictable and violent islanders, such as Robert Louis Stevenson's (1850-1894) *Island Nights Entertainment* (1893), Louis Becke's (1855-1913) *By Reef and Palm* (1894), Jack LONDON's *South Sea Tales* (1911), and Somerset MAUGHAM's *The Trembling of a Leaf* (1921); romances of idyllic tropical beaches and lubricious maidens, such as Pierre Loti's (1850-1923) *Le Mariage de Loti* (1882; The Marriage of Loti) and Charles Warren Stoddard's (1843-1909) *South Sea Idylls* (1873); novels in which the Pacific became a space for moralizing on Western society, notably Herman Melville's *Typee* (1846). James Michener (1907-1997) combined these traditions with a new subgenre of Pacific war stories in *Tales of the South Pacific* (1948) and produced the blockbuster historical romance *Hawaii* (1959), both influential because of their film treatments. Willard Price (dates n.a.), the author of *Adventures in Paradise* (1956), was perhaps the most popular producer of the many Pacific travelogues, and there were, as well, all the more solemn works of scientific study, missionary triumphalism, and memoirs of colonial officers.

Under this print coverage, indigenous cultures of oral and performance literature took a secondary place in the eyes of the outside world. It was material for ethnographic work and antiquarian interest. There is, of course, a vast literature of creation chants, myths, genealogical records, praise songs and laments for celebrated leaders, and celebrations of battles going back to the first migrations across the Pacific basin several millennia ago.

Writing by Pacific Islanders came as a result of contact with European voyagers and was connected with trade, administration, and missionary conversions. Islanders began writing letters to each other as they started to move about more widely and frequently and participate in modern commerce. In Micronesia, colonized by the Spanish, the Roman Catholic Church was the major agent for spreading literacy but it tended to exclude natives from access to European learning. Protestant missions stressed Bible reading and spread literacy more energetically. These entered Tahiti and the South Pacific from the mid-18th c. A printing press was set up in Papeete in 1817 and used to produce the King's statutes as well as scriptures and hymnbooks. King Pomare is credited with the first letter from an Islander in 1801, setting up a trade in pork with Governor King of the new colony in New South Wales. Micronesia underwent a similar modernization after the Spanish-American War in 1898. By then, Polynesians in the South were already working as catechists and preachers in Melanesia and writing reports home. Much of this writing was in local languages (including newspapers in Hawaiian in the 1800s) and some of these early works have been collected, notably in *The Works of Ta'unga* (1968) and *Maretu, Cannibals and Converts* (1983). The letters to emigrant workers in New Zealand from a Niue family in John Pule's [dates n.a.] novel, *The Shark That Ate the Sun* (1992), represent a modern offspring of this tradition.

One unique instance of writing arising from displacement is the Hindi literature of Indian caneworkers indentured to work in Fiji between 1897 and 1916. Totaram Sanadhya's (dates n.a.) *Fiji dwip men mere ikkis varsh* (1919; My Twenty-one Years in the Fiji Islands) is a celebrated exposé of the hardships of laboring life. Other writers continued traditions of poetry with an eye on Indian publication, while some explored the "girmit" experience in language that became progressively more localized. J. S. Kanwal (dates n.a.) has achieved some standing in both India and Fiji as a contemporary fiction writer in Hindi with published translations in English. Short stories in English by Subramani (b. 1943), *The Fantasy Eaters* (1988), and Raymond Pillai (b. 1942), *The Celebration* (1980), and poetry by Satendra Nandan, *Voices in the River* (1985), and Sudesh Mishra (dates n.a.), *Rahu* (1987) and *Tandava* (1992), provide more local and contemporary views of Indo-Fijian life. Indigenous Fijan writing is represented in English by Jo Nacola's (dates n.a.) *I, Native No More* (1976), Pio Manoa's (b. 1940) poems, and stories by Joseph Veramo and Vanessa Griffen as well as the plays of Larry Thomas (dates n.a.), which arise from the urban mixed-race population.

At different phases across the region, early writing by indigenes concerned itself with transcribing chants, myths and legends, usually under colonial "sponsorship." David Malo's *Moolelo Hawaii* (1898; Hawaiian Antiquities) or the collections supervised by Governor Grey in New Zealand, *Polynesian Mythology* (1855), are examples, but the process continues into preparation of school readers or publications such as Ten Tiroba's (dates n.a.) *Traditional Stories from the Northern Gilberts* (1989). Much written literature had its beginnings in adapting village oral tales and legends to the demands of new literary forms. Papua New Guinean Arthur Jawodimbari's (dates n.a.) play *The Sun* (1970) is one example, and Samoan Albert Wendt attributes his fiction to his grandmother's traditional skills as a storyteller.

The first genuinely print-literary publications in English by Pacific Islanders eventually appeared in the 1948 travelogue of Cook Islander Florence ("Johnny") Fdsbie (dates n.a.) entitled *Miss Ulysses of Puka Puka*, the 1960s poems of Alan Natachee (dates n.a.) from Papua New Guinea, and the novel by Tom and Lydia Davis (dates n.a.), *Makatu* (1960). These were isolated creations until colonial governments, spurred on by the United Nations after World War II, developed schooling and began training a generation of islanders for the professions and government service. In the educational hubs of Suva and Port Moresby (and Honolulu, though the dynamics were different), a 1960s generation being groomed for eventual national leadership with examples from Africa and the civil rights movement began to grapple with the task of expressing cultural identity in modern terms. Writing reflected a decolonizing political consciousness and found voice as radical rage against discrimination and cultural assimilation or as a sense of alienation borrowing the language of French EXISTENTIALISM—poems the "The Bush Kanaka Speaks" by Kumalau Tawali (b. 1946) and "Reluctant Flame" by John Kasaipwalova (b. 1949), both from Papua New Guinea, and Albert Leomala's bilingual bislama-English poems from Vanuatu exemplify the former, while Papua New Guinean Russell Soaba's (dates n.a.) novel *Wanpis* (1977), Subramani's stories, and Albert Wendt's fiction, notably *Sons for the Return Home* (1973) and *Leaves of the Banyan Tree* (1979), display the latter tendency. Much of the early literary production was inspired by the need to correct the images of the Pacific projected by outsiders and to repossess the imaginative space of print culture for local readers and writers.

The 1970s was the decade in which Pacific Island literature achieved international notice and the kind of "critical mass" that enabled courses to be set up. Major works like Albert Maori Kiki's autobiography *Kiki: Ten Thousand Years in a Lifetime* (1968), Papua New Guinean Vincent Eri's (dates n.a.) novel *The Crocodile* (1970), Subramani's short stories, Albert Wendt's *Sons for the Return Home* and his poem sequence *Inside us the Dead* (1976) all date from this period. Aboriginal activism also took a literary turn during this time as well, notably with the publication of first collections from Maori writers Witi lhimaera (b. 1944) and Patricia GRACE. The primary theme is identity—asserting a local viable culture, locating the place of the writer in the emerging national collective, as well as finding a style and function for English other than its official government or mission usages and consistent with an indigenous voice.

After independence (or arrival at some degree of visibility within the state, as with Maori issues or "local" writing in Hawaii), the trend has been away from anticolonial protest towards critiques of globalization and continued economic and cultural dependency, while the tensions and crossings between tradition and modernity have continued as a key theme. Tongan Epeli Hau'ofa's (dates n.a.) satiric fiction *Tales of the Tikongs* (1983) and *Kisses in the Nederends* (1988) are trenchant examples. More recently, work has emerged by and focused on migrant groups in Pacific metropoles and women championing cultural identity while questioning the traditional male bias, as illustrated in the feminist poetry of Konai Helu Thaman, Samoan Momoe von Reiche, and Vanuatu writer Grace Mera Molisa (dates n.a.). There has also been a revival of vernacular language in some parts of the Pacific that has resulted in parallel text works such as Tongan writer Pesi Fonua's *Sun and Rain* (1983) and Cook Islander Kauraka Kauraka's (dates n.a.) *Dreams of a Rainbow* (1987). New Zealand resident Alistair Campbell (dates n.a.) has also rediscovered his family origins in the Cook Islands, producing a trilogy of comic fantasy novels, *The Frigate Bird* (1989), *Sidewinder* (1991), and *Tia* (1993).

Drama is one form in which tradition and modernity can interact with little loss of audience contact. Radio plays in Papua New Guinea have been popular (nationalized Australian John Kolia [dates n.a.] being a prolific contributor of scripts), with itinerant companies such as Raun Raun Theater taking performances to villages. Key figures have been Kama Kerpi, John Kasaipwalova, Nora Vagi, and William Takaku (dates n.a.). Albert Toro (dates n.a.) scripted and acted in a feature film *Tukane* (1984), which is a problem play dealing with "drop-out" youth that anticipates the Bougainville crisis of recent years. Wan Smol Bag Theater in Vanuatu uses its plays to educate villagers in health and welfare issues. More stage-based productions have come from Fiji, notably plays by Vilsoni Hereniko and Teresa Teaiwa (dates n.a.), and the Kumu Kahua group in Honolulu.

A historical model of literary development is perforce a flexible one, since Samoa gained political independence in the 1960s before the main period of anticolonial expression, and Micronesia, only recently attaining political self-determination, has been producing "national pride" poems typical of the 1970s elsewhere. In the French Pacific continued colonialism both suppresses indigenous expression and leads to collections with a protest voice characteristic of early Papua New Guinean or Vanuatu work. New Caledonia has a body of poems and stories by settler writers, Jean Mariotti (publishing between 1929 to 1969) being perhaps the most celebrated, but in recent years Kanak works have emerged, notably from Jean-Marie Tjibaou and Déwé Gorodé (dates n.a.). In Tahiti, Henri Hiro and Charles Teri'iteanuanua Manutahi (dates n.a.) have published collections of verse. Particular circumstances such as the Free Papua movement in West Irian and tile coups in Fiji have attracted writers' attention in recent years. Likewise, Satendra Nandan's (b. 1939) autobiographical novel *The Wounded Sea* (1991) depicts the overthrow of the Bavadra parliament.

Writing is closely tied to formal education and English and French to official registers of government language, and in societies of often very low annual income, reading for pleasure is not a strongly developed culture. As a result, writers have tended to produce works during school or university years, gaining a reputation through editor-promoters such as Ulli Beier at the University of Papua New Guinea with such editions as *Black Writing from New Guinea* (1973) and *Voices of Independence* (1980) and Marjorie Crocombe in Suva/Rarotonga with the journal *Mana* and *Te Rau Maire: Poems and Stories of the Pacific* (1992). Even so, works have as a rule appeared in small magazines or in small print runs that quickly cease to be in print. Those writers who have become leading figures are generally ones who have academic careers with access to wider publishing networks. The Institute of Pacific Studies in Suva, leading publishers in New Zealand, and the University of Hawaii Press are the key sites of literary promotion for pan-Pacific writing. A critical challenge in dealing with many Pacific Island texts is to attend to the specific conditions of literary production in order to avoid patronizing assessments of a "young" literature based on an external model of "maturity." Led by Subramani, Albert Wendt, and Vilsoni Hereniko, there is an emerging quest for critical standards drawing on indigenous aesthetic traditions.

BIBLIOGRAPHY: Beier, U., ed., *Black Writing from New Guinea* (1973); Beier, U., ed., *Voices of Independence* (1980); Ihimaera, W., and D. Long, eds., *Into the World of Light* (1980); Westlake, W., and R. Hamasaki, eds., *A Pacific Islands Collection* (1984); Williams, E. W., ed., *Lisitala: A Bibliography of Pacific Writers* (1984); Simms, N., *Silence and Invisibility* (1986); Subramani, *South Pacific Literature: From Myth to Fabulation* (1985); Powell, G., ed., *Through Melanesian Eyes* (1987); Sumida, S. H., *And the View from the Shore: Literary Traditions of Hawaii* (1991);

Crocombe, M., et al., eds., *Te Rau Maire: Poems and Stories of the Pacific* (1992); Waddell, E., et al., eds., *A New Oceania: Rediscovering Our Sea of Islands* (1993); Wendt, A, ed., *Nuanua* (1995); Goetzfriedt, N. J., ed., *Indigenous Literatures of Oceania: A Survey of Criticism and Interpretation* (1995)

—PAUL SHARRAD

PADILLA, Heberto

Cuban poet, novelist, and journalist, b. 20 Jan. 1932, Puerta de Golpe, Pinar del Río

P. is one of the most controversial literary figures of the Cuban revolution. Born in the province of Pinar del Río, P. has spent a great deal of time outside of Cuba. He lived in the U.S. off and on from 1949 to 1959. After the triumph of the revolution he returned to Cuba and worked for the news agency Prensa Latina. He also collaborated with Guillermo CABRERA INFANTE on *Lunes de Revolución*, the literary supplement of the newspaper *Revolución*. He later worked as a Prensa Latina correspondent in London (1960–1961) and in Moscow (1962–1963), and directed Cubartimex (a division of the ministry of foreign commerce in charge of culture), a position which took him to eastern Europe (1964–1966). The events known as the "Padilla Affair" began in 1968 when P. won the Julián del Casal Poetry Prize from the Cuban Writers and Artists Union for his collection *Fuera del juego* (1968; out of the game). Although the judges of the contest were respected authors, all of whom were in agreement on the awarding of the prize, the book drew severe criticism on account of its supposedly antirevolutionary content. The Cuban Writers and Artists Union published the book, but with a disclaimer expressing disagreement with its ideology. P. was allowed to work as a lecturer on literature at the University of Havana from 1969 to 1970, but in 1971 he was jailed for over a month after giving a poetry reading from his new collection, *Provocaciones* (1973; provocations). After his release he read a lengthy "autocriticism" at the Cuban Writers and Artists Union, chastising himself and many other contemporary Cuban writers—including his wife, the poet Belkis Cuza Malé (b. 1942)—for their critical attitudes. After a stint as a laborer on a governmental agricultural project, P. was allowed to return to Havana, but was only able to work as a translator from 1971 to 1980, when he was given permission to emigrate to the U.S.

P. belongs to a group of poets born between 1925 and 1940 who began to publish important works during the 1960s and who initially identified with the Cuban revolution. P.'s enthusiasm for the revolution is evident in his second book of poetry, *El justo tiempo humano* (1962; just, human time). In contrast to the poetry of the *Orígenes* group which dominated the Cuban literary scene from the the mid-1940s through 1959 and which was known for its erudition and obscurity, the poems of this volume are simple in diction and relatively straightforward in their political endorsements.

When P. was arrested in 1971 he had completed a large portion of his first novel, *En mi jardín pastan los héroes* (1981; *Heroes Are Grazing in My Garden*, 1984). This novel received mixed reviews. His most recent repose work is a volume of memoirs, *Autoretrato del otro: La mala memoria* (1988; *Self-Portrait of the Other*, 1990), covering his life from the early 1950s to his departure from Cuba.

The prose is direct and engaging, and avoids the self-indulgence of the author's first novel.

P. is a fine poet and a lesser novelist. His poetry is complex and allusive, yet largely rooted in colloquial diction. A singular contribution, however, has been his very public life, which drew attention to the excessive restrictions that revolutionary Cuba placed on artistic expression in the 1960s and 1970s.

FURTHER WORKS: *Las rosas audaces* (1948); *La hora* (1964); *El hombre junto al mar* (1981). FURTHER WORKS IN ENGLISH: *Sent Off the Field: A Selection from the Poetry of H. P.* (1972); *Poetry and Politics: Selected Poems of H. P.* (1972); *Legacies: Selected Poems* (1982); *A Fountain, a House of Stone* (1991)

BIBLIOGRAPHY: Casal, L., *El caso P.: Literatura y revolución en Cuba* (n.d.); Macklin, E., "Paperweight," *Parnassus*, 10, 1 (Spring–Summer 1982): 125–39; Cohen, J. M., "Prophet," *NYRB* (30 June 1983): 32–35; Sucre, G., *La máscara, la transparencia: Ensayos sobre poesía hispanoamericana* (1985): 278–80; Zapata, M. A., "Entre la épica y la lírica de H. P.," *Inti*: 26–27 (Fall–Spring 1987–1988): 273–84

—BEN A. HELLER

PAGNOL, Marcel

French dramatist and filmmaker, b. 28 Feb. 1895, Aubagne; d. 18 April 1974, Paris

P. studied at the University of Aix-en-Provence, where in 1913 he helped found a student literary magazine, *Fantasio*. Later, as *Les cahiers du sud*, it was to become one of the most influential literary magazines of the century. From 1915 to 1927 P. taught English at various secondary schools; from then on he devoted himself wholly to writing plays, making films, and editing *Cahiers du cinéma*. In 1946 he became the first filmmaker to be elected to the French Academy.

Topaze (perf. 1928, pub. 1931; *Topaze*, 1958) was P.'s first great success. In this play he traces the metamorphosis of an obscure schoolteacher into a wily businessman. The principal themes are the lies of politicians, the venality of newspapers, the moral decline of an era in which money has become the key to success.

P.'s name is especially associated with a trilogy: the stage plays *Marius* (perf. 1929, pub. 1931; Marius) and *Fanny* (perf. 1931, pub. 1932; Fanny), also made into films; and the third, written directly for the screen, *César* (1936, pub. 1937; César). The setting of this cycle is the Vieux Port (old port) of Marseille; P. skillfully portrays its noisy, indolent life under the strong sunlight. He writes with affection about the people of Provence, their tenderness and their bravado, their dreams and their fears. The ebullient dialogue of *Marius* and *Fanny* in particular illustrates the temperament typical of the south of France—a sentimentality that easily becomes moralistic. (An American musical adaptation of the entire cycle was produced as *Fanny* in 1955.)

In his autobiography, *Souvenirs d'enfance* (4 vols., 1957–77; memories of childhood), P. describes with simplicity and charm his early years in Marseille and in the hills above the city. The first volume, *La gloire de mon père* (1957; *My Father's Glory*) is in praise of P.'s father, who was a schoolteacher. In the second volume, *Le château de ma mère* (1959; *My Mother's Castle*)—this and the first volume were published together in English as *The Days Were Too Short* (1960)—and in the third volume, *Le temps des secrets* (1960; *The Time of Secrets*, 1962), P. writes about his school years and summer vacations. The final volume, *Le temps des amours* (1977; the time of loves), incomplete and published posthumously, deals with P.'s adolescent loves.

P. will probably be better remembered as a filmmaker than as a playwright. His first two films, *Marius* (1931) and *Fanny* (1932), were actually directed by Alexander Korda and Marc Allégret respectively, but P. himself, as writer and producer, took such an active part in the coaching of the actors that subsequently he took over the full responsibility of directing *Topaze* (1932) and *César* (1936).

Besides the successful direction of movies based on his own plays, P.'s outstanding achievements are films based on texts by two other Provence writers. From Jean GIONO's novels P. made three films: *Angèle* (1934; Angèle), after *Un de Baumugnes; Regain* (1937; harvest); and *La femme du boulanger* (1938; the baker's wife). From Alphonse Daudet's (1840–1897) *Lettres de mon moulin* (letters from my windmill), P. chose three episodes for a film (1954), the screenplay of which was published in *Trois lettres de mon moulin* (1954; three letters from my windmill).

The aesthetics of P.'s films is similar to that of his plays. In both genres he is primarily concerned with a poetic or picturesque interpretation of what is real, and not with dramatic or cinematic experimentation. In both media he uses the natural settings of the city, the harbor, and the countryside as a background for the garrulous southerner, successfully conveying this character's petulance, gaiety, and optimism.

FURTHER WORKS: *Catulle* (1922); *Tonton* (1924); *Les marchands de gloire* (1924); *Ulysse chez les Phéniciens* (1925); *Un direct au cœur* (1926); *Jazz* (1926); *Pirouettes* (1932); *Merlusse* (1935); *Cigalon* (1936); *Le Schpountz* (1938); *Le premier amour* (1946); *Notes sur le rire* (1947); *Critique des critiques* (1949); *Manon des sources* (1953); *Œuvres dramatiques* (2 vols., 1954); *Judas* (1955); *Fabien* (1956); *L'eau des collines* (2 vols., 1963); *Le masque de fer* (1964); *Œuvres complètes* (6 vols., 1964–1973); *Le secret du masque de fer* (1973)

BIBLIOGRAPHY: Combaluzier, I., *Le jardin de P.* (1937); special P. issue, *Biblio*, 32, 3 (1964); Beylie, C., *M. P.* (1974); Berni, G., *M. P., enfant d'Aubagne et de la Treille* (1975); Caldicott, C. E. J., *M. P.* (1977); Castans, R., *Il était une fois M. P.* (1978)

—CHARLES G. HILL

throughout the 1960s, the high-modernist paradigm dominated and inspired the Taiwan Chinese literary production.

P.'s consistently brilliant short stories, collected in *Taipei jen* (1971; *Wandering in the Garden, Waking from a Dream: Tales of Taipei Characters*, 1982) and *Chi-mo ti shih-ch'i sui* (1976; lonely seventeen), are marked by a stylistic opulence that reminds critics of the canonized traditional 18th-c. narrative *Dream of the Red Chamber* by Ts'ao Hsüech'in (1715–1763); they skillfully employ Western fictional devices such as interior monologue, free association, and mediated narration to create psychologically rich portraitures. But unlike some of his contemporaries, P. always manages to avoid the derivative excesses often found in the overzealous imitations of the 1960s. Nearly all of P.'s stories focus on two character groups: the mainlanders who migrated with the Nationalists to Taiwan (the *Tai pei jen*, or Taipei people) and those who exiled themselves to the U.S. (the *Niu-yüeh k'e*, or New York guests). The link between the two groups is their general disenchantment with life in domestic or foreign exile and their shared nostalgia for past glories real and imagined. This psychological obsession and dependence not only paralyzes them, but also disables them from adjusting to new realities. Dramatizing such pathos and melancholy are two themes that should be familiar to readers of *Dream of the Red Chamber*, a favorite of P. himself: the ravages of time and the transience of human affairs.

A totally different group of characters emerges in P.'s first novel *Nieh-tzu* (1983; *Crystal Boys*, 1990); young gay men living in the demimonde of illicit sex and rendezvous. Besides portraying for the first time in modern Chinese fiction the young gays' incessant and arduous quests for emotional fulfillment, the novel also presents vividly the oppressive power of the Chinese partriarchy and its torturous effects on its sons. This compelling novel, as well as four memorable stories on the travails of Chinese womanhood, have been adapted into films, though predictably with uneven results. Long admired by readers in Taiwan, Hong Kong, and the overseas Chinese communities, P.'s works are now also known in mainland China.

FURTHER WORKS: *Mo-jan hui shou* (1978); *Yuyüan ching-meng* (1982); *Ming-hsing k'a-fei kwan* (1984)

BIBLIOGRAPHY: Lau, J., "Crowded Hours Revisited: The Evocation of the Past in *Yaipei jen*," *JASt*, 34, 1 (1975): 31–47; Ouyang Tzu, "The Fictional World of P," *Renditions*, 5 (1975): 79–86; Lau, J., "Celestials and Commoners: Exiles in P.'s Stories," *Monumenta Serica*, 36 (1984–1985): 409–23

—WILLIAM TAY

PAI Hsien-yung

(also romanized as Bai Xianyong) Chinese short-story writer, novelist, essayist, and screenwriter, b. 11 July 1937, Kweilin

The son of a famous general of the Anti-Japanese Resistance War (1937–1945), P. migrated to Taiwan with his father after the 1949 communist takeover of mainland China. In 1960 P. founded with a group of young writers a small magazine, *Hsien-tai wen-hsüeh*, which played an instrumental role in introducing Western MODERNISM to the Taiwan Chinese literary elites. Consequently,

PAK Tu-jin

South Korean poet, essayist, and critic, b. 10 March 1916, Ansŏng

After graduating from a local high school, P. worked as a company employee. He made his literary debut in 1939 with a group of nature poems. Between 1941 and 1945, in response to Japanese repression and the prohibition of the use of the Korean language, he refused to write anything. In 1949 P. published his first poetry collection, *Hae* (the sun). In addition to eleven volumes of poetry, he has written essays and literary criticism, including interpretations of his own poems. P. is currently a professor of Korean literature at Yonsei University in Seoul. He is also an accomplished calligrapher. His many awards include the Free Literature Prize (1956), the Culture Prize of the City of Seoul (1962), the March First Literature Prize (1970), and the Korean Academy of Arts Prize (1976).

P. is credited with having imparted a new direction to modern Korean poetry through skillful use of such elemental images as mountains, rivers, stars, the sun, the sea, and the sky. He inspires hope for a new life, a prelapsarian cosmos of perfect harmony. During the Japanese occupation (1910–45), such a world symbolized not only moral perfection of men but also independence and freedom for Korea and the Koreans. But to P., nature has always been "the source of God's love, light, truth, goodness, and beauty," and his paeans to the beauty of the created world and his Blakean innocence became imbued with a moral vision as he came to view the world in terms of moral conflict. As political corruption and repression increased in South Korea, P.'s moral consciousness came to the fore, and his poems from the mid-1960s on are imbued with a strong historical and cultural consciousness that bears testimony to contemporary reality.

P. is capable of a wide range of moods—angry accusation, fierce honesty, visionary serenity—and his language and style impart a distinctive tone to his Christian and nationalistic sentiments. Sonoric intricacies and incantatory rhythms, achieved by sporadic repetition of key words, are the hallmark of P.'s poetry. Of late, he has withdrawn into nature to perceive its creative power in water-washed stones, the topic of some two hundred of his poems. An authentic inheritor of the East Asian eremitic tradition, P. has consistently rejected the false allegiances demanded by a corrupt society.

FURTHER WORKS: *Ch'ŏgnok chip* (1946, with Pak Mogwŏl and Cho Chihun); *Odo* (1953); *P.T. sisŏn* (1956); *Ingan millim* (1963); *Kosan singmul* (1973); *Sado haengjŏn* (1973); *Susŏk yŏlchŏn* (1973); *Sok susŏk yŏlchŏn* (1976). FURTHER WORKS IN ENGLISH: *Sea of Tomorrow: Forty Poems of P. T.* (1971)

BIBLIOGRAPHY: Lee, P. H., ed., *The Silence of Love: Twentieth Century Korean Poetry* (1980): xviii–xix, 136

—PETER H. LEE

PAKISTANI LITERATURE

The demand of the Muslim League, led by Muhammad Ali Jinnah (1876–1948), for a homeland for South Asian Muslims, led to the partition of British India into India and the Islamic nation of Pakistan in 1947. Although the ideological basis for the existence of Pakistan as a state distinct from India was Islam, Islam alone did not prove sufficient to hold the two wings of Pakistan together, and East Pakistan seceded in 1971 to become the separate nation of Bangladesh. The area that now forms Pakistan has a wide variety of languages and literatures, including English, the classical languages of Arabic and Persian, the official language Urdu, the regional languages Sindhi, Punjabi, Balochi, and Pashto, and more localized languages like Brahui, Shina, Balti, and others. The most developed literature is that written in the national language, Urdu.

Although Urdu is not indigenous to the area that is now Pakistan, and is the mother tongue of only about eight percent of the population, most of them refugees from India at the time of partition and later, it is widely used as a second language and is the major language of literacy. Because each of the major languages of Pakistan is also found in neighboring countries, it is difficult to define what is specifically Pakistani about Pakistani culture and literature.

Since the creation of Pakistan in 1947, writers have been concerned with the question of Pakistani national identity and "Pakistani literature." Some, like the critic Vazir Agha (b. 1922), seek the identity of Pakistan and Pakistani literature in a synthesis of the material element of local cultures—including ancient pre-Islamic cultures—and the spiritual element of Islam. Other critics, like Jameel Jalebi (dates n.a.), go beyond the geographical limits of present-day Pakistan and see Pakistani culture as a continuation of the specifically Muslim culture that developed in the south-Asian subcontinent over the last thousand years. Some agree with Muhammad Hasan Askari (?–1974) that "Pakistani literature" should be "Islamic literature"; almost all agree that it should not be Westernized.

In English

English retains its prestige as a language of government, politics, science, and industry, but it is seldom used for creative writing. Among the very few authors writing in English are the novelist Zulfikar Ghose (b. 1935), who lives in Texas, the poetess Maki Kureishy (1924–1995), and the poets Kaleem Omar (dates n.a.) and Taufiq Rafat (dates n.a.). Rafat is noted for his use of themes derived from Pakistani culture, such as the Muslim rite of circumcision and the bride's departure from her parental home. The two novels of Ahmed ALI, *Twilight in Delhi* (1940) and *Ocean of Night* (1964), both set in British India before partition, have been widely acclaimed. *Twilight in Delhi* depicts the decline of the traditional Muslim culture of old Delhi and the growth of the nationalist movement; *Ocean of Night* describes the life of a courtesan in Lucknow. In comparison with his English works, Ahmed Ali's stories written in Urdu are more innovative in both subject and technique.

In Urdu

In the late 19th c. the poet Khwaja Altaf Husain Hali (1837–1914) protested against the cultivation of artificial diction, fixed and stereotyped themes, and borrowed imagery in classical Urdu. He felt that poetry should be natural, and should be used as a tool for reform. Among both Hindus and Muslims British influence had resulted first in an admiration for Western culture and a desire to emulate it in reforming their own cultures, and then in a reaction against the materialism of the West. Hali's revivalism coincided with the growing pan-Islamism of the Afghan Jamal al-din al-Afghani (1839–1897), who sought to unite all Islamic countries against their common enemy, the West.

Urdu prose developed during the 19th c. with the publication of a number of popular novels. Mirza Ruswa (1858–1931) is best known for his novel *Umrao Jan Ada* (1899; Umrao Jan Ada), the tale of a courtesan of Lucknow that is unusual for its considerable psychological realism.

Pan-Islamism continued in the works of Sir Muhammad IQBAL, who, however, wrote most of his poetry in Persian rather than Urdu in order to reach the Muslim audience outside of south Asia. Influenced by Henri BERGSON and Nietzsche, Iqbal preached action rather than inertia, and self-consciousness rather than the denial of self characteristic of Islamic mysticism.

The emphasis on reform became less religious and more social in nature in the Progressive Writers' Movement, which affected all the languages of south Asia and is still an important influence in the regional languages of Pakistan. The Progressives' ideals of social uplift and nationalism are found particularly in the novels and short stories of PREMCHAND. The first direct expression of Progressivism, however, was *Angare* (1932; live coals), a collection of ten stories by four writers, which was widely condemned for its criticism of Islam and its relatively open discussion of sex. It also experimented in form. STREAM-OF-CONSCIOUSNESS technique was used in short stories by Ahmed Ali and Sajjad Zaheer (1905–1973). Its effect was not to reveal the psychology of their characters but to allow the characters to express their resentment of the oppression of women and of the evils resulting from an unequal distribution of wealth. The Progressives' goals were initially broadly defined and its membership included a wide variety of writers, but under the leadership of Sajjad Zaheer the movement gradually became more dogmatic. Authors were expected to write according to the dictates of Soviet SOCIALIST REALISM, and those who did not conform were ostracized and their works censored. By the early 1950s the Progressive Movement had ceased to be an effective literary force.

The two most famous Progressive authors in Pakistan are Ahmad Nadim Qasmi (b. 1916), who writes both poetry and short stories, and the poet Faiz Ahmed FAIZ, winner of the Lenin Prize in 1962. Qasmi writes sociological stories based on village life in the Punjab. Faiz, the most popular poet in Pakistan, uses both free verse and the more traditional poetic forms. Like Iqbal, whom he admires, he reinterprets the imagery of classical Urdu poetry to express his message: the beloved of the *ghazal* becomes the longed-for new social order, the people, the country, or life itself.

In April 1939 a group of writers met at the home of Sayyid Nasir Ahmad Shah (dates n.a.) in Lahore to form the "Meeting of Story Writers." When poets also began to attend the weekly meetings, its name was changed to the "Assembly of the Men of Good Taste." Its purpose was to provide a forum for writers of every ideological bent. The poet Miraji (1913–1950) joined in 1940 and became its guiding spirit.

The first person to use free verse in Urdu was Tasaduq Hussain Khalid (b. 1900) who was inspired by Ezra POUND, D. H. LAWRENCE, and others while he was studying law in England. Free verse was developed and popularized first by Miraji, and later by N. M. Rashed (1910–1975). Miraji was one of the first to use his own symbolism rather than the traditional symbolism derived from Persian. N. M. Rashed's free-verse poems protest alien rule, religious dogmatism, and the breakdown of values.

Several important novels, including *Aisi bulandi, aisi pasti* (1948; *The Shore and the Wave*, 1971), about the upper classes of Hyderabad, were published in the 1940s by Aziz Ahmad (b. 1914), who is also a scholar and a leading authority on Islamic culture in Pakistan and India. In the 1950s the most notable fiction writers in Urdu were Qurrutulain Hyder (b. 1927) and Saadat Hasan Manto (1912–1955). Hyder's stories and novels are considered precursors of the modernist movement in their experiments with the stream-of-consciousness technique and in their subjective depiction of the loneliness and rootlessness of the individual cut off from his or her cultural moorings. Although she has now returned to India and

lives in Bombay, her novel *Ag ka darya* (1959; river of fire) was written while she was living in Karachi. Considered by many to be the best novel in Urdu, it is structurally unified by four main characters who all appear—seemingly reborn—in four historical periods encompassing 2,500 years of south Asian history. The characters identify themselves with the composite culture of India, including Hindu and Buddhist elements; thus the need for Pakistan's existence as a separate Islamic state is called into question.

Although Sadat Hasan Manto is best known for his depiction of tender-hearted prostitutes, he also wrote stories sympathetic to the oppressed members of society in general. The impassioned self-righteousness of his early political stories later gave way to a pessimistic and disillusioned view of political activity, which was described with bitter irony.

In the late 1950s and early 1960s both poets and fiction writers began to use highly metaphorical and symbolic language. This trend toward ambiguous and indirect statement may have been influenced by the declaration of martial law in 1958 and by the subsequent press censorship. In both prose and poetry, form was characterized by innovation, and subject by alienation, disillusionment, and a search for self-identity that was often combined with a questioning of national identity and purpose. The use of free verse popularized by Miraji continued, and the prose poem developed. The poet and theorist Iftikhar Jaleb (b. 1936) insisted on the indivisibility of form and content; tried to stretch the linguistic possibilities of individual words, using them in paradoxical and contradictory contexts; and juxtaposed apparently unrelated fragments of verse by free association. Zafar Iqbal (dates n.a.) has also experimented with coining new words and distorting the meanings of existing words. The poets Salimur Rahman (b. 1936) and Anis Nagi (b. 1939) are influenced by existentialism; Jilani Kamran (dates n.a.) tries to combine EXISTENTIALISM with Islamic mysticism.

The two most important modernist fiction writers are Intizar Husain (b. 1925?) and Anvar Sajjad (b. 1935). Husain's early works express nostalgic regret for the lost cultural traditions of prepartition India. Later stories show the sense of loss and the confused search for identity of the refugees who left India for Pakistan at partition. Sajjad's early concern with the symbolic and surrealistic expression of individual alienation shifted in the mid-1960s to the depiction of social and political oppression, both national and international. His stories of the 1970s often look to a new birth, brought about by previously oppressed characters.

A number of authors began writing modernist fiction in the mid-1960s, including Khalidah Asghar (dates n.a.), Masud Ashar (dates n.a.), Ahmad Hamesh (b. 1940), and Rashid Amjad (b. 1940). Asghar's early stories excel in creating an atmosphere of an unidentified impending doom. After her marriage (she now writes under the name of Khalidah Husain) her stories hint at what happens to a woman's identity in *purdah* (behind the veil). Ashar's early stories express an ambivalent search for self in which the desire to know the self is tempered by a fear of exposure of himself both to himself and to others. There is an outward turn in his stories of the 1970s, in which his search for self-knowledge is coupled with a moral concern for the actions of his countrymen, particularly in East Pakistan (now Bangladesh), and for the future direction of the country. Hamesh's stories are unusual in Urdu literature for their use of scatological references. His largely autobiographical fiction shows poverty in gruesome and bizarre detail.

In the 1970s writers began to combine the innovative literary techniques developed by the modernists in the 1960s with a concern for social problems, political repression, and the status of Third World nations, particularly in their relations with the superpowers.

In Sindhi

After the British conquest of Sind in 1843 Persian was no longer the court language. The British standardized the Sindhi script in 1852. As in Urdu, early Sindhi prose works were of two kinds: romances of adventure and magic, and didactic appeals for social reform. The prolific Mirza Qalich Beg (1853–1929) translated, compiled, or wrote over three hundred fifty works, including *Zeenat* (1890; Zeenat), the first novel in Sindhi, which advocated female education.

Sindhi poetry in the late 19th and early 20th cs. copied its forms and imagery from Persian verse and was frequently didactic. Kishin Chand Tirathdas Khatri (1885–1947), known as "Bewas," enlarged the subjects of poetry, writing about laborers and nationalism during the 1930s. The ranks of Sindhi poets today include traditionalists who continue to use the Persian style, revivalists who are bringing back the classical Sindhi forms and subjects, and those influenced by the reformist trends of the Progressive Movement.

The leading Sindhi poet in Pakistan today is Sheikh Ayaz (b. 1923), who began writing in both Urdu and Sindhi at the age of fifteen. He later switched to Sindhi alone, in protest against Urdu, which he called a symbol of exploitation because it was spoken by the refugees who flooded Karachi after partition, and whose presence was resented by some Sindhis. Ayaz has long been associated with the Progressive Writers' Movement and feels that literature should be in a language easily understood by the common man, and about subjects close to the people. Ayaz, as well as Tanvir Abbasi (dates n.a.) and Niyaz Humayuni (dates n.a.) use imagery drawn from folk legends. In prose as in poetry, the Progressive Movement is still influential, most notably in the works of Jamal Abro (dates n.a.), whose short stories protest injustice and inhumanity toward the poor.

In Punjabi

Following the British conquest of the Punjab in 1849, the second half of the 19th c. saw the growth of a concern for social change, political awareness, and nationalism. The use of literature for social reform was intensified by the Progressive Movement. During this period, however, Punjabi had begun to be considered a sectarian language of the Sikhs, and the center for Progressive literature in Punjabi was Amritsar (now in India). The cultural language of Lahore was Urdu, and Muslim Punjabi speakers frequently wrote in Urdu rather than in Punjabi.

Since partition, Punjabi writers, most of whom write in Urdu as well, have been influenced by the Progressive Movement and by modernism. Ustad Daman (dates n.a.), Joshua Fazal-ud-din (dates n.a.), and Abdul Majid Bhatti (dates n.a.) were early users of social themes in their poetry. Recently the Writers' Guild Adamjee Prize was awarded to Pir Fazal (dates n.a.), who uses the *ghazal* of the classical Persian and Urdu traditions in Punjabi. The influence of modernism is evident in the works of Muhammad Azim Bhatti (dates n.a.), Anam Adib (dates n.a.), and Munir Niyazi (dates n.a.)—also famous for his Urdu poetry—who have produced Punjabi poetry about alienation and fear in the city. The Urdu

modernists' use of symbolism in fiction is also reflected in the symbolic Punjabi novels of Mustansar Husain Tarar (dates n.a.) and Ahsan Batalvi (dates n.a.).

In Balochi

Traditional Balochi literature includes epic war ballads and love lyrics, orally transmitted by hereditary minstrels and reflecting the tribal nomadic life of Balochi society, with its emphasis on hospitality and bravery.

During the period of English influence from 1854 to 1947, Balochi poets turned to Sufism and reformist literature, and adopted literary forms from Persian and the regional languages Sindhi and Siraiki. After 1947 several literary organizations were founded, and a radio program in Balochi was started. The leading Balochi poet today is Gul Khan Nasir (b. 1910). Azah Jamaldini (b. 1919), who edited the short-lived literary journal *Balochi*, is a poet who uses free verse as well as the classical forms. He has been influenced by the Progressive Movement and writes "message" poetry decrying the economic backwardness of the Balochis.

In Pashto

Pashto is spoken in the Northwest Frontier Province of Pakistan, as well as in the east, south, and southwest of Afghanistan, where it is one of the official languages. It is also spoken by smaller numbers in Balochistan and the Punjab. The Yusufzai dialect spoken near Peshawar is considered the standard Pashto literary dialect in Pakistan.

From the 18th c. until the modern era, Pashto authors wrote poetry using Persian forms and images, and some prose historical compositions. Recent Pashto literature in Pakistan has been influenced by the reformist impulse generated by the Progressive Movement. The short stories of Zaitun Banu (dates n.a.) show the conflict between the modernized younger generation and the more traditional older generation in Pathan society. Banu has said that she feels it is her mission to write against the oppression of women.

In Other Languages

A number of the regional languages of Pakistan remained unwritten until the introduction of government-sponsored radio programs in these languages during the last two decades necessitated their use of the Urdu script. Their oral literature consists of folk tales and folk songs. The recently developed written literature of the northern languages is influenced by the relatively more developed Pashto, and by Urdu and Persian. It includes poetry using the Persian *ghazal* form, religious poetry in praise of God and the Prophet, and patriotic songs. None of these languages has a well-developed prose literature.

The regional languages Balti, Shina, Brushuski, and Khowar in the north, and the Dravidian language Brahui in the south have primarily oral literatures. Balti, a language related to Tibetan, is known for its hymns in praise of the Prophet. Shina includes love poetry with a female persona, unlike love poetry in Persian and Arabic. The most famous poet of Shina, Khalifah Rahmat Malang (1879–19??) wrote poems describing his unsuccessful love for the lady Yurmas. Literature in Brahui has existed since the middle of the 18th c., but very little has been written in it until recently. Poetry in Hindko, the form of Punjabi spoken around Peshawar, dates from the 18th c. Most Hindko poets, like those writing in Brushuski and Khowar, write in Urdu, Pashto, and Persian as well, and their literature in their native languages is influenced by the traditions of the more established literatures.

See also Bangladeshi Literature.

BIBLIOGRAPHY: Sadiq, M., *A History of Urdu Literature* (1964); Ajwani, L. H., *History of Sindhi Literature* (1970); special Pakistani issue, *Mahfil*, 7: 1–2 (1971); Kalim, S., *Pakistan: A Cultural Spectrum* (1973); Jalal, H., et al., eds., *Pakistan: Past and Present* (1977): 235–45

—LINDA WENTINK

PALACIO VALDÉS, Armando

Spanish novelist, short-story writer, and essayist, b. 4 Oct. 1853, Entralgo; d. 29 Jan. 1933, Madrid

Asturian by birth, P. V. studied in the city of Oviedo with Clarín (pseud. of Leopoldo Alas, 1852–1901), the famous author of *La regenta* (1884–1885; the regent). Subsequently he became a lawyer in Madrid. P. V. was very active at the Ateneo of Madrid, a cultural organization well known for its social gatherings. Besides editing the *Revista Europea*, he wrote for such newspapers as *El imparcial* and *La correspondecia de España*. In addition, he wrote on many contemporary writers in *Semblanzas literarias* (1871; literary biographical sketches), *Los oradores del Ateneo* (1878; the speakers of the teneo), *Los novelistas españoles* (1878; the Spanish novelists), and *Nuevo viaje al Parnaso* (1879; new journey to Parnassus). In collaboration with Clarín, he published a collection of critical essays entitled *Literatura en 1881* (1882; literature in 1881). In 1906 he was elected to the prestigious Spanish Royal Academy of the Language, an honor only afforded to well-connected figures of the cultural and political establishment in Spain (he was formally inducted as a member in 1920).

Even though P. V.'s first lengthy work of fiction, *El señorito Octavio* (1881; *Señorito Octavio*, 1896–1897), displayed aspects of his talent for character delineation and his Dickensian humor, it was with *Marta y María* (1883; *Martha and Mary*, 1896–1897) that some of his constant traits began to appear. In María de Elorza he portrays a repressive woman who reacts with a degree of physical pleasure when her maid flagellates her in the name of religion whereas she is unable to respond in a normal fashion to the affectionate advances of her fiancé and the warm feelings expressed by her family. On the surface, these traits of María seem to anticipate a disastrous ending for her, a conclusion which fails to materialize as the work finishes with a precipitous and preconceived happy ending reflecting P. V.'s unwillingness to face reality in a serious and rigorously intellectual manner.

With *La espuma* (1890; *Froth*, 1891), P. V. demonstrates his partial acceptance of naturalism as he attacks the high classes in Madrid as exploiters of Riosa's mercury miners, human beings who, by virtue of their hostile environment, remain ignorant as they provide the wealthy stockholders in the capital city with the resources they require to support their mistresses. A similar critical attitude is apparent in *La fe* (1892; *Faith*, 1892), a novel that attacks certain practices favored by the Roman Catholic church in Spain. Most of these novels, however, are not representative of P. V.'s

works in that, as stated previously, his creations often avoid serious topics as evidenced by his most famous novels: *La hermana San Sulpicio* (1889; *Sister Saint Sulpice*, 1890), *Jose* (1885; *José*, 1901), *Riverita* (1886; Riverita), and *Maxima* (1887; *Maximina*, 1888). To a large extent, entertainment for the sake of entertainment became one of P. V.'s foremost objectives in many of his works.

Overall, P. V. published twenty-four novels, along with four collections of short stories, the fictionalized memoirs of his youth—*La novela de un novelista* (1921; the novel of a novelist)—and lengthy essays. Autobiographical elements clearly predominate in some of his novels (for instance, *Riverita* and *Maximina*). His characters delighted large numbers of readers in the Spanish-speaking world for many years in that his was a relaxing art form, one deliberately wishing to avoid crude referential reality. P. V.'s value today rests primarily in his humor and his ability to create atmospheres.

FURTHER WORKS: *El cuarto poder* (1888; *The Fourth Estate*, 1901); *La alegría del capitán Ribot* (1899; *The Joy of Captain Ribot*, 1900); *La aldea perdida* (1903); *Tristán o el pesimismo* (1906; *Tristán*, 1925)

BIBLIOGRAPHY: Cruz Rueda, A., *A. P. V. Estudio biográfico* (1949); Roca Franquesa, J. M., *P. V.: técnica novelística y credo estético* (1951); Goyanes, M. Baquero, "Estudio," *Tristán o el pesimismo* (1971); Rodríguez, M. Pascuál, *A. P. V.* (1976)

—LUIS T. GONÁLEZ-DEL-VALLE

PALAMAS, Kostis

Greek poet, b. 13 Jan. 1859, Patras; d. 27 Feb. 1943, Athens

At the age of seven P. lost both his parents; he was brought up by an uncle in Missolonghi, the town his family came from. In 1875 he went to Athens to study law at the university, but instead he devoted himself to literature. He first earned his living by contributing literary articles to newspapers and periodicals, until he was appointed, in 1897, general secretary of the University of Athens, a post he held until his retirement in 1929. In Athens he lived a "life immovable," as he called it, and he died there while his country was under Nazi occupation.

P. was the central figure of the generation of the 1880s, the generation that brought Greece, which had been reborn from its ashes earlier in the 19th c., to its intellectual maturity. His wide familiarity with European literature and thought not only contributed greatly to his own originality and literary leadership; it also helped to modernize Greek literature in general and to broaden its horizons. As the leader of the group of poets known as the New Athenian School, he militantly embraced the cause of the demotic Greek language as a literary medium. He was influenced by the folk tradition; he also introduced Parnassianism to Greek poetry, and later SYMBOLISM, and was the most gifted Greek practitioner of both. His continued popularity and influence was due not only to his talent but to the fact that his work reflected the Greek spirit during years frequently disturbed by political turmoil and tragedy.

P. was a very prolific poet. His three earliest collections—*Traghoudhia tis patridhos mou* (1886; songs of my country), *Imnos is tin Athinan* (1889; hymn to Athena), and *Ta matia tis psykhis mou* (1889; the eyes of my soul)—did not truly reveal his poetic personality, although the last two won prizes and in their quality surpassed any modern poetry in Greek up to that time. P. really came into his own as a poet with the Parnassian lucidity of the twelve sonnets entitled "Patridhes" (1895; homelands). *Iamvi ke anapesti* (1897; iambs and anapests) introduced the musical, oblique, evocative suggestiveness of symbolism to Greek literature. The poems in *O tafos* (1898; *The Grave*, 1930), in lamenting the death of his five-year-old son, range from the simplicity of the folk song to the sophistication of philosophic meditation. *I asalefti zoï* (1904; Part I, *Life Immovable*, 1919; Part II, *A Hundred Voices*, 1921), the product of a decade, contains most of his best lyrical poetry on a great variety of themes and in a number of different modes. The long poem "Finikia" ("Palm Tree," 1969) in this volume is the best and also the most difficult of his symbolist poems; "Askreos" (Askreos [P.'s name for Hesiod]), another long poem in *I asalefti zoï*, is the first of what he called his "greater visions."

To these greater visions belong his next two synthesizing poems, both of epic length, *O dhodhekaloghos tou yiftou* (1907; *The Twelve Words of the Gypsy*, 1964; later tr., 1974) and *I floyiera tou vassilia* (1910; *The King's Flute*, 1967). *O dhodhekaloghos tou yiftou*, widely considered his masterpiece, is written in a variety of forms, moods, and rhythms. Its action takes place at the time preceding the fall of Constantinople to the Turks in 1453. The gypsy, who may represent the skeptical modern Greek or the poet himself reconsidering the Greek cultural experience, goes through all the stages of doubt and nihilistic negation until a violin befriends him and restores his spirits. The apparently simple symbolism of the violin becomes far more complex in its combined epic and lyrical associations. *I floyiera tou vassilia*, also epic in length and ambition, is not as successful as *O dhodhekaloghos tou yiftou*. In large part inspired by historians' recent discoveries about the cultural significance of Byzantium to modern Greece, the poem was composed and published ten years after the 1897 military débacle in which the Greek government had attempted to take possession of Crete, and shortly before the successful Balkan wars (1912–13). In this poem Emperor Basil II (958?–1025), who ruled at the time when the Byzantine Empire had reached its peak under the Macedonian dynasty, journeys through Greece to reach Athens, the ancient and modern cultural capital of Hellenism.

In his remaining books of poetry the aging P. wrote, with diminished power, lyrical verse. There are, however, exceptional moments in *O kyklos ton tetrastihon* (1919; cycle of quatrains) and elsewhere. Sadness prevails in his later verse, which reflects the impact on himself and his country of the two worlds wars. Of the few short stories he published from 1884 to 1901, "Thanatos pallikariou" (1901; "A Man's Death," 1934) is his best. He also wrote a poetic drama, *Trisevyeni* (1903; *Royal Blossom; or, Trisevyeni*, 1923), his only play. His voluminous critical writing had a considerable influence on his contemporaries and on younger writers.

P. was second only to Dionysios Solomos (1798–1857) in enriching Greek literature with a poetic language drawn from many eras, particularly the Byzantine. His poetry, in his ample drawing from Greek mythology, culture, literature, and history, encompasses the entire Greek world, both ancient and modern.

During his lifetime, his "greater visions" were deemed his major accomplishments. More recent criticism has shown a preference for the best of his shorter lyrical poetry. A duality inherent in his work—a wavering between enthusiasm and despair, affirmation and negation, action and contemplation, faith and faithlessness—has elicited many reservations from critics; what he posits beyond that wavering, however, is a faith in the capacity of art, of poetry, to transcend reality.

FURTHER WORKS: *To ergho tou Krystalli* (1894); *I heretizmi tis ilioyienitis* (1900); *Ghrammata* (2 vols., 1904, 1907); *I kaïmi tis limnothalassas ke ta satirika yimnasmata* (1912); *I politia ke i monaxia* (1912); *Ta prota kritika* (1913); *Aristoteles Valaoritis* (1914); *Vomi* (1915); *Ta parakera* (1919); *Ta dhekatetrastiha* (1919); *Dhiiyimata* (1920); *I pentasyllavi ke ta pathitika kryfomilimata* (1925); *Dhili ke skliri stikhi* (1928); *Pezi dhromi* (3 vols., 1928–1934); *Perasmata ke heretizmi* (1931); *I nihtes tou Phimiou* (1931–1932); *Dionysios Solomos* (1933); *Ta hronia mou ke ta hartia mou* (2 vols., 1933, 1940); *Vradhini fotia* (1944); *Apanta* (16 vols., 1962–1969); *Allelographia* (4 vols., 1974-86); *Evretiria Apanton* (1984); *Grammata sti Rahil* (1985). **FURTHER WORKS IN ENGLISH:** *Three Poems* (1969)

BIBLIOGRAPHY: Phoutrides, A., *A New World-Poet* (1919); Phoutrides, A., *A Living Poet of Greece: K. P.* (1921); Buck, C. D., Stevens, D. H., Skipis, S., Prior, M. E., and Argoe, K. T., Introductions (in English) to *K. P.: Dhili ke skliri stikhi* (1928); Palamas, L., *A Study on the "Palm Tree" of K. P.* (1931); Sherrard, P., *The Marble Threshing-Floor: Studies in Modern Greek Poetry* (1956): 39–81; Maskaleris, T., *K. P.* (1972); Fletcher, R., *K. P.: A Great Modeern Greek Poet* (1984)

—ANDONIS DECAVALLES

PALAZZESCHI, Aldo

(pseud. of Aldo Giurlani) Italian poet and novelist, b. 2 Feb. 1885, Florence; d. 18 Aug. 1974, Rome

P. was the only child of well-to-do parents. Although he studied accountancy, his real love since childhood had always been literature. In his youth P. spent a few years in Paris, where he was introduced to avant-garde circles.

P.'s earliest works include three volumes of poetry: *Cavalli bianchi* (1905; white horses), *Lanterna* (1907; lantern), and *Poemi* (1909; poems). *Poemi* in particular linked P. to FUTURISM. His short-lived association with that movement was based not on an acceptance of its theoretical assertions but rather on his own strong desire to "rejuvenate" Italian literature, which had come under the dominance of Gabriele D'ANNUNZIO.

Traces of futurism are present in the novel *Il codice di Perelà* (1911; *Perelà, the Man of Smoke*, 1936)—a revised edition was published as *Perelà, uomo di fumo* (1954). It is a fable about a man who has lived in a chimney for thirty-two years. When he emerges, he is at first welcomed by society and charged with the task of writing a "new code of freedom" for the state; later, rejected by the people, he is condemned to life in imprisonment but escapes and dissolves into smoke. *Il codice di Perelà* can be seen as a depiction of the crisis of values in the years preceding World War I. In this novel, as in all his other works, P. makes effective use of humor and irony.

Le sorelle Materassi (1934; *The Sisters Materassi*, 1953), one of P.'s best-known novels, recounts the story of two old-maid sisters who temporarily escape from their drab bourgeois life when their young, attractive nephew, Remo, comes to live with them. Sensing the sisters' infatuation for him, Remo exploits the situation. He eventually brings about their financial ruin, marries a wealthy American woman he has met in Venice, and leaves for a life in the U.S.

In later novels, *Il doge* (1967; the doge) and *Stefanino* (1969; Stefanino), P. returned to the fantastic mode evident in *Il codice di Peralà*. *Il doge* is a novel of Venice, which is seen in its legendary splendor; P. creates a surrealistic picture of the city through a language that combines the popular and the "cultured."

One of the most unusual figures in 20th-c. Italian literature, P. captured over fifty years of Italian life with a literary voice that was never content with conventional form. To reduce P. to a single attribute (such as the lyrical P.), as some critics have attempted to do, is to acknowledge only one aspect of his considerable and varied oeuvre. Even in his less successful works, such as *I fratelli Cuccoli* (1948; the Cuccoli brothers), whose characters are not fully developed, there are stylistic innovations, linguistic experiments, and an extraordinary imagination.

FURTHER WORKS: *Riflessi* (1908); *L'incendiario* (1910); *Il controdolore* (1914); *Due imperi mancati* (1920); *Il re bello* (1921); *Poesie* (1925; final version, 1930); *La piramide* (1926); *Stampe dell'Ottocento* (1932); *Il palio dei buffi* (1937); *Bestie del Novecento* (1951); *Roma* (1953; *Roma*, 1965); *Scherzi di gioventù* (1956); *Vita militare* (1959); *Il piacere della memoria* (1964); *Il buffo integrale* (1966); *Cuor mio* (1968); *Storia di un'amicizia* (1971); *Via della cento stelle* (1972)

BIBLIOGRAPHY: Buck, C. D., D. H. Stevens, S. Skipis, M. E. Prior and K. T. Argoe, Introductions (in English) to *K. P.: Dhili ke skliri stikhi* (1928): 19-56; Riccio, P. M., *Italian Authors of Today* (1938): 109–17; Singh, G., "A. P.: A Survey," in Pacifici, S., ed., *From Verismo to Experimentalism* (1969): 81–101; Bever, P., van, "Révolution et restauration: De P. à Ungaretti," *Revue de l'Université de Bruxelles*: 2–3 (1971): 229–37; Bergin, T. G., "The Enjoyable Horrendous World of A. P.," *BA*, 46 (1972): 55–60; Pacifici, S., *The Modern Italian Novel* (1979): 34–46

—ANTHONY R. TERRIZZI

PALESTINIAN LITERATURE

Largely a product of the 20th c., Palestinian literature forms an integral part of modern Arabic literature and partakes of most of its major thematic and formal features. Perhaps the single most crucial characteristic of Palestinian literature is its total preoccupation with national concerns. And while involvement in social and political issues is a common feature of modern Arabic literature in general, it informs Palestinian literature to a far greater degree. Political consciousness and commitment to the national cause determines not only the subject matter of Palestinian literature but also its division into periods and genres.

A general chronological division of Palestinian literature specifies three major, more or less distinct, periods demarcated by three historical events. The first period spans the years 1917–1948, from the Balfour Declaration, which promised the Jews a national homeland in Palestine, to the establishment of the state of Israel in 1948; the second from 1948 to 1967, from the first Arab-Israeli war to the June War of 1967; and the third from 1967 to the present. Like all periodization schemes, this one is useful only as a general outline.

The division into genres shows the exclusive preponderance of poetry during the first period, the emergence and rapid ascendancy of fiction during the second, and the intensification and proliferation of both during the third. The notable absence of a dramatic tradition from Palestinian literature is a direct result of the conditions of dispersion and instability that have characterized much of modern Palestinian history. All recent efforts to establish a regular Palestinian theater in East Jerusalem and the West Bank have faltered under the harsh and precarious conditions of life under Israeli military occupation. Although a number of Palestinian plays do exist, they are too few and too tentative to constitute a distinct literary tradition.

Poetry

Awareness of the unfolding Zionist schemes in Palestine impelled the first generation of Palestinian poets to devote much of their creative energy to sounding the bells of alarm. The task was made all the more urgent by the near universal ignorance of the impending danger to Palestine in the rest of the Arab world. All major Palestinian poets of the first half of this century, such as Iskandar al-Khūrī al-Baytjālī, Ibrāhīm Tūqān, 'Abd al-Rahīm Mahmūd, and 'Abd al-Karīm al-Karmiī (pseud: Abū Salmā), immersed themselves fully in the national struggle to save Palestine from Zionist colonization.

But even as they extolled the beauty of the Palestinian landscape and sought to imbue their listeners and readers with a spirit of sacrifice, these poets were profoundly pessimistic about the prospects of the homeland that was being dismembered and expropriated piecemeal before their very eyes. Palestinian national hymns, composed by these poets, were often sung collectively in public and became a common phenomenon during this period. Similarly, the image of both the martyr and the *fidā'ī* (freedom fighter) became major tropes of Palestinian poetry and through it imprinted themselves on the Palestinian collective consciousness.

In equally moving poems, both 'Abd al-Rahīm Mahmūd, who died in the battle of Sajara in 1948, and Abū Salmā simultaneously sang of Palestinian heroism and satirized official Arab impotence and treachery. Scathingly invective satire against the Zionists, the British Mandate, and the Arab kings, especially 'Abd-Allah of Jordan, provides a thematic counterpart to the panegyrics extolling heroism and patriotic virtues in this poetry.

Whatever the theme, the form of Palestinian poetry during this period is largely traditional and the language uniformly classical. To realize the intended political objective of rallying the people to the national cause, Palestinian poets availed themselves of the rich rhetorical tradition of classical poetry and fully used the intrinsic oratorical power of its established metrical and rhyme schemes. With the possible exception of Ibrāhīm Tūqān's occasional experimentation with new poetic forms, Palestinian poetry of this period shows little awareness of the revolutionary innovations that were transforming modern Arabic poetry in other parts of the Arab world, notably in Iraq.

In the wake of the Palestinian catastrophe of 1948, Palestinian poetry turned to nursing Palestinian wounds. Baffled and agonized soul-searching characterizes much of the poetry of the second phase, especially the poetry of the 1950s. The national tragedy finds its most painful expression in the fate of individual Palestinians who were transformed suddenly from citizens in their own country to refugees in foreign and often hostile lands. A mood of loss and abandonment is prevalent in much of the introspective poetry of Fadwā Tūqān, Salmā Khadrā Jayyūsiī (b. 1926), Kamāl Nāsir, and Hārūn Hāshim Rashīd (b. 1930).

This inward turn was accompanied by a greater attention to the artistic-aesthetic aspects of poetry. While many Palestinian poets went on writing in the traditional style, some adopted the new forms and innovative techniques of modernist Arabic poetry. Foremost among the pioneers in this regard was Tawfīq SĀYIGH, who introduced the prose poem into Palestinian poetry. Sāyigh's poetry often uses mythic archetypes and symbolic patterns to grapple with personal experiences and existential questions. He alone among all Palestinian poets can be said to possess a metaphysical vision. Similar interests inform much of the poetic output of Jabrā Ibrāhīm JABRĀ as well. On the whole, Palestinian poets who remained under Arab rule were far more daring and experimental than their counterparts who stayed behind in Israel.

A change in the bleak outlook and mood of Palestinian poetry begins to take form in the late 1950s and early 1960s at the hands of leftist poets like Mu'īn Bissīsū (1927–1988) and especially in the poetry of the Palestinian poets living in Israel. The distinctive quality of much of the poetry of Hannā Abū Hannā (b. 1931), Tawfīq Zayyād (b. 1932), Rāshid Husayn (1936–1977), Mahmūd DARWĪSH, and Samīh al-Qāsim is its fiercely defiant tone. In highly rhetorical poems, these poets openly challenged official Israeli policies and attitudes and launched what came to be known as "the poetry of the occupied land" or, more generally, "the poetry of the Palestinian resistance."

Initially, most of this poetry was written in traditional form to be delivered in a declamatory style during political rallies. Its declared political objective was to strengthen the resolve of the Palestinians within Israel to stay put and resist Israeli attempts to dislodge them from the land. Much of this poetry was written under constant police harassment, which often included lengthy terms of imprisonment and house arrest. The relentless pressure eventually drove two leading poets, Rāshid Husayn and Mahmūd Darwīsh, into permanent exile.

Since 1967 Palestinian poetry has developed in several simultaneous directions. While it remains uniformly committed and keenly tuned to political developments, its form and techniques have evolved considerably. This change is perhaps most clearly evident in the poetry of the leading Palestinian poet, Mahmūd Darwīsh. The structure, imagery, diction, and style of Darwīsh's poetry have grown steadily more complex since he went into exile in 1971, and rival in this regard the most experimental trends in contemporary Arabic poetry.

A similar, though less drastic, tendency is evident in the recent poetry of Samīh al-Qāsim, Hannā Abū-Hannā, and other Palestinian poets. But while al-Qāsim, like Darwīsh and others, has steadily cultivated the prophetic voice through biblical and Koranic allusion in his poetry, Abū Hannā seems to gravitate more toward ancient Canaanite history, in light of which he seeks to read contemporary Palestinian reality.

Fiction

Of the two fiction genres, the achievements of the Palestinian novel far surpass those of the Palestinian short story, though these are by no means negligible. Both genres entered Palestinian

literature in the first decades of the 20th c., but mature specimens of either began to appear only in the second half of the century. The short stories Jabrā Ibrāhīm Jabrā wrote in the 1940s but published in the 1950s, in the collection 'Araq (1956; sweat), may have been the first credible specimens of the genre in Palestinian literature.

During the 1950s and early 1960s, Samīra 'Azzām, Hannā Ibrāhīm (b. 1930), and Ghassān KANAFĀNĪ made significant contributions to this nascent genre. Their stories invariably dramatized the plight of Palestinian refugees, especially the psychological effects of dislocation on hapless Palestinian individuals. Though generally bleak, the outlook of some of these stories is occasionally brightened by a glimmer of political consciousness and the promise of change in the Palestinian condition.

With rare exceptions, these stories tend to depict Palestinian reality directly in an attempt to attract attention to the plight of the Palestinian people. As a result, the stories not infrequently subordinate literary and aesthetic considerations to political expediency. As thinly disguised commentaries on contemporary Palestinian reality, the documentary value of many of these stories may exceed their artistic merit.

A greater attention to artistic requirements is evident in much of the post-1967 output. Emile HABĪBĪ'S Sudāsiyyat al-ayyām al-sitta (1968; sextet of the six days) exemplifies this tendency. The six "tableaux" of which the work is comprised broach political issues indirectly and elliptically, primarily through the experiences of marginalized individuals.

A similar authorial restraint informs the short stories of younger writers such as Tawfīq Fayyād (b. 1939), Zakī Darwīsh (b. 1944), 'Alī Muhammad Tāhā (b. 1931), Zakī al-'Eyla (b. 1950), and Gharīb 'Asqalānī (b. 1948), among others. Much like Habībī, these writers frequently use framing devices and narrative techniques that are borrowed from the rich narrative heritage of classical Arab culture. A Thousand and One Nights is only one of many indelible sources to which these writers take frequent recourse.

The Novel

The roots of the Palestinian novel lie in journalistic writing. The two pioneers of the genre, Najīb Nassār (1862–1948) and Khalīl Baydas, were both newspaper publishers who introduced the genre by serializing their own novels in their newspapers before publishing them in book form. Intended primarily for light entertainment, these early attempts show little sophistication in form and narrative technique and possess hardly any artistic merit.

More artistically defensible specimens of the genre were written in the 1940s. Two works in particular have left a lasting impression: Mudhakkirāt dajāja (1943; diaries of a hen) by Ishāq Mūsā al-Husaynī (1904–1989) and Surākh fī layl tawīl (1955; screams in a long night) by Jabrī Ibrāhīm Jabrā. (According to the author's testimony, the latter novel was written before 1948.) The first is an allegorical work written in the style of animal fables but dealing with a philosophical issue that concerns humans, namely, how to contend with aggression. The second, far more realistic in plot, characterization, and narrative technique, deals with the perennial quest for rebirth and rejuvenation in the wasteland of modern life: the city. Neither work alludes directly to the Palestinian condition, though both evoke aspects of it indirectly.

By all accounts, the publication of Ghassān Kanafānī's first novel, Rijāl fi-al-shams (1963; Men in the Sun, 1978), was a high watermark in the development of Palestinian fiction. Though relatively short, this novel is a consummate work of art. Its plot relates the futile attempt of three Palestinian refugees to cross the Iraq-Kuwait border in search of an alternative to the abject humiliation of life in the refugee camps. All three die asphyxiated in the empty water tank of a truck that was supposed to smuggle them into Kuwait.

The rich symbolic significance of the novel's austere plot is further reinforced by adroitly sketched characters whose psychological motivation appears eminently compelling. Throughout, the pace of the narrative remains brisk, even as it shifts repeatedly from third-person omniscient narration to STREAM-OF-CONSCIOUSNESS and interior monologue. In this, as well as in his subsequent novel, *Mā tabaqqā lakum* (1966; *All That's Left to You*, 1990), Kanafānī, successfully adapts the narrative techniques of the Western psychological novel, especially as practiced by William FAULKNER, to the specifically Palestinian subject matter of his fiction.

The pervasive ramifications of the 1967 war also touched the Palestinian novel. The humiliating defeat of the regular Arab armies left a vacuum that the Palestinian guerrilla organizations rushed to fill. Their ascendancy, for as long as it lasted, significantly boosted Arab morale and irreversibly transformed Palestinian political consciousness. All the Palestinian novels written since 1967 reflect these historical facts, on which, of course, each writer puts his or her interpretive slant.

Nowhere is the change in orientation more evident than in the works of Kanafānī, the leading Palestinian novelist at the time. After having written what may possibly be the two most complex novels in all of Arabic fiction, Kanafānī abandoned the techniques of the psychological novel and turned to the simple, almost artless style of social REALISM. The two complete novels he wrote after 1967, *Umm Sa'd* (1969; the mother of Sa'd) and *'Ā'id ilā Haifā* (1969; returning to Haifa), are virtually plotless. In both, direct commentary and discursive dialogue replace artful narrative and interior monologue. Convinced of the permanence of the positive developments in the Palestinian condition, Kanafānī appears to have concluded that the time had come for Palestinian imaginative fiction to imitate Palestinian history, and not the reverse. The characters of both *Umm Sa'd* and *'Ā'id ilā Haifā* are presented in their unpolished and unadorned simplicity. In one of the posthumously published fragments of the three novels he left unfinished, Kanafānī attempted to narrow still further the gap between fiction and history by appending scholarly footnotes to the contrived fictional text.

Other major Palestinian writers responded to the new historical circumstances slightly differently. Thus Jabrā Ibrāhīm Jabrā continued to cultivate the revolutionary-cum-aesthetic sensibility of his elitist characters far from the misery of the refugee camps and the hubbub of the political street. In his masterpiece *al-Safīna* (1970; *The Ship*, 1985) the psychological effects of dislocation and homelessness on the main Palestinian character appear paradigmatic of angst-ridden and alienated modern life in general. A similar universalizing thrust informs Jabrā's subsequent novels, especially *al-Bahth 'an Walīd Mas'ūd* (1978; in search of Walid Mas'ūd), which, like Jabrā's earlier novels, uses a variety of sophisticated narrative techniques and poetic devices.

In a slightly different vein, Sahar Khalīfa's (b. 1941) novels thematize the feminist component within the political struggle for national liberation. The feminist agenda is prominently announced in the title of her first novel, *Lam na'ud jawārī lakum* (1974; no longer your maids), and is methodically pursued in both of her subsequent novels, *Alsubbār* (1976; *Wild Thorns*, 1985) and *'Abbād alshams* (1980; the sunflower).

Daring experimentation with form and narrative technique characterize Emile Habībī's fictional treatment of the experience of the Palestinians living in Israel. The five narrative works he wrote since 1967 systematically mix literary modes and confound generic distinctions. One of these, *Luka' ibn Luka'* (1980; Luka', son of Luka'), is written mostly in dialogue and is a hybrid between novel and play. Following Voltaire, Habībī takes a satirical view of human mindlessness and spares no one, least of all his fellow Arabs, the cutting edge of his biting satire. He is alone among Palestinian and Arab writers to dramatize antiheroes in lead roles. His masterpiece *Al-waqa'i' al-gharībah fī ikhifā sa'īd abī al-nahs al-mutashā'il* (1974; *The Secret Life of Saeed, the Ill-Fated Pessoptimist*, 1982) employs the style of the classical Arabic genre of *maqāma* to depict contemporary Arab reality. The lofty style of the work accentuates the wide gap between the heroic past and the lowly present.

In sum, Palestinian literature continues to be profoundly nationalistic and political, even as it strives to field universal themes and to achieve wider international recognition of its literary merits. In its relatively short life, it has made significant inroads in that direction. But to do it adequate justice, a poetics of intrinsically political literature may have to be articulated more systematically and more forcefully.

BIBLIOGRAPHY: Aruri, N., and Ghareeb, E., Introduction to *Enemy of the Sun: Poetry of Palestinian Resistance* (1970): 25–68; Abu-Ghazaleh, A. M., "The Impact of 1948 on Palestinian Writers: The First Decade," *Middle East Forum*, 66: 2–3 (1970); Peled, M., "Annals of Doom: Palestinian Literature—1917–1948," *Arabica*, 29, 2 (1982): 143–83; Sulaiman, K. A., *Palestine and Modern Arab Poetry* (1984)

—MUHAMMAD SIDDIQ

PALEY, Grace

American short-story writer and poet, b. 11 Dec. 1922, Bronx, N.Y.

Born and brought up in New York City, P. attended Hunter College for two years after graduating from Evander Childs High School. She also took various courses at New York University and the New School for Social Research where she studied poetry with W. H. AUDEN. During the 1960s P. taught at both Columbia University and Syracuse University; currently she teaches at Sarah Lawrence College in Bronxville, N.Y. She is active in feminist and antimilitary groups and was one of the founders of the Greenwich Village Peace Center. P. was awarded a Guggenheim fellowship in fiction (1961) and a National Council on the Arts grant (1966). In 1970 she received the National Institute of Arts and Letters Award for short-story writing and was elected a member of the institute in 1980.

Although P.'s early interest was in poetry, she began writing short fiction in the 1950s, and her first collection of stories, *The Little Disturbances of Man: Stories of Women and Men at Love,* was published in 1959. Segments of a novel P. never completed appeared in several periodicals during the 1960s, but P.'s second book of stories, *Enormous Changes at the Last Minute*, was not published until 1974, some fifteen years after her first. Her third collection, *Later the Same Day*, was published in 1985. P. has been accused of sacrificing her art to life, and she admits that her family, her political concerns, and her teaching are often distractions, but, as she told one interviewer, "There is a lot more to do in life than just writing." It is, however, the fact that P. has always lived her life fully and intensely that allows her to infuse her fictional world with the wry, witty glimpses of the ways in which her characters manage to live with and to love each other. P. is especially adept at exploring the turmoil that often bubbles just below the surface of what might appear to be lackluster everyday life. The influences of her childhood—the Russian and the Yiddish she heard spoken at home, the sights and sounds in the streets of The Bronx neighborhood she grew up in—her early love of poetry along with her devotion to her roles as wife and mother, all seem to have provided her with the ability to render the variety of voices, the precise inflections, the idioms, and the dialects that account for the enormous vitality of her wide range of characters.

As the title suggests, the major focus of *The Little Disturbances of Man* is on what might be viewed as commonplace issues confronting her vibrantly rendered characters. And as the subtitle hints, in these *Stories of Women and Men at Love*, the emphasis is on what happens as these ordinary people in working-class New York neighborhoods struggle with the "little disturbances" of their lives, sometimes succeeding, sometimes failing, "at love." In *Enormous Changes at the Last Minute*, some of the works move away from the traditionally structured short-story form that P. follows in her first collection. Many of the pieces are very short, almost sketches, while others seem to be plotless monologues. Yet they constitute a continuing investigation of love lost and love found, of family and of friendship, of death and of survival. *Later the Same Day* brings back many of the same characters found in the earlier collections, now somewhat older and wiser. P. still employs understatement, still avoids empty emotion and sentimentality. To be sure there is, as ever, a good deal of pathos in many of the stories, but it is always saved from any hint of melodrama by P.'s masterful use of humor and irony. Her characters' vulnerability is barely concealed by their wisecracks, but in the face of divorce, abandonment, old age, and death, they can still hope, can still see that there is possibility for change.

P. continues to hold before her readers the concept that the limitations of being human do not diminish the richness that is possible in life. If her prose has evolved into what might be considered postmodern form, her characters and their concerns transcend what seems trendy. They reinforce the importance of neighborhood, friendship, and community as antidotes to isolation and despair.

FURTHER WORKS: *Leaning Forward* (1985); *Long Walks and Intimate Talks: Poems and Stories* (1991); *New and Collected Poems* (1992)

BIBLIOGRAPHY: Mickelson, A. Z., *Reaching Out: Sensitivity and Order in Recent American Fiction by Women* (1979): 206–7, 221–34; Gelfant, B., "G. P.: Fragments for a Portrait in Collage," *NER*, 3 (Winter 1980): 276–93; DeKoven, M., "Mrs. Hegel-Shtein's Tears," *PR*, 48, 2 (1981): 217–23; Sorkin, A. J., "'What Are We, Animals?': G. P.'s World of Talk and Laughter," *SAJL*, 2 (1982): 144–54; Isaacs, N. D., *G. P.: A Study of the Short Fiction* (1990); Taylor, J., *G. P.: Illuminating the Dark Lives* (1990)

—MARGARET D. SULLIVAN

PALUDAN, Jacob

Danish novelist and essayist, b. 7 Feb. 1896, Copenhagen; d. 26 Sept. 1975, Copenhagen

P. started his studies in pharmaceutical chemistry in 1912 and received his degree in 1918. From 1920 to 1921 he lived in Ecuador and the U. S.; after his return to Denmark he worked as a literary critic for various newspapers.

P.'s stay in America affected his whole conservative and romantic outlook on life. He saw materialism and superficiality as the threatening components of "Americanization," which would eventually destroy all traditional values. This critical point of view appears in P.'s very first work, the emigrant novel *De vestlige veje* (1922; the western roads), a satirical but somewhat rhetorical attack on American urban civilization. He also satirized urban life in the novel *Søgelys* (1923; searchlight), which is set in Copenhagen. *Søgelys* contains penetrating psychological studies that recur in *En vinter long* (1924; all winter long), a lyrical novel of considerable artistic merit about loneliness and isolation that turn into defiance and frigidity.

More extroverted is P.'s next work, *Fugle omkring fyret* (1925; *Birds around the Light*, 1928), the semisymbolic, highly dramatic story of a harbor-building project in a small coastal town, illustrating the destructive forces of economic and technological progress. A more coherent character delineation is found in his most pessimistic novel, *Markerne modnes* (1927; the ripening fields). Here P. portrays two artistically gifted young men, a poet and a musician, who ultimately fail in their careers, the former because of too much popular success, which spoils him, the latter because of too much adversity in his environment, which is devoid of any true spiritual values.

P.'s most popular book—and a true masterpiece—is the two-volume novel *Jørgen Stein* (1932–33; *Jørgen Stein*, 1966). It is a social work depicting three generations: the first one is firmly rooted in the conservative pre-World War I period; the second is the "lost generation" whose values were destroyed through the war; the third is the young, disillusioned generation that takes life's emptiness for granted. At the same time, *Jørgen Stein* is a *Bildungsroman*. The individualistic but also weak and passive title character is emotionally split, at different times manifesting the attitudes of all three generations. He is unable to commit himself either to society or to a woman. The resultant catastrophe is the suicide of his girl-friend Nanna. Finally Jørgen overcomes his restlessness through resignation and by returning to nature and physical work. He gives up his illusory independence, chooses marriage, and accepts the duties of everyday life, finding at least a glimpse of hope in an otherwise meaningless world.

After *Jørgen Stein* P. turned to the essay, a genre indirectly anticipated in the numerous commentaries and reflective sections in his fictional writing. P.'s favorite targets are the American way of life and feminism, as in *Feodor Jansens jereminader* (1927; the jeremiads of Feodor Jansen). In *Året rundt* (1929; the year around), *Landluft* (1944; country air), and *Han gik ture* (1949; he took walks) contemplations on nature based on mystical experiences become predominant. Other essays pay particular attention to metapsychology, as in *Søgende ånder* (1943; searching spirits) and *Skribenter på yderposter* (1949; writers on outposts). P.'s most biting sarcasm appears in the two brilliant collections of aphorisms, *Tanker og bagtanker* (1937; thoughts and secret thoughts) and *Små apropos'er* (1943; aphorisms), which are aimed at the superficiality and vulgarization of the times and at current fashionable trends. From 1973 to 1975 P. published three volumes of anecdotal memoirs, *I høstens månefase* (1973; during the autumn moon), *Sløret sandhed* (1974; veiled truth), and *Vink fra en fjern virkelighed* (1975; waves from a distant reality). After his death another volume of memoirs, *Låsens klik* (1976; the click of the lock), was published.

P. was a sharp and critical commentator on his age. At the same time he had a deep affection for art and nature, where he discovered the harmony he could not find in the modern world. P.'s masterful style is characterized by a refined rhythm, and it maintains a subtle balance between a poetic and a purely intellectual approach. P. himself constantly strove to understand the interplay between the human mind and nature as well as man's situation in time and space.

FURTHER WORKS: *Urolige sange* (1923); *Landet forude* (1928); *Som om intet var hændt* (1938); *Mit kaktusvindue* (1944); *Bøger på min vej* (1946); *Prosa: Korte ting fra tyve år* (1946); *Facetter* (1947); *Retur til barndommen* (1951); *Fremad til nutiden* (1953); *Sagt i korthed* (1954); *Ålborg i min ungdoms vår* (1955); *Litterært selskab* (1956); *Skribent at være* (1957); *Røgringe* (1959); *En kunstsamlers meditationer* (1960); *Mørkeblåt og sort* (1965); *Siden De spørger* (1968); *Her omkring hjørnet blæser det mindre* (1969); *Dråbespil* (1971)

BIBLIOGRAPHY: Claudi, J., *Contemporary Danish Authors* (1952): 57–61; Heltberg, N., "J. P.," *ASR*, 40 (1952): 142–45

—SVEN H. ROSSEL

PANAMANIAN LITERATURE

See Central American Literature

PANAYOTOPOULOS, I(oannis) M(ichael)

Greek poet, novelist, short-story writer, critic, travel writer, and essayist, b. 23 Oct. 1901, Aitolikon; d. 17 April 1982, Athens

Educated at the University of Athens, P. combined writing with the teaching of Greek literature at private institutions. He also contributed to the cultural life of Greece by serving on the advisory board of the National Theater and as chairman of its committee on artistic affairs. In addition, he served on the editorial board of the "Basic Library," a series of books of history, literature, philosophy.

Among P.'s many honors were the Palamas Prize, awarded in 1947 for four volumes he contributed to the series known as *Ta prosopa kai ta keimena* (individuals and their works); a First National Prize in 1957 for *Ta epta koimismena paidia* (1956; the seven sleepers) as the best novel of the year; and another National Prize awarded in 1964 for his travel book *E Afriki afipnizetai* (1963; Africa awakens). Translations of his work have given P. an international reputation.

At the age of twenty P. published *To poeitiko ergo tou Kosti Palama* (1921; the poetic work of Kostis Palamas), testifying to his admiration for the great demotic poet. He followed this critical study with several poetry collections of his own, culminating in *To parathyro tou kosmou* (1962; window of the world). In 1970 he gathered and published his poetry in one large volume, *Ta poeimata* (the poems).

Like many authors of his generation, P. expresses in his poetry and fiction the moral dilemmas of man confronting an age of lost standards and eroded beliefs. His first novel, *Astrofengia* (1945; starlight), depicts the social and cultural chaos engendered by World War I. His second novel, *O aichmalatos* (1951; the captive), begins before the outbreak of World War II and describes defeated and occupied Greece. In the prize-winning *Ta epta koimismena paidia*, P. writes about 3rd-c. Rome, whose disintegration has parallels with our own time.

P. feels deeply the alienation that man suffers, a loneliness that he compares to that of God when He is abandoned by man. To be truly alive, P. believes, one must experience the agony of separation. These basic themes particularly permeate his three volumes of short stories: *To dachtilidi me ta paramythia* (1957; ring with the fairy tales), *Anthropini dipsa* (1959; human thirst), and *Flamingos* (1963; flamingos).

Like writers such as Nikos KAZANTZAKIS, Elias VENEZIS, and Petros HARIS, P. has also written about his travels. To this genre P. contributed several volumes that express his wanderlust and desire for fresh knowledge, ranging from *Ellenikoi orizondes* (1940; Greek horizons) to *Afrikaniki peripeteia* (1970; African travels). Committed to no particular politics or ideology, P. seeks in his journeys to learn what is vital for himself and for mankind.

In addition to poetry, fiction, and travel books, P. has published essays on literary and cultural subjects. His most ambitious effort consists of six volumes in the series *Ta prosopa kai ta keimena*, his last contribution being in 1956. In them he discusses both Greek and non-Greek authors. In a reminiscence touching upon his own past, *Hamozoe* (1945; "Humble Life," 1969), P. dramatizes various events in a poor section of Piraeus.

In a manner less fiery than that of Kazantzakis, P. also expresses the moral crises besetting modern man. *O synchronos anthropos* (1966; *The Contemporary Man*, 1970) is perhaps his best effort to study the "anatomy of modern reality."

FURTHER WORKS: *To biblio tis Mirandas* (1924); *Lyrika schedia* (1933); *Dromoi paralliloi* (1943); *Anisiha hronia* (1943); *Kostis Palamas* (1944); *Omilies tis yimnis psichis* (1946); *K. P. Kavafis* (1946); *O lyrikos logos* (1949); *Alcyone* (1950); *O kyklos tou zodion* (1950); *Scaravaios o ieros: E Egyptos* (1950); *Politeies tis Anatolis* (1954); *Stochasmos kai o logos* (1954); *Ta Ellenika kai ta xena* (1956); *E Kypros: Ena taxidi* (1961); *O kosmos tis Kinas* (1961); *Kerkyra: To nisi tis lyrikis Fantasias* (1975). FURTHER WORKS IN ENGLISH: *The New Barbarians and the Downfall of Authenticity* (1977)

BIBLIOGRAPHY: Gianos, M. P., ed., *Introduction to Modern Greek Literature* (1969): 21, 32–33; Hogan, M. P., Preface to *The Contemporary Man* (1970): v–xiv

—ALEXANDER KARANIKAS

PANDURO, Leif

Danish novelist and dramatist, b. 18 April 1923, Copenhagen; d. 16 Jan. 1977, Asserbo

Having finished dental school in 1947, P. moved to Sweden in 1949, where he practiced dentistry until his return to Denmark in 1956. From 1961 to 1965 he divided his time between dentistry, television journalism, book reviewing, and creative writing. In 1965 he became a full-time writer.

P. made his literary debut with a radio play, *Historien om Ambrosius* (1956; the story of Ambrosius). His first novel, *Av, min guldtand* (1957; off, my good tooth), is partly autobiographical. Dominant in his early works is the theme of the adolescent's identity crisis and the question of how to achieve maturity for the individual, as well as for society as a whole.

P.'s first major work, *Rend mig i traditionerne* (1958; *Kick Me in the Traditions*, 1961), influenced by J. D. SALINGER'S *The Catcher in the Rye*, is a humorous description of a young boy's revolt against his surroundings and his confinement in a mental hospital as a result of his refusal to accept the adult world, with its conventions, deceits, and taboos. P.'s theme of rebellion is set against the German occupation of Denmark during World War II in *De uanstændige* (1960; the immoral ones), a farcelike yet serious protrayal of the period, which focuses on the Danes' perception of one another and of morality. The protagonist has to eliminate part of his identity to fit into the so-called normal world.

Øgledage (1961; saurian days), P.'s most fantastic and modernist work, represents a determined effort to throw off the old literary bonds; it links him to the quest for linguistic liberation of the 1960s. Again, the main theme is that of the psychological problems of youth. According to P., the conventions of society force modern man to reject vitality and spontaneity, a situation that leads to schizophrenia. The author creates an inversion whereby the normal world is unbalanced and insanity is an intentional choice. The healing process for the sickness entails the assimilation into and the acceptance of bourgeois society, and these can be achieved only through the amputation of part of the self.

P.'s later novels deal with middle age. Martin Fern in *Fern fra Danmark* (1963; Fern from Denmark) rejects his limitations and the unpleasant sides of himself through loss of memory. The paranoid Marius Berg in *Fejltagelsen* (1964; the mistake) uses severe hypochondria as a shield against the demands of the outside world, and Edvard Morner in *Den gale mand* (1965; the crazy man) consciously chooses to live according to the strictest rules of society, rejecting all human emotions.

In P.'s novels of the 1970s his middle-class and middle-aged heroes are confronted with a younger generation of rebels. The main characters have isolated themselves in a self-created world of security, refusing all commitments and burdensome contacts. Yet reality intrudes upon them, bringing confusion and questions. *Daniels anden verden* (1970; Daniel's other world) depicts a society marked by chaos and dissolution. For Daniel, the title character, salvation lies in the meeting with the young, schizophrenic rebel Laila and his understanding of her world. *Amatørerne* (1972; the amateurs), as well as P.'s final two novels, *Den ubetænksomme elsker* (1973; the thoughtless lover) and *Høfeber* (1975; hay fever), also treat the problem of lack of commitment.

P.'s television dramas likewise center on the crisis of the middle class. The theme of insecurity and desperation in the supposedly well-organized modern welfare state is present in all of P.'s plays, beginning with *En af dagene* (1968; one of these days), which depicts the power struggle in an office where everybody watches everybody else because of the fear of losing the chance of advancement. *Farvel, Thomas* (1968; goodbye, Thomas) tells of a man who loses his own identity when he is abandoned by his wife. In *Hjemme hos William* (1971; at William's place) P. shows the private fiasco of a seemingly successful architect, while *Rundt om Selma* (1971; around Selma) depicts the failure of the whole middle-class life style. *Rundt om Selma* is P.'s most penetrating and also his most pessimistic analysis of bourgeois society. Every trace of humanity and love of fellow man has been displaced by callous tyranny. *I Adams verden* (1973; in Adam's world) and *Louises hus* (1974; Louise's house), among the best Scandinavian television dramas, continue P.'s attack on the "civilized" behavior of the bourgeoisie. P. became the most successful Danish dramatist of the 1970s. Paradoxically, he attacked exactly those values of the very audiences that held him in such high esteem.

As a novelist, P. occupies a central position in Danish literature; as a dramatist, his position is somewhat isolated, since, unlike most of the newer dramatists, his point of departure was not a political doctrine.

FURTHER WORKS: *Lollipop, og andre spil* (1966); *Vejen til Jylland* (1966; *One of Our Millionaires Is Missing*, 1967); *Farvel, Thomas, og andre TV-spil* (1968); *Bella, og Et godt liv: To TV-spil* (1971); *Vinduerne* (1971); *Selma, William, og Benny: Tre TV-spil* (1972); *Den store bandit* (1973); *Den bedste af alle verdener* (1974); *Bertram og Lisa, og Anne og Paul: To TV-spil* (1974); *Gris på gaflen* (1976); *Hvilken virkelighed?* (1977)

BIBLIOGRAPHY: Sokoll, G., "Mensch und Gesellschaft in L. P.s Dramatik," in Wrede, J., et al, eds., *20th Century Drama in Scandinavia: Proceedings of the International Association of Scandinavian Studies* (1978): 197–204; Hugus, F., "The King's New Clothes: The Irreverent Portrayal of Royalty in the Works of L. P. and Finn Søeborg," *SS*, 51 (1979): 162–76

—MARIANNE FORSSBLAD

PANOVA, Vera Fyodorovna

Russian novelist, dramatist, and short-story writer, b. 20 March 1905, Rostov-on-the-Don; d. 3 March 1973, Leningrad

P. began her career in her native city, where she worked as a journalist from 1922 to 1935. She returned to this profession for a period of three years while living in Perm, in the Urals, during World War II. Working for local newspapers and Komsomol (Communist Youth League) papers, she wrote sketches, feuilletons, and articles on a variety of subjects, while her stories for and about children were beginning to attract attention.

P. made her debut in the purely literary field with the publication of her first play, *Ilya Kosogor* (1939; Ilya Kosogor), which was followed by several more works for the theater. In her later years she returned to this genre and between 1956 and 1968 wrote and staged a number of plays.

It was not until shortly after the war, however, that P.'s first long story, "Semya Pirozhkovykh" (1945; the Pirozhkov family), was published, followed quickly by her first successful novel, *Sputniki* (1946; *The Train*, 1948), one of the finest Soviet books written about the war years. In this short, patriotic, and unpretentious tale of life on a hospital train P. resists presenting her characters as ideal positive heroes but strikes a genuinely human note.

Objectivity, understatement, and detachment in depicting existing Soviet reality are again present in her second novel, *Kruzhilikha* (1947; *The Factory*, 1949). These qualities earned P. the displeasure of Party critics. At a time of rampant "Zhdanovism"—after a partial liberalization of artistic and creative life immediately following the end of the war, Andrey Zhdanov, the Communist cultural "boss," had decreed a return and an undeviating adherence to SOCIALIST REALISM—P. was not spared the pressure. In her third short novel, *Yasny bereg* (1949; clear shore), set on a large state-owned stockbreeding farm, P. adhered to the dicta set forth by the Party, with all the concomitant mediocrity resulting therefrom.

P.'s first attempt at a full-length conventional novel was *Vremena goda* (1953; *Span of the Year*, 1957). Structurally, this work is less successful than her earlier books, for P.'s talent was that of a miniaturist. Nevertheless, *Vremena goda* and the novel that followed it, *Sentimentalny roman* (1958; a sentimental novel), were major literary events inasmuch as they treated controversial subjects and were harbingers of things to come. Together with Ilya EHRENBURG'S novel *The Thaw*, *Vremena goda* ushered in the post-Stalinist period in Soviet literature, marked by a bid for greater artistic freedom. In this novel, P. paints an unsavory, but truthful picture of large-scale corruption in everyday Soviet life and even dares to depict the criminal underworld.

Sentimentalny roman is a frankly autobiographical and sentimental novel in which P. uses Rostov-on-the-Don in the 1920s as background. The book is presented as the personal reminiscences of its hero, the journalist Sevastyanov, but it is based on P.'s own recollections, as was earlier the case with *Sputniki* and, partially, with *Vremena goda*. *Sentimentalny roman* is free of ideology, and the 1920s appear in it as a "golden age," seen from a distance of over thirty years. The lyricism of this almost entirely romantic work is the quality that sets it apart from other novels of the period.

P. had an extraordinary talent for writing about children, as evidenced by her novella *Seryozha* (1955; *Time Walked*, 1957) and the two complementary stories, "Valya" (1959; "Valya," 1976) and "Volodya" (1959; "Volodya," 1976). Clearly quite at home in the more limited genres of the novella and short story, P. produced in *Seryozha* a series of delightful scenes of life and events as seen from the point of view of a six-year-old boy. "Valya" and "Volodya" are set in wartime Leningrad and feature older children, with their own problems and tribulations in a time of crisis. In these stories, P. shows herself to be not only a sensitive, sympathetic, and keeneyed observer but also a master at penetrating to the depths of youthful psychology.

In her later years, P.'s long-standing interest in history resulted in a collection of stories based on old Russian chronicles published under the title *Liki na zare* (1966; faces at dawn). She was also a prolific screenwriter: between 1960 and 1967 no fewer than eight films were made from her scenarios.

P.'s feminine sensitivity toward ordinary people is evident throughout her books, as is her lucid style and detached tone, reminiscent of CHEKHOV'S. While remaining within the confines of Soviet ideology, in most of her works P. was able to retain an objectivity of characterization that complemented her writer's talent but at times earned her severe criticism from the authorities.

FURTHER WORKS: *V staroy Moskve* (1940); *Devochki* (1945); *Metelitsa* (1956); *Evdokia* (1959); *Provody belykh nochey* (1961); *Kak pozhivaesh, paren?* (1962); *Skolko let, skolko zim!* (1962); *Tredyakovsky i Volynsky* (1968); *Sobranie sochineny* (5 vols., 1969–1970); *O moey zhizni, knigakh i chitatelyakh* (1975)

BIBLIOGRAPHY: Alexandrova, V., *A History of Soviet Literature* (1963): 272–83; Brown, E. J., *Russian Literature since the Revolution* (1963): 243–45; Moody, C., Introduction to V. P., "Serezha" and "Valya" (1964): xi–xxvi; Struve, G., *Russian Literature under Lenin and Stalin, 1917–1953* (1971), 383; Holthusen, J., *Twentieth-Century Russian Literature: A Critical Study* (1972): 162–66; Slonim, M., *Soviet Russian Literature: Writers and Problems, 1917–1967* (1973), passim; Brown, D., *Soviet Russian Literature since Stalin* (1978): 177–78, 264, 270: 287–89

—NADJA JERNAKOFF

PAPADAT-BENGESCU, Hortensia

Romanian novelist and short-story writer, b. 8 Dec. 1876, Iveşti; d. 5 March 1955, Bucharest

An army officer's daughter, P.-B. married a provincial magistrate and had several children and a large household to take care of. This, in part, explains her belated literary debut: she started publishing short stories only in 1913. Although not exactly a feminist, P.-B. can be considered the most important representative to date of women's literature in Romania.

P.-B.'s literary career can be divided into two periods. The first, when she was associated with Garabet Ibrăileanu (1871–1936) and his journal *Viaţa românească*, was characterized by a lyrical, intimate prose that was a refreshing change from the objective, epic-oriented novelistic conventions of her contemporaries. Her most important work of this period is *Balaurul* (1923; the dragon), which drew upon P.-B.'s experience as a volunteer nurse during World War I. Written in diary form, the novel presents the atrocities of war through the eyes of a sheltered, sensitive woman, who initially volunteers for the medical corps not so much out of patriotism as out of a need to get over a painful romance. Confronted with the gruesome reality of her wounded patients, she comes to view her own sentimental drama as ludicrously insignificant.

The second period of P.-B.'s career, when she was associated with Eugen LOVINESCU and his review *Sburătorul*, was marked by a shift, presumably under Lovinescu's influence, from subjectivism to a soul-probing objectivism that has led critics to compare her with PROUST. It was during this period that she wrote the "Halippa cycle," which brought her the highest Romanian literary awards and a seldom-contested reputation as a master of prose. This series of novels, of which the best-known is *Concert din muzică de Bach* (1927; a Bach concert), is a loose, unstructured narrative, mostly held together by Mini, the narrator—in many ways a female counterpart of Proust's narrator, Marcel—and by her friend Nory

Baldovin, a sarcastic, upper-class feminist with whom she exchanges gossip. Like Marcel, Mini moves in upstart, pseudo-aristocratic circles whose superficiality, venality, and snobbishness she exposes with devastating irony. Nevertheless, not unlike Marcel, she is at the same time curiously fascinated by and not unsympathetic to this world. She is also the exponent of the controversial theory, which appears in much of P.-B.'s work, of the "soul as bodily form." Attributing this theory to the author, some critics see it as trite or naïve, and others as hopelessly obscure. This "psychological" theory, however, should probably not be separated from its fictional context and from its inventor, Mini, who uses it as a convenient way of "understanding" and "categorizing" her friends.

Through her psychological narrative techniques and her shift from predominantly rural to urban settings and themes, P.-B. substantially contributed to the expansion of Romanian fiction beyond conventions of naturalism and external realism that prevailed in the late 19th and early 20th cs.

FURTHER WORKS: *Ape adînci* (1919); *Sfinxul* (1920); *Bătrînul* (1920); *Femeia in faţa oglinzii* (1921); *Romanţă provincială* (1925); *Fecioarele despletite* (1926); *Desenuri tragice* (1927); *Drumul ascuns* (1933); *Logodnicul* (1935); *Rădăcini* (1938); *Sangvine* (1973); *Sărbătorile în familie* (1976)

BIBLIOGRAPHY: Munteanu, B., *Panorama de la littérature roumaine contemporaine* (1938): 237–39; Reichman, E., "Les lettres roumaines: Un lent apprentissage à la liberté," *Preuves*, No. 175 (1965): 37–47; Philippide, A., "The Spirit and Tradition of Modern Romanian Literature," *RoR*, 21, 2 (1967): 5–10; Roceric, A., "La fonction du contexte dans l'œuvre de H. P.-B.," *Cahiers de linguistique théorique et appliqué*, 6 (1969): 183–91; Mihailescu, F., "Le centenaire d'H. P.-B.," *AUB-LLR*, 26 (1977): 73–82

—MIHAI SPARIOSU

PAPADIAMANTIS, Alexandros

Greek short-story writer and novelist, b. 4 March 1851, Skiathos; d. 3 Jan. 1911, Skiathos

P., popularly called the "saint of Greek letters," was born into a pious island family; his father was a priest. P. spent most of his mature years in Athens with periodic and sometimes long extended visits to his native Skiathos. He studied literature at the University of Athens but never obtained a degree, and eventually settled down as a writer and translator for newspapers and literary journals. Humble and strongly religious, he often acted as a cantor at Greek Orthodox services in the chapels of Plaka, the district of Athens near the Acropolis, while at other times he sat and wrote his stories in modest restaurants and cafés of the same area, between glasses of wine and cups of coffee. His essential modesty shines both in the anecdote that tells of the time he felt embarrassed when he was offered a fee higher than he expected for his writings and in the fact that, in 1908, he stayed away from a public gathering in his honor at "Parnassos," a society of writers and artists.

P. began his career as a writer of historical novels at a time when the genre was going out of fashion. *I metanastis* (1879; the expatriate), *I embori ton ethnon* (1882; the merchants of nations), and *I yiftopoula* (1884; the gypsy girl) are written in purist rather than demotic Greek; they abound in romantic adventures and dramatic situations but have a loose construction and poor characterization. The novella *Christos Milionis* (1885; Christos Milionis), inspired by a folk song of the same name, suggests by its brevity and tight structure that P. was moving toward the short story.

In the following twenty-five years P. wrote about 170 short stories. Although some were set in Athens, most of them are centered around Skiathos. They are ethnographic and social stories, some very short and rapidly sketched, others longer and more elaborate, but all characterized by nostalgia, reverie, love of nature, and simple Christian piety. His characters, complex or simple, are always memorable: priests, fishermen, housewives, shepherds, sailors, described with sympathy, psychological knowledge, and an innocent kind of humor. Of the works written before 1900, the stories "I nostalghos" (1894; "She Who Was Homesick," 1920; also tr. as "The Dreamer," 1969), "O erotas sta hionia" (1896; love in the snow), and "Oloyira stin limni" (1892; all around the lake), as well as the novella *Vardhianos sta sporka* (1895; watchman of the infected ships), stand out. After 1900 P. became more lyrical and showed a greater command of language. Memorable stories from this, his last creative period, are "Oniro sto kima" (1900; dream on the waves), "Ta rhodhin'akroyalia" (1908; rosy shores), and "To miroloyi tis fokias" (1908; the dirge of the seal).

P.'s greatest work for its dramatic quality and its social significance, is the novella *I fonissa* (1903; *The Murderess*, 1977). The old lady Frangoyiannou epitomizes the subservient role a woman must play in traditional Greek society and is described by P. at the point of revolt. Contemplating her past life, during which she graduated from slavery to her father to submission to her brothers and then to her husband, the old lady loses her mind and starts murdering baby girls with the purpose of sparing them future hardships. P. portrays Frangoyiannou as a tragic rather than as an evil character, who finally dies "halfway between divine and human justice." It is probable that Dostoevsky's *Crime and Punishment*, which P. had translated from a French version, influenced P. when he wrote *I fonissa*.

P.'s language is idiosyncratic. He wrote his stories at a time when the literary movement of the vernacular (demotic) Greek over the purist was making great advances; yet he consistently used the purist in description and lyrical digression, combining purist and demotic in the narrative parts and resorting to almost pure demotic (his island's idiom) in dialogue. He used the popular language also in most of the few poems he wrote.

P. has had great admirers, but he has also been the object of strong criticism for the loose construction and lack of artistic intention of his writings. Yet, as the modern Greek literary historian Linos Politis aptly stated, "the lack of construction is usually owing to the nature of his [P.'s] nostalgia and reverie; the ideas, not bound by any predetermined plan, follow the course of reverie—and the very lack of construction is a virtue and has charm." P.'s all-encompassing interest in his native island and its people was personal and inward-looking, but it could also be seen as a positive response to the folkloristic concerns among the educated Greeks of his time. Greek and non-Greek readers who have even a mild interest in the literature about the Aegean sea and its islands certainly cannot ignore P.

On the whole, it is purity of feeling and lack of artifice that have made P. a remarkable writer and motivated the 1979 Nobel Prize winner Odysseus ELYTIS to single out P., in his poem *The Axion Esti* (1959), as one of two Greek writers (the other is the poet Dionysios Solomos, 1798–1857) from whose work and example

Greeks in distress can draw moral sustenance, and to write a lyrical commentary on P.

FURTHER WORKS: *Ta apanta* (5 vols., 1954–1956). FURTHER WORKS IN ENGLISH: *Tales from a Greek Island* (1987)

BIBLIOGRAPHY: Dimaras, C. T., *A History of Modern Greek Literature* (1972), passim; Politis, L., *A History of Modern Greek Literature* (1973), passim; Xanthopoulides, G. X., Introduction to A. P., *The Murderess* (1977): v–xv

—GEORGE THANIEL

PAPIAMENTU LITERATURE

See Dutch-Caribbean Literature

PAPUA NEW GUINEA LITERATURE

See Pacific Islands Literatures

PARAGUAYAN LITERATURE

Before 1900 literary activity in Paraguay was a peripheral part of national life. There were poets and prose writers, but they never constituted an active group of intellectuals exercising a significant influence on the country's development. A truly Paraguayan literature began with the brilliant "Generation of 1900": Cecilio Báez (1862–1925), Juan E. O'Leary (1879–1969), Manuel Domínguez (1869–1935), Alejandro Guanes (1872–1925), Manuel Gondra (1871–1927), Fulgencio R. Moreno (1872–1935), and a few other writers of comparable merit.

Essayists and poets, the writers of the Generation of 1900 were also powerful polemical journalists. They had a cause: the reassertion of national values, including a reinterpretation of the War of the Triple Alliance (1864–70), which had left Paraguay desolate and almost extinct. The combined forces of Argentina, Brazil, and Uruguay had devastated the country in a genocidal campaign, which the allied invaders justified as a "crusade of liberation": Paraguay, according to them, was a barbaric country tyrannized by a monster, Marshal Francisco Solano López (1826–1870). The Generation of 1900 tried to show that Paraguay was far more civilized than its enemies when the conflict began and that López was a great patriot and the nation's supreme hero.

Cecilio Báez, the leader of this very prolific generation, wrote more than fifty books in addition to countless essays; Blas Garay (1873–1899), O'Leary, Domínguez, and Moreno all wrote historical works. Alejandro Guanes, the great poet of the group, achieved distinction with "Las leyendas" (1910; the legends) and "Recuerdos" (1910; memories). Fiction of literary merit, however, did not flourish at the beginning of the century.

Around 1915 a new generation of talented writers appeared. The four most important essayists of this group—Justo Pasto Benítez (1895–1962), Pablo Max Ynsfrán (1894–1972), Natalicio González (1897–1966), and Arturo Bray (1898–1977)—continued the historical work of their predecessors. Benítez and Max Ynsfrán

wrote the best biographies and interpretations of recent events. By the 1930s (the period of the Chaco War with Bolivia), Paraguayan historiography attained distinction, in the writings of Julio César Chaves (b. 1907) and Efraím Cardozo (1906–1975). The first and also the most important woman prose writer of the first half of the century was Teresa Lamas de Rodríguez-Al-calá (1887–1976), while the most popular poet of this generation was Manuel Ortiz Guerrero (1897–1935), whose lyrics were set to music by a number of composers.

During the first forty years of the century the dominant literary genre was the historical essay. ("History," said one critic, "devoured literature.") During the 1940s, however, all genres began to flower with unprecedented fertility. Hérib Campos Cervera (1908–1953) won recognition throughout Spanish America for his SURREALIST poetry, which appeared in his only published volume, *Ceniza redimida* (1953; redeemed ashes). Josefina Plá (b. 1909), a dramatist, poet, and art historian, shared with Campos Cervera the leadership of the literary revival during this decisive decade. A surrealist during the 1940s, she later turned toward classical simplicity; *Rostros en el agua* (1963; faces on the water) is perhaps her greatest lyrical achievement. Among the next generation, Elvio Romero (b. 1926), a follower of Campos Cervera, became one of Latin America's outstanding contemporary poets. His *Antología poética* (1965; poetic anthology) reveals his virtuosity.

The Paraguayan novel finally achieved distinction in the 1950s and 1960s, although its two outstanding practitioners are expatriates. Gabriel Casaccia's (b. 1907) *La babosa* (1952; the driveler) caused a great stir when it was first published in Argentina. It is a searingly realistic study of a group of middleclass characters in Areguá, a resort town near Asunción, and depicts what the author sees as the corruption and vice of Paraguayan society. Augusto Roa BASTOS, also a poet, and the most distinguished writer of the Generation of 1940, is regarded as one of the leading novelists of Latin America. His novel *Hijo de hombre* (1960; *Son of Man*, 1965), one of the masterpieces of recent Latin American fiction, is a panorama of Paraguay's history, utilizing the techniques of MAGIC REALISM in its interweaving of social and religious themes. His *Yo el Supremo* (1974; I the Supreme) constitutes an extraordinary literary experiment. It is a novel narrated in the first person from the complex and contradictory point of view of Dr. José Gaspar Rodríguez de Francia (1761?–1840), dictator of Paraguay from shortly after the time it gained its independence. Roa Bastos succeeds in brilliantly combining literary invention and the Paraguayan writer's traditional preoccupation with history.

BIBLIOGRAPHY: Centurión, C. R., *Historia de las letras paraguayas* (3 vols.: 1947–57); Vallejos, R., *La literatura paraguaya como expresión de la realidad nacional* (1967); Rodríguez-Alcalá, H., *La literatura paraguaya* (1968); Pérez-Maricevich, F., *La poesía y la narrativa en el Paraguay* (1969); Rodríguez-Alcalá, H., *Historia de la literatura paraguaya* (1971)

—HUGO RODRÍGUEZ-ALCALÁ

PÁRAL, Vladimír

Czechoslovak novelist (writing in Czech), b. 10 Aug. 1932, Prague

P. was trained as a chemical engineer and, before he devoted himself full-time to literature, worked for a dozen years in the research laboratory of a textile factory in northern Bohemia. Science and technology have exerted a strong influence on his fiction.

After a false start under a pseudonym, P. achieved overnight prominence with the novel *Veletrh splněných přání* (1964; the fair of dreams fulfilled). A new kind of character in Czech fiction made his appearance: in P.'s words, he was a "statistically significant sample" of an individual molded by and conforming to the socialist variant of consumer society. Looking for an easy way to comply with demands placed on him while at the same time obviating the need for risky initiative, the protagonist, a talented young chemist, systematically transforms his life into a repetitive sequence of automatic acts. As a consequence, he also has to eliminate from his life any irregularities, including genuine love.

P.'s next novel, *Soukromá vichřice* (1966; private hurricane), presents another laboratory report on mechanized characters. They are easily interchangeable, and indeed, the plot partly consists of the swapping of partners among the couples involved. P. adapted the form of his novel to its purpose, and its short chapters are identified by a combination of letters and numbers, as in a research report.

Sophisticated stylistic and compositional devices are also apparent in *Katapult* (1967; *Catapult*, 1989). The hero, Jacek Jošt, a thirty-three-year-old chemist, attempts to escape from the banal routines of an unexciting marriage and boring work and begins several affairs simultaneously, only to find himself in a self-destructive vicious circle whose essential quality has not changed just because its diameter has increased.

P. has created in his novels a half-real world of his own, the center of which is the north Bohemian city of Ústí nad Labem, where many details of everyday life are faithfully recorded (including people on trains reading P.'s novels), but his work cannot be really described as realistic in the traditional sense. It is, in fact, a grotesquely exaggerated caricature, a schematic and analytic representation of a certain way of life.

P.'s irony is more apparent than in his earlier works in *Milenci a vrazi* (1969; lovers and murderers), in which he takes a skeptical view of the perpetual nature of the struggle between the haves and the have-nots. But the elusiveness of P.'s position, as well as his narrative virtuosity, is demonstrated in a "novel for everyone," *Profesionální žena* (1971; professional woman), a modern fairy tale that can be read as a sentimental and adventurous romance by the uninitiated and as an exhilarating spoof by more sophisticated readers. It appeared at a time when Communist Party controls over the ideological content of literature in Czechoslovakia were being tightened up, and P.'s last two novels were criticized for lack of a positive message of hope and aspiration.

The short novel *Mladý muž a bílá velryba* (1973; the young man and the white whale [Moby Dick]) seemed to be a response to such criticism. It is suffused with optimism even though its main character, a hero of labor, is killed in a work accident. The author's attitude has remained inscrutable and has made possible the interpretation voiced in the West that the novel is in fact a parody of SOCIALIST REALISM. The same view may apply to *Radost až do rána* (1975; joy until the morning), which somewhat ambiguously suggests that happiness can be found in conformity.

With *Generální zázrak* (1977; universal miracle) P. returned to the theme of searching for a full life enriched by love. *Muka obraznosti* (1980; torment of imagination) has a strong autobiographical element combined with parallels to Stendhal's *The Red and the Black*, which is often quoted.

P. managed to avoid being banned by the Czechoslovak communist authorities in the two decades after the 1968 Soviet-led invasion. During these years, he never openly spoke against the totalitarian regime. However, in the 1970s and 1980s, he wrote a number of ambiguous dystopias, which could be interpreted as being critical of the post-1968 communist rule in Czechoslovakia, notably *Pokušení A-ZZ* (1982; Temptation A-ZZ), *Válka s mnohozvířetem* (1983; A War with the Multibeast), and *Země žen* (1987; World of Women). It is now obvious that these works were intended as a direct criticism of the communist system. The most outspoken of them, *Tam za vodou* (1995; The Holiday Village on the Other Side of the River), dating from the early 1970s, was published twenty-five years after it had been written. It is a study of life in a holiday colony, whose inhabitants play games with one another and turn the colony into a totalitarian system.

P. has been a major influence on Czech fiction of the 1960s and 1970s. He was the first to submit to scrutiny the lifestyle of the new socialist middle-class; he brought attention to the industrial region of northern Bohemia, which had never been so extensively described; he infused Czech literature, traditionally inclined to lyricism, with a strong epic element. Despite the demands that its sophisticated complexity makes on readers, P.'s work has enjoyed extraordinary popularity in Czechoslovakia. It has yet to achieve wider recognition abroad, particularly in the English-speaking world. However, since the fall of communism, P. has produced mostly entertainment literature, concentrating on escapist, erotic themes.

FURTHER WORKS IN ENGLISH: *The Four Sonyas* (1993)

BIBLIOGRAPHY: Kunstmann, H., *Tschechische Erzählkunst im 20. Jahrhundert* (1974): 370–73; Hájek, I., comp., "V. P.," in Mihailovich, V.D., et al, *Modern Slavic Literatures* (1976), Vol. II: 179–82; Harkins, W. E., and P. I. Trensky, eds., *Czech Literature since 1956: A Symposium* (1980): 62-73

—IGOR HÁJEK

PARANDOWSKI, Jan

Polish novelist, essayist, and literary historian, b. 11 May 1895, Lvov; d. 26 Sept. 1978, Warsaw

While still attending secondary school in Lvov, at the time part of the Austro–Hungarian Empire, P. began to write. His first book was a literary study, *Rousseau* (1913; Rousseau). During World War I he was interned in central Russia. In 1918 P. returned to Lvov, where he resumed his university studies and received a degree in philosophy and archaeology. At that time he was also active as a journalist and theater critic.

From 1930 on P. lived in Warsaw. During World War II he was politically active in the anti-Nazi underground. After Poland was liberated by Soviet troops, he became a professor of comparative literature at Lublin Catholic University. He was president of the Polish PEN Club from 1933 to 1978, and vice-president of the International PEN Club from 1962 to 1978.

P. is perhaps best known as a devoted and erudite scholar of antiquity. *Mitologia* (1923; mythology) is a retelling of Greek myths for young readers, and the story collection *Eros na Olimpie* (1923; Eros on Olympus) is a ribald work depicting the amorous adventures of the Greek gods. *Dwie wiosny* (1927; two springs), a magnificent historical-literary travel book, was the result of his journeys to Greece in 1925 and to Sicily in 1926. Through his translations (Caesar's *Civil Wars*, Longus' *Daphnis and Chloe*, Homer's *Odyssey*), P. made a substantial contribution to Polish cultural life. In 1930 P. published the penetrating and sensitive *Król życia* (king of life), a fictionalized biography of Oscar Wilde.

After another trip to Greece P. published *Dysk olimpijski* (1932; *The Olympic Discus*, 1939). Through this depiction of the Olympic Games in 476 B.C. P. reconstructs the life of ancient Greece. His unusual ability to render physical details and his meticulous research combine to make this one of the major representations of ancient Greece in modern fiction. For this novel P. was awarded a bronze medal at the Berlin Olympic Games in 1936, despite the protests of the Germans. It is this book, which was translated into several languages, that introduced P. to the Western European reader.

Niebo w płomieniach (1936; heaven in flames), undoubtedly one of P.'s best works, is a psychological novel that treats a subject previously unknown in Polish literature—a religious crisis in the soul of a young boy. It provoked keen criticism and controversy among Roman Catholics and writers of the right. The protagonist reappears as a grown man in *Powrót do życia* (1961; return to life), but the emphasis of this later novel is primarily on the Poland of World War II. *Wrześniowa noc* (1962; September night) is P.'s account of his personal experiences during the Nazi occupation of Poland.

Ideologically, P. occupies a detached, seemingly neutral position, and he considered himself a realist; he is often called a contemporary Polish humanist. His literary style reflects his equanimity, his optimism, and his unceasing search for harmony.

FURTHER WORKS: *Aspazja* (1925); *Odwiedziny i spotkania* (1933); *Trzy znaki zodiaku* (1939); *Godzina śródziemnomorska* (1949); *Alchemia słowa* (1950); *Zegar słoneczny* (1952); *Szkice* (1953); *Pisma wybrane* (1955); *Petrarka* (1956); *Z antycznego świata* (1958; rev. ed. 1971); *Podróże literackie* (1958); *Mój Rzym* (1959; enlarged ed., 1970); *Wspomnienia i sylwety* (1960); *Juvenilia* (1960); *Kiedy byłem recenzentem* (1963; enlarged ed., 1968); *Luźne kartki* (1965); *Szkice, seria druga* (1968); *Akacja* (1968); *Pod zamkniętymi drzwiami czasu* (1975)

BIBLIOGRAPHY: Harjan, G., "J. P.: A Contemporary Polish Humanist," *BA*, 34 (1960): 261–66; Harjan, G., Introduction to *The Olympic Discus* (1964): 1–11; Backvis, C., "J. P.," *Flambeau*, 48 (1966): 281–89; Harjan, G., *J. P.* (1971); Natanson, W., "J. P.," *PolP*, 22, 2 (1979): 66–70

—GEORGE HARJAN

PARDO BAZAN, Emilia

Spanish novelist, short-story writer, critic, essayist, folklorist, and journalist, b. 16 Sept. 1851, La Coruña; d. 12 May 1921, Madrid

P. B. is an extraordinary figure in Spanish letters. Although she began life conventionally enough—albeit within the aristocracy—as daughter and then wife and mother, P. B. became a major force in Spanish letters during nearly forty years. Most closely identified with the realist-naturalist novel of social observation and criticism,

P. B. also published some 580 short stories and as many as 1,500 pieces of journalism, and founded and edited her own magazine, *Nuevo Teatro Crítico* (1891–1893). In 1916, and despite the gender-based opposition of the university council, she was named by the minister of national education to the chair of contemporary Romance literatures at the University of Madrid. During virtually all of her life she fought to make a place for women in every facet of Spanish national life; unfortunately, even such consecrated figures of national cultural life as Juan Valera (1824–1905) and Leopoldo Alas (pseud.: Clarín, 1852–1901) were early antagonists.

P. B.'s most famous works are her *La cuestión palpitante* (1882; the burning question)—a collection of diffuse articles about the naturalism that came into vogue in Spain in the late 1870s and early 1880s because of the translation of Zola's works—and her novel *Los pazos de Ulloa* (1886; *The Son of the Bondswoman*, 1908; rev. ed., 1976). But as happens with her generational companion Armando PALACIO VALDÉS, P. B. suffers from having her best-known works over-shadow the rest of her production. If one accepts that the realist-naturalist group of Spanish novelists really belong to three different cultural generations in ORTEGA Y GASSET's sense, it is clear that P. B., along with Palacio Valdés and Alas, belongs to the third generation, whereas Valera, José Marí de Pereda (1833–1906), Pedro Antonio de Alarcón (1833–1891), and Benito PEREZ GALDÓS belong to the first two. Moreover, for being a woman, P. B. probably arrives on the literary scene with even more effective years of difference than Alas and Palacio with respect to the first two generations. And this means that the aesthetics of realism-naturalism bulk much less in her production than, for example, in that of Galdós and Pereda.

This difference reveals itself thematically more than technically. Whereas the masterpieces of realism-naturalism in Spain date from the mid-1880s, notably Alas's *Le Regenta* (4 vols., 1884–1885), Galdós's *Fortunata y Jacinta* (4 vols., 1886–1887), as well as other works including P. B.'s *Los pazos de Ulloa*, P. B.'s most important novel may well be *La quimera* (1905; the chimera). Although the novel uses the standard techniques of realism-naturalism, its protagonist is a young painter who lives the artistic and spiritual conflicts and crises of end-of-the-century Madrid and Paris. As in her subsequent and penultimate novel *La sirena negra* (1907; *The black siren*), *La quimera* is a novel no longer centered on society and its issues, but on the problematic individual for whom all received values are wanting and for whom new values are not forthcoming.

A gender-related difference adds to the thematic differences between P. B. and other novelists. More than those of any other writer, P. B.'s narrators and main characters, in her longer and shorter fiction, may be masculine or feminine. In consequence the reader is usually aware of a constant subtext wherein the question of how men perceive women and women perceive men is present. This subtext is particularly compelling when the narrator is masculine and making observations about women. Hence, in one of her best novels, *Insolación* (1889; sunstroke), P. B. deftly has a male narrator tell the story of how a wealthy young woman, recently widowed, takes up her new life; in the telling the author makes important points about gender differences and roles.

P. B.'s short stories are effective narrations in which the people and problems of daily life, especially in the author's northwestern Spain, dominate. They were designated for a large, popular audience and in the main stay firmly within the realist-naturalist aesthetic of social observation and criticism. Her few works of theater are less important, but her play of social symbolism, *Cuesta abajo* (1906; downhill), compares favorably with Galdós's *El abuelo* (perf. 1904; the grandfather) and *La de San Quintín* (perf. 1895; the woman of San Quintin). As a historian and popularizer of then contemporary French and Russian literature, P. B. was a forerunner of the internationalization of Spanish culture that is actually associated with Miguel de UNAMUNO and Ortega y Gasset.

FURTHER WORKS: *Estudio crítico de Feijoo* (1876); *Pascual López* (1879); *Un viaje de novios* (1881); *San Francisco de Asís* (1882); *La tribuna* (1883); *La dama joven* (1885); *El cisne de Vilamorta* (1885); *La madre naturaleza* (1887); *Mi romería* (1888); *Obras completas* (47 vols., 1888–1922); *Morriña* (1889); *Al pie de la torre Eiffel* (1889); *Por Francia y por Alemania; Una Cristiana* (1890); *Le prueba* (1890); *La piedra angular* (1891); *Cuentos de Marineda* (1892); *Polémicas y estudios literarios* (1892); *Cuentos nuevos* (1894); *Doña Milagros* (1894); *Los poetas épicos cristianos* (1895); *Por la España pintoresca* (1895); *Memorias de un solterón* (1896); *El tesoro de Gastón* (1897); *El nino de Guzmán* (1898); *Cuentos de amor* (1898); *El saludo de las brujas* (1898); *Cuentos sacroprofanos* (1899); *Cuarenta días en la Exposición Universal de Paris* (1900); *El destripador de antaño* (1900); *En tranvía* (1901); *Cuentos de Navidad y Reyes* (1902); *Cuentos de la patria* (1902); *Cuentos antiguos* (1902); *Por la Europa católica* (1902); *Misterio* (1903); *Novelas ejemplares* (1906); *Lecciones de literatura* (1906); *El fondo del alma* (1907); *Retratos y apuntes literarios* (1907); *Sud-exprés* (1909); *La literatura francesa moderna* (3 vols., 1910, 1911, 1914); *Dulce dueño* (1911); *Belcebú* (1912); *Cuentos trágicos* (1912); *La cocina española* (1913); *Hernán Cortés y sus hazañas* (1914); *Cuentos de la tierra* (1923); *Obras completas* (3 vols., 1947, 1956, 1973)

BIBLIOGRAPHY: Hilton, R., "E. P. B.'s Concept of Spain," *Hispania*, 34 (1951): 135–48; Hilton, R., "Doña E. P. B. and the Europeanization of Spain," *Symposium*, 6 (1952): 298–307; Hilton, R., "P. B. and the Literary Polemics about Feminism," *RR*, 44 (1953): 135–48; Brown, D. F., *The Catholic Naturalism of P. B.* (1957); Kirby, H. L., "P. B., Darwinism, and *La madre naturaleza*," *Hispania*, 47 (1964): 733–37; Kronik, J. K., "E. P. B. and the Phenomenon of French Decadentism," *PMLA*, 81 (1966): 418–27; Dendle, B. J., "The Racial Theories of E. P. B.," *HR*, 38 (1970): 17–31; Pattison, W. T., *E. P. B.*, (1971); Núñez, J. Paredes, *Los cuentos de E. P. B.* (1979); Clemessy, N., *E. P. B. como novelista: de la teoría a la práctica* (1981); Scari, R. M., *Bibliografía descriptiva de estudios críticos sobre la obra de E. P. B.* (1982); Hemingway, M., *E. P. B.: The Making of a Novelist* (1983); Whitaker, D. S., "*La quimera*" *de B. P. y la literatura finisecular* (1988); Henn, D., *The Early P. B.: Theme and Narrative Technique in the Novels of 1879–89* (1988)

—STEPHEN MILLER

PAREJA DIEZCANSECO, Alfredo

Ecuadorean novelist and historian, b. 12 Oct. 1908, Guayaquil

Over his long and productive career, P. D. has gained a solid reputation and today stands out as the most important novelist his country has produced. Born of an Ecuadorean father and a Peruvian mother, both of aristocratic families, P. D. spent his formative years in Guayaquil, the port city that later served as the setting for most of his novels. He had to abandon school at an early age and go to work because the family fortunes had dwindled away. As a youth, he performed many odd jobs, including work as a cabin boy on a ship and a dock laborer. Though he never finished his formal education, he was always a voracious reader of books on philosophy, history, literature, psychology, and social science, becoming virtually an autodidact.

Disciplined, hard working, and active, P. D. also became an inveterate traveler, venturing forth when only twenty-one on his first trip abroad to New York in 1929. There he continued to suffer economic hardship during the Depression and had to seek a variety of menial jobs, such as waiting on tables, to eke out an existence. This was the first in a series of sojourns in other countries. Later he served Ecuador in many diplomatic posts, in Argentina, Chile, and Mexico, crowning his diplomatic career as ambassador to France in 1983.

P. D. also devoted many years to teaching, starting with a high-school position in Guayaquil in 1931, next at the university there in 1934, and finally for many years at the University of Quito where he specialized in Ecuadorean history. He has also taught as a visiting professor in various Latin American countries and in the U.S., most recently at the University of Texas, Austin, in 1982, where he gave classes in Spanish American literature and political science. In 1988 the University of Guayaquil conferred on him the degree of doctor honoris causa, and in 1989 he became a member of the Ecuadorean Academy of History and Language. Today, an octogenarian, he lives tranquilly in Quito, revered as elder statesman and historian.

Writing novels has been "the fundamental passion of my spirit," as P. D. puts it. He has published fourteen novels in all, though he maintains that only thirteen should be counted, disclaiming the second, *La señorita Ecuador* (1930; miss Ecuador), as negligible. Critics also tend to dismiss his first novel, *La casa de los locos* (1929; the madhouse), and the third, *Río arriba* (1931; upriver), as works of apprenticeship, though these earliest books contain virtues and the kernel of things to come. Like his major novels, they are set in the city and show P. D.'s preoccupation with political and social abuses quite graphically. The reader also realizes that P. D. does not have a political ax to grind, that he seems more interested in crafting his novels well.

The qualities just mentioned are strikingly evident in P. D.'s best works, among which one must cite *El muelle* (1933; the dock). In this naturalistic book, the first to bring him acclaim, he captures faithfully the squalid atmosphere of the coastal workers in Guayaquil, a motley group of mestizos—sailors, fishermen, stevedores, merchants, the jobless, the spoils of brothels and taverns. In this novel rife with scenes of violence, prostitution, and corruption, the descriptions are vivid and the dialogues ring with authenticity. As in most of P. D.'s novels, a feminine figure of great vitality stands out, here María del Socorro. The opening chapters, set in New York during the Depression, based on P. D.'s recent stay in that metropolis, protest against police brutality. P. D. implies that society is in bad shape, whether in New York or Guayaquil, and that the poor have no escape.

Among P. D.'s other novels, *Hombres sin tiempo* (1941; men without time), which describes the hideous conditions in a political prison, is based on the author's personal experiences during several months' incarceration, and *Las tres ratas* (1944; the three rats), which unfolds the tale of three sisters, again incorporates naturalistic Guayaquil scenes of drugs, sex, blackmail, political corruption, and tragedy. This novel met with such acclaim that a popular film version was made of it. In his more mature years, P. D. has continued to publish novels that have met with success, such as *Las pequeñas estaturas* (1970; small statures), which delves into the complexities of Ecuadorean politics, while at the same time displaying many of the technical complexities of the so-called Boom writers: long interior monologues, philosophical digressions, and baroque command over language.

P. D. has also published significant works in other fields, like his *Historia del Ecuador* (1954; history of Ecuador) in four volumes, several biographies, and literary essays, notably *Thomas Mann y el nuevo humanismo* (1956; Thomas Mann and the new humanism).

FURTHER WORKS: *La Beldaca* (1935); *Baldomera (La tragedia del cholo americano)* (1938); *Hechos y hazañas de don Balón de Baba y de su amigo Inocente* (1939); *La hoguera bábara: Vida de Eloy Alfaro* (1944); *Vida y leyenda de Miguel Santiago* (1952); *La lucha por la democracia en el Ecuador* (1956); *La advertencia* (1956); *El aire y los recuerdos* (1958); *Los poderes omnímodos* (1964); *La Manticora* (1974); *Ensayos de ensayos* (1981); *Notas de un viaje a China* (1986)

BIBLIOGRAPHY: Diez de Medina, F., "Tres libros de América. *El meulle,*" *Atenea*, 28 (1934): 35–39; Latcham, R., "A. P. D., *El muelle,*" *Atenea*, 29 (1935): 325–29; Rojas, A. F., *La novela ecuatoriana* (1948): 194–98; Schwarz, K., "A. P. D. Social Novelist," *Hispania* 42, 2 (May 1959): 220–28; Andrade, J. Carrera, *Galería de místicos y de insurgentes: La vida intelectual del Ecuador durante cuatro siglos (1555–1955)* (1959): 165–68; Pérez, G. R., *Pensamiento y literatura del Ecuador* (1972): 396–409; Pérez, G. R., *Historia y crítica de la novela hispanoamericana* (1983), Vol. 2: 158–64; Artieda, F., "Una democracia limitada. Entrevista con A. P. D.," *El secuestro del poder* (1987): 101–18; Ribadeneira, E., "La obra narrativa de A. P. D.," *RI*, 54: 144–45 (July-Dec. 1988): 763–69

—GEORGE D. SCHADE

PARISE, Goffredo

Italian novelist, screenwriter, and journalist; b. 8 Dec. 1929, Vicenza, d. 31 Aug. 1986, Treviso

Never having known his biological father, P. adopted his name at the age of fourteen after his mother married Osvaldo Parise, owner of a local newspaper. P. began his lifelong profession as a journalist by working for his father's newspaper in Vicenza, proceeding on to Milan, where he worked for the Garzanti publishing house, and later to Rome.

P.'s narrative debut, *Il ragazzo morto e le comete* (1951; *The Dead Boy and the Comets*, 1953), went relatively unnoticed; however, several prestigious reviews such as those by the poets Andrea ZANZOTTO and Eugene MONTALE were sufficient to warn critics to keep their eyes on a most unconventional and nonconformist writer to emerge from the midst of the neorealistic trends in cinema and literature. P. was in fact reacting to what he considered the repetitious and even superficial political narratives of neorealism with courageous and unorthodox expressionistic writings that

some considered too bold and scandalous. His first two novels introduce a series of eccentric characters that will return in later works, as well as the central themes and motifs that best exemplify P.'s fiction: autobiographical allusions, initiation into eros and adulthood, a nostalgic return to the years of adolescence, social and religious hypocrisies, oneirism, traumatic experiences, violence, and death. *Il ragazzo morto e le comete* ends with the death of a fifteen-year-old boy who had been befriended by Fiore. In this tragic and surreal story the two boys converse with dead people that wander around until it is time for them to disappear forever. It is a strange story about the conflict of life and death and about people who are alive and yet seem to be dead, as well as those who are dead and continue to be alive. It is also a story in which P. reveals his feelings toward God—here defined as a splendid and mysterious comet that came and went after having completed its orbit.

La grande vacanza (1953; The Big Vacation) and *Il Prete bello* (1954; *The Priest among the Pigeons*, 1955) were read by a larger public who began to appreciate the author's originality in his treatment of unusual characters, bizarre relationships, scandals, and moral corrosion specifically set in a stagnant and familiar provincial ambience. Most of P.'s stories are set around his native city of Vicenza and in the Veneto region. Combining first- and third-person accounts of events and descriptions P. is both humorous and sarcastic toward the hypocrisy of petty bourgeois characters who are often depicted as repulsive figures or as mere caricatures. In *La grande vacanza* a sixteen-year-old boy, Claudio, accompanies his grandmother on vacation in the Venetian hills. Claudio encounters several grotesque characters that lead the narration into a series of digressions and flashbacks, especially about World War II and postwar experiences. The end of "the big vacation" ends with the grandmother's death and with Claudio feeling depressed as a result of his encounters and of his awareness of having lost his adolescence as well as his innocence.

With *Il prete bello* (1954; The Beautiful Priest) P. received his first major critical attention. This rather risque novel confirmed the author's insistence on bitterly satirizing bigotry, the middle class, and the repressiveness of artificial social conventions. A small community is affected by the arrival of a young fascist priest, Don Gastone, and an attractive promiscuous woman, Fedora, who thrives on seducing and destroying men—including the priest, with whom she has a child. P.'s criticism, mixed with comical scenes, is directed against the Catholic Church, fascists, and bourgeois families all involved in hypocrisy, sex, and social scandals. The story ends with the deaths of the priest and of a young boy, called Cena, with whom the narrator Sergio befriends.

In his early novels P. masterfully depicts men and women as marionettes, animals, insects, or comic book characters. Moreover, the powerful images of conflicts between men and women in *Il prete bello* return and are reinforced in subsequent works such as *L'assoluto naturale* (1967; The Absolute Natural) and the screenplay *L'ape regina* (The Queen Bee), written in 1961 for the director Marco Ferreri. In 1960 P. left Milano and moved to Rome where he began to write film scripts—notably *8 1/2* for Federico Fellini. In addition to his script writing activities P. in the 1960s also began his frequent travels around the world on behalf of major newspapers and weekly magazines such as *Il corriere della sera* and *L'Espresso*. His superb sociopolitical reportage as a war correspondent in Vietnam and Cambodia, as well as his travel experiences in China, Biafra, the U.S., and Japan have appeared in illustrated texts such as *Cina Cina* (1966; China), *Biafra* (1968; Biafra) and *New York* (1977; New York).

P. was an excellent observer of the many changes that the Italian society was undergoing after World War II. He wrote *Il Padrone* (1965; *The Boss*, 1967) as the literary trend of "Literature and Industry" was coming to an end, and after the publication of a variety of narratives that used material from diaries and first hand accounts of the workers's experiences within an industrial setting. This is one of the most original and disturbing critiques of modern alienation linked to neocapitalism and industrialization. Rather than discuss assembly lines, strikes, or the exploitation and disillusionment of poor workers who had originally looked at industrialization as a chance to be part of progress, P. chooses to illustrate the gradual acceptance of complete submission by a worker, unnamed, to his "boss," Dr. Max. In this mordant, ironic, and grotesque presentation of psychological conditioning, conformity and total loss of identity P. mixes Darwinism, Marxism, and Freudian notions as he portrays different types of master-slave relationships in a society that seems to embrace industrialization like a new religion. The worker, for example, is forced to have unnecessary injections everyday. The various absurdities of this story are constantly accentuated by the names of the main characters—Pippo, Pluto, Urania, Minnie, and Dr. Diabete, for example—all echoing comic-book and Disney characters.

P.'s skills in narrating short stories was first demonstrated in the 1960s. With the publication of *Sillabario I* (1972; *Abecedary*, 1990) followed ten years later by *Sillabario II* (1982; *Solitudes*, 1984)—winner of the Premio Strega—the author confirms his exceptional talent in creating minimalist narrations that wish to capture the essence of life in brief but significant moments. P. had originally planned to write a short story for each letter of the alphabet. The first volume goes from "A" ("amore," "amicizia," and so on) to "F" ("famiglia"), the second from "F" ("felicità") to "S" ("solitudine"). Some critics saw a new P. focusing on common, daily, simple, but certainly not insignificant moments in people's lives. The brief stories deal mainly with spontaneous emotions, sentiments, simple perception, memories, and sensations, all written in a lyrical fashion, like long poems in prose form. The author stops at the letter "S" claiming that suddenly the lyrical voice, his poetry, left him and consequently it was time to stop writing.

P.'s most sexually explicit narrative, written and left unfinished in 1979 shortly after he suffered his first heart attack, is *L'odore del sangue* (The Smell of Blood), published posthumously in 1997. It is a story of morbid jealousy in which Filippo, a psychoanalyst in his fifties, finds a younger lover, Paloma, who is obsessed with the relationship of his wife Silvia and her younger lover, Stefano. The novel is about marital problems, sickness, visions, obsessions, and sadomasochism. The most erotic scenes involve Filippo as he often asks his wife to describe with graphic details her lovemaking with Stefano in order to have a confirmation that his visions are correct as he imagines their animalistic sexuality. P.'s familiar descriptions of scenes of adolescence, sexuality, maturing, and of a growing awareness of death are at the center of this narration just as they were in his earlier writings. And once again we see how P.'s descriptions appear to have been filtered through a distorting lens in order to produce oneiric, psychoanalytical, and surreal effects: An art form that P. mastered during his experiments with the language and techniques of cinematography in his days of script writing.

It is difficult to say if *Sillabario*, by describing from A to Z a series of significant moments, was also meant to put some order in his vision of a chaotic life. Nonetheless, these short stories are a testimonial of P.'s unusual passion for life that he continued to manifest even as he became pessimistic about a society dominated by wealth, violence and hypocrisy.

FURTHER WORKS: *Il fidanzamento* (1956); *Amore e fervore* (1959); *Gli Americani a Vicenza* (1966); *Due, tre cose sul Vietnam* (1967); *Atti impuri* (1973); *Guerre politiche: Vietnam, Biafra, Laos, Chile* (1976); *L'eleganza è frigida* (1982); *Artisti* (1984); *Arsenio* (1986); *Veneto barbaro di muschi e nebbie* (1987); *Verbo volant* (1998)

BIBLIOGRAPHY: Montale, E., "Dance of Human Insects," *Book Review Atlas* (November 1965): 312-14; Vonnegut, K., "Money Talks to the New Man," *NYT* (2 October 1966); Wardle, I., "Kafka Italianstyle," *The Observer*, 23 (July 1967); Shuttleworth, M., "The Boss," *Punch*, 26 (July 1967)

—ROCCO CAPOZZI

PARNICKI, Teodor

Polish novelist and essayist, b. 5 March 1908, Berlin, Germany; d. 5 Dec. 1988, Warsaw

P. was born into a strongly Germanized Polish family. Because of his father's travels as an engineer, P. spent his early years in Russia and China. He went to Poland in 1928 to study at the University of Lvov, where he quickly earned a reputation for his knowledge of Russian literature. His contributions to numerous magazines made him known as an essayist on the historical novel. During World War II he served as an attaché of the Polish government-in-exile at embassies in Moscow, Jerusalem, London, and Mexico City. In 1945 P. settled in Mexico, which he felt had an atmosphere favorable to his literary development. He has lived in Poland since 1967 and is the winner of several Polish literary prizes.

P. revitalized the Polish historical novel by bringing modern techniques and themes to the genre. His first novel, *Aecjusz, ostatni Rzymianin* (1937; Aetius, the last Roman), depicts the deeds of a Roman dictator during the 5th c., while *Srebrne orły* (1944; silver eagles) explores the origins of the medieval Polish state.

P.'s most important novels were written in Mexico. The uncompleted cycle known as *Światy mieszańców* (at the crossroads of civilizations), consisting of *Słowo i ciało* (2 vols., 1953, 1958; word and body) and *Koniec "zgody nardów"* (1955; the end of the "people's entente"), depicts the intrigues, customs, and ideas of ancient Mediterranean civilizations. *Twarz księżyca* (3 vols., 1961–67; the face of the moon) analyzes societies in the 3rd and 4th cs. A.D. And *Nowa baśń* (6 vols., 1962–70; the new fable) is a panorama of a medieval European culture that emerges from the confrontation between East and West. P.'s best novel is *Tylko Beatrycze* (1962; only for Beatrice), about a peasant insurrection in 12th-c. Poland. Since the publication of *Muza dalekich podróży* (1970; the muse of distant journeys) his work has evolved toward fantasy historical novels.

The two main centers of interest in P.'s work are the development of the early Catholic Church and the birth of the medieval Polish state. Erudite, P. always chooses episodes of history that highlight intellectual, social, and religious ferment. He is fascinated by the interaction between cultures and by the transformations it produces. His heroes, living in a troubled world, are full of contradictions and conflicts. P's novels reflect his effort to organize the labyrinth of the past in order to build his own spiritual and mythical genealogy. His works have a chronological, thematic, and geographical cohesiveness comparable only to that of PROUST's *Remembrance of Things Past*.

P.'s most original contribution to the historical novel is his conception of the historical fact. The past is seen through the eyes of an observer (the hero-narrator), through his beliefs and reactions; hence the work has a psychological foundation. The emphasis of the narration is on reflections about historical facts whose objectivity is questioned. Works such as *Staliśmy jak dwa sny* (1973; like two dreams) also analyze the art of writing a historical novel. This concern about theory is further demonstrated in a collection entitled *Szkice literackie* (1978; literary essays) and in a series of autobiographical lectures published as *Historia w literaturę przekuwana* (1980; making history into literature).

P.'s novels are not easy ones. Although detached from actuality, they address 20th-c. formal and moral questions, providing new insights into the problem of the extent to which the writing of history is an objective skill or imaginative, creative work. His philosophical attitude makes him akin to another specialist in the historical novel, Marguerite YOURCENAR.

FURTHER WORKS: *Trzy minuty po trzeciej* (1930); *Rozkaz nr. 94* (1930); *Opowiadania* (1958); *I u możnych dziwny* (1965); *Śmierć Aecjusza* (1966); *Koła na piasku* (1966); *Zabij Kleopatrę* (1968); *Inne życie Kleopatry* (1969); *Tożsamość* (1970); *Przeobrażenie* (1973); *Sam wyjdę bezbronny* (1976); *Hrabia Julian i król Roderyk* (1976)

BIBLIOGRAPHY: Herman, M., *Histoire de la littérature polonaise des origines á 1961* (1963): 593–761; Miłosz, C., *The History of Polish Literature* (1969): 504–07 and passim

—ALICE-CATHERINE CARLS

Nicanor Parra

PARRA, Nicanor

Chilean poet, b. 5 Sept. 1914, Chillán

P. was the eldest son of a rural elementary-school teacher who had married a farmer's daughter. He began writing poetry as a student at the Pedagogical Institute of the University of Chile in Santiago, from which he graduated in 1938 with a degree in mathematics and physics. P.'s first book, *Cancionero sin nombre* (1937; songbook without a name), won the Municipal Poetry Prize of Santiago. P. taught in Chilean high schools until 1943, when he began graduate work at Brown University in advanced mechanics. While in the U.S., P. continued to write poetry and was influenced by Walt Whitman's *Leaves of Grass*. After his return to Chile in 1945, P. was appointed director of the School of Engineering at the University of Chile. From 1949 to 1951 he studied at Oxford University under a grant from the British Council. In 1952 he was named professor of theoretical physics at the University of Chile and has held this post ever since.

P.'s early poetry emulated the ballads found in GARCÍA LORCA's *Gypsy Ballads* and was hailed by Chilean critics as marking a return to clarity and simpler poetic modes within the nation's rich lyric tradition. Today, however, P.'s first book has almost been forgotten because of the enormous success enjoyed by his *Poemas y antipoemas* (1954; *Poems and Antipoems*, 1967), which made a

profound impact on Latin American poetry. Within Chile, this book represented a creative liberation and a new direction away from the overwhelming influence of Pablo NERUDA's three volumes of *Residence on Earth*, which was written in a style typified by oneiric imagery, personal symbols, chaotic enumerations, and mythical archetypes. P.'s second book provided Latin American critics with the term "antipoem," which was an attractive name for a reaction to Nerudian surrealism and the traditionally elitist character of most lyric poetry. P. had created a tragicomic, prosaic poem characterized by biting irony, sardonic humor, and iconoclastic imagery.

Antipoetry represented more than just a dialectical reaction to the avant-garde verse in vogue up to the end of World War II. P. also attempted to refurbish lyric poetry and recapture its lost popular appeal through the incongruous juxtaposition of colloquial language and traditional poetic conceits, the employment of free verse and ironic humor, and the mordantly satirical depiction of the banal daily tribulations that afflict every 20th-c. man, including the poet himself. In short, P.'s radical departure from more conventional verse led to a thorough reexamination of the purposes and nature of the poetic art by poets and critics alike throughout Latin America.

In most of his later books P. has constantly mocked the social and literary conventions of the contemporary Western world. At the same time, P.'s own antipoetry has further evolved and replenished itself, until in *Artefactos* (1972; artifacts) he stripped poetry of all metaphorical adornments and reduced the antipoem to epigrammatic verses that still voice popular discontent with society. Almost all the characters found in P.'s poetic world are antiheroes who are obsessed with a fear of death, are prey to physical deterioration, have had disillusioning love affairs, and have a deep-felt sense of personal inadequacy and insignificance. They are trapped in the absurdly comic tragedy of daily living. Even the poet himself is presented as a pathetic figure no better off than any other man, hardly a "small god," as Vicente HUIDOBRO, another Chilean poet, once described him. Some critics view the language and form of the antipoetic texts as a reflection of the disarray of contemporary society. Religion is debunked and denigrated. Women, once the main source of poetic inspiration, are perceived as heartless, seductive adversaries of man or as his exploited sexual playmates.

P. has parodied most of the major themes and stylistic devices employed throughout the Western poetic tradition. P.'s antipoetry has now been translated into many languages. It ridicules modern man for his continued adherence to defunct myths promoted by the social establishment. It also radically subverts the established forms and language found in conventional lyric poetry. P.'s works have broadened the boundaries of poetic expression to include almost every individual and social dimension of the human experience and have made the genre more accessible to the common man.

FURTHER WORKS: *Discursos* (1962); *Versos de salón* (1962); *La cueca larga, y otros poemas* (1964); *Canciones rusas* (1967); *Obra gruesa* (1969); *Los profesores* (1971). FURTHER WORKS IN ENGLISH: *Emergency Poems* (1972, bilingual)

BIBLIOGRAPHY: Hersh, B., "The Man in the Ironic Mask," *Horizon* (May 1962): 35–41; Lerzundi, P., "In Defense of Antipoetry: An Interview with N. P.," *Review*, Nos. 4–5 (1972): 65–72; Van Hooft, K., "The *Artefactos* of N. P.: The Explosion of the Antipoem," *RevB*, 1, 1 (1974): 67–80; Grossman, E., *The Antipoetry of N. P.* (1975); Gottlieb, M., *No se termina nunca de nacer: La poesía de N. P.* (1977)

—JAMES J. ALSTRUM

PASCOAES, Teixeira de

See Teixeira de Pascoaes

PASCOLI, Giovanni

Italian poet, b. 31 Dec. 1855, San Mauro di Romagna; d. 18 Feb. 1912, Bologna

P.'s early life was darkened by a series of tragic events: at the age of eleven, by the unsolved murder of his father; later, by the deaths of his mother and three of his brothers and sisters. His university years in Bologna were marked by involvement in the socialist movement and active participation in the International. Upon graduation in 1882, he began teaching Latin and Greek in several schools and universities in southern and northern Italy, until, in 1905, he was appointed to succeed Giosuè Carducci (1835–1907), his former teacher and mentor, in the chair of Italian

literature at the University of Bologna. With the proceeds of the sale of thirteen gold medals awarded him at the Hoeuft annual competition for Latin poetry in Amsterdam, he purchased a much longed-for country home at Castelvecchio di Barga, a locale that inspired much of his poetry.

P.'s first collection of poems, published under the title of *Myricae* (1891; Latin: tamarisks), consists mostly of scenic sketches and descriptions of rural life, created by juxtaposing short phrases that add up to vivid series of pictorial and musical impressions. The choice of themes is psychologically connected to remembrances of his serene early childhood in the country and to his persistent sense of happiness forever lost. As a consequence, many lyrics that at first appear to be only idyllic descriptive fragments take on a vague and obscure symbolic meaning. Other poems are directly inspired by P.'s domestic sorrows and are highly charged with personal emotion. In the last poems of the collection, his own grief expands to a deeply melancholic view of man's destiny, and the descriptions of nature become laden with pending danger or cosmic catastrophe. The technical means by which P. achieves these effects are deceptively simple. While the logical structure of his sentence is minimal but still intact, the order of descriptive elements is very effectively handled to suggest a sense of foreboding. The use of refrains, of popular songs, of insistent onomatopoeia, of synesthesia, create the suggestion of a different, impenetrable reality in which the fates of men and of other creatures in the universe are mysteriously connected.

The poems of *Canti di Castelvecchio* (1903; songs of Castelvecchio) successfully continue the themes and manner of *Myricae*. Many poems are descriptions of his childhood or evoke the painful events of his youthful years; nonetheless, realistic evocations of daily life at Barga are dominant in the collection and give it its pervasive tone.

Primi poemetti (1904; first minor poems) and *Nuovi poemetti* (1906; new minor poems) depict the serene life of a family of farmers, with descriptions of the various phases of home and field work, of country festivities, of seasonal changes, and of animals, plants, and trees. What gives a lyrical, almost religious quality to these humble subjects is both a sense of cosmic correspondence in the destinies of men and their fellow creatures and the poet's strong belief in the sacred value of human and animal labor.

Poemi conviviali (1904; *Convivial Poems*, 1979) re-create scenes and situations of the classical world, from Homeric times to the rise of Christianity. The subject is solemn and the language highly precious and erudite; but the poet's pervasive feeling is that all things must come to an end and die, and that the dissolution of ancient myths and of history is inevitable.

Odi e Inni (1906; odes and hymns) contains poems of a civic nature. They are noteworthy as examples of the repeated attempt on the part of the poet, who never renounced his ideal of humanitarian socialism, to rationalize and harmonize his stands on the many social and political problems of contemporary Italy; among these were the massive emigration, which he felt was a heartrendingly tragic solution to unemployment, and the foreign policies of the Italian and other European governments, which he interpreted in terms of a struggle between poor and powerful nations.

Compared with the robust strains of Giosuè Carducci's poetry and with the flamboyant verse of Gabriele D'ANNUNZIO, P.'s work was long considered to be that of a homely provincial poet, a sort of bucolic Vergil in minor key. During the past decades critics have come to recognize that his emphasis on personal sensations and emotions, his persistent sense of loss, his technical innovations—connotative and evocative use of words and sounds, coherence of mood in place of logical coherence, new verse rhythms—his theory and practice of poetry as a predominantly intuitive activity place him in the mainstream of the Decadent and SYMBOLIST movements in Europe. Moreover, he is now considered the most genuine voice in Italian poetry of his time and the primary influence on all subsequent avant-garde poets.

FURTHER WORKS: *Il fanciullino* (1897); *Minerva oscura* (1898); *Sotto il velame* (1900); *La mirabile visione* (1902); *Nell'anno mille* (1902); *Miei pensieri di varia umanità* (1903); *La messa d'oro* (1905); *Pensieri e discorsi* (1907); *Canzoni di Re Enzio* (1908–1909); *Poemetti italici* (1911); *Poesie varie* (1912); *Traduzioni e riduzioni* (1913); *Poemi del Risorgimento* (1913); *Carmina* (2 vols., 1914, 1930); *Antico sempre nuovo* (1925); *Lettere agli amici lucchesi* (1960); *Lettere agli amici urbinati* (1963); *Lettere ad Alfredo Caselli* (1968); *Tutte le opere* (6 vols., 1970–1971); *Lettere a Mario Novaro e ad altri amici* (1971); *Lettere alla gentile ignota* (1972). FURTHER WORKS IN ENGLISH: *Poems of G. P.* (1923); *Poems of G. P.* (1927); *Selected Poems of G. P.* (1938)

BIBLIOGRAPHY: Valentin, A., *G. P., poète lyrique: Les thèmes de son inspiration* (1925); Purkis, G. S., Introduction to *Selected Poems of G. P.* (1938): 1–10; Wilkins, E. H., *A History of Italian Literature* (1966): 461–64; Ukas, M., "Nature in the Poetry of G. P." *KFLQ*, 13 (1966): 51–59

—RINALDINA RUSSELL

PASHTO LITERATURE

See Afghan Literature and Pakistani Literature

PASOLINI, Pier Paolo

Italian poet, novelist, essayist, and film director (also writing in Friulian), b. 5 March 1922, Bologna; d. 2 Nov. 1975, Ostia

After passing a somewhat peripatetic existence in several northern Italian cities as a young boy, a style of life occasioned by his father's military career, P. returned to his native city in 1937 and enrolled at the University of Bologna. He studied literature and art history and began writing poems in Friulian, a Rhaeto-Romanic dialect, publishing his first collection of verse, *Poesie a Casarsa* (poems to Casarsa), at his own expense in 1942. The family had spent summers for many years in the town of Casarsa, P.'s mother's birthplace northeast of Venice, and it is to this place that the poems are dedicated. In 1943 the family moved there; during the stay of six years the young poet's philological and creative interests flourished as he became more deeply involved with the dialect of the region and wrote more poetry both in Friulian and in Italian. In 1949 P. and his mother went to Rome, where he lived and worked until his brutal murder in the suburb of Ostía. In the last decade of his life P. attained international renown as a film director and became one of contemporary Italy's most outspoken and controversial figures, in political and personal as well as artistic debates.

Pier Paolo Pasolini

The richness and variety of P.'s career are equaled in magnitude only by the complexities of his inner life, which drove him to attempt a merging of his politics, metaphysics, and homosexuality into a cohesive, meaningful artistic and existential unity of intent and result. When viewed retrospectively, each work represents a piece of the mosaic, no matter how disparate the individual elements might at first appear.

P.'s first collection of verse in Friulian reflects his intense love for his mother's place of origin, a love tied to its landscapes, its peasants, and, above all, its language. The concept of an intimate "maternal tongue," one more poetically valid than standard speech, had essential resonances for P. from very early on. This intuition soon merged with his political concerns for the uneducated, dialect-speaking, marginal classes of Italy. His move to Rome opened up yet another world of experience, which both intensified his interest in the oppressed and sharpened his critical and literary skills: the former by direct contact with the Roman proletariat; the latter by collaboration on literary journals and continued study of the linguistic and artistic heritage of Italy. As P. maintained his dedication to writing poetry, he also began, in the early 1950s, to turn to fiction. In the novel *Ragazzi di vita* (1955; *The Ragazzi*, 1968), written in P.'s version of Roman dialect, P.'s goal was to describe, in their own language, the Roman street hustlers' daily struggle for survival. The protagonists are Rome's uneducated youth, who live precariously and violently in a state of permanent personal and social alienation from the bourgeois mainstream.

During this same period P. also wrote several articles in which he attempted to clarify his ideological convictions—Marxist for the most part, but already personalized by the writer's insistence on the fundamental role of culture and language in the struggle for a new Italian society. P.'s relationship to the Communist Party was always troubled and questioning; his formal association with the Party had ended shortly before his move to Rome with his expulsion "for moral and political unworthiness" because of a homosexual incident with minors for which P. was prosecuted. As in all his work, therefore, both the personal and the ideological components of his stormy politics must be kept in mind if his beliefs are to be understood correctly.

One of the clearest expressions of P.'s beliefs is found in his collection of poetry *Le ceneri di Gramsci* (1957; the ashes of Gramsci), written in standard Italian. Here he shows his ambivalence toward the political and cultural philosophy of Antonio Gramsci (1891–1937). On the one hand, he accepts the rational arguments of the great early Communist; on the other, he cannot follow the implicit exhortation to become identified passionately and intimately with the working class and to see it as an autonomous, potentially self-sufficient force for the significant transformation of society. His sense of personal, intellectual, and spiritual distance from the poor, for whom he nonetheless cared intensely, would torment him throughout his life and eventually lead him to deny the possibility of total integration he so desperately sought through his entire career.

In the late 1950s P. published many volumes that manifest his multiple interests: *L'usignolo della Chiesa Cattolica* (1958; the nightingale of the Catholic Church), a collection of the poetry written in Italian between 1943 and 1949, in which the influence of SYMBOLIST and Decadent poetry is evident; *Una vita violenta* (1959; *A Violent Life*, 1968), another novel written in Roman dialect, in which the central theme is the difficult struggle for dignity and betterment of the lower classes; *Passione e ideologia* (1960; passion and ideology), a collection of critical essays on dialect poetry, modern and contemporary Italian poets and novelists, and general literary, linguistic, and cultural topics.

P.'s debut as a film director was in 1961 with *Accattone*. As is the case of most of his films, P. wrote the script, which was also published in 1961. The film is a cinematic version of the preoccupations evident in the two dialect novels, and is distinguished by a highly effective mix of harsh realism and subtle poetic sensibility. Throughout the 1960s and up to the time of his death, P. was primarily involved in filmmaking; his best-known and most successful films are *Il vangelo secondo Matteo* (1964; the gospel according to Matthew), a moving reinterpretation of the story of Christ's life from a Marxist perspective; *Uccellacci e uccellini* (1964; hawks and sparrows), an allegorical tale also with political undertones; *Teorema* (1968; theorem), a highly symbolic story of a family seduced by a frighteningly erotic Christ-figure; *Medea* (1970; Medea, a version of the classic tragedy, starring Maria Callas; and his last film, *Salò; o, le 120 giornate di Sodoma* (1975; Salò; or, the 120 days of Sodom), a violently pornographic meditation on Italian Fascism from an eroto-political perspective provided primarily by the works of the Marquis de Sade. The scripts for all of these films were written by Pasolini and published in the same years of the films' releases. In addition, there exists an English translation of the script for the film *Edipo Re* (1967; *Oedipus Rex*, 1971), and in 1975 the scripts for *Il Decamerone* (1971; the

Decameron), *I racconti di Canterbury* (1972; the Canterbury Tales), and *Il fiore delle mille e una notte* (1974; the flower of the thousand and one nights) were published under the title *Trilogia della vita* (trilogy of life). These last three films, perhaps the most popularly successful of all P.'s cinema, are delightfully eccentric reworkings of literary classics.

P. did not, however, abandon other forms of creative expression during the last years of his life. He wrote several tragedies in verse and published another collection of poetry, *Trasumanar e organizzar* (1971; to transfigure, to organize); in 1972 his prolific critical writings were again collected and published under the title *Empirismo eretico* (*Heretical Empiricism*, 1988). P. contributed extensively to the Milanese newspaper *Corriere della sera* in the final few years of his career, writing on everything from language to current events to politics. Although filled more and more with a sense of despair, P. remained enormously productive right up to the moment of his death, intending to direct more films, complete a novel, write more poetry, and pursue his eternal goal of joining personal confession and clarification with political and cultural activism. In 1992 the massive unfinished novel *Petrolio* (*Petrolio*, 1997) was published, and other previously unpublished works have appeared since P.'s death in 1975.

The controversy surrounding P.'s death—was he murdered by one young man in a violent homosexual encounter or was he deliberately killed by prior arrangement for political reasons?—remains active to this day and adds to the mysterious, mythic dimensions of the man and his destiny. Whatever the answer to the why of his death, however, the more essential answer to the why of his life lies in his prolific and undeniably positive gifts through which he has enriched our century.

FURTHER WORKS: *Poesie* (1945); *I pianti* (1946); *Tal cour di un frut* (1953); *La meglio gioventù* (1954); *Donne di Roma* (1960); *Roma 1950, diario* (1960); *La religione del mio tempo* (1961); *Mamma Roma* (1962); *Poesia in forma di rosa* (1964); *Orgia* (1969); *Calderón* (1973); *Il padre selvaggio* (1975); *Scritti corsari* (1975); *La divina mimesis* (1975); *Lettere agli amici* (1976); *Lettere luterane* (1977); *Affabulazione; Pilade* (1977); *Le belle bandiere* (1977); *Cinema in forma di poesia* (1979); *Trilogia della vita* (1987); *Lettere 1955-1975* (1988); *Un paese di temporali e di primule* (1993); *L'Academiuta friulana e le sue riviste* (1994). FURTHER WORKS IN ENGLISH: *P. P. P.: Poems* (1982)

BIBLIOGRAPHY: Ragusa, O., "Gadda, P. and Experimentalism: Form or Ideology?," in Pacifici, S., ed., *From Verismo to Experimentalism* (1969): 239–69; O'Neill, T., "P. P. P.'s Dialect Poetry," *FI*, 9 (1975): 343–67; Anderson, L. J., "Challenging the Norm: The Dialect Question in the Works of Gadda and P.," *SHEH*, 20 (1977): 1–63; Marcus, M., "P. P. P.'s Poetics of Film," *YItS*, 1 (1977): 184–94; Friedrich, P., *P. P. P.* (1982); Siciliano, E., *P.: A Biography* (1982); White, E., on *P.: A Biography* and *P. P. P.: Poems, NYTBR*, 27 June 1982: 8–9, 14; Greene, N., *P. P. P.: Cinema as Heresy* (1990); Viano, M., *A Certain Realism: Making Use of P.'s Film Theory and Practice* (1993); Rumble, P., and B. Testa, eds., *P. P. P.: Contemporary Perspectives* (1994); Ward, D., *A Poetics of Resistance: Narrative and the Writings of P. P. P.* (1995); Rohdie, S., *The Passion of P. P. P.* (1995); Rumble, P., *Allegories of Contamination: P. P. P.'s Trilogy of Life* (1996); Gordon, R., *P.: Forms of Subjectivity* (1996)

—REBECCA J. WEST

PASTERNAK, Boris

Russian poet and prose writer, b. 10 Feb. 1890, Moscow; d. 30 May 1960, Peredelkino

Born into a family of great talent—his father, Leonid Pasternak, was a well-known painter (a friend of Leo Tolstoy and illustrator of his works), and his mother, Rosalia Kaufmann, a concert pianist—P. was early exposed to the world of art. Under the influence of the music and personality of Alexander Scriabin (another P. family acquaintance), P. spent his adolescent years preparing for a career in music, but gave it up for philosophy, which he studied at the universities of Moscow and Marburg, Germany.

His first collection of verse, *Bliznets v tuchakh* (1914; a twin in the clouds), was followed by *Poverkh barerov* (1917; over the barriers). His following two books, *Sestra moya zhizn* (1922; *Sister My Life*, 1967) and *Temy i variatsii* (1923; themes and variations), brought him critical acclaim and wide recognition; they proved to be the most influential of his works. A trip to the Caucasus in 1931 established long-term friendships and collaborations with several Georgian poets. *Vtoroe rozhdenie* (1932; second birth) marks the beginning of P.'s consciously simpler style. After the mid-1930s P. led an increasingly secluded life at his country house outside Moscow. Two slim volumes of poems, *Na rannikh poezdakh* (1943; on early trains) and *Zemnoy prostor* (1945; earth's expanse), appeared during World War II. His novel, *Doctor Zhivago* (1957; *Doctor Zhivago*, 1958), was banned in the Soviet Union, but published abroad and translated into many languages; it brought P. worldwide recognition. In 1958 P. was awarded the Nobel prize for literature, which he was forced to refuse under pressure of an attack in the Soviet press. He died two years later.

During 1914–16, without sharing in the FUTURIST poets' generally unconventional behavior or supporting their highly negative view of the art of the past, P. actively participated in Centrifuge, one of the modernist literary groups. More importantly, his handling of language and the deliberate use of nonaesthetic imagery in the poems of the period (most notably in *Poverkh barerov*) reveal P.'s more than casual relation to futurist poetics. While some critics (for example, Wladimir Weidlé) accept P.'s own retrospective view of this episode in his life as something transitory and unimportant for his development, others (such as Lazar Fleishman), although acknowledging his peripheral position, tend to view his futurist orientation as very significant until the 1930s.

Written in 1917 and 1918 respectively, but only published five years after their composition, *Sestra moya zhizn* and *Temy i variatsii* can be described as the "essential" P. The emotionally charged poems in these two books demonstrate well the fundamentals of P.'s poetry. Although the setting of the lyrics is often urban, it is through seasonal and natural changes that the emotional developments are conveyed. Transference of experiences between the subject and his surroundings—an effective device for depicting communion with nature and awareness of the surrounding physical world—testifies to a poetic point of view that embraces everything about the subject. The poet's never-failing surprise at returning spring or the joy brought by rain, for example, contribute toward the youthfulness and dynamism of this poetry. Many poems are about lovers' separations and disappointments, but the general tone is one of exaltation and exuberance. The complexity of imagery, the verbal richness, and the elliptic and unconventional syntax contribute to the appeal as well as the difficulty of this verse.

Publication of these two books established P. as a major poet of the period. The influence of his poetic manner of expression was soon seen in the work of his contemporaries and younger poets and even of some poets of the preceding generation.

One of the persistent criticisms directed at P. by establishment critics was his interest in the individual rather than in the collective. Ignoring the revolution was tantamount to rejecting it. But for P. himself, *Sestra moya zhizn* was a book about revolution, with the poet not chronicling events but conveying their essence.

During the 1920s P. published two longer narrative poems, "Devyatsot pyaty god" (1927; the year 1905) and "Leytenant Shmidt" (1927; Lieutenant Schmidt), in which he attempted to deal with the subject of the revolution. Just as in his shorter lyrics P. speaks not about himself but assigns his experiences to the surrounding world, here he speaks not about the main event but about what led to it—about the 1905 rather than the 1917 revolution. Although reprinted many times, these poems were not as successful artistically as his short lyrics.

Along with his first poems, P. started experimenting in prose, although it was not until 1925 that a collection was published, under the title *Rasskazy* (*Zhenia's Childhood, and Other Stories*, 1982). The long prose piece "Detstvo Lyuvers" (written 1918; *The Adolescence of Zhenya Luvers*, 1961), showing the world through the perception of an adolescent girl, was singled out for particular praise by the critics. Other pieces in the volume deal mainly with the problems of art and the artist.

A major prose work, *Okhrannaya gramota* (1931; "A Safe-Conduct," 1949; later tr., 1977), is an autobiography that proposes to speak about the poet's own life only when prompted by the biographies of those who were important for his development as a human being and a poet. Complex and allusive, it is one of the high points of P.'s prose works. Beginning with a chance meeting in 1900 of P.'s family with Rainer Maria RILKE, a significant influence acknowledged by P. himself, it ends in 1930, with the suicide of Vladimir MAYAKOVSKY, his contemporary, friend—and often antagonist.

P.'s simpler manner in the book of verse *Vtoroe rozhdenie* was to remain his goal until the end of his life. This programmatic desire for a less complex means of expression can be seen, at least in part, as a result of a genuine wish to become more accessible, aided, no doubt, by constant official criticism of his being incomprehensible to the mass reader. This new style, although strikingly different from his earlier work in some aspects, most notably in syntax, developed from P.'s original complexity and retained in a subdued form many of the stylistic features of his earlier poetry.

After Mayakovsky's death, P. was left the undisputed candidate for the role of the "first poet" of the Soviet state, and, indeed, his fortunes at that time stood very high. But the publication of *Okhrannaya gramota*, a highly complex and idiosyncratic work, was an indication that the poet remained his old self. Paradoxically, but consistent with P.'s temperament and position, it was at this time that he turned to translation, which became his primary occupation and main source of income until the end of his life.

P. translated Georgian poets and western European poets—Kleist, Keats, Shelley, Verlaine, Rilke. One of his last such enterprises was Goethe's *Faust*. Although prompted by the inability to publish his own works (between 1935 and 1943 no new book of his was published) and by the need to earn money to support his large family, translation, especially of Shakespeare's plays, gave P. the possibility of reaching large audiences and served as a tool for forging the simplicity of his mature work. In translating Shakespeare, P. consciously modernized the language in an attempt to make him easily comprehensible to contemporary audiences. Translations, however, were taking up most of his time and keeping him from his own work, and in his later years this complaint became one of the constant themes in his correspondence.

Doktor Zhivago, which P. considered his single greatest achievement, was conceived as a tribute to the memory of those of his friends and contemporaries who did not survive the years of Stalin's terror. From this concept stems the sense of urgency in P.'s letters of the period: in writing *Doktor Zhivago* he was paying his debt as one of the surviving witnesses of the epoch. The main conflict of the novel is between "living life" and dead ideology. The affirmation of life is couched in terms typical of P.: love and nature amid the day-to-day existence of the revolutionary and the civil-war years.

The social and economic changes brought about by the revolution initially are accepted by Zhivago without hesitation. It is the ideology that becomes an end in itself and thus turns against life that is rejected. Life is not "material" that can be shaped to fit an abstract scheme. In rejecting the regime that issued from the revolution, Zhivago defends the value of every individual and the value of life itself. In this he comes close to Christianity, the essence of which for him is precisely in its treatment of human personality as an absolute value.

The novel's protagonist, whose name means "life," is a physician and a poet. But he stops practicing his profession, is separated from his family, and is virtually unknown as a poet, and he dies in 1929 an apparent failure. But in the epilogue, his friends read Zhivago's poems and find a new significance in them: the poems speak of their time and its meaning. For P., a poet, apparently unconcerned with current events and out of step with the changing times, is in his art able to touch upon the essence of history. This is the paradox of the timelessness of art and its inevitable connection with its time.

The epilogue, set in 1943 and later, is cautiously optimistic. This was the mood of P. during World War II, when he was writing the novel and hoped that the loyalty to the regime demonstrated by the Soviet people during the war would bring about a fundamental change in the system. This hope was revived again after Stalin's death.

The final section of the novel consists of the poems attributed to Zhivago. It is in his poetry that he fulfills himself and leaves a living legacy. Immortality for Zhivago is life in the memory of others, so it is through self-sacrifice that a meaningful life is achieved. The novel and especially the poems abound in New Testament symbols of death and resurrection.

The resounding success of the novel in the West was a source of joy for P., since it brought him in contact with fellow writers and readers around the world. The success, however, was also a source of constant anxiety for him, for by allowing it to be published in the West, he defied one of the basic tenets of Soviet society.

P. was one of the most original and influential Russian poets of the century. Whatever the official pronouncements, his poetry is well known and highly valued by poets and discerning readers. In publishing *Doktor Zhivago* he took his place at the head of what is now a long list of writers to publish despite official prohibition; in writing it, he was one of the first among Soviet Russian writers to express in a clear voice the truth about Soviet society.

FURTHER WORKS: *Spektorsky* (1931); *Vozdushnye puti* (1933); *Povest* (1934; *The Last Summer*, 1959); *Avtobiografichesky ocherk*

(1961; also pub. as *Lyudi i polozhenia*, 1967; *I Remember: Sketch for an Autobiography*, 1959); *Kogda razgulyaetsya* (1959; *Poems 1955–1959*, 1960, bilingual ed.); *Sochinenia* (3 vols., 1961); *Stikhotvorenia i poemy* (1965); *Slepaya krasavitsa* (1969: *The Blind Beauty*, 1969); *Stikhotvorenia i poemy* (1976); *Perepiska s Olgoy Freydenberg* (1981; *The Correspondence of B. P. and Olga Freidenberg, 1910–1954*, 1982). **FURTHER WORKS IN ENGLISH:** *The Collected Prose Works* (1945); *Selected Poems* (1946); *Selected Writings* (1949); *Poems* (1959); *Safe Conduct: An Early Autobiography, and Other Works* (1959); *The Poetry of B. P.: 1917–1959* (1959); *In the Interlude: Poems 1945–1960* (1962); *Poems* (1964); *Letters to Georgian Friends* (1967); *Collected Short Prose* (1977)

BIBLIOGRAPHY. Conquest, R., *The P. Affair: Courage of Genius* (1962); Davie, D., and A. Livingstone, eds., *P.: Modern Judgements* (1969); special P. section, *BA*, 44 (1970): 195–243; Hughes, O. R., *The Poetic World of B. P.* (1974); Pomorska, K., *Themes and Variations in P.'s Poetics* (1975); Nilsson, N. Å., ed., *B. P.: Essays* (1976); Gladkov, A., *Meetings with P.* (1977); Gifford, H., *P.: A Critical Study* (1977); France, A. K., *B. P.'s Translations of Shakespeare* (1978); Erlich, V., ed., *P.: Twentieth Century Views* (1978); Ivinskaya, O., *A Captive of Time* (1978); Mallac, G., de, *B. P.: His Life and Art* (1981)

—OLGA RAEVSKY HUGHES

In the *Tales* there is neither the passionate intensity nor the verbal innovation [of P.'s poetry]. All attention is directed to a new manner of perception of reality and its interpretation. Liberation from the customary associations that give practical and facile explanations to the endless complexity of the world— this is the main goal of P. the prose writer.... "Childhood of Luvers" is a "psychological" history of a girl. But the "psychology" of this tale is not the least bit "psychological." It deals not with emotions or thoughts, but exclusively with perceptions . . . and a gradual formation from them of a definitive picture of the world. It is interesting to compare the sober, dry, and tight "Childhood of Luvers" with the treatment of similar subjects by Andrey Bely and by Proust. Precision, aloofness, a kind of a scientific coolness, and the quiet attentiveness of P. are the complete opposite of Bely's manner. But just as striking is his dissimilarity from Proust: instead of the endless, almost lifelike unfolding of memory, [there are] specific, very precisely and concisely presented moments, like symbols on a relief map giving a complete picture of a locality.... And all this intellectuality is directed toward exploring the most inexpressible and irrational processes, which in strange ways and judgements, eventually completely forgotten, create an original world in the child's consciousness that is afterward "related" to the world of adults.

Dmitri Svyatopolk-Mirsky, on *Rasskazy*,
Sovremennye zapiski, 25 (1925), p. 544

If his determination to maintain always a level of pure poetry sometimes makes him obscure or even awkward, it also means that he never writes below a certain standard and never wastes his time on irrelevant matter. The close texture of his verse, which at times makes it difficult to grasp all his implications at a first reading, is an essential feature of his art. It helps him to convey his intense, concentrated experience and is a true mirror of his moods. He looks at objects not in isolation but as parts of a wider unity, marks their relations in a complex whole, and stresses the dominant character of a scene as much as the individual elements in it. His work is therefore extremely personal, but not so personal as to be beyond the understanding of other men. He assumes that others will recognise the truth of his vision and come to share it with him. For, in his view, what he gives them is not a scientific, photographic transcript of an impersonal, external reality but something intensely human, since reality and value are given to things by our appreciation of them and by our absorption of them into our consciousness. Man is the centre of the universe, and human consciousness is its uniting principle.

C. M. Bowra, "B. P., 1917–1923," *The Creative Experiment* (1949), pp. 133–34

The poet himself remarked somewhere that poetry or art is the natural object informed by, or seen under, the aspect of energy—the all pervasive *vis vivida* whose flow, at times broken and intermittent, is the world of things and persons, forces and states, acts and sensations. To attempt to give more precise significance to this kind of vision may be perilous and foolish, save by discrimination from what it is not: it is neither a pathetic fallacy whereby human experience is projected into inanimate objects, nor yet is it the inversion of this, to be found, for example, in the novels of Virginia Woolf, where the fixed structure of human beings and material objects is dissolved into the life and the properties of the shifting patterns of the data of the inner and outer senses. . . . There is, on the contrary, a sense of unity induced by the sense of the pervasiveness of cosmic categories . . . which integrate all the orders of creation into a single, biologically and physiologically, emotionally and intellectually, interrelated universe. . . . Nor is this a consciously bold device or technical method of juxtaposing opposites to secure a spark or an explosion; it conveys a directly experienced vision of a single world-wide, world-long system of tensions and stresses, a perpetual ebb and flow of energy.

Isaiah Berlin, "The Energy of P.," *PR*, 7 (1950), pp. 749–50

But, although in no vulgar sense subversive, the novel certainly contains a most devastating criticism of the very foundations of official Soviet enthusiasm. The real danger it presents to the régime is that it destroys the position of moral superiority of the political "activists" and restores the confidence of those who are seeking nothing more than their right to love nature and to follow in their actions the inclinations of their heart. The compelling power of P.'s

argument is not based on any theoretical view, but on a direct poetical vision of Soviet society and of the mechanism by which its ideological foundations are maintained. . . . It is hardly probable that . . . literary bureaucrats . . . could understand and estimate all the dangers P.'s novel presents for the ideological foundations of the régime. But they must instinctively realise that once a work of art of such spontaneity has reached the public, they will not be able to look their readers in the eye when repeating the hackneyed, conventional phrases with which they fill their writings.

Max Hayward, "P.'s *Dr. Zhivago,*" *Encounter*, May 1958, p. 48

In a way quite different from Mayakovsky's, without recourse to purely tonic verse, without doing violence to classical meters, P. approximates poetry to prose, gives his verse the intonations and cadences of ordinary colloquial speech, and yet achieves wonderful musical and rhythmical effects. He is nothing if not a musical poet. Some of his best poems . . . may appear to defy normal semantic analysis, but as the reader is carried along on the waves of their sound magic, their hidden and profound meaning is revealed to him. Yet there is in P. nothing of the effeminate musicality of a Zhukovsky, a Fet, a Balmont, or a Verlaine. The texture of his verse is taut and muscular. His prosaisms, his bold enjambments, his paradoxical juxtaposition of poetic and unpoetic words and lavish use of metonymy, destroy the automatism of perception and enhance the effect of novelty and freshness. He has been compared with Donne, with Gerard Manley Hopkins (without his religion), and with Rilke (without his mysticism), but one might as well find in him parallels with T. S. Eliot and Dylan Thomas—and if poetry could develop untrammeled in the Soviet Union, his influence on the younger generation of poets would certainly be comparable to Eliot's in England and America.

Gleb Struve, *Russian Literature under Lenin and Stalin, 1917–1953* (1971), p. 182

Zhivago's vision of the wholly lived life transcends the claims of all factions and the savage meaningless wars they fight among themselves. He stands apart from this struggle, but later, as the revolution gains the upper hand, he cannot avoid total engagement in the deeper conflict between the new politics and life itself, a conflict which impinges on language, art, morality, religion, theories of history, and culture in the broadest sense: all the ceremonies, institutions, and explanations men devise to ease their earthly situation. Zhivago defines and defends his view of these entities as he discovers that the revolution corrupts or destroys some aspects of each, ignores others, and proposes spurious substitutes for still others. Nothing of the revolution's total program except its initial grievances and its long-term aspirations—its ends—remains valid for him. The fanatical actions and doctrines that brought the revolution to power—its means—will apparently endure indefinitely, certainly beyond the span of his life. The interim men, who do not contemplate their own passing, will carry out their arrogant and misguided plans, as he sees it, at the expense of most of civilization's legacy. Alone, embattled and unknown, he must stand and fight.

Rufus W. Mathewson, Jr., "P.: 'An Inward
Music,'" The Positive Hero in Russian Literature
(1975), p. 261

P. builds his New Testament scenes by blending the miraculous and the humdrum, the exceptional and the workaday, the supernatural and the ordinary. The prosiness of some of the details and the everyday quality of the proceedings serve to authenticate the miracle of which the poem tells and lend the events of sacred history an emphatically contemporary and personal stamp. The author adheres strictly to the canonical story and reproduces it at times with textual precision, but in the language and the psychological and social detail he takes bold liberties which are taken, however, not in order to violate the canvas of the legend, but to make it more exact and tangible. He approaches this theme in roughly the same way as Breughel and Rembrandt did in their time. . . . As a result the Biblical text in P.'s version appears as the most contemporary, actual reality. His poems on evangelical themes leave us with the feeling that the sacred mystery has endured to this very day.

Andrey Sinyavsky, "P.'s Poetry," in Victor Erlich,
ed., P.: Twentieth Century Views (1978), p. 101

It would be most unwise to see in the text of "Safe Conduct" a collection of veiled allusions to Lef [postrevolutionary futurism]. The work's complex philosophical meaning, which brings contradictory ideological intentions into a tragic opposition, would be overshadowed by merely clever and inventive theoretical discussions. And yet a register—as complete as possible—of [the book's] hidden polemical responses to contemporary developments and the elucidation of specific addresses, in our opinion, can explain both the meaning of a number of statements in "Safe Conduct" that have still not been explicated and their structural function in an autobiographical text. . . . [A] static and "dogmatic" expression of his own views is alien to P. in principle. Despite his distaste for public appearances, his conscious attempts to avoid organized forms of literary battles, and his avoidance of journalistic polemics, the very character of P.'s thinking (including aesthetic and theoretical problems) tended toward dynamic opposition, a kind of purgation that lays bare the internally contradictory essence of the conceptions at hand. This means that the omission of the hidden polemical (and autopolemical) intent of P.'s aesthetic declarations, the attempt to read them outside their temporal

context diminishes their profoundly personal undercurrent and, instead of demonstrating the poet's ties with his time . . . , turns the protagonist of the autobiography into a rhetorical declaimer of abstract truths.

Lazar Fleishman, B. P. v dvadtsatye gody (1981),
pp. 195–96

PATCHEN, Kenneth

American poet, novelist, and dramatist, b. 13 Dec. 1911, Niles, Ohio; d. 8 Jan. 1972, Palo Alto, California

Born and reared in Ohio's industrial Mahoning Valley, P. was the son of a steelworker and the grandson of millworkers and coal miners. P. left the mills after high school, briefly attending Alexander Meikeljohn's Experimental College, in Wisconsin, Commonwealth College, in Arkansas, and Columbia University, but he remained a largely autodidactic artist. In the habit of writing daily since age twelve P. published a sonnet in the <i>New York Times</i> while still a teenager. He spent his formative years "on the road"-style, crisscrossing the continent, working in the fields in Canada or on the Green Mountain Trail in Vermont, writing always. P. persisted in living an uprooted existence in half a dozen states—in 1938-39, living and working at the office of James Laughlin's (1914-1998) New Directions Books, in Norfolk, Connecticut, before moving into the Manhattan loft where Herman Melville had lived out his life—until settling, in the early 1950s, first in San Francisco and at last in his now familiar bungalow in Palo Alto.

P.'s original impulse was to write a proletarian poetry. He published "Lenin" in <i>Rebel Poet</i> and wrote reviews for <i>New Republic</i>. On June 28, 1934, he married his lifelong companion, Miriam Oikemus, whose parents were Finnish socialists. But by 1937, P. had already begun his withdrawal from an intuitive form of socialism to a position of anarchy. This disengagement seems to have been precipitated by the lukewarm reception by the leftist press of his first book, <i>Before the Brave</i> (1936), around the time he originally sustained debilitating and permanent injury to his spine. P.'s message of pacifism as a sane response in a world gone mad, written in the idiom of William Blake and tempered by P.'s own hard-boiled antihero's voice, made him a favorite poet among campus readers during World War II. After P. fell off the operating table while undergoing exploratory back surgery in 1959, he was left an invalid, but his poems of rage against the institutions of power, and the many recordings he made reading his poems with jazz bands, helped to sustain his reputation as a popular poet in the late 1950s and 1960s. P. once dismissed the kind of artist he called "the impatient explorer," one who only "invents a box in which all journeys may be kept." He was a patient, apparently tireless, explorer. He never stopped believing in the poem as an experiment in language, producing over forty books, in addition to a considerable body of visual art.

"Let Us Have Madness," a characteristic poem from <i>Before the Brave</i>, is designed to challenge the power of institutions and hierarchies over their victim, mankind. In P.'s proletarian poems from this earliest period, although they are always intent upon building class consciousness in its readership, the call is to "go slow" into the coming revolution and its bloody inevitability. With P.'s second book, <i>First Will and Testament</i> (1939), the poet's sense of mankind's madness is already focused on the self-destructive irrationality of individual behavior deprived of a creative release. This volume contains P.'s only written statement on the function of poetry, "A Note on 'The Hunted City,'" in which he specifies that life-supporting psychic energy must be directed into the creation of art. The poems themselves are less didactic. In "Do the Dead Know What Time It Is?" the older male speaker's telling of his "mother's / Meeting with God" is interpolated and brought to earth by the girl's flirtatious interruptions while the young man hears all. P.'s mature style features this kind of artful balance between spiritual and sexual initiations, his abstractions grounded in everydayness. P.'s masterpiece is *The Journal of Albion Moonlight* (1941), an episte-mological journal kept by one Albion Moonlight during the summer of 1940, when France fell to fascism. Moonlight's journal becomes an intersexual novel as he relates the story of his band of characters on their forced-march pilgrimage to find significance in a world at war. P. anticipates reader-response theory in this book that urges the reader to participate in the journal-keeper/novelist's struggle to create in an era of mass destruction. While P.'s poetry has been routinely likened to Blake's, *Albion Moonlight* is the book that most closely reflects P.'s reading of Blake's prophetic poems. P.'s book makes a synthesis of Blake's *Visions of the Daughters of Albion* (1793) and *The Four Zoas* (completed in 1797). Blake's heroine, Athene, embodies the spirit of the American Revolution as it inspires the revolt in France specifically and the cause against oppression of all kinds; P.'s Moonlight is what is left of illumination and the promise of the democratic experiment in the dark days of France's fall. Athene's rape is the only conventional action in Blake's poem of reasons, causes, ramifications; for P.'s book, the summer of the rape of France is the only event beyond those of perception. The motto for Blake's poem prescribes oppressed Englishwomen a way to raise their consciousness and become free, by learning to feel what they see; Blake's "The Eye sees more than the Heart knows" could serve as a gloss for P.'s *Journal*. Although Blake's *Four Zoas* and P.'s *Albion Moonlight* were fundamental formulations of the authors' mythopoetics, the books stubbornly resisted final form for their authors. The social function intended by P's Moonlight, who is after all a writer and not a warrior, is to be found in the Los of *Four Zoa's Night VII*, when Blake's hero calls up the dead of the wars of Urizen and, by his art, resurrects them into new meaning. Following the world war, in his Introduction to a 1947 edition of Blake's *Job*, P. will identify a five-fold epistemology for achieving the mystical life.

During the decade of the 1940s, P. produced two more significant prose books. Alfred Budd, the narrator of P.'s most popular work, *Memoirs of a Shy Pornographer* (1945), relates a carnival of Candide-like misadventures in a society gone insane. It is a cautionary tale of what happens to a writer who fails to take artistic control of his book. Blake was P.'s model of the writer-artist who illustrated his poems and printed his own plates; P. had edited and helped print *Albion Moonlight*. But it is a tale with a twist: Budd's manuscript is transformed beyond the author's recognition into a best-selling novel with a new title, *Spill Of Desire*. P.'s concern for controlling every printed page of his text would become crucial in his next book, as he experimented freely with concrete poetry and picture-poems. That book, *Sleepers Awake* (1946), is the most radically experimental of P.'s prose trilogy; this longest, most ambitious, and most difficult P. novel has been called his *Finnegans Wake*. Aloysious Best, the book's messianic poet, delivers himself of sermons intended for the redemption of the modern world. But

P.'s own message is often obscured by the radical layout of his book: in one twenty-five-page passage, he divides the page horizontally into one column of lyric, two columns of prose and an area of drawings. It is a book that wrestles meaning from its search for whatever form it will take next. *See You in the Morning* (1947), P.'s only conventional novel and a potboiler, follows *Sleepers Awake* like *Pierre* succeeds *Moby-Dick*.

As their titles declare, P.'s late collections, including *Hurrah for Anything* (1957), *Because It Is* (1960), and the book of picture-poems *Hallelujah Anyway* (1967), celebrate the triumph of the individual will during the postwar era when something of the social change that P. had predicted in his earliest poetry came to pass. The picture-poems of *Wonderings* (1971), the last book that P. could have seen through the press, sustain the poet's career-long insistence on the necessity for mystical wonderment in an increasingly technocratic world.

One of late modernism's and early postmodernism's outstanding U.S. iconoclasts, P. and his art defy categorization. P. made a rich career of joining none but defining many schools of writing. He explored poetry's symbiotic relationships with both jazz and the visual arts—along the way making himself one of the innovators of concrete poetry, language poetry, and performance poetry—as well as rethinking modernist gains, in the relaxation of limiting boundaries between prose and poetry, along the lines of metafiction. P. often wrote in the idiom of his beloved Blake's prophetic books, but he composed unencumbered by a unifying vision. He was never a systematic social thinker but rather a persistent and clarion voice of what is moral. God is still a player in P.'s fictive universe, only anthropomorphic to a fault. P.'s reader is treated to the romantic possibilities of an oeuvre less than a Blakean marriage of the arts but still a wild nuptial celebration of the arts on the unbounded contemporary page.

FURTHER WORKS: *The Teeth of the Lion* (1942); *The Dark Kingdom* (1942); *Cloth of the Tempest* (1943); *An Astonished Eye Looks Out of the Air* (1946); *Outlaw of the Lowest Planet*1946); *Pictures of Life and Death* (1946); *They Keep Riding Down All the Time* (1946); *Panels for the Walls of Heaven* (1946); *Selected Poems* (1946; enlarged eds., 1957, 1964); *CCLXXIV Poems* (1947); *Red Wine and Yellow Hair* (1949); *To Say if You Love Someone* (1948); *In Peaceable Caves* (1950); *Orchards, Thrones and Caravans* (1952); *The Famous Boating Party* (1954); *Fables and Other Little Tales* (1953); *Glory Never Guesses* (1955); *A Surprise for the Bagpiper Player* (1956); *Poems of Humor and Protest* (1956); *When We Were Here Together* (1957); *Poemscapes* (1958); *Selected Love Poems* (1960); *Doubleheader* (1966); *Like Fun I'd Tell You* (1966); *The Collected Poems of K. P.* (1968); *But Even So* (1968); *Love & War Poems* (1968); *Aflame and Afun of Walking Faces* (1970); *There's Love All Day* (1970); *In Quest of Candlelighters* (1972); *The Argument of Innocence* (1976); *The Argument of Innocence: A Selection from the Arts of K. P.* (1976); *P.'s Lost Plays* (1977); *Still another Pelican in the Breadbox* (1980); *What Shall We Do without Us?* (1984)

BIBLIOGRAPHY: Morgan, R. G., *K. P.: A Collection of Essays* (1977); Smith, L. R., *K. P.* (1978); Nelson, R., *K. P. and American Mysticism* (1984); Laughlin, J., *Random Essays* (1989): 226-58; Williams, J., "K. P.: 'Hiya, Ken Babe, What's the Bad Word for Today?'" *Conjunctions*, 29 (1998): 379-86

—RICHARD L. BLEVINS

Alan Paton

PATON, Alan

South African novelist, short-story writer, essayist, and poet (writing in English), b. 11 Jan. 1903, Pietermaritzburg; d. 12 April 1988, Durban

P.'s upbringing by deeply religious parents of English stock sensitized him to the moral and ethical principles underlying the racial conflicts in South Africa. He interprets the race struggle as a larger revolt of man against domination—against dominating and being dominated.

This view marked his innovations as principal of Diep Kloof Reformatory near Johannesburg, an experience that provided the material for several short stories and moved him to political action in the anti-apartheid Liberal Association, of which he was founder (1953) and president. The poles of his political views and literary themes are the same: the negative, a distrust of institutionalized power; the positive, a belief in the power of love expressed as human brotherhood.

The subject of an early, uncompleted novel—Christ's return to South Africa—anticipates the material of P.'s later fiction. His first published novel, *Cry, the Beloved Country* (1948), the story of Stephen Kumalo, a Zulu minister, and his search for his son in Johannesburg, is about racial tensions, but its primary theme is the brotherhood of man. His second, *Too Late the Phalarope* (1953), is about a white man destroyed because of an affair with a native girl. Again the primary object is to indict the inhumanity of racial

separation as institutionalized in such legislation as the Immorality Act, which prohibits sexual relations between black and white. Moving as these novels are, they are open to the charge that P. manipulates characters to conform to his thesis about the political and social situations they dramatize.

The death of P.'s wife in 1967 turned him to a self-searching analysis of domination in the complex structure of marriage in *Kontakion for You Departed* (1969). In this painful, sometimes moving account of the relationship with his wife, P. attempted to define marital communion as the sacramental point of transition from what is at best a flawed *agape* existing within society toward the perfection of the Creator's love.

Critics often overlook this thematic preoccupation when they object that humanitarian zeal sometimes reduces P.'s fiction to the level of propaganda. The charge is in any case more applicable to the volume of short stories *Debbie Go Home* (1961; Am., *Tales from a Troubled Land*) than to the novels.

The appeal of his fiction derives from the language—simple, seemingly unadorned, but modified by the rhythms of African languages and Afrikaans—and from an intricate symbolic interweaving of land, people, and theme.

In 1980 appeared *Towards the Mountain*, an account of P.'s life up to 1948. It deals largely with the public events of his life, as *Kontakion for You Departed* does with the private. The promised second part of the autobiography will likely also deal mainly with public involvements. But these have already been well documented in *The Long View* (1967), a selection of essays on political and social matters originally published in the South African journal *Contact* between 1955 and 1966, which exhibit the insistent reason of his arguments, and in *Knocking at the Door* (1976), a collection of short fiction, poems, and articles on various subjects, including politics and penal reform.

The nonfiction that P. produced in the 1960s and 1970s prepared the way for the novel *Ah, But Your Land Is Beautiful* (1981), a narrative marked by greater stylistic variety than his earlier fiction. He uses a sequence of poison-pen letters and speeches by public figures, which, although they newly dramatize his long-standing advocacy of individual freedom and racial equality, do little for characterization.

P.'s poetry is governed by the qualities so evident in his prose: feeling, reason, and clarity of expression. These qualities, however, work to disadvantage in the poetry, sometimes leaving the didactic element too apparent. The ideal medium for his characteristic intensity of feeling and simplicity of style is provided by *Instrument of Thy Peace* (1968), reflections on a prayer of Saint Francis of Assisi. In this meditative work P. confronts without equivocation the difficulties of the region in which personal and social relationships come into conflict. Wherever the uncertainties of this kind of conflict reach the danger stage, both P.'s personal commitment and his achievements in literature will be consulted as touchstones of courage and integrity.

FURTHER WORKS: *South Africa Today* (1953); *The Land and People of South Africa* (1955; rev. ed., 1972); *South Africa in Transition* (1956, with Dan Weiner); *Hope for South Africa* (1958); *Hofmeyr* (1964; Am., *South African Tragedy: The Life and Times of Jan Hofmeyr*); *Sponomo* (1965, with Krishna Shah); *Apartheid and the Archbishop: The Life and Times of Geoffrey Clayton, Archbishop of Cape Town* (1973)

BIBLIOGRAPHY: On *Cry, the Beloved Country, TLS*, 23 Oct. 1948, 593; on *Too Late the Phalarope, TLS* 28 Aug. 1953, 545; Baker, S., "P.'s Beloved Country and the Morality of Geography," *CE*, 19, 2 (1957): 56–61; Callan, E., *A. P.* (1968); Breslin, J. B., "Inside South Africa," *America*, 17 April 1976: 344–46; Sharma, R. C., "A. P.'s *Cry, the Beloved Country*: The Parable of Compassion," *LHY*, 19, 2 (1978): 64–82; Cooke, J., "'A Hunger of the Soul': *Too Late the Phalarope* Reconsidered," *ESA*, 22 (1979): 37–43

—MANLY JOHNSON

PAULHAN, Jean

French literary critic, essayist, and novelist, b. 2 Dec. 1884, Nîmes; d. 9 Oct. 1968, Melun

After receiving his degree from the Sorbonne, P. spent several years prospecting for gold and teaching on the island of Madagascar. Upon his return to Paris, he became a professor of Malagasy at the School of Oriental Languages. From 1925 to 1940 he worked for *La nouvelle revue française*, succeeding Jacques Rivière (1886–1925) as its editor in 1925. During World War II he was instrumental in launching the clandestine *Les lettres françaises* and Éditions de Minuit, and he cooperated with the French resistance movement. Later, however, he approved the return of those writers who had been collaborators.

P. was the recipient of the Grand Prize for Literature of the French Academy in 1945 and of the Grand Prize of the City of Paris in 1951. In 1953 he resumed his responsibilities as editor of *La nouvelle revue française* and as a consultant to the Gallimard publishing house. In these capacities, he exercised a profound influence on new talents, whom he discovered and encouraged. He was elected to the French Academy in 1964. It was not until the last years of his life, when his *œuvres complètes* (1966 ff.; collected works) began to be published, that his writing won for him the widespread recognition that he so well deserved.

P. wrote the preface to the scandalous *L'histoire d'O.* (1954; *The Story of O.*, 1966), which was published under the pseudonym Pauline Réage, and he was for a long time presumed to be the author of the novel. The book was, however, apparently written by a woman long associated with him as friend and secretary.

P.'s interest in and exploration of the problem of language, his lifelong preoccupation, was stimulated by his sojourn as a young man in Madagascar. He brought back from there *Les hain-tenys* (1913; Malagasy: the hains-tenys), which contains the Malagasy songs and proverbs he had been collecting.

P. continued to be dominated by the idea of language when writing *Le guerrier appliqué* (1917; the diligent warrior), *Jacob Cow, le pirate* (1922; Jacob Cow, the pirate), *Le pont traversé* (1922; the crossed bridge), *La guérison sévère* (1925; the hard recovery), and *Aytré qui perd l'habitude* (1926; Aytré who loses the habit). The early *Le guerrier appliqué*, a curious war tale inspired by P.'s experiences during World War I, illustrates, through subtle reasonings, the interplay between the realities of a soldier's life and his dreams or reveries, the search for liberation through thought and language.

Complicated and mysterious, all these tales reveal, in the subtle analysis of the subconscious, how at best language merely approximates, or screens, the essence of thought and feeling. P. saw

language as a trap, and in his demand for a means of expression that was more exact and authentic he rejected the eloquent, the commonplace, and the phrasing that reflects the thinking of acquired social habits.

Ultimately, to achieve his ideal, P. participated in what has been characterized as the "terror" of CUBISM and of SURREALISM, or, as one critic prefers to call it, "irrealism." Hostile toward the rhetorical, he favored the use of a hermetic and audacious vocabulary, one more consistent with the kind used by those who emulated Henry MILLER or the Marquis de Sade.

Reveling in paradox and always ready to correct a previous metamorphosis, P. realized that extremes breed new extremes, that the "terror" he had helped to make happen had paralyzed or handicapped the writer's creativity. To remedy this, he later did an about-face in the hope of restoring liberty to the writer, and proceeded to demonstrate, in the voluminous essay *Les fleurs de Tarbes* (1941; the flowers of Tarbes), how rhetoric could be used effectively.

À demain la poésie (1947; good-bye until tomorrow, poetry), probably P.'s best and clearest work, is a denunciation of those who renounced completely the accepted means of expression and thought to embrace whole-heartedly the dream, automatic writing, and the irrational. While words are dangerous, demonstrably so in P.'s writing, they are undeniably at the root of thought.

Absorbed with problems of language and poetics, into whose meaning and scope he inquired, P. wrote with enigmatic precision, using in his essays and tales a style that is at once, in its associations and affectations, subtle and elegant. Like Mallarmé and VALÉRY, he insisted on an absolute unity of word and meaning, of form and content. Like them, too, he fought relentlessly for the autonomy of literature. An iconoclast, he was an enemy of mediocrity, a friend to innovators, and a guardian of the avant-garde.

FURTHER WORKS: *Entretiens sur des faits divers* (1933); *Clef de la poésie* (1944); *Sept causes célèbres* (1946); *Petit guide d'un voyage en Suisse* (1947); *De la paille et du grain* (1948); *Lettre aux directeurs de la résistance* (1952)

BIBLIOGRAPHY: Toesca, M., *J. P.: L'écrivain appliqué* (1948); Carmody, F. M., "J. P.'s Imaginative Writings," *Occidental* (Nov.–Dec. 1949): 28–34; Lefèbvre, M. J., *J. P.: Une philosophie et une pratique de l'expression et de la réflexion* (1949); Judrin, R., *La vocation transparente de J. P.* (1961); Elsen, C., *J. P.: Histoire d'une amitié* (1968); Poulet, C., *J. P., l'écrivain* (1968); Hellens, F., *Adieu à J. P.* (1969)

—SIDNEY D. BRAUN

PAUSTOVSKY, Konstantin Georgievich

Russian memoirist, short-story writer, and novelist, b. 31 May 1892, Moscow; d. 14 July 1968, Moscow

Son of a railroad statistician, P. grew up in Kiev. His father encouraged him to become a writer, and at an early age his imagination was excited by the tales of his grandfather, a proud descendent of the Zaporozhian Cossacks. In 1913, after two years of study at the University of Kiev, P. moved to Moscow. Soon after, his years of wandering began; they continued until 1929. During this time P. frequently changed jobs and absorbed countless experiences. He worked as a tram conductor and driver, a medical orderly for the imperial army during World War I, a factory worker, a fisherman, a teacher, and a journalist. He went to the front, returned to Moscow, made his way to Kiev, lived for a period in Odessa, and spent time in the Caucasus. In the late 1920s he returned to Moscow, where he spent the rest of his life, although he continued to travel extensively both in the Soviet Union and abroad (after World War II). During World War II he served as a war correspondent on the southern front.

P. published his first story in 1912 but did not turn to writing as a career until the early 1920s. At that time he worked with fellow writers Isaak BABEL, Valentin KATAEV, and Edvard BAGRITSKY on the Odessa journal *Moryak*. His first collection of stories, *Morskie nabroski* (sea sketches), was published in 1925. This volume and two novels written in the same period, *Romantiki* (written 1916–23, pub. 1935; the romantics) and *Blistayushchie oblaka* (1929; shining clouds), are marked by a strong romantic coloring and by exoticism. P. writes about strange lands far across the seas and about dreamers, writers, and artists. It is not the biographies of his heroes that are important but their inner lives, their feelings.

Before long P. abandoned the exotic and began to write about everyday life. Even so, a romantic quality continued to permeate his writings. It was one of the most distinctive elements in his prose, as P. himself was later to acknowledge. P.'s short stories of the 1930s and 1940s are often marked by a wistful lyricism and by a suggestion of mysterious coincidence. Mood is heightened by evocative nature descriptions. In many stories the natural beauty of central Russia is celebrated: it is described in concise, harmonious language, conveying to the reader the simple splendor of the Russian landscape. Even in his longer historical works of the 1930s and 1940s—*Kara-Bugaz* (1932; *The Black Gulf*, 1946), *Chernoe more* (1936; the Black Sea), *Severnaya povest* (1939; a northern tale), and *Povest o lesakh* (1949; a tale of the forests)—P. plays on the reader's emotions rather than carefully reconstructing historical reality. He strives to evoke a feeling of kinship with the past and of awe before the courage and self-sacrifice of its heroes.

P.'s most important postwar work is his autobiography, *Povest o moey zhizni* (6 vols., 1946–1963; *The Story of a Life*, 6 vols., 1964–1974). The work consists of hundreds of short episodes unified by the personality of the author and by the underlying theme of Russian history on the march. P. does not simply recount his own life but evokes the turbulent times surrounding it. He captures vivid likenesses of famous contemporaries (Isaak BABEL and Mikhail BULGAKOV, just to name two) as well as many ordinary people. The first volume, *Dalyokie gody* (1946; *Childhood and Schooldays*, 1964), focuses on P.'s childhood; the second, *Bespokoynaya yunost* (1955; *Slow Approach of Thunder*, 1965), deals with the period of World War I; the third, *Nachalo nevedomogo veka* (1957; *In That Dawn*, 1967), with the Russian Revolution and the civil war; the fourth, *Vremya bolshikh ozhidany* (1959; *Years of Hope*, 1968), with P.'s adventures in Odessa in 1921. The fifth, *Brosok na yug* (1960; *Southern Adventure*, 1969), and sixth, *Kniga skitany* (1963; *The Restless Years*, 1974), treat P.'s wanderings during the 1920s.

The translation of P.'s autobiography into several European languages in the 1960s won him wide acclaim abroad. He has always been extremely popular with Russian readers because of the romantic quality of his writings, the courage and idealism of his heroes, his poignant love stories, and his descriptions of Russian nature. P. was also greatly admired by younger writers for the sincerity and warmth of his writing and for his integrity. In the 1950s and 1960s he spoke out in defense of writers who came under attack by the regime. For over ten years he ran a seminar for young writers at Tarusa, an artists' colony south of Moscow. In the semi-autobiographical *Zolotaya roza* (1956; *The Golden Rose*, 1957) P. talks about the creative process and discusses the origins of many of his own writings.

FURTHER WORKS: *Minetoza* (1927); *Vstrechnye korabli* (1929); *Sudba Charlya Lonsevilya* (1933); *Kolkhida* (1934); *Rasskazy* (1935); *Letnie dni* (1937); *Orest Kiprensky* (1937); *Isaak Levitan* (1937); *Povesti i rasskazy* (1939); *Taras Shevchenko* (1939); *Poruchik Lermontov* (1941); *Nash sovremennik: Pushkin* (1949); *Rozhdenie morya* (1952); *Perstenek* (1956); *Sobranie sochineny* (8 vols., 1967–1970). FURTHER WORKS IN ENGLISH: *The Flight of Time: New Stories* (1955); *Selected Stories* (1967)

BIBLIOGRAPHY: Bondarev, Y., "A Master of Prose," *Sovl,* No. 10 (1962): 166–69; Alexandrova, V., *A History of Soviet Literature* (1963): 302–16; Lehrman, E. H., "K. G. P.," in Simmonds, G., ed., *Soviet Leaders* (1967): 296–309; Urman, D., "K. P., Marcel Proust, and the Golden Rose of Memory," *CSS*, 2 (1968): 311–26; Kasack, W., *Der Stil K. G. P.s* (1971); Vatnikova-Prizel, Z., "P.'s *Povest o moey zhizni:* Autobiographical Techniques," *RLJ*, No. 105 (1976): 81–89; Slonim, M., *Soviet Russian Literature: Writers and Problems, 1917–1977*, 2nd rev. ed. (1977): 118–27

—SONA STEPHAN HOISINGTON

PAVESE, Cesare

Italian novelist, poet, short-story writer, and translator, b. 9 Sept. 1908, Santo Stefano Belbo; d. 27 Aug. 1950, Turin

P. was born in a village in the Piedmontese Langhe hills, where his family came on summer vacation and where P. returned all his life. He attended the University of Turin, specializing in American literature and graduating in 1930. His thesis on the poetry of Walt Whitman was first rejected for failing to follow the cultural directives of the Fascist regime and for being influenced by Benedetto CROCE's aesthetic theories. P.'s love for English and especially American literature was lifelong. His first publications were translations of Sinclair LEWIS's *Our Mr. Wrenn* and of Melville's *Moby-Dick*. He also translated works by Sherwood ANDERSON, John DOS PASSOS, William FAULKNER, James JOYCE, Gertrude STEIN, Dickens, and Defoe. Various essays on American literature were collected posthumously in *La letteratura americana, e altri saggi* (1951; *American Literature: Essays and Opinions*, 1970).

In 1932 P. enrolled in the Fascist Party ("a thing against my conscience"), but in May 1935, after a mass arrest in Turin—the same one in which Carlo LEVI was arrested—P. was exiled to Brancaleone Calabro, a southern village, for editing the anti-Fascist magazine *La cultura*, for working at the liberal publishing house Einaudi, and for the possession of some compromising letters. Sentenced to three years' confinement, he was pardoned the following year and returned to Turin, finding the woman he had loved married to another man.

In 1936 P. published his first collection of poetry, *Lavorare stanca* (*Hard Labor*, 1976) and reassumed his post as editor and translator for Einaudi. At the end of 1943 P. retreated to his sister's home in a small Piedmontese village, where he stayed until the war's end. In 1945 he became editorial director of Einaudi, joined the Italian Communist Party, and started writing for its newspaper, *L'unità*. Another romantic involvement inspired the poems of *La terra e la morte* (1947; earth and death); the collection *Verrà la morte e avrà i tuoi occhi* (1951; death will come and its eyes will be yours), written in 1950, was occasioned by another, final painful love affair. On the morning of August 27, 1950, P. was found dead, a suicide.

P. believed that "maturity is an isolation sufficient unto itself." He never reached this maturity; he wished to participate in the life around him, yet felt unable to communicate. P. thought of himself as an outsider. When he had the opportunity to fight for his ideas in the Resistance, he could not take arms. His love affairs were unsuccessful. He suffered from feelings of rejection, impotence (also in the clinical sense), and guilt.

In P.'s writings the failure to communicate takes the form of a tension between the active and contemplative life, work and idleness, country and city, nature and civilization, impulse and deliberate thought. Recurrent images—hill, tree, house, evening, bread, fruit, moon—come to signify deeprooted symbols, leading to myths.

In the first poem of *Lavorare stanca*, "I mari del sud" ("Southern Seas," 1969), P. presents the return of a sailor to his native village. This theme recurs in his last novel, *La luna e i falò* (1950; *The Moon and the Bonfire*, 1952): escape and the impossibility of escape, return and the impossibility of return. In his first collection of poems P. forges a poetic expression completely different from the HERMETICISM of Italian poetry of the time. His poems are a kind of *poesia-racconto* (poem-story), almost epic in character, free of facile lyricism. His two other books of poetry, responses to unhappy love, are limited by the outpouring of sentiment and passion.

Three of P.'s novels, *Il compagno* (1947; *The Comrade*, 1959), and the two published together under the title *Prima che il gallo canti* (1949; before the cock crows)—*Il carcere* (*The Political Prisoner*, 1959) and *La casa in collina* (*The House on the Hill*, 1961)—deal with political themes. In *Il compagno*, P.'s only "positive" novel, the protagonist sheds his indifference and becomes politically involved. *Il carcere* recounts the confinement in southern Italy of a political prisoner who proves unable to find any ties with the people around him. *La casa in collina* depicts a protagonist in flight from the war.

P. also wrote a series of novels concerned largely with how an individual can remain authentic and whole through various crises: the failure to understand conjugal love in *La spiaggia* (1942; *The Beach*, 1963); the passage from innocent adolescence to corrupt adulthood in *La bella estate* (1949; *The Beautiful Summer*, 1959); the shock of leaving natural surroundings for the sophistication of the city in *Il diavolo sulle colline* (1949; *The Devil in the Hills*, 1959); the suicidal rejection of life owing to its lack of beauty and value in *Tra donne sole* (1949; *Among Women Only*, 1959). (The last three were first published together under the title *La bella estate*.)

P.'s most original works are about the soul. In *Paesi tuoi* (1941; *The Harvesters*, 1961) he examines the intensity of unreflective life and sexual violence, including incest. The novel is set in the hills of his childhood, and images of fire, blood, and the moon abound. His use of the Piedmontese dialect filtered through standard Italian adds to the impact of the novel, which is reminiscent of VERGA in its intense realism.

In *Dialoghi con Leucò* (1947; *Dialogues with Leucò*, 1965) P. tries to penetrate the collective unconscious in order to fathom the destiny of the human race. This work is a retelling of ancient myths, charged with a modern sensibility: Orpheus, for example, intentionally looks back at Eurydice. P. wishes to share his personal anxieties—or even exorcise them—by finding their archetypal force. *Dialoghi con Leucò* is written in a poetic prose, and the sound of words often communicates as much as their meaning.

It is not enough, however, for an artist to gaze upon the timeless unconscious; one must also accept time-bound consciousness. *La luna e i falò*, P.'s final novel, is an attempt to reconcile these two dimensions. There are, as in *Paesi tuoi*, images of violence, blood, hills, destructive fire, and the white, timeless, feminine moon representing the unconscious and myth; but now there are also the controlled bonfires, symbolizing the conscious forces of history. The protagonist, who goes to America, is even able to feel a continuity between the New World to which he has escaped and the ancient world of the Langhe hills to which he returns. He cannot remain on his native soil, however, for a permanent return has become impossible.

With both his poetry and his prose P. brought a new tone to Italian literature. His originality lies in his having found a spiritual chord for the prevailing NEOREALISM of his time.

FURTHER WORKS: *Feria d'agosto* (1946; *Summer Storm, and Other Stories*, 1966); *Il mestiere di vivere: Diario 1935–1950* (1952; *The Burning Brand: Diaries 1935–1950*, 1961); *Notte di festa* (1953; *Festival Night and Other Stories*, 1964); *Fuoco grande* (1959, with Garufi Bianca; *A Great Fire*, in *The Beach*, 1963); *Racconti* (1960); *Poesie edite ed inedite* (1962); *8 poesie e quattro lettere a un'amica* (1964); *Lettere 1924–1944* (1966); *Lettere 1945–1950* (1966); *Poesie del disamore* (1968). FURTHER WORKS IN ENGLISH: *Selected Works of C. P.* (1968); *A Mania for Solitude: Selected Poems 1930–1950* (1969); *Selected Letters 1924–1950* (1969); *Told in Confidence and Other Stories* (1971)

BIBLIOGRAPHY: Milano, P., "P.'s Experiments in the Novel," *New Republic*, 4 May 1953: 18, 23; Freccero, J., "Mythos and Logos: *The Moon and the Bonfires*," *IQ*, 4, 20 (1961): 3–16; Norton, P. M., "C. P. and the American Nightmare," *MLN*, 77 (1962): 24–36; Heiney, D., *America in Modern Italian Literature* (1964): 171–86; Rimanelli, G., "The Conception of Time and Language in the Poetry of C. P.," *IQ*, 8, 30 (1964): 14–34; Hood, S., "A Protestant without God," *Encounter*, May 1966: 41–48; Sontag, S., *Against Interpretation* (1966): 39–48; Biasin, G. P., *The Smile of the Gods: A Thematic Study of C. P.'s Works* (1968); Heiney, D., *Three Italian Novelists: Moravia, P., Vittorini* (1968): 83–146; Renard, P., *P.: Prison de l'imaginaire, lieu de l'écriture* (1972); Rimanelli, G., "P.'s *Diario*: Why Suicide? Why Not?" in Rimanelli, G., and K. J. Atchity, eds., *Italian Literature: Roots and Branches* (1976): 383-405; Thompson, D., *C. P.: A Study of the Major Novels and Poems* (1982)

—EMANUELE LICASTRO

PAVIĆ, Milorad

Serbian novelist, short-story writer, poet, and literary historian, b. 15 Oct. 1929, Belgrade, Yugoslavia (now Serbia)

A native of Belgrade, P. graduated from the University of Belgrade and acquired his Ph.D. at the University of Zagreb. He now teaches history of Serbian literature at the University of Novi Sad. In that capacity, he was instrumental in bringing to attention and reevaluating some older Serbian writers and editing their neglected works. His chief occupation is writing.

P. began with a book of poetry, *Palimpsesti* (1967; palimpsests), followed by collections of short stories, *Gvozdena zavesa* (1973; iron curtain) and *Konji svetoga Marka* (1976; the horses of Saint Mark). In these early works, he showed traits that would become his trademarks: a meditative and erudite bent in poetry, and a successful merging of fantasy and a studied realistic approach, bolstered by an impeccable and controlled style.

It was not until his latest works, the novels *Hazarski rečnik* (1984; *Dictionary of the Khazars*, 1988) and *Predeo slikan čajem* (1988; *Landscape Painted with Tea*, 1990), that P. became known beyond the borders of his native land. He again mixes reality and fantasy, at times playfully but always purposefully, creating a complex world where the borders between the present, past, and future are erased and where humans seek, often unsuccessfully, to unravel the mysteries of existence. *Hazarski rečnik* is an attempt to solve the mystery of the Khazars, a tribe on the Black Sea, lost hundreds of years ago and now claimed equally by the Christians, Muslims, and Jews. In a dazzling display of fantasy, erudition, and wit, P. follows the story through the eyes of a Serbian leader, Muslim and Jewish missionaries and scholars, and an array of other characters, who all tell their version of the story in the form of a dictionary (hence, P. claims that the work can be read starting from any point in the book). The novel entails a mystery, numerous crime stories, historical forays, attempts at dream interpretation, and musing about life, death, and truth, all couched in a fashionable idiom of modern prose. Moreover, there are two versions, male and female, the difference being noticeable only on one page.

Predeo slikan čajem is equally fantastic and experimental and unbound by time and space. Even though the novel centered around a Serbian character, P. nevertheless roams through centuries and continents in his search for his roots and for the meaning of life and death, musing about the transience of time, the past and present, God, the devil, and the human being. The innovative twist in this work is that it is construed as a crossword puzzle, the solving of which is supposed to lead to the solution of the puzzle that is life. In the end, the solution depends on each individual, which, in most cases, yields no solution. P. is again dazzling in his mastery of the language and narrative techniques, which comes through in good translations.

P. has established himself as a leading Serbian writer and one of the most intriguing writers in world literature, as attested by his rising esteem all over the world and by numerous translations of his works.

FURTHER WORKS: *Istorija srpske književnosti baroknnog doba* (1967); *Mesečev kamen* (1971); *Vojislav Ilić i evropsko pesništvo* (1971); *Gavrilo Stefanović Venclović* (1972); *Istorija srpske književnosti klasicizma i predromantizma* (1979); *Ruski hrt* (1979); *Nove beogradske priče* (1981); *Duše se kupaju poslednji put* (1982); *Radjanje nove srpske književnosti* (1983); *Istorija, stalež i stil* (1985); *Izabrana dela* (1985); *Unutrašnja strana vetra ili roman o Heri Leandru* (1991)

BIBLIOGRAPHY: Livada, R., "A Book of the Future," *Relations*, 1 (1985): 73–74; Coover, R., "He Thinks the Way We Dream," *NYTBR* (20 Nov. 1988): 15–20; Golden, P. B., "The Khazars of Record," *The World and I*, 3, 11 (1988): 368–77; Mihaliovich, V. D., "Parable of Nationhood," *The World and I*, 3, 11 (1988): 378–83; Palavestra, P., "Abracadabra, a la Khazar!" *The World and I*, 3, 11 (1988): 384–89; Simic, C., "Balkan Bizarre," *The World and I*: 3, 11 (1988): 390–97; Leonard, J., "Alphabeticon," *Nation* (5 Dec. 1988): 610–11, 613; Mihailovich, V. D., "The Novel As Crossword Puzzle," *The World and I*, 4, 1 (1989): 430–33

—VASA D. MIHAILOVICH

PAVLOVIĆ, Miodrag

Yugoslav poet and essayist (writing in Serbian), b. 28 Nov. 1928, Novi Sad

After graduating from the University of Belgrade Medical School, P. practiced medicine for a short time, but then decided to devote himself to a literary career. He lives in Belgrade and works as an editor for the Prosveta publishing company.

P. appeared on the Serbian literary scene in the early 1950s, while still a university student. His first collection, *87 pesama*

Miodrag Pavlović

(1952; 87 poems), full of dark moods and nightmarish visions of destruction and the horrors of war, stirred a great deal of controversy and brought the young poet almost instant prominence. In it, P. boldly rejected the traditional poetic forms and all the stifling norms and limitations prescribed by the regime-supported literary theories, thus assuming a major role in the struggle for freedom of poetic expression waged in Yugoslavia in the early 1950s. Together with Vasko POPA, P. contributed a great deal to the successful outcome of that struggle and to the resulting integration of Serbian—and, more broadly, Yugoslav—poetry into the European and world literary mainstream.

At present, three major "chapters" can be distinguished in P.'s complex poetic corpus. In all of them, the poet is preoccupied with the fate of contemporary man, the means he possesses to resist ever-growing evil in the world, and the chances he has to preserve his humanity in the process. In the 1950s P. focused on the devastating effects of World War II on those who survived it and on the bleak prospects the future had in store for them. During the following decade (1963–71) the poet embarked on a long journey into the past in search of his nation's roots and his own, believing that the lost sense of identity must be restored before a new hope could be offered to man. Beginning with *Zavetine* (1976; country festivals), which, in P.'s own words, represents his "return to the modern world and the contemporary experience," P. once again addresses his contemporaries directly, although his preoccupations have not essentially changed. He ponders over the unity of time—past, present, and future,—and over the consistency with which human experiences repeat themselves, serving as links between generations.

P.'s verse is free and his poetic metaphor, although somewhat hermetic, is highly functional. In the collections aimed at direct communication, simple, short lines dominate. Long, solemn, and ornate verse is typical of the collections dealing with the past, which are peopled with gods and heroes.

P.'s anthologies of English, European romantic, and Serbian poetry, and his books of essays on Yugoslav poets and the art of poetry in general are a significant part of his literary output. The essays especially are a very important contribution to literary theory in Yugoslavia: they are models of erudite and objective essayistic prose that addresses itself to the rational mind of our era.

Because of its innovations, its concern with the universal problems of contemporary man, and its influence on younger Yugoslav poets, P.'s refined and humane intellectual poetry, founded on the experiences of the English poetic tradition, is one of the most impressive examples of the maturity and vitality of the contemporary Serbian—and Yugoslav—poetic art.

FURTHER WORKS: *Stub sećanja* (1953); *Most bez obala* (1956); *Oktave* (1957); *Rokovi poezije* (1959); *Igre bezimenih* (1963); *Mleko iskoni* (1963); *87 pesama: Izbor poezije* (1963); *Osam pesnika* (1964); *Velika Skitija* (1969); *Nova Skitija* (1970); *Hododarje* (1971); *Svetli i tamni praznici* (1971); *Velika Skitija, i druge pesme* (1972); *Dnevnik pene* (1972); *Poezija i kultura* (1974); *Karike* (1977); *Pevanja na viru* (1977); *Poetika modernog* (1978); *Bekstva po Srbiji* (1979); *Izabrane pesme* (1979); *Ništitelji i svadbari* (1979); *Vidovnica* (1979); *Izabrana dela* (1981). **FURTHER WORKS IN ENGLISH:** *The Conqueror in Constantinople: Poetry* (1976)

BIBLIOGRAPHY: Palavestra, P., on *Osam pesnika, LQ,* 1 (1965), 106; Simic, C., on *Velika Skitija, BA,* 44 (1970), 691; Popović, B. A., on *Hododarje, BA,* 46 (1972), 327; Mihailovich, V. D., on *Poezija i kultura, BA,* 49 (1975), 577; Eekman, T., *Thirty Years of Yugoslav Literature (1945–1975)* (1978): 201–3; Mihailovich, V. D., "The Poetry of M. P.," *CSP,* 22 (1978): 358–68; Šljivić-Šimšic, B., on *Vidovnica, WLT,* 55 (1981): 140–41

—BILJANA ŠLJIVIĆ-ŠIMSIĆ

PAYRÓ, Roberto Jorge

Argentine dramatist, short-story writer, and novelist, b. 19 April 1867, Mercedes; d. 5 April 1928, Buenos Aires

P. was brought up in Buenos Aires by his maternal grandmother. He disliked school and refused to study law, as his father wished, but he managed to educate himself and to pursue his interest in literature by his voracious reading. By the age of twenty-one he had published some stories and a novel. Even as a youth he had a passion for journalism. While visiting his father in Bahía Blanca in 1887, he contributed articles to the local newspaper and within two years had founded one of his own, *La tribuna.* Most importantly, however, he had an opportunity to observe provincial customs and manners, political mores, and character types, all of which bore fruit in his later fiction. In Buenos Aires, P. worked on the staff of *La nación;* his trips to Patagonia and Tierra del Fuego (1898) and the northern provinces (1899) resulted in two semidocumentary books, *La Australia argentina* (1898; the Argentine south) and *En las tierras de Inti* (1909; in the lands of Inti).

P. was also active in politics—he founded the Argentine Socialist Party with Leopoldo LUGONES—and took part in literary gatherings. Although a friend of Rubén DARÍO's, his own tastes in literature were in the direction of realism and naturalism rather than MODERNISM. He lectured on and translated some of the works of Émile Zola. From 1907 until 1919 P. lived in Spain and Belgium, primarily the latter, and continued to contribute to *La nación.*

Considering his dedication to newspaper columns, it is surprising that P. had time for creative writing. It is universally acknowledged, however, that even his best work suffers from a journalistic taint. P.'s first significant literary efforts were in the theater. *Sobre las ruinas* (1904; upon the ruins), his best-known play, was an important contribution to the developing Argentine National Theater. Although the play dramatizes the tragic failure of the old gaucho virtues as Don Pedro's ranch is destroyed by floods due to his stubborn refusal to accept modern engineering techniques, the hope is expressed in the end that a technologically based Argentine agricultural system will be built on the ruins of backward ways. The more melodramatic *Marco Severi* (1905; Marco Severi) is also a thesis play: should a former counterfeiter be extradited by his native Italy after he has lived his new life in Argentina as a model citizen? P.'s answer is "no," as he praises the opportunities for regeneration inherent in his native Argentina. Both plays are more valued today for their social documentation than for their intrinsic dramatic merit.

P.'s early plays are optimistic about his country; in the fiction that followed, however, there is a gradual descent into pessimism and even cynicism. To this second period belong *El casamiento de Laucha* (1906; Laucha's marriage), *Pago Chico* (1908; Pago

Chico), and *Divertidas aventuras del nieto de Juan Moreira* (1910; amusing adventures of Juan Moreira's grandson). The first is a picaresque tale in the Spanish tradition but with a rural setting and colloquial language that are distinctly Argentine. Laucha, a clever but amoral gaucho trickster, obviously delights in the telling of his story, an extended joke centering around his fraudulent marriage to a hard-working Italian widow. Upon losing his money and his "wife's" business in a horse race, he simply abandons her and departs for greener pastures. In this brief work, atmosphere, character, and language combine to create a minor classic in which the satirical intent is clearly secondary to the humor. In *Pago Chico*, a volume of loosely interrelated sketches focusing on the men and women of influence in a turn-of-the-century Argentine provincial town, P. is more biting in his satire as he ridicules graft, pomposity, and moral laxity. The picaresque tone of Laucha's story is retained, as is the locale, but the narrative voice is a more ironic third person. If the stories hold up today, it is because the characters are presented as genuinely human even in their foibles. For the most part, this is not true of the longer picaresque novel, *Divertidas aventuras del nieto de Juan Moreira*. Here the protagonist, Mauricio Gómez Herrera, a cynical opportunist who rises from small-town rogue to presidential sycophant as he betrays friends and lovers alike, is a contrived character with no redeeming qualities whatsoever. Despite its success as a satire, it suffers as a work of fiction from the manipulation of character and plot for the purpose of social criticism.

In his later years, P. returned to his earlier interest in the theater; his one-act humorous sketch (sainete), *Mientraiga* (1925; while they last), is considered to be an excellent example of the *costumbrista* genre, which satirizes popular customs and manners. P. also turned his attention to the historical novel. *El capitán Vergara* (1925; Captain Vergara) and *El mar dulce* (1927; freshwater sea) succeed in a modest way in dramatizing two significant moments in the discovery and conquest of Argentina.

P.'s universal appeal has diminished with the passing of time. Nevertheless, *El casamiento de Laucha* and *Pago Chico* can still be read for their humor, humanity, and vitality. They also immortalize a time and place in the Argentine scene that has for the most part passed away.

FURTHER WORKS: *Ensayos Poéticos* (1884); *Antígona* (1885); *Scripta* (1887); *Novelas y fantasías* (1888); *Los italianos en Argentina* (1895); *Canción trágica* (1900); *El falso Inca* (1905); *Violines y toneles* (1908); *Crónicas* (1909); *El triunfo de los otros* (1923); *Teatro: Vivir quiero conmigo, Fuego en el rastrojo, Mientraiga* (1925); *Nuevos cuentos de Pago Chico* (1929); *Chamijo* (1930); *Cuentos del otro barrio* (1931); *Siluetas* (1931); *Charlas de un optimista* (1931); *Los tesoros del rey blanco* (1935); *Alegría* (1936); *Teatro completo* (1956)

BIBLIOGRAPHY: Special P. issue, *Nosotros*, May 1928; special P. issue, *Claridad*, April 1929; Larra, R., *P.: El hombre y la obra* (1938); Anderson-Imbert, E., *Tres novelas de P., con pícaros en tres meras* (1942); Jones, C., and A. Alonso, Introduction to *Sobre las ruinas* (1943): vii-xx; García, G., *R. J. P.: Testimonio de una vida y realidad de una literatura* (1961); González Lanuza, E., *Genio y figura de R. J. P.* (1965)

—ROBERT H. SCOTT

PAZ, Octavio

Mexican poet and essayist, b. 31 March 1914, Mexico City; d. 19 Apr. 1998, Mexico City

P.'s long and productive autodidacticism began in the library of the decaying mansion of his grandfather, one of the first novelists to plead the cause of the Indians. His father, a lawyer who represented Zapata in the U.S. during the Mexican revolution, strengthened P.'s interest in social causes. Although P. attended the University of Mexico at an early age, he apparently outdistanced his professors before achieving formal degrees. His formative period was strongly shaped by his presence in Spain during the civil war. As one of the founders and most energetic editors of the literary journal *Taller* (1938–41), he had a direct influence on emerging writers. In 1943 he received a Guggenheim fellowship for travel and study in the U.S. A period of great literary activity coincided with the assumption of several high government posts (including service as Mexico's representative to UNESCO and ambassador to India), which he resigned to protest the Mexican government's handling of student demonstrations before the 1968 Olympic Games. Since then he has dedicated his time to writing and to teaching, particularly at Harvard, which awarded him an honorary degree in 1980. As the founder and chief editor first of *Plural* and then of *Vuelta*, he influences and challenges the intellectuals of Spanish America. His name is frequently cited among possible Latin American candidates for the Nobel Prize in literature. He won the prestigious Neustadt Prize in 1982.

P.'s impact as a poet preceded his accomplishments in the essay. Although he was recognized for his early poetic works, especially *A la orilla del mundo* (1942; on the world's shore), *Libertad bajo palabra* (1949; rev. eds., 1960, 1968; freedom and the word) represents the height of his talent. Employing a technique that is a mixture of SYMBOLISM and SURREALISM, the poet remains true to the necessities of his deeply personal creativity. His gift is to bridge the gap between the personal and the general, between man and society, and by defining his own alienation and anxiety to provide some solace for these universal afflictions. Although many of his poems are developed within the discipline of regular meter and rhyme, the appeal of his work rests more on their reconstruction of reality than on brilliance of form.

If one were to ask readers and critics to select P.'s most successful long poem, the likely choice would be *Piedra de sol* (1957; *Sun Stone*, 1963). Written in 584 unpunctuated endecasyllabic lines, reflecting the synodic cycle of Venus, this carefully structured work is modeled after the famous Aztec calendar stone. In the same way that the calendar stone combines interlocking circular symmetries of time and religious symbolism to suggest a cosmology, the poem joins personal reminiscence and social commentary, illustrating the truth of UNAMUNO's observation that the universal is derived from the particular. Like its model, the poem too is circular, beginning in the middle of an experience and concluding with the six introductory verses, whose meaning has been broadened, if not transformed, by the development of the poem. Its two halves, separated by the recall of the poet's experience in wartime Madrid, compare and contrast the themes of love, of the nature of man, and of his place in the world, yet leave major questions to be answered only by the reader.

Like *Piedra de sol, Blanco* (1967; *Blanco*, 1971) is an experiment in form, whose complexity, however, demands more of the reader than does *Piedra de sol*. The poet suggests in an introduction to the poem that it can be read as a succession of signs on a single page (the original edition was printed on one long page that folded out); such a reading produces a text that is in constant flux. In addition, he indicates five other ways to comprehend the text, which is composed of three columns: (1) the center column alone, whose theme is the passage of speech from silence through four stages to an ultimate silence; (2) the left column alone, divided into four sections corresponding to the four traditional elements—earth, air, fire, and water; (3) the right column alone, the counterpoint of the left, whose divisions correspond to sensation, perception, imagination, and comprehension; (4) each one of the parts consisting of two columns read separately, comprising four independent poems (that is, the left and right columns read together); (5) each of the six center sections and each of the four left and four right sections as separate poems. The effect of these multiple readings is to instruct the reader in the technique of responding in various ways to the signs that have been presented.

In *Ladera este* (1969; east slope) the lack of punctuation of *Piedra de sol* and *Blanco* and the columnar structure of *Blanco* are utilized in many of the poems. The complexity in these cases, however, suggests not so much a programmed variety of opposing and/or complementary interpretations as an independent ambiguity whose solution is not only concealed by, but may even be unknown to, the poet. A phrase or noun, for example, may be read as a part of the preceding verse, or part of the following, or as part of the poet's thought independent of both. Perhaps as a compensation for increased difficulty of comprehension, the diction is simpler. As in much of P.'s other poetry, the theme involves the reconciliation of opposites, but here, as indicated by the title and textual references, Buddhist philosophy has a noticeable influence.

In *Pasado en claro* (1975; *A Draft of Shadows*, 1979) and *Vuelta* (1976; return) P. returned to a more conventional form. The reworking of his major themes—language, love, and metaphysics—shows a constant, and perhaps futile, striving for ultimate expression. At the same time, the demands on the reader not only in interpreting the poem but also in some measure creating it, are more apparent.

The publication of twenty-three volumes of essays to date is ample evidence of P.'s productivity as a thinker. Although these can be divided broadly into the large categories of social concerns on the one hand and arts and letters on the other, it is characteristic of his approach to take every opportunity to explore the relationship between the two. In *El laberinto de la soledad* (1950; *The Labyrinth of Solitude*, 1961) P. provided a complex and controversial analysis of the Mexican character. Taking as his point of departure the *pachuco*, the hybrid Mexican-American, P. identifies concealment, the use of a mask, as the most observable feature of the Mexican character. Much "logical" social behavior is traceable to a profound individual insecurity, which is reflected in a collective identity crisis. The Mexican does not know who he is and is suspicious of others because he is suspicious of himself. In terms which are basically psychological but which P. extends to history, mythology, and social behavior, the Mexican is revealed as the defensive victim of the social rape in which he was engendered. The historical application of P.'s thesis reveals a Mexico (and, in fact, Spanish America) in quest of a national identity: America is not so much a tradition to be carried on as it is a future to be realized. In the book's final chapter on the dialectic of solitude, P. places the problems of individual integration and social communion in the center of modern existence. *Posdata* (1970; *The Other Mexico*, 1972) is an extension of his interpretation to the failure of

Octavio Paz

Mexico's ruling party to maintain communication with the people and to continue the principles on which it was established. The massacre of students in 1968 is not only symbolic of that failure, but is a modern re-creation of ritual human sacrifice on which the Aztec state was based.

Just as the meaning of history underlines P.'s analyses of society, so does the significance of language connect his numerous essays on Hispanic and French poetry and art. Ranging from *El arco y la lira* (1956; *The Bow and the Lyre*, 1973)—a brilliant analysis of poetry as language, process, and social phenomenon—to his broad history of poetic evolution in the 1972 Charles Eliot Norton lectures at Harvard—*Los hijos del limo: Del romanticismo a la vanguardia* (1974; *Children of the Mire: Modern Poetry from Romanticism to the Avant-Garde*, 1974)—he views the distillation of language not as an adornment of mankind but as a key to its comprehension. His brief but seminal study of a French surrealist artist, *Marcel Duchamp; o, El castillo de la pureza* (1968; *Marcel Duchamp; or, The Castle of Purity*, 1970), provides insights into contemporary hermetic expression, including that of the poet's own work.

P.'s poetry and prose represent two aspects of a concern for the predicament of modern man, whom P. is not unique in viewing as fragmented and mutilated. In fact, all of his work is unified by a utopian wish for the fulfillment of man's wholeness in individual creativity and in the building of society, offering an ennobling vision of man to an uneasy world. This vision underlies his attempts to reconcile opposites, especially those of passion and reason, linear and circular time, society and the individual, and word and meaning. His ideal is perhaps expressed by a line from "Himno entre ruinas" (1948; "Hymn among the Ruins," 1963): "Words that are flowers that are fruit that are acts."

FURTHER WORKS: *La hija de Rappaccini* (1956); *Las peras del olmo* (1957); *La estación violenta* (1958); *Salamandra* (1962); *Cuadrivio* (1965); *Viento entero* (1965); *Puertas al campo* (1966); *Claude Lévi-Strauss; o, El nuevo festín de Esopo* (1967; *Claude Lévi-Strauss: An Introduction*, 1970); *Corriente alterna* (1967; *Alternating Current*, 1973); *Discos visuales* (1968); *Conjunciones y disyunciones* (1969; *Conjunctions and Disjunctions*, 1974); *Los signos en rotacón, y otros ensayos* (1971); *Renga* (1971, with Edoardo Sanguineti, Tomlinson Charles, and Roubaud Jacques; *Renga: A Chain of Poems*, 1972); *Topoemas* (1971); *Traducción: Literatura y literalidad* (1971); *El signo y el garabato* (1973); *Sólo a dos voces* (1973, with Rios Julian); *El mono gramático* (1974; *The Monkey Grammarian*, 1981); *La búsqueda del comienzo* (1974); *Teatro de signos* (1974); *Versiones y diversiones* (1974); *In/Mediaciones* (1979); *Poemas (1935–1975)* (1979). FURTHER WORKS IN ENGLISH: *Configurations* (1971); *Early Poems* (1974); *The Siren and the Seashell and Other Essays on Poets and Poetry* (1974); *A Draft of Shadows* (1979); *The Labyrinth of Solitude and Other Essays*, rev. ed. (1982)

BIBLIOGRAPHY: Céa, C., *O. P.* (1965); Xirau, R., *O. P.: el sentido de la palabra* (1970); Phillips, R., *The Poetic Modes of O. P.* (1972); special P. section, *Review*, No. 6 (1972): 5–21; Gallagher, D. P., *Modern Latin American Literature* (1973): 67–81; Ivask, I., ed. *The Perpetual Present: The Poetry and Prose of O. P.* (1973); Flores, A., ed., *Aproximaciones a O. P.* (1974); Rodman, S., *Tongues of Fallen Angels* (1974): 135–61; Brotherston, G., *Latin American Poetry: Origins and Presence* (1975): 138–68; Magis, C. H., *La poesía hermética de O. P.* (1978); Roggiano, A., ed., *O. P.* (1979); Wilson, J., *O. P.: A Study of His Poetics* (1979); Chantikian, K., ed., *O. P.: Homage to the Poet* (1981)

—JOHN M. FEIN

There is no reason to require an essay to be systematic: it is enough that it be enlightening. But P. not only enlightens, he frequently arouses passion and sometimes irritates. It is interesting to follow the meanderings of his thinking with an expectant eye to the surprises his associative genius and the uniqueness of his knowledge can give us. To whom but him would it occur to note the lack of "a general history of the relations between body and soul, life and death, sex and the face?. . ."

The relationships of signs are by nature difficult. If, making use of relationships among them, one tries to establish a system of parallels and antitheses between different cultures, the exercise is hazardous and the positive results provisional. Even so, it is worth the trouble to attempt it for it is the only way to show precisely the affinities between those different cultures and the common roots shared by very different men. In sum, it is a way of showing that signs reveal a

common identity among human beings, be they Protestant Europeans of the 16th century or Buddhists of the 6th century B.C.

Ricardo Gullón, "The Universalism of O. P.," *BA*, 46 (1972), p. 587

His demand that the world be different is the demand of a healthy man, untroubled by suffering. It is just that nothing can satisfy him that is not an all-embracing, time-destroying ecstasy. His poetry, whose central topics have remained more or less constant throughout his career, constitutes a search for a single moment of dizzy ecstasy, a splendid *instante* that will annul the world that is, and germinate instead an altogether new one, where a poplar, a stone, a mountain, or a river—or, above all, O. P.—will become transfigured from what they merely are to something immeasurably more vast and magnificent.

D. P. Gallagher, *Modern Latin American Literature* (1973), p. 67

In one of his essays P. says, "When we read or listen to a poem we do not smell, taste or touch the word. All of these sensations are mental images. In order to feel a poem one must understand it; in order to understand it, hear it, see it, contemplate it, change it into an echo, into shadow, into nothing. Comprehension is a spiritual exercise." Just as the experience of man in the world, the poem is incarnation and distance, plenitude and precariousness at the same time; like the world, the poem draws its life from the dialectic between affirmation and negation. In recent years, P. proposes a more and more radical *no*: "Take negation to its limit. There contemplation awaits us: the disincarnation of language, transparency."

Thus, transparency leads to silence: that which is true reality is inexpressible. In this way P. seems to come to the same conclusion as the Igitur of Mallarmé: "Nothingness having departed, there remains the castle of purity." But will not this purity be the ultimate form in which the word is revealed to us or becomes transparent, i.e., the ultimate form in which the world becomes incarnate and fully real, so real that it cannot be named? This, I believe, is P.'s utopian vision: the appearance of the world—of the world, it is understood, in its complete original state—implies the disappearance of language and of poetry. All that is left is to live poetry: to write the world.

Guillermo Sucre, "O. P.: Poetics of Vivacity," in Ivar Ivask, ed., *The Perpetual Present: The Poetry and Prose of O. P.* (1973), p. 19

In most respects P.'s biggest "Mexican" poem, "Sun Stone," in fact belongs more properly to the collection it appeared in: *La estación violenta* . . . Complemented by P.'s first major work of criticism, *El arco y la lira* . . . these poems as a whole amount if anything to a certain scepticism about the idea of Mexico. At any event, he openly repudiates the indigenists and the social realists, and all forms of national concern with culture. Against these traditions he would set another, which had come to fascinate him more and more from the late 1940s onwards, that of the Surrealists. In a metaphor fundamental to all his writing, but especially to that of this period, he would break out of his labyrinth of solitude into new utterance. Out of empty constriction, in which man is fragmented socially and erotically, he would join the Surrealists in conjuring that marvellous instant when we truly "inhabit our names."

Gordon Brotherston, *Latin American Poetry: Origins and Presence* (1975), p. 146

Throughout P.'s writings there are many references to surrealism, especially in his *El arco y la lira* (1956). But all that he writes falls within the opposition between attitude and activity. What P. accepts and rejects follows a clear pattern of values based on that opposition. For P., surrealism as a historical movement degenerated into style and convention. All that is tainted with history, all that is subject to time's corrosion, is rejected by P.

P. has lifted surrealism out of time and social context, elevating it into an attitude of mind. This was possible because he arrived late at the surrealists' table. Sifting theory from practice also enabled P. to view surrealism as eternal, a universal constant impervious to time and change. Circumstantial involvement did not blur these clear distinctions.

First, P., like Villaurrutia and most of surrealism's detractors, rejected automatic writing, one of the theoretical and practical pillars of surrealism . . . .

In P.'s version of surrealism, all the techniques became commonplaces, or inevitable conventions because forming part of history. His attitude towards automatism became his attitude to hypnosis, dream *récits*, the mode of poem-objects, the collective games and so on.

Jason Wilson, *O. P.: A Study of His Poetics* (1979), pp. 23–24

PAZZI, Roberto

Italian poet and novelist, b. 18 August 1946, Ameglia

P. spent his formative years in Ferrara, a city that was to mark both his temperament as a man and his intellectual growth as an artist. He attended the same secondary school as two famous "ferraresi" writers, Giorgio BASSANI and Lanfranco Caretti (1915-1995), and it is here that he met the poet Vittorio SERENI. Attracted to literature at a young age, P. attended the University of Bologna, graduating in classical literature. His thesis on Umberto Saba (1883-1957) was directed by Luciano Anceschi. After graduating he returned to Ferrara and was employed as a secondary school teacher of Italian literature at the V. Monti Institute until he attained the Chair of Sociology of Art and Literature at the University of Urbino.

An established poet before he turned to narrative, P. published three collections of poety before turning to prose narrative. However, since the publication of his first novel *Cercando l'imperatore* in 1985, he has received increasing critical attention and has become a leading figure in late 20th-c. Italian literature. P.'s first poems were published in poetry journals, among these *Contrappunto*, which he eventually directed as editor (1984-85), and *Sinopia*, which he founded in 1985. An indefatigable writer, he wrote three novels in three years: *La principessa e il drago* (1986; The Princess and the Dragon), *La malattia del tempo* (1987; The Sickness of Time), *Il vangelo di Giuda* (1989; The Gospel of Judas), and *La stanza sull'acqua* (1990; The Room on the Water), as well as a collection of poetry *Calma di vento* (1987). All have been translated into English.

The appearance of these novels marked the emergence of a significant new writer. What distinguishes P. from his contemporaries is his uncanny ability to captivate the reader with an extraordinary storytelling prowess. His return to a "high style" and his condemnation of the "culture of the masses" has given new value to the communicative possiblities of literary language that moves beyond categories of descriptive realism. Since he is first and foremost a poet, P. wishes to renew the subliminal, indeed divinatory, capacity of poetic language by translating its indeterminacy into prose. He wishes to tap into humanity's archetypal imagery by presenting his own psyche as an intensely subjective starting point. In this sense P. is a more conservative author than his contemporaries. For the author life's experience is not a progression but a mandala—a circular existence where all parts relate reciprocally to all other parts. This holistic ideal runs counter to the hierarchical and depersonalized thinking of contemporary society. By clinging to this utopian model of both literature and mankind, P.'s vision of the world is both wilfully ancient in its conception yet surprisingly contemporary in its existential urgency.

In order to understand P.'s notion of literature as fulfilling man's eternal desire for a more complete and unified cosmic reality one might look at his sources. He is fond of the memorialistic literature of Marcel PROUST and Rainer Maria RILKE, he shares the same existential angst of Tasso and Giacomo Leopardi, he finds peace in the agnostic mysticism of Rosmini and the youthful poetry of Alessandro Manzoni. Yet, he is also a student of the transcendental philosophies of Schopenhauer and Nietzsche. He is interested in a wide range of literary and visual art forms but is most interested in romantic and gothic manifestations of the macabre. Consequently P.'s work relies on the basic duality of appearance versus reality. And since he possesses the sensitivity of a poet, he is able to scrutinize seemingly casual details with an eye for the subtlety that leads to epiphany. For P., then, meaning lies in the noumena of intuitive experience not in the phenomena of surface reality.

Indeed, all of P.'s images may be termed pretemporal and prehistorical, archetypal and imaginary—what we prefer to call the language of dreams and unconscious perceptions. He is able to call forth a storehouse of memories that have been freed from time. This is one of his constant themes. P. is remembering what-never-happened, pulling down thoughts and images from the realm of humanity's collective experience that form the very essence of human memory.

In this manner P.'s prose transforms history into a personal reality that is completely fictional. Characters and events "make sense" because they have acquired a sense of narrative time that gives them an authenticity that moves beyond their historical reality and into the fiction of a universal and collective text.

Leopardi, we recall, was convinced that prose nourished poetry. For P., however, the process is an anomalous one. In his first novel, *Cercando l'imperatore* (1985; Searching for the Emperor, 1989), P. places the reader in the midst of a world where everything that is familiar is dissolving. The author reconstructs the last days of Czar Nicholas II and his family under house arrest in Ekaterinbury, Siberia. Avoiding the better known and perhaps less interesting events surrounding the fall of the house of Romanov, P. focuses instead on the maddening psychological isolation of the monarchs who fill their desperate final hours with disquieting idiosyncracies.

P.'s fascination with the imperial family of Russia arises from the childhood memory of a portrait of Nicholas and Alexandra seen at the home of a neighbor. The idea of an aristocracy fascinated the urban apartment dweller as he fantasized about their royal existence in the midst of palatial opulence. As if to assuage his own loneliness, the youthful experience confirmed his vocation as an imaginary thinker. Literature became the affirmation not only of the self but the companion of his solitude. Moreover, literature made it possible to confer life to the dead; the logic of metaphor vanquished temporal structure and logical restrictions. P.'s rhetoric of ambiguity naturally gravitated to characters he could personally relate to in history. Shielded by these characters he could pursue the exploration of his own fragmented subjectivity. In all his novels P. embraces forgotten historical figures: the Imperial Romanovs, Archduke Giorge Alexandrovich Romanov (brother of the Czar), Cesarione (son of Caesar and Cleopatra), and simple, daily heroes: Doctor Malaguti, "Max," Giulio, and Ada, the same way one covets the memory of a beloved grandfather. In essence P. is searching for replicas of paternal authority, of past glory, of a sense of personal security. He is constantly falling in love with the weak and the helpless victims of history in order to find in art a source of moral instruction that neither reverts or appropriates ethics nor leads to sterile relativism. In contrast, then, to the traditional historical novel that extols the exemplary virtues of great men for the national psyche P. recuperates lost souls that have fallen through the cracks of historical memory. By not allowing history to squander their lives, he fulfills the possibilities of their existence in fiction while guaranteeing his own existence as an author.

For P. narrative space and historical time function as thematic elements that constitute the imaginative vision of the author and place him squarely within a posthistorical perspective. These postmodern themes include. the alienation of man from nature by technology, the reincarnation of spirit, social (as opposed to individual) insanity, collective memory, and historical fact and its relationship to imagination. P. believes that since history and fiction may be considered selective orderings of reality, fictive space and historical time can be organized into schematic patterns that may or may not be true but that nevertheless mutually influence each other to create a new world vision. Towards this end his writing is a mixture of ancient mysticism, folklore, fairy tale, and romance, as well as the modern myths of technology and science. These categories of experience interface as a single unifying principle of space and time and interpenetrate to transform history. Once again the poet in P. dispels weighty reality in favor of hypothetical possibilities in space and time. The multiple projections of characters and plot fulfill the author's need for literary role playing. The complex web of memories that he meticulously constructs in his poetry is played-out in his novels in a panoply of undifferentiated human (history and fiction) experience.

P. continues his experiments into narrative space and time in all his novels, but perhaps the most mythical of his characters is the historically parenthetical figure of Cesarione, son of Julius Caesar and Cleopatra, literally forgotten by time (Plutarch only briefly mentions him in his *Life of Antony*). The author descends into the capillaries of history in order to recover an imaginary Alexandrine tale of love and intrigue. In *La stanza sull'acqua* Cesarione is escaping the plottings of Ottavian Augustus Caesar by fleeing, by boat, up the Nile and into Ethiopia in order to eventually reach India. The crew, faithful to Ottavian, however, is about to mutiny against Cesarione when they meet a mysterious black boat travelling in the opposite direction. Now begins a typical Pazzian game of mirrors as the boat's inhabitant, the Ethopian princess Afra, is herself escaping similar political circumstances. The two outcasts meet, recognize their symbiotic "otherness," and decide to exchange places and roles. Despite the switch, however, both remain victims of the cruel treachery of power. Afra is killed in her sleep by agents of the emperor that mistake her for the Roman heir, while Cesarione vanishes into the wilderness, never to be heard from again. This novel contains many of P.'s favorite themes: androgeny, destiny, courtly love, and even time travel, and is written in a style that is sublime, ornate, often solemn. There is no satire in his vocabulary, no parody or irony intended; nothing detracts the reader from the quasi-religious sobriety of the prose.

P. could be called the most reluctant, yet consistent, postmodern author of late 20th-c. Italy. In his most recent novels the author takes current Italian political events and renders them into provocative historical and literary possibilities. In *Domani saro' re* (1997; Tomorrow I'll Be King), for example, a new King appears in an Italy governed by tele-democracy, threatened by secession, and burdened by an incapacitated political class. The novel's action occurs as a series of phone conversations—perhaps P.'s idea of a modern epistolary novel, perhaps symptomatic of the ironic lightness with which he allows the morass to devolve into nothingness. This novel wishes to overcome the widespread sense of isolation and fragmentation, felt by writers and critics in recent years, by invoking permanence, eternity, and history, quite in opposition to his contemporaries. Yet his postmodern tales also belie continuous change and flux. By treating contemporary events as history and history as fiction he construes all written, verbal, and visual texts as fiction. For P. history is a story with a visionary span that extends from Creation and is deterministically moving chapter by chapter, like life, towards its prophesied conclusion.

P is thus a contemporary author sponsoring a sort of marriage between "mythos" and "logos"—between history and fantasy in a way that recalls medieval beliefs in a preternatural and transcendental truth as well as a modern hermeneutical framework of discovery and disclosure of postverbal lies. In P.'s novels history becomes a general text, a geography of the mind, not a privileged authority. Beneath the fluid and frenetically sensuous imagery, the transfixing syntax, the sublime solemnity of his prose, there lies an apprehensive knowledge of the debilitating essence of here and now. P.'s narrative is thus a quest not so much for form as it is for meaning, and for lost horizons. His novels are important because they speak to the heart of today's debilitating sense of apocalypse.

FURTHER WORKS: *Le ultime notizie e altre poesie* (1969); *L'esperienza anteriore* (1973); *Versi occidentali* (1976); *Il re, le parole* (1980); *La citta' del Dottor Malagutti* (1993); *Incerti di viaggio* (1996)

BIBLIOGRAPHY: Barberi Squarotti, G., "Arriva dal futuro un nuovo Gengis Khan per rifare il mondo," *La Stampa* (12 October 1987): 3;

Barilli, R., "Delitti sul Nilo," *Corriere della sera* (5 May 1991): 23; Gramigna, G., "La sindrome del 1815," *Corriere della sera* (8 November 1987): 3; Ricci, F., "Beyond Tautology: The Cosmoconception of Time in *La malattia del tempo* by R. P.," *Italica*, 68, 1 (1991): 13-28

—FRANCO RICCI

p'BITEK, Okot

Ugandan poet, anthropologist, and social critic (writing in English and Luo), b. 1931, Gulu

Bursting onto the literary scene in the mid-1960s, p'B. drew to East Africa the attention and acclaim for literature in English that West Africa had long enjoyed. It was a fitting effect, for p'B. had all his life displayed an "unabashed commitment" to his native culture and to African standards and values.

Under the influence of his mother, a gifted singer and composer and a leader in her clan, p'B. early absorbed the rich songs, proverbs, and customs of the Luo people. He was also exposed to missionary training early, and after completing his secondary education in Gulu, attended King's College, Budo. He went abroad as a member of the Uganda national soccer team, and stayed in Britain to take a diploma in education in Bristol, a degree in law at Aberystwyth, and a further degree in social anthropology at Oxford. He returned home as lecturer at University College in Makerere, founded the Festival of African Arts in Gulu, and went on to serve as director of the National Cultural Center in Kampala. As a result of trenchant criticisms he uttered in Zambia, he made himself persona non grata to the Uganda government, and elected to move to Kenya. In 1971 he took up the post of senior research fellow at the Institute of African Studies in Nairobi.

As an administrator, p'B. has shown an intense practical involvement in the sociocultural life of East Africa, shifting the emphasis in song, dance, theater, and art from the dominant British to the basic African style. He has also emerged as an important champion of African values, in a somewhat polemical mode. He has corrected long-standing misapprehensions and created an enhanced view of African culture in such works as *African Religions and Western Scholarship* (1970), *Religion of the Central Luo* (1971), *Africa's Cultural Revolution* (1973), and the critical anthology of poetry and prose, *The Horn of My Love* (1974).

By his own testimony p'B. is less concerned with fixed "ontological definitions" than with "dynamic function," and he is at his most arresting and incisive in creative embodiments and complex dramatizations of the culture-conscious East African scene. His youthful novel in the Acholi dialect of Luo, *Lak tar miyo kinyero wi lobo* (1953; are your teeth white? then laugh), has perhaps been put into the shade by the rich suites of Songs: *Song of Lawino: A Lament* (1966), *Song of Ocol* (1970), *Song of (a) Prisoner* (1971), and *Two Songs: Song of Prisoner; Song of Malaya* (1971), which reprints the earlier title along with the new song. The first of these was composed in Acholi, and p'B. himself made the English translation that brought him international fame.

That fame has not been untouched by controversy. British observers have felt that the Songs convey animosity toward their ways and influence, while African observers have contended that African personalities and ways are exposed to satirical barbs. Access to the poems is simplified as soon as we realize they are dramatic monologues; that is, emotionally and intellectually partial utterances by characters who have silent interlocutors and who are in situations more complex than the characters directly apprehend. The reader must look through their eyes, but also into their minds—between the lines of overt statement—for the full values of the poems.

It helps further to recognize two facts: (1) that the acute social anthropologist in p'B. is not stifled in the poetry, for the main characters are really representative figures, distillations of major features of African experience in the aspiring and dislocating postindependence world; and (2) that the characters operate poetically in a kind of allegory of naïveté, where all impressions are curiously pursued by a mind too sensitive to withstand them and too fresh to organize them in a stable system.

The four Songs constitute veritable compass points of African experience. *Song of Lawino* is the plangent, minutely detailed utterance of resentment and grief by a traditional wife abandoned by her newfangled husband for a modernized woman and the new urban prosperity. *Song of Ocol* is the husband's overemphatic counterstatement, the last lines revealing his true character, one of selfish weakness and hidden anguish. *Song of a Prisoner* shows, in what appears to be a composite character, the ugly machinations and specious hopes of the new politics. And *Song of Malaya* sets forth the alternately harsh and tender world view of the new woman of pleasure in the new African town (*malaya* means "prostitute").

Song of Lawino and *Song of a Prisoner* are poems of defense; *Song of Ocol* and *Song of Malaya* are poems of attack. All are poems of seething desperation, representing points of transition and crisis not only for the individuals speaking but also for their very culture. If we want to know what p'B. thinks, we may turn to his polemical anthropological writing. But if we want to know what he apprehends and what he aspires to, then we must turn to the poetry.

BIBLIOGRAPHY: Lijong, T. Lo, *The Last Word* (1969): 135–56; Blishen, E., Introduction to *Song of Prisoner* (1971): 1–40; Cooke, M., on *Song of a Prisoner, Parnassus*, 1, 2 (1973), 115: 117–19; Heron, G., *The Poetry of O. p'B.* (1976); Asein, S. O., "O. p'B.: Literature and the Cultural Revolution in East Africa," *WLWE*, 16 (1977): 7–24; Heron, G., "O. p'B. and the Elite in African Writing," *LHY*, 19, 1 (1978): 66–93; Moore, G., *Twelve African Writers* (1980): 170–90; Heywood, A., "Modes of Freedom: The Songs of O. p'B.," *JCL*, 15, 1 (1980): 65–83

—MICHAEL G. COOKE

PEDI LITERATURE
See under South African Literature

PEDROLO, Manuel de

Spanish novelist, dramatist, short-story writer, poet, essayist, and translator (writing in Catalan), b. 1 April 1918, Aranyo; d. 22 July 1990, Cuernavaca

P., the child of middle-class landowners, earned his bachelor's degree in Barcelona in 1935. He served in the Spanish Republican Army until the end of the Spanish Civil War in 1939. After his release from a concentration camp in Valladolid he took up residence in Barcelona. In the 1950s and 1960s he ran a business and then worked in advertising and publishing; he also did translations while continuing to pursue his literary career. Since around 1970 he has been a full-time writer. Because of the publishing difficulties for Catalan writers, many of P.'s works appeared long after their composition, and a large number remain unpublished. P. was awarded the Honor Prize of Catalan Letters of 1979.

The early novel *Cendra per Martina* (written 1952, pub. 1955; cinders for Martina) is a realistic love story; it constitutes the first great testimony in Catalan fiction of a generation morally destroyed by the Spanish Civil War.

Some of P.'s plays have been acclaimed as masterpieces of the THEATER OF THE ABSURD. *Cruma* (written 1957, pub. 1958; *Cruma*, 1973)—the title is the name of an ancient unit of measurement—is a play about the EXISTENTIALIST problem of communication. Starting from the Heideggerian premise of the debatable "authenticity" of the human being, it portrays a search for scientific knowledge; the characters, however, must finally tacitly admit their inability to attain that knowledge. *Homes i no* (written 1957, pub. 1960; *Humans and No*, 1977), P.'s finest play, explores the meaning of personal freedom through the depiction of the struggle of some imprisoned people against their closed world. The play acknowledges the cosmological failure of man but concludes that man has at least succeeded in broadening his definition of freedom. Two other major plays, *Situació bis* (written 1958, pub. 1965; *Full Circle*, 1970) and *Tècnica de cambra* (written 1959, pub. 1964; *The Room*, 1972), both deal with rebellion—political and metaphysical—and the nature of freedom.

With *Un camí amb Eva* (written 1963, pub. 1968; a path with Eva) P. began a series of eleven novels called "Temps obert" (open time). In each one Daniel Bastida lives a different life—one he could have lived given new conditions and/or interests. This cycle constitutes the most ambitious mosaic of Catalan society after the civil war.

Totes les bèsties de càrrega (written 1965, pub. 1967; all the beasts of burden) is perhaps the masterpiece of contemporary Catalan fiction. It depicts, naturalistically and in a near-Kafkaesque fashion, the inhuman conditions imposed by an arbitrary state machinery and the heroism of a group of people who tenaciously fight for their human dignity.

Anònim I (written 1970, pub. 1978; anonym I) is the first of three novels that, although not a true trilogy, share the same political overtones and depict an absurd world ruled autocratically, in which an inversion of values, including especially sexual values, prevails.

In the novel, the genre that interests P. the most, he has tried all possible subgenres (including detective fiction and science fiction), frequently using a mixture of these, and employing all the modern literary techniques, including those of the NEW NOVEL. P. is the most notable literary experimenter of Catalonia—and indeed of all Spain.

FURTHER WORKS: *Addenda* (wr. 1936–1973); *Els tentacles* (wr. 1945); *Ésser en el món* (1949); *Ésser per a la mort* (wr. 1949); *Elena de segona mà* (wr. 1949, pub. 1967); *Documents* (wr. 1950); *Simplement sobre la terra* (wr. 1950); *Dimensions mentals* (wr. 1938–1951); *Reixes a través* (wr. 1944–1952); *Roba bruta* (wr. 1948–1952); *Infant dels grans* (wr. 1952); *Es vessa una sang fàcil* (wr. 1952, pub. 1954); *He provat un gest amarg* (wr. 1952); *Mister Chase, podeu sortir* (wr. 1953, pub. 1955); *L'interior és al final*

(wr. 1953, pub. 1974); *Domicili provisional* (wr. 1953, pub. 1956); *Balanç fins a la matinada* (wr. 1953, pub. 1963); *Avui es parla de mi* (wr. 1953, pub. 1966); *L'inspector arriba/fa tard* (wr. 1953, pub. 1960); *Visat de trànsit* (wr. 1952–1954); *El temps a les venes* (wr. 1953–1954, pub. 1974); *Els hereus de la cadira* (wr. 1954, pub. 1980); *Estrictament personal* (wr. 1954, pub. 1955); *Un món per a tothom* (wr. 1954, pub. 1956); *Cinc cordes* (wr. 1954, pub. 1974); *Sonda de temps* (wr. 1955); *Violació de límits* (wr. 1955, pub. 1957); *International Setting* (wr. 1955, pub. 1974); *Una selva com la teva* (wr. 1955, pub. 1960); *Nou pams de terra* (wr. 1955, pub. 1971); *Les finestres s'obren de nit* (wr. 1955, pub. 1957); *Esberla del silenci* (wr. 1956); *Crèdits humans* (wr. 1956, pub. 1957); *La nostra mort de cada dia* (wr. 1956, pub. 1958); *Introducció a l'ombra* (wr. 1956, pub. 1972); *Cops de bec a Pasadena* (wr. 1956, pub. 1972); *La mà contra l'horitzó* (wr. 1957, pub. 1961); *Pell vella al fons del pou* (wr. 1957, pub. 1975); *La terra prohibida, 1: Les portes del passat* (wr. 1957, pub. 1977); *LTP, 2: La paraula dels botxins* (wr. 1957, pub. 1977); *LTP, 3: Fronteres interiors* (wr. 1957, pub. 1978); *LTP, 4: La nit horitzontal* (wr. 1957, pub. 1979); *Entrada en blanc* (wr. 1958, pub. 1968); *Perquè ha mort una noia* (wr. 1958, pub. 1976); *Pas de ratlla* (wr. 1958, pub. 1972); *Algú a l'altre cap de peça* (wr. 1958, pub. 1975); *Darrera versió, per ara* (wr. 1958, pub. 1971); *Veus sense contacte* (wr. 1959); *Un amor fora ciutat* (wr. 1959, pub. 1970); *Tocats pel foc* (wr. 1959, pub. 1976); *Sóc el defecte* (wr. 1959, pub. 1975); *Contes fora recull* (wr. 1959–1974, pub. 1975); *Solució de continuïtat* (wr. 1960, pub. 1968); *Si són roses, floriran* (wr. 1961, pub. 1971); *Acte de violència* (wr. 1961, pub. 1975); *Si em pregunten, responc* (wr. 1961–1973, pub. 1974); *Viure a la intempèrie* (wr. 1962, pub. 1974); *M'enterro en els fonaments* (wr. 1962, pub. 1967); *Acompanyo qualsevol cos* (wr. 1962, pub. 1979); *Els elefants són contagiosos* (wr. 1962–1972, pub. 1974); *Temps obert, 2: Se'n va un estrany* (wr. 1963, pub. 1968); *L'ús de la matèria* (wr. 1963, pub. 1977); *TO, 3: Falgueres informa* (wr. 1964, pub. 1968); *TO, 4: Situació analítica* (wr. 1964, pub. 1971); *TO, 5: Des d'uns ulls de dona* (wr. 1965, pub. 1972); *Joc brut* (wr. 1965, pub. 1965); *Arreu on valguin les paraules, els homes* (wr. 1966, pub. 1975); *La sentència* (wr. 1966); *TO, 6: Unes mans plenes de sol* (wr. 1966, pub. 1972); *TO, 7: L'ordenació dels maons* (wr. 1966, pub. 1974); *A cavall de dos cavalls* (wr. 1966, pub. 1967); *Mossegar-se la cua* (wr. 1967, pub. 1968); *TO, 8: S'alcen veus del soterrani* (wr. 1967, pub. 1976); *TO, 9: Pols nova de runes velles* (wr. 1967, pub. 1977); *TO, 10: Cartes a Jones Street* (wr. 1968, pub. 1978); *Milions d'ampolles buides* (wr. 1968, pub. 1976); *Hem posat les mans a la crònica* (wr. 1969, pub. 1977); *TO, 11: "Conjectures" de Daniel Bastida* (wr. 1969, pub. 1980); *Anònim II* (wr. 1970, pub. 1980); *Obres púbiques* (wr. 1971); *Anònim III* (wr. 1971, pub. 1981); *Algú que no hi havia de ser* (wr. 1972, pub. 1974); *Aquesta nit tanquem* (wr. 1973, pub. 1978); *Espais de fecunditat irregular/s* (1973); *Mecanoscrit del segon origen* (wr. 1973, pub. 1974); *Text/Càncer* (1974); *Contes i narracions* (3 vols., 1974–1975); *Trajecte final* (wr. 1974, pub. 1975); *Dos quarts de set* (wr. 1974); *Xit* (wr. 1974); *Monòleg* (wr. 1974); *Sòlids en suspensió* (1975); *Detall d'una acció rutinària* (1975); *Procès de contradicció suficient* (wr. 1975, pub. 1976); *Lectura a banda i banda de paret* (wr. 1975, pub. 1977); *Bones notícies de Sister* (wr. 1975, pub. 1977); *D'esquerra a dreta, respectivament* (wr. 1976, pub. 1978); *Aquesta matinada i potser per sempre* (wr. 1976, pub. 1980); *Novel·les curtes* (4 vols., 1976–1982); *A casa amb papers falsos* (wr. 1976–1978, pub. 1981); *S'han deixat les claus sota l'estora* (1977); *D'ara a demà* (wr. 1977); *Baixeu a ròcules i amb les mans alçades* (wr. 1977, pub.

1979); *Reserva d'inquisidors* (wr. 1978, pub. 1979); *Apòcrif u: Oriol* (wr. 1978); *Exemplar d'arxiu/únicament persones autoritzades* (wr. 1978); *Apòcrif dos: Tina* (wr. 1979); *Successimultani* (wr. 1979, pub. 1981); *Entrem més bigues mentre dormen* (wr. 1980); *Ara (quan?) i aquí (però on?)* (wr. 1980); *Apòcrif tres: Verònica* (wr. 1981); *Crucifeminació* (wr. 1981)

BIBLIOGRAPHY: Esslin, M., *The Theatre of the Absurd* (1961): 182–85; Wellwarth, G. E., *Spanish Underground Drama* (1972): 139–47; Wellwarth, G. E., "M. de P. and Spanish Absurdism," *BA*, 46, (1972): 380–87; Wellwarth, G. E., Introduction to *3 Catalan Dramatists* (1976): 1–7; Valdivieso, T., *España: Bibliografía de un teatro silenciado* (1979): 67–72; Solanas, J. V., *Historia de la literatura catalana* (1980): 278–81

—ALBERT M. FORCADAS

PÉGUY, Charles

(pseuds.: Charles Pierre Baudouin, Pierre Deloire) French philosopher, poet, journalist, and essayist, b. 7 Jan. 1873, Orléans; d. 5 Sept. 1914, Villeroy

Born of a family of peasant craftsmen, P., an outstanding student at the lycée of Orléans, went on, after further study, to the prestigious École Normale Supérieure (1894); during 1897 he was enrolled at the Sorbonne. He took degrees in humanities and science but, having failed the *agrégation* (examination) in philosophy, abandoned academic life for journalism. His earliest works were written under pseudonyms.

His first articles expressed the utopian socialism he had adopted in place of a lost Catholic faith. By 1898 the Dreyfus affair had transformed P. into a militant for justice, and his bookshop near the Sorbonne was a rallying point for Dreyfus's socialist partisans. In 1900 he founded the *Cahiers de la quinzaine*, the journal which henceforth became the focus of his activities. Scrupulously committed to truth, it featured writers of every ideological stamp. Around 1908 P. rediscovered his faith but, for family reasons, never resumed formal practice. Intensely patriotic, he assiduously fulfilled his duties as a reserve officer, was among the first mobilized at the outbreak of World War I, and died in the Battle of the Marne.

As the major outlet for his work, the *Cahiers de la quinzaine* became the vehicle of *Péguysme*, a deeply personalist philosophy combining socialism, patriotism, and Catholicism. Less a systematic analysis than a stream of conscious meditation on the theme of the modern world, *Péguysme* constituted an organic body of thought that took shape in three distinct stages: (1) a formative period (1896–1904), culminating in a series of *Cahiers* attacking the anticlericalism and statism of modern secular society; (2) the critical middle years (1905–9), during which P. defined the situation of the modern world, while formulating in opposition to it a value system grounded in Henri BERGSON's metaphysics, classical humanism, the traditions of old France, and a spirituality free of clericalism; (3) the major phase (1910–14), when he employed all his talent as essayist, dramatist, and poet to chart for a reinvigorated nation the mystical vocation he envisaged as hers.

A masterful pamphleteer who identified issues with personalities, P. wrote lengthy polemical essays denouncing whatever deviated from his ideal: the demagoguery of erstwhile Dreyfusist

allies; the pacifism of his former mentor, the socialist politician Jean Jaurès, in *L'argent* (1913; money); a Catholicism as modernistic as its secular adversaries in *Un nouveau théologien, M. Fernand Laudet* (1911; Mr. Laudet, a new theologian); above all, the cult of science and sociology. In *Zangwill* (1904; Zangwill), the four essays, each titled *Situation* (1906–7; situation), *L'argent suite* (1913; money, continued) he focused on the party of intellectualism (Hippolyte Taine [1828–1893], Ernest Renan [1823–1892], the social and literary historians of the Sorbonne) to criticize a scientific method he deemed inadequate to describe a reality ever in process. Against them he invoked his "heroes"—the Greek poets, the historian Jules Michelet (1798–1874), and his true mentor, Bergson, whose vitalistic philosophy gave to *Péguysme* its intellectual armature. *Note sur M. Bergson et la philosophie bergsonienne* (1914; note on Monsieur Bergson and Bergsonian philosophy) and *Note conjointe sur M. Descartes et la philosophie cartésienne* (1914; added note on Monsieur Descartes and Cartesian philosophy) defended Bergson, after the Vatican had put some of his works on the Index, and reexamined, in Bergsonian terms, theological questions like freedom and grace.

Although fraught with flaws—inordinate length, endless digressions, repetitions that restate rather than developing ideas—the essays transcend their internal weaknesses to express thought in the making. *Notre patrie* (1905; our fatherland) illustrates how P. formulated an idea, the need for a national awakening, while chronicling an event. He captures the ebb and flow of life in a Paris caught up in the state visit of King Alfonso XIII of Spain, only gradually revealing to an unthinking public that the crisis at Tangiers has made a European war something that is eventually inevitable.

Rooting an idea in the concrete is basic to *Péguysme*, whose dominant motif is the insertion of the eternal in the temporal. Just as in the Incarnation the divine became incorporated with the human, so the collective cultural past of a people perdures through memory, creating across time a sense of communion. This is the theme of the posthumously published two-part dialogue composed 1909–14 and generally referred to as *Clio I–II: Véronique: Dialogue de l'histoire et de l'âme charnelle* (pub. 1955; Veronica: dialogue of history and the carnal soul; Eng. adaptation, *Clio I, in Temporal and Eternal*, 1958) and *Clio: Dialogue de l'histoire et de l'âme païenne* (pub. 1917; Clio: dialogue of history and the pagan soul). This theme is also taken up in *Victor-Marie comte Hugo* (1911; Victor-Marie Count Hugo), where P. uses Corneille's theater to illustrate how sanctity represents the transfer of temporal heroism to the plane of the eternal. His contemporaries' infidelity to the heroic ideal saddened P., leading him to write *Notre jeunesse* (1910; *Memories of Youth*, in *Temporal and Eternal*, 1958), in which he recalled what the Dreyfus affair had meant to his generation and how, from being a mystique, it had degenerated into politics.

Out of this disillusionment emerged P. the lyricist, who turned to poetry not only to exorcise pain but to take a firmer hold on reality. P. wrote a genuinely popular poetry celebrating the organic life of old France. Its hypnotic rhythms resemble incantatory verse. But P. did not simply take over older forms; his prosody evolved naturally out of his prose style. The measured beat of the essays developed, through the free verse of the *Mystères* (mysteries), into the regular verse patterns of the quatrains of *La ballade du cœur qui a tant battu* (1911–12; new ed., 1973; the ballad of the heart that has beaten so much), of the two *tapisseries* (tapestries)—*La tapisserie de Sainte Geneviève et de Jeanne d'Arc* (1912; the tapestry of Saint

Genevieve and Joan of Arc) and *La tapisserie de Notre Dame* (1913; the tapestry of Our Lady)—and of the eight thousand and more alexandrines of *Ève* (1913; Eve), the poem P. called his "Christian Iliad." At once elementary and sublime, abstract and colloquial, his poetry is written from the pseudonaïve view-point of the peasant, for whom the spiritual is firmly anchored in the carnal. P. innovated by renewing: he resurrected the medieval mystery play, infused incantatory rhythms into the classical alexandrine, and made poetry out of prayer.

All his essential motifs come together in the Joan of Arc theme. In the figure of the peasant-soldier-saint, P. fused the spiritual, humanitarian, and patriotic wellsprings of his thought. His oldest subject, it took shape initially in the three-part play in prose *Jeanne d'Arc* (1897) and was reworked, after P.'s conversion, into *Le mystère de la charité de Jeanne d'Arc* (1910; *The Mystery of the Charity of Joan of Arc*, 1950), a dialogue on heroism and saint-hood, pitting Joan against prudential wisdom embodied in Madame Gervaise. It is the latter's voice we hear in *Le Porche du mystère de la deuxième vertu* (1911; *The Portico of the Mystery of the Second Virtue*, 1970) and *Le mystère des saints innocents* (1912; *The Mystery of the Holy Innocents*, 1956), celebrating the theological virtue of hope as the principle animating not only the believer but all mankind and nature as well.

Uneven in quality and almost impossible to stage, the *Mystères* can reach extraordinary lyricism, as in God's invocation to the night to envelope in its mantle the dead Christ, or in Joan's anguish lest all men not be saved. Eschatological themes preoccupy P., and, like Hugo, he tries to capture the sweep of history so as to situate man within a sacred context. This is the goal of *Ève*, a gigantic hymn to the mother of the human race, which contains P.'s prayer for those who have died in a just war.

Prayer, the essence of P.'s poetry, was increasingly expressed in more traditional forms (sonnets, quatrains), the climax of this development being the "Presentation" poems and accompanying prayers of *La tapisserie de Notre Dame*. In presenting the Beauce region of France to Our Lady of Chartres, P. recaptures his own pilgrimages there to petition God's grace, while rooting prayer in the blood and soil of the nation.

P. wrote as an antimodernist prophet, a fact that accounts for the discordant elements in his work—the alternance between popular mysticism and controlled intellectualism; the ease with which he moved from invective, to tender lyricism, to prayer; the coexistence of a profound sympathy for the oppressed (particularly the Jewish people) and an apology for war. A seminal figure in the Catholic Literary Revival, he influenced younger writers—Georges BERNANOS, Julien GREEN—but, overall, left a varied and somewhat contradictory legacy. In the aftermath of World War I, reactionary Catholics and nationalists sought to couple him with Charles Maurras (1868–1952) and Maurice Barrès (1862–1923), but his authentic successors have been the personalist thinkers, Emmanuel Mounier (1905–1950) and Albert Béguin (1901–1957), the Resistance poets (for example, Pierre EMMANUEL), and reviews like *Esprit*. Ultimately unclassifiable, P. was a solitary, best remembered for resisting all forces seeking to make political capital out of moral issues.

FURTHER WORKS: *Œuvres complètes* (20 vols., 1916–1955); *Avec C. P., de la Lorraine à la Marne* (1916); *Lettres et entretiens* (1927); *Ébauche d'une étude sur Alfred de Vigny, suivi de L'épreuve* (1931); *Œuvres poétiques complètes* (1941; new eds., 1966, 1975); *Du rôle de la volonté dans la croyance* (1943); *La république*

(1946); *La route de Chartres* (1947); *P. et les "Cahiers": Notes de gérance 1900–1910* (1947); *Lettre à Franklin Bouillon* (1948); *Lettres à André Bourgeois* (1950); *Notes politiques et sociales* (1957); *Œuvres en prose 1909–1914* (1957); *Œuvres en prose 1898–1908* (1959); *Correspondance André Gide-C. P., 1905–1912* (1958); *C. P.-André Suarès correspondance* (1961); *Les œuvres posthumes de C. P.* (1968); *Marcel: Premier dialogue de la cité harmonieuse, accompagné d'une série d'articles publiés en 1897 et 1898 à la "Revue socialiste"* (1973); *Alain Fournier-C. P.: Correspondance 1910–14* (1973); *Pour l'honneur de l'esprit: Correspondance entre C. P. et Romain Rolland 1898–1914* (1973); *Claudel et P.: Correspondance* (1974); *Correspondance C. P.-Pierre Marcel, 1905–1914* (1980). FURTHER WORKS IN ENGLISH: *Basic Verities: Prose and Poetry* (1943), *Men and Saints: Prose and Poetry* (1944); *God Speaks: Religious Poetry* (1945)

BIBLIOGRAPHY: Servais, Y., *C. P.: The Pursuit of Salvation* (1953); Guyon, B., *P.* (1960); Nelson, R. J., *P.: Poète du sacré* (1960); Duployé, P., *La religion de P.* (1965); Jussem-Wilson, N., *C. P.* (1965); Villiers, M., *C. P.: A Study in Integrity* (1965); Schmitt, H., *P.: The Decline of an Idealist* (1967); St. Aubyn, F. C., *C. P.* (1977); Centenary Colloquium 1973 *P. écrivain* (1977); Fraisse, S., *P.* (1979)

—GEORGE E. GINGRAS

PELLICER, Carlos

Mexican poet, b. 16 Jan. 1897, Villahermosa, Tabasco; d. 15 Feb. 1977, Mexico City

P. spent his early and very formative years in the tropical state of Tabasco. When P. was eleven, his father moved the family to Mexico City because of the Mexican Revolution. There P. studied at the National Preparatory School where he was influenced by important Mexican literary figures. Upon graduation, he went to Colombia and Venezuela to organize federations of students. These trips were the first of many voyages throughout P.'s life that took him all over the world (especially Europe and Latin America) and allowed him to meet and know many international literary figures. P. occupied a variety of public posts and duties. He was a member of the Mexican Academy of the Language and served as president of the Latin American Congress of Writers. In the early 1950s, P. had turned his attention to museums, helping found several important ones in Tabasco, Sonora, Palenque, Mexico City, and the state of Morelos. In 1976 he was elected to the Mexican Senate as a representative from the state of Tabasco.

In 1921 P. published his first collection of poetry, *Colores en el mar y otros poemas* (1921; colors in the sea and other poems), dedicated to his friend Ramón López Velarde (1888–1921). *Colores* was primarily focused on landscapes and seascapes, exalting nature and its connections with humans. Although somewhat traditional in theme and form, it announced great visual evocation supported by structural and lyrical virtuosity. The next two collections, *Piedra de sacrificio* (1924; sacrificial stone) and *6, 7 poemas* (1924; six, seven poems) were published in the same year, but they were almost diametrically opposed in orientation. The latter, *6, 7 poemas*, was in many ways an extension of the lyricism and optimism of *Colores*, and it helped establish P.'s poetry as one of

major import. But *Piedra de sacrificio* was something very different. It embraced a strong voice of social protest directed primarily
against the U.S. Moreover, *Piedra de sacrificio* revealed not only a
newly discovered interest in indigenous culture, but also a clamor-
ous affirmation of Pan-Americanism, a theme generated in large
part by the ideas of P.'s close friend José Vasconcelos (1881–
1959). P.'s next important work was *Hora de junio* (1937; hour of
June), which firmly established him as an important writer. The
collection had as an organizing principle a variety of love sonnets
interspersed by landscape poems.

Although P. published two collections in 1941, *Recinto y otras
imágenes* (corner and other images) and *Exágonos* (hexagons),
they received mixed and essentially uninspired reviews. In 1949,
however, P. produced another major work, *Subordinaciones: Poemas*
(subordinations: poems). Dedicated to Gabriela MISTRAL, the
collection of twenty-six poems evidenced a continued fascination
with pre-Hispanic myth and culture, the human connection to
nature, and an exalted treatment of Hispanic heroes (Morales,
Bolívar, Justo Sierra, and others). This collection of telluric verse
mixes history, geography, flora, and fauna in a flashy, provocative
series of varied poetic forms; it is poetry of movement and
meditation, treating Greek myth, New World exoticism, and tropical musing. P.'s next important poetry collection was *Práctica de
vuelo* (1956; flight practice), a far reaching collection of verse
written from 1929 to 1952. It contained mostly devotional sonnets
in which P. affirmed his passion for the Creator and his universe.

In 1962 the National Autonomous University of Mexico honored P. by publishing *Material poético* (1982; poetic material). It
contained all of P.'s poetry written from 1918 to 1961. Two years
later, in 1964, P. was awarded the National Prize for Literature for
his poetry. In 1978 *Reincidencias* (1978; reincidences) was published posthumously. It was important because it brought together
the poet's diverse works that were written but not published from
1967 to 1976. It contained works of great color, movement,
musicality, and intimacy. Included, as well, were poems of social
protest and contemplative devotion.

Many critics have asserted that P. was Mexico's most important
poet of the 20th c. Others have cited him as one of Latin America's
greatest original voices. What is certain is that P. wrote some
twenty collections of verse spanning a period of nearly sixty years.
His poetry reflects New World lyricism and landscapes, a passionate tropical appeal, an uncanny correspondence to the plastic arts, a
nativistic Pan-Americanism, and an unbridled optimism and faith
in the message of Christianity.

FURTHER WORKS: *Oda de junio* (1924); *Bolívar* (1925); *Hora y
veinte* (1927); *Camino* (1929); *Esquemas para una oda tropical*
(1933); *Estrofas del mar marino* (1934); *Discurso por las flores:
poema* (1946; rev. ed., 1977); *Sonetos* (1950); *Museo de Tabasco*
(1959); *Con palabra y fuego* (1962); *Teotithuacán* (1965); *13 de
agosto: ruina de Tenochtitlán* (1965); *Primera antología poética*
(1969); *Noticias sobre Netzahualcóyotl y algunos sentimientos*
(1974); *Cuerdas, percusíon y aliento* (1976); *Miniantología poética*
(1977); *Breve antología* (1977); *Cosillas para el nacimiento* (1978);
Poemas (1979); *Obras* (1981); *Album fotográfico* (1982); *Cartas
de italia* (1985); *Antología breve* (1986); *Cuaderno de Viaje*
(1987); *El sol en un pesebre: nacimientos* (1987); *Esquemas para
una oda tropical (a cuatro voces)* (1987)

BIBLIOGRAPHY: Forster, M. H., "El concepto de la creación poética
en la obra de C. P.," *Comunidad*, 4 (1969): 684–88; Melnykovich,
G., "C. P. and Creacionismo," *LALR*, 2, 4 (Spring–Summer 1974):
95–111; Debicki, A., "Perspectiva y significado en la poesía de
C. P.," *Plural*, 5, 12 (1975): 33–38; Chávez, C., *Mis amigos poetas:
López Velarde, P., Novo* (1977); Mullen, E. J., *C. P.* (1977);
Mullen, E. J., *La poesía de. C. P.: Interpretaciones críticas* (1979);
Sariol, J. Prats, "La imagen en C. P.," *CasaA*, 20, 120 (May-June
1980): 3–17; Gamboa, R. A., "C. P.: Arte poética," *Káñina*, 5, 2
(July-Dec. 1981): 69–78; del Campo, D. M., *C. P.* (1987); Zaid, G.,
"Siete poemas de C. P.," *RI*, 55: 148–149 (July-Dec. 1989):
1099–118

—SAM L. SLICK

PEPETELA

(pseud. of Artur Carlos Maurício Pestana dos Santos) Angolan
novelist and essayist (writing in Portuguese), b. 29 Oct. 1941,
Moçâmedes

Born of Portuguese parents, P. adopted his *nom-guerre* when
he joined the MPLA (Popular Movement for the Liberation of
Angola) in the struggle against the Portuguese colonial regime. A
literal translation of his Portuguese surname, Pestana (eyelid), into
Umbundu, "Pepetela" defines a unique moment in the Africanization
of a white man born in Angola. It demonstrates P.'s decision to
claim Angola as the "place of the his heart" rather than just of his
birth. The concern with the notion of *Angolinidade* in his work is
itself a manifestation of "re-Africanization of the mind" proposed
by the Lusophone Guinean leader, Amílcar CABRAL. P. was
educated in Angola, Lisbon, Paris, and Algeria, graduating in 1966
with a degree in sociology. Although this peripatetic background
might be seen to account for P.'s own troubled relationship with his
homeland, it is in many ways no more complex than that of many
other postcolonial intellectuals or political activists.

Three main themes run through P.'s work, notably those of
national identity (explored metonymically through the concept of
Angolinidade), that of a recuperation of Angola's historical and
literary heritage, and—providing the backdrop for the exploration
of those concerns—a preoccupation with the place and function of
foreign ideologies within contemporary Angolan society. A well-
read, talented, and prolific writer, and one willing to experiment
with genre in his work, P. is one of the most complex and
sophisticated contemporary Lusophone authors.

P. has claimed to have been strongly influenced in his work by
Brazilian writers such as José Lins do REGO, Graciliano RAMOS,
João Guimarães ROSA, and Jorge AMADO, and American writers
such as John STEINBECK and Ernest HEMINGWAY. However, both
Muana Puó (1978; Muana Puó) and *Mayombe* (1980; *Mayombe*,
1984) already suggest a man clearly concerned with creating for
himself a distinct style. Indeed *Mayombe* provides possibly one of
the best examples of a truly polyphonic novel in the sense identified
by Mikhail BAKHTIN. More importantly, it reveals also some of the
concerns of more recent postcolonial writing, namely an awareness
of the difficulties faced by the intellectual whose praxis is also
simultaneously that of a guerrilla fighter or a politician. P.'s
treatment of Marxist ideologies, and specifically of their hegemonic
influence on the newly liberated African nations, is indicative of a
highly intellectualized attempt to rationalize the need for a unified
nation and the ability to remain in tune with the multiplicity of
voices within that same national construct.

In *Mayombe* P.'s depiction of the tribal, sexual, and ideological tensions within a guerrilla group consisting of elements drawn from the various tribes in Angola was thought to have been politically dangerous. By calling attention to the potentially fragmentary nature of Angolan society, P. in some way undermined the MPLA's claim to be the sole representative of the Angolan people in the anticolonial struggle. In fact, it was only as a result of the involvement of Agostinho Neto (1922-1979) himself, Angola's first president and best-known poet, keen to foster an active literary life in the new nation regardless of political expediency, that P.'s first novel was published. As in later works such as *Lueji* (1990; Lueji), and *A Geraçao da Utopia* (1992; The Generation of Utopia) P.'s concern with national identity, expressed more specifically in an exploration of the notion of *Angolinidade*, is both successful and highly questionable.

P.'s reliance on a close engagement with a mythopoeic framework reflects some of the difficulties in addressing the continuing problems in Angolan society. Although independent from Portugal since November 1975, Angola remains in the midst of one of the most brutal and senseless of all wars in Africa. As a one-time deputy minister of education and revolutionary ideology P. has often found himself much too close to the events his novels depict to remain consistently objective. It is true that given the internecine nature of the Angolan conflict to manage to appear even remotely detached from the society in which one operates is a truly gigantic task indeed. The fact that he is white, in a largely African society, might be seen to complicate his task as a novelist. For there is a sense in which the failure to deal with his own role within the contemporary Angolan political context may be seen to account for some of the flaws in P.'s literary work.

In *Yaka* (1984; *Yaka*, 1996), his most ambitious attempt at dealing with the whole of Angola's colonial experience, P. offers an account which, in the process of creating a narrative form capable of conveying the voice of the new nation, combines a variety of genre, ranging from the epic to MAGIC REALISM. *Yaka* moves between densely woven storytelling and a simplistic, almost pamphleteering level, where the political overtakes any aesthetic considerations, and where the novelist falls prey to the traps set up by his political activist nemesis. As the conflict in the days prior to the departure of the Portuguese deteriorates, *Yaka* begins to sound increasingly like a manifesto for the MPLA's beliefs and ideals for the new nation. As in *Lueji* and *A Geraçao da Utopia*, a sophisticated characterization is undermined by a less than subtle attempt to force upon the novel the allegorical quality that made *Mayombe* such a successful work. In P. there is a sense of the grandiose masquerading as grandeur, and for this reason the novels often fail to fulfill the scope of his own literary project, despite their effectiveness in conveying P.'s political concerns.

Significantly, however, in *Yaka*—as in the earlier fable, *Muana Puó*—it is through the use of an enigmatic statue whose status is never fully revealed that P. comes closest to presenting a truly representative portrait of *Angolinidade*. For in the inscrutability of the statues, in the Derridean tone of their supplementary quality in relation to the stories, they make real both the complexity of modern Angolan society and of P.'s own role as its most important, though problematic, narrative voice. The disruptive, apparently unreadable, or, at the very least, resistant to most possible readings, statues function in this way to suggest P.'s own ongoing struggle to find a voice of his own, and one which will transcend the limitations of both foreign political and aesthetics ideologies.

FURTHER WORKS: *As aventuras de Ngunga* (1976; *Ngunga's Adventures*, 1980); *A corda*(1978); *A revolta da casa dos ídolos* (1980); *O cao e os Caluandas* (1985); *Luandando* (1990); *O desejo de Kianda* (1995)

BIBLIOGRAPHY: Soria, G., "Intervista ad Artur Pestana (P.)," *QIA*, 61-62 (1986-87): 227-32; Guterres, M., "Lueji—O nascimento dum império: A procura de Angolinidade," *BHS*, 71, 1 (1994): 149-54; Willis, C., "*Mayombe* and the Liberation of the Angolan," *PStud*, 3 (1987): 205-14

—TONY SIMOES DA SILVA

PERCY, Walker

American novelist and essayist, b. 28 May 1916, Birmingham, AL.; d. 10 May 1990, New Orleans

After graduation from medical school and a brief career as a pathologist in New York City, P. was forced by illness to abandon the practice of medicine.

A sizable selection of his philosophical essays on man and language, *The Message in the Bottle*, was published in 1975, but his reputation rests principally upon his five novels: *The Moviegoer* (1961), *The Last Gentleman* (1966), *Love in the Ruins* (1971), *Lancelot* (1977), and *The Second Coming* (1980). All are novels of

Walker Percy

spiritual quest, part romance and part satire. Only *Love in the Ruins*—subtitled *The Adventures of a Bad Catholic at a Time near the End of the World*—is futuristic. But in the other four as well, with their more or less realistic, contemporary settings, the atmosphere is distinctly that of life in the world's last days.

The amiable, diffidently alienated, bumblingly amorous heroes of the first three novels—Binx Bolling, the stockbroker and prospective medical student of *The Moviegoer;* Will Barrett, the sometime "humidification engineer" (janitor) who becomes a paid traveling companion to a dying youth, in *The Last Gentleman;* Dr. Thomas More, the alcoholic physician of *Love in the Ruins*, who has invented a machine that can diagnose, perhaps cure, all the ills of a dying world, but who finds that his patients, including at times himself, are not really interested in being healed—have so much in common that they seem to be studies of the same man in three different "phases." The novel most recently published, *The Second Coming*, is in fact a kind of "sequel" to *The Last Gentleman*, picking up the life of Will Barrett as a middle-aged widower, who falls in love with the daughter of the woman he had, in the earlier story, thought he would marry. And even the title character of *Lancelot*, the murderer and self-ordained mad prophet Lancelot Andrewes Lamar, has curious affinities with the other more genial heroes. Yet each of the books is endlessly surprising in its wealth of invention and observation; each creates its own world.

The central settings of P.'s fiction are Southern, and, clearly, P. is surest of himself in the Southern scene and idiom. Yet he is not primarily a regionalist. The other Southern writers to whom he is discernibly indebted—among them William FAULKNER, Eudora WELTY, and Flannery O'CONNOR—are those who also, each in his or her own way, have used the South as the world's stage. And his writing has an urbanity that does not characterize his fellow Southerners of either his own or any previous generation. Both in its philosophical concerns and in its artistic form, P.'s work owes at least as much to Henry JAMES and T. S. ELIOT and to English and European writers—for instance, Evelyn WAUGH, Graham GREENE, Albert CAMUS, and Dostoevsky—as it does to any of the Southerners.

Although the effects of P.'s medical training are readily apparent in his fiction, he is interested in the science of medicine, as it is representative of all modern science, more for what it cannot tell us about man than for what it can. But his EXISTENTIALIST Catholicism provides no very clear alternative to scientism or to all the other false faiths of our demented times, which the novels so brilliantly satirize. In the three first-person narratives, *The Moviegoer, Love in the Ruins*, and *Lancelot*—only a little more obviously in *Lancelot* than in the others—the narrator-heroes are not to be identified with P. himself. And even in the two Will Barrett novels, which are narrated in the third person, it is extremely difficult at any point to identify the authorial voice. Readers expecting any kind of clear-cut "affirmation" of conventional religious values, let alone suggestions for a program of militant action to right the wrongs of the everyday world, will be disappointed and bewildered by the deliberate ambiguities, and the frequently extravagant fantasy, the mere exuberant *fictitiousness*, of P.'s tales.

On the other hand, to those who look only for proof of the continuing vitality of the novelistic form, P.'s work is wonderfully rewarding. His talent is at once solidly traditional and unmistakably original. As both the considerable popular success of his novels and the rapid development of a body of critical scholarship on all aspects of his art and thought attest, his place in American letters seems already assured, if not yet clearly defined.

BIBLIOGRAPHY: Luschei, M., *The Sovereign Wayfarer: W. P.'s Diagnosis of the Malaise* (1972); Broughton, P., ed., *The Art of W. P.: Stratagems for Being* (1979); Coles, R., *W. P.: An American Search* (1979); Tharpe, J., ed., *W. P.: Art and Ethics* (1980); Gilman, R., on *The Second Coming, New Republic*: 5–12 July 1980: 29–31; Towers, R., on *The Second Coming, NYRB*, 14 Aug. 1980: 39–41

—JOHN EDWARD HARDY

PEREC, Georges

French novelist, poet, essayist, and dramatist, b. 7 Mar. 1936, Paris; d. 3 Mar. 1982, Paris

Born into a family of Polish Jewish émigrés, P. was orphaned by World War II, an experience that would color every aspect of his literary work, if in strikingly different ways. His father, a soldier in the French army, was killed at the front in 1940; his mother was arrested in 1943 and deported to the German camps, where she was murdered. P. spent the rest of the war in a Catholic school in the unoccupied zone of France. After the war he returned to Paris, where he lived with a paternal aunt. After graduating from secondary school in 1954, he studied sociology at the Sorbonne, later working as a public-opinion pollster, a research librarian, and a crossword-puzzle maker. He died of lung cancer at the age of forty-five.

P.'s literary production includes a score of major works, and is characterized by its great diversity. Although he is principally known for his novels, he also wrote poetry, plays, essays, and film scenarios. His first novel, *Les Choses: Une histoire des années soixante* (1965; *Les Choses: A Story of the Sixties*, 1968), won the Renaudot Prize (1965), and launched P. on the literary scene. The story of a young couple living in an increasingly materialist milieu, *Les Choses* was hailed as a new "sociological" novel. It met with tremendous popular success and was eventually translated into sixteen languages.

La Disparition (1969; *A Void*, 1994) is a 300-page novel written without the letter E. It is conceived as a detective novel, the central conceit of which revolves upon the disappearance of the E from the alphabet. In a shorter novel, *Les Revenentes* (1972; the ghosts), the E is the only vowel used. P.'s work here testifies to the influence of the Oulipo (an acronym signifying Workshop of Potential Literature), a group of literary formalists he joined in 1967. P.'s contributions to the group's collective publications, such as *La Littérature potentielle: Créations, re-créations, récréations* (1973; potential literature: creations, re-creations, recreations), *Atlas de littérature potentielle* (1981; atlas of potential literature), and the three-volume *Bibliothèque oulipienne* (1987–1990; Oulipian library), are substantial.

The same sort of experimentation in form characterizes P.'s poetry. *Alphabets* (1976; alphabets), for example, is a series of heterogrammatic poems, each using only eleven letters of the alphabet. *La Clôture et autres poèmes* (1980; closure and other poems) includes bilingual poems (which can be read in French and English), palindromes, and acrostics. *Espèces d'espaces: Journal d'un usager de l'espace* (1974; species of space: journal of a user of space) is an extended essay. In it, P. reflects upon spaces of various kinds, and upon the manner in which they are represented in literature.

W ou le souvenir d'enfance (1975; *W or The Memory of Childhood*, 1988) is a hybrid text, in which chapters of autobiography alternate with chapters of fiction. It too is an exercise in literary representation; specifically, it tests the possibilities of representing the Holocaust and catastrophes, both personal and collective. The fictional narrative deals with a voyage to the island of W, where an Olympian society reveals itself as ever more oppressive; the autobiographical narrative centers upon the war years, and P.'s loss of his parents. As the two narratives alternate, it becomes clear that they are complementary, each saying things that the other cannot. They converge, moreover, upon a carceral, concentrationary locus of radical loss. In short, *W ou le souvenir d'enfance* is perhaps the most eloquent Holocaust narrative to appear in France.

P. worked on *La vie mode d'emploi* (1978; *Life: A User's Manual*, 1987), a 700-page novel, for ten years. It met with more immediate success than any of his books since *Les Choses*, and was awarded the Médicis Prize (1978). It is a work that elegantly melds the apparently irreconcilable traditions of the well-made novel and the experimental text. Recounting in minute detail the life of a Parisian apartment building. *La vie mode d'emploi* offers an astonishing multiplicity of stories, savantly interwoven. That interweaving, however, is based upon formal arcana that, although not apparent in a casual reading, constrain and order every aspect of the novel's structure. The principal image of the novel, that of the jigsaw puzzle, serves to encapsulate the novel itself, for the latter's construction, upon analysis, reveals itself to be that of a puzzle, a game studiously elaborated and offered as a participatory dynamic to the reader.

P. himself once suggested that his work responded to four concerns: a passion for the apparently trivial details of everyday life, an impulse toward confession and autobiography, a will toward formal innovation, and a desire to write "readerly" stories. It is undoubtedly in *W ou le souvenir d'enfance* and *La vie mode d'emploi* that those concerns find their most felicitous articulation, and it is those two books that have established P.'s reputation as one of the major writers in French of the 20th c. More generally, though, each of his works is a laboratory of writing, a place where the very possibilities of literature are tested. Yet the works themselves remain highly accessible, for one of the boundaries P. consistently interrogated was that between tradition and innovation. His great discovery as a writer was that those two orders were not mutually exclusive, but indeed shared many affinities and points of complementarity, and his literary production as a whole may be read as an elaborate, impassioned demonstration of that notion.

FURTHER WORKS: *Quel petit vélo à guidon chromé au fond de la cour?* (1966); *Un homme qui dort* (1967); *Petit traité invitant à la découverte de l'art subtil du GO* (1969, with Pierre Lusson and Jacques Roubaud); *Die Maschine* (1972); *La boutique obscure: 124 rêves* (1973); *Ulcérations* (1974); *Je me souviens* (1978); *Un cabinet d'amateur* (1979); *Les mots croisés* (1979); *La clôture et autres poèmes* (1980); *Récits d'Ellis Island: Histoires d'errance et d'espoir* (1980, with Robert Bober); *Théâtre* (1981); *Epithalames* (1982); *Tentative d'épuisement d'un lieu parisien* (1982); *Penser Classer* (1985); *Les mots croisés II* (1986); *"53 Jours"* (1989); *L'infra-ordinaire* (1989); *Vœux* (1989); *"53 Jours"* (1989); *Cantatrix sopranica L. et autres écrits scientifiques* (1991); *L. G.: Une aventure des années soixante* (1992); *Le Voyage d'hiver* (1993); *Beaux présents belles absentes* (1994)

BIBLIOGRAPHY: Motte, W., *The Poetics of Experiment: A Study of the Work of G. P.* (1984); Pedersen, J., *P. ou les textes croisés* (1985); Raynaud, J.-M., *Pour un P. lettré, chiffré* (1987); Burgelin, C., *G. P.* (1988); Schwartz, P., *G. P.: Traces of His Passage* (1988); Magné, B., *Perecollages 1981–1988* (1989); Bellos, D., *G. P.: A Life in Words* (1993); Béhar, S., *G. P.: Ecrire pour ne pas dire* (1995)

—WARREN MOTTE

PÉREZ DE AYALA, Ramón

Spanish novelist and poet, b. 9 Aug. 1880, Oviedo; d. 5 Aug. 1962, Madrid

Sent away to a Jesuit school at the age of eight, P. de A. received the beginnings of a solid classical education and acquired a fiercely negative attitude toward religion and authority. He set out early to explore Spanish life, but his contact with things English—he studied English early in life and served as Spanish ambassador to Great Britain in the 1930s—and his marriage to a young lady from Pennsylvania added a cosmopolitan dimension to his outlook. From the outset a writer of brilliant promise, he published his last major work in 1926; thereafter, he concentrated upon a diplomatic career, which itself was truncated by the civil war.

P. de A. began his literary career as a poet, a follower of Rubén DARÍO and perhaps Juan RAMÓN JIMÉNEZ, although the latter was, in fact, younger than he. His first book, *La paz del sendero* (1905; the peace of the path), became a part of a proposed series on the grandiose theme of man's "path" through life. In this volume the poet goes back in both theme and time to the Asturias region of his childhood memories. In general following the French poet Francis JAMMES, he concentrates upon a return to a simpler pastoral world of yesteryear. In his second volume, *El sendero innumerable* (1916; the path of infinite variations), the poet broadens his outlook by choosing the sea as an essential symbol. A third "path," entitled *El sendero andante* (1921; the flowing path), develops the symbol of the river and hence the theme of transitoriness. P. de A.'s early poetry showed great promise, but gradually his interest in fiction absorbed most of his energy.

As a novelist, P. de A. earned a certain amount of notoriety with *A. M. D. G.* (1910; A. M. D. G.), these initials being the Latin motto of the Jesuit Society: "Ad majorem Dei gloriam" (to the greater glory of God). This little novel is an emotional attack against the rigidity and cruelty of the Jesuit system of education. P. de A., who later repudiated this work, ultimately developed a much more balanced appreciation of the Christian tradition. In three other early novels—*Tinieblas en las cumbres* (1907; darkness on the heights), *La pata de la raposa* (1912; *The Fox's Paw*, 1924), and *Troteras y danzaderas* (1913; hustlers and dancers)—P. de A. developed a character, Alberto Díaz de Guzmán, who is a thinly disguised representation of the author himself. Alberto is a young man desperately seeking a philosophy of life (meaning, of course, that he had not received one). As he tests the old and explores the new, above all he intrudes in the area of the relations between the sexes (in Spain this whole area has been a problem complicated by reticence and hypocrisy). By hiding behind the device of a picaresque mode, which is frank and explicit, P. de A. is able to present sexual relations meaningfully. Although in these novels he revealed an impressive talent as a writer, he did not quite succeed in achieving a mastery of theme and form.

One of P. de A.'s enduring successes is a trilogy of short novels, each of which is subtitled *Novela poemática de la vida española* (poetic novel of Spanish life). These short novels are a showcase for P. de A.'s talents (and his weaknesses). In all three the theme is prefigured in poems placed before the prose chapters. In *Prometeo* (1916; *Prometheus*, 1920), before James JOYCE and *Ulysses*, P. de A. discovers the technique of ironically pitting the heroic or the epic against everyday life; his hero revives the epic world and sets out to raise his Prometheus as a perfect son, only to crash against the insufficiencies of life itself. In *Luz de domingo* (1916; *Sunday Sunlight*, 1920), set in a provincial town, the hopes of a simple and innocent young engaged couple are blighted when the girl is brutally raped by a group of the town bullies. In *La caída de los Limones* (1916; *The Fall of the House of Limón*, 1920) P. de A. traces the rise and subsequent fall of a *caudillo* (a local strongman) and his family. Headed by the father, the family carves out a high position in the town; later his psychotic son commits a murder that destroys the family. All three of these short novels set out to illustrate the tragic truth that life is insufficient to measure up to the dreams of man, especially in P. de A.'s Spain.

Although not very successful in his day, P. de A.'s greatest novel is now considered to be *Belarmino y Apolonio* (1921; *Belarmino and Apolonio*, 1971). This is definitely an "intellectual" novel, like Joyce's *Ulysses*, above all in the development of various levels of irony. For example, it is very Spanish in its themes and yet transcends the specifically Spanish; it attacks religion and yet it exalts religion; it is an intellectual tour de force and yet it glorifies simple love. The protagonists are both shoemakers, but the passion of Belarmino is philosophy and that of Apolonio the drama. Belarmino has developed a zany philosophical system that has its own weird logic; Apolonio thinks in dramatic verse form. The "love interest" is provided by Don Guillén (the son of Apolonio), who is now a priest, and Angustias (the daughter of Belarmino), who is now a prostitute. The way P. de A. weaves together several narrative strands and handles many levels of irony is quite impressive, although admittedly one of the complexities is that perhaps some of them remain unresolved. When the novel appeared, the Spanish reading public was not ready for it; later, critics both in Spain and in the Americas discovered its value.

P. de A.'s other truly major novel was published in two parts: *Tigre Juan* (1926; tiger Juan) and *El curandero de su honra* (1926; the healer of his honor), both parts translated into English as *Tiger Juan* (1933). This work is another treatment of the Don Juan theme, set in 20th-c. Spain. Tiger Juan is an unusual character—a bloodletter, a public scribe, and an herbal doctor in a provincial town. This Tiger Juan has a tragic past: he helped cause his wife's death in a mixup over a matter of honor. When Tiger Juan sets out to win Herminia, there is a potential for tragedy when she becomes attracted to a traveling salesman, a "superficial" Don Juan. Although she runs off with this man, when she returns Tiger Juan forgives her with understanding. Thus he becomes the "healer of his honor" in loving forgiveness, not by having his wife killed as did the protagonist in Calderón's fierce drama *The Surgeon of His Honor*. This novel is P. de A.'s most solid attempt to write about relations between man and woman based on sincere communication, rather than hypocrisy and barbaric masculine will.

P. de A. is an important novelist of the generation that falls between that of UNAMUNO, AZORÍN, VALLE-INCLÁN, and BAROJA

and that of Camilo José CELA following the civil war. After showing initial promise as a poet, he gradually saw his inspiration wane, unlike that of his friend Jiménez. In fiction, at least two of his works will surely survive: *Novelas poemáticas de la vida española* and *Belarmino y Apolonio*. In these novels slices of Spanish life are presented with unusual vividness; at the same time the author's very modern and sophisticated use of irony aptly demonstrates his talent as a novelist.

FURTHER WORKS: *Las máscaras* (2 vols., 1917, 1919); *Política y toros* (1918); *Luna de miel, luna de hiel* (1923; this and following title tr. as *Honeymoon, Bittermoon*, 1972); *Los trabajos de Urbano y Simona* (1923); *El ombligo del mundo* (1924); *Bajo el signo de Artemisa* (1924); *Divagaciones literarias* (1958); *Obras completas* (4 vols., 1964–1969)

BIBLIOGRAPHY: Madariaga, S. de, *The Genius of Spain* (1923): 71–86; Barja, C., *Libros y autores contemporáneos* (1935): 439–66; Nora, E. de, *La novela española contemporánea* (1958): 467–513; Reinink, K. W., *Algunos aspectos literarios y lingüísticos de la obra de Don R. P. de A.* (1959); Curtis, E. R., *Ensayos críticos acerca de la literatura española* (1959), Vol. II: pp. 109–21; Beck, M. A., "La realidad artística en las tragedias grotescas de P. de A.," *Hispania*, 46 (1963): 480–89; Weber, F. W., *The Literary Perspectivism of P. de A.* (1966); Rand, M. C., *P. de A.* (1971); Feeny, T., "Maternal-Paternal Attitudes in the Fiction of R. P. de A.," *Hispano*, 62 (1978): 77–85; Macklin, J. J., "Myth and Mimesis: The Artistic Integrity of P. de A.'s *Tigre Juan and El curandero de su honra,*" *HR*, 48 (1980): 15–36; Newberry, W., "R. P. de A.'s Concept of the *Doppelgänger in Belarmino y Apolonio,*" *Symposium*, 34 (1980): 56–67

—CARL W. COBB

PÉREZ GALDÓS, Benito

Spanish novelist, dramatist, and journalist, b. 10 May 1843, Las Palmas, Canary Islands; d. 4 Jan. 1920, Madrid

Raised in the somewhat remote Canary Islands, where he attended an English high school, P. G. moved to Madrid in 1862 to attend the University of Madrid. He enrolled as a student of law, a course of study he never completed—nor did he ever intend to. His time was occupied with his observations of the city, his work as a journalist for the prestigious newspaper *La nación*, and his own writing. In 1867 P. G. went to Paris, where he became familiar with the works of Balzac.

P. G. was an outspoken liberal and republican. In 1886 he was elected to Parliament; in 1907 he was again elected, as a representative for Madrid, and once more in 1914 for the Canary Islands. Although he was a member of the Royal Spanish Academy and a novelist and dramatist of great success, he died poor and broken, totally blind—and never succeeded in being nominated by the Spanish Academy for the Nobel Prize.

That P. G. is Spain's greatest novelist after Cervantes there is no debate. With *La fontana de oro* (1870; *The Golden Fountain Café*, 1989), which portrays the political struggles of the minority Liberal faction against the reactionary reign of Ferdinand VII in 1822–23, P. G. began to revitalize the Spanish novel. He also created a model

Benito Pérez Galdós

for Spanish fiction that was to be highly influential throughout the 20th c. It is difficult to imagine how the work of BLASCO IBÁÑEZ, UNAMUNO, BAROJA, PÉREZ DE AYALA, SENDER, and many others would have come into being without the legacy of P. G. Although reacted to with hostility by some of these later writers, P. G. was a strong force in their development as well as in the careers of some of the objectivist writers of the 1950s and in some of the dialectical realists of the 1960s.

When P. G. began to write, the novel in Spain was almost completely stagnant. Vacuous, mindless romantic fiction abounded. P. G. had a strong conviction that novels should be written with a keen regard for accurate observation and natural dialogue. Fiction should reflect all the good and evil in society, since it must be a moral response to reality. As a reformer and moralist who was convinced that love was the principal salvation, P. G. was fond of the dialectical process. He often proceeded along Hegelian lines, believing that only through opposition and struggle could there be growth and transcendence.

P. G.'s lifelong undertaking was the historical portrait of 19th-c. Spain, embodied in the *Episodios nacionales* (national episodes), five series comprising forty-six novels in all, beginning with *Trafalgar* (1873; *Trafalgar*, 1884), a quasi-journalistic account of that sea battle against the British, and ending with *Cánovas* (1912; *Cánovas*), a highly fictionalized account of the regime of Prime Minister Antonio Cánovas in 1906. In this mammoth undertaking P. G. sought the proper balance among fact, fiction, description, and commentary; he always tried to avoid any one ideology, lest his

panorama turn into propaganda. In doing so, he created a paradigm for the historical novel that many 20th-c. writers would later utilize.

In the category P. G. called "Novels of the First Period," *Doña Perfecta* (1876; *Doña Perfecta*, 1880; new tr., 1960) is the most popular work. Dickensian in its characterizations, it portrays Doña Perfecta, the venerable widow in Orbajosa, a backward town located somewhere in the "heart of Spain," known solely for its prodigious production of garlic. *Doña Perfecta*, a somewhat melodramatic although cogent tract against religious fanaticism, which is personified by Doña Perfecta and her cohorts, is a strong plea for scientific progress, symbolized by Pepe Rey, her nephew, who wishes to marry her daughter Rosario. The rather *imperfect* protagonist, Doña Perfecta, finds this situation totally intolerable and has Pepe murdered. Although clearly a thesis novel, *Doña Perfecta* achieves the necessary balance between abstract ideas and concrete human concerns and character development. The reader is deeply moved by the death of Pepe Rey and scornfully outraged at Doña Perfecta, one of Spanish literature's most heinous characters.

P. G.'s masterpiece is the panoramic and meticulously detailed four-volume work, *Fortunata y Jacinta* (1886–87; *Fortunata and Jacinta: Two Stories of Married Women*, 1973). The novel concerns a love triangle, in which two women are desperately in love with the same man, Juanito Santa Cruz, an idle son of a very wealthy family. He loves each woman in a different way. Jacinta, his barren wife, represents the social forces or civilization, and Fortunata, who is beautiful beyond words, the natural forces or barbarism. At the end of this many-tiered and highly symbolic novel P. G.'s Hegelian bent can be fully comprehended. When Fortunata is slowly dying after having given birth to her second child by Juanito (their first one had died young), she decides to give it to the childless Jacinta, who will become its mother. Only through dialectical opposition and struggle can there be the fusion and synthesis to insure growth and genuine progress.

Also important is the Torquemada series, comprising four novels: *Torquemada en la hoguera* (1889; *Torquemada in the Flames*, 1956), *Torquemada en la cruz* (1893; Torquemada on the cross), *Torquemada en el Purgatorio* (1894; Torquemada in purgatory), and *Torquemada y San Pedro* (1895; Torquemada and Saint Peter). This series is an exhaustive psychological portrait of a small-time usurer who tries to become a respected businessman. P. G. shows his opprobrium for materialistic values and their incompatibility with spiritual growth.

Spiritual growth, Christian charity, and the unselfish belief in others are the qualities that Benina, a self-effacing servant, possesses in P. G.'s most humanistic novel, *Misericordia* (1897; *Compassion*, 1962), in which he reached the height of his disenchantment with positivism, as he moved away from realism toward a kind of spiritual naturalism.

Although P. G. admitted that he was attracted to the drama more than to any other genre, his first play was not performed until 1892. He never became as fine a dramatist as he was a novelist, but his concerns were the same: honesty, social justice and truth, individual liberty and freedom from stultifying Spanish traditionalism and clericalism.

Electra (1901; *Electra*, 1919), one of P. G.'s most successful plays, caused a near riot at the time of its premiere, in spite of its simple, if not simplistic plot about Electra, the illegitimate daughter of a woman of "bad blood." At the end of the play Electra emerges victorious, overcoming those ill-intentioned traditionalists who desired to thwart her marriage to a man of progress. Reason, truth, and liberal ideals win out; heredity—"bad genes"—and the forces of repression lose.

P. G.'s oeuvre has a very special place in Spanish letters. His patience, tolerance, and constant striving to reform the individual are awesome. It is this legacy—the need to reform on a microcosmic, that is, an individual, scale—that the members of the Generation of 1898 received from P. G. as their mission.

FURTHER WORKS: *La sombra* (1870; *The Shadow*, 1980); *El audaz* (1871); *Bailén* (1873); *La corte de Carlos IV* (1873; *The Court of Charles IV: A Romance of the Escorial*, 1888); *El 19 de marzo y el 2 de mayo* (1873); *Cádiz* (1874); *Gerona* (1874); *Juan Martín el Empecinado* (1874); *Napoleón en Chamartín* (1874); *La batalla de los Arapiles* (1875; *The Battle of Salamanca: A Tale of the Napoleonic War*, 1895); *El equipaje del Rey José* (1875); *Memorias de un cortesano* (1875); *El Grande Oriente* (1876); *La segunda casaca* (1876); *El 7 de julio* (1876); *Gloria* (2 vols., 1876–1877; *Gloria*, 1879); *El terror de 1824* (1877); *Los cien mil hijos de San Luis* (1877); *Marianela* (1878; *Marianela*, 1883); *Un voluntario realista* (1878); *La familia de León Roch* (3 vols., 1878–1879; *Leon Roch: A Romance*, 1888); *Los apostólicos* (1879); *El amigo Manso* (1881); *La desheredada* (1881; *The Disinherited Lady*, 1957); *El doctor Centeno* (2 vols., 1883); *La de Bringas* (1884; *The Spendthrifts*, 1951); *Tormento* (1884; *Torment*, 1952); *Lo prohibido* (2 vols., 1884–1885); *Miau* (1888; *Miau*, 1963); *La incógnita* (1888–1889); *Realidad* (1889); *Crónicas de Portugal* (1890); *De vuelta de Italia* (1890); *Angel Guerra* (3 vols., 1890–1891); *La loca de la casa* (1892); *Realidad* (play, 1892); *Tristana* (1892; *Tristana*, 1961); *Gerona* (play, 1893); *La loca de la casa* (play, 1893); *La de San Quintín* (1894; *The Duchess of San Quintin*, 1917); *Los condenados* (1894); *Zaragoza* (1894; *Saragossa: A Story of Spanish Valor*, 1899); *Halma* (1895); *Nazarín* (1895); *Voluntad* (1895); *Doña Perfecta* (play, 1896); *La fiera* (1896); *El abuelo* (1897); *De Oñate a la Granja* (1898); *Zumalacárregui* (1898); *La campaña del Maestrazgo* (1899); *La estafeta romántica* (1899); *Ludana* (1899); *Vergara* (1899); *Bodas reales* (1900); *Los ayacuchas* (1900); *Montes de Oca* (1900); *Alma y vida* (1902); *Las tormentas del 48* (1902); *Narváez* (1902); *Los duendes de la camarilla* (1903); *Mariucha* (1903); *La revolución de julio* (1904); *El abuelo* (play, 1904; *The Grandfather*, 1910); *O'Donnell* (1904); *Aita Tettauen* (1905); *Amor y ciencia* (1905); *Bárbara* (1905); *Carlos VI en la Rápita* (1905); *Casandra* (1905); *La vuelta al mundo en la Numancia* (1906); *Memoranda* (1906); *Prim* (1906); *La de los tristes destinos* (1907); *Zaragoza* (play, 1907); *España sin rey* (1908); *Pedro Minio* (1908); *El caballero encantado* (1909); *España trágica* (1909); *Amadeo I* (1910); *Casandra* (play, 1910); *De Cartago a Sagunto* (1911); *La primera república* (1911); *Celia en los infiernos* (1913); *Alceste* (1914); *La razón de la sinrazón* (1915); *Sor Simona* (1915); *El tacaño Salomón* (1916); *Santa Juana de Castilla* (1918); *Arte y crítica* (1923); *Fisonomías sociales* (1923); *Nuestro teatro* (1923); *Política española* (2 vols., 1923); *Crónica* (2 vols., 1924); *Toledo: Su historia y su leyenda* (1924); *Viajes y fantasías* (1928); *Memorias* (1930); *Crónica de Madrid* (1933); *La novela en el tranvía* (1936); *Crónica de la Quincera* (1948); *Obras completas* (6 vols., 1951–1961)

BIBLIOGRAPHY: Berkowitz, H. C., *B. P. G.: Spanish Liberal Crusader* 1948); Casalduero, J., *Vida y obra de G.*, 2nd ed. (1951); Eoff, S. H., *The Novels of P. G.: The Concept of Life as Dynamic Process* (1954); Gullón, R., *G., novelista moderno* (1960); Schraibman, J., *Dreams in the Novels of G.* (1960); Nimetz, M.,</td>

Humor in G. (1968); Roger, D., ed. *B. P. G.* (1973); Pattison, W. T., *B. P. G.* (1975); Engler, K., *The Structure of Realism: The "Novelas contemporáneas" of B. P. G.* (1977); Dendle, B. J., *G.: The Mature Thought* (1980); Gilman, S., *G. and the Art of the European Novel: 1867–1887* (1981)

—MARSHALL J. SCHNEIDER

PERI ROSSI, Cristina

Uruguayan novelist, short-story writer, and poet, b. 12 Nov. 1941, Montevideo

P. R.'s father was a textile worker, her mother a school teacher. After graduation from the Artigas Institute for Teachers, P. R. started working as a journalist, and as a professor of literature in her native Montevideo: Her support of the Left, and her clear stance against a blatantly oppressive government, caused P. R. to seek political asylum in Spain, where she arrived in 1972. She still resides in Barcelona.

The noted Uruguayan essayist Angel Rama (1926–1983) includes P. R. among the writers he groups under the label "La generación crítica" (the critical generation), and suggests that some chapters of one of P. R.'s earlier texts, the novel *El libro de mis primos* (1969; the book of my cousins), represents "one of the freest examples of imagination that has been known in Uruguayan literature."

At age twenty-two, already quite a precocious member of the literary establishment, she published *Viviendo* (1963; living), a collection of three short stories that poignantly addresses the plight of women leading a life dominated by their daily boring rituals, and subtly explores lesbian relationships.

After what turned out to be the longest hiatus in P. R.'s prolific literary production—she has also been involved with journalism and criticism throughout her career—her second book of short stories, *Los museos abandonados* (1969; the abandoned museums), won the prize for young Uruguayan authors awarded by the publishing house Arca. Eroticism, the impact of social decay, and a constant feeling of sadness permeate the four stories. The first—and the longest of these—might be considered P. R.'s initial contact with the fantastic, a genre she continued to cultivate later on.

The same year, *El libro de mis primos* captured the first prize offered by *Marcha*, a weekly newspaper notorious for its incisive political analysis, but also acclaimed for its literary pages. Soon after, P. R. published *Indicios pánicos* (1970; signs of panic), a breakthrough in her production. Although she had already combined poetry and prose, and experimented with rhetorical figures and even typography in *El libro de mis primos, Indicios pánicos* is the first text where P. R. challenges conventional notions of genre. If indeed a genuine preoccupation with social issues was already evident in her work, this book is boldly politicized. Its 46 sections—allegorical vignettes, conventional short stories, poems, short essays, aphorisms—are thoroughly independent and can be read in any order. The book, however, is remarkably integrated by the underlying feeling of sociopolitical decay. P. R. makes no serious effort to hide the fact that she is referring to the Uruguayan society where she lived and worked, and plainly reiterated it a few years later in the prologue to the Spanish edition of her text. *Indicios pánicos* turned out to be a grim prophecy of the heinous

1973 coup and subsequent period of unmerciful repression in Uruguay.

With the publication of her first book of poems *Evohé* (1971; Evohé), P. R. celebrates the female body, and unabashedly expresses passion and desire. Another collection of poems, *Diáspora* (1976; diaspora), her second publication in exile, won yet another prize. A few years later P. R. published her last book of poetry to date, *Lingüística general* (1979; general linguistics), which furthers her free-verse examination of art, the intricacies of language, and lesbian love.

Seix Barral, the Barcelona-based editorial house that had previously issued *El museo de los esfuerzos inútiles* (1983; the museum of the useless efforts)—another collection of brief texts of rather difficult generic categorization—published P. R.'s second novel. *La nave de los locos* (1984; *The Ship of Fools*, 1988) is a complex text. The chaotic narration of episodes where injustice and oppression affect a cast of characters—which includes a prostitute, a *desaparecido* (a person who "disappeared" for political reasons), and a desperate woman in need of an abortion—is interwoven with an impeccable, serene, detailed description of an 11th-c. tapestry depicting creation in all its splendor.

Her most recent novel, *Solitario de amor* (1988; solitaire of love), seems to be P. R.'s most conventional text to date. It is a tightly constructed love story, but not simply that. Lost love and an almost uncontrollable passion obsess the anonymous narrator, who at a certain point exclaims "I am Melibeo!" replicating Calixto's cry in *La Celestina* (1499; the go-between), when the young nobleman, "a prisoner of Melibea's love," surrenders his religion, his patrimony, and his very identity to the object of his desires. There are enough clues in P. R.'s text to suggest the androgynous nature of Aida's yearning lover ("I am a man without a key, that is to say, a man without sex"), and explicit references to their lovemaking quite clearly portray a lesbian encounter: "We make four-hands love, like a couple playing the piano . . . like two twins." Perhaps the carefully constructed ambiguity in *Solitario de amor* suggests a vision of love so pure—and so intense-as to transcend the constraints of gender.

P. R.'s literary merits have been further recognized with two other coveted prizes in Spain: the Palma de Mallorca Prize (1979), and the Benito Pérez Galdós Prize the following year. She writes without hesitations, with total control, and with an unyielding passion for the language. Her voice is eloquent, her style is elegant, and her literature, in the opinion of Julio CORTÁZAR, "has been lived and said by a woman that knows the infernos of this earth— her own land, there in the south—and those of writing in our times—here and everywhere—."

FURTHER WORKS: *Descripción de un naufragio* (1975); *La tarde del dinosaurio* (1976); *La rebelión de los niños* (1980); *Una pasión prohibida* (1986); *Cosmoagonías* (1988); *Fantasias eróticas* (1990); *Babel bárbara* (1990); *La última noche de Dostoievski* (1992); *La ciudad de Luzbel* (1993)

BIBLIOGRAPHY: Benedetti, M., "C. P. R.: Vino nuevo en odres nuevos," *Literatura uruguaya siglo XX*, 2nd ed. (1969): 321–27; Brena, T. G., "C. P. R.," *Exploración estética: Estudio de doce poetas de Uruguay y uno de Argentina* (1974): 463–84; Pereda, R. M., "C. P. R.: la parábola de un naufragio," *Camp de l'Arp*, 13 (Oct. 1974), 27; Campos, E. Molina, "El naufragio de C. P. R.," *Camp de l'Arp*, 22 (July 1975): 26–27; Deredita, J. F., "Desde la diáspora: entrevista con C. P. R.," *Tcrit*, 9 (1978): 131–42; Mora, G., "El mito degradado de la familia en *El libro de mis primos* de C. P. R.," in Pope, R. D., ed., *The Analysis of Literary Texts: Current Trends in Methodology* (1980): 66–77; Morello-Frosch, M., "Entre primos y dinosaurios con C. P. R.," in Cunningham, L. G., ed., *Mujer y sociedad en América Latina* (1980): 193–201; Sosnowski, S., "Los museos abandonados de C. P. R.: Reordenación de museos y refugios," *Actualidades*, 6 (1980–82): 67–74; Verani, H. J., "Una experiencia de límites: la narrativa de C. P. R.," *Rl*, 48, 118–19 (Jan.-June 1982): 303–16; Verani, H. J., "La rebelión del cuerpo y del lenguaje: A propósito de C. P. R.," *Revista de la Universidad de México*, 37 (Mar. 1982): 19–22; Cosse, R., *C. P. R.: Papeles Criticos* (1995); Rowinsky, M., *Imagen y discurso: estudio de las imágenes en la obra de C. P. R.* (1997)

—HORACIO XAUBET

PERRON, Edgar du

(pseud.: Duco Perkens) Dutch novelist, poet, essayist, critic, and journalist, b. 2 Nov. 1899, Meester Cornelis, Java, Indonesia; d. 14 May 1940, Bergen

P. was descended from a well-to-do planter's family of French ancestry. He attended secondary school in Bandung, Java, but beyond that was largely self-educated. For a time he was employed on various Batavian newspapers and as a library assistant at the Royal Batavia Society of Arts and Sciences. Having left for Paris in 1921, he became a close friend of André MALRAUX—indeed Malraux dedicated his *Man's Fate* to him.

In 1930 P. went to the Netherlands, where he lived for brief periods in Amsterdam and The Hague, but most of the years 1921–36 were spent in Paris and Brussels. He collaborated on several literary journals, most notably the influential *Forum* (Rotterdam, 1932–35), which he founded together with Menno ter BRAAK and Maurice ROELANTS. In 1936 P. returned to Indonesia, where he worked for a time as a journalist for the periodical *Kritiek en opbouw*. But his stay was a keen disappointment to him; he felt himself a stranger in what he considered a materialistically attuned Dutch society in the Indies. He also recognized the just cause of Indonesians who were seeking independence; expressions of his sentiments are to be found in the posthumously published *Indies memorandum* (1946; Indies memorandum). P. returned to the Netherlands for the last time in 1939. He died of a heart attack on the day the Dutch army surrendered to the Germans.

P.'s masterpiece, *Het land van herkomst* (1935; the country of origin), is an autobiographical novel in which the East Indies of the past and the Paris of the 1930s are juxtaposed. Quite unconventional in Dutch literature, the work consists of diaries, conversations, letters, memoirs, and narration, but without any plot and with little coherence. He called it an antinovel.

P. is regarded as one of the liveliest and most stimulating Dutch critics of the 1930s. His criticism was based on a highly individualistic approach. He never wished to be regarded as a critic in the traditional sense; that is, he did not wish his views to be binding upon the reader's own judgment. P. considered his opinions to be valid for himself alone.

P. quite consciously wrote for the few; his works have never enjoyed wide popularity. They did, however, exert great influence upon his contemporaries and upon later writers in the Netherlands and Belgium. He was a notable polemicist and fiercely combated all forms of insincerity and affectation. He did not suffer fools gladly and as an individualist he remained aloof from politics but was strongly and outspokenly antifascist. P.'s role as critic and as author of *Het land van herkomst* assures him of a prominent place in Dutch letters.

FURTHER WORKS: *Manuscrit trouvé dans une poche* (1923); *Het roerend bezit* (1924, as Duco Perkens); *De behouden prullemand* (1925, as Duco Perkens); *Bij gebrek aan ernst* (1926, as Duco Perkens); *Een voorbereiding* (1927); *Poging tot afstand* (1927); *Cahiers van een lezer* (5 vols., 1928–1931); *Nutteloos verzet* (1929); *Parlando* (1930); *Micro-chaos* (1932); *Uren met Dirk Coster* (1933); *De smalle mens* (1934); *Blocnote klein formaat* (1936); *De man van Lebak* (1937); *Multatuli, tweede pleidooi* (1938); *Schandaal in Holland* (1939); *Multatuli en de Luizen* (1940); *Een lettré uit de 18e eeuw: Willem van Hogendorp* (1940); *De bewijzen uit het pak van Sjaalman* (1940); *De grijze dashond* (1941); *Een groote stilte* (1942); *Scheepsjournal van Arthur Ducroo* (1943); *Over Stendhal* (1944); *In de grootse tijd* (1947); *Verzameld werk* (7 vols., 1954–1959); *Briefwisseling Ter Braak—Du P.: 1930–1940* (4 vols., 1962–1967)

BIBLIOGRAPHY: Meijer, R. P., *Literature of the Low Countries*, new ed. (1978): 325–28

—JOHN M. ECHOLS

PERSIAN LITERATURE

See Iranian Literature; see also Afghan (Dari) Literature and Indian Literature

PERUVIAN LITERATURE

Fiction

Peruvian fiction in the 20th c.—short story and novel alike—has a readily discernible pattern. It has evolved from studiedly cosmopolitan work to writing oriented along national lines—with the distinctive rural areas of Peru providing the settings for the action—and finally to an emphasis on urban life and on the more universal problems of modern man. Throughout the first half of this century, the short story was the more cultivated and significant form of fiction, with the novel developing relatively slowly and irregularly. In the 1960s and 1970s, however, with the appearance of such gifted novelists as Mario VARGAS LLOSA, Julio RIBEYRO, and Alfredo BRYCE ECHENIQUE, a balance was achieved between the two genres.

The beginnings of 20th-c. Peruvian fiction coincide with the tardy influence of MODERNISM, a literary phenomenon that, although peculiarly Spanish American in its development, subsumes many major European artistic and philosophical preoccupations of the second half of the 19th c. The Peruvian modernists, who were well aware of prevailing fin-de-siècle themes and forms, produced their major works from the last years of the 19th c. through the first decade of the 20th. Clemente Palma (1875–1946), the most significant exponent of modernist fiction, was instrumental in giving the Peruvian narrative a more universal orientation. He is also credited

with initiating the modern short-story form in Peru. The content of most of his fiction is shocking and bizarre; its tone is ironic and pessimistic. Decadent, worldly-wise protagonists, cosmopolitan settings, and themes inspired by the disturbing implications of the scientific advances of the age characterize his best-known work, *Cuentos malévolos* (1904; malevolent stories).

Just before World War I Peruvian fiction began to lean toward national settings and characters. Abraham Valdelomar (1888–1919), Enrique López Albújar (1872–1966), and Ventura García Calderón (1886–1959) had begun writing fiction in the manner of Palma. That these three writers again coincided in the more mature phase of their careers is highly significant: their nationally oriented fiction, highlighting the coast, mountains, and jungle, marked the beginning of a rural-regional trend, which virtually dominated Peruvian fiction until the 1950s. Valdelomar's short-story collection *El caballero Carmelo* (1918; gentleman Carmelo), which beautifully depicts the landscape and inhabitants of the Peruvian seacoast, and López Albújar's *Cuentos andinos* (1920; Andean stories), a limited but unusual presentation of Indian customs and mentality, are notable examples of this period.

The novelists and short-story writers of the 1930s and 1940s continued the regional emphasis, and in general their focus was even sharper and more sensitive to surface detail as they strove to record, often with photographic accuracy, the topography, customs, speech habits, and racial types of Peru. Social protest was also an important element of many of these narratives: the Indian as a victim of cruel, unscrupulous oppressors was of particular concern to several writers.

During the 1930s two major writers, Ciro ALEGRÍA and José María ARGUEDAS, emerged. They are pivotal figures, for while sharing their contemporaries' concern for the national scene and its problems, they strove for and achieved new, more transcendent modes of expressing those realities. Their novels and short stories are, in fact, a striking synthesis of the work of their predecessors and of their own innovations. Alegría's *El mundo es ancho y ajeno* (1941; *Broad and Alien Is the World*, 1941) and Arguedas's *Los ríos profundos* (1959; *Deep Rivers*, 1978) are novels that depict in an extraordinarily powerful and profound way the complexities of the Indian and his environment.

While not forsaking rural Peru, writers during the 1950s turned with marked interest to the social, economic, and psychological problems of city dwellers. But whether detailing urban or rural Peru, they were fully aware that they were also dealing with universal moral and spiritual problems. The rejection or loss of tradition and the quest for new values in Peruvian life are understood to be a reflection of modern civilization.

The novelists and short-story writers who have emerged since 1950 also give evidence of an increased concern for the principles of the art of modern fiction. Julio Ribeyro, Carlos Zavaleta (b. 1928), Enrique Congrains Martín (b. 1932), Alfredo Bryce Echenique, and Mario Vargas Llosa are just five of a large group of talented contemporary authors. Congrains Martín is especially attuned to the desperation of the lower classes struggling to survive in *barriadas*, the peripheral slum areas that have grown up around Lima since the end of World War II. Indeed, his first short-story collection, *Lima, hora cero* (1954; Lima, zero hour), predates by two years the publication of sociological studies of the *barriada* phenomenon. Ribeyro, likewise concerned about the deprivations suffered by the poor, also provides subtle insights into the psychology of the middle class, with its own deep sense of alienation. The confusion of values afflicting that class is presented sensitively in such works as the novel *Los geniecillos dominicales* (1965; Sunday temper). Perhaps better than any modern author, Bryce Echenique understands the so-called upper class of Lima. He portrays its value system with authenticity and irony in the novel *Un mundo para Julius* (1970; a world for Julius). Zavaleta is at his best when dealing with the implications of Peru's rural traditions: How have they shaped national identity, and how do they fit within the universal beliefs and preoccupations of man? His short-story collection *La batalla* (1954; the battle) illuminates the pervasiveness of violence within the cultural tradition.

These writers have in common a thorough knowledge of narrative technique, an uncanny ear for spoken language, and a special interest in narrative structure. Within this group, however, one figure, Mario Vargas Llosa, clearly stands out. He is a stylistic innovator, a provider of striking perspectives on human experience, and a writer who devotes himself tirelessly to his craft. His first novel, *La ciudad y los perros* (1962; *The Time of the Hero*, 1966), attracted critical acclaim, stirred bitter controversy, and catapulted him into international prominence. The work examines critically and forthrightly the lives of cadets in the Lima military academy Leoncio Prado. The novel's complex structure is achieved by an extraordinary manipulation of narrative point of view.

Poetry

Peruvian poetry in the 20th c. is not quite comparable to the fiction in terms of vitality and prestige, although the work of César VALLEJO, a prominent figure in world literature, is a notable exception to this generalization.

Like fiction, the beginnings of 20th-c. poetry coincide with modernism in Peru. Although Manuel GONZÁLEZ PRADA's most significant publications are his essays, he was also important as an innovator of verse form. His poetry is generally associated with the very beginnings of the modernist movement. *Exóticas* (1911; exotics) evinces many characteristics of modernism.

José Santos CHOCANO, whose works combine a preoccupation with modernist imagery and meter and also a desire to exalt the inhabitants and landscape of Latin America, is the best-known Peruvian poet of the early part of the century. His *Alma América— Poemas indo-españoles* (1906; America soul—Indo-Spanish poems) is somewhat reminiscent of the poetry of Walt Whitman.

The next phase of Peruvian poetry was postmodernism. Two literary magazines, *Colónida* and *Contemporáneos*, were primarily responsible for introducing the major new poets during the period 1910–20. The postmodernists, while continuing to cultivate the modernist interest in euphony, reacted strongly against many of its rhetorical adornments, seeking a purer form of expression and preferring to deal more intimately and subtly with the basic problems of man. José María Eguren (1874–1942) was one of the most gifted, and until recently, underrated poets of the period.

César Vallejo must be ranked with the Chilean Pablo NERUDA in importance. He resists easy classification, but his influence on poetry has been enormous. At the risk of oversimplification, one can characterize his first collection of poetry, *Los heraldos negros* (1918; the black messengers), as postmodernist. Even in these early poems the existential problem of suffering mankind, a theme that forms the essence of his later works, can be detected. It would not be inaccurate to classify *Trilce* (1922; *Trilce*, 1973), his second book, as vanguardist. His last two collections of poetry, *Poemas humanos* (1939; *Poemas humanos/Human Poems*, 1968) and *España, aparta de mí este cáliz* (1939; *Spain, Take This Cup from*

Me, 1974), treat social themes with a deep pessimism, yet with a profound love for humanity.

During the 1930s and 1940s, SURREALISM and Indianism were the major influences, with the poets either tending toward abstract interests or nativistic concerns. Emilio Adolfo Westphalen (b. 1911) and César Moro (1903–1956) were the most prominent and productive of the surrealists. Alejandro Peralta (1896–1973), whose poetry contains much imagery associated with the Peruvian Andes, represents the nativistic vein.

Two poetic tendencies in Peru may be traced from the 1950s to the present. One is a social preoccupation, with subjects inspired by historical realities, including the mundane aspects of daily life; the other is more conceptual, even hermetic in nature. Washington Delgado (b. 1927), whose poetry ranges from a subtle lament about the alienation of modern man to strong protest, is a noteworthy example of the first tendency. Fine representatives of more conceptual poetry are Javier Sologuren (b. 1923), Francisco Bendezú (b. 1928), and Carlos Germán BELLI.

Drama

Drama is of comparatively little significance within 20th-c. Peruvian literature. For the first three decades, the plays written and staged were mainly in the costumbristic (folkloric) vein. They were of little literary interest. Since the 1930s the influence of the theater of Europe and the U.S. has been more apparent.

Two playwrights, Sebastián Salazar BONDY and Enrique Solari Swayne (b. 1915), whose works were presented with some success in the 1950s and 1960s, are worthy of mention. Salazar Bondy was intimately acquainted with and influenced by the plays of the French EXISTENTIALISTS and the American drama of social concern. *Rodil* (1951; Rodil) is an excellent example of his existentialist production, and *No hay isla feliz* (1957; there is no happy island) is reminiscent of Arthur MILLER's works. Solari Swayne is equally aware of European and North American trends in drama. In his two best-known plays, *Collacocha* (1959; Collacocha) and *La mazorca* (1965; the ear of corn), he seeks to infuse national themes with universal significance. The first play deals with the struggle of man against the Andes, and the second protrays man's efforts to accommodate himself to the jungle environment.

BIBLIOGRAPHY: Escobar, A., *La narración en el Perú* (1960); Nuñez, E., *La literatura peruana en el siglo XX* (1965); Aldrich, E., *The Modern Short Story in Peru* (1966); Luchting, W., "Recent Peruvian Fiction: Vargas Llosa, Ribeyro, and Arguedas," *RS*, No. 35 (1968): 271–90; Tamayo Vargas, A., *Literatura peruana* (1976); Luchting, W., *Escritores peruanos que piensan que dicen* (1977); Tipton, D., ed. Introduction to *Peru: The New Poetry* (1977): 11–14

—EARL M. ALDRICH, JR.

PESSOA, Fernando

Portuguese poet and critic (also writing in English), b. 13 June 1888, Lisbon; d. 30 Nov. 1935, Lisbon

After P.'s father's death in 1893, his mother married the Portuguese consul in Durban, South Africa, where P. lived from 1896 to 1905. He graduated from junior college in South Africa, winning the Queen Victoria Prize for English Composition, and went to Lisbon in 1905 to attend the university. The early British education that P. received was far different from the French culture then pervasive in Portuguese literature and made an everlasting impression on his views and his handling of language. Moreover, through his work he was to exert an anglicizing influence on subsequent poetic diction in Portugal and Brazil. Soon after 1905 he gave up his studies, using his knowledge of English to get employment as a business correspondent. For the rest of his life he lived alone in Lisbon, avoiding social life and the literary world.

At his debut in 1912—which was as a literary critic—he praised the *saudosismo* (nostalgia) movement in such extravagant terms that his articles provoked nationwide polemics. From that year on he proceeded uninterruptedly to comment on politics and literature by means of paradoxical and mystifying articles and pamphlets. He helped to launch the avant-garde movement in Portuguese literature and, through the reviews *Orpheu* and *Portugal futurista*, was its leading figure along with Mário de SÁ-CARNEIRO and José de Almada-Negreiros (1893–1970).

But it is as a poet that P. has won eminence in modern world literature. He wrote poetry under his own name as well as under at least three other names. As Fernando Pessoa he wrote poems that are marked by their startling innovations of language, although he used traditional stanza and metrical patterns. As Alvaro de Campos he was a bold modernist, tragically minded, whose forte was for dour and majestic diction in free verse. As Alberto Caeiro he was a straight-forward empiricist, a sensualist, whose free verse seems indifferent to technique. As Ricardo Reis he was a classicist, whose Horatian odes surpass the ambitions of most 18th-c. writers. These names were "heteronyms," as P. said of them, not pen names. Each persona had a distinct philosophy of life, wrote at a certain linguistic level, and worked in a distinctive style and form. P. even wrote literary discussions among them. He prepared their horoscopes to fit their lives and personalities—or he may have shaped a personality according to a horoscope. (Like other Western postsymbolist poets he had esoteric tendencies that show in his work.)

What is most impressive is that each of these "heteronyms" (and when he wrote poetry under his own name he was as much of a heteronym as when he "was" somebody else) is a great poet in his own right.

The bulk of P.'s work was published in literary magazines, especially in his own *Athena*. Editors did not begin to compile his work until 1942, and the wealth of his scattered or unpublished writings has still to be rescued, in spite of his having been recognized as a master as early as 1927.

Little of P.'s work was published in book form during his lifetime. His English poems *were* collected in books: *35 Sonnets* (1917), *Antinous* (1918), *English Poems I–II* (1921), *English Poems III* (1921). Most of them were too "metaphysical" for the time and hence very much in advance of the change of taste that was to occur in English poetry. In addition, he published *Mensagem* (1934; message), a sequence of emblematic poems in Portuguese on the history of Portugal. Although a minor work, it is still controversial today, as it can be interpreted as "nationalist" and used to present P. as an apologist for the authoritarian regime that had come into power in 1926, which he was not.

P. is admirable for his terrifying lucidity, his linguistic virtuosity, and his inventive imagery. His deeply felt intellectualism was in the best Portuguese tradition of Luís Vaz de Camões (1524?–1580) and Antero de Quental (1842–1891). (One of his best-known lines states, "What in me feels is now thinking.") Today, P.'s poetry is

still original and audacious. No one in Western literature has been more successful than he in realizing the modern dream of creating an antiromantic "objective correlative." All this qualifies him as one of the greatest poets in Portuguese, and as such he is admired in Portugal and Brazil. Translations of his poems in Spanish, French, English, German, and other languages have been appearing since the 1940s, thus opening the way for P. to be recognized as one of the most important and original masters of modern poetry.

FURTHER WORKS: *Poemas de F. P.* (1942); *Poemas de Álvaro de Campos* (1944); *A nova poesia portuguesa* (1944); *Poemas de Alberto Caeiro* (1946); *Poemas de Ricardo Reis* (1946); *Páginas de doutrina estética* (1946); *Poemas dramáticos* (1952); *Quadras ao gosto popular* (1955); *Poesias inéditas: 1919–1930* (1956); *Páginas íntimas e de auto-interpretação* (1966); *Páginas de estética e de teoria e crítica literária* (1966); *Textos filosóficos* (2 vols., 1968); *Novas poesias inéditas* (1973); *Cartas de amor de F. P.* (1978); *Sobre Portugal: Introdução ao problema nacional* (1979); *Livro do desassossego por Bernardo Soares* (1982). FURTHER WORKS IN ENGLISH: *Selected Poems by F. P.* (1971); *Selected Poems of F. P.* (1971)

BIBLIOGRAPHY: Biderman, S., "Mount Abiegnos and the Masks: Occult Imagery in Yeats and P.," *LBR*, 5 (1968): 59–74; Hamburger, M., "F. P.," *Agenda*, 6: 3–4 (1968): 104–12; Paz, O., Introduction to *Selected Poems by F. P.* (1971): 1–21; Rickard, P., Introduction to *Selected Poems of F. P.* (1971): 1–61; Jones, M. S., "P.'s Poetic Coterie: Three Heteronyms and an Orthonym," *LBR*, 14 (1977): 254–62; Bacarisse, P., "F. P.: Towards an Understanding of a Key Attitude," *LBR*, 17 (1980): 51–61; Sousa, R. W., "P.: The Messenger," *The Rediscoverers: Major Portuguese Writers in the Portuguese Literature of National Regeneration* (1981): 131–60

—JORGE DE SENA

PETERS, Lenrie

Gambian poet and novelist (writing in English), b. 1 Sept. 1932, Bathurst

In 1952 P. left Africa to study medicine at Cambridge, eventually going on to specialize in surgery. He now resides in Gambia.

P.'s one novel, *The Second Round* (1965), is important as one of the first African novels to turn from the theme of colonial protest and culture conflict to that of self-criticism—the African's criticism of his own country. In this book a doctor returns to his home in Freetown after studying and then practicing medicine for several years in England. He finds himself to be an objective observer, unable to engage himself fully in the lives of his friends, who are being torn apart as they fail to adjust to, or even to recognize, the values of their changing society. Despite several passages of a fine lyrical quality, the novel is marred by excessively sentimental scenes and a contrived plot.

P.'s forte is clearly his poetry. In *Satellites* (1967), his best collection to date, he draws together his experience of living in two worlds, the African and the Western, and analyzes both worlds in fine, almost microscopic detail. The particular confusion, frustration, and alienation he finds in his own soul is seen to be representative of Everyman's malaise in the face of technology and its suffocation of human values. P.'s medical training informs the poetry in this volume with a precision that the reader finds not only in his short, tight stanzas, but also in the incisive, at times surgical, images he employs.

This analytical introspection is continued in much of the poetry in *Katchikali* (1971), but the collection as a whole lacks the vitality of *Satellites*. Nevertheless, in a few of the poems P. made some interesting experiments with form, breaking away from the tighter structures of his earlier verse.

P.'s total output has been small, and he has published nothing since *Katchikali*. He remains, however, one of the finest contemporary African poets. No other living African poet has, in fact, so consistently displayed such control of form or created such startling images. Concerned with the spirit no less than the flesh, P. has effectively married his concerns in a poetry that addresses the social and economic problems of contemporary Africa and reasserts the aesthetic principles he finds threatened in his society.

FURTHER WORKS: *Poems* (1964); *Selected Poetry* (1981)

BIBLIOGRAPHY: Moore, G., "The Imagery of Death in African Poetry," *AfricaL* 38 (1968): 57–70; Theroux, P., "Six Poets," in Beier, U. ed., *Introduction to African Literature* (1970): 110–31; Knipp, T. R., "L. P.: The Poet as Lonely African," *SBL* 2, 3 (1971): 9–13; Larson, C. R., "L. P.'s *The Second Round* West African Gothic," *The Emergence of African Fiction* (1972): 227–41; Egudu, R. N., *Four Modern West African Poets* (1977), passim

—RICHARD PRIEBE

PETERSEN, Nis

Danish poet, short-story writer, and novelist, b. 22 Jan. 1897, Vamdrup; d. 9 March 1943, Laven

After three years as a pharmacist's apprentice, P. worked as a journalist from 1918 until 1921, when he severed all ties with the bourgeois world. He spent the rest of his life as a casual laborer, beggar, and vagabond—and writer.

Because of his break with his pietistic upbringing and its view of life in which responsibility and sin play an important part, P. became burdened with a chronic sense of guilt and a fatal irresoluteness. Similarly, many of his fictional characters feel themselves lost: they are outcasts marked by skepticism and angst. The idyll of childhood and the experience of love as well as death itself and the hope for divine grace offered the possibility of an escape from this rootlessness. But P. feared death, too; a prevalent theme in his work is death as judgment rather than as a means of salvation.

P.'s existential insecurity is most distinctly expressed in his poetry, which he began writing as early as 1915. The early verse reflects the horror of the outbreak of World War I and his own rather pathetic suicidal thoughts. These poems, written around the time of World War I, were published posthumously in *For tromme og kastagnet* (1951; for drum and castanet). His official debut was with *Nattens pibere* (1926; the pipers of the night). Here P.'s expressions of disillusion are juxtaposed to a number of nature idylls; there is a persistent dwelling on man's capacity for love and

fellowship. P.'s subsequent poetry collections, *En drift vers* (1933; a drove of verses), *Til en dronning* (1935; to a queen), and *Stykgods* (1940; mixed cargo), are variations on these themes with Rudyard KIPLING as an increasingly dominant model not only in regard to verse technique—several of the poems are long ballad-like epics—but also in regard to the worship of the heroic.

Among P.'s works of fiction *Sandalmagernes gade* (1931; *The Street of the Sandal-makers*, 1932) ranks the highest. A historical novel set in Rome during the reign of Marcus Aurelius, it is based on exhaustive use of historical sources. His true subject, however, is interwar Europe and its rootless human beings, exemplified by the weak Marcellus, and it is written in a modern, anachronistic style. Through a love affair Marcellus comes into contact with Christians and is killed through pure chance.

Sandalmagernes gade became an international best seller and was translated into ten languages. Its narrative concentration, colorful character delineation, and universal perspective are lacking in P.'s second novel, *Spilt mælk* (1934; *Spilt Milk*, 1935), set in Ireland during the civil war of the 1920s. Also less successful were P.'s last writings, which apart from a collection of moralizing aphorisms, *99 bemærkninger* (1936; 99 remarks) consist of short stories, some composed in an imaginative and witty style inspired by P. G. WODEHOUSE, and the later ones written in the fashion of modern hardboiled American prose. They are based on P.'s own experiences in the Danish provinces and were usually first printed in popular magazines before they were published in the collections: *Engle blæser på trompet* (1937; angels play the trumpet), *Dagtyve* (1941; day thieves), *Muleposen* (1942; the nose bag), and *Stynede popler* (1943; pollarded poplars), the last of which also contains a number of love poems. The subjects of P.'s short stories are often trivial and anecdotal and the characterizations deliberately sketchy. They are clearly meant to serve as expressions of P.'s own nihilism. This negative world view is a phenomenon commonly found in the writers of the chaotic interwar period, but with P. it was particularly desperate.

FURTHER WORKS: *Digte* (1942); *Brændende Europa* (1947); *Aftenbønnen* (1947); *Da seeren tav* (1947); *Memoirer: "Lad os leve i nuet"* (1948); *Samlede digte* (1949); *Mindeudgave* (8 vols., 1962)

BIBLIOGRAPHY: Claudi, J., *Contemporary Danish Authors* (1952): 115–18

—SVEN H. ROSSEL

PETRESCU, Camil

Romanian novelist, dramatist, and poet, b. 22 April 1894, Bucharest; d. 14 May 1957, Bucharest

P. studied literature and philosophy at the University of Bucharest and was later a secondary-school teacher, an influential journalist, critic, and polemicist, a director of the Bucharest National Theater (1939), and a member of the Romanian Academy.

In spite of recurrent personal differences, P. was throughout the 1930s and early 1940s close to Eugen LOVINESCU's intellectual circle, which made a stand for an art independent of political influences, one that was modern, urban, and Western-oriented. Somewhat amateurish essays on the philosophy of Henri BERGSON and on phenomenology, as well as critical essays, particularly those in *Teze şi antiteze* (1936; theses and antitheses), are evidence of his adherence to such ideas.

P. was firmly committed to an analytical rationalism, the very mechanism of which, he believed, was productive of aesthetic satisfaction. This concept is equally reflected in the tough idealism of his poems, *Versuri* (1923; expanded ed., 1957; verse), and in the theme underlying his principal dramatic works—*Suflete tari* (1925; *Those Poor Stout Hearts*, 1960), *Danton* (1931; Danton), *Act veneţian* (1931; Venetian act), and *Mioara* (1931; Mioara)—the incompatibility of a power–hungry intellect with the surrounding world.

P.'s significance rests on his novels. *Ultima noapte de dragoste, întîia noapte de război* (1930; last night of love, first night of war) probes the consciousness of the World War I generation. With subtlety and precision, parallels are drawn between individual and social psychology on the one hand, between personal, erotic suffering and failure and the cruel experience of war on the other. Even more important is *Patul lui Procust* (2 vols., 1933; Procrustes' bed), in which the series of events leading to the breakdown in sexual and social communication of a lucid and sensitive intellectual is presented from the viewpoint of several characters.

While these novels are marked by the opposition between the individual and society, *Un om între oameni* (3 vols., 1953–57; *A Man amongst Men*, 1958) is devoted to a 19th-c. Romanian revolutionary intellectual who emerges from his solitude. Although marred by a sedulous projection of abstract sociological patterns, this novel is distinguished by finely worked-out historical imagery and seems to offer the outline of a solution through action of the intellectual's dilemmas.

P.'s main strength lies in his ability to describe the psychological dimensions of conflict in Romania's increasingly urbanized social structures. His substantial influence on later prose writers was due in part to his clean factual style and innovative techniques.

FURTHER WORKS: *Jocul ielelor* (1919); *Mitică Popescu* (1926); *Transcendentalia* (1931); *Eugen Lovinescu sub zodia seninătăţii imperturbabile* (1936); *Modalitatea estetică a teatrului* (1937); *Husserl* (1938); *Rapid Constantinopol—Bioram* (1939); *Teatru* (3 vols., 1946–47); *Bălcescu* (1949); *Turnul de fildeş* (1950); *Caragiale în vremea lui* (1957); *Teatru* (2 vols., 1957–58); *Note zilnice 1927–1940* (1975)

BIBLIOGRAPHY: Munteanu, B., *Modern Romanian Literature* (1939): 242–44; Călin, V., "One of the Many," *RoR*, 9, 2 (1954): 107–19; Tertullian, N., "P.'s Plays," *RoR*, 14, 2 (1959): 138–44; Philippide, A., "The Spirit and Tradition of Modern Romanian Literature," *RoR*, 21, 2 (1967): 5–10; Alexandrescu, S., "Analyse structurelle des personnages et conflits dans le roman *Patul lui Procust* de C. P.," *Cahiers de linguistique théorique et appliqué*, No. 6 (1969): 209–24

—VIRGIL NEMOIANU

PETROV, Yevgeny

See under Ilf, Ilya

PETRUSHEVSKAYA, Ludmila

Russian dramatist and short-story writer, b. 26 May 1938, Moscow

P.'s early childhood, coinciding as it did with World War II, personally familiarized her with the bleaker aspects of life: homelessness, starvation, abject poverty, orphanages, physical brutality, and loneliness without privacy. These experiences form the psychological backbone of her oeuvre. After studying journalism at Moscow State University, P., like many Soviet youths, journeyed to the virgin lands in Kazakhstan, before she found work as a hospital nurse, a radio reporter, and an editor at a television studio. Although she began writing short stories in 1963, she waited for almost a decade before the journal *Avrora* accepted two for publication in 1972: "Rasskazchitsa" (the story-teller) and "Istoriia Klarissy" (Clarissa's story). A similar fate met her plays, a genre she first tried that same year. Financial need forced P. to undertake translation from the Polish while she continued her solitary literary activity. Until the mid-1980s only a handful of P.'s more than forty stories and plays saw the light of day. Efforts to stage her works met with continued official resistance. The theaters that succeeded in presenting her plays tended to be experimental, amateur, or provincial. The two-act *Uroki muzyki* (1973; music lessons) was performed briefly at Moscow University in 1979; the diptych *Chinzano* (1973; *Cinzano*, 1989) and *Den' rozhdeniia Smirnovoi* (1977; Smirnova's birthday) premiered in 1978 in Estonian translation in Estonia. Only her one-act play *Liubov'* (1974; love) enjoyed a long, successful run in Moscow after its inclusion in the 1979–1980 season. Two decades of professional hardships finally ended in the mid-1980s, when Gorbachev instituted his policy of glasnost. Owing to the pendulum swing in her fortunes, P. has become the most popular dramatist in Moscow, with several plays simultaneously enjoying extended runs in major theaters. Her stories likewise have become staple fare in mainstream journals and newspapers. Under glasnost both P. and her plays travel abroad, to Europe and the U.S.

P. has provoked heated controversy as both prosaist and dramatist partly because her oeuvre portrays a nightmarish life on the edge of existence, devoid of palliative reassurances. Permeated with morbid humor and grotesquerie, her harshly unidealizing works deal with the underbelly of human relations—the nasty traffic in human desires and fears, where everything carries a literal and metaphorical price. Life for P. is the penalty we pay for having been born. Everyone in her grim universe tends to be cut adrift from a reliable mooring; is ruled by appetite and self-interest; falls into seemingly irreversible patterns of (self-)destructive behavior; abrogates moral responsibility; inflicts and experiences pain in an unbroken chain of universal abuse. Suicide, alcoholism, child abuse, fictitious marriages, one-night stands, prostitution, unwanted pregnancies, abortions, crushing poverty, theft, and physical and psychological violence constitute the stuff of P.'s fiction and drama.

P.'s stories, like her plays, concentrate on the middle class, largely the urban technical intelligentsia. The majority of her protagonists and narrators tend to be women whose lives are maimed through personal weakness, uncontrollable circumstances, male mistreatment, and relatives' interference or overbearing demands—numerous female protagonists must tend simultaneously to dependent children and needy, frequently hospitalized, mothers. Alienation, betrayal, and humiliation comprise the lot of these beasts of burden, because pragmatic calculation fuels relations between family members, spouses, and lovers: "Smotrovaia ploshchadka" (1982; "The Overlook," 1990), "Temnaia sud'ba" (1988; gloomy fate), "Strana" (1988; country), or "Takaia devochka" (1988; such a girl). Romantic love is a luxury to which P.'s characters rarely have access as they battle for a place to live and, minimally, find temporary shelter, as in "Skripka" (1973; "The Violin," 1989), or for clothes, food, sex, as in "Doch' Kseni" (1988; Ksenia's daughter), or for alcohol, as in "Ali-Baba" (1988; Ali Baba). In this Darwinian struggle, painted in largely physiological hues, ethical norms fall by the wayside.

Free of nature and psychological analysis, sparse in dialogue, and stripped of imagery, P.'s prose relies for its effects on the distinctive language of its ambiguous narrators. That language, like the lives it records, is a triumph of incongruities, synthesizing urban slang, cultural clichés, malapropisms, racy colloquialisms, and solecisms. These stream forth in a relentless monologic patter that strives to camouflage, or to defer confrontation with, what is most crucial and, usually, most painful. Revelation, not action, is the pivot on which P.'s stories turn. The seamy catastrophes in which her plots abound are conveyed in a monstrously calm narrative voice whose digressive, casual chatter is a stratagem of deflection, transference, and avoidance. The most chilling aspect of the narration is precisely the discrepancy between the extraordinary horrors that multiply implacably and the flat, casual tone of reportage that reduces everything to the same level of banality. Although P. divides her narratives into stories (*istorii*) and monologues (*monologi*), they differ stylistically only in the use of free indirect discourse versus first-person narration, respectively.

"Svoi krug" (1979; "Our Crowd," 1990), P.'s longest and best narrative to date, offers the fullest, most nuanced glimpse of the ways in which the moral fabric of contemporary Russian society has unraveled. Her subsequent stories, "Novye Robinzony" (1989; "A Modern Family Robinson," 1991) and "Gigiena" (1990; hygiene), belong to the substantial body of apocalyptic visions in Soviet fiction. With her recent publication *Skazh dlia vzroslykh* (1990; fairy tales for adults) P. has made a transition to a new genre: that of gnomic allegory and Kafkaesque parable.

P.'s plays mirror essentially the concerns of her prose and contain analogous types. Family as a synecdoche for society dominates P.'s drama, its microcosm reflecting the dissolution of human bonds—of kinship, support, and responsibilities—whereby relatives and husbands are estranged and instrumentalized. In *Syraia noga, ili vstrecha druzei* (1977; a raw leg, or a gathering of friends). Serezha the boxer steals money from his old mother's savings and beats his wife Natasha senseless; in *Liubov'* Evgeniia Ivanovna's selfish hostility to her son-in-law Tolia drives him and his new bride Sveta out onto the street on their wedding night, in *Moskovskii khor* (n.d.; Moscow chorus) savage family feuds, rife with vilification, erupt when members victimized by the purges return from the camps.

As setting P. favors kitchens and overcrowded rundown apartments whose spatial limitations symptomatize the psychological claustrophobia of its occupants, their entrapment in their situation. Lack of adequate space or a roof over one's head signals an absence of psychological refuge, of belonging, exemplified by Ira's dilemma in *Tri devushki v golubom* (1980; *Three Girls in Blue*, 1988). Spatial and temporal boundaries, however, are extended through P.'s technique of reminiscence and reference, whereby hearsay characters, their words and actions, become incorporated into a play when those present quote them or refer to incidents in which they participated. In *Syraia noga, ili vstrecha druzei* Volodia suggests to Sonia that they renew their former sexual intimacy,

while blithely volunteering the information that one of his students in Kalinin supplies him with sex three times a week. While lying with his head in Ira's lap, he confesses that he cannot do without a woman for three days maximum, and recalls once propositioning ten women at a train station until one agreed to oblige him. By indirectly revealing the behavior of multiple hearsay characters, P. universalizes the moral dissoluteness of those we actually see. Fewer than twenty individuals inhabit the stage in *Tri devushki v golubom*, but over a hundred are mentioned, and the sheer volume depersonalizes people into a mass. When that technique resurrects relatives from the past, it also underscores the themes of heredity and continuity. Errors, vices, and weaknesses are one generation's legacy to the next. In *Uroki muzyki* eighteen-year-old Nina's mother, Grania, throws her parental duties, including the care of her baby, onto Nina's shoulders so as to concentrate on the violent, alcoholic ex-convict who fathered the child. When he returns uninvited to their apartment, revulsion and insufficient room force Nina to seek asylum at a neighbor's. Yet Grania's sole worry is her loss of a baby-sitter, especially when she has to check into a hospital for an abortion and fears leaving the baby with her unpredictable brute of a husband. Maternity, which serves as a key moral gauge in P.'s system of values, suffers endless violations, exemplified by Galia in *Lestnichnaia kletka* (1974; the stairwell), who plans to conceive a child with a stranger, only so as to mollify her hysterical mother.

The diversity of P.'s work for the theater is reflected in the five genres associated with her name: full-length plays, such as *Uroki muzyki, Tri devushki v goluborm, Syraia noga*, and *Moskovskii khor*, which consist of two acts and casts averaging a dozen characters; her favorite genre of the one-act play, which observes the classical unities of time, place, and action and confines the cast to between three and six characters; dialogues, such as "Izolirovannyi boks" (1988; insulated box) and "Stakan vody" (1988; a glass of water); the monologues that double as prose narratives—"Pesni XX veka" (1988; songs of the 20th c.), "Seti i lovushki" (1974; "Nets and Traps," 1989), and "Takaia devochka"—and plays for children, which draw on puppet theater and include *Dva okoshka* (1975; two windows), *Chemodan chepukhi, ili bystro khorosho ne byvaet* (1975; a suitcase of nonsense, or things don't go well quickly), and *Zolotaia boginia* (1986; golden goddess).

Critics have commented on Chekhovian elements in P.'s drama, whereas the only common features are dialogues that are essentially sequentialized monologues and the habit of calling "comedies" works that audiences perceive as devastatingly somber. Others have remarked on P.'s debt to Aleksandr Vampilov (1937–1972), whose antiheroes, indeed, do prefigure the decidedly unadmirable types that predominate in P.'s plays. In response to queries about her unremittingly gloomy vision of life, P. claims to pose problems that invite audience's self-confrontation. Optimally, that process will catalyze one's humane impulses. P. scrupulously excludes all explicit judgment, sermonizing, and hope for moral progress from her fiction and drama. In fact, it would be difficult to imagine a world more desolate and bereft of hope than that portrayed by P., which may be summarized by the famous Sartrean formula "Hell is other people."

FURTHER WORKS: *P'esy* (1983); *Bessmertnaia liubov'* (1988)

BIBLIOGRAPHY: Smith, M. T., *"In Cinzano Veritas*: The Plays of L. P.," *SEEA*, 3, 1 (1985): 119–25; Condee, N., "L. P.: How the

'Lost People' Live," *Institute of Current World Affairs Newsletter*, 14 (Feb. 1986): 1–12

—HELENA GOSCILO

PETRY, Ann

American novelist and short-story writer, b. 12 Oct. 1908, Old Saybrook, Connecticut; d. 28 Apr. 1997, Old Saybrook, Connecticut

P. is one of the few well-known African-American writers from New England. She was the only African American in her class in Old Saybrook, an experience that has informed much of her fiction. She began writing in high school, but pursued a Ph.G. degree in Pharmacy, in keeping with family tradition—both her father and her mother's sister were pharmacists, and her father owned a drugstore in Old Saybrook. However, she also lived in Harlem for a number of years, having moved there after deciding that she did not want to make pharmacy her lifework.

It is Harlem that provides the background for her first novel, *The Street* (1946). A work in the naturalist tradition and often compared to Richard WRIGHT's *Native Son*, it chronicles the fight of a woman against poverty and racism. Lutie Johnson doggedly tries to improve her economic lot, yet, in large part because men attempt to entrap her in their desires, she spirals down to murder and flight from Harlem, leaving her child behind. Praised for its metaphorical language and its absence of overt politicizing, the novel was an immediate success.

Country Place (1947) appeared only a year later but did not find a readership, no doubt in large part because it is set in a small New England town with a cast of white characters, thus not conforming to audience expectations of African-American authors. *Country Place*, which draws on P.'s own experiences, is largely told from the point of view of the town's drugstore owner. The novel exposes the hypocrisies and the materialism of its inhabitants while not being unsympathetic towards them. Johnnie Roane's return from World War II sets in motion a plot that lays bare the town's faultliness. Climaxing in a storm that coincides with a murder attempt, Johnnie's discovery of his wife's infidelity, and the revelation of her mother's relationship with the same man, the novel's most hopeful element is the budding relationship between an African-American housekeeper and a Portuguese gardener, both looked down upon by the town's less affluent whites.

P.'s epic third novel *The Narrows* (1953), also set in a New England town and written after her return to Old Saybrook, explores the relationship between Link Williams, a life-weary African-American intellectual, and Camilla Treadway Sheffield, Anglo-American heiress to ammunition company wealth, and married. Race, class, and marital status intervene in this relationship and ultimately doom it, as both characters become enmeshed in the suspicions of the outside world, the differing frames of reference that their lives provide, and distrust of each other, which ultimately leads both to reenact stereotypical expectations of their roles: he reverts to macho behavior to protect himself, and she accuses him of rape out of anger at his rejection, thus causing his death. P. shows how all of the participants in this drama, which also consists of a richly textured background providing insights into both African-American and white communities, enact their roles based in part on the history that has shaped them. A stylistic

masterpiece, *The Narrows* might well be the pinnacle of P.'s achievement.

P.'s work remains underappreciated today. Of her three novels, only *The Street* is still widely discussed and read, whereas her masterpiece, *The Narrows*, and *Country Place* have almost been forgotten. Nonetheless, the strength of her writing, its probing insight and stylistic force, will assure her a prominent place among African-American writers in particular and American writers in general.

FURTHER WORKS: *Harriet Tubman: Conductor on the Underground Railroad* (1955); *Tituba of Salem Village* (1964); *Legends of the Saints* (1970); *Miss Muriel and Other Stories* (1971)

BIBLIOGRAPHY: Bell, B. W., "A. P.'s Demythologizing of American Culture and Afro-American Character," in Pryse, M., and H. J. Spillers, eds., *Conjuring* (1985): 105-15; Clark, K., "A Distaff Dream Deferred? A. P. and the Art of Subversion," *African American Review*, 26 (Fall 1992): 495-505; Ervin, H. A., *A. P.: A Bio-Bibliography* (1993); Holladay, H., *A. P.* (1996)

—MARTIN JAPTOK

PEUL LITERATURE
See Senegalese literature

PHELPS, Anthony

Haitian poet, novelist, short-story writer, and dramatist, b. 25 Aug. 1928, Port-au-Prince

Born into a bourgeois family in Port-au-Prince, P. is one of the most prestigious representatives of the new Haitian literature that emerged in reaction to the bloody dictatorship of François Duvalier in the early 1960s. P. studied various disciplines in the U.S. and Quebec, including chemistry, photography, filmmaking, ceramics, and sculpture, before returning home and devoting himself almost entirely to literature.

P. joins to his passion for literary invention a profound disgust inspired by the political situation of his country. His impact upon the politically conscious Haitian youth set the repressive machinery of the Duvalier dictatorship against him, and he was arrested in 1963. Freed after three weeks in prison, P. was finally forced to flee to Montreal in 1964 to live in an exile that would continue until the fall of the Duvalier régime in 1986.

In 1960 P. founded the group Literary Haiti with four other young poets: Davertige (pseud. of Villard Denis, b. 1940), René Philoctête (b. 1932), Roland Morisseau, and Serge Legagneur (dates n.a.). Denouncing the barriers imposed a priori on art by ideologies and traditions, the adherents to this school make only one demand on their poetry: that it have an incontestable richness of form. In that same year, P. also published his first volume of poetry; *Été* (summer) is a thin volume, but already, in its thematic and aesthetic concerns, it announces the direction his work will take. One finds in it traces of the old Haitian aesthetic, based on the three essential principles of Indigenism, Socialism, and NÉGRITUDE. This ideological aspect is one that P. will never abjure. His work expresses a constant struggle against enemies who seek to prevent his new humanism—extolling humankind's blossoming in liberty, peace, and universal brotherhood—from realizing itself. P.'s poetry, however, would be ill-defined if it were exclusively examined from the point of view of his militancy. It is first and foremost the expression of a literature comparable to the best contemporary productions.

P.'s humanistic quest continues in *Présence* (1961; presence) and *Éclats de silence* (1962; bursts of silence), two small books of poetry, and in the texts that appeared in 1962 in *Semence*, the organ of Literary Haiti, as well as the long "Poème de la montagne" (1964; poem of the mountain), the original version of which was published in *Conjonction*, the review of the French Institute of Haiti. This poem, in which the peasants are invited to fraternize with the poet, tells much about P.'s ideological romanticism.

During his exile in Montreal, P.'s work reaches its apogee. *Points cardinaux* (1967; cardinal points), published in Montreal, focuses on P.'s situation. In this introspective work the themes of militant inspiration, even if not entirely absent, are expressed only as if in a whisper. P. looks at himself through the prism of an exiled man's fantasies; on the threshold of exile, he surveys the chaos of his mind. For the first time, he completely cultivates the abstract language of SURREALISM, before readjusting the cloak of his militancy, and altering his discourse once again to become accesible. *Mon pays que voici suivi de les dits du fou-aux-cailloux* (1968; this country of mine, followed by the sayings of the fool of the rocks), a text nearly finished at the time P. went into exile, achieves perhaps the most spectacular success a collection of poetry signed by a Haitian author has ever obtained. The poem "Mon pays que voici," which exalts patriotism and stigmatizes the shameful régime of the "tontons-macoutes," touched the most sensitive fibers of the Haitian soul.

P. is, in fact, consecrated by Haitians as the poet of exile. For years, his creativity focused itself on the theme of exile; the problem for P., however, is not how the exile confronts his material obstacles, but rather the interior drama of such a person incapable of adapting himself to his new cultural environment. Far from his country, the poet is cut off from his natural source of inspiration; progressively he loses his sense of identity. Thus, returning to his native country appears to him such a vital necessity. That is the message of *Motifs pour le temps saisonnier* (1976; motifs for seasonal time). From an artistic point of view, the poems in this collection must be rated among the best P. has written.

La bélière caraïbe (1979; the Caribbean ram), awarded the Casa de las Américas Prize (1980), begins a new cycle. In principle the period of P.'s strict exile has ended with the demise of the Duvalier régime. He can finally see the country of his birth again, and he feels the rapture of the creator recapturing the sense of his roots. From this moment on, the need to proclaim his pride in his Caribbean identity supplants the theme of exile. One finds this same thematic preoccupation in *Orchidée nègre* (1985; black orchid), which earned P. a second prize from Casa de las Américas (1987).

Même le soleil est nu (1983; even the sun is naked) is an account of the emotions of the poet struck, upon his return to Port-au-Prince, by the terrible physical and moral decay that haunted the country. The paradise of his childhood had been ravaged. The brutal physical destruction of the people vied with the extreme brutality of the government. In 1984 P. asked for and received early retirement from Radio Canada in order to return to Haiti and devote himself entirely to literature. His anticipated repatriation was, however, delayed due to the brutality of the transitional period. P.'s disappointment at his continued exile, together with the desire to reassert the value of Haiti's cultural heritage, marks the most recent of P.'s works. The publication of "La mémoire dépiegééé" (the untrapped memory) and "Femme-Amérique" (woman-America), two manuscripts completed several years ago, has been announced.

In addition to poetry, P. has always shown a great interest in theater. He has written some thirty radio plays, as yet unpublished, for Radio Cacique; he has only published one play, *Le conditionnel* (1968; the conditional), which has never been officially performed. Another manuscript, "Le mannequin enchanté" (n.d.; the enchanted mannequin), has recently resurfaced. These plays have two things in common: They are both comedies, and neither contains specific reference to Haiti. They can be performed without regard to the ethnicity of the actors, and this may account for their going nearly unnoticed on the Haitian literary scene.

P. has two major novels to his credit: *Moins l'infini* (1972; minus the infinite) and *Mémoire en colin-maillard* (1976; blindman's-buff memory). Both texts feature an elegantly turned style and are marked by all the subtleties of P.'s poetic language. Written at the time when P. was still absorbed in anti-Duvalier activism, they belong to the prolific family of tales that, throughout the 1970s, strove to denounce the horrors of the dictatorship and, a corollary, to incite Haitians to continue unflinchingly to battle until the final victory. P.'s narrative structure well demonstrates processes one finds in the NEW NOVEL, and, because of this, they may be inaccessible to many readers. But one can say about P.'s novels that, even though they may not spontaneously arouse popular enthusiasm, they possess, with respect to language and invention, everything necessary to resist the ravages of time.

P. is a complete writer. Because of the abundance, variety, and quality of his work, he represents the best that contemporary Haitian literature has to offer. He is in the advance guard of his generation of writers: engaged witnesses to one of the most dramatic periods in the history of their country, who understood they had to break through the barriers of insularity to participate equally in the fascinating literary experience of the modern world. Especially as a poet, P. must not be considered only as a Haitian writer, but also as one of the most illustrious representatives of contemporary literature written in French.

FURTHER WORKS: *Et moi je suis une île* (1973); *Haïti! Haïti!* (1985, with Gary Klang)

BIBLIOGRAPHY: Lacôte, R., "A. P.," *Lettres Françises* (19 Feb. 1969): 10; Bruner, C., "The Meaning of Caliban in Black Literature Today," *CLS*, 13 (1973): 240–53; Berrou, R., and Pompilus, P., *Histoire de la littérature haïtienne*, Vol. 3 (1977): 344–59; Bruner, C., "Haitian Poets Cross Words," *The Gar*, 33 (1979): 22–24; Dash, M., *Literature and Ideology in Haiti, 1915–1961* (1981): 213; Hoffmann, L. F., *Le roman haïtien, idéologie et structure* (1982): 334; Ferdinand, J., "The New Political Statement in Haitian Fiction," in Luis, W., ed., *Voices from Under: Black Narrative in Latin America and the Caribbean* (1984): 127–46; Souffrant, C., "Une contre-négritude caraïbe, exode rural et urbanisation chez A. P.," in CIDIHCA, ed., *L'arme de la critique littéraire, littérature et idéologie en Haïti* (1988): 217–29

—JOSEPH FERDINAND

PHENOMENOLOGY AND LITERATURE

The phenomenological movement has proliferated and diverged greatly since Edmund Husserl (1859–1938), the father of the movement, started it all with his *Logische Untersuchungen* (2 vols., 1900–1901; 2nd rev. ed., 1913; *Logical Investigations*, 1970). For example, there are the ontological phenomenology of Nicolai Hartmann (1882–1950) and Martin Heidegger (1889–1976); the phenomenological investigation of values by Max Scheler (1874–1928); the EXISTENTIALIST phenomenology of Jean-Paul SARTRE and Maurice Merleau-Ponty (1908–1961); the religious phenomenology of Mircea ELIADE, Gerhard van der Leeuw (1890–1950), and Gabriel MARCEL; the work in aesthetics of Roman Ingarden (1893–1970), André MALRAUX, and Michel Dufrenne (b. 1910); in psychology, the work of Ludwig Binswanger (1881–1966), R. D. Laing (1927–1989) and Rollo May (1909–1994); and in sociology, the work of Alfred Schutz (1899–1959). The reader who would like more background is referred to the standard history, Herbert Spiegelberg's *The Phenomenological Movement* (1960).

The objective of this essay is to handle these centrifugal developments so that an informative and meaningful relation can be established between phenomenology and literature. The procedure will be to describe those general features of phenomenology on which most adherents agree; to differentiate existential phenomenology from that of Husserl because its literary influence has been more pervasive; to discuss representative writers and critics influenced by phenomenological investigations; and finally to clarify phenomenology in its relationship to STRUCTURALISM, its near cousin and rival.

The concern of Husserl was to search out and establish the foundation of all knowledge. In *Logische Untersuchungen*, he sought the foundations of a pure logic and epistemology. In a series of lectures given in 1929 and first published in French as *Meditations cartésiennes* (1931; *Cartesian Meditations*, 1964), he wanted to provide the sciences with an absolute criterion of truth. But the novelty in his approach consisted in his finding this "objective" foundation in an analysis of subjective consciousness. Rather than trying to account for knowledge in the traditional ways of empiricism or idealism, Husserl analyzed consciousness phenomenologically. Empiricism had sought to account for knowledge by picturing consciousness as a *tabula rasa*, a passive receptor of sense data. Viewed as elementary units or building blocks, sense impressions were taken into the mind and then formed by "laws of association" into more complex edifices of knowledge. David Hume (1711–1776) had already demonstrated how questionable were the limits of knowledge built on such premises. Never acquiring the attribute of necessity, such knowledge remains only probable. Immanuel Kant (1724–1804), in trying to overcome this shortcoming, made consciousness constitutive and creative rather than a mere passive receiver. Because of universal categories within the human mind, Kant affirmed that some knowledge (the synthetic priori) could be established as necessarily true. His solution, however, gave to the mind static categories the operations of which were dependent on a world ruled by Euclidean geometry. These categories proved inadequate with the advent of non-Euclidean thinking. Husserl's phenomenology escaped the psychologism of empirical epistemology and the doctrine that objects of knowledge have no existence except in the mind of the perceiver. Husserl focused

specifically on phenomena. His famous phrase "to the things themselves" ("*zu den Sachen selbst*") is not to be interpreted in a naïve empirical way. It meant a return to objects as experienced by a subject. Phenomenology is a meditation on and description of experience understood always as a field wherein the subject and the object contribute equally. For Husserl, objects are given to the subject as a direct intuition, while simultaneously the subject constitutes that object in any meaning-giving act. Characterized this way, experience becomes a perceptual field, an "active receiving" that must include both the subject and the object as complementary poles. Husserl expressed this new understanding of experience in the term "intentionality." Consciousness is never an empty *I think,* a *cogito* without content. Consciousness always involves a something-thought-about, a *cogitatum*. This *consciousness-of* relationship, which posited the indissoluble union of the subject and object in experience, Husserl called intentionality and made the starting point of his philosophy.

The various other methods he introduced, such as the *epoche* (neither affirming nor denying existence), the eidetic reduction, and the phenomenological reduction need not concern us except for a general comment. The purpose of these methods was to lay bare the intentionality of consciousness by serving as an antidote to our habitual natural responses. They were to displace the usual acceptances of things as existing independently in-themselves by making us aware that things do not so exist but come into existence by and for a subject. For an object to exist at all, it has to exist as a meaning for a subject.

Scientists, those redoubtable empiricists, have been coming to much the same conclusions. The ideal of a science that has complete objectivity (i.e., being completely independent of man) was seen to be an illusion. The physicist Werner Heisenberg (1901–1976) pointed out that the subject, man, can never be separated from the object he observes. Jacob Bronowski (1908–1974), in an essay in *Scientific American* entitled "The Logic of Mind" (1966), more recently concluded with almost Husserlian overtones that "logical theorems reach decisively into the systematization of empirical science. It follows in my view that the aim that the physical sciences have set themselves since Isaac Newton's time can not be attained. The laws of nature cannot be formulated as an axiomatic, deductive, formal, and unambiguous system, which is also complete."

Although Husserl considered his philosophy a radical empiricism, he began his career as a mathematician. This may account for the abstract idealistic tendency in some of his writing. Wishing to give his philosophy (and science) access to transcendental (necessary) truths, he aimed at elucidating universal essences that underlay every intentional act. This abstracted universal, Husserl named the "transcendental ego." Many of Husserl's students refused to follow him in this very Kantian, too narrowly schematic procedure. The existential phenomenologists were the foremost dissenters.

Heidegger, in *Sein und Zeit* (1927; *Being and Time*, 1962), broadened Husserl's notion of intentionality to include the whole man, his feeling as well as his volitional and intellectual capacities. Husserl focused his analysis on reflecting consciousness; Heidegger turned more to the prereflective structures of consciousness. He defined human existence more generally as *Dasein*, or being-in-the-world. Because man is the only being who can and does ask questions about Being, this characteristic can serve to define his essential nature. Man is not another object among many but is the instrumental process whereby Being takes on meaning. Being reveals itself as meaning and culture in man's many and complex interrelations with the things-that-are. Being has no way of expressing itself other than through human existence *(Dasein)*. Ultimately, what makes meaning-giving possible is temporality, the human orientation toward past, present, and future. Temporality is not to be identified with some externally measured time like that of the clock or calendar. It is lived time, or better, the process whereby the intentional relationship (now expressed as being-in-the-world) operates. Man originates or "founds" the world he occupies with other things by projecting a future on the basis of an inherited past, one that gives meaning to the things-that-are in the present. Such temporalizing of intentionality leads to more awareness of history. If meaning-giving is a temporal process, then truth itself (the meaning of Being) becomes an open-ended, unfinished, historical affair. If there is no escape from having to work at truth from within time and history, the quest may become an absolute, but the truths so found must remain partial and relative. However much it is desired, an absolute vantage, or God's point of view, becomes an impossibility. This insight was to have a direct influence on post-World War II literary themes and techniques.

Of the two French existential phenomenologists, Sartre and Merleau-Ponty, the former influenced literature through his description of human existence as "dreadful freedom." Such themes as nausea, anxiety, abandonment, nothingness, and Promethean heroism fill his literary works. The same themes, or variations thereof, dominate the works of such writers as CAMUS, BECKETT, IONESCO and GENET.

Merleau-Ponty had more direct influence on critics than Sartre because he carried on the main epistemological concerns of phenomenology and remained far more concrete and empirical than either Husserl or Heidegger. For Merleau-Ponty, "lived experience," from which all analysis must begin, is now centered in the body. While the body is not identical with the subject, it is the instrument whereby the subject situates itself in a real world. By the same token, the body cannot be taken merely as a thing because it is the only object experienced from within. So the body becomes the perfect mediator between the subjective and objective poles of experience. Here is the location of the prereflective and prethematic consciousness. Fully conceptualized, or thematic, meaning takes its sense from its figure-background relation to the horizons of a prior "incarnated experience." Said another way, our body provides us with an opaque "lived experience," which in turn provides the content for and always precedes any disciplined study, the aim of which is to clarify this "lived experience" from a particular point of view.

Meaning thus becomes a dialectical movement of making explicit (bringing to foreground) what is only potentially and latently present to the inarticulate, embodied "cogito" (background). Embodied consciousness is not transparently clear like intellectual conceptions but needs ensuing reflections to become thematic and conceptualized. Basically, all knowledge is conscious reflection on prereflective experience constituted by the "perceptual" body-world relationship. Human existence becomes an expressive activity, and its proper functioning will be to give meaning to the objects around itself. Culture results from the sedimentation and accumulation of man's past symbolic or interpretative acts. This historical process will be never-ending, because the instrumentality whereby man has a perspective on the world is partial and the truth or insight thus obtained will be limited by the physical and historical environs of the creative individual. History, properly understood, is the record of our self-awareness of this symbolization process in which man articulates the world and simultaneously

gives himself an identity. What previously had been the special vocation of poets and artists—the creation of meaning—Merleau-Ponty (like Heidegger before him) presents as the generic function of human existence. As such, it constitutes a philosophic anthropology, a norm for existential psychoanalysis, and a guide to literary analysis.

From the perspective above, philosophy becomes an external but foredoomed quest. If no human expression can ever completely formulate absolute truth; if every interpretative act conceals at the same time as it reveals; if truth can establish itself only in terms of a momentary functional adequacy—then a certain ambiguity will perpetually trouble the meaning-giving function. For creative writers, this predicament often translates into self-torment, into making the creative process itself the theme of their writing. Treatments range from the bleakly tragic to self-mockery. In certain writers, occupational futility has become so exacerbated that they can keep going only by making a game of the technique of writing. Other writers, not so severely afflicted, circle around the problem of how difficult it is to stay undeluded about ourselves or the external world.

The theme of most of Jorge Luis BORGES's fiction, for example, is that there is no ordering principle given to the universe that is not arbitrary and open to doubt. All classification systems are provisional, and in order that their provisional character be kept in mind, Borges writes "self-destruct" stories. Because semblance tends to reduce the reader's disbelief, leading him to accept illusion for reality, Borges frequently exposes his fictions as a game. He quite deliberately postulates a state of affairs at the beginning of a story that the subsequent action shows to be completely impossible. With gentle, deft irony, Borges identifies total order with total disorientation. Since there is nothing of lasting value to reveal, the use of intelligence to create fictions becomes a nonserious game. To the skeptical Borges, meaning-giving provides an aesthetic pleasure, a playful exercise of the intellect that must never lose its provisional character.

A warm admirer of Borges, John BARTH, in his essay "The Literature of Exhaustion" (1967), has drawn parallels between his aims and the gameplaying of Borges. In place of Borges's lean intellectual style, however, Barth has developed a frivolous, baroque manner as thematically more suitable while also more protective of his sanity. Constantly interrupting his narrative, he destroys the reader's illusionary participation either by commenting on how badly the story is going or self-consciously calling attention to a technical point, usually a methodological inadequacy, raised by the content. In effect, the novel in his hands seems to be feeding on itself while entertaining the reader and overcoming the "insuperable" obstacle of seemingly having nothing to say. A confirmed optimist writing on nihilistic themes, Barth describes his efforts in *Lost in the Funhouse* (1968) thus: "The final possibility is to turn ultimacy, exhaustion, paralyzing self-consciousness, and the adjective weight of accumulated history . . . . To turn ultimacy against itself to make something new and valid, the essence whereof would be the impossibility of making something new."

With Borges and Barth, the style is most often satirical or ironical, in keeping with their playful-serious attitude. But when the dramatist Harold PINTER treats this epistemological theme, it becomes menacing. A world never totally amenable to human interpretation and control constantly threatens the security of his characters and sooner or later breaks down the feeble barriers they have raised in self-defense. In *A Slight Ache* (1959), Edward, a writer of theological and philosophical essays, believes he has the world and himself under control. But neither the objective nor the subjective areas in his formulated world retain the polished clear edges that his mind so cleverly imposes. Edward cannot keep objects in focus. His eyes give him "a slight ache." He feels threatened by a world that will not yield to his rational ordering. Silent nature weights like a heavy enigma on him; it undermines his integrative will and finally wears him down to hapless impotence. Such failure of the protagonist to control a momentarily secure position, be it physical or mental space, recurs as a fundamental motif in Pinter's plays. External contingencies or subconscious desires shatter the civilized proprieties erected by the ordering mind. To keep a grip on themselves and their shifting, unpredictable world, his characters hide behind familiar habits, clichéd language, and social rules. Unlike the effete and bloodless milieu of Beckett's plays, the characters of which talk compulsively to hide from a vacant universe, the destruction of verbal and social façades in Pinter's plays delivers his hero-victims to violence and animality.

Not all writers endure man's epistemological relations with reality with such bleak sufferance. Two representatives of a more positive attitude are Iris MURDOCH and Alain ROBBE-GRILLET. Murdoch studied and taught philosophy in England. Not attracted to English analytic philosophy, she went through a brief flirtation with existentialism out of which came a good book, *Sartre, Romantic Rationalist* (1953). Murdoch's novels lack the innovative brilliance of Robbe-Grillet's, but she shares his phenomenologically inspired conviction of the difficulties (and necessity) of maintaining objectivity with people and things.

Husserl's basic principle, "back to the things themselves," has as its corollary a special method, the *epoche*, which was to insure the purity of the starting point. Why was such bracketing needed? Because man has an inveterate tendency to project extraneous elements on the object he sees that do not belong to the object at all. The origin of these projections most often are subjective emotional states but can also be commitments to prior theories, hypotheses, and traditions that refract and distort experience. Secondly, no object is graspable from one point of view or from a single system. Thus, the external world should be an inexhaustible resource for thematic study and explication. To freeze the meaning-giving process, to objectify and subordinate it to one particular theoretical construction, would be intellectual bad faith. It leads to stagnation, dogmatic error, and fantasizing. Both Murdoch and Robbe-Grillet stress the need to escape delusion, and their novels illustrate the problematic nature of the subject-object encounter. In Murdoch's novel *Under the Net* (1954), Jake Donaghue blunders through a series of faulty relationships because of his own self-obsessions. The novel ends only when Jake recognizes that other people do not always surrender themselves to familiarity and classification; that contingency should not be feared but, indeed, embraced as a rich and complicated mystery; and that one finds self-knowledge (i.e., becomes a moral person) only through social interaction. A self-absorbed consciousness forms the greatest obstacle to seeing the world as it really is. To act justly one must perceive correctly—that is the lesson encountered in Murdoch's novels.

A similar message may be found in Robbe-Grillet's novels—although stated more obliquely. Like other writers of the New NOVEL, Robbe-Grillet experiments with inner lived time and dispenses with clock time. He writes in the present tense to communicate the immediacy of experience and presents the action rigorously through the sensibility of one protagonist. He has given up all authorial claims to omniscience and has publicly stated that as a literary device omniscience is outmoded and no longer

believable. A writer can no longer present plot, characters, motivations, setting, etc., as Balzac did, offering a world fully analyzed and understood to himself. Because there are no complete truths, no God, and no absolute standpoint, the reader must undergo the experience while it is happening to the protagonist. What the writer asks of the reader is that he expect not to "receive ready-made a world that is finished, full, and closed in on itself, but, on the contrary, to take part in a creation, to invent the work in his turn" (*Pour un nouveau roman* [1963; *For a New Novel*, 1965]).

To simulate the interior processes of thought or the latent desires of the subconscious, Robbe-Grillet juxtaposes and splices his protagonist's past memory, present reality, and future fantasies. As he never intrudes, it is up to the reader to follow these inner meanderings as best he can. Because the protagonists have abnormal sensibilities—for example, a sex pervert in *Le voyeur* (1955; *The Voyeur*, 1958); a jealous husband in *La jalousie* (1957; *Jealousy*, 1959); a wounded, feverish soldier in *Dans le labyrinthe* (1959; *In the Labyrinth*, 1960)—their inferiority distorts the real world. It is precisely this abnormal subjectivizing of the external world that Robbe-Grillet alternates with his *choisisme* (a neutral geometrical description of surfaces). His method very deliberately accentuates the gap between things neutrally observed and the emotionally charged world of his central characters. In essays, he has stated his aim to be the freeing of man from "tragic complicity," from his need to humanize nature. Robbe-Grillet insists on maintaining the exteriority and independence of the object. His minute description of surfaces is a limitation and hedge against projecting any kind of depth or preestablished order between things and the perceiver. If we can allow the object to maintain its independence, to remain hard, dry, impenetrable, and alien to our wishful thinking (as he believes they always should be), then there is hope that we can finally escape tragedy. Rather than contaminate objects with our hopes and fears, and then allow them to operate upon us with these accrued forces while forgetting the true origin of their power—we must refuse all complicity with objects. Robbe-Grillet wishes to end the chapter of literary history preoccupied with existential despair, alienation, and unhappiness by diagnosing the malaise as self-inflicted. He believes tragedy to be a conditioned response, and that the remedy lies in correct perception—"for once scraped clean, things relate only to themselves, with no chinks or crevices for us to slip into, and without causing us the least dizziness."

Phenomenology has influenced literary criticism in a variety of ways. In Europe it helped turn literary studies away from biographical and historical-background scholarship to a study of the creative process itself. Phenomenology had its profoundest effect on the criticism written by the Geneva School, which became prominent after World War II. Critics such as Marcel Raymond (1897–1956), Albert Béguin (1901–1957), Georges Poulet (1902–1992), Jean-Pierre Richard (b. 1922), and Jean Starobinski (b. 1920), all share the common methodology of viewing literature as an expression of a creative consciousness. Individual texts of one writer are analyzed as so many variants of a single subjectivity, whose controlling "project" may be abstracted and thematically rendered. The author's intentionality—the configuration of which can only be grasped by an examination of all his writing (literary and nonliterary)—becomes the object of analysis. Unlike American New Criticism (see Literary Criticism), which views the individual work as an autonomous and privileged object, the "critics of consciousness" impose no formal work-in-itself restriction upon their analyses. They may even move from considering the creative output of an individual author to speculating on the content of his historical subjectivity, which is akin to a *Zeitgeist*.

Georges Poulet, in his *Études sur le temps humain* (3 vols., 1949–64; Vol. 1 tr. as *Studies in Human Time*, 1956; Vol. 2, *La distance intérieure* [1952], tr. as *The Interior Distance*, 1959), employs such a wider framework to give organization to his discussion of individual writers. Using either approach, the critical analysis is not objective, but the result of a creative empathy that a critic achieves with a writer or with his age. "What must be reached," says Poulet, "is a subject, or a mental activity, that can be understood only by putting oneself in its place and perspective—by making it play again its role of subject in ourselves."

When Heidegger defined human existence as a being-in-the-world, he made possible an ontological realignment within humanistic studies that replaced a worn-out naturalism and idealism with a creative existentialism. In psychology, being-in-the-world offered an alternative to the reductive mechanistic theories of FREUD and the behaviorists. Man, in Heidegger's perspective, was not a mechanism controlled by his instincts. Life may be driven by psychobiological forces, but man utilizes these forces to create himself and history. With this new anthropology, existentialism developed its own psychoanalysis and therapy. Like its Freudian counterpart, it could and did analyze writers and their literary works. The Swiss psychologist Ludwig Binswanger appropriated from Heidegger the existentialia of temporality, spatiality, materiality, and so forth, and investigated how they are experienced by the patient. Psychoses and neuroses are not the effect of repressed instincts but are deviations of the a priori transcendental structure of *Dasein*. In his psychoanalysis of artists, that deviation most frequently occurring he called *Verstiegenheit* (eccentricity). Artists most often distort their spatial orientation by aiming too high, thereby losing their equilibrium; the result is a "tragic fall." Binswanger, in his monograph on Ibsen, saw the playwright successfully warding off this occupational hazard by bringing it to a catharsis via his tragic heroes.

Sartre applied existential psychoanalysis to a wide range of literary works and their writers. Invariably these critical writings are both application and substantiation of his own philosophy. Sartre wrote elaborate critical works on Baudelaire and Genet and published ten volumes of shorter essays from 1947 to 1976 under the general title *Situations*. In his philosophy, the prereflective consciousness is a pure nihilating power. Consciousness is not a thing—it is a continual projection into the future always breaking away or becoming unfastened from the solidified products and roles constituted by the creative process of the consciousness. Consciousness is, and should remain, an ongoing, spontaneous activity wholly self-transcending. Unfortunately it has a tendency to reify itself, to substantialize its activity and freeze itself into a role or object. Man, however, can never find rest as a thing or being. His essence is to be a continual nihilating movement over and beyond the limitations of any given situation.

Man is condemned to be free, but the exercise of this freedom will find its expression in and through the particularities of an individual's concrete historical situation. Sartre's critical essays present writers either as authentically questioning and moving beyond their situation, as a proper exercise of freedom in context, or as acting in bad faith, an example of botched opportunity and disobedience to the ethical imperative to be free and to make the right use of this freedom. His *Saint Genet: Comédien et martyr* (1952; *Saint Genet: Actor and Martyr*, 1963), without doubt, has

been the most successful and brilliant phenomenological treatment of a writer's consciousness written to date.

Other phenomenological critics who should be mentioned are Gaston Bachelard (1884–1962), Emil Staiger (b. 1908), Johannes Pfeiffer (b. 1902), Paul Ricœur (b. 1913), and Serge Doubrovsky (b. 1928). Not many critics within the Anglo-American tradition have affinities with Continental criticism, but Geoffrey Hartman (1929–1996), J. Hillis Miller (b. 1928), and Ihab Hassan (b. 1925) do owe a debt to phenomenology. Hartman, particularly, would seem to be the most influential and prolific phenomenological critic writing in the U. S.

Whereas phenomenology views the meaning-giving process as perception, as the intentionality of a subject toward an object, STRUCTURALISM replaces the subject-object relation with the unconscious ordering activity of the human mind. Although Claude LÉVI-STRAUSS repudiated phenomenology in *Tristes tropiques* (1955; *Tristes Tropiques*, 1964), the unconscious "depth structure" he has formulated has the same aim as the "transcendental ego" formulated by Husserl: both men wish to erect universal laws to govern the meaning-giving process. Thus, Lévi-Strauss's symbolic order and Husserl's transcendental ego share the identical aim of giving a structure to the empirical acts of each individual consciousness.

When Heidegger expanded intentionality to include the whole man, to include his feelings and volitions as well as his intelligence, his starting point, although experiential, was neither clear not articulate. It needed little for such a preconceptual, prereflective, preconscious intentionality to assume some of the attributes and function of an unconscious. For psychoanalysis, the relationship of unconscious to conscious was archaeological and one of cause to effect. For non-Sartrian phenomenology, "lived experience" became a pregnant latency needing deliverance into the light of conscious revelation. The midwife, or mediator, was the creative individual.

Structuralism changed this relationship with the unknown. Intentionality found itself displaced by a structured unconscious whose natural activity brings into equilibrium the contradictions and oppositions man encounters while interacting with the world. Structuralism may be said to have "naturalized" the reconciliation of opposites so prevalent in literary and religious discourse. Rather than locate this reconciliation in some transcendent unity, concrete universal, or supernatural personage, structuralism turns reconciliation into a natural attribute of how the mind unconsciously operates. Structuralism disregards all claims to a transcendent referent or presence that needs a consciousness to "speak" it. The ultimate realities of past philosophies, sciences, and literary visions have value not as truths but as various centers around which systems of meaning organized themselves. Now that we have become aware of the structuration that creates all meaning structures, these centers should be demythologized into their real function by ignoring their semantic reference (claims to truth). These claims only hide from view the structural activity that operates latently in all interpretative acts.

Existential phenomenology, on the other hand, still believed that human consciousness mediates an external otherness, or presence, and refused to subordinate intentionality to a timeless structured unconscious. While it did not object to language later being made the privileged model for understanding all our meaningful experiences, it upheld the preeminence of the speaking act (*parole*) over any semiological system (*langue*). Meaning-giving remained an original, individual act operating through human temporality and in need of the creative voice. For most phenomenologists, Orpheus, that ambiguous figure of success and failure, remained the archetypal representative of modern man in his precarious vocation.

The battle between the structuralists and phenomenologists over the "death of the subject" ended not because some universal unconscious mind eventually supplanted the conscious ego but because the individual ego was seen to be a historical consciousness made up of a matrix of social codes. The identity of any individual consciousness received its configuration from the number and range of the cultural codes in which it participated. The phenomenal world was no longer perceived as emerging from the interaction of an intentional subject with external neutral objects, but was described as a world that was always already interpreted, with its horizon rearranged and reorganized by those living within that horizon. In this dialogical process, individuals living in the present reinterpret the past, out of which comes the future—that is, new interpretations of world and self.

By the 1980s it had become clear that the most pervasive influence on the study of literature and culture in general was the later philosophy of Martin Heidegger. Instead of the temporal structures of human existence (*Dasein*) articulated in *Sein und Zeit*, language became the "house of Being," capable of bringing together Being with beings and providing man with authentic existence. The antithesis between subject and object is overcome in a language conceived not as an instrumentality operating upon the objects of the world but as the familiar horizon in which new worlds present themselves and allow Being to stand revealed. Language becomes both access and hindrance to Being, in any event an inescapable mediator. Whether positively or nihilistically, literary theorists followed this Heideggerian focus on language. As the French writer Julia KRISTEVA put it in the collection of her essays published in English translation as *Desire in Language* (1980): "Following upon the phenomenological and existentialist shock of the post-war period, the sixties witnessed a theoretical ebullience that could roughly be summarized as leading to the discovery of the determinative role of *language* in all human sciences." That statement applies to the philosophical hermeneutics launched by Hans-Georg Gadamer (b. 1900), especially in his *Wahrheit und Methode* (1960; *Truth and Method*, 1975), and which was subsequently developed into *Rezeptionsästhetik* by Hans Robert Jauss (b. 1921) and Wolfgang Iser (b. 1926). It also applies to the "deconstructive philosophy" of Jacques DERRIDA, whose three books, *De la grammatologie* (1967; *Of Grammatology*, 1976), *La voix et le phénomène* (1967; *Speech and Phenomena*, 1973), and *L'écriture et la différence* (1967; *Writing and Difference*, 1978), helped turn "scientific" structuralism into poststructuralism, a semiology of historical consciousness.

Hans-Georg Gadamer, Michel FOUCAULT, and Jacques Derrida all follow Heidegger in making language central to any understanding of human existence. All of the human sciences have become interpretive not of "phenomena" but of "meanings" seen as cultural products whose social existence have their beginnings and continuation in shared conventions or traditions. Thus, phenomenology as name or program is not often met with in current literary study; however, most of the diverging critical schools of hermeneutics, poststructuralism, *Rezeptionsästhetik*, semiotics, or reader-response operate in what can only be called a phenomenological ambience.

BIBLIOGRAPHY: Müller-Vollmer, K., *Towards a Phenomenological Theory of Literature* (1963); Duroche, L. L., *Aspects of Criticism* (1967); Lawall, S., *Critics of Consciousness* (1968); Hartman, G., *Beyond Formalism* (1970); Hassan, I., *The Dismemberment of Orpheus* (1971); Heidegger, M., *Poetry, Language, Thought* (1972); Ingarden, R., *The Literary Work of Art* (1973); Doubrovsky, S., *The New Criticism in France* (1973); Ricœur, P., *The Conflict of Interpretations* (1974); Spanos, W., ed., *Martin Heidegger and the Question of Literature* (1976); Magliola, R. R., *Phenomenology and Literature* (1977); Iser, W., *The Act of Reading* (1978); Amacher, R., and V. Lange, eds., *New Perspectives in German Literary Criticism* (1979); Tompkins, J. P., ed., *Reader-Response Criticism* (1980)

—VERNON GRAS

PHILIPPIDE, Alexandru

Romanian poet, short-story writer, essayist, and translator, b. 1 April 1900, Iași; d. 8 Feb. 1979, Bucharest

Son and namesake of a well-known linguist, classmate and lifelong friend of the writer Barbu Fundoianu (1898–1944; also known as Benjamin Fondane), P. studied law at the University of Iași, and also studied in Berlin and Paris. In Paris, Fundoianu introduced him into avant-garde circles. Upon his return to Romania he served in the Ministries of Foreign Affairs and Propaganda from 1929 to 1947.

P. began his career as a poet in 1919 with contributions to *Viața românească* in Iași and quickly became a principal in that circle. Through his friendship with Cezar Petrescu (1892–1961) he also collaborated with Gândirea (or Gîndirea), the postwar literary and philosophical movement attempting to define and express the Romanian genius—until its break with the Iași group in 1929.

His first collection of verse, *Aur sterp* (1922; barren gold), showed the influence of SYMBOLISM and a fondness for the neoromantic dream motif. *Stînci fulgerate* (1930; lightning-struck rocks) expressed violent states of mind. *Visuri în vuietul vremii* (1939; dreams amid the roar of time), uninhibitedly lyrical but also increasingly cerebral, continued philosophical queries about life and death.

His collection of tales, *Floarea de prăpastie* (1942; the flower of the precipice), blended realistic detail and the fantastic, fluctuating between infernal and paradisiac settings and Romanian townscapes.

After his blacklisting by the communist regime, and during a long hiatus, P. gave his attention to translation and collecting his earlier verse, which with the thaw of 1963 he was able to publish as *Poezii* (Short Poems) in 1964. In 1963 he was rehabilitated with election to the Romanian Academy. In 1967, however, his *Monolog in Babylon* (Monologue in Babylon) appeared, probably his masterpiece, introducing an original mythology with terrifying Dantesque landscapes and a luminous paradisiac space, reflecting an existential concern with pessimism, monstrosity, and decadence, with allegorical allusions to cultural and political conditions in Romania. In 1977 he was awarded the Grand Prize in Poetry by the Writers' Union. The posthumously published *Vis și căutare* (1979; Dream and Search) presented eighteen poems from over a half century as well as some recent verse.

P.'s translations and much of his criticism focused on writers who most affected his own work, principally German romantics, Poe, Baudelaire, and RILKE. Other essays attempted to formulate a Romanian modernism. *Considerații confortabile* (2 vols., 1970, 1972; comfortable considerations) was a series of aphorisms.

All of P.'s work is distinguished by a classicist regard for artistic discipline; romantic idealism, pathos, and love of the fantastic; and modernist techniques. Essentially his work is a Faustian search for answers about the destiny and purpose of man. Its images are oneiric, often morbid or demonic, but never sordid or ugly.

FURTHER WORKS: *Studii şi portrete literare* (1963); *Studii de literatură universală* (1966); *Scriitorul şi arta lui* (1968); *Puncte cardinale europene: Orizont romantic* (1973); *Flori de poezie străină răsădite în româeşte* (1973); *Scrieri: Studii şi eseuri* (1978)

BIBLIOGRAPHY: Eulert, D. and Avădanei, S., eds., *Modern Romanian Poetry* (1973): 88–91; Gibescu, G. "A. P.," *Romanian Bulletin*, 5, 8 (1976): 6–7; Teodorescu, A., and Bantaş, A., eds., *Romanian Essayists of Today* (1979): 59–61; Balota, N., *Introducere in opera lui A. P.* (1974); Arion, G., *A. P., sau, Drama unicitatii: incercare de portret unicitatii* (1982); Avramut, H., *A. P.: la rascrucile memoriei* (1984)

—THOMAS AMHERST PERRY

PHILIPPINE LITERATURE

For twenty years before the outbreak of the revolution of 1896, Filipinos who favored civil reform and freedom without independence published novels and newspapers in Spanish and directed them hopefully at liberals in Madrid and Barcelona. Among these were the essays of Marcelo H. del Pilar (1850–1896) and Graciano Lopez-Jaena (1856–1896), and the panoramic, accusatory novels of José Rizal (1861–1896), *Noli me tangere* (1887; *The Lost Eden*, 1961) and *El filibusterismo* (1891; *The Subversive*, 1962), which cast shadows of excellence far into the 20th c.

Yet, with the end of the Spanish-American War in 1898, virtually all Spanish literature as well as political influence ceased. Rearguard critics sometimes speak of the first half of the new century as the "golden age" of Philippine literature in Spanish. However, aside from Jesús Balmori's (pseud.: Batikuling, 1886–1948) nationalistic lyric poetry—*Rimas malayas* (1904; Malayan verses) and *Mi casa de nipa* (1941; my house made of palm leaves)—and the poems of Claro Recto (1890–1960) in *Bajo los cocoteros* (1911; under the coconut trees) and his play *Solo entre las sombras* (1917; alone among the shadows), and occasional speeches left by Recto and President Manuel Quezon (1878–1944), little that is comparable with the end-of-century flowering can be discovered. Less biased historians record, instead, a prolonged cultural pause before general education in English, which replaced education of the elite in Spanish, could produce its own literature and, by example, elevate literature in the vernacular as well.

The beginning of commonwealth status in 1935, with anticipation of full independence after ten years, gave special urgency to the search for a national identity among people with varied cultural and linguistic backgrounds. Although this was also the year of the founding of the Institute of National Language, which made Tagalog the core of various composite vernaculars, at least temporarily Filipinos found in English rather than native languages and

literary traditions the same creative challenge that Spanish once brought.

To assert some kind of continuity between otherwise alienated generations, the works of Nick JOAQUIN have attempted to recover the moral and religious orientation, which constitute the most enduring aspect of the Spanish heritage. Aside from several imitations of late-medieval saintly legends and random essays, his concern has been less with the past re-created than with its modern vestiges. Joaquin's short story "Three Generations," in *Prose and Poems* (1952), reveals irrevocable family resemblances—a rigorous Spanish sense of kinship—even in the midst of recurrent revolt against family pieties. Other stories, such as "The Summer Solstice," also in *Prose and Poems*, find in Filipinos counterparts of Spanish ambivalences: primitivistic sensuousness and Christian asceticism. His 1952 omnibus volume also contains the play *Portrait of the Artist as Filipino*, in which descendants of the declining Don Lorenzo finally confirm his inborn integrity by their own. Despite impoverishment, they refuse to sell the masterpiece which he has painted for them and which depicts Anchises being borne like a household god from burning Troy. The faces of son and father are identical. Joaquin has depicted the Filipino's need to take the burden of history on his back. However, Aeneas was not only deliverer of the past but founder of the future: and Joaquin's novel *The Woman Who Had Two Navels* (1961) respects but does not admire without qualification the ex-revolutionary, Monson, who hides in Hong Kong exile, afraid to face the trials of postwar independence.

The Spanish past is viewed with an equally discriminating eye in *The Peninsulars* (1964), Linda TY-CASPER's novel of the confusion of loyalties that made possible British occupation of Manila in the mid-18th c. Each figure of colonial authority—even those with the highest concern for the ruled—has some imperfection of motive, some overriding personal ambition that maims his magistracy. However, the *indios* too (as Spaniards called the natives) are torn between national loyalties and self-interest. Only the dying governor-general and the *indio* priest Licaros achieve a sufficient understanding of the need for mutual dependence: on one level, love; on another, the social contract. Such a novel represents an increasingly selective salvaging, by the Philippine writer, of his various usable pasts. Similarly, Ty-Casper's novel *The Three-Cornered Sun* (1979) depicts the revolution of 1896 as a series of individually motivated acts rather than as an orchestrated uprising guided by national purpose. Its sequel *Ten Thousand Seeds* (1987) continues tracing the events which led to the Philippine-American war (1899–1902) after the United States decided to retain possession of the islands they had expected to liberate. That change in national policy is experienced through the gradually enlightened eyes of an American couple honeymooning in Manila during the aftermath of the Spanish American War.

The epic impulse, the concern with rendering history as meaningful fable, has shaped the writings of poets such as Ricaredo Demetillo (b. 1920) and Alejandrino Hufana (b. 1926). *Barter in Panay* (1961) represents the first portion of Demetillo's verse adaptation of the Visayan folktale *Maragtas*, about ten groups led by *datus* (chiefs) who, in 1212, fled tyranny in Brunei. Its twenty-one cantos explain the peaceful arrangement between *Datu* Puti and the pygmy Negrito inhabitants of Panay island; and begin to explore the lust of Guronggurong for *Datu* Sumakwel's young wife, which was to test intimately the new rules of social order. Demetillo's verse–play sequel, *The Heart of Emptiness Is Black*

(1975) suggests how only love can reconcile personal desire and impersonal social codes.

Hufana's early volume *Sickle Season* (1959) deals with this same theme of the one and the many but is less restricted historically: for it, he invented Geron Munar, timeless Malayan wanderer and culture hero, mirrored in many facsimiles throughout Philippine history, legend, and myth. In *Poro Point: An Anthology of Lives* (1961), Hufana substituted for Munar personae from the author's tribal family, all Ilocanos, who, as the most migrant of Filipinos, epitomize both their countrymen's unity and their diversity.

The Philippine dream of a national identity compatible with an open, pluralistic society, evident in such adaptations from ethnohistory, has been tested severely even by Bienvenido N. Santos (b. 1911), sometimes considered a sentimentalist. The Philippine expatriates in his story collection *You Lovely People* (1956), caught in the U.S. by World War II, long passionately to return to their kinfolk. In the aftermath of war, however, many discover their homeland changed, their loved ones not inviolable; and, disillusioned, some retreat into exile once more. Similarly, his second collection, *Brother, My Brother* (1960), and his two novels, *Villa Magdalena* (1965) and *The Volcano* (1965), continue to rely on the imagery of rejection and return. However far ambition takes his characters from the ancestral home that once seemed to deprive them of personal potential, that home remains the place of least loneliness; and no satisfactory sense of self is found outside one's native community. How that problem is exacerbated among "overseas Filipinos" is encapsulated in his collection *Scent of Apples* (1979) as well as in his novels, *The Praying Man* (1982), *The Man Who (Thought He) Looked Like Robert Taylor* (1983), and *What the Hell for You Left Your Heart in San Francisco* (1987). Santos's constant affection for the common *tao* required that he describe also the growing abuse of Filipinos by their fellow countrymen, epitomized by the increased centralization of power during the prolonged rule of Ferdinand Marcos (1965-86).

Although all major Philippine writers may be said to be searching for those constants that define their identity as a people, many have avoided the historical/epic modes and have confined themselves to fundamentally agrarian aspects that are continuous in their culture. Their fiction maintains a slowness of pace and cautious simplicity appropriate to the sacred, seasonal mysteries of timeless folkways, as well as to the patient, modern search for reassurance. That pace is represented in Francisco Arcellana's (b. 1916) peasant/working-class sketches, *15 Stories* (1973), characterized by Scriptural simplicity and cyclic repetition. Manuel Arguilla (1910-1944), in the rural tales collected in *How My Brother Leon Brought Home a Wife* (1940), undercuts folk romanticism with the realism of social protest as he engages the causes of the Sakdal uprisings among tenant farmers during the 1930s. Similarly, N. V. M. GONZALEZ's tales of the frontier country, the *kaingin* (cultivated clearing burned out of forest land) ricelands— *Seven Hills Away* (1947); *Children of the Ash-Covered Loam* (1954)—as well as the novel *A Season of Grace* (1956), reveal both the hardships and enduring self-possession of his tradition-centered pioneers. In his collection *Look, Stranger, on This Island Now* (1963) the *kainginero* enjoys a kind of consoled loneliness when compared with the peasant who has migrated to the metropolis; and his restricted life is far more meaningful than that of the sophisticated *ilustrado* (a member of the "enlightened," intellectual elite) who is the protagonist of the novel *The Bamboo Dancers* (1959), a homeless international wanderer.

The provincial's life is a trial, even in Carlos Bulosan's (1914–1956) humorous tales in *The Laughter of My Father* (1941), which were intended as a satiric indictment of sharecropping penury. At the same time, Bulosan expresses admiration for the good humor, love, and other humane virtues that survive the peasant's near-penal conditions.

This capacity to endure marks each of the four major Philippine war novels—Stevan Javellana's (b. 1918) *Without Seeing the Dawn* (1947); Juan Laya's (1911–1952) *This Barangay* (1950); and Edilberto Tiempo's (b. 1917) *Watch in the Night* (1953) and *More than Conquerors* (1964)—all of them, appropriately, stories of small-scale, rural, guerrilla action supported by a kind of primitive communal interdependence.

When this close group identity is sacrificed by the ambitious provincial migrant to the city, he suffers from the anonymity of mass living without his poverty's lessening measurably. Only occasionally is adequate human warmth rediscovered among slum dwellers, as in the stories of Estrella Alfon (b. 1917)—*Magnificence* (1960)—and Andres Cristobal Cruz (b. 1929) and Pacifico Aprieto (b. 1929)—*Tondo by Two*, 1961; or in Alberto Florentino's (b. 1931) *The World Is an Apple, and Other Prize Plays* (1959).

Far less sympathy is directed toward other urban classes. The pretensions of the nouveaux riches are constantly satirized in Gilda Cordero-Fernando's (b. 1930) collections of stories *The Butcher, the Baker, the Candlestick Maker* (1962) and *A Wilderness of Sweets* (1973); as well as Wilfrido Guerrero's (b. 1917) four volumes of plays (1947, 1952, 1962, 1976). Movement from a rural area to suburbia involves risking loss of character. The consequences of social mobility unaccompanied by maturing morality are more savagely exposed in the novels of Kerima Polotan-Tuvera (b. 1925)—*The Hand of the Enemy* (1962)—and of F. Sionil Jose (b. 1924)—*The Pretenders* (1962). In both instances, the mountaineer or uprooted rural peasant is corrupted by industrialism and the new self-seeking elite, just as the agrarian revolts at the turn of the century allegedly were betrayed by the *ilustrados*, first to the Spaniards and later to the Americans. This tension between classes is central in Jose's ongoing series of novels about Rosales, an imaginary northern town: *Tree* (1978) and *My Brother, My Executioner* (1979). Social discrimination finds its parallel in the oppression of women in Polotan-Tuvera's *Stories* (1968). Wilfrido Nolledo's (b. 1933) *But for the Lovers* (1970), a parable of wartime grotesques awaiting liberation, suggests a similar situation for the masses mutilated by the forces of leftist radicals and of government by martial law.

Because, like Rizal's novels before them, they constitute assessments of agrarian values during decades of challenging cultural transition, such works will always be of historical value regardless of what other Philippine literatures emerge in the vernaculars. Even Jose Garcia VILLA's poetry, which, beginning with *Many Voices* (1939), has been criticized for not focusing on national concerns but rather offering disembodied Blakean encounters between God and the luminous poet, are in some ways relevant to the Philippine experience. Villa's dependence on devices of negation and rejection, the nearly solipsistic alienation of the protagonist, at least parallel the national passion for self-determination and the overcompensatory self-enlargement of a people reduced to colonial status for centuries.

For inventiveness and for dynamic selfhood in revolt, the counterpart of Villa in Pilipino (Tagalog) is A. G. Abadilla (1905–1969), whose volumes include *Piniling mga tula* (1965; selected poems). Sometimes as antagonist, sometimes as complement, his name is juxtaposed with the socialistically inclined Amado V. Hernandez (1903–1970), a labor leader and later premier writer in the vernacular. With his prize play *Muntinlupa* (1958; tight place; also the name of a national prison), his poems in *Isang dipang langit* (1961; a stretch of sky), and his novel *Mga ibong mandaragit* (1965; birds of prey), Hernandez revived the polemical tradition of the 19th c. and recapitulated the social protest evident in Lope K. Santos's (1879–1963) earlier novel *Banaag at sikat* (1906; false dawn and sunrise). Together with Andres Cristobal Cruz (b. 1929), author of the novel *Sa Tundo, may langit din* (1961; even in Tondo the sun shines) and the contributors to the short fiction collection *Agos sa diyerta* (1965; oasis in the desert), these writers, by avoiding the sentimentality and floridity of vernacular conventions, have made Pilipino equal to English as a reputable instrument for self-discovery.

Those conventions, derived from centuries of reducing literary function to either moral indoctrination or pure emotional expressiveness, have proven more resistant in the case of other vernacular literatures. Zarzuelas, for example, introduced as a form of concealed protest under the American occupation, deteriorated before 1930 into either musical comedies or melodramas. This predisposition toward literature as either instruction or entertainment, reinforced by the dearth of book publication and reliance on serialization of magazine fiction, has kept minimal the number of vernacular models equivalent in seriousness to their English counterparts. These would include, in the Bisayan languages, the novels of Magdalena Jalandoni (1893–1980) in the 1920s and 1930s, the political sketches of Vicente Sotto (1877–1950) throughout the 1920s, Buenaventura Rodriguez's (1893–1941) plays *Ang mini* (1921; counterfeit man) and *Pahiyum* (1935; a smile), and the prewar poetic experiments of Vicente Ranudo (1883–1930), as well as the sampling of breakthrough pieces in the 1967 anthology by the Lubasan group; and in Iloko, the early-20th-c. plays of Mena Pecson Crisologo (1844–19??), especially *Natakneng a panagsalisal* (n.d.; noble rivalry), which concerns the Philippine-American War (1898–1902), and Marcelino Pena Crisologo's (1866–1923) novel *Pinang* (1915; Pinang).

During the oppressive twenty-year rule of Marcos, the strategy of concealed protest used once by vernacular writers against foreign powers was borrowed by writers in English, to expose "internal colonialism" of Filipino by Filipino. Fiction became a subtle substitute for endangered journalistic reportage. Novels that resulted included *State of War* (1988) and *Twice Blessed* (1993) by Ninotchka Rosca (b. 1946); *Dogeaters* (1990) by Jessica Hagedorn (b. 1949); and *Awaiting Trespass* (1985), *Wings of Stone* (1986), and *A Small Party in a Garden* (1988) by Ty-Casper. Though Marcos in 1986 fled into exile and died in Hawaii, the restored voice of protest among writers became a warning against any similar abuse in the future, while their craftsmanship reinforced their seriousness.

BIBLIOGRAPHY: Bernad, M., *Bamboo and the Greenwood Tree* (1963); Del Castillo, T., and B. Medina, Jr., *Philippine Literature* (1964); Casper, L., *New Writing from the Philippines: An Anthology and a Critique* (1966); Manuud, A., ed., *Brown Heritage: Essays on Philippine Cultural Tradition and Literature* (1967); Galdon, J., ed., *Philippine Fiction* (1972); Mojares, R., *Cebuano Literature* (1975); Galdon, J., ed. *Essays on the Philippine Novel in English* (1979); Galdon, J., ed., *Salimbibig: Philippine Vernacular Literature* (1980); Mojares, R., *Origins and Rise of the Filipino Novel* (1983); Casper, L., *Sunsurfers Seen from Afar: Literary Essays 1991–1996* (1996)

—LEONARD CASPER

PHILLIPS, Caryl

English novelist and essayist, b. 13 Mar. 1958, St. Kitts, West Indies

P. was born in St. Kitts, West Indies in 1958, and in that same year his family moved to England where P. was reared in Leeds. P. went on to attend Oxford University. Celebrated as one of the leading young novelists of Britain, P. has published six novels, screenplays as well as stage and radio plays, and two important books of nonfiction. P. moved back to St. Kitts during the early 1990s and then on to teach in New York.

P.'s six novels reveal a writer of wide-reaching imagination with a literary project that seeks to explore the complex dynamic between the world of the colonizer and that of the colonized. But P.'s work does not fall easily into the realm of the typical Fanonesque postcolonial novel that establishes a simple manichaeism in the relationship between the colonized and the colonizer. Instead, P. reveals the complicated interdependency of these two groups and creates fiction that seeks above everything else to examine the naunaced relationship between two worlds and two strangely related conceptions of the meaning of human existence. P.'s writing style is almost always restrained and relies completely on the subtlety of well-constructed irony. His novels have become increasingly fragmented pieces of narrative that juxtapose characters from vastly different backgrounds and time periods in fictional episodes that daringly leap the fences of history to create a fabric of ideas.

In *A State of Independence* (1986), an early novel, P. defers the themes of slavery that will occupy his imagination in the seminal novels *Higher Ground* (1989) and *Cambridge* (1991) to recall a brief moment of self-revelation and uncertainty in the life of a character, Franci Bertram, who returns to his homeland of St. Kitts, having left the island twenty years before when he was nineteen, and arriving on the eve of that country's independence from England. Bertram is seeking his own independence, but it is clear that like that of the island, his independence is an illusion. A quality of quiet hopelessness pervades this novel that offers a sometimes caustic take on the Americanization of West Indian society, and that further exposes the nature of power's corruption among the political elite of that world. P.'s character is a failed individual without a home, without a place to call his own. In this sense P. is capturing the tortured uncertainty that surrounds the life of the British-born black who seeks a sense of belonging in the world of his parent's homeland, but finds that he does not belong to either space.

P., like many British-based black writers of the 1980s and 1990s, sees this sense of rootlessness as a kind of asset, a trope that allows him to explore ideas and themes that are sometimes unlikely fodder for a West Indian writer. It is in this sense that we must understand that P. represents a new and dominant West Indian voice—a voice of a new generation of West Indian writers that is shaping the next phase of writing from that part of the world. It is the writer of the West Indian diaspora who, somewhat divorced from the traditions of West Indian life, proceeds to write about the world of Britain (or America or Canada) from a perspective of critical ownership. Western civilization, then, becomes a space in which such a writer feels able to construct fictions of force and importance.

In *The Nature of Blood* (1998) P.'s cast of characters and shifting narratives reveal this tendency to regard the entire world view as part of his canvas. In this novel he creates a pastiche of scenarios that allow him to challenge the notions of "tribal ownership" that have come to trouble the business of imaginative writing. P. writes the novel in the voice of a Jewish girl from a 1940s concentration camp. Indeed, most of the protagonists in this work are Jewish and they include Jews from 15th-c. Venice (in a sequence that plays with the Othello narrative) and an Ethiopian Jew in modern Israel. Atypical for a West Indian novel, *The Nature of Blood* represents a shift in the freedom of the West Indian writer to explore themes that fall out of the traditional mold of anticolonialist discourse. But P.'s theoretical practice is broader and perhaps more sensible than the strict anticolonial rhetoric, for he wisely recognizes that the politics of colonial oppression reside in the larger question of Western concerns about nationalism, race, and tribalism.

It was *Crossing the River* (1993) that drew the greatest critical attention of all P.'s novels. In this work P.'s sense of the history of slavery is acutely realized, and it reveals again a broader sense of the nature and shape of slavery and the instinct towards retrieving a sense of the past among those of the African diaspora in the 20th c. The narrative is seemingly simple, a story of a man who is forced to sell his children into slavery and the complicated attempt by those enslaved to find their way back to a sense of home and belonging. Set in Africa, the U.S., and on the ocean that divides these worlds, what makes the novel stand out is P.'s ability to take a narrative that leaps across time and geographies and still construct a magical text that seems completely naturalistic. P.'s skill lies in the sheer control of his craft and the ambition of his agendas. *Crossing the River* was short listed in 1993 for the Booker Prize and received stunning reviews from critics on both sides of the Atlantic.

It is his novel *Cambridge*, however, that many regard as P.'s classic work. *Cambridge* establishes P.'s literary daring by its intriguing revisiting of the West Indian novel as a text that tries to explore the complexities of slave society and the society of the enslaver. Instead of exploring all of this through themes of the enslaved, P. takes advantage of his position at the center of the colonizing engine to construct a narrative that is "seen" through the eyes of a thirty-year-old English woman who goes to the West Indies to observe the running of her plantation. Much of the novel is told through her journal entries that seek to understand the experience of the blacks of that island through a strange amoral sensibility. But the narrative is also about a slave who has moved through several names—Olurride, Thomas, David, Cambridge—and whose relationship with this woman reveals the complex and tragic truth of a society that is shaped and driven by the business of slavery. P.'s novels are an interesting study in the business of voice, and there is a great deal here to suggest that his works amount to related stories that find novelistic unity in their capacity to construct ironies of image, metaphor, and theme rather than as novels of conventional trajectory.

P. has been widely celebrated as one of the more important novelists of the late 20th c. A writer given to careful research and an inclination to pull together the varied histories of his characters in language that is always seeking to capture the tone and mood of the culture, P. is a compelling storyteller whose writing constitutes a new direction in writing from the Caribbean.

FURTHER WORKS: *Strange Fruit* (1981); *The European Tribe* (1993); *The Final Passage* (1995); *Higher Ground: A Novel in Three Parts* (1995); *Nature of Blood* (1997); *Extravagant Strangers: A Literature of Belonging* (1997)

BIBLIOGRAPHY: Bell, R. C., "Worlds Within: An Interview with C. P.," *Callaloo*, 14 (1991): 578-606; Swift, G., "C. P.," *BOMB*, 38 (1992): 32-35; O'Callaghan, E., "Historical Fiction and Fictional History: C. P.'s *Cambridge*," *JCL*, 29 (1993): 34-47; Davison, C. M., "Crisscrossing the River: An Interview with C. P.," *ArielE*, 25 (1994): 91-99; Tiffin, C., and A. Lawson, eds., *De-Scribing Empire: Post-Colonialism and Textuality* (1994); Okazaki, H., "'Dis/Location and Connectedness' in C. P.," *JWIL*, 6 (1994): 88-96; Ledent, B., "Overlapping Territories, Intertwined Histories: Cross Culturality in C. P.'s *Crossing the River*," *JCL*, 30 (1995): 55-62; Birbalsingh, F., ed., *Frontiers of Caribbean Literatures in English* (1996)

—KWAME DAWES

PICCOLO, Lucio

Italian poet, b. 27 Oct. 1901, Palermo; d. 26 May 1969, Capo d'Orlando

P. was a member of one of the most distinguished Sicilian families and an accomplished musician and scholar. Little is known of his early life. He lived a rather cloistered life, reading extensively in classical and modern languages. His interest in the occult drew him to the works of W. B. YEATS, with whom he corresponded regularly.

In 1954, in the company of his cousin, Prince Giuseppe Tomasi di LAMPEDUSA, he met Eugenio MONTALE, who recognized P.'s talent as a poet and helped make him known. In 1956 he won the Chianciano Prize for poetry, and his reputation as a genuine and significant voice in Italian literature was established.

Religious belief, vast erudition, and an extraordinary musical sense are the hallmarks of P.'s artistry. Three thin, highly polished volumes constitute this accomplished poet's complete oeuvre: *Canti barocchi* (1956; baroque songs), *Gioco a nascondere* (1960; hide and seek), and *Plumelia* (1967; Plumelia). All his works could appropriately have been called "canti barocchi"—not "baroque" in the historical sense but as an eternal impulse of the human spirit, as an awareness of living in a world of contrasting realities—both atavistic instincts and ideas expressed through imagination and dreams.

P.'s persona is a "voice" recounting impressions, taking the multiplicity of experiences and reducing them to an undifferentiated unity of color and music. All images, all sensations are gradually transformed into incorporeal light and sound. His images, deriving from the depths of the unconscious, become visions of transfigured reality: wisps of smoke and sunbeams acquire human forms; playing cards set themselves in motion; gusts of wind become whispering voices. P.'s poetic creation is a fluctuating play between matter and spirit. Past and present coalesce. Just as the rose of June in one of his poems encompasses all the colors and fragrances that all Marches, Aprils, and Mays of the past have meticulously concocted, so, too, the poet sings with voices that come to him from past poetic experiences.

P.'s poetic instrument does not have many chords, but his voice has an extraordinary distinctiveness, and his presence in many anthologies of modern poetry is well deserved.

FURTHER WORKS: . FURTHER WORKS IN ENGLISH: *The Collected Poems of L. P.* (1972)

BIBLIOGRAPHY: Lopez, G., "The Leopard Nobody Saw," *TQ*, 14 (1971): 94–97; Cambon, G., Foreword, and E. Montale, Afterword to *The Collected Poems of L. P.* (1972): 3-9, 197-205; Ricciardelli, M., "A Baroque Life: An Interview with L. P.," *BA*, 47 (1973): 39–50; Iannace, G. A., on *The Collected Poems of L. P., FI*, 9 (1974): 312–17; Barolini, H., "The Birth, Death, and Re-life of a Poet: L. P.," *YR*, 65 (1976): 194–202

—GAETANO A. IANNACE

PIEYRE DE MANDIARGUES, André

French novelist, poet, essayist, dramatist, and art critic, b. 14 March 1909, Paris

P. de M.'s scholarly preparation includes literary studies at the Sorbonne and research in archaeology and Etruscan civilization at the University of Perugia, Italy. Extensive travels in Mexico, Europe, and the Mediterranean countries sustained P. de M.'s passion for the unconventional, the incongruous, the bizarre. Since poor health exempted him from military service during World War II, P. de M. spent that time writing in Monaco. After the war, he became associated with André BRETON and other SURREALIST writers and painters, sharing their interest in eroticism and the fantastic. Painting has played an important role in his personal and literary life, and he has written numerous exhibition catalogues and introductions to art books, including those of his wife, Bona, an Italian painter.

The themes that appear throughout P. de M.'s work are present in his first collection of fiction, *Dans les années sordides* (1943; in the sordid years). He created seaside landscapes, artificial grottoes, and dreamlike caverns peopled with anthropomorphic insects. He pursued the idea of the macrocosm reflected in the microcosm by portraying miniaturized naked women performing erotic rituals, hands tied behind their backs. And he revealed his fascination with colors, rites of initiation, the four elements, and blood and violence as they relate to sexuality, death, and regeneration.

These motifs reappear not only in M.'s major collections of short stories, such as *Le musée noir* (1946; the dark museum) and *Feu de braise* (1959; *Blaze of Embers*, 1971), but in his poetry as well. His first volume of poems, written in the 1940s but published in 1961, *L'âge de craie* (the age of chalk), takes its title from the pockmarked chalk cliffs of the Normandy coast where he spent summers as a child.

The sea figures prominently in P. de M.'s fiction. In *Le lis de mer* (1956; *The Girl beneath the Lion*, 1958), a novella of passionate intensity in which two young women go on vacation to Sardinia, the island becomes a sanctuary for the god Pan. The heroine plans her own ritualistic deflowering in a clearing by the sea, and the young man who silently performs the rite introduces her to nature as a "Pan-ic" experience. Thus P. de M. consciously relates eroticism to communion with the physical universe.

Color symbolism, particularly as it refers to black, white, and red, appears frequently in P. de M.'s work. In addition to representing alchemical substances and processes, these colors are emblematic of the Nazi flag in the novel *La motocyclette* (1963; *The Motorcycle*, 1965), in which the protagonist makes a fatal trip from France to Germany to see her lover, who had given her a motorcycle as a gift.

P. de M. began to achieve wide recognition when he received the Goncourt Prize for *La marge* (1967; *The Margin*, 1969). In this novel he spins an intricate web of references and symbols around the themes of life, desire, and death. Although he is not conventionally religious, M. decries modern materialism and seeks to reestablish correspondences between the worlds of the flesh and the spirit. This he achieves by subtly evoking arcane rituals, tarot representations, numerology, alchemy, astrology, and other esoteric lore.

P. de M. has published two plays, *Isabella Morra* (1973; Isabella Morra), and *La nuit séculaire* (1979; the last night of the century), as well as a number of translations of drama and poetry. *Le belvédère* (1958; the belvedere), *Le deuxième belvédère* (1962; the second belvedere), and *Le troisième belvédère* (1971; the third belvedere) are collections of essays dedicated to places, poets, and painters. He also wrote a sado-erotic novel in 1951 but published it only in 1979: *L'anglais décrit dans le château fermé* (the Englishman described within the enclosed chateau).

P. de M. continues the "fantastic tale" tradition of the 18th and 19th cs. His quasi-baroque narratives, rich with recondite allusions, will continue to beguile readers with their beautiful style and their multiple levels of significance.

FURTHER WORKS: *Les masques de Léonor Fini* (1951); *Soleil des loups* (1951); *Marbre* (1953); *Les monstres de Bomarzo* (1957); *Le cadran lunaire* (1958); *Sugaï* (1960); *L'âge de craie, suivi de Hédéra* (1961); *La marée* (1962); *Sabine* (1963); *Saint-John Perse: À l'honneur de la chair* (1963); *Astyanax, précédé de Les incongruités monumentales, et suivi de Cartolines et dédicaces* (1964); *Le point ùu j'en suis, suivi de Dalila exaltée et de La nuit l'amour* (1964); *Porte dévergondée* (1965); *Bcylamour* (1965); *Les corps illuminés*, photographies de Frédéric Barzilay (1965); *Larmes de généraux*, lithographies de Baj (1965); *Critiquettes*, eau-forte de Bona (1967); *Ruisseau des solitudes, suivi de Jacinthes et de Chapeaugaga* (1968); *Le marronier* (1968); *La magnanerie de La Ferrage*, gravures sur linoléum de Magnelli (1969); *Le lièvre de la lune*, eaux-fortes de Baj (1970); *Eros solaire*, dessins érotiques, lithographies d'André Masson (1970); *Bona l'amour et la peinture* (1971); *Mascarets* (1971); *La nuit de mil neuf cent quatorze* (1971); *Croiseur noir*, eaux-fortes de Wilfredo Lam (1972); *Miranda, suivi de La spirale*, eaux-fortes de Miró (1973); *Terre érotiques*, lithographies d'André Masson (1974); *Chagall* (1975); *Le désordre de la mémoire* (1975); *Parapapilloneries*, lithographies de Meret Oppenheim (1976); *Sous la lame* (1976); *Des jardins enchantés*, lithographies de Franco Gentilini (1977); *Arcimboldo le merveilleux* (1977); *Le trésor cruel de Hans Bellmer* (1979); *L'ivre œil, suivi de Croiseur noir et de Passage de l'Égyptienne* (1979)

BIBLIOGRAPHY: Temmer, M., "A. P. de M.," *YFS*, 31 (1964): 99–104; Haig, S., "A. P. de M. and 'Les pierreuses,'" *FR*, 39

(1965): 275–80; Robin, A., "A. P. de M.; ou, L'initiation panique," CS, 52 (1965): 138–50: 295–313; Campanini, S., "Alchemy in P. de M.'s 'Le diamant,'" *FR*, 50 (1977): 602–9; Bond, D., "A. P. de M.: Some Ideas on Art," *RR*, 70 (1979): 69–79; Lowrie, J., "The *Rota Fortunae* in P. de M.'s *La motocyclette*," *FR*, 53, (1980): 378–88

—JOYCE O. LOWRIE

PIGLIA, Ricardo

Argentine novelist, short-story writer, essayist, screenwriter, and critic, b. 24 Nov. 1941, Adrogué

Born in Adrogué in the province of Buenos Aires, P. and his family moved to Mar del Plata when he was fourteen. It was then that he began to read avidly and write a journal that he still keeps, and in which his published works find their initial seed. He studied history at the Universidad de La Plata and then practiced journalism in Buenos Aires. In addition to his writing, he also directed Serie Negra, which published the works of such detective fiction writers as Raymond CHANDLER and Dashiell HAMMET in Argentina. Unlike many writers of his generation, P. remained in Argentina during the violently repressive years of military dictatorship in his country, from 1976 to 1983, and this experience had a profound effect on his writing.

In P.'s early collections of stories, *La invasión* (1967; The Invasion) and *Nombre falso* (1975; *Assumed Name,* 1995), one can already perceive his "hybrid" style of fictional production in the metacritical fusion of literary history and fiction, philosophical ponderings and narrative development. Many of the stories place P. within the strong Argentine tradition of the short story, and there are clear connections with his precursors, such as Jorge Luis BORGES, Julio CORTÁZAR, and Roberto ARLT. The novella "Homenaje a Roberto Arlt" (Homage to Roberto Arlt), which appears in the latter collection, clearly gestures toward the Borgesian technique of spurious bibliographic references, false leads, and fiction's constant challenge of truth claims, while simultaneously celebrating Arlt's influential use of popular speech and hardboiled urban localities. Many of these stories have reappeared in later collections, showing P.'s constant reworking of the Argentine literary tradition in his writing. P. continually experiments with the limits of genre and blends time, space and history to fashion a cosmopolitan configuration of Argentine culture.

Respiración artificial (1980; *Artificial Respiration,* 1994) is undoubtedly one of the most important Latin American novels of the late 20th c., and especially of novels written during the Argentine dictatorship years. It has received ample critical and even popular acclaim. A difficult, complex novel, it seems to meditate on everything from nationalism, dictatorship, and memory to literature, quotation, and utopia. It is a novel that is clearly concerned with both history and historiography, and their relation to literature, as well as the Argentine psyche and its relation to more general issues of identity. Through narrative content the novel records and reinterprets certain historical "facts" and our knowledge about them. Simultaneously, its unique form of fragmented and varying types of discourses, dialogue, epistolary entries, speculative conversation, ambiguous and unnamed narrators, anachronistic references, and temporal code-switching propels the reader to question the status of the narrative and the processes by which a nation constructs itself, its history and its cultural identity.

Twelve years later P. published his second novel, *La ciudad ausente* (1992; The Absent City), which engages detective fiction techniques as the protagonist, Junior, investigates the relationship of Macedonio Fernández (an Argentine writer from earlier in this century) to his wife Elena de Obieta. He comes upon a museum that contains a machine (perhaps the preserved, technologized body of Elena) that weaves stories that represent the cultural construction of a national memory. This futuristic narrative addresses many of the same questions as *Respiración artificial*, namely, the dictatorship/post–dictatorship period and the relation between truth/reality versus possibility/fiction. As always, he focuses on the problematic of language and representation. Realism for P. is a convention, while literature is a parallel world, a counter reality; it is the attempt to create another reality when utopia is glimpsed.

P.'s novel *Plata quemada* (1997; Burned Cash) won the "Premio Planeta" literary prize of that same year. In this novel P. again contemplates the intersections between history and fiction while executing his well-developed skills in the hardboiled detective story. Basing his narrative on a true event, P. reconstructs the case of a 1965 bank robbery in San Fernando in the province of Buenos Aires through archival research combined with literary creativity. He also attaches an epilogue in which he frames the story within his own self-referential writing, claiming that, as a sixteen-year-old aspiring writer, he met the concubine of one of the perpetrators on a train as she was fleeing the country for Bolivia. There is little of his recognizable philosophical discourse in the novel, which displays instead a fast-paced and gritty narrative style.

In the tradition of many Latin American intellectuals, P.'s activities traverse a large span of cultural production. P. has been a visiting professor in the U.S. at Princeton and Harvard, and is an honorary professor at the University of Buenos Aires, where he lectures regularly. He is a critically acclaimed novelist, as well as a renowned critic and essayist. He has also written several screenplays and has collaborated on an opera based on his novel *La ciudad ausente*. His contemplative, sophisticated and critical style is an important voice in the Argentine literary tradition, and has already realized a considerable impact on Latin American cultural production.

FURTHER WORKS: *Jaulario* (1967); *Crítica y ficción* (1986); *Prisión perpetua* (1988); *Por un relato futuro: Diálogo R. P.— Juan José Saer* (1990); *Cuentos con dos rostros* (1992); *La Argentina en pedazos* (1993); *Cuentos morales* (1995)

BIBLIOGRAPHY: Morello Frosch, M., "Ficción e historia en *Respiración artificial* de R. P.," *Discurso Literario* (1984): 243-55; Balderston, D., "Latent Meaning in R. P.'s *Respiración artificial* and Luis Gusmán's *En el corazón de junio*," *RCEH*, 12 (1988): 207-19; Pons, M., "Más allá de las fronteras del lenguaje: Una historia alternativa en *Respiración artificial* de R. P.," *Inti*, 39 (1994): 153-73; Avelar, I., "Cómo respiran los ausentes: La narrativa de R. P.," *MLN*, 110 (1995): 416-32; Jagoe, E., "The Disembodied Machine: Matter, Femininity and Nation in P.'s *La ciudad ausente*," *LALR*, 23 (1995): 5-17; Grzegorczyk, M., "Discursos desde el margen: Gombrowicz, P. y la estética del basurero," *Hispamérica*, 73 (1996): 15-33

—LORI HOPKINS

PILINSZKY, János

Hungarian poet, b. 25 Nov. 1921, Budapest; d. 27 May 1981, Budapest

The event that had the most profound effect on P.'s creative life was World War II. P. grew up as the sheltered child of middle-class parents and studied law at the University of Budapest, but in late 1944 he was drafted into the Hungarian army and with the retreating Axis forces taken to Germany, where he witnessed the ravages of war as well as the mental anguish of prisoners and concentration-camp inmates. He was the first—and for a long time the only—Hungarian poet who dealt insistently with the implications of the Holocaust, seeing it as a moral disaster, a failure of civilization.

P.'s wartime experiences and their reverberations are at the center of his first two volumes of poetry, *Trapéz és korlát* (1946; trapeze and parallel bars) and *Harmadnapon* (1959; on the third day), the latter published after a decade-long silence. In the 1960s P.'s literary horizon broadened somewhat; he wrote more, became more visible, and after a number of Western poets and intellectuals—Pierre EMMANUEL and Ted HUGHES, in particular—began taking note of his achievement, he traveled abroad, spending some time in Western Europe and America, although he remained on the staff of *Új ember*, a Catholic weekly, until his death.

A Catholic poet, P. also expressed the existential agony of modern man. The ardent quest for salvation in his poems is always accompanied by a perception of solitude and despair. With radical verbal economy, although in images that are often bizarre and surrealistic, the poet conveys a sense of immobility, of utter hopelessness. P. said that for him the main purpose of poetry is not to re-create human experience but to discover, painfully, the real nature of the human condition. Many of his longer poems—for example, the celebrated "Apokrif" (1959; "Apocrypha," 1976)—are biblical in tone; in them apocalyptic visions blend with the more familiar memory flashes of wartime horrors. His later volumes, *Szálkák* (1972; splinters) and *Végkifejlet* (1974; denouement), while still spare, are a little less somber, and in his prose works he mellowed even further. *Beszélgetések Sheryl Suttonnal* (1977; conversations with Sheryl Sutton), which he subtitled "The Novel of a Dialogue," is really a series of tender and tentative monologues by and about a black American actress P. befriended in Paris.

P.'s was a lonely, distant, self-abnegating voice in an otherwise richly polyphonic literature. By Hungarian standards his total output was unusually small (in addition to poems and short prose pieces he wrote a few playlets, film scripts, and poetic oratorios), and his verse is in fact more akin to the austere objective poetry of some modern French and English poets than to the expansive, experiential lyric traditions of his native country. Yet the starkness and biblical weightiness of his poetic lines and his obsessive preoccupation with just a few themes had a stunning impact on the postwar generation of Hungarian poets. It is also true that in the 1950s Hungary's cultural leadership had no use for P.'s unwavering, self-tormenting pessimism: he became, and remained for years, an unpublishable poet. Nowadays, however, he is seen as an exemplary figure—a man of rare literary and moral sensibility.

FURTHER WORKS: *Rekviem* (1963); *Nagyvárosi ikonok* (1970); *Tér és forma* (1975); *Kráter* (1976). FURTHER WORKS IN ENGLISH: *Selected Poems* (1976); *Crater* (1978)

BIBLIOGRAPHY: Gömöri, G., "P.: The Lonely Poet," *HungQ*, 5 (1965): 43–47; Hughes, T., Introduction to J. P., *Selected Poems* (1976): 7–14; Nagy, Á. Nemes, "J. P.: A Very Different Poet," *NHQ*, No. 84 (1981): 54–59

—IVAN SANDERS

PILIPINO LITERATURE
See Philippine Literature

PILLAT, Ion

Romanian poet, essayist, dramatist, and translator, b. 31 March 1891, Bucharest; d. 17 April 1945, Bucharest

Scion of an old aristocratic family, P. studied literature and law at the Sorbonne. Destined by family tradition for a career in politics (he was the nephew of the Brătianus, a prominent Romanian political family), he chose instead poetry and a quiet private life. Between 1926 and 1937 he traveled to Spain, Italy, and Greece. He was active in Romanian cultural life, editing several journals and anthologies of poetry, and frequenting literary circles, notably that of the SYMBOLIST poet Alexandru Macedonski (1854–1920). He also translated extensively from French and German poetry. After 1924 he became closely associated with the group around the influential journal *Gîndirea*, where he published many of his poems.

Often compared to Vasile Alecsandri (1821–1890), P. actually had little in common with that 19th-c. poet-revolutionary beyond such superficial similarities as an aristocratic background, a taste for quiet country life, and a certain ease and elegance in writing verse. He was much closer, both in poetic temperament and ideology, to the Parnassian and symbolist poets. In his collection of essays *Portrete lirice* (1936; lyrical portraits) P. advocated a "pure" poetry that had "algebra and music as its limits." His own early verse drew upon such Parnassian and hermetic sources as Greek mythology and Oriental poetry, and sought a cold and studied perfection of poetic form. Throughout his career P. remained interested in poetical modernism without actually engaging in experiments himself.

His volume of poems *Pe Argeş în sus* (1923; up the Argeş river) marked his return to his national roots and was strongly influenced by the traditionalist ideology of *Gîndirea*. However, P. cast the traditional, "naïve" themes of Romanian folklore in a highly refined symbolist and neoclassicist form. He brought this curious but effective poetic blend to perfection in such volumes as *Caietul verde* (1932; the green notebook) and *Împlinire* (1942; fulfillment).

P. also wrote two plays, in collaboration with Adrian MANIU, which were adaptations from Romanian literature and folklore and which also bore a strong traditionalist mark. P. is also recognized as one of the best Romanian translators of poetry from French, English, German, Spanish, and Italian. It was P.'s poetry, however, especially the verse of his late period, that established him in Romanian literature as one of the most cerebral, cosmopolitan, and refined artistic personalities of this century.

FURTHER WORKS: *Povestea celui din urmă sfînt* (1911); *Visări păgîne* (1912); *Eternităţi de-o clipă* (1914); *Iubita de zăpadă* (1915); *Amăgiri* (1917); *Grădina între ziduri* (1919); *Satul meu*

(1925); *Dinu Paturică* (1925, with Adrian Maniu); *Tinerețe fără bătrînețe* (1926, with Adrian Maniu); *Biserica de altădată* (1926); *Florica* (1926); *Întoarcere (1908–1918)* (1927); *Limpezimi* (1928); *Scutul Minervei* (1933); *Pasărea de lut* (1934); *Poeme într-un vers* (1935); *Țărm pierdut* (1937); *Umbra timpului* (1940); *Tradiție și literatură* (1943); *Asfodela* (1943); *Cumpăna dreaptă* (1965)

BIBLIOGRAPHY: Munteanu, B., *Panorama de la littérature roumaine contemporaine* (1938): 284–87

—MIHAI SPARIOSU

PILLECIJN, Filip de

Belgian novelist and essayist (writing in Flemish), b. 25 March 1891, Hamme; d. 7 Aug. 1962, Ghent

P. started his career as a teacher, biographer, and essayist. Early creative work, the novels *Pieter Fardé* (1926; Pieter Fardé) and *Blauwbaard* (1931; Bluebeard), relied on historical or legendary sources; but in the novellas *Monsieur Hawarden* (1935; Monsieur Hawarden), *Schaduwen* (1937; shadows), and *De aanwezigheid* (1938; the presence) P. established himself as a superb stylist who gained fame for his evocation of mood and landscape, and for his subtle exploration of the psychology of eroticism.

In his novellas and the novels *Hans van Malmédy* (1935; Hans of Malmédy), *De soldaat Johan* (1939; soldier John), and *Jan Tervaert* (1947; Jan Tervaert) P. set a new standard for Flemish prose and influenced a generation of writers with his delicate yet masculine romanticism. These are works of a poetic sensibility dealing with a melancholy that found its only solace in the peaceful perpetuity of nature. The autumnal mood and an oneiric imagination found its arcadian perfection in the novel *De veerman en de jonkvrouw* (1950; the ferryman and the lady)—practically a romantic fairy tale.

Experiences of violence, social unrest, and misery during two world wars embittered P., and social considerations came to replace his earlier romanticism. The negative ramifications of man as a social and political animal are portrayed in the story "De boodschap" (1946; the message), the novella *Rochus* (1951; Rochus), and the novels *Mensen achter de dijk* (1949; people behind the dike), *Vaandrig Antoon Serjacobs* (1951; ensign Antoon Serjacobs), and *Aanvaard het level* (1956; accept life). In the last two novels, P. responds to life's pain with the resigned acceptance of an idealist purified by suffering.

Beginning with *De rit* (1927; the ride), the majority of P.'s heroes are soldiers. In conflict with conventional society and subjected to bureaucratic injustice, these outsiders—of a type that has come to dominate 20th-c. fiction—pay dearly (either by imprisonment or death) for their impotent rebellion. Only women provide solace and hope in this inhospitable and threatening world. But although physical passion is celebrated, P. insists on man's inability to establish a lasting and authentic relationship. Nature gradually emerges as mankind's only lasting joy. The farmer, in an otherwise anticlerical oeuvre, assumes the stature of a priest in P.'s telluric devotion.

P. perfected an economical prose style that is suggestive rather than explicit, lyrical rather than realistic; its melodic serenity strikes a fascinating balance between virility and refinement.

P.'s preference for historical settings—used exclusively to provide objectivity and a sense of timelessness—recalls German masters of shorter fiction such as Conrad Ferdinand Meyer (1825–1898), Gottfried Keller (1819–1890), and Adalbert Stifter (1805–1865), with all of whom he shares stylistic similarities and a preoccupation with the majesty of nature. The romantic and lyric side of P.'s work recalls the melancholy novels of the French authors Eugène Fromentin (1820–1876) and ALAIN-FOURNIER. His unsentimental devotion to nature, a characteristic shared with so many Flemish and Dutch writers, is of special interest in an age newly concerned with ecology.

FURTHER WORKS: *Onder den hiel* (1920); *Hugo Verriest* (1926); *Stijn Streuvels en zijn werk* (1932); *Dona Mirabella* (1952); *Het boek van de man Job* (1956); *Verzameld werk* (4 vols., 1959–1960); *Elizabeth* (1961).

—E. M. BEEKMAN

PILNYAK, Boris

(pseud. of Boris Andreevich Vogau) Russian novelist and short-story writer, b. 12 Sept. 1894, Mozhaysk; d. 1938

The son of a veterinarian of Volga-German origin, P. published short stories before the Russian Revolution, but attained fame later with an avant-garde novel, *Goly god* (1922; *The Naked Year*, 1927), depicting the civil war and the famine of 1919. An exceptionally popular and influential writer, he angered the Soviet authorities with his romantic view of the revolution. He incurred official disfavor for "Povest o nepogashennoy lune" (1927; "The Tale of the Unextinguished Moon," 1967), a fictionalized account of the death, believed to have been ordered by Stalin, of General Mikhail Frunze during an operation. He was expelled from the Writers' Union after the publication in Germany of *Krasnoe derevo* (1929; mahogany), which contained sympathetic portraits of old Bolsheviks. His Five-Year-Plan novel, *Volga vpadaet v Kaspyskoe more* (1930; *The Volga Falls to the Caspian Sea*, 1931), depicting the construction of a vast dam, did little to reestablish his reputation. His trips to China, Japan, and the U.S., undertaken in the late 1920s and early 1930s, resulted in the publication of several travel diaries. In 1937 he was arrested and convicted of "fascist" activities. It is believed that he died in 1938, but it is not generally known what fate he met after his arrest.

P.'s early short stories are set in rural areas and evoke the primitive, even biological, aspects of life in a lyrical style reminiscent of CHEKHOV, BUNIN, and Turgenev. Throughout his career his admiration for the instinctual and natural influenced his psychological portrayals and his thinking on culture and history.

His popularity in the early 1920s derived partly from his reputation as the first novelist of the revolution. In episodic avant-gardist narratives he eulogized the revolution as the resurgence of a Russian peasant culture which had existed before the reign of Peter the Great and which remained unadulterated by debilitating Western traits. He was, like Andrey BELY and Aleksey REMIZOV, a 20th-c. Slavophile and depicted Western Europe as moribund. His use of the novel form for the examination of philosophical ideas is also reminiscent of Dostoyevsky.

P.'s portrayals of Russia in his novels are all studies of confrontations between the new and the old. In *Mashiny i volki* (1924;

machines and wolves) the communal peasant culture he admired is shown in conflict with Marxism and technology. The complex and unconventional style of these novels, which was deplored as "Pilnyakism" by orthodox Soviet critics, features the liberal use of such devices as the frame story, the flashback, enigmatic narrative transitions, lyrical digressions, leitmotifs, symbols, insertions of documents, dialect renderings, wordplay, and typographical peculiarities. The style resembles Bely's in its musical traits and Remizov's in its antiquarianism, while its satire stems from Gogol.

In the late 1920s and 1930s P. ostensibly attempted to correct his ideology and to subdue his style, but with ambiguous results. He turned with sympathetic interest to non-European cultures. In *Rossia v polyote* (1926; Russia in flight) he depicted the Komis, a Finno-Ugric people living west of the Urals. In *Korni yaponskogo solntsa* (1927; roots of the Japanese sun) and *Kitayskaya povest* (1927; a Chinese story) he tried to capture the spirit of Oriental cultures, while in *Okey: Amerikansky roman* (1933; OK: an American novel) he denigrated capitalism. In some works of the 1930s, such as "Sozrevanie plodov" (1936; the ripening of fruit), whose subject is a craft industry, he created a new kind of mélange consisting of fiction, reportage, and autobiography. Between the late 1930s and the mid-1960s his name virtually disappeared from print in the Soviet Union. He was subsequently rehabilitated, but few of his works have been reprinted there.

Although P. defended the spontaneous and primitive, he was a bookish and derivative writer. His work was sometimes flawed by raw naturalism, shallow psychology, or an overweening didacticism. Nevertheless, his underlying compassion and intense concern for freedom associate him with the best traditions of Russian literature. His delight in the picturesque and his savoring of the eccentric rescue him from the realm of the platitudinous, and his pessimism is relieved by comic and ironic touches.

FURTHER WORKS: *Prostye rasskazy* (1923); *Ocherednye povesti* (1927); *Sobranie sochineny* (8 vols., 1930); *Izbrannye rasskazy* (1935); *Izbrannye proizvedenia* (1976). FURTHER WORKS IN ENGLISH: *Tales of the Wilderness* (1925); *The Tale of the Unextinguished Moon, and Other Stories* (1967); *Mother Earth, and Other Stories* (1968)

BIBLIOGRAPHY: Bristol, E., "B. P.," *SEER*, 41 (1963): 494–512; Wilson, P., "B. P.," *Survey*, No. 46 (1963): 134–42; Maloney, P., "Anarchism and Bolshevism in the Works of B. P.," *RusR*, 32 (1973): 43–53; Reck, V., *B. P.: A Soviet Writer in Conflict with the State* (1975); Brostrom, K., "P.'s *Naked Year*: The Problem of Faith," *RLT*, 16 (1979): 114–53; Browning, G. L., "Polyphony and the Accretive Refrain in B. P.'s *Naked Year*," *RLT*, 16 (1979): 154–70; Falchikov, M., "Rerouting the Train of Time: B. P.'s *Krasnoye derevo*," *MLR*, 75 (1980): 138–47

—EVELYN BRISTOL

PINEAU, Gisèle

Guadeloupean novelist, b. 1956, Paris, France

P. was born in Paris to Guadeloupean parents. Her father was in the French military and her mother was a housewife. She made her first visit to Guadeloupe in 1960, but lived in France until 1970. During her youth in Paris, P. witnessed firsthand the effects of racism, an experience that has shaped her fiction. She moved to Martinique with her parents in 1970, and then to Guadeloupe. P. returned to Paris to study literature at the University of Nanterre, after completing her baccalaureate in Guadeloupe. She was initially forced to abandon her studies for financial reasons, but went on to receive a degree in psychiatric nursing. After completing her nursing degree in 1980, P. returned to Guadeloupe, where she still lives and practices. She is married and the mother of two children.

P.'s first publication, a novella entitled *Un papillon dans la cité* (1992; Butterfly in the City), introduced P. as a new force in Caribbean literature. Based on the life of P.'s grandmother Julia, *Un papillon dans la cité* tells the story of a young woman from Guadeloupe who is forced to flee to France to escape an abusive husband. This novella, which serves as a prelude to P.'s later novel, *L'exil selon Julia* (1996; Exile According to Julia), introduces the autobiographical threads that wind through P.'s other works, as well as the themes of identity, exile, and alienation, which are common to them.

P.'s second publication, a novel entitled *La grande drive des esprits* (1993; The Great Drive of the Spirits) was awarded both the Reader's Prize from *Elle* magazine and the Carbet Prize for Caribbean fiction. This second work exhibits a maturity of writing style which is marked by the creolization in P.'s own fashion, of the French language. Unlike other Caribbean writers, who insert entire passages of Creole into their texts, P. uses limited Creole vocabulary, but manipulates French to reflect the pattern and flow of Creole.

Set in Guadeloupe, *La grande drive des esprits* incorporates the magic, spirituality, and supernatural of Caribbean voodoo, creating a genuine sense of the history and memory of the people of the island. The novel tells the story of Léonce, a man born with a club foot, and of his family. Set between 1928 and 1976, the novel traces the history of the family against the history of the island. Although Guadeloupe survives hurricanes and world wars, little, the novel suggests, changes for the island. French domination and exploitation remain a mainstay, and the people of Guadeloupe retain their courage and their strength.

L'espérance-macadam (1995; The Hope Road), P.'s third work, was awarded the RFO Prize. This novel, also set in Guadeloupe, takes up the spirit of the people of the island introduced in *La grande drive des esprits*, but focuses more on the particularly female experience of life that characterizes *Un papillon dans la cité*. The novel presents the lives of three women, Eliette, Rosette, and Angela, all of whom live in Savane, a small village on the island. Set against reggae music and the struggles of everyday life, this novel poignantly explores the double curse of being a woman in a poor country, but emphasizes the power of the feminine and of female community to triumph even in the most miserable of circumstances.

L'exil selon Julia functions as the narrative and thematic fusion of her first three works. This novel, which returns to the story presented in *Un papillon dans la cité*, combines the backdrops of France and Guadeloupe, and even infuses both settings with the brief, but powerful presence of Africa. The subject of this novel is not Julia, but her granddaughter—the literary representative of P. herself—who relives her own childhood memories of exile through the experiences and memories of her grandmother. More than any of the previous works, this novel presents the plight of P.'s generation, alienated both from France and from the Caribbean, and details the attempts of that generation to find itself through a return to the Caribbean culture and language that they have scarcely known.

P. has literally exploded onto the Francophone literary stage. Publishing three remarkable novels and one rich novella in the space of four years, she must be considered as one of the most talented as well as prolific female writers from the Caribbean. Her ability to embody the island of Guadeloupe through near photographic imagery and her ability to evoke the of sounds and rhythms of the island are rivaled only by her power to render the psychological and emotional portraits of the characters in her novels. A chronicler of what it means to be a women in a world which is still run by men, of what it means to be poor in a world run by money, of what it means to be Caribbean in a world run by the U.S. and Europe, P. destabilizes the assumptions of her reader, creating a literary mirror of the crisis of identity faced by the marginalized populations of the world.

—DAYNA L. OSCHERWITZ

PIÑERA, Virgilio

Cuban dramatist, short-story writer, novelist, poet, and literary critic, b. 4 Aug. 1912, Cárdenas; d. 19 Oct. 1979, Havana

P. is one of the leading and most prolific Cuban writers of the 20th c. He lived in Cuba all of his life, except for five years, from 1950 to 1955, which he spent in Argentina, where two of his major narrative works were published: the novel *La carne de René* (1953; René's flesh) and the volume of short stories *Cuentos fríos* (1956; *Cold Tales*, 1988). After the triumph of the Cuban revolution in 1959, he worked for the newspaper *Revolución* and directed the literary series "Ediciones Erre" for a number of years. He eventually fell into disgrace with the communist régime, but continued to write at a fast pace, although not a single creative piece by him was published in Cuba during the last years of his life. At his death, his apartment in Havana was sealed by Cuban authorities, and the manuscripts that he kept there were confiscated. The continued efforts of some Cuban literary critics and friends of P.'s succeeded in obtaining official permission in 1987 to publish some of these works.

As a poet, P. associated with José Lezama LIMA and those who wrote for the literary journal *Orígenes*. His poetry evolved from the symbolism and surrealist traits of his early works, such as *La isla en peso* (1943; the island's full weight) to the shockingly prosaic style apparent in the late poems of his collected verse. *La vida entera* (1969; my entire life), or in *Una broma colosal* (1988; a colossal joke), published posthumously.

P. can be considered the initiator of the literature of the absurd in Cuba, both in the narrative and in the theater. Two of his novels, *Pequeñas maniobras* (1963; minor maneuvers) and *Presiones y diamantes* (1967; pressures and diamonds), as well as many of his short stories, seem to have a common theme, that of human degradation by a concatenation of disasters that the individual cannot control and which drag him into the darkest zones of human existence. His characters, when given an option, choose to retain the miserable condition to which they have been able to adapt and in which they have found an awkward kind of happiness. Some typical features of his narrative are circular plots, macabre humor, and grotesque characterizations.

His plays follow also, with a few exceptions, the absurdist trend. *Falsa alarma* (1948; false alarm) is reminiscent of Franz

KAFKA's *The Trial*; the protagonist ends up deranged after going through a comedic process of criminal justice that brings no punishment and no acquittal. In *El flaco y el gordo* (1959; the skinny guy and the fat one), the "skinny guy" eats the "fat one" out of both a desire of revenge and desperate hunger, to face a little later another "skinny guy" who will in turn, opening a new cycle, do the same to him. *Dos viejos pánicos* (1968; two ancient panics), in the line of Samuel BECKETT's dramas about the predicament of aging, presents an old couple who play a "game of death" to prepare themselves for their impending final moments. The exceptions to the rule are *Electra Garrigó* (1943; Electra Garrigó) and *Aire frío* (1959; cold air). *Electra Garrigó* is a free adaptation of the classic tragedy, where the flaws of the Cuban bourgeoisie are depicted in a light satirical vein. Although exhibiting some distinctive grotesque elements, the very successful and much performed *Aire frío* is a departure from P.'s usual procedures; it is a realistic, semiautobiographical work, which portrays the life of a middle-class family throughout several decades. P.'s most poignant play to this date—several remain still unpublished in Cuba—is *Una caja de zapatos vacía* (1986; an empty shoe box), published posthumously in the U.S. This piece, smuggled out of Cuba in 1967, can be viewed as P.'s political testament. In it he presents, in the manner of Antonin ARTAUD's theater of cruelty, the sadistic methods that tyrants employ to rule over their subjects. He also suggests that those who are thus victimized can only earn the right to a fulfilling life through an act of liberating madness.

P. has been highly influential among the younger generations of Cuban writers. Outside Cuba his stature as a literary figure of universal appeal continues to grow.

FURTHER WORKS: *Las furias* (1941); *Poesía y prosa* (1944); *Teatro completo* (1960); *Cuentos* (1964); *El que vino a salvarme* (1970); *Un fogonazo* (1987); *Muecas para escribientes* (1987)

BIBLIOGRAPHY: McLees, A. A., "Elements of Sartrian Philosophy in *Electra Garrigó*," *LATR*, 7 (Fall 1973): 5–11; González-Cruz, L. F., "V. P. y el teatro del absurdo en Cuba," *Mester*, 5 (1974): 52–58; González-Cruz, L. F., "Arte y situación de V. P.," *Caribe*, 2 (1977): 77–86; Morello-Frosch, M., "La anatomía: mundo fantástico de V. P.," *Hispam*: 23–24 (1979): 19–34; Cabrera Infante, G., "Vidas para leerlas," *Vuelta*, 4, 41 (Apr. 1980): 4–16; Gilden, R. G., "V. P. and the Short Story of the Absurd," *Hispania*, 63, 2 (May 1980): 348–55; Arenas, R., "*La isla en peso* con todas sus cucarachas," *Mariel*, 2 (1983): 20–24; Matas, J., "Infiernos fríos de V. P.," *Linden Lane Magazine*, 4 (1985): 22–25; González-Cruz, L. F., V. P.: "*Una caja de zapatos vacía*," *Edición crítica* (1986); González-Cruz, L. F., "V. P.," in Martínez, J. A., ed., *Dictionary of Twentieth-Century Cuban Literature* (1990): 361–70

—LUIS F. GONZÁLEZ-CRUZ

PINGET, Robert

French novelist and dramatist, b. 19 July 1919, Geneva, Switzerland; d. 25 Aug. 1997, Tours

P. received a law degree in Switzerland before his interest in art led him to become a painter and an art teacher. In 1946, having made Paris his permanent residence, he studied painting at the

Academy of Fine Arts, and exhibited at the Galerie du Siècle in 1949. He then turned to prose writing in an attempt to adapt the free expression of poetry to the novel form.

P. was first attracted by the verbal acrobatics of SURREALISM and by the unbridled imagination of the French poet Max JACOB, who excelled in the spontaneous expression of his own sensibilities. The impetuous style and the burlesque ingenuity of Jacob's flights into fantasy led P. to write esoteric tales such as *Graal Flibuste* (1956; Graal Flibuste) and *Clope au dossier* (1961; Clope to the dossier), the latter dramatized as *Ici et ailleurs* (1961; *Clope*, 1963).

As early as 1957 P. also became attuned to the despairing quality of Samuel BECKETT's nihilistic philosophy, when he translated into French Beckett's drama *All That Fall*. P. himself conveyed the same feeling for the emptiness and absurdity of the modern world, as expressed by the inanity of the spoken word, in his first radio scripts, such as *La manivelle* (1960; *The Old Tune*, 1963)—the English version of which was done by Beckett.

Since 1951 P. has written short stories, plays, dialogues, a film scenario, and several radio scripts, which have been produced in France and Germany, as well as numerous novels. His works have been published in translation in thirteen different countries.

L'inquisitoire (1962; *The Inquisitory*, 1966) was awarded the Critics' Grand Prize in 1963. In this lengthy novel, the experience of the past, the endless unfolding of lost time, is conveyed through a deluge of words. An aged, deaf, broken man utters bits of broken sentences. The mumbled recollections of his rambling monologue continue without a single semicolon or period. What begins to emerge is not only the underlying insecurity of an anguished humanity, but also the elusive, often irrational quality of reality itself.

The baroque, fablelike, at times dreamlike fantasies of P.'s early books have taken on, in later years, bizarre and pessimistic undertones. The same almost poignant cries of echo voices appear in his short novel *Quelqu'un* (1965; someone), which won the Fémina Prize. Here again we find the familiar setting of P.'s geography of the imaginary. The discourse meanders afresh; there is no coherent narrative. This is because for P., literature is exclusively language, exclusively free, "gratuitous" verbal communication. He is not interested in telling a story or in developing a plot; he is concerned only with the transcription of the spoken word.

P.'s stylistic experiments have linked him to the NEW NOVEL. But his originality lies in the fact that unlike the avant-garde French novelists who perceive visually and try to render minutely, as objectively as possible, a world of things, P. listens acutely and patiently. He tries to distinguish between the textures of the many dialogues that he discerns within himself.

So, in *Le Libera* (1968; *The Libera Me Domine*, 1976), rejecting the old-fashioned stereotyped meaning of words and clichés and rigid syntax, P. searches for his own method of communication. He attempts what seems an impossible task—to pinpoint the everchanging aspect of a mobile language. The preface of *Le Libera* almost constitutes a manifesto. In it, P. defines each one of his novels as a separate quest for a particular mood, more precisely, a distinct tone of voice. He is seeking a certain inflection or a separate modulation, selected from among the many original vibrations that constitute P.'s own ways of expressing himself, each and all of them being representative of his true complex sensitivity. The right intonation for a particular novel, which he discerns within himself, is poured forth onto the page spontaneously at first. Then comes the painful labor of filtering, the conscientious effort of composing. The very process becomes a literary vein, a style; and the style in turn

determines, automatically, the intrigue. The story could have been something else; the authenticity of the speech is what constitutes, for P., his own true creation.

The search for veracity automatically implies false starts, innumerable meanderings, reversals, and culs-de-sac. Dealing with the immense and complicated palimpsest of memory—scraping, rubbing, erasing P.'s tablets of time—the author painstakingly attempts to unscramble and re-create the past in a new, "spoken" form in *Cette voix* (1975; this voice). Finally, in an effort to project, into the future, old age, and an ultimately looming death, he humbly submits to the reader his "obscure" writings of "dubious" authenticity, crowning his quest with *L'apocryphe* (1980; the apocrypha). Ambiguously written in the conditional, *L'apocryphe*, with its occasional "gray humor" undertones, unfolds P.'s maddening world of nightmares and daydreams. The engrossed reader must penetrate the many layers of meaning of this contemporary Homerian-Vergilian-Montaignian opus.

FURTHER WORKS: *Entre Fantoine et Agapa* (1951); *Mahu; ou, Le matériau* (1952; *Mahu; or, The Material*, 1967); *Le renard et la boussole* (1955); *Baga* (1958; *Baga*, 1967); *Le fiston* (1959; *Monsieur Levert*, 1961); *Lettre morte* (1959; *Dead Letter*, 1963); *Architruc* (1961; *Architruc*, 1967); *L'hypothèse* (1961; *The Hypothesis*, 1967); *Autour de Mortin* (1965; *About Mortin*, 1967); *Passacaille* (1969); *Identité, suivi d'Abel et Bela, Nuit* (1971); *Fable* (1971; *Fable*, 1981); *Paralchimie* (1973); *Amorces* (1973); *Le rescapé* (1974); *Le mois d'août* (1975); *Le vautour; Attendre; Genèse de "Fable"* (1980); *Le bifteck* (1981); *Monsieur Songe* (1982)

BIBLIOGRAPHY: Steisel, M. -G., "P.'s Method in *L'inquisitoire*," *BA*, 40 (1966): 267–71; Robbe-Grillet, A., *For a New Novel* (1965): 127–32; Steisel, M. -G., "Paroles de R. P.," *PSMLAB*, 45 (1966): 35–38; Mercier, V., *The New Novel from Queneau to P.* (1971): 363–415; Meyer, F., "P., le livre disséminé comme fiction, narration, et object," in Richdou, J., and F. Van Rossum-Guyon, eds., *Le nouveau roman: Hier, aujourd'hui* (1972), Vol. 2: 299-310, 325-50; Knapp, B., *French Novelists Speak Out* (1976): 6–14; special P. issue *Bas de casse*, No. 2 (1981)

—MARIE-GEORGETTE STEISEL

PIÑON, Nélida

Brazilian novelist and short-story writer, b. 1937, Rio de Janeiro

P. is a first-generation Brazilian, born of Spanish parents. She began serious writing in 1955, and has stated that it was not until this intense apprenticeship with the language that she truly came to identify herself as a Brazilian. Educated as a journalist at the Catholic University in Rio de Janeiro, she worked briefly for the newspaper *O Globo* before dedicating her efforts exclusively to creative writing. She has won Brazil's major literary prizes, and has taught at several universities, including Columbia and Johns Hopkins in the U.S. Her works have been translated into numerous languages, and she has traveled widely in Europe and the Americas.

P. challenges the imagination and interpretive skills of her readers. Her prose is rich with poetic devices. Narratives eschew linearity, and point of view often belongs to several different participants. Exposition of background information occurs gradually and sparingly. Shifts between interior monologue, dialogue, and narrated action are tenuously marked. Visual imagery is mimimal. Lexical, syntactic, and logical combinations tend to be unconventional. P. has stated that part of her project is to act "against official syntax."

Like most of her compatriots, P. decries social ills. Perhaps her best example of this commitment is the short-story collection *O calor das coisas* (1980; the heat of things). However, her focal point is not the streets, the fields, the factories, or the homes, but primarily the individual's consciousness. She specializes in the profound analysis of isolated characters—forceful, eccentric, and self-conscious—and causes the social dimension gradually to unfold around such interior dramas. P.'s writings show also a fascination with religiosity, or more precisely, mysticism, since she stresses the individual experience over the institutional. For example, her first novel, *Guia-mapa de Gabriel Arcanjo* (1961; guide map of Archangel Gabriel) features an extended dialogue between the female protagonist and her alter ego/guardian angel, regarding guilt, expiation, and one's relationship with deity. Another salient mark of P.'s fiction is eroticism, which is exemplified by *A casa da paixão* (1972; the house of passion). The novel is a lyrical treatment of a young woman's sexual initiation, which presents interior monologues of the woman herself, as well as of her partner and other members of her household.

P. shows a profound interest in the myths that underlie human enterprises. In particular, she seems fascinated with the myth of origination. *Fundador* (1969; founder) explores the establishment of a new society, which in some sense repeats itself through several generations of individuals. A related concern in P.'s fiction is the experience of the immigrant. *A república dos sonhos* (1984; *The Republic of Dreams*, 1989), a semiautobiographical novel, explores this experience by means of succeeding generations of a Galician family that immigrates to Brazil. The story is primarily told by the patriarch-founder of this new Brazilian family, and by his granddaughter, a writer, who pays a return visit to her ancestral home. The structure of the work is rather like William FAULKNER's *As I Lay Dying* (1930) in that the narrative content is developed as a series of flashbacks during the week in which the grandmother lies on her deathbed. This lengthy novel is generally considered to be P.'s most important work to date, as well as her most accessible to the general reader.

Because of her careful sculpting of language, her strong individualistic characters, and her orientation toward interior consciousness, critics often point out similarities between P. and Brazil's greatest female fiction writer, Clarice LISPECTOR. Feminist critics point to P.'s decentered narrations as examples of *écriture feminine* (feminine writing). Her texts are a fixture in courses on Latin American women writers; but in Brazil at least, her appeal and reputation place her squarely within the mainstream of current literary creativity.

FURTHER WORKS: *Madeira feita cruz* (1963); *Tempo das frutas* (1966); *Sala de armas* (1973); *Tebas do meu coração* (1974); *A força do destino* (1977); *A doce canção de Caetana* (1987)

BIBLIOGRAPHY: Crespo, A., and Bedate, P. Gómez, "N. P., de *Guia-mapa a Tempo das frutas*," *Revista de Cultura Brasileña*, 7 (1967): 5–27; Pontiero, G., "Notes on the Fiction of N. P.," *Review*, 17 (1976): 67–71; Riera, C., "Entrevista con N. P.: la vida es la literatura," *Quimera*: 54–55 (n.d.), 44–49; Maffre, C., "Les chemins du rêve dans *A república dos sonhos* de N. P.," *Quadrant* (1988): 165–82

—PAUL B. DIXON

PINTER, Harold

English dramatist and screenwriter, b. 10 Oct. 1930, London

P. was born in Hackney, a working-class section of London. The son of a Jewish tailor, he was at an impressionable age when he began hearing horror stories about Hitler's Germany, and was an evacuee during the blitz. In fact, he remembers seeing the family's garden in flames. After attending a local school on a scholarship, P. received a grant to study acting at the Royal Academy of Dramatic Art. He was temperamentally unsuited to the institution, however, and soon left. At about this time he also had encounters with broken-milk-bottle-wielding neofascists, declared himself a conscientious objector and stood trial for refusing to join the National Service, and published his first poems. By 1950 he had acted in BBC radio plays. He toured Ireland for eighteen months with Anew McMaster's Shakespearean repertory company and continued as a professional actor (stage name: David Baron) through the late 1950s, an experience that provided him with an important understanding of the production aspects of playwriting.

P.'s former wife, the actress Vivien Merchant, and his dramatist friend Samuel BECKETT have also advised him on the performability

Harold Pinter

of his plays. Essentially apolitical, P. occasionally works for various arts causes and sometimes directs for the National Theatre in London. His personal life generally does not enter into his works *per se*, but a six-year-long, well-publicized affair with the biographer Lady Antonia Fraser (b. 1932) ended in a divorce from Merchant in 1981 and marriage to Lady Antonia the same year. During this period, his output declined.

Over the years P. has been considered one of the most important English-language dramatists of this century. Recognition in the form of various awards and honors is one measure of how P.'s contemporaries appreciate his work. *The Caretaker* (1960) and *The Homecoming* (1965) won best-play designations on Broadway and in London, and major awards were gathered by several films for which P. wrote the screenplays. P. was made a Commander of the Order of the British Empire in 1966 and has received several other prizes and honorary degrees.

P.'s three early plays, *The Room* (1957), *The Birthday Party* (1958), and *The Dumb Waiter* (1959), have been labeled "comedies of menace." A likely outgrowth of his early experiences as a youth, the dramas are concerned with the themes of menace and dominance. The basic metaphor is of a room or some other sanctuary that is about to be invaded. The inhabitant of the room understands the existence of the menace outside, and in spite of terror and loneliness tries to communicate with the invader in an attempt to verify whether or not it is friendly. Fear of exposing a point of vulnerability, however, leads the inhabitant to be so wary that communication is impossible, even if the intruder were not so ambiguous. As a result, menace is heightened, as is the consequent need for further verification and communication, but the ability to verify or communicate is broken down, creating more menace. In *The Room* an old woman's sanctuary cannot protect her from a menacer; in *The Birthday Party* the protagonist tries to run away but is tracked down; in *The Dumb Waiter* two hired killers find that even menacers can be menaced.

Stylistically, these plays are not at all traditional. Although the dialogue is extremely realistic, P. presents his material with little or no explanation, and many theatergoers were at a loss to understand plays that neither spelled out their meaning in great detail nor conformed to the audience's preconceptions of what drama should be.

Having established the pervasive existence of menace in the modern world, P. next focused on the source of the menace. Transitional elements are obvious in the radio play *A Slight Ache* (1959) when the presence of a tramp, who never speaks, leads to the emotional breakdown of a husband and to the wife's replacing her husband with the tramp. In the dramatist's first commercial success, *The Caretaker*, two brothers and another tramp become involved in establishing or maintaining their relationships with each other. By now audiences understood what P. was doing.

In both of these plays, and the shorter works that immediately followed them (radio and television scripts included), it is clear that menace does not derive from an external, physical source; it comes from within the individual and is psychological in nature. This idea is summed up in *The Homecoming*, one of P.'s two best plays, and his most honored work. In *The Homecoming*, Teddy returns to his father's home with his wife, Ruth, only to leave, rejected by his family, while his wife stays behind. Throughout, the characters attempt to establish relationships with each other, no matter how absurd the basis for that relationship may at first seem. Desperately they grasp at anything that might be used to satisfy their needs; nonchalantly they dismiss anything that fails to meet their requirements. Teddy can leave because no one needs him and he needs no

one; Ruth stays because everyone needs her and she needs to be needed. Individual need thus is determined to be the source of the characters' terror and desperation—and they are willing to do anything and to accept everything that might fulfill their particular needs.

Completely new thematic and stylistic elements emerged in *Landscape* (1968). Given the psychological nature of the source of menace and its location—the human mind—P. began to examine how the mind functions. The intermixing of memory, time, and the nature of reality became the focal point of his interest. In *Landscape* Duff has wronged his wife, Beth, and she retreats into the world of her imagination, in which memories of the past and her romantic daydreams allow her to withdraw from reality to the extent that her husband can no longer communicate with her. In dealing with this very abstract concept, P. adopts a more lyrical style than was present in his earlier plays.

Old Times (1971), P.'s finest work to date, continues both the themes and style of *Landscape*. When Anna visits her former roommate, Kate, and Kate's husband, Deeley, a verbal battle develops between the visitor and the husband over the wife. Through a series of memories, created by the rememberer, each character tries to diminish the other in Kate's eyes. The nature of reality is such that the characters can invent tales to explain a past that will lead to a future in which their present needs and desires are fulfilled. Thus, reality, all time, and memory are shown to coexist simultaneously in the human mind and to be manipulable by it. The drama ends with Kate's deciding to remain with her husband when she remembers seeing Anna dead—and to all intents and purposes Anna ceases to exist.

P.'s screenwriting tends to parallel his playwriting: his film scripts include many of the themes that were occupying his attention in the plays written at the same time. P. has adapted several of his own works to the screen: *The Caretaker* (1963), released in the U.S. under the title *The Guest; The Birthday Party* (1969); and *The Homecoming* (1973). He has also adapted other writers' novels: *The Servant* (1963), from Robin Maugham (b. 1916); *The Pumpkin Eater* (1964), from Penelope Mortimer (b. 1918); *The Quiller Memorandum* (1966), from Adam Hall (pseud. of Elleston Trevor, b. 1920); *Accident* (1967), from Nicholas Mosley (b. 1923); *The Go-Between* (1971), from L. P. HARTLEY; *The Last Tycoon* (1976), from F. Scott FITZGERALD; *The Proust Screenplay* (pub. 1977, never filmed), from Marcel PROUST; and *The French Lieutenant's Woman* (1981; pub. 1981), from John FOWLES. (The first five of these screenplays from other writers were published together in *Five Screenplays* [1971].) Menace, interpersonal communications, psychological need, reality, and the nature of time are again his subjects. As with his radio and television writing, some of the techniques he used in the cinematic medium are carried over into his stage writing (the opening of *Old Times*, for example, incorporates a jump cut). P.'s screenplays, however, are often too wordy for the medium and on the whole are less successful than his dramas.

Throughout P.'s career, one thing has remained constant. A reader unfamiliar with the dramatist's canon would be hard pressed to conclude that *The Room* and *Landscape* were written by the same author, but an analysis of P.'s writing shows that there has been a steady thematic evolution and a concurrent and continual stylistic development from the very beginning of his career. Whereas many authors simply rewrite the same story, P. has progressed and constantly changed. The thematic movement from exposure of menace naturally led him to an investigation into the source of menace, which in turn stimulated his examination of the interconnections of memory and time and the nature of reality. Simultaneously, his form changed to reflect his content, so much so that at different times scholars have labeled him an absurdist (see THEATER OF THE ABSURD), an EXISTENTIALIST, a Freudian, and a poetic dramatist.

The elements that will ensure P.'s lasting reputation are his contributions in the areas of language (realistic dialogue, including pauses and silences) and exposition (as in real life, characters' backgrounds and motivations may be clear to them while the audience remains uninformed and must determine backgrounds and motivations purely from the characters' actions). The importance of P.'s themes and the insights into human nature he provides (often in a humorous manner, despite the seriousness of his topics), the emotional impact combined with intellectual depth, and the influence he has already had on a generation of playwrights make him a pivotal figure in the history of English drama.

FURTHER WORKS: *The Hothouse* (written 1958, pub. 1980); *A Slight Ache and Other Plays* (1961 [with *A Night Out* and *The Dwarfs*]); *The Collection and The Lover* (1963); *Dialogue for Three* (1963); *The Compartment* (1963); *The Dwarfs, and Eight Review Sketches* (1965); *The Lover; Tea Party; The Basement* (1967); *Poems* (1968); *Mac* (1968); *Night School* (1968); *Landscape and Silence, with Night* (1970); *Monologue* (1973); *No Man's Land* (1975); *Complete Works* (4 vols., 1976–1981); *Poems and Prose 1949–1977* (1978); *Betrayal* (1978); *Family Voices* (1981)

BIBLIOGRAPHY: Hinchliffe, A. P., *H. P.* (1967; rev. ed. 1981); Kerr, W., *H. P.* (1967); Taylor, J. R., *Anger and After*, rev. ed. (1969): 321–59; Esslin, M., *The Peopled Wound: The Work of H. P.* (1970; 2nd ed. *P.: A Study of His Plays*, 1973); Hollis, J. R., *H. P.: The Poetics of Silence* (1970); Sykes, A., *H. P.* (1970); Burkman, K. H., *The Dramatic World of H. P.: Its Basis in Ritual* (1971); Lahr, J., ed., *A Casebook on H. P.'s "The Homecoming"* (1971); Ganz, A., ed., *P.: A Collection of Critical Essays* (1972); Hayman, R., *H. P.* (1973); special P. issue, *MD*, 17, 4 (1974); Quigley, A. E., *The P. Problem* (1975); Dukore, B. F., *Where Laughter Stops: P.'s Tragicomedy* (1976); Gabbard, L. P., *The Dream Structure of P.'s Plays: A Psychoanalytic Approach* (1976); Gale, S. H., *Butter's Going Up: A Critical Analysis of H. P.'s Work* (1977); Gale, S. H., *H. P.: An Annotated Bibliography* (1978)

—STEVEN H. GALE

H. P.'s people are generally at cross-purposes with each other and sometimes tangled in a world of disconcerting objectivity. Mental discontinuities balance objective absurdities to arouse suspense and a sense of threat, bordering on insanity, as when in *The Dumb Waiter* mysterious orders for elaborate meals come down the lift from what had once been a restaurant to the basement kitchen where the two ambiguous ruffians are at their simultaneously flaccid and ominous talk; wherein perhaps a lucid symbolism may be felt flowering from a superficial absurdity. P.'s conversation is usually that of lower middle-class normality, and the disconcerting objects those of town life and human fabrication. In *The Caretaker* Mick reels off a speech about London districts and its various bus-routes and then one about

the legal and financial conditions of letting his property, in such a way as to make one dizzy. Questions may be left unanswered: who is the negro in *The Room*, who comes up from the basement of the tenement house, striking terror? Much of this is in the manner of Eugene Ionesco. What is so strange is that we are nowadays given the experience of nightmare, almost of the supernatural, in terms not of devils or ghosts, but of ordinary, material objects and affairs; and of people at cross-purposes with each other and with the audience in a paradoxical and dangerous world.

G. Wilson Knight, "The Kitchen Sink," *Encounter*, Dec. 1963, p. 49

Language—that common to men and of common man—is employed to make us constantly aware of the essential loneliness of the human condition. In discussing or including remedies, P. rarely indulges in overt speculation. . . . He attempts to show the constant effort of human beings to impress, confuse, or simply refuse to give answers about the problems that beset them, a refusal P. demonstrates in his plays. . . . Where [N. F.] Simpson merely exploits cliché, P.'s usage of it fascinates and evolves; and this usage makes him of all contemporary British dramatists the most poetical—more so than either [Christopher] Fry or [T. S.] Eliot. P. has looked at the whole, not merely at the language. . . . Certainly, of all contemporary British dramatists only P. manages to be topical, local, and universal—to combine the European Absurd with native wit to create a record of common inevitability. P. says, modestly, of his own work: "I am very concerned with the shape and consistency of mood of my plays. I cannot write anything that appears to me to be loose and unfinished. I like a feeling of order in what I write." This sense of order is the key to his work in any medium, and his success rests on it. In a very precise sense, among his contemporaries P. is the *miglior fabbro*.

Arnold P. Hinchliffe, *H. P.* (1967), pp. 164–65

The technique of casting doubt upon everything by matching each apparently clear and unequivocal statement with an equally clear and unequivocal statement of its contrary—used rather crudely in some parts of [*The Room*], as when Rose Hudd actually comments on the discrepancy between the Sandses' initial statement that they were on their way up and their later statement that they were on their way down when they called on her—is one which we shall find used constantly in P.'s plays to create an air of mystery and uncertainty. The situations involved are always very simple and basic, the language which the characters use is an almost uncannily accurate reproduction of everyday speech (indeed, in this respect P., far from being the least realistic dramatist of his generation, is arguably the most realistic), and yet in these ordinary surroundings lurk mysterious terrors and uncertainties—and by extension the whole external world of everyday realities is thrown into question. Can we ever know the truth about anybody or anything? Is there an absolute truth to be known?

John Russell Taylor, *Anger and After*, rev. ed. (1969), pp. 325–26

A playwright so fascinated by the difficulty, the terror, the pitfalls of communication will inevitably be fascinated by words and their multifarious uses to disclose and to disguise meaning. P.'s theatre is a theatre of language; it is from the words and their rhythm that the suspense, the dramatic tension, the laughter, and the tragedy spring. Words, in P.'s plays, become weapons of domination and subservience, silences explode, nuances of vocabulary strip human beings to the skin. Not even his severest critics have ever cast doubt on P.'s virtuosity in the use of language. His "taperecorder" ear has often been praised. And rightly: few English playwrights before him have displayed so acute an observation of the mannerisms, repetitions, and nonsensicalities of the vernacular as it is actually spoken. But there is more to P.'s use of language than merely accurate observation. In fact, what sounds like tape-recorded speech is highly stylised, even artificial. It is his ability to combine the appearance of utter reality with complete control of rhythm and nuance of meaning that is the measure of P.'s stature as a poet. P.'s dialogue is as tightly—perhaps more tightly—controlled than verse. Every syllable, every inflection, the succession of long and short sounds, words and sentences, is calculated to a nicety. And precisely the repetitiousness, the discontinuity, the circularity of ordinary vernacular speech are here used as formal elements with which the poet can compose his linguistic ballet. And yet, because the ingredients from which he takes the recurring patterns and artfully broken rhythms *are* fragments of a brilliantly observed, and often hitherto overlooked, reality, he succeeds in creating the illusion of complete naturalness, of naturalism.

Martin Esslin, *The Peopled Wound: The Work of H. P.* (1970), pp. 28–29, 30, 42–43

P.'s particular achievement has been to sustain linguistically the sort of tensions which seem to drive his characters from within. The fragmentary sentence, the phrase left hanging, the awkward pause, become outer manifestations of the inner anxiety, the deeper uncertainty. The discordant clash of language in, say, *The Caretaker*, is indicative of the discord that arises not only between character and character but within each of the characters. The fumbling efforts at conversation which ensue indicate the desperate need the characters have to make themselves known. Paraphrasing von Clausewitz's definition of "war," language becomes *a continuation of tension by other means*. On such occasions, Heidegger reminds us, language seems not so much a faculty that man possesses as that which possesses man.

But the "continuation of tension" may not always have the exchange of information as its goal. Many of

P.'s characters, on the contrary, go to some length to evade being known by others. The sounds these characters exchange are a holding action, a skirmish designed to avoid the larger confrontation. P. describes such a strategy, "communication itself between people is so frightening that rather than do that there is continual cross-talk, a continual talking about other things rather than what is at the root of their relationship." One source of this circumvention of communication may derive from opposing levels of knowledge or intelligence. In *The Birthday Party*, for example, Goldberg and McCann can badger Stanley to distraction because of their continued reference to unknown forces or significant but hidden events. Or, as in *The Caretaker*, Mick can keep ahead of Davies because of his superior intelligence and wit. But the more important source of evasion arises out of the character's fear that if he reveals himself, if he comes clean, he will be at the mercy of those who know him.

James R. Hollis, *H. P.: The Poetics of Silence* (1970), pp. 123–24

One way of looking at P.'s work is to say that it is a constant stratagem to uncover nakedness. The behavior of his characters is so seldom a reflection of the way people normally behave and so often a reflection of the way they would like to, if they weren't afraid to. Sometimes this behavior is a refraction of fears and anxieties in the form of actions. Violence occurs because animality is unleashed and, unlike the Greeks who took a high view of human dignity and kept the violence off-stage, P. peers in through the glass wall with no reverence for humanity, no belief in our lives being mapped out by divine powers. He has a keen eye for the cracks in the surface of normal conversation and normal behavior. He is always on the alert for the moments when his characters betray what is underneath and then he simply records what he sees and what he hears; but he does not do so in order to evolve theories or to warn us against ourselves. His vision and his hearing are both highly tuned instruments, invaluable in his one-man forays into the unarticulated and irrational no-man's-land inside the modern Everyman.

Ronald Hayman, *H. P.* (1973), p. 152

Attempts to categorize P.'s plays have given rise to two descriptive terms: "comedy of menace" and "Pinteresque." . . . The great danger with such terms is that they tend to become institutionalized when they are not transcended. And as they interact only minimally with the details of the plays, they tend to obscure the sublety and variety of P.'s work and contribute to the impression that his experimentation reduces to the mere repetition of a consistent formula. At a certain level of abstraction, P.'s work does deal with recurring problems: the problem of interrelational adjustment being a major one. But to give stress to less central generalizations at the expense of an acknowledgement of the great variety of his work is to promote . . . circularity of thought. . . . The point which is basic to this approach to P. is that which should be basic to any approach to language. Far from being a monolithic unity, language is an essentially pluralistic activity. Even within a certain general function, such as its interrelational use, language is characterized by variety and adaptability as well as by recurring patterns. . . . If one approaches the plays with a belief that truth, reality and communication ought to conform to certain norms, then the plays will remain tantalizingly enigmatic. But once it is realized that all of these concepts are, like any others, moves in language games, the barrier to an understanding of P. is removed.

In striving to adjust to one another, P.'s characters are negotiating not only truth and reality but their very freedom to engage their preferred identities in the environments that surround them. Their linguistic battles are not the product of an arbitrary desire for dominance but crucial battles for control of the means by which personality is created in the social systems to which they belong. As they struggle to cope, their misunderstandings and miscalculations provide a great deal of amusement for any audience, but invariably desperation and terror are eventually revealed as the linguistic warfare becomes increasingly crucial.

Austin E. Quigley, *The P. Problem* (1975),
pp. 274–77

PIONTEK, Heinz

German poet, short-story writer, novelist, editor, and essayist, b. 15 Nov. 1925, Kreuzberg

Born and raised in Upper Silesia near the Polish frontier, P. served in the armed forces toward the end of World War II. He then briefly studied German literature and held a variety of jobs before becoming a full-time writer. Among his numerous awards and honors is the Georg Büchner Prize (1976).

On the basis of his first books, the poetry collections *Die Furt* (1952; the ford) and *Die Rauchfahne* (1953; the wisp of smoke), critics praised P.'s powers of observation and originality, qualities that were to remain the hallmarks of his later works. These early poems and those of *Wassermarken* (1957; watermarks) are characterized by a variety of forms, from rhymed verse reminiscent of the poetry of Wilhelm Lehmann (1882–1968) to longer, less regular narratives. Transience is a common theme, and the mood is generally elegiac, but not without an element of Christian hope. Descriptions of nature scenes alternate with observations on human existence.

Vor Augen (1955; before our eyes) firmly established P.'s reputation as a master of short fiction. As the title suggests, the style and perspective are realistic. The war and its aftermath, the suffering of the past and its lingering presence are central to these stories, which owe their power and appeal to the interplay between past and present and between internal and external reality.

P.'s later works reflect the author's subtle and consistent development as well as his continuing respect for tradition. Some poems of *Mit einer Kranichfeder* (1962; with a crane feather) are

written in the laconic, aphoristic style that characterizes *Klartext* (1966; clear text) and *Tot oder lebendig* (1971; abridged tr., *Alive or Dead*, 1975). Nature, memories of childhood, and transience remain pervasive themes, and in *Tot oder lebendig* a concern with poetic process becomes important. P.'s long-standing interest in narrative poetry, reflected in essays and an anthology he edited, *Neue deutsche Erzählgedichte* (1964; new German narrative poems), culminated in *Vorkriegszeit* (1980; prewar period), a book-length poem set in the present.

The novels *Die mittleren Jahre* (1967; the middle years) and *Dichterleben* (1976; a poet's life) combine introspective passages, realistic vignettes, and flashbacks. The artistic consciousness and the tension between the outsider and the establishment are important themes. The generation gap—an especially significant problem in Germany—is central to P.'s third novel, *Juttas Neffe* (1979; Jutta's nephew).

P. remains one of Germany's most outstanding and versatile writers, an opponent of the radical avant-garde. His literary works, as well as his numerous essays, including those of *Männer die Gedichte machen* (1970; men who make poems), reveal a concern for poetic form and the author's quest for human values in an inhuman age.

FURTHER WORKS: *Buchstab, Zauberstab* (1959); *Weißer Panther* (1962); *Die Zwischenlandung* (1963); *Kastanien aus dem Feuer* (1963); *Windrichtungen* (1963); *Randerscheinungen* (1965); *Außenaufnahmen* (1968); *Liebeserklärungen in Prosa* (1969); *Die Erzählungen* (1971); *Klarheit schaffen* (1972); *Helle Tage anderswo* (1973); *Leben mit Wörtern* (1975); *Gesammelte Gedichte* (1975); *Die Zeit der anderen Auslegung* (1976); *Wintertage, Sommernächte* (1977); *Das Schweigen überbrücken* (1977); *Träumen, wachen, widerstehen* (1978); *Dunkelkammerspiel* (1978); *Wie sich Musik durchschlug* (1978); *Das Handwerk des Lesens* (1979); *Was mich nicht losläßt* (1981)

BIBLIOGRAPHY: Middleton, C., "The Poetry of H. P.," *GL&L*, 13 (1959): 55–57; Kügler, H., "Spur und Fährte," *Weg und Weglosigkeit* (1970): 161–86; A. K. Domandi, ed., *Modern German Literature* (1972), Vol. II: 183–87; H. P., *Leben mit Wörten* (1975): 133–224; Lubos, A., *Von Bezruč bis Bienek* (1977): 82–99; Exner, R., "H. P.," in Weissenberger, K., ed. *Die deutsche Lyrik 1945–1975* (1981): 186–97

—JERRY GLENN

PIOVENE, Guido

Italian novelist, journalist, and critic, b. 27 July 1907, Vicenza; d. 12 Nov. 1974, London, England

P. was educated in private schools and at the University of Milan, where he earned a degree in philosophy. His lifelong career in journalism began in 1927; from 1935 to 1952 he worked for *Il corriere della sera*, traveling extensively in Europe, the Soviet Union, and the U.S. During the latter part of his life, he was associated with *La stampa* of Turin.

P.'s early fiction, through 1962, reflects an intense preoccupation with deviant behavior evidenced by spiritually flawed individuals prone to violence, crime, and self-destruction. Structurally, his early work consists of retrospective, first-person narratives whose confessional tone and sustained analytical focus on behavioral motivations illuminate the characters' psychological makeup.

La gazzetta nera (written 1939, pub. 1943; the black gazette) includes five novellas whose respective protagonists, unable to repress their aversion to life, seek liberation through a criminal act. The most popular of P.'s novels, *Lettere di una novizia* (1941; *Confession of a Novice*, 1950), portrays the inner struggle of a young woman driven to murder in a desperate effort to escape convent life. The epistolary form is effectively employed to explore the manifold ways in which truth and reality are distorted to achieve selfish aims. The characters move in a climate of moral ambiguity; their sincerity and duplicity, exhaustively diagnosed, shed much light on the darker side of human consciousness.

The second stage of P.'s creative career is marked by richer introspective analysis and metaphysical reflections on the human condition. In *Le Furie* (1963; the Furies) haunting visions of the past are drawn from the author's adolescent years and youthful attraction to Fascism—also recounted in *La coda di paglia* (1962; the tail of straw). In P.'s most important work, *Le stelle fredde* (1970; the cold stars), the protagonist abandons his urban life to seek solitude and meditation. In the seclusion of his country house he discovers his insignificance in a meaningless universe and, through a visionary encounter with Dostoevsky, confronts deep perplexities about God and the afterlife. Equally revealing of P.'s despairing view of contemporary man is his last, unfinished novel, *Verità e menzogna* (1975; truth and lies), published posthumously.

P.'s distinguished activity as a journalist is represented by *De America* (1953; on America), widely regarded as a penetrating study of the U.S.; *Viaggio in Italia* (1958; traveling through Italy), a subjective account of Italian life; and *Madame la France* (1967; Madame France), a collection of articles dealing with France in the aftermath of World War II.

An original writer deeply concerned with the spiritual crisis of our time, P. brought to contemporary Italian narrative an outlook on life rich in insight, intellectual acumen, and metaphysical probing.

FURTHER WORKS: *La vedova allegra* (1931); *Pietà contro pietà* (1946); *I falsi redentori* (1949); *Lo scrittore tra la tirannide e la libertà* (1952); *Processo dell'Islam alla civiltà occidentale* (1957); *La gente che perdè Ierusalemme* (1967); *Inverno d'un uomo felice* (1977)

BIBLIOGRAPHY: Heiney, D., *America in Modern Italian Literature* (1964): 44–49; Kanduth, E., *Wesenzüge der modernen italienischen Erzählliteratur: Gehalte und Gestaltung bei Buzzati, P. und Moravia* (1968): 82–136; Goudet, J., "P., la morale et la métaphysique," *REI*, 15 (1969): 148–97

—AUGUSTUS PALLOTTA

PIRANDELLO, Luigi

Italian dramatist, novelist, short-story writer, and poet, b. 28 June 1867, Agrigento; d. 10 Dec. 1936, Rome

P. was the second of six children born to a well-to-do Sicilian family that had been deeply involved in the struggle for Italian unity. He was destined for the study of law, but from his teens

showed strong literary leanings: two manuscript notebooks of poetry date back to 1883. In 1887 he transferred from the University of Palermo to the University of Rome, where his study of Italian literature proved as short-lived as his study of law had been. He earned his doctorate in romance philology at the University of Bonn (Germany) in 1891 with a dissertation written in German on the dialect of his native region, *Laute und Lautentwickelung der Mundart von Girgenti* (facsimile ed., 1973; the sounds and their formation in the dialect of Girgenti [i.e., Agrigento]). In 1893 he settled in Rome and, aided by an allowance from his family, turned his attention to writing. He married Antonietta Portulano, a fellow Sicilian, in 1894, and in 1898 began teaching Italian language and stylistics at a teachers' college for women, a post he held until 1922. Two sons and a daughter were born between 1895 and 1899. A disaster in the sulfur mine in which his father's capital and his wife's dowry were invested cut off his private income in 1903 and forced him to turn his writing into a financially profitable activity and to stabilize his position at the college.

His first great success, the novel *Il fu Mattia Pascal* (1904; *The Late Mattia Pascal*, 1923; new tr., 1964), and two volumes of essays, *Arte e scienza* (1908; art and science) and *L'umorismo* (1908; *On Humor*, 1974), were the products of these changed circumstances. He had by that time already published four collections of poetry, his translation of Goethe's *Roman Elegies*, a narrative poem in verse, four collections of short stories—later incorporated with the many others he was to write in the two volumes of *Novelle per un anno* (1937–38; a year's worth of stories)—a full-length novel and a novelette, his first play—the one-act *L'epilogo* (1898; later retitled *La morsa; The Vise*, 1928; new tr., 1964)—and many articles on linguistic and literary topics. He was to continue to write mainly novels and short stories until 1916, at which time he was drawn to the theater.

The years of World War I were very difficult for P.: both his sons became prisoners of war and his wife's mental illness (which had first manifested itself at the time of the mine disaster) got worse to the point that she had to enter a nursing home in 1919. From the production of his first three-act play, *Se non così . . .* (1915; if not so . . . ; later retitled *La ragione degli altri* [other people's reasons]) to 1921, the date first of the spectacular failure in Rome and then the phenomenal success in Milan of *Sei personaggi in cerca d'autore* (rev. ed., 1925; *Six Characters in Search of an Author*, 1922; new tr., 1954), P. wrote and had performed sixteen plays, four of them in Sicilian dialect.

In 1922 the London and New York performances of *Sei personaggi in cerca d'autore* and the Paris performance of *Il piacere dell'onestà* (1917; *The Pleasure of Honesty*, 1923; new tr., 1962) ushered in a new period in P.'s life. More frequent and intense contacts with the theater both in Italy and abroad made him eager to try his hand at directing and producing. In 1924 he founded his own company and in 1925 inaugurated the Art Theater of Rome, for which he had won government backing. He was awarded the Nobel Prize in 1934 for "his bold and brilliant renovation of the drama and the stage." Until the very end he remained a prolific short-story writer and dramatist, renewing himself in a trajectory that had passed from the regional realism of his early work to the antitraditionalism of *teatro del grottesco* (theater of the grotesque, so called to define its combination of fantasy and seriousness), the self-reflexiveness of the plays of the theater-within-the-theater, and the symbolism of the "myth" plays.

Of P.'s seven novels, the first, *L'esclusa* (1901; *The Outcast*, 1925), is significant thematically for its unconventional treatment of adultery and historically for its subtle undermining of the assumptions of naturalism on which it appears to be based. *I vecchi e i giovani* (1908; *The Old and the Young*, 1928) is a large-scale historical novel set in 1892–94, the period that corresponds to P.'s return from Germany and his encounter with the "bankruptcy" of the new regime of united Italy. Although there is much that is "Pirandellian" in it, it was judged from the beginning to be a throwback to an earlier stage in the development of the modern novel. More original because of its protagonist—the inept "stranger in life" Mattia—and its philosophical relativism—presented as a remedy for or mitigation of the ills of existence—is *Il fu Mattia Pascal*, in which P. already plays with the idea of the "character without an author."

From a formal point of view, P.'s most interesting novels are the fragmented, kaleidoscopic, first-person narratives, *Si gira* (1915; later retitled *Quaderni di Serafino Gubbio operatore; Shoot! The Notebooks of Serafino Gubbio, Cinematograph Operator*, 1926) and *Uno, nessuno e centomila* (1926; *One, None, and a Hundred Thousand*, 1933). In *Quaderni di Serafino Gubbio* the device of the plot-within-the-plot foreshadows the later dramatic works on the theater; as a matter of fact, *Ciascuno a suo modo* (1923; *Each in His Own Way*, 1923) is based on an episode from it. In its weaving back and forth to recapture moments of the past suddenly essential to the plot, *Si gira* creates vividly the feeling of life lived without the structuring effect of a unifying concept. In its attack on the "machine that mechanizes life"—concretized in the movie camera that its protagonist operates—and in its treatment of man's alienation from his fellow men, it has lost none of its freshness.

Uno, nessuno e centomila is, on P.'s own testimony, his most important novel, the work that, had he been able to complete it when it was first begun around 1915, would have contributed to a "more exact view of my theater," for it contains the "complete synthesis of everything I have done and the source of everything I shall do." The short, discontinuous chapters of *Uno, nessuno e centomila*, with their humorous, conversational titles, are the structural counterpart of the protagonist's step-by-step discovery of the multiplicity of the personality and his final rejection of all constricting social forms in the timeless universe of madness.

P.'s short stories, the most significant body of short prose fiction in Italian literature since Boccaccio and comparable in other respects to Maupassant's, belong in any international collection devoted to the genre. They are a neglected area of his work even though rated by some critics as superior to his plays. The earliest one, "Capannetta" (1884; "The Little Hut," 1965), is a Sicilian sketch in the manner of Giovanni VERGA. Many others use the same locale and are populated by intense, tragicomic types dominated by the need to argue and dispute and embroiled in the most muddled situations: such are the crazed lawyer Zummo in "La casa del Granella" (1905; "The Haunted House," 1938), the contentious landowner Don Lollò Zirafa in "La giara" (1909; "The Jar," 1933), or Chiàrchiaro, the bearer of the "evil eye" in "La patente" (1911; the license).

Among the best known of P.'s stories are those that, like "La giara" and "La patente," were reworked as plays or are closely related to the plays: "La signora Frola e il signor Ponza, suo genero" (1915; "Signora Frola and Her Son-in-Law, Signor Ponza," 1965), for instance, in which the narrating voice prefigures the typical Pirandellian spokesman, Laudisi, in *Così è (se vi pare)* (1917; *Right You Are! (If You Think So)*, 1922), or "La tragedia di un personaggio" (1911; "A Character in Distress," 1938), in which the author's persona refuses to portray the vain Dr. Fileno, much

Luigi Pirandello

like a later author (and play director) will refuse to tell the story of the Father and his family in *Sei personaggi in cerca d'autore*.

There is also a whole group of urban stories, from "L'eresia catara" (1905; "Professor Lamis' Vengeance," 1938) about the nearsighted professor so obsessed with his esoteric research that he does not notice he is lecturing to an empty classroom, to "La carriola" (1916?; the wheelbarrow), in which a staid, respected lawyer guards against an impulse to madness by permitting himself one carefully dosed-out moment of irrationality each day, to "Il treno ha fischiato" (1914; the train whistled), in which a harried clerk finds his own private safety valve in from time to time escaping in the imagination, "between one set of figures and the other," to Siberia or the Congo.

There are, finally, the powerful, disquieting later stories, in which the major action, however violent what actually happens is, takes place in the psyche: "La distruzione dell'uomo" (1921; "Destruction of Man," 1956), whose protagonist, maddened by the horror of the overcrowded slum in which he lives, kills a pregnant woman; "Soffio" (1931; a breath of air), whose protagonist discovers that he has the power of life and death over other men; and "Cinci" (1932; "Cinci," 1959), the story of a boy who kills another boy and then simply forgets that he had ever done it.

P.'s earliest plays were one-acters reflecting distinct tendencies in the contemporary drama: *L'epilogo* and *Il dovere del medico* (1912; *The Doctor's Duty*, 1928) are classifiable as fin-de-siècle bourgeois problem plays; *Lumìe di Sicilia* (1911; *Sicilian Limes*, 1928) and *La giara* (1917; *The Jar*, 1928) belong to the regional theater and exist in dialect versions as well as in Italian; *All'uscita* (1916; *At the Gate*, 1928) is a "profane mystery" reminiscent of MAETERLINCK's kind of SYMBOLISM. In *Pensaci, Giacomino!* (1916; *Better Think Twice About It*, 1955), *Il berretto a sonagli* (1917; *Cap and Bells*, 1957), and *Liolà* (1917; *Liolà*, 1952), Sicilian motifs are combined with such basic Pirandellian themes as the triumph of the irrational, the destruction of the individual's self-constructed mask, and the conflict between appearance and reality.

But P.'s first play of fundamental importance is *Così è (se vi pare)*, a parable that uses a provincial bureaucratic milieu as a setting in which to demonstrate the relativity of truth and to plead for each man's right to his "phantom"—that private illusion he creates for himself and by which he lives "in perfect harmony, pacified." *Il piacere dell'onestà, Il gioco delle parti* (1918; *The Rules of the Game*, 1959), and *Tutto per bene* (1920; *All for the Best*, 1960) continue the trend of disassociation between the realistic foundations of P.'s art—reflected in the elements of the plot of the story being told—and its "philosophical" superstructure—the "particular sense of life" that gives the stories universal value (see P.'s preface to the 1925 edition of *Sei personaggi in cerca d'autore*; Eng. tr., 1952).

Enrico IV (1922; *Henry IV*, 1923) is without doubt P.'s masterpiece. Here alienation reaches the dimensions of madness: actual madness at first, and feigned madness later, as the only possible solution, short of suicide, by which the nameless protagonist can protect his "phantom" from the corrupt, egotistical, foolish, and vicious world about him. In the play—often called a tragicomedy, although not by P. himself, who considered it a tragedy—the tremendous and unequivocal pressure of life "on stage," which is one of the distinguishing features of P.'s dramaturgy, is given its fullest, shattering impact. *Vestire gli ignudi* (1922; *Naked*, 1923; new tr., *To Clothe the Naked*, 1962), whose protagonist *is* driven to suicide, is in many ways a companion piece to *Enrico IV*. Its middle-class setting, however, and a few stock characters from the comic repertoire account for its elegiac, rather than tragic, tone.

In the trilogy of theater-within-theater, *Sei personaggi in cerca d'autore, Ciascuno a suo modo*, and *Questa sera si recita a soggetto* (1930; *Tonight We Improvise*, 1932), the focus shifts from the existential anguish of the protagonist to the anguish of the character in search of being (compare the short story "La tragedia di un personaggio"). What these plays actually deal with is the problem of artistic creation. While ostensibly concerned with the interaction of character, actor, and spectators in achieving the illusion of life on stage—and as such they can be read as little more than amusing though brilliant theatrical experiments—within the broader framework of P.'s thought they are evidence that the theater itself was only one concretization of the concept of artistic form. This point of view is stated with uncommon cogency in the preface to *Sei personaggi in cerca d'autore*.

A second trilogy—*La nuova colonia* (1928; *The New Colony*, 1958), *Lazzaro* (1929; *Lazarus*, 1959), and *I giganti della montagna* (1937; *The Mountain Giants*, 1958), described by P. as "myths"—marks the final stage of his development. In them the frame of reference is no longer the individual whose experience is universalized, but society itself. The last play, although left unfinished at P.'s death, belongs with his masterpieces. In the figure of the magician Cotrone, who lives with his refugees from the real world in an abandoned villa that he has turned into the realm of fantasy, P. created the last projection of himself as the self-effacing artist

perceiving the abundant life swirling in never-ending movement about him.

As in the case of other artists who originally struck their public as unique and revolutionary, the passing of time has served for P., also, to reveal characteristics of his age that he shared with others. In a changing play of perspectives he has become "historicized." Yet his world view, with its pessimism, irrationalism, rebellion against convention, sympathy for the downtrodden and the misunderstood, and, at the same time, its pitiless eye for the deformed and the grotesque, continues to elicit a direct, subjective response on the part of readers and spectators that translates itself into either warm partisanship or troubled repulsion, reactions not unlike those of his first public. The controversial nature of his work—exemplarily brought out by the simultaneous official recognition accorded him by the Fascist government of Italy, the Soviet Academy that authorized the translation of his works into Russian, and the jury of the Nobel Prize—has not yet been dulled with time, and his reputation, as is true for other writers of equal stature, has grown ever stronger over the years.

FURTHER WORKS: *Pasqua di Gea* (1891); *Amori senza amore* (1894); *Elegie renane* (1895); *Il turno* (1902; *The Merry-Go-Round of Love*, 1964); *Le beffe della vita e della morte* (1902); *Quand' ero matto* (1902); *Bianche e nere* (1904); *Erma bifronte* (1906); *La vita nuda* (1908); *Suo marito* (1911); *Terzetti* (1912); *Le due maschere* (1914); *La trappola* (1915); *Erba del nostro orto* (1915); *E domani, lunedì? . . .* (1917); *L'innesto* (1917); *Un cavallo nella luna* (1918); *Il carnevale dei morti* (1919); *Tu ridi* (1919); *Berecche e la guerra* (1919); *Come prima, meglio di prima* (1921); *La signora Morli una e due* (1922); *La vita che ti diedi* (1924; *The Life I Gave You*, 1959); *Diana e la Tuda* (1927; *Diana and Tuda*, 1960); *L'amica delle mogli* (1927; *The Wives' Friend*, 1960); *O di uno o di nessuno* (1929); *Come tu mi vuoi* (1930; *As You Desire Me*, 1931); *Trovarsi* (1930; *To Find Oneself*, 1960); *Quando si è qualcuno* (1933; *When Somebody Is Somebody*, 1958); *Non si sa come* (1935; *No One Knows How*, 1960); *Novelle per un anno* (2 vols., 1956–1957); *Tutti i romanzi* (1957); *Maschere nude* (2 vols., 1958; new ed., 1973); *Saggi, poesie, scritti varii* (1960). FURTHER WORKS IN ENGLISH: *One-Act Plays* (1928); *A Horse in the Moon: Twelve Short Stories* (1932); *Better Think Twice About It and Twelve Other Stories* (1934); *The Naked Truth and Eleven Other Stories* (1934); *The Medals and Other Stories* (1938); *Four Tales* (1939); *Naked Masks* (1952); *Short Stories* (1959); *To Clothe the Naked and Two Other Plays* (1962); *The Merry-Go-Round of Love and Selected Stories* (1964); *P.'s One-Act Plays* (1964); *Short Stories* (1964)

BIBLIOGRAPHY: MacClintock, L., *The Age of P.*, (1951); Bentley, E., Introduction to *Naked Masks* (1952): vii–xxvii; Vittorini, D., *The Drama of L. P.*, 2nd ed. (1957); Bishop, T., *P. and the French Theater* (1960); Brustein, R., *The Theatre of Revolt* (1964): 281–317; Poggioli, R., "P. in Retrospect," *The Spirit of the Letter* (1965): 146–70; Starkie, W., *L. P.*, 3rd rev. ed. (1965); Büdel, O., *P.* (1966); special P. section, *TDR*, 10, 3 (1966): 30–111; Cambon, G., ed. *P.: A Collection of Critical Essays* (1967); Moestrup, J., *The Structural Patterns of P.'s Work* (1972); Matthaei, R., *L. P.* (1973); Gilman, R., *The Making of Modern Drama* (1974): 157–89; Paolucci, A., *P.'s Theater: The Recovery of the Modern Stage for Dramatic Art* (1974); Giudice, G., *P.: A Biography* (1975); Oliver, R. W., *Dreams of Passion: The Theater of L. P.* (1979); Ragusa, O., *L. P.: An Approach to His Theatre* (1980); Valency, M., *The End of*

the World: An Introduction to Contemporary Drama (1980):
84–205

—OLGA RAGUSA

. . . If the great human gift is that of words, by what
diabolic plan does it happen that words multiply
misunderstanding? The very humanity of man increases his isolation. Such is the idea "behind" one of
P.'s most famous ideas. "Multiple personality" is a
similar instance: Pirandellian man is isolated not only
from his fellows but also from himself at other times.
Further than this, isolation cannot go. This is a
"nihilistic vision" with a vengeance.

Perhaps it would nowadays be called an existentialist vision: life is absurd, it fills one with nausea
and dread and anguish, it gives one the metaphysical
shudder, yet, without knowing why, perhaps just
because one is *there*, in life, one faces it, one fights
back, one cries out in pain, in rage, in defiance (if one
is a Sicilian existentialist), and since all living, all life,
is improvisation, one improvises some values. Their
Form will last until Living destroys them and we have
to improvise some more.

P.'s plays grew from his own torment (I overlook
for the moment the few precious pages that grew from
his joy) but through his genius they came to speak for
all the tormented and, potentially, *to* all the tormented, that is, to all men. And they will speak with
particular immediacy until the present crisis of mankind—a crisis which trembles, feverishly or ever so
gently, through all his plays—is past.

Eric Bentley, Introduction to L. P., *Naked Masks*
(1952), p. xxvii

P. is a realist. In his long and great career as a writer
he has sought to portray individuals as such rather
than to present them through the concept of man,
stately but abstract. He has always molded his art
after the individuals that he has met, known, and
studied, who have touched both his sense of humor
and his heart. His powerful imagination and his
genius have done the rest in transporting them from
the tumult of life into the serenity of his art.

We are not using the term "realist" in the usual
sense of the word. P. is a realist in the sense that he
tries to encompass within the scope of his art the
basic, instinctive needs of man together with the
secret torment of his soul and the mobile life of his
intellect. Man is one in his various attributes, and P.
has pictured to us the drama of humanity as he sees it
and feels it. In so doing he has joined the ranks of the
great who have from time to time appeared under
all skies.

Domenico Vittorini, *The Drama of L. P.*, 2nd ed.
(1957), p. 9

P.'s most original achievement in his experimental
plays, then, is the dramatization of the very act of

creation. If he has not made a statue that moves, he
has made a statue which is the living signature of the
artist, being both his product and his process. The
concept of the face and the mask has become the basis
for a totally new relationship between the artist and
his work. Thus, P. completes that process of Romantic internalizing begun by Ibsen and Strindberg. Ibsen,
for all his idealization of personality, still believed in
an external reality available to all, and so did Chekhov,
Brecht, and Shaw. Strindberg had more doubts about
this reality, but believed it could be partially perceived by the inspired poet and seer. For P., however,
objective reality has become virtually inaccessible,
and all one can be sure of is the illusion-making
faculty of the subjective mind. After P., no dramatist
has been able to write with quite the same certainty as
before. In P.'s plays, the messianic impulse spends
itself, before it even fully develops, in doubts, uncertainties, and confusions.

Robert Brustein, *The Theatre of Revolt* (1964),
pp. 315–16

When all the characters of the Pirandellian universe shall have faded into thin air, the author will
nevertheless be remembered for his curious humour
made up of contradiction. In an exceedingly interesting volume on *Humour* he analyses his ideas on the
subject and makes them fit into the scheme of Italian
literature. Every true humourist, according to P., is
also a critic—a fantastic critic. For in the conception
of a work of art reflection becomes a form of sentiment, as it were a mirror in which sentiment watches
itself. And he gives many examples to show that
reflection is like icy water in which the flame of
sentiment quenches itself. Thus we can explain the
frequent digressions which occur in the novels and
plays, digressions which are always due to the disturbing effect caused by the active reflection of the
author. The Pirandellian humour arises by antithesis.
In the mind of a man a thought cannot arise without at
the same time causing a directly opposite and contrary one to appear, and so free, unfettered emotion or
sentiment, instead of soaring aloft like the lark in the
clear air, finds itself held back just at the moment that
it stretches out its wings to fly.

Walter Starkie, *L. P., 1967–1936*, 3rd rev. ed.
(1965), p. 270

If P. does explode the notion of a fixed personal
identity, this by no means implies the moral annihilation of the individual self; on the contrary, the effect
may be to dissuade human beings from taking themselves and one another for granted. In P.'s fictional
world, the elusive reality of personal existence impinges on our awareness precisely because it is felt to
be inaccessible to ready-made definitions. The capital question of whether his work is poetry or just
abstract speculation will have to be settled case by
case, and more attention to the physiognomy of his
style than has generally been applied so far should

prove very helpful here. As a result, instead of label-ing him a dramatist or novelist of ideas, we can more aptly speak of his whole work as an exploration of consciousness. It is as a drama of consciousness that it retains relevance, to the extent that the ideas operate functionally in each formal embodiment. Once this focus is established, many critical problems will become clearer. . . .

Glauco Cambon, ed., Introduction to P.: A
Collection of Critical Essays (1967), p. 9

P.'s relativism stems from his antirationalist no-tions which aim at destroying any and every illusion or fiction of man and society, tearing off the mask man fashions for himself or society forces on him. Nowhere more than in the bleak environment P. has chosen as his domain is appearance more important. The lower we get in the animal world and its species, the more important and the more effective mimicry becomes, and the lower we get in terms of social conditions, the more important fictions, fronts, and appearances become in the struggle of life. Neither the peasants, who are still close to life, to the origin of things, nor the affluent need care about appearances; they, too, do have concerns and taboos, but of a different sort. It is the bleak social segment in be-tween, that vegetates in tenement houses at the edge of cities . . . , that needs these appearances; the white collar worker who ekes out a measly existence . . . , the decrepit professional . . . , the small-time charla-tan. . . . Indeed, no social group lends itself better to a demonstration of the relative value of human appear-ances; and that is what P. set out to do.

Oscar Büdel, P. (1969), p. 58

In his last plays, P. is in effect drawing the chief meridians of his theatrical world upward to converge at a single pole. This whole business of life can be for us all no more than a tale told by an idiot unless we get deep enough below the surface of conventional val-ues to the substantive core. What blind Oedipus "saw" at Colonus, what Orestes experienced in Athene's court of ultimate appeal, what Shakespeare reveals to us in the magic art of Prospero and in Cranmer's prophecy at the christening of the child destined to become Queen Elizabeth—such is the substance of P.'s myth plays. In them he gathers up all that he had already dramatized, into a new synthesis, to show us its social, religious, and artistic reality, in its rightness, its holiness, and its beauty.

P.'s theatrical world is planted deep in the common soil of human experience, with a sturdy weathered and twisted trunk of theatrical expertise that enables him to review for us dramatically the meaning of theater, and with marvelous branches of evergreen leaves that come and go imperceptibly, laden with seasonal fruit. Just before he died, P. had a vision of such a tree—the great Saracen olive of Sicily. He explained to his son, on the morning of the day before his death, that with that tree planted in the center of

the stage, for the curtain to come down in the unwrit-ten final act of The Mountain Giants, he would solve everything he meant to show. That great tree, whose roots he had revealed in his masterful Liolà, was meant to symbolize the completion of his theater.

Anne Paolucci, P.'s Theater: The Recovery of the
Modern Stage for Dramatic Art (1974), pp. 20–21

. . . The genius of P.'s accomplishments lies in his ability to suggest the need for the movement from an avvertimento [awareness] to a sentimento del contrario [feeling of the opposite], not merely in content, but in the dramatic encapsulation of those ideas. He became a theatrical innovator in a much deeper and more important sense than the Futurists, Surrealists, and Dadaists, whose alternative vision was couched in terms that made it inaccessible to those very people who needed to be confronted with it. P.'s initial reception gives evidence that his work also met resistance. Yet his retention of aspects of convention-al realism allowed him both to draw his audience into his world in order to frustrate their old expectations and, more important, to communicate the relationship of his new vision to their everyday reality.

Roger W. Oliver, Dreams of Passion: The Theater
of L. P. (1979), p. 156

PIRES, José Cardoso

Portuguese novelist, short-story writer, essayist, and dramatist, b. 2 Oct. 1925, Pêso

P.'s birth was almost contemporaneous with that of the begin-ning of the dictatorship in Portugal (1926–74). After studying advanced mathematics in Lisbon, P. held a variety of jobs. He became involved in magazine publishing and has been the chief editor of several magazines and newspapers. His commitment to a sociopolitical literature resulted from his early literary contacts with the NEOREALIST movement. His openly avowed political beliefs during the dictatorship years not only brought great atten-tion to his writings, but also resulted in continual problems with the regime's censorship.

In the 1940s and early 1950s P. had difficulties in getting his short stories published because they vividly presented the bleaker aspects of everyday Portuguese life, such as widespread rural impoverishment, the demoralizing military life, political repres-sion, and the mistreatment of the aged. Several of these stories were collected in Jogos de azar (1963; games of chance).

O anjo ancorado (1958; the anchored angel), P.'s first novel, presented a society enduring in a centuries-old state of chaotic numbness. Its victims—the wealthy, the cultured, and the impover-ished—are no longer capable of reacting to common class confron-tations except through deceit and physical violence. The great depths and extremes of this national malaise were further devel-oped in P.'s prize-winning O hóspede de Job (1963; Job's guest), in which the recurrent metaphor for the Portuguese is that of beasts of burden, plodding along aimlessly, abusing and being abused. P.'s sophisticated use of cinematic techniques and his extremely

551

penetrating characterizations resulted in his most dynamic stylistic achievement.

P.'s treatise *Cartilha do marialva* (1960; primer for the *marialva* [rural macho male]) delved into the historical origin of the common Portuguese "macho" type. The feudal life style that reigned in Portugal well into the 20th c. is viewed as the major catalyst for the creation of this negative, hedonistic kind of person. The novel *O delfim* (1968; the dauphin) is P.'s literary investigation into the nature of a *marialva*.

The life of the late dictator Salazar was parodied in *Dinossauro excelentíssimo* (1974; most excellent dinosaur). The parliamentary debate that accompanied the publication of this "fable" was caused by P.'s exaggerated and biting satire.

P.'s works have reflected the pulse of Portugal's sociopolitical change from a purely rural society to an insignificant industrial one. Although the style of his novels is simple and direct, he attains a profundity of thought and purpose that no other contemporary Portuguese writer has approached. His ultimate goal is to discover the key to the almost masochistic national soul. His most recent collection of essays, *E agora, José?* (1977; what next, José?), reaffirms this interest. It presents, however, a rather negative, doubting tone about Portugal's future in the post-1974 revolutionary period.

FURTHER WORKS: *Os caminheiros, e outros contos* (1946); *Histórias de amor* (1952); *O render dos heróis* (1960); *O corpo-delito na sala de espelhos* (1979); *O burro-em-pé (contos)* (1979)

BIBLIOGRAPHY: Ares Montes, J., on *O hóspede de Job*, *Ínsula*, 212 (1964), 16; *TLS* (29 Jan. 1970): 115; on *O delfim*; Stern, I., on *E agora, José?*, *WLT*, 52 (1978): 611–12

—IRWIN STERN

PITTER, Ruth

English poet, b. 7 Nov. 1897, Ilford; d. 12 Feb. 1992, Long Crendon, Buckinghamshire

Oldest of three children born to two London elementary school-teachers, P. started writing verse at five and published her first poem at thirteen, in A. R. Orage's *New Age* (later *New English Weekly*). She worked as a War Office clerk in World War I; after the war she mastered various crafts (especially woodworking and painting) and worked first for a large specialty firm and later in partnership in her own shop in London until 1945; she then retired to Aylesbury, where she died in 1992. Among the awards she has received are the Hawthornden Prize (1937), the Heinemann Award (1954), and the Queen's Gold Medal for Poetry (1955).

P.'s poetry is frequently identified as reflecting a 17th-c. mind, and comparisons have been made with the work of Henry Vaughan, Thomas Traherne, and Thomas Carew, as well as with such other poets as Edmund Spenser, William Blake, John Clare, and Gerard Manley Hopkins. She wrote lyrical verse on a wide range of traditional subjects, notably the natural world and religion. Her combination of metaphysical passion and a vivid sensual awareness sprang at least in part from her identification with and precise knowledge of the English countryside, gardening, and a life of physical labor. She thus appealed to both the heart and the mind, and her "perfect ear and exact epithet" (to quote Hilaire BELLOC,

one of her first major supporters) produced a balanced, deeply felt, and often deceptively simple lyric.

She herself believed that a poem "begins and ends in mystery . . . in that secret movement of the poet's being, in response to the secret dynamism of life," and many of her poems are contemplative celebrations, such as "The Fishers" (1939) and "The Cygnet" (1945); the latter poem, one of her longest, uses two swans on the Thames to represent the soul's victory over evil. Similar poems include "Urania" (1936), "The Eternal Image" (1936), and "The Downward-Pointing Muse" (1939). But she was also capable of writing sardonic, witty verse, such as the poems in *The Rude Potato* (1941) and *R. P. on Cats* (1947), the latter less "old-maidish" (P.'s term) and rollicking than the similar volume by her acquaintance T. S. ELIOT.

P. was neither experimental nor avant-garde, and her use of traditional meters and forms set her apart from most modern poets. Nor did she reflect much topical interest in the hurried world around her (although her "The Military Harpist" [1939] is both serious and sardonic in its subdued commentary about war). Rather, her vivid, precise, always apt sensitivity celebrated silence and contemplation, especially in the contrast between ordinary life and the Christian hope, or in the personification of natural beauty and life as reflective of divine reality.

Although highly praised by some critics and many other poets, P. was never a fashionable or popular writer, was never identified with any "school" or movement, and lived in comparative but wholly unjustified obscurity. Her talent, dedication, and virtuosity warrant much higher critical esteem.

FURTHER WORKS: *First Poems* (1920); *First and Second Poems* (1930); *Persephone in Hades* (1931); *A Mad Lady's Garland* (1934); *A Trophy of Arms* (1936); *The Spirit Watches* (1939); *Poem* (1943); *The Bridge* (1945); *Urania* (1951); *The Ermine* (1953); *Still by Choice* (1966); *Poems 1926–1966* (1968 Am., *Collected Poems*, 1969); *End of Drought* (1975); *A Heaven to Find* (1987); *Collected Poems* (1996)

BIBLIOGRAPHY: Bogan, L., "A Singular Talent," *Poetry*, 51 (1937): 43–45; Swartz, R. T., "The Spirit Watches," *Poetry*, 56 (1940): 334–37; Gilbert, R., *Four Living Poets* (1944): 48–54; Watkin, E. I., *Poets & Mystics* (1953): 301–18; special P. section, *Poetry Northwest*, 1, 3 (1960): 3–20; Wain, J., "A Note on R. P.'s Poetry," *Listener*, 81 (1969): 239–40; Russell, A., ed. *R. P.: Homage to a Poet* (1969); Duncan, E., *Unless Soul Clap Its Hands: Portraits and Passages* (1984)

—PAUL SCHLUETER

PLASKOVITIS, Spyros

(born Spyros Plaskasovitis) Greek novelist, short-story writer, and essayist, b. 13 June 1917, Corfu

P. studied law at the University of Athens and philosophy of law in Paris. From 1935 to 1951 he worked as a civil servant, then joined the council of state (supreme administrative court) where he was promoted in 1959 and served until 1968 when the military dictatorship dismissed and exiled him. Charged for membership in the resistance group Democratic Defense, he was sentenced to prison. While incarcerated, he contributed a short story entitled "To radar" ("The Radar") to the antijunta miscellany *Dekaokhto Keimena* (1970; *Eighteen Texts*, 1972). Reinstated in his position after the collapse of the junta and promoted to counselor, he served until 1977, when he resigned, joined the Panhellenic Socialist Movement, and was elected member of parliament at large. He was reelected in all subsequent elections, first to the Greek and then to the European parliament, from which he retired in 1989.

P.'s first short story, "Ta sperna" (1947; memorial offerings), was published in the literary magazine *Nea Hestia*. Many stories and articles or essays have appeared to this day in prestigious periodicals, annuals, and newspapers. These were later collected in volumes. His second short-story collection, *He thyella kai to phanari* (1955; the tempest and the lantern), won a State Prize in 1956, as did his second novel, *He Poli* (1979; the city), in 1980; earlier he had received a prize from the Group of the Twelve for his first novel, *To phragma* (1960; the dam) in 1961.

P.'s diction and style are simple and straight-forward with occasional touches of lyricism. His narrative technique, however, in either stories or novels, makes frequent use of time-plane changes in passages of memory, dreaming, or vagary, which tend to give it an aura of otherworldliness or fantasy verging on the surrealistic. He retains firm control of his material thanks to his skill in making the imaginary deflate at the end in an atmosphere of believable actuality which reestablishes the initially realistic setting of his fiction. A great asset of his art is the true-to-life depiction of his characters, who are indirectly and gradually analyzed in depth. Their idiosyncratic behavior and stubborn reaction to adversities earn the sympathy of the reader and help communicate P.'s thematic concerns. These are invariably issues involving crucial choices that lead to conflict with family, community groups, or the ruling establishment in the microcosm where his heroes and heroines live and function. In *He Poli*, for instance, his two protagonists are antagonized by the selfish, unprincipled, and corrupt in family and the social milieu of Corfu, before and after World War II. Their survival or vindication is painfully achieved thanks to their inherent human decency and integrity, however eccentric these may be.

Fundamentally P. is an existential moralizer not unlike Albert CAMUS, whom he admires. His ideological stance as a moderate socialist emerges gradually but not in a doctrinaire fashion, as his spokespersons are governed by humanistic virtues that oppose the hypocrisy and moral dereliction of the conservatives or reactionaries who act as the pillars of society. This is also seen in his latest novel, *He kyria tes vitrinas* (1990; the lady of the showcase), which features the same heroine as *He Poli*. This time her vindication occurs on the personal rather than the sociopolitical level, as she finally earns the love and respect of a successful businessman who thus resists financial and sexual temptations that would only debase and destroy him. P. has the skill to elevate the personal onto a universal plane, and vice versa.

His novel *To phragma* has appeared in French, Russian, and Ukrainian. A number of his short stories were translated and included in anthologies of Greek literature in these three languages plus English, German, Italian, Romanian, and Hungarian.

FURTHER WORKS: *To gymno dentro* (1952); *Hoi gonatismenoi* (1964); *To syrmatoplegma* (1974); *To trello epeisodio* (1984); *He pezographia tou ethous kai alla dokimia* (1986)

BIBLIOGRAPHY: Raizis, M. B., on *He Poli, WLT*, 54, 4 (Autumn 1980), 678; Raizis, M. B., on *He pezographia tou ethous kai alla dokimie, WLT*, 62, 1 (Winter 1988): 167

—M. BYRON RAIZIS

PLATH, Sylvia

American poet, novelist, and short-story writer, b. 27 Oct. 1932, Winthrop, Mass.; d. 11 Feb. 1963, London, England

P. graduated from Smith College, and while on a Fulbright scholarship to Cambridge, met and married the English poet Ted HUGHES in 1956. She had suffered a nervous breakdown in 1953 while at Harvard Summer School and had twice attempted suicide. In *Letters Home* (1975), the volume of correspondence edited by her mother, there emerges a self-portrait of a young woman driven by hopes for the highest success alternating with moods of deep depression. After marital difficulties and a period of physical and psychological strain, P. committed suicide.

P.'s early poetry was somewhat derivative and academic, based on the then current styles of refined and ironic verse. Then, under the influence of her husband and the work of Dylan THOMAS and Gerard Manley Hopkins, the promise and depth of her talent developed rather suddenly and with great force. Often thought of as a "confessional" poet, since she studied with Anne Sexton (1928–1974) in Robert LOWELL's Harvard class, P. became more and more a mythic poet. Her later work, especially the volume *Ariel* (1966), was remarkable for its tight syntactic pressures and its obsessive imagery. Resembling somewhat the work of the German poet Gottfried BENN—with its EXPRESSIONIST nihilism and atavistic urgings—P.'s lyric mode was dominated by a fierce commitment to the most exalted ideal of artistic intensity: "The blood jet is poetry, / There is no stopping it."

In her well-known poems "Lady Lazarus" (1963) and "Daddy" (1963) P. pushes the traditions of self-revelation and lyric intimacy in directions not often explored in the English or American idiom. One predecessor might be Emily Dickinson, but P. has no fund of biblical or hymnbook imagery to create a sense of herself as a representative sufferer. Instead, many of the assumptions of Freudian psychology, especially with its paradigms of family conflict, self-disgust, and "split" awareness, underpin the poetry's dynamic surge toward revelation. The poetry apparently asks for no pity, and the deepest motives for its unveilings remain obscure, although clearly powerful.

P.'s poetry is not easily accessible, but she gained a considerable reputation when her novel, *The Bell Jar* (1971; English ed. published pseudonymously, 1962), appeared and won a readership drawn largely from college students. The novel is semiautobiographical, and its portraits of several characters are ripe with a controlled sense of invective (hence the use of a pseudonym). P.'s depiction of psychological disorder and the experience of recuperation in a mental hospital are especially affecting; in many ways this depiction parallels R. D. Laing's (1927-1989) account, in the popular *The Divided Self* (1960), of what he terms "ontological insecurity."

In addition to the novel, P. published several short stories, most of them in "slick" magazines. She was also occupied with writing feature stories and travel pieces, many of which were never published. *The Collected Poems* (1981) and *The Journals of S. P.* (1982), the latter with a preface by Ted Hughes, showed that her stature was still high—many reviewers praised both volumes. Unfortunately, the journals for the months immediately preceding her suicide were destroyed or lost. The questions surrounding her last, intensely creative period will still be posed, but may prove unanswerable.

Those who value P. highly see her as a starkly honest poet, often working with such contemporary themes as the woman-victim in a patriarchal society. Others find her reputation overblown, feeling that her emphasis on individual psychological disorders is finally narrow and stultifying. In part her reputation has risen and fallen with the fortunes of "confessional poetry." But her language continues to have an undeniable power, and her genius for exfoliating imagery to capture a sense of emotional distress is indeed distinctive. It will be increasingly difficult for readers and critics to separate the merits of the work from the lurid elements of the biography. But it will also be hard to ignore her considerable gift for verbalizing a certain extreme psychological reality that has been one of the chief concerns of modern literature.

FURTHER WORKS: *The Colossus, and Other Poems* (1962); *Crossing the Water* (1971); *Winter Trees* (1972); *Johnny Panic and the Bible of Dreams* (1979)

BIBLIOGRAPHY: Newman, C., ed., *The Art of S. P.* (1970); Alvarez, A., *The Savage God* (1972): 3–42; Steiner, N., *A Closer Look at "Ariel"* (1973); Holbrook, D., *S. P.: Poetry and Existence* (1976); Kroll, J., *Chapters in a Mythology: The Poetry of S. P.* (1976); Lane, G., ed. *S. P.: New Views on the Poetry* (1979); Broe, M. L., *Protean Poet: The Poetry of S. P.* (1980)

—CHARLES MOLESWORTH

Sylvia Plath

PLATONOV, Andrey Platonovich

Russian novelist and short-story writer, b. 20 Aug. 1899, Yamskaya Sloboda (near Voronezh); d. 5 Jan. 1951, Moscow

P., the son of a metalworker, had his first job at the age of thirteen. In 1924 he finished polytechnical school with an engineering degree. After several years as a specialist in land reclamation (1923–26), he permanently abandoned engineering for writing.

P. began writing in the early 1920s, with some two hundred articles of a journalistic or essayistic nature, as well as his first stories and his only book of verse, the often bombastic and undistinguished *Golubaya glubina* (1922; blue depths). Initially, P. shared with many of his fellow writers a nearly messianic faith in the power of man to transform and *defeat* nature, to reshape the world, and ultimately the universe, to suit his own ends. Yet, in one of P.'s earliest stories, "Potomki solntsa" (1921; descendants of the sun), and in "Efirny trakt" (1927; the etheric way), he warned against both the potentially destructive evil inherent in technological advance and the hypertrophy of mind at the expense of feelings and scruples. While machines would remain dear to P. the engineer, by the end of the 1920s interest in technology became secondary in his work to a focus on man's restless quest for self-knowledge and meaning in life, his battle to overcome isolation and to survive in a hostile world.

In the late 1920s and early 1930s P. became increasingly skeptical of Soviet socioeconomic experimentation, with its tendency to place bureaucratic imperatives over both the individual and collective interests of workers and peasants. This attitude can be seen in stories like "Usomnivshiisya Makar" (1929; "Makar the Doubtful," 1974) and "Vprok" (1931; for future use) and in novels like *Chevengur* (1972; *Chevengur*, 1978) and *Kotlovan* (1969; *The Foundation Pit*, 1973). *Chevengur*, which has never been published in the Soviet Union, dates from 1929 and is a satirical, folkloristic account of naïve Communist visionaries leading the masses to destitution. *Kotlovan*, which dates from the early 1930s, was P.'s answer to the call to depict new socialist construction and collectivization—which he did in a grimly phantasmagorical, and at times, surrealistic way.

P.'s reservations about the course of Soviet development earned him severe reproval from critics and caused him difficulties in getting his fiction published during the 1930s. Some of his stories were printed in journals, but only one small collection appeared separately: *Reka Potudan* (1937; *The River Potudan*, 1978), which, besides the title story, included several of P.'s best stories, "Takyr" (1934; "The Takyr," 1978), "Fro" (1936; "Fro," 1967), and "Treti syn" (1937; "The Third Son," 1969). During the "great terror" of the late 1930s P. turned to literary criticism and stories for children.

World War II offered new opportunities to write, and P. responded with six separate collections of sketches between 1942 and 1945. After his return from the front, he was once more officially rebuked, this time for the story first published under the title "Semya Ivanova"—later changed to "Vozvrashchenie"— (1936; "The Homecoming," 1970). In broken health, P. spent his last years revamping folk literature, with which many of his own works had had much in common.

P.'s artistic craft was formed by the literary experimentation of the Soviet 1920s—extreme compositional diffusion, heavy emphasis on stylistic expressiveness. Although he shared in the gray, sobering development that marked Soviet literature overall from the early 1930s until many years after Stalin's death in 1953, certain constants remained in the best of his fiction: the depiction of restless vagabonds, for whom domestic life is either not satisfying or impossible, close attention to simple, usually inarticulate people whose experiences are given an inimitable poetic quality through P.'s highly creative manipulation of roughhewn, but expressive common speech. That these experiences were usually sorrowful, even tragic, did not help P. fit into a literature that expected optimism from its writers. Still, P.'s uncommon talent, social background, and education equipped him as few others to depict the life of Russians during a particularly momentous period in their country's history. The rediscovery of P. in his homeland and the growing awareness of him abroad are among the brightest developments in post-Stalinist Russian literature.

FURTHER WORKS: *Gorod Gradov* (1926; *The City of Gradov*, 1978); *Epifanskie shliuzy* (1927; *The Epifan Locks*, 1974); *Dzhan* (written 1933–1935, pub. 1966; *Dzhan*, 1970); *Izbrannye rasskazy* (1958); *V prekrasnom i yarostnom mire: Povesti i rasskazy* (1965); *Izbrannoe* (1966); *V preskrasnom i yarostnom mire: Povesti i rasskazy* (1979. FURTHER WORKS IN ENGLISH: *The Fierce and Beautiful World: Stories by A. P.* (1970)

BIBLIOGRAPHY: Yevtushenko, Y., "Without Me, the Country's Not Complete," in *The Fierce and Beautiful World: Stories by A. P.* (1970): 7–18; Brodsky, J., Preface to *The Foundation Pit/Kotlovan* (1973): ix–xii; Jordan, M., *A. P.* (1973); Jordan, M., "A. P.," *RLT*, No. 8 (1974): 363–72; Yahushev, H., "A. P.'s Artistic Model of the World," *RLT*, No. 16 (1979): 171–88; Teskey, A., "The Theme of Science in the Early Works of A. P.," *Irish Slavonic Series*, No. 1 (1980): 3–19

—ROBERT L. BUSCH

PLOMER, William

South African novelist, poet, short-story writer, and librettist (writing in English), b. 10 Dec. 1903, Pietersburg; d. 22 Sept. 1973, London, England

After completing his education in South Africa and England, P. worked on a farm and on a trading station with his father. By the time he was nineteen, he was writing verse and had begun *Turbott Wolfe* (1925), his first novel. His writing brought him into contact with Roy CAMPBELL and Laurens van der Post (1906-1996), with whom he co-founded the significant although short-lived literary magazine *Voorslag*. In 1926 P. went to Japan, where he lived until 1929. He returned to England, where he was to spend the larger part of his life. In 1963 he was awarded the Queen's Gold Medal for Poetry; he was President of the Poetry Society from 1968 to 1971.

Of P.'s five novels, *Turbott Wolfe* is the most renowned; it has recently received renewed attention from South African and American critics. *Turbott Wolfe* shows an Africa capable of developing within its own civilization, despite the intervention of Western values. Its focus, as the eponymous narrator states, is on the "unavoidable question of colour." It is written with enormous force and descriptive power, but it is structurally uneven: there is an anecdotal quality to the events described, and the ineffectual narrator is incapable of serving as a unifying device. The novel flashes with understated wit, interspersed with a coarse humor, like the coarseness of the world he describes.

P. was a prolific poet; like his short stories, his verse is a reflection of personal experience. The strength of his poetry lies in its descriptive power, its economy of detail, and its symbolic imagery. He wrote of Africa from the colonial perspective, and in his poems written in Japan and Europe the point of view is that of a concerned foreigner. The phrase "Ballads Abroad," the title P. gave to a section of his *Collected Poems* (1960; expanded ed., 1973), suggests the position with which he was most comfortable, that of the tolerant outsider, generally observing with detached humor and ironic wit. He had a great love of landscape and used natural detail to capture impressions of local atmosphere. In two poems written in Japan, "The Aburaya" and "Hotel Magnificent," collectively labeled "Two Hotels" in the *Collected Poems*, a sense of nostalgia is expressed for a delicate and transient culture, contrasted with the hollowness of a "tradition" readymade for foreigners.

A poem that expresses many of P.'s central concerns is "The Scorpion," one of the "African Poems" in the *Collected Poems*. It speaks of the drowning of an African culture: both the traditional domestic and magical elements have been swept away. The poem focuses on two images, the corpse of a black woman and a scorpion, which P. uses to convey the demise of an Africa that was dangerous, sensuous, and noble.

P. also worked as a librettist with Benjamin Britten: their collaborations include the opera *Gloriana* (1953) for the coronation of Queen Elizabeth II. P.'s autobiography *Double Lives* (1943) describes with wit and detachment the early part of his life, in South Africa.

P. can be regarded as representing the beginnings of the "protest novel" in South Africa; however, critics now generally see him as a writer whose outlook was shaped by his world view as a liberal humanist in the tradition of Joseph CONRAD. In his writings about Africa there is a sense of his alienation from the country he lived in and loved but never fully possessed.

FURTHER WORKS: *I Speak of Africa* (1927); *Notes for Poems* (1927); *The Family Tree* (1929); *Paper Houses* (1929); *Sado* (1931; Am., *They Never Came Back*); *The Fivefold Screen* (1932); *The Case Is Altered* (1932); *The Child of Queen Victoria* (1933); *Cecil Rhodes* (1933); *The Invaders* (1934); *Visiting the Caves* (1936); *Ali the Lion* (1936; rpt. as *The Diamond of Jannina: Ali Pasha 1741–1822*, 1970); *Selected Poems* (1940); *The Dorking Thigh and Other Satires* (1945); *Curious Relations* (1945, under pseud. William D'Arfey); *Four Countries* (1949); *Museum Pieces* (1952); *A Shot in the Park* (1955); *Borderline Ballads* (1955); *At Home* (1958); *Curlew River* (libretto, 1965); *The Burning Fiery Furnace* (libretto, 1966); *Taste and Remember* (1966); *The Prodigal Son* (libretto, 1968); *Celebrations* (1972); *The Butterfly Ball and the Grasshopper Feast* (1973); *The Autobiography of W. P.* (1975); *Electric Delights* (1977)

BIBLIOGRAPHY: Margery, K., "The South African Novel and Race," *SoRA*, 1 (1963): 27–46; Doyle, J. R., Jr., *W.P.* (1969); Rabkin, D., "Race and Fiction: [Sarah Gertrude Milin's] *God's Stepchildren* and *Turbott Wolfe,* " in Parker, K., ed., *The South African Novel in English* (1978): 77–94; Marquard, J., Introduction to *A Century of South African Short Stories* (1978): 22–31; Hallet, R., "The Importance of *Voorslag:* Roy Campbell, W. P., and the Development of South African Literature," *Theoria*, 50 (1978): 29–39; Herbert, M., "The Early Writings of W. P.: Some New Material," *ESA*, 22 (1979): 13–26; Gray, S., ed., *W. P., Turbott Wolfe*, with background pieces by Laurens van der Post, Roy Campbell, Michael Herbert, Nadine Gordimer, Peter Wilhelm, David Brown, and Stephen Gray (1980)

—GILLIAN L. G. NOERO

POLGAR, Alfred

(born Alfred Polak) Austrian theater critic, journalist, short-story writer, and satirical dramatist, b. 17 Oct. 1873, Vienna; d. 24 April 1955, Zurich, Switzerland

P. was born into a petit-bourgeois family of restricted means. His father was a piano teacher; of his mother little is known. From the beginning of his career he used the pseudonym Polgar, which became his legal name in 1914. A habitué of the now legendary Vienna literary coffeehouses Griensteidl and Central, he began his career as a reporter and drama critic. As Vienna theater correspondent, he was among the first contributors to Siegfried Jacobsohn's *Weltbühne*, published in Berlin. From the mid-1920s on P. lived mostly in Berlin, where he also wrote regularly for the literary weekly *Das Tagebuch* and for its successor, *Das neue Tagebuch*. Hitler's rise to power in 1933 forced him to return to Vienna.

After the 1938 Anschluss P. lived precariously as an exile in Prague, Zurich, and Paris, before emigrating to America in 1940. For two years he held an unproductive and unrewarding post as "literary adviser" to M-G-M in Hollywood. In 1943 he moved to New York, where he contributed to *Aufbau*, the German-Jewish émigré weekly. He returned to Europe in 1949 and settled in Zurich, resuming activity as a drama critic and correspondent. The experiences of emigration and return are depicted in *Anderseits: Erzählungen und Erwägungen* (1948; on the other hand: stories and considerations) and in *Im Lauf der Zeit* (1954; in the course of time), another collection of short prose pieces.

As a master of the short form, P. followed in the Viennese tradition of Peter Altenberg (1859–1919), whom he deeply admired and whose unpublished writings he edited in 1925. Although P.'s literary stature was lastingly confirmed with *An den Rand geschrieben* (1926; written in the margins), a collection of prose sketches, and *Orchester von oben* (1926; orchestra from above), a collection of short narratives, no one title, or combination of titles, among the many he published can be designated as his major or most characteristic work. His books are almost exclusively collections of theater reviews, sketches, and short satirical-critical essays. They are typified by their originality and lucidity of expression and by a seemingly effortless stylistic brilliance.

P.'s ethical and literary kinship to Karl KRAUS is evidenced in *Kleine Zeit* (1919; small times), an anthology of sketches from the "home front" in which he exposes the "satanic imbecility" that nourishes and accompanies war. As a journalist he restored to the feuilleton a standard of excellence and responsibility it had not enjoyed in Vienna since Ludwig Speidel (1830–1906). His drama reviews and portraits of actors, first collected in the four volumes of *Ja und nein: Schriften des Kritikers* (1926–27; yes and no: the critic's papers), offer a panorama of the contemporary stage. Their strikingly artistic qualities, combined with an often biting wit, may actually work to obscure their critical substance. Of the satirical playlets he composed in collaboration with Egon FRIEDELL, the most successful was *Goethe: Eine Szene* (1908; Goethe: a scene).

The number of distinguished colleagues whose admiration P. gained during his long career testifies convincingly to his exceptional literary rank; it includes Franz KAFKA, Kurt TUCHOLSKY, Joseph ROTH, and Walter BENJAMIN, in addition to Kraus. The qualities they esteemed in him—above all, his enlightening wit and, along with the brilliance, the integrity of his language—are not, however, entirely identical with the ones that fostered his broader popularity. Beguiled by the sparkle and buoyancy of his style, readers were prone to miss his trenchant insights into social abuses and the frailty of the human condition. The characterization "master of the short form," while incontestably apt, was applied in wholesale manner to describe a P. who makes for light, entertaining reading; his skepticism and his defense of humane values were largely unnoticed.

While the case for a "political" P. must be argued with caution—he was not an activist or adherent to any doctrine—to judge his work properly one must also take account of his social-critical themes, and of their provocative intent. More recent and discriminating P. editions, from Bernt Richter's *Auswahl* (1968; selected writings) to Ulrich Weinzierl's *Taschenspiegel* (1979; pocket mirror), promise to further such recognition and thereby reveal more clearly how P. employed his mastery of the "short form" to create an oeuvre that is both artistically and ethically compelling.

FURTHER WORKS: *Der Quell des Übels* (1908); *Der Petroleumkönig; oder, Donauzauber* (1908, with Egon Friedell); *Bewegung ist alles* (1909); *Brahms Ibsen* (1910); *Talmas Tod* (1910, with Armin Friedmann); *Soldatenleben im Frieden* (1910, with Egon Friedell); *Hiob* (1912); *Max Pallenberg* (1921); *Gestern und heute* (1922); *Ich bin Zeuge* (1928); *Schwarz auf weiß* (1928); *Hinterland* (1929); *Bei dieser Gelegenheit* (1930); *Auswahlband* (1930); *Die Defraudanten* (1931); *Ansichten* (1933); *In der Zwischenzeit* (1935); *Der Sekundenzeiger* (1937); *Handbuch des Kritikers* (1938); *Geschichten ohne Moral* (1943); *Im Vorübergehen* (1947); *Begegnung im Zwielicht* (1951); *Standpunkte* (1953); *Fensterplatz* (1959); *Im Vorüberfahren* (1960); *Bei Lichte betrachtet* (1970); *Die Mission des Luftballons* (1975); *Sperrsitz* (1980); *Lieber Freund!: Lebenszeichen aus der Fremde* (1981)

BIBLIOGRAPHY: Musil, R., *Tagebücher, Aphorismen, Essays und Reden* (1957): 750–55; Schümann, K., *Im Bannkreis von Gesicht und Wirken* (1959): 135–70; Pollak, Γ., "A. P.: An Introduction," *TriQ*, 2 (1959): 35–39; Greuner, R., *Gegenspieler: Profile linksbürgerlicher Publizisten aus Kaiserreich und Weimarer Republik* (1969): 127–57; Warde, A., "A. P.," in Spalek, J. P., and J. Strelka, eds., *Deutsche Exilliteratur seit 1933* (1976), Vol. 1: 581-90; Weinzierl, U., *Er war Zeuge: A. P.* (1978); Philippoff, E., *A. P.: Ein moralischer Chronist seiner Zeit* (1980)

—SIDNEY ROSENFELD

POLISH LITERATURE

1900–18

The second part of the 19th c. was the period of the realistic novel in Poland. In this respect Polish literature displayed a development very similar to that in other literatures in both western and eastern Europe, although in relationship to the West there was the usual delay of several decades. In the same way as the works of Balzac, Stendhal, and even Flaubert in France, Dickens and Thackeray in England, and Tolstoy, Turgenev, and Dostoevsky in Russia, had their sources in romanticism but developed a distinctly different, realistic method, a realistic vision of the world, so were Boleslaw Prus (pseud. of Aleksander Głowacki, 1845–1912), Eliza Orzeszkowa (1842–1910), and Henryk SIENKIEWICZ, representatives of a similar development of this genre in Poland. Since the creative activity of all three of them carried into the 20th c., they also absorbed some later ideas. All three became quite well known outside Poland, so much so that when Sienkiewicz was awarded the Nobel Prize in literature (1905), those literary critics, in Sweden and especially in France, who had hopes for their national artists, used Sienkiewicz's enormous popularity as a possible argument against the Polish artist. His novel *Quo Vadis* (1896; *Quo Vadis*, 1896), which in France alone reached millions of copies, was considered by some as "too popular for a work of a true artistic value."

Since several trends penetrated into Poland simultaneously, the picture of Polish literature at the turn of the century is rather difficult to present in terms of this or that dominating "ism." As elsewhere, realism in Poland first began to give way to naturalism, but by the end of the 19th c. the ideas of SYMBOLISM and impressionism were also felt, so that the same artists often reacted to both trends simultaneously. In fiction Adolf Dygasinski (1839–1902) created novels and short stories in which he performed naturalistic experiments based on principles of natural science; with time, however, his "objective" descriptions of nature and the world of animals acquired certain lyrical, impressionistic qualities that were at times elevated to an almost symbolic level. His novel *Gody zycia* (1902; feast of life) was highly praised both by the adherents of realism and by adepts of the new "modernist" aesthetics. Antoni Sygietyński (1850–1923) in fiction and Gabriela Zapolska (1857–1921) in drama were above all continuators of the aesthetics of realism and naturalism, although some ingredients of the new trends found their way into their works. They were soon followed by a whole generation of artists whose creative activities began in the same vein but whose main achievements were a clear departure into the new aesthetics. It is the period popularly called "Mloda Polska" (Young Poland), embracing the last decade of the 19th c. and the first two decades of the 20th, that marks a departure from the models in which preoccupation with national or social themes and with traditional narrative structures prevailed, and a shift toward more abstract, universal themes and toward modernistic modes of expression. While the main achievements of realism and naturalism were in the field of narrative prose, the ideas of modernism manifested themselves above all in poetry and in drama. This was a natural development, which paralleled developments in other literatures, notably in France and Russia, where the trend of symbolism especially manifested itself in lyrical poetry, in the works of Verlaine, Mallarmé, Rimbaud, and of the Russian poets Valery BRYUSOV and Konstantin BALMONT, among many others.

The Polish poet who perhaps best embodies the spirit of fin de siècle, the spirit of aimless aestheticism, pessimism, frustration, punctuated with intermittent erotic extasis and expressed by means of impressionistic technique, intense "musicality," and highly emotional lyrical cadence, is Kazimierz Tetmajer (1865–1940). From the very first volume of his "series," *Poezje* (8 vols., 1891–1924; poetry), Tetmajer's fame grew rapidly, and he soon became Poland's favorite poet. His verses were known by heart, and were read and recited on every occasion, since they represented the moods and feelings of his generation. Tetmajer was also known as the author of less successful although once quite popular novels such as *Panna Mery* (1901; Miss Mery) and *Koniec epopei* (3 vols., 1913–17; end of the epic adventure). In fiction, his stories, especially the cycle *Na skalnym Podhalu* (5 vols., 1903–10; in the rocky Podhale highlands), are his really lasting achievements.

The other two important poets of the Young Poland period, although less representative of fin-de-siècle tendencies, were Jan Kasprowicz (1860–1926) and Leopold Staff (1878–1957). Kasprowicz's early poetry was conceived and couched in a realistic spirit and continued the tradition of speaking for the poor and the oppressed. Like his predecessor, Maria Konopnicka (1842–1910), he depicted in almost naturalistic style the misery of landless peasants, for example in the volume *Z chałupy* (1888; from the shanty). Gradually his poetic horizon expanded, embracing general social, moral, and philosophical themes. There is not much of the decadent spirit of the time in this poetry, but the style reflects the period quite well, with the obvious search for new modes of expression, typical archaisms, neologisms, hyperbolic metaphors and—what is rather unusual, even in modernist poetry in Poland—free verse. All this can be perhaps best observed in the volume *Hymny* (1901; hymns), where tradition and innovation blend together in a fascinating way. Leopold Staff's poetry all clearly belongs chronologically to the 20th c., since his first volume, *Sny o potędze* (dreams of power) appeared in 1901. Nevertheless, his early poetics displays most of the typical features of the Young Poland period. On the whole, the beginning of the new century is in many respects a watershed, since a number of significant literary events took place in those years, events that in some ways represented new developments, new not only in Poland but in a wider, international perspective.

The most important was the staging in Cracow in March 1901 of a play by Stanisław WYSPIAŃSKI called *Wesele* (the wedding). It is a curious, puzzling play in which the ideas of symbolist drama, operating within the primitivist basic structure of a popular Christmas play, or rather puppet show, are at the same time imbued with motifs and devices that anticipate SURREALISM and even the THEATER OF THE ABSURD. The multilevel structure of this work, the interplay of traditional realistic motifs and the "dream world" of the imaginary scenes representing the inner, deeper stream of the drama—all this was a new, challenging kind of theater. A daring confrontation of the tyranny of romantic illusion and "squelching reality" at first stunned the audiences and the critics, and many a wrong interpretation and even condemnation was made before it was realized that Wyspiański's theater simply represented certain new ideas, anticipating some of the 20th-c. experiments. In retrospect, an aura of Samuel BECKETT's *Waiting for Godot* seems to pervade this play in which national myths are exposed with a strange, ironic twist and with mastery of paradox and scenic effect. In several other plays, too, especially in *Wyzwolenie* (1903; deliverance) and *Noc listopadowa* (1904; November night), Wyspianski managed to achieve striking effect by blending historical motifs with modern and, indeed, modernistic dramatic ideas and techniques. Struggling against the romantic tradition that saw Poland as a kind of martyr, a "Christ" among European nations, he himself became a new, romantic bard. The national cause was still his obsession as it were, although at the same time he called for "deliverance" from its yoke. ("You want to make me a slave of freedom, while I am free, free, free," exclaims his hero Konrad in *Wyzwolenie*.)

An important event in Polish literary life was the establishment in 1901 of the periodical *Chimera* under the editorship of Zenon Przesmycki (pseud.: Miriam, 1861–1944). In his essays and translations in *Chimera* and in his earlier periodical *Życie*, Przesmycki acquainted Polish readers with trends and individual writers in the West. Of special importance was his study of Rimbaud and his translations and interpretations of the dramatic works of MAETER-LINCK, in which he gave a profound analysis of the main tenets of symbolism.

But the man who managed to create the most intense artistic ferment in Poland at the turn of the century was Stanisław PRZYBYSZEWSKI. Przybyszewski was the most internationally recognized figure in Polish arts of that period, a writer who was active and known in modernist circles in Germany and Scandinavia before "descending" on the Polish literary scene in 1890 surrounded by an aura of a certain fame and considerable scandal. He was known as a "Satanist," a "Chopinist," an author of a number of works written in German: novels, plays, volumes of poetic prose, and a quite widely debated and not uninfluential study *Zur Psychologie des Individuums* (1891; on the psychology of the individual), containing certain ideas that anticipated EXPRESSIONISM. Invited by a group of Young Poland artists active in Cracow, this member in good standing of the Young Germany and Young Scandinavia circles became quite an influential force in Polish literature, even though his leading role was rather short-lived. He became editor of the modernist periodical *Życie* (not to be confused with Miriam's *Życie* in Warsaw), which, however, did not last longer than about a decade (1890–1900). Przybyszewski's artistic manifesto in *Życie* was entitled "Confiteor" (Latin: I confess). It was a declaration of the absolute freedom of an artist to reject all the traditional notions of art's social, national, and moral obligations, and all the aesthetic conventions. At a time when for many groups in Poland the main preoccupation was the problem of regaining political independence, Przybyszewski's ideas were too abstract; moreover, they did not really amount to a well-thought-out, coherent aesthetic program. (Przybyszewski's obsession with "sex-drive" [*chuc*] as the source of all art overshadowed more serious considerations). His demands for artistic integrity, however, anticipated some of the slogans that the poets of the *Skamander* group would voice after Poland's rebirth in 1918.

Przybyszewski's novels and quasi-symbolist plays did not prove to be of lasting value, although they were received with considerable interest at the time. His chief merit is that through his indefatigable activities as editor, creative writer, and extremely popular and effective speaker he spread ideas of modernism all over the Slavic world, perhaps more than any other writer or critic. His works were translated and his plays staged, he lectured widely (especially in Russia, where he became the chief prophet of modernism), he corresponded with artists and editors in capitals of the East and West, securing their contributions for his periodicals and informing the world of developments in Poland. From this point of view, his position in the development of Polish letters is probably more important than generally realized.

The leading writers of fiction at the turn of the century were Stefan ZEROMSKI and Władysław Stanisław REYMONT. In spite of the general tendency toward fragmentation of the traditional "large forms," both these writers succeeded in creating impressive works. Żeromski's novels were neoromantic in spirit (in that he took up the utopian romantic note of heroism, whether in patriotic struggle or in struggle against social injustice) and neorealistic or outright modernistic, lyrical, disjointed, often symbolist in style. Żeromski's chief novels during that period were *Ludzie bezdomni* (2 vols., 1900; homeless people), one of the first European novels depicting a physician (Dr. Judym, who sacrifices personal happiness for working for the poor and the oppressed); *Popioly* (3 vols., 1904; *Ashes*, 2 vols., 1928), a Polish *War and Peace*, and *Walka z szatanem* (3 vols., 1916–19; wrestling the devil). Reymont did not attain Żeromski's stature as a moral authority and "people's conscience," but his position as an artist of international importance was assured because of his two masterpieces, *Ziemia obiecana* (2 vols., 1899; *The Promised Land*, 1927) and *Chlopi* (4 vols., 1904–9; *The Peasants*, 4 vols., 1924–25). Reymont's style is not free from the Young Poland modernistic mannerisms. Nevertheless, he did succeed in creating two of the few truly epic novels of modern time, novels in which he managed to present a collective hero, as it were: the big industrial city in the first and the backward peasant village in the second novel. While it was the general opinion in Poland that Zeromski was the writer most deserving of the Nobel Prize, it was Reymont who was awarded the prize in 1924 for his epic talent. A faithful reflection of the dilemmas of the generation torn between the traditional moral and social values and nihilistic skepticism can be found in Waclaw Berent's (1873–1940) novels: *Próchno* (1901; rotten wood) and *Ozimina* (1911; winter crop).

1918–39

On the eve of World War I Polish letters and Polish arts in general experienced quite an intense ferment of ideas penetrating from both the West and from the East and finding fertile ground. Problems of revolution and underground struggle manifested themselves in a number of prose works by such writers as Andrzej Strug (1871–1937) and Władysław Orkan (1876–1930) and in Żeromski's play *Róża* (1905; the rose). In poetry ideas of expressionism, "formism," FUTURISM, and so forth initiated experiments with new forms and themes. World War I interrupted for a while these artistic activities, but after 1918 in the reborn Poland they continued with increased intensity.

The reestablishment of the independent state brought a veritable eruption of poetry. It was a group of fresh young talents centered around the periodical *Skamander* which was the most vocal in proclaiming freedom of expression and which soon gained the status of the leading group. They were Julian TUWIM, Antoni SŁONIMSKI, Kazimierz WIERZYŃSKI, Jarosław IWASZKIEWICZ, and Jan LECHOŃ. Although they all started with very bold, seemingly antitraditional and antibourgeois declarations, their actual poetry amounted mostly to what can be called a colloquialized Young Poland tradition plus certain motifs and tropes associated with the new problems and mores in the reborn Poland. Tuwim tried to challenge the conventions in his poem "Wiosna" (1918;

spring); Wierzyński exclaimed gaily: "It is green in my head and violets bloom inside it"; Lechoń demanded: "And in the spring let me see the spring, not Poland." But all this fervor and vitalism did not lead to any real changes in poetics, and subsequently the *Skamander* poets easily joined the political establishment and they themselves became the poetic establishment. Thanks to their genuine talents, they succeeded in creating a real interest for poetry, which thus dominated the literary scene in Poland, especially during the first postwar decade.

Within the orbit of the *Skamander* group, but more independent, were a number of other poets of considerable importance. The most outstanding and influential among them were Leopold Staff, who continued to produce lyrics of clarity and suggestiveness, and Boleslaw LEŚMIAN, whose metaphysical, symbolist poetry became a source of inspiration to other poets because of the author's uncanny talent for introducing new semantic values by creative neology and metaphors. On a different level, an important place was occupied by the leader of the revolutionary "proletarian" poetry, Władysław BRONIEWSKI, whose social message was highly effective because of the author's ability to couch it in a deeply lyrical idiom of personal experience.

The dominating, generally recognized position of the *Skamander* group, popularized by the most influential literary periodical, the weekly *Wiadomości literackie*, was not completely unchallenged. It was attacked on several fronts by younger poets who felt the need of a thorough revision of the traditional aesthetics, and who gradually formed a true artistic avant-garde.

The most radical avant-garde movement was futurism, led and most articulately formulated in Poland by Bruno Jasieński (1901–1939), one of the most intriguing international figures, who left his mark in three literatures—from his start as a militant futurist in Poland with his volume of poetry *But w butonierce* (1921; boot in a buttonhole) through a political novel written in French, *Je brûle Paris* (1928; I burn Paris), to his influential role in establishing SOCIALIST REALISM in the Soviet Union, where he was highly praised for his novel in Russian, *Chelovek menyaet kozhu* (1932; man changes skin) before he disappeared in Stalin's purges. In his early struggle for Polish futurism Jasieński was joined by a number of other young writers, among whom the most active and vocal were Aleksander Wat (1900–1967) and Anatol Stern (1899–1968). No less radical, and much more extensively and coherently argued in its program of antitraditional, "functional" poetry, was the so-called Cracow avant-garde initiated by Tadeusz Peiper (1891–1969) and represented mainly by Julian PRZYBOŚ , Jalu Kurek (b. 1904), Jan Brzękowski (1903–1983) and Marian Czuchnowski (1909–1991).

In terms of popular appeal the position of *Skamander* poetry, with its eclectic character and undeniable artistic suggestiveness, remained unassailable. Nevertheless, the new avant-garde poetics gradually began to attract more and more genuine young talents, such as Józef CZECHOWICZ, Czeslaw MILOSZ, and Jerzy Zagórski (b. 1907), poets who not only were able to assert themselves as writers of integrity and originality but who in turn began to exert influence on other artists, both younger and older. Although often presented as sheer experimenters, in form many of the avant-garde poets showed deep concern with the growing social and political problems. The note of "catastrophism" was quite strong in their poems, and in certain cases one can speak of an almost prophetic quality, even in some works of a seemingly "frivolous" poet Konstanty Ildefons GAŁCZYŃSKI, for example, his long poem *Koniec świata* (1929; the end of the world).

In prose the development was much slower, and traditional forms prevailed during most of this period. The ideological tensions were still most suggestively reflected in the works of Stefan Zeromski, who continued to be regarded as the most important writer. His novel *Przedwiośnie* (1925; before the spring) was one of the most courageous and honest attempts at depicting the social conflicts and frustrations of radical socialists and liberals who wanted progress and justice but also wanted to prevent the tragedies and cruelties that followed the revolution in Russia. Contemporary problems and frustrations were also depicted in works by Zofia NAŁKOWSKA—*Romans Teresy Hennert* (1924; Teresa Hennert's love affair) and *Granica* (1935; the boundary)—and Juliusz KADEN-BANDROWSKI—*General Barcz* (1923; General Barcz) and *Czarne skrzydla* (2 vols., 1928–29; black wings), both lengthy and rather tedious attempts at creating an original style that consisted of blending supposedly realistic vulgarity with quasi-expressionistic STREAM-OF-CONSCIOUSNESS passages. A writer who gained a moral stature once afforded Stefan Zeromski was Maria DĄBROWSKA. Her volume of stories *Ludzie stamtąd* (1926; folks from over yonder) was followed by one of the few true epic novels in modern Polish literature, a tetralogy, *Noce i dnie* (1932–34; nights and days), a chronicle novel somewhat reminiscent of John GALSWORTHY's *The Forsyte Saga* and Thomas MANN's *Buddenbrooks* but basically an original, thoughtful depiction in what can be termed "modernized neorealistic style" of contemporary problems in the Polish countryside.

On the whole, literature in postwar Poland developed more and more into a "profession" rather than a "mission." There was a fast-growing number of popular and respectable belletristic writers whose works competed successfully with translations of foreign literature. A popular author of historical fiction was Zofia KOSSAK. A steady stream of more or less successful prose works comes from Andrzej Strug, Ferdynand GOETEL, Maria Kuncewiczowa (1899–1989), Jarosław Iwaszkiewicz, and others. Works that for various reasons were most frequently and heatedly discussed in intellectual circles were *Sól ziemi* (1936; *Salt of the Earth*, 1939) by Józef WITTLIN, an indictment of all militaristic mentality; Leon KRUCZKOWSKI's Marxist analysis of the historical past, *Kordian i cham* (1932; Kordian and the boor); and *Niebo w plomieniach* (1936; heaven in flames) by Jan Parandowski (1895–1978), which explored the younger generation's attitudes toward religion.

In the field of theater, this was a period of steady production of professionally respectable plays by such writers as Zofia Nalkowska, Jerzy Szaniawski (1886–1970), Ludwik Hieronim Morstin (1886–1966), Karol Hubert ROSTWOROWSKI, and many others.

A special place in this general picture is occupied by a few individual artists who were far ahead of their time and whose full significance in Polish literature and, indeed, in world literature, did not become apparent for several decades. They were Stanisław Ignacy Witkiewicz, popularly called WITKACY, Bruno SCHULZ, and Witold GOMBROWICZ. Witkiewicz's main achievement was in the field of theater, where he was a precursor of the Theater of the Absurd. His original idea was that of the theater of "pure form," that is, a totally antirealistic concept, reaching further than the futurist experiments by MARINETTI in Italy and MAYAKOVSKY in Russia and striving for a "total freedom of formal elements." Bruno Schulz's strange, haunting tales in his collections *Sklepy cynamonowe* (1934; *The Street of Crocodiles*, 1963) and *Sanatorium pod klepsydrą* (1937; *The Sanatorium under the Sign of the Hourglass*, 1978) have been quite recently "discovered" in the West as early EXISTENTIALIST prose par excellence. Witold Gombrowicz is today certainly one of the best-known names in world literature. Long ignored both in his country and abroad, Gombrowicz won international recognition after World War II, when his prewar and postwar works were translated and pronounced an important contribution to the development of avant-garde fiction and drama. His basic device is that of negating the conventional concept of descriptive narrative and instead seeing—somewhat as the futurists did—his characters undergoing constant deformation and transformation in their interaction. Gombrowicz's first novel, *Ferdydurke* (1938; *Ferdydurke*, 1961), and his first play, *Iwona, księniczka Burgundia* (1938; *Ivona, Princess of Burgundia*, 1969), already contained these main premises.

1939–56

It has yet to be fully assessed what World War II meant for Poland, its people, and its art. It is certain that after all that the people went through, their life, including their culture and art, could never be the same. The shattering experience of the new total war and of genocide defied normal expression, and writers had to resort to the biblical style of Job and Jeremiah or to sober, brutal simplicity. Some of the best-known writers—Tuwim, Wierzyński, Lechoń, Slonimski, Wittlin—found themselves in exile in the West; their works, published freely in France, England, and the U.S., became the most visible part of the literature's continued fight for their country. Some younger ones—for example, Ksawery Pruszyński (1907–1950), Wacław IWANIUK, Artur Miedzyrzecki (b. 1922)—fought as soldiers in the Polish army in the West. Of those who stayed in Poland, many were sent to German concentration camps, and only after the war those who survived gave witness to their experience: Zofia Kossak published her memoirs, *Z otchłani* (1946; from the abyss); Gustaw Morcinek (1891–1963) wrote his *Listy spod morwy* (1946; letters from under the mulberry tree); Stanisław DYGAT gave a fictionalized reaction to some of the problems of *Jezioro Bodeńskie* (1946; Lake Constance). Ironically, some of the most vocal "revolutionary" poets—Broniewski, Czuchnowski, Wat—who in prewar Poland were accused of communism and even imprisoned, were now, in turn, quickly jailed, when they found themselves in the Soviet-occupied territories.

Writers who stayed in Poland and managed to escape arrest, deportation, and concentration camps participated in the underground movement, publishing in underground presses poems, stories, and patriotic appeals and declarations, and on the whole assuming their new role as "soldiers of fighting literature." Among them were such well-known artists as Dąbrowska, Miłosz, Iwaszkiewicz and Jerzy ANDRZEJEWSKI. A number of poems and stories by Miłosz, Andrzejewski, Iwaszkiewicz, and other mostly anonymous writers were published in underground editions. A wave of the "condemned generation" poets (those born around 1920) emerged in response to the war, with most of them dying as members of the Polish Underground Army or in the Warsaw Uprising before reaching full maturity. Tadeusz Gajcy (1922–1944), Andrzej Trzebiński (1922–1943), Krzysztof K. Baczyński (1921–1944), and Zdzisslaw Stroiński (1920–1943) all died soldiers' deaths. Others perished in death camps or mass executions; a few survived to give testimony to the experience of crematoria, death commandos, burning ghettos, and total degradation of human values. Among them was Tadeusz BOROWSKI, who gave a faithful depiction of Auschwitz and on the whole of the fate of his generation, which he saw as destined to leave behind nothing but "scrap iron and hollow, jeering laughter of generations."

The first years in postwar Poland were a period of general uncertainty as to the direction of literature. It was quite clear from the beginning that the decisive voice in the lively and fairly free debates and confrontations belonged to those who took their inspiration from the U.S.S.R. Before the new directions were officially introduced, however, the field was quite wide open and writers searched for their individual solutions in trying to articulate their experiences. It was mostly felt that the traditional fabular forms of expression were no longer adequate, and that writers had to resort either to a documentary reportage form or to an antinarrative style of letting facts, thoughts, and emotions flow freely in constant interchange. Fairly conventional were Nalkowska's *Medaliony* (1946; medallions) and Andrzejewski's stories, since they were indirect, secondhand descriptions. In more personal works the style and structure were much more "convulsive," since the events depicted defied normal narrative means. Such were tales of the Jewish tragedy by Adolf Rudnicki (1912–1990) and Leopold Buczkowski's (1905–1989) "antinovel" written in 1946, *Czarny potok* (1954; *Black Torrent*, 1969).

In poetry, too, the main preoccupation for some time after the war was to find an idiom capable of expressing the experience of these years. One of the first and most important books was the volume *Ocalenie* (1945; rescue) by Czesław Milosz, in which the strongest and most profound feelings and reflections are expressed in the simplest poetic language without any aesthetic adornments or formal experimentation. It is almost frightening to realize what the years of war must have meant when one perceives the depth and the moral maturity of a poet still under thirty-five. The most striking achievements in the search for a new idiom that was free of rhetoric and exaggeration were probably those of the young poet Tadeusz RÓŻEWICZ, who started writing during the war and after the war published regularly—for example, *Niepokój* (1947; anxiety) and *Czerwona rękawiczka* (1948; red glove). Scores of other volumes appeared soon after the war by poets of such different artistic and political persuasions as Adam WAŻYK, Mieczyslaw JASTRUN, Julian Przyboś, Władysław Broniewski, Julian Tuwim, Antoni Slonimski, Jalu Kurek, and many others. In theater the wave of creative experiments was yet to come, although there were signs of the new idiom in Gałczyński's absurdist pieces in the weekly *Przekrój* called "Teatrzyk 'Zielona gesi'" (the minitheater "Green Goose"). Two serious plays by older writers had the strongest reverberations: Leon Kruczkowski's *Niemcy* (perf. 1948, pub. 1950; the Germans), which questioned some of the popular myths about the enemy, and Jerzy Szaniawski's *Dwa teatry* (1966; two theaters), which challenged the validity of materialism and realism as the only guiding light in literature.

Gradually, the implications of the new political system were becoming apparent and the tasks expected from the artists were being defined. A number of works appeared in which the scheme was to depict the prewar reality in Poland realistically but with the emphasis on the negative aspects, and to project optimism and faith in a better future under the new system. Such were the novels like Zofia Nałkowska's *Węzły Życia* (1948; knots of life), Tadeusz Breza's (1905–1970) *Mury Jerycha* (1946; the walls of Jericho), and Kazimierz BRANDYS's *Drewniany koń* (1946; the wooden horse). A prominent place is occupied by a novel that better than any other work catches the dilemmas of the postwar situation in Poland: Andrzejewski's *Popiół i diament* (1948; *Ashes and Diamonds*, 1962).

In 1949 Socialist Realism was proclaimed as the only correct artistic "method." Those unwilling to accept it had to refrain from publishing or else resort to historical or exotic themes and/or translations. Czesław Miłosz made a difficult personal decision: in 1951, while in Paris, he renounced his citizenship. The requirement of ideologically correct "socialist orientation" created a climate that proved not favorable to art. Few works of that period had much artistic value, although some of the so-called production novels and stories were of a certain documentary interest.

The historical novel was in general less subject to political interference than other genres. The most productive authors in this mode were Antoni Gołubiew (1907–1979), with his huge cycle on medieval Polish history, *Bolesław Chrobry* (7 vols., 1947–55; Bolesław the Brave), and Teodor PARNICKI, many of whose novels were devoted to the same period, although they had a much wider world perspective and were much more ambitious and accomplished than Golubiew's.

1956–1970

Although the political and cultural "thaw" of 1956 did not change the basic political system, it nevertheless led to quite a radical relaxation of the dogmatic "Stalinist" cultural policies, and the results in the field of art and in the entire cultural life of Poland were quite spectacular. To be sure, the euphoria of liberation did not last long, but a return to the previous policies proved impossible. There was a veritable eruption of original and translated works that represented all possible philosophical and aesthetic trends and schools: from existentialist novels and plays through Theater of the Absurd to NEW NOVELS and concrete poetry. Witkiewicz, Schulz, and the émigré Gombrowicz were rediscovered, and widely debated. Most (although not all) of Gombrowicz's postwar works that were brought out in Paris by the Kultura publishing house were now reissued in Poland. Other émigré writers, whose existence had been barely admitted before, were now published and discussed. To be sure, there were still restrictions, but the importance of the émigré writers as an organic part of Polish literature was recognized. On the other hand, the émigré writers—Wierzyński, Lechoń, Wittlin—took into account in their work the achievements of writers at home and thus were not seen as anachronisms in Poland. Miłosz, of course, never for a moment ceased being regarded by both young and old as a leading artistic force; his volumes, published regularly by the Paris Kultura, found their way to readers in Poland even when his name was banned. A real "second birth" could be seen in the case of poets like Lechoń and especially Wierzyński. Wierzyński proved to be able to keep pace with the postwar changes in the poetic idiom. Such volumes as *Kufer na plecach* (1964; with a trunk on my shoulders), *Tkanka ziemi* (1968; tissue of the earth), and *Sen mara* (1969; dream-phantom) were almost unanimously pronounced masterpieces by critics of various persuasions. Several editions of his selected poetry appeared in Poland within a short time and several studies were devoted to his entire work. On the other hand, some writers living in Poland, such as Brandys and Andrzejewski, openly published abroad.

On the whole, extremely lively activity took place during the first years after 1956. Poets, novelists, playwrights of all possible convictions and temperaments wrote with a real frenzy, undertaking a number of very daring and innovative experiments, especially in the theater. In poetry the search for new forms had never actually

stopped, but it now got a new impetus. Tadeusz Różewicz published regularly: *Poemat otwarty* (1956; open poem), *Formy* (1958; forms), *Rozmowa z księciem* (1960; conversation with a prince). Zbigniew HERBERT appeared as one of the most original new talents in his volumes: *Struna światła* (1956; the chord of light), *Hermes, pies i gwiazda* (1957; Hermes, dog and star), *Studium przedmiotu* (1961; study of the object). Miron BIAŁOSZEWSKI showed an uncanny linguistic inventiveness in *Obroty rzeczy* (1956; *Revolutions of Things*, 1974), *Mylne wzruszenia* (1961; mistaken emotions), and other volumes. A large number of other poets such as Tadeusz Nowak (b. 1930), Wisława SZYMBORSKA, Stanisław Grochowiak (1934–1976), and Tymoteusz Karpowicz (b. 1921) all contributed original works. Adam Ważyk, who earlier assumed the role of a teacher in the "Marxist school of emotions," now wrote his *Poemat dla dorosłych* (1955; poem for adults), in which he seemed to rediscover the individual.

It is not a coincidence that many of the young poets participated in the spectacular development of a new theatrical idiom, that of the Theater of the Absurd. It started with the establishment in 1956 by Adam Tarn (1902–1972) of a monthly, *Dialog*, which became the forum for all that was new and creative in theater. It published translations (for example, Beckett's *Waiting for Godot*), original plays, scenarios, and theoretical discussions. The author best known at home and abroad was Sławomir MROŻEK, whose plays *Zabawa* (1962; *The Party*, 1967) and *Tango* (1964; *Tango*, 1968) were perhaps the best examples of this genre in Poland. Other well-known plays by some of the above mentioned poets were *Kartoteka* (1960; *The Card Index*, 1970) by Różewicz, *Dziwny pasażer* (1964; *The Strange Passenger*, 1969) by Karpowicz, and *Chłopcy* (1964; boys) by Grochowiak.

In prose, the changes were at first mainly thematic. Maria Dąbrowska, long silenced, published her *Gwiazda zaranna* (1955; the morning star), which indeed initiated a wave of works free from political strictures. A group of young writers, mostly born after 1930, gave vent to their personal feelings of anger and frustration in face of postwar reality. Marek HŁASKO, Marek Nowakowski (b. 1939), and Ireneusz Iredyński (1939–1986) represent this generation. Hłasko's ruthlessly realistic stories, in the collection *Pierwszy krok w chmurach* (1956; first step in the clouds), were perhaps the most vocal expression of these sentiments. The author proved too restless and unruly and soon left the country to live in the West; he committed suicide at the age of thirty-five.

While controls over the political and economic life in Poland were soon tightened again, the striving for cultural and artistic independence continued with unceasing vigor and at least partial success. Although Socialist Realism was still the officially prescribed "method," nobody seemed to pay much attention to it—with the exception of a few self-admitted "stragglers" such as the novelists Jerzy Putrament (1911–1986) or Roman Bratny (b. 1921). A steady stream of novels, short stories, and poetry, some of which experiment freely with the most daring, "formalist" artistic devices, is proof of creative integrity of Polish writers. Among the most interesting works of this period are such novels as Tadeusz KONWICKI's *Sennik współczesny* (1963; *A Dreambook for Our Time*, 1969) and *Kronika wypadków miłosnych* (1974; chronicle of love events), and Tadeusz Nowak's *Obcoplemienna ballada* (1963; ballad of an alien tribe) and *A jak królem a jak katem będziesz* (1968; when you will be a king, when you will be a hangman). In all of them the basic structural pattern is the device of blending dreams and reality with a constantly changing mode of narration and swiftly shifting levels of symbolism and realism. Especially in the case of Konwicki the added element of suspense derives from the fact that some of his novels often deal with the politically sensitive theme of the Polish Underground Army's dilemma at the end of the war, when they were facing the Germans and the Communists at the same time.

An important and indeed unique development in the 1970s was the emergence of a number of independent presses—unlicensed but not openly prohibited—which put out uncensored journals, bulletins, literary magazines, and separate works in book form. The most active among them was NOWA—Niezależna Oficyna Wydawnicza (Independent Publishing House)—in Warsaw, but there were many others, such as ABC in Cracow and Młoda Polska (Young Poland) in Gdańsk. The most important literary magazine was *Zapis*, launched in 1977 by a group of mostly younger writers and critics. One of the initiators and later a true moving spirit of this and other enterprises was Stanisław BARAŃCZAK, a poetic and scholarly talent of high rank. Quite a few important works of Polish literature—important both artistically and ideologically—would have remained unpublished without these bold initiatives. Among them are such works as Tadeusz Konwicki's novels *Kompleks polski* (1977; *The Polish Complex*, 1981) and *Mała apokalipsa* (1979; small apocalypse), and Julian Stryjkowski's (1905–1996) *Wielki strach* (1980; great fear). The microcosm of both the governing circles and the opposition is explored in these novels with courage and integrity, characteristic in general of most works thus published. Further evidence of the changing mood and tone of literature can be seen in the recent works of Kazimierz Brandys. In a finely filtered but by no means ambiguous interplay of memory flashbacks and contemporary observations Brandys depicts an individual's anguish in coming to the realization of his country's "unreal" reality in his novel *Nierzeczywistość* (1977; *A Question of Reality*, 1980). More insights and narrative experiments follow in a kind of diary, *Miesiące* (1980; months).

Since August 1980 the situation in Poland has changed dramatically. Between then and the proclamation of martial law on December 13, 1981, an almost complete emancipation of Polish literature took place as the result of the astounding successes of the "Solidarity" struggle for basic social, economic, and cultural rights, which swept through the country like an avalanche. These almost revolutionary changes coincided with the award of the Nobel Prize to Czesław Miłosz. This event, of great international importance, in Poland turned out to be of truly cataclysmic consequence. Not only did Miłosz have to be restored to his rightful place as the most important creative force in Polish letters, but the event automatically created a much more favorable climate for Polish writers and publishers in general. Works previously banned were allowed to be published again, and most émigré writers were again publicly recognized. Independent publishing houses and more-or-less regularly issued magazines were thriving. NOWA and the Paris Kultura (or rather its publisher, Institut Littéraire) signed an agreement of the mutual exchange of copyrights; in *Zapis* and other magazines, poetry, short stories, and literary and political essays were published by previously banned authors and writers in exile.

By the spring of 1981 literary activities—those outside of official control and even those controlled—were marked by a complete freedom of expression. Practically every existing journal or magazine put out a special issue devoted to Miłosz; demands were made that the works of all the more important émigré writers—especially the novelist Zofia Romanowiczowa (b. 1922)

and the short-story writer Tadeusz Nowakowski (b. 1918)—be published. Plans for publication of "practically all" the works of Miłosz and of some other writers were announced. Some critics even raised the possibility of publishing the most militant writers in exile: Gustaw Herling Grudziński (b. 1919), whose short-story collection *Skrzydła ołtarza* (1960; the wings of the altar), first published in Paris, was now acknowledged as being of a high artistic value; and Józef Mackiewicz (1902–1985), who was recently nominated for the Nobel Prize by Russian émigré circles in the West for his sharply political novels *Droga donikąd* (1954; *Road to Nowhere*, 1955) and *Nie trzeba głośno mówić* (1969; one should not say it aloud). Unfortunately, before all these hopes and plans could materialize, the curtain again came down with the imposition of martial law. At the time of this writing, no exact information is available on either the official or unofficial publishing activities, no published materials are allowed to be sent abroad, and virtually all private presses are shut down. Thus, remarks on the present situation must be inconclusive.

Polish Literature since 1970

In Poland, owing to its challenging geopolitical situation, the literary process has always been strongly influenced by the country's turbulent history, and thus often motivated by political factors. Such factors have played a crucial role throughout the post-World War II period, but have acquired a new character in the 1970s, when the struggle of the Polish people against communist rule imposed by the Soviet Union led to the unusual alliance of workers, intellectuals, and the church, and culminated in the avalanche-like force called Solidarity. This spontaneous movement, spreading from cities to the countryside, embraced the entire country and, given the changes in the U.S.S.R., had to result, sooner or later, in the elimination of the oppressive régime, which became increasingly isolated from society. Indeed, as the "dissident" poet Stanislaw BARAŃCZAK stated in his article "Kto jest dysydentem" (1982; who is a dissident?) published in *Kultura*, it was rather the government that found itself by 1980 in the role of a dissident group facing virtually the entire nation.

During the 1970s Polish literary life became increasingly emancipated from the political controls and ideological inspiration of the Communist Party. The events of 1968, when the government brutally suppressed a widespread student movement demanding freedom of speech and instigated a virulent anti-Semitic campaign, and the revolt of the Baltic coast workers in 1970, suppressed by the use of force, resulted in a sharp erosion of the ideological legitimacy of communist rule. The liberalization of cultural policies that followed the workers' revolt and lasted until mid-1973, detente, and the official fostering of consumerism, contributed further to the growth of a new cultural climate, in which writers sought to take advantage of the opportunities provided by the brief period of improved economic conditions and the expanding role of the mass media, or to address the dissatisfied segments of society from a position of ideological and moral independence.

The former trend reflected as well as helped to shape a new kind of mass culture that took its inspiration and models from various Western currents, reflecting and adapting to Polish conditions and traditions such phenomena as the American and west European pop and countercultures. Manifestations of new sensibility and mores came to the fore among young writers in the 1960s and continued to spread in the 1970s, when poets found an outlet for reaching their public not only through print, but at numerous poetry readings and competitions, and through the medium of song.

One of the writers who expressed the earlier phase of the new sensibility was the poet Rafal Wojaczek (1945–1971), whose legend woven of aberrant behavior and psychological problems received tragic reinforcement as a result of his suicide. Among the most popular as well as controversial representations of the trend in the 1970s were Edward Stachura (1937–1979), also ending with suicide, and Janusz Glowacki (b. 1938). Stachura, who began his literary career as the author of highly stylized poetry and the lyrical quasi-novels *Cala jaskrawość* (1969; all the flagrance) and *Siekierezada* (1971; axerezade) became in the 1970s a singer, a youth idol, and something of a religious guru. His prose *Oto* (behold), published in 1980, after his suicide, is interesting both as an experiment in modern gospel writing and for its blending of Buddhism, Christianity, and the teachings of Lao-Tse. His last work, "Pogodzić się ze światem" (1980; to become reconciled with the world), is a day-by-day record of his embracing death as the only way of testing the slenderest of religious hopes.

Glowacki's work includes several collections of short stories, such as *Nowy taniec la-ba-da* (1970; the new dance la-ba-da), *Paradis* (1973; paradise), and *My Sweet Raskolnikow* (1977; title in English), as well as plays and film scripts, of which "Kopciuch" (1979; *Cinders*, London premiere 1981), depicting the life of delinquent girls, was a reworking of the theme of the widely acclaimed film *Psychodrama*, directed in 1969 by Marek Piwowski. Glowacki represents precisely that world which Stachura's brand of counterculture tried to reject. His stories, which in their form reflect the penetration of narrative prose by film techniques, and display a strong predilection for the grotesque and parody, show the corruption both of values and of behavior that characterized in the 1970s the "playboyland" of the communist establishment.

The trend of political contestation and opposition also surfaced in the late 1960s, but expanded considerably as the 1970s moved toward an acurte economic crisis and the Solidarity revolution. It initially comprised mostly young poets, such as Barańczak, who in 1976 gave up his party membership, Jacek Bierezin (1947–1993), Ewa Lipska (b. 1945), Krzysztof Karasek (b. 1937) Adam ZAGAJEWSKI, Ryszard KRYNICKI, and others. Many of the so-called New Wave writers found ideological inspiration in such former communists-turned-oppositionists as Leszek Kolakowski (b. 1927), philosopher and author of excellent philosophical tales, and Wiktor Woroszylski (1927–1996), poet and prose writer; they gradually found common ground with the Catholic writers around the periodicals *Więź, Znak,* and *Tygodnik Powszechny,* as well as with the émigré *Kultura* circle abroad, which, although depleted by the deaths of Witold Gombrowicz and the essayist Jerzy Stempowski (1894–1969), still included Czeslaw MILOSZ, awarded the Nobel Prize for literature in 1980, and Gustaw Herling-Grudziński (b. 1919).

The reaction of the young poets against indirectness, stylization, and abstract symbolism, which characterized much of the poetry of the 1960s, had to take into account the negative lessons of SOCIALIST REALISM, with its declaratory, rhetorical poetics and schematized imagination. The result was the adaptation of the so-called linguistic trend of the 1950s and 1960s, exemplified by Bialoszewski and Karpowicz, to the task of exposing inauthentic and manipulative speech, which found its best expression in the poetry of Barańczak and Krynicki. Distrust of public forms of speech, subversion of official and common linguistic usage,

objectivization of poetic idiom—these rather than the rhetoric of dissent became the features of the nonconformist and contestatory attitudes of the New Wave.

Although interesting as a phenomenon, the poets of the New Wave failed to challenge effectively the preeminence of the leading postwar poets: Herbert, Milosz, Różewicz, and Szymborska. The latter two consolidated their position mainly through the publication of retrospective volumes, which in Różewicz's case comprised not only his collected poems (1971; 2nd ed., 1976) but also his experimental poetic drama and prose. Herbert and Milosz developed further their respective modes of poetic discourse and reflection. In the case of Milosz, perhaps the two most significant works were a volume of poems, *Gdzie wschodzi stońce i kędy zapada* (1974; *From the Rising of the Sun,* 1974), containing a remarkable long poem of the same title, and *Ziemia Ulro* (1977; *Land of Ulro,* 1981), an essay that examines various aspects of modern religious imagination in terms of Milosz's own complex grappling with the problems of faith and unbelief. Herbert added another dimension to his ironic mode of expression by creating in *Pan Cogito* (1974; *Mr. Cogito,* 1993) a poetic persona whose multifaceted complexity enabled him not only to continue exploring in a profound way philosophical, moral, and contemporary themes, but to restate, in the famous poem "Przeslanie Pana Cognito" (1974; "Mr. Cogito's Envoy," 1977), the value of heroic idealism.

In prose the literary results of the new commitment and openness produced a number of interesting works that went beyond the allusive or naturalistic narratives of the 1950s and 1960s. Kazimierz BRANDYS's novel *Nierzeczywistość* (1977; *A Question of Reality,* 1980), published in the *Kultura* "without censorship" series; Tadeusz Konwicki's *Mala Apokalipsa* (1979; *A Minor Apocalypse,* 1983); and Jerzy ANDRZEJEWSKI'S *Miazga* (1980; pulp)—all employed new means in depicting what Zagajewski and Julian Kornhauser (b. 1946) called "the unrepresented world" of Polish life and society. Perhaps the most interesting as an artistic experiment was Andrzejewski's *Miazga* begun in the mid-1960s, and continued after 1969, it mixes various modes of discourse (narrative, essay, memoir, letters, diary, dialogues, and fictitious, yet representative, if parodic, biographical entries) in a discontinuous, patchwork fashion, in what is, in the end, an autothematic antinovel that fails to live up to the requirements of the genre in order to fulfil a complex mimetic and ideological function.

By the second half of the 1970s, a number of prominent older writers, including Andrzejewski, Konwicki, Brandys, and Marek Nowakowski, joined hands with the younger oppositionists around the Committee for the Defense of Workers (KOR, 1976), and several independent journals, such as *Zapis, Puls,* and *Spotkania.* By the late 1970s, independent journals and publishing ventures broke effectively the state's virtual monopoly on publishing.

The period of the Solidarity revolution, between August 1980 and December 1981, did not last long enough to generate new literary phenomena, but it did free the writers from some of the worst constraints of censorship and government control. Books hitherto banned began to appear, including the first book publication of Milosz's poetry in Poland since 1945—although his collections of essays, such as *Ogród nauk* (1979; the garden of knowledge) were not allowed to appear. The imposition of martial law in December 1981, arrests, internments, and suspension of professional organizations, including the Union of Polish Writers, met with considerable resistance not only on the part of the writers associated with the opposition in the 1970s, and broadly sympathetic to the Solidarity movement, but also of a fairly large segment of those who were party members. Some like Ernest Bryll (b. 1935), a poet and dramatist, renounced their party membership in protest; others, while retaining their membership, supported the efforts of the executive of the union to prevent the dissolution of the organization without compromising its autonomy. The attempt to save the organization proved, in the end, unsuccessful, and the union was dissolved by the authorities in August 1983. The subsequent creation of a party-controlled union was largely boycotted by the literary milieu, which on the whole showed a remarkable degree of solidarity.

The dissolution of the union was accompanied by the tightening of censorship, discrimination in state patronage, and the introduction of proscription lists. For instance, in March 1984 a government-controlled literary weekly published a list of twenty-eight names of writers whose works were not to be reissued by state publishing houses. Among those listed was the former president of the union, Jan Józef Szczepański (b. 1919), a fiction writer of distinction; Kornel Filipowicz (1913–1990), one of the best short-story writers in postwar Poland; Woroszylski; Konwicki; Stryjkowski; and Milosz. However, harsh government policies failed to cow the literary community, which by the mid-1980s had at its disposal alternative means of publication: In addition to the Catholic journals and publishing houses, which the government did not dare to close, there emerged numerous underground presses, and periodicals, of which the most important were *Arka, Wezwanie, Obecność*, and *Brulion*, which became the organ of the now strongly politicized counterculture trend; moreover, many writers took advantage of the émigré publishing houses and journals, such as *Kultura* and *Zeszyty Literackie* in Paris and *Puls* in London. The underground presses reprinted works by Gombrowicz, Milosz, Herling-Grudziński, Aleksander Wat—whose autobiography, *Mój wiek* (1977; *My Century*, 1990), evoked special interest—Józef Mackiewicz, and many others, and published new work written in Poland, including Jaroslaw Marek Rymkiewicz's (b. 1935) topical novel *Rozmowy polskie* (1984; Polish conversations), Konwicki's autobiographical *Wschody i zachody księżyca* (1982; *Moonrise, Moonset*, 1987), Mrożek's satirical and absurdist tales, Adam Michnik's (b. 1946) historical and literary essays, and volumes of several young poets, such as Tomasz Jastrun (b. 1950), Jan Polkowski (b. 1953), and others.

The least harmed by the consequences of martial law was poetry. In the 1980s, Milosz added to his substantial poetic achievement new work of outstanding quality, *Hymn o perle* (1981; hymn of the pearl), *Nieobjęta ziemia* (1985; *Unattainable Earth*, 1986), and *Kroniki* (1987; chronicles); the appearance of these volumes as well as of his *Collected Poems* in English translation (1988) have further enhanced his standing as a major 20th-c. poet. Herbert came with one of the most important poetic documents of the troubled time, *Report z oblężonego miasta i inne wiersze* (1983; *Report from the Besieged City and Other Poems*, 1987), in which he gives his poetic reaction to both the specifically Polish, but also universal, condition of the human being and society. The volume continues the earlier *Pan Cogito*, using the same versatile persona and developing further the philosophical and moral themes in the typically Herbertian mode of ironic complexity and intellectual integrity.

Of the poets who previously attained a level of excellence, Wislawa Szymborska's new volume *Ludzie na moście* (1986; *People on a Bridge*, 1990) has gained wide acclaim as another example of the exquisite quality of her "Mozartian" verse. Several

poets of the New Wave have now attained greater maturity and stature. Zagajewski's, Barańczak's, and Krynicki's growing to maturity received a special recognition by Miłosz, who in his diary *Rok myśliwego* (1990; a year of a humer) expressed a high opinion of their work. Adam Czerniawski's (b. 1934) *Wiek złoty* (1982; age of gold) and *Jesień* (1989; autumn) testify further to the originality of his poetic development, achieved despite the fact that he had left Poland in early childhood; and among the youngest, Bronisław Maj (b. 1953) has already made his mark as the author of *Zagłada świętego miasta* (1986; annihilation of the holy city) and other volumes. Among retrospective volumes were Jan Twardowski's (b. 1916) *Nie przyszedłem pana nawracać* (1986; I did not come to convert you), Wacław IWANIUK'S *Powrót* (1989; return), Jan Darowski's (b. 1926) *Niespodziewane żywoty* (1990; unexpected lives), and Bogdan Czaykowski's (b. 1937) *Wiatr z innej strony* (1990; wind from another side).

The most affected by the regime's policies and the economic crisis was the theater. A boycott of state-run radio and television by the actors, which lasted for nearly a year, and the considerable state interference in theatrical life affected negatively the writing of plays and the desire to be staged. Attempts to create an alternative theater (such as performances in church halls) could not replace normally functioning theater. Nevertheless, an excellent journal devoted to drama and theater—*Dialog*—on the whole managed to maintain its high standards; some good plays did get published, including Różewicz's *Pułapka* (1982; *The Trap*, 1984), and Mrożek's *Portret* (1987; portrait), possibly the best of his plays since *Emigranci* (1974; émigrés). Also, such outstanding theater directors as Tadeusz Kantor (1915–1990); the brilliant representative of the "theater-of-happening" in Poland, Zygmunt Hübner; and Jerzy Jarocki were soon able to resume their theatrical experiments despite official restrictions, while Jerzy Grotowski (b. 1929) continued to exert influence both in Poland and abroad.

Both Mrożek's and Różewicz's development seems to have been going in the same direction as the Western absurdist dramatists, namely turning back, as it were, to the more traditional forms of drama and preoccupation with philosophical and psychological questions. Różewicz's *Pułapka* tackles in a highly successful manner the difficult problem of structuring a plotless "plot" around the dilemmas of an alienated individual by means of a series of monologues and conversations situated almost exclusively within the circle of a family. Nevertheless, it can still be classified as an absurdist play, as it deals with the situation of a man (Franz Kafka) whose entire life and work is one of the sources of inspiration of the whole concept of the THEATRE OF THE ABSURD. Mrożek's case is in many respects similar.

In prose the pressure for topicality, commitment, witnessing, self-justification, affirmation of values, and painting the devil black (that is, mainly, red), thrust to the forefront paraliterary genres such as reportage, documentary fiction, diary, interview, apology, essay, polemic, and invective. One can mention here Brandys's mixture of diary, reminiscences, and commentary, *Miesiące* (3 vols., 1981–1984), *A Warsaw Diary: 1978–1981* (1983), and *Paris, New York: 1982–1984* (1988); Szczepański's report on his presidency of the Union of Writers during the Solidarity and martial-law period, *Kadencja* (1988; term of office); or fictionalized accounts of contemporary events, such as Marek Nowakowski's *Raport o stanie wojennym* (1982; *The Canary and Other Tales of Martial Law*, 1984) and his other volumes in this genre, Glowacki's story of the August 1980 strike at the Lenin shipyard, *Moc truchleje* (1982; *Give Us This Day*, 1983), Konwicki's contemporary novel *Rzeka podziemna, podziemne ptaki* (1985; underground river, underground birds), or Hanna Krall's (b. 1937) *Okna* (1987; windows), none of which, however, equaled the highly successful transformation of journalism into literary form in the much earlier *Cesarz* (1978; *The Emperor*, 1983) by Ryszard Kapuściński (b. 1932).

Contrasting with the trend of topical fiction was the work of a number of young writers, such as Grzegorz Musiał (b. 1952) and Pawel Huelle (b. 1957), whose first novel, *Weiser Dawidek* (1987; *Who Was David Weiser*, 1990), which has been translated into more than a dozen languages, is remarkable if only as an example of the advantages that "makers of fictions" have over those who find it difficult to detach themselves in their narratives from actual happenings. Finally, one should not fail to mention new work of the master of satirical and philosophical science fiction. Stanislaw Lem (b. 1921), such as *Golem XIV* (1981; included in *Imaginary Magnitude*, 1984) and *Wizja lokalna* (1982; official hearing on the spot).

Particularly popular was the genre of conversations, to mention only Ewa Czarnecka's (dates n.a.) *Podróżny świata; rozmowy z Czesławem Miłoszem* (1983; *Conversations with Czesław Miłosz*, 1987); Stanisław Nowicki's (dates n.a.) *Pół wieku czyśćca; rozmowy z Tadeuszem Konwickim* (1986; half a century of purgatory; conversations with Tadeusz Konwicki); Jacek Trznadel's (b. 1930) *Hańba domowa; rozmowy z pisarzami* (1986; native shame; conversations with writers), comprising interviews with twelve prominent writers concerning their communist past and rejection of communism; or Kazimierz Braun's (dates n.a.) and Tadeusz Różewicz's *Języki teatru* (1989; languages of theater), of considerable interest regarding the development of Różewicz's poetic drama and his literary views. There was also a great demand for diaries, a number of which by some of the most important 20th-c. writers appeared for the first time in print, offering often fascinating insights into various developments in Polish literature. Of particular value, despite some editorial deletions, are *Dzienniki* (5 vols., 1988; diaries) by Maria Dąbrowska, but mention should also be made of Jerzy Zawieyski's (1902–1969) *Kartki z dziennika, 1955–1969* (1983; pages from a diary, 1955–1969), and of the first printing in Poland of Gombrowicz's *Dziennik* (3 vols., first pub. in Paris, 1957, 1966, 1971; *Diary*, 1988–1989), with only minor deletions.

One of the major thematic concerns of the 1980s was the Jewish past, the Holocaust, and anti-semitism in Poland. Of the numerous writings dealing with this theme, Andrzej Szczypiorski's (b. 1924) *Początek* (1986; *Beautiful Mrs. Seidenman*, 1990), which deals in part with survival in Nazi-occupied Warsaw, has met with wide acclaim possibly because it is a deftly handled conventional novel; Jaroslaw Marek Rymkiewicz's *Umschlagplatz* (1988; transit place), which eludes generic classification, exemplifies the need, felt by so many writers writing on the theme of *Shoah*, to go beyond the available literary forms, so as to do justice to a subject that defies imagination; and Jerzy S. Sito's (b. 1934) play *Słuchaj, Izrealu!* (1988; listen, Israel!), which deals with life (and death) in the Warsaw ghetto, has qualities of true dramatic power and tragic pity, especially in the presentation of its main character, Adam Czerniakow. A publication of an unusual documentary value is *Antologia poezji żydowskiej* (1983; anthology of Jewish poetry), selected and edited by Arnold Slucki, and comprising translators from Yiddish of over a hundred poems by poets, many of whom died in German and Soviet camps or in ghettos or were killed on the streets or while hiding in forests.

With the collapse of communist rule in 1989, Polish history, and with it Polish literature, entered a new phase. While predictions would be unwise, it may be noted that the literary milieu has already become acutely aware of the fact that economic and political freedoms come together with the "laws of the free market" which, the pessimists say, means more demand for sex, crime, science fiction, and melodrama rather than for good literature. This may be so. But the cultural dynamics of postcommunist society, freed from ideological constraints, may yet give the lie to the pessimists, especially in a country with such literary traditions as Poland.

BIBLIOGRAPHY: Dyboski, R., *Modern Polish Literature* (1924); Scherer-Virski, O., *The Modern Polish Short Story* (1955); Heyst, A., "Poland's Contemporary Literature," *Dublin Review*, 233 (1959): 171–78; Folejewski, Z., "Socialist Realism in Polish Literature and Criticism," *CL*, 13 (1961): 72–80; Kunstmann, H., *Die moderne polnische Literatur* (1962); Csato, E., *The Polish Theatre* (1963); Herman, M., *Histoire de la littérature polonaise* (1963); Kridl, M., *Survey of Polish Literature and Culture* (1965); Kunstmann, H., *Moderne polnische Dramatik* (1965); Wirth, A., *Modernes polnisches Theater* (1967); Miłosz, C., *The History of Polish Literature* (1969); Czerwiński, E. J., "Polish Dramatists in Search of Self," *CompD*, 3 (1969): 210–17; Folejewski, Z., "The Theatre of Ruthless Metaphor: Polish Theatre between Marxism and Existentialism," *CompD*, 3 (1969): 176–82; Folejewski, Z., "Notes on the Novel in Contemporary Poland," *CSP*, 13 (1971): 299–313; Gerould, D., *Twentieth-Century Polish Drama* (1977); Krzyżanowski, J., *A History of Polish Literature* (1978); Barańczak, S., "The Gag and the Word," *Survey*, 110 (1980): 58–79; Głowiński, M., "The Grotesque in Contemporary Polish Literature," in Birnbaum, H., and Eekman, T., eds., *Fiction and Drama in Eastern and Southeastern Europe: Evolution and Experiment in the Postwar Period* (1980): 177–90; Czerwiński, E. J., "Quo Vadis? Polish Theatre and Drama in the 1980s," in Clayton, J. D., and G. Schaarschmidt, eds., *Poetica Slavica: Studies in Honour of Zbigniew Folejewski* (1981): 13–20; Levine, M. G., *Contemporary Polish Poetry, 1925–1975* (1981); Miłosz, C., *The Witness of Poetry* (1983); Ziegfeld, R. E., *Stanisław Lem* (1985); Davie, D., *Czesław Miłosz and the Insufficiency of Lyric* (1986); Barańczak, S., *A Fugitive from Utopia: The Poetry of Zbigniew Herbert* (1987); Czerwiński, E. J., *Contemporary Polish Theater and Drama* (1988); Możejko, E., ed. *Between Anxiety and Hope: The Poetry and Writing of Czesław Miłosz* (1988); Barańczak, S., *Breathing under Water and Other East European Essays* (1990); Fiut, A., *The Eternal Moment: The Poetry of Czesław Miłosz* (1990); Czerniawski, A., ed. *The Mature Laurel: Essays on Modern Polish Poetry* (1991); Donskov, A., and R. Sokoloski, eds. *Slavic Drama, the Question of Innovation* (1991)

—ZBIGNIEW FOLEJEWSKI

Kashubian Literature

The Kashubs, a Slavic people living in the region of Gdańsk (formerly Danzig), possess a rich heritage of oral literature, which serves as a primary thematic source for their written literature, launched at the close of the 19th c. by the first Kashubian poet, Jan Hieronim Derdowski (1852–1902). The author of three humorous epics, Derdowski is best remembered for *O panu Czorlińscim co do Pucka po sece jachoł* (1880; concerning Mr. Czorliński, who drove to Puck for a fishing net).

Begun when the Kashubian homeland was German territory, Kashubian literary activity has continued in contemporary Poland, where it functions as dialect literature not subsidized by funds from the central government. Consequently, it is to be found in short-lived journals and in the small printings of works published by subscription or at the author's own expense. Alexander Majkowski (1876–1938) was the first to publish Kashubian lyric poetry—*Spiewe i frańtówci* (1905; songs and lyrics)—as well as the first Kashubian novel, *Zëcé i przigodë Remusa* (1938; the life and adventures of Remus), the best-known work in Kashubian literature. His greatest contribution was the founding, in 1909, of *Gryf*, a journal of Kashubian culture. It became the organ of the Young Kashubian movement, which included Jan Karnowski (1886–1939), the foremost Kashubian lyric poet; Leon Heyke (1885–1939) and Franciszek Sędzicki (1882–1957), lyric and epic poets; and Jan Patock (1886–1940), a folklorist. The most successful Kashubian dramatist is Bernard Sychta (b. 1907), whose *Hanka sę żeni* (1935; Hanka marries) is his most popular Kashubian play.

Although Kashubian writers have always championed their ethnicity, they have never, either singly or in concert, advocated political separatism. Prior to World War I their chief goal, especially among the Young Kashubs, was resistance to the encroachment of German language and culture. During the interwar period they flourished in the so-called Polish Corridor, forming several new literary groups and journals. Nazi invasion resulted in an almost total liquidation of the Kashubian intelligentsia. Only after the end of Stalinism in the 1950s did Kashubian literature begin to flourish once again, led by the scholar Leon Roppel (b. 1912) and the poet and short-story writer Jan Piepka (b. 1926).

Although the greater part of their literary production has been poetry, the Kashubs have not produced a poet of such a stature that his language would serve as the basis for a unified literary language. Instead Kashubian writers continue in their regionalism, each writing in his own local dialect, using local themes. From its beginning Kashubian literature has been intimately tied to Kashubian folklore. Both in poetry and prose Kashubian writers sing the praise of their homeland with images of village maidens, fishermen in the perilous sea, and the exploits of local heroes during the two world wars. Aside from Majkowski's novel, only Alojzy Nagel's (b. 1930) poetry has had an impact beyond the ethnic borders.

There are now several dozen active Kashubian writers, some in their teens, who may insure the further development of Kashubian literature, at least for one more generation.

BIBLIOGRAPHY: Lorentz, et al., F., *The Cassubian Civilization* (1933); Stone, G., "The Language of Cassubian Literature and the Question of a Literary Standard," *SEER*, 1 (1972): 521–29; Neureiter, F., ed., "Übersicht über die kaschubische Literatur," *Kaschubische Anthologie* (1973): 1–19; Perkowski, J., "Kashubian Émigré Literature," *Kurier Polsko-Kanadyjski*, (6 February 1975): 33; Neureiter, F., *Geschichte der kaschubischen Literatur* (1978)

—JAN L. PERKOWSKI

POLYNESIAN LITERATURE

See Pacific Islands Literatures

PONGE, Francis

French poet, essayist, and art critic, b. 27 March 1899, Montpellier; d. 6 Aug. 1988, Le Bar-Sur-Loup

P. is a child of the Midi (Montpellier, Nîmes, Avignon) but also of Normandy (Caen), where his family moved when he was ten. He pursued his secondary studies in Caen and later in Paris, after which he began the study of law. In 1918, however, he was drafted into the army, and his formal education came to an end. His earliest extant writings date from the immediate post-World War I period.

By 1923 P. had become friendly with the *Nouvelle revue française* group—Jacques Rivière (1886–1925), Jean PAULHAN—who published several of his poems in their review. A few years later he was frequenting the SURREALISTS and in 1929 signed their second manifesto. Throughout this period he continued to write, but published little until 1942, when *Le parti pris des choses* (taking the side of things) appeared, an event that brought him a certain renown in avant-garde circles. He worked at the Hachette publishing house in the 1930s, was a member of the Communist Party between 1937 and 1947, performed various writing (and other) duties for the Resistance in occupied France during World War II, and was employed as a teacher at the Alliance Française from 1952 to 1964. Since the mid-1960s he has lectured widely in Europe and the U.S., but now spends most of the year writing at his home in Le Bar-sur-Loup (Provence).

Although one can discern an evolution or, more precisely, a shift in his writings over the last six decades, essentially P. has been producing the same kind of text since 1919. On the other hand, during that time his oeuvre has attracted strongly favorable attention from rather disparate quarters. In the early 1920s, for example, the *NRF* group admired the satirical dimension of P.'s texts; Jean-Paul SARTRE, in his laudatory 1944 study of P., extolled the phenomenologist he found at work in *Le parti pris des choses*; and in the 1960s P.'s writings were praised for their semantic materialism by figures associated with the review *Tel Quel*—Philippe SOLLERS, Jean Thibaudeau (b. 1935), Marcelin Pleynet (b. 1933). While all three views have their validity, in hindsight the *Tel Quel* approach to P.'s work seems closest to the mark. For P. is above all an explorer of the infinite resources of the French language. If he has often chosen to write of things, of objects, he has done so, as he observed in a 1969 interview, so that he "would always have a brake on [his] subjectivity." He is totally opposed to the goal of self-expression in poetry, as he is to the conception of the poet as a seeker of metaphysical truths. In his scheme of things, poets must seek out within their native language the endless interconnections (rhythmic, phonic, semantic, orthographic) that they alone are equipped to discover and celebrate. Like François de Malherbe (1555–1628), whom P. reveres, he is concerned as a poet "only with his instrument."

P.'s texts are characterized by extreme self-consciousness, by an almost exacerbated lucidity regarding their own constituent elements. They fold back on themselves in puns and other ludic devices that stress the autonomy of the text as text rather than the text's fidelity to the thing being described. With his *objeux*, his object-wordgames, P. re-creates the world piecemeal; bit by bit he is building a thoroughly demystified but perfectly habitable universe, one of rooted discourse, of world-anchored words.

His first published texts, like the short prose pieces in *Le parti pris des choses*, were not only for the most part brief, but also highly polished and tightly organized as well. From the mid-1940s onward, however, P.'s published pieces suddenly grew longer, became more loosely structured, less finished than his early pieces had been—for example, the texts collected in *Le grand recueil* (3 vols., 1961; the great collection) and *Nouveau recueil* (1967; new collection). Also, around this same time P. began to publish what appeared to be rather casually fashioned essays on the work of some contemporary painters and sculptors, essays that have been collected in *L'atelier contemporain* (1977; the contemporary atelier). P.'s "second manner," his meandering later style, represents, in fact, a freer, more comodious, less composed version of his previous mode; with it he has managed to focus steadily for the first time on a notion that has always obsessed him: the birth of form, the procedures by which a poem or a painting comes into being. The poet's preliminary notes and the artist's sketches are now put in the foreground at the expense of the finished product.

Deploying within the work the traces of its own gestation—for instance, outlines, false starts, revisions, recapitulations—the signs of the productive process that culminates in the work's creation, has been the hallmark of P.'s writing since the beginning. In recent decades an increasingly dominant metapoetic orientation has opened his writing up to a point where all distinctions in it between theory and practice, notebook (or sketch pad) and completed work, have disappeared, yielding texts of dazzling complexity and elaborateness, not incomplete, only unclosed. Today P. has emerged as France's greatest metapoet and at the same time as one of that small band of truly original writers in our century.

FURTHER WORKS: *Douze petits écrits* (1926); *L'œilet; La guêpe; Le mimosa* (1946); *Dix courts sur la méthode* (1946); *Le carnet du bois de pins* (1947); *Proêmes* (1948); *Le peintre à l'étude* (1948); *La rage de l'expression* (1952); *Tome premier* (1965); *Pour un Malherbe* (1965); *Le savon* (1967; *Soap*, 1969); *Entretiens de F. P. avec Phillipe Sollers* (1970); *La fabrique du pré* (1971; *The Making of the "Pré,"* 1979); *L'écrit Beaubourg* (1977); *Comment une figue de paroles et pourquoi* (1977). FURTHER WORKS IN ENGLISH: *The Voice of Things* (1972); *The Power of Language* (1979)

BIBLIOGRAPHY: Sollers, P., *F. P.* (1963); Thibaudeau, J., *P.* (1967); Spada, M., *F. P.* (1974), Donnefis, P., ed., *F. P. · Colloque de Cerisy* (1977); Higgins, I., *F. P.* (1979); Sorrell, M., *F. P.* (1981)

—ROBERT W. GREENE

PONIATOWSKA, Elena

Mexican novelist, short-story writer, and journalist, b. 19 May 1933, Paris, France

P.'s father, a Polish aristocrat, had emigrated to France, and her Mexican mother fled to Europe with her family during the Mexican Revolution. In 1942, during World War II, P., her mother, and her sister returned to Mexico, where her father joined them after the war. Having received her high-school education in British and American religious schools, P. learned Spanish from her family's servants, thus explaining her love of the colloquial idiom so evident in her works. In the mid-1950s P. was hired by the Mexican daily *Excélsior* to conduct interviews with a wide range of celebrities, a

position that launched her career as a journalist and eventually inspired her to write documentary fiction. In 1978 she was awarded the Mexican National Journalism Prize, and today she is perhaps Mexico's best-known writer after Octavio PAZ and Carlos FUENTES.

P. achieved fame almost overnight with the publication of *La noche de Tlatelolco* (1971; *Massacre in Mexico*, 1975), a grouping of individual eyewitness accounts of the massacre of hundreds of unarmed civilians (P.'s younger brother was one of those killed) by government troops on Tlatelolco Plaza in the heart of the capital. The tragedy, which occurred on 2 October 1968 during a peaceful protest against government policies, has been the subject of many literary texts, but P.'s is by far the most widely read, having gone through more than fifty editions to date. It consists of a montage of oral testimonies, police records, photographs, newspaper articles, and political speeches, all of which have been edited and arranged in such a way that the reader feels caught up in the swirl of the events described. Almost two decades laner P. utilized a similar technique to dramatize the earthquake that killed thousands of people in Mexico City on 19 September 1985. *Nada, nadie: Las voces del temblor* (1988; nothing, nobody: the voices of the earthquake) thrusts its readers into the center of the tragedy that, like the massacre of Tlatelolco, will remain embedded in the Mexican subconscious for generations. The searing descriptions of the terrible first-person experiences both during and after the quake are impossible to forget. Also memorable are the references to fraud on the part of contractors who had ignored building codes for personal gain, and the instances in which army and police personnel placed public order before rescue efforts. As in *La noche de Tlanelolco*, P. remains objective, allowing those she has interviewed to describe one of the major occurrences in recent Mexican history. *Nada, nadie: Las voces del temblor* reads almost like a novel, juxtaposing moments of suspense, heroism, and suffering. It is one of the most moving works ever published by a Mexican author.

P.'s best-known novel to date is *Hasta no verte, Jesús mío* (1969; *Until We Meet Again*, 1987), a testimonial of a poor, working-class woman who was born in southern Mexico about 1900, found herself caught up in the Revolution of 1910, and lived most of her life in Mexico City. P. came across her protagonist Jesusa Palancares by chance when she heard her conversing with coworkers in a laundry. With tape recorder and notebook in hand, P. spent two hours a week for many months with Jesusa, recording the old woman's recollections of her life. This novel is noteworthy for a number of reasons. Jesusa's language is a fascinating example of the colorful slang used by her class; her struggle to survive cannot fail to elicit our admiration; her everyday adventures while working for numerous employers in a wide variety of jobs liken her to a picaresque heroine; and her descriptions of the revolution and subsequent political events exude a combination of forthrightness and cynicism seldom observed in Mexican literature. While some critics see Jesusa as a feminist, a liberated woman in a *machista* society, others see her as a victim of male domination and social injustice. In a sense both opinions are correct, but one should recognize that in the course of the novel Jesusa evolves from an innocent adolescent, forced into a bad marriage at the age of fifteen, to a strong, resolute woman (she actually leads a combat unit during the revolution after her husband is killed), and she never again submits to male domination.

P.'s three other novels are *Querido Diego, te abraza Quiela* (1976; *Dear Diego*, 1986), in epistolary format; *La "Flor de Lis"* (1988; The "Flor de Lis"), an autobiographical novel and a kind of *bildungsroman* about a girl who leaves France for Mexico with her mother and sister during World War II; and *Tinísima* (1992; Tinísima), a massive nonfiction novel about Tina Modotti, an Italian-American photographer who lived in Mexico for many years before and after World War II. P.'s best collection of short fiction is *De noches vienes* (1979; You come by night), which contains sixteen stories ranging in subject matter from social protest to the complex relations between social classes and the sexes.

P. is one of today's major practitioners of documentary fiction, a genre that has become increasingly important in Spanish America. Her popularity as a writer stems from her dramatic presentations of contemporary issues, her sympathy for the downtrodden, and her emphasis on colloquial language, which makes her writings accessible to most readers. For those seeking a better understanding of modern Mexico, P.'s oeuvre provides an excellent resource.

FURTHER WORKS: *Lilus Kikus* (1954); *Palabras cruzadas: Crónicas* (1961); *Todo empezóel domingo* (1961); *Los cuentos de Lilus Kikus* (1967); *El primer primero de mayo* (1976); *Gaby Brimmer* (1979); *Fuerte es el silencio* (1980); *La casa en la tierra* (1980); *Domingo siete* (1982); *El último guajolote* (1982); *¡Ay vida, no me mereces!* (1986); *Héctor García: México sin retoque* (1987)

BIBLIOGRAPHY: Miller, B., *Mujeres en la literatura* (1978): 65–75; Fox-Lockert, L., *Women Novelists in Spain and Spanish America* (1979): 260–77; Portal, M., *Proceso narrative de la revolución mexicana* (1980): 285–92:; Fernández Olmos, M., "El género testimonial: Aproximaciones feministas," *Revl*, 11, 1 (Spring 1981): 69–75; Young, D. J. and Young, W. D., "The New Journalism in Mexico: Two Women Writers," *Chasqui*, 12: 2–3 (Feb.-May 1983): 72–80; Hancock, J., "E. P.'s *Hasta no verte, Jesús mío*: The Remarking of the Image of Woman," *Hispania*, 66, 3 (Sept. 1983): 355–59; Foster, D. W., "Latin American Documentary Narrative." *PMLA*, 99, 1 (Jan. 1984): 41–55; Chevigny, B. G., "The Transformation of Privilege in the Work of E. P.," *LALR*, 13, 26 (July-Dec. 1985): 49–62; Foster, D. W., *Alternate Voices in the Contemporary Latin American Narrative* (1985): 12–20 and passim; Friedman, E. H., "The Marginated Narrator: *Hasta no verte, Jesús mío* and the Eloquence of Repression," *The Antiheroine's Voice: Narrative Discourse and Transformations of the Picaresque* (1987): 170–87; Meyer, D., *Lives on the Line: The Testimony of Contemporary Latin American Authors* (1988): 137–38; Shea, M., "A Growing Awareness of Sexual Oppression in the Novels of Contemporary Latin American Women Writers," *Confluencia*, 4, 1 (Fall 1988): 53–59; Gazarian-Gautier, M. -L., *Interviews with Latin American Writers* (1989): 199–216; Martin, G., *Journeys through the Labyrinth: Latin American Fiction in the Twentieth Century* (1989): 344–50; Jörgensen, B. E., "E. P.," in Marting, D. E., ed., *Spanish American Women Writers: A Bio-Bibliographical Source Book* (1990): 472–82

—GEORGE R. MCMURRAY

Feminist perspectives in literary analysis have seen frequent publication in the last few years. Works by such female authors as Sor Juana Inés de la Cruz. Gertrudis Gómez de Avellaneda, Gabriela Mistral, María Luisa Bombal, Marta Lynch, and Rosario Castellanos, to name only a few, have very recently been the subject of this specific kind of investigation.

An important addition to this list is E. P.—novelist, short story and film script writer, journalist, editor, and feminist—whose production is both varied and fecund. One publication in particular, *Hasta no verte, Jesús mío* (1969), is a novel which may be considered a landmark in Mexican literature because it offers a fresh view and treatment of Latin American woman, and may represent a step toward the delineation of a new female image or role model. Intimately involved with the social realities of Mexico, the protagonist deviates radically from the commonly portrayed stereotypes of women. Her personality and conduct embody a blend of so-called feminine and masculine traits, thus approximating the androgynous figure which some feminist critics regard as essential. . . .

Hasta no verte, Jesús mío is based on the real life of Jesusa Palancares. Overhearing some vigorous statements made by a humble woman in a laundry room conversation, P. was so moved that she arranged to visit her at home in a poor neighborhood of Mexico City. This led to a series of interviews, many of them taped, which took place for more than a two-year period. . . . P. labels her work a *novela testimonial* rather than a sociological or anthropological document mainly because of what was involved in the writing. . . .

Women like Jesusa Palancares are not frequently represented in literature. In *Hasta no verte, Jesús mío*, E. P. portrays a female character whose life, attitudes, and expression invalidate the erroneous and offensive stereotypes of women that have been perpetuated. Unlike many others depicted in fiction, Jesusa is a hard-working individual who survives situations with dignity. She has a keen sense of justice that compels her to censure whatever she judges to be a social injustice. Thus, a new alternative has been established: a liberated female hero; a positive role model who is independent, self-reliant, and physically, as well as emotionally, strong.

Joel Hancock, "E. P.'s *Hasta no verte, Jesús mío*: The Remaking of the Image of Woman," *Hispania*, 66, 3 (Sept. 1983), 353–57

The evanescent or invisible, the silent or the silenced, those who elude official history or vanish from it, make the subject of the two of P.'s works from which her fame and influence chiefly derive. Her testimonial novel, *Hasta no verte, Jesús mío* . . . presents in first-person narration the story of an adventuring peasant woman, fighter in the Mexican revolution and survivor of its inhospitable aftermath. Hitherto such characters had been presented only externally, and P.'s distillation of her subject's dense and highly-colored idiom became a new literary resource. *La noche de Tlatelolco* . . . is a dramatic collage of interviews with participants in the 1968 student movement and with witnesses to the massacre of hundreds during a peaceful meeting in Mexico City, an event obfuscated by government agencies and the press alike. . . .

P.'s choosing to cast her lot with Latin America and to write in Spanish with a highly Mexican inflection, point to a deliberateness of self-formation that is reinforced by other choices. For P.'s social roots are aristocratic and her political antecedents are conservative. Generations of exile from reform and revolution in Mexico and Poland produced in France P.'s parents and P. herself. Against such a background, P.'s two most celebrated works stand in high relief; they delineate the dual trajectory of her career. In *Hasta no verte, Jesús mío*, she journeys to the opposite end of woman's world of social possibility and in *La noche de Tlatelolco* she journeys to the alternate pole of political possibility. Each journey may be seen as metaphor and impetus of the other. Like her choice of Latin America, her choosing to write of a woman with no resources but her self and of political insurgents has everything to do with her authorial self-creation.

Bell Gale Chevigny, "The Transformation of Privilege in the Work of E. P.," *LALR*, 13, 26 (July-Dec. 1985), 49–50

Since the mid 1950s, when she began writing for newspapers in Mexico City as well as writing her own poetry and prose, P. has become an author identified with the voice of the Mexican people. This authentic, clear voice speaks through her work powerfully, whether in the testimonial novel based on interviews, with the indomitable Jesusa Palancares—*Hasta no verte, Jesús mío . . .*—or in the dramatic montage of first-person accounts of the 1968 student riots in *La noche de Tlatelolco. . . .* By bringing history to life in individual portraits, P. forces her reader to reconsider the personal dimensions of otherwise distant events or situations. She is particularly adept at conveying the experiences of women; prime examples would be the paralyzed *Gaby Brimmer . . .* a woman of great courage and determination, or the artist Angelina Beloff in *Querido Diego, te abraza Quiela. . . .* whom Diego Rivera spurned after having lived with her for ten years and fathering her son.

Doris Meyer, *Lives on the Line: The Testimony of Contemporary Latin American Authors* (1988), 137

E. P. . . . is one of Latin America's most remarkable narrators. Outside of [Octavio] Paz and [Carlos] Fuentes, she is probably the most important writer in Mexico today. Her father was a French-Polish émigré aristocrat, her mother the daughter of a Mexican landowning family which fled the country during the Revolution. The family returned to Mexico when Elena was nine years old, and she was sent to an English school, largely learning Spanish from the family servants. In later life she strived desperately to integrate herself into Mexican national life, and today is the country's best known journalist and arguably Latin America's most important producer of documentary narrative. *Until We Meet Again . . .* is the

moving story of a Mexican working-class woman's experience of the 20th c., a work which makes most Social Realist novels seem artificial. *Massacre in Mexico . . .* is the single most influential record of any kind of the 1968 massacre, in which her brother Jan died, with a force reminiscent of the films of the Bouvian director Jorge Sanjinés. And her latest work, *"Nothing, No One" . . .* is a genuinely searing testimony to the experience of the [1985] earthquake. In short, P. has produced the most lasting memorials to the two most significant events of Mexican history in the last two decades, the Tlatelolco affair and the great earthquake, as well as a series of other works such as *Dear Diego . . .*, *Lilus Kilus . . .* and *"The fleur de Lys" . . .* something like a fictionalized autobiography.

Gerald Martin, *Journeys through the Labyrinth: Latin American Fiction in the Twentieth Century* (1989), 346–47

Indeed, Tlatelolco has acquired such a profound meaning in contemporary Mexican culture that it has been the subject of a book-length essay by Octavio Paz and has inspired virtually a subgenre of recent Mexican literature. *La noche de Tlatelolco . . .* by E. P. . . . is the only documentary narrative besides [Julío] Cortazar's *El libro de Manuel* and [Miguel] Barnet's *Biografía de un cimarrón* that has been translated into English. It is the most documentary of the texts studied in this essay and, consequently, the least "novelistic" if viewed in terms of fictional elements or devices. Nevertheless, it is novelistic in the sense that it sustains a complex narrative structure. And, although *Noche* has a place in a bibliography of contemporary social history, it is frequently read as a contribution to the contemporary Latin American novel. To read *Noche* as more novel than document does not detract from its quality as documentary testimonial. Rather—as is true for all recent documentary and historical fiction in Latin America—such a reading testifies to the continuity in that culture of fiction and reality and the importance of productive "mythic" factuality.

David William Foster, *Alternate Voices in the Contemporary Latin American Narrative* (1985), 13

A quick review of E. P.'s published works reveals the variety of themes and literary forms which her writing embraces. A common thread, however, connects her political and social chronicles, her novels and short stories, her interviews and her testimonial works. That common thread is the profound commitment to interpreting contemporary Mexican society, with special attention to the silenced voices and the marginalized lives that constitute the majority experience in the vast human landscape of her country. Her books record such events as the 1968 Mexican student movement, a hunger strike by mothers of the "disappeared," and the 1985 earthquake in Mexico City; they offer as protagonists street vendors, a quadriplegic woman of the middle class, student dissidents, and political prisoners. For this reason most readers concur in considering P. to be a literary champion of the oppressed. In the process of allowing the other to speak for him or herself, P. often effaces her own participation in the dialogue. . . .

> Beth E. Jörgensen, "E. P.," in Diane E. Marting, ed., *Spanish American Women Writers: A Bio-Bibliographical Source Book* (1990), 473

POPA, Vasko

Yugoslav poet (writing in Serbian), b. 29 July 1922, Grebenac; d. 4 Jan. 1991, Belgrade

During World War II P. supported the side of the partisans. He studied literature at the universities of Vienna, Bucharest, and Belgrade and received his degree at Belgrade in 1949. Since then he has worked as an editor in publishing houses. His poetry has been translated into all major languages.

When his first collection, *Kora* (1953; tree bark) was published, it was not well received by those readers and critics who resisted the modernization of Yugoslav poetry. P.'s poetry, together with that of Miodrag PAVLOVIĆ, contributed decisively to the victory of the modernists who were influenced by Western currents.

From the very first, P. showed a predilection for the concrete rather than the abstract. For him a thing is not just an inanimate object—it has a life of its own, which only the eye of a poet can discern. P. likes to use things such as quartz stone, the bark of a tree, bones, or a small box as symbols for his own concepts and attitudes. His closeness to things was undoubtedly accentuated by his war experiences as a young man, when people were primarily concerned with material things in their struggle for survival and when the language they spoke was direct and concrete.

P. combines the grotesque and the fantastic, thus dramatizing what he sees as the senselessness of the human condition. Yet there is a certain playfulness in his poetry. In his approach to reality he often eradicates the boundary between sense perceptions and even violates logic. Often he uses proverbs, puns, and witticisms, underlining the meaningless and at the same time tragicomic nature of man's existence.

P.'s preferred mode is the cycle. Each one is a self-contained entity, in which the poems deal with a common topic and are written in the same vein. Each one is related to the others. From the small seemingly insignificant objects around him in *Kora*, P. moved to the larger microcosm of his native land in *Nepočin-polje* (1956; the unrest field) and on to the macrocosm of the universe in *Sporedno nebo* (1968; the secondary sky), only to return to his native land in *Uspravna zemlja* (1972; *Earth Erect*, 1973) and to objects in *Mala kutija* (original unpub.; *The Little Box*, 1970).

P. does not use rhyme, traditional or experimental. Nor is he given to the excesses of free verse. His metrics follow a distinct, though by no means regular, pattern of groups of two or three lines, rarely four; generally it is a combination of these, interchanging freely. His style is terse, often aphoristic, even elliptic. His verse, which often resembles folk poetry, impresses by its strong rhythm.

P.'s poetry is modern in both theme and originality of expression. His concern with death, fate, the meaning of life, and love, gives his poetry universal scope. The English poet Ted HUGHES has said of P. that his "total vision is vast and one understands why he has been called an epic poet. His Cosmos is more mysteriously active and dreadful but his affection for our life is closer than ever." P. is generally recognized as the leading contemporary Serbian poet.

FURTHER WORKS: *Od zlata jabuka* (1958; *The Golden Apple*, 1980); *Pesme* (1965); *Vučja so* (1975); *Žvo meso* (1975); *Kuća nasred druma* (1975); *Rez* (1981). FURTHER WORKS IN ENGLISH: *Collected Poems 1943–1976* (1978); *The Blackbird's Field* (1979); *Homage to the Wolf: Selected Poems 1956–1975* (1979)

BIBLIOGRAPHY: Bosquet, A., "V. P.; ou, L'exorcisme populaire," *Verbe et vortige* (1961): 193–200; Hughes, T., "The Poetry of V. P.," *TriQ*, No. 9 (1967): 201–5; Mihailovich, V. D., "V. P.: The Poetry of Things in a Void," *BA*, 43 (1969): 24–29; Hughes, T., Introduction to V. P., *Collected Poems 1943–1976* (1978): 1–9

—VASA D. MIHAILOVICH

POPESCU, Dumitru Radu

Romanian novelist, short-story writer, and dramatist, b. 19 Aug. 1935, Păuşa-Bihor

P. studied medicine and the humanities in various Transylvanian colleges and obtained a degree in philology in 1961 from the University of Cluj. He became a journalist and since 1970 has been the editor of the literary weekly *Tribuna*. He was a member of the Central Committee of the Communist Party of Romania and a member of the National Assembly, and in 1981 was elected president of the Romanian Writers' Union. After 1989 he found himself often blamed for his Communist attachments.

P.'s first volumes of short stories were devoted to descriptions of the traumatic social changes in Romania after World War II, particularly urbanization and the collectivization of the villages. He depicted psychologically baffled types: humorous, tragic, and disoriented. The solemn dignity of the traditional rhythms of peasant life, intimately connected with love and death, are shown to remain at the center of a life otherwise full of comic chaos and naïve trickery in the stories in the collections *Dor* (1966; yearning) and *Duios Anastasia trecea* (1967; fondly passing Anastasia).

Gradually P. introduced two new elements in his writings. The first was the fantastic as derived from folklore and myth, but also from the traditions of the Romanian novel. The second was a moral theme: the search for an unnamed guilt by the younger generation who attempt to judge those who had effected the socialist modification of Romanian society. The main narrative section of the novel *Vînătoarea regală* (1973; the royal hunt) describes a strange drought and epidemic haunting a Danubian area. Suspicion and self-interest grow into mob terror and absurd crime. This gloomy atmosphere is lightened by the dogged search for truth by a young attorney, the son of one of the victims.

In *Ploile de dincolo de vreme* (1976; rains from beyond time) one of P.'s archvillains, a school superintendent who had formerly been a Party activist guilty of many abuses of power, is now investigated for the alleged drunken manslaughter of his common-law wife. The presumed victim (herself the former wife of an innocent purge victim) reappears, and the suspect is proved innocent. It is a grotesque and drab replay of what had been, some twenty years before, sheer pain and violence. These and other novels and short stories tend to organize themselves into a cycle, set in a specific "country," much like William FAULKNER's work (which influenced P.) and that of Gabriel GARCÍA MÁRQUEZ, which they resemble in their mixture of fantastic and satirical features. P.'s ultimate message is not pessimistic: good and truth are elusive and weak, but evil is sterile and ridiculous, while the spectacle of their inconclusive struggle is a source of joy and wisdom.

P. also wrote a number of plays in a lyrical and absurdist vein; they are somber and fantastic and have often been effective on stage.

FURTHER WORKS: *Fuga* (1958); *Zilele săptămînii* (1959); *Umbrela de soare* (1962); *Vara oltenilor* (1964; rev. ed., 1972); *Fata de la miazăzi* (1964); *Somnul pămîntului* (1965); *Prea mic pentru un război aşa de mare* (1969); *F* (1969); *Aceşti îngeri trişti* (1970); *Ploaia albă* (1971); *Cei doi din dreptul Tebei* (1973); *Teatru* (1974); *O bere pentru calul meu* (1974); *Împăratul norilor* (1976)

BIBLIOGRAPHY: Nemoianu, V., on *Vînătoarea regală*, *BA*, 48 (1974), 764; Nemoianu, V., on *Ploile de dincolo de vreme*, *WLT*, 51 (1977), 267; Kleininger, T., on *Vînătoarea regală*, *CREL*, 6, 4 (1978): 78–80

—VIRGIL NEMOIANU

PORTA, Antonio

(pseud. of Leo Paolazzi) Italian poet, novelist, short-story writer, and critic, b. 9 Nov. 1935, Vicenza; d. 12 Apr. 1989, Rome

P. resided in Milan from his early childhood, where he attended university and obtained a degree in letters. For years he worked in the publishing industry while contributing, as a literary critic, to journals and newspapers such as *Il Verri*, *Quindici*, *Il Corriere della Sera*, and *Alfabeta*.

P.'s early poems were included in the 1961 edition of *I Novissimi: poesie per gli anni '60* (*I Novissimi: Poetry for the Sixties*, 1995), a provocative and revolutionary anthology that opened the way for the formation of Gruppo 63, a movement that came to be known as the Italian Neo-avant-garde. Although poetry had been P.'s creative focus (for the collection *Invasioni* he received, in 1984, the prestigious Viareggio poetry prize), he also wrote plays, novels, and short stories.

The fundamental trait of P.'s literary production is constituted by a nomadic conception of writing that refuses any crystallization and is in constant pursuit of new forms. Writing becomes a linguistic and existential voyage marked by tension and restlessness. Literature is conceived as an open and endless project, a work in progress in which the exploration of language and the inquisitive gaze on the world always coincide.

Influenced by the general philosophical orientation provided by phenomenology and existentialism (particularly of Karl Jaspers and Maurice Merleau-Ponty), for P. experiences of reality and acts of cognition are never definitive and totalizing. Subjectivity as an expression of being-in-the-world is under constant revision. The subject is not a pregiven entity but the result of the ever-changing

dialogue with language and with external reality. Existence is inevitably marked by undisclosedness and transcendance, and consequently the desire for authenticity becomes an incessant quest.

In P.'s initial experiments—*La palpebra rovesciata* (1960; The Inside Out Eyelid) and *Aprire* (1964; To Open)—are two significant examples, external events are assembled as enigmas to be deciphered. This procedure features a visual approach to reality (close to some procedures adopted by the *ecole du regard*) and the reduction of the "I," a sort of phenomenological bracketing of one's subjectivity. P. seems to construct an apparently impassive montage of traumatic everyday occurrences whose protagonists are hallucinating and schizoid characters. These poems present a violent, nightmarish, and often absurd human natural reality that seems reminiscent of expressionistic or Beckettian representations (correlations can be also drawn with the painting of Beckmann and Bacon). The fragmented narration and the schizomorphic language produce a state of suffocation and alienation as well as a tragic vision of existence inevitably dominated by sufferance, death, and social atrocities.

A similar direction is pursued in a series of texts entitled "Rapporti umani" (Human Relationships) and "Rapporti N. 2'' (Relationships N. 2), published in *I rapporti* (1966; Relationships), in which human relations are portrayed as brutal sadomasochistic encounters, expressions of cruelty verging on the surreal. In this reified and objectified human reality P.'s gaze seems fixed exclusively on the physical and biological dimension and the horror associated with them. These poetic experiments are guided by an ethical and political viewpoint that clearly denounces the confessional and lyrical narcissism that characterized most poetry produced in the late 1950s and early 1960s. At the same time they are motivated by an existential dismay and a need to pursue an authentic knowledge of life freed from any illusion.

In this first stage P. on the one hand conceives writing as a cognitive medium and on the other as a self-reflexive process. Poetic language is employed as a mimetic tool for capturing reality and history and as a creative process aimed at uncovering alternative and utopian models of existence. However, in a number of statements of poetics P. expresses an autonomous conception of art. Poetry is intended as a world in itself and not as a metaphor of the world. The most striking example is represented by a collection entitled *Cara* (1969; Cara), which seems to hypothesize that language represents only the material presence of itself. A series of semantically unrelated linguistic segments are catalogued without any symbolic or metaphorical intent. Fixed in their synchronic and literal presence, they generate a highly provocative and terroristic notion of poetry envisioned solely as a linguistic construct, a rhythmic and syntactic space. This experiment refuses radically all traditional practices that identify poetry as the locus for transferring preconceived messages. With its metapoetic objective this collection investigates the process of writing and is totally absorbed by the specificity of poetic language.

Perhaps solicited by the profound sociopolitical changes that affected Italian society beginning in 1968, P.'s poetry also sets itself in a decisive new direction: poetic investigations of the linguistic code take the place of poetry as a self-reflexive activity. The texts written in this period, gathered in a collection entitled *Metropolis* (1971; Metropolis), display two complimentary operations: a contentious and demystifying inquiry into the reified and alienating linguistic repertory of contemporary culture (commonplaces, linguistic stereotypes, defining *topoi*, ranging from religion to sex and politics) juxtaposed to proposals for therapeutic and defalsifying language models presented as expressions of a possible recovery of communication. This collection denounces the degradation of the linguistic code to an object of consumption, subjected to falsehood and manipulation.

This shift toward a more direct probe into the sociohistorical realities reaches a transparent ideological position in *Week-end* (1974; title in English). In this collection P. explores the human condition within the structures of the capitalist society: the depersonalizing effects of automation, the anonymity of the individual, the loss of life to a product, and the atrophy and suffocation caused by the alienation of work. The dichotomies master/slave and oppression/freedom run through many of the texts. The master is identified as an expression of death within the immobility of the capitalist society to which is opposed the self-consciousness of the slave, interpreted as a liberating possibility and as a utopian tension toward alternative modes of existence. The ideological clarity reached by this collection is accompanied, as an immediate expressive correlative, by a narrative flow that has abandoned the lacerated and magmatic linguistic constructs that typify the earlier collections.

The obstinate commitment to go through the opacity of language in search of a transparency leads P. to pursue a number of new poetic models: poetry structured in the form of letter, diary, aphorism, and theater. This new stage is reached starting with *Passi Passaggi* (1980; Steps Passages) and *Invasioni* (1984; Invasions and Other Poems, 1986). The first exhibits an epistolary and diaristic style open to a more direct dialogue with the reader to whom the poet sends messages of rebirth and regeneration aimed at transforming the world; the realities of the body, the eros, and the prelinguistic gestures that precede thought and awareness constitute a constant point of reference for regaining vital signs of life. The second, far from the tragic, dimension of the collections published in the 1960s and 1970s, is charged with the luminosity and transparency produced by the lightness of intense images that capture, in a flow of surreal and dreamlike perceptions, the enchanting epiphanies of our everyday existence.

P.'s communicative project and utopian thrust continued up to his last poetic work, *Il giardiniere contro il becchino* (The Gardener Against the Undertaker). In a highly dramatic language reminiscent of the epic narrative P. recounts the struggle between life and death embodied in the figures of a grave-digger, representing the destructive forces, and a gardener who, surrounded by human catastrophes, obstinately plants the seeds of life. Against the trend of political and ethical relativism P. advocates the urgency and the courage to devise a project capable of reestablishing the fecundity of life.

P.'s tendency to experiment with forms of oral poetry close to the language of theater results also from his activities related to the latter genre. One of his first works for theater is a provocative and sarcastic one-act play, *Si tratta di larve* (1968; It Is about Larvas), in which the mockery of the bourgeois life finds inspiration in the dadaist grotesque imagination and in the absurd situations dipped in the *humour noir* of a playwright such as Eugène IONESCO. The last play written by P., *La festa del cavallo* (1986; The Horse's Feast), combines a metatheatrical slant with a plurality of linguistic registers and quotations taken from arias by Monteverdi and Gluck. Allegorical characters representing art, rationality, technology, the individual as an alienated automaton, eros, and the primordial instincts find themselves in a struggle that ends with the conviction that the world could be freed from violence, victimization, and social rituals of death. P.'s message embraces the view that the

project of emancipation proposed by the supporters of modernity is an open possibility.

As for narrative P. produced two major novels, *Partita* (1967) and *Il re del magazzino* (1978; The King of the Storeroom, 1992). The first is characterized by a radical violation of traditional narrative canons. P. assembles on the page a series of events as if observed through deforming expressionistic lenses. The result is a fragmented narration made up of displacing oneiric visions devoid of any logical progression or diachronic development, seized in the flow of an everlasting present. The formal transgression mirrors the transgression of the accepted normality of dominant bourgeois values and behaviors. The characters are in a constant state of metamorphosis and indiscriminately change their identities. P. experiments with a subjectivity unremittingly in progress as the characters experience the flowing mutation of their being in the world. Particularly the protagonist, a woman-horse, establishes a sensory immediacy with reality through bodily and erotic acts, interpretable as expressions of primordial vitality and as a disalienating and liberating revolt against established social practices.

Il re del magazzino can be classified as an apocalyptic novel whose descriptions of devastation and horror are not safely removed in a distant future but display all the menacing perils of current events. The apocalyptic theme, resulting from the stern awareness of a social and political crisis that has caused the end of a civilization, is dialectically opposed by possibilities of a new beginning entrusted to a survivor who returns to preindustrial, natural modes of existence and to a new species of wolves-men who can assure a drastically different future.

P.'s works represent some of the most dynamic and intense literary expressions of postwar Italy. The formal, existential, and social tensions that consistently accompany them are the signs of a writer who has relentlessly and courageously combined the exploration of the infinite potentialities of literary language with a search for more authentic manifestations of existence.

FURTHER WORKS: *Zero, poesie visive* (1963); *Stark* (1967); *La presa di potere di Ivan lo sciocco* (1974); *Quanto ho da dirvi. Poesie 1958-1975* (1977); *Poesia degli anni settanta* (1979); *Se fosse tutto un tradimento* (1981); *L'aria della fine. Brevi lettere 1976-1981* (1982; Kisses from Another Dream, 1987); *Nel fare poesia* (1985); *Melusina. Una ballata e un diario* (1987; Melusine, 1992); *Partorire in chiesa* (1990); *Il progetto infinito* (1991); *Los(t) Angeles* (1996)

BIBLIOGRAPHY: Carravetta, P., "Reading A. P.'s *Invasioni*," *Testuale*, 5 (1986); Moroni, M., *Essere e fare: l'itinerario poetico di A. P.* (1991); Picchione, J., *Introduzione a A. P.* (1995); Sasso, L., *A. P.* (1980); Smith, L. R., "The Poetics of A. P.," *ChiR*, 1 (1976)

—JOHN PICCHIONE

PORTER, Katherine Anne

American short-story writer and novelist, b. 15 May 1890, Indian Creek, Texas; d. 18 Sept. 1980, Silver Spring, Md.

Although her personal experience profoundly influenced P.'s art, many of the biographical facts, including the date of her birth,

Katherine Anne Porter

have not been established beyond question. On a few of the more obviously pertinent matters, however, the evidence is reasonably consistent. P. was third or fourth of a family of five children. Her mother died when P. was very young, perhaps no more than two years old, and the children's paternal grandmother, a Kentuckian who had moved to Texas shortly after the Civil War, assumed principal responsibility for their rearing. P.'s education was irregular. Rebelliously precocious as a child and adolescent, she ran away from school and was married at the age of sixteen. The first and two succeeding marriages all ended in divorce. As a young woman she made a precarious living—at occupations including those of journalist, movie extra, ballad singer, and book reviewer—in Chicago, Denver, New York City, and various places in Texas and Louisiana. Between World Wars I and II she sojourned twice in Mexico for extended periods and then in Europe, chiefly in Berlin and Paris. Later, on the strength of growing critical recognition of her work, she held appointments as lecturer and writer-in-residence at a number of colleges and universities. In old age she lived many years in College Park, Maryland. For a long time she was a fallen-away Catholic, but newspaper notices of her death referred to plans for celebration of a requiem mass.

Beyond noting her generally somber view of the human situation, which underlies even the richly comical effects of stories like "The Cracked Looking-Glass" (1932)—her recurrent emphasis upon the appalling burden of ignorant and sinful man's individual responsibility for his destiny—it is difficult to categorize P.'s work as a whole. Elements of regionalism are apparent in many of her stories; but, true to her mixed family heritage, she is not consistently classifiable as either Southerner or Southwesterner. She is propagandist for no cause or doctrine. Typically, as in "Flowering Judas" (1930), where the heroine, torn between two faiths, is loyal finally to neither, it is the psychology of apostasy and betrayal that most fascinates P. Her early and difficult experience of independent survival, artistic and financial, in the man's world of her generation, encouraged feminist leanings. Unflattering portraits of male chauvinists, feckless fools for the most part, but a few of them hideously cruel, appear often in her fiction. Yet no special sympathy for such men's female antagonists, strictly on the grounds of sex, is ever evoked.

As previously noted, much of her work is heavily autobiographical. Virtually all her fiction, from "Maria Concepción" (1922) to *Ship of Fools* (1962), even those stories centered upon the pained awakenings of childhood, involve in one way or another situations of broken or strained marriages or unhappy love affairs. The climactic events of the tragic love story "Pale Horse, Pale Rider" (1938) are a fictional account of P.'s near-fatal illness in Denver during the influenza epidemic of 1918. The heroine named Miranda, who appears as child, adolescent, or woman in a number of stories, most obviously resembles the author. But aspects of P.'s personality are discoverable in many other characters, including not only the nunish schoolteacher-revolutionary of "Flowering Judas" and at least three different women among the passengers of *Ship of Fools*, but even the male protagonist of "The Leaning Tower" (1941), which draws upon P.'s experience in Berlin during the early Nazi era.

Yet none of the stories is pure confession, of the self-therapeutic or any other design. Every persona, Miranda as much as any of the others, is fully realized as an independent dramatic agent, whose actions are explicable without necessary reference to the author's life. Always, there is a dimension of extrapersonal significance in the fiction. In some pieces—for example, "Flowering Judas" and "Hacienda" (1932) of the Mexican group, "The Leaning Tower," *Ship of Fools*, the stories of the sequence entitled (in the 1965 collected volume) "The Old Order"—there is a readily definable element of the "documentary." Nor can P. be convicted of any theoretical commitment to the necessary priority of personal values as opposed to public concerns. In all her work, however subtly, a profound consciousness of the larger cultural context of private affairs is discernible. And, finally, among P.'s many stratagems for "coming to terms with herself" in fiction—which is largely, for her, a matter of transcendence rather than either triumph or reconciliation—her uncompromising dedication to artistic *form* is most important.

For the contents of the three earlier volumes, *Flowering Judas, and Other Stories* (1930), *Pale Horse, Pale Rider: Three Short Novels* (1939), and *The Leaning Tower, and Other Stories* (1944), which with a few additional pieces were brought together in *The Collected Stories of K. A. P.* (1965), she is recognized as one of the world's great modern masters of short fiction. Her numerous honors include Guggenheim and Ford Foundation fellowships, election to the National Institute of Arts and Letters, a Pulitzer Prize and a National Book Award (both 1966, for *The Collected Stories*), and various medals. Critical opinion of her principal popular success, the long novel *Ship of Fools*, a fictional account of P.'s voyage from Mexico to Germany in 1932 aboard a German liner, has been sorely divided on a variety of issues. But the trouble may be simply that the critic is yet to appear who can satisfactorily define that book's formal principle.

FURTHER WORKS: *The Days Before* (1952); *The Collected Essays and Occasional Writings of K. A. P.* (1970); *The Never Ending Wrong* (1977)

BIBLIOGRAPHY: Mooney, H., *The Fiction and Criticism of K. A. P.* (1957); Nance, W., *K. A. P. and the Art of Rejection* (1964); Hendrick, G., *K. A. P.* (1965); Hartley, L. and G. Core, eds., *K. A. P.: A Critical Symposium* (1969); Liberman, M., *K. A. P.'s Fiction* (1971); Hardy, J., *K. A. P.: An Introduction* (1973); Kiernan, R., *K. A. P. and Carson McCullers: A Reference Guide* (1976); Warren, R., ed., *K. A. P.: A Collection of Critical Essays* (1979)

—JOHN EDWARD HARDY

PORTUGUESE CREOLE LITERATURE

See Cape Verdean, Guinea-Bissau, and São Tomé a Principe literatures

PORTUGUESE LITERATURE

The modern Portuguese intellectual's cultural inheritance from past centuries is a bizarre combination of insular ultrachauvinism and fatalism. Indeed, the writers of the much admired Portuguese Generation of 1870—José Maria Eça de Queiroz (1845–1900), Antero de Quental (1842–1891), and Joaquim Pedro de Oliveira Martins (1845–1894)—censured these national idiosyncrasies and suggested the complete "Europeanization" of Portugal to remedy them. Public events, however, superseded their desires.

A decaying monarchy was replaced in 1910 by an unmanageable republic, followed by a half-century of repressive dictatorship. The Portuguese empire was dismembered by the English Ultimatum of 1890, through which the British seized Portuguese territory in Africa for the construction of the Capetown-to-Cairo railroad. The empire gradually dwindled and finally disappeared after the 1974 revolution.

Portuguese literature was consistently ignored and/or repressed, but survived. Poetry, as throughout all of Portuguese literary history, has been dominant, but the novel and drama have also been strong and innovative. All genres have produced works of high quality and internationally respected writers.

SYMBOLIST and Parnassian poetry prevailed during the first decades of the century. Eugénio de Castro (1869–1944) was the most notable Portuguese poet after the suicide of Quental and the death of António Nobre (1867–1900). In 1890 Castro published the major Portuguese symbolist treatise as a preface to his collection of poems, *Oaristos* (1890; intimacies). His poetry revealed the influence of Baudelaire and Verlaine, while it aspired to the revitalization of Portuguese poetry through the introduction of new, shocking imagery and unusual rhyme schemes. Castro was highly esteemed by Miguel de UNAMUNO, Rubén DARÍO, and Mallarmé. A small Decadent school of poets formed around Castro, but none of them approached his expressive powers.

The verse of Florbela Espanca (1894–1930) described the fate of a woman unable to achieve the perfect love. In *Charneca em flor* (1931; the heath in flower) she admitted the impossibility of pure love and accepted instead an inner peace.

Meantime, on the other side of the world in colonial Macau, Camilo Pessanha (1867–1926) w.. also writing symbolist poetry. The poems in *Clepsidra* (1920; clepsydra) reveal the author's emotional instability through passages preoccupied with rapid time movement, flowing currents, and changing seasons. Wenceslau de Moraes (1854–1929) had spent time with Pessanha in Macau, but took up permanent residence in Japan and became a practicing Buddhist. He chronicled life there, evoking the great age of Portuguese explorations, as in *Dai Nippon* (1897; the great Japan).

The founding of the Portuguese Republic in 1910 saw the initiation of the Portuguese Renascence movement, dedicated to a national cultural rebirth. Founded by the poet TEIXEIRA DE PASCOAES, the movement's magazine *A águia* (1910–32) proffered *saudosismo*, a nebulous theory of mystical, pantheistic nostalgia, as the most adequate definition of Portuguese sociopolitical and cultural existence. Although *saudosismo* retained an influence on later Portuguese poetry—most notably in the works of Afonso Lopes Vieira (1878–1946)—it was debunked by an opposition group that had formed around the *Seara nova* review, including the historians António Sérgio de Sousa (1883–1968) and Jaime Cortesão (1884–1960).

Little literary and cultural reviews, like *A águia* and *Seara nova*, have traditionally kept the Portuguese abreast of European culture and also are publishing outlets for new writers. *Orpheu* (1915) was inspired by the concepts of FUTURISM and was initially a Luso-Brazilian undertaking. Fernando PESSOA, who had participated in *A águia*, and Mário de SÁ-CARNEIRO were contributors to the first issue and the editors of the second and final number. MODERNISM was heralded by other ephemeral reviews—*Exílio* (1916), *Portugal futurista* (1917), and *Athena* (1924–25). Jose de Almada-Negreiros (1893–1970), a poet, novelist, and artist, was the most dashing figure of Portuguese modernism. Almada-Negreiros participated in all the literary reviews and organized the movement's most remembered scandal—the bitter attack on the highly touted "commercial literature" of the historical dramatist Júlio Dantas (1876–1962).

Portuguese drama of the period included symbolist tendencies, represented by Joao da Câmara (1852–1908); the Dostoevskyan atmospheres of the dramas of Raúl BRANDÃO; and the comedy of manners, which was the forte of Eduardo Schwalbach (1860–1946). Another fine dramatist was António Patricio (1875–1930), whose *O fim* (1909; the end) was recently revived owing to its presentation of the political intrigues that led to the downfall of the monarchy. Although Pessoa and Sá-Carneiro dabbled in theater, it was Almada-Negreiros who proposed a new existential concern for drama—thus attacking the historical exaggerations of Dantas. Alfredo Cortez (1880–1946) took up some aspects of Almada-Negreiros's doctrine and created a social drama. The rural themes of Carlos Selvagem (b. 1890) have both dramatic and documentary values. Both Cortez and Selvagem presented the conflict of the individual with society, à la Ibsen.

It was not until the founding in Coimbra of the critical review *Presença* (1927–40) that the modernist ideals gained stature within Portuguese culture. Choosing as their Portuguese masters Pessoa, Sá-Carneiro, and Almada-Negreiros—the so-called lunatics of *Orpheu*—the *presencistas* brought the newer figures of European literature—APOLLINAIRE, PROUST, GIDE, VALÉRY, and PIRANDELLO—to the attention of Portuguese readers. They advocated a literature that relied on emotions rather than on intellect and rejected academic, nonartistic limits placed on culture.

The *presencistas* (like most Portuguese writers of our century) cultivated all genres, José RÉGIO and João Gaspar Simões (b. 1903) were the founders of the review. António Botto (1897–1959), whose *Canções* (1921; songs) expressed his avowedly homosexual leanings in a light, proselike form, also tangentially participated in *Presença*.

Miguel TORGA and Adolfo Casais Monteiro (1908–1972) joined the *Presença* group in the early 1930s. Monteiro's poetry, following the group's literary credo, rejected the formalities of structure. His work as a commentator and critic of literature is also significant, although it has been open to much dispute owing to its *presencista* reliance on personal judgment. The multitalented Vitorino Nemésio (1901–1978) also had his literary roots in *Presença*. His poetry expressed his sentimental attachment to his childhood in the Azores, his paradise lost. Nemésio's novel about the Azores, *Mau tempo no canal* (1944; hard times in the canal), and his role as a popularizer of Portuguese culture among the masses won him national renown. The *presencistas* also were dramatists; one of their recurrent themes (and indeed one of the most important themes in Luso-Brazilian literature) was the Sebastianic myth. Pessoa, Patricio, and Regio invoked the legend of the youthful King Sebastian, who died in battle in Africa in 1578, but who, tradition holds, would return to lead his nation on to new conquests and grandeur.

After the death of the realist Eça de Queiroz, new trends in fiction appeared, notably the symbolist novels of Raúl Brandão. When João Gaspar Simões published his novel *Eloi* (1932; Eloi), relating a common man's jealousies, he revolutionized Portuguese fiction by initiating a psychological trend, influenced by JOYCE, FREUD, and Proust. António Branquinho da Fonseca (1905–1974) wrote poetry and drama, but his thriller *O barão* (1943; the baron) and his short stories, which ever so gently remove the reader from reality, have given him an enviable place in Portuguese fiction.

Portuguese fiction was also thriving outside the *Presencista* group. Aquilino RIBEIRO revitalized regionalism. José Maria Ferreira de CASTRO published his first novels on the Portuguese emigrant experiences in the 1920s, while Manuel Teixeira Gomes (1860–1941), who was the last president of the ill-fated republic, published *Gente singular* (1909; singular people), a collection of short stories presenting disturbed, unusual characters. Irene Lisboa (1892–1958) was a fine poet, but an even more masterful narrator of the daily problems of Lisbonites in *Solidão* (1939, solitude) and of the hard existence of rural people in *Crónicas da serra* (1961; hill tales). José Rodrigues Miguéis (1901–1980), who began his impressive career as a novelist with psychological fiction, wrote novels about his childhood in Lisbon, such as *Onde a noite acaba* (1946; where night ends). His later works dealt with Portuguese immigrants in North America. Joaquim Paço d'Arcos (b. 1908) and Tomás Ribas (b. 1918) have produced popular novels detailing the personal crises of Lisbon's bourgeoisie.

Under the influence of Brazilian and North American social realism and owing to a gradual rejection of the *presencista* aesthetic, the Portuguese NEOREALIST movement was born. The Marxist orientation of the magazines *Diabo* (1934–40) and *Sol nascente* (1937–40), and others appearing between the period of the Spanish Civil War and the beginning of World War II, opened the way for doctrinal views of the social obligations of modern Portuguese literature by José Maria Ferreira de Castro, António Alves REDOL, and Mário Dionisio (1916–1992). The Salazar dictatorship's reaction to these writings was to institute a rigid censorship, which caused publication difficulties for many writers until the 1974 revolution.

Redol's novel *Gaibeus* (1939: gaibéus [field workers of the Ribatejo]) is considered to have initiated neorealism in Portuguese fiction. Joaquim Soeiro Pereira Gomes (1910–1949), who had been a member of the clandestine Portuguese Communist Party, pessimistically presented the conflict between factory owners and workers in the poor suburbs around Lisbon. For example, *Esteiros* (1941; inlets), his only novel published during his lifetime, is almost a poetic elegy on child exploitation. The fiction of Fernando NAMORA and Joé Marmelo e Silva (b. 1913) presented similar social questions. Carlos de Oliveira (1921–1981) attacked the complacent bourgeoisie as the cause of the nation's desolation, for example, in *Uma abelha na chuva* (1953; a bee in the rain).

Although Vergílio Ferreira (1916–1996) dealt with social preoccupations in his early writings, such as *Vagão J* (1942; car J), his interest in man's fate within a tradition-laden society led him to the existential themes of *Aparição* (1959; apparition) and *Nítido nulo* (1971; clear void). José Cardoso PIRES passed through social and existential themes and most recently has analyzed the almost schizophrenic Portuguese soul.

Fiction of the late 1950s and the 1960s began indirectly to challenge the dictatorship. Augusto Abelaira's (b. 1926) impressive *A cidade das flores* (1959; the city of flowers) examined the plight of young Portuguese intellectuals using as a metaphorical backdrop Mussolini's Italy of the 1930s. He follows the continued depression of these intellectuals in *Sem tecto, entre ruínas* (1979; roofless, among ruins), as they vicariously participate in the worldwide upheavals of 1968. Fernando Castro SOROMENHO presented the lives of petty Portuguese officials in Angola, and Urbano Tavares Rodrigues (b. 1923) has written a score of novels detailing rural and urban social concerns. José Almeida Faria (b. 1943) was the major voice of the NEW NOVEL. He has published a fictional trilogy about the last twenty years of Portuguese life, which encompasses the fall of the dictatorship and the confused, initial phase of the revolutionary government: *A paixão* (1965; the passion), *Cortes* (1978; cuttings), and *Lusitânia* (1980; Lusitania). *Lusitânia* is perhaps the most significant recent work of Portuguese fiction.

A number of women writers of great merit have appeared since the 1950s. Agustina Bessa Luís (b. 1921), using northern Portuguese locales, presents sociopsychological probings of her women characters in fiction about modern decadent rural aristocracy. Her *A sibila* (1953; the sibyl) and *O mosteiro* (1981; the cloister) are outstanding achievements. Maria da Graça Freire (b. 1918), Fernanda Botelho (b. 1926), and Maria Judite de Carvalho (b. 1921) also emphasize women and the woman's point of view in their fiction and short stories.

The ten volumes by different poets in the series called *Novo Cancioneiro* (1941–42; new songbook) constituted the apogee of the neorealist movement in Portuguese poetry. A lack of theoretical coherence, however, prevented the group from exerting extensive influence. Aside from Fernando Namora and Mário Dionísio, João José Cochofel (1919–1982) and Carlos de Oliveira were active participants. José Gomes Ferreira (1900–1985) has links with all the earlier Portuguese poetic movements of the 20th c. Nonetheless, his role as an "idealist militant poet" who denounces human oppression and injustice through presenting its stark reality, as in *Poeta militante* (3 vols., 1977–78; militant poet), places him ideologically closest to the neorealists. The poetry of Egito Gonçalves (b. 1922) written in the 1950s presented an outcry in code against dictatorial repression.

SURREALIST ideas had occasionally surfaced in Portuguese culture since the time of André BRETON's 1924 manifesto—for example, the poetry of António Pedro (1909–1966); it was only in 1947, however, that a group of surrealist poets appeared. Mário Cesariny de Vasconcelos (b. 1924) was the bulwark of Portuguese surrealism. His major volume, *Pena capital* (1957; capital punishment), reveals a chaotic, humorous, nonsense world. The poetry of António Maria Lisboa (1928–1953) was preoccupied with eroticism, which he viewed as the key to self-understanding and liberty. Alexandre O'NEILL presents everyday life through comic verse. The most notable work of Portuguese surrealist fiction was *A torre de Barbela* (1964; the tower of Barbela) by Ruben A[dresen Leitão] (1920–1975).

Lyric poets whose works were not directly characterized by specific sociopolitical or literary attitudes united around other little reviews. *Cadernos de poesia* was issued in three different phases between 1940 and 1953 and revealed the works of Tomaz Kim (pseud. of Joaquim Tomás Monteiro-Grillo, 1915–1967), José Blanc de Portugal (b. 1914), and Rui Cinatti (b. 1915). Sebastião de Gama (1924–1952), David Mourão-Ferreira (1927–1996), and Alberto de Lacerda (b. 1928) were associated with *Távola redonda*, which appeared between 1950 and 1954. Sophia de Mello Breyner ANDRESEN participated in both of these reviews. Her notable poetry presents maritime and aerial images suggesting a search for personal liberation, as in *O nome das coisas* (1977; the name of things). Eugénio de ANDRADE is yet another distinguished poet whose verse achieves a musical quality. Jorge de SENA, however, towers over all others since Pessoa. Recent poetic groups have included the Poetry 61 vanguard movement, which developed from concretism: E. M. de Melo e Castro (b. 1932), Fiama Hasse Pais BRANDÃO, and Maria Teresa Horta (b. 1937) are its notable figures. Horta was also one of the "Three Marias," along with Maria Isabel Barreno (b. 1939) and Maria Velho da Costa (b. 1938), who wrote the multigenre *Novas cartas portuguesas* (1973; *The New Portuguese Letters*, 1975), whose outspoken feminist viewpoint caused a worldwide sensation and resulted in its banning and the prosecution in court of its authors. Other important contemporary lyric poets include António Gedeão (b. 1906), Herberto Helder (b. 1930), and António Ramos Rosa (b. 1924).

Post-*Presença* drama has its roots in Lisbon's Salitre Studio Theater group, founded in 1946. The dramas of Bernardo Santareno (1924–1980) have a psychosexual orientation, while those of Luiz Francisco Rebello (b. 1924), a major theater critic, present the conflicts between the forces of life and death with little hope for the future, as, for example, in *Condenados à vida* (1963; condemned to life). The political criticism suggested in two plays by Luís de Sttau Monteiro (b. 1926) resulted in his imprisonment in 1967; his Brechtian drama *Felizmente há luar* (1961; luckily there's moonlight) and his novel *Angústia para o jantar* (1961; *A Man of Means*, 1965) are essential reading for the comprehension of Portuguese life during the last decades of the dictatorship.

With the collapse of the regime in April 1974, an avalanche of long-suppressed works by many of the above-cited writers and others began to appear. Literature by African-Portuguese writers was published more openly. Most notable is the fiction of the Angolan José Luandino VIEIRA. His collection of short stories *Luuanda* (1964; *Luuanda: Short Stories of Angola*, 1980), which resulted in his incarceration, viewed life in Angola during the early years of the liberation movement. Recent Portuguese fiction has also included many accounts of life under Salazar and narrations of African war experiences. Olga GONÇALVES has produced perhaps

the most original postrevolutionary body of fiction. With little of past glories to extol, Gonçalves, in *Este verão o emigrante là-bas* (1978; this summer the emigrant down there [i.e., in Portugal]) and in *Ora esguardae* (1982; hark ye now), views the sociopolitical and linguistic identity crises faced by the Portuguese in the postrevolutionary epoch.

Nuno Bragança (1929–1985) also expresses great interest in linguistic and technical aspects of narrative, as in *Directa* (1977; direct) and *Square Tolstoi* (1982; Tolstoy Square). Carlos Coutinho's (b. 1943) postrevolutionary drama, published in his *Teatro de circunstância* (2 vols., 1976–77; theater of circumstance), evokes the social atmosphere that supported both repression and resistance. The Barraca Theater Group has become an important center of theatrical revival and growth.

Portuguese literature of the 1980s has been characterized by a search for a new identity. Literary critics and historians have reviewed the national past with great skepticism about the "national myths" that were propagated in literature down through the centuries. While António José Saraiva (1917–1992) has questioned the concept of the Portuguese identity—for example, the role as the "most Catholic country"—Eduardo Lourenço (b. 1923) has reexamined the recent past and its significance for the present and future of Portugal.

Portugal's accession to the European Union, in 1986, has exacerbated the polemics over national identity and destiny. José SARAMAGO'S works, which have garnered international fame, present these dilemmas and Portuguese history as part of a metafiction of national existence. A younger generation of writers, which began publishing in the mid-1980s, seeks to liberate the literature from the artistic restraints forced on it by the years of dictatorship and the remembrances of it. Without a doubt, the novelist Lídia JORGE is the most dynamic, original voice among them.

BIBLIOGRAPHY: Bell, A., *Portuguese Literature* (1922); Moser, G., "Portuguese Literature in Recent Years," *MLJ*, 44 (1960): 245–54; Sayers, R., "Twenty-Five Years of Portuguese Short Fiction," *SSF*, 3 (1966): 253–64; Moser, G., "Portuguese Writers of This Century," *Hispania*, 50 (1966): 947–54; Stern, I., "Suppressed Portuguese Fiction: 1926–1974," *BA*, 50 (1976): 54–60; Macedo, H., Introduction to *Contemporary Portuguese Poetry* (1978): 1–18; Sayers, R., "The Impact of Symbolism in Portugal and Brazil," in Grass, R., and W. R. Risley, eds., *Waiting for Pagasus: Studies of the Presence of Symbolism and Decadence in Hispanic Letters* (1979): 125–41

—IRWIN STERN

PORZECANSKI, Teresa

Uruguayan novelist and short-story writer, b. 5 May 1945, Montevideo

P. was born in Montevideo, where she completed her secondary education and attended the university where she obtained a degree in social work as well as a certificate in anthropology. Later on she studied abroad and completed a doctorate in social work. Since 1970, P. has been teaching full-time and has done a considerable amount of research in the areas of social sciences and social work at both the University of the Republic and the Catholic University in Montevideo, Uruguay.

P. has also done an impressive amount of research in anthropology and has a long list of publications in this field. She is particularly interested in the development of communities and subcultures, and she has written extensively on both Jewish and black communities in Uruguay.

P.'s literary career started quite early and indeed quite successfully. Her first book, a collection of short stories entitled *El acertijo y otros cuentos* (1967; The Riddle and Other Stories), was awarded a prize from the Ministry of Public Instruction. Three years later P. published another intriguing collection of short stories, *Historias para mi abuela* (1970; Stories for My Grandmother), and soon after she wrote *Esta manzana roja* (1972; This Red Apple), a volume that combines prose fiction and poetry, and anticipates P.'s penchant for the fantastic and her evident concern for what might be considered an alternative view of life. *Intacto el corazón* (1976; Intact the Heart), another work combining poetry and prose, was also awarded a prize by the Ministry of Culture, followed by *Construcciones* (1979; Constructions), also short stories, and *La invención de los soles* (1981; The Invention of the Suns), P.'s first novel. P. wrote intensely in spite of—perhaps even because of—a hard-line military dictatorship (1973-85) that considerably impoverished the country's intellectual life by incarcerating many writers and driving many others into exile.

It is noteworthy that one of P.'s most significant texts, *Una novela erótica* (1986; An Erotic Novel), was published immediately after democracy was restored in Uruguay. This is indeed—as P. herself would have it—a work of "f(r)iction," and it did ruffle some feathers. In an interview with Mabel Moraña, P. revealed that during the decade of the 1960s, when she was fifteen years old, she felt the impact of the cultural and ideological rebellions unfolding in those years. "To be a woman and renounce seduction as a stepping stone to success in one's career meant to make a significant choice. To break with long-established models that would stereotype me as 'attractive and intelligent' was also a decision that weighed heavily in the process of my writing, and finally allowed me to work from the perspective of a "feminine I," from my very own discourse. Surely, from that moment on, I chose my own marginality; waiting that the generosity of some publishers would overcome their devaluation of my 'too emotional,' nonrealist, shocking literature."

In spite of the fact that P. obtained yet another award—this time from the Municipal Government—for *Ciudad impune* (1986; Unpunished City), a collection of short stories evidently linked to the period of constant, rigorous repression and disregard for human values that bred the type of indifference that—P. suggests—is "a form of savage conduct," her most remarkable achievement was yet to come. In 1992-93 the John Simon Guggenheim Foundation honored P. with its prestigious fellowship, which she used to write *Perfumes de Cartago* (1994; Scents from Carthage). A huge success, this text was reprinted four times between 1994 and 1995. It enjoyed critical acclaim both locally and internationally, and it obtained the *Bartolomé Hidalgo* Prize, undoubtedly the most coveted literary award presented in Uruguay. This novel re-creates the way of life of a Jewish immigrant family in the 1930s. The descriptions of rich Sephardic traditions, the masterful development of female characters, and the intensity of its poetic language amply justify its success. The last scene, when Lunita Mualdeb—after visiting the old, decrepit, abandoned family house—hurls the key into the sea is particularly moving.

In spite of a strenuous teaching and research schedule, P. has maintained her productivity as a writer. Published by the prestigious house Seix Barral, P.'s novel *La piel del alma* (1996; The Skin of the Soul) combines two stories, one in Montevideo—when Uruguay beats Brazil at Maracaná in the tense final of the 1950 Soccer World Cup—and the other one in 15th-c. Spain, with the protagonist being burnt at the stake. This text uses the devices of the historical novel, as well as the most conventional techniques of the thriller. As in many of P.'s works, there are subtle incursions into the fantastic.

FURTHER WORKS: *La respiración es una fragua* (1989); *Mesías en Montevideo* (1989); *Nupcias en familia y otros cuentos* (1998)

BIBLIOGRAPHY: Barros-Lemez, A., "La larga marcha de lo verosímil: narrativa uruguaya del Siglo XX," *CJLACS*, 10 (1985): 95-111; Moraña, M., *Memorias de la generación fantasma* (1988): 179-86; Burgos, F., *Antología del cuento hispanoamericano* (1991): 789-94; Valverde, E., "T. P.: La historia comienza en los ghettos," *Alpha*, 12 (1996): 123-27

—HORACIO XAUBET

POSTMODERNISM

Postmodernism is a term generally used to describe a range of specific artistic and cultural phenomena that were created approximately after 1960; by extension, postmodernism often refers to a style or a mélange of stylistic features found generally throughout the fine arts during the last thirty years. Like many such critical terms, postmodernism thus has a narrow chronological meaning and a much broader and more contested use as a term that names either a "spirit," a particular set of formal and aesthetic qualities, or even a complex social and historical epoch and its dominant form of self-understanding. Further complicating any shared or usable sense of the term is a vast array of approaches to the relationship between social forces and artistic phenomena, and also the large number of possible critical and explanatory schemes that can be used to mediate such relationships. To complete the difficulty, postmodernism is itself often understood as positing its own radically skeptical approach to the very idea of explanatory schema.

Postmodernism can nevertheless be used in a way that makes it no more imprecise, and hence no more unavoidable, a term than romanticism or neoclassicism. What usually generates disagreement about its more precise applications or analytic uses, however, is just what sort of weight or context should be given to the "post" part of the term. This conjures up in turn a field of possible disagreements about what will be understood by MODERNISM itself. What many critics who use postmodernism as an explanatory term assume—and this may be the lowest common denominator of the meanings of postmodernism—is that modernism has by now become a thoroughly accepted cultural style that no longer possesses its radical or disruptive force, and postmodernism therefore serves as the completion, replacement, successor, or final eliminator of the modernist legacy.

Just how postmodernism relates to the legacy of modernism therefore determines its meaning Fredric Jameson (b. 1934) has mapped out the various meanings of postmodernism by showing how the "post" attitude can be read as either a sign of approval or disapproval; in turn, modernism can have either a negative or positive valuation. This generates four possible variations on postmodernism: (1) a set of positive attitudes set against negatively viewed modernism; (2) a positive extension of an approved modernism; (3) a negative reaction to a modernism that is itself judged negatively; and (4) a negative reaction against an otherwise approved set of cultural values and achievements. The first position, for example, is occupied by Tom WOLFE while the fourth is occupied by Jürgen Habermas (b. 1929). Wolfe's stance, waggish and at times corrosively satirical, assumes that the classical phase of so-called "high" modernism now seems hollow, and it is all to the good that we develop new and different attitudes to replace what had become piously accepted as something like an establishment culture. On the other hand, it is one of Habermas's main points that the cultural work of modernism is essentially emancipatory, following as it does in the heritage of the Enlightenment, and postmodernism is largely dominated by those who have lost faith in modernity and modernism, its cultural expression. Jameson's map, which is very suggestive, works in part because the "post" in modernism differs from, say, the "neo" in neoclassicism. A term like neoclassicism involves more than historical revival; it usually implies a very positive, even worshipful, attitude toward the earlier values of a classical epoch. The "post" in postmodernism can be simply chronological, but it can also have a curiously judgmental stance, cautiously waiting to be filled with some sort of commitment or affectlessly avoiding it altogether.

Many critics of postmodernism, including Jameson, have remarked on its problematic relation to history itself. Postmodernism is frequently discussed as employing a pastiche of historically developed (and abandoned) styles as its own chief stylistic marker. Indeed, postmodernism can sometimes appear to be mocking the very idea of style, especially when style is considered as a guarantee of sincerity or self-expression. The pastiche of period styles was first highly evident in architecture, where the writings of Charles Jencks (b. 1939) and Robert Venturi (b. 1925) singled it out for particular praise. But such use of a formal device took place in painting as well, and throughout the visual arts, a use fomented in part by the domination of advertising and other mass media in the everyday life of postindustrial capitalist society. In the visual arts postmodernism covers a wide range of work, from the return of representational painting to the ever-increasing use of popular materials, so as to question radically the distinctions between "low" and "high" culture. Indeed, the flooding of the realm of public life with distributed and manipulated images is a phenomenon that critics often use to characterize the conflation of the postindustrial and the postmodern. These stylistic features would have analogues in literature. For example, the mixing of genres in the new journalism, and the experiments of Truman Capote and Norman Mailer with novels based on journalistic "facts," or John ASHBERY's recycling of cliches with postromantic themes, as well as Ishmael REED's inventive play with popular genres and stereotypes, are all describable as part of postmodernism.

Since the development of genres and the ranking of subject matter have generally had historical sanction, postmodernism in effect attacks history as it attacks such traditional artistic values. But, to be more precise, postmodernism attacks a specific view of history, which can be generalized as the Enlightenment view that maintains that civilization and culture are steadily upward movements away from superstition and repression. In place of the Enlightenment view, postmodernism argues that history is merely linear, without any particular pattern except what might be subjectively imposed upon it, or that it is randomly recursive, throwing up repetitions that all too often seem like gross caricatures. In the first of these possibilities, and to a lesser extent in the other as well, the figure of Nietzsche especially dominates; he may in fact be the philosopher whose influence is most pervasive in postmodernism. What postmodernism's historical sense also challenges is the belief, central to modernism, that cultural and social renewal are made possible by the discharge of revolutionary energies. Here the philosophy most immediately invoked—but only to be rejected as too subjective—is EXISTENTIALISM. The work of Jean-François LYOTARD especially makes the case against the viability of any grand narrative significance in history, whether derived from some transcendent force or the accumulated power of human will. Postmodernism is as resolute in its antiheroic feelings as in its antihierarchical attitude.

Because of its antihierarchical attitude to genres and subject matter, postmodernism may also be regarded as a certain sensibility, and in this context one of the more frequently discussed features is gross deadpan irony. Again, this can be seen as an extension of modernist irony, or its cancellation. The dark humor of Samuel BECKETT's drama and the wry anomie of Milan KUNDERA's fiction are two leading examples of this feature. Kundera, for example, while showing great respect for the historical development of the novel, employs a set of distancing devices that move the novelistic features of his work in the direction of the essay. This creates an irony like that found in many self-reflexive novels of the past, but in Kundera's case it also generates a sense that the novel, in generic terms, may be exhausted and yet remains the only available form for our cultural malaise. Set against this irony is a sense of paranoia, a feeling that the structures of ordinary experience are maintained by forces too complex to be revealed; sometimes this is extended to the point where even explanations themselves are felt to be inherently untrustworthy. Here the fiction of Thomas PYNCHON is also notable. Complexity and irony can also be combined in postmodernism to generate a sensibility that borders on nostalgia and yet refuses that response as being too easy a solution; it is as if a simple, more straightforward ethos is invoked only to show how far from such simplicities we have come. This is one of the main elements in the short fiction of Donald BARTHELME. The French novelist Georges Perec employs an exceptionally rich mixture of high and low material, but also combines a fascination with mundane and even trivial details and activities with an uncanny complexity of form, in a way that suggests that one of POSTMODERNISM's main precursors is none other than James JOYCE.

However, some currents in postmodernism instrust the very idea of a sensibility. This mistrust is grounded in a larger questioning of the notion of a unified and distinctive self. Selfhood, though a highly debated notion, has been at the heart of Western culture for centuries, underpinning as it does our sense of individuality and all our concomitant notions of personal identity and political and social rights. From such essays as Michel FOUCAULT's "Qu'est-ce qu'un auteur?" (1969; "What is an Author?" 1977) and Roland BARTHES's notion of "the death of the author," postmodernism has drawn on a complex set of arguments that claims that the sources of meaning, and even the ability to create signs, are best located in systems of signification rather than in individual subjects. These arguments have been advanced in such a way that some have defined the postmodern era as marked by "the end of humanism." The development of such arguments was aided in significant measure by what is referred to as "the linguistic turn," or "the problematic of language," a set of philosophical and semantic problems that rejected the notion that language was a transparent means of establishing a truth that could otherwise exist without being put into words. While modernists as different as William FAULKNER and T. S. ELIOT certainly raised these issues, it was postmodernism that pursued them, with a distinctive blend of thoroughness and skepticism. In some ways, postmodernism can be seen as the cultural expression of a body of thought known as "POSTSTRUCTURALISM", which includes such figures as Lyotard, Foucault, Jacques DERRIDA, Julia KRISTEVA, Jacques LACAN, Paul de Man (1919–1983), and others. Certain writers, such as George BATAILLE and Michel BUTOR, have contributed fiction and essays that have added to the complexity of the movement; for example, Bataille introduced a fascination with transpersonal erotic desire and death, and their relation to the unexpressible, that has surfaced in many other places. Other writers, such as Jean GÊNET, have used the emphasis on the insubstantial and even decreative features of language to stress the performative aspects of writing. Here the emphasis might begin with a juggling of perspectives, but would then move on to the undecidability of moral and social values, eventually calling into question most of the standard anchoring features of bourgeois epistemology. It is poststructuralism's pursuit of the linguistic turn, and its seeing the notion of a centered self as highly problematic, that allows it to contribute to postmodernism.

If postmodernism has a philosophical component it has a distinctive political understanding as well. When modernism is treated as the cultural expression of monopoly capitalism and bourgeois parliamentary democracy, then postmodernism can be understood as the cultural outgrowth of multinational capitalism and a postliberal hegemonic politics. In this light, we can approach postmodernism as the ground on which multiculturalism, with its antihierarchical attitudes, might flourish. Conversely, if one sees contemporary society as dominated by consumerism, opinion polls, media spectacles, and sophisticated techniques of mass manipulation, then the paranoid views of postmodernism have more plausibility. Postmodernism can, however, be understood positively as contributing to (or being expressed in) movements of personal resistance to oppressive social formations, from gay liberation to feminism. The wide-spread acceptance of writers such as Audre Lorde (1934–1992) and Adrienne RICH depends to a large extent on the social movements that coexist with postmodernism. Equally significant here, at least in aesthetic terms, is an increasingly direct insistence on the political force of culture itself, so that such emerging fields as cultural studies are also part of postmodernism's development. Lorde's poetry and essays claim an authority that is based on her marginalized social status—as a black lesbian—and thus she demands a rethinking of the usual understanding of the relations between the centers of political power and its peripheral subjects. This can be seen as a rejection of the apolitical formalism that was thought by some to be central to modernism. The claims made for and against postmodernism's ability to energize new possibilities take place in a tangle of opposing truths.

Postmodernism has considerably more than its share of contradictions, on every level from the philosophical to the stylistic. But it remains a cultural movement that obviously delights in contradictions, and when it embraces paradox it does so without any self-deluding claims about the tragic view of life. As such, it has been accused, with some justification, of being a cynical and empty style. Its defense against such a charge might very well be that any defense is always and only a self-serving form of evasive justification.

BIBLIOGRAPHY: Jencks, C., *The Language of Postmodern Architecture*, rev. ed. (1977); Foster, H., ed., *The Anti-Aesthetic* (1983); Lyotard, J. -F, *The Postmodern Condition* (1984); Huyssen, A., "Mapping the Postmodern," *NGC*, 33 (Fall 1984): 5–52; Ross, A., ed., *Universal Abandon: The Politics of Postmodernism* (1988); Harvey, D., *The Condition of Postmodernity* (1989); Sayre, H. M., *The Object of Performance: The American Avant-Garde since 1970* (1989); Norris, C., *What's Wrong with Postmodernism* (1990); Jameson, F., *Postmodernism, or, The Cultural Logic of Late Capitalism* (1991); McGowan, J., *Postmodernism and Its Critics* (1991); Hoesterey, I., *Zeitgeist in Babel: The Postmodernist Controversy* (1991); Rose, M. A., *The Post-Modern and the Post-Industrial: A Critical Analysis* (1991); Birringer, J. H., *Theatre, Theory, Postmodernism* (1991)

—CHARLES MOLESWORTH

POSTREALISM

During the late 19th c. realism was a goal at which to arrive; in the 20th c. it has become a platform from which to take off. Realism was not dead, as the French writer Paul Alexis (1847–1901) urgently assured the reporter Jules Huret in 1893, but it was out of favor with writers and critics alike, or rather it had reached its zenith and an inevitable reaction would lead to new interests for literary endeavor, in a ferment that would produce works that can only be called postrealistic.

There have, to be sure, been resurgences of realism as an innovating force, especially where a reexamination of actuality seemed of paramount importance or where a body of writers wished to capitalize on the positive implications of the term. In Italy after the obfuscations of the Fascist regime, there was need for an opening into contemporary reality and NEOREALISM emerged in both fiction and film. As Portugal in the 1940s showed signs of shaking off its intellectual and social torpor, a similar banner was raised. In France the Populists of the 1930s and the practitioners of the NEW NOVEL in the 1960s legitimized themselves as purveyors of a new and improved brand of realism. Such renewals of enthusiasm, however, have departed from basic doctrine and have been directed more at serving a partisan view about society or aesthetics than at forwarding what Hippolyte Taine (1828–1893) called "a great inquiry" into man and society. Indeed, the most widespread of these labels, SOCIALIST REALISM, has come to be seen (outside the communist bloc) as no realism, as a denial of the central philosophic principles on which the 19th-c. movement rested.

When it comes to depiction of social institutions and their dynamics, however, the realistic mode continues to constitute the norm in this century (see Society and Literature). Such works are legion and have a bland respectability, but they bring no surprises and have no innovative force. They are variations on a hackneyed form, having a certain interest when they explore an area of society not previously brought into view or when, more rarely, an author of compelling vision gives them at least temporary impact. They are popular perhaps because they are in a familiar vein and make no urgent demands on the reader. They tend to blend with the strictly reportorial account of sociological or anthropological cast, to move from objective selection to indiscriminate tape recording. There are no significant new worlds to conquer in this repetitive genre, and aspiring writers turn elsewhere to find models for their own vision of reality.

The most lasting and widely diffused legacy of the older realism was the massive infusion of "modern and popular subjects" that have come to dominate the literature of our time. Whereas classical writers almost automatically turned to traditional tales or exercised untrammeled imagination in their devising of illustrative actions, the contemporary author automatically turns to the here and now, to the observed scene, for his materials, such occasional tours de force as John Erskine's (1879–1951) once popular *The Private Life of Helen of Troy* (1925) or John GARDNER's *Grendel* (1971) notwithstanding. For better or worse, the stuff from which modern writers make their statement about the human condition is predominantly what they have observed, however filtered or transformed by their individual consciousness.

In large part these transformations are dictated by the very limitations imposed by realist orthodoxy. It embodied self-denying ordinances of such rigor as to proscribe for the writer much of his traditional function. He could no longer be *maker* or *seer*. He was confined to being observer and recorder, a machine, not a person. The tenet of objectivity, of an ostensibly complete authorial withdrawal, as enunciated by Gustave Flaubert (1821–1880) and reiterated even by James JOYCE in *A Portrait of the Artist as a Young Man* (1916)—was one source of limitation. The tenet that data should be accessible to all observers was another. The aspiration to a style as colorless and impersonal as that of a court transcript (Stendhal, 1783–1842) was a third. If art is an assertion and perpetuation of self—the imposition of a unique, ordering consciousness upon the disorderly and confusing data of experience—then realism as dogmatically conceived and tentatively practiced denied the artist his rightful personal role.

There had always been resistance against these restrictions; and by the end of the 19th c., Joris-Karl Huysmans (1848–1907) had forsaken Emile Zola (1840–1902), Edmond Rostand (1868–1918) had revived the romantic drama à la Victor Hugo (1802–1885), Maurice MAETERLINCK, followed by J. M. BARRIE, had made capital of the fairy tale. The romance, set in a never-never-land (Graustark or Ruritania) of swashbuckling derring-do, flourished again. None of this activity carried any hope for the future; such worn-out soil could not nurture healthy plants. The signals of change would have to come from major talents reaching their full powers, at the turn of the century. As it happened, all of them, overtly or by implication, repudiated realism, or, more properly, took from it what they needed as they set themselves new goals.

Before turning to the transformations that writers like Marcel PROUST, Thomas MANN, Hermann HESSE, Franz KAFKA, William FAULKNER, and James Joyce effected, it is instructive to consider how the realistic infusion was adapted in subliterary genres, such as the crime novel and the sex novel. Here the realist restriction had been one of sobriety, of refraining from use of the exceptional and the outré, whereas the unaligned purveyor of this kind of fare knew that the appetite of his readers was for sensationalism in increasingly hyperbolic doses. The realists had a legitimate interest in opening up the seamy side of life as part of the total human record. They fought a stubborn battle in defense of the presentation of violence and sex as part of that record, and the more responsible among them were careful not to present violence for the sake of violence or sex for the sake of sex. Predictably, however, sensation destroyed objective balance.

Zola, who always had a taste for the hyperbolic, opened the way even before the Rougon-Macquart cycle in *Thérèse Raquin* (1867;

Thérèse Raquin, 1881; later tr., 1960), where sex *and* violence were placed together in a heady mixture. Such later writers as Dashiell HAMMET, James M. CAIN, and Mickey Spillane (b. 1918) are the continuators, not the originators, of this line. In his later works Zola often went overboard in his use of sensationalism: the multiple violences of *La terre* (1887; *Earth*, 1895; later tr., 1954); Jacques Lantier running amok in his locomotive in *La bête humaine* (1890; *The Human Beast*, 1954); the alcohol-sodden body of old Antoine Macquart reduced to a heap of blue ash in *Le docteur Pascal* (1893; *Doctor Pascal*, 1893). For those disposed to read in that way, his works were a titillating *psychopathia sexualis* and *criminalis*. And they were so read.

Sensationalism, a deliberate choice of only the most heightened data, has pervaded all popular literature, even the comic book. Its hero is the sadomasochistic private detective, who exceeds the knights of old in his capacity to inflict and endure physical punishment. His recuperative powers are phenomenal; he lives in order to be beaten up another day. He is also a sexual athlete of consummate skill.

On the borderline between popular and serious novels in the exposé, the work that pleads a case. Realist objectivity forbade an author to engage in special pleading: objectively assembled fact would make its own case. Authorial withdrawal was a more effective instrument of truth than personal, and therefore suspect, bias. Because the line between such special pleading and complete objectivity was never clear, realism, from the beginning, tended to be identified with social criticism. In any event, postrealistic writers have rediscovered the joys of partisanship. Since precise truth is less important than scoring a point, they too open the doors to a form of sensationalism and see their battles in the stark colors of black and white. They surround their fables with a convincing air of verisimilitude, a specious, because selective, documentation, but their excesses of heightening and emphasis and above all of omission eventually convict them of taking sides. Upton SINCLAIR is a particularly wellknown example of this kind of writer. *The Jungle* (1906), which might have been a dispassionate and probing analysis of the life of the immigrant in the Chicago stockyards, became first a sensational exposé of meat-packing malpractices and then a gospel tract for socialism.

Less fractured but equally contrived is the whole body of Great Depression novels in the U.S. and elsewhere. Mobs do not respond to a reasoned analysis of the facts; they want to feel the bombardment of a heightened appeal in their guts.

It is in the assimilation of realist materials by serious literature that the significant transformations have taken place. The most dramatic change has been the return to expression of a unique personal vision, of a reality that is private and unduplicatable. SURREALISM is a special embodiment of this effort, although basically antirealistic, since it repudiates realistic method and most of realistic material. It was Marcel Proust, who, in his avowed intention to write the book of himself, led the main attack. He asserted that the only true reality is that which lies in the depths of memory uncorrupted by the deformations of analysis. It cannot be compared or measured against the reality that others perceive. He called into question the whole established idea of reality, finding it "not in the outward appearance of the subject," which is only "a sort of cinematographic parade." He denied that it was merely a "byproduct of existence, so to speak, approximately identical for everybody." He considered "the literature that is satisfied merely to 'describe things'" to be "the farthest removed from reality, the one that most impoverishes and saddens us . . ." by its superficiality.

Such a view may lead to a practical solipsism in which the author writes only for himself, since he is all that exists. More likely, the author attempts—but fails—to transmute personal signs and symbols into elements that convey meaning for other intelligences. What is unique and impressive in Proust is that he does not drift off into a private world of the imagination, does not revel in the chaos of the subconscious, but brings everything into the light of day by a rigorously analytical, if convoluted, method. His world is a social world. His perceptions are of people, places, and things, although he early makes the cardinal point that none of these is constant even to one observer, let alone uniform for all observers. Thus, what the mind of the narrator engages with is not a private refuge of dream removed from reality. On the contrary, it has hard, clear contours; it is apprehended by others; it exists in its own right. But that existence has no interest until it is illuminated by a unique consciousness. Space, time, and objects are elements of actuality, but only as givens. They take an inferior place to the mind that resorts them. It is the mind that gives these elements a reality that is, prior to the ordering, only contingent. So real is the world Proust evokes, so sharp is his social analysis, that Harry Levin (1912–1994), in *The Gates of Horn: A Study of Five French Realists* (1963), makes him part of the continuum of traditional realists beginning with Balzac (1799–1850). Yet Proust's essence is different from that of his predecessors. For him outward reality is merely the inescapable material on which the mind feeds, since there can be nothing in the mind that has not previously been apprehended by the senses. He stands as the unequaled practitioner of the book of oneself. Perhaps the logical direction in which to go, after his example, is toward outright poetic autobiography. Eldridge Cleaver's (1935–1998) *Soul on Ice* (1968) is in a way a successor of *Á la recherche du temps perdu* (1913–27; *Remembrance of Things Past*, 1922–32) just as *The Education of Henry Adams* (1918, privately printed 1907) by Henry ADAMS is a predecessor. At any rate, the right of the author to personal testimony has been reestablished, not in a void, but in the real world.

The glaring self-exposure of the book of oneself is not for most authors. They wish to impose themselves on their material in a less overt way. They prefer to take shelter in a degree of anonymity by way of allegory, fable, symbolic framework—some sort of analogical format—through which they impose meaning, or cause the reader to discern meaning, without mounting a pulpit. This is the high road of great literature. The realists never quite succeeded in abandoning it—witness Zola's *Germinal* (1885; *Germinal*, 1895) or Dostoevsky's (1821–1881) great novels.

The process may be only suggestive (often with ironical intent) by way of a title, such as Jules ROMAINS's *Les hommes de bonne volonté* (27 vols., 1932–46; *Men of Good Will*, 14 vols., 1933–46), in which men of good will do not prevail; John STEINBECK's appropriation of a Miltonic phrase for his *In Dubious Battle* (1936); or Robert Penn WARREN's *All the King's Men* (1946). In such cases the novel is not shaped to conform with the suggested analogue; but the meaning is implied by the title, and the reader's options of interpretation are narrowed, if not closed. A further step, as in Faulkner's *Absalom, Absalom!* (1936), is actually to conduct the narrative in broad parallel with the traditional story, although with no detailed adherence to it. The result is that a densely detailed modern story takes on breath and poignancy by reference to a suggested or lightly sketched literary analogue.

Beyond this minimal shaping for meaning is the imposition of an allegorical matrix, as a result of which the selection and position of materials of observation are determined by a preconceived idea.

Realist induction gives way to a process of deduction, just as it does in traditional allegory, but with a vastly greater density of observed data. The author (and reader) can thus have it both ways: there is the factual security of an apparent slice of life in the realist mode and the interpretive assistance of a doctrinal system that leaves no loophole of doubt as to what the author means. The most impressive writer in this vein is Thomas Mann. His first novel, *Buddenbrooks* (1901; *Buddenbrooks*, 1924), is more than a slice of life depicting existence in a German Hanseatic town, since it is dominated by the Hegelian dialectic system in its portrayal of the rise and fall of a middle-class family and, by extension, of a middle-class culture. This same Hegelian matrix is more sketchily applied to describe the nature and fate of the artist in *Tonio Kröger* (1903; *Tonio Kröger*, 1914) and *Der Tod in Venedig* (1913; *Death in Venice*, 1925). Then, in the major philosophical novel of our time, *Der Zauberberg* (1924; *The Magic Mountain*, 1927), Mann applies the dialectic on a vast scale to explain and project the history of European thought and culture. The milieu of a tuberculosis sanatorium is well documented, but both the disease and those suffering from it are pawns in a symbolic game where universal meanings are the goal. Although he abandoned the Hegelian framework in his later writings, Mann continued to use analogical devices, notably in *Doctor Faustus* (1947; *Doctor Faustus*, 1948), in which the fate of Adrian Leverkühn is in parallel with that of Nazi Germany, and the clinical metaphor of the work becomes syphilis instead of tuberculosis.

Another, although less successful, instance of this general tendency to shape by means of analogy is the work of Franz Kafka. Whatever the uncertainties about his novels in their unfinished state, the general formula is clear. *Der Prozeß* (1925; *The Trial*, 1937) is an allegory of contemporary man on three levels: religious, social, sexual. The arrest that occurs on the protagonist's thirtieth birthday is very like the sense of sin that falls upon John Bunyan (1628–1688) in *Grace Abounding to the Chief of Sinners* (1666). But it can also be read as an account of a general (and banal) sense of secular frustration or as a description of a Freudian instance of sexual inadequacy. If Kafka had carried it off, this would have been a remarkable work. As it is, it has been widely influential in showing the way to raise the individual data of everyday life to the constant universals of man's quest for meaning. Kafka, like Albert CAMUS and others, provides a wonderfully matter-of-fact texture of events, a deceptively casual and realistic narrative in pedestrian language, as a base from which to rise to cosmic questions.

The most important example of this tendency to employ analogues is James Joyce's *Ulysses* (1922), no doubt the most widely influential novel of the 20th c. His innovations, both stylistic and structural, boil down to the provision of multiple perspectives from which to view an ostensibly objective reality. The events and personalities in Dublin on June 16, 1904, are a dense assemblage of data of documentary cast. They add up to a picture of mediocrity, if not of frustration. Beyond this is the presence of the external referent of the story of Odysseus and Telemachus, which is, of course, an authorial intrusion, especially since contrivance rather than obvious similarity sustains the parallel. The result is that the all too mediocre present is to be viewed both in and for itself and *sub specie aeternitatis*. In addition to this major shaping element there are suggested parallels of Daedalus-Icarus, of Hamlet, of the Wandering Jew, and possibly of *The Divine Comedy*. As if the revisions of judgment demanded by these analogues were not enough, there are the parodic styles that begin about halfway through the novel. No major writer since Joyce has dared see reality plain. Each ingenious author has sought in his own way, by both external and internal devices, to pay tribute to the complexity, the ambiguity, and the paradoxicality of what the realists of the 19th c., in their simple faith, thought was the same for all observers.

Finally, major writers of this century have for the most part reasserted a personal style. There is a joy in language that has not been so fervent since the Renaissance. Different as they are, the styles of Joyce, Proust, Mann, and Faulkner have the indelible stamp of personality. Slang and neologism enrich the language of literature. Sentence structure after a century of radical realist pruning luxuriates once again. The heady intoxication of verbal play undoes some writers, such as Thomas WOLFE, encourages turgidity and obscurity of statement among all but the most gifted, and spurs beginners to spend themselves in verbal pyrotechnics. No doubt a new efflorescence of language was the first sign of a postrealism, but by its very excess and inappositeness on occasion it will also be the first to be curbed.

BIBLIOGRAPHY: Baumbach, J., *The Landscape of Nightmare: Studies in the Contemporary American Novel* (1965); Galloway, D., *The Absurd Hero in American Fiction* (1966); Graff, G., *Poetic Statement and Critical Dogma* (1970); Hassan, I., *The Dismemberment of Orpheus: Toward a Post-Modern Literature* (1971); Barthes, R., *Mythologies* (1973); Glicksberg, C. I., *The Literature of Commitment* (1976); Korg, J., *Language in Modern Literature: Innovation and Experiment* (1979)

—GEORGE J. BECKER

POSTSTRUCTURALISM

The term poststructuralism refers to a critical epoch and interdisciplinary movement that succeeds STRUCTURALISM but which incorporates the latter's most formal and radical features. One might begin by defining structuralism as a critical approach that explains the meaning of cultures and texts as a function of invariant structures (or constituent units) embodied in central myths and belief systems that transcend individuals but are recombined through their communications. The formalism of this approach, by which concrete social and personal phenomena would be interpreted in terms of a few stable patterns and organizing principles, would enable systematic classification. Roman Jakobson (1896–1982) and Claude LÉVI-STRAUSS are often invoked as structuralists, although to rigorously define the movement that includes the best work in formal analysis of structures in life and culture one would have to name Georg Simmel (1858–1918) and Max Weber (1864–1920). More recently, Tzvetan Todorov (b. 1939) has advocated literary structuralism as a "science of literature." The avowed radicality of structuralism would, curiously enough, reside in its capacity for generalization or abstract universalism. This radicality, joined with a denial of certitude, lives on in such categories of poststructuralist theory as difference, power, and text, which are employed in readings of cultures and historical periods very different from the ones in which the categories were formulated.

Poststructuralism, less a school or method than a mode of thought to which a number of critical methods contribute, traces the discursive effects and sign relations that organize a text or cultural phenomenon not through a central myth or structure but in institutional strategies and economies of power and difference. There are no centers, origins, or permanent truths, only strategies, and these inhabit discourses that make certain events and forms of knowledge (such as war and logic) more legitimate than others. According to Roland BARTHES, there are also no authors, these being ruses of ideologies (for example, capitalism) that produce a "human person" for purposes of control and profit. In his *Les mots et les choses* (1966; *The Order of Things*, 1971) Michel FOUCAULT proclaimed the "death of man." The distrust of central authority evinced in this approach comes from the 1968 strikes and student unrest in Paris; is epitomized in the critique of institutions carried out by poststructuralists; and is phrased philosophically as the "critique of the subject." Wherever power pools in repressive ways, poststructuralism finds a subject lurking. One "deconstructs" this subject by unmasking the rhetoric and organizing principles by which it phrases the authority of its autonomy and perceptions, all a mirage of discourse mistaking itself for the immediacy of self-evidence. Organizing centers or essences are taken by poststructuralist critics as constructions, and these include classical myths and binary oppositions that have become hierarchies such as prose/poetry, nature/culture, male/female. Gender would be a function of discursive relations that institute a system of inclusion and exclusion by which men and women are empowered and marginalized.

Although its historical background is the 1960s, poststructuralism is indebted to a much earlier "linguistic turn" showing language and interpretation as prior conditions of reality and truth. One can trace this turn back to Friedrich Nietzsche (1844–1900), and the insights of Martin Heidegger (1889–1976) in such works as *Unterwegs zur Sprache* (1959; *On The Way to Language*, 1971) that language speaks itself, that the word "bethings the thing" and allows the world to "world"—as it were verbally and not as a noun or substance. One cannot underestimate the influence of such insights upon the academic study of literature, which became even more linked to linguistic speculation through readings of Ferdinand de Saussure (1857–1913). Saussure's work described language as a system of oppositions in sign relations whose signifying power is arbitrarily grounded in static reference of words to things. Radical readings of this work would affirm the dynamism of oppositional logic and the proximity of signs to other signs that are suppressed in everyday usage, and thus would lead to the concepts of textuality and intertextuality invoked by such theorists as Jacques DERRIDA and Julia KRISTEVA. A certain linguistic idealism and "anarchy of the signifier" would ensue, as would a litany of watchwords such as rupture, effacement, undecidability. The *Lebenswelt* or "life world," which for a phenomenologist such as Maurice Merleau-Ponty (1908–1961) had been both a concrete limit and possibility of discursive freedom, would now be an infinite text. For poststructuralists the self-performance of a text would in theory be uncontainable, the border between fiction and reality erasable. But the exigencies of life draw their own lines. The act of writing itself, which for certain theorists still encounters the enigmatic density of nature and history, has its own difficult conditions. It would be fair to say that the work of rigorous postsuructuralists evinces these structural and phenomenal conditions while "playing" with their contradictions, which have been typically excluded from consideration.

The antihumanism of the viewpoint that has been sketched here, according to which language and texts dispense significance and sense as it were behind the backs of writers, speakers, readers, and audiences, has not gone unchecked. Certain theorists have claimed that the "metaphysical subject" is a pseudoproblem created solely by and for the decentralizing political arguments of many poststructuralists. In this regard the self-criticism of poststructuralism, of its own pretensions as a theory of discourse, would be immanent to its very projected aims. In his *Tropics of Discourse* (1979) Hayden White (b. 1928) says that "every discourse is always as much about discourse itself as it is about the objects that make up its subject matter." For this reason the so-called linguistic turn was perhaps more accurately a "rhetorical turn" or became consciously such as critics came to reflect on their own practices. The criticism leveled at Heidegger's theory of language by Paul de Man (1919–1983), that it gives priority to certain kinds of poetic discourse that are closest to Being and thus essentializes what is not essential but rhetorical, represents the first serious internal critique of linguistic ontology with *Jargon der Eigentlichkeit* (1964; *The Jargon of Authenticity*, 1973) by Theodor ADORNO.

Another immanent critique has come from those critics and theorists who sustain some notion of a discourse community, or of dialogue consisting of separate but ethically obligated interlocutors. Rhetoric for them does not primarily operate in an abstract field of rules and differences called Being or *langue*, as it would for the interpreters of Heidegger and Saussure, but in what Hannah Arendt (1906–1975) calls the *vita activa*, public life defined as a discursive space of exposure. The philosopher Emmanuel Levinas (b. 1906) certainly recognizes the wisdom that a Heidegger sees contained in language and which can be disclosed as an unspoken possibility of Being. Yet Levinas himself is more interested in the responsibility of speakers for each other and for their risks of utterance, their face-to-face "saying," than in the truths mystically latent in what is "unsaid." The work of Levinas in *Autrement qu'être ou au-delà de l'essence* (1974; *Otherwise Than Being or Beyond Essence*, 1981) is poststructuralist because of its abiding concern with discourse and difference, but is equally "post-Auschwitz." Like such apparently diverse writers as Arendt, Mikhail BAKHTIN, and Paul Ricœur (b. 1913), Levinas endorses notions of personal responsibility and the life of speech that link his theory to concrete experiences and encounters, including suffering.

Perhaps of the aforenamed theorists, Bakhtin, who defined discourse as "language in its concrete living totality" and whose work, like that of Roman Jakobson, sustains tacit links to the Russian oral tradition, will most leave his mark on the poststructuralist epoch. What will surely endure is Bakhtin's legacy of describing the manifold effects of voice that animate narrative as a "contact of personalities" in a context of choice amidst competing ideologies, revising our notions of social milieu and moral character. Bakhtin's critical writings on Dostoevsky have admirably brought these phenomena to our attention in a mode of interpretation Bakhtin calls "responsive understanding" in *Speech Genres and Other Late Essays* (1986).

The immanent critique (self-criticism) of poststructuralism has been shown here to have arisen from a concern with concreteness and linguistic community and personhood. Thus it has recently been argued that critics need to attend to the "embodiment" of literary discourse in expressions of bodily life and the tactile surface of signs. Other scholars have said that theory must analyze the mode of informational technology in which it and society operates. Still another concern for situational meaning has been articulated in the rise of a new critical pragmatism. All of these efforts, which represent a number of diverse viewpoints and political agendas, concur on the necessity of constraint in interpretation arising from concrete existence. A theory of constraint, which can be both an ethics and a literary materialism, comes to finally determine the possibilities of what are currently the most prominent issues in poststructuralist theory: gender, ethnic diversity, and the problem of the "canon," or body of texts that a curriculum would endorse for teaching and research. Having arisen from the problem of difference, which epitomizes the underlying political program of poststructuralism, these devisive issues remind us that the matter at stake for poststructuralist critics is above all institutional life, especially the life of radical theory. It is generally acknowledged that while conflict is positive for an institution so long as the basic values and assumptions on which its legitimacy depends are not contradicted, the life of an institution cannot be guaranteed if its members no longer share those beliefs. Thus the genuine test of poststructuralism will be its capacity to be tolerated and shared as a conflict, the capacity of its self-critique to sincerely respond to the institution of radicality.

BIBLIOGRAPHY: Sturrock, J., ed., *Structuralism and Since* (1979); Rorty, R., *Consequences of Pragmatism* (1982); Frank, M., *Was ist Neostrukturalismas?* (1984; *What is Neostructuralism?* 1989); Barthes, R., *Le bruissement de la langue* (1984; *The Rustle of Language*, 1986); Ferry, L. and A. Renaut, *La Pensée 68* (1985; *French Philosophy of the Sixties*, 1990); Weber, S., *Institution and Interpretation* (1987); Scarry, E., ed., *Literature and the Body* (1988); Tavor Bannet, E., *Structuralism and the Logic of Dissent* (1989); Fraser, N., *Unruly Practices: Power, Discourse, and Gender in Contemporary Social Theory* (1989); Fuss, D., *Essentially Speaking: Feminism, Nature and Difference* (1989); Poster, M., *Critical Theory and Poststructuralism: In Search of a Context* (1989); Simons, H. W., ed., *The Rhetorical Turn* (1990); Cadava, E., P. Connor, and J. -L. Nancy, *Who Comes after the Subject?* (1991)

—C. S. SCHREINER

POULAR LITERATURE
See Guinean Literature

POUND, Ezra

American poet, translator, and literary critic, b. 30 Oct. 1885, Hailey, Idaho; d. 1 Nov. 1972, Venice, Italy

Specializing in Romance languages and literatures, P. graduated from Hamilton College in 1905. After postgraduate work at the University of Pennsylvania and extensive travel in the Mediterranean countries, he settled in London in 1908, where for the next twelve years he was involved in prodigious literary activities. He helped initiate the IMAGIST and vorticist movements; and as foreign editor of *Poetry* (1912-18) and *The Little Review* (1917–18) he tirelessly promoted significant new work by such writers as T. S. ELIOT, James JOYCE, and William Carlos WILLIAMS. He published numerous music and art reviews and social and literary criticism as well as poetry in such journals as *The Egoist* and *The New Age*. Much of this criticism is reflected in the verse of *Hugh Selwyn Mauberley* (1920). He also began his magnum opus, *The Cantos* (1917–68). In 1920 he moved to Paris and in 1924 settled in Rapallo, Italy. For making broadcasts during World War II from

Radio Rome espousing his idiosyncratic economic and social theories and defending some Fascist policies, he was charged with treason. Arrested in 1945, he was imprisoned in the American Disciplinary Training Center at Pisa. Here he wrote the *Pisan Cantos*, the most acclaimed section of *The Cantos*, for which, amid bitter controversy, he was awarded the Bollingen Prize in 1949. P. was returned to the U.S. for trial in 1946 and was committed to St. Elizabeths Hospital for the insane in Washington, D.C., where he remained for the next twelve years. In 1958 charges against him were dismissed, and P. returned to Italy.

P.'s career was characterized by a selfless and ceaseless devotion to the art of poetry. He supported and encouraged his gifted contemporaries while endeavoring to discover and restore what he considered to be masterwork from the past. Studying the various forms and functions of poetry from other countries and other ages, P. assimilated poetic traditions from Italy, Greece, Spain, France, China, and Japan, as well as from England and America. He believed that poetry could fulfill essential functions for civilization: it provided a unique record of private sensibilities and communal values while transmitting the "tale of the tribe" (*Guide to Kulchur*, 1938). He insisted on poetry's potential importance as a linguistic and social document, a medium that could bring not only ideas and feelings, but language and historical events under scrutiny. Translation and criticism are important elements in his writing; both serve as essential guides to his poetry.

Early, major influences on P.'s work include Homer, Dante, and Confucius. From the work of these writers, P. drew techniques and themes that he developed throughout his early poetry and *The Cantos*. In the essay "Dante" in *The Spirit of Romance* (1910) P. interpreted the *Divine Comedy* both as a literal description of Dante's imagining a journey "through the realms inhabited by the spirits of men after death" and as the journey of "Dante's intelligence through the states of mind wherein dwell all sorts and conditions of men before death." P. envisaged his *Cantos* as a record of such a journey, the dramatization of individual exploration of past and present in an effort to understand our world. P. explained in *Introduzione alla natura economica degli S.U.A.* (1944; *An Introduction to the Economic Nature of the United States*, 1950; rpt., *Impact: Essays on Ignorance and the Decline of American Civilization*, 1960) that he had planned to write an epic poem that begins "in the Dark Forest, crosses the Purgatory of human error, and ends in the light." The journey in *The Cantos*, however, was "by no means an orderly Dantescan rising/but as the winds veer" (*Cantos LXXIV*). *The Cantos'* structure is more like that of a musical fugue: themes are repeated in endless variation and woven into complex patterns. Major themes include (1) the journey into the world of the dead or the past that symbolizes mankind's struggle out of ignorance into understanding; (2) the "repeat in history," the discovery of parallel or analogous events through the ages; and (3) the "magic moment," the experience of transcendent vision.

Combining his perception of Dante's work as a dramatization of states of mind with Robert Browning's use of persona and dramatic monologue, P. developed a technique of using the shifting voices of self-revelatory characters to people *The Cantos*. Mythical, historical, and contemporary figures are presented, mirroring in words and deeds their states of mind. P. relies heavily on material extracted from personal letters and literary and historical documents in *The Cantos*; he is interested not just in describing events but in revealing the motives and temperaments of those who influenced events. Historical figures such as the 15th-c. soldier and

Erza Pound

patron of the arts Sigismundo Malatesta, the Elizabethan jurist Edward Coke, Elizabeth I, John Adams, and Thomas Jefferson speak through fragments of their own writings. Embodying the ideals of personal liberty as well as ethical and responsible behavior, they represent to P. heroic figures who tried to advance civilization. P. searched through history to find those who embodied the Confucian ideals of "sincerity" and "rectitude" in contrast to those who through greed, ignorance, and malevolence worked against the common good. *The Cantos* record an endless struggle between the creators and the destroyers.

Two journeys are dramatized in *The Cantos*: one, a spiritual quest for transcendence; the other, an intellectual search for worldly wisdom. The poet's goals are for the individual and the community: personal enlightenment combined with a vision of civic order. Just as Beatrice guided Dante's pilgrim, so classical goddesses appear in *The Cantos*, signaling the advent of visionary experience: Aphrodite, Diana, Persephone, Pomona, Artemis, and other goddesses represent manifestations of divine beauty, mercy, and love. The traveler through these *Cantos* also encounters the way to the Just City. Destroyed in the past through vanity, falsehood, greed, and dissension, the ideal city appears in various guises: Wagadu, "in the mind indestructible" (*Canto LXXVII*), or Dioce, "Whose terraces are the color of stars" (*Canto LXXIV*), reminds us of continued human effort to create ordered and harmonious societies.

These themes, present throughout the *Cantos*, appear in miniature in *Canto I*. A translation of a Renaissance Latin translation of Book XI of the *Odyssey, Canto I* is itself a metaphor for renewing the poetry of the past. It recounts Odysseus' visit to the underworld to receive information that will enable him to return home. Calling the shades or spirits of the dead to life, Odysseus, like the poet, symbolically gives blood to the ghosts. The journey to the underworld parallels Dante's journey in the *Divine Comedy*; it is also analogous to the Eleusinian fertility myths, recounting the emergence of the goddess from the underworld or the sea to bring spring, the flowering of the earth.

A late section of *The Cantos*, published as *Thrones: 96–109 de los cantares* (1959), presents these themes and illustrates how P. integrated them with Confucian principles. Confucius, P. believed, represented an entire system of good government and moral order; and the dominant theme of "Thrones," conceived while P. was confined in St. Elizabeths, is Justice. Its title alludes to the seventh heaven of Dante's paradise: thrones are for the spirits of those who have been responsible for good government. Creating a mosaic of cryptic fragments extracted from various legal and philosophical documents ranging from China's *Sacred Edict* (1670) to the Magna Charta (1215) and the American Constitution, P. compares the governments, the legal and moral codes, and the linguistic systems of China, America-England, and Greece-Italy. He compares leaders who worked to establish judicious laws, encourage individual and civic responsibility, and clarify the language. Obfuscation and excessive abstraction in the language, P. believed, was one indication of corruption and tyranny in the society. A general rectification, then, had to begin with a concern with clear meanings, with the "precise definition of the word." Good laws were made by those who had respect not only for the language, but also for the processes of nature (Confucian taxes, for example, were based on a fair share of the harvest). Nature imagery forms an important part of *The Cantos*, linking Confucius, whose code leads to the Just City, with Eleusis, whose rituals lead to enlightenment. For P., the natural world is sacred, venerated in Eleusinian rites that celebrate the mysteries of nature (reproduction) and the Confucian ethos that honors the partnerships of men and nature (production).

P. has been called the "inventor" of Chinese poetry for our time. Beginning in 1913 with the notebooks of the Orientalist Ernest Fenollosa (1853–1903), P. pursued a lifelong study of ancient Chinese texts. Sinologists have disputed some of P.'s claims (for instance, that the ideogram was based on pictorial representations); nevertheless, his views are important for what they tell us about his own poetic practices. Initially, P. saw correspondences between his imagist principles and Oriental poetry. He admired the obscurity of its hidden meanings, the clarity of its directness and realism, its inclusion of mystical experiences, and its use of personae to portray states of mind. He also admired its use of nature imagery as a "metaphor by sympathy" for human emotions. His first translations appeared in *Cathay* (1915), a collection of poems by Rihaku (also known as Li Po, A.D. 701–762). Later, P. translated the writings of Confucius: *The Great Digest* (1928), *The Unwobbling Pivot* (1947), and *The Analects* (1950). His *Confucian Odes: The Classic Anthology Defined by Confucius* (1955) contains translations of over three hundred songs and narratives that represent the Confucian ethos. Often, P.'s work should not be regarded as a literal translation, but as an attempt to reproduce the ideas and the effects of the original in a modern idiom.

Of major importance to P. was the discovery of the ideogram, a more complex form of his "image." P.'s ideogrammatic method was an attempt to duplicate the graphic precision of the Chinese characters. Images and allusions were arranged in order to suggest some general concept. Names, fragments from literary and historical documents, phrases from various languages, and other references are juxtaposed as specific examples of an unstated, but unifying, idea. These examples P. called "luminous details," charged facts that supposedly illuminate an entire situation or figure. Such details arranged in a pattern become his ideograms. P. conceived of these patterns as dynamic structures that are drawn into a design by the mind perceiving the relationships between the parts. Like P.'s example of the rose formed from steel filings by the magnet, luminous details form concepts, intellectual patterns in the mind's eye. For the reader who suddenly recognizes the relationships that unify the details, the effect on the imagination can be startling and powerful. The difficulty with the method is that P. often fails to communicate because the reader does not have the information necessary to understand each reference. One name may represent a whole set of values; but it is often difficult, if not impossible, to determine its significance. This is especially true when P. cites evidence in order to challenge common opinion. Much recent scholarship has been directed toward establishing a context for *The Cantos* so that the reader will be able to interpret allusions more easily. P. believed that the ideogrammatic method allowed poetry a procedure analogous to scientific investigation: observation, collection of data, analysis, then conclusions. A theory or an abstract idea is thus always measured against observed examples. Ideas can be evaluated and qualified by how they "go into action."

Economics is another area of major importance throughout P.'s *Cantos* and in his social criticism. Influenced by the English social economist C. H. Douglas (1879–1952), P. urged monetary reforms in, for example, *Social Credit: An Impact* (1935). He railed against the evils of a private banking system that could withhold money and credit from the people and compel the government to borrow, creating a public debt. P. believed that the usurious and manipulative practices of international bankers led to scarcities for the general public, to fierce competition for foreign markets, and eventually to world war. His belief that Mussolini was instituting long-needed economic and social reforms led to his ill-advised support of Mussolini's policies. His anti-Semitic statements stemmed from his belief that the economic system was being exploited by Jewish financiers. P. proposed that the government should control the distribution of money. Congress, he maintained, had the right to determine the value of money, to regulate interest rates, and to set just prices. He opposed the gold standard, believing that money itself had no intrinsic value and should not be tied to the value of any single commodity. Rather, he believed money was merely a medium of exchange, a means to effect the orderly and equitable distribution of goods. The intrinsic wealth of the community, he believed, came from the yield of nature and human labor, and from our entire intellectual heritage. Production is affected by the enormous store of ideas and information, the invention of tools and processes, and the development of scientific formulas—all these contribute to our cultural and technological wealth: our social credit. The benefits from this heritage, P. believed, should be equitably shared among the citizens. Evidence of P.'s economic concerns, like his interest in just government, appears in condensed, often cryptic, fragments throughout *The Cantos*.

P. was one of the most influential and controversial literary figures of the 20th c. He challenged many of the political, aesthetic, and religious assumptions of his time, outraging many in the process. His criticism established some of the fundamental principles of what we now call "MODERNISM"; his translations have extended and redefined our cultural heritage. His work remains a major influence on today's writers.

FURTHER WORKS: *A Lume Spento* (1908); *A Quinzaine for This Yule* (1908); *Exultations* (1909); *Personae* (1909; rev. eds., 1926, 1949); *Provença* (1910); *Canzoni* (1911); *Ripostes* (1912); *The Sonnets and Ballate of Guido Cavalcanti* (1912, tr.); *Personae & Exultations* (1913); *Lustra* (1916); *Gaudier-Brzeska: A Memoir* (1916); *Certain Noble Plays of Japan* (1916, tr., with Ernest Fenollosa); *Noh," or Accomplishment: A Study of the Classical Stage of Japan* (1916, with Ernest Fenollosa); *Dialogues of Fontenelle* (1917, tr.); *Pavannes and Divagations* (1918); *Quia Pauper Amavi* (1919); *Umbra* (1920); *Instigations* (1921); *Poems, 1918–1921* (1921); *The Natural Philosophy of Love* (1922, tr. of Remy de Gourmont); *Indiscretions* (1923); *Antheil and the Treatise on Harmony* (1924); *Selected Poems* (1928); *Ta Hio* (1928, tr.); *Imaginary Letters* (1930); *How to Read* (1931); *Prolegomena I* (1932); *ABC of Economics* (1933); *ABC of Reading* (1934); *Make It New* (1934); *Jefferson and/or Mussolini* (1935); *Polite Essays* (1937); *If This Be Treason* (1948); *Selected Poems* (1949); *Money Pamphlets* (6 pamphlets, 1950–1951); *Patria Mia* (1950); *The Letters of E. P., 1907–1941* (1950); *The Translations of E. P.* (1953); *Literary Essays* (1954); *The Women of Trachis* (1956, tr. of Sophocles); *Love Poems of Ancient Egypt* (1962, tr. with Noel Stock); *Cavalcanti Poems* (1965, tr.); *P./Joyce Letters* (1967); *Drafts and Fragments of Cantos CX–CXVI* (1968); *Selected Prose 1909–1965* (1973); *Collected Early Poems of E. P.* (1976); *E. P. and Music: The Complete Criticism* (1977); *E. P. Speaking: Radio Speeches of World War II* (1978); *E. P. and the Visual Arts* (1981)

BIBLIOGRAPHY: Kenner, H., *The Poetry of E. P.* (1951); Leary, L., ed., *Motive and Method in the Cantos of E. P.* (1954); Espey, J., *E. P.'s Mauberley: A Study in Composition* (1955); Edwards, J. H., and W. Vasse, *Annotated Index to the Cantos of E. P.* (1957); Emery, C., *Ideas into Action: A Study of P.'s Cantos* (1958); Dembo, L. S., *The Confucian Odes of E. P.: A Critical Appraisal* (1963); Davie, D., *E. P.: Poet as Sculptor* (1964); Sullivan, J. P., *E. P. and Sextus Propertius: A Study in Creative Translation* (1964); de Nagy, N. C., *E. P.'s Poetics and Literary Tradition: The Critical Decade* (1966); Hesse, E., ed., *New Approaches to E. P.* (1969); Pearlman, D., *The Barb of Time: On the Unity of E. P.'s Cantos* (1969); Witemeyer, H., *The Poetry of E. P.: Forms and Renewal, 1908–20* (1969); Stock, N., *The Life of E. P.* (1970); Brooke-Rose, C., *A ZBC of E. P.* (1971); Kenner, H., *The P. Era* (1971); Bush, R., *The Genesis of E. P.'s Cantos* (1976); Sieburth, R., *Instigations: E. P. and Remy de Gourmont* (1978); Makin, P., *Provence and P.* (1978); Bernstein, M., *The Tale of the Tribe: E. P. and the Modern Verse Epic* (1980); Terrell, C. F., *A Companion to the Cantos of E. P.* (1980); Woodward, A., *E. P. and the Pisan Cantos* (1980); Surette, L., *A Light from Eleusis: A Study of E. P.'s Cantos* (1980); Kearns, G., *Guide to E. P.'s Selected Cantos* (1980); Bell, I. A. F., *Critic as Scientist: The Modernist Poetics of E. P.* (1981); Read, F., *'76: One World and "The Cantos" of E. P.* (1981)

—JO BRANTLEY BERRYMAN

The opinion has been voiced that P.'s eventual reputation will rest upon his criticism and not upon his poetry. (I have been paid the same compliment myself.) I disagree. It is on his total work for literature

that he must be judged: on his poetry, and his criticism, and his influence on men and on events at a turning point in literature. In any case, his criticism takes its significance from the fact that it is the writing of a poet about poetry: it must be read in the light of his own poetry, as well as of poetry by other men whom he championed. . . . P.'s great contribution to the work of other poets (if they choose to accept what he offers) is his insistence upon the immensity of the amount of conscious labor to be performed by the poet. . . . He . . . provides an ex.mple of devotion to "the art of poetry" which I can only parallel in our time by the example of Valéry.

T. S. Eliot, "E. P.," *Poetry*, 68, 6 (1946), 331–38

P. was one of the most opinionated and unselfish men who ever lived, and he made friends and enemies everywhere by the simple exercise of the classic American constitutional right of free speech. His speech was free to outrageous license. He was completely reckless about making enemies. His so-called anti-Semitism was, hardly anyone has noted, only equaled by his anti-Christianism. It is true he hated most in the Catholic faith the elements of Judaism. It comes down squarely to anti-monotheism. . . . P. felt himself to be in the direct line of Mediterranean civilization, rooted in Greece. . . . He was a lover of the sublime, and a seeker after perfection, a true poet, of the kind born in a hair shirt—a God-sent disturber of the peace in the arts, the one department of human life where peace is fatal.

Katherine Anne Porter, on *The Letters of E. P., 1907–1941, NYTBR*, 29 Oct. 1950, 4

P. should be credited with having weighted the perils of the method he elected. It pays the reader the supreme compliment of supposing that he is seriously interested: interested, among other things, in learning how to deploy his curiosity without being a dilettante. . . . His utility enters its second phase when disparate materials acquire, if only by way of his personality, a unity of tone which makes them accessible to one another. . . . In his third phase of utility . . . the poet instigates curiosity: how many people in the last thirty years have read the *Odyssey* on account of Joyce, or Donne at the encouragement of Mr. Eliot, or Dante and Confucius thanks to P.? . . . And he would consider that he was performing his maximum service for the fourth kind of reader, the one with the patience to learn and observe, within the poem, how exactly everything fits together and what exactly, page by page and canto by canto, the fitting together enunciates.

Hugh Kenner, "Homage to Musonius," *Poetry*, 90, 4 (1957), 240–41

This claim for P.—that he recovered for English verse something lost to it since Campion or at least since Waller—may get more general agreement than any other. And Charles Olson is surely right to point to this achievement as rooted in something altogether more basic and less conspicuous than, for instance, the luxurious orchestration of the choruses in *Women of Trachis*. It is something that has to do with the reconstituting of the verse-line as the poetic unit, slowing down the surge from one line into the next in such a way that smaller components within the line (down to the very syllables) can recover weight and value. When P. is writing at his best we seem to have perceptions succeeding one another at unusual speed at the same time as the syllables succeed one another unusually slowly. But succession, in any case, is what is involved—succession, sequaciousness.

Donald Davie, *E. P.: Poet as Sculptor* (1964),
p. 246

E. P.'s writings belong to the moment of experimental explosion—Stravinsky, Schoenberg, Picasso, Rilke, Joyce, Eliot, Proust. His work, like theirs, is alive with a radiant daring. . . . His *Cantos* are heroic, a poem as long as a long novel, written in a time when it seemed as if only prose fiction could bring off anything extended, important, and readable. And yet the *Cantos* are not metered fiction, nor do they go against the grain of what is possible in poetry.

Robert Lowell, "A Tribute," *Agenda*, 4, 2
(1965), 22

It's a shame he didn't get the Nobel and all the other awards at once—he was the greatest poet of the age! . . . P. told me he felt that the Cantos were "stupidity and ignorance all the way through," and were a failure and a "mess," and that his "greatest stupidity was stupid suburban anti-Semitic prejudice," he thought—as of 1967, when I talked to him. So I told him I thought that since the Cantos were for the first time a single person registering over the course of a lifetime all of his major obsessions and thoughts and the entire rainbow arc of his images and clinging and attachments and discoveries and perceptions, that they were an accurate representation of his mind and so couldn't be thought of in terms of success or failure, but only in terms of the actuality of their representation, and that since for the first time a human being had taken the whole spiritual world of thought through fifty years and followed the thoughts out to the end—so that he built a model of his consciousness over a fifty-year time span—that they were a great human achievement. Mistakes and all, naturally. [1972]

Allen Ginsberg, *Allen Verbatim: Lectures on
Poetry, Politics, Consciousness* (1974), pp. 180–81

There is a strong presence of gods and goddesses in *The Cantos* and yet P.'s poem is not "a vision." Instead, it is an attempt at an all-embracing historical

and aesthetic synthesis, a poem that praises or attacks well-known men and institutions, that proposes an economic explanation of civilization's rise and fall, and contains an explicit series of specific recommendations to both ruler and ruled. Like Dante's *Divina Commedia*, *The Cantos* demand to be taken as literally and historically true. . . . P. . . . was equally determined to endow *The Cantos* with at least the same degree (which is not identical to the same *kind*) of authority as that possessed by a historian's text.

Michael Bernstein, *The Tale of the Tribe: E. P.
and Modern Verse Epic* (1980), pp. 31–32

Although it is not possible now—nor will it ever be—to make a complete statement about all the themes in *The Cantos*, it is possible to posit a hypothesis that can help the reader, a hypothesis he can alter to his own bent as his experience dictates. To me, *The Cantos* is a great religious poem. The tale of the tribe is an account of man's progress from the darkness of hell to the light of paradise. Thus it is a revelation of how divinity is manifested in the universe: the process of the stars and planets, the dynamic energy of the seed in motion (*semina motuum*), and the kind of intelligence that makes the cherrystone become a cherry tree. Hell is darkness ("there is only the darkness of ignorance"); thus the highest manifestation of divinity flows from the mind and the spirit of man.

Carroll F. Terrell, *A Companion to the Cantos of
E. P.* (1980), p. viii

POWELL, Anthony

English novelist, b. 21 Dec. 1905, London

P. attended Eton, then studied history at Balliol College, Oxford. He worked in London for a publisher, Duckworth, and briefly wrote film scripts. Between 1931 and 1939 he published five short novels, somewhat in the vein of the early satirical novels of his friend Evelyn WAUGH. He joined the British army in 1939, serving throughout the war and rising to the rank of major; much of his time was spent in London as a liaison officer with Belgian and Polish troops headquartered there. He wrote no fiction during and immediately after the war, working instead on a biography of John Aubrey, the 17th-c. antiquary and biographer; later he also published an edition of Aubrey's *Lives*.

P.'s early accomplishments deserve attention: five good novels, a readable and reliable biography of an important figure, six years of estimable as well as engrossing war service. Still, few would on the basis of his early works accord him a place among the major writers of the modern era. Somewhat inauspiciously, then, after the war, P. began work on a twelve-volume roman-fleuve, the first volume, *A Question of Upbringing*, appearing in 1951, successor volumes following at roughly two-year intervals until the series' completion in 1975. Reading the novels as a completed sequence, however, one discovers the work of a major writer: a comprehensive social historian, with a superb sense of historical change; a master of the intricate organization of a large form; a brilliant and versatile stylist; and the creator of a comic masterpiece.

P. takes the title of the sequence, *A Dance to the Music of Time*—or sometimes just *The Music of Time*—from a Poussin painting, in which, as he describes it near the beginning of *A Question of Upbringing*, "the Seasons, hand in hand and facing outward, tread in rhythm to the notes of the lyre that the winged and naked greybeard plays." This scene suggests the sense of life's continuities and changes that the entire sequence tries to present.

Any such sequence will depend for both its inner strength and its overall continuity on its means of narration. P. uses a central character, Nicholas Jenkins, whose life resembles his own, to tell the stories. The sequence begins when Jenkins is at school, at about the age of sixteen, and, with one major and important flashback (to August 1914 in *The Kindly Ones* [1962], the sixth novel), proceeds forward chronologically, ending in the early 1970s.

A reader might expect so long a novel, and one centering on a single character, to be intolerably narcissistic. But although we spend a good deal of time with Nicholas Jenkins by the time the sequence is finished, he is, about himself, a most reticent character: to spend time with him is not necessarily to know him. The indescribability of certain relationships partly accounts for Jenkins's reticence; but he is also quite fascinated by modes of indirection. Of a member of an earlier generation, he says that she "represented to a high degree that characteristic of her own generation that everything may be said, though nothing indecorous discussed openly." Jenkins, then, is anything but forthcoming about his own life, inner thoughts, and most personal relationships; the handling of his marriage, for example, is a marvelous tour de force: there is almost no description of it, and yet it is something we feel we are well acquainted with. More than anything else, such obliquity and unforthcomingness establish Jenkins primarily as an observer, rather than as the object of our observations; but as an observer of a very complex sort.

Many readers at first find P.'s style a barrier to immediate involvement: elaborate and at times circumlocutory, often abstract in vocabulary, he particularly leans toward sudden contrasts of obliquity and directness. Among his favored constructions are those that, while displaying a certain elaborateness of description or modification, also employ an unusual economy of phrasing, especially ones in which a crucial connective is suppressed, giving the suggestion, probably accurate, of someone well trained in reading and writing Latin. P.'s stylistic range is large, made more so by the counterpointing of comically stylized dialogue with sections of narration and reflection. Several crucial characters—Charles Stringham, Ralph Barnby, Hugh Moreland—are natural epigrammatists, their remarks underscored by frequent requotation.

Such stylizations, the means and varieties of which are too numerous to mention here, accumulate over the course of the long novel, and are part of the method by which action becomes myth. Among the compensations for growing old, Jenkins says, is "a keener perception for the authenticities of mythology, not only of the traditional sort, but—when such are any good—the latterday mythologies of poetry and the novel." Mythology is perhaps the major way by which the sequence is made to hold together. Important scenes occur in front of a painting, or in connection with a musical or dramatic production, often one depicting some bit of classical mythology. For example, an important scene in *Temporary Kings* (1973), the next to the last novel, occurs beneath an apocryphal Tiepolo ceiling in Venice that depicts the story, taken from Herodotus and Plato, of Candaules and Gyges. Several ironic connections exist between the mural and the characters below; the story of the whole novel echoes that told by the painting. At the same time, individual character is illuminated by seeing it in terms of "personal mythology": each of us has his own personal myth, the key to our consciousness and actions. As the entire sequence unfolds, personal mythologies, the various stories from the sequence's own earlier volumes, frequently included snatches of those latter-day mythologies of poetry and fiction, and the classical myths alluded to and represented in the sequence in various forms all weave together to create the work's largest patterns. Mutable time becomes subsumed within the patterns of eternally recurrent mythology.

Two characters most clearly dominate the sequence (indeed only these two appear in all twelve volumes): Jenkins, and his linked opposite, Kenneth Widmerpool. Widmerpool is a laughable but unlovable grotesque, an ambitious and self-serving egotist with a genius for showing up at the wrong time and saying the wrong thing; we can count on him for several major blunders in every novel. He also represents a social class that P. depicts in increasingly ominous terms, a bureaucratic pseudomeritocracy that the sequence depicts as coming more and more to rule England. We watch Widmerpool's ascent of the ladders of power, through various businesses, the military bureaucracy, Parliament, the postwar world of left-wing politics and journalism, progressive universities, television; it plays against the far more subtly portrayed growth of Jenkins's intellectual and moral awareness. Satirically the sequence offers us the "triumph of Widmerpool" as a version of the decline of Great Britain since the end of World War I; Widmerpoolism is what replaces the traditional institutions of government and culture. Finally P. affiliates Widmerpool with large mythic forces of misrule, and yet he remains a magnificent comic character, even while carrying the increasing weight of satirized social commentary.

Widmerpool marries, after various inconsequential, extraordinary liaisons. Pamela Widmerpool is both a more compelling and a more awful character than her husband. She is a figure of death, and particularly of beauty and sexuality become thanatotic, finally destroying herself in order to be able to offer herself to a necrophiliac American professor.

Between Jenkins, cool, reserved, melancholy, ironic, and increasingly reflective, and the Widmerpools, as brilliantly and comically dreadful a pair as exists in the fiction of this century, P. offers a small multitude of highly individualized characters. Among the strengths of the roman-fleuve is the opportunity it offers the novelist to deal with minor characters in a major way, and major characters in a minor way.

Somewhat obscure characters—Jenkins's uncle-in-law Alfred Tolland, Jenkins's housemaster La Bas, Sunny Farebrother, Dicky Umfraville or Jeavons or Odo Stevens, or the literati J. C. Quiggins and Mark Members—achieve prominence in our minds simply by reappearance, without their ever having been made major in the usual novelistic sense. Meanwhile, potentially major characters like Jenkins's school friends Peter Templar and even Charles Stringham begin to recede as others survive or as other concerns begin to occupy Jenkins. Perhaps the fullest appreciation of P.'s art would demand a thorough census, particularly of characters who perform a relatively minor role in a given novel but, through return engagements, themselves not particularly noteworthy, begin to exert a surprisingly large claim on our attention. By his creation of dozens of such characters P. transforms a relatively small base of population—school friends, relatives, various members besides Jenkins of London literary circles, fellow soldiers, and other military acquaintances—into a fictional population both representative of society at large and capable of supporting a work of fiction of this size. Such a population, viewed through time, reconsidered, remembered, disappearing and occasionally reappearing, both instigates and illustrates Jenkins's increasingly frequent musings about time, mutability, recurrence, and permanence.

A case can be made for viewing this sequence as the single most important work of English fiction since World War II, and also the most important since the prewar era when the major works of modern English fiction were published—those of LAWRENCE, JOYCE, WOOLF, CONRAD, and FORD. A rival of such masters of social comedy as Evelyn WAUGH, Ronald FIRBANK, P. G. WODEHOUSE, Joyce CARY, and Henry GREEN, P., through his roman-fleuve, elevates that genre to a level of social comprehensiveness and large-scale artistry none of these writers except Waugh achieved. By this adaptation, influenced as it is by such diverse figures as PROUST and Ariosto, P. has shown himself to be both a profound traditionalist and a brilliant innovator.

FURTHER WORKS: *Afternoon Men* (1931); *Venusberg* (1932); *From a View to a Death* (1933); *Agents and Patients* (1937); *What's Become of Waring* (1939); *John Aubrey and His Friends* (1949); *A Buyer's Market* (1952); *The Acceptance World* (1955); *At Lady Molly's* (1957); *Casanova's Chinese Restaurant* (1960); *The Valley of Bones* (1964); *The Soldier's Art* (1966); *The Military Philosophers* (1968); *Books Do Furnish a Room* (1971); *Hearing Secret Harmonies* (1975); *To Keep the Ball Rolling: The Memoirs of A. P.*: Vol. I, *Infants of the Spring* (1976); Vol. 2, *Messengers of the Day* (1978); Vol. 3, *Faces in My Time* (1980); Vol. IV, *The Strangers All Are Gone* (1982)

BIBLIOGRAPHY: Mizener, A., *The Sense of Life in the Modern Novel* (1965): 79–88; Pritchett, V. S., *The Living Novel and Later Appreciations* (1964): 294–303; Morris, R., *The Novels of A. P.* (1968); Pritchard, W. H., "A. P.'s Serious Comedy," *MR*, 10 (1969): 812–19; Russell, J. D., *A. P.: A Quintet, Sextet, and War* (1970); Bergonzi, B., *A. P.*, rev. ed. (1972); Brennan, N., *A. P.* (1974); Tucker, J., *The Novels of A. P.* (1976); Jones, R., "A. P.'s *Music*: Swansong of the Metropolitan Romance," *VQR*, 52 (1976): 353–69; Wilcox, T., "A. P. and the Illusion of Possibility," *ConL*, 12 (1976): 223–39; Spurling, H., *Invitation to the Dance: A Guide to A. P.'s "Dance to the Music of Time"* (1977); Tapscott, S., "The Epistemology of Gossip: A. P.'s 'Dance to the Music of Time,'" *TQ*, 21 (1978): 104–16; Wiseman, T. P., "The Centaur's Hoof: A. P. and the Ancient World," *RRWL*, 2 (1980): 7–23

—RICHARD A. JOHNSON

The effect of *The Music of Time* is a very remarkable one for the mid-twentieth century. It is as if we had come suddenly on an enormously intelligent but completely undogmatic mind with a vision of experience that is deeply penetrating and yet wholly recognizable, beautifully subtle in ordination and yet quite unostentatious in technique, and in every respect undistorted by doctrine. Great as the achievement of many twentieth-century novelists has been, they have

been, almost to a man, novelists of ideas, in whose work experience is observed from the point of view of some more or less rationally conceived "philosophy" and functions essentially as illustration, and the writer's passion manifests itself as rhetoric rather than poetry. . . .

However powerful such novels may be—and most of the great novelists of our time have written such novels—there is something more immediately human and satisfying about an equally great novelist whose imagination apprehends all the dogmas of our time and the uses men make of them without itself being at the mercy of any of them. Such an imagination has the profound common sense, the unshakable awareness of other people, that has always given the great comic writer his sense of the discrepancies between motive and theory and allowed him to see human affairs, not as an illustration of some social or philosophical generalization, but as some kind of dance to the music of Time.

Arthur Mizener, *The Sense of Life in the Modern Novel* (1964), pp. 102–3

But these novels constitute a *roman fleuve*. The same characters reappear, with new wives, husbands, careers, fortunes and fates; they are connected intimately in their social set. They live in a whispering gallery, in a mocking music of echoes from the past. They astonish one another by their unpredictable actions and their new chummings-up. Who would have thought, in *At Lady Molly's*, that Widmerpool would fall for that brassy ex-VAD, Mrs. Haycock? Or, in a later volume, that the grand Mrs. Foxe would take up with a ballet dancer and shower him with presents? Here a difficulty arises. After the deep spate of their early flow, such novels run into shallows. What began as a panorama begins to sound like a gossip column. One noticed this in *At Lady Molly's*; in *Casanova's Chinese Restaurant*, the habit of gossip has really set in and the central interest—the examination of two marriages—is not strong enough to stop it. One has the irritating impression that Jenkins, the narrator, has no other profession but to run about collecting the news; his stability has become fitful. The characters exchange too much hearsay. This is the danger with the *roman fleuve* when it lacks a strongly sustaining idea beyond the convenience of its own existence. I am not sure that the idea of the decadence of a class, anecdotally viewed, is strong enough. I think Mr. P. has now to guard against the risk that his characters will be so familiar and real to him that he will cease to make them important to us; that they will lose their true strength, *i.e.*, that they are obsessive fictions. The constant difficulty of the novelist is to avoid the engaging demi-monde that lies between art and life. Hearsay enfeebles, if Aubrey's brief emblematic lives become Aubrey's long ones.

V. S. Pritchett, *The Living Novel and Later Appreciations* (1964), pp. 301–2

For P., however, external time (clock time) is the flux. Time is actual; its very sheerness brings about events as it relentlessly pursues the dancers who, loving, marrying, dying, are reluctant to admit that they are changing at all. P. returns to the classical conception of time: the musical old greybeard who conducts the rounds of the seasons, or the cold goddess Mutability, altering people and events from day to day. Consequently, time functions critically, not mystically. Passing because it must, it is not mysterious, only at moments indefinable. P. is concerned with time, not obsessed by it; for while he sees it as blasting the hopes of some, wasting the promises of others, he knows that it is also the sole arbiter for shaping in the future the formless formulae of the past. It is this outlook that enables him to focus on the essential aim of the novel sequence: to play changing sensibilities against the continuum of human history.

This concept is at the center of *The Music of Time*. Stated with thematic force, it resounds as a note of resignation, often melancholy or sad, sometimes even tragic, but mostly pitched to the comic stoicism of the narrator, which keeps the sequence from growing tedious, oppressive, or unwieldy.

Robert K. Morris, *The Novels of A. P.* (1968), p. 108

Later in the thirties P.'s style changed; the sentences became longer and the syntax more elaborate, and in *The Music of Time* he writes in a way quite unlike *Afternoon Men*: a complicated, leisurely, reflective and analytical manner, which unsympathetic readers have found merely longwinded. Yet whereas the style of P.'s first two novels had effectively rendered the comic disparity and randomness of experience as it unfolds moment by moment, in *The Music of Time*, P. is attempting to make aesthetic sense of a lifetime of vanished experiences, to understand them and draw out the significances that were hidden at the time. P. seems no more convinced in the sequence than he was in the early novels that order and coherence are actually part of reality, but he is prepared to allow that they may appear in the verbal patterning that the novelist imposes on his material, so that style is a necessary principle of order.

The other major aspect of P.'s method that is already quite apparent in *Afternoon Men* is his preoccupation with anecdote and gossip. To some extent such an interest is an essential part of any novelist's equipment, for he is nothing if he is not both a collector and a teller of stories. But P.'s sense of anecdote is remarkably well developed.

Bernard Bergonzi, *A. P.*, rev. ed. (1971), p. 5

What, then, is P.'s stature? It can be unfair and dangerous to blame novelists for what they have left out: the critical focus has slipped on to infinity. All the same, one does feel conscious of large gaps in P.'s work. Without joining such of P.'s justifiably guyed

figures as Guggenbühl—who heavily demands social commitment in literature ("No mere entertainment, please")—one would like to glimpse the presence now and then, or even the shadow, of that duller, poorer, grubbier world most of us inhabit. . . . Again, though P. believes in and extols feelings he is not good at igniting them on the page so that the reader feels the heat; it does happen, but the moments are exceptional. The books fall particularly short on the emotional lives of women, and a disproportionate number of his females seem brassy, shallow, restless. . . .

Possibly related to his failure to involve us in feelings is an inability, or disinclination, to deal with action as if it were taking place while we watch; the reader tends to view from afar, with the aid of first-class field-glasses, it is true, and an amusing commentary, but we are at times conscious of the distance. In P.'s work there is a general flight from immediacy, and notably in *A Dance to the Music of Time* where the narrative method is allowed to fuzz incident and situation. Often this is essential to P.'s intent, but the lack of definition and energy which can result is a disturbing weakness, just the same. . . .

What P. has is a powerful sense of life through character, caricature and period; fine humour and invention; a largely humane point of view; and unequalled competence at setting down the ways of a small, deeply interesting class of English society. Technically, he has remarkably extended what can be done through the first-person narrative; and he has the control to mix comfortably within one volume very different modes of novel writing: naturalism, fantasy, comedy, farce, occasional tragedy.

James Tucker, *The Novels of A. P.* (1976), pp. 3–5

It is paradoxical . . . that despite the great length of the novel sequence the reader is left with the impression of something small, rather delicate, a string of vignettes or miniatures, rather than a solid structure. This smallness, culminating in the refusal to end the sequence with a flourish, without valedictory passages, without giving the reader that sense of moral or spiritual growth he might have expected, finally suggests that the comparison should not be with Proust at all but with someone working on a much smaller scale: Noel Coward, whose theatrical historical pageant *Cavalcade* offered its audiences much the same pleasures as *The Music of Time*. The suggestion is not hostile (Coward was a great craftsman and entertainer) but is meant to pin down the essential quality of the sequence and to explain its hold over its devotees. P.'s ability to "hit off" the flavour of each period (up until the end of the 1940's) is celebrated justly, and readers enjoy this period detail, the popular songs, the modish paraphernalia, the new social types coming into being. And so a man with an antiquarian, rather than a historian's, feeling for the past has written a long novel that has elements in it of a parable about the decline of his class and is itself the swansong of the Metropolitan Romance. For a writer who has not believed in a general framework of ideas or historical theories, this is the greatest paradox of all.

Richard Jones, "A. P.'s *Music*: Swansong of the Metropolitan Romance," *VQR*, 52 (1976), p. 369

"Reading novels needs almost as much talent as writing them" is a favourite saying of X. Trapnel's [a character in the sequence], and one perhaps specially appropriate to the work in which he figures. For one could hardly find a work of fiction which more clearly demonstrates what Trapnel himself calls "the heresy of naturalism" than this sequence of novels in which, for the reader, the deepest satisfaction comes less from character and incident than from the structure that supports them both: a structure so contrived that, as it flows, straggles or jerks itself along, by turns farcical and grim, sombre, tumultous, absurd, reaching out through almost infinite varieties of egotism to embrace the furthest shores of crankiness and melancholia, it seems not so much to shape as to contain the disorderly process of life itself. It is not for nothing that Nicholas Jenkins takes his first name from that specialist in rhythm and design, Nicolas Poussin, whose painting provides both the title and the model for *A Dance to the Music of Time*.

Hilary Spurling, *Invitation to the Dance: A Guide to A. P.'s "Dance to the Music of Time"* (1977), p. xi

POWYS, John Cowper

English novelist, essayist, poet, and critic, b. 8 Oct. 1872, Shirley; d. 17 June 1963, Merionethshire, Wales

P. was the oldest son of a prolific literary family. Seven children of the Reverend Charles Francis and Mary Cowper Johnson P. published books, and an eighth was a book illustrator. Two of his brothers, T. F. POWYS and Llewelyn Powys (1884–1939), also achieved substantial fame. Of Welsh descent, the Powyses have been in England since 1500.

P. grew up in vicarages in Derbyshire, Dorset, and Somerset, took his degree at Corpus Christi College, Cambridge, and became a lecturer on literature. He toured England for various university-extension series, then "transferred these recitative performances, which were more like those of an actor than a lecturer, to the new world [where I spent] thirty years of my life in American railways." Turning to full-time writing in 1929, P. lived five years in upstate New York before moving "home" to Wales.

Of his six volumes of poetry, P. named *Lucifer* (written 1905, pub. 1956) "the only poem I feel [tempted] to pray that posterity may read." P.'s nonfiction smacks of the podium. *Visions and Revisions* (1915) exhorts a general audience to read, to enjoy, to share his strong literary enthusiasms. His philosophic writings, beginning with *The Complex Vision* (1920) and the best-selling *The Meaning of Culture* (1929), present a view of life consistent with his novels.

The novels center on two convictions: In P.'s words, "the deepest thing in life is the soul's individual struggle to reach an exultant peace in relation to . . . cosmic forces." And "below all the great systems of philosophic thought [and] mystical redemption stir these ultimate personal reactions to the terrible urge of sex." In "this irrational multiverse" P.'s "imaginative sensuality" is a prime tool, together with his introspective reaching for the "memories we inherit . . . from the world's remote Past." P.'s masterpieces are *A Glastonbury Romance* (1932) and *Porius* (1951). These incomparable novels and his *Autobiography* (1934), by exploring the human psyche with a deep and reckless probity, insure P.'s literary permanence.

P.'s fiction divides into three groups that engage, successively, the present, the past, and the future: the 20th-c. novels of southwestern England that culminate in the massive "Wessex novels" of 1929–35; the historical novels reaching back into ancient Wales; and the less substantial science fantasies written after 1952, when he turned eighty.

In the first Wessex novel, *Wolf Solent* (1929), the eponymous hero stops teaching history and edits pornography for an eccentric Somerset squire. He loves "androgynous" Christie, marries "voluptuous" Gerda, and finds himself, at story's end, half-way between the pigsty and the sun. The essence of the novel, P. writes, "is the necessity of opposites."

A Glastonbury Romance is of epic proportions—in time, in bulk, and in tale-telling vitality. Communists and industrialists clash in Glastonbury, but the Somerset town is a palimpsest with living traces of King Arthur and Merlin, Joseph of Arimathea, the Druids, the Fisher Kings, and "men older than the worship of gods." The novel's heroine is the Grail, P. says, and the search is for "the copulation-cry of Yes and No," and "the Self-Birth of Psyche."

Although his historical novels are as authentic as research into dark times permits, P.'s central concern in *Owen Glendower* (1941) and *Porius* (1951) remains the individual soul's quest. Prince Porius, preparing to take over the reign of his father in North Wales one October week in A. D. 499, confronts the creeds, ethnic tenets, and primitive mysticism of a medley of forces. Only a truncated *Porius* has been published, cut by one third when publishers refused to gamble on another "eleven-hundred-pager like *Glastonbury*." Even so, the novel brilliantly shows P.'s ability to imbue high drama with finely shaded introspection, to move in a page from Porius's slaughter of fifteen men using a corpse as weapon to Porius's musings on the sanctity of gray clouds.

The *Autobiography* is, for P., "a sort of Faustian Pilgrimage of the Soul." It fully confirms a rare quality—P.'s willingness to be the fool in print, to be a "ninny." Religious mystics through the ages have shamelessly shown themselves as fools; some authors can laugh at themselves; P. dares, in the intensity of pursuing his deepest thoughts and sensations, to lay himself open to all ridicule. The "ninnyism" in his personal writings and the novels puts off many readers, but it has, as he says, "a deep and subtle irony." It is a "malicious challenge," a "protest against the shallow rationality of the hour," and, ultimately, "an arraignment of the unsympathetic First Cause" in which P. finds good and evil inextricably mixed.

In the last full-length novel, *All or Nothing* (1960), written as P. approached the age of ninety, an Arch-Druid escorts earthlings to the core of the sun and the limits of the Milky Way—and back to England. The Powysian quest continues. But the mystery—the Grail mystery—yet abides. P.'s genius is in his ability to dramatize imaginatively the pursuit of ultimate questions, to probe the very souls of his questers, and to convey the sheer urgency and excitement of the eternal quest.

FURTHER WORKS: *Odes and Other Poems* (1896); *Poems* (1899); *The War and Culture* (1914); Br., *The Menace of German Culture,* (1915); *Wood and Stone* (1915); *Confessions of Two Brothers* (1916, with Llewelyn Powys); *Wolf's Bane: Rhymes* (1916); *One Hundred Best Books* (1916); *Rodmoor* (1916); *Suspended Judgments* (1916); *Mandragora* (1917); *Samphire* (1922); *Psychoanalysis and Morality* (1923); *The Art of Happiness* (1923); *The Religion of a Sceptic* (1925); *Ducdame* (1925); *The Secret of Self Development* (1926); *The Art of Forgetting the Unpleasant* (1928); *The Owl, the Duck, and Miss Rowe! Miss Rowe!* (1930); *Debate: Is Modern Marriage a Failure?* (1930, with Bertrand Russell); *In Defence of Sensuality* (1930); *Dorothy M. Richardson* (1931); *A Philosophy of Solitude* (1933); *Weymouth Sands* (1934; Br., *Jobber Skald,* 1935); *The Art of Happiness* (1935); *Maiden Castle* (1936); *Morwyn* (1937); *The Pleasures of Literature* (1938; Br., *The Enjoyment of Literature,* 1938); *Mortal Strife* (1942); *The Art of Growing Old* (1944); *Dostoievsky* (1946); *Obstinate Cymric* (1947); *Rabelais* (1948); *The Inmates* (1952); *In Spite Of* (1953); *Atlantis* (1954); *The Brazen Head* (1956); *Up and Out* (1957; includes *The Mountains of the Moon)*; *Letters of J. C. P. to Louis Wilkinson 1935–1956,* (1958); *Homer and the Aether* (1959); *Poems: A Selection* (1964); *Letters to Nicholas Ross* (1971); *Real Wraiths* (1974); *Two & Two* (1974); *You and Me* (1975); *Letters to His Brother Llewelyn* (1975); *Letters to C. Benson Roberts* (1975); *Letters to Henry Miller* (1975); *After My Fashion* (1980)

BIBLIOGRAPHY: Marlow, L., *Welsh Ambassadors: P. Lives and Letters* (1936); Knight, G. W., *The Saturnian Quest: A Chart of the Prose Works of J. C. P.* (1964); Langridge, D., *J. C. P.: A Record of Achievement* (1966); *The P. Newsletter* (1970–); Humfrey, B., ed., *Essays on J. C. P.* (1972); Cavaliero, G., *J. C. P.: Novelist* (1973); Thomas, D., *A Bibliography of the Writings of P.* (1975); *The P. Review* (1977–); Krissdotir, M., *P. and the Magical Quest* (1980)

—R. L. BLACKMORE

POWYS, T(heodore) F(rancis)

English novelist and short-story writer, b. 20 Dec. 1875, Shirley; d. 27 Nov. 1953, Mappowder

P.'s novels, stories, and fables of rural south-western England derive from a most circumscribed life. He did not follow his older brother, the novelist John Cowper POWYS, to university, but was educated at private schools and at Dorchester Grammar School. As a young man he attempted farming in Suffolk, then returned to isolated villages in the Dorset of his childhood to begin writing. He moved farther inland twice in fifty years as his first choices grew too populous.

Depending on a small paternal subsidy, he first wrote two "meditations": *An Interpretation of Genesis* (1908) and *The Soliloquy of a Hermit* (1916). "Powys believes in monotony," P. said of himself. "Writes from 11 to 1:30. Walks nearly always the same path in the afternoon, goes by the Inn to the Hill." That hill— "Madder Hill"—looks down on the several farms and hamlets of

P.'s fiction, on rapacious farmers and their sons, naïve vicars and their volatile wives, teasing girls and the men at the Inn who talk about them, gossiping women who sometimes act as pimps, and simple-minded lovers. These rustics care little for the world beyond, and rarely receive visitor—with the signal exception of God, in various guises. P.'s theme is death, and the loves, sacred and profane, that precede it. He broods deeply on religious mystery and man's fate—with realistic and ironic bitterness in the early tales, then with a gentler irony as the novels and stories become fabulistic, allegorical. His art looks back to the Bible, John Bunyan, and Thomas HARDY, and foreshadows Dylan THOMAS's *Under Milk Wood.*

Mr. Weston's Good Wine (1927) is P.'s acknowledged masterpiece. God, in the guise of Mr. Weston, a wine merchant, comes to the hamlet of Folly Down selling two vintages: a light wine (love) and a rarer dark wine of peaceful, eternal death that he, too, hopes one day to drink. Mr. Weston does business with easy dignity and humor, but can show an author's defensive pride whenever someone at the inn (which he prefers to the church) quotes from the Bible.

P.'s *Fables* (1929) are dialogues, trenchant and cryptic commentaries on profound matters by, among others, a stone, a crumb, a spittoon, a coat, a crow, a corpse, and a flea. Here, as in the novels, the humor is subtle and organic—a true yield of the topics.

P.'s last novel, *Unclay* (1931), gathers several people from the earlier novels and stories as John Death arrives, unable, at first, to carry out his duties because he has lost his list of those due to die— to be "unclayed."

Fable and allegory—ancient traditions that are patently false (a crow does not speak with courtly diction)—serve P. better than artful ambiguity. His tales are symbolically rich, but his symbols, like his humor and irony, grow naturally from his people and their actions. P.'s art is at once dark and innocent. Life in the cottages under Madder Hill is harsh; John Death is only briefly deterred from his duty. It is P.'s genius to cast a cool eye on these rural folk, and to trace their courses in unvarnished prose with deep, unsentimental compassion.

FURTHER WORKS: *The Left Leg* (1923); *Black Bryony* (1923); *Mark Only* (1924); *Mr. Tasker's Gods* (1925); *Mockery Gap* (1925); *A Stubborn Tree* (1926); *Innocent Birds* (1926); *Feed My Swine* (1926); *A Strong Girl, and The Bride* (1926); *What Lack I Yet?* (1927); *The Rival Pastors* (1927); *The House with the Echo* (1928); *The Dew Pond* (1928); *Christ in the Cupboard* (1930); *The Key of the Field* (1930); *Kindness in a Corner* (1930); *The White Paternoster* (1930); *Uriah on the Hill* (1930); *Uncle Dottery* (1930); *The Only Penitent* (1931); *When Thou Wast Naked* (1931); *The Tithe Barn and The Dove and The Eagle* (1932); *The Two Thieves* (1932); *Captain Patch* (1935); *Make Thyself Many* (1935); *Goat Green* (1936); *Bottle's Path* (1936); *God's Eyes A-Twinkle* (1947); *Rosie Plum* (1966)

BIBLIOGRAPHY: Marlow, L., *Welsh Ambassadors: P. Lives and Letters* (1936); Coombes, H., *T. F. P.* (1960); Churchill, R., *The P. Brothers* (1962); Sewell, B., ed., *Theodore: Essays on T. F. P.* (1964); Hopkins, K., *The P. Brothers: A Biographical Appreciation* (1967); Riley, P., *A Bibliography of T. F. P.* (1967); Cavaliero, G., *The Rural Tradition in the English Novel 1900–1939* (1977): 173—95; Humfrey, B., ed., *Recollections of the P. Brothers* (1980)

—R. L. BLACKMORE

PRAMOEDYA Ananta Toer

Indonesian short-story writer, novelist, essayist, and critic, b. 6 Feb. 1925, Blora, Java

The works of P., generally recognized as the master prose writer of his country, have fundamentally been shaped by his painful experiences under Dutch colonialism, Japan's occupation of Indonesia during World War II, the subsequent armed revolutionary struggle against the returning Dutch, and the many disappointments of postindependence society. The son of an embittered nationalist schoolteacher who ruined the family by obsessive gambling, P. never completed high school. As an adolescent during the Japanese occupation he worked as a stenographer; and when the revolution broke out, he joined the Indonesian armed forces. Between 1950 and 1958 he published a stream of fine novels, novellas, and short stories. After 1958 he steadily moved politically to the left and largely abandoned fiction for critical essays and historical studies.

In the wake of the October 1, 1965, coup, P. was imprisoned without trial by the ascendant military regime and was not freed until the end of 1979. In 1973 he was given access to a typewriter and began writing down a series of historical novels originally narrated orally to his fellow prisoners. In 1980 *Bumi manusia* (*This Earth of Mankind*, 1982) and *Anak semua bangsa* (child of all nations), the first two volumes of a tetralogy on the dawn of Indonesia's struggle against colonial capitalism, were published to great critical and popular acclaim. The military authorities responded to this success by banning both books and ordering thousands of copies seized and publicly burned. Typescripts of the last two volumes, *Jejak langkah* (steps forward) and *Rumah kaca* (house of glass) have been smuggled out of the country and are scheduled for publication abroad.

Initially, P.'s fame rested on three novels composed largely while he was imprisoned by the returning Dutch colonial government after the war. *Perburuan* (1950; *The Fugitive*, 1975) is a haunting description of the homeward flight of a military rebel against the Japanese, written in terms deliberately evocative of traditional Javanese legend. *Keluarga gerilya* (1950; guerrilla family), his best-known novel, depicts the agonizing destruction of a Javanese family during the national revolution. The father, a soldier in the colonial army, is killed by his own sons, who have joined the revolutionaries. Two of the sons die in battle, while the eldest is executed by the Dutch and their mother goes mad with grief. *Mereka yang dilumpuhkan* (1951; the paralyzed) depicts the strange assortment of P.'s fellow prisoners. While all three texts show P.'s narrative virtuosity, they are still couched in a semirealist style which he later abandoned for a more surrealistic one. Their prestige derived partly from their direct portrayal of grand historical themes—war and revolution—and partly on the idea, derived from Western critics of that era, that the novel was the test and confirmation of any great writer's achievement.

The passage of time, however, has shown that P.'s greatness lies, like that of another modern Asian master, the Chinese Lu HSÜN, in his short stories. Most of the tales in *Subuh* (1950: dawn) and *Percikan revolusi* (1950; sparks of revolution) are set during the revolution. *Cerita dari Blora* (1952; tales of Blora) deals with provincial Javanese society in the late colonial period, as well as with the Japanese occupation and the revolution. *Cerita dari Jakarta* (1957; tales of Djakarta) depicts an extraordinary range of postrevolutionary catastrophes in Indonesia's capital. While the key figures in these tales—maimed veterans, child-brides, failed writers, tubercular maids, careerist politicians, deracinated nouveaux riches, and so forth—are recognizable products of the breakdown of feudal Javanese society and of Indonesia's tumultuous modern political history, the peculiar power of the tales derives not from "realism," but from P.'s mature style.

Characteristic of this style is the infusion of the Indonesian language with eerily transformed images from classical Javanese culture and the use of Indonesian to describe the lower depths of Javanese-speaking communities. A polylingual living in a polylingual society, P. essentially writes "between languages," playing languages and cultures off against one another. It is characteristic that some of his best later stories are really about the marginality of the writer in Indonesian society and the problematic nature of writing itself.

The two novels published after P.'s fourteen-year imprisonment differ markedly from his earlier work. They are vast canvases of all strata of colonial society at the turn of the century. But this social and cultural complexity is conveyed in a plain, fast-paced narrative style in striking contrast to the polyphonic allusiveness of his great short stories. P. has said that he deliberately adopted some of the conventions of contemporary popular literature in order to reach the younger generation of Indonesian readers.

FURTHER WORKS: *Kranji dan Bekasi jatuh* (1947); *Bukan pasar malam* (1951; *It's Not an All Night Fair*, 1973); *Gulat di Jakarta* (1953); *Korupsi* (1954); *Midah—simanis bergigi emas* (1954); *Ditepi Kali Bekasi* (1957); *Suatu peristiwa di Banten Selatan* (1958); *Hoa Kiau di Indonesia* (1960); *Panggil aku Kartini saja* (1962). FURTHER WORKS IN ENGLISH: *A Heap of Ashes* (1975)

BIBLIOGRAPHY: Johns, A. H., "P. A. T.—The Writer as Outsider: An Indonesian Example," *Meanjin*, 22 (1963): 354–63; Johns, A. J., "Genesis of a Modern Indonesian Literature," in McVey, R., ed., *Indonesia* (1963): 410–37; Teeuw, A., "Silence at Life's Noon," *Papers of the Michigan Academy of Sciences, Arts and Letters*, 49 (1964): 245–50; Teeuw, A., *Modern Indonesian Literature* (1967): 163–80; Siegel, J., "P.'s 'Things Vanished,' with a Commentary," *Glyph*, 1 (1977): 67–100

—BENEDICT R. O'G. ANDERSON

PRATOLINI, Vasco

Italian novelist, short-story writer, and essayist, b. 19 Oct. 1913, Florence; d. 12 Jan. 1991, Rome

From a working-class background and essentially an autodidact, P. held various jobs before becoming a professional writer. Under the influence of the confusion and widespread disillusionment that affected every segment of Italian society after World War I, the young P. embraced Fascism, contributing articles to *Il Bargello*, a Fascist periodical. Although he evinces considerable sympathy for the masses even in his fiction written in the 1930s he does not reveal any inner struggle for their advancement.

By the beginning of World War II P. had become strongly anti-Fascist, and in 1943 he joined the Resistance, quickly emerging as one of its leaders. His experience with the Resistance, coupled with the political freedom in Italy during the postwar years of reconstruction, helped him to shake off spiritual isolation and to achieve a new perspective. He advanced beyond the restricted dimensions of the autobiographical short story and delicate prose poem, giving a predominantly social character to his works from 1943 to 1950. Interweaving social and personal relationships with larger, historical events in *Il quartiere* (1944; *The Naked Streets*, 1952) and *Cronache di poveri amanti* (1947; *A Tale of Poor Lovers*, 1949), as well as in his minor works of this period, P. takes the reader into his native working-class quarters of Florence to show in concrete terms that life under the Mussolini dictatorship—while not as bad as life under Hitler—was full of suffering and evil. Yet because of the author's experience in the Resistance, he is able to convey a strong confidence in man's capacity to change and to shape his own destiny.

The characters of *Il quartiere* and *Cronache di poveri amanti* evidence a strong sense of love and are motivated by principles of equality and the feeling of fellowship. They stand together not simply because they have learned about the value of solidarity from reading the *Communist Manifesto* but because the very condition of their lives forces them to close ranks behind barricades. Everything in these works—from the political and social attitudes to the profound sense of human solidarity—ultimately forms part of the natural rhythm and flow of life, which is itself a manifestation of things simple and eternal.

In 1950 P. began work on an ambitious trilogy entitled *Una storia italiana* (1955–66; an Italian story) whose aim was to represent various aspects of Italian life from 1879 to 1945. In it he sought to create social realism embedded in historically verifiable facts. *Metello* (1955; *Metello*, 1968), the first and the finest of the three parts, describes the awakening of class consciousness among the Italian proletariat at the end of the 19th c. As he does in the following two parts, *Lo scialo* (1960; the waste) and *Allegoria e derisione* (1966; allegory and derision), P., who draws many of his characters, episodes, and background material from real life, aims not at a mere reproduction of reality but at the creative and symbolic component underlying all literary realism.

P.'s commitment to the principles of realism and to political and moral dedication is also evident in *La costanza della ragione* (1963; *Bruno Santini*, 1964), the story of a worker set against the background of Italian society during the period from 1941 to 1960. As in all his major works, solidarity and interdependence in the struggle against exploitation are dominant themes. It is, indeed, primarily his moral and political commitment and the psychological insight with which he portrays his characters that distinguish P.'s work.

FURTHER WORKS: *Il tappeto verde* (1941); *Via de' Magazzini* (1942); *Le amiche* (1943); *Cronaca familiare* (1947; *Two Brothers*, 1962); *Mestiere da vagabondo* (1947); *Un eroe del nostro tempo* (1949; *A Hero of Our Time*, 1951); *Le ragazze di San Frediano* (1952; *The Girls of San Frediano*, 1954); *Diario sentimentale* (1956); *La costanza della ragione* (1963; *Bruno Santini*, 1964)

BIBLIOGRAPHY: Pacifici, S., *A Guide to Contemporary Italian Literature* (1962): 57–86; Rosengarten, F., *V. P.: The Development of a Social Novelist* (1965); Rosengarten, F., "The Italian Resistance Novel (1945–1962)," in Pacifici, S., ed., *From Verismo to Experimentalism: Essays on the Modern Italian Novel* (1969): 212–38; Kozma, J. M., "Metaphor in P.'s Novels: *Il quartiere* and *Cronache di poveri amanti*," *RomN*, 20 (1980): 298–303

—MARIO B. MIGNONE

PRATT, E(dwin) J(ohn)

Canadian poet (writing in English), b. 4 Feb. 1882, Western Bay, Newfoundland; d. 26 April 1964, Toronto, Ont.

After working with his father as a teacher and Methodist minister in the small fishing communities of Newfoundland, P. went to the University of Toronto, where he earned a Ph.D. in theology in 1917. Because of a crisis in his religious belief, he did not resume the ministry but joined the English Department at Toronto's Victoria College, where he was a much-loved teacher, poet, and raconteur until his retirement in 1953.

The central metaphor in P.'s work is evolution. He views wind, water, and rock as the sources of existence but recognizes that they can be equally destructive to life. He is particularly fascinated with primordial forms of life, with nature "red in tooth and claw," as represented by sharks, vultures, and wolves. But at the same time the poet marvels at the evolutionary process that produced man, with his fine emotions and intelligence, and above all Christ, who, for P., represents the highest point attained by evolution thus far. Man is torn between his primitive instincts to kill and the Christian ideal of compassion and self-sacrifice.

Although P. is best known for his long narrative poems on epic subjects, his evolutionary themes are central to his lyric poetry as well. His shorter poems, moreover, are often more appealing to a modern audience. In "The Shark," in *Newfoundland Verse* (1923), P. creates a symbol of something terrifying and malignant in nature, a creature more frightening than a vulture or wolf because its blood is cold. In "The Highway," in *Many Moods* (1932), P. asks whether the point of history and evolution has not been missed when man put Christ to death, but in "The Truant," in *Still Life, and Other Verse* (1943), he comes to man's defense when he sees him pitted against an amoral, mechanistic principle in the universe. Man, he contends, has frequently erred, yet evolution has created in him an ethical impulse that raises him above his savage origins. But again in his finest lyric, "Come Away, Death" (also in *Still Life*), a reflection on the bombing of Britain, he describes the possibility of man being thrown back to a state of savagery through the holocaust of war.

In his epic narratives P. deals with specific phases of the evolutionary process. In "The Great Feud" (1926), which takes place just before the Ice Age and the emergence of early man, there is a great battle between land and sea creatures over territorial rights to the shoreline. In *The Titanic* (1935) man has evolved to a point of almost complete technical mastery over his environment, but the iceberg that sinks the ship reveals that man is still vulnerable, betrayed not only by his mechanical inventions but also by his pride. P.'s finest narrative, *Brébeuf and His Brethren* (1940), is the story of the 17th-c. Jesuit mission to the Indians of New France, and in the martyrdom of Father Brébeuf P. presents the conflict between civilized man and savagery. In all his narratives he focuses on man's potential for greatness through acts of courage and compassion. His last poem was *Towards the Last Spike* (1952), which records man's struggle to build a transcontinental railway in

Canada. In this poem the enemy is the immense and formidable geography of Canada.

P. is virtually unknown outside of Canada. Technically he is an old-fashioned poet who worked outside the mainstream of modernism. Nonetheless he is a highly original, myth-making poet who wrote of the heroic phases in Canada's history with a vision of life's intractable hardness.

FURTHER WORKS: *The Witches' Brew* (1925); *Titans* (1926); *The Iron Door* (1927); *The Roosevelt and the Antinoe* (1930); *The Fable of the Goats, and Other Poems* (1937); *Dunkirk* (1941); *Collected Poems* (1944); *Behind the Log* (1947); *The Collected Poems of E. J. P.* (1958); *The Complete Poems of E. J. P.* (1989)

BIBLIOGRAPHY: Frye, N., Introduction to *The Collected Poems of E. J. P.* (1958): xiii–xxviii; Pacey, D., *Ten Canadian Poets* (1958): 165–93; Pitt, D. G., *E. J. P.* (1969); Wilson, M., *E. J. P.* (1969); Djwa, S., *E. J. P.: The Evolutionary Vision* (1974); ; Collins, R. G., *E. J. P.* (1988)

—DAVID STOUCK

PREDA, Marin

Romanian novelist, short-story writer, and essayist, b. 5 Aug. 1922, Siliştea-Gumeşti; d. 16 May 1980, Mogoşoaia

P. was born into a peasant family. He graduated from a junior college in 1941 and worked as a proofreader and editor for journals such as *Timpul* and *România liberă*. He became the editor-in-chief of the monthly *Viaţa românească* in 1957 and was director of the publishing house Carted Românească, until his death. He also held high positions in the Romanian Writers' Union. He is believed by some to have committed suicide.

P.'s talent was revealed in short stories written before 1944 as well as in his ability to maintain realistic integrity even in texts published during the repressive 1950s. His stature came to be recognized, however, in the cycle begun with *Moromeţii* (2 vols., 1955, 1967; first vol. tr. as *The Morometes*, 1957) and continued notably in *Marele singuratic* (1972; the lone wolf), although characters and situations linked to the cycle can be met in virtually all his other books. It is the saga of a peasant family from the Danubian plain; P. emphasizes their cunning and resilience in the face of changing historical circumstances. P. is an objective and unsentimental narrator who does not hide the instinctual brutality and cupidity of his characters; but he also shows how rough, redneck men react with sly wisdom and wide-awake irony to the decay of small holdings before World War II and to the simplistic cruelty of farm collectivization after it. P. pays particular attention to the complicated psychology of intellectuals who have come from and grown away from the village community, both in his novels and in the collections of essays *Imposibila întoarcere* (1971; the impossible return) and in his memoirs, *Viaţa ca o pradă* (1977; my life as a prey), which reveal some of the autobiographical sources of his works.

Eventually P. turned from peasant life to political problems. *Intrusul* (1968; the intruder) analyzes the defeat of an idealistic young worker who cannot adapt to the tough and pitiless rhythms of life in a new industrial urban township he had enthusiastically helped build. *Delirul* (1975; the delirium) describes the beginning

of World War II and the accompanying disorders in Romania through the eyes of an offspring of the Moromete clan. The novel stirred political uneasiness because of its apparent sympathy for the military dictator who crushed the fascist uprising of 1940; subsequent editions appeared with many censored passages. P.'s last novel, *Cel mai iubit dintre pămînteni* (3 vols., 1980; the most beloved among earthlings), is a sweeping and scathing criticism of Romania's present-day society as a whole; it appeared two months before P.'s death and was soon suppressed.

FURTHER WORKS: *Întîlnirea din pămînturi* (1948); *Ana Roşculeţ* (1949); *Desfăşurarea* (1952); *Ferestre întunecate* (1956); *Risipitorii* (1962; rev. ed., 1972); *Friguri* (1963); *Martin Bormann* (1966)

BIBLIOGRAPHY: Iorgulescu, M., "A New Dimension in M. P.'s Literary Craftsmanship," *RoR*, 17, 4 (1972): 76–78; Nemoianu, V., on *Imposibila întoarcere, BA*, 46 (1972), 656; Crohmălniceanu, O. S., "M. P. et ses *Moromeţii*," *CREL*, 3 (1976): 29–38; Nemoianu, V., "The Road to Bucharest," *TLS* (2 Apr. 1976): 402; Nemoianu, V., "The Innocent Abroad," *TLS* (19 Feb. 1982): 199

—VIRGIL NEMOIANU

PREMCHAND

(pseud. of Dhanpat Rai Srivastav) Indian short-story writer and novelist (writing in Urdu and Hindi), b. 1 July 1880, Lahmi; d. 8 Oct. 1936, Benares

P. was born in a town near Benares into a poor family of *Kayasthas*, or scribes, who in this case served as village accountants. P. received his early education in Urdu and Persian, and also studied English. In 1899 he became a schoolteacher, a profession he pursued for over twenty years. In 1908 he published his first volume of Urdu short stories, *Soz-e vatan* (passion for the fatherland) under the pen name Navab Rai. Because of the unabashed patriotism of these pieces, the British colonial authorities proscribed the book and ordered the unsold copies burned. The author then took the name P. and continued to write.

By 1915 he started to switch from writing in Urdu to Hindi; they are essentially the same language, sharing the same grammar and vocabulary, but written in different scripts and drawing their intellectual vocabulary, imagery, and sensibility from different literary traditions: Urdu borrows from the Persian-Arabic tradition, Hindi from the Sanskrit. As a result of this change, P.'s reading audience increased appreciably, although he continued to have his works published in Urdu versions as well.

In 1921 P. resigned his teaching position with the civil service and joined Mahatma Gandhi's nonviolent Non-Cooperation Movement, which sought to oust the British from India. P.'s commitment to Gandhian ideology is marked in a number of his novels. He also edited two literary journals, neither of which was financially successful, and wrote a number of screenplays for film companies in Bombay. Toward the end of his life P. became sympathetic to Marxism, looking to it as a possible means of solving India's myriad ills. In 1936, just a few months before his death, he served as president of the first meeting of the Marxist-oriented All India Progressive Writers' Association, which, with the help of P.'s immense literary prestige, later grew into one of the most powerful forces in nearly every major literature of India.

P. wrote about a dozen novels; the first major one was *Premashram* (1922; love retreat). The last one, *Godan* (1936; *Godan*, 1957; also tr. as *The Gift of a Cow*, 1968), is considered his best. It is notable for its evocation of the rural world of the peasant Hori, his wife Dhaniya, and their children. Here the overwhelming vicissitudes that plague the poor of India are carefully chronicled in microcosm and delineated to their final moment of tragedy. In addition, he published over three hundred short stories, collected in eight volumes as *Manasarovar* (1962; holy lake), as well as criticism, essays, plays, and translations and adaptations from Indian and European literatures.

P. is best known for his short stories, where the influence of Western writers, notably Dickens, Tolstoy, and Maupassant, is readily discernible. P. is credited in both Urdu and Hindi literatures for having single-handedly shaped the short story into its modern form. Early pieces deal with patriotic and supernatural themes; later ones depict a wide variety of characters and types from all quarters of Indian society. The best stories concentrate on village life and characters, portraying them with realism, insight, and compassion. "Mukhti marg" (1924; "The Road to Salvation," 1969), for example, depicts the bitter feud between the well-to-do farmer Jhingur and the boastful shepherd Buddhu, which ends only when each is reduced to poverty. P.'s most famous, and last, short story is "Kafan" (1936; "The Shroud," 1969), in which the untouchable Ghisu and his son Madhav witness the death of the latter's wife in childbirth. The two men then go out and beg for money with which to purchase wood for her funeral pyre and a shroud. In a fit of venality they buy liquor instead of the shroud and drink themselves into a stupor.

In some instances, especially in the novels, P. exhibits an unconvincing streak of idealism whereby unsympathetic characters have an unexplainable "change of heart" and convert to goodness. At their best, however, P.'s stories are well wrought, succinct tours de force; they are remarkable in the power of their effect. For this reason P. is considered the major writer of fiction in both Urdu and Hindi during the first half of this century.

FURTHER WORKS: *Asrar-e mabid* (1903); *Kishna* (1907); *Prema* (1907); *Ruthi rani* (1907); *Jalva-e isar* (1912); *Mahatma shaikh sadi* (1918); *Seva sadan* (1918); *Sangram: Ek samajik natak* (1923); *Karbala* (1924); *Rangabhumi* (1925); *Kayakalp* (1926); *Nirmala* (1926); *Pratigya* (1927); *Ba kamalon ke darshan* (1928); *Ghaban* (1931); *Karmabhumi* (1932); *Durga das* (1938); *Ram carca* (1941); *Mangal sutra va anya racnayen* (1948); *Citthi patri* (1962); *Gupt dhan* (1962); *Vividh prasang* (1962); *Sahitya ka uddeshya* (1967); *Kuc vicar* (1973). FURTHER WORKS IN ENGLISH: *Short Stories of P.* (1946); *A Handful of Wheat and Other Stories* (1955); *The Secret of Culture and Other Stories* (1960); *The Chess-Players and Other Stories* (1967); *The World of P.* (1969); *The Shroud and Twenty Other Stories by P.* (1972); *Twenty-Four Stories* (1980)

BIBLIOGRAPHY: Coppola, C., "A Bibliography of English Sources for the Study of P.," *Mahfil*, 1, 2 (1963): 21–24; Gopal, M., *Munshi P.: A Literary Biography* (1964); Gupta, P., *P.* (1968); Swan, R., *Munshi P. of Lahmi Village* (1969); Sharma, G., *Munshi P.* (1978); Thomas, C., *L'ashram de l'amour: Le gandhisme et l'imaginaire* (1979); Naravane, V. S., *P.: His Life and Work* (1980)

—CARLO COPPOLA

PRERADOVIĆ, Paula von

Austrian poet and novelist, b. 12 Oct. 1887, Vienna; d. 25 May 1951, Vienna

Granddaughter of the Austro-Croatian officer and poet Petar von Preradović (1818–1872), P. spent, most of her childhood in Pola (now in Yugoslavia), to which she returned after graduating from the Institute of the English Ladies, a convent school in Sankt Pölten. In 1914 she went to Vienna, where, in 1916, she married Ernest Molden (1886–1953), the future publisher of the *Neue Freie Presse*, the most prestigious Vienna daily. Their home soon became an important center of Viennese intellectual life, with P. also taking a strong, active interest in the Catholic renewal movement. In 1938, after the Nazi annexation of Austria, a time of tribulation began for the entire family. Because of their ties to the resistance movement, their lives were in constant danger. After the war, as the author of the Second Republic's national anthem, P. gave voice to the strongly emerging new national consciousness.

In her early poetry, *Südlicher Sommer* (1929; southerly summer) and *Dalmatinische Sonette* (1933; Dalmatian sonnets), P. celebrates the beloved Adriatic landscape of her lost ancestral homeland. The poems, whose melodious rhythms infuse them with a quality akin to folk songs, display P.'s instinctive flair for language and tonal color. Their expressive power, cultivated diction, and intensity of feeling imbue them with an unmistakably distinctive tone.

In *Lob Gottes im Gebirge* (1936; praise of God in the mountains), P.'s poetic discovery of her adopted "home without sea" (that is, what was left of Austria after World War I), she pays homage to the awe-inspiring mountainscape of her second home. The essentially new aspect, however, is the religious experience that pervades these poems, a Christian faith extolling nature's beauty and majesty as a revelation of its creator. The lighter, folksonglike character of her earlier poetry gives way, in keeping with the new, more reflective tone, to still melodious but more austere and contemplative lyrics.

From this point on, her work became deeply imbued with a firmly rooted religiousness. Her unshakable faith, the source of both her poetic inspiration and moral fortitude, is exemplarily expressed in *Ritter, Tod und Teufel* (1946; knight, death, and the devil), eight sonnets inspired by Albrecht Dürer's famous engraving. The true Christian, God's "pure knight," dauntlessly follows the right path, fearing neither death nor devil.

Christian motives and impulses also pervade her narrative work, especially the masterful novellas *Königslegende* (1950; legend of a king) and *Die Versuchung des Columba* (1951; Columba's temptation). Savatz, the Croatian king of *Königslegende*, whose abrupt fall from power deprives him of all he held dear, is seen not so much as a historical figure of the 11th c. but rather as a timeless poetic image of a fate experienced by many in those postwar years: the plight of the uprooted man driven from home and country. Only after bitterly quarreling with his fate does Savatz finally become reconciled to his new, humble life in exile. Accepting the inscrutable ways of the Lord—"Thy will be done"—he finds strength, comfort, and a new meaning in his existence.

In *Die Versuchung des Columba* P. dwells largely on the human side of the man who was to become the great Irish saint. Homesick and fearful of his missionary calling, he longs for the "human warmth of a life without mission." The encounter with Maurinn, to whom he was betrothed in his youth and who comes to claim him as her husband, precipitates the climactic struggle between the spirit and the flesh from which the apostle of the Picts emerges victoriously metamorphosed from man into saint. The spiritual calling proves stronger than any human ties.

P.'s poetic message is closely connected with her personal fate, making her work true "fragments of a great confession" in the Goethean sense—subjective experiences transformed into objective works of art. Although no formal innovator—song, romance, and sonnet were her preferred lyrical forms—she wrote poems that are powerfully original and display a masterful craftsmanship. The language, rich in striking imagery, is refined and melodious; some of her poems have been set to music.

FURTHER WORKS: *Pave und Pero* (1940); *Gesammelte Gedichte* (3 vols., 1951–1952); *P. v. P.: Porträt einer Dichterin* (1955); *Gesammelte Werke* (1967)

BIBLIOGRAPHY: Schoolfield, G. C., "P. v. P.—An Introduction," *GL&L*, n. s., 7, 4 (1954): 285–92; Molden, E., "Skizzen zu einem Porträt," in Molden, E., ed., *P. v. P.: Porträt einer Dichterin* (1955): 9–82; Csokor, F. T., "P. v. P.," in *Neue österreichische Biographie* (1960), Vol. XIV: 194–97; Vogelsang, H., "P. v. P.: Die Dichterin der Ehrfurcht, der Demut und des Glaubens," *ÖGL*, 10 (1965): 198–206

—FRIEDHELM RICKERT

PREVELAKIS, Pandelis

Greek poet, novelist, dramatist, and art historian, b. 18 Feb. 1909, Rethymnon, Crete; d. 15 Mar. 1986, Athens

After graduating from the University of Athens, P. studied at the University of Paris. Receiving a doctorate from the University of Thessaloniki in 1933 for his work on his illustrious fellow-Cretan Dominikos Theotokopoulos (El Greco), he served for four years as Director of Fine Arts of the Greek Ministry of Education and for thirty-five years as a professor of art history at the Higher School of Fine Arts in Athens. The recipient of several Greek and foreign awards, including the Prize of Excellence in Letters of the Academy of Athens, he was elected a member of that Academy in 1978.

The descendant of distinguished educators, clergymen, fighters, and martyrs in the long battle for Crete's liberation from Ottoman rule, P. drew from his ancestry and from his country's heroic tradition a high sense of responsibility, dignity, and pride, as well as inspiration for most of his literary work. The pupil, lifelong close friend, and collaborator of his fellow-Cretan Nikos KAZANTZAKIS, in his *O piitis ke to piima tis "Odhyssias"* (1958; *Nikos Kazantzakis and His "Odyssey,"* 1961), an exemplary critical study of his master's personality and work, P. expressed, along with his admiration, his reservations about Kazantzakis's yielding to modern Western skepticism, Nietzschean philosophy, and nihilism at the expense of his Greek and Cretan cultural heritage. To that heritage he himself has remained faithful in his creative work. He has also been unswervingly committed to the poetic beauty of demotic Greek, enriched in his masterful work by use of the Cretan idiom.

P.'s first book of verse, *Stratiotes* (1928; soldiers), a "short epic," was inspired by the tragic state of the refugees of the Greek

national disaster in Asia Minor in 1922. In the pure lyricism of his next two collections, *I yimni piisi* (1939; naked poetry) and *I pio yimni piisi* (more than naked poetry), P., as an idealized poet-lover, addresses his beloved, the complex personification of his fatherland, of poetry, of human virtue, and of natural and spiritual beauty, in the hope of a mutual transcendence, of a liberating rescue from the darkness of the ominous times—the eve of World War II.

P.'s first prose work, *To hroniko mias politias* (1930; *The Tale of a Town*, 1976), still the most popular of his works, is an affectionate, idealized, and poetic narrative about his native Rethymnon. It depicts the community when it still functioned like an industrious and harmonious beehive, shortly before that way of life succumbed to the disruptive and alienating influence of the West, which came as a result of Crete's liberation from Ottoman rule.

In order to counteract the despair of the years of war and German occupation, P. turned to studying and imaginatively chronicling the heroism of Crete's battle for freedom, more particularly the major uprising of 1866–69 that culminated in the sacrificial resistance at the Arkadhi monastery. Two "myth-histories," as he called them, *Pandermi Kriti* (1945; all-desolate Crete) and the trilogy *O Kritikos* (1948–50; *The Cretan*, 1991), as well as the later play *To ifestio* (1962; the volcano), all centered around this episode. *O Kritikos*, which blends real figures and events with imaginary ones, much in the manner of Tolstoy's *War and Peace*, besides giving expression to the Cretan spirit, traces the developments leading to the island's liberation from the Turks. Ironically enough, that final victory brought the disruption of the social harmony and the unity of spirit of the Cretan people. The resulting political conflicts and clashes of ideologies were symptomatic of what P. called the "disease of the century": man enters a "tragic stage" as an isolated, alienated individual, deprived of social and moral directives, and must face difficult choices alone.

"The disease of the century" was the theme of a trilogy of plays: *O thanatos tou Medhikou* (1939; the death of the Medici)—later revised as *To iero sfaghio* (1952; *The Last Tournament*, 1969)—*Lazaros* (1954; Lazarus), and *Ta heria tou zontanou Theou* (1955; the hands of the living God). It was followed by a novelistic trilogy, a *Bildungsroman* whose motif P. called "the paths of creation," consisting of *O ilios tou thanatou* (1959; *The Sun of Death*, 1964), *I kefali tis Medhousas* (1963; the head of Medusa), and *O artos ton angelon* (1963; the bread of the angels). Here P. used an autobiographical first-person narrator in order to give an imaginative yet true account of the three stages of his intellectual development. In the first volume the narrator, orphaned early in life, is nurtured by the spirit of his native soil, where the reality of death is omnipresent. In the second volume he is alienated by the impact of Western skepticism. In his despair he attempts a return to his roots in the last volume, in order to find himself again, and also possibly to rescue the traditions of his people and enlighten them about the value of the old ways. The result of his quest, however, is frustration and failure: the protagonist reaches the spiritual impasse of modern man.

A romance of love and heroism, *Erotokritos* (a name meaning "the one tested and judged by love") by Vitzentzos Kornaros, the poetic masterpiece of the 17th-c. Cretan literary renascence; the ethics and lore of Byzantine Christianity; Cretan history; and P.'s personal experience all served as the mythical and spiritual foundations and framework for a lyrical, allegorical epic, *O neos Erotokritos* (1973; rev. ed., 1978; the new Erotokritos), which was to integrate and crown P.'s oeuvre by endowing his intellectual enterprise with the power of mythic universality. It is a highly complex work of great poetic beauty, moving in the realm of the spirit where suffering and death are accepted for their promise of transcendence and because of the possibility of resurrection: beauty, virtue, and love are transformed, through the tree of life, into freedom, man's supreme and eternal good, accomplishment, and reward.

FURTHER WORKS: *Dominikos Theotokopoulos* (1930); *Dhokimio yenikis isaghoyis stin istoria tis tehnis* (1934); *O Greco sti Romi* (1941); *Tetrakosia ghrammata tou Kazantzaki ston P.* (1965); *O angelos sto pighadhi* (1970; *The Angel in the Well*, 1974); *To heri tou skotomenou* (1971; *The Hand of the Slain*, 1974); *Mousafireï sto Stepantsikovo* (1972); *I antistrofi metrisi* (1974); *Dhio Kritika dhramata* (1974); *Arhea themata stin Italiki zoghraphiki tis Anayiennisis* (1975); *Mnimosino stous iroes ke tous martires tou meghalou sikomou tou 66* (1976); *To Rethemnos os ifos* (1977; *Rethymno as a Style of Life*, 1981); *O piitis Yiannis Ritsos* (1981); *Loghodhosia kritikou singhrafea stous sinpatriotes tou* (1981); *Monaxia* (1981); *Angelos Sikelianos* (1984); *Dihtes poreias* (1985). FURTHER WORKS IN ENGLISH: *The Cretan* (1991)

BIBLIOGRAPHY: Chamson, A., "P. et la Crête," *Mercure de France* (April 1959): 577–88; Laourdas, B., "Introduction to P. P.," *Odyssey Review* (June 1962): 148–55; Coavoux, P., "Réflexions sur *La chronique d'une cité*" *BalSt*, 9 (1968): 429–50; "P. P. Talks to Peter Mackridge: An Interview," *Omphalos 1*, 1 (1972): 34–39; Decavalles, A., "P. P.: An Introduction," *The Charioteer*: 16–17 (1974–1975): 10–40; Decavalles, A., *P. P. and the Value of a Heritage* (1981)

—ANDONIS DECAVALLES

PRÉVERT, Jacques

French poet and screenwriter, b. 4 Feb. 1900, Neuilly-sur-Seine; d. 12 April 1977, Paris

P.'s father came from Brittany, his mother from the Auvergne. At fifteen he left school and tried various occupations. At twenty he did his military service, first in Lorraine, then in Turkey with the French occupation forces. In 1925 he was introduced by Raymond QUENEAU to the group of French SURREALISTS, including Louis ARAGON, André BRETON, Robert DESNOS, and Michel LEIRIS. P.'s first published texts appeared in *Commerce*, a surrealist monthly. Starting in 1930 he went to work with a theatrical group, writing playlets in which he also performed. In 1933 the group, called October, went to Moscow, and one of P.'s playlets, *La bataille de Fontenoy* (the battle of Fontenoy) was premiered in an international workers' theater Olympiad. Besides film scripts, he also wrote songs. In 1948, while at the offices of the French national radio, P. fell out of a second-floor window onto the pavement and remained in a coma for several weeks. He spent months convalescing at Saint-Paul-de-Vence, where he was to stay, with his family, until 1955, when he moved back to Paris. He had a number of collages exhibited at the Galerie Maeght in 1957.

Surrealism had influenced the young P. but he soon broke away from its formulas to establish his own style. He did use some

surrealist devices over the years, without, however, observing the nonpolitical stance of most surrealists. P.'s brand of surrealism, or what survived of it, strongly resembles the paintings of René Magritte: in an airy yet concrete way he thumbs his nose at society and defies logic and the laws of physics.

In his seemingly artless yet moving descriptions, P. communicates the immediacy of man's experience of everyday life. A radical anarchist, acutely critical of society and passionately opposed to authority and coercion, P. remained aloof from party politics even though he often espoused the causes of antimilitarism, anticlericalism, and social justice.

When *Paroles* (1946; *Paroles*, 1978) appeared, it was an immediate popular success. While academic critics remained indifferent or hostile toward much of P.'s writing, the initial success of *Paroles* was confirmed through dozens of subsequent editions, and P. is still the best known and most widely read poet in France. Although P.'s poems are usually a mating of laughter and tears, a few of them are indeed tragic. His humor, which is both subtle and ferocious, is at all times put at the service of serious social and human ideals. His endeavor to use laughter to combat many social and political evils as well as the absurd and degrading frailties man is heir to in such abundance may well stem from a desire to free himself of anguish.

P. scrupulously abides by the literal meaning of words, but he makes those words bear a meticulous responsibility. In these days when vagueness is rampant, this is an especially admirable quality. Like Christian MORGENSTERN he is alert to the absurdity of pompous language, and his merciless precision effectively underscores the insincerity of much that is uttered at solemn occasions. He punctures pretentious speech and caricatures those who misuse language to deceive others.

P. also exploded conventional word patterns and juggled with neologisms. He ridiculed meaningless clichés, but he also proved, by his ability to instill fresh meaning into stale expressions, that old adages still have significance for mankind. Many of his poems contain gruesome images; P. is obviously haunted by bloodshed. These images—used concretely, not symbolically—frequently depict animals (he shows a marked preference for donkeys and giraffes), birds of all kinds, flowers, and fruit. As P. shows the world through his lenses, animals can peacefully coexist, but as soon as man enters the picture, war breaks out, animals are mistreated, even murdered, and the balance of nature is upset.

In P.'s view, all men are not evil. Simple, nature-loving people are exempted from his condemnation. The political slant in his poems clearly is directed against capitalism, military commanders, the clergy, and the whole middle class in its rigid system of values. Artists, workers, children, innocent bystanders in the social struggle are viewed with friendly interest and sympathy. Oddballs and social outcasts are looked upon fondly, and the pathetic fight for daily bread is illustrated by the hopeless monotony of a lonely person's breakfast. P. looks on approvingly at every nonconformist's protest against the rules of bourgeois society.

P. created his own mythology around existing names. His great men may coincide with history's, but they usually turn out to represent the exact reverse of grandeur, as in *Histoires* (1946; stories), where an odd assortment of names familiar through literature or history threaten to step out of the book and start autonomous lives of their own. Mixed metaphors, in P.'s poetry, become tidbits of insane humor, but of an incisive, purposeful kind loaded with iconoclastic meaning and aimed at old taboos. His humor disintegrates age-old prejudice and creates a liberating atmosphere in which true humanism flourishes.

Although P. sometimes seems to be playing around with mere words loosely strung together, he is actually working in dead earnest to get his message across—a message of warmth and love of life, of delight in people, places, things, and beings, of faith in eventual progress. P.'s famous dunce in the poem "Le cancre" (1946; the dunce) shakes his head to say "no," but his heart says "yes," and "despite the teacher's threats . . . he draws on the board the face of happiness."

P. also wrote numerous widely acclaimed screenplays, some of the most notable being *Le crime de Monsieur Lange* (1935; the crime of Monsieur Lange), directed by Jean Renoir, and those for films directed by Marcel Carné: *Drôle de drame* (1937; pub. 1974; a peculiar drama; known in Eng. as *Bizarre, Bizarre*); *Quai des brumes* (1938; quay of fogs); *Le jour se lève* (1939; pub. 1965; day is dawning; pub. in Eng. as *Le Jour Se Lève*, 1970); *Les visiteurs du soir* (1942; pub. 1974; the night visitors); *Les enfants du paradis* (1944; pub. 1974; *Children of Paradise*, 1968); and *Les portes de la nuit* (1946; the gates of night).

FURTHER WORKS: *C'est à Saint-Paul-de-Vence* (1945); *Le cheval de Trois* (1946, with André Verdet and André Virel); *L'ange garde-chiourme* (1946); *Contes pour enfants pas sages* (1947); *Le petit lion* (1947); *Des bêtes . . .* (1950); *Spectacle* (1951); *Vignette pour les vignerons* (1951); *Le grand bal du printemps* (1951); *Bim, le petit âne* (1952, with Albert Lamorisse); *Charmes de Londres* (1952); *Guignol* (1952); *Lettres des Îles Baladar* (1952); *Tour de chant* (1953); *L'opéra de la lune* (1953); *La pluie et le beau temps* (1955); *Lumière d'homme* (1955); *Miró* (1956); *Images* (1957); *P. vous parle* (1958); *Portraits de Picasso* (1959); *Couleur de Paris* (1961); *Diurnes* (1962); *Histoires et d'autres histoires* (1963); *Les chiens ont soif* (1964); *Fatras* (1966); *Arbres* (1967, with Georges Ribemont-Desaignes); *Imaginaires* (1970); *Fromanger* (1971, with Alain Jouffroy); *Hebdromadaires* (1972, with André Pozner); *Choses et autres* (1972); *Cinquante chansons* (1977, with Joe Kosma); *Soleil de Nuit* (1980); *Collages* (1982); *La cinquième Saison* (1984); *Paroles* (1990); *Blood and Feathers* (1993). FURTHER WORKS IN ENGLISH: *Selections from "Paroles"* (1958); *Poems I* (1967); *Poems II* (1968); *Words for All Seasons: Collected Poems of J. P.* (1979)

BIBLIOGRAPHY: Quéval, J., *J. P.* (1955); Guillot, G., *Les P.* (1966); Bergens, A., *J. P.* (1969); Baker, W. E., *J. P.* (1967); Sadeler, J., *À travers P.* (1975); Greet, A. H., Introduction to *Words for All Seasons: Collected Poems of J. P.* (1979): 3–11; Mancini, M., "P.: Poetry in Motion Pictures," *Film Comment* (Nov.–Dec. 1981): 34–37

—KONRAD BIEBER

PRICE, Reynolds

American novelist, short-story writer, poet, essayist, and dramatist, b. 1 Feb. 1933, Macon, North Carolina

The child of a traveling salesman father and a loving but eccentric mother, P. developed a deep affection for his home region of eastern North Carolina—the setting for most of his fiction. He attended Duke University, where one of his teachers for a writing workshop was Eudora WELTY. After receiving a B.A. degree in 1955, he studied at Merton College, Oxford, as a Rhodes Scholar. Since 1958, P. has been a faculty member at Duke, except for brief periods when he served as writer-in-residence at other universities.

P.'s first novel, *A Long and Happy Life* (1962), begins his saga of the Mustian family and explores ironic tensions between love and duty. Rosacoke Mustian's lifelong love for Wesley Beavers is not reciprocated, but he agrees to marry her after she becomes pregnant with his child. One selection from *The Names and Faces of Heroes* (1963), P.'s first collection of short stories, also focuses on Rosacoke. While visiting a relative in a hospital, she spontaneously leaves a bouquet for another patient dying of lung cancer. Although her gesture goes unnoticed, it clearly displays her loving and generous nature. The novel *A Generous Man* (1966) portrays the sexual maturation of Rosacoke's brother Milo. The plot—involving searches for an errant circus python, for Milo's retarded brother, and for a pet dog wrongly diagnosed as rabid—verges on the grotesque. In the character of a sheriff named Rooster, who is usually impotent, P. continues his depiction of life's pervasive ironies.

All the stories in *Permanent Errors* (1970), P.'s second collection, explore a similar theme. In varied characters and contexts P. examines a central error of understanding or action that sorely limits an individual's life. P. suggests, however, that perceiving and addressing the error can bring hope for the future. The story "Waiting at Dachau" illustrates such a process. During a tour of Europe, a young woman refuses to visit the former Nazi concentration camp with her boyfriend. This action and the young man's yearning for more personal freedom pull the couple apart. Eventually, though, he comprehends the folly of his earlier attitude and understands that relationships imply obligations.

In *The Surface of Earth* (1975) P. introduces the Kendal and Mayfield families and shows the sins of parents visited upon children through three generations. After Eva Kendal elopes with Forrest Mayfield, her mother commits suicide. Trying to atone for this tragedy, Eva leaves her husband and initiates a series of further misfortunes. *The Source of Light* (1981) focuses on a single descendant of Eva and Forrest, who offers hope for reconciliation. Hutchins Mayfield is an aspiring poet who flees North Carolina to study at Oxford University, but he returns home to bury his father.

Kate Vaiden (1986) is the most highly praised of P.'s novels, and its protagonist is his most fully realized female character. Through animated first-person narration P. presents a picaresque tale often compared to that of Moll Flanders. An orphan who abandoned her own illegitimate son, Kate suffers many years later from cervical cancer and seeks a reunion with her lost child.

The Tongues of Angels (1990) examines the brief but intense friendship between a summer camper and his counselor. Drawn together by aesthetic sensitivity and shared pain (from the recent deaths of parents), they seek mystic insight. Years later the counselor (now a successful artist) reflects on his possible complicity in the camper's death. In *The Promise of Rest* (1995) P. revisits the Mayfield clan and examines a contemporary tragedy that can sever or unite families. By the early 1990s Hutchins Mayfield is a distinguished writer and professor at Duke University, and his own son is an architect in New York City near death from AIDS. Depicting a painful reunion of parent and child, P. acknowledges the individual desire for independence but also affirms the power of family to shelter and comfort.

P.'s own lengthy battle with cancer and the self-hypnosis that he used initially to relieve pain have inspired two notable nonfiction works. In *Clear Pictures* (1989) P. reflects upon his life up to the age of twenty-one. This memoir offers sharp depictions of small-town life and revealing commentary about his mother—the inspiration for the character of Kate Vaiden. *A Whole New Life: An Illness and a Healing* (1994) is both a candid documentary of the progress of a disease and a thoughtful essay on how one copes with its indignities.

Although P. has produced significant works in several genres, he remains best known for his fiction. Here, his persistent focus on family sagas—on the tension between duty and freedom—within a limited but vividly realized Southern domain has led to comparisons with William FAULKNER. P. portrays flawed characters and ignoble behavior, but his vision remains positive and frequently comic.

FURTHER WORKS: *Love and Work* (1968); *Late Warnings: Four Poems* (1968); *Things Themselves* (1972); *Presence and Absence* (1973); *Early Dark* (1977); *Lessons Learned. Seven Poems* (1977); *A Palpable God* (1978); *Nine Mysteries* (1979); *The Annual Heron* (1980); *Country Mouse, City Mouse* (1981); *Vital Provisions* (1982); *Mustian: Two Novels and a Story* (1983); *Private Contentment* (1984); *The Laws of Ice* (1985); *Good Hearts* (1988); *A Common Room* (1988); *Real Copies* (1988); *Back before Day* (1989); *The Foreseeable Future* (1990); *New Music* (1990); *The Use of Fire* (1990); *Night Dance* (1991); *Better Days* (1991); *August Snow* (1991); *Blue Calhoun* (1992); *An Early Christmas* (1992); *The Collected Stories* (1993); *Full Moon and Other Plays* (1993); *The Honest Account of a Memorable Life* (1996)

BIBLIOGRAPHY: Stevenson, J., "The Faces of R. P.'s Short Fiction," *SSF*, 3 (1966): 300-6; Shepard, A., "Love (and Marriage) in *A Long and Happy Life*," *TCL*, 17 (Jan. 1971): 29-35; Kimball, S., ed., *R. P.: From A Long and Happy Life to Good Hearts* (1989); Humphries, J., ed., *Conversations with R. P.* (1991); Schiff, J. A., *Understanding R. P.* (1996)

—ALBERT WILHELM

PRIESTLEY, J(ohn) B(oynton)

English novelist, dramatist, essayist, and critic, b. 13 Sept. 1894, Bradford; d. 15 Aug. 1984, Stratford-on-Avon

Son of a schoolmaster, P. attended a local grammar school, and at seventeen began working as a clerk in a wool firm. World War I changed his life; after four years in the army, he went to Cambridge after demobilization, graduating in 1921. He then became a journalist in London; by 1925 he had published five books and established himself as a professional writer. He produced nine more books in the next three years.

P.'s early works included critical studies like *The English Comic Characters* (1925) and *George Meredith* (1926), together with several collections of essays. Kenneth Young has described his early essays as diverting and charming, the later ones as tough as old boots. P. is sharply observant, and often polemical. In *English Journey* (1934) he showed an acute perception of social problems and social changes. In *Literature and Western Man* (1960) he saw not merely England but the whole Western world in crisis, and he tried to remind it of what it had created through its literature. Some fifty volumes of nonfiction, few of them negligible, constitute only one side of his remarkable output; they contain some of his best writing.

P.'s first novel, *Adam in Moonshine* (1927), was, in P.'s words, "all fine writing and nonsense, a little coloured trial balloon"; it was an experiment that failed. Resembling modernists like Virginia WOOLF in looking deeply inside his characters, he still wanted to tell a straightforward story. With *The Good Companions* (1929) he achieved a major success; its warmheartedness and vitality won it favor, and it is still the single book by which he is best known. Centering his story around a group of traveling entertainers touring England, P. brings in a wide variety of characters, many of them portrayed with Dickensian humor and gusto, and illustrates a theme he had borrowed from H. G. WELLS: "You can change your life." Surprisingly, his next novel, *Angel Pavement* (1930), deals with people whose lives would never change, except for the worse; it tells of the impact the mysterious and predatory Mr. Golspie has on the lives of people working for a small veneer firm. Among many other humorous or satirical novels, *Festival at Farbridge* (1951) gives an amusing account of a Midland town responding to the Festival of Britain, and *Sir Michael and Sir George* (1964) tells of the rivalry between the heads of two government cultural agencies. The latter novel was a forerunner of the major work of P.'s later years, *The Image Men*, which appeared in two volumes—*Out of Town* (1968) and *London End* (1969)—an account of the effects of media on society told through the story of the founding of an "Institute of Social Imagistics."

While writing novels, P. was carving out a substantial reputation as a dramatist. His first play, *Dangerous Corner* (1932), he himself called an "ingenious box of tricks;" it cleverly exploited the device of George Bernard SHAW of turning half a dozen apparently pleasant people inside out. Several of his plays during the 1930s experimented with concepts of time, notably *Johnson over Jordan* (1939), the story of a man who has recently died. His dramatic works cover a very wide range, from farces like *When We Are Married* (1938) to plays in the manner of CHEKHOV like *Eden End* (1934) and *The Linden Tree* (1947). Critics who consider his novels diffuse sometimes think that the discipline of the theater has been good for him; a play like *An Inspector Calls* (1947) is enigmatic, tense, and tightly constructed.

Many English critics consider P. undervalued; they think of him as a thoroughly professional writer, who has done work of distinction in a number of fields, and whose oeuvre coheres into a unity marked by a strong and inimitable personality. In 1940, during the low point of the war for Britain, his radio broadcasts touched a national nerve; similarly, in his writing he has a strong sense of what the public will respond to. As he himself once said, he may not have been a genius but he had "a hell of a lot of talent."

FURTHER WORKS: *The Chapman of Rhymes* (1918); *Brief Diversions, Being Tales, Travesties and Epigrams* (1922); *Papers from Lilliput* (1922); *I for One* (1923); *Figures in Modern Literature* (1924); *Talking* (1926); *The English Novel* (1927); *Open House* (1927); *Benighted* (1927; Am. *The Old Dark House*, 1928); *Thomas Love Peacock* (1927); *Apes and Angels* (1928); *Too Many People* (1928); *Farthing Hall* (1929, with Hugh Walpole); *English*

Humour (1929); *The Balconinny* (1929); *The Town Major of Miraucourt* (1930); *The Works of J. B. P.* (1931); *Faraway* (1932); *Self-Selected Essays* (1932); *I'll Tell you Everything: A Frolic* (1933, with Gerald Bullett); *The Roundabout* (1933); *Albert Goes Through* (1933); *Wonder Hero* (1933); *Laburnum Grove* (1934); *Four-in-Hand* (1934); *Cornelius* (1935); *Duet in Floodlight* (1935); *Spring Tide* (1936, with George Billam); *Bees on the Boat Deck* (1936); *They Walk in the City* (1936); *Midnight on the Desert: A Chapter of Autobiography* (1937); *Mystery at Greenfingers* (1937); *People at Sea* (1937); *Time and the Conways* (1937); *The Doomsday Men* (1938); *Let the People Sing* (1939); *Rain Upon Godshill: A Further Chapter of Autobiography* (1939); *Britain Speaks* (1940); *Out of the People* (1941); *Britain at War* (1942); *Black-Out in Gretley* (1942); *Britain Fights* (1943); *British Women Go to War* (1943); *Daylight on Saturday* (1943); *Desert Highway* (1944); *They Came to a City* (1944); *Three Men in New Suits* (1945); *How Are They at Home?* (1945); *The Secret Dream: An Essay on Britain, America, and Russia* (1946); *Bright Day* (1946); *Russian Journey* (1946); *Jenny Villiers* (1947); *The Long Mirror* (1947); *The Rose and Crown: A Morality Play* (1947); *The Plays of J. B. P.* (3 vols., 1948); *The Golden Fleece* (1948); *The High Toby: A Play for the Toy Theatre* (1948); *Ever Since Paradise* (1949); *Home Is Tomorrow* (1949); *Delight* (1949); *Bright Shadow* (1950); *Going Up with Other Stories and Sketches* (1950); *Summer Day's Dream* (1950); *The P. Companion: A Selection* (1951); *Dragon's Mouth* (1952, with Jacquetta Hawkes); *Private Rooms* (1953); *Mother's Day* (1953); *The Other Place and Other Stories of the Same Sort* (1953); *Try It Again* (1953); *Treasure on Pelican* (1953); *A Glass of Bitter* (1954); *Low Notes on a High Level* (1954); *The Magicians* (1954); *Journey Down a Rainbow* (1955, with Jacquetta Hawkes); *All About Ourselves* (1956); *The Scandalous Affair of Mr. Kettle and Mrs. Moon* (1956); *The Writer in a Changing Society* (1956); *The Art of the Dramatist* (1957); *Thoughts in the Wilderness* (1957); *Topside; or, The Future of England* (1958); *The Glass Cage* (1958); *The Story of Theatre* (1959); *William Hazlitt* (1960); *Saturn over the Water* (1961); *Charles Dickens* (1961); *The Thirty-First of June* (1961); *The Shapes of Sleep* (1962); *Margin Released* (1962); *Man and Time* (1964); *A Severed Head* (1964, with Iris Murdoch); *Lost Empires* (1965); *The Moment, and Other Pieces* (1966); *Salt Is Leaving* (1966); *It's an Old Country* (1967); *Essays of Five Decades* (1968); *Trumpets over the Sea* (1968); *All England Listened: The Wartime Broadcasts of J. B. P.* (1968); *The Prince of Pleasure and his Regency, 1811–1820* (1969); *Anton Chekhov* (1970); *The Edwardians* (1970); *Snoggle* (1971); *Victoria's Heyday* (1972); *Over the Long High Wall: Some Reflections and Speculations on Life, Death and Time* (1972); *The English* (1973); *A Visit to New Zealand* (1974); *Outcries and Asides* (1974); *Particular Pleasures* (1975); *The Carfitt Crisis, and Two Other Stories* (1975); *English Humour* (1976); *Found, Lost, Found; or, The English Way of Life* (1976); *The Happy Dream: An Essay* (1976); *Instead of the Trees: A Final Chapter of Autobiography* (1977); *The English Novel* (1977)

BIBLIOGRAPHY: Hughes, D., *J. B. P.: An Informal Study* (1958); Evans, G. L., *J. B. P., the Dramatist* (1964); Cooper, S., *J. B. P.: Portrait of an Author* (1970); Young, K., *J. B. P.* (1977); Braine, J., *J. B. P.* (1978); De Vitis, A., and Kalsen, A. E. *J. B. P.* (1980); Atkins, J., *J. B. P.: The Last of the Sages* (1981)

—D. J. DOOLEY

PRISCO, Michele

Italian novelist and short-story writer, b. 18 Jan. 1920, Torre Annunziata

After graduating from law school in 1942, P. decided to follow his literary vocation and began to write for leading newspapers and reviews such as *Risorgimento, Il messaggero,* and *La fiera letteraria.* His first collection of short stories, *La provincia addormentata* (1949; the sleepy province), and his first novel, *Gli eredi del vento* (1950; *Heirs of the Wind,* 1953), were early indications of his major concerns as a writer, particularly of his keen perception of the human, social, psychological, and psychopathological makeup of the people he knew best, the middle class of the small towns of the Vesuvian hinterland.

While P.'s subsequent novels did show a gradual widening of the historical perspective, along with a new sense of the social reality of the postwar years, his main works of fiction—the novels *Una spirale di nebbia* (1966; a spiral of fog), which won the Strega Prize; *I cieli della sera* (1970; evening skies); and *Gli ermellini neri* (1975; black ermines)—focused again, with growing lucidity and slow but intense narrative pace, on the study of human nature as a consistent source for the portrayal of types and characters, on the complex world of family life, and on the moral decline of the provincial middle class. P.'s persistent and keenly analytical observations reveal the disturbing forces that motivate from within the actions and reactions that constitute human behavior. Cowardice and dissimulation, greed and ambition, hatred and violence are constant manifestations of the human condition, which are to be viewed within the wider spectrum of good and evil. The reader is invited to consider these observations in order to gain some understanding of the roots of the problems of contemporary history as reflected by provincial society: the disintegration of the traditional family structure, the continuing disarray in the social system, and the resulting displacement and degradation of the natural order of things and of the basic values of human existence.

The author himself has provided some valuable insights into the themes and issues of his writing in a book he is particularly fond of: *Punto franco* (1965; duty-free point), a collection of stories and narratives, substantially autobiographical in inspiration.

FURTHER WORKS: *Figli difficili* (1954); *Fuochi a mare* (1957); *La dama di piazza* (1961); *Il colore del cristallo* (1977).

—A. ILLIANO

PRISHVIN, Mikhail Mikhailovich

Russian short-story writer, essayist, nature writer, and novelist, b. 4 Feb. 1873, Krushchevo; d. 16 Jan. 1954, Moscow

Born on the estate of his parents in the Orel district, P. studied agronomy in Riga and Leipzig. Finding work as a journalist in St. Petersburg, he published his first story in 1906. After brief service in World War I, he moved to the countryside, the setting for nearly all his subsequent works. Early in the 1930s P. made excursions to the Urals, to the northern regions of Russian and to the far east of the Soviet Union. He devoted the last years of his life largely to juvenile literature and his memoirs.

P.'s writings are marked by an optimism and idealism typical of 19th-c. Russian populism. Fascinated by nature, hunting, and rural life, which he knew from earliest childhood, P. can be compared with gentry writers such as Konstantin Aksakov (1817–1860), Turgenev, and Tolstoy. Unlike them, however, P. expanded his rural interests with systematic studies in agronomy and ethnography.

P.'s earliest books describing his journey to the White Sea region, *V krayu nepugannykh ptits* (1907; in the land of unfrightened birds) and *Za volschebnym kolobkom* (1908; following the ginger-bread man), combine poetic, informed nature lore and a fascination with primitive peoples. After the revolution P. published what is perhaps his most characteristic work, *Kalendar prirody* (1939; *The Lake and the Woods; or, Nature's Calendar*, 1951), a collection of essays on natural history, hunting, and peasant life, in which he speaks with the voice of an educated, cosmopolitan artist isolated in the remote Russian countryside. Soviet exploitation of the country's natural resources is reflected in P.'s *Zhen-shen* (1933; *Jen Sheng: The Root of Life*, 1936), describing the establishment of a game farm in the Soviet far east.

Toward the end of his life P. published a charming juvenile tale, *Kladovaya solntsa* (1947; *The Treasure Trove of the Sun*, 1952), to great acclaim. From 1923 until his death P. labored intermittently over his fictionalized autobiography. *Kashcheeva tsep* (1956; Kashcheev's chain). The title refers to the monster in a Russian folktale who holds his victims in chains; P. saw this tale as a metaphor for the social and psychological limitations that restrain human potentialities.

Very popular in the Soviet Union, P.'s works are marked by a deft stylistic touch and fine poetic sensibility. Highly typical are his love and knowledge of the natural world and his earnest striving to fit man into the greater scheme of things.

FURTHER WORKS: *Adam i Yeva* (1909); *Cherny arab* (1910; *The Black Arab*, 1947); *Krutoyarsky zver* (1911); *Nikon Starokolenny* (1912); *Slavny bubny* (1913); *Okhotnichi byli* (1926); *Zhuravlinaya rodina* (1929); *Vesna sveta* (1938); *Fatselia* (1940); *Lesnaya kapel* (1940); *Korabelnaya chashcha* (1954; *Ship-Timber Grove*, 1957); *Sobranie sochineny* (6 vols., 1956–1957); *Glaza zemli* (1957). FURTHER WORKS IN ENGLISH: *The Black Arab and Other Stories* (1947); *The Sun's Storehouse: Short Stories* (1955)

BIBLIOGRAPHY: Huxley, J. S., Foreword to *Jen Sheng* (1936): v–vii; Alexandrova, V., *A History of Soviet Literature* (1963): 191–202; Struve, G., *Russian Literature under Lenin and Stalin* (1971): 146; Slonim, M., *Soviet Russian Literature* (1977): 109–15; Parrott, R., "Evolution of a Critical Response: M. P.," *RLJ*, 109 (1977): 101–23; Parrott, R., "Questions of Art, Fact, and Genre in M. P.," *SlavR*, 36 (1977): 465–74

—LELAND FETZER

PRITCHETT, V(ictor) S(awdon)

English critic, novelist, short-story writer, and journalist, b. 16 Dec. 1900, Ipswich; d. 21 Mar. 1997, London

In two volumes of memoirs, *A Cab at the Door* (1968) and *Midnight Oil* (1971), P. has given a fascinating account of the

V. S. Pritchett

middle-class suburban London atmosphere in which he grew up. His father's life, he says, was blighted by Christian Science and extravagant ambition; the cab was often at the door, to move the family after a business failure. Although P. showed an aptitude for languages, he had to leave school at age fifteen to go into the leather trade. He found its mysteries fascinating, and through it he met a whole gallery of memorable eccentrics. Nevertheless, he had his vocation fixed in his mind: he wanted to pursue a writing career. From 1920 to 1927 he lived abroad. Back in England, he struggled to become a journalist; eventually he became a book reviewer for the *New Statesman*, for which he was to write a literary column over a period of several decades.

His first volume, *Marching Spain* (1928), was a travel book. Three works of fiction, described by one critic as "highly wrought tales of highly intellectualized passion," came in swift succession after it—the novel *Clare Drummer* (1929), *The Spanish Virgin, and Other Stories* (1930), and another novel, *Shirley Sanz* (1932; Am., *Elopement into Exile*). *Dead Man Leading* (1937), dealing with an expedition into the Brazilian jungle, was an ambitious combination of psychological novel and adventure story. But P. found the novel too ruminative and discursive, and too time-consuming. His best-known novel, *Mr. Beluncle* (1951), illustrates his difficulties with the form; despite its verbal brilliance, its successful capturing of atmosphere, and its memorable characters, especially its profound imaginative insight into an extreme puritan, it lacks the interior dynamics a good novel must have. P. was to put the same material—basically the story of his own father—to far better use in his autobiographical works.

During World War II he developed a considerable reputation in a form much more congenial to him—the short story. It has been said that he has a remarkable ability to convey a freighterful of implication in a skiff of words. A few strokes of the pen establish a setting; a few more, the people and their situation. Another fine short-story writer, Eudora WELTY, commends him for his ability to distill each story's truth through a pure concentration of human character. Often there is a note reminiscent of CHEKHOV, emphasizing the place of illusion and obsession in life. In "The Camberwell Beauty" (1974) the world of antique dealers is vividly realized: their main aim, it becomes apparent, is not to sell but to possess. P. has always defended the short story as a distinct art form; it can no longer be viewed as the refuge of writers unequal to the demands of the novel.

His method in criticism is inductive: he wants to describe accurately "the new point in life from which any given novel started." Although he has written a biography, *Balzac* (1973), and a study of Turgenev, *The Gentle Barbarian* (1977), he prefers the short incisive essay to the long discursive work. His comment that literary criticism does not add to its stature by opening an intellectual hardware store reveals his opinion of academic criticism and theorizing. He is, however, anything but insular; in fact his book *The Myth Makers* (1979), a "plain man's guide to world fiction," contains essays on nineteen writers, none of whom wrote in English. Although he has not written the major work that would rank him among the leaders in an age of criticism, he has established a substantial reputation because of his ability to strike at the heart of a book and explain whether or not it should last, to set English novels against Continental ones, and to produce striking capsule judgments.

In his travel books, he said, he took a lesson from D. H. LAWRENCE and selected the short, compact subject, made personal. Most of his writing shows a similar desire to get at the essence of a thing and describe it precisely, clearly, and economically. He also writes that in prose he found the common experience and the solid world in which he could firmly tread. He wants to describe the world around him, in all its solidity, but not to rise above it. Therefore some critics find him unduly limited in outlook: one complains that he fiddles while literature burns. His autobiography—that is, his two volumes of memoirs—has been called one of the best of our time, but about some incidents in his life he remains curiously reticent; he does not allow us very far inside himself. Still, if he gives us the impression of coming close to the highest reaches of art but not quite getting there, he has won distinction as a short-story writer, critic, and autobiographer. It is not surprising that he was knighted for his services to literature (1975).

FURTHER WORKS: *This England* (1930); *Nothing Like Leather* (1935); *In My Good Books* (1942); *It May Never Happen and Other Stories* (1945); *Build the Ships* (1946); *The Living Novel* (1946); *Why Do I Write? An Exchange of Views between Elizabeth Bowen, Graham Greene, and V. S. P.* (1948); *Books in General* (1953); *The Spanish Temper* (1954); *Collected Stories* (1956); *The Sailor, Sense of Humor and Other Stories* (1956); *When My Girl Comes Home* (1961); *London Perceived* (1962); *The Key to My Heart: A Comedy in Three Parts* (1963); *Foreign Faces* (Am., *The Offensive Traveller*, 1964); *The Living Novel, and Later Appreciations*

(1964); *New York Proclaimed* (1965); *The Working Novelist* (1965); *Shakespeare: The Comprehensive Soul* (1965, with others); *Blind Love and Other Stories* (1969); *George Meredith and English Comedy* (1970); *The Camberwell Beauty and Other Stories* (1974); *Autobiography* (Presidential Address to the English Association) (1977); *Selected Stories* (1978); *On the Edge of the Cliff* (1979); *The Tale Bearers: Literary Essays* (1980); *Collected Stories* (1982); *The Turn of the Years: As Old as the Century* (1982)

BIBLIOGRAPHY: "Mr. P.'s Novels," *TLS* (19 Oct. 1951): 660; Mellors, J., "V. S. P.: Man on the Other Side of a Frontier," *London* (April—May 1975): 5–13; Reid, B. L., "Putting in the Self," *SR*, 75 (1977): 262–85; Welty, E., "A Family of Emotions," *NYTBR* (25 June 1978): 39–40; Theroux, P., "V. S. P.'s Stories: His Greatest Triumph" *SatR*, (May 1982): 56–57; Raban, J., "Going Strong," *NYRB* (24 June 1982): 8–12; Cunningham, V., "Coping with the Bigger Words," *TLS* (25 June 1982): 687

—D. J. DOOLEY

PROUST, Marcel

French novelist, b. 10 July 1871, Auteuil; d. 18 Nov. 1922, Paris

P. was born in what was then a suburb of Paris, although the family soon returned to Paris. P.'s father was a professor of medicine; his mother came from a prosperous Alsatian Jewish family. At the age of nine, P. suffered his first attack of asthma, and this affliction, aggravated by nervous disorders, would make of him a lifelong invalid. The death of his father in 1903, and particularly that of his mother two years later, left P. stricken with grief and obliged to undertake the first of several retreats to a sanatorium. Living virtually as a recluse from the age of thirty-four to his death at fifty-one, P. had constructed for himself the celebrated "cork-linked chamber" where he worked through long nights to complete the vast novel he had conceived. Occasionally he would make forays into the social world about which he was writing, and be seen at the opera, the new Russian ballet, or dining at the Ritz, wrapped in furs and looking like a waxen ghost.

As a young man, P. had sporadically contributed society notes and articles to the newspaper *Le Figaro*, but his first published literary work was a collection of bizarre tales called *Les plaisirs et les jours* (1896; *Pleasures and Regrets*, 1948; enlarged ed., *Pleasures and Days, and Other Writings*, 1957). Although the book received a polite critical reception, it was steeped in typically fin-de-siècle "hothouse" prose and bore little resemblance to the majestic style and sweep of his later masterpiece, *À la recherche du temps perdu* (1913–27; *Remembrance of Things Past*, 1922–32; rev. tr., 1981). Despite his uncertain English, P. next turned to translating the art criticism of John Ruskin. After P.'s death, it was discovered that during the first decade of the century he had already written a full-length novel bearing the title of its hero, *Jean Santeuil* (1952; *Jean Santeuil*, 1956) and also a substantial collection of literary criticism.

In 1913 the first volume of *À la recherche du temps perdu* was printed at P.'s own expense; it would take a decade for him to complete the seven-volume, four-thousand-page novel, and fifteen years before it was published in full: I, *Du côté de chez Swann* (1913; *Swann's Way*, 1922); II, *À l'ombre des jeunes filles en fleur* (1918; *Within a Budding Grove*, 1924); III, *Le côté de Guermantes* (1920–21; *The Guermantes Way*, 1925); IV, *Sodome et Gomorrhe* (1921–22; *Cities of the Plain*, 1927); V, *La prisonnière* (1923; *The Captive*, 1929); VI, *Albertine disparue* (1925; *The Sweet Cheat Gone*, 1930); VII, *Le temps retrouvé* (1927; *The Past Recaptured*, 1932).

The English phrase "remembrance of things past" (taken from a Shakespeare sonnet) does not convey the novel's central theme as expressed in the French title: "in search of lost time." Far more than writing a mere "remembrance," P. was profoundly concerned with the metaphysics of time and the function of human memory, and he developed the radical relativistic thesis that, contrary to common acceptance, it is not the fleeting present or the uncertain future that has true reality for man but rather the *past*, and that the past is never "gone" but an accessibly present phenomenon. Writing in the first person throughout, P. demonstrates his theory by reproducing a narrative sequence that closely resembles his own life struggle to become a writer. It seems to him a wasted life, spent in a glittering but hollow social world; his personal and emotional pursuits he can only judge to be vain until he discovers that his very quest for understanding and meaning is in itself the theme and subject of a novel. He thus transcends time by deciding to "recapture the past" in words and endow it with the greater permanence of art. Readers are thus faced with the enticing conceit that the novel P. is about to start writing is the novel they have just finished reading!

The pivotal scene, one of the most memorable and literally evocative in Western fiction, is one in which P. dips a *madeleine* cake into a cup of tea and finds that the physical sensations evoked transport him back in time to an identical experience of childhood and enable him to experience the past completely as a simultaneous part of his present existence: " . . .the whole of Combray and its surroundings, all this came forth with shape and solidity, town, gardens and everything, from my cup of tea." We then follow the narrator as his universe expands from the provincial town of Combray to a seashore resort for the socially prominent to the most elegant and fashionable drawing rooms of Paris at the turn of the century, and even into the shadowy labyrinth of the homosexual world, where duke and workingman meet as peers.

The characters P. depicts are among the most vivid and complex in literature, rivaling those of Shakespeare and Balzac in their gigantic proportions. There is the Jewish bourgeois Charles Swann, who scales the Parisian social ladder, introduces the adolescent narrator to the arts, but loses his personal dignity and ruins his life through jealousy of a woman he does not really even love. In contrast, an uncouth but ambitious bourgeois couple named Verdurin successfully claw their way to the top and are not only accepted by, but ultimately supersede, the old nobility of France. That titled upper class, represented primarily by the Duke and Duchess de Guermantes, is portrayed by P. with both affection and satire; he conveys their human weaknesses and follies yet admires the traditions they embody. As a boy, he is "in love" with the duchess—meaning that he seeks to become a part of her world. P.'s most monumental portrait is the Baron de Charlus, another member of the illustrious Guermantes family, who is cultivated and socially powerful but leads the secret "double life" of a homosexual. Like Swann, he is a slave to passion; for love of a young musician of the lower classes, he frequents a level of society beneath his station, is

Marcel Proust

consumed by jealousy, and courts disaster. At the novel's end, the aged and dying baron can still summon his powers to bow deeply to a "grande dame" in a passing carriage; ironically, she is a mere social climber who once insulted him.

À la recherche du temps perdu can be read simply as a compelling narrative, but also at a variety of other levels: sociohistorical, psychological, philosophical. With great insight and awareness of social change, P. traces the decline and fall of Parisian society and the rise of the bourgeoisie during the Third Republic. Many critics felt that this was his principal intention; P., however, also sought to demonstrate what he considered to be the governing laws of human behavior. Paramount among these is his concept of "successive selves." In keeping with his relativistic theory of time and memory, P. shows that no individual is a permanent reality but a series of different, changing persons throughout life, and that some of our apparent "selves" depend chiefly on how we are perceived by others.

The brilliant climax of the novel occurs at a great social gathering at which the narrator fails to recognize many of the people he has known for decades because the ravages of time have so transformed them physically. It is there that he realizes that he too is no longer young—no longer any *one* self from the past but the present accumulation of these. But he can still recapture the past and all past "selves" in a book, and thereby defy the metamorphoses of time through the metamorphosis of literature. Just as individuals and society may be transformed by time, P.'s quest for self-identity culminates in his discovery of his vocation as a writer—an artist who can transform life into the relatively more permanent reality of art.

À la recherche du temps perdu is not easy to classify. Although P. necessarily "paints from life," his novel is no roman à clef wherein real people are thinly disguised as fictional characters. Nor is it a roman-fleuve, a series of separate novels with continuing characters; this is a single cohesive work of fiction. Finally, it is not autobiography in the usual sense. P. himself was homosexual and part-Jewish; his first-person narrator is neither. What P. sought to communicate was not so much the *events* of his life but the essence of his spiritual quest.

Previously unpublished manuscripts found in the 1950s shed great light on the nature of that quest and on his method of composition. The novel *Jean Santeuil* had been written in the traditional third person, and the objective omniscient narrator clearly could not accommodate P.'s subjective need for interaction with the characters of his creation. The essays composed in 1908 and collected as *Contre Sainte-Beuve* (1954; *On Art and Literature*, 1958) yield another important clue. The 19th-c. critic Sainte-Beuve contended that thoroughly investigating a writer's personal life illuminates his work, and that notion held sway for many years. P. was among the first to attack this theory, claiming that the person and the artist are separate beings, that the writer becomes "another" when recreating experience in terms of fiction. It is believed that this conceptual breakthrough is the key to *À la recherche du temps perdu*: P. needed to speak not with his own voice but with the voice of P. the *artist*.

P. himself consciously set about writing with three very different models in mind. Just as the memoirs of Saint-Simon had pictured in minute detail the vast panorama of 17th-c. court life under Louis XIV, P. sought to re-create a social tapestry of his own era. He also wished to emulate Balzac, whose seventy-volume "Human Comedy" captures the sweep of Parisian and provincial life in the early 19th c. and conjures a total vision of mankind. Oddest of all, P. wanted to weave into his monumental work the color and the fantastic proportions of the legendary Arabian saga, *A Thousand and One Nights*.

One editor, little dreaming that P.'s novel was destined to become one of the classics of world literature, rejected the first volume, *Du côté de chez Swann*, as wordy, boring, wandering, and diffuse. However, the second volume, *À l'ombre des jeunes filles en fleurs*, won the prestigious Goncourt Prize in 1919. P.'s elaborate style, ideally suited to the complexity of his thought and to the sweep of his undertaking, is not an easy style. A single sentence may run to well over a page, yet each sentence, like the novel in its totality, is harmoniously balanced, frequently digressive but never meandering, and precisely structured to the idea or image conveyed. P. spoke often of the "architectural design" of his work, ambitiously likening it to a cathedral of prose. P.'s "digressions," whether on painting, music, psychology, or philosophy, actually illuminate his aesthetics and enable the reader more fully to appreciate the form and pattern of the novel.

Early critics and readers, for the most part, could not see, until the final volume appeared after P.'s death, the complete and complex design he had envisioned from the very start. Because of the richness of its texture, both stylistically and thematically, *À la recherche du temps perdu* has become one of the most abundantly analyzed literary achievements of all time. P. has been acclaimed as a master social historian and the creator of characters as memorable as those of Dickens, Balzac, and Dostoevsky. His serious presentation of homosexuality, however primitive and naïve it may seem today, was a pioneering accomplishment for its time. Ultimately, however, it is perhaps P.'s bold metaphysical concept of "time lost, time recaptured and transcended" that has earned for *À la recherche du temps perdu* not only enduring distinction among the great works of fiction but an important place in the realm of philosophical literature.

FURTHER WORKS: *Portraits de peintres* (1896); *Pastiches et mélanges* (1921); *Chroniques* (1927); *Morceaux choisis* (1928); *Comment parut "Du côté de chez Swann": Lettres de M. P.* (1930; repub. as *P. et la stratégie littéraire, avec des lettres de M. P. à René Blum, Bernard Grasset et Louis Brun*, 1954); *Correspondance générale* (6 vols., 1930–1936); *À un ami: Correspondance inédite, 1903–1922* (1948; *Letters to a Friend*, 1949); *Lettres à André Gide, avec trois lettres et deux textes d'André Gide* (1949); *Lettres de M. P. à Antoine Bibesco* (1949; *Letters to Antoine Bibesco*, 1955); *Correspondance avec sa mère* (1954; *Letters to His Mother*, 1956); *Choix de lettres* (1965); *Lettres retrouvés* (1966); *Correspondance de M. P.* (1970 ff.); *Textes retrouvés* (1971). FURTHER WORKS IN ENGLISH: *The Maxims of M. P.* (1948); *M. P.: A Selection from His Miscellaneous Writings* (1948); *Letters* (1949)

BIBLIOGRAPHY: Beckett, S., *P.* (1931); Spagnoli, J. J., *The Social Attitudes of M. P.* (1931); March, H., *The Two Worlds of M. P.* (1948); Green, F. C., *The Mind of P.* (1949); Maurois, A., *P.: Portrait of a Genius* (1950); Hindus, M., *The Proustian Vision* (1954); Painter, G., *M. P.: A Biography* (2 vols., 1959–1965); Girard, R., ed., *P.: A Collection of Critical Essays* (1962); Moss, H., *The Magic Lantern of M. P.* (1962); Shattuck, R., *P.'s Binoculars* (1963); Bersani, L., *M. P.: The Fictions of Life and Art* (1965); Brée, G., *M. P. and Deliverance from Time* (1969); Bucknall, B. J., *The Religion of Art in P.* (1969); Fowlie, W., *A Reading of P.* (1969); Kopp, R., *M. P. as a Social Critic* (1971); Wolitz, S., *The Proustian Community* (1971); Deleuze, G., *P. and Signs* (1972); Revel, J. -F., *On P.* (1972); Stambolian, G., *M. P. and the Creative Encounter* (1972); Rivers, J. E., *P. and the Art of Love* (1980)

—JAMES ROBERT HEWITT

P. was both a realist and an idealist.

As a realist he observed carefully the world about him and with scientific accuracy noted the details which, according to the latest nineteenth-century thought, enter into the composition of the character. This compelled him to treat each of his characters as a social being, belonging to a particular class with distinctive traits which play an important part in his behavior. From such observation of individuals, P. charted the flux of late nineteenth-century French society and drew general conclusions regarding the different social classes.

However, his observation soon reaches a point where it ceases to be scientific and is colored by his abnormal temperament. Unattached to any social institution, he can criticize every one of them with the intransigence of an idealist. He is sensitive to all of the faults of society and refuses to see any spiritual values in it. He therefore depicts a world in which the upper classes have no intellectual, artistic or moral principles, in which the middle classes are interested only in making money and in rising to the social position of the upper classes, and in which the lower classes have the same social ambition as the others and the greed that springs from such ambition.

John J. Spagnoli, *The Social Attitudes of M. P.*
(1931), p. 157

P. has several conceptions of time—which are not contradictory but are merely different views of the same reality. These divergences may give the impression that his ideas are more complicated than they really are. Sometimes he considers Time as an enemy, eager to destroy everything that is dear and precious to us, perpetually changing each one of us into another being. It kills our affections, subtly undermines our health, slowly but surely ruins our minds, turns pretty maidens into decrepit old hags. A great part—perhaps the greatest part—of P.'s writings is intended to show the havoc wrought in and round us by Time; and he succeeded amazingly not only in suggesting to the reader, but in making him actually feel, the universal decay invincibly creeping over everything and everybody with a kind of epic and horrible power. This conception of Time is a reflection of P.'s own experience. His whole life was a fight against Time—an endless struggle to last out a few more moments in spite of tremendous physical odds. He felt, especially in the latter part of his existence, more than ever threatened by the danger of having his thread of life cut short before he could express all that he had to say. Then the idea of Time became like a haunting nightmare and all his writings of that period bear the stamp of the ever-present, hostile obsession.

Georges Lemaitre, *Four French Novelists* (1938),
pp. 92–93

But a part of P.'s special savor comes from his invalidism and neuroticism. His world is that of the man in bed, seen at one remove, and this fact is his strength and his weakness. Imagination and memory play larger rôles than in the case of a more normal writer. He remembers and he imagines slights, deceptions, tricks; he projects his idiosyncrasies beyond his cork-lined walls and fastens them on to others. But from his claustration, too, he drew his extraordinary acuity of vision and the rich quality of his memory. "Never," he wrote, long before he could realize how fully the statement was to apply to himself, "was Noah able to see the world so well as from the Ark."

His great achievement as a psychologist is his description of himself. No one, not even Stendhal, has told himself so fully; and no one has probed more patiently and more exhaustively into the dark corners

of the neurotic personality. To do this, it was not enough to be himself the neurotic introvert; he needed, and he had, a remarkable power of detachment and a strong analytic talent. The result is that from his own highly special psychology he was able to abstract a general truth.

Harold March, *The Two Worlds of M. P.* (1948),
pp. 245–46

These memories [of his early childhood and youth] had lain undisturbed in the depths of his mind for a certain necessary gestative period of time, when they were delivered fresh and unretouched to the surface by a strong sensory impression like that made upon the narrator by the taste of the little madeleine dipped into a cup of tea, out of which, like the goddess Venus, Combray sprang in full bloom. Commonplace experiences and memories recalled after many years had passed were commonplace no longer. Something magical had happened to them. They were transmuted as if by alchemy, and, simply from having lain imbedded for so long in the mysterious caves and recesses of the mind, they came forth once more into the light of an unfading day, completely emblazoned and covered over with the golden imagery of his genius.

Milton Hindus, *The Proustian Vision* (1954),
pp. 277–78

The confrontation between Marcel and the world is thus re-created in the details of the narrator's style; the dramatic tensions of the Proustian sentence repeat stylistically the conflicts between the self and the world. It is easy to see the significance of certain characteristics of the narrator's style—for example, the seemingly endless proliferations around any starting point of description. It is as if this could do away with the memory of the world as distinct from the self, as if, under the melting pressure of analysis and comparison, objects could be thoroughly de-objectified and everything made to appear as a metaphor for everything else. The galleys of *À la recherche du temps perdu* came back to Gallimard covered with additions, and P.'s publishers understandably felt some panic when they saw how a job of correction inevitably became the occasion for uncontrollable elaboration. In looking over his text, P. apparently never found things sufficiently "digested"; the way to conquer their resistance, their opaqueness, was not to revise or cut out passages, but to inflate them, to "cover" every aspect of the elusive world with a continuously dense reflection on the world.

Leo Bersani, *M. P.: The Fictions of Life and Art*
(1965), pp. 230–31

On tasting the crumbs of the *madeleine* in a spoonful of tea, the narrator is invaded by a powerful joy . . . This rapture might be compared, if one wished, to that of a saint taking communion. The *madeleine* resembles the Host, in that a metaphysical ecstasy has been induced as a result of the physical act of eating, without the ecstasy's being limited to the taste of the food or of the same nature as that taste. We could say that like the ecstatic who goes so far as to doubt whether God is in him or whether he is not himself God, the narrator feels that the precious essence with which he has been filled is actually himself. But again, it might be safer to understand this statement about the "precious essence" with which the narrator has been filled as a warning not to confuse that essence with God or with the Infinite or any transcendental entity. P. goes on, after this, to speak of the tea as a "breuvage" whose "vertu" is diminishing. No longer would the reader be justified in thinking of the tea as a communion cup: these are rather the terms in which one speaks of a magic potion whose effects can wear off, like the love philter of Tristan and Yseult. Then the narrator says that the answer is not in the cup but in his mind: what he is seeking is something, as yet undiscovered, within his mind, which his mind, to discover, will have to create.

> Barbara J. Bucknall, *The Religion of Art in P.*
> (1969), pp. 155–56

In his seemingly excessive preoccupation with the world: the worldliness of social groups, time, love, snobbism, painting, music, the prestige of names, P. never forgets the real subject of his novel: the literary vocation of his protagonist. This spiritual theme dominates all others and bears a relationship with all others. It is the framework of the novel and pervades the matinée scene at the end. Throughout the final pages, all the dramas announced and developed in the novel are transcended and fused into the one taking place in Marcel's mind. The struggle is that being waged by the esthete in Marcel, the artist, the potential novelist, and the terrified human observer of the immense changes brought about by time. More discreet than other themes in the novel, but never absent for long from any of the volumes, the two themes—Marcel's literary vocation and his obsession with death—assume the greatest importance and form both symbolically and in fact the conclusion of *À la recherche du temps perdu*.

> Wallace Fowlie, *A Reading of P.* (1975), p. 288

How does the narrator's statement that homosexually oriented people are as numerous as "the sands of the earth" accord with his position that they are sick, mentally deranged, suffering from a hereditary affliction, and, in general, physically and psychologically different from the rest of the population—"[belonging] not to common humanity but to a strange race which mixes with it, hides within it, but never merges with it"? These ideas do not, of course, accord at all. When the narrator says people with homosexual tastes are found everywhere, in great numbers, and in all walks of life, he seems to forget that elsewhere he says they are grotesque anomalies who are radically, ontologically different from the general run of humanity. It may be that P. uses the former idea because he knows from personal experience it is true and the latter idea because it is the expected and the socially acceptable thing to say. In any case, the extremely high incidence of homosexuality depicted in *À la recherche* is one of the most original aspects of P.'s treatment of the theme, owing very little to—in fact, directly contradicting—both the scientific and the popular thinking of his era.

> J. E. Rivers, *P. and the Art of Love* (1980), p. 177

PROVENÇAL LITERATURE

See French Literature: Occitan Literature

PRZYBOŚ, Julian

Polish poet and critic, b. 5 May 1901, Gwoźnica; d. 6 Oct. 1970, Warsaw

P. was raised in a provincial backwater of what was then the Austro-Hungarian Empire. During the 1920s and 1930s, while earning his living as a schoolteacher, he was affiliated with a number of avant-garde literary journals. From 1937 to 1939 he lived in Paris: this was his first sustained contact with life in a major cosmopolitan city. P. spent most of World War II in his native region, having assumed for his protection the identity of a peasant laborer. In 1944 he offered his services to the Soviet-backed Polish government; thus began a long career as a trusted member of the Communist literary establishment. From 1947 through 1951 P. served as Polish ambassador to Switzerland. The last two decades of his life were spent in Warsaw.

When P. came to Cracow—itself a rather sleepy medieval town, albeit an intellectual center—to pursue his university education after World War I, he was swept off his feet by the dynamics of city life. He enthusiastically endorsed the manifestos of the Polish FUTURIST movement, especially the "three M's" proclaimed by Tadeusz Peiper (1891–1969): *miasto, masa, maszyna* (metropolis, masses, machinery). His earliest poetry collections, *Śruby* (1925; screws) and *Oburącz* (1926; with both hands), are aggressive celebrations of technology and urban life. They merge calls for social revolution with paeans of praise to dynamos, generators, and other manifestations of industrialized society. Rich sound instrumentation, insistent repetition, and the use of verbs dynamic in both meaning and form (for example, imperatives and active participles) combine with images of power and motion to create hymns to human and mechanical energy. In P.'s work of this time one can discern similarities to both MARINETTI and MAYAKOVSKY.

In the 1930s, beginning with the volume *W głąb las* (1932; into the forest depths), a private lyrical strain entered P.'s poetry, coexisting with the more strident political theme of revolution, which remained prominent throughout the decade. The lyrical poems merge contemplation of nature, particularly the rural landscape, with meditations on death and the meaning of life. Metaphors and language are designed to concentrate as many layers of meaning as possible into a single image. The majority of these poems are suffused with enthusiasm for life. Images of light, usually radiant and life-giving, although at times threatening destruction, are a characteristic feature. A series of annual poems in celebration of spring, beginning with spring 1934 and ending in 1970, exemplify P.'s delight in life coupled with his insatiable yearning for experience.

A new theme, which reveals as it were the terrors shoved aside in the dynamic poems of affirmation and revolution, appeared in the late 1950s. The poems of the last decade of P.'s life are more introspective than anything previous. They combine the insights of psychoanalysis with the poet's license to create his personal myth, and are attempts at probing the singular obsessions that had driven him for much of his life. The best of these poems, written under the cloud of serious illness, achieve a delicate balance between the expansiveness of the poet's response to nature's abundance and man's inventiveness, and the private grief attendant upon recognition of his mortality.

P.'s literary career of almost half a century was marked by paradox. His ideological stance and avant-garde poetic practices made him a rather marginal figure in prewar Poland, but his fortunes were reversed by the Communist accession to power. His virulent attacks on the avant-garde of the late 1950s and early 1960s defended both his own poetic values and the social needs of the state. Nonetheless, P. remained an aesthete whose difficult poetry demands a higher level of sophistication from its audience than is normally tolerated under even the loose Polish guidelines of SOCIALIST REALISM.

FURTHER WORKS: *Sponad* (1930); *Równanie serca* (1938); *Póki my żyjemy* (1944); *Miejsce na ziemi* (1945); *Czytając Mickiewicza* (1950; rev. ed., 1956); *Rzut pionowy* (1952); *Najmniej słów* (1955); *Narzędzie ze światła* (1958); *Linia i gwar* (1959); *Poezje zebrane* (1959; 2nd ed., 1967); *Próba całości* (1961); *Więcej o manifest* (1962); *Sens poetycki* (1963); *Nike i słowik* (1964); *Na znak* (1965); *Liryki 1930–1964* (1966); *Kwiat nieznany* (1969); *Zapiski bez daty* (1970); *Wiersze i obrazki* (1970); *Utwory poetyckie* (1975)

BIBLIOGRAPHY: Milosz, C., *The History of Polish Literature* (1969): 401–4; Levine, M. G., *Contemporary Polish Poetry 1925–1975* (1981): 21–35; Carpenter, B., "J. P.: The Double Image," *PolR*, 26, 2 (1981): 23–34

—MADELINE G. LEVINE

PRZYBYSZEWSKI, Stanisław

Polish novelist, dramatist, and critic (also writing in German), b. 7 May 1868, Łojewo, Poland; d. 23 Nov. 1927, Jaronty, Poland

Until he was thirty years old, P. moved almost exclusively in German cultural circles. Born in the Prussian-ruled area of partitioned Poland, he went to Berlin to study architecture and medicine, but

never finished. Extremely popular with the intelligentsia of that city as a pianist, writer, and bon vivant, P. quickly came to typify for them fin-de-siècle decadence: he was cosmopolitan, scandalous (alcohol, sex, and satanism were among his principal interests), refined (his renditions of Chopin brought him much fame), and cerebral (his novels in German were highly regarded). In 1898 he left Berlin to take a position as the editor of the literary journal *Życie* in Cracow, where he worked largely in Polish and even began to put his earlier German works into his native language. After a fruitful although brief period (until 1906), he returned once again to Germany, remaining there until the end of World War I. When Poland was reconstituted as a nation in 1918, he settled first in the Free City of Danzig (now Gdańsk) and then in Warsaw; no longer a professional litterateur, he served as a minor clerk in a government office. He died near Warsaw in relative obscurity.

Although hailed as a genius when he was at the height of his career (approximately 1893–1907), P. today is regarded more as a promoter of literature than a great writer. His novels, prose poems, and plays are all characterized by his insistence on the principle of art for art's sake. In this regard he became the most visible and vocal exponent of his time of the neoromantic movement in Polish literature known as Young Poland. As the editor of *Życie* from 1898 to 1900, he published many fine young poets and, albeit in exaggerated and excessive terms, outlined a literary program that postulated not only the absoluteness of art for its own sake but also the primacy of sexuality in determining human conduct, the superiority of the neurotic over the "healthy" psyche, and the bankruptcy of the older generation of utilitarian, positivist, and, to his mind, tendentious writers. Most of these notions he summarized in his manifesto *Confiteor* (1899; Latin: I confess), which many considered at the time a kind of charter of Polish neoromanticism. Even today his theoretical formulations are occasionally cited to underscore points in contemporary Polish literary controversies.

The practical result of P.'s beliefs as embodied in his fiction was a vehement style seemingly weighty with new ideas, but in the final analysis unoriginal. His three-part novel *Homo sapiens* (German original, 1895–96; Polish version, 1901; *Homo Sapiens*, 1915), for example, examines at great length the psychological states (P.'s famous "naked soul") of the hero, Eric Falk, as he destroys the lives of several women in order to assert his superiority over them. The details of mood and feeling, richly developed in the novel, contrast sharply with the work's colorless settings and plotless construction. P.'s goal here as elsewhere was to focus attention on his theories of art, sexuality, psychology, and the power of the will.

While his views were in vogue, his writings were both popular and influential. But as those theories became dated, P.'s fiction also suffered, for it had few literary qualities to offer audiences grown bored with his notions. Moreover, his indebtedness to other writers, particularly Schopenhauer, Nietzsche, Tolstoy, Dostoevsky, Ibsen, MAETERLINCK, and the French SYMBOLISTS, soon became obvious. Only a few essays on music—for example "Chopin und Nietzsche" (1891; Chopin and Nietzsche)—also included in the collection *Zur Psychologie des Individuums* (1892; on the psychology of the individual) and "Szopen a naród" (1910; Chopin and the nation)—in which he displays genuine sensitivity to the art; and memoiristic pieces like "Z gleby kujawskiej" (1902; from the soil of Kujawy) and *Moi współcześni wśród obcych* (1926; my contemporaries abroad) and the unfinished, posthumously published *Moi współcześni wśród swoich* (1930; my contemporaries at home), in which he vividly recalls the many literary and artistic personalities with whom he was intimate, are read with any frequency today.

On the whole, P.'s position in Polish literature is secure, if not outstanding, for he worked indefatigably to bring to the public eye the works of the best Young Poland writers, like Stanisław WYSPIAŃSKI and Jan Kasprowicz (1860–1926). "A genius without portfolio," as Henryk SIENKIEWICZ called him, he was a powerful influence in his time. And although his bold theoretical statements and even bolder attempts to embody them in fiction have for the most part aged badly, nonetheless the charismatic hold he had on his generation makes him a figure to be reckoned with in Polish literary history to the present day.

FURTHER WORKS: *Totenmesse* (1893; Polish, *Requiem aeternam*, 1901); *Vigilien* (1894; Polish, *Z cyklu Wigilii*, 1899); *De profundis* (German, 1895; Polish, 1899; rev. ed., 1922); *Pro domo mea* (German, 1895); *Die Synagoge des Satan* (1896; Polish, *Synagoga Szatana*, 1899); *Satans Kinder* (1897; Polish, *Dzieci Szatana*, 1899); *Das große Glück* (1897; Polish, *Dla szczęścia*, 1900; *For Happiness*, 1912); *Androgyne* (1899); *Na drogach duszy* (1900); *Nad morzem* (1901); *Złote runo* (1901); *Goście* (1901); *Synowie ziemi* (Part I, 1901; Part II, *Dzień sądu*, 1909; Part III, *Zmierzch*, 1910); *Die Mutter* (1902; Polish, *Matka*, 1903); *Śnieg* (1903; *Snow*, 1920); *Odwieczna baśń* (1906); *W godzinie cudu* (1906); *Gelübde* (1906; Polish, *Śluby*, 1907); *Dzieci nędzy* (Part I, 1913; Part II, *Adam Drzazga*, 1914); *Gody życia* (1910); *Mocny człowiek* (Part I, 1911; Part II, *Wyzwolenie*, 1912; Part III, *Śięty gaj*, 1913); *Topiel* (1912); *Miasto* (1914); *Krzyk* (1914–1915); *Polen und der heilige Krieg* (1915); *Von Polens Seele* (1917; Polish, *Szlakiem duszy polskiej*, 1917); *Il regno doloroso* (in Polish, 1924); *Mściciel* (1927); *Listy* (3 vols., 1937, 1938, 1954)

BIBLIOGRAPHY: Czaykowski, B., "Poetic Theories in Poland: Przesmycki and P.," *PolR*, 11 (1966): 45–55; Miłosz, C., *The History of Polish Literature* (1969): 329–33; Schluchter, M., *S. P. und seine deutschsprachigen Prosawerke*: 1892–1899 (1969); Stammler, H., "S. P. and Antonio Choloniewski: Two Interpreters of the Meaning of Polish History" *Jahrbücher für die Geschichte Osteuropas*, 20 (1972): 42–59; Jaworska, W., "Edvard Munch and S. P." *Apollo*, 100 (1974): 312–17; Klim, G., "S. P.'s Expressionism: Between Philosophy and Mysticism," in Sussex, R., ed., *Polish Colloquium of the University of Melbourne* (1976): 45–62

—HENRY R. COOPER, JR.

PSAILA, Carmelo

Maltese national poet, lexicographer, essayist, and critic, b. 18 Oct. 1871, Ħaż-Żebbuġ; d. 13 Oct. 1961, St. Julians

Better known as Dun Karm, P. studied philosophy and theology and was ordained priest on May 18, 1894. He became a teacher at the seminary in Malta and then a librarian at the Malta National Library. The death of his mother in 1909 left an indelible mark on his psychology that was reflected in some of his best poems. In 1921 P. was a founding member of the Academy of Maltese writers and six years later he was elected its president until 1942. In 1945,

when he had already established a literary career, the University of Malta conferred on him the degree D. Litt. (Hon. Causa) for his unstinting dedication to Maltese literature.

P. wrote several articles on criticism scattered in the Academy's journal between 1927 and 1942 and was later commissioned by the government to complete a much-needed bilingual dictionary, *English-Maltese Dictionary* (1947-55). His reputation, however, rests primarily upon his expressive poetry. He composed the "Innu Malti" (1923; The Maltese National Anthem), and in his lifetime he was honored as the National Poet of Malta, a title that he still retains. P. wrote numerous poems that deal with subjectivity within a Christian conscience, and he wrote others that contain a social commitment to promote the national identity and dignity of the Maltese people during colonial times. His first two collections of poems, *L-Ewwel Ward* (1914; The First Roses) and *Ward Leħor* (1920; Other Roses), established him immediately as a major Maltese poet. Then he published a translation of Ugo Foscolo's (1778-1827) poem, *L-Oqbra* (1936; The Graves), which was followed by his masterpiece *Il-Jien u Lihinn Minnu* (1938; The Self and Beyond It), a poem of 520 hendecasyllabic lines depicting the journey of the human soul from intellectual pride to utter Christian humility. Then he published *X'Ħabb u X'Ħaseb il-Poeta* (1939, What the Poet Felt and Thought), *X'Emmen il-Poeta* (1939, What the Poet Believed), and *X'Għmel Iżjed il-Poeta* (1940; What Else the Poet Did), which include his essential poetic qualities.

Stylistically and thematically *Il-Jien u Lilninn Minnu* is the representative Maltese poem of the 20th c. It contains a profundity of schematized philosophical insight and a disciplined intellectual creativity. Its ambition is to teach the essence of Christian living and to explain what makes humanity so hard to endure. A spiritual reviewer, P. seeks not to quarrel with reason but only to show how inadequate it is in matters of faith. William Blake believed that the imagination was the real man; for P., a poet's imagination was the real Christian man. His imaginative vision reverently elevated poetry to philosophical and theological levels. To write about soul-stirring matters was in line with the historical period in question. The first half of the 20th c. was full of wars, political disputes, and industrial uncertainty. In the face of such situations, the privilege accorded by P. to poetry is considerably more than mere escapism. Now poetry appears an enclave of Maltese society that celebrates the creative values and affirms morality. Imaginative creation became a nonalienated task in which the transcendental scope of the priestly poet's mind provided some criticism of ideologies enslaved to facts. If society appeared fragmented, poetry appeared organically coherent. In P.'s hands creativity became associated with spontaneity and rationality, and poetry (far from being identified with idle escapism) assumed the deep social and philosophical implications of an ideology. One can even say that poetic imagination gained so much power that it almost became a social force, transforming the people's mentality in the name of Catholic values. There is in P. continuity, never conflict, between his poetic and social commitments.

Historically considered, the poet-priest remains the most important figure in Maltese literature for he emphasized the significance of the inner self. His poetry of the maturing inner self is located in his Catholic thinking. With the growth of the inner self, landscape grew too, for landscape often conspired with thematic implications for the enhancement of the inner self. Thus landscape became more visible in P. and had a sort of therapeutic spiritualism.

It was from landscape that he very often entered the self. Then as the self grew inward, landscape retreated to the background. The immense burden P. had to carry is dual: the subject of some of his poems is his own subjectivity, and the subject of some others is collectivism. In the former the poet sees spiritual life in himself, and in the latter he interprets nationalistic feelings (encased in Malta's National Anthem). In his poetry that promoted the national spirit of the Maltese there was continuity with the previous generations of romantic poetry rife in the 19th c., and in his poetry of the maturing inner self there was an anticipation of the needs of the new poetry rife in postindependence Malta.

BIBLIOGRAPHY: Arberry, A. J., ed., Introduction to *A Maltese Anthology* (1960): xi-xxxvii; Friggieri, O., "In Search of a National Identity: A Survey of Maltese Literature," in Hopkins, K., and R. van Roekel, eds., *Crosswinds: An Anthology of Post-War Maltese Poetry* (1980): i-xxxiv; Friggieri, O., *Movimenti Letterari e Coscienza Romantica Maltese* (1980): i-xxxiv; Friggieri, O., *Storia della Letteratura Maltese* (1986)

—CHARLES BRIFFA

PUERTO RICAN LITERATURE
See Spanish-Caribbean Literature

PUIG, Manuel

Argentine novelist, b. 1932, General Villegas; d. 22 July 1990, Cuernavaca

P.'s youthful experiences left an indelible mark on his work. The drab existence of a typical middle-class family in a small town in the province of Buenos Aires—offset by the glamour of distant urban life, embodied in American films—has been the core of much of his fiction. In 1951 he began studies at the University of Buenos Aires. Unable to define a career for himself, he went to Rome in 1957 with a scholarship to study at the Experimental Film Center. For the next ten years he lived abroad, collaborating in the direction of several films and beginning to write. He returned to Buenos Aires briefly in 1967 but has lived abroad since then, mostly in Rome and New York. Since the publication of his first novel he has dedicated himself exclusively to writing fiction and to teaching writing.

With the publication of his first novel, *La traición de Rita Hayworth* (1968; *Betrayed by Rita Hayworth*, 1971), P. was immediately acclaimed as one of Latin America's most talented writers. Although the quality of P.'s fiction is remarkably even, most critics consider this first novel his masterpiece. It was followed by *Boquitas pintadas* (1969; *Heartbreak Tango*, 1973), a story of two love triangles written in the form of a serialized novel. The structural model for *The Buenos Aires Affair* (1973 [title in English]; *The Buenos Aires Affair*, 1976) is the detective story. *El beso de la mujer araña* (1976; *Kiss of the Spider Woman*, 1979) deals with a political prisoner and a homosexual who share a cell in a prison. Politics and sexuality, and their mutual relationship, are

Manuel Puig

also evident in the two novels, *Pubis angélical* (1979; angelic pubis) and *Maldición eterna a quienes lean estas páginas* (1980; *Eternal Curse on the Reader of These Pages*, 1982), the latter written first in English and translated into Spanish by the author.

P. has been called the chronicler of middle-class Argentina. His fiction describes the devastating emptiness of this life, the frustrations of those who desire to get beyond it, and the disappointments of failure. His novels, however, are far more than social documents portraying everyday reality. They penetrate and probe the complexities of human emotion and psychology. A pattern emerges among these complexities: although P.'s characters suffer from their empty daily existence, they live rich and full inner lives, often through fantasy. This creative aspect of existence is commonly expressed through cinematic metaphors.

In *La traición de Rita Hayworth* much of the mundane reality is filtered through the young protagonist, Toto Casals. It relates his story from infancy in 1933 to adolescence in 1948. The structure is typical of P.'s novels: it features eight chapters in each of the work's two parts, and the order of the chapters is not completely chronological. Rather than understanding all the circumstances surrounding Toto's life from the outset, the reader gradually fits the pieces of the puzzle together. It becomes apparent that Toto is a sensitive and intelligent person surrounded by mediocrity. Argentine society obviously does not accommodate those who do not fit into its structures and conform to its traditional values.

La traición de Rita Hayworth offers a variety of changing narrative situations with different narrators, written documents, and extensive dialogue. P. is a master of diverse writing styles, using several of them in each of his works. Some of the technical devices he employs are adopted from films, such as close-ups and the presentation of one-sided conversations. Among his other techniques are the use of shifting points of view and streams of sensory impressions.

The problems P.'s characters confront follow a chronological trajectory in the first three novels: *La traición de Rita Hayworth* deals with youth, *Boquitas pintadas* with late adolescence and early adulthood, and *The Buenos Aires Affair* with adulthood. In each of these novels sexual frustration and the ways a dominating society can limit human potential are major themes.

P. is one of Latin America's major writers and one of the most widely read. He has created a body of fiction that is highly sophisticated technically and thematically, yet at the same time quite accessible.

FURTHER WORKS: *Sangre de amor correspondido* (1982)

BIBLIOGRAPHY: Rodríguez Monegal, E., "A Literary Myth Exploded," *Review*: 4–5 (1971–72): 56–64; Hazera, L., "Narrative Technique in M. P.'s *Boquitas pintadas*," *LALR*, 2, 3, (1973): 45–51; Brushwood, J., *The Spanish American Novel* (1975): 305–8; Christ, R., "An Interview with M. P." *PR*, 44 (1977): 52–61; Luchting, W. A., "Betrayed by Education: M. P.'s *La traición de Rita Hayworth*," *PPNCFL*, 28, 1 (1977): 134–37; Lindstrom, N., "The Problem of Pop Culture in the Novels of M. P.," *TAH*, 4: 30–31 (1978): 28–31

—RAYMOND L. WILLIAMS

PUNJABI LITERATURE
See Indian Literature and Pakistani Literature

PURDY, James

American novelist, short-story writer, dramatist, and poet, b. 14 July 1923, near Fremont, Ohio

P., a child of divorced parents, spent his formative years moving about his native state. Finally graduating from a Chicago high school, P. attended the University of Chicago and the University of Puebla in Mexico. His linguistic abilities earned him a position teaching English in a private boys' school in Havana, Cuba. In 1953, after graduate study, traveling abroad, and four years on the faculty at Lawrence College in Wisconsin, he devoted himself to writing full-time. Rejected for years by American publishers, P.'s early stories were printed privately in 1956 and publicly, thanks to the support of Dame Edith SITWELL, in England in 1957 under the title *63: Dream Palace*. The collection was then published in the U.S. under the title *Color of Darkness* (1957). A recipient of Guggenheim and Ford Foundation grants, P. now lives in New York.

P.'s first collection of macabre tales, *Color of Darkness*, signals the major themes, characteristics, and discernments of American

society that permeate his later works and properly link him to a Southern Gothic tradition. Loveless, barren marriages and family lives abound in the stories, estranged children strive to communicate and find identity, while the spiritually deprived seek fulfillment through perverse love and violent sexuality. These subjects find their fullest expression in P.'s first and most popular novel, *Malcolm* (1959), an elusive allegory/fable/parable of Black HUMOR structured as a picaresque tale through which an innocent boy in search of his father moves progressively toward his own death, encountering the false, empty values of America that are emblematized in marriages, sexual attitudes, science, wealth, and art.

Satire functions as the dominant mode in two major novels. *The Nephew* (1961) turns to traditional realism to expose gently the small-town life of the Middle West and its underlying human darkness. More vitriolic and savage, *Cabot Wright Begins* (1964) scathingly portrays the brutal, immoral heart of American culture, where rape becomes a release from boredom and ennui, where the institutions of Wall Street and the New York publishing industry alienate and dehumanize; thus the corrupting ethos of commerce and the failure of art to engage reality are revealed.

P.'s works often explore the theme of homosexuality in order to show the anguish and suffering of the human condition, the dual curse of love as healer and betrayer. In *Eustace Chisholm and the Works* (1967) the hero, unable to accept his love for another man, escapes to the army, where he meets his human nemesis. The sadomasochistic relationship of hero and nemesis culminates in a horrific, ferocious scene of disembowelment and suicide.

P. regularly employs bizarre incident to underscore his ideas. The maimed soldier of *In a Shallow Grave* (1976) attempts to heal psychic wounds through love, for example, by drinking his lover's blood, spilled in a Christlike act by his lover's own hand. Similarly, *Narrow Rooms* (1978) concerns the love-hate, fear-submission bonds that bring four men to mystical absolution and murder. The protagonist purifies himself at the end by being crucified on a barn door as the disinterred body of his lover lies before him.

Jeremy's Version (1970) and *The House of the Solitary Maggot* (1974), parts of the incomplete trilogy *Sleepers in Moon-Crowded Valleys*, are regional in character and evoke a nostalgia for the Midwest of the 1920s and 1930s, but they also focus on a final and familiar P. theme: metaphysical preoccupation with the relation of language to reality. Through layers of narrative, stories within stories, memoirists, feeding on memoirists, these novels imply a madness in the American psyche that substitutes dreams for life itself.

Despite the eccentric nature of P.'s works, the originality and power of his dour vision into the blackness of the human soul, as well as his highly wrought style and unique symbolist techniques, will secure his position as an outstanding American craftsman.

FURTHER WORKS: *Children Is All* (1962); *An Oyster Is a Wealthy Beast* (1967); *Mr. Evening: A Story and Nine Poems* (1968); *On the Rebound: A Story and Nine Poems* (1970); *The Running Sun* (1971); *I Am Elijah Thrush* (1972); *Two Plays* (1979); *Mourners Below* (1981)

BIBLIOGRAPHY: Pomeranz, R., "The Hell of Not Loving: P.'s Modern Tragedy", *Renascence*, 15 (1963): 149–53; Skerrett, T., "J.P. and the Works: Love and Tragedy in Five Novels", *TCL*, 15 (1969): 25–53; Baldanza, F., "Playing House for Keeps with J. P.,"

ConL, 11 (1970): 489–510; Tanner, T., *City of Words* (1971): pp.85–108; Chupack, H., *J.P.* (1975); Adams, S., *J. P.* (1976)

—LYNN DEVORE

PUTINAS, Vincas

See Mykolaitis, Vincas

PYM, Barbara

(born Barbara Mary Pym Crampton) English novelist, b. 6 June 1913, Oswestry, Shropshire; d. 11 Jan. 1980, Oxford

P. received a B.A. in English literature from St. Hilda's College, Oxford, and spent most of her life in the Oxford area. During World War II she worked in Postal and Telegraph Censorship and served a year in Italy with the Women's Royal Naval Service. Her most productive writing years, from 1946 until her retirement in 1958, were spent as a research assistant for the International African Institute and as assistant editor of the organization's journal, *Africa*.

P.'s novels of manners are filled with the social details of the ordinary, usually uneventful lives of rather well-off unmarried women involved in church life. Excitement and adventure are rare in the novels; characters are more often interested in observing the lives of others than in creating events in their own lives. The novels emphasize eating, drinking, and thinking about clothes; the pleasures of Earl Gray tea, and food that is well prepared. P. consistently provides exact observations of a limited scene, whether domestic, academic, or clerical. Her middle-aged protagonists cope with loneliness by filling their lives with observation and contemplation. Influenced by her years with the African Institute, P. displays the detachment of an anthropologist, yet sympathizes with her characters' peculiarities or failures.

P.'s characters often cherish a secret love; their affections are unannounced and unrequited, usually because the loved one is somehow "unsuitable," either too young, already married, or of an inappropriate class. P.'s first novel, *Some Tame Gazelle* (1950), begins the pattern that continues in many of the novels. Two middle-aged sisters, modeled on P. and her sister Hilary, love men unsuitable for marriage: Belinda faithfully loves a former sweetheart now married to someone else, while Hilary loves a succession of young curates. In comparing their feelings with those of married people, the sisters conclude that remaining single is the way to preserve love. P. reverses the typical marriage plot so that the two women decide not to accept the proposals that come their way, but to remain unmarried and thus keep their love alive.

Characters satisfy their need for love in ways not necessarily associated with marriage or sexuality; characters love animals, young curates, church activities, persons who become surrogate children, or particular kinds of church services. *Excellent Women* (1952) and *Jane and Prudence* (1953) demonstrate that marriage is not necessarily any more fulfilling than the life of a "spinster" who does "good works" or has a succession of mild love affairs.

The ironic tone of P.'s work recalls Jane Austen (1775–1817). Protagonists maintain an ironic distance from the world; with

James Purdy

independence of thought and a keen ability to observe and evaluate society, P.'s women rarely take themselves or their work very seriously; they see humor and irony associated with even their own favorite habits, and they find fulfillment in observation and a heightened consciousness of the society around them. In contrast, P.'s men, often anthropologists or clergymen, are usually selfish, vain, or arrogant, taking themselves seriously and expecting the devotion "excellent women" shower upon them. The novels often imply feminist subtexts, but P.'s characters rarely depart from proscribed behavior—the women see the ironies inherent in patriarchal culture, but they never rebel.

After publishing P.'s first six novels, Jonathan Cape in 1963 rejected *An Unsuitable Attachment* (1982) and inaugurated a period of sixteen years during which P. published nothing. The novels written after the mid-1960s, during the long period when her work was rejected, differ from the earlier ones; while the early work centers on English village life, with characters concerned about the habits and lives of their neighbors, the later novels are set in the city, where characters have more trouble admitting or expressing affection for one another. The later characters prefer to mind their own business rather than interfere; nor do they want their own freedom limited by neighbors, as when Leonora of *The Sweet Dove Died* (1978) is careful not to be seen by the woman who rents an upstairs apartment from her. In *Quartet in Autumn* (1977), four elderly office workers secretly care about one another, but their interaction is confined to the office; only after two of them retire and their routine avoidance of one another concludes do they attempt friendship. Although a village setting returns for *A Few Green Leaves* (1980), the intimacy of the early novels is absent, as is the emphasis on the church.

Despite the difference in the early and late novels, P.'s entire oeuvre is remarkable in its portrayal of daily life in 20th-c. England. P.'s attention to uneventful lives allows her to capture the essence of daily life. Her characters may lead what some consider dull existences, but through them P. displays the extraordinary capacity for observation and perception that accompanies an examined life.

FURTHER WORKS: *Less Than Angels* (1955); *A Glass of Blessings* (1958); *No Fond Return of Love* (1961); *A Very Private Eye: An Autobiography in Diaries and Letters* (1984); *Crampton Hodnet* (1985); *An Academic Question* (1986); *Civil to Strangers and Other Writings* (1987)

BIBLIOGRAPHY: Brothers, B., "Women Victimized by Fiction: Living and Loving in the Novels by B. P.," in Staley, T. F., ed., *Twentieth-Century Women Novelists* (1982): 61–80; Calisher, H., "Enclosures: B. P.," *NewC*, 1, 3 (Nov. 1982): 53–56; Nardin, J., *B. P.* (1985); Schofield, M. A., "Well-Fed or Well-Loved?: Patterns of Cooking and Eating in the Novels of B. P.," *UWR*, 18, 2 (Spring/Summer 1985): 1–8; Stetz, M. D., "*Quartet in Autumn*: New Light on B. P. As a Modernist," ArQ, 41, 1 (Spring 1985): 24–37; Salwak, D., ed., *The Life and Work of B. P.* (1987); Liddell, R., *A Mind at Ease: B. P. and Her Novels* (1989); Wyatt-Brown, A. M., *B. P.: A Critical Biography* (1992)

—KAREN WILKES GAINEY

PYNCHON, Thomas

American novelist, b. 8 May 1937, Glen Cove, New York

P.'s family traces back to a colonial magistrate who presided over a witchcraft trial and who wrote a theological tract that was burned on Boston Common. Like Nathaniel Hawthorne P. has made literary capital out of his Puritan antecedents. He also has mined the vast resources of Western culture, particularly its recent history, science, and technology.

P. began writing while an undergraduate at Cornell University, where he studied engineering and English, receiving a B.A. degree in 1959 after a two-year interval in the Navy. While working at an aircraft company in Seattle, and later living in Mexico, he wrote *V.* (1963), which won the William Faulkner Prize for the best first novel of the year. For his second novel, *The Crying of Lot 49* (1966), he received the Rosenthal Foundation Award of the National Institute of Arts and Letters. *Gravity's Rainbow* (1973) was denied the Pulitzer Prize for its alleged obscenity and obscurity, despite the unanimous recommendation of the committee's judges. In 1975 P. declined the William Dean Howells gold medal for the best fiction of the previous five years. P. today lives a reclusive life, refusing to be interviewed or photographed.

Meanwhile, critical interest in P.'s work accelerates. Reviewers have been succeeded by scholars who log into the vast data bank that comprises P.'s five novels and a few short stories, each critic attempting to extract new meanings from the profusion and confusion of signals input by the author. P.'s stylistic virtuosity has been both praised as awesome and damned as tedious. Unquestionably, he has exploited, with brilliance and originality, the entire range of the novelistic tradition, drawing inspiration from Sterne and Voltaire, from Melville and Mark Twain, and from 20th-c. masters like Joseph CONRAD, James JOYCE, Vladimir NABOKOV, and Jorge Luis BORGES. No doubt he owes something to the example of work like William GADDIS's *The Recognitions* (1955).

P. changes modes and moods with disconcerting speed—shifting from romance to satire, from burlesque and slapstick to poignant lyricism. He seems to have overlooked no literary precedents—Anatole FRANCE's missionary to the penguins, for example, is matched by Father Fairing and his parish of rats in the sewers of Manhattan in *V.* His pages abound with mandalas, carbon rings, limericks, and notes on art history and musicology. With a wildness of tone and taste, he applies the tricks of cinematography, comic books, and other forms of popular culture. His most powerful and subversive weapon is parody.

P.'s work bears evidence of his knowledge of an esoteric assortment of world myths and other cultural traditions, of the intellectual and aesthetic products of a wide range of thinkers and artists from past and present. His offbeat erudition enables him to utilize history and anthropology in startling ways, addressing, for example, the 1898 Fashoda Crisis in the Sudan, the death of the composer Anton von Weber, Ojibwa customs, the Kyrgyz language, martial arts, the Tibetan Book of the Dead, or Lombroso's misoneism, although readers must remain on guard against invented peoples, persons and places, concepts, and institutions.

Perhaps P.'s most stunning achievement is the use he makes of science and technology in the creation of his metaphors. An early short story, "Entropy" (1960), revealed P.'s fascination with the Second Law of Thermodynamics. The entropy concept, in its dual application in physics and in information theory, pervades all of P.'s novels—iterating a theme of the general breakdown of the contemporary sociocultural order.

P.'s prose is strewn with scientific and mathematical allusions—Gödel's Theorem, Maxwell's Demon, Poisson's Distribution. Such concepts, together with discourses on cybernetics, chemistry, and electronics, are implanted in the very tissue of the fiction, and they grow into symbolic significance that sets P. apart from practitioners of science fiction and fantasy. Equipped as he is with the latest and most specialized scientific and technical lore and the most innovative literary techniques, P. seems fitted to provide his readers with a complete Baedeker's guide through the 20th c.

The novel *V.*, set in the 1950s, traverses the previous half-dozen decades in a bewildering itinerary across continents and cultures, to the frontiers of reality and beyond. The novel's overriding form is a doubling of the ancient quest motif. One plot focuses on Herbert Stencil and his obsessive search for the identity of the title symbol: *V.* is at once a person, a place, and a mental construct—she/he metamorphoses through several identities, ending finally in an assortment of prosthetic attachments. Stencil's career is counterpointed by the aimless peregrinations of Benny Profane, whose freedom dissipates into the mechanical motions of a human yo-yo.

The protagonist of *The Crying Lot 49* is a California housewife named Oedipa Maas who is doomed as the pursuer pursued through Kafkaesque horrors of contemporary American civilization.

The paranoia of this slim book spills over into *Gravity's Rainbow*, a novel of enormous proportions populated by over three hundred characters who operate on an international scale near the close of World War II and in the Allied Zones of Occupation in 1945. Among these characters is an American lieutenant named Tyrone Slothrop, comically and ironically both quester and quarry. Slothrop, it turns out, was the unwitting subject of scientific manipulation during childhood and now he is the experimental target of competing military factions, one of which attempts to correlate a Poisson distribution of the lieutenant's sex encounters with the pattern of V-2 bombs that fall on London. As the book progresses, Slothrop is the victim of multiple intrigues from all directions. His paranoia is paradigmatic of the hostility and suspicion in all ranks. The rage to control and the terror of being controlled are doubled and redoubled on both sides of the Channel. Over and over again we are brought to the threshold of cosmic conspiracy.

Underneath a metaphysical cloud of doubt and suspicion P.'s multitudes of men and women move in and out of the Zone, dabbling in their own puddles of purpose, puddles that are iridescent with the slime of humanity. And over all—beyond good and evil?—arches the trajectory of the rocket: the vapor trail of the V-2, caught in the light of the sun whose image dominates the pages of *Gravity's Rainbow*. The rocket is P.'s candidate for apocalyptic successor to Henry Adams' Virgin and Dynamo.

In the 1970s the critic Edward Mendelson proposed a new literary genre, the encyclopedic narrative; and into this exclusive category he admitted *Gravity's Rainbow* along with works of Dante, Rabelais, Cervantes, Goethe, Melville, and Joyce. It is astonishing how often the book has been compared to *Moby-Dick* and *Ulysses*.

After *Gravity's Rainbow* nothing was heard of P. For seventeen years, except for a slender collection of short stories, *Slow Learner* (1984). Then, in 1990, appeared P.'s fourth novel, *Vineland*. Its title refers to a mythical town in northwest California, ironically named to remind readers of Leif Ericson's Vinland dating a millennium earlier, P. has populated his Vineland with an assorted collection of refugees from the 1960s—the novel opens in the Orwellian year 1984. These refugees, some of whom are now semi dead Thanatoids, include leftover Wobblies from the union wars, aging hippies and other products of the drug scene, and a novel mix of people who may use weapons ranging from cameras to guns.

But reader's sympathies flow toward these social misfits as it becomes clear that they are victims of a great betrayal. For government agents, fouled in their own paranoia and lusts, are an even greater threat to family and community in Vineland. The novel's characters on both sides of the war are vividly realized, and P.'s plot is full of helical twists that bear strands of reality and fantasy. Cultural symbols appear decade by decade, from movies to radio to recordings to television and computers, all worked by P. into high-tech fantasy. Television viewers, for example, have become so addicted that they retreat to Tube detoxification centers. And one character wonders whether humans are not zeroes and ones in a vast computer's digital system, all lying "beneath the notice of the hacker we call God."

And yet *Vineland* ends with hints of hope, as the Vineland citizens have read to them a golden text from Ralph Waldo

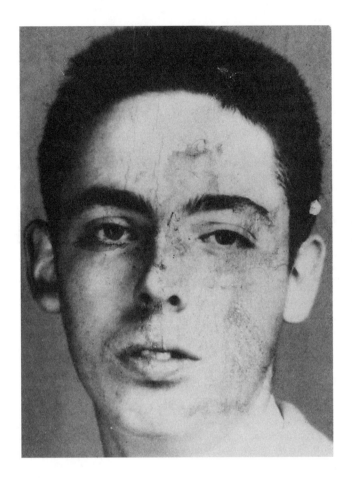

Thomas Pynchon

Emerson, found by one of their number in a jailhouse copy of William James's *Varieties of Religious Experience*: "Secret retributions are always restoring the level, when disturbed, of the divine justice."

In 1997, after years of rumors concerning the reclusive author's next project, appeared *Mason and Dixon*, another encyclopedic novel filled with P.'s characteristic wit and density. Into a vast 18th-c. milieu, created in the spirit of Laurence Sterne and Henry Fielding, P. presents the picaresque meanderings of the legendary pair remembered for plotting the historic line that bears their names. Charles Mason, astronomer, and Jeremiah Dixon, surveyor, first are teamed together in South Africa, where they report on the Transit of Venus and, incidentally, observe the depredations of colonialism and slavery. Then, a third of the way through the novel, they are assigned to survey the disputed boundary between land grants of the Penns of Pennsylvania and the Calverts of Maryland. Mason, a melancholy widower, and Dixon, a quirky member of the Quaker faith, recruit a force of axmen and other workers for the years-long expedition that eventually moves westward as far as Ohio.

Before and during the journey P. arranges for encounters with familiar pre-Revolutionary personages, including an inventive Franklin, a hemp-smoking Washington, and a young Virginian who hears Dixon use a phrase, "the pursuit of happiness," and jots it down for future use. The book abounds with P.'s usual blend of esoterica and wild inventions, reinforced here with humorous anachronisms and with the archaic spellings and idioms of the Rev.

Wicks Cherrycoke, whose anecdotal accounts supply what plot line is visible in the novel. Its pages are populated by Chinese Jesuits, feuding religious sects, and genocidal frontiersmen as well as talking animals and clocks, giant vegetables, and four-ton cheese. There is talk of golems, feng shui, and the eleven days that vanished from the calendar in 1752.

Underneath all the tomfoolery P. has carefully defined a series of judgments regarding human nature as it has expressed itself in American history. Mason and Dixon may wander clownlike through the landscape, but each achieves moments of moral insight. Dixon, who once snatched a whip from a slaver and gave him a dose of his own cruelty, remarks to Mason that they have seen slaves everywhere, at the Cape and on St. Helena, "and now, here we are again, in another Colony, this time having drawn a Line between their Slave-Keepers, and their Wage-Payers." And Mason, at the last wonders, "Shall wise Doctors one day write History's assessment of the Good resulting from this Line, *vis-a-vis* the not-so-good? I wonder which List will be longer." So much for a manmade slash across the pristine wilderness, an abstraction that has haunted America down to the present.

All art is a matter of the artist's selecting and arranging what he finds in his world. P.'s powers of assimilation have proved prodigious; his world is fabulous, his fabrications are splendid. In the process of creating his fables, he has teased the old questions, especially those of freedom and determinism (his is not a binary view), and enlarged our view of human nature.

BIBLIOGRAPHY: Slade, J., *T. P.* (1974); Levine, G., and Leverenz, D., eds., *Mindful Pleasures: Essays on T. P.* (1976); Mendelson, E., ed., *P: A Collection of Critical Essays* (1978); Cowart, D., *T. P.: The Art of Illusion* (1980); Mackey, D. A., *The Rainbow Quest of T. P.* (1980); Stark, J. O., *P.'s Fictions: T. P. and the Literature of Information* (1980); Pearce, R., ed., *Critical Essays on T. P.* (1981); Schaub, T. H., *P.: The Voice of Ambiguity* (1981); Cooper, P., *Signs and Symptoms: T. P. and the Contemporary World* (1983); Hite, M., *Ideas of Order in the Novels of T. P.* (1983); Bloom, H., *T. P.* (1986); Seed, D., *The Fictional Labyrinths of T. P.* (1988); Madsen, D. L., *The Postmodernist Allegories of T. P.* (1991); Chambers, J., *T. P.* (1992); Berressem, H., *P.'s Poetics: Interfacing Theory and Text* (1993); Green, G., *The Vineland Papers: Critical Takes on P.'s Novel* (1994)

—CARL D. BENNETT

Q

QABBĀNĪ, Nizār

Syrian poet, b. 21 March 1923, Damascus; d. 1 May 1998, London, England

Son of a rich merchant, Q. joined the Syrian foreign service after finishing his law studies in 1945. As a diplomat he was posted successively to Egypt, Turkey, the United Kingdom, Lebanon, Spain, and China, and he traveled widely. He resigned from the foreign service in 1966 and settled in Beirut, Lebanon, where he worked in literary journalism and eventually started a publishing house.

Q. is perhaps the most popular poet in the Arab world, his collections having run into several printings. Since the early 1940s, when he began writing poetry, to the present day, love and women have continued to be his major themes. Whether or not he is an irresponsible intellectual locked up in an adolescent sensuality that wastes his talent, as some critics think, his achievement is astounding in that for over thirty-five years his creativity has never ceased exploring ever new ways of expressing his love for woman's beauty and portraying women in ever different love situations.

His early poems, such as those in *Qālat lī al-samrā'* (1944; the brunette said to me) and *Anti lī* (1950; you are mine), exhibit a stark physical craving for woman, as he dwells on parts of her body, which he paints in thrilling, evocative images of great beauty. In later poems, as in *Qasā'id* (1956; poems), *Habībatī* (1961; my sweetheart), and *Al-Rasm bi-al-kalimāt* (1966; painting in words), his sensuality becomes refined as he portrays the elegance of high-society women. But Q. has become increasingly aware of the complexities of love relations, especially of woman's vulnerability in man's world, and he has written several poems expressing woman's disgust with man's crass insensitivity to her. The love poems of his more mature years, as in *Qasā'id mutawahhisha* (1970; wild poems) and *Ash'ār khārija 'alā al-qānūn* (1972; law-breaking poems), treat the experience of love and see it ideally as an honest relation of two reciprocating equals free from social taboos.

Q. has occasionally dealt with other social themes, as in his poem "Khubz wa hashīsh was qamar" (1955; "Bread, Hashish, and Moon," 1972), in which he castigated Arab society for its languor, superstitiousness, and quiescence. But it was not until 1967, after the humiliating defeat of the Arabs by Israel in the Six Day War, that Q. produced a series of politically motivated poems criticizing repressive Arab regimes and their submissive citizenry, and supported the Palestine Liberation Movement as a hope for wider Arab liberation and transformation. These poems, mostly collected in his *Al-A'māl al-styāsiyya* (1974; political works), are characterized by the same naturalness and spontaneity that mark his love poems.

FURTHER WORKS: *Tufūlat nahd* (1948); *Sāmbā* (1949); *Al-Shi'r qindīl akhdar* (1964); *Yawmiyyāt imra'a lā mubāliya* (1969); *Kitāb al-hubb* (1970); *Lā* (1970); *Al-Kitāba 'amal inqilābī* (1978)

BIBLIOGRAPHY: Loya, A., "Poetry as a Social Document: The Social Position of the Arab Woman as Reflected in the Poetry of N. Q.," *MW*, 63, 1 (1973): 39–52; Gabay, Z., "N. Q., the Poet and His Poetry," *MES*, 9, 2 (1973): 207–22; Badawi, M. M., *A Critical Introduction to Modern Arabic Poetry* (1975): pp.221–22; Jayyusi, S. K., *Trends and Movements in Modern Arabic Poetry* (1977), Vol. II: 563, 664–65

—ISSA J. BOULLATA

QADIRIY, Abdullah

(pseud.: Julqunbay) Uzbek novelist, short-story writer, dramatist, and satirist, b. 1894, Tashkent; d. 1940

Q.'s Muslim education combined Persian, Arabic, and Chaghatay (a Turkic literary language) classics with post-1900 "new method" instruction introduced into Turkistan by the modernizing reformers known as the Jadids. His father, a bankrupt merchant turned winegrower, was a firsthand source for the 19th-c. history of the khanate of Qoqan, the setting for Q.'s novels. Q., arrested in 1939 as an "enemy of the people," died in prison; since his 1956 rehabilitation some of his works have been republished, although in altered form.

Q. began writing as early as 1910. He produced some poetry and won early success with his innovative prose: satires, sketches, short stories like "Ulaqudä" (1916; at a horsemen's goat-snatching contest) and "Juwanbaz" (1915; the pederast), and plays, including the much-performed *Bäkhtsiz kuyaw* (1915; the unlucky son-in-law).

Q. brought his dramatist's skills—lively dialogue and vivid episodic style—to his major venture: replacing Central Asian folk epics with the first Uzbek novel. Q., who was acquainted with works of Jurjī Zaydān (1861–1914), an Arab historical novelist, used court intrigues, harem politics, and merchant and clerical households as backdrop for his novels: *Otgän kunlär* (1925–26; days gone by), a tragedy of an arranged polygamous marriage, and *Mehrabdän chäyan* (1929; scorpion from the pulpit), the true story of a poor orphan who rose to be chief secretary to the khan. Both books, written in modern literary language laced with folk humor, were best sellers, reprinted often, and later translated into other Central Asian languages and Russian. Avoiding both the stereotyped beautiful women of Oriental literature and the tractordriving heroines of much Soviet fiction, Q. presents subtle characterizations, psychologically motivated, of both sexes.

In satirical story cycles published between 1923 and 1927 in *Mushtum* one of several periodicals with which Q. was associated, the comical portraits of the self-important characters Kälwäk Mähzum and Aunty Shärwan were popular.

Q.'s belated recognition as creator of the Uzbek novel filled an awkward void in Soviet Uzbek literary history, for except for his work there was little of note in this genre by Uzbeks before AYBEK'S novel *Näwaiy* in 1944. Q.'s influence on succeeding writers as mentor and model has been gratefully and openly acknowledged by Aybek, by the Kazakh author Mukhtar Omarkhanuli AUEZOV, by the Turkmen novelist Berdi Kerbaba-oghli (1894–1974), and by many others.

FURTHER WORKS: *Abid ketman* (1934)

BIBLIOGRAPHY: Hayit, B., "Die jüngste özbekische Literatur," *CAsJ*, 7 (1962): 119–52; Allworth, E., *Uzbek Literary Politics* (1964), passim; Benzing, J., "Die usbekische und neu-uigurische Literatur," *Philologiae Turcicae Fundamenta*, 2 (1965): 700–20; "Kadyri, Abdulla," *Great Soviet Encyclopedia*, 3rd ed. (1976), Vol. 11: 334

—SUSANNA S. NETTLETON

QANOAT, Mu'min

Tajik poet and critic, b. 20 May 1923, Badakhshan

Q. grew up in a family of kolkhoz farmers in the autonomous Badakhshan region of the Pamirs. As a young man, he worked on the farm and participated in kolkhoz activities. His first poems were published in the 1940s in a local newspaper in the neighboring Gharm region of Tajikistan. Upon his graduation in 1956 from Tajikistan State University, where he studied philology and history, Q. worked for the *Sado-i Sharq* journal, contributing to its poetry section. Between 1961 and 1966 he was the main editor for that section. Q. joined the Writers Union of Tajikistan in 1961 and served as its First Secretary between 1977 and 1991.

Q.'s first poetry collection, *Sharora* (1960; Flame), set the mood and the tone for his poetic career. His knowledge of the classical poetic traditions of the Perso-Tajik peoples and of the world at large enable him to paint imagery that is at once delightful and compelling.

Two of his works, *Surush-i Istolingrod* (1971; The Stalingrad Anthem) and *Tojikiston—Ism-i Man* (1974; Tajikistan—My Name), brought Q. to the attention of the Moscow critics and authorities. In 1977 he was recognized as a Poet Laureate of the U.S.S.R. Meanwhile, his longer poems, *Mawjho-i Dniper* (1964; Dnieper Waves) and *Doston-i Otash* (1971; The Story of Fire), having been translated into Russian, made him well known outside the republic of Tajikistan. In Tajikistan he was recognized as the State Poet Laureate in 1978.

The themes of Q.'s poems are varied. But whether dealing with everyday events, philosophical speculation, or human suffering, Q. finds representative characters to communicate his exact thoughts. Furthermore, he chooses his characters carefully from among the working classes. For *Doston-i Otash,* for instance, he spent time at Norak, getting to know the individuals who built the hydroelectric station. From among them he chose to tell the story of Anna, a war widow with a child. We learn that Anna had worked for a long time on the Volga, waiting for her husband. We hear her son continuously asking for his father, and we enter Anna's own ruminations as she builds up hope each night as she lies down only to face yet another day of lonely labor. At Norak she is promoted to a managerial position and her talented son grows up and begins taking care of her. Mawjgul, from *Nur dar Qullaho* (1976; Light on the Summits), has a similar story. She escapes from her family and village to avoid an arranged marriage. She is accepted by the workers at Norak, where she begins a new, exciting, and meaningful life.

One of the major themes on which Q. draws a great deal is war. This theme, which he often generalizes, touches him personally so that the reader can feel the pain of separation brought about by war. For instance, in the poem entitled "Barodaram" (n.d.; My Brother) the character's distress at the loss of his brother is intense. After he searches among thousands of dead youth, he becomes convinced that he will never see or hear his brother again and that he will never again smell the smell of his brother. But then he has a sudden change of attitude. He realizes that while he has lost one mortal brother he has found thousands of immortal brothers.

Q.'s major work, *Surush-i Istolingrod*, glorifies the untiring efforts of the Soviet men and women who defended that city. Consisting of an introduction and nine chapters, the work gives an account of the lives of soldiers, workers, fathers, and mothers who liberated the city. The mother-image is the most prominent. In fact, the work begins and ends by monologues glorifying motherhood and, by extension, the motherland. *Surush-i Istolingrod* combines a number of positive features; it mixes epic and lyricism with drama, is composed of interconnected but mostly independent stories, and each chapter tells a different story. The entire poem explains a tragedy that must not be repeated. For example, Matvei Putilov—after having been mortally wounded—uses his teeth to reestablish a much needed disconnected telephone line. He dies holding the line. Similarly, Misha, the Black Sea sailor, having been set on fire by a broken Molotov cocktail, runs all the way and throws himself under the enemy tank, blowing it up.

These haunting images, however, are surface realizations of higher and more profound conflicts arising from the clash of social, political, and ideological values. Life and death, justice and injustice, and bravery and cowardice form the fabric of Q.'s epical work. In his "Gahvora-i Sino" (1980; The Cradle of Ibn-i Sina), for which he won Tajikistan's Rudaki Prize in literature, a similar battle is waged by Ibn-i Sina. The epitome of benevolence, humanism, and love for his fellow man, Ibn-i Sina wages an unending war against disease, poverty, and suffering. But while he prevents death from reaching others, he himself succumbs to death.

The most prominent features of Q.'s poetry are innovation, precision, and realism. He actually places the reader within the frame of the poem so that the reader can see and hear the very sights and sounds that have inspired the poem. This feeling is tangible, especially when Q. recites his own poetry.

FURTHER WORKS: *Golosa Stalingrada* (1977); *Osor-i Muntakhab* (2 vols., 1982)

BIBLIOGRAPHY: Qodiri, A., *Adibon-i Tojikiston* (1966): 274-76; Akbarov, U., *Talab-i Hayot ve Qismat-i Adabiyyot* (1977); Akbarov, U., *Qismat-i Inson ve Qismat-i Shi'r* (1980); Hakimov, A., *Dar Qalamrav-i Sukhan* (1982); Sattorov, A., *Nuqta-i Paivand* (1982); Saifullaev, A., "M. Q.," *Ensaiklopidio-i Soveti-i Tojik* (1984), Vol. 5: 23-24; Akbarov, U., *Shi'r-i Ihsos ve Tafakkur* (1985); Saifullaev, A., *Arkon-i Sukhan* (1985); Akbarov, U., "M. Q.," *Ensaiklopedio-i Adabiyyot ve San'at-i Tojik* (1989), Vol. 2: 394-97; Mirzozoda, Kh., *Adabiyyot-i Soveti-i Tojik*, (1990): 228-35

—IRAJ BASHIRI

QUASIMODO, Salvatore

Italian poet, translator, and essayist, b. 20 Aug. 1901, Modica, Sicily; d. 14 June 1968, Naples

Q. was born into a family of modest means. His father was a stationmaster whose transfers allowed the boy to know various Sicilian scenes, which were later to appear in his poetry. He pursued technical studies in Palermo and Rome, and became a civil

Salvatore Quasimodo

engineer with the Ministry of Public Works (1926–38). Thereafter he moved into the more congenial field of letters, contributing to literary journals, serving as editor of the weekly *Il tempo* several times, and from 1940 on teaching Italian literature at the Milan Conservatory of Music. He was always an assiduous student of ancient and modern languages and literatures. His poetry brought him several literary awards, including the Etna-Taormina Prize for Poetry (1953, shared with Dylan THOMAS [q.v.]), the Viareggio Prize (1958), and the Nobel Prize for literature (1959).

Q.'s literary production consists of a dozen slender volumes of poetry; fifteen or more volumes of excellent translations of Greek and Latin classics, Shakespeare, and modern poets of various nationalities; two volumes of critical essays; numerous (partly uncollected) articles and reviews; and several librettos for music.

His first volume of verse, *Acque e terre* (1930; water and land), contains features that were to recur throughout his work: vivid memories of his youth, compassion and concern for the humble folk from whom he came, a deep sense of the solitude of the individual, a personal seriousness and melancholy, a generally negative view of life. This early collection contains at least one authentic masterpiece, "Vento a Tíndari" ("Wind at Tíndari," 1960). Q.'s forceful and evocative style was immensely attractive despite its initial "difficulty," and was quickly acclaimed by the public and the critics. Several other volumes appeared in quick succession. His whole prewar output was pruned, revised, and republished in the volume *Ed è subito sera* (1942; and suddenly it is evening), which remains his most widely read book.

World War II broadened Q.'s human sympathy and the horizon of his poetry. *Giorno dopo giorno* (1947; day after day) reflects his country's hardships. The poems in it are intense, deeply felt; their eloquence is achieved less through rhetoric than through a precise directness of language, brief realistic notations, a humane commentary. A less closed and less intimate style, a more "public" utterance, are appropriately used here to deal with Italy's woes, in poems such as "Alle fronde dei salici" ("On the Willow Branches," 1960) and "Uomo del mio tempo" ("Man of My Time," 1960). This may be Q.'s best work, and perhaps the best volume of poetry to come out of World War II in any country.

Q.'s last four volumes of verse show a continuing concern for social justice, fond memories of past friends and past loves, probings into the meaning of life, and ponderings on illness and death. They are somewhat uneven collections, but with a preponderance of fine poems.

Q.'s overall production is impressive in its uncommon originality and its high quality. One of its most attractive features is the great sensitivity to the look and feel of the poet's native Sicily and a constant awareness of its cultural heritage from Greeks, Romans, Arabs, and other invaders. He recalls certain landscapes, his experience of them, what they meant to him; he notes literary associations ("my Homeric childhood," "Ulysses' isle,"), historical relics, the physical environment—its harshness and its Mediterranean beauty ("earth and sky and gentle gift of water"). The voluntary exile in the northern metropolis remembers his island as a brave, bright Eden, situated on storied ground; he inevitably poetizes it, viewing it through the prisms of love, memory, time and distance. The "myth" of Sicily that he creates adds much to the richness and flavor of Q.'s poetry. He is also keenly interested in the island's present-day economic and political problems; these he notes with harsh realism.

In style and language Q. avoids the "classical" and the ornate in favor of a condensed, lean, and forceful utterance that is nonetheless flexible and varied. He is sober in the expression of feeling. He manages a fine affectionate poem to his mother, and another to his father, that have none of the usual sentimental effusions. Everywhere the superfluous or vague is pared away, and the word is given its essential meaning in an essential role. This is the mark of Q.'s modernity and places him in the current of HERMETICISM that dominated his time. The critics speak of the "tension" and "intensity" of the word, of his "poetics of the word," of a process of "essentialization" resulting in a spare and "naked" language. His poems are brief; the short lines conform only loosely, if at all, to traditional meters. They have a natural harmony and a sustained literary dignity. Q. has assumed his rightful place among the three or four best Italian poets of the century.

FURTHER WORKS: *Oboe sommerso* (1932); *Odore di eucalyptus* (1933); *Erato e Apòllion* (1936); *Poesie* (1938); *Con il piede straniero sopra il cuore* (1946); *La vita non è sogno* (1949); *Il falso e vero verde* (1956); *La terra impareggiabile* (1958; *The Incomparable Earth*, 1958); *Il poeta e il politico, e altri saggi* (1960; *The Poet and the Politician, and Other Essays*, 1964); *Tutte le poesie* (1960); *Dare e avere* (1966; *To Give and to Have, and Other Poems*, 1969); *Poesie e discorsi sulla poesia* (1971); *The Selected Writings of S. Q.* (1960); *Selected Poems* (1965); *To Give and to Have and Other Poems* (1969)

BIBLIOGRAPHY: Cambon, G., "A Deep Wind: Q.'s Tíndari," *IQ*, 3 (1959): 16–28; Rossi, L. R., "S. Q.: A Presentation," *ChiR*, 14

(1960): 1–21; Cambon, G., "Q.," *Chelsea*, 6 (1960): 60–67; Pacifici, S., "S. Q.," *Cesare Barbieri Courier*, 3 (1960): 10–16; Jones, F. J., "Poetry of S. Q.," *IS*, 16 (1961): 60–77; Beall, C. B., "Q. and Modern Italian Poetry,"*NorthwestR*, 4 (1961): 41–48; Dutschke, D., "S. Q.," *IQ*, 12 (1969): 91–103; Molinaro, J. A., "Q. and the Theme of the Willow Trees," *RomN*, 18 (1977): 32–37; Danesi, M., "Some Observations on Information Theory and Poetic Language, with Illustrations from the Poetry of S. Q.," *CJItS*, 1 (1978): 224–30

—CHANDLER B. BEALL

QUEIROZ, Rachel de

Brazilian novelist, dramatist, and journalist, b. 17 Nov. 1910, Fortaleza

Q. started her literary career in 1927 as a journalist in her native city. She made a sensational debut as a novelist with *O quinze* (1930; 'fifteen [i.e., 1915]), which was received with enthusiastic critical acclaim throughout Brazil. The fact of her youth contributed to this success, but more important was the fact that the novel was one of the first, after *A bagaceira* (1928; sugar mill) by José Américo de Almeida (1887–1980), to introduce to Brazil a new social-minded literature of the 1930s. Although the periodic droughts in northeastern Brazil had been the theme of a few earlier novels, the literary school initiated with the books of Almeida and Q. substituted social and even socialist intentions and preoccupations for the traditional sentimental approach to that tragedy. The novel's title refers to the year of 1915, in which one of the most catastrophic droughts occurred. All these circumstances explain the immense interest awakened by *O quinze*, which was awarded the Graça Aranha Foundation literary prize in 1931.

Q.'s second novel, *João Miguel* (1932; João Miguel), was a tentative effort toward a proletarian novel. Its hero is in fact an anti-hero, the common man of northeast Brazil. In terms of Q.'s development as a novelist, it marks a transition from a social to a psychological approach.

Indeed, after a five-year period of silence, Q. published *Caminho de pedras* (1937; road of stones), which was followed by *As três Marias* (1939; *The Three Marias*, 1963). Both are clearly individualist in accent and purpose. With the exception of *O galo de ouro* (the golden rooster)—not yet published in book form—which appeared in installments in 1950 in a Rio de Janeiro publication, Q. stopped writing narratives until 1975, when the novel *Dôra Doralina* (Dôra Doralina) was published.

In the 1940s Q. began to write columns for several newspapers and particularly for the periodical *O cruzeiro*. Her *crônicas* gained widespread popularity in Brazil and assured her reputation as one of Brazil's outstanding writers. Many of those *crônicas* were subsequently collected into books—for example, *100 crônicas escolhidas* (1958; 100 selected chronicles).

In the 1950s she became interested in the theater. Her first play, *Lampião* (1953; Lampião), is about the life and deeds of the famous rural outlaw nicknamed Lampião. It was well received in Rio de Janeiro and São Paulo, where it was awarded the Saci Prize as the year's best play. Five years later, another play, *A beata Maria do Egito* (1958; blessed Mary of Egypt), was awarded two other prizes.

In addition, Q. is a highly respected translator, having brought out in Portuguese works by Dostoevsky, Jane Austen, Emily Brontë, and John GALSWORTHY.

What can be said about Q. without hesitation is that she is to be credited with writing a Portuguese that is highly expressive and that she handles colloquial Portuguese masterfully. In 1957 she was awarded the Brazilian Academy of Letters prize for her total work, and was elected to this academy in 1977.

FURTHER WORKS: *Três romances* (1948); *A donzela e a moura torta* (1948); *Quatro romances* (1960); *O Brasileiro perplexo* (1964); *O caçador de tatu* (1967); *O menino mágico* (1969)

BIBLIOGRAPHY: Ellison, F. P., *Brazil's New Novel: Four Northeastern Writers* (1954): 135–54; Schade, G. D., "Three Contemporary Brazilian Novels: Some Comparisons and Contrasts," *Hispania*, 39 (1956): 391–96; Woodbridge, B. M., Jr. "The Art of R. de Q.," *Hispania*, 40 (1957): 139–48; Reynolds, C. R., "The Santa María Egipciaca Motif in Modern Brazilian Letters," *RomN*, 13 (1971): 71–76

—WILSON MARTINS

QUENEAU, Raymond

French novelist and poet, b. 21 Feb. 1903, Le Havre; d. 25 Oct. 1976, Paris

As a young writer, Q. was attracted to SURREALISM and participated actively in the movement between 1924 and 1929. He became a reader for Gallimard in 1938 and was the principal editor of their encyclopedias and histories of literature published in the Pléiade series beginning in the late 1940s. Q. engaged in a broad range of activities, including painting and film, and he wrote of these as well as on literature and many other subjects, including mathematics. He was elected to the Goncourt Academy in 1951.

Q.'s first novel, and perhaps his best, was *Le chiendent* (1933; *The Bark-Tree*, 1968). It was one of the first books to reveal, through the use of slangy speech, a crisis in the language of the novel. Q., who was at that time still close to surrealism, seems to have reenacted the surrealist rebellion here, insisting that the real subject of his work is language itself, language that is being endlessly created.

Pierrot mon ami (1942; *Pierrot*, 1950), whose hero moves about an amusement park in a manner reminiscent of Charlie Chaplin, is also a clever exercise in words, a detective story in which one can never be sure whether a crime has been committed.

Loin de Rueil (1944; *The Skin of Dreams*, 1948) is very much admired by sophisticated readers. The protagonist, Jacques L'Aumône, leads a complex fantasy life as well as a mundane existence; he becomes the hero of films he sees, a boxing champion, a bishop, a nobleman, until finally neither he nor the reader is sure who he is. *Loin de Rueil* presents a half-mad, half-poetic vision of the world.

Zazie dans le métro (1959; *Zazie*, 1960) was an immediate popular success, perhaps because Zazie is a sort of farcical French Lolita, but its ultimate value lies in Q.'s use of a popular, if salacious, style of dialogue, often reproduced phonetically. As in his earlier novels, he thus questions the nature and value of language itself, and here the banal setting stresses the meaninglessness of action and speech.

Q. had already experimented explicitly with language in *Exercices de style* (1947; *Exercises in Style*, 1958), in which he presents ninety-nine different versions of the same totally insignificant anecdote. In fact, Q.'s entire work could be characterized as an exercise in style intended to reveal the absurdity of human activity.

This expression of the gratuitousness of life through experimentation with language is especially apparent in his poems. They are often built on plays on words and on the repetition of key words, as in the collection with the meaningless title of *Les ziaux* (1943; the ziaux). *Cent mille milliards de poèmes* (1961; one hundred trillion poems) carries this tendency several steps further, and also reflects Q.'s mathematical bent, by presenting ten sonnets in which any line can be substituted for any other line, thereby creating the number of poems in the title.

In his efforts to rejuvenate literary forms and to develop new means of literary communication, Q. often employed traditional forms—the novel, the sonnet, the alexandrine—but always parodying them, using the vocabulary and tempo of popular speech. He does not attempt to provide an exact transcription of contemporary life and society; rather, he creates a new view of it based on the language forged from his observations.

Q.'s view of language shows his affiliation with surrealism; yet he was also close to EXISTENTIALISM in his creation of a sense of the absurd, of the hopelessness and ridiculousness of the contemporary world. Q. has not reached the vast public of SARTRE and CAMUS, however, because he did not attempt to go beyond the meaninglessness he expressed, but, rather, enjoyed it. His readership will remain those who can share his joy without demanding more.

Many writers, including Henry MILLER and Boris VIAN, have found affinities with Q. and admitted his influence. Perhaps Q., of all modern French writers, comes closest to James JOYCE, in the breadth of his learning and his creation of new literary structures through his linguistic virtuosity. But again, his seemingly frivolous attitude toward literature and life precludes his being treated critically with as much seriousness as his Irish predecessor.

FURTHER WORKS: *Gueule de Pierre* (1934); *Les derniers jours* (1936); *Odile* (1937); *Chêne et chien* (1937); *Les enfants du limon* (1938); *Un rude hiver* (1939; *A Hard Winter*, 1948); *Les temps mêlés* (1941); *En passant* (1944); *Foutaises* (1944); *L'instant fatal* (1946); *Pictogrammes* (1946); *À la limite de la forêt* (1947; *At the Edge of the Forest*, 1954); *Bucoliques* (1947); *Une trouille verte* (1947); *On est toujours trop bon avec les femmes* (1947, under pseud. Sally Mara; *We Always Treat Women Too Well*, 1981); *Monuments* (1948); *Saint Glinglin* (1948); *Bâtons, chiffres et lettres* (1950); *Petite cosmogonie portative* (1950); *Journal intime* (1950, under pseud. Sally Mara); *Si tu t'imagines* (1952); *Le dimanche de la vie* (1952); *Le chien à la mandoline* (1958); *Sonnets* (1958); *Texticules* (1961); *Entretiens avec Georges Charbonnier* (1962); *Les œuvres complètes de Sally Mara* (1962; reprint of *On est toujours trop bon avec les femmes* and *Journal intime*) *Bords* (1963); *Les fleurs bleues* (1965; *Blue Flowers*, 1967); *Une histoire modèle* (1966); *Courir les rues* (1967); *Battre la campagne* (1968); *Le vol d'Icare* (1968; *The Flight of Icarus*, 1973); *Fendre les flots* (1969); *Morale élémentaire* (1975)

BIBLIOGRAPHY: Bens, J., *R. Q.* (1962); Bergens, A., *R. Q.* (1963); Guicharnaud, J., *R. Q.* (1965); Gayot, P., *R. Q.* (1966); Klinkesberg,

J.-M, *Jeu et profondeur chez R. Q.* (1967); Queval, J., *R. Q.* (1971); Baligand, R., *Les poèmes de R. Q.* (1972)

—CHARLES G. HILL

QUIROGA, Horacio

Uruguayan short-story writer, b. 31 Dec. 1878, Salto; d. 19 Feb. 1937, Buenos Aires, Argentina

Certain thematic designs run through Q.'s life and work. His life was crammed with adventure, hazardous enterprise, and recurrent tragedy. When he was an infant, his father was accidentally killed when a shotgun went off; later, his stepfather shot himself. His first wife, unable to endure the hardships in the jungle where Q. insisted on living, committed suicide by taking poison. The singular amount of violence marring Q.'s personal life doubtless explains a great deal about the obsession with death so marked in his stories.

Q.'s zest for adventure and the magnetic attraction the jungle hinterland of northern Argentina held for him are also biographical details that have great impact on his work. His first trip to Misiones province occurred in 1903, and in 1906 he bought land there and from then on divided his time between Misiones and Buenos Aires. (Although born and raised in Uruguay, he spent most of his years in Argentina.)

Q. began writing under the aegis of MODERNISM, which dominated Spanish American literary life at the turn of the century. Soon, however, he reacted against the highly artificial mode of his first book, *Los arrecifes de coral* (1901; coral reefs), a collection of prose poems and poetry, and turned to writing tales firmly rooted in reality, although they often emphasized the bizarre or the monstrous. Many of these early stories are reminiscent of Poe and show a skillful handling of gothic elements.

For three decades Q. continued publishing short stories in great quantity, many of them also of impressive quality. (His few attempts at the novel were failures.) Two collections should be singled out as high points: *Los desterrados* (1926; the exiled) and *Cuentos de amor, de locura, y de muerte* (1917; stories of love, madness, and death). The latter title sets forth Q.'s major themes and could properly be the heading for his entire work.

He also achieved renown with *Cuentos de la selva* (1918: *South American Jungle Tales*, 1959), a volume cast in fable mold, with talking animals, for children of all ages, which is permeated with tenderness and humor; and with *Anaconda* (1921; anaconda), whose title story describes a world of snakes and how they battle men and also one another. This long tale moves at a leisurely pace, with a spun-out plot. Its ophidian characters are more compelling than believable, and the animal characterization is not as striking as that of his shorter narratives.

If we examine Q.'s stories closely, we will find moments full of vision concerning mankind. He has an astute awareness of the problems besetting man on every side—not only the pitfalls of savage nature but also those pertaining to human relationships. His comments on illusions can be withering. Althrough he never palliates man's faults and weaknesses, the heroic virtues of courage, generosity, and compassion also emerge in many of his stories.

Q. at his best was a master craftsman. He described his technique in "Manual del cuentista perfecto" (1927; manual for the perfect short-story writer), a succinct decalogue filled with cogent advice. Usually Q. practiced the economy he preaches in this shortstory manual. Wonderful feats of condensation are common, as in "El hombre muerto" (1934; the dead man), where he shows his powers in dramatic focus on a single scene, or in "A la deriva" (1917; drifting), a stark story in which everything seems reduced to the essential, where the brief opening scene of a man bitten by a viper contains the germs of all that comes afterward. The language is terse and pointed, the situation of tremendous intensity, the action straightforward and lineal.

Q. does not have a social axe to grind, but some of the most trenchant social commentary in Spanish American fiction can be perceived in his stories, particularly those concerned with the exploitation of Misiones lumberjacks, like "Los mensú" (1917; "The Contract Workers," 1962). Setting, as well as narrative technique, is vitally important to Q., because it is inseparable from the real, day-to-day experience of human existence. Q.'s feelings are bound up in place, especially in Misiones, where the majority of his best stories take place. He makes us feel the significance of this setting, the symbolic strength of the rivers, and the hypnotic force of its snake-infested jungles.

Q. continues to rank as one of Latin America's finest short-story writers. He knew his trade in and out, and was universal in scope. He subjected his themes to dramatic form, transmitting to his readers all their virtues and ferment. He wrote tautly and described with intensity so that the story would make its mark on the reader.

FURTHER WORKS: *El crimen del otro* (1904); *Los perseguidos* (1905); *Historia de un amor turbio* (1908); *El salvaje* (1920); *El desierto* (1924); *Pasado amor* (1929); *El más allá* (1934); *Cuentos* (7 vols., 1937); *Diario de viaje a París* (1950); *Obras inéditas y desconocidas* (7 vols., 1967–1968). FURTHER WORKS IN ENGLISH: *The Decapitated Chicken and Other Stories* (1976)

BIBLIOGRAPHY: Delgado, J., *H. Q.* (1939); Etcheverry, J., *H. Q.* (1957); Martínez Estrada, E., *El hermano Q.* (1957); Rodríguez Monegal, E., *El desterrado: Vida y obra de H. Q.* (1968); Bratosevich, N., *El estilo de H. Q. en sus cuentos* (1973); Schade, G., Introduction to *The Decapitated Chicken and Other Stories* (1976): ix–xviii; Flores, À., et al. *Aproximaciones a H. Q.* (1976)

—GEORGE D. SCHADE

R

RABE, David

American playwright, novelist, and screenwriter, b. 10 Mar. 1940, Dubuque, Iowa

R. was born and reared in the largely Catholic town of Dubuque, Iowa. His childhood was classically American: He attended parochial schools and was a football star in high school. As an undergraduate at Loras College, the local Catholic college, he changed direction and began focusing on writing. After graduating, he nearly completed an M.A. in theater at Villanova University before quitting to take a series of odd jobs. Then, in 1965, he was drafted. Although he never saw combat in Vietnam, his eleven months of active duty attached to a hospital unit changed his life.

Upon his return, R. began working on his plays under the auspices of a Rockefeller Foundation playwriting grant. The first to see production was *The Basic Training of Pavlo Hummel* (perf. 1971, pub. 1973), the story of a bland character foolishly attached to idea of being a soldier. With the encouragement of the Public Theater's Joseph Papp, R. was immediately established as an important American playwright. Pavlo was the first of what would become a motif in R.'s plays: the character drawn to false models for self-creation in the absence of a strong sense of identity.

Sticks and Bones (perf. 1971, pub. 1973), the companion piece to *The Basic Training of Pavlo Hummel*, deals with the callous reception a blinded soldier receives upon his return from Vietnam. Unable to communicate with his all-American family, the main character David is as brutalized by his return as by the war itself. Made into a teleplay, the piece generated a controversy when CBS refused to air it for several months for fear of offending veterans' families. In *The Orphan* (perf. 1973, pub. 1993) R. tried to contemporize a Greek myth by retelling it as the story of the Manson murders. Most critics thought the play failed to live up to its ambition. A better reception met *In the Boom Boom Room* (perf. 1973, pub. 1975), a semirealistic account of the downward spiral taken by a Philadelphia go-go girl, Chrissy, tormented by her past and victimized by a series of men. Feminists disagreed about the play: some saw it as a scathing critique of the commodification of women, while others argued that the playwright failed to make his female character a real person.

With *Streamers* (perf. 1976, pub. 1977) R. returned to the war as subject, this time telling the story of three recruits in a training camp who must come to terms with each others' racial and sexual differences. *Hurlyburly* (perf. 1984, pub. 1985) saw a similar disturbing violence in the shallow, callous world of Hollywood. Here the humor was successful, even as the play presented a bleak and disturbing view of a contemporary culture empty of human feeling. The American dream appears little more than rampant drinking, drug use, violence, and bad sex, and the characters' failure to communicate is expressed in the play's use of bizarre syntax and nonsense words. Again critics argued about whether the play critiqued or partook in the misogyny and racism it portrayed.

One of *Hurlyburly*'s characters, the struggling actor Phil, became the protagonist of R.'s next play, *Those the River Keeps* (1991). Meant to take place before *Hurlyburly*, *Those the River Keeps* follows Phil's attempts to put his mobster past behind him and become an actor.

R. has explored other genres, writing the screenplays for *Casualities of War* (1989) and John Grisham's *The Firm* (1993, with Robert Towne and David Rayfiel). His original novel, *Recital of the Dog* (1993), was not deemed as strong as his plays.

R.'s work is powerful and often brutally honest, depicting many ugly facts of American life. As a playwright he gave voice to an important era in the evolution of American consciousness: the time of disillusionment. Refusing to provide solutions or even understanding for their characters, his plays stand testament to the feelings of loss and betrayal that dominated the time when, in the opinion of many people, America lost its innocence.

FURTHER WORKS: *Two Plays by D. R.* (1973); *I'm Dancing as Fast as I Can* (1982); *Goose and TomTom* (1986); *The Vietnam Plays* (2 vols., 1993); *The Crossing Guard* (1995)

BIBLIOGRAPHY: Werner, C., "Primal Screams and Nonsense Rhymes: D. R.'s Revolt," *ETJ*, 30 (1978): 517-29; Homan, S., "American Playwrights of the 1970s: R. and Shepherd," *CritQ*, 24, 1 (1982): 73-82; Zinman, T. S., *D. R.: A Casebook* (1991); Radavich, D., "Collapsing Male Myths: R.'s Tragicomic *Hurlyburly*," *AmerD*, 3, 1 (1993): 1-16; Hebel, U. J., "The Epic Core of D. R.'s *Streamers*: A Case of Brechtian Conventions in Contemporary American Drama," *LWU*, 26 (1993): 203-12; Andreach, R. J., "Unredeemed Savagery in *The Orphan*: D. R.'s Contemporary *Oresteia*," *CML*, 15, 4 (1995): 329-44

—GINGER STRAND

RABEARIVELO, Jean-Joseph

Malagasy poet, playwright, novelist, and translator, b. 4 Mar. 1901, Antananarivo; d. 22 June 1937, Antananarivo

Writing in the 1920s and 1930s, R. holds the position of Madagascar's first major French language author. His work mirrors the impact of colonial rule on Madagascar's nationalistic intelligentsia, and the problematic transition from writing in Malagasy to writing in French.

R. owes much of his reputation to his poetry. The early collections, *La coupe de cendres* (1924; Cup of Ashes), *Sylves* (1927; Woods), *Volumes* (1928), and *Chants pour Abéone* (1936; Songs for Abeone) form one cluster in his writing. Images of early death, dethroned kings, and the journey away from the native land symbolize the loss of Malagasy independence in these collections of poetry. However, allusions in these early works are deliberately European and foreign. A strict adherence to the rules of classical French prosody is evident in the meticulous rhyme schemes and sonnets of the poems. R.'s early poetry reveals his mastery of French models, and a desire to conform to a standard of poetry largely defined by the French romantic and symbolist schools. In *Presque-songes* (1935; Near Dreams) and *Traduit de la nuit* (1936; Translations from the Night), composed in the 1930s, R. adopts a new and distinctive style. R.'s later verse draws as much upon the traditional Malagasy poetic form known as hain teny, as on the French Symbolist heritage. The terse language of these two collections, the dialogic format, and reliance on a select stock of constantly reinvented images can be traced to the world of the colonized writer. Nonetheless, R. cannot be described as a political poet. Overt criticism of colonial rule is clearly absent from both his early and later works of poetry. By temperament, he disliked the identification of the writer with the political militant; besides, the authorities of the time still regarded undisguised Malagasy nationalism with considerable suspicion.

R. reserved his most direct criticism of the French for his prose works, *L'aube rouge* (1925; Red Dawn), *L'interférence* (wr. 1928, pub. 1988; Interference). Both texts are works of historical fiction with a strongly nationalistic bias that remained unpublished in his lifetime. In a third text, a short story, "Un conte de la nuit" (1934; A Tale of the Night), R. focuses on a more personal theme as he recounts the events leading to the tragic death of one of his children. R. is at his most distant from the political context of his times in his two plays, *Imaitsoanala, fille d'oiseau* (1935; Imaitsoanala, Daughter of a Bird) and *Aux portes de la ville* (1936; At the City Gates). The staging of these plays with the financial assistance of the colonial administration required R. to be even more circumspect in the expression of his political opinions. Accordingly, these plays concentrate on a simple representation of Malagasy myths and customs.

Nonetheless, the colonial setting cast a wide shadow over all of R.'s writing and life. In particular, his lifelong preoccupation with translation reflected a desire to compensate for the subordinate position of the Malagasy language in the colonial period. R. wrote in Malagasy as well as in French, and produced several translations of French poems into Malagasy for the small literary magazines associated with Malagasy literary life in the early decades of the 20th c. His translation of well-known hain teny into French, was published posthumously as *Vielles chansons des pays d'Imerina* (1967; Old Songs of the Merina Country). He presented many of his French-language works as translations and supported the claim by producing bilingual works. His plays and last two collections of poetry were written in bilingual French-Malagasy formats. At a time when other Malagasy writers refused to give up writing in Malagasy as a sign of opposition to colonial rule, R. sought to reconcile the French and the Malagasy languages in the ideal of a bilingual literature. However, his efforts did not earn him the expected recognition and remuneration. Confronted with financial problems and career disappointments, he committed suicide in 1937.

FURTHER WORKS: *Lova* (1957); *Des stances oubliées* (1959); *Amboara poezia sy tononkalo malagasy* (1965); *L'interference suivi d'Un conte de la nuit* (1988); *Poèmes* (1990). **FURTHER WORKS IN ENGLISH:** *Translations from the Night: Selected Poems* (1975)

BIBLIOGRAPHY: Adejunmobe, M., "History and Ideology in R.'s Prose Works," *CJAS*, 28, 2 (1995): 219-35; Adejunmobe, M., "The Francophone Anti-Colonialist Novel," in Losambe, L., ed., *Introduction to African Prose Narrative* (1979): 99-104; Wake, C. "J.-J. R.—A Poet before Négritude," in Wright, E., ed., *The Critical Evaluation of African Literature* (1973): 149-72; Wake, C., "Madagascar," in Gérard, A., ed., *European Language Writing in Sub-Saharan Africa* (1986): 141-51

—MORADEWUN A. ADEJUNMOBI

RABEMANANJARA, Jacques

Malagasy poet and playwright, b. 23 June 1913, Maroantsetra

R.'s writing and stature in Malagasy literature extends from the late colonial period to the decades after independence in 1960. If writers like Jean-Joseph RABEARIVELO belong firmly in the colonial period, while those like Michèle RAKOTOSON exemplify Malagasy writing in the late 20th c., R. remains Madagascar's most active writer with experience in both periods. R. was also the only Malagasy writer of the colonial period to identify himself with the main figures of the African literary movement, NÉGRITUDE, during his student days in Paris. Indeed, when a change of government in Madagascar led him into exile in the 1970s, he returned to France where he later assumed leadership of the publishing house associated with the Négritude movement, Présence Africaine. Like several writers from Francophone Africa in the colonial period, R. participated in the colonial and postindependence politics of his nation. He joined nationalist movements pressing for independence, and was even accused by the colonial authorities of involvement in an insurrection that led to the deaths of thousands of Malagasy in 1947. Some of his early collections of poetry, notably *Antsa* (1956; Eulogy), *Lamba* (1956; Malagasy Shawl), and *Antidote* (1961), were in fact written during the nine-year confinement in prison that he served following this incident.

R.'s nationalism provides both the backdrop and central concern to his early works of poetry. *Antsa* was reportedly written in a single night, after he had been informed that he would be executed the following morning for his involvement in the 1947 insurrection. However, it is far from being a reflection on death and imprisonment. It is, on the contrary, a work in which he reaffirms his commitment to Madagascar, and his convictions concerning Madagascar's ultimate liberation from colonial rule. In *Antidote* he focuses on the constraints facing "natives" in colonial society, while *Lamba* is a hymn of triumph dedicated to Malagasy womanhood and ultimately to the Malagasy nation. He pursues the conflation between the nation and the female in *Les ordalies* (1972; Testing), which also marks his return to a more classical form of prosody.

R. has published three plays in French: *Les dieux malgaches* (1947; Malagasy Gods), *Les boutriers de l'aurore* (1957; Vessels of the Dawn), and *Agape des dieux Tritriva* (1957; Feast of the Tritriva Gods). All three plays are tragedies and reflect in varying degrees the influence of classical French dramaturgy on the author. As to be perhaps expected, given R.'s long association with other African writers in Paris in his student days, these plays share much in common with the dramatic tradition of Francophone Africa in the colonial period. Reference to local history or myth and the adoption of the rules of classical French dramaturgy are some of the significant elements of this tradition. *Agape des dieux Tritriva*, for example, elaborates on a Malagasy legend in which a young couple commits suicide in order to preserve a relationship rejected by their families. *Les dieux malgaches* takes its inspiration from Malagasy history, and combines the use of alexandrines with a formal register of speech. No conflict exists as such between R.'s plays and his poetry, even if the militant nationalism of his poetry seems absent from his plays. R.'s intention may have been to demonstrate that Malagasy myth and history offered comparable resources to the Greek and Latin settings of most classical French tragedies. To this extent his plays bring a cultural dimension to his writing that is less palpable in his poetry.

The interest in Malagasy history continues in R.'s *Le Prince Razaka* (1997; Prince Razaka), a historical narrative based on 19th-c. Malagasy history. Nor has R. stopped producing an increasingly lyric and symbolic poetry as an expression of his commitment to his homeland. In so doing he reveals the difference in manner and style between his writing and that of a new generation of Malagasy writers as implicated in the unfolding events in their country, as was R. before he went into exile in the 1970s.

FURTHER WORKS: *Rites millénaires* (1955); *Thrènes d'avant l'aurore* (1985); *Rien qu'encens et filigrane* (1987)

BIBLIOGRAPHY: Koenig, J.-P., "R. et les différentes influences de la littérature française," *PA*, 15 (1977): 47-55; Wake, C., "Madagascar," in Gérard, A., *European Language Writing in SubSaharan Africa* (1986): 141-51; Koenig, J.-P., "Introduction a l'ouvrage: le théâtre de J. R.," *PA*, 148, 4 (1988): 99-103

—MORADEWUN A. ADEJUNMOBI

RABON, Israel

(original surname: Rubin) Yiddish poet, novelist, and translator, b. 1900, Gewerczew, Poland; d. 1941, Ponary, Lithuania

When R. was two years old, his family settled in Łódź, in a section called the Balut, a ghetto of continual unemployment and deprivation. His father died soon afterward, and the extreme penury in which R. grew up led an angry talent to become a masterful portrayer of the impact of persistent material poverty on the spirit of an extraordinary individual. In the midst of a productive artistic life, he was arrested by the Nazis, taken to Ponary in Lithuania, and murdered in 1941.

When R. was fifteen, he began to publish humorous poems on topical themes. These appeared in Lazar Kahan's *Fraytik* and later in the *Folksblat*, under the pseudonym Yisroylik der Kleyner. With Khaim L. Fuks (b. 1897), R. edited the journal *Shveln* which published his first story, "Shneyland" (1923; snowland). His poems were first accepted by *Gezangen;* soon the leading Łódź Yiddish literary journals, *Vegn*, *Oyfgang* and *S'feld,* welcomed his striking bohemian verse. The best of these poems were included in his *Hintern ployt fun der velt* (1928; behind the fence of the world) and *Groer friling* (1933; gray spring), collections whose mood is bleak and existential. Having abandoned the attempt to make sense of violence and horror, R. in these two volumes uses irony and allusion. The strands of folk literature in these poems make them compelling and accessible to the general reader.

During a brief sojourn in Warsaw R. edited the monthly *Oys*, the organ of the Yiddish literary vanguard. Like many Yiddish writers of this century, R. was barely able to live on the income from his writing. A bitter pauper most of his life, he composed several *shundromanen,* potboilers appearing serially in newspapers, under a variety of pseudonyms. For his own satisfaction, he published literary-critical articles and splendid translations of French and German poets.

In the novels *Di kale fun Balut* (1926; the bride from the Balut), published under the pseudonym Y. Rozental, and *Balut: Roman fun a forshtot* (1934; Balut: a novel about a suburb), R. succeeded in

conveying the unremitting bleakness of life in the lower depths, relating it to the grossness and bestiality of pretension and counterfeit morality.

An iconoclast and rebel, R. focused on the deprived strata of the Jewish community. In his angry, explosive prose and poetry there are elements of unrealized creative greatness. R. stands in the tradition of protest and compassion that permeates much of contemporary Yiddish literature, his idiosyncratic experimentation reflecting the tiredness of an age. Arguably Yiddish literature's preeminent black humorist, R. coupled the need to shock the complacent burgher with a demonstrable capacity for capturing the bizarre and ribald elements of everyday life and the potential for fantasy of the human imagination. Although his particularity of outlook and brutally realistic shock techniques led to his being unappreciated and neglected during his lifetime, he has come to be recognized as one of the most original writers in modern Yiddish literature—a minor master.

FURTHER WORKS: *Di gas* (1928; *The Street*, 1985); *Lider* (1938)

BIBLIOGRAPHY: Dobzynski, C., *Le miroir d'un peuple: Anthologie de la poésie yidich 1870–1970* (1971): 341

—THOMAS E. BIRD

RACHILDE

(pseud. of Marguerite Eymery Vallette) French novelist, editor, and critic, b. 11 Feb. 1860, Château-l'Evêque; d. 4 Apr. 1953, Paris

The fate of R.'s brilliant, beautiful mother, who demanded political equality for women and ended her life in an insane asylum, remained for her a cautionary tale with the moral that women should confine their social roles to those of the housewife or artist. Her witty conversation and her unremitting labor kept her at the center of Parisian letters for forty-five years.

A precocious, prolific writer of keen intelligence, R. had a literary vocation as a storyteller from the beginning. She quickly became the leading French woman decadent writer during La Belle Époque (1880-1914), the period of prosperity, colonial expansion, and intense artistic creativity that was ended by World War I in France. Whereas the male decadents such as the early Joris-Karl Huysmans (1848-1907) frequently stress the cult of the aesthetic object and withdrawal from relationships with others, R. often depicts protagonists who seek sexual satisfaction in defiance of conventional social and moral codes. They are absorbed by morbid delectation, and have no other interests.

R. sometimes treats solitary perversions such as implied bestiality (*L'animale* [1893; The Female Animal]), necrophilia (*La tour d'amour* [1899; The Tower of Love]), or masturbation (*La jongleuse* [1900; The Juggler,* 1990]), but her most provocative works consistently use gender interchanging and inversion to suggest that gender often is a social construction independent of anatomy. Several of her titles make such inversion obvious: *Monsieur Vénus, roman matérialiste* (1884; Mister Venus, A Materialistic Novel), *La Marquise de Sade* (1887; *The Marquise de Sade*, 1994), or *Madame Adonis* (1888; Madame Adonis). In *Monsieur Vénus* a wealthy, domineering woman enslaves a poor working man, and feminizes him to the point where she suffers intense jealousy when he falls in love with one of her suitors. She arranges his death in a duel, and then makes a mechanical sex doll with her victim's hair, teeth, and nails embedded in wax. As a result of such morbid subjects, and because before her marriage R. wore men's clothes more easily to pursue her profession as a journalist, she was nicknamed "Mademoiselle Baudelaire," after the poet whose *Fleurs du mal* (1857; *The Flowers of Evil*, 1861) more than any other work anticipated the decadent movement.

Refuting the popular impression that decadent style consists of embedded layers of narration, long, tortuous sentences, contrived syntax, and an abuse of rare words, R.'s prose is lucid and simple. Her plot lines are straightforward. Her noteworthy linguistic experiments, particularly in *Monsieur Vénus*, are lexical: they extend gender confusion to the details of language.

R.'s fictions consistently find the origins of love in emotional pathology. Despite her sensational subjects, her personal life was probably drug-free, and chaste before her marriage to the writer Alfred Vallette in 1889. Eventually, she became a cult figure for young gay men, with whom she liked to go out late in outlandish costumes. Together she and Vallette founded the famous journal *Le Mercure de France*, whose first number was dated January 1, 1890. It adopted a libertarian position, opposing the criminalization of consensual sexual acts, and military service. They had one daughter, Gabrielle, in 1890. R. wrote the book review column, reading forty titles a month until 1914, and fewer until 1925. From 1890 to 1930 she hosted a famous literary salon. Her "mardis" (Tuesdays) ran from the first of the year until Easter, and gathered major symbolist and decadent writers such as Remy de Gourmont (1858-1915), Alfred JARRY, Henri de Régnier (1864-1936), and Paul VALÉRY. Vallette died in 1935. R. stayed in their apartment in the building that housed the offices of *Le Mercure* (which continued under other editorship until 1965), but was almost totally forgotten during the twenty years before her death. FEMINIST CRITICISM has revived interest in her novels during the last decade, although her pungent *Pourquoi je ne suis pas féministe* (1928; Why I Am Not a Feminist) is strongly misogynistic, claims no rights for women, and says that they are incapable of sustained rational thought.

FURTHER WORKS: *Monsieur de la Nouveauté* (1880); *La femme du 199e Régiment (fantaisie militaire)* (1881); *Histoires bêtes pour amuser les petits enfants d'esprit* (1884); *Nono, roman de moeurs contemporaines* (1885); *Queue de poisson* (1885); *A mort* (1886); *La virginité de Diane* (1886); *Le tiroir de Mimi-Corail* (1887); *L'homme roux* (1888); *Minette* (1889); *Le mordu. Moeurs littéraires* (1889); *Nono* (1889); *La sanglante ironie* (1891); *Théâtre* (1891); *L'animale*, (1893); *Mon étrange plaisir* (1893); *Le démon de l'absurde* (1894); *La princesse des Ténèbres* (1895); *Les hors nature. Moeurs contemporaines* (1897); *L'heure sexuelle* (1898); *Contes et nouvelles, suivis du théâtre* (1900); *L'imitation de la mort, nouvelles* (1903); *Le dessous* (1904); *Le meneur de louves* (1905); *Son printemps* (1912); *La terre qui rit* (1917); *Dans le puits ou la vie inférieure 1915-1917* (1918); *La découverte de l'Amérique, nouvelles* (1919); *La maison vierge* (1920); *La souris japonaise* (1921); *Les rageac* (1921); *Le grand saigneur* (1922); *L'Hôtel du Grand Veneur* (1922); *Le château des deux amants* (1923); *Le parc du mystère* (1923, with F. de Homem Christo); *Au seuil de l'enfer* (1924, with F. de Homem Christo); *La haine amoureuse* (1924); *Le théâtre des bêtes* (1926); *Alfred Jarry ou le surmâle des lettres* (1928); *Le prisonnier* (1928, with André David); *Madame de*

Lydone, assassin (1928); *Refaire l'amour* (1928); *La femme aux mains d'ivoire* (1929); *Le val sans retour* (1929, with Jean-Joë Lauzach); *Portraits d'hommes* (1929); *L'homme aux bras de feu* (1930); *Les crocs* (1931; rev. ed., *L'amazone rouge*, 1932); *Les voluptés imprévues* (1931); *Notre-Dame des rats* (1931); *Jeux d'artifices* (1932); *La femme dieu* (1934); *La mort de la Sirène* (1934, with Francis Carco); *L'aérophage* (1935, with Jean-Joë Lauzach); *L'autre crime* (1937); *Les accords perdus* (1937, poems); *La fille inconnue* (1938); *L'anneau de Saturne* (1939); *Face à la peur* (1942); *Duvet-d'Ange. Confession d'un jeune homme de lettres* (1943); *Survie* (1945); *Quand j'étais jeune* (1947). FURTHER WORKS IN ENGLISH: *Madame la Mort and Other Plays* (1998)

BIBLIOGRAPHY: Mauclair, C., "Eloge de la luxure," *Le Mercure de France*, 8 (1893): 43-50; Coulon, M., "L'imagination de R.," *Le Mercure de France*, 142 (1920): 545-69; Hawthorne, M., "*Monsieur Vénus*: A Critique of Gender Roles," *NCFS*, 16 (1987-88): 162-79; Kelly, D., *Fictional Genders: Role and Representation in 19th-Century French Narrative* (1989): 143-55; Dauphiné, C., *R.* (1991); Hawthorne, M., "R. (1860-1953)," in Sartori, E. M., and D. W. Zimmerman, eds., *French Women Writers: A Bio-Bio-graphical Source Book* (1991): 346-56; Hawthorne, M., "To the Lighthouse: Fictions of Masculine Identity in R.'s *La tour d'amour*," *L'Esprit Créateur*, 32 (1992): 41-51; Kingcaid, R., *Neurosis and Narrative: The Decadent Short Fiction of Proust, Lorrain, and R.* (1992): 111-45; Lukacher, M., *Maternal Fictions: Stendhal, Sand, R., and Bataille* (1994): 109-60; Porter, L. M., "Decadence and the *fin-de-siècle* Novel," in Unwin, T., ed., *The French Novel from 1800 to the Present*(1997): 101-8

—LAURENCE M. PORTER

RADAUSKAS, Henrikas

Lithuanian poet, b. 23 April 1910, Cracow, Austro-Hungarian Empire (now in Poland); d. 27 Aug. 1970, Washington, D.C., U.S.A.

R. studied literature in Kaunas and later worked as a radio announcer and as an editor on the Commission on Book Publishing of the Lithuanian Ministry of Education. He left Lithuania in 1944 to escape the Soviet occupation. In 1949 he came to the U.S. and worked at the Library of Congress from 1959 to the time of his death.

R. stood aloof from the main movements in Lithuanian literature because his purposes in art were not subject to literary fashion or ideological trend. For him, genuine poetic achievement was always the result of a single individual's encounter with the infinite promise of language, both in its "natural" state and as shaped, or cultivated, by any given tradition in art.

R.'s poetry acquires form and substance as it projects the interplay between life and death, the absolute entities, in terms of concrete but relative manifestations, such as colors, shapes, and movements, as well as ideas and emotions. Thus, if the purpose of art is to "hold a mirror up to nature," the poem "Sekmadienis" (1965; "Sunday," 1978) is an imitation of life as reflected in a mirror of death. The poem resembles a perverse genre painting in which the cozy images of everyday life are represented in terms of their dead counterparts.

The image of death may possess the attributes of living things; or conversely, the violent exuberance of life may be expressed in sets of metaphors and symbols signifying death. In one of R.'s poems, "Veneros gimimas" (1955; "The Birth of Venus," 1976), the birth of Venus is shown as a catastrophe—it is a sea storm that engulfs the villages of fishermen and ruins the fruits of their gardens. Life and death, depicted in terms of each other and deprived of their philosophical or metaphysical messages, ultimately come to represent complex structures of metaphorical transformations in concrete reality, thus establishing the poet's art itself as a third absolute entity.

R.'s poetry is sometimes quite theatrical, resembling a grotesque and humorous carnival where the mundane and the fantastic, the cruel and the beautiful, blend together under the carefully measured control of the artist. R. often uses themes from classical mythology, and has a particular fondness for those myths in which the act of dying is extended into a frozen infinity, as for instance in the poem "Lotofagų šalis" (1955; "The Land of the Lotus-Eaters," 1970), where old men must lie dying forever under the hot sun because in this land, akin to Paradise, time does not exist.

Other poems are based upon descriptions of landscapes. There again, the verbal structures—contrapuntal arrangements of colors and transformations of physical shapes in direct response to the patterns of sound and of rhythm that follow the hidden lines of emotion—matter much more than any direct representations of nature.

The thrust of R.'s poetic language often tears up the fabric of reality, producing new forms, comprehensible only in terms of their own logic. Yet, even his most "explosive" poems fully reveal themselves only to the reader who is sensitive to their subtle nuances and delicate shadings, their fresh and fragile metaphors, such as the description of rain "running around in the garden on thin and brittle legs of glass." Most importantly, however, his kaleidoscopic festival of words does ultimately speak to us with the tragic and the comic human voices in all their simplicity and truth.

Some of R.'s bold metaphorical constructions are reminiscent of Boris PASTERNAK and the Russian Acmeist poets, or of Polish modernists, such as Julian TUWIM. At other times one hears the echoes of western European experimental poetry. Generally, however, R. was very much an authentic individual voice, a lonely alchemist who combined and recombined the elements of life and death in a search for the substance of art.

FURTHER WORKS: *Fontanas* (1935); *Strėlė danguje* (1950); *Žiemos daina* (1955); *Žaibai ir vėjai* (1964); *Eilėraščiai* (1965); *Eilėraščiai, 1965–1970* (1978); *Chimeras in the Tower: Selected Poems of H. R.* (1986)

BIBLIOGRAPHY: Ivask, I., "The Contemporary Lithuanian Poet H. R.," *Lituanus*, 5, 3 (1969): 86–90; Šilbajoris, R., "H. R.: The Passion of the Intellect," *Perfection of Exile: Fourteen Contemporary Lithuanian Writers* (1970): 25–55; Šilbajoris, R., "H. R.: Timeless Modernist," *BA,* 43 (1969): 50–54; Silbajoris, R., "The Arts as Images in the Poetry of H. R.," in Ziedonis, A., et al, eds., *Baltic Literature and Linguistics* (1973): 29–35; Zdanys, J., "The Applied Aestheticism of H. R.," *Lituanus*, 23, 1 (1977): 23–24; Blekaitis, J., "R.," *Lituanus*. 25, 3 (1979): 37–69

—RIMVYDAS ŠILBAJORIS

RADIGUET, Raymond

French novelist, b. 18 June 1903, Parc Saint-Maur; d. 12 Dec. 1923, Paris

R. grew up in a pleasant suburb located only a short train ride from Paris, on the banks of the Marne, and his two novels are structured around the journey between those two worlds, which in his fiction as in his life represent naïveté and sophistication. The fifteen-year-old narrator of *Le diable au corps* (1923; *The Devil in the Flesh*, 1932) takes a day off from attending school in Paris to accompany a nineteen-year-old woman, who is about to be married, while she shops for furniture. After her marriage, when her husband is shipped off to the war, the narrator begins an affair with her back in the suburbs, in the room whose furniture he selected himself. Eventually the lovers take a trip to Paris that proves disastrous: the young man cannot muster up the courage to ask for a hotel room, and his mistress literally catches her death of cold wandering the streets in the rain.

François de Séryeuse in *Le bal du comte d'Orgel* (1924; *Ball at Count d'Orgel's*, 1929) is both higher on the social scale and somewhat older than R.'s first hero, and he is able to rent lodgings in a fashionable part of Paris. He is eager to get back to his family home on the Marne, however, and to introduce his new friends the Count and Countess d'Orgel to his mother. When his unspoken love for the countess is finally reciprocated—only in a letter, however, not by any overt action—François's mother, who "never goes anywhere," is drawn to Paris for once to resolve the situation. That neither of R.'s heroes can successfully break free from home and family is not surprising, in view of the fact that R. himself was only twenty years old when he died of typhoid, in the fast-moving city that was the antithesis of the idyllic setting where he had lived during his adolescence.

Many accounts have been offered of the autobiographical background behind R.'s first novel, especially since 1952, when an irate reader stepped forward and presented himself as the cuckolded soldier in question. While *Le diable au corps* thus seems to have grown from the ruthless self-evaluation that followed a real experience in R.'s youth, *Le bal du comte d'Orgel* is closer to a fantasized projection of R. into the upper-class Parisian world to which his acquaintance with poets and painters later gained him access. The models for most of the characters are quite clear, and so is the model for the style: the polished 17th-c. prose of Madame de la Fayette, whose *The Princess of Cleves* presents the same mixture of suppressed passion and close psychological analysis.

The most important living influence on R., however, was Jean COCTEAU, with whom the young man was intimately associated for almost five years. The question of which of the pair owed the most to the other will probably never be definitively settled. Cocteau called R. his "master" and credited the younger man with leading him away from SURREALISM and back to the classical style represented so well by R.'s second novel. On the other hand, Cocteau probably made more than minor revisions in both of R.'s novels, which would not have been completed in the first place without Cocteau's constant prodding. What is certain is that the two men spent several summer vacations writing side by side, collaborated on three short works for the theater, and had enormous influence upon one another.

While Cocteau's work extends over many uneven volumes, however, R., after an early career as a poet, produced only two substantial works—and both are novels that rank among the handful of permanent masterpieces in modern French literature. *Le diable au corps* is usually rated more highly by critics, but *Le bal du comte d'Orgel* contains a brilliant exploration of its own central metaphor. The masked ball of the title is never described; the novel ends as the count, oblivious to his wife's confession of her love for François, continues planning costumes and entrances. Yet the novel itself has been a masked ball, with all the characters hiding their true feelings, from themselves as well as from others, under a variety of socially acceptable disguises. Claude-Edmonde Magny, in a classic study, faults R.'s second novel for being overly epigrammatic, overly prone to the expression of allegedly universal truths. Yet the first-person narrator of R.'s first novel generalizes almost as much as the omniscient narrator of his second. What saves both novels from being sententious is that so many of their insights *are* universally true, and that R.'s pose of Olympian detachment and infinite wisdom is justified by the acuteness of his insights. If R. had been able to continue his tragically brief career as a novelist, his style would perhaps have evolved considerably, but he would never have known more about the intricacies of human emotions than he knew at the very beginning.

FURTHER WORKS: *Les joues en feu* (1920); *Devoirs de vacances* (1921); *Les Pélican* (1921; *The Pelicans*, 1964); *Les joues en feu* (1925; *Cheeks on Fire*, 1976); *Œuvres complètes* (1952); *Œuvres complètes* (2 vols., 1959); *Gli inediti* (1967; bilingual, French and Italian); *Paul et Virginie* (1973, with Jean Cocteau)

BIBLIOGRAPHY: Magny, C. -E., *Histoire du roman français depuis 1918* (1950): 92–111; Goesch, K. J., "R. R. and the Roman d'Analyse," *AUMLA*, 4 (1956): 1–10; Cocteau, J., *Professional Secrets* (1970): 94–99; Steegmuller, F., *Cocteau* (1970): 245–317; Bouraoui, H. A., "R.'s *Le diable au corps* Beneath the Glass Cage of Form," *MLQ*, 34 (1973): 64–77; Crosland, M., *R. R.: A Biographical Study with Selections from His Work* (1976); Turnell, M., *The Rise of the French Novel* (1978): 259–96; McNab, J. P., *R. R.* (1984)

—MICHAEL POPKIN

RADNÓTI, Miklós

Hungarian poet and translator, b. 5 May 1909, Budapest; d. 8 Nov. 1944, Abda

R.'s life was overshadowed by tragedy: his mother died while giving birth to him, and the young R., born into a Jewish family, was raised by relatives. He received a university education, but in the economically depressed and intolerant Hungary of the 1930s he could not find employment as a teacher of literature. He eked out a living as a freelance writer, translator, and tutor. Yet this mild-mannered, melancholy poet managed to secure a place for himself on the lively prewar literary scene. He turned his back on his petit-bourgeois background and embraced the ideals of the intellectual left, although not the more aggressive, organized political and artistic "isms" of his day. He also came under the influence of leading Catholic intellectuals, and in 1943 he formally converted.

Although his literary career was rather brief and his total output not that large, R. is regarded as one of the most significant Hungarian poets of the 20th c. For his fellow poets who survived

him, as well as for the generation that followed him, R. has become a model—the modern poet who clung with stoic serenity to the humane values of the Western tradition at the very moment the forces of inhumanity tried frantically to destroy them. R., at the age of thirty-five, fell victim to these forces; in late 1944, during a forced march westward across Hungary, he, along with other members of his forced-labor company, was shot to death by Hungarian guards. After the war his body was exhumed from a mass grave, and his last poems, his most gripping, written days before he was killed, were discovered in his coat pocket.

R.'s tragic fate lends a special poignancy to his work. But what makes his mature poetry even more extraordinary is that he intimated the horrors to come long before Europe was engulfed in war. Whereas his first two collections of verse, *Pogány köszöntő* (1930; *Pagan Salute*, 1980) and *Újmódi pásztorok éneke* (1931; *Song of Modern Shepherds* 1980), are full of affirmation and celebration, poems written just a few years later, and included in *Járkálj csak, halálraítélt!* (1936 *Walk On, Condemned!* 1980), and *Meredek út* (1938; *Steep Road* 1980), contain disquieting premonitions about the future. They proved to be prophetic because so many of them foreshadow the poet's own violent death. What may have seemed at the time little more than the anxieties and obsessions of a hypersensitive artist strike the postwar reader as sober preparations, mental training, for that long forced march, that summary execution. But even in his darkest moments R. was sustained by his faith in the human spirit, in love, and in reason. In fact, it is in his last poems, in his celebrated eclogues, and in lines addressed to his wife, Fanni, that despair, resignation, nostalgia yield most readily to defiant hope.

R. was a true European—mindful of his native heritage but always eager to look beyond it, always ready to respond to new cultural stimuli. He was among the first in his country to translate the poems of Guillaume APOLLINAIRE, Blaise CENDRARS, and Georg TRAKL. And his own poetry is filled with subtle allusions and echoes, revealing just how thoroughly he assimilated the Western poetic tradition. Profoundly modern in spirit, R.'s poems are for the most part traditional in form, and for him, as for many other Hungarian poets, form is as important a carrier of the poem's message as content. He may have become a committed poet but he remained devoted to his craft; even his "activist" verses transcend the here and now. In R.'s greatest works a 20th-c. poet's despair is tempered by the aesthetic ideals of antiquity and the moral imperatives of the Judeo-Christian tradition.

FURTHER WORKS: *Lábadozó szél* (1933; *Convalescent Wind*, 1980); *Tajtékos ég* (1946; *Sky with Clouds* 1980); *R. M. összes versei és műfordításai* (1970); *Próza* (1971); *R. M. művei* (1978). FURTHER WORKS IN ENGLISH: *Subway Stops* (1977); *The Witness: Selected Poems by M. R.* (1977); *Forced March* (1979); *The Complete Poetry* (1980); *Under Gemini: A Prose Memoir and Selected Poetry* (1985)

BIBLIOGRAPHY: Adams, B. S., "The Eclogues of M. R.," *SEER*, 43 (1965): 390–99; Adams, B. S., "The Lager Verse of M. R.," *SEER*, 45 (1967): 65–75; Gömöri, G., and Wilmer, C., Introduction to M. R., *Forced March* (1979): 7–13; George, E., Introduction to M. R., *The Complete Poetry* (1980): 13–46; Sanders, I., "Training for the *Forced March*," *Commonweal* (22 October 1982): 571–72; Birnbaun, M. D., *M. R.* (1983)

—IVAN SANDERS

RADZINSKY, Edvard

Russian dramatist, b. 23 Sept. 1936, Moscow

R. was born into a Moscow family of the intelligentsia. His father was a prominent man of letters who translated from the French and adapted works of fiction for the stage. R. graduated from the Moscow State Historical-Archival Institute in 1960.

Probably no Soviet writer better deserves the title of "chronicler of his generation" than R. He made his stage debut in 1960 when his play, *Mechta moia, Indiia . . .* (1960; India, my dream . . .), written in collaboration with Liia Geraskina (dates n.a.), was performed at the Theater of the Young Spectator in Moscow. It was followed by *Vam 22, stariki!* (1962; you're 22, fellows!), a first in introducing the vernacular language of the younger generation into the Soviet theater. R.'s first critical success came in 1964 with his *104 stranitsy pro liub'vi* (1964; 104 pages about love). The play, which brought an ordinary love story onto the Soviet stage for the first time in the post-Stalin era, proved extremely popular in the Soviet Union where it was staged in 120 theaters as well as being made into a film and a ballet. Critical acclaim abroad followed as the play joined the repertory of major theaters in eastern Europe, West Germany, and Japan.

Snimaetsia kino . . . (1966; making a movie), an exposé of movie censorship, and *Obol'stitel' Kolobashkin* (1982; the seducer Kolobashkin), a savage satire of the Moscow intelligentsia (banned in 1968 after the dress rehearsal), led to the blacklisting of all R.'s plays for a period of seven years. During that time, R. returned to his first profession, history, and began working on a trilogy of historical dramas. In *Besedy s Sokratom* (1982; conversations with Socrates), *Lunin ili smert' Zhaka, zapisannaia v prisutstvii khoziana* (1982; I, Mikhail Sergeevich Lunin, 1982), and *Teatr vremen Nerona i Seneki* (1982; theater in the time of Nero and Seneca) R. used historical fact to explore the plight of the intellectual in a totalitarian society. A masterpiece of Aesopean innuendo, the trilogy brought R. notoriety at home—where parallels were easily drawn between his historical characters and leading dissidents, including Aleksandr SOLZHENITSYN and Andrei Sakharov—as well as international renown in the late 1970s.

With *Sportivnye stseny 1981 goda* (1981; *Jogging [Sporting Scenes, 1981]*, 1988), R. directly confronted contemporary Soviet life, this time depicting the privileged and corrupt youth of the Kremlin leaders (the heroine and her husband are loosely based on Galina Brezhneva and her recently convicted husband, Yuri Churbanov). Its staging in 1986 at the Moscow Ermolova Theater was one of the first productions to usher in the new Gorbachev era of glasnost. It was followed by *Ub'em muzhchinu?; "Ya stoiu a restorana: zamuzh—pozdno, sdokhnut'—rano"* (1987; shall I kill the man?; I'm standing by a restaurant: too late to get married, too early to croak), about a neurotic actress and a philandering theater director; and *Nash Dekameron* (1988, Nash dekameron), a satire about a Moscow prostitute who becomes queen of an African nation.

During the 1980s, R. had as many as nine plays running simultaneously in Moscow. Equally successful abroad, he has become probably the most frequently staged Russian dramatist, second only to Anton CHEKHOV. R.'s *Lunin*, about the Decembrist dissident, was widely performed in Europe to great critical acclaim. When his *Staraia aktrisa na rol' zheny Dostoevstogo* (n.d.; *An Old Actress in the Role of Dostoevsky's Wife*, 1986) was staged at the Odeon in Paris, the French press hailed R. as a "Russian Pirandello." New York audiences also had an opportunity to see R.'s work in performance at the Jean Cocteau Repertory Theatre's productions of his historical trilogy.

In the late 1980s, R. put aside dramaturgy and turned to writing "novellas in dialogue." Among the works in his first collection, published in 1989, are prose versions of a number of his dramas, including his trilogy of historical plays, as well as his first historical novella, *Posledniaia iz doma Romanovykh: Povesti v dialogakh (Toroplivaia proza)* (the last of the house of Romanovs: novellas in dialog [hasty prose]). Set in the 18th c. during the reign of Catherine the Great, it recounts one of the most enigmatic episodes in Russian history. This book was followed by the publication of a collection of short stories based on anecdotal versions of episodes from the life of Stalin.

R.'s great popularity as a dramatist is equally rooted in his mastery of language and in his ability to create tightly constructed plays susceptible to a variety of scenic interpretations. In his choice of themes and in their interpretation, R. has in the course of his career moved from writing about his own generation to exploring more universal historical, philosophical themes. While frequently banned by the authorities, R.'s plays have consistently won a following among leading directors and actors as well as audiences in the former Soviet Union.

FURTHER WORKS: *Teatr vremen . . . teatr "pro liubov": . . . teatr v teatre . . .* (1986). FURTHER WORKS IN ENGLISH: *A Pleasant Woman with a Geranium and Windows Facing North* (1985)

BIBLIOGRAPHY: Golub, S., "E. R.'s Masters of History, Servants to Illusion," *Newsnotes on Soviet and East European Drama and Theatre*, 3, 3 (1983): 9–14; Abensour, G., "Lorsque le roi est nu," *Slovo*, 6 (1984): 169–87; Kipp, M., "E. R.'s *Don Juan Continued*: The Last Return of Don Juan?," *SEEA*, 3, 1 (1985): 109–18; Leverett, J., "Worlds Apart: A Soviet Voice on the American Stage," *American Theatre*, 1 (1986): 26–27; Dementyeva, M., "E. R.'s Main Hero," *Culture And Life*, 12 (1987): 30–32

—ALMA H. LAW

RAINE, Kathleen

English poet, editor, critic, and translator, b. 14 June 1908, London

Daughter of two London schoolteachers, R. received an M.A. in natural sciences from Girton College, Cambridge, in 1929. She had two brief marriages to Cambridge professors. Along with her second husband, Charles Madge (b. 1912), and William EMPSON, she was a member of the Cambridge group of poets in the 1930s.

R.'s earliest verse was praised for its precise observations of nature, at least in part the result of her scientific studies. All her poetry is distinguished by a lucid, introspective awareness of the physical universe as it affects human life, by a sometimes austere and archaic diction, and by a meditative quality. She has self-consciously chosen to use the "symbolic language" identified with the English romantic poets, and her Neoplatonic concern with such universal themes as birth and death, nature and eternity, distinguish her from most other modern poets.

R.'s emphasis on the natural world's transcendence over mere human concerns has led to many volumes of what she calls "soul-poetry," verse that reflects Platonic reality and objectivity. She has never emphasized wittiness or self-conscious confessionalism in her verse; rather, her smooth, graceful, lyricism and precise diction subordinate "mere human emotion" to the "Perennial Philosophy," to an expression of ancient truths in a modern world. Those writers with whom she has the greatest affinities include Edmund Spenser, William Blake, and William Butler YEATS.

Her major critical work, *Blake and Tradition* (1968), is an exhaustive analysis of Blake's visionary language and cosmology, in which she shows how his symbolic language derives from and is in the line of antimaterialistic philosophy from Plotinus and Plato. *In Defending Ancient Springs* (1967) R. argues that genuine poets "learn" a symbolic language as a means of grasping the "beautiful order of 'eternity.'" Her three-volume autobiography—*Farewell Happy Fields* (1973), *The Land Unknown* (1975), and *The Lion's Mouth* (1978)—is important not only for further expansion of her literary theories but also for vivid depictions of her rural youth and Cambridge in the 1930s, her marriages and other relationships, and her incessant seeking after transcendent truth that led to a brief conversion to Catholicism.

Both R.'s verse and her criticism reflect a visionary attempt to return to the roots of modern experience and thought. Some of her best poetry, such as "The Speech of Birds" in *Living in Time* (1946), is especially successful in depicting man's separation from nature, and the universal, even Jungian symbols and images she uses (as in her dream or meditational poems) are constant reminders of this separation. At her worst, she relies too heavily upon wistful, escapist, and self-consciously mystical experience; at her best, she effectively reminds the reader of those poets she considers her masters.

FURTHER WORKS: *Stone and Flower* (1943); *The Pythoness, and Other Poems* (1949); *William Blake* (1951; rev. eds., 1965, 1969); *Selected Poems* (1952); *The Year One* (1952); *Coleridge* (1953); *Collected Poems* (1956); *Poetry in Relation to Traditional Wisdom* (1958); *Christmas 1960; An Acrostic* (1960); *Blake and England* (1960); *The Hollow Hill, and Other Poems* (1965); *The Written Word* (1967); *Six Dreams, and Other Poems* (1969); *Life's a Dream* (1969); *On the Mythological* (1969); *Poetic Symbols as a Vehicle of Tradition* (1970); *William Blake* (1971); *The Lost Country* (1971); *Yeats, the Tarot, and the Golden Dawn* (1972; rev. ed., 1976); *Hopkins, Nature, and Human Nature* (1972); *Faces of Day and Night* (1972); *On a Deserted Shore* (1973); *Three Poems Written in Ireland* (1973); *Death-in-Life and Life-in-Death* (1974); *David Jones, Solitary Perfectionist* (1974); *A Place, a State* (1974); *The Inner Journey of the Poet* (1976); *Waste Land, Holy Land* (1976); *Berkeley, Blake, and the New Age* (1977); *Blake and Antiquity* (1977); *The Oval Portrait, and Other Poems* (1977); *Fifteen Short Poems* (1978); *From Blake to "A Vision"* (1978); *David Jones and the Actually Loved and Known* (1978); *Blake and the New Age* (1979); *Cecil Collins; painter of Paradise* (1979); *What Is Man?* (1980); *The Oracle in the Heart* (1980); *Collected Poems: 1935–80* (1981); *The Human Face of God* (1982); *The Inner Journey of the Poet* (1982)

BIBLIOGRAPHY: Owen, E., "The Poetry of K. R.," *Poetry*, 80 (1952): 32–36;; Adams, H., "The Poetry of K. R.: Enchantress and Medium," *TxSE*, 37 (1958): 114–26; Foltinek, H., "The Primitive Element in the Poetry of K. R.," *ES*, 42 (1961): 15–20; Grubb, F., *A Vision of Reality: A Study of Liberalism in Twentieth Century Verse* (1965): 105–16; Mills, R. J., Jr., *K. R.* (1967); Grigson, G., The Contrary View (1974): 166–76; Adams, M. V., "The New Age: An

Interview with K. R.," *Spring 1982: An Annual of a Archetypal Psychology and Jungian Thought* (1982): 113–32

—PAUL SCHLUETER

RAINIS, Jānis

(pseud. of Jānis Pliekšāns) Latvian poet, dramatist, and translator, b. 11 Sept. 1865, Rubene County; d. 12 Sept. 1929, Majori (near Riga)

The son of a well-to-do estate overseer, R. was brought up in the country. After attending secondary school in Riga, he obtained a law degree from the University of St. Petersburg. In 1891 he became editor of the influential political newspaper *Dienas lapa* and a staunch champion of the New Current group, which the first Latvian democrats and socialists rallied around in the 1890s. In 1897 R. was arrested as dangerous to imperial Russia and exiled—first to Pskov, then to Slobodsk, in the Urals—for six years, during which he finished translating Goethe's *Faust* and wrote poetry.

As one of the central figures in the 1905 revolution (which in Latvia developed into a nationalist movement), he had to flee from Latvia. Like many other eastern Europeans of the age, R. and his wife Aspazija (pseud. of Elza Rozenberga-Pliekšāne, 1868–1943), a well-known Latvian poet and a feminist leader, emigrated to Switzerland. During fourteen years of exile R. wrote his major literary works and became the ideologist of an autonomous Latvian state, envisioning it as neither a slave to the East nor a servant to the West. In 1920 R. returned to the newly proclaimed independent Republic of Latvia, where he held prominent positions in the government (including that of Minister of Education) and in the Social Democratic party. He was instrumental in founding the Riga Art Theater in 1920, and directed the Latvian National Theater from 1921 to 1925.

R.'s translations gave great literary works their footing in Latvia and proved that the Latvian language was a vehicle by which emotional and intellectual experiences could be communicated.

The publication of R.'s *Tālas noskaņas zilā vakarā* (1903; distant moods in a blue evening) and *Vētras sēja* (1905; sowing the storm) heralded a new age in Latvian verse and established R.'s preeminence as a lyric poet. In the poems in these volumes R. revealed his mastery of technique, form, and diction. He liked to use an abbreviated sonnet form consisting of nine lines in iambic pentameter (the "Rainis stanza"). Because they were unrivaled in Latvia for their passionate and rebellious protest against oppression, R.'s poems evoked a strong response in his readers.

In his next three volumes—*Jaunais spēks* (1906; new strength), *Klusā grāmata* (the silent book; officially banned, 1909; repub., 1910, as *Vēja nestas lapas* [leaves driven by the wind]), and *Tie, kas neaizmirst* (1911; those who do not forget)—R.'s objective was to strengthen the national spirit of his compatriots who took part in the abortive 1905 revolution.

Into his most intellectual poetry collection, *Gals un sākums* (1912; end and beginning), R. projected the spiritual and social crisis of his own individuality and that of his nation, which in turn was indicative of the underlying restlessness of a whole civilization. One solution, R. suggested, is the acceptance of perpetual change and flexibility, a theme that often appeared in his dramas.

R. greeted Latvia's attainment of independence in 1918 with two memorable volumes, *Sveika, brīvā Latvija!* (1919; I salute you, free Latvia!) and *Daugava* (1919; [the river] Daugava).

Although most of R.'s fifteen excellent dramas (all but two written in verse) espoused national causes (they drew heavily on Latvian history and particularly folklore), R. was equally interested in appealing to universal human emotions. R.'s play *Uguns un nakts* (1907; *Fire and Night*, 1983), one of the most esteemed works in Latvian literature, is based on an ancient legend about the epic hero Lāčplēsis (the name means bear-slayer) and his struggle with the Black Knight. Actually, its theme is freedom.

Perhaps R.'s most original drama is *Spēlēju, dancoju* (1919; I played, I danced), a poetic drama full of fairies and demons, witches and hobgoblins. It is characterized by somber mysticism and numerous elusive symbols and allegories. *Jāzeps un viņa brāli* (1919; *The Sons of Jacob*, 1924) is usually considered R.'s greatest drama because of the handling of the emotions and psychology of its characters. Based on the biblical story of Jacob and his sons, it expresses the irreconcilable conflict between the individual and society of which R. was so aware.

Since the Soviet takeover of the Baltic countries in 1940, R. has been elevated to a supranational level. Most Soviet critics are willing to accord deserved praise to certain parts of his work for their progressive spirit, but they have largely overlooked his more poetic qualities. Moreover, those of R.'s works that contradict the official view were suppressed until the 1980s—for example, *Rīgas ragana* (1928; the witch from Riga), *Daugava, and Sveika, brīvā Latvija!* Although these and other works have now been reissued, the text of *Sveika, brīvā Latvija!* was bowdlerized.

R.'s place is unquestionable as the greatest Latvian poet, and perhaps the greatest Latvian writer. He was also the key figure in Latvian literary and intellectual history during the period 1900–30. Brilliant and strongly individualistic, R. was independent of any specific literary school. Spiritually and aesthetically he is the best example in modern Latvian literature of the organic relationship between talent shaped by tradition and talent creating tradition.

FURTHER WORKS: *Mazie dunduri* (1888); *Apdziedāšanās dziesmas 3. Vispārīgiem latvju dziesmu svētkiem* (1889); *Pusideālists* (1904); *Ģirts Vilks* (1905); *Ave, sol!* (1910); *Zelta zirgs* (1910; *The Golden Steed*, 1979); *Indulis un Ārija* (1911); *Kopoti raksti* (2 vols., 1912–1914); *Pūt, vējiņi!* (1913); *Addio bella* (1920); *Cūsku vārdi* (1920); *Uz mājām* (1920); *Zelta sietiņš* (1920); *Kopoti raksti* (5 vols., 1920–23); *Krauklītis* (1920); *Ilja Muromietis* (1922); *Sudrabota gaisma* (1922); *Mušu ķēniņš* (1923); *Puķu lodziņš* (1924); *Vasaras princīši un princītes* (1924); *Lellīte Lollīte* (1924); *Jaunā strāva* (1925); *Novelas* (1925); *Putniņš uz zara* (1925); *Mēness meitiņa* (1925); *Dzīve un darbi* (11 vols., 1925–1931); *Mīla stiprāka par nāvi* (1927); *Saulīte slimnīcā* (1928); *Suns un kaķe* (1928); *Kastaņola* (1928); *Sirds devējs* (1935); *Dvēseles dziesmas* (1935); *Rakstu izlase* (4 vols., 1935–1937); *Lielās līnijas* (1936); *Aizas ziedi* (1937); *R. un Aspazija dzīvē un mākslā: Sarakstīšanas* (2 vols., 1937); *Mūza mājās* (1940); *Kalnā kāpējs* (1940); *Kopoti raksti* (14 vols., 1947–1951); *Raksti* (17 vols., 1952–1965); *Kopoti raksti* (30 vols., 1977 ff.)

BIBLIOGRAPHY: Andrups, J., and Kalve, V., *Latvian Literature* (1954): 118–21; Ziedonis, A., *The Religious Philosophy of J. R.* (1969); Gāters, A., "J. R.: Sein Leben und sein Werk," *BHe*, 19 (1973): 84–152; Ehlert, W., "R. und seine Lyrikzyklen," in J. R., *Nachtgedanken über ein neues Jahrhundert: Gedichte* (1974): 161–81; Ekmanis, R., *Latvian Literature under the Soviets*: 1940–1975 (1978): 69–73 and passim

—ROLFS EKMANIS

RAKESH, Mohan

Indian dramatist, short-story writer, novelist, and essayist (writing in Hindi), b. 8 Jan. 1925, Amritsar; d. 3 Dec. 1972, New Delhi

R. earned M.A. degrees in both Sanskrit and Hindi, and between 1945 and 1957 held teaching positions in a number of colleges and schools in Bombay, Simla, and Jullundur. In 1962 he assumed the editorship of the prestigious and highly influential Hindi literary journal, *Sarika*, a position he resigned within a year's time to devote himself entirely to writing. From 1963 until his death from a heart attack, R. was one of a minuscule number of Indians who made their living exclusively by writing.

R. came to prominence in the 1950s with the publication of his first collection of short stories, *Insan ke khandhar* (1950; ruins of mankind), and through his leadership role in the so-called "New Short Story" movement that emerged in Hindi literature during this period. This group of young writers explored the alienation and insecurity of the middle classes in postindependence India. Their stance in a number of ways resembles that of French EXISTENTIALIST writers of the post-World War II period.

R.'s best short stories appear in later collections, including *Janwar aur janwar* (1958; animals and animals), *Ek aur zindagi* (1961; another life), and *Faulad ka akash* (1966; the sky of steel). In these stories characters experience a gradual or sudden sense of disillusionment; and in spite of a great deal of talk, they fail to communicate with one another, a fact underscored in the stories, and later in R.'s dramas, by a highly effective use of interrupted speech and incomplete utterances.

R. also wrote three novels, the first and most important of which is *Andhere band kamre* (1961; *Lingering Shadows*, 1970). Over five hundred pages in length in its original Hindi version, this work was heavily edited by the author for translation into English. It deals with the love-hate relationship between Nilima, an attractive, ambitious woman with artistic pretentions, and her ordinary, ineffectual husband, Harbans, who constantly thwarts her attempts at artistic success because of his own inability to achieve.

R.'s plays include three full-length works. *Ashadh ka ek din* (1958; *A Day in Ashadh*, 1969) is based on the myth of the great Sanskrit poet Kalidasa (c. 4th c. A.D.). *Lahron ke rajhans* (1962; *The Swans of the Great Waves*, 1973) presents the conflict faced by Nand, half-brother of Lord Buddha, as to whether he should continue to live as a prince or follow his half-brother's path of renunciation of the world. Some critics, and R. himself, consider the last major play, *Adhe adhure* (1969; *Half-way House*, 1971; later tr., *Adhe Adhure*, 1973), as his finest literary creation. Set in modern-day Delhi, it depicts the gradual disintegration of a contemporary Indian family, most notably the mother, who functions as the group's central focus and support.

R. will probably be best remembered for his contributions to the development of modern Hindi drama. His plays were highly controversial when first produced because of their innovations in theme, structure, and language. R. is considered not only as one of the major dramatists of Hindi literature, but of Indian literature generally.

FURTHER WORKS: *Naye badal* (1952); *M. R.: Shresth kahaniyan* (1966); *Aj ke saye* (1967); *Kahaniyan* (1967); *Parivesh* (1967); *Akhiri cattan tak* (1968); *Na ane wala kal* (1968); *Royen reshe* (1968); *Ek ek duniya* (1969); *Mile jule cehre* (1969); *Meri priya kahaniyan* (1971); *Antral* (1972); *Kvartar* (1972); *Pahcan* (1972); *Warish* (1972); *Ande ke chilke aur anya ekanki tatha bijnatak* (1973); *Bina har-mans ke admi* (1973); *Baklam khud* (1974); *Ek ghatna* (1974); *Rat bitne tak tatha anya dhvani natak* (1974); *M. R.: Sahityik aur sanskrtik drshti* (1975); *Pair tale ki zamin* (1975). **FURTHER WORKS IN ENGLISH:** *JSoAL*, 9, 2–3 (1973) and 14, 3–4 (1979)

BIBLIOGRAPHY: Special R. issue, *Enact*, 73–74 (1973); Taneja, G., "M. R.: The Story Teller," *IndL*, 17: 1–2 (1974): 104–11; Williams, R., "*Jivan* and *Zindagi*: An Analysis of M. R.'s Short Story 'Savorless Sin,'" *JSoAL*, 13: 1–4 (1977–78): 39–43; Blackwell, F. and P. Kumar, "M. R.'s *Lahrom ke rajhams* and Ashvaghosha's *Saundarananda*," JSoAL, 13: 1–4 (1977–78): 45–52; Weir, A., "Behind the Facade: Communication between Characters in the Stories of M. R.," *JSoAL*, 13: 1–4 (1977–78): 53–63; Sinha, R., "M. R.: A Visionary Short-Story Writer," *IndL*, 20, 1, (1978): 93–114

—CARLO COPPOLA

RAKOTOSON, Michèle

Malagasy novelist, dramatist, and journalist, b.14 June 1948, Antananarivo

R.'s writing is typical of the perspective adopted by a generation of Malagasy writers seeking to come to terms with the initial euphoria and later disillusion that accompanied a change of government in Madagascar in the early 1970s. As colonialism had impacted the writing of earlier Malagasy writers, so also was the experience of military dictatorship and economic decline in the 1980s to leave its imprint on the prose and plays by R. and a host of other Malagasy authors.

Before R. emerged as a writer, Malagasy authors like Jean-Joseph RABEARIVELO and Jacques RABEMANANJARA had been best known for their poetry. Writing in a time of growing social dislocation, R. and those Malagasy authors that followed her example sought immediacy and interaction with the public. Consequently, they turned to genres that were more likely to find quick access to performance or publication such as drama and the short story. R. first started writing plays in the 1970s, but her earliest publications date from the 1980s. The pattern has continued through her writing career, and almost invariably her plays have existed as dramatic performances before they were published—illustrated in the performance in 1997 of the unpublished play *Sur la crête des vagues* (1997; On the Crest of Waves).

Following her studies of Malagasy language and literature, R. initially began writing plays in Malagasy, and only later turned to French. Her plays, like most Malagasy dramatic texts produced in the 1980s and 1990s, do not refer to ancient myths or distant history. They often provide reflection on contemporary events and personal challenges. *Un jour ma mémoire* (1991; Remembrance, One Day) was apparently inspired by R.'s recollection of personal responses and responsibility during the tumultuous events of 1972. It reviews the question of individual complicity with institutional

violence as the two main characters remember their own abdication of responsibility at a previous time of social unrest. *La maison morte* (1991; The Dead Home) is a play parodying the frequent and bloody takeovers of power by men in the military that are described as revolutions needed to sanitize a corrupt political system. But as R. demonstrates in the play, the so-called reformers are rarely more principled than their predecessors in government. In her plays R. endeavors to bring drama closer to real life by recapturing the quality of everyday dialogue through the use of a conversational register of speech drawing upon popular slogans and allusions.

Although she is better known for her plays, R. has also published three prose texts: *Dadabé et autres nouvelles* (1984; Dadabé and Other Stories), *Le bain des reliques* (1988; Awash with Relics), and *Elle, au printemps* (1996; She, in the Spring). In addition, several of her short stories have appeared in a variety of magazines. While the setting is different in each of her full-length narratives, all three are permeated by a crushing sense of angst and disquiet that has become the hallmark of Malagasy prose writing at the close of the 20th c. The tales in *Dadabé* and the narrative in *Le bain des reliques* take place in Madagascar, while *Elle, au printemps* recounts the experience of Sahondra, a Malagasy student in search of a better life who has come to France to pursue her studies. There are no simple and happy endings in any of these narratives, and the main characters in each text share in common the experience of some form of disillusion with life. R.'s narratives are not as overtly political as some of her plays, however, there is no doubt that disappointment with political developments in the country indirectly accounts for a large measure of the personal tragedies facing the protagonists in R.'s prose. R. expresses her commitment to her country through other media, besides creative writing. As a journalist, she also has several professional opportunities to engage in commentary on Madagascar. However, she has lived in exile in France since the 1980s. And while she remains in close contact with the Malagasy diaspora in France, it remains to be seen whether exile and physical distance from Madagascar will ultimately lead, as it has with Rabemananjara, to the emergence of a different and less politically motivated focus to her future writing.

—MORADEWUN A. ADEJUNRNOBI

RAMÍREZ, Sergio

Nicaraguan novelist, short-story writer, and essayist, b. 5 Aug. 1942, Masatepe

R. studied law at the University of León, where he was a student activist opposed to the dictatorial régime of Anastasio Somoza. His interest in politics led to his fascination with the Nicaraguan patriot Augusto César Sandino (1895–1934), the subject of several of his best essays. But R. has also had a lifelong dedication to literature, which has at times conflicted with, and at times been enhanced by, his political career. After receiving his law degree in 1964, R. worked for several years in Costa Rica as a member of the Central American Inter-University Council. Soon thereafter he moved to West Berlin where he was supported by a grant from the German government. In 1977 he joined the Sandinista revolt against Somoza, who was overthrown in 1979. R. served as vice president of his homeland until the Sandinistas were defeated at the polls in 1990.

R.'s most important collection of stories is *Charles Atlas también muere* (1976; *Stories*, 1986), the unifying theme of which is the dependency of Nicaragua on the U.S. In the title story the puny narrator improves his physique after enrolling in Charles Atlas's course on physical culture, but upon traveling to the U.S. to meet the self-made Hercules, he discovers his hero to be a moribund old man. This portrait of demythification is enhanced by a subtle irony characteristic of the entire collection.

"Nicaragua es blanca" ("Nicaragua Is White") satirizes the influence, both cultural and economic, of the U.S. on the author's native land. In this absurd tale a meteorologist predicts snow for Managua on Christmas day, triggering elaborate preparations for the unprecedented event: fur coats, sweaters, and blankets are imported; heating systems are installed; and sleighs clog the streets. But the snow never materializes except in the backward areas of the country where subzero temperatures cause untold suffering.

Equally absurd, "A Jackie, con nuestro corazón" ("To Jackie with All Our Hearts") targets the social elite. The narrator is the president of the Virginia Country Club who, upon learning of Jackie (Kennedy) Onassis's trip to Nicaragua, pulls all strings to enable his organization to control every phase of her visit. Having been authorized by his club to purchase a boat to meet Jackie's yacht (and thus prevent other less prestigious groups from sharing the limelight), the narrator acquires the *Queen Elizabeth* and has it completely refurbished. The story ends with the image of the luxury liner filled with disgruntled passengers skirting the coast and anxiously scanning the horizon.

R.'s first novel, *Tiempo de fulgor* (1970; time of splendor), is set in the 19th c. in the city of León. Several plots are skillfully interwoven, the most important involving two families. Although this work emerges as something akin to the novel of customs, it differs from this traditional genre in that it is laced with fantasy and thereby shows unmistakable similarities to *Cien años de soledad* (1967; *One Hundred Years of Solitude*, 1970), by Colombia's Nobel laureate Gabriel GARCÍA MÁRQUEZ.

¿Te dio miedo la sangre? (1977; *To Bury Our Fathers*, 1983), R.'s second novel, is considerably more complex than his first, its major theme being the armed struggle against the Somoza régime between 1930 and 1961, just before the foundation in 1962 of the National Sandinista Liberation Front. A tangle of six interrelated plot threads informs this densely populated work, whose characters in their entirety embody the collective voice of a nation in travail. Just as resonances of García Márquez are discernible in *Tiempo de fulgor*, narrative strategies perfected by Peruvian novelist Mario Vargas LLOSA have left their mark on *¿Te dio miedo la sangre?* These include the weaving of numerous plot threads into an artistically integrated whole; the frequent shifts in the narrative perspective; and the use of interior monologues, dreams, and abrupt temporal and spatial dislocations to keep the reader alert.

In the early 1930s the most sensational criminal case in Nicaraguan history focused the nation's attention on the city of León, where a law student from Guatemala was accused of poisoning his wife and two members of a prominent local family. *Castigo divino* (1988; *Divine Punishment*, 1991), R.'s most engrossing novel, dramatizes this case. The work is an excellent example of documentary fiction, that is, a combination of historical fact and authorial imagination, the former creating an air of authenticity and the latter generating dramatic tension. In *Un baile de máscaras* (1995; A Mascarade), the birth of a child in a Nicaraguan pueblo is celebrated and given universal and mythical dimensions

R. is Nicaragua's leading writer of prose fiction and one of Latin America's most important men of letters of his generation.

Despite his well-known commitment to socialism, his political convictions never mar his art, which in general terms can be described as poetic realism. Thus he makes use of figurative language, innovative techniques, and fantasy to condemn U.S. imperialism and depict the appalling conditions in his native land. He is not only a gifted storyteller but also a sensitive spokesman for the Third World.

FURTHER WORKS: *Cuentos* (1963); *Mis días con el rector* (1965); *Nuevos cuentos* (1969); *Mariano Fiallos* (1971); *De tropeles y tropelías* (1972); *El pensamiento vivo de Sandino* (1974); *Viva Sandino* (1976); *Biografía de Sandino* (1979); *El muchacho de Niquinohomo* (1981); *Los no alineados* (1981); *El alba de oro* (1983); *Balcones y volcanes y otros ensayos y trabajos* (1983); *Sandino, su ideología y los partidos políticos* (1984); *Estás en Nicaragua* (1985); *Seguimos de frente* (1985); *Julio, estás en Nicaragua* (1986); *Sandino* (1986); *Las armas del futuro* (1987); *Sandino siempre* (1988); *La marcha del Zorro* (1990)

BIBLIOGRAPHY: Arellano, J. E., "La primera novela de un joven cuentista," *PrensLit*, 20 (12 Sept. 1970); Arellano, J. E., *Panorama de la literatura nicaragüense* (1977): 138–39; Foster, D. W., on *Charles Atlas también muere*, *WLT*, 51, 2 (Spring 1977): 260; Rama, A., ed., *Novísimos narradores hispanoamericanos en marcha, 1964–1980* (1981): 34, 271; Dauster, F., on *¿Te dio miedo la sangre?*, *WLT*, 58, 4 (Autumn 1984): 573; Morales, A., "S. R.: 'Gobernar con el mismo esmero con que escribo,'" *CasaA*, 25, 151 (July–Aug. 1985): 70–74; Schaefer, C., "La recperación del realismo: ¿Te dio miedo las sangre" de S. R.," *TCrit*, 13: 36–37 (1987): 146–52; Fuertnes, C., "Una novela centroamericana." *Suplemento Literario, La Nación* (Buenos Aires) (26 June 1988): 6; Santos, R., ed., *And We Sold the Rain: Contemporary Fiction from Central America* (1988): 9–24, 207; McMurray, G. R., on *Castigo divino, Chasqui*, 18, 1 (May 1989): 75–77; Beverley, J., and Zimmerman, M., *Literature and Politics in the Central American Revolutions* (1990): 40–48, 79–80, 182–88; McMurray, G. R., "S. R.'s *Castigo divino* as Documentary Novel," *Confluencia*, 5, 2 (Autumn 1990): 155–59

—GEORGE R. MCMURRAY

RAMOS, Graciliano

Brazilian novelist and short-story writer, b. 27 Dec. 1892, Quebrângulo; d. 20 March 1953, Rio de Janeiro

R. was the first child in the large family of a businessman and occasional farmer living in the state of Alagoas in the Northeast. He attended secondary school in Maceió and published his early poetic efforts under a pseudonym. Living briefly in Rio, he worked on a variety of newspapers and began writing short stories. He then moved back to the Northeast and went into the dry-goods business, gaining his early reputation not in literature but in politics.

Like most Brazilian writers, R. never managed to live by the pen; he spent most of his adult life in public service in various capacities. His writing talents, in fact, were discovered when a report he wrote while mayor of the town of Palmeira dos Indios reached the poet and publisher Augusto Frederico Schmidt (1906–1965), who encouraged R. to publish the manuscript Schmidt was sure R. had tucked away. Such a manuscript did indeed exist and was the first novel of the four that constitute the bulk of his fictional work. He gained national prominence in the 1930s both for his novels and for his politics—his novels were publicly burned at least once and their author imprisoned at least twice because the government of President Getúlio Vargas considered R. a communist and his books subversive. Oddly, there is little but circumstantial evidence of leftist politics in the novels; more concrete proof of R.'s political sympathies appears in his *Memórias do cárcere* (1953; prison memoirs) and in his travel books and miscellaneous publications.

R. is known as the most literate, or at least the most literary, member of a generation of Brazilian novelists who began writing about 1930. Most of the works produced by this group are set in the poverty-ridden Northeast and are at least vaguely political, but R. is by far the subtlest of the group and probably the most skeptical. His novels are relatively tightly controlled, the language reserved, and the psychological dimension rich; hence, they are the most "English" in Brazil since those of Joaquim Maria Machado de Assis (1839–1908). A careful stylist, R. is an excellent writer to read closely, because of his nuances and turns of phrase.

Although the scenarios of all four novels are clearly localistic, only one, *Vidas secas* (1938; *Barren Lives*, 1965), is sufficiently region-bound as to require explanatory notes; the others are neither so rooted in place as to be unintelligible to outsiders nor so concerned with local color as to be provincial. Even *Vidas secas*, arguably his masterpiece, is as intelligible to the sensitive reader as John STEINBECK's *The Grapes of Wrath*, although the historical situation is less than familiar to non-Brazilians.

The first two novels, *Caetés* (1933; Caetés [the name of an Indian tribe]) and *São Bernardo* (1934; *São Bernardo*, 1975), are obliquely metafictional. *Caetés* is self-referential in the sense that the book which the protagonist, a small-town bookkeeper, is writing (a book about Indians) carries the title of the volume the reader has in his hands. In *São Bernardo* the narrative itself is ostensibly a book called *São Bernardo*, written by a ruthless and cynical rancher to explain and justify his life. The third, *Angústia* (1936; *Anguish*, 1946), is a sort of hallucinatory monologue by a Brazilian John Doe in which the narrator's obsessions and failures are gradually exposed. The first-person exposition in each necessarily reduces the scope of characterization to a focus on the narrator's own obsessions, the most important of which are amorous and materialistic. In all three cases the protagonist is involved in a love triangle, and in each case one member of the triangle is eliminated by death. Each protagonist is brought to eventual ruin by his egotism, whether that egotism takes the form of lust for a woman or for possessions and status.

Vidas secas, R.'s final novel, is a short but penetrating study of the lives of a peasant family forced by drought to relocate. The book consists of thirteen apparently independent chapters, each dealing with a single character or topic, and is presented in a combination of third-person narration and indirect free discourse. The apparent randomness of the narrative structure is negated in the end, where it becomes clear that the beginning and end are merely points on a circle, the pattern of settling and relocation a grim and inexorable cycle.

R. is probably the only novelist of his generation whose works of the 1930s have survived well into the present: among others, only Jorge AMADO, who completely refurbished his technique in the 1950s, is still widely read. A master stylist and a writer keenly attuned to man's persistent capacity to fool himself, R. is not only

technically but also philosophically adept, and his artistic but depressing representations of the perversities of self can stand with some of the best existential writing of the century, even as it provides glimpses into a cultural milieu almost unknown outside Brazil.

FURTHER WORKS: *Histórias de Alexandre* (1944); *Infância* (1945); *Dois dedos* (1945); *Insônia* (1947); *Viagem* (1954); *Linhas tortas* (1962); *Viventes das Alagoas* (1962)

BIBLIOGRAPHY: Ellison, F., *Brazil's New Novel* (1954): 111–32; Hamilton, R., "Character and Idea in R.'s *Vidas secas*," *LBR*, 5, 1 (1968): 86–92; Mazzara, R., "New Perspectives on G. R.," *LBR*, 5, 1 (1968): 93–100; Martins, W., *The Modernist Idea* (1970): 300–306; Sovereign, M., "Pessimism in G. R.," *LBR*, 7, 1 (1970): 57–63; Mazzara, R., *G. R.* (1974); Hulet, C., *Brazilian Literature* (1975), Vol. 3: 207–15; Vincent, J., "G. R.: The Dialectics of Defeat," in Martins, H., ed., *The Brazilian Novel* (1976): 43–58; De Oliveira, C. L., *Understanding G. R.* (1988)

—JON S. VINCENT

RAMUZ, Charles-Ferdinand

Swiss poet and novelist (writing in French), b. 24 Sept. 1878, Cully-sur-Lausanne; d. 23 May 1947, Lausanne

R. grew up in Lausanne, where his father had a small business, but R. never lost touch with the rural life of his peasant ancestry. Convinced early of his literary vocation, he went to study in Paris, where he felt painfully isolated. In 1913 he married and then decided to return to the lake shores of Switzerland, where he had first experienced serenity and fulfillment.

There are three distinct periods in R.'s career. The first one corresponds to the years of exile in the French capital, between 1902 and 1914, when he became intensely conscious of his roots and of his true identity as a writer. Once aware that he could only write about his own people and in an appropriate manner, he started on the arduous task of developing a personal style steeped in the speech of his countrymen, even though such a style challenged all the established rules of French literary tradition and contributed to the critics' prolonged neglect of his work. In his first novels, centered on individual destinies, R. kept his imagination in check, since he felt unable to resolve the emotional duality that tormented him: his feeling of solitude and of communion; his anguish when facing the inexorability of death, and his rapture over beauty, nature, and life. Love and death, the two spiritual poles of R.'s work, reflect this inner conflict, which is emphasized by his placing his early protagonists in alienating surroundings. R. reached artistic maturity with *Aimé Pache, peintre vaudois* (1911; Aimé Pache, painter of Vaud) and *La vie de Samuel Belet* (1913; *The Life of Samuel Belet*, 1951), in which the semi-autobiographical protagonists surmount this state of separation to reach plenitude, communion with the universe, and reconciliation with their destiny.

The second period reveals a change of direction foreshadowed in *Adieu à beaucoup de personnages* (1914; farewell to many characters), and confirmed by the outbreak of World War I. For the next ten years, R. was interested in symbolic themes and collective destinies; he perfected his narrative technique, expanded the scope of his plots, added color to his imagery, and gave free rein to his lyricism. His novels of this period present apocalyptic visions of disaster and death, resolved by the redemptive love of a young girl in *Le règne de l'esprit malin* (1914; *The Reign of the Evil One*, 1922) and *La guérison des maladies* (1917; the cure of illnesses). In *La séparation des races* (1923; the separation of the races) R. even tried to eliminate narration altogether. The most technically daring of R.'s works, these were also the least successful because he failed in his attempt to transform stories into written paintings.

The third period began with the very original *Passage du poète* (1923; the poet's passage), which affirmed the universality of true poetic experience. From then on, the fate of individuals was once more prevalent, but R.'s technique, style, and vision were greatly enriched by his previous experimentation. Working in depth, R.'s imagination transforms a bare fact into a living reality, while the repetition of certain words or events serves as a leitmotif and lends an aura of popular tale to *La grande peur dans la montagne* (1926; *Terror on the Mountain*, 1968), which reaches epic grandeur. In *Derborence* (1934; *When the Mountain Fell*, 1947), perhaps R.'s masterpiece, a poignant drama is created from a tenuous plot devoid of intellectual or psychological complexity. Turning up alive two months after disappearing in an avalanche, a man is saved from his morbid desire to return to the mountain by his wife's love and courage. The originality of the novel is in its truly authentic atmosphere, its architectural composition, its strongly delineated characters, its metaphorical and evocative language, and its double mood of sweetness and sadness.

Recognized as the leading Swiss writer, R.'s fame has steadily grown in France since his death, although he is still not well known in the English-speaking world, despite a number of translations. The structural solidity and the elemental simplicity of R.'s works evoke Cézanne (whom he so greatly admired), while the heavily accented, repetitive rhythm of his prose calls to mind Charles PÉGUY and Paul CLAUDEL. Authenticity and sincerity are the hallmarks of his oeuvre. Also noteworthy are R.'s technical experiments with time, point of view and cinematic devices. Before Louis-Ferdinand CÉLINE and Raymond QUENEAU, R. rejected literary conventions to write fiction in an oral style. The regionalist label, which the majority of critics assign to him, does not fit R.'s scope or his accomplishment: despite the narrow geographical confines of all his novels, R.'s peasants represent primitive man close to the soil and the essential realities of life, devoid of social mask. Born of inner necessity and inseparable from the language that gives it expression, R.'s creation is essentially poetic and has a profoundly human accent.

FURTHER WORKS: *Le petit village* (1903); *Aline* (1905); *La grande guerre du Sondrebond* (1906); *Les circonstances de la vie* (1907); *Jean-Luc persécuté* (1909); *Nouvelles et morceaux* (1910); *Raison d'être* (1914); *La guerre dans le Haut-Pays* (1915); *Le grand printemps* (1917); *Les signes parmi nous* (1919); *Histoire du soldat* (text for music by Stravinsky, 1920; *The Soldier's Tale*, 1924); *Chant de notre Rhône* (1920); *Salutation paysanne* (1921); *Terre du ciel* (1921); *Présence de la mort* (1922; *The End of All Men*, 1944); *L'amour du monde* (1925); *La beauté sur la terre* (1927; *Beauty on Earth*, 1929); *Souvenirs sur Igor Strawinsky* (1929); *Farinet ou la fausse monnaie* (1932); *Adam et Ève* (1932); *Une main* (1933); *Taille de l'homme* (1933); *Questions* (1935); *Le garçon savoyard* (1936); *Besoin de grandeur* (1937); *Si le soleil ne revenait pas* (1937); *Paris: Notes d'un Vaudois* (1938); *Découverte du monde* (1939); *La guerre aux papiers* (1942); *Pays de Vaud* (1943); *La Suisse romande* (1943); *René Auberjonois* (1943); *Vues*

sur le Valais (1943); *Nouvelles* (1944); *Les servants, et autres nouvelles* (1946); *Journal, 1896–1942* (1945); *Journal, 1942–1947* (1949); *Le village brûlé: Derniers récits* (1951); *Lettres, 1900–1918* (1956); *Lettres, 1919–1947* (1959); *Œuvres complètes* (20 vols., 1967). FURTHER WORKS IN ENGLISH: *What Is Man?* (1948)

BIBLIOGRAPHY: Zermatten, M., *Connaissance de R.* (1947; rev. ed., 1964); Tissot, A., *C.-F. R.* (1948); Béguin, A., *Patience de R.* (1950); Guisan, G., *R.* (1958); Parsons, C. R., *Vision plastique de C.-F. R.* (1964); Guers-Villate, Y., *R.* (1966); Guisan, G., ed. *C.-F. R., ses amis et son temps* (4 vols., 1967–68); Auberjonois, F., "C.-F. R. and the Way of the Anti-Poet," in Natan, A., ed. *Swiss Men of Letters* (1970): 37–55; Bevan, D., *C.-F. R.* (1979)

—YVONNE GUERS-VILLATE

RANNIT, Aleksis

Estonian poet, scholar, and art critic (also writing in English), b. 15 Oct. 1914, Kallaste; d. 5 Jan. 1985, New Haven, Conn.

R. studied art history and literature at the universities of Tartu (Estonia) and Vilnius (Lithuania); after World War II, classical archaeology and aesthetics at Freiburg (Germany). In 1953 he settled in the U.S., studying literature and library science at Columbia University. He holds honorary doctorates from the universities of Stockholm and Seoul, Korea. R. has pursued various occupations, always linked with the arts. Since 1960 he has been curator of Russian and East European Studies at Yale University. He was elected a member of the International Academy of Arts and Letters in Paris in 1962.

R.'s poetry is best understood in the context of his lifelong devotion to art. A respected art critic, he has organized exhibitions, compiled catalogues, given many lectures, and written extensively on mostly, although not exclusively, 20th-c. art. As a literary critic, R. combines a broad historical-comparative erudition (he knows every European literature) with a unique synesthetic approach, viewing poetry always in context with other art forms. He has used this approach successfully in essays on various poets: the Estonians Marie UNDER and Heiti TALVIK, the Russians Anna AKHMATOVA and Nikolay ZABOLOTSKY, the Lithuanian Henrikas RADAUSKAS, the Austrian Rainer Maria RILKE, among others. Also a connoisseur of music, the theater, and architecture, R. translates experiences in all these art forms into the language of his poetry.

R.'s poems tend to be built around ingenious conceits, realized in vividly stylized imagery: landscapes and seascapes as a painter would see them, paintings, sculptures, and musical compositions as they strike a poet's imagination. Many of R.'s poems are, explicitly or implicitly, chapters of an *ars poetica*, ever new attempts to define poetry. R.'s poetry exemplifies the condition of every purely lyric poet: his naturally soft, vague, and fluid impressions (pure color and nuance) require the self-imposed discipline of a strict rhythm and pointedly difficult structure (line) to assume shape. R.'s conscious emphasis is on line, although he is also a master of delicate nuances of color. An eminently conscious craftsman, R. cultivates the euphonic aspect of his verse, developing intricate patterns of alliteration and inner rhyme, vowel assonance and vowel modulation. He is a master of difficult rhymes.

R. has added to Estonian poetry a distinctly Parnassian and classicist strain. This is important for a literature that started, essentially, with romanticism. R.'s poetry has appeared in book form in translations into English, German, Russian, Hungarian, and Lithuanian.

FURTHER WORKS: *Akna raamistuses* (1937); *Käesurve* (1945); *Suletud avarust* (1956); *Kuiv hiilgus* (1963); *Kaljud* (1969); *Sõrmus* (1972); *Helikeeli* (1982). FURTHER WORKS IN ENGLISH: *Line* (1970); *Dry Radiance: Selected Poems in New Directions 25: An International Anthology in Prose and Poetry* (1972); *Donum Estonicum: Poems in Translation* (1976); *Cantus Firmus* (1978, bilingual); *The Violin of Monsieur Ingres: Some Hieratic and Some Erratic Estonian Lines in English* (1983)

BIBLIOGRAPHY: Willmann, A., "The Perceptional World of A. R.'s Poetry," *Estonian Learned Society in America Yearbook* IV, 1964–1967 (1968): 32–50; Rubulis, A., *Baltic Literature* (1970): 97–104; Lyman, H., Introduction to A. R., *Dry Radiance*, in Laughlin, J., ed. *New Directions* 25 (1972): 146–50; Terras, V., "The Poetics of A. R.: Observations on the Condition of the Émigré Poet," *JBalS*, 5 (1974): 112–16; Leitch, V. B., "Modernist Poetry: A Phenomenological Reading of A. R.'s English Works," *JBalS*, 10 (1979): 187–204; Saagpakk, P., "The Apollonian Impulse: A. R. and Wallace Stevens," *MR*, 21 (1980): 157–73; Weidlé, W., "Beneath the Surface of Foreign Words and/or A. R.," *JBalS*, 11 (1980): 187–98

—VICTOR TERRAS

RANSOM, John Crowe

American poet, critic, and editor, b. 30 April 1888, Pulaski, Tenn.; d. 3 July 1974, Gambier, Ohio

R., the son of a Methodist missionary and a schoolteacher, attended Vanderbilt University in Nashville, Tennessee, and Oxford as a Rhodes Scholar. In 1914 he began to teach English and literature at Vanderbilt. After serving in France in World War I, R. returned to Vanderbilt.

In 1919 an undistinguished volume, *Poems about God*, was published at the recommendation of Robert FROST. Soon after, R. joined a group of teachers, students, and townsmen who gathered regularly to talk about poetry and to read their own verse. Out of this group emerged *The Fugitive* (1922–25), a little magazine that is said to have initiated the Southern renascence in poetry. The contributors, who came to be known as the "Fugitives," included R. Allen TATE, Robert Penn WARREN, and Donald Davidson (1893–1968).

R. wrote most of his poetry between about 1916 and 1928, publishing *Chills and Fever* (1924) and *Two Gentlemen in Bonds* (1927). Most of the poems in *Selected Poems* (1945; rev. ed., 1963) and in *Poems and Essays* (1955) appeared originally in these two volumes.

R.'s finely wrought poetry achieves ironic effects through subtle combinations of incongruous strains of diction: he freely mixes Latin elegance and Anglo-Saxon simplicity, the pedantic and the commonplace, the archaic and the colloquial. He seems both involved in and remote from his personae, who most often are failures in a world that has lost its capacity to act as a stabilizing

agent. R.'s most frequent theme is decay: of belief, of the order of society, or of the individual life.

In 1925, as a result of the ridicule heaped upon the South because of the Scopes "monkey trial" (which revolved around the teaching of evolution in the schools), R. became a defender of the agrarian traditions of the South. Although the "Southern Agrarians" had different aims from those of the Fugitives, R., Tate, Warren, and Davidson were active in both groups.

The agrarian defense of the South and the attack upon encroaching industrialism culminated in the intellectually important but practically ineffective book of essays *I'll Take My Stand* (1930), for which R. wrote the "Statement of Principles" and the lead essay. R. defended the South as a traditionalist society, which, he said, through manners and rituals and a life close to the soil, gave fuller scope to existence than could an industrialized and urbanized society.

In *God without Thunder* (1930) R. ascribes the decline of religion and poetry to the influence of science and its abstractionism. The God of modern religions had been deprived of his mystery, had lost his terrible thunder.

In the early 1930s R. turned his attention to poetics. As a theorist and editor, he was a major influence in the New Criticism, which focused upon the aesthetic as opposed to the philological, biographical, and historical aspects of the poem. The New Criticism revolutionized the teaching of poetry in college classrooms and had a marked effect on close textual analysis in practical literary criticism.

R.'s main poetic theme, the dissociation of sensibility, is related to his principal concern in his criticism and critical theory. R. holds that experience is dualistic, a rich mixture of the particular and the general. The dissociation of sensibility, according to R., is a modern malady caused by scientific abstractionism. Science reduces experience to general patterns, abstracts the universal from the particular, tries to remove the mystery from delightfully unique beings. R. believes that art reminds us of concreteness and particularity. He argues repeatedly that poetry has both structure and texture. By structure he means the logic or theme; by texture, the concrete, the individual, the "irrelevant," which cannot be reduced to paraphrase. The texture is inviolable; it makes poetry different from scientific discourse. R.'s critical point is manifested in his poems through his many portraits of frustrated and failed lovers, those who are so confused by modernist compartmentalization of experience that they cannot savor the grand particularity of the unique beloved object.

In 1937 R. went to teach at Kenyon College in Gambier, Ohio, where he founded and edited until 1959 the prestigious *Kenyon Review*. Through his editing, his numerous essays, and his books *The World's Body* (1938) and *The New Criticism* (1941), R. is a voice to be reckoned with in the academic debates over the nature and value of poetry. In his poetry he is at best an exemplary craftsman who left perhaps a dozen splendid poems that will defy the ravages of time.

FURTHER WORKS: *Armageddon* (1923); *Grace after Meat* (1924); *Selected Poems*, 3rd ed., rev. and enlarged (1969); *Beating the Bushes: Selected Essays, 1914–1970* (1972)

BIBLIOGRAPHY: Knight, K. F., *The Poetry of J. C. R.* (1964); Stewart, J. L., *The Burden of Time: The Fugitives and Agrarians* (1965); Buffington, R., *The Equilibrist: A Study of J. C. R.'s Poems, 1916–1963* (1967); Young, T. D., ed., *J. C. R.: Critical Essays and a Bibliography* (1968); Parsons, T. H., *J. C. R.* (1969); Williams, M., *The Poetry of J. C. R.* (1972); Young, T. D.,

Gentleman in a Dustcoat: A Biography of J. C. R. (1976); Quinlan, K., *J. C. R.'s Secular Faith* (1989)

—KARL F. KNIGHT

RAO, Raja

Indian novelist and short-story writer (writing in English), b. 8 Nov. 1908, Hassan

Born a Brahmin in the state of Mysore in south India, R. received his education at Muslim schools. In 1929 he was awarded a government scholarship for study in France, and he attended the University of Montpellier. He married a French woman in 1931 and did research in history at the University of Paris. During 1931–32 he contributed four articles written in Kannada to *Jaya Karnataka*, an influential journal. When his marriage disintegrated in 1939, he returned to India and began his first period of residence in an ashram. In 1942 he was active in an underground movement against the British. He returned to France in 1948 and alternated between France in and India from then on. He first visited America in 1950 and later spent some more time living in an ashram. R. lectured on Indian philosophy at the University of Texas beginning in 1963. Now retired, he is married to an American.

R. is perhaps the most sophisticated and philosophically complex Indian novelist writing in English. His first novel, *Kanthapura* (1938), is a small masterpiece dealing with nonviolent resistance against the British in a village in south India. Told through the persona of a garrulous old woman, the novel echoes the style and structure of Indian vernacular tales.

In *The Serpent and the Rope* (1960), an avowedly autobiographical novel that won the Sahitya Akademi Award, R. explores his Brahmin heritage in the context of marriage to a Frenchwoman. As the hero struggles with commitments imposed on him by his Hindu family, his wife becomes a Buddhist and renounces worldly desires. Both this novel and R.'s third, *The Cat and Shakespeare* (1965), celebrate his preference for Advaita Vedanta, or unqualified nondualism. The enigmatic third novel, a sequel to the second, is a metaphysical comedy that answers philosophical questions posed in the earlier book. The hero's guru is a neighbor who offers devotional Hinduism through passive union with God (the way of the cat). Once the narrator is able to grasp the notion of "play," with its absence of distinction making, he discovers that there is no dichotomy between himself and God.

These three novels are R.'s major works; they are rather demanding but are marked by superb narrative skill and masterful diction, remarkable in one whose native tongue was Kannada. His short stories, first collected in *The Cow of the Barricades, and Other Stories* (1947), seven of which were reprinted in *The Policeman and the Rose* (1978), together with three new pieces, are experiments in style and subject matter. Among the collected stories, "Javni" (1944), "Akkayya" (1944), and "Nimka" (1978) are exceptionally fine. *Comrade Kirillov* (1976), a novella written early in R.'s career and first published in French (1965), explores communism as an ideological misunderstanding of man's ultimate aims. R.'s novel entitled *The Chessmaster and His Moves* (1988) is a massive work, surely influenced by Proust, in which Sivaram Sastri, an Indian mathematician in Paris, recounts, with characteristic R. intensity, his love affairs and friendships. A post-colonial novel in some ways, and a paean to elitism in others, it is crowned

by a remarkable dialogue between Sastri, who explains evil, and Michel, a Polish Jew who conducts a litany to expiate the holocaust. The metaphor of the chess game animates a novel so philosophically rich with ideas of East and West as to continually astonish and exasperate the most devoted reader.

R. stands out as a strong intelligence in both Indian and Commonwealth literary traditions. Moreover, he has achieved independence and significance by using powerful images derived from the Western literary tradition to express an overwhelming commitment to Advaita Vedanta and the Sanskrit language. His are essentially ideological novels rooted in Brahmanism and Hinduism. They convey, more powerfully than the work of any other Indo-English writer, the essence of Indian thought.

FURTHER WORKS: *On the Ganga Ghat* (1993)

BIBLIOGRAPHY: Amur, G. S., "R. R.: The Kannada Phase," *Journal of Karnataka University*, 10 (1966): 40–52; Gemmill, J. P., "Rhythm in *The Cat and Shakespeare*," LE&W, 13 (1969): 27–42; Narasimhaiah, C. D., R. R. (1970); Naik, M. K., R. R. (1972); Westbrook, P., "Theme and Inaction in R. R.'s *The Serpent and the Rope*," WLWE, 14 (1976): 385–99; Guzman, R. R., "The Saint and the Sage: The Fiction of R. R.," VQR, 56 (1980): 32–50; Niranjan, S., "Myth as a Creative Mode: A Study of Mythical Parallels in R. R.'s Novels," ComQ, 4, 13 (1980): 49–68; special R. issue, WLT, 62 (1988); Perera, S., "Towards a Limited Emancipation: Women in R. R.'s *Kanthapura*," Ariel, 23 (1992): 99-110; Dey, E., *The Novels of R. R.* (1992)

—JANET M. POWERS

RASPUTIN, Valentin

Russian novelist, short-story writer, and essayist, b. 15 Mar. 1937, Atalanka

R. is one of the most artistically talented and politically controversial of Russia's postwar writers. Born in a village on the Angara River in Siberia, R. studied at Irkutsk University. From his college years until the mid-1960s, he worked as a journalist, reporting on such diverse topics as construction projects and the native peoples of Siberia. After 1966 he devoted his time primarily to fiction, with numerous forays into ethnographic and political essay writing. His primary home has remained Irkutsk in Siberia. In 1980 R. was severely beaten by thieves, an attack that interrupted his career for several years. Since the beginning of the Gorbachev era, R. has become increasingly involved in the "burning questions" of the day, from protection of the environment to the fate of Russia in the disintegrating U.S.S.R. Through his glasmostera statements on nationalism, R. has been perceived both at home and abroad as belonging to the right-wing political camp, though not to its most extreme faction. R. served briefly in Gorbachev's government in 1990. Over the years he has played an active role in the Writers' Union of the Russian Republic and of the U.S.S.R., and has served on the editorial board of the influential conservative journal *Nash sovremennik*.

R. is primarily known for a series of four short novels: *Dengi dlya Marii* (1967; *Money for Maria*, 1981), *Posledniy srok* (1970; *Borrowed Time*, 1981), *Zhivi i pomni* (1974; *Live and Remember*, 1978), and *Proshchanie s Matyoroy* (1976; *Farewell to Matyora*,

1979). All of these works are set in the Siberian countryside and all focus on a moment of crisis in a peasant family or community. In *Dengi dlya Marii*, an innocent woman is faced with prison if her husband cannot collect enough money to cover losses at the government store where she works; what concerns the author most is the community's response to the crisis faced by one of its members. *Posledniy srok* focuses on a dying peasant woman who tries to reunite her family during her final days. *Zhivi i pomni* tells the story of a World War II deserter who secretly returns to his village, bringing tragedy in his wake. *Proshchanie s Matyoroy*, the best known of all R.'s works, shows an ancient village on an island in the Angara River just before it is to be flooded to make way for a new hydroelectric project. In all these works R. displays a talent for weaving together very specific details of life in the Siberian countryside with narratives of universal appeal. While avoiding the excessive folk stylization of some ruralists, R. has been remarkably successful in capturing the voices of contemporary peasants, especially the old women of the village. His longer narratives owe a great deal to the influence of 19th-c. writers, especially Dostoevsky, and virtually nothing to Soviet literature. Indeed, in R.'s work we see one of the best examples of the undermining of Socialist REALISM in published literature during the period before glasnost.

Since the mid-1960s, R. has also written a number of shorter works that have gained a wide readership in Russia. Among his better-known stories are "Ekh, starukha" (1966; "The Old Woman," 1985), "Vasilii i Vasilisa" (1966; "Vasily i Vasilisa," 1989), "Vniz i vverkh po techeniyu" (1972; "Downstream," 1982), "Vek zhivi—vek lyubi" (1981; "Live and Love," 1986; rev., ed. 1989), and "Pozhar" (1985; "The Fire," 1989). "Vniz i vverkh po techeniyu," one of R.'s most autobiographical works, follows a writer traveling by boat down the Angara River to his native regions; it is a finely wrought story and an interesting companion piece to the novel *Proshchanie s Matyoroy*. "Pozhar" was one of the first major literary works to appear in the Gorbachev era, and while its somber tone seemed out of place in the euphoric early glasnost years, by the end of the 1980s it seems to have foreseen all too accurately the chaotic nature of post communist Russia. Like Dostoevsky, Aleksandr SOLZHENITSYN and many other conservative Russian writers before him, R. sees his latter works as both a prophecy of the nation's decline and a plea to return to traditional ways.

In the second half of the 1980s, R. returned to the essay form that marked the beginning of his career, but with a far different focus. If, in the 1960s, he described with some enthusiasm the development of Siberia, twenty years later he was distraught over the same kind of development. And, while his earlier ethnographic work had concentrated on the non-Russian peoples of Siberia, by the 1980s he was concerned with the long history of Russian involvement in that region. These twin themes of the cost of progress and the need for recovering national roots came together in his campaign to save Lake Baikal, whose restoration he saw as being crucial not just to the environment, but to Russia's cultural and spiritual health as well.

R.'s work has marked important stages in Russia's political and literary life. He began in the Socialist Realist style, but abandoned it for a more traditional realism that was enriched by the rural idiom and universal themes. His novel *Proshchanie s Matyoroy* defines the end of the all-important Village Prose movement in 1976, and his story "Pozhar" marks the beginning of glasnost literature in 1985. His rhetorical shift to a more publicistic and less lyrical tone in the late 1980s reflects a process that was taking place throughout Russian literature. It is R.'s nonfractional statements from this

latter period—specifically those that blame Russia's weakened state on Westerners and a host of non-Russians including Soviet Jews—that have gained him a prominence in the West that eluded him as a novelist and short-story writer. He has had the misfortune, mostly of his own making, to become well-known abroad as a Russian chauvinist, rather than as one of the finest writers of the post-Stalinist period.

FURTHER WORKS: *Kray vozle samogo neba* (1966); *Kostrovye novykh gorodov* (1966); *Chelovek s etogo sveta* (1967); *Dengi dlya Marii. Povest i rasskazy* (1968); *Posledniy srok. Povest i rasskazy* (1970); *Zhivi i pomni. Povest i rasskazy* (1975); *Vek zhivi-vek lyubi. Rasskazy* (1982); *Povesti i rasskazy* (1984); *Izbrannye proizvedeniya v dvukh tomakh* (1984). FURTHER WORKS IN ENGLISH: *You Live and Love and Other Stories* (1986); *Siberia on Fire: Stories and Essays* (1989)

BIBLIOGRAPHY: Shneidman, N. N., *Soviet Literature in the 1970s* (1979): 75–87; Corten, I., "Solzenitcyn's Matrena and R.'s Darĵa: Two Studies in Russian Peasant Spirituality," *RLJ*, 114(1979): 85–98; Hosking, G., *Beyond Socialist Realism* (1980): 70–81; Brown, E. J., *Russian Literature since the Revolution*, rev. ed. (1982): 305–11; Gillespie, D., *V. R. and Soviet Russian Village Prose* (1986); Mikkelson, G., and Winchell, M., "V. R. and His Siberia," Introduction to *Siberia on Fire* (1989): ix–xxii; Polowy, T., *The Novellas of V. R.: Genre, Language and Style* (1989); Parthé, K., "Master of the Island," Introduction to *Farewell to Matyora* (1991): vii–xxii; Parthé, K., "The Good Soldier's Wife," Introduction to *Live and Remember* (1992): v–xx

—KATHLEEN PARTHÉ

REA, Domenico

Italian short-story writer, novelist, essayist, and critic, b. 8 Aug. 1921, Nocera Inferiore

Self-taught and an attentive reader of classical and modern literature, R. began to write during World War II. His early collections of stories, *Spaccanapoli* (1947; the street that cuts through Naples) and *Gesù, fate luce* (1950; Jesus, make light), established him as one of the foremost interpreters of the temper and vitality, the emotions and expectations, of the people of Naples and of the south, the people with whom he had lived through the difficult years of the war and the American occupation. His writing in this period is characterized by a brisk, eclectic, and dense style, which also utilized the Neapolitan dialect, and by a mood of detachment that was able to transcend immediate historical facts and blend levels of reality and fantasy. In the 1950s, however, he shifted toward a committed portrayal of the social reality of the south in its more painfully obvious manifestations. The stories of *Ritratto di maggio* (1953; May portrait) are indicative of this development.

The issues and objectives of R.'s fiction are also the object of his critical writings, particularly of *Le due Napoli* (1950; the two Naples), a dispassionate analysis of the history, traditions, environment, and modern conditions of the city, whose inhabitants are not unaware of their own misery. He shows the human degradation and desperation that other writers have covered up or disguised with the falling image of a city blissfully joyous in its traditional role of showplace for the benefit of the unsuspecting outsider or of the misguided tourist in search of spectacle and titillation. Some of his specting outsider or of the misguied more incisive work as critic, essayist, and columnist has been collected in *Diario napoletano* (1971; Neapolitan diary).

In writing his first and only novel (to date), *Ina vampata di rossore* (1959; *A Blush of Shane*, 1963), R. was apparently yielding to a desire for recognition as a novelist, but the work was a true challenge, a conscious test of his skill in the longer narrative. The pressing need to expose the myth of the happy Naples is a constant preoccupation and is clearly evidenced in this novel. In some of his subsequent works, however, R. gave expression to other important social concerns and was among those perceptive Italian writers who closely followed the evolution of the middle class in the years of the economic boom.

FURTHER WORKS: *La figlia di Casimiro Clarus* (1945); *Le formicole rosse* (1948); *La signora scende a Pompei* (1952); *Quel che vide Cummeo* (1955); *Il re e il lustrascarpe* (1961); *I racconti* (1965); *L'altra faccia* (1965); *Gabbiani* (1966); *Questi tredici* (1968); *La signora è una vagabonda* (1968); *Tentazione, e altri racconti* (1976); *Fate benealle anime del purgatorio, illuminazioni napoletane* (1977).

—A. ILLIANO

READ, Herbert

English poet, critic, and essayist, b. 4 Dec. 1893, Kirbymoorside; d. 12 June 1968, Malton

The boyhood R. spent on his father's farm in Yorkshire, recounted in *The Innocent Eye* (1932), remained throughout his life a dominant influence, Wordsworthian in the power of its innocence and beauty. He attended Leeds University, was commissioned in 1915, fought in France and Belgium 1915–18, and left the army a convinced pacifist. He had a high position in the Treasury from 1919 to 1922, and then, in an abrupt change of occupation, was a curator at the Victoria and Albert Museum from 1922 to 1931.

His real vocation, however, had always been literary. First known as a war poet, writing short, graphic poems reflecting the futility and brutality of combat, R. quickly established himself in the 1920s as a literary critic and editor. He was creditors of the short-lived but influential *Art and Letters*, and contributed reviews and essays to *The Criterion*, edited by T. S. ELIOT, and to many other literary journals, English and American. His museum position led to studies in the plastic arts, which bore fruit in the 1930s in much art criticism, including *The Meaning of Art* (1930; rev. eds., 1936, 1951; first Am. ed., *The Anatomy of Art*, 1932), *Art Now* (1933), *Art and Industry* (1934), *Surrealism* (1935), and *Art and Society* (1937). To the general public R. was best known as an art critic, especially as a defender of abstract and SURREALIST art, and an authority on industrial design.

In the 1930s R. also emerged as an articulate advocate of anarchism, in *Poetry and Anarchism* (1938) and other works, abandoning his earlier adherence to Marxist socialism. From these interests in literature, art, society, and the relations among them, R. continued to produce until his death a large quantity of critical writing, as well as a much smaller amount of poetry. In addition, he

was active in practical affairs, serving as director of the publishing firm of Routledge and Kegan Paul, president of the Institute of Contemporary Arts, president of the British Society of Aesthetics, trustee of the Tate Gallery, among other positions. He held many fellowships and lectureships. He was knighted in 1953.

R.'s early poetry was much influenced by IMAGISM, the tenets of which remained always of great importance to him. His poems, however, despite original and striking images, are seldom imagist, many being meditative or dramatic, with complicated patterns of thought. R.'s poetry is probably underrated. He was a minor poet, but his best work-such as "The Analysis of Love" (1923), "The End of a War" (1933), and "A World within a War" (1943)—is good by any standards. Yet it is a prose work, his fantasy *The Green Child* (1935), that is his most notable and original creative work. This complex and strangely luminous story, an allegory of a journey through the self to an aesthetic source of life, ends in the underground realm of the green people, an elaborately worked out and unforgettable image of that point in the psyche where personal becomes impersonal, where inner and outer order are finally the same.

Most of R.'s critical books are collections drawn from his prolific output of essays, lectures, and reviews, often grouped around a central theme. Essays are sometimes reprinted in several different collections, early writings occasionally being revised to conform to later views.

R.'s early critical work is difficult to classify. He appeared to want to adhere to the antiromantic "reason" and "classicism" espoused by Eliot and T. E. Hulme (1883–1917), the latter of whose posthumous papers, *Speculations* (1924), R. edited; and at the same time he wished not to deny the claims of "emotion"—a position expressed in the title of his first collection of literary criticism, *Reason and Romanticism* (1926). In the 1930s, however, he gradually began calling himself a romantic. In *From in Modern Poetry* (1932) he set forth an "organic" position derived from Coleridge by way of FREUD: "personality" determines "form." Hence, the primary concern of criticism must be with the poetic personality, not the poet's technique, and R.'s own critical writings took this direction, especially in *Wordsworth* (1930) and *In Defense of Shelley* (1936).

By 1938, in *Collected Essays in Literary Criticism*, he could announce his aim, quite accurately, as the "rehabilitation of romanticism." R. thus remained outside the mainstream of Anglo-American literary criticism in the 1930s and 1940s, which ran in the direction of the kind of close technical analysis advocated by the New Critics. But he was one of the earliest to practice psychoanalytical criticism, at first Freudian, and later mostly Jungian (see Jung), as in *The Origins of Form in Art* (1965). From the 1940s on, R.'s varied interests came together in an attempt to establish a philosophy of life in which the laws of nature and the social order are grounded on principles ultimately aesthetic, as in *Education through Art* (1943), *Icon and Idea* (1955), and *The Forms of Things Unknown* (1960).

Never a fashionable critic or the leader of a critical school, R. was nonetheless widely known during his lifetime, in academic circles and by the general public. He was particularly discerning in his views on the essential romanticism of "modern" poetry—as in *Phases of English Poetry* (1928), *The True Voice of Feeling* (1953), and *The Tenth Muse* (1958)—the history of which he had himself lived through. Since his death his reputation has somewhat declined, although a very considerable number of his many books remain in print.

FURTHER WORKS: *Naked Warriors* (1919); *Eclogues* (1919); *Mutations of the Phoenix* (1923); *In Retreat* (1925); *English Stained Glass* (1926); *Collected Poems, 1913–1925* (1926); *English Prose Style* (1928); *Staffordshire Pottery Figures* (1929); *The Sense of Glory: Essays in Criticism* (1929); *Ambush* (1930); *Poems, 1914–34* (1935); *Annals of Innocence and Experience* (1940); *Thirty-five Poems* (1940); *The Politics of the Unpolitical* (1943); *Paul Nash* (1944); *A Coat of Many Colors: Occasional Essays* (1945); *Collected Poems* (1946); *The Grass Roots of Art* (1947); *Klee* (1948); *Education for Peace* (1949); *Gauguin* (1949); *Coleridge as Critic* (1949); *Existentialism, Marxism and Anarchism* (1949); *Contemporary British Art* (1951); *The Philosophy of Modern Art: Collected Essays* (1952); *Moon's Farm and Poems Mostly Elegiac* (1955); *The Art of Sculpture* (1956); *A Concise History of Modern Painting* (1959); *Kandinski* (1959); *The Parliament of Women: A Drama in Three Acts* (1960); *Truth Is More Sacred* (1961, with Edward Dahlberg); *A Letter to a Young Painter* (1962); *To Hell with Culture* (1963); *The Contrary Experience: Autobiographies* (1963); *Selected Writings: Poetry and Criticism* (1963); *A Concise History of Modern Sculpture* (1964); *Henry Moore* (1965); *Collected Poems* (1966); *Poetry and Experience* (1967); *Art and Alienation* (1967); *Arp* (1968); *The Cult of Sincerity* (1969); *The Redemption of the Robot* (1970)

BIBLIOGRAPHY: Treece, H., ed., *H. R.: An Introduction to His Work by Various Hands* (1944); Berry, F., *H. R.* (1953); Fishman, S., "Sir H. R.: Poetics vs. Criticism" *JAAC*, 13 (1954): 156–62; Skelton, R., ed., *H. R.: A Memorial Symposium* (1970); Harder, W., A *Certain Order: The Development of H. R.'s Theory of Poetry* (1971); Woodcock, G., *H. R.: The Stream and the Source* (1972); Harder, W., "Crystal Source: H. R.'s *The Green Child,*" *SR*, 81 (1973): 714–38; Savage, D., "Unripeness Is All: H. R. and *The Green Child,*" *DUJ*, 70 (1979): 205–24; King, J., *The Last Modern: A Life of H. R.*(1990)

—WORTH T. HARDER

RÈBORA, Clemente

Italian poet and translator, b. 6 Jan. 1885, Milan; d. 1 Nov. 1957, Stresa

R. graduated from the Accademia Scientifico-Letteraria in Milan and obtained a teaching position in the province of Milan, but he failed several times to qualify for tenure. Between 1914 and 1918 R.'s critical writings, essays, and poems appeared in *Lavoce* and other literary journals. He also published a number of translations of works by Leonid ANDREEV, Tolstoy, and Gogol.

R.'s friendships with prominent artists and writers, his romantic involvement with the concert pianist Lydia Natus, and his traumatic experiences in World War I are recorded in his many letters to friends and relatives published in *Lettere* 1893–1930 (1976; letters, 1893–1930), which, together with his creative writings, constitute a spiritual diary showing R.'s artistic growth as he moved to more universal concerns and finally to asceticism. In 1929 he abandoned atheism and entered the Catholic Church; in 1931 he became a novice of the Rosmini Fathers and was eventually ordained as a priest.

R. is one of the most sincere and powerful poets of 20th-c. Italy, expressing anxiety and a search for an assuaging force within the Christian promise. The publication of his first collection of poems, *Frammenti lirici* (1913; lyrical fragments) immediately established his reputation. His second collection was called *Canti anonimi* (1922; anonymous poems). Even in many of the poems in these two volumes a definite sense of movement toward the spiritual is already discernible.

R.'s religious conversion brought about a change in his style from a rather hermetic EXPRESSIONISM to a classic linearity: he wanted to translate his spiritual experience into lucid form. R.'s mature work, collected in the volume *Le poesie, 1913–1947* (1947; poems, 1913–1947)—later included in *Le poems, 1913–1957* (1961; poems, 1913–1957)—and in *Canti dell'infermità* (1957; poems of sickness), is a poetic transfiguration of Christian belief into everyday words, the creation of a new grammar to express mystical experiences. While his poems reflect the various artistic modes of Italian poetry, from FUTURISM to Christian EXISTENTIALISM, his voice remains independent.

R.'s poetry is not marked by the crisis of purpose that led many avant-garde movements either to sterile protest or to esoteric expressionism. He discovers new meaning in the reality of everyday experience and finds the presence of a moral dimension.

FURTHER WORKS: *Curriculum vitae* (1955); *Via crucis* (1955); *Iconografia: Prose e poesie inedite* (1959)

BIBLIOGRAPHY: Marchione, M., *C. R.* (1979); Kingcaid, R. and C. Klopp, "Coupling and Uncoupling in R.'s 'O carro vuoto,'" *Italica*, 56 (1979): 147–71

—GAETANO A. IANNACE

REBREANU, Liviu

Romanian novelist and short-story writer, b. 27 Nov. 1895, Tîrlisiua; d. 1 Sept. 1944, Valea Mare

Son of a poor rural schoolteacher, R. graduated from the Budapest Military Academy in 1906. After a short career in the Austro-Hungarian army, he left his native Transylvania for Bucharest, where he earned his living as a journalist and as a literary secretary for several theaters. During World War I R. was arrested by the Germans in occupied Bucharest; when he managed to escape to Iasi, he was in turn suspected of espionage by the Romanian authorities. He described this difficult period in the autobiographical novel-diary *Calvarul* (1919; Calvary). When Soviet troops occupied Romania just before the end of World War II, R. committed suicide.

R. began his literary career by writing short stories. The first important collections were *Golanii* (1916; the muggers) and *Răfuiala* (1919; the settling of accounts). While the stories in *Golanii* present an idealized picture of Romanian village life, those in *Răfuiala* are more objective and naturalistic.

With the publication of *Ion* (1920; *Ion*, 1967) R. came to be regarded as Romania's foremost novelist. Ion, the central figure, appears at first as a ruthless peasant, governed by animal instincts and an obsession for land and material possessions, but he later seeks love, with tragic consequences. A parallel plot centers around Titu Herdelea, a largely autobiographical figure, who is torn between his desire for social and financial success within the political framework of the Austrian Empire and his ideal of ethnic and national reintegration. In fact most of R.'s major fiction dramatizes the conflict between material and spiritual aspirations in modern society.

In *Răscoala* (1932; *The Uprising*, 1964), regarded by many as R.'s masterpiece, the conflict between the materialistic drive and the ideal of social and national unity is presented on an epic scale and is placed in the context of the Romanian peasant revolt of 1907. As in *Ion*, the Romanian peasant is neither idealized nor condemned for this natural instincts, and the uprising is presented in all its gruesome excesses. Titu Herdelea is again one of the main characters and functions as a sort of objective center of consciousness in the narrative. In this respect he becomes a linking figure in a trilogy, of which the last novel, *Gorila* (1938; the gorilla), is a presentation of the corrupt and decadent Romanian ruling class.

For R., there was no economic or political solution to the conflict between the violent nature of man and his idealistic aspirations. He believed this conflict could be overcome only through the Christian principle of universal love and unconditional renunciation of violence. R. introduced this utopian theme in *Pădurea spînzuraţilor* (1922; *The Forest of the Hanged*, 1930), where Apostol Bologa, a Romanian officer in the imperial army, is torn between his rational sense of duty toward the Empire and the irrational call of his ethnicity. He becomes a half-hearted deserter, and when he is caught and sentenced to death he eagerly accepts his "martyrdom."

R.'s achievement is perhaps not so much his epic breadth as his impressive attempt to come to terms with the conflicts of a society that wavers between religious, transcendental values and secular, materialist modernization.

FURTHER WORKS: *Frămîntări* (1912); *Mărturisire* (1916); *Cadrilul* (1919); *Răscoala moţilor* (1919); *Catastrofa* (1921); *Norocul* (1921); *Nuvele şi schiţe* (1921); *Plicul* (1923); *Adam şi Eva* (1925); *Apostolii* (1926); *Cîntecul lebedei* (1927); *Cuibul visurilor* (1927); *Ciuleandra* (1927); *Cîntecul iubirii* (1928); *Crăişorul* (1929); *Metropole* (1931); *Iţic Ştrul, dezertor* (1932); *Jar* (1934); *Oameni de pe Someş* (1936); *Calea sufletului* (1936); *Amîndoi* (1940); *Amalgam* (1943)

BIBLIOGRAPHY: Dima, A., "Zur zeitgenössischen rumänischen Literaturkritik und Literaturgeschichte," *BRP*, 3, 1 (1964), 80–87; Philippide, A., "The Spirit and Tradition of Modern Romanian Literature," *RoR*, 21, 2 (1967): 5–10; Mandescu, N., "L. R.; or, The Tragic Novel," *RoR*, 33, 9 (1979): 111–23

—MIHAI SPARIOSU

REDOL, António Alves

Portuguese novelist, short-story writer, and dramatist, b. 29 Dec. 1911, Vila Franca de Xira, Portuguese; d. 29 Nov. 1969, Lisbon

From a family of modest means, R. worked as a grocer's helper in his small home town when he was growing up; the life of the town later was a source of material for his novel *A barca dos sete lemes* (1958; *The Man with Seven Names*, 1964). At other times he was employed in an office, as a salesman, and as manager of a printing firm. His formal education was limited to elementary

school and a business course. At sixteen R. went to Angola, where he remained three years and earned his living teaching shorthand in a private school. After returning to Portugal in 1930, he became involved in opposition politics, for which he was twice imprisoned.

He describes his first book, *Glória: Uma aldeia no Ribatejo* (1938; Glória a village in the Ribatejo province), as an ethnographic essay. His second was *Gaibéus* (1939; gaibéus [field workers of the Ribatejo]), a novel depicting the subhuman conditions of life of field workers in the Tagus river region. It marks the beginning of the school of NEOREALISM, which was to dominate Portuguese literature for years to come. At first it was concerned with the portrayal of life in rural Portugal not for its picturesqueness but rather in protest against the exploitation of the peasants and migratory workers. This material was explored again in *Marés* (1941; tides), *Avieiros* (1942; avieros [river boatmen]), and *Fanga* (1943; fanga [an old measure of land]), all about the Ribatejo region. R. moved north in his books of the Port wine cycle: *Horizonte cerrado* (1949; clouds on the horizon), *Os homens e as sombras* (1951; men and shadows), and *Vindima de sangue* (1953; bloody vintage).

R.'s early works reflect the influence of Jorge AMADO in their ideological orientation, lyric interpretation of character, and poetic prose. Like Aquilino RIBEIRO and other novelists of rural life, he uses an extensive vocabulary of regional terms and archaisms. The poetic effects diminish gradually in his later novels, and the focus shifts from the group to the individual. *Uma fenda no muralha* (1959; a crack in the wall) and *O cavalo espantado* (1960; the frightened horse) deal with ethical problems and are written in a subdued, simpler style. R.'s masterpiece, *Barranco dos cegos* (1962; the chasm of the blind), is again about the Tagus region and the theme of social inequality, but the center of action is a family of landowners rather than peasants and especially the dominant figure of the family group.

In the 1950s the scope of neorealism broadened to include all exploitation—not only exploitation of workers, but more generally, exploitation that resulted from the existence of privilege and deprivation—and psychological consequences and ethical problems were brought into focus. R.'s career followed this trajectory as his work increased in strength and originality; when he died he was at the height of his creative power.

FURTHER WORKS: *Nasci com passaporte de turista* (1940); *Porto Manso* (1946); *Olhos de água* (1954); *Constantino guardador de vacas e de sonhos* (1962); *Histórias afluentes* (1963); *O muro branco* (1966); *Teatro* (1966–67)

BIBLIOGRAPHY: Korges, J., "A Masterpiece from Portugal: A. R.'s *The Man with Seven Names*," *Crit*, 8, 1 (1965): 17–20

—RAYMOND S. SAYERS

REED, Ishmael

American novelist and poet, b. 22 Feb. 1938, Chattanooga, Tenn.

Although he was born in the South, R.'s formative years were spent in New York State: he grew up in Buffalo, attended the State University of New York at Buffalo, and worked briefly on a number of New York City newspapers, most prominently on the

East Village Other. He now teaches creative writing at the University of California at Berkeley and is founding editor and co-publisher of *The Yardbird Reader.* He has published several volumes of poetry and collections of essays, as well as the novels on which his reputation is based. But he considers himself as much a publisher as a writer, and he has done much to foster the publication of minority-group literatures.

R. thinks of his work as running counter to the mainstream of literary modernism, for he attempts to write within a black aesthetic derived largely from his study of Vodoun. Because Vodoun is a Haitian amalgam of a number of African tribal cultures, it has a metaphoric value for the multiculture of America, he argues, and because it reflects the imposition of an individual vision on universal forms, it is an appropriate aesthetic for the American who must preserve his identity in the melting pot of his country. These principles are not unique to Vodoun art, of course, and R.'s work has many affinities with the work of such contemporary writers as Thomas Pynchon and William Gaddis. His exaggerated parodies, his cartoonlike characters, and his esoteric allusiveness are all staples of contemporary absurdist fiction, in fact, and his work embodies a black tradition chiefly in its references to Vodoun and Egyptology.

Indeed, the most successful of R.'s effects are parodic and have little to do with his black aesthetic. *The Free-Lance Pallbearers* (1967) is a parody of the black *Bildungsroman; Yellow Back Radio Broke-Down* (1969) is a parody of the Western dime-novel; *Mumbo Jumbo* (1972) and *The Last Days of Louisiana Red* (1974) are parodies of thrillers, both with a necromantic detective named Papa LaBas as their central character; *Flight to Canada* (1976), generally regarded as his best novel, is a parody of the escaped-slave narratives of 19th-c. America; and *The Terriable Twos* (1982) is a parody of many things, but especially the Saint Nicholas legend. One might even speculate that R.'s black aesthetic has served his talent badly, for *Mumbo Jumbo* (1972) and *The Last Days of Louisiana Red*, both insistently Vodounistic, are generally thought inferior to his other novels. R.'s real contribution to the tradition of black literature consists in his breaking with the pseudoautobiographical mode of such writers as James Baldwin, Ralph Ellison, and Richard Wright, and in his substituting an iconoclastic, impish humor for the sobriety of classic black fiction.

And R.'s claim to literary significance survives his dubious aesthetic. He is important to the world of letters as an accomplished craftsman, as a deft satirist, and as a major spokesman for the black artist in America.

FURTHER WORKS: *Catechism of D NeoAmerican HooDoo Church* (1970); *Conjure* (1972); *Chattanooga* (1973); *Shrovetide in Old New Orleans* (1978); *Secretary to the Spirits* (1978); *God Made Alaska for the Indians* (1982); *Reckless Eyeballing* (1986); *New and Collected Poems* (1988); *Writin' is Fightin': Thirty-Seven Years of Boxing on Paper* (1988); *The Terrible Threes* (1989); *Airing Dirty Laundry* (1993); *Japanese by Spring* (1993)

BIBLIOGRAPHY: Ford, N. A., "A Note on I. R.: Revolutionary Novelist," *SNNTS,* 3 (1971): 216–18; Schmitz, N., "Neo-HooDoo: The Experimental Fiction of I. R.," *TCL,* 20 (1974): 126–40; Uphaus, S. H., *"I. R.'s Canada,"* *CRevAS,* 8 (1977): 95–99; Mackey, N., "I. R. and the Black Aesthetic," *CLAJ,* 21 (1978): 355–66; Northouse, C., "I. R.," in Bruccoli, M. J., and C. E. Clark, Jr., eds., *Conversations with Writers,* 11 (1978): 213–54; Harris, N., "Politics as an Innovative Aspect of Literary Folklore: A Study

of I. R.," *Obsidian,* 5, 1–2 (1979), 41–50; McConnell, F., "I. R.'s Fiction: Da Hoodoo Is Put on America," in Lee A. R., ed., *Black Fiction: New Studies in the Afro-American Novel since 1945* (1980): 136–48; Martin, R., *I. R. and the New Black Aesthetic Critics* (1988); McGee, P., *I. R. and the Ends of Race* (1997)

—ROBERT F. KIERNAN

RÉGIO, José

(pseud. of José Maria dos Reis Pereira) Portuguese poet, dramatist, novelist, and essayist, b. 17 Sept. 1901, Vila do Conde; d. 22 Dec. 1969, Vila do Conde

While studying Romance philology in Coimbra to prepare himself for a teaching career, R. published, at his own expense, his first book of poetry, *Poemas de Deus e do diabo* (1925; poems of God and the devil). Two years later he, João Gaspar Simões (b. 1903), and *António Branquinho da Fonseca* (1905–1974) founded the literary magazine *Presença,* which marks the begining of the second period of MODERNISM in Portuguese poetry. After leaving Coimbra he dedicated himself to teaching and writing, first in Porto and then in Portalegre.

Thematically, technically, and stylistically R.'s works form an integrated whole and do not lend themselves to a genre-by-genre study. "Everyone else had a father and a mother," he says in "Cântico negro" (1925; black chant), "but I was born of the love that exists between God and the Devil." His *fado* (fate), or what he calls pre-experience, made R. highly sensitive to this moral duality. His protagonists constantly struggle between madness and sanity, good and evil, perversity and purity. This duality forms parts of their vital existence, and when one side triumphs over the other they both cease to exist. In the novel *O príncipe com orelhas de burro* (1942; the prince with the donkey ears), for example, Leonel conquers evil, becomes perfect and purified—a purification symbolized by the loss of the floppy ears—and then becomes nonexistent. A similar process takes place in the play *Benilde; ou, A Virgem Mãe* (1947; Benilde, or, the Virgin Mother), the basis for a film of the same title (1975). Too innocent and pure, the protagonist cannot live in the real world.

R. implements these moral conflicts and heightens their dramatic intensity by playing free with chance and reality. Both the Prince's ears and Benilde's pregnancy, the symbols of their conflicts, stem from some sort of contract with the devil, or with God, or both.

Time in R.'s works moves at a leisurely, day-by-day pace; people grow up, fall in love, get married, have children, and die. The simplicity of the established patterns enables R. effortlessly to capture the timelessness behind a specific moment in the big house, the little village, and the small, half-forgotten country called Portugal.

R. injects a note of lyrical, psychological *costumbrismo* (local color) into all his works, especially the ambitious *A velha casa* (5 vols., 1945–66; the old house), which comprises *Uma gota de sangue* (1945; a drop of blood), *As raízes do future* (1947; the roots of the future), *Os avisos do destine* (1953; the warnings of destiny), *As monstruosidades vulgares* (1960; common monstrosities), and *Vidas são vidas* (1966; lives are lives).

R.'s characters, like those in the novels of the Spaniard Juan Valera (1824–1905), are the important inhabitants of the small village—those who live in or belong to the "big house." Like Valera, R. felt he was more successful in depicting women than men. Letícia in *O príncipe com orelhas de burro*, Benilde in *Benilde; ou, A Virgem Mãe*, and Rosa in the story "A Rosa brava" (brave Rosa) in *Histórias de mulheres* (1946; stories about women) belong to the literary tradition of the heroine of Flaubert's classic short story "A Simple Heart."

Many aspects of R.'s style—his long, flowing sentences in the style of Cervantes, his images, his use of language—belong to past centuries. His didacticism, his preoccupation with moral questions, and his concern over the real values and virtues of Portuguese literature also tend to place his works in an older literary tradition.

R.'s contribution to literature rests on his study of man—quite often grotesque in his abnormality—and his relation to himself. Although he focuses on the young man or woman from a small village, like so many other writers of our century he achieves universality by capturing the essence of his native land and its people.

FURTHER WORKS: *Biografia* (1929); *Jogo de cabra cega* (1934); *As encruzilhadas de Deus* (1936); *Críticos e criticados* (1936); *António Botto e o amor* (1938); *Em torno da expressão artística* (1940); *Primeiro volume de teatro* (1940); *Pequena história da moderna poesia portuguesa* (1941); *Davam grandes passeios aos domingos* (1941); *Mas Deus é grande* (1945); *El-Rei Sebastião* (1949); *A salvação do mundo* (1954); *Três peças em um acto* (1957); *Filho do homem* (1961); *Há mais mundos* (1962); *Ensaios de interpretação crítica* (1964); *Três ensaios sobre arte* (1967); *Cântico suspenso* (1968); *Música ligeira* (1970); *Colheita da tarde* (1971); *16 poemas dos não incluídos na "Colheita da tarde"* (1971); *Confissão dum homem religioso* (1971)

BIBLIOGRAPHY: Bell, Aubrey F. G., ed., *The Oxford Book of Portuguese Verse* (1952): 374; Parker, J. M., *Three 20th-Century Portuguese Poets* (1960): 48–64

—LEO L. BARROW UPDATED BY IRWIN STERN

REGLER, Gustav

German novelist, essayist, and poet (writing in German and English), b. 25 May 1898, Merzig; d. 14 Jan. 1963, New Delhi, India

R. had a strict Catholic upbringing, but his experiences in World War I, where he was wounded, and the subsequent chaotic years of inflation and mass unemployment in Germany, turned him into a socialist and a foe of organized religion. He joined the Communist Party in 1928. In 1923 he earned his doctorate in literature at the University of Heidelberg. He then worked at various jobs, such as managing a large department store and editing a liberal newspaper. He gradually turned to writing to express his social commitment. With the coming of Hilter in 1933 he was forced into exile, first to the Saarland and then to Paris. In 1934 he participated at the International Writers Congress in Moscow. Moved by a strong sense of justice, he fought against Franco in the Spanish Civil War between 1936 and 1937, where he was again wounded. Shortly thereafter, he was locked up in a French internment camp, but managed to emigrate to Mexico in 1940, where he renounced his communism and turned to a mystical, spiritual approach to life. In

1952 he returned to West Germany, but continued to write in this religious vein. He died of apoplexy in India, where he was doing research for a planned book on mysticism and the occult.

R.'s use of literature to effect social change is apparent from the start. One of his first works, the novel *Wasser, brot und blaue bohnen* (1932; water, bread, and blue beans), is a brutal critique of the German prison system. *Der verlorene sohn* (1933; the prodigal son) is an attack on the Catholic church, which he views as an oppressive institution. *Die saat* (1936; the sowing), which was written in exile and published in Amsterdam, is a historical novel about the medieval Peasants' Revolt and stresses the need for citizens to rise up against political suppression, an obvious parallel to Nazi Germany.

For several years, R. could write little because of his direct political activity and his injury. In 1940, however, he published in English *The Great Crusade*, which deals with the activity of the International Brigades during the Spanish Civil War. In it he describes the heroism of the troops, the atrocities of war, and the feeling of moral rectitude that enabled the poorly equipped soldiers to hold out against great odds.

R. gradually became disenchanted with communism (the failure of Stalin to support the Republican cause in Spain, the Hitler-Stalin pact) and was ostracized by his fellow exiles in Mexico because of his new apolitical stance. He turned for solace to natural and supernatural phenomena, whereby he tried to synthesize the opposites of life. In several volumes of poetry (some written in English in an attempt to find a niche in the American market) he uses a plethora of nature symbols to stress the mystical, cosmic oneness of all matter. His poems are contained in *The Hour 13* (1943; the 13th hour), *Der brunnen des abgrunds* (1943; the bottomless pit), *Jungle Hut* (1946; title in English), and *Marielouise* (1946; Marielouise). In his prose works of the time he follows a similar bent. *Amimitl oder die geburt eines schrecklichen* (1947; Amimitl, or the birth of a monster) discusses Aztec prehistory and attributes war to the breakdown of cosmic harmony (women were deprived of their influence); *Vulkanisches land mexiko* (1947; volcanic Mexico), which was enlarged as *Verwunschenes land mexiko* (1954; *A Land Bewitched*, 1955), describes evil and suffering as part of the natural order and as a necessary component of progress.

Back in Germany R. expanded his new philosophy. The novel *Sterne der dämmerung* (1948; stars of twilight) seeks to find a confirmation of life beyond war and death through the unification of the male and female principles. His last novel, *Aretino* (1955; Aretino), a fictional biography of the Renaissance poet and libertine, is a diatribe against traditional religion as well as a harsh warning on the evils of excess.

R.'s life and works are fascinating for their diversity and for the way they document some of the most important and tumultuous upheavals of the 20th c. Since much of his work was first published outside of Germany, he is also an excellent example of German exile literature.

FURTHER WORKS: *Die ironie im werk goethes* (1923); *Zug der hirten* (1929); *Hahnenkampf—abenteuer eines französischen mädchens* (1931); *Im kreuzfeuer* (1934); *Der letzte appell* (1939); *Wolfgang Paalen* (1946); *Der turm und andere gedichte* (1951); *Das ohr des malchus* (1958; *The Owl of Minerva*, 1960)

BIBLIOGRAPHY: Acker, R., "G. R. and Ramon Sender: A Comparative View of Their Mexican Exile," in Moeller, H.-B., ed., *Latin*

America and the Literature of Exile (1983): 311–22; Diwersy, A., *G. R.: Bilder und Dokumente* (1983); Schock, R., *G. R.—Literatur und Politik (1933–1940)* (1984); Grund, U., R. Schock, and G. Scholdt, eds., *G. R.—Dokumente und Analysen* (1985); Pohle, F., *Das mexikanische Exil* (1986): 140–67

—ROBERT ACKER

REGO, José Lins do

Brazilian novelist, b. 3 June 1901, Pilar; d. 12 Sept. 1957, Rio de Janeiro

R. was born on his grandfather's sugar plantation in the state of Paraíba in northeast Brazil. His mother died in his first year of life, and his father moved away to take care of another plantation, leaving the infant R. in the care of a maiden aunt. When R. was ten, his aunt died, and he was sent off to a boarding school and later to a Catholic secondary school. In 1919 he went to Recife to study law. It was there that he met and was deeply impressed by the sociologist and writer Gilberto FREYRE, who introduced him to the "region-tradition" movement of which he would become the principal exponent in fiction. He worked briefly as a district attorney and later as a bank inspector in Maceió, writing criticism and occasional pieces for newspapers all the while. After the publication of his third novel he moved to Rio to dedicate himself more fully to writing.

R. published a dozen novels and another dozen volumes of memoirs, speeches, and sketches, but he is best known for the six novels usually identified as the "Sugarcane Cycle." The basic components of the cycle, which is the visibly autobiographical chronicle of the life of Carlos de Melo, like R. the son of an old planter family, are *Menino de engenho* (1932; *Plantation Boy*), *Doidinho* (1933; *Doidinho*), *Bangüê* (1934; *Bangüê*)—these three published together in English translation under the title *Plantation Boy* (1966)—and *Usina* (1936; sugar refinery). Many critics also include *O moleque Ricardo* (1935; black boy Ricardo) and *Fogo morto* (1943; dead fire), generally considered his masterpiece.

Menino de engenho deals with the first years of the lonely, fearful protagonist and *Doidinho* with his coming of age in a boarding school. *Bangüê* finds Carlos a law student in Recife, and *O moleque Ricardo* recounts the adventures of Carlos's childhood companion when he grows up and moves to the city. *Usina* recounts the deaths of both the friend and the old plantation system and the emergence of an impersonal, mechanized system that displaces both the aristocracy and the poor laborers.

With the exception of *O moleque Ricardo*, all the narrative lines in these novels derive directly from the author's own past, but this autobiographical element has the effect of making incident and character believable, since everything is seen from the convincing viewpoint of an eyewitness. There is no doubting the documentary nature of the works, but R. felt that the MODERNISTS of Rio and São Paulo were too artificially cosmopolitan, and that the best way to tell about the world was to tell about that part of it best known to the author himself. Since the protagonist keeps reappearing, there is also some repetition of theme, and such motifs as fear of death, sexuality, the power of the planter class, and the conflict of folk and cultured world views keep recurring. But the real theme of the collective work is based on a nostalgic view of a vanishing life

style, and R.'s novels thus have the incantatory potential of romance and legend. The literal chronology involves the gradual decline of the old rural aristocracy and its labor-intensive plantation system (*bangüêue*) and the parallel emergence and flourishing of the industrialized machine-powered sugar refinery (*usina*).

Fogo morto is in some senses the culmination of the cycle and a rewrite of it. Carlos de Melo is a secondary figure, and his first-person voice is replaced by that of a more perceptive and more literary narrator with an eye for fine detail and a flair for characterization. The external structure of the novel, in fact, makes the narrative appear to be three characters studies sewn together. The three characters are an embittered and feared saddlemaker, the degenerate planter on whose estate he lives, and the resident eccentric, whose resilient moral fiber is accompanied by a totally impractical view of reality.

Although some of R.'s writing seems dated today, his portrait of Brazil's plantation economy is one of the fullest available. The portrayal is also an examination of weakness and decadence, however, and the characters made in the telling, from the introverted Carlos to the dissipated and quixotic characters in later works, are both imaginative and suggestive creations whose forlorn oddness still holds appeal.

FURTHER WORKS: *Histórias da velha Totônia* (1936); *Pureza* (1937; *Pureza*, 1948); *Pedra bonita* (1938); *Riacho doce* (1939); *Água-maẽ* (1941); *Gordos e magros* (1942); *Pedro Américo* (1943); *Poesia e vida* (1945); *Conferências no Prata* (1946); *Eurídice* (1947); *Bota de sete léguas* (1951); *Homens, seres e coisas* (1952); *Cangaceiros* (1953); *A casa e o homem* (1954); *Roteiro de Israel* (1955); *Meus verdes anos* (1956); *Presença do Nordeste na literatura brasileira* (1957); *Gregos e Troianos* (1957); *O vulcão e a fonte* (1958); *Dias idos e vividos: Antologia* (1981)

BIBLIOGRAPHY: Ellison, F., *Brazil's New Novel* (1954): 45–79; Martins, W., *The Modernist Idea* (1970): 285–88; Hulet, C., *Brazilian Literature* (1975), Vol. 3: 271–74

—JON S. VINCENT

REICH, Ebbe Kløvedal

Danish novelist, short-story writer, and essayist, b. 7 Mar. 1940, Odense

Since the late 1960s, R. has had a high profile in Denmark; not only is he a prolific writer, but he has also quite consciously assumed the role of a public figure with a message for his country. He seemed headed for a career as a politician in a moderate party, switched then to assume the editorship of a leftist magazine, but moved on to become one of the most eloquent and least predictable leaders of the so-called "'68-generation," That group of youthful rebels—one that had originated in the antinuclear movement—demonstrated not only against the American presence in Vietnam, but also against imperialism in general. The "'68-generation," mainly consisting of university students—a small, but influential, group that through dress, hair length, and language (often combined with experimentation with drugs) symbolically declared its distinct identity—tended to be quite dogmatically Marxist, but was reacting as well against the preceding generations' lack of any substantial idealism. Denmark became a stage for virulent disputes, violent demonstations, a very active feminist movement—and a blatant generation gap. R. was a frequent speaker at rallies and mass meetings, and some of his speeches and pieces of journalism were gathered in *Svampens tid* (1969; the age of the mushroom).

During those years R. lived with his friends in a commune called "Mao's Joy." R., however, was an "odd man out" among rigid Marxists, for he was profoundly fascinated with the occult, the cabala, astrology, and, to boot, Christianity. At that point R.'s worldview may seem obscure and fragmented, but it was headed for a synthesis of social radicalism, a sense of Christian solidarity, and a mysticism with a strong antiauthoritarian or anarchistic bent. The middle name "Kløvedal," a translation of J. R. R. Tolkien's (1892–1973) Rivendale from the *The Lord of the Rings* (3 vols., 1954–1955), was one he assumed, together with a group of like-minded contemporaries in 1970.

R. has contributed to all genres, but in the early 1970s, he began to settle into a role as a historical novelist who saw it as his mission to use fiction to send strong warnings to his compartriots about the impending loss of their national character. In *Holger danske* (1970; Holger the Dane) he composed a series of tales about a legendary Danish hero who is supposed to awaken from his slumber when the Danish nation is in distress. Thereby, R. established a method for his historical fiction; he operates with strong analogies between past and present and conjures up historical figures that serve as role models—they are intendedly without much depth—and have, as a rule, much in common with the free-spirited, antiauthoritarian "'68-generation."

This series of historical novels started in earnest with *Frederik* (1972; Frederik), which recorded how a prominent Danish preacher, poet, and pedagogue gained through love the personal strength that enabled him to become a mythmaker who would sustain his troubled nation. The book was a hit. It was followed by *Rejsen til Messias* (1974; the journey of Messiah), which records the disastrous rise of the repressive absolute monarchy. *Fæ of fræznde* (1977; kith and kin) takes its readers back to the Iron Age and contrasts democratic, egalitarian Denmark with the rising Roman empire; and in *Festen for Cæcilie* (1979; the feast for Cæcilia), which is set in the Middle Ages, it is made obvious how greatly supranational organizations, such as the Catholic church, have intervened in Danish national affairs. Those novels have been followed up with a series of short-story collections tracing Danish history, *De forste* (1981; the first ones) and *Ploven og sværdet* (1982; the plough and the sword).

Through a contemporary setting, the novel *Bygningen af en bro* (1988; The building of a bridge) expresses heartfelt resistance to a bridge that would connect the main island of Denmark (the location of Copenhagen) with, for all practical purposes, the continent. The bridge becomes a metaphor for Europe's growing domination of Denmark. The problems of contemporary political and intellectual independence are at the center of *Kontrafej af den danske ånd* (1991; Portrait of the Danish spirit) and of *Morgendagens mand* (1993; The man of tomorrow). In these works R. cannot refrain from hearkening back to the glorious past of Denmark, and in *En engels vinger* (1990; The wings of an angel) his conclusion is that Scandinavia's happiest days were during the union of the North in late medieval times.

These books, many of which are filled with those fast-paced action scenes one expects in a historical romance, emerge as R.'s opposition to all attempts—such as making Denmark a member of the European Common Market—to interfere with his ideal nation. R. is a severe critic of his times, but one who always sees hope for the future. He is an energetic mythmaker, who sees myth as a tool for personal and national growth.

FURTHER WORKS: *Vietnam. Krigen i perspekniv* (1965, with Preben Dollerup); *Kina. Den ideologiske stormagt* (1967); *Billedalmanak fra en rejise i det fremmede* (1967); *Retning mod venstre* (1968); *Hvem var Malatesta* (1969); *Eventyret om Alexander 666* (1970); *Svampen og korset* (1973); *Du danske svamp* (1974); *Henry George* (1975); *Til forsvar for masselinien og den rette tro* (1976); *Svaneøglen* (1978); *Mediesvampen* (1980); *Viljen til Hanstholm* (1981); *David, de fredløses konge* (1982); *David, Guds udvalgte konge* (1983); *Kong Skildpadde* (1985); *Billeder og fortællinger fra Biblen* (1986); *Nornen fra Ygdrasil* (1988, with Gerhard Kaimer)

BIBLIOGRAPHY: Borum, P., *Danish Literature* (1979): 111–12; Kopp-Sievers, S., *Die Wieder-entdeckung des Nationalen in Dänemark: Eime Analyse von E. K. Rs "Frederik"* (1985); Houe, P., in Rossel, S., *A History of Danish Literature* (1992): 534-36

—NIELS INGWERSEN

REID, Christopher

British poet, b. 13 July 1949, Hong Kong

R. achieved fame as one of the so-called "Martian" school of poets that emerged in the late 1970s and was lauded for introducing a new note of self-awareness, experimentation, and fun into the often dour precincts of British poetry. Far more than being the product of a once-trendy poetic movement, however, R.'s production reveals an original talent that deserves to be evaluated on its own merits.

R. was born in Hong Kong, the son of a Shell oil executive. He attended Oxford, where one of his tutors was Craig Raine (b. 1944), who became his poetic mentor as he wrote his first collection, *Arcadia* (1979). *Arcadia* has been rather facetiously characterized as being influenced by Wallace STEVENS; this is true only if any self-conscious verse is somehow diagnosed as Stevensian. R.'s approach is homegrown, whimsical, yet somehow intent on seeing the world anew, starting from first principles. In the title poem of the volume, R. uses techniques of estrangement, defamiliarization, and metaphor that link him with the Martian school of poetry, named after Raine's poem "A Martian Sends A Postcard Home," a school comprised basically by R. and Raine, although their techniques influenced other poets of their generation. However, other poems in *Arcadia* such as "Maritime Liverpool" and "The Old Soap Opera" show R. going beyond bejeweled, out-of-this-world artifice to investigate the confluences of the uncanny and the ordinary, of memory and the imagination.

Katerina Brac (1985) assumes the persona of an Eastern European woman poet. In this way, the local artifices of R.'s previous poems are magnified into a general conceit. The advantage this has is that strangeness no longer has to be the end product of each individual poem, but can lay at the root of the poem's utterance itself because of the artificiality of the persona. In "Annals," for instance, the persona proposes that the annals of her village be written not by a flowery poet but by a lucid prose stylist; there is some irony here, but overriding this is a sense that for the fantastic to come across into the world it has to be responsibly recorded. If poems like "What the Uneducated Old Woman Told Me" have a nonsensical, almost surrealistic aspect, "History and Parody" and "When the Bullfrogs are In Love" reveal the shimmering byplay of a lover's musings with the often melancholy exuberance of the poetic imagination. Critical reaction to *Katerina Brac* was somewhat muted, even though R. was clearly trying to expand out of the potentially straitjacketing Martian mode by writing in persona. Even the book's use of Eastern European motifs, then tremendously in vogue among middlebrow critics, did not evoke much response despite the poems' revelation of R.'s genuine, if self-limiting, receptivity to poets such as Zbigniew HERBERT and Miroslav HOLUB. This set the tone for the relative critical neglect R. was to experience from this point on.

In The Echoey Tunnel (1991) is distinguished by "For Art's Sake," a set of poems on the ironies of careers in the creative arts. In "Go, Little Book" a middle-class poet from the north of England labors to produce a book of verse in spite of grueling and discouraging personal conditions, only to find the book dismissed in a brief review by a slick urban reviewer recently up from Oxford. R. reveals both his cynicism about careerist opportunism in the arts and his deep sympathy for those who pursue their aesthetic vocations in spite of daunting obstacles against success—whether moral of financial. "Arbiter" savagely limns the psyche of a trendy critic, and "Howl, Howl" nimbly skewers the pretensions of modern art that seeks to rise above commercialism. Two long sequences rounded out the book, "Survival: A Patchwork," dedicated to R.'s wife and structured in short, elegant six-line stanzas, and "Memres of Alfred Stoker," a poem written in a north England vernacular and told by a young boy in the Victorian age, which is intriguing if somewhat opaque.

Expanded Universes (1996) continues with the artistic career motif in "One for the Footnotes," which by describing R.'s own "achievement" as a baby parodies how writers' lives are summed up while also addressing deeper issues of the inadequacies of writing. R. continues to explore the potentialities of metaphor, but in this book metaphor is structured as a kind of anecdote, a tale-telling which reveals an unexpected development or meaning. R.'s metaphoricity is thus far less static than in his earlier books, showing a capacity to be startling and provocative, not just merely burnished and ornamental. A particularly fine example of this is "Second Genesis," which succinctly manages to conflate the Greek and Hebrew flood-myths in a moving fashion. R.'s ability to tackle political issues abstractly is displayed in "The Thing and the Book," while "Two Dogs on a Pub Roof" combines humor, an outrageous extension of a single rhyme, and a philosophical consideration of what it means to be alive.

Although R. is mainly known for his brief currency in the early 1980s, a thorough reading of his work reveals a productive, consistent, and still evolving career that cannot be constrained within merely one period or poetic idiom.

FURTHER WORKS: *Pea Soup* (1982)

BIBLIOGRAPHY: Haffenden, J., "An Interview with C. R.," *PoetryR*, 72 (Sept. 1982): 16-24; Hulce, M., "The Dialectic of the Image: Notes on the Poetry of Craig Raine and C. R.," *MHRev*, 64 (Feb. 1983): 20-27; Waterman, A., "Martian Invasion," *Helix*, 17 (1984): 42-28; Robinson, A., *Instabilities in Contemporary British Poetry* (1988)

—NICHOLAS BIRNS

Erich Maria Remarque

REMARQUE, Erich Maria

(pseud. of Erich Paul Remark) German novelist, b. 22 June 1898, Osnabrück; d. 25 Sept. 1970, Locarno, Switzerland

While preparing to become a teacher, R. was drafted into the German army; during World War I he was wounded in action. After the war he taught school and then became a journalist in Berlin, where he edited the magazine *Sport im Bild* for nine years. In 1931 he emigrated to Switzerland. Two years later the Nazis banned and burned his books for ideological reasons and took away his German citizenship. He moved to New York in 1939 and became a U.S. citizen in 1947. He later returned to Switzerland. In 1967 he received the Great Service Cross of the Federal Republic of Germany in recognition of his literary works and his commitment to humanism in political life.

Using a direct and honest journalistic style, R. created a series of novels about basic human experiences in the turmoil of the major social and political problems and events of the 20th c. In painfully vivid detail he documented the impact of wars, inflation, persecution, racism, nationalism, and other horrors upon individual lives. His sagas of survival amid suffering, misery, and frustration underscore the vitality of the human spirit and the continued existence of virtues such as friendship, kindness, loyalty, and love.

R.'s first successful novel, *Im Westen nichts Neues* (1929; *All Quiet on the Western Front*, 1929), became the best-known novel ever written about World War I and set a pattern for the antiwar novel in Germany. It was made into a film in 1930 and was eventually translated into more than forty languages. In its portrayal of the terrors of war as experienced by a young draftee and his companions, *Im Westen nichts Neues* focuses on the physical, spiritual, and emotional desolation that caused youthful soldiers to become aliens in their own society. Detailed, vivid, realistic descriptions of the daily routine of men who exist only in the trenches, without past or future, allow the reader to experience the making of a "lost generation." Emphasis is placed on the humanity of individuals measured against the inhumanity of the war. The limited perspective of a small group of characters gives the work a strong sense of immediacy. Even though some figures are only hastily sketched, they become a precise, if terse statement of R.'s view of their world.

Der Weg zurück (1931; *The Road Back*, 1931), a sequel to *Im Westen nichts Neues,* and *Drei Kameraden* (1937; *Three Comrades*, 1937) present R.'s perceptions of social and political problems in Germany after World War I. Der Weg zurück describes the collapse of Germany in 1918 as experienced by returning soldiers. Although less effective than *Im Westen nichts Neues*, it was an important forerunner of similar novels and stories that pervaded German literature after World War II. *Drei Kameraden* examines the specific woes of unemployment and political tension in post-World War I Berlin. In the lives of three ex-soldiers immersed in the troubles of the times, R. stressed once more the values of self-sacrifice and lasting comradeship.

Several of R.'s novels treat problems generated by the rise of the Nazis. Included in this group are *Liebe deinen Nächsten* (1941; *Flotsam*, 1941), a story about political refugees who are driven from country to country, and *Der Funke Leben* (1952; *Spark of Life*, 1953), a documentary novel that illustrates the will to survive amid extremes of human suffering in a concentration camp. The most important and successful of these novels is *Arc de Triomphe* (1946; *Arch of Triumph*, 1946), which tells of a German doctor who escapes from the Gestapo and lives as a refugee in the Paris underworld. Like *Im Westen nichts Neues*, *Arc de Triomphe* achieves its narrative success through stark realism and immediacy resulting from the deep psychological penetration of a limited cast of characters. Subsequent novels about Nazi Germany and the World War II era achieved some popularity, but none had the literary strength or success of R.'s earlier writings.

R. is often criticized for a tendency to moralize, for observations about God and the world that are not really integrated structurally and psychologically into his novels. Whatever validity such criticism may have, it cannot negate the force, the directness, the effective realism of R.'s documentary portraits of major 20th-c. events.

FURTHER WORKS: *Die Traumbude* (1920); *Zeit zu leben und Zeit zu sterben* (1954; *A Time to Live and a Time to Die*, 1954); *Die letzte Station* (1956; *Full Circle*, 1974); *Der schwarze Obelisk* (1956; *The Black Obelisk*, 1957); *Der Himmel kennt keine Günstlinge* (1961; *Heaven Has No Favorites*, 1964); *Die Nacht von Lissabon* (1964; *The Night in Lisbon*, 1965); *Schatten im Paradies* (1971; *Shadows in Paradise*, 1972); *Der Feind* (1998); *Die großen Romane* (1998); *Der Pazifist* (1998); *Stationen am Horizont* (1998); *Das unbekannte Werk* (1998)

BIBLIOGRAPHY: White, J. S., R.'s *"All Quiet on the Western Front"* (1966); Taylor, H. U., "Autobiographical Elements in the Novels of E. M. R.," *WVUPP*, 17 (1970): 84–93; Bernhard, H. -J, "E. M.

R.'s Romane nach dem zweiten Weltkrieg," *ADP*, 7 (1973): 35–49; Baumer, F., E. M. R. (1976); Bance, A. F., "*Im Westen nichts Neues* A Bestseller in Context," *MLR*, 72 (1977): 359–73; Cernyak, S. E., "*The Life of a Nation* The Community of the Dispossessed in E. M. R.'s Emigration Novels," *PCL*, 3, 1 (1977): 15–22; Firda, R. A., "Young E. M. R.:*Die Traumbude,*" *Monatshefte*, 71 (1979): 49–55; Wagner, H., *Understanding E. M. R.* (1991); Schneider, T., *E. M. R.* (1996)

—LOWELL A. BANGERTER

REMIZOV, Alexey Mikhaylovich

Russian novelist, short-story writer, dramatist, and poet, b. 24 June 1877, Moscow; d. 26 Nov. 1957, Paris, France

Born into a pious merchant family, R. was raised according to strict Russian Orthodox tradition. R. studied natural science at Moscow University until his arrest and expulsion in 1896 for participating in a student demonstration. During his subsequent eight years of repeated imprisonment and exile, R. developed an avid interest in Russian and Finno-Ugric folklore. Settling in St. Petersburg in 1905, he frequented SYMBOLIST circles, but retained a highly personal literary orientation. In 1921 he emigrated to Berlin and two years later settled permanently in Paris.

Both of R.'s full-length novels, the autobiographical *Prud* (1908; the pond) and *Chasy* (1908; *The Clock*, 1924), provide vivid descriptions of a grim Dostoevskyan world of pain, brutality, and self-laceration, where chance misfortune at times appears to be the manipulation of a malignant demon. Devoid of humor and marred by excesses of vagueness, lyric fragmentation, abstractness, and verbosity, the two novels anticipated R.'s highly successful short novels that established his distinctive narrative style, which, in the tradition of Gogol and Nikolay Leskov (1831–1895), uses a first-person narrator to cloak the author's personality and point of view while making full use of the resources of popular language. In *Krestovye syostry* (1910; sisters of the cross) R. creates a microcosm of man's suffering and humiliation by depicting the inhabitants of a single tenement house, while in *Neuyomny buben* (1910; repub. [1922] as *Povest to Ivane Semyonoviche Stratilatove: Neuyomny buben; The History of the Tinkling Cymbal and Sounding Brass: Ivan Semyonovich Stratilatov*, 1927) he skillfully interweaves pain and humiliation with humor, grotesque fantasy, and the profane in the extraordinary character of the provincial clerk Stratilatov. Literary parody, philosophic polemic, and commentary on current political events emerge most clearly in *Pyataya yazva* (1912; *The Fifth Pestilence*, 1927), in which a scrupulously honest magistrate perishes in expiation for his inhuman integrity.

Some of R.'s best short stories focus on a child protagonist, exploring the psychology of disillusionment in "Tsarevna Mymra" (1908; Princess Mymra) or of hope culminating in senseless death in "Petushok" (1911; the little cock). Later, in the collections *Vesennee poroshie* (1915; spring trifles) and *Sredi murya* (1917; amid the swarm), the stories become mood pieces in which the author-narrator's ability to communicate with the child provides a unifying perception of events.

R.'s re-creative writing, which had begun with fairy tales and descriptions of children's games in *Posolon* (1907; sunward) and canonical and apocryphal narratives in *Limonar: Lug dukhovny* (1907; Limonar: a spiritual meadow), assumed an ever-increasing role in his work, focusing on legends and folktales about highly revered Saint Nicholas in *Nikoliny pritchi* (1918; Saint Nicholas's parables), the character of women in Russkie *zhenshchiny* (1917; Russian women), various indigenous peoples of Siberia, the Caucasus, and Tibet in collections such as *Sibirsky pryanik* (1919; a Siberian cookie), and even blasphemy humorously rendered in *Zavetnye skazy* (1920; forbidden tales). Also worthy of mention are his painstakingly researched recreations of folk dramas such as *Tsar Maximilian* (1920; Tsar Maximilian), which was performed by soldiers during the revolution.

The Russian Revolution profoundly affected R., whose immediate response in the poem "Krasnoe znamya" (1917; the red banner) anticipated Alexandr BLOK'S "The Twelve" and was followed by the poignantly lyrical "Slovo o pogibeli zemli russkoy" (1917; the lay of the ruin of the Russian land), cast in the form of an ancient Russian rhythmic prose lament. R. convincingly portrayed the atmosphere of Petersburg at war in a number of short stories included in the collections *Shumy goroda* (1921; the sounds of the city) and *Mara* (1922; specter), but more significant was his development of a hybrid memoir that combined biographical sketches, letters, reminiscences, subjective essays on life and literature, autobiography and a fantastic dreamworld best exemplified in *Vzvikhrennaya Rus* (1927; Russia in a whirlwind), an unmatched, deeply personal chronicle of the revolution. He refined the complex amalgam of reality and dream in the surrealistic autobiographies *Podstrizhennymi glazami* (1951; with clipped eyes) and *Myshkina dudochka* (1953; a flute for mice), considered by some critics to be the apogee of R.'s art in emigration. His lifelong fascination with dreams culminated in an astute critical commentary on major Russian writers in *Ogon veshchey* (1954; the fire of things) and an extensive collection of his own dreams in *Martyn Zadeka* (1954; Martyn Zadeka).

One of the most versatile, prolific, and erudite writers of the 20th c., R. is little known today in Russia. The intrinsic value of his remarkable memoirs is appreciated only by Slavic specialists, but the influence of his early fiction and varied narratives was readily apparent in the Soviet Union throughout the 1920s in the works of ZAMYATIN, PILNYAK, PRISHVIN, Vyacheslav Shishkov (1873–1945), and many others. The interest in R. that has arisen in the West recently will undoubtedly continue to increase and will be reflected, albeit to a limited extent, in the former Soviet Union, where *Izbrannoe* (1973; selections) by R. recently appeared.

FURTHER WORKS: *Morshchinka* (1907); *Chto yest tabak* (1908); *Chortov log i polunoshchnoe solntse* (1908); *Rasskazy* (1910); *Sochinenia* (8 vols., 1910–1912); *Podorozhie* (1913); *Dokuka i balagurie* (1914); *Za svyatuyu Rus* (1915); *Ukrepa* (1916); *Nikola Milostivy* (1918); *Strannitsa* (1918); *O sudbe ognennoy* (1918); *Snezhok* (1918); *Elektron* (1919); *Besovskoe deystvo* (1919); *Tragedia o Iude* (1919); *Tsar Dodon* (1921); *Yo: Zayashnye skazki tibetskie* (1921); *Ognennaya Rossia* (1921); *Skazki obezyanego tsarya Asyki* (1922); *Chakkhchygys-Taasu* (1922); *Lalazar* (1922); *V pole blakitnom* (1922; *On a Field of Azure,* 1949); *Rossia v pismenakh* (1922); *Krashenye ryla* (1922); *Akhru* (1922); *Travamurava* (1922); *Plyas Irodiady* (1922); *Koryavka* (1922); *Bespriyutnaya* (1922); *Gore-zloschastnoe* (1922); *Rusalia* (1922); *Kukkha* (1922); *Skazki russkogo naroda* (1923); *Zvenigorod oklikanny* (1924); *Zga* (1925); *Olya* (1927); *Zvezda nadzvyozdnaya* (1928); *Po Karnizam* (1929); *Tri serpa* (2 vols., 1929); *Obraz Nikolaya Chudotvortsa* (1931); *Golubinaya kniga* (1946); *Plyashushchy demon* (1949); *Povest o dvukh zveryakh* (1950); *Besnovatye* (1951); *Melyuzina*

(1952); *V rozovom bleske* (1952); *Tristan i Isolda* (1957); *Krug schastya* (1957)

BIBLIOGRAPHY: Mirsky, D., *Contemporary Russian Literature,* 1881–1925 (1926): 281–91; Shane, A., "R.'s *Prud*: From Symbolism to Neo-Realism," *CalSS,* 6 (1971): 71–82; Shane, A., "A Prisoner of Fate: R.'s Short Fiction," *RLT,* 4 (1972): 303–18; Lampl, H., "A. R.'s Beitrag zum russischen Theater," *WSJ,* No.17 (1972): 136–83; Bialy, R., "Parody in R.'s Pjataja jazva," *SEEJ,* 19 (1975): 403–10; Sinany, H., Bibliographie des oeuvres d'A. R. (1978); Slobin, G., "Writing as Possession: The Case of R.'s 'Poor Clerk,'" in Nilsson, N. A., ed., Studies in 20th Century Russian Prose (1983): 59–79

—ALEX M. SHANE

RENAULT, Mary

(pseud. of Mary Challans) British novelist, b. 9 Apr. 1904, London; d. 13 Dec. 1983, Cape Town, South Africa

Of French Huguenot descent, R. studied English literature at Oxford, then trained and made a career as a nurse. Her first published novel, *The Purposes of Love* (1939; pub. in the U.S. as *Promise of Love,* 1939) is set in a provincial hospital in England, the milieu she knew best. Its success made it possible for her to consider writing as a full-time occupation. But with the outbreak of

Mary Renault

World War II she returned to nursing for the duration. After the war, she settled in Durban, South Africa, and became an opponent of her adopted country's expanding system of apartheid and censorship laws. Nonetheless, she remained and over the next decade published several other novels with contemporary settings, generally in England, and contemporary themes, generally about interpersonal relations. One of these novels, *Return to Night* (1947), won the $150,000 MGM prize, although it was never made into a movie.

But it is with ancient Greece and its themes that her name is irretrievably linked. Beginning in 1956 with *The Last of the Wine*, in a series of novels spanning more than a quarter of a century, she virtually created the modern reader's image of Bronze Age and Classical and Hellenistic Greece. Through impeccable research and imaginative reconstruction, she created an age and an ethos that to modern readers remain totally convincing. Whether she is writing of actors or of emperors, of hero kings or common people, of Greeks at home or abroad, whether her characters are drawn from history or from myth or from her own imagination, she has total empathy for them and for their culture. Her concern is with institutions and people alike. R. has frequently been praised for the historical accuracy of her novels. But she is more than an historical novelist. We might more accurately speak of her as a novelist of myth, even as the creator of a new novel form that merges history and myth.

The Last of the Wine only begins to set the pattern; it is more a historical novel in the manner perfected by Sir Walter Scott: characters and events based on history in the background, invented characters to the fore. The setting is Athens and the Aegean; the sources included Plato's *Phaedo* and Xenophon's *Memorabilia*; the principal historical figure is Alkibiades, and the principal events drawn from history are those leading to the defeat of Athens by Sparta in 404 B.C. We see everything through the eyes of the fictional Alexias, son of a noble Athenian family and witness to the events leading to the downfall of the city and loss of her freedom, it is a Greek tragedy of folly and excessive pride, taking place, ironically, in the midst of a magnificent cultural era. The tragic hero is the city itself.

The King Must Die (1958) and *The Bull from the Sea* (1962) form together one of the most evocative mythic narratives ever constructed, bearing comparison in this respect to such modern masterworks as James JOYCE's *Ulysses* (1922) and Nikos KAZANTZAKIS's *The Odyssey: A Modern Sequel* (1958). In *The King Must Die*, Theseus, prince of Troizen, undergoes the adventures attributed to him in myth, but R. adds to this tradition knowledge derived from archaeology (down to the jewelry worn by King Minos of Crete), close familiarity with *The Golden Bough* (her very title taken from one of its basic, archetypal concepts), and a penchant for logical explanations of events that must once have seemed totally illogical.

The principal source of *The Bull from the Sea* is Euripedes's *Hippolytus*, but R. has again made characteristic changes. The fringe myth of Hippolyta, queen of the Amazons, is made the romantic core of the story. Hippolytus is an acolyte of Artemis, following his dead mother. His own death has been foreshadowed from early in *The King Must Die*, and if forms part of a seamless, fateful web: The power of the feminine principal, which the young Theseus thought he had displaced at Eleusis, is reasserted here, and Theseus's tragic fate is worked out in the death of his son. With *The Mask of Apollo* (1966) R. returns to history. The time is the final years of Greek democracy; the political plot revolves around the

civil war in Syracuse; the characters include Plato and members of his Academy, and the young Alexander of Macedon appears in a scene ominous for the old Hellenic ways but promising continuity for Hellenistic culture. Much of this is R.'s reconstruction, and the result is compelling—even if it seems more scholarly at time than poetic. A similar pattern is followed in *The Praise Singer* (1978), whose subject is poetry and whose time is the Lyric Age of Pisistratos (with Persian invasion hovering in the future), and whose protagonist is Simonides, a name known to us from history, champion singer of odes at the great festival at Delos. History, culture, politics, and personal charateristics—as in every R. narrative—are part here of a unified, inseparable whole.

Most of the last decade and a half of R.'s career was devoted to her study of Alexander the Great, resulting in a trilogy of novels—*Fire from Heaven* (1969), *The Persian Boy* (1972), and *Funeral Games* (1981)—and a history of sorts, *The Nature of Alexander* (1975). This last provides us, in a sense, with the remnants of her research and the rationale for her fictional interpretations. It is thus a splendid companion to the novels, although it perhaps does not stand very well by itself for those who know little of R.—it may tell us more about R. than about her subject.

There is much in the trilogy to remind us of R.'s earlier Theseus series. Even the natures of the protagonists and their backgrounds (both raised by their mothers, devotees of the old religion, both inadvertent causes of the deaths of their fathers) are similar. Many of the old themes too are here; a responsiveness to foreign cultures, an acceptance of almost all forms of sexuality (here the hero's great love is not an Amazon but a eunuch); the recognition of the role played by fate in all human lives, but an insistence at the same time on individual responsibility in the working out of those lives. Much of the first two volumes of the triology is predictable, albeit never dull. Her major imaginative leap occurs in the second novel: the Persian Boy of the title is Bagoas, Alexander's lover, and he serves as narrator. He provides the international viewpoint (he is writing in Egypt, many years later) that historians associate with the nature Alexander. He also provides a powerful mix of involvement and of distance, a vision at once intimate and universal.

The final volume of the trilogy, *Funeral Games*, begins with the death of Alexander and traces in human terms the disintegration of the empire he created. His heirs are given personalities that are consistent with their roles in recorded events. But there is a sense here also of larger events that goes well beyond the historical record (the rhythms of nature and of the individual psyche) and of the interaction of individuals with the patterns of history. Everything comes together in the end; human aspirations and fate, history and myth, imagination and scholarship. It is a fitting conclusion to R.'s distinguished career.

FURTHER WORKS: *Kind Are Her Answers* (1940); *The Friendly Young Ladies* (1944; pub. in the U.S. as *The Middle Mist*, 1945); *Return to Night* (1947); *North Face* (1948); *The Lion in the Gateway: The Heroic Battles of the Greeks and Persians at Marathon, Salamis and Thermopylae* (1948); *The Charioteer* (1953)

BIBLIOGRAPHY: Herbert, K., "The Theseus Theme: Some Recent Versions," *Crit*, 6, 3 (1960): 175–85; Burns, L. C., Jr., "Men Are Only Men: The Novels of M. R.," *Crit*, 6 (1963–1964): 102–21; Casey, B., "Nurse Novels," *SWR*, 49, 4 (1964): 332–41; Wolfe, P., *M. R.* (1969); Dick, B. F., *The Hellenism of M. R.* (1972); Hartt,

J. N., "Two Historical Novels," *VQR*, 49, 3 (1973): 450–58; Dick, B. F., "The Herodotean Novelist," *SR*, 81, 4 (Oct.-Dec. 1973): 864–69

—MORTON P. LEVITT

RÉUNION LITERATURE

In the 19th c. two Réunion-born poets achieved prominence in Paris: Charles-Marie-René Leconte de Lisle (1818–1894), leader of the Parnassians, and Léon Dierx (1838–1912), elected "prince of poets" after the death of Mallarmé. In the first half of the 20th c., however, there was little literary activity, although two Réunion-born literary historians, Joseph Bédier (1864–1938) and Louis Cazamian (1877–1944?), who lived and worked in Paris, became well known for their scholarly publications.

A few Réunion writers began publishing in the 1950s, and in the 1960s a new generation gave evidence of an underlying literary vitality. This phenomenon seems linked to an improved economy and to access to education by all social classes. Until then, poetry had been the only field in which Réunion writers excelled, and French the only acceptable language.

Nowadays, writers no longer regard French literature as the only model to imitate. Aware of their multiracial culture, with roots in Madagascar, Africa, India, China, as well as France, they see themselves as a distinct entity, the specificity of which should be reflected in their works. They have started to write, in Creole and French, novels and plays deriving from oral tales or reflecting striking historical events and the quest for their own heritage. Creole is no longer looked down on, nevertheless, writers are aware that any publication in Creole has a very limited readership.

Poetry is still the dominant genre. Some twenty-five writers have published between one and seven volumes of poetry. Most prominent are Boris Gamaleéya, (b. 1930), Jean Albany (b. 1917), and Jean Azéma (dates n.a.), who write in French. The island of Réunion is their focus. Gamaléya, in *Vali pour une reine morte* (1972; vali [a Malagasy musical instrument] for a dead queen) and *La mer et la mémoire* (1978; sea and memory), sees the island from a passionately political viewpoint; he advocates independence, so as to achieve an integration of the past with present aspirations and the creation of a distinct country. Albany, in such works as *Miel vert* (1966; green honey), *Outre-mer* (1967; overseas), *Bleu mascarin* (1969; mascarene blue), *Bal indigo* (1976; indigo dance), and *Percale* (1979; percale), presents the people in vivid settings, depicting delightful scenes of everyday life full of humor and tenderness. Some of Albany's poems have been set to music and have become very popular. He writes in Creole as well as French. Azéma, in *Olographes* (1978; holographs) and *D'azur á perpétuité* (1979; of azure forever), looks at the island with the eye of a lover and makes it part of himself. His elaborate and sophisticated style conveys his pure lyricism and sensuousness.

Other highly regarded poets are Gilbert Aubry (b. 1942), Alain Lorraine (b. 1946), and Jean-Francçois Sam-Long (b. 1949), all of whom write in French.

BIBLIOGRAPHY: Cornu, M. -R., "Les poètes réunionnais du XXe siècle: Vue d'ensemble," PFr, 13 (1976): 129–37; Joubert, J. -L., "L'Océan Indien," in A. Reboulet and M. Tétu, ed., *Guide culturel:* *Civilisations et litteréres d'expression française* (1977): 321–25; Aubry, G. and J. -F. Sam-Long, Introduction to *Créolies: Poésies réunionnaises* (1978): 9–21; Sam-Long, J. -F., "Écrivains d'aujourd'hui," in *Le mémorial de la Réunion* (1980), Vol. VII: 136–47; Marimoutou, C., *L'île écriture* (1982)

—MARIE-RENÉE CORNU

REVERDY, Pierre

French poet, essayist, critic, novelist, and short-story writer, b. 13 Sept. 1889, Narbonne; d. 21 June 1960, Solesmes

Son of a highly literate wine merchant, R. was educated in Narbonne. In 1910 he arrived in Paris, where he met Guillaume APOLLINAIRE, Max JACOB, Pablo Picasso, and Georges Braque. He became editor of the journal *Nord-Sud* in 1917. From 1926 until his death he lived in seclusion near the Benedictine monastery of Solesmes.

R.'s writings are deeply rooted in SYMBOLISM. Although he shared with his predecessors a preoccupation with pure poetry, he differed from them in his rejection of all forms of mediation, such as dreams and myths. His involvement with and study of CUBIST paintings not only influenced his poetry but led him to deny any fundamental difference between literature and the visual arts, and also to substitute for a directly mimetic view of art an analytical and transformational approach. In his 1924 essay *Pablo Picasso* R. claims that his friend completely reinvented art after having swept aside all accepted traditions, thus rivaling Descartes's *tabula rasa* in philosophy.

In *Une aventure méthodique* (1950; a methodical adventure), he discusses Braque's search for his own visual "language," his continuous, yet anguished confrontation with the unknown, his courage to stand alone. This work is profusely illustrated by the painter. Other works with original graphics include *Cravates de chanvre* (1922; hangman's nooses), with etchings by Picasso, and *Au soleil du plafond* (1955; at the ceiling's sun), with lithographs by Juan Gris.

An acutely self-conscious poet in the tradition of Baudelaire and Mallarmé, R., in his numerous essays, notably in the collections *Self defence* (1919; title in English) and *Le gant de crin* (1927; the horsehair glove), stresses the significant changes that were taking place in the arts and in aesthetics. His often-quoted theory that the striking image is based not on comparison but on the juxtaposition of two distant or clashing referents was later adopted by the SURREALISTS.

Outer reality is neither accessible nor acceptable to the poet who rejects mimesis in his quest of essence. In *La lucarne ovale* (1916; the oval skylight) the poet, in looking through a window, crosses the threshold between the outer and the inner world without exploring or even contemplating his self. His quest, which often does not go beyond the realm of abstractions, gives his poetry a metaphysical quality. He evokes the constant frustrations and obstacles of this search in a collection of stories appropriately entitled *Risques et périls* (1930; risks and perils). Poetry has led him on an arduous and obscure path, bereft of that inexpressible reward so devoutly sought by mystics.

R.'s poems strike the reader as impersonal, almost anonymous. Yet, although the poet even as a persona remains absent, anguish pervades his world. This impersonal quality does not diminish as the poem progresses, for erosion rather than density appears to prevail. A narrator, usually an impersonal *on* (one), moves through a spatial expanse as if it were a haunted place where long corridors alternate with the unexpected encounters of walls, imprisoning the subject who pursues freedom. He, or perhaps she, seeks an opening that would provide an escape, an answer that would eliminate fear. Creatures and objects that emerge are mere fragmentary replicas of the subject's mutilated self, unable to possess any elements of reality or to discover any stable order amid a constantly shifting world. Because of the discrepancy between aspiration and results, between hope and frustration, paradoxes recur throughout.

R. eschews punctuation in his verse, which is usually characterized by discontinuity: brief statements placed separately on the page, syntactical fragments. Rarely does he flesh out his images, and any attempt to link the discontinuous lines into a chain would do violence to his conception of poetry by reintroducing discursive reasoning into texts that rely on immediacy. The poet makes interchangeable abstract and concrete, animate and inanimate elements. His language consists of simple everyday expressions, and he frequently introduces banal statements or cliché into his poetry in such a way that they regain their lost powers.

Between his prose poems—Poèmes *en prose* (1915; poems in prose), *Étoiles peintes* (1921; painted stars)—and his verse there is no fundamental difference. True, the prose poems may adhere more closely to their cubist model, as they make more consistent use of spatial concepts in their structure. The same poetic principles govern his poetry and his fiction. The prose of *Risques et périls* and the novel *Le voleur de Talan* (1917; the thief of Talan) is often given the typographical configuration of verse, similar to such poetry collections as *Les ardoises du toit* (1918; roof slates) or *Sources du vent* (1929; sources of the wind). *Risques et périls* and *Le voleur de Talan* are generally free of narrative features and abound in imagery.

R. introduced into poetry the splintered persona, the multiple perspective, and other forms of discontinuity that have become central to postmodernist poetics.

FURTHER WORKS: *Quelques poèmes* (1916); *Les jockeys camouflés* (1918); *La guitare endormie* (1919); *Cœur de chêne* (1921); *Les épaves du ciel* (1924); *Grande nature* (1925); *Écumes de la mer* (1925); *La peau de l'homme* (1926); *La balle au bond* (1928); *Flaques de verre* (1929); *Pierres blanches* (1930); *Ferraille* (1937); *Plein verre* (1940); *Plupart du temps* (1945); *Visages* (1946); *Le livre de mon bord* (1948); *Le chant des marts* (1948); *Main d'œuvre* (1949); *Cercle doré Chanson dont l'air est encore á trouver* (1955); *En vrac* (1956); *La liberté des mers* (1959); *Sables mouvants* (1966); *Note eéternelle du présent: Écrits sur l'art 1923–1960* (1973); *Lettres à Jean Rousselot* (1973); *Œuvres* (1973 ff.); *Cette émotion appelée poésie: Écrits sur la poésie 1932–1960* (1974); *Nord-Sud, Self defence, et autres écrits sur l'art et la poésie* (1975); *Ancres* (1977); *Roof Slates, and Other Poems* (1981; bilingual); *Selected Poems* (1991)

BIBLIOGRAPHY: Greene, R., *The Poetic Theory of P. R.* (1967); Balakian, A., *Surrealism: The Road to the Absolute*, rev. ed. (1970): 100–120; Rizzuto, A., *The Style and Themes of P. R.'s "Les ardoises du toit"* (1971); Bishop, M., "P. R.'s Conception of the Image," *FMLS*, 12 (1976): 25–36; Bishop, M., "The Tensions of Understatement: P. R.'s *Poémes en prose*," AJFS, 14 (1977): 105–18; Caws, M. A., *La main de P. R.* (1979); Greene, R., *Six French Poets of Our Time* (1979): 23–58

—RENÉE RIESE HUBERT

REVUELTAS, José

Mexican novelist, short-story writer, dramatist, and essayist, b. 20 Nov. 1914, Durango; d. 14 April 1976, Mexico City

R.'s life was passionately dedicated to writing and politics. He was largely self-educated, his formal education having ended at fourteen, when he was sent to a reformatory for participating in a left-wing demonstration. In 1932, and again in 1934, he was exiled to the penal colony of Las Islas Marías for subversive activities. After his release he began writing short stories for journals, and from 1940 to 1943 he worked as a reporter for the then Marxist-oriented daily *El popular*. He also worked with experimental theater groups and later became a successful writer of screenplays. From 1968 to 1973 he was in prison for his leading role in the protests against the killing of students at Tlatelolco in October 1968.

Although a Marxist, R. was not an orthodox party-line follower. His views combined the teachings of FREUD with a Marxist-Leninist interpretation of history and literature to formulate a broad concept of human brotherhood.

Most critics consider R.'s second novel, *El luto humano* (1943; *The Stone Knife*, 1947, also pub. as *Human Mourning*, 1990), his best. This book demonstrates his use of interior monologue, SURREALISM, and cinematic techniques. The narrative focuses on six rural workers, vainly trying to flee their home because of a flood. A montage of images is used to convey to the reader the story of the previous life of each character. Also communicated by means of these images is the story of the Mexican revolution (1910–20), of the ravages of the Cristero rebellion (1926–28), and of an abortive attempt to organize a cooperative in the village. The themes—death, the search for Mexican identity, disillusionment with the revolution—become a psychological mosaic of man's suffering, solitude, and anguish as he faces the meaninglessness of his existence.

El apando (1969; solitary confinement) deals with the futile attempt of three men in solitary confinement to obtain drugs. This novella, written in one continuous paragraph, is technically the most successful of R.'s fictional works. The physical confinement of the prison is a symbolic expression of the psychological confinement of each prisoner's mind.

R.'s short stories are artistically more effective than his novels. Most of them have been collected in *Dios en la tierra* (1944; God on earth) and *Dormir en la tierra* (1960; sleep on earth). They are remarkable for their simplicity and starkness. In *Dormir en la tierra* R. reveals himself again as one of the major exponents of *tremendismo*, the "literature of terror." There is no understanding between people, no love, no tenderness. The world R. offers is a world distorted by hostility and gloom. Only in facing death, in killing or dying, does the individual comprehend something of himself.

R.'s importance lies in his role as an innovator. His early novels foreshadow those of Juan RULFO and Carlos FUENTES. As a transitional figure he contributed greatly to the apogee of the contemporary Mexican novel by experimenting with new novelistic techniques. He also focused on the broad and complex problems of mankind sifted through the Mexican reality, an approach that necessitated his rejection of the "novel of revolution," whose writers had been exclusively preoccupied with Mexico's social and economic conditions.

FURTHER WORKS: *Los muros de agua* (1941); *Ausentes* (1942); *Israel* (1947); *Los días terrenales* (1949); *El cuadrante de soledad* (1950); *El realismo en el arte* (1956); *En algún valle de lágrimas* (1956); *Los motives de Caín* (1957); *México, una democracia bárbara* (1958); *Ensayo sobre un proletariado sin cabeza* (1962; partial tr., "A Headless Proletariat in Mexico," in L. E. Aguilar ed., *Marxism in Latin America*, 1968); *Los errores* (1964); *El conocimiento cinematográfico y sus problemas* (1965); *Apuntes para una semblanza de Silvestre Revueltas* (1966); *Obra literaria* (2 vols., 1967); *Los procesos de México* (1968); *Material de los sueños* (1974); *Conversaciones con J. R.* (1977); *México 68: Juventud y revolución* (1978); *Cuestionamientos e intenciones* (1978); *Obras completas* (1978 ff.); *Cartas a María Teresa: La nave de los locos* (1979); *Las cenizas* (1981); *Dialética de la conciencia* (1981); *Tierra y libertad* (1981)

BIBLIOGRAPHY: Paz, O., "Letras de México: Una nueva novela mexicana," *Sur,* 12 (1943): 93–96; Menton, S., *El cuento hispano-americano* (1964): 262–72; Brushwood, J. S., *Mexico in Its Novel* (1966): 26–28, 222–26, 231; de Goémez, A. M. and E. Prado, *Diccionario de escritores mexicanos* (1967): 316–18; Sommers, J., *After the Storm: Landmarks of the Modern Mexican Novel* (1968): 174–76; Ruffinelli, J., *J. R.: Ficción, política y verdad* (1977); Murad, T., "Before the Storm: J. R. and Beginnings of the New Narrative in Mexico," *MLS,* 8, 1 (1977–1978): 57–64; Slick, S., *J. R.* (1983)

—KRISTYNA P. DEMAREE

REXROTH, Kenneth

American poet, critic, and dramatist, b. 22 Dec. 1905, South Bend, Ind.; d. 6 June 1982, Montecito, Cal.

Reared mainly in Chicago, where he attended the Art Institute, R. was precociously active in avant-garde poetry, painting, theater, and radical politics. After traveling widely as a young man across America, to Mexico, and to Europe, R. emerged as a personality of vast culture. He was associated with major poetic movements—the Chicago revolution of the 1920s, the objectivism of the 1930s, the anarchism of the 1940s. He became the mentor of the San Francisco renaissance and the Beat generation, and received numerous literary awards.

A contemplative reverie, *The Homestead Called Damascus* (written 1920–25; pub. 1957), serves to introduce R.'s common poetic themes of erotic mysticism and the search for communal transcendence, just as the poetry collection *The Art of Worldly Wisdom* (1949) offers his initial experiments in CUBISM and in creating dissociative, abstracting images. Additional, more intense lyric exploration of love and philosophical dilemmas is found in the collection *The Signature of All Things* (1950) and in the long poem *The Dragon and the Unicorn* (1952). Perhaps the culmination of R.'s images and passionate melodies in this vein is rendered in

Kenneth Rexroth

Beyond the Mountains (1951), a tetralogy of plays based on Greek and Japanese Nō models.

R.'s recurrent sense of social and political outrage found its first expression in the poems of *In What Hour* (1940) and, obscurely, in the long philosophical poem *The Phoenix and the Tortoise* (1944), where the horror of World War II intensifies a pacifist ethic of universal responsibility. During the Beat years, R. unleashed his vatic denunciation of the antipersonal structures of capitalism and the military-industrial complex in the poetry collection *In Defense of Earth* (1956). "Thou Shalt Not Kill," R.'s homage in this volume to Dylan THOMAS, is most exemplary of his protest. R.'s resistance to the "social lie" is witnessed, too, in *An Autobiographical Novel* (1966; rev. and expanded ed., 1991), which covers his youthful days in and around Chicago, and in several prose collections: *Bird in the Bush* (1959), *Assays* (1961), *The Alternative Society* (1970), and *The Elastic Retort* (1973). R.'s essays, written in the tradition of H. L. MENCKEN and Edmund WILSON, reveal his conversational style, brilliance, and range of intellect.

In *The Heart's Garden, the Garden's Heart* (1967) R. turned away from the dialectics of Western philosophy to fulfill and complete his long journey of following the sensuous music of poetry toward contemplative illumination. R. uses the gardens of Japan as a matrix in this perfectly realized meditation for conveying the visionary experience of Taoist-Zen Buddhism, the attainment of *satori*. Eastern values continued to shape and occupy R.'s poetry and are especially recognized in the countless Chinese and Japanese passages or influences seen in such collections as *Sky Sea*

Birds Trees Earth House Beasts Flowers (1971), *New Poems* (1974), and *On Flower Wreath Hill* (1977). In *The Love Poems of Marichiko* (1978), R.'s most intense poems of desire and bliss, passion and contemplative realization coalesce while R. implies the union of the pre-Buddhist goddess Marichi with the Buddha Dainichi.

Translation constitutes yet another area of R.'s immense talent. Working in his early years in French, Spanish, Greek, and Latin, after 1962 he concentrated solely on Chinese and Japanese. R. promoted the poetry of more Eastern women, living and dead, than any other man, as in *The Orchid Boat: Women Poets of China* (1972) and *The Burning Heart: Women Poets of Japan* (1977). As a translator R. was erudite, sensitive, and a master of facility in the American idiom. Some have compared his work to that of Ezra POUND.

R. was a superior man of letters who helped to shape the contours of American art through a personal, visionary poetry that moves within the traditional American subjects of individualism and communion with nature. The accomplished record of R.'s long spiritual growth sustains both the truths and insights of an ever-enduring craftsman.

FURTHER WORKS: *A Bestiary for My Daughters Mary and Katherine* (1955); *One Hundred Poems from the Japanese* (1955, trs.); *Thirty Spanish Poems* (1956, trs.); *One Hundred Poems from the Chinese* (1956, trs.); *Natural Numbers* (1963); *The Collected Shorter Poems* (1967); *The Collected Longer Poems* (1968); *The Classics Revisited* (1968); *Pierre Reverdy: Selected Poems* (1969, trs.); *With Eye and Ear* (1970); *Love in the Turning Year: One Hundred More Poems from the Chinese* (1970, trs.); *American Poetry in the Twentieth Century* (1971); *Communalism, from the Neolithic to 1900* (1975); *The Silver Swan* (1976); *Seasons of Sacred Lust: The Selected Poems of Kazuko Shiraishi* (1978, trs.); *The Morning Star* (1979); *Li Ch'ing-chao: Complete Poems* (1979, trs.); *The Buddhist Writings of Lafcadio Hearn* (1983); *World Outside the Window: The Selected Essays of K. R.* (1987); *More Classics Revisited* (1989); *Sacramental Acts: The Love Poems of K. R.* (1997)

BIBLIOGRAPHY: Lipton, L., "Notes toward an Understanding of K. R., with Special Attention to *The Homestead Called Damascus,*" *QRL,* 9 (1957), 37–46; Foster, R., "With Great Passion, A Kind of Person," *HudR,* 13 (1960), 149–54; Foster, R., "The Voice of the Poet: K. R.," *MinnR,* 2 (1962), 377–84; Gibson, M., *K. R.* (1972); Gardner, G., ed., *For R.* (1980); Hamalian, L., *A Life of K. R.* (1991); Gutierrez, D., *The Holiness of the Real: The Short Verse of K. R.* (1996)

—LYNN DEVORE

REYES, Alfonso

Mexican poet, literary critic, and scholar, b. 17 May 1889, Monterrey; d. 27 Dec. 1959, Mexico City

R. was educated in his native Monterrey, as well as in Mexico City, where he attended the famed National Preparatory School and the National University, from which he received a law degree in 1913. He worked closely with the Dominican Republic critic Pedro Henríquez Ureña (1884–1946) in Mexico City, where they founded the Atheneum of Youth, a group that had a strong influence in

revivifying Mexican intellectual life. In 1913 he went to France as Undersecretary of the Mexican legation. The following year he moved to Madrid, where he studied under Ramón Menéndez Pidal (1869–1968), the dean of Spanish literary scholars, and became an authority on the Spanish Golden Age. There followed a long series of diplomatic appointments in Spain (1922–24) and France (1924–27); he was ambassador to Argentina (1927–30, 1936–37) and to Brazil (1930–36). On his return to Mexico in 1939, he was named president of the House of Spain—the forerunner of the College of Mexico, the country's most distinguished center for higher education—and was elected to the Mexican Academy of Language. In 1945 he was awarded the National Prize for Arts and Letters.

R. was a Renaissance man of enormous learning and dazzling productivity. As early as 1906 he was publishing verse. Although at first inspired by the MODERNIST aesthetic, he quickly achieved his own poetic independence, an attitude of freedom one sees in the collection *Pausa* (1921; pause). His first important book of criticism, *Cuestiones estéticas* (1911; questions on aesthetics), which grew out of the literary discussions of the members of the Atheneum, shows an indebtedness to William James and Oscar Wilde.

One of R.'s persistent attempts was to rediscover the world through the eyes of a classicist. An early and very important essay, *Visión de Anáhuac* (1917; vision of Anáhuac), is a lyrical description of the ancient city of Mexico as it was seen by the Spanish conquistadors. In this essay R. suggests that there is a link between the 20th-c. Mexican and the pre-Columbian Indian. His concern with the relationship between Spanish American nativism and Old World culture were similar to those articulated by other thinkers of the period, for example, the American Waldo Frank (1889–1967) and the Argentine Ricardo Rojas (1882–1957). This concern was central in some of his most important essays. In *Discurso por Virgilio* (1933; discourse for Vergil) R. relates a plan of the Mexican government to develop local viniculture industries, using motifs similar to those in Vergil's *Georgics*. R.'s most important observations on the theme of Americanism are found in "Notas sobre la inteligencia Americana" (1937; "Thoughts on the American Mind," 1950) and "Posición de América" (1942; "The Position of America," 1950), two essays in which he posits an American cultural synthesis that would fuse Old World and native American values.

R.'s versatility as a writer is reflected in his tragic poem *Ifigenia cruel* (1924; cruel Iphigenia). Here, as in his historical-philosophical essays, his training as a classicist emerges in his re-creation of the legend of Iphigenia in Tauris. In addition to his work as a creative writer, R. also translated works by Robert Louis Stevenson (1850–1894), G. K. CHESTERTON, Anton CHEKHOV, and Jules Romains, among others, and edited a number of valuable scholarly editions of important writers, such as Francisco de Quevedo (1580–1645), Baltasar Gracián (1601–1658), Lope de Vega (1562–1635), and Amado NERVO.

R. is justly ranked among the finest essayists in 20th-c. Spanish America and is considered to have trained an entire generation of Mexican intellectuals. Through his voluminous writings he set forth the important thesis that the discovery and cultivation of the uniquely Mexican is essential to the development of a truly universal national culture.

FURTHER WORKS: *Los poemas rústicos de Manuel José Othón* (1910); *El paisaje en la poesía mexicana del siglo XX* (1911); *Cartones de Madrid* (1917); *El suicida* (1917); *El plano oblicuo*

(1920); *Retratos reales e imaginarios* (1920); *El cazador* (1921); *Simpatías y differencias* (5 vols., 1921–26); *Huellas* (1922); *Cuestiones gongorinas* (1927); *El testimonio de Juan Peña* (1930); *La saeta* (1931); *En el Ventanillo de Burgos* (1931); *A vuelta de correo* (1932); *Horas de Burgos* (1932); *Las vísperas de España* (1937); *Mallarmé entre nosotros* (1938); *Algunos poemas* (1941); *La experiencia literaria* (1942); *El deslinde* (1944); *La casa del grillo* (1945); *Cortesía* (1948); *Letras de la Nueva España* (1948); *La X en la frente* (1952); *Homero en Cuernavaca* (1952); *Berkeleyana* (1953); *Trayectoria de Goethe* (1954); *Marginalia* (1954); *Parentalia* (1954); *Hipócrates y Asclepio* (1954); *Presentación de Grecia* (1955); *Obras completas* (13 vols., 1955–61). FURTHER WORKS IN ENGLISH: *The Position of America and Other Essays* (1950); *Criticism and the Roman Mind* (1963); *Mexico in a Nutshell, and Other Essays* (1964)

BIBLIOGRAPHY: Bara, W., "Aspects of A. R.," *Hispania*, 34 (1951), 378–80; Olguín, M., *A. R. ensayista* (1956); Robb, J. W., *Patterns of Image and Structure in the Essays of A. R.* (1958); Robb, J. W., "A. R.," *Américas*, 18 (1966), 17–23; Stabb, M. S., *In Quest of Identity: Patterns in the Spanish American Essay of Ideas 1890–1960* (1967): 81–86; Aponte, B., "The Dialogue between A. R. and Spain," *Symposium*, 22 (1968), 5–15; Carter, S. Y., "A. R.: Critic and Artist," *CarQ*, 21, 4 (1975), 30–42; Wild, G., *C. C. R. G.: "La raza de Caín"* (1992)

—EDWARD MULLEN

REYLES, Carlos

Uruguayan novelist, b. 30 Oct. 1868, Montevideo; d. 24 July 1938, Montevideo

Born into a wealthy family of Irish descent (original name, O'Reilly), R. belonged to Uruguay's landed aristocracy. After studying at the Colegio Hispano-Uruguayo, he came into a substantial inheritance that permitted him to travel to Europe in 1886 and to live for a while in Spain.

R.'s first novel, *Por la vida* (1888; for life), which contains a good deal of autobiographical data, attacks the social and economic class to which he belonged. The publication of *Beba* (1894; Beba) secured for R. his position as one of the great writers of the *mester de gauchería* (gaucho literature of Latin America). Conceived in the tradition of French naturalism, its blatant determinism evoked a storm of protest both in Uruguay and Argentina.

La raza de Caín (1900; the race of Cain), whose action takes place in an urban setting, is another venture in determinism. In it R. attempts to examine the psychological defects of his weak characters, all of whom are destined to meet failure at the hands of stronger adversaries. In *El terruño* (1916; native soil) R. continued to develop his characters from a deterministic point of view. This is the story of the confrontation between two headstrong brothers that ends in the destruction of both. The novel also contains a subplot in which the regeneration of an impractical idealist is traced.

R.'s best-known work is *El embrujo de Sevilla* (1922; *Castanets*, 1929), in which he uses a distinct MODERNIST style to convey the heady atmosphere of Andalusia and to evoke the Spanish soul as it is revealed in the popular ballad, dance, and the traditional bullfight. This novel represents R.'s greatest success both from the standpoint of popular international acclaim and from that of

technical mastery. Here the sometimes crude realism and the naturalistic determinism of previous novels gives way to the blending of impressionistic scenes of fire, color, and passion.

R.'s last novel, *El gaucho Florido* (1932; the gaucho Florido), contains a precisely observed rendering of rural mores in the style of *Beba*. This tale of violent love and death is marred by its excessive use of melodramatic situations.

All of R.'s novels are based on previously published short stories. This technique enabled R. to develop carefully the psychological and sociological aspects of a tale after he had crystallized the plot. In the minds of a number of critics R. is considered the outstanding Uruguayan novelist of his generation.

FURTHER WORKS: *Primitivo* (1896); *Academias* (3 vols., 1896–98); *El extraño* (1897); *El sueño de la rapiña* (1898); *El ideal nuevo* (1903); *La muerte del cisne* (1911); *Diálogos olímpicos* (1924); *El nuevo sentido de la narración gauchesca* (1930); *Ego sum* (1939); *A batallas de amor . . . campos de pluma* (1939); *Cuentos completos* (1968); *Diario, seguido de La conversación de C. R. por Gervasio Guillot Muñoz* (1970)

BIBLIOGRAPHY: Lerna Acevedo de Blixen, J., *R.* (1943); Menafra, L. A., *C. R.* (1957); Englekirk, J., et al., *An Outline History of Spanish American Literature* (1965): 209–10; Englekirk, J., and Ramos, M. *La narrativa uruguaya* (1967): 261–66; Benedetti, M., *Literatura uruguaya siglo XX*, rev. ed. (1969): 46–59; Foster, D., *The 20th Century Spanish-American Novel: A Bibliographic Guide* (1975): 163–66; Bollo, S., *Literatura uruguaya* (1976): 147–54; Wild, G., *C. C. R. Gutiérrez: "La raza de Caín"* (1992)

—HARLEY D. OBERHELMAN

REYMONT, Władysław Stanisław

Polish novelist, b. 2 May 1867, Kobiele Wielkie; d. 5 Dec. 1925, Warsaw

The son of an organist, R. was partly of peasant stock. The novelist has fascinated his biographers. An actor in a wandering troupe, a railway employee, a spiritualist medium, a candidate for a religious order, and finally, a passionate although volatile lover, R. was a writer who relied on experience, and he used his multifarious adventures as raw material for his fiction. The notes he scrupulously kept for ten years (1884–94) served as a literary apprenticeship and substitute for the formal education he lacked. In 1925 R. won the Nobel Prize for literature.

R.'s first literary success, a book of travel reportage, *Pielgrzymka do Jasnej Góry* (1894; pilgrimage to Jasna Góra) attracted the attention of the critics with its portrayal of the collective psychology of a group of people—those on a pilgrimage: its moods, reflexes, and modes of behaviour, as well as its internal divisions and stratifications.

His first two novels, *Komediantka* (1896; *The Comedienne*, 1920) and *Fermenty* (1897; fermentation), form a diptych. They tell the story of the rebellion of a determined young woman against her family and provincial milieu, and represent a fictional reminiscence of the author's own conflicts with his father. The heroine is the first in a series of strong personalities driven by a passion and at odds with the conventions of the society in which they live. These characters are temperamentally close to their author; the passion—whether it is for the theater, art, money, sex, or spiritualism—is an answer to the grayness of everyday life, and the rebellion is an attempt to escape it. At the same time, R. the realist was aware that revolt against the laws of society must end in failure or self-destruction, and the wisdom gained by some of his characters, like the heroine of *Fermenty*, is an understanding and acceptance of necessity.

Ziemia obiecana (2 vols., 1899; *The Promised Land*, 1927) is a stark and cruel novel, one of the strongest antiurban statements in literature. The protagonist of the book is the city of Łódź. This rapidly growing industrial metropolis created its own special type of men—and imposed upon them its own morality dictated by money. The novel presents a kaleidoscopic variety of places, situations, and characters representing different generations, social strata, races, and nationalities, all of them appearing as mere parts in a huge, complex mechanism. The narrative technique, similar to that of a film—fragmentary and constantly moving from one scene to another—foreshadows many novelistic techniques developed later in the 20th c.

Chłopi (4 vols., 1904–9; *The Peasants*, 4 vols., 1924–25), R.'s magnum opus, is both a realistic novel about the life of Polish peasants in the second half of the 19th c. and an epic of peasant life true for any place or time. One of the central themes of the novel is time, which controls the existence of the peasant to a far greater degree than anything else. The narrative structure of the novel—divided into four parts: "Jesień" ("Autumn"), "Zima" ("Winter"), "Wiosna" ("Spring"), and "Lato" ("Summer")—as well as its internal rhythm, is determined by the natural, immutable sequence of the seasons. They impose on the peasants definite jobs. Another rhythm, that of church holidays and religious rituals, overlaps the rhythm of nature. The holidays raise the life of the peasants to a higher, more sacred level. A third kind of time, ominously present throughout the work, is that of human life, different for each person and pertaining thus to the individual rather than the collectivity. Unlike the other two temporal modes it is noncyclical. The presentation of biology and religion as the only forces in man's life, coupled with the historical timelessness of the work, lead toward generalization. The characters and their problems become eternal and universal. Against the mythic background of nature, religion, and human existence, R. presents the life of a village, Lipce, and the novel's protagonists: the family of a wealthy peasant, Maciej Boryna. The plot follows the love affair of Maciej's son, Antek, with his young and sensual stepmother, the love-hate relationship of father and son, who are caught in an insoluble situation. A great epic of the life of peasants written in their own diction, the only weakness of the book is the lyrical, metaphorical language of some passages typical of the style of "Young Poland," in which R. was paying tribute to the literary fashion of his day.

R. was a writer of experience, not an intellectual or a visionary. His virtues were those of a realist: the gift of close observation, objectivity toward his subject matter, and straightforwardness in the presentation of tragic conflict. The source of R.'s realism was not literary doctrine but his own predisposition. His novels offer a vast panorama of Polish life in the last quarter of the 19th c. Their central themes are the clash between a strong personality and a collectivity, between passion and common sense, between adventure and tradition, as well as the conflict between the instincts of destruction and preservation, death and life.

FURTHER WORKS: *Spotkanie* (1897); *Lili* (1899); *Sprawiedliwie* (1899; *Justice*, 1925); *W jesienną noc* (1900); *Przed świtem* (1902); *Komurasaki* (1903); *Z pamiętnika* (1903); *Burza* (1907); *Na krawędzi* (1907); *Marzyciel* (1910); *Z ziemi chełmskiej* (1910); *Wampir* (1911); *Rok 1794* (3 vols., 1913–18); *Przysięga* (1917); *Za frontem* (1919); *Osądzona* (1923); *Bunt* (1924); *Legenda* (1924); *Krosnowa i świat* (1928); *Pisma* (20 vols., 1921–25); *Pisma* (48 vols., 1930–34); *Pisma* (20 vols., 1948–57); *Wybór nowel* (1954); *Dzieła wybrane* (11 vols., 1955–56); *Nowele wybrane* (1958); *Pisma* (7 vols., 1968 ff.)

BIBLIOGRAPHY: Schoell, F. L., *Les paysans de Ladislas R.* (1925); Borowy, W., "R.," *SlavonicR*, 16 (1938), 439–48; Kridl, M., *A Survey of Polish Literature and Culture* (1956): 435–43; Milosz, C., *The History of Polish Literature* (1969): 369–71; Krzyzanowski, J. R., *W. S. R.* (1972); Krzyzanowski, J., *A History of Polish Literature* (1978): 536–42

—BOGDANA CARPENTER

RHODESIAN LITERATURE

See Zimbabwean Literature

RHONE, Trevor

Jamaican dramatist and screenwriter, b. 24 Mar. 1939, Kingston

Born in Jamaica, R. studied in England, gaining experience in broadcasting and theater during his years there in the 1960s. He returned to Jamaica in 1967 determined to play a significant role in the development of theater in the newly independent nation. In that same year R. joined with other writers and performers to create the Barn Theater, which would establish itself as one of the most important theater companies in Jamaica. R. would divide his time between teaching high school and writing for the theater. However, by the mid-1970s he was able to devote himself full time as a dramatist and director.

In 1971 R. collaborated with film director Perry Henzel in writing the screenplay for the hit cult film *The Harder They Come*, which still remains one of the most insightful examinations of the frenetic and unpredictable life of the Kingston dweller to be made into film. *The Harder They Come* tells a simple story of a young man's move from the country to the city to try and make it big in music. He ends up going afoul of the law because of his inability to secure legal work in the class-stratified society. Ultimately, his artistic inclinations are thwarted by exploitative producers who fail to give him a chance to reap the benefits of his musical talents. In effect, R. and Henzel managed to explore the hero as trickster in Jamaican culture. There are paradigms at work in this film that speak to a strong understanding of the social and political context of Jamaican society. In many ways, then, *The Harder They Come* is an emblematic film, replete with symbols and a strong reliance of reggae music for its ethos that would become increasingly important in Jamaican literature.

Ironically, R.'s work has never truly explored the complex world of the reggae aesthetic with any significant conviction.

Instead, he has relied on the values of a rural Jamaican world that is constantly being assailed by the encroachment of modernization, colonial and postcolonial classism, and the difficulties of political violence. R.'s Jamaica begins as a paradasical one that does not situate itself within the history of slavery and exploitation, but in a rural world of deep wisdom, strong community values, and the centrality of spirituality—almost Christian spirituality—at the core of these values. It is the disruption of this paradasial world that supplies R. with his dramatic moments that are always at once comic and deeply tragic. But R.'s work is never ultimately tragic. R. is fixated on the idea of a comic ending—an ending full of hope and possibility.

His first major success as a dramatist was his play *Smile Orange* (perf. 1970), set in the tourist infested North Coast of Jamaica. *Smile Orange* is a slapstick comedy with many elements of farce running through it. R. makes use of the figure of the hero as trickster and treats the encroachment of tourism as a metaphor for the alteration of Jamaican society by Western values. Yet it is hard to regard *Smile Orange* as a political work. R. has always had a penchant for comic dialogue and for language that captures the punning and sharp repartee of the Jamaican language. These elements, coupled with his capacity to explore issues of sexuality and power, allow him, in *Smile Orange*, to write a piece that is wholly Jamaican and that finds it political center in the very act of speaking about Jamaican themes on the stage. Indeed, the basic template used for *Smile Orange* would be repeated in another popular play by R. of similar structure and intent, *School's Out* (1986).

However, it was with *Old Story Time* (1981) that R. would establish himself as one of the most important dramatists in the Caribbean. In this work R. explores with very economical and imaginative use of the stage the politics of class and race in Jamaican society through an intimate study of the life of one family—a family with deep rural roots and a growing and uncomfortable entry into the urban world of modern Jamaica. R. makes use of folk idioms, folk myths, and folk spirituality to tell the story of a family that must ultimately free itself of the past and try and find some order and hope in the future. R.'s bitterness about the racism of Jamaican society is tackled in this work, and while there remains some ambivalence about how he resolves this dilemma, it is clear that R. holds to a relatively conservative view of Jamaican social politics that locates a sense of belonging and place not in the evocation of Africa, but in a faith in the essential goodness and richness of Jamaican society.

This disinterest in history as it is normally cast by writers like Dennis SCOTT, Edward Kamau BRATHWAITE, and Derek WALCOTT makes R. a deeply contemporary writer. For insight into the trauma and anxiety that surrounded the life of everyday Jamaicans in the politically volatile 1970s one must turn to R.'s *Two Can Play* (perf. 1983, pub. 1986), which offers a disturbing but quite accurate exploration of the twisted nature of Jamaican politics. *Two Can Play* is a play with just two characters who are trying to decide whether to stay in Jamaica through the siege of gunshots and violence or whether to try and escape to the U.S. The play is also about the relationship between a husband and wife who are starting to face the realities of women's liberation and the alteration of male roles in the society. Typically, *Two Can Play* is a wonderful comic tour de force that offers hope and a strong nationalism at the end of the narrative. But its dramatic form is largely conventional, and R. never truly departs from this pattern in his later works.

Old Story Time is R.'s most important play and its influence on the work of other Caribbean playwrights cannot be overstated. The play has had numerous revivals in the Caribbean, in the United Kingdon, in Canada, and in the U.S., and it has established R. as an important figure in Caribbean literature. Unfortunately, the limited publishing of plays remains a major problem in Caribbean society and very few of the plays written by writers such as R. and his contemporaries can be encountered outside of productions. However, what R. and his contemporaries reveal is that dramatists—forced to be relevant to capture the interest of the audience—are some of the most innovative writers in the Caribbean today, writers who have, like the reggae artists and the Deejays, a finger on the pulse of the society, the language, and the changes in social and political norms.

BIBLIOGRAPHY: Okagbue, O., "Identify, Exile, and Migration: The Dialectics of Content and Form in West Indian Theater," *NLitsR*, 19 (1990): 14-23; King, B., ed., *Post-Colonial English Drama: Commonwealth Drama Since 1960* (1992); Gainor E. J., ed., *Imperialism and Theatre: Essays on World Theatre, Drama and Performance* (1995)

—KWAME DAWES

RHYS, Jean

(pseud. of Ella Gwendolen Rees Williams) English novelist and short-story writer, b. 24 Aug. 1890?, Roseau, Dominica; d. 14 May 1979, Exeter

R., the daughter of a Welsh doctor, was educated in the Roseau convent school and went to England in 1907. After one term at the Perse School, Cambridge, and one at the London Academy of Dramatic Arts (now RADA), she worked as a chorus girl in a touring musical company. In 1919 she married the French-Dutch journalist Jean Langlet and went to the Continent with him. While he was serving a prison sentence for illegal financial transactions, she lived with Ford Madox FORD. This affair ended with much bitterness, and she and her husband were divorced. Such personal experiences in the pre-World War I demimonde and in postwar Europe provide the main subjects of the fiction R. began publishing in 1927. She was married two more times. From 1939 to 1957 she dropped from public attention; upon her "rediscovery" she found an appreciative audience for her bittersweet tales focusing on the subjection of women in a male-dominated society. She received various literary awards for her last novel, *Wide Sargasso Sea* (1966).

R.'s stories, collected in *The Left Bank, and Other Stories* (1927), *Tigers Are Better Looking* (1968), and *Sleep It Off Lady* (1976), are highly compressed, impressionistic vignettes. Although the stories in *The Left Bank* are apprentice work, strongly influenced by the tutoring of Ford (who contributed a preface to the volume), they announce themes and subjects that figure in all of the later writings. There is the aging woman who gives herself into the hands of her young lover ("La Grosse Fifi"); the intimacy that a woman knows only with another woman ("Illusion"); the senseless cruelty that society inflicts on the weak ("From a French Prison" and "The Sidi"). Often the warmth of Caribbean life is contrasted to the coldness and sterility of English life.

Although the stories show a keen observation of human behavior and social customs and a compassionate view of individuals rejected by society, it is in the novels that R. made her greatest contribution to literature through her delineation of a certain type of woman. In her first four novels she portrays four women who are actually the same character seen at different stages of life. The youngest heroine is Anna, in *Voyage in the Dark* (1934), followed chronologically by Marya, in *Quartet* (1928), Julia, in *After Leaving Mr. Mackenzie* (1930), and Sasha, in *Good Morning, Midnight* (1939). Like the novelist herself, this woman is an expatriate from a tropical world; she is beautiful and sensitive; and her life is controlled by forces outside herself. Unlike R., who successfully transformed experience into art, this woman is uncreative and generally self-destructive. Feeling and sentiment, never logic, rule her life. Anna, the young chorus girl, gives herself completely to her older lover, has an abortion for which he pays, and, helpless to stand up for herself, becomes the passive victim of other men and women. In *Quartet*, R.'s first novel, initially entitled *Postures*, Marya appears to be more active. Actually the mechanics of the plot—the story is that of a woman who is seduced by a friend while her husband is in prison—give this impression of activity; the character of Marya is essentially that of the typical R. heroine. Julia is the most passive and downtrodden manifestation of this character: she particularly shows the contrast between an individual's concept of herself and the identity that society forces upon her. This identity is largely based upon her economic situation; and R.'s equation of personal identity with weath links the novel to other writings of the Depression years.

Good Morning, Midnight is R.'s masterpiece. In it, Sasha, the now aging woman, returns to Paris, scene of her earlier days. Seeking to understand who she is and how she has become this person, she achieves a realization of her relationship to society and to herself. All of R.'s writings exemplify craftsmanship and awareness of literary technique; and *Good Morning, Midnight* marks the high point of R.'s technical development. The first-person narration controls the personal vision and understanding of Sasha and delineates the precise limits of the novel. Within this necessarily restricted area R. provides a complete study of Sasha and perfects the form of the novel.

Although well received by contemporary reviewers, R.'s novels were not widely read at the time of publication, and the publishing exigencies of World War II restricted the growth of R.'s literary reputation. Discouraged by this lack of success, R. published nothing more until 1966, when, encouraged by readers who saw her as a forerunner of the emancipated woman, she brought out her romantic tour de force, *Wide Sargasso Sea*. In it she takes the character Edward Rochester from Charlotte Brontë's *Jane Eyre* and tells the story of his first marriage to the mad Bertha Mason. R.'s "reconstruction" ends with the burning of Thornfield and the death of Bertha. Yet while *Jane Eyre* provides characters and a situation for *Wide Sargasso Sea*, the main character, Antoinette Cosway (R.'s name for Bertha Mason), is again the typical R. protagonist: the sensitive, loving woman frustrated and driven to madness by her domineering and cold-blooded English husband. Again R. successfully creates her characters by allowing them to tell different parts of the story through their first-person narration. She also stresses the problems caused by the conflicting cultures of the Caribbean and of England.

The wry, ironic tone of R.'s work continues in her last stories and in *Smile Please: An Unfinished Autobiography* (1979). This attitude of outrage and puzzlement over a world that constantly threatens her, combined with an indomitable spirit expressed through a passive character, has given R. special appeal to readers who seek a new understanding of male-female relationships. R. was several decades ahead of her time in her sexual attitudes and understandings; her knowledge of human psychology and her artistry are now causing her work to be praised in the highest terms.

FURTHER WORKS: *My Day* (1975); *Voyage in the Dark* (1982); *The Letters of J. R.* (1984); *J. R., the Complete Novels* (1985); *Tales of the Wide Caribbean* (1985); *The Collected Short Stories* (1987)

BIBLIOGRAPHY: Alvarez, A., "The Best Living English Novelist," *NYTBR*, 17 March 1974, 6–7; Mellown, E., "Character and Themes in the Novels of J. R.," in Spacks, P., ed., *Contemporary Women Novelists*, (1977): 118–36; James, L., *J. R.* (1978); Bender, T. K., "J. R. and the Genius of Impressionism," *SLitI*, 11 (1978), 45–53; Dash, C. M. L., "J. R.," in King, B., ed., *West Indian Literature* (1979): 196–209; Staley, T., *J. R.*(1979); Annan, G., on *Smile Please, TLS* (21 December 1979); 154; Wolfe, P., *J. R.* (1980); Hynes, S., on *Smile Please, New Republic* (31 May 1980); 28–31; Rose, P., on *Smile Please, YR*, 69 (1980), 596–602; Howells, C. A., *J. R.* (1991); Malcolm, C. A., *J. R.: A Study of the Short Fiction* (1995); Sternlicht, S., *J. R.* (1997)

—ELGIN W. MELLOWN

RIBA, Carles

Spanish poet, short-story writer, literary critic, and translator (writing in Catalan), b. 23 Dec. 1893, Barcelona; d. 12 July 1959, Barcelona

R. established himself early as a literary figure: in 1911 he was awarded a prize for his "Egloga" (eclogue), and by 1919 he had translated Virgil and Homer. From 1925 to 1933 he was a professor of Greek at the Bernat Metge Foundation, where he added to his reputation as a leading scholar. R. went into exile in France in 1939 after Franco's victory, but returned to Barcelona in 1943 to resume his academic pursuits. He was instrumental in the diffusion of Catalan culture abroad and also contributed importantly to furthering the dialogue in Spain between Catalan and Castilian writers.

R.'s *Primer llibre d'estances* (1919; first book of stanzas) is highly personal poetry within the framework of the Catalan cultural movement known as Noucentisme. With great originality he applied the prescriptions of the Noucentista critic Eugeni d'Ors (1881–1954), setting forth a concept of poetry as an expression of culture. One of the work's outstanding features is its attempt to explore psychological states through abstractions going back as far as Homer: mind, soul, desire, and the senses.

The six poems comprising *La paraula a lloure* (written 1912–19, pub. 1965; the word at ease), a deeply felt work in which R. struggles to find his definitive lyrical voice, adapted to the Catalan language the *canzone libera* of Leopardi. Also present is the influence of the Catalan poet Joan Maragall (1860–1911).

Segon llibre d'estances (1930; second book of stanzas) shows the influence of the German romantics and the French SYMBOLISTS. In these poems, moving explorations of the vulnerability of human love, R.'s mastery of fixed forms is complemented by an extraordinary flexibility in syntax.

The thirty sonnets of *Tres suites* (1937; three suites) explore the tensions between the senses and the mind when a man faces the sensual aspects of woman. R.'s voice here is hermetic, the usual personal tone being sublimated.

Elegies de Bierville (1943; enlarged ed., 1949; elegies of Bierville), for many critics R.'s poetic materpiece, reflects his experience of the Spanish Civil War and his years of exile, tinted with the yearning to return home. The individual's suffering in exile, reduced to its basic elements, can represent collective experience. The exploration of physical isolation and spiritual deprivation, as well as the hope arising from the poet's new understanding of life, is developed through motifs from classical mythology. These motifs gradually lead R. to a recognition of the Christian God.

In *Del joc i del foc* (1946; about play and about fire), experimental poems written in the late 1930s and early 1940s, R. essayed the Japanese tanka form. The book is a powerful exercise in style, but R. also develops his earlier idea of poetry as comprised of ingenuity and passion.

Salvatge cor (1953; wild heart), profoundly religious in tone, is a spiritual chant with resonances of Christian Neoplatonic thought. In *Esbós de tres oratoris* (1957; sketch of three oratories), narrative poetry with subtle mythical overtones, the patient speculation of *Elegies de Bierville* gives way to a more dramatic questioning of the possibilities of religious belief.

R.'s work—mainly metaphysical in essence, based on a personal synthesis of the Noucentista literary outlook, and enriched by his profound knowledge of the European classics, ancient and modern (of the latter he translated CAVAFY, RILKE, KAFKA, Poe, and Hölderlin, among others)—brought Catalan poetry to new heights. He was also the best literary critic in Catalonia of his time. Like his poetry, his criticism falls within the European postsymbolist framework. His concept of literary analysis evolved to an approach to the work as a function of the creator's sensibility. This critical technique, which "re-creates" a work while explaining it and which allows the critic to analyze himself in the process, has had many worthy followers in Catalonia.

FURTHER WORKS: *Aventures d'En Perot Marrasquí* (1917); *Guillot, bandoler* (1920); *Escolis, i altres articles* (1921); *Verdaguer* (1922); *L'ingenu amor* (1924); *Els marges* (1927); *Nocions de literatura grega* (1927); *Nocions de literatura llatina* (1927); *Sis Joans* (1928); *Resum de literatura llatina* (1928); *Per comprendre* (1937); *Versions de Hölderlin* (1944); . . .*Més els poemes* (1957); *Poemes de Kavafis* (1962); *Obres completes* (2 vols., 1965–1967). FURTHER WORKS IN ENGLISH: *Poems* (1964, bilingual)

BIBLIOGRAPHY: Aleixandre, V., "C. R., los discípulos, el campo," *Los encuentros* (1958): 77–84; Terry, A., "Some Sonnets of C. R.," in Pierce, F. W., ed., *Hispanic Studies in Honour of I. González Llubera* (1959): 403–13; special R. section, *PSA*, 23, 68 (1961): 133–219; Gili, J. L., Introduction to C. R., *Poems* (1964): 9–10; Barjau, E., "C. R.: La poesía como potenciación del lenguaje," *Convivium*, 27 (1966): 41–53; Goytisolo, J. A., *Poetas catalanes contemporáneos* (1968): 11–16, 49–50; Terry, A., *A Literary History of Spain: Catalan Literature* (1972): 101–3 and passim.

—ALBERT M. FORCADAS

RIBEIRO, Aquilino

Portuguese novelist, short-story writer, and essayist, b. 13 Sept. 1885, Carregal da Tabosa, Beira Alta; d. 27 Sept. 1963, Lisbon

R.'s life and works are intimately related to the Beira provinces—the hill country of central Portugal—where he was born and spent his first twenty years. After studying briefly for the priesthood, R. went to Lisbon in 1906 and worked as a journalist and translator. His outspokenness about his antimonarchist, prorepublican views resulted in his exile in Paris. After his return in 1914 to a Portugal that had been declared a republic in 1910, he became a teacher, a member of the group around the journal *Seara nova*, and later a librarian at the National Library. His subsequent role in revolts against the new dictatorship caused his repeated flights into exile in France and Germany. In 1932 he returned to Portugal and concentrated on his writing. He was decorated by the Brazilian government in 1952 for his contributions to Luso-Brazilian culture. In 1960 R. was brought before a military tribunal charged with having "insulted the state" through the publication of *Quando os lobos uivam* (1958; *When the Wolves Howl*, 1963). An international outcry resulted in his acquittal.

R.'s first collection of regional stories, *Jardim das tormentas* (1913; garden of storms) is characterized by the themes and techniques he developed in his later fiction. Nature is all-embracing, pure, but sensually corrupting. Village life—its character types, its popular traditions, and its foibles—and the overpowering role of the Church are presented in a very vivid, satiric, and verbose style. In his juxtaposition of Portuguese archaisms, rural terminology, and slang, R. was admittedly indebted to the 19th-c. Portuguese master novelist Camilo Castelo Branco (1825–1890).

R.'s version of the *pícaro*, Malhadinhas, is perhaps the most memorable figure in his work and one of the best-known characters in modern Portuguese fiction. Malhadinhas is a sly muleteer, who skillfully uses his knife or his tongue to resolve his difficulties.

R.'s novels often involve the resolution of religious or political dilemmas, in a manner similar to that of Anatole FRANCE, whom R. greatly admired. *A via sinuosa* (1918; the winding path) presents Libório Barradas's (one of R.'s many autobiographical protagonists) personal crises, as he justifies his revolutionary attitudes in the face of his traditional Catholic upbringing. *O homem que matou o diabo* (1930; the man who killed the devil) was inspired by one of R.'s flights from political imprisonment. The repercussions of the failure of the First Portuguese Republic are viewed from the perspective of the Portuguese and Spanish peasantry.

The city was a foreign, incomprehensible place for R. His novels about the bourgeoisie of Lisbon, such as *Mónica* (1939; *Monica*, 1961), thus lack sufficient psychological depth. His novels about peasants are much stronger. *Quando os lobos uivam* recounts an actual incident of peasant rebellion against the government and was thus considered "insulting to the state."

R. was also a popular historian, folklorist, and literary critic. His translation of *Don Quixote* into Portuguese was highly praised. Although he studied under Henri BERGSON and lived in Paris at the height of the avant-garde movements of the early 20th c., R. maintained complete literary independence, and to this independence is owed his standing as one of the most distinguished and admired Portuguese writers of this century.

FURTHER WORKS: *Terras do demo* (1919); *Filhas da Babilónia* (1920); *Estrada de Santiago* (1922); *Andam faunos pelo bosque*

(1926); *A batalha sem fim* (1931); *As três mulheres de Sansão* (1932); *Maria Benigna* (1933); *É a guerra* (1934); *Quando ao gavião caiu a pena* (1935); *Aldeia: Terra, gente e bichos* (1935); *Alemanha ensangüentada* (1935); *Aventura maravilhosa de D. Sebastião* (1936); *S. Bonaboião, anacoreta e mártir* (1937); *Anastácio da Cunha, o lente penitenciário* (1938); *O Cavaleiro de Oliveira: Estudo crítico e biográfico* (1938); *O servo de Deus e a casa roubada* (1940); *Por obra e graça* (1940); *Os avós de nossos avós* (1942); *Brito Camacho: Vida e obra* (1942); *Volfrâmio* (1944); *O livro de Menino Deus* (1945); *Lápides partidas* (1945); *Caminhos errados* (1947); *Constantino de Bragança, 7° vice-rei da Índia* (1947); *Cinco reis de gente* (1948); *Uma luz ao longe* (1948); *Camões, Camilo, Eça e alguns mais* (1949); *Geografia sentimental* (1951); *Portugueses das sete partidas* (1951); *Humildade gloriosa: História prodigiosa do Padre S. António* (1954); *Abóboras no telhado* (1955); *O romance de Camilo* (1955); *A casa grande de Romarigães* (1957); *No cavalo de pau de Sancho Pança* (1960); *De Meca a Freixo de Espada à Cinta* (1960); *Tombo no inferno e o Manto de Nossa Senhora* (1963); *Casa do escorpião* (1964); *Um escritor confessa-se* (1972)

BIBLIOGRAPHY: West, A., on *When the Wolves Howl, New Yorker* (28 Dec. 1963): 73–76; Moser, G., "A. R.," *Hispania*, 47 (1964): 339–42; Moser, G., Portuguese Writers of This Century," *Hispania*, 50 (1967): 947–54

—IRWIN STERN

RIBEIRO, Darcy

Brazilian novelist and prose writer, b. 26 Nov. 1922, Montes Claros, Minas Gerais; d. 17 Feb. 1997, Brasília

R. is his nation's premier investigator of the indigenous populations, publishing extensively, from a decidedly Marxian perspective, on underdevelopmental issues germane to the Brazilian subcontinent and to Latin America as a whole. Early on, his expertise and dedication brought him to the attention of reformist elements within several pre-1964 central governments, where he served as cofounder and head of the University of Brasilia, minister of education and culture, and presidential chief of staff. A lengthy exile followed—in Uruguay, Venezuela, Chile, and Peru—precipitated by the 1964 rightest coup that was to impose successive military regimes on the nation. In 1978, with an end to overt oppression, R. returned permanently to Brazil, first getting elected as vice governor of Rio de Janeiro State and, most recently, as its senator. At the same time, he began a late-blooming and highly successful novelistic career. Indeed, in a decade marked by intense extraliterary pursuits, he penned four narratives, three of which are quite lengthy and involved.

In *Matra* (1976; *Maíra*, 1984) the author goes further than anyone, before or since, in redefining fictionally the Native American experience, pinpointing autochthonous ethnography within defined boundaries and exposing irreversible sociological tendencies. In so doing, he goes about allegorizing and synthesizing the dichotomy between European and indigenous populations, but from the viewpoint of a tribal nation. While the distressing findings are not surprising, nor the reasons new, R.'s empathy produces an explosive indictment of aboriginal mistreatment. The author's updated, factual, scientific New Indianism exposes a torrent of collateral ills, from continuing ecological abuse to governmental malfeasance and detrimental missionary work. The sometimes weighty approach, however, is tempered and embellished by the mock-heroic tone of omnipresent native deities. Much as in the classically inspired *Os lusíadas*, the supernatural dramas of the deities run parallel to, and intervene with, those of the earthly adversaries, further enriching Indian legends.

Externally, the novel is divided into four parts, titled to mirror those of the Catholic mass, itself so symbolic of death and sacrifice. Internally, structure draws mostly on the indigenous myths and traditions, whose spontaneous arrangement makes for a fragmented narrative, unfolding through an endless array of counterpoint. Thus, what immediately comes into focus is the schism between the red and white nations, a pervasive thesis that polarizes every aspect of *Maíra* The author presents *Maíra*, as well, through linguistic duality: colloquial Portuguese, enhanced by copious *Maírum* vocabulary for which no exact translation exists. Use of the indigenous tongue, along with its speech patterns, solidifies an autochthonous atmosphere already pregnant with native flora and fauna. The rhythmic prose, multiple levels of symbolism, and lively descriptions all proved R. to be a competent, first-time novelist, while the committed tone and dialectic development of the novel make for convincing polemics.

O mulo (1982; the mule) is his first confessional novel. Its more than five hundred pages project the backward psyche of an old land baron whose *goiano* rusticity is encased in layers of somber eroticism, machismo, brutishness, violence, and intolerance. The novel has an oral spontaneousness heightened by the intimate and informal nature inherent in any dying person telling all, as well as by the rambling prolixity of its very opinionated and self-serving character.

In *Utopia selvagem* (1982; savage utopia) R. subverts genres, blending legends, (un)official history, essay, polemics, and pamphleteering into a loosely structured, satirical discussion of, and attack on current Brazilian society, its values and identity. R. juxtaposes luxuriant indigenous settings with echoes of concrete and steel metropolises. He sets his fable, as inferred in the title, around the sights, sounds, smells, and tastes of autochthonous nations still largely unscathed by *caraíba*, or white contact. Meanwhile, an obtrusive, humorous, and sardonic first-person narrator shortens the distance between himself, the reader, and the reluctant antihero. His constant intrusions, in an informal language studded with slang, foreign neologisms, indigenous terminology, and explicit sexual epithets, succeed in interpreting extraneous goings-on as much as they propel the protagonist forward. Such is the comedic intent of the piece, in fact, that even the hallowed tenants of traditional Indianism are relegated to providing little more than contrast in the form of a colorful if catalytic backdrop. The protagonist, on the other hand, is a passive and vulnerable main character-victim, definitely more comic than tragic. His major comedic thrust is the way in which his virility is progressively erased. His carnivalized reversal of the traditional, composite macho role is made that much more ironic, given his race, region of origin, and profession. He is apt to appear reluctantly and more often naked than clothed; Amazons first depilate his body, then reduce him to being a humiliated, zoomorphic appendage of his genitalia—a sort of ritualistic male rape that may also be seen as a metaphoric reversal. Unlike in the real world, the Indians possess the upper hand as well as the secret to societal success.

Although uniquely autobiographical, R.'s *Migo* (1988) shares with *O mulo* the presence of an aging and overbearing male narrator-character, a prolixity in keeping with spontaneous, informal and repetitive mental meanderings, and a pervasive sense of ribald earthiness. Nonetheless, *Migo* is, in fact, a sophisticated cross section of the views, left and right, held by that generation of Brazil's intelligentsia most responsible for the nation's dismal state of affairs. A multiplicity of focus is elaborated throughout nearly two hundred short, titled chapter entries, many of which conclude with a brief, unidentified if often famous quote that serves as a kind of posterior motif. These fragmented entries are then arranged in six blocks, all but the first prefaced by the progressing dialectic discord surrounding a colossal womblike construction. The individual blocks may also be read out of conventional order, through an imaginative pattern, or *roteiro*, outlined at the beginning.

Rather than subverting style to fit the oftentimes radical notions that characterize his intellectual trajectory, R. has turned his works into a fictional and expository celebration of national consciousness. Telluric epic and allegory combine with scatology and eroticism; political treatise joins tragicomedy, farce, and parody; and ethnological essay is fleshed out through pulsating figures whose varying autobiographical bents aptly evoke, as well, facets of the Brazilian character. Indeed, for those willing to look, the author's fiction, to date, reinforces and synthesizes the numerous essays for which he is best known worldwide.

FURTHER WORKS: *Religião e mitologia Kadiwéu* (1950); *Linguas e culturas indigenas no Brasil* (1951); *A poética indígena brasileira* (1962); *A universidade necessária* (1969); *As Américas e a civilização* (1970); *Os índios e a civilização* (1970); *Configurações histórico-culturais dos povos americanos* (1975); *Uirá sai a procura de Deus* (1976); *O dilema da América Latina* (1978); *Ensaios insólitos* (1979); *Aos trancos e barrancos; como o Brasil deu no que deu* (1985); *Sobre o óbvio* (1986); *Testemunho* (1990); *A gestação do Brasil* (1995)

BIBLIOGRAPHY: Johnson, R., "D. R.," in Stern, I., ed., *Dictionary of Brazilian Literature* (1988): 287–88; Silverman, M., on *Migo, WLT*, 63, 2 (Spring 1989): 287–88; Columbus, C. K., "Mother Earth in Amazonia and in the Andes: D. R. and Jose Maria Arguedos," in Dennis, P. A., and W. Aycock, eds., *Literature and Anthropology* (1989); Lucas, F., "Memoirs Told to the Mirror," *Tropical Paths: Essays on Modern Braziliam Literature* (1993): 162-82

—MALCOLM SILVERMAN

RIBEIRO, João Ubaldo

Brazilian novelist and short-story writer, b. 23 Jan. 1940, Itaparica

R. was born and still resides in Itaparica, a large island across All Saints' Bay from the city of Salvador, the colonial capital of Brazil from 1549 to 1763. Proud of its multiracial heritage and its respect for tradition, Bahia, as Salvador and its surrounding areas are commonly known, is regarded as the place where the present and the past of Brazil meet, and where the roots of Brazilian culture are most authentically preserved. Although R. is by no means a regionalist writer, his work reflects the sense of both national history and national pride deeply ingrained in the Bahian mind. Trained as a lawyer at the University of Bahia, R. later attended the University of Southern California, where he earned his M. A. in

political science and public administration and perfected his command of English to the point that he has been able to translate his own novels. Returning to Bahia upon completion of his degree, R. resumed his career as a journalist, taught for some time at the Federal University, and has dedicated increasingly larger amounts of time to writing fiction.

Although individually R.'s works are characterized by a great diversity of subject matter, settings, tone, and styles, they are linked by an awareness of the past history and present problems of Brazil, and by a concern for the controversial question of national identity.

R.'s first novel, *Setembro não tem sentido* (1968; September has no meaning), is a semiautobiographical account of the trials and tribulations of a group of young intellectuals in a still provincial city of Salvador. Although the novel is ostensibly set during the political turnoil that followed the abrupt resignation of President Jânio Quardros on 25 August 1961, it evokes the anxiety, insecurity, and hopelessness of R.'s generation as Brazil is about to enter the most authoritarian phase in the country's modern history, the dark years from 1969 to 1974 known as *sufoco* (choking). Written in a harsh poetic prose, R.'s next work, *Sargento Getúlio* (1971; *Sergeant Getulio*, 1978), is a rambling monologue by the title character, a gunman who has been hired by a political boss to capture and deliver one of the boss's enemies. Ordered by his boss to set the prisoner free when political conditions abruptly change, Getulio refuses to bend and vows to carry out his assignment even as federal troops are sent after him and eventually kill him. Although Getulio is capable of the most savage actions against his fellow human beings, he is also somewhat of a tragic hero, who remains completely faithful to his principles, and whose unshakable sense of duty lies above opportunism and political expediency. *Sargento Getúlio*, is thematically and formally R.'s most subversive work. *Vencecavalo e. o outro povo* (1974; Overcomes-Horses and the other people), a collection of five interconnected short stories, is an irreverent and iconoclastic satire, whose light tone masks a serious examination of a host of important national issues, ranging from government corruption and ineptitude to the consequences of colonialism and economic dependence. Published when censorship was just beginning to be relaxed, this work relies on parody, allegory, allusion, and a Rabelaisian delight in linguistic excess to create an antihistory of Brazil, which demystifies and deconstructs official history.

R.'s three most recent novels are products of both the growing liberalization that began in the late 1970s and of the increasing doubts of Brazilians about the prospects for their country. Rejecting the symbolism and stylization of the two preceding works, *Vila Real* (1979; Vila Real) is a straightforward incursion into the old problem of economic deprivation in the Brazilian Northeast. *Viva o povo brasileiro* (1984; *An Invincible Memory*, 1989) is a massive historical novel, intertwining imagined situations with well-known historical events, and spinning stories about the interconnections of dozens of characters from different segments of Brazilian society over a period ranging from 1647 to 1977. R.'s next novel, the more somber and bitter *O sorriso do lagarto* (1989; *The Lizard's Smile*, 1994), is a biting satire depicting a corrupted society that has lost its moral bearings. Parodying many of the devices used in soap operas, pornographic films, and popular fiction, this story of decadence can be viewed as a literary counterpart to the pessimism brought about by the aimlessness of José Sarney's government (1985–1990) and the worsening economic crisis of the late 1980s.

A masterful storyteller and an impeccable stylist, R. is one of the most talented contemporary writers from Brazil. As more translations of his works become available, R. is sure to gain the international recognition he unquestionably deserves.

FURTHER WORKS: *Livro de histórias* (1981); *Política* (1981); *Vida e paixão macro de Pandonar, o cruel* (1983); *Sempre aos domingos* (1988); *A vingança de Charles Tiburone* (1990); *Já podes da pàtria filhos* (1991)

BIBLIOGRAPHY: Solomon, B. P., "Dupes of Authority," *NYTBR* (9 April 1978): 11; Amado, J., Introduction to *Sergeant Getulio* (1978): ix–xii; Bumpus, J., on *Sergeant Getulio, PR*, 46, 4 (1979): 634–35; DiAntonio, R., "Chthonian Visions and Mythic Redemption in J. U. R.'s *Sergeant Getulio,*" *MFS*, 32, 3 (Autumn 1986): 449–58; Valente, L. F., on *An Invincible Memory, WLT*, 64, 2 (Spring 1990): 288–89; Stern, I., on *O sorriso do lagarto, WLT*, 64, 2 (Spring 1990): 286; Valente, L. F., "Fiction as History: The Case of J. U. R.," *LARR*, 28, 1 (1993): 41-60

—LUIZ FERNANDO VALENTE

RIBEYRO, Julio Ramón

Peruvian novelist, short-story writer, dramatist, and essayist, b. 31 Aug. 1929, Lima

Like many other contemporary Latin American writers, R. has lived outside his native country for much of his adult life. He was born and raised in Lima, but after graduating from Catholic University he traveled to Europe, attracted by the opportunity to study and work there. Since 1960 he has lived in Paris, where, in addition to his literary endeavors, he has worked for the France-Presse Agency and UNESCO.

Although R. has published significant works in all genres except poetry, it is in fiction that he excels. His first work, *Los gallinazos sin plumas* (1955; buzzards without feathers), a collection of short stories, was one of the first in Peru to focus on the special problems of post-World War II urban dwellers, especially those who suffer from economic and emotional deprivation. Without in any way lecturing or shrilly condemning anyone, he is able to strip away the impersonal mask that tends to obscure the individual tragedies of large-scale poverty in the city. In his second book, *Cuentos de circunstancias* (1958; stories of circumstances), R. subtly fuses mundane reality with the magical and inexplicable. His other two short-story collections, *Tres historias sublevantes* (1964; three stories of revolt) and *Las botellas y los hombres* (1964; bottles and men), present characters and concerns similar to those treated in the first book.

Rounding out his major fictional production are two novels: *Crónica de San Gabriel* (1960; chronicle of San Gabriel) and *Los geniecillos dominicales* (1965; Sunday temper). It is unfortunate that *Crónica de San Gabriel*, a novel of subtle insights and intriguing symbolism, has not received wider attention. Although R. is primarily an interpreter of urban life, his depiction of a decaying feudal system in rural Peru demonstrates a profound understanding of the historical forces at work there. Focusing on the confusion, melancholy, and sordid vices of the descendants of formerly powerful and rich land barons of the Peruvian sierra, R. captures the spiritual and economic poverty of a social system now clearly in the throes of death. In *Los geniecillos dominicales* R. turns his attention to the search for values by youths of university

age in Lima. The youngsters are disillusioned by the moral shortcomings and hypocrisy of their elders, but at the same time they inevitably encounter their own lack of courage and discipline.

Alienation, in fact, is the dominating theme in all of R.'s fiction. The reader is introduced to characters from the lower and middle classes who live as victims on the fringes of a world that ultimately shuts them out. R. has an uncanny ability to convey the rhythm and nuances of spoken language and to capture the most subtle and complex psychological states. Although he has been overshadowed by Mario Vargas LLOSA, it seems likely that R. will be recognized as one of Peru's most gifted writers.

FURTHER WORKS: *Santiago el pajarero* (1959); *La palabra del mudo* (1972); *La juventud en la otra ribera* (1973); *Dos soledades* (1974); *La caza sutil* (1975); *Teatro* (1975); *Cambio de guardia* (1976); *Prosas apátridas aumentadas* (1978); *Atusparia* (1981)

BIBLIOGRAPHY: Aldrich, E. M., Jr., *The Modern Short Story in Peru* (1966): 146–47; Luchting, W., "Recent Peruvian Fiction: Vargas Llosa, R., and Arguedas," *RS*, No. 35 (1968): 277–83; Luchting, W., *J. R. R. y sus dobles* (1971); Losada Guido, A., *Creación y praxis: La producción literaria como praxis social en Hispanoamérica y el Perú* (1976): 82–94; Tamayo Vargas, A., *Literatura peruana* (1976): 594–608; Luchting, W., *Escritores peruanos que piensan que dicen* (1977): 45–61

—EARL M. ALDRICH, JR.

RICARDO, Cassiano

Brazilian poet and essayist, b. 25 July 1895, São José dos Campos; d. 15 Jan. 1974, São Paulo

Born on a small farm outside São Paulo, R. began to compose his first poems around the age of ten. Later, as a law student, he published his first book of verse, *Dentro da noite* (1915; inside of night), a lyrical and melancholy work written in the SYMBOLIST vein. After a brief experiment with Parnassianism, *Evangelho de Pã* (1917; Gospel of Pan; expanded ed., *A frauta de Pã*, 1925; Pan's pipe), and political activism (of a nationalistic bent), R. began to take an active interest in the incipient MODERNIST revolt then getting under way in Brazil. In 1923 R. formed a literary group, Anta (Tapir), and began to espouse a sociologically grounded theory of art, one that exalted authentic indigenous values and types. An active and prolific writer, by 1936, R. was regarded as one of Brazil's most significant modernist poets. In 1937 he was elected to the Brazilian Academy of Letters, and in 1971 he won the National Prize for Literature.

R. is remembered, above all else, as a leading proponent of literary nationalism in Brazil. His politics, literary and aesthetic in nature, were, after the revolution of 1930, often confused with the overtly fascist stance adopted by one of R.'s literary colleagues, Plínio Salgado (b. 1895). *Vamos caçar papagaios* (1926; let's go parrot hunting), R.'s best known early work, utilizes the language of the people and emphasizes purely Brazilian themes. *Deixa estar, jacaré* (1931; let it be, crocodile), a later effort, gives free rein to an artistically and theoretically refined nationalism.

R.'s greatest literary achievement is *Martim Cererê* (1928; Martim Cererê), a comprehensive view of Brazil and Brazilian civilization which is epic in scope and which celebrates what the poet feels are the most salient and unique characteristics of the Brazilian people, who, in a collective sense, constitute the hero of the poem. Focusing on the story of São Paulo's growth into the dynamic metropolis it is today, R. sings of the virtues of racial mixing, which is presented as a singularly positive Brazilian attribute, and of the untapped reservoirs of strength that reside deep within a people formed out of a blending of three distinct racial stocks. The title is, in fact, a portmanteau name composed of the following elements: "Saci Pererê," the Indian; "Saci Cererê," the black African; and "Martins Pereira," the white European, or Portuguese. Colorful and boisterous, highly mythic and metaphorical, *Martim Cererê* grew out of a children's poem into a paean not only to the diversity of Brazil's ethnic and cultural makeup but to its potentially great future as well.

Although in *O sangue das horas* (1943; the blood of the hours) R. had proved that he could write verse that speaks more directly to social problems, he never strayed far from his foremost preoccupation as a poet: how to discover and bring to the attention of his fellow citizens all that was uniquely, truly, and unmistakably Brazilian in their land. Innovative in technique but consistent in his basic theme, R., by the end of his life, had succeeded in developing a poetic voice that was at once distinctive in style and totally Brazilian in subject matter.

FURTHER WORKS: *Jardim das Hespérides* (1920); *Atalanta (A mentirosa de olhos verdes)* (1923); *Borrões de verde e amarelo* (1926); *Canções da minha ternura* (1930); *O Brasil no original* (1936); *O negro na bandeira* (1938); *A Academia e a poesia moderna* (1939); *Pedro Luís visto pelos modernos* (1939); *Marcha para o oesta* (1940); *A Academia e a língua brasileira* (1943); *Um dia depois do outro* (1947); *A face perdida* (1950); *Poemas murais* (1950); *Vinte e cinco sonetos* (1952); *A poesia na técnica do romance* (1953); *O Tratado de Petrópolis* (2 vols., 1954); *Meu caminho até ontem* (1955); *O arranha-céu de vidro 1954* (1956); *Pequeno ensaio de bandeirologia* (1956); *João Torto e a fábula* (1956); *Poesias completas* (1957); *O homem cordial* (1959); *A difícil manhã* (1960); *Montanha russa* (1960); *Algumas reflexões sobre poesia de vanguarda* (1964); *Antologia poética* (1964); *Jeremias sem chorar* (1964); *O Indianismo de Gonçalves Dias* (1964); *22 e a poesia de hoje* (1964); *Poesia praxis e 22* (1966); *Viagem no tempo e no espaço* (1970); *Os sobreviventes* (1971). FURTHER WORKS IN ENGLISH: *Marginal Voices: Selected Stories* (1993)

BIBLIOGRAPHY: Nist, J., *The Modernist Movement in Brazil* (1967), passim; Martins, W., *The Modernist Idea* (1970): 184–99 and passim; Foster, D., and V. R. Foster, *Modern Latin American Literature* (1975), Vol. 2: 249–53

—EARL E. FITZ

RICARDOU, Jean

French novelist and critic, b. 17 June 1932, Cannes

Until 1977 R. was a full-time schoolteacher. He received a Ph.D. for his published works in 1975, twenty years after he had taken his last university degree. Since 1970 he has taught often in Canadian and American universities.

R.'s career is a telling illustration of the convergence that took place in France during the 1960s and 1970s of the practice of fiction and the theoretical activity engaged in by the writers themselves. The appearance of R.'s theoretical work coincided with the development of semiotics in European and American universities and thus helped in shaping analytical concepts basic to the formal methodology of literary studies. In fact, R. became known as much for his theoretical assessment of the NEW NOVEL and its antecedents as for his own literary works. Associated at first with the influential literary journal *Tel Quel*, R. later acquired his own distinctive identity and became a major theoretician of the New Novel with *Problèmes du nouveau roman* (1967; problems of the new novel), *Pour une théorie du nouveau roman* (1971; for a theory of the new novel), and *Le nouveau roman* (1973; the new novel). He also organized three significant colloquia and edited their proceedings: *Nouveau roman: Hier, aujourd'hui* (2 vols., 1972), *Claude Simon: Analyse, théorie* (1975), and *Robbe-Grillet: Analyse, théorie* (2 vols., 1976).

This aspect of R.'s work has somewhat obscured his own fiction, too often understood to be a mere application of his theories. Beyond the technical interest, however, there is also in his work a strong political and philosophical emphasis, exemplified by his fight against the two "dogmas" of "expression" and "representation" in literature and by his assertion that writing is a "production" designed to resist ideology and unconscious repression.

L'observatoire de Cannes (1961; the Cannes observatory) is clearly in the New Novel tradition, with its reliance on optical effects and the permutations among elements of the narrative (themselves typical of the period: trains, postcards, photographs, optical instruments, dispassionate eroticism). In *Les lieux-dits: Petit guide d'un voyage dans le livre* (1969); place names: a little guide for a trip through the book), the self-representation of the writing process and the exploration of its ambiguous effects borrow some formal aspects from detective stories—another feature of many New Novels. *Révolutions minuscules* (1971; minuscule revolutions) is a collection of brief pieces that explore the fictional effects produced by minimal displacements within the system of textual elements. R.'s most ambitious work, however, is *La prise de Constantinople* (1965; the capture of Constantinople), which carries the alternate title *La prose de Constantinople* (the prose of Constantinople). In this work many features of his other fictions are rearranged in an even more complex fashion. *La prise de Constantinople* is inseparable from the detailed analysis of it provided by R. in *Nouveaux problèmes du roman* (1978; new problems of the novel).

R.'s novels do not purport to refer to the "real" world, and they do not partake of the traditional function of literature as a means to explore interiority. While achieving this severance from tradition, R.'s fictions make his theoretical positions a necessary reference for understanding them. His novels require the reader to become an active partner. If they make for good reading, they seem to do so more because of their uncanny character than because of the ideological self-examination they are supposed to induce on the part of the reader.

FURTHER WORKS: *Paradigme* (1976); *Albert Ayme* (1976); *Le théâtre des métamorphoses* (1982)

BIBLIOGRAPHY: Rice, D. B., "The Excentricities of J. R.'s *La prise/prose de Constantinople*," *IFR*, 2 (1975): 106–12; Ricardou, J., "Composition Discomposed," *CritI*, 3 (1976): 79–91; Ricardou, J., "Birth of a Fiction," *CritI*, 4 (1977): 221–30; Higgins, L. A.,

"Typographical Eros: Reading R. in the Third Dimension," *YFS*, 57 (1979): 180–94; Higgins, L. A., *Parables of Theory: J. R.'s Metafiction* (1984)

—M. PIERSSENS

RICE, Elmer

(pseud. of Elmer Leopold Reizenstein) American dramatist, b. 28 Sept. 1892, New York, N.Y.; d. 8 May 1967, Southampton, England

R., whose grandparents were immigrants, worked his way through night school and law school. Success came elsewhere, however, with his play *On Trial* (perf. 1914, pub. 1919). Drawing on his experience as a clerk and on his legal training, R. launched a career in the theater noteworthy for its commitment both to experimentation and to ideology. On *Trial* was the first American play to utilize the cinematic technique of flashback in order to highlight a well-crafted plot in which a miscarriage of justice is averted. It was an overnight hit. Fifteen years later he won a Pulitzer Prize for *Street Scene* (1929), a play R. regarded as experimenting with a more intricate formula than that of *On Trial*.

One of America's most prolific playwrights, R. was determined to fuse form and content in both his life and his work. This principle motivated his film scripts from two of his own plays (*Street Scene*

Elmer Rice

in 1931; *Counsellor-at-Law* [1931] in 1933), his choice of plays to direct, his desire to establish repertory theater groups, his teaching, his helping to found the Dramatists' Guild in 1937, his serving as regional director for the WPA's Federal Theater Project during the Depression, and his involvement with organizations for social change—he attacked censorship throughout his life and blacklisting in the 1950s.

Thus, he could confidently assert that all his plays confirmed his conviction that nothing was "as important in life as freedom." An early play that deals with social and individual freedom directly is *The Adding Machine* (1923). The stylized form that R. devised borrows EXPRESSIONIST devices from European drama. But R. localized them in a prattling, homey speech rooted in the American idiom. Although frequently overshadowed by Eugene O'NEILL, R. proved in *The Adding Machine* not only that he could create in the symbolic mode but also that he could evoke real human beings—even in fantastic settings. Mr. Zero, a nowhere man whose job is replaced by a machine that out performs him, is not a likable character. But despite R.'s mixture of vulgarity and sardonic pity, we become intensely aware of Mr. Zero's lack of external and internal freedom. The tragicomical form assails society unequivocally.

That we possess the capacity to solve the problem of freedom is the argument of *Street Scene*. The scene is a tenement street in New York City, a neighborhood of ethnic multiplicity interacting with prejudice and love. The play's swirling realism renders the elusive sense of place. Yet for all its qualities of a genre painting, the play's interlaced plot hammers out a pulsating denunciation of the city's monolithic power to oppress. Rose Maurrant refuses to succumb to this force: tempted to follow her heart and marry Sam Kaplan, she opts to go it alone. In 1947 *Street Scene* was transformed into an opera with R. providing the spoken dialogue, Kurt Weill the score, and Langston HUGHES the lyrics.

Form did not always follow content in several of R.'s later plays, particularly as he became more engaged by social issues and zigzagged between melodrama and comedy. *Counsellor-at-Law*, however, the story of a rags-to-riches lawyer threatened with disbarment, artfully connects the implications of the outer world—shown in the vistas of New York City looming through the set's huge office windows—with the microcosm of the beleaguered hero victimized by "high" society. *We, the People* (1933), an amalgam of techniques from Street Scene and the novels of John Dos PASSOS, seeks a different kind of panorama, a social one, in order to politicize the audience. Melodramatic touches exist in these plays, but the comic effects of the more narrowly focused *Left Bank* (1931) and *Dream Girl* (1945) successfully satirize America's cultural sterility. Whether dealing with expatriates or a dreamy heroine, R.'s ultimate faith rests in the potential for the self to take control of its chimeras, not to be dominated by them.

R. deserves more respect than he has received. When his vision meshes with its expression, his plays are impressive achievements. Too often he settled for re-creating only his ideas. But he was a mirror of his times, reflecting in innovative structures the social changes America was experiencing during his lifetime.

FURTHER WORKS: *The House in Blind Alley* (perf. 1914, pub. 1932); *The Iron Cross* (perf. 1917, pub. 1965); *Wake Up, Jonathan* (perf. 1921, pub. 1928, with Hatcher Hughes); *Close Harmony; or, The Lady Next Door* (perf. 1924, pub. 1929, with Dorothy Parker); *Cock Robin* (perf. 1928, pub. 1929, with Philip Barry); *The Subway* (1929); *See Naples and Die* (perf. 1929, pub. 1935); *A Voyage to*

Purilia (1930); *Black Sheep* (perf. 1932, pub. 1938); *Judgment Day* (1934); *Between Two Worlds* (perf. 1934, pub. 1935); *Three Plays without Words*, (1934); *Not for Children* (pub. 1935, prod. as *Life Is Real*, 1937; rev. and pub. 1951); *Imperial City* (1937); *American Landscape* (perf. 1938, pub. 1939); *Two on an Island* (1940); *Flight to the West* (1941); *A New Life* (perf. 1943, pub. 1944); *The Show Must Go On* (1949); *The Grand Tour* (perf. 1951, pub. 1952); *The Winner* (1954); *Cue for Passion* (perf. 1958, pub. 1959); *Love among the Ruins* (perf. 1958, pub. 1963); *The Living Theatre* (1959); *Minority Report: An Autobiography* (1963)

BIBLIOGRAPHY: Levin, M., "E. R.," *Theatre Arts* (Jan. 1932): 54–63; Rabkin, G., *Drama and Commitment: Politics in the American Theater of the Thirties* (1964): 237–59; Hogan, R., *The Independence of E. R.* (1965); Durham, F., *E. R.*(1970); Palmieri, A. F. R., *E. R.: A Playwright's Vision of America* (1980)

—JAMES B. ATKINSON

RICH, Adrienne

American poet and theorist, b. 16 May 1929, Baltimore, Md.

R.'s parents were cultivated upper-middle-class Southerners. Her father was Jewish and a professor of medicine, her gentile mother a former concert pianist and composer. This ethnic mixture and its cultural and emotional meanings for R.'s life have been a subject of her writings since the late 1970s. R.'s parents, particularly her mother, devoted a great deal of time and energy to her early education in literature and music. After graduation from Radcliffe College (1951), R. entered into her professional career as a writer, uneasily combining this work, in the early years, with her roles as Harvard faculty wife and mother of three young sons. The tensions inherent in this dual life are reflected in her collection of poems *Snapshots of a Daughter-in-Law: Poems, 1954–1962* (1963; rev. ed., 1967). From 1966 to 1979, after leaving Cambridge, R. lived in the New York area, where she taught at Columbia's School of the Arts, the City College of New York, and Rutgers University. She lived for several years in western Massachusetts, where she edited the lesbian feminist journal *Sinister Wisdom*, and since the mid-1980s has been established in California, where she holds a professorship in English and feminist studies at Stanford University.

R. is widely regarded as one of the major American poets and the single most important American woman poet of the second half of the 20th c. As her work has come increasingly to reflect the influence of feminism and to contribute to that movement, she has retained the recognition and respect that her mastery of poetic craft won her in literary circles; this situation is extremely rare for American writers who are identified as "ideological," especially those whose ideology tends to the left of center.

R.'s career as an author spans more than forty years from her first published collection of poems, *A Change of World* (1951), to the recent *Dark Fields of the Republic* (1995); hers is an exceptionally long and rich production. Despite the conflicts and frustrations that many poems themselves record. R.'s is also a career in which recognition came early. *A Change of World* was selected for the Yale series of Younger Poets Award in 1951 by W. H. AUDEN, who wrote respectfully—if somewhat condescendingly—in the collection's preface of R.'s stylistic acumen. This elegance is mentioned

Adrienne Rich

by most of the critics who commented on her first several volumes. As early as her second collection. *The Diamond Cutters and Other Poems* (1955), however, Donald Hall (b. 1928) was able to contrast its immersion in lived experience with what he called the "smug" detachment of her first book; here, he claims, "the wolf is inside and is busy writing poems about its successful campaign."

Feminist themes began to emerge with *Snapshots of a Daughter-in-Law: Poems, 1954–1962*, published before there was an organized social or literary movement around such issues. Those themes became more explicit and more in touch with the collective insights of the women's movement in *The Will to Change* (1971) and *Diving into the Wreck: Poems, 1971–1972* (1973). By the time of the publication of *The Dream of a Common Language: Poems, 1974–1977* (1978). R.'s poetry had itself become a source for a feminist theory, and this volume has been described as a mythic feminist manifesto. R.'s feminism has also served her, from the 1970s on, as a way of apprehending and writing poems about the condition of other oppressed and colonized groups.

R.'s prose includes essays in feminist literary criticism—notably the essays "When We Dead Awaken" (1972) and "*Jane Eyre*: Secrets of a Motherless Daughter" (1978)—as well as contributions to social theory. The book-length study *Of Woman Born: Motherhood as Experience and Institution* (1976) examines motherhood, as its subtitle indicates, as both experience and institution and has become a landmark in feminist analysis of the maternal condition; the essay "Compulsory Heterosexuality and Lesbian Existence" (1980), with its key notion of the "lesbian continuum," is equally central to the development of radical feminist and lesbian theory.

One of the hallmarks of R.'s writing, throughout, has been her concern for language as both a tool and a conceptual universe. As her poetry and her life have become more explicitly political, she has managed neither to abandon that concern not to identify discourse with action. Rather, as she maintains in her first volume of collected prose pieces, *On Lies, Secrets, and Silence: Selected Prose, 1966–1978* (1979): "Poetry is, among other things, a criticism of language. Poetry is, above all, a concentration of the power of language, which is the power of our ultimate relationship to everything in the universe."

FURTHER WORKS: *Necessities of Life: Poems, 1952–1955* (1960); *Selected Poems* (1967); *Leaflets: Poems, 1965–1968* (1969); *Poems: Selected and New, 1950–1974* (1974); *Twenty-One Love Poems* (1976); *A Wild Patience Has Taken Me This Far: Poems, 1978–1981* (1981); *Sources* (1983); *The Fact of a Doorframe: Poems Selected and New, 1950–1984* (1984); *Blood, Bread, and Poetry: Selected Prose, 1979–1986* (1986); *Time's Power, Poems 1985–1988* (1989); *An Atlas of the Difficult World: Poems 1988-1991* (1991); *What is Found There: Notebooks on Poetry and Politics* (1993); *Dark Fields of the Republic: Poems 1991-1995* (1995)

BIBLIOGRAPHY: Gelpi, B. C. and Gelpi, A., *A. R.'s Poetry* (1975); Juhasz, S., *Naked and Fiery Forms* (1976): 177–204; DuPlessis, R. B., "The Critique of Consciousness and Myth in Levertov, R., and Rukeyser," in Gilbert, S. M., and Gubar, S., eds., *Shakespeare's Sisters* (1979): 280–300; Ostriker, A., "Her Cargo: A. R. and the Common Language," *APR*, 8, 4 (July-Aug. 1979): 6–10; Cooper, J. R., *Reading A. R.* (1984); Martin, W., *An American Triptych: Anne Bradstreet, Emily Dickinson, and A. R.* (1984); Keyes, C., *The Aesthesics of Power: The Poetry of A. R.* (1986); Werner, C. H., *A. R.: The Poet and the Critics* (1988); Templeton, A., *The Dream and the Dialogue: A. R.'s Feminist Poetics* (1994)

—LILLIAN S. ROBINSON

RICHARDS, I(vor) A(rmstrong)

English critic, educator, and poet, b. 26 Feb. 1893, Sandbach; d. 7 Sept. 1979, Cambridge

R. was educated at Magdalene College, Cambridge. In 1922 he became Lecturer in English and moral sciences and four years later a Fellow of Magdalene College. In 1929–30 he taught at the Tsing Hua University, Peking, and in 1939 he joined the faculty at Harvard. After his retirement in 1963 he continued his varied and prolific career as a writer, producing poetry and verse drama as well as studies in literature, language, education, and philosophy.

In his early critical works—*The Foundations of Aesthetics* (1922, with C. K. Ogden and James Wood), *Principles of Literary Criticism* (1924), *Science and Poetry* (1926), and *Practical Criticism* (1929)—R. examined aesthetic questions in the light of recent developments in psychology and linguistics. His criticism was more systematic and tough minded than much that preceded it, but it suffered in places from R.'s excessive faith in the methods and assumptions of science. He sometimes seemed ready to reduce

aesthetic questions to problems in neuropsychology and aesthetic experience to a means of psychotherapy.

Moreover, R.'s distinctions between "emotive" and "referential" language seemed to undercut his claims for the value and importance of poetry. The "referential language" of science, R. wrote, makes statements about matters of verifiable fact. These statements may be true or false, depending upon whether the references are correct; but the "emotive language" of poetry makes "pseudo statements" whose only function is "to bring about and support attitudes," and "it matters not at all" whether the references are correct. The term "truth," R. argued, should be restricted to science. What is "true" in poetry is simply what "completes or accords with the rest of the experience" to arouse the desired response in the reader.

Although R.'s early criticism was attacked for "psychologistic" or "scientistic" bias, it was widely influential. His theory that the "equilibrium, of opposed impulses" is the "ground plan of the most valuable aesthetic responses" laid the basis for the doctrine of New Criticism that irony is the defining characteristic of poetic structure and the source of poetry's unique value. R.'s experiment, described in *Practical Criticism*, of having students comment on poems without their knowing the authors or titles, is often regarded as a major influence upon the New Critical emphasis on close reading of individual poems and the resulting revolution in the criticism and teaching of literature that took place in American universities during the second quarter of this century.

R.'s later criticism was less influential, but it exhibited his continued openness to new ideas and his willingness to revise his thinking. In *The Philosophy of Rhetoric* (1936) R. turned from psychology to rhetoric for the basis of his poetic theory. R. now argued that scientific language, where "words have, or should have" clearly defined, stable meanings, does not provide an adequate model for the study of other forms of discourse, where words "incessantly change their meanings with the sentences they go into and the contexts they derive from." Celebrating this ambiguity as the source of the "subtlety" and "suppleness" of language and of "its power to serve us," R. now developed theoretical grounds for the close verbal analysis of poetry that he had already advocated in *Practical Criticism*.

R.'s continued interests in language and education made him an influential figure in those fields as well as in literary criticism, and after the 1930s those subjects, along with his own poetry, almost entirely supplanted literary theory in his writing. Beginning with *The Meaning of Meaning: A Study of the Influence of Language upon Thought and of the Science of Symbolism* (1923, with C. K. Ogden) R. published numerous studies of language and its relationships to thought and learning. He argued the value of Ogden's Basic English, a simplified language with an 850-word vocabulary, in such books as *Basic in Teaching: East and West* (1935), *Interpretation in Teaching* (1938), *How to Read a Page: A Course in Efficient Reading with an Introduction to a Hundred Great Words* (1942), and *Basic English and Its Uses* (1943). He also developed a pictorial method of teaching foreign languages and a number of elementary language textbooks based upon it.

R.'s early books on literary theory did much to determine the course of English and American literary studies in this century. More than any other writer, he bridged the gap between the two cultures of science and literature and offered a convincing defense of literary study as a necessary pursuit in the modern world. R.'s early criticism provided the foundation for a monumental edifice of formalist literary criticism, but R. was never willing to enclose himself within any intellectual edifice—even one of his own construction. The multiplicity of R.'s interests and his continued openness to new ideas led him to explore new intellectual frontiers while other critics were following paths he had earlier charted. As a result, R.'s influence upon the study of language and literature seems likely to reach farther and last longer than that of any other critic of his age.

FURTHER WORKS: *Mencius on the Mind: Experiments in Multiple Definition* (1932); *Basic Rules of Reason* (1933); *Coleridge on Imagination* (1934); *Plato, The Republic: A New Version, Founded on Basic English* (1942); *Nations and Peace* (1947); *Speculative Instruments* (1955); *Goodbye Earth, and Other Poems* (1958); *Coleridge's Minor Poems* (1960); *The Screens and Other Poems* (1960); *Tomorrow Morning, Faustus!* (1962); *Why So, Socrates? A Dramatic Version of Plato's Dialogues* (1964); *Design for Escape: World Education through Modern Media* (1968); *So Much Nearer: Essays toward a World English* (1968); *Poetries and Sciences* (1970); *Internal Colloquies* (1971); *Beyond* (1974); *Poetries: Their Media and Ends* (1974); *Complementarities: Uncollected Essays* (1976); *New and Selected Poems* (1978); *R. on Rhetoric: I. A. R., Selected Essays* (1991)

BIBLIOGRAPHY: Ransom, J. C., *The New Criticism* (1941): 3–101; Crane, R. S., "I.A.R. on the Art of Interpretation," in Crane, R. S., ed., *Critics and Criticism, Ancient and Modern* (1952): 27–44; Krieger, M., *The New Apologists for Poetry* (1956): 57–63, 113–22 and passim; Wimsatt, W. K. and C. Brooks, *Literary Criticism: A Short History* (1957); Hotopf, W. H. N., *Language, Thought and Comprehension: A Case Study of the Writings of I. A. R.* (1965); Rackin, P., "Hulme, R., and the Development of Contextualist Poetic Theory," *JAAC*, 25 (1967): 413–25; Wellek, R., "On Rereading I. A. R.," *SoR*, 3 (1967): 533–54; Schiller, J. P., *I. A. R.'s Theory of Literature* (1969); Brower, R., Vendler, H. and Hollander, J. eds., *I. A. R.: Essays in His Honor* (1973); Russo, J. P., *I. A. R.: His Life and Work* (1989)

—PHYLLIS RACKIN

RICHARDSON, Dorothy Miller

English novelist, short-story writer, and essayist, b. 17 May 1873, Abingdon, Berkshire; d. 17 June 1957, Beckenham, Kent

R. was the third of four daughters in a nonconformist family. Her father, who inherited his tradesman father's fortune, devoted himself to the life of a gentleman patron of science until he was overtaken by financial disaster. Her mother, from the yeoman-landholding class, fostered what R. would call her own deep-rooted suspicion of "facts." Thus R.'s early experiences were dominated by sharp contrasts in outlook and mood as family life changed from order and comfort to actual penury.

Ultimately R.'s mother committed suicide, and R.'s three sisters escaped into marriage. But R., at seventeen, had secured a post as pupil-teacher in Hanover, Germany. After six months she returned to England and took various jobs as teacher, as governess, and eventually as clerk-assistant in a London dental office.

These and other autobiographical details are incorporated in the story of Miriam Henderson's "pilgrimage," a fictional transmutation of R.'s life from adolescence through the years when she was working in London, making friends with—and debating—avant-garde artists and intellectuals, anarchists, Russian Jews, suffragists, and Fabian socialists, including George Bernard SHAW and H. G. WELLS.

In her early school years, R. had been a close friend of Amy Catherine Robbins, who was the wife of Wells. In 1907 R. had an affair with Wells, became pregnant, but miscarried. The relationship is mirrored in *Pilgrimage* when Miriam for a brief time becomes the mistress of Hypo G. Wilson, but somehow manages to maintain her friendship with her former classmate Alma. The parallel was not noticed at first because R. introduced Wells into the novel under his own name as well. With her multivolume *Pilgrimage*, an important example of modern psychological fiction, R. was one of the first writers to exploit the technique known as STREAM-OF-CONSCIOUSNESS.

Leaving London for a time, R. lived on a Sussex farm with a Quaker family, an episode reflected in the twelfth part of *Pilgrimage*. One result of the appeal that mysticism had to her was the publication in 1914 of her first two books: *The Quakers Past and Present* and *Gleanings from the Works of George Fox*.

R. had been writing for publication since 1906, and she continued to supplement her limited income by writing reviews, essays on dentistry, cinema, and other topics, as well as translations of French and German works. In 1917, at age forty-four, she took on the domestic burdens of marriage to Alan Odle, an obscure artist-illustrator, fifteen years younger but in frail health. For more than thirty years they divided their time between London and Cornwall, often living in primitive conditions, but their life together was mutually supportive in spite of illness and other hardships, including the theft of many of Odle's prized artworks. Friends frequently rescued them from actual privation, and eventually secured for R. a Civil List pension.

R. began writing *Pilgrimage* in 1913. The first "chapter," *Pointed Roofs*, published in 1915, introduces Miriam Henderson as the young woman whose inner consciousness would dominate succeeding volumes produced over the next quarter century: *Backwater* (1916), *Honeycomb* (1917), *The Tunnel* (1919), *Interim* (1919), *Deadlock* (1921), *Revolving Lights* (1923), *The Trap* (1925), *Oberland* (1927), *Dawn's Left Hand* (1931), *Clear Horizon* (1936), and the twelfth "chapter," *Dimple Hill*, first published in the omnibus four-volume edition of *Pilgrimage* (1938). *March Moonlight*, a posthumous fragment, was included in the 1967 edition.

In her use of a single-viewpoint character, R. was influenced by Henry JAMES and Joseph CONRAD. She was proud of the fact that both she and Conrad had been "discovered" by Edward Garnett (1868–1937), who denominated her innovative technique "feminine impressionism." But in a foreword to the 1938 edition of *Pilgrimage* R. declared her own intention had been to create "a feminine equivalent of the current masculine realism." And in that foreword she acknowledged what critics were doing in comparing her with Marcel PROUST, Virginia WOOLF, and James JOYCE.

May SINCLAIR, in a 1918 essay on R., was the first to apply in a literary discussion the metaphor "stream-of-consciousness," a term invented by William James (1842–1910) to suggest the complexities of human thought. R. herself seemed to prefer the terms "interior monologue" or "slow-motion photography."

Other critics found in her fiction qualities of imagist poetry. Joyce's epiphanies and Woolf's intense moments of illumination are paralleled in R.'s mystical perceptions of reality. Woolf herself, as evidenced in a 1919 review of *The Tunnel*, respected R.'s technical achievements although she saw dangers of solipsistic formlessness in a long work focused exclusively on the consciousness of a single individual. Woolf praised R. for crafting "the psychological sentence of the feminine gender."

Not all R.'s contemporaries were unqualified admirers of *Pilgrimage*. Graham Greene called her work "ponderous," and C. P. SNOW pronounced the "moment-by-moment" novel to be the most hopeless "cul-de-sac" in the history of fiction.

From her wide reading and associations R. gained perspective on literary art and on more abstruse problems like freedom and time. She found philosophers "more deeply exciting than the novelists." Bergsonian concepts of time find expression in her handling of the subtleties of Miriam Henderson's mingling of memory with perceptions of immediate reality.

But R.'s skill in conveying thoughts, sensations, and memories in a welter of moments past and present, occasionally punctuated by flashes of mystical illumination, is not the only basis for critical consideration.

Winifred Bryher (1894–1983), who befriended R. when she was in financial need, felt that *Pilgrimage* was the book to read for understanding transitions in English society between 1890 and World War I. R.'s fiction is undoubtedly useful for understanding the intellectual and political forces of her day.

Although R. followed the activities of Mrs. Pankhurst and other suffragettes with interest, even visiting a friend who was confined in Holloway Gaol, she was her own kind of feminist. Through Miriam Henderson's consciousness she accurately depicted the evolution of a feminine mind in a time when women were striving for a new identity. Miriam's and her creator's struggle against masculine domination and against the psychocultural structures that contribute to women's self-abasement has timeless relevance.

FURTHER WORKS: *John Austen and the Inseparebles* (1930); *Journey to Paradise: Short Stories and Autobiographical Sketches* (1989)

BIBLIOGRAPHY: Sinclair, M., "The Novels of D. R.," *Egoist*, 5 (April 1918): 57–59; Powys, J., *D. M. R.* (1931); Blake, C., *D. R.* (1960); Gregory, H., *D. R., An Adventure in Self-Discovery* (1967); Rosenberg, J., *D. R., The Genius They Forgot: A Critical Biography* (1973); Staley, T. F., *D. R.* (1976); Fromm, G. G., *D. R.: A Biography* (1977); Fromm, G. G., *Windows on Modernism: Selected Letters of D. R.* (1995)

—CARL D. BENNETT

RICHARDSON, Henry Handel

(pseud. of Ethel Florence Lindesay Richardson Robertson) Australian novelist, b. 3 Jan. 1870, Melbourne; d. 20 Mar. 1946, Fairlight, England

R. lived outside of Australia after 1887. Having studied music in Leipzig, Germany, for three years, she began her writing career with articles on music and Scandinavian authors. After her marriage in 1895 she and her husband lived in Germany for seven years, and then settled permanently in England. In 1896 her translations of Jens Peter Jacobsen's (1847–1885) *Niels Lyhne (Siren Voices)* and Bjørnstjerne Bjørnson's (1832–1910) *Fiskerjenten (The Fisher Lass)* were published. From Niels Lyhne R. formulated her lifetime literary aesthetic: she would adhere to a "romanticism imbued with the scientific spirit and essentially based on realism."

All of R.'s works of fiction (except her last book) are ultimately founded on some aspect of her personal life. Her first novel, *Maurice Guest* (1908), set in the bohemian music world of Leipzig in the 1890s, pictures love as a destructive passion and suggests that success in art and love depends on a Nietzschean genius for transcending the ordinary. An apprenticeship work, it shows the combined influences of Jacobsen, Flaubert, Turgenev, Dostoevsky, Tolstoy, Nietzsche, and D'ANNUNZIO.

The Getting of Wisdom (1910), her second novel, is based on R.'s adolescent years at the Presbyterian Ladies' College in Melbourne in the 1880s. With realism and comic irony, she traces a girl's growth to worldly wisdom through struggles with the problems of truth, sin, sex, and art. The work shows the influence of Bjørnson, Charlotte Brontë, and Nietzsche.

R. achieved artistic independence with *The Fortunes of Richard Mahony* (rev. completeed., 1930), a cycle of three biographical novels: *Australia Felix* (1917), *The Way Home* (1925), and *Ultima Thule* (1929). *Ultima Thule* is widely regarded as her as her best work. A naturalistic narrative based on R.'s father's life, this trilogy is the history of a hypersensitive Anglo-Irish physician, a social and psychological misfit in Australia and, indeed, in the entire human world. The tension between established colonials and English immigrants from the 1850s through the 1870s forms the background of the trilogy. The protagonist's unsuccessful battle with his environment and himself, in which he is mentally and physically destroyed, has the inevitability, irony, and unrelieved seriousness of Greek tragedy.

The End of a Childhood (1934) is a collection of short stories, the longest of which centers on Mahony's young son. Eight of its sketches depicting young girls are written in the same vein as *The Getting of Wisdom*.

In *The Young Cosima* (1939), a heavily documented but unsuccessful biographical novel, R. returned to the questions of *Maurice Guest*—the nature of genius and the motives of a woman who flouts convention. Here disastrous love is presented as it affected the famous triangle of Richard Wagner, Cosima Liszt von Bülow, and Hans von Bülow.

Despite faults of style and limitations of imagination in all of her fiction, R. is a superior Australian novelist in the English European tradition.

FURTHER WORKS: *Two Studies* (1931); *Myself When Young* (1948); *Letters of H. H. R. to Nettie Palmer* (1953)

BIBLIOGRAPHY: Robertson, J. G., "The Art of H. H. R.," in R. H. H., *Myself When Young* (1948): 153–210; Palmer, N., *H. H. R.: A Study* (1950); Gibson, L. J., *H. H. R. and Some of Her Sources* (1954); Purdie, E. and O. Roncoroni, eds., *H. H. R.: Some Personal Impressions* (1957); Howells, G., *H. H. R., 1870–1946: A Bibliography to Honour the Centenary of Her Birth* (1970); Green, D., *Ulysses Bound: H. H. R. and Her Fiction* (1973); Elliott, W. D., *H. H. R.* (1975)

—VERNA D. WITTROCK

RICHLER, Mordecai

Canadian novelist, essayist, and short-story writer (writing in English), b. 27 Jan. 1931, Montreal

The grandson of Jewish immigrants, R. disappointed his grandfather, a writer of Hasidic texts, by rejecting this heritage at thirteen. In partial expiation, perhaps, he decided at fourteen to become a writer himself. In 1951 he dropped out of Montreal's Sir George Williams College, cashed an insurance policy, and went to Paris to measure his talent against the best. While reading MALRAUX, CAMUS, SARTRE, and CÉLINE, R. wrote a derivative first novel, *The Acrobats* (1954), set in the wasteland of post-civil-war Spain. It is structured around such themes as expatriate isolation, the existential necessity of action even at the cost of self-destruction, and Jewish animus against Nazis.

Returning to Canada in 1952, R. worked at various jobs, including television journalism. Between 1954 and 1972 he lived in England, supporting himself by writing short stories, articles, book reviews,and film and television scripts, and excelling as an inveterate anti-Canadian for the mass media. He returned to Canada in 1968 and in 1972 to teach at universities. He is now living in Montreal.

In its careful realism and autobiographical portrait of the writer when young, *Son of a Smaller Hero* (1955) focuses on the struggle of its Jewish protagonist to escape the mental and physical ghetto of his upbringing as well as the WASP alternative outside. In a country consisting of invisible ghettos and cultural solitudes, the book takes on broad significance.

Like *The Acrobats, A Choice of Enemies* (1957) is concerned with the moral problem of choice in life. The protagonist must choose between his bohemian friends, a group of American expatriates fleeing the McCarthy purges of the 1950s, and the spineless bourgeoisie that made McCarthyism possible. His conclusion is that both camps are equally given to vanity, covetousness, and lust for power. R.'s plague-on-both-your-houses attitude, and the satirical dissection of the Jew re-creating himself as non-Jew, were to become staples of his later fiction.

Like *Son of a Smaller Hero*, the milieu of *The Apprenticeship of Duddy Kravitz* (1959)—made into a film in 1974—expands from Montreal's Jewish ghetto to take in the wider ghetto beyond. A pimply, narrow-chested punk when we meet him, Duddy is success-driven to acquire land. To this end he struggles out of the stultifying ghetto only to discover that people everywhere are motivated by the same ignoble goals and lusts. The fact that the novel marks the full flowering of R.'s comic talents, notably in the cinematic set-piece scenes, is apt to obscure a deeper ironic purpose: to show that Duddy's ruthlessness, at least when compared with the practiced venality of those who get in his way, stems from natural, almost innocent desires. Symbolizing the ethical dilemmas of a generation, Duddy seems likely to remain one of the most memorable characters in Canadian literature.

Cocksure (1968) debunks an exotic collection of *idées fixes* that R. found flourishing in London in the 1960s. Those under the spell of their own manias include deviants posing as sexual liberationists, Jews hunting out anti-Semites, and advocates of world brotherhood who set themselves the task of demonstrating virtue in the lives of Nazi extermination-camp guards. The other characters, however, are little more than puppets agitated by the strings of R.'s innumerable antipathies. Although its grotesque fantasies are often hilarious, the book suffers from a thinness of invention, and lacks the

Mordecai Richler

consistent moral base requisite for satire. In effect, the salacious attacks on the pop generation serve as a kind of defense of the establishment.

St. Urbain's Horseman (1971) and the earlier *The Apprenticeship of Duddy Kravitz* are R.'s best novels to date. An extravagant, virtuoso performance, *St. Urbain's Horseman* revisits, with ambivalent nostalgia, the Jewish neighborhood of R.'s youth and the expatriate theme. It is a raconteur's novel that goes after familiar targets: the 1950s, modern London and Toronto, the sexual tribulations of the middle-aged rich, and, inevitably, the Jews and the Germans. The book is, nevertheless, R.'s most serious examination of the anxiety and malaise, the hypocrisy and self-deceit at the roots of modern society. It transcends the dead-end cynicism and caricature of *Cocksure* with a wiser tolerance and with characters full of sympathetic frailties.

Joshua Then and Now (1980) also has its origin on St. Urbain Street, and suggests that, although his writing and outlook have matured considerably since *The Apprenticeship of Duddy Kravitz*, R. has never really left home. A chronological mosaic of different periods in its hero's life that alternates in mood between savage anger and exuberant fun, the novel deals with the experience of growing older and the disappointments and compromises it entails.

R.'s achievement has not gone unrecognized in Canada. Beginning as a narrow realist, he has gradually developed a distinctive mode of satirical fantasy to serve as a formidable vehicle for his Swiftian, BLACK HUMOR vision. He is a leading literary interpreter of the North American Jewish experience, to be ranked with Saul

BELLOW, Bernard MALAMUD, and Philip ROTH. His masterful analyses of the psychological and cultural tensions between his characters' formative environments and the several wildernesses beyond provide an important perspective on the Canadian experience as well.

FURTHER WORKS: *The Incomparable Atuk* (1963; Am., *Stick Your Neck Out*, 1963); *Hunting Tigers under Glass* (1968); *The Street* (1969); *Shovelling Trouble* (1973); *Notes on an Endangered Species* (1974); *Jacob Two-Two Meets the Hooded Fang* (1975); *Images of Spain* (1977); *The Great Comic Book Heroes and Other Essays* (1978); *Home Sweet Home: My Canadian Album* (1984); *Solomon Gursky Was Here* (1984); *Oh Canada! Oh Quebec! Requiem for a Divided Country* (1992)

BIBLIOGRAPHY: Woodcock, G., *M. R.* (1970); Sheps, G. D., ed., *M. R.* (1971); Ower, J., "Sociology, Psychology and Satire in *The Apprenticeship of Duddy Kravitz*," *MFS*, 22 (1976): 413–28; Marshall, T., "Third Solitude: Canadian as Jew," and Moss, J., "R.'s Horseman," in Moss, J., ed., *The Canadian Novel: Here and Now* (1978): 147–55, 156–65; Pollock, Z., "The Trial of Jake Hersh," *JCF*, 22 (1978): 93–105; McSweeney, K., "Revaluing M. R.," *SCL*, 4, 2 (1979): 120–31; Davidson, A. E., *M. R.* (1983); Darling, M., ed., *Perspectives on M. R.* (1986)

—JOHN H. FERRAS

RIERA, Carme

Spanish novelist and short-story writer (writing in Catalan and Castilian), b. 12 Jan. 1948, Palma de Mallorca

Born into an affluent family, R. studied first at a religious school, where the nuns stressed good manners as much as book learning, and later at the University of Barcelona. She is now a full professor of Spanish literature at the Autonomous University of Barcelona. Her literary criticism, written in Castilian, has focused on 20th-c. poetry, and her doctoral dissertation, *La Escuela de Barcelona* (1988; The Barcelona School), was awarded the Anagrama Essay Prize. R. writes her fiction in Catalan. Castilian versions or translations of her novella, three novels, and all but one of her four volumes of short stories have appeared, and various works have been translated into Czech, Dutch, English, German, Greek, and Russian.

Both R. and the writer characters she has created emphasize that the first thing authors must do is seduce their readers; the crux of the matter is to do so without resorting to cheap tricks. In her desire to establish contact with readers, awaken their interest, and ensure their continuing attention, R. often resorts to ambiguity and surprise, explaining that what is obvious holds no interest for her as a writer or as a reader. Since seduction is both theme and strategy in her fiction, it is logical that the letter is one of her favorite literary forms, inasmuch as epistolary literature abounds in stories of seduction. Another distinguishing feature of R.'s work is a concern with voice and marginality. She has spoken of her own triple marginalization—as a woman, as a writer who forms part of a minority literature (Catalan rather than Castilian), and as one who within this minority literature is not from the center (Barcelona) but from an island. Her sensitivity to marginality and silencing has led

her to give a voice to those who have not had one, be they the crypto-Jews of her novel, *Dins el darrer blau* (1994; In the Furthest Blue), or the desiring, despairing, and designing women of a host of shorter narratives. Her privileging of the ex-centric highlights what is off center and makes readers reexamine the notions of margin and center, of outside and inside.

R.'s work is remarkably coherent, and her first two collections of short stories contain, in embryonic form, almost all the elements found in her subsequent books. The titular narrative of the first volume, *Te deix, amor, la mar com a penyora* (1975; I Leave You, My Love, the Sea as a Token), consists of a farewell letter written by a young married woman to her first love. It is not revealed until the final paragraph that the addressee is not a man but another woman. The text is doubly transgressive in that the lesbian relation described contravenes social and religious codes, and the narrating of this relation is a further act of aggression against patriarchal norms. Doubling and mirror images are frequent in R.'s writing, and the titular narrative of her second volume, *Jo pos per testimoni les gavines* (1977; I Call on the Seagulls as Witness), presents the other side of *Te deix, amor, la mar com a penyora*, and its narrator purports to be the lover referred to in the earlier work. Both tales transform the canonical heterosexual love plot, with its conventionally happy ending, and underscore the importance of that which is relegated to the margins of texts and of society. R.'s preference for first-person narration and the confessional mode is again evident in the "Bisti de Càrrega" (Beast of Burden) stories of *Jo pos per testimoni les gavines*. The protagonists are working-class women who speak from a position of sexual, social, and economic inferiority. The fact that their interlocutors are silent while the women come to voice inverts the usual situation, in which the latter are silent. The stories of *Epitelis tendríssims* (1981; Most Tender Epithelia) represent another type of subversion of reader expectations. Erotic literature has typically been written by and for men, and has been taken quite seriously by them. The ludic spirit and irreverent tone of *Epitelis tendríssims* and the fact that its author is a woman are a break with tradition.

The book that has received most critical attention is *Qüestió d'amor propi* (1987; A Question of Self-Love), which is the scene of multiple seductions and is filled with references to famous literary seductions, including those of Margarete by Faust and of Ana Ozores by Alvaro Mesía in *La Regenta* (1884 85; *La Regenta*, 1984) by Leopoldo Alas (1852-1901). R.'s most ambitious novel to date, *Dins el darrer blau*, has been honored with four prizes, among them the National Prize for Narrative, never before awarded to a novel written in Catalan. It is at one and the same time a historical account, a rousing adventure tale, a love story, and a reflection upon the horrors committed against those who are "different," in this instance a group of Majorcan crypto-Jews who attempted to flee the island in 1687, were imprisoned in the dungeons of the Inquisition, and were burned at the stake. The novel, a striking blend of eroticism, religiosity, lyricism, sarcasm, and humor, offers a gallery of portraits of memorable characters, depicts daily life in Palma at the end of the 17th c. in vivid detail, and recreates the claustrophobic atmosphere of the city.

By endowing characters of the "wrong" sex, class, or religion with a voice and permitting them to speak out, R. brings these eccentrics to life and draws them into the limelight. Her powers of seduction are manifest in the skill with which she captures readers' attention and entices them to attend to voices of marginality. The fact that R.'s first volume of stories has gone through over thirty printings and her work is receiving increasing critical attention attests to her standing as one of the most important contemporary Catalan writers.

FURTHER WORKS: *Una primavera per a Domenico Guarini* (1981); *La obra poética de José Agustín Goytisolo* (1987); *La molt exemplar història del Gos Màgic i la seva cua* (1988); *Joc de miralls* (1989); *La obra poética de Carlos Barral* (1990); *Contra l'amor en companyia i altres relats*(1991); *Hay veneno y jazmín en tu tinta: Aproximación a la poesía de J. A. Goytisolo* (1991). **FURTHER WORKS IN ENGLISH:** *Mirror Images* (1993)

BIBLIOGRAPHY: Ordóñez, E. J., "Beginning to Speak: C. R.'s *Una primavera para Domenico Guarini*," in Paolini, G., ed., *La Chispa '85: Selected Proceedings* (1985): 285-93; Nichols, G. C., *Escribir, espacio propio: Laforet, Matute, Moix, Tusquets, R. y Roig por sí mismas* (1989): 187-227; Aguado, N., "Epístolas de mar y de sol: Entrevista con C. R.," *Ouimera*, 105 (1991): 32-37; Cotoner, L., Introduction to *Te dejo el mar* (1991): 11-34; Johnson, R., "Voice and Intersubjectivity in C. R.'s Narratives," in González-del-Valle, L. T., and J. Baena, eds., *Critical Essays on the Literatures of Spain and Spanish America* (1991): 153-59; Tsuchiya, A., "The Paradox of Narrative Seduction in C. R.'s *Cuestión de amor propio*," *Hispania*, 75 (1992): 28-86; Epps, B., "Virtual Sexuality: Lesbianism, Loss, and Deliverance in C. R.'s 'Te deix, amor, la mar corn a penyora,'" in Bergmann, E. L., and P. J. Smith, eds., *¿Entiendes?: Queer Readings, Hispanic Writings* (1995): 317-45

—KATHLEEN M. GLENN

RIFBJERG, Klaus

Danish poet, novelist, short-story writer, dramatist, screenwriter, critic, and journalist, b. 15 Dec. 1931, Copenhagen

R. spent a year at Princeton University in the U.S. (1950–51) before he began to study literature at the University of Copenhagen (1951–55). He became a film instructor from 1955 to 1957, contributed to the newspaper *Information* (1957–59), and built a reputation as a book, theater, and film critic for the newspaper *Politiken* (1959–71). From 1959 to 1963 he coedited the literary periodical *Vindrosen*, which served as a forum for debates on MODERNISM. R. was made a member of the Danish Academy in 1967.

R.'s use of various genres—in addition to fiction, poetry, and drama, he has written revues and screenplays—represents differing approaches to an essentially coherent thematic content with a psychological orientation. His works are autobiographical insofar as they are based on personal experience, but they are also social in that they capture a broad spectrum of life in contemporary Denmark.

The private side is naturally most dominant in R.'s poetry, and R. first became known as a poet. In the collection of modernist poems *Konfrontation* (1960; confrontation) he is an unprejudiced explorer of reality through the application of all the senses. In *Camouflage* (1961; camouflage), R.'s most complex lyrical work, he tries to raise deep, unconscious memories to the level of awareness through the guidance of physical impulses. The dissection of the subconscious causes guilt feelings to emerge, although new insights may bring about a feeling of redemption.

In *Amagerdigte* (1965; Amager poems) the complicated modernist techniques are replaced by a simple, everyday realism. This turn, however, was reversed with the publication of the metaphorically complex collection of poems *Livsfrisen: Fixérbillede med satyr* (1979; the life frieze: puzzle picture with satyr).

The psychological penetration in R.'s novels and short stories centers on states of crisis in the characters' development. *Den kroniske uskyld* (1958; chronic innocence) is a novel of adolescence, dealing with the impossibility of maturing into adulthood without losing childhood innocence. *Operaelskeren* (1966; the opera lover), which treats the "second puberty," is about a middle-aged mathematics professor faced with his unrecognized subconscious in the shape of a vivacious opera singer. The liaison fails because of the professor's fear of the irrational.

A common feature in R.'s works is his stressing the banal in the portrayal of ordinary people in everyday settings. In *Arkivet* (1967; the archives) unpretentious, exact realism is employed to describe the anonymous "briefcase people." The radio play *De beskedne* (1976; the modest ones) covers the life of three generations at home and at work during the economic boom of the postwar period, illustrating the changing social structures: a bookstore manager gradually loses his independence while becoming more affluent, while his wife and daughter are faced with the need to redefine their social roles. faced with the need to redefine their social roles. R. displays a fine ear for the vernacular and uses dialogue to reveal social conditions and their psychological impact.

R. has always been in close touch with ongoing social transformations, and topical issues and current attitudes find their way into his works. Notable is R.'s interest in women's psychological conflicts. The protagonist of *Anna (jeg) Anna* (1969; *Anna (I) Anna*, 1982) is a middle-aged woman who has failed to integrate part of her unconscious self into her personality during her social climb. Her unrecognized self is symbolized by her young daughter, toward whom she develops pathological aggressions. The success of the novel may be traced to the balanced blend of psychological description and exciting action—action that also serves as an externalization of inner problems.

R.'s tone may be one of political commitment, as in *Dilettanterne* (1973; the dilettantes); or it may be humorous, as in *Tak for turen* (1975; thanks for the trip). His style ranges from descriptive "neutral" prose to image-filled stream of CONSCIOUSNESS. He is, however, predominantly a lyrical writer whose strength lies in the illustrative and mimetic rather than the reflective or philosophical. Because of his vast and varied oeuvre, his technical mastery and topical relevance, R. has become the most representative and significant author in Denmark during the second half of the 20th c.

FURTHER WORKS: *Under vejr med mig selv* (1956); *Efterkrig* (1957); *Voliere* (1962); *Weekend* (1962); *Hva' skal vi lave* (1963, with Jesper Jensen); *Portræt* (1963); *Og andre historier* (1964); *Boi-i-ing 64!* (1964); *Diskret ophold* (1965, with Jesper Jensen); *Udviklinger* (1965); *Der var engang en krig* (1966); *Hvad en mand har brug for* (1966); *Rif* (1967); *Fædrelandssange* (1967); *Voks* (1968); *Lonni og Karl* (1968); *Rejsende* (1969); *Mytologi* (1970); *År* (1970); *I skyttens tegn* (1970); *I medgang og modgang* (1970, with Lilli Friis); *Marts 1970* (1970); *Narrene* (1971); *Leif den lykkelige jun.* (1971); *Ferien* (1971); *Til Spanien* (1971); *Lena Jørgensen, Klintevej 4, 2650 Hvidovre* (1971); *Svaret blæser i vinden* (1971); *Dengang det var før* (1972); *Den syende jomfru* (1972); *R.s lytterroman* (1972); *Brevet til Gerda* (1972); *R.R.* (1972); *Spinatfuglene* (1973); *Gibs* (1973); *Scener fra det daglige liv* (1973); *Privatlivets fred* (1974); *Du skal ikke være ked af det, Amalia* (1974); *Sommer* (1974); *En hugorm i solen* (1974); *25* *desperate digte* (1974); *Vejen ad hvilken* (1975); *Den søndag* (1975); *Kiks* (1976); *Stranden* (1976); *Det korte af det lange* (1976); *Twist* (1976); *Et bortvendt ansigt* (1977); *Drengene* (1977); *Deres Majestæt!* (1977); *Tango; eller, Syv osmotiske fortællinger* (1978); *Dobbeltgænger eller den korte, inderlige, men fuldstændig sande beretning om K.R.s liv* (1978); *Joker* (1979); *Voksdugshjertet* (1979); *Vores år 1-4* (1980); *Det sorte hul* (1980); *De hellige aber* (1981); *Spansk motiv* (1981); *R. rundt* (1981); *Kesses krig* (1982); *Mænd og kvinder* (1982); *Jus; og/eller, Den gyldne middelvej* (1982); *Hvad sker der i kvarteret?* (1983). **FURTHER WORKS IN ENGLISH:** *Selected Poems* (1976)

BIBLIOGRAPHY: Mitchell, P. M., *A History of Danish Literature* (1971): 306–9; Gray, C. S., "K. R.: A Contemporary Danish Writer," *BA*, 49 (1975): 25–28; Borum, P., *Danish Literature* (1979): 93–98; Rossel, S. H., *A History of Scandinavian Literature* (1982): 330–32

—CHARLOTTE SCHIANDER GRAY

RILKE, Rainer Maria

Austrian poet, novelist, and short-story writer, b. 4 Dec. 1875, Prague, Austro-Hungarian Empire; d. 29 Dec. 1926, Valmont, Switzerland

Among R.'s early formative experiences were a childhood inhibited by the collapse of his parents' marriage, a fragmentary education in military schools and a business academy unsuited to his sensitive personality, a brief encounter with university life in Prague, and participation in art groups, lectures, literary readings and other cultural activities. While still in school he published his first book of poetry, wrote naturalistic dramas and reviews for newspapers, and even founded a literary journal in an attempt to make a name for himself.

In 1896 R. began a life of restless wandering. While in Munich he met Lou Andreas-Salomé, whom he later followed to Berlin. She introduced him to important philosophical currents of the time, as well as cultural and historical ideas of the Italian Renaissance. With Lou and her husband R. traveled twice to Russia. There he became acquainted with Tolstoy and other Russian writers. He grew enamored of the Russian landscape and people, drawing from them impressions and inspiration that shaped his verse for many years.

After living for a time in an artists' colony near Bremen, R. left his wife, the sculptress Clara Westhoff, and moved to Paris. From 1902 until the outbreak of World War I Paris was the focus of his life and work. Important for his development during this period were friendships with Auguste Rodin, from whom he learned rigid artistic discipline, and Paul Cézanne, whose approach to painting strongly influenced visual elements in R.'s poetry. The experience of Paris as a center of poverty, fear, and human misery provided much of the substance for several significant works. Even the language had an impact on him, and he began to write poetry in French. Visits to Duino Castle near Trieste as a guest of Princess Marie von Thurn und Taxis, in 1911 and 1912, changed R.'s life and provided key stimuli for poems of his late period.

R. spent most of the relatively unproductive war years in Munich. In 1915 and 1916 he served briefly in the Austrian army. After the war he moved to Switzerland, where he spent most of the rest of his life. In the splendid solitude of the Château de Muzot in the Rhone Valley he completed his finest cycles of poems.

R. is perhaps best described as a poet of inner experience. In language that is often musical and sometimes playful, in melodic poems that abound with internal and end rhyme, alliteration, assonance, and consonance, R. Captured his own internal life. Common elements of his poetry are the experience of suffering, intense infatuation with individual objects, a peculiar harmony of love and death, and overpowering loneliness. It is an evolving landscape that changes with external experience of places and people. The respective influences of Russia, Paris, and Duino were molding forces that provided a framework for his inner vision. Succeeding poems and cycles describe R.'s efforts to refine the mural of the inner world, to secure what remains uncertain and clarify what is unclear. For R., the poetic task was a religious one. Individual poems reflect a deep humility when contemplating the secrets of existence. His work as a whole documents the awareness of a poetic calling that arises from fear of life that is transformed into jubilant affirmation of it.

The poems of R.'s student years in Prague, which appeared in the collections *Leben und Lieder* (1894; life and songs), *Larenopfer* (1895; offering to the Lares) and *Traumgekrönt* (1896; dream-crowned), exhibit naïveté and a sentimentality that are not found in later works. Influenced by the Danish poet Jens Peter Jacobsen (1847–1885), R. framed poems around sensitive observations of nature and psychological descriptions of people, especially women and children. Visual imagery prevails, although the poetic focus is often not what is described, but the movement of the soul caused by the perceptual experience.

In *Mir zur Feier* (1899; celebrating me) R. began the creative transition to forms and poetic approaches that became more visible in *Das Stundenbuch* (1905; *The Book of Hours*, 1961). As the title suggests, the poems of *Mir zur Feier* center on the poet. With reflections of religious ecstasy, they present longings and prayers in soft, yet rich and pleasing language, celebrating the things that are not grasped by human will but can only be revealed in their true form and essence through poetry.

The celebration of self is also an important element in *Das Stundenbuch*, a three-part work written during the years 1899–1903 and molded by a variety of influences and experiences that include R.'s relationship to Lou Andreas-Salomé, the plays of Henrik Ibsen and Maurice MAETERLINCK, the philosophy of Nietzsche, ideas from the Italian Renaissance, and R.'s impressions of Russia and Paris. Viewed as a whole, the three cycles document R.'s progress toward a poetry devoted to assimilating things for their own sake into the poet's inner world. When compared with earlier works, the poems reveal a new kind of brotherly rapport between the poet and the external realm of God's creation. As R.'s first major representation of the religious meaning of experience, *Das Stundenbuch* presents and refines the idea that God is not a constant perfect entity but an eternally developing creation of the artist.

The first part of *Das Stundenbuch*, "Das Buch vom mönchischen Leben" (written 1899; "Of the Monastic Life"), is a young monk's outpourings of the spirit in prayer to a God who embodies life per se. The music of R.'s language and the richness of metaphor and of visual imagery are combined with powerful imagination to reveal the poet's almost Franciscan sympathy with the world.

The intensity of the portrayal of inner ecstasy increases in the second cycle, "Das Buch von der Pilgerschaft" (written 1901; "Of Pilgrimage"). This section of *Das Stundenbuch* is R.'s strongest development of themes derived from his impressions of Russian piety. The poems are dominated by his view that the Russian people are the incarnation of humble submissiveness and deep spirituality. Spatial relationships reflect the poet's perception of the Russian landscape as the archetype of divine creation. At the same time, individual phenomena melt into the portrayal of the inner landscape, and peaks of religious fervor are achieved in poems that glorify the mystical union between man and woman in homage to R.'s love for Lou Andreas-Salomé.

"Das Buch von der Armut und vom Tod" (written 1903; "Of Poverty and Death"), the final cycle of *Das Stundenbuch*, emphasizes R.'s impressions of Paris during his first year there. Its poems offer variations on the theme of human misery, laying bare the world of the outcast, the sick, and the fearful. Although Christian motifs and themes appear, the cycle as a whole presents R.'s rejection of the Christian God. In rich imagery the poet affirms his perception of God as his own poetic creation.

Another work of the same period, *Das Buch der Bilder* (1902; expanded ed., 1906; the book of pictures), is regarded by some critics as poetically stronger than *Das Stundenbuch*. It is especially important for what it reveals of R.'s progress toward the perfection of a poetic harmony of visual impression and visual elements of the language. In *Das Buch der Bilder* R.'s creative process becomes a refinement of the act of seeing, in which the observer creates the world of the visual image through subjective perception of his surroundings.

The most important poetic development of R.'s Paris period, and his most significant contribution to German poetry was the *Dinggedicht*, or object poem. A reflection of R.'s receptiveness to impressions from the visual art of Rodin and *Cézanne*, the *Dinggedicht* is a product of concentrated and detailed examination of its model. It attempts to present the nature and essence of an object that is portrayed for its own sake in carefully cultivated language. Some of the poems are literary translations of paintings and works of sculpture. Others examine landscapes, animals, plants, human figures, structures, and even themes from the Bible and mythology, in a new kind of interpretation of the world and clarification of existence. The *Dinggedicht* contrasts with R.'s earlier lyric forms in its renunciation of the devotion to musical sound associations and related chains of images. By precisely identifying the poem's object and reducing it to its essence, R. placed it into an absolute realm of pure symbol.

In the poems of *Neue Gedichte* (2 vols., 1907–8 *New Poems*, 1964), the most representative of the *Dinggedichte*, R. combined extreme subtlety and refinement of language with worldly elegance to create symbolic portraits of a broad variety of models. Among the best are poems based on impressions from the Jardin des Plantes. "Der Panther" ("The Panther," 1940), the most famous work of the group, presents its object as a symbol for a heroic life, while "Karussel im Jardin du Luxembourg" ("Merry-Go-Round," 1960) is a symbolic representation of the world as a whole. As a group, these poems are R.'s affirmation of the validity of physical existence and a declaration of his belief that the primary task of the modern poet is the employment of the artistic creative process to analyze and master the world.

The creative attitudes and poetic forms that R. introduced in *Neue Gedichte* were given their most intense and masterful development in two cycles of poetry that he completed in 1922 and 1923, *Duineser Elegien* (1923; *Duinese Elegies*, 1930; four later trs. through *Duino Elegies*, 1978) and *Sonette an Orpheus* (1923; *Sonnets to Orpheus*, 1936). In these mature poems R. responded to

a variety of stimuli—the war, Freud's psychology, writings of Friedrich Gottlieb Klopstock (1724–1803), Kleist, and Goethe, among others—to create an intricately detailed synthesis of his poetic philosophy. In free rhythms, dactylic and iambic forms, questions and exclamations, R. framed keen images that emphasize once more the basic themes of his work as a whole.

Duineser Elegien, molded in part by R.'s impressions of the Duino Castle landscape, offer a refined definition of his perception of the poet's calling. Strongly affirming the idea that man, as the final, most extreme possibility of existence, can preserve the world by transforming it to a realm of timeless "inner space," R. tried to create an alternative to temporal decay. By gathering life, death, earth, and space, all dimensions of time and reality into a single inner hierarchical unity, he sought to insure the external existence of man. According to the elegies, the movement of external reality into a world within is accomplished most completely by lovers, heroes, children, and animals. The poems feature themes such as the mountain landscape experienced as motion, the flight of birds, and dance. All these are presented so as to reveal the sharp tension between physical perception and visionary images. The cycle is ordered in a conscious progression from lament to praise, affirming both life and death, and celebrating man's promise to preserve existence. The elegies are especially notable for the sharpness with which basic existential questions are raised, and for their pregnant imagery.

Inspired in part by the death of a young dancer, *Sonette an Orpheus* consists of fifty-five poems that are closely related to *Duineser Elegien* in mood and theme. Equating the artistic task with a human responsibility to retard the collapse of existence, R. symbolized the poet in the singer Orpheus, making of him a new, non-Christian messiah. Orpheus, as the ordained representative of humanity, brings to pass the preservation of external reality by making "things" eternal. The sonnets celebrate the transformation of objects that occurs in poetry, and present a vision of the resulting new state of the world. In so doing, they reflect R.'s final realization of the basic demands of the *Duineser Elegien*: the development of an ability to see and present things in constellations, and the creation of a poetic song that transcends all boundaries between internal and external, between life and death. The singer Orpheus is R.'s ultimate poetic symbol for change, creativity, and the ability to perceive objects in an absolute harmony of time and timelessness.

Although R. is most famous for his poetry, he also wrote several works of narrative prose. In *Vom lieben Gott und Anderes* (1900; repub. as *Geschichten vom lieben Gott*, 1904; *Stories of God*, 1963), R. imbued memories of his childhood and youth with an almost romantic fairy-tale quality, representing God as a meticulous sculptor similar to Rodin. Like the poems of R.'s early Paris period, the *Geschichten vom lieben Gott* reject Christian views of God in reaction to the misery of the Paris environment.

R.'s most important prose work is *Die Aufzeichnungen des Malte Laurids Brigge* (1910; *The Notebooks of Malte Laurids Brigge*, 1949). A product of the same molding influences, this novel complements the poems of *Neue Gedichte*. It takes the form of a series of almost random sketches written by a Danish expatriate in Paris. Specific external and internal events reflect R.'s attempt to come to grips with his own disastrous childhood, simultaneously exploring from an existential perspective major themes of his literary works as a whole: love, death, fear, idolization of women, God viewed as a creation of the poet's heart. Intensely negative elements of the Paris experience are revealed in a literary substance of illnesses, different forms of death, strange events, nightmares, and spiritualistic visions. Although the content is not unified, each scene focuses on the message of the work. Ugly, negative physical objects reflect the psychological essence of man, while ultimate resolution of the problem of the individual who must cope with life's horrors is given in the concept of love that transcends the individual and encompasses the world in all its variety.

To the extent that R.'s writings accurately represent his special inner landscape, they lay bare the soul of a poet who believed that his works could effect a positive transformation in his readers' view of the world. In their affirmation of life and their elevation of individual man to the status of creator of his own world, R.'s poems have earned him a rightful place among the truly great poets of German literature.

FURTHER WORKS: *Wegwarten* (1896); *Jetzt und in der Stunde unseres Absterbens* (1896); *Christus—Visionen* (written 1896–98, pub. 1950; *Visions of Christ*, 1967); *Im Frühfrost* (1897); *Ohne Gegennwart* (1898); *Am Leben hin* (1898); *Advent* (1898); *Zwei Prager Geschichten* (1899); *Die Letzten* (1902); *Das tägliche Leben* (1902); *Worpswede* (1903); *Auguste Rodin* (1903; *Auguste Rodin*, 1919); *Die Weise von Liebe und Tod des Cornets Christoph Rilke* (1906; *Lay of the Love and Death of Cornet Christopher Rilke*, 1959); *Requiem* (1909; *Requiem*, 1949); *Die frühen Gedichte* (1909); *Das Marienleben* (1913; *The Life of the Virgin Mary*, 1947); *Die weiße Fürstin* (1920); *Vergers, suivi des Quatrains Valaisans* (1926); *Les fenêtres* (1927; *The Windows*, 1980); *Les roses* (1927; *The Roses*, 1980); *Gesammelte Werke* (6 vols., 1927); *Erzählungen und Skizzen aus der Frühzeit* (1928); *Briefe an Auguste Rodin* (1928); *Ewald Tragy* (1929; *Ewald Tragy*, 1959); *Verse und Prosa aus dem Nachlaß* (1929); *Briefe an einenjungen Dichter* (1929; *Letters to a Young Poet*, 1954); *Briefe an eine junge Frau* (1930); *Über Gott: Zwei Briefe* (1933); *Späte Gedichte* (1934); *Briefe an seinen Verleger* (1934); *Poèmes français* (1935); *Gesammelte Briefe* (6 vols., 1936–39); *Tagebücher aus der Frühzeit* (1942); *Gedichte in französischer Sprache* (1949); *Nachlaß, vier Teile* (1950); *Briefe* (2 vols., 1950); *Die Briefe an Gräfin Sizzo 1921–1926* (1950); *Aus dem Nachlaß des Gräfen C. W.: Ein Gedichtkreis* (1950; *From the Reminiscences of Count C. W.*, 1952); *Briefwechsel mit Marie von Thurn und Taxis* (1951; *The Letters of R. M. R. and Princess Marie von Thurn und Taxis*, 1958); *Briefwechsel* (R. M. R. and Lou Andreas-Salomé) (1952); *André Gide: Correspondance 1909–26* (1952); *Briefe an Frau Gudi Nölke* (1953; *Letters to Frau Gudi Nölke*, 1955); *Gedichte 1909–1926* (1953); *Briefwechsel in Gedichten mit Erika Mitterer* (1954; *Correspondence in Verse with Erika Mitterer*, 1953); *R. M. R. an Benvenuta* (1954; *Letters to Benvenuta*, 1954); *R. M. R. et Merline: Correspondance 1920–1926* (1954); *Briefwechsel* (R. M. R. und Katharina Kippenberg) (1954); *R. M. R. et Andrée Gide/Émile Verhaeren: Correspondance inédite* (1955); *Sätliche Werke* (6 vols., 1955–66); *Lettres Milanaises, 1921–26* (1956); *R. M. R. und Inga Junghanss: Briefwechsel* (1959); *Briefe an Sidonie Nádherny von Borutin* (1969); *Über Dichtung und Kunst* (1974); *Wladimir, der Wolkenmaler, und andere Erzählungen* (1974); *Das Testament* (1975); *R. M. R. und Helene von Nostitz: Briefwechsel* (1976); *Briefe an Nanny Wunderly-Volkart* (1977); *R. M. R. und Hugo v. Hofmannsthal: Briefwechsel* (1978); *Briefe an Axel Juncker* (1979).

FURTHER WORKS IN ENGLISH: *Poems by R. M. R.* (1918; enlarged ed., 1943); *The Journal of My Other Self* (1930); *Translations from the Poetry of R. M. R.* (1938); *Wartime Letters of R. M. R., 1914–1921* (1940); *Fifty Selected Poems* (1940; bilingual); *Primal Sound,*

and Other Prose Pieces (1943); *Letters* (2 vols., 1945–48); *Thirty-One Poems by R. M. R.* (1946); *Selected Letters of R. M. R., 1902–1926* (1946); *Five Prose Pieces* (1947); *Requiem, and Other Poems* (1949); *R. M. R.: His Last Friendship: Unpublished Letters to Mrs. Eloui Rey* (1952); *Selected Works* (2 vols., 1954, 1960); *Poems 1906–26* (1957); *Selected Works: Prose and Poetry* (2 vols., 1960); *Poems* (1971); *R. on Love and Other Difficulties* (1975); *Holding Out: Poems* (1975); *Possibility of Being* (1977); *The Voices* (1977); *Nine Plays* (1979); *Requiem for a Woman and Selected Lyric Poems* (1981); *Selected Poems* (1981); *The Astonishment of Origins* (1982, bilingual French/English); *Selected Poetry* (1982, bilingual); *Letters on Cezanne* (1985); *R.: Between Roots: Selected Poems* (1986); *Two Stories of Prague* (1994); *Uncollected Poems* (1995); *R.'s Book of Hours: Love Poems to God* (1996); *The Rose Window and Other Verse form New Poems* (1997); *Diaries of a Young Poet* (1997)

BIBLIOGRAPHY: Mason, E. C., *R.'s Apotheosis* (1938); Kunisch, H., *R. M. R.* (1944); Buddeberg, E., *R. M. R.* (1953); Belmore, H. W., *R.'s Craftsmanship* (1954); Wood, F., *R. M. R.: The Ring of Forms* (1958); Fürst, W., *Phases of R.* (1958); De Salis, J. R., *R. M. R.: The Years in Switzerland* (1964); Mandel, S., *R. M. R.: The Poetic Instinct* (1965); Graff, W. L., *R. M. R.* (1969); Rolleston, J., *R. in Transition* (1970); Wood, F. H., *R. M. R.* (1970); Holthusen, H. E., *Portrait of R.* (1971); Bauer, A., *R. M. R.* (1972); Purtscher, N. W., *R.: Man and Poet* (1972); Stephens, A., *R. M. R.s Gedichte an die Nacht* (1972); Jephcott, E. F. N., *Proust and R.* (1972); Butler, E. M., *R. M. R.* (1973); Rose, W., and G. C. Houston, eds., *R. M. R.: Aspects of His Mind and Poetry* (1973); Calbert, J. P., *Dimensions of Style and Meaning in the Language of Trakl and R* (1974); Casey, T. J., *R. M. R.* (1976); Heller, E., *The Poet's Self and the Poem* (1976): 51–72; Peters, H. F., *R. M. R.* (1977); Webb, K. E., *R. M. R. and Jugendstil* (1978); Schwarz, E., *Poetry and Politics in the Work of R. M. R.* (1981); Kleinbard, D., *The Beginning of Terror: A Psychological Study of R. M. R.'s Life and Work* (1993)

—LOWELL A. BANGERTER

R . . . appears here as the patron-saint of the loneliness of modern man; not as an advocate of a spurious retreat into other worldliness, but as the authentic opposite of the mass-mind and of the civilisation of machines and ideologies; as a poet who, though his words are separated by an immense gulf from what today passes for "Public opinion" and from the ways of thinking common in our world, remains inseparably linked with this world as the prophet and interpreter of its other, its secret nature.

Hans Egon Holthusen, *Rainer Maria Rilke* (1952), p. 7

There are very few prose works by great poets which are at once as exacting and exciting to read as this slender notebook [*Malte Laurids Brigge*] of R.'s. Though its form is roughly that of a novel, and though it purports to be the diary of a Danish poet living in Paris, it is anything but fiction in the accepted sense of the word; it is an extended prose poem which borrows the tonalities of prose in order to weave, with deceptive precision and coolness, a poetic reality. I can think of few little books so densely packed with the matter of poetic observation, few books where every line counts so heavily. Moreover, the nature of the poetry in it is so unwaveringly accurate in its vision and so coolly, surgically presented to the reader that one hesitates to use the world at all . . . No, this is something very different—the tracing of a fugitive reality which lies underneath those deluding appearances we call Time, History, and Memory . . . Our poet does not take up attitudes, does not allow the temperature of his language to rise to the consciously "Poetic" in the bad sense of the phrase. On the contrary he places himself before his inner vision and quietly fills his notebook with accurate transcriptions of what he sees . . . This almost scientific detachment gives the poetry a unique kind of resonance. It evokes the past without nostalgia, it creates the present without regret or disdain, it peers into the curvature of the future without fear.

Lawrence Durrell, "*Malte Laurids Brigge*," *GL&L*,
16 (1963), p. 138

The *Duino Elegies* and the Sonnets to Orpheus constitute in their entirety one coherent poetic statement . . . The *Sonnets* that flowed from R.'s pen almost as a piece of automatic writing during a few January days in 1922 provided the catalyst that brought the *Elegies* to completion within a very short time . . .

As their title implies, the *Elegies* are written in a minor key. They sound a note of heartbreak, of infinite anxiety, anguish, doubt, and fear, although strains of ecstatic jubilation frequently interrupt the throb of the despairing heart. The *Sonnets* are written in a major key, sounding a theme of praise that brooks no qualification. They proclaim a pan-ecstatic view of life. In the explicit language of the *Sonnets*, even lament is nothing but a muted form of praise. Praise of existence is a total musical statement as it were, requiring the minor themes of wailing and lament for its development . . .

Hermann J. Weigand, "The Poet's Dilemma: An
Interpretation of R.'s. Second *Duino* Elegy, "
PMLA, 82 (1967), p. 3

In the early poems the child motif predominates over all others, because R.'s childhood or lack of it is almost his only authentic experience; but it is not so much a theme as a pervasive atmosphere. Before turning to the development of the child image from a mere word into a mature poetic symbol, I should like to examine briefly the figure into which R. pours so much of his feeling in these years: the adolescent girl. This figure, which remained an important symbol for him until the *Sonette an Orpheus*, was central to him in the 1890s for more subjective reasons. With a past rapidly losing its meaning and a future longed for yet feared, the girl symbolizes that "Unentschlossenheit" which characterizes R.'s poetry in these years. Like

him, all she can do is state the paradoxes of her position and ask questions of the future.

James Rolleston, *R. in Transition* (1970), p. 3

It is tragic that R. was never to find Christ—the Word Incarnate—who would have been the door and the way in the poet's life-long despairing search for God. Like so many a Catholic whose early religious education lay exclusively in the hands of a silly, sentimental woman, he was repelled by the anthropomorphic figure of "Gentle Jesus, meek and mild" when he reached the age of criticism; during his formative years he was surrounded by intellectuals who were—to say the least—agnostics, and he did not meet a Christian of really mature intellect until it was too late. So he had to pursue his hard quest alone. But during the period we are now studying, the quest for God ran parallel to the seeking of his own soul, for which he groped when he looked into the brown eyes of the fair-haired painter and admired the clear-cut strength of the dark, vivacious sculptress.

Nora W. Purtscher, *R.: Man and Poet* (1972),
p. 72,

R.'s theory, then, might be regarded as an attempt to harmonise and combine two different views of poetry. On the one hand it demanded the fullness which comes from living in the imagination, from yielding to every impression, and in this it recalls the Romantics with their eager quest of sensations and their belief in the unique nature of the poet's calling. On the other hand it recalls Mallarmé's conception of the ideal poem as something absolute in itself and free from anything that might be called the private tastes of its maker. The two views are not easily reconciled; for the one asserts the importance of everything that the poet feels, the other demands that the poet's individuality must be omitted from the actual poem, which exists in its own world of pure art. But R.'s attempt to combine the two views is intelligible in the light both of his time and of his own development. He saw, as others saw, that the Romantic personality was in many ways destructive to poetry, while the impersonal art of the Parnassians omitted too much. And in his own experience he had both known the ardours of an intense inner life and felt the majesty of works of art which were somehow complete in themselves. In his last years he turned again to the poetry of self-revelation, but before that he went through a time when he deliberately tried to lose himself in impressions, hoping that out of them he would create an objective and self-sufficient art.

C. M. Bowra, "The *Neue Gedichte*," in William
Rose and G. C. Houston, eds., *R. M. R.: Aspects
of His Mind and Poetry* (1973), pp. 92–93

If R. is merely a latecomer in this pilgrimage towards poetic self-lessness, he has added not merely a new episode to its history but given it a new quality: he raised this poetic fate to the level of an aesthetic philosophy, a conscious method, that he expressed nowhere more firmly than in the "Requiem" he wrote in the autumn of 1908 in Paris. It mourns a young man, Wolf Graf von Kalckreuth who, at nineteen, had put an end to his life because of an unhappy love. He had made attempts at writing poetry, and it is this that provided R. with the pretext for stating his idea of the "thing-poem" with a precision never before achieved. The unhappy young man might have been saved, R. believes, had he endured as a poet, a poet, that is, who would have learned the lesson that the maker of the "thing-poems" could have taught him, one who had outgrown the Romantic belief that poetry is the proper vehicle for communicating personal emotions, be they sad or joyful.

Erich Heller, *The Poet's Self and the Poem*
(1976), pp. 62–63

RINGUET

(pseud. of Philippe Panneton) Canadian novelist, short-story writer, historian, and essayist (writing in French), b. 30 April 1895, Trois-Rivières, Que.; d. 28 Dec. 1960, Lisbon, Portugal

The controversy that surrounded R. manifested itself in his turbulent schooling, when he was expelled from a series of colleges for his freethinking. R. ultimately became a doctor, like his father, after studies in Paris, later becoming a professor of otolaryngology at the University of Montreal. Simultaneously, he was an active writer, spoke often on Radio-Canada, was a much-solicited public speaker and journalist, and served as president of the French-Canadian Academy. He was appointed Canadian ambassador to Portugal in 1956. Had R.'s views been known, this appointment might not have been made, for in the 1920s he had advocated Quebec separatism.

The young R. admired the 18th c.: he emulated its critical spirit, its anticlericalism, and its literary forms, and published some poems written in Alexandrines in newspapers beginning in 1915. He was also active in the theater as an actor, a critic, and the writer of two curtain raisers in verse, *Idylle au jardin* (1919; idyll in the garden) and *Je t'aime . . . Je ne t'aime pas* (1927; I love you . . . I love you not). A journal kept during his European years furnished material for the unpublished "Le carnet du cynique" (cynic's notebook). His maxims in this journal, which have been quoted in studies of R., reveal his reading of Zola and his anticlericalism. Fear of the all-powerful Index of the Catholic Church perhaps led to the decision not to publish this book and to the adoption of the pseudonym for 30 *arpents* (1938; *Thirty Acres*, 1940), a novel incorporating these ideas.

Littérature . . . à la manière de . . . (1924, with Louis Francœur; literature . . . in the style of . . .) exhibits this 18th-c. spirit in a lighter mood. The series of pastiches of Quebec's literary classics won the David Prize for humor. R.'s books of popular history also attacked sacred cows. *Un monde était leur empire* (1943; the world was their empire) reveals the riches of the pre-Columbian civilization in America and suggests the limited value of the arrival of European Catholicism, while *L'amiral et le facteur* (1954; the admiral and the postman) advances the claim that Amerigo Vespucci was the discoverer of America. A series of radio talks, collected

after his death in *Confidences* (1965; confidences), exposes another facet of R., as he recalls his youth with much emotion.

This personal note mars much of R.'s fiction. He writes lyrically from his own experience in novels exploring the influence of place on people, whether it be the effect of the country on a group of city dwellers, as in *Fausse monnaie* (1947; counterfeit money), or the opportunities of the city for self-advancement in Horatio Alger style in *Le poids d'un jour* (1949; one day's burden).

Nevertheless, R.'s masterpiece, *30 arpents*, which won numerous prizes, is resolutely detached and objective in tone. In this novel R. scrutinizes the life of Euchariste Moisan as he struggles to develop the family farm in Quebec province in order to pass it on to the next generation. Implicitly denouncing earlier "rural idylls," R. shows the farmer to be subject to the exigencies of a sometimes cruel nature. He demonstrates that rural life is far from perfect and cannot support families. Euchariste is forced to emigrate to the U.S. to work in a factory and dies alienated, uprooted from the soil. Although a typical 19th-c. novel in terms of its narrative techniques, buildup of extensive detail, and method of characterization, *30 arpents* had a revolutionary impact in Quebec, since it was the first French-Canadian novel using the techniques of naturalism to reach a wide public and introduced a new pessimism into French-Canadian literature. A companion piece, the short story "L'héritage" ("The Heritage," 1960), in the collection *L'héritage, et autres contes* (1946; the heritage, and other tales), which was made into a film, is a complementary study, relating the efforts of a city dweller to move to the country and completing the debunking of the pastoral myth and the idealized view of man that had a powerful sway for so long in Quebec. The iconoclast R. thus opened the way for developments in French-Canadian fiction that took place after 1945, when it became possible to write without the pressure to conform to those religious and nationalistic ideologies that had previously hampered Quebec writers.

FURTHER WORKS: *La princesse mauve* (1920); *Histoire véridique d'un plombier, d'une gantière et d'un siphon d'évier; ou, La grossièrté est toujours punie* (1926); *Le devoir* (1927); *Jean Nolin* (1928)

BIBLIOGRAPHY: Robidoux, R., and Renaud, A. *Le roman canadien-français du vingtième siècle* (1966): 44–48; Panneton, J., R (1970); Viens, J., *La terre et "Trente arpents"* (1970); Sutherland, R., *Second Image* (1971): 6–10; Urbas, J., *From "Thirty Acres" to Modern Times* (1976): 19–25; Hoekema, H., "The Illusion of Realism in *Thirty Acres*," *ECW*, 17 (1980): 102–12

—BARBARA GODARD

RINSER, Luise

German novelist and essayist, b. 30 Apr. 1911, Pitzling

Die glasernen Ringe forged a path for the female narrative to be recognized in contemporary German literature. R. uses the genre of the *Bildingsroman* to disclose the journey of a woman, pursuing her individuality, inhibited by the hostility and pressures of conventional family and societal standards toward that realization. This theme was to shape R.'s fiction, and was at the core of her diaries and essays.

In 1944 the Nazis condemned R. to death for high treason. In prison she detailed her ordeal in her diary, *Gefangnisagebuch* (1946; Prison Diary). R. fused diary writing and fiction in her most successful novel, *Mitte des Lebens* (1950; republished as *Nina*, 1956), which gave her national recognition.

This novel and its sequel, *Abenteuer der Tugend* (1957; The Virtuous Adventurer), depicts a woman's confrontation with oppression and her search for autonomy in wartime Germany. The protagonist, Nina, like R., puts her survival secondary to her ideals as she assists in saving the lives of Jews. She must also liberate herself from unfulfilling romantic relations to attain independence and success.

After 1959, R. took a second residence in Italy. For the next three decades she produced political essays that explored world issues as well as women's condition within them and generated six volumes of diaries in which she advanced her beliefs against violence, war, and oppression. In 1974 her novel *Der schwarze Esel* (The Black Donkey) critically examined the internal conflicts within Germany, confronting the atrocities of the Nazi period, from the first-person perspective of six women. R. judged this novel as her finest work, and its theme would reappear in her immensely popular autobiography, *Den Wolf umarmen* (1981; The Wolf's Embrace).

A distinguished and prolific West German writer, R. remained committed throughout her career to her art and to her struggle against political and social oppression. Later in life her political activity gained acknowledgment as she became the presidential candidate for the Green Party.

BIBLIOGRAPHY: McInnes, E., "L. R. and the Religious Novel," *GL&L*, 32 (Spring 1978): 40-45; Frederiksen, E., "L. R.'s Autobiographical Prose: Political Engagement and Feminist Awareness," in Kessler-Harris, A., and W. McBrien, eds., *Faith of a (Woman Writer)* (1988): 165-71

—LISA TOLHURST

RISTIKIVI, Karl

Estonian novelist, poet, and critic, b. 16 Oct. 1912, Paadrema; d. (probably) 19 July 1977, Stockholm, Sweden

R. received a degree in geography from the University of Tartu in 1942, and geography along with history, psychology, and comparative religion remained his principal areas of interest throughout his life. In 1942–43 he was an assistant in the Department of Geography in Tartu and in 1943 escaped from Nazi-occupied Estonia to Finland, going from there to Sweden in 1944. As an insurance company clerk in Stockholm, he lived the isolated life of an introspective and reserved person, his activity, besides passionate reading, being extensive wandering in the Mediterranean countries.

R.'s juvenilia consist of children's books and two light novels published in the newspaper *Perekonnaleht* in 1934 and 1936. Soon after that he produced *Tuli ja raud* (1938; fire and iron), the story of an industrial worker, a vigorous realistic novel that was an immediate success and at once placed him among the masters of Estonian prose. The work has indubitable power because of its fluent narration, terseness of structure, and psychological insight. These

qualities are even more strongly present in the novel *Rohtaed* (1942; the grassy garden), with which he achieved the full creative maturity of his first period. Its hero is an alienated semi-intellectual who can neither realize his pseudoclassical ideals nor find happiness in his personal life.

In the EXISTENTIALIST novel *Hingede öö* (1953; all souls' night), R. moved into the surreal neighborhood of Kafka's *The Trial* and *The Castle*. By his own testimony, however, he did not read KAFKA until critics pointed out the similarity. The hero of *Hingede öö* is a man obsessed by an anxiety neurosis and experiencing a nightmare of frustration, an Estonian exile who hopelessly goes around in circles in a vain effort to clarify his situation and his mission.

In the 1960s R. once more changed his world view as well as his style, which could be called poetic realism. Moving away from Estonian regionalism, he now selected his subjects, sometimes using them allegorically, from the history and civilization of Western Europe, especially of the Middle Ages. In his late novels—among them *Viimne linn* (1962; the last city), *Rõõmulaul* (1966; song of joy), and his last, highly imaginative book, *Kaspar von Schmerzburgi Rooma päevik* (1977; Roman diary of Kaspar von Schmerzburg)—R. succeeded in suppressing personal sentiment far more than before; he had no social or other pretensions, but stated phenomena without comment and accepted the given logic of natural and historical laws.

The technique of R.'s late novels is that of acute observation, his art being visual rather than intellectual. His extreme economy of means sometimes reduced the work to almost a skeleton. An illegitimate child, he treated themes taken from his own search for a father and mother, but his turmoil found resolution in meditation on and gratitude for what had not even been given him R. had a profound religious sense, and to him writing was a form of prayer. It is in this atmosphere of ultimate piety that R. interrupts the life of his last hero, Schmerzburg, who dies at his writing desk unable to finish his diary, in the same peaceful way R. himself departed from life (his body was discovered several days after his death).

Perhaps the best poems R. wrote are those included in his Schmerzburg novel. Intentionally composed in the 18th-c. lyric style, they have an air of devotional taciturnity and detachment from everyday turmoil. A few of the pieces in R.'s only, somewhat uneven verse collection, *Inimense teekond* (1972; man's journey), have similar quality and harmony, but in general his poems cannot compete with the formal finesse and simple serenity of his prose. As a critic, R. was distinguished by kindliness, attentiveness, understanding of style, and contemplation of spirit.

Both in content and form, R.'s late work is pietist throughout; this is, in fact, its predominant character, and it makes his art one of unsullied purity.

FURTHER WORKS: *Võõras majas* (1940; repub. as *Õige, mehe koda*); *Ei juhtunud midagi* (1947); *Kõik, mis kunagi oli* (1946); *Eesti kirjanduse lugu* (1954); *Põlev lipp* (1961); *Imede saar* (1964); *Mõrsjalinik* (1965); *Nõiduse õpilane* (1967); *Bernard Kangro* (1967); *Kahekordne mäng* (1972); *Lohe hambad* (1970); *Eesti kirjandus paguluses* (1973, with Bernard Kangro and Arvo Mägi)

BIBLIOGRAPHY: Jänes, H., *Geschichte der estnischen Literatur* (1965): 168–70; Mägi, A., *Estonian Literature* (1968): 63–66; Nirk, E., *Estonian Literature* (1970): 364–68, 396; Kurman, G., on

Lohe hambad, Ba, 46 (1972): 142–43; Jörma, M., on *Kaspar von Schmerzburgi Rooma päevik*, *WLT*, 52 (1978): 148–49

—ALEKSIS RANNIT

RITSOS, Yannis

Greek poet, b. 1 May 1909, Monemvasia, Greece; d. 11 November 1990, Athens

The youngest of four children born to a ruined landowner of southern Peloponnesus, R., at the age of seventeen, was stricken with tuberculosis, the same disease that five years earlier had killed both his mother and his older brother. That same year his father was confined to a mental institution (a fate that was to befall his older sister ten years later). From 1927 to 1938 R. found himself frequently referred to sanatoriums. While continuing to write poetry, he managed at the same time intermittent stints as a professional actor and dancer. With the outbreak of war in 1941, he joined the Greek Democratic Left and by 1945 was directing the Popular Theater of Macedonia, a propaganda troupe supporting the work of the partisans. Interned by a succession of right-wing regimes in a number of detention camps from 1948 to 1952 for his leftist political activities, he was thereafter provided fifteen years of respite, from which period date half his poetic works. The Papadopoulos coup on April 21, 1967, led to further arrests, imprisonment, and exile on various Greek islands. Hospitalized at intervals during four years of the right-wing military junta, he spent considerable time in military hospitals for his recurring tubercular condition. Later free to travel under a freely elected government, R. divided his time between Athens and the island of Samos, where his wife practiced medicine.

One of modern Greece's most prolific poets, R. published over eighty books of poetry, a book of criticism, two plays, and ten books of translation, largely of eastern European poetry. His poetry consists of short lyrics, long dramatic poems (dramatic monologues and choral pieces with a number of voices), and long narrative poems (ranging from several pages to over a hundred). Whatever the mode, however, R.'s basic concern is with the world of the Greek worker and peasant—approached through some contemporary event or statement, or masked by some classical incident or persona.

A conventional socialist in his first book of poetry, *Trakter* (1934; tractor), R. reached maturity as a political poet in his expression of the agony of his people and their devotion to freedom in *Romiosini* (1954; *Romiosini*, 1969), a long poem composed between 1945 and 1947, during his years of partisan involvement in the Greek civil war (which ended in 1949). Here the poet finds in the continuity of the past and present a source for modern heroism. Thus, the contemporary sailor "drinks the bitter sea from the wine cup of Odysseus" and the Greek mother, Niobe-like, "wrings her heart-strings for her seven butchered sons."

In the poetry of his post-civil war years, particularly since 1963, R. left behind the pathos and sentiment of a poetry tied to temporal events, turning his gaze inward through short lyrical confessional pieces. These "testimonies," as R. describes them, descend into a nightmarish world of reality-rooted abstractions. *Ghrafi tyflou* (1979; *Scripture of the Blind*, 1979), a collection of short poems, presents its bootblacks, hags, street people, mutes, dwarfs, and the blind as experiences essential to any statement of the human

condition. Like the earlier poetry, these short lyrics arise out of the landscape of the peasant and the urban worker; but their wonder, their style, their irony, their fluidity, their universality have now reached fullness. The importance of R.'s short poetry lies, however, in neither its message nor its style; rather, it lies in the transmutation of message into style, in R.'s ability to see through his role as a social poet and revolutionary to achieve a poetry of instinct and inspiration.

R.'s movement from descriptive socialist verse to an abstract poetry led him increasingly, in his long dramatic poems, to themes that permitted exploitation of the classical Greek past through its intersection with present reality. The mask of the classical persona (taken largely from Greek tragedy) alienates events, distances them from the poet's own experience, and thus objectifies them. Still, the poet's insistence on maintaining the moment of present time allows the reader to take such a work as his dramatic monologue, *Aias* (1972; Ajax), written between 1967 and 1969, as a cry of anguish against those friends who forsook him. A mask protecting the poet from prying eyes, Ajax permits R. to confess freely.

As R.'s themes in both the short and long poems matured from purely humanitarian concerns to existential problems, his prosody also changed from the strict meter and rhyme of the quatrain, couplet, and the traditional fifteen-syllable line to a disavowel of traditional metric pattern. Early in the 1940s R. adopted a free verse of short, staccato lines; his later long poems capitalized on long, undulating lines. Having initially seen poetry as a tool of political purpose and having at first used the traditional meters of his age, R. came to create a poetry in free verse marked by a suffering detached from its most immediate meaning to permit a universal statement. From 1982 to 1986 R. released nine volumes of lyrical prose, which he called "novels," that constituted a surrealistically articulated autobiographical narrative under the seies entitled *Dkonostasic anonymon ayion* (Icononstasis of Anonymous Saints).

FURTHER WORKS: *Pyramidhes* (1935); *Epitafios* (1936); *To traghoudhi tis adhelfis mou* (1937); *Earini symfonia* (1938); *To emvatirio tou okeanou* (1940); *Palia mazourka se rythmo vrohis* (1943); *Dhokimasia* (1943); *O syntrofos mas* (1945); *O anthropos me to gharyfalo* (1952); *Aghrypnia* (1954); *Proino astro* (1955); *I sonata tou selinofotos* (1956); *Hroniko* (1957); *Apoheretismos* (1957); *Ydhria* (1957); *Himcrini dhiaughia* (1957); *Petrinos hronos* (1957); *I ghitonies tou kosmou* (1957); *Otan erhete O xenos* (1958); *Anypotahti politia* (1958); *I arhitektoniki tou dhentron* (1958); *Pera ap' ton iskio ton kyparision* (1958); *I gherontises k'i thalasa* (1959); *Mia ghyneka plai sti thalasa* (1959); *To parathyro* (1960); *I ghefyra* (1960); *O mauros aghios* (1961); *Piimata I* (1961); *Piimata II* (1961); *To nekro spiti* (1962); *Kato ap ton iskio tou vounou* (1962); *To dhentro tis fylakis ke i ghynekes* (1963); *12 piimata ghia ton Kavafy* (1963); *Martyries I* (1963); *Piimata III* (1964); *Pehnidhia t'ouranou ke tou nerou* (1964); *Filoktitis* (1965); *Orestis* (1966); *Martyries II* (1966); *Ostrava* (1967); *Petres, Epanalypseis, Kigklidhoma* (1972); *I Eleni* (1972); *Heironomies* (1972); *Tetarti dhiastasi* (1972); *I epistrofi tis Ifighenias* (1972); *Hrysothemis* (1972); *Ismini* (1972); *Dhekaohto lianotraghoudha tis pikris patridhas* (1973; *Eighteen Short Songs of the Bitter Motherland*, 1974); *Dhiadhromos ke skala* (1973; *Corridor and Stairs*, 1976); *Gkragkanta* (1973); *Septiria kedhafniforia* (1973); *O afanismos tis Milos* (1974); *Ymnos ke thrinos ghia tin Kypro* (1974); *Kapnismeno tsoukali* (1974); *Kodhonostasio* (1974; *Belfry*, 1980); *Hartina* (1974); *O tihos mesa ston kathrefti* (1974); *Meletimata* (1974); *I kyra ton ampelion* (1975); *The Lady of the Vineyards*, (1981); *I teleutea pro anthropou ekatontaetia* (1975); *Ta epikerika* (1975); *Piimata IV* (1975); *To ysteroghrafo tis dhoxas* (1975); *Imerologhia exorias* (1975); *Mantatofores* (1975); *Thyrorio* (1976); *To makrino* (1977); *Ghignesthe* (1977); *Volidhoskopos* (1978); *Tihokolitis* (1978); *Trohonomos* (1978); *I pyli* (1978); *To soma ke to ema* (1978); *Monemvasiotisses* (1978); *To teratodhes aristourghima* (1978); *Fedhra* (1978); *Lipon* (1978); *To roptro* (1978); *Mia pygholampidha fotizi ti nyhta* (1978); *Ghrafi tyflou* (1979; *Scripture of the Blind*, 1979); *Oniro kalokerrinou mesimeriou* (1980); *Monohordha* (1980); *Dhiafania* (1980); *Parodhos* (1980); *Erotika* (1981); *Erotica*, 1982); *Selected Poems* (1981); *The Lady of the Vineyards* (1981); *The House Vacated* (1989); *Selected Poems* (1989). **FURTHER WORKS IN ENGLISH:** *Gestures, and Other Poems* (1971); *Selected Poems* (1974); *Chronicle of Exile* (1977); *The Fourth Dimension* (1977); "Selected Poems: 1938–1975," special issue, *Falcon*, 9, 16 (1978); *R. in Parenthesis* (1979); *Subterranean Horses* (1980); *Exotica* (1982); *Y. R.: Repetitions, Testimonies, Parentheses* (1991); *The Fourth Dimension* (1993)

BIBLIOGRAPHY: Friar, K., Introduction to *Modern Greek Poetry* (1973): 88–93; Bien, P., Introduction to Y. R., *Selected Poems* (1974): 11–38; Myrsiades, K., "The Classical Past in Y. R.'s Dramatic Monologues," *PLL*, 14 (1978): 450–58; Myrsiades, K., "R. and Greek Resistance Poetry," *JHD*, 5, 3 (1978): 47–56; Keeley, E., Introduction to *R. in Parenthesis* (1979): xiii–xxvi; Friar, K., and Myrsiades, K., Introduction to Y. R., *Scripture of the Blind* (1979): xi–xxvi; Myrsiades, K, ldquo;Y. R.," *Durak,*, (Dec. 1980): 22–49

—KOSTAS MYRSIADES

RIVE, Richard

South African novelist, short-story writer, and editor (writing in English), b. 1 Mar. 1931, Cape Town; d. 6 June 1989, Cape Town

R. received his teacher's diploma in 1951 from Hewat Training College and his B.A. and B.Ed. from the University of Cape Town (1962). He earned his M.A. from Columbia University (1966) and his doctorate from Oxford University (1973). R.'s brutal and unexplained murder ended the important career of this man of letters. In a sense this more general title is a better accolade of his achievement than novelist, for his editorial enterprise was significant in bringing South African writing to the attention of an international audience. *Quartet: New Voices from South Africa* (1963) was an anthology in which he introduced four major new talents, including his own. His often anthologized short story "The Bench" (1952) exemplified all the qualities that would direct African writing from that country. It became a metaphor for the sense of belligerent resentment that determined political resistance throughout the following decades. There were a number of other publications, of short stories, essays, and, since he was at heart an academic, the important project of editing the letters of Olive SCHREINER. Many titles are listed in his bibliography, but his reputation may ultimately rest on one major novel, *Emergency* (1964).

The term "emergency" in this context is specific and relates to the South African government's declaration of a state of emergency, which permitted it to withdraw all the constraints of the legal constitution. The actual events happened in Cape Town between 28 and 30 March 1960. This was the high point of the campaign

against the odious Pass Laws that required all nonwhites to carry identity papers. The government response to the upsurge of protest was immediate and harsh: arbitrary arrests of individuals, bullets and tear gas against the demonstrating crowds. The confrontation culminated in the infamous shootings at Sharpeville. At one level, this is a realistic novel drawing upon actual events. If it were only that, however, it would be journalism. However, the incidents form the background against which a series of carefully developed fictional characters react to the intense political intolerance that conditions their existence. Their survival depends upon their courage and their ingenuity. The central people are "colored." The whites are at the periphery. They sometimes show real kindness, but their liberal convictions are questioned by others since they do not suffer the same persecution. Somewhat surprisingly, the blacks are portrayed as a threatening majority. They exhibit, albeit from the opposite pole, a racism as virulent as the white version and equally destructive to harmonious social change. The coloreds feel excluded from both sides. The characters are convincing in their variety. Altmann the dedicated teacher, Abe the idealist intellectual, Mrs. Hanslo the kindly landlady, Braam the self-consciously dirty hippie, and, inevitably, the tough, sadistic police. The main character, Andrew, is seeking an advanced education, which requires his dependence on the hospitality of his resentful, brutal brother-in-law. Andrew is drawn into a more radical stance by circumstance as much as by conviction. His ambitions are genuine. He is not by nature a radical. He is forced into that attitude in response to the persecutions of the Special Branch. They show no mercy when they discover that he is breaking the Immorality Act by having a love affair with Ruth, a white woman.

In spite of following the precise dates of the days of increasing social violence, R. creates his own fictional rhythm. Against the background of events the characters move with inescapable urgency toward their own tragic catastrophes. The conclusion suggests that a stoic determination to survive is the only weapon against the state. Abe decides upon the rational solution of exile. Andrew chooses to make the absurd gesture of remaining, knowing he will inevitably be arrested. In this way he exhibits the same defiance as the man in "The Bench." R.'s final moral is that commitment, rather than successful outcome, is the true measure of heroism.

It was twenty years before the next major work appeared: *Buckingham Palace* (1986), the rather improbable name for a series of shabby cottages, one of which is a thriving whorehouse. The book presents a series of intriguing characters who live within the boundaries of District Six, the area of Cape Town reserved for coloreds. In this book R. again draws upon the region of his own upbringing. He records, with a very touching fondness, a life no longer permitted, for the apartheid bulldozers have razed this amiable community where pigmentation did not match the patterns of city planners. These vignettes are conceived with mature skill. The language is sensitive and accurate—with lively patois and sometimes poetry: "the apricot warmth of a summer Sunday morning." What is most remarkable is the style, so wonderfully tongue-in-cheek innocent, as R. subtly makes his wry observations. The episodes are wildly comic, even satiric, yet depict no unkindness or overt criticism. A wife discovers her husband's adultery when he pretends he must go to band practice but leaves his huge visible bass drum at home. Milton September follows his namesake by writing satiric verse, including a complaint against the prison warder, who becomes so incensed he threatens that either he or Milton must leave and "as Milton had two more years to serve . . . he was granted a transfer." There are the adventures of Dubaas who, commanded to paint all the house, obeys precisely, and the walls inside and out and all the furniture and the refrigerator are coated in a hideous pink. There are riches here that beg recounting and a shared delight.

Ultimately R.'s greatest claim to recognition is *Emergency*, with its passionate commitment to a nonracial and liberated South Africa. *Buckingham Palace* indicates his advance as a writer and makes us more aware of how much was lost by his sadly premature decease.

FURTHER WORKS: *African Songs* (1963); *Modern African Prose* (1964); *Make Like Slaves* (1973); *Selected Writings* (1977); *Advance, Retreat: Selected Short Stories* (1983); *Olive Schreiner Letters* (1987); *Emergency Continued* (1990)

BIBLIOGRAPHY: Gorman, G. E., *The South African Novel in English since 1950* (1978), 15, 19, 21, 40; Gray, S., *Southern African Literature* (1979): 9, 133, 137–38, 196; Bamett, U. A., *A Vision of Order: A Study of South African Literature in English* (1914–1980) (1983): 129–31, 246–49, 264–66, and passim; "An Interview with R. R.," *Current Writing: Text and Reception in Southern Africa*, 1, 1 (Oct. 1989): 45–55; Raju, J. and C. Dubbeld, "R. R.: A Select Bibliography," *Current Writing: Text and Reception in Southern Africa*, 1, 1 (Oct. 1989): 56–65

—JOHN POVEY

RIVERA, José Eustasio

Colombian poet and novelist, b. 19 Feb. 1889, Neiva; d. 1 Dec. 1928, New York, N.Y., U.S.A.

After finishing teachers' college, R. went on to the National University, receiving a law degree in 1917. Most of his life was subsequently spent in political service to his country. Diplomatic missions took him to Peru and Mexico. While a member of Congress, R. participated in two important investigations. In 1925 he was chairman of a committee sent to study problems relating to Colombia's oil lands. More importantly, he had earlier been sent to the swamp infested jungle region in the southeast as a member of a government commission whose purpose it was to look into a boundary dispute between Colombia and Venezuela. It was while on this expedition that he became familiar with the geography of the region as well as the socioeconomic problems connected with the exploited rubber gatherers. Extensive notes that he took at that time were later used as a basis for his novel, *La vorágine* (1924; *The Vortex*, 1935).

R.'s literary works consist of a volume of poetry, *Tierra de promisión* (1921; land of promise), in addition to *La vorágine*. In this volume of sonnets, R. paints word pictures of the tropical Colombian landscape. There are echoes of Rubén Darío and other MODERNISTS in the rhythms and especially the Parnassian plasticity. But perhaps the most salient effect produced by R., especially through the poetic device of personification, is that of a pantheistic relationship between the poet and nature.

It is for *La vorágine*, however, one of the great regional novels of Latin America, that R. is best known. Up until a few years ago, critics and literary historians focused their attention on R.'s poetic description of the Amazon jungle and on his concern for the exploited rubber workers. While these critics applauded R.'s

descriptive powers, for the most part they maintained that the novel lacked aesthetic unity. On the one hand, it seemed to portray the struggle of man against nature, with the former shown to be powerless against the overwhelming destructiveness of the latter. On the other hand, the novel was seen as a social-protest work, an exposé of the debt bondage of the rubber workers and a plea for justice. But this is clearly a limited reading of the novel. Recently some critics have given more attention to the novel's thematic unity and universality, focusing on the protagonist, Arturo Cova, from whose point of view the events are narrated. From this angle, the struggle is not so much man against a nature that is exterior to him—although to be sure this struggle is still present—as man's struggle against the all consuming baseness of his natural self. Cova's quest for his lover Alicia, kidnapped and taken by the evil Narciso Barrera from the Colombian plains into the Amazon jungle, is on a deeper level a metaphorical quest for ideal love, psychic wholeness, and true human identity. It is also a mythical journey to the underworld by a hero to rescue a damsel from the clutches of a monster. Cova is a failed hero, however, dragged down by his unredeemed egotism (pride), sensuality, greed, and concupiscence. His descent from Bogotá to the plains and eventually into the jungle traces the pattern of the vortex. It is this poetic image, reinforced over and over again in external nature, folk legends, economic exploitation, and especially the women Cova meets along the way—all of them projections of his inner struggle—that gives the novel not only its profound thematic unity but its unusual power as well.

BIBLIOGRAPHY: Neale-Silva, E., "The Factual Bases of *La vorágine*," *PMLA*, 54 (1939): 316–31; Neale-Silva, E., *Estudios sobre J. E. R.* (1951); Olivera, O., "El romanticismo de J. E. R.," *RI*, 17 (1952): 41–61; Valente, J. A., "La naturaleza y el hombre en *La vorágine* de J. E. R." *CHA*, 24 (1955): 102–8; Neale-Silva, E., *El horizonte humano: Vida de J. E. R.* (1960); Franco, J., "Image and Experience in *La vorágine*," *BHS*, 41 (1964): 101–10; Callan, R. J., "The Archetype of Psychic Renewal in *La voágine*," *Hispania*, 54 (1971): 470–76; Menton, S., "*La vorágine*:, Circling the Triangle," *Hispania*, 59 (1976): 418–34

—ROBERT H. SCOTT

ROA BASTOS, Augusto

Paraguayan novelist and short-story writer, b. 13 June 1917, Iturbe

Born in the Guairá region of Paraguay, R. B. grew up among the peasantry, speaking both Spanish and Guaraní. When he was eight years old, he was sent to military school in Asunción. He did not ultimately follow a military career, but he did see action in the Chaco War against Bolivia. After the war R. B. visited the *yerba mate* plantations as a journalist. In 1944 he was awarded a fellowship by the British Council to study journalism in London. There and in Paris R. B. witnessed the upheaval of the last days of World War II. On returning to Paraguay he soon found his country caught up in a bloody civil war, which eventually forced him into political exile. Since 1947 he has lived and worked in Argentina. In addition to short stories and novels, he has written film scenarios, lectured widely, and directed numerous writers' workshops.

R. B. began his career by writing verse, but he soon discovered that the short story was a more promising medium for dramatizing his social concerns. He has published three volumes of stories to date: *El trueno entre las hojas* (1953; thunder among the leaves); *El baldío* (1966; the empty field); and *Moriencia* (1967; slaughter). Most of R. B.'s stories are set in rural or small-town Paraguay and deal with the oppressed poor; others have as their protagonists members of the middle class and take place in Asunción or Buenos Aires. R. B.'s main themes are those of the postmodernist social realists and documentary regionalists: economic and political oppression, war and revolution, the stifling effects of small-town life. In general, his earlier efforts tend to sentimentalize the plight of the common man, to idealize his heroism, and to portray the capitalist or government oppressor in an exaggerated negative light. In his better stories R. B. demonstrates a mastery of sophisticated narrative technique and an indirection that suggest the ambiguities of the human condition without sacrificing social commitment. What stands out in these stories is man's heroic struggle for freedom, authenticity, and spiritual redemption in the face of what are seemingly hopeless circumstances. Tragically trapped by nature, society, and self, R. B.'s men and women are capable of self-redemption through solidarity and sacrificial death.

R. B.'s first novel, *Hijo de hombre* (1960; *Son of Man*, 1965), won first prize in an international competition sponsored by Editorial Losada in 1959. Since its publication it has received universal acclaim as one of the best novels of the Latin-American "boom" era. Thematically and structurally it is an extension of the short stories, but its profoundly sensitive portrayal of human struggle, its symbolic and mythical qualities, and its understated style raise it to a higher artistic level. On the one hand, *Hijo de hombre* is the national novel of Paraguay. It embraces the country's history from the days of the Francia dictatorship in the 19th c. to the present, includes each of the important geographical regions, and portrays both indigenous and European characters. The seven individual narratives of the novel are connected by various subtle means, but the deeper unity stems from the centrality of the Christ myth and the accompanying motifs of crucifixion-resurrection, heroism-betrayal, and the redeemed prostitute by which R. B. is able to transmute Paraguayan reality into universal myth. Indigenous heroes like Gaspar Mora, Casiano Jara, and the latter's son Cristóbal are idealized but not sentimentalized archetypal figures who incarnate the undeterred human will to endure, to overcome suffering and injustice, and to have abundant life in solidarity with their fellows; their deaths in the face of apparently absurd circumstances that recur cyclically are both sacrificial and redemptive. By contrast, the more intellectual Miguel Vera, from whose viewpoint much of the novel is narrated, is forever caught in a tangle of moral ambiguity, unable to give himself completely to any cause. Unlike the deaths of heroic Christ figures, Vera's is a sterile suicide. Despite his Judas-like betrayal of social causes and of his fellowman, however, Vera is portrayed with sympathy and understanding, not as a villain but as a tragic figure.

R. B.'s novel, *Yo el Supremo* (1974; *I, the Supreme*, 1986), is considered to be his greatest work. It is without question his most complex. *Yo el Supremo* is one of many excellent novels that have recently come out of Latin America on the subject of the dictator, but whereas most of the other novelists, Alejo CARPENTIER and Gabriel GARCÍA MÁRQUEZ among them, offer a composite portrait, R. B.'s protagonist is a specific historical person, Dr. José Gaspar Rodríguez de Francia (1761?–1840). One comes away from this novel with a feeling for the times and a knowledge of historical events as Francia assumes power shortly after independence, astutely removes his tiny nation from Brazilian and Argentine

influence, brings under control the Church and the military, and in general governs as an absolute incarnation of the will of the Paraguayan people. By letting Francia tell his own story (either as he approaches death or from beyond the tomb), R. B. avoids the artistic pitfall of openly passing judgment on the man. Instead, what we have is a self-portrait—rambling, circular, fragmentary— of a contradictory and complex mind. In his efforts to justify his life, Francia reveals himself as enlightened and superstitious, democratic and totalitarian, a torturer and a defender of the rights of the people, but above all obsessed and paranoid. The novel's power, given this mixture, lies not in the presentation of historical material—and this despite the pseudodocumentary paraphernalia—but in the reader's having experienced the demented thought process through which the historical times are viewed.

Among the many outstanding writers in Latin America today, R. B. has not received the recognition of some of the more brilliant lights. But few have probed so deeply man's tragic destiny while at the same time revealing the paradox of man's eternal hope.

FURTHER WORKS: *El ruiseñor de la aurora, y otros poemas* (1942); *El naranjal ardiente, nocturno paraguayo* (1960); *Madera quemada: Cuentos* (1967); *Los pies sobre el agua* (1967); *Moriencia* (1969); *Cuerpo presente y otros cuentos* (1971); *El pollito de fuego* (1974); *Visita del almirante* (1992); *Fiscal* (1993); *Contravida* (1995); *Madama Sui* (1995)

BIBLIOGRAPHY: Rodríguez-Alcalá, H., "Hijo de hombre y la intrahistoria del Paraguay," *CA*, 121 (1963): 221–34; Menton, S., "Realismo mágico y dualidad en *Hijo de hombre*", *RI*, 33 (1967): 55–70; Foster, D. W. *The Myth of Paraguay in the Fiction of A. R. B.* (1969); Luchting, W. A., "Time and Transportation in *Hijo de hombre*", *RS*, 41 (1973): 98–106; Aldana, A. L., *La cuentística de A. R. B.* (1975); Foster, D. W., "A. R. B.'s *I the Supreme*: The Image of a Dictator," *LALR*, 7 (1975): 31–35; Foster, D. W., *A. R. B.* (1978); Marcos, J. M., *R. B., precursor del post-boom* (1983); Sosnoski, s., *A. R. B. y la producción cultural americana* (1986); Burgos, F., *Las voces del karai* (1988); Weldt-Basson, H. C., "A. R. B.'s *I the Supreme*: A Diologic Perspective* (1993)

—ROBERT H. SCOTT

ROBAKIDSE, Grigol

Georgian poet, dramatist, novelist, short-story writer, and essayist (also writing in German), b. 28 Oct. 1884, Sviri; d. 19 Nov. 1962, Geneva, Switzerland

After secondary education in his native country, R. studied in universities in Germany, France, and Russia before returning to Tbilisi, the Georgian capital. His influence was very strong on the young generation of Georgian writers by way of his introducing them to European modes of literary thought and style. R. himself was never a literary model, as his work was *sui generis*: a remarkable synthesis of Georgian folk tradition and the archetypes of universal mythology philosophically interpreted.

R.'s first work, a play entitled *Londa* (Londa), was produced in 1919. It combined theater and music in a way reminiscent of a Greek tragedy. Romain ROLLAND, who was present at its performance, wrote, "I find this art closer to our great musicians than to our poets."

R.'s first novel, *Gvelis perangi* (1926; the snake-skin shirt), combined the essence of ancient Caucasian and Indo-Iranian epic mythology with the conflicts inherent in the encounter of the traditional way of life in the Caucasus and the revolutionary awakening in Russia. *Megi—kartveli kali* (1929; Megi—a Georgian woman) is a novel in praise of women's contributions to the culture of the Caucasus through a depiction of the life of Medea. The long story *Engadi* (1929; Engadi) is a mystical interpretation of the sacred eroticism of the Khevsur mountain tribe.

Lamara (Lamara), R.'s most famous theatrical work (actually a choral drama), was first produced in Tbilisi in 1926. It deals with the life of the Khevsurs as seen through the lens of their mythology. The success of this drama was enormous. It played in Moscow in 1930 to universal critical acclaim and in 1931 it gave R. the opportunity to leave Georgia. Stalin had been so impressed by the work—although there was not even a trace in it of Bolshevik ideology (in common with all R.'s work produced in Soviet Georgia)—that he sent the national Rustaveli Theater of Georgia abroad to perform it. R. went along with the troupe and then defected.

R. settled in Berlin in 1931. His first novel in exile was written in German: *Die gemordete Seele* (1931; the murdered soul), a devastating condemnation of Bolshevism from the viewpoint of an apolitical, creative metaphysician. In the years that followed, R. wrote many prose works in German, including *Der Ruf der Göttin* (1933; the call of the goddess), based upon a myth of the Svan tribe of Georgia. *Die Hüter des Grals* (1937; the guardians of the Grail), R.'s last novel, is about a future hero of the Georgian people, while its basic idea is a consideration of the meaning and worth of humanity.

R. was fascinated with the conception of the "hero" as expressed in mythology and in contemporary life. His interest led him to write studies (in German) of Hitler—*Adolf Hitler* (1939)—and Mussolini—*Mussolini* (1941)—both viewed not from the political but from the mythological standpoint.

In 1945 R. moved to Geneva, Switzerland, where he wrote a series of philosophical essays on subjects ranging from Nietzsche to Georgian mythology. He also continued to write poetry in both Georgian and German. His Georgian poetry is marked by a depth of metaphysical insight never before or since approached in the language.

R.'s work remains banned in his native Georgia, where he is officially considered a "traitor." Although works such as *Lamara* and *Londa* are completely apolitical, they are never performed.

FURTHER WORKS: *Kaukasische Novellen* (1939).

—LEONARD FOX

ROBBE-GRILLET, Alain

French novelist, essayist, and filmmaker, b. 18 Aug. 1922, Brest

Educated in Paris, R.-G. received the French equivalent of a Ph.D. in 1945 from the National Institute of Agronomy. Subsequently he worked in Morocco, Guinea, Guadeloupe, and Martinique as an agronomist specializing in exotic fruits. In 1955 he gave up scientific research to become literary director of the publishing house Éditions de Minuit. R.-G. has traveled and lectured in Europe, Asia, and North and South America, with extended teaching assignments at New York University and the University of California at Los Angeles.

R.-G. came to the fore in the 1950s, along with Michel BUTOR, Nathalie SARRAUTE, Claude SIMON, Robert PINGET, and other writers who were published by éditions de Minuit and who were known collectively as the New Novelists. Like the other practitioners of the NEW NOVEL, R.-G. refused to follow traditional concepts of plot and characterization, engaging himself in a systematic devaluation and desacralization of literary convention—a demythification that has continued until the present and that has involved him in collaborations with filmmakers, painters, photographers, and educators.

R.-G.'s artistic theories and innovations, although controversial, established him, nevertheless, as the leader of the new literary movement frequently referred to as *l'école du regard* (the school of sight), *l'écriture objective* (objective writing), *le chosisme* (thingism or thingishness), and *le stylo caméra* (the pen camera). This emphasis on sight, along with visually detailed descriptions of objects, is a technique that defines in a very general way his first four published novels—*Les gommes* (1953; *The Erasers*, 1964), awarded the Fénéon Prize; *Le voyeur* (1955; *The Voyeur*, 1958), awarded the Critics' Prize; *La jalousie* (1957; *Jealousy*, 1959); and *Dans le labyrinthe* (1959; *In the Labyrinth*, 1960)—all of them New Novels or antinovels belonging to the first of R.-G.'s two main literary periods. The second, referred to as the period of the New New Novel, began with the publication of *La maison de rendez-vous* (1965; *La Maison de Rendez-vous*, 1966) and includes all of R.-G.'s subsequent novels.

When he was not writing fiction or essays R.-G. wrote scenarios and directed films. His career in films began in 1961 with the screenplay for *L'année dernière è Marienbad* (pub. 1961; *Last Year at Marienbad*, 1962), directed by Alain Resnais, a film that changed the course of cinema as much as Picasso's *Demoiselles d'Avignon* changed the course of painting. After *L'année dernière à Marienbad*, R.-G. both wrote and directed his films. Most popular was *Trans-Europ-Express* (1966), a pseudo-Hitchcock whodunit comedy spoofing all manner of conventional gangster movies, James Bond films, and skin flicks. His next film, *L'homme qui ment* (1968; the man who lies), was even more ambitious in its efforts to redirect traditional filmmaking. *L'Éden et après* (1971; Eden and after)—the first of a color trilogy also comprising *Glissements progressifs du plaisir* (pub. 1974; slow slide into pleasure) and *Le jeu avec le feu* (1975; playing with fire)—is also the first film based on a series of twelve themes that R.-G. himself has compared to Arnold Schönberg's twelve-tone musical system.

While R.-G.'s devaluation of conventional artistic norms belongs to his two literary periods and to his films, what distinguishes the New New Novel from the New Novel is a proliferation of names and pronouns in a context of contradictory and conflicting situations, specifically designed to undermine all accepted standards of realism and verisimilitude. A generative theme, such as the color red in *Projet pour une révolution à New York* (1970; *Project for a Revolution in New York*, 1972)—a color signifying rape, arson, and murder—or the mirroring effects of *Topologie d'une cité fantôme* (1975; *Topology of a Phantom City*, 1976), in addition to polysemy, intertextuality, and verbal play, stresses the foregrounding of language, the autonomy of the text, the literariness of self-reflexive writing. All these processes emphasize the adventures *of* writing as opposed to the adventures *in* writing.

This dramatization of the creative process uses *play*, connoting and denoting both theater and games, to generate a novel's existential thereness as well as its ludic structure. The New New Novel's destruction of the traditional hero and dissolution of privileged

points of view also coincides with the partial retreat of EXIS-
TENTIALISM and PHENOMENOLOGY and the emergence of
STRUCTURALISM. But R.-G.'s New New Novels are also organized
in a manner that contests the determinism of structuralism. His
ludic fiction, referred to by some as "flaming fiction," is a liberating force insomuch as playing with language, ideology, and myth
(hence the title of his film *Le jeu avec le feu*) is a game designed to
combat all imposed and predetermined social structures.

While R.-G.'s art seems to be a radical break with the past, the
frequently used labyrinth theme links him with the tradition of
KAFKA and BORGES. R.-G.'s ritualized preoccupations with sex
link him to the Marquis de Sade; his mistrust of the Natural, to
Raymond ROUSSEL; his dislocation of time to FAULKNER and
PROUST; his fascination with mirroring effects, to GIDE; his preoccupation with form and the poetry of fiction to Flaubert, along with
Flaubert's dislike of encoded bourgeois values. Last, although by
no means least, R.-G.'s interest in art as a reality mirroring itself
has distant ties linking him with Diderot's *Jacques the Fatalist* and
Sterne's *Tristram Shandy*.

These connections with self-reflexive works have led a number
of commentators to conclude that R.-G.'s writing is a nonmimetic
art with nothing to say. Others believe that his emphasis on objects
corresponds to the reification of man, that his novels are sociopolitical commentaries, testimonials to modern man's profound
disorientation and dehumanization. Still others believe that R.-G.
uses fragments of contemporary myth, embodying them in scenes
of ritualized fear, eroticism, and violence, as, for example, in *Projet
pour une révolution à New York*, or in eroticized mysticism, as in
Souvenirs du triangle d'or (1978; memories of the golden triangle)
and the film *Glissements progressifs du plaisir* and that by inflating
contemporary mythic elements he exposes the arbitrariness of all
codes, systems, and ideologies. This exaggeration of certain clichéd
images drawn from advertising, psychotherapy, pulp magazines,
and erotic films, this dramatization of social, religious, and sexual
taboos, this subversion of the sacred cows of the establishment are
important dimensions of R.-G.'s New New Novels and films. For
example, in *Le jeu avec le feu* he juxtaposes naked girls and wild
game in an elegant salon. Other similar neosurrealist images
confirm R.-G.'s desire to escape from the "prison-house of language" and the straitjacket of convention into the unfettered realm
of the imaginary, where his freedom as an artist vies with the
bondage of the ready-made, the accepted, the standard.

Like Gide, R.-G. is in constant motion, emphasizing not what he
is, but what he is becoming. He himself stresses the *Aufhebung* of
an *Aufhebung*, that is, the transcendence of a transcendence, a
going beyond that is not the usual notion of Hegel's synthesis but is
instead the perpetual and inevitable dialectical movement between
the inside and the outside, between the self and the other, between
the subjective and the objective. Thus, rooms, cells, cellars, corridors, and attics communicate mysteriously and spontaneously and
with no visible openings or transitions to justify the connection,
with streets, cafés, buildings, cities, beaches, and forests on
the outside.

R.-G.'s art is a point of contact for the phenomenological
subjectivity of the self and the determinism of language which
structures the meaning of the world outside the self. The title of a
novel like *La jalousie* (the French word signifies both jealousy and
window blind) exemplifies this fusion of two realities that, for
philosophers, have always remained separate entities. The window
blind opens and closes, allowing the narrator's and the reader's
perceptions to move both inside and outside the house. The

Alain Robbe-Grillet

window blind is a functional object, but it also describes the
feelings of the unnamed narrator spying on his wife—a wife whose
disorderly behavior threatens the Cartesian order of the husband's
inner world.

This same dialectical process is at work in *L'immortelle* (pub,
1963; *The Immortal One*, 1971), the first film R.-G. directed
himself. Istanbul, where the action occurs, is a real city, but it is also
an imaginary labyrinth for Professor N., who is unable to distinguish between his fantasy and the city's objective reality. His
"love" for Leila, like the husband's jealousy, traps him inside the
maze of his skewed responses. But since R.-G.'s novels and films
are all fictions to begin with, they annihilate themselves, leaving
the reader/viewer with the uneasy feeling that creative acts in art
and in life, like the task of building reality and determining its
meaning, have to be begun anew each time by every one of us. This
ideal and free artistic collaborator is the New Man R.-G. so ardently
advocates in *Pour un nouveau roman* (1963; *For a New Novel*,
1965), a collection of polemical essays in which he describes both
the purpose and the aesthetic of his innovative fiction. In the final
analysis, R.-G.'s art is an existential triumph emphasizing freedom
and thus fulfilling the philosophical premises laid down earlier by
SARTRE, the philosopher, novelist, and existentialist.

FURTHER WORKS: *Instantanés* (1962; *Snapshots*, 1968); *Rêves de
jeunes filles* (1971, with David Hamilton); *Les demoiselles d'Hamilton* (1972, with David Hamilton); *N. a pris les dés* (1975);
Construction d'un temple en ruines à la déesse Vanadé (1975, with

Paul Delvaux); *La belle captive* (1976, with René Magritte); *Traces suspectes en surfaces* (1978, with Robert Rauschenberg); *Un régicide* (1978); *Temple aux miroirs* (1979, with Ionesco Irina); *Djinn: Un trou rouge entre les pavés disjoints* (1981; *Djinn*, 1982); *Le rendez-vous* (1981, with Yvone Lenard). FURTHER WORKS IN ENGLISH: *Generative Literature and Generative Art: New Essays by A. R.-G.* (1983); *Recollections of the Golden Triangle* (1984); *Ghosts in the Mirror* (1991); *La Belle Captive* (1995)

BIBLIOGRAPHY: Sturrock, J., *The French New Novel: Claude Simon, Michel Butor, A. R.-G.* (1969): 1–41, 170–240; Heath, S., *The Nouveau Roman: A Study in the Practice of Writing* (1972): 15–43, 67–152; Ricardou, J., and van Rossum-Guyon, F. eds., *Nouveau roman: Hier, aujourd'hui* (2 vols., 1972), passim; Roudiez, L. S., *French Fiction, Today* (1972): 206–36; Ricardou, J., *Le nouveau roman* (1973), passim; Morrissette, B., *The Novels of R.-G.* (1975); O'Donnell, T., "Thematic Generation in R.-G.'s *Projet pour une révolution à New York,*" in Stambolian, G., ed., *Twentieth Century French Fiction: Essays for Germaine Brée* (1975): 184–97; special R.-G. issue, *Obliques*: 16–17 (1978); Mistacco, V., "The Theory and Practice of Reading Nouveaux Romans: R.-G.'s *Topologie d'une cité fantôme,*" in Suleiman, S., and Crosman, I., eds., *The Reader in the Text: Essays on Audience and Interpretation* (1980): 371–401; Armes, R., *The Films of A. R.-G.* (1981); Stoltzfus, B., "R.-G.'s Labyrinths: Structure and Meaning," *ConL*, 22 (1981): 292–307; Leki, I., *A. R.-G.* (1983)

—BEN STOLTZFUS

For R.-G., the function of language is not a raid on the absolute, a violation of the abyss, but a progression of names over a surface, a patient unfolding that will gradually "paint" the object, caress it, and along its whole extent deposit a patina of tentative identifications, no single term of which could stand by itself for the presented object.

On the other hand, R.-G.'s descriptive technique has nothing in common with the painstaking artisanry of the naturalistic novelist. Traditionally, the latter accumulates observations and instances qualities as a function of an implicit judgment: the object has not only form, but odor, tactile properties, associations, analogies—it bristles with *signals* that have a thousand means of gaining our attention, and never with impunity, since they invariably involve a human impulse of appetency or rejection. But instead of the naturalist's syncretism of the senses, which is anarchic yet ultimately oriented toward judgment, R.-G. requires only one mode of perception: the sense of sight. For him the object is no longer a commonroom of correspondences, a welter of sensations and symbols, but merely the occasion of a certain optical resistance. [1954]

Roland Barthes, "Objective Literature: A. R.-G.," in A. R.-G., *Jealousy: A Novel* (1959), pp. 14–15

In *À la recherche du temps posthume* (remembrance of posthumous time) [Jean-Louis Curtis] describes Marcel Proust's return to earth to conduct an inquiry into the state of modern literature. In the milieu where the master of the psychological novel had expected to hear discussions of Henry James and his disciples, Marcel is astonished to find even Gilberte Swann agreeing that "today we ask something quite different of the novel," and that "psychology nowadays is out of style, obsolete, no longer possible," since modern readers have only scorn for the sacrosanct "characters" of the traditional novel. To prove to Marcel *redivivus* that the modern novel "can no longer be psychological, it *has* to be phenomenological, Mme. de Guermantes introduces him to R.-G. ("with hair and mustache the color of anthracite") who promptly recites, in parodied style, the "new doctrine." One could also cite to illustrate the uneasiness caused in certain literary quarters by this disturbing new force, a cartoon showing the Tree of Literature with numerous well-known Novelists and Critics clinging to its branches, while below, sawing away at the trunk, stands a smiling R.-G.

Bruce Morrissette, "Surfaces and Structures in R.-G.'s Novels," in A. R.-G., *Jealousy: A Novel* (1959), pp. 3–4

Reification. . . on a much more radical level is the subject matter of R.-G.'s third novel, *Jealousy*. This is the very term used by [Georg] Lukács to signal the disappearance of all importance and all significance from the actions of individuals and their transformation into voyeurs, into purely passive entities—this being nothing more nor less than the peripheral manifestation of a fundamental phenomenon—reification—the transformation of human beings into things. . . . It is on this level that R.-G., in *Jealousy*, undertakes the analysis of contemporary society. . . The book demonstrates the progressive autonomy of objects that are the only concrete reality, outside of which human realities and feelings have no independent existence. The presence of the jealous [husband] is indicated only by a third chair, a third glass, etc. . . . the novel's passages affirming the impossibility of separating what is perceived, known, and felt from the object itself. . . .

What matters, however, more than such details, is the structure of a world in which objects have acquired their own autonomous reality; in which men, far from dominating these objects, are assimilated to them; in which feelings exist only to the extent that they manifest themselves through reification. . . . If we define realism as the creation of a world whose structure is analogous to the essential structure of the social reality in which and from which the work was written . . . then R.-G. is one of the most realistic writers of contemporary French literature.

Lucien Goldmann, *Pour une sociologie du roman* (1964), pp. 204–5, p. 209

The play of the mind as it is embodied in the *nouveau roman* [New Novel] is constituted by our freedom to rearrange the images or memories of the past without reference to a perceived reality. The images are irreducible facts, the patterns that are made with them are fictions. The relationship between facts and fiction is also paralleled on the linguistic plane. Here the rules of the game which the sovereign consciousness must recognize are the rules of language, those governing the meaningful combination of words. In respect of language as in respect of reality the powers of the mind are truly combinatory and not inventive; we cannot add to the stock of language (except by neologisms based on existing formations) any more than we can add to the stock of matter. The freedom of the individual speaker is perfectly defined in the terms first introduced by [Ferdinand de] Saussure; the necessity that he must accept as the guarantee of his being able to communicate at all is the *langue* [shared language], what he is free to invent is his *parole* [individual utterance]. More simply, the speaker, or the writer, invents a message by selection from a pre-existent code.

John Sturrock, *The French New Novel* (1969),
p. 22

The critique of what R.-G. refers to as the essentialist conceptions of man does indeed link him at one level not simply to the work of [Roland] Barthes but to the whole focus of contemporary research that has called into question the received notions of Man, Human Nature, and so on. . . When [Michel] Foucault writes: "There is comfort nevertheless, and a sense of profound tranquility in thinking that man is only a recent invention, a figure only two centuries old, a simple crease in our knowledge that is destined to disappear the moment a new form is found" (*Les mots et les choses*, p. 15), the conception of *l'homme* [man] he is there discussing is that essentialist conception at the basis of the bourgeois mythology analyzed by Barthes, and there is no need to stress the tonal relation between Foucault's statement . . . and R.-G.'s stress on the necessity for the abandonment of humanisms centred on essentialist conceptions of man.

Stephen Heath, *The Nouveau Roman: A Study in
the Practice of Writing* (1972), pp. 84–85

[R.-G.'s] films, thanks to his close collaboration with Michel Fano, evolve on two levels: one is visual, the other auditory. Subtle relationships are established between the two. Sound and image separate from each other, then come together, mingle, and separate again, generating redundant, contradictory effects; the pulsating movement produces a rhythm without literary equivalent.

Far from authenticating the image, the sound track definitely destroys its realism; thus, in the opening scene of *L'homme qui ment*, the illusion of a real pursuit by real soldiers in a real forest is completely annihilated by the progressive exaggeration of sound: isolated shots multiplied, machine guns, grenades, then everything together.

However, the most original consequence of this is, without a doubt, the birth of a new film time: with this

dialectic, a past, a present, and a future are created that have nothing to do with the duration of lived experience. In *L'homme qui ment* sounds are heard that have no connection with the image, and, inversely, certain images are not accompanied by corresponding sounds (Boris drops a glass, which breaks in silence); further on the two come together. Once this complex structure is understood, two simultaneous readings of the film occur: superimposed on the image on the screen is the mental image generated by the sound. The arrival of Boris on the riverbank, where Maria is doing the laundry, is announced in the preceding sequence by the sound of water; the alert spectator is thus projected into an immediate future.

André Gardies, "Nouveau roman et cinéma:
Une expérience décisive," in Jean Ricardou
and Françoise van Rossum-Guyon, eds., *Nouveau
roman: Hier, aujourd'hui* (1972), Vol. I,
pp. 196–97

The *First New Novel* forces a *tendentious division within the diegetic Unity* [that is a time-space narrative unity], thereby initiating a period of *contestation*. The story is contested, either by an excess of constructions that are too knowledgeable, or by the abundance of descriptive slippages, or by multiplied mirroring effects and the weakening, already, of different variants; nevertheless, by hook or by crook, it manages to retain a certain unity. The next stage, which some . . . have named the *New New Novel*, dramatizes the *impossible assemblage of a diegetic Plural*, thus initiating a *subversive* period. From the eminently multiple and unstable domain of generalized variants, from the clash of stories, from the conflict of rhetorics, it is in vain that one tries to construct a unitary narrative. *We have passed from the stage of an assaulted Unity, to the stage of an impossible Unity.* The story has not disappeared: in the course of its trial it has multiplied and this plurality is now in conflict with itself.

Jean Ricardou, *Le nouveau roman* (1973), p. 139

Thus the game that R.-G. plays is supposedly indifferent to content, and is designed simply to draw attention to its own procedures. "All my work is precisely engaged in the attempt to bring its own structures to light," he says. The elements or counters in this game are what he calls "generative themes"; and he draws attention to the important parallel between his method and that of the other arts, based as they so often are in the postmodern period, upon combinatorial logic. [As R.-G. says in the "Flier" for *Projet pour une révolution à New York*]: "From now on it is indeed the themes of the novel themselves (objects, events, words, formal movements, etc.) which become the basic elements engendering all the architecture of the story and even the adventures which unfurl within it; this is according to a mode of development comparable to that employed by serial music or modern art and sculpture. . . . Far from disappearing, the anecdote thus sets about growing; discontinuous, plural, mobile, subject to chance, pointing out its own fictitiousness, it becomes a 'game' in the strongest sense of the word."

These burgeoning anecdotal units aim at a deliberate banality, and this for interesting ideological reasons. For the "generative themes," simple objects or incidents though they may be, are frequently enough selected for their cliché-ridden "mythological" status, and this gives their manipulator a clear mimetic commitment: "I take them quite freely so far as I am concerned, from the mythological material which surrounds me in my daily life" [says R.-G. in his "Flier"].

Christopher Butler, *After the Wake: An Essay on the Contemporary Avant-Garde* (1980), p. 46

ROBERT, Shaaban

Tanzanian poet, novelist, and essayist (writing in Swahili), b. 1 Jan. 1909, Vibambani; d. 20 June 1962, Tanga

Since his death from tuberculosis a year after Tanganyika gained its independence from Great Britain, R. has become known as the "Shakespeare of East Africa." He had only four years of formal education (during the colonial era a Muslim child was not allowed to go beyond grade five unless he converted to Christianity). R. worked as a minor government clerk, never learning more than a smattering of English, and devoted himself to the twofold task of rescuing Swahili literature from the decline colonialism had brought to it and of developing the potential of the Swahili language as a unifier and lingua franca of a vast African population by bringing modern ideas and popular language into a formerly esoteric, elitist written literature.

In 1934 R. began writing Swahili verse in a conservative vein, but his third-class position beneath Europeans and Asians brought him rapidly around to progressive writing, often on nationalist themes. In order to promote his own work, he started a publishing house in Tanga. It failed, and most of his works were not published until after his death, since the British would tolerate no criticism, even in abstruse fairy tales.

R. was more than the first national poet in Swahili; in his works he looked beyond the borders of his country to the rest of Africa and the world, anticipating in his ethical vision of work as a source of salvation and in his antipathy to money some of the basic principles of the 1967 "Arusha Declaration," in which Tanzania's aspirations for "socialism" were outlined. His *Utenzi wa vita vya uhuru, 1939 hata 1945* (1967; the epic of the war for freedom, 1939–1945), a global epic about World War II, shows how vast a change in scope he brought to a literature previously preoccupied with local and metaphysical issues. He even introduced the "insha" (essay) form into Swahili. However, he also continued the nonreligious tradition of Swahili verse in homiletic poems such as "Adili" (c. 1947; good conduct), a didactic poem for his son on the value of hard work, good manners, obedience to parents, God, government, and so forth, and in "Hati" (c. 1947; document), a similar poem for his daughter that enumerates the virtues she should embody.

R.'s most enduring works will probably be his anticolonial verse novels like *Kufikirika* (1946; Kufikirika), *Kusadikika* (1951; Kusadikika)—both are names of imaginary countries—and *Utubora mkulima* (1968; Utubora the farmer), and his utopian works such as the verse novel *Siku ya watenzi wote* (1968; the day of all workers), which looks beyond independence to an ideal state whose description often resembles the programmatic dreams of Tanzania's President Julius Nyerere.

R.'s love for his nonethnic language is largely responsible for Swahili's status as his country's national language today.

FURTHER WORKS: *Adili na nduguguze* (1952); *Marudi mema* (1952); *Tenzi za marudi mema, na Omar Khayyam* (1952); *Kielezo cha insha* (1954); *Insha na mashairi* (1959); *Diwani ya Shaaban* (14 vols. to date, 1959 ff.); *Koja la lugha* (1969); *Pambo la lugha* (1969)

BIBLIOGRAPHY: Allen, J., "The Complete Works of the Late S. R., MBE," *Kiswahili*, 33, 2 (1963): 128–42; Mgeni, A., "Recipe for a Utopia," *Kiswahili*, 41, 2 (1971): 91–94; Mulokozi, M., "Two Utopias: A Comparative Examination of William Morris' *News from Nowhere* and S. R.'s *Siku ya watenzi wote*," *Umma*, 5, 2 (1975): 134–58; Arnold, R., *Afrikanische Literatur und nationale Befreiung: Menschbild und Gesellschafts-konzeption im Prosawerk S. R.s* (1977); Knappert, J., *Four Centuries of Swahili Verse* (1979): 266–75; Senkoro, F. E. M. K., "Ngombe Akivundika Guu. . . : Preliminary Remarks on the Proverb-Story in Written Swahili Literature," in Dorsey, D. et al, eds. *Design and Intent in African Literature* (1982): 59–69

—STEPHEN H. ARNOLD

ROBINSON, Edwin Arlington

American poet, b. 22 Dec. 1869, Head Tide, Maine; d. 6 April 1935, New York, N.Y.

After a normal boyhood in the small city of Gardiner, Maine, and two happy years as a special student (not a degree candidate), at Harvard University, R.'s life was clouded by family tragedy—the sudden death of his mother and the ruin of his two older brothers' lives by drug addiction and alcoholism—and by many years of poverty resulting from his uncompromising and unrewarded dedication to a literary career, first in Gardiner and then, after 1899, in New York City.

His first volume, *The Torrent and The Night Before* (1896), privately printed and reissued in 1897, with some additions and omissions, as *The Children of the Night,* attracted some critical attention but few readers; and the more substantial and mature achievement in *Captain Craig* (1902) sank from sight with still less notice. For mere physical survival he was forced to depend on occasional uncongenial jobs, such as timekeeper on the New York subway project, and, reluctantly, on the charity of friends.

Rescued by Theodore Roosevelt, who liked his poetry and in 1905 gave him a position in the New York Customs House, R. found that the creative urge had deserted him; and *The Town Down the River* (1910), a thin volume that appeared a year after he followed Roosevelt out of public service, was all he had to show for eight years of effort. This, also, was largely ignored by critics and readers, and there followed another period of desperate struggle against poverty, discouragement, and alcohol, during which, however, he found a saving influence at the MacDowell Colony in Peterborough, New Hampshire, where he spent each summer, beginning in 1911, for the rest of his life. These years were also marked by misdirected efforts to write for the stage. Only two plays were published: *Van Zorn* (1914) and *The Porcupine* (1915).

Finally, however, the poems of the collection *The Man against the Sky* (1916) won him an acknowledged place in the first rank of American poets; and during the next dozen productive years he achieved preeminence, although only *Tristram* (1927), which brought him his third Pulitzer Prize, was a sensational success. But the long poems that followed—really novels in blank verse—had progressively less popular appeal, and after his death in 1935 his reputation suffered a sharp decline, which has been only partly reversed in recent decades.

A likely cause of this lowered status is that R. is essentially a 19th-c. poet—although efforts to trace specific influences are unconvincing. His is a poetry of statement rather than metaphor; its movement is governed by traditional meters and stanzas and not exclusively by internal tensions; and its first concern is substance—thought, action, character—rather than structure. Moreover, long verse narratives had definitely ceased to be fashionable; and so had R.'s choice of an artistic middle ground between overt social comment and pure aestheticism. So, too, had his underlying preoccupation with religious faith, especially when coupled with his rejection of what seemed to him the easy alternatives, on the one hand, of embracing some particular form of orthodoxy or, on the other, of dismissing the whole issue as irrelevant. Finally, he wrote too much; and at times he did not always—especially in his last years—write as well as he did at others.

Taken on its own terms, however, as all art finally must be, R.'s poetry offers rich rewards. Its special appeal is the power to envision distinctive human beings and bring them to life in words, a power in which R. has surpassed all other 20th-c. poets writing in English. No treatment of the Arthurian legend, for instance, by any other poet has conferred on most of the main characters such credibility for modern readers as *Merlin* (1917), *Lancelot* (1920), and *Tristram*. Other memorable character studies are the title character in "Captain Craig" (1902) and Fernando Nash in *The Man Who Died Twice* (1924). For readers seeking briefer but equally compelling verbal portraits, there are such medium-length blank verse pieces as "Isaac and Archibald" (1902), "Ben Jonson Entertains a Man from Stratford" (1916), and "Rembrandt to Rembrandt" (1921). And in still shorter poems, in lyric or sonnet form—"Richard Cory" (1897), "Miniver Cheevy" (1910), "Mr. Flood's Party" (1921), "For a Dead Lady" (1910), "Eros Turannos" (1916), "Reuben Bright" (1897), and "Karma" (1925), to name a few of many brilliant pieces—we find portraits that no other writer of English verse or prose has etched so indelibly in so confined a space.

In these and other poems that are successful—even an admirer must admit that more than a few are uninspired—the effect is enhanced by R.'s mastery of style, whether simple and direct or rich and resonant, according to the subject and mood. At its best, also, R.'s writing is brightened by humor, strengthened by irony, made compelling by pathos—which never descends to sentimentality.

Many of his characters, as the world sees them, are failures, and R. has often been labeled a pessimist. But although his view of life

Edwin Arlington Robinson

is often somber, it is never despairing. Even life's victims retain a measure of dignity, and even those who triumph—the fortunate few—remain magnanimous; it is only a handful that R.'s unflinching realism compels him to condemn as irredeemable. Similarly, when the poet speaks in his own person or obviously identifies himself with one of his characters, as in the exalted meditation of "The Man against the Sky" (1916) or the lavish philosophizing of Captain Craig, the mood is almost unfailingly, if soberly, affirmative.

When a final judgment is rendered, uninfluenced by temporary trends in taste, R.'s psychological insight, his scrupulous and sometimes inspired verbal artistry, and his clear-eyed but compassionate observance of the human drama will make secure his standing as a major American poet.

FURTHER WORKS: *The Three Taverns* (1920); *Avon's Harvest* (1921); *Collected Poems* (1921; expanded eds., 1929, 1937); *Roman Bartholow* (1923); *Dionysus in Doubt* (1925); *Cavender's House* (1929); *The Glory of the Nightingales* (1930); *Matthias at the Door* (1931); *Nicodemus* (1932); *Talifer* (1933); *Amaranth* (1934); *King Jasper* (1935); *Selected Letters of E. A. R.* (1940); *Letters of E. A. R. to Howard George Schmitt* (1943); *Untriangulated Stars* (1947; letters of R. to Harry de Forest Smith); *Tilbury Town* (1953); *Selected Early Poems and Letters* (1960); *Selected Poems of E. A. R.* (1965); *E. A. R.'s Letters to Edith Brower* (1968)

BIBLIOGRAPHY: Cestre, C., *An Introduction to E. A. R.* (1930); Winters, Y., *E. A. R.* (1946); Neff, E., *E. A. R.* (1948); Barnard, E.,

E. A. R.: A Critical Study (1952); Anderson, W. L., *E. A. R.: A Critical Introduction* (1967); Coxe, L. O., *E. A. R.: The Life of Poetry* (1968); Franchere, H., *E. A. R.* (1968); Barnard, E., ed. *E. A. R.:Centenary Essays* (1969); Cary, R., ed. *Appreciation of E. A. R.* (1969); Barnard, E., "E. A. R.," in Bryer, J. R., ed., *Sixteen Modern American Authors*, rev. ed. (1973): 473–98; Joyner, N. C., *E. A. R.: A Reference Guide* (1978)

—ELLSWORTH BARNARD

ROBLÈS, Emmanuel

French novelist, dramatist, and editor, b. 4 May 1914, Oran, Algeria

From childhood poverty as the posthumous son of a Spanish mason, through language studies on scholarships at schools in Oran and Algiers, R. evolved a three-dimensional life of writing, traveling, and teaching. During World War II he worked in the Resistance and as a military meteorologist, interpreter, and journalist. Like his close personal and literary friend Albert CAMUS, R. reluctantly left Algeria to settle in Paris as one of the postwar North African Group of Writers. He was founding editor of the reviews *Le profane* and *Forge*, and of the Mediterranean Writers Series for Éditions du Seuil. In 1973 he was elected to the Goncourt Academy.

With varying social levels and geographical backgrounds, one major theme permeates R.'s works regardless of genre: the dignity and worth of humankind. All values emanate from and apply to living persons in whom R. places his faith. His protagonists find themselves opposed to whatever divisive elements impede fraternity or elevate any one person or group at the expense of others.

L'action (1938; action), a novel about an abortive strike in Algiers, and *La croisière* (1968; the cruise), a novel dealing with Franco-German businessmen and their relationship with a proletarian crew on board a yacht, focus on economic exploitation, on class distinction between the wealthy and the workers, and on the exploiters; solidarity, which in *La croisière* transcends even international borders and a war. Likewise, the boy protagonist of the largely autobiographical *Saison violence* (1974; violent season) is a victim of prejudice, exploitation, and social injustice in Oran because he is the very poor son of a widowed laundry woman and half Spanish. Yet all the well-off in R.'s works are not oppressors. Although the poor are often treated like animals by rich landowners in *Cela s'appelle l'aurore* (1952; *Dawn on Our Darkness,* 1954), the novel's doctor-hero, well-to-do himself, clearly sides with the underdogs.

Having closely observed and opposed colonialism through most of his life, R. exposed its evils in three of his best works: the prophetic novel *Les hauteurs de la ville* (1948; the heights of the city), which astutely recognized the early signs of the coming Algerian revolution; his dramatic masterpiece *Montserrat* (1948; *Montserrat*, 1950), a drama set against the background of the South American struggle led by Simon Bolívar for independence from Spain; and *Plaidoyer pour un rebelle* (1965; *Case for a Rebelle,* 1977), a play dealing with the morality of terrorism.

R. also translated the horrors of war from personal experience into fiction. *Un printemps d'Italie* (1970; a springtime in Italy), depicts a massacre of Italian patriots by the Germans and refers to the bombing of innocent civilians; *Le Vésuve* (1961; *Vesuvius*, 1970) forcefully describes battles, death, and destruction. In R.'s works the virtual worthlessness of human life in wartime paradoxically creates favorable circumstances for fraternity among combatants mobilized for a common purpose, and for love between men and women as a refuge from the horrors of war.

The typical R. hero, through action, forges a morality that essentially argues that only man justifies man. The protagonists of *La remontée du fleuve* (1964; going back up the river) and *Les sirènes* (1977; the sirens), however, traumatized by the absurdity of death, offer a mystical and challenging foil to R.'s ultimately triumphant philosophy of life.

A superb writer of fiction and powerful dramatist, R. shares the humanist views of a character in *Venise en hiver* (1981; Venice in winter), a novel set against the backdrop of terrorism in present-day Italy: "In the final analysis all evil stems from the fact that men do not feel bound together and interdependent on this ridiculous little planet."

FURTHER WORKS: *Île déserte* (1941; *Desert Isle*, 1975); *Vallée du paradis* (1941); *Travail d'homme* (1943; *The Angry Mountain*, 1948); *García Lorca* (1950); *La mort en face* (1951); *La vérité est morte* (1952); *Porfirio* (1952; *Porfirio*, 1977); *Fédérica* (1954; *Flowers for Manuela*, 1958); *Les couteaux* (1956; *Knives*, 1958); *L'horloge* (1958; *The Clock*, 1977); *L'homme d'avril* (1959); *Mer libre* (1965); *L'ombre et la rive* (1970); *Un amour sans fin* (1976; *A Love without End*, 1976); *Les horloges de Prague* (1976); *L'arbre invisible* (1979)

BIBLIOGRAPHY: special R. issue, *Simoun,* No. 30 (1959); Depierris, J.-L, *Entretiens avec E. R.* (1967); Landi-Bénos, F., *E. R. ou, Les raisons de vivre* (1969); Peyre, H., Afterword to *Vesuvius* (1970): 201–8; Astre, G.-A, *E. R.; ou, L'homme et son espoir* (1972); Rozier, M., *E. R. ou, La rupture du cercle* (1973); Kilker, J., Introduction to E. R., *Three Plays* (1977): pp. xixxiii; Chéze, M.-H, *E. R., témoin de l'homme* (1979)

—MARIE J. KILKER

RODÓ, José Enrique

Uruguayan essayist and critic, b. 15 July 1872, Montevideo; d. 1 May 1917, Palermo, Italy

R.'s childhood and youth were quite uneventful. Born of upper-middle-class parents, he was educated in Montevideo, where he attended the university, studying literature and history. Reserved, perhaps even timid, he never married, although his biographers have uncovered letters and poems that indicate several early romantic attachments. Except for some political activity, which saw him elected as national deputy on three occasions, the bulk of R.'s life was devoted to literary and pedagogical pursuits.

R. began writing while still in his twenties; with a literary friend, Víctor Pérez Petit (1871–1947), he founded the short-lived but important journal *Revista national de literature y ciencias sociales*, in which he published his first major essay, "El que vendrá" (1896; he who is to come). This piece was followed by several literary articles and, at the turn of the century, the book-length *Ariel* (1900; *Ariel* 1922), his most celebrated essay and a work that has become particularly identified with him. Several years later an important work dealing with questions of religious freedom, *Liberalismo y jacobinismo* (1906; liberalism and Jacobinism), appeared, and was followed by *Motivos de Proteo* (1909; *The Motives of Proteus*, 1928) and *El migrator de Próspero* (1913; Prospero's watchtower), the last of what may be considered R.'s major essays.

Ariel is not only R.'s most definitive book, but also one of the basic texts for understanding the Spanish American mind of the period. The author begins by adopting the tone of a venerated teacher addressing a group of youthful disciples. He warns his listeners of the dangers posed by the rising tide of materialism—symbolically rendered by Shakespere's Caliban—of a vulgarly interpreted concept of democracy, and of the perils inherent in abandoning the idealism and spirituality of Latin civilization, epitomized by the figure of Ariel. Although R. frequently points out that it is the culture of the United States that most clearly threatens the best of the Latin tradition, it would be oversimplifying to consider *Ariel* a mere exercise in literary anti-Yankeeism. Rather, R. exhorts his readers to hold fast to such values as the disinterested love of art, respect for the "inner" person, and a concept of democracy that provides the machinery for selecting an aristocracy of merit.

At least two other works of R.'s reveal essential facets of his thought. *Liberalismo y jacobinismo* grew out of a heated discussion surrounding the placing of crucifixes in the rooms of public, secular hospitals. While many argued that religious symbols were inappropriate in such institutions, R. maintained that the cross and representations of Jesus should be viewed simply as symbols of charity and humanitarianism, rather than as expressions of Christian dogmas. In *Motivos de Proteo*, a much less polemical essay, R. takes the multiform mythological figure of Proteus as a metaphor for Renaissance versatility, which he contrasts with the modern emphasis on specialization. As one might expect, R. urges his contemporaries to transcend the tendencies toward narrowness and to emulate Renaissance man, who succeeded in developing all aspects of his being—the scientific, the artistic, and the philosophical.

Although he has been occasionally criticized for providing a convenient justification for the status quo and for presenting only a partial view of the continent's culture—one that ignores, among other things, the indigenous element—R. remains one of the most eloquent champions of Latin American civilization during a period when the humanistic values underlying this society were being challenged from within and without.

FURTHER WORKS: *La nueva novea* (1897); *Rubén Darío* (1899); *Parábolas* (1909); *Cinco ensayos* (1915); *El camino de Paros* (1918); *Epistolario* (1921); *Nuevos motivos de Protoe* (1927); *Los últimas motivos de Proteo* (1932); *Los escritos de "La revista national de literature y ciencias sociales"; Poesias dispers* (1945); *Obras completas* (1956)

BIBLIOGRAPHY: Ellis, H., Introduction to *The Motives of Proteus* (1928): v–xv; Oribe, E., *El pensamiento vivo de R.* (1944); Pereda, C., R.'s *Main Sources* (1948); Rodríguez Monegal, E., *J. E. R. en el novecientos* (1950); Albarrán Puente, G., *El pensamiento de J. E. R.* (1953); Costable de Amorín, H. and Fernández Alonso, M. del R., *R.: Pensador y estilista* (1973); Aken, M. Van, "R., *Ariel*, and Student Militants of Uruguay," and Whitaker, A. P., "*Ariel* on Caliban in Both Americas," in Chang-Rodríguez, R. and Yates,

D. A., ed., *Homage to Irving A. Leonard: Essays on Hispanic Art, History and Literature* (1977): 153–60: 161–71

—MARTIN S. STABB

RODOREDA, Mercè

Spanish-Catalan novelist and short-story writer (writing in Catalan), b. 1909, Barcelona; d. 22 Apr. 1983, Barcelona

R. is the most famous Catalan novelist of the post-Civil War period (and is often considered to be the most important female writer of the entire Mediterranean region in many centuries). She participated fully in the great cultural flowering of Spain in general and of Barcelona in particular before that war. Even before publishing her well-received first novel, *Sóc una dona honrada?* (1932; am I an honest woman?), the young R. was associated with the so-called Sabadell group, and her name was a familiar one in the pages of prestigious Catalan literary reviews such as *La Rambla, Mirador*, and *La Publicitat*. In 1937 she won one of the major Catalan literary prizes, the Creixelles. With the imminent entrance of victorious Francoist forces into Barcelona in 1939, she went into a thirty-year exile. She stayed in Paris until the advent of the Germans during World War II, and then established herself with the Spanish exile community in southern France along the border with Spain. In 1954 she began to place her life on a new footing by going to live in Geneva and by gaining economic security as a translator for the many international groups headquartered there. With much of the worst of her experience of war and exile now under control, she was able to return to literature and published *Vint-i-dos contes* (1958; twenty-two stories). In 1962 R. published *La plaça del Diamant* (*The Pidgeon Girl*, 1967; repub. as *The Time of Doves*, 1980), the novel that is considered her masterpiece, and which has been both widely translated and made into versions in film and television.

This novel exhibits what is probably R.'s most characteristic element of style: the continuous, at times lyrical, interior monologue of a female protagonist, in which the details of daily experience dominate over the sociohistorical context favored by 19th-c. realist-naturalists. This practice leads critics to place R. in world literature by studying her in relation to James JOYCE, Virginia WOOLF, and Gertrude STEIN among others. Nevertheless, R. does have male narrators and protagonists, and does portray directly larger sociohistoric canvases, especially with reference to the Barcelona of her pre-exile life. In this she may be similar to her illustrious predecessor Emilia Pardo BAZÁN; the reader of both novelists senses a need in them to see the world from a masculine point of view, almost as if they lacked confidence in or were not satisfied solely with their feminine one. R., in a 1982 television interview, went so far as to express conformity with the version of the basic male-female relationship given in Genesis: real and necessary subordination of the so-called second to the first sex. In this light the resilient strength in suffering and solitude of R.'s protagonists such as Natalia/Colometa of *La plaça del Diamant* and Cecilia of *El carrer de les Camèlies* (1966; Camellia Street) is ambiguous. It is probably for the reader to decide if those women have a worthwhile life and how their and their fellow women's prospects appear.

ING

Some of R.'s shorter fiction is strikingly different from these long narratives. At times R. gives free rein to her fantasy and imagination to create tales that bear comparison to Franz KAFKA and to works of mainstream horror and science fiction. In other stories, those more thematically related to her novels and often involving some kind of exile, R. explores the uncertain boundary between the feminine and the masculine in men and women.

R.'s place in literature is, so soon after her death, still being mapped out. As with certain other contemporary writers whose first language is Catalan, her fame is such that virtually all her important work has been translated into Spanish, especially in paperback collections of fine reputation and wide circulation. Moreover, contemporary female Hispanists especially read R in Catalan, but then go on to include her in the broader contexts of Hispanic and Western literature. It seems, therefore, that R.'s wide and at the same time select present audience will guarantee continued reputation.

FURTHER WORKS: *Del que hom no pot fugir* (1934); *Un día en la vida d'un home* (1934); *Crim* (1936); *Aloma* (1938; rev. ed., 1969); *Jardí vora del mar* (1967); *La meva Cristina i altres contes* (1967); *Mirall trencat* (1974); *Obres completes* (2 vols., 1976, 1978); *Viatges i flors* (1980); *Quanta quanna guerra . . .* (1980); *Una campana de vidre: amtologia de contes* (1984); *Cartas a I' Anna Muria: 1939–1956* (1985); *Mort i la primavera* (1986). FURTHER WORKS IN ENGLISH: *Two Tales* (1983); *My Christina and Other Stories* (1984)

BIBLIOGRAPHY: Arnau, C., "La obra de M. R.," *CHA*, 383 (May 1982): 239–57; Ortega, J., "Mujer, guerra y neurosis en dos novelas de M. R. (*La plaza del Diamante y La calle de las Camelias*)," in Pérez, J. W., ed. *Novelistas femeninas de la post-guerra española* (1983): 71–83; Wyers, F., "A Woman's Voices: M. R.'s *La plaça del diamant*," *KRQ*, 30 (1983): 301–9; Nichols, G. C., "Exile, Gender, and M. R..," *MLN* 101, 2 (1986): 405–17; Galerstein, C. L., ed., *Women Writers of Spain: An Annotated Bio-Bibliographical Guide* (1986): 273–75; Martí-Olivella, J., ed., *Homage to M. R.* (1987); Nichols, G. C., "Sex, the Single Girl, and Other Mésalliances in R. and Laforet," *ALEC*, 12 (1987): 123–40; Pérez, J., "M. R.," *Contemporary Women Writers of Spain* (1988): 74–85

—STEPHEN MILLER

RODRIGUES, Nelson

Brazilian dramatist, short-story writer, and journalist, b. 23 Aug. 1912, Recife

At the age of five, R. was taken to Rio de Janeiro to live with his father, a polemical journalist, and he himself entered that profession at the age of fifteen. When he was seventeen, the murder of his brother by someone enraged at an article by his father and the father's death a short time later deeply affected him. The only support of his family, he was stricken with tuberculosis, which caused his prolonged confinement in a sanatorium far from Rio. After his recovery, he went back to journalism and began a second career as a dramatist. Later he turned to fiction. His hard life as a youth and the influence of his violent but courageous father made him an aggressive journalist willing to support unpopular ideas.

R.'s first dramas shocked the middle-class theater-going public accustomed to plays with no intellectual or artistic pretensions. To a stage from which any serious discussion or presentation of sex was banned, he introduced FREUD in his first play, *A muther sem pecado* (perf. 1939, pub. 1944; the woman without sin). His next play, *Vestido de noiva* (perf. 1943, pub. 1944; the wedding dress), was innovative in every sense; it was Freudian and fraught with sexual symbolism and implications, and it laid bare ugly family relationships. Presented on the three planes of reality, memory, and fantasy, it is surrealistic theater. Working with a minimum of scenery and stage props and depending on lighting for scene changes, R. was able to bring to the theater cinematic techniques such as fadeouts and rapidly shifting focus.

The violence, sex, and morbid humor, as well as the technical innovations of *Vestido de noiva*, are recurring elements in his later plays. Sex is frequently sadistic; sexual and family relationships are often incestuous, and their presentation is distorted or exaggerated in an EXPRESSIONIST manner. The philosophy is the cynical, cruel disillusionment of expressionism, with its scorn of conventional morality and attitudes. In *O beijo no asfalto* (1961; the kiss on the asphalt pavement) an expression of innocent kindness to a dying man is willfully misinterpreted by a journalist and family members as an indication of homosexuality and leads to the protagonist's ostracism. *Boca de ouro: Tragédia carioca em três atos* (1959; the man with the gold teeth: a Carioca tragedy in three acts) depicts a powerful numbers-racket broker as seen through the shifting perspective of a former mistress. The locale of this play, like that of most of the others, is a lower-middle-class suburb of Rio populated by historical housewives or widows, journalists, pimps, lazy civil servants, and others who live on the fringe of society. These characters speak in the colloquial, slangy language of their section of the city. This use of ordinary spoken Portuguese represents one of the most important of all R.'s theatrical innovations.

R. is considered one of Rio's better journalists. But his journalism, some of it autobiographical, and his fiction are insignificant compared to his plays. Perhaps even more important than the intrinsic merit of his dramas are their innovations, which opened the way for the new Brazilian theater.

FURTHER WORKS: *Anjonegro* (1946); *Doroteia* (1948); *A valsa no. 6* (1951); *A falecida* (1953); *Senhora dos afogados* (1954); *Asfalto selvagem* (1960); *Cem contos escolhidos: A vida como ela é* (2 vols., 1961); *Bonitinha mas ordinária* (1965); *Teatro quase completo* (4 vols., 1965–1966); *O casamento* (1966); *Memórias* (1967); *Confissões* (1968); *A cabra vadia* (1969); *O óbvio ululante* (1969); *Eles gostam de apanhar* (c. 1970); *Toda nudez será castigada* (1973); *O reacionário* (1977); *Teatro completo* (1981ff.).

—RAYMOND S. SAYERS

ROELANTS, Maurice

Belgian novelist, short-story writer, poet, and journalist (writing in Flemish), b. 19 Dec. 1895, Ghent; d. 25 April 1966, St. Martens-Lennik

R., son of a laborer, received a degree from a teachers college and was an elementary schoolteacher from 1915 to 1922. During this period he also turned to journalism, becoming chief editor of the Catholic weekly *De Spectator*. With Richard Minne (1891–1965), Karel Leroux (1895–?), and Raymond Herreman (1896–1971), he founded the influential literary journal *'t Fonteintje* (1921–24). In 1922 he accepted the position of literary adviser to the Department of Education, but soon after he became curator of the historic castle of Gaarbeek near Brussels and thus could devote most of his time to writing. In 1932 R. started the literary monthly *Forum* with his fellow Flemings Marnix GIJSEN, Gerard WALSCHAP, and Herreman, and with Menno ter BRAAK and Edgar du PERRON of the Netherlands. Turning away from nationalism, these writers aimed at being true Europeans. R. advanced the cause of literature by setting up the first mail-order bookshop in Flanders, planning the Antwerp book fair, and starting a festival of Flemish literature in 1937. He also founded the first film club in Flanders.

R. the creative writer began as a lyric poet, with the collection *Eros* (1914; Eros). In the late 1920s, however, he turned to fiction. His first novel, *Komen en gaan* (1927; coming and going), was also the first Flemish psychological novel. In *Het Leven dat wij droomden* (1931; the life we were dreaming of) R. analyzes the mind of a young woman who, wanting to devote herself to medical studies to help her physician father, has banished all thoughts of love and marriage. But, against her will, she falls deeply in love with her girl friend's fianceé. R. closely examines the painful conflict of love and duty. The resolution, in which love triumphs, is convincing. For R., inner harmony is the primary law of life.

In the innovative *Alles komt terecht* (1937; everything turns out right) R. relates the same events twice, first as seen by the heroine's hypochondriac husband and then as seen by herself and her rather lighthearted male friend. R.'s best work is the title story of the collection *De jazz-speler* (1928; *The Jazzplayer*, 1947), in which a middle-aged, well-to-do married man tries to suppress his longing for the more adventurous life led by young bachelors.

For R., who placed great value on quiet and harmony, the most important quest was for happiness, based on moral balance. Happiness can be obtained through positive thought and practical action, and above all through self-knowledge. Thus, R. embraced pascal's theory that knowing oneself brings man close to God. The Pascalian philosophy was expressed in the autobiographical novel *Gebed om een goed einde* (1944; prayer for a good death), in which the narrator prays to God not to let him die through lack of courage, as did his mother and his grandfather, both of whom lost their belief in human happiness. This work was R.'s last novel. Because of his doubts about the value of fiction as such and of his own work in particular, R. withdrew his books from circulation for about ten years. During this time he returned to lyric poetry.

R. Contributed greatly to the revival of Flemish literature with his psychological novels and his stimulating contributions to *'t Fonteintje* and *Forum*. His greatest attribute was his warm regard for human life, expressed in a melodious language and a simple, almost classical style.

FURTHER WORKS: *De driedubbele verrassing* (1917); *De kom der loutering* (1918); *De twee helden* (1928); *Van de vele mogelijkheden om gelukkig te zijn* (1929); *Het verzaken* (1930); *Schrijvers, wat is er van den mensch* (continuing series, 1942–1957); *De weduwe Becker* (1943); *Drie romanellipsen* (1943); *Gun goede wijn een kans* (1947); *Pygmalion* (1947); *Lof der liefde* (1949); *Vuur en dauw* (1965); *Kritisch en essayistisch proza* (1965); *Roman van het tijdschrift "Forum"; of, Les liaisons dangereuses* (1965)

BIBLIOGRAPHY: Mallinson, V., *Modern Belgian Literature* (1966): 97–98

—JUDICA I. H. MENDELS

ROEMER, Astrid H.

Surinamese novelist, short-story writer, and dramatist (writing in Dutch), b. 27 Apr. 1947, Paramaribo

Born and reared in Paramaribo, R. at the age of nineteen emigrated to the Netherlands to study elementary education. She has lived in the Netherlands since that time. In addition to writing, she has studied sociology and law and has been a family therapist since 1988. In 1990 she joined the City Council of Den Haag. She founded a theater group that focuses on migrant issues; she writes and speaks on issues of racism and women, and she makes regular contributions to a news bulletin for women. She made her debut as a poet with the publication of *Sasa* in 1970. Since that time, she has published ten volumes of poems, ten plays, and eleven books of prose fiction. She says that she does not have a favorite genre, rather, she loves the act of writing, and that "some things want to be told in a certain genre, and I must listen to that strange inner voice."

A veritable renaissance woman, R. has written poetry, novels, plays, radio plays, and essays, among other creative projects, though she is perhaps best known for her novels. In her works, R. experiments with narrative perspective, style, and theme, and by doing so, she has invited criticism levied at her use of the Dutch language, sexual-orientation sensationalism, and overuse of metaphors. Central to her works are the issues of race, gender, the Caribbean character in exile, and relationships, especially between mother and daughter. These issues are firmly embedded in the knowledge of the historical past and present reality of the politics of the Dutch Caribbean.

To date she has published thirteen novels, many of which have been translated into English. The breadth of issues and concerns of her novels are not easily classified. In her novel *Neem mij terug Suriname* (1974; Take Me Back, Surinam) R. explores the effects of racism on young black intellectuals in a Dutch society. *De wereld heeft gezicht verloren* (1975; The World Has Lost Face) is set in Paramaribo and explores the intense feelings of a narrator affected by the death of her mother. In the ironical, short work *Waarom zou je huilen mijn lieve lieve* (1987; Why Should You Cry, My Darling Darling) a lottery seller wins it big only to have rats eat his ticket before he can claim the prize money. In the novel *Levenslang Gedicht* (1987; Lifelong Poem), R. eradicates the myth of the "happy multicultural society" that is equated with the Surinamese identity, and in *De orde van de dag* (1988; The Order of the Day) R. explores the world of a paranoid dictator of a small country. In *Lijken op Liefde* (1997; Looks like Love) R. gives voice to a Surinamese domestic who is neither expected or encouraged to speak.

At the heart of her works is the idea that the Afro-Caribbean writer must draw on the trickster tradition inherited from Africa to counter the effects of the colonial legacy. R. deftly manipulates the language of the metropolis and the written traditions as well as its techniques to illuminate her "neighborhood" as it exists both within and outside of the Caribbean. She resists easy categorization in her works as she creates space for the engagement of national orientation.

FURTHER WORKS: *Over de gekte van een vrouw* (1982); *Nergens ergens* (1983); *Het spoor van de jakhals* (1988); *De achtentwintigste dag* (1988); *Alles wat gelukkig maakt* (1989); *Niets wat pijn doet* (1993); *Gewaagd Leven* (1996)

BIBLIOGRAPHY: van Kempen, M., "De beweging is gebleven, mar het zwarte punt ligt anders: De poëzie van Astrid Roemer," *Kalá*, 1, 1 (1986): 9-14; Paravisini-Gebert, L., and O. Torres-Seda, eds., *Caribbean Women Novelists: An Annotated Critical Bibliography* (1993): 336-43; Phaf, I., "Women and Literature in the Caribbean," in Schipper, M., ed., *Women and Literature in Africa, the Arab World, Asia, the Caribbean, and Latin America* (1984): 168-200; Newson, A., and L. Strong-Leek, eds., *Winds of Change: The Transforming Voices of Caribbean Women Writers and Scholars* (1998)

—ADELE S. NEWSON

ROETHKE, Theodore

American poet, b. 5 May 1908, Saginaw, Mich.; d. 1 Aug. 1963, Seattle, Wash.

R. was born and raised in Saginaw, Michigan, where his German-American parents were half-owners of one of the largest, most successful greenhouses in the Midwest. The rich, minimal

Theodore Roethke

world of roots and plants, weeds and moss, ordinary and exotic flowers was at the center of R.'s childhood universe. Subsequently, the terrifying and beautiful "tropical" world of the greenhouse came to stand for the lost world of his childhood and, at the same time, to serve as the central symbol—both the heaven and hell—of his poetry. R. was educated at the University of Michigan and at Harvard University. Through the years he pursued an important double career of writing and teaching poetry at Lafayette College, Pennsylvania State College, Bennington College, and finally, the University of Washington. He won a number of major poetry prizes (a Pulitzer Prize, two Guggenheim Fellowships, a National Book Award, a Bollingen Prize) and in 1953 achieved a measure of domestic happiness by marrying a former student. Nonetheless, R.'s adult life (and consequently his poetry) continued to be marked and informed by a series of manic episodes and mental breakdowns. As both a manic depressive and a superbly gifted American romantic poet, R. associated himself with other joyous and mystical poets of romantic madness: Christopher Smart (1722–1771), John Clare (1793–1864), and William Blake (1757–1827).

R.'s first book, *Open House* (1941), consists of strictly controlled, technically traditional individual lyrics. The book's title poem announces that "my secrets cry aloud" and "my heart keeps open house," but in fact R.'s first poems never wholly break loose from the formal lyricism, witty neo-Meta-physical manner, and chill austerity of his early poetic. The impress of lyrical models like Emily DICKINSON, W. H. AUDEN, and Leonie Adams (1899-1988) is too heavy on his work, and his imaginative struggle to find a correspondence between interior and exterior worlds is undermined and constricted by the limited range of his diction and the narrowness of his formalism.

The great moment in R.'s poetic life was his breakthrough from the aesthetic straitjacket of his first book into the mature organicism of his second book. *The Lost Son, and Other Poems* (1948). In the fourteen "greenhouse poems" of the book's opening sequence R. returns to his childhood and explores the paradoxical nature of his family greenhouse. The greenhouse was for him both a natural and an artificial world, a locale of generation and decay, order and chaos. His poems explore the instinctual sources of life from the dank minimal world of roots ("Root Cellar") to the open, flowering reality of young plants ("Transplanting"). The discovery of the greenhouse as the central symbol of his poetry was tied to two other discoveries R. was making in the 1940s. Through the critic Kenneth Burke's (b. 1897) influence, he began to explore at first the Freudian and then the Jungian possibilities for poetry, plunging into his own unconscious for personal and archetypal symbols. Simultaneously, he recognized that the organic life of plants could serve as a metaphor for the creative process itself, each poem taking on its own sensuous form and shape. This poetic expressionism is the key to R.'s American romanticism.

R.'s central sequence of dramatic interior monologues begins with the title poem of *The Lost Son*, continues through *Praise to the End!* (1951), and concludes with the opening lyric of *The Waking* (1953). In this narrative sequence (as in his later and less important nonsense poems, *I Am! Says the Lamb* [1961]) R. shows himself to be a major poet of the regressive imagination. The sequence is R.'s *Prelude* (Wordsworth) and charts the spiritual progress of the individual psyche from its first struggles to be born to its wholly separated adult state. Technically, the poems move forward by rapid associations and radical rhythmic shifts. They rely heavily on fairy tales and myths, nursery rhymes, Elizabethan songs, Blakean precedents, and biblical rhythms to chart in direct sensory terms the individual's (and the race's) mythic journey of physical and spiritual growth.

Throughout his carrer R. tirelessly experimented with traditional meters, stanzas, and styles. In *The Waking* and in a key sequence, "Love Poems," in *Words for the Wind* (1958) he again returned to traditional forms, in particular mastering the device of the endstopped line. Rhythms like YEATS's occasionally seem to overwhelm R.'s style, and poems like "Four for Sir John Davies" (1953) and "The Dying Man" (1958) show R.'s anxiety about and his indebtedness to the Irish master. But in his best metrical poems—for example. "The Waking" (1953) and "I Knew a Woman" (1958)—he was able to fuse the Yeatsian influence with the influence of the Elizabethan plain stylists to create a unique musical style. In his sensual love poems R. was again concerned with using poetry for the direct—as opposed to the abstract—apprehension of reality. In "I Knew a Woman" and in his own favorite poem. "Words for the Wind," R. celebrated his beloved and expressed the poet's joy at moving out of the self and living in the dynamic presence and light of another. Love is in these poems a way of triumphing over the self's anxiety about nonbeing and nothingness. It is consequently a way of transcending isolation and mystically uniting body and spirit. R.'s "Love Poems" provide a thematic intimation of the mystical ascent from the flesh to the spirit that predominates in his posthumous book, *The Far Field* (1964).

R.'s spiritual autobiography culminates in the opening "North American Sequence" and the closing "Sequence, Sometimes Metaphysical" of his final volume. Written under the presiding spirit of Walt Whitman, the six poems of the "North American Sequence" show a new meditative openness and discursive energy. The sequence follows an epic-like journey from R.'s origins in the Midwest to his mature years in the Pacific Northwest. The journey also represents a symbolic quest to transcend the sensual emptiness of the phenomenal world through a mystical participation in reality. In the thirteen poems of "Sequence, Sometimes Metaphysical" R. again takes up the subject of the reality of physical appearances. These poems illuminate the mystic path toward a final union of physical and spiritual realities.

R. is one of the major American poets of the postwar decades. His best work shows him to be a poet celebrating and moralizing the American landscape. This work also places him in the central Emersonian and visionary tradition of American literature.

FURTHER WORKS: *Party at the Zoo* (1963); *On the Poet and His Craft: Selected Prose of T. R.* (1965); *The Collected Poems of T. R.* (1966); *Selected Letters* (1968); *Straw for the Fire: From the Notebooks of T. R., 1943–1963* (1972)

BIBLIOGRAPHY: Burke, K., "The Vegetal Radicalism of T. R.," *SR*, 58 (1950): 68–108; Mills, R. J., Jr. ed., *T. R.* (1963); Stein, A., ed., *T: R.: Essays on the Poetry* (1965); Malkoff, K., *T. R.: An Introduction to the Poetry* (1966); Seager, A., *The Glass House The Life of T. R.* (1968); Blessing, R., *T. R.'s Dynamic Vision* (1974); Sullivan, R., *T. R.: The Garden Master* (1975); Kunitz, S., "Four for R.," *A Kind of Order, A Kind of Folly* (1975): 77–127; La Belle, J., *The Echoing Wood of T. R.* (1976); Parini, J., *T. R.: An American Romantic* (1979); Stiffler, R., *T. R.: The Poet and His Critics* (1986); Balakian, P., *T. R.'s Far Fields: The Evolution of His Poetry* (1989)

—EDWARD HIRSCH

ROJAS, Manuel

Chilean novelist and short-story writer, b. 8 Jan. 1896, Buenos Aires, Argentina; d. 14 March 1973, Santiago

R. was born in Argentina of Chilean parents; his father died when the boy was four years old. He subsequently lived in Buenos Aires, Rosario, and Mendoza, Argentina, with his mother before going alone to Chile at the age of seventeen. Having left school earlier, at the age of fourteen, R. worked at a variety of jobs: grape picker, construction laborer on the Trans-Andean Railroad, stevedore on the Valparaiso docks, linotype operator, prompter with itinerant theater groups, and journalist. As a youth he was active as an anarchist; but because of the violence perpetrated by certain factions, he repudiated such activities. As a writer, he has never espoused political causes. In 1957 he received the Chilean National Prize for Literature.

R.'s first book was *Hombres del sur* (1926; men of the south). In this volume of short stories his emphasis is on rugged outdoor types and dramatic, fast-paced action in a regional Andean setting. The story "Laguna" (Laguna), a character sketch of a poor man haunted by bad luck, is a literary embellishment of a personal experience R. had while working on the railroad; the quiet humor mixed with pathos used in this character portrayal is a constant in almost all of R.'s works.

Two subsequent volumes, *El delincuente* (1929; the delinquent) and *Travesía* (1934; west wind), contain a variety of stories, both serious and humorous, about characters mostly from the poorer social classes. Those that have best stood the test of time are "El vaso de leche" (the glass of milk), "El delincuente," and "El mendigo" (the beggar), all from *El delincuente*. Slower in their movement than the stories in his first collection, and with a minimum of action, these stories convey subtle changes in moods and mental states as they depict lonely, alienated men searching for companionship in a bewildering urban environment. R. is by no means an experimental short-story writer, but in his direct style and conventional technique he is certainly a master of the genre.

In his first novel, *Lanchas en la bahía* (1932; boats in the bay), R. exploited his personal experiences as a young stevedore. Employing visual and auditory imagery to great effect, he paints an impressionistic picture of the dock area of Valparaiso at night as well as the atmosphere of a low-class brothel. More importantly, the novel is an exploration of the character of a youth in late adolescence. While the pain of this ambivalent stage in life between boyhood and manhood is clearly present, R. prefers to stress the humorously ironic aspects of the young man's dilemma. The novel is little more than an expanded short story, similar in its conventional structure to his earlier works.

In *Hijo de ladrón* (1951; *Born Guilty*, 1955) R. reached his full maturity as a novelist. It remains without a doubt his greatest literary achievement. Like his previous work, this too is highly autobiographical. But the central character, Aniceto Hevia, from whose retrospective point of view the novel is narrated, transcends the autobiographical—his experiences are representative of those of modern man in a broken world. Condemned to his past because of his father's profession as a thief, young Aniceto is a man in search of an authentic role in life and at least a modicum of freedom in what might be called a "tragic fellowship" with others. Following the breakup of his family upon his mother's death and his father's imprisonment, Aniceto is thrown into the chaos of the world of the lower depths to find his own way. Underlying his varied experiences and the fragmentary nature of the events as they follow the zig-zag course of recollection is a substructure that gives unity to apparent chaos—the mythical pattern of man's fall from innocence into the discovery of a world of suffering, solitude, and death, and the quest for salvation that naturally follows. Without writing a religious novel, R. uses subtle Christian symbolism as Aniceto's rites of passage from boyhood to manhood are narrated. From the solidarity of family through the inferno of loneliness, sickness, and social upheaval, Aniceto by the novel's end has found friendship and a degree of liberation from the past; the wounds inflicted by the world have been healed to a great extent, and the ultimate vision is one of hope.

Three later novels, *Mejor que el vino* (1958; better than wine), *Sombras contra el muro* (1963; shadows against the wall), and *La oscura vida radiante* (1971; this dark but radiant life), continue the adventures of Aniceto Hevia. The first explores the psychophysiological maze of Aniceto's sexual-romantic relationships, moving from the depths of loveless, sterile couplings to the rapturous heights of spiritual and sexual love with one of the women he marries. The second novel is a kaleidoscopic burlesque of Aniceto's anarchist friends, whose efforts at human solidarity for the most part are seen in the light of their absurdity. Both are good novels although at times burdened by an experimental style that fails to express the profundity and genuine humanity of the earlier *Hijo de ladr´n*. The last novel of the tetralogy is unfortunately far inferior to the others; repetitious and composed of undisguised autobiographical material from R.'s life, it reveals only a writer whose inspiration has finally gone dry.

In general, R.'s works, while almost entirely autobiographical, are of high artistic quality. A master of ironic understatement, tongue-in-cheek humor, genuine pathos, and a style that evokes the spoken word, his novels and stories exude life and authentic human experience.

FURTHER WORKS: *Tonada del transeunte* (1927); *La ciudad de los Césares* (1936); *De la poesía a la revolución* (1938); *Imágenes de infancia* (1955); *Punta de rieles* (1960); *El árbol siempre verde* (1960); *Obras completas* (1961); *Pasé por México un día* (1964)

BIBLIOGRAPHY: Cannizzo, M., "M. R., Chilean Novelist and Author," *Hispania*, 41 (1958): 200–201; González Vera, J. S., *Algunos* (1959): 175–205; Goic, C., "*Hijo de ladrón*: Libertad y lágrimas," *Atenea* 389 (1960): 103–13; Silva Castro, R., "M. R., novelista," *CHA*, 44 (1960): 5–9; Alegría, F., *Fronteras del realismo* (1962): 83–112; Lichtblau, M., "Ironic Devices in M. R.'s *Hijo de ladrón*," *Symposium*, 19 (1965): 214–25; Scott, R., "The Dialectic of Hope: The Unifying Theme in *Hijo de ladrón*", *Hispania*, 61 (1979): 626–34

—ROBERT H. SCOTT

ROJO, Antonio Benítez

Cuban short-story writer, novelist, essayist, and critic, b. 14 Mar. 1931, Havana

A mathematician by training, R. wrote his first short story at the age of thirty-three, an act that changed his career and his life forever. Today, he is an internationally recognized writer and literary critic. In spite of his "nonliterary background," R.'s first short stories were masterpieces of precision and complexity. His view of literature from a scientific perspective together with his refined sensitivity for the arts and music, makes him a unique writer, and his narratives, intricate puzzles with an uncanny insight into the cultures and history of the Caribbean.

R. was born in Havana, Cuba, but spent periods of his childhood in Panama, in the Canal Zone, where he learned English, and also in Puerto Rico. When he returned to Cuba, he began to study business. He won a scholarship to study in Washington D.C. where he spent a year, before returning once more to Cuba and taking a job with de Cuban Telephone Company in the Department of Statistics. In 1959, with the triumph of the Cuban revolution, a historical moment that changed the life of all Cubans, major changes occurred that would change his future. The new socialist regime confiscated and nationalized foreign companies and investments in the island, among these, the Telephone Company. R. was then transferred to the Department of Labor. From the onset of the revolution the new socialist government highly encouraged cultural activities and supported the enhancement of art, literature, and music. Encouraged by these opportunities, in 1965 R. ventured into writing a short story that was immediately acclaimed and published in *La gaceta de Cuba*. It was a simple experiment that changed his life. From this moment on R. continued to write and win awards. That same year, as a result of his literary success, he was offered the position of vice-director of the sector of theater and dance in the Department of Culture. In 1970, while serving as the director of the Center for Literary Research at Casa de las Américas, he was offered the prestigious position of Director of the Center for Caribbean Studies in Casa de las Américas, a position that put him in contact with writers and scholars and that allowed him to travel.

In spite of his apparent success and integration to the revolution, R. experienced difficult periods due to his unresolved differences with the philosophy of the revolutionary system. His wife and two children had been allowed to leave the island and settle in Boston seeking medical help for his daughter, and his known desire to visit them created at times open tension with the system and placed him, intermittently, in an "out of grace" state with the government. It is possible, as Roberto González Echevarría has stated in his introduction to R.'s *Estatuas sepultadas y otros relatos* (1984; Buried Statutes and Other Stories), that "Just as Scheherazade narrated stories to save her own life, R. wrote them to be able to leave Cuba." His position and his success as a writer allowed him for several years to travel to other countries, always under close scrutiny and watch; however, in June 1980, at the height of his career, while in Paris, accompanying a Cuban delegation, early one morning R. walked down the steps of the hotel, alone, and disappeared unnoticed in the Parisian streets. With the help of a friend also exiled in Paris he reached West Berlin, requested political asylum, and eventually joined his family in Boston.

R.'s defection was a road to freedom he had carved with his writing; however, it was also an act of dispossession, since he had to leave all of his unfinished and published manuscripts behind. By this time he had already published two novels; five collections of short stories, the first two of them being the best known of his early work, *Tute de reyes* (1967; Set of Four Kings), awarded the 1967 Literary Award for the best collection of short stories by Casa de las Américas, and *El escudo de hojas secas* (1969; Dried Leaves Coat of Arms); and three movie scripts—including *Los sobrevivientes* (The Survivors), directed by Tomás Gutiérrez Alea and presented at the Cannes Festival in 1979. It can be said with no doubt that R.'s international reputation as a mature and complex writer was established in the 1960s with the publication of *Tute de reyes* and *El escudo de hojas secas*. Ironically, several of these short stories were written with such precision that they seem to conform to the strictest aesthetic dictates of the revolutionary system, yet they also unfolded into other alternative readings, palimpsests of two or more ways of readings different significations. Perhaps one of the most unique characteristics of R.'s work is that the text is always trying to escape its own boundaries. R. plays with multiple dimensions and parallel realities, as can be found in his Cortaza-like structure of "La tijera" (The Scissors) in *Tute de reyes*. He often constructs self-contained worlds in which the codes to unlock a hidden secret can only be found in the religious beliefs of Afro-Cuban sects versus—and already always within—the dominant Western materialistic pre and postrevolutionary Cuban society. In these short stories the reader encounters a dance between the inner self, the most hidden patterns of the psychic, as well as the collective unconscious of a people versus the official world—the world of the law created for, and imposed on, a people. R.'s characters are often caught between these unreconciliable worlds and are left with no solutions. R.'s work unveils the many faces of prejudice whether political, social, and racial as in "Recuerdos de una piel" (Memories of a Skin) where the reader enters the complex world of deep rooted racial differences in the complex dynamics of the intimate relationship between two lovers, the narrator, an apolitical white man, and Mariana, a black woman with whom he has been living for years. Ironically, in this story, what makes Mariana aware of the "differences" and makes her conscious of her otherness in her lover's eyes, is the revolutionary ideals of equality presented by Máximo, a black employee in the house. By leaving the narrator and going with Máximo, Mariana asserts her independence but also her difference, leaving to the reader the task of explaining the many faces of difference and equality.

In an intricate dance between incarceration and freedom, escape is often a frustrated desire for most of R.'s characters. In "La tijera," for example, the character is condemned to dream the same dream for the rest of his life, and in "El cielo y la tierra" (Heaven and Earth) Pedro Limón, now a new revolutionary man, is isolated and different from his own people. Now bound to a revolutionary freedom that sets him aside, sequestered by a new reality with new and different laws. However, in "Estatuas sepultadas" (Buried Statues) a highly symbolic short story he dedicated to his wife, escape is uncanny and magical, but possible.

In 1979 R. published *El mar de las lentejas* (1979; *The Sea of Lentils*, 1990), a novel immediately well acclaimed in Cuba but soon banned by the government after his defection. It is a historical novel that interweaves four moments of the history of America: the death of Ferdinand II, the first years of the conquest of Hispanola, the conquest of what is now Florida by Pedro Meléndez de Alivés, and the entrance of John Hawkins in the Caribbean, whose presence marked the beginning of the intense market of African slaves in América. The title of the novel refers to a mistranslation from Antilla to the French Lentil made by the cosmographer Guillaume Le Testu of the first map of this area where a name other than North Sea was given, a symbolical error for R. of the entire conquest experience. Much like his short stories, *El mar de Las lentejas* creates a close world—this time a historical world, with historical characters and protagonists incarcerated by their own actions and thoughts. In this novel those who create history are always at the end defeated by the same history they help create, and the powerful often fall victim of their own power. The novel dismantles the official version of the historical events to leave the characters

naked before their own fears, weaknesses, and desires. The conqueror is always a victim of his own actions, conquered by history, and destroyed by his own violence. Although the novel is staged in the 16th c., and it is faithfully true to the history it rewrites, it is also an allegory of the Caribbean from the arrival of Columbus to the present. For R., history in the Caribbean repeats itself, an idea he explores at depth in his collection of essays, *La isla que se repite* (1989; *The Repeating Island*, 1992; rev. ed., 1996).

Experimenting with and meditating on the theory of Chaos, and applying it to the social sciences, art, music, and literature, R. suggests that in the Caribbean, as in the closed worlds of his short stories, the plantation system became a way of thought and of life, giving way to a Plantation system imprinted in the political, economic, and social fabrics of the Caribbean. It is in essence always already the same system in operation regardless of the political philosophy or economic structures said to dictate the lives of the different Caribbean societies. It is a system so ingrained in the patterns of life that changes of governments cannot break. History then, in the Caribbean, cannot be explained through a hegelean dialectics, but as a dance, always the same, a rhythmic movement between dance partners, like an erotic duel, always repeating the same steps, ending only to start again. It is a unique and uncanny reading of the Caribbean as seen through its literary production that pushes the margins of literature into those of science, humanity, and the social sciences. It is perhaps the most unique and complex gaze at Caribbean cultures written to date. As in many of his short stories, R. offers an insightful analysis of the Caribbean as a close world that traps its characters, where escape seems to be an illusion, and change a simple justification for the same.

Soon after his arrival to the U.S., R. was offered a position at Amherst College in Massachusetts. He has traveled extensively and lectured in many universities. After a long pause in his fictional production, during which he established a solid reputation in the U.S. as a literary critic, he published another collection of short stories, *Paso de los vientos*, first in an English version with the title of *A View from the Mangroves* (1997). Staged in the Caribbean, in different periods, most of these short stories follow many of the same techniques he had mastered in *El mar de las lentejas* to explore again, from a different historical perspective, the history of the Caribbean, as well as themes like treason and honor, illegality and resistance, and, again, Afro-Caribbean presence and beliefs, as well as the motifs of escape, exile, and condemnation.

FURTHER WORKS: *Tres relatos panameños* (1974); *Los inquilinos* (1976); *Heroica* (1976); *Siglo del relato latinoamericano* (1976). FURTHER WORKS IN ENGLISH: *Magic Dogs and Other Stories* (1990)

BIBLIOGRAPHY: González-Echevarría, R., "A. B. R.," *NER*, 6 (Summer, 1984): 575-78; Artalejo, L. "Creación y subversión: La narrativa histórica de A.B.R.," *RI*, 56 (July-Dec. 1990): 152-53, 1027-1030; Forns-Broggi, R., "Una lectura vertical de "Estatuas sepultadas" de A. B. R.: Apuntes sobre la política del cuento," *Torre de Papel*, 3 (Fall 1993): 29-40; Sklodowska, E., "Literary Invention and Critical Fashion: Missing the Boat in the Sea of Lentils," *StTCL*, 19 (Winter, 1995): 61-79; Bracho, E., "El Caribe y la teoría del caos," *Quimera*, 131-32 (1994): 55-61; Colas, S., "'There's No Place Like Home': or, The Utopian, Uncanny Caribbean State of Mind of A.B.R.," *Siglo*, 13 (1995): 207-17; Bromberg, S. J. "The New Story of the Caribbean: Quantum Mechanics and

Postmodem Theory in A.B.R.'s *La isla que se repite: El Caribe y la perspectiva posmoderna,*" *Ometeca,* 3-4 (1996): 142-53; Cuervo Hewitt, J. "Crónica de un deseo: Re(in)sistencia, subversión y re-escritura en *El mar de las lentejas,*" *RI,* 63 (April-June 1996): 461-76

—JULIA CUERVO HEWITT

ROLAND HOLST, Adriaan

Dutch poet and essayist, b. 23 May 1888, Amsterdam; d. 6 Aug. 1976, Amsterdam

The son of a stockbroker, and the nephew of the painter Richard Roland Holst and the Christian-socialist poet and activist Henriëtte ROLAND HOLST-VAN DER SCHALK, R. H. was a student at Oxford from 1908 to 1911. There he familiarized himself with the poetry of the English romantics, especially Shelley, and was attracted to the poetry of the Irish Revival, in particular to the work of YEATS. A very sociable and yet distant person, R. H. spent most of his life in the artists' village of Bergen, North Holland. Living soberly as a country gentleman, he never sought employment. He was an associate editor of *De gids,* the magazine of the Dutch literary establishment, from 1920 to 1934. After World War II he spent several months in South Africa as an unofficial literary envoy, in a doomed attempt to revitalize the cultural bonds between the Netherlands and South Africa. In 1959 he was awarded the prestigious Netherlandic Literature Prize.

R. H.'s first volume of poems, *Verzen* (1911; verses), reveals a neoromantic, nostalgic dreamer, who in a highly stylized poetic idiom expresses his innermost feelings. Wind, waves, and islands are the symbols of his isolation. He sets himself apart from mankind much as the true believer sets himself apart from those who do not have faith. R. H. was particularly fond of symbolism drawn from the Trojan War. He saw Helen's beautiful smile as the doom of materialistic Troy. His celebration of the power of beauty is perhaps best expressed in his greatest poetic achievement, *Een winter aan zee* (1937; a winter at sea), a series of more than sixty poems.

R. H. translated Shakespeare's *King Lear* (1914) and *Richard III* (1929). He also published a brilliant Dutch rendering of Yeats's *The Countess Cathleen* in 1941. The best of R. H.'s prose writings is *Deirdre en de zonen van Usnach* (1916; *Deirdre and the sons of Usnach*), a doom-shadowed account of the Celtic legend that shows the influence of Yeats. As a critic, R. H. was instrumental in establishing the reputation of J. H. LEOPOLD with his article "Over den dichter Leopold" (1926; on the poet Leopold). In "Shelley, een afscheid" (1928; Shelley, a farewell) he repudiated his former idol.

Although R. H.'s verse is sometimes obscure, indeed deliberately so, it is always melodious. Addressed to the senses rather than to the mind of the reader, it reveals a vision of the springtime of human existence before what R. H. considered the corruption of civilization.

FURTHER WORKS: *De belijdenis van de stilte* (1913); *Voorbij de wegen* (1920); *De wilde kim* (1925); *De afspraak* (1925); *Het elysisch verlangen* (1928); *De vagebond* (1931); *Tussen vuur en maan* (1932); *De pooltocht der verbeelding* (1936); *Voortekens* (1936); *Uit zelfbehoud* (1938); *Onderweg* (1940); *Eigen achtergronden* (1945); *In memoriam Herman Gorter* (1946); *Sirenische kunst* (1946); *De twee planeten* (1947); *Tegen de wereld* (1947); *In*

ballingschap (1947); *Verzamelde werken* (4 vols., 1948–1949); *Van erts tot arend* (1948); *Swordplay, wordplay* (1950, with Simon Vestdijk); *Woest en moe* (1951); *Bezielde dorpen* (1957); *In gevaar* (1958); *Omtrent de grens* (1960); *Het experiment* (1960); *Onder koude wolken* (1962); *Onderhuids* (1963); *Uitersten* (1967); *Verzamelde gedichten* (1971); *Voorlopig* (1976)

BIBLIOGRAPHY: Meijer, R. P., *Literature of the Low Countries* (1971): 294–98

—FRANCIS BULHOF

ROLAND HOLST-VAN DER SCHALK, Henriëtte

Dutch poet, dramatist, and biographer, b. 24 Dec. 1869, Noordwijk; d. 21 Nov. 1952, Amsterdam

R. H. came from a well-to-do background, but her idealistic tendencies soon found an outlet in the socialism that swept up many Dutch poets of the turn of the century. She married the painter Richard N. Roland Holst and became active in socialist politics after 1897. Eventually, with the outbreak of the Russian Revolution, she became a communist, but a visit to the Soviet Union in 1921 led to a gradual disillusionment with the totalitarian nature of Soviet communism, and from 1925 on she became a prominent advocate of a Christian socialism that integrated the spiritual sensitivity always evident in her poetry with a socialism that had originally derived more from the English writer William Morris (1834–1896) than from Marx.

As a poet, R. H. began as a protégé of Albert VERWEY; Plato, Spinoza, and especially Dante are important influences on her work. Her first volume was the earnest and energetic *Sonnetten en verzen in terzinen geschreven* (1895; sonnets and verses written in tercets), but she found her characteristic tone and subject matter in the series of volumes beginning with *De nieuwe geboort* (1902; the new birth). As with many of her contemporaries, sonnets predominate in her early work, but her often unrestrained exuberance and her passionate energy give her work in this form a very individual character. Typical of her poetry is a long, breathless, flowing sentence that runs through many verses. R. H. also wrote dramas and numerous prose works, including a noteworthy series of biographies.

R. H.'s voluminous work is generally thought to be uneven, but at her best she is a strong feminine voice, recording a ceaseless striving and reaching out toward a social vision of a brighter future for the humble who now have only fleeting intuitions of what they potentially can be. For a woman these aspirations are made concrete in the child, and R. H. effectively gives voice to the special difficulty of the woman whose social consciousness will not let her be content with the domestic satisfactions of being a wife and mother: "It is no good fortune to come at the turn of the tide, and to be born a woman." What makes her best verse interesting is a frank and open-hearted exploration of the conflicts and disappointments that arise out of the poet's commitment to a social ideal.

FURTHER WORKS: *Kapitaal en arbeid in de 19de eeuw* (1902); *Generalstreik und Sozialdemokratie* (1906); *Opwaartsche wegen* (1907); *De opstandelingen* (1910); *De vrouw in het woud* (1912); *Thomas More* (1912); *Rousseau* (1912); *Het feest der gedachtenis*

(1915); *Verzonken grenzen* (1918); *De held en de schare* (1920); *Het offer* (1921); *De kinderen* (1922); *Tusschen twee werelden* (1923); *Arbeid* (1923); *De voorwaarden tot hernieuwing der dramatische kunst* (1924); *Heldensage* (1927); *Verworvenheden* (1927); *Vernieuwingen* (1929); *Tolstoi* (1930); *Kinderen van deze tijd* (1931); *Wij willen niet* (1931); *Gustaaf Landauer* (1931); *Guido Gezelle* (1931); *De moeder* (1932); *De roep der stad* (1933); *Herman Gorter* (1933); *Rosa Luxemburg* (1935); *Gedroomd gebeuren* (1937); *R. N. Roland Holst* (1941); *Uit de diepte* (1946); *Romain Rolland* (1946); *Van de schaduw naar het licht* (1946); *In de webbe der tijden* (1947); *Gandhi* (1947); *Wordingen* (1949); *Het vuur brandde voort* (1949); *Romankunst als levensschool* (1950); *Bloemlezing* (1951)

BIBLIOGRAPHY: Meijer, R. P., *Literature of the Low Countries*, new ed. (1978): 263–66; Zweers, A. F., "Leo Tolstoj's Role in H. R. H.'s Quest for Brotherhood and Love," *CRCL*, 7 (1980): 1–21

—FRED J. NICHOLS

ROLLAND, Romain

French novelist, dramatist, biographer, and musicologist, b. 29 Jan. 1866, Clamecy; d. 30 Dec. 1944, Vézelay

R. was born into a provincial Catholic family, which moved to Paris in 1880 so that R. could complete his studies there; in 1886 he was admitted to the École Normale Supérieure. Life in the capital had a deeply disturbing effect on the young student; long an eager reader of Tolstoy, he wrote to him for guidance. Tolstoy's reply left a deep impression on him, and he vowed never to leave any letter unanswered. Trained in history and a sensitive musician, Fellow of the École Française de Rome, he completed his thesis, *Histoire de l'opéra en Europe avant Lully et Scarlatti* (history of opera in Europe before Lully and Scarlatti), in 1895. In Rome he formed a lasting friendship with Malwida von Meysenbug, confidante of Nietzsche and Wagner, who encouraged his first attempts at writing. He held the first chair in musicology at the Sorbonne and gave courses on art and music there, as well as at the École des Hautes Etudes Sociales and the École Normale, until his resignation in 1912. Married in 1892 and divorced in 1901, he was a rather solitary man, closely attached to his mother.

As a young man, R. had a strong sense of social responsibility, believing that art has a duty to society. Eager to participate in the political and intellectual life of his time, he wished to bring courage, faith, hope, and vigor to his contemporaries. With this intention he wrote first for the stage. He began several dramas on Italian subjects, but most of his published dramas were set during the French Revolution. One of them, *Les loups* (pub. 1898; *The Wolves*, 1937), a barely veiled version of the Dreyfus case, brought him into conflict with part of the public, a situation that was to continue throughout his life.

Frustrated by the exigencies of the stage, R. began to write biographies of famous men—*Vie de Beethoven* (1903; *Beethoven*, 1917), *Vie de Tolstoï* (1911; *Tolstoy*, 1911)—to bring the same message of strength and hope, but he also turned to fictitious biography and wrote the novel *Jean-Christophe*, (10 vols., 1904–12; *Jean-Christophe*, 4 vols., 1910–13). This cyclical novel traces the development of a German musician, in whom can be discerned elements of Beethoven, Mozart, and Wagner. Forced to leave Germany, Jean-Christophe struggles to develop his art in France, Switzerland, and Italy. The novel, among other things an attempt to bring about greater understanding between France and Germany, is a pan-European work. Jean-Christophe is the heroic example of the lifetime struggle of a genius with himself, his society, and his art, the example of a man who remains true to his ideals. Naive, blundering, intensely sincere, warmly sympathetic to those around him, full of contradictions, a somewhat romantic hero—the misunderstood artist in a hostile society—he is an appealing and even unforgettable figure, especially but not solely to younger readers. Through Jean-Christophe and a second major character, the Frenchman Olivier, R. criticized the failings of both French and German artistic and social life, thereby making many enemies. For this and other works he received the 1915 Nobel Prize for literature.

Although he knew little of the theoretical bases of socialism, R. looked upon this movement as one almost religious in nature; he also found such qualities in the French and Russian revolutions. Disillusioned by the socialists' failure in 1914, he hailed the Russian Revolution in 1917. At the outbreak of the war in 1914 he was in Switzerland, where he often sojourned. There he remained, not to stay out of the battle, but to stay above it and to try to mitigate the hatred and hysteria of the combatants, an attempt that earned him the distrust of many and the approval of only a few.

In 1922 R. began publication of another cyclical novel, *L'âme enchantée* (7 vols., 1922–33; *The Soul Enchanted*, 6 vols., 1925–35), whose protagonist is a female counterpart of Jean-Christophe. The novel portrays the development of a young woman and of her son; both move from intransigent individualism toward a more collective ideal. Annette's enchantment is the process of stripping away false ideas and illusions. Except for her maternity, Annette has no creative life; her struggles are to raise her son and to free herself, psychologically and socially, from the bonds of the past and the present. A vague proponent of women's rights, she becomes active in the defense of the Soviet Union. Her half-sister Sylvie profits from a sexist society to advance her own fortunes. The final volumes are filled with the chaos and conflicts of Europe of the 1920s; they are at times almost documentary in character.

After World War I R. kept up the struggle for truth and justice; he opposed Fascism and Nazism, and was a staunch defender of the U.S.S.R.; he was a proponent of a pacifism that was nonviolent but not nonresistant. Nonviolence, congenial to his character, was strongly influenced by his contacts with Eastern thinkers, such as Gandhi and Rabindranath TAGORE. His perception of the U.S.S.R. was also formed by his contacts with Russian revolutionaries in Switzerland, his friendship with Maxim GORKY, and his marriage in 1934 to the half-French widow of a Russian gentleman. But he was never a member of the Communist Party.

R.'s life and his work are reflected in the precepts he set down in *Le théâtre du peuple* (1903; *The People's Theatre*, 1918): that art must bring joy, energy, and intelligence to the people; that it must portray genuine emotions and be of a true realism and simple morality; that it must combat the lethargy of the mind. Art and all intellectual life must engage in this struggle for the enlightenment of the people. These noble qualities in the two long novels and many of his other works have made them part of world literature.

FURTHER WORKS: *Saint-Louis* (1897); *Aërt* (1898); *Le triomphe de la raison* (1899); *Danton* (1900; *Danton*, 1918); *Millet* (1902; *Millet*, 1902); *Le quatorze juillet* (1902; *The Fourteenth of July*, 1918); *Le temps viendra* (1903); *La Montespan: Drame en trois actes* (1904; *The Montespan: Drama in Three Acts*, 1923); *Michel-Ange* (1905; *The Life of Michael Angelo*, 1912); *Théâtre de la Révolution: Le quatorze juillet; Danton; Les loups* (1906; *Musiciens d'aujourd'hui* (1908; *Musicians of Today*, 1914); *Musiciens d'autrefois* (1908; *Some Musicians of Former Days*, 1915); *Haendel* (1910; *Handel*, 1916); *Les tragédies de la foi: Saint-Louis; Aërt; Le triomphe de la raison* (1913); *Au-dessus de la mêlée* (1915; *Above the Battle*, 1916); *Le triomphe de la liberté* (1917); *Empédocle d'Agrigente et l'âge de la haine* (1918); *Liluli* (1919; *Liluli*, 1920); *Colas Breugnon* (1919; *Colas Breugnon, Burgundian*, 1919); *Les précurseurs* (1919; *The Forerunners*, (1920); *Voyage musical aux pays du passé* (1919; *Musical Tour through the Land of the Past*, 1923); *Clerambault: Histoire d'une conscience libre pendant la guerre* (1920; *Clerambault: The Story of an Independent Spirit during the War*, 1921); *Pierre et Luce* (1920; *Pierre and Luce*, 1922); *La révolte des machines; ou, La pensée déchaînée* (1921; *The Revolt of the Machines; or, Invention Run Wild: A Motion Picture Fantasy*, 1932); *Les vaincus* (1922); *Mahatma Gandhi* (1924; *Mahatma Gandhi*, 1924); *Le jeu de l'amour et de la mort* (1925; *The Game of Love and Death*, 1926); *Pâques fleuries* (1926; *Palm Sunday*, 1928); *Les Léonides* (1928; *Les Léonides*, 1929); *Beethoven: Les grandes époques créatrices* (7 vols., 1928–1945; new enlarged ed., 1966; partial tr., *Beethoven the Creator*, 1929); *Essai sur la mystique et l'action de l'Inde vivante* (3 vols., 1929–1930; *Prophets of the New India*, 1930); *Goethe et Beethoven* (1930; *Goethe and Beethoven*, 1931); *La musique dans l'histoire générale; Gretry; Mozart* (1930); *Quinze ans de combat* (1919–1934) (1935; *I Will Not Rest*, 1935); *Par la révolution, la paix* (1935); *Compagnons de route: Essais littéraires* (1936); *Les pages immortelles de Rousseau* (1938; *The Living Thoughts of Rousseau*, 1939); *Valmy* (1938); *Robespierre* (1939); *Le voyage intérieur* (1942; expanded ed., 1959; *The Journey Within*, 1947); *Péguy* (1945); *Le seuil, précédé du Royaume de T.* (1946); *De Jean-Christophe à Colas Breugnon: Pages de journal* (1946); *Lettres de R. R. à un combattant de la Résistance* (1947); *Souvenirs de jeunesse* (1866–1900) (1947); *Choix de lettres à Malwide von Meysenbug* (1948; *Letters, 1890–1891, R. R. and Malwide von Meysenbug*, 1933); *Correspondance entre Louis Gillet et R. R.* (1949); *Richard Strauss et R. R.* (1951); *Le cloître de la rue d'Ulm: Journal de R. R. à l'École Normale* (1952); *Printemps romain: Choix de lettres de R. R. à sa mère* (1954); *Une amitié française. Correspondance entre Charles Péguy et R. R.* (1955); *Mémoires* (1965); *Retour au Palais Farnèse: Choix de lettres de R. R. à sa mère* (1956); *R. R.-Lugné-Poe: Correspondance 1894–1901* (1957); *De la décadence de la peinture italienne au XVI siècle: Thèse latine* (1957); *Chère Sofia: Choix de lettres de R. R. à Sofia Bertolini Guerrieri-Gonzaga* (2 vols., 1959–1960); *Inde: Journal 1915–1943* (1960); *Rabindranath Tagore et R. R.: Lettres et autres écrits* (1961); *Ces jours lointains: Alphonse Séché et R. R.* (1962); *Fräulein Elsa: Lettres de R. R. à Elsa Wolff* (1964); *Deux hommes se rencontrent: Correspondance entre Jean-Richard Block et R. R.* (1964); *R. R. et le mouvement florentin de "La Voce": Correspondance et fragments du journal* (1966); *Lettres de R. R. à Marianne Czeke* (1966); *Un beau visage à tous sens: Choix de lettres de R. R.* (1967); *Salut et fraternité: Alain et R. R.* (1969); *Gandhi et R. R.: Correspondance, extraits du journal et textes divers* (1969); *Je commence à devenir dangereux: Choix de lettres de R. R. à sa mère* (1914–1916) (1971); *D'une rive à l'autre: Hermann Hesse et R. R.: Correspondance et fragments du journal* (1972); *Pour l'honneur de l'esprit: Correspondance entre Charles Péguy et R. R.* (1973); *Bon voisinage: Edmond Privat et R. R. Lettres et documents*

(1977); *Monsieur le Comte: Correspondance entre R. R. et Léon Tolstoï* (1978). **FURTHER WORKS IN ENGLISH:** *Essays on Music* (1948)

BIBLIOGRAPHY: Bonnerot, J., *R. R.: Sa vie, son œuvre* (1921); Zweig, S., *R. R.* (1921); Sénéchal, C., *R. R.* (1933); Aronson, A., *R. R.: The Story of a Conscience* (1944); Doisy, M., *R. R.* (1945); Descotes, M., *R. R.* (1948); Starr, W. T., *A Critical Bibliography of the Published Writings of R. R.* (1950); Starr, W. T., *R. R. and a World at War* (1956); Robichez, J., *R. R.* (1961); Starr, W. T., *R. R.* (1971); issue, special *R.*, *RHL*, 76, 6 (1976); Fisher, D. J., *R. R. and the Politics of Intellectual Engagement* (1987)

—WILLIAM T. STARR

ROMAINS, Jules

(pseud. of Louis Farigoule) French novelist, dramatist, poet, and essayist, b. 26 Aug. 1885, Saint-Julien-Chapteuil; d. 14 Aug. 1972, Paris

R. grew up and was educated in Paris. An only child, he early acquired the habit of long walks through the city. He also read the French classics as well as Hugo and Goethe, both of whom served as models. He may also have been influenced by Henri BERGSON'S philosophy of intuition and the *élan vital* and *Émile* Durkheim's (1858–1917) theories of social groups. Although R.'s first book of poems appeared in 1904, he combined teaching with his writing until 1919, when he left teaching to devote himself entirely to literature.

R.'s initial venture into "unanimism," which grew out of his early sense of group dynamics in Paris and his association with GEORGES DUHAMEL and the Groupe de l'Abbaye gained him considerable notoriety. Besides publishing many volumes of poetry, plays, and fiction through the 1920s and 1930s, he played an active role in political affairs and was president of the International P.E.N. Club, aiding writers in countries with oppressive regimes during the 1930s. R. spent World War II in the U.S. and Mexico; he returned after the war and was elected to the French Academy in 1946. He continued to write prolifically, mainly fiction and essays on world affairs, until shortly before his death.

R.'s first important work was *La vie unanime* (1908; unanimist life), a series of long poems that illustrate his unanimist vision. This emphasizes the collective consciousness of a group—a household, a city, even a nation—which, once animated by an outsider, is transformed from dormant individual consciousness into a unified and efficiently functioning group. The move from individual to collective consciousness is an instinctive one, with the collectivity becoming a kind of god replacing in part the God of R.'s childhood faith.

These poems contain a number of technical innovations, which R. considered essential to the revitalization of French poetry, such as adding a complex system of assonance and near-rhyme, which he called *accords*, to the traditional resources of rhyme. His most eloquent later poem is the long *Europe* (1916; Europe), which expresses his horror of what he considered a European civil war. Here the continent more than the nation has become the unanimist group at a higher level, but is now bent on its own destruction.

L'homme blanc (1937; the white man), an epic sequel to *Europe*, uses Hugo as a model, but is less effective, merely extolling the expansion of European civilization throughout the world.

R.'s early fiction and drama are also illustrations of unanimism, particularly the novels *Mort de quelqu'un* (1911; *The Death of a Nobody*, 1914) and *Les copains* (1913; *The Boys in the Back Room*, 1937). In *Mort de quelqu'un* the death of an unattached apartment-house dweller gives the other tenants a new sense of solidarity, which is, however, dissipated after a year's time. *Les copains* presents a group of practical jokers reminiscent of R.'s student days, who descend on two small towns, reviving one out of its torpor and causing the inhabitants of the other to flee in terror. They claim to have restored the "pure act," a foreshadowing of ANDRÉ GIDE'S "gratuitous act."

R. had initially conceived of unanimism as usually a benevolent force, but the wholesale destruction of World War I led him to consider more seriously the dangers and abuses of group dynamism. This is a key element in most of his important plays, beginning with the verse drama *Cromedeyre-le-Vieil* (1920; Cromedeyre-le-Vieil), the name of an isolated mountain village whose nearly all-male population kidnaps a group of women from a neighboring village. In this retelling of the rape of the Sabine Women it is violence that predominates.

In the play *Donogoo-Tonka; ou, Les miracles de la science* (1920; Donogoo-Tonka; or, the miracles of science), the physical violence becomes relatively harmless fraudulence. A town in South America that does not exist (Donogoo-Tonka) is created in order to cover up the stupidity of the geographer Le Trouhadec, who became the hero of two later comedies. In *Knock; ou, Le triomphe de la médecine* (1924; *Doctor Knock*, 1925), R.'s greatest dramatic success (due in part to his collaboration with the actor-director Louis Jouvet), Dr. Knock takes over an unpromising practice in a mountain village and "animates" the town to his advantage through his power of suggestion, creating a group of well-organized hypochondriacs.

The play *Le dictateur* (1926; the dictator) raises the question of the uses and abuses of political power, but R. found the essay more effective for the expression of political ideas, as in *Problèmes européens* (1933; European problems), *Le couple France-Allemagne* (1934; the Franco-German couple), and later *Le problème no. 1* (1947; the number one problem).

Although R. continued to write poetry and plays, fiction eventually became his primary creative vehicle. His major work is his monumental *Les hommes de bonne volonté* (27 vols., 1932–46; *Men of Good Will*, 14 vols., 1933–46). He intended the series as a vast panorama telling the story of French society between 1908 and 1933. In various novels he concentrated on different characters and segments of society, bringing them together to form a complete picture. He intended also to create a new novel form, but he remains essentially the traditional omniscient author, broadening his narrative, however, by adding to it the unanimist perspective of the group.

For instance, the first novel, *Le 6 October* (1932; *The Sixth of October*, 1933), which covers that single day in 1908 when the political crisis in the Balkans that eventually led to World War I was in the Paris newspapers, first presents the Parisian crowds going to work as a unanimist group, then characters from various segments of society, some of whom will later play important roles.

The two most important characters, Jerphanion and Jallez, meet and become good friends in volumes two and three—*Crime de Quinette* (1932; *Quinette's Crime*, 1933) and *Les amours enfantines*

(1932; *Childhood's Loves*, 1934). The two young men represent two sides of R.'s own character, real or potential-the practical and the sensitive. This device permits discussion of a wide variety of contemporary topics and the introduction of much autobiographical material throughout the series. The next few volumes introduce the themes of sentimentality and sexuality and new groups of characters, some in contrast, like Haverkamp in *Les superbes* (1933; *The Proud*, 1934) and Louis Bastide in *Les humbles* (1933; *The Meek*, 1934).

The most searching of the earlier novels is *Recherche d'une église* (1934; *The Lonely*, 1935), which treats the theme of metaphysical solitude and the search for a faith to replace outmoded religious values. Politics begins to dominate in the middle volumes, especially the 1910 general strike and the threat of war, but private concerns and the problems of artistic creation are well integrated with these public matters.

The best novels of the series are *Prélude à Verdun* (1938; *Verdun: The Prelude*, 1939) and *Verdun* (1938; *Verdun: The Battle*, 1939), where R. epitomizes the horrors and the courage of war in one key battle. The battle itself is seen through very few characters, but R. also maintains the unanimist perspective of entire armies functioning as units, now negating individuals rather than enhancing their value.

The later volumes deal with the disillusion of postwar France, the utopian vision in Russia, the negative collective threat of fascism, and finally incipient Nazism in Germany, all against the background of individual destinies. These later volumes were written under the shadow of and during World War II and reflect a flagging of the optimism expressed in the general title. It has been noted, in fact, that some of the characters, even in the earlier volumes, are singularly lacking in good will.

Les hommes de bonne volonté remains one of the great fictional achievements of the century. R.'s creative energy, his breadth of vision, and his analytical powers in his best novels bring him close to Balzac, Hugo, and Zola, his spiritual predecessors, but the quality of his work is less uniform, and he does not equal them as a creator of character. *Knock and Cromedeyre-le-Vieil* are also lasting contributions to the French stage, but they and the novels can be appreciated today with little reference to his original theories of unanimism.

FURTHER WORKS: *L'âme des hommes* (1904); *Le bourg régénéré* (1906); *À la foule qui est ici* (1909); *Premier livre de prières* (1909); *Deux poèmes* (1910); *Manuel de déification* (1910); *Un être en marche* (1910); *Puissances de Paris* (1911); *L'armée dans la ville* (1911); *Odes et prières* (1913); *Sur les quais de La Villette* (1914; 2nd ed., *Le vin blanc de La Villette*, 1923); *Les quatre saisons* (1917); *Le voyage des amants* (2 vols., 1920); *La vision extra-rétinienne* (1920; *Eyeless Sight*, 1924); *Amour couleur de Paris* (1921); *M. Le Trouhadec saisi par la débauche* (1921); *Psyché* (3 vols., 1922–1929; *The Body's Rapture*, 1933); *Petit traité de versification* (1923); *Théâtre* (7 vols., 1924–1935); *Le marriage de Le Trouhadec* (1925); *La scintillante* (1925; *The Peach*, 1933); *Ode génoise* (1925); *Amédée et les messieurs en rang* (1926; *Six Gentlemen in a Row*, 1927); *Démétrios* (1926); *Jean le Maufranc* (1927); *La vérité en bouteilles* (1927); *Chants des dix années* (1928); *Volpone* (1929); *Le déjeuner marocain* (1929); *Musse* (1929); *Pièces en un acte* (1930); *Donogoo* (1931); *Boën; ou, La possession des biens* (1931); *Problèmes d'aujourd'hui* (1931); *Le roi masqué* (1932); *Eros de Paris* (1932; *Eros in Paris*,

1934); *Province* (1934; *Provincial Interludes*, 1935); *Montée des périls* (1935; *Flood Warning*, 1936); *Les pouvoirs* (1935; *The Powers That Be*, 1936); *Zola et son exemple* (1935); *Recours à l'abîme* (1936; *To the Gutter*, 1937); *Les créateurs* (1936; *To the Stars*, 1937); *Visite aux Américains* (1936); *Mission à Rome* (1937; *Mission to Rome*, 1938); *Le drapeau noir* (1937; *The Black Flag*, 1938); *Pour l'esprit et la liberté* (1937); *Cela dépend de vous* (1938); *Vorge contre Quinette* (1939; *Vorge against Quinette*, 1941); *La douceur de la vie* (1939; *The Sweets of Life*, 1941); *Sept mystères du destin de l'Europe* (1940; *Seven Mysteries of Europe*, 1940); *Messages aux Français* (1941); *Cette grande lueur à l'est* (1941; *Promise of Dawn*, 1942); *Le monde est ton aventure* (1941; *The World Is Your Adventure*, 1942); *Stefan Zweig, grand Européen* (1941; *Stefan Zweig, Great European*, 1941); *Une Vue des choses* (1941); *Grâce encore pour la terre* (1941); *Mission ou démission de la France* (1942); *Salsette découvre l'Amérique* (1942; *Salsette Discovers America*, 1942); *Journées dans la montagne* (1942; *Mountain Days*, 1944); *Les travaux et les joies* (1943; *Work and Play*, 1944); *Nomentanus le réfugé* (1943); *Tu ne tueras point* (1943; *Thou Shalt Not Kill*, 1943); *Actualité de Victor Hugo* (1944); *Bertrand de Granges* (1944); *Retrouver la foi* (1944); *Naissance de la bande* (1944; *The Gathering of the Gangs*, 1945); *Comparution* (1944; *Offered in Evidence*, 1945); *Le tapis magique* (1946; *The Magic Carpet*, 1946); *Françoise* (1946; *Françoise*, 1946); *Le sept octobre* (1946; *The Seventh of October*, 1946); *Le colloque de novembre* 1946); *L'an mil* (1947); *Choix de poèmes* (1948); *Pierres levées* (1948); *Le moulin et l'hospice* (1949); *Lettre à A. O. Barnabooth* (1950); *Violation des frontières* (1951; *Tussles with Time*, 1952); *Interviews avec Dieu* (1952); *Saints de notre calendrier* (1952); *Confidences d'un auteur dramatique* (1953); *Maisons* (1953); *Examen de conscience des Français* (1954; *A Frenchman Examines His Conscience*, 1955); *Passagers de cette planète, où allons-nous?* (1955); *Le fils de Jerphanion* (1956); *Une femme singulière* (1957; *The Adventuress*, 1958); *Souvenirs et confidences d'un écrivain* (1958); *Situation de la terre* (1958; *As It Is on Earth*, 1962); *Cinquantenaire du 6 octobre* (1958); *Le besoin de voir clair* (1958); *Mémoires de Madame Chauverel* (2 vols., 1959–1960); *Hommes, médecins, machines* (1959); *Pour raison garder* (3 vols., 1960–1967); *Les hauts et les bas de la liberté* (1960); *Un grand honnête homme* (1961); *Landowski: La main et l'esprit* (1961); *Portraits d'inconnus* (1962); *Barbazouk* (1963); *Napoléon par lui-même* (1963); *Ai-je fait ce que j'ai voulu?* (1964); *Lettres à un ami* (2 vols., 1964–1965); *Lettre ouverte contre une vaste conspiration* (1966; *Open Letter against a Vast Conspiracy*, 1967); *Marc-Aurèle; ou, L'empereur de bonne volonté* (1968); *Amitiés et rencontres* (1970); *Correspondance J. R.-André Gide* (1976)

BIBLIOGRAPHY: Cuisenier, A., *J. R. et l'unanimisme* (1935); Blaser, H., *De l'influence alternée et simultanée des éléments sensibles et intellectuels dans les œuvres de J. R.* (1941); Cuisenier, A., *L'art de J. R.* (1949); Berry, M., *J. R.: Sa vie, son œuvre* (1953); Cuisenier, A., *J. R. et "Les hommes de bonne volonté"* (1954); Norrish, P., *Drama of the Group: A Study of Unanimism in the Plays of J. R.* (1958); Maurois, A., *From Proust to Camus* (1966): 252–78; Moore, H. T., *Twentieth Century French Literature to World War II* (1966): 61–66, 137–43; O'Brien, J., The French Literary Horizon (1967): 221–44; Boak, D., *J. R.* (1974)

—CHARLES G. HILL

ROMANIAN LITERATURE

At the beginning of the 20th c. and until shortly before the outbreak of World War I, Romanian literature was in a state of stagnation. The great achievements of romanticism and realism in poetry, prose, and drama—as illustrated by Mihai Eminescu (1850–1889), Ion Creangă (1839–1889), Ion L. Caragiale (1852–1912), and Ioan Slavici (1848–1925)—lay behind, and the great critical-intellectual mentors, the aestheticist Titu Maiorescu (1840–1917) and the Marxist Constantin Dobrogeanu-Gherea (1855–1920) were long past their prime. The SYMBOLIST group centered around the flamboyant and talented Alexandru Macedonski (1854–1920) no longer provided intellectual excitement. Only Ion Minulescu (1881–1944), an able manipulator of grandiloquent images and verse combinations, maintained, for a while, genuine appeal in the symbolist tradition. A lot of hope was invested in the broad populist movement, which expressed itself in *Viaţa românească, Sămănătorul*, and a dozen other literary journals. Its proponents were trying to produce a literature written in simple language, with themes taken from local rural life and national history and geared to the emotional needs of a broad unsophisticated audience.

Some talented writers had emerged, such as the fiction writers Ion Agirbiceanu (1882–1962) and Gala Galaction (1879–1961), in both of whose work a sentimental Christian humanism is mixed with shrewd social observations, and Calistrat Hogaş, (1847–1917), a master of the long serpentine sentence, whose descriptions of travels in the Carpathian mountains are enlivened by comical touches and allusions to classical mythology. The lively poetic parodies of Gheorghe Topîrceanu (1886–1937) and the mournful nature descriptions, fervent social yearnings, and national prophetic tones of Octavian Goga (1881–1938) and Ştefan O. Iosif (1875–1913) made them into some of the most popular poets ever to write in Romanian. But the populist literary movement expressed itself particularly through some important thinkers. Nicolae Iorga (1871–1940) was a prodigious figure—a historian, politician, journalist, poet, and playwright who was immensely prolific; as a critic, he pioneered research into 18th- and early-19th–c. Romanian literature and proclaimed the need for a national rebirth through an ethical literature that should unify the body politic. Garabet Ibrăileanu (1871–1936) and Constantin Stere (1865–1936) emphasized the importance of social awareness and the need for radical reform; both also wrote important novels, Ibrăileanu a psychological one, Stere a satire of political life with revolutionary implications.

The social and political changes that came with World War I, as well as an increased awareness of Western modernism, paved the way for one of the richest literary ages in Romanian history. Virtually all areas inhabited by Romanians were unified after World War I, a radical land reform accompanied strong efforts at industrial development, and introduction of universal suffrage created conditions for a full democracy. While welcomed by many, such changes uprooted others and led to resentment and nostalgia. In spite of social dissatisfaction, fascist violence, and the ominous approach of World War II, freedom of expression was preserved and permitted a wide variety of opinions and styles.

The literary circle around Eugen LOVINESCU provided encouragement and intellectual support for aesthetic experimentation, liberal attitudes, and a choice of urban and psychological themes, as well as for the expression of a more sophisticated and ambiguous sensitivity; the group was seen as supportive of minorities and sympathetic to the West. The literary journal *Gîndirea*, which often promoted right-wing and even fascist ideologies, also encouraged EXPRESSIONIST writings, a search for a spiritually oriented literature, and complex statements in favor of a genuinely native and traditional literary identity. At the same time a fusion of literary scholarship and criticism was achieved in the works of George CĂLINESCU, Perpessicius (pseud. of Dimitrie S. Panaitescu, 1891–1971), Tudor Vianu (1897–1964), Şerban Cioculescu (1902–1988), and others, which stimulated literary production. Among the philosophers of the day, Constantin Noica (1909–1987) combined EXISTENTIALIST views with some Gnostic and Eastern Orthodox traditions in an irrationalist synthesis; along with Lucian BLAGA, the historian Vasile Pârvan (1882–1927), and the poet Dan Botta (1907–1958), Noica was among those who tried to provide a metaphysical definition of Romanian culture. Meanwhile, Mihai Ralea (1896–1964), an essayist, critic, psychologist, and historian, emerged as the chief standard-bearer of the radical tradition in social and aesthetic thinking.

The greatest achievements of the interwar period are to be found in poetry. George BACOVIA opened the door to modernism through his dryly melancholic poems, full of hopelessness and morbid obsessions. Tudor ARGHEZI radically renewed poetic language; his lyrical themes range from the search for faith in god to gross sexuality and violence, and his prose mixes precise realism with fantasy; his polemical verve is unparalleled; when, in his old age, he tried his hand at long historical and philosophical poems, he was less than successful. Ion BARBU provided tightly structured versions of philosophical or mathematical truths, obscure and brilliant; he shrewdly mixed with these touches of Balkan color and allusions to stock folk characters. Lucian Blaga was fascinated by the connections between natural realities and transcendent mystery, which he explored in his poetry as well as in his plays and philosophical works.

Prominent traditionalist poets who nevertheless were capable of using modern techniques and who were often men of exquisite taste include Adrian MANIU, who hid a cruel sense of decaying reality by imitating in a sophisticated way the naïve manner of folk art; Vasile VOICULESCU, who was working toward a natural mysticism; and Ion PILLAT, a polished and delicate neoclassicist. Aron Cotruş (1891–1957) turned his feelings of social revolt and his messianic nationalist thunderings into rolling free verse, which has a strong impact through its racy concrete vocabulary and its sonorous range. Nichifor Crainic's (1889–1972) religious verse and Radu Gyr's (1905–1974) vigorous balladry won them temporary popularity.

The Romanian avant-garde was in lively contact with its European counterparts and was often involved in initiating decisive movements through such writers as Tristan Tzara, Eugène IONESCO, and URMUZ, the last the author of preposterously funny short pieces of prose. Some of its members, such as Barbu Fundoianu (1898–1944; also pub. in French as Benjamin Fondane) and Ilarie Voronca (1903–1946), wrote poetry in French also, bringing to both languages a specific contribution through a mixture of SURREALIST play and earthy primitive imagery. Others, including Ştefan Roll (b. 1903) and Saşa Pană (b. 1902), were preoccupied with combining a radical political message with surrealist experiments. Camil Baltazar (1902–1977) was capable of melting words into a totally fluid, soft, and melodious verse, suggestive of paradisiacal innocence and an almost morbid yearning for unearthliness. Ion Vinea (1895–1964) was perhaps the most distinguished of all the poetic anarchists; in his work jazz rhythms and stridently prosaic passages alternate with refined lyricism. It is very difficult to place Alexandru PHILIPPIDE, a neoromantic whose poetry between the two world wars was dynamic, full of spectacular cosmic imagery, while his later work is more restrained and pessimistic, and often opposes the restraint of culture to the cruelty of history; he is the only great interwar poet who produced major lyrical poetry after 1945 and who renewed his writing by introducing into it demonic landscapes and existentialist anxieties.

Romanian drama produced little of value in the same period. Some historical and poetic drama was written by Lucian Blaga, Mihai Sorbul (1885–1967), and Victor Eftimiu (1887–1972), and the sentimental comedies of Mihai Sebastian (1907–1945) enjoyed a deserved success, as did his psychological novels and his essays dealing with the situation of the Jewish intellectuals in Romania. Sebastian's posthumously published diaries contain moving testimony as to the intellectual and emotional sufferings of a Jewish-Romanian intellectual under fascism. Prose writing was more varied and more distinguished. The great masters of, respectively, poetic and objective realism, Mihail SADOVEANU and Liviu REBREANU, who had started writing before World War I, now published their most important works. Sadoveanu moved from historical novels to parabolic ahistoric tales exploring the relationship between nature and the spirit; his realistic tales of provincial life are less remarkable. Rebreanu dealt not only with the cruelties and conflicts of peasant life, but also with the dilemmas of World War I and of its political aftermath.

A bittersweet criticism of the social alienation of the 1920s and nostalgia for the decency of a patriarchal society pervade many of the novels of Cezar Petrescu (1892–1961). Ionel Teodoreanu (1897–1954) likewise deplored the loss of innocence and of an Edenic rural world, while describing in sentences strewn with perfumed metaphors the sentimental intrigues of the new bourgeoisie. The prose of George Călinescu dealt with somewhat similar matters, but he worked within a classicist tradition of moral and typological characterization. Meanwhile, the influence of Marcel PROUST, André GIDE, Aldous HUXLEY, and others was strongly felt. Camil PETRESCU and Anton Holban (1902–1937) tried to combine psychological analysis with modern writing techniques; M. BLECHER and Hortensia PAPADAT-BENGESCU produced startling anatomies of the soul and portrayed grotesque combinations of subliminal pressures and social pretense. Gib Mihăescu (1894–1935) offered a melodramatic version of the psychosocial changes in interwar Romania. Pavel Dan (1907–1937) knew how to introduce fantastic elements in his solidly realistic tales about Transylvanian peasants. Mircea ELIADE won a leading position among younger novelists by adding mythical patterns and gothic horror to his probings of tumult among young intellectuals; his greatest works were written in postwar exile. Mateiu CARAGIALE and Dinu Nicodin (1886–1943) occupy a somewhat special place owing to their mixture of brutal naturalism with unyielding devotion to aesthetic purity.

Among the many minor authors who enlivened the period, Panait Istrati (1884–1935), who lived in France and usually wrote in French, won renown as a Balkan GORKY; Ion Marin Sadoveanu (1893–1964) wrote a carefully drawn family saga; Felix Aderca (1891–1962), Constantin Fîntîneru (b. 1907), and H. Bonciu (1893–1950) indulged in intimate psychiatric probings and a fantastically absurd humor; Emanoil Bucuta (1887–1946) displayed exquisite descriptive refinement; and Damian Stănoiu (1893–1956) wrote guffawing descriptions of monastic life. Ion Călugaru (1902–1956) wrote touching descriptions of provincial life in a Jewish Moldavian milieu, and George Mihail Zamfirescu (1892–1939) evoked with sentimental empathy the colorful existence in the shantytowns around Bucharest.

World War II and the ensuing Communist takeover brought a massive disruption of literary evolution. Accelerated social and technological changes altered Romanian society: large numbers of people moved to the cities, private farming all but disappeared, traditional ways of thinking tried to accommodate newer Leninist views, and industry began to play the leading part in economic life. Large-scale political persecutions and the suppression of freedom of speech and the press accompanied these changes. For over a decade after 1948 the literary landscape was stricken with a blight owing to censorship, the incarceration of writers, flight into exile by numerous literary figures, and the rigid imposition of the dogmas of Socialist REALISM. Horia Stamatu (1912–1989), Vintilă Horia (1915–1992), and Ştefan Baciu (1918–1993) belonged to a generation of promising existentialist lyric poets who had to continue their work abroad. Together with Dan Botta, Emil Botta (1912–1977), Simion Stolnicu (1905–1966), and others, they had tried in different ways to react to the great preceding generation, by accepting impulses from western European poetry and by claiming the right to more personal initiatives.

Two poetic groups emerged in the mid 1940s and shaped the early postwar period, although for a while they were silenced. One was the Bucharest group, which included Ion CARAION, Geo Dumitrescu (b. 1920), Constant Tonegaru (1919–1952), and Dimitrie Stelaru (1917–1971); they were ironic pessimists who had all assimilated the avant-garde tradition. They clamored for total poetic freedom, for an adventurous life, and for the need to demolish philistine traditions. The other was the Sibiu group, including Ştefan Augustin DOINAŞ and Radu Stanca (1920–1962), author of lyrical tragicomedies and playful ballads. With the support of excellent critics, such as Cornel Regman (b. 1919) and Ion NEGOIŢESCU, they stated eloquently the need for humanistic traditions, cultural autonomy, and aesthetic values as part of any viable social structure in Romania. Inspired by Schiller's humanist aestheticism and Lucian Blaga's metaphysics, they strove to establish a set of values and a traditional literary canon that would eliminate intolerance and petty nationalism in favor of an enlightened opening-up toward the world.

Meanwhile, the 1950s witnessed how some gifted writers tried in vain to produce valid literature out of sloganeering material; among them were Zaharia Stancu (1902–1974), with his rhapsodic peasant novels; Mihai Beniuc (b. 1907), with his proletarian verse; Eugen Jebeleanu (1911–1991), with his political rhymes; and Petru Dumitriu (b. 1924), with his novelistic chronicles of the decaying nobility. A few managed to survive this period with their artistry intact, among them Virgil Teodorescu (1909–1988), who had started as a surrealist in the 1930s and who later maintained his stance, although with somewhat more moderation. Miron Radu Paraschivescu (1911–1971) used his Communist underground credentials to encourage younger poets toward uncharted poetic territories; of his own poems, those inspired by gypsy folklore are the best known. Nina Cassian (b. 1924) wrote feminist lyrics, often cynical and bantering, although sometimes with emotional intensity. Iulia Soare (1920–1971) evoked the life of the prewar Jewish bourgeoisie.

The 1960s brought about a more liberal cultural environment, massive literary change, and the emergence of a new poetic generation. Nichita Stănescu and Nicolae Labiş (1935–1956) became the standard-bearers of a large group devoted to establishing

a metaphorical version of reality, without ideological interference—Labiş through his acute sensory awareness and Stănescu through his extraordinary visionary ability. Ion Gheorghe's (b. 1935) uneven production mixes crass primitivism with sophisticated Joycean language games and strives to set up a personal mythology. Ioan Alexandru's (b. 1941) best verse moves from tragic existentialism to religious fulfillment. Marin SORESCU's metaphysical irony and Mircea Ivănescu's (b. 1931) monotonously gray elegies brought intellectual tones to the poetry of their generation, as well as a relaxed, colloquial poetic language. Sorescu's poetry enjoyed wide recognition and has been translated into many languages. His popularity derives from his casual, jocular debunking of the common-places of life. Petre Stoica (b. 1931), Florin Mugur (1934–1991), and Ilie Constantin (b. 1938) dwell with refined lyrical discretion upon the gestures and objects of everyday life. Leonid Dimov (1926–1987) launched the "oneiric" movement (based on musical word association and dream imagery), to which the younger prose writers Dumitru Ţepeneag (b. 1936) and Virgil Tănase (b. 1940) also belonged. This group tried to renew surrealism by injecting some narrative lines and by striving toward a harmonious irrationality. Constanta Buzea (b. 1941) is probably the most gifted among a large group of younger women poets. Other promising poets included Sorin Mărculescu (b. 1936), Dan Laurenţiu (b. 1937), Mihai Ursachi (b. 1941), Emil Brumaru (b. 1939), and Mircea Dinescu (b. 1950).

A similar flourishing in fiction occurred slightly later. It had been preceded by the new realism of Marin PREDA and by the picturesque and grotesque writings of Eugen Barbu (1924–1993), who excelled in describing the underworld of Bucharest, as well as the teeming and colorful social landscapes of 18th-c. Wallachia. From the mid-1960s on, three main trends can be distinguished in Romanian prose. The first is illustrated by writers who, much like the great South American masters of magic REALISM, discover the structures of the fantastic (comically bizarre or sensational and horrifying) inside reality itself. Ştefan Bănulescu (b. 1929) depicts often nightmarish and disastrous situations in which the fantastic develops naturally. Fănuş Neagu (b. 1932) has little narrative energy, but he excels in the picturesque stridency of his episodes and imagery. Nicolae Velea (1936–1987) writes short stories and sketches that abound in uncanny, strange characters originating in Romania's changing rural world. Sorin Titel (1935–1985) acknowledges the influence of Franz KAFKA and Samuel BECKETT on his gloomy, delicate novels. George Bălăiţă (b. 1935) is a versatile writer, whose main strength is his ability to render the concrete feel of reality.

The second trend is concerned with political and historical judgments of Romania's present and recent past. While Paul Goma (b. 1935) went all the way to open dissidence and wrote powerful indictments of the Communist system, Alexandru Ivasiuc (1933–1977) tried to explain in a Marxist framework the power mechanisms of the system's representatives. Constantin Ţoiu (b. 1923) and Augustin Buzura (b. 1938) exposed the price paid by those who were the target of the pressures of historical change. Petru Popescu (b. 1943) described with sincerity and accuracy the state of mind and interests of the disaffected young generation in the urban areas. Nicolae Breban (b. 1934) explored the pitfalls of the strong individual when he is faced with the temptations of an egalitarian system. Ion Lăncrănjan (1928–1991), although clumsy in his writing technique, received some attention for his satirical attacks against corruption in high places. Dumitru Radu POPESCU was the only one who managed to combine the strengths of both these trends.

The third trend is more intellectual, devoted to light, fantastic arabesques, and characterized by psychological experiment, cultural allusions, and passages of essayistic prose. Mircea Horia Simionescu (b. 1928) writes jocular and mystifying short texts in which social mechanisms are parodied. Matei Călinescu's (b. 1936) ironic parables expose the fallacies of rationalistic inertia. Mircea Ciobanu (1940–1996), Alice Botez (b. 1914), and Radu Petrescu (1927–1982) are among those who distorted traditional narrative forms in a modernistic way to obtain new literary effects.

While drama after 1945 is almost totally insignificant, solid scholarship and shrewd criticism is abundant. Among young critics, the most acute is Nicolae Manolescu (b. 1939); he, along with Mircea Martin (b. 1940), Ion Pop (b. 1941), and Mihai Zamfir (b. 1940), integrates in his work deconstructionist, archetypal, and STRUCTURALIST influences.

On the whole, while probably not reaching the level of the interwar period, Romanian postwar literature shows, in spite of tremendous political obstacles, a surprising vigor and diversity. The 1970s brought renewed efforts by governmental authorities to encourage a sloganeering, cliché-ridden literature, often with blatantly nationalist overtones, while experimentation has been largely suppressed. In fact, circumstances compelled literature to accommodate social and intellectual debate in a coded way—not a healthy situation, but one that made literature more interesting. There was and there still is a widespread feeling that the maintenance of high aesthetic standards is somehow decisive for the survival of a small nation in the modern world.

For other writing in Romanian, see Moldovian Literature and under Yugoslav Literature.

BIBLIOGRAPHY: Munteanu, B., *Modern Rumanian Literature* (1939); Ierunca, V., "Littérature roumaine," in Queneau, R., ed., *Histoire des littératures* (1956), Vol. II: 1389–1403; Schroeder, K. H., *Einführung in das Studium des Rumänischen* (1967): 122–47; Ciopraga, C., *La personalité de la littérature roumaine* (1975): 187–289; Gabanyi, U., *Partei und Literatur in Rumänien seit 1945* (1975); Nemoianu, V., "Recent Romanian Criticism: Subjectivity as Social Response" WLT, 51 (1977): 560–63; Hitchins, K., "*Gîndirea*: Nationalism in a Spiritual Guise," in Jowitt, K., ed., *Social Change in Romania, 1860–1940: A Debate on Development in a European Nation* (1978): 140–73; Călin, V., "Postwar Developments of the Prewar Tradition in Romanian Prose," in Birnbaum, H., and T. Eekman, eds., *Fiction and Drama in Eastern and Southeastern Europe: Evolution and Experiment in the Postwar Period* (1980): 87–101; Perry, T. A., "The Point of View in the Novel (with Reference to the Contemporary Romanian Novel)," *Synthesis*, 7 (1980): 107–13

—ANN DEMAITRE

In German

German literature has been written in Romania by three different groups: the Saxons of southern Transylvania (who were colonized in the 12th c.); the Catholic and rural Swabians of Banat (after 1700); and the largely urban German-Jewish population of Bukovina. The first of these had a long cultural history and wrote literature both in standard German and in local dialect, particularly after the Reformation. The other two developed a literary consciousness by the end of the 19th and in the early 20th c.

After 1918, in the context of a Romanian-speaking community, the chief writers often seem preoccupied with the dialectics of ethnic identity and national or European trends. There was always the temptation to solve this conflict by moving to one of the German-speaking countries. Thus, Adam Müller-Guttenbrunn (1852–1923), the greatest Swabian writer after Nikolaus Lenau (1802–1850), although he dealt in his novels almost exclusively with problems of his native province, chose to live most of his life in Vienna. Adolf Meschendörfer (1877–1963) brought out the journal *Die Karpathen* (1907–14) in order to familiarize his readers with modern literary trends such as naturalism and Scandinavian psychological realism; his main works, among them *Die Stadt im Osten* (1937; city in the east), show the influence of Gerhart HAUPTMANN's later novels. Heinrich Zillich (b. 1898) continued this work of modernization in his journal *Klingsor* (1924–38) but did not always avoid nationalist tones in his novels. Erwin Wittstock (1899–1962) wrote mildly pessimistic and ironic or nostalgic short stories on the slow decline of the Saxon community. The magic REALISM of Oskar Walter Cisek's (1897–1966) historical novels was a conscious attempt to combine German literary traditions with Romanian literary influence; he was close to Lucian BLAGA and Mihai SADOVEANU. Similarly, Wolf von Aichelburg (1912–1995) shared in some of the aesthetic and neoclassical ideals of Ion NEGOIȚESCU and his group; he wrote essays, plays, and short stories.

Some of the best lyrical poetry of the interwar period was written by German-Jewish authors of Bukovina, such as Alfred Margul-Sperber (1898–1967) and Alfred Kittner (b. 1906), under the influence of EXPRESSIONISM. From the same cultural environment came the younger Paul CELAN, whose first poems were written in Romanian and who later moved to Paris via Vienna and wrote in German.

Emigration gradually depleted the ranks of a promising younger generation, which included the witty satirical novelist Paul Schuster (b. 1930), the refined and hermetic lyricist Oskar Pastior (b. 1927), and essayists such as Dieter Schlesak (b. 1934) and Dieter Fuhrmann (b. 1938). German literature in Romania had its own share of banal sloganeering production; George Scherg (b. 1917) is one of the few political writers who, under the influence of Bertolt BRECHT, occasionally reached aesthetic achievement. Young writers, faced with a dwindling readership, often concentrate on translations, strive to become bilingual (or to publish often in Romanian-language journals), or concentrate on essay writing. Such are Dieter Roth (b. 1936), Claus Stephani (b. 1938), Gerhardt Csejka (b. 1945), Werner Söllner (b. 1951), Anemone Latzina (b. 1942), and Peter Motzan (b. 1946).

BIBLIOGRAPHY: Klein, K. K., *Literaturgeschichte des Deutschtums im Ausland* (1939): 238–64, 384–434; Stiehler, H., *Nachrichten aus Rumänien; Rumäniendeutsche Literatur* (1976); Reichroth, E., ed., *Reflexe: Kritische Beiträge zur rumäniendeustchen Gegenwartsliteratur* (1977); Stiehler, H., *Paul Celan, Oskar Walter Cisek und die deutschsprachige Gegenwartsliteratur Rumäniens* (1979)

—VIRGIL NEMOIANU

In Hungarian

The development of modern Hungarian literature in Transylvania, the home of a Hungarian minority of almost two million, reflects the political and social tensions generated by the territorial rearrangements that took place after World War I. Throughout the centuries Transylvania had produced many outstanding writers, scientists, and statesmen who had greatly contributed to Hungarian culture. In continuing the work of their predecessors, Transylvanian poets and writers of recent decades thus sought to maintain a centuries-old literary tradition and to promote the Hungarian minority's cultural autonomy.

In 1926 twenty-seven Hungarian writers formed a group called the Transylvania Helicon. Their platform stressed commitment to "Transylvanism," defined as the recognition of a historically and geographically determined specific conscience and spirituality.

The most prominent poets belonging to this group were Lajos Áprily (1887–1967) and Sándor Reményik (1890–1941), whose oeuvre reflected the influence of the French SYMBOLISTS and of the poets of the Hungarian Nyugat group. Although these influences are manifest in their cultivation of strict artistic forms and their poetic discipline, both writers succeeded in giving a seductively original coloration to their poetry. Ámacrprily found meaning and consolation in a Rousseau-like communion with nature. The hallmark of Reményik's poetry is an associative symbolism, which he used with exquisite skill to express his faith in moral values. The return to nature and peasant simplicity is the leitmotif of János Bartalis's (1893–1976) poetry. Known as the Hungarian Walt Whitman, Bartalis experimented for a while with EXPRESSIONIST techniques, as did Jenő Dsida (1907–1938), who found in mystical introspection a soothing antidote to his melancholic view of the world.

The literary scene in Transylvania was further enlivened by the emergence of outstanding writers of fiction. The works of *Áron Tamási* (b. 1897), such as the novels *Ábel a rengetegben* (1932; Abel in the trackless forest), the first book of his "Abel trilogy" (1932–34), and *Elvadult paradicsom* (1958; paradise run wild), provide colorful insight into the robust but cheerful existence of Székely (Sekler) peasantry of southeastern Transylvania. Enlivened by sly humor and fascinating flights of imagination, Tam´si's writings are delicately tinged with the moodiness of Transylvanian folk ballads. Relying on a dense, expressionistic style that reflected his vitalistic world view, József Nyirő (1889–1953) excelled in myths that brought into high relief both the tragic and the comic aspects of village life in novels such as *Isten igájában* (1926; in God's yoke), and *Uz Bence* (1933; Bence Uz). In Gémarcza Tabéemacrcry's (1890–1958) historical novels—*Szarvasbika* (1925; stag), *Vértorony* (1929; tower of blood)—the well-designed plots are developed against the backgrounds of social and ideological conflicts. Hungarian and Transylvanian history provided the subject matter for the novels of Sándor Makkai (1890–1952) and Irén Gulácsi (1894–1945). Makkai's *Ördöszékér* (1925; chariot of the devil) and Gulácsi's *Fekete vólegények* (1927; black bridegrooms) are skillfully woven historical tapestries. Aladár Kuncz's (1886–1931) novel *A fekete kolostor* (1931; *Black Monastery*, 1934), based on the author's own experiences in an internment camp in France during World War I, is now considered one of the masterpieces of modern Hungarian fiction.

While "Transylvanism" provided the main ideological inspiration for Hungarian literature in Transylvania between the two world wars, there also developed a literature with markedly "socialist" or "internationalist" coloration. The latter trend is manifested in the poetry of Ernő Salamon (1912–1943) and Viktor Brassai (dates n.a.), both of whom perished during World War II. Among the socialist prose writers, István Nagy (b. 1904), András Szilágyi

(b. 1904), and István Asztalos (b. 1909) produced works of merit both before and after the war.

Despite the restrictions imposed by a Communist regime, there has been considerable literary activity since World War II. Jenă Kiss (b. 1912) displayed a robust lyricism in affirming an optimistic world view. The poetry of József Miliusz (b. 1909) reflects an impassioned interest in the problems of contemporary life. Gábor Gáal (1891–1954), the editor of the literary periodical *Korunk*, wrote critical essays of high quality, which contributed greatly to the effervescence of Hungarian literature in Transylvania. And the short stories of András Sütă (b. 1927), in the collections *Októberi cseresznye* (1955; October cherry) and *Tártkarú világ* (1959; open-armed world), are distinguished by quiet humor and stylistic artistry.

BIBLIOGRAPHY: Sivirsky, A., *Die ungarische Literatur der Gegenwart* (1962); Klaniczay, T., et al., *History of Hungarian Literature* (1964); Reményi, J., *Hungarian Writers and Literature* (1964)

—ANN DEMAITRE

Romanian Literature since 1980

In the late 1970s and throughout the 1980s, Romanian literature and intellectual life had to function under the most oppressive dictatorship in Europe, centered on Nicolae Ceauşescu and his relatives. The country's living standards fell to unprecedented lows, isolation from Europe and the world was consciously fostered, and normal social communication was impeded by pervasive government supervision and invasion of privacy. Official pressure was exerted to encourage the growth of a nationalist-communist synthesis in writing, which ended up producing an ideology not unlike right-wing populism. Its leading spokesmen were the novelist Eugen Barbu and the poet Adrian Paunescu (b. 1943). The speculative theories of Edgar Papu (b. 1908) on the temporal priority of Romanian stylistic, cultural, and literary phenomena over Western ones (known as "protochronism") were used to bolster nationalist ideology. The novel *Căderea în lume* (1987; fall in the world) by Constantin Toiu suggested that before World War II only communists and *legionari* (fascists) represented true social consciousness and that, at a deeper level, these were twin brothers. Anti-Semitic tones found their way into the magazines closest to officialdom. Luxurious volumes flattering the regime and its leader were constantly edited. Nevertheless it is striking to note that the best Romanian literary production of the 1970s and 1980s adopted a socially critical stance.

Prose writing, despite heavy censorship, often sent messages of disagreement, anger, and despair to the readers. Augustin Buzura emerged as the most prominent novelist to depict contemporary Romania as a land of darkness and injustice, particularly in *Vocile nopţii* (1980; voices of the night) and *Refugii* (1984; kinds of refuge). Others, either inside Romania or in emigration, also developed the nightmare mode, using fantasy and allegory, among them Bujor Nedelcovici (b. 1936), Ioana Orlea (b. 1936), and Constantin Eretescu (b. 1938). Paul Goma, living in Paris since 1977, wrote a sequence of novels portraying the growth of a young man from the 1940s on, under constantly renewed strata of communist persecution and threat; although written in Romanian, many of his novels have been published so far only in their French translation. Long short stories or short novels by the younger writers Ioan Groşan (b. 1954). Mircea Nedelciu (b. 1950), and the postmodernist

Ştefan Agopian (b. 1947) suggested the indirect but dire impact of dictatorship upon everyday lives, sometimes using the camouflage of historical distance. Even more impressive were the works by women novelists such as Gabriela Adameşteanu's (b. 1942) *Dimineaţa nimănui* (1983; nobody's morning) and Dana Dumitriu's (1943–1987) *Sărbătorile răbdării* (1980; the feasts of patience) in which the cruelty and tensions of male-female relationships in a warped society were pointed out with precision and subtlety, as well as with a clear feminist consciousness. Norman Manea (b. 1936) described movingly the sufferings of a concentration-camp Jewish childhood in his early short stories and devised later a complicated and insinuating modernist idiom to portray the anguishes and half-truths of the society surrounding him, most notably in *Plicul negru* (1986; black envelope). Ioan D. Sîrbu (1919–1989), in the collection of short stories *Şoarecele B* (1983; mouse B), but much more forthrightly and powerfully in his underground novel of ideas *Adio Europa* (1986; a farewell to Europe), pointed to the very roots of the system as one designed to destroy individual options and personal identity. Petre Creţia (b. 1927) provided in his highly original *Norii* (1979; the clouds) a series of meditations on nature, intended as a record of social sensitivity and a defense of personal privacy.

The best poets of the 1970s and 1980s were in the forefront of dissidence. The poems of Ana BLANDIANA, who had been known earlier for delicate eroticism and mild lyricism, had an explosive effect and circulated throughout the country. Mircea Dinescu (b. 1950), indirectly in *Proprietarul de poduri* (1976; the bridge owner) and *Exil pe o boabă de piper* (1983; exile on a peppercorn), and, in the end openly, in the banned *Moartea citeşte ziarul* (1989; death reading the newspaper), challenged dictatorship and Ceauşescu in a very personal style, blending elements of SURREALISM and street rap. Dorin Tudoran (b. 1945) picked up the the parodic and parabolic style that had been invented by Marin SORESCU and others, but gave it moral rectitude, a sarcastic edge, and combative immediacy, as seen perhaps best in his volumes *Semne particulare* (1979; distinguishing features) and *De bună voie* (1986; of my own free will). His activities as a relentless investigative journalist impelled the government to exile him in 1985.

A new poetic generation arose after 1980, abruptly altering the prevailing poetic idiom by opting for a tough colloquial language, cynical and disenchanted imagery, a tragic or hopeless view of life, and brooding over the asperities of the concrete. Among its prominent figures were Florin Iaru (b. 1955), Ion Stratan (b. 1954), Bogdan Ghiu (b. 1956), Mariana Marin (b. 1955), Liviu Ioan Stoiciu (b. 1950), and particularly Mircea Cărtărescu (b. 1955). The latter's novel in verse *Levantul* (1990; Levantine realm) is a postmodernist exercise in recuperating early romantic vision and meter in an ironic perspective.

Ştefan Augustin DOINAŞ, now generally recognized as the greatest living Romanian poet, offered in *Vînătoare cu şoim* (1985; a-hawking) and in *Interiorul unui poem* (1991; a poem's insides) metaphoric statements of rage and resentment, often using the corruption and erosion of freedom in imperial Rome as a referential level. Ileana Mălăncioiu (b. 1940) emerged—along with Blandiana—as the leading woman poet within Romanian literature, particularly in volumes such as *Linia vieţii* (1982; life-line) and *Urcarea muntelui* (1985; climbing the mountain), which displayed enormous lexical variety and skillfully used the lyrical intensities of love and death as suggestions for political and social conflict.

Perhaps the most characteristic feature of Romanian literature in the 1970s and the 1980s was the fact that, because of dictatorial constraints on political and social debate, literary criticism and essay writing had to take over the functions of the former, in a coded manner. The most influential philosophical figure of the 1980s was Constantin Noica (1909–1987), who advocated a platonic detachment from social life and an option for the exclusive creativity of cultural elites, and at the same time urged the rejection of Western civilization and thinking patterns in favor of local and nationally identifiable styles. His disciples Andrei Pleşu (b. 1948) and, more markedly, Gabriel Liiceanu (b. 1943) have tended to modify Noica's teachings to allow for more openness toward modernist and humanist possibilities, as seen in Liiceanu's *Jurnalul de la Păltiniş* (1983; the Păltiniş diary) and in the collective volume *Epistolar* (1987; epistolary).

Others, unconnected with Noica, were presenting even more consistently the argument for Western and democratic values. Mihai Şora (b. 1917) used models drawn from aesthetics as an underpinning for epistemology and showed that any antimaterialist stance must be rooted in the respect for the individual person, rather than in tribal or ethnic patterns and frameworks. Nicolae Steinhardt (1912–1989), a Jewish-born Eastern Orthodox monk, maintained that true spiritual liberation and even national identity can be achieved only by firmly placing Romanian literature in its European contexts. The need for personal ethical responsibility and for a closer connection between the workings of imagination and desire and the practices of social behavior was pointed out by Alexandru Paleologu (b. 1919) and by Octavian Paler (b. 1926), one of the latter's more significant works being the autobiographical novel *Un om fericit* (1985; a happy man). Paler and Paleologu outlined a case for democratic development with social and liberal overtones. All these essayists were subjected over the years to imprisonment or house arrest, and their works were banned for longer or shorter periods of time.

Ileana Vrancea (b. 1929), who emigrated in the 1980s to Israel, and Mircea Martin formulated their theories regarding the conflict between nativist and Westernizing trends in Romanian history by using as a vehicle a discussion about the literary criticism of George CĂLINESCU. Adrian Marino (b. 1921), a comparatist and literary theoretician, often promoted principles of democratic pluralism cloaked in the idiom of literary criticism; and Alexandru George (b. 1930) consistently defended the liberal tradition in Romanian literature. More than any of the above, Nicolae Manolescu, the country's leading critical voice, insisted on professionalism and aesthetic and ethical standards against an encroaching totalitarianism. His efforts were often supported by émigré critics such as Monica Lovinescu (b. 1923) and Virgil Ierunca (b. 1920), who castigated forcefully the political and ethical compromises of writers and highlighted genuine literary achievements. A deeper revision of the self-understanding of Romanian culture is now being advanced in the sociocultural studies of Z. Ornea (b. 1930), a moderate Marxist, and in the new histories of Romanian literature written by Manolescu and Ioan Negoiţescu, the latter living in Germany since 1979.

One remarkable new phenomenon of the last two decades has been the emergence of regional intellectual, literary, and political movements in a number of Romanian larger cities. In a form less obvious before than after 1989, groups of young writers assumed the initiative of shaping public opinion and organizing efforts toward change. The dissident essayist Dan Petrescu (b. 1949), an acute diagnostician of Romanian social psychology, provided a focus for a larger number of socially conscious writers in the eastern city of Iasi. Novelists and scholars such as Vasile Popovici (b. 1956), Serban Foarţă (b. 1942), and Mircea Mihăieş (b. 1954) emerged as revolutionary leaders in the western city of Timisoara. Other young philosophers and writers constituted themselves as a group of articulate media leaders, among them Stelian Tănase (b. 1951), Dan C. Mihăilescu (b. 1953), and Radu feposu (b. 1954). As political changes in Romania created the need for alternative political elites, the intellectual categories that had, to a certain point, preserved rational sociopolitical discourse showed themselves willing to switch over to a much more active political role.

BIBLIOGRAPHY: Cornis-Pope, M., "A Long Rehearsed Revolution of Sensibility: Post-Modernism and the Historical Romanian Avantgarde," *South-Eastern Europe*, 11 (1984): 129–48; Spiridon, M., "Ideology and Fiction," *CREL*, 2 (1986): 85–96; Cornis-Pope, M., "Narration across the Totalistic Gap: On Recent Romania Fiction," *Symposium*, 43, 1 (Spring 1989): 3–19; Moraru, C., "Poetical Subject and Ontological Precariousness," *CREL* (1989): 102–9; Nemoianu, V., "Mihai Sora and the Traditions of Romanian Philosophy," *Review of Metaphysics*, 43 (Mar. 1990): 591–605

—VIRGIL NEMOIANU

ROMANSH LITERATURE

See under Swiss Literature

ROMERO, José Rubén

Mexican novelist and poet, b. 25 Sept. 1890, Cotija de la Paz; d. 4 July 1952, Mexico City

R. spent most of his adolescence and early adulthood in his native state of Michoacán. Although his formal education was limited to primary school, he enjoyed a reputation as an intellectual, particularly in the field of government, which was his main vocation. Beginning with minor posts in Michoacán, he advanced to federal positions in Mexico City in the 1920s. In 1930 he entered the diplomatic corps, eventually serving as Mexican ambassador to Brazil and Cuba. During his distinguished political career he was named to the prestigious Mexican Academy of Language. After retiring from government service in 1945 he spent his remaining years writing, lecturing, and managing his own publishing company.

Although R. cultivated various literary genres, including the short story, essay, and newspaper writing, his literary career was devoted primarily to poetry and the novel. At the age of eighteen he published his first collection of poems, *Fantasías* (1908; fantasies). This was followed by numerous other collections, only one of which, *Tacámbaro* (1922; Tacámbaro), rates as an important contribution to Mexican poetry.

After writing poetry for many years R. abandoned it in favor of the novel, the genre in which he gained his literary fame. His first novel, *Apuntes de un lugareño* (1932; the notes of a villager), was an instant success. In it R. established the style and themes that appear repeatedly in most of his seven subsequent novels. Plot and novelistic form are relegated to minor importance in favor of a series of loosely connected anecdotal episodes in which the author relates his many experiences in Michoacán. The novel vividly

displays R.'s fondness for the people, settings, and life styles of provincial Mexico through the use of local color, colloquial language, and humor.

Other novels quickly followed *Apuntes de un lugareño*, including *Desbandada* (1934; at random), *El pueblo inocente* (1934; the innocent village), and *Mi caballo, mi perro y mi rifle* (1936; my horse, my dog and my rifle). The author's masterpiece, *La vida inútil de Pito Pérez* (1938; *The Futile Life of Pito Pérez*, 1967), deserves particular mention, for it is a classic in Mexican literature. Picaresque in both flavor and structure, the novel chronicles the hapless life of a Mexican rogue. Poignant characterization, sympathetic portrayal, and a biting realism tempered with a lyrical style are successfully forged to create an outrageous but lovable antihero. The novel—a frank, bittersweet examination of Mexico, its society, and its revolution—continues to enjoy immense popularity in Mexico. Although R. published several novels after *La vida inútil de Pito Pérez*, none ever achieved its stature.

Even though R., a poet turned novelist, produced novels that lacked many of the more traditional or formal components of fiction, he was a major contributor to the development of Mexican narrative. R. may best be described as a regionalist writer who provided his countrymen with candid portraits of their provincial society.

FURTHER WORKS: *Rimas bohemias* (1908); *Cuentos rurales* (1915); *La musa heroica* (1915); *La musa loca* (1917); *Sentimental* (1919); *Mis amigos, mis enemigos* (1921); *Versos viejos* (1930); *Anticipación a la muerte* (1939); *Una vez fui rico* (1942); *Algunas cosillas de Pito Pérez que se me quedaron en el tintero* (1945); *Rosenda* (1946); *Obras completas* (1957); *Cuentos y poesías inéditos* (1964)

BIBLIOGRAPHY: Stanton, R., "R., Costumbrista of Michoacán," *Hispania*, 24 (1941): 423–28; Arreola Cortés, R., "J. R. R.: Vida y obra," *RHM*, 12 (1946): 7–34;; Moore, E. R., "J. R. R. bibliografia," *RHM*, 12 (1946): 35–40; Castagnaro, R. A., "R. and the Novel of the Mexican Revolution," *Hispania*, 36 (1953): 300–304; Brushwood, J., *Mexico in Its Novel* (1964): 211–13, 222–24; Phillips, E. E., "The Genesis of Pito Pérez," *Hispania*, 47 (1964): 698–702; Franco, J., *An Introduction to Spanish-American Literature* (1969): 204–8

—SAM L. SLICK

RONGA LITERATURE

See Mozambican Literature

ROSA, João Guimarães

Brazilian novelist and short-story writer, b. 27 June 1908, Cordisburgo; d. 19 Nov. 1967, Rio de Janeiro

R. studied medicine and practiced in the *sertão* of Minas Gerais (*sertão*, as used by Brazilians, means simply the sparsely populated wilderness beyond the areas of permanent settlement). He entered the diplomatic service in 1934 and was attached to embassies in Germany, Colombia, and France until 1951. His work and experience in the *sertão* provided him with settings and characters for his fiction. Unlike that of other Brazilian regional writers, R.'s treatment of the *sertão* and its inhabitants transcends the purely regional, as he explores, in search of basic human truths, the complex relationships between man's inner world and the world that he lives in.

In 1937 R. wrote his first important work, *Sagarana* (1946; *Sagarana*, 1966), a collection of nine independent short stories unified by style, language, and setting. The stories deal with the *sertão* inhabitants' everyday activities and their emotions. Each story is preceded by an epigraph from Brazilian folklore, which functions as a summing-up of the narrative line and suggests the symbolic meaning. Most unusual in these stories is the expression of R.'s almost mystical sense of the oneness of man and nature; equally unusual is the way in which the joy of being alive is communicated. What makes the stories especially impressive is R.'s mastery of form. The writing leads the reader to feel that the *sertão* is rendered in a new language, one liberated from worn-out conventions, a language so graphic and forceful that it seems to be an expression of nature itself.

R.'s only novel, *Grande sertão: Veredas* (1956; *The Devil to Pay in the Backlands*, 1963), is a remarkable achievement on every level. Structurally, it is one gigantic monologue, in which the protagonist Riobaldo unburdens his soul to an unidentified listener, to whom he is turning for enlightenment because of his respect for the listener's deep understanding of life. Now a respectable property owner, Riobaldo is obsessed by the past. In his youth, having been a bandit in the *sertão*, he lived in the midst of violence, brutality, and misery. Unable to come to terms with this past, he now suffers anguish because of the pact he had made with the devil to avenge the death of the bandit leader and because of his homoerotic love for Diadorim, his closest companion. Torn by the paradoxes of the human condition and the protean shapes that reality assumes, Riobaldo is not even sure whether his pact with the devil was indeed concluded, or whether the devil exists at all.

Riobaldo's ruminations on his past ultimately become a quest for identity, and the novel assumes existential overtones. This quality is reflected in the title: the *sertão* symbolizes life, the *veredas* (paths, trails), the various attempts man makes in his quest for identity. *Grande sertão: Veredas* is a mixture of multiple realities: the personal world of Riobaldo, who, in search of himself, struggles between good and evil; the past and the present; the real, concrete world of the *sertão* and its fantasy, myths, and legends.

The rhythm of the prose is erratic at first, as Riobaldo rambles through his past, but it becomes more rapid as the intensity of the narrative increases. The time sequence becomes blurred, as Riobaldo's drive to express everything that oppresses him dominates the character of the narrative.

As in R.'s previous work, the world of this novel is communicated in a highly personal idiom of great freshness and vigor. With consummate control, with infinite attention to the power of each word, R. ranges freely over the resources of the Portuguese language—European and Brazilian Portuguese, scientific terms, the idiom of the *sertão* inhabitant—as well as devised neologisms, striking images, invented proverbs. By these means hc has created a fictional world of an artistic authenticity not surpassed by other novelists.

Primeiras estórias (1962; *The Third Bank of the River, and Other Stories*, 1968) is a collection of twenty-one short narratives that reveal the author's continued preoccupation with language and style. The volume is characterized by R.'s extremely personal use

of the Portuguese language (unusual deformations of syntax, the creation of new words by making verbs from adjectives and by combining parts of different words) and his variation in narrative points of view. These innovations underscore the writer's view of the multiplicity of human reality as it comes into being through language. The perception of self and the external world, the search for fulfillment and for authenticity of existence, are basic concerns of R. in this rich cosmos of narratives where various types of characters, including children, perceive and act in the complex worlds of interior and exterior realities. The story "A terceira margem do rio" ("The Third Bank of the River") illustrates well R.'s understanding of life and the human being's complex, almost absurd existence. The principal character, referred to simply as the father, severs his connections with the world and spends the rest of his days rowing around in the middle of the river. The only person who understands him is his son, who narrates the story. The son, feeling a great need to be with his father, is torn between remaining on shore and taking his father's place on the river. The "third bank," which may be interpreted as a higher level of reality where the individual encounters his identity and authenticity, is lost for the son, who at the last minute becomes afraid and decides to remain on shore.

Tutaméia (1967; an invented word meaning "trifle") is a collection of forty vignette-like short stories on rural subjects. In four prefaces interspersed throughout the book, R. discusses his concept of the short story and the linguistic and stylistic techniques he has introduced to Brazilian fiction. He sees the short story as a work of art that the reader must understand intuitively and into which he must project himself. Language should express the diverse facets of life—hence his linguistic innovations and his often highly poetic prose characterized by alliteration, onomatopoeia, rhyme, and rhythm.

Ave, palavra (1970; hail, word), published three years after R.'s death, contains eighteen pieces written over the course of his career. The book has received increasing critical attention in the last few years, not so much for the narrative element (which is almost completely missing) as for the author's comments on language. As the title indicates, the emphasis is on the word itself, the mystery of this linguistic entity, and the innumerable possibilities it offers within the context of the narrative. The book contains a wealth of information that may be used to understand the entire fictive world and manner in which R. conceived and constructed his narratives.

Becoming progressively more hermetic, as his language became more complex, and as he began to fuse the myths and legends of the *sertão* with those of foreign origin, R. has been criticized for the burden his writing places on the reader. Nevertheless, the grandness of his achievement is such that he is recognized today as the outstanding fiction writer of 20th-c. Brazil.

FURTHER WORKS: *Corpo de baile* (1956; reprinted in 3 vols., 1969: *Manuelzão e Miguilim; No urubùquaquá, no pinhém; Noites do sertão: Estas estórias*)

BIBLIOGRAPHY: Oliveira, F., de, "Introduction to the Epigraphs in *Sagarana*," in *Sagarana* (1966): vii–xiv; Rodriguez Monegal, E., "The Contemporary Brazilian Novel," in Peyre, H., ed. *Fiction in Several Languages* (1968): 8–13; Harss, L., and Dohmann, B., *Into the Mainstream: Conversations with Latin American Writers* (1969): 137–72; Daniel, M. L., "J. G. R.," *SSF*, 8 (1971): 209–16; Martins,

W., *Structural Perspectivism in G. R.* (1973); Vincent, J. S., *J. G. R.* (1978)

—FRED M. CLARK

ROSEI, Peter

Austrian novelist, short-story writer, and poet, b. 17 June 1946, Vienna

R. studied law at the University of Vienna and earned his doctorate in 1968. He then held a variety of jobs, including working as the secretary for the artist Ernst Fuchs. In 1972 he moved to Bergheim (near Salzburg) to devote himself entirely to his writing. In 1981 he returned to Vienna, where he still lives.

R. began his career by writing dark and negative antihomeland literature, where scenes of death and inhuman conditions prevail. The stories of *Landstriche* (1972; tracts of land) and *Wege* (1974; paths) are populated by characters who succumb to the tyranny and domination of others. The persons in *Bei schwebendem verfahren* (1973; pending proceedings) are so driven by sex and avarice that the president of the country wishes to destroy all individuality through comprehensive legislation. In all these works any attempt to subjugate and control others ends in disaster.

R. entered a second stage of his writing with *Entwurf für eine welt ohne menschen, entwurf zu einer reise ohne ziel* (1975; plan for a world without people, plan for a trip without a goal). In this and in subsequent works the protagonists take long trips that are without purpose or direction. In the first story of this book the narrator makes a long journey where he does not encounter a single human being; in the second, a group of people travel endlessly through a country populated by quasi-barbarians. In *Wer war edgar allen?* (1977; who was Edgar Allen?) the protagonist travels to Italy where he tries to learn more about his psyche through drugs and alcohol. Karl, in *Von hier nach dort* (1978; *From Here to There*, 1991), takes a long motorcycle trip, returns home, makes a lucrative drug deal, and then flies to a large city in the south, where he goes on long walks. Finally, Ellis, in *Die milchstrasse* (1981; the Milky Way), a compendium of R.'s ideas to date, is constantly on the move meeting friends and acquaintants. Everyone here seems to be lonely and isolated, and any type of happiness appears to be elusive.

R. explains his rather bizarre thematics in a series of essays collected under the title *Versuch, die natur zu kritisieren* (1982; attempt to criticize nature). Here he postulates that we are all on the journey of life, in search of happiness, which we can never achieve as long as we try to dominate nature and other individuals. Instead we should accept our isolation, try to be at one with nature, and look for happiness within ourselves and in our sense experiences.

The achievement of a modicum of happiness is the theme of a cycle of six prose pieces written between 1984 and 1988; *Mann & frau* (1984; man & woman), *Komödie* (1985; comedy), *15.000 seelen* (1985; 15,000 souls), *Die wolken* (1986; the clouds), *Der aufstand* (1987; the rebellion), and *Unser landschaftbericht* (1988; our landscape report). R. likens this project to a Gothic winged altar that portrays a central religious theme in a series of individual paintings. In all these works we learn that happiness cannot be achieved through human relationships or religion but by working hard, by living alone, and by assimilating nature.

R. is extremely prolific (averaging one or two works a year), and has developed into one of the most important and respected contemporary Austrian writers. He has conceived a unique vision of the postmodern world, which shocks, fascinates, and entertains his readers at the same time.

FURTHER WORKS: *Klotz spricht mit seinem rechtsanwalt* (1975); *Der fluss der gedanken durch den kopf* (1976); *Nennt mich tommy* (1978); *Alben* (1979); *Regentagstheorie: 59 gedichte* (1979); *Das lächeln des jungen: 59 gedichte* (1979); *Chronik der versuche, ein märchenerzähler zu werden* (1979); *Das schnelle glück* (1980); *Frühe prosa* (1981); *Reise ohne ende: aufzeichnungsbücher* (1983); *Rebus* (1990)

BIBLIOGRAPHY: Schirnding, A. Von, "Schreiben, weil Schweigen qualvoller ist: Über P. R.," *Merkur*, 33, 7 (1979): 714–20; Greiner, U., *Tod des Nachsommers* (1979): 139–54; Exner, R., "Stifter und die Folgen—Schreiben ohne Menschen, ohne Ziel? Reflexionen zu P. R.'s Prosa," *MAL*, 13, 1 (1980): 63–90; Bormann, A. Von, "'Es ist, als wenn etwas wäre': Überlegungen zu P. Rs Prosa," in Zeman, H., ed., *Studien zur österreichischen Erzählliteratur der Gegenwart* (1982): 156–88

—ROBERT ACKER

ROSENBERG, Isaac

English poet, b. 25 Nov. 1890, Bristol; d. 1 April 1918, Fampoux, France

In 1897 R.'s family moved to London. After eight years of elementary schooling, R. became an apprentice engraver while attending evening art classes at Birbeck College. In 1911 he entered the Slade School for advanced training in painting. In 1914 he went to South Africa for his health. On his return in early 1916 R. enlisted in the army and was killed in action two years later.

R. had been writing poetry from an early age. Three pamphlets, published between 1912 and 1916, show a strong interest in dialogue and dramatic form. *Night and Day* (1912) relates, in the manner of Shelley, the poet's yearning for the absolute and charts this fiery quest to its euphoric and triumphant conclusion. R., however, remains an outcast in a strange land. In *Youth* (1915) he is assaulted by visions of chaos and continually awakened by sneers that rob him of a sense of self. *Moses: A Play* (1916), a drama in verse, provides the persona through which he begins to speak with new vigor and muscularity. All of these self-published works demonstrate the moral earnestness and predilection for sonorous language that give R.'s work its richness yet, when in excess, detract from its effectiveness. The inclusion of the fine pieces written in the trenches (1916–18) in the posthumous collection *Poems* (1922), edited by Gordon Bottomley (1874–1948), aroused renewed interest in a poet who, quite obviously, had found a subject equal to his fiery spirit just before his untimely death.

At his death R. had been working on a verse drama to be called *The Unicorn*. The fragments of his work that survive reveal that he was developing a more direct, often monosyllabic way of writing that can be seen in the best of his war poems. He had also employed this style in *Adam*, a preceding unfinished work that includes many of the poems of his two years in the war.

R.'s earliest work, written before 1912, and that written between 1912 and 1915 but not published by him at the time, is marred by poeticisms ("silvern," "loathing to desist"), a rhetoric that attempts to compel emotional response ("sad shuddering forest"), and abstract imagery ("tomb of buried hours," "dark pools of brooding care").

Tracing R.'s evolving treatment of Old Testament heroes and stories throughout his poetic career reveals a development toward a poetry that is taut and vivid. In the early poems, like "Ode to David's Harp," R.'s recourse to Jewish history is not so much in the interest of an ideology or religion as it is for a set of images and characters with dramatic color and content. In the later poems that deal with Jewish themes (1916–18), he breaks with the merely decorative and imitative and in hammering rhythms and economical language uses Old Testament heroes and tales to evoke his concept of life as agon in which the soul struggles to rise above its imperfections. Particular poems (such as "The Jew," 1916) also reflect upon the mutability of all men and ask why the Jew should be singled out for scorn, or project a historical movement ("The Destruction of Jerusalem by the Babylonian Hordes") as the incarnation of the eschatological mood of the World War I period. "Through These Pale Cold Days," however, is a powerful evocation of Jewish identity as it affected the quality of R.'s own life.

R.'s reputation since 1964 is partly the consequence of renewed attention paid the handful of war poems, with their truly poetic immediacy and, in part, a tardy tribute to the courage and commitment of a man, a soldier, and an artist.

FURTHER WORKS: *The Collected Works of I. R.: Poetry, Prose, Letters and Some Drawings* (1937; rev. ed., 1979); *The Collected Poems of I. R.* (1949)

BIBLIOGRAPHY: Leavis, F. R., "The Recognition of I. R.," *Scrutiny*, 6 (1937): 229–30; Daiches, D., "I. R.: Poet," *Commentary*, July 1950: 91–93; Johnston, J. H., *English Poetry of the First World War* (1964): 210–49; Bergonzi, B., *Heroes' Twilight: A Study of the Literature of the Great War* (1965): 109–21; Silk, D., "I. R. (1890–1918)," *Judaism*, 14 (1965): 562–74; Silkin, J., *Out of Battle: The Poetry of the Great War* (1972): 249–314; Cohen, J., *Journey to the Trenches: The Life of I. R. 1890–1918* (1975)

—FRANCINE RINGOLD

ROSTWOROWSKI, Karol Hubert

Polish dramatist, b. 3 Nov. 1877, Rybna; d. 4 Feb. 1938, Cracow

From an aristocratic family, R. studied agriculture in Halle, Germany, and music and philosophy in Leipzig and Berlin. In 1933 he was elected to the Polish Academy of Literature.

R. came into prominence because of the success of two plays, *Judasz z Kariothu* (1913; Judas Iscariot) and *Kaius Cezar Kaligula* (1917; Gaius Caesar Caligula). Both plays offer a reinterpretation of their protagonists by probing the psychological forces at work. R.'s Judas is not an evil but a petty man. He is the owner of a small store, unable to understand the meaning of Revelation; he sees Christ's mission as the imposition of social and material equity. Judas's spiritual limitations lead not only to deception and treason but also to his own defeat, insanity, and the loss of his wife. The great number of characters are divided into groups and factions

(Christ's followers, apostles, members of the Sanhedrin), providing an impressive background that both reinforces and contrasts with the internal drama of the protagonist.

Similar in conception is *Kaius Cezar Kaligula*. R. challenges the stereotype by presenting not a tyrant but a tortured and insane man. In R.'s play Caligula's courage and frankness put him above the petty, cowardly, and hypocritical crowd of courtiers and state dignitaries who disguise their selfishness behind ideals of patriotism, public interest, justice, and freedom. This psychological interpretation, however, is inconsistent with the historical evidence accepted by R. and followed in the course of the action of the play. The central event—the murder of the emperor—appears unwarranted and gratuitous. A similar disparity mars *Niespodzianka* (1929; the surprise), in which a horrified mother learns she has murdered her own son. A drama that has started as a psychological study ends as a morality play.

Greatly admired in his own time, R. is largely forgotten today. The themes of his plays are obsolete for the contemporary reader, his historical figures not truly updated or revalued. His language—artificial, symbolic, and obscure—recalls the stylistic mannerisms of the "Young Polland" movement. No productions of R.'s plays have been staged since World War II, and this lack of performances has contributed to the unfavorable verdict of posterity. For R.'s strength is precisely the theatricality of his dramas. It is a theater not only of strong emotions, but also—as the copious stage directions accompanying the texts reveal—of striking, carefully arranged visual and auditory effects.

FURTHER WORKS: *Tandeta* (1901); *Pro Memoria* (1907); *Maya* (1908); *Ante lucis ortum* (1908); *Saeculum solutum* (1909); *Carmen saeculare* (1910); *Pod górę* (1910); *Miłosierdzie* (1920); *Straszne dzieci* (1922); *Zmartwychwstanie* (1923); *Antychryst* (1925); *Czerwony marsz* (1930); *Przeprowadzka* (1932); *U mety* (1932); *Zygzaki* (1932); *Pisma* (2 vols., 1936–37); *Pisma wybrane* (1966); *Dramaty* (2 vols., 1967)

BIBLIOGRAPHY: Borowy, W., "Fifteen Years of Polish Literature," *SlavonicR*, 12 (1933–34): 670–90; Czachowski, K., "R.—Polish Tragic Dramatist," *SlavonicR*, 17 (1938–39): 677–88; Kridl, M., *A Survey of Polish Literature and Culture* (1956): 502–3; Milosz, C., *The History of Polish Literature* (1969): 360; Krzyżanowski, J., *A History of Polish Literature* (1978): 515–16

—BOGDANA CARPENTER

ROTH, Henry

American novelist and short-story writer, b. 8 Feb. 1906, Tysmenitsa, Austro-Hungarian Empire; 13 Oct. 1995, Albuquerque, N.M.

R. was born in Galicia but was brought to New York by his mother when he was eighteen months old; his father had arrived earlier to earn the money to bring them over. His parents became bitterly estranged because R.'s birth date and paternity were in question. He recalled his father as a "despicable" and "most unadmirable guy." His mother, in her sensitive, noble, contemplative, and loving aspects, was Genya in his *Call It Sleep* (1934); "in her irritations, anxieties, and angers she was Bertha."

From 1908 to 1910 the family lived in the Brownsville section of Brooklyn; in 1910 they moved to the Lower East Side, to a homogeneous environment. The move from this milieu to rowdy, heterogeneous Harlem in 1914 produced a shock, says R., from which he never recovered. Withdrawing into himself, he read fairy tales, and everything from Sir James Frazer's *The Golden Bough* to T. S. ELIOT'S *The Waste Land*, from Mark Twain to James JOYCE.

While a student at the City College of New York (1924–28) R. began writing. During this period he met Eda Lou Walton, a New York University professor several years his senior, who subsidized him. He married Muriel Parker in 1938 and worked during the next decades as a teacher, precision grinder, psychiatric aide, and breeder of ducks and geese in Maine. Since 1968 he has lived in New Mexico. Besides *Call It Sleep* R. has published (since 1925) stories and articles in *The New Yorker, Commentary*, and other magazines.

Call It Sleep was written in three and a half years, beginning in 1930 in "sort of general mystical state . . . part of having been an orthodox Jew." Its publication met with a favorable reception, but R. never finished his second novel. In *The American Scholar*, in 1956, the critic Alfred Kazin (b. 1915) described *Call It Sleep* as a "wonderful novel" and Leslie A. FIEDLER referred to its "astonishing, sheer virtuosity." Since it was published in 1964, the paperback edition has sold over a million copies.

Call It Sleep is a psychological novel. Its events are seen through the eyes of seven-year-old David Schearl. Living in fear of his father, who doubts that David is his son and is tormented by his lack of success in America and his inability to adjust to the New World's values, David comes to associate evil and darkness with his cellar and the neighborhood, and sex with "playing dirty." At *heder* (Hebrew school), searching for a sign, he is electrified by Reb Yidel Pankower's reading of a passage from Isaiah in which an angel touches Isaiah's lips with a fiery coal, purifying him. Forced by three anti-Semitic youths to poke a metal dipper into a streetcar third rail, he is almost electrocuted. Overhearing fragments of a conversation in Polish and Yiddish between his mother and aunt, he misunderstands the details of his mother's affair with a gentile in the Old Country. After dropping a rosary given to him by a Polish American boy, for whom he had provided access to his aunt's stepdaughter, he flees his enraged father, who is now convinced that David is not his son. This time, seeking resolution of his troubles and fears, David purposely thrusts a milk ladle into the third rail. His near-electrocution reunites his parents, and as he closes his eyes, with his mother beside him, we are told, "one might as well call it sleep." This somewhat ambiguous phrase seems to signify the end of David's creative life, his reconciliation to, in R.'s words, "a more ordinary form of existence."

Call It Sleep is an immigrant novel, a quest novel, an initiation novel, a work about Jewish identity and one about helplessness in the face of adversity. The theme of redemption plays a major role. R.'s techniques include Joycean STREAM OF CONSCIOUSNESS, rich symbolism, and carefully delineated gradations of language from Yiddish to English. In Fiedler's words, "no one has ever distilled such poetry and wit from the counterpoint between maimed English and the subtle Yiddish of the immigrant. No one has reproduced so sensitively the terror of family life in the imagination of a child caught between two cultures."

FURTHER WORKS: *The Cruz Chronicle* (1989); *Boundaries of Love and Other Stories* (1990); *Mercy of a Rude Stream* (1994); *Shifting Landscape* (1995); *From Bondage* (1996); *Requiem for Harlem* (1997)

BIBLIOGRAPHY: Marsh, F., "A Great Novel about Manhattan Boyhood," *NYHT* (17 Feb. 1935): 6; Fiedler, L., and Kazin, A., "The Most Undeservedly Neglected Books of the Past Twenty-five Years," *ASch*, 25 (1956): 478, 486; Fiedler, L., "H. R.'s Neglected Masterpiece," *Commentary* (Aug. 1960): 102–7; Lyons, B., *H. R.: The Man and His Work* (1976); Sheres, I., "Exile and Redemption in H. R.'s *Call It Sleep, MarkhamR*, 6 (1977): 72–77; Walden, D., "H. R.'s *Call It Sleep*: Ethnicity, 'The Sign,' and the Power," *MFS*, 25 (1979): 268–72; special R. issue, *SAJL*, 5, 1 (1979); Wirth-Nesher, H., ed., *New Essays on Call It Sleep* (1996)

—DANIEL WALDEN

ROTH, Joseph

Austrian novelist, short-story writer, and journalist, b. 2 Sept. 1894, Brody, Austro-Hungarian Empire (now in Ukrainian S.S.R.); d. 27 May 1939, Paris, France

R. was raised by his mother amid the ethnically diverse surroundings of his native Brody, in Galicia; of his father, who died insane, he knew nothing. After completing his secondary education, he studied from 1914 to 1916 at the University of Vienna. From 1916 to 1918 he served in the Austrian army. (R.'s claim to have been taken as a prisoner of war by the Russians seems to be one of the many legends with which he embroidered his biography.) He began his journalistic career in 1920 and became one of the foremost feuilleton writers of his day, traversing Europe between 1925 and 1928 as an esteemed contributor to the *Frankfurter Zeitung*. Upon Hitler's ascent to power in 1933, he emigrated to Paris. From this time on, his life was marked by restless travel and, after the final, guilt-ridden separation from his schizophrenic wife, by chronic financial distress and severe alcoholism. The physical ruination that led to his death in a Paris hospital was a form of gradual suicide.

R.'s early novels *Hotel Savoy* (1924; Hotel Savoy) and *Die Rebellion* (1924; the rebellion) both depict the attempt of a war returnee to secure his identity and personal existence in a changed society characterized by the loss of traditional values. While the shadowy Galician backdrop of *Hotel Savoy* accentuates the unsettled state of its protagonist, Gabriel Dan, the central figure of *Die Rebellion*, the crippled Andreas Pum, suffers the injustices of an unfeeling social order in postwar Vienna.

The protagonists of R.'s next three novels, *Die Flucht ohne Ende* (1927; *Flight without End*, 1930), *Zipper und sein Vater* (1928; Zipper and his father), and *Rechts und Links* (1929; right and left), also belong to a wartime generation that cannot find its place in a new society and is burdened by the knowledge of its own superfluousness. In style, these works testify to R.'s attraction during the late 1920s to the documentary realism of the literary movement *Neue Sachlichkeit* (new factualism).

R. first achieved wide prominence with *Hiob* (1930; *Job: The Story of a Simple Man* 1931), a modern-day analogue of the biblical story. The novel is both a deeply moving realistic depiction of East European Jewish existence and a legend about the piety of a simple man, his loss of faith, and its eventual restoration. R.'s Job, Mendel Singer, is an indigent children's religion teacher in tsarist Russia. As the fabric of his family is rent by the afflictions of fate—a condition that remains his lot in America also—Singer despairs of God's justice. In the growing void created by the loss of his loved ones, he is faced with a crisis of belief, which is finally overcome through the "miracle" of the novel's conclusion: the discovery of his son, previously believed dead in Russia. Despite its somewhat contrived "happy ending," *Hiob* is a convincing lyrical evocation of humaneness in a world in which man's transcendent vision is increasingly obscured.

If *Hiob* represents R.'s tribute to his Jewishness, *Radetzkymarsch* (1932; *Radetzky March*, 1933), the work that won him lasting renown, was his profession of faith as an Austrian. In the family saga of the Trottas, who rise from Slovene peasants to Austrian nobility in the service of the Emperor Franz Joseph, R. glowingly memorialized Hapsburg Austria. The fate of the family's last member, Carl Joseph von Trotta, symbolically mirrors the end of the monarchy, which the author attributes to the evil of nationalism. Trotta's nostalgic quest for a homeland that could be for him the all-embracing imperium that the monarchy was for his grandfather, the "hero of Solferino," and for his father, the loyal civil servant, leads him inwardly to negate Austria. The elder Trotta, who is unable to live without Austria, dies on the same day as the emperor; Carl Joseph, who finds no spiritual home within Austria, sacrifices himself in the Great War. To the end, he is unable to cross the invisible border that separates him from his family's Slovene past. The peoples of the monarchy, however, in creating their own nation-states, drew the new boundaries that dissolved Austria. R.'s narrative achievement lies in the poetic illumination of the Austrian historical theme within the individual history of the Trottas.

In *Die Kapuzinergruft* (1938; The Emperor's Tomb, 1985), a sequel to *Radetzkymarsh*, R. ascribes the fall of the monarchy and the fatal weakness of the First Republic to pan-German nationalism. But the novel does not convincingly blend its political thesis with the story of its protagonist, Franz-Ferdinand Trotta, who vainly seeks to escape from the decadence of his Viennese world in the period after 1918. At the conclusion of the narrative—Austria has just been annexed by Nazi Germany—Trotta stands bewildered and without refuge before the symbol of Austria's irretrievable past, the imperial graves in the Capuchin crypt.

Other works of R.'s exile years are akin in subject, atmosphere, and character types to the Russian psychological novel. *Tarabas* (1934; *Tarabas*, 1934), *Beichte eines Mörders* (1936; *Confessions of a Murderer*, 1937), and *Das falsche Gewicht* (1937; the false weight) draw their figures and, fully or in part, their setting from the Slavic borderlands whose life the author knew intimately from childhood on. These works evidence R.'s growing occupation with the religious themes of evil, penance, and forgiveness, themes that received their most expressly Christian treatment in *Die hundert Tage* (1936; *Ballad of the Hundred Days*, 1936), a lyrical novel on Napoleon's triumphant return from banishment and his final defeat at Waterloo, and in the masterful short story "Die Legende vom heiligen Trinker" (1939; "The Legend of the Holy Drinker," 1943).

In his last novel, *Die Geschichte von der 1002. Nacht* (1939; the story of the thousand-and-second night), R. took doleful leave of his Austrian theme. Although the story is set in the still-untroubled period before the turn of the century, its writing was overshadowed by the calamity of the Third Reich. In the course of the narrative, the three principal figures—Baron Taittinger, the brothel keeper Frau Matzner, and the prostitute Mizzi Schinagl—fall victim to the rewards they had reaped from a visit to Vienna by the Persian Shah (an episode that is depicted with subtle irony in the "Arabian Nights" framework plot). All three are confronted with the emptiness and falsehood of their existence; shorn of their sustaining illusions, they succumb to despair. Although R. drew his characters

and their world with empathy and affection, the novel probes and condemns the moral languor, callousness, and self-deception that lay below the surface of Gay Vienna and were to explode in barbarism in the author's final years.

From the start, the novelist R. was also a prolific political journalist. But while his articles and feuilletons show greater sagacity—and in the 1920s, a firmer socialist conviction—than has generally been acknowledged, he was not a political thinker. Above all, he was a storyteller, whose decisive break through occurred when, in 1929, he renounced documentary realism in favor of the poetic imagination. But he had hardly attained distinction when his books were banned in Germany and he was subjected to the fate of a writer in exile. The nostalgia for a lost world, in which a traditional, hierarchical order remained intact, had already informed *Hiob* and *Radetzkymarsch*; hence forth it was to underlie R.'s entire work and outlook. In the despondency of his exile years, he professed Catholicism (while stressing his origins as an East European Jew), and passionately espoused the Hapsburg monarchist cause. As an artist, however, he was able to resolve the contradictions of his personality and beliefs in the humane vision, the graceful sweep and poetic twilight glow that characterize his finest novels and stories.

FURTHER WORKS: *Das Spinnennetz* (1923); *April: Die Geschichte einer Liebe* (1925); *Der blinde Spiegel: Ein kleiner Roman* (1925); *Juden auf Wanderschaft* (1927); *Panoptikum: Gestalten und Kulissen* (1930); *Der Antichrist* (1934; *Antichrist*, 1935); *Der Leviathan* (1940); *Werke* (3 vols., 1956); *Romane, Erzählungen, Aufsätze* (1964); *Der stumme Prophet* (1966; *The Silent Prophet*, 1980); *Briefe 1911–1939* (1970); *Der Neue Tag: Unbekannte politische Arbeiten 1919 bis 1927—Wien, Berlin, Moskau* (1970); *Die Erzählungen* (1973); *Werke* (4 vols., 1975–1976); *Perlefter: Die Geschichte eines Bürgers* (1978)

BIBLIOGRAPHY: Linden, H., ed., *J. R.: Leben und Werk* (1949); Scheible, H., *J. R.* (1971); Bronsen, D., "Austrian versus Jew: The Torn Identity of J. R.," *Yearbook XVIII of the Leo Baeck Institute* (1973): 219–26; Arnold, H. L., ed., *J. R.* (1974); Bronsen, D., *J. R.: Eine Biographie* (1974); Magris, C., *Weit von wo* (1974); Williams, C. E., *The Broken Eagle: The Politics of Austrian Literature from Empire to Anschluss* (1974): 91–112; Bronsen, D., ed., *J. R. und die Tradition* (1975); Sültemeyer, I., *Das Frühwerk J. R.s 1915–1926* (1976); Browning, B. W., "J. R.'s *Legende vom heiligen Trinker*: Essence and Elixir," in Strelka, J. P., Bell, R. F., and Dobson, E., eds., *Protest—Form—Tradition: Essays on German Exile Literature* (1979): 81–95; Bronsen, D., "The Jew in Search of a Fatherland: The Relationship of J. R. to the Habsburg Monarchy," *GR*, 54 (1979): 54–61; Muller-Funk, W., *J. R.* (1989)

—SIDNEY ROSENFELD

ROTH, Philip

American novelist, short-story writer, and essayist, b. 19 March 1933, Newark, N.J.

Among the most controversial of current American writers, R. in his early works examined the urban Jewish experience and the tragicomic contradictions of cultural assimilation. His handling of these subjects seemed to suggest a degree of ambivalence toward

Philip Roth

his ethnic heritage, thereby alienating a large segment of the reading public. In his essays of the same period, however, R. maintained that he wished neither to condemn nor to romanticize, but simply to render his material fully and objectively. In the attempt, he has repeatedly drawn upon certain details of his personal background: childhood in Newark, graduate studies at the University of Chicago, a brief military stint, sudden literary success, a tumultuous marriage, university teaching, psychonalysis, and European travel.

Many commentators still consider R.'s first book, *Goodbye, Columbus, and Five Short Stories* (1959), to be his best, while *Portnoy's Complaint* (1969) remains his most hotly debated. The former, a National Book Award winner and the basis for a successful film, revolves around a young man's summer romance. His wealthy Radcliffe girlfriend's crass, nouveau-riche suburban surroundings contrast sharply with the youth's stereotyped, old-world home life in Newark, and Roth acidly lampoons both extremes. In *Portnoy's Complaint* R. focuses on the protagonist's masturbatory exploits, thereby producing a notoriously tasteless yet exceptionally humorous work. Narrating from his analyst's couch, Portnoy blames his neuroses on what he considers a too-rigid upbringing, and directs his most vituperative remarks at his mother. *Portnoy's Complaint* firmly established R. not only as a writer but as something of a popular curiosity as well. Described as the literary heir to stand-up comedian Lenny Bruce, R. with this novel helped to create the burst of "confessional" literature that has flourished since the book's publication.

Although primarily a realist and a novelist of manners, R. embarked during the early 1970s on a phase of misdirected experimentation that yielded three rather inferior books. Of these, only *The Great American Novel* (1973) warrants serious notice. R. constructs a bizarre fable involving an imaginary baseball league, and uses this framework to comment upon our national tendency to mythologize and falsify history. The novel is a fictive demonstration of R.'s comment, "Sheer Playfulness and Deadly Seriousness are my closest friends," and reflects his conception of American life as fundamentally absurd.

In recent years R.'s novels have become increasingly autobiographical, scrutinizing situations obviously based on the author's experience. In the lengthiest of these books, *My Life as a Man* (1974), the protagonist says, "All I can do with my story is tell it. And tell it. And tell it." This seems to have become R.'s own situation, as each new volume covers essentially the same territory: a sensitive, questioning young Jewish novelist combats the combined forces of marriage, family, the academic establishment, and his own self-doubts and erotic yearnings to wage a lonely, unsatisfying war of emotional and artistic independence.

But if R.'s works are somewhat repetitious, they are also quite accomplished. With each retelling of his basic plot, his underlying preoccupations are given clearer expression. His main theme is a weighty one: the difficulty of reconciling the opposed demands of the self and the social contract, particularly in the context of interpersonal relationships. Parents and children, husbands and wives, lovers and friends encounter problems because they are unable to achieve a balance between license and repression. Usually this failure is linked to sexual avidity, and the resulting dilemmas are played out against the complex background of conflicting ethnic and cultural mores.

As R.'s career has unfolded, his treatment of his subject matter has moderated, evincing greater maturity and restraint. His latest books are neither as symbolic as *Goodbye, Columbus* nor as uproarious as *Portnoy's Complaint*. But in their far more affirmative attitude toward the reinforcing aspects of interdependency, commitment, and love, they achieve a broader, more universal scope of implication.

The ethnic component, in particular, has undergone a notable redefinition. Whereas earlier works were often sharply satiric, novels such as *The Professor of Desire* (1977), *The Ghost Writer* (1979), *Zuckerman Unbound* (1981), and *The Anatomy Lesson* (1983) adopt a wryly celebratory approach to the characters' Jewishness. Frequent references to the Holocaust, for example, and R.'s ongoing fascination with Franz KAFKA not only link him to the European tradition but also make former allegations of anti-Semitism almost amusing in retrospect.

Principal among R.'s technical strengths is his narrative voice, an uncommonly skillful blend of colloquial and literary effects. A master of the vernacular idiom, he also possesses an acute social eye and good descriptive powers, and, of course, an excellent sense of humor. Whether indulging broad burlesque or mining the text with more subtly farcical incongruities, R. is always entertaining. Prolific, probing, and problematic, R. is an important contemporary writer despite some critics' claims that he has not yet fulfilled his early promise.

FURTHER WORKS: *Letting Go* (1962); *When She Was Good* (1967); *Our Gang* (1971); *The Breast* (1972); *Reading Myself and Others* (1975); *A. P. R. Reader* (1980); *Zuckerman Unbound* (1981); *The Anatomy Lesson* (1983); *Zuckerman Bound* (1985);

The Counterlife (1986); *The Facts: A Novelist's Autobiography* (1988); *Deception* (1990); *Patrimony* (1991); *Operation Shylock: A Confession* (1993); *Sabbath's Theatre* (1995); *American Pastoral* (1997)

BIBLIOGRAPHY: Leer, N., "Escape and Confrontation in the Short Stories of P. R.," *Christian Scholar*, 49 (1966): 132–46; Spacks, P. M., "About Portnoy," *YR*, 58 (1969): 623–35; Tanner, T., *City of Words: American Fiction 1950–1970* (1971): 295–321; McDaniel, J. N., *The Fiction of P. R.* (1974); Pinsker, S., *The Comedy That "Hoits": An Essay on the Fiction of P. R.* (1975); Siegel, B., "The Myths of Summer: P. R.'s *The Great American Novel*," *ConL*, 17 (1976): 171–90; Rodgers, B. F., *P. R.* (1978); Weil, H., "P. R.: Still Waiting for His Masterpiece," *SatR* (June 1981): 26–31; Jones, J. P., and Nance, G. A., *P. R.* (1981); Lee, H., *P. R.* (1982); Baumgarten, M., *Understanding P. R.* (1990); Wade, S., *The Imagination in Transit: The Fiction of P. R.* (1996)

—GEORGE J. SEARLES

ROTIMI, Ola

(born Emmanuel Gladstone Olawale Rotimi) Nigerian dramatist (writing mostly in English), b. 13 Apr. 1938, Sapele

R.'s family background brought him into contact with the English language, with the diversity of Nigeria, and with the performing arts from an early age. He spent part of his youth in the most cosmopolitan city in Nigeria, Lagos, and there, since his father was playing a leading role in the trade-union movement, he had firsthand contact with political activity. On completing his secondary education, he went to the U.S. and obtained his B.A. from Boston University and his M.F.A. from Yale University. He returned to Nigeria in 1966 and has held appointments at the universities of Ife and Port Harcourt.

Since the late 1950s Nigeria has been swept by a variety of political and intellectual movements, and these provide the background to R.'s approach to the theater. The intense nationalism of the independence movement was accompanied by an anxiety to affirm the vitality and validity of Nigerian cultural traditions and a concern that the historical experiences of the nation should be made familiar to generations emerging from a colonial educational system. Today there is in Nigeria, it appears, a spirit of vitality and excess that finds expression both creatively and destructively in politics, business, music, art, crime, fashions, the press, celebrations, and the very style in which people express themselves. It is appropriate that such a society should have produced a dramatist with R.'s commitment to plays on a grand scale in which monumental emotions are unleashed.

R.'s early foray into political drama, *Our Husband Has Gone Mad Again* (1974), first performed at Yale in 1966, reflected the intensity of nationalist feelings, and revealed the dramatist's desire to exploit various means of communication within the "two-hour traffic of the stage." His next major work was characteristically ambitious: Seeking to exploit similarities between the cultures of Yorubaland and Ancient Greece, R. prepared an adaptation of *Oedipus Rex*, with the provocative title *The Gods Are Not To Blame* (1971). He created a compelling theatrical event in which issues of concern to all communities, such as incest and political stability,

are explored through a drama rich in ritual, spectacle, and movement. The play is written in English, but an English heavily interlaced with elements from several Nigerian languages and rhetorical traditions, replete with incantations, proverbs, riddles, and direct translations of Yoruba verse forms. At the end of the 1960s, R. toured his production of the play to various theaters in Nigeria and Ghana; it attracted large audiences, and was appreciated even by those who had only a limited knowledge of English.

During the late 1970s and the 1980s, R. turned to history for his sources and wrote *Kurunmi* (1971) and *Ovonramwen Nogbaisi: An Historical Tragedy in English* (1974). He found his material in the Yoruba conflicts that preceded colonial rule and that affected the Kingdom of Benin—events in which he found conflicts that appealed to his taste for full-blooded theater and that had relevance for his contemporaries.

R.'s recent work focuses on suffering humanity in a contemporary setting. *If* (perf. 1979, pub. 1983), subtitled "A Tragedy of Our Times," is set in a crowded and poverty-stricken row of "quarters" whose residents lives and experiences are representative of the pressures on "the wretched of the earth." Over the course of a weekend they go through what R. calls "the giddy gamut of survival imposed by the sociopolitical truths of present-day Nigeria."

In *Hopes of the Living Dead* (1989), set in a hospital for lepers during the 1930s, R. extends his pioneering experiments in communicating with audiences unfamiliar with English, even Pidgin English. The hospital patients are from different language groups, and important statements, particularly those made by the central character. Ikoli Harcourt White, are translated for their benefit. With this device, R. has found a way of keeping a substantial proportion of his audience informed about developments. The device inevitably slows the play down, but R. provides so much incident and action, so much broad comedy and high drama, that the necessary momentum is maintained.

R. has been accused of cultural and theatrical opportunism, as well as attacked on political grounds, by detractors who hold narrower views of what theater should be and who do not share his ideological perspectives. But R.'s true importance should be measured by the extent to which he has contributed to a popular and dynamic Nigerian theater tradition. His plays speak to large audiences in a variety of languages and, as they are intended to do, take the audience through the "giddy gamut" of emotions.

FURTHER WORKS: *Holding Talks* (1977); *Statements towards August 1983* (1983); *Everyone His Own Problem* (1987); *When Criminals Turn Judges* (1990)

BIBLIOGRAPHY: Adedeji, J., "Oral Tradition and the Contemporary Theatre in Nigeria," *RAL*, 2, 2 (1971): 135–49; Sekoni, O., on *Kurunmi, Ba Shiru*, 7, 1 (1976): 80–81; Adelugba, D., "Wale Ogunyemi, Zulu Sofola and O. R.: Three Dramatists in Search of a Language," in Irele, A. and O. Ogunba, eds., *Theatre in Africa* (1978): 201–20; Jeyifo, B., "The Search for a Popular Theatre," in Ogunbiyi, Y., ed., *Theatre and Drama in Nigeria* (1981): 411–21; Crow, B., "Melodrama and the 'Political Unconscious' in Two African Plays," *ArielE*, 14, 3 (1983): 15–31; Lalude, O. O., *Theatre Arts: O. R. and his Works—An Annotated Bibliography* (1984); Osofisan, F., *Beyond Translation: Tragic Paradigms and the Dramaturgy of O. R. and Wole Soyinka* (1986)

—JAMES GIBBS

ROUMAIN, Jacques

Haitian novelist, short-story writer, poet, and essayist, b. 4 June 1907, Port-au-Prince; d. 18 Aug. 1944, Port-au-Prince

R.'s maternal grandfather, Tancrède Auguste, was president of the Haitian Republic (1912–13), and R. might easily have followed in his grandfather's footsteps. But R. helped launch the Haitian Communist Party, was imprisoned three times for political reasons, and spent five years in exile, during which he studied ethnology. In 1942 he was named Haitian *chargé d'affaires* to Mexico. After suffering from ill health for several years he died at the age of thirty-seven while on a visit home.

From a wealthy landowning family, R. began his literary career as a rebel, alienated from Haiti's ruling class. His collection of short stories *La proie et l'ombre* (1930; the prey and the darkness) portrays the aimlessness of Haitian bourgeois existence. The final story in the collection, "Préface à la vie d'un bureaucrate" (preface to the life of a bureaucrat), depicts a day in the life of Michel Rey, a suicidal failure given to drink, who seems to represent the negative side of the author. Michel Rey reappears in the novel *Les fantoches* (1931; the puppets) as an older, more mellow, and more cynical writer to whom the young protagonist Marcel Basquet is mysteriously attracted.

The Haitian scholar Roger Gaillard has indicated the similarities between *La montagne ensorcelée* (1931; the bewitched mountain) and *Hill of Destiny* by Jean GIONO, published in 1929, only one year before R. began to write what was the first peasant novel to appear in Haiti. In both novels, a series of calamities befalls the inhabitants of a small village, who blame these happenings on the supernatural and seek revenge by punishing someone they believe to be guilty of witchcraft. R.'s novel is original, however, in its emphasis on voodoo. The style of *La montagne ensorcelée*, with its use of Creole expressions to convey the peasants' natural speech and its shifting point of view from third-person narrator to first-person protagonist, anticipates the haunting, lyrical style of R.'s masterpiece, *Gouverneurs de la rosée* (1944; *Masters of the Dew*, 1947).

Gouverneurs de la rosée is a mature treatment of themes that were important to R. throughout his diplomatic and literary career: nationalism, communism, nostalgia for the Haitian peasant woman, romantic love, the plight of the leader, agricultural reform, and the cult of perfect friendship. Whereas the protagonists of *Les fantoches* and *La proie et l'ombre* were intellectuals unable to take action, in this novel R. created a hero capable of gaining the respect and support of his fellow townspeople. Manuel is a Christ figure who rejects traditional religion-both that of the French clergy and that of the voodoo priests, since those leaders only encourage passivity and resignation.

A posthumously published collection of poems, *Bois d'ébène* (1945; *Ebony Wood*, 1972), written in exile in 1938–39, reveals the anger, violence, and bitterness with which R. experienced the black revolt, and influenced Aimé CÉSAIRE, Léon-Gontran DAMAS, and David Diop (1927–1960). All the major themes of NEGRITUDE are expressed in this collection: slavery, exile, forced labor, lynching, segregation, anticlericalism, colonial oppression, and a nostalgia for Africa.

During his brief lifetime, R. failed to fulfill his potential as a political leader, but his literary works are powerful cries of protest on behalf of Haitians, blacks, and all the oppressed of the earth. His masterpiece, *Gouverneurs de la rosée*, is the most beautiful, tender, and moving novel to come out of the Caribbean.

FURTHER WORKS: *Analyse schématique: 32–34* (1934); *À propos de la campagne "anti-superstitieuse"* (1942); *Contribution à l'étude de l'ethnobotanique précolombienne des Grandes Antilles* (1942); *Le sacrifice du tambour-assoto* (1943). FURTHER WORKS IN ENGLISH: *When the Tom-Tom Beats: Selected Prose and Poems* (1995)

BIBLIOGRAPHY: Price-Mars, J., Preface to *La montagne ensorcelée* (1931): 9–13; Cook, M., "The Haitian Novel," *FR*, 19 (1946). 406–12; Gaillard, R., *L'univers romanesque de J. R.* (1965); Achiriga, J., *La révolte des romanciers noirs de langue française* (1973): 119–41; Dixon, M., "Towards a World Black Literature and Community," *MR*, 18 (1977): 750–69; Fowler, C., *A Knot in the Thread: The Life and Work of J. R.* (1980); Dorsinville, R., *J. R.* (1981)

—DEBRA POPKIN

ROUSSEL, Raymond

French novelist, poet, and dramatist, b. 20 Jan. 1877, Paris; d. 14 July 1933, Palermo, Italy

R., whose father was a wealthy stockbroker, left school at thirteen, tried writing songs and poems at sixteen, and soon felt certain that he was akin to Shakespeare and Dante. After experiencing hallucinations, he became the patient of the famous French psychiatrist Pierre Janet. R. translated his "pyrotechnic" visions into writing and worked painstakingly to "outshine the glory of Napoleon." Living an eccentric life, he traveled around the world, took up chess, and turned to alcohol and barbiturates. Having tried to open his veins, he later died under mysterious circumstances.

R. has been praised by André BRETON, Jean COCTEAU, Michel LEIRIS, and Roger Vitrac (1899–1952) and has been recognized by Alain ROBBE-GRILLET, Michel BUTOR, and Eugène IONESCO as perhaps the most prominent precursor of both SURREALISM and the NEW NOVEL. Experimenting with language, he wrote novels in "free" verse, published them at his own expense, and then turned them into plays. An example is *Locus solus* (1914; *Locus Solus*, 1970), dramatized in 1922.

His first work in verse, the long poem *Monâme* (1897; my soul), was written when he was seventeen; he republished it later under a new title, *L'âme de Victor Hugo* (1932; the soul of Victor Hugo). In it he attempted to describe his own literary genius and the essence of the soul as a "vacuum," as the pit of a coal mine belching forth the fires of imagination. This second metaphor is reminiscent of Zola's *Germinal*, but R.'s originality lies in the fact that the multitude of "realistic" visions become the core of poetic creation.

R.'s second work was *La doublure* (1897; the understudy), a novel in alexandrine couplets, which PROUST praised as a "forceful" literary endeavor. The word *doublure* can also be translated as the "lining of a garment." The dual meaning of the title points to R.'s attempt to reveal the inner self of the pathetic actor who, having failed, sheds his pitiful frayed coat. Amid images of floats during the Nice carnival and clowns at the Neuilly fair are minute descriptions of sights, sounds, movement, and colors.

In a posthumously published work, *Comment j'ai écrit certains de mes livres* (1935; *How I Wrote Certain of My Books*, 1963) R. hailed his own "unforeseen" literary creation—due, he claimed, to phonic combinations—as a very special poetic procedure akin to a rhyming technique. Using the "metagrammic" word-ladder method (for example, bald, bold, boot), he wrote fiction in which the impact of the opening sentence reverberates in the last line of the novel. The word-association method and some automatic-writing devices are examplified in his *Impressions d'Afrique* (1910; *Impressions of Africa*, 1967).

Mallarmé before him had also striven to achieve pure poetry. Often abstruse, R.'s works do not spring from external factors; they are essentially constructed from within. His humor and fantasy make him the Marcel Duchamp of French literature. His overflowing, completely alogical imagination turns his own strange world into a deluge of vocables until nothing else remains but R.'s powerful, deceptive, opaque, and fascinating world of words.

FURTHER WORKS: *Chiquenaude* (1900); *La vue* (1904); *L'étoile au front* (1925); *La poussière de soleils* (1927); *Nouvelles impressions d'Afrique* (1932); *Épaves* (1972)

BIBLIOGRAPHY: Foucault, M., *R. R.* (1963); special R. issue, *Bizarre*, No. 34–35 (1964); Heppenstall, R., *R. R.* (1967); Caburet, B., *R. R.* (1968); Caradec, F., *Vie de R. R.* (1972); special R. issue *L'arc*, No. 68 (1977); Hill, L., "R. R. and the Place of Literature," *MLR*, 74 (1979): 823–35; Foucault, M., *Death and the Labyrinth: The World of R. R.* (1986)

—MARIE-GEORGETTE STEISEL

ROVINSKI, Samuel

Costa Rican dramatist, novelist, and short-story writer, b. 13 Nov. 1932, San José

R. was born in San José in 1932 and was educated there until going to the Universidad Autónoma in Mexico City, where he obtained his degree in civil engineering (1956). He pursued the engineering profession until 1971. R. lived in Paris for a time, where he studied filmmaking, and was an advising minister of the Costa Rican embassy in Paris from 1972 to 1975. He has held several important cultural positions in Costa Rica, including the presidency of the Association of Costa Rican Authors (1976) and, in addition to writing, is currently the president of the film enterprise ICARO Productions.

The Teatro National of Costa Rica has premiered several of R.'s works, which have brought him to a position of prominence in Costa Rican theater. R. has also worked significantly in the novel, his only published work in that genre, *Ceremonia de casta* (1976; caste ceremony), receiving critical acclaim, and in the short story. His theater has wide range, from THEATER OF THE ABSURD to Brechtian experimentation to plays concerning conflicts within typical Costa Rican families. He attained great popular success in Costa Rica with *Las fisgonas de Paso Ancho* (1971, the eavesdroppers

of Paso Ancho), a farce about social mores in San José, the Costa Rican capital.

The primary concerns of the work of R. have included the impact of modernity on Costa Rican society and the concomitant loss of traditional values, as detailed in *Ceremonia de casta*. This novel recalls *All My Sons* (1947) by Arthur MILLER as well as the Sartoris novels of William FAULKNER with its focus on a dying patriarch and his loss of influence over his resentment-ridden family, whose conflicts and historical faults are concentrated in the figure of his outcast bastard son, the narrator of the novel. The house which Juan Matías, the patriarch, tries to keep in the family becomes a metaphor for the changes in Costa Rican society, and which is surrounded by the modern San José. Other concerns important to R. have been political corruption and dictatorship, central to his plays *El laberinto* (1986; the labyrinth), *Gobierno de alcoba* (1986; bedroom government), and *El martirio del pastor* (1983; the martyrdom of the pastor), the latter dramatizing the murder of Archbishop Oscar Arnulfo Romero of El Salvador on 24 March 1980.

R.'s plays are usually experimental, although not forbiddingly so. In *El martirio del pastor*, for example, two film screens are placed on the stage, projecting newsreels showing scenes of noting, public speaking, and inaugurations that form a counterpoint to the action in the text. *El laberinto* uses sound effects, while *Un modelo para Rosaura* (1974; a model for Rosaura) features an on-stage argument between some of the actors, the director and the author, with direct address of the audience, about how to interpret and present the second part of the play.

The short stories of R., which have included those collected in *La hora de los vencidos* (1963; the hour of the vanquished). *La pagoda* (1968: the pagoda), and *Cuentos judíos de mi tierra* (1982; Jewish stories of my land), are varied in form and content. Some are relatively traditional in narrative style; others are more adventurous, recalling the intricate texture of his novel. The pieces in *La hora de los vencidos*, as the title indicates, present different protagonists who undergo forms of defeat, but who often—though not always—find some redemption or catharsis through their frustration. *Cuentos judíos de mi tierra* is a collection with apparent autobiographical content. R.'s approach to the Jewish experience is generally more concerned with issues of personal integrity, family survival, and economic problems than with the questions of historicity and political involvement dealt with by Mario SZICHMAN or with the problems of identity emphasized by Isaac GOLDEMBERG. R. has also worked with Jewish material in his play *La víspera del sábado* (1984; Saturday [Sabbath] eve).

R. has detailed his coming of age as a writer in the interesting *Cuarto creciente* (1964; growing quarter), an autobiographical narrative that presents the young R. as a rather introverted potential artist who began his first novel, never finished, as an homage to the doomed World War II struggle of the Jews in the Warsaw ghetto against Nazi occupiers. The book won the National Prize for Essay in Costa Rica in 1964 and was reissued with a new preface in 1987.

R. has been an important cultural force in Costa Rica because of his triple positions as businessman, politician, and writer. He brings to his work a wide and judicious experience, allowing him to deal with numerous themes, especially in his surprisingly varied short stories. In more recent years, he has been heavily involved in the cinema but has continued to produce literary works. R. is a literary presence deserving of more attention from critics and readers abroad.

FURTHER WORKS: *La Atlántida* (perf. 1960); *Los agitadores* (perf. 1965); *Política cultural de Costa Rica* (1976; *Cultural Policy in Costa Rica*, 1978); *Los pregoneros* (1978); *La guerra de los filibusteros* (film script, 1981); *Los intereses compuestos* (1981); *Gulliver dormido* (1985); *Eulalia* (film script, 1987); *El embudo de Pandora* (1991)

BIBLIOGRAPHY: Herzfeld, A. and Salas, T. Cajiao, *El teatro de hoy en Costa Rica: perspectiva crítica y antología* (1973): 47–54; Gallegos, D., Introduction to *Tres obras de teatro* (1985): 7–9; Souza, R. D., "Novel and Context in Costa Rica and Nicaragua," *KRQ*, 33, 4 (Nov. 1986): 453–62; Allen, R. F., ed., *Teatro hispano-americano: una bibliografía anotada/Spanish American Theatre: An Annotated Bibliography* (1987), 71; Vallbona, R. de, "Costa Rica," in Foster, D. W., comp., *Handbook of Latin American Literature* (1987): 191–202; Rojas, M. A., "*Gulliver dormido* de S. R.: Una parodía del discurso del poder," *LATR*, 24, 1 (1990): 51–63

—KENNETH E. HALL

ROY, Arundhati

Indian novelist (writing in English), b. 1961 in Shillong, Bengal

Though born in Bengal, R. grew up in the Syrian Christian community of her mother's native village, Aymanam, near the town of Kottayam, in the southern Indian state of Kerala. From an early age she attended classes in a school founded by her mother; then, at age ten, she was sent to a boarding school in the Ootacamund Hills. R.'s mother had defied community traditions first by marrying a Bengali Hindu, then by divorcing him, and finally by challenging the Travencore Christian Succession Act in a precedent-setting case decided by the Indian Supreme Court that established the inheritance rights of Christian women as equal to that of their men. Feeling shunned by her community as a result, and encouraged to be independent by her mother, R. left home to study at the Delhi School of Architecture and live there in a hut within the Ferozshah Kotla ruins. She had a five-year relationship with fellow student Gerard da Cunha, including a period living on the beach in da Cunha's native Goa. Da Cunha eventually established himself as a noted Indian architect; but R., after studying architectural restoration on a scholarship in Italy, quit school and took a position in Delhi with the National Institute of Urban Affairs. Soon afterwards, she met the film director Pradip Krishen, whom she later married, and acted in his film *Massey Sahib*. R. went on to write scripts for an ITV serial, *The Banyan Tree*, which was never completed, and two films on Indian television's Channel Four, *In Which Annie Gives It to Those Ones* (in which she also acted) and *Electric Moon*. R.'s first publication described the making of the latter film, and soon after she began nearly five years of work on her novel. The finished draft attracted an inordinate amount of attention from publishers and agents, due in part to its promotion by Pankaj Mishra, at that time an editor for Harper Collins in India. Media attention over the enormous advance she received from her British publishers, in 1996, was followed by even more publicity when *The God of Small Things* (1997) won the 1997 Booker Prize,

Britain's most prestigious literary award—the only time an author's first book has ever received that prize.

Comparisons seem inevitable between R.'s *The God of Small Things* and another Booker Award-winning novel from India, Salman RUSHDIE's *Midnight's Children* (1980). Some of the apparent connections, however, such as children with extrasensory abilities and a connection to historical events, are standard features of postcolonial magical realism, while others, including the pickle factory, have an autobiographical basis for R. Indeed, the novel's setting and characterizations, if not its plot, are drawn largely from R.'s childhood. The story is set in the Aymanam-like village of Ayemenem, where the twins, Rahel and Esthappen, live with their single mother, Ammu. The plot turns on the coincidence of Ammu's risky love affair and the visit of a cousin. The cousin, Sophie Mol, is drowned when the twins' boat capsizes while the three are fleeing an adult world seemingly filled with betrayal and indifference. Ammu's lover, Velutha—identified in the novel as "The God of Small Things"—is as kind with the children as he is passionate with Ammu, though these two sides of his love can never meet: he is a Paravan, untouchable by Brahmin Hindus and Syrian Christians alike; and he is also a Marxist, though of a different stripe from the twins' uncle Chacko, for whom he works, or the local party official Comrade Pillai, the "professional omeletteer" who does not mind breaking a few eggs. In Velutha, R. creates a hero of gentle idealism, while in the outraged and outrageous reaction to the affair in Ayemenem, from Ammu's own family to the policemen from whose beating Velutha dies, she attacks the evils of personal intolerance and public injustice.

But the nonchronological progression of the novel—it begins, for example, with Sophie Mol's funeral—allows R. to end with two disturbingly beautiful love scenes, occurring years apart but meaningfully paired. In the first, the twins, adults now and separated since the events of the novel, find each other in an apparently sexual as well as emotional union. Then, in the final chapter of the novel, the narrative returns to the night of the first encounter between Ammu and Velutha when, overpowered by their love and aware that it has no future, they instinctively stick "to the Small Things."

Few first novels have ever garnered the combined critical and financial success of *The God of Small Things*. The question now is whether R. will be burdened by that success and its possibly unmatchable performance, or liberated by it to enhance and experiment with her art.

BIBLIOGRAPHY: Brijnath, R., and B. K. John, "A. R.: Flowering of a Rebel," *India Today*, 15 Apr. 1997: 114-24. Jaggi, M., "An Unsuitable Girl," *The Guardian*, 24 May 1997: 12

—DAVID MESHER

ROY, Claude

(pseud. of Claude Orland) French poet, novelist, essayist, critic, journalist, and writer of children's books, b. 28 Aug. 1915, Paris; d. 13 Dec. 1997, Paris

R.'s presence in the literary life of post-World War II France is a ubiquitous one. Having published copiously in just about every genre imaginable: poetry, novels, short stories, literary and art criticism, autobiography and memoirs, travel documentaries, monographs on well-known personalities, and children's literature, he displayed in his approximately fifty published volumes and in his countless articles both a protean talent and a chameleon-like personality. Because few of his books have been translated into English, his reputation in monolingual America is limited mainly to cognoscenti of French literature. But in the French-speaking nations he has always enjoyed a justly merited reputation as one of the most intelligent and perceptive writers of his generation.

Of Charentes (southwestern coastal France) background, R. divided his early years between life in Paris and the Charentes region (near Angoulême). Having studied both at the Lycée in Angoulême and the prestigious Lycée Montaigne in Paris, where he received his baccalaureate degree, he entered the Sorbonne at the University of Paris at the age of twenty. At the beginning of World War II, he enlisted in the army and took part in active armed combat as an officer in a tank battalion. Decorated with the military honor Croix de Guerre, R. was captured by the Germans and imprisoned in a military camp near Metz. This painful incarceration left indelible scars in his memory and influenced his literary texts. Eventually he escaped and fled to the so-called Free Zone in southern France. At first, R. joined the ultra-right wing of the extremist patriotic movement called L'Action Française. Quickly disillusioned by the fascistic tendencies of this movement, he briskly transformed himself from an ultra-conservative into a card-carrying member of the Communist Party, the leaders of which he admired because of their prominent role in the anti-Nazi resistance movement struggling to liberate his beloved France from the humiliating German Occupation. A courageous militant, he became a close friend of the radical poets Louis ARAGON, Paul ÉLUARD, and Roger VAILLANT.

Following the liberation of France R. continued to advocate Communist causes. Inspired by an insatiable wanderlust, he undertook a number of important trips: to the U.S. in 1949, to China and Korea in 1951, to the Soviet Union in 1952, and soon thereafter to French North Africa, Czechoslovakia, and Poland. His exposure to the excesses of communism in Eastern Europe soon undermined his Socialist proclivities. Revolted by the harsh annihilation by the Russians of Hungary's revolutionary uprising, R. denounced communism with the result that he was soon expelled from the Communist Party. That R. could undergo such a drastic political transformation—from the right-wing extremism of L'Action Française to the left-wing radicalism of communism—attests to his intellectual dexterity. He ultimately rejected all enslavement to a single political position. For the remainder of his life R. stressed the importance of intellectual freedom and the right to assume whatever political position he chose, provided that it faithfully reflected his personal conviction of right and wrong.

Following a second trip to the Soviet Union in 1966, R. was even more convinced that the only political position that he could defend was that of total independence. This willingness to alter ideologies mirrors his flexibility in adapting himself to new ideas. This same flexibility explains his ability to write in various literary styles and to express himself within the realm of all sorts of art-forms. He could even effortlessly pastiche the style of any writer that he chose to emulate.

From the early 1970s until his death at the end of 1997, R.'s entire existence was devoted to writing, reflection, and traveling.

When not in residence at his Left Bank Paris address, he spent most of his time at his country home of Le Haut Bout, in the southern outskirts of Paris, or else on the picturesque island of Belle-Ile, off the Britanny coast, frequently in Venice, one of his favorite cities, or in travels to the Orient, the U.S., and wherever else his restless soul led him. Each of these venues plays a significant role in his writing. During much of his career, he was affiliated with the House of Gallimard, one of France's most prestigious publishing firms, where he served on the jury of readers who decided on the manuscripts to accept or to reject. Significantly, R.'s second wife, the noted dramatist Loleh Bellon (b. 1925), played a key role as a highly respected advisor in the composition of his books.

Several years before his death, R.'s health was severely affected by cancer: one of his lungs was removed. He had earlier been a heavy smoker. Out of this dramatic event he forged one of the major themes of his later work, the importance of cherishing the time allotted to one's fragile life and the appreciation of each precious moment. R. realized then the extent to which all human beings live on the precipice of death.

Aware that his lifetime coincided with virtually all of the major dramas of the 20th c. including World War II, R. made the conscious decision that as the result of all of these cataclysmic events he would compose literature that reflected these events and that would also serve as a reminder to humanity that all of us must conduct our lives so that human injustice is either reduced or brought to an end.

R. regarded poetry as his favored arena of activity. Much of his volumes of poetry are colored by his exposure to and love for SURREALISM. His verse is particularly reminiscent of the poems of Aragon, Éluard, Guillaume APOLLINAIRE, and Jules SUPERVIELLE, all leading poets of the most modern movements of contemporary French poetry. His major titles include *Le poète mineur* (1949; The Poet in Minor Key), *Poésies* (1970; Poetry), *A la lisière du temps* (1984; At the Edge of Time), and *Le noir de l'aube* (1990; The Blackness of the Dawn). Although many of his poems border on being undecipherable, others are entirely lucid. With their colorful imagery and varied allusions, his richly musical and charming poetry expresses his passion for natural phenomena: flowers, tiny birds, animals (especially his cats), blades of grass, plants, trees, the wind and breeze, the sea and the coastline. An avid bird watcher, his poetry is replete with verbal sketches of ornithological antics he observed on his property at Le Haut Bout and on Belle-Ile. With minutial detail he delineates the slightest details of his various encounters with his animal and bird friends.

As a novelist R. ranks among the writers who composed novels strongly tied to the politico-social causes to which he had dedicated his life. These novels reverberate with R.'s passionate commitment to alleviate the suffering of the downtrodden of this world: the poor, the hungry and homeless, minorities that have been persecuted throughout the ages—Jews, people of color, Gypsies—R. wrote several important novels, notably *Léone et les siens* (1963; Léone and Her Own People), *La traversée du Pont des Arts* (1979; The Crossing of the Bridge of the Arts), and *L'ami lointain* (1987; The Distant Friend, 1990). In *Léone* R. assembles a disparate assortment of characters (a young American couple, a group of Indonesian immigrants, a Latin American revolutionary leader, a French photographer, a German singer, and an elderly French painter), all of whom are brought together in the midtown-Manhattan boarding house apartment of Léone, their hostess. Their cultural and age differences and their mutual tolerance for each other having been subjected to the supreme test, they ultimately unite around Léone and celebrate the marriage of their hospitable and generous landlady. In *La traversée du Pont des Arts*, possibly R.'s best-known novel, the author departs from his usual subjects of sociopolitical themes in order to analyze in intricate detail the love affair between a musical composer and his devoted wife. In a parallel theme he deals with the subject of a composer who struggles during his entire life to achieve absolute musical perfection and truth. In *L'ami lointain* R. returns to his more common theme, that of the way in which two drastically dissimilar young men, a Catholic with totally French traditions and a Jew devoid of national roots and quite untraditional in his daily behavior, become indispensable friends to each other. Each offers the other the ingredients lacking in the life of the other. The two develop a beautiful, mutually enriching relationship that gives great meaning to their lives.

A substantial amount of R.'s literary productivity falls under the rubric of autobiographical writing. He recaptured the significant events that he had witnessed and in which he participated directly, notably in *Moi je* (1969; I Myself), *Somme toute* (1976; In Sum), *Nous* (1972; We), *Les chercheurs de dieux* (1981; The Seekers of Gods), *Permis de séjour* (1983; Residence Permit), *La fleur du temps* (1988; The Flower of Time), *L'etonnement du voyageur* (1990; The Astonishment of the Traveler), and *Le rivage des jours* (2 vols., 1990, 1992; The Shore of the Days). Together these volumes constitute a vast compendium of R.'s life, his travels, a dazzling array of portraits of the luminaries, writers, artists, and statesmen he knew very well, and a collective statement containing his philosophy of life.

One of the most perceptive art and literary critics of his day, he wrote a host of volumes with riveting interest for the literary and art connoisseur; R. devoted whole volumes to his penetrating diagnoses of primitive art, classicism, romanticism, the baroque, rococo, and contemporary art. In other volumes he dealt authoritatively with writers like Marivaux, Aragon, Stendhal, and Supervielle, and directors and personalities of the French theater like Gérard Philippe and Jean Vilar. His total bibliography is further enhanced by a number of volumes that chronicle his extensive travels throughout the world; notable are those works in which he paints his impressions of and experiences in the U.S., China, and the French provinces.

R., who regarded himself primarily as a poet, saw life around him through the prism of poetry. Unusually sensitive to the natural phenomena surrounding his universe, he formulated metaphors and imagery that described the smallest as well as the most titanic forms of life: blades of grass, tiny birds, animals, flowers, the clouds in the sky, the wind, streams and rivers, shores and seas. He tried to drape his images in musical or sonorous tonalities. He also depicted the characters in his novels with subtle nuances and sensitive attentiveness. He learned to describe characters with the same degree of concentrated finesse as was the case with animals and birds. R.'s books are filled with cosmopolitanism. His books take place in many lands, and even when they are restricted to a single venue, he manages to introduce into the texture of his story a number of foreigners. R. involved himself in virtually all of the major sociopolitical events of his day and freely expounded on his feelings about warfare, the Holocaust, fascism, communism, capitalism, and revolution. R. identified with all of the underdogs of his time: ethnic, racial, and religious minorities, the elderly, the sick, the famished, the homeless, and the poor. And in his books he

pleads for more fairness and a higher degree of justice for those who, in his view, are the victims of rampant injustice. Above all, R.'s texts are eminently readable and lucid for an author who wrote during an era of sometimes regrettable ambiguity and Byzantine complexity.

FURTHER WORKS: *Aragon* (1945); *Lire marivaux* (1947); *La nuit est le manteau des pauvres* (1949; rev. ed., 1983); *Clefs pour l'Amérique* (1949); *Descriptions critiques* (1950); *La France de profit* (1952); *Stendhal par lui-même* (1952); *Clefs pour la Chine* (1953); *La famille Quatre-Cents Coups* (1954); *L'amour de la peinture* (1955); *Un seul poème* (1955); *L'amour du théâtre* (1956); *Le Malheur d'aimer* (1958); *Le journal des voyages* (1960); *Supervielle* (1964); *Jean Vilar* (1968); *Le soleil sur la terre* (1968; rev. ed., 1974); *La dérobée* (1968); *Les soleils du romantisme* (1974); *La maison qui slenvole* (1977); *Nouvelles enfantasques* (1978); *Sur la Chine* (1979); *Proverbes par tous les bouts* (1980); *Le chat qui parlait malgré lui* (1982); *Les animaux très sagaces* (1983); *Le voyage d'automne* (1987); *La cour de recreation* (1991); *Le voleur de poèmes: Chine* (1991); *L'art à la source* (2 vols., 1992); *L'ami qui venait de l'an mil* (1994)

BIBLIOGRAPHY: Grenier, R., *C. R.* (1971); Koster, S., *C. R., un poète* (1985); Kolbert, J., Introduction to *A Distant Friend* (1990), v-xxiii; Descamps, C., "Poète et ami des poètes," *QL*, 15-30 June 1993: 17; Orizet, J., "La Conversation des poètes," *RDM*, 9 (Sept. 1993): 176-80; Rinaldi, A., "Dans le subtil empire de R.," *Express*, 12 May 1994: 65; Roudaut, J., "C. R., Les Rencontres des jours," 1992-1993, *Magazine Littéraire*, 331 (April 1995): 113-14; Weightman, J., "Birdsong at Dusk," *TLS*, 7 July 1995: 33

—JACK KOLBERT

ROY, Gabrielle

Canadian novelist and short-story writer (writing in French), b. 22 March 1909, St. Boniface, Man.; d. 13 July 1983, Quebec, Que.

R. was the youngest of eight children born to Quebecois parents established in St. Boniface, a French-speaking suburb of Winnipeg, Manitoba. After a French-Catholic education she entered the Winnipeg Normal School, graduating in 1929. For the next eight years she taught in a boys' school in Winnipeg and in northern Manitoba. From 1937 to 1939 she traveled in France and studied acting in England. On her return to Canada she settled in Montreal and for the following eight years traveled widely in Quebec as a freelance journalist. *Bonheur d'occasion* (1945; The Tin Flute, 1947), her first novel, won her immediate fame. In 1947 she married a Quebec physician and returned to Europe for three years while he completed postgraduate studies. She lived in Quebec City until her death.

With her novels and volumes of short stories, R. established herself as the major French-Canadian fiction writer of her generation. She was as well known in the rest of Canada, through numerous translations of her work, as she was in Quebec. *Bonheur d'occasion* is Quebec's first urban novel. It traces the fortunes of a handful of characters from the Saint-Henri slum of Montreal during the first year of World War II. With a fine sense of drama, humor, and compassion R. paints realistic portraits of Rose-Anna, the long-suffering mother; Florentine, her brittle daughter; the reluctant suitor, Jean Lévesque; and the vainglorious ineffectual father, Azarius Lacasse. The novel not only delineates the trials of the urban poor but suggestively exposes the rift between English and French speakers in Quebec.

Several more of R.'s novels are set in the Province of Quebec. *Alexandre Chenevert* (1954; *The Cashier*, 1955) is another city novel, the story of a timid clerk locked in his teller's cage who dreams of making contact with the larger world and of achieving some kind of spiritual release. *La montagne secrète* (1961; *The Hidden Mountain*, 1961) is an allegorical novel about a painter who travels through northern Quebec and Labrador and finally to Paris in search of his ultimate vocation. *La rivière sans repos* (1970; *Windflower*, 1970) is a series of stories about Eskimos' contact with white civilization, and *Cet été qui chantait* (1972; *Enchanted Summer*, 1976) a collection of sketches on a summer in Charlevoix County.

Alternating with these Quebec-based works are an equal number set in the Canadian west. *Rue Deschambault* (1955; *Street of Riches*, 1957) and *La route d'Altamont* (1966; *The Road Past Altamont*, 1966) are autobiographical fictions evoking R.'s childhood. *La Petite Poule d'Eau* (1950; *Where Nests the Water Hen*, 1951) is drawn from R.'s experience teaching school to an isolated family in northern Manitoba. *Un jardin au bout du monde* (1975; *Garden in the Wind*, 1977) is a collection of stories dealing with Quebecois, Chinese, Doukhobor (Christian sect of Russian origin), and Polish settlers in the west, while *Ces enfants de ma vie* (1977; *Children of My Heart*, 1979) is based on R.'s memories of teaching immigrant children in Manitoba. She also published a children's book, *Ma vache Bossie* (1976; my cow Bossie) and a collection of journalism, *Fragiles lumières de la terre* (1978; *Fragile Lights of Earth*, 1982).

The major characteristics of R.'s work are its lyric quality, its deep humanity, and its gentle nostalgia, backed by a keen eye for detail and a sure narrative gift. Although she is not innovative or experimental, her insight into the lives of women, of children, and of humble people in Quebec, the Arctic, and the West made her one of the most representative of Canadian novelists.

A solitary and modest person, R. lived a very private life reflecting principally on the experiences of her first thirty years. This reflection, transposed into her fiction, achieves the universal without ever sacrificing the vividly particular, and her insight, at once compassionate and dispassionate, allowed her to penetrate the secret lives of her characters with tenderness, justice, and wonder.

FURTHER WORKS: *Courte-Queue* (1979; *Cliptail*, 1980); *Enchantment and Sorrow: The Autobiography of G. R.* (1987)

BIBLIOGRAPHY: Genuist, M., *La création romanesque chez G. R.* (1966); Samson, J. -N., *G. R.* (1967); Grosskurth, P., *G. R.* (1972); Cameron, D., *Conversations with Canadian Novelists* (1973), Vol. 2: 128–45; Gagné, M., *Visages de G. R.* (1973); Hind-Smith, J., *Three Voices: The Lives of Margaret Laurence, G. R., Frederick Philip Grove* (1975): 63–128; Ricard, F., *G. R.* (1975); Mitcham, A., *The Literary Achievement of G. R.* (1983); Hesse, M. G., *G. R.* (1984)

—PHILIP STRATFORD

ROZANOV, Vasily Vasilyevich

Russian autobiographer, philosopher, journalist, and critic, b. 2 May 1856, Vetluga; d. 23 Jan. 1919, Sergiev-Posad (now Zagorsk)

Under the influence of a domineering mother, R. grew into an inner-directed, eccentric personality who developed unconventional views on family, religion, and sex early in life. After graduating in law and philosophy from Moscow University in 1881, R. taught in provincial secondary schools until 1893, when he entered the St. Petersburg civil service. While still a student, he expressed his fascination with Fyodor Dostoevsky's fictional psychology by marrying Dostoevsky's former mistress Polina Suslova. Her refusal to divorce R. after six tempestuous years forced him to spend the rest of his life in a common-law relationship with Varvara Rudneva, the mother of his five children. As a result, illegitimacy and divorce figure prominently in R.'s polemics.

For many years, as a contributor to the conservative *Novoe vremya*, R. supported government policy, including its anti-Semitic attitude and Tolstoy's excommunication. At the same time, he expressed in other writings dissatisfaction with the state of society and wrote for the liberal *Russkoe slovo* under the pseudonym Varvarin. The authorities considered him a blasphemer and pornographer despite his sometime ultrarightist orientation. Impoverished in youth, R. earned enough from his writings to travel to western Europe, but died in extreme poverty after revolutionary leaders, who labeled him a literary prostitute, deprived him of his livelihood. He remained a maverick to the end. While still at work on his final anti-Christian treatise, he sought and received refuge at the Troitsky monastery near Moscow, one of Russia's renowned holy places.

R. first gained critical attention with a long essay, *O ponimanii* (1886; on understanding), a polemic against the agnosticism, liberalism, and positivism then dominant at the University of Moscow. This essay was followed by a radical reinterpretation of Dostoevsky's ideas in *Legenda o velikom inkvizitore* (1890; *Dostoevsky and the Legend of the Grand Inquisitor*, 1972). All of R.'s subsequent work echoes his belief in the importance of the individual psyche and his absolute faith in personal instinct. In *Krasota v prirode i ee smysl* (1894; beauty in nature and its meaning) R. voices disdain of prevailing Russian social morality and advocates glorification of human animal drives instead. When he commented on the reaction of his readers in irreverent and daring words, in *V mire neyasnogo i nereshennogo* (1901; in the world of the unclear and undecided), he suffered the first of many censorial deletions. R. denounced Russia's rigidly enforced laws against divorce and the rights of illegitimate offspring in *Semeyny vopros v Rossii* (1903; the family problem in Russia).

R. has been called the Russian Nietzsche because he too engaged in a lifelong polemic with Christianity. The most important books on this topic are *Okolo tserkovnykh sten* (1906; around the walls of the church), *Russkaya tserkov* (1909; the Russian church), *Tyomny lik* (1911; the dark face), *Lyudi lunnogo sveta* (1913; moonlight people), and *Apokalipsis nashego vremeni* (1918; apocalypse of our time). In these works R. attacks Christianity's emphasis on chastity and its supposed sexlessness, which he sees as a denial of the source of life. In vivid and provocative language, without parallel in language and thought for that time, he offers his preference for less inhibited, more natural religions.

In another group of books—*Uedinennoe* (1912; *Solitaria*, 1927), *Opavshie listya* (1913; *Fallen Leaves, Bundle One*, 1929), and *Opavshie listya: Korob vtoroy* (1915; fallen leaves: second basket)—R. developed his belief that the mysteries of the flesh contain mythico-spiritual significance into a highly personal philosophy. To emphasize the subjective nature of these writings, R. employs a confessional, sometimes poetic language marked by unconventional typography.

Because of his unorthodox views and often journalistic, disjointed style, R. stands some-what estranged from Russian literary tradition in general, and from the Silver Age, in which he wrote, specifically. Yet his discussions of many taboo topics, coupled with his insight into Dostoevsky's psychology, give him a rather modern aspect. His challenges forced contemporary writers, philosophers, and theologians to reevaluate and defend their positions. He thus contributed greatly to the intellectual climate of the time.

FURTHER WORKS: *Mesto khristianstva v istorii* (1890); *Sumerki prosveshchenia* (1899); *Religia i kultura* (1899); *Literaturnye ocherki* (1899); *Priroda i istoria* (1900); *Oslabpuvshy fetish* (1906); *Kogda nachalstvo ushlo* (1909); *Italyanskie vpechatlenia* (1909); *Bibleyskaya poezia* (1912); *Literaturnye izgnanniki* (1913); *Sredi khudozhnikov* (1914); *Obonyatelnoe i osyazatelnoe otnoshenie evreev v krovi* (1914); *"Angel Iegovy" u evreev* (1914); *Evropa i evrei* (1914); *Apokalipsicheskaya sekta: Khlysty i skoptsy* (1914); *Voyna 1914 goda i russkoe vozrozhdenie* (1915); *Voyna i germanskaya sotsialdemokratia* (1916); *Iz vostochnykh motivov* (1916–1917); *Pisma R. k E. Gollerbakhu* (1922)

BIBLIOGRAPHY: Arseniev, N., *Die russische Literatur der Neuzeit und Gegenwart* (1929): 226–40; Pozner, V., *Panorama de la littérature russe contemporaine* (1929): 47–65; Poggioli, R., *The Poets of Russia: 1890–1930* (1960): 76–78; Poggioli, R., *R.* (1962); Edie, M. et al., eds., *Russian Philosophy* (1965), Vol. II: 281–84; Roberts, S., *Essays in Russian Literature: The Conservative View: Leontiev, R., Shestov* (1968): 357–83; Mirsky, D., *A History of Russian Literature*, rev. ed. (1973): 418–24

—MARGOT K. FRANK

RÓŻEWICZ, Tadeusz

Polish poet, dramatist, and short-story writer, b. 9 Oct. 1921, Radomsko

From a middle-class family, R. had to interrupt his studies because of the outbreak of World War II. Later he took an active part in the underground movement against the Nazis. After the war he enrolled at the Jagiellonian University in Cracow to study art history. While at the university, he began his literary career. In 1955, 1962, and 1966 he was awarded the Polish State Prize, and in 1966 the Jurzykowski Foundation Prize in the U.S.

The impact of the war is clearly visible in his early collections of poems, *Niepokój* (1947; anxiety) and *Czerwona rękawiczka* (1948; red glove), in which R. expresses in his own poetic idiom the anxieties and obsessions resulting from his war experiences. The poems come close to an objective prose account, because R.

abandons such traditional forms as regular meter, rhyme, and stanzas. Full of juxtaposed images, these poems are distinguished by R.'s skill in maintaining an emotional tension under the surface of seemingly detached narration. Widely imitated, R.'s early collections established a new trend in postwar Polish poetry.

After a brief period of succumbing to the dictates of Socialist REALISM, which was imposed stringently in Poland during the years 1949–55—work from this period includes *Pięć poematów* (1950; five poems) and *Czas który idzie* (1951; time that comes)—R. was able to return to his own way of searching for answers to the philosophical and moral dilemmas created by the postwar chaos. The resulting poems are collected in *Poemat otwarty* (1956; open poem), *Rozmowa z księciem* (1960; conversation with a prince), and *Regio* (1969; mons). His imaginative power and lyricism came to the fore. He further developed his poetic art by defying traditional patterns of versification. These poems, often described as "antipoetic," were stripped of metaphors but became metaphoric in a new way, since bare words created new, powerful poetic images. His style became rigid, cool, yet charged with concealed intense lyricism.

R. turned to drama in the 1960s with the grotesque *Kartoteka* (1961; *The Card Index*, 1969). The protagonist of the play, whose identity keeps changing all the time, is visited by a number of people who represent a cross section of contemporary society. Under the surface of some seemingly absurd situations R. expresses his deep concern with the superficiality of the social fabric, often juxtaposing this concern with his yearning for some true values. Strong satirical overtones are mixed here with slapstick humor, and criticism of moral and social postures is presented with bitter irony, while war memories contrast sharply with the banality of present-day life. The characters in the play are, according to Czesław MIŁOSZ, "symbols of common humanity, everymen, although they move within a given time and space." *Świadkowie albo nasza mała stabilizacja* (1962; *The Witness*, 1970) represents a more serious and dramatic type in R.'s drama. Composed of three dialogues (between Him and Her, Husband and Wife, and Number Two and Number Three), the play focuses on the gap in communication between people who cannot comprehend each other or face the cruelty of the surrounding world, and who seek escape in meaningless words and phrases, which cannot express their innermost emotions.

Closely related to the avant-garde theater of the 1920s and to the modern THEATER OF THE ABSURD, R.'s dramas are grotesque and tragic at the same time. In them he explores the condition of modern man while satirizing the peculiarities of socialist society in contemporary Poland. By making them more universal than local, however, R. has achieved a wide appeal, and has earned a reputation as a diligent social critic. Formally, R.'s dramas transcend existing theatrical forms and demand of the director, the actors, and the public that they cocreate some new form of performance.

R.'s short stories, written mostly in the 1960s and 1970s, often present his reminiscences of the war, as in the collection *Wycieczka do muzeum* (1966; excursion to a museum), and reflect upon the new generation incapable of understanding those horrors that shaped the author's world. The past, heavy with cruel memories, recurs as an ever-present motif in R.'s poetry, drama, and narratives.

R. is one of the most original writers in modern Polish literature. His philosophical themes, combined with his artistic vision and his individual style, have gained him international recognition. In Poland he had been considered an innovator of literary forms and, perhaps more importantly, a courageous spokesman for the unrestricted freedom of expression. But during the 1970s he dissociated himself from the active literary opposition and withdrew into his private world, thus losing the leading position he had been enjoying for almost twenty years.

FURTHER WORKS: *W łyżce wody* (1949); *Wiersze i obrazy* (1952); *Wybór wierszy* (1953); *Kartki z Węgier* (1953); *Równina* (1954); *Srebrny kłos* (1955); *Uśmiechy* (1955); *Opadły liście z drzew* (1955); *Poezje zebrane* (1957); *Formy* (1958); *Zielona róża* (1961); *Głos Anonima* (1961); *Nic w płaszczu Prospera* (1962); *Akt przerwany* (1964; *The Interrupted Act*, 1969); *Wyszedł z domu* (1964; *Gone Out*, 1969); *Twarz* (1964); *Śmieszny staruszek* (1966; *The Funny Old Man*, 1970); *Utwory dramatyczne* (1966); *Poezje wybrane* (1967); *Wiersze i poematy* (1967); *Stara kobieta wysiaduje* (1968; *The Old Woman Broods*, 1970); *Twarz trzecia* (1968); *Opowiadania wybrane* (1968); *Przyrost naturalny* (1968; *Birth Rate: The Biography of a Play for the Theatre*, 1977); *Wybór poezji* (1969); *Wiersze* (1969); *Śmierć w starych dekoracjach* (1970); *Teatr niekon-sekwencji* (1970; rev. enlarged ed., 1979); *Przygotowanie do wieczoru autorskiego* (1971); *Poezje zebrane* (1971); *Sztuki teatralne* (1972); *Poezja; Dramat; Proza* (1973); *Proza* (1973); *Wiersze* (1974); *Białe małżeństwo i inne utwory sceniczne* (1975); *Poezje zebrane* (1976); *Duszyczka* (1977); *Próba rekonstrukcji* (1979); *Niepokój* (1980); *Pułapka* (1982; *The Trap*, 1984). **FURTHER WORKS IN ENGLISH:** *Faces of Anxiety* (1969); *The Card Index and Other Plays* (1969); *The Witness and Other Plays* (1970); *Selected Poems* (1976); *The Survivor and Other Poems* (1976); *Unease* (1980); *Conversations with the Prince, and Other Poems* (1982); *Mariage Blanc and The Hunger Artist Departs* (1983); *T. R.'s Bas-Relief and Other Poems* (1991)

BIBLIOGRAPHY: Lourie, R., "A Contest for T. R.," *PolR*, 12 (1967): 97–104; Leach, C., "Remarks on the Poetry of T. R.," *PolR*, 12 (1967): 105–26; Miłosz, C., *The History of Polish Literature* (1969): 462–70; Gerould, D., *Twentieth Century Polish Avant-Garde Drama* (1977): 88–95; Levine, M. G., *Contemporary Polish Poetry, 1925–1975* (1981): 73–91; Filipowicz, H., *A Laboratory of Impure Forms: The Plays of T. R.* (1991)

—JERZY R. KRZYŻANOWSKI

RUDENKO, Mykola

Ukrainian poet, novelist, literary critic, journalist, and dramatist, b. 19 Dec. 1920, Yurivka, Luhansk region

Born into a miner's family, R. completed his secondary education in 1939, and began studies at the philosophical faculty of the Kiev University. He served in the Soviet army, survived the blockade of Leningrad, was severely wounded, recovered, and spent the last moments of World War II again at the front. For his war efforts, R. was awarded various medals including the Order of the Red Star and admitted to the Communist Party. Discharged from the army in 1946, he worked as poetry editor for the journal *Radyansky pysmennyk*, and from 1947 to 1950 he served as editor in chief of the literary journal *Dnipro*.

R.'s early poetic work such as the collection of poetry *Z pokhodu* (1947; from the campaign), his *Nezboryme plemya: Leninhradtsi* 1948; the unvincible tribe, the people of Leningrad), as well as his early novels, *Viter v oblychchya* (1955; wind in the face) and *Ostannya shablya* (1959; the last sword) are informed by

his war experiences and written, for the most part, according to the tenets of Socialist REALISM. A somewhat more liberal spirit pervades his science-fiction works, the novels *Charivny bumeranh* (1966; the magical boomerang) and *Slidamy kosmichnoyi katastrofy* (1962; on the tracks of a cosmic catastrophe), and his poetry of the early 1960s. Like many other Ukrainian writers of his generation. R. was influenced by the *shestydesyatnyky*, the young storm-and-stress generation of Ukrainian poets of the 1960s, whose entrance on the literary scene he heartily welcomed in an article published on 30 January 1962, in *Literaturna hazela*, at that time the official organ of the Union of Ukrainian Writers.

The repression of Ukrainian writers in the 1970s caused R. to revolt. In his writings and his personal appearances he began to lodge various protests against the persecution of the Ukrainian intelligentsia. He was warned several times and finally arrested and tried. On 30 June 1977, R. was convicted of "anti-Soviet agitation and propaganda" and sentenced to seven years of imprisonment and five years of exile. Released in 1987, R. was allowed to emigrate to the West. On 27 January 1988, he arrived in the U.S., where he lived in New York and in Jersey City, N.J., working for the Ukrainian daily *Svoboda* and contributing to Radio Liberty. In 1991 R. returned to his native Ukraine.

R.'s poetry of the 1970s reflects the transition of his weltanschauung from Marxism to what may be termed a Christian humanism. R. realized that "a soulless world is the creation of a bureaucrat," and that the task of the poet, in these spiritless times, is to seek "the human being and the way," and to strive for "goodness and light." In his prison poetry, for instance in "Tak prosto vse: napyshesh kayattya" ("Prison Poem," 1978) dated 18 August 1977, he rejects any kind of compromise, preferring the prison walls to "the prison hidden in the human being." His poetry, such as the collections *Prozrinnya* (1978; enlightenment) and *Za gratamy* (1980; behind bars), both published in the West, rejects all totalitarian coercion of the human spirit and restores human conscience to its position of primacy. R.'s metaphysical poetry reached its zenith in the long narrative poem *Khrest* (1979; *The Cross*, 1987), a philosophical attempt to explain the problem of evil, in which the author developed a poignant parallel between the Stalin-made famine in Ukraine (1932–1933) and the crucifixion of Christ.

Most important of R.'s prose works are the *Künstlerroman* entitled *Orlova balka* (1982; eagle's ravine), a search for the meaning of human existence, written under the influence of Dante and the Ukrainian philosopher Hryhory Skovoroda (1722–1794), and a study entitled *Ekonomichni monology* (1978; economic monologues), a trenchant critical analysis of Marxist economics based on his own thinking and on the work of François Quesnay (1694–1774).

R.'s philosophic poetry and imaginative prose, while influenced by such thinkers as Pascal, Kant, and Hegel, are steeped in the Ukrainian poetic tradition. A profound Christian mysticism coupled with a semiotic pantheism inform his work, which bears witness to a tragic period in his country's history.

FURTHER WORKS: *Poeziyi* (1949); *Muzhnist* (1952); *Svitli hlybyny* (1952); *Pereklyk druziv* (1954); *Poeziyi* (1956); *Bila akatsiya* (1962); *Vsesvit u tobi* (1968); *Ya vilny* (1977); *Na dni morskomu* (1981)

BIBLIOGRAPHY: Rudnytzky, L., Introduction to *The Cross* (1987): 7–10; Zyla, W. T., on *The Cross, WLT*, 62, 3 (Summer 1988), 478; Rudnytzky, L., "A Miracle in Continuity: Christian Themes and

Motifs in Soviet Ukrainian Literature," *UQ*, 46 (1990): 34–44; Black, H., "By Way of Golgotha: Notes on M.R.'s *The Cross*," *America* (19 & 26 Sept. 1991)

—LEONID RUDNYTZKY

RUKEYSER, Muriel

American poet, translator, and biographer, b. 15 Dec. 1913, New York, N.Y.; d. 12 Feb. 1980, New York, N.Y.

"What would happen if one woman told the truth about her life?" asks R. in her 1968 poem "Käthe Kollwitz," answering herself laconically in the next line. "The world would split open." Throughout an exceptionally prolific forty-five-year career as a poet, R. was notable for trying to tell the truth—not always as a feminist, but always as an honest and clear-eyed commentator on society and on the connection between historical forces and the inner life of individuals.

R.'s career as a writer, and an outspoken one, began early. While she was still at Vassar College, she joined with other students who were also to leave their mark on American literature—Elizabeth BISHOP, Mary MCCARTHY, and Eleanor Clark (1913-1996)—to found an experimental alternative to the official campus literary magazine. At twenty-one, she received the Yale Series of Younger Poets Award, entailing publication of her first collection of poems, *The Theory of Flight* (1935). From that time until her death, R. remained involved as a writer and a social activist, supporting herself by teaching at Sarah Lawrence College and helping to run New York's House of Photography.

From the first, R.'s poems were recognized as a rare combination of the two meanings of "avantgarde": They showed a mastery of technique, an assimilation of MODERNISM's formal explorations, but they addressed subjects of social concern. Philip Blair Rice in his review of *The Theory of Flight* pointed out that the poems in this collection "are among the few so far written in behalf of the revolutionary cause which combine craftsmanship, restraint, and intellectual honesty." In the 1930s and 1940s R. wrote poems in support of the labor movement and the antifascist struggle in Spain and eventually throughout Europe. In the postwar period, as such topics became less modish, she continued to speak out—in person and in poetry—about human-rights abuses and against war and imperial aggression. Always sensitive to gender as it intersected with other social issues, her poems became more explicitly feminist in the 1970s.

Another aspect of R.'s modern sensibility was her interest in science and technology, particularly her adoption for poetic purposes of figurative language drawn from contemporary achievements in these areas. As her work developed, she continued to use such metaphors, but tended increasingly to place them at the service of what one reviewer called her "oracular, soothsaying quality." The two come together, for example, in the title of her collection *The Speed of Darkness* (1968), as well as in a number of the poems it contains.

R.'s social and scientific interests are also reflected in her biographies of Willard Gibbs (1942), Wendell Wilkie (1957), and Thomas Hariot (1971). She also published fiction and criticism, the latter in the essays collected in *The Life of Poetry* (1949) and her Clark Lectures, *Poetry and Undeniable Fact* (1968). R. was a sensitive translator and was responsible for making the work of Mexican poet Octavio PAZ and Swedish poet Gunnar EKELÖF available to readers of English.

R.'s involvement with social issues was never restricted to her writing. She was active in support of the causes to which she was committed and took part in protest demonstrations, as well as more decorous efforts. In her later years, she visited Hanoi to express her opposition to the U.S. role in the Vietnam War and, as president of P.E.N. American Center, led a vigil in Seoul in support of South Korean poets imprisoned for their writings. This continued commitment, along with the content of her poems exploring the condition of women, won her a new audience in those years among younger feminists—activists, writers, and critics.

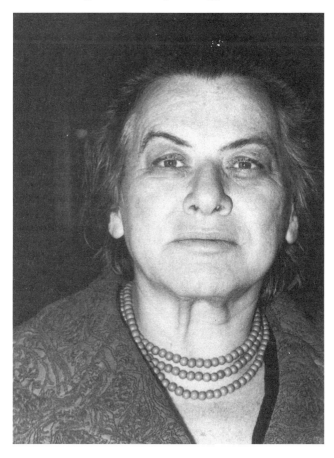

Muriel Rukeyser

FURTHER WORKS: *Mediterranean* (1938); *U.S. 1* (1938); *A Turning Wind* (1939); *The Soul and Body of John Brown* (1940); *Wake Island* (1942); *Beast in View* (1944); *The Children's Orchard* (1947); *The Green Wave* (1948); *Elegies* (1949); *Orpheus* (1949); *Selected Poems* (1951); *Come Back Paul* (1955); *Body of Waking* (1958); *I Go Out* (1961); *Waterlily Fire: Poems 1932–1962* (1962); *The Orgy* (1966); *Bubbles* (1967); *The Outer Banks* (1967); *Mages* (1970); *Twenty-Nine Poems* (1970); *Breaking Open* (1973); *Early Poems, 1935–1955* (1973); *Brecht's Uncle Eddie's Moustache* (1974); *The Gates* (1976); *The Collected Poems of M. R.* (1978); *More Night* (1981); *A M. R. Reader* (1994)

BIBLIOGRAPHY: Coles, R., "M. R.'s *The Gates*," *APR.* 7, 3 (1978), 15; DuPlessis, R. B., "The Critique of Consciousness and Myth in

Levertov, Rich, and R.," in Gilbert, S. M., and Gubar, S., eds., *Shakespeare's Sisters* (1979): 280–300; Kertesz, L., *The Poetic Vision of M. R.* (1980); Kalaidjian, W., "M. R. and the Poetics of Specific Critique: Rereading 'The Book of the Dead,'" *Cultural Critique*, 20 (1991-92); Gardinier, S., "A World that Will Hold All People: On M. R.," *KenR*, 14, 3 (1992): 88-105; Cooper, J., "Meeting Places: On M. R.," *APR*, 25, 5 (April 1996): 11-16

—LILLIAN S. ROBINSON

RULFO, Juan

Mexican novelist and short-story writer, b. 16 May 1918, Sayula; d. 7 January 1986, Mexico City

R. was born into a family of landowners that suffered financial ruin during the Mexican Revolution (1910–20) and the *cristero* wars, a series of church-led rebellions against the government during the late 1920s. After completing a minimal education in Guadalajara, the capital of his native state of Jalisco, R. moved to Mexico City, where he studied law and literature briefly. The bulk of his education, however, has come from his widespread reading. For approximately twenty years he worked as an editor for the National Indian Institute and served as an adviser at the government-sponsored Mexican Writers' Center.

Although R. is one of Spanish America's most esteemed authors, he published only two books: a collection of short stories, *El llano en llamas* (1953; *The Burning Plain, and Other Stories*, 1967), and a novel, *Pedro Páramo* (1955; *Pedro Páramo*, 1959). The setting of all his work is the southern part of Jalisco, an arid region inhabited by poverty-stricken peasants whose lives are marked by violence and the omnipresent threat of death. The hallmarks of R.'s style are his sparse, incisive language and his incursions into experimental techniques.

El llano en llamas consists of fifteen tales, whose protagonists are tormented by guilt, poverty, and despair. Reacting against the convention of authorial omniscience, R. relied on dialogue and the interior monologue to create the impression of objectivity and enhance dramatic effect. He also utilized flashbacks, shifting points of view, and circular structures, devices that lend a timeless, static quality to his fictional universe. Indeed, time all but stops in the minds of his characters, for whom the burdens of the past have absorbed the present and demolished all hope for the future. By probing the depths of their psyches R. exposed the core of all humanity, thus transcending the borders of Mexico and achieving universal status.

R.'s most memorable stories include "El hombre" ("The Man"), which describes in contrapuntal monologues the relentless pursuit of a murderer; "Es que somos muy pobres" ("We're Very Poor"), the rambling soliloquy of a child whose sister is destined to become a prostitute because the cow given to her for her dowry drowns in a flood; "Talpa" ("Talpa"), in which remorse plagues two lovers after they deliberately hasten the death of the woman's ailing husband; and "No oyes ladrar los perros" ("No Dogs Bark"), the stark drama of a law-abiding old man carrying his wounded bandit son to a distant town for medical assistance.

The setting of *Pedro Páramo*, R.'s undisputed masterpiece, is the ghost town of Comala, where a young man named Juan Preciado is sent to search for his father, Pedro Páramo. Anticipating

Juan Rulfo

a kind of paradise described to him by his mother, Juan Preciado is literally frightened to death by the eerie voices of phantoms who recount their mortal sins of the distant past. Perhaps the two most salient features of the book are its fragmented structure and its colloquial but poetically stylized language. Pedro Páramo emerges as the prototype of the Latin American *cacique* (a corrupt small-town despot), whose character gradually takes shape through his own interior monologues and the dialogues of other characters. A curious blend of brutality and sentimentalism, he is referred to at the beginning of the novel as being pure hate, the reasons for which, the reader gradually discerns, are the murder of his father and disrespect shown by the citizens of Comala following the death of his beloved wife. His murder by one of his many illegitimate sons can be read as the metaphoric demise of *caciquismo* (political bossism) in Mexico, but *Pedro Páramo* is much more than a vehicle for social protest. It is, above all, a lyrical, architectonic novel with strong mythical overtones, that is, a novel whose poetic imagery and complex structural arrangement serve to convey the archetypal theme of man's fall from grace.

R.'s dramatic portraits of Jalisco reflect the existential dilemma of 20th-c. man, whose vain search for self-fulfillment in a chaotic world beyond comprehension has led him to solitude and despair. Although bordering on nihilism, this view of the human endeavor is redeemed by the consistently fine artistry in which it is cloaked.

FURTHER WORKS IN ENGLISH: *Pedro Páramo: A Novel of Mexico* (1990)

BIBLIOGRAPHY: Brushwood, J. S., *Mexico in Its Novel* (1966): 31–34; Harss, L., and Dohmann, B., *Into the Mainstream* (1966): 246–75; Schade, G. D., Introduction to *The Burning Plain and Other Stories* (1967); Sommers, J., *After the Storm* (1968): 68–94; Langford, W. M., *The Mexican Novel Comes of Age* (1971): 88–102; Foster, D. W., and Foster, V. R., eds., *Modern Latin American Literature* (1975), Vol. II: 295–304; Brotherston, G., *The Emergence of the Latin American Novel* (1977): 71–80

—GEORGE R. MCMURRAY

RUNYANKORE LITERATURE
See Ugandan Literature

RUSHDIE, Salman

Indian novelist, short-story writer, and critic (writing in English), b. 19 June 1947, Bombay

R. is perhaps the most controversial novelist of the late 20th c.; he lives under sentence of death at the hands of Islamic fundamentalists and the government of Iran, and thus remains in hiding, presumably somewhere in the British Isles. His books, moreover, have been banned in India, South Africa, and most of the Muslim world. Born in Bombay of Muslim parents, R. has spent most of his

Salman Rushdie

adult life in Great Britain but retains ties to three countries: India, Pakistan, and England. He graduated from the Cathedral School in Bombay and took an M.A. (honors) degree in history from King's College, Cambridge in 1968. He has one son from his first marriage in 1976. R. worked as an actor in London from 1968 to 1969 and as a freelance advertising copywriter there from 1970 to 1980. His second marriage, to an American, ended in divorce during his forced underground exile.

In his first novel, *Grimus* (1975), R. introduced his own distinctive narrative technique of magic REALISM, which has been compared to the narratives of Gabriel García MÁRQUEZ. The hero of *Grimus* is Flapping Eagle, a Native American who discovers the meaning of life through a series of bizarre encounters with eccentric characters and supernatural experiences. Myth dominates the lives of all who live on Calf Island, where a Dantesque figure named Virgil serves as guide for Flapping Eagle's journey up Paradise Mountain. However, it was R.'s second novel. *Midnight's Children* (1981), that catapulted him to international literary attention and earned him the Booker McConnell Prize (1981), the English-Speaking Union Award (1981), and the James Tait Black Memorial Prize (1982).

Midnight's Children takes its title from Nehru's speech delivered at the stroke of midnight, 14 August 1947, as India gained its independence from England (coincidentally the year R. was born). R.'s central narrative device is a network of one thousand and one babies, born during the first hour of renascent India, all of whom share the ability to communicate with each other through extrasensory perception. This device permits the author to range widely across geography, caste, and class, as well as employ a multiplicity of perspectives as he handsprings his way through Indian history. Protagonist Saleem Sinai, a man in his early thirties, is both prematurely old and impotent, and must be taken as an allegory for India itself. R.'s fiction is funambulistic—an exhilerating admixture of languages, historical moments, and fantasy. His style, full of puns, allusions, autobiographical elements, satire, and slang, is perfectly suited to the task of plummeting through India's astonishing first three decades.

Having presented India's exuberant history as a historical farce, R. did much the same thing for Pakistan in *Shame* (1983), using an altogether darker lens. As the author admits, in one of many authorial intrusions, he experienced Pakistan in so many fragments that he tends to reflect it in bits of broken mirrors. Through an array of preposterous characters living outrageous lives, R. explores themes of shame and shamelessness, polar opposites that lead to violence. The story evolves into a thinly disguised allegory of two historical figures in the characters of Iskander Harappa, playboy turned politician, modeled on former Prime Minister Zulfikar Ali Bhutto, and General Raza Hyder, Iskander's valued associate and later his executioner, who stands for real-life military dictator Zia-al-Huq. With hyperbole, R. depicts the neglected wives and daughters of the two rivals and cruelly works through the triple whammy of being born a girl-child in an elite family of a patriarchal Islamic society. *Shame* won for R. election to the Royal Society of Literature (1983) and France's Foreign Book Prize (1985).

When *The Satanic Verses* (1988) appeared, it was clear that all of R.'s earlier novels had been merely rehearsals for this chef d'oeuvre that was to cause so much controversy worldwide and earn the Whitbread Award for Fiction (1988).

England, the obvious milieu for an exploration of the immigrant experience, is the setting for this brilliant and disturbing fantasy. The immigrant heroes are Gibreel Farishta, a Bombay film actor who plays Hindu gods, and Saladin Chamcha, a voice dubber who has been successful at "translating" himself into British culture. Victims of an airplane bomb explosion, both men fall to earth and soon after begin their respective physical and moral transformations into the Archangel Gibreel and Satan. These characters allow R. to explore not only the question of what it means to be fully human, but also what it feels like to change cultures abruptly. Although he briefly considers the encounter between different ethnic communities in London, it is R.'s own Islamic heritage that evokes extravagant satire and casts the two heroes in dualistic opposition.

R.'s Islamic critics insist that his creation of the character Mahound, a thinly veiled parody of the prophet Muhammad, is sheer blasphemy. But they would do well to look closely at what R. has chosen to ridicule: the prophet's nine wives, mullahs who refuse to countenance competing orthodoxies, and extreme sects that lead their followers into dangerous waters. These, R. insists, are elements of Islam that no educated Muslim can honestly acknowledge. To treat the prophet so cavalierly may be against the tenets of Islam, but R.'s exaggerated humanization of Mahound is a plea for Islam to make peace with the contemporary world by recognizing the prophet Muhammad as a historical figure and diminishing the rigidity of its belief system. R.'s satire has clearly found a target, for the Muslim world has reacted to his demand for self-scrutiny by rejecting all discussion and sentencing the heretic. To examine *The Satanic Verses* only in its religious dimensions, however, is to do injustice to what is a densely patterned Oriental carpet: boisterous language, film archetypes, autobiographical experience, and highspirited plots and subplots. Moreover, as with James JOYCE's *Ulysses* (1922), a strong human truth emerges from R.'s multilingual welter: Chamcha/Satan regains his humanness only upon returning to Bombay to care for his dying father and to recognize the integrity of South Asian culture.

Haroun, and the Sea of Stories (1990) is a very different sort of novel, a fantasy of simple dimensions that begs to be read aloud and savored as a tale of good outwitting evil. Emerging from R.'s painful experience of having to live as a hunted criminal, this story depicts a kingdom of darkness that has stopped the motion of the earth so that it may forever keep its people unenlightened and miserable. (In this allegory born of R.'s private hell, read Iran). The heroes, Rashid, a storyteller who has temporarily lost his gift, and his son Haroun, together with Butt the Hoopoe and Iff the Water Genie, manage to defeat Khattam-Shud, Arch-Enemy of Stories and Foe of Speech, and rescue the princess. Weaving together strands from the *Ramayana* and classical Sanskrit story literature, as well as characters from Satyajit Ray films and houseboat life in Kashmir, R. produces an enchanting moral tale studded with puns and artifacts of classical Indian culture. *The Moor's Last Sigh* tells the story of a Christian-Jewish family, four generations worth, involved in the spice trade in India. In a boisterous verbal tapestry, R. paints Moorish Spain and Mughal India as similarly complex, highly productive, and religiously tolerant societies. Linking his novel to *Don Quixote*, he celebrates, through identically-named paintings by the narrator's mother and his madman captor, the cultural achievements possible in such complex worlds. It is a full-fledged argument that R. delivers in this novel: when properly nurtured by imperialism, cultural hybridity can become a genuine and powerful synthesis of contradictory components. As for contemporary forms, R. has only contempt, both for cultural artifacts handled as commodities and for aesthetic effort stopped dead in its tracks by religious fundamentalism. R., like Thomas PYNCHON, Gabriel García MÁRQUEZ, and Günter GRASS, is a fabulist whose

apocalyptic visions of a disenchanted world both terrify and fascinate. R.'s diction, however, is the most densely exotic, for he stirs in bits of five or six languages, as well as a multitude of disparate contemporary voices. Yet this blend of eclecticism and energy is fully equal to the task of presenting a postcolonial world undergoing unpredictable transformations. In deconstructing the old stabilities and rewriting them, R. generates new cultural confluences awesome in their richness and promise of redemption. Because he does not apologize for the intrusion of an irrepressible South Asian culture, but instead revels in it, R.'s locutions and vision have gained a prominent place in contemporary literature, bringing to the forefront the global dimensions of POSTMODERNISM.

FURTHER WORKS: *The Jaguar Smile: A Nicaraguan Journey* (1987); *In Good Faith* (1990); *Is Nothing Sacred* (1990); *Imaginary Homelands: Essays and Criticism (1981–1991)* (1991); *The Wizard of Oz* (1992); *East, West: Stories* (1995); *Mirrorwork: Fifty Years of Indian Writing, 1947-1997* (1997)

BIBLIOGRAPHY: Couto, M., "*Midnight's Children* and Parents," *Encounter*, 58, 2 (1982): 61–66; Gorra, M., "Laughter and Bloodshed," *HudR* 37, 1 (1984): 151–64; Grewal, I., "S. R.: Marginality, Women, and *Shame*," *Genders*, 3 (1988): 24–42; Mukherjee, B., "Prophet and Loss: S. R.'s Migrations of Souls," *Village Voice Literary Supplement*, 72 (1989): 9–12; Leithauser, B., "Demoniasis," *New Yorker* (15 May 1989): 124–28; Pipes, D., "The Ayahtollah, the Novelist, and the West," *Commentary*, 87, 6 (1989): 9–17; Mazrui, A., "Is *The Satanic Verses* a Satanic Novel? Moral Dilemmas of the Rushdie Affair," *MQR*, 28, 3 (Summer 1989): 347–71; Tyssens, S., "*Midnight's Children* or the Ambiguity of Impotence," *CE&S*, 12, 1 (1989): 19–29; Srivastava, A., "The Empire Writes Back: Language and History in *Shame* and *Midnight's Children*," *ArielE*: 20, 4 (Oct. 1989): 62–78; Malak, A., "Reading the Crisis: The Polemics of S. R.'s *The Satanic Verses*," *ArielE*, 20, 4 (Oct. 1989): 176–86; Amanuddin, S., "The Novels of S. R.: Mediated Reality in Fantasy," *WLT*, 63, 1 (Winter 1989): 42–45; Edmundson, M., "Prophet of a New Postmodernism: The Greater Challenge of S. R.," *Harper's*, 297 (Oct. 1989): 62–71; King, B., "Satanic Verses and Sacred Cows," *SR*, 98, 1 (Winter 1990): 144–52; special R. issue, *SARev*, 16 (1992); Cantor, P. A., "Tales of the Alhambra: R.'s Use of Spanish History in *The Moor's Last Sigh*," *SNNTS*, 29 (1997): 323-41

—JANET M. POWERS

It is generally recognized that the modern novelist is "a special master of language in whom the energies of idiomatic usage, of etymological implication, declare themselves with obvious force," and that the main impulse of current literature is the search for ethnicity. *Midnight's Children* evokes this "lost centre" in language that conveys the ineffable and inescapable "Indianness" of the novelist. He dips into the rich store of religious and social customs, into the physical aspects of identity . . . for a splendid array of metaphor drawn from Indian reality. The rhythmic flow and the high figurative content of Indian languages, myth, fable, belief and superstition are integrated into English prose in joyful profusion to suggest India's many-tongued diversity. In its meandering interpolations, its paradoxical statements, its parabolic patterns, the novel strives to suggest the formlessness of India's all-encompassing form, its ability to "swallow the lot," "to encapsulate the whole of reality." Traditionally, the women of North India were in purdah, and from within its confines peered at a limited view of the world. The metaphor of the hole drawn from this custom suggests the development of a fractured self, and the manner in which the novel is written—gradually, in vignettes of finely observed detail—reveals a mosaic of experience spread over three generations.

Maria Couto, "*Midnight's Children* and Parents,"
Encounter, 58, 2 (1982), pp. 61–66

Shame is in some small degree a *roman à clef* about the relationship between Pakistan's last two dictators, Zulfikar Ali Bhutto and General Zia ul-Haq, but any *clef* is strictly secondary to R.'s consideration of Pakistan itself as a failed act of the imagination. The country's very name is an acronym, he writes, meant to denote the peoples and regions of its western portion-while ignoring the Bengalis who comprised the bulk of its population until the founding of Bangladesh. That irony makes the country's history grotesque from the start, and yet R. hesitates before assaulting it. . . "Is history," he asks, in one of the many passages in his own voice interpolated into, and commenting on, *Shame's* narrative line, "to be considered the property of the participants solely?" Well, perhaps—but if so, R. can take certain liberties with it, can avoid the "reallife material" that would otherwise "become compulsory," in favor of a symbolic version. R.'s compromise with history is to write about a country that is "not quite" Pakistan, one that occupies the "same space" but exists at "a slight angle to reality," an angle that gives him the freedom upon which this "modern fairy tale" is predicated. . . . His prose prances, a declaration of freedom, an assertion that *Shame* can be whatever he wants it to be, coy and teasing and ironic and brutal all at once. He's been compared to Sterne, but the 18th-c. novelist who comes to my mind is Fielding. To read R. is to re-experience the novel as novel, as new, to recapture Fielding's claim, in *Tom Jones*, to be "the founder of a new province of writing [in which] I am at liberty to make what laws I please." *Shame* is, like *Tom Jones*, full of narrative games, a fiction about fiction that is nevertheless crammed, and finally most concerned with, the vibrant stuff of life.

Michael Gorra, "Laughter and Bloodshed," *HudR*
37, 1 (Spring 1984), p. 162

The Satanic Verses is in love with metamorphosis. The best-known of R.'s metamorphoses is, of course, his rather cruel rewriting of the political, personal, and religious life of the prophet Muhammad, who comes off, to the horror of the Islamic devout, looking like a shrewd opportunist. But what R. is trying to do with traditional narratives is what time itself inevitably does. As time separates us further from our

stories, they're transformed, they come *to mean* differently. R. with no little presumption, wants to be ahead of time, doing some of history's work for it. (And history, of course, is what those who believe they possess the Word most want to resist: "History is the blood-wine that must no longer be drunk," thinks R.'s exiled imam.) In the case of his rewriting of Muhammad, that means speeding up the work of secularization by vaporizing—in good, negative postmodern fashion—the prophet's holy aura.

But I'm more affected by the kind of *positive* transforming work that *The Satanic Verses* undertakes. Shuttling from London to Bombay, the book dramatizes the blending of two cultures, conjuring a new version of England as a land of immigrants and of India as the potential site of a world culture, at once appalling and exhilarating. R.'s objective is to stand between these two worlds and encourage their fusion; he wants to persuade people on both sides to open themselves to each other, though he's not unsophisticated about the risks involved in such an opening. The book's visions of cultural conjoining tend to be executed with gisto and high good humor. . . .

The prose of *The Satanic Verses* is indescent, fugre like: It strives to outspeed as well as out-envision the camera. Perspectives supplant one another and idioms alternate ceaselessly. But the book is also dense, full of layered, striving meanings that sometimes work in clear collaboration, sometimes not.

Mark Edmundson, "Prophet of a New
Postmodernism: The Greater Challenge of S. R.,"
Harper's, 297 (Dec. 1989), p. 66

R.'s imagination is cyclically Hindu and dualistically Muslim, with an extravagant inventiveness that seems pan-Indian. Certainly the Hindu and Islamaic cosmogonies are richer, fictionally speaking, than the Jewish Genesis, and R. uses them both for modern fictional purposes. According to Islam, humanity was brought into a world already seething with dangers, displacing the angels, who remain jealous, yet still subject to corruption by the subhuman, shape-changing djinns. *The Satanic Verses*, in spite of its much-reported brush with Islamic orthodoxy, is a *very* Muslim book. . . .

R. humanizes Mohammed—whose nondivinity is one of the pillars of the faith—but in decidedly contemporary terms. R.'s Mohammed patronizes whores, tolerates a few Arabian tribal gods, and splits the territory with the local competition, Jews and Christians, who've been expanding their franchises on Arabian turf. It's not Mohammed who comes out badly; it's his traditional interpreters, the mullahs, those who've institutionalized Mahound's own fear of self-scrutiny into an aggressive, fortressed denial of all criticism. . . .

One of R.'s more appealing notions (which I hope is not an unfounded flattery) is that immigration, despite losses and confusions, its sheer absurdities, is a net *gain*, a form of levitation, as opposed to Naipaul's loss and mimicry. Of course, the gain is equivocal.

Many of us, R. included, trade top-dog status in the homeland for the loss-of-face meltdown of immigration. He dramatizes the pain, that confusion, with a thousand inventions and some very shrewd, dead-on observations. R.'s language is a mask, a way of projecting all the forms of Indian speech at once (bombastic, babu, bureaucratic, Vedantic, vehement, servile, and Sellersish, without mocking or condescending) while remaining true to the essentially damaged, ego-deficient, postcolonial psyche.

> Bharati Mukherjee, "Prophet and Loss: S. R.'s Migrations of Souls," *Village Voice Literary Supplement*, 72 (1989), pp. 9–12

Writers . . . are naturally committed to free speech and to personal freedom; they expect justice and equality. Within nationalism there is increasingly a conflict between free thought and political and cultural unity, a conflict between two forms of modernization, the one experimental and open to change, the other looking to the past as a model. Fundamentalism is a radical traditionalism imposing orthodoxy and order on people who feel threatened by rapid change.

The Satanic Verses shows the conflict between modernization and traditionalism within the Islamic and Third World in the contrast between the exiled imam with his eyes continually on the past and the various immigrants, such as Saladin, who live in a multicultural changing world. But it also embodies the conflict by investigating and questioning traditionalism and the past. We live in an age of large movements of population through immigration, rapid international transportation and communication, global politics, and a world economy in which goods and people continually cross borders. Cultural movements or periods represent significant social, demographic, economic, or political changes . . . and the international controversy concerning *The Satanic Verses* tell[s] us much about what may be truly significant to our culture and time.

> Bruce King, "Satanic Verses and Sacred Cows," *SR*, 98, 1 (Winter 1990), p. 151

RUSSELL, George William

(pseud.: AE) Irish poet, critic, short-story writer, and novelist, b. 10 April 1867, Lurgan; d. 17 July 1935, Bournemouth, England

R.'s Protestant parents moved with him to Dublin when he was thirteen. He soon enrolled in art school there. He became a close friend of W. B. YEATS and began a life-long interest in theosophy: for seven years (1890–97) his life centered around the Theosophical Society in Dublin, as he wrote poetry, stories, essays, and made Blake-like illustrations for the society's journals, which he also edited. A few years after R.'s first book of poems appeared, Yeats urged the Irish Agricultural Organisation Society to employ R., his only rival as an Irish poet, R. having practical talents as accountant, speaker, and editor. After observing R.'s skill in organizing cooperatives, the I.A.O.S. appointed him editor of its weekly, *Irish*

George William Russell

Homestead in 1905, and, when the paper dropped its agricultural orientation in 1923 and became the *Irish Statesman*, R. continued as editor until its demise in 1930.

Much of R.'s best poetry was written before he became editor of the *Homestead, Homeward: Songs by the Way* (1894), poems of man's exile from his spirit, ranked R. alongside the early Yeats. But that volume's reflections of R.'s visions in jewellike images of twilights and dawns so pleased him that he repeated them for almost thirty years, rather than using his poems to explore his visions. During those years, however, his prose for the *Homestead* and *Statesman* became tough and straightforward, and this prose writing strengthened his later verse, much as Yeats's playwriting strengthened his. This is seen most clearly in R.'s *Selected Poems* (1935), beginning about halfway through the selections from *Voices of the Stones* (1925) and continuing to the end. But R.'s best nature poems always glow like an impressionist's canvas because of his treatment of light as a transfiguring, supernatural being.

Most of R.'s stories, among them his semi-autobiographical "Strange Awakening" (1894), are scattered throughout early theosophical journals that he edited before joining the I.A.O.S. The stories he included in *The Mask of Apollo* (1905), like those of Yeats's poems in *Crossways*, are set in Egypt, Greece, and Ireland. More fables than stories, most stress the awakening of children and men to the god within them, whether that god be Apollo or Angus Oge (a Celtic god).

Throughout his editorial and critical work for the *Homestead* and *Statesman*, R. kept the best of Ireland's creative artists and thinkers before his readers. R. became the spiritual, artistic, and cooperative director of the Irish people. His own spiritual and artistic experiences, especially his honest explorations of the origins of his visions and his poems, are the subject of *The Candle of Vision* (1918) and the much more lucid *Song and Its Fountains* (1932).

R. set forth his vision of a cooperative Ireland in *The National Being* (1916), perhaps his most solidly written work. In the dialogues of *The Interpreters* (1922) representative Irish leaders of the 1916 uprising spend the night dispassionately explaining to each other the visions for which they will face the firing squads in the morning. Having suffered through the destruction of his own dream of a slowly evolving cooperative Ireland, R. created the legend of *The Avatars: A Futurist Fantasy* (1933). This novel re-creates R.'s vision of Irish gods who come to earth to bring about a revolution, their crucifixion, and their resurrection in the people's hearts.

Those who know R. only through the fictions of George MOORE, James JOYCE, or Sean O'CASEY do not know R. Like Joyce's Bloom, R. was more of an "all-around man" than any other Irishman. All of his writing comes from what he called his own "center of being," a term familiar to readers of Thomas Merton (1915–1968) as "own being," And R. did more than any other Irish man of letters to help his fellow Irishmen by holding up their creative work with charity and knowledge to the critical light of the world community.

FURTHER WORKS: *The Earth Breath* (1897); *Literary Ideals in Ireland* (1899, with W. B. Yeats and John Eglinton); *The Nuts of Knowledge* (1903); *Deirdre* (1903); *The Divine Vision* (1904); *By Still Waters* (1906); *Some Irish Essays* (1906); *Co-operation and Nationality* (1912); *Collected Poems* (1913; rev. eds., 1919, 1926, 1931, 1935); *Gods of War* (1915); *Imaginations and Reveries* (1915; rev. ed., 1921); *Midsummer Eve* (1928); *Enchantment* (1930); *Vale* (1931); *The House of the Titans* (1934); *Some Passages from the Letters of AE to W. B. Yeats* (1936); *AE's Letters to Mínanlábáin* (1937); *The Living Torch* (1937); *Letters from AE* (1961); *Selections from the Contributions to "The Irish Homestead"* (2 vols., 1978)

BIBLIOGRAPHY: Denson, A., *Printed Writings of George W. Russell (AE)* (1961); Daniels, W., "AE: 1867–1967," *DUR*, 4 (1967): 106–20; Summerfield, H., *That Myriad-Minded Man: A Biography of G. W. R.* (1976); Daniels, W., "AE: Some Critical Perspectives," *IUR*, 2 (1976): 223–28; Summerfield, H., "AE as Literary Critic," in Ronsley, J., ed., *Myth and Reality in Irish Literature* (1977): 41–61; Daniels, W., "Glory and Shadow: AE's Supernatural Imagery," *Éire*, 13 (1978): 46–53

—WILLIAM DANIELS

RUSSIAN LITERATURE

Censorship, ill-treatment of writers, and geographical dislocation helped to determine the Russian literary climate well before the 20th c., but for most of the Soviet era (1917-91) these three factors played a far greater role than at any earlier time. Censorship, relaxed in the years 1905-14, became draconian after Stalin consolidated power (1929-53). It then mitigated after his death, but did not disappear until the twilight of the Soviet era. Because of censorship, all writers raised in the Soviet Union came to practice

self-censorship, and the sociopolitical significance that Russian writers and readers attributed to literature became grossly inflated. Mikhail Gorbachev's rise to leadership in 1985 and his policy of glasnost, usually defined as "openness," gradually led to the elimination of official censorship, while the collapse of the Soviet Union in 1991 brought about the rapid commercialization of Russian culture as a whole and of literature in particular. The censorship of the marketplace has now replaced that of official-dom, with the predictable results that the literary community has grown highly fragmented; writers in general have been marginalized; and poetry, literary criticism, scholarly editions, and literary journals have fallen on particularly hard times.

Official harassment of Russian writers dates at least to the 18th c., and such 19th-c. figures as Alexandr Pushkin (1799–1837), Ivan Turgenev (1818–1883), and Fyodor Dostoevsky (1821–1881) provoked the government's displeasure and paid dearly for it. In the post-1917 period, however, the litany of arrests, trials, deportations, exiles, campaigns of official vilification, executions, and suicides staggers the Western mind and would require an entire volume for adequate description. The present article dispenses with the roll call of horrors that characterizes most non-Soviet surveys of Russian literature in the 20th c. Readers interested in this tragic aspect of Russian literary history are urged to consult any of several works listed in the bibliography.

The phenomenon of Russian writers living and publishing abroad first occurred in the 19th c., when Alexandr Herzen (1812–1870) established his Free Russian Press in London. In the 20th c. the number of Russian writers who have emigrated and the activities of Russian-language presses outside Russia immeasurably exceed 19th-c. precedents. After the Bolshevik coup d'état in 1917 scores of literati (and millions of nonliterati) left Russia, settling for the most part in France, Germany, and the U.S., some of them later to return to their homeland. World War II witnessed a lesser wave of emigration as far as literature was concerned, but the so-called third wave, dating from the 1960s and 1970s, has included many of the most talented and best-known Soviet Russian writers of the postwar era. Moreover, several Russian authors, beginning with Boris PASTERNAK, have published abroad "illegally" while continuing to live in the U.S.S.R.

The geographical dislocation of Russian literature in the 20th c. led until recently to a not very useful distinction between Soviet Russian literature and an émigré offshoot. A broader historical view renders such a categorization invalid, and developments over the last two decades have simply made it unworkable. Russian literature of the 20th c., much of it unavailable to Soviet readers, remains a single entity.

Russian Literature since 1980

With the election of Mikhail Gorbachev as secretary-general of the Communist Party of the U.S.S.R. in 1985 and his subsequent proclamation of perestroika, a policy of announced reform and renewal, Russian literature entered the age of glasnost. Usually defined as "openness," glasnost has affected Russian literature in a number of ways. First, it has gradually brought about the elimination of official censorship. There are no guarantees that governmental control over the printed word will not be reinstated, but for the time being the role of censor seems to have passed to editors and, in a sense, to Russian consumers.

The concept of the reader as a consumer leads to a second major consequence of perestroika and the disappearance of censorship, namely, the rapid commercialization of Russian culture as a whole and of literature in particular. Russian publishers now have to think about sales and profits. As a result, poetry, literary criticism, and scholarly editions have fallen on hard times, a situation that many writers and critics naturally view with alarm. As could have been predicted, popular culture is rapidly crowding out the pious high-brow literature that the Soviet state so long subsidized.

In a third significant development, glasnost has firmly resolved the question of whether Russian émigré literature and Russian literature originally written and published in the U.S.S.R. or Russia belong to the same body of writing. Clearly they do, although only now, for the first time since 1917, may one plausibly argue that the most significant Russian-language presses are all in Russia. There, with ever increasing zeal, publishers of newspapers, magazines, and books have been making available to readers works to which they lacked easy or indeed even legal access before the age of glasnost.

Now that glasnost has erased distinctions between writing published in Russia and writing published abroad, Russian literature has reemerged as a single but variegated literature. Naturally, its competing branches, schools, and tendencies reflect both Russian and Soviet tendencies and processes. Consequently, there exists an overtly didactic and ideological mainstream paralleled by a competing but less voluminous countertradition of Russian writing.

Finally, by way of a paradoxical disclaimer, it should be noted that future historians of Russian literature may conclude that glasnost, at least in its early stages, did not fundamentally alter the overall literary landscape that had been visible to commentators abroad well before 1985. After all, many of the works published in Russia within the last few years cannot count as new. Russian journals and publishing houses have been zealously filling in the "blank spots" in their literary history, but many of those spots were blank only in the Soviet Union. Not surprisingly, given the amount of writing only now being published in Russia but already known in *samizdat* or *tamizdat*, at least one critic has argued that Russian literature's present is actually its past.

Poetry

The turn of the century coincided with the rise of Russian SYMBOLISM, or Decadence, a MODERNIST movement that influenced all the arts but first emerged with full force in poetry. A complex and contradictory school that defies easy categorization, symbolism in its earliest stages represented a rejection of much of the positivism and civic mindedness that characterized the Russian literary ethos in the second half of the 19th c. Under the combined influence of Western European modernists and such rediscovered Russian masters as Fyodor Tyutchev (1803–1873) and Afanasy Fet (1820–1892), Russian symbolists asserted the artist's right to create his own world, however solipsistic, and to meditate on the most intimate and irrational aspects of human experience, especially sex and religion.

The origins of Russian symbolism date from the last decade of the 19th c. Dmitry MEREZHKOVSKY, a writer whose works have generally faded into obscurity, gave early notice of a new literary orientation with his manifesto *O prichinakh upadka i o novykh techeniakh sovremennoy russkoy literatury* (1893; "On the Reasons for the Decline and the New Tendencies in Contemporary Russian Literature," 1975). Valery BRYUSOV and Konstantin BALMONT translated the new sensibility into poetry that aroused the public's interest and sometimes its ire. Bryusov's anthologies

Russkie simvolisty (3 vols., 1894–95; Russian symbolists) scandalized decorous readers, although the poet later produced coldly classical verses and ended his career singing the praises of proletarian labor. Balmont's neoromantic *Pod severnym nebom* (1894; under the northern sky) immediately aroused enthusiasm with its facile melodiousness, and *Budem kak solntse* (1903; let us be like the sun) established the ecstatic tone and mastery of form that mark his mature work.

By the turn of the century symbolism had passed from a fledgling movement into a significant cultural force, all the while picking up new adherents. With her religious and metaphysical verse in *Sobranie stikhov* (2 vols., 1904, 1910; collected poems), Zinaida HIPPIUS foreshadowed the out-and-out mystical bent that some symbolists would pursue. An erudite interest in philosophy and religion characterizes the work of Vyacheslav IVANOV, whose ornate, cerebral poetry carries on the romantic tradition of the artist as seer. The most purely aesthetic symbolist poetry is that of Fyodor SOLOGUB. In collections such as *Plamenny krug* (1908; circle of fire) he created an exotic, hermetic world in which aggressive ugliness wages war on vulnerable beauty.

Maximilian Voloshin (1877–1932) voiced his mystical hopes for Russia in his last major publication, *Demony glukhonemye* (1919; deaf-mute demons). Two representatives of the second generation, Andrey BELY and Alexandr BLOK, wrote verses that continue to inspire the Russian literary imagination. For all their mystical coloration, Bely's early collections *Zoloto v lazuri* (1904; gold in azure) and *Pepel* (1909; ashes) display verbal and metrical invention that has rarely been equaled. Blok, by general consensus the greatest Russian symbolist, produced an autobiographical oeuvre in which one can trace the poet's successive love affairs, his progressive disenchantment with mysticism, and his enduring concern for Russia's past, present, and future. His crowning achievement, the long poem "Dvenadtsat" (1918; "The Twelve," 1920), with its vision of Jesus Christ marching at the head of a band of rampaging Red Guards, startles and bewilders readers to this day.

Taken as a totality, the Russian symbolists made their greatest contribution to Russian literature by making lyric poetry respectable again in Russia, as it had not been since the 1840s, and by expanding its thematic and technical range. An honest assessment of their achievement, however, demands that one note the absence of truly great poets from among the symbolist ranks. Nonetheless, with its attention to form, which 19th-c. positivist criticism had denigrated, Russian symbolism created the preconditions for sustained poetic activity. Moreover, when viewed in a historical light, most of the schools of poetry that arose as a reaction to symbolism, and which included many of Russia's greatest 20th-c. poets, look very much like organic outgrowths of symbolism.

The first indication of a movement "to overcome symbolism" came in 1912 with the creation of the Guild of Poets, soon renamed the Acmeists. The distinctly minor poet Sergey Gorodetsky (1884–1967) and the much better known Nikolay GUMILYOV founded the group and wrote its manifestos, which rejected symbolist "otherwordliness," ignoring the fact that the symbolists themselves had already largely abandoned mysticism. Ironically, in such a hallucinatory poem as "Zabludivshysya tramvay" (1921; "The Lost Streetcar," 1967), Gumilyov committed some of the same alleged sins of which he had earlier accused the symbolists. Georgy Ivanov (1894–1958), one of the youngest Acmeists, found his true voice in poetry of despair and alienation, gathered in such collections as *Rozy* (1931) [first pub. in Paris]; roses) and *Raspad atoma*

(1938 [first pub. in Paris]; the decay of the atom). Georgy Adamovich (1894–1972) wrote little verse himself, but his call for a spare, unadorned style influenced such later poets as Igor Chinnov (b. 1909).

Although a small group, the Acmeists boasted two of Russia's most outstanding modern poets, Anna AKHMATOVA and Osip MANDELSHTAM. Akhmatova's first collection of verse, *Vecher* (1912; evening), revealed the distinctly feminine voice, simplicity of diction, concreteness of detail, and restrained pathos that characterize all her work. Mandelshtam, whose reputation among critics now approaches that of Pushkin, created a corpus of challenging poetry in which the theme of art itself predominates. This thematic interest informs even his earliest collections, *Kamen* (1913; *Stone*, 1973) and *Tristia* (1922; Latin: sad things [from Ovid]).

Two poets of note, Innokenty ANNENSKY and Mikhail KUZMIN, influenced the Acmeists but did not formally belong to the group. Annensky's posthumously published *Kiparisovy larets* (1910; *The Cypress Chest*, 1982), with its bleak, finely crafted lyrics, greatly impressed Akhmatova and Gumilyov. Kuzmin's essay "O prekrasnoy yasnosti" (1910; on beautiful clarity) sounded programmatic notes that appealed to the Acmeists, and the tidy Epicurean verse in his *Seti* (1908; nets) foreshadowed proclaimed Acmeist ideals. In later collections, such as *Nezdeshine vechera* (1921; otherworldly evenings), Kuzmin evolved a much denser, hermetic style.

A second major challenge to symbolism was that of FUTURISM, a movement even more complex and contradictory than symbolism, with a dizzying history of groupings and regroupings. Generally speaking, Russian futurism, which had little direct connection with the Italian movement of the same name headed by Filippo MARINETTI, professed a rejection of all tradition. In fact, however, most futurist experimentation merely rang variations on Bely's poetic theories and practice. Many of the futurists felt an attraction to the graphic arts, an interest that led them to devote great attention to book design and layout. In this connection one might well argue that the works of such primitivists as Alexey Kruchonykh (1886–1968), Vasily Kamensky (1884–1961), and David Burlyuk (1882–1967) possess greater visual appeal than literary merit.

The futurist movement produced three incontestably major poets: Vladimir MAYAKOVSKY, Velemir KHLEBNIKOV, and Boris Pasternak. In prerevolutionary works such as *Oblako v shtanakh* (1915; "The Cloud in Trousers," 1933) Mayakovsky couched intensely lyrical love poetry in a brash, hyperbolic style that reeked of the street. After 1917 love lyrics alternated with agitprop in Mayakovsky's opus. His poetic manner greatly influenced Nikolay Aseev (1889–1963), and his manner of declamation, high-decibeled and fiercely rhythmic, haunts Russian poetry readings to this day. Khlebnikov, who along with Kruchonykh created the notion of *zaum* (transrational language), left a chaotic body of poetry in which linguistics, mathematics, and history blend in an intoxicating brew. Although Pasternak soon parted company with futurism, his early collections *Sestra moya zhizn* (1922; *Sister My Life*, 1967) and *Temy is variatsii* (1923; themes and variations), whose style he later repudiated, abound in the sort of daring wordplay associated with futurism. Certain formal aspects of futurist practice bring the poetry of Marina TSVETAEVA close to the movement, but her passionately romantic themes are quite at odds with the futurist ambience. The volumes *Remeslo* (1923; craft) and *Posle Rossii: 1922–25* (1928; after Russia: 1922–25) exemplify the mature Tsvetaeva, who ranks as one of Russia's four or five greatest 20th-c. poets.

Futurism soon generated its own superficially antithetical movements, the first of them the "imaginists." Led by the ex-futurist Vadim Shershenevich (1893–1942), this tiny but vocal troupe proclaimed the value of the striking image above all other poetic criteria, thus only proving its debt to futurism. Sergey YESENIN, the best-known imaginist and probably the most genuinely popular Russian poet of the 20th c., penned maudlin verse lamenting the disappearance of the traditional Russian village and the poet's own corruption by fame and the city. Yesenin's early mentor, Nikolay KLYUEV, also a peasant poet, specialized in ornate poetry on folkloric and religious themes.

In the early Soviet period, politically involved futurists such as Mayakovsky and Aseev, organized around the journals *LEF* (1923–25) and *Novy LEF* (1927–28), found themselves opposed by a number of so-called proletarian groups: the Proletkult, the Smithy, the Cosmists, and others. Proletarian poets such as Alexey Gastev (1882–1941), Vladimir Kirillov (1890–1943), and Mikhail Gerasimov (1889–1939) sang the mystical praises of labor and the collective, all the while relying on established symbolist and futurist techniques.

A short-lived offshoot of futurism, constructivism (1922–30), hoped for the creation of a socialist art linked to technology. Vera Inber (1890–1972) briefly experimented with technological imagery, but her mature work, most of it patriotic, displays traditional versification. The leading constructivist, Ilya Selvinsky (1899–1968), displayed formal virtuosity and a colorful language in his first and best volume of poetry, *Rekordy* (1926; records). Edvard BAGRITSKY, whose association with constructivism had more to do with friendship than with ideology, won followers with his exuberantly romantic verse, especially *Duma pro Opanasa* (1926; the lay of Opanas), an epic about the civil war that followed the revolution.

The most pronouncedly modern school of Russian poetry arose in Leningrad and called itself OBERIU, an acronym for Obedinie Realnogo Iskusstva (Union of Real Art). Absurdist leanings linked all the members of this informal group, which reached its apogee in the late 1920s. Their most important poet, Nikolay ZABOLOTSKY, gave a phantasmagorical depiction of everyday Leningrad life in *Stolbtsy* (1929; *Scrolls*, 1971). Daniil Kharms (1905–1942), known in his lifetime as a writer of children's books, additionally wrote grotesque verse filled with black humor that has yet to be published in the U.S.S.R. Equally absurd but considerably more accessible than Kharms's poetry is that of Alexandr Vvedensky (1904–1941). Konstantin Vaginov (ca. 1899–ca. 1934) revealed his taste for the fragmentary and alogical in *Puteshestvie v khaos* (1921; journey into chaos).

During the period of high Stalinism (1929–53) very little original poetry of merit appeared in the Soviet Union. The best poets simply fell silent, not always of their own will, and hacks such as Alexandr Prokofiev (1900–1971) and Stepan Shchipachov (b. 1899) achieved dubious distinction. A grisly respite from cultural desolation came during World War II, when Akhmatova and Pasternak published poignant verses occasioned by patriotism of the loftiest sort. Alexandr TVARDOVSKY, a relative newcomer, earned enormous popularity with his folksy epic about a common soldier, *Vasily Tyorkin* (1945; *Vasily Tyorkin*, 1975).

Abroad, established poets such as Adamovich, Georgy Ivanov, Vyacheslav Ivanov, Balmont, Hippius, and Tsvetaeva continued to enrich the body of 20th-c. Russian poetry. Vladislav KHODASEVICH gathered most of his small opus, much of it with EXISTENTIALIST overtones, in *Sobranie stikhov* (1927; collected poems). The most significant new émigré voice belonged to Boris Plavsky (1903–1935), whose *Flagi* (1931; flags) portrayed post-World War I Europe in vivid, surrealistic images. After World War II several other important poets arose in emigration. Ivan Yelagin (1918-1987) combined traditional forms and modern imagery to dramatize the psychology of displacement. The laconic verse of Valery Pereleshin (b. 1913) builds on Acmeist practices. Igor Chinnov creates innovative forms for his skeptical observations on life and religion.

Soon after Stalin's death, with the advent of the thaw period (1955–64), there occurred a general poetic revival in Russia, with poets acquiring the status and popularity that movie actors and rock stars have in the West. In retrospect, it is clear that much of the public's interest was aroused not by aesthetic concerns, but by the explicit or implicit anti-Stalinist sentiments that characterized the poetry of the thaw.

Two of Russia's most distinguished modern poets survived Stalin: Akhmatova and Pasternak. Akhmatova's haunting, elusive *Poema bez geroya* (1960; *Poem without a Hero*, 1973) dwells on memory, time, and Russia's tragic history. Pasternak's late poetry, notably the poems from *Doktor Zhivago* (1957 [first pub. in Milan]; *Doctor Zhivago*, 1958), although tinged with tragic notes, celebrates the beauty and mystery of life and nature. Other long-established poets such as Semyon Kirsanov (1906–1972), Pavel Antokolsky (b. 1896), and Leonid Martynov (1905–1982) published verses during the thaw period criticizing the Stalinist past. Tvardovsky delighted readers with *Tyorkin na tom svete* (1963; Tyorkin in the other world), a satire in which hell greatly resembles the Soviet bureaucracy.

Many of the poets who came to the fore in the 1950s and 1960s had in common the memories of World War II as the central experience of their youth. Yevgeny Vinokurov (b. 1925) began his career with poetry exclusively about the war, but has since expanded his thematics, often reveling in the simple pleasures of everyday life. The early poetry of Boris Slutsky (1919-1986), also on war themes, sears the emotions, but his more recent verse shows a cold, probing intelligence at work. Semyon LIPKIN, a gifted translator, writes reflective poetry in which he often induces philosophical truths from the observation of seemingly minor moments. Also philosophical, but more challengingly so, are the works of Arseny Tarkovsky (b. 1907), one of the most cerebral of contemporary Russian poets. Naum Korzhavin (b. 1925), the most impassioned of the war-generation poets, frequently dwells on Russia's past in order by implication to condemn her present. David Samoylov (1920-1990) also writes about history, usually in a philosophical vein.

Of the youngest poets to enter literature during the thaw, Yevgeny YEVTUSHENKO and Andrey VOZNESENSKY attracted the greatest attention, both at home and abroad. The stylistically versatile Yevtushenko lacks any true originality as a poet or thinker, and he is probably best read as a chronicler of his own life and of the currents of his age. Voznesensky, a much more erudite and imaginative poet than Yevtushenko, has produced flashy verse on a wide range of topics, one of his favorites being art and the artist. Viktor Sosnora (b. 1936) often strikes readers as a Voznesensky in a lower key. Another poet who won popularity in the 1960s, Bella AKHMADULINA, writes highly polished, emotional verse, often about her own vulnerability. Classically precise meditations on cultural artifacts ranging from doorbells to the city of Leningrad characterize the poetry of Alexandr Kushner (b. 1936). The most politically active poet of her generation, Natalya Gorbanevskaya

(b. 1936), creates a world of isolation and despair in her intensely personal poetry.

Although the poets who achieved renown in the 1950s and 1960s provided an invaluable service to Russian literature by resurrecting language itself and by returning lyric poetry to a position of preeminence, only Joseph BRODSKY achieved the stature of a classic. Arguably the most intellectual Russian poet now writing, in such collections as *Ostanovka v pustyne* (1970 [first pub. in New York]; a stop in the desert) and *Chast rechi* (1977 [first pub. in Ann Arbor, Mich.]; a part of speech) Brodsky relies on largely traditional forms for his bleak pieces on life and history, both of which for him can be made bearable only through art.

Of the younger poets, Yury Kublanovsky (b. 1947) and Alexey Tsvetkov (b. 1947) give the greatest promise. In *Sbornik pies dlya zhizni solo* (1978 [first pub. in Ann Arbor, Mich.]; a collection of pieces for the solo life) and *Sostoyanie sna* (1981 [first pub. in Ann Arbor, Mich.]; the condition of sleep) Tsvetkov often meditates on mortality, while Kublanovsky's *Izbrannoe* (1981) [first pub. in Ann Arbor, Mich.]; selected poems) depicts Leningrad and the Russian north with masterly imagery and orchestration.

A unique feature of literary life in the Soviet Union over the last two decades has been the emergence of a school of tape-recorder bards. Throughout the country people gather privately to listen to tapes of poets singing their works. The largely apolitical Novella Matveeva (b. 1934) and Bulat OKUDZHAVA, with their gentle, wistful lyricism, offer Soviet listeners an escape from the implacably heroic and optimistic world of official culture. The songs of Vladimir Vysotsky (1937–1980) and Alexandr Galich (1919–1977), on the other hand, generally have implicit or explicit overtones of political protest.

Several of the most interesting poets now publishing were in fact known earlier, if only to the select few who read their verses in limited copies. Now the broader public is making the acquaintance of these poets, several of whom have organized themselves in informal groups.

The two most acclaimed groups of poets, both of them quite heterogeneous in their makeup, are the Conceptualists and the Metaphorists. The Conceptualists number among their ranks Lev Rubinshteyn (b. 1947), Dmitry Prigov (b. 1940), Vsevolod Nekrasov, and Timur Kibirov (dates n.a.). Because of the sense of playfulness and high irony characteristic of Conceptualist verses, critics find in them echoes of such Russian schools of the 1920s as the Futurists and the Oberiu (the latter a Leningrad-based absurdist group).

The Metaphorists, also sometimes referred to as Metarealists or Presentalists, are represented by Aleksey Parshchikov (b. 1954), Aleksandr Yeryomenko (b. 1950), and Viktor Krivulin (dates n.a.), among others. Close to this movement, but younger than any of its members, is Tatyana Shcherbina (dates n.a.). An even less coherent school than the Conceptualists, the Metaphorists nonetheless reveal many of the same influences. On the whole, however, their verses are much less accessible than those of the Conceptualists, and in general the work of the Metaphorists invites the classification of postmodern.

Not associated with any group, but a poet who has recently attracted considerable attention both at home and abroad, is Olesya Nikolaeva (b. 1956). In her poetry, startlingly rich in its stylistic diversity, Nikolaeva shows a concern for spiritual and moral questions. All the poets mentioned here reveal a greater affinity with the techniques and concerns of Russian poets of the early part of the 20th c. than with those of their contemporaries and immediate predecessors.

Fiction and Other Narrative Prose

Although Russian symbolism arose as a movement in poetry, it can be argued that the symbolists made their most lasting contribution in prose. Many consider Bryusov's masterpieces his historical novels *Ognenny angel* (1908; *The Fiery Angel*, 1930) and *Altar pobedy* (1913; the altar of victory), which focus on intellectual and erotic dilemmas. Sologub's *Melky bes* (1907; *The Little Demon*, 1916; later tr., *The Petty Demon*, 1962), a hilariously perverse chronicle of provincial life, ranks among the very best 20th-c. Russian novels. Bely represents an altogether special case. His early novels, *Serebryany golub* (1909; *The Silver Dove*, 1974), *Peterburg* (1916; rev. ed., 1922; *Petersburg*, 1959), and *Kotik Letaev* (1922; *Kotik Letaev*, 1971), written under the spell of apocalyptic mysticism and Rudolf Steiner's (1861–1925) anthroposophy, invite stylistic comparison with the works of James JOYCE. Bely's verbal invention and formal play have exerted an influence on almost all of Russia's modernist writers. The idiosyncratic, quilted style of Vasily ROZANOV, especially in *Opavshie listya* (2 vols., 1913–15; Vol. I tr. as *Fallen Leaves, Bundle One*, 1929), made itself felt in much modernist writing, too, particularly during the 1920s.

Works carrying on the venerable traditions of 19th-c. Russian realism competed with symbolist prose. Curiously, however, the two greatest living realists at the turn of the century, Lev Tolstoy (1828–1910) and Anton CHEKHOV, pointed out directions for symbolist and realist prose alike. The taboo shattering discussion of sex and death in Tolstoy's late stories opened the door for the physiological orientation of much early 20th-c. writing across the board, while Chekhov's rejection of traditional civic-mindedness coincided with early symbolist practice.

The most popular prose writers of the first decade of the 20th c. initially allied themselves with Maxim GORKY and his publishing house Znanie. Sympathy for the downtrodden characterizes all of Gorky's prose. Nowhere is this attitude clearer than in his influential but lackluster novel about revolutionaries, *Mat* (1907; *Mother*, 1907). An infinitely better work, *Detstvo* (1913; *My Childhood*, 1914), the first part of an autobiographical trilogy, shows Gorky at his remarkable best. Gorky's only serious rival for popular attention, Leonid ANDREEV, titillated sensation seekers with shrill tales of madness and mayhem such as *Krasny smekh* (1904; *The Red Laugh*, 1905). Alexandr KUPRIN holds a modest but secure place in literary history thanks to his *Poedinok* (1905; *The Duel*, 1916), a novel about decency and idealism trampled by military life. Ivan Shmelyov (1873–1950) attracted attention with his *Chelovek iz restorana* (1911; the man from the restaurant), a novel about a waiter in a philanthropic tradition of the young Dostoevsky. The influence of Turgenev and Chekhov revealed itself in the early stories of Boris ZAYTSEV. Far and away the most talented member of the Znanie group was Ivan BUNIN, the first Russian to receive the Nobel Prize for literature (1933). Although most of his mature writing treats the intimate themes of love, death, and memory, Bunin scandalized the public with his novel *Derevnya* (1910; *The Village*, 1923), in which he portrayed the peasantry, one of the intelligentsia's most sacrosanct cows, as brutish and bestial. Bunin's elegant, controlled style remains a model of its kind.

A much smaller prose school, Zavety (Behests), gathered together writers who shared an interest in life outside the city. Alexey REMIZOV wrote in various genres and styles, many of them derivative. His folktales influenced Mikhail PRISHVIN, who ultimately earned renown for his acute and joyous observations of Russian nature. Yevgeny ZAMYATIN began his career with

"Uezdnoe" (1913; "A Provincial Tale," 1967), a stylized portrait of brutality in the provinces.

As a result of the economic chaos and geographical displacement produced by world war, revolution, and civil war, the publication of Russian literature in the years 1917–21 virtually came to a halt. By the early 1920s, however, Russian prose was once again thriving, both at home and abroad. During that decade the revolution itself, as well as the conflict between the old and the new in nascent Soviet society, provided the major themes for prose writing. Certain prerevolutionary literary tensions remained, particularly the interplay between tradition and modernism in various guises and the often acrimonious dialogue between politically committed artists and those who wished to retain a clear distinction between art and propaganda.

Russian modernism in the 1920s had its own Russian roots, especially in the so-called ornamental line of writing best exemplified in the works of Nikolay Gogol (1809–1852) and Nikolay Leskov (1831–1895) in the 19th c. and Bely in the 20th. First place among Russian modernists in the 1920s belonged to Boris PILNYAK, whose *Goly god* (1922; *The Naked Year*, 1928) depicted the October Revolution as an elemental conflict between East and West and whose motley style inspired many of his contemporaries. Nearly as popular a writer as Pilnyak, Vsevolod Ivanov (1895–1963) offered a nihilistic vision of the revolution in works such as *Bronepoezd 14–69* (1922; *Armored Train 14–69*, 1933). Andrey PLATONOV, a modernist in his reliance on irony, offered an idiosyncratic portrait of the revolution in *Chevengur* (1972 [first pub. in Paris]; *Chevengur*, 1978). The quixotic heroes of that sprawling novel take the metaphorical slogans of the revolution literally and act accordingly, often with results that both amuse and horrify. Early stories by Boris Lavrenyov (1891–1959) rely on exciting, complex plots to cast a romantic light on the events of the revolution and civil war. The most archly experimental work of the period, *Sentimentalnoe puteshestvie* (1923; *A Sentimental Journey: Memoirs, 1917–1922*, 1971), by Viktor Shklovsky (b. 1893), blends literary criticism and reportage. In his *Konarmia* (1926; *Red Cavalry*, 1929) Isaak BABEL produced the single most artistically brilliant portrayal of revolutionary violence. In these disturbing sketches Babel uses an exquisitely taut metaphorical style and aesthetic irony to depict a Darwinian maelstrom.

One of the earliest modernist treatments of the new Soviet society came from Fyodor GLADKOV. Although he soon abandoned avant-garde practices, his novel *Tsement* (1925; *Cement*, 1929), a tale of postrevolutionary reconstruction, revealed in its first published version distinct echoes of Pilnyak and Bely. The conflict between traditional humanistic values and Soviet utilitarianism received an ambivalent treatment in the richly metaphorical *Zavis* (1927; *Envy*, 1936) by Yury OLESHA. Konstantin FEDIN, another writer who soon retreated from formal experimentation, relied on a rather gimmicky confusion of chronology in his *Goroda i gody* (1924; *Cities and Years*, 1962) to explore the quandaries facing intellectuals in the early Soviet period.

Any discussion of traditionalist writers who treated the revolution must begin with the classic *Tikhy Don* (4 vols., 1928–40; *And Quiet Flows the Don*, 1934; *The Don Flows Home to the Sea*, 1941) by the Nobel laureate Mikhail SHOLOKHOV. In this truly epic novel, one that does not especially flatter the Bolsheviks, Sholokhov portrays the devastating effects of war and revolution on Cossack life. Sholokhov's literary roots lie in Tolstoy's *War and Peace*, as do those of Alexandr FADEEV, whose *Razgrom* (1927; *The Nineteen*, 1929), a short novel about a detachment of partisans, reads like a catalogue of Tolstoyan techniques. Mikhail BULGAKOV reveals a similarly Tolstoyan orientation in his *Belaya gvardia* (incomplete, 1925; complete, 1966; *The White Guard*, 1971), wherein the reader follows the events in the lives of members of a single family in Kiev during the civil war. Mikhail Osorgin (1878–1942) also portrayed the fate of a family, in this case a Moscow professor's, in *Sivtsev vrazhek* (1928; *Quiet Street*, 1930). On a distinctly lower literary plane than any of the works mentioned above stands *Chapaev* (1923; *Chapaev*, 1935) by Dmitry Furmanov (1891–1926), a documentary novel about the interplay between the revolutionary commander of the title and the commissar assigned to him.

Leonid LEONOV is the most overtly Dostoevskian of modern Russian writers. In his *Barsuki* (1925; *The Badgers*, 1947), Leonov depicts the capitulation of rural Russia to the new urban culture. His *Vor* (1927; *The Thief*, 1931), dealing with a conscience stricken former commissar, represents a not very imaginative reworking of Dostoevsky's *Crime and Punishment*. Veniamin KAVERIN, a great admirer of E. T. A. Hoffmann and Edgar Allan Poe, addressed the problems of the older intelligentsia in revolutionary Russia in *Devyat desyatykh subdy* (1925; nine-tenths of fate). His most interesting novel, *Khudozhnik neizvesten* (1931; *The Unknown Artist*, 1947), treats the conflicts between two artists, one an idealist and one a pragmatist.

Much of the best writing of the 1920s took a satirical bent, usually poking fun at the habits of émigré life or mocking the entrepreneurs who profited from the capitalistic New Economic Policy, otherwise known as NEP. Arkady Averchenko (1881–1935) published many collections of humorous short stories in emigration, but the best-known émigré humorist was N. A. Teffi (pseud. of Nadezhda Lokhvitskaya, 1875–1952), whose collections such as *Chorny iris* (1921 [first pub. in Stockholm]; the black iris) and *Gorodok* (1927 [first pub. in Paris]; a small town) revealed sympathy for human frailty along with an eye for the ironies of everyday émigré life.

Ilya ILF and Yevgeny PETROV collaborated on the classic satire of the NEP period, *Dvenadtsat stulev* (1928; *Diamonds to Sit On*, 1930). Its hero, Ostap Bender, ranks as one of the most inventive con artists in world literature. Petrov's brother, Valentin KATAEV, contributed *Rastratchiki* (1926; *The Embezzlers*, 1929), a grotesque account of a cashier and a bookkeeper on a decadent spree. Mikhail ZOSHCHENKO, one of the most original humorists of the period and the despair of translators, wrote short stories in which semieducated and not very perceptive narrators skewer themselves and the foibles of the Soviet system. Bulgakov satirized unscrupulous scientists and boorish proletarians in the story "Rokovye yaytsa" (1925; "The Fatal Eggs," 1965) and in the much more satisfying *Sobachie serdtse* (1968 [first pub. in Paris]; *The Heart of a Dog*, 1968). Less specifically Soviet in their targets were *Neobychaynye pokhozhdenia Khulio Khurenito i ego uchenikov* (1922; *The Extraordinary Adventures of Julio Jurenito and His Disciples*, 1930) by Ilya EHRENBURG and Zamyatin's *My* (corrupt text, 1924 [first pub. in Prague]; full text, 1952; *We*, 1924). Ehrenburg's novel, his first and best, mounts a nihilistic attack on civilization itself, while Zamyatin drew on Dostoevsky's Grand Inquisitor and modernist techniques for an antiutopian satire that inspired George Orwell's *1984*.

Many writers in the 1920s were drawn to the historical novel. Olga Forsh (1873–1961) made one of the first contributions to the genre with the serially published *Odety Kamnen* (1924–25; *Palace and Prison*, 1958), about a young revolutionary in the 19th c. who

lost his mind in the Peter-Paul Fortress. The critic and scholar Yury Tynyanov (1894–1934) put his research to good use in *Kyukhla* (1925; *Kyukhla*), a lively novel about Pushkin's friend, the Decembrist poet Vilgelm Karlovich Kyukhelbeker (1797–1846), and *Smert Vazir-Makhtara* (1929; *Death and Diplomacy in Persia*, 1938), an account of the tragic fate of the poet and dramatist Alexandr Sergeevich Griboedov (1795–1829), who was literally torn to pieces by a mob in Tehran.

With Stalin's ascent to power in the late 1920s, the creation of the Union of Soviet Writers in 1932, and the promulgation of the vague but noxious dogma of Socialist REALISM in 1934, original literature published in the U.S.S.R. began a headlong dive into pompous dreariness and mendacity, from which it did not emerge—and then only partially—until after Stalin's death. The so-called production novel, in which recognizable human emotions, motivations, and concerns were replaced by industrial or agricultural impulses, ruled the day. The heroes in such novels were invariably good, honest communists who unmasked spies and saboteurs. Among the classics of this genre are Leonov's *Skutarevsky* (1932; *Skutarevsky*, 1936), Gladkov's serially published *Energia* (1932–38; energy), and Sholokhov's *Podnyataya tselina* (2 vols., 1932, 1960; *Seeds of Tomorrow*, 1935, *Harvest on the Don*, 1961). A variation on the production novel came with *Kak Zakalyalas stal* (1932–34; rev. ed., 1935; *The Making of a Hero*, 1937; also tr. as *How the Steel Was Tempered*, 1960) by Nikolay OSTROVSKY. The novel's hero, Pavel Korchagin, who overcomes all manner of obstacles and afflictions on his own path to communism, is force-fed to Soviet schoolchildren to this day. Of all the production novels that gushed forth, however, only Kataev's *Vremya, vperyod!* (1932; *Time Forward!*, 1933), with its cinematic technique, and Pilnyak's *Volga vpadaet v Kaspyskoe more* (1930; *The Volga Falls to the Caspian Sea*, 1931) demonstrated any literary imagination.

So as to help forge a new Soviet patriotism, writers of historical novels were encouraged to treat larger-than-life figures from the prerevolutionary past. Alexey TOLSTOY succeeded brilliantly in this venture in his serially published, unfinished *Pyotr Pervy* (1929–45; *Peter the First*, 1959), a masterpiece of its kind. Alexey Chapygin (1870–1937) contributed his sprawling, serially published *Stepan Razin* (1926–27; *Stepan Razin*, 1946), about the leader of a Cossack uprising in the 17th c. Many of the best writers of the period practiced what Babel called the "genre of silence," not always of their own volition.

Literature based on the experience of World War II is vast. Ehrenburg wrote about the war in the West, from a procommunist perspective, in *Padenie Parizha* (1941; *The Fall of Paris*, 1943). *Fadeev's Molodaya gvardia* (1945; *The Young Guard*. 1959), a dismal work of literature, portrays the heroic activities of members of the Young Communist League under German occupation. A few novels about World War II rose above mediocrity. Konstantin SIMONOV published serially *Dni i nochi* (1943–44; *Days and Nights*, 1945), about the Armageddon at Stalingrad. A much less heroic, more human account of the same battle came from Viktor Nekrasov (b. 1911) in his *V okopakh Stalingrada* (1946; *Front-Line Stalingrad*, 1962). In the short novel *Sputniki* (1946; *The Train*, 1948) Vera PANOVA offered a Chekhovian treatment of human relations on a hospital train.

The two most important writers of fiction in emigration were Bunin and Vladimir Nabokov. Bunin's autobiographical *Zhizn Arsieneva* (1927–39; partial tr., *The Well of Days*, 1933) reminds one of Lev Tolstoy's *Childhood, Boyhood, and Youth*. The nine novels that Nabokov wrote in Russian, among them *Zashchita*

Luzhina (1930; *The Defense*, 1964) and *Otchayanie* (1934; *Despair*, 1937; rev. ed., 1966), all deal with the theme of artistic creation in one way or another, often in unexpected contexts.

With the death of Stalin in 1953 the thematic and formal range of Russian literature broadened considerably. The best writing in the post-Stalin era, much of it in the short form, has centered on the Soviet past and present. The revolution, the terror of the 1930s and the camp system, and World War II are the major topics from the past. Writers who treat the present divide their attention and sympathies between the village and the city, whose cultures differ to an extent unimaginable for most Western readers. A quest for truth and morality characterizes all the best post-Stalinist writing, bringing much of it in line with the grand traditions of 19th-c. Russian literature, both stylistically and ethically.

The general tendency in writing about World War II has been to strip the war of the heroic patina that it had acquired in literature before 1953. *Yul 41-go goda* (1965; July 1941) by Grigory Baklanov (b. 1923) describes the panic and poor preparation attending the early stages of the war. Okudzhava's novella *Bud zdorov, shkolyar!* (1961; "Lots of Luck, Kid!," 1964) depicts the resentment and terror that a young soldier experiences. Yury Bondarev (b. 1924), the most orthodox of the war novelists, describes intense battle scenes from the point of view of haggard participants. With his *Zhizn I neobychaynye priklyuchenia soldata Ivana Chonkina* (1969 [first pub. in Paris]; *The Life and Extraordinary Adventures of Private Chonkin*, 1977) and its continuation, *Pretendent na prestol* (1979 [first pub. in Paris]; *Pretender to the Throne: The Further Adventures of Private Ivan Chonkin*, 1981), Vladimir VOYNOVICH turns traditional heroic treatments of the war inside out and portrays it as a grotesque farce. These two books have not been published in the Soviet Union.

Literature dealing with the Stalinist past, much of it published outside the U.S.S.R., is rich and varied. The first major allusion to GULAG came in Pasternak's *Doktor Zhivago*, whose heroine disappears, probably perishing "in one of the innumerable mixed or women's concentration camps in the north." In her searing memoirs, *Krutoy marshrut* (1967 [first pub. in Milan]; *Journey into the Whirlwind*, 1967) and *Krutoy marshrut II* (1979 [first pub. in Milan]; *Within the Whirlwind*, 1981), Yevgenia Ginzburg (1896–1977) describes the very camps at which Pasternak hinted. Aleksandr SOLZHENITSYN, Russia's third Nobel laureate, has created the most impressive single body of labor-camp literature, beginning with the short novel *Odin den Ivana Denisovicha*, (1962; *One Day in the Life of Ivan Denisovich*, 1963) and reaching its apogee in the massive nonfictional study *Arkhipelag GULAG* (3 vols., 1973–75 [first pub. in Paris]; *The Gulag Archipelago*, 3 vols., 1974–78). One of Solzhenitsyn's campmates, Lev Kopelev (b. 1912), has written a trilogy of his own memoirs: *Khranit vechno* (1975; rev. ed., 1978 [both first pub. in Ann Arbor, Mich.]; *To Be Preserved Forever*, 1977), *I sotvoril sebe kumira* (1978 [first pub. in Ann Arbor, Mich.]; *The Education of a True Believer*, 1980), and *Utoli moya pechali* (1981 [first pub. in Ann Arbor, Mich.]; *Ease My Sorrows*, 1983). *Kolymskie rasskazy* (1969–75 [first pub. serially in New York]; *Kolyma Tales*, 1980) by Varlam Shalamov (1907–1982) documents an experience much harsher than Solzhenitsyn's or Kopelev's, namely, forced labor in the Kolyma gold fields. Yury Dombrovsky (b. 1909) combines prison memoirs and philosophical meditations in his extraordinary novel *Fakultet nenuzhnykh veshchey* (1976 [first pub. in Paris]; the department of unnecessary things). In his *Verny Ruslan* (1975 [first pub. in Frankfurt]; *Faithful Ruslan*, 1979) Georgy Vladimov (b. 1931) has created one of the

indisputable literary masterpieces about the psychological effects of the camps.

Several writers have taken as their theme the domestic atmosphere during the terror of the 1930s. The memoirs *Vospominania* (1970 [first pub. in Paris]; *Hope against Hope*, 1970) and *Vtoraya kniga* (1972 [first pub. in Paris]; *Hope Abandoned*, 1974) by Nadezhda Mandelshtam (1899–1981), widow of Osip Mandelshtam, vividly and mercilessly re-create the atmosphere among writers of the time. Lidia Chukovskaya (b. 1907) gives a moving account of a woman's agony in the wake of her son's arrest in the novel *Opustely dom* (1965 [first pub. in Paris]; *The Deserted House*, 1967). The black comedy of terror as it affects a provincial archaeological museum is portrayed in Dombrovsky's *Khranitel drevnostey* (1964; *The Keeper of Antiquities*, 1969). Pavel Nilin (b. 1908) in *Zhestokost* (1958; *Comrade Venka*, 1959), Yury TRIFONOV in *Starik* (1979; the old man), and Sergey Zalygin (b. 1913) in *Na Irtyshe* (1964; on the Irtysh) go back to the early days of the Soviet regime to question any system that fails to discriminate between means and ends.

Much of the literature about the past has taken the form of memoirs. Important works by Nadezhda Mandelshtam, Kopelev, and Ginzburg have already been mentioned. Ehrenburg's disjointed *Lyudi, gody, zhizn* (1960–65; *People and Life*, 1891–1921, 1962; *Memoirs: 1921–1941*, 1964; *The War, 1941–1945*, 1964; *Post-war Years, 1945–1954*, 1966) resurrected significant cultural figures from the 1920s and 1930s. The six-volume *Povest o zhizni* (1945–63; *The Story of a Life*, 6 vols., 1964–74) by the venerable Konstantin PAUSTOVSKY offers a lively portrayal of picturesque figures and events from the early part of the century. Lidia Chukovskaya has recently published two splendid volumes of memoirs, *Zapiski ob Anne Akhmatovoy* (1976, 1980 [first pub. in Paris]; notes about Anna Akhmatova). The most controversial of recent works, Kataev's *Almazny moy venets* (1979; my diamond crown), has struck many readers as offensively coy, especially in its flippant treatment of such tragic figures as Yesenin and the poet Vladimir Narbut (1888–1914).

The most prominent theme in works about contemporary life is the village. The grimness of village life, along with the endurance of the peasants and their traditions, has led some critics to speak of village prose as an analogue of Western EXISTENTIALISM. *Derevensky dnevnik* (1958–70; a village diary), a massive series of sketches surveying the conditions of peasant life by Yefim Dorosh (1908–1972), first sounded this major new theme in post-Stalinist literature, one that boasted such 19th-c. exponents as Turgenev and Dmitry Grigorovich (1822–1899). *Vologodskaya svadba* (1962; Vologda wedding) by Alexandr Yashin (1913–1968) straddles the genres of exposé and elegy. A three-volume chronicle, *Pryasliny* (1974; the Pryaslins), by Fyodor ABRAMOV follows village life through collectivization and world war. One of the most compassionate writers about the village, as evidenced in his *Privychnoe delo* (1968; the usual affair), is Vasily Belov (b. 1932). Valentin RASPUTIN is one of the most talented of village writers. His haunting novella *Proshchanie s Matyoroy* (1976; farewell to Matyora) focuses on old people in a village slated for submergence as part of a hydroelectric project, and implicitly attacks soulless Soviet planning and the abuses of technology in general. Yury NAGIBIN, a writer whose thematics do not often embrace the village, depicted the plundering of natural resources in the countryside in his early story "Khazarsky ornament" (1956; the Khazar ornament). Vladimir TENDRYAKOV, a first-class storyteller, often treats moral crises in a rural setting. Vladimir SOLOUKHIN finds beauty in village traditions, including Christianity. His *Chornye doski* (1969; *Searching for Icons in Russia*, 1972), describes a phenomenon that swept the Soviet Union in the 1960s and 1970s. Some of the most poetic descriptions of the Russian countryside have come from the short-story writer Yury KAZAKOV. The sometimes whimsical, sometimes genuinely tragic tales of Vasily Shukshin (1929–1974), best known for the novel *Kalina Krasnaya* (1973; *Snowball Berry Red*, 1979), often portray peasants trying to cope with city life. The most pessimistic account of rural life is to be found in *Nezhelannoe puteshestvie v Sibir* (1970 [first pub. in New York]; *Involuntary Journey to Siberia*, 1970) by Andrey Amalrik (1938–1981).

Some very talented writers have chosen rural life as their theme but fall outside the school of village writing as such. Sasha SOKOLOV, the most daringly imaginative writer of his generation and the most gifted stylist working today, uses a country setting for his novels *Shkola dlya durakov* (1976 [first pub. in Ann Arbor, Mich.]; *School for Fools*, 1977) and *Mezhdu sobakoy i volkorn* (1980 [first pub. in Ann Arbor, Mich.]; between the dog and the wolf). The stories of Fazil ISKANDER, an Abkhazian writing in Russian, range from humorous tales of childhood to hair-raising stories of epic violence and poignant accounts of love and betrayal; examples may be found in his *Sandro is Chegem* (1979; additional chapters, 1981 [first pub. in Ann Arbor, Mich.]; *Sandro of Chegem*, 1983), a chronicle of Abkhazian life from the turn of the century to the present day. The primary theme for Chïngï z AYTMATOV, a Kirgiz, is cultures in conflict. A recent work, *I dolshe veka dlitsya den* (1980, and the day lasts longer than forever), created quite a stir because of its frankly religious overtones.

Urban fiction, generally taking as its locus either Moscow or Leningrad, tends to focus on moral issues in a society that looks more bourgeois with every passing year. The former Muscovite Vasily AKSYONOV has produced a body of work that ably chronicles the experiences of his own postwar generation. His novel *Zvyozdny bilet* (1961; *A Starry Ticket*, 1962), which introduced teenage slang into the literary language, earned Aksyonov the reputation of a Russian J. D. SALINGER. *Ozhog* (1980 [first pub. in Ann Arbor, Mich.]; *The Burn*, 1983) offers a modernistic account of midlife crises among Moscow's Western-oriented intelligentsia in the post-thaw period. Another early leader of urban fiction, Anatoly Gladilin (b. 1935), shares both Aksyonov's thematic interests and his slangy style, as evidenced by his best story, "Pervy den novogo goda" (1965; the first day of the new year), a frank treatment of the generation gap. Yury Trifonov, a writer who did not come into his own until the 1970s, produced masterful portraits of disintegrating urban family life in his novellas *Obmen* (1969; *The Exchange*, 1977), *Predvaritelnye itogi* (1970; *Taking Stock*, 1977), *Dologe proshchanie* (1971; *The Long Goodbye*, 1977), and *Drugaya zhizn* (1975; another life). *Sem dney tvorenia* (1971 [first pub. in Frankfurt]; *Seven Days of Creation*, 1974) by Vladimir Maximov (b. 1932) depicts the unpleasantness of everyday Soviet life. I. Grekova (pseud. of Yalena Venttsel, b. 1907), writing from the point of view of a middle-aged widow or divorcé, offers stories that abound in witty dialogue, a rare feature in Russian prose. Her best work, "Damsky master" (1963; "The Ladies' Hairdresser," 1973), recounts the tribulations of a naïvely ambitious coiffeur. The two most important satirists with Muscovite roots are Venedikt Yerofeev (b. 1947) and Yuz Aleshkovsky (b. 1929). Yerofeev's *Moskva-Petushki* (1977 [first pub. in Paris]; *Moscow to the End of the Line*, 1980), already a classic of its kind, recounts a grimly hilarious alcoholic spree, while Aleshkovsky's *Nikolay Nikolaevich*

(1980 [first pub. in Ann Arbor, Mich.]; Nikolay Nikolaevich) makes poetry out of gutter language in its account of the hero's experiences as a sperm donor at a genetics laboratory.

The most distinguished Leningrad urbanist, Andrey Bitov (b. 1937), simultaneously surveys contemporary life among the intelligentsia and Russian cultural history in a work of impressive psychological depth, *Pushkinsky dom* (1978 [first pub. in Ann Arbor, Mich.]; Pushkin House). Another Leningrader, Daniil Granin (b. 1918), often explores parallels between artistic and scientific creativity, as in his novel *Idu na grozu* (1972; I face the storm). Boris Vakhtin (1930–1983) reveals a remarkable gift for characterization in such stories as "Dublyonka" (1979 [first pub. in Ann Arbor, Mich.]; "The Sheepskin Coat," 1983) and "Odna absolyutno shchastlivaya derevnya" (1982 [first pub. in Ann Arbor, Mich.]; "An Absolutely Happy Village," 1983). Vladimir Maramzin (b. 1934), one of the most innovative stylists in contemporary prose, stretches the Russian language to its limits and challenges traditional Russian sexual prudishness in *Blondin obeego tsveta* (1975 [first pub. in Ann Arbor, Mich.]; "The Two-Toned Blond," 1982). Sergey DOVLATOV delights in dramatizing the manifold absurdities of Soviet life, especially in the field of journalism. Several of his humorous stories have appeared recently in *The New Yorker*. Another Leningrader, Viktor Konetsky (b. 1929), usually takes his readers out to sea, where in such works as *Zavtrashnie zaboty* (1961; tomorrow's cares) and *Kto smotrit oblaka* (1967; he who looks at the clouds) he meditates on the human condition.

Recent Russian literature has displayed a strong current of fantasy. Orthodox critics who disapprove of this trend like to blame it on Bulgakov's posthumously published masterpiece, *Master i Margarita* (written 1928–40; pub. [U.S.S.R. censored text] 1966–67; full text pub. in West Germany, 1969; *The Master and Margarita*, 1967), a stunning novel about art and morality whose characters include a gunslinging cat. Predating the publication of *Master i Margarita*, however, are *Fantasticheskie povesti* (1961 [first pub. in Paris]; *Fantastic Stories*, 1963) by Andrey SINYAVSKY, who calls his own style "fantastic realism." One of the few true modernists among contemporary Russian writers, Sinyavsky has recently published a short novel, *Kroshka Tsores* (1980; little Tsores), his tribute to E. T. A. Hoffmann. Aksyonov's *Ostrov Krym* (1981; the island of Crimea) offers an amusing and instructive fantasy about a non-Soviet Crimea. *Ziyayushchie vysoty* (1976 [first pub. in Lausanne]; *The Yawning Heights*, 1979) by Alexandr Zinoviev (b. 1922) provides a withering allegorical satire on the Soviet system. His criticism of the Soviet Union is no less potent in *Svetloe budushchee* (1978 [first pub. in Lausanne]; *The Radiant Future*, 1981).

Science fiction has found hosts of admirers among Russian readers. The genre counts Alexandr Belyaev (1884–1942) its Russian father, and two of the most popular writers in the Soviet Union today are the team of Arkady Strugatsky (b. 1925) and his brother Boris Strugatsky (b. 1933), who blend satire, detection, and adventure for science-fiction novels that often question Soviet values and practices.

Broadly speaking, most genuinely new works of prose represent one of two traditions—the overtly ideological mainstream or the nonmainstream, nonideological countertradition. The mainstream itself consists of two competing but complementary orientations—conservative and liberal. Conservative writers, usually Russophiles opposed to liberal democracy, have grouped themselves around the journals *Nash Sovremennik*, *Molodaya Gvardia*, and *Moskva*. The liberals publish in such journals as *Druzhba*

Narodov, Znamia, Yunost, and the venerable *Novy Mir.* The last two journals additionally provide a home for most of the nonmainstream, countertraditional writing.

Both conservatives and liberals admire. Aleksandr SOLZHENITSYN, in whose works one finds nearly all the themes that typify the literature of glasnost. At the nexus of those concerns lies the Stalinist past and its impact on Russian life today. Solzhenitsyn's aesthetics and ethics grow out of his fellow Russian writers, whether conservatives or liberals. The result is a decidely monologic mainstream literature not always easily distinguishable from monochrome journalism.

No new names have arisen among the conservatives, many of whom represent village prose. The insularity and xenophobia that always marked much of the writing of that school have now evolved into undisguised Russian chauvinism, antidemocratism, anti-Westernism, and anti-Semitism. These aspects of conservative literary ideology are most apparent in the novella *Pechalny detektiv* (1986; a sad detective story) and the story "Lovlia peskarei v Gruzii" (1986; gudgeon fishing in Georgia) by Viktor Astafev (b. 1924); the novel *Vsyo vperedi* (1986; *The Best Is Yet To Come,* 1989) by Vasily Belov (b. 1932); the movel *Sudny den* (1988; judgment day) by Viktor Ivanov (b. 1932); and published remarks by the novelist Valentin RASPUTIN.

Many of the liberals are no less overtly ideological than the conservatives, and their prose is often no less monologic, especially in such major works of glasnost as *Deti Arbata* (1987; *Children of the Arbat,* 1988) by Anatoly Rybakov (b. 1911), *Zubr* (1987; *The Bison,* 1990) by Daniil Granin (b. 1919), and *Belye odezhdy* (1987; *White Garments,* 1989).

Several of the most interesting writers of the liberal traditionalist school, in fact, began publishing much earlier but did not really make their mark until the era of glasnost. Thus, most of the "new names" among the liberals are not particularly young or inexperienced writers. Several of these authors, each in his own way, write most of all about history. In *Nepridumannoe* (1989; true stories) Lev Razgon (b. 1908) reminisces about leading figures in the arts and politics both inside and outside the camps during the Stalin period. Boris Yampolsky (dates n.a.) shares Razgon's interest in depicting the Stalinist terror; his *Moskovskaya ulitsa* (1988; a Moscow street) paints a terrifying portrait of someone awaiting arrest in the late 1940s. In *Kapitan Dikshteyn* (1987; "Captain Dikshtein," 1990), *Nochnoy dozor* (1989; the night watch), and "Petya po doroge v Tsarstvie Nebesnoe" (1991; Pete on the way to the Heavenly Kingdom), Mikhail Kuraev (b. 1939) narrates Soviet history from the point of view of average people largely unable to make sense of the quite fantastic events transpiring around them. Vyacheslav Petsukh (b. 1946) offers witty, but ultimately superficial commentary on manifold aspects of Russian and Soviet history in his *Novaya moskovskaya filosofia* (1989; the new Moscow philosophy) and *Rommat* (1990; Rommat).

Other "new" authors identified with glasnost write about contemporary life. Of them, Anatoly Genatulin (b. 1925) is the most conventional. His favorite theme is the moral and physical rigors of life in the Bashkirian village. When not writing as a professional economist, Nikolay Shmelyov (b. 1936) pens straightforward tales about contemporary urban mores and morals. Gennady Golovin (b. 1941), whose most recent collection of stories bears the title *Terpenie i nadezhda* (1988; patience and hope), draws on the style's and themes of classical Russian writers for his tales of people hard-pressed by the vicissitudes of life today.

Critics have dubbed the current countertradition in Russian prose "the other prose." On the whole, this extremely heterogenous school of writing tries to ignore seventy years or so of Soviet Russian literature and to take up where the experimentalists and countertraditionalists of the 1920s left off. Some of the writers associated with "the other prose" evoke the greatest interest because of their stylistics, others because of their thematics. The brightest star among the former, Tatyana TOLSTAYA, writes philosophical stories whose richly metaphorical style calls to mind Yury OLESHA. Several of Tolstaya's narratives are collected in the volume *Na zolotom kryltse sideli* (1987; *On the Golden Porch,* 1989). Valeria Narbikova (b. 1960) shares Tolstaya's love of metaphor, while her intoxication with language itself suggests an affinity with the futurist poet Velemir KHLEBNIKOV. A very different sort of writer, Tatyana Nabatnikova (dates n.a), treats the age-old battle of the sexes with verve and insouciance.

The second group have caused the greatest stir not because of their styles, also nontraditional and worthy of comment, but because of their thematics. Their works consistently treat aspects of social and personal life generally excluded from the Russian literary tradition until now. As a consequence, such works are often referred to collectively as *chernukha,* a word that suggests unrelieved darkness and gloom. In his *Smirennoe kladbishche* (1987; *The Humble Cemetery,* 1990), Sergey Kaledin (b. 1949) portrays grave diggers at work and rest, for instance. Viktor Yerofeev (b. 1947) shocks readers with physiological detail and the depiction of mindless violence. The characters in the short stories of Lyudmila PETRUSHEVSKAYA seem to have emerged from a social worker's case book. Svetlana Vasilenko (b. 1956) writes of women and death in tragic tones. All in all, because of its exploration of new possibilities for theme, language, and style, many critics, both at home and abroad, feel that the future of Russian literature now lies with "the other prose."

Drama

In an article written in 1923, the playwright and critic Lev Lunts (1901–1924) argued that Russian drama as such had never existed. Were he alive today, Lunts would have little reason to tone down his hyperbolic assessment, since although Russians have made significant contributions to world theater in the 20th c., especially through the influential directors Konstantin Stanislavsky (1863–1938) and Vsevolod Meyerhold (1874–1940), the achievement in Russian drama as such falls far short of that in poetry and fiction. Individual plays of interest have appeared, but no dramatist of high international reputation has emerged since Chekhov. His last two plays, *Tri sestry* (1901; *Three Sisters,* 1916) and *Vishnyovy sad* (1904; *The Cherry Orchard,* 1908), with their plotlessness and subtle, multileveled dialogue, pointed the way toward symbolist drama and perhaps even to the THEATER OF THE ABSURD.

Gorky wrote over a dozen plays, all of them firmly rooted in Russian reality, static in construction, more concerned with sociopolitical ideas than with recognizable emotions, antibourgeois, antiintellectual, and deadly serious. His *Na dne* (1901; *The Lower Depths,* 1912), a disquisition on the relative merits of the painful truth versus the noble lie, is perhaps Gorky's best effort for the theater.

Many symbolists and modernists indulged in writing for the stage. Blok's *Balaganchik* (1906; *The Puppet Show,* 1963), a satire on Petersburg mysticism, enjoyed a brief vogue, as did Andreev's

Tot, Kto poluchaet poshchochinu (1916; *He Who Gets Slapped*, 1921), a violent love story with a circus setting.

In the 1920s and early 1930s the most noteworthy dramatists were Bulgakov, Mayakovsky, Nikolay Yevreynov (1879–1953), and Nikolay Erdman (1902–1970). Bulgakov's *Dni Turbinykh* (perf. 1926, pub. 1970; *The Days of the Turbins*, 1934), based on his novel *Belaya gvardia*, provided one of the Moscow Art Theater's few triumphs in the postrevolutionary period. Mayakovsky's *Klop* (1929; *The Bedbug*, 1960) and *Banya* (1929; *The Bathhouse*, 1963) satirize nascent Soviet conservatism, while Erdman's *Mandat* (1925; *The Mandate*, 1975) takes as its target acquisitive instincts and political pragmatism in the NEP period. Erdman's *Samoubystvo* (1928; *The Suicide*, 1973) features a hero who considers suicide as a protest against the Soviet regime. Yevreynov's *Samoe glavnoe* (1921; *The Chief Thing*, 1926) projects a vision of life made happier through illusion.

The Stalinist period witnessed predictably dismal plays about socialist construction and anti-Soviet sabotage. Nikolay Pogodin (1900–1962) has the dubious distinction of having written *Aristokraty* (1934; *Aristocrats*, 1937), a four-act "comedy" set at the White Sea-Baltic Canal, a work project accomplished with forced labor. The popular *Strakh* (1931; *Fear*, 1934) by Alexandr Afinogenov (1904–1941) showed an old scientist falling into the hands of anti-Soviet elements. Of the many plays occasioned by World War II, Leonov's *Nashestvie* (1942; *The Invasion*, 1944), a drama about life under the German occupation, is probably the best of the lot. The only outstanding dramatist of the time, Yevgeny Shvarts (1896–1958), wrote allegorical dramas such as *Goly Korol* (1934; *The Naked King*, 1968) and *Drakon* (1943; *The Dragon*, 1966), which make Soviet theater censors nervous to this day.

The best post-Stalinist dramatic writing has come from Alexandr Vampilov (1937–1972) and Mikhail Roshchin (b. 1933). Vampilov's last and best play, *Proshlym letom v Chulimske* (1973; *Last Summer in Chulimsk*, 1977), traces the lives of several people in a small Siberian town, gradually revealing subtle, Chekhovian webs of passion and tension. Roshchin, the "slickest" of contemporary Russian playwrights, has had his greatest success with *Valentin i Valentina* (1971; *Valentine and Valentina*, 1977), a drama about young love sorely tested by parental interference.

As with prose fiction, Russian dramas and dramatists working in the glasnost era fall into two general categories: traditionalist and alternative. The new plays published by the traditionalists in Russia since 1985 generally explore the past or expose the present. The dramatist who has shown the greatest interest in the early days of the Soviet regime is Mikhail Shatrov (pseud. of Mikhail Marshak, b. 1932). His *Brestsky mir* (1987; the peace of Brest-Litovsk) and *Vperyod, vperyod, vperyod* (1988; forward, forward, forward) explode many of the clichés of preglasnost official Soviet history while nonetheless leaving intact the Lenin cult.

The veteran dramatists Aleksandr Galin (b. 1947), Aleksandr Gelman (b. 1933), and Igor Gorin (b. 1940) have all had plays staged and published that reflect various aspects of perestroika. Representative is Galin's *Zvyozdy na utrennem nebe* (1988; *Stars in the Morning Sky*, 1988), which portrays the life of prostitutes, whose very existence as social group was officially denied before glasnost.

Petrushevskaya remains the most significant alternative dramatist. Such plays of hers as *Tri devushki v golubom* (1980; *Three Girls in Blue*, 1988) and *Chinzano* (1973; *Cinzano*, 1989) depict aimless lives in moral voids. Other noteworthy alternative dramatists include Nikolay Kolyada (b. 1957) and Viktor Korkia (dates

n.a.). Like Petrushevskaya, Kolyada shocks Russian audiences with depictions of milieus previously unimaginable on the Soviet or Russian stage. Kolyada's *Rogatka* (1989; the slingshot), for instance, portrays a gay relationship between an older alcoholic cripple and a much younger man. Korkia's absurdist leanings are apparent in his *Cherny chelovek, ili ya bedny Soso* (1988; the black man, or, I am poor Soso), whose protagonists are Stalin and Beria. In both language and theme, plays by Petrushevskaya and other nontraditional dramatists invite comparison with "the other prose."

Criticism

The most incisive Russian LITERARY CRITICISM in the 20th c. has come from the so-called formalists, formalism being a movement that flourished during the 1920s. Pioneering studies of versification by Bely, whom Nabokov deemed a "meddler of genius" in this regard, prefigured the formalists' rejection of the sociological traditions of 19th-c. Russian criticism and the impressionism of certain modern critics. The formalists themselves, with their linguistic attention to the text itself and to its organization, anticipated American New Criticism and French STRUCTURALISM.

Most of the formalists applied their theories of verse and prose to specific authors, movements, or genres, often producing landmark studies in the process. Boris Eikhenbaum (1886–1959) wrote unsurpassed monographs on Tolstoy: *Molodoy Tolstoy* (1922; *The Young Tolstoy*, 1972), *Tolstoy v 50-kh godakh* (1928; Tolstoy in the fifties); *Tolstoy v 60-kh godakh* (1931; *Tolstoy in the Sixties*, 1982), and *Tolstoy v 70-kh godakh* (1960; *Tolstoy in the Seventies*, 1982). Eikhenbaum's *Lermontov* (1924; *Lermontov*, 1981) also ranks as a classic study. With *Dostoevsky i Gogol* (1921; *Dostoevsky and Gogol*, 1979) Yury Tynyanov forced readers to examine those two authors as well as the notion of parody in a radically new light. His *Problemy stikhotvornogo yazyka* (1924; *Problems of Verse Language*, 1981) brings him close to modern structuralism. Viktor Zhirmunsky (1891–1971) made a valuable contribution to the field of comparative literature with his *Bayron i Pushkin* (1924; Byron and Pushkin). Viktor Shklovsky offered insightful readings of Pushkin and Tolstoy, among others. A critic who was molded by formalist thought, Mikhail Bakhtin (1895–1975), left a substantial body of theoretical writings and applied criticism that only now is receiving its due, both in the U.S.S.R. and abroad. Dostoevsky studies have been profoundly influenced by the notion of "polyphony" that Bakhtin introduced in his *Problemy tvorchestva Dostoevskogo* (1929; expanded version, *Problemy poetiki Dostoevskogo*, 1963; *Problems of Dostoevsky's Poetics*, 1973). *Voprosy literatury i estetiki* (1975; *The Dialogic Imagination*, 1981) presents a theory of literature in line with contemporary semiotics.

Marxist and Freudian criticism have had precious few capable Russian exponents in the 20th c. Vladimir Pereverzev (1882–1968), the best and most extreme of the Marxists, wrote such intriguing socioeconomic interpretive studies as *Tvorchestvo Dostoevskogo* (1912; the art of Dostoevsky) and *Tvorchestvo Gogolya* (1914; the art of Gogol). Ivan Yermakov (1875–19??) wrote Freudian analyses of Pushkin and Gogol.

Structuralism has not bypassed the Russian critical consciousness. Indeed, in the 1960s Tartu State University (in Estonian S.S.R.) boasted a constellation of critics who practiced a Russian brand of semiotics. The head of that group was Yury Lotman (b. 1922), whose *Struktura khudozhestvennogo teksta* (1970; the structure of the artistic text) and *Analiz poeticheskogo teksta* (1972; *The Analysis of the Poetic Text*, 1976) provide both a general semiotic theory and its practical application. Lotman himself has recently turned to more traditional literary scholarship, but many of his students who are now outside the Soviet Union continue to experiment with structuralist modes of criticism. As a general rule, Russian structuralists have shown a greater inclination toward interpretation than toward theory, which makes their studies considerably less opaque than those by some of their western European counterparts.

Although one can point to such notable exceptions as Iskander, Trifonov, Bitov, and Aytmatov, the merit of most recent creative writing published in the U.S.S.R. is less than negligible. The range of topics excluded by censorship embraces nearly every subject that one traditionally associates either with world literature or Soviet life. By far the most interesting writing in Russian now issues from outside the U.S.S.R., but it remains to be seen how much longer the Soviet authorities will allow Soviet citizens to publish abroad "illegally" and whether those Russian writers now in emigration can sustain their present level of activity.

Judged by Western standards, Russian literary criticism in the age of glasnost remains primarily a boundary genre in which history, philosophy, sociology, and polemical journalism sometimes commingle. Critics for whom literature is indisputably a matter of ideology fall, predictably, into two camps—conservatives and liberals. The most influential conservative critics, many of them opposed to liberal reform, include Vadim Kozhinov (b. 1930), Sergey Vikulov (b. 1922), and Mark Lyubomudrov (dates n.a.), the latter a theater critic.

The critic most identified with reform and glasnost is the talented Natalya Ivanova (b. 1945), whose articles are collected in *Tochka zrenia* (1988; point of view) and *Voskreshenie nuzhnykh veshchey* (1990; the resurrection of needed things). Other critics who treat literature in a way and tone congenial to Western liberals are Tatyana Ivanova (dates n.a.), author of *Krug chtenia* (1988; circle of reading); Igor Dedkov (b. 1934), a recent volume of whom bears the title *Obmovlyonnye zrenie* (1988; renewed vision); Igor Zolotussky (b. 1930), recent pieces by whom may be found in *Ispoved Zoila* (1989; Zoilus's confession); and the extraordinarily witty Natalya Ilina (b. 1914). Representing the countertradition of Russian criticism, what the 19th c. called "aesthetic criticism," is Viktor Yerofeev. His efforts to draw a line between literature and didacticism, imaginative writing and prophecy, often enrage Russian readers.

During the twilight years of the Soviet empire critics from both extremes of the ideological spectrum used journals and newspapers as soap boxes. In post-Soviet Russia, given the elimination of censorship and the marginalization of high culture, engaged literary criticism has lost the considerable force it once had. Interesting alternate writing has come from those critics and scholars who elaborate the premises of Russian postmodernism, Vyacheslav Kuritsyn (b. 1965), Mark Lipovetsky (b. 1964), and Mikhail Epshtein (b. 1950) the most notable among them. Many older readers and writers register extreme hostility to postmodern critical practice and assumptions, but as long as Russian literature continues to reside firmly outside the domain of official control and firmly within the marketplace, traditional kinds of engaged Russian literary criticism will have difficulty finding much of an audience. The future finally seems to lie with a less rigidly ideological criticism than has ever been the case before.

BIBLIOGRAPHY: Mirsky, D., *Contemporary Russian Literature,* 1881–1925 (1926); Brown, R., *The Proletarian Episode in Russian Literature,* 1928–1932 (1953); Simmons, E. J., ed., *Through the Glass of Soviet Literature* (1953); Donchin, A., *The Influence of French Symbolism on Russian Poetry* (1958); Zavalishin, V., *Early Soviet Writers* (1958); Muchnic, H., *From Gorky to Pasternak* (1961); Rogers, T. F., *"Superfluous Men" and the Post-Stalin Thaw* (1962); Alexandrova, V., *A History of Soviet Literature* (1963); Hayward, M., and L. Labedz, eds., *Literature and Revolution in Soviet Russia* (1963); Hayward, M., and E. L. Crowley, eds. *Soviet Literature in the Sixties* (1964); Maguire, R., *Red Virgin Soil* (1968); Markov, V., *Russian Futurism* (1968); Struve, G., *Russian Literature under Lenin and Stalin,* 1917–1953 (1971); Holthusen, J., *Twentieth-Century Russian Literature* (1972); Brown, E. J., ed., *Major Soviet Writers: Essays in Criticism* (1973); Barooshian, V., *Russian Cubo-Futurism* 1910–1930 (1974); Erlich, V., ed., *Twentieth-Century Russian Literary Criticism* (1975); Mathewson, R., *The Positive Hero in Russian Literature* (1975); Kasack, W., *Lexikon der russischen Literatur ab* 1917 (1976); Slonim, M., *Soviet Russian Literature: Writers and Problems, 1917–1977,* 2nd ed. (1977); Brown, D., *Soviet Russian Literature since Stalin* (1978); Hingley, R., *Russian Writers and Soviet Society 1917–1978* (1979); Segel, H. B., *Twentieth-Century Russian Drama: From Gorky to the Present* (1979); Shneidman, N., *Soviet Literature in the 1970s* (1979); Chapple, R., *Soviet Satire of the Twenties* (1980); Erlich, V., *Russian Formalism* (1980); Hosking, A., *Beyond Socialist Realism* (1980); Kasack, W., *Die russische Literatur* 1945–1976 (1980); Markov, V., *Russian Imaginism* (1980); Clark, K., *The Soviet Novel: History as Ritual* (1981); Hingley, R., *Nightingale Fever: Russian Poets in Revolution* (1981); Svirsky, G., *A History of Post-war Soviet Writing: The Literature of Moral Opposition* (1981); Proffer, C., "A Disabled Literature," *New Republic,* 14 Feb. 1981, 27–34; Brown, E. J., *Russian Literature since the Revolution,* rev. ed. (1982); special Russian literature issue entitled *Perestroika and Soviet Culture: The New Soviet Prose, MQR,* 28, 4 (1989); Zalygin, S., ed., *The New Soviet Fiction* (1989); Goscilo, H., and B. Lindsey, eds., *Glasnost: An Anthology of Russian Literature under Gorbachev* (1990); E. Brystol, *A History of Russian Poetry* (1991); Moser, C., *The Cambridge History of Russian Literature* (1992); Parthé, K., *Russian Village Prose* (1992); Brown, D., *The Last Years of Soviet Russian Literature* (1993)

—DAVID A. LOWE

RYLSKY, Maxym

Ukrainian poet, critic, and translator, b. 19 March 1895, Kiev; d. 24 July 1964, Kiev

The son of a peasant woman and a well-known social historian and leader of a movement whose purpose was to persuade the Polonized Ukrainian gentry to return to Ukrainian ideals and to serve the Ukrainian people, R. as a child became imbued with love for the Ukrainian language, traditions, and folklore. He studied at the University of Kiev, then taught Ukrainian in various rural schools (1919–23); and at the university (1923–29); during this time he became one of the leaders of Ukrainian intellectual life.

R. was a member of a group of poets known as neoclassicists, who advocated the cult of the refined word expressed with aesthetic simplicity and classical clarity. Persecuted during Stalin's reign of terror, R. witnessed the liquidation of hundreds of his fellow poets and intellectuals, but remained firm in his Parnassian convictions until his arrest and imprisonment in 1931. He was released from prison upon writing "Deklyaratsya obovyazkiv poeta in hromadyanyna" (1931; a declaration concerning the duties of a poet and citizen) and resumed his career as a man of letters broken in spirit but unimpaired in talent. From that time on, R. served the Party, writing according to the Party line, and was rewarded with several literary prizes.

R.'s career may be divided into three periods: (1) the SYMBOLISTS period, which began with his precocious collection *Na bilykh ostrovakh* (1910; on white islands) and ended with his return to Kiev in 1921, following a two-year sojourn in the provinces; (2) the neoclassicist period, the transition to which began with the collection *Synya dalechin* (1922; the blue distance) and ended with his conversion to communism in 1931; and (3) his communist period (1931 until his death).

R.'s poetry, especially that of the early period, has a static quality. It seems to have been written by a dreamer standing on lofty heights gazing into the distance and envisioning the peace of eternity. R. continued to worship beauty even when he sensed the inevitability of his doom. His second period is characterized by the same aloofness and aesthetic tranquillity, but by a greater refinement of form and a more pronounced tendency toward escapism.

Throughout his life R. remained a master of the poetic word. Even when he wrote paeans to Stalin and the Communist Party during his final period, his poetry remained pure and pristine in its lyric expression and classical form. The long poem *Zhaha: Poemavydinnya* (1943; *Thirst: A Poem-Vision*, 1963), written under the tension of the German invasion of the Ukraine, is full of vitality.

R. also made a significant contribution to the development of the Ukrainian language through his translations from Dante, Shakespeare, Molière, Voltaire, the French Parnassians, the Polish writer Adam Mickiewicz (1798–1855), among others. In his later years R. wrote essays on Ukrainian and other literatures, tried to "rehabilitate" his friend Mykola Zerov (1890–1941), who was liquidated by Stalin, and courageously defended the writers of the Generation of the 1960s from the attacks of zealous Party-line critics.

FURTHER WORKS: *Pid osinnimy zoryamy* (1918); *Na uzlissi* (1918); *Poemy* (1924); *Kriz buryu i snih* (1925); *Trynadtsyata vesna* (1926); *Homin i vidhomin* (1929); *De skhodyatsya dorohy* (1929); *Znak tereziv* (1932); *Maryna* (1933); *Kyyiv* (1935); *Lito* (1936); *Vybrani virshi* (1937); *Ukrayina* (1938); *Vybrani virshi* (1939); *Zbir vynohradu* (1940); *Vybrani poeziyi* (1940); *Za ridnu zemlyu* (1941); *Slovo pro ridnu matir* (1942); *Narod bessmerten* (1942); *Svitla zbroya* (1942); *Vybrani poeziyi* (1943); *Velyka hodyna* (1943); *Mandrivka v molodists* (1944); *Neopalyma kupyna* (1944); *Chasha druzhby* (1946); *Poeziyi* (3 vols., 1946); *Virnists* (1947); *Den yasny* (1948); *Mosty* (1948); *Poeziyi* (3 vols., 1949); *Braterstvo* (1950); *Poemy i liryka* (1950); *Vesnyana pisnya* (1952); *Nasha syla* (1952); *Pid zoryamy Kremlya* (1953); *Virshi* (1954); *Kvity druzyam* (1954); *300 lit* (1954); *Orlyna simya* (1955); *Velyky polsky poet Adam Mickiewicz* (1955); *Heroyichny epos ukrayinskoho narodu* (1955); *Pro poeziyu Adama Mickiewicza* (1955); *Sad nad morem* (1955); *Na onovleny zemli* (1956); *Tvory* (3 vols., 1956); *Poemy* (1957); *Velyky podvyh* (1957); *Troyandy i vynohrad* (1957); *Kobzar Yegor Movchan* (1958); *Khudozhny pereklad z odnieyi slovyanskoy movy na inshu* (1958); *Slovo pro rindu matir* (1958); *Illich i divchynka* (1958); *Daleki neboskhyly* (1959); *Nasha krovna sprava* (1959); *Holosiyivska osin* (1959); *Pryroda i literatura* (1960); *Trudy i dni* (1960); *V zatinku zhayvoronka* (1961); *Poezia Tarasa Shevchenka* (1961); *Poetyka Shevchenka* (1961); *Vohni* (1961); *Tvory* (10 vols., 1960–62); *Vechirni rozmovy* (1962); *Pro lyudynu dlya lyudyny* (1962); *Pro mystetstvo* (1962); *Zymovi zapysy* (1964); *Taras Shevchenko* (1964); *Slovo pro literaturu* (1974); *Mystetstvo perekladu* (1975); *U bratersky spivdruzhnosti: Literaturno-krytychni statti* (1978); *Statti pro literaturu* (1980); *Poetychni pereklady* (1984); *Zibrannya tvoriv y dvadsyaty tomakh* (20 vols., 1990). FURTHER WORKS IN ENGLISH: *Taras Shevchenko: A Biographical Sketch* (1964, with Alexandr Deutsch; rev. ed., 1974); *Selected Poetry* (1980)

BIBLIOGRAPHY: Andrusyshen, C. H., and W. Kirkconnel, eds., *The Ukrainian Poets, 1189–1962* (1963): 337–39; Chikovani, S., "M. R. (1895–1964)," *SovL*, 9 (1968): 158–61; Lupiy, O., "In Search of New Words," *Digest of the Soviet Ukrainian Press*, 17, 9 (1973): 14–15; Mihailovich, V. D., et al., eds., *Modern Slavic Literatures* (1976), Vol. II: 501–3

—LEONID D. RUDNYTZKY